WILLMINGTON'S
GUIDE TO THE BIBLE

Willmington's
GUIDE
to the
BIBLE

Dr. H. L. Willmington

TYNDALE HOUSE
PUBLISHERS, INC.
CAROL STREAM, ILLINOIS

Visit Tyndale's exciting Web site at www.tyndale.com

TYNDALE and Tyndale's quill logo are registered trademarks of Tyndale House Publishers, Inc.

Library of Congress Catalog Card Number 80-53295
ISBN-13: 978-0-8423-8804-7 Hardcover
ISBN-10: 0-8423-8804-4 Hardcover

Printed in the United States of America

13 12 11 10 09 08
29 28 27 26 25 24

DEDICATION

The enclosed material is in reality a number of combined books and study sections. I therefore have taken the privilege of making a fivefold presentation. This book, the greatest accomplishment (for better or worse) of my life, is gratefully dedicated to the following:

1. To my wonderful wife Sue, and our beloved son Matthew.
2. To the blessed memories of two departed men of God, Paul Willmington (my father), and Charles Ransom (Sue's father).
3. To Valma and Gladys, their wives, and our mothers.
4. To Dr. Jerry Falwell, my boss, pastor, and friend.
5. To all my students who have patiently endured my jokes, overlooked my weaknesses, absorbed my material, and accepted my challenge to become scriptural giants for God.

NOTE:

Honesty would force me to admit that some mistakes will certainly be found in the many Scripture references in this book. Although the editors and I have sought to eliminate inconsistencies and errors, some will have crept in, for which I take full responsibility. The considerate reader would render me a great service by calling my attention to any such errors.

NOTE ON THE CHARTS:

To obtain the maximum benefit from the illustrations and charts it is suggested that they be allowed to function as both a *preview* and a *review* of each chronological stage. For example, before reading the printed content dealing with the Creation Stage, one should first allow the charts corresponding to this stage to give him a preview of the material to be studied. After this, the content itself can be read. Following this, the charts may be once again consulted to serve as a general review of the stage.

Contents

FOREWORD

Because of the sheer volume of material in this book, three vital questions need to be answered concerning the *why, who,* and *what* of its contents.

I. The *why* of the book. The roots of this volume can be traced back to my days at Dallas Theological Seminary in the late fifties. During that time God placed in my heart a love for his Word that I had never known before. It was then I began building my library in earnest, always looking for that book, or books which would give me the most Bible information in the least amount of time. In fact, I sought for a book that might in itself provide me with a basic overall scriptural summary. Finding none, I entertained the possibility of someday attempting to author such a book. In brief, this book is my best effort to supply that need. My goal has been to publish an all-inclusive one-volume concise summary of basic Bible information. The two key words to be noted here are *concise* and *summary.* Thus, my supreme objective is to make available in abbreviated form to our "Now Generation" a complete Bible education in a single book. The reader alone will determine whether I have accomplished this.

II. The *who* of the book. I have kept in mind four special groups of individuals while preparing this book. It is intended for:

A. Pastors, attempting to provide for their preaching purposes a rapid, accurate, and workable outline analysis of those great scriptural facts they learned in college and seminary. In some cases this book may be a substitute for the formal education a pastor did not receive.

B. Sunday school teachers, offering to them quick fingertip scriptural facts geared for effective teaching purposes.

C. High school and college groups, presenting a "no-nonsense" historical, scientific, and theological summary of God's timeless Book for their uncertain age.

D. Bible lovers everywhere, supporting their already-held convictions that the Bible is still the most exciting, practical, and inspirational Book ever written!

III. The *what* of the book. How does one go about this task? What methods are employed in the manuscript? It will be noted that this book consists of two general divisions. The first division is entitled Main Curriculum, and the second division is called Supporting Curriculum.

I. MAIN CURRICULUM

There are two basic methods of Bible study absolutely vital if one is to truly acquire and apply the great truths within God's Word. The first of these is the chronological method, and the second is the theological approach.

A. The chronological method. This consists of informative and inspirational paragraph outlines of the twelve main chronological stages of Bible history from Genesis through Revelation. These stages are:

1. The Creation Stage: Genesis 1–11
2. The Patriarchal Stage: Genesis 12–50; Job
3. The Exodus Stage: Exodus; Leviticus; Numbers; Deuteronomy
4. The Conquest Stage: Joshua
5. The Judges Stage; Judges; Ruth; 1 Samuel 1–7
6. The United Kingdom Stage: 1 Samuel 8–31; 2 Samuel; 1 Kings 1–11; 1 Chronicles; 2 Chronicles 1–9; Psalms; Song of Solomon; Proverbs; Ecclesiastes
7. The Chaotic Kingdom Stage: 1 Kings 12–22; 2 Kings 1–25; 2 Chronicles 10–36; Jonah; Amos; Hosea; Joel; Obadiah; Nahum; Isaiah; Micah; Habakkuk; Zephaniah; Jeremiah; Lamentations
8. The Captivity Stage: Ezekiel; Daniel
9. The Return Stage: Ezra; Esther; Nehemiah; Haggai; Zechariah; Malachi

    10. The Gospel Stage: Matthew; Mark; Luke; John
    11. The Early Church Stage: Acts
    12. The Epistle Stage: Remaining books in the New Testament
These then are the twelve basic stages in the Book of Ages. The Old Testament has nine stages and the New Testament has three. The reader will find many helpful charts throughout the Old Testament and New Testament sections.

B. The theological method. This includes an analytical study of twelve major doctrinal themes. These are:
    1. The doctrine of the Trinity
    2. The doctrine of the Father
    3. The doctrine of the Son
    4. The doctrine of the Holy Spirit
    5. The doctrine of man
    6. The doctrine of the Church
    7. The doctrine of sin
    8. The doctrine of salvation
    9. The doctrine of Satan
    10. The doctrine of angels
    11. The doctrine of the Bible
    12. The doctrine of prophecy

II. SUPPORTING CURRICULUM

To undergird and amplify the two above methods in the main curriculum, the following supporting phases of Bible study are offered.

A. A topical summary of the Bible. This includes a summary list of approximately 135 biblical topics. A sample of these topics would feature:
    1. All the cities mentioned in the Bible
    2. All the recorded conversions in the Bible
    3. All the miracles in the Bible
    4. All the occupations in the Bible
    5. All the parables in the Bible
    6. All the prophecies in the Bible, etc.

B. Historical study summaries:
    1. A historical summary of the nine most important Old and New Testament peoples. These are:
        a. The Canaanites
        b. The Sumerians
        c. The Philistines
        d. The Egyptians
        e. The Babylonians
        f. The Assyrians
        g. The Persians
        h. The Greeks
        i. The Romans
    2. A listing in related categories of the 613 Old Testament commands.
    3. A historical summary of the most important archaeological discoveries.
    4. A summary of the nation Israel's history from the destruction of the second Temple in September A.D. 70, to the Yom Kippur War in October 1973. These nineteen centuries can be historically divided into ten main periods. These are:
        a. The Roman Period (A.D. 70-325)
        b. The Byzantine Period (325-614)
        c. The Persian Period (614-634)
        d. The Arab Period (634-1072)
        e. The Seljuk Period (1072-1099)
        f. The Crusaders Period (1099-1291)
        g. The Mamluk Period (1291-1517)
        h. The Turkish (Ottoman) Period (1517-1917)
        i. The British Period (1917-1948)
        j. The Independent Period (1948-present day)
    5. A listing in related categories of the 300 most important Old Testament and New Testament individuals.
    6. A complete cross reference of every single Old Testament verse quoted in the New Testament.
    7. Holy Land Statistics.

HEBREW BIBLE
OLD TESTAMENT
ARRANGEMENT

LAW *5 books*	GENESIS EXODUS LEVITICUS NUMBERS DEUTERONOMY		
PROPHETS *8 books*	*4 FORMER* JOSHUA JUDGES SAMUEL KINGS	*4 LATTER* ISAIAH JEREMIAH EZEKIEL THE TWELVE	
WRITINGS *II books*	*3 POETICAL* PSALMS PROVERBS JOB	*5 ROLLS* SONG OF SOLOMON RUTH LAMENTATIONS ESTHER ECCLESIASTES	*3 HISTORICAL* DANIEL EZRA NEHEMIAH CHRONICLES

ENGLISH BIBLE
OLD TESTAMENT
ARRANGEMENT

LAW *5 books*	• GENESIS • EXODUS • LEVITICUS • NUMBERS • DEUTERONOMY		
HISTORY *12 books*	• JOSHUA • JUDGES • RUTH • 1 SAMUEL • 2 SAMUEL • 1 KINGS	• 2 KINGS • 1 CHRONICLES • 2 CHRONICLES • EZRA • NEHEMIAH • ESTHER	
POETRY *5 books*	• JOB • PSALMS • PROVERBS • ECCLESIASTES • SONG OF SOLOMON		
PROPHECY *17 books*	*5 MAJOR* • ISAIAH • JEREMIAH • LAMENTATIONS • DANIEL • EZEKIEL	*12 MINOR* • HOSEA • JOEL • AMOS • OBADIAH • JONAH • MICAH	• NAHUM • HABAKKUK • ZEPHANIAH • HAGGAI • ZECHARIAH • MALACHI

Why the Child of God Should Study the Word of God

At first glance it would seem totally unnecessary to discuss reasons for studying God's Word. One might assume that, upon conversion, the most natural thing for a new believer to do would be to begin a lifelong study of that Book which originally brought him to Christ. But personal observation, as well as church history, proves the facts to be quite the opposite. The truth is, most Christians know very little about the Bible! Here then are some sound reasons for studying the Scriptures.

    I. Because of its Author.

        Often God is thought of as a Creator, a Redeemer, a Shepherd, a Judge, etc. This is correct thinking, of course, for he does indeed function in all these roles. But there is one great accomplishment of God which is almost always left off the divine attribute lists compiled by men. This wonderful but forgotten role is that of Author! God has written a book, and that profound and priceless book is the Bible. As testified to by any human author, the nicest thing one can say to an author is, "Oh, yes, I've read your book."

        It is a tragic but true fact that many of the Christians who will someday (along with all believers) stand before the judgment seat of Christ will be sadly forced to admit that, while they were saved by heeding the salvation message in God's Book, they nevertheless failed to take the time to read it. Thus, if for no other reason, the Bible should be carefully read to allow the believer to proclaim to Christ on that day: "Dear Jesus, there were many things I did not do on earth that I should have done, as well as other things I did do that I should not have, but one thing I did—I read your book!"

    II. Because of the often-repeated command to read it.

        "This book of the law shall not depart out of thy mouth; but thou shalt meditate therein day and night, that thou mayest observe to do according to all that is written therein: for then thou shalt make thy way prosperous, and then thou shalt have good success" (Josh. 1:8).

        "Study to shew thyself approved unto God, a workman that needeth not to be ashamed, rightly dividing the word of truth" (2 Tim. 2:15).

        "But he answered and said, It is written, Man shall not live by bread alone, but by every word that proceedeth out of the mouth of God" (Mt. 4:4).

        Especially to be noted is this last verse. Jesus said *every word.*

    III. Because the Bible is God's chosen way to accomplish his divine will.

        A. Sinners are saved through the message of the Bible.

            "For whosoever shall call upon the name of the Lord shall be saved.

            How then shall they call on him in whom they have not believed? and how shall they believe in him of whom they have not heard? and how shall they hear without a preacher? And how shall they preach, except they be sent? as it is written, How beautiful are the feet of them that preach the gospel of peace, and bring glad tidings of good things! But they have not all obeyed the gospel. For Esaias saith, Lord, who hath believed our report? So then faith cometh by hearing, and hearing by the word of God" (Rom. 10:13-17).

            "But Peter, standing up with the eleven, lifted up his voice, and said unto them, Ye men of Judaea, and all ye that dwell at Jerusalem, be this known unto you, and hearken to my words" (Acts 2:14).

            "Now when they heard this, they were pricked in their heart, and said unto Peter and to the rest of the apostles, Men and brethren, what shall we do?" (Acts 2:37).

            "Therefore they that were scattered abroad went every where preaching the word. Then Philip went down to the city of Samaria, and preached Christ unto them. And the people with one accord gave heed unto those things which Philip spake, hearing and seeing the miracles which he did. For unclean spirits, crying with loud voice, came out of many that were possessed with them: and many taken with palsies, and that were lame, were healed. And there was great joy in that city" (Acts 8:4-8).

"Being born again, not of corruptible seed, but of incorruptible, by the word of God, which liveth and abideth for ever" (1 Pet. 1:23).

"Of his own will begat he us with the word of truth—that we should be a kind of firstfruits of his creatures" (Jas. 1:18).

B. Saints are sanctified through the message of the Bible.

"Sanctify them through thy truth: thy word is truth" (Jn. 17:17).

"As newborn babies, desire the sincere milk of the word, that ye may grow thereby" (1 Pet. 2:2).

"For this is the will of God, even your sanctification, that ye should abstain from fornication" (1 Thess. 4:3).

"Wherewithal shall a young man cleanse his way? by taking heed thereto according to thy word. With my whole heart have I sought thee: O let me not wander from thy commandments. Thy word have I hid in mine heart, that I might not sin against thee" (Ps. 119:9-11).

"Every word of God is pure: he is a shield unto them that put their trust in him. Add thou not unto his words, lest he reprove thee, and thou be found a liar" (Prov. 30:5, 6).

"If ye abide in me, and my words abide in you, ye shall ask what ye will, and it shall be done unto you" (Jn. 15:7).

"And now, brethren, I commend you to God, and to the word of his grace, which is able to build you up, and to give you an inheritance among all them which are sanctified" (Acts 20:32).

IV. Because our enemy the devil has read it.

During the account in Matthew 4, Christ is tempted three times by the devil. On each occasion the Savior answered Satan with the phrase, "It is written," and then proceeded to quote from the Word of God as found in the book of Deuteronomy. But what is almost always overlooked is the fact that the phrase "it is written" is repeated four times in Matthew 4, and that the fourth time it is the devil using it to quote Scripture to Christ! Note the background at this point.

"Then the devil taketh him up into the holy city, and setteth him on a pinnacle of the temple, and saith unto him, If thou be the Son of God, cast thyself down: for it is written, He shall give his angels charge concerning thee: and in their hands they shall bear thee up, lest at any time thou dash thy foot against a stone" (Mt. 4:5, 6).

Here Satan quotes from Psalm 91:11, 12. It is taken completely out of context, to be sure, but how did Satan know about it in the first place? The answer is painfully obvious. One day when the devil had nothing better to do, he must have sat down and studied Psalm 91. Many Christians today have probably never even read this Psalm, but the devil apparently has it memorized! Thus, we need to read God's Word lest Satan get an advantage upon us.

V. Because of the example of Paul.

Paul was probably the greatest Christian that ever lived. His spiritual accomplishments are nothing short of staggering. Here was a man who made the first three missionary journeys, who founded and pastored the first fifty or more Bible-believing churches, who wrote over half of the New Testament, and who on five occasions saw the resurrected Christ, and at least once was actually caught up into the third heaven itself! But then he was arrested, condemned to death, and placed in prison. Note carefully his final words to Timothy just prior to his execution.

"For I am now ready to be offered, and the time of my departure is at hand. I have fought a good fight, I have finished my course, I have kept the faith: Henceforth there is laid up for me a crown of righteousness, which the Lord, the righteous judge, shall give me at that day: and not to me only, but unto all them also that love his appearing. The cloak that I left at Troas with Carpus, when thou comest, bring with thee, and the books, but especially the parchments" (2 Tim. 4:6-8, 13).

What were these parchments? They were his copies of the Old Testament scrolls. The point to be made here is that in spite of all his marvelous achievements, the old apostle still felt he could profit from studying the Word of God on the eve of his death.

VI. Because the Bible alone provides answers to life's three sixty-four-trillion-dollar questions. These questions, pondered by every generation, are:

A. Where did I come from?

"And God said, Let us make man in our image, after our likeness: and let them have dominion over the fish of the sea, and over the fowl of the air, and over the cattle, and over all the earth, and over every creeping thing that creepeth upon the earth. So God created man in his own image, in the image of God created he him; male and female created he them" (Gen. 1:26, 27).

"Know ye that the Lord he is God: it is he that hath made us, and not we ourselves; we are his people, and the sheep of his pasture" (Ps. 100:3).

B. Why am I here?

"Let us hear the conclusion of the whole matter: Fear God, and keep his commandments: for this is the whole duty of man" (Eccl. 12:13).

"Thou are worthy, O Lord, to receive glory and honour and power: for thou hast created all things, and for thy pleasure they are and were created" (Rev. 4:11).

C. Where am I going?

"For God so loved the world, that he gave his only begotten Son, that whosoever believeth in him should not perish, but have everlasting life. For God sent not his Son into the world to condemn the world; but that the world through him might be saved. He that believeth on him is not condemned: but he that believeth not is condemned already, because he hath not believed in the name of the only begotten Son of God" (Jn. 3:16–18).

"The Lord is my shepherd; I shall not want. Surely goodness and mercy shall follow me all the days of my life: and I will dwell in the house of the Lord for ever" (Ps. 23:1, 6).

"And whosoever was not found written in the book of life was cast into the lake of fire" (Rev. 20:15).

VII. Because we'll never have the opportunity to apply many of its verses after we leave this earth.

A. There will be no opportunity to apply 1 Corinthians 10:13 in heaven.

"There hath no temptation taken you but such as is common to man: but God is faithful, who will not suffer you to be tempted above that ye are able; but will with the temptation also make a way to escape, that ye may be able to bear it" (1 Cor. 10:13).

Reason: In heaven there will be no temptation.

B. There will be no opportunity to apply 1 John 1:9 in heaven.

"If we confess our sins, he is faithful and just to forgive us our sins, and to cleanse us from all unrighteousness" (1 Jn. 1:9).

Reason: In heaven there will be no sin.

C. There will be no opportunity to apply Philippians 4:19 in heaven.

"But my God shall supply all your need according to his riches in glory by Christ Jesus" (Phil. 4:19).

Reason: In heaven there will be no need.

D. There will be no opportunity to apply John 14:1–3 in heaven.

"Let not your heart be troubled: ye believe in God, believe also in me. In my Father's house are many mansions: if it were not so, I would have told you. I go to prepare a place for you. And if I go and prepare a place for you, I will come again, and receive you unto myself; that where I am, there ye may be also" (Jn. 14:1–3).

Reason: In heaven there will be no sorrow.

E. There will be no opportunity to apply Psalm 23:4 in heaven.

"Yea, though I walk through the valley of the shadow of death, I will fear no evil: for thou art with me; thy rod and thy staff they comfort me" (Ps. 23:4).

Reason: In heaven there will be no death.

VIII. Because the only ultimate proof for our faith is the Bible.

To introduce the eighth and final reason for studying God's Word, the following imaginary situation is proposed. Often the unbeliever hurls the following accusation at the believer: "Oh, you Christians—you're all alike! You're so dogmatic. You think you alone are right and everybody else is dead wrong. How can you possibly be so sure what you believe is true?" This question, though often asked in a scoffing manner, is nevertheless a fair one. How *does* the child of God know his faith is the only correct one?

Let us suppose that you are invited to an important social function in your hometown. Attending this gathering are people from all over the world. As the introductions are being made, it slowly dawns upon you that the only professing Christian there is yourself. You are subsequently introduced to a Buddhist, a Confucianist, a Shintoist, a Moslem, and other individuals, all belonging to various non-Christian religions. After a pleasant dinner, the conversation gradually turns to matters of religion. Your hostess, realizing this subject to be of general interest, suddenly announces:

"I have a wonderful idea! Since everyone here seems to have a great interest in religion, may I suggest that we share with one another by doing the following: Each person will be allowed to speak uninterrupted for ten minutes on the subject, 'Why I feel my faith is the right one.' "

The group quickly agrees with this unique and provocative idea. Then with no warning she suddenly turns to you and exclaims, "You go first!" All talk immediately ceases. Every eye is fixed on you. Every ear is turned to pick up your first words. What would you say? How would you start? Let us quickly list a few arguments which you could *not* use.

1. You *couldn't* say, "I know I'm right because I *feel* I'm right! Christ lives in my heart!"

This, of course, is a wonderful truth experienced by all believers, but it would not convince the Buddhist, who would doubtless *feel* that he was right too.

2. You *couldn't* say, "I know I'm right because Christianity has more followers in this world than any other religion."

    This is simply not true today. Actually, the sad truth is that evangelical Bible-believing Christianity is a distinct minority in the world today. The Moslem would doubtless quickly point this out to you.

3. You *couldn't* say. "I know I'm right because Christianity is the oldest of all religions.

    Ultimately, of course, this is true. But the Confucianist might contend that Confucius presented his teachings centuries before the Bethlehem scene. Of course, he would not understand the eternal existence of our Lord Jesus Christ. These then are arguments you could *not* use. What *could* you say? In reality you would have at your disposal only one single argument. But that argument, that weapon, used in the right way, would be more than enough to overwhelmingly convince any honest and sincere listener at that social gathering. That wonderful weapon, that unanswerable argument, is one's own personal copy of the Bible! What could you say? Well, you could hold up your Bible and confidently proclaim the following:

    "Look at this! I know I'm right because the Author of my faith has given me a Book which is completely unlike any of the books of your faiths."

    You could then continue (until your time ran out) by pointing out the unity, the indestructibility, and the universal influence of the Bible. You could discuss its historical, scientific, and prophetical accuracy. Finally, you might relate exciting examples of perhaps the greatest single proof of the supernatural nature of the Bible, that is, its marvelous life-transforming power!

    Of course, it must be pointed out that neither the Word of God nor the God of the Word can be scientifically analyzed in a laboratory test tube. The divine Creator still desires and demands faith on the part of his Creation. (See Heb. 11:1-6.) But he has presented us with a heavenly textbook to aid us in this needed faith. In fact, the Gospel of John was specifically written ". . . that ye might believe that Jesus is the Christ, the Son of God; and that believing ye might have life through his name" (Jn. 20:31).

THE FORTY-EIGHT MOST IMPORTANT CHAPTERS IN THE OLD TESTAMENT

The Old Testament has 929 chapters. The following forty-eight chapters have been selected because of their historical, prophetical, theological, or practical significance.

GENESIS
1—**Creation** of all things
3—**Fall** of man
6—The universal **flood**
11—The Tower of **Babel**
12—The call of **Abraham**
15—The confirmation of the **Abrahamic Covenant**

EXODUS
3—The call of **Moses**
12—The **Passover**
14—The **Red Sea** crossing
16—The giving of the **Sabbath**
20—The giving of the **Law**
40—The completion of the **tabernacle**

LEVITICUS
8—The anointing of **Aaron** as Israel's first high priest
23—The **feasts** of Israel

NUMBERS
14—The **rebellion** at Kadesh-barnea
21—The serpent of **brass**

DEUTERONOMY
28—**Israel's future** predicted by Moses

JOSHUA
4—Israel enters the **Promised Land**

RUTH
4—The marriage of Boaz and **Ruth**

I SAMUEL
9—The anointing of **Saul** as Israel's first king
16—The anointing of **David**

2 SAMUEL
6—**Jerusalem** becomes the capital of Israel
7—The giving of the **Davidic Covenant**

I KINGS
8—The dedication of the **Temple** by **Solomon**
12—The **divided kingdom** of Israel

2 KINGS
17—The **capture** of the northern kingdom by Assyria
19—The **saving** of Jerusalem by the death angel
24—The **capture** of the southern kingdom by Babylon

EZRA
1—The decree of Cyrus and the **return** to Jerusalem

JOB
1—The confrontations between **God and Satan** (see also Job 2)

PSALMS
22—The Psalm of **Calvary**
23—The Psalm of the **Good Shepherd**
51—The great confession of **sin** chapter
119—The Psalm of the **Word of God**

ISAIAH
7—The **prophecy** of the virgin birth
14—The fall of **Satan**
35—The **Millennium**
53—The sufferings of **Christ**

JEREMIAH
31—The **promise** of the new covenant to Israel

EZEKIEL
10—The **departure** of the glory cloud from Israel
28—The prehistorical life of **Satan**
37—The dry bone **vision** of Israel's restoration
38—The **future** Russian invasion into Palestine (see also Ezekiel 39)
40—The **future millennial temple**

DANIEL
2—The **dream** of the future Gentile world powers (see also Daniel 7)
9—The **vision** of the seventy weeks

JONAH
2—The **great fish** and Jonah

ZECHARIAH
14—The **Second Coming** of **Christ**

THE MOST IMPORTANT OLD TESTAMENT EVENTS

1. Creation of **Adam** and **Eve** (Gen. 1:26, 27; 2:7, 21, 22)
2. Institution of **marriage** (Gen. 2:23–25)
3. **Fall** of man (Genesis 3:6)
4. Promise of the **Redeemer** (Gen. 3:15)
5. Universal **flood** (Gen. 6–8)
6. Institution of human **government** (Gen. 9:1–19)
7. Tower of **Babel** (Gen. 11:1–9)
8. Conversion and call of **Abraham** (Gen. 12:1–3)
9. Giving of Abrahamic **Covenant** (Gen. 12:7; 13:14–17; 15:1–21)
10. Abraham's marriage to **Hagar** (Gen. 16:1–16)
11. The birth of **Isaac** (Gen. 21:1–8)
12. The flight of **Jacob** (Gen. 28)
13. The selling of **Joseph** into Egyptian slavery (Gen. 37)
14. The enslavement of **Israel** in **Egypt** (Ex. 1)
15. The call of **Moses** (Ex. 3:1–10)
16. The ten **plagues** (Ex. 7–12)
17. The institution of the **Passover** (Ex. 12)
18. The appearance of the **glory cloud** (Ex. 13:21, 22)
19. The **Red Sea** crossing (Ex. 14)
20. The giving of the **manna** (Ex. 16:4)
21. The institution of the **Sabbath** (Ex. 16:29)
22. The giving of the **Law** (Ex. 20:1–17)
23. The completion of the **tabernacle** (Ex. 40:33, 34)
24. The anointing of **Aaron** (Lev. 8:1–12)
25. The **unbelief** at Kadesh-barnea (Num. 14)
26. The death of **Moses** (Deut. 34:5–8)
27. The **Jordan River** crossing into Palestine (Josh. 3)
28. The victory over **Jericho** (Josh. 6)
29. The death of **Joshua** (Josh. 24:29)
30. The marriage of **Ruth** to Boaz (Ruth 4)
31. The capture of the **ark** by the Philistines (1 Sam. 4)
32. The rejection of **Samuel** by Israel (1 Sam. 8:1–9)
33. The anointing of **Saul** (1 Sam. 9, 10)
34. The rejection of **Saul** (1 Sam. 15:23)
35. The anointing of **David** (1 Sam. 16:13)
36. The capture of **Jerusalem** by David (2 Sam. 5:9)
37. The recovery of the **ark** by David (2 Sam. 6:15, 16)
38. The giving of the Davidic **Covenant** (2 Sam. 7:8–17)
39. The anointing of **Solomon** (1 Ki. 1:39)
40. The completion of **Solomon's Temple** (1 Ki. 6:38)
41. The Israeli **civil war** (1 Ki. 12)
42. The deliverance of **Joash** from murderous Queen Athaliah (2 Chron. 22:10–12)
43. The **Assyrian captivity** of the northern kingdom (2 Ki. 17:6)
44. The **deliverance** of **Jerusalem** from the Assyrians (2 Ki. 19:32–35)
45. The death of **Josiah** (2 Ki. 23:29, 30)
46. The departure of the **glory cloud** (Ezek. 10:18)
47. The **destruction** of the **Temple** of Solomon (2 Ki. 25:8, 9)
48. The **Babylonian captivity** of the southern kingdom (2 Ki. 25:11)
49. The return under **Cyrus'** decree (Ezra 1)
50. The completion of the new Temple under **Zerubbabel** (Ezra 3)
51. The salvation of the Jews by **Esther** (Est. 4–7)

The Chronological Method

Nearly every Bible institute and Christian college offers courses in Old Testament and New Testament survey. The usual approach is to briefly examine the sixty-six books, suggesting a key thought, verse, truth, character, etc., for each book. The main problem with this method is the difficulty in connecting the many "keys" with the proper biblical "locks."

A simpler method would be to place every book into twelve logical and historical divisions. This we have done in this *Guide to the Bible.*

Each stage describes a particular and unique period of time in God's progressive revelation to man. These twelve divisions are historical, *not* dispensational in nature.

A quick survey of these twelve reveals the following:

Creation Stage	1. Creation
	2. Fall
	3. Flood
	4. Tower of Babel
Patriarchal Stage	1. Lives of Abraham, Isaac, Jacob, Joseph, and Job
	2. Beginning of Hebrew nation
	3. Arrival of Jews in Egypt
Exodus Stage	1. Deliverance from Egypt
	2. Giving of Law
	3. Building of tabernacle
	4. Failure at Kadesh
Conquest Stage	1. Invasion of the land
	2. Subjection of the land
	3. Division of the land
Judges Stage	1. Ministry of twelve military reformers
	2. Marriage of a Moabite girl
	3. Call and ministry of Samuel
United Kingdom Stage	1. Reigns of Saul, David, and Solomon
	2. Recovery of the ark and capture of Jerusalem
	3. Construction of first Temple
Chaotic Kingdom Stage	1. Civil War
	2. Capture of ten tribes by Assyria
	3. Capture of two tribes by Babylon
Captivity Stage	1. Ministry of Daniel and Ezekiel
	2. Fall of Babylon
	3. Rise of Persia
Return Stage	1. Decree of Cyrus
	2. Construction of second Temple
	3. Deliverance of Jews in Persia
Gospel Stage	Birth, life, death, resurrection, and ascension of Christ
Early Church Stage	1. Birth of Church at Pentecost
	2. Ministry of Peter, Stephen, and Philip (Acts 1–12)
	3. Ministry of Paul, Barnabas, and Silas (Acts 13–28)
Epistle Stage	Letters of Paul, Peter, John, James, and Jude

OLD TESTAMENT BASIC STAGES

	MAIN ACTORS	MAIN ACTION
From the undated past up to **2165 B.C.** **CREATION STAGE** GENESIS 1–11	ADAM, ABEL, ENOCH, NOAH	• CREATION • FLOOD • FALL • TOWER OF BABEL
2165–1804 B.C. **PATRIARCHAL STAGE** GENESIS 12–50 JOB	ABRAHAM, ISAAC, JACOB, JOSEPH JOB, ELIPHAZ, BILDAD, ZOPHAR, ELIHU	• BEGINNING OF HEBREW NATION • GIVING OF ABRAHAMIC COVENANT • JEWS MOVE INTO EGYPT • GOD ALLOWS SATAN TO TEST JOB
1804–1405 B.C. **EXODUS STAGE** EXODUS LEVITICUS NUMBERS DEUTERONOMY	MOSES, AARON, MIRIAM, ELEAZER KORAH, BALAAM, PHINEHAS	• DELIVERANCE FROM EGYPT • BUILDING OF THE TABERNACLE • GIVING OF THE LAW • THE FAILURE AT KADESH-BARNEA
1405–1382 B.C. **CONQUEST STAGE** JOSHUA	JOSHUA, CALEB, RAHAB, ACHAN	• INVASION OF THE LAND • SUBJECTION OF THE LAND • DIVISION OF THE LAND
1382–1043 B.C. **JUDGES STAGE** JUDGES RUTH 1 SAMUEL 1–7	EHUD, BARAK, DEBORAH, GIDEON, JEPHTHAH, SAMSON RUTH, NAOMI, BOAZ HANNAH, ELI, SAMUEL	• THE MINISTRY OF 12 MILITARY REFORMERS • THE MARRIAGE OF A MOABITE GIRL • THE PRAYER OF A MOTHER • THE DEATH OF A PRIEST

1043–931 B.C.
UNITED KINGDOM STAGE
 	
1 SAMUEL 8–31
2 SAMUEL
1 KINGS 1–11
1 CHRONICLES
2 CHRONICLES 1–9
PSALMS
PROVERBS
ECCLESIASTES
SONG OF SOLOMON
	SAUL, DAVID, SOLOMON, JOAB, ABNER, ABSALOM, GOLIATH, ZADOK, BATH-SHEBA, WITCH OF ENDOR, NATHAN, JONATHAN, QUEEN OF SHEBA	• THE THREEFOLD ANOINTING OF DAVID
		  IN BETHLEHEM BY SAMUEL
		  IN HEBRON BY 2 TRIBES
		  IN HEBRON BY ALL 12 TRIBES
		• THE CAPTURE OF JERUSALEM BY DAVID
		• THE BRINGING OF THE ARK INTO JERUSALEM
		• THE GIVING OF THE DAVIDIC COVENANT
		• THE CONSTRUCTION OF THE FIRST TEMPLE

931–605 B.C.
CHAOTIC KINGDOM STAGE
 	
1 KINGS 12–22
 	
2 KINGS
 	
2 CHRONICLES 10–36
 	
OBADIAH (850–840)
JOEL (841–834)
JONAH (785–750)
AMOS (760–753)
HOSEA (760–700)
ISAIAH (739–681)
MICAH (735–700)
NAHUM (650–620)
	NORTHERN KINGS: JEROBOAM, OMRI, AHAB, JEHU, JEROBOAM II, HOSHEA
	
	SOUTHERN KINGS: REHOBOAM, ASA, JEHOSHAPHAT, UZZIAH, AHAZ, HEZEKIAH, MANASSEH, JOSIAH, JEHOIAKIM, ZEDEKIAH
	
	ORAL PROPHETS: ELIJAH, MICAIAH, ELISHA
	VARIOUS FIGURES: JEZEBEL, NAAMAN, ATHALIAH
	
	AMAZIAH
	GOMER, JEZREEL, LO-RU-HA-MAH, LO-AM-MI
		• ISRAEL'S TRAGIC CIVIL WAR
		• THE CAPTURE OF THE NORTHERN KINGDOM BY
		  THE ASSYRIANS
		• THE SALVATION OF JERUSALEM FROM THE
		  ASSYRIANS
		• THE GREAT PREACHING MINISTRY OF THE ORAL
		  PROPHETS
		• THE GREAT PREACHING MINISTRY OF THE
		  WRITING PROPHETS
		• THE GIVING OF THE NEW COVENANT

ZEPHANIAH (640–620) **JEREMIAH (627–575)** **HABAKKUK (609–606)** **LAMENTATIONS (586)**	BARUCH, GEDALIAH, ISHMAEL, JOHANAN	• THE CAPTURE OF THE SOUTHERN KINGDOM BY THE BABYLONIANS

605–538 B.C.
CAPTIVITY STAGE

DANIEL (605–536) **EZEKIEL (593–560)**	DANIEL, NEBUCHADNEZZAR, SHADRACH, MESHACH, ABEDNEGO, BELSHAZZAR, DARIUS	• PERSONAL DELIVERANCE OF DANIEL AND HIS FRIENDS • DESTRUCTION OF FIRST TEMPLE • DESCRIPTION OF THE FUTURE MILLENNIAL TEMPLE • A PANORAMA OF GENTILE WORLD POWERS • A PREVIEW OF ISRAEL'S FUTURE • THE FALL OF BABYLON

538–400 B.C.
RETURN STAGE

EZRA (438–440) **ESTHER (478–463)** **NEHEMIAH (445–415)** **HAGGAI (520–504)** **ZECHARIAH (520–488)** **MALACHI (427–400)**	CYRUS, JOSHUA, ZERUBBABEL, EZRA AHASUERUS, ESTHER, MORDECAI, HAMAN NEHEMIAH, ARTAXERXES, SANBALLAT	• THE DECREE OF CYRUS • THE CONSTRUCTION OF THE SECOND TEMPLE • THE REBUILDING OF THE WALLS • THE DELIVERANCE OF THE JEWS IN PERSIA

NEW TESTAMENT BASIC STAGES

5 B.C.–A.D. 30
GOSPEL STAGE

	MAIN ACTORS	MAIN ACTION	
MATTHEW *KING AND LIONLIKE* **MARK** *SERVANT AND OXLIKE* **LUKE** *PERFECT MAN AND MANLIKE* **JOHN** *MIGHTY GOD AND EAGLELIKE*	• TWELVE APOSTLES • MARY AND JOSEPH • MARY AND MARTHA • PILATE AND HEROD • JOHN THE BAPTIST • NICODEMUS • LAZARUS • MARY MAGDALENE	• BIRTH • FLIGHT INTO EGYPT • TEMPTATION • CHOOSING THE TWELVE • UPPER ROOM EVENT • TRIALS AND DEATH • DEDICATION • TEMPLE VISIT AT AGE TWELVE • INTRODUCTION AS LAMB OF GOD	• TRANSFIGURATION • GETHSEMANE • RESURRECTION • WISE MEN VISIT • BAPTISM • FIRST TEMPLE CLEANSING • TRIUMPHAL ENTRY • GREAT HIGH PRIESTLY PRAYER • ASCENSION

A.D. 30–A.D. 68
EARLY CHURCH STAGE

ACTS	PETER, PHILIP, STEPHEN, PAUL, BARNABAS, SILAS, JAMES	• PENTECOST • DEATH OF ANANIAS AND SAPPHIRA • SELECTION OF THE FIRST DEACONS • MARTYRDOM OF STEPHEN • CONVERSION OF ETHIOPIAN EUNUCH • CONVERSION OF SAUL • CONVERSION OF CORNELIUS • ESTABLISHMENT OF ANTIOCH CHURCH • DELIVERANCE OF PETER • THREE MISSIONARY JOURNEYS OF PAUL • JERUSALEM COUNCIL • PAUL'S MACEDONIAN VISION • PAUL'S ARREST AND TRIP TO ROME

45–A.D. 100
EPISTLE STAGE

JAMES (45)	GALATIANS (49)	1 PETER (68)
	1 THESSALONIANS (51)	2 PETER (68)
JUDE (68)	2 THESSALONIANS (51)	
	1 CORINTHIANS (56)	
	2 CORINTHIANS (56)	1 JOHN (95)
	ROMANS (57)	2 JOHN (95)
	EPHESIANS (60)	3 JOHN (95)
	COLOSSIANS (61)	REVELATION (95)
	PHILIPPIANS (61)	
	PHILEMON (62)	
	1 TIMOTHY (62)	
	TITUS (66)	
	2 TIMOTHY (67)	
	HEBREWS (59)	

These then are the twelve stages, nine in the Old Testament, and three in the New Testament. It has been my undeserved privilege to have presented this twelve-stage Bible survey approach to over 10,000 students during the last decade at Thomas Road Church in Lynchburg. Both written and oral testimonies from many of these students have amply supported its helpfulness. For this I am profoundly grateful.

THE CREATION STAGE

INTRODUCING THE CREATION STAGE (Genesis 1-11)

These eleven chapters are absolutely vital in rightly understanding the remaining 1178 in the Bible. If one accepts them at face value, he will have no difficulty concerning the rest of the Old and New Testament.

THE CREATION STAGE

GENESIS, CHAPTERS ONE THROUGH ELEVEN

The three important men of this stage are Adam, Enoch, and Noah.

The four important events are, the Creation, the Fall, the Flood, and the Tower of Babel.

The Creation account includes everything, from electrons to galaxies, from dinosaurs to dandelions, and from Adam to angels!

This stage is the only one which describes God as resting (Gen. 2:2, 3).

It gives us the first human to be created (Adam) and the first human to be born (Cain) (Gen. 1:26; 4:1).

It records the first man to die (Abel) and the first not to die (Enoch) (Gen. 4:8; 5:24).

We are introduced to a serpent, a raven, and a dove (Gen. 3:1; 8:7, 10)

The glory of God in creation (Gen. 1:1) and the grace of God in salvation (Gen. 6:8) are both clearly seen.

We see the world's earliest civilization (Cainite) and the world's oldest citizen (Methuselah) (Gen. 4:17; 5:27).

This stage describes the first marriage, the first murder, and the first promise of the Messiah (Gen. 2:23-25; 4:8; 3:15).

It gives us the first illustration of human religion (the fig leaves), and the first example of divine redemption (the coats of skin) (Gen. 3:7, 21).

In its pages sinners are drowned, and a saint is drunken (Gen. 7:21; 9:20, 21).

A ship settles on a mountain and a tower rises on a plain (Gen. 8:4; 11:1-4).

AN OVERALL VIEW OF GENESIS 1-11

I. The *Creation* of All Things (Gen. 1-2)
  A. First day
  B. Second day
  C. Third day
  D. Fourth day
  E. Fifth day
  F. Sixth day
  G. Seventh day
II. The *Corruption* of All Things (Gen. 3-5)
  A. The subtlety of Satan (3)
  B. The sin of Adam (3)
  C. The redemption of God (3)
  D. The story of Cain and Abel (4)
  E. The ministry of Enoch (5)
III. The *Condemnation* of All Things (Gen. 6-9)
  A. The conditions prior to the flood (6)
  B. The salvation through the flood (7-8)
  C. The tragedy following the flood (9)
IV. The *Confusion* of All Things (Gen. 10-11)
  A. The arrogance of man
  B. The judgment of God
  C. The origin of nations

THE GEOGRAPHY OF GENESIS 1-11

THE CREATION STAGE

I. The Creation of All Things (Gen. 1-2).
  "In the beginning God created the heaven and the earth" (Gen. 1:1). The word *heaven* is plural in the Hebrew. There are three heavens mentioned in the Bible. God created all three.

GENESIS 1–11: "IN THE BEGINNING...

GOD

CREATION

ORIGIN OF ALL THINGS—GEN. 1–2

- SIX DAYS OF CREATION
- ONE DAY OF REST

CORRUPTION

SIN OF ADAM—GEN. 3–5

- SUBTLETY OF SATAN
- SIN OF ADAM
- REDEMPTION OF GOD
- MARTYRDOM OF ABEL
- MINISTRY OF ENOCH

CONDEMNATION

FLOOD OF NOAH—GEN. 6–9

- CONDITIONS BEFORE THE FLOOD
- SALVATION THROUGH THE FLOOD
- THE TRAGEDY AFTER THE FLOOD

CONFUSION

TOWER OF BABEL—GEN. 10–11

- THE ARROGANCE OF MAN
- THE JUDGMENT OF GOD
- THE ORIGIN OF NATIONS

First Heaven—home of the birds and clouds.

"The leaves thereof were fair, and the fruit thereof much, and in it was meat for all: the beasts of the field had shadow under it, and the fowls of the heaven dwelt in the boughs thereof, and all flesh was fed of it" (Dan. 4:12).

"Behold the fowls of the air: for they sow not, neither do they reap, nor gather into barns; yet your heavenly Father feedeth them. Are ye not much better than they?" (Mt. 6:26).

Second Heaven—home of the sun, moon, and stars.

"The heavens declare the glory of God; and the firmament sheweth his handiwork" (Ps. 19:1).

Third Heaven—home of the angels and departed saints.

"I knew a man in Christ above fourteen years ago, (whether in the body, I cannot tell; or whether out of the body, I cannot tell: God knoweth;) such an one caught up to the third heaven" (2 Cor. 12:2).

Note now the work of the first six days.

A. First day: the creation of light (1:2–5).

The Holy Spirit moved (vibrated) upon the earth. From this omnipotent, vibrating energy source began to flow our energy waves—waves of heat and sound magnetism. Thus, the created uni-verse was energized. The earth rotating on its axis also began at this time. Both energy and matter were now present in the space, mass, time framework. The three basic types of force fields were now in effect.

1. gravitational—the force between two objects
2. electro-magnetic—the force between the electron and the nucleus of an atom
3. nuclear—the force between the proton and neutron within the atom.

Some mistakenly believe that the Holy Spirit first came to earth at Pentecost in Acts 2, and that he will leave at the rapture. But here he is pictured in the second verse in the Bible.

"In the Beginning GOD Created the Heaven and the Earth"

THIS IS A SUMMARIZATION STATEMENT	THIS IS A REFUTATION STATEMENT	
1:1 TELLS US **WHAT** GOD DID.	PHILOSOPHY REFUTED	HOW REFUTED
	ATHEISM	THERE IS A GOD
1:2–2:25 TELLS US **HOW** HE DID IT.	POLYTHEISM	THERE IS BUT ONE GOD
	EVOLUTION	HE CREATED ALL THINGS
	PANTHEISM	HE IS APART FROM HIS CREATION
	MATERIALISM	THERE WAS A BEGINNING TO CREATION
	FATALISM	THERE WAS A PURPOSE TO CREATION

B. Second day: the separating of the waters (1:6–8). This water was in two forms:
  1. regular land-based water in shallow ocean, river, and lake beds
  2. atmospheric water—in the form of invisible translucent vapor

C. Third day: the creation of plant life (1:9–13). Lush green vegetation and exotic flowers now grace the newly emerged dry ground.

These verses alone totally refute the harmful doctrine of theistic evolution which says life began aeons ago from a glob of scum floating on some remote ocean surface. But to the contrary, Moses tells us life was supernaturally created on the third day of Creation and began on dry ground.

D. Fourth day: the creation of the sun, moon, and stars (1:14–19). On the first day God created physical light. He now creates special light sources. These heavenly bodies were to function in a threefold manner:
  1. As signs—they teach and remind men of God's creative work.

  "When I consider thy heavens, the work of thy fingers, the moon and the stars, which thou hast ordained" (Ps. 8:3).

  "Because that which may be known of God is manifest in them; for God hath shewed it unto them. For the invisible things of him from the creation of the world are clearly seen, being understood by the things that are made, even his eternal power and Godhead; so that they are without excuse" (Rom. 1:19, 20).

THE THREE HEAVENS OF CREATION

(See Gen. 1:1; 2:1)

THIRD HEAVEN
(2 COR. 12:2)

SECOND HEAVEN
(PS. 19:1)

FIRST HEAVEN
(DAN. 4:12; MT. 6:26)

EARTH

FATHER SON
GOD
HOLY SPIRIT

2. As seasons—they function as a calendar, dividing seasons, days, and years, enabling men to accurately plan their work.
3. As lights—they replace the temporary light source of the early days.

It may be asked why God created the earth on the first day, but waited until the fourth day before establishing the sun, stars, and moon. Two possible reasons are suggested for this, one dealing with *priority*, the other with *prevention*.

  a. That of priority. God created the earth first because it was the most important in his mind. It was upon *planet earth* that he planned to create on the sixth day a creature made in his own image. This creature, man, would live on earth, and not the moon. Then, plans had already been made in the fullness of time for the second person in the Trinity to wrap human flesh and bone about him and come to planet earth. Finally, it will be upon the earth, not Pluto or Venus, that the King of kings shall someday touch down upon the Mount of Olives to establish his millennial Kingdom.

  b. That of prevention. Almost without exception every ancient civilization has worshiped the sun. But God wanted his people to worship its Creator, namely, himself. Thus, he informs us that life and light existed before the sun, and that "every good gift and every perfect gift is from above and cometh down from the Father of lights . . ." (Jas. 1:17).

E. Fifth day: the creation of fish and fowl (1:20–23).

What a contrast is seen here, from the tiny hummingbird to the massive blue sperm whale. It is not generally known, but the blue sperm whale is longer and heavier than a modern 737 Boeing jet passenger plane. It can reach a length of 110 feet, and weigh 150 tons.

THE DAYS OF CREATION

THE LENGTH OF THESE DAYS
QUESTION: **ARE THESE LITERAL TWENTY-FOUR-HOUR DAYS?**
ANSWER: **YES, BECAUSE:**
1. THE NUMERICAL ADJECTIVE USED WITH THE WORD "DAY" (HEBREW *YOM*) INDICATES THIS.
2. MOSES BELIEVED IT (EX. 20:11; 31:17)
3. DAVID BELIEVED IT (PS. 33:6–9)
4. MOST HEBREW LANGUAGE SCHOLARS BELIEVE IT.
5. HEBREW STRUCTURE ITSELF SEEMS TO TEACH IT.

THE CORRELATION OF THESE DAYS
FIRST THREE DAYS **PROVIDE THE BACKDROP FOR THE CREATION DRAMA**

LAST THREE DAYS **PROVIDE THE ACTUAL ACTORS IN THE CREATION DRAMA**

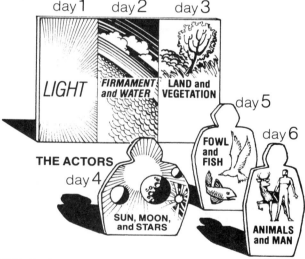

THE BACKDROP
day 1   day 2   day 3
LIGHT   FIRMAMENT and WATER   LAND and VEGETATION
THE ACTORS
day 4
SUN, MOON, and STARS
day 5
FOWL and FISH
day 6
ANIMALS and MAN

THE TWOFOLD ACCOUNT OF THESE DAYS
THE FLOODLIGHT ACCOUNT (GEN. 1)
A GENERAL DESCRIPTION OF THE CREATION OF THE UNIVERSE.
A CHRONOLOGICAL ACCOUNT
THE SPOTLIGHT ACCOUNT (GEN. 2)
A SPECIFIC DESCRIPTION OF THE CREATION OF MAN
A TOPICAL ACCOUNT

F. Sixth day: the creation of land creatures and man (1:24–31). Man immediately becomes the highlight of this day and of the entire creation week.

Note the divine account of this act. "And God said, Let us make man in our image, after our likeness . . ." (Gen. 1:26). This is the first strong evidence of the Trinity in the Old Testament. (See also Gen. 11:7; Ps. 2:7; 45:7; 110:1; Isa. 48:16.)

"Come ye near unto me, hear ye this; I have not spoken in secret from the beginning; from the time that it was, there am I: and now the Lord God, and his spirit, hath sent me" (Isa. 48:16).

1. He was made in the image of God and possessed the highest kind of life.
   a. Plant life possessed *unconscious* life.
   b. Animal life possessed *conscious* life.
   c. Man alone possessed *self-conscious* life.
   Thus, here was a creature who could not only eat of Eden's delicious food, but would glance heavenward first and thank that One who created both eater and food. No dandelion or dinosaur could do this.
2. He was to subdue the earth and fill it (1:28).
3. He was encouraged to enjoy the Tree of Life and all other trees of creation except one (2:9, 16).
4. He was forbidden to partake of the Tree of the Knowledge of Good and Evil (2:17).
5. He was to name all the animals (2:19).
6. He was given a wife (2:18-25). Here is the first of three great institutions given by God to man, that of *marriage, human government* (Gen. 9), and the *church* (Mt. 16).
   This records the second of four methods used by God to bring human beings into this world.
   a. a man without mother or father (Adam)
   b. a woman without a mother (Eve)
   c. a man without a father (Christ)
   d. individuals having both mothers and fathers (all other human beings)

G. Seventh day: God rests (2:1-3).

This is the only place where God is described as resting. Sin would soon enter the picture and the entire Trinity will become involved in redemption.

The first law of thermodynamics is now in effect. This law says that energy can be changed from one form to another, but it cannot be created or destroyed.

Here we have in fifty-six simple but sublime verses (Gen. 1 and 2) the concise but complete account of creation. The first of these verses (1:1) should be looked upon as a summary statement. God here tells us just *what* he did. The remaining fifty-five verses then become detailed statements informing us just *how* he went about doing all he said he did.

The creation of angels is not mentioned in the original week. However, in the book of Job (38:7) the Bible seems to place their creation at the same time as that of the stars. If this is correct, the angels came into being on the fourth day. Others feel this same chapter (38:4) indicated angels were present at the creation of the earth. If this is true, then angels must have been created sometime during the very first day of the Creation week.

II. The Corruption of All Things (Gen. 3-5).

At a later place in this study we will consider a popular (but in our opinion erroneous) position known as the Gap Theory. In a nutshell this theory locates the fall of Satan between Genesis 1:1 and 1:2. To the contrary, however, Moses seems to place it between the second and third chapters of Genesis. Helpful background material concerning the events transpiring between these two chapters can be found in Isaiah 14 and Ezekiel 28.

A. The subtlety of Satan (3:1).

1. He speaks through the serpent. Eve is tempted to disobey God by the devil who talks with her through the serpent's body. Adam and Eve could apparently communicate with the animal kingdom prior to the Fall in ways totally unknown to us today.

   Prior to the Fall, the serpent was not only the most intelligent creature of all, but perhaps the most beautiful also. It is clear from the later account (see 3:14) that the serpent did not crawl as it does today. It may even have had wings and stood upright. The serpent is the first of three creatures besides man which speaks in the Bible. (For the other two, see Num. 22:28, where an ass speaks; and Rev. 8:13, where an eagle talks.) From this point on, the serpent becomes a symbol for treachery and sin.

   "Their poison is like the poison of a ser-

THE CREATION WEEK

DAY	ACTION	COMMENT
1	CREATION of earth, light and probably angels	• Created universe now energized. • Earth's rotation on its axis begins. • Gravitational electro-magnetic and nuclear force fields now in effect.
2	SEPARATION of the upper and lower waters by space	• Upper atmosphere may have had more water vapor than today. • Would help explain longevity before the flood. • Would help explain the flood itself.
3	CREATION of plant life	• Totally refutes theistic evolution. • Darwin said life began in ancient ocean. • MOSES said it began on dry ground.
4	CREATION of the sun, moon, and stars	Why was the EARTH created before the SUN? • TO SHOW GOD'S PRIORITY. • To prevent sun worship.
5	CREATION of fish and fowl	• Included the tiny humming bird. • Included the mighty blue whale.
6	CREATION of land animals and man	Included all land animals from the dog to the dinosaur.
7	CREATION COMPLETED. GOD RESTS	• The seventh day now becomes a symbol of a finished creation. • The only time God is pictured as resting.

THE GAP THEORY

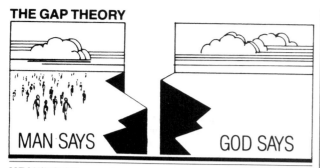

MAN SAYS   GOD SAYS

MEANING OF • In Gen. 1:1 God created a perfect and complete universe. • Between 1:1 and 1:2 Satan's rebellion marred this perfect universe. • From 1:2 on, God remolds this sin-marred creation.

POPULARITY OF Made popular and well known by two men: • George H. Pember in 1876 • C.I. Scofield in 1917

CONSIDERATION OF

Arguments FOR Gap Theory		Arguments AGAINST Gap Theory
WORDS	"Without form and void" always indicate judgment. (See Isa. 34:11; 45:18; Jer. 4:23.)	FALSE. Words can often simply refer to lifelessness and empty space. (See Job 26:7; Deut. 32:10.)
VERB	"Was" in 1:2 should be translated "became."	FALSE. Hebrew word *hayetha* (was) is almost always translated "was." It is used 264 times in the Pentateuch. Of these, it is translated "was" 258 times. See Jonah 3:3 for an example.
THERE IS A DIF-FERENCE BETWEEN CREATED (*BARA*) AND MADE (*ASAH*)		FALSE. Words are used interchangeably. EXAMPLE: 1. GOD created (*bara*) the great sea monsters (1:21). 2. GOD made (*asah*) the beast of the earth (1:25). 3. "Let us make [*asah*] man" (1:26). 4. "So God created [*bara*] man" (1:27).
WORD "DARKNESS" INDICATES JUDGMENT. (SEE 1:2.)		FALSE. Darkness here is simply the absence of light and is sometimes spoken of as being good. (See Ps. 104:20, 24.)
WORD "REPLENISH" IN 1:28 INDICATES THE WORLD WAS ONCE FILLED.		FALSE. Hebrew word *male* almost always means simply "to fill." (See Ex. 40:34; 1 Ki. 18:33; Ps. 107:9.)

pent: they are like the deaf adder that stoppeth her ear" (Ps. 58:4).

"Ye serpents, ye generation of vipers, how can ye escape the damnation of hell" (Mt. 23:33).

"And the great dragon was cast out, that old serpent, called the Devil, and Satan, which deceiveth the whole world: he was cast out into the earth, and his angels were cast out with him" (Rev. 12:9).

"And he laid hold on the dragon, that old serpent, which is the Devil, and Satan, and bound him a thousand years" (Rev. 20:2).

2. He begins by doubting God's Word.

"Yea, hath God said . . .?" (3:1). Eve now foolishly attempts to match her wits with the devil. No child of God should even try this. We are to resist him (1 Pet. 5:8, 9; Jas. 4:7), but never to debate him!

"Be sober, be vigilant; because your adversary the devil, as a roaring lion, walketh about, seeking whom he may devour: Whom resist stedfast in the faith, knowing that the same afflictions are accomplished in your brethren that are in the world" (1 Pet. 5:8, 9).

"Submit yourselves therefore to God. Resist the devil, and he will flee from you" (Jas. 4:7).

To make matters worse, Eve adds to God's Word during the debate (3:3). God did not tell her not to touch the fruit. The devil laughs with hellish glee when he can trick someone into either adding to or subtracting from God's Word.

"Every word of God is pure: he is a shield unto them that put their trust in him. Add thou not unto his words, lest he reprove thee, and thou be found a liar" (Prov. 30:5, 6).

"For I testify unto every man that heareth the words of the prophecy of this book, If any man shall add unto these things, God shall add unto him the plagues that are written in this book: And if any man shall take away from the words of the book of this prophecy, God shall take away his part out of the book of life, and out of the holy city, and from the things which are written in this book" (Rev. 22:18, 19).

3. He ends by denying God's Word.

"And the serpent said . . . ye shall not surely die" (3:4). Are there any lies in the Bible? There are indeed and here is the first one. God told Adam and Eve they would die if they disobeyed, but Satan says they will not. It should, of course, be quickly noted here that while the Bible certainly *teaches* no lies whatsoever, it does, on occasion, faithfully *record* the lies of both sinners (Saul, for example—see 1 Sam. 15:20) and saints (David, see 1 Sam. 21:2).

Many centuries later the apostle John would warn all believers to beware of three deadly temptations. These are (1) the lust of the flesh, (2) the lust of the eyes, and (3) the pride of life. See 1 John 2:15-17. In the Garden, Satan now subjects Eve to all three.

a. "The woman saw the tree was good for food" *(lust of the flesh)*.

b. "And that it was pleasant to the eyes" *(lust of the eyes)*.

c. "And a tree to . . . make one wise" *(pride of life)*.

Our Lord would later be tempted in a similar manner by the devil in the wilderness. (See Mt. 4:3-10.)

a. "Command that these stones be made bread" *(lust of the flesh)*.

b. "He showeth him all the kingdoms of the world" *(lust of the eyes)*.

c. "Cast thyself down [from the pinnacle of the temple] . . . for he shall give his angels charge concerning thee . . ." *(pride of life)*.

Note Satan's work in Genesis 3:5—"for God doth know that in the day ye eat thereof, then your eyes shall be opened, and ye shall be as God, knowing good and evil."

In one sense, Satan's promises were true. Their eyes *were* opened, and they *did* know good and evil, *but not as God did!* Thus, a half-truth presented as the whole truth is an untruth. God wanted Adam to know what the good *is* and what the evil *would* be, but instead he now would discover what the evil *was* and what the good *would have been!*

Instead of recognizing the evil from the summit of the good, they now must recognize the good from the abyss of evil. Often, experience is *not* the best teacher, for sometimes the tuition is too expensive!

- THE HIGHLIGHT OF GOD'S CREATION
- ABSOLUTELY UNIQUE
- MADE IN GOD'S IMAGE
- DECLARED KING OF CREATION
- COMMANDED NOT TO EAT OF THE TREE OF THE KNOWLEDGE OF GOOD AND EVIL
- ENCOURAGED TO EAT OF ALL OTHER TREES
- GIVEN A WIFE

SEVEN FACTS ABOUT ADAM

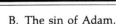

B. The sin of Adam.

1. He becomes the first human sinner.

Chronologically, Eve ate first, but theologically, Adam is declared by the New Testament to be the original sinner. The reason for this is that Adam was the head of the human race, and, therefore, responsible for its actions.

"Wherefore, as by one man sin entered into the world, and death by sin; and so death passed upon all men, for that all have sinned" (Rom. 5:12).

"But I fear, lest by any means, as the serpent beguiled Eve though his subtilty,

so your minds should be corrupted from the simplicity that is in Christ" (2 Cor. 11:3).

"And Adam was not deceived, but the woman being deceived was in the trangression" (1 Tim. 2:14).

2. He attempts (at first) to hide his nakedness before God (3:7). Apparently some drastic change occurred concerning Adam's physical as well as his spiritual condition. It may be that the bodies of Adam and Eve were, at creation, covered with a soft light of innocence. Our Lord was clothed with a light brighter than the sun during his transfiguration. (See Mt. 17:2.)

But now this protection is gone. In a desperate effort to correct the situation, they "sewed fig leaves together and made themselves aprons" (3:7).

We now have the first example of man-made religion in history. Religion is any attempt to clothe ourselves apart from the righteousness of Christ. Adam and Eve tried it with fig leaves. Men today try it with education, church membership, baptism, tithing, confirmation, good works, etc. But all to no avail.

"But we are all as an unclean thing, and all our righteousnesses are as filthy rags; and we all do fade as a leaf; and our iniquities, like the wind, have taken us away" (Isa. 64:6).

3. He attempts (at last) to hide himself from God.

"Adam and his wife hid themselves from the presence of the Lord . . ." (3:8).

This is the ultimate tragic result of sin. It not only separates man from God, but makes him actually desire to hide from God. But this cannot be done!

"O God, thou knowest my foolishness; and my sins are not hid from thee" (Ps. 69:5).

"Whither shall I go from thy spirit? or whither shall I flee from thy presence?" (Ps. 139:7).

"Fear them not therefore: for there is nothing covered, that shall not be revealed; and hid, that shall not be known" (Mt. 10:26).

"And the kings of the earth, and the great men, and the rich men, and the chief captains, and the mighty men, and every bondman, and every free man, hid themselves in the dens and in the rocks of the mountains; And said to the mountains and rocks, Fall on us, and hide us from the face of him that sitteth on the throne, and from the wrath of the Lamb: For the great day of his wrath is come; and who shall be able to stand?" (Rev. 6:15-17).

C. The redemption of God.

Up to this point we have seen only those attributes of God directly involved in his *creative* acts. These would include his power and wisdom. In this chapter, however, after man's sin, we are in-

Genesis 3

THE FIVEFOLD JUDGMENT UPON SIN

UPON MAN
Wearisome toil

UPON WOMAN
Suffering in childbirth
Subordination to man

UPON NATURE
Thorns and thistles
Aimlessness

UPON THE SERPENT
To crawl upon its belly

UPON SATAN
To suffer a fatal head wound

HE PROMISED ADAM A SAVIOR

HE SOUGHT ADAM OUT

HE CLOTHED ADAM

HE REMOVED ADAM FROM THE GARDEN

THE FOURFOLD GRACE OF GOD

troduced to his *redemptive* attributes, those of his holiness and his grace.

1. His holiness, as God deals with *sin*. God now pronounces a fivefold judgment sentence.
    a. Upon the man (3:17).
    "Cursed is the ground for thy sake." God is careful never to put a curse on Adam. He curses the serpent, Satan, and the soil, but not mankind. The reason, of course, is that he desired to redeem man and, therefore, would not curse that which he planned to later save. Even so, the unsaved man can expect nothing good in this life apart from Christ.
    "Yet man is born unto trouble, as the sparks fly upward" (Job 5:7).
    "Man that is born of a woman is of few days, and full of trouble" (Job 14:1).
    b. Upon the woman (3:16).
    "In sorrow thou shalt bring forth children." It should be noted that the suffer-

ing of childbirth is not so much a direct judgment from God, but rather an indirect result of sin. Sin always causes suffering, sickness, separation, and sorrow.
    c. Upon all nature (3:18).
    "Thorns . . . and thistles shall it bring forth." From this point on, man's paradise becomes a wilderness. The roses now contain thorns and the docile tiger suddenly becomes a hungry meat eater! This will continue to be the case until the curse is lifted during the millennium. In the New Testament Paul writes about all this in Romans 8:19–22:
    "For the earnest expectation of the creature waiteth for the manifestation of the sons of God. For the creature was made subject to vanity, not willingly, but by reason of him who hath subjected the same in hope, because the creature itself also shall be delivered from the bondage of corruption into the glorious liberty of the children of God. For we know that the whole creation groaneth and travaileth in pain together until now."
At this point, that immutable scientific principle called the Second Law of Thermodynamics came into being. This law states that when energy is being transformed from one state to another, some of it is turned into heat energy which cannot be converted back into useful form. In other words, this universe may be looked upon as a wound-up clock that is slowly running down. This law is expanded in Psalm 102:26 and Hebrews 1:10–12.
    "And, Thou, Lord, in the beginning hast laid the foundation of the earth; and the heavens are the works of thine hands: They shall perish; but thou remainest; and they all shall wax old as doth a garment; And as a vesture shalt thou fold them up, and they shall be changed: but thou art the same, and thy years shall not fail" (Heb. 1:10–12).

THE VICIOUS VOCABULARY OF SIN

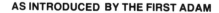

AS INTRODUCED BY THE FIRST ADAM		AS DEALT WITH BY THE SECOND ADAM	
BY **GEN. 2:17**	*HE INTRODUCED...* **DEATH**	*BY* **HEB. 2:9**	*HE DEALT WITH...* **DEATH**
BY **GEN. 3:7**	*HE INTRODUCED...* **NAKEDNESS**	*BY* **JN. 19:23**	*HE DEALT WITH...* **NAKEDNESS**
BY **GEN. 3:14**	*HE INTRODUCED...* **CURSE**	*BY* **GAL. 3:13**	*HE DEALT WITH...* **CURSE**
BY **GEN. 3:17**	*HE INTRODUCED...* **SORROW**	*BY* **ISA. 53:3**	*HE DEALT WITH...* **SORROW**
BY **GEN. 3:18**	*HE INTRODUCED...* **THORNS**	*BY* **JN. 19:5**	*HE DEALT WITH...* **THORNS**
BY **GEN. 3:19**	*HE INTRODUCED...* **SWEAT**	*BY* **LK. 22:44**	*HE DEALT WITH...* **SWEAT**
BY **GEN. 3:24**	*HE INTRODUCED...* **SWORD**	*BY* **JN. 19:34**	*HE DEALT WITH...* **SWORD**

d. Upon the serpent (3:14).

"And . . . God said unto the serpent . . . upon thy belly shalt thou go."

The serpent is not offered a chance to explain its actions as God allowed Adam and Eve to do. Judgment is passed out immediately. For lending its body to Satan, the serpent was cursed to crawl in the dust from that point on. Isaiah indicates that this judgment will continue to be binding upon the serpent even during the millennium!

"The wolf and the lamb shall feed together, and the lion shall eat straw like the bullock: and dust shall be the serpent's meat. They shall not hurt nor destroy in all my holy mountain, saith the Lord" (Isa. 65:25).

e. Upon the devil (3:15).

"And I will put enmity between thee and the woman, and between thy seed and her seed; it shall bruise thy head, and thou shalt bruise his heel" (Gen. 3:15).

At first glance this verse would merely seem to predict the natural hatred of man for snakes. But for centuries devout Bible students have seen a far more precious and profound truth underlying these words. For in this verse they claim to see no less than a thrilling prediction of the Cross and the resurrection, of the Savior's great victory over Satan. Theologically, then, verse 15 may be translated as follows:

"And there will be intense hatred between Satan and Christ. Eventually Christ will crush the head of Satan, while suffering a heel wound in the process."

This all-important verse is known as the "Proto-Evangel," the first Gospel.

See also:

"And the God of peace shall bruise Satan under your feet shortly. The grace of our Lord Jesus Christ be with you. Amen" (Rom. 16:20).

"But he was wounded for our transgressions, he was bruised for our iniquities: the chastisement of our peace was upon him; and with his stripes we are healed" (Isa. 53:5).

2. His grace, as God deals with sinners.

a. In seeking out Adam (3:9).

"And the Lord God called unto Adam." Sometimes foolish and wicked college professors tell their students that the Bible is simply a record of man's search after God; but it is instead the opposite. The Bible is a record of God's search after man! Here God takes the first step in reconciling man back to himself.

"Come now, and let us reason together, saith the Lord: though your sins be as scarlet, they shall be as white as snow; though they be red

like crimson, they shall be as wool" (Isa. 1:18).

"Ho, every one that thirsteth, come ye to the waters, and he that hath no money; come ye, buy, and eat; yea, come, buy wine and milk without money and without price. Wherefore do ye spend money for that which is not bread? and your labour for that which satisfieth not? hearken diligently unto me, and eat ye that which is good, and let your soul delight itself in fatness. Incline your ear, and come unto me: hear, and your soul shall live; and I will make an everlasting covenant with you, even the sure mercies of David" (Isa. 55:1-3).

"In the last day, that great day of the feast, Jesus stood and cried, saying, If any man thirst, let him come unto me, and drink. He that believeth on me, as the scripture hath said, out of his belly shall flow rivers of living water" (Jn. 7:37, 38).

"And the Spirit and the bride say, Come. And let him that heareth say, Come. And let him that is athirst come. And whosoever will, let him take the water of life freely" (Rev. 22:17).

"For the Son of man is come to seek and to save that which was lost" (Lk. 19:10).

b. In promising them a Savior (3:15).

c. In clothing them (3:21).

"God made coats of skins and clothed them."

Although we are not specifically told so, it would seem probable that some innocent animal had to die so that Adam and his wife might be clothed. Thus, here we have the first example of that great biblical doctrine, the innocent dying for the guilty.

"But he was wounded for our transgressions, he was bruised for our iniquities: the chastisement of our peace was upon him; and with his stripes we are healed. All we like sheep have gone astray; we have turned every one to his own way; and the Lord hath laid on him the iniquity of us all" (Isa. 53:5, 6).

"For Christ also hath once suffered for sins, the just for the unjust, that he might bring us to God, being put to death in the flesh but quickened by the Spirit" (1 Pet. 3:18).

Note: We have already seen the first symbol in the Bible when the serpent became a type for sin. We now observe the second symbol—righteousness and salvation are likened to right clothes. (Compare Isa. 64:6 with Rev. 19:7, 8.)

"But we are all as an unclean thing, and all our righteousnesses are as filthy rags; and we all do fade as a leaf; and our iniquities, like the wind, have taken us away" (Isa. 64:6).

"Let us be glad and rejoice, and give honour to him: for the marriage of the Lamb is come, and his wife hath made herself ready. And to her was granted that she should be arrayed in fine linen, clean and white: for the fine linen is the righteousness of saints" (Rev. 19:7, 8).

d. In removing them from the Garden of Eden (3:24).

"So he drove out the man."

Man's expulsion from Eden by God was really an act of mercy rather than judgment. As we are told in 3:22, God did this to prevent mankind from partaking of the tree of life and living forever in immorality. Adolf Hitler killed himself a few days after reaching his fifty-sixth birthday. Yet during his brief life span, he was directly responsible for the slaughter of literally millions of human beings by shooting, bombing, hanging, burning, gassing, and other forms of torture and death too horrible to mention. But what if this Nazi monster had lived to be 500 or even 5000? Or worse still, what if he could have lived forever? This is why God drove Adam from Eden.

"He placed . . . cherubims and a flaming sword" (3:24).

The cherubims are apparently a special kind of angelic being who concern themselves with matters relating to the holiness of God. (See Ex. 25:18–22; Ezek. 10:1–20; Rev. 4:6–8.) This is the first of two kinds of angels mentioned in the Bible. The other kind are known as the seraphims. (See Isa. 6.)

"In the year that king Uzziah died I saw also the Lord sitting upon a throne, high and lifted up, and his train filled the temple. Above it stood the seraphims: each one had six wings; with twain he covered his face, and with twain he covered his feet, and with twain he did fly. And one cried unto another, and said, Holy, holy, holy, is the Lord of hosts: the whole earth is full of his glory. And the posts of the door moved at the voice of him that cried, and the house was filled with smoke" (Isa. 6:1–4).

"To keep the way of the tree of life" (3:24).

At this point, the tree of life disappears from the pages of the Bible. It reappears once again during the millennial and eternal age.

"And he shewed me a pure river of water of life, clear as crystal, proceeding out of the throne of God and of the Lamb. In the midst of the street of it, and on either side of the river, was there the tree of life, which bare twelve manner of fruits, and yielded her fruit every month: and the leaves of the tree were for the healing of the nations" (Rev. 22:1, 2).

D. The Martyrdom of Abel (Gen. 4).

1. Eve gives birth to Cain and exclaims, "I have gotten a man from the Lord" (4:1). Here she apparently felt this baby was the fulfillment of Genesis 3:15. She would soon know differently. Abel is then born (4:2).

The birth of these two babies illustrates the fourth of four methods God has chosen to bring human beings into this world.

a. Adam—born without father or mother.
b. Eve—born without a mother.
c. Christ—born without a father.
d. All others—both with father and mother.

2. Cain brings a bloodless offering to God and is rejected (4:5). Not only was the sacrifice bloodless, but it had already been cursed by God; therefore, Cain added insult to injury. (See 3:17.) Cain may have thought it to be far more refined and cultured to bring fresh fruit and vegetables rather than a bloody animal offering, but not so!

"There is a way which seemeth right unto a man, but the end thereof are the ways of death" (Prov. 14:12).

We have in this verse the first plank of that great scriptural platform of truth that without the shedding of blood there is no remission of sin. (See Lev. 17:11; Heb. 9:22.)

"And almost all things are by the law purged with blood; and without shedding of blood is no remission" (Heb. 9:22).

Abel offers a lamb sacrifice and is accepted (4:4).

Dr. Barnhouse has written the following:

"The highway to the cross was now firmly established. Here the first lamb is seen, one lamb for one man. Later, at the Passover, there will be one lamb for one household (Ex. 12). Then, on the Day of Atonement, there will be one sacrifice for the nation (Lev. 16). Finally, it is Christ who takes away the sin of the world" (Jn. 1:29).

This was God's way then of illustrating the awesome power of the bleeding Lamb. One Lamb saves a man, then a household, then a nation, and finally is available through the Lamb of God for the whole world.

3. Cain slays his brother. Cain now becomes the first murderer (4:8). He also becomes the first human liar (see 4:9).

4. Cain is driven from the blessings of God. He marries one of his sisters (4:17; 5:4) and dwells in the land of Nod. Let us observe some recorded facts concerning earth's first civilization.

a. *Cain* builds the first city and names it Enoch (after his own son), which means "dedication." This urban project was no doubt an attempt to counteract God's curse in 4:12.

b. *Lamech,* Cain's great-great-great-grandson becomes:

(1) the first recorded polygamist (4:19)
(2) the first recorded songwriter (the word "speech" in 4:23 may refer to a poem or ballad)
(3) the second recorded murderer (4:23)

c. *Jabal* becomes the inventor of the tent and developer of the Nomadic life style. He also devised formal systems for domesticating and commercially producing animals apart from sheep. His name means "wanderer" (4:20).

d. *Jubal* becomes the inventor of both stringed and wind musical instruments. His name means "sound" (4:21).

e. *Tubal-Cain* becomes the inventor of metallurgy both in bronze and iron (4:22).

E. The ministry of Enoch.

1. He is one of two men who was said to have walked with God before the flood. (The other was Noah—see 6:9.) Note: It does not say he walked with God, however, until his first son, Methuselah, was born. In the Hebrew language, the name Methuselah literally means, "When he is dead it shall be sent." Why did Enoch walk with God? Because God had apparently told him that when Methuselah died the world was going to be destroyed by the terrible flood. This is probably why Methuselah lived longer than any man in the history of the world (969 years), for God was not willing that any should perish and was giving sinful mankind as much time for repentance as possible.

"The Lord is not slack concerning his promise, as some men count slackness; but is longsuffering to us-ward, not willing that any should perish, but that all should come to repentance" (2 Pet. 3:9).

"Who will have all men to be saved, and to come unto the knowledge of the truth" (1 Tim. 2:4).

2. Enoch was the first recorded preacher and he preached on the coming judgment. In Jude 1:14, 15 we actually have his recorded message:

"And Enoch also, the seventh from Adam, prophesied of these, saying, Behold, the Lord cometh with ten thousands of his saints, To execute judgment upon all, and to convince all that are ungodly among them of all their ungodly deeds which they have ungodly committed, and of all their hard speeches which ungodly sinners have spoken against him."

3. Enoch was a man of great faith (Heb. 11:5). "By faith Enoch was translated that he should not see death; and was not found, because God had translated him: for before his translation he had this testimony, that he pleased God."

But just how did Enoch demonstrate this great faith ascribed to him? Well, here was a preacher who fervently spoke of Christ's *second* coming centuries before his *first* coming had taken place.

4. Enoch was one of two human beings who got to heaven without dying physically. (For the other, see 2 Ki. 2:11.) Someday, however, millions of Christians will experience the same thing.

"Behold, I shew you a mystery; We shall not all sleep, but we shall all be changed, in a moment, in the twinkling of an eye, at the last trump: for the trumpet shall sound, and the dead shall be raised incorruptible, and we shall be changed" (1 Cor. 15:51, 52).

"For the Lord himself shall descend from heaven with a shout, with the voice of the archangel, and with the trump of God: and the dead in Christ shall rise first: Then we which are alive and remain shall be caught up together with them in the clouds, to meet the Lord in the air: and so shall we ever be with the Lord" (1 Thess. 4:16, 17).

III. The Condemnation of All Things (Gen. 6–9).

A. The conditions prior to the Flood.

1. A great population explosion took place (6:1). Man has consistently broken every single command given by God with the exception of the very first one. This one he has consistently obeyed! "Be fruitful, and multiply, and fill the earth . . ." (Gen. 1:28).

2. There was an outpouring of satanic activity (6:2).

3. All humanity had become depraved. Wickedness, both in word and deed, was both universal and unparalleled (6:5, 11).

4. As a result of all this, "it repented the Lord that he had made man on earth, and it grieved him at his heart" (6:6). The Hebrew *(nacham)* and Greek *(metanoia)* words for repentance have both a literal and a theological meaning.

a. the literal meaning—to be eased, to be comforted *(nacham)*

b. the theological meaning—to change one's mind *(metanoia)*

Combining both meanings, it may be said that God's original creation had ceased to reflect his glory (see Rev. 4:11) to the extent that he was no longer comforted by it. He, therefore, changed his previous course of action toward humanity and determined to destroy it by a mighty universal flood.

5. The Flood would occur 120 years from this point (6:3).

B. The salvation through the Flood.

1. God informs Noah (who had found grace in his sight) to construct a 450 × 75 × 45-foot floating barge.

Some have limited the word *law* to the Old Testament, and the word *grace* to the New Testament. But this is a serious error. Here in Genesis 6, early in Old Testament history, and long before the Mosaic Law, Noah experiences the marvelous *grace* of God. A more correct summary of the Old and New Testament would thus be:

a. The Old Testament is the account of how God *in grace* dealt with the nation of Israel and sinners.

b. The New Testament is the account of

how God in grace deals with the church and sinners.

2. Noah was to cover both the outside and inside of the ark with pitch. The Hebrew word here translated pitch is *kaphar*. In almost every other instance in the Old Testament *kaphar* is translated by the word *atonement*. (See Ex. 30:10.) To atone is to cover with blood. As the oily pitch protected the ark from the Flood judgment, so the blood of Christ protects the believer from the sin judgment. Thus far, we may note the following Old Testament types:
   a. Enoch is a type of the church, being saved *from* the Flood judgment. (The church will not go through the great tribulation.)
   b. Noah is a type of Israel, being saved *through* the Flood judgment. (Israel will go through the great tribulation.)

3. Noah gathered a male and female of all earth's animals (including seven pairs of clean animals, such as the ox and lamb) and, along with his wife, three sons, and their wives, at the command of God, boarded the ark.

   This passage (Gen. 7:1) is the first to record the word *come* in the Bible.
   "And the Lord said unto Noah, Come thou and all thy house into the ark. . . ."
   The final reference to this word is:
   "And the Spirit and the bride say, Come. And let him that heareth say, Come. And let him that is athirst come. And whosoever will, let him take the water of life freely" (Rev. 22:17).

4. God "remembered" Noah during the flood as he later would remember:
   a. Lot in Sodom.
      "And it came to pass, when God destroyed the cities of the plain, that God remembered Abraham, and sent Lot out of the midst of the overthrow, when he overthrew the cities in the which Lot dwelt" (Gen. 19:29).
   b. Israel in Egypt.
      "And God heard their groaning, and God remembered his covenant with Abraham, with Isaac, and with Jacob" (Ex. 2:24).
      "And I have also heard the groaning of the children of Israel, whom the Egyptians keep in bondage; and I have remembered my covenant" (Ex. 6:5).
   c. The thief on the cross.
      "And he said unto Jesus, Lord, remember me when thou comest into thy kingdom" (Lk. 23:42).

5. The flood passes and the ark rests upon the mountains of Ararat. Noah is told by God to "be fruitful and multiply upon the earth" (8:17; 9:1). Adam had once heard similar words (1:28), but here after the flood the word *subdue* is left out. Scofield writes the following concerning Genesis 1:28.
   "This is the divine magna charta for all true scientific and material process. Man

began with a mind that was perfect in its finite capacity for learning, but he did not begin knowing all the secrets of the universe. He is commanded to 'subdue,' i.e., acquire a knowledge and mastery over his material environment, to bring its elements into the service of the race." (*New Scofield Bible*, p. 4)
But now Eden's sin and the Flood judgment had so radically changed man's environment that he would find it quite impossible to fully subdue anything.

These verses in Genesis, if rightly understood, help explain a rather strange miracle performed by Christ in the New Testament. It all began when Simon Peter came to Jesus concerning the needed payment of a certain tribute tax. The Savior responded by ordering his apostle to "go thou to the sea, and cast a hook, and take up the fish that first cometh up; and when thou hast opened his mouth thou shalt find a piece of money: that take, and give unto them for me and thee" (Mt. 17:27). This miracle, if properly considered, demonstrates more clearly the Savior's perfect *humanity* than his *deity*, for Adam could have (and possibly did) exercised this same power over both fish and fowl. Again, consider the divine command given to Adam:
   "Be fruitful, and multiply, and fill the earth, and subdue it; and have dominion over the fish of the sea, and over the fowl of the air, and over every living thing that moveth upon the earth" (Gen. 1:28).

6. God now establishes a rainbow covenant with Noah. The covenant elements are as follows:
   a. God would never again destroy the earth of men through a flood (8:21, 22; 9:9–17). But the earth will be destroyed again, this time through a fire. (See 2 Pet. 3:1–13.)
      "But the day of the Lord will come as a thief in the night; in the which the heavens shall pass away with a great noise, and the elements shall melt with fervent heat, the earth also and the works that are therein shall be burned up" (2 Pet. 3:10).
   b. God would require the life of a man who murdered another man (9:6).
   c. The order and seasons of nature are confirmed (8:22).
   d. The fear of animals for man is prophesied (9:2).
   e. The flesh of animals for man's diet is permitted (9:3).

C. The tragedy following the Flood (9:20–29).
   1. Noah becomes drunken from his own vineyard and exposes himself within his tent.
   2. His son Ham and grandson Canaan view this nakedness. Canaan especially, incurs the wrath of his grandfather for the part he played in this.
   3. Noah predicts the future physical and spiritual life style of his three sons and their descendants.

4. Noah dies at the age of 950. The ultimate tragedy in his life may be seen by the fact that no spiritual accomplishments whatsoever are recorded during his final 350 years. He apparently experienced that thing so dreaded by Paul—being set on a shelf by God. (See 1 Cor. 9:19-27.)

> "But I keep under my body, and bring it into subjection: lest that by any means, when I have preached to others, I myself should be a castaway" (1 Cor. 9:27).

IV. The Confusion of All Things (Gen. 10-11).

A. The arrogance of man.

A rebel named Nimrod (grandson of Ham) instigates a religious building program (consisting of both an astrological tower and a city) on the plains of Shinar near Babylon (11:1-4).

B. The judgment of God.

God punishes this evil attempt and separates mankind into small ethnic groups by confusing their once universal language into many dialects (11:5-9).

C. The origin of nations.

The ancient world is now settled by the descendants of Noah's three sons.

1. The descendants of Japheth (10:2-5).
Some of his descendants and the peoples they founded would be:
   a. Gomer (Germany)
   b. Magog, Tubal, and Mechech (Russia)
   c. Madai (Persia)
   d. Javan (Greece)
   e. Tiras (Italy)
   f. Togarmah (Armenia)
   g. Tarshish (Spain)
   h. Kittim (Cyprus)
2. The descendants of Ham (10:6-20).
Some of his descendants and the peoples they founded would be:
   a. Cush (Ethiopia)
   b. Mizraim (Egypt)
   c. Phut (Africa)
   d. Canaan (the Canaanites of Palestine)
   e. Nimrod (Babylon and Assyria)
   f. Sidon (Phoenicia)
   g. Heth (Hittites)
   h. Jebus (the Jebusites, the occupants of Jerusalem prior to David's reign)
   i. Pilistim (the Philistines)
   j. Sin (possible founder of the oriental peoples, China, Japan, India, etc.)
3. The descendants of Shem (10:21-32; 11:10-32).
   a. Through Abraham, Isaac, and Jacob: the nation Israel.
   b. Through Abraham, Ishmael, and Esau: the Middle East Arab countries.

Anthropologist Arthur Custance writes:

> "And thus we conclude that from the family of Noah have sprung all the peoples of the world, prehistoric and historic. The events described in connection with Genesis 6 to 10 and particularly the prophetic statements of Noah himself in Genesis 9:25-28 with respect to the future of his three sons, Shem, Ham, and Japheth, together combine to provide us

NOAH—GENESIS 9:20–27

THE FAILURE OF NOAH: DRUNKENNESS
THE SIN OF CANAAN: UNKNOWN, PERHAPS THAT OF HOMOSEXUALITY

THE THREEFOLD PROPHECY OF NOAH

CONCERNING HAM AND CANAAN:	CONCERNING JAPHETH:	CONCERNING SHEM:
General servitude to seed of Shem and Japheth.	"God shall enlarge Japheth, and he shall dwell in the tents of Shem."	
"A SERVANT OF SERVANTS"	**"GOD SHALL ENLARGE JAPHETH"**	**"BLESSED BE THE LORD GOD OF SHEM"**
• Joshua, David, and Solomon subdued them. • Alexander the Great subdued them. • The Romans subdued them.	• Since 539 B.C., with the defeat of the Babylonians by Cyrus the Great, no Semitic or Hamitic race has succeeded in breaking the world supremacy of the Japhethic race.	• Here is obviously a reference to the special favor bestowed upon Shem's descendants, beginning with Abraham, and ending in a Bethlehem manger.
TECHNICAL PROFICIENCY	**"AND HE SHALL DWELL IN THE TENTS OF SHEM."**	
The famous Christian anthropologist Arthur C. Custance states that all the earliest civilizations of note were founded and carried to the highest technical proficiency by Hamitic peoples.	This glorious prophecy is fully explained by Paul in Rom. 11:13-25.	

THE THREEFOLD CONTRIBUTION OF NOAH'S SONS

HAM	JAPHETH	SHEM
• Technical proficiency. • Responsible for man's physical well-being.	• Application of philosophy. • Development of the scientific method. • Responsible for man's mental well-being.	• Religious insights. • Responsible for man's spiritual well-being.

with the most reasonable account of the early history of mankind, a history which, rightly understood, does not at all require us to believe that modern man began with the stature of an ape and only reached a civilized state after a long, long evolutionary history, but made a fresh start as a single family who carried with them into an unpeopled earth the accumulated heritage of the pre-flood world.

In summary, then, what we have endeavored to show in this paper may be set forth briefly as follows:

(1) The geographical distribution of fossil remains is such that they are most logically explained by treating them as marginal representatives of a widespread and, in part, forced dispersion of people from a single multiplying population, established at a point more or less central to them all, which sent forth successive

waves of migrants, each wave driving the previous one further towards the periphery.

(2) The most degraded specimens are representatives of this general movement who were driven into the least hospitable areas where they suffered physical degeneration as a consequence of the circumstances in which they were forced to live.

(3) The extraordinary physical variability of their remains stems from the fact that they were members of small, isolated, strongly inbred bands; whereas the cultural similarities which link together even the most widely dispersed of them indicate a common origin for them all.

(4) What is true of fossil man is equally true of vanished and of living primitive societies.

(5) All these initially dispersed populations are of one basic stock—the Hamitic family of Genesis 10.

(6) They were subsequently displaced or overwhelmed by the Indo-Europeans (i.e., Japhethites) who nevertheless inherited, or adopted and extensively built upon, their technology and so gained the upper hand in each geographical area where they spread.

(7) Throughout this movement, both in prehistoric and historic times, there were never any human beings who did not belong within the family of Noah and his descendants.

(8) Finally, this thesis is strengthened by the evidence of history, which shows that migration has always tended to follow this pattern, has frequently been accompanied by instances of degeneration both of individuals or whole tribes, and usually results in the establishment of a general pattern of cultural relationships, which are paralleled to those that archaeology has since revealed from antiquity." (*Genesis and Early Man*, pp. 56, 57)

QUESTIONS AND ANSWERS ABOUT GENESIS 1-11

1. How vast is our universe?

It is so vast that it takes a beam of light (which travels some 700 million miles per hour) over 100,000 years just to cover the distance length of our galaxy called the Milky Way. But our galaxy is only one among many billions in the known universe. To illustrate the size of our universe, consider the following four examples:

a. paper stack model

(1) Let us say the thickness of a sheet of paper represents the distance from the earth to the sun (some ninety-three million miles).

(2) To represent the distance to the nearest star

we would need a seventy-one-foot high stack of paper.

(3) To cover the diameter of our Milky Way galaxy would require a 310-mile high stack.

(4) To reach the edge of the *known* universe would demand a pile of paper sheets thirty-one *million* miles high.

b. orange and grain of sand model

(1) Here an orange would represent the sun.

(2) A grain of sand is the earth, circling the orange at a distance of thirty feet.

(3) Pluto (most remote planet in our solar system) is another grain of sand, circling the orange at ten city blocks away.

(4) Alpha Centauri (the nearest star) is 1300 miles away from the orange.

c. hollow sun illustration

(1) If the sun were hollow, one million, three hundred thousand earths could fit inside.

(2) A star named Antares (if hollow) could hold sixty-four million of our suns.

(3) In the constellation of Hercules there is a star which could contain 100 million of Antares.

(4) The largest known star, Epsilon, could easily swallow up several million stars the size of the one in Hercules!

d. the relative speed illustration

(1) Our earth is traveling around its own axis at 1000 m.p.h.

(2) It moves around the sun at 67,000 m.p.h.

(3) It is carried by the sun across our galaxy at a speed of 64,000 m.p.h.

(4) It moves in orbit around our galaxy at 481,000 m.p.h.

(5) It travels through space at one million, three hundred and fifty thousand m.p.h.

(6) Every twenty-four hours we cover 57,360,000 miles.

(7) Each year we travel 20,936,400,000 miles across empty space.

All the above is, of course, but a feeble attempt to illustrate the magnitude of space and of a universe which contains as many stars as there are grains of sand on all the seashores of the world. Furthermore, in Psalm 147:4 (also Isa. 40:26), we are told that God has both numbered and named each star.

"He telleth the number of the stars; he calleth them all by their names" (Ps. 147:4).

"Lift up your eyes on high, and behold who hath created these things, that bringeth out their host by number: he calleth them all by names by the greatness of his might, for that he is strong in power; not one faileth" (Isa. 40:26).

But more glorious than all this is the statement that this same omnipotent and omniscient God "healeth the broken in heart and bindeth up their wounds" (Ps. 147:3).

"Great is our Lord, and of great power: his understanding is infinite" (Ps. 147:5).

2. How minute is our universe?

Simply stated, it is as unbelievably small as it is big. Consider the following:

a. All material in the universe consists of *atoms*. Atoms in turn are made up of three "building blocks," which are *protons* and *neutrons* (which two go to make up the center of an atom called the nucleus), and *electrons* (which circle the nucleus as our earth does the sun).

b. On the tip of a ball point pen are so many atoms that if they were carried by an army, marching four abreast, an atom to a man, it would take over 20,000 years for a march-past.

c. It would take 25 trillion protons laid side by side to span a linear inch.

d. There are as many protons in a cubic inch of copper as there are drops of water in the oceans of the world, or grains of sand on the seashores of our earth.

e. The size of an electron is to a dust speck as the dust speck is to the entire earth.

f. The *space* between an electron and the nucleus is 10,000 times as great as the size of that nucleus. For example, if the outer shell of electrons in an atom were the size of the Houston Astrodome, the nucleus would be the size of a Ping-Pong ball in the center of that stadium.

Question: If most of the atom is empty space, why does a table top offer so much resistance when you push at it with your finger?

Answer: The surface of the table (like the tip of one's finger) consists of a wall of electrons, belonging to the outermost layer of atoms in both objects. Both the speed and force attraction of these electrons thus prohibit your finger from going through the table as a fast-moving bicycle wheel would prevent you from placing your finger through the spokes.

3. How much energy exists within our universe?

a. The protons and neutrons within the nucleus of an atom are held together with a density of one billion tons per cubic inch. This is around forty pounds of energy between each proton.

b. This energy force is one followed by thirty eight zeros times stronger than regular gravitational forces. How big is this number? It is over 100 trillion times larger than the number of all the grains of sand on earth's seashores.

c. German physicist Otto Gail has calculated that a single drop of gasoline, if totally utilized in an automobile, would be sufficient for 400 journeys around the world (a trip involving ten million miles).

d. Albert Einstein estimated the total amount of energy released from one ounce of water could easily lift 200 million tons of steel one mile above the earth.

e. The various stars and galaxies were created by the conversion of energy into mass. It has been determined that the amount of energy used in the creation of only one gram of matter (1/450th of a pound) is equal to 2.5 times the amount of energy generated by Niagara Falls in one entire day. This would be ten million kilowatts.

4. What mysterious secrets lie within our universe?

A prominent scientist once said that man's universe is both unknown and unknowable. Consider:

a. Quasars: These are light sources discovered by Dr. M. Schmidt of the California Institute of Technology in 1963. They are relatively small, yet produce more energy than a cluster of ten trillion stars!

b. Super novaes: These are stars that suddenly increase their luminosity by more than ten million times.

c. Neutron stars: This is a star that implodes (falls in on itself) rather than exploding. The gravitational forces would crush the atoms into nuclear particles called neutrons. A neutron star would have an unbelievable density, as a teaspoon of its material would weigh a billion tons on earth. In fact, its weight would be sufficient to drive itself all the way through our earth. If we collapsed the whole earth to neutron star density, it would be approximately 300 feet in diameter. If you took all the human beings in the world today and put them in one raindrop, you would have such density as exists in a neutron star.

d. Black holes: A black hole occurs when an imploding star continues beyond the neutron stage. Its gravitational forces thus become so strong that even light itself cannot escape. Dr. Kip Thorne, of the California Institute of Technology, writes:

"A black hole is the end product of the catastrophic collapse of a really large star, the ultimate concentration of matter. We believe a black hole is an extremely smooth structure; it can never have ripples or mountains. Anything it traps can never escape. The black hole can neither split nor decrease in size; it can only grow, and nothing can prevent it from growing. Ultimately if the universe itself does not collapse and die first, the black holes will eat up all the matter in our galaxy. Already, as much as one ten thousandth of the universe might be down black holes. We would like to sweep this fact under the rug, but occasionally we drag it out and look it in the face and shudder." (*National Geographic,* May, 1974)

e. Time-light mysteries: As an object reaches the speed of light, time (we are told) slows down. Thus, a rocket ship manned by several men sets out to explore the universe traveling at near the speed of light.

Destination	Years lapsed aboard ship	Years lapsed on earth
(1) Alpha Centauri (our closest star)	3 years, 6 months	ten years
(2) Center of our Milky Way	21 years	50,000 years
(3) Andromeda Galaxy (our nearest galaxy)	28 years	2 million years

f. Length and weight-time mysteries: Not only does time on a space craft (moving at near the speed of light) slow down, but its length and weight are also affected. Imagine a space ship which is 1000 feet long and weighs 1000 tons. At 162,000 miles-per-second, it would measure only 500 feet, but weigh 2000 tons.

It has furthermore been speculated that if a thirty-year old man could somehow remove himself to a planet exactly thirty light years away from our earth and from there point a telescope back to earth, he could actually watch himself being born.

5. How complex is our universe?

Here we refer to life itself. The wonders of the atom

and the glory of the galaxies are but drab tinker toys when compared to the miracle of living organisms.

a. The smallest insect on this earth is made up of millions of living cells. There are some seventy-five trillion such cells in the body of an average man. But each individual cell is unbelievably complex. It has been demonstrated that the simplest living cell is vastly more complicated than the most sophisticated giant computer on earth.

b. Each cell is a world brimming with as many as 200 trillion tiny groups of atoms called protein molecules. It is a micro-universe in itself.

c. The largest molecule is called the DNA (deoxyribonucleic acid). The DNA strand carries the hereditary information from the parent to the offspring in all living things. It contains the genetic code and determines whether you will turn out to be a man, mushroom, dandelion, or dinosaur.

INDICATIONS OF A RECENT CREATION DATE

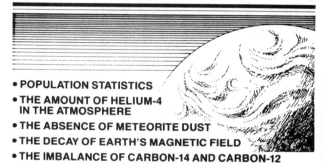

- **POPULATION STATISTICS**
- **THE AMOUNT OF HELIUM-4 IN THE ATMOSPHERE**
- **THE ABSENCE OF METEORITE DUST**
- **THE DECAY OF EARTH'S MAGNETIC FIELD**
- **THE IMBALANCE OF CARBON-14 AND CARBON-12**

d. The total length of the DNA strand in one cell is six feet. If all the DNA strands in the body were bunched up they could fit into a box the size of an ice cube. But if unwound and joined together, the string could stretch from the earth to the sun and back more than 400 times.

e. Each of the seventy-five trillion cells in a man's body contains the information found in all other cells. Thus, a cell in a man's little toe has all the data in its DNA for making another man physically identical to himself.

f. If the coded DNA instructions of a single human cell were put into English, they would fill a 1000-volume encyclopedia.

g. During cell division, two strands of DNA (called the double helix), which have been interwoven around each other in ladder-like fashion, separate to form a new cell. It is believed that the rotation during this unwinding occurs at the rate of more than seventy-five turns a second. This would be somewhat like attempting in a split second to uncoil and separate a huge cathedral packed from top to bottom with twisted and intertwined microphone cord. After the double helix is separated it then duplicates itself into a new cell. This duplication is so accurate that it would correspond to a rate of error of less than one letter in an entire set of the *Encyclopedia Britannica.*

h. A human cell in a laboratory, free from bodily influence, may divide some fifty times before dying. If all of our cells divided that often, we would eventually reach a weight of more than eighty trillion tons.

6. When was the universe created?

Some scientists would confidently tell us its origin occurred via a big bang from five to fifty billion years ago. How are these dates arrived at? One time calendar is called radiometric dating—the dating of rocks. In certain rocks the element uranium 238 decays into lead 206 with a half-life of 4.5 billion years (that is, the decay involves 50% of the original uranium each 4.5 billion years). It is claimed, therefore, that the age of a rock may be determined through this method.

However, there are serious problems at times with radiometric dating. For example, radiometric dating has shown certain rocks from volcanoes in Russia to be five billion years old, whereas it is known they were formed within the last 200 years.

In opposition to the above radical ancient dates, a number of creation scientists now feel there is mounting evidence that our earth may be much younger than supposed, perhaps less than 12,000 years old. These indications are as follows:

a. Population statistics. If man appeared over one million years ago, the present world population would be thousands of times greater than it actually is. In fact, our entire galaxy could not provide the needed space for so many.

The present world population is around 4.3 billion. Assuming the average life span to be seventy years and the average generation length to be thirty-five years, then starting with one family, the present world population would result in about thirty doublings. These doublings would carry us back in history from today to around 3500 B.C. This date is suggested by several creationist scientists to mark the time of the Flood.

Thus, the creation model dovetails beautifully with known world population statistics. But what of the evolutionary model? Morris writes:

"Now, if the first man appeared one million years ago, and these very conservative growth rates applied during that period, the world population would be at present 10 (27000 zeros following) people. However, no more than 10 (with 100 zeros) people could be crammed into the known universe!" (*Science and Creation,* p. 154)

b. The amount of helium-4 in the atmosphere. This suggests that our atmosphere is less than 15,000 years old.

c. The absence of meteorite dust. Some fifteen million tons of nickel meteorite dust settle to earth each year. If the earth has indeed existed for five billion years, then there should now be a layer of this dust at least 200 feet thick all over the planet. Of course, no such layer is found.

d. The decay of earth's magnetic field. This field, it has been shown, has a half-life of 1400 years. This means it is weakened by 50 percent each fourteen centuries. It also means the magnetic field was twice as strong 1400 years ago as it is now, four times as strong 2800 years ago, and so on. Only 7000 years ago it must have been thirty-two times as strong. It is very doubtful that it could have been much stronger than this.

e. The imbalance of carbon-14 and carbon-12. It can be shown that it would take a period of 30,000

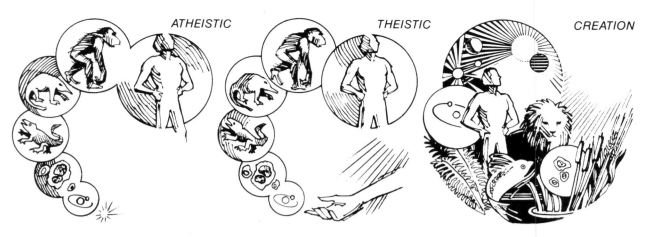

ATHEISTIC   THEISTIC   CREATION

THREE VIEWS ON THE ORIGIN OF LIFE

BELIEF	ATHEISTIC MATERIALISM	THEISTIC EVOLUTION	SPECIAL CREATION
Source	Accidental arrangement of molecules	God through evolution	God in six literal days
Time	One billion years ago	One billion years ago	Less than 10,000 years
Method	Mutations	Mutations	Supernatural act from the hand of God
Purpose	No purpose	To glorify God	To glorify God
First Man	Some remote, sub-human male ape	Some remote, sub-human male ape	Adam
First Woman	Some remote sub-human female ape	Some remote sub-human female ape	Eve
View of Gen. 1–3; Rom. 5:12–21	Pure myth	Spiritual allegory	Historical fact
Proponent	Darwin and his followers	Those who would attempt to reconcile Moses and Darwin	Moses
Reason for View	Contempt for supernatural possibility	Mistaken view that evolution has been proven and must be accepted	Literal interpretation of Genesis 1; 2
Problem	First law of thermodynamics, second law of thermodynamics, law of biogenesis	Cannot take at face value (Gen. 1–2; Rom. 5:12-21)	No real problem
Scriptural Proof	None	None	Gen. 1:31; 2:1–3; Ex. 20:11; 31:17; Ps. 33:6–9; I Cor. 11:8–9; 15:39; I Tim. 2:13
Scientific Support	None	None	First law of thermodynamics, second law of thermodynamics, law of biogenesis

years to attain an equilibrium between these two. However, at present C-14 still exceeds C-12 by some 50 percent.

The above are but five of over eighty facts which would indicate a recent creation date.

  f. Another time calendar is known as the radiocarbon method. This method, unlike the first three, is used only in determining the age of organic fossils. Radioactive carbon is formed in the earth's upper atmosphere resulting from the incoming cosmic radiation and atmospheric nitrogen-14. It then unites with oxygen to form carbon dioxide and is absorbed by all plants and animals. At the moment of death, plants and animals cease to absorb C-14. It then begins to decay back into nitrogen 14. This has a half-life of 5730 years. Five "half-lives" of C-14 would equal 29,000 years, and would leave only $^1/_{32}$ of the original C-14 content. Therefore, the C-14 method becomes increasingly weak past a few thousand years. As with the other dating methods, C-14 has its problems. Many living systems are not in equilibrium for the C-14 exchange. It has been found that the shells of living mollusks may show radiocarbon ages up to 2300 years.

The amount of natural carbon may have varied in the past. It is known that the earth once had far more vegetation than today. This is indicated by the vast amounts of coal deposits now known all over the world. Consequently, organisms living at that time would be subjected to only a very small C-14/C-12 ratio, and their remains now would contain no radio carbon at all, even if they had lived 6000 years ago. On the other hand, during the ice age there would have been much less C-12 than during the vegetation age.

However, one must exercise care in attempting to pinpoint exactly a recent creation date. For example, the Irish seventeenth century theologian Archbishop James Ussher and his contemporary Dr. John Lightfoot stated that creation week occurred on October 18-24 in the year 4004 B.C., and that the creation of Adam took place on Friday of that week, October 23, 4004 B.C., at 9:00 A.M., forty-fifth meridian time!

7. How did life come into being?

The real question today is not the survival of the species, but rather the *arrival* of it. Three theories have been advocated to explain the problem of origin.

a. Atheistic materialism.

This interesting theory boldly assures us that everything once came from nothing. In other words, if one gives enough mud enough time, it will, all by itself, produce the music of a Beethoven, the paintings of a Raphael, the writings of a Shakespeare, and the teachings of a Christ.

Question: How long would it take one million monkeys typing away day and night on one million typewriters for just one monkey to accidentally type out the first ten words in the Bible? ("In the beginning God created the heaven and the earth.")

Answer: Consider a rock which reached from the earth to the nearest star (some twenty-six trillion miles away). Once every million years a tiny bird flies to this massive rock and removes the smallest grain of sand from it. When four rocks this size have been completely carried away, then one of those monkeys will have accidentally typed out Genesis 1:1.

But this accomplishment would be absolutely nothing as compared to the probabilities that a living cell would by random processes be formed. Consider the following: Dr. Harold Morowitz of Yale estimated the theoretical limits for the smallest free-living thing which could duplicate itself. It would require 239 individual protein molecules. What are the chances that the first protein molecule would form all their amino acids into left-handed chains? (For some unknown reason all life consists only of these left-handed protein molecule chains). Well, the minimal number of amino acids in a protein is 410. This then would be like flipping a coin 410 times and coming up with heads *every* time! The answer is one chance in 10^{123} (the figure 1 followed by 123 zeros). But then even *if* this occurred in one protein, it would have to be repeated in at least 238 other proteins also. The chances are now one in 10^{29345} (one followed by 29,345 zeros). This would be about twenty $8\frac{1}{2} \times 11$ pages of typed zeros! How big is this number? Consider the following:

There are 10^{18} seconds in 15 billion years.
The known universe weighs 7×10^{41} pounds.
The universe contains 5×10^{78} atoms.
The universe contains 10^{130} electrons.

Conclusions: Suppose each atom could expand until it was the size of the present universe. There would then be 3×10^{157} atoms in the universe.

By comparison, the odds against a single protein forming by chance in earth's entire history is 4000 times larger than the number of atoms in this super-universe. Imagine an amoeba traveling a line stretched across our known universe, some fifteen billion light years in length. Its speed is one inch per year. It has one task, to carry one atom across and come back for another. Each trip takes 2×1^{28} years. The time it would take to carry all the atoms across the entire diameter of the known universe is the expected time it would take for one protein to

form by chance. Suppose the amoeba has only traveled one inch since the universe has existed (fifteen billion years to cover one inch). He could still carry 6×10^{53} universes while one protein is forming.

From time to time sensational claims are made concerning attempts to create life in a laboratory. But has this actually been done?

Stanley Miller (University of California) showed that certain amino acids (which are basic components of proteins) could be generated by discharging electricity through a mixture of methane, water vapor, and ammonia.

Sidney Fox (Florida State University) heated a dry mixture of amino acids at 175°C for six hours and showed that under certain artificial conditions a number of amino acids could be randomly linked together. He called them "coacervates" and thought them to be similar to protein molecules.

Arthur Kornberg (Stanford) was able to make DNA replicate itself after extracting it from a living cell and placing it in a bath of the four nucleotides which constitute DNA, provided the proper enzymes and other constituents were also present. He also showed that virus DNA could be made to reproduce outside a host cell, contrary to usual virus behavior, provided the proper enzymes were present. A virus, however, is *not* a living cell.

H. G. Khorana (University of Wisconsin) was successful in the synthesis of a gene. He started with a certain simple DNA structure, considered to be a particular gene, and with the presence of enzymes again, was able to copy this gene. In 1970 J. P. Danielli (Buffalo University) claimed to have accomplished the first artificial synthesis of a living and reproducing cell. However, he had started with living amoebas in the first place, then partially dismantling and finally reassembling them, using components from different amoebas.

However, if life is to be defined as a self-contained, self-sufficient, and self-reproducing unit, such as in a cell, then we see the experiments above have yet to take the first tiny step in the journey of a billion light years in the creation of life. Thus, the theory of atheistic materialism is not only interesting, but idiotic and impossible also.

b. Theistic evolution.

This theory may be thought of as the Mosaic-Darwinian theory, for it earnestly attempts to unify two seemingly irreconcilable philosophies. It is known as the molecule-to-man theory. Theistic evolution says we must look to Darwin for the *when* and *how* of creation, and then learn from Moses concerning the *who* and *why* of all things. There are, however, two serious flaws in this theory. One is a *scientific* problem. Evolution runs contrary to the Second Law of Thermodynamics which describes this universe as a wound-up clock which is slowly running down. Instead, evolution has all life being built up from the simple to the complex.

The second problem confronting evolution is a scriptural one. For example, Moses informs us that life began on dry land during the third day of creation (Gen. 1:9-13), while evolution says it originated in some slimy sea. Furthermore, evolution is in direct contradiction to the creation of Eve. Finally, evolution would reduce Adam to a spiritually transformed ape, but the Scripture says he was originally and suddenly made in the very image of God.

In an attempt to get around this, it is claimed by some that our world in this area is not governed by the Second Law, for it receives the necessary energy from the sun to account for evolution. But the complexity of life calls for more than a source of energy. It also demands a purposeful direction of that energy. As an example, a builder might expose bricks, sand, nail, paint, wires, wood, and other building materials to the heat and energy of the sun and to the refreshing gentle rains, but these objects would never by themselves unite and form a house! In the light of all this many have concluded with Dr. Henry Morris that evolution is clearly, strongly, and completely refuted by the Bible. Morris observes:

"*Genesis* teaches that life began on dry land (Gen. 1:11, 12) while evolution says it began in some remote sea bottom.

Genesis declares birds existed before insects while evolution reverses this order (Gen. 1:20, 24).

Genesis states that birds and fishes were created at the same time (Gen. 1:21) but evolution says fishes evolved hundreds of millions of years before birds developed.

Genesis stresses ten times that the entities created were to reproduce "after their kinds," while evolution postulates the slow ascent of all organisms from a common ancestor.

Genesis says that Adam was made from the dust of the ground into the image of God, while evolution claims Adam descended from a sub-ape creature.

Genesis records woman coming from man's side, while evolution teaches both man and woman developed simultaneously.

Genesis tells us that man was originally a vegetarian (Gen. 1:29) while evolution teaches he was probably a head-hunting cannibal!"

c. Special creation.

This simply affirms that God said just what he meant and meant just what he said in the first two chapters of the Bible, as he did in the remaining 1187 chapters.

8. How many false philosophies does the first verse in the Bible refute?
   a. It refutes *atheism*, for creation is the work of God's hand.
   b. It refutes *evolution*, for the universe was created and did not evolve.
   c. It refutes *materialism*, for the universe did not always exist.
   d. It refutes *polytheism*, for there is only one God.
   e. It refutes *pantheism*, for God is apart from and independent of his creation.

9. Why was the earth made on the first day but the sun, moon, and stars not until the fourth day of creation? We have already briefly touched upon this.
   a. To emphasize the importance of this earth. God would soon (during the sixth day) place a creature created in his own image upon the earth. Years later his only Son would be born upon this planet and die upon it. Furthermore, upon this earth the King of kings will someday once again return.
   b. To discourage the worship of the sun. All ancient civilizations worshiped the sun. It gave them light and warmth. But God wanted his people to know that light and life come from him—that the earth existed *before* the sun, and that *he* created both.

   Dr. John Witcomb writes:

   "But if the sun, moon, and stars are not ultimately essential to the earth's existence, then why did God create them? Three basic reasons are listed in Genesis 1:14. They are for lights, for seasons (a calendar), and for signs.

   As lights, they replaced the special and temporary light of the early days.

   As a calendar, dividing seasons, days, and years, they enable men to plan their work accurately into the distant future, thus reflecting the purposive mind of God.

   As signs, they teach and ever remind men of vastly important spiritual truths concerning the Creator.

   David learned from the heavens the transcendence of God and his own comparative nothingness. 'When I consider the heavens, the work of thy fingers, the moon and the stars which thou hast ordained, what is man that thou art mindful of him?' (Ps. 8:3). The Apostle Paul insisted that men are utterly without excuse for their idolatry." (*The Early Earth*, pp. 58, 59)

10. Are the days of Genesis 1 really literal twenty-four-hour days?
    There is strong scholarly and scriptural evidence that the days are indeed literal.
    a. The use of a numerical adjective with the word "day" in Genesis 1 would limit it to a normal day.
    b. The natural reading of the Genesis account would suggest it.
    c. Moses believed it. See Exodus 20:11; 31:17.
    d. Edward Young (outstanding Hebrew scholar) believed it.
    e. Benjamin Warfield (one of the great Orthodox theologians of all time) believed it.
    f. Departmental professors of Oriental language in nine leading universities were once asked the following question by a research scholar:

    "Do you consider that the Hebrew word Yom (day) as used in Genesis 1 accompanied by a numeral should properly be translated as (a) a day, as commonly understood, (b) an age, or (c) either a day or an age without preference?"

    The nine universities polled were: Oxford, Cambridge, London, Harvard, Yale, Columbia, Toronto, McGill, and Manitoba. Of these, seven universities responded that it should be translated as a day as commonly understood.
    g. As indicated by the genealogies found in Genesis 5 and 11. If evolution is correct and man is really a million years old, then we would be forced to allow a fifty-thousand-year gap between each name in these two chapters. Furthermore, if life itself is nearly five billion years old, then each day in Genesis 1 would have to stand for approximately seven hundred million years!

11. Did something horrible take place between the first and second verse in the Bible? Many believe something terrible indeed occurred, and that something was the fall of Satan. The following arguments are offered to support this.

a. The phrase in Genesis 1:2, "without form and void" (Hebrew: *tohu wa-bohu*), appears elsewhere in Isaiah 34:11; 45:18; and Jeremiah 4:23 and speaks of judgment. However, in other passages it simply means space. (See Job 26:7; Deut. 32:10; Job 6:18; 12:24; Ps. 107:40.)

b. The verb translated "was" in Genesis 1:2 (Hebrew: *hayetha*) should be translated "became." Scriptural evidence, however, would deny this. The Hebrew verb *hayetha* is found 264 times in the Pentateuch, and of these, in 258 instances the word is correctly translated *was*. See, for example, Jonah 3:3.

c. There is a difference between the verbs *bara* (created, Genesis 1:1) and *asah* ("made," Genesis 1:7). But, to the contrary, these verbs are used synonymously. Note:

"And God *created [bara]* the great sea monsters . . ." (1:21).

"And God *made [asah]* the beast of the earth . . ." (1:25).

"Let us *make [asah]* man in our image . . ." (1:26).

"So God *created [bara]* man in his own image . . ." (1:27).

d. Genesis 1:2 says "darkness was upon the face of the deep," and darkness is a symbol of evil.

This is not always the case, as seen in Psalm 104:20, 24: "Thou makest darkness, and it is night, wherein all the beasts of the forest do creep forth. . . ."

Although traces of this theory can be traced back in Christian writings as early as the fourth century A.D., it was not until the ministries of Dr. Thomas Chalmers, Scottish scholar, and George H. Pember (1876) that the theory really caught on. In 1917 C.I. Scofield included it in his notes and its popularity was assured. These last two dates are significant, for by 1880 Darwin's theory of evolution, as propounded in his book, *The Origin of the Species*, was universally accepted by the scientific world. This theory taught that the world was many millions of years old, as indicated by the vast fossil record and the claims of uniformitarian geology. The Christian theologian was then confronted with a serious problem. How could all this be reconciled with Genesis 1? An answer was found—uncounted millions of years could be conveniently tucked into that bottomless hole which was thought to exist between Genesis 1:1 and 1:2. Thus the gap theory may be viewed in part as an attempt by the Christian theologian to appease the non-Christian evolutionist.

In summary, the gap theory faces a real problem in the New Testament, for Paul states in Romans 5:12 and 8:20–22 that man's sin brought about death, even of animals. But the gap theory would have Adam walking on top of a gigantic fossilized animal graveyard! One may thus conclude that Genesis 1:1 is a summary statement for the first two chapters. In this verse God tells us *what* he originally did. In the remaining verses he then informs us *how* he did it!

In conclusion at this point it may be asked: "If Satan did not fall between Genesis 1:1 and 1:2, then where do we place his fall?" A probable answer is somewhere between Genesis 2:25 and 3:1. We do know that Lucifer had become the devil at the time of Genesis 3:1. Bible students have pondered for centuries over why Lucifer sinned in the first place. Two suggestions have been offered: One, Satan may have doubted God's word that he had been created. Maybe God was lying. Second, he was no doubt jealous over man's nature (especially his ability to reproduce himself—something angels cannot do), and the responsibilities given to Adam. (See Gen. 1:26–28; Ps. 8:3–6; Heb. 2:5–9.) This last suggestion would of course indicate that Lucifer did not sin until *after* the creation of Adam.

12. What was God doing before he created man?

a. He was having fellowship with his Son. (See Prov. 8:22–30; Jn. 17:5, 24.)

"The Lord possessed me in the beginning of his way, before his works of old. I was set up from everlasting, from the beginning, or ever the earth was. When there were no depths, I was brought forth—when there were no fountains abounding with water. Before the mountains were settled, before the hills, was I brought forth; while as yet he had not made the earth, nor the fields, nor the highest part of the dust of the world. When he prepared the heavens, I was there; when he set a compass upon the face of the depth; when he established the clouds above; when he strengthened the fountains of the deep; when he gave to the sea its decree, that the waters should not pass his commandment; when he appointed the foundations of the earth, then I was by him, as one brought up with him; and I was daily his delight, rejoicing always before him" (Prov. 8:22–30).

"And now, O Father, glorify thou me with thine own self with the glory which I had with thee before the world was" (Jn. 17:5).

"Father, I will that they also, whom thou hast given me, be with me where I am, that they may behold my glory, which thou hast given me; for thou lovedst me before the foundation of the world" (Jn. 17:24).

THE THREEFOLD PROBLEM OF THE GAP THEORY

IT IS UNSCIENTIFIC
- THE GAP THEORY WAS (IN PART) A CHRISTIAN ATTEMPT TO RECONCILE THE CREATION ACCOUNT WITH THE LONG PERIODS OF TIME IN THE THEORY OF EVOLUTION.
- BUT EVOLUTION ITSELF AS A THEORY IS TOTALLY UNSCIENTIFIC, DEFYING THE SECOND LAW OF THERMODYNAMICS.

IT IS UNSCRIPTURAL
- THE GAP THEORY WOULD DESCRIBE ADAM WALKING ATOP A GIGANTIC FOSSILIZED ANIMAL GRAVEYARD.
- PAUL, HOWEVER, IN ROM. 5:12 AND 8:20–22 STATES THAT MAN'S SIN BROUGHT ABOUT DEATH, EVEN OF ANIMALS.

IT IS UNNECESSARY
- THE MOST NATURAL INTERPRETATION OF GEN. 1 AND 2 IS TAKING IT AT FACE VALUE, WITHOUT ADDITION OR SUBTRACTION.
- GEN. 1:1 THUS BECOMES A SUMMARY STATEMENT OF CREATION.
  1. IN THE FIRST VERSE GOD TELLS US *WHAT* HE DID.
  2. IN THE REMAINING VERSES HE TELLS US *HOW* HE DID IT.

Why did God make man in the first place? Well, whatever else may be involved, he did not create Adam because he was lonely. God had, he has, and always will have a beloved Son called Jesus Christ.

b. He was creating angels and stars.

"Where wast thou when I laid the foundations of the earth? declare, if thou hast understanding" (Job 38:4).

"When the morning stars sang together, and all the sons of God shouted for joy" (Job 38:7).

Both were there at the creation of Adam. The starlight fell upon that beautiful garden and the angels hovered over it.

c. He was choosing the elect.

"According as he hath chosen us in him before the foundation of the world, that we should be holy and without blame before him, in love" (Eph. 1:4).

"Who hath saved us, and called us with an holy calling, not according to our works, but according to his own purpose and grace, which was given us in Christ Jesus before the world began" (2 Tim. 1:9).

Theologians may argue over the reason *for* this election, but not the fact *of* the matter!

d. He was planning for a church.

"Unto me, who am less than the least of all saints, is this grace given, that I should preach among the Gentiles the unsearchable riches of Christ, and to make all men see what is the fellowship of the mystery, which from the beginning of the ages hath been hidden in God, who created all things by Jesus Christ" (Eph. 3:8, 9).

Before God created the upper atmosphere he had in mind the Upper Room.

e. He was preparing for a kingdom.

"Then shall the King say unto them on his right hand, Come, ye blessed of my Father, inherit the kingdom prepared for you from the foundation of the world" (Mt. 25:34).

Thus, in God's mind the thousand-year period of the millennium preceded the one-week period of Creation.

f. God was planning for a Savior.

"Forasmuch as ye know that ye were not redeemed with corruptible things, like silver and gold, from your vain conversation received by tradition from your fathers; but with the precious blood of Christ, as of a lamb without blemish and without spot: Who verily was foreordained before the foundation of the world, but was manifest in these last times for you" (1 Pet. 1:18–20).

"And all that dwell upon the earth shall worship him, whose names are not written in the book of life of the Lamb slain from the foundation of the world" (Rev. 13:8).

Long before he placed the first Adam in the Garden, God prepared the second Adam for the cross.

13. Why did God create man in the first place?

We have already stated that he did not create Adam because he was lonely! Some have suggested that prior to man's creation God had ample opportunity to express many of his attributes. In creating the stars, his omnipotence was shown. In fashioning angels, his omniscience was seen. In judging Lucifer (Ezek. 28; Isa. 14) his holiness was demonstrated. But one attribute very close to his heart had not been exercised. This was his grace. It is therefore not unreasonable to suggest that God created Adam knowing full well he would sin (but in no way encouraging him to do so) and then, in the fullness of time, he planned to send his only Son to die in man's place and thus display his marvelous grace! All this is indicated in the following verses:

"Thou art worthy, O Lord, to receive glory and honour and power: for thou hast created all things, and for thy pleasure they are and were created" (Rev. 4:11).

"Moreover the law entered, that the offence might abound. But where sin abounded, grace did much more abound" (Rom. 5:20).

"That in the ages to come he might shew the exceeding riches of his grace in his kindness toward us through Christ Jesus" (Eph. 2:7).

"For we are his workmanship, created in Christ Jesus unto good works, which God hath before ordained that we should walk in them" (Eph. 2:10).

14. How was man made in the image of God?

a. Perhaps because of man's trinity—man consists of spirit, soul, and body.

"And the very God of peace sanctify you wholly; and I pray God your whole spirit and soul and body be preserved blameless unto the coming of our Lord Jesus Christ" (1 Thess. 5:23).

"For the word of God is quick, and powerful, and sharper than any two-edged sword, piercing even to the dividing asunder of soul and spirit, and of the joints and marrow, and is a discerner of the thoughts and intents of the heart" (Heb. 4:12).

b. Perhaps because man (like God) knows the differences between good and evil. Only man, among all creatures, has self-consciousness.

c. Perhaps God had in mind the future work of Jesus when he took upon himself the body of a man.

"And the Word was made flesh, and dwelt among us, (and we beheld his glory, the glory as of the only begotten Father,) full of grace and truth" (Jn. 1:14).

"And without controversy great is the mystery of godliness: God was manifest in the flesh, justified in the Spirit, seen of angels, preached unto the Gentiles, believed on in the world, received up into glory" (1 Tim. 3:16).

"Let this mind be in you, which was also in Christ Jesus: Who, being in the form of God, thought it not robbery to be equal with God: But made himself of no reputation, and took upon him the form of a servant, and was made in the likeness of men: And being found in fashion as a man, he humbled himself, and became obedient unto death, even the death of the cross" (Phil. 2:5–8).

d. Perhaps God had in mind the future life of the believer when all Christians shall be like Jesus.

"Who shall change our vile body, that it may be fashioned like unto his glorious body, according to the working whereby he is able even to subdue all things unto himself" (Phil. 3:21).

"For whom he did foreknow, he also did predestinate to be conformed to the image of his

Son, that he might be the firstborn among many brethren" (Rom. 8:29).

"Beloved, now are we the sons of God, and it doth not yet appear what we shall be: but we know that, when he shall appear, we shall be like him, for we shall see him as he is" (1 Jn. 3:2).

15. What was Adam really like?
   a. Adam was the highlight of God's creation. It has been estimated that the most brilliant genius uses but one tenth of 1 percent of his total potential brain ability. This means Adam was at least one thousand times superior to today's intellectuals. We are probably 95 percent blind to the total color scheme displayed by nature and 98 percent deaf to her many sound patterns. But Adam's five senses were tuned to absolute perfection. He may even have possessed E.S.P. He perfectly understood both himself and his environment. He apparently was able to communicate with animals (Gen. 3:1, 2) and perhaps all nature also!

   The following article appeared in the April 1977 issue of *Reader's Digest:*

   "Six-Million-Dollar Original

   Tired of hearing that the human body is worth only about three dollars? And of the humbling and humiliating realization that a chicken or a salmon sells for more than you are worth? There's news to heal our bruised egos.

   Yale University biophysicist Harold J. Morowitz says that the human body is actually worth $6 million. And that price covers only the raw materials—hormones, proteins, enzymes, etc. The intricate work of fashioning the material into human cells might cost six thousand trillion dollars. And assembling these cells into a functioning human being would drain all the world's treasures. 'Each human being is price-less' is the professor's understatement" (p. 144).

   b. Adam was absolutely unique. Over the years a pile of shattered skulls and moldy bones have been dug up and presented by the evolutionist to "prove" the existence of ancient subhuman creatures who finally evolved into man. Again, one must either choose between Moses or Darwin on this subject. Some of the more "important" of these lost links in man's chronological chain are:

   Neanderthal man—Found in Neander Valley, near Dusseldorf, Germany, in 1856 by Johann C. Fuhlrott. The find consisted of a skull and several bones. He was first portrayed as a semi-erect brutish subhuman. It is now believed these "creatures" were real people who suffered severely from rickets, caused by a deficiency of vitamin D. This condition results in the softening of bones and consequent malformation.

   "It is now known that Neanderthal man was fully erect and in most details was indistinguishable from modern man, his cranial capacity even exceeding that of modern man. It is said that if he were dressed in a business suit, and were to walk down one of our city streets, he would be given no more attention than any other individual. Today he is classified *Homo Sapiens*—full human" (*Evolution? The Fossils Say No,* Duane T. Gish, p. 103).

   Java man (Pithecanthropus erectus, "erect ape man")—Found in Trinil, Java, in 1891, by Eugene Dubois, a Dutch physician. The "find" consisted of a single skull cap. One year later a thigh bone, along with two molar teeth, was discovered fifty feet from where the skull cap had been. Dubois estimated they all belonged together, and dated back one-half million years! He did not reveal, however, until thirty-one years later, that he had also found two obviously human skulls at the same time and in the same level. Most evolutionists of the day were convinced of the validity of this 500-thousand-year-old creature. But prior to his death, Dubois sadly concluded his Java man was actually the remains of a large gibbon.

   Piltdown man (Eanthropus dawsoni, "Dawn Man")—Found in Piltdown, England, in 1912, by Charles Dawson. The find was a skull part and a few teeth. Soon the consensus of the world's greatest authorities was that here indeed was a genuine link in the evolution of man. It was dated to be from 500 to 750 thousand years old! The praises of the Piltdown man were sung by Dr. Arthur Smith Woodward, eminent paleontologist at the British museum, and Dr. Henry Fairfield Osborn, paleontologist of the American Museum of Natural History. However, in 1950 the Piltdown bones were carefully examined by fluoride tests and discovered to be a colossal hoax. The "skull" had been stained with iron salts and the teeth filed down to give it the appearance of age. Thus, the world-famed Piltdown man was simply the doctored remains of a recent age.

   Peking man—Found near Peking, China, in 1912 (and 1937) by Davidson Bolack. Find consisted of the fragments of thirty skulls and 147 teeth. This find disappeared in 1941 when it was moved from Peking by a U.S. Marine detachment to escape the oncoming Japanese invasion. It is now believed by some that this find was simply the remains of some large monkeys or baboons killed and eaten by workers in an ancient lime-burning quarry!

   Nebraska man ("Western ape man")—Found in western Nebraska in 1922 by Harold Cook. The find was exactly one tooth! It was immediately declared by Dr. H. F. Osborn of the American Museum to be the vaunted missing link. He placed it at the very bottom of the tree of man's ancestry. Dr. William K. Gregory, curator of the American Museum of Natural History and professor of Paleontology at Columbia University, called it "the million dollar tooth." Sir Grafton Elliott Smith of the *London Illustrated News* assigned an imaginative artist to draw the ape man that once carried the tooth around in his mouth some six thousand centuries ago. During the famous Scopes evolutionary trial in Dayton, Tennessee, William Jennings Bryan (Bible defender) was confronted and ridiculed for his ignorance concerning this tooth and other "facts" of evolution by a delegation of authorities, led by Professor H. H. Newman of the University of Chicago. In 1927, to the supreme embarrassment of many, the tooth was discovered to be that of an extinct pig.

   East Africa ape (zinjanthropus)—Found in 1959 in Olduvia, Tanzania, by Louis S. B. Leakey. Find consisted of a skull cap and a few bone fragments.

This "discovery" was sensationalized through the *National Geographic Magazine,* which society had sponsored Leakey. His find was dated from two to four million years in age, thus making East Africa man by far the oldest "link" known at the time. However, prior to his death, Leakey indicated he felt his vaunted discovery was but a variety of *australopithecus* (Southern ape) found in 1924.

One of the most respected scholars of the twentieth century is Dr. Mortimer J. Adler, co-editor of the monumental fifty-four-volume set, *Great Books of the Western World.* In one of his many books, *Great Ideas from the Great Books,* Adler answers a question asked him concerning the difference between men and animals.

"Dear Dr. Adler,

Is there any basic difference between man and animals, or is man an animal like all the others? Some people say that man is the only creature that can think and learn. But I don't regard this as a real distinction, since biologists and psychologists have demonstrated that animals can construct things and solve problems. I have known some very intelligent dogs and some very thoughtless human beings. What is the essential difference between man and the animals? A.M.P.

Dear A.M.P.

Until comparatively recent times, few philosophers doubted that man was essentially different from all other animals. In the great tradition of Western thought, from Plato right down to the nineteenth century, it was almost universally held that man and man alone is a rational animal. This philosophical view of man's distinctive nature accords with the Biblical view that man and man alone is created in the image of God—a person, not a thing.

Since the time of Darwin, the opposite view has come to prevail, not only among scientists but among the educated classes generally. The Darwinian theory of man's origin, as you know, is that man and that anthropoid apes have descended from a common ancestral form; and along with this view of man's evolutionary origin goes the view that man and the higher mammals differ only in degree. Thus, for example, instead of regarding man alone as rational, the evolutionists find the same kind of intelligence in man and other animals. Man simply has more of it.

You say in your letter that you think the traditional arguments for man's distinctive nature are weak, because animals as well as men can reason, because animals as well as men can make things, etc. Let me answer your question by defending the traditional point of view about man as a very special creature.

The strongest evidence that men have certain powers which no other animals possess in any degree whatsoever consists in the thing which men can do but which other animals cannot do at all. One such indication is man's power of making things.

I know that bees make hives, birds make nests, and beavers make dams. But such productions are entirely instinctive on their part. A given species of bird makes its nests in the same way generation after generation. This shows that the nest is a product of instinct not of art, which involves reason and free will. In making houses, bridges, or any other of their artifacts, men invent and select. They are truly artist, as animals are not.

In addition, only men build machines which are themselves productive. Other animals may use rough tools, but no other animal makes a die press which stamps out an indefinite number of a product when the raw materials are fed into it. This is another indication of man's special power as a maker of things.

You say that other animals can reason. In my opinion it is more correct to say that other animals can solve problems when they are confronted by the biological urgency of finding a way of getting what they need. All so-called 'thinking' by animals is on this level. But no animal ever sits down to think, the way a philosopher or a mathematician does when he has no biologically urgent need to do so.

The fact that human thinking is discursive and involves language is another indication that it is quite different from animal problem-solving. Animals, of course, do make sounds and communicate their emotions or impulses to one another. But no animal communicates thought; no animal ever utters a sentence which asserts something to be true or false. Only a rational animal can do that.

I could go on and give you many other items of evidence that man has certain powers which no other animal possesses in the least degree. But I shall content myself with one more fact.

Man is the only animal with an historical development. Other animals may change in their biological constitution over the course of hundreds of thousands of generations; but such changes result entirely from changes in the germ plasm, which is the only thing that is transmitted from one generation to another. Men transmit ideas and institutions, a whole tradition of culture, from one generation to another, and it is this which accounts for the history of the human race.

In my opinion the empirical evidence is overwhelmingly in favor of the view that men are essentially different in kind from the brutes. Like the brutes, they, too, are animals. But unlike them, men are rational. This, of course, if true, would require us to reject Darwin's theory of man's evolutionary origin. But theories after all must be made to fit the facts, not facts theories."

(*Great Ideas from the Great Books,* pp. 173–275)

c. Adam was declared the king of creation, commanded to subdue the earth, to name the animals, and to care for his beautiful home in Eden's garden (Gen. 1:28–31; 2:8–15, 19, 20).
d. He was commanded to abstain from the tree of the Knowledge of Good and Evil, lest he die (Gen. 2:17). The Hebrew language indicates here that if Adam sinned he would die twice. This phrase can also be translated, "and in dying thou shalt surely

die." In the Bible there are two kinds of death and both can be defined by a single word. The word is separation. The two kinds of death are physical and spiritual. When a person dies physically, his soul is separated from his body. The body is put in the ground, but the soul lives on. It can never die. The more serious kind of death, however, is spiritual death. This will occur when the unsaved sinner will someday be forever separated from God. This is sometimes called the second death.

"And then I will profess unto them, I never knew you: depart from me, ye that work iniquity" (Mt. 7:23).

"Then shall he say also unto them on the left hand, Depart from me, ye cursed, into everlasting fire, prepared for the devil and his angels" (Mt. 25:41).

"And I saw a great white throne, and him that sat on it, from whose face the earth and the heaven fled away; and there was found no place for them. And I saw the dead, small and great, stand before God; and the books were opened: and another book was opened, which is the book of life: and the dead were judged out of those things which were written in the books, according to their works. And the sea gave up the dead which were in it; and death and hell delivered up the dead which were in them: and they were judged every man according to their works. And death and hell were cast into the lake of fire. This is the second death. And whosoever was not found written in the book of life was cast into the lake of fire" (Rev. 20:11–15).

"But the fearful, and unbelieving, and the abominable, and murderers, and whoremongers, and sorcerers, and idolaters, and all liars, shall have their part in the lake which burneth with fire and brimstone: which is the second death" (Rev. 21:8).

With this background in mind, let us ponder this tremendous truth: to be born once means to die twice, but to be born twice means to die once (and maybe not even once, if one is alive at the rapture). (See 1 Cor. 15:51–53; 1 Thess. 4:16, 17.)

e. Adam was encouraged to participate in the Tree of Life and all other trees (the trees of music, literature, art, etc.?). (See Gen. 1:29; 2:9, 16.)

Even though Adam had a perfect body at creation, it was apparently necessary for him to partake of this fruit tree in order to assure that his body continued in top running order. Many centuries later the early Spanish explorers in America looked in vain for the fountain of youth. But they searched for the wrong thing!

f. Adam was given a wife (2:22–24). The first wedding in history was conducted in Eden and performed by God himself. Note the account:

(1) "And the rib . . . from man made he a woman" (2:22). It has often been noted that God did not take Eve from Adam's feet, that she might be his slave, nor did he take her from Adam's head, that she might be his master, but rather from under his heart, that she might love and be loved by Adam.

"For the man is not of the woman; but the woman of the man. Neither was the man

created for the woman; but the woman for the man" (1 Cor. 11:8, 9).

The word rib should be translated side. The Hebrew here is *tsela* and is almost always translated side.

"And thou shalt cast four rings of gold for it, and put them in the four corners thereof; and two rings shall be in the one side of it, and two rings in the other side of it" (Ex. 25:12).

"His strength shall be hunger-bitten, and destruction shall be ready at his side" (Job 18:12).

16. What seven words were missing from Adam's vocabulary? We are told in Genesis 2:19 that "Adam called every living creature . . . the name thereof." Adam must have had a tremendous vocabulary. Today there are over 3500 different mammals, 8600 birds, 5500 reptiles and amphibians. Doubtless there existed many more in Adam's day. And he named them all! In spite of this, however, there were seven simple words unknown and unexperienced by Adam prior to his fall. These words were:

Death:
"But of the tree of the knowledge of good and evil, thou shalt not eat of it: for in the day that thou eatest thereof thou shalt surely die" (Gen. 2:17).

Nakedness:
"And the eyes of them both were opened, and they knew that they were naked; and they sewed fig leaves together, and made themselves aprons" (Gen. 3:7).

Cursed:
"And unto Adam he said, Because thou hast hearkened unto the voice of thy wife, and hast eaten of the tree, of which I commanded thee, saying, Thou shalt not eat of it: cursed is the ground for thy sake; in sorrow shalt thou eat of it all the days of thy life" (Gen. 3:17).

Sorrow:
(Gen. 3:17)

Thorns:
"Thorns also and thistles shall it bring forth to thee; and thou shalt eat the herb of the field" (Gen. 3:18).

Sweat:
"In the sweat of thy face shalt thou eat bread, till thou return unto the ground; for out of it wast thou taken, for dust thou art, and unto dust shalt thou return" (Gen. 3:19).

Sword:
"So he drove out the man; and he placed at the east of the garden of Eden Cherubims, and a flaming sword which turned every way, to keep the way of the tree of life" (Gen. 3:24).

After the Fall, Adam soon added these bitter and bloody words to his vocabulary. The echo of these wicked words would haunt Adam and mankind for over forty long centuries. Then came the Second Adam. He successfully met and dealt with each word.

Death:
"Jesus said unto her, I am the resurrection, and the life: he that believeth in me, though he were dead, yet shall he live" (Jn. 11:25).

Nakedness:
"Then the soldiers, when they had crucified Jesus, took his garments, and made four parts, to every soldier a part; and also his coat: now the coat was

without seam, woven from the top throughout" (Jn. 19:23).

Cursed:
"Christ hath redeemed us from the curse of the law, being made a curse for us: for it is written, Cursed is every one that hangeth on a tree" (Gal. 3:13).

Sorrow:
"He is despised and rejected of men; a man of sorrows, and acquainted with grief: and we hid as it were our faces from him; he was despised, and we esteemed him not" (Isa. 53:3).

Thorns:
"Then came Jesus forth, wearing the crown of thorns, and the purple robe. And Pilate saith unto them, Behold the man!" (Jn. 19:5)

Sweat:
"And being in an agony he prayed more earnestly: and his sweat was as it were great drops of blood falling down to the ground" (Lk. 22:44).

Sword:
"But one of the soldiers with a spear pierced his side, and forthwith came there out blood and water" (Jn. 19:34).

Paul shouts out the glorious results of Christ's mission. "Blotting out the handwriting of ordinances that was against us, which was contrary to us, and took it out of the way, nailing it to his cross" (Col. 2:14).

17. How long were Adam and Eve in the Garden?
In Genesis 4:1 we are told that Adam "knew his wife." This is a reference to sexual union. Inasmuch as this is the first time it is mentioned, it would appear they spent a very short time in Eden, perhaps only a few hours or days.

18. Will we see Adam in heaven?
We know he was created perfect and we know he sinned. But was he saved later? There are two verses that indicate he was saved.
   a. Genesis 3:21—God clothed Adam and Eve in coats of animal skins. Doubtless some innocent animal died to provide this clothing. This act is a type of salvation.
   b. Genesis 4:4—Abel knew the right way to God was by the blood of a lamb. It seems reasonable to assume this knowledge came from Adam.

19. Where did Cain get his wife?
Perhaps no other question concerning the Bible has been asked more than this one. To say the least, it is absolutely insignificant as compared to the one asked by a Philippian jailor, "What must I do to be saved?" (Acts 16:30). According to Genesis 5:4, Adam and Eve had sons and daughters. Thus, Cain doubtless married one of his sisters. This verse also explains what Cain was afraid of after he had murdered his brother in Genesis 4:14. He no doubt assumed his parents would bear other sons and daughters and that one of them might someday come looking for him.

20. Do the genealogies in Genesis 5 and 10 contain any gaps?
   a. The names in Genesis 5 are repeated in exact order in 1 Chronicles 1:1-4 and Luke 3:36-38, so it might seem there are none. However, if this is true, then one must conclude the following:
      (1) That Creation took place around 4000 B.C.
      (2) That the Flood occurred around 2400 B.C. (1656 years after Creation).

   (3) That Adam was a contemporary with Enoch for 308 years and died fifty-seven years before his translation.
   (4) That Seth (Adam's son) lived to see Enoch's translation and died just fourteen years before the birth of Noah.
   (5) That Noah was a contemporary with Abraham for fifty-eight years.
   (6) That Shem (Noah's son) actually outlived Abraham by thirty-five years. However, few conservative Bible scholars would concur with all these conclusions.
   b. In Genesis 10 there is at least one gap. Note:
      (1) Genesis 10:24 tells us that Arpachs begat Shelah who begat Eber.
      (2) Luke 3:34, 36 informs us that Arpachs begat Cainan who begat Shelah, who begat Eber.
   c. In Matthew chapter one three names are left out.
      (1) Matthew 1:8, 9 tells us that Asa begat Jehoshaphat, who begat Jehokam, who begat Uzziah.
      (2) In 2 Chronicles chapters 17-26 we are told that Asa begat Jehoshaphat, who begat Jehoram, who begat Ahaziah, who begat Joash, who begat Amaziah, who begat Uzziah.

21. Who were those mysterious sons of God in Genesis 6? Much controversy has surrounded these verses. Who were the sons of God who married the daughters of men? There are two basic approaches to this. The simple interpretation is that the sons of God were those individuals belonging to the line of Seth while the daughters of men were the unsaved girls who belonged to the line of Cain. The second and more involved interpretation holds that the sons of God were wicked and fallen angelic beings of some kind who committed immoral and unnatural physical acts with women in general.
   a. Basic arguments for the first view.
      (1) This is the most natural way to interpret the passage.
      (2) It is supported by Jesus' statement in Matthew 22:30:
         "For in the resurrection they [saved human beings in heaven] neither marry, nor are given in marriage, but are as the angels of God in heaven."
      (3) Because of the law of biogenesis, life begets similar life. (Note the statement "after its kind" in Gen. 1:11, 12, 21, 24, 25.)
      (4) Paul's statement in 1 Corinthians 15:38-40, "There are also celestial bodies, and bodies terrestrial," would indicate these two can never co-join.
      (5) Moses did not use the regular Hebrew word for angel (malak) which he later employs at least twenty-eight times in the Pentateuch.
      (6) "Mighty men" (supposed offspring of angels and women) is the Hebrew word gibbor (Gen. 6:4) which is used dozens of times in the Old Testament and always refers to human men (see Jdg. 6:12).
   b. Basic arguments for the second view:
      (1) The Hebrew language seems to favor it.
         (a) The Hebrew phrase "bne-elohim" (Sons of God) always refers to angels in the Old

Testament. (See Job 1:6; 2:1; 38:7; Dan. 3:25.)

(b) The Hebrew word *"nephilim"* (translated "giants" in 6:4) actually should be rendered "fallen ones." The normal word for a huge man is *rapha*. Thus, men like Og and Goliath were described by the word *rapha*. (See Deut. 3:11; 1 Chron. 20:6.)

(2) There is almost always a basis for commonly held ancient legends, however weird and distorted they might have become. In 6:4 we read concerning the "men of renown," which some believe is the historical basis for the legends of Hercules and other children of the gods of mythology. This later corresponds to such Babylonian figures as Gilgamesh, the supposed son of a goddess and a mortal. He was called "two-thirds god and one-third man."

(3) The common opinion of Jewish scholars: Josephus, the great Jewish historian, brings this out in his writings. The Septuagint (the Greek translation of the Hebrew Old Testament and the Bible used by Jews) translates Genesis 6:2 as the "angels of God."

(4) The interpretation of the early church: it was not until the fourth century that another view opposed to the angels of God theory was offered. Dr. James M. Gray (past President of Moody Bible Institute) writes, "There is reason to believe this view would not have changed . . . had it not been for certain erroneous opinions and practices of Christendom" (from his book, *Spiritism and the Fallen Angels*). Gray then suggests two such reasons:

(a) One of these was angel worship. The church sometime after the fourth century began worshiping angels, so the natural thing would be to deny any angel could do such vile things with humanity.

(b) The other reason was celibacy. If indeed these sons of God were human men, then the monks would have scriptural justification for indulging in sexual activities in spite of their official vows of celibacy.

(5) Various New Testament passages support this view. For example: 1 Peter 3:18-20—"For Christ also hath once suffered for sins, the just for the unjust, that he might bring us to God, being put to death in the flesh but quickened by the Spirit: By which also he went and preached unto the spirits in prison; which sometime were disobedient, when once the long-suffering of God waited in the days of Noah, while the ark was a preparing wherein few, that is, eight souls were saved by water."

It is thought by some that these spirits here were those sons of God in Genesis 6. The reason for their iniquity was a satanic attempt to corrupt human flesh and thus prevent the promised Incarnation (Gen. 3:15) from taking place. But here Peter describes Christ as telling them their foul plan didn't work! For another suggested passage along this line, see Jude 1:5-7.

(6) Two kinds of fallen angels exist: the unchained and those already chained. The *unchained* now have access to high places and to the bodies of unsaved men. (See Eph. 6:12; Lk. 8:27; Mk. 1:23.) The *chained* are at present already incarcerated. (See 2 Pet. 2:4; Jude 1:5-7.) The thought is that these are chained because of their involvement in Genesis 6.

In conclusion it should be noted that in recent times a third view has been advocated which says the sons of God were indeed fallen angels who totally controlled and possessed all the evil men living before the flood. These demons may have even attempted to change (by genetic engineering, as we see today) the DNA code of future babies, as would some deadly virus.

22. What was the pre-flood world like? Life prior to the flood was doubtless very different than today.
   a. It was probably universally warm, with a pleasant and mild climate.
   b. It may have had no deserts or ice caps.
   c. The land surface was more extensive and the oceans much smaller.
   d. The topography was gentle, without the rugged mountains or deeper canyons which affect our weather so much today.
   e. Lush vegetation may have thrived worldwide.
   f. There was apparently no rainfall, the earth being watered by early ground dews and from artesian springs. In addition to scriptural inferences, the presence of great oil deposits and plant fossils found near both North and South Poles give conclusive evidence that the world's climate was once temperate or even sub-tropical.

23. How advanced was the pre-flood civilization? One of the most popular books of the early seventies was *Chariots of the Gods?* by Erich Von Daniken. He attempts to prove by the following data that our earth was once visited by "little green men":
   a. a landing strip, built many centuries ago, in Peru
   b. long, ancient concrete constructions in Bolivia
   c. drawings of space ships in Mexico

THE PHYSICAL FEATURES OF THE ANCIENT WORLD

- **UNIVERSALLY WARM WITH PLEASANT AND MILD CLIMATE**
- **NO DESERTS OR ICE CAPS**
- **MORE LAND SURFACE THAN TODAY**
- **SMALLER AND SHALLOWER OCEAN BASINS**
- **NO RUGGED MOUNTAINS OR DEEP CANYONS**
- **CONSTANT, GENTLE WEATHER CONDITIONS**
- **WORLDWIDE LUSH VEGETATION**
- **NO RAINFALL, EARTH PROBABLY WATERED BY GROUND DEWS AND FROM ARTESIAN SPRINGS**

d. glass-like bits of rocks called "tektites" in which radioactive aluminum isotopes have been discovered in Lebanon

e. finds of cut crystal lenses, indicating electro-chemical activity

f. electric dry batteries found in Baghdad

g. ornaments of smelted platinum in Peru

h. parts of a belt made of aluminum in an ancient grave in China

While one would immediately reject Von Daniken's unscriptural conclusions, there is nevertheless a remote possibility that the above objects are but faint evidences of a highly sophisticated (and, alas, highly sinful) pre-flood society.

24. How much spiritual light did the pre-flood world have?
    a. They had the witness of nature.
       "Because that which may be known of God is manifest in them; for God hath shewed it unto them. For the invisible things of him from the creation of the world are clearly seen, being understood by the things that are made, even his eternal power and Godhead; so that they are without excuse" (Rom. 1:19, 20).
    b. They had the witness of conscience.
       "For when the Gentiles, which have not the law, do by nature the things contained in the law, these, having not the law, are a law unto themselves: Which shew the work of the law written in their hearts, their conscience also bearing witness, and their thoughts the mean while accusing or else excusing one another" (Rom. 2:14, 15).
    c. They had the promise of a Redeemer.
       "And I will put enmity between thee and the woman, and between thy seed and her seed; it shall bruise thy head, and thou shalt bruise his heel" (Gen. 3:15).
    d. They had the knowledge of the sacrifice.
       "And Abel, he also brought of the firstlings of his flock and of the fat thereof. And the Lord had respect unto Abel and to his offering" (Gen. 4:4).
    e. They had the preaching of Enoch.
       "And Enoch also, the seventh from Adam, prophesied of these, saying, Behold, the Lord cometh with ten thousands of his saints, to execute judgment upon all, and to convince all that are ungodly among them of all their ungodly deeds which they have ungodly committed, and of all their hard speeches which ungodly sinners have spoken against him" (Jude 1:14, 15).
    f. They had the preaching of Noah.
       "And spared not the old world, but saved Noah the eighth person, a preacher of righteousness, bringing in the flood upon the world of the ungodly" (2 Pet. 2:5).
    g. They had the ministry of the Holy Spirit.
       "And the Lord said, My spirit shall not always strive with man, for that he also is flesh: yet his days shall be an hundred and twenty years" (Gen. 6:3).
    But all this *light* produced *life* for only eight human beings.

THE MORAL FAILURES OF THE ANCIENT WORLD

- **PREOCCUPATION WITH PHYSICAL APPETITES (LK. 17:27)**
- **RAPID ADVANCES IN TECHNOLOGY (GEN. 4:22)**
- **GROSSLY MATERIALISTIC ATTITUDES AND INTERESTS (LK. 17:28)**
- **UNIFORMITARIAN PHILOSOPHIES (HEB. 11:7; 2 PET. 3:4)**
- **INORDINATE DEVOTION TO PLEASURE AND COMFORT (GEN. 4:21)**
- **NO CONCERN FOR GOD IN EITHER BELIEF OR CONDUCT (2 PET. 2:4; JUDE 15)**
- **DISREGARD FOR THE SACREDNESS OF MARRIAGE RELATIONSHIP (MT. 24:38)**
- **REJECTION OF THE INSPIRED WORD OF GOD (1 PET. 3:19)**
- **POPULATION EXPLOSION (GEN. 6:1, 11)**
- **WIDESPREAD VIOLENCE (GEN. 6:11, 13)**
- **CORRUPTION THROUGHOUT SOCIETY (Gen. 6:12)**
- **PREOCCUPATION WITH ILLICIT SEX ACTIVITY (GEN. 4:19; 6:2)**
- **WIDESPREAD WORDS AND THOUGHTS OF BLASPHEMY (JUDE 1:15)**
- **ORGANIZED SATANIC ACTIVITY (GEN. 6:1–4)**
- **PROMULGATION OF SYSTEMS AND MOVEMENTS OF ABNORMAL DEPRAVITY (GEN. 6:5, 12)**

25. How did their age compare with ours? Our Lord once said:
    "And as it was in the days of Noah, so shall it be also in the days of the Son of man. They did eat, they drank, they married wives, they were given in marriage, until the day that Noah entered into the ark, and the flood came, and destroyed them all" (Lk. 17:26, 27).
    Dr. Henry Morris suggests some fifteen similarities between their age and ours:
    a. preoccupation with physical appetites (Lk. 17:27)
    b. rapid advances in technology (Gen. 4:22)
    c. grossly materialistic attitudes and interests (Lk. 17:28)
    d. uniformitarian philosophies (Heb. 11:7; 2 Pet. 3:3-6)
       "Knowing this first, that there shall come in the last days scoffers, walking after their own lusts, and saying, Where is the promise of his coming? for since the fathers fell asleep, all things continue as they were from the beginning of the creation. For this they willingly are ignorant of, that by the word of God the heavens were of old, and the earth standing out of the water and in the water: Whereby the world that then was, being overflowed with water, perished" (2 Pet. 3:3-6).
    e. inordinate devotion to pleasure and comfort (Gen. 4:21)
    f. no concern for God in either belief or conduct (2 Pet. 2:4; Jude 1:15)
    g. disregard for the sacredness of the marriage relationship

"For as in the days that were before the flood they were eating and drinking, marrying and giving in marriage, until the day that Noe entered into the ark" (Mt. 24:38).

FLOOD FACTS

WHEN DID THE FLOOD BEGIN?	It began in November. This month is lamented by many people around the world as the day of the dead.
HOW LONG DID THE FLOOD LAST?	**371 DAYS**
WHAT MAY HAVE TRIGGERED THE FLOOD?	**A.** An earthquake may have released vast and pressured water reservoirs in the earth's mantle (Gen. 7:11) **B.** This may have blown immense amounts of dust skyward which would then initiate the condensation and precipitation of the watery canopy.
WAS THE FLOOD WORLDWIDE? YES!	**A.** Because of the need for the ark **B.** Because of the wide distribution of man before the flood. (See Gen. 4:16.) **C.** Because of the comparison made in 2 Peter 3:3–7 **D.** Because of the universal flood traditions **E.** Because of the marine fossils found on mountains **F.** Because of the many fossil fish beds **G.** Because of the worldwide animal fossil graveyards **H.** Because of the evidence of recent water bodies in present desert areas **I.** Because of the evidence of a recent drastic rise in the sea level **J.** Because of the evidence from the geologic column

HOW BIG WAS THE ARK?

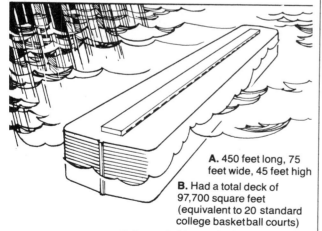

A. 450 feet long, 75 feet wide, 45 feet high

B. Had a total deck of 97,700 square feet (equivalent to 20 standard college basketball courts)

C. Largest ship ever built until 1884 A.D.

D. Nearly one half the length of the Queen Mary

HOW DID NOAH FIND ROOM FOR ALL THE ANIMALS?	**A.** Total animal population would not have exceeded 35,000 vertebrates **B.** Average size would be that of a sheep **C.** Modern train of 150 boxcars could carry this **D.** Ark had carrying capacity of over 520 boxcars!

h. rejection of the inspired Word of God

"But there were false prophets also among the people, even as there shall be false teachers among you, who privily shall bring in damnable heresies, even denying the Lord that bought them, and bring upon themselves swift destruction" (2 Pet. 2:1).

i. population explosion (Gen. 6:1, 11)

j. widespread violence

"The earth also was corrupt before God, and the earth was filled with violence" (Gen. 6:11).

"And God said unto Noah, The end of all flesh is come before me; for the earth is filled with violence through them; and, behold, I will destroy them with the earth" (Gen. 6:13).

k. corruption throughout society (Gen. 6:12)

l. preoccupation with illicit sex activity

"And Lamech took unto him two wives: the name of the one was Adah, and the name of the other Zillah" (Gen. 4:19).

"That the sons of God saw the daughters of men that they were fair; and they took them wives of all which they chose" (Gen. 6:2).

m. widespread words and thoughts of blasphemy (Jude 1:15)

n. organized satanic activity (Gen. 6:1–4)

o. promulgation of systems and movements of abnormal depravity (Gen. 6:5, 12)

26. How could men live so long at that time? The average age of the patriarchs mentioned in Genesis 5 was 912 years. Several factors doubtless contributed to this amazing phenomenon.

a. As a slow developing cancer will often take several years to destroy a healthy body, so the physical results of sin settled down upon the bodies of men.

b. Prior to the flood there apparently existed many times the amount of water vapor in the upper atmosphere that there is today. (Compare Gen. 1:7 with 7:11.) This vapor, although invisible to the eye, would nevertheless function as a filtering protection and shield against the amount of intense radiation falling upon the earth from the sun. Scientific research is now demonstrating that radiation can appreciably reduce the life span of living tissue and actually cause the cells to speed up the process. Of course, after the flood that protective watery canopy disappeared as it fell upon the earth in the form of rain.

27. When did the flood begin? Creation scientist F. Filby suggests that it began in November (the seventeenth day of the second month on Noah's calendar; Gen. 7:11). He points out that this fact and date is indelibly enshrined in the memory of the human race, pointing out that to many people around the world, November brings the Day of the Dead (in the western world, November 2 is All Soul's Day).

28. How long did the flood last? It is believed that 371 days elapsed from the time Noah entered the ark (Gen. 7:11) until the day he stepped out (8:18).

29. What may have triggered the flood? Dr. Henry Morris suggests the following:

a. A secondary source of water is postulated, existing in vast subterranean heated and pressurized reservoirs in the earth's mantle.

b. The actual trigger to unleash these stored waters may have been an earthquake.

c. This earthquake would not only allow the underground waters to surface through the fractured earth, but would also result in immense amounts of dust blown skyward which would then initiate the condensation and precipitation of the water canopy.

30. Was the flood really worldwide? Both scriptural and secular evidence would strongly support that it was indeed universal.
This is verified by:
   a. The need for the ark. God commanded Noah to build an ark to save both a remnant of humanity and the animal creation. But if the flood were local, then all the effort to build it would be totally unnecessary and the whole story becomes ridiculous. Noah could have just trotted down the road a few miles and escaped.
   b. The wide distribution of man before the flood. In Genesis 4:16, Cain "went out from the presence of the Lord and dwelt in the land of Nod, on the east of Eden." Some believe this to be a reference to China.
   c. The comparison between the historical flood judgment and the coming fire judgment. The Apostle Peter (2 Pet. 3:3-7) states definitely that as God once destroyed the world by a flood, he will someday do likewise through a fire. As the Bible clearly teaches, the entire earth will be burned (2 Pet. 3:10; Rev. 21:2), we logically conclude that the entire earth was once flooded. Few local flood advocates would propose a "local-fire" theory.

   "And as it was in the days of Noe, so shall it be also in the days of the Son of man. They did eat, they drank, they married wives, they were given in marriage, until the day that Noe entered into the ark, and the flood came, and destroyed them all. Likewise also as it was in the days of Lot; they did eat, they drank, they bought, they sold, they planted, they builded; but the same day that Lot went out of Sodom it rained fire and brimstone from heaven, and destroyed them all. Even thus shall it be in the day when the Son of man is revealed" (Lk. 17:26-30).

   d. If the flood was local, then God lied to Noah when he promised never to send a destructive flood again (Gen. 9:11). But there have been, of course, many local destructive floods since.
   e. Flood traditions can be found in the history of every ancient civilization culture. The early aborigines of nearly every country of the world have preserved records of the universal flood. Dr. Richard Andree collected forty-six flood legends from North and South America, twenty from Asia, five from Europe, seven from Africa, and ten from South Sea islands and Australia.
   f. Marine fossils have been found atop mountains. Scientists of the nineteenth century were dismayed to find that, as high as they climbed, the rocks yielded skeletons of marine animals, ocean fish, and shells of mollusks. Thus, in ancient days, flood waters streamed over Mount Everest and all other mountains. A whale's skeleton was once found on the top of Mount Sanhorn on the Arctic Coast, and other similar skeletons a mile high on California's coastal range.
   g. Many fossil "fish beds" exist all over the world. The *Science Magazine,* January 9, 1959, states:
   "More than a billion fish averaging 6 to 8 inches in length died on 4 square miles of bay bottom off the California Coast line."
   Ivan Velikovsky writes:
   "When a fish dies its body floats on the surface or sinks to the bottom and is devoured rather quickly, actually in a matter of hours, by other fish. However, the fossil fish found in sedimentary rocks is very often preserved with all its bones intact. Entire shoals of fish over large areas, numbering billions of specimens, are found in a state of agony, but with no marks of a scavenger's attack." (*Earth in Upheaval,* p. 222)
   h. Because of the worldwide animal fossil graveyards. Robert Broom, South African paleontologist, estimated 800 *billion* skeletons of vertebrate animals exist in the Karroo formation alone. To this can be added the tens of thousands of fossils of all kinds found in the LaBrea tar pits in Los Angeles, California.
   i. Evidence of water bodies in present desert areas.
   j. Evidence of a recent drastic rise in the sea level.
   k. The universal occurrence of rivers in valleys too large for the present system.
   l. Evidence from the geologic column suggests two things:
      (1) That there was a continuous deposition of the stratum layers from beginning to end. There is no erosion in between the layers. In fact, in some layers there are actual ripple marks. In other stratums there exists one or more vertical tree trunks, with the same tree making its way up from top to bottom!
      (2) That fossils from supposed different "ages" in the evolutionary theory actually lived at the same time!

31. How destructive would a worldwide flood be? In his book entitled, *Disasters,* author John Godwin related the following terrifying information concerning just one kind of power which can spring from the ocean. This is called Tsunami or "killer waves." He lists three examples.
   a. Hilo, Hawaii, May, 1960. At this time a hundred-foot wave traveling at 550 m.p.h. hit the coast, drowning 665 people and causing property damage of 50 million dollars.
   b. Lisbon, Portugal, Nov. 1, 1755. This city was hit by a seventy-foot wave which drowned 65,000 people.
   c. Indonesia, May 20, 1883. On this date the volcano Krakatoa exploded and caused a 150-foot wave to rush ashore. It sunk thirty-three European vessels, buried many islands beneath a nine-foot layer of mud, destroyed over 1000 coastal cities, and left over 50,000 dead in its terrible wake. One of the most descriptive summaries of the destruction wrought by a worldwide flood is from the pen of Dr. Henry Morris, Ph.D., and expert in hydrology (the nature of moving water). Morris writes:
   "Visualize, then, a great hydraulic cataclysm bursting upon the present world, with currents of water pouring perpetually from the skies and erupting continuously from the earth's crust, all over the world, for weeks on end, until the entire globe was submerged, accompanied by out-

pourings of magma from the mantle, gigantic earth movements, landslides, tsunamis, and explosions.

Sooner or later all land animals would perish. Many, but not all, marine animals would perish. Human beings would swim, run, climb, and attempt to escape the floods but, unless a few managed to ride out the cataclysm in unusually strong watertight sea-going vessels, they would eventually all drown or otherwise perish.

Soils would soon erode away and trees and plants be uprooted and carried down toward the sea in great mats on flooding streams. Eventually, the hills and mountains themselves would disintegrate and flow downstream in great landslides and turbidity currents. Slabs of rock would crack and bounce and gradually be rounded into boulders and gravel and sand. Vast seas of mud and rock would flow downriver, trapping many animals and rafting great masses of plants with them.

On the ocean bottom, upwelling sediments and subterranean waters and magmas would entomb hordes of invertebrates. The waters would undergo rapid changes in heat and salinity, great slurries would form, and immense amounts of chemicals would be dissolved and dispersed throughout the seaways.

Eventually, the land sediments and waters would commingle with those in the ocean. Finally, the sediments would settle out as the waters slowed down, dissolved chemicals would precipitate out at times and places where the salinity and temperature permitted, and great beds of sediment, soon to be cemented into rock, would be formed all over the world.

The above, of course, is only the barest outline of the great variety of phenomena that would accompany such a cataclysm." (*Scientific Creationism*, pp. 117, 118)

32. How big was Noah's Ark? The size of the ark was approximately 450 feet long, seventy-five feet wide, and forty-five feet high. It had a deck total of 97,700 square feet, or the equivalent to more than an area of twenty standard college basketball courts. Its total volume was around 1,500,000 cubic feet and the gross tonnage exceeded some 14,000 tons. (See Gen. 6:14-16.) It was not until 1884 A.D. that this huge boat was exceeded by modern man (when the Italian vessel, *Eturia*, was built). The *Queen Mary* ocean liner had a total length of 1018 feet, so the ark was nearly half this size. Author Frederick Filby writes:

"The Ark was, according to the specifications laid down, to be 300 cubits long by 500 cubits wide by 30 cubits high. The ratios of these numbers are very interesting. They obviously reflect an advanced knowledge of ship building. The Babylonian account which speaks of the Ark as a cube betrays complete ignorance. Such a vessel would spin slowly around. But the Bible ratios leave nothing to be desired." (*The Flood Reconsidered*, p. 90)

33. How did Noah possibly gather all the needed animals from the various remote areas and nations of the world? In the first place, we are told that God himself gathered these animals (Gen. 7:8, 9). In addition, the indication is strong that prior to the flood the conti-

nents of the earth were not separated by vast bodies of water as they are today.

34. How did Noah possibly pack all those animals on board? First it must be asked how many animals were involved here? Millions? Hundreds of thousands? Hardly. One of America's leading systematic taxonomists lists the following numbers for animal species according to the best estimates of modern taxonomy:

Mammals	3,500
Birds	8,600
Reptiles and amphibians	5,500
Worms	25,500

Taking this into consideration, one may reasonably conclude that no more than 35,000 individual vertebrate animals the size of a sheep (overall average) boarded the Ark. It has been estimated that a modern train hauling 150 boxcars could easily handle these animals. But the Ark had a carrying capacity of more than 520 stock cars! In other words, there was more than enough room in the Ark. Noah and his family could have played shuffleboard on deck had they chosen to do so.

35. How did Noah feed and keep these animals for an entire year? Of course, we may only speculate. A possible solution might have involved that mysterious and remarkable factor of animal physiology known as hibernation. Hibernation is generally defined as a specific physiological state in an animal in which normal functions are suspended or greatly retarded, enabling the animal to endure long periods of complete inactivity. This suggestion would not seem to be unreasonable, for the animals went aboard two by two (the clean animals by sevens) and came off the same way—including the rabbits.

36. Were there dinosaurs on board the Ark? Perhaps no other single question concerning the flood will more quickly bring out the agnostic's sneers and the believer's fears than will this one. But there is now mounting evidence that man and dinosaurs did indeed live on earth at the same time.

a. In Rhodesia paintings on cave walls by bushmen known to have left the caves in 1500 B.C. include paintings of brontosaurs. According to the nature of their art, cavemen only painted from what they could actually see. Thus, they would have had to see a brontosaur in order to paint one.

b. Evidence of these large reptiles has been found since the flood. Dinosaur footprints have been located in the same strata with human footprints in Glen Rose, Texas.

c. To conclude this argument, we quote again from Henry Morris:

"The Book of Job is one of the oldest in the Bible and reflects living conditions in the early centuries after the flood. The climax of the book is when God speaks directly to Job and his friends in Job 38, 39, 40, and 41. God is calling attention to His great power in creating and sustaining all things (exactly the message urgently needed by the world today.)

Finally, He calls attention to His two greatest creations in the animal kingdom, behemoth (Job 40:15-24) and leviathan (Job 41:1-34). Most commentators today suggest behemoth is either the elephant or hippopotamus and that leviathan is the crocodile. However, the actual descriptions (and these, coming as they do from the mount of God Himself, certainly refer to real animals) obviously do not apply to any animals known today. The most reasonable interpretation, therefore, is that they refer to extinct animals. Perhaps, then behemoth is a land dinosaur and leviathan a marine dinosaur. Suddenly these chapters become very much alive and meaningful! These great animals were still living in Job's day, even though they may have become extinct since.

In reading God's description of behemoth, one can clearly visualize a giant brontosaur, with his long neck projecting out to eat the swamp vegetation and to wash it down with great quantities of water, with his powerful legs and tail easily capable of demolishing his enemies with their overwhelming blows. 'Behold now behemoth,' God remarks . . . 'he eateth grass as an ox . . . his strength is in his loins, and his force is in the navel of his belly. He moveth his tail like a cedar.' (Ever see an elephant's tail?) His bones are as strong pieces of brass, his bones are like bars of iron (no wonder so many fossil dinosaur bones have been preserved so long). Finally, God states, 'He is the chief of the ways of God' (thus the greatest animal God ever made); 'He that made him can make his sword to approach unto him' (thus God Himself can destroy the dinosaurs, even though man could not). 'Behold he drinketh up a river . . . his nose pierceth through snares.' " (*The Remarkable Birth of the Planet Earth*, pp. 32, 33)

Thus, to answer the question concerning whether dinosaurs were on the ark, it may be said that inasmuch as they definitely existed with man prior to the flood, the chances are good that a young pair of these huge reptiles may well indeed have been aboard!

37. Why do we not find animal fossils in Asia Minor, the place where the Ark landed? Both agnostics and local flood advocates have often pointed out this fact to those who hold the universal flood view. Dr. Russell L. Mixter, professor of Zoology at Wheaton College, writes:

"If kangaroos were in the ark and first touched land in Asia, one would expect fossils of them in Asia. According to Romer, the only place where there are either fossil or living kangaroos is in Australia. What shall we conclude? If the fossil evidence means that there never have been kangaroos in Asia, then kangaroos were not in the ark or if they were, they hurried from Australia to meet Noah, and as rapidly returned to their native land. Is it not easier to believe that they were never in the ark, and hence were in an area untouched by the flood, and that the flood occurred only in the area inhabited by man?" (*Creation and Evolution*, p. 15)

This objection, however, may be quickly refuted by pointing out the fact that fossils are only formed under unusual conditions and that, apart from these conditions, all dead animals rapidly decompose and disappear. Note the following examples to undergird this:

a. Concerning lions in Palestine: There is no fossil evidence of lions in Palestine, but the Old Testament informs us that the land was once infested with these animals. (See Jdg. 14:5; 1 Sam. 17:34; 2 Sam. 23:20; 1 Ki. 13:24; 20:36; 2 Ki. 17:25.)

b. Concerning buffalo (or bison) in the American West:

"The Buffalo carcasses strewn over the plains in uncounted millions two generations ago have left hardly a present trace. The flesh was devoured by wolves and vultures within hours or days after death, and even the skeletons have now largely disappeared, the bones dissolving and crumbling into dust under the attack of the weather." (Carl Dunbar, *Historical Geology*, p. 39)

38. How did the animals get from Asia Minor to their present location? Professor Paul A. Moody of the University of Vermont writes:

"In times of flood, large masses of earth and entwining vegetation, including trees, may be torn loose from banks of rivers, and swept out to sea. Sometimes such masses are encountered floating in the ocean out of sight of land, still lush and green, with palms twenty to thirty feet tall. It is entirely probable that land animals may be transported long distances in this manner. Mayr records that many tropical ocean currents have a speed of at least two knots; this would amount to fifty miles in a day, 1000 miles in three weeks." (*Introduction to Evolution*, p. 262)

"It seems certain that land animals do at times cross considerable bodies of water where land connections are utterly lacking . . . floating masses of vegetation, such as are sometimes found off the mouths of the Amazon, may be one means of effecting this type of migration." (Alfred S. Romer, Harvard University, *Vertebrate Paleontology*)

"One glance at a world map will show that, with the exception of the narrow break at the Bering Strait, a dryland path leads from Armenia to all lands of the globe except Australia. In the case of the latter (Australia) the East Indies even today form a fairly continuous bridge of stepping-stones to that southern continent. As regards the Bering Strait, there is no doubt that a land connection once existed between Asia and North America." (Frank L. Marsh, *Evolution, Creation, and Science*)

39. Where did all the flood waters go? Hebrew scholar John Whitcomb writes:

"Even as the beginning of the flood year was characterized by supernatural intervention, so also the end of the flood was brought about by a stupendous miracle of God. Apart from this, the waters would have covered the earth forever, and all terrestrial-like would soon have come to an end.

Two passages of Scripture, in widely separated Old Testament books, deal with this particular activity of God. The first, in Genesis 8:2-3, tells us that 'the fountains . . . of the deep . . . were stopped . . . and the waters returned from off the earth continually.' Since the breaking up of the fountains of the great deep involved the uplift of ocean floors, the stopping of these 'fountains' must refer to a reversal of this action, whereby new and much deeper ocean basins were formed to serve as vast reservoirs for the two oceans which were separated from each other by the atmospheric expanse before the flood (Gen. 1:7). A natural result of this subsidence was that 'the waters returned from off the earth continually' permitting continents to emerge from the oceans again, as they had done on the third day of creation.

A second passage that sheds important light upon the termination of the flood is Psalm 104:6-9.

'Thou coveredst it with the deep as with a garment: the waters stood above the mountains. At thy rebuke they fled; at the voice of thy thunder they hasted away. They go up by the mountains; they go down by the valleys unto the place which thou hast founded for them. Thou hast set a bound that they may not pass over; that they turn not again to cover the earth' (Ps. 104:6-9).

Though it contains several figures of speech, the passage is clearly historical in its reference to the flood. Note, for example, the statement of verse 6—'the waters stood above the mountains' and that of verse 9—'thou hast set a bound that they may not pass over; that they turn not again to cover the earth.' The latter is obviously a reference to the rainbow covenant of Genesis 9, in which God assured mankind that there would never again be a universal flood (cf. Isa. 54:9).

Now the key statement in this passage (Ps. 104:8) for our purposes is in the beginning of verse 8: 'The mountains rose, the valleys sank down' (ASV; cf. RSV, Berkeley, Amplified, NASB). We have already seen in Genesis 8:2 that the ocean basins were lowered at the termination of the flood, and with this concept the phrase 'the valleys sank down' is in agreement. God supernaturally depressed various parts of the earth's crust, and into those places which God 'founded for them' the waters 'fled' and 'hasted away,' there to abide while this earth exists (cf. Rev. 21:1), never again to cover the continents.''
(*The World That Perished*)

40. Has the Ark been sighted since it landed on Mt. Ararat? Introduction: On the evening of June 2, 1840, a terrific earthquake shook the highest mountain of the Armenian plains, located north of Lake Van in Turkey. The name of this shattered mountain was Aghri Dagh, better known as Mt. Ararat. The power released was beyond that of hundreds of atomic bombs. It totally wiped out the little village of Ahora and the monastery of St. Jacob.

Since 1840, a number of reports have come to the world's attention concerning the sighting of an ark-like structure of hand-tooled timber on treeless Mt. Ararat. Even prior to this there have been many ancient reports about this very thing, which includes the testimonies of Herodotus (the Greek historian), Josephus (the Jewish historian), the Koran (sacred book of the Islamic faith), and Marco Polo (famous European explorer).

A summary of the eyewitness reports since 1840 proves fascinating reading indeed. Their testimonies bear striking similarities.

a. The ship is half buried in a partly melted lake.
b. Its altitude is around 13 thousand feet.
c. The inside of the ark is filled with wooden separators (like bars in a cage).
d. The outside and inside are covered with a heavy varnish or lacquer.
e. The wood is extremely hard, almost petrified.
f. The main door is missing.

The witnesses themselves are an interesting lot:

g. Haji Yearman (date of Ark sighting, 1865). He was an Armenian who lived at the base of Mt. Ararat. He died in Oakland, California, in 1916.
h. John Joseph. The Archbishop of Babylon and head of the Christian Nestorian Church. Joseph reported his experience at the World's Fair in Chicago in 1893.
i. W. Roskovitsky. A Russian airman. The sighting was in 1915 during World War I. Later, in 1917, a Russian expedition numbering 150 men saw it.
j. Carveth Wells. A popular radio commentator over KFI in Los Angeles reported seeing wood from the Ark while at the site in 1933.
k. Various airmen (both Russian and American) during World War II. Mount Ararat was on a direct flight between the allied base in Tunisia and the Russian base at Brivan. One of the Russians claiming to have seen it was Major Jasper Maskelyn, wartime chief of Camouflage (1941-1945).
l. Resit. A Kurdish farmer. His experience was published in an Istanbul newspaper on November 13, 1948.
m. Dr. Donald M. Liedman. Dr. Liedman is a Jewish scientist and medical doctor. He has given sworn testimony that he was shown actual snapshots of the Ark on two occasions while in Hamburg, Germany, by a Russian air force major who had personally taken the pictures during World War II.
n. George Jefferson Greene. Greene was on a helicopter research mission for his company in 1953. While flying over Mt. Ararat he spotted a strange object and took a number of pictures from ninety feet. When developed, they showed a large wooden object. These pictures were seen by many. Greene was later found murdered. The pictures were never located.
o. Bernard Navarra. This French explorer visited Mount Ararat and later wrote a book on the subject entitled, *Noah's Ark, I Touched It*. Navarra cut some wood from an object on Mt. Ararat and subjected it to C-14 testings at two universities.

"This fossilized wood was derived from an epoch of great antiquity." (official statement from the University of Bordeaux)

"Our analysis estimated the age of the fragment at 5000 years." (from the Forest Institute in Madrid)

Concluding statements:

p. In the thirties, Dr. Alexander A. Koor, Russian Colonel, scholar, researcher, author, historian, and etymologist of ancient languages discovered and translated an ancient Sumerian inscription found at Karada Pass near Mt. Ararat. It read:

"God sowed the seeds of the world into the waters . . . the waters filled the earth, descending from above . . . His children came to rest on the mountain peak."

q. The following quotes are taken from Viola Cumming's book, *Noah's Ark, Fable or Fact?*

"Silhouetted against the sky at the crest of a rocky eminence some distance away, the sharply-carved outlines of a nobly-proportioned patriarchal head rose perhaps eight to ten feet above the top of the hill. For some reason, the ancient sculptor had faced the bearded, turbaned profile so that its sightless gaze would forever rest on the towering heights of Mt. Ararat. Did the same hand that recorded the story of the Deluge on the Karada Cliff not far away also carve the majestic patriarchal head atop a hill facing the heights of Mt. Ararat?

One of the still greater wonders of Ararat is the rainbow which can frequently be seen in the afternoon from the north and north-eastern slopes."

41. Was there an Ice Age?

Author Reginald Daly writes the following:

"The Ice Age automatically follows the Universal Flood. There could not have been a universal flood without a glacial age following. The deserts were sopping wet for centuries following the flood. There were lakes everywhere. Evaporation kept humidity at 100%. There was rain every day in the north country. Winds carried moisture-laden clouds, super-saturated, to northern Canada, Scotland, Norway, Sweden, where snow poured down every day and every hour from November until April, probably five hundred or a thousand feet thick the first winter. Multiply 500 feet of snow by 100 years of wet weather. This makes 50,000 feet of snow which would settle down into approximately 5000 feet of ice—the glacial age. The tops of these mountains, a mile high, would be so cold that snow would continue to pile up all spring and early fall as well as all winter, leaving such a brief, chilly July-August summer that only a small amount of snow would melt. The small amount melting in July would be many times over-balanced by the prodigious winter snowfall. The effect would be cumulative: the higher the mountain, the colder the temperature, the shorter the summers, and the greater the snowfall. The weight of a mile or two of ice would cause it to flow outwards, across the Baltic Sea, depositing boulders all over the north German plain, as we find them today. Also downward over North America, across Lake Erie, leaving moraines, eskers, drumlins and boulders across Ohio and Missouri as far south as the Missouri River." (*Earth's Most Challenging Mysteries*, p. 142)

Few other men have written as extensively on the Ice Age from a Christian viewpoint as has Donald Patten. He writes:

"Mammoths were, along with mastodons, the largest members of the elephant family. They have become mummified in two manners, both of which suggest cataclysm and suddenness. In Alaska and Siberia mammoths have been mummified, apparently by the millions, both in ice and in sedimentary strata. It is as if they had been deposited in watery graves in some areas, but encased in ice in other areas, ice which has remained unmelted. Their entombment and refrigeration have been so effective that mammoth carcasses have been thawed to feed sled dogs, both in Alaska and Siberia; in fact, mammoth steaks have even been featured on restaurant menus in Fairbanks.

Every indication is that the mammoths died suddenly, in intense cold, and in great numbers. Death came so quickly that the swallowed vegetation is yet undigested in their stomachs and their mouths." (*The Ice Age*, p. 105)

42. What was involved in Noah's prophecy concerning his three sons after the flood?

Noah became drunk and exposed his nakedness to Ham. Upon awaking he pronounced a judgment upon Ham's son, Canaan. He then issued a prophecy concerning all three sons, Ham, Shem, and Japheth.

"And Noah began to be an husbandman, and he planted a vineyard: And he drank of the wine, and was drunken; and he was uncovered within his tent.

And Ham, the father of Canaan, saw the nakedness of his father, and told his two brethren without.

And Shem and Japheth took a garment, and laid it upon both their shoulders, and went backward, and covered the nakedness of their father; and their faces were backward, and they saw not their father's nakedness. And Noah awoke from his wine, and knew what his younger son had done unto him. And he said, Cursed be Canaan; a servant of servants shall he be unto his brethren. And he said, Blessed be the Lord God of Shem; and Canaan shall be his servant.

God shall enlarge Japheth, and he shall dwell in the tents of Shem; and Canaan shall be his servant.

And Noah lived after the flood three hundred and fifty years. And all the days of Noah were nine hundred and fifty years: and he died" (Gen. 9:20-29).

a. What was this horrible sin which prompted a curse?

Some believe the crime involved here was homosexuality. Reasons for holding this view are:

(1) The Hebrew language seems to suggest it.

(2) The phrase "nakedness of his father" in 9:22 is definitely connected with sexual immorality in Leviticus 18 and 20.

(3) Ham's son, Canaan, was the progenitor of the Canaanite people who later populated Palestine and who were noted for their horrible habits of sexual perversion.

"And the border of the Canaanites was from Sidon, as thou comest to Gerar, unto Gaza; as thou goest, unto Sodom, and Gomorrah, and Admah, and Zeboim, even unto Lasha" (Gen. 10:19).

"And there came two angels to Sodom at even; and Lot sat in the gate of Sodom: and Lot seeing them rose up to meet them; and he bowed himself with his face toward the ground; and he said, Behold now, my lords, turn in, I pray you, into your servant's house, and tarry all night, and wash your feet, and ye shall rise up early, and go on your ways. And they said, Nay; but we will abide in the street all night. And he pressed upon them greatly; and they turned in unto him, and entered into his house; and he made them a feast, and did bake unleavened bread, and they did eat.

But before they lay down, the men of the city, even the men of Sodom, compassed the house round, both old and young, all the people from every quarter:

And they called unto Lot, and said unto him, Where are the men which came into thee this night? bring them out unto us, that we may know them.

And Lot went out at the door unto them, and shut the door after him, and said, I pray you, brethren, do not so wickedly. Behold now, I have two daughters which have not known man; let me, I pray you, bring them out unto you, and do ye to them as is good in your eyes: only unto these men do nothing; for therefore came they under the shadow of my roof.

And they said, Stand back. And they said again, This one fellow came in to sojourn, and he will needs be a judge: now will we deal worse with thee, than with them. And they pressed sore upon the man, even Lot, and came near to break the door.

But the men put forth their hand, and pulled Lot into the house to them, and shut to the door.

And they smote the men that were at the door of the house with blindness, both small and great: so that they wearied themselves to find the door'' (Gen. 19:1-11).

"And there were also sodomites in the land: and they did according to all the abominations of the nations which the Lord cast out before the children of Israel'' (1 Ki. 14:24).

"Wherefore God also gave them up to uncleanness through the lusts of their own hearts, to dishonour their own bodies between themselves: Who changed the truth of God into a lie, and worshipped and served the creature more than the Creator, who is blessed for ever. Amen.

For this cause God gave them up unto vile affections: for even their women did change the natural use into that which is against nature: And likewise also the men, leaving the natural use of the woman, burned in their lust one toward another; men with men working that which is unseemly, and receiving in themselves that recompence of their error which was meet'' (Rom. 1:24-27).

b. Why was Canaan cursed (9:25) when it would appear that Ham, "his younger son," had instigated the crime?
Lange's Commentary suggests that the phrase "his younger son" should be translated "his youngest one," and was actually a reference to Noah's youngest grandson, which was Canaan. To lend weight to this, if the account in Genesis 5:32 can be taken at face value, Japheth was Noah's youngest son, and not Ham.

c. What was involved in Noah's threefold prophecy?
(1) To Ham and Canaan—"a servant of servants shall he be unto his brethren."
    (a) Negative—it did not result in a special curse upon black people. Ham had four sons. These were:
    Cush—the progenitor of the Ethiopians
    Mizriam—of the Egyptians
    Phut—of the Libyans and peoples of Africa
    Canaan—of the Canaanites

Thus, as the curse was specifically leveled at Canaan and not Phut (who may have founded the African nations), there exist absolutely no racial implications whatsoever within the curse. In fact, the skin texture of Israelites and Canaanites at the time of Joshua's invasion was probably very similar. The problem concerning the Canaanites was not in the color of their *skin* but rather in the condition of their *hearts*.
    (b) Positive—but the wider scope of Noah's words accurately foretells that the descendants of Ham would be in some measure subjected to the descendants of both Shem and Japheth. History attests to this.
    Joshua, David, and *Solomon* had subdued them by 1000 B.C.
    Alexander the Great (a descendant of Japheth) defeated the Phoenicians in 331 B.C.
    The Romans (of Japheth) defeated Hannibal of Carthage (founded by the Hamitic Phoenicians in 850 B.C.) during the Second Punic War in 202 B.C. at Zama. German theologian Eric Sauer writes:
    "With Nimrod began, with Hannibal ended the drama of Hamitic World Empire, and Rome's brilliant victory sealed conclusively the . . . establishment of the world-rule of the Japhetic race. 'Let Canaan be his servant'—this it is which stands as written, as with letters of fire, over the battlefield of Zama.'' (*Dawn of World Redemption,* p. 80)

(2) To Shem—"Blessed be the Lord God of Shem." Here is obviously a reference to the special favor bestowed upon Shem's descendants, beginning with Abraham, Isaac, and Jacob, and ending in a Bethlehem manger.

(3) To Japheth—"God shall enlarge Japheth." Some nineteen centuries later this prophecy came to pass. During those centuries the Hamites ruled in the Nile Valley and the Semites reigned in Mesopotamia. But in October of 538, the decisive hour struck, as Cyrus the Persian (a descendant of Japheth) defeated Belshazzar (Dan. 5) and the proud Semitic capital fell. Since then no Semitic or Hamitic race has succeeded in breaking the world supremacy of the Japhetic race. Shortly after this, Cambyses, successor of Cyrus, conquered Egypt and ended the Hamitic rule. As recent as A.D. 732 Japhethic descendant Charles Martel defeated the combined hordes of both Semitics and Hamitics at the historic battle of Tours.

It should also be noted that the second part of the prophecy concerning Japheth reads, "and he shall dwell in the tents of Shem." Paul himself would later explain this glorious fulfillment in Romans 11:13-25.

"For I speak to you Gentiles, inasmuch as I am the apostle of the Gentiles, I magnify mine office: If by any means I may provoke to emulation them which are my flesh, and might save some of them. For if the casting away of them be the reconciling of the world, what shall the receiving of them be, but life from the dead?

For if the firstfruit be holy, the lump is also holy: and if the root be holy, so are the branches.

And if some of the branches be broken off, and thou, being a wild olive tree, wert grafted in among them, and with them, and with them partakest of the root and fatness of the olive tree; boast not against the branches. But if thou boast, thou bearest not the root, but the root thee.

Thou wilt say then, The branches were broken off, that I might be grafted in.

Well; because of unbelief they were broken off, and thou standest by faith. Be not highminded, but fear: For if God spared not the natural branches, take heed lest he also spare not thee. Behold therefore the goodness and severity of God: on them which fell, severity, but toward thee, goodness, if thou continue in his goodness: otherwise thou also shalt be cut off. And they also, if they abide not still in unbelief, shall be grafted in: for God is able to graft them in again. For if thou wert cut out of the olive tree which is wild by nature, and wert grafted contrary to nature into a good olive tree; how much more shall these, which be the natural branches, be grafted into their own olive tree? For I would not, brethren, that ye should be ignorant of this mystery, lest ye should be wise in your own conceits; that blindness in part is happened to Israel, until the fulness of the Gentiles be come in" (Rom. 11:13-25).

43. How have the descendants of each of Noah's three sons contributed to mankind?

Dr. Arthur C. Custance, renowned scholar and anthropologist writes the following:

"In the case of Ham and his descendants, history shows that they have rendered an extraordinary service to mankind from the point of view of the physical developments of civilization. All the earliest civilizations of note were founded and carried to their highest technical proficiency by Hamitic people. There is scarcely a basic technological invention which must not be attributed to them. As we shall show later, neither Shem nor Japheth made any significant contribution to the fundamental technology of civilization, in spite of all appearance to the contrary. This is a bold statement but it is not made in ignorance of the facts.

The contribution of Japheth has been in the application of philosophy to technology and the consequent development of the scientific method. As the application of Japheth's philosophy to the technology of Ham produced science, so the application of his philosophy to the religious insights of Shem produced theology. The Hamitic people never developed science and the Semitic people did not develop theology, until the influence of Japhetic philosophy was brought to bear . . . most of us have been brought up to believe that we, Indo-Europeans, are the most inventive people in the world. It is exceedingly difficult to escape from this culturally conditional prejudice to take a fresh objective look at the origins of our technological achievements. One may take almost any essential element of our highly complex civilization—aircraft, paper, weaving, metallurgy, propulsion of various kinds, painting, explosives, medical techniques, mechanical principles, food, the use of electricity, virtually anything technological in nature—and an examination of the history of its development leads us surely and certainly back to a Hamitic people and exceedingly rarely to Japheth or Shem. The basic inventions which have been contributed by Shem or Japheth can, it seems, be numbered on the fingers of one hand. This seems so contrary to popular opinion, yet it is a thesis which can be supported—and has been documented—from close to 1000 authoritative sources.

What we have been trying to show is that the historical process reflects the interaction between three families of people descended respectively from the three sons of Noah whom God appears to have apportioned specific responsibilities and equally specific capabilities for the fulfillment of them; to Shem, responsibility for man's religious and spiritual well-being; to Japheth, his mental well-being; and to Ham, his physical well-being . . . all the great religions of the world—true and false—had their roots in the family of Shem, all true philosophical systems have originated within the family of Japheth, and the world's basic technology is a Hamitic contribution . . . when these three work together in balanced harmony, civilization as a whole has advanced.

It is important to observe that all three are necessary for this. If any one element is given overemphasis the ultimate effect is detrimental! No society prospers which is over materialistic, or overly intellectual, or overly spiritual." (*Noah's Three Sons*, pp. 26, 37, 38, 263, 264)

In another book, Custance has written:

"I believe that in Adam and his descendants, until the Flood brought an end to the old world, these three capacities were by and large combined within each person individually though, of course, not always in exactly the same measure, just as not everyone now has the same level of intelligence. But each man carried within himself a threefold potential which after the Flood was very greatly reduced and more often than not was limited to a capacity chiefly in one direction. In another work, the thesis has been examined rather carefully that *science* results only where philosophy (the contribution of Japheth) is wedded to technology (the contribution of Ham), just as *theology* only arises where philosophy is wedded to spiritual insight based upon revelation (which was the specific contribution of Shem). On the whole, those who are highly inventive and mechanically minded are rarely of a philosophical turn of mind, and philosophers tend to be rather impractical. Whenever these two capacities do happen to appear in one man, we have the scientific individual. Unfortunately, scientifically minded people tend to be somewhat indifferent about spiritual things that are matters of faith. And since man is primarily a spiritual creature, science has often tended to be one-sided and inadequate, sometimes rather futile, and frequently dangerous because it encourages a sceptical attitude. But consider what would happen if every man had within himself a large capacity for invention and could extend the application of his own inventiveness as greatly as scientists have recently extended the basic technology of the previous 6,000 years of civilization. The progress of the past 100 years might have been crowded into the first few centuries of human history, and Adam's grandson might have seen the development of city life, the erection of very large buildings, the appearance of the arts including all kinds of music, the extended use of metals, and the establishment of cattlemen and farmers on a large scale—as evidently Cain's children did (Gen. 4:17-22).

But, as always seems to have been the case, man's spiritual capacity tended to suffer from disuse, or even abuse, and the evil in man was fortified very rapidly to an extraordinary degree by the exercise of the other capabilities, until the Lord looked down from Heaven and saw that it was too dangerous for the individual to be endowed so fully. After the Flood, what had been combined in Adam was thenceforth divided between Shem, Ham, and Japheth. During pre-flood times, however, it seems that the capacity of the individual was so much greater that the processes of civilization were all enormously accelerated." (*Genesis and Early Man*, pp. 138, 139)

44. What really took place at the Tower of Babel?

"And the whole earth was of one language, and of one speech. And it came to pass, as they journeyed from the east, that they found a plain in the land of Shinar; and they dwelt there. And they said one to another, Go to, let us make brick, and burn them throughly. And they had brick for stone, and slime had they for morter. And they said, Go to, let us build us a city and a tower, whose top may reach unto heaven; and let us make us a name, lest we be scattered abroad upon the face of the whole earth" (Gen. 11:1-4).

The passage in Genesis 11 does not teach that early mankind stupidly attempted to build a tower which would reach into outer space! Especially to be noted are the words in verse four "may reach." They are in italics to show they are supplied by the translators and therefore not in the original Hebrew text. In reality the phrase should read: "whose top is heaven."

Archaeological evidence suggests that the Tower of Babel was in reality a building given over to astrology, or the heathen worship of the heavens. Among the ruins of ancient Babylon is a building 153 feet high with a 400 foot base. It was constructed of dried bricks in seven stages, to correspond with the known planets to which they were dedicated. The lowermost was black, the color of Saturn, the next orange, for Jupiter, the third red, for Mars, and so on. These stages were surmounted by a lofty tower, on the summit of which were the signs of the Zodiac. Dr. Barnhouse writes:

"It was an open, definite turning to Satan and the beginning of devil worship. This is why the Bible everywhere pronounces a curse on those who consult the sun, the moon, and the stars of heaven."

"Lest we be scattered abroad" (11:4).

Years prior to this, the world's first murderer, Cain, heard God say, "A fugitive and a vagabond shalt thou be in the earth" (Gen. 4:12). Now Cain's spiritual children were rebelling against the same God, but were anxious to stay together, lest they share Cain's fate.

German theologian Erich Sauer has written:

"The original language in which Adam in Paradise had named all the animals was, as it were, a great mirror in which the whole of nature was accurately reflected. But now God shattered this mirror, and each people retained only a fragment of it, the one a larger, the other a smaller piece, and now each people sees only a piece of the whole, but never the whole completely." (*Dawn of World Redemption*, p. 82)

Thus, the many earphones and translation booths at the United Nations in New York today give eloquent testimony to the tragic episode at Babel. "Therefore is the name of it called Babel" (11:9). This tower project may have been named by Nimrod himself. Babel literally means "gate of God." Thus, while mankind had rejected the true God, they nevertheless attempted to assuage their uneasy consciences by acknowledging some vague and impersonal "grand architect of the universe." But it didn't work! God changed the meaning of the word Babel to mean "confusion."

45. When, where, and how did the distinct racial characteristics of modern mankind begin?

Dr. Henry Morris writes:

"As each family and tribal unit migrated away from Babel, not only did they each develop a distinctive culture, but also they each developed distinctive physical and biological characteristics. Since they would communicate only with members of their own family unit, there was no further possibility of marrying outside the family. Hence, it was necessary to establish new families composed of very close relatives, for several generations at least. It is well established genetically that variations take place very quickly in a small inbreeding population, but only very slowly in a large interbreeding population. In the latter, only the dominant genes will find common expression in the outward physical characteristics . . . even though the genetic factors for specifically distinctive characteristics are latent in the gene pool of the population. In a small population, however, the . . . genes will have opportunity to become openly expressed and even dominant under these circumstances. Thus, in a very few generations of such inbreeding, distinctive characteristics of skin color, height, hair texture, facial features, temperament, environmental adjustment, and others, could come to be associated with particular tribes and nations." (The *Genesis Record*, p. 176)

THE PATRIARCHAL STAGE

INTRODUCING THE PATRIARCHAL STAGE (Genesis 12-50; Job)

1. The important men who appear during this stage are Abraham, Isaac, Jacob, Joseph, and Job. Abraham is considered to be the second of the seven greatest men who ever lived. These are: Adam, Abraham, Moses, David, John the Baptist, Peter, and Paul.

2. In the Creation Stage God dealt with the entire earth in general. For example, Genesis 1-11 deals with the world of men as a whole. Now, however, in the Patriarchal Stage, he will employ the rifle instead of the shotgun. The floodlight will give way to the spotlight. Our attention is now drawn from the world to a nation (Israel), then to a tribe in that nation (Judah), then to a family within that tribe (Jesse), and finally to an individual within the family (Jesus Christ).

3. This stage spans a period of some 350 years.

4. Here a city is destroyed on the plains (Sodom) and a boy is spared on a mountain (Isaac) (Gen. 19, 22).

5. Here a son (Jacob) deceives his father (Isaac) and is later himself deceived by his sons (brothers of Joseph) (Gen. 27, 37).

6. Here we read of the first barren wife (Sarah) and the first dying mother (Rachel) (Gen. 16, 35).

7. This stage records how God's friend (Abraham) speaks to him concerning a city (Sodom), and how his enemy (Satan) speaks to him concerning a saint (Job) (Gen. 18; Job 1-2).

8. Jerusalem (a type of the heavenly) and Egypt (a type of the worldly) are first mentioned in this stage (Gen. 13-14).

9. Here we first learn of a king called Melchizedek and a cave named Machpelah (Gen. 14, 25).

10. Here the first of three great biblical covenants is introduced.
    a. The Abrahamic Covenant, promising a goodly land (Gen. 15).
    b. The Davidic Covenant, promising a glorious king (2 Sam. 7).
    c. The new covenant, promising a godly people (Jer. 31).

THE PATRIARCHAL STAGE

The remaining thirty-nine chapters of Genesis (12-50) summarize the lives of Abraham, Isaac, Jacob, and Joseph. Although there is some overlapping, the following chapter division may be noted:

Genesis 12-24—The story of Abraham
Genesis 24-27—The story of Isaac
Genesis 28-36—The story of Jacob
Genesis 37-50—The story of Joseph

THE PATRIARCHAL STAGE

ABRAHAM ISAAC JACOB JOSEPH
GENESIS 12-50   JOB

The Old Testament World

I. Abraham (Gen. 12-24).
   A. His conversion (Acts 7:2).
      The God of glory appeared unto our father, Abraham, when he was in Mesopotamia . . .
      1. Abraham was born around 2166 B.C. We know nothing of his early life or how he was led to God. It has been speculated that either Job, Shem, or even Melchizedek showed him the way of salvation. The importance of his life cannot be underestimated. He is mentioned some 308 times in the Bible; 234 times in the Old Testament; and seventy-four in the New Testament. These quotes came from twenty-seven books: sixteen in the Old Testament and eleven in the New Testament. Abraham was the reason the southern kingdom was spared as long as it was. (See 2 Ki. 13:23.)

The book of Genesis spans a period of around 2350 years. The first eleven chapters, which describe the Creation of the universe, the Fall, Flood, and Tower of Babel, cover a period of 2000 years. The last thirty-nine chapters concern themselves with Abraham and his seed, covering some 350 years. In other words, God gave us more detail about Abraham than about the origin of the universe!

2. Abraham was born and raised in the city of Ur of the Chaldees. Ur was a seaport on the Persian Gulf, at the mouth of the Euphrates River, some twelve miles from the traditional site of the Garden of Eden. But preceding the time of Abraham, it was the most magnificent city in all the world; a center of manufacturing, farming, and shipping, in a land of fabulous fertility and wealth, with caravans going in every direction to distant lands, and ships sailing from the docks of Ur down the Persian Gulf with cargoes of copper and hard stone. For years the skeptic ridiculed the actual existence of Ur. But during the years of 1922-1934 C. T. Wooley of the British museum thoroughly explored the secrets of these ruins.

The most conspicuous building of the city in Abraham's day was the ziggurat, or the temple tower, which was probably patterned after the Tower of Babel. This tower was square, terraced, and built of solid brick. Each successive terrace was planted with trees and shrubbery. The city had two main temples, one dedicated to Nannar, the Moon-god, and the other to his wife, Ningal.

(The information concerning Ur was gleaned in part from *Halley's Handbook*, pp. 88, 89.)

B. His calling (Gen. 11:31; 12:1; Josh. 24:3; Acts 7:2). He was to leave Ur and his father's house for a land that God would show him.

C. His commission (Gen. 12:2, 3; Acts 7:3) was sevenfold:
1. I will make of thee a great nation.
2. I will bless thee.
3. I will make thy name great.
4. Thou shalt be a blessing.
5. I will bless them that bless thee.
6. I will curse him that curseth thee. (See the book of Esther.)
7. In thee shall all families of the earth be blessed. (A reference to Christ; see Mt. 1:1.)

D. His caution (11:31, 32).
God had told Abraham to leave his father's house and proceed to Canaan. But he was disobedient concerning both matters in that he took his father with him, and allowed himself to get bogged down in Haran. Haran was the last green outpost of civilization before one entered the vast desert of Arabia. The city was 700 miles northwest of Ur and about sixty miles from the Euphrates River. It was located on a main caravan road connecting the cities of the east with Damascus and Egypt. This was considered a strategic location. The city also worshiped the moon god and goddess as did Ur.

Abram might have been content to settle in Haran permanently, but once more God stepped in and Terah his father died. After that, Abram quickly moves on! The name "Terah" means "delay." Only God knows the multitudes of Christians that have left Ur, bound for Canaan, only to get bogged down in Haran.

E. His Canaan (12:4-9).
1. He entered the Promised Land and pitched camp near Shechem, some thirty miles north of Jerusalem.
2. God again appeared to him. It should be noted that the Lord had simply promised to show him a land when he was in Ur, but now adds the words, "Unto thy seed will I give this land." (Compare 12:1 with 12:7.)
3. Abram built his first recorded altar here.
4. He then moved on to Bethel, a place meaning "house of God" which would later become a very sacred place in Canaan. (See Gen. 28:1-22; 35:7.) At Bethel he built his second altar to the Lord.

F. His carnality (12:10-20).
1. After a short while, the land was hit with famine. Thus far, he had obeyed God and was dwelling victoriously in the Promised Land. But now comes the temptation from Satan. There was a famine in the land.
2. He then left Palestine and went to Egypt. This is the first mention of Egypt in the Bible. Egypt in the Scriptures is pictured as a symbol or type of the world, an instance of dependence upon some human source or help apart from God. As God himself once warned: "Woe to them that go down to Egypt for help . . . and trust in chariots . . . and in horsemen . . . but . . . look not unto the Holy One of Israel, neither seek the Lord" (Isa. 31:1). The Christian therefore "goes to Egypt," spiritually speaking, when he depends upon something or someone else for guidance instead of God. (Carefully read Prov. 3:5, 6; 2:6, 8; Mt. 6:31-33.)
3. Pharaoh planned to marry Sarai, but was plagued by God and eventually found out the deception of Abraham. The angry king rightfully took Abram to task for this. After a frustrating, dangerous, and embarrassing time, Abram returned to Palestine, where he should have stayed in the first place. Notice the tragic results of his disobedience:
   a. He grieved God—Abram's sin (and our sin) always grieves God. (See Ps. 78:40; Eph. 4:30; Ps. 95:10; Mk. 3:5.)
   b. He weakened his own faith—later Abram failed God in this same matter of lying about his wife. (See Gen. 20.) After we once commit a sin, the second time becomes much easier.
   c. He became a poor testimony to his nephew Lot—some of Abram's worldliness rubbed off on Lot, with tragic results. (See Gen. 13, 19.)
   d. He caused the Pharaoh to be afflicted. (See 12:17.) Sometimes the children of the world suffer for the sins of Christians.

We note Pharaoh's rebuke to Abram here. There is no sadder situation in the world than when an unbeliever rebukes a Christian for some wrong action.

e. He picks up Hagar the Egyptian handmaid (Gen. 16:3). Hagar would later become Abram's mistress and would give birth to Ishmael, the father of the modern Arabs. Thus the agony of the world's most troubled hot spot, the Middle East, has been caused in part by Abram's sin some thirty-nine centuries ago.

f. He provided a bad example for his son, Isaac. Even though unborn at the time of the sin, Isaac doubtless was told of it as a young man; he failed God likewise by lying about his wife Rebekah. (See Gen. 26.)

Lest we forget—our sins always affect others.

G. His condescension (13:1-18).

1. Upon returning to Palestine he once again worshiped the Lord at Bethel—right where he had left God's blessing by going to Egypt. (See Isa. 30:15; Rev. 2:4, 5.)

2. The servants of Abraham and his nephew Lot began arguing over grazing rights. Abraham was concerned about this and graciously allowed the younger man to pick his choice of land. Lot foolishly selected that area near Sodom. Lot now left the Promised Land, never to return.

3. God appeared to Abraham for the third time and reassured him of a mighty posterity and of their eventual rights to Palestine.

H. His courage (14:1-16).

1. This chapter records the first war in the Bible. The last great battle can be found in Revelation 19:11-21. Until that time human wars will continue. On the headquarters of the United Nations there is inscribed the words of Micah 4:3: " . . . and they shall beat their swords into plowshares, and their spears into pruning hooks; nation shall not lift up a sword against nation, neither shall they learn war any more." This, of course, will be literally realized some glorious day. But not until the Prince of Peace comes to reign on this earth. Until that day, both Daniel (Dan. 9:26) and Jesus (Mt. 24:6) warned of continued war. It has been pointed out by the Society of International Law at London that there have been only 268 years of peace during the past 4000 years of human history, despite the signing of more than 8000 separate peace treaties. So then, until the coming of Christ, the United Nations should have more correctly inscribed the fearful words of Joel 3:9, 10: "Proclaim ye this among the Gentiles; Prepare war, wake up the mighty men; let all the men of war draw near; let them come up; beat your plowshares into swords, and your pruning hooks into spears."

2. Nine nations were involved in this war. It began when five kings, located in the Dead Sea area, revolted against Ched-or-Laomer, King of Elam, and his three allies. The Dead Sea Confederation, which included Sodom, was wiped out during a pitched battle. Lot, who had moved into the wicked city, was taken captive along with thousands of others. God would scarcely have bothered to record this pagan dog fight between nine heathen cities were it not for these four little words, "and they took Lot!" Lot still belonged to God. He didn't act like it, he didn't look, talk, dress, or walk like it, but God knows his own. (See 2 Tim. 2:19; 2 Pet. 2:7.)

3. Abraham learned of this and immediately armed his 318 trained servants for battle. We learn a number of things about Abraham's character from this single action.

a. He was a man of sympathy.
He could have said, "It serves him right," or, "He had it coming to him," but he didn't. Abram was fulfilling the truth that would later be written in Matthew 7:1 and Galatians 6:1.

b. He was prepared.
Abram kept in shape, spiritually, socially, mentally, and physically. God often cannot use a Christian, not because he is unclean, but because he is unprepared. The Bible has much to say about preparation. (See 2 Chron. 12:14; 19:3; 27:6; Mt. 3:3; Lk. 12:47; 2 Tim. 2:21.)

4. After a forced night march, Abraham caught up with them just north of Damascus and defeated them after a sudden surprise attack.

I. His communion (14:17-24).

1. As Abram returned from defeating Ched-or-Laomer, he was met by Melchizedek, the King of Salem (Jerusalem), who was also a priest of God. Who was this mysterious king-priest? There are three main theories as to his identity:

a. That he was Shem. This is the Hebrew tradition. If so, he would have been the world's oldest living person at the time. Shem died at the age of 600.

b. That he was Christ himself. This is referred to by theologians as a Christophany (a pre-Bethlehem Old Testament appearance of the Savior). Those who advocate this theory offer Hebrews 7:1-4 to support their claim.

c. That he was simply the first mentioned king of Jerusalem. Melchizedek literally means "King of Righteousness," and Salem is thought to be an early name for Jerusalem. Melchizedek is mentioned again in Psalm 110. (In the New Testament, he is found in Heb. 5:6-10; 7:1-22.)

2. Melchizedek brought him bread and wine and blessed him. This is the first mention of bread and wine in the Bible, and depicts the future work of Christ on the cross.

3. The word priest first appears in the Bible at this time. (See 14:18.) At this point it is appropriate to point out briefly the three great offices in the Old Testament. These are: The offices of prophet, priest, and king.

a. The prophet was one who represented God to man (1 Ki. 19:16).

    b. The priest was one who represented man to God (Lev. 8:12; Ps. 133:2).

    c. The king was one who under God ruled over man (1 Sam. 10:1; 16:13)

       In the New Testament, however, all three of these offices belong to our Lord Jesus Christ.

    a. He was a prophet (his past ministry) (Jn. 1:18; Mt. 21:11; Lk. 7:16; Jn. 4:19; Heb. 1:1, 2).

    b. He is a priest (his present ministry) (Rom. 8:34; Heb. 4:14-16; 7:24, 25; 1 Jn. 1:1).

    c. He will be a king (his future ministry) (Rev. 19:11-16).

4. After Melchizedek had blessed him, Abram gave him tithes of all he had. Some believe the practice of tithing (giving one's money to God) was only to be done by the nation Israel under the Law and therefore is not for us now. But this is not the case. Abram tithed long before Israel became a nation, and some 400 years before the Law was given. When we come to the New Testament, we are told that not just a tenth, but everything the Christian has belongs to God. (See 1 Cor. 6:19, 20.) This includes his *time* (Eph. 5:16; Ps. 90:12); his *talents* (Rom. 12:6; 1 Cor. 7:7; 2 Tim. 1:6); and his *treasures* (1 Cor. 16:1, 2; 2 Cor. 9:7).

5. Abram refused the materialistic offer of the ungodly Bera, who was King of Sodom. Bera wanted him to split the loot from the war.

J. His covenant (15:1-21).

1. God spoke to Abram in a vision, saying, "Fear not, Abram: I am thy shield, and thy exceedingly great reward" (15:1). Here we read for the first time those two wonderful little words, "fear not." Abram needed this reassurance at this time, for he had made some powerful enemies as a result of his actions in Genesis 14.

2. Abram "reminded" God that he and Sarai were still childless and suggested that a young servant boy named Eliezer of Damascus become his adopted heir. But this request was refused. Eliezer would later be used to aid Abram in another way. (See Gen. 24:1-4.)

3. God once again promised his old servant a child, this time adding the words, "Look now toward heaven, and count the stars, if thou be able to number them: and he said unto him, So shall thy seed be" (15:5). Here is another little proof of the Bible as God's Word. Today we know there are probably as many stars in the heavens as there are grains of sand on the seashores of the world. But in Abram's time men believed the total number of stars to be less than twelve hundred.

4. When God had finished, we are told that Abram "believed in the Lord; and he counted it unto him for righteousness" (15:6). This is the first biblical mention of three great words and each deserves our consideration.

    a. Believed.

      (1) This does not mean that Abram was the first man to believe in God, but rather that his faith is to be a pattern for all future believers. (See Rom. 4; Gal. 3:6-9; Heb. 11:8-10, 17, 19.)

      (2) It does not say Abram pleased God or appeased him, but that he *believed* in God.

    b. Counted. In the New Testament, this word is translated "imputed." To impute means to add to one's account. There are three main imputations in the Bible.

      (1) The imputation of Adam's sin upon the human race (Rom. 3:23; 5:12).

      (2) The imputation of the race's sin upon Christ (Isa. 53:5, 6; Heb. 2:9; 2 Cor. 5:14-21; 1 Pet. 2:24).

      (3) The imputation of God's righteousness upon the believing sinner (Phil. 3:9; Jas. 2:23; Rom. 4:6, 8, 11, 22, 23, 24).

    c. Righteousness—This word, simply defined, means "right clothing." The Bible teaches that all sinners are naked before God (Gen. 3:10; Heb. 4:13; Rev. 3:17). Some realize this and attempt to make their own set of spiritual clothes, but God looks upon such clothes as filthy rags (Isa. 64:6). Therefore, whenever a sinner realizes his nakedness and calls on the mercy of God, he gets a new suit of clothes. (See 2 Cor. 6:7; Eph. 6:14; Rev. 19:7, 8.)

5. When Abram asked how he could be sure all these things were true, especially the promise concerning the land, God ordered him to gather some animals and birds. Dr. Donald Barnhouse writes concerning this answer in 15:9:

"This is one of the strangest answers ever given to a question. Yet, it was the only possible answer. The question was, 'How am I to know that I shall possess the promised land?' The answer is, 'Bring me a heifer!' One might think that the dial of the radio had slipped from one program to another. The question is asked on a program of legal advice. The answer comes from a broadcast of a department of agriculture. But as we shall soon see, both the heifer and the inheritance are bound together in the mind of God." (*Genesis*, Vol. 1)

6. Abram gathered the creatures as ordered. In our culture today, whenever two parties determine to enter an agreement, a contract is drawn up and signed by both parties. But in Abram's time it was different. Back then the two parties would slaughter some animals, carve them up, and arrange the pieces in two lines. Then both parties would join hands and solemnly walk together down the middle path. By so doing they would pledge in the presence of blood and suffering and death, their intention to keep the terms of the contract. This is the first of three kinds of legal convenants in the Bible. These are:

    a. The covenant of blood (Gen. 15:10; Jer. 34:18, 19).

b. The covenant of a shoe (Ruth 4:7, 8).
c. The covenant of salt (Num. 18:19; 2 Chron. 13:5).

7. Just prior to God's physical presence upon this scene (in the form of a smoking fire-pot and a flaming torch), Abram was put into a deep sleep. As he slept, God's presence passed through these bloody pieces alone, thus indicating that the promises of Jehovah concerning Abram's salvation and his possession of Palestine were both unconditional, with no heavenly strings attached whatsoever. Thus, the Abrahamic Covenant which was *announced* in Genesis 12:1-4, and *confirmed* in 13:14-17; 15:1-7, is now officially and legally *ratified* here in 15:8-18.

8. In Genesis 15:13-16 God utters a sevenfold prophecy to Abram. *All seven have eventually come to pass.*
   a. That Abram's descendants would be strangers in a foreign land. (See Gen. 46:2-4.)
   b. That they would be servants in that land. (See Ex. 1:7-14.)
   c. That this servitude would last some 400 years. (See Ex. 12:40.)
   d. That God himself would later judge that nation which enslaved Israel. (See Ex. 7-12.)
   e. That Abram would be spared all of this. (See Gen. 25:7, 8.)
   f. That after spending four long generations in Egypt, Israel would return to Canaan. (See Ex. 6:16-20. Here we learn that Levi, Abram's great-grandson, was the first generation. Levi's son Kohath, was the second; Kohath's son, Amram, was the third; and Amram's son, Moses, was the fourth.)
   g. That Israel would come out of Egypt with great substance. (See Ex. 12:35, 36; Ps. 105:37.)

9. God would take a long time to accomplish this, however, "for the iniquity of the Amorites is not yet full" (15:16). Here we have another expression of that important principle first discussed in Genesis 6:3. Sin accumulates until the time when God's anger and judgment explode down upon it. In this case the Amorites were those wicked descendants of Canaan (Gen. 10:16) who had been dwelling in Palestine for some 400 years at the time of Abraham. But God would allow them yet another four or five hundred years before destroying them. (See Josh. 10.) (This truth is brought out by Paul in Rom. 2:4, 5. See also 2 Pet. 3:1-9; 2 Chron. 36:15, 16.) Thus, while God's patience and forgiveness have no *depth* limit (Rom. 5:20), they *do* have a *length* limit (Prov. 27:1).

K. His compromise (16:1-15).
   1. Sarai persuaded Abram to father a child through her Egyptian maiden girl Hagar. They would then adopt this child as their own.
   2. Hagar became pregnant and her arrogant attitude soon caused trouble, resulting in her dismissal from Abram's household by Sarai. This one verse alone refutes the doctrine of polygamy. God permitted it, but never approved it. (See Gen. 2:23; 1 Tim. 3:2.)
   3. Hagar was found by the angel of the Lord beside a desert spring and commanded to return to Abram and Sarai. The sex (male) and name (Ishmael) of her unborn child were prophesied by this angel. This is the first mention of the angel of the Lord. Some theologians believe that when this title is found in the Old Testament, it is actually another name for the Lord Jesus Christ. At any rate, this special angel played an important part in the history of Israel.
      a. The angel of the Lord wrestles with Jacob (Gen. 32:24-30).
      b. The angel of the Lord redeems Jacob (Gen. 48:16).
      c. The angel of the Lord speaks to Moses from a burning bush (Ex. 3:2).
      d. The angel of the Lord protects Israel at the Red Sea (Ex. 14:19).
      e. The angel of the Lord prepares Israel for the Promised Land (Ex. 23:20-23; Ps. 34:7; Isa. 63:9; 1 Cor. 10:1-4).
      f. The angel of the Lord commissions Gideon (Jdg. 6:11).
      g. The angel of the Lord ministers to Elijah (1 Ki. 19:7).
      h. The angel of the Lord reassures Joshua (Josh. 5:13-15).
      i. The angel of the Lord saves Jerusalem (Isa. 37:36).
      j. The angel of the Lord preserves three Hebrew young men (Dan. 3:25). In this verse the angel of the Lord locates and comforts a pagan Egyptian woman named Hagar. Hagar does not fare well in the Bible, for she possesses little or no spirituality, is brazen, hateful, proud, disrespectful, and is a poor mother. Yet God loves her, and sends his blessed messenger to help her.
   4. Ishmael is born. Abram was eighty-six years old at this time.

L. His circumcision (17:1-27).
   1. As chapter 16 ends, Abram is at his lowest spiritual point. He has sinned and is out of fellowship with both his God and his family. But the Lord seems to do nothing to his erring child. Is Abram going to get away with all this?
      To answer we need only note that he was eighty-six years old when Ishmael was born (16:16), but is 99 when God again speaks with him. Abram thus apparently suffered a thirteen-year period of God's grieved silence. Here the words of the Psalmist concerning Israel's history comes to mind: "And he gave them their request; but sent leanness into their soul" (Ps. 106:15).
   2. In spite of this, a gracious God now forgives and restores him (Ps. 51) back into fellowship. The title "Almighty God" in the Hebrew is *El Shaddai.* The word *Shadd* refers to

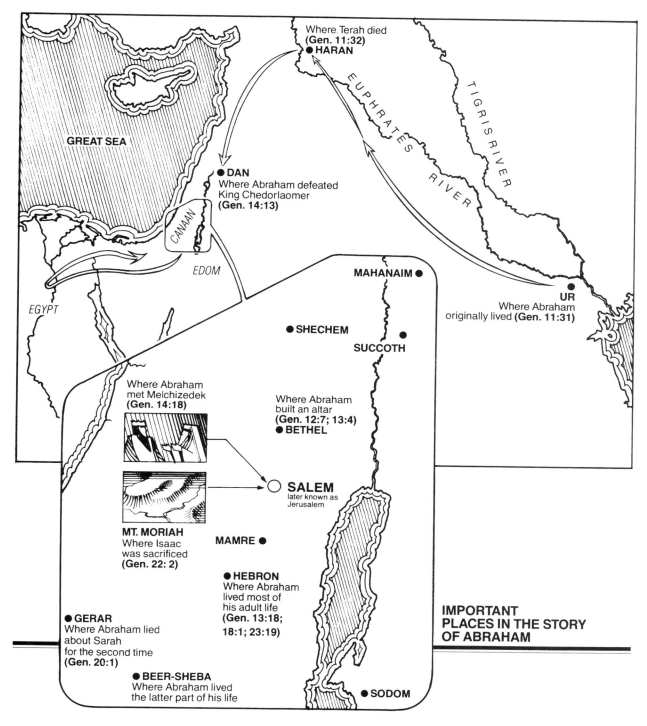

IMPORTANT PLACES IN THE STORY OF ABRAHAM

the bosom of the nursing mother. The word *El* means "the strong one."

a. God comforts Jacob with his name (Gen. 35:10, 11).

b. He reassures Moses with this name (Ex. 6:3).

c. Jacob blesses Joseph with this name (Gen. 49:25).

This title is found more often in the book of Job (thirty-one times) than in any other Old Testament book. And that suffering patriarch needed it. Perhaps the most sublime passage in which it is used is Psalm 91:1: "He that dwelleth in the secret place of the most High shall abide under the shadow of the Almighty."

3. His name was now changed from Abram, which means "exalted father," to Abraham, which means, "Father of a great multitude." Dr. Donald Barnhouse has summarized Abram's life at this time in a wonderful and witty way:

"And the point of the story lies in the fact that Abram had no seed. This may not be

41

a disaster in our western lands, but in the Orient it must have been particularly galling.

There are some things in the Bible that cause me to chuckle, and there is a thought in connection with this verse that always has had that effect on me. I cannot help think of what must have happened when Abraham broke the news to his family and servants that he was now changing his name. They all knew that his former name was Abram, father of many, and they knew it had been somewhat of a thorn to him. So we can imagine the stir of interest and curiosity when he announced, 'I am going to change my name.' 'The old man couldn't take it. It finally got under his skin.' After all, to be father of nobody for eighty-six years, and then to be father of only one, with a name like he has—father of many—must have its rough moments. So he is going to change his name. I wonder what it will be."

And then the old man spoke, 'I am to be known as Abraham—father of a multitude.' We can almost hear the silence of the stunned moment as the truth breaks upon them. Father of a multitude? Then the laughter broke forth behind the scenes. 'The old man has gone crazy. He had one child when he was eighty-six and now at ninety-nine he is beginning to get ideas. Father of a multitude! Was there anything more ridiculous for a man of his age?' " (*God's Remedy*, Vol. III, p. 316)

4. For the fourth time now God reaffirms the land and seed covenant to his old servant. (See Gen. 12:2, 3, 7; 13:14-17; 15:5.) On this occasion (17:9-14), God commanded Abraham to circumcise himself, all the males of his household, and each future male baby on the eighth day of birth. Following is a brief summary of circumcision as found in the Bible.

a. Abraham was the first man to be circumcised.
   This in itself was a real act of faith, for it rendered completely helpless all the males in the camp.

b. Circumcision was to be the seal (or sign) of God's promise, but not the source.

c. Faith in God's Word was the source.

d. Circumcision of the flesh without circumcision of the heart was absolutely worthless.
   Years later, Moses would remind Israel: "And now, Israel, what doth the Lord thy God require of thee, but to fear the Lord thy God, to walk in all his ways, and to love him, and to serve the Lord thy God with all thy heart and with all thy soul. Circumcise therefore the foreskin of your heart, and be no more stiffnecked" (Deut. 10:12, 16).

e. Circumcision was set aside in Acts 15:29.

5. Abraham's wife's name is now changed from Sarai (contentious) to Sarah (a princess).

6. Abraham laughs for joy (Rom. 4:19-21) at the thought of his own physical heir and asks God to bless Ishmael.

7. God promises to bless Ishmael and then commands Abraham and Sarah to name the future heir of the covenant, Isaac.

8. Abraham obeys God's command to circumcise all males.

M. His compassion.

1. Abraham is personally visited by the Lord and two angels. As he ministers to them, God again promises him an heir, and this time sets a date (18:10, 14).

2. Sarah overhears this conversation and laughs in disbelief. God rebukes Abraham for his wife's unbelief. Sarah then denies that she laughed (18:10-15).

3. Both Sarah and Abraham then hear God's thrilling words (18:14): "Is anything too hard for the Lord?" (See also Lk. 1:26-37; Mt. 19:23-26.)

4. The two angels depart to complete a secret mission to Sodom. God then reveals to Abraham his intention to destroy that wicked cesspool of sin on the desert sand (18:16-22).

5. Abraham then begins his remarkable plea for Sodom. This is one of the most compassionate and persistent prayers in all the Bible.

   a. It was definite. He did not pray for "that soul nearest hell," or for "the missionaries around the world," or for "Aunt Tilly's sore toe."

   b. It was reverent. "I . . . am but dust and ashes" (v. 27).

   c. It was mixed with faith. "Shall not the Judge of all the earth do right?" (v. 25).

6. At first he asks God to spare the city if but fifty righteous persons can be found there. God agrees. Then the request is for forty-five; then forty; then thirty; then twenty; and finally ten. Here Abraham stops. Why did he not press for five? The answer is that he probably felt there were at least ten saved people. There were, after all, Lot, Lot's wife, their two unmarried daughters, and the married daughters and their husbands. This group he thought would surely total more than ten! But Abraham was to be heartbroken, for it would appear that only Lot and his two unmarried daughters were saved.

N. His corrupted kin (19:1-38).

1. In this chapter we have the dramatic account of the destruction of Sodom, which is the second of two Old Testament events referred to by our Lord as illustrations of the coming day of judgment. The first event was the flood in Noah's day. Note Christ's words in Luke 17:26-30.

2. The angels find Lot at the gate of Sodom. He was probably an alderman of some sort, with delegated authority. He has now come the full circle of compromise. Note the sad order of his tragic fall:

a. He first looked longingly at Sodom (Gen. 13:10).

b. He then chose the area of ground near Sodom (Gen. 13:11).

c. He next pitched his tent toward Sodom (Gen. 13:12).

d. He thereupon moved into the city of Sodom (Gen. 14:12).

e. He finally gives both his daughters and his energies to Sodom (Gen. 19). Surely the New Testament words apply here: "Behold, how great a matter a little fire kindleth!" (Jas. 3:5). Sin is like cancer and leprosy. It starts off ever so small, but winds up eating at the vital organs of the body.

In the New Testament Simon Peter's great sin of cursing the Lord Jesus also began very small. He warmed his hands at the camp of the enemy (Lk. 22:54-56).

f. He began by boasting of his loyalty (Mk. 14:29)

g. He then slept when he should have prayed (Mk. 14:37)

h. He thereupon followed Christ from afar off (Mt. 26:58)

i. He next is found associating with Christ's enemies (Mt. 26:69)

j. He finally curses the Savior (Mt. 26:70-74)

Lot makes a feast for these two angels and prepares unleavened bread. This action suggests two facts: The fact that he served them unleavened bread indicates he recognized the identity of his heavenly guests. The fact that he and not his wife did the baking suggests her unconcern for her husband's position or the things of God.

3. The angels tell Lot of the impending destruction of Sodom. Conditions were so corrupt that they were forced to blind some sexual perverts who had surrounded Lot's home where they were staying. These men had absolutely no respect for the backslidden Lot.

4. Lot had become so carnal that he attempted to appease those Sodomite sinners by offering them his two virgin daughters. He also refers to them as "brethren." (See 2 Jn. 10, 11.)

5. He spends the rest of the night in a frantic but fruitless attempt to convince his married daughters to flee to the city with him.

6. At daybreak the angels literally drag Lot, his wife, and their two daughters out of Sodom, telling them to flee to the mountains.

7. Lot begins arguing, begging that they allow him to settle in a nearby little city called Zoar instead of the mountains.

8. Lot's family receives one final warning: "Haste thee, escape there; for I cannot do anything till thou be come there" (19:22). Sodom's destruction is a foreshadow of the coming tribulation, and Lot's departure may be pictured as a type of the Rapture of all believers. (See 2 Thess. 2:6, 7.)

9. The Lord then "rained upon Sodom and upon Gomorrah brimstone and fire from . . . out of heaven" (19:24). Brimstone is often used in the Bible to denote punishment and destruction (Deut. 29:23; Job 18:15; Ps. 11:6; Isa. 30:33; Ezek. 38:22; Lk. 17:29; Rev. 9:17). Some feel it to be a reference to sulphur. We are told in Genesis 14:10, that the surrounding area of Sodom was "full of slime pits" (or asphalt pits).

10. Lot's wife looked back and she became a pillar of salt. In Luke 17:32, the Lord Jesus admonishes all men to "remember Lot's wife." And so we should. Her life is proof of the saying: "You can take the boy out of the farm, but not the farm out of the boy." In her case the proverb would read: "You can take a worldly person out of the world, but you can't take the world out of a worldly person."

The unbeliever has often ridiculed the account of Lot's wife turning into a hundred-pound bag of salt! Of course God could have literally done this, but a more reasonable explanation would be that a flaming glob of sulphur fell upon her and encrusted her with its salty substance.

God remembered Abraham, and sent Lot out. A gracious God has promised to forget the confessed sins of all believers (Heb. 8:12), but in his faithfulness he does remember at least two things:

a. The prayers of a believer (see Gen. 18:23; Rev. 5:8).

b. The works of a believer (Heb. 6:10).

Thus carnal and worldly Lot was saved through the faithful prayers of Abraham. Perhaps Jude had Lot in mind when he later wrote:

"And of some have compassion, making a difference: And others save with fear, pulling them out of the fire; hating even the garment spotted by the flesh" (Jude 1:22, 23).

11. In his terrible fear, Lot bypasses Zoar and takes refuge in a cave with his two unmarried daughters. Here the ultimate is shown of the high cost of low living. Lot's daughters, fearing they will never marry, get their own father drunk, and have sexual relations with him. Both bear him children. The oldest daughter names her son Moab (father of the Moabites) and the younger daughter calls her boy Ben-ammi (father of the Ammonites). Both nations would later cause Israel much heartache. (See Gen. 19:30-38.)

O. His carnality (20:1-17).

1. Abraham falls into the same sin pattern here as he had once done in Egypt. On this occasion he moves into the land of the Philistines and lies to Abimelech concerning Sarah as he previously lied to Pharaoh.

2. God warns Abimelech in a dream not to touch Sarah.

3. Abimelech rebukes Abraham for lying to him.

Abraham

EVENT	DETAILS	SCRIPTURE REFERENCE
1. **CONVERSION AT UR**	**SEVENFOLD PROMISE** 1. I will make of thee a great nation. 2. I will bless thee. 3. I will make thy name great. 4. Thou shalt be a blessing. 5. I will bless them that bless thee. 6. I will curse him that curseth thee. 7. In thee shall all the families of the earth be blessed.	**Acts 7:2** **Gen. 11:31** **Gen. 12:1-4** **Josh. 24:3**
2. **AT HARAN**	PARTIAL OBEDIENCE: He takes his father and settles in Haran	**Gen. 11:31, 32**
3. **ARRIVAL IN CANAAN**	He builds an altar and is promised the land	**Gen. 12:4-9**
4. **TRIP TO EGYPT**	**REASON:** A famine in Canaan **SIN:** Doubt (concerning God) and deceit (concerning Sarai) **TYPE:** Egypt is a type of the world **RESULTS:** 7 tragic consequences: 1. He grieved God 2. He weakened his own faith 3. He weakened the faith of Sarai 4. He became a poor testimony to his nephew Lot 5. He caused the Pharaoh to be afflicted 6. He picked up Hagar, the Egyptian handmaid 7. He provided a bad example for his son, Isaac	**Gen. 12:10-20**
5. **MEETS MELCHIZEDEK**	**BACKGROUND:** Abram had won a war and rescued his nephew **IDENTITY OF MELCHIZEDEK:** Christ? Shem? Unknown priest? **IMPORTANCE OF MEETING:** Four firsts recorded: 1. FIRST COMMUNION (bread and wine) 2. First mention of HOLY CITY (Salem) 3. First mention of PRIEST 4. First example of TITHING	**Gen. 13, 14**
6. **RATIFICATION OF HIS COVENANT**	**BACKGROUND:** This covenant was: 1. Announced in Genesis 12:1-4 2. Confirmed in Genesis 13:14-17; 15:1-7 3. Ratified in Genesis 15:8-18 **METHOD EMPLOYED:** A blood agreement **FEATURES:** A land (Palestine) and a people (Israel) **TERMS:** Unconditional, no strings attached **LANGUAGE:** Three key words: **BELIEVED, COUNTED, RIGHTEOUSNESS** **PROPHECY INVOLVED:** The 400-year Egyptian captivity and deliverance of Israel	**Gen. 15**
7. **MARRIAGE TO HAGAR**	The **PLAN** of Sarai The **PLIGHT** of Hagar The **AID** of an angel The **BIRTH** of Ishmael	**Gen. 16**

  4. Abraham prays for God's blessing to fall upon Abimelech.
 P. His celebration (21:1-34).
  1. Isaac is born as God had promised. His name meant "laughter."
  2. A great celebration is held to mark the weaning of Isaac.
  3. Hagar and her fourteen-year-old son Ishmael are sent away from Abraham's household for mocking Isaac during this happy occasion. (Paul discusses the significance of this event in Gal. 4:22-31.)
  4. God graciously ministers to Hagar and Ishmael after they are lost in the wilderness of Beer-sheba, by pointing her to a fresh well. Ishmael later marries an Egyptian girl and becomes an expert archer.
 Q. His "calvary" (22:1-24).
  1. God "tempts" Abraham by ordering him to "take now thy son, thine only son Isaac, whom thou lovest, and get thee into the land of Moriah: and offer him there for a burnt offering . . . " (22:2) This was in reality a *test* to help Abraham grow spiritually. (Contrast Gen. 22:2 with Jas. 1:13.)
  2. The land of Moriah was that district around Jerusalem where the Temple was much later built (see 2 Chron. 3:1). Just what did God

Abraham

8.	**ABRAM AT 99**	**SOME NEW NAMES** 1. Abram changed to Abraham (father of nations) 2. Sarai changed to Sarah (a princess) 3. God introduced as *El Shaddai* (the fruitful one) **A NEW SEAL:** circumcision now becomes the sign of God's covenant	**Gen. 17**
9.	**GOOD NEWS AND BAD NEWS**	**ABRAHAM** is visited by the Lord and two angels The **GOOD** news: His long-promised heir would be born the next spring The **BAD** news: God planned to destroy Sodom, Lot's home city **SODOM** is destroyed. Only Lot and his two daughters survive	**Gen. 18, 19**
10.	**ABRAHAM IN PHILISTIA**	During a famine he again leaves Canaan and lies about Sarah	**Gen. 20**
11.	**THE HEIR OF THE COVENANT**	Isaac is born Hagar and Ishmael are sent away	**Gen. 21**
12.	**FORESHADOWS OF CALVARY**	The **TYPE:** 1. Sacrifice of Isaac 2. Substitute for Isaac The **LOCATION:** Mt. Moriah, thought to be Golgotha The **REVELATION:** A new name for God, Jehovah-Jireh ("the Lord will provide")	**Gen. 22**
13.	**DEATH OF SARAH**	Sarah dies at 127 and is buried in the cave of Machpelah	**Gen. 23**
14.	**COMMANDING HIS SERVANT**	**ABRAHAM'S COMMAND:** To fetch a bride for Isaac **THE SERVANT'S PRAYER:** Show me the right girl **THE LORD'S ANSWER:** Rebekah is the one **THE SCRIPTURAL TYPES:** This is the most type-filled chapter in the Bible 1. Abraham is a type of the Father 2. Isaac is a type of the Son 3. The servant is a type of the Holy Spirit 4. Rebekah is a type of the Church	**Gen. 24**
15.	**HIS MARRIAGE TO KETURAH**	She bore him six sons **The fourth was Midian, father of the Midianites**	**Gen. 25:1-6**
16.	**HIS DEATH**	**AGE:** 175 Place of **BURIAL:** The cave of Machpelah **EPITAPH:** **HEB. 11:8-10** "By faith Abraham, when he was called to go out into a place which he should after receive for an inheritance, obeyed; and he went out, not knowing whither he went. By faith he sojourned in the land of promise, as in a strange country, dwelling in tabernacles with Isaac and Jacob, the heirs with him of the same promise: For he looked for a city which hath foundations, whose builder and maker is God."	**Gen. 25:7-10; Heb. 11:8-10**

BY FAITH ABRAHAM... BY FAITH ABRAHAM... BY FAITH

order Abraham to do to Isaac? (Later, in Lev. 1:1–9, Moses is given instructions about the burnt offering.)

a. The offering had to be a male animal without blemish.

b. It had to be offered voluntarily by the owner.

c. It was killed and the blood sprinkled.

d. It was then cut into pieces.

e. Finally, it was washed and burned.

How much of this was known to Abraham, we are not told. But this the old man did know: God was ordering him to slaughter his beloved son.

3. They arrived on the third day. Abraham left a day after God commanded him, and it took three days to get to Moriah, thus making a total of four days. This corresponds perfectly to Exodus 12:3, where the Passover Lamb was to be kept for four days before killing it. (See Gen. 22:3, 4.)

4. Abraham then instructs his servants, saying: "Abide ye here with the ass; and I and the lad will go yonder and worship, and come again to you" (22:5). Here we see a glimpse of Abraham's faith. Notice he tells the men that both he and his son would come back again. Thus even though Abraham fully

meant to sacrifice Isaac, he believed God would raise him from the dead! So then the two highest points in this grand old man's life would be:

   a. Believing God concerning the supernatural birth of his son (Rom. 4:18–21).
   b. Believing God concerning the supernatural resurrection of his son (Heb. 11:17–19).

5. Isaac then asked, "Behold the fire and the wood: but where is the lamb for a burnt offering?" (22:7). This question is still being asked by a frightened and confused world today. Where is that lamb? Where do we look for our salvation? The world asks the right question, but looks for the wrong thing. Some look for this lamb in various directions:

   a. The lamb of education.
   b. The lamb of good works.
   c. The lamb of the U.N.
   d. The lamb of baptism.
   e. The lamb of church membership.

   But the salvation lamb cannot be found in any of these.

6. The heartbroken old patriarch softly answers his son: "My son, God will provide himself a lamb for a burnt offering . . ." (22:8). This one sentence is a complete summary of the Bible. Theologically we could read it in either of the following ways:

   a. God will provide *for* himself a lamb—that is, the lamb will come from God.
   b. God will provide himself *for* a lamb—that is, the lamb offered will be God.

   Either way is correct, for in the New Testament, both meanings come true.

7. Abraham builds an altar and binds his only son to it. This little statement speaks highly of Isaac, for he was not the small boy some have pictured him to be, but probably a full grown man. Yet he willingly allows his old father to tie and bind him to a death altar (22:9).

8. The Spirit of God records for us in dramatic phrases the breathtaking action which now takes place on that windswept hill: "And Abraham stretched forth his hand, and took the knife to slay his son" (Gen. 22:10).

   However, before he can do this, God shows him a nearby ram and orders this animal to be sacrificed in place of Isaac. A grateful Abraham obeys and names this place Jehovah-jireh.

9. The title Jehovah-jireh is one of God's great names in the Old Testament, and it literally means, "the Lord will provide." Does it really pay to serve God? Just for the record, God had already provided Abraham with the following "fringe benefits."

   a. eternal salvation (Gen. 15:6)
   b. guidance (Gen. 12:1)
   c. courage (Gen. 14:15)
   d. spiritual blessings (Gen. 14:19)
   e. earthly needs (Gen. 13:2)
   f. social security (Gen. 15:15)
   g. forgiveness (Gen. 20:17)

   h. a son in his old age (Gen. 21:3)
   i. continued protection (Gen. 15:1)
   j. the promise of a heavenly city (Heb. 11:10)

10. Before leaving this chapter, let us notice some striking similarities between Abraham the father and God the Father:

   a. Both had a beloved son (Mt. 3:17; 17:5). Both were born miraculously (Lk. 1:35).
   b. Both had willing sons—that is, sons that were willing to be offered up (Jn. 10:18).
   c. Both offered up their sons (Jn. 3:16; both on the same spot).
   d. Both received their sons back with great joy (Ps. 24:7–10).
      (Note: Some believe this Psalm refers to the Lord Jesus' coming back to the glory of heaven after his death and resurrection.)
   e. Both made careful preparations for their sons' weddings. In Genesis 24, Abraham sends his trusted servant out to find a bride for Isaac. In the New Testament, we read, of course, of the Heavenly Father's preparation for his Son's wedding (Mt. 22:1, 2).

11. The angel of the Lord again announces the features of the Abrahamic Covenant.

12. Upon returning home Abraham learns a message has arrived bringing him up to date concerning his brother Nahor, whom he apparently had not seen since leaving Ur. Nahor had moved into Haran and God had blessed him and his wife Milcah with eight sons. The fifth son, Bethuel, would become important in the biblical record, for he had a daughter named Rebekah and a son named Laban. Rebekah would, of course, later marry Isaac; and Laban's daughters, Rachel and Leah, were to be Jacob's wives (22:19–24).

R. His cave (23:1–20).

   1. Sarah dies at the age of 127. There are those today who would advocate the adoration of Mary, but in the New Testament it is the life of Sarah that is called to our attention. (See 1 Pet. 3:1–6.)

   2. Abraham buys a cave at Machpelah for 400 pieces of silver and buries his beloved wife there. Later he himself will be laid there.

S. His command (24:1–67).

   1. Abraham commands his trusted servant (Eliezer) to go to Haran and choose a wife for Isaac.

   2. Upon reaching his destination, the servant kneels down outside the city and prays for wisdom. This is one of the most remarkable prayers in all the Bible, not only because of its great faith, but because it was answered even before the prayer was finished. The servant asks God to show which girl he desired for Isaac by causing her to offer both him and the thirsty camels some water. Note the result:

      "And it came to pass, before he had done speaking, that, behold, Rebekah came out, who was born to Bethuel, son of Milcah, the wife of Nahor, Abraham's

brother, with her pitcher upon her shoulder" (24:15).
3. Rebekah unknowingly fulfills his prayer by offering water both to the servant and his camels.
4. The servant is introduced to Rebekah's mother and her brother Laban. He informs them of his mission, and also of the amazing answer to his prayer.
5. Rebekah agrees to go with the servant and become Isaac's wife.
6. Isaac anxiously awaits his bride in a field near Hebron. They become husband and wife.
This is one of the great typical chapters in all the Bible. Note:
a. Abraham is a perfect type of the Heavenly Father. It is the Father who is planning a marriage for his beloved Son (see Mt. 22:2).
b. Isaac is a perfect type of the Lord Jesus Christ. Isaac, like Jesus, had been offered up as a sacrifice (compare Gen. 22 with Mt. 27) and seeks his bride. Isaac, like Christ, had been given all things of his father. (Compare 24:36 with Phil. 2:9, 10.) Finally Isaac, like Christ, loves his bride dearly. (Compare 24:67 with Eph. 5:25.)
c. Eliezer is a perfect type of the Holy Spirit. Abraham's servant came to Mesopotamia for one sole reason—to take a bride for Isaac. Years later (Acts 2) the Holy Spirit would come at Pentecost for one purpose—to gather a bride for the Son. While at Mesopotamia, Eliezer gave honor constantly to the father and son. Today the Holy Spirit does likewise. (See Jn. 15:26.)
d. Rebekah is a perfect type of the church. Before anyone can enter God's true church, he or she must first favorably answer the question of the Father's servant: "And they called Rebekah, and said unto her, Wilt thou go with this man? And she said, I will go" (24:58).
T. His Keturah (25:1-6).
1. Abraham marries a woman named Keturah, who bears him six sons.
2. The most important son was Midian, the fourth boy, who became the father of the Midianites. This nation would later cause Israel much grief.
U. His city (25:7-10; Heb. 11:8-10).
"And these are the days of the years of Abraham's life which he lived, an hundred threescore and fifteen years.
Then Abraham gave up the ghost, and died in a good old age, an old man, and full of years; and was gathered to his people.
And his sons Isaac and Ishmael buried him in the cave of Machpelah, in the field of Ephron, the son of Zohar the Hittite, which is before Mamre;
The field which Abraham purchased of the sons of Heth: There was Abraham buried, and Sarah his wife" (25:7-10).
"By faith Abraham, when he was called to go out into a place which he should after receive for an inheritance, obeyed; and he went out, not knowing whither he went. By faith he sojourned in the land of promise, as in a strange country, dwelling in tabernacles with Isaac and Jacob, the heirs with him of the same promise: For he looked for a city which hath foundations, whose builder and maker is God" (Heb. 11:8-10).

II. Isaac (Gen. 25—27).
Isaac has been described as the mediocre son of a great father (Abraham) and the mediocre father of a great son (Jacob). The main action of his life occurs at the following five places: on a mountain, by a field, alongside some desert wells, in a Philistine apartment, and at a supper table.
A. On a Jerusalem mountain (22:1-14).
The submissive son. Isaac meekly submits to being used as a burnt offering.
B. By a Hebron field (24:61-67; 25:9-11, 19-26); *the gentle groom.*
1. He meets Rebekah for the first time (24:61-67).
2. He and Ishmael his brother bury their father Abraham (25:9).
Abraham had lived thirty-eight years after the death of Sarah.
3. Ishmael dies at the age of 137 (25:17).
4. Isaac prayed that God would give him and his wife children (25:21).
This is the second of five recorded biblical prayers for a child. Note:
a. Abraham's prayer (Gen. 15:2).
b. Isaac's prayer (Gen. 25:21).
c. Rachel's prayer (Gen. 30:1, 22).
d. Hannah's prayer (1 Sam. 1:10, 11; 2:1-10).
e. Zachariah's prayer (Lk. 1:5-7, 13-17).
5. Rebekah gives birth to twin boys. They are named Esau and Jacob (25:24-26).
C. In a Philistine home (26:1-14); the copy cat.
1. Isaac repeats the sin of his father many years back. (See 1 Cor. 10:13.)
a. In time of famine, he forsakes Palestine and moves into the Philistine area (as Abraham had once gone to Egypt).
b. He lies to King Abimelech concerning Rebekah, saying she is his sister.
2. Abimelech discovers the truth of the matter and reproves a totally embarrassed Isaac about his lying.
3. In spite of his carnality, God reaffirms the Abrahamic Covenant to Isaac and blesses him greatly in material things.
D. Alongside some desert wells (26:15-34); the willing worker.
1. The Philistines soon became jealous of his great success and retaliated by filling up with earth some old wells once dug by his father, Abraham. Isaac spends a great deal of time clearing the debris from these clogged water holes.
The young minister of God can derive some profitable lessons from these verses. Throughout history our spiritual forefathers had, with patience and pleasure, dug down deep into the Word of God and beautifully exposed those clear, fresh cold water wells of the virgin birth, the sinless life of Christ, his

death, resurrection, ascension, and future second coming. But of late these wells have been clogged in the minds of many because of the hateful actions of false critics. Therefore, the main job of the young man of God today is to clean out these wells, that the life-giving fluids may once again satisfy the parched hearts of humanity.

2. Isaac (as did once his father Abraham) enters into a nonaggressive pact with King Abimelech (Prov. 16:7).
3. God appears to Isaac again.
4. Isaac and Rebekah are grieved over the marriage of Esau, who at forty years of age, picks a pagan girl for his wife.

E. At a supper table in his own home (27:1-46); the frustrated father.

1. Isaac, at age 137, felt he was at the point of death. Actually, he would live another forty-three years and reach 180 (Gen. 35:28). His brother Ishmael had died at 137 (25:17) and this may have influenced his thinking. In addition, he was half-blind at this time.
2. He instructs Esau to kill a deer and prepare him a venison meal that he might eat and bless him before he dies. At the very point of death (or so he thought) Isaac's last thoughts were on his stomach! His spiritual condition had apparently seriously deteriorated (see Phil. 3:18, 19).
3. Rebekah overhears this conversation and immediately enters a plot with Jacob to deceive Isaac, that he (Jacob) might obtain the blessing. Rebekah was right in concluding that God desired the blessing to go to Jacob (Gen. 25:23), but she was totally wrong by taking matters into her own hands. The end never justifies the means. It is never right to do wrong that right might be done (see Rom. 3:8). Jacob feels the plot will never work. In spite of being half-blind, the lad knew his father would want to lay hands on him, and he complains: "Behold, Esau, my brother, is a hairy man, and I am a smooth man" (27:11). He surely was, and in more ways than one. You would not have wanted to buy a used car from Jacob!
5. His mother reassures him, "Upon me be thy curse, my son" (see Mt. 27:24, 25), and prepares Jacob for his deceitful action by cooking a dish similar to that of venison. She then dressed him in Esau's rough clothing and put "the skins of the kids of the goats upon his hands, and upon the smooth of his neck" (27:16).
6. Jacob then presents himself to Isaac as Esau. When asked how he found the venison so quickly, Jacob lies, "Because the Lord thy God brought it to me" (27:20).
7. After some initial doubts concerning his identity, Isaac gives the blessing.
8. Jacob kisses his father. This is the first of three kisses of treachery in the Bible.
   a. Jacob kisses Isaac in order to deceive him (Gen. 27:27).

Isaac

The Submissive Son
GEN. 22:1-4
● He is offered up by his father Abraham

The Gentle Groom
GEN. 24:62-67
● He meets Rebekah for the first time

The Praying Parent
GEN. 25:19-26
● He prays that God would bless them with children
● Rebekah gives birth to twins—Esau and Jacob

The Copy-Cat
GEN. 26:1-11
● Like his father, he leaves Palestine during a famine
● Like his father, he lies about his wife

The Willing Worker
GEN. 26:17-33
● Some jealous Philistines had filled up Abraham's wells with debris
● Isaac redigs and cleans out those wells

The Frustrated Father
GEN. 27:1-45
● At ninety-seven Isaac feels his death is near
● Esau is instructed to prepare him a meal and receive the patriarchal blessing
● Rebekah arranges to deceive the dim-eyed Isaac by substituting Jacob
● Jacob receives the blessing intended for Esau
● Rebekah sends Jacob away that he might escape Esau's revenge

   b. Joab kisses Amasa in order to murder him (2 Sam. 20:9).
   c. Judas kisses Christ in order to betray him (Mt. 26:49).
9. Jacob had no sooner walked out than Esau came in and the plot was discovered. Esau wails aloud over this deception (Heb. 12:16, 17) and determines to kill him after his father's funeral (27:41).
10. Rebekah learns of this plot and asks Isaac that Jacob might be sent to Haran to seek a wife. Her main reason, however, was to save his life.
11. Isaac calls in Jacob, blesses him, and sends him to Haran, saying: "Thou shalt not take a wife of the daughters of Canaan" (28:1). At this point Isaac drops out of the biblical account, even though he lived another forty-three years. Isaac was not a man who dreamed dreams and conquered continents. A summary of his rather uneventful life, listing both strong and weak points, would include:
   a. He was a submissive son.
      (1) As shown by his willingness to be sacrificed (Gen. 22:7-10).
      (2) As shown by his willingness to allow a bride to be picked for him (Gen. 24).
   b. He was a sensual man.
      (1) As shown by the "window" passage (Gen. 26:8).
      (2) As shown by his craving for food (Gen. 27:1-4).
   c. He was an indulgent father and husband.

(1) He had little control over Esau, who married two heathen girls (Gen. 26:34).

(2) He had little control over Rebekah, who felt free to deceive him at will (Gen. 27:5-13).

(3) He had little control over Jacob, who looked to his mother instead of him for authority (Gen. 27:13).

d. He was, nevertheless, at times a man of faith (Gen. 28:1-4; 22:7-10; Heb. 11:20).

III. Jacob (Gen. 25; 27-36; 38).

A. The devising brother (25:27-34).

1. Jacob was the second born of twins. The birth of these boys is vividly paraphrased for us by *The Living Bible* (25:25, 26).

"The first was born so covered with reddish hair that one would think he was wearing a fur coat! So they called him 'Esau.' Then the other twin was born with his hand on Esau's heel! So they called him Jacob (meaning 'grabber')."

2. Both these boys had the same background. But one grew to love God, while the other looked down upon spiritual things.

3. Esau became a skilled hunter and the favorite of Isaac's while Jacob was the quiet type and appealed more to his mother.

4. Jacob connives to get his famished brother to trade his birthright. This applied to certain advantages, privileges, and responsibilities of firstborn baby boys during Old Testament Israelite history. Note:

a. The *advantages* and privileges were that this baby became the object of special affection and would legally receive a double portion of his father's estate.

b. The *responsibilities* were that he was expected to assume the spiritual leadership of the family. He also was required to provide food, clothing, and other necessities for his mother until her death and all unmarried sisters until their marriage. But, we are told, "Esau despised his birthright" (25:34). In the New Testament we read the following concerning Esau and this birthright: "Lest there be any fornicator, or profane person, as Esau, who, for one morsel of meat, sold his birthright" (Heb. 12:16).

5. With all this background in mind, much light can be thrown upon the character of Esau, who counted as nothing his birthright.

a. He was apparently not interested in any double-portion slice of his father's estate. While Isaac his father would gather much wealth later (Gen. 26:12-14), he may have possessed very little of this wealth during these early days. At any rate, Esau was not interested in the material advantages of his birthright.

b. He certainly was not interested in maintaining any spiritual responsibilities. Nor was he concerned with providing for his mother. He may have sensed her special affection for Jacob (Gen. 25:28).

c. His actions reflected his carnal attitude for as we have already seen, he was both a fornicator and a profane person. The term fornicator refers to his immorality, while the word profane calls attention to his utter disregard for spiritual things. It literally means, "one outside the temple."

B. The deceitful son (27:1-46).

1. Rebekah overhears Isaac's plan to bestow the patriarchal blessing upon Esau.

2. She immediately plots with Jacob to obtain this for him.

3. Isaac is deceived by Jacob and he receives that blessing meant for Esau.

4. Esau discovers this trickery and vows revenge. The question may be raised as to why Esau who once had despised his birthright now is so concerned with the blessing. The answer seems to be in the nature of the two. As we have previously noted, Esau was not interested at all in assuming the spiritual responsibilities of the birthright. But the blessing was something different, for it carried with it a good and wholesome prophecy concerning the future.

C. The dreaming pilgrim (28:1-22).

1. Jacob leaves Beer-sheba and starts toward Haran. After a long hard journey he arrives at Bethel, some forty miles from Beer-sheba.

2. Using a stone for a pillow, Jacob soon falls into an exhausted sleep.

3. As he sleeps, he dreams, "and behold a ladder set up on the earth, and the top of it reached to heaven: and behold the angels of God ascending and descending on it" (28:12). According to Hebrews 1:14, angels are the ministering spirits to the heirs of salvation. Jacob's grandfather Abraham had received their blessed ministry (Gen. 18:1-16) as had Lot (Gen. 19:1). Now Jacob would also share in this experience.

4. At the top of this ladder Jacob sees the presence of God himself, and (for the first time) hears the Lord's voice confirming to him the Abrahamic Covenant. (See 28:1-15.) Especially thrilling are the words, "I will not leave thee" (28:15).

"Most precious of all promises is that of the presence of the Lord. It was made here to Jacob in pure grace; to Moses for all the people before they crossed the Jordan with Joshua (Deut. 31:6); to Joshua as he assumed leadership and faced battle (Josh. 1:5, 8); and to Solomon for the building of the Temple (1 Chron. 28:20). It was made to the disciples just before the Lord ascended into heaven (Mt. 28:20), and confirmed to us here today" (Heb. 13:5, 6). (*Genesis*, Vol. 2, p. 86, D. G. Barnhouse)

5. Jacob awakens and makes a vow (Gen. 28:20-22).

In spite of the rather pitiful conditions of this carnal prayer, a sovereign God graciously chose to answer it.

D. The love-struck suitor (29:1-20).
1. Jacob arrives in Haran and meets his cousin (and future wife) Rachel. After rolling away a heavy well stone, which allowed her to water her sheep, Jacob introduces himself, accompanied by kissing and crying (29:1-12). This is the first of several important meetings in the Bible which took place beside wells. (See Ex. 2:15; Jn. 4:6, 7.)
2. Jacob then meets Laban (his uncle) and future father-in-law. Jacob agrees to work seven years for the hand of Rachel in marriage (29:13-15). Here begins one of the great love stories of all time.
E. The frustrated family man (29:21—30:24).
1. Jacob is deceived on his wedding night by a crafty Laban who had secretly substituted his oldest girl named Leah in place of Rachel, his youngest (29:16-24). Jacob, the deceiver, is now himself deceived.
2. Jacob is furious, but agrees to work another seven years for Rachel without pay. He is, however, permitted to marry her within a week (29:25-30).
3. Jacob now has two wives and would gather two more, as Leah and Rachel each present him their personal handmaidens for child-bearing purposes. These four women will bear Jacob twelve sons and one daughter.
   a. From Leah:
      (1) Reuben ("see, a son"), his first son (29:32).
      (2) Simeon ("hearing"), his second son (29:33).
      (3) Levi ("joined"), his third son (29:34).
      (4) Judah ("praise"), his fourth son (29:35).
      (5) Issachar ("he brings wages"), his ninth son (30:18).
      (6) Zebulun ("dwelling"), his tenth son (30:20).
   b. From Bilhah (Rachel's handmaiden):
      (1) Dan ("judge"), his fifth son (30:6).
      (2) Naphtali ("wrestling"), his sixth son (30:8).
   c. From Zilpah (Leah's handmaiden):
      (1) Gad ("troop"), his seventh son (30:11).
      (2) Asher ("gladness"), his eighth son (30:13).
   d. From Rachel:
      (1) Joseph ("adding"), his eleventh son (30:24).
      (2) Benjamin ("son of my right hand"), his twelfth son (35:18).
4. The following interesting conclusions may be drawn at this point:
   a. Half of Jacob's sons were born to a wife (Leah) he had no intention or knowledge of marrying. This included:
      (1) Levi—from which tribe all priests would eventually come.
      (2) Judah—from which tribe the Lord Jesus would eventually come.
   b. Leah gave Jacob his only recorded daughter, whose name was Dinah (30:21).
   c. Rachel bore him his two final and favorite sons. Joseph would later, of course, become the most famous of all.
   d. After her first four children, Leah becomes temporarily barren and attempts to stimulate her womb by eating some mandrakes, a leafy plant (sometimes referred to as love apples), eaten by peasant women in the Near East in the belief that this would aid them in becoming pregnant. Leah was now attempting to bear children with the aid of artificial methods. The mandrake fruit, as used here, serves as an example of the various artificial and Christ-dishonoring methods used by some to fill the house of God, such as church bazaars, bingo parties, rock-and-roll sessions, etc. Earthly children are only born when the bride comes into contact with her bridegroom. So it is with souls. When the Bride prays Rachel's prayer, "Give me children, or else I die" (30:1), the Bridegroom will bless.
F. The enterprising employee (30:25—31:55).
1. After the birth of his children, Jacob wants to return home but is persuaded by Laban to remain for awhile (30:25-28).
2. He agrees under the condition that he be allowed to keep as his own all speckled or spotted goats, and all black sheep (30:29-36).
3. Jacob then attempts to increase the size of his herd by removing some of the bark from certain kinds of tree branches and placing them in that area used by the animals for mating purposes (30:37-39).
4. After a period of six years Jacob becomes a very wealthy man. Jacob is commanded by God to return to Palestine again (30:43; 31:3).
5. Jacob quickly breaks camp and leaves for home without bothering to inform Laban (31:17-21).
6. Laban, upon hearing of the flight three days later, sets out in hot pursuit and catches up with them, after a week's journey, at Mt. Gilead. God had already warned the angry father-in-law not to harm Jacob (31:22-25).
7. Laban rebukes Jacob for sneaking off without saying goodbye, and accuses him of stealing his household gods (31:26-30). *The New Scofield Bible* offers the following comment concerning these gods:

   "This incident has long been a puzzle. Why was Laban so greatly concerned about recovering these images which Rachel had stolen? Attempting to recapture them he conducted a long (275 miles) and expensive expedition.

   Excavations at Nuzi in northern Mesopotamia, in the region in which Laban lived, show that the possession of the household gods of a father-in-law by a son-in-law was legally acceptable as proof of the designation of that son-in-law as principal heir. . . . It is no wonder that Jacob was angry that he should be accused of such a deed, and that the two men set up a boundary and promised not to cross it to injure one another. Jacob never made evil use of these images which Rachel had stolen, but ordered that they should be buried at Shechem" (Gen. 35:2-4). (*New Scofield Bible*, p. 46)

8. Jacob angrily denies stealing these images (unaware of Rachel's actions) and directs a tirade against Laban, accusing him of grossly inconsistent and inhuman treatment during their twenty-year employment relationship (31:36-42).

9. These idols, hidden in Rachel's camel saddle, were never discovered. She remained seated during the search, saying, "I cannot rise up before thee, for the custom of women is upon me" (31:35).

10. At Laban's suggestion, the two men entered a covenant by building a pile of stones and calling it Mizpah, or "the watchtower." Laban then added these words upon completion: "The Lord watch between me and thee, when we are absent one from another" (31:49).

Dr. Donald Barnhouse writes:

"Careless reading of the Word of God has made this statement familiar to millions in a totally false application. That it should be engraved on rings, made the motto of a youth organization, and used for a benediction to close a meeting is preposterous. It did not stand for blessing, communion and fellowship; rather, it indicates armistice, separation, menace, and warning. In effect the pillar of Mizpah meant, 'If you come over on my side of this line, . . . I'll kill you!' The covenant-breaker would need God to take care of him, because the other would shoot to kill!" (*Genesis, Vol. 2*, p. 110).

G. The determined wrestler (32:1—33:20).

1. Jacob is again ministered to by angels on his route homeward as he had been when leaving home some twenty years before. (See Gen. 28:12 and compare with 32:1, 2.) Jacob here mentions for the first time in the Bible the armies of heaven. That is what he meant by the phrase "God's host." This host is composed of angels. There are many instances in the Scripture showing this divine army in action.

a. *Joshua* was visited by the captain of this host (Josh. 5:14).

b. *Elisha* and his young servant were reassured by this mighty army (2 Ki. 6:13-17).

c. *The Savior* announced to Peter that he could call upon this divine army to save him from the Cross, had he wanted to. But thank God he did not choose to do so. (See Mt. 26:52, 53 where he states he could easily call down twelve legions, or seventy-two thousand, angels!)

As David would write in Psalm 34:7: "The angel of the Lord encampeth round about them that fear him and delivereth them."

2. At this time he learns the terrifying news that Esau his brother was en route to meet him with 400 men. Jacob is petrified with fear. He immediately does three things:

a. He divides his household into two groups, saying, "If Esau comes to the one company, and smite it, the other company which is left shall escape" (32:8).

b. He cries out to God in prayer (32:9-11). At this time Jacob acknowledges, perhaps for the very first time that: "I am not worthy of the least of all the mercies, and of all the truth, which thou hast shown unto thy servant" (32:10).

Paul would testify to this truth also. (See 1 Tim. 1:12-15.)

c. He sends out a bribe gift to Esau consisting of 550 animals (32:13-21).

3. There occurred that night by the river Jabbok one of the most mysterious and wondrous events in all the Bible. (See 32:24-29.)

4. Whatever theology one may glean from these strange verses of God and man engaged in an all-night wrestling match, two facts clearly emerge:

a. His name is changed from Jacob (the crooked heel-catcher) to Israel, which signifies "one who has power with God" (32:28).

b. He never walked the same after this soul-struggling session with God (32:31, 32).

5. Afterward Jacob called the name of this place Peniel (the Face of God). God had touched his heart at Bethel, but here at Peniel God claimed his life. The former place saw his conversion and salvation, but this place witnessed his consecration and sanctification. The first had *introduced him* to the peace of God; the second freely *gave him* that peace of God. He now possessed not only life, but abundant life. (See Rom. 5:1; Phil. 4:7; Jn. 10:10.)

6. Jacob, bowing and trembling, meets Esau. To his surprise and immense relief, Esau embraces him (33:1-4).

7. Esau wanted Jacob to accompany him to the land of Seir. This was the farthest thing from Jacob's mind, but instead of simply telling Esau this, he hides behind his children: "My lord knoweth that the children are tender, and the flocks and herds with young are with me: and if men should overdrive them one day, all the flock will die" (33:13).

8. Jacob promises, however, to meet him in Seir. This was, of course, a brazen lie. Jacob was headed for Succoth, which was northwest, while Seir was southeast. One wonders what Esau thought about Jacob's glowing testimony concerning God's grace when he learned his brother had once again deceived him. (See 33:14-16.)

H. The enraged father (34:1; 38:1-30).

1. Over the sin of murder, committed by Levi and Simeon (34:1-31).

a. Jacob allows his daughter Dinah to run loose, resulting in her being seduced by

Shechem, the son of King Hamor of the Hivites. Jacob, like his father Isaac, had little idea what his children did or whom they saw. It was an accepted assumption among the Egyptians and Canaanites that unmarried and unattended women were legitimate prey. (See Gen. 12:14; 20:2; 26:7.) Dinah was approximately fourteen years of age at this time.

b. Shechem then determines to marry Dinah and asks Jacob for the necessary permission. In fact, the Hivites suggested to Jacob, "Make ye marriages with us and take our daughters unto you. And ye shall dwell with us . . ." (34:9, 10).

c. This line of reasoning is, of course, one of Satan's favorite tactics. The Christian is urged to raise his tolerance level and lower his standards, to appease his flesh and to abandon his faith. (For the answer to this satanic suggestion, see 1 Cor. 6:15-20; 2 Cor. 6:14-18.)

d. Dinah's brothers, inwardly boiling with anger, cruelly deceived Shechem by agreeing to his request with the stipulation that all male Hivites circumcise themselves (34:13-24).

e. On the third day, when their wounds were sore and sensitive to every movement, Levi and Simeon walked boldly into the camp and slaughtered every man there, including Shechem and his father. They then plundered the city, taking all its spoil, including the widows and orphans (34:25-30).

f. Jacob was furious and soundly rebuked his two murderous sons: "Ye have troubled me to make me stink among the inhabitants of the land, among the Canaanites and the Perizzites: and I being few in number, they shall gather themselves together against me, and slay me; and I shall be destroyed, I, and my house" (34:30).

Even at this late stage in Jacob's life we sadly note:

(1) He expresses no sorrow over the defilement of his only daughter Dinah.

(2) He voices no regrets over an entire town being exterminated.

(3) He apparently is unconcerned about God's feelings in all this.

(4) His main (perhaps only) concern is that he be hurt because of his sons. He assumes no personal responsibility whatsoever.

2. Over the sin of adultery, committed by Judah (38:1-30).

Although Jacob's name does not occur in this chapter, we may assume he was well aware of the tragic facts and disapproved of them.

a. Judah, Jacob's fourth son, marries a Canaanite girl, who bears him three sons, Er, Onan, and Shelah (38:1-5).

b. His oldest son, Er, marries a girl named Tamar, but God soon kills him for an un-

recorded act of wickedness. Judah then commands his second son, Onan, to marry her. He also is soon slain for wickedness.

c. Judah promises Tamar to give her his youngest son Shelah in due time, although he secretly had no intention of doing this (38:11, 12).

d. After awhile Tamar realizes this and, disguising herself as a common harlot, entices Judah into her tent for sexual purposes. For payment she demands and receives his signet, bracelets, and staff (38:13-19). Tamar soon becomes pregnant from this relationship.

e. Some three months later an indignant Judah orders her to be burned to death. Tamar then shows him his signet, bracelets, and staff. A remorseful and doubtless red-faced Judah immediately sets her free (38:24-26).

f. Tamar has twins and calls them Perez and Zerah. Both this Canaanite prostitute woman and her illegitimate firstborn son would later be included through the amazing grace of God in the sacred genealogy of the Lord Jesus Christ! (See Mt. 1:3.)

I. The obedient patriarch (35:1-7).

1. God again reminds Jacob of his previous command to return to Bethel (35:1). (See also 31:11-13.) Jacob had been living in Shechem for ten years, and Bethel was only thirty miles away. How tragically easy it is to move toward surrender and yet fall short of it. (See Heb. 4:1, 9, 11.)

2. Jacob instructs his entire household to destroy their idols, to wash themselves, and to put on fresh clothing in preparation for the Bethel trip. These idols and earrings are then collected and buried under an oak tree near Shechem. This is the first recorded revival in God's Word.

3. Jacob arrives at Bethel and builds an altar there, naming it El-Bethel. As we have already seen, the name Bethel means "House of God," but El-Bethel means, "The God of the House of God." The difference between these two concepts is the difference between knowing the Word of God and of knowing the God of the Word! We are to read the pages of the first to acquaint us with the Person of the second (35:7).

J. The sorrowing saint (35:8-29).

1. Jacob loses, in rapid succession, three loved ones.

a. His old nurse, *Deborah* (35:8). This woman, first mentioned here, apparently came to live with Jacob after the death of her mistress (and Jacob's mother) Rebekah.

b. His beloved wife *Rachel* dies giving birth to her second (and Jacob's twelfth) son, who is named Benjamin, "Son of my Right Hand" (35:16-20).

c. His father *Isaac* (35:27-29) dies at age of 180 and is buried by Jacob and Esau

Jacob

THE DEVISING BROTHER
GEN. 25:27-34
- He pressures Esau into trading his birthright.

THE DECEITFUL SON
GEN. 27:6-29
- He tricks his father to receive the blessing.

THE DREAMING PILGRIM
GEN. 28:10-22
- He sees a ladder set up from earth to heaven at Bethel.
- Angels are ascending and descending upon it.
- God confirms to him the Abrahamic Covenant.
- Upon awakening he anoints a rockpile and vows to serve God.

THE LOVE-STRUCK SUITOR
GEN. 29:1-20
- He meets Rachel, his cousin and future wife, beside a well.
- Here begins one of history's great love stories.
- He promises Rachel's father Laban (Jacob's uncle and future father-in-law) he will work seven years for her hand in marriage.

THE FRUSTRATED FAMILY MAN
GEN. 29:21—30:24
- He is deceived on his wedding night by Laban who secretly substitutes Leah (Rachel's older sister) for Rachel.
- Jacob is furious, but agrees to work yet another seven years for Rachel.
- He now has two wives and would gather yet another two, for both Rachel and Leah present to him their personal handmaids for childbearing purposes.
  These four women would bear Jacob twelve sons and one daughter.

wife	**Leah**	**Bilhah** (Rachel's handmaid)	**Zilpah** (Leah's handmaid)	**Rachel**
son	1. Reuben			
	2. Simeon			
	3. Levi			
	4. Judah			
		5. Dan		
		6. Naphtali		
			7. Gad	
			8. Asher	
	9. Issachar			
	10. Zebulun			
				11. Joseph
				12. Benjamin
daughter	Dinah			

THE ENTERPRISING EMPLOYEE
GEN. 30:25—31:55
- Jacob goes into business with Laban and becomes a wealthy man.
- Upon being ordered by God to return home, he breaks camp without telling Laban.
- Laban chases him down and accuses Jacob (among other things) of stealing his household gods.
- Laban and Jacob come to a truce and build a memorial pile of stones.

THE DETERMINED WRESTLER
GEN. 32:1—33:20
- Jacob learns that Esau is on his way to meet him, riding with 400 men.
- Filled with fear, Jacob wrestles with God in prayer all night long by the Brook Jabbok.
- He is reassured by God for this and his name is changed from Jacob to Israel.
- The ensuing meeting between Israel and Esau is very friendly.

THE ENRAGED FATHER
GEN. 34:1-31; 35:22; 38:1-30
- Over the sin of murder, committed by Levi and Simeon
  1. These boys trick a group of desert men (whose leader had seduced Dinah, their sister) into circumcising themselves.
  2. On the third day when they are helpless to defend themselves because of their self-inflicted wounds, Jacob's two sons slaughter them like animals.
- Over the sin of adultery, committed by Reuben
  "And it came to pass, when Israel dwelt in that land, that Reuben went and lay with Bilhah, his father's concubine: and Israel heard it . . ." (Gen. 35:22).
- Over the sin of adultery, committed by Judah
  1. To seek revenge upon Judah (for refusing a request of hers) Tamar, his daughter-in-law, disguises herself as a common harlot and entices him into her tent for sexual purposes.
  2. Tamar becomes pregnant and Judah orders her death for immorality until he learns who the father of the child really is!

THE OBEDIENT PATRIARCH
GEN. 35:1-15
- Jacob is ordered by God back to Bethel.
- In preparation for this trip, Jacob instructs his household to destroy their idols and prepare their hearts.
- He builds an altar at Bethel and calls it "El-Bethel"—the God of the house of God.

THE SORROWING SAINT
GEN. 35:16-20; 37:31-35
- He loses his beloved wife, Rachel, in childbirth.
- He buries his father Isaac.
- He is led to believe that Joseph has been killed and eaten by a wild beast

alongside Abraham in the Cave of Machpelah at Hebron.

2. There are two important "first mentions" in these verses.
   a. The first mention of the drink offering (35:14).
   b. The first reference to Bethlehem (35:19). Here Rachel dies giving birth to the son of Jacob's right hand. Many centuries later a young virgin would give birth to another baby in Bethlehem. This Babe would be known as the Son of God's Right Hand.

IV. Joseph (Gen. 37, 39–50).
   A. The favored son (37).
      1. The dreams of Joseph.
         a. The remaining chapters in Genesis now describe the life of Joseph, Jacob's second youngest son, born to him of his beloved Rachel. (See Gen. 30:24.)
         b. Joseph had brought down upon him the wrath of his ten half-brothers. Three factors had led to this sad situation.
            (1) Because he had reported to his father some of the bad things the ten were doing (37:2).

(2) Because he had become Jacob's favorite son. To show this special affection, the old man gave Joseph a long-sleeved brightly colored tunic (37:3).

(3) Because of Joseph's strange dreams.

    (a) In one of his dreams they were all in the field binding sheaves, when suddenly his sheaf stood up and their sheaves all gathered around it and bowed low before it.

    (b) During his second dream he saw the sun, moon, and eleven stars bow low before him (37:9).

c. Joseph is sent from his home in Hebron to Shechem to check on his half-brothers and their grazing flocks. He finally finds them at Dothan, some fifteen miles from Shechem, and sixty-five miles from Hebron.

2. The deceit of his brothers.

a. His ten brothers see him in the distance and determine to kill him (37:18).

b. Reuben, Jacob's firstborn (Gen. 29:32), apparently had second thoughts, however, for he suggested that they simply throw him in a pit and let him die. Reuben was then planning to secretly return him to his father (37:21, 22).

c. Joseph is stripped of his coat and cast into a pit (37:24).

d. Ignoring his pitiful cries (Gen. 42:21), the cruel brothers sat down to eat. Suddenly a slave caravan of Ishmaelites and Midianites came into view en route to Egypt. The nine brothers made a hasty and heartless decision to sell Joseph as a slave (37:25-27). Reuben was apparently not present at the time. Judah is the ringleader in this disgraceful deal.

e. Joseph is sold for twenty pieces of silver (the going price of a slave) and carried into Egypt (37:28). Reuben returns and weeps over the action his brothers have taken (37:29).

3. The despair of his father.

a. To conceal their horrible crime, they take Joseph's coat, smear it with goat's blood, and deceive Jacob into believing his beloved son has been slain and eaten by a wild animal (37:31-35).

b. Joseph is sold as a slave to Potiphar, a captain in Pharaoh's Egyptian palace guard (37:36). That immutable law of retribution which runs so strongly throughout the Bible (see Gal. 6:7) is clearly seen here in this chapter. Jacob, who once deceived his father by using the skin of a kid (Gen. 27:16), is himself now deceived in a similar manner. Other examples would include:

    (1) Pharaoh, who ordered the destruction of Israel by the waters of the Red Sea, was himself drowned there. (Compare Ex. 14:5 with 14:28.)

    (2) Korah, who caused a division in the congregation of Israel, was swallowed by a division in the ground. (Compare Num. 16:1-3 with 16:31, 32.)

    (3) Haman, who built the gallows to execute a godly Hebrew, later himself was hanged from the same gallows. (Compare Est. 5:14 with 7:10.)

B. The faithful steward (39).

1. His service.

a. Joseph is sold as a slave to Potiphar, an officer in Pharaoh's Egyptian palace guard (38:30; 39:1).

b. Under the blessings of God, he was quickly entrusted with the entire administration of Potiphar's household (39:2-6).

2. His self-control.

a. Joseph is enticed to commit immorality by the wife of Potiphar, but refuses her continued advances (39:7-10).

b. In an act of revenge, she accuses Joseph of rape (39:11-18).

3. His sufferings.

Joseph is thrown into prison (39:9-20).

C. The forgotten servant (40).

1. The jailor, like Potiphar, soon recognized Joseph's beautiful and talented character and put him in charge of the entire prison administration (39:21-23).

2. For some reason, the anger of Pharaoh is aroused against both his chief baker and butler and he sends them to Joseph's prison (40:1-4).

3. While in prison these two men have mysterious dreams. God gives Joseph the ability to correctly interpret each dream.

a. The *details* of the butler's dream. He had seen a vine with three branches that began to bud and blossom and soon produced clusters of ripe grapes. In his dream, the butler then squeezed the juice from the grapes and served it to Pharaoh in the royal wine cup (40:9-11).

b. The *meaning* of the butler's dream. The three branches meant that within three days Pharaoh would free him and restore him to his old employment. Joseph then asked the butler to mention him to Pharaoh, and ask him to remember the injustices he suffered (40:12-15).

c. The *details* of the baker's dream. He saw himself carrying upon his head three baskets of pastries. The top basket contained special goods for the Pharaoh. But suddenly some birds flew down and ate this food (40:16, 17).

d. The *meaning* of the baker's dream. It meant that within three days the Pharaoh would take off the baker's head and impale his body on a pole, and that the birds would come and pick off his flesh (40:18, 19).

4. Three days later, on his birthday, the Pharaoh dealt with the butler and baker exactly as Joseph had predicted he would do. But the

butler forgot to mention anything about Joseph (40:20-23).

D. The famed statesman (41-44).

1. The revelation of Joseph.

   a. One night two years later Pharaoh experienced two mysterious dreams.

      (1) The contents of the first dream. He was standing on the bank of the Nile River when suddenly seven sleek, fat cows came up out of the river and began grazing in the grass. Then seven other cows came up, but they were very skinny and all their ribs stood out. Suddenly the skinny cows ate the fat cows (41:1-4).

      (2) The contents of the second dream. He saw seven heads of grain on one stalk, with every kernel well formed and plump. Then suddenly seven more heads appeared on the stalk, but these were shriveled and withered by the east wind. The dream ended as the thin heads devoured the plump ones (41:5-7).

   b. Pharaoh consults his magicians about these dreams the next morning but they are unable to interpret them (41:8).

   c. The butler suddenly remembers the amazing talent of Joseph and relates to the Pharaoh those events which occurred in prison two years back (41:9-13).

   d. Joseph is cleaned up, shaven, and brought before Pharaoh. After hearing the contents of the dreams, he immediately interprets them, giving God the glory. According to Joseph, both dreams meant the same thing (41:14-25).

      (1) The seven fat cows and the seven plump heads of grain meant that there were seven years of prosperity ahead (41:26).

      (2) The seven skinny cows and the lean heads of grain meant that a seven-year famine period would follow the years of plenty (41:27).

   e. Joseph then advises Pharaoh to appoint a capable administrator over a nationwide farm program, and divide Egypt into five districts. The officials of these districts should then gather into the royal storehouses all the excess crops of the next seven years (41:33-36).

2. The elevation of Joseph (41:37-57).

   a. The Pharaoh appoints Joseph to this high office on the spot.
      He then:

      (1) Places his own signet ring on Joseph's finger.

      (2) Dresses him in beautiful clothing.

      (3) Hangs the royal golden chain about his neck.

      (4) Gives him the chariot of his second-in-command.

      (5) Decrees that all shall bow down to him.

      (6) Changes his name to Zaph-enath-paneah, which means, "the one who

furnishes the sustenance of the land."

      (7) Presents him with a wife, Asenath, the daughter of Potiphera, priest of Heliopolis. Joseph thus marries into a family of high nobility, his father-in-law being a major priest-politician of the time.

   b. Joseph is now thirty years of age (41:46). In one day he has been elevated from the prison to the palace. But it has taken God thirteen years to bring him to this place of service, for he was seventeen when he first arrived in Egypt. (See Ps. 105:17-21.)

   c. Joseph's wife presents him with two boys. The first is named Manasseh (meaning "made to forget"), and the younger Ephraim (meaning "fruitful"). (See 41:50, 52.)

   d. As Joseph had predicted, the seven fat years were followed by seven lean ones, causing people from many lands to buy their food in Egypt (41:53-57).

3. The consternation of Joseph's brothers (Gen. 42-44).

   a. Jacob sends his ten older sons into Egypt from Hebron to buy food (42:1-5).

   b. They arrive in Egypt and bow low before Joseph, but do not recognize him, thus fulfilling his dream some twenty years back (42:6).

   c. Joseph does not reveal himself at first but accuses them of being foreign spies. The frightened brothers attempt to convince him otherwise (42:7-13).

   d. He throws them into jail for three days and then releases them, but keeps Simeon as a hostage until they can return with Benjamin, as he demands they bring him to him (42:14-20).

   e. The terrified brothers acknowledge to each other that their present misfortunes have doubtless been caused by the terrible sin committed twenty years back, not realizing that Joseph can understand every word (42:21-23).

   f. After leaving the room to weep, he orders his servants to fill the men's sacks with grain and also to put each brother's payment at the top of his sack. The nine then start for home (42:24-26).

   g. En route home, one of the men discovers his payment, and when they reach Hebron the rest find theirs and are filled with fear concerning the safety of Simeon. In spite of their earnest pleas, Jacob at first refuses to allow Benjamin to accompany them on a future trip into Egypt (42:27-38).

   h. The famine intensifies in Hebron and Jacob is forced to allow Benjamin to go back with them into Egypt for food. Judah attempts to guarantee the safety of Benjamin (43:1-14).

   i. They again present themselves to Joseph, who takes them to his palace for a feast.

The brothers attempt to convince Joseph's household manager that they have not stolen the payment of their former trip. Simeon is released and joins the group. For the first time in twenty years all twelve brothers are together, but only one is aware of it (43:15-25).

j. The brothers are fed at a separate table from that of Joseph. But to their amazement he seats them in order of their ages, giving Benjamin five times as much food as the others (43:23-34).

k. Before they return the next morning Joseph once again secretly places the payment money in each man's sack, along with Joseph's own silver cup at the top of Benjamin's sack (44:1, 2).

l. The brothers have but left the city when they are arrested (at Joseph's command) and accused of stealing his silver cup (44:4-6).

m. They quickly deny this charge and agree to serve as slaves if any stolen loot can be found on them. A search quickly reveals the cup in Benjamin's sack (44:7-12).

n. Standing before Joseph for the third time, Judah steps forward and begs him to accept his life in place of Benjamin. He tearfully reminds Joseph that their old father Jacob would simply die if anything happened to Benjamin (44:13-34).

E. The forgiving saint (45-48).
  1. Joseph and his brothers.
    a. Joseph cannot contain himself any longer and reveals his identity to his brothers (45:1-3).
    b. After a time of tearful reuniting, Joseph informs them that the two-year drought they have already experienced will continue another five years and urges that they bring Jacob back with them and all make plans to live in Egypt (45:4-15).
    c. Joseph reassures his brothers (still in semi-shock) he has no hard feelings, but feels God has overruled their evil plot so as to guarantee Israel will indeed be a great nation (45:5-8).
    d. Pharaoh rejoices along with Joseph over his restored brethren and also invites the entire clan to live in Egypt (45:16-20).
  2. Joseph and his father.
    a. The old patriarch, Jacob, at first cannot comprehend the thrilling news concerning Joseph, but then believes the report and plans his trip to Egypt (45:26-28).
    b. En route at Beer-sheba, God reassures Jacob he will still bless him, even in Egypt. Jacob is told he is to die there, but God will bring his descendants back to Palestine someday (46:1-4).

      Note: There has been some controversy as to whether Jacob's trip to Egypt was God's perfect will or his permissive will. One benefit, however, was the fact that Egypt was a country in which Jacob's descendants would be forced to remain a separate and distinct people, for they were shepherds, and shepherds were an abomination to the Egyptians (Gen. 43:32; 46:34). There would thus be no intermarriage. In Canaan, this had apparently occurred. Simeon had married a girl from Canaan (46:10).

    c. Jacob enters Egypt with his entire household. Here three separate numbers are given.
      (1) Sixty-six (Gen. 46:26). This was the number of those going to Egypt, his own descendants, not counting his son's wives.
      (2) Seventy (Gen. 46:27). This was the number after adding Jacob himself, Joseph, and Joseph's two sons, Ephraim and Manasseh.
      (3) Seventy-five (Acts 7:14). Here Stephen refers to the "kindred," a probable reference to the five surviving wives of Jacob's sons.
    d. Joseph and Jacob meet in Goshen for the first time in twenty-two years. The son is now thirty-nine and the father 130 (46:28-30).
    e. Joseph introduces his father to the Pharaoh and Jacob is given choice land to live upon (47:1-12).
    f. As the famine continues, Pharaoh becomes richer and Joseph's wise food administration plan saves untold thousands from outright starvation (47:13-26).
    g. The population of Israel in Goshen rapidly expands in spite of the famine everywhere else (47:27).
    h. At the age of 147 Jacob realizes his time is near and thus calls for his beloved son Joseph and his favorite grandsons, Ephraim and Manasseh (48:1).
    i. Joseph promises his father he will not be buried in Egypt (47:29-31).
  3. Joseph and his sons.
    a. Joseph's two sons stand before their grandfather waiting to be blessed. The old man adopts them as his own sons and assures them of an equal inheritance (48:3-9).
    b. Jacob lays his right hand on Ephraim's head and his left hand on Manasseh's head. A displeased Joseph attempts to reverse this, pointing out that Manasseh is the older and therefore should have the right hand on his head (48:10-18).
    c. Jacob refuses to change hands, however, for he predicted the tribe of Ephraim would be even greater than the tribe of Manasseh (48:19-22).

F. The fruitful shade tree (49-50).
  1. Joseph receives his father's blessing (49). (See also Heb. 11:21.) Jacob gathers his twelve sons around his bedside just before his death, "that I may tell you that which shall befall you in the last days" (49:1). The *New Scofield Bible* has the following note on this verse:

"This is the first occurrence of the term 'the last days,' a most important concept in Biblical prophecy. In general, the expression refers to that terminal period in the history of a particular group of people or nations when God's announced purpose for them is about to be consummated" (p. 68).

Jacob then pronounces the following prophecies:

a. Upon Reuben (49:3, 4)
  (1) He was as unruly as the wild waves of the sea. As the first-born he was entitled to a double share of honor and inheritance (Deut. 21:17), but Jacob passes him over because of his immorality with Bilhah, Jacob's own concubine (Gen. 35:22).
  (2) The Reubenites later settled east of Jordan (along with the tribe of Gad and half-tribe of Manasseh). (See Josh. 1:12-16.)
  (3) They unintentionally almost caused a civil war by putting up a large monument on the west bank of Jordan (Josh. 22:10).
  (4) They later refused to help the armies of Israel, led by Barak and Deborah, in their war against a pagan named Sisera and his 900 iron chariots. (See Jdg. 4:1-3; 5:15, 16.)
b. Upon Simeon and Levi (49:5-7).
  (1) These were men of violence and injustice. They slaughtered the inhabitants of Shechem by deceit (Gen. 34:25). Jacob also bypasses them both.
  (2) Their descendants would thus be scattered throughout Israel. This meant that they would not be given regular land holdings as were their brother tribes. Levi's children dwelled in various cities throughout Palestine, and the Simeonites had to share that portion of land given to Judah. (See Num. 18:24; Josh. 19:1-9.)
c. Upon Judah (49:8-12).
  (1) The other brothers were to praise Judah and bow before him.
  (2) Judah would destroy his enemies, and would be left undisturbed, like a young lion.
  (3) The scepter would not depart from Judah until Shiloh (Christ) came. (See Num. 24:17; Rev. 5:5.) With the anointing of David (1 Chron. 28:4; 5:2; 2 Sam. 7:13), this was assured.
d. Upon Zebulun (49:13).
  (1) He would dwell near the seashore.
  (2) His borders would extend to Sidon.
e. Upon Issachar (49:14, 15).
  (1) He would be a strong beast of burden.
  (2) He would give up liberty for security.

f. Upon Dan (49:16-18).
  (1) Dan would become a serpent in the pathway that bit horses' heels, causing the riders to fall off. An old tradition has it that the antichrist will come from this tribe.
  (2) Samson was from Dan (Jdg. 13:2, 24).
g. Upon Gad (49:19).
  Gad would be the opposite of Issachar, and would often bravely fight for liberty. (See 1 Chron. 5:18; 12:8-15.)
h. Upon Asher (49:20).
  "Asher would produce rich food, fit for kings." Anna was from the tribe of Asher (Lk. 2:36).
i. Upon Naphtali (49:21).
  He would become known for his mobility and swiftness (as a released deer) and for his eloquence with words.
j. Upon Joseph (49:22-26).
  (1) He would be a fruitful tree beside a fountain whose branches shaded the wall.

Joseph

The Favored Son
(GEN. 37)
● The dreams of Joseph
● The deceit of his brothers
● The despair of his father

The Faithful Steward
(GEN. 39)
● His service
● His self-control
● His sufferings

The Forgotten Servant
(GEN. 40)
● Joseph finds himself in the same cell with the Pharaoh's butler and baker who were also imprisoned.
● These two men experience strange dreams. Joseph interprets both, predicting that within three days the king will free the butler but execute the baker.
● All this comes true. However, upon his release, the butler forgets all about Joseph.

The Famed Statesman
(GEN. 41-44)
● The revelation by Joseph
● The elevation of Joseph
● The frustration of Joseph's brothers

The Forgiving Saint
(GEN. 45-48)
● Joseph and his brothers
● Joseph and his father
● Joseph and his sons

The Fruitful Shade Tree
(GEN. 49-50)
● He receives his father's blessing
  "Joseph is a fruitful bough . . . by a well, whose branches run over the wall. . . . His hands were made strong by . . . the mighty God . . .
  . . . the Almighty . . . shall bless thee with the blessings of heaven above . . ." (Gen. 49:22-25).
● He returns his father's body

(2) He would be severely injured by vicious archers, but their weapons were shattered by the mighty one of Jacob, the Shepherd, the Rock of Israel.

(3) Jacob predicts and pronounces the richest divine blessing of all the twelve (with the exception of Judah) upon Joseph.

k. Upon Benjamin (49:27).

(1) He was to be as a wolf on the prowl.

(2) He would devour his enemies in the morning and divide the spoils in the evening. For examples of this trait, see Judges 20.

(3) Both the Saul of the Old Testament (1 Sam. 9:1, 2) and the Saul of the New Testament (Phil. 3:5) were from this tribe.

2. Joseph returns his father's body (50).

a. Jacob dies at age of 147 (47:28; 49:33).

b. His body is embalmed in Egypt during a forty-day preparation period (50:2, 3).

c. All Egypt mourns over him for seventy days (50:3).

d. He is carried by his sons in Palestine and buried alongside Abraham and Isaac in the Cave of Machpelah (50:13).

e. Joseph reassures his troubled brothers that favorable conditions would remain as before the funeral (50:15-21). He gently reminds them: "Ye thought evil against me; but God meant it unto good, to bring to pass, as it is this day, to save much people alive" (50:20).

f. Joseph dies at age of 110 (50:26).

G. The foreshadow of the Savior.

Joseph is the most complete type of Christ in all the Bible. Note the amazing similarities between these two:

1. Both were beloved by their fathers (37:3; Mt. 3:17).

2. Both regarded themselves as shepherds (37:2; Jn. 10:11-14).

3. Both were sent to their brethren by their fathers (37:13, 14; Lk. 20:13; Jn. 3:17; Heb. 10:7).

4. Both were hated by their brethren without cause (37:4, 5, 8; Jn. 1:11; 7:5; 15:25).

5. Both were plotted against by their brethren (37:20; Jn. 11:53).

6. Both were severely tempted (39:7; Mt. 4:1).

7. Both were taken to Egypt (37:36; Mt. 2:14, 15).

8. Both were stripped of their robes (37:23; Jn. 19:23, 24).

9. Both were sold for the price of a slave (37:28; Mt. 26:15).

10. Both were bound (39:20; Mt. 27:2).

11. Both remained silent and offered no defense (39:20; Isa. 53:7).

12. Both were falsely accused (39:16-18; Mt. 26:59, 60).

13. Both experienced God's presence through everything (39:2, 21, 23; Jn. 16:32).

14. Both were respected by their jailors (39:21; Lk. 23:47).

JOSEPH .. THE FORESHADOW OF THE SAVIOR

JOSEPH GENESIS	Note the amazing similarities between these two	JESUS
37:3	Beloved by their fathers	MT. 3:17
37:2	Regarded themselves as shepherds	JN. 10:11-14
37:13, 14	Sent by their fathers to their brethren	LK.20:13; HEB. 2:12
37:4, 5, 8	Hated by their brethren without a cause	JN. 1:11; 7:5; 15:25
37:20	Plotted against by their brethren	JN. 11:53
39:7	Severely tempted	MT. 4:1
37:26	Taken to Egypt	MT. 2:14, 15
37:23	Stripped of their robes	JN. 19:23, 24
37:28	Sold for the price of a slave	MT. 26:15
39:20	Bound	Mt. 27:2
39:20	Remained silent and offered no defense	ISA. 53:7
39:16-18	Falsely accused	MT. 26:59, 60
39:2, 21, 23	Experienced God's presence through everything	JN. 16:32
39:21	Respected by their jailors	LK. 23:47
40:2, 3	Placed with two prisoners, one of which was later lost, the other saved	LK. 23:32
41:46	Both around thirty at the beginning of their ministry	LK. 3:23
41:41	Both highly exalted after their sufferings	PHIL. 2:9-11
41:45	Both took non-Jewish brides	EPH. 3:1-12
42:7, 8	Both lost to their brethren for awhile	ROM. 10:1-3; 11:7, 8
45:1-15	Both forgave and restored their repentant brothers	ZECH. 12:10-12
41:57	Both visited and honored by all earthly nations	ISA. 2:2, 3; 49:6

15. Both were placed with two prisoners, one of which was later lost, and the other saved (40:2, 3, 21, 22; Lk. 23:32, 39-43).

16. Both were around thirty when their ministry began (41:46; Lk. 3:23).

17. Both were highly exalted after their sufferings (41:41; Phil. 2:9-11).

18. Both took Gentile brides (41:45; Eph. 3:1-12).

19. Both were lost to their brothers for awhile (42:7, 8; Rom. 10:1-3; 11:7, 8).

20. Both forgave and restored their repentant brothers (45:1-15; Micah 7:18, 19; Zech. 12:10-12; Rev. 1:7).

21. Both were visited and honored by all earthly nations (41:57; Isa. 2:2, 3; 49:6).

V. Job (Job 1–42). Introduction:

1. This is one of the most ancient books of the entire Bible.
   Note:
   a. The ancient historical allusions, e.g., the pyramids (3:14), the cities of the plains (15:28), and the Flood (22:16).
   b. The mission of Israel's history. No reference is made to the Law, the Exodus, the Red Sea crossing, Canaan, or any of the kings of Israel.

2. Job was a historical character, mentioned later by both Ezekiel (Ezek. 14:14, 20) and James (5:11).

3. The Greek Septuagint identifies Job with Jobab, the second king of Edom (Gen. 36:33).

4. The land of Uz may have been located northeast of the Sea of Galilee, running toward the Euphrates River. (See Gen. 36:28; Lam. 4:21.)

5. Job's disease may have been leprosy, complicated with elephantiasis, one of the most loathsome and painful diseases known in the world of his time.

6. Job's sufferings are intensified by three false friends, a bitter wife, and an impetuous youth.
   a. Eliphaz, who bases his advice on personal experience. (See 4:8, 12–16; 5:3, 27; 15:17.) Eliphaz was a descendant of Esau. (See Gen. 36:11.)
   b. Bildad, who bases his advice on tradition. (See 8:8–10; 18:5–20.) Bildad was a descendant of Abraham and Keturah. (See Gen. 25:2.)
   c. Zophar, who bases his advice on pure dogmatism. (See 11:6; 20:4.) Zophar was from the land of Naamah.
   d. Elihu, who seems to base his advice on youth alone. (See 32:6–10.) Elihu was a descendant of Nahor, Abraham's brother. (See Gen. 22:21.)
   e. Job's wife, who bases her advice on sheer unbelief. (See 2:9.)

7. The statements from Job's various "friends" cannot be used for doctrinal purposes, for they are often wrong.
   a. God rebukes them for not speaking the truth about him; see 42:7.
   b. They were also wrong in calling Job a hypocrite. (See 8:12; 15:34; 20:5; 34:30.) God, however, had found *no fault* in him. (See 1:8; 2:3.)

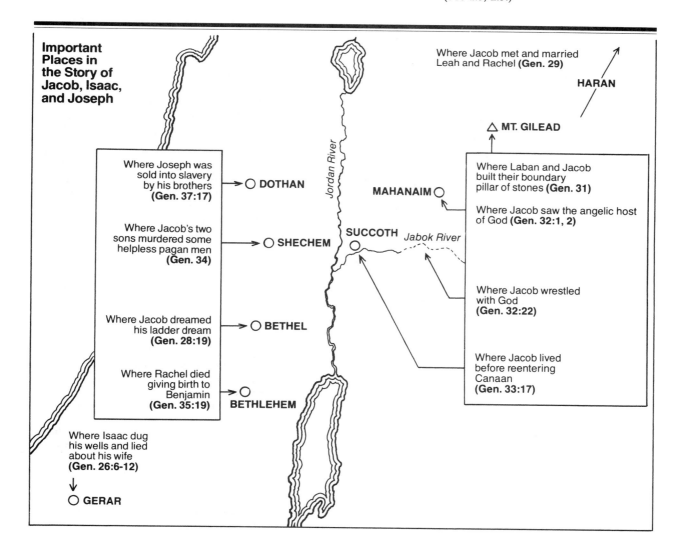

Important Places in the Story of Jacob, Isaac, and Joseph

Where Jacob met and married Leah and Rachel **(Gen. 29)**

HARAN

△ MT. GILEAD

Jordan River

Where Joseph was sold into slavery by his brothers **(Gen. 37:17)** → ○ DOTHAN

Where Laban and Jacob built their boundary pillar of stones **(Gen. 31)**

MAHANAIM ○

Where Jacob saw the angelic host of God **(Gen. 32:1, 2)**

Where Jacob's two sons murdered some helpless pagan men **(Gen. 34)** → ○ SHECHEM

SUCCOTH ○   *Jabok River*

Where Jacob wrestled with God **(Gen. 32:22)**

Where Jacob dreamed his ladder dream **(Gen. 28:19)** → ○ BETHEL

Where Jacob lived before reentering Canaan **(Gen. 33:17)**

Where Rachel died giving birth to Benjamin **(Gen. 35:19)** → ○ BETHLEHEM

Where Isaac dug his wells and lied about his wife **(Gen. 26:6-12)**
↓
○ GERAR

8. The book of Job is an extended commentary on Luke 22:31, 32 and Hebrews 12:7-11.
9. The following opinions have been given concerning the book of Job.
   a. Victor Hugo: "The book of Job is perhaps the greatest masterpiece of the human mind."
   b. Thomas Carlyle: "Call this book . . . one of the grandest things ever written. There is nothing written, I think, of equal literary merit."
   c. Alfred, Lord Tennyson: "The greatest poem, whether of ancient or modern literature."

A. Job's terrible trials (Job 1-2).
1. The nature of these trials.
   a. First trial: His oxen and donkeys are stolen and his farm hands are killed by a Sabean raid.
   b. Second trial: His sheep and herdsmen are burned up by fire.
   c. Third trial: His camels are stolen and his servants killed by a Chaldean raid.
   d. Fourth trial: His sons and daughters perish in a mighty wind.
   e. Fifth trial: Job himself is struck with a terrible case of boils.
2. The reason for these trials.
   A conversation takes place in the heavenlies between God and Satan concerning Job. The devil sneeringly charges that Job only worships God because of two selfish benefits:
   a. Because God has given his servant much wealth.
   b. Because God has given his servant good health. Satan argues that if he could but remove these two elements, that Job would curse God to his face. Thus, to shut the devil's mouth, God gives him permission to remove both Job's wealth and health. It should be noted here that Satan cannot tempt a believer apart from God's specific permission.

B. His whimpering wife (2:9, 10).
   "Then said his wife unto him, Dost thou still retain thine integrity? Curse God, and die. But he said unto her, Thou speakest as one of the foolish women speaketh. What? Shall we receive good at the hand of God, and shall we not receive evil? In all this did not Job sin with his lips."

C. His fickle friends (4-37).
   It has been pointed out that his friends came to sympathize, but stayed on to sermonize. At any rate, Job's three "friends" delivered eight full-blown messages, all with three points and a poem, to the long-suffering patriarch. Eliphaz preached three of these (Job 4-5; 15; 22); Bildad, three (ch. 8; 18; 25); and Zophar, being less-winded, came up with two (11; 20). No sooner, however, had this tiresome trio finished than the filibuster began again by a young "preacher boy" named Elihu who drones on for six chapters (32-37). Perhaps at no other Bible conference in history have so many preachers preached to so few in attendance where the congregation enjoyed it less!

Following is a brief summary of their speeches and of Job's defense.
The speeches of Eliphaz (ch. 4, 5, 15, 22).
See Genesis 36:10.
1. He claimed Job was suffering for his sins. "Remember, I pray thee, who ever perished, being innocent? Or where were the righteous cut off? Even as I have seen, they that plow iniquity, and sow wickedness, reap the same" (4:7, 8).
   "Thine own mouth condemneth thee, and not I: yea, thine own life testify against thee" (15:6).
   He then accuses Job of the following:
   a. That he had cheated the poor (22:6).
   b. That he had withheld bread from the hungry (22:7).
   c. That he had mistreated widows and orphans (22:9).
   d. That he was a windbag (15:2).
2. He bases his conclusions on personal experience. (See 4:8, 12-16; 5:3, 27; 15:17.)
3. He relates his night vision "ghost story" (4:12-17).
4. He urges Job to repent and turn back to God (22:21-28). "If thou return to the Almighty, thou shalt be built up, thou shalt put away iniquity very far from thy tents" (22:23).
The speeches of Bildad (ch. 8; 18; 25).
5. He claimed Job was suffering for his sins. "Behold, God will not cast away a perfect man, neither will he help the evildoers" (8:20).
6. He bases his conclusions on tradition. "For inquire, I pray thee, of the former age, and prepare thyself to the search of their fathers" (8:8). (See also 8:9, 10.)
7. He urges Job to repent and turn back to God. "If thou wouldest seek unto God betimes, and make thy supplication to the Almighty; If thou wert pure and upright; surely now he would awake for thee, and make the habitation of thy righteousness prosperous" (8:5, 6).
The speeches of Zophar (11:4, 5).
8. He claimed Job was suffering for his sins. "For thou hast said, My doctrine is pure, and I am clean. . . . But oh, that God would speak, and open his lips against thee. . . . Know, therefore, that God exacteth of thee less than thine iniquity deserveth" (11:4-6).
   "Knowest thou not this of old, since man was placed upon the earth, that the triumphing of the wicked is short, and the joy of the hypocrite but for a moment" (20:4, 5).
9. He bases his conclusions on sheer dogmatism. (See 11:6; 20:4.)
10. He urges Job to repent and turn back to God. "If thou prepare thine heart, and stretch out thine hands toward him. If iniquity be in thine hand, put it far away, and let not wickedness dwell in thy tents. For then shalt thou lift up thy face without spot; yea, thou shalt be steadfast, and shalt not fear" (11:13-15).
The speech of Elihu (ch. 32-37).
11. He waits awhile before speaking because of his youth (32:4-7).

12. However, once begun, he feels as confident and qualified to straighten out Job as the former three did. In fact, he actually suggests that he is the one whom Job seeks! "Behold, I am according to thy wish in God's stead; I also am formed out of the clay" (33:6).

13. Elihu is angry at all four, at Job because of his self-righteousness, and at the three friends because they had "found no answers, and yet had condemned Job" (32:3).

14. He accuses Job of both foolish speaking (34:35–37; 36:16) and false righteousness (35:2).

15. He exhorts Job to consider God's glory and his greatness (37:14–24).

D. The defenses and dialogues of Job.

The suffering patriarch responds to his accusers in nine separate speeches.

First: chapter 3; Second: 6–7; Third: 9–10;
Fourth: 12, 13, 14; Fifth: 16–17; Sixth: 19;
Seventh: 21; Eighth: 23–24; Ninth: 26–31

During these nine speeches Job discusses fourteen topics. These are:

1. I am righteous, and therefore not suffering for my sin (27:6; 31:1–30). "My righteousness I hold fast, and will not let it go; my heart shall not reproach me as long as I live" (27:6).

2. In the past I have performed many good works (29:12–17; 30:25).

3. Oh, for those good old days when I enjoyed health, wealth, and respect (29:1–11, 20–25).

4. But now I am being unfairly punished by God (9:16, 17, 30, 31, 32, 33; 13:26, 27; 10:2, 7, 8; 19:6–11; 30:20, 21).

5. My three so-called friends are miserable comforters (12:2; 13:4; 16:2; 19:3).

6. If they were in my place I would help them and not unjustly accuse them (16:4, 5).

7. Even my neighbors, associates, and servants have turned against me (19:13–22; 30:1, 9, 10).

8. I wish I could find the answers for all this (28:12–28).

9. I wish I could find God (23:8, 9).

10. My flesh is clothed with worms (7:5; 30:17, 18, 30).

11. I wish I had never been born (3:3–11, 16; 10:18).

12. I wish I were dead (6:8, 9; 7:15, 16).

13. I have no hope (10:20–22).

14. In spite of all, I'll trust God (13:15; 16:19; 23:10).

E. His glorious God (38–41).

Suddenly from out of a whirlwind comes the mighty voice of God. The sullen Job is then subjected to a sixty-question quiz. Note God's first series of questions (Job 38–40).

1. Job 38:4: "Where wast thou when I laid the foundations of the earth? Declare, if thou hast understanding."

2. Job 38:18: "Hast thou perceived the breadth of the earth? Declare if thou knowest it all."

3. Job 38:19: "Where is the way where light dwelleth? and as for darkness, where is the place thereof?"

4. Job 38:24: "By what way is the light parted, which scattereth the east wind upon the earth?"

5. Job 38:28: "Hath the rain a father? or who hath begotten the drops of dew?"

6. Job 40:2: "Shall he that contendeth with the Almighty instruct him? He that reproveth God, let him answer it."

Job's reply (40:4, 5): "Behold, I am vile; what shall I answer thee? I will lay mine hand upon my mouth. Once have I spoken; but I will not answer: yea, twice; but I will proceed no further." God's second series of questions (40:6–41:34).

7. Job 40:15: "Behold now behemoth, which I made with thee; he eateth grass as an ox."

8. Job 41:1: "Canst thou draw out leviathan with an hook? Or his tongue with a cord which thou lettest down?"

Note: These two creatures may very well refer to a land dinosaur and a sea dinosaur.

Job's reply (42:1–5):

"I know that thou canst do every thing, and that no thought can be witholden from thee. Who is he that hideth counsel without knowledge? Therefore have I uttered that I understood not; things too wonderful for me, which I knew not. Hear, I beseech thee, and I will speak: I will demand of thee, and declare thou unto me. I have heard of thee by the hearing of the ear; but now mine eye seeth thee: Wherefore I abhor myself, and repent in dust and ashes."

F. His bountiful blessings (42:7–17).

Job has been subjected to five fiery trials and has participated in five painful debates, but now he receives at the hand of God a tenfold blessing.

1. He is allowed to see the glory of God.

2. He sees himself as God sees him. (This is always a blessing.)

3. He is vindicated by God before the eyes of his three critical friends.

4. He discovers the joy of praying for these three friends.

5. His former health is fully restored.

6. He is comforted by his brothers and sister.

7. He is given double his former wealth.

8. He is given seven more sons and three more daughters.

9. He lives to enjoy his grandchildren and great-grandchildren.

10. He is given an additional 140 years—twice the number normally accorded a man. (See Ps. 90:10.)

CLASSIC STATEMENTS IN JOB

1. "He taketh the wise in their own craftiness . . ." (5:13). Quoted by Paul in 1 Corinthians 3:19.

2. "Behold, happy is the man whom God correcteth; therefore, despise not thou the chastening of the Almighty" (5:17). Quoted in Hebrews 12:5, 6.

3. "Neither is there any daysman between us that might lay his hand upon us both" (9:33). The word daysman refers to a mediator. In the New Testament of course, all this would change. See 1 Timothy 2:5.

4. "Man that is born of a woman is of few days, and full of trouble. He cometh forth like a flower, and is cut

Job

HIS TERRIBLE TRIALS

Nature of trials (1-2)
1. Oxen and donkeys stolen and farmhands killed
2. Sheep and herdsmen burned by fire
3. Camels are stolen and servants killed
4. Sons and daughters die in a mighty wind
5. Job himself is struck with boils

Background of trials
Job's motives for worshiping God had been challenged by Satan during a confrontation in the heavenlies.

A sovereign God thereupon allows the five trials.

HIS WHIMPERING WIFE

"Then said his wife unto him, Dost thou still retain thine integrity? Curse God. and die" **(2:9).**

HIS FICKLE FRIENDS

ELIPHAZ
SERMON LOCATION 4, 5, 15, 22
SERMON AUTHORITY PERSONAL EXPERIENCE 4:8, 12-16
SERMON CONCLUSION
"You are suffering because of your sin!" **(4:7, 8; 15:6)**
1. You have cheated the poor **(22:6)**
2. You have not fed the hungry **(22:7)**
3. You have mistreated widows and orphans **(22:9)**
4. You are a windbag **(15:2)**
"My advice: Repent and turn back to God!" **(22:21-28)**

BILDAD
SERMON LOCATION 8, 18, 25
SERMON AUTHORITY TRADITION 8:8-10
SERMON CONCLUSION
"You are suffering because of your sin!" **(8:20)**
"My advice: Repent and turn back to God!" **(8:5, 6)**

ZOPHAR
SERMON LOCATION 11, 20
SERMON AUTHORITY DOGMATISM 11:6; 20:4
SERMON CONCLUSION
"You are suffering because of your sin!" **(11:4-6; 20:4, 5)**
"My advice: Repent and turn back to God!" **(11:13-15)**

ELIHU
SERMON LOCATION 32-37
SERMON AUTHORITY Elihu thought he was God's answer to Job's problem 33:6
SERMON CONCLUSION
1. You are guilty of foolish speaking **(34:35-37; 36:16)**
2. You are guilty of false righteousness **(35:2)**
3. Consider God's glory and greatness **(37:14-24)**

HIS DEFENSES and DIALOGUES

The suffering patriarch responds to his accusers in nine separate speeches.

ONE **CHAPTER 3**	FOUR **12, 13, 14**	SEVEN **21**
TWO **6-7**	FIVE **16, 17**	EIGHT **23, 24**
THREE **9-10**	SIX **19**	NINE **26-31**

During these nine speeches Job discusses fourteen topics. These are:
1. Righteousness and suffering (27:6; 31:1-40)
2. Good works (29:12-17; 30:25)
3. Health, wealth, and respect (29:1-11, 20-25)
4. Unfair punishment (9:16, 17, 30-33; 13:26, 27; 10:2, 7, 8; 19:6-11; 30:20, 21)
5. So-called friends (12:2; 13:4; 16:2; 19:3)
6. "If they were in my place" (16:4, 5)
7. False neighbors, associates, and servants (19:13-22; 30:1, 9, 10)
8. Answers (28:12-28)
9. God (23:8, 9)
10. The flesh (7:5, 13, 14; 30:17, 18, 30)
11. "I wish I had never been born" (3:3-11, 16; 10:18)
12. "I wish I were dead" (6:8, 9; 7:15, 16)
13. "I have no hope" (10:20-22)
14. "In spite of all, I'll trust God" (13:15; 16:19; 23:10)

HIS GLORIOUS GOD

Suddenly from out of a whirlwind comes the mighty voice of God. The sullen Job is then subjected to a quiz:

GOD'S FIRST SERIES OF QUESTIONS: JOB 38-39

1. **JOB 38:4** "Where wast thou when I laid the foundations of the earth? Declare, if thou hast understanding."
2. **JOB 38:18** "Hast thou perceived the breadth of the earth? Declare if thou knowest it all."
3. **JOB 38:19** "Where is the way where light dwelleth? And as for darkness, where is the place thereof?"
4. **JOB 38:24** "By what way is the light parted, which scattereth the east wind upon the earth?"
5. **JOB 38:28** "Hath the rain a father? Or who hath begotten the drops of dew?"
6. **JOB 40:2** "Shall he that contendeth with the Almighty instruct him? He that reproveth God, let him answer it."

JOB'S REPLY: 40:4, 5

GOD'S SECOND SERIES OF QUESTIONS: JOB 40:6—41:33

1. **JOB 40:15** "Behold now the behemoth, which I made with thee; he eateth grass as an ox."
2. **JOB 41:1** "Canst thou draw out leviathan with an hook? or his tongue with a cord which thou lettest down?"

   NOTE: These two creatures may very well refer to a land dinosaur and a sea dinosaur.

JOB'S REPLY: 42:1-5

HIS BOUNTIFUL BLESSINGS

JOB 42:7-17

Job has been subjected to five fiery trials and has participated in five painful debates, but now he receives at the hand of God a tenfold blessing
1. He is allowed to see the glory of God.
2. He sees himself as God sees him. (This is always a blessing.)
3. He is vindicated by God before the eyes of his three critical friends.
4. He discovers the joy of praying for these three friends.
5. His former health is fully restored.
6. He is comforted by his brothers and sister.
7. He is given double his former wealth.
8. He is given seven more sons and three more daughters.
9. He lives to enjoy his grandchildren and great-grandchildren.
10. He is given an additional 140 years—twice the number normally accorded a man. **(See Ps. 90:10.)**

Some reasons for Job's sufferings
1. That Satan might be silenced **(1:9-11; 2:4, 5)**.
2. That Job might see God **(42:5)**.
3. That Job might see himself **(40:4; 42:6)**.
4. That Job's friends might learn not to judge **(42:7)**.
5. That Job might learn to pray for, rather than to lash out against, his critics **(42:10)**.
6. To demonstrate that all God's plans for his own eventually have happy endings **(42:10)**.

down; he fleeth also as a shadow, and continueth not" (14:1, 2).

5. "They have gaped upon me with their mouth; they have smitten me upon the cheek reproachfully; they have gathered themselves together against me. God hath delivered me to the ungodly, and turned me over into the hands of the wicked" (16:10, 11).

These words are repeated (in paraphrase fashion) in Psalms 22:13; 35:21, in reference to the sufferings of Christ on the cross.

6. "Also now, behold, my witness is in heaven, and my record is on high" (16:19).

7. "But he knoweth the way that I take; when he hath tested me, I shall come forth as gold" (23:10).

8. "He stretcheth out the north over the empty place, and hangeth the earth upon nothing" (26:7).

9. "Oh, that I knew where I might find him, that I might come even to his seat!" (23:3). This problem was solved through the *incarnation* of Christ. See John 1:18, 45.

10. "How then can man be justified with God? Or how can he be clean that is born of a woman?" (25:4). Problem solved through the *death* of Christ. See Romans 4:24, 25; 5:1.

11. "If a man die, shall he live again?" (14:14). Problem solved through the *resurrection* of Christ.

12. "For I know that my redeemer liveth, and that he shall stand at the latter day upon the earth: And though after my skin worms destroy this body, yet in my flesh shall I see God" (19:25, 26).

SOME REASONS FOR JOB'S SUFFERINGS

1. That Satan might be silenced (1:9–11; 2:4, 5).
2. That Job might see God (42:5).
3. That Job might see himself (40:4; 42:6).
4. That Job's friends might learn not to judge (42:7).
5. That Job might learn to pray for, rather than to lash out against his critics (42:10).
6. To demonstrate that all God's plans for his own eventually have happy endings (42:10).

THE EXODUS STAGE

INTRODUCING THE EXODUS STAGE
(Exodus, Leviticus, Numbers, Deuteronomy)

1. The four most important men during this stage are: Moses, Aaron, Caleb, and Joshua.
2. The Exodus Stage covers a period of some 325 years.
3. It includes the following key events:
   a. The captivity and deliverance of Israel from Egypt by Moses (Ex. 1-14).
   b. The failure of Israel to enter the Promised Land because of unbelief (Num. 13-14).
   c. The appearance of the manna (Ex. 16:14), the institution of the Sabbath (Ex. 16:23-30), and the giving of the Ten Commandments (Ex. 20:3-17).
   d. The building of the tabernacle (Ex. 40).
   e. The aimless wandering in the wilderness (Num. 14:33, 34).
   f. The sin and death of Moses (Num. 20:7-13; Deut. 34:5-8).
   g. The choice of Joshua as Israel's new leader (Num. 27:15-23; Deut. 34:9).
4. Here we read of a bloody river, a backed up sea, and a bitter brook (Ex. 7, 14, 15).
5. We are told of a golden calf, a talking ass, and a bronze snake (Ex. 32; Num. 22; 21).
6. We see a burning bush in the desert and a bright cloud in the sky (Ex. 3, 13).
7. Here Moses ascends to the pleasures of heaven (Ex. 33) while Korah descends to the pits of hell (Num. 16).

THE EXODUS STAGE

I. Israel, Enslaved in Egypt (Ex. 1:1—12:36).
   A. God's people.
      1. After the death of Joseph there arose a new king over Egypt, "which knew not Joseph" (1:8).
      2. This king cruelly persecuted Israel, enslaved them, and ordered the death of all male Hebrew babies (1:10-16).
   B. God's grace.
      "And God heard their groaning, and God remembered his covenant with Abraham, with Isaac, and with Jacob. And God looked upon the children of Israel, and God had respect unto them" (2:24, 25).
   C. God's man.
      1. The prince of Egypt.
         a. Moses is born of godly parents, hidden for three months, and then set afloat in a basket on the Nile River (2:3).
         b. Moses is discovered by Pharaoh's daughter and, upon the advice of Miriam (Moses' sister, who had watched all this), secures the nursing services of his own mother (2:8, 9).
         c. Moses grows up in Pharaoh's court, but at the age of forty flees the land of Egypt. This he does:
            (1) Because of his involvement in murder. Moses slays an Egyptian who is beating a Hebrew slave (2:12).
            (2) Because of his involvement with the Messiah—Hebrews 11:24-26: "By faith Moses, when he was come to years, refused to be called the son of Pharaoh's daughter; choosing rather to suffer affliction with the people of God, than to enjoy the pleasures of sin for a season."
      2. The shepherd of Midian.
         a. Moses finds refuge in Midian and marries Zipporah, the daughter of Jethro, and lives the next forty years as a shepherd (2:21).
         b. Moses receives his divine call from the burning bush to deliver Israel (3:1-10).
         The command was: "Draw not nigh hither: put off thy shoes from off thy feet, for the place whereon thou standest is holy ground" (3:5).
         Note: Moses was told to take his shoes off at this time, for he was on holy ground. This he did. But it should be observed that he later put them back on again. All too often Christians hear God speak to them concerning special service for him. They take their spiritual shoes off at some church altar, perhaps, but then do nothing about that call. God needs individuals who will both take off and put back on their shoes today. A worship experience should be followed by a working experience.
         c. He resisted this call, listing five lame excuses why he could not perform God's command:
            (1) I have no ability (3:11).
            (2) I have no message (3:13).
            (3) I have no authority 4:1).
            (4) I have no eloquence (4:10).
            (5) I have no inclination (4:13).
         d. God answered all these arguments for Moses, just as he does today for those whom he calls for service. Thus:
            (1) The objection, "I have no ability" is answered by Philippians 4:13.

(2) The objection, "I have no message" is answered by 1 Corinthians 15:3, 4.

(3) The objection, "I have no authority" is answered by Matthew 28:18-20.

(4) The objection, "I have no eloquence" is answered by Philippians 2:13.

(5) The objection, "I have no inclination" is answered by Philippians 2:13.

e. God answers all these arguments and gives Moses a twofold demonstration of his powers (4:2-7).
   (1) His shepherd's rod temporarily becomes a snake.
   (2) His right hand temporarily becomes leprous.

f. God graciously allows Moses to take his older brother Aaron with him (4:14, 15).

g. Moses had carelessly neglected to circumcise his own son, Gershom, which was a serious blunder on his part. Zipporah finally steps in at the last minute and saves Moses from divine judgment (4:24-26).

D. God's enemy.

1. Pharaoh not only refuses to free Israel, but puts more work upon the slaves, making them gather their own straws to make the bricks (5:1-9).

2. Pharaoh's treatment embitters the leaders of Israel against Moses, who complains to God and is reassured (5:20—6:8).

E. God's plagues.

1. Moses (now eighty) and Aaron (eighty-three) work their first miracle against Pharaoh, causing a rod to become a snake (7:10).

2. The Pharaoh's magicians (Jannes and Jambres—see 2 Tim. 3:8) perform the same trick, but see their snakes swallowed up by Moses' snake (7:12).

3. Moses calls down the ten plagues.
   a. First plague—water into blood (7:20).
   b. Second plague—a frog invasion (8:6).
   c. Third plague—lice (8:17).
   d. Fourth plague—flies (8:24).
   e. Fifth plague—cattle disease (9:6).
   f. Sixth plague—boils (9:10).
   g. Seventh plague—hail mingled with fire (9:24).
   h. Eighth plague—locusts (10:13).
   i. Ninth plague—a three-day darkness (10:22).
   j. Tenth plague—slaying of the firstborn (12:29).

4. Pharaoh offers Moses four compromises during these plagues, but all are refused.
   a. First compromise—don't leave, but do your thing here in Egypt (8:25).
   b. Second compromise—leave, but don't go too far (8:28).
   c. Third compromise—leave, but allow your children to remain here (10:10).
   d. Fourth compromise—leave, but without your flocks and herds (10:24).

5. Pharaoh's heart is hardened some eleven times during this period. We note that on at least seven occasions in the book of Exodus we are told that God hardened the heart of Pharaoh (see 4:21; 7:3; 9:12; 10:1, 20, 27; 11:10). How are we to understand this? A partial (and only partial) answer may be found in the following observation: The manner in which a given object will react when confronted by an outside influence is wholly dependent upon the nature of that object. For example, imagine a winter scene. Yonder is a frozen river. On either side is a bank of yellow clay. Suddenly the sun comes from behind the clouds and shines brightly down upon the river and the banks. What happens next? The reaction is this—the ice will melt but the clay will harden. Thus we see in nature the same outside and heavenly influence softening one object but hardening the other. Furthermore it should be pointed out that on four occasions we are informed that Pharaoh hardened his own heart. (See Ex. 7:22; 8:15, 19; 9:35.)

F. God's salvation (Ex. 11-12).

At this point let us summarize briefly both the nature and purpose of these plagues.

1. The nature of the plagues:
   a. The turning of the Egyptian waters into blood (7:20). Some have attempted to view this plague as the result of a natural event, such as the polluting of the Nile by excessive red soil or the sudden increase of certain bacteria microcosms, but it is doubtful if such natural occurrences would make the slightest impression upon the watching Pharaoh.
   b. The vast horde of frogs (8:2).
      Dr. John David quotes Harry Rimmer, who writes: "Like the blanket of filth the slimy, wet monstrosities covered the land, until men sickened at the continued squashing crunch of the ghastly pavement they were forced to walk upon. If a man's feet slipped on the greasy mass of putrid uncleanness, and when he sought water to cleanse himself, the water was so solid with frogs, he got no cleansing there." (*Moses and the Gods of Egypt,* p. 101)
   c. The lice (8:16).
      Some Hebrew scholars believe a more accurate translation here is "gnats," or "mosquitoes." Small insects have always been a problem in Egypt. Many devices were constructed by the ancient Egyptians in an attempt to get relief from them (such as ostrich plumes on the end of a stick which would be waved by servants to keep such insects away from the faces of the king and lords; floors and walls were often washed with a solution of soda).
   d. The swarm of flies (8:24).
      This may have been the large bloodsucking dog fly.

e. The grievous murrain cattle disease (9:3).
This plague doubtless had grave economic and religious consequences for the Egyptians. Oxen were depended upon for heavy labor in agriculture, while camels, asses, and horses were used for transportation. Cattle not only provided milk, but the bull was one of the most sacred objects in the worship services of the land.

f. The blains and boils (9:10).
The Hebrew language indicates these were leprous, pus-filled, open, and running sores.

g. The hail mingled with fire (9:24).
This crushing hailstorm was possibly accompanied by severe lightning which set fires to the Egyptian fields already ruined by the massive icy pellets from heaven. Because of the first of six plagues, some of the Egyptians apparently believed the word of God and brought their cattle and slaves in from the field (9:20).

h. The invasion of locusts (10:13).
A locust is capable of eating its own weight daily and one square mile of a swarm will normally contain up to 200 million of the creatures. Swarms covering more than 400 square miles have been recorded. A plague this size would carry some eighty billion locusts.

i. The three-day darkness (10:22).
This plague was surely the most frightening of all that had previously fallen. The darkness was so complete it could actually be felt. For seventy-two agonizing hours this horrifying blackness deprived its victims of food, water, and the slightest freedom of movement. More than one mind must have snapped under its terrible torture.

j. The death angel visitation (12:29).
God instructs Israel on preparing for that first Passover. An unblemished year-old male lamb was to be selected by each family on the tenth of April. This animal was to be killed on the fourteenth day. Its blood was to be drained into a basin. A cluster of hyssop branches was to be dipped into the basin and blood smeared against the lintel and two side panels of the door. The flesh of the lamb was to be roasted and eaten on the night of the fourteenth along with bitter herbs and unleavened bread.
Note: This is the first mention of leaven in the Bible, and from this point on it becomes a symbol of evil. In the New Testament, leaven stands for:
(1) Hypocrisy (Lk. 12:1)
(2) Rationalism (Mt. 16:6, 12)
(3) Worldliness (Mk. 8:15)
(4) Evil conduct (1 Cor. 5:6)
(5) False doctrine (Gal. 5:9)
The Passover lamb was of course a beautiful type and foreshadow of the Lord Jesus Christ. (See Jn. 1:29; 1 Cor. 5:6, 7; 1 Pet. 1:18, 19.) The hyssop here may represent faith. It was a common plant of the field. As the hyssop plant was used to apply the lamb's blood in the Old Testament, so faith applies the blood to the human heart in the New Testament. (See Eph. 2:8, 9.) It should be observed, however, that the mere death of the lamb did not automatically save anyone *until* the shed blood was applied.

Israel ate unleavened bread that night, and were to do this each April to remind them of their great deliverance (12:39–51).

2. The purpose of the plagues.
The purpose of the plagues was apparently twofold:
a. To demonstrate to Israel the strength of their God.
b. To show the Egyptians the total inability of their gods. It may be observed that each plague was directed against a particular Egyptian god. Thus:

ISRAEL, ENSLAVED IN EGYPT

GOD'S PEOPLE: Persecuted by a Pharaoh who did not know Joseph **(Ex. 1)**

GOD'S GRACE: He remembered his covenant with Abraham and heard their cries **(2:23-25)**

GOD'S MAN:

MOSES

HIS FIRST FORTY YEARS AS A PRINCE IN EGYPT (2:1-14)
● He is rescued by an Egyptian princess as a baby
● Later he rescues an Israeli slave

HIS SECOND FORTY YEARS AS A SHEPHERD IN MIDIAN (2:15—4:31)
● He marries a girl named Zipporah
● He receives his "burning bush" call

GOD'S ENEMY: Pharaoh refuses to free the Jews and increases their work burden **(Ex. 5:2, 4-9)**

GOD'S PLAGUES: EXODUS 7-10

PURPOSE
1. To show Israel their true God.
2. To show Egypt their false gods.

NATURE	EGYPTIAN GOD DEFEATED	
1. Water into blood	OSIRIS	Exodus 7:20
2. A frog invasion	HEKT	8:6
3. Lice	SEB	8:17
4. Flies	HATKOK	8:24
5. Cattle disease	APIS	9:6
6. Boils	TYPHON	9:10
7. Hail with fire	SHU	9:24
8. Locust	SERAPIA	10:13
9. Three-day darkness	RA	10:22
10. Death of firstborn	ALL gods	12:29

GOD'S CHOICE

FACT	REASON
● That the firstborn be sanctified	● He wanted a nation of priests.
● That the southern route be taken	● Israel needed to spend time with him.

(1) The first plague of bloody waters was directed against Osiris, the god of the Nile.

(2) The second plague of frogs was against the frog goddess Hekt.

(3) The third plague of lice was against Seb, the earth god.

(4) The fourth plague of beetles (or flies) was against Hatkok, the wife of Osiris.

(5) The fifth plague of cattle disease was against Apis, the sacred bull god.

(6) The sixth plague, boils, was against Typhon.

(7) The seventh plague, hail and fire, was against Shu, the god of the atmosphere.

(8) The eighth plague, locusts, was against Serapia, the god who protected Egypt against locusts.

(9) The ninth plague, darkness, was against Ra, the sun god.

(10) The tenth plague, the death of the firstborn, was an attack on *all* gods.

3. The result of the final plague.

a. At midnight, April 14, the death angel passes over Egypt, taking the firstborn sons from all unprotected homes, including the household of Pharaoh himself.

b. During the early morning hours of the fifteenth, all Israel (600,000 men plus their families) cross the border of Egypt.

c. They are accompanied by a mixed multitude.

G. God's selection.

1. The sanctification of the firstborn—God originally planned for a nation of priests, but finally, due to Israel's constant sin, limited his selection to the tribe of Levi (Ex. 13:2; 19:6; Num. 8:16).

2. The selection of the safer route (13:17).

II. Israel, En Route to Mt. Sinai (Ex. 12:37—18:27).

Ten key events took place between Rameses, their departure city in Egypt, and the arrival at the base of Mt. Sinai. The distance was approximately 150 miles. These events are:

A. The appearance of God's shekinah glory cloud (13:21, 22).

From Succoth to Etham. At Etham the pillar of cloud and fire is manifested to lead Israel by day or night. This marks the first appearance of the shekinah, that visible and luminous indication of God's presence (13:21, 22). Other Old Testament and New Testament appearances would include:

1. At the Red Sea (Ex. 10:19, 20).

2. In the tabernacle Holy of Holies (Lev. 16:2).

3. In the Temple Holy of Holies (2 Chron. 5:11-13).

4. Disappearance in Ezekiel's time (Ezek. 10).

5. At the birth of Christ (Lk. 2:9-11).

6. On the Mount of Transfiguration (Mt. 17:5).

7. At the Ascension (Acts 1:9).

8. At the rapture (1 Thess. 4:17).

9. At the Second Coming (Mt. 24:30; Mk. 8:38).

10. During the millennium (Isa. 4:5, 6; 60:19).

B. The chase by Pharaoh, who had regretted his action of letting Israel go (14:5-10).

From Etham to Pi-hahiroth (14:1-4).

1. The decision of Pharaoh—to follow up. Pharaoh regrets his decision to free Israel and determines to fall upon them and recapture them in the desert near the Red Sea through his crack chariot corps.

2. The despair of the people (Ex. 14:11, 12) to give up.

3. The declaration of the prophet (Ex. 14:13, 14) to look up.

C. The parting of the Red Sea (14:13-31).

D. The subsequent celebration of Israel over their deliverance and the destruction of Pharaoh's armies (15:1-21).

From Pi-hahiroth through the Red Sea (14:15—15:21).

1. The cloudy pillar—protecting. This is the second greatest miracle in all the Bible. The greatest of course is the resurrection of Christ from the dead—see Ephesians 1:20. The Red Sea crossing is mentioned many times in the Word of God. See Psalm 78:53; 106:11, 12, 22; Hebrews 11:29. This miracle was actually threefold in nature:

a. The first part was the shift in position of the glory cloud which placed itself between the camp of the Israelites and that of the Egyptians. It then settled down upon Pharaoh's armies like a fog, but gave light to God's people.

b. The second part was the actual dividing of the waters, clearing a path of perhaps a mile wide. Concerning this, Dr. Leon Wood writes:

"A marching line of 2,000,000 people, walking ten abreast with an average five feet separating each rank, would be 190 miles long. Had this path been only as wide as a modern highway, the first Israelites through would have been in Canaan before the last started, and several days would have elapsed." (*A Survey of Israel's History*, p. 133)

c. The third part was the actual closing of the water.

2. The Red Sea parting.

"And Moses stretched out his hand over the sea; and the Lord caused the sea to go back by a strong east wind all that night, and made the sea dry land, and the waters were divided" (14:21).

3. The Egyptian army perishing.

"And the waters returned, and covered the chariots, and the horsemen, and all the host of Pharaoh that came into the sea after them; there remained not so much as one of them" (14:28).

4. The Lord's people praising.

"Then sang Moses and the children of Israel this song unto the Lord, and spake, saying, I will sing unto the Lord, for he hath triumphed gloriously: the horse and his rider hath he thrown into the sea" (Ex. 15:1).

E. Marah's bitter waters made sweet by the casting in of a tree (15:22-26). God at this time promised them freedom from sickness if they would but obey him.

From the Red Sea to Marah (15:22-26).
1. The galling water.
"And when they came to Marah, they could not drink of the waters of Marah, for they were bitter: therefore the name of it was called Marah" (15:23).
2. The goodly tree.
"And he cried unto the Lord; and the Lord shewed him a tree, which when he had cast into the waters, the waters were made sweet: there he made for them a statute and an ordinance, and there he proved them" (Ex. 15:25).
3. The Great Physician.
"And said, If thou wilt diligently hearken to the voice of the Lord thy God, and wilt do that which is right in his sight, and wilt give ear to his commandments, and keep all his statutes, I will put none of these diseases upon thee, which I have brought upon the Egyptians: for I am the Lord that healeth thee" (Ex. 15:26).
From Marah to Elim (Ex. 15:27).
"And they came to Elim where were twelve wells of water and threescore and ten palm trees: and they encamped there by the waters."
F. The giving of the manna (16:4, 14, 35).
This heavenly bread would become their staple diet for the next forty years.
From Elim to the Wilderness of Zin (16:1-36).
1. The complaining crowd.
"And the whole congregation of the children of Israel murmured against Moses and Aaron in the wilderness: And the children of Israel said unto them, would to God we had died by the hand of the Lord in the land of Egypt, when we sat by the flesh pots, and when we did eat bread to the full; for ye have brought us forth into this wilderness, to kill this whole assembly with hunger" (Ex. 16:2, 3).
2. The miraculous manna (16:14, 15).
Beginning now and continuing for the next forty years God would feed them six days a week with manna, a white, flat, coriander-like seed which tasted like honey bread. It would only cease when Israel entered the Promised Land. (See Josh. 5:12.)
It was to be picked up each morning and eaten that same day for six days, and on the sixth, a double portion was to be taken for the seventh, when no manna would fall. The word manna in the Hebrew literally means, "What is it?" This is what the people said when they first saw it, and the name stuck. Jesus would later apply this event to his own ministry. (See Jn. 6:30-63.) Dr. John David writes the following helpful words on the subject of manna:
"It should not be assumed from these passages that manna constituted the only part of the diet of the Hebrews during the forty-year period. We know that the Is-

raelites had sheep and cattle (12:38; 17:3) and they continued to possess these not only in Sinai (34:3) but had them when they reached Edom and the country east of the Jordan (Num. 20:19; 32:1). It appears that on some occasions the Hebrews bought food and even water from the Edomites (Deut. 2:6, 7). That wheat and meats were available is clearly implied in such references as Exodus 17:3; 24:5; Leviticus 8:2, 26, 31; 9:4; 10:12; 24:5; and Numbers 7:13, 19." (*Moses and the Gods of Egypt,* p. 181)
G. The institution of the Sabbath (16:23, 26-30; 31:13).
The solemn Sabbath (16:23-30).
"See, for that the Lord hath given you the sabbath, therefore he giveth you on the sixth day the bread of two days; abide ye every man in his place, let no man go out of his place on the seventh day. So the people rested on the seventh day" (Ex. 16:29, 30).
Following is a brief summary on the biblical teaching concerning the Sabbath:
1. Sabbath first mentioned in Exodus 16:23. For the first 2500 years of human history no one observed it but God himself. (See Gen. 2:2.)
2. Sabbath was then given to Israel (Ex. 31:13, 17) who previously knew *nothing* about it whatsoever. (See Ex. 16:29.) This day was never given to the church (see Col. 2:16; Gal. 4:9-11).
3. Sabbath is not a Hebrew word for seven but means "Rest or cessation." Hebrew words for seven are *sheba* and *shibah*. Thus, a literal translation of the fourth commandment would read, "Remember the rest day, to keep it holy."
4. There were many "Sabbaths" given to Israel:
a. The weekly seventh day Sabbath (Ex. 20:8-11).
(1) It began at sundown on Friday and ended at sundown Saturday.
(2) It was a day of absolute rest, with no services or gatherings.
b. The first day of the seventh month Sabbath (Lev. 23:24, 25), feast of trumpets.
c. The tenth day of the seventh month Sabbath (Lev. 16:29, 30), day of atonement.
d. The fifteenth day of the seventh month Sabbath (Lev. 23:34), feast of tabernacles.
e. The seventh year Sabbath (Lev. 25:1-4), land was to be idle for entire year.
f. The fiftieth year Sabbath (Lev. 25:8).
The seventy-year Babylonian captivity was primarily due to Israel's disobedience to observe these rest years. In approximately 500 years they had accumulated until Israel owed the Promised Land seventy rest years. (See Lev. 26:27-35; 2 Chron. 36:21; Jer. 25:11.)
5. Sabbath had never been changed but has been set aside because the nation Israel has been set aside. (See Mt. 21:43.)
6. The Sabbath will be observed again during the kingdom age. (See Isa. 66:23.)

Question: Where then does the church receive authority to worship on Sunday?

Answer: This authority was laid out in pattern form through the resurrection, which occurred on the first day—Sunday. This fact is reported by all four Gospels (Mt. 28:1; Mk. 16:2, 9; Lk. 24:1, 13; Jn. 20:1, 19). Thus, as the seventh day commemorates a finished creation (Ex. 20:8-11), so the first day commemorates a finished redemption. (See Acts 20:7; 1 Cor. 16:1, 2; Heb. 7:12.) It is true that Paul often preached to the Jews on the Sabbath (Acts 13:14; 16:13; 17:2; 18:4), but he only did so because this was the day the Jews regularly gathered together. (See 1 Cor. 9:19, 20.)

H. Striking the rock at Rephidim (17:1-7).

This was done to provide water, which God supernaturally gave from the side of that rock. Nearly forty years later Moses will strike another rock in a distant place, but at that time he will be out of God's will. (See Num. 20:7-13.)

From the Wilderness to Rephidim (Ex. 17:1-18:27).

Moses strikes the rock (17:6). The fickle Israelites were almost ready to stone Moses because of their thirst when God stepped in. "Behold, I will stand before thee there upon the rock in Horeb; and thou shalt smite the rock, and there shall come water out of it that the people may drink. . . ."

2 ISRAEL, EN ROUTE TO MT. SINAI   EXODUS 12-18

A. APPEARANCE OF GLORY CLOUD (EX. 13:21, 22)
The first of ten biblical appearances

B. CHASE BY PHARAOH (14:5-10)
The decision of the Pharaoh—to follow up
The despair of the people—to give up
The declaration of the prophet—to look up

C. THE MIRACLE AT THE RED SEA (14:13—15:21)
The cloudy pillar—*PROTECTING*
The Red Sea—*PARTING*
The Egyptian army—*PERISHING*
The Lord's people—*PRAISING*

D. THE EPISODE AT MARAH (15:22-26)
The galling waters
The good tree
The Great Physician

E. THE GIVING OF MANNA (16:4, 14, 35)
The sarcastic crowd
The supernatural food

F. THE INSTITUTION OF THE SABBATH (16:23, 26-30)
Given to Israel as a spiritual wedding ring
Commemorated a finished creation

G. THE WATER-FILLED ROCK (17:1-7)
In obedience Moses strikes this rock
In disobedience he will later strike another rock
(See **Num. 20:7-13**)

H. VICTORY OVER THE AMALEKITES (FOUR "FIRSTS" NOW OCCUR) (17:8-16)
First mention of Joshua
First intercession of Moses for Israel
First part of Bible to be written (?)
First reference to God as *Jehovah-Nissi*

I. MOSES REUNITED WITH HIS FAMILY (18:5)
He greets his father-in-law, wife, and two sons

I. Israel's Victory over the Amalekites (Ex. 17:8-16). Here four important "firsts" should be noted:
1. The first mention of Joshua, who was selected by Moses to lead the armies of Israel (17:9).
2. The first prayer of Moses for Israel (17:11, 12).
3. The first part of the Bible to be written (17:14).
4. The first reference to one of God's great names—*Jehovah-nissi* (the Lord is my banner). (See 17:15.)

Moses smites an enemy (17:11). The enemy—the Amalekites. These descendants of Esau (Gen. 36:12), a roving and raiding desert band, had probably been tracking Israel for some time now, and chose this moment to strike (17:8).

The general—Joshua. This is the first mention of one of the most remarkable military men who ever lived. In spite of his youth (probably in his early twenties), Moses chose him to head up Israel's fighting forces. His ability and bravery were matched by his love for God (17:9).

The intercessor—Moses. This grand old man ascends a nearby hill, extends his arms upward, and begins praying for Joshua and Israel fighting below (17:11).

The helpers—Aaron and Hur. These two aided Moses in keeping his weary arms heavenward so that God could give victory below. Israel is victorious, one of the first sections of the Bible is written, and Moses builds an altar to God, calling it *Jehovah-nissi*, meaning "Jehovah is my Flag."

J. The meeting of Moses with his family (18:5).
Moses salutes his family (18:7).
1. He is greeted by Jethro, Zipporah, and his two sons Gershom and Eliezer.
2. At Jethro's advice, Moses appoints capable men to help him judge the problems of Israel (18:17-27).

III. Israel, Settled down at Sinai (Ex. 19:1—Num. 10:10). On June 15, 1445 B.C., Israel arrived at Mt. Sinai. They would be there for eleven months and five days (Num. 10:11). Three major events took place during this time. These are:

The commandment of the law (requirement for fellowship).

The corruption of the golden calf (ruination of that fellowship).

The construction of the tabernacle (restoration of that fellowship).

We shall now look at an introduction *to* and a consideration *of* these three events.
A. An introduction to the action at Mt. Sinai.
1. Israel arrives at Mt. Sinai and is given notice that God will meet with them in three days. They are therefore to wash their clothes and prepare their hearts (Ex. 19:9, 10).
2. On the third day, God manifests himself on Mt. Sinai, accompanied by thunderings, lightnings, a thick cloud, the voice of a trumpet, an earthquake, smoke, and fire (Ex. 19:16-18).

3. Moses is ordered to climb Mt. Sinai to meet God. At this time, God gives him orally both the Ten Commandments and the seventy laws which compose the Book of the Covenant. Moses then descends the mountain and repeats God's words to Israel (Ex. 19:20—23:33).

4. The people agree to all that God has told Moses (24:3).

5. Moses then writes down for Israel's record all that he has told them, builds an altar of twelve pillars, and sacrifices blood upon it to satisfy this covenant agreement (24:4-8).

6. Moses once again ascends the mountain and this time is accompanied part way by Joshua (24:13).

7. Here he will spend the next forty days, at which time he will receive the pattern for the tabernacle and two tables of stone written by God himself and containing the Ten Commandments. During this entire period, Moses fasts (Ex. 24:18; 31:18; 34:28; Deut. 9:9).

8. He then is warned to get down immediately to deal with the golden calf episode below (Ex. 32:7).

9. He prays for Israel that God would not destroy her (Ex. 32:11-13).

10. He picks up Joshua halfway down (Ex. 32:17).

11. Upon viewing Israel's terrible immorality, he breaks into pieces the stones containing the Ten Commandments (Ex. 32:19).

12. He rebukes Aaron and judges Israel the second time (32:20-29).

13. He prays for Israel the second time (32:30-32).

14. He then fasts for the next forty days (Deut. 9:18).

15. He again ascends the mountain and is ordered by God to carve out two new rocks, upon which the Lord rewrites the Ten Commandments (Deut. 10:2).

16. He is commanded to make an ark-box of shittim wood and to place the two tablets of stone in this box. Moses then returns to the valley below with the ark (Deut. 10:5).

17. Moses asks to see the glory of God. The Lord replies:

"And he said, I will make all my goodness pass before thee, and I will proclaim the name of the Lord before thee; and I will be gracious to whom I will be gracious, and will shew mercy on whom I will shew mercy. And he said, Thou canst not see my face: for there shall no man see me, and live. And the Lord said, Behold there is a place by me, and thou shalt stand upon a rock. And it shall come to pass, while my glory passeth by, that I will put thee in a clift of the rock, and will cover thee with my hand while I pass by. And I will take away mine hand, and thou shalt see my back parts: but my face shall not be seen" (Ex. 33:19-23).

B. A consideration of the action at Mt. Sinai.
The Commandment of the Law. There were three basic sections of the Mosaic Law.

1. The moral code. This section is commonly known as the Ten Commandments (Ex. 20:3-17; Deut. 5:7-21).
   a. Thou shalt have no other gods before me.
   b. Thou shalt not make unto thee any graven image.
   c. Thou shalt not take the name of the Lord thy God in vain.
   d. Remember the Sabbath day to keep it holy.
   e. Honor thy father and thy mother.
   f. Thou shalt not kill.
   g. Thou shalt not commit adultery.
   h. Thou shalt not steal.
   i. Thou shalt not bear false witness.
   j. Thou shalt not covet.

2. The spiritual code. This section deals with the ordinances, all of which foreshadow Christ and salvation. (See Heb. 10:1.) It includes the Levitical feasts, offerings, etc. (Ex. 35-40; Lev.).

3. The social code. This section deals with the judgments and divine laws of God's new establishment for Israel. It includes rules for diet, sanitation, quarantine, soil conservation, taxation, military service, marriage, divorce, etc.

   There are some seventy basic regulations in the social code. Of these, twenty of the more important are as follows:
   a. "And if a man smite his servant, or his maid, with a rod, and he die under his hand; he shall be surely punished (Ex. 21:20).
   b. "And he that smiteth his father, or his mother, shall surely be put to death" (21:15).
   c. "And he that stealeth a man, and selleth him, or if he be bound in his hand, he shall surely be put to death" (21:16).
   d. "Eye for eye, tooth for tooth, hand for hand, foot for foot" (21:24).
   e. "And he that curseth his father, or his mother, shall surely be put to death" (21:17).
   f. "And if a man smite the eye of his servant, or the eye of his maid, that it perish; he shall let him go free for his eye's sake" (21:26).

3
ISRAEL, SETTLED DOWN AT SINAI

Three main events occurring at Sinai

1. **EXODUS 20:3-17**
   THE COMMANDMENTS OF THE LAW
   Requirement for divine fellowship

2. **EXODUS 32**
   THE CORRUPTION OF THE CALF
   Ruination of divine fellowship

3. **EXODUS 25-31, 35-40**
   CONSTRUCTION OF THE TABERNACLE
   Restoration to divine fellowship

g. "If a man shall steal an ox, or a sheep, and kill it, or sell it; he shall restore five oxen for an ox, and four sheep for a sheep" (22:1).

h. "And if a man entice a maid that is not betrothed, and lie with her, he shall surely endow her to be his wife" (22:16).

i. "Thou shalt not suffer a witch to live" (22:18).

j. "Whosoever lieth with a beast shall surely be put to death" (22:19).

k. "He that sacrificeth unto any god, save unto the Lord only, he shall be utterly destroyed" (22:20).

l. "Thou shalt neither vex a stranger, nor oppress him: for ye were strangers in the land of Egypt" (22:21).

THE THREEFOLD DIVISION OF THE LAW

Moral Code
1. Thou shalt have no other gods before me.
2. Thou shalt not make unto thee any graven image.
3. Thou shalt not take the name of the Lord thy God in vain.
4. Remember the Sabbath day to keep it holy.
5. Honor thy father and thy mother.
6. Thou shalt not kill.
7. Thou shalt not commit adultery.
8. Thou shalt not steal.
9. Thou shalt not bear false witness.
10. Thou shalt not covet.

The Revelation from Christ
(1 CORINTHIANS 10:4)

Spiritual Code

This section dealt with those special ordinances which foreshadowed Christ and his full redemption. It included:

1. The seven **Levitical feasts.**
2. The five **Levitical offerings.**

EXODUS 35-40; LEVITICUS

The Realization in Christ
(MATTHEW 5:17, 18; ROMANS 10:4; 1 CORINTHIANS 5:7)

Social Code

This section included rules governing Israel's diet, sanitation, quarantine, soil conservation, taxation, military service, marriage, childbirth, divorce, etc.

BOOK OF LEVITICUS

The Regulation Until Christ
(GALATIANS 3:24)

m. "Ye shall not afflict any widow, or fatherless child" (22:22).

n. "If thou lend money to any of my people that is poor by thee, thou shalt not be to him as an usurer, neither shalt thou lay upon him usury" (22:25).

"If thou at all take thy neighbour's raiment to pledge, thou shalt deliver it unto him by that the sun goeth down" (22:26).

"For that is his covering only, it is his raiment for his skin: wherein shall he sleep? and it shall come to pass, when he crieth unto me, that I will hear; for I am gracious" (22:27).

o. "Thou shalt not revile the gods, nor curse the ruler of thy people" (22:28).

p. "Thou shalt not delay to offer the first of thy ripe fruits, and of thy liquors: the firstborn of thy sons shalt thou give unto me" (22:29).

q. "If thou meet thine enemy's ox or his ass going astray, thou shalt surely bring it back to him again" (23:4).

"If thou see the ass of him that hateth thee lying under his burden, and wouldest forbear to help him, thou shalt surely help with him" (23:5).

r. "Thou shalt not wrest the judgment of thy poor in his cause" (23:6).

s. "And six years thou shalt sow thy land, and shalt gather in the fruits thereof: But the seventh year thou shalt let it rest and lie still; that the poor of thy people may eat: and what they leave the beast of the field shall eat. In like manner thou shalt deal with thy vineyard, and with thy oliveyard" (23:10, 11).

t. "Behold, I send an Angel before thee, to keep thee in the way, and to bring thee into the place which I have prepared" (23:20).

Simply stated, the moral code acted as the *revelation* of God's law, the social code as the *regulation* of that law, and the spiritual code as the *realization* of that law—in Christ. (See Mt. 5:17, 18; Rom. 10:4.)

C. The corruption of the golden calf (Ex. 32).

1. During the final days of Moses' first forty-day meeting with God atop Mt. Sinai, the fickle Israelites in the valley below demand that Aaron make them a god.

2. Aaron agrees, and, using their own golden earrings, forms a golden calf god.

3. After the "worship service" the people throw a wild party and indulge in sexual immorality. The verb translated "to play" in 32:6 means to sexually caress. (See Gen. 26:8 for a similar situation.)

4. God informs Moses of all this on the mountain and declares his intention to destroy the entire bunch. A trembling Moses then begins his respectful "debate with deity." He pleads for God to turn his wrath away for two reasons:

a. Because of his enemies (32:12).
b. Because of his friends (32:13).

5. Moses and Joshua return to the camp and in righteous anger Moses breaks the Ten Commandment tablets of stone. He then burns the golden calf, grinds it into powder, mixes it with water, and makes the people drink it.

6. He reprimands Aaron and demands to know who is on the Lord's side. The tribe of Levi, to a man, declare themselves to be, and from that day are chosen to become the priests of God.

7. God then sends a plague to punish Israel and orders the execution of 3,000 troublemaking ring leaders.

D. The construction of the tabernacle (Ex. 25–31: 35–41; Lev.).

1. A general description of the tabernacle:

a. The three sections—the outer court, the inner court, and the Holy of Holies. The outer court, a glorified picket fence construction, measured 150 feet in length, seventy-five feet wide, and seven-and-a-half feet high. In the center of the "picket fence" was a tent, forty-five feet long, fifteen feet wide, and fifteen feet high.

There were two rooms in this tent, separated by a thick veil. The eastern room section of this tent (the entire tabernacle faced east) was the holy place, and the western section was the Holy of Holies. The tent was made of forty-eight upright boards and was covered by four kinds of cloth. Three of these were animal skins, and the fourth was a fine linen. The colors involved were white, blue, purple, and scarlet.

b. The various materials used—gold (3,140 pounds), and silver (9,575 pounds), bronze (7,540 pounds), animal cloth, acacia wood, olive oil, spices, onyx stones.

c. Overall supervisor, Bezaleel, grandson of Hur, from tribe of Judah.

d. Time of construction, approximately six months.

e. Method of construction—the tabernacle was the production of willing hands and hearts. God's house was financed by God's people, and not through suppers,

THE CONSTRUCTION OF THE TABERNACLE

DESCRIPTION AND SIZE

Consisted of three sections: (1) outer court (2) inner court (3) holy of holies
Outer court: similar to a picket fence—150 ft. long, 75 ft. wide, 7½ ft. high
Tent within the outer court—45 ft. long, 15 ft. wide, 15 ft. high
Tent had two rooms which were separated by a thick veil
Eastern tent room known as the inner court or Holy Place
Western tent room known as the Holy of Holies

BUILDING MATERIALS

Gold, silver, bronze, animal cloth, acacia wood, onyx stones

FURNITURE
EX. 25, 27, 30, 37, 38

In outer court: a bronze altar and a bronze laver
In inner court: shewbread table, lampstand, and incense altar
In Holy of Holies: the Ark of the Covenant

TIME OF CONSTRUCTION

Six months

METHOD OF CONSTRUCTION

Made by willing hands and hearts (See **Ex. 35; Num. 7**)

THE PRIESTS
EX. 28-29

Had to come from the tribe of Levi
Were anointed with water, oil, and blood

THE HIGH PRIEST

Had to come from the line of Aaron of the tribe of Levi
Clothing: two ephods (outer and inner robes) breastplate, mitre, Urim and Thummim
Duties: to care for the physical needs of the tabernacle and the spiritual needs of the people

OFFERINGS

BURNT OFFERING **Lev. 1**	Offered primarily to **maintain**
MEAL OFFERING **Lev. 2**	fellowship with God.
PEACE OFFERING **Lev. 3**	
SIN OFFERING **Lev. 4**	Offered primarily to **restore**
TRESPASS OFFERING **Lev. 5**	fellowship to God.

HOLY FEASTS
(LEV. 23, 25)

WEEKLY SABBATH	These three speak of God's
SEVEN-YEAR SABBATH	first great work, that of **creation.**
FIFTY-YEAR SABBATH	(See **Rev. 4:11**)
PASSOVER Speaks of Calvary	These six speak of God's
FIRST FRUITS The resurrection	second great work, that of
PENTECOST Coming of Holy Spirit	**redemption.** (See **Rev. 5:9.**)
TRUMPETS Rapture and Second Coming	
ATONEMENT The tribulation	
TABERNACLE The millennium	

THE PURPOSE OF THE TABERNACLE

To provide for Israel a visible center of worship.
To preview the work of Christ. Note similarities between the language of Moses and John.

MOSES	JOHN
Describes the brazen altar	Describes the Lamb of God (**Jn. 1:29**)
Speaks of the brazen laver	Speaks of the water of life (**Jn. 4:14**)
Writes of the table of shewbread	Writes of the bread of life (**Jn. 6:35**)
Talks of the lampstand	Talks of the light of the world (**Jn. 9:5**)
Presents the altar of incense	Presents the great prayer of Christ (**Jn. 17**)
Witnesses of the mercy seat	Witness of Christ our mercy seat (**1 Jn. 2:2**)

DEDICATION OF TABERNACLE

THE TRIUMPH: God's glory cloud fills the place (**Ex. 40:33-38**)
THE TRAGEDY: God's judgment falls upon Aaron's two wicked sons (**Lev. 10:1-11**)

CENSUS OF TABERNACLE

The first Exodus census (of two) now takes place (**Num. 1**) (For second census see **Num. 26.**)

NAZARITE VOW

THREE RULES: (1) not to drink wine (2) not to cut hair (3) avoid contact with dead objects (**Num. 6**).

junk sales, and bingo parties. Some of the most inspiring verses in the Old Testament speak of this sweet and sacrificial spirit (35:5, 21, 22, 29).

Another precious truth involved in the tabernacle project was the fact that God personally observed each gift which was given, no matter how small. This is dramatically brought out in Numbers 7, where twelve tiny gold boxes of incense are given by twelve different individuals. In spite of the fact that the gifts were identical and inexpensive (approximately $6.50 per box) God nevertheless achnowledged each person and each gift. (See also Rev. 2:2, 9, 13; 3:1, 8, 15.)

2. The furniture of the tabernacle.
There were six main objects:
a. The brazen (or bronze) altar—Exodus 27:1-8; 38:1-7.

This was the first piece of furniture as one enters the tabernacle from the east. It was a box-like structure made of acacia wood overlaid with bronze. It was approximately seven-and-a-half feet wide and three feet high. There was a grate midway between the top and the bottom. A horn was located on each corner of the altar to help hold the animal sacrifices which were offered at this altar.

b. The brazen (or bronze) laver—Exodus 30:18; 38:8.

A brass basin which was filled with water, resting on a pedestal, covered by mirrors. It was used by the priests for actual and ceremonial cleansing of both hands and feet.

c. The table of shewbread—Exodus 25:23-30; 37:10-16.

A table was made of acacia wood and covered with gold. On this table were placed twelve cakes of bread, renewed each week, one for each tribe in Israel. This table was approximately one-and-a-half feet wide by two-and-a-half feet high. This table, unlike the first two pieces of furniture, was on the inside of the tent, resting on the northern side of the first room.

d. The lampstand—Exodus 25:31-40; 37:17-24.

One of the most ornate objects in the tabernacle. It was made of pure gold and consisted of an upright shaft from each side of which three branches extended upward in pairs. The lamps were trimmed every morning and evening and were never to be extinguished all at one time. The lamp had to be regularly supplied with pure olive oil. The entire lamp required 107 pounds of gold and cost approximately $175,000. Jewish tradition says the lampstand was five feet high and three-and-a-half feet wide. It rested on the south side of the first room (also called the holy place).

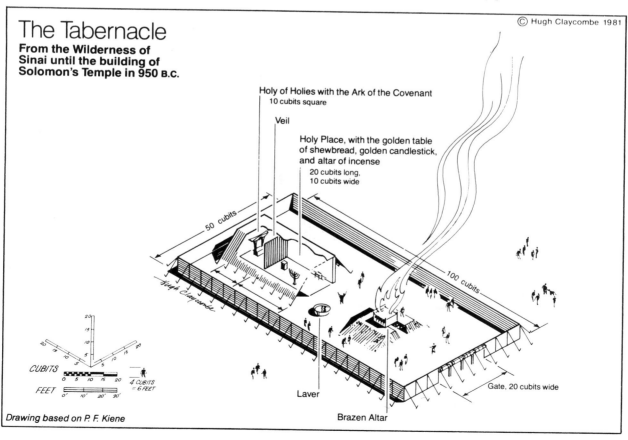

The Tabernacle

From the Wilderness of Sinai until the building of Solomon's Temple in 950 B.C.

© Hugh Claycombe 1981

Holy of Holies with the Ark of the Covenant
10 cubits square

Veil

Holy Place, with the golden table of shewbread, golden candlestick, and altar of incense
20 cubits long,
10 cubits wide

50 cubits

100 cubits

CUBITS

4 CUBITS = 6 FEET

FEET

Laver

Gate, 20 cubits wide

Brazen Altar

Drawing based on P. F. Kiene

e. The altar of incense—Exodus 30:1-10; 37:25-28.

This foot-and-a-half square by three feet high acacia wood table overlaid with gold was symbolic of prayer. Sweet spices were burned on this table each morning and evening. (See Rev. 8:3, 4.) Once each year the horns on this altar were smeared with blood. The incense table occupied the western position of the holy place.

f. The Ark of the Covenant—Exodus 25:10-22; 37:1-9.

The most important piece in all the tabernacle, also made of acacia wood covered with gold. It resembled a cedar chest, and was approximately four feet long and two feet high. It contained several objects, the most important being the two stones upon which was written the Ten Commandments. The lid of this box was made of solid gold and called the mercy seat. On top of the box stood two golden angelic cherubims. Once each year during the great day of atonement in October, the high priest would enter the Holy of Holies (which was separated from the holy place by a thick veil) and sprinkle blood upon the mercy seat for the sins of Israel. Above the entire ark dwelled the Shekinah Glory cloud of God. Perhaps the most thrilling truth of the tabernacle is seen here: the one thing that stood between the broken law that man could not keep and the holy and righteous wrath of God was the blood of the lamb.

3. The priesthood of the tabernacle.

a. Their ordination—one of the most impressive ceremonies in the Old Testament world was undoubtedly the consecration of a young Levite boy to the Israelite priesthood. The sacred procedure was as follows:

(1) He was first washed with water (Ex. 29:4).

(2) He was then clothed (29:5).

(3) He was then anointed with oil (29:7).

(4) He was finally to identify himself with a sacrifice (29:15-20). This was done by the placing of his hand upon a dying lamb. The blood of this lamb was then placed upon his right ear, his right thumb, and his right big toe.

b. Their clothing. Following is a description of the garments worn by the high priest (Ex. 28:2-43).

(1) The ephod—a sleeveless outer garment reaching from the shoulders to below the knees. It consisted of two pieces, one covering the back and the other the front side of the body, fastened on each shoulder by a golden clasp on the top of which were two onyx stones with the names of six tribes on each stone. The ephod was woven of blue, purple, scarlet, and fine linen yarn, embroidered with figures of gold and held to the body by a girdle.

(2) The breastplate of judgment (28:15-20)—a square piece of cloth

THE FURNISHINGS OF THE TABERNACLE AND THE BRAZEN ALTAR

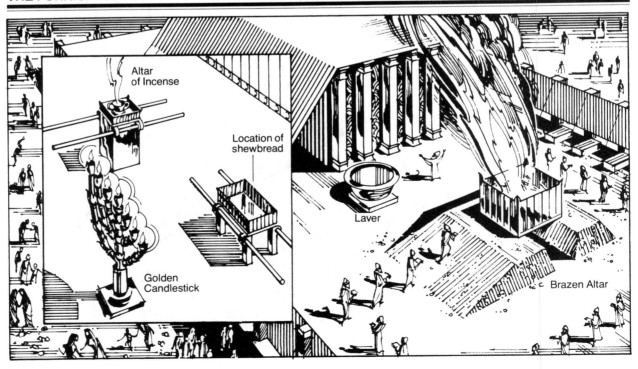

Altar of Incense

Location of shewbread

Laver

Golden Candlestick

Brazen Altar

THE ARK OF THE COVENANT

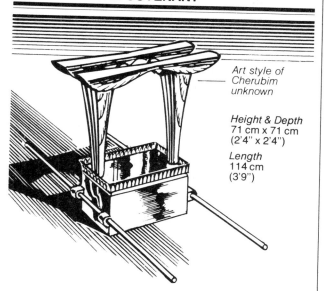

Art style of Cherubim unknown

Height & Depth
71 cm x 71 cm
(2'4" x 2'4")

Length
114 cm
(3'9")

attached to the ephod over the priest's heart upon which were twelve precious stones set in gold and arranged in four rows. On top of the stones were engraved the names of the twelve tribes of Israel.

(3) The Urim and Thummim (28:30).
The nature of this apparel is not certain. The Hebrew words literally mean "lights" and "perfection." They could have been two especially costly stones. It is thought by some that they were used by the high priest in times of crisis to determine the will of God. (See Num. 27:21; 1 Sam. 28:6.)

(4) The robe of the ephod (28:31–35).
This was a blue seamless garment worn under the ephod and was a lit-

THE HIGH PRIEST AND HIS GARMENTS

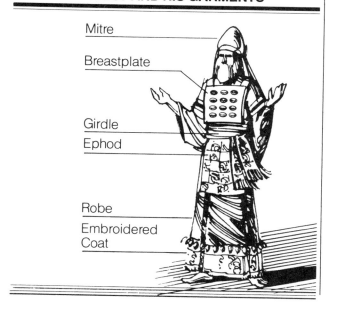

Mitre

Breastplate

Girdle

Ephod

Robe

Embroidered Coat

tle longer than the ephod. Along its hem were blue, purple, and scarlet pomegranates and golden bells which tinkled as the priest served in the tabernacle.

(5) The mitre (28:36–38).
The fine white linen turban headdress of the high priest. On its front was a golden nameplate with the words "Holiness to the Lord" engraved on it.

c. Their duties. The various responsibilities of the priesthood would fall into two basic categories:
(1) That of Temple service—this would include the burning of incense, the care of the lamps, the placing of the bread, and the sacrificial offerings (Num. 3:5–9).
(2) That of personal service—to inspect unclean persons, especially lepers, to instruct the people of Israel in the law of God, and to take a general interest in the spiritual welfare of the people (Num. 6:23–27; Deut. 17:8, 9).

d. Their personal obligations.
(1) They must not consume strong drink (Lev. 10:9).
(2) They must not clip bald spots on their heads, beards, or flesh (Lev. 21:5).
(3) They must not marry a harlot, divorced woman, widow, or someone from another tribe. Their wife must be a virgin from Levi (Lev. 21:7, 14).
(4) They could not have any bodily defects such as blindness or lameness (Lev. 21:16–21).

4. The offerings of the tabernacle.
a. There were five main offerings and each kind is described by a separate chapter in Leviticus 1–5.
(1) The burnt offering (Lev. 1).
(2) The meal offering (2).
(3) The peace offering (3).
(4) The sin offering (4).
(5) The trespass offering (5).

b. These five offerings can be placed into two general categories:
(1) Those offerings to be used for the purpose of restoring broken fellowship. This would include the sin and trespass offerings.
(2) Those offerings to be used for the purpose of maintaining fellowship. These would include the burnt, the meal, and the peace offerings. The special red heifer offering of Numbers 19 would also be included in this category.

5. The holy feasts of the tabernacle. There were nine special feasts and rest times in Israel's calendar. The first three were to remind the believers of God's creative work and the last six of his redemptive work.

a. His creative work.
  (1) The weekly Sabbath (Ex. 20:8-11; Lev. 23:1-3).
  (2) The seven-year Sabbath feast (Ex. 23:10, 11; Lev. 25:2-7).
  (3) The fiftieth year Sabbath feast (Lev. 25:8-16).

Note: These three speak of God's creation, as they come in endless cycles of seven, just as God rested on the seventh day.

b. His redemptive work.
  (1) The Passover feast (Lev. 23:4-8). This speaks of *Calvary* (1 Cor. 5:7).
  (2) The feast of the first fruits (Lev. 23:9-14) speaks of the resurrection (1 Cor. 15:23).
  (3) The feast of Pentecost (Lev. 23:15-25). This speaks of the coming of the Holy Spirit (Acts 2).
  (4) The feast of trumpets (Lev. 23:23-25). This speaks of the rapture and Second Coming (1 Thess. 4:13-18).
  (5) The day of atonement feast (Lev. 23:26-32). This speaks of the tribulation (Rev. 6-19). In the Hebrew this is *Yom Kippurim* and it occurred on October 10 of each year. The order of service on this all-important day is detailed for us in Leviticus 16.
    (a) The high priest would offer a bull sacrifice for himself. Preachers need to be saved and cleansed too!
    (b) Lots would then be cast over two goats to determine which one would become a scapegoat, and which would be killed.
    (c) The high priest would then sprinkle the blood of the slaughtered bull and goat seven times upon the mercy seat.
    (d) He would finally place his hands upon the scapegoat, confess over it all the sins of Israel, and then appoint a man to lead the goat into the desert.
  (6) The feast of tabernacles (Lev. 23:33-44). This speaks of the *millennium* (Rev. 20:1-6).

c. To picture the entire program of salvation.

6. The handbook of the tabernacle. The remaining chapters in Leviticus are given over to various dos and don'ts which cover the religious, social, and physical life of each Israelite.

a. Certain foods may be eaten, while other kinds must be avoided. The general invitation to eat all animals given to Noah (Gen. 9:3) is now being restricted.

b. Two chapters (12; 15) are given over to the ceremonial cleansing involved in sex and childbirth. Here it should be pointed out that nowhere does the Bible in any remote way equate sin with sex and childbirth. What God was undoubtedly attempting to do through these laws was to teach the tragic truth that all men are born with sin natures (see Rom. 5:12).

c. The subject of leprosy occupies two chapters (13-14). This is the first mention of the word, and from this point on, leprosy becomes a symbol of sin. Among the many thousands of lepers in the Old Testament only two were healed by God. In Numbers 12, Miriam is healed, and in 2 Kings, Naaman is cured.

d. Blood is discussed in chapter 17 to explain that great biblical principle: "It is the blood that maketh an atonement for the soul" (17:11; see also Heb. 9:22).

e. Chapters 18-21 involve themselves with personal separation. Note the following commands as taken from *The Living Bible:* "None of you shall marry a near relative . . ." (18:6).

"Homosexuality is absolutely forbidden, for it is an enormous sin" (18:22).

"A medium or a wizard . . . shall surely be stoned to death . . ." (20:27).

A specific listing of the regulations in this handbook would include the following:

(1) concerning diet
    (a) animal life (Lev. 11:2, 3)
    (b) marine life (11:9)
    (c) bird life (11:20)
    (d) insect life (11:21, 22)
(2) concerning motherhood (Lev. 12)
(3) concerning leprosy (13-14)
    (a) recognizing the leper (13:2, 3)
    (b) rules for the leper (13:45-56)
    (c) restoring the leper (14:2, 3)
(4) concerning issues from the body (Lev. 15)
(5) concerning morality among one's kin (18)
    (a) the father (18:7)
    (b) the mother (18:8)
    (c) the sister (18:9)
    (d) the daughter-in-law (18:10)
    (e) the aunt (18:12)
    (f) the uncle (18:14)
    (g) the sister-in-law (18:16)
(6) concerning benevolence (Lev. 19)
(7) concerning apostasy (20:1-9)
    (a) worshiping Molech (20:3)
    (b) consulting wizards (20:6)
    (c) cursing one's parents (20:9)
(8) concerning perversion (20:10-21)
    (a) adultery (20:10)
    (b) incest (20:12)
    (c) sodomy (20:13)
    (d) polygamy (20:14)
    (e) indecent exposure (20:17)
(9) concerning kinsman redemption (25:47-49)
(10) concerning disobedience (Lev. 26)
    (a) the principle stated (26:1-13)
    (b) the punishment cited (26:14, 15)
        [1] first punishment (26:14, 15)

[2] second punishment (26:14, 15)

[3] third punishment (26:21, 22)

[4] fourth punishment (26: 23–26)

[5] fifth punishment (26:27–31)

(c) the punishment certain (26: 32–39)

(11) concerning dedication (Lev. 27)

7. The dedication of the tabernacle. (Ex. 30:22-33; 40:32-35).

Thus was dedicated the most important building ever constructed on this earth. There was however one tragic event which marred the otherwise happy celebration, and that was the death of Nadab and Abihu, Aaron's two priest sons. These two foolish and wicked young men had offered unholy fire before the Lord. Furthermore, the account indicates (see Lev. 10) that both were drunk at the time.

8. The census of the tabernacle (Num. 1:1-54). There are two occasions when Israel was numbered during their march from Egypt to Palestine. The first occurred here at Sinai on April 15 (see Num. 1-2), and the second took place some thirty-eight years later in the desert of Moab (Num. 26). The census here counted all the men twenty years of age and up. The total was 603,550 men.

It is sad to know that of these men, 603,550 in number, 603,548 would later perish in the wilderness (cf. Num. 14:29). The only two men who would later enter Canaan were Joshua and Caleb.

Much speculation has centered around this census figure. If taken literally it would strongly suggest a total Israelite population of over two million. The problem therefore arises concerning the care and feeding of this multitude for nearly forty years; much of it spent in a desolate and arid desert. For example, it has been estimated that it would require nearly fifty railway box cars of manna per day just to feed the people. This would not take into account the physical needs of the thousands of animals which accompanied them. The water needs would likewise be immense: some twelve million gallons per day. In fact the ground area needed to accommodate this multitude when they camped at night would exceed one hundred square miles.

Some have attempted to solve these problems by a watering down of the text. For example, it is suggested that the Hebrew word 'elep translated by the King James Version as "thousand" could as easily be rendered by the word "family" or "clan."

Thus, we would have six hundred and three families with each family contributing perhaps an average of five fighting men each for a total of 3,015 soldiers. Assuming each man was married with two children we then would arrive at the figure of some fifteen thousand or the grand total of Israel's camp.

But this approach raises far more problems than it solves. Gleason Archer writes:

"It is true that there is an 'elep which means family or clan (1 Sam. 10:19, etc.); but it is very clear from the numeration chapters (Num. 1-4; 26) that 'elep is intended in the sense of 'thousand,' for the smaller unit below this 'elep is me' ot, 'hundreds' (cf. Num. 1:21, 23, 25, etc.). The most that a 'family' could contribute to the national army would be four or five men on the average, and it would be absurd to suppose that 'hundreds' would be mentioned or the next lower numerical unit after an average contingent of five men each.

Further corroboration is given by the total amount of ransom money—at the rate of half shekel apiece—recorded in Exodus 38:25 as 100 talents, 1775 shekels. Since there were 3000 shekels to the talent, this comes out to exactly 603,550 contributors. It is therefore safe to say that no objective handling of the textual evidence can possibly sustain the thesis that 'elep in Numbers signifies anything less than a literal thousand." (Gleason Archer, *A Survey of Old Testament Introduction*, pp. 246, 247)

This number did not include the men of Levi, which was the tribe to be excluded from the census. The total number of the Levitical priesthood is given as 8,580 in 4:48. If the estimated Israelite population of that time, some two million, is divided by the number of the priesthood—8,580—it comes out that each priest was responsible for around two-hundred-thirty-three people. The largest tribe was Judah (74,600) and the smallest was Manasseh with 32,200. The descendants of Gershon, Kohath, and Merari, Levi's three sons, were placed in charge of the entire tabernacle. God's original plan, of course, was to have the eldest sons of all the tribes act as priests (see Ex. 13:1), but because of Israel's constant sin, he had limited his choice to the Levites (Num. 3:11-13). The priest had to be thirty years of age before he could fully enter into the service of God. (See Num. 4:3; Lk. 3:23.)

9. The arrangement of the tribes around the tabernacle (Num. 2:1-34). Especially to be noted are the actual location arrangements of the various tribes. On the east were Issachar, Judah, and Zebulun. On the west were the tribes of Benjamin, Ephraim, and Manasseh. On the north were Asher, Dan, and Naphtali, while the south was occupied by Gad, Reuben, and Simeon. Rabbinical tradition suggests that Judah (leader of the eastern section) carried with it a standard of green because it was on an emerald that the name of Judah was engraved upon the breastplate of the high priest, and that its emblem was that of a lion because of the prophecy in Genesis 49:9.

Reuben, leader of the southern flank, flew a red standard to commemorate their name

TRIBAL ENCAMPMENT POSITION

ASHER	**DAN** EAGLE Red and White	NAPHTALI
BENJAMIN	MERARITES	ISSACHAR
EPHRAIM OX Yellow	GERSHON-ITES / SONS OF AARON *Tabernacle*	**JUDAH** LION Green
MANASSEH	KOHATHITES	ZEBULUN
GAD	**REUBEN** HUMAN HEAD Red	SIMEON

written on a sardius stone. Their emblem was that of a human head. The chief tribe of the western side was Ephraim. It displayed a golden flag, for it was upon a golden stone that their name was engraved. Ephraim's emblem was a calf, it is said, because Joseph (their founder) was elevated to power in Egypt through a calf vision. (See Gen. 41:1-32.) Finally the color of Dan (northern leader) was red and white, for their stone was the jasper. An eagle was the emblem of this tribe. We are not sure, of course, just how much of all this is based on fact. If it is true, however, it blends in beautifully with the visions of both Ezekiel and John (see Ezek. 1 and Rev. 4).

10. The Nazarite vow of the tabernacle (Num. 6:1-21).

This especially concerned itself with that individual (man or woman) who desired to consecrate himself to the Lord in a special way, either for life or for a certain period of time. The rules were:

a. He could not taste the fruit of the vineyard in any manner.

b. He could not cut his hair.

c. He could not come in contact with any dead person.

The most well-known Old Testament Nazarite of course was Samson. (See Jdg. 13:7).

11. The great benediction of the tabernacle (Num. 6:22-27).

"And the Lord spake unto Moses, saying, Speak unto Aaron and unto his sons, saying, On this wise ye shall bless the children of Israel, saying unto them, The Lord bless thee, and keep thee: The Lord make his face shine upon thee, and be gracious unto thee: The Lord lift up his countenance upon thee, and give thee peace. And they shall put my name upon the children of Israel; and I will bless them" (Num. 6:22-27).

12. The two silver trumpets of the tabernacle

(Num. 10:1-9). These trumpets were to be sounded on four specific occasions.

a. To summons (v. 2). If both trumpets were blown, then the entire congregation was to gather at the tabernacle (v. 3). If, however, but one trumpet blew, only the heads of the divisions were to appear (v. 4).

b. To give warning in case of attack (v. 5).

c. When Israel itself would go to war (v. 9).

d. At Israel's appointed feasts (v. 10).

IV. Israel, from Sinai to Kadesh-barnea (Num. 10:11—12:16).

This was also a distance of 150 miles.

A. En route to Kadesh (10:11—12:16).

1. A balking brother-in-law. Moses attempts to secure the scouting services of Hobab, his brother-in-law, but the offer is refused (10:29-32).

2. A continuing cloud (10:34-36).

"And the cloud of the Lord was upon them by day, when they went out of the camp. And it came to pass, when the ark set forward that Moses said, Rise up, Lord, and let thine enemies be scattered; and let them that hate thee flee before thee. And when it rested, he said, Return, O Lord, unto the many thousands of Israel" (Num. 10:34-36).

The distance between Mt. Sinai and Kadesh is less than two hundred miles. In Numbers 33:16-36 Moses lists some twenty stops from these two places. The Sinai area is dotted with mountains, rugged valleys, and sandy ground. But their journey was never too long or difficult for "the cloud of the Lord was upon them."

3. A murmuring multitude (11:4-6).

a. Once again this unsaved Egyptian-controlled group stirred up the people to complain, this time about their food. Note their words:

"We remember the fish, which we did eat in Egypt freely; the cucumbers, and the melons, and the leeks, and the onions, and the garlick: But now our soul is dried away; there is nothing at all, beside this manna, before our eyes" (11:5, 6).

b. God sends a fire to punish this rebellion. The people cry to Moses who again intercedes for them and the plague is stopped.

4. A provoked prophet (11:10-15).

a. Moses concludes that God has simply given him too heavy a burden in leading Israel and demands additional help. The despair grows so severe that Moses demands from God either deliverance or death. (See v. 15.) Elijah the prophet would later require a similar thing from God in a moment of despondency (cf. 1 Ki. 19:4).

It is tragic that in his great hour of need Moses did not respond as the Apostle Paul would do when facing an unbearable burden.

"And lest I should be exalted above measure through the abundance of

THE EXODUS STAGE

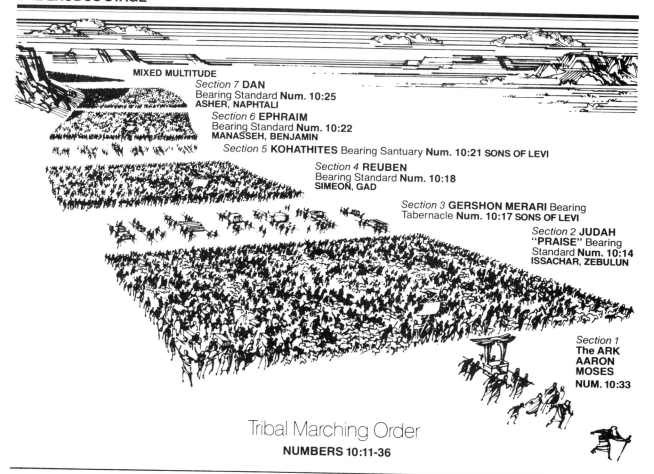

MIXED MULTITUDE

Section 7 **DAN**
Bearing Standard **Num. 10:25**
ASHER, NAPHTALI

Section 6 **EPHRAIM**
Bearing Standard **Num. 10:22**
MANASSEH, BENJAMIN

Section 5 **KOHATHITES** Bearing Santuary **Num. 10:21 SONS OF LEVI**

Section 4 **REUBEN**
Bearing Standard **Num. 10:18**
SIMEON, GAD

Section 3 **GERSHON MERARI** Bearing
Tabernacle **Num. 10:17 SONS OF LEVI**

Section 2 **JUDAH**
"PRAISE" Bearing
Standard **Num. 10:14**
ISSACHAR, ZEBULUN

Section 1
The **ARK**
AARON
MOSES
NUM. 10:33

Tribal Marching Order

NUMBERS 10:11-36

the revelations, there was given to me a thorn in the flesh, the messenger of Satan to buffet me, lest I should be exalted above measure. For this thing I besought the Lord thrice, that it might depart from me. And he said unto me, My grace is sufficient for thee; for my strength is made perfect in weakness. Most gladly, therefore, will I rather glory in my infirmities, that the power of Christ may rest upon me" (2 Cor. 12:7-9).

b. God grants this regrettable request by taking some of the power of the Holy Spirit from Moses and distributing it equally to seventy chosen Hebrew elders (11:25).

c. Two of these men, Eldad and Medad, begin prophesying (11:26-29).

5. A deadly diet (11:31-34).
To silence the people's constant bickering, God sent an immense flock of quail over the camp, flying approximately three feet in the air. Millions of these birds were knocked down and eaten, but with the meat God sent a plague also. (See Ps. 106:15.)

6. A suffering sister (Num. 12:1-15).

a. Aaron and Miriam criticize their younger brother Moses on two counts:
   (1) Because of his wife. They could have been referring to Zipporah, but it is possible that she had died and this Cushite wife was his second one. It is indeterminate from the text as to whether the criticism was because she was a Gentile or because of her color (if indeed she was of different color). At any rate, the marriage was not contrary to the law which forbade marriage only to Canaanites. (See Gen. 24:37.)
   (2) Because of his strong leadership. How often has this sin been committed by deacons and officials in a local church since this time. Aaron and Miriam would soon learn the truth of Psalm 105:15: "Touch not mine anointed, and do my prophets no harm."

b. God rebukes them for their criticism, telling them that Moses was his special friend.

c. Miriam, the ring leader, is suddenly struck with leprosy. Aaron begs forgiveness and asks Moses to plead with God concerning her restoration.

ISRAEL, EN ROUTE TO KADESH-BARNEA

A Balking Brother-In-Law
NUM. 10:29-31
Moses unsuccessfully attempts to secure the services of his brother-in-law as a guide.

A Continuing Cloud
NUM. 10:34-36
God's faithful guide continues to show them the way.

A Murmuring Mixed Multitude
NUM. 11:1-3
God sends a fiery plague to stop the bitter and blasphemous complaints of Israel.

A Provoked Prophet
NUM. 11:14-25
At Moses' request, God sends seventy men to help him.

A Deadly Diet
NUM. 11:31-34
To show their hatred for the manna, the people turn to a diet of quail meat. A deadly plague follows.

A Suffering Sister
NUM. 12
For criticizing both Moses and his wife, Miriam is punished with leprosy.

ISRAEL, AT KADESH-BARNEA

The Two-Fold Report
TEN-MAN MAJORITY REPORT
"We are not able to go up against the people; for they are stronger than we." **(Num. 13:31)**
"And there we saw giants . . . and we were . . . as grasshoppers . . . in their sight." **(Num. 13:33)**

TWO-MAN MINORITY REPORT
"Let us go up at once, and possess it; for we are well able to overcome it." **(Num. 13:30)**
" . . . Neither fear ye the people of the land . . . for . . . the Lord is with us . . ." **(Num. 14:9)**

The Two-Fold Reaction
THE REACTION OF THE PEOPLE
"Would God that we had died in the land of Egypt!" **(Num. 14:2)**
"Let us make a captain, and let us return into Egypt." **(Num. 14:4)**

THE REACTION OF GOD
This marked their tenth rebellion against him. **(Num. 14:22)**
Their carcasses would fall in the wilderness. **(Num. 14:29)**
No one over twenty (Joshua and Caleb excepted) would enter Palestine. **(Num. 14:29)**
They would wander forty years, a year for each day the spies spent in the land. **(Num. 14:34)**
The majority-report members would die of a plague. **(Num. 14:37)**

---

d. Moses does this, and after a period of seven days she is restored to fellowship and health.

V. Israel at Kadesh-barnea (Num. 13-14).
   A. The penetration.

Moses is instructed to send a leader from each of the twelve tribes to spy out the land of Canaan. Among these leaders were Joshua, from the tribe of Ephraim, and Caleb, from Judah.

In Numbers 13 it would seem that this command of God was indicative of his perfect will that Canaan be spied out first, but Moses adds more information as recorded in Deuteronomy 1:19-24, which gives the entire background. "And ye came near unto me, every one of you, and said, we will send men before us, and they shall search out the land, and bring us word again . . ." (Deut. 1:22).

Thus it would seem that the original expedition idea came from man and not from God.

   B. The lamentation.

After forty days of searching out the land, the twelve return with these reports:

1. The majority report—composed of the leaders of ten tribes: "We can't take the land!" (13:32, 33).
2. The minority report—by Joshua and Caleb: "Let us go up at once and possess it, for we are well able to conquer it" (Num. 13:30).
3. The vote of the people: "We won't go!" (14:1-3). This sad episode marked the tenth occasion when Israel rebelled against God. He had graciously brought them out of captivity through ten mighty plagues only to have them turn against his grace ten times (14:22).

These ten occasions of rebellion are as follows:

a. At the Red Sea (Ex. 14:11, 12).
b. At Marah (Ex. 15:24).
c. In the wilderness of Sin (Ex. 16:2, 3).
d. At Rephidim (Ex. 17:1-3).
e. At Sinai (Ex. 32:1-6).
f. En route to Kadesh (three occasions) (Num. 11:1-3; 4-9; 31-34).
g. At Kadesh (two occasions) (Num. 14:1-4; 14:10).

   C. The condemnation.

God determined that not one person twenty years or over would be allowed to enter Canaan. "Since the spies were in the land for forty days, you must wander in the wilderness for forty years—a year for each day, bearing the burden of your sins" (Num. 14:34).

During the next four decades, then, Israel was to linger in the desert until the last person twenty years and older died and was buried. Dr. Leon Wood makes the following observation:

"Figuring 1,200,000 (600,000 of both men and women) as having to die in 14,508 days (38½ years), gives 85 per day. Figuring 12 hours per day maximum for funerals, gives an average of seven funerals per hour for all 38½ years, a continuous foreboding reminder of God's punishment upon them." (*A Survey of Israel's History*, p. 159)

Thus, the sad period of Kadesh ends with these words:

"Then the ten spies who had incited the rebellion against Jehovah by striking fear into the hearts of the people were struck dead before the Lord. Of all the spies, only Joshua and Caleb remained alive" (Num. 14:36-38, TLB).

VI. Israel, from Kadesh-barnea to the Eastern Bank of Jordan (Num. 15-36).

During this period of aimless wanderings, the following events transpire:

A. A futile attack stopped (Num. 14:40-45).

The fickle and foolish Israelites suddenly change their minds and attempt to push their way into the land, but are quickly defeated by the Canaanites.

B. A Sabbath-breaker stoned (15:32-36).

C. A troublemaker swallowed (16:1-32).

1. A very influential descendant of Levi named Korah led a 250-strong conspiracy against the authority of Moses.

2. The entire matter led to a showdown on the following day at which time God stepped in and caused the ground to open up and swallow the troublemakers. In spite of this terrible object lesson, Israel continued to murmur, actually accusing Moses of killing God's people. Before the tragic incident was over, 14,700 more people would be killed by a special judgment plague from God. The New Testament writer Jude (1:11) mentions this event in his epistle as a stern warning against apostasy.

D. A stick that sprouted—the budding of Aaron's rod (17:1-13).

To emphasize the authority he had invested in Moses and Aaron, the Lord ordered the leaders from each tribe to place a rod in the tabernacle with his personal name inscribed on it. Aaron was commanded to do the same. The next morning it was discovered that Aaron's rod had budded, was blossoming, and had ripe almonds hanging from it!

E. A red heifer slain (Num. 19:1-22).

1. The rite of the red heifer (19:1-10). Laws had already been given whereby a living person coming in contact with a corpse would be considered unclean (disqualified from religious life and service) for a period of seven days. But a crisis had probably now arisen. Due to the recent plague (Num. 16:49) no less than 14,700 corpses had come upon the scene. This event alone had, doubtless, contributed to the defilement of tens of thousands of people. What could be done about this? The rite of the red heifer was God's answer to this problem.

2. The rules for cleansing (19:11-32). "He who toucheth the dead body of any man shall be unclean (v. 11)." The cleansing of a defiled Israelite was fourfold.

a. Eleazar was to slaughter an unblemished red heifer outside the camp (vs. 2, 3).

b. Its blood was to be sprinkled toward the tabernacle seven times (v. 4).

c. The red heifer was to be burned along with cedar, wood, hyssop, and some scarlet cloth material (vs. 5, 6).

d. Finally water was to be added to the ashes of the heifer and sprinkled upon the defiled Israelite (vs. 17-19).

F. An angry man snared (20:1-13).

1. Miriam died and was buried near Kadesh (20:1).

2. After years of hard work, the devil finally snared Moses, the meekest man on earth (Num. 12:3), into the trap of anger and pride. The wicked and fickle Israelites were, as usual, complaining about the lack of water (it would seem they held a protest meeting against God at least once a day). God thereupon instructed Moses to speak to a certain rock and order it to pour out its water.

3. But the longsuffering Moses suddenly "blew his cool," and in an act, due partly to unbelief and anger, screamed at the people and disobeyed the Lord by striking the rock twice instead of speaking to it once as God had commanded (20:8).

4. God sent water in spite of Moses' disobedience, but told him this sin would keep him from the Promised Land (20:12).

5. Evidently Moses petitioned God later about going to Palestine until the Lord finally ordered him not to even mention it again (Deut. 3:26, 27).

G. A simple request scorned (20:14-22).

The Edomites, descendants of Esau, refused to allow Israel to march through their land, thus forcing God's people to trek an additional 180 miles in a hot and hostile desert.

H. A high priest stripped (20:23-29).

1. God ordered Moses to strip Aaron of his priestly garments and place them upon his son, Eleazar.

2. Aaron died at the age of 123 and was buried on Mt. Hor.

3. C. I. Scofield observes that the death of Aaron marks the end of Israel's wanderings. From this point the nation either marched or halted, but did not wander (*New Scofield Bible*, p. 195). It should be noted here that the wilderness experience, but not the wanderings, was originally in the perfect will of God for Israel (Ex. 13:17, 18).

I. A serpent problem solved (21:5-9).

1. God sent poisonous serpents to punish rebellious Israel.

2. The people repented and a cure was provided.

3. A serpent of brass was placed atop a pole where all could view it.

4. Anyone bitten needed only to look upon the brass serpent to be healed. Jesus used this event as an illustration to win Nicodemus. (See Jn. 3:14, 15.) Years later, in 700 B.C., King Hezekiah destroyed this serpent, for the people were worshiping it. (See 2 Ki. 18:4.)

J. The Amorites slaughtered (21:21-24).

As did the Edomites, the Amorites refused Israel passage, but on this occasion the armies of Moses fought and won a great victory.

K. A perverted prophet (Num. 22-24).

1. Balak, the frightened King of Moab, offers Balaam, a pagan diviner from Mesopotamia, tempting riches if he will put a hex on the advancing Israelites and thus save Moab (22:1-8).

2. God warns Balaam not to accept this bribe (22:9-12).

3. The offer is increased and Balaam agrees to go with Balak's men (22:15-21).

4. En route to Moab, Balaam is soundly re-

buked by the very animal he rode and narrowly escapes death at the hand of God's angel (Num. 22:22-35).

5. Balaam arrives in Moab and, looking down upon Israel's armies in a nearby valley, attempts to curse them on four occasions. But, in every case, words of blessing proceed from his mouth, to his amazement and Balak's anger. These four blessings are as follows: Numbers 23:8-10; 23:22-24; 24:5-9; 24:7.

Especially to be noted is the language found in some of Balaam's prophecies. "How shall I curse, whom God hath not cursed? or how shall I defy, whom the Lord hath not defied? For from the top of the rocks I see him, and from the hills I behold him: lo, the people shall dwell alone, and shall not be reckoned among the nations. Who can count the dust of Jacob, and the number of the fourth part of Israel? Let me die the death of the righteous, and let my last end be like his!" (Num. 23:8-10).

"I shall see him, but not now: I shall behold him, but not nigh: there shall come a Star out of Jacob, and a Sceptre shall rise out of Israel, and shall smite the corners of Moab, and destroy all the children of Sheth. And Edom shall be a possession for his enemies; and Israel shall do valiantly" (Num. 24:17-19).

Of the thousands of characters in the Old Testament, surely Balaam is the most mysterious, and in some ways, the most tragic. He is mentioned by no less than three New Testament writers, each of whom writes concerning a particular aspect of his character.

His way—". . . the *way* of Balaam . . . who loved the wages of unrighteousness . . ." (2 Pet. 2:15).

His error—". . . the *error* of Balaam . . ." (Jude 1:11). His error was his conclusion that God would simply have to curse Israel because of their many sins. M. F. Unger writes:

"He was ignorant of God's election of Israel as a nation, and the immutability of God's choice (Rom. 11:29) and the nation's preservation. He failed to see how God can be 'Just and the Justifier' of the believing sinner through the cross, to which all Israel's tabernacle ritual pointed." (*Unger's Bible Dictionary*, pp. 133, 134)

His doctrine—". . . the *doctrine* of Balaam who . . . cast a stumbling block before the children of Israel, to eat things sacrificed unto idols, and to commit fornications" (Rev. 2:14). Even though this wicked prophet failed in his attempts to curse Israel, his corrupt and clever suggestions that God's people mix with the Moabites was highly successful. Before it was all over, this perverted preacher would cause the death of 24,000 Israelites (Num. 25:9), resulting in a punishment from God. Balaam was later killed by the invading armies of Israel (Num. 31:8). Thus, even though Balaam could not turn God away

from Israel, he did, for a while, turn Israel away from God. The hero of this tragedy was Phinehas, the grandson of Aaron. A controversy had been imagined between the number Moses gives here (24,000), and the number Paul later gives in the New Testament (23,000) (see 1 Cor. 10:8), but the solution would seem to be a simple one—Moses gives the entire number while Paul gives the number who died on the first day.

L. A patriotic priest (Num. 25).
1. In spite of his failure to curse Israel, Balaam nearly succeeded in destroying that nation by craftily arranging for the Moabite women to sexually seduce the Israelite men (Num. 25:1; 31:16).
2. Phinehas, godly grandson priest of Aaron, averted the full wrath of Almighty God by his drastic action in executing an especially brazen sexual couple, a prince from the tribe of Simeon and his harlot lover from Midian. In spite of this, 24,000 died (25:7-18).

Because of his faithfulness and fearlessness, God promised Phinehas his covenant of peace (v. 12), and from his family was to come Israel's high priest, and two priestly sons (two had already died through a divine punishment because of their sin). These were Eleazar and Ithamar. Phinehas was the son of Eleazar. But for some unknown reason the high priesthood was later switched from Eleazar to Ithamar in the person of Eli (1 Sam. 1), a descendant of Ithamar. However, in the days of David it returned to the promised line here through Zadok, a descendant of Eleazar. (See 1 Ki. 1:8.)

M. The second census (Num. 26).
1. The total of the second census is given as 601,730. (See v. 51.) This census, about thirty years after the first (1:46) was 1820 fewer.
2. Not one individual was alive who had been over twenty at the Kadesh rebellion, except for Moses, Caleb, and Joshua (26:64, 65).
3. The greatest decrease from the first census was in Simeon's tribe (37,100) and the greatest increase was in Manasseh (20,500).

N. Five determined daughters (27:1-11).
Zelophehad, a man from the tribe of Manasseh, had died, leaving five daughters but no sons. Those daughters then appealed to Moses and received the right to inherit their father's land when Palestine was later divided.

O. A change in commanders (27:12-23).
1. Eleazar the high priest is instructed to lay hands upon Joshua in a public ceremony, thus transferring Moses' authority over to him.
2. Joshua then becomes the new leader. Moses himself delivers the ordination address.

P. The mortification of Midian (31).
1. Moses' final order from God as Commander was to defeat and judge the Midianites for their former sin in refusing Israel passage through their land (25:6-18; 31:1, 2).
2. This Moses does by picking a thousand choice warriors from each of Israel's twelve tribes (31:3-7).

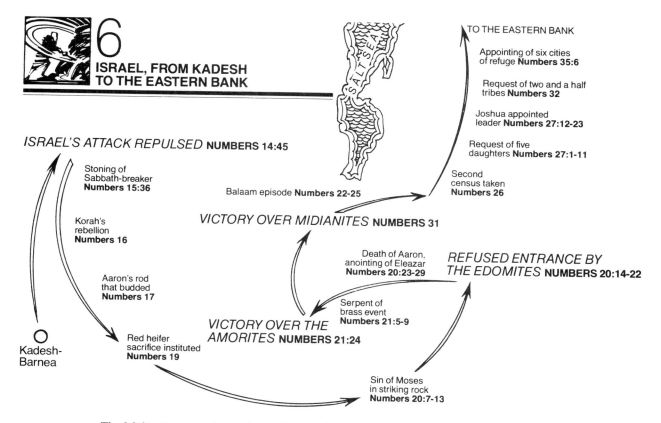

6
ISRAEL, FROM KADESH TO THE EASTERN BANK

TO THE EASTERN BANK

Appointing of six cities of refuge **Numbers 35:6**

Request of two and a half tribes **Numbers 32**

Joshua appointed leader **Numbers 27:12-23**

Request of five daughters **Numbers 27:1-11**

Second census taken **Numbers 26**

ISRAEL'S ATTACK REPULSED **NUMBERS 14:45**

Stoning of Sabbath-breaker **Numbers 15:36**

Balaam episode **Numbers 22-25**

Korah's rebellion **Numbers 16**

VICTORY OVER MIDIANITES **NUMBERS 31**

Death of Aaron, anointing of Eleazar **Numbers 20:23-29**

REFUSED ENTRANCE BY THE EDOMITES **NUMBERS 20:14-22**

Aaron's rod that budded **Numbers 17**

Serpent of brass event **Numbers 21:5-9**

VICTORY OVER THE AMORITES **NUMBERS 21:24**

Kadesh-Barnea

Red heifer sacrifice instituted **Numbers 19**

Sin of Moses in striking rock **Numbers 20:7-13**

The Midianites were descendants of Abraham through his wife Keturah (Gen. 25:2). Some forty years back Moses (a descendant of Abraham through Sarah) had married a Midianite, Zipporah. But in the ensuing years, this tribe had degenerated until they were no different from a dozen other pagan desert people.

A great contrast can be seen at this point, as one compares the account here with that described in the tribulation. In the first (Num. 31) God sends out 12,000 Israelite soldiers to consume their enemies, but in the second (Rev. 7) he will send out 144,000 Israelite preachers to convert their enemies.

Q. Some worldly warriors (Num. 32).
1. The Reubenites, Gadites, and half-tribe of Manasseh come to Moses and ask permission to settle in Gilead, an area east of Palestine, just across the Jordan River.
2. Moses sadly issues the requested permission, providing these two-and-a-half tribes would cross over with the remaining tribes and help defeat the Canaanites. To this they agree.

R. A summary of the sojournings (33).
In this chapter Moses lists each camp site of Israel from Rameses, Egypt, to Shittim, Moah. They made no less than forty-two stops, thus moving to a new location every eleven months for forty years.

S. Six cities of salvation (35).
1. These cities were: on the eastern side of Jordan—Bezer, Golan, and Ramoth. On the western side (in Palestine itself)—Kadesh, Shechem, and Hebron (Num. 35:10-14; Deut. 4:43; Josh. 20:7-9).

2. These six were part of the forty-eight cities given to the Levites who did not receive a regular section of land as did the other tribes when the land was later divided by Joshua.
3. The six were designated as refuge for all accidental manslayers to avoid the dead man's avenging relatives.
4. The manslayer was safe as long as he remained in one of these six cities until the death of the high priest, at which time he could safely return home (35:25-28).

VII. Israel, on the Eastern Side of the River Jordan (Deuteronomy).
On the banks of the Jordan Moses delivers three sermons to Israel, issues a challenge to Joshua, pronounces a blessing upon the individual tribes, composes a song, and departs for heaven.
A. His three sermons.
First sermon (Deut. 1-4).
1. He relates the splendor of God they had experienced while at Mt. Sinai (4:10-19, 32, 33).
2. He reviews their tragic sin at Kadesh-barnea (1:27). Thus a trip that should have taken but eleven days (from Mt. Sinai to Canaan) actually took some thirty-eight years (1:2).
3. He reminds them of his own sin which would keep him from the Promised Land (3:23-27; 4:21, 22). (See also 31:1.)
4. He urges Israel to encourage their new leader Joshua (1:38; 3:28). (See also 31:7, 8, 23.)
5. He sets apart the three eastern cities of refuge (4:41-43).
Second sermon (5-26).
6. The Ten Commandments are repeated (5:7-21).

7. A warning is issued against immorality (23:17), compromise (7:1-5), and witchcraft (18:9-14).

8. Moses gives a description of Canaan (8:7, 8).

9. He reviews his personal experiences with God while upon Mt. Sinai (9:9-21).

10. He reminds them of their financial obligations to God (26).

11. Laws concerning clothing (22:5), divorce (24:1-4), woman's rights (21:10-17; 22:13-20), and warfare (20) are given.

12. He summarizes God's overall purpose and plan for that generation of Israelites. "And he brought us out from there [Egypt] that he might bring us in [Canaan] . . . ." (See 6:23.)

Third sermon (27-30).

13. He orders the blessings and judgments (curses) of the law to be read by the Levites upon two mountains when Israel entered the Promised Land. The blessings were to be read on Mt. Gerizim, and the curses upon Mt. Ebal. (See 11:26-29; 27:1-14.) The specific blessings are referred to in 28:1-14, and the curses in 27:15-26; 28:15-68.

14. Deuteronomy 28-30 records in seven parts the features of the Palestinian Covenant.

    a. Israel to be dispersed for disobedience (28:36, 49-53, 63-68; 30:1). This takes in the Assyrian, Babylonian, and Roman captivities, in addition to Israel's trials during the past twenty centuries. It would almost seem that Moses had Hitler's armies in mind when he wrote 28:64-67. During this time Israel would become a byword (28:37), and be the tail instead of the head (cf. 28:13 with 28:44).

    b. Israel will repent while in dispersion (30:2).

    c. The return of Christ will occur (30:3).

    d. Israel will be restored to the land (30:5).

    e. The nation will receive a new heart (30:6).

    f. Israel's oppressors will be judged (30:7).

    g. The nation will experience prosperity (30:9).

15. Moses offers his generation a choice between God's judgment or blessing (30:15-20). During these three sermons Moses expounds upon the following great theological themes:

    a. The faithfulness of God (2:7; 4:33-38; 7:6-8; 8:3, 4; 9:4-6; 29:5, 6; 32:9-14).

    b. The Word of God (4:1, 2, 7, 9; 11:18-21; 30:11-14).

    c. The Person of God (6:4, 5; 7:9; 32:39).

    d. The love of God (7:13).

    e. The glory of God (4:39; 10:17, 18).

    f. The grace of God (7:6-9; 9:4-6).

    g. The coming great prophet of God (18:15-20).

    h. The will of God (10:12-16).

    i. The kings of God (17:14-20).

    j. The Israel of God (4:25-31; 11:16, 17).

7

ISRAEL, AT THE EASTERN BANK

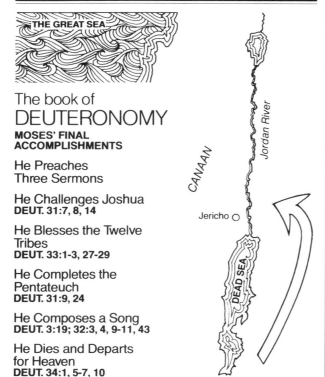

The book of DEUTERONOMY

MOSES' FINAL ACCOMPLISHMENTS

He Preaches Three Sermons

He Challenges Joshua
DEUT. 31:7, 8, 14

He Blesses the Twelve Tribes
DEUT. 33:1-3, 27-29

He Completes the Pentateuch
DEUT. 31:9, 24

He Composes a Song
DEUT. 3:19; 32:3, 4, 9-11, 43

He Dies and Departs for Heaven
DEUT. 34:1, 5-7, 10

MOSES **THE THEOLOGIAN**

During these three sermons Moses expounds upon ten great theological themes.

1. THE **FAITHFULNESS** OF GOD
DEUTERONOMY 2:7; 4:33-38; 7:6-8; 8:3, 4; 9:4-6; 29:5, 6; 32:9-14

2. THE **WORD** OF GOD
4:1, 2, 7, 9; 11:18-21; 30:11-14

3. THE **PERSON** OF GOD
6:4, 5; 7:9; 32:39

4. THE **LOVE** OF GOD
7:13

5. THE **GLORY** OF GOD
4:39; 10:17, 18

6. THE **GRACE** OF GOD
7:6-9; 9:4-6

7. THE COMING **GREAT PROPHET** OF GOD
18:15-19

8. THE **WILL** OF GOD
10:12-16

9. THE **KINGS** OF GOD
17:14-20

10. THE **ISRAEL** OF GOD
4:25-31; 11:16, 17

B. His challenges to Joshua (31). See especially 31:7, 8, 14, 23.

C. His song. See 31:19-22, 30; 32:1-47.
At this time Moses also completes the Pentateuch (first five books of the Bible). (See 31:9, 24.)

D. His blessings upon the individual tribes (33).

E. His departure for heaven (31:2, 14-18; 32:48-52; 34:1-12).

THE EXODUS STAGE

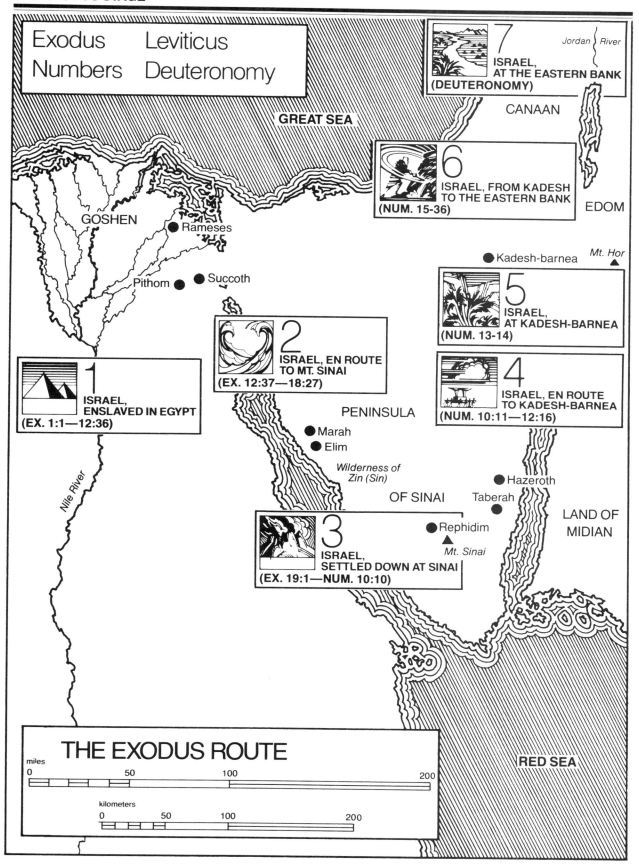

Exodus   Leviticus
Numbers   Deuteronomy

GREAT SEA

Jordan River

7
ISRAEL,
AT THE EASTERN BANK
(DEUTERONOMY)

CANAAN

6
ISRAEL, FROM KADESH
TO THE EASTERN BANK
(NUM. 15-36)

EDOM

GOSHEN

● Rameses

● Kadesh-barnea   *Mt. Hor* ▲

Pithom ● ● Succoth

5
ISRAEL,
AT KADESH-BARNEA
(NUM. 13-14)

2
ISRAEL, EN ROUTE
TO MT. SINAI
(EX. 12:37—18:27)

PENINSULA

4
ISRAEL, EN ROUTE
TO KADESH-BARNEA
(NUM. 10:11—12:16)

1
ISRAEL,
ENSLAVED IN EGYPT
(EX. 1:1—12:36)

● Marah
● Elim

*Wilderness of
Zin (Sin)*

● Hazeroth
Taberah
●

OF SINAI

Nile River

3
ISRAEL,
SETTLED DOWN AT SINAI
(EX. 19:1—NUM. 10:10)

● Rephidim
▲
Mt. Sinai

LAND OF
MIDIAN

THE EXODUS ROUTE

miles
0   50   100   200

kilometers
0   50   100   200

RED SEA

THE CONQUEST STAGE

INTRODUCING THE CONQUEST STAGE (Joshua)

1. The three most important individuals in this stage are Joshua, Caleb, and Rahab.
2. It covers a period of about twenty-five years.
3. The book describes the invasion, conquest, and settlement of Palestine by the nation Israel.
4. The book of Joshua is the counterpart of Exodus. *Exodus* records how God led his people *out of* the land of *bondage,* while Joshua tells us how he led his people *into* the land of *blessing.* Moses summarizes both books in Deuteronomy 6:23: "And he brought us out from there, that he might bring us in, to give us the land which he swore to give unto our fathers."
5. In Exodus God had parted the waters of the Red Sea to bring his people out of Egypt. Now in Joshua he will part the waters of the Jordan River to bring his people into Canaan. God performs whatever is necessary to assure both the exit and entrance of his people (Ex. 14:21, 22; Josh. 3:13-17).
6. Joshua has been called the Ephesians of the Old Testament.
7. In this stage we see the salvation of a harlot from the town of Jericho (Rahab) and the condemnation of a Hebrew from the tribe of Judah (Achan) (Josh. 6:25; 7:24-26).
8. We view a prince from glory and some beggars from Gibeon (Josh. 5:13-15; 9:3-15).
9. Joshua records the twin miracles of the falling walls and a standing sun (Josh. 6:20; 10:12-14).

THE CONQUEST STAGE

I. The Invasion of the Land—Israel claims its possessions (1-5).
   A. The preparation (1:1-9).
      1. God speaks to Joshua.
         a. He was to lead Israel across the Jordan into Palestine.
         b. He was to be strong and courageous.
         c. He was to observe and meditate upon the Law of God.
         d. He could then be absolutely confident that, "The Lord thy God is with thee wherever thou goest" (1:9).
      2. Joshua speaks to Israel.
         "Prepare you victuals; for within three days ye shall pass over this Jordan . . ." (1:11).
   B. The penetration (2:1).
      1. Two men are sent to spy out Jericho.
      2. The King of Jericho learns of their mission and sends out a search party.

3. The spies are hidden by a newly converted ex-harlot named Rahab. Rahab had not only heard of the mighty power of God (2:9-11), but apparently come to trust him also. She must have possessed some kind of testimony, for it was to her house the spies first went, and later the King of Jericho guesses they might be hiding there also. This converted harlot is mentioned in three New Testament passages (Mt. 1:5; Heb. 11:31; Jas. 2:25). She later married a Hebrew man named Salmon, who may have been one of the spies. At any rate, this former pagan would later become the great-great-grandmother of King David. This is perhaps one of the most beautiful illustrations of the grace of God in the Bible.
   C. The passage (3:13).
      1. The priests were to lead the way to the Jordan River, carrying the Ark of God.
      2. The congregation was to follow them about a half-mile behind.
      3. When the priests put their feet into Jordan, the river immediately stopped flowing, thus allowing Israel to cross on dry ground.
   D. The pile of stones (4:1, 8, 9, 21).
      1. Upon crossing, Israel was to construct two memorial piles of twelve stones each. One pyramid was to be placed in the middle of the river and the other on the west side of Jordan.
      2. The pyramid on the western bank was there as a silent witness to future generations of God's faithfulness in rolling back Jordan's waters.
   E. The purification of the people (5:3).
      Upon reaching the western side of Palestine, God ordered the males of Israel to be circumcised. This was done, and the name of the place was called Gilgal, which means, "to roll away."
   F. The Passover (5:10).
      "And the Children of Israel encamped in Gilgal, and kept the passover on the fourteenth day of the month at even in the plains of Jericho."
   G. The passing diet (5:11, 12).
      "And they did eat of the old corn of the land on the morrow after the passover, unleavened cakes, and parched corn in the selfsame day. And the manna ceased on the morrow after they had eaten of the old corn of the land; neither had the children of Israel manna anymore; but they did eat of the fruit of the land of Canaan that year."

THE CONQUEST STAGE

The book of JOSHUA

INVASION OF THE LAND

Israel CLAIMS Its Possessions
JOSHUA 1-5

The PREPARATION 1:1-9
God speaks to Joshua: I will be with you.

Joshua speaks to Israel: Get prepared, for we move out in three days.

The PENETRATION 2:1-24
Two Israeli spies search out Jericho. Upon being discovered, they are hidden by a newly converted harlot named Rahab.

The PASSAGE 3:1-17
The message from God: Step out as if the Jordan was solid rock.

The miracle from God: The waters of the Jordan are rolled back.

The PILE OF STONES 4:1-24
Israel was to place twelve huge stones on the western bank as a memorial reminder of the supernatural crossing.

The PURIFICATION 5:2-9
Upon reaching the western bank, the Israeli males are circumcised.

The PASSOVER 5:10
The Passover is observed upon the plains of Jericho.

The PASSING DIET 5:11-12
The manna ceases and they eat the food of the Promised Land.

The PRINCE FROM HEAVEN 5:13-15
Joshua is visited and reassured by Jesus himself.

    H. The prince from heaven (5:13–15).
        1. Joshua receives a heavenly visitor, apparently Jesus himself on the eve of the battle against Jericho.
        2. Joshua is reassured of victory and is told (as once was Moses—Ex. 3:5) to remove his shoes.
  II. The Subjection of the Land—Israel conquers its possessions (6–12).
    A. The central campaign (Josh. 6–8).
      1. Jericho—a city shouted down (6:20).
        a. This was the first recorded example of psychological warfare in history. Dr. John Davis writes the following about the actual march:

> "A single march around the nine-acre mound area probably took twenty-five to thirty-five minutes. It should not be concluded that every Israelite took part in this march. Such a feat would not only be impractical, but would be impossible. It is more probable to assume that the march was carried out by tribal representation." (*Conquest and Crisis,* p. 45)

        b. The command to destroy all the humanity in Jericho except Rahab and her household has been a problem to both saved and unsaved. Why would the God of love and grace order this wholesale destruction? While God owes no living man an explanation for anything he does, there are nevertheless, certain factors undoubtedly involved.

        (1) When a culture or a city (like that of Sodom, Gen. 19) reaches a certain point of perversion, the holiness and justice of God demand that he step in and destroy it. The entire Canaanite society had long since reached that point. According to 1 Kings 14:24, the entire land was populated with loathsome sexual perverts.

        (2) God desired to keep Israel as pure as possible for as long as possible to assure the future purity of the line of Christ. Had Mary been an immoral woman, God would not and could not have used her.

        c. In verse 26 of this chapter, Joshua makes an amazing threefold prophecy about this fallen city. He predicted:
           (1) That Jericho would be rebuilt again by one man.
           (2) That the builder's oldest son would die when the work on the city had begun.
           (3) That the builder's youngest son would die when the work was completed.

        d. Joshua uttered these words around 1406 B.C. Did all this happen? Some five centuries later, in 930 B.C., we are told the following:
           (1) That a man named Hiel from Bethel rebuilt Jericho. That as he laid the foundations, his oldest son, Abiram, died.
           (2) That when he had completed the gates, his youngest son, Segub, died. (See 1 Ki. 16:34.)

      2. Ai—arrogance knocked down (7:3).
        a. After Jericho, Israel became overconfident and determined to send out only a token fighting force to subdue the next enemy, a little city called Ai.
        b. Israel's armies are totally routed by Ai and suffer a great loss of troops.
      3. Achan—a sinner sought (7:19).
        a. Joshua is told that this defeat was due to sin in the camp. Someone had disobeyed God and stolen some forbidden loot from Jericho.
        b. A divinely conducted manhunt begins and eventually points to Achan, from the tribe of Judah, as the criminal.
        c. He confesses to stealing a Babylonian robe, some silver, and a bar of gold.
        d. Achan is executed for this in the Valley of Achor.
      4. Gerizim and Ebal—the law handed down (8:30-35). As Moses had previously commanded, the blessings and curses of the law are read from Mt. Gerizim and Ebal.

B. The southern campaign (Josh. 9–10).

1. Gibeon—the wool pulled over (9:3–6).
   a. When news of Jericho and Ai reached Gibeon, the people resorted to trickery to save themselves. They sent to Joshua ambassadors wearing worn-out clothing, as though they had come on a long journey. They had patched shoes, weather-worn saddle bags on their donkeys, old and patched wine skins, and dry moldy bread.
   b. Upon arriving, they persuaded Joshua to make a nonaggression treaty. They probably were aware of the Law of Moses (Deut. 7:1, 2; 20:10–15) which permitted Israel to make peace with far-off cities when Joshua entered Palestine, but not with the Canaanite nations living in close proximity to them.

2. Ajalon—the sun shone down (10:12, 13).
   a. When the King of Jerusalem heard of the Gibeonite alliance with Israel, he formed a pact with four other kings for the purpose of destroying both Israel and Gibeon.
   b. Upon hearing this, Joshua is instructed to attack this alliance before they can attack him. During the battle, he is aided by a divinely sent hailstorm.
   c. Joshua then prayed God would allow the sun to give prolonged additional light for the mopping-up exercises. This happened, for the sun stopped in the heavens and stayed there for almost twenty-four hours.

Apart from the whale and Jonah, perhaps no other biblical miracle has caused such ridicule from unbelievers and so much uncertainty among believers. What really happened here? Three basic views can be found in the writings of sound Bible scholars.

   d. The total eclipse view. Dr. John Davis writes: "The essence of this view is that God brought darkness rather than light on this occasion" (*Conquest and Crisis*, p. 66).

   This prayer was then a petition from Joshua to shade his weary troops from the fierce Mideast sun. God, it would seem, answered this prayer by sending a massive hailstorm which not only cooled off Joshua's weary troops, but killed their enemies. No less a scholar than Dr. Robert Dick Wilson of Princeton advocates this theory, pointing out that the Hebrew word *dom*, translated "stand thou still" in the KJV, can also be correctly rendered "be silent," "cease," and "leave off." However, two serious objections would seem to discredit this view.
   (1) The account in Joshua 10:11 would indicate that the hailstorm occurred *before* Joshua's petition, and not after.
   (2) In verse 14, we are told that this day was absolutely unique in history, which simply would not be true if the miracle here involved only a massive hailstorm.

   e. The slowing down of the earth's rotation. The late scientist and Bible student Dr. Harry Rimmer held this view and cited Professor Pickering of Harvard Observatory along with Dr. Totten of Yale among those who favored this position. Another believer in this view is Immanuel Velikovsky, who suggests in his famous book, *Worlds in Collision,* that the miracle was caused by a comet which came near the earth, exerted its gravitational pull, and disrupted normal movement. The comet's icy tail, according to Velikovsky, could have provided the hailstones. Finally, in listing the various points which favor the second view, it may be said that research has brought to light reports from Egyptian, Chinese, and Hindu sources of such a long day. But the second view is not without its problems.
   (1) One consideration is the sheer staggering power it would take to slow down or stop the earth on its own axis. Our planet weighs some six trillion tons and at the equator is moving about a thousand miles an hour. It has been estimated that it would take roughly twenty million billion of our largest hydrogen bombs to stop the earth. Of course, God is capable of anything, but compared to this the impressiveness of the universal flood (the greatest Old Testament miracle) would shrink significantly. In fact, this would require more raw power than anything God had ever done since creation, either before or after. If this really occurred, however, it would seem strange that the only other reference to it is found in Habakkuk 3:11.
   (2) If the second view is correct, then God would be required to do this same stupendous thing again for Hezekiah. Dr. John Davis writes:
       "It is extremely doubtful that such a miracle was performed on that occasion. In fact, the parallel passage found in 2 Chronicles 32:24–31 seems to imply that it was a local miracle. Verse 24 of this passage indicates that God gave a special sign to Hezekiah. That sign was evidently witnessed only in Palestine, for verse 31 records the fact that ambassadors from Babylon were sent down to Hezekiah to 'inquire of the wonder that was done in the land'! If the miracle performed in the days of Hez-

ekiah was universal, there would be little need for ambassadors to come all the way from Babylon to inquire of the miracle." (*Conquest and Crisis*, p. 69)

   f. The extension of refraction of the sun's rays on a local level. Taking everything into consideration, this would seem to be the most scriptural approach. At least two other instances come to mind when God did a similar thing concerning light and darkness on a local level. These are:

     (1) The three-day darkness upon the land of Egypt (Ex. 10:21–23).

     (2) The three-hour darkness surrounding the area of the cross (Mk. 15:33).

  3. Makkedah—five kings cut down (10:10, 28).

    a. During the battle, the king of Jerusalem, the one who organized and led the southern campaign against Israel, and four other kings took refuge in a cave at Makkedah.

    b. Joshua had these kings taken from the cave and, in a victory celebration, ordered the captains of his army to put their feet on the kings' necks. They were then executed.

C. The northern campaign (Josh. 11–12).

  1. Hazor—a capital burned down (11:13).

    Jaban, King of Hazor, organized and led the northern attack against Israel. He was soundly defeated and had his capital burned to the ground.

  2. Merom—the horses slowed down (11:6, 9). Here, Joshua hamstrung the horses, thus rendering them useful for farm work but useless for warfare.

III. The Distribution of the Land—Israel colonizes its possessions (13–24).

  A. The land divided.

    The land was now partitioned under the supervision of Joshua, Eleazar, and the key tribal leaders by the casting of lots (14:1, 2; 19:51).

    1. The land east of Jordan: Reuben, Gad, and one half tribe of Manasseh.

    2. The land west of Jordan: Judah, Ephraim, one half tribe of Manasseh, Benjamin, Simeon, Zebulun, Issachar, Asher, Naphtali, Dan.

    3. The land for Levi: Levi was given no land, as God himself would be its portion (13:33). However, the tribe was given forty-eight special cities from the remaining eleven tribes (21:41).

  B. A warrior excited.

    Caleb visits with Joshua and gives one of the most thrilling testimonies in all the Bible. Note his challenging words in 14:7–12.

  C. An altar indicted (22).

    1. After the land was divided, Israel set up the tabernacle at Shiloh (18:1).

    2. Joshua called together the armies of the two

SUBJECTION OF THE LAND

Israel CONQUERS Its Possessions
JOSHUA 6-12

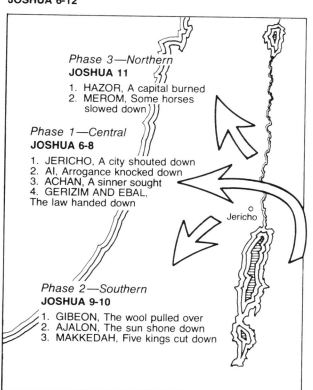

Phase 3—Northern
JOSHUA 11
1. HAZOR, A capital burned
2. MEROM, Some horses slowed down

Phase 1—Central
JOSHUA 6-8
1. JERICHO, A city shouted down
2. AI, Arrogance knocked down
3. ACHAN, A sinner sought
4. GERIZIM AND EBAL, The law handed down

Jericho

Phase 2—Southern
JOSHUA 9-10
1. GIBEON, The wool pulled over
2. AJALON, The sun shone down
3. MAKKEDAH, Five kings cut down

DISTRIBUTION OF THE LAND

Israel COLONIZES Its Possessions
JOSHUA 13-24

● **THE LAND DIVIDED (14:1, 2; 19:51)**

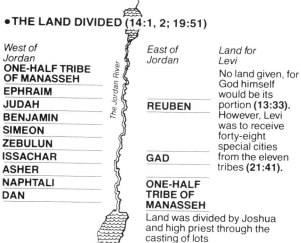

West of Jordan	East of Jordan	Land for Levi
ONE-HALF TRIBE OF MANASSEH		No land given, for God himself would be its portion **(13:33)**. However, Levi was to receive forty-eight special cities from the eleven tribes **(21:41).**
EPHRAIM		
JUDAH	**REUBEN**	
BENJAMIN		
SIMEON		
ZEBULUN		
ISSACHAR	**GAD**	
ASHER		
NAPHTALI	**ONE-HALF TRIBE OF MANASSEH**	
DAN		

Land was divided by Joshua and high priest through the casting of lots

● **A WARRIOR EXCITED (14:7-12)**
Caleb visits Joshua and relates one of Scripture's most thrilling testimonies.

● **AN ALTAR INDICTED (chapter 22)**
1. The tabernacle was set up in Palestine at Shiloh (18:1).
2. The two-and-one-half eastern tribes set up an altar on the Jordan bank as a reminder of their common heritage with the western tribes.
3. This was at first misinterpreted as an act of rebellion and a civil war was narrowly averted.

● **A FINAL SERMON RECITED (23-24)**
Joshua's last words to Israel

and a half tribes at Shiloh, blessed them, and sent them to their chosen home on the east side of Jordan.

3. Before crossing the river, these two and a half tribes erected a large monument in the shape of an altar to remind them and their unborn children of their common heritage with the tribes on the west side of Jordan.

4. This was misinterpreted by the nine and a half tribes as an act of rebellion and an ugly civil war was threatened.

5. The misunderstanding was cleared up just in time by an eleven man delegation from the nine and a half tribes led by Aaron's grandson, Phinehas.

D. A final sermon recited (23–24).
   Joshua's last words to Israel.
   1. He reminds them of God's goodness (23:3).
   2. He warns them concerning disobedience (23:11–13).
   3. He reviews this history (24:1–13).
   4. He challenges them to serve God (24:14–18).

THE JUDGES STAGE

INTRODUCING THE JUDGES STAGE
(Judges; Ruth; 1 Samuel 1-7)

1. This stage records the saddest and most sordid period in the entire history of Israel. It is the dark ages of that nation.
2. Important names in this period would include Gideon, Samson, Naomi, Ruth, Boaz, Eli, and Samuel.
3. The book spans a period of some 300 years.
4. In brief, it records seven apostasies on Israel's part, seven servitudes to seven heathen nations, and seven deliverances.
5. The following two outlines have been suggested which summarize the Judges Stage.
   a. Rebellion, retribution, repentance, and restoration (or)
   b. Sin, servitude, supplication, and salvation.
6. Counting Eli and Samuel, there were fifteen judges in all. One was a woman, Deborah. These judges were not so much legal experts, as military reformers.
7. The root of Israel's problem was that when Joshua died, God could find no man to take his place as he did when Moses died. The statement, "In those days there was no king in Israel; every man did that which was right in his own eyes," is repeated on four separate occasions in the book of Judges. (See 17:6; 18:1; 19:1; 21:25.) This period is thus the antithesis of the millennium when King Jesus will rule with a rod of iron (see Ps. 2).
8. The fruit of Israel's problems could be seen in her:
   a. Compromise—not doing what God told her to do, that is, to drive out the enemy. (See 1:21, 27-33; 2:1-5.)
      "And an angel of the Lord came up from Gilgal to Bochim, and said, I made you to go up out of Egypt, and have brought you unto the land which I sware unto your fathers; and I said, I will never break my covenant with you. And ye shall make no league with the inhabitants of this land; ye shall throw down their altars: but ye have not obeyed my voice; why have ye done this? Wherefore I also said, I will not drive them out from before you; but they shall be as thorns in your sides, and their gods shall be a snare unto you."
   b. Apostasy—doing what God told her not to do, that is, to worship the gods of her enemies. (See 2:11-15; 6:8-10.)
      "And the children of Israel did evil in the sight of the Lord, and served Baalim: And they forsook the Lord God of their fathers, which brought them out of the land of Egypt, and followed other gods, of the gods of the people that were round about them, and bowed themselves

unto them, and provoked the Lord to anger. And they forsook the Lord, and served Baal and Ashtaroth" (Jdg. 2:11-13).

9. In spite of all this God still loved Israel. In the Old Testament the angel of the Lord is mentioned eighty times. It is thought by most theologians that the angel of the Lord in the Old Testament was none other than Christ himself. No less than twenty of these instances are in the book of Judges. Thus, during no other stage does God so minister to his people.
10. The final part of Galatians 5 provides an excellent summary of the books of Joshua and Judges. (See 5:22-26 concerning Joshua and 5:17-21 concerning Judges.)
      "Now the works of the flesh are manifest, which are these; Adultery, fornication, uncleanness, lasciviousness, idolatry, witchcraft, hatred, variance, emulations, wrath, strife, seditions, heresies, envyings, murders, drunkenness, revellings, and such like: of the which I tell you before, as I have also told you in time past, that they which do such things shall not inherit the kingdom of God. But the fruit of the Spirit is love, joy, peace, longsuffering, gentleness, goodness, faith, meekness, temperance: against such there is no law" (Gal. 5:19-23).
   Note the overall contrast between these two stages:

Joshua	Judges
a. victory	defeat
b. freedom	slavery
c. faith	unbelief
d. progress	declension
e. obedience	disobedience
f. heavenly vision	earthly emphasis
g. joy	sorrow
h. strength	weakness
i. unity among tribes	disunity among tribes
j. strong leader	no leader

11. Judges is the classic example of Hosea 8:7 and Galatians 6:7.
      "For they have sown the wind, and they shall reap the whirlwind" (Hosea 8:7a).
      "Be not deceived; God is not mocked: for whatsoever a man soweth, that shall he also reap. For he that soweth to his flesh shall of the flesh reap corruption; but he that soweth to the Spirit shall of the Spirit reap life everlasting" (Gal. 6:7, 8).
   Note especially Judges 6:3.
      "And so it was, when Israel had sown, that the Midianites came up, and the Amalekites, and the children of the east, even they came up against them" (Jdg. 6:3).
   This almost seems to be a play on words. Read it again carefully.

12. Judges also offers seven illustrations of 1 Corinthians 1:27.

"But God hath chosen the foolish things of the world to confound the wise; and God hath chosen the weak things of the world to confound the things which are mighty."

In Judges, God used:

a. an oxgoad (3:31)
b. a nail (4:21)
c. some trumpets (7:20)
d. some pitchers (7:20)
e. some lamps (7:20)
f. a millstone (9:53)
g. the jawbone of an ass (15:15)

13. In Judges we thus see:

a. The first Nazarite recorded in history (Jdg. 13:2–5).
b. The strongest man recorded in history (15:15).
c. A bloodthirsty son (Abimelech) and a heartbroken father (Jephthah) (9, 11).
d. An evil spirit and the Spirit of God (9:23; 13:24, 25).
e. An army put to death for mispronouncing a word (12).
f. Three hundred victorious men and 600 desperate men (7:7; 20:46, 47).
g. One of the two fables in the Bible (9:7–15).
h. A new name for God (6:24).
i. Fox catching, riddle telling, fleece throwing, and hair cutting (15:4; 14:14; 6:36–40; 16:19).

14. The book of Ruth in brief.

a. It is the first of two biblical books to bear the name of a woman.
b. Ruth becomes the third of four women to be included by Matthew in his genealogy of Christ (See Mt. 1.)
c. The history of this book, which took place during the Judges Stage, is like a pure lily floating on the vast cesspool of sin.
d. It records the first of three all-important trips to the little city of Bethlehem in the Bible (Ruth 1:19). (For the other two, see 1 Sam. 16:4; Lk. 2:4.)
e. It offers the greatest example of Christ as our Kinsman Redeemer in the entire Bible.
f. Ruth becomes the second of two women in the Old Testament who foreshadow the church in the New Testament. (The other is Rebekah; see Gen. 24.)

15. The first seven chapters of 1 Samuel in brief.

a. We find one of the greatest dedicatory prayers for one's child ever uttered.

"And she said, Oh my lord, as thy soul liveth, my lord, I am the woman that stood by thee here, praying unto the Lord. For this child I prayed; and the Lord hath given me my petition which I asked of him: Therefore also I have lent him to the Lord; as long as he liveth he shall be lent to the Lord. And he worshipped the Lord there" (1 Sam. 1:26–28).

b. The description of one of Israel's saddest moments—the capture of their beloved Ark of the Covenant (1 Sam. 4:10, 11).
c. A divine midnight call to a young boy (1 Sam. 3:1–10).
d. The agony of a dying mother and the ecstasy of a grateful prophet.

(1) The agony is seen in the word *Ichabod.*

"And his daughter in law, Phinehas' wife, was with child, near to be delivered: and when she heard the tidings that the ark of God was taken, and that her father in law and her husband were dead, she bowed herself and travailed; for her pains came upon her.

And about the time of her death the women that stood by her said unto her, Fear not; for thou hast born a son. But she answered not, neither did she regard it.

And she named the child Ichabod, saying, The glory is departed from Israel: because the ark of God was taken, and because of her father in law and her husband.

And she said, The glory is departed from Israel: for the ark of God is taken" (1 Sam. 4:19–22).

(2) The ecstasy is seen in the word *Eben-ezer.*

"And as Samuel was offering up the burnt-offering, the Philistines drew near to battle against Israel: but the Lord thundered with a great thunder on that day upon the Philistines, and discomfited them; and they were smitten before Israel.

And the men of Israel went out of Mizpeh, and pursued the Philistines, and smote them, until they came under Beth-car.

Then Samuel took a stone, and set it between Mizpeh and Shen, and called the name of it Eben-ezer, saying, Hitherto hath the Lord helped us" (1 Sam. 7:10–12).

THE JUDGES STAGE

"In those days there was no king in Israel, but every man did that which was right in his own eyes" (17:26). See also 19:1; 21:25.

"And the children of Israel did evil in the sight of the Lord, and served Baalam" (2:11).

"And the anger of the Lord was hot against Israel, and he delivered them into the hands of the spoilers . . ." (2:14).

"Nevertheless the Lord raised up judges, who delivered them out of the hand of those who spoiled them" (2:16).

The main action of the Judges stage. The key events during this period center around the following individuals or groups of individuals.

I. Twelve Military Reformers.
II. A Bloody Butcher.
III. An Idol-Worshiping Son.
IV. A Cowardly Levite.
V. A Moabite Girl.
VI. A Dedicated Mother.
VII. An Undisciplined Priest.
VIII. Some Frustraed Philistines.
IX. A Circuit-riding Preacher.

We shall now examine in some detail each of these nine.

I. Twelve Military Reformers—The Judges.
    A. First judge: Othniel (1:12, 13; 3:8–11).
        1. Oppressing nation: Mesopotamia
        2. Length of oppression: eight years
        3. Years of peace he gave: forty
        4. Accomplishments:
            Othniel was both the nephew and the son-in-law of Caleb (1:13). He won his wife by

successfully defeating a strong enemy city which his tribe Judah was attempting to capture (1:12). Othniel had already proven his bravery. (See Josh. 15:15-20.) He was one of the many judges said to be filled with the Holy Spirit (3:10). He defeated the King of Mesopotamia (3:10) which had plagued Israel for eight long years (3:8). The land now had rest for forty years (3:11).

B. Second judge: Ehud (3:12-30).
　1. Oppressing nation: Moab
　2. Length of oppression: eighteen years
　3. Years of peace: eighty years
　4. Accomplishments:

Ehud was a left-handed Benjaminite (Jdg. 3:15). In Old Testament times God often especially blessed left-handed warriors. (See Jdg. 20:16; 1 Chron. 12:2.)

Ehud was chosen to carry Israel's annual (and hated) tax money to the Moabite capital. Israel had been doing this for eighteen years (3:14, 15).

After paying the tax, Ehud secured a private meeting with Eglon, the fat Moabite king, claiming he had a "message from God" for the king. He thereupon stabbed Eglon with a double-edged eighteen-inch dagger (Jdg. 3:16-23). We note however that the Bible does not say he did this by the Spirit of God.

He then fled to the hill country of Ephraim where he sounded the war trumpet, raised an army, attacked the Moabites (killing 10,000), and gave rest to the land for the next eighty years (Jdg. 3:26-30).

C. Third judge: Shamgar (3:31).
　1. Oppressing nation: Philistia
　2. Length of oppression: unrecorded
　3. Years of peace: unrecorded
　4. Accomplishments: With an ox goad this soldier killed 600 Philistines.

D. Fourth judge: Barak (as helped by Deborah, Jdg. 4-5).
　1. Oppressing nation: northern Canaanites
　2. Length of oppression: twenty years
　3. Years of peace: forty years
　4. Accomplishments:

Israel (at this time) had been in bondage to King Jaban of Hazor (a Canaanite ruler) for twenty years (4:3). Jaban had a five-star general named Sisera, who commanded 900 iron chariots plus a huge marching army (4:2, 3).

At this time Israel was judged by a woman whose name was Deborah (4:4, 5). She informed Israel's army commander, a man named Barak, that God had chosen him to mobilize 10,000 men from the tribes of Naphtali and Zebulun. He was then to lead them to Mt. Tabor and do battle with Sisera (4:6, 7).

At his insistence, Deborah agrees to go with him, but warns him that the honor of conquering Sisera will not be credited to him, but to another woman (4:8, 9).

Barak leads his 10,000 men down the slopes of Mt. Tabor and, through God's intervention, totally routs and defeats Sisera (4:14, 15).

Sisera escapes and takes refuge in the tent of a Kenite housewife named Jael. Pretending to befriend him, she lulls him to sleep and kills him by driving a peg through his brain (4:17-21). Deborah and Barak thereupon sing their "duet of deliverance" hymn of praise to God.

The land then was to enjoy rest for forty years (5:31). Barak is later included in the New Testament hall of fame (Heb. 11:32). This fifth chapter of Judges is the third great song of praise in the Bible thus far. The other two are Exodus 15 and Deuteronomy 32.

E. Fifth judge: Gideon (6-8).
　1. Oppressing nation: Midian
　2. Length of oppression: seven years
　3. Years of peace: forty years
　4. Accomplishments:

After Barak's death, Israel returned to idolatry and God delivered them into the hands of the cruel Midianites for seven years. (Note their sad plight: Jdg. 6:2-6.)

A nameless (and fearless) prophet reminded Israel that their terrible circumstances were due to sin (6:8-10). An angel of the Lord (Jesus?) appeared at this point to Gideon, who was threshing wheat by hand in the bottom of a grape press to hide it from the Midianites (6:11).

Gideon is divinely commissioned to defeat the Midianites, and thereupon builds an altar to God, calling it *Jehovah-shalom* ("the Lord send peace," Jdg. 6:12-24).

Note: In spite of his many doubts, Gideon shows real faith at this time of famine by offering a young goat and baked bread sacrifice. Gideon thus, like Abraham, prepared a meal for God himself. (See Gen. 18.)

That very night, at God's command, Gideon pulls down the family altar of Baal and replaces it with an altar to Jehovah (6:25-27). Gideon's father, Joash, calms down an angry crowd the next morning who would have killed Gideon for his brave act. God's Spirit then comes upon Gideon. Gideon blows a trumpet and sounds a call to arms (6:34, 35).

He then throws out the fleece (twice) and is thus reassured concerning his call by God (6:36-40). Was Gideon justified in doing this? Is it ever God's will for a believer to throw out a fleece? Is the old cliche "testing is not trusting" correct? Let us consider the following:
　5. Biblical examples of fleece throwing:
　　a. The servant of Abraham (Gen. 24:14). He was sent to find a bride for Isaac in a foreign land. Upon arriving, he prayed and threw out a fleece. God obviously accepted this fleece prayer. Especially thrilling are the words, "and it came to pass, before he had done speaking, that, behold, Rebekah came out" (v. 15).
　　b. King Ahaz (Isa. 7:11).
　　　"Moreover the Lord spake again unto Ahaz saying, Ask thee a sign of the

Lord thy God; Ask it either in the depth, or in the height above. But Ahaz said, I will not ask, neither will I tempt the Lord" (Isa. 7:10-12).

In this instance, God himself invited this wicked Judean king who was threatened by outside enemies to ask for any sign he wanted and God would perform it to prove that Jerusalem would be saved from her enemies. But the evil ruler refused.

c. King Hezekiah (2 Ki. 20:10, 11).
God caused the sundial shadow to go back ten degrees, showing he would be healed. Again, it may be observed that God honored this requested sign.

d. Satan (Mt. 4:6).
"Then the devil taketh him up into the holy city, and setteth him on a pinnacle of the temple, And saith unto him, If thou be the Son of God, cast thyself down: for it is written, He shall give his angels charge concerning thee: and in their hands they shall bear thee up, lest at any time thou dash thy foot against a stone. Jesus said unto him, It is written again, Thou shalt not tempt the Lord thy God" (Mt. 4:5-7).
Here the Savior rightly refused to perform the perverted fleece-throwing as suggested by the devil.

e. Gideon (Jdg. 6:37).
Several facts may be immediately seen:
(1) The Lord had already on two previous occasions clearly assured Gideon of what he was to do. (See 6:14, 16.)
(2) The Lord had on one occasion actually given a sign that Gideon had requested. (See 6:17-21.)

6. Basic conclusions on fleece-throwing:
a. On certain occasions the believer may rightfully seek God's will through a fleece of some sort. This may be done:
(1) *If* the Scriptures have not already answered his request. In other words, it would be totally in error to throw out a fleece concerning whether God desired a believer to quit body-harming habits, for to do so is clearly implied in many passages. (See 1 Cor. 6:19, 20.)
(2) *If* the immediate circumstances are indefinite and unclear. Let us suppose a missionary feels strongly about entering a country whose doors have just been closed to all Christian work. He then would be perfectly justified in asking God to open those doors if it is his perfect will.
(3) *If* his fleece does not limit the action God must take. To illustrate this, it would be unwise for a pastoral candidate, when preaching a trial sermon, to pray that God would show

him this was the church he should accept by having exactly seven come forward during the invitation for salvation. What if there were eight present that morning whom God desired to save? Or what if there were indeed seven there under conviction, all being dealt with by the Holy Spirit, but it was not God's perfect will for the pastoral candidate to accept that church?

b. In Gideon's case, while God did honor his fleece-prayer, it was nevertheless unnecessary (for he already knew what he should do), and unprofitable, for he later needed reassurance again. (See Jdg. 7:10.)

God thereupon cut down his army from 32,000 to 22,000, and finally down to 300 (7:2-7). With these 300 he would face 135,000 enemy troops (see 8:10). Gideon and his servant made their way behind enemy lines on the eve of the battle and were once again reassured of victory by overhearing an enemy conversation (7:10-15). Gideon divided his army into three companies, and upon the signal, each man blew a trumpet, broke a clay jar, raised up a blazing torch, and shouted, "The sword of the Lord, and of Gideon" (7:16-20). The army of Midian was thrown into panic and completely routed (7:21-24). Gideon pursued them across the Jordan River where he finished defeating them. He thereupon returned to Palestine and severely punished two towns which had refused to feed his 300 hungry troops (8:4-17).

Gideon then executed the two pagan Midianite kings for killing his brothers at Tabor (8:18-21). He refused an offer by Israel to become king over them, but requested the gold earrings captured in battle, plus other war booty (8:22-26).

From this gold he made an ephod. Soon Israel began worshiping this, and it became a snare for the nation (8:27).

Note: An ephod was part of the apparel worn by the high priest. Gideon had previously declined to offer to become king, but he may have had aspirations for the priestly office.

Gideon eventually settled down, married many wives, and raised seventy-one sons (and doubtless many daughters also). One of these sons was named Abimelech, who would later cause much bloodshed after Gideon's death (8:29-31). Because of Gideon's work the land would enjoy rest for forty years (8:28).

F. Sixth judge: Tola (10:1).
1. Oppressing nation: unrecorded
2. Length of oppression: unrecorded
3. Years of peace: twenty-three
4. Accomplishments: unrecorded

G. Seventh judge: Jair (10:3-5).
1. Oppressing nation: unrecorded
2. Length of oppression: unrecorded
3. Years of peace: twenty-two

4. Accomplishments: He and his thirty sons delivered thirty Israeli cities from oppression.
H. Eighth judge: Jephthah (10:6—12:17).
   1. Oppressing nation: Ammon
   2. Length of oppression: eighteen years
   3. Years of peace: six
   4. Accomplishments:
   After Abimelech's death, Israel was judged
by Tola for twenty-three years. The clan of
Tola was later known in David's time for its
men of valor (1 Chron. 7:1, 2). After Tola's
death, God raised up a man called Jair, who
judged for twenty-two years. When Jair died,
Israel once again "did evil in the sight of the
Lord," and was turned over to the Philistines
and Ammonites for a period of eighteen
years (10:6-8). Fickle and foolish Israel once
again turned to God in their hour of great
need. As usual, he was filled with compassion and promised deliverance, but not before delivering a soul-searching message.
Note its content: Judges 10:10-16. This passage in Judges should be compared with Isaiah 63:7-9. God now raised up Jephthah, the
son of a harlot. He had been rejected by his
own brethren due to his illegitimate birth
(11:1-11).

Jephthah attempts to negotiate with the
Ammonites concerning some disputed land
east of Jordan. He argues that:
a. The land was originally the Amorites'
   and not the Ammonites' (Num.
   21:21-30).
b. God gave the land to Israel and she had
   been there for the last 300 years.

At this statement a state of war existed between the two countries. God's Spirit came
upon him, and Jephthah prepared for battle
(11:28, 29). On the eve of the battle, however, Jephthah did something which would
later cause him much pain and anguish. We
read in Judges 11:30, 31:

"And Jephthah vowed a vow unto the
Lord, and said, If thou shalt without fail
deliver the children of Ammon into mine
hands, then it shall be, that whatsoever
cometh forth of the doors of my house to
meet me, when I return in peace from the
children of Ammon, shall surely be the
Lord's, and I will offer it up for a burnt
offering."

God delivered the Ammonites into Jephthah's hands (11:32, 33). But his real problem
was just beginning. We read in Judges 11:34,
35:

"And Jephthah came to Mizpeh unto his
house, and, behold, his daughter came
out to meet him with timbrels and with
dances: and she was his only child; beside
her he had neither son nor daughter.

And it came to pass, when he saw her,
that he rent his clothes, and said, Alas, my
daughter! Thou hast brought me very
low, and thou art one of them that trouble
me: for I have opened my mouth unto the
Lord, and I cannot go back."

Much ink has been used throughout the
years by theologians concerning this passage.
What was involved in Jephthah's vow here?
Dr. John J. Davis writes:

"There are, therefore, today, two prevailing interpretations of this portion of chapter 11. The *first* is that he did not kill his
daughter. This view is suggested by a
number of conservative writers. The arguments for this view are as follows: (1)
Jephthah was too well acquainted with
the law to be ignorant of God's condemnation of human sacrifices (11:15-27). (2)
He must have known that a human being
would come out of the home. Furthermore, an animal would have been too
small a sacrifice for such a victory. (3)
Jephthah must have been a godly man, or
his name would not have appeared in Hebrews 11. (4) If his daughter were to be
slain, there would be no point in empha-
sizing her virginity (37-39). (5) Jephthah
could not have done this, especially after
the Spirit of God came upon him (29). (6)
There were women at this time who gave
their lives to serving the Lord in the tabernacle at Shiloh (1 Sam. 2:22). Thus, Jephthah could have vowed that in case of
victory, he would dedicate to God for tabernacle service one member of his household. The fact that it turned out to be his
daughter was tragic for him. Because she
was his only child, he would never expect
to see grandchildren; and he would seldom, if ever, see her again. (7) It is argued
that the conjunction which appears in the
vow in verse 31 should be translated 'or'
rather than 'and.' In other words, Jephthah is thought to have said, 'Whatever
comes from the doors of my home to
meet me as I return shall be devoted to
the Lord's service if it is human, or if it is
a clean animal, I will offer it up as a whole
burnt offering. (8) It is argued by those
holding this view that the expression 'to
lament' in verse 40 should be translated
'to talk to,' indicating that the daughter
remained alive.

The *second* view with regard to Jephthah's vow and its fulfillment is that he
did offer his daughter as a human sacrifice. Again this view is supported by
many well-known writers. The arguments
for this view are as follows: (1) The Hebrew word for burnt offering is *olah* which
always has the idea of a burnt sacrifice in
the Old Testament. (2) Jephthah was the
son of a common heathen prostitute
Zonah and spent a great deal of time with
various peoples on the east side of the Jordan (11:1-3). Furthermore, it should be
observed that later individuals engaged in
such human sacrifice. Second Kings 3:26,
27 records the action of the king of Moab
in offering his eldest son for a burnt offering on the wall of his city. Second Chron-

icles 28:3 tells of Ahaz's burning of his children, and 2 Kings 21:6 tells of Manasseh's sacrifice of his son. If such practices were followed by leaders in Israel at the later period, it is not impossible that they could have been introduced at this earlier period. (3) The fact that Jephthah was a judge of Israel does not remove the possibility of his making a rash vow. The dominant philosophy of this day was a moral and spiritual relativism in which 'every man did that which was right in his own eyes' (Jdg. 21:25). Many of Israel's leaders were affected by this attitude. Recall that Gideon made a golden ephod which led Israel to idolatry, and Samson engaged in activities that were obviously in opposition to the law of Moses. (4) If Jephthah could lead in the slaughter of 42,000 Israelites (Jdg. 12), he would therefore be capable of this vow and its fulfillment. (5) The fact that her virginity is bewailed in verses 36-40 seems to imply that there was no hope for children in the future because of her impending death. This discussion 'is probably mentioned to give greater force to the sacrifice, as it would leave him without issue, which in the east was considered a special misfortune.' Finally, the argument based upon the Hebrew word for 'lament' in verse 40 by those holding the dedication view is rather tenuous. The verb *tanah* occurs only once elsewhere in the Hebrew Bible (Jdg. 5:11). The best translation of this form appears to be 'to recount.'" (*Conquest and Crisis*, pp. 125-128)

After all this, Jephthah's troubles were not yet over, for he was provoked into battle by the jealous tribe of Ephraim (Jdg. 12:4-7). This tragic battle, won by Jephthah, resulted in the loss of 42,000 Ephraimite troops. It was one of the strangest ever fought, because many of those troops lost their lives due to their inability to pronounce the word *Shibboleth* (Hebrew for "stream") correctly.

I. Ninth judge: Ibzan (12:8-10).
   1. Oppressing nation: unrecorded
   2. Length of oppression: unrecorded
   3. Years of peace: seven
   4. Accomplishments: unrecorded
J. Tenth judge: Elon (12:11, 12).
   1. Oppressing nation: unrecorded
   2. Length of oppression: unrecorded
   3. Years of peace: ten
   4. Accomplishments: unrecorded
K. Eleventh judge: Abdon (12:13-15).
   1. Opposing nation: unrecorded
   2. Length of oppression: unrecorded
   3. Years of peace: eight
   4. Accomplishments: unrecorded
L. Twelfth judge: Samson (13-16).
   1. Opposing nation: Philistia
   2. Length of oppression: forty
   3. Years of peace: twenty (16:31)
   4. Accomplishments:
      Prior to Samson's birth, Israel had been in bondage to the Philistines for forty years (13:1).
      Samson's mother is visited by the angel of the Lord, who tells her of his future birth (13:2, 3). She thus becomes one of the four biblical women who received such a pre-birth angelic promise. The three others were:
      a. Sarah (Gen. 18:10-14)
      b. Elisabeth (Lk. 1:13)
      c. Mary (Lk. 1:30, 31)
      This heavenly messenger instructed the parents that their child was to be raised a Nazarite (13:4, 5). According to Numbers 6:1-6, the Nazarite had three restrictions placed upon him.
      d. He was not to touch wine.
      e. His hair was to remain untouched by a razor.
      f. He must not touch a dead body.
      (Note: Samson's mother was also commanded not to drink wine, 13:4, 14.)
      On this occasion Samson's parents prayed a prayer all expectant Christian parents should pray (Jdg. 13:8, 12). Who was this angel of the Lord: The parents attempted to discover his name, but were told, "it is secret" (v. 17). The Hebrew word here translated "secret," can also be rendered "wonderful," and is very similar to the word used in Isaiah 9:6, where we are told concerning Christ's birth that, "his name shall be called Wonderful, Counsellor, The Mighty God, The Everlasting Father, The Prince of Peace." This would strongly indicate a pre-Bethlehem appearance of the Lord Jesus Christ.
      Samson was born and empowered by the Holy Spirit even as he grew up (13:24, 25).
      He determined to marry an unbelieving Philistine girl, to the dismay of his parents. Already Samson's carnal nature is seen coming to the surface. In spite of his sensuality, God used him for his glory (14:1-4).
      En route to Philistia Samson kills a lion. Later he discovers that a swarm of bees had chosen the carcass of the lion to make honey in. At his wedding feast Samson uses this experience as a basis for a riddle (Jdg. 14:12-14).

THE JUDGES STAGE

The books of
JUDGES; RUTH; 1 SAMUEL (1-7)
THE JUDGES

Othniel	Gideon	Ibzan
Ehud	Tola	Elon
Shamgar	Jair	Abdon
Deborah	Jephthah	Samson
Barak		

The guests eventually would dishonestly solve this riddle, getting the answer from Samson's bride. He becomes furious at this and pays his debt to the wedding guests, but only at the expense of thirty Philistine victims (14:15-19).

He returns only to find that the girl's father had given his bride to Samson's best man! In an act of revenge, the Hebrew strong man does the following:

"And Samson went and caught three hundred foxes, and took firebrands, and turned tail to tail, and put a firebrand in the midst between two tails. And when he had set the brands on fire, he let them go into the standing corn of the Philistines, and burnt up both the shocks, and also the standing corn, with the vineyards and olives" (Jdg. 15:4, 5).

He then killed many Philistines (15:8). After this, the Philistines threaten to destroy the tribe of Judah unless Samson is bound and delivered to them. Samson meekly allows himself to be tied up, but as the enemy comes in view he breaks the ropes, grabs the jawbone of an ass, and slaughters 1,000 Philistines (15:9-17).

He then prays one of his only two recorded prayers. Both are totally carnal and self-centered. (Compare 15:18 with 16:28.)

At Gaza (a Philistine city) Samson once again avoids capture, this time by ripping apart the iron gate of the city (16:1-3). Samson is finally done in by a Philistine woman named Delilah, who discovers the source of his great strength (16:4-20).

Note: At this point, Samson has violated

TWELVE MILITARY REFORMERS

Othniel JUDGES 1:12, 13; 3:8-11
Oppressing nation—**Mesopotamia**
Length of oppression—**8 years**
Years of peace **40 years**
He was both nephew and son-in-law of Caleb.
He captured a strong Canaanite city.

Ehud (3:12-30)
Oppressing nation—**Moab** Length of oppression—**18 years**
Years of peace **80 years**
He assassinated a fat Moabite enemy king named Eglon.
He organized an Israeli army which killed 10,000 enemy troops.

Shamgar (3:31)
Oppressing nation—**Philistia** Length of oppression—**unrecorded**
Years of peace **unrecorded**
He killed 600 Philistines with an oxgoad.

Barak (4-5)
Oppressing nation—**Canaanites**
Length of oppression—**20 years**
Years of peace **40 years**
He raised an army of 10,000 at Deborah's encouragement.
He defeated enemy general named Sisera at base of Mt. Tabor.
Sisera is killed later by Jael while in her tent sleeping.
Barak and Deborah sang a duet of praise over their victory.

Gideon (6-8)
Oppressing nation—**Midian** Length of oppression—**7 years**
Years of peace **40 years**
He was commissioned by God to defeat the Midianites.
He prepared for this by destroying the family idols.
He threw out the fleece twice.
He raised an army of 10,000.
He saw this army reduced to 300 by God.
He defeated 135,000 enemy troops with his 300.
He caused Israel to sin by making a golden ephod.

Tola (10:1)
Oppressing nation—**unrecorded** Length of oppression—**unrecorded**
Years of peace **23 years**
Unrecorded

Jair (10:3-5)
Oppressing nation—**unrecorded** Length of oppression—**unrecorded**
Years of peace **22 years**
He and his 30 sons delivered 30 Israeli cities from oppression.

Jephthah (10:6—12:17)
Oppressing nation—**Ammon** Length of oppression—**18 years**
Years of peace **6 years**
He was a harlot's son who became a mighty warrior.
On the eve of battle he made a rash vow to God: if victorious he would offer the first thing that greeted him. His daughter met him and he sadly performed his vow.
He is later provoked into battle with the jealous tribe of Ephraim.

Ibzan (12:8-10)
Oppressing nation—**unrecorded** Length of oppression—**unrecorded**
Years of peace **7 years**
Unrecorded

Elon (12:11, 12)
Oppressing nation—**unrecorded** Length of oppression—**unrecorded**
Years of peace **10 years**
Unrecorded

Abdon (12:13-15)
Oppressing nation—**unrecorded** Length of oppression—**unrecorded**
Years of peace **8 years**
Unrecorded

Samson (13-16)
Oppressing nation—**Philistia** Length of oppression—**40 years**
Years of peace **20 years**
He was to be raised as a Nazarite.
He killed a lion en route to his wedding.
He killed 30 Philistines to pay off a clothing debt.
Upon losing his wife, he burned the wheat fields of the Philistines.
He killed 1000 Philistines with the jawbone of an ass.
He ripped off an iron gate at Gaza.
He was betrayed into the hands of the Philistines by Delilah.
He was shaven, blinded, and enslaved.
He was supernaturally empowered to destroy many Philistines in their own temple by pulling it down.
He himself was killed at this time.

THE JUDGES STAGE

The action during this period centers around nine individuals or groups of individuals.

TWELVE MILITARY REFORMERS

A BLOODY BUTCHER

AN IDOL-WORSHIPING SON

A COWARDLY LEVITE

A MOABITE GIRL

A DEDICATED MOTHER

AN UNDISCIPLINED PRIEST

SOME FRUSTRATED PHILISTINES

A CIRCUIT-RIDING PREACHER

all three Nazarite vows. He had touched the carcass of a lion (14:8, 9). He had drunk wine (14:10). He had allowed his hair to be cut (16:19).

Samson now learns the high cost of low living (Jdg. 16:21).

"But the Philistines took him, and put out his eyes, and brought him down to Gaza, and bound him with fetters of brass; and he did grind in the prison house."

In prison he regains his strength as his hair grows out again. He is then allowed by God to destroy thousands of Philistines who had gathered in their heathen temple for a drunken orgy. In the following destruction Samson himself perished (Jdg. 16:22–31).

II. A Bloody Butcher—Abimelech (9).

A. Abimelech was the son of Gideon by a concubine in Shechem (8:31). He arranged for the brutal murder of sixty-nine of his seventy half-brothers and was crowned "king" of his mother's home-town, Shechem (9:1–5).

Jotham, the half-brother who escaped, relates one of the two fables in the Bible (for the other, see 2 Ki. 14:9), and directs it at Abimelech, whom he ridicules as a "thornbush bramble king." Note his dripping sarcasm in Judges 9:8–14.

Three years later God stirred up trouble between King Abimelech and the citizens of Shechem. In the ensuing struggle, Abimelech was killed (Jdg. 9:22–57). Some Christians have been bothered concerning the statement recorded in Judges 9:23:

"Then God sent an evil spirit between Abimelech and the men of Shechem; and the men of Shechem dealt treacherously with Abimelech."

This is the first of at least three Old Testament instances when such action took place. Let us briefly examine each occasion.

1. Saul (1 Sam. 16:14, 23)
2. Ahab (2 Chron. 18:18–22)

How are we to understand these verses? Two basic interpretations have been offered:

a. That these were angelic messengers sent from God to do his works of judgment as the seven elect angels will one day do during the coming tribulation. (See Rev. 8:2.)

b. That these were demonic fallen angels. The context, it would seem, favors this view. They are described as evil, and the word used is the same Hebrew word found in Genesis 6:5, where we are told God destroyed mankind for their evil hearts. But why would evil spirits request to be used of God, and why would the Lord comply? Here one should carefully read Job 1 and 2. Satan himself had requested permission to torment Job. God allowed it, but only to fulfill his divine purpose.

In Abimelech's case, God had pronounced doom upon this mad dog through a woman of Shechem, thus making way for a godly ruler named Tola, who would defend the sheep of Israel, and not butcher them as Abimelech had done. (See Jdg. 10:1.) The evil spirit obviously had a different motive in mind for the removal of Abimelech. He had proven to be an inept bungler who for three years had failed to extend his wicked reign beyond the city boundaries of Shechem. Perhaps the evil spirit had hoped to work through another wicked man. But it didn't succeed! In Saul's case, the evil spirit apparently hoped to totally control him in an attempt to remove from the scene the hated David. But again, it would fail, for God had already set in motion those plans which would lead to his death on a Philistine battlefield.

In Ahab's case, the evil spirit may have wanted the wicked king to go into battle, willing to sacrifice this faithful devil worshiper in order to get to Jehoshaphat. As things turned out, had not God stepped in, the foolish Jehoshaphat would indeed have fallen in battle (see 2 Chron. 18:28–32).Thus, God often uses the wrath of wicked men and even demons for his glory (Ps. 76:10). For two New Testament instances in which God will use both wicked men and demons for his glory, consider the following passages:

(1) Revelation 16:13, where he will use demons to entice men to Armageddon.

(2) Revelation 17:16, 17, where he will cause the antichrist to destroy the false church.

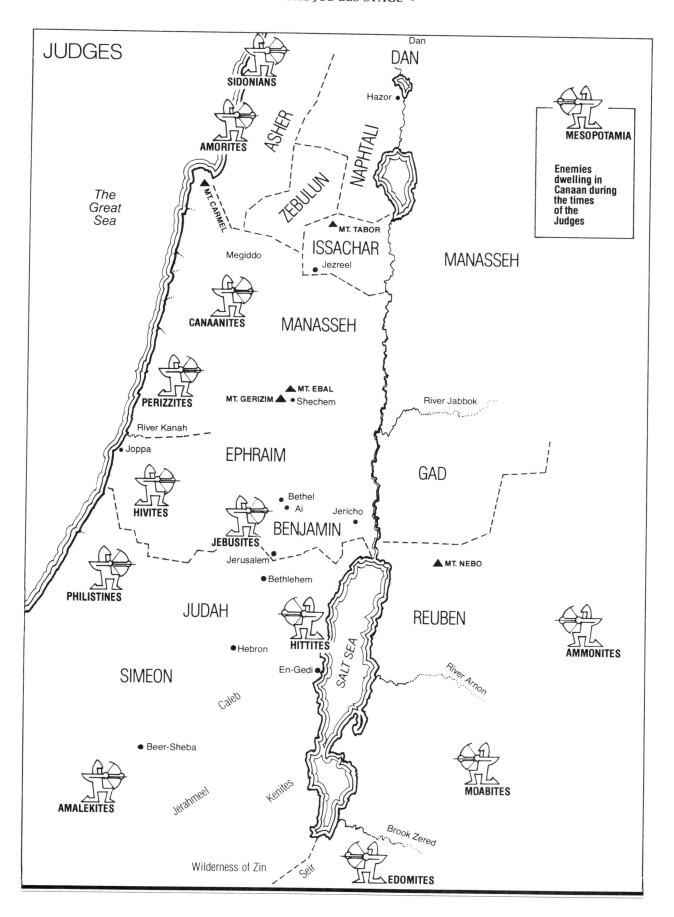

JUDGES

SIDONIANS

DAN

Dan

ASHER

AMORITES

NAPHTALI

Hazor

ZEBULUN

MESOPOTAMIA

Enemies
dwelling in
Canaan during
the times
of the
Judges

The
Great
Sea

MT. CARMEL

MT. TABOR

ISSACHAR

MANASSEH

Megiddo

Jezreel

CANAANITES

MANASSEH

MT. EBAL

PERIZZITES

MT. GERIZIM

Shechem

River Jabbok

River Kanah

Joppa

EPHRAIM

GAD

HIVITES

Bethel

Ai

Jericho

JEBUSITES

BENJAMIN

Jerusalem

MT. NEBO

PHILISTINES

Bethlehem

JUDAH

HITTITES

REUBEN

AMMONITES

Hebron

En-Gedi

River Arnon

SIMEON

Caleb

SALT SEA

Beer-Sheba

Kenites

Jerahmeel

MOABITES

AMALEKITES

Brook Zered

Wilderness of Zin

Seir

EDOMITES

A TERRIBLE TRIO

Abimelech, the bloody butcher— Judges 9

1. He was the mad-dog son of Gideon.
2. He arranged for the murder of sixty-nine of his half-brothers. Only a man named Jotham escaped.
3. He set up his "kingdom" at Shechem.
4. He was later killed by God, who used an evil spirit and an old woman to perform his will.

Micah, a mother-spoiled thief and idol worshiper— Judges 17-18

1. He is encouraged by his indulgent mother to "start his own religion."
2. He does this by hiring his own personal priest, a money-hungry Levite from Bethlehem.
3. This perverted "private pastor" is later enticed by the tribe of Dan to become their official priest.

A cowardly and emotionally sick Levite— Judges 19-21

1. A Levite and his concubine are threatened by a mob of sex perverts while visiting in the land of Benjamin.
2. He saves his miserable hide by allowing this corrupt crowd to sexually murder the woman.
3. He then cuts up her dead body into twelve pieces and sends a bloody chunk to each tribe in Israel.
4. An army of 450,000 is raised, but the Benjamin tribe officials refuse to hand over the guilty men.
5. A civil war breaks out, which leaves but 600 Benjaminite soldiers alive.
6. A plan is effected by the eleven tribes to provide wives for these 600, lest the tribe of Benjamin disappear.

III. An Idol-Worshiping Son—Micah (17-18).
Micah, a thief and idol worshiper, is encouraged by his indulgent mother to "start his own religion." This he does by (among other things) hiring his own personal priest, a money-grabbing Levite from Bethlehem (17:1-13). This perverted "private pastor" is later enticed by the tribe of Danites to become their official priest (18:1-31).

IV. A Cowardly Levite (19-21).
  A. These three chapters are among the most depressing in all the Bible. The story began when a Levite and his unfaithful concubine wife stopped overnight in Gibeah, a city located in the tribal territory of Benjamin (19:1-15).
  B. The couple stayed with an old man. That night his house was surrounded by a group of sex perverts who demanded the Levite come out and partake of their disgusting and degrading actions. The cowardly Levite saved himself by giving his wife over to this miserable mob. By morning time the perverts had sexually murdered her (19:16-27).
  C. The Levite (who apparently was emotionally sick himself) thereupon cut her dead body into twelve pieces, and sent a bloody chunk to each tribe in Israel along with the story of what happened (19:28, 29).
  D. Israel was enraged at this sexual crime and gathered an army of some 400,000 troops to punish the guilty perverts of Gibeah (19:30—20:11).
  E. The citizens of Benjamin, however, refused to surrender the criminals and a civil war broke out. After an especially bloody three-battle war in which Israel lost 40,000 men, Benjamin was defeated. When the body "dead count" was in, only 600 out of some 26,000 soldiers of Benjamin were left alive. A sobered and saddened Israel then provided wives for these 600, lest the very name of Benjamin disappear from the face of the earth (20:12—21:25).

V. A Moabite Girl—Ruth (Ruth 1-4).
  A. Chapter one: Ruth renouncing.
    1. During a famine, a Bethlehem citizen named Elimelech (which means, "God is King"), his wife Naomi ("the sweet one") and their two sons, Mahlon and Chilion ("sick" and "pining") leave Palestine and go into Moab (Ruth 1:1, 2).
    2. The two boys marry, but soon tragedy strikes, for at first the father dies, and then both sons, leaving three saddened widows (1:3-5).
    3. Naomi decides to return to Palestine and is accompanied by her older daughter-in-law, Ruth. Naomi attempts to persuade Ruth to go back to her own home. Ruth's answer must be counted as one of the most beautiful statements ever to come from the human throat. She says (in Ruth 1:16, 17):
      "And Ruth said, Intreat me not to leave thee, or to return from following after thee: for whither thou goest, I will go; and where thou lodgest, I will lodge: thy people shall be my people, and thy God my God: where thou diest, will I die, and there will I be buried: the Lord do so to me, and more also, if ought but death part thee and me."
    4. Ruth and Naomi begin their difficult trip, walking nearly 100 miles and crossing mountains a mile high. Upon their return, a disillusioned Naomi instructs her old neighbors to call her "Mara," which means, "bitter," and not Naomi (1:20-22).
  B. Chapter two: Ruth requesting.
    1. Ruth goes out to glean wheat and, in the providence of God, picks a field belonging to Boaz, a near relative of Elimelech (2:1-3). Boaz was the son of the ex-harlot, Rahab (Mt. 1:5).
    2. Boaz sees her, and apparently falls in love with her. He treats her kindly and orders his hired hands to do the same (2:15, 16).
    3. Ruth brings home some thirty pounds of barley and reports the kindness of Boaz to Naomi, who immediately begins planning a wedding (2:19-23).
  C. Chapter three: Ruth resting.
    1. Naomi sends Ruth to Boaz with instructions for her to assume a position at his feet. This has been looked upon by some as an immoral act, but no one who knew the custom of Israel and the ancient oriental world would make such a claim. According to Hebrew law, Ruth was entitled to call upon her nearest of kin to fulfill the various duties of a kinsman redeemer. By this course of action, Ruth was doing just this. Boaz understood fully her request to: "spread therefore thy

skirt over thine handmaid; for thou art a near kinsman" (3:9).

From this point on, Boaz took the necessary steps to marry Ruth. This custom is still practiced to some extent among the Arabs today.

2. Boaz then explains to Ruth why he had not proposed marriage to her before this time: "There is a kinsman nearer than I" (3:12).
3. Ruth returns home to Naomi with a full report. Naomi reassures her concerning Boaz by the following words:

"Then said she, Sit still, my daughter, until thou know how the matter will fall: for the man will not be in rest, until he have finished the thing this day" (3:18).

D. Chapter four: Ruth reaping.
  1. Boaz called a council meeting to determine whether the nearest kinsman (who may have been a brother to Elimelech) wanted to assume his obligations (4:1-4).

    Note: Boaz's heart must have dropped to his knees when the man said, "I will redeem

RUTH
A Moabite Girl

Chapter One
Ruth Renouncing

- A citizen from Bethlehem named Elimelech, his wife Naomi, and their two sons move to Moab during a famine.
- The boys marry Moabite girls, but soon both father and sons die, leaving three widows.
- Naomi returns to Bethlehem, accompanied by one of her daughters-in-law, named Ruth, who had renounced her Moabite gods for the true God of Israel.

Chapter Two:
Ruth Requesting

- In the providence of God Ruth gleans wheat in a field owned by Boaz, a near relative of Elimelech.
- At their first meeting, Boaz falls in love with Ruth.
- Upon learning of this, Naomi begins planning for the wedding.

Chapter Three:
Ruth Reaping

- Naomi sends Ruth to Boaz, that she might request of him to fulfill his responsibility as a kinsman redeemer.
- Boaz is thrilled with Ruth's request, but tells her there is a kinsman redeemer closer than he.
- Ruth returns home and leaves the matter with God.

Chapter Four:
Ruth Rejoicing

- Boaz arranges a meeting with the closer kinsman redeemer.
- Upon hearing the facts, he steps aside and allows Boaz to fulfill the kinsman redeemer responsibilities, including marriage to Ruth.
- Ruth presents Boaz with a male baby which is named Obed.

it" (4:4). But Boaz continues the meeting, saying:

"What day thou buyest the field of the hand of Naomi, thou must buy it also of Ruth the Moabitess, the wife of the dead, to raise up the name of the dead upon his inheritance" (4:5).

With a great sigh of relief, and no doubt a silent prayer of thanksgiving to God, Boaz hears the nearest kinsman conclude:

"I cannot redeem it for myself, lest I mar mine own inheritance: redeem thou my right to thyself; for I cannot redeem it" (4:6).

2. The issue was no longer in doubt. Boaz would now marry Ruth. To confirm this decision, the man plucked off his shoe. It was the custom at that time in Israel for a man transferring a right of purchase to pull off his sandal and hand it to the other party. This publicly validated the transaction (4:7-10).
3. In time, God gave Boaz and Ruth a son named Obed. Obed would grow up and father a boy named Jesse, who would in turn have a son called David. Thus a Moabite girl who was once heathen would become the great-grandmother of King David, and be included in the New Testament genealogy of the Lord Jesus Christ. (See Mt. 1:5). This is perhaps one of the most thrilling examples of God's marvelous grace in all the Bible.

IV. A Dedicated Mother—Hannah (1 Sam. 1:1—2:11, 18-21).

A. The account begins when a barren woman stands weeping and praying at the altar in Shiloh. Her name was Hannah. We note her prayer in 1 Samuel 1:11.

We observe several factors in this request:
  1. Part of Hannah's sorrow was due to constant ridicule from her husband's other wife, Peninnah (1:6). God never sanctioned polygamy, for it always brought grief and frustration. (See Gen. 21:9-11; 30:1.)
  2. Dr. John Davis writes concerning this prayer of Hannah:

    "In great bitterness of soul she prayed to the Lord and the essence of this prayer is wrapped up in two words found in verse 11, 'remember me.' These words have a familiar ring to them. One is reminded of the simplicity of Samson's prayer recorded in Judges 16:28. In blindness and helplessness he cried out to his God and asked to be 'remembered.'

    This prayer was also found on the lips of a man being crucified at Calvary. One of the malefactors who was hanged with Jesus looked to Him with faith and said, 'Lord remember me when thou comest into thy kingdom.'" (See Lk. 23:42.) (*Conquest and Crisis*)
  3. Hannah vows that if a son is given to her, she will raise him as a Nazarite. Thus her boy, Samuel, would become one of the three Nazarites mentioned in the Bible. The other two were Samson (Jdg. 13) and John the Baptist (Lk. 1).

THE SORROWING, SINGING SAINT

Hannah

Her Sorrow 1 SAMUEL 1:1-19

● Hannah was a barren and ridiculed woman.
● Even her anguished prayer was misinterpreted in the Temple by Eli the priest.
● She promised God that any son given her would be raised as a Nazarite.
● She is reassured about this from God through Eli.

Her Song 1 SAMUEL 1-2

● Hannah gives birth to Samuel.
● Upon weaning him she brings him to Eli for Temple service unto God.
● She sings a hymn of praise to God for:
  1. Blessing the poor and humble over the rich and proud
  2. Keeping the feet of his saints
  3. Rightfully judging the earth
● In her hymn she utters a Messianic prophecy: "He shall give strength unto his king, and exalt the horn of his anointed" **(2:10)**.
● Hannah later has three additional sons and two daughters. **(1 SAM. 1:20—2:11, 18-21).**

4. In her soul's agony, Hannah moves her lips, but makes no audible sound, which causes the old high priest Eli (who has been secretly watching her) to conclude that she is drunk (1:12, 13).

B. Upon being rebuked for this supposed drunkenness, Hannah immediately denies the charge and then shares with Eli the true nature of her heartache. The old priest thereupon reassures her that God will indeed answer her prayer (1:14-18).

C. In the course of time God did "remember" Hannah (compare with Gen. 8:1) with a son whom she called Samuel. When he was weaned (probably at two or three years of age) Hannah brought him to Eli to dedicate him to God (1 Sam. 1:26-28).

D. After the dedication, Hannah utters a beautiful ode of praise which appears to be the basis of Mary's song found in Luke 1:46-55. (See 1 Sam. 2:1-11.)

VII. An Undisciplined Priest—Eli (1 Sam. 2:12-17, 22-36; 4:1-22).

A. A sad note is now introduced concerning the priestly sons of Eli. According to the sacred account:
1. They were unsaved (2:12).
2. They regarded Belial as the true God (2:12).
3. They stole the offerings from God (2:14).
4. They bullied the people of God (2:14).
5. They committed adultery right in the tabernacle (2:22).
6. They caused God's people to transgress (2:17, 24).

B. Eli attempts to correct this by a mild and weak "slap on the wrist," but his wicked sons remain unmoved and unrepentant (2:22-25).

C. Eli was warned by an unnamed prophet of God concerning the following:
1. That his two wicked sons would both die on the same day (2:34).
2. That God would raise up a faithful priest (2:35).
   Note: There has been some speculation concerning the identity of this "faithful priest." Let us briefly examine this:
3. God originally instituted the priesthood through Aaron, who was a descendant of Levi (Ex. 28:43; 29:9).
4. Aaron had four sons. Two were slain by God due to their wickedness (Lev. 10). The other two were Eleazar and Ithamar. The line of the high priest was apparently to continue through Eleazar. At his death, Phinehas took office (Num. 25:11-13).
5. However, after this, for some unexplained reason, the line was shifted from Eleazar's line to that of Ithamar in the person of Eli.
6. Some Bible students feel that the verse in 1 Samuel 2:35 is a reference to Zadok, from the line of Eleazar, who would later be the faithful spiritual advisor to King David (1 Ki. 1:7, 8). This prophecy also indicates that there would never lack a descendant of Zadok to walk before God's anointed kings. Zadok's seed will walk before Christ in the millennium temple (Ezek. 44:15; 48:11; 43:19).

D. God revealed himself to Samuel one night as the boy lay in his bed in the Temple. The bulk of this divine message was the future judgment of Eli's household. The next morning a reluctant Samuel relates all this to Eli (3:1-18).

E. Samuel is now elevated by God to the office of a prophet (3:19-21).

Eli
THE UNDISCIPLINED PRIEST FATHER

SINS OF HIS SONS
They were unsaved **(1 Sam. 2:12)**
They regarded Belial as the true god **(2:12)**
They stole the offerings from God **(2:14)**
They bullied the people of God **(2:14)**
They committed adultery right in the tabernacle **(2:22)**
They caused God's people to transgress **(2:17, 24)**

WARNINGS TO HIS SONS
By God through an unnamed prophet **(2:34)**
By God through the boy Samuel **(3:1-18)**

DEATH OF HIS SONS
Israel is defeated by the Philistines **(1 Sam. 4:1-10)**
The ark is captured **(4:11)**
Eli's sons are killed **(4:11)**
Eli learns of this, falls from his seat, and dies **(4:12-18)**
His daughter-in-law dies in childbirth, but not before naming her baby boy Ichabod **(4:19-22)**

F. After this, Israel is soundly defeated by the Philistines. During the battle, the Ark of the Covenant is captured, and Eli's two sons, Hophni and Phinehas, are killed (4:1–11).

G. The tragic news is brought back to Shiloh, which results in the death of Eli and the total despair of his daughter-in-law (1 Sam. 4:14, 18–22).

VIII. Some Frustrated Philistines (1 Sam. 5–6).

A. The captured Ark of the Covenant proved a curse among the Philistines wherever it was taken.

1. At Ashdod, it destroyed the statue of the idol god Dagon and smote the people with boils (5:1–7).

2. At Gath it wrought great destruction and similar boils (5:8, 9).

3. At Ekron it brought great fear and more boils (5:10).

Note: Dr. John Davis writes the following concerning the various plagues suffered by the Philistines:

"Many feel that this is one of the first references to the 'black death,' or bubonic plague. This is inferred from the mention of tumors and mice (possibly rats) that 'marred the land.'" (See 6:4, 5.) (*Conquest and Crisis*)

B. The ark is then placed by the Philistines on a wooden cart hitched to two cows. On this cart are also placed five golden mice (6:1–11).

C. The ark is carried to an Israelite town called Beth-shemesh, where it is first received with great rejoicing, but later brings great sorrow, for some foolish men look into the ark and cause a divine punishment from God (6:12–19).

D. From Beth-shemesh, the ark is taken to another Israelite town named Kirjath-jearim. Here it was to remain for twenty years (7:1, 2).

IX. A Circuit-riding Preacher—Samuel (1 Sam. 7).

"And Samuel grew, and the Lord was with him, and did let none of his words fall to the ground. And all Israel from Dan even to Beer-sheba knew that Samuel was established to be a prophet of the Lord. And the Lord appeared again in Shiloh . . . [and] revealed himself to Samuel" (1 Sam. 3:19–21).

A. At this time the great prophet and priest Samuel gathers all of Israel at Mizpeh (another town in Palestine) for a great revival (7:3–6).

B. When the Philistines hear of this gathering, they mobilize their armies and prepare to attack. But at Samuel's cry, God steps in and utterly routs the Philistines (7:7–14).

"So the Philistines were subdued, and they came no more into the coast of Israel: and the hand of the Lord was against the Philistines all the days of Samuel" (7:13).

"And Samuel judged Israel all the days of his life. And he went from year to year in circuit to Bethel, and Gilgal, and Mizpeh, and judged Israel in all those places. And his return was to Ramah; for there was his house; and there he judged Israel; and there he built an altar unto the Lord" (7:15–17).

SAMUEL, THE CIRCUIT-RIDING PREACHER

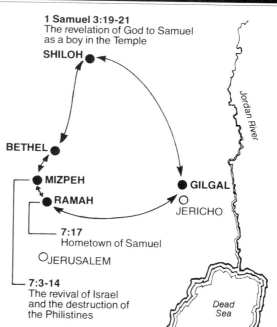

1 Samuel 3:19-21
The revelation of God to Samuel as a boy in the Temple

SHILOH

BETHEL

MIZPEH

RAMAH

GILGAL

JERICHO

7:17
Hometown of Samuel

JERUSALEM

7:3-14
The revival of Israel and the destruction of the Philistines

Jordan River

Dead Sea

"And Samuel judged Israel all the days of his life. And he went from year to year in circuit to Bethel, and Gilgal, and Mizpeh, and judged Israel in all those places. And his return was to Ramah; for there was his house, and there he judged Israel, and there he built an altar unto the Lord"
1 SAMUEL 7:15-17

THE TRAVELING ARK

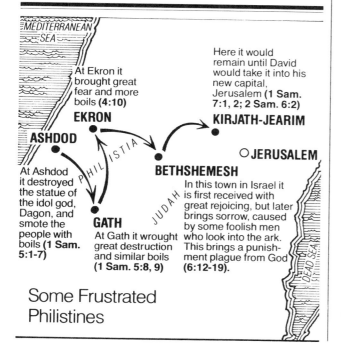

MEDITERRANEAN SEA

At Ekron it brought great fear and more boils (4:10)

EKRON

ASHDOD

At Ashdod it destroyed the statue of the idol god, Dagon, and smote the people with boils (1 Sam. 5:1-7)

GATH
At Gath it wrought great destruction and similar boils (1 Sam. 5:8, 9)

BETHSHEMESH
In this town in Israel it is first received with great rejoicing, but later brings sorrow, caused by some foolish men who look into the ark. This brings a punishment plague from God (6:12-19).

Here it would remain until David would take it into his new capital, Jerusalem (1 Sam. 7:1, 2; 2 Sam. 6:2)

KIRJATH-JEARIM

JERUSALEM

PHILISTIA

JUDAH

DEAD SEA

Some Frustrated Philistines

THE UNITED KINGDOM STAGE

INTRODUCING THE UNITED KINGDOM STAGE (1 Samuel 8–31; 2 Samuel; 1 Kings 1–11; 1 Chronicles; 2 Chronicles 1–9; Psalms; Proverbs; Ecclesiastes; Song of Solomon)

1. This stage, covering a period of approximately 120 years, records the history of Israel's first three kings. Each ruled for forty years. The kings are Saul, David, and Solomon.
2. Most of Israel's beautiful songs and words of wisdom were composed during this period. These would include: Psalms, Proverbs, Song of Solomon, and Ecclesiastes.
3. The period begins with the selection of a ruler (Saul, 1 Sam. 9) and ends with the rejection of another ruler (Rehoboam, 1 Ki. 12).
4. It includes a visit to the witch of En-dor (1 Sam. 28) and a visit by the Queen of Sheba (1 Ki. 10).
5. The death of two babies is noted. The first (2 Sam. 12) pointed out the wages of sin, while the second (1 Ki. 3) pointed out the wisdom of Solomon.

   "And David said unto Nathan, I have sinned against the Lord. And Nathan said unto David, The Lord also hath put away thy sin; thou shalt not die. Howbeit, because by this deed thou hast given great occasion to the enemies of the Lord to blaspheme, the child also that is born unto thee shall surely die" (2 Sam. 12:13, 14).

   "And the king said, Divide the living child in two, and give half to the one, and half to the other. Then spake the woman whose the living child was unto the king, for her bowels yearned upon her son, and she said, O my lord, give her the living child, and in no wise slay it. But the other said, Let it be neither mine nor thine, but divide it. Then the king answered and said, Give her the living child, and in no wise slay it: she is the mother thereof. And all Israel heard of the judgement which the king had judged; and they feared the king: for they saw that the wisdom of God was in him, to do judgement" (1 Ki. 3:25–28).

6. During this period a city is saved (1 Sam. 11), some animals are spared (1 Sam. 15), and a giant is slain (1 Sam. 17).
7. It describes a fearless prophet (Nathan, 2 Sam. 12), and a faithful priest (Zadok, 2 Sam. 15).
8. The Ark of God on two occasions is carried to Jerusalem, once during a celebration (2 Sam. 6), and again during a revolution (2 Sam. 15).

   "So David and all the house of Israel brought up the ark of the Lord with shouting, and with the sound of the trumpet. And they brought in the ark of the Lord, and set it in his place, in the midst of the tabernacle that David had pitched for it: and David offered burnt-offerings and peace-offerings, he blessed the people in the name of the Lord of hosts" (6:15, 17).

   "And David said unto all his servants that were with him at Jerusalem, Arise, and let us flee; for we shall not else escape from Absalom: make speed to depart, lest he overtake us suddenly, and bring evil upon us, and smite the city with the edge of the sword. And lo Zadok also, and all the Levites were with him, bearing the ark of the covenant of God:

THE UNITED KINGDOM STAGE

1 SAMUEL 8-31   PSALMS

2 SAMUEL   PROVERBS

1 KINGS 1-11   ECCLESIASTES

1 CHRONICLES   SONG OF

2 CHRONICLES 1-9   SOLOMON

and they set down the ark of God; and Abiathar went up, until all the people had done passing out of the city. And the king said unto Zadok, Carry back the ark of God into the city: if I shall find favour in the eyes of the Lord, he will bring me again, and shew me both it, and his habitation" (15:14, 24, 25).

9. A sister is raped (2 Sam. 13) and a son is hanged (2 Sam. 18).
10. A father's son (Jonathan) protects young David from the son's father (Saul, Sam. 20).
11. A heathen city becomes the Holy City (2 Sam. 5).
"And the king and his men went to Jerusalem unto the Jebusites, the inhabitants of the land: which spake unto David, saying, Except thou take away the blind and the lame, thou shalt not come in hither: thinking, David cannot come in hither. Nevertheless David took the strong hold of Zion: the same is the city of David. And David said on that day, Whosoever getteth up to the gutter, and smiteth the Jebusites, and the lame and the blind, that are hated of David's soul, he shall be chief and captain. Wherefore they said, The blind and the lame shall not come into the house" (2 Sam. 5:6–8).
12. Solomon is instructed (1 Ki. 2) and the Temple is constructed (1 Ki. 6).

THE UNITED KINGDOM STAGE

"And the Lord said to Samuel, hearken unto their voice, and make them a king" (1 Sam. 8:22).

The Rulers of This Stage

I. Saul, Israel's First King.
  A. The selection of Saul.
    1. The circumstances leading to his selection.
      a. Israel's elders gather at Ramah and demand that Samuel give them a king (8:3–20).
      b. Samuel is displeased and lists the many disadvantages of having a king (8:11–18).
      c. God nevertheless informs Samuel of his decision to give Israel a king and that he can expect the new leader at his doorstep in twenty-four hours (1 Sam. 9:16).
      d. The next day Saul unknowingly fulfills this prophecy by seeking Samuel's help in locating some lost animals (1 Sam. 9:18–20).
    2. The chronology of his selection.
      a. He is privately anointed by Samuel at Ramah (10:1).
      b. He is publicly acclaimed by Samuel at Mizpeh (10:24).
        Note: At this stage Saul was a very humble man. He felt he was unworthy of being king (9:21) and actually had to be brought out of hiding when Samuel officially proclaimed him king (10:21).
    3. The confirmation of his selection.
      a. Following his inaugural service, Saul returns to his farm in Gibeah (10:26).
      b. He later raises an army of 330 thousand to rescue a surrounded Israelite city called Jabesh-Gilead from a cruel enemy and thus establishes his ability to lead the kingdom (11:8–15).
      c. Samuel then gathers Israel to Gilgal, and

there delivers his final recorded sermon to the people.
        (1) He warns both people and their king of the follies of disobeying God (12:25).
        (2) God emphasizes this warning by the miracle of thunder and rain (12:18).
  B. The rejection of Saul (1 Sam. 13:1—15:9). This Saul caused:
    1. By offering the sacrifice of a priest (13:9).
    2. By ordering the death of his own son. Saul had foolishly ordered no food to be eaten by his troops until the Philistines were defeated. Jonathan, his son, unaware of the command, ate some honey. The people, however, refused to let Saul carry out his foolish law and thus saved Jonathan (14:45). God saved Israel that day; this was done in spite of Saul's stupidity, through three things:
      a. Jonathan's battle plan and personal courage (14:6)
      b. a divine earthquake (14:15)
      c. panic among the Philistine troops (14:19)
    3. By opposing the command of God to destroy a pagan named Agag and his city (15:9). This event was significant because:
      a. It marked the total rejection of Saul by God (15:11).
      b. It illustrated a great biblical principle. When Saul lamely excused his actions in not killing the animals as instructed, but in saving them for sacrificial reason, he heard the stern rebuke of Samuel:
        "And Samuel said, Hath the Lord as great delight in burnt offerings and sacrifices, as in obeying the voice of the Lord? Behold, to obey is better than sacrifice, and to hearken than the fat of rams. For rebellion is as the sin of witchcraft, and stubbornness is as iniquity and idolatry. Because thou hast rejected the word of the Lord, he hath also rejected thee from being king" (1 Sam. 15:22, 23).
        In other words, it is better to obey than to sacrifice (for sins) because when one obeys God in the first place, he need not offer a sacrifice. (It is therefore better to apply the principle laid down in Eph. 6:13 than the one found in 1 John 1:9.)
      c. It was the last meeting between Saul and Samuel until Samuel died (15:35).
II. David, Israel's Finest King (1 Sam. 16—2 Sam. 31; 1 Chron. 11–29).
  A. David the shepherd (16:1–13).
    1. Samuel is instructed to visit the house of Jesse in Bethlehem and anoint one of his eight sons as King of Israel.
    2. Samuel is furthermore admonished to, "Look not on his countenance, or on the height of his stature . . . for the Lord seeth not as man seeth; for man looketh on the outward appearance, but the Lord looketh on the heart" (16:7).
    3. After God rejects the first seven sons, David is fetched from the sheep pasture and anointed by Samuel (16:11–13).

B. David the singer (16:14-23).
   1. King Saul is from this point on troubled by an evil spirit.
   2. The fame of David's skill as an accomplished harpist causes Saul to issue a "command performance," and David readily agrees.
   3. David's beautiful music helps the troubled Saul.
C. David the soldier (17).
   1. Jesse sends David with some food for his brothers who are soldiers in Saul's army.
   2. Israel at this time was engaged in battle with the Philistines.
   3. Upon arriving, David views a giant Philistine warrior who had for forty days (17:16) brazenly insulted the armies of Israel and their God, taunting them to send forth a soldier to do battle with him and thus determine the war. The giant's name was Goliath; he was approximately ten feet high. He wore a bronze helmet, a 200-pound coat of mail, bronze leggings, and carried a bronze javelin several inches thick, tipped with a twenty-five-pound iron spearhead.
   4. David accepts this challenge and, armed with only the sling of a shepherd, kills the giant with a stone which he hurls into his forehead.
D. David the sought (1 Sam. 18-31).
   1. He now begins his lifelong friendship with Jonathan, Saul's son (1 Sam. 18:1-4).
   2. He is made commander-in-chief of Saul's armies (1 Sam. 18:5).
   3. He receives the praise of the Israelite women for slaying Goliath (1 Sam. 18:6, 7). These women sang concerning how Saul had slain his thousands, but David his ten thousands. Apparently the Philistines would also later hear of this song. (See 1 Sam. 21:11; 29:5.)
   4. He incurs the wrath of Saul (1 Sam. 18:8).
   5. Saul makes his first attempt to kill David (1 Sam. 18:11).
   6. He is demoted from general to a captain in Saul's armies (1 Sam. 18:13).
   7. Saul attempts to have the Philistines kill David, by falsely promising his daughter to wife for defeating the enemy (1 Sam. 18:19).
   8. Saul then promises his second daughter, Michal, to David if he can kill 100 Philistines. David thereupon goes out and kills 200 (1 Sam. 18:20-27).
   9. David marries his first of many wives, Michal (1 Sam. 18:27, 28).
   10. Saul attempts to kill him again with a javelin (1 Sam. 19:10).
   11. David escapes Saul's next murderous attempt by being lowered down through his own bedroom window with the help of Michal (1 Sam. 19:12).
   12. David goes to Ramah and reports all this to Samuel (1 Sam. 19:18).
   13. Jonathan warns David of Saul's renewed efforts to kill him (1 Sam. 20:18-22, 35-42).
   14. David goes to Nob and (after lying about the nature of his visit) receives bread and a sword from Ahimelech, the high priest (1 Sam. 21:1-9).

15. He then goes to the Philistine city of Gath and fakes insanity before King Achish (1 Sam. 21:10-15).
16. David makes the Cave of Adullam his headquarters and begins gathering his "outlaw army." This army at first totaled 400 men (1 Sam. 22:1, 2).
17. During this period three of his mighty men slipped through enemy lines to bring David the drink of water from the well in Bethlehem he had so longed for. David was so impressed that he refused to drink it, but poured it out as an offering to God (1 Chron. 11:16-19).
18. David goes to Moab, but is ordered back to Judah through the mouth of Gad, the prophet of the Lord (1 Sam. 22:3-5). God had already gone to the trouble of bringing David's great grandmother from Moab into Judah. (See Ruth 1.)
19. A vicious Edomite named Doeg betrays Ahimelech to Saul, whereupon the insane king orders the slaughter of eighty-five priests at Nob simply because Ahimelech had offered some bread to David (22:12-19).
20. David receives Abiathar, one of Ahimelech's sons, who alone had escaped Saul's bloody slaughter of the priests at Nob (1 Sam. 22:20-23).
21. David saves the Israelite city of Keilah from the Philistines (1 Sam. 23:5).
22. He then is warned by God to flee the city, for the fickle citizens were preparing to hand him over to Saul (1 Sam. 23:10-12).
23. He now has an army of 600 men (1 Sam. 23:13).
24. Jonathan and David meet in the woods of Ziph and renew their friendship (1 Sam. 23:16-18).
25. Saul surrounds David in the wilderness of Maon, but upon hearing the report of a Philistine invasion, is forced to leave before capturing him (1 Sam. 23:26-28).
26. David spares Saul's life in a cave in the wilderness of En-gedi, by cutting off a piece of Saul's coat when he could have sliced off his head (1 Sam. 24:1-15).
27. David's heart immediately smote him for this act of disrespect (1 Sam. 24:5). (This "smiting" was to be recorded on two future occasions, as well.)
    a. After his sin with Bath-sheba (2 Sam. 12:13).
    b. After numbering the people of Israel (2 Sam. 24:10). (Psalm 7 may have been written at this time.)
28. Saul acknowledges both his stupidity and the fact that he knew God had chosen David to rule Israel (1 Sam. 24:16-22).
29. David marries his second wife, Abigail. She was the widow of an arrogant and rich Judean sheepherder who had refused to help David in his time of need and for this reason was slain by the Lord ten days later (25:1-42). (Just prior to this, Samuel had died and was buried at Ramah.)
30. David marries his third wife, Ahinoam

(1 Sam. 25:43). Note: His first wife, Michal, had been given by Saul to another man (25:44). Ahinoam would later give birth to Amnon (see 2 Sam. 3:2).

31. David spares Saul's life the second time on a hillside in the wilderness of Ziph. To prove this to Saul, he orders one of his men to take the spear and water canteen while the king lies sleeping (1 Sam. 26:1-16).

32. Saul once again acknowledges his wickedness and promises no more to seek his life (1 Sam. 26:17-24). Note: The wicked and frustrated king, apparently, this time, kept his word.

33. David backslides and moves to the Philistine city of Ziklag (1 Sam. 27:1).

34. David now completes his army of mighty men. These men were known for:
    a. their strength (1 Chron. 12:2, 8)
    b. their spiritual perception (1 Chron. 12:18)

35. During this time, a period of sixteen months, David carries out numerous plundering raids upon various non-Israelite cities, but convinces the Philistine king, Achish, that the cities are indeed Israelite ones. (See 1 Sam. 27:8-12.)

36. Saul visits the witch of En-dor in a desperate attempt to call up Samuel from the dead in order to receive advice concerning a fearful Philistine military threat (28:1-11).

37. Samuel appears, apart, however, from any actions of the evil witch, and predicts Saul's defeat and death on the battlefield the following day (28:12-25).

Note: The appearance of Samuel on this occasion has created a great deal of discussion among Bible scholars and has produced a number of viewpoints with regard to the precise nature of this event. They are as follows:

a. "The appearance of Samuel was not a literal one, but merely the product of psychological impressions. According to this view, the woman had permitted herself to become emotionally involved and psychologically identified with the prophet, so that she was convinced that he had actually appeared when called. Two objections can be raised against this view. The first is derived from verse 12, which indicates that when Samuel did appear, the medium cried out with a loud voice, apparently surprised or startled by his appearance. Such would not be the case if she were merely seeking a vision produced by 'psychological excitement.' Second, the general reading of the text leads one to the conclusion that not only did the woman speak with Samuel, but Saul spoke with him as well (cf. v. 15).

b. A demon or Satan impersonated Samuel. Those holding this view argue for the idea that a visible form of Samuel himself appeared, which was in reality merely an impersonation of him. Many who defend this view argue that God would not permit a woman of this type to actually disturb the rest of a godly man. The whole affair is therefore considered a satanic or demonic deception of Saul. The advocates of this view remind us that Satan can appear as 'an angel of light' (2 Cor. 11:14) and, therefore, has the ability to carry out such deceptions. In evaluating this view, it should be pointed out that the basic reading of the biblical text leads one to the conclusion that this was actually Samuel and not an impersonation. While it is true that Satan can perform such deception, it is highly doubtful that he has the prophetic knowledge necessary to reveal that which was given to Saul in this chapter. Furthermore, if this were a demon or an evil spirit, it is improbable that he would have given the prediction found in this passage. More likely, in the light of the godly character of David and the wickedness of Saul, the demonic power would have flattered Saul with a positive prophecy.

c. The whole thing was a deliberate imposture practiced upon Saul. The witch really did not see Samuel, but fooled Saul into believing that her voice or that of someone else was that of Samuel. Those maintaining this view point out that only the woman saw Samuel and reported his words. Saul heard and saw nothing. A number of objections may be raised against this view. In the first place, the Bible does not specifically say that the woman reported Samuel's words; on the contrary, it makes it clear that Samuel spoke directly to Saul. Orr's statement that the king 'saw and heard nothing' is in direct conflict with the obvious reading of the text (cf. v. 15ff). It is also highly doubtful that she was in a position to predict the outcome of the battle and specifically forecast the death of Saul's sons. It is also unlikely, from a practical point of view, that she would give such a forecast to a man obviously aligned with the Israelite camp.

d. The most popular view and that which is maintained by most orthodox commentators is that this was a genuine appearance of Samuel brought about by God himself. In favor of this proposal is the Septuagint reading of 1 Chronicles 10:13 which is as follows: 'Saul asked counsel of her that had a familiar spirit to inquire of her, and Samuel made answer to him.' Furthermore, the fact that she cried out when she saw Samuel indicated that she did not bring up Samuel and did not expect him to appear in this manner. The fact that Saul bowed himself to the ground and did obeisance is a further indication that this was a real appearance of Samuel. It is doubtful that he would have reacted merely on the grounds of a verbal description or a false impression.

Samuel's statement to Saul in verse 15 should not be regarded as a proof of the fact that the witch of En-dor or Saul brought him back from the dead. What, then, was the purpose of God in bringing Samuel back for this appearance? This unusual act on the part of God was certainly designed to emphasize the doom of Saul and God's displeasure for his coming to a necromancer. Robert Jamieson suggests three additional reasons: (1) To make Saul's crime an instrument of his punishment, (2) To show the heathen world God's superiority in prophecy, and (3) to confirm a belief in a future state after death. Two other men who made an appearance on the earth after death were Moses and Elijah at the transfiguration of Christ (Mt. 17:3; Lk. 9:30, 31). They, however, appeared 'in glory,' but Samuel ap-

peared in the mantle which he had worn while on earth. Therefore, in a real sense the appearance of Samuel after death was a completely unique event." (*The Birth of a Kingdom,* John J. Davis, pp. 96–99)

King Saul, HIS RISE AND FALL

RISE

1 SAMUEL 8
Israel demands a king. Reasons for this:
Samuel was getting old.
His sons were wicked.
Israel wanted to be like all other nations.

1 SAM. 9
Saul is chosen by Samuel at God's command.
Saul seeks Samuel's advice concerning some lost animals.
Samuel tells him of God's plans.

1 SAM. 10
Saul is anointed at Ramah and acclaimed at Mizpah.
He begins as a humble and somewhat reluctant ruler.
See 9:21; 10:22, 27; 11:12-15.

1 SAM. 11-12
His leadership is confirmed at the rescue of Jabesh-Gilead.
This Israelite city is surrounded by the Ammonites.
Saul raises an army and delivers the city.
He is urged by Samuel to always serve God.

FALL

STEP ONE:	He intrudes into the office of the priesthood **(1 Sam. 13)**.
STEP TWO:	He orders the death of his own son **(1 Sam. 14)**.
STEP THREE:	He spares Amalek, God's enemy **(1 Sam. 15)**.
STEP FOUR:	He is possessed by an evil spirit **(16:14; 18:10; 19:9)**.
STEP FIVE:	He attempts to kill David **(18:11, 21, 25; 19:1, 10, 15)**.
STEP SIX:	He curses and attempts to kill his own son **(20:30-33)**.
STEP SEVEN:	He slaughters eighty-five priests of God at the city of Nob **(22:17-19)**.
STEP EIGHT:	He goes to the witch of Endor and is slain on a battlefield **(1 Sam. 28, 31)**.

38. David foolishly volunteers to join the Philistines as they march to fight with Israel at Jezreel. But he is not fully trusted by the Philistine leaders, and his offer is refused (1 Sam. 29:1-11).

39. David avenges the sudden destruction of his adopted Philistine city Ziklag by totally slaughtering the guilty Amalekites (1 Sam. 30:1-18).

40. After this successful battle, David institutes an important statute and ordinance in Israel, which reads:
    "But as his part is that goeth down to the battle, so shall his part be that tarrieth by the stuff: they shall part alike" (1 Sam. 30:21-25).

41. Saul is defeated by the Philistines and is sorely wounded. He thereupon falls upon his sword to avoid torture at the hands of the enemy. His sons, including Jonathan, are also killed in battle (31:1-7).

E. David the sovereign (2 Sam. 1-10; 1 Chron. 11-19).

1. David hears the news of the death of Saul and Jonathan and grieves for them in Ziklag (2 Sam. 1:1-27). He orders the execution of an Amalekite soldier who attempted to take the credit for Saul's death.

2. At God's command, he returns to Palestine and is anointed at Hebron by the men of Judah as their king. This was his second anointing (2 Sam. 2:1-4). David is now around thirty and he will rule over Judah for the next seven and a half years (2 Sam. 5:5).

3. Abner, Saul's general, makes Ish-bosheth, Saul's son, king over the eleven tribes (2:8-10).

4. Joab arranges a meeting with Abner and murders many of his men. Abner is forced to kill Joab's brother Asahel in self-defense (2:18-23).

5. After a long war between Saul's house and David's house, Abner breaks with Ish-bosheth and attempts to negotiate with David (3:1, 21). David agrees to cooperate.

6. Joab hears of this and murders Abner (3:30).

7. At this time David gets Michal, his first wife, back. He then marries four more women, for a grand total of seven wives, while in Hebron (2 Sam. 3:2-5; 1 Chron. 3:1-4). It was in Hebron that four (of his many) children were born who would later bring sorrow to his life. They were:
   a. Amnon, who would rape his half-sister Tamar (2 Sam. 13:1-14)
   b. Tamar (2 Sam. 13:1)
   c. Absalom, who would kill Amnon for this and later lead a revolt against the king himself (2 Sam. 13:28; 15:13, 14)

d. Adonijah, who also would later attempt to steal David's throne while the old king lay dying (1 Ki. 1)

8. David learns of and bitterly laments the brutal murder of Abner (Saul's ex-captain) by Joab (David's captain) (2 Sam. 3:31-39). David would never forget this vicious act of revenge done by Joab to Abner. Nor did Joab stop here, for the king's beloved (and prodigal) son, Absalom, would later be murdered by Joab (see 2 Sam. 18:14). The viciousness of this crime was intensified in that it was done in Hebron, a city of refuge (see Josh. 21:13). In such a city not even the avenger of blood might slay the murderer without a trial (Num. 35:22-25). Joab probably murdered Abner for two reasons:

a. To avenge the slaying of his brother Asahel (2:23) by Abner. However, Abner had done this only in self-defense.

b. To protect his own position as commander-in-chief of David's armies.

Joab was the son of David's half-sister, Zeruiah (1 Chron. 2:16; 2 Sam. 17:25) and was therefore his nephew.

9. David avenges the murder of Ish-bosheth, Saul's fourth son, by executing his two murderers (2 Sam. 4:9-12). This was the turning point, for after the death of Ish-bosheth, nothing could stop David from having the kingdom of Israel. Much blood had now been shed to purchase David's throne. Death had claimed eighty-five priests, Saul, Jonathan, an Amalekite, Asahel, many Israelite soldiers, Abner, Ish-bosheth, and two captains. David was indeed (even though at that time unintentionally so) a bloody man. (See 1 Chron. 22:8.) How different would be David's perfect Son who shed only his own blood to obtain his eternal throne! (See 1 Pet. 1:18, 19.)

10. David is anointed king over all Israel at Hebron. This marked his third anointing. It was a fantastic three-day celebration with nearly 400 thousand honor troops from the twelve tribes of Israel taking part (2 Sam. 5:1-5; 1 Chron. 12:23-40). Especially helpful must have been those soldiers from the tribe of Issachar, for we are told they were: "Men that had understanding of the times, to know what Israel ought to do" (1 Chron. 12:32).

11. David then captured Jerusalem and made it his permanent capital. He enlarges his kingdom, hires Hiram, the King of Tyre, to build him a palace, and marries more wives and concubines (5:6-16).

12. He is victorious over the Philistines twice during this time. Both victories were at the hand of God (2 Sam. 5:17-25).

13. David brings the Ark of the Covenant (2 Sam. 6:1-19; 1 Chron. 13:1-14; 15:1—16:43).

a. His method of carrying the ark (in a new cart) displeases God, resulting in the death of a man called Uzzah, and brings a three-month delay (2 Sam. 6:3, 7, 11).

b. Finally, with much shouting, singing, and making of music, the ark enters the city. A history of the ark up to this time is as follows:

(1) It was first made by Moses at God's command (Ex. 25:10-22).

(2) It was then transported along with the other tabernacle furniture through the forty-year wilderness journey.

(3) It was eventually set up in Shiloh, the first Israelite capital (Josh. 18:1).

(4) It was carried into battle and captured by the Philistines (1 Sam. 4:11).

(5) It was passed on among the Philistine cities like a hot potato (1 Sam. 5).

(6) It was brought to the city of Bethshemesh, where it caused a fearful plague (1 Sam. 6:19).

(7) It was brought to Kirjath-jearim where it resided twenty years (1 Sam. 7:1, 2).

c. David then appointed some of the Levites to "minister before the ark of the Lord, and to record, and to thank and praise the Lord God of Israel" (1 Chron. 16:4; 25:7). This choir, numbering 288, was to do nothing but praise and thank the Lord.

d. David now delivers his first recorded Psalm (1 Chron. 16:7-36).

14. Upon returning home, he is severely rebuked for all this "religious emotional nonsense" by his wife Michal (2 Sam. 6:20-23).

15. He desires to build a temple, but this request is not allowed by God (2 Sam. 7:17; 1 Chron. 17:4).

16. He is now given the Davidic Covenant from God (2 Sam. 7:8-17). This all-important covenant stated:

a. David is to have a child, yet to be born, who will succeed him and establish his kingdom.

b. This son (Solomon) shall build the Temple instead of David.

c. The throne of his kingdom shall be established forever.

d. The throne will not be taken away from him (Solomon) even though his sins justify chastisement. (See Ps. 89:33-37.)

e. David's house, throne, and kingdom shall be established forever. (See also Lk. 1:28-33, 68-75; Acts 15:13-18.)

17. He responds to this by offering a beautiful prayer of thanksgiving (2 Sam. 7:18-29).

18. He now consolidates his kingdom by defeating in rapid succession the Philistines, the Moabites, the Syrians, and the Edomites (2 Sam. 8:1-14).

19. He seeks out and shows kindness to Mephibosheth, Jonathan's lame son (2 Sam. 9:1-13).

20. The Ammonites spurn his act of kindness by humiliating his ambassadors and are soundly punished for this (2 Sam. 10:1-19).

The life of
DAVID

1. The Shepherd 1 SAMUEL 16:1-13
1. David, the eighth son of Jesse, is brought from a sheep field near Bethlehem and anointed by Samuel (1 Sam. 16:1-12).
2. The Spirit of God comes upon David (16:13).

2. The Singer 1 SAM. 16:14-23
1. King Saul is troubled by an evil spirit.
2. David's beautiful music on the harp helps soothe the troubled king (1 Sam. 16:14-25).

3. The Soldier 1 SAM. 17:1-58
1. A giant Philistine warrior named Goliath had defied the armies of Israel for forty days (17:16).
2. With but a sling and a stone, David kills this mighty soldier (17:49).

"The Lord hath sought him a man after his own heart...." 1 SAM. 13:14

4. The Sought 1 SAM. 18-31
1. He begins his lifelong fellowship with Jonathan (1 Sam. 18:1-4; 20:41, 42; 23:16-18).
2. His growing popularity incurs Saul's insane jealousy. Saul attempts to do him in by:
   A. Jonathan (compare 18:5 with 18:13)
   B. Private attempts on his life (18:11, 21, 25; 19:1, 10, 15)
   C. Trickery (18:25-27)
   D. Openly hunting him as a wild animal (23:15, 26; 24:2; 26:2, 17-20)
3. He marries Michal, the first of many wives (18:27).
4. He flees to the city of Nob, and in desperation lies to the high priest there (21:1-9).
5. He then travels to the Philistine city of Gath and fakes insanity (21:10-15).
6. He begins gathering his army of "spiritual outlaws" (22:1, 2; 23:13).
7. He goes to Moab but is ordered to Judah by God (22:3-5).
8. He spares the life of Saul on two occasions:
   A. In a cave in En-gedi (24:1-15)
   B. In a wilderness in Ziph (26:1-16)
9. He marries his second wife, a widow named Abigail (25:1-42).
10. Again he backslides and settles in the Philistine city of Ziklag (27:1-6).

5. The Sovereign 2 SAM. 1-10 1 CHRON. 11-19

1. Upon the death of Saul, by God's command he comes to Hebron and is anointed by the men of Judah as their king (2 Sam. 2:1-4).
2. After a seven-year war, David is successful over the house of Saul and is anointed at Hebron by all twelve tribes (2 Sam. 3-5).
3. He captures the city of Jerusalem and makes it his new capital (2 Sam. 5:6-10).
4. He then brings the Ark of the Covenant into Jerusalem (2 Sam. 6:1-19; 1 Chron. 15-16).
5. He desires to build a Temple for God, but is not allowed to do so (2 Sam. 7:17; 1 Chron. 17:4).
6. He now receives the all-important Davidic Covenant from God (2 Sam. 7:8-17; 1 Chron. 17:7-15). This covenant in essence predicted the millennial reign of Christ, the seed of David, upon the earth someday.
7. He seeks out and shows kindness to Mephibosheth, Jonathan's lame son (2 Sam. 9:1-13).

6. The Sinner 2 SAM. 11
1. David commits adultery with Bath-sheba.
2. He then arranges to have her husband, Uriah, killed on a battlefield (2 Sam. 11).

7. The Sorrowful **2 SAM. 12–21**
1 CHRON. 20, 21

1. Nathan the prophet confronts David about this, and the king confesses **(2 Sam. 12:1-12; Ps. 32, 51)**.
2. God forgives him, but determines David will pay back fourfold. **(Compare 12:5, 6 with 12:9-12.)** This will involve:
   A. The death of his infant son **(12:18)**
   B. The rape of Tamar, his daughter, by Amnon, his son **(13:14)**
   C. The murder of Amnon by his half-brother (and David's son) Absalom **(13:29)**
   D. The rebellion of Absalom against his father's own throne **(15-18)**

8. The Statesman **2 SAM. 21:1-14**

1. God had sent a three-year plague upon Israel to punish them for Saul's past sins against the nation Gibeon.
2. He stays the plague by negotiating with the Gibeonites, who agree justice can only be served by permitting them to execute seven of Saul's guilty sons **(2 Sam. 21:1-14)**.

9. The Statistician **2 SAM. 24**

1. He succumbs to the temptation of Satan and numbers Israel **(1 Chron. 21:1-6)**.
2. A divine plague occurs, which is finally stopped by David as he pleads with the death angel **(2 Sam. 24:15-25; 1 Chron. 21:18-30)**.

10. The Sponsor **1 CHRON. 22-29**

1. He presides over a great dedicatory service for the future Temple **(1 Chron. 22:5, 9, 10)**.
2. He himself contributes millions of dollars and helps raise additional millions **(1 Chron. 29:4, 6, 7)**.
3. He gives the Temple blueprints he received from God to Solomon **(28:19)**.
4. He then offers one of Scripture's most beautiful prayers **(29:10-19)**.

11. The Scribe **2 SAM. 22:1; 23:1-3**

David writes over half of the Psalms in the Word of God. "The spirit of the Lord spoke by me, and his Word was in my tongue" **(2 Sam. 23:2)**. See also **23:1-3; 22:1**.

12. The Sage **1 KINGS 2**

On his deathbed David exhorts Solomon to do the following:
1. Act like a man of God **(1 Ki. 2:2)**
2. Be true to the Word of God **(2:3)**
3. Rely on the promises of God **(2:4)**
4. Execute the judgment of God **(2:5)**

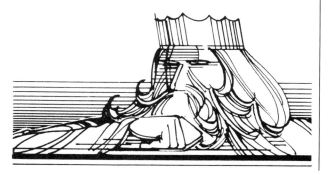

F. David the sinner (2 Sam. 11).
   1. The indulgent king lusts after and lies with Bath-sheba, the wife of Uriah, one of his soldiers.
   2. Bath-sheba becomes pregnant and reports this to David.
   3. Uriah is hurriedly called home from the battlefield under a pretext that he might visit his wife and thus later believe that the unborn child would be his.
   4. Uriah apparently realizes the truth of the situation and refuses to cooperate.
   5. In an act of desperation, David sends him back with a sealed letter to Joab to arrange for his death in battle.
   6. Uriah is killed and David marries Bath-sheba.
G. David the sorrowful (2 Sam. 12–21; 1 Chron. 20, 21).
   1. After Bath-sheba's child is born, Nathan the prophet relates to David a story of how a rich farmer who owned thousands of sheep stole a little pet lamb from a poor farmer, his only one, butchered and ate it (12:1–4).
   2. David's anger knows no limit and he vows that the cruel rich man will pay back fourfold for his sin (12:5, 6).
   3. Nathan then boldly points out to David that he, the king, is that man.
   4. David confesses his sin and repents (12:13).
   5. God forgave David, but would require his servant to pay back fourfold, the same price the king would have made the rich man pay.
   6. Seven days after David's confession, the first installment comes due, for the child dies (12:18).
   7. The king accepts this by faith, believing he will someday see him again (12:23).
   8. Solomon is born (12:24).
   9. David fights his last recorded battle against an outside enemy and defeats Rabbah, the capital city of Ammon (12:29).
   10. David's son, Amnon, lusts after and eventually rapes his own half-sister, Tamar. The second installment on David's debt had come due (13:14).
   11. Absalom, the full brother of Tamar, begins plotting the murder of Amnon and kills him two years later. This would be installment number three (13:29).
   12. Absalom flees into the desert and stays with his pagan grandfather for three years (13:38).
   13. Joab employs a crafty woman from Tekoah to trick David into permitting Absalom to return to Jerusalem.
   14. Absalom returns, but is refused an audience with his father for two years. Finally, after Absalom burned a barley field to get attention, David agrees to see him (14:33).
   15. Absalom begins planning a revolt against his father. After four years, he is ready, and instigates the plot in Hebron (15:12).
   16. The rebellion gathers strength and David is forced to leave Jerusalem. God had now exacted the fourth installment (15:14).

17. David is accompanied into the wilderness by Ittai (a foreign guest who, along with his 600 soldiers, sides in with him) (2 Sam. 15:18–22).
18. Abiathar and Zadok also accompany him. However, David orders these joint high-priests back to Jerusalem. They return, carrying God's ark with them (2 Sam. 15:24–29).
19. David walks up the road to the Mount of Olives and weeps (2 Sam. 15:30).
20. Upon learning that his advisor Ahithophel has joined Absalom's rebellion, the king prays, "O Lord, I pray thee, turn the counsel of Ahithophel into foolishness" (2 Sam. 15:31).
21. David then orders another advisor, Hushai, also to pretend to sell out to Absalom, that he might frustrate and counter Ahithophel's advice (2 Sam. 15:34). Absalom listens to both counselors. Ahithophel advises an immediate "hit-'em-where-they-aren't" frontal attack, before David can muster his forces. Hushai, however, appeals to the vain pride of Absalom by suggesting that they wait until a larger army can be raised and that Absalom himself lead the attack. This inferior advice was heeded, whereupon Ahithophel went home and hanged himself (17:1–23).
22. He now meets Ziba, the manager of Mephibosheth's household, who brings him food, but who lies about his master to feather his own nest (2 Sam. 16:1–4).
23. David is cursed out and has stones thrown at him by Shime-i, a member of Saul's family (2 Sam. 16:5–8). In spite of this, David refuses to order his execution (16:10–12).
24. Absalom enters Jerusalem and possesses David's concubines (16:22).
25. David is warmly greeted by Shobi (an Ammonite), and others, who offer him mats to sleep upon and food to eat (2 Sam. 17:27–30).
26. Out of loving concern, David's armies refuse to allow him into the battle with Absalom (2 Sam. 18:3).
27. He sends his troops into battle in the woods of Ephraim, but orders the life of Absalom to be spared (2 Sam. 18:5, 6).
28. Absalom's green soldiers are no match for David's seasoned troops and they quickly lose some twenty thousand men and the entire battle (18:7).
29. Absalom attempts to escape, but is caught in some underbrush and killed by Joab (18:14).
30. David learns of Absalom's death at Joab's hand and grieves over his dead son (18:33; 19:1–4).
31. Joab severely rebukes him for this (19:5–7).
32. He begins his trip back to Jerusalem and promises to appoint his nephew Amasa as head of his armies if Amasa can get the people of Judah (who had been miffed at David) to back his return to power (19:13, 14).
33. He spares the life of Shime-i, who falls at his feet at the river Jordan and begs forgiveness (19:23).
34. He meets Mephibosheth and hears why his lame friend did not join him in the wilderness (19:24–30).
35. He meets Barzillai, who had befriended him in the wilderness, and invites the old man to accompany him to Jerusalem and live there (19:34–37).
36. Upon crossing Jordan, David is confronted with yet another rebellion, this one led by Sheba, a Benjaminite. Ten tribes now desert David. Only Judah and Benjamin remain loyal (20:1–3).
37. David instructs Joab to crush this revolt. This Joab does at a city called Abel, but prior to this, Joab brutally murders Amasa, thus eliminating a dangerous rival (20:6–22).
38. David thereupon once again returns to Jerusalem, a sadder and wiser man. He would have more troubles later, but they would not include wars and rebellions. He could now burn the mortgage on his sin-debt with Bathsheba.

H. David the statesman (2 Sam. 21:1–14).
1. A three-year plague from God had settled down upon Israel. David is told it was because of the bloody house of Saul in the past when he slew the Gibeonites.
2. In Joshua 9, Israel had made a covenant with these Gibeonites that they would not be harmed. This sin was now being punished.
3. David negotiates with the Gibeonite leaders, and they determine that justice can be done only by allowing them to execute seven of Saul's sons, all of whom doubtless had participated in the former Gibeon massacre. This is done and the plague is stayed.

I. David the statistician (2 Sam. 24).
1. David succumbs to the temptation of Satan and numbers Israel (1 Chron. 21:1–6).
2. He later repents of this and is offered by God one of three kinds of punishment:
   a. seven years of famine
   b. to flee ninety days before his enemies
   c. a three-day pestilence
3. He chooses the third (2 Sam. 24:15).
4. As a result, 70,000 men die. The plague is stopped by David at a threshing floor as he pleads with God's death angel. David later buys this floor (2 Sam. 24:15–25; 1 Chron. 21:18–30).

J. David the sponsor (1 Chron. 22–29).
1. David is now nearly seventy. When he was but thirty-seven, he determined to build the Temple for God, but was forbidden by the Lord to do so (22:7, 8).
2. The old king is, however, allowed to lead in the preparations for the Temple which Solomon will construct (22:5, 9, 10).
3. David therefore makes the following preparations:
   a. the blocks of squared stone which will be used in the Temple (22:2)
   b. great quantities of iron for the Temple nails (22:3)
   c. a huge supply of cedar logs (22:4)
   d. three million dollars in gold bullion (22:14)
   e. two million dollars' worth of silver (22:14)

f. 24,000 Levites to supervise the Temple work (23:4)

g. 6,000 Levites to be Temple bailiffs and judges (23:4)

h. 4,000 Levites to act as Temple guards (23:5)

i. 4,000 Levite musicians to head up the praise service (23:5)

j. a special Temple choir of 288 skilled singers (25:1, 7)

4. David then calls a special dedicatory service and does the following:

a. He hands over the Temple blueprints to Solomon, which plans he received directly fom God's hand (28:19).

b. He personally contributes to the work of an offering totaling 85 million dollars of gold and 20 million dollars of silver (29:4).

c. His action immediately prompts Israel's leaders to pledge $145 million in gold, $50 thousand in foreign currency, $30 million in silver, 800 tons of bronze, and 4600 tons of silver, in addition to great amounts of jewelry (29:6, 7). Thus the total of David's preparation must have exceeded $200 million.

d. He then offers one of the most beautiful prayers in all the Bible (1 Chron. 29: 10-19).

e. This dedicatory service was ended by a massive sacrificial service, which included a thousand young bulls, a thousand rams, and a thousand lambs, all offered up as burnt offerings (29:21).

K. David the scribe: Of the 150 Psalms, David wrote seventy-seven. The Psalms are discussed at the end of this stage.

L. David the sage (1 Ki. 2:2-5).

III. Solomon, Israel's fabulous king (1 Ki. 1-11; 2 Chron. 1-9).

A. His triumph over his enemies (1 Ki. 1:1—2:46).

1. Over Adonijah.

a. While David is on his deathbed, his oldest living son, Adonijah, attempts to steal the throne from his half-brother, Solomon. He is supported by Joab and Abiathar (1:7).

b. Solomon, however, is supported by Nathan, the Prophet; Bath-sheba, his mother; Zadok, the high priest; and Benaiah, one of David's mighty men of old (1:8-11).

c. Bath-sheba visits her dying husband, and arranges for Solomon to be anointed by Zadok (1:39).

d. Adonijah is placed on probation, but later executed when he makes a power play for the throne by attempting to marry Abishag, who had been David's last concubine (1:3; 2:17, 25).

2. Over Abiathar (2:26, 27). Because of his faithfulness to David, Abiathar is allowed to live but is banished from the priesthood.

3. Over Joab (2:28-34). This bloody general is finally executed, not only for his part in Adonijah's rebellion, but for many past crimes which included the murders of Abner and Amasa.

4. Over Shimei (2:36-46). Shimei, like Adonijah, is for a while placed on parole, but he breaks this trust and suffers the death penalty for it. At the execution of Shimei, David's dying request has been fulfilled by Solomon, for he had asked that justice be done to both Joab and Shimei (2:5, 8).

B. His talent from God (3:4-28).

1. Solomon is visited by the Lord in a dream while in Gideon to make sacrifice. God tells him he may have anything he desires and the new king asks for wisdom (3:6-9).

2. When he returns to Jerusalem, he is immediately confronted with a situation which tests his newly acquired wisdom. Two harlot mothers approach him concerning two babies, one dead and the other living. Both mothers claim the living one as theirs. Solomon suggests he divide the living child with a sword and give half to each woman. The real mother, of course, is horrified at this, and thus her true identity is revealed (3:16-28).

C. His total and tranquil reign over all Israel (1 Ki. 4:1-34). Solomon's reign at this time is a beautiful foreshadowing of Christ's perfect millennial reign. Thus we see:

1. Solomon had twelve cabinet members to aid in his reign (1 Ki. 4:7). Jesus will confer this upon his twelve disciples (Mt. 19:28).

2. Solomon ruled "over all kingdoms" in the Holy Land area (1 Ki. 4:21), while Christ will rule over all kingdoms everywhere (see Rev. 11:15).

3. Solomon's subjects served him as we will serve Christ (1 Ki. 4:21; Rev. 22:3).

4. Solomon brought in local peace (1 Ki. 4:24), as Christ will usher in universal peace (Isa. 2:2-4).

5. Judah and Israel dwelt safely, "every man under his vine" (1 Ki. 4:25). So will it be during Christ's reign (Jer. 23:6; Micah 4:4; Zech. 3:10).

D. His Temple of worship (1 Ki. 5-8; 2 Chron. 2-7).

1. The preparation.

a. It was begun in May during Solomon's fourth year and completed in November of his eleventh year, thus making a total of seven years (1 Ki. 6:38).

b. It was exactly twice the size of Moses' tabernacle, ninety feet long, thirty feet wide, and forty-five feet high. (Compare with Ex. 26:16, 18.)

c. It was built by the partial slave labor project instituted by Solomon, which consisted of 100,000 Israelites, 80,000 stone cutters, and 3,600 foremen.

d. The floors and walls were made of stone covered with cedar and overlaid with gold (1 Ki. 6:16, 21, 22).

e. It was built without the sound of hammer, axe, or any other tool (1 Ki. 6:7).

f. It had ten lampstands and ten tables of shewbread (1 Ki. 7:49), as opposed to one each in Moses' tabernacle.

g. Solomon paid King Hiram of Tyre nearly a million bushels of wheat and some 840 gallons of pure olive oil for the timber alone from the forest of Lebanon to construct the Temple shell (5:8-11).

h. There were two golden cherubim in the Holy of Holies (1 Ki. 8:7).

2. The dedication. Solomon briefly reviews the historical circumstances which led up to this glad day (1 Ki. 8:12-21; 2 Chron. 6:1-11).

3. The supplication (1 Ki. 8:22-53; 2 Chron. 6:12-42). Solomon prays that the influence of this beautiful Temple will extend itself in a threefold manner:

a. Over the individual (1 Ki. 8:31, 32).
   (1) That sinners will be judged.
   (2) That the righteous will be justified.
b. Over the nation.
   (1) That its sins might be forgiven (vs. 33-35).
   (2) That its land might be healed (vs. 36, 37).
   (3) That Israel might be preserved in captivity (vs. 44-50).
c. Over the heathen (vs. 41-43).

4. The benediction (1 Ki. 8:54-61).

5. The manifestation (2 Chron. 7:1-3). "Now when Solomon had made an end of praying, the fire came down from heaven and consumed the burnt offering and the sacrifices; and the glory of the Lord filled the house."

6. The presentation (1 Ki. 8:62-66; 2 Chron. 7:4-10). This offering, consisting of 120 thousand sheep and twenty-two thousand oxen, was the largest in the Bible, and perhaps of all time.

E. His treasury of riches.

1. He had 700 wives and 300 concubines (1 Ki. 11:3).

2. He had fantastic quantities of gold.
   a. from Hiram he acquired three and a half million (9:14)
   b. from his navy, 420 talents of gold (9:27, 28)
   c. from the Queen of Sheba, three and a half million (10:10)
   d. from yearly taxes and revenue, upwards of 20 million (10:14)

3. He owned 40,000 horses (4:26).

4. He owned 1400 chariots, each costing $400 apiece (10:26).

5. He commanded 12,000 cavalrymen (10:26).

6. He owned an extensive fleet of ships (1 Ki. 9:26-28; 10:22; 2 Chron. 8:17, 18).

7. He built a huge ivory throne and overlaid it with pure gold. It had six steps and a rounded back with arm rests. It was surrounded by twelve lions, two resting on each step (10:18-20).

8. He constructed an iron-smelting industry at Ezion-Geber (1 Ki. 9:17).

F. His testimony throughout the land (1 Ki. 4:29-34; 10:1-13).

1. The ruler of Arabia came to see for herself the riches of Solomon and also to test his

Solomon

Triumph over his enemies
1 KINGS 1-2
- Adonijah
- Abiathar
- Joab
- Shimei

Talent from God
1 KINGS 3:4-28
- The talent—wisdom
- The test—a baby and a sword

Total and tranquil reign
1 KINGS 4
A beautiful type of Christ's millennial rule

Temple of worship
1 KINGS 5-8; 2 CHRONICLES 2-7
- Twice the size of the tabernacle
- Seven years in construction

Treasury of riches
4:26; 9:17, 26-28; 10:22, 26; 11:3
- Much gold
- Many horses and chariots
- A fleet of ships

Testimony throughout land
4:29-34; 10:1-13
As testified by the Queen of Sheba

Transgressions against God
1 KINGS 11
He disobeyed **(Deut. 17:14-17)** and accumulated:
- Much gold
- Many wives
- Many horses

universally famed wisdom. She entered Jerusalem a skeptic, but left with this testimony: "I believed not the words, until I came and mine eyes had seen it: and behold, the half was not told me: thy wisdom and prosperity exceedeth the fame which I heard" (1 Ki. 10:7).

Some nine centuries later the Savior would refer to this historic visit. (See Mt. 12:42.)

2. Solomon's wisdom was testified to universally in matters of:
   a. jurisprudence (1 Ki. 3:28)
   b. administration (1 Ki. 4:29; 5:12)
   c. poetry (1 Ki. 4:32) (Solomon's writings are discussed at the end of this stage.)
   d. natural science (1 Ki. 4:33)
   e. architecture and engineering (1 Ki. 5:1-7; 9:15-22)
   f. commercial enterprise (1 Ki. 9:26—10:29)
   g. philosophy (Eccles. 2:3)
   h. horticulture (Eccles. 2:5)

G. His transgressions against God:
1. The warnings to Solomon against transgressing.
   a. from David
      (1) first warning (1 Chron. 22:13)
      (2) last warning (1 Ki. 2:3)
   b. from God
      (1) first warning (1 Ki. 3:14)
      (2) second warning (9:6, 7)
      (3) last warning (11:11)
2. The nature of Solomon's transgressions. Some four and one-half centuries before Solomon, God had written the following qualifications concerning all future kings of Israel:

"When thou art come unto the land which the Lord thy God giveth thee, and shalt possess it, and shalt dwell therein, and shalt say, I will set a king over me, like as all the nations that are about me; thou shalt in any wise set him king over thee, whom the Lord thy God shall choose: one from among thy brethren shalt thou set king over thee: thou mayest not set a stranger over thee, which is not thy brother. But he shall not multiply horses to himself, nor cause the people to return to Egypt, to the end that he should multiply horses: forasmuch as the Lord hath said unto you, Ye shall henceforth return no more that way. Neither shall he multiply wives to himself, that his heart turn not away: neither shall he greatly multiply to himself silver and gold" (Deut. 17:14-17).

But Solomon disobeyed in all three areas.
   a. He had much gold and silver (1 Ki. 10:14-27).
   b. He owned thousands of horses (4:26).
   c. He gathered hundreds of wives and concubines (11:3).
3. The results of Solomon's transgressions:
   a. That he would, for the first time in his reign, be plagued with troublemakers and minor revolts (11:14-25).
   b. That after his death, God would take the kingdom from Solomon's son and give a large portion of it to another (11:9-13, 26-40).

The Writings of This Stage

I. The Psalms. There are three basic ways to study the Psalms: (1) by book division, (2) by authorship, and (3) by subject matter.
   A. By book division (each ends with a doxology).
      1-41 (corresponds to Genesis) Key word is *man*.
      "Blessed is the man that walketh not in the counsel of the ungodly, nor standeth in the way of sinners, nor sitteth in the seat of the scornful" (1:1).
      "What is man, that thou art mindful of him? and the son of man, that thou visitest him?" (8:4).
      "What man is he that feareth the Lord: him shall he teach in the way that he shall choose" (25:12).
      "O taste and see that the Lord is good: blessed is the man that trusteth in him" (34:8).
      "What man is he that desireth life, and loveth many days, that he may see good?" (34:12).
      "The steps of a good man are ordered by the Lord: and he delighteth in his way" (37:23).
      "Mark the perfect man, and behold the upright: for the end of that man is peace" (37:37).
      "Blessed is that man that maketh the Lord his trust, and respecteth not the proud, nor such as turn aside to lies" (40:4).
      42-72 (corresponds to Exodus) Key word is *deliverance*.
      "And call upon me in the day of trouble: I will deliver thee, and thou shalt glorify me" (50:15).
      "For he hath delivered me out of all trouble: and mine eye hath seen his desire upon mine enemies" (54:7).
      "For thou hast delivered my soul from death: wilt not thou deliver my feet from falling, that I may walk before God in the light of the living?" (56:13).
      "Deliver me from mine enemies, O my God: defend me from them that rise up against me" (59:1).
      "Deliver me out of the mire, and let me not sink: let me be delivered from them that hate me, and out of the deep water" (69:14).
      "Deliver me in thy righteousness, and cause me to escape: incline thine ear unto me, and save me" (71:2).
      "For he shall deliver the needy when he crieth; the poor also, and him that hath no helper" (72:12).
      73-89 (corresponds to Leviticus) Key word is *sanctuary*.
      "Until I went into the sanctuary of God; then understood I their end" (73:17).
      "They have cast fire into thy sanctuary, they have defiled by casting down the dwelling place of thy name to the ground" (74:7).
      "Thy way, O God, is in the sanctuary: who is so great a God as our God?" (77:13).
      "And he built his sanctuary like high palaces, like the earth which he hath established for ever" (78:69).
      90-106 (corresponds to Numbers) Key words are *unrest, wanderings*. (See chapters 90 and 106.)
      107-150 (corresponds to Deuteronomy) Key phrase is *Word of God*. (See chapter 119.)

B. By authorship.
  1. David
     a. The Shepherd Psalms: 8, 19, 23, 29, 144
     b. The Sinner Psalms: 32, 51, 38
     c. The Suffering Psalms: 3, 4, 5, 6, 7, 11, 12, 13, 14, 17, 22, 25, 26, 27, 28, 31, 34, 35, 39, 40, 41, 53, 54, 55, 56, 57, 58, 59, 61, 62, 63, 64, 69, 70, 86, 109, 140, 141, 142, 143
     d. The Satisfied Psalms: 2, 9, 15, 16, 18, 20, 21, 24, 30, 36, 37, 52, 60, 65, 68, 72, 95, 101, 103, 105, 108, 110, 122, 124, 131, 133, 138, 139, 145
  2. Korah: 42, 44, 45, 46, 47, 48, 49, 84, 85, 87
  3. Asaph: 50, 73, 74, 75, 76, 77, 78, 79, 80, 81, 82, 83
  4. Heman: 88
  5. Ethan: 89
  6. Solomon: 127
  7. Moses: 90
  8. Hezekiah: 120, 121, 123, 125, 126, 128, 129, 130, 132, 134
  9. Anonymous: 1, 10, 33, 43, 66, 67, 71, 91, 92, 93, 94, 96, 97, 98, 99, 100, 102, 104, 106, 107, 111, 112, 113, 114, 115, 116, 117, 118, 119, 135, 136, 137, 146, 147, 148, 149, 150
C. By subject matter.
  1. The Devotional Psalms: 4, 9, 12, 13, 14, 16, 17, 18, 19, 22, 23, 24, 27, 30, 31, 33, 34, 35, 37, 40, 42, 43, 46, 50, 55, 56, 61, 62, 63, 66, 68, 69, 71, 73, 75, 76, 77, 80, 81, 84, 85, 88, 90, 91, 94, 95, 100, 103, 106, 107, 111, 115, 116, 118, 119, 122, 123, 126, 133, 136, 138, 139, 141, 142, 144, 147, 148, 149, 150
  2. The Penitential Psalms: 6, 32, 38, 51, 102, 130, 143
  3. The Imprecatory Psalms: 35, 55, 58, 59, 69, 83, 109, 137, 140
  4. The Degree or Ascent Psalms: 120 through 134
  5. The Hallel (Hallelujah) Psalms: 113 through 118
  6. The Historical Psalms: 78, 105, 106
  7. The Acrostic Psalms: 9, 10, 25, 34, 37, 111, 112, 119, 145
  8. The Messianic Psalms: 2, 8, 16, 22, 23, 24, 31, 34, 40, 41, 45, 55, 68, 69, 72, 89, 102, 109, 110, 118, 129

We shall now study the Psalms by the subject matter method.

The Devotional Psalms

These seventy Psalms have been titled "devotional" because they contain (among other things) precious and personal promises which all believers can feed upon. In dealing with these, sometimes only the promise itself will be quoted with no comment. On other occasions, a word or so may be added. These Psalms include both sobbing and singing. The authors will at times pout, doubt, and shout. They review the past and preview the future. Here the naked soul of man is manifested as perhaps in no other writings.

  1. Psalm 4
     Selection:
     "But know that the Lord hath set apart him that is godly for himself; the Lord will hear when I call unto him" (4:3).

"I will both lay me down in peace, and sleep: for thou, Lord, only makest me dwell in safety" (4:8).
     Reflection:
     Here David's praying brought him peace and sleep. One of the sweetest fringe benefits of the Christian life is peace. Note: "The Lord . . . will bless his people with peace" (Ps. 29:11).
     "Great peace have they which love thy law: and nothing shall offend them" (Ps. 119:165).
  2. Psalm 9
     Selection:
     "The wicked shall be turned into hell, and all the nations that forget God" (9:17).
     Reflection:
     This will someday become a horrible reality. (See Ps. 11:6; Mt. 25:31–46; Rev. 14:10; 19:20; 20:11–15; 21:8.)
  3. Psalm 13
     Selection:
     "How long wilt thou forget me, O Lord? for ever? how long wilt thou hide thy face from me?" (v. 1).
     "How long shall I take counsel in my soul, having sorrow in my heart daily? How long shall mine enemy be exalted over me?" (v. 2).
     Reflection:
     One popularly held misconception about the Bible is that its heroes were men who differed entirely from other men; they never suffered defeat, they never became discouraged, they were at all times successful, saintly, and supremely happy. Absolutely nothing could be further removed from the truth. The fact is that all of them were "subject to like passions as we are" (Jas. 5:17). These men had all borne the bitter burden of defeat on many occasions. They were at times overwhelmed with despair as the sons and daughters of Adam are today. This despondency was often evident in their praying. Psalm 13 is such an example of soul-suffering supplication. Other notable examples are as follows:
     David's prayer in Psalms 6:1–7; 31:1–14
     Asaph's prayer in Psalm 77:1–20
     Heman's prayer in Psalm 88:1–18
     Unknown author's prayer in Psalm 102:1–11
     Jewish prisoner's prayer en route to Babylon in Psalm 137:1–6
     Moses' prayer in Numbers 11:1, 12, 14, 15
     Joshua's prayer in Joshua 7:6–9
     Elijah's prayer in 1 Kings 19:4, 10, 14
     Job's prayers in Job 3:3–12; 10:18–22
     Jeremiah's prayers in Jeremiah 4:10; 20:7–9, 14–18
     Jonah's prayer in Jonah 4:1–3
     Habakkuk's prayer in Habakkuk 1:2–4
     Korah's prayer in Psalms 42:3–11; 44:8–26
  4. Psalm 14
     Selection:
     "The fool hath said in his heart, there is no God. They are corrupt, they have done abominable works, there is none that doeth good" (14:1).
     Reflection:
     David here describes the atheistic fool. In biblical terms, a fool is a person with heart trouble, not head trouble. Note other kinds of fools in the Bible.
     a. The sin-mocking fool (Prov. 14:9).
     b. The wisdom-hating fool (Prov. 15:5).
     c. The strife-causing fool (Prov. 20:3).
     d. The glory-seeking fool (1 Sam. 26:21).
     e. The money-loving fool (Lk. 12:20).

f. The Christ-honoring fool (1 Cor. 4:10; the only "wise" fool in the bunch).

5. Psalm 17
Selection:
"Keep me as the apple of the eye, hide me under the shadow of thy wings" (17:8).
Reflection:
Here David uses two tender terms depicting God's affection for the believer.
   a. Apple of the eye. (See also Deut. 32:10; Zech. 2:8.)
   b. Shadow of thy wings. (See also Deut. 32:11, 12; Ps. 36:7; 57:1; 91:1, 4; Mt. 23:37.)

6. Psalm 18
Selection:
"He sent from above, he took me, he drew me out of many waters" (18:16).

"He brought me forth also into a large place: he delivered me, because he delighted in me" (18:19).

"For thou wilt light my candle: the Lord my God will enlighten my darkness" (18:28).

"Thou hast also given me the shield of thy salvation: and thy right hand hath holden me up, and thy gentleness hath made me great" (18:35).
Reflection:
In verse 16 he speaks of being drawn out of many waters. Water is often employed in the Psalms as a symbol for trouble and anguish. (See Ps. 69:1, 2; 144:7; Isa. 43:2.) In a very real sense, the daughter of Pharaoh, upon fetching a baby from the Nile, unconsciously nicknamed every child of God when she "called his name Moses . . . because I drew him out of the water" (Ex. 2:10). David here claims the Lord drew him out of many waters. Years later the Apostle John would write: "The Lamb . . . shall lead them unto living fountains of waters . . ." (Rev. 7:17).

7. Psalm 23
Selection:
(The entire Psalm) "The Lord is my shepherd; I shall not want."
Reflection:
This is undoubtedly the most famous prayer of all times, with the possible exception of the so-called Lord's prayer in Matthew 6:9–13.

David says the Lord is his Shepherd. Because of this, he continues, "I shall not want." Thus:
   a. When his soul needed spiritual refreshment, the Shepherd provided green pastures.
   b. When his soul was weary, the Shepherd provided still waters.
   c. When his soul needed revival, the Shepherd restored him.
   d. When his soul needed guidance, the Shepherd led him in right paths.
   e. When his soul was confronted with death, the Shepherd went with him.
   f. When his soul was confronted with enemies, the Shepherd provided his victory table.
   g. When his soul was wounded, the Shepherd anointed his head with oil.
   h. When his soul needed companionship, the Shepherd appointed goodness and mercy to accompany him.
   i. When David would leave this temporary earthly dwelling place, the Shepherd would provide a permanent heavenly dwelling place. Thus David's testimony was, "I shall not want." What a contrast to

compare this statement with the one that would later be written on a Babylonian banquet wall addressed to Belshazzar.
   The message was:
   ". . . God hath numbered thy kingdom, and finished it" (Dan. 5:26).
   "Thou art weighed in the balances, and art found wanting" (Dan. 5:27).
j. At this point, it is appropriate to consider what is known as the trilogy of the Psalms, that is, a comparison of Psalms 22, 23, 24. Note:
   Psalm 22 (Jn. 10:11)
   (1) the Good Shepherd
   (2) the Savior
   (3) the Foundation
   (4) Christ dying
   (5) the Cross
   (6) he gives his *life*
   (7) Grace
   Psalm 23 (Heb. 13:20)
   (8) the Great Shepherd
   (9) the Satisfier
   (10) the manifestation
   (11) Christ living
   (12) the Comforter
   (13) he gives his *love*
   (14) guidance
   Psalm 24 (1 Pet. 5:4)
   (15) the Chief Shepherd
   (16) the Sovereign
   (17) the expectation
   (18) Christ coming
   (19) the crown
   (20) he gives his *light*
   (21) glory

8. Psalm 34
Selection:
"This poor man cried, and the Lord heard him, and saved him out of all his troubles. The angel of the Lord encampeth round about them that fear him, and delivereth them. O taste and see that the Lord is good: blessed is the man that trusteth in him. O fear the Lord, ye his saints: for there is no want to them that fear him (34:6-9).
Reflection:
Our gracious heavenly Father often uses his angelic messengers to aid, protect, and encourage his earthly children. (See 2 Ki. 6:17; Heb. 1:14; Acts 12:7.)

9. Psalm 35
Selection:
"False witnesses did rise up; they laid to my charge things that I knew not. They rewarded me evil for good to the spoiling of my soul. But as for me, when they were sick, my clothing was sackcloth: I humbled my soul with fasting; and my prayer returned into mine own bosom" (35:11-13).
Reflection:
This type of praying is indeed difficult—to intercede for those in their need who perhaps do not even want to be prayed for and who would rejoice if the same calamity overtook you. But the believer is nevertheless commanded to pray such a prayer.

10. Psalm 37
Selection:
"Fret not thyself because of evildoers, neither be thou envious against the workers of iniquity. For they shall

soon be cut down like the grass, and wither as the green herb. Trust in the Lord, and do good; so shalt thou dwell in the land, and verily thou shalt be fed" (37:1-3).

"Delight thyself also in the Lord; and he shall give thee the desires of thine heart" (v. 4).

"Commit thy way unto the Lord; trust also in him; and he shall bring it to pass" (v. 5).

"Rest in the Lord, and wait patiently for him: fret not thyself because of him who prospereth in his way, because of the man who bringeth wicked devices to pass" (v. 7).

"The wicked plotteth against the just, and gnasheth upon him with his teeth" (v. 12).

"The Lord shall laugh at him: for he seeth that his day is coming" (v. 13).

"The Lord knoweth the days of the upright: and their inheritance shall be for ever" (v. 18).

"The steps of a good man are ordered by the Lord: and he delighteth in his way" (v. 23).

"Though he fall, he shall not be utterly cast down: for the Lord upholdeth him with his hand" (v. 24).

"I have been young, and now am old; yet have I not seen the righteous forsaken, nor his seed begging bread" (v. 25).

"For the Lord loveth judgment, and forsaketh not his saints; they are preserved for ever; but the seed of the wicked shall be cut off" (v. 28).

Reflections:

This prayer Psalm could be called "the climb to the sublime," or, "from frustration (v. 1) to exaltation" (v. 34). There are five rungs in this ladder of ascent as given in the first several verses. Fret not—I have a problem.

Trust—I believe God can answer my problem.

Delight—I believe he will answer my problem.

Commit—I bring my problem to him.

Rest—I leave my problem with him.

In the Psalms God is pictured as laughing at two things:

a. the attempts of the wicked to dethrone his son (Ps. 2:2-4)

b. the attempts of the wicked to destroy his saints (Ps. 37:13; 59:8)

Often in the Psalms the one praying will ask the Lord to impress upon him the brevity of this life, so that he might commit each precious day to his Creator. This is referred to here (37:18) and in other prayers:

"My times are in thy hand . . ." (Ps. 31:15).

"Lord, make me to know mine end, and the measure of my days, what it is: that I may know how frail I am" (Ps. 39:4).

"So teach us to number our days, that we may apply our hearts unto wisdom" (Ps. 90:12).

"How many are the days of thy servant?" (Ps. 119:84) In this Psalm verses 23, 24, 25 and 28 describe God's Social Security plan for his workers along with all its fringe benefits.

11. Psalm 40

Selection:

"I waited patiently for the Lord; and he inclined unto me, and heard my cry. He brought me up also out of an horrible pit, out of the miry clay, and set my feet upon a rock, and established my goings. And he hath put a new song in my mouth, even praise unto our God: many shall see it, and fear, and shall trust in the Lord" (40:1-3).

"Many, O Lord my God, are thy wonderful works which thou hast done, and thy thoughts which are to us-ward: they cannot be reckoned up in order unto thee: if I would declare and speak of them, they are more than can be numbered" (v. 5).

Reflections:

Verses 1-3 illustrate the differences between Christianity and all other religions. Consider this story: Here is a man who has fallen into a dark and foul pit, breaking his legs and arms as he lands. Soon his helpless and pain-wracked cries for air proceed from the pit. In this illustration, Confucius comes by, looks down, and says: "Friend, let me give you this sage advice: If you ever get out of there, take heed where you walk, that you fall not again into such a place." With this, the Chinese philosopher walks on.

Awhile later, Buddha passes by and views the helpless man. He says: "Friend, you need help. If you can meet me halfway, I'll aid in your escape. Just climb a bit and stretch your hands toward me." But the broken and bleeding victim cannot move. Buddha then sadly walks away. The desperate man huddles in his prison of pain, his hope almost gone. But he utters one final cry for salvation. Then the Savior of all men gazes down upon him with loving compassion. Without a word of advice or admonishment, he slips down into the pit, tenderly places the fallen traveler over his strong shoulders, and climbs out of the pit with him. He then sets the broken bones, points the man's feet toward heaven, and puts a song in his heart! This is *salvation*. In verse 5 of this prayer, David mentions God's wonderful works performed for him, and God's countless thoughts about him. Other passages bring this precious truth into focus (see Ps. 92:5; 139:17, 18; Jer. 29:11).

12. Psalm 42

Selection:

"Why art thou cast down, O my soul? and why art thou disquieted in me? Hope thou in God: for I shall yet praise him . . . (42:5). (See also 42:11; 43:5.)

Reflection:

These three verses are mentioned here because of their remarkable repetition. It is often rather jokingly observed by the world that it is all right for a man to talk to himself, but if he answers himself—this is bad. But not according to Korah! He both asks *and* answers his own questions. This self-assurance of one's own soul is a good practice. Sometimes it is helpful for a person to lecture and console himself as he would another.

13. Psalm 46

Selection:

"God is our refuge and strength, a very present help in trouble. Therefore will not we fear, though the earth be removed, and though the mountains be carried into the midst of the sea: Though the waters thereof roar and be troubled, though the mountains shake with the swelling thereof" (46:1-3).

"The heathen raged, the kingdoms were moved: he uttered his voice, the earth melted. The Lord of hosts is with us; the God of Jacob is our refuge. Selah. Come, behold the works of the Lord, what desolations he hath made in the earth. He maketh wars to cease unto the end of the earth; he breaketh the bow, and cutteth

the spear in sunder; he burneth the chariot in the fire" (vs. 6-9).
Reflection:
This may become a favorite Psalm of that frightened Israelite remnant which may hide from the antichrist in Petra during the last terrible period of the great tribulation. (Isa. 26:19, 20; Rev. 6:12-14; especially Mt. 24:15, 16; Rev. 12:14).

14. Psalm 50
Selection:
"Gather my saints together unto me; those that have made a covenant with me by sacrifice" (50:5).

"For every beast of the forest is mine, and the cattle upon a thousand hills. I know all the fowls of the mountains: and the wild beasts of the field are mine. If I were hungry, I would not tell thee: for the world is mine, and the fulness thereof. Will I eat the flesh of bulls, or drink the blood of goats? Offer unto God thanksgiving; and pay thy vows unto the most High" (50:10-14).
Reflections:
There are those critics that have charged the Old Testament with presenting a bloodthirsty Hebrew tribal god who was more interested in gory sacrifices than in helping men. In this Psalm, Asaph lays the axe to that lie. He says God was more interested in the man's soul than in his sacrifices. Burning devotion was far more precious to him than bloody beasts. It was not the outward brazen altar that pleased the Lord, but the inward, heart altar. Moses had reminded Israel some four centuries previous to this of the same great principle. (See Deut. 10:12-16.)

15. Psalm 56
Selection:
"Thou tellest my wanderings: put thou my tears into thy bottle: are they not in thy book?" (56:8).

"For thou hast delivered my soul from death: wilt not thou deliver my feet from falling, that I may walk before God in the light of the living?" (56:13).
Reflections:
The sweet words in verse 8 here should comfort and cheer the most despondent heart. David asks God to preserve his tears. The author once traced the trail of human tears across the pages of the Bible during a personal study of his own. What a study it was. This sea of soul sorrow begins in Genesis and flows through every book, finally to crest itself in the Revelation of John.

One of the first instances of a believer weeping occurred when Abraham buried his beloved Sarah in a lonely and desolate cave somewhere in Hebron (Gen. 23:2).

This trickle continues and becomes a current as it is fed by the tears of Jacob for Joseph (Gen. 37:35), of Moses for Miriam (Num. 12:13), of Hannah for a son (1 Sam. 1:10), of Samuel for Saul (1 Sam. 15:11, 35), and of David for Absalom (2 Sam. 18:33). By this time the current has become a torrent, but is still growing. Hezekiah weeps for himself (2 Ki. 20:2, 3), Nehemiah for Jerusalem (Neh. 1:4), a father for his little girl (Mk. 5:39), and two sisters over their dead brother (Jn. 11).

This torrent, now an uncontrollable river, finds itself carrying the most precious tears of all, those belonging to our Savior. He weeps over Lazarus (Jn. 11:35) and over Jerusalem (Lk. 19:41). But at last, in the Book of Revelation, this swollen sea is dramatically and decisively stopped! The last recorded instance of a believer weeping is found in Revelation 5:5. Finally, God himself mops up all remaining traces (in Rev. 21:4).

16. Psalm 63
Selection:
"When I remember thee upon my bed, and meditate on thee in the night watches" (63:6).
Reflection:
In the Psalms we read of David praying at various times of the day. But especially did he enjoy seeking his Shepherd in the still of the night, as he relates here in verse 6. Consider his midnight messages to God: "Commune with your own heart upon your bed, and be still" (Ps. 4:4).

"Thou hast visited me in the night . . ." (Ps. 17:3).
"I cry . . . in the night season . . ." (Ps. 22:2).
"In the night his song shall be with me, and my prayer . . ." (Ps. 42:8).
"I call to remembrance my song in the night . . ." (Ps. 77:6).
"To shew forth . . . thy faithfulness every night" (Ps. 92:2).
"I have remembered thy name, O Lord, in the night . . ." (Ps. 119:55).
"Let the saints be joyful in glory: let them sing aloud upon their beds" (Ps. 149:5).

17. Psalm 66
Selection:
"If I regard iniquity in my heart, the Lord will not hear me" (66:18).
Reflection:
This absolute prayer principle is stated throughout the entire Bible and refers to both sinners and saints alike. The blood of Christ will forgive us of all our confessed sins, but will not cover even one of our miserable excuses. (See Prov. 15:29; 28:9; Isa. 1:15; 59:1, 2; Jn. 9:31; Jas. 4:3.)

18. Psalm 68
Selection:
"The chariots of God are twenty thousand, even thousands of angels" (68:17).
Reflection:
In verse 17 David numbers the angels in heaven among the thousands. This estimate is undergirded by other biblical references such as in Daniel 7:10, Mt. 26:53, and Revelation 5:11. Some five centuries later, a lonely and broken prophet would sit amid the debris of a dying and desolate Jerusalem, only recently leveled by the invading Babylonians. As he sat there he may have recalled David's testimony here in Psalm 68:19. At any rate, the prophet with the pierced heart wrote his testimony, based upon David's earlier one: "This I recall to mind, therefore have I hope. It is of the Lord's mercies that we are not consumed, because his compassions fail not. They are new every morning: great is thy faithfulness" (Lam. 3:21-23).

19. Psalm 69
Selection:
"But as for me, my prayer is unto thee, O Lord, in an acceptable time: O God, in the multitude of thy mercy hear me, in the truth of thy salvation" (69:13).
Reflection:
When is this "acceptable time"? A teacher once said to his Sunday school class: "Boys, the best time for a fella to prepare to meet God is the day before he dies." This at first seemed to be acceptable to the class, but then

one small boy raised his hand and exclaimed: "But teacher, sometimes a guy doesn't know about it twenty-four hours before he dies! What should he do then?" The teacher wisely replied: "Then boys, the *next* best time for a fella to prepare to meet God is today!" One of the most important theological concepts in the Scriptures is the doctrine of the present tense—of today.

God desires:

a. That the sinner give his heart to Christ today (2 Cor. 6:2).

b. That the saint give his body to Christ today (Rom. 6:19; 12:1–3; Heb. 3:7, 13, 15).

The obvious reason for all this haste is found in the following verses: Proverbs 27:1; James 4:13–15.

20. Psalm 71

Selection:

"For thou art my hope, O Lord God: thou art my trust from my youth" (71:5).

"Cast me not off in the time of old age; forsake me not when my strength faileth" (71:9).

"O God, thou hast taught me from my youth: and hitherto have I declared thy wondrous works" (71:17).

"Now also when I am old and grayheaded, O God, forsake me not; until I have shewed thy strength unto this generation, and thy power to every one that is to come" (71:18).

Reflection:

This could rightly be called, "The Psalm of the Old Man." One of the greatest "fringe benefits" afforded to the believer is that old age simply brings him all the closer to that glorious goal of being like Christ. This is totally different from all other earthly goals, such as in the field of sports and other professional careers, where youth, brains, strength, and looks are cruel taskmasters, and the unfortunate individual is crudely and rudely cast aside in his old age (see Ps. 25:7; 37:25; Eccles. 11:9, 10; 12:1).

21. Psalm 73

Selection:

"But as for me, my feet were almost gone; my steps had well nigh slipped" (73:2).

"For I was envious at the foolish, when I saw the prosperity of the wicked" (v. 3).

"They are not in trouble as other men; neither are they plagued like other men" (v. 5).

"Their eyes stand out with fatness: they have more than heart could wish" (v. 7).

"Behold, these are the ungodly, who prosper in the world; they increase in riches" (v. 12).

"Verily I have cleansed my heart in vain, and washed my hands in innocency" (v. 13).

"For all the day long have I been plagued, and chastened every morning" (v. 14).

"When I thought to know this, it was too painful for me; until I went into the sanctuary of God; then understood I their end. Surely thou didst set them in slippery places: thou castedst them down into destruction. How are they brought into desolation, as in a moment! They are utterly consumed with terrors" (73:16–19).

Reflections:

Asaph here asks a question that has bothered countless Christians throughout history: Why do the wicked prosper while the righteous suffer? Lazarus must have pondered it as he sat ill-clothed, ill-fed, and covered with running sores beside the gates of a heartless and thoughtless millionaire (Lk. 16:19–31). Samuel was

doubtless pained by the thought as he watched the anointed David fleeing from the arrogant Saul.

It is reported that some years ago an editor wrote in a farm magazine that while he was not a particularly religious man, yet he did see the wisdom of the biblical command to work six days and rest on the seventh. Soon after the publication of the article, an irate farmer wrote the editor, informing him that his article was pure hogwash! To prove this, he pointed out that that very year he had planted his crops on Sunday, cared for them on Sunday, and harvested them on Sunday. He closed gleefully with the words: "Now here it is October already and I have made more money this year than any of my so-called Christian farmer friends who did not work on Sunday!" The editor, upon receiving his letter, published it in the following issue along with his own terse observation which read:

"Dear Sir, God does not settle all his accounts in October!"

22. Psalm 75

Selection:

"For promotion cometh neither from the east, nor from the west, nor from the south. But God is the judge: he putteth down one, and setteth up another" (75:6, 7).

Reflection:

Perhaps no other king in all history attested more to the fearful accuracy of these words than did the mighty Babylonian monarch Nebuchadnezzar. He had dreamed of a mighty tree which had been cut down at God's command. Daniel rightly prophesied that God was warning the proud ruler to humble himself, lest he be cut down to size. Not only would this happen, but he would also suffer a seven-year period of insanity. But the haughty king refused to bend or bow. Then, the storm broke. (See Dan. 4:29–37.)

23. Psalm 76

Selection:

"Surely the wrath of man shall praise thee" (76:10).

Reflection:

Scriptural illustrations abound which prove the prayer statement found here. Consider:

a. The wrath of Esau caused Jacob to flee afar off, where he met Rachel—to the praise of God (Gen. 27:41–45; 29:10).

b. The wrath of eleven brothers sent Joseph to Egypt as a slave, where he later became prime minister—to the praise of God (Gen. 37:23–28; 41:38–44).

Later Joseph would remind his brothers of all this:

"But as for you, ye thought evil against me; but God meant it unto good, to bring to pass, as it is this day, to save much people alive" (Gen. 50:20).

c. A Moabite king in wrath attempted to curse Israel through a hireling prophet, but this resulted in a beautiful prophecy about Christ—to the praise of God (Num. 22:1–6; 24:17).

d. The wrath of Haman built a gallows to destroy a Jew but was himself hanged upon that same gallows—to the praise of God (Est. 5:12–14; 7:10).

e. The wrath of an Israelite king burned a book from God, but the book was thereupon rewritten with an addition which prophesied his own doom—to the praise of God (Jer. 36:22, 23, 27, 28, 29, 30, 31, 32).

   f. The wrath of the Pharisees placed Christ on the cross between two thieves, which resulted in the salvation of the dying thief—to the praise of God (Lk. 23:39–43).

   g. The wrath of a Roman emperor banished the Apostle John to a lonely isle to prevent him from preaching the gospel, resulting in the book of Revelation—to the praise of God (Rev. 1:9).

24. Psalm 80

Selection:

"Give ear, O Shepherd of Israel, thou that leadest Joseph like a flock; thou that dwellest between the cherubims, shine forth" (80:1).

"Thou hast brought a vine out of Egypt: thou hast cast out the heathen, and planted it" (80:8).

Reflection:

Here a reference is made to the cherubim. The two golden cherubim statues, some fifteen feet high, which stood over the mercy seat of the Ark of the Covenant in the Holy of Holies, were apparently meant to be representative of actual beings. They are mentioned some sixty-four times in the Bible. Note:

   a. Both Moses and Solomon placed them in the Holy of Holies (Ex. 25:19; 1 Ki. 6:27).

   b. God spoke to Moses from between the cherubim (Num. 7:89).

   c. Hezekiah spoke to God through the cherubim (2 Ki. 19:15).

   d. Ezekiel sees the glory of the Lord amid four flying cherubim (Ezek. 10).

   e. The millennial Temple is described as featuring the cherubim (Ezek. 41:17–20).

Aside from what has already been said about the cherubim, this psalm prayer of Asaph could rightly be titled "The Dying Vine Psalm." The vine is often used in the Bible as a symbol for Israel. Note what Asaph says about this vine. He declares:

   f. God brought it out of Egypt (v. 8).

   g. He planted this vine in his chosen land (v. 8).

   h. He cleared the ground and tilled the soil for his vine (v. 9).

   i. The vine took root and grew for awhile (v. 9).

   j. The vine covered the mountains and grew as high as cedar trees (v. 10).

   k. It traveled from the Great Sea to the Euphrates River (v. 11).

   l. But then God broke down the hedge protecting his vine (v. 12).

   m. Strangers then took their plunder of its grapes (v. 12).

   n. The wild boar rooted it and the wild beast ate it (v. 13).

   o. Its enemies chopped it and burned it (v. 16).

Why did God treat his vine like this? The answer is given very clearly. (See Isa. 5:1–4; Jer. 2:21; Hos. 10:1.) God desired that his chosen vine bear fruit to feed the hungry nations around it. But it did not do so. In the fullness of time, therefore, God set aside this wild and wicked and wasted vine. Our Lord Jesus solemnly and sadly declared this rejection in a lecture to the wicked Pharisees. He said: "Therefore I say unto you, The kingdom of God shall be taken from you, and given to a nation bringing forth the fruits thereof" (Mt. 21:43).

While he was upon earth, the Lord Jesus was God's blessed vine (Isa. 53:2), and bore goodly fruit through his miracles, parables, prayers, and sermons. But then it came time for the crucified and resurrected vine to ascend back into his Father's heavenly vineyard. Who then would bear the Father's fruit on earth? This thrilling plan is spelled out in detail for us in John 15:1–8. The believer is therefore to do that which Israel would not do—to bear fruit, more fruit, much fruit. This can only be done through abiding in him (prayer) and allowing his words to abide in us (Bible study). He is the vine, we are the branches. A branch exists for one sole purpose—to bear fruit. It cannot produce it, it simply bears it. It is good for nothing else. Its wood is not used for building or furniture making, nor can it be employed for fuel material. It is simply to bear and share its fruit.

25. Psalm 81

Selection:

"I am the Lord thy God, which brought thee out of the land of Egypt; open thy mouth wide, and I will fill it. But my people would not hearken to my voice; and Israel would none of me. So I gave them up unto their own hearts' lust: and they walked in their own counsels. Oh that my people had hearkened unto me, and Israel had walked in my ways! I should soon have subdued their enemies, and turned my hand against their adversaries" (81:10–14).

Reflection:

Nearly ten centuries later the rejected Redeemer of Israel would stand on Mt. Olive overlooking Jerusalem and powerfully voice similar words. (See Mt. 23:37–39.)

26. Psalm 84

Selection:

"Blessed is the man whose strength is in thee; in whose heart are the ways of them. Who passing through the valley of Baca make it a well; the rain also filleth the pools. They go from strength to strength, every one of them in Zion appeareth before God" (84:5–7).

Reflection:

Verse 7 speaks of growing in strength. This word *strength* is very important in the biblical vocabulary of prayer and sanctification. Note the statement describing man's inward strength as opposed to God's imparted strength.

Man's strength:

"My strength is dried up . . ." (Ps. 22:15).

"My strength faileth because of mine iniquity . . ." (Ps. 31:10).

"I retained no strength" (Dan. 10:8).

God's strength:

"Hast thou not known? hast thou not heard, that the everlasting God, the Lord, the Creator of the ends of the earth, fainteth not, neither is weary? There is no searching of his understanding. He giveth power to the faint; and to them that have no might he increaseth strength. Even the youths shall faint and be weary, and the young men shall utterly fall: But they that wait upon the Lord shall renew their strength; they shall mount up with wings as eagles; they shall run, and not be weary; and they shall walk, and not faint" (Isa. 40:28–31).

"Fear thou not; for I am with thee: be not dismayed; for I am thy God: I will strengthen thee; yea, I will help thee; yea, I will uphold thee with the right hand of my righteousness" (Isa. 41:10).

(See also Ps. 27:1; 28:7; 29:11; 43:2; 46:1; 81:1; 118:14; 119:28; Phil. 4:13; 1 Pet. 5:10; Eph. 3:16; Rom. 5:6; 2 Tim. 4:17; 2 Cor. 12:9.)

27. Psalm 85
Selection:
"Wilt thou not revive us again: that thy people may rejoice in thee?" (85:6).

"I will hear what God the Lord will speak: for he will speak peace unto his people, and to his saints: but let them not turn again to folly. Surely his salvation is nigh them that fear him . . ." (85:8, 9).

"Mercy and truth are met together; righteousness and peace have kissed each other" (85:10).

Reflections:
Perhaps no other prayer is more welcome in the ears of God than the one for revival, as expressed here in verse 6. Only a child of God can be revived. Sinners cannot be revived; they need to be resurrected. A dead person cannot be revived; only a live person can be or should be revived. Later, Habakkuk would pray a similar prayer for himself and the Israelite remnant:

". . . O Lord, revive thy work in the midst of the years, in the midst of the years make known; in wrath remember mercy" (Hab. 3:2). As millions of Christians throughout church history have discovered, God will hasten to answer the prayer of that soul who desires revival. But as Korah suggests in the last few words of verse 8, a true desire for revival carries with it a determination to abandon that sin which necessitated it in the first place.

There are many revivals recorded in the Bible. All of them were prompted by either prayer or Bible study or both. Consider these scriptural reforms and revivals:
  a. under Jacob (Gen. 35:2-4)
  b. under Moses (Ex. 14:31—15:21)
  c. under David (1 Chron. 15:25-28; 16:1-43; 29:10-25)
  d. under Solomon (2 Chron. 7:4-11)
  e. under Elijah (1 Ki. 18:21-40)
  f. under Asa (1 Ki. 15:11-15)
  g. under Jehu (2 Ki. 10:15-28)
  h. under Jehoiada (2 Ki. 11:17-20)
  i. under Josiah (2 Ki. 22, 23)
  j. under Jehoshaphat (2 Chron. 20)
  k. under Hezekiah (2 Chron. 29-31)
  l. under Manasseh (2 Chron. 33:11-20)
  m. under Ezra (Ezra 9, 10)
  n. under Nehemiah (Neh. 13)
  o. under Jonah (Jonah 3)
  p. under Esther (Est. 9:17-22)
  q. under John the Baptist (Lk. 3:2-18)
  r. under the Savior (Jn. 4:28-42)
  s. under Philip (Acts 8:5-12)
  t. under Peter (Acts 9:32-35; 2:1-47)
  u. under Paul (Acts 13:14-52; 17:10-12; 18:8; 19:18)

The amazing power of prayer is seen in verse ten. Here are two pairs of irreconcilables, mercy and truth, and righteousness and peace. Mercy looks at the sinner and says, "Spare him," but truth demands, "For the wages of sin is death." Peace viewed the troubled soul of the sinner and longed to soothe it, but righteousness pointed out that the soul that sinneth shall surely die. What could be done? Then came the miracle—love found a way, in Christ.

Thus these two opposites could be reconciled and kiss each other.

28. Psalm 88
Selection:
"For my soul is full of troubles: and my life draweth nigh unto the grave" (88:3).
Reflection:
This is by far the darkest and most despondent prayer in the entire Bible. Not one ray of hope appears.

29. Psalm 90
Selection:
"The days of our years are threescore years and ten; and if by reason of strength they be fourscore years, yet is their strength labour and sorrow; for it is soon cut off, and we fly away" (90:10).

"So teach us to number our days, that we may apply our hearts unto wisdom" (90:12).

Reflection:
This has often been called "The Psalm of Death" or "The Psalm of the First Adam." It was written by Moses. Note the seventy-year average span of man statement in verse 10, a tragic drop from the early patriarchal age found in Genesis 5. But as the first Adam would discover, one of the bitter fruits of sin is physical death. With this background, man's only logical conclusion is stated in verse 12. A sinner should accept Christ today (for this is the beginning of wisdom), and the believer should spend his days as wisely as he is exhorted to spend his money. In fact, more so, for wasted time can never be reclaimed.

30. Psalm 91
Selection:
"He that dwelleth in the secret place of the most High shall abide under the shadow of the Almighty" (91:1).

"For he shall give his angels charge over thee, to keep thee in all thy ways" (91:11).

"They shall bear thee up in their hands, lest thou dash thy foot against a stone" (91:12).

Reflection:
This is known as "The Psalm of Life," or "The Psalm of the Second Adam." It is primarily one which describes the keeping power of the Father concerning the Son while he walked this earth. Verse 11 speaks of giving "his angels charge over thee." Note the ministry angels performed for our Lord Jesus while he was upon this earth:
  a. They worshiped him (Heb. 1:6).
  b. They announced his birth (Lk. 1:26-38; 2:8-14; Mt. 1:20-23).
  c. They ministered to him:
     (1) in the wilderness (Mt. 4:11)
     (2) in the garden (Lk. 22:43)
  d. They rolled away the tombstone (Mt. 28:2).
  e. They announced his resurrection (Mt. 28:6).
  f. They were present at his ascension (Acts 1:10, 11).
  g. They will accompany his Second Coming (2 Thess. 1:7, 8)

During Jesus' awful temptations, Satan quoted verse 11 of this Psalm (Mt. 4:6). Shakespeare was right when he declared, "The devil doth quote Scripture."

31. Psalm 94
Selection:
"When I said, my foot slippeth; thy mercy, O Lord, held me up" (94:18).
Reflection:
This verse, like others in the Psalms, teaches the eternal security of the believer. It describes not the child of God desperately "hanging on" to the Father for dear

life, but rather having his frail hand securely clasped by that strong heavenly grasp. (See also Ps. 37:23, 24.)

32. Psalm 100
Selection:
"Make a joyful noise unto the Lord, all ye lands" (100:1).
Reflection:
This has been known as "The Old One Hundredth," and for style, beauty and content, deserves to be placed alongside Psalm 23.

33. Psalm 103
Selection:
"Bless the Lord, O my soul: and all that is within me, bless his holy name" (103:1).
Reflection:
This Psalm is possibly the greatest, grandest, and most glorious poem of praise to Jehovah God ever composed. In it David's zeal reaches its zenith. His reach is higher, his thoughts are deeper, his song is sweeter, and his heart is more moved than in any other prayer of praise in the Bible.

34. Psalm 107
Selection:
"For he satisfieth the longing soul, and the hungry soul he filleth with goodness. Such as sat in darkness and in the shadow of death, being bound in affliction and iron. . . . He maketh the storm a calm, so that the waves thereof are still" (vs. 9, 10, 29).
Reflection:
While he was upon this earth our Lord literally and lovingly fulfilled these verses:
 a. He fulfilled 107:9, 10, in Matthew 4:16 and Hebrews 2:14, 15.
 b. He fulfilled 107:29, in Matthew 8:26.

35. Psalm 111
Selection:
"The fear of the Lord is the beginning of wisdom . . . " (111:10).
Reflection:
The word "fear" in the Bible, especially in the Psalms, where it is used over a hundred times, is closely connected with prayer and praise. This particular kind of fear is not the sickening dread type, but that of reverential respect. This holy breed of fear is obviously missing in the world today. As Paul would say when describing the wickedness of the human race: "There is no fear of God before their eyes" (Rom. 3:18). Note the usage of the word fear as it relates to prayer and fellowship with God.
 "And now, Israel, what doth the Lord thy God require of thee, but to fear the Lord thy God, to walk in all his ways, and to love him, and to serve the Lord thy God with all thy heart and with all thy soul" (Deut. 10:12).
 "Now therefore fear the Lord, and serve him in sincerity and in truth . . . " (Josh. 24:14).
 "Serve the Lord with fear . . . " (Ps. 2:11).
 "In thy fear will I worship . . . " (Ps. 5:7).
 "Then they that feared the Lord spake often one to another: and the Lord hearkened, and heard it, and a book of remembrance was written before him for them that feared the Lord, and that thought upon his name" (Mal. 3:16).

36. Psalm 118
Selection:
"[Jehovah] hath chastened me sore: but he hath not

given me over unto death. This is the Lord's doing; it is marvellous in our eyes. This is the day which the Lord hath made; we will rejoice and be glad in it" (Ps. 118:18, 23, 24).
Reflection:
The life and experiences of Job serve as an entire commentary on verse 18. Verses 23 and 24 can be rightfully claimed by all believers on the basis of Romans 8:28, even on the day of the funeral of a loved one.

37. Psalm 119
Selection:
"Thy word have I hid in my heart, that I might not sin against thee" (119:11).
 "It is good for me that I have been afflicted; that I might learn thy statutes" (119:71).
 "I know, O Lord, that thy judgments are right, and that thou in faithfulness hast afflicted me" (119:75).
 "For ever, O Lord, thy word is settled in heaven" (119:89).
 "I have more understanding than all my teachers: for thy testimonies are my meditation" (119:99).
 "Thy word is a lamp unto my feet, and a light unto my path" (119:105).
 "The entrance of thy words giveth light; it giveth understanding unto the simple" (119:130).
Reflection:
We now come to the longest Psalm and by far the most lengthy prayer in all the Bible. The sole theme of this prayer is the Word of God. It is referred to in every one of the 176 verses with the exception of five. The psalmist gives the Bible nine titles in this Psalm and ascribes some twelve ministries to it.
 a. The nine titles
  (1) his law (v. 1)
  (2) his testimonies (v. 2)
  (3) his ways (v. 3)
  (4) his precepts (v. 4)
  (5) his statutes (v. 5)
  (6) his commandments (v. 6)
  (7) his righteous judgments (v. 7)
  (8) his Word (v. 9)
  (9) his ordinances (v. 91)
 b. The twelve ministries
  (1) it cleanses (v. 9)
  (2) it quickens (v. 25)
  (3) it strengthens (v. 28)
  (4) it establishes (v. 38)
  (5) it defends (v. 42)
  (6) it comforts (v. 50)
  (7) it instructs (vs. 98, 99)
  (8) it enlightens (v. 105)
  (9) it assures (v. 114)
  (10) it upholds (v. 116)
  (11) it brings peace (v. 165)
  (12) it delivers (v. 170)
Concerning verse 11, D. L. Moody said that the Bible would keep one from sin or sin would keep one from the Bible. Concerning verse 71, God often afflicts us with woes in order to acquaint us with his Word (see also Ps. 94:12). The author of the book of Hebrews builds upon verse 75. (See Heb. 12:5-15.)
 Concerning verse 89, our Lord once said:
"Heaven and earth shall pass away, but my words shall not pass away" (Mt. 24:35). (See also Mt. 5:18; 1 Pet. 1:23, 25).

Concerning verse 99, the psalmist is not boasting of his brain-power, nor is he belittling all instructors. He is simply saying that in matters of God's will for his life, more can be gleaned from a study of the Scriptures than from all well-meaning, but nevertheless human, advisors. Sometimes even the godliest instructor can give another believer the wrong advice. A classic example of this was Nathan's encouragement concerning David's plan to build the Temple (see 1 Chron. 17:1-4). In his first letter, the Apostle John writes concerning this (see 1 Jn. 2:27).

Concerning verse 105, it can be pointed out that Satan too is described as a light-displayer of some type. But there is this difference: God's light is directed at the man's feet, thus guiding his eyesight. Satan's light is aimed at the man's eyes, thus blinding his eyesight. As Paul would later declare: "The god of this world hath blinded the minds of them which believe not, lest the light of the glorious gospel of Christ, who is the image of God, should shine unto them" (2 Cor. 4:4). (See also Ps. 97:11.)

Concerning verse 130, it can be pointed out that the Word of God is simple enough to bless the heart of the densest believer and at the same time profound enough to challenge the brain of the wisest believer. It is both milk for the babe and meat for the man.

38. Psalm 123
Selection:
"Unto thee lift I up mine eyes, O thou that dwellest in the heavens. Behold, as the eyes of servants look unto the hand of their masters, and as the eyes of a maiden unto the hand of her mistress; so our eyes wait upon the Lord our God, until that he have mercy upon us" (123:1, 2).
Reflection:
A citizen of Western civilization, whose society advocates (at least on paper) the equality of all men, who reads these words in this Psalm cannot but faintly comprehend their full meaning, as he knows nothing of the absolute submission and loyalty which existed in the oriental servant-master and maid-mistress relationships. We are told that when in the presence of his master, the servant should fix his gaze upon the hand of that master. Thus, the lightest movement or gesture from that hand would rouse the servant into immediate and total action. This eye-to-hand service was likewise true with the maid and her mistress. This meaning may certainly be attached to God's words to David in Psalm 32:8, 9: "I will instruct thee and teach thee in the way which thou shalt go: I will guide thee with mine eye. Be ye not as the horse, or as the mule, which have no understanding: whose mouth must be held in with bit and bridle, lest they come near unto thee." In Romans 1:1, Paul refers to himself as a bond-slave of Jesus Christ. This was no doubt the secret underlying his mighty works for God.

39. Psalm 136
Selection:
"O give thanks unto the Lord; for he is good: for his mercy endureth forever" (Ps. 136:1).
Reflection:
This is Scripture's great mercy refrain Psalm. The phrase, "for his mercy endureth forever," appears twenty-six times, once for each verse. Note other biblical prayers in which mercy is the outstanding element:

a. Jacob's prayer (Gen. 32:10)
b. Abraham's prayer (Gen. 24:27)
c. Moses' prayer (Ex. 15:13)
d. David's prayer (2 Sam. 22:26; 24:14)
e. the remnant's prayer (Neh. 9:19)
f. Jonah's prayer (Jonah 4:2)
g. the publican's prayer (Lk. 18:13)
h. other Psalms (25:6; 40:11; 51:1; 69:16; 79:8; 103:4; 119:77, 156; 145:9)

40. Psalm 139
Selection:
"O Lord, thou hast searched me, and known me" (139:1).
Reflection:
Within this Psalm of David is more about the omniscience of God than can be found in any other prayer in the Bible. According to David:
a. God knew when he sat or stood (v. 2).
b. God knew his every thought (v. 2).
c. God knew his every habit (v. 3).
d. God knew his every word (v. 4).
e. God knew his every step (v. 5).
f. God knew him before he was born (v. 16).
Because of this wonderful wisdom, David thanked God:
g. For creating him (vs. 13-16).
h. For keeping him.
(1) Even if he ascended into heaven (v. 8).
(2) Even if he descended into the grave (v. 8).
(3) Even if he visited the furthest ocean (v. 9).
(4) Even if he covered himself with the blackest night (vs. 11, 12).
i. For thinking about him (vs. 17, 18).

The Penitential Psalms (6, 32, 38, 51, 102, 130, 143)

No less than five out of the seven penitential Psalms were written by David. He wrote 6, 32, 38, 51, and 143. We will here consider Psalms 32, 38, and 51.
1. Psalm 32
This Psalm should be connected with Psalm 51. The latter describes David's emotions as he confesses his sin of adultery and murder (2 Sam. 11), while this Psalm depicts his feelings before such confession was made, when the awful burden of guilt still bore heavy upon him. In the book of Romans (4:7, 8) Paul quotes the first two verses of this Psalm to illustrate one of Scripture's great doctrines, that of imputation. Imputation is that act of one person adding something to another person's account. There are three main imputations in the Bible:
a. That of Adam's sin nature upon mankind (Rom. 3:23; 5:12).
b. That of man's sin upon Christ (Isa. 53:5, 6; Heb. 2:9; 2 Cor. 5:14-21; 1 Pet. 2:24).
c. That of Christ's righteousness upon the believing sinner (Phil. 3:9; Jas. 2:23; Rom. 4:6-24).
2. Psalm 51
We have already seen the background from which David wrote this Psalm.
a. He begins this great confessional by doing what God expects every sinning saint to do—freely acknowledging his sin. The Father will accept our tears, but not our excuses. David refuses to blame his failure on society, heredity, poverty, or environment.

b. In verse 4 he states that he has sinned "against . . . thee only." In a technical sense, of course, this was not true. David had sinned against himself, against Bath-sheba, against Uriah, and against all Israel who looked up to their beloved king. But his sin against God was so serious and stupendous that all other parties involved faded away. The last part of this verse is quoted by Paul to prove the universal condemnation of mankind (Rom. 3:4).

c. In verse 7 David pleads to be purged (or cleansed) with hyssop. Perhaps his mind slipped back to his nation's first Passover night some five centuries before. Doubtless he had read the account many times:

> "Then Moses called for all the elders of Israel, and said unto them, Draw out and take you a lamb according to your families, and kill the passover. And ye shall take a bunch of hyssop, and dip it in the blood that is in the bason, and strike the lintel and the two side posts with the blood that is in the bason. . . . For the Lord will pass through to smite the Egyptians; and when he seeth the blood . . . the Lord will pass over the door, and will not suffer the destroyer to come in unto your houses to smite you" (Ex. 12:21–23).

So God purged him. Later, David's greater Son would perform this ministry for all believers everywhere. We are told:

> " . . . When he had by himself purged our sins, sat down on the right hand of the Majesty on high" (Heb. 1:3b).

David wanted this ministry that he might be whiter than snow. Some three centuries later God would use David's words in addressing sinful Israel. Through the mouth of Isaiah, Jehovah said: "Come now, and let us reason together, saith the Lord: though your sins be as scarlet, they shall be as white as snow . . ." (Isa. 1:18).

d. In verse 11 David prays a prayer, however, which no believer need or should request today. Regardless of the seriousness of our sin, we need not concern ourselves over losing the indwelling Holy Spirit. In the upper room our Lord promised:

> "And I will pray the Father, and he shall give you another Comforter, that he may abide with you forever" (Jn. 14:16).

e. However, every child of God will sometime need to pray David's words in verse 12. The entire church at Ephesus needed to pray these words, as Jesus told them: "Nevertheless I have somewhat against thee, because thou hast left thy first love" (Rev. 2:4). When this joy and first love returns, the conversion of sinners will indeed take place as mentioned in verse 13.

f. This confession Psalm brings out many precious truths, but perhaps the greatest of all is found in verses 16 and 17. The reason for this was very simple—there existed no sacrifice for the sin of adultery. Rather, the one guilty of adultery was to be taken out and stoned to death (Lev. 20:10). So then, David bypasses the Levitical offerings and throws himself completely upon the mercy and grace of God.

3. Psalm 38

Surely this must rank among the most remarkable passages in the entire Bible, if for no other reason, because of its absolute frankness. This pitiful prayer ought to demonstrate that the Bible is not only a Book that man could not write if he would, but would not write if he could! Here is David, the sweet singer of Israel, the anointed of the Lord, the man after God's own heart. Yet as one carefully studies the language of this prayer, it becomes impossible to escape the shocking possibility that David was plagued with that kind of disease which often accompanies immoral living and activities (see vs. 3–11).

The Imprecatory Psalms
(35, 55, 58, 59, 69, 83, 109, 137, 140)

A. The definition of these Psalms: To imprecate is to pray against, or to invoke evil upon someone or something.

B. The fact of these Psalms: There are many instances where the Psalmist calls down judgment upon his enemies, asking God to:
1. fight against them (35:1)
2. bring them into confusion (35:4)
3. scatter them as chaff (35:5)
4. allow the Lord's angel to chase and persecute them (35:5)
5. cause their way to be dark and slippery (35:6)
6. allow death to seize upon them (55:15)
7. pull them down into hell (55:15)
8. break their teeth (58:8)
9. cut up their defense (58:7)
10. withhold all mercy to them (59:5)
11. consume them in wrath (59:13)
12. set a trap for them (69:22)
13. darken their eyes (69:23)
14. make their loins to shake (69:23)
15. let their habitation be desolate (69:25)
16. blot them out of the book of the living (69:28)
17. make them as the dung of the earth (83:10)
18. persecute them (83:15).
19. give them over to Satan (109:6)
20. let their days be few (109:8)
21. let their children be beggars (109:10)
22. let burning coals fall upon them (140:10)
23. cast them into a deep pit (140:10)

C. The problems involved in these Psalms: How can we reconcile these phrases with the New Testament admonition of Jesus in Matthew 5:44:
> "But I say unto you, love your enemies, bless them that curse you, do good to them that hate you, and pray for them which despitefully use you, and persecute you"?

D. The suggested answers for these Psalms. (The following material is taken from Dr. Roy L. Aldrich's booklet, *Notes for Lectures on the Psalms*.)
1. The Psalms are inspired and the Holy Spirit has a right to denounce sin and sinners.
2. This is in harmony with the law (Ps. 28:4; Jer. 50:15).
3. Such judgment against evil and evildoers is in harmony with the teachings of Christ and the epistles (Mt. 18:6; 23:33; 26:24; Gal. 1:8, 9; 5:12; Jas. 5:3; Jude 13, 15; 2 Pet. 2:12, 22; 2 Thess. 2:10–12; Rev. 14:10, 11).
4. The Scriptures pronounce maledictions against the Israelites also for falling into sin and idolatry (Lev. 26; Deut. 27–28; Isa. 5:24, 25; 28:13, etc.).

5. David in private exercised great forbearance, but in the Psalms he makes God's cause his cause (Ps. 5:10, 11).
6. The Oriental was accustomed to using stronger language than the Westerner. His denunciations were more exaggerated and his praise more vehement.
7. Many of the imprecations are uttered out of sympathy for the injured and the oppressed (Ps. 10:8-10).
8. Some of these Psalms are prayers for success on the battlefield (Ps. 144:5-7). Many of Israel's wars were definitely approved of God.
9. Some of the petitions have reference to scriptural predictions (Ps. 137:8, 9). The Psalmist has before him a direct prophecy where the fall of Babylon is predicted in these same terms (Isa. 13:16; also Jer. 50:15; 51:6, 36).
10. Some concern Christ and his betrayers (Ps. 40; 55; 60). Psalm 69:22-25 gives us the punishment meted out to Judas. Psalm 109 has been called the "Iscariot Psalm."
11. The wicked in the Psalms are looked upon as confirmed or apostate wicked. This is in keeping with the sovereignty of God and also with the prophetic character of the Psalms. Many of the Psalms look forward to the final earthly judgments against the wicked.
12. Grace is manifest in frank and repeated warnings to the wicked (Ps. 2:12).
13. The imperative may be changed to the future without violence to the Hebrew: Instead of, "Let them be confounded" we have, "They shall be confounded." The prayer thus becomes a prophecy. (See Ps. 109:8-10.)
E. A brief examination of these Psalms:
1. Psalm 35. This is the first of the nine imprecatory Psalms. (See vs. 1-8.) But it should also be kept in mind that David had at first fervently prayed for his fierce enemies in spite of their cruelty toward him. (See vs. 12-16.) This is also the first of four Iscariot Psalms, that is, Psalms which prophetically depict the treachery of Judas in the New Testament. The other three are: 41:9; 55:12-14; 109:6-8. See the following verses for the imprecatory prayer in each:
2. Psalm 55:9
3. Psalm 58:6-9
4. Psalm 59:11-15
5. Psalm 69:22-28
6. Psalm 83:9-17
7. Psalm 109:6-20
8. Psalm 137. Here is a twofold imprecatory prayer:
   a. That God would judge Edom for their treachery during the fall of Jerusalem by the Babylonians (v. 7).
   b. That God would judge Babylon. (See vs. 8, 9.) Note, however, that these words do not describe an army of Israelite "G.I. Joes" running around and bashing the bodies of little Babylonian babies, for, historically speaking, the Babylonians conquered Israel, and not the opposite. This may then be regarded as a prophecy referring to the Persians who did indeed defeat Babylon. (See Dan. 5; Isa. 12:16.) The divine law of retribution was involved here, as

it was in Exodus 32:34; Psalm 7:16; Proverbs 11:19, 21; and Galatians 6:7.
9. Psalm 140. See verses 8-10 for the imprecatory prayer.

The Degree or Ascent Psalms

A. Who wrote them? A commonly held theory is that they were composed by three men.
   1. Hezekiah wrote ten of them (120, 121, 123, 125, 126, 128, 129, 130, 132, 134).
   2. Solomon wrote one of them (127).
   3. David wrote four of them (122, 124, 131, 133).
B. Why were they written? Many believe it was because of the following: Around 728 B.C., God healed a Judean king named Hezekiah of a fatal illness. Isaiah (ch. 38) records the prayer of thanksgiving of the grateful king, composed after his recovery. In verse 20 he exclaims:
   "The Lord was ready to save me: therefore we will sing my songs to the stringed instruments all the days of our life in the house of the Lord."
   Some scholars (including Thirtle, Lightfoot, Scroggie) believe that these songs of Hezekiah are the ten anonymous "Songs of Degrees" in the group of fifteen (120-134). These Psalms do have a certain similarity of style. Hezekiah may have written ten of these anonymous degree Psalms in memory of the ten steps of the shadow on the sundial (2 Ki. 20:9-11), and then added five appropriate hitherto unpublished Psalms from the pens of (David and) Solomon (see Prov. 25:1), to bring the total to fifteen, in honor of the fifteen years God added to his life. (See 2 Ki. 21:6.)
C. How were they to be sung? Here there are various theories:
   1. An old Jewish tradition explains that they were sung when the choir ascended the semicircular flight of stairs leading up to the court of men in the Temple.
   2. The ascents may have referred to the stages of pilgrimage to Jerusalem, to be sung along the way by travelers en route to the various annual feast days.
   3. Ascent means "a song in the higher choir," the singers being on the stairs of some high place.
   4. The reference may be musical, signifying that the notes rose by degrees in succession.

The Hallel (Hallelujah) Psalms (113—118)

These six Psalms were sung on the night of the Passover.
A. Psalms 113 and 114 at the beginning of the meal.
B. Psalms 115 and 116 at the close. These were sung by the Savior and his disciples in Matthew 26:30. They are still recited in Palestine eighteen times a year at various occasions, and twenty-one times yearly by those Jews outside the Holy Land.

The Historical Psalms (78, 105, 106)

These three Psalms, which depict the history of Israel, may be summarized as follows:
A. The sins of Israel.
   1. They refused to walk in God's law (78:10).
   2. They forgot his works (78:11, 42; 106:13).
   3. They spoke against him (78:19).

4. They didn't trust his salvation (78:22).
5. They lied to him (78:36).
6. They grieved him (78:40).
7. They limited him (78:41).
8. They worshiped graven images (78:58; 106:19).
9. They envied his leader Moses (106:16).
10. They despised the Promised Land (106:24).
11. They murmured in their tents (106:25).
12. They ate the sacrifices of the dead (106:28).
13. They mingled among the heathen (106:35).
14. They sacrificed their sons and daughters to devils (106:37).
15. They shed innocent blood (106:38).

B. The grace of God.
1. He remembered his covenant when they cried unto him (105:8–11).
2. He divided the sea (78:13).
3. He led them with a cloud by day (78:14).
4. He led them with a fire by night (78:14).
5. He provided water for them out of rocks (78:15).
6. He rained down manna for them (78:24).
7. He was full of compassion and forgave their iniquity (78:38).
8. He wrought signs for them in Egypt (78:43; 105:27–36).
9. He brought them to the border of the Promised Land (78:54).
10. He cast out the heathen before them (78:55).
11. He chose David to lead them (78:70, 71).
12. He allowed no man to hurt them (105:14).
13. He fed them (78:72).
14. He reproved kings for their sake (105:14).
15. He elevated them through Joseph (105:17).
16. He gave them the riches of Egypt (105:37).
17. He kept them all strong (105:37).
18. He continually forgave them (106:43).
19. He continually heard their cry (106:44).

The Acrostic Psalms (9, 10, 25, 34, 37, 111, 112, 119, 145)

These nine Psalms are also called the alphabetical Psalms. This is so because each line of these Psalms begins with a successive letter of the twenty-two letters in the Hebrew alphabet.

Psalm 119 is of course the most famous of the acrostic Psalms. It has twenty-two stanzas. Each stanza has eight verses, for a total of 176. Each of these stanzas begins with one of the twenty-two Hebrew letters. Not all of these Psalms are complete in this arrangement; that is, some are missing a letter or more. Thus we find:
A. Psalms 9, 10, 25 are missing several letters.
B. Psalms 34, 45 have all but one letter.
C. Psalms 37, 111, 112, 119 have all the letters.

It is reasonable to suppose that the acrostic device was designed to assist the memory.

The Messianic Psalms

We shall consider these all-important Psalms in a twofold manner. First, in the order that Christ fulfilled them in the New Testament. Second, in the order that they appear in the book of Psalms.
A. In the order that Christ fulfilled them in the New Testament.
1. his obedience (40:6–10).
"Sacrifice and offerings thou didst not desire . . .

then said I, Lo, I come: In the volume of the book it is written of me" (compare Heb. 10:5–7).
2. his zeal (69:9).
"The zeal of thine house hath eaten me up" (Jn. 2:17).
3. his rejection (118:22).
"The stone which the builders refused is become the headstone of the corner" (see Mt. 21:42).
4. his betrayal.
"Yea, mine own familiar friend, in whom I trusted, which did eat of my bread, hath lifted up his heel against me" (41:9).
"For it was not an enemy that reproached me; then I could have borne it: neither was it he that hated me that did magnify himself against me . . . but it was thou, a man mine equal, my guide, and mine acquaintance. We took sweet counsel together, and walked unto the house of God in company" (55:12–14).
(See Mt. 26:14–16, 21–25.)
5. his sufferings (22:1, 6, 7, 8, 16, 18).
"They gave me also gall for my meat; and in my thirst they gave me vinegar to drink" (69:21). (See Mt. 27:34, 48.)
"Into thine hand I commit my spirit" (Ps. 31:5). (See Lk. 23:46.)
"He keepeth all his bones: Not one of them is broken" (34:20). (See Jn. 19:33–36; also 129:3.)
6. his false witnesses.
"For the mouth of the wicked and the mouth of the deceitful are opened against me: They have spoken against me with a lying tongue. They compassed me about also with words of hatred; and fought against me without a cause" (109:2, 3). (See Mt. 26:59–61; 27:39–44.)
7. his prayers for his enemies.
"[In return] for my love they are my adversaries: but I give myself unto prayer" (109:4). (See Lk. 23:34.)
8. his resurrection.
"For thou wilt not leave my soul in hell; neither wilt thou suffer thine Holy One to see corruption" (16:10; compare with Acts 13:35).
"I will declare thy name unto my brethren: in the midst of the congregation will I praise thee" (22:22; compare with Jn. 20:17).
9. his ascension.
"Thou hast ascended on high, thou hast led captivity captive: thou hast received gifts for men . . ." (68:18; compare with Eph. 4:8).
10. his triumphal entry.
"Lift up your heads, O ye gates; and be ye lifted up, ye everlasting doors; and the King of Glory shall come in. Who is this King of Glory? The Lord strong and mighty, the Lord mighty in battle" (24:7, 8). (See Acts 1.)
11. his high priestly work.
"The Lord hath sworn, and will not repent, thou art a priest forever after the order of Melchizedek" (110:4). (See Heb. 5–7.)
12. his marriage (45:2, 6, 8, 13, 15). (See Rev. 19.)
13. his destruction of the heathen.
"The Lord said unto my Lord, sit thou at my right hand, until I make thine enemies thy footstool" (Ps. 110:1). (See also Ps. 2.)
"He shall judge among the heathen . . ." (110:6). (See Rev. 6–19.)

Whither shall I go from thy spirit?
or whither shall I flee from thy presence?
If I ascend up into heaven, thou art there:
if I make my bed in hell, behold thou art there.

If I take the wings of the morning and dwell in the uttermost parts of the sea;
even there shall thy hand lead me,
and thy right hand shall hold me. **PSALM 139:7-10**

PSALMS

BY BOOK DIVISION

CHAPTERS	HOW SIMILAR TO PENTATEUCH
1-41	Key word is man (corresponds to **Genesis**)
42-72	Key word is deliverance (corresponds to **Exodus**)
73-89	Key word is sanctuary (corresponds to **Leviticus**)
90-106	Key words are wandering, unrest (correspond to **Numbers**)
107-150	Key word is word of God (corresponds to **Deuteronomy**)

BY SUBJECT MATTER

SUBJECT	PSALMS
PENITENTIAL	6, 32, 38, 51, 102, 130, 143
IMPRECATORY	35, 55, 58, 59, 69, 83, 109, 137, 140
DEGREE OR ASCENT	120-134
HALLELUJAH	113-118
HISTORICAL	78, 105, 106
ACROSTIC	9, 10, 25, 34, 37, 111, 112, 119, 145
MESSIANIC	16, 22, 24, 31, 34, 40, 41, 45, 55, 68, 69, 89, 102, 109, 110, 118, 129

BY AUTHORSHIP

AUTHOR	PSALMS
DAVID: 77	Shepherd Psalms—**8, 19, 23, 29, 144** Sinner Psalms—**32, 51, 38** Suffering Psalms—**3, 4, 5, 6, 7, 11, 12, 13, 14, 17, 22, 25, 26, 27, 28, 31, 34, 35, 39, 40, 41, 53, 54, 55, 56, 57, 58, 59, 61, 62, 63, 64, 69, 70, 86, 109, 140, 141, 142, 143** Satisfied Psalms—**2, 9, 15, 16, 18, 20, 21, 24, 30, 36, 37, 52, 60, 65, 68, 72, 95, 101, 103, 105, 108, 110, 122, 124, 131, 133, 138, 139, 145**
KORAH: 10	42, 44, 45, 46, 47, 48, 49, 84, 85, 87
ASAPH: 12	50, 73, 74, 75, 76, 77, 78, 79, 80, 81, 82, 83
HEMAN: 1	88
ETHAN: 1	89
SOLOMON: 1	127
MOSES: 1	90
HEZEKIAH: 10	120, 121, 123, 125, 126, 128, 129, 130, 132, 134
ANONYMOUS: 37	1, 10, 33, 43, 66, 67, 71, 91, 92, 93, 94, 96, 97, 98, 99, 100, 102, 104, 106, 107, 111, 112, 113, 114, 115, 116, 117, 118, 119, 135, 136, 137, 146, 147, 148, 149, 150

MESSIANIC PSALMS

PSALM REFERENCE	FEATURE OF CHRIST DESCRIBED	NEW TESTAMENT FULFILLMENT
40:6-10	**His Obedience**	Hebrews 10:5-7
69:9	**His Zeal**	John 2:17
118:22	**His Rejection**	Matthew 21:42
41:9; 55:12-14	**His Betrayal**	Matthew 26:14-16, 21-25
22:1, 6-8, 16, 18; 31:5; 34:20; 69:21; 129:3	**His Sufferings**	Matthew 27:34, 48; Luke 23:46; John 19:33-36
109:2, 3	**His False Witnesses**	Matthew 26:59-61; 27:39-44
109:4	**His Prayer for His Enemies**	Luke 23:34
16:10	**His Resurrection**	Acts 13:35
68:18	**His Ascension**	Ephesians 4:8
24:7, 8	**His Triumphal Entry into Glory**	Philippians 2:9-11
110:4	**His High Priestly Work**	Hebrews 5-7
45:2, 6, 8, 13, 15	**His Marriage to the Church**	Revelation 19:7-10
110:1, 6	**His Destruction of the Heathen**	Revelation 6-19
89:27; 102:16-21; 72:17	**His Millennial Reign**	Matthew 23:39; Revelation 11:15

14. his millennial reign (89:27; 102:16–21).

"Thou madest him to have dominion over the works of thy hands: thou hast put all things under his feet" (8:6; compare with Heb. 2).

"His name shall endure forever: his name shall be continued as long as the sun, and men shall be blessed in him. All nations shall call him blessed" (72:17). (See Mt. 23:39; Rev. 11:15.)

B. In the order they appear in the book of Psalms.

1. Psalm 2: Predicts the tribulational destruction of the heathen and the millennial reign of Christ. This Psalm is in four parts:
   a. the rebellion of man (vs. 1–3)
   b. the reaction of God (vs. 4–6)
   c. the rule of the Son (vs. 7–9)
   d. the recommendation of the Psalmist (vs. 10–12)

   Messianic passages:

   Verse 2: "The kings of the earth set themselves, and the rulers take counsel together, against the Lord, and against his anointed . . . ." (Quoted in Acts 4:26.)

   Verse 7: "I will declare the decree: The Lord hath said unto me, Thou art my Son; this day have I begotten thee." (Quoted in Acts 13:33.)

2. Psalm 8: Predicts the millennial reign of Christ. One may well compare the statement in this Psalm (v. 6) which says it took God's fingers to create man with Isaiah 53:1 where we are told it cost God his arms to redeem us! Thus, salvation is infinitely more costly than creation.

   Messianic passage:

   Verse 6: "Thou madest him to have dominion over the works of thy hands; thou hast put all things under his feet."

3. Psalm 16: Predicts the death and resurrection of Christ.

   Messianic passage:

   Verse 10: "For thou wilt not leave my soul in hell; neither wilt thou suffer thine Holy One to see corruption." (Quoted in Acts 2:27.)

4. Psalm 22: Predicts the intense sufferings of Christ. The Psalm is in two parts:
   a. the sob of the crucified (vs. 1–21)
   b. the song of the glorified (vs. 22–31)

   It has been suggested that Peter had this Psalm in mind when he wrote 1 Peter 1:10, 11:

   "Of which salvation that prophets have inquired and searched diligently, who prophesied of the grace that should come unto you: searching what, or what manner of time the Spirit of Christ which was in them did signify, when it testified beforehand the sufferings of Christ, and the glory that should follow."

   If this is true, then verses 1–21 speak of the sufferings, while verses 22–31 depict the glory.

   Messianic passages:

   Verse 1: "My God, my God, why hast thou forsaken me?" (Quoted by Christ on the cross, Mt. 27:46.)

   Verse 8: "He trusted in the Lord that he would deliver him: let him deliver him, seeing he delighted in him." (Quoted by the wicked Israelite rulers at the cross, Mt. 27:43.)

   Verse 16: "They pierced my hands and my feet." (Fulfilled by the Roman soldiers at the cross, Mt. 27:35.)

   Verse 18: "They part my garments among them, and cast lots upon my vesture." (Fulfilled by the Roman soldiers at the cross, Mk. 15:24.)

   Verse 22: "I will declare thy name unto my brethren: in the midst of the congregation will I praise thee." (Quoted in Heb. 2:12.)

5. Psalm 23: Predicts the tender shepherding ministry of Christ.

   Messianic passage:

   Verse 1: "The Lord is my shepherd; I shall not want." (Although this exact quotation does not appear in the New Testament, it is nevertheless referred to by Jesus himself in Jn. 10:1–18).

   This is known as the Pearl of the Psalms. It is in three parts:
   a. The Sheep and the Shepherd (vs. 1–3; speaks of provision).
   b. The Guide and the Traveler (vs. 3, 4; speaks of direction).
   c. The Host and the Guest (vs. 5, 6, speaks of communion).

6. Psalm 24: Predicts Christ's triumphal entry into heaven. This Psalm, although originally written to celebrate David's entrance into the newly captured city of Jerusalem, and his subsequent inauguration as King, may also speak of that victorious entry of the Savior into glory after he had finished his work of redemption and ascended from the Mount of Olives. The Psalm was sung by two choirs:
   a. Verses 1–6 were sung at the foot of the hill on which Jerusalem stood.
      (1) Choir A would sing 1–3.
      (2) Choir B would respond with 4–6.
   b. Verses 7–10 were sung in front of the gates of the city.
      (1) Choir A would sing verse 7.
      (2) Choir B would sing the first part of verse 8.
      (3) Choir A would sing the second part of verse 8.
      (4) Choir A would sing verse 9.
      (5) Choir B would sing the first part of verse 10.
      (6) Choir A would sing the second part of verse 10.
   c. Certain Psalms were sung at the morning service in the Temple worship each day of the week:
      (1) On Monday the choir sang Psalm 48. Then, each day as follows:
      (2) Tuesday, Psalm 82
      (3) Wednesday, Psalm 94
      (4) Thursday, Psalm 81
      (5) Friday, Psalm 93
      (6) Saturday, Psalm 92
      (7) Sunday, Psalm 24

   Messianic passages:

   Verses 7–10: "Lift up your heads, O ye gates; and be ye lift up, ye everlasting doors; and the King of glory shall come in. Who is this King of glory? The Lord strong and mighty, the Lord mighty in battle. Lift up your heads, O ye gates; even lift them up, ye everlasting doors; and the King of glory shall come in. Who is this King of glory? The Lord of hosts, he is the King of glory."

(Although these verses are not directly quoted in the New Testament, they are nevertheless generally spoken of in Acts 2:32, 33.)

7. Psalm 31: Predicts the Savior's thoughts and words on the cross.
   Messianic passage:
   Verse 5: "Into thine hand I commit my spirit . . . ."
   (This was directly quoted by Jesus just prior to his death on Calvary in Lk. 23:46.) The Apostle Paul would later refer to verse 19 of this Psalm in 1 Corinthians 2:9.

8. Psalm 40: Predicts the obedience of Christ while on this earth.
   Messianic passage:
   Verse 6: "Sacrifice and offerings thou didst not desire: mine ears hast thou opened. . . ." (Quoted in Heb. 10:5, 6.)
   Verse 7: "Then said I, Lo, I come: in the volume of the book it is written of me." (Quoted in Heb. 10:7.)

9. Psalm 41: Predicts the betrayal of the Savior by Judas. This is the first of three Psalms which speak of that treachery. The others are Psalms 55 and 109.
   Messianic passage:
   Verse 9: "Yea, mine own familiar friend, in whom I trusted, which did eat of my bread, hath lifted up his heel against me." (A reference to Judas. See Jn. 13:18.)

10. Psalm 45: Predicts the beauty and marriage of Christ. This Psalm probably had its historical roots in Solomon's marriage to the King of Egypt's daughter (1 Ki. 3:1), but it certainly lends itself to the marriage of Christ passage in Revelation 19:7–9. The Psalm is in two parts:
    a. Part one: The characteristics of the Bridegroom (1–8a).
       (1) He is the fairest of all.
       (2) His words are filled with grace.
       (3) He enjoys the fullest possible blessings of God.
       (4) He is a defender of truth, humility, and justice.
       (5) He defeats all his enemies.
       (6) His throne will exist forever.
       (7) Justice is his royal scepter.
       (8) He loves the good and hates the wrong.
       (9) His robes are perfumed with myrrh, aloes, and cassia.
    b. Part two: The privileges of the Bride (8b–17).
       (1) She will live in an ivory palace filled with lovely music.
       (2) She will be fitted with the finest of clothing and most costly jewelry.
       (3) She will be loved throughout all eternity by her Bridegroom.
          Messianic passage:
          Verse 6: "Thy throne, O God, is for ever and ever: The sceptre of thy kingdom is a right sceptre." (Quoted in Heb. 1:8.)
          Verse 7: "Thou lovest righteousness, and hatest wickedness: therefore God, thy God, hath anointed thee with the oil of gladness above thy fellows." (Quoted in Heb. 1:9.)

11. Psalm 68: Predicts the glorious victory of Christ and his triumphal entry into heaven.
    Messianic passage:
    Verse 18: "Thou hast ascended on high, thou hast led captivity captive: Thou hast received gifts for men." (Quoted in Eph. 4:8.) Where was the abode of the departed righteous prior to Calvary? It is held by a number of Bible students that before Jesus died, the souls of all men descended into an abode located somewhere in the earth known as Hades in the New Testament, and Sheol in the Old Testament. Originally, there were two sections of Hades, one for the saved and one for the lost. The saved section is sometimes called "paradise" (see Lk. 23:43), and other times referred to as "Abraham's bosom" (See Lk. 16:22).

    There is no name given for the unsaved section apart from the general designation of Hades. In Luke 16:19-31 the Savior relates the account of a rich man who died and went to the unsaved section. However, many believe that all this changed after Christ made full payment for the believer's sins on Calvary. The *Scofield Bible* suggests that during the time of his death and resurrection, our Lord descended into Hades, depopulated paradise, and led a spiritual triumphal entry into the heavenlies with all the saved up to that time. Ephesians 4:8-10 is offered as proof of this. In his book, *Revelation*, the late Dr. Barnhouse writes:

    "When He ascended on High (Eph. 4:8) He emptied Hell of Paradise and took it straight to the presence of God. Captivity was taken captive. . . . From that moment onward there was to be no separation whatsoever for those who believe in Christ. The gates of Hell would never more prevail against any believer." (See Mt. 16:18.)

12. Psalm 69: Predicts the zeal and sufferings of Christ.
    Messianic passages:
    Verse 9: "For the zeal of thine house hath eaten me up." (Quoted in Jn. 2:17.)
    Verse 21: "They gave me also gall for my meat; and in my thirst they gave me vinegar to drink." (Fulfilled in Mt. 27:34, 48.)

13. Psalm 72: Predicts the millennial reign of Christ. It is not absolutely certain whether this Psalm is a prayer of Solomon to God or a prayer of David concerning Solomon. At any rate, it vividly describes the glorious millennial reign of David's greater Son, the Lord Jesus Christ. Note the following characteristics of his reign:
    a. The poor will receive righteousness (v. 2).
    b. The mountains and hills will flourish (v. 3).
    c. All oppressors will be crushed (v. 4).
    d. His rule will be as gentle and fruitful as the springtime rains upon the grass (v. 6).
    e. All good men will prosper exceedingly (v. 7).
    f. His reign will extend to the ends of the earth (v. 8).
    g. All nations will give him gifts and serve him (vs. 10, 11).
    h. All peoples will bless and praise him (v. 15).
    i. His name will be honored and will continue forever (v. 17).

Messianic passage:

Verse 8: "He shall have dominion also from sea to sea, and from the river unto the ends of the earth." (Referred to by John in Rev. 11:15.)

14. Psalm 89: Predicts the unchanging faithfulness of God upon David's dynasty through Christ, in spite of continued disobedience within that dynasty. This Psalm was written by Ethan the Ezrahite, who was a noted wise man during Solomon's reign (1 Ki. 4:31). While we cannot be certain, the Psalm may express the thoughts of Solomon during his latter years when, because of his sin, he underwent hard times. (See 1 Ki. 11.)

Messianic passage:

Verse 27: "Also I will make him my firstborn, higher than the kings of the earth." (Referred to by Paul in Phil. 2:9–11.)

15. Psalm 102: Predicts the eternality of Christ. This Psalm may be assigned to the closing years of the Babylonian exile, and its design was to encourage the Jews to return and rebuild Jerusalem. It also refers to the second coming of Jerusalem's great King. (See v. 16.)

Messianic passage:

Verses 25–27: "Of old hast thou laid the foundation of the earth: and the heavens are the work of thy hands. They shall perish, but thou shalt endure: yea, all of them shall wax old like a garment; as a vesture shalt thou change them, and they shall be changed: But thou art the same, and thy years shall have no end." (Quoted in Heb. 1:10–12.)

16. Psalm 109: Predicts the betrayal of Judas and his frightful punishment.

Messianic passage:

Verse 8: "Let his days be few; and let another take his office." (Quoted by Peter in Acts 1:20.)

17. Psalm 110: Predicts the eternal priesthood of Christ.

a. Note the fivefold description of Christ in this Psalm.

(1) He is God (v. 1).

(2) He is King (v. 2).

(3) He is a Priest (v. 4).

(4) He is a Judge (v. 6).

(5) He is a mighty Warrior (v. 6).

b. Note the twofold description of Christ's people in this Psalm.

(1) They are priests: "Thy people shall be willing" (literally, "They shall offer up freely offerings," v. 3). (Compare with Rev. 1:6.)

(2) They are soldiers: "In the day of thy power" (literally "Thy army," v. 3). (Compare with Eph. 6:11.)

Messianic passages:

Verse 1: "The Lord said unto my Lord, Sit thou at my right hand, until I make thine enemies thy footstool."

This verse is quoted more times in the New Testament than any other single Old Testament verse. On at least four occasions it is repeated.

(3) In Matthew 22:41–46 (to point out the deity of Christ).

(4) In Acts 2:34, 35 (to point out the identity of Christ).

(5) In Hebrews 1:13 (as a question, to point out the superiority of Christ).

(6) In Hebrews 10:12, 13 (to point out the finished work of Christ).

Verse 4: "The Lord hath sworn, and will not repent, Thou art a priest forever after the order of Melchizedek."

This verse is found no less than three times in the New Testament, and all three deal with his high priesthood.

(7) In Hebrews 5:6 (to give the qualifications of this High Priesthood after the order of Melchizedek).

(8) In Hebrews 6:20 (to give the immutability of this High Priesthood).

(9) In Hebrews 7:21 (to give the necessity for the High Priesthood).

18. Psalm 118: Predicts Christ to be the vital stone in God's building, rejected by men but chosen by the Lord. This Psalm, often used during the Feast of Tabernacles, may have been sung by the Savior en route to Gethsemane.

Messianic passages:

Verse 22: "The stone which the builders refused is become the headstone of the corner."

This "Supreme Stone of the Scriptures" is referred to in many Old Testament and New Testament passages.

a. It is the cornerstone (Mt. 21:42; Eph. 2:20).

b. It is the headstone (Zech. 4:7; Acts 4:11).

c. It is the smitten stone (1 Cor. 10:4).

d. It is the stumbling stone (1 Cor. 1:23).

e. It is the crushing stone (Dan. 2:34).

f. It is the living, chosen, and precious stone (1 Pet. 2:4–7).

Verse 26: "Blessed be he that cometh in the name of the Lord." (Quoted by the triumphal entry crowd in Mt. 21:9.)

In concluding this section, here are a few suggested names and titles for some of the Psalms.

1. Psalm of the Godly Man (1)
2. Psalms of Creation (8, 104)
3. The Good Shepherd Psalm (22)
4. The Great Shepherd Psalm (23)
5. The Chief Shepherd Psalm (24)
6. The Unity Psalm (133)
7. Psalms of Jerusalem (48, 122, 126, 132, 137)
8. Family Psalms (127, 128)
9. The Security Psalm (121)
10. Psalm of the Only True God (115)
11. Psalm of the Exodus (114)
12. Psalm of Refuge (46)
13. The Ladder of Faith Psalm (37)
14. Psalms of Supreme Praise (103, 148, 150)
15. The Psalm of Old Age (71)
16. The Old One Hundredth Psalm (100)
17. The Psalm of Death (90)
18. The Psalm of Life (91)
19. The Deliverance Psalms (31, 116)
20. The House of God Psalm (84)
21. The Wealth of God Psalm (50)
22. The Word of God Psalms (19, 119)
23. The Voice of God Psalm (29)
24. The Mercy of God Psalm (136)
25. The Goodness of God Psalms (27, 107)
26. The Omniscience and Omnipresence of God Psalm (139)

27. The Omnipotence of God Psalm (147)
28. The Psalm of the Davidic Covenant (89)
29. The History of Israel Psalms (78, 105, 106)
30. The Psalms of the "Why?" (42, 73)
31. Psalms of Deepest Despair (69, 88)

II. The Book of Proverbs.
   Introduction:
   1. A proverb is a short sentence drawn from long experience.
   2. There are several authors of the Book of Proverbs.
      a. Solomon (1–24). We are told in 1 Kings 4:32 that he wrote three thousand proverbs and composed over one thousand songs. However, chapters 1–24 contain only a fraction of this number.
      b. the men of Hezekiah (25–29)
      c. Agur (30)
      d. Lemuel (31)
   3. The book tells a story. It is a picture of a young man starting out in life. His first lesson is given in 1:7. Two schools bid for him and both send out their literature. One is the school of wisdom , and the other, the school for fools.
   4. The key word of Proverbs is, of course, wisdom.
      a. Wisdom will protect her students (2:8).
      b. Wisdom will direct her students (3:5, 6).
      c. Wisdom will perfect her students (4:18).
   5. There are several classic passages in this book.
      a. the warnings of wisdom (1:20–31)
      b. the rewards of wisdom (3:5, 6)
      c. the energy of wisdom (6:6–11)
      d. the godless whore (7:1–27)
      e. the godly wife (31:10–31)
      f. the sovereign Savior (8:22–31)
      g. fifteen famous facts (30:18–31)
      h. the riotous rebel (30:11–14)
   6. Proverbs is the Old Testament equivalent of the epistle of James. It is impossible to offer a chronological outline of this book. At least eleven main subjects are discussed.
      a. A good name:
         (1) "The memory of the just is blessed: but the name of the wicked shall rot" (10:7).
         (2) "A good name is rather to be chosen than great riches, and loving favour rather than silver and gold" (22:1).
      b. Youth and discipline:
         (1) A man with a level headed son is happy, but a rebel's mother is sad (10:1; 17:21, 25; 19:13).
         (2) A wise youth will listen to his father but a young mocker won't (13:1).
         (3) "He that spareth his rod hateth his son: but he that loveth him chasteneth him betimes" (13:24).
         (4) "Chasten thy son while there is hope, and let not thy soul spare for his crying" (19:18).
         (5) "Train up a child in the way he should go: and when he is old, he will not depart from it" (22:6).
         (6) "Foolishness is bound in the heart of a child; but the rod of correction shall drive it far from him" (22:15; 29:15, 17).

         (7) "Withhold not correction from the child: for if thou beatest him with the rod, he shall not die. Thou shalt beat him with the rod, and shalt deliver his soul from hell" (23:13, 14).
         (8) See 23:15–25.
         (9) See 30:11–14.
      c. Business matters:
         (1) God hates a dishonest scale and delights in honesty (11:1; 16:11; 20:10, 23).
         (2) Don't sign a note for someone you barely know (6:1–5; 11:15; 17:18).
         (3) Don't withhold repayment of your debts (3:27).
         (4) God will not let a good man starve to death (10:3).
         (5) Lazy men are soon poor; hard workers have an abundant supply (10:4; 22:29).
         (6) A lazy fellow is a pain to his employer—like smoke in his eyes or vinegar that sets the teeth on edge (11:26).
         (7) He that trusts in his riches shall fall (11:28).
         (8) It is wrong to accept a bribe to twist justice (17:23).
         (9) Develop your business first before building your house (24:27).
         (10) "Riches can disappear fast. And the king's crown doesn't stay in his family forever—so watch your business interests closely. Know the state of your flocks and your herds; then there will be lamb's wool enough for clothing, and goat's milk enough for food for all your household after the hay is harvested, and the new crop appears, and the mountain grasses are gathered in" (27:23–27, *The Living Bible*).
      d. Marriage:
         (1) Drink waters out of your own cistern (5:15).
         (2) Rejoice with the wife of your youth (5:18).
         (3) A beautiful woman lacking discretion and modesty is like a fine gold ring in a pig's snout (11:22).
         (4) He that troubles his own house shall inherit the wind (11:29).
         (5) A virtuous woman is a crown to her husband: but she that makes ashamed is as rottenness in his bones (12:4).
         (6) Every wise woman builds her house; but the foolish one plucks it down with her hands (14:1; 19:13).
         (7) Whoever finds a wife finds a good thing, and obtains favor of the Lord (18:22).
         (8) It is better to dwell in a corner of the housetop, than with a brawling woman in a wide house (21:9; 25:24).
         (9) It is better to dwell in the wilderness, than with a contentious and angry woman (21:19).
         (10) Who can find a virtuous woman?
            Note: The most detailed answer to this question is given in the last chapter of Proverbs (31).

e. Immorality:
  (1) It means to flout the law of God (2:17).
  (2) It leads along the road to death and hell (2:18; 7:27; 9:18).
  (3) It pollutes the conscience (5:4).
  (4) It causes one to groan in anguish and shame when disease consumes the body (5:11).
  (5) It leads to bitter remorse (5:12, 13).
  (6) It will be judged by God (5:21).
  (7) It will bring a man to poverty (6:26).
  (8) It will burn the soul as surely as fire burns the skin (6:27, 32).
  (9) It can be compared to (7:22, 23):
    (a) an ox going to the butcher
    (b) a trapped stag awaiting the death arrow
    (c) a bird flying into a snare
f. Evil companions:
  (1) Refuse them, for in attempting to trap others they only trap themselves (1:10–19).
  (2) Refuse them, for they eat the bread of wickedness and drink the wine of violence (4:17).
  (3) Refuse them, for their kindness is a trick; they want to use you as their pawn (23:6–8).
  (4) Refuse them, for a man's true character is reflected by the friends he chooses (27:19).
g. Wisdom:
  (1) The fear of God is its root (1:7; 9:10).
  (2) It will gain one many honors (1:9).
  (3) It will keep one from immorality (2:16).
  (4) It will direct all one's paths (3:6).
  (5) It will give one renewal, health, and vitality (3:8).
  (6) It will (as one wisely tithes) fill one's barns with wheat and barley and overflow the wine vats with the finest wines (3:9, 10).
  (7) It is better than silver, gold, and precious rubies (3:14; 8:11, 19).
  (8) It gives a long life, riches, honor, pleasure, and peace (3:16, 17; 9:11).
  (9) It was God's method in creation (3:19, 20).
  (10) It is the principal thing (4:7).
  (11) It should be loved like a sweetheart (7:4).
  (12) It brings the favor of God (8:35).
h. Self-control:
  (1) It is better to have self-control than to capture a mighty city (16:32).
  (2) An uncontrolled man often begins something he can't finish (25:8).
  (3) A man without self-control is as defenseless as a city with broken down walls (25:28).
i. Strong drink:
  (1) It gives false courage and leads to brawls (20:1).
  (2) It fills the heart with anguish and sorrow (23:29).
  (3) It causes bloodshot eyes and many wounds (23:29).
  (4) It bites like a poisonous serpent and stings like an adder (23:32).
  (5) It leads to hallucinations and delirium tremens (23:33).
  (6) It makes one say silly and stupid things (23:33).
  (7) It causes one to stagger like a sailor tossed at sea (23:34).
  (8) It allows one to be beat up without even being aware of it (23:35).
  (9) It causes leaders to forget their duties and thus pervert justice (31:5).
j. Friendship:
  (1) A true friend is always loyal and is born to help in time of need (17:17).
  (2) Wounds from a friend are better than kisses from an enemy (27:6).
  (3) Never abandon a friend—either yours or your father's (27:10).
  (4) Friendly suggestions are as pleasant as perfume (27:9).
  (5) A friendly discussion is as stimulating as the sparks that fly when iron strikes iron (27:17).
  (6) A man who would have friends must himself be friendly (18:24).
  (7) A true friend sticks closer than a brother (18:24).
k. Words and the tongue:
  (1) The tongue of the just is as choice silver (10:20).
  (2) He that refrains from speaking is wise (10:19; 11:12).
  (3) The lips of the righteous feed many (10:21).
  (4) A hypocrite with his mouth destroys his neighbor (11:9).
  (5) A talebearer reveals secrets; but one of a faithful spirit conceals the matter (11:13).
  (6) Some speak like the piercings of a sword; but the tongue of the wise is health (12:18).
  (7) He who keeps his mouth keeps his life; but he who opens wide his lips shall have destruction (13:3).
  (8) A true witness delivers souls (14:25).
  (9) A soft answer turns away wrath; but grievous words stir up anger (15:1).
  (10) A wholesome tongue is a tree of life; but perverseness is a breach in the spirit (15:4).
  (11) A word spoken in due season is good (15:23).
  (12) The heart of the righteous studies to answer (15:28).
  (13) Pleasant words are like a honeycomb: sweet to the soul, and health to the bones (16:24).
  (14) A froward man sows strife; and a whisperer separates chief friends (16:28; 17:9).
  (15) The beginning of strife is like letting out water. Therefore, leave off contention, before it is meddled with (17:14).

(16) He who has knowledge spares his words (17:27).

(17) The words of a talebearer are wounds (18:8).

(18) He who answers a matter before he hears it, it is folly and shame unto him (18:13).

(19) Death and life are in the power of the tongue (18:21).

(20) He that speaks lies shall not escape (19:5).

(21) A word fitly spoken is like apples of gold in pictures of silver (25:11).

(22) By long forebearing is a prince persuaded, and a soft tongue breaks the (hard) bone (25:15).

(23) He who passes by, and meddles with strife not belonging to him, is like one who takes a dog by the ears (26:17).

(24) Where no wood is, there the fire goes out; so where there is no talebearer, strife ceases (26:20).

(25) Let another man praise you, and not your own mouth (27:2).

PROVERBS

ELEVEN TIMELY THEMES

A Good Name
10:7; 22:1

Youth and Discipline
13:24; 19:18; 22:6, 15; 23:13, 14

Business Matters
11:1; 6:6-11; 10:4, 26

Marriage
5:15, 18; 11:22, 29; 12:4; 14:1; 19:13; 21:9, 19; 31:10

Immorality
5:3-5; 6:24-32

Evil Companions
1:10-19; 4:17; 23:6-8; 27:19

Wisdom
3:13-18; 8:35

Self-Control
16:32; 25:28

Strong Drink
20:1; 23:29-32

Friendship
17:17; 18:24; 26:6

Words and the Tongue
15:1, 23, 28; 16:24; 17:27; 18:21; 25:11; 26:17, 20, 22

CLASSICAL PASSAGES

A WORD SPOKEN IN DUE SEASON, HOW GOOD IS IT! (15:23).

CHAPTER	VERSES	CHAPTER	VERSES
1	24-28	24	16, 17, 28, 29
3	5, 6, 9, 10-12, 19-26	25	19-22
6	16-19	27	1
8	22-31	28	13
11	30	29	1, 18
14	12, 34	30	4-9, 11-14
16	3, 7, 18	31	10-12, 28, 30
18	10		

l. Various groupings:

(1) Seven things that God hates (6:16-19):
   (a) a proud look
   (b) a lying tongue
   (c) hands that shed innocent blood
   (d) a wicked, plotting heart
   (e) eagerness to do wrong
   (f) a false witness
   (g) sowing discord among brothers

(2) Four things which are never satisfied (30:15, 16):
   (a) the grave
   (b) the barren womb
   (c) a barren desert
   (d) fire

(3) Four wonderful and mysterious things (30:18, 19):
   (a) how an eagle glides through the sky
   (b) how a serpent crawls upon a rock
   (c) how a ship finds its way across the ocean
   (d) the growth of love between a man and a woman

(4) Four things which the earth finds unbearable (30:21-23):
   (a) a slave who becomes a king
   (b) a fool when he is filled with meat
   (c) a bitter woman when she finally marries
   (d) a servant girl who marries her mistress' husband

(5) Four small but wise things (30:24-28):
   (a) ants (They aren't strong, but store up food for the winter.)
   (b) cliff badgers (delicate little animals who protect themselves by living among the rocks)
   (c) the locust (Though they have no leader, they stay together in swarms.)
   (d) spiders (They are easy to catch and kill, yet are found even in kings' palaces.)

(6) Four stately monarchs (30:29-31):
   (a) the lion, king of animals (He won't turn aside for anyone.)
   (b) the greyhound
   (c) the he-goat
   (d) a king as he leads his army

(7) Two things Agur requests of God (30:7-9):
   (a) Remove from me vanity and lies.
   (b) Give me neither poverty nor riches—feed me with food convenient for me:
      Lest I be full, and deny thee and say, who is the Lord?
      Lest I be poor, and steal, and take the name of my God in vain.

In addition to all this, there are a number of classical passages in this book. Some of the more important are as follows:

"Because I have called, and ye refused; I have stretched out my hand, and no man regarded; but ye have set at nought all my counsel, and would none of my reproof: I also will laugh at your calamity; I will mock when your fear cometh; when your fear cometh as desolation, and your destruction cometh as a whirlwind; when distress and anguish cometh upon you. Then shall they call upon me, but I will not answer; they shall seek me early, but they shall not find me" (1:24–28).

"Trust in the Lord with all thine heart; and lean not unto thine own understanding. In all thy ways acknowledge him, and he shall direct thy paths. Honour the Lord with thy substance, and with the first-fruits of all thine increase: So shall thy barns be filled with plenty, and thy presses shall burst out with new wine.

My son, despise not the chastening of the Lord; neither be weary of his correction: For whom the Lord loveth he correcteth; even as a father the son in whom he delighteth.

The Lord by wisdom hath founded the earth; by understanding hath he established the heavens. By his knowledge the depths are broken up, and the clouds drop down the dew.

My son, let not them depart from thine eyes: keep sound wisdom and discretion: So shall they be life unto thy soul, and grace to thy neck. Then shalt thou walk in thy way safely, and thy foot shall not stumble.

When thou liest down, thou shalt not be afraid: yea, thou shalt lie down, and thy sleep shall be sweet. Be not afraid of sudden fear, neither of the desolation of the wicked, when it cometh. For the Lord shall be thy confidence, and shall keep thy foot from being taken" (3:5, 6, 9–12, 19–26).

"These six things doth the Lord hate: yea, seven are an abomination unto him: A proud look, a lying tongue, and hands that shed innocent blood, an heart that deviseth wicked imaginations, feet that be swift in running to mischief, a false witness that speaketh lies, and he that soweth discord among brethren" (6:16–19).

"The Lord possessed me in the beginning of his way, before his works of old. I was set up from everlasting, from the beginning, or ever the earth was. When there were no depths, I was brought forth; when there were no fountains abounding with water.

Before the mountains were settled, before the hills was I brought forth: while as yet he had not made the earth, nor the fields, nor the highest part of the dust of the world.

When he prepared the heavens, I was there: when he set a compass upon the face of the depth: when he established the clouds above: when he strengthened the fountains of the deep: when he gave to the sea his decree, that the waters should not pass his commandment: when he appointed the foundations of the earth: then I was by him, as one brought up with him: and I was daily his delight, rejoicing always before him; rejoicing in the habitable part of his earth; and my delights were with the sons of men" (8:22–31).

"The fruit of the righteous is a tree of life; and he that winneth souls is wise" (11:30).

"There is a way which seemeth right unto a man, but the end thereof are the ways of death. Righteousness exalteth a nation: but sin is a reproach to any people" (14:12, 34).

"Commit thy works unto the Lord, and thy thoughts shall be established. When a man's ways please the Lord, he maketh even his enemies to be at peace with him. Pride goeth before destruction, and an haughty spirit before a fall" (16:3, 7, 18).

"The name of the Lord is a strong tower: the righteous runneth into it, and is safe" (18:10).

"For a just man falleth seven times, and riseth up again: but the wicked shall fall into mischief. Rejoice not when thine enemy falleth, and let not thine heart be glad when he stumbleth: Be not a witness against thy neighbour without cause; and deceive not with thy lips. Say not, I will do so to him as he hath done to me: I will render to the man according to his work" (24:16, 17, 28, 29).

"Confidence in an unfaithful man in time of trouble is like a broken tooth, and a foot out of joint. As he that taketh away a garment in cold weather, and as vinegar upon nitre, so is he that singeth songs to an heavy heart. If thine enemy be hungry, give him bread to eat; and if he be thirsty, give him water to drink: for thou shalt heap coals of fire upon his head, and the Lord shall reward thee" (25:19–22).

"Boast not thyself of tomorrow; for thou knowest not what a day may bring forth" (27:1).

"He that covereth his sins shall not prosper: but whoso confesseth and forsaketh them shall have mercy" (28:13).

"He, that being often reproved hardeneth his neck, shall suddenly be destroyed, and that without remedy. Where there is no vision, the people perish: but he that keepeth the law, happy is he" (29:1, 18).

"Who hath ascended up into heaven, or descended? who hath gathered the wind in his fists? who hath bound the waters in a garment? who hath established all the ends of the earth? what is his name, and what is his son's name, if thou canst tell? Every word of God is pure: he is a shield unto them that put their trust in him.

Add thou not unto his words, lest he reprove thee, and thou be found a liar. Two things have I required of thee; deny me them not before I die: Remove far from me vanity and lies: give me neither poverty nor riches; feed me with food convenient for me: Lest I be full, and deny thee, and say, Who is the Lord? or lest I be poor, and steal, and take the name of my God in vain. There is a generation that curseth their father, and doth not bless their mother. There is a generation that are pure in their own eyes, and yet is not washed from their filthiness.

There is a generation, O how lofty are their eyes! and their eyelids are lifted up. There is a generation, whose teeth are as swords, and their jaw-teeth as knives, to devour the poor from off the earth, and the needy from among men" (30:4-9, 11-14).

"Who can find a virtuous woman? for her price is far above rubies. The heart of her husband doth safely trust in her, so that he shall have no need of spoil. She will do him good and not evil all the days of her life. Her children arise up, and call her blessed; her husband also, and he praiseth her. Favour is deceitful, and beauty is vain: but a woman that feareth the Lord, she shall be praised" (31:10-12, 28, 30).

III. The Book of Ecclesiastes.
Introduction:
1. The meaning of the word is to address an assembly.
2. The purpose of the book:
   a. "To convince men of the uselessness of any world view which does not rise above the horizon of man himself. It pronounces the verdict of 'vanity of vanities' upon any philosophy of life which regards the created world of human enjoyment as an end in life." (Gleason L. Archer, *A Survey of Old Testament Introduction*, p. 459)
   b. "You do not have to go outside the Bible to find the merely human philosophy of life. God has given us in the book of Ecclesiastes the record of all that human thinking and natural religion has ever been able to discover concerning the meaning and goal of life. The arguments in the book, therefore, are not God's arguments, but God's record of man's arguments. This explains why such passages as 1:15; 2:24; 3:3, 4, 8, 11, 19, 20; 8:15 are at positive variance with the rest of the Bible." (*What the Bible Is All About*, Henrietta Mears, p. 200)
3. Did Solomon teach there is no life after death? The answer is no! (See 3:16; 11:9; 12:14.)
4. The key words in Ecclesiastes are man (used forty-seven times), labor (thirty-six), under the sun (thirty), and vanity (thirty-seven).
5. The book of Ecclesiastes may be summarized by two statements, one made by a sewer worker in Chicago, and the other by a well-known agnostic lawyer. Both statements were in response to a question concerning their personal philosophy of life.
   "There is a statement in the Bible which summarizes my life. It says, 'We have toiled all night, and have taken nothing . . .'" [Lk. 5:5]. —Clarence Darrow
   "I digge de ditch to gette de money to buye de food to gette de strength to digge de ditch!" — Cook County Sewer Employee
A. The quest—man's problems stated (1-2).
   Even before he starts the search, Solomon has doubts. In his opinion:
   Everything seems so futile (1:2).
   Generations come and go, but it seems to make no difference (1:4).

The sun rises and sets, the wind twists back and forth, but neither seems to get any place or accomplish any purpose (1:5, 6).
The river runs into the sea, but the sea is never full. The water returns again to the rivers and flows again to the sea (1:7).
Everything appears so unutterably weary and tiresome (1:8).
No man seems satisfied, regardless of what he has seen or heard (1:8).
History merely repeats itself—absolutely nothing new ever occurs under the sun (1:9, 10).
One hundred years from now everything will have been forgotten, regardless what occurs today (1:11).
Was life truly this way everywhere? Could a wise and healthy man, by searching the length and breadth of the land, find peace and purpose? Solomon would try. This he diligently did by drinking deeply at the wells of the following:
1. Human wisdom.
   "I communed with mine own heart, saying, Lo, I am come to great estate, and have gotten more wisdom than all they that have been before me in Jerusalem: yea, my heart had great experience of wisdom and knowledge. And I gave my heart to know wisdom, and to know madness and folly: I perceived that this also is vexation of spirit" (1:16, 17).
   Solomon had more natural capacity to accumulate and apply raw facts than any man who ever lived (apart from Christ), but he sadly concluded:
   "For in much wisdom is much grief: and he that increaseth knowledge increaseth sorrow" (1:18).
2. Pleasure (2:1-3).
   "Philosophy has failed, says the preacher, so let merriment be tried. Music, dance, wine (not to excess), the funny story, the clever repartee: these are now cultivated. Clowns are now welcomed to the court where only grave philosophy had been. The halls of the palace resounded with laughter and gaiety." (Henrietta C. Mears, *What the Bible Is All About*, p. 201).
   But laughter and liquor could in no way soothe man's soul.
   Note the king's sad conclusion: "I said of laughter, It is mad: and of mirth, What doeth it?" (2:2). (See also 8:15.)
3. Alcohol (2:3).
   "I sought in mine heart to give myself unto wine . . . ."
4. Great building projects (2:4).
   "I made me great works; I builded houses . . . ."
   Solomon now attempts to plug that "hole in his soul" by inaugurating a great public works program. Aqueducts, pools, palaces, and gleaming buildings soon grace the Syrian skyland. The court comedians give way to the great architects. But all too soon the building campaign wears thin and is quietly dropped.

5. Beautiful gardens and parks (2:4–6).

"I planted vineyards; I made me gardens and orchards, and I planted trees in them of all kinds of fruits; I made pools of water, to water therewith the wood that bringeth forth trees" (2:4–6).

Now luscious vineyards, graceful gardens, exotic and rare flowers, tropical plants, and other gems of green suddenly sprout up. Jerusalem and the vicinity bloom like the original Garden of Eden. But, alas, before long the frost of disinterest puts the blight to this bloom also!

6. Personal indulgences (2:7).

"I got me servants and maidens, and had servants born in my house" (2:7).

The king now had an individual servant for every wish. But none could serve up his wish for inward peace and purpose.

7. Sex.

"And he had seven hundred wives, princesses, and three hundred concubines . . ." (1 Ki. 11:3).

8. Massive wealth.

"I had great possessions of herds and flocks above all that were in Jerusalem before me: I gathered also silver and gold, and the peculiar treasure of kings and the provinces . . ." (2:7, 8).

9. International reputation.

"And she [the Queen of Sheba] said to the king, it was a true report that I heard in mine own land of thy acts and of thy wisdom. Howbeit, I believed not the words, until I came, and mine eyes had seen it: and behold, the half was not told me: thy wisdom and prosperity exceedeth the fame which I heard" (1 Ki. 10:6, 7).

10. Cattle breeding (2:7).

Great herds of cows, sheep, oxen, goats, and other animals would now graze upon the green Palestinian pastures. But while the skin and meats of these animals might clothe and feed the outer man, the inner person remained naked and starving.

11. Music (2:8).

"I got me men singers and women singers, and the delights of the sons of men, as musical instruments, and that of all sorts."

But the missing chord of contentment was not to be found through music, however beautiful the song and talented the singers.

12. Literature.

"And he spoke three thousand proverbs, and his songs were a thousand and five" (1 Ki. 4:32).

13. Natural science.

"And he spake of trees, from the cedar tree that is in Lebanon even unto the hyssop that springeth out of the wall: he spake also of beasts, and of fowl, and of creeping things, and of fishes" (1 Ki. 4:33).

14. Military power.

"And Solomon had forty thousand stalls of horses for his chariots, and twelve thousand horsemen" (1 Ki. 4:26).

"And King Solomon made a navy of ships . . . on the shore of the Red Sea . . ." (1 Ki. 9:26).

B. The digest—man's problems studied (3–10).

After completing an exhaustive (and doubtless exhausting) journey, Solomon returns home (4:1) and contemplates his travels. He concludes the following about life apart from God:

1. It is utterly futile (2:11).
2. It is filled with repetition (3:1–8).
3. It is permeated with sorrow (4:1).
4. It is grievous and frustrating (2:17).
5. It is uncertain (9:11, 12).
6. It is without purpose (4:2, 3; 8:15).
7. It is incurable (1:15).
8. It is unjust (7:15; 8:14; 9:11; 10:6, 7).
9. It is on the level of animal existence (3:19).

C. The best—man's problem solved (11–12).

Solomon concludes that even with God, life is a mystery, but apart from him it becomes a horrible nightmare. Therefore, it is best if man:

1. Finds God early in his life (11:9, 10; 12:1, 2).
2. Fears God throughout his life (12:13, 14).

J. Vernon McGee aptly summarizes verses 1–7 in the following way:

Verse 2: "Failing eyesight makes it appear that the sun, moon, and stars are getting dimmer. Time flies and one sad experience follows another—clouds return after rain."

Verse 3: "Keepers of the house shall tremble" refers to the legs. The old person begins to totter. "Strong men" are the shoulders that are no longer erect. "Grinders" are the teeth. "Those that look out of the windows" refers to failing eyesight.

Verse 4: "Doors shut in the street" refers to being hard of hearing. "Sound of grinding is low" refers to the tongue. The voice of old age gets thin.

"Shall rise up at the voice of the bird"—it took an alarm clock to wake him before, now the chirping of a bird disturbs his sleep.

"Daughters of music shall be brought low" indicates that he can no longer sing in the choir, cannot carry a tune anymore.

Verse 5: "Afraid of that which is high"—things that formerly did not frighten him. "Fears shall be in the way"—he no longer enjoys traveling. "Almond tree shall flourish"—our senior citizen is getting gray-haired, if his hair has not fallen out. "Grasshoppers shall be a burden"—little things annoy him. "Desire shall fail"—romance is gone. "Man goeth to his long home"—death comes.

Verse 6: "Silver cord"—the spinal cord.

"Golden bowl"—the head.

"Pitcher"—the lungs.

"Wheel"—the heart.

IV. The Song of Solomon.

Background of the story:

A. Act One—The Shulamite Cinderella.

1. Solomon had a vineyard in the hill country of Ephraim, just outside the little town of Shunam, about fifty miles north of Jerusalem (8:11).

137

2. This vineyard was rented out to a family of sharecroppers consisting of a mother, two sons, and two daughters. The oldest of these girls was the Shulamite, and the youngest, her little sister (6:13; 8:8).
3. The Shulamite was the Cinderella of the family, having great natural beauty, but unnoticed by the world.
4. Her brothers made her work very hard tending the vineyards, so that she had little opportunity to care for her personal appearance (1:6).
   a. She pruned the vines.
   b. She set traps for the little foxes (2:15).
   c. She also kept the flocks (1:8).
5. From being out in the open so often, she became sunburned (1:6).

B. Act Two—The Shepherd Stranger.
1. One day a mysterious, handsome stranger comes to the vineyard and soon wins the heart of the Shulamite girl. Unknown to her, he is really Solomon, disguised as a lowly shepherd.
2. She asks about his flocks (1:7).
3. He answers evasively, but is very definite concerning his love for her (1:8-10).
4. He leaves her, but promises he will someday return to her.
5. During his absence she dreams of him on two occasions.
   a. First dream—that they are already married and that one night she awakens to find him missing from her bed. She quickly dresses and goes out looking for him (3:2-4).
   b. Second dream—that her beloved has returned and besought her to open the door and let him in. But she refuses for she is unwilling to reclothe herself and soil her feet going to the door. Soon however, her heart smites her for this shabby action and she leaps for the door. But alas, he has gone!
      We read:
      "My beloved put in his hand by the hole of the door . . . I rose up to open to my beloved; and my hands dropped with myrrh, and my fingers with sweet smelling myrrh, upon the handles of the lock" (5:4, 5).
      Dr. J. Vernon McGee informs us that a lovely custom of that day was for the lover to place sweet-smelling myrrh inside the handle of the bride's door. The bride then began her frantic search for the lover she had so carelessly ignored. During her search the guards of the city mistreated her, and the watchman on the wall tore off her veil. She then pleaded with the women of Jerusalem to aid her in finding her lover and informing him of her love for him (5:6-8).
      Suddenly and joyfully she discovers his whereabouts.
      "My beloved is gone down into his garden, to the beds of spices, to feed in the gardens, and to gather lilies. I am my beloved's and my beloved is mine: he feedeth among the lilies" (6:2, 3).
6. These then, are her two dreams concerning the mysterious shepherd lover of the Shulamite girl. But why did he leave her? Where did he go? Would he ever return?

C. Act Three—The Mighty Monarch.
1. One day the little town of Shunam receives some electrifying news. King Solomon himself is approaching their city. But the lovesick and lonely maiden is not interested, and takes no further notice until word is brought to her that the powerful potentate himself desires to see her.
2. She is puzzled until she is brought into his presence, where she recognizes him as her beloved shepherd. He then gently explains to her that although he has already gathered sixty wives, eighty concubines, and unnumbered virgins, that she will be his choice bride and true love (6:8). He invites her to come with him and promises to care for her little sister (8:8, 9).
3. The bride is then placed in the king's chariot, made from the wood of Lebanon, with silver posts, a golden canopy, and purple seating (3:9, 10).
4. Together they ride off to the royal palace in Jerusalem, accompanied by sixty mighty swordsmen and experienced body guards (3:7, 8).

D. The bride of the story (as described by the bridegroom).
1. She was the most beautiful girl in the world (1:8).
2. Her eyes were as soft as doves (1:15).
3. She was as a lily among the thorns as compared to his other wives (2:2).
4. Her hair fell across her face like flocks of goats which frisked across the slopes of Gilead (4:1).
5. Her teeth were as white as sheep's wool (4:2).
6. Her lips were like a thread of scarlet (4:3) and made of honey (4:11).
7. Her neck was as stately as the Tower of David (4:4).
8. Her bosom was as twin fawns of a gazelle, feeding among the lilies (4:5).
9. She was like a lovely orchard, bearing precious fruit (4:13).
10. She was as a garden fountain, a well of living water, refreshing as the streams from the
11. Lebanon mountains (4:15).
    Her thighs were like jewels, the work of the most skilled of craftsmen (7:1).
12. Her navel was as lovely as a goblet filled with wine (7:2).
13. Her waist was like a heap of wheat set about with lilies (7:2).
14. Her nose was shapely like the Tower of Lebanon overlooking Damascus (7:4).
15. He was completely overcome by a single glance of her beautiful eyes (4:9).

E. The bridegroom of the story (as described by the bride).

1. He was like a bouquet of flowers in a garden (1:14).
2. He was as swift as a young gazelle leaping and bounding over the hills (2:9).
3. He was ruddy and handsome, the fairest of ten thousand (5:10).
4. His head was as purest gold, covered by wavy, raven hair (5:11).
5. His eyes were as doves beside the water brooks, deep and quiet (5:12).
6. His cheeks were like sweetly scented beds of spice (5:13).
7. His lips were as perfumed lilies and his breath like myrrh (5:13).
8. His arms were as round bars of gold set with topaz (5:14).
9. His body was bright ivory encrusted with jewels (5:14).
10. His legs were pillars of marble set in sockets of finest gold, like cedars of Lebanon (5:15).

THE CHAOTIC KINGDOM STAGE

THE CHAOTIC KINGDOM STAGE
(1 Kings 12-22; 2 Kings 1-17;
2 Chronicles 10-36; Obadiah; Joel;
Jonah; Amos; Hosea; Micah; Isaiah;
Nahum; Zephaniah; Habakkuk;
Jeremiah; Lamentations)

1. This stage covers a period of around 325 years, from 930 b.c. to 605 b.c. The key events take place in Jerusalem and Samaria.
2. The period begins with a tragic civil war which splits the nation Israel into two opposing kingdoms. The period ends with the capture of both these kingdoms by two enemy Gentile nations (1 Ki. 12; 2 Ki. 17, 25).
3. The chaotic stage would feature the following:
   a. One king (Josiah) discovering God's Word in the Temple and another king (Jehoiakim) attempting to destroy it in the fire (2 Ki. 22; Jer. 36).
   b. The writing of at least twelve Old Testament books by eleven human authors. These are: Obadiah, Joel, Jonah, Amos, Hosea, Micah, Isaiah, Nahum, Zephaniah, Habakkuk, and Jeremiah (who also wrote Lamentations).
   c. The second of four great miracle-working periods in the Bible.
      (1) The first was during the time of Moses and Joshua.
      (2) The second was during the time of Elijah and Elisha.
      (3) The third was during the time of Daniel and Ezekiel.
      (4) The fourth was during the time of Christ and the apostles.
   d. All three of the individuals who were raised from the dead in the Old Testament: (1) 1 Kings 17, (2) 2 Kings 4, and (3) 2 Kings 13.
   e. The only Old Testament man ever to be healed of leprosy (Naaman, 2 Ki. 5).
   f. The salvation of Samaria (northern capital) by four lepers, and the salvation of Jerusalem (southern capital) by the death angel (2 Ki. 7, 19).
   g. The beginning of the Samaritan race (2 Ki. 17).
   h. The second and third of three occasions when God rolled back the waters of the Jordan river (2 Ki. 2). (For the first, see Josh. 3.)
   i. The account of a singing choir defeating an enemy on a battlefield.
      "And they rose early in the morning, and went forth into the wilderness of Tekoa: and as they went forth, Jehoshaphat stood and said, Hear me, O Judah, and ye inhabitants of Jerusalem;

Believe in the Lord your God, so shall ye be established; believe his prophets, so shall ye prosper. And when he had consulted with the people, he appointed singers unto the Lord, and that should praise the beauty of holiness, as they went out before the army, and to say, Praise the Lord; for his mercy endureth for ever. And when they began to sing and to praise, the Lord set ambushments against the children of Ammon, Moab, and mount Seir, which were come against Judah; and they were smitten" (2 Chron. 20:20-22).
   j. The sight of water being burned by fire (1 Ki. 18). "Then the fire of the Lord fell and consumed the burnt-sacrifice, and the wood, and the stones, and the dust, and licked up the water that was in the trench" (1 Ki. 18:38).
   k. The sight of an axe head floating on water (2 Ki. 6).
   l. The second of two men who went to heaven without first dying (2 Ki. 2).
      "And it came to pass, as they still went on, and talked, that, behold, there appeared a chariot of fire, and horses of fire, and parted them both asunder; and Elijah went up by a whirlwind into heaven" (2 Ki. 2:11).
   m. The only time in the Old Testament where men are allowed to see God's mounted army of angels (2 Ki. 6).
      "And when the servant of the man of God was risen early, and gone forth, behold, an host compassed the city both with horses and chariots. And his servant said unto him, Alas, my master? how shall we do? And he answered, Fear not: for they that be with us are more than they that be with them. And Elisha prayed, and said, Lord, I pray thee, open his eyes, that he may see. And the Lord opened the eyes of the young man; and he saw: and, behold, the mountain was full of horses and chariots of fire round about Elisha" (2 Ki. 6:15-17).
   n. Seven prayers on a mountain, seven dips in a river, and seven sneezes on a bed (1 Ki. 18; 2 Ki. 5; 4).
      Elijah did the praying on Carmel.
      Naaman did the dipping in Jordan.
      A resurrected child did the sneezing in Shunem.

THE CHAOTIC KINGDOM STAGE

This stage is the most interwoven, fast-moving, and detailed period in all the Bible. It will be considered under three main divisions.
   I. An Introduction to the Chaotic Kingdom Stage.
   II. The Rulers of the Chaotic Kingdom Stage.
      At this point we will employ a twofold method:

THE CHAOTIC KINGDOM STAGE

1 Kings 12-22
2 Kings
2 Chronicles 10-36
Obadiah
Joel
Jonah
Amos
Hosea
Micah
Isaiah
Nahum
Zephaniah
Habakkuk
Jeremiah
Lamentations

THE SOUTHERN KINGDOM

REHOBOAM	JOTHAM
ABIJAM	AHAZ
ASA	HEZEKIAH
JEHOSHAPHAT	MANASSEH
JEHORAM	AMON
AHAZIAH	JOSIAH
ATHALIAH	JEHOAHAZ
JOASH	JEHOIAKIM
AMAZIAH	JEHOIACHIN
UZZIAH	ZEDEKIAH

THE NORTHERN KINGDOM

JEROBOAM	JEHOAHAZ
NADAB	JEHOASH
BAASHA	JEROBOAM II
ELAH	ZECHARIAH
ZIMRI	SHALLUM
OMRI	MENAHEM
AHAB	PEKAHIAH
AHAZIAH	PEKAH
JEHORAM	HOSHEA
JEHU	

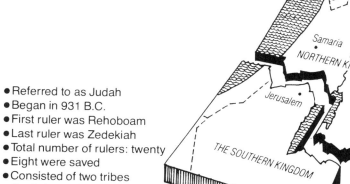

- Referred to as Judah
- Began in 931 B.C.
- First ruler was Rehoboam
- Last ruler was Zedekiah
- Total number of rulers: twenty
- Eight were saved
- Consisted of two tribes
- Capital was Jerusalem
- Captured by the Babylonians in 606 B.C.
- Three separate returns from captivity
- Lasted 325 years: 931—606 B.C.

- Referred to as Israel and Ephraim
- Began in 931 B.C.
- First ruler was Jeroboam
- Last ruler was Hoshea
- Total number of rulers: nineteen
- Not one was saved
- Consisted of ten tribes
- Capital was Samaria
- Captured by the Assyrians in 721 B.C.
- No return from captivity
- Lasted 210 years: 931—721 B.C.

A. The floodlight, shotgun approach. Here the reign of every king will be briefly outlined.

B. The spotlight, rifle approach. Here the reign of the more important kings will be expanded upon.

III. The Old Testament Books Written During the Chaotic Kingdom Stage.

I. An Introduction to the Chaotic Kingdom Stage.
After the death of Solomon, a tragic civil war split Israel into two opposing kingdoms, the north and the south.

A. The northern kingdom:
1. It began in 931 B.C. and lasted 210 years.
2. The first ruler was Jeroboam.
3. The last ruler was Hoshea.
4. The total number of kings was nineteen. Not one was righteous.
5. It consisted of ten tribes.
6. Its capital later became Samaria.
7. It was captured by the Assyrians in 721 B.C.
8. There was no return from captivity.

B. The southern kingdom:
1. It began in 931 B.C. and lasted 326 years.

NORTHERN RULERS

1. Jeroboam
DATES **931-909** DURATION **22 YEARS**
SCRIPTURE **1 KINGS 11:26—14:20;**
2 CHRONICLES 9:29—13:22

1. He served as a cabinet member under Solomon, but fled to Egypt to escape the king's wrath.
2. He led the revolt of the ten tribes at Shechem.
3. His false religion caused Israel to sin.
4. His pagan altar was destroyed, his arm paralyzed, and his son stricken by God due to his sin.
5. He was defeated in battle by Abijam, the second king of the south.
6. He was stricken with a plague from God and died.

2. Nadab
DATES **910-908** DURATION **2 YEARS**
SCRIPTURE **1 KINGS 15:25-28**

1. He was the son of Jeroboam.
2. He was assassinated by a rebel named Baasha.

3. Baasha
DATES **909-885** DURATION **24 YEARS**
SCRIPTURE **1 KINGS 15:27—16:7;**
2 CHRONICLES 16:1-6

1. He killed Nadab and thus fulfilled Ahijah the prophet's prediction. Compare 1 Kings 14:4 with 15:29.
2. He fought with Asa (third king of the south) and built a wall to cut off trade to Jerusalem.
3. His seed was predicted to suffer the same judgment as that of Jeroboam.

4. Elah
DATES **885-883** DURATION **2 YEARS**
SCRIPTURE **1 KINGS 16:6-14**

1. He was the son of Baasha.
2. He was assassinated by a soldier rebel while drunk.

5. Zimri
DATES **885** DURATION **7 DAYS**
SCRIPTURE **1 KINGS 16:9-20**

1. He fulfilled prophecy by slaughtering Baasha's seed.
2. He was trapped by rebel soldiers in his own palace, resulting in a fiery suicidal death.

6. Omri
DATES **885-873** DURATION **12 YEARS**
SCRIPTURE **1 KINGS 16:15-28**

1. He made Samaria the northern capital.
2. He was the most powerful king up to his time.
3. He arranged the marriage of his son Ahab to Jezebel.

2. The first ruler was Rehoboam.
3. The last ruler was Zedekiah.
4. The total number of rulers was twenty: nineteen kings and one queen. Eight of the twenty were righteous.
5. It consisted of two tribes (Judah and Benjamin).
6. Its capital remained Jerusalem.
7. It was captured by the Babylonians in 606 B.C.
8. There were three separate returns from captivity.

Note: The Chaotic Kingdom Stage may thus be divided into two time periods:
a. The divided kingdom (both north and south) (931-721 B.C.).
b. The single kingdom (only the south) (721-605 B.C.).

II. The Rulers of the Chaotic Kingdom Stage.
The Floodlight, Shotgun Approach:
Northern rulers:
A. Jeroboam (1 Ki. 11:26—14:20; 2 Chron. 9:29—13:22).
1. He served as a cabinet member under Solomon, but fled to Egypt for awhile to escape the king's wrath (1 Ki. 11:28, 40).
2. He led the revolt of the ten tribes at Shechem.
3. His false religion caused Israel to sin.
4. His false altar was destroyed, his arm was paralyzed, and his son stricken by God, all as punishment for his sin.
5. He was defeated in battle by Abijam, the second king of the South.
6. He was stricken with a plague from God and died.
7. He ruled for twenty-two years (931-909 B.C.)
B. Nadab (1 Ki. 15:25-28).
1. He was the son of Jeroboam.
2. He was assassinated by a rebel named Baasha.
3. Nadab was thus the first of six northern kings to be murdered while in office.
4. He ruled for two years (910-908).
C. Baasha (1 Ki. 15:27—16:7; 2 Chron. 16:1-6).
1. He unknowingly fulfilled the prophecy given to Jeroboam's wife by Ahijah the prophet, in killing Nadab and his relatives. (Compare 1 Ki. 14:14 with 15:29.)
2. He declared war on Asa (third king of Judah) and began building a wall fortress at Ramah to control the road to Judah, thus hoping to cut off all trade to Jerusalem (2 Chron. 16:1).
3. He was rejected by God because of his sin. Jehu, the prophet, predicted that Baasha's descendants would suffer the same judgment God placed on Jeroboam.
4. Baasha ruled for twenty-four years (909-885 B.C.).

Note: It can be seen already that some of the reigns overlapped each other—that is, on occasion both father and son may have ruled at the same time. This explains the difference in the total number of years of all the northern kings *as given in the Bible,* which is 252 years; and the *actual time involved,* around 208 years (beginning with Jeroboam in 931 B.C., and ending with Hoshea in 721 B.C.).

D. Elah (1 Ki. 16:6-14).
1. He was the son of Baasha.
2. He was assassinated by the commander of his royal chariot troops, a man named Zimri.
3. Elah was drunk at the time.
4. He ruled for two years (885-883 B.C.).

E. Zimri (1 Ki. 16:9-20).
1. He fulfilled Jehu's prophecy by slaughtering all the seed of Baasha. (Compare 1 Ki. 16:7 with 16:12.)
2. Zimri was then trapped by Omri, Israel's new commander-in-chief, in the palace, which resulted in a fiery suicidal death.
3. He reigned but seven days (885 B.C.).

F. Omri (1 Ki. 16:15-28).
1. He moved the northern capital from Tirzah to Samaria.
2. He arranged the political marriage of his son Ahab to Jezebel, daughter of Ethbaal, king of the Sidonians.
3. He ruled for twelve years (885-873 B.C.).

G. Ahab (1 Ki. 16:28—22:40; 2 Chron. 18:1-34).
1. He married Jezebel.
2. He was allowed to defeat the Syrians on two occasions.
3. He was denounced often by Elijah.
   a. for encouraging Baal-worship
   b. for his part in the murder of Naboth
   c. for sparing the life of a godless Syrian king
4. He tricked godly king Jehoshaphat (fourth king of Judah) into a twofold compromise:
   a. a matrimonial alliance, whereby his wicked daughter, Athaliah, is given to Joram, son of Jehoshaphat
   b. a military alliance, whereby Jehoshaphat and Ahab go to war against Syria
5. The death of his wicked wife was predicted by Elijah.
6. His own death was predicted by both Elijah and the prophet Micaiah.
7. He was slain in battle with the Syrians.
8. He ruled for twenty-two years (874-852 B.C.).

H. Ahaziah (1 Ki. 22:40—2 Ki. 1:18; 2 Chron. 20:35-37).
1. He was the oldest son of Ahab and Jezebel.
2. He persuaded Jehoshaphat to enter into a shipbuilding enterprise with him at Ezion-geber (2 Chron. 20:35-37).
3. He suffered a severe (and later fatal) fall in his palace at Samaria.
4. He turned to the pagan god Baal-zebub for healing, but received instead the condemnation of Elijah, whom he unsuccessfully attempted to arrest.
5. He ruled for two years (853-851 B.C.).

I. Jehoram (2 Ki. 3:1—9:25; 2 Chron. 22:5-7).
1. He was the youngest son of Ahab and brother of Ahaziah.
2. He also (like father and brother) persuaded Jehoshaphat to enter into an alliance, this time a military campaign against the Moabites. The prophet Elisha at this time worked a miracle on the battlefield (for Jehoshaphat's

NORTHERN RULERS

7. Ahab
DATES 874-852   DURATION 22 YEARS
SCRIPTURE 1 KINGS 16:28—22:40;
2 CHRONICLES 18:1-34
1. He married Jezebel.
2. His Baal-worshiping practices caused a great famine to fall upon the land.
3. He was allowed to defeat the Syrians on two occasions to prove a point.
4. He tricked godly King Jehoshaphat (fourth king of Judah) into a twofold compromise—matrimonial and military.
5. His death for his many sins was predicted by three prophets (1 Ki. 20:42; 21:19; 22:17, 28).
6. The death of Jezebel, his wife, was also predicted by Elijah.
7. He experienced a brief (but temporary) fox-hole type conversion (1 Ki. 21:29).
8. He was killed in a battle with Syria.

8. Ahaziah
DATES 853-851   DURATION 2 YEARS
SCRIPTURE 1 KINGS 22:40—2 KINGS 1:18;
2 CHRONICLES 20:35-37
1. He was the oldest son of Ahab and Jezebel.
2. He persuaded Jehoshaphat to enter into a ship-building enterprise with him at Ezion-Geber.
3. He suffered a severe fall (which proved fatal) in his palace in Samaria.
4. He turned to the pagan god Baal-Zebub for healing.
5. He was rebuked for this by Elijah, whom he unsuccessfully attempted to arrest.

9. Jehoram
DATES 852-840   DURATION 12 YEARS
SCRIPTURE 2 KINGS 3:1—9:25;
2 CHRONICLES 22:5-7
1. He was the youngest son of Ahab and Jezebel.
2. He persuaded Jehoshaphat to ally with him against Syria.
3. Elisha the prophet performed a miracle (for Jehoshaphat's sake) which won the battle.
4. Elisha later helped Jehoram by warning him of several planned Syrian ambushes.
5. Elisha would, however, prevent him from slaughtering some supernaturally blinded Syrian troops.
6. He was on the throne when Naaman came to be healed of leprosy.
7. He was on the throne when God used four lepers to save Samaria from starvation.
8. He was finally murdered by Jehu in the Valley of Jezreel.

10. Jehu
DATES 841-813   DURATION 28 YEARS
SCRIPTURE 2 KINGS 9:1—10:36;
2 CHRONICLES 22:7-12
1. He was anointed by a messenger from Elisha.
2. He was known for his bloodletting. He executed:
   Judah's King Ahaziah (not to be confused with Ahab's oldest son), grandson of Jehoshaphat
   The northern king Jehoram
   Jezebel
   Ahab's seventy sons, relatives, and friends
   Forty-two royal princes of Judah
   The Baal-worshipers

NORTHERN RULERS

11. Jehoahaz
DATES **814-797**   DURATION **17 YEARS**
SCRIPTURE **2 KINGS 13:1-9**

1. He was the son of Jehu.
2. He saw his army almost wiped out by the Syrians.
3. He experienced a brief period of remorse over his sins, but apparently not genuine repentance.

12. Jehoash
DATES **798-782**   DURATION **16 YEARS**
SCRIPTURE **2 KINGS 13:10—14:16;**
        2 CHRONICLES 25:17-24

1. He visited Elisha on his deathbed.
2. He defeated Amaziah (eighth king of Judah) on the battlefield.
3. He related one of the two Old Testament fables to ridicule the arrogant claims of Amaziah.
4. He plundered Jerusalem, taking many hostages and much wealth.

13. Jeroboam II
DATES **793-752**   DURATION **41 YEARS**
SCRIPTURE **2 KINGS 14:23-29**

1. He ruled longer than any other northern king.
2. He was one of the most powerful kings of the north.
3. He recovered much of Israel's lost territory.

14. Zechariah
DATES **753**   DURATION **6 MONTHS**
SCRIPTURE **2 KINGS 14:29—15:12**

1. He was the great-great-grandson of Jehu, and fourth ruler in his dynasty.
2. He was murdered by a rebel named Shallum, thus fulfilling God's prophecy against Jehu. See 2 Kings 10:30; 14:29; 15:8-12.

15. Shallum
DATES **752**   DURATION **1 MONTH**
SCRIPTURE **2 KINGS 15:10-15**

He was murdered by a cruel soldier named Menahem.

16. Menahem
DATES **752-742**   DURATION **10 YEARS**
SCRIPTURE **2 KINGS 15:14-22**

1. He was one of Israel's most brutal dictators.
2. He bought off Assyrian king Tiglath-Pileser with a two-million-dollar bribe.

17. Pekahiah
DATES **742-740**   DURATION **2 YEARS**
SCRIPTURE **2 KINGS 15:22-26**

1. He was the son of Menahem.
2. He was killed by his army commander, Pekah.

sake) which resulted in an allied victory over the Moabites.
3. Elisha later helped Jehoram by warning him of several planned Syrian ambushes.
4. Elisha then refused to allow him to slaughter some enemy Syrian soldiers who had been supernaturally blinded by God.
5. Jehoram was on the throne when God used the four lepers to save the city of Samaria from starvation.
6. He was also the king with whom the Syrian leper Naaman met.
7. He was later murdered by Jehu in the Valley of Jezreel.
8. He ruled for twelve years (852–840 B.C.).

J. Jehu (2 Ki. 9:1—10:36; 2 Chron. 22:7-12).
1. He was anointed by Elisha and ordered to execute the dynasty of Ahab, which included Jehoram and Jezebel.
2. He rode his chariot to the valley of Jezreel, where he executed both Jehoram and Ahaziah, the sixth king of Judah (not to be confused with the Ahaziah who was Jehoram's older brother).
3. He then made his way to the city of Jezreel and killed Jezebel.
4. After this he demanded and received the heads of the seventy sons of Ahab who were living in the city of Samaria.
5. He continued his blood purge by slaying even the descendants and friends of Ahab.
6. He finally, by trickery, assembled all the priests of Baal in a large convention hall in Jezreel, where he ordered the slaughter of each priest.
7. He ruled for twenty-eight years (841–813 B.C.).

K. Jehoahaz (2 Ki. 13:1-9).
1. He was the son of Jehu.
2. He was oppressed by the Syrian king Hazael during his entire reign, and his army was finally reduced to fifty mounted troops, ten chariots, and ten thousand infantry men.
3. He briefly displayed remorse (as Ahab had once done, see 1 Ki. 21:27-30), but apparently it was not true repentance.
4. He ruled for seventeen years (814–797 B.C.).

L. Jehoash (2 Ki. 13:10—14:16; 2 Chron. 25:17-24).
1. He was the son of Jehoahaz.
2. He visited Elisha on his deathbed.
3. He defeated Amaziah (sixth king of Judah) on the battlefield.
4. He related the second of two Old Testament fables to ridicule the arrogant claims of Amaziah.
5. He led Amaziah back to Jerusalem as a captive and left the city, taking both wealth and hostages.
6. He ruled for sixteen years (798–782 B.C.).

M. Jeroboam II (2 Ki. 14:23-29).
1. He was the son of Jehoash.
2. He ruled longer than any other northern ruler.
3. He was also one of the most powerful kings of the north.
4. He recovered the lost territories of Israel surrounding the Dead Sea. God thus allowed

him to prosper and enlarge his kingdom in spite of his wicked ways, because of divine mercy upon the pitiful condition of Israel at that time (2 Ki. 14:25, 26).

    5. Jonah the prophet lived and ministered during this time.

    6. Jeroboam II ruled for forty-one years (793-753 B.C.).

N. Zechariah (2 Ki. 14:29—15:12).
    1. He was the son of Jeroboam II.
    2. He was murdered by a rebel named Shallum.
    3. Zechariah was the great-great-grandson of Jehu, and the fourth ruler in his dynasty. With his death the line would cease, thus fulfilling God's prophecy to Jehu. (See 2 Ki. 10:30; 14:29; 15:8-12.)
    4. He ruled for six months (753 B.C.).

O. Shallum (2 Ki. 15:10-15).
    1. He was murdered by a cruel warrior named Menahem.
    2. He ruled for one month (752 B.C.).

P. Menahem (2 Ki. 15:14-22).
    1. He was one of the most brutal dictators to sit upon the northern throne.
    2. He rewarded any opposition on the part of his subjects by a wholesale slaughter, including the ripping open of pregnant women.
    3. He bought off the Assyrian king Tiglath-pileser, who had invaded Israel at that time with a two-million-dollar bribe.
    4. He ruled for ten years (752-742 B.C.).

Q. Pekahiah (2 Ki. 15:22-26).
    1. He was the son of Menahem.
    2. He was assassinated by his army commander, Pekah.
    3. He ruled for two years (742-741 B.C.).

R. Pekah (2 Ki. 15:27-31; 2 Chron. 28:5-8).
    1. He joined Syria in an unsuccessful attack against the Judean king Ahaz to punish the southern kingdom for refusing to team up with them in an effort to stop the growing Assyrian threat.
    2. During his reign Tiglath-pileser, the Assyrian king, invaded Israel and captured some of its northern and eastern cities.
    3. Pekah was assassinated by Hoshea.
    4. He ruled for twenty years (740-732 B.C.).
    Note: It will be noted that only eight years are in view here (740-732). It is thought that the first twelve years (752-740) were shared by a co-regency arrangement with both Menahem and Pekahiah.

S. Hoshea (2 Ki. 15:20—17:6).
    1. He was the last ruler of the northern kingdom.
    2. After becoming a vassal to the Assyrian king, Shalmaneser, Hoshea joined with Egypt in rebelling against Assyria.
    3. For this he was imprisoned and the people were exiled to Assyria (2 Ki. 17:4-6). Hoshea thus became the last of the northern kings. Eight died natural deaths, seven were murdered, one died a suicide, one in battle, one under judgment of God, one in a fall. Not a single ruler turned to God. From this captivity, the ten tribes have never been restored to Palestine. In fact, they would soon lose

NORTHERN RULERS

18. Pekah
DATES **740-732**   DURATION **20 YEARS**
SCRIPTURE **2 KINGS 15:27-31;**
          2 CHRONICLES 28:5-8

1. Only eight years are in view here (740-732). It is thought that the first twelve years (752-740) were shared by a co-regency arrangement with both Menahem and Pekahiah.
2. He joined Syria in an unsuccessful attempt to punish Judah for their refusal to team up against Assyria.
3. He saw Assyria capture some of Israel's northern and eastern cities.
4. He was assassinated by Hoshea.

19. Hoshea
DATES **732-723**   DURATION **9 YEARS**
SCRIPTURE **2 KINGS 15:30—17:6**

1. He was Israel's final king.
2. He joined with Egypt in rebelling against Assyria.
3. For this he was imprisoned in Assyria.

their very tribal identity (but not their ancestry). The future restoration of all twelve tribes of Israel will be consummated at the Second Coming of Christ. (See Mt. 24:27-31.) The righteous God had to cut off Israel for their sin. (See 2 Ki. 17:7-18.)

    a. The King of Assyria then transplanted colonies of people from various foreign countries into the depopulated land of northern Israel (2 Ki. 17:24).
    b. Soon after their arrival, a plague of man-eating lions, sent by God, terrified the land. In desperation, the colonists sent a message to the Assyrian ruler, asking for the ministry of a Jehovah prophet, that the plague be stopped (17:25, 26). This lion plague had been predicted by Moses centuries back. (See Ex. 23:29; Lev. 26:21, 22.)
    c. A prophet arrived and began his ministry from Bethel. The lion plague disappeared and a form of Jehovah-worship appeared, but only in form, as the people continued with their idol-worship as well (2 Ki. 17:27-34). This is the beginning of the Samaritan race and religion which was prevalent in the time of Jesus. (See Jn. 4.)

    4. Hoshea ruled for nine years (732-723 B.C.).
Southern rulers:

A. Rehoboam (1 Ki. 11:42—14:31; 2 Chron. 9:31—12:16).
    1. He was the son of Solomon.
    2. His stupidity caused the civil war of Israel.
    3. He had eighteen wives and sixty concubines. They gave him twenty-eight sons and sixty daughters.
    4. His favorite wife was Maachah, the evil daughter of Absalom.
    5. He was invaded by Shishak of Egypt.
    6. He ruled seventeen years (931-914 B.C.).

SOUTHERN RULERS

1. Rehoboam
DATES **931-914**   DURATION **17 YEARS**
SCRIPTURE **I KINGS 11:42—14:31;**
         2 CHRONICLES 9:31—12:16

1. He was the son of Solomon.
2. His stupidity and tactlessness sparked the civil war.
3. He had eighteen wives and sixty concubines.
4. His favorite wife was Maachah, the evil daughter of Absalom.
5. He sees his capital, Jerusalem, invaded by Shishak, Pharaoh of Egypt.

2. Abijam
DATES **914-911**   DURATION **3 YEARS**
SCRIPTURE **1 KINGS 14:31—15:8;**
         2 CHRONICLES 13:1-22

1. He defeated (by supernatural intervention) the northern king Jeroboam on the battlefield.
2. In spite of God's help, he degenerated into a wicked king.

3. Asa
DATES **911-870**   DURATION **41 YEARS**
SCRIPTURE **1 KINGS 15:8-14;**
         2 CHRONICLES 14:1—16:14

1. He was Judah's first saved king.
2. He led Judah in a revival.
3. He was a great builder.
4. He saw God answer his prayer by delivering Jerusalem from a massive Ethiopian attack (2 Chronicles 14:11).
5. He deposed Maacah (his grandmother) because of her idolatry.
6. He later backslid and threw into prison a prophet who had rebuked his sin.
7. He died of a foot disease, which problem he refused to take to God.

4. Jehoshaphat
DATES **873-848**   DURATION **25 YEARS**
SCRIPTURE **1 KINGS 22:41-50;**
         2 CHRONICLES 17:1—20:37

1. He instituted a national religious education program by sending out teachers of the Word of God.
2. He later marred his testimony by compromising with three ungodly northern kings.
3. He appointed a religious director and a civil director, thus recognizing the separation of church and state.
4. When Jerusalem was threatened by a massive Moabite invasion, God heard his prayer and supernaturally intervened.

5. Joram
DATES **853-845**   DURATION **8 YEARS**
SCRIPTURE **2 KINGS 8:16-24;**
         2 CHRONICLES 21:1-20

1. He married Athaliah, daughter of Ahab and Jezebel.
2. He began his reign by murdering his six brothers.
3. He received a posthumous message from Elijah predicting judgment upon him because of his wicked and murderous reign.
4. He was attacked and defeated by the Philistines and Arabians.
5. He died of a horrible disease and was unmourned at the funeral.

B. Abijam (1 Ki. 14:31—15:8; 2 Chron. 13:1-22).
   1. He defeated (by supernatural intervention) the northern king, Jeroboam, on the battlefield.
   2. In spite of God's help at this time, he later degenerated into a wicked king.
   3. He ruled three years (914-911 B.C.).
C. Asa (1 Ki. 15:8-14; 2 Chron. 14:1—16:14).
   1. He was Judah's first righteous king.
   2. He led Judah in a revival and was a great builder.
   3. God answered his prayer and delivered him from a massive Ethiopian attack.
   4. He even deposed his own grandmother Maachah because of her idolatry.
   5. He later was rebuked by a prophet for his sin and responded by throwing him in prison.
   6. He died with a foot disease which problem he refused to take to God.
   7. He ruled forty-one years (911-870 B.C.).
D. Jehoshaphat (1 Ki. 22:41-50; 2 Chron. 17:1—20:37).
   1. He was the second righteous king of Judah.
   2. He instituted a nationwide Bible education program.
   3. He compromised with Ahab and his two sons, Ahaziah and Jehoram.
   4. He ruled for twenty-five years (873-848 B.C.).
E. Joram (2 Ki. 8:26-29; 2 Chron. 21:1-20).
   1. He married Athaliah, daughter of Jezebel and Ahab.
   2. He began his reign by murdering his six brothers.
   3. He received a posthumous message from Elijah predicting judgment upon him because of his wicked and murderous reign.
   4. He was attacked and defeated by the Philistines and Arabians.
   5. He died of a horrible disease and was unmourned at the funeral.
   6. He ruled for eight years (853-845 B.C.).
F. Ahaziah (2 Ki. 8:24—9:29; 2 Chron. 22:1-9).
   1. He was killed by Jehu (tenth northern king).
   2. He ruled for one year (841 B.C.).
G. Athaliah (2 Ki. 11:1-20; 2 Chron. 22:1—23:21).
   1. She was the mother of the slain Ahaziah.
   2. At his death she slaughtered all his children except one who was hidden from her.
   3. She herself was later executed.
   4. She ruled for six years (841-835 B.C.).
H. Joash (2 Ki. 11:1—12:21; 2 Chron. 22:10—24:27).
   1. He was the surviving heir of Athaliah's bloodbath.
   2. For awhile he lived for God but later became a cruel leader.
   3. He sanctioned the stoning of Zechariah, the godly Jewish high priest who had rebuked Judah's sin and called for national repentance.
   4. He was executed by his own palace guard.
   5. He ruled for forty years (835-795 B.C.).
I. Amaziah (2 Ki. 14:1-20; 2 Chron. 25:1-28).
   1. He was a good king for awhile, and executed the men who had assassinated his father, Joash. But he did not kill their children, obeying the Mosaic law which said the sons

were not to be killed for the sins of their fathers (Deut. 24:16; Ezek. 18:4, 20). (See 2 Chron. 25:1-4; 2 Ki. 12:21; 14:1-6).

2. Amaziah then organized the army of Judah and found he had an army of 300,000. He then hired 100,000 experienced mercenary soldiers from Israel for $200,000 to help him fight against Edom (2 Chron. 25:5, 6).

3. He was warned against this by a prophet. The king reluctantly sent these mercenaries home, bitterly resenting the lost money he had paid them. But the prophet reassured him, "The Lord is able to give thee much more than this" (2 Chron. 25:9). Here is a precious spiritual gem that should be carefully considered whenever God requires us to give up our time, talent, treasure, or anything close and precious to us. See Jesus' stirring words to Peter in Matthew 19:27-29.

4. The Israelite troops returned home, also angry and frustrated. On the way they raided several cities of Judah and killed 3000 people (2 Chron. 25:13).

5. Amaziah went into battle with only his own troops and soundly defeated Edom, killing 20,000 enemy soldiers (26:11). But the foolish king brought back with him some Edomite idols and began worshiping them. God warned the king, through a prophet, of his divine anger. Amaziah refused to listen and curtly dismissed him, but not before the king's doom was predicted (25:14-16).

6. The overconfident Amaziah then declared war on northern king Jehoash, for the disgraceful action of the returning Israelite mercenaries (25:17). Northern king Jehoash responded to Amaziah's challenge by relating the second (and final) Old Testament fable. (For the first one, see Jdg. 9:8-15.) Note the language of this fable:

"The thistle that was in Lebanon sent to the cedar that was in Lebanon, saying, Give thy daughter to my son to wife: and there passed by a wild beast that was in Lebanon, and trode down the thistle" (2 Chron. 25:18).

7. Jehoash was at this point warning Amaziah not to let his Edomite victory blind him to reality but to withdraw his arrogant declaration of war. But the plea fell on deaf ears.

Amaziah was soundly defeated by Jehoash at Beth-shemesh and was led as a common prisoner back to his own capital in Jerusalem. Upon arriving, Jehoash dismantled 200 yards of the city walls to effect an impressive victory celebration. He then carried off all the treasures of the Temple and palace. Finally the northern king left, taking with him many hostages (2 Chron. 25:21-24).

8. He ruled for twenty-nine years (796-767 B.C.).

J. Uzziah (2 Ki. 15:1-7; 2 Chron. 26:1-23).

1. He was a mighty warrior and builder.
2. He attempted to intrude into the office of the priest.
3. He was punished for this sin by leprosy.
4. He ruled for fifty-two years (792-740 B.C.).

SOUTHERN RULERS

6. Ahaziah
DATES **841** DURATION **1 YEAR**
SCRIPTURE **2 KINGS 8:24—9:29;**
2 CHRONICLES 22:1-9

1. He was the son of Joram and Athaliah.
2. He was killed by Jehu (tenth northern king)

7. Athaliah
DATES **841-835** DURATION **6 YEARS**
SCRIPTURE **2 KINGS 11:1-20;**
2 CHRONICLES 22:1—23:21

1. At the death of Ahaziah, her son, she took over the throne of Judah, slaughtering all the royal seed but one (Joash) who was hidden from her.
2. After a rule of six years, she herself was executed.

8. Joash
DATES **835-795** DURATION **40 YEARS**
SCRIPTURE **2 KINGS 11:1—12:21;**
2 CHRONICLES 22:10—24:27

1. He alone had survived Athaliah's bloody purge.
2. For awhile he lived for God, but later became a cruel tyrant.
3. He sanctioned the stoning of Judah's own high priest, Zechariah, who had fearlessly rebuked the sin among the people.
4. He was executed by his own palace guard.

9. Amaziah
DATES **796-767** DURATION **29 YEARS**
SCRIPTURE **2 KINGS 14:1-20;**
2 CHRONICLES 25:1-28

1. He was a good king for awhile, executing the killers of his father, Joash.
2. He was rebuked by a prophet for hiring some mercenary Israeli soldiers to help him fight against Edom.
3. He reluctantly dismissed these paid soldiers and, with God's help, defeated Edom with his own soldiers.
4. He foolishly brought back some of the Edomite gods for worshiping purposes.
5. The reckless king then declared war on northern Israel and was soundly defeated.

10. Uzziah
DATES **792-740** DURATION **52 YEARS**
SCRIPTURE **2 KINGS 15:1-7;**
2 CHRONICLES 26:1-23

1. He was a mighty warrior and builder.
2. He attempted, however, to intrude into the office of the priesthood and was punished for this by leprosy.

11. Jotham
DATES **750-736** DURATION **16 YEARS**
SCRIPTURE **2 KINGS 15:32-38;**
2 CHRONICLES 27:1-9

1. He was a good king.
2. He built the upper gate of the Temple and erected fortresses and towers.
3. He defeated his enemies and received huge annual tribute from them.

SOUTHERN RULERS

12. Ahaz
DATES **735-719**   DURATION **16 YEARS**
SCRIPTURE **2 KINGS 16:1-20;**
2 CHRONICLES 28:1-27

1. He was perhaps the second worst king of Judah.
2. He sacrificed his own children to devil gods.
3. He was the first person to hear about the virgin birth. (See Isa. 7:1-25.)
4. He ordered the construction of a pagan Assyrian altar and placed it in the Temple to appease Tiglath-Pileser.

13. Hezekiah
DATES **716-687**   DURATION **29 YEARS**
SCRIPTURE **2 KINGS 18:1—20:21;**
2 CHRONICLES 29:1—32:33

1. He was Judah's second best king and the richest of all.
2. He repaired the Temple, organized an orchestral group, and appointed a Levitical singing choir.
3. He carried out the greatest Passover celebration since Solomon.
4. He saw the death angel defeat the Assyrian enemies which had surrounded Jerusalem.
5. He was supernaturally healed of a terminal disease and given an additional fifteen years to live.
6. He added fifteen Psalms to the Old Testament Canon.
7. He foolishly showed the wealth of Judah to some nosy Babylonian ambassadors.

14. Manasseh
DATES **697-642**   DURATION **55 YEARS**
SCRIPTURE **2 KINGS 21:1-18;**
2 CHRONICLES 33:1-20

1. He ruled longer than any other king of north or south.
2. He was the most wicked king of all.
3. He experienced the new birth while in an enemy prison.

15. Amon
DATES **643-641**   DURATION **2 YEARS**
SCRIPTURE **2 KINGS 21:19-26;**
2 CHRONICLES 33:21-25

1. He was wicked like his father, Manasseh, but did not repent as did his father.
2. He was executed by his own household servants.

16. Josiah
DATES **641-610**   DURATION **31 YEARS**
SCRIPTURE **2 KINGS 22:1—23:30;**
2 CHRONICLES 34:1—35:27

1. He was the godliest king since David.
2. He was Judah's last godly king.
3. The book of Moses was accidentally discovered among the debris in the Temple at the beginning of his reign.
4. He used this to lead Judah in a great revival.
5. He also conducted a larger Passover celebration than that of Hezekiah his great-grandfather.
6. He fulfilled a three-hundred-year-old prophecy. Compare 1 Kings 13:1, 2 with 2 Kings 23:15.
7. He was killed in a battle with the Egyptians.

K. Jotham (2 Ki. 15:32-38; 2 Chron. 27:1-9).
1. He was a good king (2 Chron. 27:6).
2. He built the upper gate of the Temple and erected fortresses and towers.
3. He defeated the Ammonites and received a huge annual tribute of silver and wheat from them.
4. He ruled for sixteen years (750–732 B.C.).

L. Ahaz (2 Ki. 16:1-20; 2 Chron. 28:1-27).
1. He was perhaps the second worst king of Judah.
2. He sacrificed his own children to devilish gods.
3. He was the first person to hear about the virgin birth.
4. He ruled sixteen years (732–716 B.C.).

M. Hezekiah (2 Ki. 18:1—20:21; 2 Chron. 29:1—32:33).
1. He was the second best king of Judah.
2. He was also the richest of all.
3. He organized the greatest Passover celebration since the days of Solomon.
4. He saw the death angel defeat the Assyrian enemies which had surrounded Jerusalem.
5. He was supernaturally healed and given an additional fifteen years to live.
6. He ruled for twenty-nine years (716–687).

N. Manasseh (2 Ki. 21:1-18; 2 Chron. 33:1-20).
1. He ruled longer than any northern or southern king.
2. He was the worst of all the kings.
3. He experienced the new birth prior to his death.
4. He ruled fifty-five years (697–642 B.C.).

O. Amon (2 Ki. 21:19-26; 2 Chron. 33:21-25).
1. He was, like his father Manasseh, a wicked sinner.
2. He was, unlike his father Manasseh, unrepentant.
3. He was executed by his own household servants.
4. He ruled two years (643–641 B.C.).

P. Josiah (2 Ki. 22:1—23:30; 2 Chron. 34:1—35:27).
1. He was the best king since David.
2. The book of Moses was discovered in the Temple during his reign.
3. He led his people in a great revival.
4. He was the last good king of Judah.
5. He was killed in a battle with the Egyptians.
6. He ruled for thirty-one years (641–610 B.C.).

Q. Jehoahaz (2 Ki. 23:31-33; 2 Chron. 36:1-4).
1. This middle son of Josiah had both a sinful (2 Ki. 23:32) and short-lived (2 Ki. 23:30, 31) reign. He was deposed by Pharaoh Necho (who had previously killed his father, Josiah, in battle), after but ninety days on the throne (2 Ki. 23:33). Necho then leveled a tax against Judah totaling $230,000. Jehoahaz was eventually carried into Egypt where he died in captivity (2 Ki. 23:34).
2. Jehoahaz's younger brother, Eliakim (renamed Jehoiakim by Necho), was chosen by the Egyptian king to succeed him on the throne of Judah (2 Ki. 23:34). Things were now at rock bottom when the devil's man could pick the king over the Lord's people!
3. He ruled for three months (609 B.C.).

R. Jehoiakim (2 Ki. 23:34—24:5; 2 Chron. 36:5-7).
1. He was the brother of Jehoahaz.
2. He was probably Judah's third worst king.
3. He persecuted Jeremiah the prophet.
4. He experienced the first of Nebuchadnezzar's fearsome "visits" to Jerusalem.
5. During this time Daniel and other Hebrew young people were taken to Babylon by Nebuchadnezzar.
6. He died, and as Jeremiah had predicted, received the burial of an ass.
7. He ruled for eleven years (609-598).

S. Jehoiachin (2 Ki. 24:6-16; 2 Chron. 36:8-10).
1. He was the son of Jehoiakim, and grandson of Josiah. Jehoiachin was also called Coniah (Jer. 22:24, 28; 37:1).
2. He began ruling at eighteen (2 Ki. 24:8). Note: There is a textual problem here, for 2 Chronicles 36:9 informs us he was eight years old.
3. He was an evil king (2 Ki. 24:9). Because of this:
   a. Both Ezekiel (19:5-9) and Jeremiah (22:24-26) predicted that he would be carried off into the Babylonian captivity.
   b. He was to be regarded as childless, as none of his children would ever sit upon the throne of David or rule in Judah.
   The *New Scofield Bible* observes:
   "This declaration does not mean that he would have no children, for in 1 Chron. 3:17, 18, some are named (Cf. Mt. 1:12). By divine judgment, this king was to be written childless, i.e., no physical descendant would occupy a place in the list of Israel's kings. Consequently, if our Lord Jesus, who is to occupy David's throne (Lk. 1:32, 33), had been begotten by Mary's husband, Joseph, who was of the line of Jeconiah (Mt. 1:12, 16), it would have contradicted this divine prediction. Christ's dynastic right to the throne came through his foster father, Joseph, from Jeconiah, but the physical descent of Jesus from David came through Mary, whose genealogy is traced to David through Nathan, rather than through Solomon." (Compare Lk. 3:31 with Mt. 1:17.) (pp. 793, 794)
4. Jehoiachin was captured during the eighth year of Nebuchadnezzar's reign (2 Ki. 24:12) and carried into Babylon, along with 10,000 other Jewish captives (Jer. 24:1; 29; 2 Ki. 24:14, 15). Ezekiel was also carried away at this time.
5. He then appointed Zedekiah (Jehoiachin's great uncle) to occupy the throne of Judea (2 Ki. 24:17).
6. Jehoiachin was placed in a Babylonian prison, where he remained for thirty-six years, until the death of Nebuchadnezzar. He was then released by the new Babylonian monarch, Evil-Merodach, who not only freed him, but gave him a seat at the king's own table and an allowance for his support (2 Ki. 25:27-30; Jer. 52:31-34).
7. He ruled for three months (598 B.C.).

SOUTHERN RULERS

17. Jehoahaz
DATES 609 DURATION 3 MONTHS
SCRIPTURE 2 KINGS 23:31-33;
2 CHRONICLES 36:1-4
1. He was the middle son of Josiah.
2. He was deposed after only ninety days by the Pharaoh who had killed his father.
3. He was carried into Egyptian captivity where he eventually died.

18. Jehoiakim
DATES 609-598 DURATION 11 YEARS
SCRIPTURE 2 KINGS 23:34—24:5;
2 CHRONICLES 36:5-7
1. He was the oldest brother of Jehoahaz.
2. He was put on the throne by the Egyptian Pharaoh.
3. He was later made vassal by Nebuchadnezzar after the Babylonians had defeated the Egyptians.
4. He was totally materialistic and self-centered. He can be considered Judah's third worst king.
5. He murdered the innocent and often persecuted Jeremiah.
6. He burned a copy of a part of God's Word. (See Jer. 36:22-32.)
7. He experienced the first of three fearful "visits" Nebuchadnezzar made to the city of Jerusalem.
8. During this visit (606 B.C.) Daniel and other Hebrew young people were carried off into captivity.
9. At his death he received the burial of an ass, as Jeremiah had predicted.

19. Jehoiachin
DATES 598 DURATION 3 MONTHS
SCRIPTURE 2 KINGS 24:6-16;
2 CHRONICLES 36:8-10
1. He was the son of Jehoiakim and grandson of Josiah.
2. He incurred a curse from God, stating that his sons would not sit upon Judah's throne.
3. Both Ezekiel (19:5-9) and Jeremiah (22:24-26) predicted he would be carried off into Babylonian captivity.
4. This happened during Nebuchadnezzar's second "visit" (597) to Jerusalem. Ezekiel was also carried away at this time.
5. He eventually died in Babylon.

20. Zedekiah
DATES 597-586 DURATION 11 YEARS
SCRIPTURE 2 KINGS 24:17—25:30;
2 CHRONICLES 36:11-21
1. He was the youngest son of Josiah and uncle to Jehoiachin.
2. Jeremiah was persecuted during his reign.
3. He rebelled against Babylon along with Egypt.
4. He was captured, blinded, and carried off into Babylonian captivity by Nebuchadnezzar.
5. Jerusalem was burned to the ground and the Temple destroyed at this time.

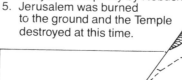

T. Zedekiah (2 Ki. 24:17—25:30; 2 Chron. 36:11-21).
1. He was the youngest son of Josiah.
2. He rebelled against Nebuchadnezzar. For this he was blinded and carried off as a captive to Babylon.
3. He ruled for eleven years (597-586 B.C.).

The Spotlight, Rifle Approach:

The Chaotic Kingdom Stage can be best summarized by examining in some detail the lives of twenty individuals. This number does not include the writing prophets such as Jonah, whose life will be considered along with his book. Of the twenty, six are northern rulers, twelve are southern rulers, and two are prophets. These are: Jeroboam, Omri, Ahab, Jehu, Jeroboam II, Hoshea (northern), Rehoboam, Asa, Jehoshaphat, Athaliah, Joash, Uzziah, Ahaz, Hezekiah, Manasseh, Josiah, Jehoiakim, Zedekiah (southern), Elijah and Elisha (prophets).

The important northern rulers:

A. Jeroboam (first king). He began in 930 B.C. and ruled for twenty-two years.

To properly consider the reign of Jeroboam, it is necessary to know something of the circumstances which put him into power. It all began with Solomon's arrogant young son named Rehoboam.
1. Rehoboam comes to Shechem to be crowned king over all Israel (1 Ki. 12:1; 2 Chron. 10:1).
2. He is issued an ultimatum by a delegation led by Jeroboam (who had returned from Egyptian exile after Solomon's death) which stated simply that the people demanded a better life under him than they had known under Solomon (1 Ki. 12:3, 4; 2 Chron. 10:2-4).
3. Rehoboam asks for a three-day recess to consider their demands. During this period he consults with his arrogant young friends and, favoring their advice over the older and wiser men, retorts to waiting Israel at the end of the three-day period:
   "My Father made your yoke heavy, and I will add to your yoke: my Father also chastised you with whips, but I will chastise you with scorpions" (1 Ki. 12:14).
4. Upon hearing this, ten of the twelve tribes heed Jeroboam's cry to strike their tents, and Israel's sorrowful secession story has begun (1 Ki. 12:16).
5. Rehoboam's tax collector is stoned to death and the frightened king runs for his life to Jerusalem (12:21, 22). (Rehoboam would continually disobey this command throughout his reign; see 1 Ki. 15:6.)
6. Jeroboam, the new leader of the ten-tribe confederation, is immediately faced with a serious threat. Three times a year, as commanded by God (see Lev. 23; Ex. 23:17), the entire nation is to go to Jerusalem and worship God. Jeroboam knows the priests will doubtless use these opportunities to bring all Israel back into the fold of Rehoboam. Jeroboam therefore attempts to resolve all this by adopting a fourfold plan.
   a. He changes the religious symbols of Israel. Instead of the two golden cherubims above the ark, he substitutes two golden calves. Here he could point to the action of the first high priest Aaron for a historical example. (In fact, he stole Aaron's text in introducing these calves to Israel. Compare Ex. 32:4 with 1 Ki. 12:28.)
   b. He changes the religious worship center from Jerusalem to Bethel and Dan. This is in direct disobedience to God's clear command to him. (See 1 Ki. 11:36.)
   c. He degrades the Levitical priesthood, by making "priests of the lowest of the people, which were not of the sons of Levi" (12:31). Because of this, the vast majority of priests and Levites flee southward to Judah, leaving behind them a situation of near-total apostasy. (See 2 Chron. 11:13-17.) (This explains the tragic fact that not one of the nineteen Israelite kings beginning with Jeroboam and ending with Hoshea—over a period of approximately 210 years—turned his heart and kingdom to God!)
   d. He changes the religious calendar, from October to November. According to Leviticus 23, Israel was to observe six main yearly feasts, beginning in April and ending in October. These six feasts, three of which would fall in October, foreshadowed the Cross (unleavened bread), the resurrection (firstfruits), Pentecost (feast of fifty days), the rapture (feast of trumpets), the tribulation (day of atonement), and the millennium (feast of tabernacles). It is evident, however, that Jeroboam has little use for any of this, for we are told that he devises this November feast after his own heart. (See 12:33.)
7. Jeroboam visits the altar in Bethel to burn incense. He now becomes the second of three Israelite kings who dared to take upon themselves the office of a priest also. All three were severely punished. The other two were:
   a. Saul (1 Sam. 13:9-14)
   b. Uzziah (2 Chron. 26:16-21)
8. For his idolatry, Jeroboam is prophesied against and punished by a man of God.
   a. The prophecy. That years later a king of Judah named Josiah would totally destroy Jeroboam's false religion, even burning the bones of his dead priests upon the very altar where Jeroboam stood sacrificing. This amazing prophecy was fulfilled exactly some 300 years later. (Compare 1 Ki. 13:2 with 2 Ki. 23:15, 16.)
   b. The punishment. Jeroboam's altar was destroyed and his arm was paralyzed, both supernaturally from God (1 Ki. 13:3-6). The prophet then prayed and the king's hand was restored.
9. On his route home, the prophet foolishly heeds the words of a lying old prophet from Bethel, and thus forfeits his life for disobeying God.

a. God had told him to return home immediately.

b. The old Bethel prophet told him God had changed his mind and desired him to stay and eat in Bethel.

c. When he finally left for home he was attacked and killed by a lion.

10. Soon after this sad event, Jeroboam's son, Abijah, becomes very ill. Ahijah the prophet sadly relates God's message to Jeroboam's wife (who had attempted to disguise herself), which is that because of his extreme wickedness he will suffer terrible judgment (14:10-14). All this, of course, did take place. The child soon died (14:17) and a few years later Nadab, Jeroboam's son who succeeded him, was murdered along with all his relatives by a rebel named Baasha, who took over his throne (15:29). At this time God also issued the first chilling warning of the future Assyrian captivity, which occurred some 200 years later (14:15).

11. God strikes Jeroboam with a plague and he dies, after a wicked reign of twenty-two years. No less than twenty-one times it is recorded that he "made Israel to sin." He is succeeded by his son Nadab (1 Ki. 14:20; 2 Chron. 13:20). Nadab was murdered by a rebel named Baasha, after a reign of only two years. He thus became the first of six northern kings to be assassinated. These are: (2) Elah, (3) Jehoram, (4) Zechariah, (5) Shallum, and (6) Pekahiah. In killing him and his relatives, Baasha unknowingly fulfills the prophecy given to Jeroboam's wife by Ahijah the prophet. (Compare 1 Ki. 14:14 with 15:29.)

B. Omri (sixth king).
1. He began in 885 B.C. and reigned for twelve years.
2. Omri made the city of Samaria the new northern capital (1 Ki. 16:24).
3. He was the most wicked king of the north up to that time (16:25).

C. Ahab (seventh king).
1. He began in 874 and reigned for twenty-two years.
2. Ahab marries Jezebel and builds a temple to Baal in Samaria (1 Ki. 16:31, 32).
3. He was more wicked than his father Omri (16:33). (See also 21:25, 26.)
4. At the beginning of his reign a 500-year-old prophecy is fulfilled concerning the rebuilding of Jericho (16:34; compare with Josh. 6:26).
5. He is confronted by Elijah and warned that, due to his sin and Israel's wickedness, a three-and-a-half-year famine will occur (1 Ki. 17:1; Jas. 5:17).
6. Ahab sees his priests of Baal defeated and destroyed by Elijah on Mt. Carmel (18:40).
7. He is allowed by God to defeat the arrogant Syrians on two occasions to prove a point, the point being that Jehovah is Lord over all (20:23, 28).

At this time King Ben-hadad of Syria declares war on Ahab, who at first attempts to appease with a bribe to the greedy Syrian Monarch, but when this fails, Ahab is determined to fight (1 Ki. 20:1-11). A nameless prophet (perhaps Elijah) reassures Ahab of victory over the Syrians, which victory soon takes place (20:13-19). After their defeat, the Syrians conclude it was due to a geographical factor, as the battle had taken place on hilly ground, thus giving the Israeli troops a tremendous advantage. The Syrians believed that the God of Israel was a hill God. Plans were then made to fight again, but this time they would meet Israel on the plains. They could not have been more mistaken. Israel's God is indeed the God of the hills, but he is also:
a. the God of the valley (Ex. 17:8-13; 1 Sam. 17:3, 49)
b. the God of the mountain (1 Ki. 18:19, 40)
c. the God of the plain (Jdg. 11:33)
d. the God of the water (Ex. 14:27, 28)
e. the God of the fire (Dan. 3:19-26)

The Syrians attack and are again soundly defeated, losing 127,000 infantrymen. The victorious Ahab disobeys God's command and spares Ben-hadad's life (as Saul had once done with Agag, 1 Sam. 15:31-33). The prophet of God then announces that because Ahab has done this, the Lord will require his life for Ben-hadad's life (1 Ki. 20:32-43). This will happen some three years later (see 1 Ki. 22:29-37).

8. Ahab attempts unsuccessfully to purchase a choice vineyard near his palace owned by a man from Jezreel named Naboth. Years back Samuel had warned against land grabbing by Israel's kings. (See 1 Sam. 8:14.) Even had Naboth wanted to sell his vineyard, the Levitical law would have forbidden him. (See Lev. 25:23; Num. 36:7; Ezek. 46:18.)

Ahab returns home in a sullen mood. Jezebel is told of Naboth's refusal and informs her pouting potentate to cheer up, as he will soon possess that vineyard. She then writes letters in Ahab's name, seals them with his seal, and addresses them to the civic leaders of Jezreel where Naboth lives. She commands them to call the citizens together for prayer and fasting. They are then to summon Naboth and pay two lying witnesses to accuse him of cursing God and the king. He then is to be taken out and murdered. This horrible order is carried out to the letter (1 Ki. 21:4-14). His sons are also stoned. (See 2 Ki. 9:26.) Wicked Jezebel, herself a rabid worshiper of Baal, now cleverly appeals to the Mosaic law in obtaining two witnesses against the accused (Lev. 24:17).

This mock trial would have its ultimate counterpart some nine centuries later on an early Friday morning in April as the mighty Creator is judged by his miserable creatures. (See Mt. 26:59-68.) Jezebel is told the news, and Ahab gleefully goes down to the vineyard to claim it (1 Ki. 21:15, 16). God now orders Elijah to confront Ahab in Naboth's vineyard and pronounces heaven's curse upon him and his household. An angry and doubtless fearful Ahab then hears Elijah's stern words of judgment (21:19, 21-24). All this literally came true.

a. The dogs did lick Ahab's blood, as they had done with Naboth's blood (1 Ki. 22:38).

b. His descendants were destroyed. Ahaziah, his oldest son, died in a fall (2 Ki. 1:17), and Jehoram, his youngest son, was murdered by Jehu (2 Ki. 9:24), and his body thrown in the same field where Naboth was buried.

c. His wicked wife Jezebel was eaten by the wild dogs of Jezreel (2 Ki. 9:30-36).

Upon hearing these terrible prophecies, Ahab humbles himself, and God spares him from at least seeing his sons killed. But his repentance is only temporary and shallow (1 Ki. 21:27-29).

9. At this time Ahab desires the reigning Judean monarch of the southern kingdom (whose name was Hezekiah) to join with him in fighting against Syrian king Ben-hadad, who has betrayed a three-year convenant (1 Ki. 22:1), and is still stationing Syrian troops at Ramoth-gilead. Had Ahab executed him as God had commanded some time back, this serious situation would not have arisen. Jehoshaphat had nothing materially to gain, and much morally to lose. His response is tragic:

"I am as thou art, my people as thy people, my horses as thy horses" (1 Ki. 22:4). Jehoshaphat evidently has second thoughts concerning this alliance right away, for he desires Ahab to, "Enquire, I pray thee, at the word of the Lord today" (2 Chron. 18:4).

Ahab immediately summons 400 prophets, all of which were in his pay, and each possessing a spineless back and a lying tongue. They arrive and, to a man, loudly predict victory (2 Chron. 18:5, 6). These were the kind of men Jeremiah would later speak about. (See Jer. 23:21.) Jehoshaphat, still bothered with doubts, asks if there is any other prophet around. Ahab bitterly relates that, yes, "There is yet one man, Micaiah the son of Imlah, by whom we may enquire of the Lord: but I hate him; for he doth not prophesy good concerning me, but evil" (1 Ki. 22:8). Perhaps the greatest compliment that could be paid to Micaiah is that he was hated by Ahab. The wicked king hated this prophet the way a foolish man might despise the doctor who told him he had cancer!

At the gentle urging of the southern king, Ahab reluctantly sends for the imprisoned Micaiah, but privately instructs the messenger to warn his prison prophet not to contradict the majority report. Micaiah listens to the message and retorts: "As the Lord liveth, what the Lord saith unto me, that will I speak" (1 Ki. 22:14).

As the two kings await the arrival of Micaiah, Zedekiah, the puppy-dog prophet spokesman for the rest, performs a few little tricks for his master Ahab. He grabs some horns and prances around, attempting to demonstrate Ahab's victory over the Syrians. He may have learned this little act by taking Deuteronomy 33:17 completely out of context. Finally Micaiah stands before Ahab, and no doubt with a twinkle in his eye, and with sarcasm in his voice, imitates the other prophets: "Go, and prosper: for the Lord shall deliver it into the hand of the king" (1 Ki. 22:15). The dripping sarcasm must have been painfully evident to both, for Ahab turns livid with rage and screams out: "How many times shall I adjure thee that thou tell me nothing but that which is true in the name of the Lord?" (22:16). Ahab wanted this about as much as a guilty criminal desires to hear the judge pronounce sentence upon him. The words were doubtless said to impress Jehoshaphat.

The twinkle from Micaiah's eye suddenly disappears and the scorn turns to sobering words of judgment as he says: "I saw all Israel scattered upon the hills, as sheep that have not a shepherd: and the Lord said, These have no master: let them return every man to his house in peace" (22:17).

Upon hearing this, Ahab explodes again, saying to Jehoshaphat: "Did I not tell thee that he would prophesy no good concerning me, but evil?" (22:18).

Micaiah continues however, but stating that God has allowed a lying spirit to deceive Ahab's prophets, in order to kill the wicked king in battle. As he finishes this true prophecy, he is slapped by Zedekiah, Ahab's house pet. This stinging insult would later be experienced by both our Lord (Jn. 18:22) and the Apostle Paul (Acts 23:2). Ahab orders Micaiah back to prison and puts him on a diet of bread and water until he returns home safely from the battle. As he leaves, Micaiah states that if indeed Ahab returns safely, it will mean God has not spoken through him (1 Ki. 22:28).

10. Ahab and Jehoshaphat hurriedly proceed to Ramoth-gilead. On the eve of the battle, Ahab suggests that Jehoshaphat wear his royal robes, but that he, Ahab, put on the garment of an infantry soldier. The southern king agrees. Sometimes, it would seem, Jehoshaphat can be downright stupid (1 Ki. 22:29, 30).

Jehoshaphat is immediately spotted in battle and mistaken by the Syrians for Ahab. The foolish and frightened Judean king cries out to God for deliverance, and is unharmed by the Syrians when they realize he is not Ahab (1 Ki. 22:31-33; 2 Chron. 18:30-32). One of the Syrian soldiers, however, shoots an arrow haphazardly into the air at the Israeli troops and it strikes the disguised Ahab at the openings where the lower armor and the breastplate meet. The wound is a mortal one. At his gasping order, Ahab is propped up in his chariot and hurriedly driven home. Just as the sun sinks in the western skies, he dies (1 Ki. 22:34-37; 2 Chron. 18:33, 34). Ahab is buried in Samaria and his blood-caked chariot is taken down to be cleaned at a nearby pool, where it is licked by the dogs, just as Elijah predicted (1 Ki. 22:38, 39). Ahab is succeeded by his oldest son, Ahaziah, who continues in the evil ways of his father (1 Ki. 22:52, 53).

D. Jehu (tenth king).
   1. He began in 841 B.C. and reigned for twenty-eight years.
   2. Elijah had been commanded to anoint Jehu as king (1 Ki. 19:16), but for some reason had not done so. Therefore, Elisha anoints him, using the services of a young preacher boy (2 Ki. 9:1).
   3. Jehu becomes notorious for his chariot riding (9:20) and bloodletting. He would execute:
      a. the Judean king, Ahaziah, grandson of Jehoshaphat (9:27)
      b. the northern king, Jehoram, who was in power at the time (9:24)
      c. Jezebel (9:30-37)
      d. Ahab's seventy sons (10:1, 11)
      e. forty-two royal princes of Judah (10:14)
      f. the Baal worshipers (10:25)
   God orders him to execute the dynasty of Ahab, including Jezebel, whom the dogs would later eat (2 Ki. 9:1-10), but does not sanction these other assassinations. Let us now consider his bloody activities in brief manner.

   Upon being anointed, Jehu mounts his chariot and drives furiously toward Jezebel to execute King Jehoram, Ahab's youngest son, who was at this time recovering from some wounds he had received in a recent battle. On that fateful day he had received a visitor, the Judean king, Ahaziah, who was Jehoshaphat's grandson, and Jehoram's nephew. It is doubtful in all history that two conferring heads of state have had more wicked mothers than did this pair. Jehoram's mother was Jezebel, and Ahaziah's mother was Athaliah.

   Jehu is spotted while still on the valley road, and both Jehoram and Ahaziah, fearing an impending rebellion, ride out to meet Jehu, hoping to settle any demands in a peaceful manner. Jehu spurns Jehoram's pleas and executes both uncle and nephew kings by a shower of deadly arrows. Jehoram's lifeless body is thrown into the field of Naboth, where Ahab (the dead king's father) had once dumped Naboth himself. The birds were indeed coming home to roost (2 Ki. 9:25-29).

   Jehu enters Jezreel, spots the painted hag, Jezebel, taunting him from an upstairs window, and orders her cast down. She is immediately thrown to her death and soon eaten by the wild city dogs who leave only her skull, feet, and hands. Thus Elijah's sober prophecy to Ahab is literally fulfilled. (Compare 1 Ki. 21:23 with 2 Ki. 9:30-36.)

   Jehu then writes a letter to the city council of Samaria, demanding the heads (literally) of the seventy sons of Ahab who were all living in that city. The frightened officials immediately obey this bloody order, pack the separated heads into baskets, and deliver this gory mass to Jehu in Jezreel (10:11-14).

   Jehu continues his blood purging by slaying every descendant and friend of Ahab, including forty-two kinsmen of Ahaziah who have just arrived in Jezreel to visit Jezebel (10:11-14). The brutal charioteer then orders all the priests of Baal to attend a special religious convention in Jezreel, pretending that he too has become a Baal worshiper. However, secret plans are laid to slaughter the whole bunch once they can be herded into a central meeting place.

   Eventually the house of Baal in Jezreel is packed with pagan priests. It is then that Jehu gives the order and the false Phoenician god stands helplessly by while his worshipers are systematically slaughtered. Jehu then burns their altar, wrecks the temple, and converts it into a public toilet. Because of his obedience to God concerning the destruction of Ahab's dynasty, Jehu is promised a continuation of his own dynasty up through the fourth generation (2 Ki. 10:30).
   4. In spite of his reforms, Jehu continues worshiping the golden calves set up by Jeroboam (10:29-31), and dies an unsaved king.

E. Jeroboam II (thirteenth king).
   1. He began in 793 and reigned forty-one years.
   2. Jeroboam was the most powerful of all the northern kings.
   3. He restored much of Israel's land which previously had been taken by the Syrians (2 Ki. 3:5; 14:25-27).
   4. This was prophesied by Jonah, who lived during the reign of Jeroboam II (14:25).

F. Hoshea (nineteenth king).
   1. He began in 732 and reigned nine years.
   2. After becoming a vassal to the Assyrian king, Shalmaneser, Hoshea joined with Egypt in rebelling against that empire.
   3. For this he was imprisoned by Shalmaneser (2 Ki. 17:4, 5).
   4. It was at this time that Samaria fell and the citizens of the northern kingdom were carried away into Assyrian captivity (2 Ki. 17:6).

The important southern rulers:
   A. Rehoboam (first king).
      1. He began in 930 B.C. and reigned seventeen years.
      2. His cruel and tactless answer to the demands of some of Israel's leaders help trigger the tragic civil war (1 Ki. 12:1-16).
      3. He is unknowingly helped by Jeroboam who has driven the faithful Levite priests from the north to Jerusalem. These godly men were responsible in the main for Judah's continuation a century after Assyria had captured the northern kingdom (2 Chron. 11:16, 17).

4. Rehoboam's failure doubtless began by his polygamous actions, which involved eighteen wives and sixty concubines; they bore him twenty-eight sons and sixty daughters. Another factor in his downfall was his favorite wife, whose name was Maachah. This woman, the daughter of Absalom, apparently exercised an evil influence upon both Rehoboam and Abijam, their son, who succeeded his father. Finally, her wicked power was curbed by her own grandson, King Asa, who deposed her for idol-worshiping (2 Chron. 11:18-23; 12:1, 14; 2 Ki. 15:13). As his power grew, so his evil increased. Judah built shrines and obelisks and idols on every high hill and under every green tree. In addition to all this, there was homosexuality throughout the land. This vile and perverted sexual crime had possibly been introduced to the inhabitants of Palestine by Canaan, grandson of Noah. (See Gen. 9:20-25.)

Now the people of Israel had allowed this sickness of the soul to degrade them also. In the New Testament the Apostle Paul lashes out against sodomy perhaps more severely than against any other single sin. (Read Rom. 1:18-32.)

5. During the fifth year of Rehoboam's reign, Judah is invaded by King Shishak of Egypt with a powerful force. Because of Rehoboam's wickedness, Jerusalem is now invaded by a foreign power for the first time in nearly 100 years. Shishak conquers the fortified cities of Judah and comes to Jerusalem. Shemaiah, the prophet, then leads Rehoboam and the frightened people in a revival. God thus spares Jerusalem, but allows the city to pay tribute to Shishak, that they might realize it is far better to serve their Heavenly King than an earthly one. Shishak plunders the Temple treasury, including the golden shields placed there by Solomon. Rehoboam then replaces them with bronze shields, symbolizing the rapidly deteriorating spiritual condition of Judah. Already the trace of Ichabod could be seen gathering over the southern kingdom (2 Chron. 12:2-12; 1 Sam. 4:21).

6. After a reign of seventeen years, Rehoboam dies and is succeeded by his son, Abijam (1 Ki. 14:31).

7. Abijam soon finds cause to do battle with his father's old enemy, Jeroboam. They meet in the field, but Abijam has only 400,000 troops, as opposed to Jeroboam's 800,000 Israeli soldiers. Just prior to the fighting, Abijam gives a long lecture to Jeroboam and his soldiers concerning the folly of rebelling against the house of David, and the wickedness of their golden calf worship. He contrasts all this to the true Temple worship still carried on in Jerusalem. Upon completing his message, however, Abijam discovers that Jeroboam has secretly outflanked him and they are surrounded. He immediately cries out to God for mercy and the priests blow

their trumpets. God then turns the tide of battle their way and Jeroboam is dealt a severe defeat which costs him 500,000 men (2 Chron. 13:1-17).

8. In spite of his heaven-sent victory on the battlefield, Abijam degenerates into a wicked king (1 Ki. 15:3, 4). After a reign of three years, Abijam dies and is succeeded by his son Asa (1 Ki. 15:8).

B. Asa (third king).
1. He began in 911 B.C. and reigned forty-one years.
2. During the first ten years of his reign, the land was at peace. Asa used the time wisely.
   a. He led the people in a great revival (2 Chron. 14:2-5).
   b. He built up and fenced in the cities of Judah (14:6, 7).
3. This peace is suddenly shattered, however, when he is threatened with invasion by a million Ethiopian troops (14:9).
4. Hopelessly outnumbered, Asa cries out to God:
   "Lord, it is nothing with thee to help, whether with many, or with them who have no power: help us, O Lord our God; for we rest on thee, and in thy name we go against this multitude. O Lord, thou art our God; let not man prevail against thee" (14:11).
5. God graciously answers this prayer and personally smites the Ethiopians (14:12).
6. A thankful Asa returns home and continues his reforms (15:8-15).
   "And they entered into a covenant to seek the Lord God of their fathers with all their heart and with all their soul" (15:12).
7. The zealous king even deposes Maachah (his grandfather Rehoboam's wife) because of her idolatry (1 Ki. 15:13).
8. In the thirty-sixth year of Asa's reign, the northern king, Baasha, declares war on him and begins building a wall fortress at Ramah to control the road to Judah, thus hoping to cut off all trade to Jerusalem (2 Chron. 16:1). Instead of trusting God, as he did during the Ethiopian threat some years back, Asa bribes the Syrian king to ally with him against Israel (2 Chron. 16:2-6).
9. Asa is severely rebuked for this by the prophet Hanani and warned that he would be plagued with wars from that point on due to his faithlessness. He eloquently reminds the foolish king of past history (2 Chron. 16:8, 9).
   Hanani then says:
   "For the eyes of the Lord run to and fro throughout the whole earth, to show himself strong in the behalf of them whose heart is perfect toward him. Herein thou hast done foolishly: therefore, from henceforth thou shalt have wars" (16:9).
   Asa responds by throwing Hanani in prison (2 Chron. 16:10). This is a favorite but futile trick of sinful monarchs toward uncooperative preachers. Ahab had done it to Mi-

caiah (2 Chron. 18:7), Zedekiah did it to Jeremiah (Jer. 32:3), and Herod did it to John the Baptist (Mt. 14:3). He then ended the good reign he began by oppressing the people. Two years prior to his death he became seriously diseased in his feet, but refused to take this problem to God. After a reign of forty-one years he died and was succeeded by his son Jehoshaphat (2 Chron. 16:10— 17:1).

C. Jehoshaphat (fourth king).
1. He began in 873 and reigned twenty-five years.
2. He began by continuing the moral reforms and building projects his father Asa had started (2 Chron. 17:3-6).
3. During his third year in power he instituted a nationwide religious education program, sending out Bible teachers to all important Judean cities who lectured to the people from the Law of Moses (17:7-9).
4. He grew in power and accepted tribute from the Philistines (17:11).
5. In the latter years of his reign, however, he marred his testimony by compromising with three ungodly northern kings, Ahab and his two sons, Ahaziah and Jehoram.
   a. His matrimonial alliance with Ahab: He foolishly allowed his son Joram to marry Athaliah, the wicked daughter of Ahab and Jezebel (2 Chron. 18:1).
   b. His military alliance with Ahab against Syria (2 Chron. 18:2, 3).
   c. His trading alliance with Ahaziah, Ahab's oldest son (2 Chron. 20:35-37).
   d. His military alliance with Jehoram, Ahab's youngest son, against Moab (2 Ki. 3:6, 7).
6. Jehoshaphat returns home after the Syrian fiasco and is soundly rebuked for his foolishness and compromise by the prophet Jehu (2 Chron. 19:1-3).

   A chastened Jehoshaphat once again resumes his spiritual reforms, this time going out himself among the people, encouraging them to worship God, and appointing godly men to judge them. His admonition to these Jewish dispensers of justice is noteworthy indeed. (See 2 Chron. 19:6, 7.)
7. Jehoshaphat also appoints the high priest, Amariah, to act as a court of final appeal in religious matters, and Zebediah, a ruler of Judah, to determine all important civil cases. Here is another example of the "separation of church and state" principle often found in the Old Testament (as well as in the New Testament) (2 Chron. 19:11).
8. At this time the Moabites and their allies declare war upon Judah, and word reaches Jerusalem that a vast army is marching toward the Holy City. Jehoshaphat is badly shaken by this terrifying news and calls for a national time of fasting and praying. People from all across the nation flock to Jerusalem to join their king as he himself leads in public prayer beside the Temple. He prays:

   "O Lord God of our fathers, art not thou God in heaven? And rulest not thou over all the kingdoms of the heathen? And in thine hand is there not power and might, so that none is able to withstand thee? O our God, wilt thou not judge them? for we have no might against this great company that cometh against us; neither know we what to do: but our eyes are upon thee" (2 Chron. 20:6, 12).
9. Suddenly the Spirit of God came upon a Levite named Jahaziel who proclaimed the following thrilling words:

   "Hearken ye, all Judah, and ye inhabitants of Jerusalem, and thou King Jehoshaphat, thus saith the Lord unto you, Be not afraid nor dismayed by reason of this great multitude; for the battle is not yours, but God's. Ye shall not need to fight in this battle: set yourselves, stand ye still, and see the salvation of the Lord with you, O Judah and Jerusalem. . . . Tomorrow go out against them: for the Lord will be with you" (2 Chron. 20:15, 17).
10. The king falls down and leads all the people in a worship and praise service to God. The service ends as the Levitical choir stands and sings joyful songs of thanksgiving (20:18, 19).

    Early the next morning the army of Judah marches forth to meet the enemy. After a consultation with his associates, Jehoshaphat determines to let the choir lead the march, clothed in sanctified garments and singing, "His mercy endureth for ever" (v. 21). And so they meet the enemy. Almost immediately God causes consternation among the troops of the foe, and they begin fighting among themselves. Surely no other battle in all history was won like this battle. Here songs defeated spears, and hosannas proved stronger than horses. Four days after the battle, after gathering all the immense loot discarded by their enemies (money, garments, jewels), all the Judeans gathered in a valley called Berachah, which means "blessings" and again had a heavenly hallelujah hour of praising God (20:26-30).

D. Athaliah (seventh ruler).
1. She began in 841 b.c. and reigned six years.
2. It has already been noted that Athaliah (Jezebel's daughter) has married Joram (Hezekiah's son). They had one son and named him Ahaziah. When he was killed by Jehu, Athaliah mounted the throne (2 Chron. 22:10).
3. This murderous woman then ordered the slaughter of all of the royal seed of the house of Judah.
4. But Athaliah's own daughter, Jehosheba (along with her husband Jehoiada, who was high priest at that time) hid one sole survivor of the bloodbath, a small boy named Joash (22:11).
5. After hiding the lad for six years, Jehoiada planned a coup to dethrone Judah's only queen. He was aided by the army and the Levitical priests. When all was ready, Joash

was brought out of hiding and publicly proclaimed king. When the astonished and infuriated queen rushed out to crush this revolt, she was arrested and executed. It is ironic to note that this murderous mother, who had once attempted to wipe out David's seed, was herself slain by one of David's own spears (2 Ki. 11:4-16).

E. Joash (eighth king).

1. He began in 835 B.C. and reigned forty years.
2. The young king first cooperates with Jehoiada the high priest in ushering in a time of revival, which includes, among other things, the destruction of the temples of Baal (2 Chron. 23:16-21; 24:1, 2).

   Joash then determines that the Temple of God needs repairs and orders Jehoiada to carry it out. Jehoiada constructs a special offering box to finance the work (2 Ki. 12:4-16). This was the first free-will offering taken since the construction of the tabernacle under Moses. (See Ex. 35 and Num. 7.)
3. After the death of Jehoiada, the high priest, Judah would experience difficult days. As long as Jehoiada was living, Joash walked the line, but with his death, a tragic transformation took place. It was doubtless in the grace of God that the high priest lived as long as he did—130 years. But now he was dead and without him Joash became as a Lot without an Abraham (2 Chron. 24:2, 15, 16).
4. We note with sadness the events which took place during the final years of Joash's reign.
   a. Soon after Jehoiada's funeral, the leaders of Judah induce the king to abandon God and worship idols. Joash now makes the same foolish and fatal error that his forefather, Rehoboam, once made; he allows himself to be counseled by the corrupt. (See 1 Ki. 12:8; 2 Chron. 24:17-19.)
   b. The Syrian king, Hazael, began a move to enlarge his throne by capturing the Philistine city of Gath. He then started toward Jerusalem, but was for awhile bribed away by Joash, who hurriedly sent him all the gold and treasuries of the Temple (2 Ki. 12:17, 18).
   c. The Spirit of God at this time came upon Zechariah, Jehoiada's son, and this fearless high priest boldly denounced Judah's idolatry and called for national repentance. Finally, at Joash's order, Zechariah was stoned to death. This is perhaps the darkest moment in Judah's history, the brutal murder of her own high priest. Our Lord would refer to this some eight-and-a-half centuries later. (See Mt. 23:35.)

      Zechariah thus becomes the Old Testament Stephen, as both of them were stoned for speaking the truth. (See Acts 7:51-59.) His last words were: "The Lord look upon it, and require it" (2 Chron. 24:22).

      Here the high priest asked that his death be avenged by God. We have already noted the favorable comparison between Zechariah and Stephen's ministry. But there is a significant difference in that Zechariah dies demanding that God judge his murderers, while Stephen asks the Lord to forgive them (see Acts 7:60). New Testament grace goes much further than Old Testament law.
5. A few months after the murder of Zechariah, God sent the Syrian army all the way into Judah. Jerusalem was captured, the chief leaders executed, and the Holy City looted and spoiled. Joash himself was severely wounded at this time and was finally murdered by his own palace officials.

F. Uzziah (tenth king).

1. He began in 790 B.C. and reigned for fifty-two years.
2. Uzziah had the second longest rule of all Judah's kings. Uzziah was a good ruler and was helped much by a godly prophet named Zechariah (2 Chron. 26:5). We marvel at his accomplishments:
   a. He rebuilt the city of Eloth and restored it to Judah.
   b. He subdued the strong cities of the Philistines.
   c. He was victorious against the Arabians.
   d. He made the Ammonites give him annual tribute.
   e. His fame spread down to Egypt and other nations.
   f. He built fortified towers in Jerusalem.
   g. He constructed forts in the Negeb.
   h. He built many water reservoirs.
   i. He raised great herds of cattle.
   j. He laid out many farms and vineyards.
   k. He organized his army into regiments. This army consisted of 307,500 men, all elite troops. These men were led by 2600 commanders.
   l. He equipped them with the finest weapons of war.
   m. He produced great engines of war which shot arrows and huge stones from the towers and battlements (2 Chron. 26:6-15).
3. But in the midst of his strength he was cut down by pride. We are told: "But when he was strong, his heart was lifted up to his destruction" (26:16). The first creature in God's universe who sinned had these same tragic words said against him. (See Isa. 14:12-15; Ezek. 28:12-17.)
4. His sin was intrusion into the office of the priesthood by burning incense upon the golden altar.
5. Caught in the very act of doing this, the king was soundly and severely rebuked by the high priest, Azariah, and eighty other brave priests. He was warned that this action was only to be done by the descendants of Aaron. Uzziah became furious and refused to budge. He suddenly was divinely struck with leprosy even as he held the incense burner (26:17-21). Uzziah was the third and final

biblical king to make the fatal error of assuming the office of the priesthood. God rejected the first (Saul; 1 Sam. 13:11-14), took the son of the second (Jeroboam; 1 Ki. 14:17), and here struck the third with leprosy.

6. Uzziah later died, still in this tragic condition. "And Uzziah, the king, was a leper unto the day of his death, and dwelt in a separate house . . . for he was cut off from the house of the Lord" (2 Chron. 26:21).

G. Ahaz (twelfth king).

1. He began in 735 B.C. and reigned sixteen years.

2. This young, arrogant twenty-year-old king experienced troubles almost from the start.

   a. He was threatened by an enemy alliance of Rezin (the Syrian king), and Pekah (the Israelite king) (2 Ki. 15:37; 16:5, 6).

   b. He was attacked separately, and then cojointly (2 Chron. 28:5, 6; 2 Ki. 16:5). They wanted to punish him for his refusal to join them in an alignment to stop the growing power of Assyria, Rezin, and Pekah.

   c. The terrified young king was visited by Isaiah, who assured him not to worry, for the Syrian-Israelite plot would fail and those nations themselves would soon (within sixty-five years) be destroyed (Isa. 7:1-9).

   d. God then (through Isaiah) invited Ahaz to ask him for a divine sign to prove his enemies would indeed be destroyed as prophesied. The unbelieving king refused (having apparently already determined to enlist Israel) and Isaiah then predicted that a sign would be forthcoming from God himself to the entire house of David (and not just to Ahaz), proving God's might and love to all Abraham's seed. Note the eloquent language:

   "Therefore the Lord himself shall give you a sign; Behold a virgin shall conceive, and bear a son, and shall call his name Immanuel" (Isa. 7:14).

   Thus did Isaiah predict the virgin birth of Christ! Seven centuries later the angel Gabriel would remind a heartbroken carpenter living in Nazareth concerning these words. (See Mt. 1:18-25.)

   e. Ahaz not only refused to heed God's word, but turned his wicked heart to Baal worship, which included offering up his own children as burnt sacrifices to this devil-god in the valley of Hinnom, right outside Jerusalem (2 Chron. 28:1-4).

   f. Because of all this, God allowed many enemies to spoil Ahaz's kingdom.

   g. In sheer desperation, Ahaz turned to the Assyrian king, Tiglath-pileser, for help against these foes. He bribed him by sending along the gold and silver of the Temple with his request (2 Chron. 28:16-21; 2 Ki. 16:7, 8).

   h. Tiglath-pileser agreed and captured Damascus, killing Rezin, one of Ahaz's enemies. The Judean king then hastened to Damascus to lick the hand of the Assyrian king. While he was there, he saw a special pagan altar. He jotted down its dimensions and sent it back to Urijah, the high priest, with orders to have a model ready for him upon his return. This false altar then replaced the old bronze one in the Temple (2 Ki. 16:10-16). He thus continued his vile pagan worship (2 Chron. 28:22).

   i. Tiglath-pileser continued his conquest by carrying away into captivity some of the cities of northern Israel, including the land east of Jordan (2 Ki. 15:29).

H. Hezekiah (thirteenth king).

1. He began in 715 B.C. and reigned for twenty-nine years.

2. His reforms. By God's estimation, Hezekiah was the best king of Judah up to his time. His spiritual record would only be exceeded by his grandson, Josiah (2 Ki. 18:5). He broke the shrines on the hills, destroyed the idols of Asherch and the serpent of brass made by Moses (Num. 21:9), which were being worshiped by the people.

3. His wealth. Among all the kings of both North and South, Hezekiah's vast wealth was exceeded only by Solomon (2 Chron. 32:27-30).

4. His Temple ministry. During the very first month of his reign, Hezekiah ordered the re-institution of animal sacrifices, realizing that great Mosaic law which stated, "It is the blood that maketh an atonement for the soul" (Lev. 17:11; see also Heb. 9:22). The king then organized the Temple orchestral group consisting of harps, psalteries, cymbals, and a special trumpet corps of priests. A Levitical singing choir was also formed, which featured the Psalms of David in their repertoire. When all was ready, the public was invited to come (2 Chron. 29:20-30). This simply had to be one of the great worship services of all time.

5. His great Passover celebration. Hezekiah began planning for the grandest Passover celebration since Solomon's dedication of the Temple over three centuries back (2 Chron. 30:26). Letters were sent throughout all Judea and parts of Israel inviting people to repent, return, and rejoice, all of which could be accomplished by attending the Passover. Many of the northern peoples laughed and scorned such an invitation (for a New Testament example, see Luke 14:16-24), but others joyfully responded (2 Chron. 30:3-11).

The celebration was originally scheduled to last seven days, but it was unanimously decided to continue it for another seven days. A fantastic number of animals were offered during these days which included 20,000 young bulls and 17,000 sheep (2 Chron. 30:21-27). Eventually the worshipers returned home and the revival continued, as household idols were destroyed (2 Chron.

31:1). Hezekiah then organized his priests and Levites into service corps, appointing some to offer animal sacrifices to God, and others simply to thank and praise him (2 Chron. 31:2, 3). Years before, David had appointed a special choir numbering 288 to do nothing but praise and thank the Lord (1 Chron. 16:4; 6:31, 32.) Time and again we read of this consecrated choir:

a. As the Temple was dedicated under Solomon (2 Chron. 5:12, 13).
b. As the Lord defeated a great host of Israel's enemies under Jehoshaphat (2 Chron. 20:21).
c. As wicked Queen Athaliah was deposed under Jehoiada the high priest (2 Chron. 23:13).
d. During Hezekiah's revival (2 Chron. 29:25-28).
e. During the Passover celebration under Josiah (2 Chron. 35:15, 16).
f. As the returning remnant laid the Temple foundation under Ezra (Ezra 3:11, 13).

The tithes now began to roll in from God's revived people. Azariah, the high priest, put the surplus in specially prepared rooms in the Temple. Note his testimony:

"Since the people began to bring the offering into the house of the Lord, we have had enough to eat, and have left plenty: for the Lord hath blessed his people; and that which is left is this great store" (2 Chron. 31:10).

This glorious truth is further amplified in the final Old Testament book. (See Mal. 3:8-10.)

6. His military achievements. Under the reign of Ahaz, Judah had paid tribute to the Assyrians, but in the fourth year of his rule Hezekiah rebelled against the Assyrian monarch, Shalmaneser, and no longer did this (2 Ki. 18:7). He also conducted a successful Philistine campaign at this time (2 Ki. 18:8).

7. His sickness and recovery. Hezekiah was stricken with a fatal boil-like disease and told by God through Isaiah that he would not recover. The reason for this sickness may have been his pride (2 Chron. 32:24, 25; Isa. 38:17).

The broken king turned his face to the wall and pleaded for God to spare him. God heard and promised to add fifteen more years to his life (2 Ki. 20:1-6). Thus Hezekiah was the only human being who ever lived who could (for fifteen years) absolutely count on seeing another sunrise when he retired at night.

Isaiah prepared a fig paste to put upon Hezekiah. This plaster, of course, had no more healing power than did the clay with which Jesus anointed the eyes of the blind man (Jn. 9:6). Both healings were accomplished by faith in the power and promise of God's Word (2 Ki. 20:7). Hezekiah asked for a supernatural sign to prove this treatment would really work. God granted him this,

and, at the king's own request, moved the shadow on the royal sundial back ten points (2 Ki. 20:8-11). Dr. John Davis writes the following concerning this miracle:

"The sign that God gave to Hezekiah was certainly one of the most spectacular miracles in Old Testament history. In the courtyard of the palace there was apparently a series of steps (not necessarily a sundial as we would think of it) so arranged that the shadow cast by the sun would give an approximation of the time. At the request of the kings, and, doubtless, in the presence of a large group of officials (including foreign ambassadors?), the shadow moved backward ten steps (or degrees)! How did God actually accomplish this miracle? Did He cause the earth to stop its rotation and turn backwards a little? All true Christians would agree that He could have done such a thing, for by Him all things consist, or hold together (Col. 1:17). But the Bible makes it rather clear that this was not God's method; for, in referring to this miracle, 2 Chronicles 32:24 states that Hezekiah 'prayed unto Jehovah; and he spake unto him, and gave him a sign (Hebrew: *mopheth*).' But in verse 31 we are told that the Babylonians sent ambassadors to Hezekiah 'to inquire of the wonder (*mopheth*) that was done in the land.' Obviously, then, it was a geographically localized miracle, which did not involve a reversal of the earth's rotation, with shadows retreating ten degrees all over the Near East. Instead, the miracle occurred only 'in the land' (of Judea); and, to be even more specific, it was only in the king's courtyard that 'the sun returned ten steps of the dial whereon it was gone down' (Isa. 38:8). It is the writer's conviction that a proper understanding of the nature of this great miracle helps us to understand what happened in the miracle of Joshua's long day (Josh. 10:12-14). Since Joshua's need was a prolongation of light (not a slowing down of the earth's rotation), his need could be met by a supernatural continuation of sunlight and moonlight in central Palestine for 'about a whole day' until Joshua's army could follow up its great victory and completely destroy the enemy." (*Solomon to the Exile*, pp. 128-129)

In his book, the prophet Isaiah includes for us a page in Hezekiah's diary written during this terrible sickness. It makes a gloomy reading indeed. (See Isa. 38:9-20.)

Some believe that Hezekiah spent the last fifteen years of his life putting the Old Testament Scriptures in order, for we often find the Hebrew letters "H Z K" at the end of many Old Testament books in the Hebrew manuscripts.

8. His Babylonian visitors. Hezekiah received an envoy from a rising power which would

soon meet and defeat mighty Assyria. The Babylonians may have come for several reasons:

a. To pay their respects to a king who had been raised from his very deathbed.
b. To inquire as to how this happened. The Babylonians were indeed fascinated by astronomic signs, for their national life revolved around the movement of heavenly bodies. (See Isa. 47:13; Dan. 2:27; Jer. 10:2.)
c. To determine how much loot they could take from Jerusalem after coming into power (2 Ki. 20:12, 13).

Hezekiah foolishly showed them all his treasures. He was soundly rebuked by Isaiah for this. The prophet then predicted that years after the king's death, Judah would be carried into captivity by the Babylonians, partly to obtain the very wealth Hezekiah had so freely shown them. The king's answer is a classic study in total selfishness:

"Good is the word of the Lord which thou hast spoken. And he said, Is it not good, if peace and truth be in my days?" (2 Ki. 20:19). (See also Rom. 7:18.)

We are told that God allowed the Babylon visit as a test for Hezekiah. But he flunked. (See 2 Chron. 32:31.)

9. His ordeal with Sennacherib. As we have already observed, Hezekiah had rebelled against paying tribute to Assyria during the fourth year of his reign. But as he began his fourteenth year in office, the powerful successor of Shalmaneser began to threaten Jerusalem. Hezekiah attempted to patch up his previous rebellion by sending a $1,500,000 bribe to the Assyrian warrior. This sad attempt to appease the bloodthirsty Sennacherib reminds one of England's prime minister, Neville Chamberlain, meekly going to Munich in the late thirties to hand over to Hitler half of Europe! But it didn't work, as both Hezekiah and Chamberlain would sadly discover.

Sennacherib soon surrounded the city of Jerusalem (2 Ki. 18:17; Isa. 36:1). Hezekiah made a desperate effort to defend himself by reinforcing the walls and recruiting an army. He even delivered a challenging message to inspire them, but apparently the king had serious personal doubts concerning the outcome of the crisis (2 Chron. 32:1-8).

Sennacherib now sent his Rabshakeh (title for his chief of staff) who attempted at first to break down Jerusalem's walls by the sheer power of his big mouth alone. He spewed out his terrible threats near the water supply source of the city, a place where he knew the greatest number of Jews could be reached. He lists seven arguments why Jerusalem should surrender immediately (2 Ki. 18:17-35).

a. Their ally Egypt was powerless to help them (v. 21).

b. They had "offended" Jehovah their God by destroying all the worship places except in Jerusalem (v. 22).

Those Jews who heard this argument must have laughed out loud at its stupidity. It was quite true that Hezekiah had removed the high places (see 18:4), but only because these were centers of Baal worship.

c. Jerusalem had a weak army (v. 23). Rabshakeh even offered to furnish 2000 horses, but doubted if they would muster up the soldiers to ride them.
d. It was God's will that Jerusalem be conquered (v. 25). It is true that Isaiah did predict the invasion of Assyria into Palestine (Isa. 10:5, 6), but not because this was his perfect will. It was a divine punishment for their sins.
e. Assyria had a massive army (v. 24).
f. Pleasant surrender conditions were proposed (v. 31). No one but an absolute fool would swallow this lie, for the Assyrians treated their prisoners in a most horrible way.
g. The absolute inability of Jehovah to save Jerusalem was pointed out (v. 35). This loudmouth would soon learn firsthand just how "weak" Jehovah really was!

During all this Assyrian arrogance, Rabshakeh was interrupted only once by Hezekiah's three-man truce delegation. They timidly asked that the "peace talks" be conducted in Aramaic (Syrian), and not in Hebrew, to prevent the listening crowd from understanding. The Judean negotiators were afraid a panic would follow if the seriousness of the situation was fully realized. Rabshakeh not only refused, but lifted his voice to a shout, so all could hear. But a panic did not take place. The people remained silent. This was wise, for how does a sheep answer the grunts and snorts of a wild hog? (2 Ki. 18:27, 28, 36).

10. His prayer for the city of Jerusalem. The three-man delegation immediately reported all Rabshakeh's threats to Hezekiah. The king then earnestly besought God in prayer. Hezekiah immediately heard from that grand prophet Isaiah, who reassured him that God had already determined to slay Sennacherib; and that he had nothing to fear from the Assyrian sneers. (See 2 Ki. 19:1-7; also Phil. 4:6, 7.)

11. His answer from the Lord. God at this point addressed both Hezekiah and Sennacherib through the prophet Isaiah (2 Ki. 19:20-33). To Hezekiah, God said:

a. I have heard you (v. 20). This by itself would have surely comforted the king's heart. (See Ps. 20:1; 34:4; 120:1; Jonah 2:2; 1 Jn. 5:14.) How different are the deaf idols of the pagan gods. (See Ps.135:15-21; 115:2-7.)
b. The fields which the Assyrians have destroyed will be resown and replanted (v. 29).

c. By the third year the normal agricultural cycle will function again (v. 29).

d. This time of testing will produce a strong remnant of spiritual believers in Jerusalem (v. 29).

To Sennacherib, God said:

e. My "daughter" Zion is not afraid of you (v. 21).

f. She scorns and mocks you (v. 21).

g. The only reason you have conquered anything is because I let you do so (v. 25).

h. I know every rotten thing you think, say, and do (v. 27).

i. I will put a hook in your nose and a bridle in your mouth and drag you from Jerusalem (v. 28).

Note: This was a cruelty which the Assyrians frequently inflicted upon their captives. Another pagan nation will suffer this same kind of judgment during the tribulation. (See Ezek. 38:4.)

j. You will not enter Jerusalem nor even shoot an arrow into the city (v. 32).

k. You yourself will be murdered by members of your own household (v. 7).

Note: Archaeological findings indicate that Sennacherib was crushed to death by his own sons. This they did by creeping into his private prayer chapel and pushing over upon him a gigantic statue of Nisrich, his god! Dr. John Davis writes: "And thus the great and proud king of Assyria, who boasted that Hezekiah's God was utterly helpless, not only lost his army at one flick of Jehovah's finger but was himself crushed to death by the idol of a non-existent deity to whom he had devoted his life." (*Solomon to the Exile*, p. 124)

l. I will save this city both for my sake, and for David's sake (v. 34).

m. All this will happen because when you mocked Jerusalem, you also mocked me.

God not only promised to save Jerusalem, but assured the king that not one enemy arrow would fall into it. That very night the angel of the Lord killed 185,000 Assyrian troops, and dead bodies were seen all across the landscape in the morning. Some believe this angel was Christ himself. At any rate, the powers of an angel are fantastic. In Matthew 26:53 our Lord said he could, if he so desired, even then call for twelve legions of angels to help him. A legion in those days was 6000 soldiers. Thus Christ had at his immediate disposal at least 72,000 heavenly warriors. The Assyrians now experienced that which the Egyptians had suffered some eight centuries previously. (See Ex. 12:29.) Sennacherib immediately returned to Nineveh and was soon murdered, just as God predicted (2 Ki. 19:36, 37). Hezekiah died after a glorious twenty-nine-year reign, and was succeeded by his son, Manasseh (2 Ki. 20:20, 21; 2 Chron. 32:32, 33).

I. Manasseh (fourteenth king).

1. He began in 695 B.C. and reigned for fifty-five years.

2. The fourteenth ruler of Judah was, without doubt, the most unique king ever to sit upon either the northern or southern throne. Note the following:

a. He was king longer than any other of either kingdom.

b. He had the godliest father up to that time of all Judean kings.

c. His grandson Josiah was finest of all.

d. He was the only wicked king to genuinely repent prior to his death.

e. He was the most wicked of all kings prior to his salvation!

3. The preconversion reign of Manasseh (as recorded in 2 Ki. 21:2-6; 2 Chron. 33:1-20) would probably have surpassed that of Stalin and Hitler in terms of sheer wickedness. Consider the following items of information:

a. He rebuilt all the altars of Baal his father had destroyed (2 Chron. 33:3).

b. He set up a Zodiac center for the heathen worship of the sun, moon, and stars in every house of God (2 Chron. 33:4, 5).

c. He sacrificed his own children to satanic gods in the Valley of Hinnom as his grandfather Ahaz had done (33:6).

d. He consulted spirit-mediums and fortune-tellers (33:6).

e. Tradition says he murdered Isaiah by having him sawn asunder (Heb. 11:37).

f. God said he was more wicked than heathen nations which had once occupied Palestine (2 Ki. 21:11).

g. He shed innocent blood from one end of Jerusalem to another (2 Ki. 21:16).

h. He totally ignored repeated warnings of God in all this (2 Chron. 33:10).

i. He was imprisoned temporarily by the king of Assyria.

j. He repented while in prison and was forgiven by God.

k. He was later allowed to return as king of Judah.

l. He ruled for fifty-five years and was succeeded by his son, Amon.

J. Josiah (sixteenth king).

1. He began in 640 B.C. and reigned for thirty-one years.

2. Josiah was the finest king since Solomon.

"And like him was there no king before him, that turned to the Lord with all his heart, and with all his soul, and with all his might, according to all the law of Moses; neither after him arose there any like him" (2 Ki. 23:25).

His achievements stagger the mind. One wonders just when he arranged to eat and sleep!

3. The reforms of Josiah.

a. He began to seek after God while he was yet very young, only sixteen (2 Chron. 34:3).

b. At the age of twenty, he began his massive reform work (34:3).

c. He destroyed all the altars of Baal (34:4).

d. He then ground them into dust and scattered it over the graves of those who had sacrificed to them (34:4).

e. He burned the bones of heathen priests upon their own altars (34:5).

f. He carried out these actions in distant Israelite cities as well as in his own kingdom (34:6).

g. At the age of twenty-six, he began to repair the Temple (34:8).

h. He led his people in a massive "repentance service" upon the discovery of the law of Moses (2 Ki. 23:1-3, 18-21, 29-32). He then had this book read to all his people.

i. He planned for and presided over one of the greatest Passover services of all time (2 Chron. 35:1, 18).

j. He killed heathen priests whom previous kings of Judah had appointed (2 Ki. 23:5).

k. He removed the shameful idol of Asherah from the Temple (23:6).

l. He tore down the houses of male prostitutes (23:7).

m. He brought back to Jerusalem the priests of God who were living in other cities in Judah (23:8).

n. He destroyed the altar of Topheth in the Hinnom Valley so no one could offer human sacrifices upon it (23:10).

o. He tore down the statue of horses and chariots (which were dedicated to the use of the sun god) located near the entrance of the Temple (23:11).

p. He tore down Ahaz's pagan altars on the palace roof (23:12).

q. He destroyed those altars which Manasseh had built in the two courts of the Temple (23:12).

r. He removed the shrines of Ashtoreth (god of Sidon), Chemosh (god of Moab), and Milcom (god of Ammon), which Solomon had built for his many wives (23:13).

s. He tore down the altar and shrine at Bethel which Jeroboam I had made (23:15), thus fulfilling a 300-year-old prophecy. (See 1 Ki. 13:1, 2.)

t. He demolished the shrines on the hills of Samaria (23:19).

u. He exterminated mediums, wizards, and soothsayers (23:24).

4. The scriptural ministry of Josiah.

a. In cleansing the Temple, Hilkiah the high priest discovered an old scroll which turned out to be a copy of the Law of Moses (2 Ki. 22:8).

b. Josiah was informed of this and tore his clothes in terror, realizing how the Old Testament laws had been so ridiculed and ignored during the wicked reign of both his father and grandfather (22:9-13). Apparently under Manasseh's wicked reign the Word of God had been all but totally destroyed. It was probably a capital offense to possess a copy of the Mosaic Law. Thus some faithful priest may have hidden a copy of this precious law in the Temple to await better days.

c. The young king then ordered Hilkiah to seek the counsel of a godly woman prophetess concerning all this. Her name was Huldah, and she may have been Jeremiah's aunt. (See 2 Ki. 22:14; Jer. 32:7.) God had often spoken to his people through a woman, and would do so after this also (22:14).

(1) He spoke through Miriam, the sister of Moses (Ex. 15:20).

(2) He worked through Deborah (Jdg. 5).

(3) Zacharias' wife was a prophetess (Lk. 2:36).

(4) Philip's four daughters were called prophetesses (Acts 21:9).

d. Huldah's message was a twofold prophecy. It stated that:

(1) Because of Judah's tragic and shameful spiritual failure, God had already determined to judge his people. She pronounced upon the Holy City the fearful divine words of the Lord (see 22:17).

(2) Because of Josiah's love of God, he would be spared all this, as judgment would not fall until after his death. He himself would be "gathered into thy grave in peace" (2 Ki. 22:20).

We are not to understand this to mean that Josiah would die a quiet death on his royal bed (he was actually killed in battle), but that he would be spared the wrath of the Babylonian capitivity and subsequent destruction of Jerusalem.

e. Josiah then gathered all his people at the Temple and personally read aloud the Law of Moses and urged them all to obey God's Word (2 Ki. 23:1-3).

5. The great Passover celebration of Josiah. This feast, which had begun in Egypt nearly 900 years back (Ex. 12) had evidently not been celebrated since the days of Hezekiah, over sixty years ago. But now Josiah determines to amend for this delay. We note with amazement the tremendous number of animals offered up at this time (2 Chron. 35:7, 8).

a. Animals.

(1) thirty thousand lambs

(2) three thousand young bulls

(3) seventy-six hundred sheep

(4) three hundred oxen

b. Ark of the Covenant.

According to 2 Chronicles 35:18, this was the greatest Passover of all time. During the Passover celebration, Josiah elevated the sacred Ark of the Covenant to its proper place in the Temple

(2 Chron. 35:3). Here is the final Old Testament mention of this, the most sacred piece of furniture ever built, the Ark of the Covenant. Its history makes fascinating reading indeed.

(1) It is first mentioned in Exodus 25:10.
(2) It was put in the tabernacle by Moses (Ex. 40:21).
(3) It was carried throughout Israel's forty-year wilderness experiences (Num. 10:35; 14:44).
(4) It followed the people of Israel across the Jordan River (Josh. 4:5).
(5) It was carried around Jericho (Josh. 6:13).
(6) It was placed beside Joshua on Mt. Ebal as he read the law to all Israel (Josh. 8:33).
(7) It was formally placed in the new tabernacle, set up at Shiloh (Josh. 18:1).
(8) It was carried into battle with the Philistines by wicked Hophni and Phinehas (1 Sam. 4:4).
(9) It was captured by the Philistines for seven months (1 Sam. 4:11; 6:1). During this time
  (a) It was taken to Ashdod where it defeated Dagon (1 Sam. 5:1).
  (b) It was taken to Ekron, where it caused a great plague (1 Sam. 5:10).
(10) It was carried by two "Milch Kine" into Bethshemesh. Here God smote a number of the citizens of this city for looking inside (1 Sam. 6:12).
(11) It was taken to Kirjath-jearim. Here it remained for twenty years (1 Sam. 7:1).
(12) It was brought to Gibeah by Saul. Here it saved Israel from the Philistines (1 Sam. 14:18).
(13) It was carried from Gibeah toward Jerusalem by David on a new cart. En route, Uzzah was slain for touching it (2 Sam. 6:3).
(14) It rested at the house of Obed-edom for three months (2 Sam. 6:11).
(15) It was brought into Jerusalem by David (2 Sam. 6:16).
(16) It was carried by Zadok the high priest over the brook Kidron to David during his escape from Absalom's rebellion (2 Sam. 15:24).
(17) It was carried back to Jerusalem by David's order (2 Sam. 15:25, 29).
(18) It was placed in Solomon's Temple (1 Ki. 8:1).
(19) We do not know what eventually became of it.

6. The tragic death of Josiah.
  a. Necho, the king of Egypt, planned to lead an army through Judah to aid the Babylonians against the Assyrians at Carchemish (2 Chron. 35:20).

  b. Josiah declared war upon Necho for this. In vain, the Egyptian king attempted to convince the Judean ruler that he had no quarrel with him whatsoever, and warned him not to interfere, lest God destroy him in battle (35:20, 21).
  c. Josiah refused the peace offers and attacked Necho in the Valley of Megiddo. This particular encampment located in the plain of Esdraelon had already seen many battles.
    (1) It was here that Deborah and Barak defeated the Canaanites (Jdg. 4–5).
    (2) It was here that Gideon defeated the Midianites (Jdg. 7).
    (3) It was here that David defeated Goliath (1 Sam. 17).
    (4) It was here that the Philistines killed Saul (1 Sam. 31).
    (5) It was here that Josiah was killed (2 Chron. 35:22).
    (6) It will be in this area that the mighty battle of Armageddon will someday be fought (Zech. 12:11; Rev. 16:16).
  d. Josiah was tragically slain in spite of an attempt to disguise himself (as did another king once). (See 1 Ki. 22:30.) He was carried back to Jerusalem and buried with much ceremony and sorrow. Jeremiah himself attended the funeral (2 Chron. 35:23-25). At his death, Judah would see no more good kings. It was all spiritual degeneration from this point on. Josiah was succeeded by his son, Jehoahaz (2 Chron. 36:1).

K. Jehoiakim (eighteenth king).
  1. He began in 609 B.C. and reigned for eleven years.
  2. With the exception of Manasseh (his great-great-grandfather), Jehoiakim may be regarded as Judah's most evil king. Note this sordid record:
    a. He built a plush palace, with huge rooms, many windows, paneled throughout with a fragrant cedar, and painted a beautiful red. This he accomplished with forced slave labor while his own people were suffering (Jer. 22:13, 14).
    b. He was full of selfish greed and dishonesty (22:17).
    c. He murdered the innocent, oppressed the poor, and reigned with ruthlessness (22:17).
    d. He butchered with a sword a godly and fearless prophet named Uriah, having him first tracked down in Egypt and brought back to Jerusalem (26:33).
    e. He often attempted to silence the prophet, Jeremiah (26:24; 36:19, 26).
    f. On one occasion he burned a scroll which contained the inspired writings and prophecies of Jeremiah. But this backfired, as the prophet rewrote all the king had burned and added a chilling prophecy against Jehoiakim (36:22, 23, 27–32).

3. Jehoiakim was made a vassal by Nebuchadnezzar after the Babylonians had defeated the Assyrians and Egyptians at the battle of Carchemish. During the last part of his reign, Nebuchadnezzar captured Jerusalem and took some of the sacred Temple vessels to Babylon. He also bound Jehoiakim, intending to carry him along, but apparently, for some reason, restored him to the throne of Judah as his puppet king (2 Ki. 24:1; Jer. 25:1; 2 Chron. 36:6, 7). He did, however, carry into captivity some royal Jewish youths, one of which was Daniel (Dan. 1:3, 4).

4. After three years of this, Jehoiakim was induced by the Egyptian party in his court to rebel against Nebuchadnezzar.

5. Although Nebuchadnezzar apparently could not rise up immediately at that time to crush this rebellion, God punished the wicked Judean king by allowing the land to be invaded by the Syrians, Moabites, and Ammonites (2 Ki. 24:2, 3).

6. Jehoiakim died, and, as prophesied by Jeremiah (22:18, 19; 36:30), received the burial of a wild animal. He was dragged out of Jerusalem and thrown on the garbage dump beyond the gate, unmourned even by his immediate family. He was succeeded by his son, Jehoiachin (2 Ki. 24:5, 6).

L. Zedekiah (twentieth king).

1. He began in 597 and reigned for eleven years. This youngest son of godly King Josiah was the last to rule, and, like his two brothers, Jehoahaz and Jehoiakim, Zedekiah was wicked. He has been called "the fickle puppet" (2 Ki. 24:18, 19; 2 Chron. 36:12).

2. At first, Zedekiah showed signs of an intention to obey the Law of Moses (Jer. 34:8-10).

3. He went to Babylon in his fourth year, probably to reassure Nebuchadnezzar of his loyalty (51:59).

4. He returned and was forced to muzzle the "loud-mouth" prophet, Jeremiah (27-29).

5. Jeremiah suffered much under the reign of Zedekiah.

   a. He was hated and plotted against because of his message of divine judgment (Jer. 11:8-10).

   b. He was arrested by the Temple priest Pashhur, whipped, and put in stocks for one night (20:1-3).

   c. He was almost murdered by a wild mob by Judah's false priests and prophets after one of his messages (26:7-9).

   d. In the fourth year of Zedekiah's reign, a false prophet named Hananiah publicly rebuked Jeremiah, saying Babylon would be overthrown in two years (28:1-4).

   e. He was arrested and thrown into prison, charged with treason (27:11-16).

   f. He was then removed from there and placed in the palace prison by the fickle Zedekiah (37:21).

   g. He was soon taken from here, however, and placed into an empty cistern in the prison yard by some Jewish hotheads.

There was no water in it, and Jeremiah sank down into the thick layer of mire at its bottom (38:1-6).

   h. He was again set free and, in vain, attempted to convince Zedekiah to submit to the Babylonian threat as God's divine punishment (38:14-26).

   i. During the final two years of Zedekiah's pitiful and perverted rule, Jeremiah was again confined to prison. At this time, he was ordered to purchase a farm from his cousin, Hanamel (32:6-15).

6. Zedekiah foolishly refused the counsel of Jeremiah and rebelled against Nebuchadnezzar, even though he had taken an oath of loyalty (2 Chron. 36:13). Rising to this revolt, Nebuchadnezzar came against him. For some thirty months, Jerusalem held out, but on July 18, 586 B.C., it totally collapsed. During the final night, Zedekiah attempted to escape, but was captured near Jericho and brought back to Nebuchadnezzar for punishment. He was forced to witness the execution of his own sons and then his eyes were gouged out. He was finally taken in chains to Babylon where he died (Jer. 52:4-11; 39:1-7).

Note: Jeremiah had warned Zedekiah that he would look into the very eyes of Nebuchadnezzar (32:4; 34:3), but Ezekiel prophesied that he would not see Babylon with his eyes (12:6, 12, 13). These horrible prophecies came true.

7. During the latter part of July, 587, Nebuchadnezzar's captain of the guard, Nebuzaradan, burned the Temple, along with most private and public buildings. The walls of the city were torn down (Jer. 52:12-23).

8. Nebuchadnezzar then ordered the execution of Seraiah the high priest along with seventy-three other important officials. Judah's exile was now complete (Jer. 52:24-27). From this date on, until May 14, 1948 A.D., Israel as a nation would cease to exist.

The important oral prophets:

A. Elijah.

The ministry of Elijah, one of the most colorful and courageous prophets who ever lived, will be considered first in outline subject-matter form, and then presented in actual chronological fashion.

An outline, subject-matter consideration of his life:

1. Elijah and King Ahab:

   a. announcing the three-and-a-half year drought (1 Ki. 17:1)

   b. challenging him to a contest on Mt. Carmel (18:17-20)

   c. predicting the end of the drought (18:41-46)

   d. pronouncing the death sentence upon him and his wife (21:17-24)

2. Elijah and the ravens at Cherith (17:2-7)

3. Elijah and the widow at Zarephath (17:8-15)

4. Elijah and Obadiah (18:1-16)

5. Elijah and the people of Israel (18:20-24)

Elijah

ELIJAH AND KING AHAB
Announcing the three-and-a-half year drought (1 Ki. 17:1)
Challenging him to a contest on Mt. Carmel (17:17-19)
Predicting the end of the drought (18:41-46)
Pronouncing the death sentence upon him and his wife (21:17-24)

ELIJAH AND THE RAVENS OF CHERITH
He is supernaturally fed by some ravens beside a drying brook (1 Ki. 17:2-7)

ELIJAH AND A WIDOW AT ZAREPHATH
He is supernaturally fed by God through a widow (1 Ki. 17:8-16)
He raises the dead son of that widow (17:17-24)

ELIJAH AND A BACKSLIDER NAMED OBADIAH
Obadiah was a secret believer who had ministered to 100 prophets (1 Ki. 18:1-15)
He reluctantly and fearfully arranges a meeting between Elijah and Ahab (1 Ki. 18:16)

ELIJAH AND THE NATION ISRAEL
He rebukes and challenges Israel on Mt. Carmel (1 Ki. 18:20-24)

ELIJAH AND THE PRIESTS OF BAAL
The priests of Baal are unable to pray down the fire (1 Ki. 18:25-29)
He has them killed for their paganism (18:40)

ELIJAH AND THE LORD GOD
He flees Israel to escape Jezebel's revenge (1 Ki. 19:1-3)
He is ministered to by an angel (19:4-7)
He hears God's still small voice in a cave (19:8-18)

ELIJAH AND ELISHA THE PROPHET
He calls Elisha to special service (1 Ki. 19:19-21)
He prepares Elisha for special service (2 Ki. 2:1-10)

ELIJAH AND NORTHERN KING AHAZIAH
He predicts wicked Ahaziah will die from a fall (2 Ki. 1:1-18)
He prays down fire to destroy two companies of soldiers sent to arrest him (1:9-12)
He spares the third company, led by a captain who begs for mercy (1:13-16)

ELIJAH AND A CHARIOT OF FIRE
He parts the River Jordan and stands on the eastern bank (2 Ki. 2:1-8)
He receives a last request from Elisha (2:9, 10)
He is carried into heaven without dying (2:11)

6. Elijah and the priests of Baal (18:25-40)
7. Elijah and God (19:1-18)
8. Elijah and Elisha
   a. calling him to special service (1 Ki. 19:19-21)
   b. preparing him for special service (2 Ki. 2:1-10)
9. Elijah and King Ahaziah (2 Ki. 1:1-17)
10. Elijah and the chariot of fire (2 Ki. 2:11)

A chronological consideration of his life:
1. Dr. John Whitcomb introduces this mighty Tishbite as follows:
   "Like a meteor suddenly flashing across the darkened sky, Elijah appears on the scene without historical background, and without warning!" (*Solomon to the Exile*, p. 50)
2. He announces to wicked King Ahab that a long drought can be expected as a punish-

ment for sin (1 Ki. 17:1). The New Testament writer James refers to this terrible drought as an example of the tremendous power of prayer (Jas. 5:17). James says the drought lasted three-and-a-half years. The lack of rain was a divine punishment for sin. (See Deut. 11:13-17; 28:24; 2 Chron. 7:12-15.)
3. God then orders his prophet to hide himself (from the king's wrath) by the Brook Cherith at a place east of where it enters the Jordan (17:2). Here he would be fed supernaturally by some ravens.
4. Elijah is now ordered to proceed to a city in Jezebel's own backyard, called Zarephath, where God has commanded a widow to feed him. After what must have seemed an eternity (possibly a year or longer), Elijah finally graduates from the D.B.I. (Drying Brook Institute). The brook experience almost always precedes the Mt. Carmel challenge in the plan of God for his chosen servants. Paul spent three years in the A.B.I. (Arabian Bible Institute, Gal. 1:18) and Moses passed some forty years on the campus of the S.B.I., Sinai Bible Institute. (See Ex. 3:1; 1 Ki. 17:8, 9.)

   Again God does the unexpected thing. His prophet who has been fed by some ravens now has his needs met by a lonely and poverty-stricken old widow. Elijah asks the starving widow and her son to share their last available meal with him and promises them that God himself will see to it that their oil and flour containers will always be full until it rains and the crops grow again. By faith the widow shares with him and finds God's promise to be true (17:10-16).
5. Suddenly, with no warning whatsoever, the widow's son dies. In her grief-stricken statement at this time, the widow brings out two significant things (1 Ki. 17:18):
   a. The testimony of Elijah. Note her phrase, "O thou man of God." Here was a woman who had seen the prophet out of his pulpit and before he had drunk his first cup of coffee in the morning. She saw him as he really was, and still could call him a man of God. The acid test of a man's true religion is the home test.
   b. Her own uneasy conscience. She asks him if he was sent to call her sin to remembrance. Perhaps some shameful and secret deed in her past had constantly plagued her conscience.
6. Elijah carries the lad upstairs, stretches himself upon the lifeless body three times, and prays that God will raise the boy. God hears his prayer. This marks the first of eight body resurrections in the Bible (not counting the resurrection of Christ). These are:
   a. Elijah raises the widow's boy (1 Ki. 17:22).
   b. Elisha raises the son of a Shunammite woman (2 Ki. 4:35).
   c. Elisha's bones raise a man whose dead body touches them during a graveyard burial (2 Ki. 13:21).

d. Christ raises the daughter of Jairus (Mt. 9:25).

e. Christ raises the son of a widow (Lk. 7:14).

f. Christ raises Lazarus (Jn. 11:43, 44).

g. Peter raises Dorcas (Acts 9:40, 41).

h. Paul raises Eutychus (Acts 20:12).

7. Elijah is promised by God that he will soon send rain and orders his prophet to confront Ahab again. En route to the palace, Elijah is met by Obadiah, a backslidden believer, who served as household administrator under Ahab. Obadiah attempts to impress Elijah with his good works (he has hidden 100 prophets in a cave from the murderous wrath of Jezebel) and reluctantly and fearfully agrees to inform Ahab of Elijah's presence (1 Ki. 18:1-16).

8. At their summit meeting, Ahab blames Elijah for all Israel's trouble.

9. Elijah, however, refuses to accept Ahab's stupid accusation and challenges Ahab and pagan priests of Baal to a "fire-consuming sacrifice" contest on Mt. Carmel, with the following rules:

a. Two bullocks would be sacrificed and laid upon two altars, one dedicated to Baal, the other to God.

b. Both deities would be prayed to, and the real god could prove himself by sending down fire from heaven to consume his sacrifice (1 Ki. 18:23-25).

10. The priests of Baal pray first, agonizing, screaming, dancing, and even cutting themselves to attract their god's attention, but all in vain. During this time Elijah mocks them. We read that about noontime, Elijah began mocking them.

" 'You'll have to shout louder than that,' he scoffed, 'to catch the attention of your god! Perhaps he is talking to someone, or is out sitting on the toilet, or maybe he is away on a trip, or is asleep and needs to be awakened' " (1 Ki. 18:27, *The Living Bible*).

11. Then it was evening, and Elijah's turn. He took twelve stones and rebuilt an old torn-down altar of God in that very area. He then dug a three-foot wide trench around the altar and dumped twelve barrels of sea water into it. Finally, he stepped back and prayed (18:36, 37).

12. The fire immediately fell from heaven and consumed the sacrifice. Note the order in which the things at the altar were consumed:

a. The burnt-sacrifice. This speaks of ourselves! (See Rom. 12:1-3.)

b. The wood. This speaks of our efforts. It is tragically possible for a pastor on a Sunday morning to experience either fire without wood or wood without fire. The first occurs when he isn't studied up, and the second when he isn't prayed up.

c. The stones. This speaks of the difficult things in our lives.

d. The dust. This speaks of the useless things in our lives.

e. The water. This speaks of the impossible things in our lives (18:38).

13. Elijah then executed the prophets of Baal.

14. Finally, after a sevenfold prayer meeting, there was a great rain (18:45). God often works in a roundabout way, but he does so to accomplish certain specific things. Thus, through all this:

a. Elijah received valuable training for his future ministry.

b. A disrespectful king learned the fear of the Lord.

c. A heathen woman believed on the name of the Lord.

d. A young man was raised from the dead.

e. A backslidden believer was restored to fellowship.

f. The nation Israel experienced a temporary revival.

g. A large number of God's enemies were destroyed.

15. Upon hearing of Elijah's action, Jezebel vowed to kill him in twenty-four hours, and Elijah ran for his life (19:2). This points out two important spiritual truths:

a. The infallibility of the Word of God. No mere human author would have included the sad account we read here. This part in the life of a fearless man of God would have simply been denied or ignored.

b. The fallibility of the man of God. Elijah, like David, was a man who failed God in what was supposedly his strongest point. In David's case it was his purity and in Elijah's situation it was his courage. But both fell on their faces. They needed the lesson God taught Paul in 2 Corinthians 12:1-10.

16. Elijah fled eastward and after a day's journey he fell exhausted under a juniper tree, praying that God would kill him (19:4). This was prayed some twenty-eight centuries ago and God had yet to answer it. Elijah, like Enoch, participated in God's first and second space shot. (Compare Gen. 5:24 with 2 Ki. 2:11.) But someday the Lord will allow his prophet to lay down his life for Jesus. (Compare Mal. 4:5, 6 with Rev. 11:3-12.) Both Moses (Num. 11:15) and Jonah (4:3) had also prayed this despondent prayer.

17. As he slept, an angel touched him and fed him (19:5). God often allows his angels to participate in his dealing with man. (See Heb. 1:14; 1 Pet. 1:12.)

Elijah was by now totally exhausted, having traveled 150 miles from Jezreel to Beersheba. But now he desperately needed food. Our spiritual and physical natures are so closely entwined that one automatically affects the other. Part of his terrible soul depression was due to the mistreatment of his body. The stomach can affect the soul. (See Ps. 127:2.)

18. God himself finally spoke through a still, small voice to Elijah in a cave, perhaps the same one where Moses had viewed God's glory some five centuries before. (Compare 19:9 with Ex. 33:21-23.) In spite of his objections to the contrary, Elijah was ordered immediately to perform four tasks:

   a. Get back and start preaching again. Besides, he was not alone as he claimed, for God still had 7000 followers in Israel who had not bowed to Baal (19:15, 18).

   b. Anoint a man named Hazael to be king of Syria (19:15).

   c. Anoint a man named Jehu to be king of Israel (19:16).

   d. Begin training Elisha to succeed him (19:16). In passing, it should be noted (19:10) that Elijah's prayer here is the only example of an Israelite believer making intercession against his own beloved nation Israel. Paul specifically states that this was indeed the case. (See Rom. 11:1-4.) Needless to say, God has never and will never honor this kind of praying. James and John later expressed the same vindictive spirit concerning some unbelieving Samaritans. (See Lk. 9:55.)

19. Elijah returned and found Elisha plowing in a field. Elijah went over to him and threw his coat across his shoulders. Elisha thereupon prepared a farewell feast for his family and servants and followed Elijah (19:19-21).

20. Elijah confronted wicked Ahab in the vineyard of Naboth. There he predicted the divine death penalty judgment upon both Ahab and Jezebel for their part in the cold-blooded murder of godly Naboth (1 Ki. 21:17-24).

21. Sometime later, King Ahaziah, wicked northern ruler (and eldest son of Ahab) suffered a severe fall off the upstairs porch of his palace in Samaria. Fearing the worst, he sent messengers to the Philistine temple dedicated to Baalzebub at Ekron to ask this pagan god whether he would recover (2 Ki. 1:1-3). This ungodly son of Ahab was apparently unaware of Israel's history, for had he been aware, he certainly would not have trusted in a pagan god who was utterly powerless to save his own worshipers against the wrath of the Ark of God (in 1 Samuel 5:10-12). Elijah was instructed by God's angel to intercept these messengers and send them back to Ahaziah with his prophecy, that due to the king's idolatry, he would indeed soon die (1:3-6).

Ahaziah correctly guessed the identity of this fearless hairy man with the wide leather belt and sent out a captain with fifty men to arrest him. As the soldiers approached him, Elijah called down fire from heaven and they were consumed. Another fifty were sent out and suffered the same fate. The captain of the third group fell to his knees and begged Elijah to spare their lives and come with them. The prophet agreed and soon stood before the king where he repeated similar words he had once said to Ahab, Ahaziah's father. Shortly after this, Ahaziah died and was succeeded by his younger brother Jehoram (2 Ki. 1:7-17). He had reigned for but two short years.

22. Elijah's magnificent ministry had now come to a close and he would soon be taken heavenward by means of a whirlwind, without dying. He quickly traveled his circuit for the final time, moving rapidly from Gilgal to Bethel to Jericho to the Jordan River. At the first three stops he tested the determination of Elisha by suggesting that he might want to drop the hectic life of the prophet and return to his quiet farm. But on each occasion (2:2, 4, 6) he refused by uttering these five fearless words: "I will not leave thee!" Elisha, like Ruth, thus proved worthy for the blessings of God! (See Ruth 1:15-17.) Both at Bethel and Jericho Elisha spoke with the sons of the prophets living in those areas. These men may have been able to trace their heritage back to the prophetic schools of Samuel's day (1 Sam. 19:20). But what a sorry lot they were.

   a. They were cowardly (1 Ki. 18:4).

   b. They attempted to discourage Elisha (2 Ki. 2:3, 5).

   c. They lacked faith (2 Ki. 2:16-18).

When they came to the Jordan River, Elijah folded his cloak together and struck the water with it; and the river divided, allowing them to cross on dry ground (2:8).

23. Elijah then asked Elisha what wish he would have granted before his heavenly departure. Elisha asked for a double portion of his master's power. He was told this was a hard thing, but that if he were present at Elijah's translation the request would be granted (2:9, 10).

24. Suddenly a chariot of fire, drawn by horses of fire, appeared and drove between them, separating them, and Elijah was carried by a whirlwind into heaven (2:11). He thus became the second of two individuals who saw glory without the grave. (See Gen. 5:24 for the other person.)

B. Elisha.

   1. Parting the waters at Jordan (2 Ki. 2:14).

When Elijah had disappeared from view, Elisha picked up his master's cloak and returned to the Jordan River bank to see if his request for power had been granted. Striking the river with Elijah's cloak, he thundered out, "Where is the Lord God of Elijah?" Immediately the Jordan waters parted. This marked the third time such a miracle had happened in Israel's history. (Compare Josh. 3:17; 2 Ki. 2:8, 14.) Today, in our desperate world, the cry is: "Where are the Elijahs of the Lord God?"

All this was watched by the students from the J.B.I. (Jericho Bible Institute), but these pessimistic prophets found it difficult to believe Elijah really went all the way to heaven and therefore suggested that some of their best athletes form a search party; "Lest peradventure the Spirit of the Lord hath taken him up, and cast him upon some mountain, or into some valley" (2 Ki. 2:16). After repeated urging, Elisha agreed to the search. After the fifty men combed the entire area for three days, the hunt was called off (2 Ki. 2:17, 18).

Elisha now employed his supernatural powers to their greatest extent. No other Old or New Testament individual (apart from the Savior), with the possible exception of Moses, could match the sheer number of his miracles.

2. Purifying the waters at Jericho (2:19-22).
At Jericho Elisha purified a polluted city well, which was believed by the citizens to be causing miscarriages, by pouring a bowl of salt into the noxious water (2 Ki. 2:19-22). Moses did a similar miracle at Marah centuries before. (See Ex. 15:23-25.)

3. Judging some hoodlums at Bethel (2:23, 24).
En route to Bethel he was surrounded by a gang of young hoodlums from that city who ridiculed his bald head and mocked the recent translation of Elijah. Elisha caused two female bears to appear, and forty-two of these arrogant rebels were clawed as a divine punishment (2 Ki. 2:23-25). The Hebrew word *yeled*, translated "little children," should doubtless be rendered "young lads." The same word is found in 1 Samuel 16:11, referring to David, and by then David had already established a reputation as "a mighty man of valor" (1 Sam. 16:18), having killed a lion and a bear (1 Sam. 17:34-37). Note their taunt, "Go up, thou bald head," an obvious effort to ridicule the rapture of Elijah. (See Lev. 26:21, 22.)

4. Causing some empty ditches to fill with water (2 Ki. 3:16-27).
This took place during the days of Jehoshaphat, king of Judah. Jehoshaphat was again tricked by the Ahab dynasty into an unholy alliance. This time (the fourth and final), King Jehoram, Ahab's youngest son, persuaded him into a fighting alliance to defeat the Moabites, who had rebelled against Israel by refusing to pay their tribute after Ahab's death (3:1-8).

The two allied armies met in the wilderness of Edom and immediately were faced with the problem of water. In desperation both kings turned to Elisha when it was discovered he was secretly traveling with them. Elisha utterly spurned the pleas of wicked Jehoram, but agreed to help for Jehoshaphat's sake. At his order, great trenches were dug and the next day God had filled them all with water (3:9-20).

The Moabites were now aware of the impending attack and began to marshal their forces along the frontier. On the day of the battle, the Moabites mistook the rays of the sun shining across the water-filled trenches for blood, and immediately attacked, concluding that their enemies were fighting a bloody battle among themselves (3:21-23).

This reckless action led them into a trap which resulted in their total defeat. The Moabite king made one last effort to break through the siege by leading an attack of 700 swordsmen. When this failed, he took his oldest son and, to the horror of the watching allied armies, killed and sacrificed him as a burnt offering to his pagan god (3:22-27).

5. Creating oil in empty vessels (4:1-7).
At Samaria he rescued a poverty-stricken widow of a God-fearing man from her creditor, who was threatening to enslave her two sons for non-payment. Elisha ordered the woman to borrow every possible container from her neighbors and then pour her remaining jar of olive oil into these vessels. She did this and every container was supernaturally filled, thus solving her indebtedness problem (2 Ki. 4:1-7). God loves to use little things.
   a. He used Moses' rod (Ex. 4:2).
   b. He used Aaron's rod (Num. 17:8).
   c. He used David's sling (1 Sam. 17:49).
   d. He used Gideon's trumpet (Jdg. 7:18).
   e. He used the widow's handful of meal (1 Ki. 17:12).
   f. He used a little boy's lunch (Jn. 6:9-11).

6. Raising a dead boy at Shunem (4:18-21, 32-37).
In Shunem he was given a sleeping room by a prominent woman of that city and her husband. To reward her kindness for his prophet's chamber, Elisha promised she would have a son. The son was born, but fell sick some years later and died. In desperation the mother found Elisha and begged him to do something. He then sent his carnal servant Gehazi who laid the prophet's staff upon the dead child's face, but all in vain. Elisha then arrived and stretched his body across the child. The lad became warm, sneezed seven times, and opened his eyes (2 Ki. 4:8-37). Elisha would later advise this woman to leave the land during a divinely sent seven-year famine. Upon return, she went to the northern king (Jehoram) to get her land back. Gehazi happened to be there and was relating to the king how Elisha had once raised a boy from the dead. At that very moment she walked in. The king was so impressed he restored all her land (2 Ki. 8:1-6).

7. Purifying a poisonous stew at Gilgal (4:38-41).
In Gilgal a student prophet had unknowingly prepared some harmful stew for the students' lunch hour by adding some poisonous wild gourds. Upon discovering this, Elisha purified the soup by throwing some meal into it (2 Ki. 4:38-41).

8. Feeding 100 men by supernaturally increasing twenty loaves of bread and a sack of corn (4:42-44).

Near Baal-shalishah he fed one thousand men supernaturally from a sack of fresh corn and twenty loaves of barley bread. Again the prophet's servant Gehazi displayed his carnality by doubting this could be done. He acted here as Philip and Andrew would later respond prior to the feeding of the 5000 performed by our Lord in John 6:5-13. (See 2 Ki. 4:42-44.)

9. Healing of Naaman (5:1-19).
The Syrian king at this time had an army commander whose name was Naaman. This general was honorable, brave, and successful, but he had a problem, for he was also a leper (2 Ki. 5:1). A little Israeli slave girl who was serving in the Naaman household told her master about the miraculous power of the prophet Elisha in Israel. Acting upon her testimony, the Syrian king sent Naaman to Jehoram (Israel's ruler) carrying $20,000 in silver, $60,000 in gold, and ten units of clothing, along with a personal royal letter requesting healing (5:2-6).

Jehoram was filled with both wrath and fear at this impossible request and concluded Syria demanded this as an excuse to invade the land again. However, Elisha soon learned the purpose of Naaman's visit, and bid the leprous general to visit him (5:7, 8). Naaman arrived and waited outside Elisha's home where he was instructed by a servant to wash seven times in the Jordan River, which would cure his leprosy. The Syrian soldier was furious at such "impersonal treatment" but finally was persuaded by his own servants to obey. This he did and was immediately healed (5:9-14).

Naaman arrived back at Elisha's home and was this time greeted by the prophet, but his offered reward was refused. Elisha's servant, Gehazi, coveted the money and later told Naaman that his master had changed his mind. Naaman gave him $4,000 and two expensive robes. Elisha discovered this, and Gehazi was divinely punished by being afflicted with the kind of leprosy of which Naaman was cured (5:15-27).

10. Predicting the judgment of leprosy upon Gehazi (2 Ki. 5:15-27).
11. Recovering a lost axehead (6:1-7).
At the river Jordan, Elisha caused an axehead which had accidentally fallen into the water to float on top (2 Ki. 6:1-7).
12. Revealing the secret war plans of Syria (6:8-12).
Elisha the prophet, who had once refused to help Jehoram, the northern king, now aided him by warning the monarch of several planned Syrian ambushes (2 Ki. 6:8-10).
The Syrian king concluded a traitor in his camp must be informing Israel of their plans, but was told by one of his officers that Elisha was supernaturally revealing these plans (6:11, 12). Syrian troops were immediately dispatched to arrest Elisha at Dothan. The

prophet awakened the next day and found himself surrounded by a great army of chariots and horses (6:13-15).
13. Praying that his servant could see an invisible angelic army and blinding the Syrian army (6:15-23).
His servant, Gehazi, was terrified, but was soon reassured by Elisha.
"And he answered, Fear not: for they that be with us are more than they that be with them. And Elisha prayed, and said, Lord, I pray thee, open his eyes, that he may see. And the Lord opened the eyes of the young man; and he saw: and, behold, the mountain was full of horses and chariots of fire round about Elisha. And when they came down to him, Elisha prayed unto the Lord, and said, Smite this people, I pray thee, with blindness. And he smote them with blindness according to the word of Elisha" (6:16-18).

Elisha then led these sightless Syrian soldiers into Samaria, where their eyes were opened. King Jehoram (the northern king) determined to slay his helpless enemies, but was forbidden to do so by Elisha (6:19-23). This little account by itself totally refutes the devilish claim of liberals and unbelievers that the Old Testament is one huge bloody "eye-for-an-eye" slaughter story. Here an entire Syrian army was defeated by sheer kindness. (See Rom. 12:20, 21; Prov. 25:21, 22; Mt. 5:43-45.)
14. Blinding the entire Syrian army (2 Ki. 6:18-23).
15. Predicting the salvation of Samaria from starvation (2 Ki. 7).
Some years later (perhaps after Naaman's death) the Syrians invaded Israel and besieged the city capitol of Samaria, causing a great famine. This must have been indescribably horrible, for even a donkey's head sold for $50.00 and a pint of dove's dung brought $3.00. Things became so desperate that even cannibalism was practiced (6:29).

All this was tragically prophesied over five centuries before by Moses. (See Lev. 26:27-29.) The southern kingdom of Judah would later be reduced to this same pit of despair during the destruction of Jerusalem. (Compare Deut. 28:53 with Lam. 4:10; see 2 Kings 6:25-29.) The northern king, Jehoram, bitterly remembered how Elisha had once refused to allow him to kill the blinded Syrian soldiers some years back, and vowed to execute the prophet, blaming him for the present terrible situation (6:31). The unruffled Elisha ignored the king's threats and predicted that within twenty-four hours food would be so plentiful that two gallons of flour and four gallons of barley grain would only bring a dollar in the Samaritan market. He also prophesied that the king's chief officer, an especially arrogant man, would see this food but never live to eat it (7:1, 2).

Outside the gate of the city sat four starving lepers who decided in desperation to surrender to the Syrians and began walking toward their camp (7:3, 4). But God caused their very footsteps to resemble the clatter of speeding chariots and horses. In panic, the Syrians fled, concluding that Samaria must have hired the Hittites and Egyptians to attack them (7:5-7).

God had employed this method before. (See 2 Sam. 5:23, 24; Jdg. 7:16-21; 2 Chron. 20:20-25.) After looting the camp, the four lepers reported the good news to Samaria. Soon thousands of frantically happy men and women were rushing out from the main gate to gather food. In their mad drive, the king's official, attempting to control the traffic, was knocked down and crushed to death, just as Elisha had predicted. That very day two gallons of flour and four gallons of barley grain did indeed sell for a dollar (7:8-20).

16. Predicting the death of Ben-hadad, King of Syria, and the subsequent reign of Hazael over Syria (2 Ki. 8:7-15).

Elisha went to Damascus to visit Ben-hadad, the ailing Syrian king. En route he was greeted by Hazael, an important Syrian official who presented the prophet with forty camel loads of the best products of the land. Hazael was instructed to inquire whether Ben-hadad would recover from his illness. Elisha gave the strange answer that he would indeed get well, but would still die (2 Ki. 8:7-10).

Elisha then predicted that Hazael would become the next king of Syria and that his reign would shed much Israelite blood. Hazael denied this, but the very next day he smothered to death his master, Ben-hadad (8:11-15).

Hazael would later oppress Israel without mercy. (See 2 Ki. 13:22.) Elisha instructed one of his young prophets to locate a professional charioteer in Ramoth-gilead named Jehu and anoint him the next king over Israel. This was done and Jehu was ordered by God to execute the dynasty of Ahab, including Jezebel, whom the dogs would later eat (2 Ki. 9:1-10). Note: The anointing of both

Elisha

ELISHA AND EIGHTEEN EXCITING EVENTS

1. Parting the waters at Jordan— **2 KINGS 2:14**
2. Purifying the waters at Jericho— **2 KINGS 2:19-22**
3. Judging some hoodlums at Bethel— **2 KINGS 2:23, 24**
4. Causing some empty ditches to fill with water— **2 KINGS 3:16-27**
5. Creating oil in empty vessels— **2 KINGS 4:1-7**
6. Raising a dead boy at Shunam— **2 KINGS 4:18-21; 32-37**
7. Purifying a poisonous stew at Gilgal— **2 KINGS 4:38-41**
8. Feeding 100 men by supernaturally increasing twenty loaves of bread and a sack of corn— **2 KINGS 4:42-44**
9. Healing of Naaman from leprosy— **2 KINGS 5:1-14**
10. Predicting the judgment of leprosy upon Gehazi— **2 KINGS 5:15-27**
11. Recovering a lost axehead from the Jordan— **2 KINGS 6:1-7**
12. Revealing the secret war plans of Syria to Israel— **2 KINGS 6:8-12**
13. Praying that his servant would see an invisible angelic army— **2 KINGS 6:13-17**
14. Blinding the entire Syrian army— **2 KINGS 6:18-23**
15. Promising deliverance to the starving citizens of Samaria— **2 KINGS 6:24—7:20**
16. Predicting the death of Benhadad, king of Syria, and the subsequent reign of Hazael over Syria— **2 KINGS 8:7-15**
17. Predicting three victories by Israel over Syria— **2 KINGS 13:14-19**
18. Raising a dead man years after Elisha himself had died— **2 KINGS 13:20, 21**

Hazael and Jehu was ordered by God to be performed by Elijah, but for some reason he did not accomplish this. (See 1 Ki. 19:15, 16.)

17. Predicting Israel's three victories over Syria (2 Ki. 13:14–19).

On his deathbed Elisha was visited by Jehoash, a wicked northern king of Israel. In spite of his evil ways he did apparently have some affection for Elisha. Jehoash visited the dying prophet and wept over his impending death. Following Elisha's strange command, the king shot an arrow from his bedroom window. This was to symbolize Israel's victory over the Syrians. He was then instructed to strike the floor with some arrows, which he timidly did three times, thus angering Elisha, who told him he should have hit the ground five or six times, for each strike assured him of a victory over Syria (2 Ki. 13:14–19).

During the period that followed, Jehoash reconquered the cities his father had previously lost, and defeated the Syrians on three specific occasions, just as Elisha had predicted (13:22–25).

18. Raising a man from the dead years after the prophet himself had died (13:20, 21).

Elisha died and was buried. After some years, a corpse was being buried near the prophet's grave and was accidentally allowed to touch the bones of Elisha. The dead man suddenly revived and jumped to his feet (13:20, 21).

OBADIAH (around 848 B.C.)

INTRODUCTION:

1. Obadiah is the shortest and smallest Old Testament book.
2. We know nothing about the author except his name, which means, "The servant of the Lord."
3. Obadiah has only one theme, and that concerns the destruction of the nation, Edom, for its treachery toward Judah.
4. There were at least four instances when Edom helped in the plunder of Jerusalem and Judah. These were:
   a. during the reign of Joram (853 B.C.) (2 Chron. 21:8, 16, 17; Amos 1:6)
   b. during the reign of Amaziah (796 B.C.) (2 Chron. 25:11, 12, 23, 24)
   c. during the reign of Ahaz (735 B.C.) (2 Chron. 28:16–21)
   d. during the reign of Zedekiah (597 B.C.) (2 Chron. 36:11–21; Ps. 137:7)

I. The House of Edom—to be reviled by God (1:1–16).
   A. Because of their thankless heart (1:1–9).
      1. They had become proud and arrogant because they lived in those high, inaccessible, mountainous cliffs, which surrounded their capital, the city of Petra.
         Note: These unique ruins, cut out of the solid cliffs of rose-colored rock and long hidden in the arid regions of the Dead Sea, were discovered in A.D. 1812.
      2. Esau had founded and fathered this proud people. (See Gen. 25:30; 36:1.)

THE WRITING PROPHETS OF THE CHAOTIC KINGDOM STAGE

AUTHOR	YEARS OF MINISTRY	DATES	DESTINATION
1. Obadiah	10	850-840	EDOM
2. Jonah	35	785-750	NINEVEH
3. Nahum	30	650-620	NINEVEH
4. Amos	7	760-753	NORTH (Israel)
5. Hosea	60	760-700	NORTH
6. Joel	7	841-834	SOUTH (Judah)
7. Isaiah	58	739-681	SOUTH
8. Micah	35	735-700	SOUTH
9. Zephaniah	20	640-620	SOUTH
10. Habakkuk	3	609-606	SOUTH
11. Jeremiah	52	627-575	SOUTH
12. Lamentations	—	586	SOUTH

3. God prophesied every nook and cranny of Petra would be searched and robbed, and every treasure found and taken.
4. Edom's allies would turn against them.
5. Their wise men would be filled with stupidity. Edom was noted for her wise men. Eliphaz, the wisest of Job's three friends, was from Teman, five miles east of Petra in Edom. (See Job 2:11; Obad. 1:8.)
6. The mightiest soldiers of Teman would be confused and helpless to prevent this awful slaughter.
   B. Because of their treacherous hand (1:10–16).
      1. They deserted their blood brothers (Judah) in time of great need. Both peoples were, of course, related, for two twin brothers, Jacob and Esau, were their forefathers.
      2. They stood aloof, refusing to lift even one finger to help.
      3. They actually rejoiced over Judah's agony.
      4. They mocked them.
      5. They occupied their lands after the captivity.
      6. They stood at the crossroads and killed those trying to escape.
      7. Those they did not murder were returned to Judah's enemies, or became prisoners of war.
II. The House of Jacob—to be revived by God (1:17–21).
   A. In spite of their terrible persecutions and punishments, some deserved and others undeserved, Judah will someday be fully restored to Palestine.
   B. The Israelites will then control tremendous land areas never before occupied, including the land of Edom.
   C. Judges will rule over Edom and Petra from Jerusalem during the millennium.
      Note: Some of these prophecies concerning Edom have already come to pass, at least in part.
      1. By 312 B.C., the Nabataeans, an Arab people, had displaced the Edomites living in Petra.

2. They then fled to Southern Palestine and were later subdued by the Jewish military hero, John Hyrcanus, during the Maccabean period (134–104 B.C.).
3. Wicked King Herod came from this displaced group of Edomites.
4. They were destroyed in A.D. 70, along with the Jews, when they revolted against the Roman empire.
5. Other Scripture verses which foretell the doom of Edom are:
Isaiah 34:5–15; Ezekiel 25:12–14; 35:1–15; Amos 1:11, 12.
6. In spite of the nation's sins, a gracious God will someday restore Edom. (See Isa. 11:14.)

JOEL (835–796 B.C.)
INTRODUCTION:
1. As with Obadiah, almost nothing is known concerning the prophet Joel. He was the son of Pethuel, and his name means, "Jehovah is God."
2. Sometime during Joel's ministry, the land of Judah was struck by a ferocious locust plague, more intense than any experienced before.
3. Joel, under divine inspiration, compares that terrible locust plague to the coming tribulation period.
4. Joel is also known as the prophet of Pentecost, because his words about the Holy Spirit were later quoted by Simon Peter on the day of Pentecost.

I. Israel and God's Judgment: A review of the past (1:1–20).
   A. The severity of the locust judgment.
   "That which the palmer worm hath left hath the locust eaten; and that which the locust hath left hath the cankerworm eaten; and that which the cankerworm hath left hath the caterpillar eaten" (1:4).
   Some expositors interpret these words as describing the four stages in the development of the caterpillar, while others consider them to be four different kinds of insects. Locusts were often sent as a judgment from God. (See Deut. 28:38–42; Ex. 10:12–15; 1 Ki. 8:37; Rev. 9:1–12.)
   B. The title name for the locust judgment.
   "Alas for the day! For the day of the Lord is at hand, and as a destruction from the Almighty shall it come" (1:15).
   This is the second mention in the minor prophets of the term, "The day of the Lord." It can be found in many passages, both in the Old and New Testaments. (See Isa. 2:12; 13:6, 9; Ezek. 13:5; 30:3; Joel 2:1, 11, 31; 3:14; Amos 5:18, 20; Obad. 1:15; Zeph. 1:7, 14; Zech 14:1; Mal. 4:5; Acts 2:20; 1 Thess. 5:2; 2 Thess. 2:2; 2 Pet. 3:10.) The phrase is almost always a reference to the seven-year tribulation period, but here in Joel 1:15, the prophet uses it to refer to the judgment then going on.

II. Israel and God's Judgment: A preview of the future (2:1—3:21).
   A. The identity of this invasion. What nation or enemy is Joel speaking of here in chapters 2 and 3? He may be referring to several in general, giving special emphasis to the last in particular.
   1. The Assyrian invasion in 701 B.C., led by Sennacherib and crushed at the very gates of Jerusalem by God's death angel (2 Ki. 19). See Joel 2:20.
   2. The Babylonian invasion in 586 B.C., led by Nebuchadnezzar (2 Ki. 24).
   3. The Russian invasion, during the middle of the tribulation, to be led by Gog (Ezek. 38, 39).
   4. The final invasion, at the end of the tribulation, to be led by the antichrist at the battle of Armageddon (Rev. 16:13–16; 19:11–21).
   B. The gathering place of this invasion.
   "I will also gather all nations, and will bring them down into the Valley of Jehoshaphat, and will judge them there" (3:2). (See also 3:9–14.)
   Note: This battle, the biggest, boldest, bloodiest, and most brazen of all time, will stretch from the city of Megiddo on the north (Zech. 12:11; Rev. 16:16), to Edom on the south (Isa. 34:5, 6; 63:1), a distance of some 200 miles. It will reach from the Mediterranean Sea on the west to the hills of Moab on the east, a distance of 100 miles. Thus, the total fighting area will exceed twenty thousand square miles. The center of the action will apparently be the Valley of Jehoshaphat, located just east of Jerusalem, between the Holy City and the Mount of Olives. It is also known as the Kidron Valley.
   C. The twofold purpose for this invasion gathering.
   1. The purpose of the antichrist—to destroy Israel and her God. (See Ps. 2.)
   2. The purpose of God—to destroy antichrist and his allies.
   D. The outcome of this invasion.
   "The sun and the moon shall be darkened, and the stars shall withdraw their shining. The Lord also shall roar out of Zion, and utter his voice from Jerusalem; and the heavens and the earth shall shake: but the Lord will be the

Joel

The prophet used an event contemporary in his day to describe coming events

CONTEMPORARY EVENTS—Joel 1
A Review of Israel's Current Insect Invasion
- Nature: A terrible locust plague had settled down upon the land (1:4, 12)
- Reason: Because of Israel's sin (1:5)
- Suggested cure: Call for a special meeting, pray, and repent (1:14)

COMING EVENTS—Joel 2-3
A Preview of Israel's Coming Enemy Invasion
- Identity: Probably twofold:
  1. The Russian invasion during the middle of the tribulation, led by Gog (Ezek. 38-39)
  2. The final invasion at the end of the tribulation, led by the antichrist (Rev. 16:13-16; 19:11-21)
- Location: Valley of Jehoshaphat (3:2, 9-14)
- Purpose:
  1. The purpose of Satan—to destroy Israel and her God (Ps. 2)
  2. The purpose of God—to destroy Satan and his allies (Rev. 16:16)
- Results:
  1. The salvation of Israel (3:15-21)
  2. The sanctification of Israel (2:21-32)

hope of his people and the strength of the children of Israel" (Joel 3:15, 16). (Also see Rev. 19:11-21.)
E. The blessings after this invasion has been crushed.
1. God's Spirit will be poured out upon all flesh. (See 2:28-32.) It should be noted that this passage event will mark the fulfillment of Moses' desire. (See Num. 11:29.)
Peter would later quote this passage in Joel on the day of Pentecost. (See Acts 2:16-21.) This he did, not to indicate that Pentecost was the *fulfillment* of Joel's prophecy (for it was not), but, rather, as an *example* of it.
2. All human needs will be provided for (2:21-27).
3. Nature itself will be transformed (3:18).
4. Christ himself will reign in Zion (3:21). Mount Zion is the height which rises close to the southwest corner of the old walled city. It was once within the walls of ancient Jerusalem. It is held to be one of the most sacred places in Israel, because there is located the traditional tomb of King David. Above it is an upper room believed to be on the site of that upper room in which Jesus and his disciples ate the last Passover together and where he established the Communion service (Mk. 14:12-16; Lk. 22:7-13). This upper room has also been considered to be the place where the twelve disciples were gathered when the Holy Spirit came upon them on the day of Pentecost (Act 1:12-14; 2:1-4).

JONAH (780-750)
INTRODUCTION:
A. The book of Jonah is one of three Old Testament books especially hated by Satan. These are:
1. Genesis, which predicts the incarnation of Christ as the seed of the woman (Gen. 3:15).
2. Daniel, which predicts the glorious Second Coming of Christ (Dan. 7:9-12) to destroy his enemies.
3. Jonah, which predicts (in type form) the death and resurrection of Christ. (Compare Jonah 2 with Mt. 12:38-41.)
B. There are three basic interpretations of the book of Jonah.
1. The *mythological* approach. This is the liberal view, which would look upon Jonah as it would Robinson Crusoe, Gulliver (of *Gulliver's Travels*), or Hercules.
2. The *allegorical* (or parabolic) approach. In this view the book is merely an extended parable. Thus:
a. Jonah is really Israel.
b. The sea is Gentile nations in general.
c. The fish is the Babylonian captivity.
d. The regurgitation is the return during Ezra's time.
"Surely this is not the record of actual historical events nor was it ever intended as such. It is a sin against the author to treat as literal prose what he intended as poetry . . . His story is thus a story with a moral, a parable, a prose poem like the story of the Good Samaritan." (Julius Bewer, *International Critical Commentary*)

3. The *literal-historical* approach. This, alone, is the correct view.
a. The account presents itself as actual history.
b. The Jews and early church believed it to be literal.
c. The author of 2 Kings (14:25) refers to Jonah as a historical person. His hometown is given, along with the name of his father, and the king he served under.
d. Jesus testified to the literal account of Jonah (Mt. 12:38-41; 16:4; Lk. 11:29-32).
4. Jonah was from Gath-heper of Zebulun (Josh. 19:13), north of Nazareth in Galilee. Thus, the Pharisees were in error concerning their statement recorded in John 7:52—"Search, and look; for out of Galilee ariseth no prophet."

I. Jonah Protesting (demonstrating God's patience)—chapter 1:
A. The command of God—Go! (1:1, 2).
God orders his prophet to proceed to Nineveh and preach out against the city's exceeding wickedness.
B. The action of the minister—No! (1:3).
1. The futility of his action. Jonah foolishly attempts the impossible—to flee from God's presence! (See Ps. 139:7-12.) He purchases a fare to Tarshish (ancient name for Spain) from the Port of Joppa. This port is significant, for some eight centuries later, another Jewish preacher would receive a similar command to share the Gospel with some Gentiles! (See Acts 10:5.)
2. The reason for his action. Why did he disobey? Several reasons have been offered.
a. Because he was a coward. This is definitely in error, as seen by 1:12.
b. Because he was an extreme nationalist. This seems to be the logical answer. At this time in history, Assyria was on the rise and many felt it would only be a matter of time before her blood-covered boots came marching toward Palestine. The cruelty of the Assyrian armies was unparalleled in ancient history. Consider the following testimonies from various authors:
"Some of the victims were held down while one of the band of torturers, who are portrayed upon the monuments gloating fiendishly over their fearful work, inserts his hand into the victim's mouth, grips his tongue, and wrenches it out by the roots. In another spot, pegs are driven into the ground. To these, another victim's wrists are fixed with cords. His ankles are similarly made fast, and the man is stretched out, unable to move a muscle. The executioner then applies himself to his task; and beginning at the accustomed spot, the sharp knife makes its incision, the skin is raised inch by inch till the man is flayed alive. These skins are then stretched out upon the city walls, or otherwise disposed of so as to terrify the people

and leave behind long-enduring impressions of Assyrian vengeance. For others, long, sharp poles are prepared. The sufferer, taken like all the rest from the leading men of the city, is laid down; the sharpened end of the pole is driven in through the lower part of the chest; the pole is then raised, bearing the writhing victim aloft; it is planted in the hole dug for it, and the man is left to die."

"Pyramids of human heads marked the path of the conqueror; boys and girls were burnt alive or reserved for a worse fate; men were impaled, flayed alive, blinded, or deprived of their hands and feet, or their ears and noses, while the women and children were carried into slavery, the captured city plundered and reduced to ashes, and the trees in its neighborhood cut down."

C. The hand of God—Blow! (1:4-12).
1. God suddenly flings a terrific wind over the sea, causing a great storm.
2. The frightened sailors pray to their various pagan gods and frantically throw the cargo they are carrying overboard to lighten the ship.
3. During this time, Jonah is sound asleep in the ship's hold. Upon hearing this, the captain awakes him and orders that he, too, make prayer to his God for salvation.
4. In desperation, the sailors cast lots to determine who among them had brought the storm by offending his God. The lot falls upon Jonah.
5. Jonah admits to them his nationality and sin of disobeying God. He then advises them to throw him overboard.

D. The action of the mariners—Throw! (1:13-17).
1. After further useless strugglings, the sailors cry out a prayer for forgiveness for what they have to do with Jonah and quickly throw him overboard into the boiling sea.
2. Immediately, the raging waters become calm as the storm ceases. The amazed sailors give thanks to Jehovah God.
3. Jonah is swallowed by a huge fish, which God had previously arranged for.

Of all the miracles in the Bible, none is better known or has raised more eyebrows, than this one.

Dr. J. Vernon McGee writes:
"The fish here is not the hero of the story, neither is it its villain. The book is not even about a fish. The fish is among the props and does not occupy the star's dressing room. Let us distinguish between the essentials and the incidentals. Incidentals are the fish, the gourd, the east wind, the boat, and Nineveh. The essentials are Jehovah and Jonah—God and man."

The question is often asked as to whether a whale could actually swallow a man. In the first place, it should be pointed out that nowhere in the original Old Testament or New Testament language does it say a whale swallowed Jonah. The word "whale" does not even appear in the King James Version in the book of Jonah. The Hebrew word for fish is *dag,* and refers to a great sea monster. In Matthew 12:40, the word translated *whale* by the King James Version is the Greek word, *ketos,* which again refers to a sea monster. In the second place, God *could* have used a whale, had he chosen to. Dr. Gleason Archer writes the following paragraph:

"Numerous cases have been reported in more recent times of men who have survived the ordeal of being swallowed by a whale. The *Princeton Theological Review* (Oct., 1927) tells of two incidents, one in 1758 and the other in 1771, in which a man was swallowed by a whale and vomited up shortly thereafter with only minor injuries.

One of the most striking instances comes from Francis Fox, *Sixty Three Years of Engineering* (pp. 298-300), who reports that this incident was carefully investigated by two scientists (one of whom was M. DeParville, the scientific editor of the *Journal Des Debats* in Paris). In February, 1891, the whaling ship, *Star of the East,* was in the vicinity of the Falkland Islands, and the lookout sighted a large sperm whale three miles away. Two boats were lowered and in a short time, one of the harpooners was enabled to spear the creature. The second boat also attacked the whale, but was then upset by a lash of its tail, so that its crew fell into the sea. One of them was drowned, but the other, James Bartley, simply disappeared without a trace. After the whale was killed, the crew set to work with axes and spades removing the blubber. They worked all day and part of the night. The next day they attached some tackle to the stomach, which was hoisted on deck. The sailors were startled by something in it which gave spasmodic signs of life, and inside was found the missing sailor, doubled up and unconscious. He was laid on the deck and treated to a bath of sea water, which soon revived him. At the end of the third week, he had entirely recovered from the shock and resumed his duties . . . His face, and neck and hands were bleached to a deadly whiteness and took on the appearance of parchment. Bartley affirms that he would probably have lived inside his house of flesh until he starved, for he lost his senses through fright and not through lack of air." (*A Survey of Old Testament Introduction*), p. 302

II. Jonah Praying (demonstrating God's pardon)—chapter 2:
A. The petition (2:1-8).
1. Jonah immediately begins an earnest and all-out one-man prayer meeting. His altar was

perhaps the strangest ever used, the slippery slopes of a fish's stomach!

2. Some believe Jonah's language seems to indicate he actually died and was later resurrected by God. Note his phrases:
   a. "Out of the belly of hell (*sheol*)" (v. 2).
   b. "Thou brought up my life from corruption" (v. 6).
   c. "My soul fainted within me" (v. 7).
   While there is no question that God could have done this, the simple context approach would suggest Jonah did not die, but was at the point of death.

3. On two occasions, Jonah refers to "thine holy temple." (See vs. 4, 7.) In fact, he points his prayer in this direction. Jonah was no doubt calling to remembrance Solomon's Temple dedication some 150 years back (1 Ki. 8:38, 39).

   "What prayer and supplication soever be made by any man, or by all thy people Israel, which shall know every man the plague of his own heart, and spread forth his hands toward this house: Then hear thou in heaven thy dwelling place, and forgive, and do, and give to every man according to his ways, whose heart thou knowest; (for thou, even thou only, knowest the hearts of all the children of men)."

4. One can almost picture the pathetic and praying prophet as he sloshed and slid around with the seaweeds wrapped around his head. The backslider is often forced to wear a strange halo!

5. Jonah mentions a scientific fact totally unknown by human resources in that day when he speaks of the mountains which rise from off the ocean floor (see v. 6). This is just another little proof that the Bible is, indeed, the very Word of God!

6. Jonah renounces his sin, remembers his vow of service, and reconsecrates his life to God (vs. 8, 9).

B. The pardon (2:9, 10).
   1. He ends his prayer with a five-word summary of the entire Bible and, indeed, the very plan and purpose of God: "Salvation is of the Lord!" (v. 9).
   2. He is then vomited up on dry land by the fish.

III. Jonah Preaching (demonstrating God's power)—chapter 3:
   A. The warning —(3:1-4).
      1. His mission field:
      "Nineveh lay on the eastern side of the Tigris, and was one of the greatest—if not the greatest—of the cities of antiquity. It had 1,200 towers, each 200 feet high, and its wall was 100 feet high, and of such breadth that three chariots could drive on it abreast. It was 60 miles in circumference, and could, within its walls, grow corn enough for its population of 600,000. Zenophon says the basement of its wall was of polished stone, and its width 50

feet. In the city was a magnificent palace, with courts and walls covering more than 100 acres. The roofs were supported by beams of cedar, resting on columns of cypress, inlaid and strengthened by bands of sculptured silver and iron; its gates were guarded by huge lions and bulls sculptured in stone; its doors were of ebony and cypress encrusted with iron, silver, and ivory, and panelling the rooms were sculptured slabs of alabaster, and cylinders and bricks with cuneiform inscriptions. Hanging gardens were filled with rich plants and rare animals, and served with other temples and palaces, libraries and arsenals, to adorn and enrich the city; and all was built by the labor of foreign slaves."

   2. His message:
   "Yet forty days and Nineveh shall be overthrown" (v. 4). Forty is often the number of testing in the Bible, as indicated by the following:
      a. The flood rains continued forty days in Noah's time (Gen. 7:17).
      b. Moses spent forty days on Mt. Sinai (Ex. 24:18).
      c. The twelve spies searched out Palestine for forty days (Num. 13:25).
      d. Israel wandered for forty years in the wilderness (Num. 14:33).
      e. Jesus was tempted for forty days (Mt. 4:2).
      f. Forty days elapsed between his resurrection and ascension (Acts 1:3).

   B. The mourning—(3:5-9).
      1. This chapter describes the greatest revival in all recorded history. No other physical miracle in this book (or any other Old Testament book) compares with the marvel and extent of this spiritual miracle! In the New Testament, Jesus later warned that his entire generation (in general) would someday be drastically affected because: "The men of Nineveh shall rise in judgment with his generation and shall condemn it: because they repented at the preaching of Jonah; and behold, a greater than Jonah is here" (Mt. 12:41).
      2. The critic, however, always anxious to knock the Bible, has gleefully pointed out that secular history records no such revival in Nineveh as described here. Dr. H. Freeman writes:

      "The complaint that there is no record of Nineveh's repentance in secular history is not only a valueless argument from silence, but ignores the fact that the event *is* recorded in Biblical history in the book of Jonah. Remember the Hittites! They were an ancient people mentioned in more than a dozen Old Testament books. Of the Hittites no trace could be found, leading some critics to view these Old Testament references with suspicion. Archaeological discoveries in the early part of the twentieth century, however, not only confirmed the Biblical references as accurate, but also revealed the Hittites to be an important people with an extended empire during the fourteenth and thirteenth centuries B.C." *(Introduction to the Old Testament)*

However, secular history may, indeed, hint to this sacred revival recorded in Jonah after all. It is known that about this time there was a religious movement in Nineveh, which resulted in a change from the worship of many gods to that of one God whom they called Nebo. Nebo was the son in the Babylonian trinity. His name meant, "The Proclaimer, the Prophet."

He was the proclaimer of the mind and will of the trinity head. Nebo was the god of wisdom, the creator, the angelic overseer. Some believe Nebo had been worshiped in earlier days as the only supreme God. It is known that the Ninevite ruler Adal-Nirari III (810-783) had advocated a monotheistic worship system of some kind. *If* the revival took place at this time as a result of Jonah's preaching, then the use of their national name for the Son of God is what we might possibly expect. Jonah did not preach repentance to the Ninevites in the name of Yahweh (the Hebrew God of the Covenant), but in the name of Elohim (the triune Creator of the Universe; Gen. 1:1). Some believe, however, that the revival took place a little later, under the reign of King Assurdan III (771-754 B.C.) If so, then God had even more time to prepare the Ninevites, for:

a. A great plague had occurred in 765 B.C.

b. A total eclipse of the sun took place on June 15, 763 B.C..

c. Another plague fell in 759 B.C.

C. The transforming (3:10).

"And God saw their works, that they turned from their evil way; and God repented of the evil that he had said that he would do unto them, and he did it not."

Two phrases in this verse deserve a brief comment:

1. "God repented"—that is, God changed his previously intended course of action. (See also Gen. 6:6; Ex. 32:14; 2 Sam. 24:16.)

2. "Of the evil." While it is true the Hebrew word *ra* (here translated evil) is usually connected with sin, it can also be (and is often) translated by such words as affliction, calamity, distress, grief, harm, trouble, and sorrow. The context would show that the latter meaning is meant here in Jonah 3:10. See also Jonah 1:7, 8 and Isaiah 45:7 for similar examples.

IV. Jonah Pouting (demonstrating God's pity)— chapter 4:

A. Lamenting over a city (4:1-5).

1. This chapter, along with 2 Samuel 11; 1 Kings 19; Genesis 9, 13, and others, demonstrates beyond any reasonable doubt that the Bible is not a book man would write if he

could: Here God's chosen minister is presented as a petty and pouting prophet, sitting on a hill outside Nineveh and hoping the city will refuse his previous message and be destroyed! Surely Jeremiah's sober words apply here:

"The heart is deceitful above all things, and desperately wicked: who can know it?"

2. He reluctantly acknowledges the grace, mercy, and goodness of God, and then in brazen desperation and disappointment dares to pray:

"Therefore now, O Lord, take, I beseech thee, my life from me; for it is better for me to die than to live" (4:3).

See Numbers 11:15 (Moses); Jeremiah 20:14-18 (Jeremiah); 1 Kings 19:4 (Elijah) for similar requests.

3. God then attempted to reason with Jonah as he once did with Cain (Gen. 4:6, 7) and as he still does with sinners everywhere (Isa. 1:18).

B. Learning under a gourd (4:5-11).

1. Jonah makes a leafy lean-to shelter and continues to sit sulking on the hillside.

2. When the sun has withered the leafy shelter, to Jonah's surprise and relief, God arranges for a vine to grow quickly and shade him.

3. But God also prepares a worm, which soon eats through the vine's stem and kills it.

4. Finally, the Lord subjects his prophet to a scorching east wind, until he once again cries out for God to kill him.

5. Jonah is asked then if he regretted the destruction of the vine. The prophet loudly assures God he did, indeed, and the divine trap is sprung. God's final recorded words to Jonah must have softened his stubborn and carnal heart:

"Then said the Lord, Thou hast had pity on the gourd, for which thou hast not laboured, neither madest it grow; which came up in a night, and perished in a night: And should not I spare Nineveh, that great city, wherein are more than sixscore thousand persons that cannot discern between their right hand and their left hand; and also much cattle?" (4:10, 11).

AMOS (765-750)

INTRODUCTION:

1. The name Amos means "burden." As Middle Eastern names are usually meaningful, this name may have referred to his unwelcome birth, or been given as a prophecy of his future ministry to describe his burdened heart over Judah and Israel's sin.

2. He was from the little town of Tekoa, some five miles from Bethlehem in Judea.

3. Amos was a herdsman (1:1; 7:14, 15) and a gatherer of sycamore fruit (7:14). He had not graduated from the school of the prophets, but was called by God to become a layman evangelist.

4. He was called to be a prophet to the whole house of Jacob (3:1, 13), but chiefly to the northern kingdom (7:14, 15) at the main sanctuary at Bethel (7:10). Here

he conducted his "Greater Samaritan Revival Campaign," and thundered away on the subjects of sin, separation, and sanctification.

5. Amos ministered during the reigns of Uzziah (King of Judah) and Jeroboam II (King of Israel), beginning his ministry some two years before a mighty earthquake had struck Palestine (1:1). This earthquake was so severe that Zechariah (a later Hebrew prophet) referred to it some 250 years later. (See Zech. 14:5.) Josephus, the Jewish historian, tells us the earthquake happened at the time when God punished King Uzziah with leprosy for his intrusion into the office of the priesthood. (See 2 Chron. 26:16-21.)

6. At the time of Amos' ministry, Israel, under powerful King Jeroboam II, was at its zenith of success. (See 2 Ki. 14:25.) But along with the nation's prosperity had come religious perversion!

I. Eight Nations Denounced (1-6).
   A. Syria—capital city, Damascus (1:1-5).
      1. This nation had often harassed Israel, especially under Ben-hadad I and King Hazael. (See 2 Ki. 10:32, 33; 1 Ki. 20:1; 2 Ki. 6:24.)
      2. God would thus:
         a. Burn down the palace of the capital city.
         b. Break down their strongholds.
         c. Cause many Syrians to die and others to be carried back into Kir, the land of their former slavery. (Compare 1:5 with 9:7.) Kir was located in Mesopotamia. See also 2 Kings 16:9.
   B. Philistia—capital city, Gaza (1:6-8).
      Philistia's four chief cities, Gaza, Ashdod, Ashkelon, and Ekron were to be judged because they sold Israelites into slavery to Edom. (See 2 Chron. 21:16, 17; Joel 3:4-8.)
   C. Phoenicia—capital city, Tyre (1:9, 10).
      1. They had broken their covenant of brotherhood with Israel (referring to the agreement David and Solomon had made with Tyre. See 1 Ki. 9:13).
      2. Israel had been attacked by Tyre and its citizens led into slavery to Edom. (See also Joel 3:4-8.)
      3. God would thus burn down the forts and palaces of Tyre.
   D. Edom—capital cities, Teman and Bozrah (1:11, 12).
      1. Teman was located southeast of Petra, and Bozrah was in north central Edom.
      2. Even though the Edomites and Israelites were closely related (one people from Esau, the other from Jacob, see Gen. 25:30), Israel had suffered grievously at the hands of Edom. (See also Mal. 1:2; Obad. 1:1-21.)
      3. Their strongholds would thus be burned.
   E. Ammon—capital city, Rabbah (1:13-15).
      1. The Ammonites, descendants of Lot's youngest daughter (Gen. 19:38) had committed cruel crimes, ripping open pregnant Israelite women with their swords during their expansion wars in Gilead.
      2. God would thus destroy their cities and enslave their people.
   F. Moab—capital city, Kirioth (2:1-3).
      1. These people (from Lot's older daughter, Gen. 19:37) had, among other crimes, dese-

crated the tombs of the kings of Edom, with no respect for the dead. (See 2 Ki. 3:26, 27.)
      2. Moab would be defeated in battle and its palaces burned.
   G. Judah—capital city, Jerusalem (2:4, 5).
      1. Judah had rejected the Word of God, and disobeyed the God of the Word.
      2. They had hardened their hearts as their fathers had done.
   H. Israel—capital city, Samaria (2:6-16).
      1. They had perverted justice by accepting bribes.
      2. They had sold the poor into slavery, trading them for a pair of shoes.
      3. Both fathers and sons were guilty of immorality with the same harlot.
      4. They were lounging in stolen clothing from their debtors at religious feasts.
      5. They had offered sacrifices of wine in the Temple, which had been purchased with stolen money.
      6. They were absolutely unthankful for God's past blessings.
      7. They caused Nazarites to sin by tempting them to drink wine.
      8. Because of all this, God would:
         a. Make them groan as a loaded-down wagon would groan.
         b. Cause their swiftest warriors to stumble in battle.
   I. The Whole House of Jacob (both Israel and Judah) (3:1—6:14).
      1. Jacob's punishment must equal her past privileges (3:1-3)
         "Hear this word that the Lord hath spoken against you, O children of Israel, against the whole family which I brought up from the land of Egypt, saying, You only have I known of all the families of the earth: therefore I will punish you for all your iniquities. Can two walk together, except they be agreed?"
      2. God was issuing them one final warning through his prophets (3:7).
      3. Jacob's enemies are called upon to attest to her wickedness (3:9).
         a. Her women had become cruel and demanding (4:1-3).
         b. Her formal and empty religious ceremonies had become an insult to divine holiness (4:4, 5; 5:21-26).
         c. They had surrounded themselves with gross luxury, with ivory beds to lie upon, and the choicest food to eat (6:4).
         d. They thought more of worldly music than their own Messiah (6:5).
         e. They had drunk wine by the bucketful, perfumed themselves with sweet ointments, and totally neglected the poor and needy (6:6).
      4. God had tried everything to bring his people to their senses (4:6-13). But they had refused. Thus, their former Savior would now become their Judge.
         "Therefore, thus will I do unto thee, O Israel; and because I will do this unto

thee, prepare to meet thy God, O Israel" (4:12).

5. One final invitation is extended by God (5:4-15).

"Seek him who maketh the . . . stars . . . and turneth the shadow of death into the morning, and maketh the day dark with night: that calleth for the waters of the sea, and poureth them out upon the face of the earth: The Lord is his name."

6. This invitation was rejected and judgment would fall.

a. Jacob would be consumed as a lion devours a sheep (3:12).

b. There would be crying in the streets and every road (5:16).

c. In that day they would be like a man who escaped from a lion, only to meet a bear. They would be as one who leans against a wall in a dark room and puts his hand upon a snake! (5:19).

d. Ninety percent of their soldiers would fall in battle (5:3).

II. Five Visions Announced (7-9).

A. The locust plague (7:1-3).

1. In a vision God revealed to Amos his intentions to destroy all the main crops that sprang up after the first mowing.

2. Amos interceded for Israel and a merciful God changed his course of action.

B. The vision of the great fire (7:4-6).

1. Amos saw a destructive fire, the heat from which was so fierce that it consumed the very waters of Palestine. This was to fall upon the land to punish sin.

2. Again the prophet pled for mercy, and again God set aside this deserved judgment.

C. The vision of the plumb line (7:7-16).

1. Amos viewed the Lord as he stood beside a wall built with a plumb line to see if it was straight.

2. God informed Amos:

a. That he would continue testing Israel with the plumb line of heavenly justice.

b. That he would no longer turn away from punishing.

c. That he would destroy the dynasty of Jeroboam II by the sword. This, of course, literally happened (as do all of God's prophecies). Jeroboam II was succeeded by his son Zechariah, who was assassinated by a rebel named Shallum after a reign of only six months. (See 2 Ki. 15:10-12.) God would later use this same plumb line on Judah during the days of wicked King Manasseh. (See 2 Ki. 21:13-15.)

3. At this point in his preaching ministry, Amos was confronted by Amaziah, the chairman of the Bethel ministerial association, who quickly issued two messages.

a. One was to King Jeroboam II, warning him against the "Bible banging" activities of Amos.

b. The other was to Amos himself, ordering him to leave Bethel and go back to his own land of Judah.

Amos quickly responded that, in spite of his lowly background (he was not a prophet, nor a prophet's son) he had been called by God and would not allow any middle-of-the-road spokesman to stop him. Amos then related to Amaziah from the Lord one of the most terrifying prophecies ever pronounced upon a human being, because of the false priest's attempts to silence God's true prophet.

(1) Amaziah's wife would become a common Bethel street prostitute.

(2) His sons and daughters would be killed.

(3) His land and possessions would be divided up.

(4) He, himself, would die as a captive in a heathen land.

D. The vision of the basket of summer fruit (8:1-14).

1. The meaning of this vision: God showed Amos a basket filled with ripe fruit, explaining that it symbolized Israel, which was now ripe for judgment.

2. The reason for this judgment vision. The cruel and totally materialistic merchants of the northern kingdom had:

a. robbed the poor (by selling them moldy food) and trampled upon the needy

b. longed for the Sabbath to end and various religious holidays to be over that they could once again start cheating, using their weighted scales and undersized measures

c. made slaves of the poor, buying them for their debt of a piece of silver or a pair of shoes

3. The results of this judgment vision:

a. The riotous sound of singing in the Temple would be turned to weeping.

b. Dead bodies would be scattered everywhere.

c. Fearful heavenly signs would occur:

"And it shall come to pass in that day, saith the Lord God, that I will cause the sun to go down at noon, and I will darken the earth in the clear day" (8:9). This frightening punishment will have its ultimate fulfillment during the coming great tribulation. (See Mt. 24:22, 29.)

d. There would be no comforting words from God (8:11, 12).

"Behold, the days come, saith the Lord God, that I will send a famine in the land, not a famine of bread, nor a thirst for water, but of hearing the words of the Lord: And they shall wander from sea to sea, and from north even to the east, they shall run to and fro to seek the word of the Lord, and shall not find it."

E. The vision of the Lord at the altar (9:1-15).

1. The condemnation of Israel's transgressors (9:1-10).

"Though they dig into hell [sheol] there shall mine hand take them; though they

climb up to heaven, from there will I bring them down; and though they hide themselves in the top of [mount] Carmel, I will search and take them out from there; and though they be hidden from my sight in the bottom of the sea, there will I command the serpent and he shall bite them" (9:2, 3).
2. The restoration of David's Tabernacle (9:11-15).
  a. The Davidic monarchy was in a degraded condition with ten out of the twelve tribes refusing to give homage to it. But during the glorious millennium all this would change. James quotes Amos 9:11, 12 at the Jerusalem Council (Acts 15:14-17) and bases an important decision upon it, namely, should saved Gentiles be circumcised? His answer was a resounding *no!*
  b. The blessings of this restored monarchy (under Christ, the rightful seed of David) would be manifold:
    (1) The harvest time will scarcely end before the farmer starts again to sow another crop.
    (2) The terraces of grapes upon the hills of Israel will drip sweet wine.
    (3) Israel's faithful will have their fortunes restored and be permanently regathered in the glorious land.

Amos

PART ONE

Eight Nations Denounced Amos 1-6

NATION	CRIME	PUNISHMENT
SYRIA (1:1-5)	Had often harassed Israel	• The capital at Damascus to be burned • Their strongholds to be broken • Their citizens to be enslaved
PHILISTIA (1:6-8)	Had sold Israelites into slavery to Edom	• The burning of their four main cities: Gaza, Ashdod, Ashkelon, Ekron
PHOENICIA (1:9, 10)	Had broken their peace covenant with Israel	• The burning down of the forts and palaces in Tyre, their chief city.
EDOM (1:11, 12)	Had murdered many Jews	• The destruction of their cities
AMMON (1:13-15)	Had murdered Jewish women	Their cities to be burned • Their citizens to be enslaved
MOAB (2:1-3)	Had desecrated the tombs of the dead	• They would be defeated in battle
JUDAH (2:4, 5)	• Had rejected the Word of God • Had disobeyed the God of the Word	• Their Temple in Jerusalem to be destroyed
ISRAEL (2:6-16)	• Had accepted bribes • Had enslaved the poor • Had committed adultery • Had stolen • Were totally unthankful • Had caused the innocent to sin	• Their punishment would make them groan as a loaded-down wagon • Their armies would stumble in battle

Additional indictments upon the whole house of Israel —both southern and northern kingdoms **(3-6)**

PART TWO

Five Visions Announced Amos 7-9

THE LOCUST PLAGUE (7:1-3)

THE GREAT FIRE (7:4-6)

THE PLUMB LINE (7:7-16)

THE BASKET OF SUMMER FRUIT (8:1-4)

THE LORD AT THE ALTAR (9:1-15)

HOSEA (755-715 B.C.)

INTRODUCTION:
1. Hosea's name means "salvation." He was a prophet to the northern kingdom, and wept over their sins, as Jeremiah later wept over Judah's sins.
2. Hosea is perhaps the strangest book in all the Bible, for God instructed his prophet to "take unto thee a wife of whoredoms."
  There were several reasons why God did this.
  a. The experimental reason. By marrying an unfaithful wife, Hosea could, as perhaps no other single prophet, understand somewhat the anguish in God's own heart over the northern kingdom, whose people were constantly committing spiritual fornication and adultery against Jehovah.
    God had often compared his relationship to Israel to that of a marriage. (See Isa. 62:5; Hos. 2:19; Jer. 3:14.)
  b. The illustrative reason. His own marriage would become a walking and visible example of his message to Israel.
  c. The prophetical reason. God would command him to name his children by those titles which would describe the future punishment and eventual restoration of all Israel.
3. He may have ministered longer than any other prophet.
4. Hosea predicted the Assyrian invasion, and later lived to see these prophecies fulfilled in 721 B.C.
5. In his book he refers to the northern kingdom as Ephraim constantly. Ephraim was the first of the twelve tribes of Israel to backslide.
6. Hosea is quoted more times for its size in the New Testament than any other Old Testament book, for a total of some thirty times. Compare:
  a. Hosea 11:1 with Matthew 2:15
  b. Hosea 6:6 with Matthew 9:13
  c. Hosea 10:8 with Luke 23:30
  d. Hosea 2:23 with Romans 9:25
  e. Hosea 13:14 with 1 Corinthians 15:55

I. A Grieving Husband and His Grievous Wife (Hosea vs. Gomer) (1-3).
  A. Hosea's wife, ill-famed. His wife Gomer was apparently a harlot before marriage and an adulteress after marriage. Hosea attempts in vain to save this marriage by:

1. Barring her from the markets of the world. "Therefore, behold I will hedge up thy way with thorns, and make a wall that she shall not find her paths" (2:6).

   Hosea thought he could force her to remain home in this manner. He even sought the help of his first son, Jezreel, asking him to reason with his mother concerning the folly of her ways.

   "Plead with your mother, contend; for she is not my wife, neither am I her husband. Let her, therefore, put away her harlotry out of her sight, and her adulteries from between her breasts" (2:2).

   But all this was to no avail. Gomer apparently continues to run off at the first opportunity.

2. Buying her out of the markets of the world. It was not long before Gomer had been used, abused, and abandoned by her lustful lovers, and found herself in a slave market.

   God ordered Hosea to find and redeem her from this market. "So I bought her for myself for fifteen pieces of silver, and for an homer of barley, and an half homer of barley" (3:2).

B. Hosea's children, ill-named. The prophet fathered three children through Gomer. Each child (at God's command) was given a name which carried with it prophetical meaning. The first child, a boy, named *Jezreel* (1:4), meaning "to be scattered," predicted two future events.

1. The setting aside of the dynasty of a northern king named Jehu. This brutal and bloody king had slain many in and around the city of Jezreel. Among his victims were:

   a. the northern king Jehoram and the Judean king Ahaziah on the same day (2 Ki. 9:14-28)

   b. Jezebel (2 Ki. 9:33)

   c. Ahab's seventy sons (2 Ki. 10:1-10)

   d. Ahab's distant relatives and political friends (2 Ki. 10:11, 17)

   e. the royal princes of Judah (2 Ki. 10:12-14)

   f. the priests of Baal (2 Ki. 10:18-28)

   While God did indeed order him to avenge Naboth, whose innocent blood Ahab had shed (1 Ki. 21), the brutal Jehu went too far in his bloodletting. Because of this, Jehu would be allowed only four generations upon Israel's throne (2 Ki. 10:30). These were:

   first generation, Jehoahaz, his son

   second generation, Jehoash, his grandson

   third generation, Jeroboam II, his great-grandson

   fourth generation, Zechariah, his great-great-grandson

   At the time of the birth of Hosea's son, Jehu's third generation was ruling, in the person of Jeroboam II. Thus, it would not be long until the dynasty would end. This, of course, happened in the days of Zechariah, who was murdered after a reign of but six months (2 Ki. 15:12).

2. The Assyrian invasion, at which time the entire northern kingdom would be scattered (1:5).

   The second child, a girl, named *Lo-ruha-mah* (1:6). This name literally meant, "no more mercy," indicating that God's judgment was just around the corner. Along with this baby, however, came the promise that God would spare Judah, the southern kingdom, of this coming Assyrian invasion. (See 1:7.) This, of course, happened as recorded in 2 Kings 19:35.

   The third child, a boy, named *Lo-ammi* (1:9). Here the name means "not my people."

II. A Grieving Husband and His Grievous Wife (God vs. Ephraim) (4:14).

   A. Ephraim denounced:

   1. Because of her ignorance:

      "My people are destroyed for lack of knowledge; because thou hast rejected knowledge, I will also reject thee, that thou shalt be no priest to me; seeing thou hast forgotten the law of thy God, I will also forget thy children" (4:6).

   2. Because of her idolatry:

      "My people ask counsel of their idols . . . they sacrifice upon the tops of the mountains, and burn incense upon the hills . . . Ephraim is joined to idols; let him alone" (4:12, 13, 17).

   3. Because of immorality:

      "I know Ephraim, and Israel is not hidden from me; for now, O Ephraim, thou committest whoredoms, and Israel is defiled" (5:3).

   B. Ephraim desired: In spite of her wickedness, God still loved her.

      "O Ephraim, what shall I do unto thee? O Judah, what shall I do unto thee? For your goodness is like a morning cloud, and like the early dew it goeth away" (6:4).

   C. Ephraim described:

   1. She was aflame with lust like a baker's hot oven (7:4). God said the hearts of the people smolder with evil plots during the night, and burst into flaming fire the next morning.

   2. They mingled with the heathen and had become as useless as a half-baked cake (7:8).

   3. They were as a silly dove, calling to Egypt, and flying to Assyria for help (7:11).

   4. They were as a crooked bow, always missing the target, which was God's glory (7:16).

   5. They lay among the nations as a broken pot (8:8).

   6. They were as a wandering and lonely wild ass (8:9).

   7. They were as a dried up root (9:16).

   8. They were as an empty vine (10:1).

   9. They were as a backsliding heifer (4:16).

   D. Ephraim disciplined: God declared,

      "For they have sown the wind, and they shall reap the whirlwind" (8:7). (See also 10:13.)

   1. God would therefore (for awhile) withhold his mercy from them (2:4).

   2. They would be many days without (3:4):

      a. A king: In 721 B.C. Hoshea, Israel's last king, was dethroned, and in 587 B.C.,

Zedekiah, Judah's final king, was deposed. Some six centuries later Israel's only true king was rejected (Jn. 19:15). Thus, this tragic situation will continue until he comes again (Rev. 19:11–16).

b. A prince: The next recorded prince in Israel's future will not minister until the millennium. (See Ezek. 44:3.)

c. A sacrifice: In A.D. 70 Titus destroyed the Temple and all animal sacrifices ceased. During the tribulation they will once again be instituted, only to be stopped by the antichrist (Dan. 9:27).

d. An image: This literally means, "the pillars," and may refer to the Temple. A temple will be rebuilt during the tribulation (Rev. 13), destroyed (Zech. 14:2), and again raised during the millennium (Ezek. 40:48).

e. An ephod: A reference to Israel's high priesthood. The ephod was a garment he wore. Her last high priest personally

planned the murder of the nation's own Messiah. (See Jn. 11:49–51; Mt. 26:57–68.)

f. Teraphim: These were normally figurines, or images in human form. (See Gen. 31:34.) It is not known what Hosea had in mind here.

3. They would go off as slaves into Assyria (10:6).

4. They would be (for awhile) swallowed up among the nations (8:8; 9:17).

E. Ephraim delivered. Someday this glorious event will indeed take place. Note the following passages:
1. Hosea 2:19, 23
2. Hosea 3:5
3. Hosea 6:1–3
4. Hosea 11:1, 4, 8, 9
5. Hosea 13:10, 14
6. Hosea 14:4–7

Hosea

A GRIEVING HUSBAND AND HIS GRIEVOUS WIFE

HOSEA AND GOMER   HOSEA 1-3

His Wife—Ill-Famed
Gomer was a harlot before marriage and an adulteress after marriage.
Hosea attempts to save his marriage by:
1. Barring Gomer from the markets of the world.
2. Buying her out of the markets of the world.
3. Asking his own son to reason with his mother.

His Children—Ill Named
NAME	MEANING
JEZREEL	"To be scattered" This predicted two things: 1. Scattering of Jehu's seed. 2. Scattering of the northern kingdom.
LO-RUHA-MAH	"No more mercy"
LO-AMMI	"Not my people"

Ephraim Denounced
1. Because of her ignorance (4:6)
2. Because of her idolatry (4:12, 13, 17)
3. Because of her immorality (5:3)

Ephraim Desired (6:4)
In spite of all this, God still loved her!

Ephraim Described
1. A backsliding heifer (4:16)
2. A baker's hot oven (7:4)
3. A half-baked cake (7:8)
4. A silly dove (7:11)
5. A crooked bow (7:16)
6. A broken pot (8:8)
7. A wandering and lonely wild animal (8:9)
8. A dried up root (9:16)
9. An empty vine (10:1)

Ephraim Disciplined (3:4)
To be many days without:
1. A king   3. A sacrifice   5. An ephod
2. A prince   4. An image   6. Teraphim

Ephraim Delivered
1. 2:19, 23   3. 6:1–3   5. 13:10, 14
2. 3:5   4. 11:1, 4, 8, 9   6. 14:4–7

MICAH (740–690 B.C.)

INTRODUCTION:

1. Micah lived on the Philistine border at a town called Moresheth, about twenty-five miles southwest of Jerusalem.

2. He was a contemporary with Isaiah. Micah was a country preacher, while Isaiah was a court preacher.

3. Micah was God's final prophet to the northern kingdom.

4. He was the only prophet sent to both the southern and northern kingdoms. He ministered especially to the capitals of these kingdoms, Jerusalem and Samaria.

5. He includes an amazing number of prophecies in his short book.
a. the fall of Samaria (1:6, 7)
b. the invasion of Judah by the Assyrians (1:9–16)
c. the eventual fall of Jerusalem and destruction of its Temple (3:12; 7:13)
d. the exile in Babylon (4:10)
e. the return from captivity and future restoration of Israel (4:1–8, 13; 7:11, 14)
f. the birth of Christ in Bethlehem (5:2)
g. the future reign of Christ (2:12, 13; 4:1, 7)

6. Micah is quoted on three occasions:
a. by the elders of Judah (Jer. 26:18, quoting Micah 3:12)
b. by the Magi coming to Jerusalem (Mt. 2:5, 6, quoting Micah 5:2)
c. by Jesus, when sending out the twelve (Mt. 10:35, 36, quoting Micah 7:6)

I. The Outward Look: Micah's public sermons (1–6).
A. Proclaiming the retribution upon Israel (1:3).
1. First sermon (1):
a. God himself would soon respond in judgment because of the sins found in Samaria and Jerusalem (1:1–5).
b. Samaria would be utterly destroyed (1:6). This, of course, happened during the Assyrian invasion. (See 2 Ki. 17:1–18.)
c. The enemy will come up to the very gates of Jerusalem (1:9). But God would spare his beloved city for yet another 115 years before allowing the Babylonians to destroy it. (See 2 Ki. 19:35.)

2. Second sermon (2):
   a. God condemns those who lie awake at night, plotting wickedness, and rise at dawn to perform it (2:1).
   b. He promises to reward their evil with evil (2:3).
   c. Israel rejects her true prophets, telling them God would never do such things (2:6).
   d. Their punishment will only end when the Messiah (the Breaker and King of 2:13) leads them out of exile through the gates of their cities of captivity, back to their own land.

3. Third sermon (3):
   a. Israel's leaders are especially rebuked by God. They were supposed to know right from wrong, but were themselves the vilest sinners of all (3:1–5).
   b. Their corrupt and crowd-pleasing messages would lead to the destruction of the people (3:6, 7).
   c. Micah alone of the prophets at that time was "full of power by the Spirit of the Lord, and of judgment, and of might, to declare unto Jacob his transgression, and to Israel his sin" (3:8).
   d. Because of those false prophets, Jerusalem would later be plowed as a field and become a heap of rubble. The very spot on Mt. Moriah where the Temple stood would be overgrown with brush (3:12).

B. Prophesying the restoration of Israel (4–5). In spite of her terrible sins, God would someday, after her punishment had been consummated, restore her to Palestine.
   1. The chronology leading to this restoration:
      a. Judah must first suffer the seventy-year Babylonian captivity (4:10). This was a remarkable passage indeed, for at the time Micah wrote, Babylon was anything but a world power. Assyria was the strong nation then.
      b. Judah's Messiah would be born in Bethlehem (5:2).
      c. God would set them aside awhile as a nation until their spiritual rebirth during the tribulation (5:3).
      d. The nations would gather together against Israel at Armageddon (4:11). (See also Rev. 16:13–16; 19:17.)
      e. These nations would be utterly destroyed (5:15).
   2. The final results of this restoration (Micah 4:1–6).

C. Pleading for the repentance of Israel (6). See Micah 6:3–8.

II. The Inward Look: Micah's personal contemplations (7:1–6).
   "Woe is me! For I am as when they have gathered the summer fruits, as the grape gleanings of the vintage; there is no cluster to eat; my soul desired the first ripe fruit" (7:1).

III. The Upward Look: Micah's prayerful petitions (7:7–20).
   A. His decision for God:

Micah

 ## His Public Messages   MICAH 1-6

Proclaiming retribution upon Israel (three sermons)
Chapters **1-3**
Prophesying restoration of Israel (1 prediction)
Chapters **4-5**
1. Chronology of restoration
   - Seventy-year captivity **(4-10)**
   - Bethlehem **(5:2)**
   - Divine rejection **(5:3)**
   - Armageddon **(4:11)**
   - Gentile destruction **(5:15)**
2. Results of restoration **(4:1-6)**
Pleading for repentance from Israel **(6:3-8)**

 ## His Personal Contemplations   7:1-6

"Woe is me! For I am as when they have gathered the summer fruits, as the grape gleanings of the vintage; there is no cluster to eat; my soul desired the first-ripe fruit" **(7:1)**.

His Prayerful Petition   7:7-20

His decision for God **(7:7, 9)**
His description of God **(7:18-20)**

"Therefore, I will look unto the Lord; I will wait for the God of my salvation; my God will hear me" (7:7).

"I will bear the indignation of the Lord, because I have sinned against him, until he plead my cause, and execute judgment for me; he will bring me forth to the light, and I shall behold his righteousness" (7:9).

B. His description of God (7:18–20):
   "Who is a God like unto thee, that pardoneth iniquity, and passeth by the transgression of the remnant of his heritage? he retaineth not his anger for ever, because he delighteth in mercy. He will turn again, he will have compassion upon us; he will subdue our iniquities; and thou wilt cast all their sins into the depths of the sea. Thou wilt perform the truth to Jacob, and the mercy to Abraham, which thou hast sworn unto our fathers from the days of old."

ISAIAH

INTRODUCTION:
1. The book of Isaiah may be compared to the Bible. The Bible has sixty-six books; Isaiah has sixty-six chapters. The Old Testament has thirty-nine books; the first section of Isaiah has thirty-nine chapters. The New Testament has twenty-seven books; the last section of Isaiah has twenty-seven chapters. The Old Testament covers the history and sin of Israel, as does Isaiah 1–39. The New Testament describes the person and ministry of Christ, as does Isaiah 40–66. The New Testament begins with the ministry of John the Baptist. The second section in Isaiah (chapter 40) begins by predicting this ministry. The New Testament ends by referring to

the new heavens and the new earth. Isaiah ends his book by describing the same things. (Compare Isa. 66:22 with Rev. 21:1–3.)

2. The book of Isaiah is generally regarded as one of the six greatest in the Bible. The others are: Romans, John, the Psalms, Genesis, and Revelation.

3. A copy of this book was among the famous Dead Sea scroll discovery in 1947 in cave one at Qumran. It was copied in the second century, B.C., and consisted of seventeen sheets which were twenty-four feet in length by ten inches high. This copy was amazingly similar to the standard masoretic text of the twelfth century, A.D.

4. Isaiah was the greatest of the Old Testament prophets, and one of the most eloquent writers who ever lived, at times even surpassing the literary abilities of a Shakespeare, a Milton, or a Homer.

5. He prophesied during the reigns of five kings of Judah (Uzziah, Jotham, Ahaz, Hezekiah, and Manasseh).

6. He is called the Messianic prophet. Only the Psalms have more material about Christ than Isaiah.

7. Jesus said Isaiah saw the glory of Christ, and "spoke of him" (Jn. 12:41).

8. Isaiah was married and had two sons.

9. It is believed that his father, Amoz, was the brother of King Amaziah of Judah. This then would make Isaiah of the royal seed.

10. Isaiah wrote other books which have not been preserved, such as:
    a. The life of Uzziah (2 Chron. 26:22).
    b. A book of the kings of Israel and Judah (2 Chron. 32:32).

11. Isaiah is quoted more times in the New Testament than any other Old Testament prophet. These passages quote his words in reference to:
    a. the ministry of John the Baptist (Mt. 3:3; Lk. 3:4; Jn. 1:23)
    b. the ministry of Christ to the Gentiles (Mt. 4:14, 15; 12:17, 18)
    c. the future rule of Christ over the Gentiles (Rom. 15:12)
    d. the healing ministry of Christ (Mt. 8:17)
    e. the blindness of Israel (Mt. 13:14; Acts 28:25–27)
    f. the hyprocrisy of Israel (Mt. 15:7)
    g. the disobedience of Israel (Rom. 10:16, 20)
    h. the saved remnant of Israel (Rom. 9:27, 29)
    i. the sufferings of Christ (Acts 8:28, 30)
    j. the anointing of Christ (Lk. 4:17)

The Book of Isaiah
   I. General Outline
   II. A Summary of Isaiah's Prophecies
   III. The Various Personalities Mentioned in Isaiah
   IV. The Greatness of God
   V. The Messiah
   VI. The Sins of Israel
   VII. The Gentile Nations
   VIII. The Tribulation
   IX. The Millennium

General Outline
   I. Israel, God's Faithless Servant (and her various enemies) (1–35).
      A. Her sins listed (1, 3, 5).
      B. Her future predicted (2, 4, 9, 11, 12, 25–35).
         C. Her great prophet's vision (6).
         D. Her wicked king's unbelief (7).
         E. Her enemies judged (13–23).
            1. Babylon (Isa. 13, 14, 21)
            2. Assyria (14:24–27)
            3. Philistia (14:28–32)
            4. Moab (15–16)
            5. Damascus (17)
            6. Ethiopia (18)
            7. Egypt (19–20)
            8. Edom (Idumea) (34:5–15)
            9. Arabia (21:13–17)
            10. Tyre (23)
            11. The entire world (24–25)
   II. Hezekiah, God's Frightened Servant (36–39).
      A. Hezekiah and the king of Assyria (36–37).
      B. Hezekiah and the King of heaven (38).
      C. Hezekiah and the king of Babylon (39).
   III. Christ, God's Faithful Servant (40–66).
      A. The deliverance—the comfort of Jehovah (40–48).
         1. God and the idols (40–46).
         2. God and the nations (47–48).
      B. The Deliverer—the salvation of Jehovah (49–57).
      C. The delivered—the glory of Jehovah (58–66).

A Summary of Isaiah's Prophecies
   I. Prophecies Fulfilled During His Own Lifetime.
      A. Judah would be saved from the threatened Syrian and Israelite invasion (7:4, 16).
      B. Syria and Israel later to be destroyed by Assyria (8:4; 17:1–14; 28:1–4).
      C. Assyria would invade Judah (8:7, 8).
      D. Jerusalem would be saved during this invasion (37:33–35).
      E. Moab would be judged by the Assyrians within three years (15–16).
      F. Egypt and Ethiopia would be conquered by the Assyrians (18–20).
      G. Arabia would be destroyed (21:13–17).
      H. Tyre to be destroyed (23:1–12).
      I. Hezekiah's life would be extended by fifteen years (38:5).
      J. Assyria to be judged by God (10:5–34; 14:24–27; 30:27–33; 37:36).
   II. Prophesies Fulfilled After His Lifetime.
      A. The Babylonian captivity (3:1–8; 5:26–30; 22:1–14; 39:5–7).
      B. Babylon to be overthrown by Cyrus (13:17–22; 14:1–23; 21:2; 46:11; 48:14).
      C. Babylon to suffer perpetual desolation (13:20–22; 47:1–15).
      D. The conquests of a Persian named Cyrus (41:2, 3; 44:28; 45:1–4).
      E. The return to Jerusalem decree of Cyrus (44:38; 45:13).
      F. The joy of the returning remnant (48:20; also compare with Ps. 126).
      G. The restoration of Tyre (23:13–18).
      H. The perpetual desolation of Edom (34:5–17).
      I. The birth, earthly life, sufferings, death, resurrection, ascension, and exaltation of Jesus Christ (7:14, 15; 9:1, 2, 6; 11:1, 2; 35:5, 6; 42:1–3; 50:4–6; 52:13–15; 53:2, 10–12, 15; 61:1, 2).
      J. The ministry of John the Baptist (Isa. 40:3–5).

III. Prophecies Yet to Be Fulfilled.
  A. The tribulation (Isa. 2:10-22; 13:6-13; 24:1-23; 26:20, 21; 34:1-10; 51:6).
  B. The battle of Armageddon (Isa. 34:1-10; 42:13, 14; 63:1-6; 66:15, 16).
  C. The millennium (Isa. 2:2-4; 4:2-6; 11:6-10, 12; 14:3, 7, 8; 19:18-25; 29:18; 30:19, 23-26; 32:18; 35:1-10; 40:4, 5; 42:13, 14, 16; 44:23; 49:10-13; 51:3, 11; 52:1, 6-10; 56:6-8; 59:20, 21; 60:1-3, 11-13, 19-22; 62:1-4; 63:1-6; 65:18-25; 66:10, 12, 15, 16, 23).

The Various Personalities

I. Isaiah.
  A. The greatest Old Testament prophet and author of this book (1:1).
  B. He viewed the glory of God as few other men have ever experienced (6:1-13). For other experiences, see the accounts of:
    1. Moses (Ex. 33:18-23)
    2. Ezekiel (Ezek. 1:1-28)
    3. Daniel (Dan. 7:9-14)
    4. Zechariah (Zech. 3:1-9)
    5. Stephen (Acts 7:55-60)
    6. Paul (2 Cor. 12:1-4)
    7. John (Rev. 4-22)
  C. He was ordered to offer wicked King Ahaz a sign concerning God's faithfulness (7:3).
  D. He fathered two children (*Shear-jash-ub*, 7:3; and *Ma-her-shalal-hash-baz*, 8:3), giving them names which depicted coming events in prophecy.
  E. He was ordered to walk barefooted and naked (perhaps from the waist up) for three years to symbolize the troubles God would bring upon the Egyptians and the Ethiopians (20:1-6).
II. Ahaz—the wicked father of Hezekiah who refused God's gracious sign of his faithfulness to Judah in their hour of need (7:1-25).
III. Lucifer—that powerful and perverted angel, who rebelled against God, became known as Satan and the devil (Isa. 14:12-14).
  "How art thou fallen from heaven, O Lucifer, son of the morning! How art thou cut down to the ground, which didst weaken the nations! For thou hast said in thine heart, I will ascend into heaven, I will exalt my throne above the stars of God: I will sit also upon the mount of the congregation, in the sides of the north: I will ascend above the heights of the clouds, I will be like the most high" (14:12-14).
  We note these five foolish and fatal "I wills" of the devil:
  A. "I will ascend into heaven"—obviously Satan had the third heaven in mind here, the very abode of God! (See 2 Cor. 12:1-4.)
  B. "I will exalt my throne above the stars of God"—this is probably a reference to angels. Satan desired the worship of angels!
  C. "I will sit also upon the mount of the congregation, in the sides of the north"—Lucifer now sought to enter God's "executive office" somewhere in the north and sit at God's very desk. He would attempt to control not only the angels, but the size and number of the starry galaxies.
  D. "I will ascend above the heights of the clouds"—this may well refer to that special Shekinah glory cloud of God found so frequently in the Bible.
  E. "I will be like the most high"—it is revealing to note the name for God that Satan uses here. He wanted to be like *El-Elyon,* the most High. This name literally means, "the strongest strong one." The devil could have picked other names for God. He could have used *El-Shaddai,* which means, "the breasted one, the one who feeds his children," but he didn't. He might have selected *Jehovah-Rohi,* which means, "the shepherd God," but he avoided this title also. The reason is obvious—Satan coveted God's strength, but was not the least bit interested in his feeding and leading attributes.
IV. Shebna (22:15-25).
  He was the indulgent and utterly self-centered palace administrator (perhaps during Hezekiah's early reign) who was rebuked and set aside by God.
V. Eliakim (36:3).
  He replaced the selfish Shebna and was Hezekiah's spokesman during the Assyrian crisis led by Sennacherib.
VI. Rabshakeh (36:2).
  The personal (and arrogant) loudmouthed Assyrian spokesman during the siege of Sennacherib.
VII. Sennacherib (37:21).
  The Assyrian Commander-in-chief whose efforts to destroy Jerusalem were totally blocked by God's death angel.
VIII. Hezekiah (36:1).
  The thirteenth king of Judah who was on the throne when God saved Jerusalem, and also extended the king's own life by fifteen years.
IX. Mero-dach-bal-adan (39:1).
  The King of Babylon who sent spies (disguised as good-will ambassadors) to congratulate Hezekiah after his recovery. Their real mission was to discover the amount and location of Jerusalem's wealth.
X. John the Baptist (40:3-5).
  Compare these verses with: Matthew 3:1-3; Mark 1:2, 3; Luke 3:2-6; John 1:23.
XI. Cyrus (44:28; 45:1).
  The Persian monarch whose name and ministry to the Jewish remnant (in allowing them to return and rebuild the Temple) Isaiah prophesied some two centuries before he was even born.

The Greatness of God

I. Isaiah 1:18:
  "Come now, and let us reason together, saith the Lord; though your sins be as scarlet, they shall be as white as snow; though they be red like crimson, they shall be as wool."
  Scarlet—a reference to the deep-dyed character of sin. (See Num. 19:2, 6, 9.)
  Snow—Psalm 51:7
  Reason together
  God appeals to man's intellect as well as his emotions. We are not to simply put our brains into neutral in our dealing with God. (See Isa. 43:26; Rom. 12:1; Mt. 22:37; 2 Pet. 3:1.)
II. Isaiah 12:2-5:
  "Behold, God is my salvation; I will trust, and not be afraid: for the Lord Jehovah is my strength and my song; he also is become my salvation. Therefore with joy shall ye draw water out of the wells of salvation. And in that day shall ye say, Praise

the Lord, call upon his name, declare his doings among the people, make mention that his name is exalted. Sing unto the Lord; for he hath done excellent things; this is known in all the earth."

These blessed waters had formerly been rejected. (See 8:6. See also Jn. 4:10, 14.)

III. Isaiah 25:1, 4, 8, 9:

"O Lord, thou art my God; I will exalt thee, I will praise thy name; for thou hast done wonderful things; thy counsels of old are faithfulness and truth. For thou hast been a strength to the poor, a strength to the needy in his distress, a refuge from the storm, a shadow from the heat, when the blast of the terrible ones is as a storm against the wall. He will swallow up death in victory; and the Lord God will wipe away tears from off all faces; and the rebuke of his people shall he take away from off all the earth: for the Lord hath spoken it. And it shall be said in that day, Lo, this is our God; we have waited for him, and he will save us: this is the Lord; we have waited for him, we will be glad and rejoice in his salvation."

Swallow up death. (See 1 Cor. 15:54; Hos. 13:14; Rev. 20:14.)

Wipe away tears. (See Rev. 7:17; 21:4.)

IV. Isaiah 40:1-31:

A. Concerning verses 1, 2.
  1. God orders the prophet to speak tenderly to and comfort the hearts of his people. The message of comfort is threefold.
    a. Their term of forced service is complete.
    b. Their guilt is pardoned.
    c. They had received ample punishment for their sins.

B. Concerning verses 3-5.
  1. This voice had its partial fulfillment at his first coming through the mouth of John the Baptist (Mt. 3:3), but will only see its ultimate consummation at his Second Coming. (See Isa. 35:2.) Note the main features of this proclamation:
    a. A straight highway in the desert was to be made for the King.
    b. Every valley was to be filled in.
    c. Every mountain and hill should be leveled off.
  2. When all this was accomplished (spiritually, in the hearts of Israelites), then the glory of the Lord would be revealed to all flesh.

C. Concerning verses 6-8.
  A heavenly voice orders an earthly voice to cry out concerning the greatness of God and the insignificance of man, saying:
  1. The beauty and duration of man is as a flower and grass, which would soon fade and wither away (Jas. 1:10; 1 Pet. 1:24, 25).
  2. The Word of our God by contrast would stand forever.

D. Concerning verses 9-11.
  The voice now orders Zion's messengers upon a high mountain where they are to boldly proclaim the following:
  1. Behold the coming of your mighty God!
  2. He comes as a King to rule over you and to reward you.
  3. He comes as a Shepherd to tenderly feed you and lead you.

E. Concerning verses 12-31.
  This coming King-Shepherd had all power.
  1. As seen in his dealing with nature (vs. 12-14).
    a. He holds the oceans in his hands.
    b. He measures off the heavens.
    c. He knows the weight of the earth and mountains.
    d. He needs no advice from angels, demons, or men. (See Rom. 11:34; 1 Cor. 2:16.)
  2. As seen in his dealing with the nations (vs. 15-17).
    a. All peoples are as a drop in the bucket and dust on the scales.
    b. He picks up the islands as if they had no weight at all.
    c. All of Lebanon's forests do not contain sufficient fuel to consume a sacrifice large enough to honor him, nor all its animals enough to offer God.
  3. As seen in his dealing with vain idols (vs. 18-20).
    a. God cannot be even remotely depicted by a wooden or golden idol.
    b. Man can create a false idol, but only God can create man. (See also 41:6, 7, 21-24, 29; 44:9-20; 46:1, 5-7.)
  4. As seen in his dealing with the mighty of this earth (vs. 21-24).
    a. Man's willful ignorance of God's greatness is inexcusable. (See Rom. 1:18-23; 2 Pet. 3:5.)
    b. God sits enthroned above the circle of the earth and views its inhabitants as grasshoppers. (Compare Num. 13:33.)
    c. He spreads out the heavens like a veil.
    d. He brings the great men of the world to naught (1 Cor. 1:26-29).
    e. They are scarcely planted until he removes them. (See Ps. 103:15, 16.)
  5. As seen in his dealings with the stars (vs. 25, 26).
    a. He originally created all the stars.
    b. He knows their number.
    c. He has named each one. (See Ps. 147:4.)
  6. As seen in his dealing with the elect (vs. 27-31).
    a. In light of all this, God's children are not to question his dealing with them. (See also Isa. 54:7, 8.)
    b. The eternal God has unending strength and unfathomable insight.
    c. He therefore gives power to the faint who wait upon him.
    d. This allows them to walk, run, and fly as eagles.

V. Isaiah 41:8-10.

"But thou, Israel, art my servant, Jacob whom I have chosen, the seed of Abraham my friend. Thou whom I have taken from the ends of the earth, and called thee from the chief men thereof, and said unto thee, Thou art my servant; I have chosen thee, and not cast thee away. Fear thou not; for I am with thee: be not dismayed; for I am thy God: I will strengthen thee; yea, I will help thee, yea, I will uphold thee with the right hand of my righteousness."

"Israel . . . my servant." Scofield notes the following:

Three servants of the Lord mentioned in Isaiah: (1) David (Isa. 37:35); (2) Israel the nation (Isa. 41:8-16; 43:1-10; 44:1-8; 21; 45:4; 48:20); and (3) Messiah (42:1-12; 49:5-7; 50:4-6; 52:13-15; 53:1-12).

VI. Isaiah 42:8-12:

"The former things are come to pass"—a possible reference to the fall of Babylon (Isa. 13:17-22; 21:1-10) and destruction of Assyria (10:5-34; 14:24-27; 30:27-33; 31:8)

"New things do I declare"—the sufferings, death, resurrection, and ascension of Jehovah's Servant, Jesus Christ! (See 52:13-15; 53:1-12.)

"Let the inhabitants of the rock sing"—a possible reference to the hiding remnant in Petra during the tribulation. (See Zech. 14:5; Dan. 11:41.)

VII. Isaiah 43:2, 5, 6, 11, 25:

"When thou passest through the waters, I will be with thee; and through the rivers, they shall not overflow thee; when thou walkest through the fire, thou shalt not be burned; neither shall the flame kindle upon thee. Fear not: for I am with thee: I will bring thy seed from the east, and gather thee from the west; I will say to the north, Give up; and to the south, Keep not back: bring my sons from far, and my daughters from the ends of the earth; I, even I, am the Lord; and beside me there is no Saviour. I, even I, am he that blotteth out thy transgressions for mine own sake, and will not remember thy sins."

"through the waters" (Ex. 14:19-31).

"through the fire" (Ps. 66:12; Dan. 3:25-27).

"from the east . . . west . . . north . . . south." (See Mt. 24:31.)

"beside me there is no Saviour" (Acts 4:12).

"who blotteth out thy transgressions" (Isa. 44:22; Acts 3:19).

"and will not remember thy sins" (Ps. 103:10-12; Isa. 38:17; 44:22; Micah 7:19; Heb. 8:12).

VIII. Isaiah 44:3:

"For I will pour water upon him that is thirsty, and floods upon the dry ground: I will pour my spirit upon thy seed, and my blessing upon thine offspring."

(See Joel 2:28-32; Acts 2:16, 17.)

IX. Isaiah 45:5-12, 18-23:

"I girded thee" (v. 5). This passage describes the work of Cyrus, who would allow the Jews in Babylon to return. God reminds all here that he allowed Cyrus to capture Babylon.

"I . . . create evil" (v. 7). God is of course not the author of sin! (See Hab. 1:13; 2 Tim. 2:13; Titus 1:2; Jas. 1:13; 1 Jn. 1:5.) One of the meanings of the Hebrew word ra carries the idea of adversity or calamity, which is obviously the intended meaning here.

"Woe to him that striveth with his maker" (v. 9). (See Isa. 10:15; 29:16; Rom. 9:19-21.) Sinful Israel is here pictured as questioning God's dealing with her, accusing him of being all thumbs! (Note the expression, "He hath no hands.") This of course was sheer insanity, for God points out later that those same hands made the earth and created man (see v. 12).

"I have not spoken in secret" (v. 19). God never dealt in esoteric knowledge which was available only for a select few. (See Jn. 18:19, 20.)

"Look unto me, and be saved, all the ends of the earth" (v. 22). This was the verse that led the great Charles H. Spurgeon to Christ according to his testimony.

"Every knee shall bow." (See Rom. 14:11; Phil. 2:10.)

X. Isaiah 46:9, 10:

"Remember the former things of old: for I am God, and there is none else; I am God, and there is none like me. Declaring the end from the beginning, and from ancient times the things that are not yet done, saying, My counsel shall stand, and I will do all my pleasure."

"Remember the former things of old" (v. 9). Perhaps God had in mind those things such as the Passover salvation, the Red Sea deliverance, the sweetened waters of Marah, the heavenly manna, etc.

"Declaring the end from the beginning" (v. 10). Bible prophecy is simply history written in advance!

XI. Isaiah 49:13-16:

"Sing, O heavens; and be joyful, O earth; and break forth into singing, O mountains: for the Lord hath comforted his people, and will have mercy upon his afflicted. But Zion said, The Lord hath forsaken me, and my Lord hath forgotten me. Can a woman forget her sucking child, that she should not have compassion on the son of her womb? yea, they may forget, yet will I not forget thee. Behold, I have graven thee upon the palms of my hands; thy walls are continually before me."

XII. Isaiah 55:1-3:

This chapter may rightly be entitled, "The Incredible Invitation."

A. The Host of the invitation (v. 1):
God himself! Here the Father is depicted as standing behind a booth in an eastern market place, seeking the attention of those who pass by.

B. The guests of the invitation (v. 1):
Who are those invited? All the thirsty and penniless.

C. The menu of the invitation (vs. 1, 2).
These items constitute the original soul food of man.
1. Water and wine—a reference to the Spirit of God. (See Jn. 7:37-39; Eph. 5:18; 1 Thess. 1:6.)
2. Milk—a reference to the Word of God. (See 1 Pet. 2:2.)
3. Bread—a reference to the Son of God. (See Jn. 6:35.)

D. The terms of the invitation (vs. 6, 7):
1. Seek the Lord.
2. Call upon him.
3. Let the wicked forsake his way.
4. Let him return unto the Lord.

E. The time limit of the invitation (vs. 6, 7):
1. While he may be found.
2. While he is near.

F. The necessity of the invitation (vs. 8, 9):
"For my thoughts are not your thoughts, neither are your ways my ways, saith the Lord.

For as the heavens are higher than the earth, so are my ways higher than your ways, and my thoughts than your thoughts."

G. An example of the invitation (vs. 9, 10). Rain! "For as the heavens are higher than the earth, so are my ways higher than your ways, and my thoughts than your thoughts. For as the rain cometh down, and the snow from heaven, and returneth not thither, but watereth the earth, and maketh it bring forth and bud, that it may give seed to the sower, and bread to the eater."

H. The promise of the invitation.
1. To Israel:
    a. the blessings of the Davidic Covenant (v. 4)
    b. the acceptance of all nations (v. 5)
    c. the fullness of joy and peace (v. 12)
2. To nature:
    the removal of the curse (vs. 12, 13)
3. To all:
    a. sublime soul satisfaction (v. 2)
    b. mercy and abundant pardon (v. 7)

XIII. Isaiah 57:15, 19–21:
"For thus saith the high and lofty One that inhabiteth eternity, whose name is Holy; I dwell in the high and holy place, with him also that is of a contrite and humble spirit to revive the spirit of the humble, and to revive the heart of the contrite ones. I create the fruit of the lips; Peace, peace to him that is far off, and to him that is near, saith the Lord; and I will heal him. But the wicked are like the troubled sea, when it cannot rest, whose waters cast up mire and dirt. There is no peace, saith my God, to the wicked."
"A contrite and humble spirit" (v. 15). (See Ps. 34:18; 51:17; Isa. 66:2; 2 Cor. 7:10; 1 Pet. 5:6.)
"Peace to him . . . far off" (v. 19). (See Heb. 13:15; Acts 2:39; Eph. 2:17.)
"There is no peace . . . to the wicked" (v. 21). (See Isa. 48:22.)

XIV. Isaiah 61:10:
"I will greatly rejoice in the Lord, my soul shall be joyful in my God; for he hath clothed me with the garments of salvation, he hath covered me with the robe of righteousness, as a bridegroom decketh himself with ornaments, and as a bride adorneth herself with her jewels."
"robe of righteousness" (see Isa. 64:6; Gen. 3:21; Mt. 22:2–13; Rev. 19:8; Jer. 33:11; Rev. 21:2.)

XV. Isaiah 63:7–9:
"I will mention the loving kindnesses of the Lord, and the praises of the Lord, according to all that the Lord hath bestowed on us, and the great goodness toward the house of Israel, which he hath bestowed on them according to his mercies, and according to the multitude of his loving kindnesses. For he said, Surely they are my people, children that will not lie: so he was their Saviour. In all their affliction he was afflicted, and the angel of his presence saved them: in his love and in his pity he redeemed them; and he bare them, and carried them all the days of old."
"he was afflicted." (See Jdg. 10:16.)
"the angel of his presence." (See Gen. 16:9; 22:11; 48:16; Ex. 3:2; 14:19; Num. 22:22; Jdg. 2:4; 6:11; 13:3; 2 Ki. 19:35; Zech. 1:12; 12:8.)

The Messiah

I. His Incarnation:
A. Isaiah 7:14, 15:
"Therefore the Lord himself shall give you a sign; Behold, a virgin shall conceive, and bear a son, and shall call his name Immanuel. Butter and honey shall he eat, that he may know to refuse the evil, and choose the good."
It should be noted that three children are mentioned in connection with Isaiah's visit to King Ahaz and the wicked ruler's refusal to ask God for a sign. Two of these children were yet unborn. The three are:
1. Immanuel, meaning, "God with us." There are six major implications within 7:14:
    a. This sign was to be given by God. (Note the phrase, "the Lord himself.")
    b. It was given to the entire house of David and not to Ahaz (the word "you" here is plural).
    c. It involved a miraculous sign (God had just invited Ahaz to ask of him any fantastic miracle he desired, whether "in the depth or in the height above." (See v. 11.)
    d. It concerned a virgin birth. The Hebrew word almah was a common term for an unmarried and sexually undefiled girl. (See Gen. 24:43; Ex. 2:8; Ps. 68:25; Song of Solomon 1:3; Prov. 30:19.) Were the promised babe not to have been virgin born, this could scarcely have been considered a mighty sign. (See Mt. 1:22, 23 for the fullfillment of this where the Greek word parthenos is used, a term depicting absolute virginity.
    e. This mighty miracle sign would result in the very incarnation of God himself into human flesh, for the baby's name was to be Immanuel, meaning "God with us."
    f. This divine baby would also be completely human, eating what other children ate, and growing to maturity like other children. (Compare Isa. 7:16 with Lk. 2:52.)
2. Shear-jashub, meaning, "a remnant shall return" (7:3). This tiny child was Isaiah's son who accompanied him to Ahaz's palace. Isaiah told the unbelieving king that before this young boy reached the age to know right from wrong, both of Ahaz's enemies, Pekah and Rezin, would be destroyed. This was literally fulfilled by the Assyrian monarch Tiglath Pileser, who slew the Damascus King Rezin in 732 B.C. (2 Ki. 16:9), and by Hoshea, who murdered Pekah shortly after this (2 Ki. 15:30).
3. Maher-shalal-hash-baz, meaning "hasten to the booty, hurry to the prey" (8:1–4). This child, also the son of Isaiah, was called by this name to indicate the Assyrian captivity of the northern Israelite kingdom.
B. Isaiah 9:6:
"For unto us a child is born, Unto us a son is given, and the government shall be upon his shoulder; and his name shall be called Won-

derful, Counsellor, The mighty God, the ever-lasting Father, The Prince of Peace."

1. Both his humanity and deity are seen here.
   a. The phrase, "A child is born" refers to his humanity (Lk. 2:7; Heb. 2:14; 1 Jn. 4:9).
   b. The phrase, "a son is given" refers to his deity (Jn. 3:16).
2. Five great names are ascribed to this child-son of Mary and God.
   a. "Wonderful"—this is a noun in the Hebrew, and therefore a real name. (See Jdg. 13:18 where it is translated "secret.")
   b. "Counsellor." This child-son would never need an advisory board, for, "Who hath known the mind of the Lord? or who hath been his counsellor?" (Rom. 11:34). (See also Jn. 2:24, 25.)
   c. "The mighty God"—here is *El-Gibbohr*, "God's strong Hero"!
   d. "The everlasting Father"—literally, Avi-ad, "The Father of eternity." (See Jn. 1:3; Col. 1:16; Heb. 1:2.)
   e. "The Prince of Peace"—this is *Sar-Sha-lohim,* as described in Isaiah 57:15-19.
3. From the very dawn of history this wicked world has desperately sought to employ the services of someone (or something) who could heal the hurt of the human soul and usher in the long dream of universal righteousness. Many persons have applied for this position, and numerous methods have been employed, but all have led to bitter disappointment and despair. But here the prophet Isaiah introduces a special candidate. What are his qualifications? Can he satisfy the five key questions?
   a. What about his personality and character? Answer—it is *wonderful.*
   b. What about his education? Answer—he knows all things and is therefore the supreme *Counselor.*
   c. What about his nationality? Answer—he is the *mighty God,* and the only Son of the living God.
   d. What about his previous work experience? Answer—he both planned for and carried out the creation of this universe and is therefore the *Father of eternity.*
   e. What is his special talent? Answer—as the God-man, he is able to reconcile man with God, and is therefore the *Prince of Peace.*

   In view of all this, Isaiah (along with Peter, Paul, John, and a host of others) earnestly exhorts all sinners to hire this heavenly Candidate immediately. (See Isa. 1:18.)

II. His Lowliness and Youth in Nazareth:
   A. Isaiah 11:1, 2:
   "And there shall come forth a rod out of the stem of Jesse, and a Branch shall grow out of his roots; and the Spirit of the Lord shall rest upon him, the Spirit of Wisdom and Understanding, the Spirit of Counsel and Might, the Spirit of Knowledge and of the Fear of the Lord."

1. This passage describes what is left of a once mighty tree after it has been cut down—a stump. That mighty tree, the kingdoms of David and Solomon, would be cut to the ground by the Assyrian and Babylonian axemen.
2. But this stump stands in obvious contrast to the vast number of dead stumps that covered the ground after God had hewn down the huge Assyrian forest described by Isaiah in chapter 10 (as he will eventually do to all ungodly nations). But there is an important difference in that this stump is not dead! First, a rod (or sprig) will spring from that supposed dead stump, and then that rod will branch out into fruit. (See Rev. 5:5.)
3. The Hebrew word for branch is *netser,* and was probably what Matthew referred to when he stated that Christ, "Came and dwelt in a city called Nazareth: that it might be fulfilled which was spoken by the prophets, He shall be called a Nazarene" (Mt. 2:23).
4. The Holy Spirit of God was to rest upon this Babe of Bethlehem and citizen of Nazareth, thus giving to him:
   a. The spirit of wisdom—that ability to discern the nature of things.
   b. The spirit of understanding—the ability to discern their differences.
   c. The spirit of counsel—the ability to adopt right conclusions.
   d. The spirit of power—the ability to carry them out.
   e. The spirit of knowledge—the ability to personally know the very essence of the Father himself. This characteristic can be considered the *root* of his ministry, and the first four its *fruit.*
   f. The spirit of the fear of the Lord—because of this knowledge, the ability to always refrain from displeasing him. (See Jn. 8:29.)

   Thus these seven (counting the Holy Spirit and his gifts) correspond to the seven-lighted lampstand, with its main shaft and the three pairs of branches from its side (Ex. 25:31, 32; Rev. 1:4; 4:5; 5:6).

   B. Isaiah 53:2:
   "For he shall grow up before him like a tender plant, and like a root out of a dry ground; he hath no form nor comeliness, and when we shall see him, there is no beauty that we should desire him."

   (This verse is only quoted here. It will be dealt with under the aspect of his suffering in connection with Isaiah 53.)

   C. Isaiah 7:15:
   "Butter and honey shall he eat, that he may know to refuse the evil, and choose the good."

   This refers to the relative poverty of the Savior's family. Thickened milk and honey were the food of desert wanderers. They were, of course, not the only articles of food, but provided the staples.

III. His Relationship to the Father:

A. Beloved by the Father

"Behold my servant, whom I uphold; mine elect in whom my soul delighteth; I have put my Spirit upon him; he shall bring forth justice to the nations" (Isa. 42:1).

This was quoted in Matthew 12:18 and demonstrated in Matthew 3:17 and 17:5.

B. Obedience to the Father

"The Lord God hath given me the tongue of the learned, that I should know how to speak a word in season to him who is weary; he awakeneth morning by morning; he waketh mine ear to hear like the learned. The Lord God hath opened mine ear, and I was not rebellious, neither turned backward" (Isa. 50:4, 5).

(See Jn. 7:16; 8:28, 38; 12:49; 14:10. 24; Phil. 2:8; Heb. 10:5.)

IV. His Specific Ministry to the Gentiles:

"Nevertheless, the dimness shall not be such as was in her vexation, when at the first he lightly afflicted the land of Zebulun and the land of Naphtali, and afterward did more grievously afflict her by the way of the sea, beyond Jordan, in Galilee of the nations. The people that walked in darkness have seen a great light; they that dwell in the land of the shadow of death, upon them hath the light shined" (Isa. 9:1, 2).

Here Isaiah points out that the very region where Assyrian armies brought darkness and death would be the first to rejoice in the light brought by the preaching of Christ. Matthew refers to the fulfillment of this prophecy. (See Mt. 4:12–16.)

V. His Gracious Ministry to All:

"He shall not cry, nor lift up, nor cause his voice to be heard in the street. A bruised reed shall he not break, and the smoking flax shall he not quench; he shall bring forth justice in truth" (Isa. 42:2, 3).

Here we are told three things God's righteous servant would not do during the course of his ministry:

A. He would not scream out in the streets. Unlike other worldly and noisy warriors, this gentle conqueror would not allow his voice to be shouted out in the streets. Our Lord would bear absolutely no similarity to wild-eyed, shrieking rebels.

B. He would not break the bruised reed. This he demonstrated when he freely forgave and restored an immoral woman whose sin had twisted and torn her soul. (See Jn. 8:1–11.)

C. He would not quench the smoking flax. This he demonstrated by releasing an army of evil spirits which had all but snuffed out the light of sanity and hope from the maniac of Gadara. (See Mk. 5:1–20.)

The fulfillment of this prophecy is recorded in Matthew 12:14–21 and amplified in 11:28–30.

VI. His Miracles:

"Then the eyes of the blind shall be opened, and the ears of the deaf shall be unstopped. Then shall the lame man leap as an hart, and the tongue of the dumb sing . . ." (Isa. 35:5, 6).

Although this passage will have its ultimate fulfillment in the millennium, it does nevertheless refer in part to the first earthly ministry of Christ.

A. The eyes of the blind were opened. (See Mt. 9:29; Mk. 8:25; Jn. 9:7; Mt. 12:22; Mt. 20:34.)

B. The ears of the deaf were unstopped. (See Mt. 11:5; Mk. 7:34.)

C. The crooked limbs of the lame were straightened. (See Mt. 9:2; Mk. 12:13; Jn. 5:8.)

VII. His Message:

"The Spirit of the Lord God is upon me, because the Lord hath anointed me to preach good tidings unto the meek; he hath sent me to bind up the brokenhearted, to proclaim liberty to the captives, and the opening of the prison to those who are bound; to proclaim the acceptable year of the Lord, and the day of vengeance of our God; to comfort all that mourn" (Isa. 61:1, 2).

Scofield has the following helpful note at this point:

"Observe that the Lord Jesus suspended the reading of this passage in the synagogue at Nazareth (Lk. 4:16–21) with the words 'Year of the Lord.' The first advent, therefore, opened the day of grace, 'the acceptable year of the Lord,' but does not fulfill the day of vengeance that will be accomplished when Messiah returns."

(See 2 Thess. 1:7–10 and compare with Isa. 34:8; 35:4.)

VIII. His Sufferings and Death:

In three key passages Isaiah describes in accurate and awesome detail the crucifixion of Christ some 700 years before it took place.

A. Isaiah 50:6:

"I gave my back to the smiters, and my cheeks to them that plucked off the hair; I hid not my face from shame and spitting."

This was, of course, literally fulfilled:

1. the smiters—see Matthew 27:26, 30; John 18:22

2. the spitters—see Matthew 26:67; 27:30; Mark 14:65; 15:19

B. Isaiah 52:14:

"As many were astounded at thee—his visage was so marred more than any man, and his form more than the sons of men."

Scofield notes:

"The literal rendering presents a shocking picture: so marred from the form of man was his aspect that his appearance was not that of a son of man, i.e., not human. This was the effect of the brutalities described in Matthew 26:67, 68; 27:27–30."

If this passage be taken at face value it means that Christ suffered more on the cross than any other human being ever suffered anywhere, anytime.

C. Isaiah 53:1–10a:

1. Concerning verses 1–3.

a. These opening statements may be the voices of the believing Israelite remnant of all ages as they discuss his death. The first verse is literally, "Who believed what we heard?"

Leupold writes:

"So to speak, here we seem to hear two disciples standing on a street-corner in Jerusalem reviewing the things that happened on Good Friday in the light of the better insight that came after Pentecost. They express especially their amazement at the complete misunderstanding they were guilty of in regard to the remarkable figure that appeared as the great Sufferer in their midst . . . they still marvel as they reflect on this blindness." (*Exposition on Isaiah*, p. 225)

An example of this can be seen through the testimony of the two Emmaus disciples as they comment on their former unbelief. See Luke 24:13-32.

b. The question, "And to whom is the arm of the Lord revealed?" should be compared with Psalm 8:3. In this passage David says it took only the fingers of God to create us, but Isaiah states it took his arms to redeem us.

c. Verses 2 and 3 tell the life story of the Savior from the cradle to the cross.

   (1) He was despised (counted as nothing) because of his lowly background (v. 2). See also John 1:46.

   (2) He was rejected because of his message (v. 3). See also Luke 4:16-30.

   (3) He was a man of sorrows and acquainted with grief because of his earthly mission (v. 3). See also Luke 19:10.

d. His humble beginning seemed so unimportant. Who really noticed him as a stripling lad in Nazareth? He could be likened to an insignificant "shoot," a bit of vegetation that is scarcely noticed.

e. What about the personal appearance of Christ? There is no biblical description of our Lord, for there was no need of this. He came as the suffering Servant of Jehovah and the only qualification of a servant is that he be able to do the job. This is why Mark's Gospel account (which pictures Christ as the ox-servant of God) has no genealogy. We may conclude that our Lord was humble, healthy, wholesome, but not handsome. He probably did not exude charisma, nor display a flashy and striking life style. The late-night talk show hosts never would have considered booking him for an interview.

2. Concerning verses 4-6.

a. *The Scofield Bible* notes the following about verse 4:

> "Because Matthew quotes this passage and applies it to physical disease (8:17) it has been conjectured by some that disease as well as sin was included in the atoning death of Christ. But Matthew asserts that the Lord fulfilled the first part of Isaiah 53:4 during the healing ministry of his service on earth. Matthew 8:17 makes no reference to Christ's atoning death for sin" (p. 759).

b. The last part of verse 4 informs us that the nation Israel in general looked upon the cross as a righteous sentence imposed by God himself upon a blasphemer named Jesus Christ! (See Mt. 27:38-44.) Thus Israel here looked upon Jesus as Job's wife and friends looked upon Job, as a man suffering for his sins. (See Job 2:9; 4:7; 8:3.)

c. Verse 5 tells us he was wounded (translated *tormented* by *Lang's Commentary*) and bruised (*crushed*) for our iniquities. These two words "wounded" and "bruised" are the strongest terms to describe a violent and agonizing death.

d. Verse 6 is the "all" verse, as it begins and ends with this word. "*All* we like sheep have gone astray . . . the Lord hath laid on him the iniquity of us *all.*" Thus Christ took our hell that we might partake of his heaven. The blessed Son of God became the Son of Man that sons of men might become sons of God.

3. Concerning verses 7-9.

a. Some might ask how we can know that Isaiah is really referring to Christ in chapter 53, since the Savior is not mentioned by name. But his identity is clearly brought out in two New Testament passages which link him directly to Isaiah 53.

   (1) The testimony of John the Apostle—John 12:37, 38. (Here Isa. 53:1 is quoted.)

   (2) The testimony of Philip—Acts 8:32, 33. (Here Isa. 53:7, 8 is quoted.)

b. We are told that although he was oppressed (treated unsparingly), yet he opened not his mouth. Not once during his seven unfair trials before Annas, Caiaphas, the Sanhedrin, Pilate, Herod, Pilate again, and the Roman soldiers did our Lord attempt to justify himself, or demand a mistrial. (See v. 7.) John the Baptist was doubtless thinking of the phrase "as a lamb to the slaughter" when he first introduced Jesus as "the Lamb of God" (Jn. 1:29).

c. Verse 8 might be rendered: "By oppression and an unjust sentence he was taken away; and as to his fate, who gave it any thought?"

d. Verse 9 tells us the religious officials planned to dump him into a potter's field along with the two thieves. Of course, God stepped in and he was placed in a new tomb owned by a rich man (see Mt. 27:57). Scofield notes the following concerning verse 9:

> "In the Hebrew the word rendered 'death' is an intensive plural. It has been suggested that it speaks of the violence of Christ's death, the very pain of which made it like a repeated death" (p. 759).

4. Concerning verse 10a.

Who really killed Christ? Many of course played a part in his death. This would include Judas, Caiaphas, Annas, the wicked Jewish religious leaders, Pilate, Herod, the

Roman soldiers, the devil, and the sins of all sinners! But who actually masterminded the original plan? Here we are told it was God himself! See the following: Acts 2:23; 1 Peter 1:18-20; Revelation 13:8.

IX. His Resurrection, Ascension, and Exaltation:

A. Isaiah 52:13:

"Behold, my servant shall deal prudently; he shall be exalted and extolled, and be very high."

The word "prudent" here means to prosper, to be successful (see Josh. 1:7, 8; Jer. 23:5, where the same Hebrew word occurs) and what a success story we have here in this verse.

Note the predicted threefold accomplishments of God's Servant:

1. He would be exalted (literally, to be high). This is a reference to his resurrection. (See Mt. 28:1-10.)
2. He would be extolled (meaning, to be lifted up). This is a reference to his ascension. (See Acts 1:9, 10.)
3. He would be very high (or, greatly exalted). This is a reference to his exaltation. (See Phil. 2:5-11.)

All this is even more significant because of what follows in Isaiah 53, for here we see the Servant of the Lord resurrected, ascended, and exalted even before he was crucified! Who but God himself could possess that kind of glorious confidence?

B. Isaiah 53:10b-12; 52:15:

"When thou shalt make his soul an offering for sin, he shall see his seed, he shall prolong his days, and the pleasure of the Lord shall prosper in his hand. He shall see of the travail of his soul, and shall be satisfied; by his knowledge shall my righteous servant justify many; for he shall bear their iniquities. Therefore will I divide him a portion with the great, and he shall divide the spoil with the strong, because he hath poured out his soul unto death; and he was numbered with the transgressors; and he bore the sin of many, and made intercession for the transgressors" (53:10b-12).

"So shall he sprinkle many nations; the kings shall shut their mouths at him; for that which had not been told them shall they see, and that which they had not heard shall they consider" (52:15).

These final verses give us a grand summary of both the sufferings and the ultimate satisfaction of Jehovah's servant. Doubtless Peter had this in mind when he wrote:

"Of which salvation the prophets have inquired and searched diligently, who prophesied of the grace that should come unto you: Searching what, or what manner of time the spirit of Christ which was in them did signify, when it testified beforehand the sufferings of Christ, and the glory that should follow" (1 Pet. 1:10, 11).

1. The sufferings of God's Servant.
   a. He poured out his soul unto death as a trespass offering unto God. (See Jn. 10:11, 15, 18.)
   b. He was counted as a common criminal.
   c. In spite of this, he bore the sins of the world and prayed for his tormentors. (See Heb. 2:9; Lk. 23:34.)
2. The satisfaction of God's Servant.
   a. He shall see the spiritual children he died to save. (Compare Heb. 12:1, 2 with Jude 1:24.)
   b. He would fulfill the will and pleasure of his Father.
   c. He will receive from his Father the spoils of victory. (See Rev. 11:15.)
   d. He will be the supreme source of blessing to many nations. (See Rev. 21:22-26.)

CHRIST in ISAIAH

1. His Incarnation **7:14, 15; 9:6**

2. His Youth in Nazareth **11:1, 2; 53:2; 7:15**

3. His Relationship with the Father **42:1; 50:4, 5**

4. His Miracles **35:5, 6**

5. His Message **61:1, 2**

6. His Specific Ministry to the Gentiles **9:1, 2**

7. His Gracious Ministry to All **42:2, 3**

8. His Suffering and Death **50:6; 52:14; 53:1-10**

9. His Resurrection, Ascension, and Exaltation **52:13; 53:10-12**

10. His Millennial Reign **9:7; 42:4-7; 59:16-21; 11:3-5; 49:1-12; 32:1; 33:22**

e. He will enjoy this satisfaction throughout all eternity. (See Rev. 1:8; 1 Pet. 1:1, 2; Heb. 10:22.)

X. His Millennial Reign:
A. Isaiah 9:7:
"Of the increase of his government and peace there shall be no end, upon the throne of David, and upon his kingdom, to order it, and to establish it with judgment and with justice from henceforth even for ever. The zeal of the Lord of hosts will perform this."
B. Isaiah 42:4-7
C. Isaiah 59:16-21:
1. These verses describe God's search for a man, and his choice of Christ as the only acceptable Redeemer. Isaiah here depicts a sight later described by the Apostle John in Revelation 5:1-14.
2. Paul informs us that the armor pieces worn by this Warrior-Redeemer are now available to all his redeemed warriors. (See Eph. 6:13-17.)
D. Isaiah 11:3-5:
"And shall make him of quick understanding in the fear of the Lord: and he shall not judge after the sight of his eyes, neither reprove after the hearing of his ears: But with righteousness shall he judge the poor, and reprove with equity for the meek of the earth: and he shall smite the earth with the rod of his mouth, and with the breath of his lips shall he slay the wicked. And righteousness shall be the girdle of his loins, and faithfulness the girdle of his reins."
E. Isaiah 49:1-12
F. Isaiah 32:1:
"Behold, a king shall reign in righteousness, and princes shall rule in judgment."
G. Isaiah 33:22:
"For the Lord is our judge, the Lord is our lawgiver, the Lord is our king; he will save us."

The Sins of Israel

I. Her Stupidity.
A. She did not even have the common sense of a brute animal (1:3).
B. God had to tell them everything over and over again (line upon line; here a little, there a little) and still they could not understand (28:9-13).
II. Her Hypocrisy.
A. God was sick of their sacrifices which were offered without any sorrow for sins (1:11-14).
B. Because of this, he would refuse to see their outstretched hands or hear their pious words during prayer time (1:15).
C. Israel's worship services amounted to mere words learned by rote memory (29:13).
III. Her Women (3:16-26).
A. Before God judged them (3:16-23):
1. They were haughty with their noses in the air.
2. They had wanton eyes.
3. They wore ornaments about their feet and chains around their ankles.
4. They had necklaces and bracelets.

5. They had veils of shimmering gauze.
6. They wore head bands.
7. They wore nose jewels and earrings.
8. They sported party clothes, negligees, and capes.
9. They wore ornate combs and carried purses. How far removed all this was from Peter's description of real beauty and adornment. (See 1 Pet. 3:1-4.)
B. After God judged them (3:24-26):
1. Instead of sweet fragrance, there would be rottenness.
2. Instead of a girdle (sash), a rope.
3. Instead of well-set hair, baldness.
4. Instead of beauty, shame, disgrace, and widowhood.
IV. Her Fruitlessness (5:1-7). The parable of the Lord's vineyard.
This parable employs one of the two figures taken from the botanical world to represent the nation Israel. The other figure is a fig tree. (See Mt. 21:33-46.)
A. What God did for his vineyard (5:1, 2).
1. He planted it on a very fertile hill with the choicest vine.
2. He plowed it and took out all the rocks.
3. He built a watchtower and cut a winepress in the rocks.
4. He waited patiently for the harvest.
B. What God received from his vineyard—nothing but wild and sour grapes (5:2).
C. What God would do to his vineyard (5:3-7).
1. He would tear down the fences and let the vineyard go to pasture, to be trampled by cattle and sheep.
2. He would not prune nor hoe it, but let it be overgrown with briars and thorns.
3. He would even command the clouds not to rain on it anymore.
V. Her Six-Count Indictment (5:8-22).
A. She denied others their own property rights.
B. She had become a nation of drunkards. (See also 28:1-8.)
C. She had mocked God and dared him to punish her.
D. She had called right wrong, and wrong right. Her black was white, her white was black, her bitter was sweet, and her sweet was bitter! Here is a classic example of today's "new morality" practiced by Israel some seven centuries B.C.
E. She was wise and shrewd in her own eyes.
F. She took bribes which resulted in freeing the guilty and imprisoning the innocent.
VI. Her False Leaders.
A. 9:15, 16:
"The ancient and honourable, he is the head; and the prophet that teacheth lies, he is the tail. For the leaders of this people cause them to err; and they that are led of them are destroyed."
B. 28:14, 15:
"Wherefore hear the word of the Lord, ye scornful men, that rule this people which is in Jerusalem. Because ye have said, We have a covenant with death, and with hell are we at agreement; when the overflowing scourge shall pass through, it shall not come unto us:

for we have made lies our refuge, and under falsehood have we hid ourselves."

VII. Her Dependence upon Egypt (Isa. 30:1-7; 31:1-3).
31:1, 3:
"Woe to them that go down to Egypt for help; and stay on horses, and trust in chariots, because they are many; and in horsemen because they are very strong; but they look not unto the Holy One of Israel, neither seek the Lord! Now the Egyptians are men, and not God; and their horses flesh, and not spirit. When the Lord shall stretch out his hand, both he that helpeth shall fall, and he that is holpen shall fall down, and they all shall fail together."

VIII. Her Tragic Overall Condition.
A. 1:5, 6:
"Why should ye be stricken any more? Ye will revolt more and more: the whole head is sick, and the whole heart faint. From the sole of the foot even unto the head there is no soundness in it; but wounds, and bruises, and putrifying sores: they have not been closed, neither bound up, neither mollified with ointment."

B. 59:1-8

C. 64:6:
"But we are all as an unclean thing, and all our righteousnesses are as filthy rags; and we all do fade as a leaf; and our iniquities, like the wind, have taken us away."

D. 65:2, 3:
"I have spread out my hands all the day unto a rebellious people, which walketh in a way that was not good, after their own thoughts; A people that provoketh me to anger continually to my face; that sacrificeth in gardens, and burneth incense upon altars of brick."

The Gentile Nations

I. Babylon (Isa. 13-14, 21).
The *New Scofield Bible* notes the following:
"This prophecy concerning Babylon announces the doom of the nation and city at the hands of the Medes (13:17-22), but applies the word Babylon to the totality of Gentile world power beginning with Nebuchadnezzar (Dan. 2:31, 32, 37, 38) and culminating in the fourth world empire (Dan. 2:34, 35, 40-45) at the return of Jesus Christ to the earth as the Smiting Stone. This is the time of the Gentiles. See Luke 21:24."

A. Babylon was to be destroyed by the Medes (13:17-22).

B. Their armies would be chased back to their own land as a wild dog would pursue a frightened deer (13:14).

C. Their soldiers would be butchered, their children murdered, and their wives raped (13:15, 16).

D. The prophet Isaiah is horrified and becomes physically ill at God's description of Babylon's punishment (21:3-5).
The last passage was no doubt fulfilled to a T when Darius took Babylon. (See Dan. 5.) This all reads as if it were an eyewitness account of the destruction as recorded by Daniel. Yet Isaiah wrote about this some 200 years before it actually transpired. (See also Jer. 51:8, 9.)

Isaiah also vividly describes the watchman as he brings word to the king that the city had fallen. (See 21:6-10. Also see Jer. 51:31-33.)

E. Babylon was to become a desolate land of porcupines and swamps (14:23); the wild animals would make it their home, and demons would come there to dance (13:21).

F. Babylon was never to be rebuilt on that site. Here it should be pointed out that some believe the ultimate fulfillment of these verses must await the tribulation period, when ancient Babylon will be rebuilt on the Euphrates. (See Rev. 18.) This is advocated because some of the prophecies concerning Babylon's destruction were not all fulfilled when the city fell to the Medes. (See also Jer. 25:17-26; 51:26.)

G. The rulers of two Gentile nations are used by God as a basis of describing the person and ministry of Satan. One is Tyre (Ezek. 28:1-19) and the other is Babylon (Isa. 14:12-16).
For other examples of this addressing Satan through another, see the following:
1. Genesis 3:15, where Satan is addressed through the serpent.
2. Matthew 16:22, 23 where Satan is addressed through Simon Peter.

II. Assyria (14:24-27).
A. God had determined to crush the Assyrian army on the mountains of Israel (14:25).
B. This would be done to remove the awful Assyrian yoke from his people.

III. Philistia (14:28-32).
A. Philistia was warned not to rejoice over the death of King Ahaz of Judah, who had smote them while alive (14:29).
B. His son (Hezekiah) would be even more demanding (14:29).
C. Finally, Philistia was to suffer total doom under the cruel attack of Sargon, the Assyrian king.

IV. Moab (15-16).
A. Moab was the nation which came from Lot through the incestuous relationship with his eldest daughter. The illegitimate son of this sordid affair was the father of the Moabites. Their people became the persistent enemies of the nation Israel. Balak, their king, hired Balaam, the prophet, to curse them. But Ruth also came from this land! (See Num. 22:2-4; Ruth 1:4.)
B. Moab was to be punished by God, with its chief cities destroyed in one night (15:1).
C. The whole land would be filled with weeping from one end to another (15:8).
D. Lions would hunt down the survivors (15:9).
E. Moab's refugees were invited by God to avail themselves of his mercies. They were enjoined to pay tribute to Israel according to their past arrangement (2 Ki. 3:4-9; Isa. 16:1).
F. However, pride kept Moab from doing this (16:6).
G. Isaiah wept because of God's judgment upon this stubborn pride (16:11).
H. Judgment was officially set to fall within three years. The Assyrians at that time invaded Moab (16:14).

V. Damascus (17).
A. Damascus was the capital of Syria and is the oldest living city in the world today. Ephraim (an-

other title for the Israelite northern kingdom) and Damascus had allied together against Judah, thus linking that kingdom with the divine judgment. Partners in crime meant partners in punishment (17:3).

B. Both allies were later besieged by Tiglath-Pileser (2 Ki. 15:29) and were finally deported by Shalmaneser (2 Ki. 17:6).

VI. Ethiopia (18).

A. This "land shadowing with wings" is thought to be African Ethiopia (18:1). Missionaries to that land tell us that it is known as the land of birds and is called "the Land of Wings."

B. This nation marches against Israel (historically or prophetically?) but is cut off by God himself. Their army will be left dead on the field for the birds and animals to eat (18:4-6).

C. After this (the tribulation?) Ethiopia will bring gifts to the Lord of Hosts in Jerusalem (18:7).

VII. Egypt (19-20).

A. No nation is so prominent in the Bible as Egypt. It is first mentioned when Abraham visited there (Gen. 12). Later Joseph lived and died there (Gen. 39-50). There Israel became a nation.

B. Egypt was to be severely punished because of her idolatry (19:1). Her people were originally monotheistic but gradually lapsed into the basest idolatry. They worshiped the bull, the frog, the

fish, and various birds. The contest in Exodus was a battle of the gods versus Jehovah. (See Ex. 7-12. Note Isaiah's prophecies in chapters 19-20.)

1. Egypt was to be given over to a cruel ruler (19:4) who may have been the Ottoman Turk who reduced Egypt to a poverty-stricken nation.

2. Egyptian would fight against Egyptian (19:2). A pharaoh arose about the time of Isaiah who could not control this great kingdom and the army no longer obeyed him.

3. The channels along the Nile River would be filled and fouled with rotting reeds. This is true even today.

4. The paper reeds by the brooks would wither away (19:7), a reference to the papyri which was used in that day as paper. This was one of the main industries of Egypt and afforded a great volume of wealth. It disappeared, though, and no longer grows along the banks where Moses was once hidden.

5. Egypt's fishing industry was to disappear (19:8, 10).

6. Her linen industry was also to disappear (19:9). The linen of Egypt was world-renowned. The linen taken from mummies is superior to any linen that is made by the mills of Ireland. The fine twined byssus linen

PROPHECIES CONCERNING GENTILE NATIONS IN ISAIAH

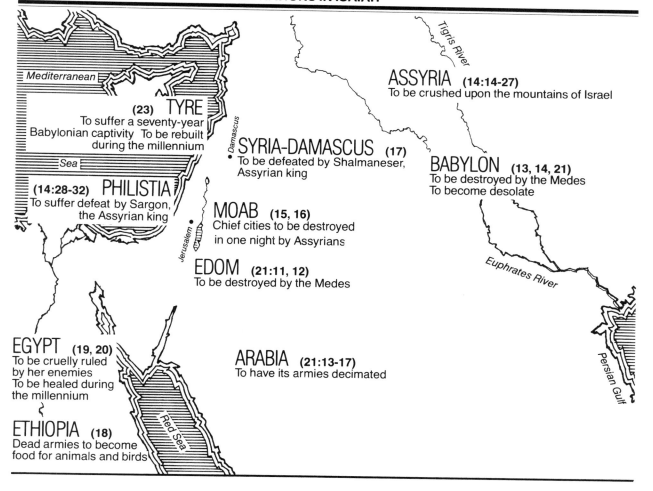

ASSYRIA (14:14-27)
To be crushed upon the mountains of Israel

(23) TYRE
To suffer a seventy-year Babylonian captivity To be rebuilt during the millennium

SYRIA-DAMASCUS (17)
To be defeated by Shalmaneser, Assyrian king

BABYLON (13, 14, 21)
To be destroyed by the Medes
To become desolate

(14:28-32) PHILISTIA
To suffer defeat by Sargon, the Assyrian king

MOAB (15, 16)
Chief cities to be destroyed in one night by Assyrians

EDOM (21:11, 12)
To be destroyed by the Medes

EGYPT (19, 20)
To be cruelly ruled by her enemies
To be healed during the millennium

ARABIA (21:13-17)
To have its armies decimated

ETHIOPIA (18)
Dead armies to become food for animals and birds

was used in the construction of the tabernacle. All this, however, has gone.

7. Egypt was to stagger along in world history as a "drunken man staggereth in his vomit" (19:14).
8. Judah would be a terror to Egypt (19:17).
9. Egypt was to be invaded within three years by Assyria (20:1–6).

C. But all this would someday gloriously change.
1. God would smite Egypt in the tribulation, but would then graciously heal her (19:22).
2. Egypt and Iraq will be connected by a highway, thus allowing both nations to freely travel to Jerusalem to worship God (19:23–25).

VIII. Edom (21:11, 12). This passage includes a question and an answer:
A. The question: "Watchman, what of the night?"
B. The answer: "The morning cometh, and also the night."
Both morning and night are coming. What will be glory for some (the Medes, who would overrun Edom), would be shame for others (the Edomites). The New Testament likewise presents Christ's glorious coming as night for some (the unsaved, see Jn. 9:4) and morning for others (the saved, see Rom. 13:11, 12).

IX. Arabia (21:13–17).
A. Arabia was the land of the Ishmaelites, the Bedouin tribes of the desert, the modern Arabs.
B. They would be so severely judged that only a few of their stalwart archers would survive (21:17).

X. Tyre (23).
This is the tenth and last burden against the nations. J. Vernon McGee suggests that each of these great nations represents or symbolizes some principle, philosophy, or system which God must judge.
Thus:
Babylon—false religion, idolatry
Assyria—utter ruthlessness
Philistia—extreme pride
Moab—a formal religion
Damascus—compromise
Ethiopia—an industrial-military complex
Egypt—the world
Edom—the flesh
Arabia—war
Tyre—big business

Tyre and Sidon were the two great cities of the Phoenicians. Their ships entered all ports of the Mediterranean Sea; they even penetrated the uncharted ocean beyond the pillars of Hercules. Their vessels brought tin from Great Britain. They settled the North African city of Carthage.
A. Tyre was to be destroyed by the Babylonians and carried into captivity for seventy years (23:15).
B. This was to be done because of its pride and utter materialism (23:8). (For several remarkable similarities in the history of Judah and the life of Nebuchadnezzar, see Jer. 25:11; 29:10; Dan. 9:24; 4:28–37.)
C. Nebuchadnezzar would lay siege to the coastland city, raze its palaces, and make it a heap of ruins (23:13).
D. Egypt, its ally, would sorrow over its swift destruction, along with its own sailors, who would not even be able to return home to port (23:5–7). For another remarkable similarity, see the sorrow of this world over the destruction of Babylon during the tribulation (Rev. 18).
E. After seventy years Tyre would be rebuilt (as was Jerusalem), but would soon degenerate into the same gross materialism and pride of former days (23:17).
Note: At this point the student should carefully examine Ezekiel 26 where the historical account is completed. Alexander the Great utterly destroys both the coastal and the island cities of Tyre in 332 B.C.
F. In the millennium, Tyre will be rebuilt and be blessed by God (23:18). (See also Ps. 45:12.)

The Tribulation

I. The Main Passages:
A. Isaiah 2:10–22
B. 13:6–13
C. 24:1–23
D. 26:20, 21
E. 34:1–10
F. 42:13, 14
G. 51:6
H. 63:1–6
I. 66:15, 16

II. The Main Action:
A. The earth.
1. Shall be terribly shaken (2:21).

THE TRIBULATION IN ISAIAH

EARTH

MAIN PASSAGES

2:10-22	13:6-13	24:1-23

MAIN ACTION

To be shaken
To be moved out of its place
To be made waste and turned upside down
To be burned with fire
To be broken and dissolved
To reel to and fro like a drunkard
To be unable to cover its dead

HEAVENS

MAIN PASSAGES

26:20, 21	34:1-10	42:13, 14

MAIN ACTION

Stars, sun, and moon to be darkened
Hosts of heaven to be dissolved and rolled up like a scroll
Stars to fall as figs from a tree when shaken

SINFUL MANKIND

MAIN PASSAGES

51:6	63:1-6	66:15, 16

MAIN ACTION

To hide in caves and holes of the earth
To faint with fear and hearts to melt
To suffer the pain of childbirth
To experience no joy whatsoever
To cover the mountains with their dead
To overpower the valleys with their stench
To be trampled by God like overripe grapes

2. To be moved out of its place (13:13).
3. To be made waste and turned upside down (24:1).
4. To be burned with fire (24:6).
5. To be broken down and dissolved (24:19).
6. To reel to and fro like a drunkard (24:20).
7. To be unable to cover its dead (26:21).

B. The heavens.
  1. The stars, sun, and moon to be darkened (13:10).
  2. The hosts of heaven to be dissolved and rolled up as a scroll (34:4; 51:6).
  3. The stars shall fall as figs from a tree when shaken (34:4).

C. Sinful mankind.
  1. To hide in the caves and holes of the earth (2:19).
  2. Will faint with fear and their hearts will melt (13:7; 24:17).
  3. To suffer the agonies of childbirth (13:8).
  4. To experience no joy whatsoever (24:8-10).
  5. To cover the mountains with their blood and to overpower the valleys with the stench of their dead (34:3).
  6. To be utterly trampled by a wrathful God like overripe grapes (63:3).

The Millennium.

I. The Salvation of Gentile Nations:
  A. Isaiah 2:2-4:
    "And it shall come to pass in the last days, that the mountain of the Lord's house shall be established in the top of the mountains, and shall be exalted above the hills; and all nations shall flow into it. And many people shall go and say, Come ye, and let us go up to the mountain of the Lord, to the house of the God of Jacob; and he will teach us of his ways, and we will walk in his paths: for out of Zion shall go forth the law, and the word of the Lord from Jerusalem. And he shall judge among the nations, and shall rebuke many people: and they shall beat their swords into plowshares, and their spears into pruninghooks: nation shall not lift up sword against nation, neither shall they learn war any more."
    Isaiah 2:4 is inscribed upon the foundation of the U.N. building in New York City. This glorious truth will, of course, be literally realized during the millennium. But until that day, the fearful words of Joel 3:9, 10, the exact reverse of this passage, will hold true.
  B. 11:10:
    "And in that day there shall be a root of Jesse, which shall stand for an ensign of the people; to it shall the Gentiles seek: and his rest shall be glorious."
  C. 19:18-25:
    Israel suffered perhaps more under the various brutal reigns of Assyria and Egypt than any other two nations. But during the millennium God will supernaturally unite these three into a beautiful trio of fellowship.
    1. The Egyptians will speak the Hebrew language.
    2. They will build an altar and monument to the Lord.
    3. God will answer their prayers and heal them.
    4. Both Egypt and Assyria (Iraq) will be connected by a highway.
    5. Both shall worship Jehovah and receive his rich blessings.
  D. 52:10:
    "The Lord hath made bare his holy arm in the eyes of all the nations; and all the ends of the earth shall see the salvation of our God."
  E. 56:6-8
  F. 66:23:
    "And it shall come to pass, that from one new moon to another, and from one sabbath to another, shall all flesh come to worship before me, saith the Lord."
  These glorious verses are condensed by John in Revelation 21:23-27.

II. The Salvation of Israel and Jerusalem:
  A. 4:2-6
    1. They will be washed and rinsed of all their moral filth.
    2. They will once again be blessed by the fiery and cloudy pillar.
  B. 11:12:
    "And he shall set up an ensign for the nations, and shall assemble the outcasts of Israel, and gather together the dispersed of Judah from the four corners of the earth."
  C. 14:3:
    "And it shall come to pass in the day that the Lord shall give thee rest from thy sorrow, and from thy fear, and from the hard bondage wherein thou wast made to serve."
  D. 30:19:
    "For the people shall dwell in Zion at Jerusalem: thou shalt weep no more: he will be very gracious unto thee at the voice of thy cry; when he shall hear it, he will answer thee."
  E. 32:18:
    "And my people shall dwell in a peaceable habitation, and in sure dwellings, and in quiet resting places."
  F. 44:23:
    "Sing, O ye heavens; for the Lord hath done it: shout, ye lower parts of the earth: break forth into singing, ye mountains, O forest, and every tree therein: for the Lord hath redeemed Jacob, and glorified himself in Israel."
  G. 49:10-13
  H. 51:3, 11:
    "For the Lord shall comfort Zion: he will comfort all her waste places; and he will make her wilderness like Eden, and her desert like the garden of the Lord; joy and gladness shall be found therein, thanksgiving, and the voice of melody. Therefore the redeemed of the Lord shall return, and come with singing unto Zion; and everlasting joy shall be upon their head: they shall obtain gladness and joy; and sorrow and mourning shall flee away."
  I. 52:1, 6-9
  J. 59:20, 21:
    "And the Redeemer shall come to Zion, and unto them that turn from transgression in Jacob, saith the Lord. As for me, this is my covenant with thee, saith the Lord; my spirit that

is upon thee, and my words which I have put in thy mouth, shall not depart out of thy mouth, nor out of the mouth of thy seed, nor out of the mouth of thy seed's seed, saith the Lord, from henceforth and for ever."

   K. 60:1–3, 11, 12, 13, 19–22
   L. 62:1–4
   M. 65:18–24
   N. 66:10, 12:

"Rejoice ye with Jerusalem, and be glad with her, all ye that love her: rejoice for joy with her, all ye that mourn for her: For thus saith the Lord, Behold, I will extend peace to her like a river, and the glory of the Gentiles like a flowing stream: then shall ye suck, ye shall be borne upon her sides, and be dandled upon her knees."

These glorious verses are condensed by Paul in Romans 11:1, 26, 27.

III. The Salvation of the Afflicted:
   A. 29:18:

"And in that day shall the deaf hear the words of the book, and the eyes of the blind shall see out of obscurity, and out of darkness."

   B. 35:3–6
   C. 42:16:

"And I will bring the blind by a way that they knew not; I will lead them in paths that they have not known: I will make darkness light before them, and crooked things straight. These things will I do unto them, and not forsake them."

These glorious verses are condensed by John in Revelation 22:1–5.

IV. The Salvation of All Nature
   A. 11:6–9
   B. 14:7, 8:

"The whole earth is at rest, and is quiet: they break forth into singing. Yea, the fir trees rejoice at thee, and the cedars of Lebanon, saying, Since thou art laid down, no feller is come up against us."

   C. 30:23–26
   D. 35:1, 2, 7–10:

"The wilderness and the solitary place shall be glad for them; and the desert shall rejoice, and blossom as the rose. It shall blossom abundantly, and rejoice even with joy and singing: the glory of Lebanon shall be given unto it, the excellency of Carmel and Sharon, they shall see the glory of the Lord, and the excellency of our God. And the parched ground shall become a pool, and thirsty land springs of water: in the habitation of dragons, where each lay, shall be grass with reeds and rushes. And an highway shall be there, and a way, and it shall be called The way of holiness; the unclean shall not pass over it; but it shall be for those: the wayfaring men, though fools, shall not err therein. No lion shall be there, nor any ravenous beast shall go up thereon, it shall not be found there; but the redeemed shall walk there: And the ransomed of the Lord shall return, and come to Zion with songs and everlasting joy upon their heads: they shall obtain joy and gladness, and sorrow and sighing shall flee away."

THE MILLENNIUM IN ISAIAH

Fourfold Salvation

Of Gentile Nations
2:2-4; 11:10; 19:18-25; 52:10; 56:6-8

Of Israel and Jerusalem
4:2-6; 11:12; 14:3; 30:19; 32:18; 44:23; 49:10-13; 51:3, 11; 52:1, 6-9; 59:20, 21; 60:1-3, 11-13, 19-22; 62:1-4; 65:18-24; 66:10, 12

Of the Afflicted   **29:18; 35:3-6; 42:16**

Of All Nature
11:6-9; 14:7, 8; 30:23-26; 35:1, 2, 7-10; 40:4, 5; 65:25

   E. 40:4, 5:

"Every valley shall be exalted, and every mountain and hill shall be made low: and the crooked shall be made straight, and the rough places plain: And the glory of the Lord shall be revealed, and all flesh shall see it together: for the mouth of the Lord hath spoken it."

   F. 65:25:

"The wolf and the lamb shall feed together, and the lion shall eat straw like the bullock; and dust shall be the serpent's meat. They shall not hurt nor destroy in all my holy mountain, saith the Lord."

These glorious verses are condensed by Paul in Romans 8:18–25.

NAHUM (630–612 B.C.)

INTRODUCTION:

1. The name Nahum means "the comforter."
2. The New Testament Galilean headquarters of Jesus was a city named Capernaum, which literally means, "the village of Nahum." Many thus believe Capernaum was named after this prophet.
3. The book has only one theme, the terrible and total coming destruction of Nineveh. At the time of this prophecy, Nineveh appeared to be impregnable, with its walls 100 feet high and broad enough for chariots to drive upon them. It had a circumference of some sixty miles and was adorned by more than 1200 towers.

4. Nineveh fell in 612 (some eighteen years after this prophecy), being completely destroyed by the Medes from the north and the Babylonians from the south.

5. Nahum not only predicted the fall of Nineveh, but the very manner in which it would fall. (Note 1:8: "an overrunning flood he will make an utter end of the place.")

   History tells us that Nabopolassar, King of the Babylonian invasion forces, besieged the city for three years, leading three massive attacks against it, and failing each time. Because of this, the Assyrians inside Nineveh rejoiced and began holding drunken parties. But suddenly the Tigris River overflowed its banks and sent its wildly churning waters against the walls of the city. Soon it had washed a hole, into which rushed Babylonians, and the proud city was destroyed.

6. The destruction of Nineveh was so great that Alexander the Great marched his troops over the same desolate ground which had once given support to her mighty buildings and did not even know there had once been a city there! The city itself was not excavated until as recently as A.D. 1845.

7. God had once used Jonah (150 years before) to ward off his judgment. But now because of the city's relapse into gross sin, he calls upon Nahum to pronounce judgment.

I. The Patience of God (1:1-8).
   "The Lord is slow to anger, and great in power . . ." (see Gen. 15:16; Ps. 103:8.)
   For over 500 years Nineveh and the Assyrians were feared as the terror of Western Asia. But while God's patience is infinite in depth, it is not eternal in duration. The time for judgment would soon come.

II. The Pride of Sennacherib (1:9-14).
   "There is one come out of thee, that imagineth evil against the Lord, a wicked counselor" (1:11).
   It is generally agreed that the wicked counselor here is Sennacherib, the evil Assyrian king who invaded Judah and surrounded Jerusalem in 701 B.C. Although Sennacherib's armies had been smashed at Jerusalem's gates and the monarch himself murdered years before (see 2 Ki. 19:35-37), the arrogant ruler seemed to symbolize the pride of Nineveh, and is therefore used here.
   Sennacherib had made Nineveh a truly magnificent city, laying out its streets and squares, and built within a famous "palace without a rival." The dimensions of this palace were fantastic, 600 × 630 feet! It comprised at least eighty rooms, many of which were lined with sculpture.

III. The Promise of Judah (1:15).
   "Behold upon the mountains the feet of him that bringeth good tidings, that publisheth peace! O Judah, keep thy solemn feasts, perform thy vows: for the wicked shall no more pass through thee; he is utterly cut off."
   Judah would need no longer fear this cruel nation.

IV. The Punishment of Nineveh (2-3).
   A. The certainty of this terrible punishment (3:11-19).
      Nahum compared Nineveh to Thebes (No-Amon, see 3:8), that great capital of upper Egypt. It too boasted that no power on earth could subdue it. However, both Jeremiah (46:25) and Ezekiel (30:14-16) predicted its destruction, which

Nahum

THE DESTRUCTION OF NINEVEH

Source of the Destruction—
GOD HIMSELF

Reason for the Destruction—
SIN

Cruelty   Wickedness   Evil

Tool used in the Destruction—
BABYLON

1. The Patience of God (1:8)
   God had once stayed his hand of judgment upon Nineveh through Jonah's ministry. But now his patience was exhausted.

2. The Pride of the Assyrian King (1:9-14)

3. The Promise to Judah (1:15)
   Judah need no longer fear this cruel nation.

4. The Punishment of Nineveh (2-3)
   The certainty of it (3:11-19)
   The description of it (2:3-9)

was fulfilled later by Sargon of Assyria in his campaign against Egypt. Now Nineveh's hour had come.
   B. The description of this terrible punishment.
      "Shields flash red in the sunlight! The attack begins! See their scarlet uniforms! See their glittering chariots moving forward side by side, pulled by prancing steeds! Your own chariots race recklessly along the streets and through the squares, darting like lightning, gleaming like torches. The king shouts for his officers; they stumble in their haste, rushing to the walls to set up their defenses. But too late! The river gates are open! The enemy has entered! The palace is in panic! The queen of Nineveh is brought out naked to the streets, and led away, a slave, with all her maidens weeping after her; listen to them mourn like doves, and beat their breasts! Nineveh is like a leaking water tank! Her soldiers slip away, deserting her; she cannot hold them back. 'Stop, stop,' she shouts, but they keep on running. Loot the silver! Loot the gold! There seems to be no end of treasures. Her vast, uncounted wealth is stripped away. Soon the city is an empty shambles; hearts melt in horror; knees quake; her people stand aghast, pale-faced and trembling" (Nahum 2:3-10, *The Living Bible*).

ZEPHANIAH (625-610 B.C.)

INTRODUCTION:
1. The name Zephaniah means, "the Lord hides or protects."
2. He was the great-great-grandson of King Hezekiah and, therefore, of royal blood.

3. He ministered during the days of King Josiah, Judah's last godly ruler. The prophet was kin to Josiah.
4. His ministry may well have helped prepare for the great revival of 621 B.C., which occurred under Josiah's reign when the law of Moses was rediscovered during the repair of the Temple. (See 2 Chron. 34-35.)

I. A Bad Day—The prophet pronounces judgment (1:1—3:8).
   A. Upon the land of God:
      1. The fact of this judgment: God would sweep away everything in the land and destroy it to the ground. This would include man, birds and even fish (1:2-4).
      2. The reason for this judgment: Judah had worshiped Baal (the great god of the Canaanite pantheon), and Milcom (chief Ammonite deity), thus ignoring the only true God (1:5, 6).
      3. The name of this judgment: the prophet calls it "the day of the Lord." This term is used no less than seven times. See 1:7, 8, 14, 18; 2:2, 3.
      4. The results of this judgment (1:14-18).
      Note: Zephaniah evidently had in mind not only the historical Babylonian invasion of 605-586 B.C., but also the yet future Great Tribulation. (See Rev. 6:12-17.)
   B. Upon the enemies of God:
      1. The Philistine cities of Gaza, Ashkelon, Ashdod, and Ekron would be rooted out and left in desolation (2:4-6).
      2. Moab and Ammon would be destroyed as Sodom and Gomorrah, for mocking Judah and invading her land (2:8-11). (See Gen. 19.)
      3. Ethiopia would be slain by God's avenging sword (2:12).
      4. Assyria and its capital Nineveh were to be made utterly desolate (2:13-15).
   C. Upon the city of God:
      1. A cry of alarm would begin at the fish gate in Jerusalem. It would be heard from gate to gate until it reached the highest part of the city (1:10).
      2. God planned to search with lanterns in Jerusalem's darkest corners to find and destroy all sinners (1:12, 13).
      3. The city's leaders were like roaring lions and ravenous wolves, devouring any and all victims (3:1-7).
II. A Glad Day—the prophet announces justice (3:8-20).
   A. Upon the (once) enemies of God (3:9, 10):
      "For then will I turn to the people a pure language, that they may call upon the name of the Lord, to serve him with one consent. From beyond the rivers of Ethiopia my suppliants, even the daughters of my dispersed, shall bring mine offering."
      Note: The "pure language" of 3:9 may refer to two things:
      1. It may indicate a reversal of the language curse at Babel (Gen. 11:9), thus allowing redeemed man to once again enjoy a universal language, perhaps composed of the best from all known existing human languages.

Zephaniah

Judgment

The Prophet Pronounces Judgment (1:1—3:8)
UPON THE LAND OF GOD
The facts of **(1:2-4)**
The reason for **(1:5, 6)**
The name of **(1:7, 8, 14, 18; 2:2)**
The results of **(1:14-18)**
UPON THE ENEMIES OF GOD
Philistia **(2:4-6)**
Moab and Ammon **(2:8-11)**
Ethiopia **(2:12)**
Assyria **(2:13-15)**
UPON THE CITY OF GOD
Its gates **(1:10)**
Its citizens **(1:12, 13)**
Its leaders **(3:1-7)**

Justice

The Prophet Announces Justice (3:9-20)
UPON THE (FORMER) ENEMIES OF GOD
During the millennium all nations will worship God **(3:9)**
UPON THE LAND OF GOD
Israel will dwell in peace **(3:13)**
UPON THE CITY OF GOD
Jerusalem to be filled with singing **(3:14, 15)**
God himself to lead the songs **(3:17)**

      2. It doubtless carries with it a morality purity. In other words this new language will have no filthy four-letter words.
   B. Upon the land of God (3:13):
      "The remnant of Israel shall not do iniquity, nor speak lies; neither shall a deceitful tongue be found in their mouth: for they shall feed and lie down, and none shall make them afraid."
   C. Upon the city of God (3:14-20):
      1. Jerusalem will once again be filled with singing, for the theme of their song, the King of Israel will be there (3:14, 15).
      2. God himself will lead this happy song (3:17).

HABAKKUK (620-610 B.C.)

INTRODUCTION:
1. His name means, "embrace."
2. Habakkuk was the last of the minor prophets writing to the southern kingdom before the Babylonian captivity in 606 B.C., just as Micah was the final prophet to the northern kingdom prior to the Assyrian captivity in 721 B.C.
3. He was apparently one of the Levitical choristers in the Temple. His closing statement, "for the chief musicians on my stringed instrument" reveals that this is actually a song.
4. It is a book of deepest doubt. Habakkuk has been called the Doubting Thomas of the Old Testament. His doubts centered around two painful problems.
   a. How could God allow the sins of Israel to go unpunished? God then tells him Judah would indeed be punished by the Babylonians.

b. How then, he asks, could God justify allowing a godless nation to punish Judah, which nation at least believed in God and had some good men left?

5. Habakkuk sees one of the greatest manifestations of God's glory and power in all the Bible (3:1-16). It is reminiscent of that at Mount Sinai as viewed by Moses. (See Ex. 19.)

6. Habakkuk's great theological declaration, "the just shall live by faith" (2:4) is quoted no less than three times in the New Testament. (See Rom. 1:17; Gal. 3:11; Heb. 10:38.)

7. It has been noted that the book opens with gloom but ends with glory. The doubts of the prophet turn into shouts.

I. The Doubts (1-2).
 A. His question: "Will you punish our nation?" The prophet was grieved over the wickedness of Judah.
  1. Wherever he looked he saw oppression and bribery (1:3).
  2. The laws were not enforced and in the courts unrighteousness prevailed (1:4).
 B. God's answer: "I will, through Judah's foes." This would be done even during Habakkuk's lifetime (1:5).
  1. He was raising a new force on the world scene, the Chaldeans, a tribe of Semites living between Babylon and the Persian Gulf who began to assert themselves against the Assyrians around 630 B.C. (1:6).
  2. They would become notorious for their cruelty (1:7).
   a. Their horses were swifter than leopards (1:8).
   b. Their warriors were more fierce than wolves at dusk (1:8).
 C. His question: "Will you punish these Chaldeans also?" Habakkuk could not comprehend why God would let this pagan nation punish his own people, even though they were admittedly guilty of gross sin (1:12-17).
  "Thou art of purer eyes than to behold evil, and canst not look on iniquity: wherefore lookest thou upon them that deal treacherously, and holdest thy tongue when the wicked devoureth the man that is more righteous than he?"
  Habakkuk continues to probe for answers. He wants to know:
  1. Will God's people be caught and killed like fish? (1:14).
  2. Would they be strung upon hooks and dragged along in nets? (1:15).
  God then answers his question concerning whether he would punish the Chaldeans.
 D. God's answer:, "I will, through my woes!" Habakkuk climbs upon his watchtower to await God's answer. Soon it comes.
  1. God tells him the Chaldeans would indeed be punished, but only at his appointed time (2:3). This later took place, for some seventy-five years later Babylon fell to the Medes and Persians. (See Dan. 5.)
  2. Babylon was to be judged for their many sins.

Habakkuk

The Doubts (HABAKKUK 1-2)
HIS QUESTIONS *Will you punish our nation?*
GOD'S ANSWERS *I will, through your foes!*
Habakkuk wonders if God will allow Judah's sins to go unpunished. *The Babylonian captivity was the answer.*
HIS QUESTIONS *Will you punish our foes?*
GOD'S ANSWERS *I will, through my woes!*
God informs Habakkuk that Babylon, Judah's foe, would herself be punished for her sins.

"The just shall live by faith" **2:4**

The Shouts (3)
The soul of the prophet is revived **(3:2).**
The eyes of the prophet are reassured **(3:3-16).**
The heart of the prophet is rejoiced **(3:18).**
The feet of the prophet are renewed **(3:9).**

   a. They had destroyed many nations without a shred of pity (2:8).
   b. They had degenerated into a nation of drunkards (2:5).
   c. They had worshiped various pagan idols (2:18, 19).
   d. All this would surely take place, for "The Lord is in his holy temple; let all the earth keep silence before him" (2:20). In other words, the trial is to begin, the Judge is on his bench, therefore, let the court remain silent!

II. The Shouts (3).
 A. The soul of the prophet is revived. Habakkuk had even before this, concluded that, "the just shall live by faith" (2:4).
  But now he probes deeper into the grace and glory of God.
  "O Lord, I have heard thy speech, and was afraid; O Lord, revive thy work in the midst of the years, in the midst of the years make known; in wrath remember mercy" (3:2).
 B. The eyes of the prophet are reassured. In 3:3-16 Habakkuk sees an awesome manifestation of God's majestic glory.
  1. He sees him moving across the deserts from Mount Sinai.
  2. His brilliant splendor fills the earth and sky.
  3. From his hands flash rays of brilliant light.
  4. Habakkuk sees him stop for a moment, gazing upon the earth. He then shakes the nations, scattering the everlasting mountains.
  5. He sees him (in a historical vision) part the waters of the Red Sea. (See Ex. 14.)
  6. He sees him lead Israel across the hostile desert into Palestine.
 C. The heart of the prophet rejoices.
  "Yet I will rejoice in the Lord, I will joy in the God of my salvation" (3:18).
 D. The feet of the prophet are renewed.
  "The Lord is my strength, and he will make my feet like hinds' feet, and he will make me to walk upon mine high places" (3:19).

JEREMIAH (Destination southern kingdom)

I. The Rulers Under Whom Jeremiah Ministered.
   A. Josiah. Jeremiah was called by God during the reign of Josiah, Judah's last good king.
   B. Jehoiakim. This wicked king burned Jeremiah's original written prophecy scroll.
   C. Jehoiachin. This ninety-day wonder is soundly condemned by Jeremiah.
   D. Zedekiah. The prophet suffered much under the reign of Zedekiah, Judah's final king.
   E. Nebuchadnezzar. Jeremiah is treated with respect by the great Babylonian conqueror.
   F. Gedaliah. He was appointed by Nebuchadnezzar to govern the fallen city of Jerusalem.
   G. Johanan. He took over after the tragic assassination of Gedaliah and later forced Jeremiah to accompany a Jewish remnant to Egypt.

II. The Threefold Ministry of Jeremiah.
   A. He warned the majority still in Judah about the coming Babylonian captivity.
   B. He comforted the minority already captive in Babylon (ch. 29). Jeremiah wrote a letter of encouragement to the Jewish exiles in Babylon (29:1-32).
      1. They were to settle down for a long seventy-year stay.
      2. They were to pray for the peace and prosperity of Babylon, that their own lives might be peaceful.
      3. They were to ignore the lies of these false prophets and mediums in Babylon, lest they be punished along with them.
      4. Jeremiah pronounced God's death sentence upon two of these prophets named Ahab and Zedekiah for their lying messages and their sin of adultery (29:20-23).
      5. He also warned the exiles concerning a man named Shemaiah, who was sending poison pen letters from Babylon to the influential leaders in Jerusalem against Jeremiah (29:23-32).
      6. God still loved them and would someday bring them back to Jerusalem (29:14).
   C. He pronounced judgment upon nine Gentile nations (46-51). These nations were:
      Egypt (46:1-27)
      Philistia (47:1-6)
      Moab (48:1-47)
      Ammon (49:1-6)
      Edom (49:7-22)
      Damascus (49:23-27)
      Kedar and Hazor (49:28-33)
      Elam (49:34-39)
      Babylon (50-51)
      After listing these nations, Jeremiah dealt with each one in a specific way:
      1. Egypt (46:1-27).
         a. Egypt would be defeated by Nebuchadnezzar at the Battle of Carchemish (46:2).
         b. Their armies would flee in terror and fill the Euphrates with corpses (46:5, 6).
         c. Their sin wound (like Judah's) was incurable (46:11).
         d. Pharaoh Hophra, the Egyptian leader, is ridiculed as a man of plenty of noise, but no power (46:17).
         e. Egypt would be occupied by Nebuchadnezzar (46:26).
      2. Philistia (47:1-6).
         a. It was to be overrun by the Egyptians. This occurred in 606 B.C., the year King Josiah died (47:1).
         b. Strong Philistine men would scream and fathers would flee, leaving behind their helpless children (47:2, 3).
         c. Philistia's allies, Tyre and Sidon, would be destroyed at the same time (47:4).
         d. The two chief Philistine cities of Gaza and Ashkelon would be totally destroyed (47:5).
      3. Moab (48:1-47).
         a. Nebuchadnezzar's armies would overrun Moab (48:1, 2).
         b. Their god Chemosh was to be carried away with priests and princes (48:7).
         c. Prior to this time, Moab had been relatively undisturbed, from various invasions (48:11).
         d. In the end, Moab will be as ashamed of her national idol god Chemosh as Israel was of her calf-god at Bethel (48:13).
         e. The ancestor of the Moabites (Moab) was born in a cave (Gen. 19:37). During the fearful Babylonian invasion, the Moabites will once again flee into caves (48:28).
      4. Ammon (49:1-6).
         a. This nation would be punished for occupying the cities of Israel after the captivity and worshiping the false god Milcom (49:1).
         b. Milcom, along with the Ammonite princes and priests, would be carried away (49:3).
         c. Ammon will be reestablished during the millennium (49:6).
      5. Edom (49:7-22).
         a. Edom's cities would become as silent as Sodom and Gomorrah (49:18).
         b. Their cry will be heard as far away as the Red Sea (49:21).
         c. God will, however, be merciful to her widows and orphans (49:11).
      6. Damascus (49:23-27).
         a. Her entire army would be destroyed in one single day (49:26).
         b. A fire would start at the edge of the city and eventually burn up the palaces of Benhadad (49:27).
      7. Kedar and Hazor (49:28-34).
         a. Kedar was the name of an Arab tribe living in the desert east of Palestine which was to be destroyed by Nebuchadnezzar (49:28).
         b. God himself ordered Nebuchadnezzar to destroy these wealthy, materialistic, and arrogant Bedouin tribes (49:31).
         c. Hazor, another Arabian tribe located nearby, was to be leveled also, never again to be rebuilt (49:33).

8. Elam (49:34-39).
   a. Elam was east of the Tigris-Euphrates country, with its capital at Susa and overrun by Nebuchadnezzar in the winter of 596 B.C. Zedekiah, Judah's last king, began ruling in Jerusalem at that time (49:34).
   b. Elam is to be reestablished during the millennium (49:39).
9. Babylon (50:1—51:64).
   a. Two Babylons seem to be referred to in these verses. One is the historical Babylon, captured by Darius the Persian in October of 539 B.C. (see Dan. 5) and the other is future Babylon, which will be destroyed by God himself. (See Rev. 18:18.)
   b. After the destruction of both Babylons, Israel would seek their God. This happened historically (Ezra 1) and it will occur in the future (Zech. 13:9-11).
   c. After the final destruction of Babylon (Rev. 18) the city will never be inhabited again (51:26).
   d. The ungodly nations would weep over the destruction of both Babylons (Rev. 18; Jer. 50:46).
   e. The Israelites were to flee from both Babylons (Rev. 18:4; Jer. 51:6).
   f. Both cities are depicted as golden cups filled with iniquities from which the nations have drunk and become mad (Rev. 17:1-6; Jer. 51:7).
   g. All heaven rejoices over the destruction of both (Jer. 51:10, 48; Rev. 18:20).
III. A Personal History of Jeremiah.
   A. He is called into full-time service during the reign of Josiah (1:1-10). He was to remain unmarried (16:2).
      1. Jeremiah was the son of Hilkiah, a priest living in Anathoth, some three miles northeast of Jerusalem in the land of Benjamin (1:1).
      2. He received his call to full-time service during the thirteenth year of godly King Josiah (1:6).
         a. Jeremiah at first protested this call (as Moses once did—see Ex. 3-4) pleading his youth as an excuse (1:6).
         b. He was quickly reassured by God, however, that:
            (1) The Lord had already chosen him prior to his birth as a divine spokesman to the nations (1:5).
            (2) God would therefore give his chosen messenger the message (1:7-10).
      3. Because of his fearless sermons on the coming judgment, Jeremiah was persecuted by his own family (12:6), the townspeople of Anathoth (11:21), and eventually the entire nation of Judah.
      4. As he began his ministry, God showed him two things which underlined the nature and importance of his call.
         a. He was shown an almond tree rod (1:11). Because it flowers earlier than the other trees, the almond signified the near fulfillment of God's proposed judgment.
         b. He saw a pot of boiling water, tipping southward from the north. This symbolized the Babylonian invasion (1:13).
      5. Jeremiah weeps over Judah's coming destruction (4:19-21). He would often do this (see 8:18, 21; 9:1, 2, 10; 13:17; 14:17).
      6. He is commanded (like the Greek Diogenes who once ran through the streets of Athens with a lantern trying to find an honest man) by God to "run to and fro through the streets of Jerusalem, and see now, and know, and seek in its broad places, if ye can find a man, if there be any that executeth justice, that seeketh the truth, and I will pardon her" (5:1). God had once made a similar arrangement with Abraham concerning Sodom (see Gen. 18:23-33).
      7. Jeremiah admits that this dreadful condition existed among the poor and ignorant, but that he felt he could find honest men within the ranks of Judah's educated and rich rulers. However, they too had utterly rejected God (5:4, 5).
      8. After a fruitful thirty-one-year reign, Josiah dies. A weeping prophet attends his funeral (2 Chron. 35:25). Judah's last good king had gone and it would be downhill spiritually from that point on.
   B. He pleads with Judah to return to God (3:12-14; 26:1-7).
      1. God would repeatedly invite Israel back to himself (2:9).
      2. He would receive Israel even after her immorality with other lovers (3:1). This was prohibited under the Mosaic Law (see Deut. 24:1-4).
      3. Jeremiah pleaded with them to plow up the hardness of their hearts, lest all be choked up by thorns (4:3, 4).
      4. They could still escape judgment by cleansing their hearts and purifying their thoughts (4:14).
      5. To repent meant they could remain in the land (7:3).
      6. To refuse meant to be covered by thick darkness (13:16).
   C. He fearlessly pronounces coming judgment at the hands of the Babylonians. He then lists Judah's sins.
      1. Judah had forsaken the fountain of divine water and built broken cisterns which could not hold water (2:13).
      2. The nation had become a race of evil men (2:21).
      3. No amount of soap or lye could make them clean (2:22).
      4. The rulers had stained their clothes with the blood of the innocent and poor (2:34).
      5. They were as an unashamed prostitute (3:3).
      6. They worshiped false gods upon every hill and under every shade tree (3:6).
      7. They had killed their prophets as a lion would slaughter his prey (2:30).
      8. They were as insolent as brass, and hard and cruel as iron (6:28).

9. They had set up idols right in the Temple and worshiped the pagan "queen of heaven" goddess (7:18; 44:17).
10. They had actually sacrificed their little children as burnt offerings to devil gods (7:31; 19:5).
D. He finally warns them concerning the terrible results of their disobedience.
1. Great armies would march upon Jerusalem.
2. Neither Assyria or Egypt could help Judah against Babylon (2:18, 36).
3. People will flee from Judah's cities as one runs from a hungry lion (4:5-7).
4. Jerusalem will be surrounded as by hunters who move in on a wild and wounded animal (4:17; 6:3-5).
5. They will cry out as a woman in delivery (4:31; 6:24; 13:21).
6. Jerusalem's own trees would be cut down and used against her walls as battering rams (6:6).
7. The Temple would be destroyed (7:14).
8. Enemy troops would then move among the people like poisonous snakes (8:17).
9. Many would die by sword (15:3), disease (16:3, 4), and starvation (21:9).
10. Some would be scattered as chaff by the fierce desert winds (13:24).
11. Unburied corpses would litter the valleys outside Jerusalem, and become food for wild animals and birds (7:32, 33; 9:22; 12:8, 9).
12. Judah's enemies would break open the sacred graves of her kings, priests, and prophets, and spread out their bones on the ground before the sun, moon, and stars (8:1, 2).
13. Thousands would be carried away into Babylon for a period of seventy years (7:15; 25:11; 29:10).
14. The severity of Judah's punishment would astonish the onlooking pagan Gentile nations (19:8; 22:8; 25:11).
E. When the people ridicule and reject his message, the warning prophet becomes the weeping prophet (4:19; 8:21; 9:1, 2, 10; 13:17; 14:17).
F. Because of his sermons and stand, Jeremiah suffers much.
1. He is persecuted by his own family (12:6).
2. He is plotted against by the people of his hometown (11:21).
3. He is rejected and reviled by his peers in the religious world.
a. Pashhur, the chief Temple priest, has him whipped and put in stocks (20:1-3).
b. He is almost murdered by a wild mob of priests and prophets after one of his messages (26:7-9).
c. He is ridiculed by a false prophet named Hananiah (28).
4. He is threatened by King Jehoiakim (26:21-24; 36:26).
5. He is arrested, flogged, and accused of treason (37:11-16). Zedekiah sends to Jeremiah asking for his prayers after Nebuchadnezzar had declared war on Judah (21:1, 2). Jeremiah sends word back to the wicked king stating prayers were useless on this subject, for God would use the Babylonians to punish Jerusalem, and Zedekiah himself was to be given over to Nebuchadnezzar (21:3-7). Jeremiah tells Zedekiah that Jerusalem will be burned and he is to be captured and carried into Babylon (34:1-5).

Jeremiah rebukes those rich Jewish home owners who violated the Mosaic Law which demanded all Hebrew servants to be set free after serving six years (34:8-16).

Pharaoh Hophra's Egyptian armies had arrived to aid Judah in fighting Nebuchadnezzar. Jeremiah warns Zedekiah that their political alliance would fail, for Nebuchadnezzar would defeat the Egyptians (37:5-10).

Jeremiah attempts to visit the land of Benjamin at this time to inspect some property he had bought (37:11, 12). However, a guard named Irijah arrests him at the city gate and accuses him of defecting to the Babylonians (37:13). Jeremiah denies this, but is flogged and thrown into prison (37:14-16). He is soon secretly sent for by Zedekiah, and once again predicts the defeat of Jerusalem (37:17). Zedekiah places him in the palace prison instead of returning him to the dungeon he was formerly in (37:21).

In the palace, however, pressure from the religious officials who despised Jeremiah eventually force Zedekiah to return the prophet to a more crude confinement. This time he is lowered by ropes into an empty cistern in the prison yard where he soon sinks down into a thick layer of mire at the bottom (38:1-6). Eventually, an Ethiopian friend, Ebed-melech, persuades Zedekiah to remove him from this filthy place. It takes thirty men to haul him from the cistern. He is returned to the palace prison (38:7-13). Jeremiah again predicts the fall of Jerusalem (38:14-17). See also 32:1-5. He would remain in prison until the city was taken (38:28).

6. He sees his original manuscript burned by wicked King Jehoiakim (36:21-23). He is ordered to have his scribe Baruch write down all those oral messages he had been given for the past twenty-three years (36:1, 2). Baruch does this and reads them to the people in the Temple (36:8). He then is invited to read them to the religious officials. When he finishes, they are badly frightened and decide King Jehoiakim should also hear them (36:14-16).

An official named Jehudi thereupon reads them to Jehoiakim as the sullen king sits in front of his fireplace. As Jehudi finishes reading three or four columns, Jehoiakim will take his knife, slit off the section of the roll, and throw it into the fire. Finally, the entire scroll is destroyed (36:21-23). Jeremiah is then commanded to rewrite the burned sections plus a good deal of additional material, including these fearful words about Jehoiakim:

"Therefore thus saith the Lord of Jehoiakim king of Judah; he shall have none to sit upon the throne of David: and his dead body shall be cast out in the day to the heat, and in the night to the frost. And I will punish him and his seed and his servants for their iniquity; and I will bring upon them, and upon the inhabitants of Jerusalem, and upon the men of Judah, all the evil that I pronounced against them; but they hearkened not. Then took Jeremiah another roll, and gave it to Baruch the scribe, the son of Neriah; who wrote therein from the mouth of Jeremiah all the words of the book which Jehoiakim king of Judah had burned in the fire: and there were added besides unto them many like words."

After Jehoiakim burns the scroll, Baruch becomes despondent. It had probably taken him a year to write the material. God then both warns and encourages him through Jeremiah (45:1-5).

7. He is now commanded by God not to pray for Judah (7:16, 11:14; 14:11; 16:5).

8. He experiences frustration and depression (20:7-9, 14-18). Jeremiah had become so frustrated over his inability to call Judah back to God that he determines to quit the ministry!

"Then I said, I will not make mention of him, nor speak any more in his name. But his word was in mine heart like a burning fire shut up in my bones, and I was weary with forebearing, and I could not refrain" (20:9). (See also 1 Ki. 19:3, 4; Jonah 1:1-3; 1 Cor. 9:16.)

At this time he utters one of the most despondent prayers in all the Bible (see also Job 3):

"Cursed be the day wherein I was born: let not the day wherein my mother bare me be blessed. Cursed be the man who brought tidings to my father saying, A man child is born unto thee; making him very glad. And let that man be as the cities which the Lord overthrew, and repented not: and let him hear the cry in the morning, and the shouting at noontide. Because he slew me not from the womb; or that my mother might have been my grave, and her womb to be always great with me. Wherefore came I forth out of the womb to see labour and sorrow, that my days should be consumed with shame?" (20:14-18).

9. He writes a letter of encouragement to those Jewish exiles already in Babylon (29).

10. While in prison, he is ordered by God to buy a field from his cousin Hanamel. This was to illustrate that in spite of the advancing Babylonian armies, "Houses and fields and vineyards shall be possessed again in this land" (32:15). The background of all this is interesting: God tells Jeremiah that his cousin, Hanamel, was soon to visit him, attempting to sell the prophet a farm he owned in Anathoth. Jeremiah was to buy it for seventeen shekels of silver (32:6-13). Baruch was then to place the sealed deed in a pottery jar and bury it. All this was to demonstrate that someday people would once again own property in Judah, and buy and sell (32:14, 15).

Jeremiah is comforted during this time in prison by God's gracious promise:

"Call unto me, and I will answer thee, and show thee great and mighty things, which thou knowest not" (33:3).

These tremendous and thrilling "things" are listed in chapters 30, 31, and 33. They include the following:

a. In spite of the impending Babylonian captivity, the time was coming when God would heal Jerusalem's hurt and give her prosperity and peace (33:4-6).

b. He still loved Israel with an everlasting love (31:3).

c. Israel would be gathered into Palestine from the earth's farthest ends (31:8). See also 30:3, 10, 11.

"They shall come with weeping, and with supplications will I lead them; I will cause them to walk by the rivers of water in a straight way, in which they shall not stumble; for I am a father to Israel. . . . Therefore they shall come and sing in the height of Zion . . . to the goodness of the Lord . . . and their soul shall be like a watered garden, and they shall not sorrow any more at all" (31:9, 12).

Note: In 31:15, 16, Jeremiah predicts that the loud wails and bitter weeping of Rachel for her children in Ramah will disappear. Ramah is an ancient reference to the area in and around Bethlehem. It was here that Nebuchadnezzar killed many sick and feeble exile captives who would not be able to endure the long trip to Babylon. Rachel, who was the wife of Jacob, is of course symbolic of all weeping Israelite mothers. In Matthew 2:18 this sad verse is linked to that occasion when Herod murdered the babies of Bethlehem in an attempt to kill Christ.

d. During the millennium Israel will understand the necessity for and the purpose of all their sufferings (31:18, 19).

e. The cities of Israel will be rebuilt and Jerusalem is to become the praise and power center of all the earth (33:7-9; 31:38, 39; 30:18-21).

11. Jeremiah sees two baskets of figs in the Temple. One basket has fresh, well-ripened figs, but the other contains rotten ones (24:1-3). God explains that the fresh figs represent the Jewish exiles in Babylon (men such as Daniel and Ezekiel), while the rotten fruit depicts Zedekiah and his corrupt officials (24:4-8).

Jeremiah is ordered to make a yoke and fasten it upon his neck with leather thongs. He is then to send messages to the kings of Edom, Moab, Ammon, Tyre, and Sidon, through their ambassadors in Jerusalem,

Jeremiah

HIS PERSONAL LIFE

1. Was the son of a priest **(Jeremiah 1:1)**
2. Was commanded to remain unmarried **(16:2)**
3. Protested his call by God at first, pleading youth as an excuse **(1:6)**
4. Was assured that God had already chosen him prior to birth **(1:5)**
5. Attempted to find one honest man in Jerusalem **(5:1-5)**
6. Pleaded with Judah to return to God **(3:12-14; 26:1-7)**
7. Fearlessly denounced Judah's sin and was persecuted by:
   - His family **(12:6)**
   - Hometown people **(11:21)**
   - Religious world **(20:1-3; 26:7-9; 37:11-16)**
8. Listed Judah's many sins
   - Their worship of the queen of heaven **(7:18; 44:17)**
   - Their sacrifice of their own children to devil gods **(8:31; 9:15)**
   - Their murder of Judah's own prophets **(2:30)**
9. Warned them about coming Babylonian captivity
   - Jerusalem to be surrounded **(4:17; 6:3-5)**
   - Her own trees to be used against her **(6:6)**
   - Temple to be destroyed **(7:14)**
   - Corpses to feed animals **(7:32; 9:22; 12:8, 9)**
   - Captivity for seventy years **(7:15; 25:11; 29:10)**
10. Wept over this captivity **(4:19-21; 8:18, 21; 9:1, 2, 10; 13:17; 14:17)**
11. Had his original manuscript burned by King Jehoiakim **(36:21-23)**
12. Threatened to resign **(20:7-9, 14-18)**
13. Ordered to buy a field while in prison to prove a point **(32:6-15)**
14. Was freed by Nebuchadnezzar **(40:1-6; 39:14)**
15. Helped newly appointed governor Gedaliah **(40:6)**
16. Advised Johanan when Gedaliah was killed **(42:1-5)**
17. Was carried by force to Egypt by Johanan **(43:1-7)**
18. Continued to preach out against sin **(43-44)**
19. Probably died in Egypt

"I ordained thee a prophet

unto the nations"

Jeremiah

RULERS HE MINISTERED UNDER

JOSIAH Judah's last godly king

JEHOIAKIM Ungodly, Bible-burning king

JEHOIACHIN A ninety-day wonder judged by God

ZEDEKIAH Judah's final king

NEBUCHADNEZZAR Great Babylonian conqueror

Gedaliah Babylonian appointed governor of occupied city of Jerusalem

JOHANAN Successor of Gedaliah who was assassinated.

PEOPLE HE MINISTERED TO

1. To the majority in Judah about the coming captivity—a warning 2. To the minority already captive in Babylon—an encouragement (see chapter **29**)

NATIONS HE PROPHESIED AGAINST

EGYPT **46:1-27**
To be defeated by Nebuchadnezzar at battle of Carchemish

PHILISTIA **47:1-6**
To be overrun and destroyed by the Egyptians

MOAB **48:1-47**
To be conquered by Babylon

AMMON **49:1-6**
To be destroyed for sinning against Israel
To be reestablished during the millennium

EDOM **49:7-22**
To become as Sodom and Gomorrah

DAMASCUS **49:23-27**
To be destroyed in a single day

KEDAR AND HAZOR **49:28-35**
To be destroyed by Nebuchadnezzar

ELAM **49:34-39**
To be overrun by Nebuchadnezzar
To be reestablished during the millennium

BABYLON **50:1—51:64**
These prophecies concern two Babylons. (See next outline.)

warning them that God has given their nations over to Babylon. Those who submit and wear the yoke of punishment with true repentance will be spared, but those who refuse will be destroyed (27:1-11). After God had used Nebuchadnezzar to punish Judah and his neighbor nations, he would chastise Babylon itself (27:7). Judah is reassured that after the Babylonian captivity she will be gathered back to Jerusalem (27:22).

Jeremiah is accused of lying by a false prophet named Hananiah who had predicted the Babylonian captivity would last for only two years and that those already in exile (such as King Jehoiachin, Daniel, Ezekiel, etc.) would be returned along with all the Temple treasury which had been taken (28:1-4). To dramatize his accusation, Hananiah breaks the yoke worn by Jeremiah (28:10, 11).

Jeremiah predicts Hananiah's death by God's hand in the near future because of the prophet's lying ministry. Within two years he was dead (28:13-17).

12. Jeremiah visits the settlement where the Rechabite families live. These individuals belonged to a religious order founded by Jonadab, son of Rechab, during the reign of Jehu (841-814 B.C.). They assisted in the eradication of Baalism from Israel. Avoiding city life, they lived as shepherds, drinking no wine (35:2).

   a. Jeremiah is commanded to test the people by offering them wine. They immediately refuse, saying:

> "We will drink no wine; for Jonadab, the son of Rechab, our father, commanded us, saying, Ye shall drink no wine, neither ye, nor your sons forever" (35:6).

   b. Jeremiah then relates this sterling example to Judah, and contrasts the obedience of the Rechabites to the disobedience of Jerusalem (35:12-19).

13. He preaches a sermon at the Temple gate and is nearly killed by an angry mob for predicting the Temple will be destroyed (26:6-9). He is defended by some of Judah's wise old men, who remind the angry mob that Jeremiah's message is like that of the prophet Micah (Micah 3:12). See Jeremiah 26:17-19.

G. Jeremiah under Nebuchadnezzar.
  1. Zedekiah attempts to escape the doomed city, but is captured near Jericho and brought back to Jerusalem. Here he is forced to witness the execution of his own sons, and then submit to the agony of his eyes being gouged out (39:4-7; 52:6-11).
  2. Nebuchadnezzar instructs his chief-of-staff, Nebuzaradan, to treat Jeremiah with kindness (39:11, 12).
  3. Jeremiah is released from prison and taken by Nebuzaradan to Ramah. Here he is offered his choice of going on to Babylon, or returning to Jerusalem. Jeremiah chooses to

return and is placed under the protection of the new Jewish governor of Jerusalem, a man named Gedaliah (40:1-6; 39:14).

H. Jeremiah under Gedaliah.
  1. Gedaliah attempts to institute a moderate post-war administration over the devastated city of Jerusalem (40:7-12).
  2. This soon arouses the fury of a Jewish rebel leader named Ishmael, who plots to assassinate Gedaliah. The governor is warned of this plot by a man named Johanan, but refuses to take it seriously (40:13-16).
  3. Gedaliah is murdered by Ishmael, along with many other Jewish officials, pilgrims, and some Babylonian soldiers. Some of their bodies are hurled down an empty cistern (41:1-9).
  4. Johanan arrives upon the scene of the massacre and soon restores order (41:11-17).

I. Jeremiah under Johanan.
  1. Johanan asks Jeremiah to determine God's will for the tiny Jewish remnant still in Jerusalem (42:1-5).
  2. After a ten-day prayer session with God, Jeremiah is told the Lord desired the remnant to remain in Jerusalem and not go to Egypt, as some were already planning to do (46:6-22).
  3. Upon hearing this unwelcome report, Johanan and other leaders accuse Jeremiah of lying. They then disobey the clearly revealed word of God by going to Egypt. Jeremiah is forced to accompany them (43:1-7).
  4. Upon reaching Egypt, many of the Jews resort to their old habits of idolatry. They begin burning incense to the "queen of heaven" (this was another name for Ishtar, the pagan Mesopotamian goddess of love and war, 44:8-10, 15-19).
  5. Jeremiah pronounces the divine death penalty upon all who refuse to repent and return to Jerusalem (44:7-14, 28).
  6. To dramatize this bitter truth, he buries some large rocks between the pavement stones at the entrance of Pharaoh's palace. This signified that Nebuchadnezzar would occupy Egypt and set his throne upon those stones. Jeremiah predicted he would then kill many of the Jewish remnant who refused to return. The others would die of various plagues or be enslaved (43:9-13).

IV. The Prophecies of Jeremiah.
  A. The fall of Jerusalem (1:14-16; 3; 4:5-9; 5:15-17; 6:1-6; 32:2, 3; 38:17, 18).
  B. The destruction of the Temple (7:11-15; 26:6-9).
  C. The death of the deposed Judean king, Jehoahaz, in Egypt (22:10-12).
  D. The ignoble and unlamented death of King Jehoiakim (36:27-30). He soundly condemns Jehoiakim for his wicked reign (22:13-19). He was constructing an extravagant palace with forced labor. He had murdered the innocent and oppressed the poor. He was filled with selfish greed and dishonesty.

About this time one of Jeremiah's fellow prophets, Uriah, is murdered by Jehoiakim for his fearless preaching (26:20-23). Therefore, Jeremiah predicts that the king will die unlamented and be buried like a dead donkey, dragged out of Jerusalem, and thrown on the garbage dump beyond the gate.

E. The cutting off from the royal line of King Jehoiachin (22:24-30).

1. This young son of Jehoiakim ruled only three months, but so aroused the divine wrath of heaven that, Jeremiah is told, had he been the signet ring of God's right hand, he would still have been cast off and given to the Babylonians (22:24, 25).

2. Jeremiah predicted that this ninety-day wonder would:
   a. Be given over to Nebuchadnezzar.
   b. Be cast out of the land along with his mother.
   c. Die in a foreign land.
   d. Be regarded as a discarded and broken dish.
   e. Be considered childless (even though he had offspring) as far as the throne of David was concerned (22:25-29).

F. The death of two false prophets (Zedekiah and Ahab) and the punishment of another (Shemiah) who were ministering among the first Jewish captive exiles in Babylon (29:20-32).

G. The death of a false Jerusalem prophet named Hananiah (28:13-17).

H. The captivity of Seraiah.
   Jeremiah warns a man named Seraiah that he will be taken captive by Nebuchadnezzar at a later date. (This literally happened some six years later, 51:59.) Seraiah is then given a scroll containing Jeremiah's prophecies against Babylon. When he arrives there the prophet commands him to publicly read it and then tie a rock to the scroll and throw it into the Euphrates River. This symbolized that Babylon would sink, never to rise again (51:60-64).

I. The failure of the Egyptian-Judean military alliance against Babylon (37:5-10).

J. The defeat of Egypt by Babylon (46:1-26).
   Jeremiah describes in vivid detail the world-famous battle at Carchemish at the very moment when it is being fought. Egypt suffers a resounding defeat at the hands of Nebuchadnezzar (46:1-12).

K. The eventual occupation of Egypt by Babylon (43:9-13).

L. The seventy-year captivity of Judah into Babylon (25:11; 29:10).

M. The restoration after the seventy years to Jerusalem (27:19-22; 30:3, 10, 11, 18-21; 31:9, 12, 38, 39; 33:3-9).
   Jeremiah promises ultimate restoration.

1. Israel will be gathered back from all over the world (3:14; 31:10; 32:37-43).

2. God will appoint leaders after his own heart (3:15).

3. Palestine will once again be filled with the glory of God, and the people of God (3:16-18). This will be a far greater event than the original Exodus, when God brought them out of Egypt (16:14, 15; 23:7).

4. A righteous Branch (the Savior) will occupy King David's throne, ruling with wisdom and justice (23:5, 6; 30:21; 33:17).

5. Jerusalem will be rebuilt and filled with joy and great thanksgiving (38:18-20; 31:4, 7-9, 12-14, 23-25; 33:10-12).

N. The defeat of Babylon after the seventy years (25:12; 27:6).
   Note: The punishment Babylon would receive from God as found in Jeremiah 50-52 evidently refers not only to the historical judgment (see Dan. 5), but also that future judgment (see Rev. 18).

THE TWO BABYLONS OF JEREMIAH 50-51

Historical Babylon
Was captured by Darius the Persian in 539 B.C.

Future Babylon
Will be destroyed by God the Father during the tribulation **(See Rev. 18:18.)**

● After the final destruction of Babylon (Rev. 18) the city will never be inhabited again **(51:26)**.
● The ungodly nations would weep over the destruction of both Babylons **(Rev. 18; Jer. 50:46)**.
● The Israelites were to flee from both Babylons **(Rev. 18:4; Jer. 51:6)**.
● Both cities are depicted as golden cups filled with iniquities from which the nations have drunk and become mad **(Rev.17:1-6; Jer. 51:7)**.
● All heaven rejoices over the destruction of both **(Jer. 51:10, 48; Rev. 18:20)**.
● After the destruction of both Babylons, Israel would seek their God. This happened historically (Ezra 1) and it will occur in the future **(Zech. 13:9)**.

THE EIGHTEEN PROPHECIES OF JEREMIAH

1. Fall of Jerusalem **(1:14-16; 4:5-9; 5:15-17; 6:1-6; 32:2, 3; 38:17, 18)**
2. Destruction of the Temple **(7:11-15; 26:6-9)**
3. Death of deposed King Jehoahaz in Egypt **(22:10-12)**
4. Unlamented death of King Jehoiakim **(36:27-30)**
5. Cutting off of the royal line of King Jehoiachin **(22:24-30)**
6. Death of two false prophets and punishment of another—all three living in Babylon **(29:20-32)**
7. Death of a false Jerusalem prophet **(28:13-17)**
8. Capture and exile of a friend named Seraiah **(51:59)**
9. Failure of the Egyptian-Judean military alliance against Babylon **(37:5-10)**
10. Defeat of Egypt by Babylon at Carchemish **(46:1-12)**
11. Babylonian occupation of Egypt **(43:9-13)**
12. Seventy-year captivity of Judah in Babylon **(25:11; 29:10)**
13. Restoration to Jerusalem after the seventy years **(27:19-22; 30:3, 10, 11, 18-21; 31:9, 12, 38, 39; 33:3-9)**
14. Defeat of Babylon after the seventy years **(25:12; 27:7)**
15. Capture of Zedekiah **(21:3-7; 34:1-5; 37:17)**
16. Kindly treatment of the godly exiles in Babylon **(24:1-7)**
17. Final regathering of people of Israel **(30:3, 10; 31:8-12)**
18. Final rebuilding of the land of Israel **(30:18-21; 31:38, 39; 33:7-9)**

O. The capture of Zedekiah (21:3-7; 34:1-5; 37:17). (See 39:4-7; 52:6-11 for fulfillment.)

P. The kindly treatment of the godly exiles in Babylon (24:1-7).

V. The New Covenant of Jeremiah.

A. The nature of the new covenant (31:31-34).

1. It would embrace the entire house of Israel.
2. It would be totally unlike the old Mosaic Covenant.
3. God would inscribe his laws upon their hearts. Israel had always suffered with self-inflicted spiritual heart trouble. Note the divine diagnosis:

"The sin of Judah is written with a pen of iron and with the point of a diamond; it is engraved upon the tablet of their hearts . . ." (Jer. 17:1).

But under the new covenant the heavenly Physician would offer them perfect and guaranteed successful heart transplants.

4. This nation with the new hearts would then once again become God's people, and he their God.

B. The time of the new covenant. It will go into effect "after those days" (31:33), and following the "time of Jacob's trouble" (30:7). Both these terms refer to the coming great tribulation. Thus, the new covenant will begin to function after the time of Jacob's trouble, at the start of the glorious millennium.

C. The superiority of the new covenant. It will be immutable, unconditional, and eternal, as opposed to the Mosaic Covenant (Ex. 19:5-8). M. F. Unger writes:

"The Old Covenant was the law covenant grounded in legal observance. The New Covenant (Heb. 8:8-12) will be entirely on the basis of grace and the sacrificial blood of Christ, which will be the foundation of Israel's future inward regeneration and restoration to God's favor. Israel's entering into the blessings of the New Covenant (Rom. 11:1-26) will insure her being an everlasting nation." (*Unger's Bible Dictionary*, p. 352)

God himself assures Israel of the duration of this new covenant when he declares: "If the heaven above can be measured, and the foundations of the earth searched out beneath, I will also cast off all the seed of Israel . . ." (31:37). (See also 33:20-26.)

D. The Mediator of the new covenant: the Son of David himself (33:15-18; 30:9).

VI. Classic Passages in Jeremiah.

A. "They have healed also the hurt of the daughter of my people slightly, saying, Peace, peace; when there is no peace" (6:14).

B. "Is this house, which is called by my name, become a den of robbers in your eyes? Behold, even I have seen it, saith the Lord" (7:11).

C. "The harvest is past, the summer is ended, and we are not saved. Is there no balm in Gilead; is there no physician there? why then is not the health of the daughter of my people recovered?" (8:20, 22).

D. "Who would not fear thee, O King of nations? for to thee doth it appertain: forasmuch as

among all the wise men of the nations, and in all their kingdoms, there is none like unto thee. He hath made the earth by his power, he hath established the world by his wisdom, and hath stretched out the heavens by his discretion" (10:7, 12).

E. "But I was like a lamb or an ox that is brought to the slaughter; and I knew not that they had devised devices against me, saying, Let us destroy the tree with the fruit thereof, and let us cut him off from the land of the living, that his name may be no more remembered" (11:19).

F. "Can the Ethiopian change his skin, or the leopard his spots? then may ye also do good, that are accustomed to do evil" (13:23).

G. "Then said the Lord unto me, Though Moses and Samuel stood before me, yet my mind could not be toward this people: cast them out of my sight, and let them go forth. Thy words were found, and I did eat them; and thy word was unto me the joy and rejoicing of mine heart: for I am called by thy name, O Lord God of hosts" (15:1, 16).

H. "Therefore, behold, the days come, saith the Lord, that it shall no more be said, The Lord liveth, that brought up the children of Israel out of the land of Egypt; but, the Lord liveth, that brought up the children of Israel from the land of the north, and from all the lands whither he had driven them; and I will bring them again into their land that I gave unto their fathers" (16:14, 15).

I. "Thus saith the Lord; Cursed be the man that trusteth in man, and maketh flesh his arm, and whose heart departeth from the Lord. For he shall be like the heath in the desert, and shall not see when good cometh; but shall inhabit the parched places in the wilderness, in a salt land and not inhabited. Blessed is the man that trusteth in the Lord, and whose hope the Lord is. For he shall be as a tree planted by the waters, and that spreadeth out her roots by the river, and shall not see when heat cometh, but her leaf shall be green; and shall not be careful in the year of drought, neither shall cease from yielding fruit. The heart is deceitful above all things, and desperately wicked: who can know it? I the Lord search the heart, I try the reins, even to give every man according to his ways, and according to the fruit of his doings" (17:5-10).

J. "The word which came to Jeremiah from the Lord saying, Arise and go down to the potter's house, and there I will cause thee to hear my words. Then I went down to the potter's house, and, behold, he wrought a work on the wheels. And the vessel that he made of clay was marred in the hand of the potter; so he made it again another vessel, as seemed good to the potter to make it. Then the Lord came to me saying, O house of Israel, cannot I do with you as this potter? saith the Lord. Behold, as the clay is in the potter's hand, so are ye in mine hand, O house of Israel" (18:1-6).

K. "O Lord, thou hast deceived me, and I was deceived: thou art stronger than I, and hast prevailed: I am in derision daily, everyone mocketh me. For since I spake, I cried out, I cried violence and spoil; because the word of the Lord was made a reproach unto me, and a derision, daily. Then I said, I will not make mention of him, nor speak any more in his name. But his word was in mine heart as a burning fire shut up in my bones, and I was weary with forebearing, and I could not stay" (20:7-9).

"Sing unto the Lord, praise ye the Lord: for he hath delivered the soul of the poor from the hand of evildoers. Cursed be the day wherein I was born: let not the day wherein my mother bare me be blessed. Cursed be the man who brought tidings to my father, saying, A man child is born unto thee; making him very glad" (20:13-15).

L. "And unto this people thou shalt say, Thus saith the Lord; Behold, I set before you the way of life, and the way of death" (21:8).

M. "Is not my word like as a fire? saith the Lord; and like a hammer that breaketh the rock in pieces?" (23:29).

N. "For I know the thoughts that I think toward you, saith the Lord, thoughts of peace, and not of evil, to give you an expected end. Then shall ye call upon me, and ye shall go and pray unto me, and I will hearken unto you. And ye shall seek me, and find me, when ye shall search for me with all your heart. And I will be found of you, saith the Lord: and I will turn away your captivity, and I will gather you from all the nations and from all the places whither I have driven you, saith the Lord; and I will bring you again into the place whence I caused you to be carried away captive" (29:11-14).

O. "Alas! for that day is great, so that none is like it; it is even the time of Jacob's trouble; but he shall be saved out of it" (30:7).

P. "The Lord hath appeared of old unto me, saying, Yea, I have loved thee with an everlasting love: therefore with loving kindness have I drawn thee. Behold, I will bring them from the north country, and gather them from the coasts of the earth, and with them the blind and the lame, the woman with child and her that travaileth with child together; a great company shall return thither. They shall come with weeping, and with supplications will I lead them: I will cause them to walk by the rivers of waters in a straight way, wherein they shall not stumble: for I am a father to Israel, and Ephraim is my firstborn. Thus saith the Lord: A voice was heard in Ramah, lamentation, and bitter weeping; Rachel weeping for her children refused to be comforted for her children, because they were not. How long wilt thou go about, O thou backsliding daughter? for the Lord hath created a new thing in the earth, a woman shall compass a man" (31:3, 8, 9, 15, 22).

Q. "Ah Lord God! behold, thou hast made the heaven and the earth by thy great power and stretched out arm, and there is nothing too hard for thee: Behold, I am the Lord, the God of all flesh: is there anything too hard for me?" (32:17, 27).

R. "Call unto me, and I will answer thee, and shew thee great and mighty things, which thou know-est not. As the host of heaven cannot be numbered, neither the sand of the sea measured: so will I multiply the seed of David my servant, and the Levites that minister unto me" (33:3, 22).

S. "But fear not thou, O my servant Jacob, and be not dismayed, O Israel: for, behold, I will save thee from afar off, and thy seed from the land of their captivity; and Jacob shall return, and be in rest and at ease, and none shall make him afraid" (45:27).

T. "O thou sword of the Lord, how long will it be ere thou be quiet? put up thyself into thy scabbard, rest, and be still" (47:6).

LAMENTATIONS (586 B.C.)

INTRODUCTION:

1. This book is composed of five elegies, all of them lamenting the tragic destruction of Jerusalem by the Babylonians.

2. The literary form is alphabetical, somewhat like Psalm 119.

   a. A different Hebrew letter of the alphabet begins each of the twenty-two verses of chapters 1, 2.

   b. In chapter 3 there are sixty-six verses, arranged in twenty-two groups of three verses, each of which in succession begins with a different letter.

3. Tradition says Jeremiah sat weeping outside Jerusalem's north wall under the knoll called Golgotha, where our Lord was later to die.

4. J. Vernon McGee writes:

   "The book is filled with tears and sorrow. It is a paean of pain, a poem of pity, a proverb of pathos, a hymn of heartbreak, a psalm of sadness, a symphony of sorrow. . . . It is the wailing wall of the Bible." (*Briefing the Bible*, p. 232)

I. The Provocation Against God (Lam. 1). Around 1000 B.C. David had established his capital in Jerusalem. (See 2 Sam. 6.) Thus, God had blessed this beloved city for nearly 400 years. He had allowed the northern kingdom to be carried away by the Assyrians in 721 B.C. But Jerusalem had been spared for another 115 years. All this mercy and longsuffering, however, had been in vain, for Judah continued provoking the Holy One of Israel through constant sinning. The end had now come.

Note the following verses of indictment.

A. 1:1:

   "How doth the city sit solitary, that was full of people! how is she become as a widow! She that was great among the nations, and princess among the provinces, how is she become tributary!"

B. 1:3:

   "Judah is gone into captivity because of affliction, and because of great servitude: she dwelleth among the heathen, she findeth no rest: all her persecutors overtook her between the straits."

C. 1:8:

   "Jerusalem hath grievously sinned; therefore she is removed: all that honoured her despise her, because they have seen her nakedness: yea, she sigheth, and turneth backward."

D. 1:9:

   "Her filthiness is in her skirts; she remembereth not her last end; therefore she came down wonderfully: she had no comforter. O Lord, behold my affliction: for the enemy hath magnified himself."

E. 1:17:

"Zion spreadeth forth her hands, and there is none to comfort her: the Lord hath commanded concerning Jacob, that his adversaries should be round about him: Jerusalem is as a menstrous woman among them."

II. The Punishment from God (Lam. 2).

A. He had destroyed every home in Judah (2:2).

B. Every fortress and wall was broken (2:2).

C. He bent his bow of judgment across the land (2:4).

D. He allowed his own Temple to fall as though it were a booth of leaves and branches in a garden (2:6).

E. Judah's enemies were given full freedom to ridicule and destroy her citizens (2:16).

F. Her people, old and young alike, choked the streets of Jerusalem with their lifeless bodies (2:21).

III. The Prophet of God (Lam. 3). The tears of Jeremiah fell like a spring rain over the destruction of Jerusalem and its suffering people.

A. The affliction of the prophet. All through Lamentations, Jeremiah shares the agony of his soul with us, as the following verses bring out.

1. 1:12:

"Is it nothing to you, all ye that pass by? behold, and see if there be any sorrow like unto my sorrow, which is done unto me, wherewith the Lord hath afflicted me in the day of his fierce anger."

2. 1:16:

"For these things I weep; mine eye, mine eye runneth down with water, because the comforter that should relieve my soul is far from me: my children are desolate, because the enemy prevailed."

3. 2:11:

"Mine eyes do fail with tears, my bowels are troubled, my liver is poured upon the earth, for the destruction of the daughter of my people; because the children and the sucklings swoon in the streets of the city."

4. 3:1-19:

Jeremiah then relates the sufferings he endured at the hands of his own countrymen even prior to the Babylonian invasion. (See 3:52-66.)

B. The assurance of the prophet. In the midst of the terrible storm there shines a ray of reassurance.

"This I recall to my mind, therefore have I hope. It is of the Lord's mercies that we are not consumed, because his compassions fail not. They are new every morning: great is thy faithfulness. The Lord is my portion, saith my soul; therefore will I hope in him. The Lord is good unto them that wait for him, to the soul that seeketh him. It is good that a man should hope and quietly wait for the salvation of the Lord. It is good for a man that he bear the yoke in his youth; for the Lord will not cast off for ever: But though he cause grief, yet will he have compassion according to the multitude of his mercies. For he doth not afflict willingly nor grieve the children of men" (3:21, 22, 23, 24, 25, 26, 27, 31, 32, 33).

C. The advice of the prophet (3:40, 41).

"Let us search and try our ways, and turn again to the Lord. Let us lift up our heart with our hands unto God in the heavens."

IV. The People of God (Lam. 4).

A. The children's tongues stuck to the roof of their mouths for thirst (4:4).

B. The cream of Judah's youth were treated as earthenware pots (4:2). See also 5:13.

C. The rich and pampered were in the streets begging for bread (4:5).

D. Their mighty princes, once lean and tan, were now but skin and bones, and their faces black as soot (4:7, 8). See also 5:12.

E. Tender-hearted women had cooked and eaten their own children (4:10).

F. The false prophets and priests were blindly staggering through the streets, covered with blood (4:14).

G. The king, himself (Zedekiah), had been captured, blinded, and carried off into captivity (4:20).

V. The Prayer to God (Lam. 5). Jeremiah's prayer contained four elements:

A. That of remembrance

"Remember, O Lord, what is come upon us; consider, and behold our reproach" (5:1).

B. That of repentance

"The crown is fallen from our head; woe unto us, that we have sinned" (5:16).

C. That of recognition

"Thou, O Lord, remainest forever, thy throne from generation to generation" (5:19).

D. That of renewal

"Turn thou us unto thee, O Lord, and we shall be turned; renew our days as of old" (5:21).

THE CAPTIVITY STAGE

INTRODUCING
THE CAPTIVITY STAGE

1. Psalm 137 describes the beginning of this period, while Psalm 126 describes the end.
2. Israel is cured of the *sin* of idolatry while in the *city* of idolatry.
3. Two eyewitnesses write of this era. One was a prime minister, the other a priest.
4. This historical period includes:
   a. Three men who wouldn't bend or burn (Dan. 3).
   b. A *review* of Babylon's greatest king (Nebuchadnezzar, Dan. 1–4) and a *preview* of Greece's greatest king (Alexander the Great, Dan. 7:6; 8:5–8, 21, 22; 11:3, 4).
   c. A fight between a Persian ram and a Greek goat (Dan. 8).
   d. An aimless hand (of God) that wrote and a lifeless band (of men) that walked (Dan. 5; Ezek. 37).
   e. The only description of God the Father in the Bible (Dan. 7:9–14).
   f. Great prophecies revealed through the falling of a stone (Dan. 2) and the felling of a tree (Dan. 4).
   g. The second of three attempts to consolidate religion around an image (1) Genesis 11 (2) Daniel 3 (3) Revelation 13.
   h. The real story of when the Bear comes over the mountain (Ezek. 38–39).
   i. The future and final earthly temple (Ezek. 40–48).
5. God blesses a basic diet and curses a blasphemous feast (Dan. 1, 5).
6. Both archangels, Gabriel and Michael, are referred to during this period (Dan. 8, 12).
7. This era has more to say about the ministry of the heavenly cherubim than any other period (Ezek. 1, 10).
8. This era has more to say about the ministry of the hellish antichrist than any other period (Dan. 7, 8, 9, 11).
9. Ezekiel denounces the materialistic city of Tyre (ch. 26) and describes the millennial city of God (ch. 48).
10. Ezekiel begins by describing the removal of God's glory cloud (Ezek. 10:18), and concludes by predicting the return of this glory cloud (Ezek. 43:2).

THE CAPTIVITY STAGE
Ezekiel (around 597 B.C.)

INTRODUCTION:
1. Ezekiel was the son of a Zadokite priest. He was deported to Babylon in 597 B.C. with King Jehoiachin. His wife died the day the siege began in 588 B.C. (Ezek. 24:1, 15–18).

2. He was thirty when he began writing and resided at a town on the Chebar, a canal which flowed from the Euphrates River.
3. His ministry was twofold, to *remind* the exiles of their sins and to *encourage* them concerning God's future blessings.
4. Ezekiel may be compared with other Old Testament books as follows:
   a. Isaiah speaks of God's salvation.
   b. Jeremiah speaks of God's judgment.
   c. Daniel speaks of God's kingdom.
   d. Ezekiel speaks of God's glory.

I. The Sanctification of the Man of God—Ezekiel (1, 2, 33).
   A. Ezekiel sees the vision of the living creatures (1:1–28).
      1. The description of these creatures. (See 1:4–28.)
      2. The identity of these living creatures. Who are they? These magnificent beings are identified later by Ezekiel (10:20) as the cherubim, angels of high ranking order. They make their appearance on three distinct occasions in the Word of God.
         a. In the Garden of Eden, to keep Adam from the Tree of Life after his sin (Gen. 3:22–24).
         b. To Ezekiel here in Babylon (1:4–28).
         c. In heaven, during John's vision (Rev. 4:6–8).
      3. The duties of these living creatures.
         a. To guard and vindicate the righteousness of God (Gen. 3:24; Ex. 26:1; 36:8, 35).
         b. To symbolize the mercy of God (Ex. 25:22; 37:9).
         c. To aid in the administration of the government of God (1 Sam. 4:4; Ps. 80:1; 99:1; Ezek. 1:22, 26).
         d. To be eternal reminders of the blessed earthly ministry of the Lord Jesus Christ. This is seen by the following summary of the four gospel accounts:
            (1) Matthew (writing to the Jews), pictures Christ as a Lion, the Messiah.
            (2) Mark (writing to the Romans), pictures Christ as an Ox, the Servant.
            (3) Luke (writing to the Greeks), pictures Christ as the perfect Man.
            (4) John (writing to the whole world), pictures Christ as the Eagle, the mighty God.

(For a description of another kind of special angelic beings, called the seraphim, see Isaiah 6:1–7.)

B. Ezekiel hears the voice of the living God (2:1—8:27; 33:1–22).
1. He was commissioned as Israel's watchman in Babylon.
2. He was to warn the wicked that if they abandoned their wicked ways, God would not physically destroy them.
3. He was to warn the righteous that if they abandoned their righteous ways, God would physically destroy them.
4. He was to do all this without fear or favor.
5. He was to totally absorb the message of God (3:1, 2). (See also Rev. 10:8–11.)

II. The Desolation of the City of God—Jerusalem (4–24). There were three distinct phases in the Babylonian captivity and the siege of Jerusalem.

In 605 B.C. At this time Daniel and other individuals of noble birth were carried away (Dan. 1:3, 4; 2 Chron. 36:6, 7).

In 597 B.C. During this phase both King Johoiachin and Ezekiel, along with many others, were taken into Babylon (2 Ki. 24:10–16).

In 586 B.C. At this final time Judah's last king, Zedekiah, was carried away, the walls of Jerusalem were destroyed, and both Temple and city were burned (2 Ki. 25:1–7).

The events recorded here in Ezekiel 4–24 took place between the second and third phase. Apparently there were false prophets, both in Jerusalem and in Babylon, who brazenly assured the Jews that God would not dare destroy his own city, even though it had already suffered two bitter sieges. But Ezekiel knew otherwise and he attempted through symbolism, parables, visions, and messages to warn all that the Holy City would indeed suffer desolation and destruction.

A. Ezekiel's twelve symbolic acts.
1. He drew a map of Jerusalem on a large flat tablet of soft clay, showing siege mounds being built against the city. He then added more details, portraying the enemy camps around it, and the placement of the battering rams. He finally placed an iron plate between the map and himself. This was to indicate the impenetrable wall of the Babylonian army, and also to show the impossibility of escape (4:1–3).
2. He lay on his left side a few hours each day for 390 days, to symbolize the iniquity of the northern kingdom. Each day was to represent a year (4:4, 5).
3. He then lay on his right side a few hours each day for forty days, to depict the iniquity of Judah, the southern kingdom. Again, each day was to represent a year (4:6). It must be admitted that the full meaning of these time periods cannot be known. Unger writes:

"His discomfort for 390 days on his left side and 40 days on his right side (total 430 years, symbolically a year for a day), recalled the Egyptian servitude (Ex. 12:40, 41). A similar captivity would engulf both Israel and Judah. The captivity of the Northern Kingdom was to be longer, however." (*Unger's Bible Handbook*, p. 367)

4. He prepared bread made with mixed grains and baked it over dried cow dung which had been set afire. This was to indicate the scarcity of food in Jerusalem (4:9–17).
5. He shaved his head and beard with a sharp sword, and then divided the hair into three equal parts (5:1–4).
   a. One third he burned.
   b. One third he cut up with the sword.
   c. One third he scattered to the wind.

   All this was to indicate what was in store for Judah and Jerusalem. One third of her citizens would die by fire in the Jerusalem siege. One third of her citizens would fall by the sword, and the remaining third would be scattered to the wind.
6. He was to stamp his feet and clap his hands to get their attention (6:11).
7. He set some scant baggage outside his home. Then, in the evening he dug an entrance through the city wall. As he went through it carrying the baggage, he also covered his face. This was to vividly symbolize the following (12:1–16):
   a. The few articles of baggage represented the exiles hurriedly departing their homes.
   b. The entrance in the wall symbolized their desperation to leave the doomed city of Jerusalem.
   c. The covered face depicted Zedekiah, Judah's last king, who was blinded by Nebuchadnezzar because of his rebellion, and led captive into Babylon (2 Ki. 25:1–7).
8. He was to tremble as he ate his food and to ration out his water as though it were his last (12:17–20).
9. He was to slash about in the air a gleaming sword, and with sobbings, beat upon his thigh (21:9–17).
10. He drew a map of the Middle East and traced two routes for the King of Babylon to follow. One led to Jerusalem, and the other to Rabbath-Ammon. Both cities had rebelled against Nebuchadnezzar in 593 B.C. Ezekiel pictured the king here at the crossroads. Which city would be destroyed first? The sad answer is immediately forthcoming (21:18–22):

    "He will call his magicians to use divination; they will cast lots by shaking arrows from the quiver; they will sacrifice to idols and inspect the liver of their sacrifices. They will decide to turn toward Jerusalem!" (21:21, 22, TLB).
11. He filled a pot of boiling water with the choicest meats and cooked it until the flesh fell off the bones. He then threw it all out and allowed the pot to bake itself dry to eliminate the scum and rust (24:1–14). Here, of course, the symbolism is clear. The judgment fire of God would utterly consume even the rich and noble of Jerusalem. All of

its citizens would be cast out of the land, that his holy city might be cleansed of their moral scum and rust.

12. He was forbidden to express any outward sorrow over the sudden death of his beloved wife (24:15-18). Charles Feinberg has written:

"The covered head (2 Sam. 15:30); the bare feet (Isa. 20:2); and the covered lip (Lev. 13:45; Micah 3:7) were prohibited Ezekiel. Priests could mourn for their near kin (Lev. 21:1-3), but Ezekiel was an exception for a special purpose. It was customary in ancient times to have a funeral feast; the friends of the bereaved sent the food as a token of sympathy (Deut. 26:14; Jer. 16:7; Hosea 9:4). Faced with this directive, Ezekiel exhibits complete subordination of his own will and feelings to his prophetic office in the will of God. In spite of the fact that he knew his wife's hours were numbered, he went about the ministry committed to Him. What an example of obedience!" (*The Prophecy of Ezekiel*, pp. 139, 140)

One of the most emotion-filled verses in all the Bible is his testimony at this time:

"So I spoke unto the people in the morning and at evening my wife died; and I did in the morning as I was commanded" (24:18).

God ordered him not to mourn over the death of his wife to emphasize that he, the Lord, would not mourn over Jerusalem's death. It is especially significant to observe that she died the very day that Nebuchadnezzar began his third and final assault upon Jerusalem (24:2).

B. Ezekiel's twelve judgment messages.

A brief summary of Ezekiel's main points in these sermons would include:

1. God had often held back his divine wrath in spite of Israel's brazen disobedience (20:7-10, 14, 21, 22).
2. God took no joy in judging his people even at this desperate stage and again called for Judah's repentance (18:31, 32).
3. But Judah would not listen and her hour of doom was now at hand (7:6, 12).
4. Judah would then be destroyed, *not* because of the sins of their fathers, but because of their own vile wickedness (18:1-4, 20).
5. Even the presence of such godly men as Noah, Daniel, and Job could not spare the City of Jerusalem (14:14, 20).
6. Her armies would be absolutely helpless in defending her (7:14).
7. Her wealth could not purchase one additional minute of freedom (7:19).
8. The Holy City of God had now become the harlot city of Satan.
9. God would therefore bring into Jerusalem the worst of nations and people to occupy their lands and homes (7:24).
10. Judah's cities would be burned and her idols smashed (6:4, 6).

11. Four great punishments would fall upon her citizens, that of war, famine, ferocious beasts, and plagues (14:21).

C. Ezekiel's six parables.

1. A fruitless vine tree (15:1-8).
   a. The vine is a common symbol for the nation of Israel in the Bible. (See Deut. 32:32; Ps. 80:8-12; Isa. 5:1-7; Jer. 2:21; Hosea 10:1; Mt. 21:33.)
   b. The only value and purpose of a vine is to bear fruit. It is not good for house building (the wood is too crooked), or furniture making (the wood is too soft), or for fuel (the wood burns too rapidly).
   c. Because the vine had refused to perform its only prescribed duty, it would be burned. (See Jn. 15:6.)

2. The adopted girl who became a harlot (16:1-63).

Dr. Charles Feinberg writes the following to introduce this parable:

"Here, in the longest chapter in Ezekiel, the story is told in detail in all its sordid, loathsome character, so that God's infinite abhorrence of Israel's sin may be clearly seen. According to Rabbi Eleizer ben Hyrcanus in the mishna, the chapter was not to be read nor translated in public." (*The Prophecy of Ezekiel*, p. 85)

   a. God had found in a field an abandoned, despised, and dying baby girl. Her name was Israel (16:1-5). This is a reference to Israel's bondage to the Egyptians in the first few chapters of Exodus. (See especially Ex. 1:13, 14; 2:23; 3:7.)
   b. God graciously adopted this ragged little girl. When she became of age, he entered into the sacred rite of marriage with her, and she legally became his elected wife (16:8). This, of course, all took place at Mt. Sinai when God ratified his covenant with Israel. (See Ex. 19:5. Also, compare Ezek. 16:9 with Ex. 19:14.)
   c. After the marriage God dressed her in the most beautiful clothes, adorned her with the most costly jewels, and provided the finest food available for his beloved (16:10-14). This occurred in Israel's history during the reign of David and Solomon. (See 2 Sam. 8:11; 1 Ki. 3:13; 10:4-7.)
   d. But this little ex-orphan soon spurned all his love and faithfulness and became a common harlot of the streets (16:15-34).
   e. This intolerable action could not continue unpunished, for the beloved Husband was also the righteous Judge. He would, therefore, turn her over to her own murderous lovers to be abused and punished (16:36-41).
   f. Her wickedness by this time had surpassed even that of her older sister (Samaria, the capital of the northern kingdom) and that of her younger sister (Sodom). (See Ezek. 16:46-50.)
   g. After he had chastened her, God would once again restore her to himself (along

with her two sinning sisters) because of his love for her and his promise to Abraham (16:53, 60, 63).

3. The two eagles (17:1-21). The events mentioned in this parable narrate the international affairs of Judah, Babylon, and Egypt between 597 and 588 B.C. The figures involved are Jehoiachin, Zedekiah, and Nebuchadnezzar. For the recorded history of this period, see 2 Kings 24:8-20; 2 Chronicles 36:9-13; Jeremiah 37; 52:1-7.

4. The tender twig (17:22-24).
   a. God himself stated he would someday plant the finest and most tender twig of all upon Israel's highest mountain (17:22).
   b. This twig would grow into a noble tree, blessing all who came near it by its fruit and shade (17:23).
   c. Through all this, the entire world would know the plan and power of God (17:24).
   d. These verses without question introduce a messianic prophecy. (See Isa. 2:2-4; Micah 4:1-4.) The tender twig is the Messiah (see Isa. 11:1; 53:2; Jer. 23:5, 6; 33:15; Zech. 6:12; Rev. 22:16) and the high mountain is Mount Zion. (See Ps. 2:6.)

5. The mother lioness and her cubs (19:1-9).
   a. A mother lioness had some cubs. One of her whelps grew up and learned to devour men. For this he was trapped and taken into Egypt (19:1-4).
   b. Another of her cubs did the same thing. He also was captured and carried away into Babylon (19:5-9).
   c. Some believe the mother lioness here was Hamutal, the wife of Josiah, and mother of three Judean kings. The first cub was Jehoahaz (2 Ki. 23:31-34) who was carried away into an Egyptian prison by Pharaoh Necho. The other cub was Zedekiah (Hamutal's youngest son). He was Judah's last king and was carried away by Nebuchadnezzar into Babylon (2 Ki. 24:18).

6. Two harlot sisters (23:1-49).
   a. Two sisters begin their sad history of prostitution by engaging in immorality with the Egyptians (23:1-3).
   b. The names of these girls are Aholah and Aholibah and are identified as Samaria and Jerusalem (23:4).
   c. The word Aholah means "her tent" and may be a reference to the fact that God never approved of the false religion of Samaria (capital of the northern kingdom) as instituted by its first king, Jeroboam. (See 1 Ki. 12:25-33.) Thus, "her tent" meant she had her own religion which did not include God.
   d. The word Aholibah means "my tent is in her," indicating perhaps that God's presence still dwelt in the Jerusalem Temple in spite of Judah's sin.
   e. It is said here both these girls became harlots because of their Egyptian immo-

rality. This may refer to the fact that both cities were impressed with the religious and political structures of Egypt.
   f. Aholah then began illicit relations with Assyria (23:5). This happened under northern king Menahem, who allied himself with Assyria. (See 2 Ki. 15:13-20.)
   g. Aholibah did the same thing with Babylon (23:11). King Hezekiah treated the Babylonian representatives almost as if they were gods. (See 2 Ki. 20:12-19; 2 Chron. 32:31.)
   h. God therefore determined to turn both these sisters over to the full brutality of their respective lovers (23:9, 22, 24).

D. Ezekiel's extended Temple vision (8:1—11:25).
   1. The departure of Judah from the glory of God.
      a. Ezekiel is caught away in a vision and transported from Babylon to the Jerusalem Temple during September of 592 B.C. Here he witnesses those things which are transpiring in the Holy City at that very moment (8:1-3).
      b. He first sees an idol just north of the altar gate (8:5).
      c. He then enters into a hidden room in the Temple court, where he sees the walls covered with pictures of all kinds of snakes, lizards, and hideous creatures. In this room are seventy Israelite elders who stand, each with his censer of burning incense, and worshiping these vile drawings. They are being led in their depraved devotions by a Jew named Jaazaniah, the son of Shaphan. Ezekiel must have gasped in shock, for it was Shaphan who had read the book of the law to King Josiah during the great Jerusalem revival some thirty years back (2 Ki. 22:8-11). But his son now led in this awful apostasy (Ezek. 8:7-11). (See also Rom. 1:21-23.)

      Dr. Feinberg writes:
      "The seventy men were obviously not the Sanhedrin which was not organized until the restoration from Babylon. The reference is probably to the pattern given in Exodus 24:9, 10 and Numbers 11:16. These seventy, in the time of Ezekiel, represented the laity . . . the Lord had appointed seventy leaders in years past and their chief duties were to guard against idolatry. What a perversion this was of their high calling!" (The Prophecy of Ezekiel, p. 51)

      d. After this repulsive experience, the prophet goes to the northern gate of the Temple. Here he sees Jewish women weeping for Tammuz, their god (8:14). A history of the religion of Tammuz makes sordid reading indeed:
      (1) Satan's church began officially at the tower of Babel in Genesis 11:1-9, nearly twenty-four centuries B.C.

Here, in the fertile plain of Shinar, probably very close to the original Garden of Eden, the first spade of dirt was turned for the purpose of devil-worship.

(2) The first full-time minister of Satan was Nimrod, Noah's wicked and apostate grandson (Gen. 10:8-10).

(3) Secular history and tradition tell us that Nimrod married a woman who was as evil and demonic as himself. Her name was Semerimus. Knowing God's promise of a future Savior (Gen. 3:15), Semerimus brazenly claimed that Tammuz, her first son, fulfilled this prophecy.

(4) Semerimus thereupon instituted a religious system which made both her and her son the objects of divine worship. She herself became the first high priestess. Thus began the mother-child cult which later spread over the world.

(5) What was the teaching of Semerimus' satanic church?

(a) That Semerimus herself was the way to God. She actually adopted the title "queen of heaven."

(b) That she alone could administer salvation to the sinner through various sacraments, such as the sprinkling of holy water.

(c) That her son Tammuz was tragically slain by a wild boar during a hunting trip.

(d) That he was, however, resurrected from the dead forty days later. Thus, each year afterward the temple virgins of this cult would enter a forty-day fast as a memorial to Tammuz's death and resurrection.

(e) After the forty-day fast, a joyful feast called Ishtar took place. At this feast colored eggs were exchanged and eaten as a symbol of the resurrection. An evergreen tree was displayed and a yule log was burned. Finally hot cakes marked with the letter "T" (to remind everyone of Tammuz) were baked and eaten.

Jeremiah also spoke against this vile religion. (See Jer. 7:18; 44:25.)

e. Ezekiel continues his journey and views twenty-five men with their backs to the Temple, facing east and worshiping the sun (8:16). Again, Dr. Feinberg writes:

"Ezekiel saw the crowning insult to the Lord of heaven and earth. Twenty-five men in that hallowed place were worshiping the sun, the object of Persian idolatry. Moses had warned them against this ever present danger (Deut. 4:19) . . . The twenty-five men represent the twenty-four Levitical priestly courses with the high priest at their head. The apostasy of the laity and of the women has already been noted; now it is revealed in the ranks of the priesthood. Like priests, like people. Think of it! That which was intended best to manifest the glory of God in creation (Ps. 19), is perverted to detract from the glory of God . . . while they faced toward the sun in adoration, they turned their backs toward the temple of God. It was an attitude of defiance toward God and rejection of his worship. This was as complete a repudiation of the Lord as possible (see 2 Chron. 29:6), the cup of their iniquity had been filled to the brim." (The Prophecy of Ezekiel, p. 52)

f. As he stands there shocked by all this blasphemy, which literally surrounds him, he sees six heavenly beings appear, each one carrying a sword. They were led by another being dressed in linen clothing and carrying a writer's case (9:1, 2). This leader-angel may have been God's recording angel, and the writing case the Book of Life. (See Ex. 32:32; Ps. 69:28; 139:16; Isa. 4:3; Dan. 12:1; Phil. 4:3.)

g. The leader is commanded by God to walk through Jerusalem's streets and mark the forehead of those individuals whose hearts are grieved over Judah's sin (9:3, 4). Their sealing was for the purpose of insuring safety. (See also Rev. 7:1-3; Gal. 6:17; Rev. 13:16-18; 14:1; 2 Tim. 2:19.)

h. The sword-bearing angels are then commanded to follow this leader and slay all those unmarked individuals (9:5-11). They were to begin at the Temple. This is where God's judgment starts. (See 1 Pet. 4:17.)

i. Ezekiel prays over Jerusalem (as Abraham once did over Sodom. Compare Gen. 18:23-33 with Ezek. 9:8), but is told the situation is now beyond the praying stage (9:8-10).

j. The leaders of Judah have ignored all God's warnings and actually convinced themselves that those already taken captive (including Daniel and Ezekiel) were removed because of their sins (11:14, 15).

2. The departure of the glory of God from Judah.

a. Ezekiel views the glory cloud over the mercy seat (9:3).

b. It then stood over the door of the Temple (10:4).

c. From there it moved to the east gate (10:18, 19).

d. Finally it hovered over the Mount of Olives and disappeared (11:23).

From this point on, that terrible word Icha-bod could have been written across the Jerusalem skies —The glory of the Lord is departed from Israel. (See 1 Sam. 4:22.) But, from those blackened skies of despair and doom, comes a dazzling beam of hope, for the prophet hears the voice of God. (See 11:17-20.)

III. The Condemnation of the Enemies of God (25:1—32:32; 35:1-15).

  A. Ammon (25:1-7).

    1. The nation Ammon (occupying that area east of the Jordan and north of Moab) came from the incestuous relationship between Lot and his youngest daughter. (See Gen. 19:38.)

    2. Ammon had often displayed its hostility toward Judah. (See 2 Sam. 10; Amos 1:13-15.) It had joined the Babylonians against Judah about 600 B.C. (2 Ki. 24:2). Previous to this, it had seized the territory belonging to the tribe of Gad after the Assyrian captivity (Jer. 49:1).

    3. Ammon's chief sin, however, was the devilish glee it openly displayed over the destruction of the Jerusalem Temple, the slaughter and enslavement of Judah's citizens (Lam. 2:15).

    4. Because of this, God would allow various fierce Bedouin desert tribes to overrun her land. Their capital city, Rabbath (the present day Amman) would be turned into a pasture for camels.

  B. Moab (25:8-11).

    1. These people originated from Lot and his oldest daughter. Their child was named Moab (Gen. 19:37).

    2. Their main sin was in degrading Judah's Jehovah as just another national and tribal god.

    3. The same desert tribes which overran Ammon would also occupy the main Moabite cities.

  C. Edom (25:12-14; 35:1-15).

    1. This nation stemmed from Esau, the brother of Jacob (Gen. 25:33). Because of their common ancestry, Israel was not to fight with Edom en route to the Promised Land (Deut. 23:7). The Edomites settled that territory south of Moab from the Dead Sea to the Gulf of Aqaba.

    2. In spite of their common heritage, Edom was considered as Israel's most bitter enemy. (See Obad. 1:10; Mal. 1:2-5.)

    3. Their sins were manifold:

      a. They had rejoiced over Judah's fall (Ps. 137:7; Lam. 4:21, 22; Obad. 1:10-14). See also Ezekiel 35:15.

      b. They butchered helpless Jews during the Babylonian invasion (35:5).

      c. They planned to occupy the entire land of Palestine and drive the Lord God from it (35:10).

    4. God would punish them by allowing various nations to fill the land with unburied Edomite corpses (35:5-9).

  D. Philistia (25:15-17).

    1. If Edom topped Israel's enemy list, Philistia would certainly rank a close second. This hostile nation is mentioned in the Old Testament more than any other.

    2. They constantly harassed and oppressed Israel until the reign of King David. (See 1 Sam. 13-14.)

    3. Because of this long-standing hatred and persecution, God would execute terrible vengeance upon them (25:17).

  E. Tyre (26:1—28:19).

    1. The history of Tyre.

      a. Tyre was the ancient city of the Phoenicians, appearing for the first time in the Bible in Joshua 19:29. It was the greatest commercial city in Old Testament times. Tyre means "rock" and was the center of the Mediterranean world.

      b. According to both Ezekiel (26:13), and Isaiah (23:16), Tyre was a city of great music lovers and musicians.

      c. The city exerted great influence during the reigns of David and Solomon. Hiram, King of Tyre was a devoted friend of David (2 Sam. 5:11). He later helped both David and Solomon in their building operations, especially that of the Temple (1 Ki. 5:1-12; 1 Chron. 14:1; 2 Chron. 2:3, 11).

      d. Perhaps here it should be noted that Tyre was actually two cities, one on the coastline, some sixty miles northwest from Jerusalem, and the other on an island, a half mile out in the Mediterranean Sea.

      e. At the time of Ezekiel's prophecy, the Tyrians were in open revolt against Babylon.

    2. The sin of Tyre.

      a. Tyre had rejoiced over the fall of Judah (26:2). The reason was that this meant free passage for her trade caravans going from north to Egypt in the south. With Judah's demise, she need no longer pay an interstate tax.

      b. She had sold Jews as slaves to the Greeks and Edomites (Joel 3:4-8; Amos 1:9, 10).

        (1) The ruler at this time was Ithobal II, who boasted he was as strong as a god and wiser than a Daniel (28:2, 3). History of course is filled with others whose pride became their downfall. See especially the examples of Sennacherib (2 Ki. 18:33-35), Nebuchadnezzar (Dan. 3:15; 4:30), and Herod (Acts 12:21-23).

        (2) In his claim to be a god, the Tyrian ruler becomes a foreshadow of the future antichrist. (See 2 Thess. 2:4.)

      c. The city was totally corrupted with gross materialism (27:4-25).

    3. The punishment of Tyre.

      a. Various nations were to come up against Tyre like ocean waves (26:3).

        (1) The Assyrian king, Sennacherib, in 701-696 B.C. had taken part of the city on the mainland, but did not capture the island fortress.

(2) The Babylonian king, Nebuchad-nezzar, also tried to take both cities for thirteen years (585–573 b.c.), but like Sennacherib, failed to take the island.

b. In spite of this strong watery protection, Ezekiel predicted her walls would be torn down, her very soil would be scraped, making her as bare as a rock, and both cities would become a place for the spreading of fishing nets (26:4, 5).

Over 225 years passed without this prophecy being fulfilled. But in 332 b.c., Alexander the Great arrived upon the scene and the island city was doomed. He built a land bridge leading from the coastline to the island by throwing the debris of the old city into the water. In doing this, he literally scraped the coast-line clean. Some years ago an American archaeologist named Edward Robinson discovered forty or fifty marble columns beneath the water along the shores of an-cient Tyre. After a seven-month siege, Alexander took the island city and de-stroyed it. From this point on, the sur-rounding coastal area has been used by local fishermen to spread and dry their nets.

c. Ezekiel furthermore stated the city would never again be inhabited (26:20, 21). Tyre has never been rebuilt, in spite of the well-known nearby fresh water springs of Roselain, which yields some 10,000 gallons of water daily.

d. Many of her ships would be destroyed by fierce hurricanes (27:26, 27).

e. The entire known western world would lament and wail over her destruction (26:16–18; 27:28–36). In the tribulation, the world will do the same over the de-struction of Babylon. (See Rev. 18.)

4. The sinister force behind Tyre (28:11–19).

a. The identity of this force. We have al-ready noted that in 28:1–10 Ezekiel de-scribes the pride of Ithobal II, who was ruler of Tyre at that time. But the prophet now moves beyond the earthly scene and describes for us the creation and fall of a vile and vicious non-human angelic creature. This fearful being is Sa-tan himself, the real force behind the wickedness of Tyre. God often speaks to Satan through another indirect source. For example:

(1) He spoke to the devil through the serpent (Gen. 3:14, 15).

(2) He spoke to the devil through Si-mon Peter (Mt. 16:23).

b. The characteristics of this force.

(1) The perfection of wisdom and beauty (v. 12).
No human being is ever described in these terms, but rather the contrary! (See Rom. 3:23.)

(2) You were in Eden, the garden of God (v. 13).

Some have speculated that Ezekiel had Adam in mind here, but the Genesis account nowhere speaks of Adam's clothing being "bejeweled with every stone," and then fitted "in beautiful settings of finest gold."

(3) "The workmanship of thy tabrets and of thy pipes" (v. 13, as trans-lated by the KJV).
Here Dr. J. Dwight Pentecost writes: "Musical instruments were origi-nally designed to be means of praising and worshiping God. It was not necessary for Lucifer to learn to play a musical instru-ment in order to praise God. If you please, he had a built-in pipe organ, or, he was an organ. That's what the prophet meant when he said 'the workmanship of thy tabors and of thy pipes. . .' Lucifer, because of his beauty, did what a musical instrument would do in the hands of a skilled musician, bring forth a paean of praise to the glory of God. Lucifer didn't have to look for someone to play the organ so that he would sing the doxol-ogy—he was a doxology!" (*Your Adversary, the Devil*, p. 16)

(4) The anointed guardian cherub (v. 14).

(a) He was anointed—in the Old Testament, there were three anointed offices, that of the prophet, priest, and king. Here is a suggestion that Lucifer may have originally been created to function (under Christ) as heav-en's prophet-priest and king but he failed! This may be the reason why God separated these offices. (See 1 Sam. 13; 2 Chron. 26.)

(b) He was a guardian cherub—a cherub was a special kind of an-gelic being whose purpose was to protect God's holiness. (See Gen. 3; Ex. 25; 1 Ki. 6; Ezek. 1; Rev. 4.) Both archaeological and biblical evidences suggest they bore the likeness of a lion, calf, eagle, and man. Apparently Lu-cifer was created (among other purposes) to demonstrate the earthly work of Christ, as pic-tured by the four Gospel writ-ers.
Matthew—presents Christ as the lion-like king.
Mark—presents him as the calf-like servant.
Luke—presents him as the perfect man.
John—presents him as the eagle-like God.

(5) Your heart was filled with pride because of all your beauty (v. 17). Here is the first sin and the self-creation of the first sinner in all the universe.

F. Sidon (28:20–24).

1. Sidon was twenty miles north of Tyre and was founded by Canaan's firstborn (Gen. 10:15).
2. This city seemed to be the headquarters of the Baalite idolatry. The princess Jezebel, Scripture's most vicious woman, was a fanatical Baal-worshiper from Sidon. (See 1 Ki. 16:31–33.) In addition, Sidon was the center of Ashtaroth and Tammuz worship.
3. Because of her horrible influence, Sidon was likened to a pricking brier and a hurting thorn to the house of Israel.
4. God would thus punish Sidon by sending an epidemic of disease and an army to destroy her. This occurred in 351 B.C., at which time the city was put to the torch by the Persians.

G. Egypt (29:1—32:32).

1. Her historical punishment (by Nebuchadnezzar).

   a. Egypt's sin, like that of so many other nations, was pride (29:3).
   b. Pharaoh Hopha (the king referred to here in Ezek. 29) of the twenty-sixth dynasty had apparently convinced Judean King Zedekiah that Egypt could be of more help against Nebuchadnezzar than God himself (29:6). (See also 30:21–26.)
   c. Ezekiel, therefore, pronounces doom upon Pharaoh, people, and even the animals (29:8–12).
   d. In chapter 31 Egypt is described as a mighty cedar of Lebanon, towering above all other trees. The birds rested in its branches, and animals gave birth under its shade. But soon the tree was corrupted by pride and God ordered the Babylonian wood choppers to hew it down.

Ezekiel
THE DESOLATION OF THE CITY OF GOD

JERUSALEM (4-9, 11-24)

Twelve Symbolic Acts
Drawing a map of Jerusalem (**Ezekiel 4:1-3**)
Lying on his left side for a portion of 390 days (**4:4, 5**)
Lying on his right side for a portion of 40 days (**4:6**)
Preparing a scant meal (**4:9-17**)
Shaving his head and beard (**5:1-4**)
Stamping his feet and clapping his hands (**6:11**)
Digging through a wall (**12:1-16**)
Trembling as he ate his food (**12:17-20**)
Slashing about with a sword (**21:9-17**)
Drawing a map of the Middle East (**21:18**)
Boiling a pot of water dry (**24:1-14**)
Remaining tearless at his wife's funeral (**24:15-18**)

Six Parables
A fruitless vine tree (**15:1-8**)
The adopted girl who became a harlot (**16:1-63**)
The two eagles (**17:1-21**)
The tender twig (**17:22-24**)
The mother lioness and her cubs (**19:1-9**)
The two harlot sisters (**23:1-49**)

His Extended Temple Vision 8-11
He sees the departure of Judah from the glory of God.
He sees the departure of the glory of God from Judah.

Twelve Messages

6:1-14	14:13-23	21:1-7
7:1-27	18:1-32	22:1-16
13:1-23	20:1-44	22:17-22
14:1-12	20:45-49	22:23-31

NOTE: While in exile, Ezekiel warns his fellow captives that Jerusalem, already occupied by the Babylonians, will later be totally destroyed. He uses drama, parables, and sermons to emphasize this warning.

TYRE (26-28)

HISTORY	Was the greatest commercial city in Old Testament times
	The king of Tyre helped both David and Solomon during their reigns
LOCATION	Tyre was actually two cities, one on the Mediterranean, and the other nearly a mile out on an island
SIN	Pride and gross materialism
RULER	Ethbaal II (during Ezekiel's time)
PUNISHMENT	Both cities to be destroyed, never to be rebuilt
	Areas then to become bare, a place for the spreading of fishing nets
SINISTER FORCE BEHIND TYRE	Many believe God is actually condemning and describing Satan in 28:11-19
	He was the real power behind its sin

EGYPT (29-32)

To be desolate for forty years
To remain a minor kingdom
To never be sought out by Israel for help again
To be punished during the tribulation

e. Ezekiel informs us that Nebuchadnezzar conquered Egypt for its wealth in order to pay his soldiers after their long siege of Tyre (Ezek. 29:17-21).

f. Egypt was to be desolate for forty years (29:9, 11); the period when the Babylonians held sway over Egypt was about this length of time. Berosus, historian of Babylon, states that Nebuchadnezzar took great numbers of Egyptians into captivity after he occupied their land.

g. After the forty-year punishment period, Egypt would be restored somewhat, but would forever remain a minor kingdom (Ezek. 29:13-15).

h. Israel would never again depend upon Egypt (29:16).

2. Her future punishment (30:1-19).

a. Although the name Nebuchadnezzar appears once in this passage (v. 10), it is thought that the final fulfillment of the judgments mentioned here would transpire during the tribulation. Ezekiel indicates this when he uses the prophetical term "the day of the Lord" (see v. 3). This phrase almost always refers to the seven-year tribulation. (See Isa. 13:6, 9; Joel 1:15; 2:1, 11; 3:14; Amos 5:18; Obad. 1:15; Zeph. 1:7, 14; Zech. 14:1; 1 Thess. 5:2; 2 Thess. 2:2; 2 Pet. 3:10.)

b. According to Daniel 11:40-43, Egypt will indeed be destroyed during the tribulation.

c. At that time she will experience God's judgments. (See 30:4-17.)

To complete this section, it may be observed that Ezekiel's words in 32:17-21 have been characterized as the most solemn eulogy over a heathen people ever composed. In it he pictures Egypt slowly descending into the dark and fearful underworld of Sheol in the heart of the earth. She will then make her bed next to various other once-powerful, but now crumbling and decaying people, such as Assyria, Elam, the Hittites, Edom, and Sidon.

IV. The Presentation of the Shepherd of God—Jesus Christ (34).

A. The many false shepherds.

1. They fed themselves instead of the flock (34:2, 3).

2. They had not taken care of the weak, nor tended the sick, nor bound up the broken bones, nor sought the lost (34:4).

3. The sheep were then scattered, having no shepherd (34:5).

4. They had become prey to the wild animals (34:5).

5. Therefore, the shepherds would be punished (34:9).

a. Their positions as shepherds would be removed (34:10).

b. They would themselves not be fed by the Great Shepherd (34:9, 10).

c. They would be judged and destroyed (34:16).

B. The only true Shepherd. (See Ps. 23; Jn. 10:11; Heb. 13:20; 1 Pet. 5:4.)

1. He would search out the lost sheep (34:11).

2. He would deliver them from their enemies (34:12).

3. He would gather them from all nations (34:13).

4. He would feed them upon the mountains of Israel (34:14).

5. He would give them rest in green pastures (34:15).

6. He would put splints and bandages upon their broken limbs (34:16).

7. He would heal their sick (34:16).

8. He would establish David as his trusted undershepherd (34:23). (See also Ezek. 37:24; Jer. 30:9; Hos. 3:5.)

9. He would make an eternal pact with them (34:25).

10. He would guarantee their safety and place them in a perfect paradise (34:25-28).

V. The Restoration of the Nation of God—Israel (36-37).

A. The necessity of this restoration. Israel had previously been driven from Palestine because of her sin (36:17-19).

B. The reasons for this restoration.

1. To shame those Gentile nations which had sneered at Israel's tragedy (36:1-7).

2. To exonerate the great name of God (36:20-23, 32). The rumor was being spread around that the God of Israel was unable (or unwilling) to protect and purify his own people.

C. The vision of this restoration (37:1-14).

1. Ezekiel is commanded to prophesy over a valley filled with old dry human bones, scattered everywhere (37:1-6).

2. Suddenly there was a rattling noise from all across the valley and the bones of each body came together and attached to the other as they had once been (37:7).

3. After this, the muscles and flesh formed over the bones, and skin covered them (37:8).

4. But the completed bodies had no breath. Ezekiel was then commanded to:

"Prophesy unto the wind, prophesy, son of man, and say to the wind, thus saith the Lord God: Come from the four winds, O breath, and breathe upon these slain, that they may live. So I prophesied as he commanded me, and the breath came into them, and they lived, and stood up upon their feet, an exceedingly great army" (37:9, 10).

D. The symbol of this restoration (37:15-22).

1. Ezekiel was to carve the following words on two wooden sticks:

a. The first stick read: "For Judah, and for the children of Israel, his companions."

b. The second stick read: "For Joseph, the stick of Ephraim, and for all the house of Israel, his companions."

2. Dr. Charles Feinberg writes the following concerning these two sticks:

"The sticks are here equivalent to scepters, reminiscent of those in the days of

"The thief cometh not, but for to steal, and to kill, and to destroy: I am come that they might have life, and that they might have it more abundantly.

I am the good shepherd . . ."

JOHN 10:10, 11

**THE PRESENTATION OF THE
SHEPHERD OF GOD
—JESUS CHRIST (EZEK. 34)**

The Many False Shepherds

They fed themselves instead of the flock **(34:2, 3)**

They had not taken care of the weak, tended the sick, bound up the broken bones, nor sought the lost **(34:4)**

The sheep were then scattered, having no shepherd **(34:5)**

They had become prey to the wild animals **(34:5)**

Therefore, the shepherds would be punished **(34:9)**

Their positions as shepherds would be removed **(34:9)**

They would not themselves be fed by the Great Shepherd **(34:9, 10)**

They would be judged and destroyed **(34:16)**

The Only True Shepherd

He would search out the lost sheep **(34:11)**

He would deliver them from their enemies **(34:12)**

He would gather them from all nations **(34:13)**

He would feed them upon the mountains of Israel **(34:14)**

He would give them rest in green pastures **(34:15)**

He would put splints and bandages upon their broken limbs **(34:16)**

He would heal the sick **(34:16)**

He would establish David as his trusted undershepherd **(34:23)** (see also **Ezek. 37:24; Jer. 30:9; Hos. 3:5**)

He would make an eternal pact with them **(34:25)**

He would guarantee their safety and place them in a perfect paradise **(34:25-28)**

Moses (see Num. 17:1-2). 'Judah, and . . . his companions' (v. 16) showed that the southern kingdom included, in addition to Judah, the greater part of Benjamin and Simeon, the tribe of Levi, and godly Israelites who had come at different times from the northern kingdom with its idolatry and false priesthood into the kingdom of Judah (see 2 Chron. 11:12; 15:9; 30:11, 18; 31:1). In connection with the other stick, Joseph was mentioned. In all probability he was chosen because the house of Joseph, comprising the two powerful tribes of Ephraim and Manasseh, formed the main body of the northern kingdom." (*The Prophecy of Ezekiel*, p. 215)

THE RESTORATION OF THE NATION OF GOD

ISRAEL EZEKIEL 36, 37

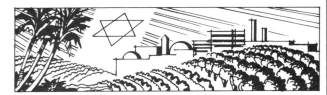

NECESSITY OF
Israel was out of the Promised Land because of sin **(36:17-19)**

REASONS FOR
To punish the foes of Israel **(36:1-7)**
To exonerate the name of God **(36:20-23)**

VISION EXPLAINING
Ezekiel speaks to a valley filled with dried Israeli bones **(37:1-6)**
The bones join together and are covered with flesh **(37:7, 8)**
He speaks again and the breath of life enters their bodies **(37:9-14)**

SYMBOL OF
Ezekiel carves the name Judah on one stick and Ephraim on another **(37:15, 16)**
He then holds both sticks in one hand, indicating God would someday reunite all twelve tribes **(37:17-20)**

RESULTS OF
Israel to once again become God's people **(36:28; 37:27)**
To be sprinkled with clear water **(36:25)**
To possess the indwelling Holy Spirit **(36:27)**
To be given new hearts **(36:26)**
To have a new Temple **(37:26, 28)**
To be ruled over by David **(37:24)**
To be justified among the nations **(36:30)**
To have abundant crops **(36:29; 30, 34, 35)**
To repopulate Jerusalem and other waste cities **(36:38)**
To occupy the Holy Land forever **(37:25)**

3. Ezekiel was then to hold both sticks together in one hand, indicating that God intended to reunite once again in Palestine the divided kingdoms of Israel (37:17-20).
E. The results of this restoration.
   1. To once again become God's people (36:28; 37:27).
   2. To be sprinkled by clear water (36:25, 29, 33). This, of course, is an allusion to the Mosaic rite of purification. (See Num. 19:17-19.)
   3. To possess the ministry of the indwelling Holy Spirit (36:27; 37:14). (See also Ezek. 39:29; Isa. 44:3; 59:21; Joel 2:28, 29; Acts 2:16-18.)
   4. To be given new hearts and right desires (36:26).
   5. To enjoy the blessings of the new Temple (37:26, 28).
   6. To be ruled over by David (37:24).
   7. To be justified among the nations (36:30).
   8. To have abundant crops (36:29, 30, 34, 35). (See also Isa. 35:1, 2; 55:13; Zech. 8:12.)
   9. To repopulate the cities of Israel, especially Jerusalem (36:38).
   10. To occupy the Holy Land forever (37:25).
VI. The Demonstration of the Wrath of God— Russia (38, 39).
   In these two remarkable chapters, Ezekiel describes for us an invasion into Palestine by a wicked nation north of Israel in the latter days.
   A. The identity of the invaders. Where is the land of Magog? It seems almost certain that these verses in Ezekiel refer to none other than that Red Communistic bear, the U.S.S.R. Note the following threefold proof of this.
      1. Geographical proof.
         Ezekiel tells us in three distinct passages (38:6, 15; 39:2) that this invading nation will come from the "uttermost part of the north" (as the original Hebrew renders it). A quick glance at any world map will show that only Russia can fulfill this description.
      2. Historical proof.
         The ancient Jewish historian Josephus (first century A.D.) assures us that the descendants of Magog (who was Japheth's son and Noah's grandson) migrated to an area north of Palestine. But even prior to Josephus, the famous Greek historian Herodotus (fifth century B.C.) writes that Meshech's descendants settled north of Palestine (Gen. 10:2).
      3. Linguistic proof.
         Dr. John Walvoord writes concerning this:
         "In Ezekiel 38, Gog is described as 'the prince of Rosh' (ASV). The Authorized Version expresses it as the 'chief prince.' The translation 'the prince of Rosh' is a more literal rendering of the Hebrew. 'Rosh' may be the root of the modern term 'Russia.' In the study of how ancient words come into modern language, it is quite common for the consonants to remain the same and the vowels to be changed. In the word 'Rosh,' if the vowel 'o' is changed to 'u' it becomes the root of the modern word 'Russia' with the suffix

added. In other words, the word itself seems to be an early form of the word from which the modern word 'Russia' comes. Gesenius, the famous lexicographer, gives the assurance that this is a proper identification, that is, that Rosh is an early form of the word from which we get Russia. The two terms 'Mesheck' and 'Tubal' also correspond to some prominent words in Russia. The term 'Mesheck' is similar to the modern name 'Moscow' and 'Tubal' is obviously similar to the name of one of the prominent Asiatic provinces of Russia, the province of Tobolsk. When this evidence is put together, it points to the conclusion that these terms are early references to portions of Russia; therefore the geographic argument is reinforced by the linguistic argument and supports the idea that this invading force comes from Russia." (*The Nations in Prophecy*, p. 107, 108)

B. The allies in the invasion.

Ezekiel lists five nations who will join Russia during her invasion. These are Persia, Ethiopia, Libya, Gomer, and Togarmah. These may (although there is some uncertainty) refer to the following present-day nations:

1. Persia—modern Iran
2. Ethiopia—black African nations (South Africa)
3. Libya—Arabic African nations (North Africa)
4. Gomer—East Germany
5. Togarmah—southern Russia and the Cossacks, or perhaps Turkey.

C. The reasons for the invasion.

1. To cash in on the riches of Palestine (Ezek. 38:11, 12). To control the Middle East. Ancient conquerors have always known that he who would control Europe, Asia, and Africa must first control the Middle East bridge which leads to these three continents.
2. To challenge the authority of the antichrist (Dan. 11:40-44).

D. The chronology of the invasion.

Here it is utterly impossible to be dogmatic. The following is therefore only a suggested possibility, based on Ezekiel 38 and Daniel 11:40-44.

1. Following a preconceived plan, Egypt attacks Palestine from the south (Dan. 11:40a).
2. Russia thereupon invades Israel from the north by both an amphibious and a land attack (Dan. 11:40b).
3. Russia does not stop in Israel, but continues southward and double-crosses her ally by occupying Egypt also (Dan. 11:42, 43).
4. While in Egypt, Russia hears some disturbing news coming from the East and North and hurriedly returns to Palestine. We are not told what the content of this news is. Several theories have been offered:
   a. That it contains the electrifying news that the antichrist has been assassinated, but has risen from the dead! (See Rev. 13:3.)
   b. That it concerns itself with the impending counterattack of the western leader (the antichrist).
   c. That it warns of a confrontation with China and India ("kings of the East"), who may be mobilizing their troops.

It should be noted at this point, however, that some Bible students identify the "he" of Daniel 11:42 as being the antichrist, and not the Russian ruler. If this is true, then the above chronology would have to be rearranged accordingly.

E. The destruction of the invaders.

Upon her return, Russia is soundly defeated upon the mountains of Israel. This smashing defeat is effected by the following events, caused by God himself:

1. A mighty earthquake (Ezek. 38:19, 20).
2. Mutiny among the Russian troops (Ezek. 38:21).
3. A plague among the troops (Ezek. 38:22).
4. Floods, great hailstones, fire, and brimstone (Ezek. 38:22; 39:6).

F. The results of the invasion.

1. Five-sixths (83 percent) of the Russian soldiers are destroyed (Ezek. 39:2).
2. The first grisly feast of God begins (Ezek. 39:4, 17, 18, 19, 20). A similar feast would seem to take place later, after the battle of Armageddon (Rev. 19:17, 18; Mt. 24:28).
3. The communistic threat will cease forever.
4. Seven months will be spent in burying the dead (Ezek. 39:11-15).
5. Seven years will be spent in burning the weapons of war (Ezek. 39:9, 10).

Dr. John Walvoord writes the following concerning this seven-year period:

"There are some . . . problems in the passage which merit study. A reference is made to bows and arrows, to shields and chariots, and to swords. These, of course, are antiquated weapons from the standpoint of modern warfare. The large use of horses is understandable, as Russia today uses horses a great deal in connection with their army. But why should they use armor, spears, bows and arrows? This certainly poses a problem. There have been two or more answers given. One of them is that Ezekiel is using language with which he was familiar—the weapons that were common in his day—to anticipate modern weapons. What he is saying is that when this army comes, it will be fully equipped with the weapons of war. Such an interpretation, too, has problems. We are told in the passage that they used the wooden shafts of the spears and the bow and arrows for kindling wood. If these are symbols, it would be difficult to burn symbols. However, even in modern warfare there is a good deal of wood used . . . A second solution is that the battle is preceded by a disarmament agreement between nations. If this were the case, it would be necessary to resort to primitive

THE DEMONSTRATION OF THE WRATH OF GOD

RUSSIA EZEKIEL 38, 39

1. IDENTITY OF THE INVADERS
- Geographical proof
- Historical proof
- Linguistic proof

2. ALLIES IN THE INVASION

PERSIA	Modern Iran
ETHIOPIA	South African Nations
LIBYA	North African Nations
GOMER	Eastern Europe
TOGARMAH	Turkey

3. REASONS FOR THE INVASION
- To cash in on the riches of Israel **(38:11, 12)**
- To challenge the authority of the antichrist **(DAN. 11:40-44)**

4. RESULTS OF THE INVASION
- Russia totally defeated by God **(38:21-23)**
- Five-sixths of the Russian troops destroyed on the mountains of Israel **(39:2)**
- Seven years to be spent in burning the war weapons **(38:9)**
- Seven months to be spent in burying the dead **(39:12)**

weapons easily and secretly made if a surprise attack were to be achieved. This would allow a literal interpretation of the passage. A third solution has also been suggested based on the premise that modern missile warfare will have developed in that day to a point where missiles will seek out any considerable amount of metal. Under these circumstances, it would be necessary to abandon the large use of metal weapons and substitute wood such as is indicated in the primitive weapons." (*The Nations in Prophecy*, pp. 115, 116)

VII. The Manifestation of the Glory of God—the Temple (40-48).
    A. Its biblical order.
       The millennial temple is the last of seven great scriptural temples. These are:
        1. the tabernacle of Moses—Exodus 40 (1500-1000 B.C.)
        2. the Temple of Solomon—1 Kings 5-8 (1000-586 B.C.)
        3. the Temple of Zerubbabel (rebuilt later by Herod)—Ezra 6; John 2 (516 B.C. TO A.D. 70)

        4. the Temple of the Body of Jesus—John 2:21 (4 B.C. to A.D. 30)
        5. the spiritual temple, the church—Acts 2; 1 Thess. 4 (from Pentecost till the rapture)
          a. the whole church (Eph. 2:21)
          b. the local church (1 Cor. 3:16, 17)
          c. the individual Christian (1 Cor. 6:19)
        6. the tribulational temple—Revelation 11 (from the rapture till Armageddon)
        7. the millennial temple—Ezekiel 40-48; Joel 3:18; Isaiah 2:3; 60:13; Daniel 9:24; Haggai 2:7, 9

    B. Its holy oblation.
       Palestine will be redistributed among the twelve tribes of Israel during the millennium. The land itself will be divided into three areas. Seven tribes will occupy the northern area and five the southern ground. Between these two areas there is a section called "the holy oblation," that is, that portion of ground which is set apart for the Lord. Dr. J. Dwight Pentecost quotes Merrill F. Unger on this:

       "The holy oblation would be a spacious square, thirty-four miles each way, containing about 1160 square miles. This area would be the center of all the interests of the divine government and worship as set up in the Millennial earth . . . The temple itself would be located in the middle of this square (the holy oblation) and not in the City of Jerusalem, upon a very high mountain, which will be miraculously made ready for that purpose when the temple is to be erected. (See Isa. 2:3; Micah 4:1-4; Ezek. 37:26.) (*Things to Come*, pp. 510, 514)

    C. Its dimensions (40:1—42:20; 46:21-24).
    D. Its purpose:
       1. To provide a dwelling place for the cloud of glory (43:1-17).
       2. To provide a center for the King of glory (43:7). (See also Isa. 2:2, 3; Micah 4:2.)
    E. Its priesthood (44:5-31).
       On four specific occasions, we are told that the sons of Zadok will be assigned the priestly duties (Ezek. 40:46; 43:19; 44:15; 48:11).
       Zadok was a high priest in David's time (the eleventh in descent from Aaron). His loyalty to the king was unwavering. Because of this, he was promised that his seed would have this glorious opportunity (1 Sam. 2:35; 1 Ki. 2:27, 35).
    F. Its prince (45:7, 8, 17; 46:1-20).
       In his description of the temple, Ezekiel refers to a mysterious "prince" some seventeen times. Whoever he is, he occupies a very important role in the temple itself, apparently holding an intermediary place between the people and the priesthood. We are sure that he is not Christ, since he prepares a sin offering for himself (Ezek. 45:22), and is married and has sons (Ezek. 46:16). Some suggest that the prince is from the seed of King David, and that he will be to David what the false prophet was to the antichrist.
    G. Its unique features.
       Several articles and objects present in the temples of Moses, Solomon, and Herod will be absent from the millennial temple.

1. There will be no veil. This was torn in two from top to bottom (Mt. 27:51) and will not reappear in this temple. Thus there will be no barrier to keep man from the glory of God.
2. There will be no table of shrewbread. This will not be needed, for the Living Bread himself will be present.
3. There will be no lampstands. These will not be needed either, since the Light of the World himself will personally shine forth.
4. There will be no Ark of the Covenant. This will also be unnecessary, since the Shekinah Glory himself will hover over all the world, as the glory cloud once did over the ark.
5. The east gate will be closed. Observe the words of Ezekiel: "This gate shall be shut, and no man shall enter in by it; because the Lord, the God of Israel, hath entered in by it; therefore, it shall be shut" (Ezek. 44:2).

   This gate, it has been suggested, will remain closed for the following reasons:
   a. This will be the gate by which the Lord Jesus Christ enters the temple. As a mark of honor to an eastern king, no person could enter the gate by which he entered.
   b. It was from the eastern gate that the glory of God departed for the last time in the Old Testament (Ezek. 10:18, 19). By sealing the gate, God reminds all those within that his glory will never again depart from his people.

H. Its sacrifices.

As we have already seen, several pieces of furniture in the Old Testament Temple will be missing in the millennial edifice. However, the brazen altar of sacrifice will again be present. There are at least four Old Testament prophecies which speak of animal sacrifices in the millennial temple: Isaiah 56:6, 7; 60:7; Zechariah 14:16-21; Jeremiah 33:18. But why the need of these animal blood sacrifices during the golden age of the millennium?

To answer this, one must attempt to project himself into this fabulous future period. Here is an age of no sin, sorrow, sufferings, sickness, Satan, or separation. During the millennium even the vocabulary will be different. For example, today respectable and decent society shuns certain filthy four-letter words, and well they should! This will doubtless also be practiced during the millennium. But how the words will change! Below is a sampling of some four-letter words to be shunned during the thousand-year reign: fear, pain, jail, hate, dope. These words are so much a part of our sinful society that it is utterly impossible to avoid or ignore them. The point is simply this: during the millennium millions of children will be born and reared by saved Israelite and Gentile parents who survived the tribulation. In spite of their perfect environment, however, these "kingdom kids" will need the new birth. As sons and daughters of Adam they, too, like all others, will require eternal salvation (Rom. 3:23; Jn. 3:3). But how can these children be reached? What object lessons can be used?

Here is a generation which will grow up without knowing fear, experiencing pain, witnessing hatred, taking dope, or seeing a jail.

This is one reason that the sacrificial system will be reinstituted during the millennium. These sacrifices will function as:
1. A reminder to all of the necessity of the new birth.
2. An object lesson of the costliness of salvation.
3. An example of the awfulness of sin.
4. An illustration of the holiness of God.
I. Its business office.
1. General business, such as standard weights and measurements, temple tax, etc. (45:9-16).

THE MANIFESTATION OF THE GLORY OF GOD

THE TEMPLE EZEKIEL 40-48
DISTRIBUTION OF THE LAND

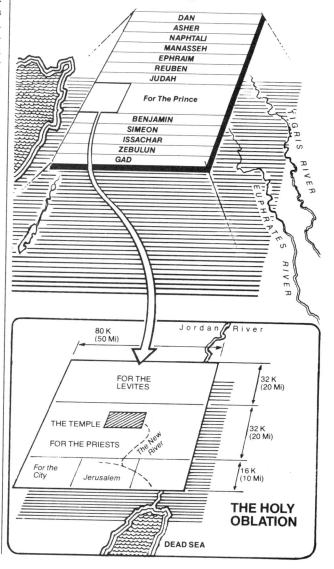

FACTS ON THE MILLENNIAL TEMPLE

●ITS BIBLICAL ORDER

1. The tabernacle of Moses **(Ex. 40)**
   Dates: 1444—1100 B.C.
2. The Temple of Solomon **(1 Ki. 6)**
   Dates: 959—586 B.C.
3. The Temple of Zerubbabel **(Ezra 6)**
   Note: This was later greatly enlarged by Herod. **(See Jn. 2.)**
   Dates: 516 B.C.—A.D. 70
4. The temple of Christ's body **(Jn. 2)**
   Dates: 4 B.C.—A.D. 30
5. The spiritual temple, the church **(Acts 2)**
   Dates: Pentecost—rapture
   - ● The whole church **(Eph. 2:21)**
   - ● The local church **(1 Cor. 3:16, 17)**
   - ● The individual believer **(1 Cor. 6:19)**
6. The tribulational temple **(Rev. 11)**
   Dates: Rapture—Armageddon
7. The millennial temple **(Ezek. 40-48)**
   Dates: Through the millennium

●ITS PURPOSE

1. To provide a place for the glory cloud of God **(Ezek. 43)**
2. To provide a center for the King of glory **(43:7)**

●ITS PRIESTHOOD

Those priests from the line of Zadok **(40:46)**

●ITS PRINCE

1. Definitely not Christ **(45:22; 46:16)**
2. Perhaps someone from the line of David.

●ITS UNIQUE FEATURES

1. No veil
2. No table of shewbread
3. No lampstands
4. No Ark of the Covenant
5. East gate to be closed **(44:2)**

●ITS SACRIFICES
(Isa. 56:7; 60:7; Jer. 33:18; Zech. 14:16-21)

1. As a *reminder* to all of the necessity of the new birth
2. As an *object lesson* of the costliness of salvation
3. As an *example* of the awfulness of sin
4. As an *illustration of the* holiness of God

●ITS RIVER
(47:1-12)

1. The *source:* proceeding from beneath the temple
2. The *course:* flows to Dead Sea and Mediterranean Sea
3. The *force:* waters to swim in

●ITS CITY

1. Circumference: six miles **(48:35)**
2. Name: the millennial Jerusalem will be named "Jehovah-Shammah," meaning, "the Lord is there" **(48:35)**

---

2. Specific affairs, such as land allotment (47:13—48:34). This total area land is about the size God promised Abraham. (See Gen. 15:18-21.)
   J. Its river (47:1-12).
   1. The source of the river—proceeding from beneath the temple (47:1).
   2. The course of the river—flowing eastward and then south through the desert and Jordan River to the Dead Sea where its sweet waters will purify that lifeless body of polluted water (47:2, 6, 12).
   3. The force of the river—at first it reached Ezekiel's ankles, then his knees, after this his waist, and finally he swam across its unknown depths (47:3-5).
   K. Its glory cloud (43:1-5).
   L. Its city.
   1. Jerusalem will become the worship center of the world and will occupy an elevated site (Zech. 14:10). (See also Isa. 2:2, 3.)
   2. The city will be six miles in circumference (Ezek. 48:35). In the time of Christ the city was about four miles.
   3. The city will be named "Jehovah-Shammah," meaning "The Lord is there" (Ezek. 48:35).

DANIEL (605-536 B.C.)

INTRODUCTION

1. Daniel was a teenager taken captive by Nebuchadnezzar during the first siege of Jerusalem in 605 B.C.
2. He was of royal blood.
3. While in captivity without the slightest compromise he faithfully served under the administration of three kings, Nebuchadnezzar, Belshazzar, and Darius.
4. He was himself ministered to by both of heaven's recorded archangels, Gabriel and Michael (9:21; 10:13).
5. He has more to say about the coming antichrist than any other Old Testament writer.
6. One of his contemporaries, Ezekiel, refers to:
   a. The righteousness of Daniel, comparing him with Noah and Job (Ezek. 14:14).
   b. The wisdom of Daniel (Ezek. 28:3).
7. Jesus quoted Daniel during his Mt. Olivet discourse (Mt. 24:15).
8. The unusual feature of his book is that Daniel wrote the central portion (2:4—7:28) in the Aramaic language.
9. He may be compared to Joseph, for both men had the gift of interpreting dreams. (Compare Gen. 37:5, 9; 40:8; 41:25 with Dan. 2:24; 4:19.)
10. His book marks the third of five great periods of miracles in the Bible. The periods are:

a. the time of Moses and Joshua
b. the time of Elijah and Elisha
c. the time of Daniel
d. the time of Christ and his disciples
e. the time of Peter and Paul
11. Daniel's life may be characterized by purpose, prayer, and prophecy.

I. A Divine Diet
  A. The resolution of Daniel (1:1-8).
    1. Nebuchadnezzar had selected some choice Hebrew youths to enroll in the special three-year B.D. course (Babylonian Development). Daniel and his three friends were a part of that student body (v. 4).
    2. These youths were assigned the best of the king's food and wine (1:5).
    3. Their brainwashing began when the superintendent changed their names (v. 7).
      a. *Hananiah* (the Lord is gracious) becomes *Shadrach* (illumined by the sun-god).
      b. *Mishael* (who is the Lord) becomes *Meshach* (who is Ishtar).
      c. *Azariah* (the Lord is my help) becomes *Abednego* (the slave of Nabu). Nabu was the Babylonian god of wisdom and education.
      d. *Daniel* (God is Judge) becomes *Belteshazzar* (Bel's prince). Bel was ruling god of the Babylonian pantheon, equivalent to Zeus or Jupiter.
    4. Daniel submits to his new name, but determines not to accept the king's menu (1:8). Three factors may have entered into his decision:
      a. The meat and wine had probably been sacrificed to false gods.
      b. The food may have been prohibited under Mosaic Law (Lev. 11:44-47).
      c. He may have previously taken the Nazarite vow (Num. 6:3).
    5. Satan doubtless attempted to get Daniel to rationalize through various ways. He may have considered:
      a. The king had ordered it, therefore it was a law.
      b. To disobey might bring severe punishment.
      c. It would probably spoil all chances of advancement.
      d. When in Rome (or Babylon), simply do as the natives do.
      e. He was a long way from home and no one would ever know.
      f. God had failed him anyway in permitting his capture.
  B. The recommendation of Daniel (1:8-14).
    1. Daniel seeks permission of the superintendent to eat other food instead. But in spite of his great affection for Daniel, the request is denied for fear of what Nebuchadnezzar might do.
    2. Daniel then proposes a test to the steward under the superintendent. He suggests a ten-day diet of only vegetables and water. At the end of this short time the steward could compare Daniel and his friends with the oth-

ers who ate the king's rich food (1:11-13). The terms of this test are granted.
  C. The rewards of Daniel (1:15-21).
    1. At the hand of God.
      a. Daniel and his friends look healthier and better nourished at the end of the ten-day period. This is the first of a number of miracles in the book of Daniel (1:15).
      b. Daniel and his friends are ten times smarter at the end of the three-year period. In addition to this, God imparts to Daniel the supernatural ability to understand dreams and visions, a gift he will greatly use (see Dan. 2:31; 4:19).
    2. At the hand of Nebuchadnezzar (1:21). This Babylonian king appoints Daniel to a political career which will span some seventy years under the reign of various Babylonian and Persian kings.

II. A Statue and a Stone.
  A. The frustration of the Babylonians (2:1-13).
    1. Nebuchadnezzar has a terrifying nightmare and calls in his entire cabinet to interpret his dream (2:1-3).
    2. The king is assured that if he will but relate the details of the dream, an interpretation will immediately be given (2:4). From this verse on through 7:28, the book of Daniel is written in Aramaic, the language spoken at Nebuchadnezzar's court. (Daniel wrote this section in Aramaic because it was a Gentile language and that part of his book deals with four great Gentile world powers.)
    3. Nebuchadnezzar refuses to tell them about his dream, and retorts: "the thing is gone from me" (v. 5). Here it should be noted that he is not telling them he has forgotten the dream, that it has gone from his mind, but rather that the command has gone from him and he wants action.
    4. He then issues his decree of punishment if they fail, but promises great rewards if they succeed (2:5, 6).
    5. The frightened cabinet admits its total inability to perform this, sadly concluding that: "There is no other that can show it before the king, except the gods, whose dwelling is not with flesh" (v. 11).
      Some six centuries later an amazing event transpiring in Bethlehem would gloriously and forever change all this (see Jn. 1:14; Gal. 4:4).
    6. Nebuchadnezzar, his face purple with rage, orders his entire State Department slaughtered for this shameful failure (2:12, 13). This, of course, included Daniel and his three friends who had only recently entered the Babylonian diplomatic service.
  B. The revelation of God (2:14-30).
    1. Daniel learns of this insane decree and immediately assures Arioch (head of the Babylonian F.B.I.) that the king's bloody order need not be carried out, for his dream will soon be revealed.
    2. Daniel then relates the same information to the king (2:14-16).
    3. He returns home and leads his three friends

in a prayer and praise service (2:17–23). We note here for the first time the phrase "the God of heaven," as found in 2:18. This expression is peculiar to the books of the captivity (see Neh. 1:4). Now that Jerusalem was destroyed and the Temple burned, God no longer dwelt between the cherubim. Ezekiel saw the departure of the Shekinah glory to heaven (see Ezek. 9:3; 10:4, 18; 11:23). He is now the God of heaven.

4. That very night God allows Daniel to see in a vision the same events Nebuchadnezzar had previously dreamed (2:19).

5. Daniel then offers praise to the God of heaven (2:21–23).

6. Daniel is ushered into Nebuchadnezzar's presence. Before he interprets the dream he makes it perfectly understood that:

"There is a God in heaven who revealeth secrets, and maketh known to the king . . . But as for me, this secret is not revealed to me for any wisdom that I have more than any living . . . " (2:28, 30).

C. The interpretation of Daniel (2:30–45).

1. A chronology of the dream (what did the king see?) (2:31–35).

   a. He saw a huge and powerful statue of a man. It was made up of various materials.

      (1) Its head was gold.

      (2) Its breast and arms were silver.

      (3) Its belly and thighs were brass.

      (4) Its legs were iron and its feet part iron and clay.

   b. This statue was then utterly pulverized into small powder by a special rock, supernaturally cut from a mountainside, which fell upon it.

   c. The rock then grew until it filled the entire earth (2:34, 35).

2. A theology of the dream (what did this all mean?) (2:36–45).

   a. The statue represented four Gentile world powers.

      (1) The golden head was Babylon.

      (2) The silver chest and arms were Persia.

      (3) The brass belly and thighs were Greece.

      (4) The iron legs and iron and clay feet were Rome.

   b. In the days of the final world power, the God of heaven would shatter all earthly kingdoms through his Rock (the Lord Jesus Christ) and set up an eternal kingdom (2:44, 45).

   c. The final Gentile power (Rome) will be revived during the tribulation and will consist of ten nations. This is implied, for the great prophecies concerning the fourth power were not fulfilled in the history of ancient Rome. The smiting Rock did not shatter those earthly kingdoms. On the contrary, he was put to death by the sentence of an officer of the fourth empire. During his Olivet discourse our Lord uttered the following words concerning Jerusalem. His message was both historical and prophetical in its scope. He proclaimed:

" . . . and Jerusalem shall be trodden down of the Gentiles until the times of the Gentiles be fulfilled" (Lk. 21:24).

Concerning this, Scofield observes:

"The 'times of the Gentiles' began with the captivity of Judah under Nebuchadnezzar (2 Chron. 36:1–21), since which time Jerusalem has been under Gentile overlordship." (*Scofield Bible*, p. 1106)

The same powers that Nebuchadnezzar dreamed about were later depicted in the prophecy of Daniel (7:1–27) as four wild animals.

   (1) Babylon was a winged lion.

   (2) Persia was a bear.

   (3) Greece was a winged leopard.

   (4) Rome was an indescribably brutal and vicious animal.

Thus God views man in a far different light than man views himself.

3. A summary of the dream (important dates in the history of the four kingdoms).

Babylon (key dates: 626–556 B.C.).

   a. The religious roots of Babylon were sown at the tower of Babel by Nimrod and his followers (Gen. 11:9).

   b. By 1830 B.C. the city began its rise to prominence.

   c. Hammurabi (1704–1662 .B.C.) would later make it world famous through his code of law.

   d. Babylon was controlled by the Assyrians from 900–722 B.C.

   e. Around 722 B.C. a Babylonian named Merodach-Baladan (mentioned in 2 Ki. 20:12 and Isa. 39:1) revolted against the Assyrians.

   f. In 626 B.C. another strong man named Nebopalassar founded the dynasty which was flourishing in Daniel's day.

   g. In 612 he finished off the remaining Assyrian threat near the city of Haran.

   i. In 605 B.C. he sent his world-famous son Nebuchadnezzar to do battle with the Egyptians at a place called Carchemish. The Babylonians emerged the masters of the world.

   j. Nebuchadnezzar (who reigned from 606–561 B.C.) was a vigorous and brilliant commander and the greatest man of his time in the non-Jewish world. He was a soldier, statesman, and architect. He married a Median princess named Amyhia and built for her the famous Hanging Gardens of Babylon, considered by the Greeks the seventh wonder of the ancient world.

   k. Nebuchadnezzar pursued the fleeing Egyptians as far west as Jerusalem. His first visit to Jerusalem was short, for he hurried home in 605 B.C. because of the sudden death of his father. But before he finished, he would lay siege to the Holy City on at least three occasions and ultimately burn it to the ground. These occasions were:

(1) 605 B.C. He occupies the city, allows Jehoiakim (Josiah's son) to rule as his puppet king, takes some of the Temple treasures, and key royal seed to Babylon. Among this group of teenagers were Daniel and his three friends (2 Chron. 36:6, 7; Dan. 1:1–3).

(2) 597 B.C. He comes again and takes the rest of the treasures to Babylon along with Ezekiel the prophet, King Jehoiachin (Jehoiachim's son), and 10,000 princes, officers, and chief men (2 Ki. 24:14–16).

(3) 586 B.C. He once more returns to punish the rebellion led by Zedekiah, Judah's last king. This time the walls are broken, the Temple destroyed, and the city burned. Zedekiah's sons are killed and he himself is blinded and carried into Babylon where he dies.

l. Nebuchadnezzar dies in 562 B.C.

m. Evil-merodach, his son, begins a short rule in 562 B.C. (2 Ki. 25:27). He released King Jehoiachin and treated him as a royal foreign guest.

n. In 556 an Assyrian nobleman named Nabonidus somehow managed to gain the throne. After a short while, however, he semi-retired and put up his young son Belshazzar as Babylonian co-regent.

o. Belshazzar ruled until the fateful night of October 13, 556 B.C., when the Medes and Persians entered Babylon and took the city (Dan. 5).

Persia (key dates: 539–331 B.C.).

a. Cyrus the Great founded the mighty Persian Empire in 559 B.C. He is mentioned often in the Old Testament (Ezra 1–5; Isa. 44:28; 45:1; Dan. 1:21; 6:28; 10:1).

b. In 546 he defeated King Croesus of Lydia, a ruler of fantastic wealth.

c. In 539 he took the city of Babylon and had Belshazzar executed.

d. Cyrus allowed the Jewish remnant to return a few years later.

e. He died in battle in 529 B.C.

f. He was then succeeded by his son Cambyses II (529–522) who conquered Egypt. Soon after this, he committed suicide. A civil war then began.

g. Darius the Great (522–486) succeeded Cambyses II and saved the crumbling empire by restoring law and order.

h. Darius was defeated by the Greeks during the great sea battle at Marathon in 490 B.C.

i. Xerxes (486–465), the son of Darius, then reigned. He was the King Ahasuerus of the book of Esther. Xerxes, like his fa-

ther, also suffered defeat by the Greeks in 480 at Salamis.

j. Artaxerxes I (465–423) was king during Nehemiah's palace service.

k. Darius III (335–331)—the Persian Empire was destroyed by Alexander the Great during his short reign.

Greece (key dates: 331–323 B.C.).

a. From 546–479 B.C. the Greek states were constantly threatened by Persian invasions. But all this ended after the victorious battles of Salamis and Platoea.

b. Shortly after these battles, Greece entered into its Golden Age, led by an Athenian democratic leader named Pericles (461–429 B.C.) A number of its citizens would become some of the most famous who ever lived.

(1) Herodotus (485–425), the father of history

(2) Hippocrates (460–370), the father of modern medicine

(3) Socrates (469–399), philosopher

(4) Plato (427–347), philosopher

(5) Aristotle (384–322), philosopher

(6) Demosthenes (385–322), one of history's greatest composers of oration

c. However, the Golden Era was short lived, for two of the leading Greek city states, Sparta and Athens, began fighting among themselves. Their three armed conflicts are known as the Peloponnesian wars (from 459–404 B.C.). Sparta came out ahead after these wars.

d. In 338 B.C. a man from Macedonia conquered Greece. He was assassinated two years later, in 336 B.C. His name was Philip of Macedon (380–336 B.C.).

e. Philip was succeeded by his son, Alexander the Great, who would soon become one of the world's most famous conquerors. He was twenty at the time. He immediately prepared to carry out his father's orders to invade Persia.

f. In 334 B.C. he crossed the Hellespont (which separated Asia Minor from the Middle East).

(1) He defeated the Persians at Granicus in 334 B.C.

(2) He routed them again at Issus in 333 B.C.

(3) He destroyed Tyre, spared Jerusalem, and was welcomed by Egypt. Here he founded the city of Alexandria.

(4) He forever crushed the Persians at Arbela in 331 B.C.

g. In 327 he invaded India. At this time he also laid plans to rebuild the city of Babylon to its former glory. But in India he died in 323 B.C. at the age of thirty-two.

h. His mighty empire was soon divided by his four generals.

(1) Ptolemy—who ruled Egypt. Cleopatra came from this line.

THE CAPTIVITY STAGE

Daniel, Ezekiel

1. The Divine Diet

Resolution:
Not to eat the king's food
Recommendation:
That a ten-day diet be conducted
Reward:
Daniel graduates ten times smarter

2. A Statue and a Stone

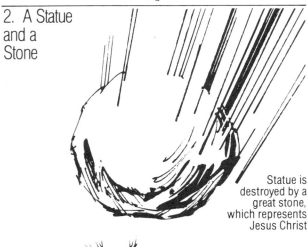

Statue is destroyed by a great stone, which represents Jesus Christ

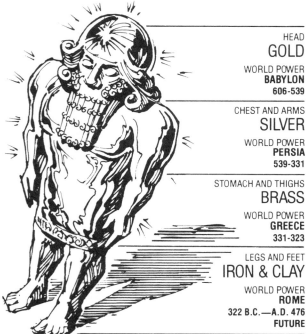

HEAD
GOLD
WORLD POWER
BABYLON
606-539

CHEST AND ARMS
SILVER
WORLD POWER
PERSIA
539-331

STOMACH AND THIGHS
BRASS
WORLD POWER
GREECE
331-323

LEGS AND FEET
IRON & CLAY
WORLD POWER
ROME
322 B.C.—A.D. 476
FUTURE

● The frustration of the Babylonians: the king's aides cannot interpret his dream and are sentenced to death.
● The revelation of the Lord: God reveals the dream to Daniel.
● The interpretation of the prophet: Daniel explains the dream.
● The prostration of the king: upon hearing their interpretation, Nebuchadnezzar falls down and worships Daniel.

In Daniel 7 the same four nations are described, but from a heavenly view, which looks upon them as four wild animals.

WORLD POWER	DESCRIPTION
Babylon	Lion
Persia	Bear
Greece	Leopard
Rome	Monster

(2) Seleucus—who took Syria. From here came the notorious Antiochus Epiphanes IV (176–163 B.C.)
(3) Cassander—who took Greece and Macedonia.
(4) Lysimachus—who ruled Asia minor.

Rome (key dates: 58 B.C. to A.D. 476).

a. The traditional date for the founding of Rome is April 21, 753 B.C. Cicero says the name came from its founder, Romulus. He ruled for thirty-nine years and then mysteriously disappeared, having been supposedly taken up into heaven.

b. By the year 338 B.C. Rome controlled central Italy.

c. Then came the historic Punic Wars between Rome and Carthage, with the latter being destroyed in 146 B.C.
(1) First war (264–241 B.C.)
(2) Second war (218–202 B.C.):
Hannibal appeared during this war. He terrified the Romans when he marched a herd of elephants over the Alps in 218 B.C. and defeated two large Roman armies. He also routed his enemy at Cannae in 216 B.C. Finally a Roman general named Scipio defeated Hannibal at Zama in 202 B.C. Rome then became the mistress of the Mediterranean.
(3) Third war (149–146): The city of Carthage was taken and burned.

d. Pompey, the famous Roman General, conquered Palestine in 63 B.C. This was followed by a period of civil wars and uncertainty.

e. The empire was then saved and consolidated by Julius Caesar during his famous Gallic wars (58–51 B.C.). On the Ides of March, 44 B.C., Caesar was assassinated in Rome.

f. The empire was then taken over by Octavius (also known as Augustus) Caesar. He defeated Brutus and Cassius (two of the rebels who murdered Julius Caesar) at Philippi in 42 B.C. In 31 B.C. Octavius defeated the forces of Antony and Cleopatra at Actium, and made Egypt into a Roman province. The Roman empire now entered its zenith of power and glory. It was during Octavius' rule that our Lord was born (Lk. 2:1). Octavius ruled from 31 B.C. to A.D. 14.

g. Octavius was succeeded by Tiberius Caesar (A.D. 14–37). The ministries of both John the Baptist and the Savior took place at this time.

h. Caligula (A.D. 37–41), also known as Little Boots. He became a ruthless maniac and was assassinated. Caligula was in power during the early part of the book of Acts.

i. Claudius (41–54) was poisoned by his own wife. Paul conducted his great missionary trips during his reign.

j. Nero (54–68)—after a normal eight-year reign Nero degenerated into an insane monster. He had Rome burned and murdered many Christians by falsely blaming them for the fire. Peter and Paul were martyred during his reign. In A.D. 68 Nero committed suicide.

k. The Roman General Vespasian (68–79) became ruler. He ordered his son Titus to destroy Jerusalem. This was done in A.D. 70.

l. Upon his death, Titus took the throne. He ruled from 79–81. During his rule Pompeii was destroyed by Mt. Vesuvius.

m. In 81 Domitian ascended into power. He banished John the apostle to the Isle of Patmos (Rev. 1:9).

n. The ten or more Roman emperors had one thing in common—they all hated Christians.

o. Finally in 284 Diocletian came into power. He is known as the last emperor to persecute believers, but also the most ruthless. Diocletian separated the Eastern empire from the Western and appointed a man named Maximian to rule the eastern part. In 305 he resigned.

p. When Diocletian left the throne two men immediately began contending for it. One was the son of Maximian, and the other was Constantine. The issue as to who would rule Rome was settled in 312 just outside the city at a place called Milvian Bridge. Here Constantine soundly defeated his rival to power.

q. In 313 Constantine issued the famous Edict of Toleration which in effect made Christianity his state religion. He also presided over the Council of Nicaea in 325.

r. Julian the apostate, the nephew of Constantine, became ruler after the death of his uncle. He attempted to replace Christianity but failed. His dying words on a battlefield in 363 were: "Oh Galilean, thou hast conquered at last!"

s. Theodosius the Great (378–395), a champion of Christianity, once more divided the empire into Eastern and Western sections (as Diocletian had previously done).

t. During the years of 450–455 Attila the Hun and the Vandals plundered Italy and Rome.

u. In 476 Romulus Augustulus, the last Roman Emperor, was dethroned.

D. The prostration of Nebuchadnezzar (2:46–49).
  1. The king bows down to Daniel and commands his people to offer sacrifices and burn sweet incense before him (2:46).
  2. He acknowledges the God of Daniel as being "God of gods" (2:47).
  3. He elevates Daniel to the highest office in Babylon, as chief magistrate in the king's court (2:48).
III. A Fiery Furnace.
  A. The king's command (3:1–7).
    1. Nebuchadnezzar constructs a golden statue ninety feet high and nine feet wide. This is set up in the Plain of Dura near Babylon.

3. A Fiery Furnace

The king's command: That all his leaders fall down and worship a ninety-foot golden image. Reasons for this:
1. To elevate his person
2. To consolidate his empire

The Hebrews stand: Shadrach, Meshach, and Abednego refuse to kneel and are thrown into the fiery furnace.

The Lord's own man: Christ himself joins the trio and delivers them out unhurt.

4. A Tree in Turmoil

The tree (Nebuchadnezzar) corrupted through vanity
1. Nebuchadnezzar relates his dream to Daniel
2. Daniel reveals the dream to Nebuchadnezzar

The tree (Nebuchadnezzar) corrected through insanity
1. The pride of Nebuchadnezzar
2. The punishment of Nebuchadnezzar
3. The praise from Nebuchadnezzar

5. The Heavenly Hand

The Ball **DANIEL 5:1**   The Call **DAN. 5:7-23**
The Gall **DAN. 5:2-4**   The Scrawl **DAN. 5:24-29**
                                 (writing)
The Wall **DAN. 5:5, 6**   The Fall **DAN. 5:30, 31**

6. The Lions and the Lion-Hearted

AN EVIL PLAN (6:1-9)
A plan is instigated by some jealous Chaldeans to trap Daniel by his daily prayer life.

A KNEELING MAN (6:10-20)
Daniel continues to pray and is cast into a den of hungry lions.

A HEAVENLY BAN (6:21-28)
Daniel is delivered by God's angel, who shuts the mouths of the lions.

There were several reasons behind this project.

 a. To elevate Nebuchadnezzar. Daniel had designated Nebuchadnezzar as the head of gold as he explained the meaning of his statue dream in chapter two. But the vain king wanted to be the whole thing! Bible teacher Bob Thieme writes the following:

 "Let us assume for a moment that the image was half as thick as it was wide, or four and a half feet. Using these three dimensions (90 $\times$ 9 $\times$ 4 $^1/_2$), we find the volume to be 3645 cubic feet or 4,400,000 pounds! Even at the pre-inflation price of $33 an ounce, this spectacular statue would have cost about $2,315,000,000! Not only does this give us an idea of the fantastic wealth of Nebuchadnezzar's empire, but it reveals the extent of his egomania." (*Daniel*, p. 3)

 b. To consolidate his empire through a common religion. This is the second of three great attempts of man to institute a one-world religion. The first occurred at the Tower of Babel (Gen. 11) and the last will take place in Jerusalem during the tribulation (Rev. 13).

2. The king then requires every VIP in all the empire to assemble in the Plain of Dura on a scheduled day (3:2).

3. When dedication day arrived, an orchestra was on hand (3:5).

4. At the sound of the music, all those assembled were commanded to fall down and worship the statue (3:4, 5).

5. Failure to comply would result in instant death by being thrown into a burning furnace. There is little doubt that the entire crowd could see this furnace and watch it belch forth its fierce yellow and orange flames high into the Babylonian sky. The Romans executed criminals through crucifixion, the Jews by stoning, and the Babylonians by burning. (See Jer. 29:22.) This doubtless was the most persuasive altar call of all times—bow or burn.

B. The Hebrews' stand (3:8–23).

1. Shadrach, Meshach, and Abednego remain standing during the "invitation." This was immediately reported to the king by some jealous petty Babylonian officials (3:8–12).

2. The three young men are brought to Nebuchadnezzar himself and offered a final chance to bow down. (Daniel apparently was not present at the dedication service. His duties as prime minister doubtless required him to travel extensively.) All three refuse, saying:

 "O Nebuchadnezzar, we are not careful to answer thee in this matter. If it be so, our God whom we serve, is able to deliver us from the burning fiery furnace, and he will deliver us out of thine hand, O king. But if not, be it known unto thee, O king,

that we will not serve thy gods, nor worship the golden image which thou hast set up" (3:16–18).

Especially noteworthy are the words "our God . . . is able." This phrase is often found in the New Testament. (See Heb. 7:25; 2:18; Jude 1:24; Eph. 3:20; 2 Tim. 1:12.) Their testimony was similar to that of Job. (See Job 13:15.)

The three youths were no doubt aware of the many excuses available to them for bowing down at this private meeting.

For example:

a. Why not join the system. You can't fight city hall!

b. We'll cooperate with old Neb and win him to Christ!

c. A living dog is better than a dead lion—better red than dead! "He who fights and runs away lives to fight another day!"

d. Daniel our leader is not here to make the right decision for us.

All these excuses *could* have been used. But they weren't, for Shadrach, Meshach, and Abednego had been brought up on the Ten Commandments of Moses. Especially burned in their minds was the second law:

 "Thou shalt not make unto thee any graven image . . . Thou shalt not bow down thyself to them, nor serve them . . ." (Ex. 20:4, 5).

3. In an insane rage Nebuchadnezzar (who has now totally lost control of himself) orders the furnace to be heated seven times hotter and the three Hebrew heroes bound and cast in (3:19–21).

4. The horrible decree is done, resulting in the deaths of those soldiers who are accidentally burned themselves while throwing the three men in (3:22).

5. All three are seen falling headlong into the hellish fires.

C. The Lord's own man (3:24–30).

1. Finally the furnace has cooled down somewhat and the angry monarch sees something that nearly shocks him senseless. In utter amazement he turns and asks his counselors.

 "Did not we cast three men, bound, into the midst of the fire?" (3:24).

Upon being immediately assured that this is indeed the case, the baffled Babylonian then exclaims:

 "Lo, I see four men loose, walking in the midst of the fire, and they have no hurt; and the form of the fourth is like the Son of God" (3:25).

Here we note the following:

a. He sees them walking. Thus the only thing the fire burned was their shackles, for they were all bound when thrown in.

b. He sees one like the Son of God, or literally, "One like a son of the gods." Nebuchadnezzar was unaware of the Trinity, but he was looking upon the Son of God himself, the Lord Jesus Christ.

IV. A Tree in Turmoil.
   A. The tree (Nebuchadnezzar) corrupted through vanity (4:1–27).
      1. Nebuchadnezzar relates his dream to Daniel (4:1–18)
         a. This chapter could rightly be entitled "Nebuchadnezzar's Tract," as it contains his personal testimony of those events which led him to repentance.
         b. The tree-dream of Nebuchadnezzar occurred probably during the thirtieth and thirty-fifth year of his reign. Daniel was around forty-eight at the time. Some twenty-eight years had elapsed since the fiery furnace event.
         c. "I thought it good" (v. 2), literally, "It was beautiful before me." The king wanted all to know what had happened. (See Isa. 52:7.)
         d. I . . . was at rest (v. 4). The Hebrew here is *raan*, and is an idiom for prosperity. It literally means, "to grow green, to be covered with leaves."
         e. It was during this peaceful time that he experienced this fearful dream. The main features are as follows:
            (1) He saw a large and leafy tree increasing in size until it reached the heavens and was viewed by all. The wild animals and birds were shaded and sheltered by its leafy branches and the entire world was fed from its generous fruit supply (4:10–12).
            (2) Suddenly a heavenly figure appeared and ordered the tree cut down and its fruit scattered. Only the stump was to be left, banded with a chain of iron and brass. This felled tree represented a man who would be given the mind of an animal and remain in this pitiful condition for seven years (4:13–16).
            (3) This all was to be done so the entire world might know that "the most High ruleth in the kingdom of men, and giveth it to whomsoever he will, and setteth up over it the basest of men" (4:17).
      2. Daniel reveals the dream to Nebuchadnezzar (4:19–27).
         a. The interpretation was so frightful that Daniel observed an hour of shocked silence (4:19).
         b. He then revealed the details:
            (1) The tree indeed stood for a man, and that man was Nebuchadnezzar. (Compare Dan. 4:22 with 2 Sam. 12:7.) Often in the Bible trees symbolize various things. A tree can represent a man (Ps. 1:3; Jer. 17:8; Isa. 56:3). It can represent Christendom (Mt. 13:31, 32). It can represent judgment (Deut. 21:23; Gal. 3:13; Heb. 12:2; 1 Pet. 2:24).
            (2) The heavenly visitor was a reconnaissance angel which pronounced judgment upon the tree. (Compare 4:23 with Mt. 3:10; Lk. 13:7.)
            (3) The destruction, however, was not to be total, for the tree was ordered banded about with iron and brass. In the ancient world this was done to keep the stump of a felled tree from splitting, thus making it possible for the tree to grow again. God still had a purpose for Nebuchadnezzar.
            (4) The king would nevertheless suffer a seven-year period of insanity for his pride. During this time he would act and think like a wild animal. This mental illness is not uncommon and is known as zoanthropy or lycanthropy. Often the victim pictures himself as a wolf. As has already been observed, this psychosis would last seven years. The word "times" (Dan. 4:25) is used for units of years both in Daniel (7:25; 12:7) and in Revelation (12:14).
            (5) This affliction would only end when Nebuchadnezzar realized "the powers that be are ordained of God." (Compare 4:25 with Rom. 13:1.)
         c. Daniel then begs the proud monarch to "break off thy sins," but all to no avail (4:27).
   B. The tree (Nebuchadnezzar) corrected through insanity (4:28–37).
      1. The pride of Nebuchadnezzar (4:28–30).
         a. Twelve months after the dream the king is strolling on the roof of the royal palace in Babylon. We note his arrogant boast.
            "Is not this great Babylon, that I have built for the house of the kingdom by the might of my power, and for the honor of my majesty?" (4:30).
         Certainly the ancient city of Babylon was all this, as the following description (taken from Lehman Strauss and others) will bear out:
         Babylon was founded by Nimrod, the great-grandson of Noah (Gen. 10:8–10). Surviving a series of conflicts, it became one of the most magnificent and luxurious cities in the known world. Superbly constructed, it spread over an area of fifteen square miles, the Euphrates River flowing diagonally across the city. The famous historian Herodotus said the city was surrounded by a wall 350 feet high and eighty-seven feet thick—extending thirty-five feet below the ground to prevent tunneling, and wide enough for six chariots to drive abreast.
         Around the top of the wall were 250 watchtowers placed in strategic locations. Outside the huge wall was a large ditch, or moat, which surrounded the city and was kept filled with water from the Euphrates River. The large ditch was meant to serve as an additional protection

against attacking enemies, for any attacking enemy would have to cross this body of water first before approaching the great wall. Within this wall were one hundred gates of brass. But in addition to being a bastion for protection, Babylon was a place of beauty. The famous hanging gardens of Babylon are on record yet today as one of the seven wonders of the world. Arranged in an area 400 feet square, and raised in perfectly cut terraces one above the other, they soared to a height of 350 feet. Viewers could make their way to the top by means of stairways, which were ten feet wide.

From a distance these hanging gardens presented an imposing sight. The tower itself sat on a base 300 feet in breadth and rose to a height of 300 feet. The great temple of Marduk, adjoining the Tower of Babel, was the most renowned sanctuary in all the Euphrates Valley. It contained a golden image of Bel and a golden table which together weighed not less than 50,000 pounds. At the top were golden images of Bel and Ishtar, two golden lions, a golden table forty feet long, fifteen feet wide, and a human figure of solid gold eighteen feet high. Babylon was literally a city of gold! (See Isa. 14:4.) The city had fifty-three temples and 180 altars to Ishtar.

2. The punishment of Nebuchadnezzar (4:31-33).
   a. Even while the king spoke his proud words, the judgment of God fell from heaven and he was driven from the palace (4:31).
   b. We note the sad results of his vanity:
      "He was driven from men, and did eat grass like oxen, and his body was wet with the dew of heaven, till his hairs were grown like eagles' feathers, and his nails like bird claws" (4:33).

      In spite of his helpless condition, he was not harmed during those years of insanity. This was doubtless due to the divine protection of God. In addition to this, it was considered bad luck in the ancient world to kill an insane person. Nebuchadnezzar's malady protected him from physical injury, just as David's feigned madness at Gath spared his life. (See 1 Sam. 21:10-15.)
   c. The king's insanity is corroborated by history. Josephus quotes from a Babylonian historian named Berasus who mentions a strange malady suffered by the king. There is also the testimony of Abydenus, the Greek historian of 268 B.C.

3. The praise of Nebuchadnezzar (4:34-37). Nebuchadnezzar humbles himself and receives the manifold blessings of God. Note these heavenly gifts.
   a. His reason returns ("my reason returned").
   b. His reign is returned ("the glory of my kingdom").
   c. His reputation is returned ("mine honor").
   d. His resplendence is returned ("mine . . . brightness").
   e. His rapport is returned ("my counselors sought unto me").
   f. His rhetoric is returned ("now I, Nebuchadnezzar praise, and extol, and honor").
   g. His redemption is accomplished. (Was Nebuchadnezzar a saved man? The three words praise, extol, and honor are active verbs, indicating continued action. In other words, Nebuchadnezzar continued praising and glorifying God long after his restoration. This would hardly be the action of a pagan.)

V. A Heavenly Hand.
   A. The ball (5:1).
      1. Belshazzar the king stages a huge dinner and drinking party and invites his top 1000 officers to attend. For many years the historical fact of Belshazzar's very existence was doubted by historians. According to the known records, the last king of Babylon was Nabonidus. But recent findings have definitely authenticated Belshazzar's reign over Babylon. Here are the findings of archaeologist Sir Herbert Rawlinson who confirmed Belshazzar's existence in A.D. 1854.
         a. Nebuchadnezzar's only son Amel-Marduk (also called Evil-Merodach in 2 Ki. 25:27; Jer. 52:31-34) succeeded him in 562 B.C.
         b. He was murdered by his brother-in-law Nergal-Sharezer (Jer. 39:3, 13) in August of 560 B.C.
         c. Nergal-Sharezer died and was succeeded by his young son Labashi-Marduk in 556 B.C.
         d. This boy was murdered shortly after his ascension by Nabonidus. Nabonidus married one of Nebuchadnezzar's daughters. Belshazzar was born of this union. Nabonidus, who ruled from 556-539 B.C., for some reason chose not to make Babylon his capital, but left that dazzling city and resided in Tema of Arabia. Belshazzar was thus made the co-regent of Babylon by his father. This fact is brought out several times in Daniel 5 when Belshazzar offers to elevate Daniel to third ruler in the kingdom (see 5:7, 16, 29).
      2. His feast was ill-timed, to say the least, for Babylon had been under attack by the Medes and Persians for some time. Perhaps the feast was to build morale.
   B. The gall (5:2-4).
      1. Belshazzar sits at his table, drunk, depraved, and demon-possessed. Suddenly he is seized with a wild and wicked idea. He is reminded of the gold and silver cups taken by his grandfather Nebuchadnezzar from the Jerusalem Temple. He orders them brought to

the feast and proposes to his guests that they drink wine from them and praise the Babylonian gods.

2. These sacred vessels were originally made by Solomon (1 Ki. 7:48–51), shown by Hezekiah (2 Ki. 20:13), and taken by Nebuchadnezzar (2 Chron. 36:10).

C. The wall (5:5, 6).

1. Suddenly in the midst of this drunken toast, they see the fingers of a man's hand writing on the wall next to the king's table. Belshazzar is terrified! We are told: "Then the king's countenance was changed" (5:6). This is, literally, "his brightness changed." In other words he immediately turned from a drunken pink to a frightened white!

2. Belshazzar "cried aloud" (literally, "in great earnest") for some kind of help, but it was already too late. He would soon experience the fearful warning of Proverbs 1:24–27. Some ten centuries before this a group of Egyptian magicians had testified concerning this heavenly hand in connection with the terrible plagues which had befallen them.

We read:

"Then the magicians said unto Pharaoh, this is the finger of God!" (Ex. 8:19).

D. The call (5:7–23).

1. In his hour of great need, Belshazzar turns to astrology. How little human nature has changed. The United States alone has over fifteen million serious students of astrology.

2. But Belshazzar soon discovers that astrology is no balm in Gilead. No horoscope ever written can heal the hurt in the human heart. His wise men could not help him. This marks their third failure in the book of Daniel.

3. Finally at the suggestion of the queen (probably his mother, Nitocris) Belshazzar summons Daniel (5:10–15).

4. The king offers him the third ruling position if he will interpret the mysterious writing (5:16).

5. Daniel agrees to do so, but spurns the king's bribe. However, before he interprets the message, the aged prophet reviews Belshazzar's wicked past.

a. Belshazzar's grandfather, Nebuchadnezzar, had set a good example for his young grandson when he turned to God after his period of insanity (5:18–21).

b. Belshazzar knew all this, but had deliberately rejected and hardened his heart (5:22, 23). (See also Prov. 29:1.)

c. Belshazzar was thus gambling with his immortal soul, for the very air he breathed came from this God he had so recklessly spurned (5:23).

E. The scrawl (scroll) 5:24–29.

1. The writing contained a threefold message from God to Belshazzar.

a. "Mene, Mene"—God has numbered your kingdom and finished it! His number was up. Belshazzar had not followed the wise advice of Moses when he prayed: "So teach us to number our days, that we may apply our hearts unto wisdom" (Ps. 90:12). Belshazzar's sad end here should be contrasted to Paul's thrilling testimony before his death. (See 2 Tim. 4.)

b. "Tekel"—You are weighed in the balances, and found wanting. Again, by way of contrast, see David's testimony in Psalm 23:1. The words "found wanting" mean literally "found too light." Belshazzar's morality didn't weigh enough!

c. "Peres" ("Upharsin" is the plural of this word)—your kingdom is divided and given to the Medes and Persians.

F. The fall (5:30, 31).

1. The Greek historian Herodotus tells us that the Babylonian armies at first moved north to challenge the advancing Persian troops, but were soon driven back behind the walls of Babylon. Cyrus then proceeded to divert the Euphrates River from its normal bed, under the walls of the city, channeling the waters to a nearby reservoir he had dug. Another Greek historian, Xenophon, states that entrance was made into the city at a time when the Babylonians were feasting at a drunken orgy.

2. Belshazzar is slain that very night and the city is ruled by a sixty-two-year-old Mede named Darius.

3. The prophet Isaiah predicted the fall of Babylon over two hundred years in advance. (See Isa. 21:1–10.)

VI. The Lions and the Lion-hearted.

A. An evil plan (6:1–9).

1. Darius, the Mede, immediately sets about to reorganize and consolidate his fantastic new kingdom called Babylon. He divides the kingdom into 129 provinces, each under a governor. These governors are accountable to three presidents, with Daniel being one of the three. There has been some historical question raised concerning the identity of Darius. Three main explanations have been offered:

a. That he was really Cyrus under a different name.

b. That he was Cambyses, the son of Cyrus.

c. That he was a special "presidential assistant" named Gubaru, who was appointed by the great Persian king, Cyrus, to rule over this city for him. The third view seems the most logical one.

2. Daniel, now over eighty, was still blessed with so much skill and ability that Darius was considering elevating him over the other two presidents (6:3).

3. This so infuriated both the presidents and the governors that they plotted to take away his life (6:4).

4. Being unable to see the slightest flaw in his secular life, they determine to trap him in his religious life (6:5).

5. Darius is tricked into signing a thirty-day decree which says that all praying during that time is to be directed to the king himself (6:6–9).

B. A kneeling man (6:10–20).

1. Daniel learns of this and doubtless immediately sees through its clumsy effort to trap him. But the old warrior continues worshiping God as before. We note:

   a. He kept his windows opened. To close them would have been cowardly. To open them (had this not been his custom) would have been foolhardy.

   b. He continued praying three times a day, in the morning, at noon, and in the evening.

   c. He knelt down. This is perhaps the most common prayer posture depicted in the Bible.

   d. He faced Jerusalem. Solomon had given this procedure in his dedicatory prayer of the Temple. (See 1 Ki. 8:44–48; 2 Chron. 6:36–39.)

2. Those vicious hunters who had set their trap now see the prey inside and gleefully rush to Darius to deliver the death blow. Darius realizes he has been had and desperately seeks to find a loophole in the immutable law of the Medes and Persians, but all to no avail (6:11–15).

3. Daniel is arrested and thrown down into a den of hungry man-eating lions. In the Bible the devil is often likened to a lion. (See Ps. 10:9; 57:4; 2 Tim. 4:17; 1 Pet. 5:8; Dan. 6:16.)

4. After sealing the mouth of the den with his own signet ring, Darius returns and spends a sleepless and miserable night in the royal palace (6:17, 18).

5. At daybreak the next morning he rushes to the den, orders the cap stone removed, and calls out in anguish:

   "O Daniel, servant of the living God, is thy God, whom thou servest continually, able to deliver thee from the lions?" (6:20).

C. A heavenly ban (6:21–28).

1. Out of the blackness of that den of doom there comes a cheerful and clear voice:

   "O king, live for ever. My God hath sent his angel, and hath shut the lions' mouths, that they have not hurt me; forasmuch as before him innocency was found in me; and also before thee, O king, have I done no hurt" (6:21, 22).

   Peter and Paul doubtless had this thrilling event in mind when they later wrote:

   "Who, through faith, subdued kingdoms, wrought righteousness, obtained promises, stopped the mouths of lions" (Heb. 11:33).

   "Wherefore, let them that suffer according to the will of God commit the keeping of their souls to him in well-doing, as unto a faithful Creator" (1 Pet. 4:19).

   That same heavenly messenger who had saved Daniel's three friends in the furnace now protected the prophet in the den.

2. The king's reaction to all this was twofold; he was both glad and mad!

   a. He rejoiced at the salvation of Daniel and issued a decree ordering all the citizens of his kingdom to consider this almighty Judean God (6:23, 25–27).

   b. He took immediate vengeance upon those who had tricked him in the first place and ordered them along with all their families thrown into this same den. Their bodies were instantly torn apart by the lions (6:24). Persian law was much more cruel than Hebrew law. (See Ezek. 18:20; Deut. 24:16; 2 Ki. 14:6; 2 Chron. 25:4; Jer. 31:29, 30.)

VII. Godless Kingdoms and the Kingdom of God.

A. Nebuchadnezzar, the Babylonian lion (7:4)—also the head of gold in 2:32.

1. In this vision Daniel sees the same four godless kingdoms and the final kingdom of God that Nebuchadnezzar had dreamed of in chapter 2. But he sees it from an entirely different viewpoint. As has already been brought out, man may see his kingdoms as gleaming metals such as gold and silver, but God looks upon them as wild and ravenous beasts.

2. Daniel sees a great storm on a mighty ocean with four winds blowing from every direction. (See Rev. 7:2; Eph. 2:2; 6:12.) These winds may indicate satanic forces.

3. The first beast symbolized Nebuchadnezzar and Babylon.

   a. It was like a lion. (See Jer. 4:7; 49:19; 50:17, 43, 44.)

   b. It had eagle's wings. (See Jer. 48:40; 49:22; Lam. 4:19; Ezek. 17:3; Hab. 1:8.) Nebuchadnezzar showed these wings at the Battle of Carchemish in 605 B.C.

   c. Those wings were plucked. See Daniel 4:33 (Nebuchadnezzar's wings), and Daniel 5:31 (Babylon's wings).

B. Cyrus, the Persian bear (7:5)—also the silver breast and arms in 2:32.

1. This bear raised itself up on one side, probably referring to the stronger Persian part of the Mede and Persian dual alliance.

2. It had three ribs in its mouth, a reference to Babylon, Egypt, and Lydia, three nations Persia had just conquered.

3. It would devour much flesh. The Persian King Xerxes led a force of over one and one half million men and 300 ships into Greece alone.

C. Alexander, the Grecian leopard (7:6)—also the bronze stomach and thighs of 2:32.

1. It was like a leopard. Alexander traveled faster and conquered more land than any other man in all recorded history.

2. It had four heads. After his untimely death at 32, his kingdom fell to four of his generals.

D. Little horn, the Roman monster (7:7, 8)—also the iron legs and clay and iron feet of 2:33.

1. In A.D. 476 this monster "retired" to its den for awhile to hibernate.

2. It will awaken in the form of ten nations during the tribulation by the little horn, who is none other than the antichrist! He is called

the man of sin in 2 Thessalonians 2:3, 4 and the sea beast in Revelation 13:1.

   3. The antichrist will defeat three of these ten kingdoms (horn) in his rise to power (7:8).

   4. He will have a universal rule during the final three-and-a-half years of the tribulation (7:25). (See also Rev. 13:5; Mt. 24:21.)

   5. He will shed blood upon his earth in an unprecedented manner (7:7, 19).

   6. He will wear out the saints of God (Israel) (7:25). (See also Rev. 12:13.)

   7. He will attempt to change seasons and laws (7:25).

   8. He will blaspheme God (7:25). (See also Rev. 13:5, 6.)

   9. He will be defeated at the coming of Christ and his body given over to the flames of hell (7:11).

E. Jesus Christ, the King of kings (7:13, 14)—also the smiting Stone of 2:34.

   1. He comes in the clouds to claim his rightful earthly inheritance (7:13). Our Lord warned Israel's wicked high priest of this very coming during the unfair trial that led him to Calvary. (See Mk. 14:61, 62.)

   2. He is given his universal and eternal throne by his Father, the Ancient of Days (7:9, 13, 14). This is the only description of the Father in the Bible, and corresponds to John's description of Jesus in Revelation 1:9–18. Both David (Ps. 2:6–9) and the angel Gabriel (Lk. 1:32) predict this throne Christ receives from his Father.

   3. Daniel sees a continuous river of fire gushing from the throne (7:10). This stream of judgment (Heb. 12:29; Isa. 66:15, 16; 2 Thess. 1:8) will later turn into a fountain of blessing after the Great White Throne Judgment is completed. (See Rev. 22:1.)

   4. Millions of angels stand and minister to the Ancient of Days and his Son (7:10). (A similar immense number of angels is mentioned in Rev. 5:11; Ps. 68:17; Heb. 12:22.)

   5. Hundreds of millions stand before him ready to be judged and the books are opened (7:10). (See also Rev. 20:11–15.)

VIII. The Horns of the Heathen.

A. A two-horned ram (Persia, as represented by Darius III) (8:1–4).

   1. In this vision Daniel sees himself in the fortress of Shushan (or Susa), a city some 230 miles east of Babylon and 120 miles north of the Persian Gulf.

   2. He sees a victorious ram, coming from the east, and pushing its way westward, northward, and to the south. This, of course, represented the Persian conquests which included Syria (west), Armenia (north), and Egypt (south). Marcellinus, a fourth-century historian, states that the Persian ruler bore the head of a ram as he stood in front of his army.

B. A one-horned goat (Greece, as represented by Alexander the Great) (8:5–8).

   1. Daniel then sees a goat from the west which rushes toward the ram, smashes it to the ground, and stomps it to pieces.

7. Godless Kingdoms and the Kingdom of God

"And four great beasts came up from the sea . . ." (7:3)

"Behold, one like the Son of man came with the clouds . . ." (7:13)

KINGDOM	SYMBOL	REPRESENTATIVE
BABYLON 7:4 (2:37, 38)	A LION	Nebuchadnezzar
PERSIA 7:5 (2:39)	A BEAR	Cyrus
GREECE 7:6 (2:39)	A LEOPARD	Alexander the Great
ROME 7:7, 8 (2:40-43)	A ONE-HORNED MONSTER WITH TERRIBLE TEETH	HISTORICAL: Roman Caesars PROPHETICAL: Antichrist
EVERLASTING KINGDOM 7:9-14 (2:44, 45)	THE SON OF MAN	The Lord Jesus Christ

   2. This prophecy of the ram and goat places a microscope down on the conflict between the second and third world empire in the struggle of East and West, of Orient and Occident, of Asia and Europe. Historical drawings have been discovered which depict a one-horned goat as the symbol for the ancient Greek armies.

   3. We are told the goat was "moved with choler" against the ram. The driving energy and holy crusade of Alexander was to crush the hated Persian who had invaded Greece. As we have previously seen, he totally routed the Persians on three separate occasions:

    a. at Granicus, in 334 B.C.

    b. at Issus, in 333 B.C.

    c. at Arbela, in 331 B.C.

An interesting footnote of history may be added here. Josephus tells us that Alexander was met outside Jerusalem by Juddua, Israel's high priest, who came dressed in all his magnificent apparel, and showed the Greek conqueror how a Hebrew prophet, Daniel by name, had predicted his defeat over the Persians some 225 years ago. The high priest then proceeded to read Daniel 8, whereupon Alexander fell down and worshiped him.

   4. Daniel sees this powerful horn suddenly broken and its might divided fourfold. Alexander died in Babylon during a drunken orgy at the age of thirty-two, in 323 B.C. His kingdom was then divided among his four leading generals.

a. Ptolemy took the southern part, Egypt
b. Seleucus, the eastern section, Syria
c. Cassander, the western division, Greece
d. Lysimachus, the northern area, Asia Minor

C. Two little-horned kings (Syria and the revived Roman Empire and represented by Antiochus Epiphanes and the antichrist) 8:9-27. We note that the archangel Gabriel interpreted all this to Daniel. This is the first mention of him in the Bible. (See also 9:21; Lk. 1:19, 26.)

1. The historical little horn—Antiochus Epiphanes.
   a. He was a Syrian.
   b. He came to the throne in 175 B.C. and ruled until 164 B.C.
   c. He was anti-Semitic to the core. He assaulted Jerusalem, murdering over 40,000 in three days, and selling an equal number into cruel slavery. It is thought that on September 6, 171 B.C., he began his evil actions toward the Temple.
   d. On December 15, 168, his Temple desecration reached its ultimate low, for on that day this idolater sacrificed a giant sow on an idol altar he had made in the Jewish Temple. He then forced the priests to swallow its flesh, made a broth of it, and sprinkled all the Temple. He finally carried off the golden candlesticks, table of shrewbread, altar of incense, various other vessels, and destroyed the sacred books of the Law. A large image of Jupiter was placed in the Holy of Holies. All this was termed by the horrified Jews as "the abomination of desolation," and is referred to by Jesus in Matthew 24:15 as a springboard to describe the activities of the future antichrist.
   e. All through Palestine altars to Jupiter were set up and the Jews were forced to sacrifice on them. But at a little Jewish town called Modin (seventeen miles northwest of Jerusalem) there lived a Jewish priest named Mattathias, of the House of Hasmon. He had five sons and this brave old man not only refused to worship Antiochus' idols, but boldly slew the king's religious ambassador. The Jewish revolt was on. One of his sons was named Judas and he was called the Maccabee (meaning, the hammer).

   For the next few years Judas successfully led an army of Jews against the Syrians. Their brave exploits are described in two Apocrypha books, first and second Maccabees. On December 25, 165 B.C., the Jewish patriots cleansed and rededicated the Temple Antiochus had defiled. This later became a Jewish holiday known as the Feast of Dedication (see Jn. 10:22).

   Note: In 8:14 there is a time period of 2300 days mentioned. This apparently began on September 6, 171 B.C. and ended on December 25, 165 B.C. It was, however, on the basis of this period that William Miller, founder of the modern Seventh Day Adventist movement, went astray. He made the days stand for years and arrived at the date of October 22, 1844, for the return of Christ!
   f. Antiochus died in Babylon in 164 B.C. after being soundly defeated in battle.

2. The prophetical little horn—the antichrist. The future enemy of Israel will do all his forerunner did and much more. The following comparisons can be seen between the two:
   a. Both would conquer much (Dan. 8:9; Rev. 13:4).
   b. Both would magnify themselves (Dan. 8:11; Rev. 13:15).

---

8. The Horns of the Heathen

KINGDOM	SYMBOL	REPRESENTATIVE
MEDES AND PERSIANS	A TWO-HORNED RAM 8:1-4, 20	Darius III
GREECE	A ONE-HORNED GOAT 8:5-8, 21, 22	Alexander
PAST		
SYRIA	TWO LITTLE HORNED KINGS 8:9-20, 23-27	Antiochus Epiphanes
FUTURE		
REVIVED ROMAN EMPIRE		Antichrist

Darius III and Alexander

Some 250 years in advance, Daniel predicts the resounding defeat of Darius III at the hands of Alexander in 332 B.C.

At Alexander's death (age 32) his kingdom was divided by his four generals.

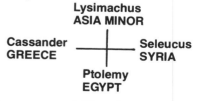

Both to conquer much (**Dan. 8:9; Rev. 13:4**)
Both to magnify themselves (**8:11; Rev. 13:15**)
Both deceitful (**8:25; 2 Thess. 2:10**)
Both offer a false peace program (**8:25; 1 Thess. 5:2**)
Both hate and persecute Israel (**8:25; Rev. 12:13**)
Both profane the Temple (**8:11; Mt. 24:15**)
Both energized by Satan (**8:24; Rev. 13:2**)
Both active in Middle East for seven years (**8:14; 9:27**)
Both to speak against God (**8:25; 2 Thess. 2:4**)
Both to be destroyed by God (**8:25; Rev. 19:19, 20**)

c. Both would be masters of deceit (Dan. 7:25; 2 Thess. 2:10).

d. Both would offer a false "peace program" (Dan. 8:25; 1 Thess. 5:2, 3).

e. Both would hate and persecute Israel (Dan. 8:25; Rev. 12:13).

f. Both would profane the Temple (Dan. 8:11; Mt. 24:15).

g. Both would be energized by Satan (Dan. 8:24; Rev. 13:2).

h. Both would be active in the Middle East for about seven years (Dan. 8:14; 9:27).

i. Both would speak against the Lord God (Dan. 8:25).

j. Both would be utterly destroyed by God (Dan. 8:25) (Rev. 19:19, 20).

IX. The Secret of the Seventy Sevens

A. Daniel—the prayer of a prophet (9:1-19).

1. This is one of the greatest chapters in all the Bible. It has a double theme, that of prayer and prophecy. At this time Daniel was about eighty-five.

2. Daniel was reading from the book of Jeremiah (the old prophet had probably become the official custodian of various Old Testament books after the destruction of the Temple) and was reminded that God had determined Jerusalem must lie desolate for seventy years. (See Jer. 25:11; 29:10.)

3. He then began an intense and prolonged prayer to God, concerning both his personal sins and those national sins of Israel which had caused the captivity in the first place. His prayer was accompanied by fasting, sackcloth, and ashes (9:1-3). These three actions were customary for the day when genuine contriteness of heart was felt. (See Ezra 8:23; Neh. 9:1; Est. 4:1, 3, 16; Job 2:12; Jonah 3:5, 6.)

4. He reminds God of his covenants (9:4), possibly thinking of the Abrahamic Covenant (which promised Israel the land of Palestine forever) (Gen. 12:7; 13:14, 15-17; 15:7; 18-21; 17:8), and the Davidic Covenant (which guaranteed Israel an everlasting king and kingdom) (2 Chron. 13:5; 2 Sam. 7:12-16; 23:5).

5. He contrasts the grace and goodness of God with the immorality and idolatry of Israel (9:5, 7, 8, 9).

6. He mentions Judah's kings (9:8). Two of them had been carried off into the Babylonian captivity along with the Jewish people.

7. He fully agreed that Judah had gotten just what she deserved and that God meant just what he said when he warned them about disobedience and punishment (9:12-14). (See Lev. 26.)

8. He ends his prayer by throwing both himself and his people completely upon the manifold grace of God:

"For we do not present our supplications before thee for our righteousness, but for thy great mercies" (9:18).

B. Gabriel—the prophecy of an angel (9:20-27). Even while Daniel was praying, God sent Gabriel the archangel to both minister to him and explain the most important, the most amazing, and the most profound single prophecy in the entire Word of God! For another example of God answering even while his child was praying, see Genesis 24:15. Note the message of this mighty angel in 9:24-27. We will now consider this prophecy by asking and attempting to answer six key questions.

1. To whom does this prophecy refer? It refers to Israel.

2. What is meant by the term "seventy weeks"? In his correspondence course on the book of Daniel, Dr. Alfred Martin of Moody Bible Institute writes the following helpful words:

"The expression translated 'seventy weeks' is literally 'seventy sevens.' Apart from the context one would not know what the 'sevens' were. One would have to inquire, 'seven' of what? This expression in Hebrew would be as ambiguous as if one were to say in English, 'I went to the store and bought a dozen.' A dozen of what? One of the basic principles of interpretation is that one must always interpret in the light of the context, that is, in the light of the passage in which a given statement occurs. As one searches this context, remembering that the vision was given in answer to the prayer, one notes that Daniel had been reading in Jeremiah that God would 'accomplish seventy years in the desolations of Jerusalem' (Dan. 9:2). This is the clue. Daniel is told in effect, 'Yes, God will accomplish seventy years in the captivity; but now He is showing you that the whole history of the people of Israel will be consummated in a period of seventy sevens of years.' " (*Daniel, the Framework of Prophecy*, pp. 85, 86)

To further clarify the meaning of the seventy weeks, it should be noted that Israel had in its calendar not only a week of seven days (as in Ex. 23:12) but also a "week" of seven years (Lev. 25:3, 4, 8-10; Gen. 29:27, 28). In other words, God is here telling Daniel that he would continue to deal with Israel for another 490 years before bringing in everlasting righteousness.

To summarize this particular point:

a. Israel was to allow its land to remain idle every seventh year (Lev. 25:1-4).

b. This command was disobeyed (Lev. 26:33-35; Jer. 34:12-22; 2 Chron. 36:21).

c. Finally, over a total period of 490 years, the nation had built up a land rest debt of seventy years.

d. Daniel knew of all this and was praying about it. He recognized that the seventy years of captivity represented seventy sevens of years in which those violations had transpired.

e. Gabriel now tells him that another period, similar in length (490 years) to that which had made the exile necessary, was coming in the experience of the people.

3. When was the seventy-week period to begin? It was to begin with the command to

rebuild Jerusalem's walls. The first two chapters of Nehemiah inform us that this command was issued during the twentieth year of Artaxerxes' accession. The *Encyclopedia Britannica* sets this date on March 14, 445 B.C.

4. What are the distinct time periods mentioned within the seventy-week prophecy and what was to happen during each period?

9. The Secret of the Seventy Sevens

DANIEL: THE PRAYER OF A PROPHET

TIME OF THE PRAYER	First year of Persian rule 538 B.C. **(9:2)**
OCCASION FOR THE PRAYER	Daniel's understanding of Jeremiah's prophecy **(9:2)**
BASIS FOR THE PRAYER	The promise of God **(9:4)** The mercy of God **(9:9, 18)**
CONFESSION IN THE PRAYER	"We have sinned!" **(9:5, 8, 9, 11, 15, 16)**
REQUESTS IN THE PRAYER	That God would bring them out of Babylon as he once did out of Egypt **(9:15)** That God would forgive **(9:19)** That God would allow the Temple to be rebuilt in Jerusalem **(9:16, 17)**
ANSWER TO PRAYER	"Yea, while I was . . . in prayer . . . Gabriel . . . touched me . . ." **(9:21)**.

GABRIEL: THE PROPHECY OF AN ANGEL

QUESTIONS	ANSWERS	
TO WHOM DOES THE PROPHECY REFER?	Israel **(9:24)**	
WHAT ARE THE SEVENTY WEEKS?	They refer to seven years of years, or 490 years.	
WHEN WOULD THIS PERIOD BEGIN?	At the rebuilding of Jerusalem's walls. March 14, 445 B.C.	
WHAT ARE THE THREE TIME PERIODS WITHIN THE SEVENTY WEEKS? WHAT HAPPENED DURING EACH PERIOD?	Seven "weeks" or forty-nine years	**FROM 445-396 B.C.** Walls of Jerusalem to be rebuilt in troublous times.
	Sixty-two "weeks" or 434 years	**FROM 396 B.C. TO 32 A.D.** Messiah to be crucified

CHURCH AGE

One "week" or seven years	From rapture to Armageddon
	Ministry of antichrist and return of true Christ.

(Taken from *Daniel's Prophecy of The Seventy Weeks*, By A. J. McClain, pages 30-31)

a. First period.
Seven weeks (forty-nine years), from 445 B.C. to 396 B.C. The key events during this time were the building of the streets and walls of Jerusalem "even in troublous times." This literally took place! (See Neh. 2-6.)

b. Second period.
Sixty-two weeks (434 years), from 396 B.C. to A.D. 30. At the end of this second period the Messiah was crucified! (See Mt. 27; Mk. 15; Lk. 23; Jn. 19.)

The brilliant British scholar and Bible student, Sir Robert Anderson, has reduced the first two periods into their exact number of days. This he has done by multiplying 483 (the combined years of the first two periods) by 360 (the days in a biblical year, as pointed out in Gen. 7:11, 24; 8:3, 4).

The total number of days in the first sixty-nine weeks (or 483 years) is 173,880. Anderson then points out that if one begins counting on March 14, 445 B.C., and goes forward in history, these days would run out on April 6, A.D. 32.

It was on this very day that Jesus made his triumphal entry into the city of Jerusalem! Surely our Lord must have had Daniel's prophecy in mind when he said:
"If thou hadst known, even thou, at least in this thy day, the things which belong to thy peace! But now they are hid from thine eyes" (Lk. 19:42).
Of course, it was on this same day that the Pharisees plotted to murder Christ (Lk. 19:47).

Thus Daniel, writing some five and one-half centuries earlier, correctly predicted the very day of Christ's presentation and rejection.

c. Third period—one week (seven years) from the rapture until the millennium. At the beginning of this period the antichrist will make his pact with Israel and will begin his terrible bloodbath. At the end of the last week (and of the entire seventy-week period), the true Messiah will come and establish his perfect millennium.

5. Do the seventy weeks run continuously? This is to say, is there a gap somewhere in these 490 years, or do they run without pause until they are completed?

Dispensational theology teaches that these "weeks" do not run continuously, but that there has been a gap or parenthesis of nearly 2000 years between the sixty-ninth and seventieth week. The chronology may be likened to a seventy-minute basketball game. For sixty-nine minutes the game has been played at a furious and continuous pace. Then the referee for some reason calls time out with the clock in the red and showing one final minute of play. No one knows for sure when the action will start again, but at some point the referee will step in and blow his whistle. At that time the teams will gather to play out the last minute of the game.

God has stepped in and stopped the clock of prophecy at Calvary. This divine "time out" has already lasted some twenty centuries, but soon the Redeemer will blow his trumpet and the final "week" of action will be played upon this earth.

6. Does the Bible offer any other examples of time gaps in divine programs? It does indeed. At least three instances come to mind in which gaps of many centuries can be found in a single short paragraph.

   a. Isaiah 9:6, 7.

     In the first part of verse 6 a gap of at least twenty centuries is separated by a colon. The phrase "unto us a son is given" refers to Bethlehem, while the words "and the government shall be upon his shoulder" look forward to the millennium.

   b. Zechariah 9:9, 10.

     Verse 9 is a clear reference to the triumphal entry of our Lord, but verse 10 looks ahead to the millennium.

   c. Isaiah 61:1, 2.

     In verse 2 of this passage Christ's earthly ministry (to "proclaim the acceptable year of the Lord") and the tribulation (the "day of vengeance of our God") are separated by only a comma. It is extremely important to note that when Jesus read this passage during his sermon in Nazareth, he ended the reading at this comma, for "the day of vengeance" was not the purpose of his first coming. (See Lk. 4:18, 19.)

As a final brief review of the seventy weeks, we may note:

7. The six main accomplishments of the seventy weeks.

   a. To bring to an end all human transgressions and sins, especially those of the nation Israel (Acts 3:13-16; 28:25-31; Ezek. 37:23; Rom. 11:26, 27).

   b. To make reconciliation for iniquity. This was done at Calvary when the Messiah was cut off (2 Cor. 5:18-20).

   c. To vindicate by fulfillment all true prophets and their prophecies.

   d. To prove the inability of the devil to rightfully rule this world.

   e. To destroy him and his chief henchman, the antichrist (Rev. 19:20; 20:10).

   f. To usher in the millennium (Ps. 45:3-7; Isa. 11:3-5; Jer. 23:3-8).

8. The three main time-periods of the seventy weeks (490 years).

   a. First period—(forty-nine years, or seven weeks) from 445 to 396 B.C.

   b. Second Period—(434 years, or sixty-two weeks) from 396 B.C. to A.D. 32.

   c. A time out period (which has already lasted almost twenty centuries). This time gap between the sixty-ninth and seventieth week was unrevealed and therefore unknown to the Old Testament prophets. (See Eph. 3:1-10; 1 Pet. 1:10-12.)

   d. Third period (seven years, or one week) from the rapture until the millennium.

9. The two main individuals of the seventy weeks.

   a. Messiah—the Lord Jesus Christ.

   b. The prince that shall come—the wicked antichrist.

X. The Conflict Above the Clouds.

  A. A man in mourning (10:1-4).

    1. Daniel had set aside a period of three weeks to be alone with God. During that time, he refrained from eating food, drinking wine, and anointing himself. The latter was usually done daily with oil to guard oneself against the fierce desert sun.

    2. There may have been several reasons which prompted this season of sorrow.

     a. because of the sins of his people

     b. because of the long period (490 years) of suffering his people must still go through (chapter 9)

     c. because of the paltry few (around 40,000) Jews who had elected to return under Zerubbabel. Some two years had already gone by since Cyrus issued his decree (Ezra 1:1-4) allowing them to return to Jerusalem.

     d. because of the hardships those returning Jews were experiencing.

      Note: God had apparently denied Daniel this opportunity to return. This was due perhaps to his advanced age (around ninety) and also the fact that his high governmental position could be used in helping the returning remnant.

  B. An angel in attendance (10:5-21).

    1. The description of the angel (10:5-9).

     a. Daniel immediately grows pale and weak with fright at such a dazzling sight. Some believe this angel to have been Jesus.

10. The Conflict Above the Clouds

A MAN GREATLY BELOVED
THE MAN OF GOD

- Daniel had been fasting and praying for three weeks on the banks of the River Tigris.
- Several possible reasons for this:

1. Because so few were elected to go back to Jerusalem.
2. Because of the heartaches of those who did go back.
3. Because of Israel's future sufferings, implied in the seventy-week prophecy.

A MAN CLOTHED IN LINEN
THE ANGEL OF GOD

- The description of the angel **(10:5-9)**
- The declaration of the angel **(10:10-17)**

1. He had been *hindered* by the prince of Persia.
2. He had been *helped* by the archangel Michael.

- The duty of the angel **(10:18, 19)**—to strengthen and to encourage Daniel.
- The determination of the angel **(10:20, 21)**—to again fight against the prince of Persia.

While a similar description is found in Revelation 1:12-16, it would not appear that the angel in Daniel can be identified with Christ. In 10:13 the angel had to call upon Michael, another angel, to help him. It is obvious that the Savior would have needed no help.

b. The men with Daniel were also filled with terror, although they did not actually see the vision as did Daniel (10:7). (See a similar event in Acts 9:7, 8.)

2. The declaration of the angel (10:10-19).

a. He had been hindered by the prince of Persia (10:13). Who was this prince? We quickly note that:

(1) He was powerful—he singlehandedly blocked one of heaven's mightiest angels for twenty-one days.

(2) He was perverted—he withstood God's divinely appointed messenger. Thus, he must have been a high ranking demon assigned by Satan to Persia to control the demonic activities in that kingdom. (See also Jn. 12:31; 14:30; 16:11; Mt. 9:34; 12:24; Isa. 24:21.)

b. He had been helped by the archangel Michael (10:13). This is the other archangel mentioned in the Bible. He is mentioned three times in the Old Testament (Dan. 10:13, 21; 12:1) and twice in the New Testament (Jude 1:9; Rev. 12:7). This was a mutual thing, however, for the angel here had once helped Michael. (See Dan. 11:1.)

Here the veil is momentarily lifted upon the heavenly warfare which believers, demons, and angels are engaged in. (See the following passages: 2 Cor. 10:3-5; Eph. 6:12; Rom. 8:38; Eph. 1:21; 3:10; Col. 2:15.)

This angel then proceeds to comfort, reassure, strengthen, and instruct Daniel concerning the end times.

3. The duty of the angel (10:18, 19).

4. The determination of the angel (10:20, 21). As he returned to God, the angel was aware that not only would he be once again confronted by the Persian demon, but also the demon of Greece. Apparently Satan was throwing in new support by sending into battle his future appointee over the Grecian empire. But the angel was confident, knowing he could again count on the help of Michael.

XI. A Chronology of Ungodly Kings. This chapter gives the most detailed account of history in all the Bible. It covers events occurring from approximately 529 to 164 B.C. It also describes many things which will yet transpire during the future tribulation. But the amazing thing is that Daniel wrote it all down in 540 B.C.

A. Alexander the Great (11:1-20), including his predecessors and successors.

1. Four Persian kings would rule after Cyrus (who was ruling when Daniel wrote this) and the fourth would be the richest of all. This happened (11:2).

a. Cambyses (529-522)
b. Smerdis (522-521)
c. Darius Hystaspes (521-486)
d. Xerxes (486-465) (He was by far the richest, see Est. 1:1-12)

2. After this, a mighty king would rule (11:3). This was Alexander the Great (336-323).

3. This king would suddenly die in his prime. His kingdom would not be given to his posterity, but would be divided up by outsiders into four sections (11:4). This is what happened. Shortly after his death, Philip, his half-brother; Alexander II, his legitimate son; and Hercules, his illegitimate son, were all three murdered and Alexander's four generals took over.

4. One of the generals, Ptolemy, would begin a southern dynasty in Egypt, and another general, Seleucus, would do the same through a northern dynasty in Syria. Ptolemy ruled from 323-283 B.C. and Seleucus from 304-281 B.C. (11:5).

5. These two kings would fight but later their countries would enter into an alliance (11:6). Egypt and Syria did make an alliance in 250 B.C. It happened after both generals had died when Ptolemy II Philadelphus (283-246), the son of Ptolemy I, gave his daughter Bernice in marriage to Antiochus II Theos (262-246), the grandson of Seleucus.

6. Two years later her father, Ptolemy II, died, and her husband Antiochus divorced her and remarried his former wife, whose name was Laodice.

7. Laodice, still bearing a grudge, poisoned Antiochus and had Bernice murdered. She then appointed her son, Seleucus II to become King of Syria.

8. Meanwhile, in Egypt, Bernice's brother, Ptolemy III, succeeded his father on the throne. He ruled from 246-221 B.C.

9. Ptolemy III invaded Syria and revenged his sister's death by executing Laodice. Seleucus II hid out in Asia Minor during this Egyptian invasion.

10. Ptolemy III then carried away much Syrian loot, including 40,000 talents of silver, and 2500 precious vessels (11:8-11).

11. In 240 B.C. Seleucus II attempted unsuccessfully to counterattack Ptolemy III in Egypt. Seleucus died and was succeeded by his son Antiochus III (also known as the Great). Antiochus ruled Syria from 223-187 B.C.

12. Ptolemy III died and was succeeded by his son, Ptolemy IV Philopaton (221-204).

13. These two kings (Antiochus III and Ptolemy IV) met head on in a crucial battle at Raphia in 217 B.C. This battle, where both sides used massive elephants, was won by Ptolemy IV.

14. In 203 B.C. Ptolemy IV died and was succeeded by Ptolemy V Epiphanes (203-181).

15. In 198 B.C. Antiochus the Great wrestled control of Palestine from Ptolemy V at a battle outside Sidon.

16. In 193 Antiochus the Great gave his daughter Cleopatra to marry Ptolemy V. (Note: This was not the famous Cleopatra of history, for

she would not come along until 69 B.C.) The reason for this marriage was to keep Egypt off his flank when he pursued warfare against Rome. Antiochus the Great also hoped Cleopatra would foster Syrian interests in Egypt, for he still secretly planned to conquer Egypt. But Cleopatra turned out to be a loyal wife.

17. Antiochus the Great was at this point joined by the renowned self-exiled Hannibal from Carthage. Together they invaded Greece, but in 188 B.C. were completely driven out of that part of the world by Rome.

18. Antiochus' grandiose plans failed utterly. He died in 187 B.C. (11:19).

19. His older son, Seleucus IV Philopator (187-176), then ruled, but was later murdered by his own prime minister (11:20).

B. Antiochus Epiphanes (11:21-35).

1. He was the youngest son of Antiochus the Great and is immediately classified as a vile (or contemptible) person by the Word of God (11:21).

2. He was nicknamed "Epimanes" ("madman") by those who knew him best.

3. He practiced deceit and pretended to be a second century Robin Hood (1 Macc. 3:29-31).

4. In 170 he defeated the Egyptian King Ptolemy Philometor (181-145) at a battle just east of the Nile delta. This young king was his own nephew, for his mother, Cleopatra, was Antiochus' sister.

5. Ptolemy lost this battle because he was betrayed by some of his friends who sat at his own table (11:26).

6. Antiochus then took his young nephew to Syria and pretended to befriend him. But neither the uncle nor the nephew trusted each other (11:27).

7. Antiochus had hoped to capture Egypt, but was stopped coldly by the mighty Romans (11:30).

8. He took out his insane rage on the city of Jerusalem (11:28-35).

C. Antichrist (11:36-45).

1. He shall do everything according to his own selfish will (11:36). (See also Rev. 13:7; 17:13.)

2. He shall magnify himself and malign God (11:36). (See also 2 Thess. 2:4; Rev. 13:6.) The word meaning "marvelous things" in this verse is literally "astonishing, unbelievable." The antichrist will scream out unbelievable blasphemies against God, insults no one else could ever think of, or would dare say if they could!

3. He will be allowed by God to prosper (given full rope) during the tribulation (the indignation) 11:36. (See also Rev. 11:7; 13:4, 7, 10.) The phrase "that which is determined shall be done," however, reminds us that God is still in absolute control, even during the terrible reign of this monster.

4. He will not regard "the gods of his fathers" (11:37). The word for God is plural. The antichrist will carry out a vendetta against all organized religion. In fact it is he who will

destroy that great harlot, bloody Babylon, which is the super world church. (See Rev. 17:5, 16.)

5. He will not have the desire for (or of) women (11:37). Here three theories are offered to explain this phrase.
   a. the normal desire for love, marriage, sex (see 1 Tim. 4:3)
   b. those things characteristic of women, such as mercy, gentleness, and kindness
   c. that desire of Hebrew women to be the mother of the Messiah (1 Tim. 2:15)

11. A Chronology of Ungodly Kings
DANIEL 11:1-20
Alexander and Predecessors

This amazing chapter contains no less than thirty-eight fulfilled prophecies. Some are as follows:

The rule of four Persian kings (v. 2)
The war of the fourth with Greece
The rise and fall of Alexander (v. 3, 4)
The fourfold division of his empire (v. 4)
The eventual alliance of two of these two kingdoms (v. 6)
The Egyptian plunder of Syria (v. 8)
The unsuccessful retaliation of Syria (v. 9)
The civil war in Egypt (v. 14)
The Syrian occupation of Palestine (v. 16)
The Temple desecration by a Syrian king (vs. 31, 32)
The Maccabean revolt (v. 32)
The eventual defeat of the Maccabeans (v. 33)

DANIEL 11:21-35
Antiochus Epiphanes

He was a cruel, Jew-hating Syrian king who occupied Jerusalem for awhile, ruling from 175-164 B.C.

On September 6, 171 B.C., he began his blasphemous actions against the Temple.

The supreme insult took place on December 15, 168, when he sacrificed a huge sow on the Jewish Temple altar.

In three days he murdered over 40,000 Jews.

On December 25, 165 (2300 days after the September 6, 171, date; see Dan. 8:9-14) some Jewish heroes called the Maccabees recaptured Jerusalem and the Syrian occupation ended.

DANIEL 11:36-45
Antichrist

Will be totally self-willed
Will magnify himself and malign God
Will prosper for awhile
Will not regard the gods of his fathers
Will have no desire for women
Will honor the god of fortress
Will be attacked by two southern and northern kings
Will occupy the Holy Land
Will occupy Egypt
Will hear frightful news while in Egypt
Will return to the Holy Land and wage war
Will be destroyed by Christ on Mt. Zion

6. His god will be the god of fortresses (11:38). The antichrist will spend all his resources on military programs.
7. In the latter days of the tribulation, he shall be attacked by the king of the south (Egypt) and the king of the north (Russia—11:40). According to Ezekiel (38–39) these two nations, especially Russia, are destroyed upon the mountains of Israel by God himself.
8. After the defeat of Russia, the antichrist will occupy Palestine (11:41). Edom and Moab will not be occupied by him. Some believe God will not allow him dominion over these areas, because Petra is located there, the mountainous city where the Jewish remnant will take shelter from the antichrist during the last part of the tribulation. (See Rev. 12:14.)
9. Upon establishing control in Palestine, the antichrist marches into Egypt and controls that land (11:42, 43).
10. While he is in Egypt he hears alarming rumors from the east and the north (11:44). The exact nature of these rumors is uncertain. Several suggestions have been offered:
    a. This concerns a report about a Jewish uprising. Dr. Leon Wood advocates this position in his book, *A Commentary on Daniel* (p. 313).
    b. It concerns an invasion of a vast horde of some 200,000,000 warriors from the far east (Rev. 9:16) under the leadership of "kings of the east" (Rev. 16:12), who now challenge him for world leadership. These nations would include China, India, and others. Dr. J. Dwight Pentecost suggests this possibility (*Things to Come*, p. 356).
    c. It concerns a report that thousands of Jews are escaping Jerusalem and fleeing into Petra. This theory is offered as a possibility by the author.
11. He quickly returns and in great fury destroys many (11:44). Here again the identity of those who are destroyed cannot be dogmatically stated.
12. He apparently successfully deals with the threat and establishes his worldwide headquarters on Mt. Zion. Here he remains until his total destruction by the King of kings at the end of the tribulation (11:45). (See also Rev. 19:11-21.)

XII. Closing Conditions.
A. The ministry of Michael (12:1).
    1. Michael is Israel's guardian angel.
    2. He will help deliver Israel through the worst period of human history since the creation of the world. Jesus quoted this verse when he spoke of that future hellish hour. (See Mt. 24:21, 22.) It is Michael who will cast Satan out of the heavenlies during the middle of the tribulation (Rev. 12:7), and then this heavenly hero apparently helps the escaping one-third Israelite nation into Petra. (See Zech. 13:8, 9; Rev. 12:14.)
    3. These Israelites already have their names in the Lamb's Book of Life. (See also Ex. 32:32; Ps. 69:28; Lk. 10:20; Mt. 24:22; Rev. 20:12.)
B. The two resurrections (12:2, 3). Other Old Testament and New Testament passages make it clear that these two resurrections are not at the same time, but rather are separated by a period of 1000 years. Neither resurrection here refers to the rapture.
    1. The resurrection of those to eternal life. This will occur at the beginning of the millennium and will include all Old Testament and martyred tribulational saints. (See Job 19:25, 26; Ps. 49:15; Isa. 25:8; 26:19; Hosea 13:14; Heb. 11:35; Rev. 20:4, 6.) The reward of all righteous soul-winners is mentioned in Daniel 12:3.
    2. The resurrection of those to shame and everlasting contempt. This will transpire after the millennium and will include all unsaved people who have ever lived. (See Rev. 20:5.) Our Lord summarizes these two resurrections in John 5:28, 29.
C. The two prophecies (12:4).
   "But thou, O Daniel, shut up the words, and seal the book, even to the time of the end: many shall run to and fro, and knowledge shall be increased."
After reading this passage many years ago, the great scientist (and Christian), Sir Isaac Newton, is reported to have said:
   "Personally I cannot help but believe that these words refer to the end of the times. Men will travel from country to country in an unprecedented manner. There may be some inventions which will enable people to travel much more quickly than they do now."
This was written around A.D. 1680. Newton went on to speculate that this speed might actually exceed fifty m.p.h. Some eighty years later, the famous French atheist, Voltaire, read Newton's words and retorted:
   "See what a fool Christianity makes of an otherwise brilliant man! Here a scientist like Newton actually writes that men may travel at the rate of 30 or 40 m.p.h. Has he forgotten that if man would travel at this rate he would be suffocated? His heart would stand still!"
One wonders what Voltaire would have said had he known that some two centuries after he wrote this, an American astronaut, Edward H. White, on June 3, 1965, would climb out of a space craft a hundred miles in the sky and casually walk across the continental United States in less than fifteen minutes, strolling along at 17,500 m.p.h.? Or that during the moon landings, man exceeded a speed some twelve times faster than a twenty-two-caliber rifle bullet travels? In this same prophecy, Daniel predicted an intensification of knowledge. Our country is just over two hundred years old. Yet, during this time, we have developed the public educational system from absolutely nothing to its present level. We have now over sixty million students in America alone, attending some 72,000 public elementary schools, 27,000 secondary schools, and 1200 colleges and universities. Each year we spend thirty-six billions of dollars to finance all this.

D. The three time periods (12:5-13).
1. 1260 days ("a time, times and a half." See 12:7.)
a. Daniel sees two other angels who had been listening to this private prophecy conference the mighty angel was conducting for the old statesman. Angels are very much interested in God's program of salvation (1 Pet. 1:12) and one of the two suddenly asks how long this terrible tribulational period will last (12:6). Neither of these angels had apparently overheard the details of the seventy-week vision in 9:24-27.
b. The mighty angel informs them that the duration of this final horrible half of the tribulation will last as long as it takes for the pride and power of the Jews to be broken, or three-and-a-half years (12:7).
2. 1290 days (12:11). This period refers to the same as mentioned above, but includes an additional thirty days. Although we cannot be dogmatic, it would seem reasonable to conclude that an additional month will be needed here to carry out the sheep and goat judgment mentioned in Matthew 25:31-46.
3. 1335 days (12:12). Here again a period of time is added, forty-five days. What will be the need of these forty-five days? It may be the time necessary for setting up the governmental machinery for carrying on the rule of Christ. Dr. Franklin Logsdon has written the following helpful words concerning the seventy-five additional days beyond the three-and-a-half year period.

"We in the United States have a national analogy. The President is elected in the early part of November, but he is not inaugurated until January 20. There is an interim of 70 plus days. During this time, he concerns himself with the appointment of cabinet members, foreign envoys and others who will comprise his government. In the period of 75 days between the termination of the Great Tribulation and the Coronation, the King of Glory will likewise attend to certain matters." (*Profiles in Prophecy*, p. 81)

E. The four final conclusions
1. The mighty angel raises both hands into heaven as he attests to the veracity of all this (12:7). The regular gesture of raising one's hand to heaven showed solemnity and importance (see Gen. 14:22; Deut. 32:40), but here both hands are raised. (See also Rev. 10:1-6.)
2. Many shall be cleansed (saved) during the tribulation (12:1); this includes both Jews and Gentiles. (See Rev. 7:1-17.)
3. The wicked, however, will continue their evil ways (12:10). (See Rev. 9:20, 21; 11:9, 10.)
4. Daniel was to carefully preserve his writings (12:4), but all their meaning would not be revealed to him until that glorious day when he would stand alongside the righteous awaiting his inheritance lot (12:9, 13).

12. Closing Conditions

"*. . . A time of trouble, such as never was . . .*" (12:1)

● THE HELPER IN THE TRIBULATION
Michael the Archangel (12:1)

● THE LENGTH OF THE TRIBULATION
There are three specific time periods listed here concerning the tribulation and following events.

1260 DAYS (12:7)
A reference to the final and worst part of the tribulation, some three-and-a-half years.

1290 DAYS (12:11)
A reference to the first time period plus thirty days. This time may be needed to conduct the various Jewish, Gentile, and angelic judgments.

1335 DAYS (12:12)
A reference to the second time period plus forty-five days. This may be spent in preparing for the millennial government.

● THE INTEREST CONCERNING THE TRIBULATION
Both angels and Old Testament prophets (12:5-8)

● THE SALVATION DURING THE TRIBULATION
". . . Every one . . . written in the book" (12:1).
"Many shall be purified, and made white . . ." (12:10).

● THE SIGNS PRECEDING THE TRIBULATION

An Increase in Speed (12:4)

An Increase in Knowledge (12:4)

● THE RESURRECTIONS FOLLOWING THE TRIBULATION (12:2, 3)
At the Beginning of the Millennium
Resurrection of Old Testament and tribulation saints
At the End of the Millennium
Resurrection of all unsaved dead

THE RETURN STAGE

INTRODUCING THE RETURN STAGE

1. This period describes Satan's attempts to harass the Jews in Palestine (the book of Nehemiah) and hang them in Persia (the book of Esther).
2. It covers the construction of the second Old Testament Temple, and the completion of the Old Testament canon.
3. Its duration is approximately 140 years.
4. It begins with the historical ministry of Ezra the scribe (Ezra 7:6-10), and ends with the prophetical ministry of Elijah the prophet (Mal. 4:5, 6).
5. We read of the spirit-induced midnight mission of Nehemiah (Neh. 2) and the satanic-induced midnight mission of Haman (Est. 6).
6. We are told of a plot against a pagan king (Est. 2:21-23) and one against the King of kings (Zech. 11:12, 13).
7. This era includes the restoration of the feast of tabernacles (Neh. 8:13-18) and the institution of the feast of Purim (Est. 9:20-32).

THE RETURN STAGE
EZRA; ESTHER; NEHEMIAH;
HAGGAI; ZECHARIAH; MALACHI

EZRA (445 B.C.)

INTRODUCTION:

1. Zedekiah, Judah's last king, was carried away into captivity by Nebuchadnezzar in 597 B.C. The city of Jerusalem was destroyed and the Temple burned on July 18, 586, B.C. (see 2 Ki. 24).
2. Many citizens of Judah along with Daniel and Ezekiel were also transported to Babylon. Both ministered and wrote there. One was a priest, the other a prime minister.
3. On October 29, 539 B.C., Babylon fell to the invading armies of the Medes and Persians, led by Cyrus the Great. The Babylonian king at that time, Belshazzar, was executed. (See Dan. 5.)
4. Cyrus then placed his able general, Darius the Mede (also the Gobryas of history) as king over the city of Babylon.
5. During Cyrus' first year reigning, he issued the decree which permitted the Jews to return and rebuild their temple at Jerusalem.
   a. Jeremiah had predicted the length of the captivity. (See 25:11, 12; 29:10.)
   b. Isaiah had actually called Cyrus by name some 170 years before. (See Isa. 44:28; 45:1.)
6. There were three separate returns by the Jewish remnant.

a. Zerubbabel led the first in 536 B.C.
b. Ezra led the second in 455 B.C.
c. Nehemiah led the third in 445 B.C.

7. In 535 B.C. the construction on the Temple began. For a while it was halted by various satanic activities.
8. During this time Haggai and Zechariah ministered to the discouraged remnant.
9. In October of 516 the Temple was completed and dedicated.
10. There were at least five Persian kings associated in some way with the period of the return. They are:
   a. Cyrus the Great (539-530), the victor over Babylon, and king who issued the decree (Ezra 1:1-4).
   b. Cambyses (530-522 B.C.), the son of Cyrus.
   c. Smerdis (522-520 B.C.).
   d. Darius the Great (520-486 B.C.). This was not the same as Darius the Mede. Darius the Great established order and saved the Persian empire after the chaos which followed Cambyses' death. He allowed the Temple work to continue.
   e. Xerxes I (486-465 B.C.). He was the son of Darius the Great, and also the Ahasuerus of the book of Esther.
   f. Artaxerxes (465-424). He was the son of Xerxes I, and on the throne when both Ezra and Nehemiah returned (Ezra 7:1, 8; Neh. 2:1).

I. The Period Under Zerubbabel (Ezra 1-6).
   A. The king, proclaiming.
      1. The writing (1:1-4)
         a. God places a desire in Cyrus' heart to issue his return decree.
         b. The king freely acknowledges God's sovereignty in giving him his kingdom.
         c. The language of the decree suggests that Daniel himself may have drafted it for Cyrus.
      2. The rising (1:5-11)
         a. God plants a holy desire in the hearts of many Hebrew people to return. Although only three tribes are mentioned (Judah, Benjamin, and Levi), we know from other passages that there were doubtless representatives from all twelve who returned.
         Note:
         (1) In 2 Chronicles 11:13-17 we are told at the time of Israel's civil war that various individuals from all twelve tribes moved to Jerusalem.
         (2) Jesus said he came to minister to the entire house of Israel (Mt. 10:6).
         (3) The tribes of Zebulun and Naphtali are referred to in Matthew 4:13, 15.

THE RETURN STAGE

Ezra   Esther

Nehemiah   Haggai

Zechariah   Malachi

"For thus saith the Lord, after seventy years are accomplished at Babylon, I will visit you, and perform my good word toward you, in causing you to return even unto this place"

A CHRONOLOGY OF THE RETURN STAGE

Jer. 29:10.

FOREIGN KING	DATE	EVENT	SCRIPTURE	OLD TESTAMENT BOOK	LOCATION
Cyrus the Great	539—530	Conquers Babylon Issues return decree	Dan. 5 Ezra 1-3	• Ezra 1-6	
Cambyses	530-522	Not referred to in Old Testament	—	• Haggai	Jerusalem
Smerdis	522-520	Stops work on the Temple	Ezra 4:1-23	• Zechariah	
Darius the Great	520-486	Orders work to continue	Ezra 4:24; 6:1-22	(See Ezra 5:1; 6:14)	
Ahasuerus	486-465	Makes Esther his queen	Esther 1-10	• Esther	Persia
Artaxerxes	465-424	Allows Ezra to return Allows Nehemiah to return	Ezra 7-12 Nehemiah 1-13	• Ezra 7-12 • Nehemiah	Jerusalem

(4) Anna was from the tribe of Asher (Lk. 2:36).

(5) Paul speaks of "our twelve tribes" (Acts. 26:7).

These verses alone refute the false doctrine of British Israelism, which teaches the ten "lost tribes" are really Americans and Englishmen.

  b. Those Hebrews remaining in Babylon contributed toward this venture.

  c. King Cyrus donated the golden vessels Nebuchadnezzar had taken from the Jerusalem Temple some sixty years before. This totaled 5,469 gold and silver items.

B. The people, reclaiming.

  1. Their genealogy (2:1-57). The family trees of those who returned were carefully recorded for posterity. Especially to be noted was their leader, whose name was Zerubbabel. This humble man was the grandson of Jehoiachin (Ezra 3:2; 1 Chron. 3:19). He faced a difficult task in rebuilding the Temple and was often personally encouraged by God himself. (See Hag. 1:14; 2:4, 21, 23; Zech. 4:6, 7, 9, 10.) The total number of those returning was 42,360.

  2. Their theology (3:1-13).

  a. After they reached Jerusalem the altar was built and the sacrificial system reinstituted, led by Jeshua, grandson of Israel's last high priest before the Babylonian captivity. This Jeshua (called Joshua by Haggai and Zechariah) became the first high priest of the return period.

  b. The first sacred feast to be observed was the Feast of the Tabernacles.

  c. In June of 535 B.C. work was begun on the Temple.

  d. When the foundation was laid a great ceremony was held. It may be concluded, however, that this ground-breaking program was different from any other either before or after. Note the unusual account in 3:10-13.

C. The devil, defaming. Satan tried his best to prevent the Temple from going up.

  1. He tried compromise (4:1-3). Judah's enemies suggested they all have a part in building some kind of universal house of worship. Zerubbabel and Jeshua refused.

  2. He tried slander (4:4, 5). Their enemies then wrote lies concerning them to the Persian officials. They reminded the king (Cambyses)

SIX SOVEREIGN TRIPS

"By the rivers of Babylon, there we sat down, yea, we wept, when we remembered Zion" **(Ps. 137:1).**

Three Trips from Jerusalem to Babylon

DATE	CAPTIVES	OLD TESTAMENT PROPHETS		FOREIGN KINGS	
606	**Daniel**	In Babylon	**Daniel**	Before 539	Nebuchadnezzar
597	**Ezekiel**		**Ezekiel**		Belshazzar
586	**Zedekiah**	In Jerusalem	**Jeremiah**	After 539	King Cyrus and his General Darius

"When the Lord turned again the captivity of Zion, we were like them that dream" **(Ps. 126:1).**

Three Trips from Babylon to Jerusalem

DATE	LEADER	FOREIGN KING	OLD TESTAMENT PROPHET
536	**Zerubbabel** and **Joshua**	● Cyrus the Great ● Cambyses ● Smerdis ● Darius the Great	**Haggai** **Zechariah**
455	**Ezra**	Artaxerxes	**Ezra**
445	**Nehemiah**	Artaxerxes	**Nehemiah**

of Jerusalem's history as a hotbed of rebellion and suggested he stop all building action. Cambyses agreed and issued the order to halt (4:18–23).

    D. The Lord, sustaining. In spite of all this, God was at work!

        1. Both Haggai and Zechariah begin their comforting ministry at this time (5:1, 2).

        2. The new Persian king, Darius the Great, takes a personal interest in the matter. A search soon reveals the original title decree of Cyrus, which gave the Jews permission to rebuild their Temple. Darius therefore orders the work to continue and decrees the construction cost to be paid from the treasury of some of his own officials (6:1–12).

        3. On February 18, 516 B.C., the Temple was completed (6:15). In April the Passover was celebrated in Jerusalem, the first time in over sixty years (6:19).

II. The Period Under Ezra (Ezra 7–10). Between chapters 6 and 7 of Ezra there is a period of some sixty years. We have no biblical record concerning those events which transpired during this time. J. Vernon McGee writes the following about Ezra:

    "He is one of the characters who has not received proper recognition. Ezra was a descendant of Hilkiah, the high priest (Ezra 7:1), who found a copy of the law during the reign of Josiah (2 Chron. 34:14); Ezra, as a priest, was unable to serve during the captivity, but he gave his time to a study of the Word of God—he was 'a ready scribe in the law of Moses' (Ezra 7:6). Ezra was a revivalist and reformer. The revival began with the reading of the Word of God by Ezra (see Neh. 8). Also, he probably was the writer of 1st and 2nd Chronicles and of Psalm 119, which exalts the Word of God. He organized the synagogue, and was the founder of the order of scribes, helped settle the canon of Scripture and arranged the Psalms." (*Through the Bible*, p. 117)

    A. The cooperation from the king (Ezra 7). The Persian monarch Artaxerxes greatly aided Ezra in his plans to leave Babylon and lead a pilgrimage to Jerusalem. The king issued an official letter addressed to three parties.

        1. To all Jews in Babylon: Artaxerxes invited as many as desired to return to Jerusalem with Ezra. He also encouraged them to give liberally to the special offering Ezra was collecting (7:11–20).

        2. To all Persian officials west of the Euphrates River: They were to furnish Ezra with all he needed.

        3. To Ezra himself: He was to select and appoint his own officials, and to rule the Jewish people west of the Euphrates River (7:25, 26).

    B. The preparation for the trip (8).

        1. Ezra leaves from Babylon in mid-March of 455 B.C. with approximately 1500 men and their families.

        2. En route the group assembles at the Ahava River (a tributary of the Euphrates River) for a roll call. Ezra is amazed to discover that not one Levite has volunteered to come (8:15).

        3. He then hurriedly sends a delegation to return and persuade some Levites to make the trip. God's Spirit works, for soon nearly 300 Levites join the group (8:16–20).

        4. Ezra then proclaims a fast there by the river, praying God will grant them a safe journey. His confession here is interesting (8:22).

        5. Ezra then appoints twelve leaders to be in charge of transporting the monies received from the offering he had taken in Babylon. This was a considerable sum, totaling over

Ezra

Period under Zerubbabel EZRA 1-6

THE KING
PROCLAIMING

- Cyrus signs the return decree **(1:1-4)**.
- A spiritual Jewish minority responds to this **(1:5-11)**. Some 40,000 now leave for Jerusalem

THE PEOPLE
RECLAIMING

- They reclaim their genealogy **(2)**.
- They reclaim their theology **(3)**.
Upon reaching Jerusalem they build the altar and keep the feasts.

THE DEVIL
DEFAMING

- He attempts compromise **(4:1-3)**.
- He attempts slander **(4:4-24)**.

THE LORD
SUSTAINING

- Through the ministry of Haggai and Zechariah **(5:1; 6:14)**.
- Through the title deed search by King Darius **(6)**.

SIXTY YEAR GAP

Events in the book of
ESTHER take place

Period under Ezra EZRA 7-10

COOPERATION
FROM THE KING (7)

- Ezra is helped by King Artaxerxes, who encourages the Jews to go and writes letters in their behalf.

PREPARATION
FOR THE TRIP (8)

- Ezra gathers 1500 families plus 300 Levitical priests.
- He collects five million dollars.
- He observes a time of prayer and fasting.

SUPPLICATION
BY THE SCRIBE (9)

- He learns that the people have already compromised their testimony.
- He pours out his soul in prayer to God over their sin.

PURIFICATION
OF THE PEOPLE (10)

- They are convicted of their sins.
- The people put away their sins.

---

five million dollars in gold and silver (8:24–29).

    6. In August of 455 B.C., the little group arrives safely in Jerusalem (7:9; 8:31, 32).

C. The supplication of the scribe (9:1–15).

    1. Ezra soon learns that the Jews already in the Holy City have compromised their testimony by practicing heathen customs and even marrying their pagan women (9:1, 2).

    2. The great Bible teacher immediately goes into deep mourning and pours out his soul to God concerning this tragic situation. Ezra's prayer in 9:5–15 may be favorably compared to that of Daniel (Dan. 9) and also Nehemiah (Neh. 9).

D. The purification of the people (Ezra 10).

    1. Soon conviction of sin settles down upon the hearts of the leaders and they agree something must be done immediately.

    2. A proclamation goes out throughout all Judah, ordering all male citizens to appear in Jerusalem on the fifth day of December.

    3. Upon hearing Ezra's sermon, the men agree to dismiss their heathen wives. Ezra appoints various leaders to handle the legal matters connected with this. By March 15 of the following year the thing had been resolved.

NEHEMIAH (445 B.C.)

INTRODUCTION:

1. The year was 445 B.C. The Jews had already been in Jerusalem for some ninety years. A number had remained in Babylon and Persia.

2. One of the Jews still living in Persia was Nehemiah. This capable man had been elevated to the position of cup bearer (personal press secretary and valet) to King Artaxerxes, monarch of all Persia.

3. Upon being saddened and then challenged concerning the desperate need about Jerusalem's wall-less and defenseless city, Nehemiah goes to the Holy City and builds the necessary walls.

4. Nehemiah was a younger contemporary of Ezra.

    a. Ezra was a priest and Bible teacher. His main job concerned the purification of the people of Jerusalem.

    b. Nehemiah was a politician and builder. His main job concerned the protection of the people of Jerusalem.

5. King Artaxerxes had shown kindness to Ezra some ten years before, and would also honor Nehemiah's request to return to Jerusalem. This king was the son of Xerxes and therefore the stepson of Esther. His stepmother no doubt had much influence upon Artaxerxes' attitude toward Ezra and Nehemiah.

6. Nehemiah is the last historical book in the Old Testament.
7. The book of Nehemiah is the autobiography of his "call to the wall."

I. The News Concerning the Wall (Neh. 1).
   A. In December of 446 b.c., Nehemiah learns from a returning Jew named Hanani (and his own brother—see 1:2; 7:2) of the pitiful state of Jerusalem. The report breaks his heart (1:3).
   B. Upon hearing this, Nehemiah begins a time of:
      1. Confession to God over the deeds of his people (1:6, 7).
      2. Intercession to God over the needs of his people (1:8–11).

II. The Request to Build the Wall (2:1–8).
   A. In April of 445 b.c., after a prayer period of four months, Nehemiah asks the king to "send me unto Judah, unto the city of my fathers' sepulchers, that I may build it" (2:5).
   B. Artaxerxes agrees and gives Nehemiah two letters.
      1. One was to the Persian officials west of the Euphrates, giving him passport permission.
      2. The other was to Asaph, manager of the king's forest, instructing him to issue the necessary timber for the construction job.

III. The Necessity for the Wall (2:9–20). Soon after reaching Jerusalem, Nehemiah makes a secret midnight ride around the city itself. The next morning he assembles Judah's leaders and shares with them the burden of his heart (2:17, 18).

It may be concluded that there were at least two compelling reasons for building the wall.
   A. It was necessary for protection, that is, to keep the outsiders out. This would protect against sneak attacks.
   B. It was necessary for separation, to keep the insiders in. This would cut down upon the growing worldliness of the Jews who had been associating freely with the surrounding pagan people.

IV. The Gates in the Wall (Neh. 3). The various gates mentioned here are in themselves a beautiful picture summary of the Christian life. Note:
   A. The sheep gate (3:1). This speaks of the cross. (See Jn. 10:11.)
   B. The fish gate (3:3). This speaks of soul-winning. (See Mt. 4:19.)
   C. The old gate (3:6). This speaks of our old nature. (See Rom. 6:1–23.)
   D. The valley gate (3:13). This speaks of sufferings and testing. (See 2 Cor. 1:3–5.)
   E. The dung gate (3:14). This speaks of the works of the flesh. (See Gal. 5:16–21.)
   F. The fountain gate (3:15). This speaks of the Holy Spirit. (See Jn. 7:37–39.)
   G. The water gate (3:26). This speaks of the Word of God. (See Jn. 4:10–14.)
   H. The horse gate (3:28). This speaks of the believer's warfare. (See Eph. 6:10–17.)
   I. The east gate (3:29). This speaks of the return of Christ. (See Ezek. 43:1, 2.)
   J. The Miphkad gate (3:31). This was thought to be the judgment gate and therefore speaks of the judgment seat of Christ. (See 1 Cor. 3:9–15; 2 Cor. 5:10.)

V. The Opposition to the Wall. A work for God will always be met by both human and satanic opposition. These combined forces did their perverted best to halt the wall building. Many methods were employed to accomplish this.
   A. Ridicule (2:19; 4:1–3). Nehemiah had but begun when he was opposed by a hellish trinity. This consisted of:
      1. Sanballat (the governor of Samaria)
      2. Tobiah (an Ammonite leader)
      3. Geshem (an Arab chief)
   These troublemakers scoffed at the work. Tobiah sneered, "Even that which they build, if a fox go up, he shall break down their stone wall" (4:3). But Nehemiah took his case before God and continued the good work (4:4, 5).
   B. Wrath (4:1, 6–9). In spite of this ridicule, however, the wall was soon half its intended height all around the city. The sneers of this terrible trio soon disappeared. In their fury they plotted to lead an army against Jerusalem. But once again Nehemiah would testify: "We made our prayer unto our God, and set a watch against them day and night, because of them" (4:9).
   C. Discouragement (4:10). After awhile many of the workers became weary in the heavy work of removing the debris which had piled up for so many years.
   D. Fear (4:11–23). The builders were aware of the impending attack planned by their combined enemies to murder them en masse. Once again the mighty Nehemiah was equal to the occasion.
      1. He stationed armed guards behind the walls.
      2. He inspired them with his own confidence in God.
      3. He appointed a trumpeter to sound an alarm if needed.
      4. He prepared his men by issuing both weapons and working tools to every man. Then the wall was constructed.
      5. He scheduled the work from sunrise to sunset. During that hectic but heroic period neither the guards or the workers ever removed their clothes.
   E. Internal strife (5:1–5). Some of the rich Jews were profiteering at the expense of their poorer brethren by forcing them into slavery and acquiring their properties. Nehemiah was furious upon hearing of this and called a public trial to deal with those materialistic men. At this hearing he demanded and received their promise to restore their dishonest gain to their victims (5:6–13).
   F. Laziness (4:10). We are told that some of the leaders were lazy and of no help whatsoever.
   G. Satanic subtlety (6:1–8). On four separate occasions Nehemiah's enemies attempted to set up a "dialogue" session with him. But he refused, knowing they actually were planning to kill him. Note:
      1. Their invitation of compromise:
      "Come now, therefore, and let us take counsel together" (6:7).
      2. His answer of conviction:
      "I am doing a great work, so that I cannot come down. Why should the work cease, while I leave it, and come down to you?" (6:3).

H. Lying prophets (6:10–14). A false prophet named Shemaiah, in the hire of Sanballat, attempted to frighten Nehemiah into hiding by claiming God had revealed to him Nehemiah would be murdered that very night.

VI. Blessings of the (Completed) Wall. In spite of all the persecution and hardships, Nehemiah had the wall up and completed in early September, just fifty-two days after they had begun (6:15). This project resulted in many blessings, including:

A. The reading of the Word of God (8:1–8; 9:3).
B. The restoration of the feast of tabernacles (8:13–18).
   1. This feast had not been properly observed since the time of Joshua, over 900 years back.
   2. The feast was instituted in Leviticus 23. Its purpose and method of observation are found in 23:40–43.
   3. With great joy the people carried this out. Ezra read from the scroll on each of the seven days of the feast.
C. The prayer recitation of Israel's History (9:6–38). In this remarkable public prayer, Ezra summarized the entire history of the faithfulness of God bestowed upon Israel.
D. The ratification of a special covenant (9:38; 10:1–29).
E. The repopulating of the city of David (11:1, 2).
F. The denouncing of sins:
   1. of ungodly alliances (9:1, 2; 10:30; 13:3)
   2. untithed possessions (10:32–39; 12:44–47; 13:10, 11)
   3. unlawful Sabbath work (10:31; 13:15–22)
   4. unequal marriages (13:23, 24)
   5. unauthorized usage of the Temple (13:1–9)
   Nehemiah's fantastic zeal and fearless actions helped bring into being all this repentance over sin.
   1. He had gone back to Persia for awhile (13:6), but upon returning he discovered several very disquieting things.
      a. The Temple custodian had actually converted a storage room into a beautiful guest room for (of all people) his friend Tobiah.
      b. Nehemiah ordered him to leave and threw out all his belongings from the room (13:9).
      c. He then had to regather the Temple choir which had dissolved during his absence (13:10).
   2. His zeal simply knew no limits, as the following account brings out. (See 13:23–25.)
   3. His last recorded act was to excommunicate Joiada (the very son of Eliashib, the high priest) because of his unlawful marriage to Sanballat's daughter (13:28).
G. The rejoicing of all the remnant. When God's work is done in God's way, joy will follow. Note the various references to this.
   1. The people sent presents to each other and ate festive meals (8:12).
   2. The Levitical choir sang and played with cymbals, psalteries, and harps (9:4; 12:27, 28).
   3. Nehemiah divided the people into two groups. Each walked in opposite directions

upon the completed wall singing their songs of praise to God (12:31–34).
   4. Ezra led a special corps of trumpet-playing priests (12:35–37).
   5. The result of all this was that "the joy of Jerusalem was heard even afar off" (12:43).

ESTHER (478–464 B.C.)
INTRODUCTION:
1. Esther is one of the two Old Testament books named after a woman. (The other is Ruth.)
2. The name Esther means "star."
3. The books give the story of those Jews living in Persia who did not return to Jerusalem after Cyrus' decree. To pinpoint the historical account here, consider the following:
   a. The Jews first went back to Jerusalem under Zerubbabel in 536 B.C.
   b. The Temple was completed in 516 B.C.
   c. Esther became queen in 478 B.C.
   d. She saved her people in 473 B.C.
   e. Ezra returned to Jerusalem in 455 B.C.
   f. Nehemiah returned in 445 B.C.
   Thus Esther appears upon the scene about sixty years after the decree of Cyrus and approximately thirty-five years before Nehemiah returned.
4. The name of God never appears in this book. It is also not to be found in the Song of Solomon. For this reason the early church at first was somewhat reluctant to accept the book of Esther as a part of the inspired canon, but soon it was regarded as such.
5. In spite of the omission of any name for deity, there is no other book in all the Bible where God is more evident, working behind the scenes, than in this book.
6. The key in understanding Esther is the word "providence," literally meaning, "to provide in advance." Providence has been defined by the great theologian Strong as follows:
   "Providence is that continuous agency of God by which He makes all events of the physical and moral world fulfill the original design with which He created it."
   Providence has also been defined as "the hand of God in the glove of history." Providence is the last of three great facts which make up the sovereignty of God as witnessed by man. These are:
   a. Creation—which accounts for the existence of this universe (Gen. 1:1).
   b. Preservation—which accounts for the continuation of this universe (Heb. 1:3; Col. 1:16, 17).
   c. Providence—which accounts for the progress and development of this universe (Ps. 135:6–10; Dan. 4:35).
7. One may with full justification pen the words of Romans 8:28 across the book of Esther.

I. The Rise of Esther (Est. 1–2).
   A. The rejection of Vashti (1:2–21).
      1. In the third year of his reign, the Persian monarch Ahasuerus (Xerxes) gave a fantastic feast which lasted 180 days. It was attended by thousands of his kingdom officials, coming from every one of the 127 provinces, stretching from India to Ethiopia (1:1–4).

2. Although it is not specifically stated so, the probable reason for the festivities was to raise the morale of his leaders and psychologically prepare them for his planned expedition against Greece. Here a little background is necessary.
   a. In 490 B.C., Xerxes' father, Darius the Great, had led a huge fleet of 600 ships carrying some 60,000 Persian crack cavalry and foot soldiers to capture Athens and subdue the Greek civilization. But he was soundly defeated on a small plain called Marathon by the brilliant Greek general Miltiades. In spite of the vastly numerical superiority of the Persians, the Greeks out-circled their foes and cut them down as overripe wheat.
   b. The battle of Marathon is listed as number six in the book, *History's 100 Greatest Events*, by William A. DeWitt.
3. During the final week of the feasting the king called for his wife, Vashti, to come in and parade her beauty before some of his important, but half-drunk friends. The queen curtly refused to display herself in this cheap manner (1:5-12).
4. Burning with anger, the king acted upon the advice of his crony friends and banished his wife forever from his presence, lest the other women of the kingdom get ideas from her insubordination (1:13-21).

B. The selection of Esther (2:1-20).
1. After his anger had cooled, the king regretted his hasty action, but was unable to change the strict Persian law even though he himself had decreed it (2:1).
2. At the suggestion of his aides, he allowed an empire-wide beauty search to begin, with the winner of the contest to become his new wife (2:2-4).
3. Among the beauties brought to the palace was a Jewish girl named Hadassah, also known as Esther. The beautiful young maiden had been raised by her older cousin, whose name was Mordecai, of the tribe of Benjamin (2:5-8).
4. Esther gained immediate favor with Hegai, the headmaster of the Miss Persian pageant. However, upon the advice of Mordecai, Esther did not reveal her Jewish identity at this time (2:9-11).
5. The contest lasted some four years, but after the king had seen all the available "finalists," he wholeheartedly chose Esther to become his next queen (2:12-17).
6. To celebrate this event, Ahasuerus threw another big party, and even went so far as to lower taxes in his province.

Note: The reason for all this was also, in part, to compensate for his recent defeat at the hands of the Greeks. It should be understood that a period of some four years elapsed between the divorce of Vashti and the marriage to Esther. The following is a summary of the events which took place during that period.

a. In the spring of 480 B.C., Xerxes crossed the Dardanelles with over 100,000 men and hundreds of ships. History tells us Xerxes wept while watching the dazzling display of his smartly marching armies, all carrying their brightly colored flags and banners. When asked why he wept, the king replied, "Because I know all this military glory is but for a moment and will soon fade away forever. Because in much less than one hundred years from now every man present here today will have died, myself included."
b. Disaster struck soon after, for he lost 400 ships in a severe spring storm at sea. In blind frustration and anger, Xerxes beat upon the stormy waters with his belt.
c. Upon landing in Greece, his proud Persian troops were stopped for an entire day at the mountainous pass called Thermopylae. Here, a Greek captain named Leonidas and his 300 brave Spartan soldiers held back the entire invading army for twenty-four hours, inflicting great losses on them, and allowing the much smaller Greek army to carry out an orderly retreat to safety.
d. Xerxes eventually broke through and burned Athens to the ground. But most of its citizens had escaped to the island of Salamis. The king then set sail for Salamis, confident of victory, for he outnumbered his enemy at least three to one. But the smaller and swifter Greek fighting boats had mastered the art of ramming. Soon, before his horrified eyes, Xerxes viewed the slaughter of his proud navy.
e. He left for Persia a defeated man. The remaining troops were put under the command of General Nardonius. One year later, Nardonius was defeated and killed in a pitched battle at Plataea in 479 B.C. The Persian Empire was then dealt the final death blow. J.F.C. Fuller's well-known book, *The Decisive Battles of the Western World*, lists the battles at Salamis and Plataea among the most important in recorded history.

C. The detection of Mordecai (2:19-23).
1. Mordecai, who had become a palace official, overhears at the gate a plot of two guards to assassinate Xerxes.
2. He reports this to Queen Esther, who in turn informs the king. Both guards are executed. This was all duly recorded in the book of the history of King Xerxes' reign. Note: Later, in 465 B.C., Xerxes would be assassinated in a similar plot.

II. The Lies of Haman (3-5).
A. Infernal servitude.
1. Soon after Esther had become queen, Xerxes appointed as his prime minister a vicious politician named Haman. Haman was an Amalekite, and a descendant from a former king of that nation named Agag, who ruled in the days of Saul and Samuel. It will be

remembered that Saul disobeyed God and spared King Agag in battle. (See 1 Sam. 15.) The Amalekites had been the bitter enemies of Israel. They had attacked them while en route to the Promised Land (Ex. 17:14; Deut. 25:17-19).

2. The arrogant Haman soon learned a Jew named Mordecai was refusing to bow before him, as had been commanded. Mordecai had simply stood for his faith, as once did three other Jewish captives in a foreign land (see Dan. 3).

3. Haman hatched a plot to exterminate not only Mordecai, but every other Jew living in the Persian Empire. Here is the ultimate of anti-Semitic action in the Old Testament. In his satanic strategy, he approached the king with the following "recommendations."

   a. That there is a "certain people scattered abroad and dispersed among the people in all the provinces of thy kingdom, and their laws are different from all people; neither keep they the king's laws. Therefore, it is not for the king's profit to tolerate them" (3:8). This, of course, was a brazen lie!

   b. That he, Haman, would be happy to contribute the sum of twenty million dollars into the royal treasury for the expense involved in this purge (3:9). Haman had doubtless counted on confiscating far more than this sum, which would be taken from those hundreds of thousands of innocent people he planned to butcher like cattle.

   c. The careless and heartless king agreed to this, without even checking the identity of this "certain people," to say nothing of their guilt (3:10, 11).

   d. Several weeks later Haman had prepared his murderous manifestation in the various languages and dialects of each province in the empire. Royal riders were sent forth to announce this edict of execution which decreed that all Jews would be killed on February 28 of the following year—473 B.C. (3:12-15).

B. Intestinal fortitude (4-5).

1. As seen in Mordecai (4:1-14).

   a. Upon learning of the decree of death, Mordecai immediately identified with his people and went into deep mourning.

   b. Unaware of the new law, Esther learned of her cousin's sorrow and inquired concerning the reason behind it.

   c. Mordecai informed her and advised that she visit the king immediately.

   d. Esther pointed out to him that she had not been summoned to Xerxes' inner court for thirty days and to walk in uninvited would very possibly bring instant death.

   e. Mordecai answered with what is, perhaps, the key statement in the entire book. (See 4:13, 14.)

   f. Two phrases are especially significant here:

      (1) "Then shalt . . . deliverance arise to the Jews from another place." Even though the name God as such is not mentioned in Esther, surely Mordecai had his deliverance in mind here.

      (2) "Thou art come to the kingdom for such a time as this." This would indeed be the case. Not only did Esther later save the Jews in Persia, but also those living in Palestine, for the death decree included them too. In addition to this, Esther no doubt exercised a great influence upon her step-son, Artaxerxes, who later proved to be so kindly disposed toward Ezra and Nehemiah.

2. As seen in Esther (4:15—5:14).

   a. Esther immediately ordered a three-day fast among the Jews, and determined that she would "go in unto the king, which is not according to the law. And if I perish, I perish" (4:16). (See also Dan. 3:17, 18.)

   b. Three days later Esther entered the king's inner court, uninvited, but to her relief, she was warmly received. Xerxes, realizing his wife must have been desperate to take such a risk, said:

      "What wilt thou, queen Esther? And what is thy request? It shall be even given thee to the half of the kingdom" (5:3).

      (See Dan. 5:16 and Mk. 6:22, 23. See also Prov. 21:1; 19:12.)

   c. The queen did not reveal her request at this time, but simply asked that both the king and Haman attend a banquet she was preparing the next day. Xerxes quickly agreed.

   d. Upon learning of his invitation, the vain Haman became puffed up with pride. But when he saw Mordecai standing at the palace gate, still refusing to bow, he was furious.

   e. He related both his joy and frustration to Zeresh and his friends at home. Note the following account which revealed perhaps the true character of Haman (and indeed his wife) in the strongest light possible. (See 5:12-14.)

III. The Prize of Faith (6-10).

A. The execution of a beast—Haman (6-8).

1. Scene one—the king's bedroom (6).

   a. Xerxes experienced a case of royal insomnia and ordered the reading of some historical records, hoping perhaps that this dull material would put him to sleep (6:1).

   b. The reader, by "chance," just happened to begin reading at the place which related how Mordecai had once saved the king's life by exposing an assassination plot. The king, now fully awake, asked: "What honor and dignity hath been bestowed upon Mordecai for this?" (6:3). The answer from his advisor was: "There has nothing been done for him."

c. At this exact moment Haman arrived at Xerxes' palace, seeking the king's permission to hang Mordecai. The king, still determined to reward Mordecai (neither Xerxes nor Haman, of course, knew what the other was thinking) used Haman as a sounding board and inquired:

"What shall be done for the man whom the king delighteth to honor?" (6:6).

d. The arrogant and self-centered Haman immediately thought Xerxes had him in mind and brazenly suggested the following:

(1) That the man to be honored be clothed in the king's own royal robes.

(2) That he be placed upon Xerxes' personal horse.

(3) That he be allowed to wear the king's crown.

(4) That the king's most noble prince lead this hero, seated upon the horse, through the streets of the city, shouting his praises for all to hear (6:7-9).

e. The king quickly agreed to all this and then turned to Haman and ordered his wicked prime minister to perform all this for Mordecai. The totally dumb-struck Haman stumbled out to obey Xerxes' command and later hurried home, utterly humiliated! Even there he received no comfort, but heard his wife say:

"If Mordecai is of the seed of the Jews, before whom thou hast begun to fall, thou shalt not prevail against him, but shalt surely fall before him" (6:13).

f. While they yet spoke, he received the message to attend Esther's banquet (6:14).

2. Scene two—the king's banquet hall (7).

a. The treachery learned (7:1-6).

(1) Esther warned the king that a plot was underway to slaughter both her and all her people. The king, filled with astonishment and then anger, asked: "Who is he, and where is he, who would presume in his heart to do so?" (7:5).

(2) Esther pointed to Haman and replied: "The adversary and enemy is this wicked Haman" (7:6). (See also 1 Pet. 5:8; 1 Jn. 2:13; 2 Thess. 2:8.)

b. The tables turned (7:7—8:17).

(1) Xerxes, unable to speak because of his fury, walked outside into his palace garden for a moment (7:7).

(2) Filled with horrible fear, the cowardly Haman begged Esther to intercede to the king for him. In his terrible fright he accidentally fell upon the couch where Esther was reclining (7:8).

(3) At this point Xerxes walked back in and viewed what he interpreted to be a rape attempt on the part of Ha-

man. Upon learning of the nearby gallows that Haman had built for Mordecai, the king roared out in his wrath for Haman himself to be hanged that very night. The order was immediately carried out (7:9, 10).

Note: Haman had violated that fearful warning of God to Abraham which said:

"And I will bless them that bless thee, and curse him that curseth thee" (Gen. 12:3).

For this violation he would forfeit his life. (See Prov. 26:27; Gal. 6:7, 8; Isa. 54:17.) Pharaoh learned that Esther's people couldn't be drowned (Ex. 14). Nebuchadnezzar learned

Esther

The Rise of Esther

CHAPTERS 1-2

The rejection of Vashti:	King Ahasuerus divorces his wife Vashti.
The selection of Esther:	Esther is the winner of a beauty contest and becomes his new queen.
The detection of Mordecai:	He overhears and reports a plot to assassinate the king.

The Lies of Haman

CHAPTERS 3-5

Infernal servitude:	Haman is appointed prime minister and instigates a plot to kill all the Jews.
Intestinal fortitude:	Upon hearing of this wicked plot, both Mordecai and Esther display great courage and wisdom. ● As seen by Mordecai's advice to Esther. ● As seen by Esther's appearance before the king.

The Prize of Faith

CHAPTERS 6-10

The execution of a "beast"—Haman
● Scene one: The king's bedroom. He learns of Mordecai's loyalty.
● Scene two: The king's banquet hall. He learns of Haman's treachery.
The institution of a feast—Purim

they couldn't be burned (Dan. 3). Darius learned they couldn't be eaten (Dan. 6). Haman learned they couldn't be hanged (Est. 7).

(4) After his execution, Xerxes gave Esther Haman's estate and appointed Mordecai his new prime minister (8:1, 2).

(5) Both now begged the king to reverse Haman's order. But the law of the Medes and Persians once made, was immutable, and not even Xerxes himself could change it. Xerxes then did the next best thing. He ordered the Jews to defend themselves. Mordecai immediately sent copies of this new decree to all of the 127 provinces (8:3–14).

B. The institution of a feast—Purim (9–10).

1. The Jews prepared themselves and were able to slaughter their enemies on February 23, execution day (9:1–19).

2. Mordecai and Esther then instituted a new memorial feast called Purim, to commemorate yearly their great salvation from Haman (9:20–32).

3. Mordecai became a great and godly statesman, respected by both Jews and Gentiles for his abilities and actions (10).

Note: Some 2400 years after the events in the book of Esther had transpired, an amazing twentieth century replay was enacted in Russia:

On March 1, 1953—a bare eight years after the holocaust that took the lives of six million Jews—Josef Stalin unveiled a proposal to liquidate the Jews of the Soviet Union—another three million. The proposal was due to go into effect on March 9, but it never did, for a day after Stalin presented it, he unexpectedly dropped dead of a stroke.

The amazing story, often rumored, has been officially confirmed by a non-Jewish Soviet librarian, Ludmila Lufanov, who worked for years in top-secret Soviet archives in Moscow. She managed relatively recently to leave the USSR and now lives in the United States. A short while ago, in a Soviet Russian language journal, she told the incredible story and a copy reached the Jewish Press in Jerusalem.

Stalin, a paranoid Jew-hater, had liquidated thousands of Jews in the 1930s, including many who had been his most loyal and trusted comrades from the beginning of the Bolshevik movement. He liquidated not only the infamous Jewish community party section—Yevesektzia—which did more to wipe out Judaism and Jewish culture than anyone else, but also exterminated the heads of the Yevesektzia. After the war, which interrupted his plans for the Jews, Stalin was infuriated at the reception given to Israel's first ambassador to Moscow, Golda Meir, by Soviet Jews. He moved ruthlessly.

Jewish poets, writers, and artists were liquidated (most of whom had been loyal communists who had never complained when Stalin liquidated religious and Zionist Jews). He demanded that the satellite states do the same and the world was stunned to see Czechoslovak Community Party boss—Slansky—a loyal Stalinist, and a number of other top Jews, tried on charges of "cosmopolitanism" and "treason" and hanged. But it was the infamous "doctor's plot" that was to mark the climactic moment of Jewish genocide.

In 1953 Stalin suddenly announced that a "plot" had been discovered to kill him. It was a devious and clever one, planned by doctors—all of whom happened to be Jewish. The controlled press gave the "plotters" and the "plot" non-stop first-page treatment. Denunciations from puppet Communists came in from all over the Soviet Union. It was clear that the key word here was "Jewish" or the code names "Cosmopolitanism" and "Zionism." Stalin decided that the hanging of the doctors would serve as a pretext for mass rioting on the part of Soviet masses that would last three days and would eliminate two thirds of the three million Soviet Jews. The rest would be sent to Siberia to concentration camps where they would also die.

On March 1, 1953, at 12 noon, Stalin called a meeting of the Politburo in the Kremlin and read to the Soviet leaders his plan for the extermination of the Jews. According to the secret transcript, he said:

"The murderers in the white jackets have admitted their guilt. On the ninth of March they will be hanged in Red Square before all to see, but not even this punishment will satisfy our people. . . . The masses' anger will not be satisfied and there will be three days when we will be unable to stem the righteous wrath of the people who will pour out their fury on the Jewish heads."

Stalin concluded by saying that after three days, the heads of the Jewish community will admit in writing their collective guilt against the Russian people and will plead with the government to save them from total annihilation.

"After receiving this request to intervene, the government will not be able to remain aloof, and in order to separate the racist Jews from the Russian people, the Jews will be placed on special railroad cars and sent to the Far North and the Siberian plains. However, only a third of the passengers on the special trains will arrive at their destinations. The other two-thirds will fall victim to the anger of the masses at every stop along the way."

According to the librarian, when Stalin finished reading the proposal there was dead silence in the room. Stalin, furious, cursed his cabinet minister and walked out, slamming the door.

On March 2, the day after outlining the plans and exactly a week before the extermination of the three million Jews was to have taken place—Stalin died of a stroke. He lay in state for a week and was buried on March 9, which was the Jewish holiday—Purim.

HAGGAI (520 B.C.)

INTRODUCTION:

1. The name Haggai means, "my feast."

2. His book is the second smallest in the Old Testament (Obadiah is the shortest), and consists of but thirty-eight verses.

3. Haggai was a contemporary of Zechariah. Both are mentioned in the book of Ezra (5:1; 6:14) as that dynamic duet who functioned as God's spiritual cheerleaders in erecting the Temple under Zerubbabel.

4. Haggai's prophecies are the most precisely dated ones in all the Bible.

5. His book has been compared to the epistle of James in the New Testament.

6. A chronology of this period may be seen by the following:

a. 536 B.C.: 50,000 Jews under Zerubbabel return to Jerusalem.

b. 536 B.C.: seventh month, they build the altar and offer sacrifice.

c. 535 B.C.: second month, work on the Temple begins, and is stopped.

d. 520 B.C.: sixth month (September), first day, Haggai's call to build.
   (1) sixth month, twenty-fourth day, building begins
   (2) seventh month (October), twenty-first day, Haggai's second appeal
   (3) eighth month (November), Zechariah's opening address
   (4) ninth month (December), twenty-fourth day, Haggai's third and fourth
   (5) eleventh month (February), twenty-fourth day, Zechariah's visions

e. 518 B.C.: ninth month (December), fourth day, Zechariah's visions

f. 516 B.C.: twelfth month (March), third day, the Temple is completed.

g. 515 B.C.: first month (April), fourteenth—twenty-first days, joyful Passover.

h. 455 B.C.: Ezra comes to Jerusalem and makes certain reforms.

i. 445 B.C.: Nehemiah rebuilds the wall. Period of Malachi.

7. Thus, his book is actually a record of four sermons.
   a. His first is found in 1:1-11.
   b. His second, in 2:1-9.
   c. His third, in 2:10-19.
   d. His fourth, in 2:20-23.

8. The New Testament passage found in 1 Corinthians 15:58 may appropriately be written over the book of Haggai.

I. A September Message: Directed to the hands of the people. It said, "Perform!" (1:1-15).
   A. The people had just about given up concerning the building of their Temple. After fifteen years it remained unfinished. Their lame excuse was,
      "The time is not yet come, the time that the Lord's house should be built" (1:2).
      Because of this carelessness, God could not and would not bless them with either spiritual or financial prosperity.
   B. God's advice to them was therefore to:
      "Go up to the mountain, and bring wood, and build the house; and I will take pleasure in it, and I will be glorified, saith the Lord" (1:8).
   C. The spirits of Zerubbabel (the governor) and Joshua (the high priest) were then stirred up by the Lord. This godly pair thus led the people to finish building the Temple.

II. An October Message: Directed to the hearts of the people. It said, "Patience!" (2:1-9).
   A. In spite of the insignificant Temple they had just built, as we have already seen (Ezra 3:8-13), there was weeping as well as joy at the dedication during Zerubbabel's time as some of the old men remembered the glories of Solomon's Temple. The new Temple was far inferior in size and cost.
   B. Patience was needed because of the magnificent temple that would someday be built.
      "The glory of this latter house shall be greater than of the former, saith the Lord of hosts; and in this place will I give peace, said the Lord of hosts" (2:9).

Haggai

PERFORM:
● DON'T GIVE UP—on the Temple.
● DO GO UP—on the mountain.
● GET ALL STIRRED UP—about the Lord.

PATIENCE:
● IN SPITE OF the insignificant Temple they had just built
● BECAUSE OF the magnificent Temple they someday would build

PONDER:
● THE FACT OF JUDAH'S CONTAMINATION (2:10-17)
● THE FACT OF GOD'S DETERMINATION (2:18, 19)
● THE FACT OF THE GREAT TRIBULATION (2:20-22)
● THE FACT OF ZERUBBABEL'S ELEVATION (2:23)

This, of course, is a reference to the beautiful new millennial temple, yet to be built. (See Ezek. 40-48.)

III. A December Message: Directed to the head of the people. It said, "Ponder!" (2:10-23).
   A. The fact of Judah's contamination (2:10-17). God asked Judah to answer two questions.
      1. "If one of you is carrying a holy sacrifice in his robes, and happens to brush against some bread, or wine, or meat, will it too become holy?" (2:12, The Living Bible).
         The answer of course, was, "No holiness does not pass to other things that way."
      2. "If someone touches a dead person, and so becomes ceremonially impure, and then brushes against something, does it become contaminated?" (2:13).
         Here the answer was yes! The point God was making here is that whatever righteousness the nation Israel might have once possessed was not automatically transferred upon them at this time. But their own unrighteousness was affecting both them and their children.
   B. The fact of God's determination (2:17-19). God promised them that because of their decision to finish the Temple, he would bless them from that day on, even before the structure was completed.
   C. The fact of the great tribulation (2:20-22). Someday God would destroy all those Gentile nations which had afflicted Israel throughout the years.
      ". . . I will shake the heavens and the earth; and I will overthrow the throne of kingdoms, and I will destroy the strength of the kingdoms of the nations; and I will overthrow the chariots, and those who ride in them; and the horses and their riders shall come down, every one by the sword of his brother" (2:21, 22). (See also Heb. 12:26; Rev. 16:18-20.)
   D. The fact of Zerubbabel's elevation (2:23).
      "In that day, saith the Lord of hosts, will I take thee, O Zerubbabel, my servant . . . and will make thee as a signet; for I have chosen thee. . . ."
      Some believe that Zerubbabel will be God's prime minister during the millennium.

ZECHARIAH (520 B.C.)

INTRODUCTION:

1. Zechariah means, "Jehovah remembers." He was of priestly descent (as were Jeremiah and Ezekiel).
2. Josephus tells us he was later slain in the Temple, thus becoming a martyr for Christ.
3. He was a younger contemporary of Haggai (see 2:4).
4. Zechariah's writings resemble those of Daniel. Note also:
   a. Daniel was born in Palestine but wrote his prophecies in Babylon.
   b. Zechariah was born in Babylon, but wrote his book in Palestine.
5. Zechariah also reminds one of the book of Revelation.
6. His book contains more messianic passages than any other minor prophet. He speaks of the following:
   a. Christ as the Branch (3:8)
   b. Christ as God's Servant (3:8)
   c. Christ as God's smitten Shepherd (13:7)
   d. The triumphal entry (9:9)
   e. The betrayal for thirty pieces of silver (11:12, 13)
   f. The piercing of Jesus' hands and feet (12:10)
   g. His return to Mount Olivet (14:3-8)

I. The Visions of the Prophet (1-6). Zechariah receives ten visions, all apparently during the same night.
   A. The rider on the red horse (1:7-17).
      1. Zechariah sees a heavenly rider on a red horse, surrounded by other riders, all mounted also upon various colored horses.
      2. This special rider on the red horse is probably Christ.
      3. The other riders are angels who have been sent by God to "walk to and fro through the earth" (1:10). Thus, it is comforting to know that God also has his "spiritual spies" out checking upon this old sinful earth, as does Satan (see Job 1:7; 2:2; 1 Pet. 5:8).
      4. The angel of the Lord (Jesus) then prays over the troubled state of Jerusalem and is reassured by the Father that "the Lord shall yet comfort Zion, and shall yet choose Jerusalem" (1:17).
   B. The four horns (1:18, 19). Zechariah sees four animal horns and is told that they represent the four world powers that have scattered Judah, Israel, and Jerusalem. These horns may have symbolized the following:
      1. Assyria—which captured the northern kingdom of Israel. (See 2 Ki. 17.)
      2. Babylon—which captured the southern kingdom of Judah. (See 2 Ki. 24.)
      3. Persia—which planned on one occasion to destroy all Jews. (See the book of Esther.)
      4. Rome—which controlled and heavily taxed the city of Jerusalem during the days of Christ.
      These horns could, of course, also symbolize the four world powers mentioned by Daniel. (See 2:37-45; 7:2-8, 17-28.) Here they would be identified as Babylon, Persia, Greece, and Rome.
   C. The four artisans (1:20, 21). An artisan is a worker in wood, stone, or metal.
      1. The identity of these artisans: two suggestions have been offered here.
         a. That they refer to the four judgments spoken of by both Ezekiel (14:21) and John (Rev. 6:1-8). These judgments are war, famine, wild animals, and pestilence.
         b. That they refer to the powers which defeated those four nations.
            (1) Cyrus would be one, for he defeated Babylon (Dan. 5).
            (2) Alexander the Great would be one, for he defeated Persia (Dan. 8).
            (3) The various Roman generals would be one, for they subdued Greece.
            (4) Christ is one, for he will totally destroy the revived Roman Empire (Rev. 19).
      2. The purpose of the artisans:
         "These are come to terrify them, to cast out the horns of the nations, which lifted up their horn over the land of Judah to scatter it" (1:21).
   D. The man with a measuring line (2:1-13).
      1. Zechariah sees a man carrying a yardstick in his hand en route to measure Jerusalem. This is the second of four instances in the Bible in which either Jerusalem or its Temple is measured. Note:
         a. The Temple is measured in Jerusalem during the tribulation. (See Rev. 11:1, 2.)
         b. The Temple and city are measured during the millennium. (See Ezek. 40:3, 5; 37:26.)
         c. The eternal New Jerusalem is measured after the millennium. (See Rev. 21:15.)
      2. Zechariah is assured of the following thrilling facts concerning the millennial Jerusalem.
         a. That Jerusalem would someday be so full of people that some would have to live outside its city walls, yet dwelling in perfect safety.
         b. That God himself would be a wall of fire protecting them.
         c. That he would be the glory of the city.
         d. That the one who harmed them, touched the apple of his eye! (See also Deut. 32:7, 10; Ps. 17:8.)
      3. In verses 8, 9 of this chapter we have a remarkable Old Testament proof concerning the Trinity. Here the Lord of Hosts says he was sent by the Lord of Hosts.
      4. Palestine is referred to as "the holy land" in verse 12. This is the only place in Scripture where it is called by this name.
   E. The confrontation in heaven (3:1-10). The clothing of Joshua, the high priest. This is undoubtedly the greatest single chapter on the subject of salvation in all the Old Testament. In this vision Zechariah sees Joshua, the high priest, dressed in filthy clothing, and standing before God in heaven. He is being accused by Satan because of his soiled clothing. Christ, however, rebukes Satan, removes Joshua's dirty clothing, and dresses him in clean apparel. Joshua then is challenged to serve God with his whole heart. He is promised that someday God's Branch will appear to

cleanse the land of its sin. The following facts concerning salvation are brought out here:

1. The enemy of salvation. Contrary to popular opinion, Satan is not in hell today, but has accesss to God's very throne, where he constantly makes accusations against believers. (See also Job 1, 2; Rev. 12.)
2. The Person of Salvation. He is, of course, the Savior. Again in verse 2 we have proof of the Trinity, for the Lord (Jesus) calls upon the Lord (the Father) to rebuke Satan.
   a. His names: the Branch (3:8). He is called by this title in four Old Testament passages.
      (1) The branch of David. (Isa. 11:1; Jer. 23:5; 33:15). This corresponds to Matthew, who presents him as the King of the Jews.
      (2) My servant the Branch (Zech. 3:8). This corresponds to Mark, who presents him as the lowly slave.
      (3) The Man whose name is the Branch (Zech. 6:12, 13). This corresponds to Luke, who presents him as the perfect Man.
      (4) The Branch of Jehovah (Isa. 4:2). This corresponds to John, who presents him as the mighty God.
      (5) The Cornerstone (3:9). (See Isa. 28:16; Ps. 118; 22; Mt. 21:42; Acts 4:11; Eph. 2:20, 21.) Thus:
         (a) To the Gentiles, he is the Stone of crushing (Dan. 2:34, 35, 44, 45).
         (b) To Israel, he is the stumbling Stone (Rom. 9:31-33).
         (c) To the believer, he is the salvation Cornerstone (Eph. 2:19-22).
   b. His ministry:
      (1) To clothe all believers in robes of righteousness. (See Prov. 30:12; Isa. 64:6; 4:3, 4; Rom. 10:1-4; Phil. 3:9.)
      (2) To make intercession for the believer against Satan's lies. (See Lk. 22:31; Rom. 8:34; Heb. 7:25; 9:24; 1 Jn. 2:1.)
      (3) To bring in and rule over the millennium. (See Rev. 11:15-19.)
3. The purpose of salvation (3:6, 7). These verses may be paraphrased as follows: "If you will walk in my ways and keep my charge, you [Joshua] shall not only have the honor of judging my house, and keeping my courts, but when your walk on earth is done, you shall be transplanted to higher service in heaven, and have places to walk among these pure angelic beings who stand by me, harkening unto the voice of my word." (See also Ps. 103:20, 21; Eph. 2:4-10.)

F. The golden lampstand and the two olive trees (4:1-14). Here Zechariah sees a sevenfold golden lampstand, supplied by a reservoir of olive oil. On either side of the lampstand was a carved olive tree.

1. A lampstand in the Bible represents God's witnesses in this world.
   a. It can refer to Israel (as it does here).
   b. It can refer to the church (as it does in Rev. 1-3).
2. The olive oil is, of course, a symbol for the Holy Spirit. (See Lk. 4:18; Acts 10:38; Heb. 1:9; 1 Jn. 2:20.) We note the words of God in Zechariah 4:6 at this point:
   "Not by might, nor by power, but by my Spirit, saith the Lord of Hosts."
3. The olive trees refer to two famous teams:
   a. The historical team of Zerubbabel and Joshua.
   b. The prophetical team of Elijah and Moses. (See Rev. 11.)

G. The flying scroll (5:1-4). Zechariah sees a flying scroll, fifteen feet wide by thirty feet long. This represented the words of God's curse going out over the entire land of Israel.

1. The scope of this judgment. Although only two of the original commandments are mentioned here, that of swearing (the third, Ex. 20:7) and stealing (the eighth, Ex. 20:15), they nevertheless covered the entire moral code of God.
   a. The sin of swearing (using God's name falsely) represents all crimes against God and is vertical in nature.
   b. The sin of stealing represents all crimes against man, and is horizontal in nature.
2. The accused at this judgment. All unsaved Israelites throughout history. (See Rom. 9:6; Mt. 23; 1 Thess. 2:15, 16; Ezek. 11:21; 20:38.)
3. The time of this judgment. After the tribulation and just prior to the millennium. (See Mt. 25:1-30.)
4. The penalty of this judgment. It will apparently include both physical and spiritual death.

H. The woman in the ephah (5:5-11). The prophet views a flying bushel basket (ephah) covered by a heavy lead top piece. When the lid is lifted he sees a woman seated inside. He is then told:

1. The woman inside represents sin and wickedness. Often in the Bible iniquity is symbolized by a woman. (See Mt. 13:33; Rev. 2:20; 17:1-7.)
2. The heavy lead cover probably symbolizes the restraining power of God over evil.
3. The destination is said to be Babylon where it (evil and wickedness) would "be established, and set there upon its own base" (5:11). This statement may carry with it both historical and prophetical implications. Thus:
   a. Historical—the Tower of Babel, where organized rebellion against God began. (See Gen. 11:1-9.)
   b. Prophetical—the city of Babylon, which may actually be rebuilt during the tribulation. (See Rev. 18.)

I. The four chariots (6:1-8). Zechariah sees four chariots driven by four heavenly spirits proceeding from two brass mountains. Each chariot is pulled by a different colored team of horses. These colors are red, white, black, and gray. The various symbols here would seem to be as follows:

Zechariah

- The Tenfold
Vision of the Prophet Zechariah 1-6
- The Manifold
Vanities of the People Zechariah 7-8
- The Twofold
Visitation of the Prince Zechariah 9-13

THE TEN VISIONS

1. RIDER ON A RED HORSE (1:7-17)

- An appearance of Christ himself, along with some angels, keeping watch over Jerusalem.

2. THE FOUR HORNS (1:18, 19)

- May represent the four Gentile world powers which scattered (or would scatter) Israel

1. Assyria (Captured northern kingdom.)
2. Babylon (Captured southern kingdom.)
3. Persia (Plot against all Jews. See **Esther**.)
4. Rome (Has scattered and will scatter Israel.)

3. THE FOUR ARTISANS (1:20, 21)

- A probable reference to the first four sealed judgments in **Revelation 6:1-8**

4. MAN WITH A MEASURING LINE (2:1-13)

- Reference to the measuring of Jerusalem during the millennium (**Ezek. 40:1-5; 48:30-35**)

5. THE CONFRONTATION IN HEAVEN (3:1-10)

The Charge	The wearing of filthy garments
The Charged	Joshua and the people of Jerusalem
The Prosecutor	Satan
The Defender	The Branch—called this four times in the Old Testament

The Branch of David (**Isa. 11:1; Jer. 23:5; 33:15**)	Gospel fulfillment—Matthew
My Servant, the Branch (**Zech. 3:8**)	Gospel fulfillment—Mark
Joshua Cleansed and Reassured	The man Branch (**Zech. 6:12**)	Gospel fulfillment—Luke
	The Branch of Jehovah (**Isa. 4:2**)	Gospel fulfillment—John

6. THE GOLDEN LAMPSTAND AND THE TWO OLIVE TREES (4:1-14)

- Historical meaning — May refer to the anointed team of Zerubbabel and Joshua.
- Prophetical meaning — May refer to the anointed team of Elijah and Moses. (**See Rev. 11:3-12.**)

7. THE FLYING SCROLL (5:1-4)

- Meaning — God's judgment upon the land. Man had broken his entire moral law.
- Reason

Sin of swearing	Against God	Vertical
Sin of stealing	Against man	Horizontal

8. THE WOMAN IN THE EPHAH (5:5-11)

- The woman — A type of sin and rebellion
- The cover — A type of God's restraining power
- The destination — To establish itself in Babylon

Organized rebellion	Had begun here (**Gen. 11**)
Organized rebellion	May end here (**Rev. 18**)

9. THE FOUR CHARIOTS (6:1-8)

- Four heavenly spirits (angels) are driving these chariots, proceeding from two brass mountains
- The chariots may represent the first four plagues of **Revelation 6** and the mountains the judgment of God

10. THE CROWNING OF JOSHUA (6:9-15)

- Zerubbabel does this to illustrate the threefold ministry of the coming Messiah

1. He would build the Temple
2. He would minister as a Priest
3. He would rule as a King

---

1. The two brass mountains speak of God's judgment. (See Num. 21:9; John 3:14.)
2. The angel-driven chariots represent God's agents to effect various judgments upon Gentile nations. (See Rev. 7:1-3; 8:2, 7, 10, 12; 9:14, 15; 11:15; 15:1; 16:1-3.)
3. The various colored horses doubtless tie in with those mentioned in Revelation 6.
   a. The red ones speak of war and bloodshed. (See Rev. 6:4.)
   b. The black ones speak of famine and starvation. (See Rev. 6:5, 6.)
   c. The white ones speak of false peace. (See Rev. 6:2.)
   d. The gray ones speak of death. (See Rev. 6:8.)
      Note: We are told that those who proceeded "toward the north country have quieted my spirit . . . " (6:8).
      This may be a reference to the future divine judgment upon Russia during the tribulation. (See Ezek. 38, 39.)
J. The crowning of Joshua (6:9-15).
   1. Zechariah is told that three Jewish exiles will soon return to Jerusalem from Babylon, carrying gifts of silver and gold from the remnant there. Zechariah is instructed to make a golden crown from these gifts and place it upon Joshua, explaining to him that he rep-

resents the future Branch of Israel, the Messiah himself.

2. This blessed Messiah will someday function both as Priest and King. He will also build the Temple of God.

3. Zechariah is told the three returning exiles represent many others who will someday come from distant lands back to Palestine. (See also Isa. 56:6-8.)

II. The vanities of the people (7-8).

A. A group of Jews had come to Jerusalem from Bethel to ask the priests there if they could set aside their traditional custom of fasting and mourning each year during the month of August. The *New Scofield Bible* (p. 969) says in a footnote: "The mission of these Jews of the Captivity concerned a fast day instituted by the Jews in commemoration of the destruction of Jerusalem, wholly of their own will and without warrant from the Word of God. In the beginning there was doubtless sincere contrition in the observance of the day; now it had become a mere ceremonial. The Jews of the dispersion would be rid of it, but seek authority from the priests. The whole matter, like much in modern pseudo-Christianity, was extra-Biblical, formal and futile."

B. God tells them through the priests that it doesn't really make much difference what they do, for their hearts are insincere. He admonishes them to be honest in their dealings with both their God and their neighbors.

C. He promises that, because of his grace, their fast days will someday be feast days, and their sorrow turned into singing. (See 8:3, 4, 5, 8, 22, 23.)

III. The Visitation of the Prince (9-14).

A. The first coming of the Prince.

1. He came to feed the flock as his Father had instructed him to do (11:7).

2. The false shepherds of Israel, however, rejected him (11:8).

3. He thus broke one of his two staffs and set Israel aside for awhile (11:10). (See also Mt. 21:19, 42-46; 23:37-39.)

4. He finished his ministry by the triumphal entry into Jerusalem. "Rejoice greatly, O daughter of Zion; shout, O daughter of Jerusalem; behold, thy King cometh unto thee; he is just, and having salvation; lowly, and riding upon an ass, and upon a colt, the foal of an ass" (9:9). This was dramatically fulfilled, of course, in Matthew 21:1-11.

5. He was sold for thirty pieces of silver (11:12), the price of a slave which had been gored by an ox. (See Ex. 21:32.) This was fulfilled in Matthew 26:15.

6. This price, contemptuously given, was then cast aside with additional contempt, for the word "cast" used here is a gesture of disgust (as seen from Ex. 22:31; Isa. 14:19; 2 Sam. 18:17; 2 Ki. 23:12). This prophecy was fulfilled in Matthew 27:3-10.

7. He then broke his second staff, signifying perhaps the destruction of Jerusalem by Titus in 70 A.D. This tragedy ended all unity which existed in Israel.

8. He was finally crucified (12:10).

B. The Second Coming of the Prince:

1. The blood-letting of the false shepherd.

a. Because they rejected their Good Shepherd at his first coming, Israel will be given over for awhile to the cruel antichrist shepherd just prior to the second appearing of their glorious shepherd (11:15-17).

b. Two out of three will die in this horrible purge (13:8).

2. The bereavement of Israel (12:10-14). When he comes again, Israel will finally recognize him and mourn their heinous national crime of rexicide, the killing of one's own King. "And they shall look upon me whom they have pierced, and they shall mourn for him, as one mourneth for his only son . . ." (12:10).

3. The battle of Armageddon (12:1-9; 14:1-3, 12-15).

4. The bow of victory (10:4). This bow is, of course, the Son of God. We are assured of his deity because of the Father's statement in 13:7: "The man who is my fellow, said the Lord of hosts." This is literally translated, "the man who is my *equal*." From the bow of God this avenging arrow comes to earth.

ZECHARIAH AND THE PRINCE

The Two Visitations of the Prince

HIS FIRST COMING

● He comes to feed the flock of God (11:7)

● He is rejected by Israel's leaders (11:8)

● He thus set aside Israel **(11:10)**
(Possible meaning of his breaking the staff called beauty)

● He makes his triumphal entry into Jerusalem **(9:9)**

● He is sold for thirty pieces of silver **(11:12)**

● He predicts the destruction of Jerusalem **(11:14)**
(Possible meaning of his breaking the staff called band)

● He is crucified **(12:10)**

HIS SECOND COMING

● The cruel reign of the antichrist **(11:16)**

● Jerusalem to be surrounded and taken **(14:2)**

● Two thirds of the Jews to perish **(13:8)**

● One third of the Jews to be saved **(13:9)**

● Christ to appear upon the Mount of Olives **(14:4, 8)**

● Armageddon to be fought **(12:3; 14:2, 3)**

● God's enemies to be destroyed **(12:4, 9; 14:12-15)**

● Israel to recognize Christ **(12:10-14)**

● Israel to be cleansed **(13:1)**

● Israel to be settled in the land **(10:6-12; 8:8)**

● Gentiles to worship the Lord **(14:16-19)**

● Jerusalem to be filled with happy boys and girls **(8:5)**

● Christ to build the temple **(6:13)**

● Christ to rule as the Priest-King over all the world **(6:13; 9:10)**

a. He punishes those nations which have persecuted Israel. (See 9:1–8, 12–16.)

b. He will then strengthen the house of Judah, and "hiss [whistle] for them, and gather them" (10:8).

Note: God had previously said he would summon their enemies against them by hissing (Isa. 7:18, 19). Now, in the same way, he summons his people back to their own land.

c. He will finally "speak peace unto the nations; and his dominion shall be from sea even to sea, and from the river even to the ends of the earth" (9:10).

d. He will personally and visibly perform all this (14:4, 8).

5. The blessings of God (9:16, 17; 13:1, 9; 14:9, 10, 11, 16, 20, 21).

MALACHI (435–396 B.C.)

INTRODUCTION:

1. Malachi means "my messenger."

2. Absolutely nothing is known of Malachi beyond his name and the fact that he was the last Old Testament prophet.

3. Malachi may be looked upon as a miniature summary of the entire Old Testament, for the prophet briefly covers those five key truths found in the other books. These are:

a. The *selection* of Israel by God (1:2; 2:4–6, 10).

b. The *transgression* of Israel against God (1:6; 2:11, 17).

c. The *manifestation* of the Messiah (3:1; 4:2).

d. The *tribulation* upon the nations (4:1).

e. The *purification* of Israel at last (3:2–4, 12, 16–18; 4:2–6).

4. Malachi may be compared to Moses.

a. Moses gives us the first Old Testament prophecy concerning the Messiah. (See Gen. 3:15.)

b. Malachi lists the last Old Testament prophecy concerning the Messiah. (See 4:2.)

5. Malachi's book may be considered as a partial fulfillment of Daniel's prophecy in 9:24–27. This great prediction, known as the seventy-weeks (actually a 490-year period) began in 445 B.C. and was divided into three main segments. The first covered a period of forty-nine years. This would thus bring it to 396, or the approximate date many feel Malachi completed his book.

I. The Love of God Stated (1:1–5).

A. In the second verse of his book Malachi lists the first of seven rather flippant questions the carnal Israelites had required of God. Each question was the result of a previous clear statement from God. These were:

1. In what way hast thou loved us? (1:2).

2. In what way have we despised thy name? (1:6).

3. In what way have we polluted thee? (1:7).

4. In what way have we wearied thee? (2:17).

5. In what way shall we return? (3:7).

6. How have we robbed thee? (3:8).

7. What have we spoken so much against thee? (3:13).

B. S. Franklin Logsdon writes the following concerning this first question:

"The question, "Wherein hast thou loved us?" indicates an irritation on the part of the people which led them to accuse the Lord of failure to prove his love. They had a bitter recollection of the attitudes and actions of the Edomites when Jerusalem was plundered by the Philistines and Arabians (2 Chron. 21:16, 17). These descendants of Esau were there aiding and abetting the enemy in the defeat of their brethren, and the Lord did not restrain them (Obad. 11).

They showed sadistic pleasure over Judah's misfortune by mocking at her calamities (Obad. 12). They shared the spoils with the enemy when the city was captured (Obad. 13). They assisted the enemy by blocking the retreat of refugees (Obad. 14). They turned over to the insurgents those that could not escape (Obad. 14). Thus, in Judah's trying hours, the Edomites looked, laughed, insulted, robbed, trapped, and murdered because of their inherited hatred toward Jacob (and his posterity) for fraudulently obtaining the blessing.

The Lord's people carried a painful grievance concerning this. It was a festering sore in their memory. They recalled how their fathers, as captives, sitting along the rivers of Babylon, cried out, 'Remember, O Lord, the children of Edom in the day of Jerusalem; who said, Rase it, rase it, even to the foundation thereof' (Ps. 137:7). The question in Malachi's day is, in substance. 'Why did God permit this if He loved us?' " (*Malachi, or, Will a Man Rob God?* pp. 14, 15)

C. God answers their first question by pointing out two facts.

1. He would never allow Edom to prosper because they had mistreated the apple of his eye, Israel.

2. He had already preferred Israel over Esau. Some have been greatly troubled over God's statement that he *loved* Jacob and *hated* Esau. Here several factors must be observed.

a. The Genesis account which gives us the history of both boys never records that God actually and personally hated Esau and loved Jacob. (See Gen. 25, 27.)

b. The statement may have well referred to those *nations* founded by the two men. God definitely did abhor the sinful attitudes and actions of the Edomites, as spoken of by the prophet Obadiah.

c. The name *Jacob* here is a plural noun, which may indicate the entire nation of Israel.

d. The Hebrew word for hate is *sane*, and sometimes is used to indicate preference or priority instead of abhorrence. This is also the case with the Greek word for hate which is *misco*. Note the following example:

(1) "And when the Lord saw that Leah was *hated*, he opened her womb: but Rachel was barren" (Gen. 29:31). In no way does the record indicate that Jacob hated his first wife, but simply that he preferred his second.

(2) "The poor is *hated* even by his own neighbor, but the rich hath many friends" (Prov. 14:20).

"If any man come to me, and *hate* not his father, and mother, and wife, and children, and brethren, and sisters, yea, and his own life also, he cannot be my disciple" (Lk. 14:26).

Here it is perfectly obvious that our Lord was not teaching an individual to despise and abhor his own flesh and blood, but simply that God must be given first priority in a believer's life!

e. The real problem in Malachi's passage, however, is probably not the fact that God "hated" Esau, but that he could *love* Jacob. The fact is that he did indeed love his sinful nation. During his final address to Israel, Moses reminds them of this love no less than seven times. (See Deut. 4:37; 7:8, 13; 10:15; 15:16; 23:5; 33:3. Other passages stating this fact are: Isa. 43:4; 48:14; 63:9; Jer. 31:3; Hosea 3:1; 11:1, 4; 14:4.)

II. The Love of God Scorned.
  A. By the prophets.
    1. Who cheated the Lord through their shabby offerings (1:6—2:9).
      a. They had offered lame and sick animals to God. These cheap sacrifices were refused by the Lord, who challenged them if they dared to "offer it now unto thy governor; will he be pleased with thee, or accept thy person?" (1:8).
        (See also David's testimony in 2 Sam. 24:24.)
      b. They had not offered that proper honor and respect to God that:
        (1) a child should give to his father (1:6)
        (2) a servant should render to his master (1:6)
        (3) a citizen should pay to his king (1:14)
    2. Who cheated the people through their shabby example (2:7-9).
  B. By the people.
    1. through their *inequalities* (2:10)
    2. through their *intermarriages* (2:11)
    3. through their *immorality* (2:14)
    4. through their *insincerity* (2:17)
    5. through their *indebtedness* (3:8-10)
    6. through their *incriminations* (3:13-15)
III. The Love of God Shown.
  A. By remembering his own saints (3:16, 17). Especially to be noted are the last five words in 3:16, "that thought upon his name." This no doubt included the various names for God given in the Old Testament, along with their meanings. A summary of God's names would include:
    1. *Elohim*—used 2,570 times, refers to God's power and might (Gen. 1:1; Ps. 19:1).
    2. *El*—four compounds of this name—
      a. *Elyon*, the strongest strong One (Gen. 14:17-20; Isa. 14:13, 14)

      b. *Roi*, the strong One who sees (Gen. 16:13)
      c. *Shaddai*, the breasted One (used forty-eight times in Old Testament; see Gen. 17:1; Ps. 91:1)
      d. *Olam*, the everlasting God (Isa. 40:28)
    3. *Adonai*—Master, Lord. God owns all his creation (Mal. 1:6).
    4. *Jehovah*—most common name. Occurs 6,823 times. The Self-existent One, the God of the covenant (Gen. 2:4).

    There are nine compound names of this name:

Malachi

The Love of God
HIS LOVE STATED

"I have loved you, saith the Lord . . . I loved Jacob, and I hated Esau" **MALACHI 1:2, 3.**

A twofold problem is seen in these verses:

● WHY GOD "HATED" ESAU. NOTE:

1. The Genesis account **(25, 27)** never records God hating Esau.

2. The Hebrew word here translated hate can also mean preference (see **Gen. 29:31; Prov. 14:20; Lk. 14:26).**

3. The name Esau also doubtless stood for the entire wicked nation of Edom, whose ways God did indeed hate.

● WHY GOD LOVED JACOB: THIS IS THE REAL PROBLEM IN THE PASSAGE.

HIS LOVE SCORNED

● BY THE PRIESTS

1. Who cheated *the Lord* through their shabby offerings **(1:7, 8).**

2. Who cheated *the people* through their shabby example **(2:7-9).**

● BY THE PEOPLE:

1. Through their inequalities **(2:10)**
2. Through their intermarriages **(2:11)**
3. Through their immorality **(2:14)**
4. Through their insincerity **(2:17)**
5. Through their indebtedness **(3:8-10)**
6. Through their incriminations **(3:13-15)**

HIS LOVE SHOWN

● BY REMEMBERING HIS SAINTS **(3:16).**

● BY SENDING HIS OWN SON.

1. His first coming was introduced by John the Baptist **(3:1a).**

2. His Second Coming will be introduced by Elijah the prophet **(4:5).**

THE PURPOSE OF HIS SECOND COMING

● REGARDING THE GENTILES:

To consume them as chaff in his oven **(4:1, 3).**

● REGARDING THE JEWS:

They will accept Christ **(3:1b).**
They will be gathered by Christ **(3:17).**
They will be purified by Christ **(3:2, 3).**
They will be healed by Christ **(4:2).**

a. *Jireh*—the Lord will provide (Gen. 22:13, 14)

b. *Nissi*—the Lord, my banner (Ex. 17:15)

c. *Shalom*—the Lord is Peace (Jdg. 6:24)

d. *Sabbaoth*—the Lord of Hosts (1 Sam. 1:3; Isa. 6:1–3)

e. *Maccaddeshoem*—the Lord thy Sanctifier (Ex. 31:13)

f. *Rohi (Raah)*—the Lord my Shepherd (Ps. 23:1)

g. *Tsidkenu*—the Lord our Righteousness (Jer. 23:6)

h. *Shammah*—the Lord who is present (Ezek. 48:35)

i. *Rapha*—the Lord our Healer (Ex. 15:26)

B. By sending his own Son

1. His first coming was introduced by John the Baptist (3:1). The *New Scofield Bible* observes: "The first part of verse one is quoted by John the Baptist (Mt. 11:10; Mk. 1:2; Lk. 7:27) but the next words, 'The Lord, whom ye seek,' etc., are nowhere quoted in the New Testament" (p. 980).

The reason for this omission is tragically apparent—Israel did not anticipate nor accept Christ at his first coming. (See Jn. 1:11.)

J. Vernon McGee writes:

"Malachi announced the coming of John the Baptist as my messenger. John was the Malachi of the New Testament and began where Malachi of the Old Testament left off. Malachi was the first radio announcer who said, 'The next voice you will hear will be that of the Lord's messenger.' "

2. His Second Coming will be introduced by Elijah the prophet (4:5, 6). (See also Rev. 11:3–14.)

Elijah thus will be awarded the privilege of preparing this cruel, corrupt, and cursed old world for its greatest, grandest, and most glorious moment—the personal and visible appearance of the King of kings and Lord of lords!

a. He shall come to punish the Gentiles (4:1, 3).

b. He shall come to purify Israel (3:2–4).

IMPORTANT EVENTS BETWEEN THE TESTAMENTS

YEAR B.C.

1. **334 B.C.**—Alexander crosses the Hellespont
2. **331 B.C.**—Alexander defeats the Persians
3. **323 B.C.**—Alexander dies at age thirty-two in Babylon
4. **260 B.C.**—The translation of the Septuagint

5. **214 B.C.**—The Great Wall of China begun
6. **175 B.C.**—Apocryphal literature completed
7. **169 B.C.**—Epiphanes defiles the Temple on December 15
8. **166 B.C.**—The revolt of the Maccabees

9. **165 B.C.**—The cleansing of the Temple on December 25

10. **146 B.C.**—Destruction of Carthage by Rome and the end of the Punic Wars
11. **63 B.C.**—Pompey conquers Jerusalem
12. **44 B.C.**—Julius Caesar is assassinated in March

13. **37 B.C.**—Herod is appointed to govern Jerusalem
14. **20 B.C.**—The rebuilding and enlargement of the Temple

THE GOSPEL STAGE

INTRODUCING THE GOSPEL STAGE
(Matthew, Mark, Luke, John)

This stage covers a period of approximately thirty-five years. It opens with an announcement in the Temple of God (Lk. 1:11–20) and closes with the ascension of the Son of God (Lk. 24:51). As the Old Testament began with man made in the image of God (Gen. 1:26), this stage begins with God in the image of man (Jn. 1:14). The man made in the image of God would be defeated by Satan in a beautiful garden (Gen. 2:8), but the God made in the image of man would soundly defeat Satan in the barren desert (Mt. 4:1).

Prior to this stage sheep had died for shepherds (Ex. 12:1–13), but now the Shepherd will die for the sheep (Jn. 10:11).

At his birth he was offered gold, frankincense, and myrrh by wise men who worshiped him (Mt. 2:11), while at his death he was offered thorns, vinegar, and spittle by wicked men who ridiculed him (Mt. 27:29, 34; 26:67).

The record describes him saving sinners under a tree (Jn. 1:48), up a tree (Lk. 19:4, 5), and on a tree (Lk. 23:43).

In its pages a foaming sea is calmed (Lk. 8:24), and a fruitless tree is cursed (Mt. 21:19).

Three of the eight biblical resurrections occur during this period. These are: Jairus' daughter (Mk. 5:41), the widow's son (Lk. 7:14), and Lazarus (Jn. 11:43, 44). As the story unfolds, a dreaming carpenter is reassured (Mt. 1:20, 21), and a denying disciple is restored (Jn. 21:15–17).

We overhear conversations coming from the heavens above (Mt. 17:1–5) and from the grave beneath (Lk. 16:19–31). Harlots are forgiven (Jn. 4:39; 8:11), and hypocrites are condemned (Mt. 23).

Here the concepts of the church (Mt. 16:18), communion (Mt. 26:26–30), and the Great Commission (Mt. 28:19, 20), are first presented.

MOST IMPORTANT NEW TESTAMENT EVENTS

A. Gospel Events (Matthew—John)
THE MAIN HIGHLIGHTS OF CHRIST'S LIFE:

1. His birth (Lk. 2:1-7)
2. The adoration by the shepherds (Lk. 2:8-20)
3. The dedication in Jerusalem (Lk. 2:21-38)
4. The worship by the wise men (Mt. 2:1-12)
5. Flight into Egypt (Mt. 2:13-23)
6. Temple visit at age twelve (Lk. 2:41-50)
7. His baptism (Mt. 3:13-17)
8. His temptation (Mt. 4:1-11)
9. Introduction by John the Baptist (Jn. 1:29)
10. First Temple cleansing (Jn. 2:13-25)
11. Conversion of Nicodemus (Jn. 3:1-21)
12. The choice of the twelve (Mt. 10:1-4)
13. Imprisonment and execution of John (Mt. 14:1-12)
14. Peter's great confession (Mt. 16:13-20)
15. The transfiguration (Mt. 17:1-13)
16. His triumphal entry (Mt. 21:1-11)
17. Weeping over Jerusalem (Mt. 23:37-39; Lk. 19:41)
18. In the upper room (Jn. 13-14)
19. In Gethsemane (Jn. 18:1-11)
20. His arrest and trials (Jn. 18:12—19:15)
21. The crucifixion (Jn. 19:16-18)
22. The resurrection (Mt. 28:1-7)
23. The ten appearances
24. The ascension (Lk. 24:51)

B. Early Church and Epistle Events (Acts—Revelation)

1. Pentecost (Acts 2:1-4)
2. Sermon of Peter (2:14-40)
3. Healing of a lame man (3:1-11)
4. Death of Ananias and Sapphira (5:1-11)
5. Election of the first deacons (6:1-8)
6. Martyrdom of Stephen (7:1-60)
7. Conversion of the Ethiopian eunuch (8:26-39)
8. Conversion of Saul (9:1-19)
9. Conversion of Cornelius (10:1-48)
10. Establishment of the Antioch church (11:19-26)
11. Deliverance of Peter (12:1-19)
12. Paul's first missionary trip (13:2—14:28)
13. The Jerusalem Council (15:1-35)
14. Paul's second missionary trip (15:36—18:22)
15. Paul's third missionary trip (18:23—21:16)
16. Paul's imprisonment in Rome (28:30)
17. The exile of John to Patmos (Rev. 1:9)

THE 27 NEW TESTAMENT BOOKS

The **Christ** of God   4 BOOKS

author MATTHEW   Matthew

author MARK   Mark

author LUKE   Luke

author JOHN   John

The **Church** of God   1 BOOK

author LUKE   The Book of the Acts

The **Correspondence** of God   22 BOOKS

author PAUL

Galatians	Romans	Philippians
1 Thessalonians	Hebrews (?)	1 Timothy
2 Thessalonians	Ephesians	Titus
1 Corinthians	Colossians	2 Timothy
2 Corinthians	Philemon	

author JOHN

1 John	3 John
2 John	Revelation

author PETER

1 Peter	2 Peter

author JAMES

Book of James

author JUDE

Book of Jude

In short, the blind see, the deaf hear, the mute speak, the lame walk, the dead rise, the possessed are freed, and the lost are saved!

THE GOSPEL STAGE
A Review of the Savior's Steps

Any serious student of the life of Christ soon discovers one cannot be dogmatic concerning either the duration of our Lord's earthly ministry, or the exact sequence of events which transpired during that duration. In preparing this study I have been strongly influenced by Johnston M. Cheney's *The Life of Christ in Stereo,* a harmony of the Gospels. It suggests, among other things, a four-year duration for his public ministry. Cheney writes:

"The generally accepted chronology of Jesus' ministry is based on the references in John's Gospel to the Passover

THE FIFTY-THREE MOST IMPORTANT CHAPTERS IN THE NEW TESTAMENT

The New Testament has 260 chapters. The following fifty-three chapters have been selected because of their historical, prophetical, theological, or practical significance.

MATTHEW
1—The baptism of Jesus
4—The temptation of Jesus
5—The Sermon on the Mount
6—The Lord's Prayer
13—The parable of the sower
16—The promise of the church
17—The transfiguration of Jesus
21—The rejection of Israel by Jesus
27—The crucifixion of Jesus
28—The resurrection of Jesus

LUKE
1—The birth of John the Baptist
2—The birth of Jesus

JOHN
2—The first miracle of Jesus
3—Jesus and Nicodemus
11—The resurrection of Lazarus
13—The Lord's Supper
14—The Father's House sermon
15—The abiding chapter
17—The prayer of Jesus

ACTS
1—The ascension of Jesus
2—Pentecost
9—The conversion of Saul
13—The call of Saul and Barnabas
15—The Jerusalem Council
16—The Macedonian vision

ROMANS
5—The justification chapter
6—The sanctification chapter
8—The glorification chapter
11—The dispensation chapter
12—The consecration chapter

1 CORINTHIANS
3—The judgment seat of Christ
7—The marriage chapter
11—Teachings on the Lord's Supper
12—The gifts of the Spirit
13—The love chapter
14—The tongues chapter
15—The resurrection chapter

GALATIANS
5—The fruit of the Spirit

EPHESIANS
5—The love of Christ for his church
6—The protection of the believer

PHILIPPIANS
2—The Kenosis (emptying) of Christ

1 THESSALONIANS
4—The rapture

2 TIMOTHY
3—Duties of pastors and deacons

HEBREWS
11—The faith chapter
12—The chastisement chapter

JAMES
3—The gossip chapter

1 JOHN
1—The fellowship chapter

JUDE
1—The apostasy chapter

REVELATION
6—Beginning of tribulation
13—The ministry of the antichrist
19—Second Coming of Christ
20—Great white throne judgment
21—New heaven and new earth

feasts. Three Passovers are noted in John 2:12; 6:4, and 11:55, and another is assumed from the reference in 5:1 to an unnamed feast. These four Passovers thus span a period of three years, from the first temple cleansing to Passion Week. . . .

Accepting then the historical accuracy of John's documentations, it is quite clear that Jesus' ministry had to span two or three years at the least. But that it should be limited to three years is nowhere required by the texts. This limitation has merely been assumed from the silence on John's part with reference to a fifth Passover. The view assumes that John referred to every Passover of Jesus' ministry. . . .

One of the most questionable features of the traditional three-year chronology is that it compresses too many events into the last six months of His ministry . . . the logical alternative suggested is that Jesus had a four-year ministry." (Johnston M. Cheney, *The Life of Christ in Stereo* [Portland: Western Baptist Seminary Press, 1969, pp. 226–228])

Jesus' parable in Luke 13:6–9 also strongly suggests a four-year ministry.

"He spake also this parable; A certain man had a fig tree planted in his vineyard; and he came and sought fruit thereon, and found none. Then said he unto the dresser of his vineyard, Behold, these three years I come seeking fruit on this fig tree, and find none: cut it down; why cumbereth it the ground? And he answering said unto him, Lord, let it alone this year also, till I shall dig about it, and dung it: And if it bear fruit, well: and if not, then after that thou shalt cut it down."

A TV singing commercial advertising a soft drink cola once ran:

"Dr. Pepper, so misunderstood!
If anyone would try you, they'd know you taste good."

By simply substituting the words Jesus Christ for Dr. Pepper, one would immediately have a tragic but nevertheless true twentieth-century religious picture. Certainly Jesus is misunderstood. A little girl once misquoted John 3:16: "For God so loved the world that he gave his only *forgotten* son. . . ."

I. Jesus Christ Is Misunderstood by the Liberals.
   Note the following sordid statements on the Savior:
   A. Albert Schweitzer:
      "He was a deluded fanatic who futilely threw away his life in blind devotion to a mad dream. There is nothing more negative than the critical study of the life of Christ."
   B. George Bernard Shaw:
      "A man who was sane until Peter hailed him as the Christ and who then became a monomaniac . . . his delusion is a very common delusion among the insane . . . quite consistent with the [cunning] which Jesus displayed in Jerusalem after his delusion had taken complete hold of him."
   C. Rudolf Bultmann:
      "I do indeed think we can now know almost nothing concerning the life and personality of Jesus."
   D. Hugh Schonfield:
      "A conspiracy had to be organized of which the victim himself was the principal instigator. It was a night-marish conception and undertaking, the outcome of the frightening logic of a sick mind. . . ."

II. Jesus Christ Is Misunderstood by the Cults.
    A. The opinion of the Jehovah's witnesses:
       "The man Jesus is dead, forever dead" (Charles Russell).
    B. The opinion of the Mormon Church:
       "Jesus Christ was a polygamist; Mary and Martha, the sisters of Lazarus, were his plural wives, and Mary Magdalene was another. Also, the bridal feast of Cana of Galilee, where Jesus turned the water into wine, was the occasion of one of his own marriages" (Brigham Young).
    C. The opinion of Christian Science:
       "God is indivisible. A portion of God could not enter man; neither could God's fulness be reflected by a single man" (Mary Baker Eddy).

III. Jesus Christ Is Misunderstood by Bible-believing People. There is today almost a total absence of strong exegetical preaching on the life of Christ from fundamentalist pulpits. The reason seems to be that the liberals have majored so much and so long on his life, that believers often avoid it and only concern ourselves with his death. Certainly no sincere student of the Bible would deny for one second that it was indeed his death on Calvary which redeemed us. Nothing could be more clearly stated in the Bible than this precious truth. But as one studies the truths presented concerning this blessed Savior from the book of Acts through Revelation, he is amazed at how many times the epistles drive him back to the Gospels! Note some of these references, all of which emphasize his *life* as well as his death on Calvary.
     A. Hebrews 12:1–3:
        "Wherefore, seeing we also are compassed about with so great a cloud of witnesses, let us lay aside every weight, and the sin which doth so easily beset us, and let us run with patience the race that is set before us. Looking unto Jesus, the author and finisher of our faith, who for the joy that was set before him endured the cross; despising the shame, and is set down at the right hand of the throne of God. For consider him [think about and weigh his worth] that endured such contradiction of sinners against himself, lest ye be wearied and faint in your minds."
     B. Philippians 2:5–8:
        "Let this mind be in you, which was also in Christ Jesus, who, being in the form of God, thought it not robbery to be equal with God, but made himself of no reputation, and took upon him the form of a servant, and was made in the likeness of men; and being found in fashion as a man, he humbled himself and became obedient unto death, even the death of the cross."
     C. 2 Corinthians 4:8–11:
        "We are troubled on every side, yet not distressed; we are perplexed, but not in despair; persecuted, but not forsaken; cast down, but not destroyed; always bearing about in the body the dying of the Lord Jesus, that the life also of Jesus might be made manifest in our body. For we who live are always delivered unto death for Jesus' sake, that the life also of Jesus might be made manifest in our mortal flesh."

D. 2 Corinthians 3:18:

"But we all, with unveiled face beholding as in a mirror the glory of the Lord are changed into the same image from glory to glory, even as by the Spirit of the Lord."

Consider Paul's argument here in this chapter. He says:

1. The message of the law had a glory, but it faded away. This was the reason Moses wore a veil as he came down from Mt. Sinai, so Israel would not see this fading glory. (See 3:13.) This glory was represented by Moses.

2. The message of grace also has a glory, which will never fade away. Therefore, no veil is needed. This glory is represented by Christ.

3. As a believer therefore studies the *life* of Christ (the "glory of the Lord" referred to here in 3:18 is Christ, as proved by Jn. 1:14) he is changed (Greek, *metamorphoomai*) bit by bit into the image of Christ.

4. Thus the supreme goal of the believer on this earth is to become as much like Jesus as possible! This, of course, is God's ultimate goal throughout all eternity, but he wants to start this process now! Dr. H. A. Ironside writes in his book on 2 Corinthians:

"You remember Hawthorne's story of 'The Great Stone Face.' He tells of a lad who lived in the village below the mountain, and there upon the mountain was that image of the great stone face, looking down so solemnly, so seriously, upon the people. There was a legend that some day someone was coming to that village who would look just like the great stone face, and he would do some wonderful things for the village and would be the means of great blessing. The story gripped this lad, and he used to slip away and hour after hour would stand looking at that great stone face and thinking of the story about the one that was coming. Years passed, and that one did not come, and still the young man did what the boy had done, and went to sit and contemplate the majesty, the beauty of that great stone face. By and by youth passed away and middle age came on, and still he could not get rid of that legend; and then old age came, and one day as he walked through the village someone looked at him and exclaimed, 'He has come, the one who is like the great stone face!' He became like that which he contemplated. If you want to be Christlike, look at Jesus. If you want to grow in grace, contemplate Jesus. You find Him revealed in the Word, so read your Bible and meditate upon it.

We sing the song,

'Take time to be holy,
Speak oft with thy Lord.'

Dr. Lewis Sperry Chafer almost always interrupts when this hymn is given out, and says, 'Please let me change that first line; let us sing it, Take time to behold Him.'

As we behold Him we will become holy, for, 'We all, reflecting as in a mirror the glory of the unveiled face of the Lord, are changed, are transfigured, and transformed into the same image from glory to glory, even as by the Spirit of the Lord.' " (pp. 92, 93)

E. Romans 5:8-10:

"But God commendeth his love toward us in that, while we were yet sinners, Christ died for us. Much more then, being now justified by his blood, we shall be saved from wrath through him. For if, when we were enemies, we were reconciled to God by the death of his Son, much more, being reconciled, we shall be saved by his life!"

F. 1 Peter 2:21:

"For even hereunto were ye called, because Christ also suffered for us, leaving us an example, that ye should follow his steps."

One of the most famous religious books ever written has taken this verse for its foundation and, I believe, misinterpreted it. The book, of course, is *In His Steps*, by Charles M. Sheldon. It has sold over eight million copies. In the novel the author describes a situation in which a group of Christians are determined to do and say only those things Jesus would have said and done for a period of time. But, of course, Peter does not refer to this practice here. If for no other reason, because of Jesus' supernatural life, this would be totally impossible. For example, here is a Christian strolling along the Atlantic seaboard one day when he suddenly sees a boat threatened by an unexpected ocean storm. He hears the terrified cries of the helpless passengers. Quickly he thinks—what would Jesus have done? We know of course exactly what he did do in similar circumstances on at least two other occasions (see Jn. 6:19; Mt. 8:26), but who could do this today? Furthermore, it should be noted that Peter does *not* tell us to follow *in* his steps, but to *follow* his steps.

When Peter used the Greek word here translated "example" he went back to his boyhood classroom days for an illustration. The word means literally "to write under." It was used of words given children to copy and study. The child could then learn to write by tracing his finger over the written example above. Thus, Peter was admonishing all believers to study and to trace out the various steps of the blessed Savior while he was on this earth.

These steps make interesting reading indeed. His first step was from glory to Bethlehem. The second was from Bethlehem to Jerusalem when he was eight days old, and so on. The final step was from the Mount of Olives back to glory, from whence he came.

The following study of the life of Christ is an attempt to present these steps, some seventy-two in number, in a geographical and chronological way. To aid in this effort, a simple topical scheme of symbols has been employed (see chart). For example, while on this earth, our Lord performed thirty-six recorded miracles. These miracles are

ASPECTS OF CHRIST'S MINISTRY

 Symbol for Christ's miracles

 Symbol for Christ's parables

 Symbol for Christ's prayers

 Symbol for Christ's sermons

 Symbol for Christ's predictions

 Symbol for Old Testament prophecies fulfilled by Christ

located and are properly placed under the exact chronological step. They are accompanied by the symbol of a starburst. The thirty-eight parables Christ told are treated in a similar way and carry the symbol of an open mouth. His nineteen prayers are indicated by folded hands, while his sixteen sermons have the symbol of an open book. Finally, his forty-five predictions are accompanied by the symbol of an eye. To all this may be added the thirty-seven Old Testament prophecies that our Lord fulfills, which are located and symbolized by a crown.

It is earnestly hoped that through this method of study, a student of the life of Christ will be able to easily locate by these symbols any and all the important things Jesus said and did in the Gospel accounts. At the very end of the study is a summary list of Jesus' life, as gleaned from the seventy-two steps. These subjects, some already mentioned, cover such areas as:

1. The thirty-six miracles of the Savior
2. The thirty-eight parables of the Savior
3. The nineteen prayers of the Savior
4. The forty-five predictions of the Savior
5. The sixteen sermons of the Savior
6. The thirty-six dialogues of the Savior
7. The sixteen Old Testament references of the Savior
8. The twenty-two Old Testament quotes of the Savior
9. The tenfold proof of the deity of the Savior
10. The thirtyfold proof of the humanity of the Savior
11. The thirty-seven names and titles of the Savior

THE MOST IMPORTANT EVENTS IN THE LIFE OF CHRIST

1. His Birth (LK. 2:1-7)
2. The Adoration by the Shepherds (LK. 2:8-20)
3. The Dedication in Jerusalem (LK. 2:21-38)
4. The Worship by the Wise men (MT. 2:1-12)
5. Flight into Egypt (MT. 2:13-23)
6. Temple Visit at Twelve (LK. 2:41-50)
7. His Baptism (MT. 3:13-17)
8. His Temptation (MT. 4:1-11)
9. Introduction by John the Baptist (JN. 1:29)
10. First Temple Cleansing (JN. 2:13-25)
11. Conversion of Nicodemus (JN. 3:1-21)
12. The Choice of the Twelve (MT. 10:1-4)

13. Imprisonment and Execution of John (MT. 14:1-12)
14. Peter's Great Confession (MT. 16:13-20)
15. The Transfiguration (MT. 17:1-13)
16. His Triumphal Entry (MT. 21:1-11)
17. Weeping over Jerusalem (MT. 23:37-39; Lk. 19:41)
18. In the Upper Room (JN. 13-14)
19. In Gethsemane (JN. 18:1-11)
20. His Arrest and Trials (JN. 18:12—19:15)
21. The Crucifixion (JN. 19:16-18)
22. The Resurrection (MT. 28:1-7)
23. The Ten Appearances
24. The Ascension (LK. 24:51)

12. The thirty-seven Old Testament prophecies fulfilled by the Savior
13. The twenty-seven souls converted by the Savior
14. The fifteen kinds of sufferings experienced by the Savior
15. The seven last statements of the Savior
16. The ten resurrection appearances of the Savior
17. The political and religious parties in the days of the Savior
18. The various places visited by the Savior
19. The many individuals who met the Savior
We shall now consider an introduction *to,* a presentation *of,* and a summarization *from* the life of our blessed Lord.

I. The Two Prefaces.
   A. Luke's preface (Lk. 1:1-4).
      1. Many had already drawn up a narrative of Christ's life.
      2. Luke proposed to do the same, obtaining his facts from various eyewitnesses.
      3. He then planned to forward his narrative to his friend Theophilus. Luke would also later write his second book, the book of Acts to Theophilus (Acts 1:1).
   B. John's preface (Jn. 1:1-5).
      1. Jesus Christ was with the Father in eternity past. (See Prov. 8:22-31; Jn. 17:5, 24.)
      2. Jesus Christ was the Creator of all things. (See Col. 1:16, 17; Eph. 3:9; Heb. 1:2.)
      3. Jesus Christ is both the light and the life of men. (See Jn. 5:26; 1 Jn. 5:11; Jn. 8:12; 9:5; 12:35, 46.)
      4. Jesus Christ shone in the darkness of this world and the darkness could not extinguish him.
      5. These first five verses in John are the most profound in the Bible and are worthy to have been written in gold.

II. The Two Genealogies.
   A. Matthew's genealogy (Mt. 1:1-17).
      1. His account has forty-one names in it.
      2. He traces the line forward in time from Abraham, the father of the Hebrew race, to Joseph. (See Gal. 3:16.)
      3. He traces the line from David through his son Solomon (2 Sam. 12:24).
      4. He gives the line of Joseph.
         Study note: This genealogy is remarkable for several reasons.
         a. It contains the names of four women. Oriental and Mid-Eastern genealogies rarely do this.
         b. All four women had questionable backgrounds.
            (1) Tamar was an ex-harlot (Mt. 1:3; Gen. 38:13-30).
            (2) Rahab was an ex-harlot (Mt. 1:5; Josh. 2:1).
            (3) Ruth was a former pagan (Mt. 1:5; Ruth 1:4).
            (4) Bath-sheba was a former adulteress (Mt. 1:6; 2 Sam. 11:1-5).
         But through the manifold and marvelous grace of God, the first woman (Tamar) became the distant removed grandmother of King David; the second (Rahab) became his great, great grandmother; the third (Ruth) was his great grandmother; and the fourth (Bath-sheba) became his beloved wife and mother of Solomon. (See Ruth 4:18-22.)
   B. Luke's genealogy (Lk. 3:23-38).
      1. His account has seventy-four names in it.
      2. He traces the line backward in time from Joseph to Adam, the Father of the human race.
      3. He traces the line from David through another son named Nathan (2 Sam. 5:14).
      4. He gives the line of Mary.
         Special note: Several problems are involved in both these genealogies.
         a. Joseph's father is said to be Jacob by Matthew (1:16), while Luke says he was Heli's son (Luke 3:23). The ancient world often referred to their sons-in-law as their own sons. Thus Heli was really the father of Mary (many believe) and the father-in-law of Joseph.
         b. Satan was keenly aware of the fact that the line leading to Christ would go through David's seed. He thus apparently attempted to break a link in his royal chain somewhere. With the advent of King Jeconiah (the nineteenth "link" from David), it appeared that the devil had succeeded, for God pronounced the following curse upon this wicked young ruler:
            "Thus saith the Lord, write this man childless, a man that shall not prosper in his days: for no man of his seed shall prosper, sitting upon the throne of David, and ruling any more in Judah" (Jer. 22:30).
         This declaration did not mean he would have no children, for in 1 Chronicles 3:17, 18 some are named. (See also Mt. 1:12.) What it did mean is that by divine judgment this king would be considered childless as far as the throne of Judah was concerned. Whatever it meant, it seemed the royal line of David and Solomon had ground to a stop with Jeconiah (also called Coniah and Jehoiachin in the Old Testament). (See Jer. 22:24; 2 Ki. 24:8.) But what a rude shock when the devil learned God was not limited to one line! David had another son named Nathan, and it was through this line that Mary, the mother of Jesus, came.

III. The Three Annunciations.
   A. To Zacharias, about the birth of John, the Messiah's forerunner (Lk. 1:5-25).
      1. The archangel Gabriel appears to Zacharias the priest as he burns incense at the golden altar in the Jerusalem Temple. (See Ex. 30:7; 2 Chron. 29:11.)
         Note: This is the first spoken message from heaven in over 400 years. Radio station Old Testament went off the air with Malachi 4. But now God resumes broadcasting. Radio New Testament is officially on the air!

2. Zacharias is informed that his prayers have been heard and that his aged wife Elisabeth will bear him a son. This is the eighth of nine biblical births in which God himself intervened. They are:
   a. The birth of Isaac to Abraham and Sarah (Gen. 21:1)
   b. The birth of Jacob and Esau to Isaac and Rebekah (Gen. 25:21)
   c. The birth of Reuben to Jacob and Leah (Gen. 29:31)
   d. The birth of Issachar to Jacob and Leah (Gen. 30:17, 18)
   e. The birth of Joseph to Jacob and Rachel (Gen. 30:22-24)
   f. The birth of Samuel to Elkanah and Hannah (1 Sam. 1:19)
   g. The birth of Samson to Manoah and his wife (Jdg. 13:1, 2)
   h. The birth of John to Zacharias and Elisabeth (Lk. 1:57)
   i. The birth of Jesus to Mary (Lk. 2:7)
3. Gabriel tells Zacharias that this son:
   a. Would be named John.
   b. Would abstain from all strong drink. Thus, he was to be a Nazarite (Num. 6:3), as Samson was supposed to be (Jdg. 13:4).
   c. Would be great in the sight of the Lord. (See Mt. 11:11.)
   d. Would be filled with the Holy Spirit from his mother's womb. This is said about two other men.
      (1) Jeremiah (see Jer. 1:5).
      (2) Paul (see Gal. 1:15).
   e. Would turn many Israelites to the Lord. This he did at the Lord's first coming, as Elijah will someday do at Christ's Second Coming. (See Mal. 4:5, 6.)
   f. Would preach in the style and spirit of Elijah. (See Mt. 11:14; Mk. 9:12.)
   g. Would prepare the way for the coming Messiah. He thus would fulfill Isaiah 40:3.
4. As both he and his wife were advanced in years, Zacharias had some difficulty believing all this. (As once did Abraham and Sarah. See Gen. 17:17; 18:12.)
5. Gabriel gently rebukes the old priest for his unbelief and warns him he will be mute until the day of John's birth.
6. The waiting crowd outside soon realizes something very strange has happened to Zacharias and that he cannot pronounce the expected blessing upon them. No doubt many in that waiting crowd were there to help Zacharias celebrate a very special event, the burning of incense upon the golden altar. A priest could only do this once in his entire life. Others in the multitude were expecting to hear him pronounce the great Levitical blessing. In Numbers 6:22-27 we read:

   "And the Lord spoke unto Moses, saying, Speak unto Aaron and unto his sons, saying, In this way ye shall bless the children of Israel, saying, the Lord bless thee, and keep thee; the Lord make his face shine upon thee, and be gracious unto thee; the Lord lift up his countenance upon thee, and give thee peace. And they shall put my name upon the children of Israel; and I will bless them."

   But on that day there is no celebration or benediction. Something far more exciting and eternal is about to happen. Zacharias returns home and soon his old and barren wife conceives a child.
7. The name Zacharias means "God remembers" and the name Elisabeth means, "his oath." With the birth of John the Baptist, God was remembering his covenant made in Psalm 89:34-37.

B. To Mary, about the birth of Jesus (Lk. 1:26-38).
   1. During the sixth month of Elisabeth's pregnancy, the archangel Gabriel appears to a Nazareth virgin (and espoused wife-to-be of Joseph) named Mary.
   2. He announces that God has chosen her to bear his blessed Son into the world. (See Gal. 4:4.) Especially to be observed are the words in Luke 1:28:

      "And the angel came in unto her, and said, Hail, thou who art highly favored, the Lord is with thee; blessed art thou *among* women."

      The angel did not say *above* women, but *among* women. Note also in 1:47 that the first recorded person to call Jesus Savior was his mother. Mary needed salvation like all others. See Romans 3:23.
   3. Old Testament Prophecy Fulfillment Number 1, That he would be born of a virgin. (Compare Isa. 7:14 with Mt. 1:22, 23.)
   4. The archangel predicted that this Babe:
      a. Would be called Jesus.
      b. Would be called the Son of the Highest. A demon later referred to him by this very name. (See Mk. 5:7.)
      c. Would inherit the throne of David.
      d. Old Testament Prophecy Fulfillment Number 2, That he would be given the throne of David. (Compare 2 Sam. 7:11, 12; Ps. 132:11; Isa. 9:6, 7; 16:5; Jer. 23:5 with Lk. 1:31, 32.)
      e. Would occupy this throne forever. (See Dan. 2:44; 7:14, 27; Micah 4:7.)
      f. Old Testament Prophecy Fulfillment Number 3, That this throne would be an eternal throne. (Compare Dan. 2:44; 7:14, 27; Micah 4:7 with Lk. 1:33.)
   5. Mary is perplexed: "How shall this be, seeing I know not a man?" (Lk. 1:34).
   6. The archangel is reassuring: "The Holy Ghost shall come upon thee, and the power of the Highest shall overshadow thee" (Lk. 1:35). These verses (Lk. 1:31, 35) teach two powerful things about the incarnation.
      a. Jesus was conceived of the Holy Spirit.
      b. The supernatural element in the incarnation was not the *birth* of Christ, but rather his *conception*. He was born as all humans are born. It is vital to make this distinction, for he was not only as completely

THE BIRTH AND EARLY YEARS OF CHRIST

THE TWO PREFACES

> **Luke's preface (Lk. 1:1-4)**
> **John's preface (Jn. 1:1-5)**

THE THREE ANNUNCIATIONS

To Zacharias	**CONCERNING JOHN'S BIRTH**	**(Lk. 1:5-25)**
To Mary	**CONCERNING JESUS' BIRTH**	**(Lk. 1:26-38)**
To Joseph	**CONCERNING MARY'S PURITY**	**(Mt. 1:18-25)**

THE THREE SONGS OF PRAISE

PRAISE OF ELISABETH TO MARY	**(Lk. 1:39-45)**
PRAISE OF MARY TO GOD	**(Lk. 1:46-56)**
PRAISE OF ZACHARIAS TO GOD	**(Lk. 1:57-79)**

THE FIRST THIRTY YEARS OF THE GLORY STORY

From Glory to Bethlehem (Lk. 2:1-21) . . . . **Birth**

From Bethlehem to Jerusalem (Lk. 2:22-38) . . . . **Dedication**

From Jerusalem back to Bethlehem (Mt. 2:1-12) . . . . . . **Visit of Magi**

From Bethlehem to Egypt (Mt. 2:13-18) . . . . **Escape Trip**

From Egypt to Nazareth (Mt. 2:19-23; Lk. 2:40) . . . . **Boyhood Days**

From Nazareth to Jerusalem (Lk. 2:41-50) . . . . **Temple Quiz**

From Jerusalem back to Nazareth (Lk. 2:51, 52) . . . . **Preparation Years**

God as though he had never been man, but also as completely man as though he had never been God.

7. Gabriel predicts Mary's Son will also be called the Son of God. (See Mt. 14:33; Mk. 1:1; Jn. 1:34; 20:31; Acts 8:37; Rom. 1:4.)

8. He then informs her of her cousin Elisabeth's pregnancy.

"For with God nothing shall be impossible" (Lk. 1:37). (See also Gen. 18:14; Jer. 32:17; Mt. 19:26; Lk. 18:27.)

9. Mary sweetly and simply submits to God's will. "Behold the handmaid of the Lord; be it unto me according to thy word" (Lk. 1:38).

C. To Joseph, about the purity of Mary (Mt. 1:18-25).

1. Upon learning of her pregnancy, Joseph, "being a just man, and not willing to make her a public example, was minded to put her away privily" (Mt. 1:19).

2. That very night however, he is assured in a dream by Gabriel concerning the impending virgin birth of Christ.

3. This Babe, Joseph is told, "shall save his people from their sins" (Mt. 1:21). (See also Acts 4:12; 5:31; 13:23, 38; Heb. 7:25.)

4. Gabriel refers to this future Babe as Emmanuel, meaning, "God with us" (Mt. 1:23).

5. Old Testament Prophecy Fulfillment Number 4, That he would be called Emmanuel. (Compare Isa. 7:14 with Mt. 1:23.)

"Behold, a virgin shall be with child, and shall bring forth a son, and they shall call his name Emmanuel, which being interpreted is, God with us" (Mt. 1:23).

This prophecy was of course a fulfillment of Isaiah 7:14 (see Mt. 1:22). Some have questioned (unsuccessfully) the Hebrew word *almah* in Isaiah 7:14, saying it does not always mean virgin. However, there is absolutely no doubt whatsoever about the Greek word for virgin, which is *parthenos,* and always, without exception, refers to a young girl totally devoid of sexual experiences.

6. Joseph arranges to make Mary his fully legal wife. Joseph must be considered by all standards of measurement as a truly just man, with the spiritual maturity of a David, Moses, Peter, or Paul. In fact the New Testament Joseph may be favorably compared to the Old Testament Joseph. Both had fathers named Jacob. Both had amazing maturity. Both received visions from God. Both were in Egypt. One was a type of Christ, the other was his legal guardian.

In fact, had it not been for Judah's sin, Joseph would have been ruling from Jerusalem as the rightful king when Christ was born. It was he and not Herod who had the proper credentials to sit upon the throne of Israel.

IV. The Three Songs of Praise.

A. The praise of Elisabeth to Mary (Lk. 1:39-45), often called the *"Magnificat."*

Note: This apparently happened prior to Joseph's learning of Mary's condition. Mary, upon the departure of the archangel, had hurriedly and perhaps secretly left Nazareth to visit Elisabeth somewhere near Jerusalem. Joseph did not know of her condition until she returned some three months later.

1. John leaps in the womb upon hearing Mary's greeting, and Elisabeth is filled with the Holy Spirit.

2. Elisabeth blesses Mary: "Blessed art thou among women, and blessed is the fruit of thy womb" (Lk. 1:42). (See also Lk. 1:28.)

B. The praise of Mary to God (Lk. 1:46-56).

1. Mary responds, "My soul doth magnify the Lord and my spirit hath rejoiced in God my Saviour" (1:46, 47).

2. She realizes history will accord her favored of the Lord.

3. She praises the Father for putting down the mighty, exalting the meek, filling the hungry, and displaying the strength of his mighty arm. (See Isa. 52:10; Ps. 33:10; 1 Sam. 2:6-8; Isa. 53:1.)

4. After three months Mary returns to Nazareth.

C. The praise of Zacharias to God (Lk. 1:57-79).

1. Zacharias' son is born and circumcised on the eighth day.

2. His friends and kindred assume the baby will be named after him. The old priest, however, still mute, writes that his name will be John.

3. He immediately regains his speech and praises God in the power of the Holy Spirit, thanking him for:

a. Keeping his promises made to Abraham and David.

b. Visiting and redeeming his people. (See also Ps. 111:9; Lk. 7:16.)

4. Zacharias then speaks concerning John.

a. He will be Christ's forerunner. (See Isa. 40:3; Mt. 11:10.)

b. He will give the knowledge of salvation. (See Jn. 1:29.)

c. He will preach repentance. (See Lk. 3:3.)

d. He will introduce the Savior. "The dayspring from on high hath visited us" (1:78). (See also Num. 24:17; Mal. 4:2.)

Upon reaching maturity, John retires to the desert and begins preparing for his future as a Nazarite evangelist.

V. The Four Biographers (Matthew, Mark, Luke, John). Each presents a different picture of the Savior.

A. Matthew: the King, lionlike. Written to the Hebrews.

B. Mark: the Servant, oxlike. Written to the Romans.

C. Luke: the Perfect Man, manlike. Written to the Greeks.

D. John: the Mighty God, eaglelike. Written to all the world. Thus:

1. There is a genealogy in Matthew, for a king *must* have one.

2. There is a genealogy in Luke, for a perfect man *should* have one.

3. There is no genealogy in Mark, for a servant does not *need* one.

THE FOURFOLD GOSPEL ACCOUNT

	Matthew	Mark	Luke	John
PORTRAIT of CHRIST	KING AND LIONLIKE	SERVANT AND OXLIKE	PERFECT MAN AND MANLIKE	MIGHTY GOD AND EAGLELIKE
Angelic reminder Rev. 4; Ezek. 1	FIRST CREATURE LIONLIKE	SECOND CREATURE OXLIKE	THIRD CREATURE MANLIKE	FOURTH CREATURE EAGLELIKE
Style of writer	**TEACHER**	**PREACHER**	**HISTORIAN**	**THEOLOGIAN**
Emphasis by writer	*His Sermons*	*His Miracles*	*His Parables*	*His Doctrines*
CULTURE OF ORIGINAL READERS	JEWS	ROMANS	GREEKS	THE WORLD
Genealogical record	YES: **Matthew 1:1-17**	NO	YES: **Luke 3:23-38**	NO
REASON	A king must have one	A servant needs none	A perfect man should have one	God has none
ROOT	Traces the regal line of David through his son Solomon		Traces the physical line of David through another son, Nathan	
FRUIT	Leads to Joseph, the legal stepfather of Jesus		Leads to Mary the physical mother of Jesus	
Place of main action	*C A P E R N A U M I N G A L I L E E*			*JERUSALEM IN JUDEA*
Twofold division	Synoptic Gospels—stress the humanity of Christ			Fourth Gospel— stresses the deity of Christ

4. There is no genealogy in John, for the mighty God does not *have* one. Dr. Van Dyke once said:

"If four witnesses should appear before a judge to give an account of a certain event, and each witness should tell exactly the same story in the same words, the judge would probably conclude, *not* that their testimony was exceptionally valuable, but that the only event which was certain beyond a doubt was that they had agreed to tell the same story! But if each man had told what he had seen, as he had seen it, then the evidence would be credible. And when we read the four gospels, is not that exactly what we find? The four men tell the same story in their own way."

It should be furthermore noted that the four Gospel accounts should not be consid-

ered a *biographical* summary of Christ's life, but rather a *theological* summary. Almost all of his early life from birth to age thirty is left out.

VI. The Message and Ministry of John the Baptist (Mt. 3:1–12; Mk. 1:1–8; Lk. 1:80; 3:1–18; Jn. 1:6–28).

Note: Although John's full ministry would not transpire until some thirty years later, it nevertheless did precede and prepare for the Messiah and is therefore placed here at this point of our study.

A. John's purpose would be to go forth at the proper time as a witness for Christ, who alone was the earth's true Light (Jn. 1:6–18).

  1. This Light would offer salvation to all men (1:9).

  2. This Light would, however,

    a. Be ignored by the world he created (Jn. 1:10).

    b. Be rejected by the nation he called (Jn. 1:11). (See also Lk. 19:14; Acts 13:46.)

John the Baptist

HIS OFFICE **(Jn. 1:6-18)**	A Nazarite forerunner of and witness to earth's true light
HIS CLOTHES AND FOOD **(Mt. 3:4)**	*CLOTHES*—made of camel's hair and leather *FOOD*—locusts and wild honey

HIS MESSAGE	Predicted by both Isaiah (40:3-5) and Malachi (3:1)				
	THE CROWDS **Mt. 3:2-6** **Lk. 3:3-6**	THE PHARISEES **Mt. 3:7-10**	THE PUBLICANS **Lk. 3:13**	THE SOLDIERS **Lk. 3:14**	THE WORLD **Jn. 1:29**

HIS TESTIMONY TO ALL	1. That he was not the Christ **(Jn. 1:20)** 2. That he was not Elijah or Moses' Prophet **(Mal. 4:5; Deut. 18:15-18)** 3. That he was simply a voice in the wilderness **(Jn. 1:23)** 4. He was unworthy to unloose the shoe latchet of the Messiah **(Jn. 1:27)** 5. He was only a friend of the Bridegroom **(Jn. 3:29)** 6. He must decrease but Christ must increase **(Jn. 3:30)**

HIS TWOFOLD PREDICTION	That the Messiah would enjoy the ministry of the spirit and love of the Father in an unprecedented manner **(Jn. 3:34, 35)**	That the Messiah would someday baptize believers with the Holy Spirit at Pentecost, and unbelievers with fire during the tribulation **(Lk. 3:16; see also Acts 2; Rev. 6)**

HIS REASSURANCE AND TRIBUTE FROM CHRIST	*REASSURANCE*—That Christ was indeed the Messiah **(Mt. 11:2-6)** *TRIBUTE*—There was no greater man than John **(Mt. 11:7-11)**

HIS MARTYRDOM FOR CHRIST	**The events leading to his death** He had denounced Herod's marriage to Herodias, former wife of the king's own brother	**The vixen behind his death** Herodias demanded and received the head of John on a platter

It has been said that John 1:11 is the "saddest" verse in the Bible, and that 1:12 is the "gladdest"!

"He came unto his own, and his own received him not."

"But as many as received him, to them gave he power to become the sons of God, even to them that believe on his name."

3. This Light, incarnated in human flesh, full of grace and truth, would turn into sons of God all repenting sinners. Thus, the Son of God became the Son of Man, that sons of men might become sons of God (Jn. 1:11–14). We note from 1:13 that salvation is not of *generation* (not of blood), *reformation* (nor of the will of the flesh), nor *confirmation* (nor of the will of man), but *regeneration* (of God!).

B. John's clothes (made of camel's hair and leather), and his food (locusts and wild honey) reflect singlemindedness devotion to his holy calling (Mt. 3:4).

C. John's message to the crowds in general was:

1. Repent, for the kingdom of God is at hand (Mt. 3:2).
2. Make ready the way of the Lord (Lk. 3:4–6).
3. Submit to baptism in the River Jordan as proof of your repentance (Mt. 3:6; Lk. 3:3).

D. John's message to the specific groups was:

1. To the Pharisees and the Jewish rulers (Mt. 3:7–10):

"But when he saw many of the Pharisees and Sadducees come to his baptism, he said unto them, O generation of vipers, who hath warned you to flee from the wrath to come? Bring forth therefore fruits meet for repentance: And think not to say within yourselves, We have Abraham to our father: for I say unto you, that God is able of these stones to raise up children unto Abraham. And now also the ax is laid unto the root of the trees: therefore every tree which bringeth not forth good fruit is hewn down, and cast into the fire."

2. To the publicans:

Exact no more than that which is appointed you (Lk. 3:13).

3. To the soldiers:

Do violence to no man, neither accuse any falsely; and be content with your wages (Lk. 3:14).

4. To new converts:

He that hath two coats, let him impart to him that hath none; and he that hath meat, let him do likewise (Lk. 3:11).

5. To the world: "Behold the Lamb of God, which taketh away the sin of the world" (Jn. 1:29).

E. John's testimony to all:

1. That he was not the Christ (Jn. 1:20).
2. That he was not Elijah the prophet nor that prophet spoken of by Moses (1:21). (See also Mal. 4:5; Deut. 18:15, 18.) The priests and Levites were well within their rights in questioning John, for it was their responsibility to check on all religious teachers. (See Deut. 13:1–5; 18:20–22.)

3. That he was simply a voice crying in the wilderness (Jn 1:23).
4. That he was unworthy to unloose the shoe latchet of the true Messiah (1:27).
5. That he was the friend of the true Bridegroom (3:29).
6. That all flesh would soon see God's salvation (Lk. 3:6).
7. That this incarnate salvation (Christ) would reveal the Father (Jn. 1:18).
8. That this Savior would enjoy the ministry of the Spirit and the love of the Father in an unprecedented manner (Jn. 3:34, 35).
9. That he would baptize men with the Holy Spirit in grace at his first coming, but with fire in judgment at his Second Coming (Lk. 3:16). (See Acts 2 and Rev. 6.)
10. That Christ must increase, but John must decrease (Jn. 3:30).
11. Old Testament Prophecy Fulfillment Number 5, That he would have a forerunner. (Compare Isa. 40:3–5; Mal. 3:1 with Lk. 1:76–78; 3:3–6; Mt. 3:1–3.) John thus becomes the last of the great biblical prophets, as Samuel in the Old Testament was the first. Samuel introduced Israel's first king, Saul (1 Sam. 10), while John would present its eternal King, Jesus (Jn. 1:29).

His Seventy-two Steps from Glory to Glory

Step One: From Glory to Bethlehem (Lk. 2:1–21)

Step Two: From Bethlehem to Jerusalem (Lk. 2:22–38)

Step Three: From Jerusalem to Nazareth (Lk. 2:39)

Step Four: From Nazareth to Bethlehem (Mt. 2:1–12)

Step Five: From Bethlehem to Egypt (Mt. 2:13–18)

Step Six: From Egypt to Nazareth (Mt. 2:19–23; Lk. 2:40)

Step Seven: From Nazareth to Jerusalem (Lk. 2:41–50)

Step Eight: From Jerusalem to Nazareth (Lk. 2:51, 52)

Step Nine: From Nazareth to Bethabara on the Jordan River (Mt. 3:13–17)

Step Ten: From Bethabara to the temptation wilderness (Mt. 4:1–11; Mk. 1:12, 13; Lk. 4:1–13)

Step Eleven: From the temptation wilderness to Bethabara (Jn. 1:29–42)

Step Twelve: From Bethabara to Bethsaida (Jn. 1:43–51)

Step Thirteen: From Bethsaida to Cana (Jn. 2:1–11)

Step Fourteen: From Cana to Capernaum (Jn. 2:12)

Step Fifteen: From Capernaum to Jerusalem (Jn. 2:13—3:21)

Step Sixteen: From Jerusalem to the Jordan River (Jn. 3:22–36)

Step Seventeen: From the Jordan River to Sychar in Samaria (Mt. 4:12; Lk. 3:19, 20; Jn. 4:1–42)

Step Eighteen: From Sychar to Cana (Jn. 4:43–54)

Step Nineteen: From Cana to Nazareth (Lk. 4:16–30)

Step Twenty: From Nazareth to Capernaum (Mt. 4:13–22; 8:14–17; Mk. 1:14–38; Lk. 4:31–42)

Step Twenty-one: From Capernaum to his first preaching tour of Galilee (Mt. 4:23; 8:2–4; Mk. 1:39–45; Lk. 4:43—5:16)

Step Twenty-two: From the first Galilean preaching tour to Capernaum (Mt. 9:2–9; Mk. 2:1–14; Lk. 5:17–28)

Step Twenty-three: From Capernaum to a Galilean grain field (Mt. 12:1–8; Mk. 2:23–28; Lk. 6:1–5)

Step Twenty-four: From a Galilean grain field to a Galilean synagogue (Mt. 12:9–14; Mk. 3:1–6; Lk. 6:6–11)

Ministry of the FATHER
in the life of Christ

1 The Father sent his Son
   (Jn. 3:16; 6:57; 8:16-18; 12:49; Gal. 4:4)

2 The Father sealed his Son
   (Jn. 6:27)

3 The Father taught his Son
   (Jn. 8:28)

4 The Father anointed his Son
   (Lk. 4:18; Isa. 61:1; Acts 10:38)

5 The Father honored his Son
   (Jn. 8:54)

6 The Father commanded his Son
   (Jn. 10:18)

7 The Father bore witness to his Son
   (Jn. 8:18)

8 The Father loved (and loves) his Son
   (Jn. 10:17)

9 The Father delighted in his Son
   (Isa. 42:1; Mt. 3:17; 17:5; 2 Pet. 1:17)

10 The Father heard his Son
   (Mt. 26:53; Jn. 11:41, 42; 12:27, 28)

11 The Father offered up his Son
   (Jn. 3:16; 18:11; Rom. 8:32; 1 Jn. 4:9, 10)

12 The Father raised his Son
   (Eph. 1:20)

13 The Father exalted his Son
   (Eph. 1:20; Phil. 2:9-11)

14 The Father glorified his Son
   (Jn. 12:28; 17:1)

15 The Father has made his Son head
   of the church
   (Eph. 1:22)

16 The Father has committed judgment
   to his Son
   (Jn. 5:22, 27)

Ministry of the HOLY SPIRIT
in the life of CHRIST

1 He was begotten by the Holy Spirit
   (Lk. 1:35)

2 He was anointed by the Holy Spirit
   (Mt. 3:16; Heb. 1:9)

3 He preached in the power of the Holy Spirit
   (Lk. 4:18)

4 He was sealed by the Holy Spirit
   (Jn. 6:27)

5 He was led by the Holy Spirit
   (Mt. 4:1)

6 He worked miracles through the Holy Spirit
   (Mt. 12:28; Acts 10:38)

7 He was filled by the Holy Spirit
   (Jn. 3:34; Lk. 4:1)

8 He sorrowed in the Holy Spirit
   (Jn. 11:33)

9 He rejoiced in the Holy Spirit
   (Lk. 10:21)

10 He offered up himself through
   the Holy Spirit
   (Heb. 9:14)

11 He was raised from the dead by the
   Holy Spirit
   (Rom. 1:4; 1 Pet. 3:18)

12 He commanded his apostles through
   the Holy Spirit
   (Acts 1:2)

Step Twenty-five: From a Galilean synagogue to Mount Tabor (Mt. 5:1—7:29; 4:24, 25; 10:2-4; 12:15-21; Mk. 1:12; 3:7-19; Lk. 6:12-49; 12:22-31, 57-59; 16:17)

Step Twenty-six: From Mount Tabor to Capernaum (Mt. 8:1, 5-13; Lk. 7:1-10)

Step Twenty-seven: From Capernaum to Nain (Lk. 7:11-17, 36-50)

Step Twenty-eight: From Nain to the second Galilean preaching tour (Mt. 12:46-50; 13:1-52; Mk. 3:19-35; 4:1-34; Lk. 8:1-21; 12:10; 13:18-21)

Step Twenty-nine: From the second Galilean preaching tour to the country of the Gerasenes (Mt. 8:18, 23, 34; Mk. 4:35—5:20; Lk. 8:22-39)

Step Thirty: From the Gerasenes to Capernaum (Mt. 9:1; 10:34; 11:2-19; Mk. 1:21-43; 2:15-22; Lk. 8:40-56; 5:29-39; 7:18-35; 16:16)

Step Thirty-one: From Capernaum to Jerusalem (Jn. 5:1-47)

Step Thirty-two: From Jerusalem to Nazareth (second visit) (Mt. 13:53-58; Mk. 6:1-6)

Step Thirty-three: From Nazareth to his third Galilean preaching tour (Mt. 9:35—10:1, 5-16, 24-33, 37—11:1; 14:1-13; Mk. 6:6-29; Lk. 9:1-9)

Step Thirty-four: From his third Galilean preaching tour to a wilderness near Bethsaida (Mt. 14:13-23; Mk. 6:30-47; Lk. 9:10-17; Jn. 6:1-18)

Step Thirty-five: From the Bethsaida wilderness to the Plain of Gennesaret (Mt. 14:24-36; Mk. 6:48-56; Jn. 6:19-21)

Step Thirty-six: From the Plain of Gennesaret to Capernaum (Mt. 15:1-20; Mk. 7:1-23; Jn. 6:22-71; 7:1)

Step Thirty-seven: From Capernaum to the Tyre and Sidon area (Mt. 15:21-28; Mk. 7:24-30)

Step Thirty-eight: From Tyre and Sidon to the Decapolis region (Mk. 7:31-37)

Step Thirty-nine: From Decapolis to Mt. Tabor (Mt. 15:29-38; Mk. 8:1-9)

Step Forty: From Mt. Tabor to Magdala (Mt. 15:39—16:12; Mk. 8:9-21)

Step Forty-one: From Magdala to Bethsaida (Mk. 8:22-26; Jn. 7:2-9)

Step Forty-two: From Bethsaida to Jerusalem (Jn. 7:10—10:39)

Step Forty-three: From Jerusalem to Perea (Jn. 10:40-42)

Step Forty-four: From Perea to Caesarea Philippi (Mt. 16:13-28; Mk. 8:27—9:1; Lk. 9:18-27)

Step Forty-five: From Caesarea Philippi to Mt. Hermon (Mt. 17:1-23; Mk. 9:2-31; Lk. 9:28-45)

Step Forty-six: From Mt. Hermon to Capernaum (Mt. 17:24—18:35; Mk. 9:33—10:1; Lk. 9:46-50)

Step Forty-seven: From Capernaum to Perea (Mt. 8:19-22; 11:20-30; 19:1, 2; Lk. 9:51—10:37; Mk. 10:1)

Step Forty-eight: From Perea to Bethany and surrounding area (Mt. 10:34-36; 12:22-38; 42-45; 19:3—20:28; 24:43-51; Mk. 10:2-45; Lk. 10:38—12:9; 13:22, 32-36; 13:1-17, 22, 33; 14:1—16:15, 18-31; 17:1-37; 18:1-34; Jn. 11:1-54)

Step Forty-nine: From Bethany to Jericho (Mt. 20:29-34; Mk. 10:46-52; Lk. 18:35—19:28)

Step Fifty: From Jericho to Bethany (Mt. 26:6-13; Mk. 14:3-9; Lk. 22:1; Jn. 11:55—12:11)

Step Fifty-one: From Bethany to Bethphage (Mt. 21:1-7; Mk. 11:1-7; Lk. 19:29-35)

Step Fifty-two: From Bethphage to the upper room (Mt. 10:17-23; 21:8—23:39; 24:1-42; 25:1-46; 26:1-5; 14-38; Mk. 11:8—13:37; 14:1, 2, 10-25; Lk. 19:36—20:1-8, 20-40, 45-47; 21:1-38; 13:34, 35; 12:11, 12; 22:2-34; Jn. 12:12)

Step Fifty-three: From the upper room to Gethsemane (Mt. 26:31-56; Mk. 14:26-52; Lk. 22:35-53; Jn. 15:1—18:12)

Step Fifty-four: From Gethsemane to Annas' house (Jn. 18:12-14; 19-24)

Step Fifty-five: From Annas' house to Caiaphas' palace (Mt. 26:57—27:1; Mk. 14:53-72; Lk. 22:54-71; Jn. 18:15-18, 25-27)

Step Fifty-six: From Caiaphas' palace to Pilate's hall (Mt. 27:2, 11-14; Mk. 15:1-5; Lk. 23:1-6; Jn. 18:28-38)

Step Fifty-seven: From Pilate's hall to Herod's palace (Lk. 23:7-12)

Step Fifty-eight: From Herod's palace to Pilate's hall (Mt. 27:15-26; Mk. 15:6-15; Lk. 23:13-25; Jn. 18:39—19:16)

Step Fifty-nine: From Pilate's hall to the Praetorium court (Mt. 27:27-31; Mk. 15:16-20)

Step Sixty: From the Praetorium court to Calvary (Mt. 27:32-56; Mk. 15:21-41; Lk. 23:26-49; Jn. 19:16-37)

Step Sixty-one: From Calvary to Joseph's tomb (Mt. 27:57-66; Mk. 15:42-47; Lk. 23:50-56; Jn. 19:31-42)

Step Sixty-two: From Joseph's tomb to the heart of the earth (1 Pet. 3:18-20)

Step Sixty-three: From the heart of the earth to the resurrection garden (Mt. 28:2-4; Mk. 16:9-11; Lk. 24:12; Jn. 20:1-18)

Step Sixty-four: From the resurrection garden to the Father (Jn. 20:17)

Step Sixty-five: From the Father to a road near Jerusalem (Mt. 28:5-15; Mk. 16:2-8; Lk. 24:1-11)

Step Sixty-six: From a road near Jerusalem to the Emmaus Road (Mk. 16:12, 13; Lk. 24:13-35)

Step Sixty-seven: From Emmaus to the upper room (Lk. 24:36-43; Jn. 20:19-23)

Step Sixty-eight: From the upper room back to the upper room (a week later) (Jn. 20:24-29)

Step Sixty-nine: From the upper room to the Sea of Tiberias (Jn. 21:1-25)

Step Seventy: From the Sea of Tiberias to Mount Tabor (Mt. 28:16-20)

Step Seventy-one: From Mt. Tabor to the upper room (Mk. 16:14-18; Lk. 24:44-49)

Step Seventy-two: From the upper room to the Mount of Olives (Mk. 16:19, 20; Lk. 24:50-53; Acts 1:4-11)

HIS SEVENTY-TWO STEPS FROM GLORY TO GLORY

Step One: From Glory to Bethlehem
(Lk. 2:1-21).

A. Joseph and Mary are brought to Bethlehem because of an enrollment decree which commanded each Hebrew citizen to be counted from that town where he or she was born. Note: This is the third all-important trip made to Bethlehem. Ruth and Naomi made the first journey. (See Ruth 1:22.) Samuel the prophet made the second. (See 1 Sam. 16.)

B. Mary gives birth to the Savior. She "wrapped him in swaddling clothes, and laid him in a manger; because there was no room for them in the inn" (Lk. 2:7).

    1. This was the *fourth* greatest day in human history.

    2. The *third* greatest day in human history occurred some thirty-four years later when this Babe grew into glorious manhood, only to be put to death between a pair of thieves on Calvary's cross.

LAND OF THE GOSPELS

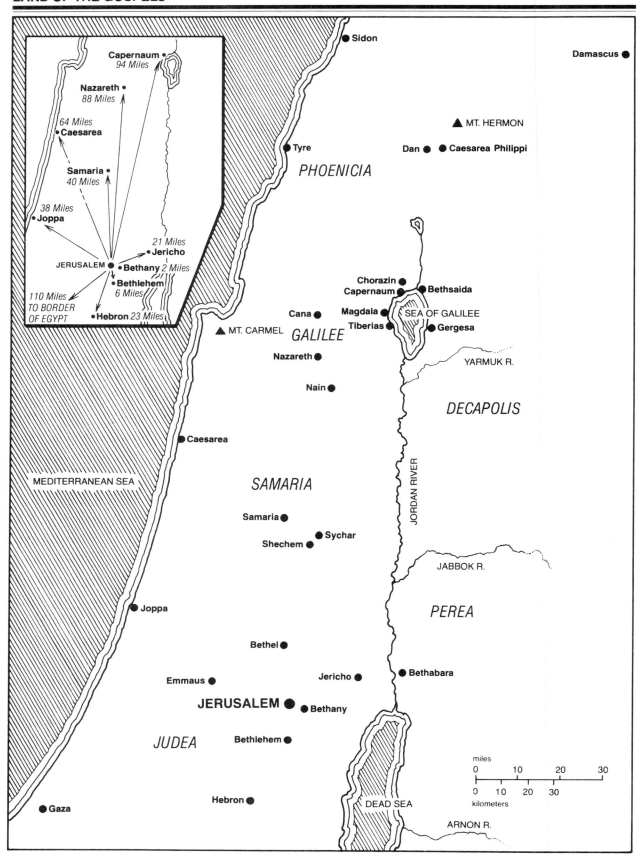

"And when they were come to the place which is called Calvary, there they crucified him, and the malefactors, one on the right hand, and the other on the left" (Lk. 23:33).

3. The *second* greatest day in human history occurred three days later, when an angel told some sorrowing women:

"Fear not ye; for I know that ye seek Jesus, who was crucified. He is not here; for he is risen as he said. Come, see the place where the Lord lay" (Mt. 28:5, 6).

4. The *greatest* day in human history is yet to happen. The Apostle John tells us of this:

"And the seventh angel sounded; and there were great voices in heaven, saying, The kingdoms of this world are become the kingdoms of our Lord, and of his Christ, and he shall reign forever and ever" (Rev. 11:15).

One may favorably contrast Luke 2:7 with Daniel 2:11. In this Old Testament passage King Nebuchadnezzar had just ordered the death of his wise men because of their inability to relate a dream he had just experienced. These astrologers thereupon protested, exclaiming:

"And it is a rare thing that the king requireth, and there is no other that can reveal it before the king, except the gods, whose dwelling is not with flesh."

But at the advent of the fourth greatest day in history all this would change.

In John 1:14 we read that the Word was made flesh. One of the most glorious truths of the incarnation was its eternality. This simply means that the results of the fourth day will last forever. He *still* has and always *will* have a body of flesh and bone (see Lk. 24:39).

C. Old Testament Prophecy Fulfillment Number 6, That he would be born in Bethlehem. (Compare Micah 5:2 with Lk. 2:4-6; Mt. 2:5, 6.)

D. The angel of the Lord announces all this to a group of nearby shepherds.

"I bring you good tidings of great joy, which shall be to all people" (Lk. 2:10). See Genesis 12:3; Matthew 28:19; Luke 2:31, 32; 24:47; Colossians 1:23. "For unto you is born this day in the city of David a Saviour, which is Christ the Lord. . . . Ye shall find the babe wrapped in swaddling clothes, lying in a manger" (Lk. 2:11, 12).

E. The angel is then joined by a multitude of heavenly hosts, praising God and saying: "Glory to God in the highest, and on earth peace, good will toward men" (Lk. 2:14). (See also Lk. 19:38.)

F. The shepherds then come and worship Jesus and return praising God.

G. The Babe is circumcised on the eighth day and officially named Jesus. (See Gen. 17:12; Lev. 12:3.) It has been claimed by a few that, apart from the New Testament writers, there exists no secular proof whatsoever concerning the historicity of Jesus. This is simply not true. Both the ancient Roman and Jewish world make mention of his life and death. The following quotes prove this:

"On the eve of the Passover, Jesus of Nazareth was hung. During the previous 40 days a herald went before him crying aloud: 'He ought to be stoned because he has practiced magic, has led Israel astray, and caused them to rise in rebellion. Let him who has something to say in his defence come forward and declare it!' But no one came forward, and he was hung on the eve of the Passover." (From *The Babylonian Jewish Talmud*)

The Talmud also reported that Jesus was an illegitimate child born of Mary and a Roman soldier named Ben-Panther.

"And there arose about this time Jesus, a wise man, if indeed we should call him a man. For he was a doer of marvelous deeds, a teacher of men who received the truth with pleasure. He led away many Jews, and also many of the Greeks. This man was the Christ. And when Pilate had condemned him to the cross on his impeachment by the chief men among us, those who had loved him at first did not cease; for he appeared to them on the third day alive again, the divine prophets having spoken these and thousands of other wonderful things about him: and even now the tribe of Christians so named after him, has not yet died out." (*Antiquities of the Jews*, by Josephus, Jewish historian)

"Christus, the founder of the name, had undergone the death penalty in the reign of Tiberius, by sentence of the procurator Pontius Pilate, and the superstition was checked for a moment, only to break out once more, not merely in Judaea, the home of the deceased, but in the Capital (Rome) itself. . . ." (*The Annals*, by the Roman writer Tacitus)

"To say that antiquity was in the habit of ascribing supernatural births to its great personages and that Christianity has followed the conventional pattern is misleading. Are so-called Virgin births of antiquity the same kind as that ascribed to Jesus in the gospels? The words of Louis Matthew Sweet are worth recalling:

'After a careful, laborious, and occasionally wearisome study of the evidence offered and the analogies urged, I am convinced that heathenism knows nothing of Virgin births. Supernatural births it has without number, but never from a virgin in the New Testament sense and never without physical generation, except in a few isolated instances of magical births on the part of a woman who had not the slightest claim to be called Virgin. In all recorded instances which I have been able to examine, if the mother was a virgin before conception took place she could not make that claim afterwards.' " (*A Short Life of Christ*, E. Harrison, p. 45)

Scripture says nothing about the time of year of his birth. The first known observance of December 25 is associated with the church at Rome about the middle of the fourth century, but the practice may go back to the second century. January 6 was observed in Eastern churches. Many have concluded that it would have been impossible for his birth to have happened in December on the grounds of cold weather. Shepherds would hardly have had their flocks exposed on the hills. But the traditional date is not at all impossible, for the great drop in temperature which sometimes occurs in the winter generally makes itself felt only after Christmas.

Special study note: At this point let us stop and ponder six questions that may be raised concerning the events leading up to the birth of the Savior.

ANGELS AND DEMONS IN THE LIFE OF CHRIST

Angels

- They were made by and for him
  (Col. 1:16)

- They worship him
  (Heb. 1:6)

- They predicted his birth
  (Mt. 1:20, 21; Lk. 1:31)

- They announced his birth
  (Lk. 2:9-13)

- They protected him from Herod
  (Mt. 2:13; Ps. 91:11)

- They ministered to him in the wilderness
  (Mt. 4:11)

- They ministered to him in the garden
  (Lk. 22:43)

- They rolled away the tombstone
  (Mt. 28:2)

- They announced his resurrection
  (Mt. 28:6)

- They predicted his Second Coming
  (Acts 1:10, 11)

- They will accompany his Second Coming
  (2 Thess. 1:7, 8)

DEMONS

- They knew him
  (Mk. 3:11; Lk. 4:34; Acts 16:15)

- They feared him
  (Lk. 8:28)

- They obeyed him
  (Mk. 5:13)

- They were cast out of humans by him

  1. *A CAPERNAUM DEMONIAC*
     (Mk. 1:25; Lk. 4:35)

  2. *A GADARENE DEMONIAC*
     (Mt. 8:32; Mk. 5:8; Lk. 8:33)

  3. *A DUMB DEMONIAC*
     (Mt. 9:33)

  4. *A DEMONIAC GIRL*
     (Mt. 15:28; Mk. 7:29)

  5. *A DEMONIAC BOY*
     (Mt. 17:18; Mk. 9:25; Lk. 9:42)

  6. *A BLIND AND DUMB DEMONIAC*
     (Mt. 12:22; Lk. 11:14)

  7. *A WOMAN WITH AN EIGHTEEN-YEAR INFIRMITY*
     (Lk. 13:10-17)

  8. *MARY MAGDALENE* **(Mk. 16:9; Lk. 8:2)**

---

1. Why did the angel Gabriel rebuke Zacharias for his question and not rebuke Mary for her question?
   a. Zacharias: "How shall I know this? For I am an old man, and my wife well stricken in years" (Lk. 1:18).
   b. Mary: "How shall this be, seeing I know not a man?" (Lk. 1:34). Answer: Zacharias had for many years been praying for a son (Lk. 1:13) but when the announcement came he doubted God's power to do this. When something wonderful happens sometimes the most surprised individual on earth is that very Christian who had been fervently praying for it to happen! However, there is no reason to believe Mary had been praying to become the mother of Jesus.

   A classic example of this is found in the book of Acts. Peter was in prison awaiting execution, and when the Jerusalem believers heard of it, "prayer was made without ceasing of the church unto God for him" (Acts 12:5). At God's command an angel staged a spectacular jail break. Upon being set free, Peter hurried to the prayer meeting to announce the good news. Note the amusing account:
   "And when he had considered the thing, he came to the house of Mary the mother of John, whose surname was Mark; where many were gathered together praying. And as Peter knocked at the door of the gate, a damsel came to hearken, named Rhoda. And when she knew Peter's voice, she opened not the gate for gladness, but ran in and told how Peter stood before the gate. And they said unto her, thou art mad. But she constantly affirmed that it was even so. Then said they, It is his angel. But Peter continued knocking: and when they had opened the door, and saw him, they were astonished" (Acts 12:12-16).
   Peter had a harder time getting into that prayer meeting than getting out of his prison house!

2. Why did Joseph and Mary wait so long before coming to Bethlehem? We know both believed the angel's message about the Babe in Mary's womb and they doubtless were well aware of the prophecy in Micah 5:2 which stated Christ was to be born in Bethlehem. Why did they wait until the last moment to come? In fact, one is somewhat led to believe that had it not been for the decree of Caesar Augustus they might not have come at all.
   Answer: No satisfactory answer has been found by this author. It is best to conclude that Joseph (man of God that he was) had good reasons for acting in the manner he did. The reader may desire to explore this further.

3. Why didn't Mary and Joseph stay with their relatives in Bethlehem? The inns of those days were rather notorious, and Joseph must have been desperate to subject his pregnant wife to the sin and noise of such a place. But of course they were even denied this.

Answer: It would have been too difficult to explain (or to expect them to understand) the nature of the virgin birth. Every gossip in town doubtless knew by this time that Joseph and Mary had only been married six months, and there she was, expecting a baby at any moment. Was it Joseph's? Did it belong to some stranger? Thus, to spare his beloved wife all this, Joseph did not call upon their relatives!

4. Why was Jesus born in a place which apparently housed animals?

Answer: Because lambs are usually born in barns. This was God's Lamb.

5. Why did the angels appear to the shepherds first?

Answer: Because what other earthly group would better understand what God had just accomplished than these men who raised lambs and later sold them for sacrificial purposes in the Temple. (See Jn. 1:29; 10:11.)

Note: They would eventually understand that in the past the sheep had died for the shepherd, but soon now the Shepherd planned to die for the sheep. (See Jn. 10:11.)

When the shepherds heard the glad tidings they "came with haste" (Lk. 2:16). After finding Jesus they "made known abroad the saying which was told them . . . glorifying and praising God for all things that they had heard and seen . . ." (Lk. 2:17-20).

6. Why did God use the angels in the first place?

Answer:

a. Because angels are interested in the things of salvation. (See 1 Pet. 1:12; Ex. 25:20; Dan. 12:5, 6; Lk. 15:10; Eph. 3:10.)

b. Because they were present at the creation of this world and shouted for joy (Job 38:7). It is only logical, therefore, that God would allow them to be on hand at the presentation of the Savior of this world.

Step Two: From Bethlehem to Jerusalem
(Lk. 2:22-38).

A. Jesus is brought to the Temple to be dedicated to the Lord.

1. He was at least forty days old at this time, for Mary would have been considered ceremonially impure until this time had elapsed following childbirth. (See Lev. 12:2-4; Ex. 13:2.)

2. Two offerings were to be brought (Lev. 12:6).

a. A yearling lamb as a burnt offering.

b. A young pigeon or turtledove as a sin offering.

3. However, if the family was poor, God would accept two birds (Lev. 12:8).

4. Joseph and Mary offered these birds in place of the lamb.

B. The Holy Spirit had promised an old man named Simeon that he would live to see God's Messiah. When Jesus is brought to the Temple, Simeon immediately recognizes this forty-day-old Babe as the one.

C. Simeon takes the tiny Savior in his arms.

1. He thanks the Father for what he has done.

2. He foretells what the Savior will do.

a. He will be a Light to the Gentiles.

b. He will be the Glory of Israel.

c. He will be the cause of the fall and rise of many in Israel. (See Mt. 21:44; 1 Cor. 1:23; 2 Cor. 2:16; 2 Pet. 2:7.)

d. His sufferings to accomplish all this will be as a sword in Mary's soul. (See Jn. 19:25, 26.)

D. Anna, a godly eighty-four-year-old widow, at this point came in and also thanked the Father for his gift to the world.

1. She "departed not from the temple, but served God with fastings and prayers night and day" (Lk. 2:37). (See also 1 Tim. 5:5.)

2. Anna was one of the prophetesses mentioned in the Bible.

a. Miriam, Moses' sister, was one (Ex. 15:20).

b. Deborah, who judged Israel, was one (Jdg. 4:4).

c. Huldah was one (2 Ki. 22:14).

d. Philip's four daughters were prophetesses (Acts 21:8, 9).

Step Three: From Jerusalem to Nazareth
(Lk. 2:39).

Step Four: From Nazareth to Bethlehem
(Mt. 2:1-12). (This is implied in the text.)

A. The wise men arrived in Jerusalem and inquired of Herod about the recent birth of the King of the Jews. Here are several questions that may be asked.

1. Who were these wise men? It is thought that they were perhaps a group of religious astronomers living in the Mesopotamia area.

2. How did they associate the star with Christ? There are several possibilities. In the fourteenth century, B.C., a prophet from their area named Balaam had spoken of this star. (See Num. 24:17.) They also had the writings of Daniel, who had been prime minister of both Babylon and Persia some six centuries before Christ. Daniel, of course, wrote much about the Second Coming.

3. Why did they come? These men were doubtless acquainted with the various religions of the East and knew the emptiness of them all. It would seem they followed this star to find peace and purpose for their lives.

4. When did they arrive in Bethlehem? It was perhaps not until some two years after the angels announced his birth to the shepherds. He is referred to as "the young child" (2:9, 11, 13, 14) and is not a tiny babe at this time. When Herod later attempted to destroy this unknown Babe, he had all children in the Bethlehem area two years and under slain. (2:16).

5. How many wise men came? There is absolutely no evidence that there were three. On the contrary, the group may have numbered from two to several hundred or more.

6. Was the star a regular star? Perhaps it was a special heavenly light created by God for this specific purpose and not some remote fiery globe of gas a million light years removed from our earth.

B. King Herod, troubled and agitated, asks the chief priest and scribes about the magis' request and is told Bethlehem was to be the Messiah's birthplace. (See Mal. 2:7; Micah 5:2.)

C. Herod sends the wise men there and asks them to report back to him, pretending to be desirous of worshiping him also. In reality he was already planning to kill him.

Note: The Jewish leaders had degenerated to such a level that they were unwilling to trot down the road a few miles from Jerusalem to Bethlehem and see if their Messiah had really come! But here was a group of sincere Gentiles who had traveled across a hostile and extended desert to find him.

D. Upon being led by the star to his very home, they fell at his feet and offered him their gifts.
 1. They gave him gold, which spoke of his deity.
 2. They gave him frankincense, which spoke of his humanity.
 3. They gave him myrrh, which spoke of his future sufferings.
 4. Old Testament Prophecy Fulfillment Number 7, That he would be worshiped by wise men and presented with gifts. (Compare Ps. 72:10 and Isa. 60:3, 6, 9 with Mt. 2:11.) This prophecy, given by Isaiah, was only partly fulfilled at his first coming. The gift of myrrh (symbol of his suffering) was not included by Isaiah. The reason is that the prophecy will have its ultimate fulfillment during the Second Coming, when all nations will offer him presents which speak of his glorious humanity and unblemished deity. Myrrh will *not* be offered, however, at that time, for his sufferings will be done forever.

E. God warns them of Herod's real plans for Jesus, and the magi depart another way for their land.

Step Five: From Bethlehem to Egypt

(Mt. 2:13–18).
 A. Joseph is instructed by the archangel in a dream to flee to Egypt.
 B. Old Testament Prophecy Fulfillment Number 8, That he would be in Egypt for a season. (Compare Num. 24:8; Hosea 11:1 with Mt. 2:15.)
 C. Herod, discovering he has been tricked, orders the death of all babies in the Bethlehem area two years old and under.
 D. Old Testament Prophecy Fulfillment Number 9, That his birthplace would suffer a massacre of infants. (Compare Jer. 31:15 with Mt. 2:17, 18.)

Note: A divine irony is seen here. In the Old Testament God led his chosen people out of Egypt to escape Satan's wrath, but in the New Testament he leads his beloved Son into Egypt to escape this same wrath.

Step Six: From Egypt to Nazareth

(Mt. 2:19–23; Lk. 2:40).
 A. After Herod's death, Joseph is instructed to come back to Israel by the archangel. (See Isa. 51:12.)
 B. Joseph obeys, but because of Archelaus, Herod's son, who is Judea's new ruler, he is afraid to move into Bethlehem, so he settles the family at Nazareth in Galilee (Mt. 2:22, 23).
 C. Old Testament Prophecy Fulfillment Number 10, That he would be called a Nazarene. (Compare Isa. 11:1 with Mt. 2:23.)
 D. At Nazareth Jesus grows and becomes strong, filled with wisdom, with God's favor resting upon him (Lk. 2:40).

Step Seven: From Nazareth to Jerusalem

(Lk. 2:41–50).
 A. Jesus attends his first recorded Passover when he is twelve.
 B. He is found missing on the way home and is finally located in the Temple discussing theology with the priests. (See Isa. 11:1-4; 49:1, 2; 50:4.)
 C. The learned doctors are astonished at his understanding. (See also Mt. 7:28; Mk. 1:22; Lk. 4:22, 32; Jn. 7:15.)
 D. He speaks his first recorded words: "How is it that ye sought me? Wist ye not that I must be about my Father's business?" (Lk. 2:49). Contrast this with his words en route from heaven to Bethlehem. (See Heb. 10:5-7.)

Step Eight: From Jerusalem to Nazareth

(Lk. 2:51, 52).
 A. He returns with Mary and Joseph and subjects himself to them. (See Phil. 2:5-8.)
 B. He increases in wisdom and stature, and in favor with God and men.

Jesus as a lad doubtless learned Hebrew, Aramaic, and Greek. He later would read from a Hebrew scroll in Nazareth (Lk. 4), teach the multitudes in Aramaic, and converse with Pilate in Greek.

He may have read The Testaments of the Twelve Patriarchs, which was a noncanonical account relating the testimony of Jacob's twelve sons. He surely also would have been familiar with well-known Jewish books on the sacred law and writings.

Note: His fourfold increase as stated in Luke 2:52:
 1. in wisdom (mental maturity)
 2. in stature (physical maturity)
 3. in favor with God (spiritual maturity)
 4. in favor with man (social maturity)

JESUS' BOYHOOD
"This hamlet of Nazareth in northern Palestine was a miniature of the whole country in the sense that its situation afforded ready contact with the outside world, yet considerable separation from it, the very features Israel historically had enjoyed. Their land lay at the crossroads of the world but was detached by its peculiar topography, which confined the flow of travel largely to the lowlands, passing by the plateau where the life of the nation centered.

From the hill back of Nazareth, Jesus as a boy must often have scanned the horizon in all directions. Travelers attest the magnificence of the view from this spot. The panorama would include the Mediterranean Sea to the west, Mount Carmel and the plain of Sharon south of it, the broad valley of Esdraelon, with Mount Tabor on the north, the hill of Moreh and Mount Gilboa on the south, and Samaria beyond—all of these in an almost perfect line north and south. To the east, beyond the depression made by the Sea of Galilee and the Jordan, rose the hills that marked the beginning of the Bashan-Gilead country. To the north lay the somewhat broken terrain of Galilee, rising to plateau proportions in the distance, with glistening Mt. Hermon to the northeast capping the scene.

No patriotic son of Israel could allow his eye to sweep these vistas without being reminded of the stirring events of history that would forever be associated with them: Elijah's triumph over the prophets of Baal, the victory of Deborah and Barak, the crushing of the Midianites by Gideon and his band, the lamented death of Saul and Jonathan—these and other episodes would easily rise out of the past and in fancy be reenacted. Yes, Nazareth was secluded, but just beyond its sheltering quiet lay the world of affairs. Its immediate gift to Jesus was an opportunity to live a life of simplicity. More remotely, it provided a door of entrance to the busier and more complex life in which he would minister.

Nazareth depended for its livelihood upon the tillage of its grainfields and the cultivation of its vineyards and groves, which ranged up and down the neighboring hills. Though his labor kept him in the village, Jesus loved the out-of-doors, and must often have tramped through the countryside enjoying its sights and sounds. Years later, when he chose to slip away from human companionship to commune with the Father, he was remaining true to the influence of the environment of the early days.

Judging from his parables Jesus must have cultivated early in life the habit of observing what went on around him. He saw that not all the sower's seed fell on good ground. He knew that a good tree was needed to insure good fruit.

He had many times stuffed dried grass into his mother's stove to heat it for baking, grass that only a short time before had been growing in the field. Perchance he had watched Mary light a lamp and look carefully for the coin that had slipped from her hand and rolled out of view. Whether indoors or out he was alert to all that was going on. This panorama of early days furnished him with many a true-to-life illustration as he stood before the multitude and taught." (Everett F. Harrison, *A Short Life of Christ*, pp. 56, 57)

Step Nine: From Nazareth to Bethabara on the Jordan River

(Mt. 3:13–17; Mk. 1:9–11; Lk. 3:21, 22). He is now thirty years of age (Lk. 3:23). (See also Num. 4:1–3.)
A. Jesus is baptized by John (who protested he was unworthy to do so) to fulfill all righteousness. There are a number of baptisms mentioned in the Gospel account. The word baptism means to identify with.
  1. The baptism of John the Baptist. This was national baptism. (See Mk. 1:4.)
  2. The baptism of Jesus.
     a. With water by John (Mt. 3:15).
     b. With the Holy Spirit by the Father (Mt. 3:16).
  3. The baptism of sin upon Christ at Calvary (Lk. 12:50; Mt. 20:22).
  4. The baptism of the Holy Spirit upon believers at Pentecost (Mt. 3:11b).
  5. The baptism of God's wrath upon sinners during the tribulation (Mt. 3:11b; 3:12; 13:30).

THE BAPTISM OF CHRIST

The Reasons for the Baptism of Christ

IDENTIFICATION

ONE: To identify with the three **Old Testament** offices and anointings

OFFICES	ANOINTINGS	FULFILLMENT
Prophet—Oil only	1. With water (Lev. 8:6)	By John (Mt. 3:15)
Priest—All three	2. With oil (Lev. 8:12)	By the Holy Spirit (Mt. 3:16)
King—Oil only	3. With blood (Lev. 8:23)	By himself (Mt. 26:28)

TWO: To identify with the **MESSAGE OF JOHN** (Jn. 1:31-34)

THREE: To identify with **ISRAEL** (Jn. 1:11)

FOUR: To identify with **SINNERS** (Isa. 53:12; 2 Cor. 5:21)

The Trinity in the Baptism of Christ

Christ is anointed by the Holy Spirit	"And, lo, the heavens were opened unto him, and he saw the spirit of God descending like a dove, and lighting upon him" (Mt. 3:16).
Christ is approved by the Father	"And lo a voice from heaven saying, This is my beloved Son, in whom I am well pleased" (Mt. 3:17).

THREEFOLD APPROVAL OF CHRIST BY GOD

FIRST (Mt. 3:17)   SECOND (Mt. 17:5)   THIRD (Jn. 12:28)

6. The baptism of believers (Mt. 28:19).

Why was Christ baptized? Four reasons have been offered.

7. To identify himself with the office of the prophet, priest, and king. In the Old Testament all three were anointed. In Leviticus 8 we have described the threefold anointing of a priest. He was first washed with water, then anointed with oil, then finally with blood. Christ submitted to the first two of these (water baptism and the oil of the Spirit) but not the third.
8. To identify himself to John the Baptist. (See Jn. 1:31-34.)
9. To identify himself with Israel (Jn. 1:11).
10. To identify himself with sinners (Isa. 53:12; 2 Cor. 5:21).

B. First prayer: At his baptism (Lk. 3:21).
C. The Holy Spirit descends upon him as a dove and the Father voices his delight. Here we see the entire Trinity in action. Note John's statement at this time:
"I saw the Spirit descending from heaven like a dove, and it abode upon him. And I knew him not: but he that sent me to baptize with water, the same said unto me, Upon whom thou shalt see the Spirit descending and remaining on him, the same is he which baptizeth with the Holy Ghost" (Jn. 1:32, 33). (See also Isa. 11:2; 42:1.)

1. The ministry of the Holy Spirit in the life of Jesus:
   a. He was begotten by the Holy Spirit (Lk. 1:35).
   b. He was here anointed by the Holy Spirit (Mt. 3:16). (See Heb. 1:9.)
   c. He preached in the power of the Holy Spirit (Lk. 4:18).
   d. He was sealed by the Holy Spirit (Jn. 6:27).
   e. He was led by the Holy Spirit (Mt. 4:1).
   f. He worked his miracles through the Holy Spirit (Mt. 12:28; see also Acts 10:38).
   g. He was filled by the Holy Spirit (Jn. 3:34; Lk. 4:1).
   h. He sorrowed in the Holy Spirit (Jn. 11:33).
   i. He rejoiced in the Holy Spirit (Lk. 10:21).
   j. He offered up himself at Calvary through the Holy Spirit (Heb. 9:14).
   k. He was raised from the dead by the Holy Spirit (Rom. 1:4; 1 Pet. 3:18).
   l. He commanded his disciples after his resurrection through the Holy Spirit (Acts 1:2).
   m. He will someday return and raise the dead in Christ through the Holy Spirit (Rom. 8:11).
2. The ministry of the Father in the life of Jesus.
   a. He sends his Son (Jn. 3:16; Gal. 4:4; Jn. 6:57; 8:16, 17, 18; 12:49).
   b. He seals his Son (Jn. 6:27).
   c. He teaches his Son (Jn. 8:28).
   d. He honors his Son (Jn. 8:54).
   e. He commands his Son (Jn. 10:18).
   f. He bears witness to the Son (Jn. 8:18).
   g. He loves his Son (Jn. 10:17).
   h. He glorifies his Son (Jn. 12:28; 17:1).
   i. He raises his Son (Eph. 1:20).
   j. He exalts his Son (Phil. 2:9-11; Eph. 1:20).
   k. He makes his Son Head of the Church (Eph. 1:22).
   l. He anoints his Son (Isa. 61:1; Acts 10:38).
   m. He delights in his Son (Isa. 42:1; Mt. 3:17; 17:5; 2 Pet. 1:17).

n. He hears his Son (Mt. 26:53; Jn. 11:41, 42; 12:27, 28).
o. He offers his Son (Jn. 3:16; 18:11; Rom. 8:32; 1 Jn. 4:9, 10).
p. He commits judgment unto his Son (Jn. 5:22, 27).

Note: This is the first of at least three occasions on which the Father speaks from heaven concerning his beloved Son. (See Mt. 17:5 and Jn. 12:28.) Although the doctrine of the Trinity is hinted at and foreshadowed in the Old Testament, it was on the occasion of Christ's baptism that it was first clearly manifested.

Step Ten: From Bethabara to the temptation wilderness
(Mt. 4:1-11; Mk. 1:12, 13; Lk. 4:1-13).

A. The fact of his temptation: He is led by the Spirit into a wilderness and remains for forty days with the wild beasts, fasting all the while.
B. The nature of his temptations: After forty days, Satan appears and tempts him.
   1. First temptation—to turn stones into bread.
   2. Second temptation—to jump off the pinnacle of the Temple.
   3. Third temptation—to fall down and worship Satan.
C. The theology involved in his temptations:
   1. Did Satan know whom he was tempting? He did indeed. The account in Matthew 4:3 and 4:6 is in the indicative mode in the Greek and should be rendered, "Since you are the Son of God."
   2. What benefits did Satan offer him?
      a. First temptation—to fill his stomach (and thus depend upon his own resources).
      b. Second temptation—to jump off the Temple (and thus force the hand of the Father).
      c. Third temptation—to grasp the kingdoms of this world (and thus refuse Calvary).
   3. What method did Satan use during the second temptation? He attempted to confuse Christ by quoting Scripture out of context. (Compare Mt. 4:6 with Ps. 91:11, 12.)
   4. Did Satan really have the right to offer Christ "all the kingdoms of the world and the glory of them" (Mt. 4:8)? He did indeed! (See Rev. 13:7; Jn. 14:30.)
   5. How did Christ answer Satan? By the Word of God.
      a. First temptation: "It is written, man shall not live by bread alone, but by every word that proceedeth out of the mouth of God." (Compare Mt. 4:4 with Deut. 8:3.)
      b. Second temptation: "It is written again, Thou shalt not tempt the Lord thy God." (Compare Mt. 4:7 with Deut. 6:16.)

      This temptation was probably an attempt for him to prematurely (and wrongly) fulfill Malachi 3:1.

      "Behold, I will send my messenger, and he shall prepare the way before me; and the Lord, whom ye seek, shall suddenly come to his temple, even the messenger of the Covenant, whom ye delight in; behold, he shall come, saith the Lord of hosts."

Satan's supreme object in the temptation ordeal was to cause Christ to act by himself, independent of the Father. Just what does it mean to tempt God? Israel is said to have tempted God on ten specific occasions en route to the Promised Land. (See Num. 14:11, 22; Heb. 3:9.) It means simply to presume upon the goodness of God. It refers to using this goodness in a selfish way. It means to force God's hand on something. Had Christ actually jumped from this Temple pinnacle, God would have been forced to step in and save Christ from smashing his physical body on the ground below.

c. Third temptation: "Get thee hence, Satan: for it is written, thou shalt worship the Lord thy God, and him only shalt thou serve." (Compare Mt. 4:10 with Deut. 6:13.) (See also Jas. 4:7.)

Dr. Everett F. Harrison writes the following about the third temptation:

"In this final episode Satan is unmasked. Gone is any suggestion that he is working for the best interests of the Son of God. No citation from Scripture is offered. Satan reveals the inmost secret of his being. Much as he enjoys the distinction of being the prince of this world, a distinction only sin has enabled him to achieve, he covets something else infinitely more. He would be like the Most High. He would receive to himself what is most characteristically and exclusively the prerogative of God, namely, worship. A true angel abhors the very thought of being worshiped (Rev. 22:8, 9), but this fallen angel fiercely, cravenly covets it.

That such an offer was extended to Jesus is a testimony to his greatness. The stakes are high. When Satan made Judas his victim, his bait was a mere thirty pieces of silver. Indeed Satan could not well offer a lesser inducement to our Lord, for the nations were the promised inheritance of the Messiah and the uttermost parts of the earth were his anticipated possession (Ps. 2:8). In Psalm 2 this passage follows immediately the divine recognition of the sonship of the Messiah, the focal point of the temptation. 'Ask of me,' says God, but Satan brazenly usurps the place of the Almighty." (*A Short Life of Christ*, p. 90)

As it can be seen here, Christ quotes from the book of Deuteronomy each time. It is no accident that higher criticism in Germany began with Deuteronomy in its vicious attack against the Bible.

6. Is this the only time Satan tempted Christ? No; in Luke 4:13 we are told: "And when the devil had ended all the temptation, he departed from him for a season." Note especially the last three words. Satan tempted Christ all through his ministry (see Mt. 16:23).

7. What happened after the wilderness temptation? "Then the devil leaveth him, and behold, angels came and ministered unto him" (Mt. 4:11). Heaven's angels played an important part in the earthly ministry of Christ.
   a. They worshiped him (Heb. 1:6).
   b. They announced his birth (Lk. 1-2; Mt. 1).
   c. They ministered to him
      (1) in the wilderness (Mt. 4:11)
      (2) in the garden (Lk. 22:43)
   d. They rolled away the tombstone (Mt. 28:2).
   e. They were present at his ascension (Acts 1:10, 11).
   f. They announced his resurrection (Mt. 28:6).

THE WILDERNESS TEMPTATIONS

Gen. 3:6	1 John 2:16	Mt. 4:1-11; Lk. 4:1-13
AS EXPERIENCED BY THE FIRST ADAM	**AS DESCRIBED BY JOHN**	**AS EXPERIENCED BY THE SECOND ADAM**
"The tree was good for food"	"The lust of the flesh"	"Command that these stones be made bread."
"It was pleasant to the eyes"	"The lust of the eyes"	"The devil . . . showeth him all the kingdoms of the world, and the glory of them."
"A tree desired to make one wise"	"The pride of life"	"Cast thyself down; for . . . he shall give his angels charge concerning thee . . ."

The SATANIC SUBTLETY of Christ's Temptations

First temptation—
Fill your belly
—And thus depend upon your own resources

Second temptation—
Jump off the Temple
—And thus force the hand of God

Third temptation—
Grasp for the world's kingdoms
—And thus bypass Calvary

g. They will accompany his Second Coming (2 Thess. 1:7, 8).

8. Could Christ have sinned during the temptation experience? He could not; God cannot sin. The Bible declares:
   a. He knew no sin (2 Cor. 5:21).
   b. He did no sin (1 Pet. 2:22; Heb. 4:15).
   c. He had no sin (1 Jn. 3:5; Jn. 14:30). (See also Heb. 7:26.)

9. What then was the purpose for the temptation?
   a. The purpose was not to see if he would, but to prove that he could not sin.

   During the settling of the West a railroad company faced a problem. A bridge spanning a deep chasm gained the reputation of being unsafe. Careful examination by railroad officials showed this to be totally unfounded but the rumor persisted. Finally, a train was formed made up of only heavy locomotives. For an entire day as hundreds watched, this train crossed and recrossed the bridge. Why was this done? Did the railroad engineers arrange the experiment to see *if* the bridge would hold, or did they do it to prove it *would* hold? The obvious answer here may be applied to the purpose of Christ's temptations.

   b. The purpose was to provide the believer with an experienced high priest. (See Heb. 4:15; 2:18.)

Step Eleven: From the temptation wilderness to Bethabara

(*Jn. 1:29–42*).

A. John the Baptist introduces the Messiah as the Lamb of God (1:29).

   "Behold the Lamb of God, which taketh away the sin of the world" (Jn. 1:29).

   Perhaps without being fully aware of it, John was here answering the question asked by a young lad some twenty centuries prior to this.

   "And Isaac spoke unto Abraham, his father, and said, My father: and he said, Here am I, my son. And he said, Behold the fire and the wood: but where is the lamb for a burnt offering?" (Gen. 22:7).

   For the glorious conclusion of this wonderful theme, hear the cry of heaven's angels who exclaim:

   "Worthy is the Lamb that was slain to receive power and riches, and wisdom, and strength, and honor and glory and blessing" (Rev. 5:12).

   (See Gen. 22:7; Ex. 12:3; Isa. 53:7; 1 Pet. 1:19; Rev. 5:6.)

B. John relates how he recognized the Messiah when the Spirit in the form of a dove descended upon him.

C. John, the son of Zebedee, and Andrew, younger brother of Peter, two of John the Baptist's disciples, now leave the Baptist and follow Christ.

D. Soon Andrew brings his brother Peter to Christ. Without realizing it, Andrew answered Job's perplexing question.
   1. Job: "Oh that I knew where I might find him!" (23:3).
   2. Andrew (to Peter) "We have found the Messiah, which is, being interpreted, the Christ" (Jn. 1:41).

E. Jesus calls Peter "Cephas" which is translated, "a stone." God's purpose is to change men's names (and character). (See Rev. 3:12.)

1. He changed Abram to Abraham (Gen. 17:5).
2. He changed Sarai to Sarah (Gen. 17:15).
3. He changed Jacob to Israel (Gen. 32:28).
4. He changed Saul to Paul (Acts 13:9).

Step Twelve: From Bethabara to Bethsaida

(*Jn. 1:43–51*).

A. Jesus meets Philip and calls him to follow.

B. Philip locates his friend Nathanael and tells him of that one "of whom Moses in the law, and the prophets, did write, Jesus of Nazareth, the son of Joseph" (Jn. 1:45).

C. Nathanael is skeptical: "Can there any good thing come out of Nazareth?" (Jn. 1:46).

D. Philip is positive: "Come and see" (Jn. 1:46).
   1. We note Philip, a new convert, did not have a full understanding of the virgin birth, but he was still an effective witness.
   2. Nathanael was hung up on Philip's "Jesus of Nazareth" title. He doubtless realized the Messiah would be born in Bethlehem. In addition, he probably had a low view of Galileans.
   3. Philip refused to argue, however, but invited him to "Come and see."

E. Nathanael confesses Christ as the Son of God and King of Israel.
   1. He was amazed that Jesus knew he had been sitting under a fig tree when Philip talked to him. The Savior always dealt with men on their own level.
      a. He dealt with Nathanael *under* a fig tree (Jn. 1:48).
      b. He dealt with Zacchaeus *up* a sycamore tree (Lk. 19:4, 5).
      c. He dealt with a dying thief *on* a cruel tree (Lk. 23:39–43).
   2. Nathanael is promised he will someday see heaven open and the angels ascending and descending upon Christ. This happened at the ascension. (See Acts 1:9-11.)

      Although Nathanael addresses him as the King of Israel (1:49), our Lord refers to himself as the Son of Man (1:51). This is by far his favorite title for himself. He will use it more times than any other name. Nathanael and Philip are the first to hear it.
   3. First prediction: Concerning his ascension (Jn. 1:50, 51).

      Note: It is thrilling to observe that our Lord's first recorded prediction was not concerning his suffering, death, or even resurrection but that he would someday ascend. As Isaiah once declared of God:

      "Remember the former things of old: for I am God, and there is none else; I am God, and there is none like me, Declaring the end from the beginning, and from ancient times the things that are not yet done, saying, my counsel shall stand, and I will do all my pleasure" (46:9, 10).

Step Thirteen: From Bethsaida to Cana

(*Jn. 2:1–11*).

A. Jesus, Mary, and his disciples attend a wedding in Cana.

B. Mary informs Jesus that they have run out of wine.

C. He plans to solve this embarrassing problem, but gently reminds Mary that the purpose of his coming to earth was not simply to work miracles. (Compare Jn. 2:4 with 12:23.)

D. Mary instructs the servants that "whatsoever he saith unto you, do it" (Jn. 2:5). (See also Lk. 5:5, 6; Acts 9:6; Heb. 5:9, 11:8.)

E. They were instructed to fill six eighteen-gallon stone waterpots with water.

F. First miracle: Changing of water into wine (Jn. 2:7-9). It is significant that our Lord chose a wedding at which to perform his first recorded miracle. The oldest and greatest of three grand institutions given by God to man is that of marriage. God himself performed the first wedding in Eden. (See Gen. 2:20-25.) The Father would later choose that relationship between a man and wife to illustrate the love of Christ for his church. (See Eph. 5:22-33.) Finally, the great event of the ages, yet to come, is a wedding—the marriage of God's Son to his chosen Bride. (See Rev. 19:6-9.)

Jesus used waterpots to accomplish his first miracle. He desires to do the same today, but now he uses living, earthly vessels. If we allow him, he fills us with the water of God's Word and when we pour it out (give it out) it becomes the wine of the Spirit.

G. The head of the feast testifies to the excellent quality of the wine.

Step Fourteen: From Cana to Capernaum
(Jn. 2:12). This is soon to become his home city.

Step Fifteen: From Capernaum to Jerusalem
(Jn. 2:13—3:21).

A. Jesus attends the Passover and visits the Temple. All males were required to go to Jerusalem three times a year, at the time of the Feasts of Passover, Pentecost, and Tabernacles.

B. He performs his first Temple cleansing as he drives the materialistic money changers out. He would later repeat this at the end of his ministry. (Compare Jn. 2:15 with Mt. 21:12.)

C. Old Testament Prophecy Fulfillment Number 11, That he would be zealous for the Father. (Compare Ps. 69:9; 119:139 with Jn. 2:13-17.)

Note the statement: "The zeal of thine house hath eaten me up" (Jn. 2:17). This is taken from Psalm 69, which is one of the six most quoted Psalms in the New Testament. (The others are 2, 22, 89, 110, and 118.)

D. The Jews demand a sign from him to justify what he has done.

E. Second prediction: Concerning his death and resurrection (Jn. 2:19-22).

1. He said his Temple would be destroyed.

2. He said that he would raise it again after three days.

3. The Jews thought he spoke of Herod's temple, which took forty-six years to build. Later they would twist this statement completely out of context during Jesus' trial and even while he was on the cross. (See Mt. 26:61; 27:40; Mk. 15:29.)

4. He was, of course, referring to his body. (See 1 Cor. 3:16; 6:19; 2 Cor. 6:16.) The Jews should have known this, for Jesus used two separate words here. He used the word *hieron* when referring to

the temple of Herod, and the word *naos* when describing his body.

5. His disciples would remember this conversation after the resurrection (Lk. 24:8).

6. Fickle crowds begin to flock to him after his miracle in Cana and display of strength in the Temple, but he avoids them, being fully aware of their carnal motives. (Compare Jn. 2:24, 25 with Mt. 9:4; Mk. 2:8; Jn. 6:64.)

F. Nicodemus comes to Jesus by night (Jn. 3:1-21).

1. Although this man was both a ruler and religious teacher, he needed the new birth. Note Jesus' question in 3:10, "Art thou a master of Israel, and knoweth not these things?" In the Greek the definite article is used, meaning, "Are you *the* teacher in Israel?" Nicodemus may have been the most famous teacher of his day.

2. Jesus illustrated his visitor's need by referring to Moses and the brazen serpent. (Compare Jn. 3:14 with Num. 21:9.) On this occasion in the Old Testament account God had sent poisonous serpents to punish rebellious Israel. The people repented and a cure was provided. A serpent of brass was placed atop a wooden pole where all could view it. Anyone bitten needed only to look upon the brass serpent to be healed.

To paraphrase, here is what Jesus tells Nicodemus:

"Nicodemus, like those Old Testament Israeli individuals, you have been bitten by a serpent—the serpent of sin. It is an incurable and fatal bite. But soon God is going to erect a cross-like pole just outside Jerusalem. And on that cross he will place a Savior."

It may be said that one cannot fully grasp the most famous verse in the Bible, John 3:16, unless he has some understanding of its background, which is found in John 3:14.

"And as Moses lifted up the serpent in the wilderness, even so must the Son of man be lifted up."

3. Nicodemus is told of God's great love for the world (Jn. 3:16).

4. Several questions may be raised here.

a. Why did he come by night? We do not know, and it is unfair to brand him a coward. Perhaps the heavy schedules of both men required this.

b. What did Nicodemus know about Jesus? He knew he was from God because of his supernatural miracles. (Compare Jn. 3:2 with 20:30, 31.)

c. What did Jesus mean by his expression, "except a man be born of water and of the Spirit, he cannot enter into the Kingdom of God" (Jn. 3:5)? Here four main views have been offered.

(1) He was referring to baptismal regeneration. This, of course, is totally refuted by other biblical passages. (See Eph. 2:8, 9; 1 Cor. 1:17; Rom. 5:1.)

(2) He was referring to that watery sac which accompanies physical birth and thus contrasts physical birth with spiritual birth. He was saying that the one requirement to live on this earth is to have had a physical birthday; and likewise, the one requirement to someday live in heaven is to

have a spiritual birthday. Those who hold this view point to 3:6 where they feel Jesus clarifies his position.

(3) He was referring to John's baptism of repentance in the Jordan, which baptism the Pharisees had rejected. (Compare Lk. 3:3 with 7:30.)

(4) He was referring to the Word of God (the water) and the Spirit of God (Spirit), without which no man can ever be saved. (See Jn. 16:8-11; Rom. 11:6-15.) Advocates of this position point out that water in the Bible is often the recognized symbol for the Word of God. (See Ps. 119:9; Jn. 4:14; Eph. 5:25, 26; Titus 3:5.)

d. Did Nicodemus accept Christ? There is strong evidence that he did, although he was apparently not the most vocal witness for Christ who ever lived. (See Jn. 7:50; 19:39.)

5. Third prediction: Concerning his death (Jn. 3:14).

6. In 3:13 Jesus said: "And no man hath ascended up to heaven, but he that came down from heaven, even the Son of man who is in heaven." How can this statement be reconciled to the one describing Elijah's homegoing, where we are told: "And Elijah went up by a whirlwind into heaven" (2 Ki. 2:11)?

A suggestion is that Jesus was referring to the third heaven of 2 Corinthians 12:2, while the heaven Elijah was taken to was actually Paradise (or Abraham's bosom) which, prior to the cross, is believed to have been located in the heart of the earth.

Step Sixteen: From Jerusalem to the Jordan River

(Jn. 3:22-36).
A. Jesus baptizes in the Jordan River.
B. John the Baptist gives a faithful witness about Jesus to his (John's) own disciples.

Step Seventeen: From the Jordan River to Sychar in Samaria

(Mt. 4:12; Lk. 3:19, 20; Jn. 4:1-42).
A. John the Baptist is placed in prison for denouncing Herod's unlawful marriage (Mt. 4:12; Lk. 3:19, 20; Mk. 1:14).
B. Jesus realizes the Pharisees are putting him in a baptismal contest with John, so he departs Judea for Galilee (Jn. 4:1-3).
C. Jesus witnesses to and wins over an immoral Samaritan woman en route (Jn. 4:4-42).
   1. He asks her for a drink of water from the well Jacob once gave to Joseph, and is immediately reminded of a serious racial problem. (Compare Jn. 4:9 with 2 Ki. 17:24; Ezra 4:3; Lk. 9:52.)
   2. He overlooks her taunts and offers her living water. (Compare Jn. 4:10 with Isa. 12:3; Rev. 22:17.)
   3. She asks him if he is greater than Jacob the patriarch.
   4. He again passes over her terse words and for the second time offers her living water.
   5. When she asks for this special water he gently reminds her of her sinful past, pointing out her

five previous marriages, and noting the fact she is at the present living in adultery with a sixth man.

6. In a desperate attempt to avoid this painful issue, she asks him a theological question concerning whether men should worship in Jerusalem or on Mt. Gerizim in Samaria.

7. Jesus points out that God is Spirit and that they who worship him must do so in spirit and in truth.

8. He reveals to her that he is the Messiah (4:26). (See also Jn. 9:37; Mk. 14:61, 62.)

9. The disciples return from buying food and Jesus lectures them on soul-winning. (Compare 4:35 with Mt. 9:37.)

10. The woman returns, leading a great crowd of Samaritans out to meet Christ. Many of them are saved.

D. This passage contains one of the greatest examples for soul-winners in the entire Bible. Note a few of its practical points.
   1. Jesus refused to argue with the woman.
   2. He avoided getting entangled by various theological concepts.
   3. He never browbeat her, even though she was a great sinner.
   4. He repeatedly spoke of the living water, which was the real (and only) issue.
   5. He concluded by pointing her to himself (4:26).
   6. The Christian has only to lift up his eyes to see the bountiful harvest of lost souls all around him.
   7. Christians sometimes sow seed which will be reaped by others, but they often reap seed planted by another. God alone gives the increase. (See 1 Cor. 3:5-9.)

Step Eighteen: From Sychar to Cana

(Jn. 4:43-54).
A. Jesus enters Galilee, but bypasses his own hometown of Nazareth and proceeds to Cana because, "a prophet hath no honour in his own country" (Jn. 3:44).
B. He is approached by a nobleman from Capernaum who desires him to heal his dying son.
C. Second miracle: Healing of the nobleman's son (Jn. 4:50).
   1. Jesus sends the man home with the promise that he will find his boy cured.
   2. He returns home and finds this true. He and his entire household accept Christ.

Step Nineteen: From Cana to Nazareth

(Lk. 4:16-30).
A. Jesus is asked to read the Scriptures in his hometown synagogue.
B. He takes his text from Isaiah 61:1, 2 where the prophet predicted the Holy Spirit would anoint the future Messiah to do marvelous things.
   1. He would preach the gospel to the poor.
   2. He would heal the brokenhearted.
   3. He would preach deliverance to the captives.
   4. He would restore sight to the blind.
   5. He would set the bruised at liberty.
   6. He would proclaim the acceptable year of the Lord.
C. First sermon: From Isaiah 61; in Nazareth (Lk. 4:16-30). Note: Jesus stopped his reading with the words "the acceptable year of the Lord," and did not read the last

OLD TESTAMENT EVENTS AND PEOPLE
MENTIONED BY CHRIST

OLD TESTAMENT REFERENCE	EVENT	NEW TESTAMENT REFERENCE
1. **GENESIS 1:27; 2:24**	CREATION OF ADAM AND EVE	**MARK 10:6-8**
2. **GENESIS 4:10**	MURDER OF ABEL	**LUKE 11:51**
3. **GENESIS 6:5-13**	CORRUPTION OF NOAH'S DAY AND FLOOD	**LUKE 17:26, 27**
4. **GENESIS 18:20; 19:24**	CORRUPTION OF LOT'S DAY AND THE FIRE	**LUKE 17:28, 29**
5. **GENESIS 19:26**	WORLDLINESS OF LOT'S WIFE	**LUKE 17:32**
6. **EXODUS 3:1-6**	MOSES AND THE BURNING BUSH	**LUKE 20:37**
7. **EXODUS 16:15**	MOSES AND THE HEAVENLY MANNA	**JOHN 6:31**
8. **NUMBERS 21:8**	MOSES AND THE BRAZEN SERPENT	**JOHN 3:14**
9. **1 SAMUEL 21:6**	DAVID AND THE SHEWBREAD	**MATTHEW 12:3, 4**
10. **1 KINGS 10:1**	SOLOMON AND THE QUEEN OF SHEBA	**MATTHEW 12:42**
11. **1 KINGS 17:1, 9**	ELIJAH, THE WIDOW, AND THE FAMINE	**LUKE 4:25, 26**
12. **2 KINGS 5**	NAAMAN AND HIS LEPROSY	**LUKE 4:27**
13. **2 CHRONICLES 24:20, 21**	THE MURDER OF ZECHARIAH	**LUKE 11:51**
14. **DANIEL 9:27; 11:31; 12:11**	DANIEL AND THE ABOMINATION OF DESOLATION	**MATTHEW 24:15**
15. **JONAH 1:17**	JONAH AND THE FISH	**MATTHEW 12:40; 16:4**
16. **JONAH 3:4-10**	THE REPENTANCE OF NINEVEH	**LUKE 11:30; MATTHEW 12:41**

half of the sentence in Isaiah 61:2 which said: "and the day of vengeance of our God." This he did, for the "acceptable year" belongs to his first coming, and the "day of vengeance" relates to his second appearance.

D. Jesus then identifies himself as the promised Messiah in Isaiah 61.

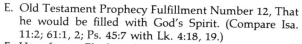

E. Old Testament Prophecy Fulfillment Number 12, That he would be filled with God's Spirit. (Compare Isa. 11:2; 61:1, 2; Ps. 45:7 with Lk. 4:18, 19.)

F. He refers to Elijah and Naaman in an attempt to convict his hometown people of their unbelief.
1. There were many hungry Jewish widows in Elijah's time, but God fed only one, the widow at Zarephath in Sidon. (See 1 Ki. 17:9-16.)
2. There were many Jewish lepers in Elisha's time, but God healed only one, Naaman the Syrian. (See 2 Ki. 5:14.)

G. The Jews are filled with wrath at all this and actually attempt to murder him, but "he, passing through the midst of them, went his way" (Lk. 4:30). This marks the first of numerous instances when the Jews attempted to kill him. (See Jn. 5:16; 7:30; 8:40, 59; Lk. 11:53, 54.) One of the reasons for their insane hatred was his illustration of the faith of two Gentiles. The Jews looked upon Gentiles as dogs and hogs. This is the first of two recorded visits by Christ to Nazareth. (For the other visits see Mt. 13:54-58; Mk. 6:1-6.)

Step Twenty: From Nazareth to Capernaum
(*Mt. 4:13-22; 8:14-17; Mk. 1:14-38; Lk. 4:31-42*).
A. Jesus now begins to emphasize the kingdom of heaven and the doctrine of repentance in his ministry (Mt. 4:17; Mk. 1:14, 15).
B. He makes Capernaum his preaching headquarters (Mt. 4:13).
C. Old Testament Prophecy Fulfillment Number 13, That he would be a light to the Gentiles. (Compare Isa. 9:1, 2; 42:1-3, 6, 7; 60:1-3 with Mt. 4:13-16; Acts 13:47.)
D. He calls into full-time service Peter, Andrew, James, and John as they cast their nets into the Galilean Sea.
1. His request: "Follow me, and I will make you fishers of men" (Mt. 4:19).
2. Their response: "And they straightway left their nets, and followed him" (Mt. 4:20).

E. Third miracle: Healing of a Capernaum demoniac (Mk. 1:25; Lk. 4:35).
   1. The demon: "Let us alone; what have we to do with thee, thou Jesus of Nazareth? Art thou come to destroy us? I know thee who thou art, the Holy One of God" (Mk. 1:24).
   2. The Savior: "Hold thy peace, and come out of him" (1:25).
   3. The crowd: "What thing is this? What new doctrine is this? For with authority commandeth he even the unclean spirits, and they do obey him" (1:27).
   4. Note: This is the first instance of Christ exorcising a demon from a human being. There would be many other occasions. (See Mt. 8:32; 9:33; 12:22; 15:28; 17:18; Lk. 8:2; 13:10–17.) Demons are fallen angels who sided in with Lucifer (who became the devil) during the rebellion in heaven before the creation of man. (See Isa. 14:12–15; Ezek. 28:15–17; Rev. 12:4; Eph. 6:12.) Their activities are manifold and malice-filled.
      a. They oppose God's purpose (Dan. 9:11–14).
      b. They execute Satan's program (1 Tim. 4:1; Rev. 16:12–14)
      c. They afflict earth's people. Some cause:
         (1) insanity (Mt. 8:28; 17:15)
         (2) muteness of speech (Mt. 9:33)
         (3) blindness (Mt. 12:22)
         (4) the person to harm himself (Mk. 5:5)
         (5) paralysis (Lk. 13:11)
         (6) deafness (Mk. 9:25)
   The number of demons is apparently very high. Jesus cast out seven from Mary Magdalene (Mk. 16:9; Lk. 8:2) and possibly as many as 6000 from the maniac at Gadara (Mk. 5:9).

F. Fourth miracle: Healing of Peter's mother-in-law (Mt. 8:15; Mk. 1:31; Lk. 4:39).
G. He healed many that day by laying his hands on them (Lk. 4:40, 41; Mk. 1:32–34; Mt. 8:16, 17).

H. Old Testament Prophecy Fulfillment Number 14, That he would heal many. Compare Isaiah 53:4 with Matthew 8:16, 17. Was physical healing promised in the atonement? It was indeed, but was fulfilled during Christ's earthly ministry. Note:
   "When the even was come, they brought unto him many that were possessed with devils: and he cast out the spirits with his word, and healed all that were sick: that it might be fulfilled which was spoken by Isaiah the prophet, saying, Himself took our infirmities, and bore our sicknesses" (Mt. 8:16, 17).
   This, of course, does not mean that God cannot and does not heal the bodies of believers today. But it does mean that no child of God can demand total physical healing on the basis of Isaiah 53:4.

I. Second prayer: On the eve of his first Galilean preaching tour (Mk. 1:35; Lk. 4:42).
   1. This was prayed in a desert place.
   2. It was to prepare him for the first preaching tour of all Galilee.

Step Twenty-one: From Capernaum to his first preaching tour of Galilee
(Mt. 4:23; 8:2–4; Mk. 1:39–45; Lk. 4:43—5:16).

A. He begins this tour by speaking to a crowd from Peter's boat.

B. Fifth miracle: Catching a great number of fish (Lk. 5:5, 6).
   1. He tells Simon to launch out in deep waters and let down their nets.
   2. Simon is skeptical: "Master, we have toiled all the night, and have taken nothing: nevertheless at thy word I will let down the net" (Lk. 5:5).
   3. The net suddenly becomes so filled with fish that it begins to sink.
   4. Upon seeing this, Peter falls at Jesus' feet and confesses his sinfulness.
   5. Jesus calms his fears and again assures him he will be used as a fisher of men. J. Vernon McGee writes:
      "What a pulpit! I believe this illustration is both figurative and suggestive. Every pulpit is a fishing boat; a place to give out the Word of God and attempt to catch fish.
      Simon Peter did catch men. Remember how well he did on the day of Pentecost. The Lord's answer to Peter is certainly significant; 3000 souls came to Christ after his first sermon! Peter was fishing according to God's instruction. There is another lesson here. Do you know there is another fisherman? Do you know that Satan also is a fisherman? See 2 Timothy 2:26. Satan has his hook out in the water too. God is fishing for your soul, and Satan also is fishing for your soul with a hook baited with the things of the world. You might say God's hook is a cross." *(Luke,* pp. 69, 72)

C. Sixth miracle: Healing a leper (Mt. 8:3; Mk. 1:41).

   1. The leper fell at Jesus' feet and asked to be healed.
   2. Jesus was moved with compassion and touched him.
   3. He then ordered the cured man to present himself to the priest for the Mosaic cleansing. (See Lev. 14:3, 4, 10, 22.) Note: This excited request from a healed leper doubtless caused much confusion and amazement in the Temple among the priests. Up until this point there was no need for the cleansing ceremony, for no Israelite had ever been healed of leprosy until Jesus came! (With the single exception of Miriam, see Num. 12:13–15.) (Naaman, of course, was a Syrian. See 2 Ki. 5:1, 14.)
   4. The Jews instructed him to say nothing about his healing in the market places, but the healed leper could not be restrained.
D. Jesus heals many during his tour (Mt. 4:23).
E. Third prayer: After healing a leper (Lk. 5:16). Although he was becoming famous, he withdrew to pray, realizing his real task was not the healing of men's bodies, but rather of their souls.

Step Twenty-two: From the first Galilean preaching tour to Capernaum
(Mt. 9:2–9; Mk. 2:1–14; Lk. 5:17–28).

A. Seventh miracle: Healing a paralytic (Mt. 9:2, 6, 7; Mk. 2:5, 10–12; Lk. 5:20, 24, 25).
   1. This man is lowered from the roof by his friends at the feet of Jesus.
   2. Jesus forgives the man of his sins.
   3. The Pharisees accuse him of blasphemy for doing this.

4. Jesus then heals the cripple of his sickness, that the man might know of his authority to forgive sins.

5. The watching crowds are amazed at all this and praise God for it. Again, J. Vernon McGee writes: "There are many people who are not going to receive the message of salvation unless you lift a corner of their stretcher and carry them to the place where they can hear the word of the Lord. They are paralyzed—immobilized by sin and by many other things the world holds for them. Some are paralyzed by prejudice and others by indifference. They are never going to hear Jesus say to them, 'Son, thy sins be forgiven thee,' unless you take the corner of their stretcher and bring them to Him." (*Luke*, p. 74)

B. Jesus calls Matthew (Levi) as his disciple (Mt. 9:9; Mk. 2:13, 14; Lk. 5:27, 28).
   1. The Savior simply walks into Levi's place of business and says "follow me" (Lk. 5:27).
   2. Levi "left all, rose up, and followed him" (Lk. 5:28).

END OF THE FIRST YEAR

Step Twenty-three: From Capernaum to a Galilean grain field

(Mt. 12:1–8; Mk. 2:23–28; Lk. 6:1–5).

A. Jesus is involved in his first Sabbath controversy with the Pharisees because he allowed the disciples to pluck grain and eat it on the seventh day.

B. Jesus justifies this by reminding them of David's actions in the Old Testament when he ate bread to gain strength.
   1. The bread David ate was in the Temple (1 Sam. 21:3–6).
   2. The bread David ate was only for the priests.

C. He calls their attention to the fact that God made the Sabbath for man, and not man for the Sabbath (Mk. 2:27).

Step Twenty-four: From a Galilean grain field to a Galilean synagogue

(Mt. 12:9–14; Mk. 3:1–6; Lk. 6:6–11).

A. Eighth miracle: Healing a withered hand (Mt. 12:13; Mk. 3:5; Lk. 6:10).
   1. Jesus notices a man in the synagogue with a withered right hand.
   2. The Pharisees wait to see if he will heal on the Sabbath.
   3. Knowing their evil thoughts he asks them if it is lawful to do good or evil on the Sabbath.
   4. He reminds them they doubtless would help a sheep out of a ditch on the Sabbath and he feels a man is better than a sheep.
   5. Jesus heals the man and is filled with anger at their hard hearts.

B. The Pharisees are consumed with fury to the point of madness at his actions and consult how they might kill him.

Step Twenty-five: From a Galilean synagogue to Mount Tabor (?)

(Mt. 5:1—7:29; 4:24, 25; 10:2–4; 12:15–21; Mk. 1:12; 3:7–19; Lk. 6:12–49; 12:22–31, 57–59; 16:17).

A. He heals many along the route (Mt. 4:24, 25; Mk. 3:7–12).

B. The evil spirits acknowledge him as the Son of God when he casts them out (Mk. 3:11).

C. He continues to fulfill the prophecy of Isaiah (Mt. 12:17–21).
   1. That he would be God's chosen, beloved, and Spirit-filled servant.
   2. That his justice would be shown to the nations.
   3. That he would not be clamorous or a street yeller.
   4. That he would not break the bruised reed nor quench the smoldering wick.
   5. That his very name would mean victory and hope for the nations.

D. Old Testament Prophecy Fulfillment Number 15, That 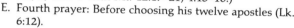 he would deal gently with the Gentiles. (Compare Isa. 9:1, 2; 42:1–3 with Mt. 12:17–21; 4:13–16.)

E. Fourth prayer: Before choosing his twelve apostles (Lk. 6:12).

F. After a night in prayer for guidance, our Lord chooses his twelve-disciple band.
   1. Simon Peter
   2. Andrew
   3. James, Son of Zebedee
   4. John
   5. Philip
   6. Bartholomew
   7. Thomas
   8. Matthew
   9. James, Son of Alphaeus
   10. Judas (Thaddaeus)
   11. Simon the Zealot
   12. Judas Iscariot
   See Matthew 10:2–4; Mark 3:13–19; Luke 6:13–16 for the lists.

G. He continues the next day to heal people (Lk. 6:17–19).

H. Second sermon: On the characteristics of the kingdom (Mt. 5–7; Lk. 6:20–49; 12:22–31, 57–59; 16:17). According to our Lord, a citizen of the kingdom should possess the following traits:
   1. He should be lowly in spirit, knowing God has promised him a kingdom.
   2. He should mourn and weep if necessary, knowing he will someday laugh and be comforted.
   3. He should be meek, for in the future he is to inherit the earth.
   4. He should hunger and thirst after righteousness and will then be satisfied.
   5. He should be merciful that he might himself obtain mercy.
   6. He should be pure in heart, realizing he shall see God.
   7. He should be a peacemaker in order to be called a Son of God.
   8. He should rejoice in persecutions, knowing his reward will be great.
   9. He is to be the salt of the earth and the light of the world.
   10. His righteousness is to far surpass that of the scribes and Pharisees.

The Sermon on the Mount MATTHEW 5-7

The Eightfold Highway to Happiness (Mt. 5:1-12)

BEATITUDE	EXEMPLIFIED BY CHRIST	EXEMPLIFIED BY OTHERS	REWARD
THOSE PURE IN SPIRIT (5:3)	1 PETER 2:22	THE NEW TESTAMENT JOSEPH (Mt. 1:18-20)	The kingdom of heaven
THOSE THAT MOURN (5:4)	MATTHEW 26:37, 38	JOB	To be comforted
THE MEEK (5:5)	MATTHEW 11:28-30; JOHN 13:4, 5	MOSES (Num. 12:3)	To inherit the earth
THOSE WHO HUNGER AND THIRST FOR RIGHTEOUSNESS' SAKE (5:6)	JOHN 4:34	PAUL (Phil. 1:21; 3:7-14)	To be filled
THE MERCIFUL (5:7)	LUKE 23:43; HEBREWS 2:17	DAVID	To obtain mercy
THE PURE IN HEART (5:8)	LUKE 2:40, 52	OLD TESTAMENT JOSEPH	To see God
THE PEACEMAKERS (5:9)	EPHESIANS 2:14-17	BARNABAS	To be called the sons of God
THOSE PERSECUTED FOR RIGHTEOUSNESS' SAKE (5:10)	ACTS 13:28	DANIEL	The kingdom of heaven

The Law of God and the Son of God

THE RELATIONSHIP OF CHRIST TO THE LAW

"Think not that I am come to destroy the law or the prophets: I am not come to destroy, but to fulfill. For verily I say unto you, till heaven and earth shall pass, one jot or one tittle shall in no wise pass from the law, till all be fulfilled" (Mt. 5:17, 18).

THE AMPLIFICATION BY CHRIST OF THE LAW

. . . the OLD and the NEW . . .

"YE HAVE HEARD IT SAID . . ."	"BUT I SAY UNTO YOU . . ."
5:21 Thou shalt not kill.	**5:22** Whosoever is angry with his brother without a cause shall be in danger of judgment.
5:27 Thou shalt not commit adultery.	**5:28** Whosoever looketh on a woman to lust after her hath committed adultery with her in his heart.
5:31 Whosoever shall put away his wife, let him give her a writing of divorcement.	**5:32** Whosoever shall put away his wife except for the cause of fornication causeth her to commit adultery.
5:33 Thou shalt not perjure thyself, but shall perform unto the Lord thine oaths.	**5:34, 37** Swear not at all . . . but let your communication be, Yea, yea; Nay, nay.
5:38 An eye for an eye, and a tooth for a tooth.	**5:39** Resist not evil, but whosoever shall smite thee on thy right cheek, turn to him the other also.
5:43 Thou shalt love thy neighbor, and hate thine enemy.	**5:44** Love your enemies, bless them that curse you, do good to them that hate you, and pray for them who despitefully use you, and persecute you.

The Sermon on the Mount **Matthew 5, 6, and 7**

Rules for the Redeemed

The Money Rule

"Lay not up for yourselves treasures upon earth, where moth and rust doth corrupt, and where thieves break through and steal:

But lay up for yourselves treasures in heaven, where neither moth nor rust doth corrupt, and where thieves do not break through and steal" **(Mt. 6:19, 20).**

The Golden Rule

"Therefore all things whatsoever ye would that men should do to you, do ye even so to them: for this is the law and the prophets" **(Mt. 7:12).**

The Judgment Rule

"Judge not, that ye be not judged" **(Mt. 7:1).**

The Worry Rule

"Therefore take no thought, saying, What shall we eat? or, What shall we drink? or, Wherewithal shall we be clothed? (For after all these things do the Gentiles seek:) for your heavenly Father knoweth that you have need of all these things.

But seek ye first the kingdom of God, and his righteousness, and all these things shall be added unto you" **(Mt. 6:31-33).**

The Prayer Rule

"Ask, and it shall be given you; seek, and ye shall find; knock, and it shall be opened unto you:

For every one that asketh receiveth; and he that seeketh findeth; and to him that knocketh it shall be opened" **(Mt. 7:7, 8).**

Duets

Two Metaphors 5:13, 14	*YE ARE THE SALT OF THE EARTH (5:13).*	*YE ARE THE LIGHT OF THE WORLD (5:14).*
Two Gates 7:13, 14	*THE WIDE GATE* *LEADS TO DESTRUCTION* *MANY TAKE THIS WAY*	*THE NARROW GATE* *LEADS TO SALVATION* *FEW TAKE THIS WAY*
Two Trees 7:15-23	*THE GOOD TREE . . . MUCH FRUIT* A type of the true teacher PROFESSING AND POSSESSING	*THE BAD TREE . . . NO FRUIT* A type of the false teacher PROFESSING ONLY
Two Builders 7:24-27	*THE WISE BUILDER* *BUILT HIS HOUSE UPON A ROCK* *SURVIVED THE STORM*	*THE FOOLISH BUILDER* *BUILT HIS HOUSE UPON THE SAND* *WAS DESTROYED BY THE STORM*

11. He should not become unduly angry with his brother, but should constantly seek reconciliation.
12. He shall not desire his brother's wife.
13. He shall give proper honor to his own wife.
14. His yes and no answers can be taken literally and trusted completely.
15. He is to love those who hate him and pray for those who curse him.
16. He is to be compassionate.
17. He is to work his works, fast his fasts, and pray his prayers in secret.
18. His prayer life should include the following elements:
    a. A personal relationship with God: "Our Father." The word *our* signifies the believer's brotherly relationship with all other Christians. While the Bible nowhere presents the universal Fatherhood of God, it does declare

NOTEWORTHY PRAYERS

The Model Prayer—Matthew 6:9-13

LANGUAGE	TEACHING
"Our Father"	● A personal relationship with God and other believers
"Which art in heaven"	● Faith
"Hallowed be thy name"	● Worship
"Thy kingdom come"	● Expectation
"Thy will be done in earth as it is in heaven"	● Submission
"Give us this day our daily bread"	● Petition
"And forgive us our debts"	● Confession
"As we forgive our debtors"	● Compassion
"And lead us not into temptation, but deliver us from evil"	● Dependence
"For thine is the kingdom, and the power, and the glory forever"	● Acknowledgment

the universal brotherhood of believers. The word *Father* signifies the relationship between God and the believer.

b. Faith: "which art in heaven." Paul declares that without this element our prayers are useless. (See Heb. 11:6.)

c. Worship: "Hallowed be thy name." David felt this part of prayer to be so important that he appointed a select group of men who did nothing else in the Temple but praise and worship God. (See 1 Chron. 23:5; 25:1, 7.) In the book of Revelation John sees four special angels who exist solely to worship God and who "rest not day and night, saying Holy, holy, holy, Lord God Almighty, which was, and is, and is to come" (Rev. 4:8). See also Christ's statement to the Samaritan woman (Jn. 4:23, 24).

d. Expectation: "thy kingdom come." This kingdom is that blessed millennial kingdom spoken of so much in the Old Testament. (See Isa. 2:2–4; 25:8; 35:1, 8, 10; 65:20, 25) and later previewed by John in the New Testament (Rev. 20:1–6).

e. Submission: "thy will be done in earth, as it is in heaven." Jesus would later give the finest example of this element in Gethsemane. (See Mt. 26:39.)

f. Petition: "Give us this day our daily bread." This suggests that our praying should be as our eating—daily.

g. Confession: "and forgive us our debts." The blood of Christ will forgive us of every sin, but not one excuse! Only confessed sin can be forgiven (see 1 Jn. 1:9).

h. Compassion: "as we forgive our debtors." (See Mt. 18:21–35 and 1 Jn. 4:20.)

i. Dependence: "And lead us not into temptation, but deliver us from evil." It should be understood that while God has never promised to keep us *from* temptation, he has promised to preserve us *in* and *through* temptation. (See 1 Cor. 10:13.)

j. Acknowledgment: "For thine is the kingdom, and the power, and the glory forever." (See David's great prayer in 1 Chron. 29:10-19 where he actually anticipates the final part of Jesus' model prayer.)

19. He will lay up treasure in heaven and prefers God to gold on earth.

20. He will ever seek God's kingdom and his righteousness.

21. He will trust God to feed, lead, and clothe him.

22. He will never critically judge nor condemn his brother.

23. He will be careful in discussing holy things before depraved men.

24. He will ask, seek, and knock at the door of his Father, believing he will receive, find, and gain entrance.

25. He will always do for others that which he would have them do for him.

26. He will beware of false teachers, identifying them by their corrupt fruit.

I. Fourth prediction: Concerning the great white throne judgment (Mt. 7:21-23).

 1. Many unbelievers in that day will pretend to have done marvelous things in Jesus' name.
   a. "We have prophecied in your name."
   b. "We have cast out demons in your name."
   c. "We have done many wonderful works in your name."

 2. The Savior, however, knowing the true hearts of all men, will say:
   a. "I never knew you."
   b. "Depart from me, ye workers of iniquity."

J. First parable: Two houses in a hurricane (Mt. 7:24-27; Lk. 6:47-49).

 1. One was built on a rock and stood straight.
 2. One was built on the sand and fell flat.

K. Jesus finishes his sermon and the crowds are amazed at his teaching, authority, and crystal clear illustrations.

Step Twenty-six: From Mount Tabor (?) to Capernaum

(Mt. 8:1, 5–13; Lk. 7:1–10).

A. Ninth miracle: Healing a centurion's servant (Mt. 8:13; Lk. 7:10).

B. He is amazed at the amount of faith shown by this Gentile official.

1. "Trouble not . . . to . . . come under my roof."
2. "Speak but a word, and my servant will be healed."

C. He is saddened at the fact that many such Gentiles will someday fellowship with Abraham (the father of faith) in heaven while many Jews will be cast into hell.

On two specific occasions Jesus marveled at the faith of individuals, and both persons were Gentiles. One was the Roman centurion here (Mt. 8:10) and the other was a Syro-phoenician woman (Mt. 15:28). However, the only thing he could marvel over concerning the nation Israel was its tragic unbelief (see Mk. 6:6).

Step Twenty-seven: From Capernaum to Nain
(Lk. 7:11–17, 36–50).

A. Tenth miracle: Raising a widow's son (Lk. 7:14).
  1. He is moved with pity and tells the widow to cease her weeping.
  2. He touches the bier and commands the young man to arise.
  3. He presents the boy to his mother.
  4. He is recognized as a great prophet from God after performing this miracle.

B. Second parable: Forgiving the fifty and the five hundred (Lk. 7:41, 42).
  1. Our Lord is eating in the home of a Pharisee named Simon.
  2. An immoral woman quietly comes in and (to the astonishment of the Pharisees) does the following things:
    a. She begins to weep, thus wetting the feet of Jesus.
    b. She kisses his feet and wipes them with her hair.
    c. She anoints them with ointment.
  3. Knowing Simon was condemning him in his thoughts for allowing such actions, our Lord gives the parable of a moneylender who forgave two of his debtors, one of them 500 denarii, and the other fifty.
  4. He then asks Simon which one will love the moneylender more.
  5. Finally he relates all this to both Simon and the immoral woman.

a. Simon had given him no kiss of welcome, but she had kissed his feet.
b. Simon had not anointed his head with oil, but she was anointing his feet with ointment.

Step Twenty-eight: From Nain to the second Galilean preaching tour
(Mt. 12:46–50; 13:1–52; Mk. 3:19–35; 4:1–34; Lk. 8:1–21; 12:10; 13:18–21).

A. He is accompanied on this tour by his disciples plus some older and godly women, such as Mary Magdalene, Joanna (the wife of Herod's steward), and a woman named Suzanna (Lk. 8:1–3).
B. He is accused of insanity and becomes a source of embarrassment to his kinfolk (Mk. 3:21).
C. Third parable: Subduing a strong man (Mk. 3:22–30).
  1. He is accused of casting out demons through Beelzebub, the prince of demons.
  2. He points out the stupidity of this accusation by asking the question, "How can Satan cast out Satan?"
  3. He continues by reminding them that a house divided against itself cannot stand.
  4. He concludes by stating that no man can enter into a strong man's house unless he first subdue that strong man. This, of course, our Lord had done to Satan.
  5. He finally warns that to accuse him of working with Satan is unpardonable in God's sight and will never be forgiven.
D. He is told his brothers and mother are waiting to see him and uses this opportunity to explain that anyone hearing and obeying God's Word is his brother, and sister, and mother (Mk. 3:31–35; Mt. 12:46–50; Lk. 8:19–21).
E. Third sermon: On the examples of the kingdom (Mt. 13:1–52; Mk. 4:1–34; Lk. 8:4–18; 13:18–21). Note: The term "kingdom of heaven" as used by Jesus can refer to one (or both) of the following concepts:
  1. That general rule of the Father from heaven over the affairs of men from creation to the millennium. Thus, both saved and unsaved belong to this kingdom. (See Dan. 4:17.)

MATTHEW 13

A Panoramic View of the Kingdom of Heaven

1. DEFINITION OF THE KINGDOM OF HEAVEN

FIRST MEANING

That general rule of the Father from heaven over the affairs of men from creation to the millennium. Both saved and unsaved belong to this kingdom. **(See Dan. 4:17, 32; Mt. 8:12; 22:2; 25:1.)**

Christ had this general meaning in mind in **Matthew 13.**

SECOND MEANING

That specific rule of the Son from Jerusalem over the affairs of men during the millennium. Only saved people will enter this kingdom. **(See Mt. 6:10, 13; 25:34; 26:29.)**

2. DISTINGUISHED FROM THE KINGDOM OF GOD

FIRST MEANING

On rare occasions the kingdom of God is used interchangeably with the kingdom of heaven (millennial meaning). **(Compare Mk. 1:14, 15 with Mt. 3:1, 2. See also Acts 1:3, 6.)**

SECOND MEANING

The most common meaning is a reference to the new birth. **(See Jn. 3:3, 5; Acts 8:12; 19:8; 20:25; 28:23, 31; 1 Cor. 15:50.)**

2. That specific rule of the Son from Jerusalem over the affairs of men during the millennium. At this time the curse of sin is removed and all men shall dwell in a perfect environment. (See Rev. 11:15.)

In his sermon here our Lord refers primarily to the first general concept. The sermon consists of nine main parabolic examples.

F. Fourth parable: The sower, the seed, and the soil (Mt. 13:1-9, 18-23; Mk. 4:1-20; Lk. 8:4-15).
   1. He relates the parable: A sower went out and sowed seed.
      a. Some fell on the roadside and was soon trampled by men and devoured by birds.
      b. Some fell on rocky areas where there was little earth. The seed separated immediately but soon wilted in the sun because of the lack of root and moisture.
      c. Some fell in thorn-infested ground and was soon choked by the thorns.
      d. Some fell into good soil and produced thirty-fold, sixtyfold, and some even one-hundred-fold fruit.
   2. He explains the parable: He is the Sower and the seed is his Word.
      a. There are those who receive the Word without really understanding it. Almost immediately Satan tramples and devours it. This is the roadside example.
      b. There are those who receive the Word in a very shallow way. When persecutions and trials arise, they just fall away. This is the rocky area example.
      c. There are those who receive the Word but attempt to mix it with the pleasures of this life. However, the worldly things eventually choke it. This is the thorn-infested ground example.
      d. There are those who receive the Word with honest, sincere, and understanding hearts. These alone will bear much fruit. This is the thirty, sixty, and one-hundredfold example.
G. At this point in his ministry, our Lord privately explains to the disciples his reason for telling parables. It was to reveal spiritual truths to the sincere but to hide them from the skeptical (Mt. 13:10-17; Mk. 4:10-12; Lk. 8:9, 10).
H. Fifth parable: Satan's tares in the Savior's field (Mt. 13:24-30, 36-43).
   1. He relates the parable.
      a. A man scatters good seed in his field and retires for the night.
      b. During the night his enemy comes and sows tares in that field.
      c. The man decides not to dig up the tares, lest he root up the wheat.
      d. His plan is to await the harvest and then have the reapers burn the tares in his furnace as he collects the wheat in his granary.
   2. He explains the parable.
      a. He is the man, the field is the world, and the good seed are believers.
      b. The enemy is Satan and tares are unbelievers.
      c. The harvest is the consummation of this age, and the reapers are his angels.
      d. The furnace is hell and the granary is heaven.

I. Sixth parable: From scattering to sickling (Mk. 4:26-29).
   1. The growth of the kingdom is steady but mysterious.
   2. First the seed sprouts, then the blade, then the ear, then the full grain.
J. Seventh parable: The mighty mustard seed (Mt. 13:31, 32; Mk. 4:30-32; Lk. 13:18, 19).
   1. The kingdom, like a mustard seed, is very small when planted.
   2. However, when it grows up, it produces the largest plant of the garden, large enough for birds to roost in its shade.
K. Eighth parable: The cook's leaven and the kingdom of heaven (Mt. 13:33; Lk. 13:20, 21).
   1. Here the kingdom is likened to leaven which a woman took and hid in three measures of flour.
   2. Soon the entire mass was leavened.
      The *New Scofield Bible* says the following concerning leaven:
      "Leaven, as a symbolic or typical substance, is always mentioned in the Old Testament in an evil sense. The usage of the word in the New Testament explains its symbolic meaning. It is malice and wickedness as contrasted with sincerity and truth (1 Cor. 5:6-8). It is evil doctrine (Mt. 16:12) in its threefold form of Pharisaism, Sadduceeism, and Herodinism (Mt. 16:6; Mk. 8:15). The leaven of the *Pharisees* was externalism in religion (Mt. 23:14-16, 23-28); of the *Sadducees,* skepticism as to the supernatural and as to the scriptures (Mt. 22:23, 29); of the *Herodians,* worldliness (Mt. 22:16-21; Mk. 3:6)." (p. 1016)
L. Ninth parable: Finding a fortune in a field (Mt. 13:44).
   1. A man finds a great treasure buried in a field.
   2. With joy he sells all he has and buys the field.
M. Tenth parable: The price of a pearl (Mt. 13:45, 46).
   1. A pearl merchant discovers a pearl of extremely great value.
   2. He therefore sells all his possessions and buys it. Note: A number of Bible students believe the hidden treasure is Israel and the pearl of great price is the church. If that is so, this is the first reference to the church in the Bible.
N. Eleventh parable: Sorting out a sea catch (Mt. 13:47-50).
   1. A great dragnet is cast into the sea and gathers in all kinds of creatures.
   2. Fishermen then sort the catch, saving the good and throwing out the bad.
O. Twelfth parable: A trained man and his treasure (Mt. 13:52).
   1. A man who understands the kingdom is like a master of a house.
   2. He can bring forth out of his treasure things new and old.
P. Old Testament Prophecy Fulfillment Number 16, That he would speak in parables. (Compare Isa. 6:9, 10 with Mt. 13:10-15.)
   Dr. M. F. Unger aptly summarizes seven of these parables as discussed in Matthew 13. He writes:
   "The Seven Parables (Mysteries) of the Kingdom (3-52). They are called 'mysteries' because they contain truth previously not revealed. The seven

PARABLES

MATTHEW 13

ILLUSTRATION	INFORMATION	INTERPRETATION	
THE SOWER, THE SEED, AND THE SOIL **MATTHEW 13:1-9, 18-23**	A SOWER SOWS SEED UPON FOUR KINDS OF SOIL ● Roadside soil. This seed was trampled by men and devoured by birds. ● Shallow rock-based soil. Seed sprouted but soon wilted because of the lack of root and moisture. ● Thorn-infested soil. Seed was soon choked by the thorns. ● Fertile soil. Seed sprouted and bore fruit, producing (in some areas) thirtyfold, sixtyfold, and even a hundredfold.	SOWER SEED SOILS	The sower is *CHRIST* The seed is the *WORD OF GOD* **Roadside soil** A person who receives the Word without really understanding it. Seed soon stolen by both Satan and his false ministers. **Shallow Soil** A person who receives the Word without acting fully upon it. Thus, when persecutions and trials arise, he falls away. **Thorn-infested soil** A person who receives the Word but attempts to mix it with the pleasures of this life. However, worldly things soon choke it. **Fertile soil** A person who receives the Word with an honest, sincere, and understanding heart. This one alone will bear fruit.
SATAN'S TARES IN THE SAVIOR'S FIELD **MATTHEW 13:24-30, 36-43**	● A MAN SCATTERS GOOD SEED IN HIS FIELD. ● DURING THE NIGHT HIS ENEMY SOWS TARES (WEEDS) IN THAT FIELD. ● THE MAN'S DECISION WAS TO AWAIT THE HARVEST, AT WHICH TIME HE WOULD COLLECT THE WHEAT AND BURN THE TARES.	THE MAN THE ENEMY THE FIELD THE WHEAT THE TARES THE HARVEST THE REAPERS THE GRANARY THE FURNACE	*CHRIST* is the man The enemy is the *DEVIL* The field is the *WORLD* The wheat are *BELIEVERS* The tares are *UNBELIEVERS,* especially false teachers. See Acts 20:29, 30 The harvest is the *CONSUMMATION OF THE AGE* The reapers are *ANGELS* The granary is *HEAVEN* The furnace is *HELL*
THE MUSTARD SEED AND THE BIRDS **MATTHEW 13:31, 32**	● A SMALL MUSTARD SEED IN A GARDEN GREW INTO A GREAT TREE. ● VARIOUS BIRDS CAME AND ROOSTED IN ITS BRANCHES.	THE SEED THE TREE THE BIRDS	Here the seed, as in the first parable, seems to stand for the Word of God. This tree is unnatural, for a mustard seed always develops into a plant. The tree thus becomes a symbol of professing Christendom. The birds, as in the first parable, probably represent false teachers. **(See also Rev. 18:2.)**
THE LEAVEN IN THE MEAL **MATTHEW 13:33**	A WOMAN PLACES LEAVEN IN THREE MEASURES OF MEAL. SOON THE ENTIRE BATCH IS PERMEATED WITH IT.	THE LEAVEN	In both the Old Testament and New Testament, leaven (like leprosy) is always a type and symbol of evil. There are five kinds of sin leaven can stand for. *PHARISAISM* — Hypocrisy, ritualism **(Mt. 16:6-12; Lk. 12:1)** *SADDUCEEISM* — Rationalism, liberalism **(Mt. 16:6-12)** *HERODIANISM* — Materialism, worldliness **(Mk. 8:15)** *CORINTHIANISM* — Immorality, adultery **(1 Cor. 5:6-8)** *GALATIANISM* — Legalism **(Gal. 5:1, 9)**
		THE THREE MEASURES OF MEAL	In the Old Testament an offering to God of three measures of meal was for the purpose of communion and fellowship. **(See Gen. 18:6; Lev. 14:10; Num. 15:9; 28:12.)**
		THE WOMAN	The woman represents false doctrine, that is, the mixing of evil with the sacrifice of pure fellowship with God. **(See Zech. 5:5-11; Rev. 2:20; 17:1-6; 18:1-8.)**

parables deal with the present age when Israel, the vineyard, is untended (Isa. 5:1-7). *Parable 1* reveals that our Lord sows the seed of the Word in the field (the world), 3-23. *Parable 2,* the good seed and the tares, 24-30, interpreted in 36-43, shows Satan's activity and deception during this age in counterfeiting the wheat, the true children of the kingdom with false professors (Mt. 7:21-23). *Parable 3,* the mustard seed, 31-32, symbolizes the rapid growth of the mystery form of the kingdom. *Parable 4,* the leaven hidden in three measures of meal, 35, warns of the permeation of the truth of the Word with the error of leaven by false teaching (the woman) during this age (cf. Mt. 16:11, 12; Mk. 8:15; 1 Cor. 5:6; Gal. 5:9). *Parable 5* portrays our Lord who gave all He had to possess the treasure (Israel) hid in the field, 44 (cf. Isa. 53:4-10; Ps. 22:1; 2 Cor. 8:9). He will reinstate this treasure on the basis of His atoning death. *Parable 6* shows our Lord as a merchant, who found 'one pearl of great price' (the Church, Eph. 5:25-27) and sold all at Calvary to purchase it, 45-46. *Parable 7* presents the net gathering both good and bad, 47-52, which will remain together during this age until separated at its consummation." (*Unger's Bible Handbook,* p. 478)

Step Twenty-nine: From the second Galilean preaching tour to the country of the Gerasenes

(Mt. 8:18, 23-34; Mk. 4:35—5:20; Lk. 8:22-39).

A. Eleventh miracle: Calming the stormy sea (Mt. 8:26; Mk. 4:39; Lk. 8:24).
  1. A great windstorm hits the sea of Galilee while Jesus and the disciples are crossing it.
  2. He is asleep in the stern but awakens to their fearful cries for help.
  3. He rebukes the winds and calms the sea.
B. Twelfth miracle: Healing the Gerasene demoniac (Mt. 8:32; Mk. 5:8; Lk. 8:33).
  1. Jesus is confronted with a wild, bleeding, crying, and naked man who falls at his feet.
    a. He cannot be held by chain or shackle.
    b. He has lived among the tombs, uttering cries and cutting himself with stones.
  2. The maniac's demon recognizes Jesus as God's Son and implores him not to torment it, and the many other evil spirits within the man, before their time.
    a. "What are you doing to us, Jesus, Son of the most high God?"
    b. "Did you come here to torment us before the time?"
    c. "Before God, I implore you, torment me not!"
  3. Jesus permits the evil legion, upon coming out of the man, to enter a nearby herd of swine.
  4. This they do and the whole herd of some two thousand stamp down a steep slope into the sea where they drown.
  5. Soon the entire city hears of all this and, being seized with fear, requests that Jesus leave their area.
  6. As he boards his boat, the cured maniac asks to go with him.
  7. Our Lord, however, has him go back to his own family and give his testimony to them.

Step Thirty: From the Gerasenes to Capernaum

(Mt. 9:1, 10-34; 11:2-19; Mk. 2:15-22; 5:21-43; Lk. 5:29-39; 7:18-35; 8:40-56; 16:16).

A. Levi (Matthew) holds a banquet for Jesus and invites some unsaved friends.
  1. Jesus is criticized by the wicked Pharisees for eating with publicans and sinners.
  2. He rebukes them, explaining that he came to call sinners to repentance, and not the so-called righteous (Mt. 9:10-15; Mk. 2:15-20; Lk. 5:29-35).
B. Thirteenth parable: A rent cloth and a ruptured container (Mt. 9:16, 17; Mk. 2:21, 22; Lk. 5:36-39).
  1. Some disciples of John the Baptist ask Jesus why they fast and neither he nor his disciples are required to do this.
  2. Jesus explains that the friends of the bridegroom do not fast, but rather feast while he is with them.
  3. He relates this parable, to further clarify, stating that no one would sew a piece of new, unshrunk cloth on an outworn garment, or would put new wine into old wine skins, else both articles be ruined. What he is saying here is that the new wine of the Spirit-controlled life would not fit into the old skins of legalistic Judaism.
C. Thirteenth miracle: Healing a woman with internal bleeding (Mt. 9:22; Mk. 5:29; Lk. 8:44).
  1. Our Lord is en route to perform another miracle when this one occurs.
  2. His garment border is touched by a sick woman.
    a. The woman: "If I may but touch his clothes, I shall be cured."
    b. Jesus, to the disciples: "Who touched my clothing? . . . Somebody touched me; for I know that power went forth from me."
    c. Jesus to the woman (after she has confessed to touching him): "Be of good courage, daughter; your faith has healed you."
D. Fourteenth miracle: Raising Jairus' daughter (Mt. 9:25; Mk. 5:41; Lk. 8:54).
  1. Jairus, a synagogue official, receives word that his daughter is dead.
  2. Jesus comforts the father and asks him to keep his faith.
  3. Jesus takes Peter, James, and John and enters the little girl's room with her parents.
  4. He ignores the ridicule of the funeral guests outside, and taking her hand, restores her to life and commands that she be given something to eat.
E. Fifteenth miracle: Healing two blind men (Mt. 9:29).
  1. Jesus: "Do you believe that I can do this?"
  2. The men: "Yes, Lord."
  3. Jesus: "According to your faith, be it done to you."
F. Sixteenth miracle: Healing a dumb demoniac (Mt. 9:33).
  1. This miracle fills the crowd with wonder.
  2. But the Pharisees continue to accuse him of doing this through the Prince of Demons.
G. He answers the doubts of the imprisoned John by healing many (Mt. 11:2-6; Lk. 7:18-23).
  1. John has sent his disciples to Jesus, asking if he is indeed the Messiah, or are they to look for another.
  2. In their presence he proceeds to restore sight to the blind, hearing to the deaf, cleansing to the lep-

er, mobility to the cripple, and life to the dead.

3. He then instructs them to return and tell John the things they have seen and heard. (See Isa. 35:4–6.)

H. Fourth sermon: On John the Baptist (Mt. 11:7–15; Lk. 7:24–30). Our Lord pays profound tribute to John. According to Jesus:

1. John was not a reed tossed about by the wind, but was a rough and ready preacher.

2. John was the greatest of all prophets.

"Verily I say unto you, among them that are born of women there hath not risen a greater than John the Baptist; not withstanding, he that is least in the Kingdom of heaven is greater than he" (Mt. 11:11).

To whom did Jesus refer by his statement, "least in the Kingdom . . . is greater"? Two theories have been offered:

a. That he had the Apostle Paul in mind. (See Eph. 3:8; 1 Cor. 15:9.)

b. That he had the millennium in mind, when the least citizen of that glorious kingdom would experience more of God's majesty than any prophet, priest, or king had previously done.

3. John was heard gladly by the common folk and sinners but was disregarded by the ungodly Jewish rulers.

4. John's fearless ministry marked the beginning of satanic opposition to the kingdom.

5. John came in the spirit of the Old Testament Elijah.

"For this is he, of whom it is written, Behold I send my messenger before thy face, which shall prepare thy way before thee" (Mt. 11:10).

Here Jesus links the prophecy in Malachi 3:1 with John the Baptist. However, it is significant to note that he left out the last part of this verse which says, "and the Lord whom ye shall seek, shall suddenly come to his temple. . . ."

According to Habakkuk 2:20, when this happens, Christ comes to judge. However, his first coming was marked by grace, thus the final part was omitted.

I. Fourteenth parable: A generation of gripers (Mt. 11:16–19; Lk. 7:31–35).

1. Jesus compares his generation to a group of fickle children playing.

a. One group said: "We fluted to you, and you did not dance."

b. Another group said: "We wailed to you, and you did not weep."

2. He states that this fickleness can be seen in Israel also.

a. John practiced fasting and the Pharisees claimed he had a demon.

b. Jesus did not fast and he was accused of being a glutton and wine drinker.

Step Thirty-one: From Capernaum to Jerusalem

(Jn. 5:1–47).

A. Seventeenth miracle: Healing of a thirty-eight-year invalid (Jn. 5:8).

1. Jesus asks an invalid if he desires healing.

2. The man replies he does indeed, but cannot step into a pool of water in time, which he believes would heal him.

3. Jesus ignores his misdirected faith, and heals him.

4. Jesus is soon confronted with the wicked Pharisees, as this miracle is performed on the Sabbath.

5. Jesus later meets the healed man in the Temple and admonishes him to sin no more.

6. The Jews keep seeking to kill him, not only because of his Sabbath actions, but because he calls God his own Father (Jn. 5:16–18).

B. Fifth sermon: On judgment and resurrection (Jn. 5:19–47).

1. Jesus says that the Father loves him and instructs him in his actions.

2. He claims the Father has given over all judgment to him and desires that men honor the Son as they do the Father.

3. He promises everlasting life to all who will believe this.

4. He assures them that they will someday be raised from the dead by the Son. Note his statement:

"Marvel not at this: for the hour is coming in the which all that are in the graves shall hear his voice, and shall come forth, they that have done good, unto the resurrection of life; and they that have done evil, unto the resurrection of damnation" (Jn. 5:28, 29).

Other verses in the Bible make it clear that there are two distinct resurrections in mind here, each separated by one thousand years. The *first* resurrection will occur just prior to the millennium and will include all saved Old Testament and tribulational saints. The *second* will take place after the millennium and will consist of all unbelievers who have ever lived. (See Dan. 12:2 and Rev. 20:5, 6, 11–15.)

5. He points out that his deity is attested to by at least four truthful witnesses:

a. John the Baptist

b. his own miracles (seventeen up to this time)

c. the Father himself (at his baptism)

d. the Old Testament (especially the writings of Moses)

6. He sadly observes, however, that in spite of all this, most of Israel will not accept him.

C. Fifth prediction: On the future resurrection (Jn. 5:28, 29).

1. The just will be resurrected for eternal bliss.

2. The unjust will be resurrected for eternal damnation.

Step Thirty-two: From Jerusalem to Nazareth (second visit)

(Mt. 13:53–58; Mk. 6:1–6).

A. He preaches there and is a source of embarrassment to his half-brothers and sisters.

B. He sadly observes that a prophet is not without honor except in his own hometown, as he hears the crowd ask:

1. "Is this not the carpenter, the son of the carpenter?"

2. "Is not his mother called Mary, and his brothers James and Joseph and Simon and Jude?"

3. "And his sisters, are they not all here with us?"

C. He performs a few miracles but marvels over the unbelief of the town.

Step Thirty-three: From Nazareth
to his third Galilean preaching tour
*(Mt. 9:35—10:1, 5-16, 24-33, 37—11:1; 14:1-13;
Mk. 6:6-29; Lk. 9:1-9).*
 A. He shares his burden for the lost with his disciples
   (Mt. 9:36-38).
    1. He tells them of a plentiful harvest but of a scar-
      city of laborers.
    2. He encourages them to ask the Father to send out
      laborers.

 B. Sixth sermon: To the departing twelve (Mt. 10:5-16,
   24-33, 37-42; Lk. 9:3-5; Mk. 6:8-11).
    1. Their field of service was confirmed to Israelite
      people alone.
    2. Their ministry was to be manifold. They were to:
      a. Preach that the kingdom of heaven is at hand
        and that people should repent (Mk. 6:12).
      b. Heal the sick.
      c. Cleanse the leper.
      d. Raise the dead.
      e. Cast out demons.
    3. They were to do all this without pay, but would be
      fed and clothed by those to whom they minis-
      tered.
    4. They were to stay only in the homes of those who
      loved God.
    5. They were to shake the dust from their feet while
      leaving any city rejecting their message.
    6. They would often be sheep among wolves, and
      therefore were to be wise as serpents and guileless
      as doves.
    7. They were to expect persecutions, but should take
      heart, for the Father had already numbered the
      very hairs of their head.
    8. They were to confess Christ before men that he
      might confess them someday before his Father.
    9. They were to always put him first and bear their
      own cross.
    10. They would be treated as prophets by some who
       would then someday share in their rewards.
 C. He himself goes out to preach alone after sending out
   the twelve in six teams (Mt. 11:1).
 D. He is informed of the murder of John the Baptist and
   retires with his twelve (Mt. 14:1-13; Mk. 6:14-29; Lk.
   9:7-9).
    1. Herod had imprisoned John for fearlessly de-
      nouncing the king's unlawful marriage to Hero-
      dias, the former wife of Herod's brother Philip.
    2. Herodias was furious and demanded the execution
      of John, but Herod feared him and for awhile even
      seemed somewhat interested in his message.
    3. Herodias, however, aided by the dancing charms
      of her beautiful daughter and the king's own sen-
      sual nature, demanded and received the head of
      John the Baptist on a platter.
    4. Herod, troubled and perplexed, later feared that
      Jesus was really John the Baptist resurrected.
    5. Thus the greatest New Testament prophet passes
      from the earthly scene. Jesus had previously com-
      mented on the greatness of this man of God. (See
      Mt. 11:1-11.) One of the final statements we have
      about John reveals that this fearless prophet was
      also a powerful prayer warrior.
        We read of Jesus' disciples coming to the Savior
      and asking: "Lord, teach us to pray, *as John* also
      taught his disciples" (Lk. 11:1).

Step Thirty-four: From his third
Galilean preaching tour to a
wilderness near Bethsaida
*(Mt. 14:13-23; Mk. 6:30-47;
Lk. 9:10-17; Jn. 6:1-18).*
 A. Jesus withdraws with his disciples for a much-needed
   rest but is soon recognized and surrounded once again
   by the ever-present crowds.
 B. He is moved with compassion and heals many, in-
   structing them concerning the Kingdom of God.
 C. Eighteenth miracle: Feeding 5000 men and their fam-
   ilies (Mt. 14:19; Mk. 6:41; Lk. 9:16; Jn. 6:11).
    1. Jesus tests Philip, asking how such a crowd can be
      fed. Philip feels the situation is hopeless.
    2. Andrew finds a young lad with five barley loaves
      and two small fishes, but he too agrees sadly with
      Philip.
    3. The twelve finally realize the only solution is to
      dismiss the crowd, hoping they may fend for
      themselves in the surrounding villages.
    4. Jesus, however, has the crowd seated in groups of
      fifty.
    5. He then takes the lad's meager lunch, blesses it,
      and feeds everybody.
    6. His disciples later gather up twelve baskets full of
      the remains. In reality he probably fed over
      15,000, for the 5000 mentioned were the *men* of the
      crowd. Doubtless many hundreds of women and
      children were also present. This is one of only two
      miracles recorded by all four Gospel writers. The
      other is the restoration of a severed ear in the Gar-
      den of Gethsemane.
 D. Fifth prayer: On a mountain near the sea after feeding
   the 5000 (Mt. 14:23; Mk. 6:46; Jn. 6:15).
    1. Jesus realizes the 5000 fed men are so impressed
      they are planning to force him into being their
      king.
    2. He therefore orders the disciples to leave without
      him and retires to a mountain to pray.

Step Thirty-five: From the Bethsaida
wilderness to the Plain of Gennesaret
(Mt. 14:24-36; Mk. 6:48-56; Jn. 6:19-21).
 A. Nineteenth miracle: Walking on the sea (Mt. 14:25;
   Mk. 6:48, Jn. 6:19).
    1. Jesus sees his disciples battling for their lives on a
      stormy sea and walks toward them.
    2. They become terrified upon seeing him but he
      calms their fears and permits Peter's request to
      walk to him.
    3. Peter takes his eyes off Jesus after walking a few
      steps and is rescued from certain drowning by
      Jesus.
      a. Peter: "Lord, save me!" (Mt. 14:30). (The short-
        est prayer in the Bible.)
      b. Jesus: "Ye of little faith, what made you
        doubt?"
    4. Jesus and Peter climb into the boat and he receives
      worship and awe from the amazed twelve. "Truly
      thou art the Son of God."
 B. Jesus disembarks at Gennesaret and enters into the
   villages nearby, healing many.

END OF SECOND YEAR.

Step Thirty-Six: From the Plain
of Gennesaret to Capernaum
(Mt. 15:1–20; Mk. 7:1–23: Jn. 6:22–71; 7:1).

A. Seventh sermon: On the bread of life (Jn. 6:26–59).
   1. Part of the crowd he previously fed now gathers around him.
   2. He knows their carnal motives and admonishes them to seek the living bread rather than more physical bread. (See Jn. 2:23–25.)
   3. He tells them that the Father has sealed him and desires that all men believe on him.
   4. He states that he alone is the Bread of Life and all those whom the Father directs will come to him and never hunger.
   5. The Jews who know Mary and Joseph ridicule his claim to have come from heaven, but ignoring this, he says he alone has seen the Father.
   6. He promises to raise all believers from the dead at the last day.
   7. He says he will soon give his flesh for the life of the world.
   8. He concludes by stating the absolute necessity of partaking of his flesh and blood to be assured of eternal life.
B. Some of his followers are confused and offended at his sermon, and many leave him at this point, never to return (Jn. 6:60–66).
C. Jesus asks the twelve if they, too, desire to leave. Peter immediately responds (Jn. 6:67–69):
   1. "Lord, to whom shall we go?"
   2. "Thou hast the words of eternal life."
   3. "And we believe and are sure that thou art that Christ, the Son of the living God."
D. Sixth prediction: his betrayer (Jn. 6:70, 71).
   Note: Some believe Judas will be the future antichrist because of this passage, and others which refer to him.
   1. In Luke 22:3 and John 13:27, it is recorded that Satan enters Judas. This is never said of any other individual in the Bible.
   2. There are two instances in the New Testament where the title "Son of Perdition" is used. In the first instance, Jesus used it to refer to Judas (Jn. 17:12), and on the second occasion, Paul refers to the antichrist (2 Thess. 2:3).
E. Eighth sermon: Concerning the source of defilement (Mt. 15:1–20; Mk. 7:1–23).
   1. The Pharisees accuse Jesus of lawbreaking when he allows his disciples to eat with unpurified hands.
   2. He points out that they are the real lawbreakers in God's sight, as was prophecied by Isaiah (Isa. 29:13). This they do:
      a. by their big mouths and cold hearts
      b. by emphasizing their own traditions and ignoring God's commandments
      c. by the disgraceful manner in which they treat their own parents
   3. He teaches that the real source of defilement comes from within, and consists not of dirty hands but of dirty hearts. He then lists some of these things:

a. murder, adultery, sex vices
b. thefts, false testifying, blasphemies
c. envyings, malicious deeds, deceit
d. licentiousness, a sinful eye, conceit, and foolishness

Step Thirty-seven: From Capernaum
to the Tyre and Sidon area
(Mt. 15:21–28; Mk. 7:24–30).

A. He seeks solace in a house but is found by a desperate Gentile mother.
B. Twentieth miracle: Healing a demoniac girl (Mt. 15:28; Mk. 7:29).
   1. Jesus at first listens in total silence to her pitiful cries concerning her daughter.
   2. He then gently reminds her that his miracle ministry is primarily for Israel.
   3. She points out, however, that even the little dogs eat of the children's crumbs that fall from their master's table.
   4. He is thrilled at her faith and heals her daughter.

Step Thirty-eight: From Tyre and Sidon
to the Decapolis region
(Mk. 7:31–37).

A. He is asked to lay his hands on a deaf man who also has a speech impediment.
B. Twenty-first miracle: Healing of a deaf man with a speech impediment (Mk. 7:34, 35).
   1. Our Lord goes about this miracle in the following unusual way;
      a. He places his fingers in the deaf man's ears.
      b. He spits on the ground and touches the man's tongue.
      c. He looks up into the heavens and groans.
   2. The nearby crowds are amazed beyond measure, saying, "He has done all things well! He makes even the deaf to hear and the dumb to speak."

   "O for a thousand tongues to sing
      My great Redeemer's praise.
   The glories of my God and King,
      The triumphs of His grace.

   Hear Him, ye deaf; His praise, ye dumb,
      Your loosened tongues employ:
   Ye blind, behold your Saviour come;
      And leap, ye lame, for joy."
                    —Charles Wesley

Step Thirty-nine: From Decapolis
to Mt. Tabor (?)
(Mt. 15:29–38; Mk. 8:1–9).

A. He heals great multitudes on this Galilean mountain.
B. Twenty-second miracle: Feeding 4000 men and their families (Mt. 15:36; Mk. 8:6).
   1. He is moved with compassion with these families who have been with him for the past three days and are all very hungry.
   2. The twelve can only find in their search for food seven loaves and a few little fish.
   3. Jesus takes this food, blesses it, and abundantly feeds everyone present.
   4. The twelve then gather up seven baskets full of the fragments that remain.

Step Forty: From Mt. Tabor (?) to Magdala
(Mt. 15:39—16:12; Mk. 8:9-21).

A. He is confronted with the Pharisees and Sadducees who demand he show them some miraculous sign.
  1. He rebukes this hypocrisy and points out a glaring inconsistency on their part.
    a. They accept the signs of the sky as it tells them of the weather.
    b. They reject the sign of the Son as he tells them of the Father. (Note: Here they were, still demanding a sign from him, when he had just completed his twenty-second recorded miracle!)
      He states that only a wicked and adulterous generation would make such a demand.

B. Seventh prediction: His resurrection (Mt. 16:4).
  1. The only generation to demand such signs is a wicked and adulterous one.
  2. The only sign to be given to such a generation is the sign of Jonah. This is the reason Satan hates the book of Jonah so much. Throughout history he has attempted to downplay and deny it by having his followers ridicule the fish swallowing Jonah. It is not the *fish* but the *foreshadow* that the devil despises.

C. Jesus warns his disciples against the leaven (traditionalism) of the Pharisees, of the Sadducees (skepticism), and of Herod (materialism).

Step Forty-one: From Magdala to Bethsaida
(Mk. 8:22-26; Jn. 7:2-9).

A. Twenty-third miracle: Healing a blind man (Mk. 8:25).
  1. Jesus puts spittle on the man's eyes and lays his hands on him.
  2. He asks if he can see anything.
  3. The man claims to see men appear as walking trees. The *Scofield Bible* has the following note on this miracle:
    "Our Lord's action here is significant. Having abandoned Bethsaida to judgment (the blind man was from Bethsaida) Matthew 11:21-24, He would neither heal in that village nor permit further testimony to be borne there (Mk. 8:26). The probation of Bethsaida as a community was ended, but He would still show mercy to individuals. (Compare Rev. 3:20.) Christ is outside the door of the Laodicean Church, but 'If any man hear my voice' . . ." (p. 1059)
  4. Jesus touches his eyes again and he now sees clearly. As believers, we often need a second touch by the Savior, lest we see those around us as impersonal statistics instead of needy human beings.

B. Jesus is rebuked by his half-brothers (Jn. 7:2-9).
  1. They suggest he is avoiding publicity because of insincerity.
  2. He attempts to penetrate this dull thinking with the fact that when his hour of Calvary comes there would be plenty of publicity. The names of four of his half-brothers are listed in Matthew 13:55. They are: James, Joses, Simon, and Judas.

C. Old Testament Prophecy Fulfillment Number 17, That he would be rejected by his own. (Compare Isa. 53:3 and Ps. 69:8 with Jn. 1:11; 7:5.)

D. In John 7:6 our Lord says: "My time is not yet come." The "time" in mind here, of course, is his crucifixion. He was always acutely aware of this time and hour. Note:
  "Jesus saith unto her [his mother at the marriage feast in Cana], woman, what have I to do with thee? Mine *hour* is not yet come" (Jn. 2:4).
  "Then they [a murderous crowd in Jerusalem] sought to take him; but no man laid hands on him, because his *hour* was not yet come" (Jn. 7:30).
  "And Jesus answered them [some Greeks who wanted to see him] saying, the *hour* is come, that the Son of man should be glorified" (Jn. 12:23). (See also 12:27.)
  "Now before the feast of the passover . . . Jesus knew that his *hour* was come that he should depart out of this world unto the Father . . ." (Jn. 13:1).
  "Father, the *hour* is come . . ." (Jn. 17:1).
  Especially should be noted the statements found in John 7:30 and 8:20. These verses teach that the servant of God is indestructible until the will of God has been accomplished in his life. (See also Rev. 11:7.)

Step Forty-two: From Bethsaida to Jerusalem
(Jn. 7:10—10:39).

A. Jesus attends the Feast of Tabernacles in Jerusalem and is the object of much speculation (7:12, 43).
  1. Some thought he was just a good man (7:12).
  2. Some thought he was a deceiver (7:12).
  3. Some recognized him as a master teacher (7:14, 15, 46).
  4. Some looked upon him as a Sabbath breaker (especially after healing the man with the thirty-eight-year infirmity) (7:19-25).
  5. Some viewed him as a Prophet (7:40).
  6. Some accepted him as their Messiah (7:31, 41).

B. Eighth prediction: His ascension (Jn. 7:33, 34).
  1. He says they will seek him unsuccessfully.
  2. He says he will then be where they cannot come.

C. Ninth prediction: Pentecost (Jn. 7:37-39).
  1. That the Holy Spirit will come after the glorification of Jesus.
  2. That the Holy Spirit will produce within all believers rivers of living water.
    "In the last day, that great day of the feast, Jesus stood and cried, saying, If any man thirst, let him come unto me, and drink. He that believeth on me, as the scripture hath said, out of his belly shall flow rivers of living water" (7:37, 38).
    Dr. Homer Kent of Grace Seminary suggests the following:
    "The custom had developed of having the priests bring a vessel of water daily during the festival from the Pool of Siloam and come with it in procession to the Temple. Here the water would be poured on the altar of burnt offering as a reminder of how God supplied Israel's need in the wilderness. On the eighth day the ceremony was omitted, signifying Israel's presence in the land. If this event occurred on the eighth day, Christ's invitation to men to come to him for living water was especially dramatic, as he claimed to be the fulfillment of the typol-

ogy carried out at the feast. He was the supplier of the spiritual living water! (See also Jn. 4:10 and 1 Cor. 10:4.)"

D. Nicodemus attempts to defend Jesus and is ridiculed by the Pharisees (7:50–53).

   1. Nicodemus: "Doth our law judge any man before it hear him, and know what he teacheth?"

   2. The Pharisees: "Art thou also of Galilee? Search, and look: for out of Galilee ariseth no prophet."

      Note: The Pharisees were wrong in their contention that no prophet ever came from Galilee. Jonah was from there; Nahum may also have been.

E. He forgives an adulterous woman (Jn. 8:1–11).

   1. This incident is used by the Pharisees in a theological attempt to pit Jews against Moses and thus trap Jesus.

   2. The Savior, however, turns the tables on them and the accusers shuffle away accused, while the accused walks away forgiven and free.

     a. The Pharisees to Jesus: "This woman was taken in adultery . . . Moses commanded us that such should be stoned; what therefore do you say?" (See Lev. 20:10; Deut. 22:23, 24.)

     b. Jesus to the Pharisees (after writing something on the ground): "He that is without sin among you, let him cast the first stone at her."

     c. Jesus to the woman: "Where are those who accused you?" (She responds that her accusers have left.) "Neither do I condemn you. Go and sin no more."

 F. Tenth prediction: His ascension (Jn. 8:14, 21).

 G. Eleventh prediction: His death (Jn. 8:28).

H. He speaks about his Father and many believe on him (Jn. 8:30–32).

   1. He encourages them to continue in his Word (8:31).

   2. He promises them this truth will make them free (8:32).

I. Ninth sermon: On the devil and his children (Jn. 8:33–59).

   1. Jesus refutes the Pharisees' boastful claims to be the real children of Abraham.

     a. They are not doing the kind of things Abraham would do (8:37–43).

     b. They are doing the kind of things Satan would do (8:44).

   2. They once again accuse him of being demon possessed (8:48, 52). Note also their sneering insinuation, "We be not born of fornication" (8:41). This is but one of several occasions on which the Jews make snide remarks questioning the unusual circumstances surrounding Christ's birth. When our Lord later heals a blind man, the Pharisees refuse to believe it, telling the cured man to "Give God the praise: We know that this man [Jesus] is a sinner" (Jn. 9:24).

   3. Jesus claims to have existed prior to Abraham (8:56–58). "Your father Abraham rejoiced to see my day: and he saw it, and was glad" (8:56). When did this happen in the life of Abraham? (See Gen. 22 and Heb. 11:17–19.)

     "Then said the Jews unto him, Thou art not yet fifty years old, and hast thou seen Abraham?" (8:57).

Their statement here gives us an insight concerning the awesome pressure and burden carried by our Lord. Here he is, barely thirty-three, and yet mistaken for nearly fifty.

     "Jesus said unto them, Verily, verily, I say unto you, Before Abraham was, I am" (8:58).

     Notice he does not say, "I was," but I *am!* (See Ex. 3:14.)

   4. The Jews attempt unsuccessfully to stone him (8:59).

J. Twenty-fourth miracle: Healing of the man born blind 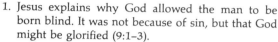 (Jn. 9:7).

   1. Jesus explains why God allowed the man to be born blind. It was not because of sin, but that God might be glorified (9:1–3).

   2. He spits on the ground, mixes it with clay, anoints the eyes of the blind man, and orders him to wash in a pool called Siloam (9:6, 7).

   3. The man does this and sees.

   4. The following six dialogues now take place:

     a. Between the blind man and his neighbors (9:8–12).

       (1) Some think it is the same man, while others doubt.

       (2) He assures them who he is and witnesses about Jesus.

     b. Between the blind man and the Pharisees (9:13–17).

       (1) The Pharisees are incensed as this was done on the Sabbath.

       (2) They refuse to accept the blind man's testimony.

     c. Between the Pharisees and the man's parents (9:18–23).

       (1) The parents acknowledge the fact that the man in question is indeed their son who was born blind.

       (2) But they do not give Jesus the proper credit, for they fear excommunication.

     d. Between the blind man and the Pharisees (9:24–34).

       (1) The blind man repeats his testimony.

       (2) The Pharisees ridicule him and accuse him of being Jesus' disciple.

     e. Between the blind man and Jesus (9:35–38).

       (1) Jesus asks him if he believes on God's Son.

       (2) The man desires to, but wants more information.

       (3) Jesus declares his deity and receives the worship of the blind man.

     f. Between Jesus and the Pharisees (9:39–41).

       (1) He states that he is the Light of the world.

       (2) He warns them of their awful spiritual blindness.

   5. This remarkable miracle:

     a. Corrects two errors.

       (1) That an individual can sin prior to birth. (See vs. 1, 2.)

       (2) That all suffering is a direct result of sin. (See v. 3. Also see Jn. 11:4, 14, 15.) The disciples here made the same grievous error that Job's three "friends" made and

some modern faith healers make today, namely, assuming that all suffering comes from sin.

b. Confirms three facts.
  (1) That religious men are often the blindest of all. (See vs. 16, 24, 39-41.)
  (2) That the fear of man keeps many from accepting Christ. (See vs. 18-23. Also see Jn. 12:42, 43.)
  (3) That Jesus claimed to be the very Son of God. (See vs. 35-38.)

K. Tenth sermon: On the Good Shepherd (Jn. 10:1-18).
  1. The Good Shepherd knows his sheep (10:3, 14).
  2. The Good Shepherd leads his sheep (10:3, 4, 27).
  3. The Good Shepherd talks with his sheep (10:3, 4, 27).
  4. The Good Shepherd saves his sheep (10:9, 28).
  5. The Good Shepherd satisfies his sheep (10:10).
  6. The Good Shepherd dies for his sheep (10:11, 15).
  7. The Good Shepherd unites his sheep (10:16).

L. Summary of the tenth sermon. One of the best summaries of John 10 has been written by Dr. Homer Kent. He writes:

1. The Shepherd forms his flock (10:1-6).

Palestinian sheep folds were usually walled enclosures near the village. Numerous shepherds would place their flocks in the fold at night, and then each would gather his own sheep in the morning and lead them out to pasture for the day. It is this morning activity of forming the flock around the shepherd that is the theme of the first part of the discourse.

The shepherd in the story represents Christ, and the fold is a picture of Judaism, the religious system in which God's people were kept until Christ came. This seems clear from 10:16, where Jesus called the Gentiles "other sheep I have, which are not of this fold." It must also be remembered that Jesus was talking to representatives of Judaism who had just seen the blind man removed from its communion. Thus he was explaining how Judaism is related to Messiah and his followers. The fold does not picture heaven, for there can be no thieves or robbers there (Mt. 6:20). Nor is it a picture of salvation or the church, for the shepherd found his sheep already in this fold and then led them out of it (10:3).

a. He comes the proper way (10:1, 2).

The shepherd who has a right to the sheep does not need to sneak into the fold or climb over the wall. He can enter through the door. So Christ could come to his people because he had the right. The Old Testament prophecies pointed to him (and to no one else). He was born of a virgin, as Isaiah had foretold (Isa. 7:14). He had the title to the throne of David from Joseph, his legal father (Mt. 1:1-16).

b. He is received by the porter (10:3a).

The porter or doorkeeper was the person who was in charge of the fold until the shepherd came, and then admitted him to the sheep. This seems to picture John the Baptist, the one who officially introduced this Shepherd to the nation (1:26-34).

c. He calls his sheep by name (10:3b).

Many flocks were kept in a Palestinian fold but would be separated by their own shepherds, who gave their special call. So when Christ came to the nation of Israel, not every Jew recognized him as the Messiah. Though most gave allegiance to the religious system of Judaism, they were not all the true spiritual flock of God. Some, however, were his true flock. There were some who were truly waiting for the redemption of Israel (e.g., Zacharias, Elisabeth, Simeon, Anna, Mary, and Joseph) and received with joy the Savior who came. The blind man in the context was one. When the true Shepherd came, he recognized his voice.

d. He leads his sheep out of the fold (10:3c-6).

As Jesus presented himself to his nation, the leaders rejected him. Eventually they persecuted not only him, but also all who followed him. This is our Lord's explanation of his relation to the blind man. He had been removed from Judaism because he had responded to Christ. The fold of Judaism had fulfilled its function. It had kept the nation under the protection of the Mosaic Law and separate from the idolatrous nations of the world. But now that Christ had come, a new order was beginning (cf. Gal. 3:24, 25). The Pharisees might object that Jesus did not lead the man out, but that they had cast him out. However, God in his sovereignty often uses the acts of men to accomplish his purposes. Messiah was forming his flock in fulfillment of the ancient prophecies. It is of interest that the passage nowhere states that the flock is led back into this fold again.

The audience of Jesus was composed largely of unbelieving Pharisees (9:40), and they failed to grasp the truth embodied in this figure (10:6).

2. The Shepherd feeds his flock (10:7-10).

Jesus proceeded to describe a second scene which gave additional instruction. The scene is midday, with the sheep having been led away from the village fold and out to the grassy slopes and running brook for pasture and drink. Jesus called himself the "door" to teach the truth about his provision for his own. We should not think of him as the door of the fold, however (for he has already been differentiated from the fold door by being called the Shepherd who entered through the door, 10:2). Rather we must understand the door as representing the entrance perhaps to a wooded thicket where a sheep would enter to find shade and water and from which it would pass to find pasturage.

a. He is the door to salvation (10:7-9a).

Perfect safety for the sheep lay in being near the shepherd. So with Christ, spiritual salvation is provided by one's union with him. By faith in him as Lord and Savior, the believer is introduced to the realm of salvation. Christ becomes our Shepherd and assumes the responsibility for supplying all our needs.

b. He is the door to nourishment (10:9b).

Shepherds took the responsibility for locating pasture for their flocks, a task not always easy in that largely arid land. So Christ is the nourisher of believers, and their spiritual growth occurs as they "feed" upon him by hearing his word and following it (Acts 20:32; 1 Tim. 4:6; 2 Pet. 3:18). To "go in and out" is a common Biblical idiom to depict the idea of living and carrying on one's affairs (Deut. 31:2; 2 Chron. 1:10; Acts 1:21).

c. He is the door to abundant life (10:10).

The life the believer receives from Christ is eternal. It is not merely an extension of mortal life, but a far richer life than he has ever known before. And he begins to experience it the moment he puts his faith in Christ. Access to God in prayer, knowledge of full pardon for sin, possession of God's Spirit to illuminate God's Word and guide him in daily life—all these and many more give abundance to the Christian life.

3. The Shepherd protects his flock (10:11-18).

The scene now shifts to evening. Often Palestinian shepherds took their flocks so far from the village in search of pasture and water, especially in the dry season, that they could not get back to the fold at night. Thus they spent the night outdoors. But this was the time when danger lurked and when the shepherd's protection was most needed.

a. He dies for his sheep (10:11-13).

Many shepherds died while defending their flocks. There were knives and clubs of robbers to be faced, as well as the attacks of wild animals. In their cases, however, death was always unintended. Christ, on the other hand, was also to die for his sheep in order to save them, but he was going to do so voluntarily. He would "give his life." His sheep were in danger of the greatest kind. "All we like sheep have gone astray" (Isa. 53:6). Jesus was thus predicting his own death which would occur the following spring.

Such sacrificial action of the shepherd is in stark contrast to the hireling, whose only real interest was his personal gain. Hired hands may have watched over the sheep when it was to their advantage, but they would not risk their lives for someone else's property. The reference would seem to be to the religious leaders who profited from

The Good Shepherd Sermon JOHN 10:1-28

"The thief cometh not, but for to steal, and to kill, and to destroy: I am come that they might have life, and that they might have it more abundantly.

I am the good shepherd . . ."

JOHN 10:10, 11

A MORNING SCENE

THE GOOD SHEPHERD ORGANIZES HIS FLOCK

THE MESSAGE	THE MEANING
● He is the only true Shepherd **10:1, 2**	● A condemnation of all other religions
● He is recognized by the porter **10:3**	● A possible reference to John the Baptist
● He calls his sheep by name **10:3**	● Something a stranger would never do
● He leads them out of the fold **10:3-6**	● The fold of Judaism

A MIDDAY SCENE

THE GOOD SHEPHERD FEEDS HIS FLOCK

The door and food of salvation **10:9**	"I am the door: by me if any man enter in, he shall be saved."
The door and food of sanctification **10:10**	"I am come that they might have life, and that they might have it more abundantly."

AN EVENING SCENE

THE GOOD SHEPHERD PROTECTS HIS FLOCK

He gives his life for the sheep **10:11**
He knows the sheep and the sheep know him **10:14, 27**
He gathers his sheep **10:16**
He is raised again for the sheep **10:18**
He gives his sheep eternal life **10:28, 29**

their professional labors but had no real concern for the "sheep."

b. He knows his sheep (10:14, 15).

This Shepherd protects his sheep because he has perfect knowledge of them. He knows their proneness to wander and their infirmities. Thus he can preserve them as members of his flock. None of them can wander away and be lost because he knows all about them. "Those that thou gavest me I have kept, and none of them is lost" (17:12). This knowledge of his sheep is as complete as the knowledge of Christ and the Father about each other.

c. He gathers his sheep (10:16-18).

As the Good Shepherd, Christ also has an interest in gathering "other sheep" which were never a part of the "fold" of Judaism. The reference seems clearly to be to Gentiles whom the Shepherd would be gathering from all parts of the world wherever the gospel would be proclaimed. When his sheep respond to his voice in the gospel, they become "one flock" with "one shepherd." Following Christ's death and the establishment of the New Testament Church at Pentecost, all who respond to Christ, whether Jew or Gentile, are members of one flock with Christ as the Shepherd. The apostle Paul wrote of it as one body, with both Jew and Gentile a part of it (Eph. 3:6; Col. 3:11). (*Light in the Darkness*, pp. 138-142)

M. Twelfth prediction: His death (Jn. 10:17, 18).
   1. That the Father loved him, because he would lay down his life.
   2. That no man would take it from him.

N. His sermon once again causes people to decide either for or against him (10:19-21).

O. He is confronted again by the Pharisees (10:22-39).
   1. They attempt to stone him for his claim to be one with the Father (10:30-33).
   2. He retorts that the proof of the pudding is in the eating, that is, he invites them to check the validity of his words by his miraculous works (10:34-38).

P. They attempt to seize him but once again he escapes out of their hands (10:39). Israel has now rejected both his *works* (Jn. 5:16) and his *words* (Jn. 8:58, 59; 10:30, 31).

Step Forty-three: From Jerusalem to Perea

(Jn. 10:40-42).

A. He crosses the Jordan and dwells briefly in the area where John once baptized.

B. Many from that area believe on him.

END OF THIRD YEAR.

Step Forty-four: From Perea to Caesarea Philippi

(Mt. 16:13-28; Mk. 8:27—9:1; Lk. 9:18-27).

A. Sixth prayer: Near Caesarea Philippi (Lk. 9:18).

B. Jesus asks his disciples what others think of him.
   1. Some, he is told, were saying he was John the Baptist.

2. Others felt he was Elijah.
3. Some thought he was Jeremiah.

C. He asks his disciples what they think of him. Peter answers (Mt. 16:16).
   1. That he is the Messiah.
   2. That he is the Son of the living God.

D. Jesus points out that his confession was prompted by the Father.

E. Thirteenth prediction: The church (Mt. 16:18, 19). Our Lord promises the following things concerning his future church:
   1. That he will build it upon such confessions as Peter has just given.
   2. That the very gates of Hades will not prevail against it.
   3. That believers will be given the keys of the kingdom of heaven.
   4. That heaven and earth will cooperate in the binding and loosening of spiritual matters. Note: This passage immediately raises questions.
      a. Was Jesus building his church upon Peter and planning to make him its first pope? It may be clearly stated that he was not.
         (1) Because Christ later gave the same responsibilities to the other apostles which he here gives to Peter. (Compare Mt. 16:19 with Jn. 20:22, 23.)
         (2) Because the New Testament clearly presents Christ and Christ only as the Foundation of his church. (See Acts 4:11, 12; 1 Cor. 3:11; 1 Pet. 2:4-8.)
         (3) Because the New Testament clearly presents Christ and Christ only as the Head of his church. (See Eph. 1:20-23; 5:23; Col. 1:18; 2:18, 19.)
         (4) Because of the Greek language. There is a play upon words here. Jesus said, "Thou art Peter [*petros*, a little stone], and upon this rock [*petra*, a massive cliff of rock] I will build my church."
         (5) Because of Peter's personal testimony. (See 1 Pet. 5:1-4.)
         (6) Because James and not Peter later officiated at the Jerusalem church. (See Acts 15:13, 19.)

      What then, was Christ doing? The answer is given in Ephesians 2:19-22; Revelation 21:14. What did he mean by "The gates of hell shall not prevail against it?" J. Vernon McGee writes:

      "The gates of hell refer to the 'gates of death.' The word used here is the hades and sheol of the Old Testament which refers to the unseen world and means death. The gates of death shall not prevail against Christ's church. (*Matthew*, Volume II, p. 23)

      This glorious event is called the rapture. (See 1 Thess. 4:13-18; 1 Cor. 15:51-57.)

      What were the "keys of the kingdom of heaven" that Jesus gave Peter? A key, of course, unlocks doors and makes available something which was previously closed.

   5. Jesus here predicts that Peter would be given the privilege of opening the door of salvation to various peoples. This he later did.

a. He opened the door of Christian opportunity to Israel at Pentecost (Acts 2:38-42).

b. He did the same thing for the Samaritans (Acts 8:14-17).

c. He performed this ministry to the Gentiles at Cornelius' house at Caesarea (Acts 10).

6. What did Christ mean by the binding and loosing of Matthew 16:19? This authority was given to all the apostles and even other believers. (See Mt. 18:18; Jn. 20:22, 23.) W. A. Criswell writes:

"In Greek the future perfect tense is used to express the double notion of an action terminated in the past but whose effects are still existing in the present. 'Having been bound and still bound,' and 'having been loosed and still loosed.' The meaning is: if the disciples act in their proper capacity as stewards, they will be acting in accordance with the principles and elective purposes ordained beforehand in heaven." (*Expository Notes on Matthew*, p. 101)

In other words, all the actions of the Spirit-filled believer, whether positive or negative in nature, will carry with it the awesome authority of heaven itself.

F. Fourteenth prediction: His resurrection (Mt. 16:21; Mk. 8:31; Lk. 9:22).

1. The Son of man will suffer many things.

2. He will be rejected by the elders, chief priests, and scribes.

3. He will be killed and on the third day rise again.

G. He is reproved by Peter and in turn rebukes him (Mt. 16:22, 23; Mk. 8:32, 33). On several occasions God rebukes Satan through others. (See Gen. 3:14, 15 and Ezek. 28:11-19.)

H. He comments on the true value of a man's life (Mt. 16:24-26; Mk. 8:34-37; Lk. 9:23-25).

1. To keep it at all costs is eventually to lose it.

2. To lose it (for his sake) is eventually to gain it.

3. To gain the world but to lose one's soul is a tragic exchange of values.

I. Fifteenth prediction: His Second Coming (Mt. 16:27; Mk. 8:38; Lk. 9:26).

1. He will return to this earth someday.
   a. in the glory of his Father
   b. in the company of his angels

2. He will render to every man according to his words and deeds.

J. Sixteenth prediction: His transfiguration (Mt. 16:28; Lk. 9:27).

Step Forty-five: From Caesarea Philippi to Mt. Hermon

(Mt. 17:1-23; Mk. 9:2-32; Lk. 9:28-45).

A. Seventh prayer: On the Mount of Transfiguration (Lk. 9:28, 29).

B. He is transfigured (Mt. 17:2; Mk. 9:3; Lk. 9:29).

1. Peter, James, and John accompany Jesus atop Mt. Hermon to pray, but soon fall asleep.

2. Jesus' face suddenly shines like the sun and his garments become white as snow.

3. He receives two heavenly visitors, Moses and Elijah, and they talk concerning his death, resurrection, and ascension in Jerusalem.

4. The three now awaken and Peter declares (from the top of his head):

"It is good for us to be here: if thou wilt, let us make here three tabernacles; one for thee, and one for Moses, and one for Elias."

5. The Father now speaks from a bright cloud that overshadows them:

"This is my beloved Son, in whom I am well pleased; hear ye him" (Mt. 17:5).

6. The three disciples fall on their faces in terror, but are calmed by Jesus.

7. Thoughts on the transfiguration:

a. The Scriptures suggest this may have been a night scene, for the three disciples had just awakened from a deep sleep. (See Lk. 9:32.)

b. Note that the light was from within, and not from some giant cosmic spotlight suddenly focusing down upon Jesus. His countenance was affected first, then his garments. Saul would later see this shining Savior (Acts 9) as did John (Rev. 1). Satan has tried (unsuccessfully) to imitate the inward splendor of Christ. (See 2 Cor. 11:14.)

c. The word "transfigured" is *metamorphoo* in the Greek language. We get our word "metamorphosis" from this. It brings to mind a caterpillar in the cocoon coming forth as a butterfly.

d. The transfiguration of Christ does not set forth his *deity*, but rather his *humanity*. Transformation is the goal of humanity. We shall experience this at the rapture. Adam and Eve may well have been clothed by a light of innocence proceeding from within. But all this was lost through sin.

e. Both Moses and Elijah appear. Both had previously experienced a special revelation from God (see Ex. 33:17-23 and 1 Ki. 19:9-13), and at the same place (Mt. Sinai/Horeb). The transfiguration answered Moses' twofold request:

(1) "To see the glory of God." (See Ex. 33:18.)

(2) "To enter the Promised Land." (See Deut. 3:23-25.) Some believe these two men will once again team up to minister for God during the great tribulation. (See Mal. 4:5 and Rev. 11:3-14.)

8. Peter here (thoughtlessly) suggests the building of three booths. It may be that at this time the Feast of Tabernacles (booths) was being celebrated in Jerusalem. This was to be a type of the coming millennium as well as a reminder of Israel's redemption from Egypt. (See Lev. 23:34-44.) But before this could happen (the millennium), *another* feast would take place—the Passover. (See Lev. 23:4-8 and Mt. 26-27.) "For even Christ, our passover, is sacrificial for us" (1 Cor. 5:7).

9. Peter would never forget this great event. He later writes about it. (See 2 Pet. 1:16-18.)

10. Jesus spoke to Moses and Elijah concerning his "decease" (Lk. 9:31). The word here is actually "exodus" and is used by Peter at a later date in describing his approaching death. (See 2 Pet. 1:13, 14.)

C. Seventeenth prediction: His resurrection (Mt. 17:9; Mk. 9:9).

D. Jesus comments on the ministry of Elijah as they descend the mountain (Mt. 17:10-13; Mk. 9:11-13).
  1. He says John the Baptist has already come in the spirit of Elijah.
  2. He says Elijah himself will come again during the tribulation. (See Mal. 4:5.)
E. Eighteenth prediction: His suffering (Mt. 17:12; Mk. 9:12).
  1. He will suffer much.
  2. He will be despised.
F. Twenty-fifth miracle: Healing a demoniac boy (Mt. 17:18; Mk. 9:25; Lk. 9:42).
  1. Jesus descends the mountain and is confronted by a heartbroken father.
    a. The father had a son possessed of a demon.
      (1) The demon caused the lad intense suffering.
      (2) It brought on epileptic fits.
      (3) It would seize him and throw him down in convulsions.
      (4) It caused the boy to foam at the mouth and grind his teeth.
      (5) It often bruised him.
      (6) It had attempted to kill him by forcing him into fire and water.
      (7) It had entered and controlled him since childhood.
    b. The father had brought this son to the disciples but they could not help him.
  2. Jesus orders the lad to be brought to him.
    a. Jesus asks the father if he believes he (Jesus) can cure the boy.
    b. The father cries out: "Lord, I believe; help thou my unbelief."
  3. Jesus rebukes the foul spirit, commanding it to depart and never return.
  4. The spirit comes out shrieking and convulsing the lad into unconsciousness.
  5. Jesus tenderly revives him and presents the cured boy to his grateful father.
  6. The disciples inquire why they could not help the lad and are told by Jesus:
    a. That they were lacking in faith.
    b. That this kind of demon would only respond to prayer and fasting.
  7. What a contrast can be seen here as one compares what had just happened on the mountain (a picture of what God intended man to be) with the scene below (what man had become because of sin.)
  8. This is perhaps the most fearful description of demon possession in the entire Bible. A summary of demons would include:
    a. Their *origin:* Angels who sided against God with Satan during the heavenly rebellion. (See Isa. 14:12-15; Ezek. 28:11-17; Rev. 12:4.)
    b. Their *classification:* Chained angels (Jude 1:6, 7; 2 Pet. 2:4), and unchained angels (Eph. 6:12). It is held by some that the reason some evil angels are already in chains of darkness was due to their activity in Genesis 6 before the flood.
    c. Their *activity:*
      (1) They oppose God's purpose (Dan. 10:10-14).

      (2) They execute Satan's program (1 Tim. 4:1; Rev. 9; 16:12-14).
      (3) They afflict earth's people. Some cause insanity (Mt. 8:28), others cause muteness of speech (Mt. 9:33), while a certain kind cause immorality (Mk. 1:23-26) and finally, some produce deafness (Mk. 9:25).
    d. Their *destiny* (Mt. 25:41).
G. Nineteenth prediction: His betrayal (Lk. 9:44; Mt. 17:22).
H. Twentieth prediction: His resurrection (Mk. 9:31; Mt. 17:23).
  1. The Son of man will be killed.
  2. He will be raised up on the third day.

Step Forty-six: From Mt. Hermon to Capernaum

(Mt. 17:24—18:35; Mk. 9:33—10:1; Lk. 9:46-50).
A. Twenty-sixth miracle: Catching a fish with a coin in its mouth (Mt. 17:27).
  1. Peter promises a Temple collector that Jesus will pay the half-sheckle Temple tax.
  2. Jesus then asks Peter from whom kings should collect taxes.
    a. Should they be paid by his citizens?
    b. Should they be paid by his own household?
  3. Peter understands his mistake but our Lord agrees to pay the tax, lest he become a stumblingblock to the people.
  4. Jesus then instructs Peter to depart for the Sea of Galilee.
    a. He is to cast a hook in and take the first fish that comes up.
    b. He is to open its mouth and take out a silver coin.
    c. He is to take the coin and pay both Jesus' and his own tax dues.
  5. Here the second Adam demonstrates that he has recovered what the first Adam had lost—the "dominion over the fish of the sea, and over the fowl of the air, and over the cattle, and over all the earth, and over every creeping thing that creepeth upon the earth" (Gen. 1:26).
B. Eleventh sermon: On humility and hell (Mt. 18:1-20; Mk. 9:33—10:1; Lk. 9:46-50).
  1. Jesus answers the question concerning who is greatest in the kingdom of heaven.
    a. He sets a little child in their midst.
    b. He teaches that the greatest in the kingdom is the one with that child's humility.
    c. He promises that to receive a little child in his name is also to receive him (Mt. 18:5).
    d. He warns all who will hear to never weaken the faith of a child lest they be better off drowned in the sea (Mt. 18:6).
    e. He states that their angels in heaven minister for them in the presence of his father (Mt. 18:10).
  2. Jesus answers the question concerning sectarianism (Mk. 9:38-41).
    a. John the apostle had rebuked a man for casting out demons in Jesus' name simply because the man was not one of the original twelve.

b. Jesus rebukes him for this, saying that (in a sense) if the man was not against him, he was in truth for him. (Also vice versa. See Lk. 11:23; 9:50; Mk. 9:40.)

c. He promises a reward to all outsiders who would render kind treatment to his disciples.

3. Jesus preaches on hell (Mt. 18:8, 9; Mk, 9:43–48).

a. If you are in danger of hell, because of what you might go and do, then cut off your hands and feet.

b. If you are in danger of hell because of what you look upon, pluck out your eye.

c. It is better to enter into heaven maimed than to go to hell whole, where the fires never die.

4. Jesus states his purpose for coming in the first place.

a. He came to seek and save lost people (Mt. 18:11).

b. As a shepherd would leave his fold of ninety-nine and seek the one sheep which had gone astray, so he would do (Mt. 18:12, 13).

c. He then rejoices over that one more than over the ninety-nine which did not go astray.

5. Jesus speaks on reconciliation.

a. Attempt to reconcile a sinning brother privately if you can (Mt. 18:15–17).

b. If this fails, take one or two others and try again.

c. If this fails, bring him before the assembly.

d. If this fails, excommunicate him.

e. When two people agree concerning this matter and ask the Father, it shall be done for them.

f. When two people meet together in Jesus' name on this matter, he is in their midst.

C. Peter asks Jesus a question about forgiveness (Mt. 18:21–35).

1. The question: "Lord, how often shall my brother sin against me and I forgive him? Till seven times?" (Mt. 18:21).

2. The answer: "I say to you, not till seven times, but till seventy times seven" (Mt. 18:22). An old Jewish tradition said three times was enough, based on Amos 1:3 and 2:6. For a contrast to this, see Genesis 4:24.

D. Fifteenth parable: The forgiven who wouldn't forgive (Mt. 18:23–35).

1. A bondman owed his king a great debt of ten thousand talents.

2. His king had planned to sell all the man's goods and put him in prison but was moved with compassion and freely forgave him.

3. The forgiven bondman was owed a very small debt of one hundred pence by a fellow servant.

4. The servant could not pay and was cast into prison by the bondman.

5. The king learns of this and in his fury orders the unforgiving bondman cast into prison.

Step Forty-seven: From Capernaum to Perea
(*Mt. 8:19–22; 11:20–30; 19:1, 2; Mk. 10:1; Lk. 9:51—10:37*).

A. He heals and teaches many (Mt. 19:1, 2; Mk. 10:1).

B. He attempts to enter a village in Samaria but is rebuffed because his face is set for Jerusalem (Lk.

9:51–53). We often think of the Samaritans in the light of the Good Samaritan story (Lk. 10:30–37), but they, like the Jews, would reject Jesus.

1. James and John urge him to call down fire from heaven and burn the village (Lk. 9:54–56).

2. Jesus rebukes them and reminds them he did not come to destroy men's lives but to save them.

C. He interviews three would-be disciples, but all three fail the test (Mt. 8:19–22; Lk. 9:57–62).

1. A scribe to Jesus: "Master, I will follow thee whithersoever thou goest." Jesus answers: "The foxes have holes, and the birds of the air have nests, but the Son of man hath not where to lay his head" (Mt. 8:20).

2. Jesus to a disciple: "Follow me." The disciple answers: "Lord, let me first go and bury my Father" (Mt. 8:21). Jesus to the disciple: "Leave the dead to bury their own dead" (8:22).

3. A disciple to Jesus: "I will follow you, Lord, but first let me bid farewell to those in my home" (Lk. 9:61). Jesus answers: "No one who has put his hand to the plow and looks back is fit for the kingdom of God" (Lk. 9:62).

D. Twelfth sermon: To the departing seventy (Mt. 11:20–24; Lk. 10:1–16).

1. He reminds them of the plentiful harvest, but of the shortage of laborers, and urges their prayers concerning this matter.

2. He issues the following instructions:

a. They were to abide in the home of a believer upon entering a city.

b. They were to heal the sick.

c. They were to preach the kingdom of God.

d. They were to wipe the dust from hostile villages from off their feet.

3. He pronounces woes upon three cities.

a. Chorazin and Bethsaida

(1) Tyre and Sidon would have repented, had they witnessed the mighty works done in these two Galilean cities.

(2) Tyre and Sidon will therefore fare better in judgment than they.

b. Capernaum

(1) Capernaum had been exalted to heaven, but because of unbelief, would be hurled to Hades. One of the most familiar sights in Israel today is the ruins of Capernaum.

(2) Sodom, that wicked Old Testament city, will be better off in the judgment than Capernaum.

4. He tells them that all who receive them, receive him, and to reject them was to reject both him and his Father.

E. Our Lord, after sending out the seventy (two by two), goes out and preaches (Mt. 11:28–30).

1. He invites all who labor and are heavy-laden to come to him for soul rest.

2. He desires them to take his yoke and learn of him.

3. He is meek and lowly in heart.

4. His yoke is easy and his burden is light.

"Come unto me, all ye that labor and are heavy laden, and I will give you rest. Take my yoke upon you, and learn of me; for I am meek and lowly in heart, and ye shall find rest unto your souls. For my yoke is easy and my burden is light" (Mt. 11:28–30).

These beautiful words give us the only self-description of Christ found in the Gospel account. (See also Phil. 2:5-8.) This also marks a pivotal point in the ministry of Jesus. The rejected King now turns from the rejecting nation and offers, not the kingdom, but rest and service to all who are in need of his help. Many of these will be Gentiles. Note:

"Behold my servant, whom I have chosen; my beloved, in whom my soul is well pleased; I will put my spirit upon him, and he shall show justice to the Gentiles" (Mt. 12:18).

This new ministry should be contrasted with his previous instructions to the twelve apostles.

"These twelve Jesus sent forth, and commanded them, saying, Go not into the way of the Gentiles, and into any city of the Samaritans enter not; But go, rather, to the lost sheep of the house of Israel" (Mt. 10:5, 6).

F. He meets and greets the returning seventy (Lk. 10:17-20).
   1. Their testimony: "Lord, even the demons are subject to us through your name."
   2. His advice:
      a. "I saw Satan falling like lightning out of heaven." (See Isa. 14:12-15.)
      b. "I give you authority to tread on serpents and scorpions, and over the power of the enemy. . . ." (See also Mk. 16:18.)
      c. "Nevertheless rejoice not in this, that the spirits are made subject to you, but rather rejoice because your names are written in heaven."

G. Eighth prayer: Upon hearing the report of the returning seventy (Mt. 11:25-27; Lk. 10:21, 22).
   1. He praises his Father for hiding spiritual truths from the materialistic and revealing them to the childlike in faith.
   2. He knows this is all well-pleasing in the Father's sight.
H. He reminds the seventy of their priceless privilege because many prophets and kings had desired in vain to see and hear the things his disciples had seen and heard (Lk. 10:23, 24). (See also 1 Pet. 1:10-13; Heb. 11:30-40.)
I. Sixteenth parable: How to know your neighbor (Lk. 10:25-37).
   1. A lawyer asks Jesus the way of eternal life and is told to love God with all his heart and his neighbor as himself.
   2. The lawyer then asks: "Who is my neighbor?" (Lk. 10:25-37).
   3. Jesus accepts his challenge and relates this parable, describing three basic attitudes of the human heart toward his neighbor.
      a. A man traveling from Jerusalem to Jericho is robbed and severely beaten by thieves. Here the attitude reflected is: "What is thine is mine."
      b. A priest and then a Levite soon come along, but both refuse to stop and help him. Now the attitude is: "What is mine is mine."
      c. A Samaritan eventually comes by.
         (1) He is moved with compassion and dresses the man's wounds with oil and wine.

         (2) He sets the man upon his own beast and carries him to an inn.
         (3) He stays with him for a day and upon leaving pays the innkeeper enough to keep him until his health returns. The final attitude then is: "What is mine is thine."
   4. Jesus then asks the lawyer who the victim's neighbor really was and, of course, is told that the Samaritan was.

Step Forty-eight: From Perea to Bethany and surrounding area

(Mt. 10:34-36; 12:22-38; 42-45; 19:3—20:28; 24:43-51; Mk. 10:2-45; Lk. 10:38—12:9; 13:1-17, 22-35; 14:1—16:15, 18-31; 17:1-37; 18:1-34; Jn. 11:1-54).

Note: From this point until his triumphal entry, it is impossible to trace Jesus' exact route except to say that he moves freely about in the Bethany, Jericho, and Perea area.

A. He visits the home of Mary and Martha in Bethany (Lk. 10:38-42).
   1. Martha is disturbed and complains to Jesus that Mary is listening to him and not helping her.
   2. Jesus explains to Martha that it is more needful for a person to hear him (first) before laboring for him.
B. Ninth prayer: Just prior to teaching others how to pray (Lk. 11:1).
C. He repeats his model prayer again (see also Mt. 6:9-13) and comments on the subject of prayer (Lk. 11:1-13).
   He observes that no earthly father will give his son a stone or a serpent in place of bread or fish and neither will the heavenly Father.
D. Twenty-seventh miracle: Healing a blind and dumb demoniac (Mt. 12:22; Lk. 11:14).
   1. The Pharisees again accuse him of working such miracles through Beelzebub.
   2. He repeats his earlier parable, "Subduing a strong man." (See Mk. 3:22-30; Mt. 12:23-32; Lk. 11:15-21.)
   3. He says the one who is not for him is in reality against him (Lk. 11:23).
   4. He warns again against the unpardonable sin (Mt. 12:31, 32).
      a. "Whoever speaks a word against the Son of man . . . will be forgiven."
      b. "Whoever speaks against the Holy Spirit . . . will not be forgiven, either in this age or the age to come."
   What is the nature of the unpardonable sin? Taken in its proper context it involves crediting the works Christ performed through the Holy Spirit during his earthly ministry to the devil. Here the wicked Pharisees had actually seen the Savior's mighty works with their own eyes and had heard his marvelous words with their own ears. After experiencing this dazzling display of deity, what was their reaction? They claimed both he and his ministry were from hell! To sin against such light was unpardonable. What more could God himself do to convince them?

Can the unpardonable sin be committed today? Taking into consideration what has already been said, it cannot. Christ is no longer walking this earth in his physical body performing miracles and preaching oral sermons.

5. He condemns the Pharisees as a generation of snakes and warns they will someday answer for their horrible words in the judgment (Mt. 12:33-37.)

E. Seventeenth parable: "Seven spirits and a deserted house" (Mt. 12:43-45; Lk. 11:24-26).

1. He describes in this parable the tragedy of reformation without regeneration.
2. He pictures an evil spirit who leaves an unsaved man.
3. The man is relieved and decides to clean up his life.
4. The demon, however, eventually returns and discovers the changes and reforms.
5. He (the demon) therefore invites seven spirits, more wicked than himself, and all eight possess the man.

F. Jesus informs a woman that the one hearing and doing God's word is even more blessed than his earthly mother (Lk. 11:27, 28).

G. Twenty-first prediction: His resurrection (Mt. 12:38-40; Lk. 11:29, 30).

1. The Pharisees are still pestering him for a sign after he has already performed twenty-seven recorded miracles!
2. Jesus says the only sign for their evil generation is the sign of Jonah.
   a. Jonah was in the belly of a sea monster for three days and three nights.
   b. Jesus will be in the heart of the earth for three days and three nights.

H. Twenty-second prediction: The great white throne judgment (Mt. 12:41, 42; Lk. 11:31, 32).

1. In the judgment, the men of Nineveh will stand and condemn this generation.
   a. They repented at Jonah's preaching (Jonah 3).
   b. He is greater than Jonah, but the Pharisees were not repenting.
2. In the judgment, the Queen of Sheba will stand and condemn this generation (1 Ki. 10).
   a. She came from afar to hear the wisdom of Solomon.
   b. He is greater than Solomon, but the Pharisees were not listening.

I. He condemns the Pharisees and lawyers for various acts of wickedness (Lk. 11:37-52).

1. The Pharisees are condemned:
   a. for having clean hands but dirty hearts
   b. for elevating their traditions and disregarding the justice and love of God
   c. for their vanity and corrupted inward nature
2. The lawyers are condemned:
   a. for weighing men down with intolerable burdens
   b. for boasting in their tomb building for the prophets that their fathers killed
   c. for taking away the key of knowledge

J. He is violently assailed by both groups when he finishes these comments (Lk. 11:53, 54).

K. Twenty-third prediction: The great white throne judgment (Lk. 12:2, 3). (See also Rev. 20:11-15.)

1. All secret deeds ever done will someday be revealed.
2. All secret words ever said will someday be heard.

L. Eighteenth parable: "A fool in a fix" (Lk. 12:16-21).

1. A rich farmer makes the following decisions after a bumper crop.
   a. I do not have room for all my goods.
   b. I will tear down my old barns and build bigger ones.
   c. I will there bestow all my produce and my goods.
   d. I will then seek only pleasure, for I have much goods laid up for many years.
2. A sovereign God also makes some decisions concerning the foolish farmer.
   a. "Thou fool, this night thy soul shall be required of thee."
   b. "Then whose shall those things be, which thou hast provided?"
   Note: This marks the only occasion in the Bible on which God himself personally calls an individual a fool. The man was a fool:
   c. Because he thought he could satisfy his eternal soul with materialistic goods. Note this statement, "and I will say to my soul, Soul, thou hast much goods laid up . . ." (12:19).
      See Jesus' statement in Matthew 4:4; 16:26. The only *real* soul food is the Word of God.
   d. Because he smugly assumed he would naturally live to a ripe old age. Again, observe his misplaced confidence: "Thou hast much goods laid up for many years." (See Prov. 27:1; 29:1; Ps. 90:12; Isa. 4:13-15.)

M. Nineteenth parable: Keep the home fires burning (Lk. 12:32-40; Mt. 24:43, 44).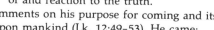

1. The believer has been promised the kingdom of his Father.
2. He should, therefore, store up his treasures in heaven, which is both theft and rust proof.
3. He should keep his clothing adjusted and his lamps burning, as he awaits the Bridegroom.
4. He will then be served personally by the Bridegroom.
5. He must be constantly ready, for the Bridegroom will come at the least expected time.

N. Twentieth parable: "A sinning servant and a returning ruler" (Mt. 24:45-51; Lk. 12:42-48).

1. The sinning servant
   a. He assumes his master will prolong his coming indefinitely.
   b. He abuses his fellow servants.
   c. He associates and drinks with the drunken.
2. The returning ruler
   a. He returns suddenly at a totally unexpected hour.
   b. He consumes the wicked servant in his anger.
   c. He appoints his portion with the hypocrites.
   d. He punishes him according to his knowledge of and reaction to the truth.

O. He comments on his purpose for coming and its reaction upon mankind (Lk. 12:49-53). He came:

1. to cast fire upon the earth

2. to be baptized with a special baptism (the cup of our sin upon the cross)

3. to bring division

4. to divide homes
   a. to set a man against his father
   b. to set a daughter-in-law against her mother-in-law
   c. to set a daughter against her mother
   d. to set a father against his son
   e. to set a mother against her daughter
   f. to set mother-in-law against daughter-in-law

P. He warns through two current events that unless all repent, all will perish (Lk. 13:1–5).
   1. the event of Pilate murdering some Galileans
   2. the event of the tower of Siloam falling upon eighteen people

 Q. Twenty-first parable: A fruitless fig tree (Lk. 13:6–9).
   1. A vineyard owner orders his caretaker to chop down a fig tree which had been fruitless for three years.
   2. The caretaker asks for one more year to fertilize it.

 R. Twenty-eighth miracle: Healing a woman with an eighteen-year infirmity (Lk. 13:10–17).
   1. Jesus heals a bent-over woman in a synagogue who suffers with an eighteen-year spirit of infirmity. Note: Although Satan cannot *possess* a believer, he can nevertheless *oppress* and physically *afflict* a child of God (see Job 1–2; 2 Cor. 12:7). "And ought not this woman, being a daughter of Abraham, *whom Satan hath bound,* lo, these eighteen years, be loosed from this bond on the Sabbath day?"
   2. The synagogue ruler criticizes Jesus for doing this on the Sabbath.
   3. Jesus rebukes him as a hypocrite and receives praise from the synagogue crowd.

S. He refers to that narrow gate leading to heaven (Lk. 13:22–30).
   1. Many will seek to enter heaven unsuccessfully.
   2. Some of these will be citizens from the very cities in which Jesus has ministered.
   3. All will weep and gnash their teeth as they are separated from Abraham, Isaac, Jacob, and other prophets in the kingdom of God.

T. Jesus sends a message to Herod (calling him a fox) and warns him that even the king cannot keep him from Calvary outside Jerusalem (Lk. 13:31–33).

 U. Twenty-ninth miracle: Healing a man with dropsy (Lk. 14:4).

 V. Twenty-second parable: Choosing the least at a wedding feast (Lk. 14:7–11).
   1. He says the one who exalts himself will be humbled—that is, a guest who demands a place next to the host may be asked to move down in favor of a more important guest.
   2. He says the one who humbles himself will be exalted—that is, the guest who assumes the lowest place will doubtless be asked by the host to move higher.

W. Jesus advises his Pharisee host to also include some poor, cripple, lame, and blind folk in his future supper feasts (Lk. 14:12–14).

 X. Twenty-third parable: Two fools and a hen-pecked husband (Lk. 14:15–24).

1. The invited guests: Three men are invited to a great feast. All refuse for various reasons.
   a. The first fool: "I can't come, for I must go and check out a field I just purchased." Only a fool would buy a field unseen!
   b. The second fool: "I can't come for I must go try out some oxen I have just purchased." Only a fool would buy untried oxen!
   c. The hen-pecked husband: "I can't come, as I have just married me a wife." No comment necessary.

2. The angry host:
   a. He orders his servants to visit the streets and lanes, the highways and hedges of the city, and to bring in all the poor and sick they can find.
   b. He vows that none of the originally invited guests will taste of his banquet.

Y. Jesus tells the throngs that all would-be disciples of his should first count the cost (Lk. 14:25–35).
   1. Not to do this would be as unwise as a builder would be to lay a foundation for a tower and then find he cannot finish it.
   2. Not to do this would be as unwise as a king who engages another king and discovers that he has but half the army of his enemy.

On this occasion Christ makes a strange statement. He says:

"If any man come to me, and hate not his father, and mother, and wife, and children, and brethren, and sisters, yea, and his own life also, he cannot be my disciple" (Lk. 14:26).

This has bothered some people. However, it should be kept in mind that the Greek word *misco* can also mean a preference for one thing over another. Greek scholar W. E. Vine points to two other passages where this preference meaning is obviously intended.

"No man can serve two masters: for either he will hate [prefer] the one and love the other; or else he will hold to the one, and despise [count as nothing] the other. Ye cannot serve God and mammon" (Mt. 6:24).

"He that loveth his life shall lose it; and he that hateth his life [counts it less than Christ] in this world shall keep it unto life eternal" (Jn. 12:25).

In reality, Christ taught a man to *love* his family. (See Eph. 5:25, 28.)

Z. Twenty-fourth parable: The missing sheep, the misplaced silver, and the miserable son (Lk. 15:1–32). Jesus tells this threefold parable when he is accused by the ungodly Pharisees of mingling and eating with known sinners.
   1. The missing sheep (Lk. 15:3–7)
      a. A shepherd has one hundred sheep but discovers one is missing.
      b. He leaves the ninety-nine and searches until he finds the lost one.
      c. He carries it home and calls in his friends to rejoice with him.
      d. Jesus says there is similar joy in heaven at the repentance of a lost sinner, more than over ninety-nine self-righteous ones who feel no need of repentance.

2. The misplaced silver (Lk. 15:8–10).
   a. A woman has ten silver pieces and loses one.
   b. She lights a lamp and sweeps her house until she finds it.
   c. She calls her friends inside to rejoice with her.
   d. Jesus says there is similar joy in heaven at the repentance of a lost sinner, more than over ninety-nine self-righteous men who feel no need of repentance.
3. The miserable son (Lk. 15:11–32).
   a. A younger son demands his share of his father's property and leaves home.
   b. He soon wastes it all in sinful living and begins to suffer hunger.
   c. He hires out a swine feeder, and finally coming to himself, decides:
      (1) To go back home to his father.
      (2) To confess his sin.
         Note the boy's statement:
         "I will arise and go to my father, and will say unto him, Father, I have sinned against heaven, and before thee" (Lk. 15:18).
         This boy becomes the seventh of eight individuals in the Bible to say those three difficult words, "I have sinned." The remaining seven are: *Pharaoh* (Ex. 9:27; 10:16); *Balaam* (Num. 22:34); *Achan* (Josh. 7:20); *Saul* (1 Sam. 26:21); *David* (2 Sam. 12:13; 24:10); *Job* (7:20); and *Judas* (Mt. 27:4).
         As can be seen, some of these who said it didn't really mean it.
      (3) To request a job as a hired servant.
   d. The boy is seen by his watching father while a long distance down the road.
   e. The father, moved with compassion, runs to meet him, kisses him repeatedly, and orders the following:
      (1) a robe for his back
      (2) a ring for his finger
      (3) sandals for his feet
      (4) a fatted calf for a celebration
   f. The son's older brother is jealous over all this and complains to his father.
      (1) The elder son's complaint:
         "I have always served you and obeyed you. But you have never even given me so much as a kid to celebrate with my friends. Now this sinful son of yours comes home and you kill the fatted calf."
      (2) The father's answer:
         "Son, all that I have is yours, as you are always with me. But now your lost brother is alive and home. It is therefore fitting that we rejoice and be merry."
   g. We may observe the following concerning this passage in Luke 15.
      (1) General observations:
         (a) This is really one basic parable with three illustrations.
         (b) The entire Trinity is symbolized in this parable. The *Son* (the shepherd)
is seen in the first, the *Holy Spirit* (the light) in the second, and the *Father* in the third.
         (c) There is a mathematical progression seen here concerning that which was lost. The account moves from one out of a hundred, to one from ten, to one out of two.
         (d) The thrust of the parable is that restoration results in rejoicing.
      (2) Specific observations—concerning the third part:
         (a) This account is not primarily a picture of the conversion of a sinner, but rather the restoration of a believer.
         (b) The tragic figure of the account is not the repentant younger son, but rather the self-righteous older brother.
         (c) The main character of this account is the forgiving Father.

AA. Twenty-fifth parable: The stewings of a steward (Lk. 16:1–13).
   1. A wasteful steward is informed he will soon be dismissed from his position.
   2. He is loath to work and ashamed to beg, so he prepares for the future in the following manner.
      a. He reduces by 50 percent a bill owed to his master, and thus gains the friendship of an oil merchant.
      b. He reduces by 20 percent another bill, thus receiving the friendship of a wheat merchant.

BB. Twenty-sixth parable: When Hades petitioned Paradise (Lk. 16:19–31).
   1. Jesus describes the life of a certain rich man.
      a. He was clothed in purple and fine linen.
      b. He lived daily in merriment and splendor.
      c. He died, was buried, and awakened in Hades.
   2. Jesus describes the life of a certain poor man (named Lazarus).
      a. He lay at the rich man's gates, covered with sores.
      b. He longed for the crumbs which daily fell from the rich man's table.
      c. He died and was carried by the angels to Paradise (Abraham's bosom).
   3. Jesus describes the plight of the rich man.
      a. He saw Abraham and Lazarus in Paradise afar off.
      b. He was tormented by fire and asked Abraham to allow Lazarus to cool his tongue with a drop of water.
      c. He is informed this cannot be done because of the great chasm separating where he was from where they were.
      d. He asked Abraham to send Lazarus to warn his five brothers, lest they join him in his misery.
      e. He was refused this request also on the ground that his brothers would have ample opportunity to repent if they so desired.

In Luke 16:31 Abraham says: "If they hear not Moses and the prophets, neither will they be persuaded, though one rise from the dead."

This statement has a prophetic ring to it, for a few months later Jesus would perform his greatest single miracle, the resurrection of a decaying corpse, and his name happened to be Lazarus. (See Jn. 11:53; 12:10.)

This verse (Lk. 16:31) indirectly answers a question asked by many, and that is, "Do the departed saints in glory know what is happening back on earth?" Apparently, up to a point, they do, for here Abraham speaks of a man (Moses) who would not even be born until some six centuries *after* the "father of the faithful" had departed this earth.

This is the reason why God does not do mighty miracles today. God's will is accomplished through faith and not through signs. After the rapture many miracles and signs will occur during the tribulation, but sinful men will not believe (see Rev. 9:20, 21). Note: It is held by a number of Bible students that before Jesus died, the souls of all men descended into an abode located somewhere in the earth, known as Hades in the New Testament and Sheol in the Old Testament.

Originally, there were two sections of Hades, one for the saved and one for the lost. The saved section is sometimes called "paradise" (see Lk. 23:43), and other times referred to as "Abraham's bosom" (see Lk. 16:22). There is no name given for the unsaved section apart from the general designation of Hades.

In Luke 16:19–31 the Savior relates the account of a poor believer who died and went to the saved part of Hades and of a rich unbeliever who died and went to the unsaved section. However, many believe that all this changed after Christ had made full payment for the believer's sins on Calvary. The *Scofield Bible* suggests that during the time of his death and resurrection, our Lord descended into Hades, depopulated Paradise, and led a spiritual triumphal entry into the heavenlies with all the saved up to that time. Ephesians 4:8–10 is offered as proof of this.

In his book *Revelation,* the late Dr. Donald Grey Barnhouse writes:

"When he ascended on High (Eph. 4:8) He emptied Hell of Paradise and took it straight to the presence of God. Captivity was taken captive. . . . From that moment onward there was to be no separation whatsoever for those who believe in Christ. The gates of hell would never more prevail against any believer (Mt. 16:18). But what of the lost? The state of the unsaved dead remained (and re-mains) unchanged after the cross. They remain in Hades awaiting the final Great White Judgment Throne (Rev. 20:11-15). But a glorious change has occurred concerning the state of those who fall asleep in Jesus."

Note the following Scriptures:

"But he, being full of the Holy Ghost, looked up steadfastly into heaven, and saw the glory of God, and Jesus standing on the right hand of God. And they stoned Stephen, calling upon God, and saying Lord Jesus, receive my spirit. And he kneeled down, and cried with a loud voice, Lord, lay not this sin to their charge. And when he had said this, he fell asleep" (Acts 7:55, 59, 60).

"For to me to live is Christ, and to die is gain. For I am in a strait betwixt two, having a desire to depart, and to be with Christ; which is far better" (Phil. 1:21, 23). ". . . to be absent from the body [is to be] present with the Lord" (2 Cor. 5:8).

CC. Twenty-seventh parable: When our best is but the least (Lk. 17:7–10).
1. The master of a bondservant expects him to perform certain duties without demanding to be praised or thanked.
   a. He is to tend his master's field.
   b. He is to prepare his food.
   c. He is to serve him at all times.
2. The servant of God is likewise expected to perform certain duties without insisting upon special recognition.
   a. He is to accomplish all God's commandments.
   b. He is then to admit that the very best he can do is but the very least he should do.

DD. Thirtieth miracle: Healing ten lepers (Lk. 17:11–19).
1. Jesus heals the lepers and directs them to the priest for ceremonial cleansing.
2. One of the ten, a Samaritan, returns and falls at his feet to worship.
3. Jesus marvels that out of the ten he healed, only a "foreigner," the Samaritan, returns to thank him. Jesus healed many people of physical infirmities during his earthly ministry. Did all of these also experience spiritual salvation at the time of their healing? The Savior's statement here to the one thankful leper would suggest this was *not* the case.
   "And he said unto him, Arise, go thy way; thy faith hath made thee whole" (Lk. 17:19). (See also Jn. 5:8, 14.)
   At any rate, the arrival of these healed lepers at the Temple for ceremonial cleansing must have caused considerable confusion among the priests as they dusted off the old Levitical regulations governing this, for in the Old Testament not *one* single Israeli (apart from Miriam; see Num. 12) was ever healed of leprosy. Naaman, of course, was a Syrian. (See 2 Ki. 5.)

EE. Twenty-fourth prediction: His sufferings (Lk. 17:25).

FF. Twenty-fifth prediction: The last days (Lk. 17:26-30).
   1. Sensual conditions similar to those in *Noah's* day will prevail. (See Gen. 6.)
      a. humanity eating and drinking
      b. humanity marrying and being given in marriage
      c. humanity unprepared for the flood
   2. Materialistic conditions similar to those in *Lot's* day will prevail. (See Gen. 19.)
      a. humanity buying and selling
      b. humanity planting and building
      c. humanity unprepared for the fire

GG. Twenty-sixth prediction: Concerning Armageddon (Lk. 17:34-37).
   1. Some will be taken while in bed.
   2. Some will be taken while in a mill.
   3. Some will be taken while in a field.
   4. All will be destroyed and their bodies eaten by vultures.
      Note: This passage has often been used to refer to the saved being taken at the rapture, but the context indicates a reference to the unsaved being taken for judgment at Armageddon. It also indicates the scientific accuracy of the Bible. We note some will be in bed (at nighttime) while some will be in the fields (daylight). Thus Luke, under inspiration, was aware of the shape of our earth.

HH. Twenty-eighth parable: A widow and a weary judge (Lk. 18:1-8).
   1. Jesus describes an unconcerned judge.
      a. This judge is confronted daily by a persistent woman who desires justice against her adversary.
      b. The judge finally submits, lest he be worn out by her continual pleas.
   2. Jesus compares this judge with his heavenly Father.
      a. The earthly judge rendered justice in spite of his unconcern.
      b. The heavenly Father will do even more because of his great concern.
   3. Jesus concludes that men ought always to pray and not to faint.

II. Twenty-ninth parable: A haughty Pharisee and a humble Publican (Lk. 18:9-14).
   1. Two men enter the Temple to pray.
      a. A Pharisee and his prayer:
         (1) "I'm glad I'm not like all others."
         (2) "I'm not avaricious, unrighteous, or adulterous."
         (3) "I fast twice each week."
         (4) "I pay tithes of everything I get."
      b. A Publican and his prayer:
         (1) He stands afar off and lowers his eyes.
         (2) He beats his breast.
         (3) He confesses his sin.
         (4) He begs for mercy.

   2. The two men leave the Temple.
      a. God has received and exalted the Publican.
      b. God has rejected and humbled the Pharisee.

JJ. Jesus comments on divorce (Mt. 19:3-12; Mk. 10:2-12; Lk. 16:18).
   1. He explains God's original intentions:
      a. That a man should leave his parents when he takes a bride.
      b. That the man and his wife are now considered to be as one flesh.
      c. That no outsider has the right to break this spiritual union.
   2. He explains God's later provision because of man's hard heart—a writ of divorcement.
   3. He explains God's general attitude concerning remarriage:
      a. The man who remarries a second woman commits adultery (unless his first wife has been sexually untrue to him).
      b. The man who marries a divorced woman commits adultery.
      c. The woman who remarries a second man commits adultery (unless her first husband has been sexually untrue to her).
      d. The woman who marries a divorced man commits adultery.
   4. He explains God's general attitude on non-marriage.
      a. There are eunuchs who were born so from their mother's womb.
      b. There are eunuchs who were made so by men.
      c. There are eunuchs who have made themselves so for the sake of the kingdom of heaven.

KK. Tenth prayer: After receiving some small children (Lk. 18:15-17; Mt. 19:13-15; Mk. 10:13-16).
   1. A number of small children and infants are brought to Jesus to be prayed for.
   2. His disciples attempt to prevent this intrusion upon the Savior's time.
   3. Jesus rebukes their efforts and gladly receives the little ones, saying:
      a. "Let the little children come to me; and forbid them not."
      b. "The kingdom of heaven is such as this."
      c. "All that would enter that kingdom must receive it as a little child."

LL. Thirty-first miracle: Raising of Lazarus (Jn. 11:43, 44).
   1. Jesus is informed that a dear friend, Lazarus of Bethany, is near death.
   2. He decides to attend his funeral in spite of the objections of his disciples.
      a. They are afraid he will be stoned if he goes that close to Jerusalem.
      b. Jesus tells them he must work his works while it is still day.
         (1) Jesus: "Lazarus is dead, and I go to awaken him."

(2) Thomas: "Let us go that we may die with him" (not a great amount of faith shown here).

3. He is met by Martha, Lazarus' sister, as he nears their home in Bethany.
   a. Martha: "Lord, if thou hadst been here, my brother had not died."
   b. Jesus: "Thy brother shall rise again."
   c. Martha: "I know that he shall rise again in the resurrection at the last day."
   d. Jesus: "I am the resurrection, and the life: he that believeth in me, though he were dead, yet shall he live: And whosoever liveth and believeth in me shall never die. Believest thou this?"
   e. Martha: "Yea, Lord: I believe that thou art the Christ, the Son of God, which should come into the world."

4. Martha goes inside the house and tells her sister Mary that Jesus has come.

5. Jesus sees her weeping and weeps himself as he stands outside the tomb.

6. He orders the stone taken away over the objections of Martha.
   a. Martha: "Lord, he's been there four days and by now he is offensive."
   b. Jesus: "Didn't I tell you to believe and see the glory of God?"

7. Eleventh prayer: Before raising Lazarus (Jn. 11:41, 42).
   a. "I thank you, Father, that you always hear me."
   b. "I pray that this crowd may believe that you have sent me."

8. Jesus then cries out: "Lazarus, come forth!"

9. The enemies of Jesus make formal plans to kill both him and Lazarus if necessary after the accomplishment of this miracle (Jn. 11:45–54).
   a. The Pharisees fear all will believe on him, causing the Romans to set them aside.
   b. Caiaphas, the high priest, states that it is expedient for Israel that Jesus die. This marks the final prophecy uttered by a high priest of Israel. Note its contents: "And this spake he not of himself; but being high priest that year, he prophesied that Jesus should die for that nation; and not for that nation only, but that also he should gather together in one the children of God that were scattered abroad" (Jn. 11:51, 52).

   The *Wycliffe Bible Commentary* observes:
   "The words, so to speak, were put into his mouth. Here is a Balaam (see Num. 22–24) who would curse Jesus, but out of the prophecy comes the realization of the purpose of God that Christ should die for the *nation* in a redemptive, vicarious sense, and even for a larger group, that all the dispersed children of God (in a prospective sense) would be brought together. How fitting it was that one who filled the office of high priest should un-

wittingly set forth the work of Christ as the Lamb who takes away sin!" (p. 331)

Note also the high priest's fear which prompted this prophecy:
"If we let him thus alone, all men will believe on him: and the Romans shall come and take away both our place and nation" (Jn. 11:48).

The divine irony of history is of course that both things did happen. Men *did* believe on him and the Romans *did* come. Comments on this miracle:

1. This is usually regarded as the greatest of all the miracles of our Lord.

2. It marks the first instance where the death of a believer is likened to sleep. (Compare Jn. 11:11 with Mt. 9:24; 27:52; Acts 7:60; 1 Cor. 11:30; 15:50, 51; 1 Thess. 4:14.)

3. We note he waited until Lazarus had been dead four days. He may have done this because of the superstition among the Jews that after death the spirit hovered over the body for three days and a resurrection up to that time was at least remotely possible. But after this period, all hope was gone.

4. Martha, and not Mary, is the heroine of this story. (See Lk. 10:38–42 where the opposite was true.)
   a. It was Martha who went to meet Jesus while Mary remained in the house (11:20).
   b. Martha's great testimony here ranks equally as important as that given by Simon Peter on another occasion. (Compare Jn. 11:27 with Mt. 16:16.)

5. This passage records the first of four instances where Christ wept. (For the other occasions, see Heb. 5:7; Lk. 19:41; Mt. 23:37–39.)
   a. He wept because of his true humanity. (See Heb. 4:14–16.)
   b. He wept because of the wicked men he saw around him. (See 11:37, 46.)

6. The Savior desired human help in performing his great miracle.
   a. He ordered someone to roll the stone back. (See 11:39.)
   b. He ordered someone to unbind the resurrected Lazarus. (See 11:44.)

MM. Jesus talks to the rich young ruler (Mt. 19:16–26; Mk. 10:17–27; Lk. 18:18–27).
   1. Our Lord is confronted by a young Jewish leader who runs to meet him, kneels, and inquires concerning eternal life.
   2. Jesus tells him to observe the commandments.
   3. The young man claims to have always done this.
   4. Jesus tells him one final thing is lacking, that he is to:
      a. Sell all he has and give it to the poor.
      b. Come and follow Jesus.
   5. The young man walks away sadly, unwilling to do these two things.
   6. Jesus comments on wealthy people and the kingdom of God.
      a. He says it is easier for a camel to pass through the eye of a sewing needle than for a rich man to enter the kingdom of God.

b. He says that, humanly speaking, salvation would be hopeless, but with God all things are possible.

7. The rich young ruler was guilty of three grievous errors.

   a. Concerning the person of Christ. He merely concluded him to be a "good teacher."

   b. Concerning the plan of salvation. He felt he could earn it through good works.

   c. Concerning the pride of his own heart. He thought he had earned it. We are told that "the disciples were astonished at his words" (Mk. 10:24). To the Jewish people, temporal prosperity was considered a token of divine favor. (See Deut. 28:1-12.) Some people today feel the same way.

 NN. Twenty-seventh prediction: Concerning future rewards (Mt. 19:27-30; Mk. 10:28-31; Lk. 18:28-30).

1. Jesus promises the twelve future rewards if they sacrifice for him.

   a. They shall sit on twelve thrones.

   b. They shall judge the twelve tribes of Israel.

2. Jesus promises all believers future rewards if they sacrifice for him.

   a. They shall receive a hundredfold more in this present age.

   b. They shall receive eternal life in the ages to come.

3. Note his statement here:

"Verily, I say unto you that ye who have followed me, in the regeneration, when the Son of man shall sit on the throne of his glory, ye also shall sit upon twelve thrones, judging the twelve tribes of Israel" (Mt. 19:28).

The word "regeneration" is found only one other time in the New Testament apart from here. It occurs in Titus 3:5 where it refers to the Christian's new birth. Here in Matthew 19:28 it also has a new birth in mind—the conversion of sinful old Mother Nature. This glorious new birth will usher in the millennium. (See Isa. 11:6-9; Rom. 8:19-23; Acts 3:21.)

 OO. Thirtieth parable: When the last was first and the first was last (Mt. 20:1-16).

1. The master of a house recruits workers for his vineyard.

   a. He hires some at sunrise, offering a penny for the day.

   b. He hires some at 9:00 A.M. for the same.

   c. He hires some at noon for the same.

   d. He hires some at 3:00 P.M. for the same.

   e. He hires some at 5:00 P.M. for the same.

2. He settles up at the day's end, giving all their promised pay, beginning with the 5:00 P.M. workers and finishing with the sunrise workers.

3. The sunrise workers expect more than the 5:00 P.M. workers and complain to the master.

4. The master points out:

   a. That they were not wronged, for each had gotten the promised amount.

b. That it was his business if he chose to be generous.

PP. Twenty-eighth prediction: Concerning his resurrection (Mt. 20:17-19; Mk. 10:32-34; Lk. 18:31-34).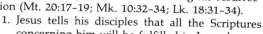

1. Jesus tells his disciples that all the Scriptures concerning him will be fulfilled in Jerusalem.

   a. He will be betrayed to the chief priests and scribes.

   b. He will be condemned to death by them.

   c. He will be delivered up to the Gentiles for crucifixion.

   d. He will be mocked.

   e. He will be treated shamefully.

   f. He will be spit upon.

   g. He will be scourged.

   h. He will be put to death.

   i. He will rise again on the third day.

2. The disciples are filled with awe and fear, but do not comprehend his solemn words.

QQ. Jesus hears a request from the mother of James and John (Mt. 20:20-28; Mk. 10:35-45).

1. The request: "Allow my sons to be seated on your left and right side in the kingdom."

2. The denial: "It is not mine to grant what you ask, but only that of the Father."

3. The lesson:

   a. The Son of man did not come to be ministered to, but to minister and to give his life as a ransom for many.

   b. His disciples should likewise minister to others, for love is the secret of greatness.

On this occasion Jesus said:

"Ye know not what ye ask, can ye drink of the cup that I drink of; and be baptized with the baptism that I am baptized with? And they said unto him, we can. And Jesus said unto them, ye shall indeed drink of the cup that I drink of; and with the baptism that I am baptized shall ye be baptized" (Mk. 10:38, 39).

The cup here was that of suffering. Both of these brothers would indeed drink of that cup. One was beheaded (Acts 12:2), and the other exiled for Christ (Rev. 1:9).

Step Forty-Nine: From Bethany to Jericho
(Mt. 20:29-34; Mk. 10:46-52; Lk. 18:35—19:28).

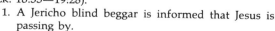

A. Thirty-second miracle: Healing a blind man (Mt. 20:34; Lk. 18:35—19:28).

1. A Jericho blind beggar is informed that Jesus is passing by.

2. He cries out (in spite of the crowd's rebuke) for the Son of David to have pity on him.

3. Jesus asks: "What do you wish me to do for you?"

4. He answers: "Lord, that I may receive sight."

5. The Savior, filled with compassion, touches the beggar's eyes and opens them.

6. The ex-blind man follows him, glorifying God.

B. Jesus greets and saves Zacchaeus (Lk. 19:1-10).
  1. The sinner:
     a. Zacchaeus was a chief Publican.
     b. He was rich and somewhat dishonest.
     c. He was small of stature.
     d. He climbs a sycamore tree to watch Jesus.
  2. The Savior:
     a. Looks up the tree and sees Zacchaeus.
     b. Informs him that he plans to visit his home.
     c. Is criticized by the watching crowd for associating with such sinners.
  3. The saint (Zacchaeus):
     a. Accepts Christ as his Messiah-Savior.
     b. Determines to give half of his possessions to the poor.
     c. Plans to make a fourfold restitution to all he had previously cheated.
     d. He becomes a true son of Abraham.

 C. Thirty-first parable: Three stewards and their silver (Lk. 19:11-27).
  1. A man of noble birth prepares to leave for a far country to receive a kingdom.
  2. He calls in ten of his bondmen before departing.
     a. Each is given a pound of silver.
     b. Each is ordered to do business until he returns.
  3. He later returns and calls in the ten bondmen for a personal accounting.
     a. The first man:
        (1) Had increased his pound tenfold.
        (2) Was given the rule over ten cities.
     b. The second man:
        (1) Had increased his pound fivefold.
        (2) Was given the rule over five cities.
     c. A third man:
        (1) Had ignored his pound completely.
        (2) Was severely punished and loses his pound to the first man.

 D. Thirty-third miracle: Healing a blind man (Mt. 20:34; Mk. 10:46, 52). Note: Although there are many similarities between the thirty-second and thirty-third miracles, they are not the same. The first blind man, unnamed, was healed as our Lord entered Jericho, while the second man, Bartimaeus by name, was healed as he left Jericho.
  1. Bartimaeus: "Jesus, Son of David, have pity on me."
  2. The crowd: "Have courage; rise up, he is calling you."
  3. Jesus: "What do you wish me to do for you?
  4. Bartimaeus: "Dear Rabbi, let me receive my sight."
  5. Jesus: "Go; your faith has healed you."
     This marks Jesus' final visit to Jericho. He will now leave for Jerusalem. (See Mt. 20:29.) Before this, he had told the story of a man who left Jerusalem for Jericho (the parable of the Good Samaritan, Lk. 10:25-37). But now the original Good Samaritan will reverse the trip, leaving Jericho for Jerusalem where he would soon, "fall among thieves."

END OF JESUS' PUBLIC MINISTRY.

Step Fifty: From Jericho to Bethany
(Mt. 26:6-13; Mk. 14:3-9; Lk. 22:1; Jn. 11:55—12:11).

SATURDAY

A. Jesus is anointed by Mary of Bethany (Mt. 26:6-13; Mk. 14:3-9).
  1. Lazarus, his two sisters, and Jesus are invited to supper at the Bethany home of Simon, the leper (Jn. 12:1, 2).
  2. Mary approaches Jesus during dinner with an alabaster flask of costly ointment and a pound of pure nard (Jn. 12:3).
  3. Mary is criticized for this by the disciples in general and by Judas Iscariot in particular.
     a. The disciples felt the ointment should have been sold and given to the poor (Mt. 26:8, 9).
     b. Judas, treasurer for the twelve, wanted control of the money, for he was a thief (Jn. 12:4-6).
  4. Jesus rebukes the rebukers, pointing out that:
     a. Mary had performed a good thing. Note Jesus' statement: "Let her alone: against the day of my burying hath she done this" (12:7). This was the only anointing his body would receive. In spite of the many times Christ had warned of his suffering and death (see Mt. 16:21; 20:18, 19), apparently the only person to take him seriously was Mary. (See also Jn. 10:11, 17, 18.)
     b. They could always minister to the poor, but not to him.
     c. Her devotion to him would always be remembered wherever the gospel was preached (Mt. 26:10-13; Mk. 14:6-9; Jn. 12:7, 8).
     The chief priests now begin planning how they might kill Lazarus along with Jesus, since his resurrection had led to so many converts (Jn. 12:9-11).

Step Fifty-one: From Bethany to Bethphage
(Mt. 21:1-7; Mk. 11:1-7; Lk. 19:29-35).

SUNDAY

A. Jesus sends two of his disciples to fetch a colt.
  1. The owners of the colt ask: "What are you doing, untying the colt?"
  2. The disciples answer: "The Lord has need of it."

B. Jesus is set on the colt by his disciples.

Step Fifty-two: From Bethphage to the upper room
(Mt. 10:17-23; 21:8—23:39; 24:1-42; 25:1-46; 26:1-5, 14-30; Mk. 11:8—13:37; 14:1, 2, 10-25; Lk. 12:11, 12; 13:34, 35; 19:36—20:8, 20-40, 45-47; 21:1-38; 22:2-34; Jn. 12:12).

A. He enters Jerusalem and receives the glad shouts of the crowds (Mt. 21:9-11; Mk. 11:9, 10; Lk. 19:38; Jn. 12:12-15).
1. "Blessed is the king of Israel, who is coming in the name of the Lord."
2. "Hosanna in the highest to the Son of David."

B. He defends their cries, telling the critical Pharisees that had the crowd been silent, the very stones would have cried out (Lk. 19:39, 40).

 C. Old Testament Prophecy Fulfillment Number 18, That he would make a triumphal entry into Jerusalem. (Compare Zech. 9:9 with Mt. 21:4, 5.) The palm branches used during the triumphal entry (Jn. 12:13) were a token of rejoicing (Lev. 23:40; Neh. 8:15; Rev. 7:9). They may also have carried a political significance, since they had been used at the feast of tabernacles when Judas Maccabeus' recapture of the Temple from the Syrians was celebrated. (See 2 Maccabees 10:7.)

D. He weeps over Jerusalem (Lk. 19:41, 42).
Note his words:
   "If thou hadst known, even thou, at least in this thy day, the things which belong unto thy peace! But now they are hid from thine eyes."
The famous Bible student, Sir Robert Anderson, has attached great meaning to the three words, "this thy day." According to the prophecy in Daniel 9:24-27 (often called the seventy-week prophecy) God told Daniel he would deal with Israel for yet another seventy "weeks," which is usually interpreted as 490 years. The prophecy continued that after sixty-nine of these "weeks," or 483 years, the Messiah would be "cut off" (rejected and crucified). The prophecy was to start on March 14, 445, B.C. Mr. Anderson suggests that if one begins counting forward from that day, he discovers that the 483 years (173,880 days) runs out on April 6, A.D. 32. It was on this exact day that Jesus rode into Jerusalem on the foal of an ass and, although welcomed by the masses, was officially rejected by Israel's leaders. According to Sir Robert, all this was in mind when our Lord uttered the words of this statement.

 E. Twenty-ninth prediction: Concerning the destruction of Jerusalem (Lk. 19:43, 44).
1. That the city would be surrounded by her enemies.
2. That her children would be killed and her Temple leveled.

MONDAY

 F. Thirty-fourth miracle: Destroying a fig tree (Mt. 21:19; Mk. 11:14).
1. He examines a leafy but fruitless fig tree.
2. He pronounces a curse upon it: "Let there be no fruit from you hereafter." Immediately the fig tree dries up. Note: Of all his miracles, this doubtless was the only one which would fill him with sadness, for in this symbolic act he was setting aside the nation Israel (often pictured as a fig tree) because of its fruitlessness. See Matthew 21:42-45 where this is confirmed.

G. Thirtieth prediction: Concerning the setting aside of Israel (Mt. 21:43, 44).

H. He performs the second cleansing of the Temple (Mt. 21:12, 13; Mk. 11:15-17; Lk. 19:45, 46). Note his statement at this time: "It is written, my house shall be called the house of prayer; but ye have made it a den of thieves" (Mt. 21:13). Our Lord here quotes from Jeremiah 7:12-15, which recalls the destruction of the original tabernacle of Moses at Shiloh by the Philistines, and predicts the destruction of the Temple of Solomon in Jerusalem by the Babylonians. Jesus of course knew that in less than forty years the Temple of Herod would be leveled and burned by the Romans. In the midst of the storm clouds gathered at this verse, a bright ray suddenly appears, for its words are associated with yet a final and future temple. Isaiah speaks about this.
   "Even them [Israel, during the millennium] will I bring to my holy mountain, and make them joyful in my house of prayer: their burnt offerings and their sacrifices shall be accepted upon mine altar; for mine house shall be called an house of prayer for all people" (Isa. 56:7).

I. He heals many blind and lame and receives the worship of some children (Mt. 21:14-16).

J. Old Testament Prophecy Fulfillment Number 19, That he would be praised by little children. Compare Psalm 8:2 with Matthew 21:16.

TUESDAY

K. He is asked about the withered tree and comments on the faith that removes mountains (Mt. 21:20-22; Mk. 11:20-26).

L. He is challenged by the Pharisees concerning the source of his authority (Mt. 21:23-27; Mk. 11:27-33; Lk. 20:1-8).
1. They demand that he tell them the source of his authority.
2. He agrees to do so, but first wants to know if they feel that the source of John's baptism came from man or God.
3. The Pharisees immediately realize they have a problem.
   a. If they answer, "From God," he will doubtless say, "Then why don't you believe him?"
   b. If they answer, "From men," the people will attempt to stone them, for John is their hero.

4. The Pharisees cannot answer his question and he, therefore, will not answer theirs.

M. Thirty-second parable: "Two sons who changed their minds" (Mt. 21:28-32).
  1. A vineyard owner had two sons.
  2. He asked both boys to work in his vineyard.
    a. The first son said he would not, but later repented and did.
    b. The second son said he would, but did not do so.

N. Thirty-third parable: The vicious vine keepers (Mt. 21:33-46; Mk. 12:1-12; Lk. 21:9-19).
  1. A house master leases his vineyard to some men and leaves the country.
  2. He later sends a bondman to gather his fruit.
  3. The keepers beat the servant and send him away empty-handed.
  4. The master continues to send bondmen, but all are beaten and some killed.
  5. He finally sends his own son, hoping the keepers will respect him, but he too, is cruelly murdered.
  6. The house master thereupon comes in fury and destroys the miserable vinekeepers.
  7. Jesus relates this parable to himself, and states that he is rejected as the cornerstone" (Mt. 21:42).

O. Old Testament Prophecy Fulfillment Number 20, That he would be the rejected Cornerstone. (Compare Ps. 118:22, 23 with Mt. 21:42.)

P. Thirty-fourth parable: A wedding guest with no wedding garment (Mt. 22:1-14).
  1. A king prepares a wedding feast for his son and invites a select few.
    a. Those invited refuse to come and insult or kill the king's messengers.
    b. The angry king dispatches troops which destroy them and burn their cities.

Q. He is confronted by the Pharisees and Herodians concerning the payment of tribute money (Mt. 22:15-22; Mk. 12:13-17; Lk. 20:20-26).
  1. Their crafty questions: "Is it lawful for us to give tribute to Caesar or not?"
  2. His wise answer: "Render, therefore, to Caesar the things which are Caesar's; and to God the things which are God's."
    Dr. Charles Ryrie comments:
    "The tribute tax was a poll tax imposed by Rome on every Jew. The burning question in the minds of many Jews of that day was simply this: If God gave the land of Israel to the Hebrews, and if God meant them to live there, and if He received their sacrifices and offerings in achnowledgement of His relationship to them, how could they pay tribute to any other powers, king or person? If Christ said that they should pay, they could then charge Him with disloyalty to Judaism; if He said no, they could denounce Him to the Romans."

R. He is confronted by the liberal Sadducees concerning the resurrection (Mt. 22:23-33; Mk. 12:18-27; Lk. 20:27-40).
  1. Their stupid illustration:
    a. A man who had six brothers married but died shortly after, leaving his wife childless.
    b. The second brother, fulfilling the Mosaic Law, married her, but he, too, died without children.
    c. Eventually, all seven brothers married the woman and died.
    d. In the resurrection, then, whose wife would this woman be?
  2. His straightforward answers:
    a. They were in serious error concerning the scriptural *fact* of the resurrection.
    "Have you not read what was spoken to you by God in the book of Moses, in the part about the bush, when he called the Lord the God of Abraham, and the God of Isaac, and the God of Jacob? He is not the God of the dead, but the God of the living. . . ."
    b. They were in serious error concerning the scriptural *nature* of the resurrection.
    ". . . the resurrected dead neither marry nor are given in marriage, but are as angels in heaven."

S. He is questioned about the greatest commandment of them all (Mt. 22:34-40; Mk. 12:28-34).
  1. The question: Which commandment in the law is first and greatest? The scribes had divided the whole law into 613 precepts.
  2. The answer:
    a. The greatest is: "You shall love your neighbor as yourself" (on these two commandments hang all the law and the prophets).
  3. The scribe (who asked the original question): "Teacher you have well said the truth . . . these are better than all burnt offerings and sacrifices."
    a. The Savior: "You are not far from the kingdom of God."

T. Jesus questions the Pharisees concerning the promised Messiah (Mt. 22:41-46; Mk. 12:34-37; Lk. 20:41-44).
  1. Her question: "Whose son is the Messiah?"
  2. Their answer: "He is the son of David."
  3. His question: "If the Messiah is David's Son, why did David then call him Lord in the Psalms?"
  4. Their answer: They not only had no answer for his question, but from that day on, ceased their wicked efforts to trap him theologically.

U. Thirteenth sermon: Indicting the Jewish rulers on twelve counts (Mt. 23:1-36; Mk. 12:38-40; Lk. 20:45-47).
  1. They dressed proud and sat high.
  2. They devoured the homes of widows.
  3. They made a mockery of prayer.
  4. They weighed men down with their vain traditions.
  5. They shut up the kingdom of heaven against men.

6. They taught converts all their evil ways.
7. They uttered their oaths of promise with forked tongues.
8. They ignored things such as justice, mercy, and fidelity.
9. They strained out the gnat while swallowing the camel.
10. They had polished exteriors but rotten interiors.
11. They revered the memories of their murderous fathers.

> "That upon you may come all the righteous blood shed upon the earth from the blood of righteous Abel unto the blood of Zechariah. . . . Whom ye slew between the temple and altar" (23:35).

> This number is recorded in 2 Chronicles 24:20-22. Since Abel's death is recorded in Genesis (chapter 4) and since 2 Chronicles is the last book in the Hebrew Bible, Christ was saying in effect, "from the first to the last murder in the Bible."

12. They would later themselves beat and kill God's prophets.

V. Jesus weeps over Jerusalem again (Mt. 23:37-39; Lk. 13:34, 35).

> "O Jerusalem, Jerusalem, thou that killeth the prophets, and stonest them which are sent unto thee, how often would I have gathered thy children together even as a hen gathereth her chickens under her wings, and ye would not! Behold your house is left unto you desolate. For I say unto you, ye shall not see me henceforth, till ye shall say, Blessed is he that cometh in the name of the Lord" (Mt. 23:37-39).

Note especially Jesus' reference to *your* house (the Temple) here as contrasted to the *"my* house" statements of John 2:16 and Matthew 21:13. At this point Israel is set aside for the duration of the church age (see Mt. 21:33-46). Jesus' statement in 23:39 will someday be gloriously fulfilled. (See Ps. 118:26; Zech. 12:10.)

Note that this chapter (Mt. 23), which contains the most severe indictment of the leaders of Israel, ends with Jesus weeping over the city of Jerusalem.

W. He observes a poor widow giving her all (two tiny copper coins) to the Temple offering chest (Mk. 12:41-44; Lk. 21:1-4).

 X. Thirty-first prediction: Concerning his death (Jn. 12:20-26).
1. Philip tells him of the desire of some Greeks to see him.
2. He comments on his death.
   a. That the hour had come for him to be glorified.
   b. That he would eventually bare much fruit by this death, as a grain of wheat does by falling into the ground.

 Y. Twelfth prayer: When some Greeks desired to see him (Jn. 12:27, 28).

1. The Son's prayer
   a. "Shall I pray, Father, save me from this hour?"
   b. "No! This is why I came."
   c. "Father, glorify thy name!"
2. The Father's answer: "I both glorified it and will glorify it again."

Z. Thirty-second prediction: Concerning his death (Jn. 12:32). "And I, when I am lifted up from the earth, will draw all men to myself."

AA. He is rejected by many Jewish rulers, even though they believe his message (Jn. 12:37-43).
1. Because they are afraid of excommunication.
2. Because they love men's approval more than God's approval.

BB. Old Testament Prophecy Fulfillment Number 21, That his miracles would not be believed. (Compare Isa. 53:1 with Jn. 12:37, 38.)

CC. Fourteenth sermon: On the coming tribulation (Mt. 24:1-42; 10:17-23; 25:1-46; Mk. 13:1-37; Lk. 21:5-36; 12:11, 12).
1. The destruction of Jerusalem (Mt. 24:1, 2; Lk. 21:20-24).
   a. Jerusalem will be completely encircled by armies. (See also Lk. 19:43, 44.)
   b. The Temple will be leveled down to the last stone.
   c. Her people will be killed and some led captive to all nations.
   d. Jerusalem will be trodden down by the Gentiles until the times of the Gentiles are fulfilled. Note: Our Lord apparently is referring to two separate destructions of Jerusalem in these verses.
      (1) The first is now historical, occurring when Titus leveled the city in A.D. 70. Our Lord warned that not one Temple stone would be left upon another. This prophecy was remarkably fulfilled on September 8, A.D. 70. On this day the Roman general Titus broke down the Jerusalem walls and captured the city. A false rumor had been spread among the Roman troops that the Jews had used gold instead of mortar to hold together the beautiful marble stones of the Temple. The soldiers thus literally pried apart every stone in their fruitless search to discover this gold.
      (2) The second is yet future, and will occur sometime during the tribulation.
2. Thirty-third prediction: Concerning the tribula- tion (Mt. 24:1-42; 10:17-23; 25:1-46; Mk. 13:1-37; Lk. 21:5-36; 12:11, 12).
3. The tribulation: First half (Mt. 24:3-14; 10:17-23; Mk. 13:4-13; Lk. 21:7-19; 12:11, 12).
   a. False prophets and messiahs will arise and deceive many.
   b. Wars and war rumors will intensify.

The Mount Olivet Discourse MATTHEW 24

A TWOFOLD QUESTION (24:3)

"Tell us, when shall these things be?"

THE DESTRUCTION
OF THE TEMPLE

OCCURRED IN A.D. 70

*"What shall be the sign of thy coming
and of the end of this age?"*

THE COMING TRIBULATION

YET TO OCCUR

THE COMING TRIBULATION

FIRST THREE-AND-A-HALF YEARS (24:1-14)	*The Seventieth Week of Daniel*	LAST THREE-AND-A-HALF YEARS (24:15-31).
● Intensification of wars ● Famines ● Pestilences ● Earthquakes ● Persecution of Israel ● Rise of many false teachers *"ALL THESE ARE THE BEGINNING OF SORROWS"* (24:8).		● The abomination of desolation ● The rise of antichrist and the false prophet ● Armageddon ● The angelic regathering of Israel *"FOR THERE SHALL BE GREAT TRIBULATION"* (24:21).

c. There will be famines, pestilences, earthquakes, and great signs from heaven.

d. Believers will be scourged, imprisoned, hated, betrayed by their own families.

e. Wickedness will be multiplied and the love of many shall grow cold. Note: Many of these things, of course, have taken place throughout the entire church age on a lesser scale, and will doubtless continue right up to the rapture.

4. The tribulation: Last half (Mt. 24:15-31; 36-42; Mk. 13:14-27; 32-37; Lk. 21:25-28; 34-36).

a. The abomination of desolation (a statute of the antichrist) will be unveiled in the Temple Holy of Holies.

b. The world's most severe tribulation and persecution will begin.

c. The sun and moon will be darkened.

d. The sea tides will rise and roar out much destruction.

e. The hearts of men will experience terror as never before.

f. The battle of Armageddon will take place.

g. Christ will return to earth.

5. Thirty-fourth prediction: Concerning his Second Coming (Mt. 24:29-41).

a. His elect will be gathered by angels from everywhere.

b. The unsuspecting wicked will suddenly be removed and destroyed just as they were in Noah and Lot's day.

DD. Thirty-fifth parable: A fig tree and the future (Mt. 24:32-35; Mk. 13:28-31; Lk. 21:29-33).

1. He pictures Israel here (and in other places) as a fig tree.

2. He says that when Israel begins to show signs of life, tremendous events will occur.

a. That the kingdom of God will be near at hand.

b. That the very generation which views the beginning of the budding will live to see the consummation of all things.

EE. Thirty-sixth parable: Five lamps that went out (Mt. 25:1-13).

1. Ten maidens take their lamps and go out to meet the bridegroom.

2. The bridegroom suddenly comes in the dead of the night.

3. Five of the maidens find their lamps need oil and leave to obtain some.

4. They return only to find the door leading to the wedding feast shut.

FF. Thirty-seventh parable: Three stewards and their talents (Mt. 25:14-30).
1. A master turns over his substance to his three bondmen and leaves the country.
   a. He gives one man five talents.
   b. He gives another two talents.
   c. He gives the third one talent.
2. The master returns and requires a stewardship report.
   a. The man with five talents has gained five more and is rewarded.
   b. The man with two talents has gained two more and is likewise rewarded.
   c. The man with the one talent has wasted his and is punished. This parable is similar to that of the pounds in Luke 19:11-27. The difference seems to be that the *pounds* represent the equal opportunities of life while the *talents* speak of the different gifts God gives each individual.

GG. Thirty-eighth parable: Separating the sheep from the goats (Mt. 25:31-46).
1. At his Second Coming Jesus will place the sheep (believers) at his right hand.
   a. His words of praise:
      (1) "You are blessed by the Father and will inherit his eternal kingdom."
      (2) "You fed me and gave me water when I was hungry and thirsty."
      (3) "You welcomed me as a stranger."
      (4) "You clothed me when I was naked."
      (5) "You visited me when I was sick and in prison."
   b. Their question: "When did we do all these things for you?"
   c. His answer: "Inasmuch as you did it to one of the least of these my brothers, you did it to me."
2. At his Second Coming Jesus will place the goats (unbelievers) at his left hand.
   a. His words of condemnation:
      (1) "Depart from me you cursed, into the devil's fire."
      (2) "I was hungry and thirsty but received nothing from you."
      (3) "I was a stranger and received no welcome from you."
      (4) "I was naked but you made no offer to clothe me."
      (5) "I was sick and in prison, but received no visit from you."
   b. Their question: "When did we treat you like this?"
   c. His answer: "Inasmuch as you did it not to one of the least of these, you did it not to me."

HH. Thirty-fifth prediction: Concerning his death (Mt. 26:2).
II. Old Testament Prophecy Fulfillment Number 22, That his friend would betray him for thirty pieces of silver. (Compare Ps. 41:9; 55:12-14; Zech. 11:12, 13 with Mt. 26:14-16, 21-25.)

1. The Jews assemble at Caiaphas' palace and plot to kill Jesus (Mt. 26:3-5; Mk. 14:1, 2; Lk. 22:2).
2. Satan enters Judas and he joins this plot for thirty pieces of silver (Mt. 26:14, 15; Mk. 14:10, 11; Lk. 22:3-6).

THURSDAY

JJ. Jesus sends Peter and John into Jerusalem to prepare for the Passover (Mt. 26:17-19; Mk. 14:12-16; Lk. 22:7-13).
1. They are to follow a man carrying a pitcher of water.
2. He will lead them to the Passover in the upper room.

KK. Jesus enters the room with his disciples (Mt. 26:20-29; Mk. 14:17-25; Lk. 22:14-34; Jn. 13:1—14:31).
1. He comments on the supper (Lk. 22:14-18).
   a. That he desires to eat with them before he will suffer.
   b. That he will celebrate no other Passover until things are fulfilled in the kingdom of God.
2. He washes the feet of his disciples (Jn. 13:1-17).
   a. Peter to Jesus: "Lord, are you washing my feet?"
   b. Jesus to Peter: "What I am doing you do not know now, but you will know hereafter."
   c. Peter to Jesus: "Never may you wash my feet."
   d. Jesus to Peter: "If I do not wash you, you have no part with me."
   e. Peter to Jesus: "Lord, not my feet only, but also my hand and my head."
   f. Jesus to Peter: "He who has bathed needs not to wash, except his feet, but is clean over all."
      Here in John 13:10 Jesus uses two separate Greek words.
      "Jesus saith to him, he that is washed [*louo*, to bathe completely] needeth not save to wash [*nipto*, to splash one's feet, hands, or face] his feet."
      The background here is that of a Jewish person returning from the public baths. On the way home his feet may become dirty and require cleansing, but not his entire body.
      Thus, when a sinner repents, he is forever clean. (See Heb. 10:1-12.) This corresponds to the *louo* bath. However, during his earthly walk, the believer will, on occasion, allow sin to defile certain parts of his body. Sometimes it is his hands, other times his feet, and often his tongue. He now needs a *nipto* cleansing. This is provided in 1 John 1:9:
      "If we confess our sins, he is faithful and just to forgive us our sins, and to cleanse us from all unrighteousness."
   g. Jesus to the twelve:
      (1) That they ought to follow his example and wash one another's feet.

(2) That a bondman is not greater than his master.

3. Thirty-sixth prediction: His betrayal (Jn. 13:18-33; Mt. 26:21-25; Mk. 14:18-21; Lk. 22:21-23).

a. The disciples are shocked and inquire as to who it would be.

b. Jesus states it will be the one to whom he gives the morsel when he dips it.

c. Jesus tells Judas privately that he knows he is the betrayer.

d. Satan enters Judas and he departs from the upper room.

e. The disciples believe Judas is on an errand for Jesus.

4. He institutes the Lord's Supper (Mt. 26:26-29; Mk. 14:22, 25; Lk. 22:19, 20).

a. The bread: "Take eat; this is my body, which is given for you. This do in remembrance of me."

b. The cup: "This cup which is poured out for you is my blood of the new covenant, which is poured out for many for the remission of sins."

Note his statement at this point:

"But I say unto you, I will not drink hereafter of this fruit of the vine, until that day when I drink it new with you in my Father's kingdom" (Mt. 26:29).

We learn from this that the Passover will be reinstated during the millennium.

5. He rebukes the disciples' strife (Lk. 22:24-27; Jn. 13:34, 35).

a. They were arguing concerning who was greatest among them.

b. Jesus tells them the greatest one is the one who is the most humble.

6. Thirty-seventh prediction: The death of Peter (Jn. 13:36).

a. "You cannot follow me now."

b. "You shall follow me afterward."

7. Thirty-eighth prediction: Concerning Peter's first three denials (Jn. 13:38; Lk. 22:34). Note: The Gospel chronology, as arranged by *The Life of Christ in Stereo*, clearly indicates Peter would betray his Lord not three times on one occasion, but six times on two occasions. Thus:

a. In the upper room Jesus predicted the first occasion, saying Peter would deny him three times before the cock crowed at all. (See Jn. 13:38; Lk. 22:34.)

b. En route to Gethsemane, Jesus predicted the second occasion, saying Peter would deny him before the cock crowed twice. (See Mt. 26:34; Mk. 14:30.)

8. The order of the Passover is probably as follows:

a. Jesus gives thanks and they drink from the cup.

b. The bitter herbs are introduced, symbolizing their previous life of bondage in Egypt.

c. The Passover lamb is introduced and explained.

d. The singing of the Hallel, Psalms 113, 114, took place.

e. Jesus probably ceremonially washed his hands, then, taking two cakes of bread, went through the ceremony of breaking one cake.

f. The entire group then partook of the roasted lamb and bitter herbs.

9. Observe the conversation that took place when Jesus announced the first denials in the upper room.

a. Peter: "I will lay down my life for your sake."

b. Jesus: "Simon, Satan demanded that he might have you disciples, that he might sift you like wheat; but I prayed for you Peter, that your faith may not fail. And when you have turned back, strengthen your brethren."

c. Peter: "Lord, I am ready to go with you, both to prison and to death." He would, of course, later do both after Pentecost. (See Acts 12:1-18; 2 Pet. 1:14.)

d. Jesus: "Peter, the cock will not at all crow this day till you have denied three times that you know me!"

Note: The devil once requested permission from God to test and torment another choice servant of God, Job by name. (See Job 1-2.) Here Satan apparently asked for the same power over Simon Peter. The apostle may have had this very event in mind when he wrote concerning the devil and the believer in one of his epistles. (See 1 Pet. 5:7-11.) At any rate, it should be a great comfort for all believers to know that the resurrected Savior is even today, at this very moment, praying for them in glory! (See Rom. 8:34; 1 Jn. 2:1; Heb. 7:25; 9:24.)

LL. Fifteenth sermon: On his Father's house (Jn. 14:1-31).

1. He speaks about heaven.

a. His Father's house has many abodes.

b. He is going there to prepare places for them.

c. Thirty-ninth prediction: Concerning his return (Jn. 14:2, 3).

"In my Father's house are many mansions [dwelling places]: if it were not so, I would have told you. I go to prepare a place for you. And if I go and prepare a place for you, I will come again, and receive you unto myself; that where I am, there ye may be also."

Note the phrase, "I will come again, and receive you unto myself." This is the only reference to the rapture in the four-Gospel account, and the first time in Scripture that God promises to take people off this earth.

2. He is questioned by Philip and Thomas.

a. Thomas: "How can we know the way?"

b. Jesus: "I am the way, the truth, and the life."

c. Philip: "Show us the Father."

d. Jesus: "He who has seen me has seen the Father."

3. He speaks about the Holy Spirit (14:16–21).
   a. The Holy Spirit will come and dwell with them forever.
   b. The Holy Spirit will come and teach them all things.
4. He is questioned by Judas (not Iscariot) (14:22, 23).
   a. Judas: "How will you manifest yourself to us and not to the world?"
   b. Jesus:
      (1) "If anyone loves me, he will keep my Word."
      (2) "My Father will love him, and we will come to him and make our abode with him."
5. He speaks about peace (14:26, 27):

a. He promised to leave his peace with them.
b. This peace would keep their hearts from trouble and fear.
6. He suggests they leave the upper room and make their way to Gethsemane. Matthew tells us that, "When they had sung a hymn, they went out into the Mount of Olives" (Mt. 26:30).

Six Psalms are called the "Hallel" Psalms. There are: 113, 114, 115, 116, 117, 118. All of these were to be sung on the eve of the Passover. This is what Jesus and the disciples sang. Note some of the verses in these Psalms:

"The sorrows of death compassed me, and the pains of hell got hold upon me: I found trouble and sorrow" (116:3).

The Thursday Night Passover Sermon of Christ JOHN 14-16

The Savior

CHRIST HIMSELF
- The mystery of his return—first mention of rapture **14:3**
- The mystery of his body **14:20 (See also Eph. 3:1-7; Col. 1:24-27.)**

CHRIST AND THE FATHER
- He declares him **14:7-9**
- He is inseparably linked to him **14:10, 11**
- He glorifies him **14:13**
- He goes to him **14:2, 12, 28; 16:10, 16, 28**

CHRIST AND THE HOLY SPIRIT
- He comes at Christ's prayer **14:16**
- He comes to honor and testify concerning Christ **15:26; 16:13-15**
- He comes to perform a threefold work **16:7-11**

CHRIST AND THE BELIEVER
- He is the Vine **15:1-8, 16**
- They are the branches

The Saint

THE BELIEVER AND THE FATHER
- Indwelled by the Father **14:23**
- Loved by the Father **14:21; 16:27**
- Empowered to do greater works than Christ **14:12**

THE BELIEVER AND THE HOLY SPIRIT
- To teach believers all things **14:26; 16:14, 15**
- To abide forever with believers **14:16**

THE BELIEVER AND PERSECUTIONS
- To expect many persecutions **14:27; 15:18-21**
- To rejoice in all persecutions **16:1-4, 20-22, 33**

THE BELIEVER AND OTHER BELIEVERS
- To love them **15:12-14, 17**

"I will take the cup of salvation, and call upon the name of the Lord" (Ps. 116:13).

"The stone which the builders refused is become the head stone of the corner. This is the Lord's doing; it is marvelous in our eyes. This is the day which the Lord hath made; we will rejoice and be glad in it" (118:22-24).

"Blessed is he that cometh in the name of the Lord . . ." (118:26).

Step Fifty-three: From the upper room to Gethsemane

(Mt. 26:31-56; Mk. 14:26-52; Lk. 22:35-53; Jn. 15:1—18:12).

A. Sixteenth sermon: On the vine and branches (Jn. 15:1—16:33).
  1. He is the vine and all believers are branches in his Father's vineyard.
    a. If a branch is to bear fruit:
      (1) It must be cleansed by the Father.
      (2) It must abide in the Son (15:1-5).
      Note the progression of this: *Fruit, more* fruit, and *much* fruit (15:1-5). This fruit can signify *converts* (Rom. 1:13), Christian *character* (Gal. 5:22, 23), or *conduct* (Phil. 1:11; Rom. 6:21, 22).
    b. If a branch fails to bear fruit, it is rejected and cast aside (15:6). There is a problem concerning these fruitless branches that are removed from the vine (15:2, 6). Three theories are offered at this point.
      One, that the removed branches represent Christians who lose their salvation.
      Two, that they are Christians who commit the sin unto death as described in Acts 5:1-11; 1 Corinthians 11:27-34; 1 John 5:16. The burning, according to this theory, would be their works, as seen in 1 Corinthians 3:11-15.
      Three, that they represent mere professing Christians (religious people) who are finally severed from their superficial connection with Christ. This had already happened with Judas. (See Jn. 13:27-30; 17:12.)
  2. He has been unjustly hated by the world, and his disciples will be likewise hated (15:18-25).
    a. They will be banished by religious groups.
    b. They will be murdered in the "name" of God.
  3. He must depart to the Father so that the Holy Spirit may come (15:26; 16:7-15).
    "Nevertheless I tell you the truth; It is expedient for you that I go away" (16:7).
    Prior to this the high priest had also used the word "expedient" as did Jesus here. (See Jn. 11:50; 18:14.)
    a. The Holy Spirit will testify of and glorify the Son.
    b. The Holy Spirit will convict the world of sin, righteousness, and judgment.
      (1) Of sin, because men did not believe on him.
      (2) Of righteousness, because he was going to his Father.
      (3) Of judgment, because the world's ruler (Satan) has been judged.
    c. The Holy Spirit will guide believers into all truth.
  4. He issues a fourfold promise to his followers (16:20-33).
    a. That their present sorrow would turn into joy (as the sorrow of a travailing woman blends into joy at the birth of her child).
    b. That they can freely ask of the Father concerning their needs in the Son's name.
    c. That they will have peace in tribulation.
    d. That they will have courage to overcome the world.
    Note his statement in John 16:28, which is really a summary of his ministry.
    "I come forth from the Father [the incarnation], and am come into the world [the manifestation]: again I leave the world [the crucifixion], and go to the Father [the resurrection and ascension]."

B. Thirteenth prayer: After leaving the upper room (Jn. 17:1-26).
  1. He offers a ninefold review of the past: what the Son had done.
    a. He had given eternal life to all the elect (v. 2).
    b. He had glorified the Father (v. 4).
    c. He had completed his assignment (v. 4).
    d. He had revealed the Person of God to man (vs. 6, 26).
    e. He had declared the Word of God to man (vs. 8, 14).
    f. He had kept the elect (v. 12; see also 18:9).
    g. He had sent them into the world (v. 18).
    h. He had sanctified (separated) himself for them (v. 19).
    i. He had shared with them his glory (v. 22).
  2. He offers a ninefold recommendation for the future: what the Father should do.
    a. He asks the Father to glorify the Son (vs. 1, 5).
    b. He asks the Father to keep the elect (v. 11).
    c. He asks the Father to unify the elect (v. 11).
    d. He asks the Father to fill them with joy (v. 13).
    e. He asks the Father to protect them (v. 15).
    f. He asks the Father to sanctify them (v. 17).
    g. He asks the Father to guide them in the world (v. 23).
    h. He asks the Father to gather them in the heavenlies (v. 24).
    i. He asks the Father to fill them with love (v. 26).
    In this prayer Jesus prays for himself (17:1-5), for the disciples (17:6-19), and for the church (17:20-26).
    Note: What a blessed "Father and Son" business meeting this prayer was! Now the Son is in his Father's house and the Holy Spirit is busily at work carrying out those "recommendations of redemption" as laid down by the Son and agreed upon by the Father.

C. He advises his disciples to plan for the future (Lk. 22:35-38).

The Great High Priestly Prayer—JOHN 17

A Report of the Past

What the Son had done

He had completed his mission

- By glorifying the Father **(17:4)**
- By providing salvation, security, and service for the elect **(17:2, 12, 18)**
- By revealing the person of God to men **(17:6, 26)**
- By revealing the Word of God to men **(17:8, 14)**

He was ready to die **(17:19)**

A Recommendation for the Future

What the Father should do

Glorify the Shepherd **(17:1, 5)**

Edify the sheep

- By keeping them **(17:11)**
- By unifying them **(17:11)**
- By filling them with joy **(17:13)**
- By protecting them **(17:15)**
- By sanctifying them **(17:17)**
- By perfecting them **(17:23)**
- By someday receiving them **(17:24)**
- By filling them with love **(17:26)**

---

1. In the past they were sent forth without purse or provision.
2. In the future they were to make full provision for themselves. At this point Christ says:

   "For I say unto you that this that is written must yet be accomplished in me, and he was reckoned among the transgressors; for the things concerning me have a fulfillment" (Lk. 22:37).

   Here Christ emphatically applies to himself a portion of Isaiah 53. (See also Acts 8:32–35.)

D. He sings a hymn with his disciples en route to the Mt. of Olives (Mk. 14:26; Mt. 26:30).

E. Fortieth prediction: That his disciples would forsake him (Mt. 26:31).

F. Forty-first prediction: That he would see them in Galilee after his resurrection (Mt. 26:32; Mk. 14:28; 16:7).
   1. All will be caused to stumble because of him.
   2. The shepherd will be smitten and the flock will be scattered.

G. Forty-second prediction: Concerning Peter's second set of three denials (Mt. 26:33–35; Mk. 14:29–31).
   1. Peter: "Even if all are made to stumble because of you, yet not I; I will never be made to stumble."
   2. Jesus: "During this night, before the cock crows twice, you will deny me three times."
   3. Peter: "Even if I must die with you, I will not at all deny you."

H. He crosses the brook Kidron and enters Gethsemane (Mt. 26:36; Mk. 14:32; Jn. 18:1). Some ten centuries earlier King David had made a similar night walk across the Kidron. (See 2 Sam. 15:23, 30.) Both men had suffered rejection by their own flesh and blood and both had wept over this.

I. He asks Peter, James, and John to watch and pray with him (Mt. 26:37, 38; Mk. 14:33; Lk. 22:40).

J. He experiences the agony of the hour (Mt. 26:37, 38; Mk. 14:33, 34).
   1. He was sorrowful, amazed, and deeply distressed.
   2. He said his soul was near death.

K. Old Testament Prophecy Fulfillment Number 23, That he would be a man of sorrows. (Compare Isa. 53:3 with Mt. 26:37, 38.)

L. Fourteenth prayer: His first garden prayer (Mt. 26:39; 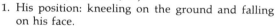 Mk. 14:35, 36; Lk. 22:41, 42).
   1. His position: kneeling on the ground and falling on his face.
   2. His prayer:
      a. "My Father, if it be possible, let this cup pass from me."
      b. "Nevertheless, not as I will, but as thou wilt."

M. He returns and finds the disciples sleeping (Mt. 26:40, 41; Mk. 14:37, 38).
   1. "Simon, are you asleep?"
   2. "So you could not watch with me one hour!"
   3. "Watch and pray, that you enter not into temptation."
   4. "The spirit indeed is willing, but the flesh is weak."

N. Fifteenth prayer: His second garden prayer (Mt. 26:42; Lk. 22:44; Mk. 14:39).
   1. His position: Kneeling, with his sweat dropping as great drops of blood.

2. His prayer:
   a. "My Father, if thou art willing, take away this cup from me."
   b. "Nevertheless, if this cannot pass from me unless I drink it, not my will, but thine, be done."

      Contrast the "not my will" of Jesus with the self-will of Satan. See Isaiah 14:12-14. Gethsemane thus becomes his preparation for Calvary. At Golgotha he yielded up his *body*, but here in Gethsemane he offered up his *will*.

O. He is strengthened by an angel from heaven (Lk. 22:43).

P. He finds his disciples sleeping for the second time (Mt. 26:43; Mk. 14:40).

Q. Many artists and songwriters have depicted this prayer for us, and their descriptions usually show a hushed and tranquil scene, with the light from heaven falling upon a kneeling Savior, his hands clasped devoutly in front, his eyes cast heavenward, and his lips moving faintly as he prays his "cup of suffering" prayer. All is silent, subdued, and serene. But this is not the biblical account at all. The careful student can almost hear the shrieks of demons and the crackling flames which filled the gentle Garden of Gethsemane that awful night. Notice our Lord's own description of his feelings during that hour. He says he was:
   1. "Sore amazed"—that is, he was suddenly struck with surprised terror (Mk. 14:33).
   2. "Very heavy"—that is, he experienced the totally unfamiliar which bore down upon his soul and filled it with uncertainty and acute distress (suggested exegesis here by the late Kenneth S. Wuest, Greek Instructor, Moody Bible Institute).
   3. "Exceeding sorrowful unto death"—that is, he was so completely surrounded and encircled by grief that it threatened his very life.

      From all this it becomes evident that the devil made an all-out effort to murder the Savior in the garden in order to prevent his blood being shed a few hours later on the cross. Our Lord realized this and responded accordingly, as we are told in Hebrews 5:7:

      "Who in the days of his flesh, when he had offered up prayers and supplications with strong crying and tears unto him that was able to save him from death, and was heard in that he feared."

      The Father heard his cry for aid and sent angels to strengthen him. (See Lk. 22:43.) We are told that he wrestled his way through three prayer sessions in the garden and he referred to "the cup" during each prayer. What was this cup his soul so dreaded to drink from? Some say it was the cup of human suffering, but our Lord was no stranger to suffering and pain, for he had known these things throughout his ministry. Others claim it was the cup of physical death that our Lord abhorred here.

      But again, it must be realized that he was the Prince of life, and therefore, death would hold no terror for him.

What then, was the nature of this cursed cup? We are not left groping in the dark here, for the Scriptures plainly inform us that the Gethsemane cup was filled with the sins of all humanity! Our Lord looked deeply into the cesspool of human sin that dark night and groaned as he smelled its foul odor and viewed the rising poisonous fumes.

Was there no other way to redeem man than by drinking this corrupt cup? There was no other way. In a few short hours he would drain that container of its last bitter drop of human depravity.

Hebrews 2:9: "But we see Jesus, who was made a little lower than the angels for the suffering of death, crowned with glory and honour; that he by the grace of God should taste death for every man."

(See also Isa. 53; Rom. 4:25; 1 Pet. 2:24; 3:18; 2 Cor. 5:21.)

R. Sixteenth prayer: His third garden prayer (Mt. 26:44).

S. He finds his disciples sleeping for the third time (Mt. 26:45, 46; Mk. 14:41; Lk. 22:45, 46).
   1. "Are you sleeping even now, and taking your rest?"
   2. "It is enough! Behold, the hour has come, and the Son of man is being betrayed into the hands of sinners."
   3. "Rise, let us be going. Lo, my betrayer is at hand."

T. He is betrayed by the kiss of a turncoat (Mt. 26:47-56; Mk. 14:43-52; Lk. 22:47-53; Jn. 18:2-12).
   1. Judas leads a band of soldiers and Jewish rulers to Gethsemane. A band of men equaled one tenth of a Roman legion. A legion was 6000 men. Then some 600 soldiers appeared here in the garden to arrest him.
   2. He approaches Jesus.
      a. Jesus: "Friend, for what purpose have you come?"
      b. Judas: "Master, Master, hail, Master!"
      c. Jesus: "Judas, are you betraying the Son of man with a kiss?"
   3. Jesus approaches the soldiers.
      a. Jesus: "Whom do you seek?"
      b. The soldiers: "Jesus of Nazareth!"
      c. Jesus: "I am he."

         (At this, the amazed soldiers fall to the ground and must be assured once again that he is indeed the one they seek.) (See Ps. 27:1, 2; 40:14.)
      d. Jesus: "If, therefore, you are seeking me, let those go away." (He said this that the Scripture prophecy might be fulfilled: "Of them which thou gavest me I have lost none" (Jn. 18:9).
   4. Jesus is seized by the soldiers.

U. Thirty-fifth miracle: Restoring a severed ear (Mt. 26:51; Mk. 14:47; Lk. 22:50, 51; Jn. 18:10).
   1. Peter draws his sword and cuts off the right ear of Malchus, a servant of the high priest.
   2. Jesus quickly restores the severed ear, saying, "Permit even this."

V. Jesus rebukes Peter concerning his violent act (Mt. 26:52–54; Jn. 18:11).
   1. "Put back your sword into its sheath; for all who take the sword will perish by the sword."
   2. "Or do you think that I cannot now pray to my Father, and he will presently give me more than twelve legions of angels?"
      Compare this with the power of just one angel. (See 2 Ki. 19:35.)
   3. "But how then would the scripture be fulfilled, that it must be so?"
   4. "The cup which the Father has given me, shall I not drink it?" There are many "cups" in the Bible: The cup of *salvation* (Ps. 116:13), of *consolation* (Jer. 16:7), of *joy* (Ps. 23:5), and of *judgment* (Ps. 11:6; Jer. 25:15; Rev. 14:10).

W. Jesus rebukes his captors concerning their violent act (Mt. 26:55; Mk. 14:48, 49; Lk. 22:52, 53).
   1. "Have you come out as against a robber, with swords and clubs to seize me?"
   2. "Daily I sat with you, teaching in the temple, and you did not arrest me, you stretched forth no hands against me."
   3. "But this has all come to pass that the scriptures of the prophets may be fulfilled."
   4. "This is your hour, and the power of darkness."

X. He is forsaken by all (Mt. 26:56; Mk. 14:50–52).
   1. The disciples flee.
   2. A certain young man (John Mark?) who has been following him flees.

 Y. Old Testament Prophecy Fulfillment Number 24, That he would be forsaken by his disciples. (Compare Zech. 13:7 with Mt. 26:31, 56.)

FIRST UNFAIR TRIAL

Step Fifty-four: From Gethsemane to Annas' house
(Jn. 18:12–14; 19–24).

A. Jesus is questioned by Annas concerning his disciples and his teaching.

B. Jesus answers:
   1. "I spoke openly to the world."
   2. "I taught in the synagogues and in the Temple."
   3. "I said nothing in secret."
   4. "Question those who have heard me as to what I said."

C. Jesus is slapped by an officer of Annas.

D. This marks the first of seven trials our Lord was subjected to. The *New Scofield Bible* aptly summarizes these terrible trials.
   "There were two legal systems that condemned Christ: the Jewish and the Roman, the very two which underlie modern jurisprudence. The arrest and proceedings under Annas, Caiaphas, and the Sanhedrin were under Jewish law; those under Pilate and Herod were under Roman law. The Jewish trial was illegal in several particulars:

   1. The judge was not impartial and did not protect the accused. There is no evidence that the quorum of twenty-three judges took part in the arrest; and they were hostile (Mt. 26:62, 63).
   2. The arrest was unlawful because it was carried out under no formal accusation.
   3. In criminal trials all sessions had to be started and carried on only during the day. Night sessions were illegal.
   4. A verdict of guilty could not be rendered on the same day as the conclusion of the trial. It had to be given on the next day.
   5. The search for hostile testimony was illegal (Mt. 26:59; Mk. 14:56; Jn. 11:53).
   6. No accused could be convicted on his own evidence, yet the accusers sought replies and admissions from Christ to condemn him (Mt. 26:63–66; Jn. 18:19).
   7. No valid legal evidence was presented against him.
   After Pilate declared Christ innocent (Mt. 27:24), his subsequent acts were all contrary to the letter and spirit of Roman law." (p. 1042)

SECOND UNFAIR TRIAL

Step Fifty-five: From Annas' house to Caiaphas' palace
(Mt. 26:57—27:1; Mk. 14:53–72; Lk. 22:54–71; Jn. 18:15–18, 25–27).

A. Peter and John follow Jesus afar off.

B. Caiaphas and the assembled Sanhedrin make a miserable but unsuccessful attempt to condemn Christ through the testimony of false witnesses.
   1. The attempt: "We heard this man say, I will destroy this temple of God that is made with hands, and in three days I will build another, not with hands."
   2. The results: "For even though many false witnesses came forward and testified against him, their testimony did not agree."

C. Caiaphas questions Jesus.
   1. The high priest: "Are you the Messiah, the Son of God?"
   2. The Savior:
      a. "It is as you have said: I am."
      b. "Hereafter you will see the Son of man sitting at the right hand of power and coming upon the clouds of heaven."

D. Forty-third prediction: Concerning his Second Coming (Mt. 26:64).

E. Caiaphas tears his clothes at Christ's answer. By doing this he breaks the Levitical law (see Lev. 21:10).
   1. "He has spoken blasphemy."
   2. "Why need we any more witnesses?"

F. Caiaphas and his group condemn Christ to die and turn on him like vicious wolves.
   1. They spit in his face (see also Mt. 27:26, 30).
   2. They strike him with their fists.

3. They blindfold him and mock him: "Prophesy to us, you Messiah!"
4. "Who is it that struck you?"

 G. Old Testament Prophecy Fulfillment Number 25, That he would be scourged and spat upon. (Compare Isa. 50:6 with Mt. 26:67; 27:26.)

H. Peter denies his Lord (Mt. 26:58, 69-75; Mk. 14:54, 66-72; Lk. 22:54-62; Jn. 18:15-18, 25-27). We have already observed the possibility that Christ predicted Peter would deny him six times, three times before the cock crowed at all, and three times before it crowed twice. It is, of course, impossible to be dogmatic here. The following is but a suggested chronological outline of these denials.
1. Peter and John arrive (after following him afar off) at the courtyard of the high priest.
2. John (who knew the high priest) apparently enters the trial room itself where Jesus stands before Annas and Caiaphas.
3. Peter stands outside, frightened and frustrated over the events of the past few hours.
4. To warm himself, he walks up to a fire which has been built for the bondservants and Temple guards.
First denials:
a. A servant girl who attends the door: "You are not also one of this man's disciples, are you?" Peter: "I am not!"
b. The guards (same question): Peter: "I am not!"
c. A servant girl of the high priest: "This man, too, was with Jesus of Nazareth . . . you, too, were with the Galilean."
Peter: "Woman, I know him not. I do not know or even understand what you are talking about."
(At this moment a cock suddenly crows.)
Second denials (perhaps an hour or so later);
d. A man and a woman: "This man, too, was with Jesus of Nazareth!"
Peter: Once again, he denies this relationship.
e. A man and a servant girl: "Of a truth, this man also was with him, for, he too, is a Galilean!"
Peter: Denies all this.
f. A bondservant relative of Malchus: "Did not I see you in the garden with him? Surely you also are one of them! For you are a Galilean and even your speech confirms it and betrays you."
Peter: He begins to curse and swear, "I know not this man of whom you speak; man, I know not what you are talking about."
(While he is yet speaking, the cock crows a second time.)

I. The Lord turns and looks upon Peter (Mt. 26:75; Mk. 14:72; Lk. 22:61, 62). Note: Somehow the Lord overhears Peter cursing and denying him, and looks sadly upon his disciple.
1. Peter remembers the prophecy of the crowing cock and his own denials.
2. He is stricken in his thoughts and goes out weeping bitterly. It is not our sin that causes us to weep. It is rather seeing the Savior that we have sinned against that causes us to weep.

J. Jesus is formally convicted by the Sanhedrin (Mt. 27:1, 2; Mk. 15:1; Lk. 22:66—23:1).
1. The Sanhedrin: "If you are the Messiah, tell us."
2. The Savior:
a. "If I should tell you, you would not at all believe."
b. "Hereafter will the Son of man be seated at the right hand of the power of God."
c. Forty-fourth prediction: Concerning his Second Coming (Lk. 22:69).
3. The Sanhedrin: "So you are the Son of God?"
4. The Savior: "It is as you are saying, for I am."
5. The Sanhedrin: "What need have we for more testimony? For we have heard it ourselves from his own mouth."

K. Judas commits suicide (Mt. 27:3-10).
1. Judas is overcome with remorse and returns to the priests the thirty pieces of silver.
a. Judas: "I have sinned by betraying innocent blood." Judas' "repentance" was not the godly repentance of 2 Corinthians 7:10.
b. The priests: "What is that to us? You see to that."
2. Judas leaves and hangs himself.
3. The priests take the money and buy a potter's field as a burying ground for strangers.
"Then was fulfilled that which was spoken by Jeremiah the prophet, saying, And they took the thirty pieces of silver . . ." (Mt. 27:9).
There is a problem here, for this is a quote from Zechariah 11:12, 13.
Dr. John Walvoord suggests:
"Perhaps the best explanation is that the third section of the Old Testament began with the book of Jeremiah and included all that followed. Just as the first section was called the law, after the first five books, and the second section was called the Psalms, although other books were included, so that third part began with Jeremiah, and the reference is related to this section of the Old Testament rather than to the book of Jeremiah."

L. Old Testament Prophecy Fulfillment Number 26, That his price money would be used to buy a potter's field. (Compare Zech. 11:12, 13; Jer. 18:1-4; 19:1-4 with Mt. 27:9, 10.)

Step Fifty-six: From Caiaphas' palace to Pilate's hall
(Mt. 27:2, 11-14; Mk. 15:1-5; Lk. 23:1-6; Jn. 18:28-38).

A. Pilate and the Jews:
1. Pilate demands to know what Jesus has done.
2. The Jews evade the question, saying only that he is an evil-doer.

3. Pilate refuses to take any action unless specific charges are made.
4. The Jews then relate their grievances, realizing that no death penalty can be incurred without Pilate's permission.
5. Jesus is thereupon indicted on a threefold count.
   a. That he perverted the nation Israel. This was false. (See Mt. 5:17.)
   b. That he forbade the giving of tribute to Caesar. This too was false. (See Mt. 22:21.)
   c. That he claimed to be the promised Messiah. This was true. (See Jn. 4:26.)

B. Pilate and the Savior:
   1. Pilate asks him if he is the King of the Jews.
   2. Jesus answers that he is, but that his kingdom is not of this world, else his attendants would fight to save his life.
   3. Jesus tells Pilate that he came into the world to bear winess to the truth.
   4. Pilate asks Jesus, "What is truth?" but walks out before the Savior can answer.

C. Pilate and the Jews:
   1. Pilate reports to the waiting Jews that he can find no fault with Jesus.
   2. The Jews retort that he has stirred up trouble from Galilee down to Jerusalem.
   3. Pilate, upon hearing that Jesus is a Galilean, turns him over to the jurisdiction of Herod, who is also in Jerusalem at this time.

FIFTH UNFAIR TRIAL

Step Fifty-seven: From Pilate's hall to Herod's palace
(Lk. 23:7–12).

A. Herod is extremely glad to see Jesus.
   1. He had heard so much and had desired to see him for a long time.
   2. He hoped Jesus would perform some miraculous sign for his amusement.

B. Herod asks Jesus many questions, but the Savior answers him not a word.

C. Herod thereupon ridicules and mocks him by dressing him in gaudy apparel.

D. Jesus is finally sent back to Pilate at Herod's command.

E. Pilate and Herod use this incident to erase an enmity that has existed between them and become friends from this day on.

SIXTH UNFAIR TRIAL

Step Fifty-eight: From Herod's palace to Pilate's hall
(Mt. 27:15–26; Mk. 15:6–15; Lk. 23:13–25; Jn. 18:39—19:16).
A. Pilate sets Jesus before the Jews, offering to chastise and release him.

THE FINAL DAYS OF CHRIST'S MINISTRY

SATURDAY
Anointed by Mary
(Jn. 12:1-11)

SUNDAY
The triumphal entry
(Jn. 12:12-19)

MONDAY
Second Temple cleansing
Cursing of the fig tree
(Mt. 21:12-22)

TUESDAY
Confrontation with the Pharisees
● About his authority **(Mt. 21:23-27)**
● About paying of tribute **(Mt. 22:15-22)**
● About the resurrection **(Mt. 22:23-33)**
● About the greatest commandment **(Mt. 22:34-40)**
Denunciation of the Pharisees
(Mt. 23)
Request by the Greeks
(Jn. 12:20-50)
Mt. Olivet discourse
(Mt. 24-25)

WEDNESDAY
DAY OF SILENCE

THURSDAY
Preparation for the Passover
(Mk. 14:12-16)
Events in the upper room
(Jn. 13-14; Mt. 26:20-35)
En route to Gethsemane
(Jn. 15-16)
The great high priestly prayer
(Jn. 17)
In Gethsemane
(Mt. 26:36-56)
Final pre-Calvary miracle
(Lk. 22:50, 51)

FRIDAY Unfair trials and Crucifixion

1. He reminds them that neither he nor Herod could find any fault with him.
2. He reminds them of their Passover custom whereby a Jewish prisoner is released.
3. He is himself reminded of his wife's sobering message: "Do nothing to that righteous man, for I suffered many things today in a dream because of him."

B. Pilate sets Jesus and Barabbas before the Jews, offering to release one of them.
  1. The Jews desire Barabbas over Jesus. It is ironic that the name Barabbas means "son of the father." Pilate then set two men before the howling Jews. Both of them were "sons of the father."
    a. Barabbas was a notable prisoner.
    b. He was a robber, murderer, and insurrectionist.
  2. The Jews demand the crucifixion of Jesus.
C. Pilate still desires to free Jesus and reminds them for the third time that no fault could be discovered in him.
  1. He thereupon has Jesus scourged by the soldiers in an attempt to appease the Jews.
  2. The soldiers ridicule him and place a crown of thorns on his head, striking him as they do.
D. The bloodthirsty Jews are unmoved and continue to demand his death, claiming he made himself the Son of God.
E. Pilate is filled with fear and privately questions Jesus.
  1. He reminds the Lord that he had the power to release or crucify him.
  2. He is, himself, reminded by the Lord that he has no power at all except what was given him from above.
F. The impatient Jews waiting outside now cry out: "If you release this man you are not a friend of Caesar."
  1. Pilate retorts: "Shall I crucify your king?"
  2. The Jews respond: "We have no king but Caesar!"
G. Pilate realizes the hopelessness of the situation and, sensing a riot, washes his hands before the multitude.
  1. Pilate: "I am innocent of the blood of this righteous man."
  2. The Jews: "His blood be on us! And on our children!"
H. Pilate officially condemns Jesus and frees Barabbas.

SEVENTH UNFAIR TRIAL

Step Fifty-nine: From Pilate's hall to the Praetorium court

(Mt. 27:27-31; Mk. 15:16-20).

A. The soldiers gather together to confront Jesus.
  1. They strip him.
  2. They clothe him with purple and place around him a crimson cloak.
  3. They put a crown of thorns on his head.
  4. They place a reed in his right hand.
  5. They bow their knees in mock homage to him.
  6. They ridicule him saying, "Hail, King of the Jews."
  7. They spit on him and strike his head with the reed.
B. The soldiers put his own clothes on him and lead him out for crucifixion.

Step Sixty: From the Praetorium court to Calvary

(Mt. 27:32-56; Mk. 15:21-41; Lk. 23:26-49; Jn. 19:16-37).

A. The soldiers force a man named Simon to bear Jesus' cross to Calvary (Mt. 27:32; Mk. 15:21; Lk. 23:26).
B. A group of sorrowing women follow Jesus and hear his sobering words (Lk. 23:27-31).
  1. "Daughters of Jerusalem, do not weep for me, but for yourselves and for your children."
  2. Forty-fifth prediction: The destruction of Jerusalem (Lk. 23:28-31).
  3. "Then will they begin to say to the mountains, 'Fall on us!' and to the hills, 'Cover us!'"
  4. "For if they do these things in the tree that is green, what will happen in the dry?"
C. Jesus is crucified (Mt. 27:34, 35; Mk. 15:24; Lk. 23:33; Jn. 19:18).
  1. He is placed between two thieves (Mk. 15:27; Lk. 23:32, 33; Mt. 27:38).
  2. He is offered drugged vinegar, but refuses it (Mk. 15:23; Mt. 27:34).
D. Old Testament Prophecy Fulfillment Number 27, That he would be crucified between two thieves. (Compare Isa. 53:12 with Mt. 27:38; Mk. 15:27, 28; Lk. 22:37.)
E. Old Testament Prophecy Fulfillment Number 28, That he would be given vinegar to drink. (Compare Ps. 69:21 with Mt. 27:34, 48; Jn. 19:28-30.)
F. Old Testament Prophecy Fulfillment Number 29, That he would suffer the piercing of his hands and feet. (Compare Ps. 22:16; Zech. 12:10 with Mk. 15:25; Jn. 19:34, 37; 20:25-27.)
G. Seventeenth prayer: First prayer on the cross (Lk. 23:34).
H. Pilate writes an inscription in Hebrew, Greek, and Latin above his head on the cross: "This is Jesus of Nazareth, The King of the Jews" (Mt. 27:37; Mk. 15:26; Lk. 23:38; Jn. 19:19-22).
  1. The Jews are displeased and demand that Pilate change the sign.
  2. Pilate refuses, saying: "What I have written I have written."
The soldiers cast lots for his seamless tunic (Mt. 27:35; Lk. 23:34; Jn. 19:23, 24).

According to the commonly accepted time table, our Lord was placed on the cross on an April Friday at 9 A.M. Here he suffered for some six hours and gave up his spirit at 3:00 in the afternoon. Surely these were the most important six hours of all human history, spent upon a lonely hill outside a city.

I. First cross utterance: "Father, forgive them; for they know not what they do" (Lk. 23:34).

Note: This prayer has bothered some, as it seems to be a blanket pardon for all involved in Jesus' crucifixion. Of course, we know this is not the case. Forgiveness can only come through faith (Eph. 2:8, 9). It has been pointed out by some that the word "forgive" here can also mean "to allow," and is actually translated thereby on at least thirteen other occasions in the New Testament. If this should be the case here, Christ then would pray, "Father, *allow them* to crucify me." Thus the prayer would be a plea to stay the wrath of a righteous Father as he viewed his beloved Son being murdered by sinful and wicked men. (See Mt. 3:15;

19:14; Mk. 1:34.) However, most Bible students would accept the word "forgive" at face value and interpret his prayer as a request for God not to add this horrible crime of regicide (the killing of one's own king) to the personal accounts of those individuals who killed him. Peter and Paul would amplify on this in later sermons (Acts 3:14, 15, 17):

> "But ye denied the Holy One and the Just, and desired a murderer to be granted unto you; and killed the Prince of life, whom God hath raised from the dead; whereof we are witnesses. And now, brethren, I wot that through ignorance ye did it, as did also your rulers."

See also 1 Corinthians 2:8: "Which none of the princes of this world knew: for had they known it, they would not have crucified the Lord of glory." The sinlessness of our Savior is again proven here, for he did *not* pray, "Father, forgive me." He needed no forgiveness for he knew no sin. In summary, the first cross utterance did not mean that men are excusable, but rather forgivable. (Contrast Rom. 2:1 with 1 Tim. 1:13.)

J. Jesus is cruelly mocked by various viewing groups (Mt. 27:39-44; Mk. 15:29-32; Lk. 23:35-39).
   1. Those passing by:
      a. "Aha! You who would destroy the Temple and build it in three days, save yourself!"
      b. "If you are the Son of God, come down from the cross!"
   2. The Jewish rulers:
      a. "He 'saved' others; himself he cannot save!" This was true!
      b. "Let him save himself, if he is the Christ, the chosen one of God."
      c. "He trusted in God; let him deliver him now, if he desires him, for he said, I am the Son of God."
   3. The soldiers: "If you are the king of the Jews, save yourself!"
   4. The two thieves: "If you are the Messiah, save yourself and us."

K. Old Testament Prophecy Fulfillment Number 30, That his garments would be parted and gambled for. (Compare Ps. 22:18 with Lk. 23:34; Jn. 19:23, 24.)

L. Old Testament Prophecy Fulfillment Number 31, That he would be surrounded and ridiculed by his enemies. (Compare Ps. 22:7, 8 with Mt. 27:39-44; Mk. 15:29-32.)

M. One of the dying thieves accepts Christ as his Savior (Lk. 23:40-43).
   1. He repents over his own foolish charges.
   2. He rebukes the unrepentant thief.
      a. "Do you not even fear God, since you are under the same condemnation?"
      b. "We indeed justly, for we are receiving due reward for our deeds, but this man did nothing amiss."
   3. He looks upon Jesus.
      a. The dying robber: "Lord, remember me when you come in your kingdom."
      b. The dying Redeemer: "Verily, I say to you, to-day shall you be with me in Paradise."

N. Second cross utterance: "Verily, I say to you, today shall you be with me in Paradise" (Lk. 23:43).
   Note: This statement emphasizes several facts concerning salvation.

1. That salvation is offered to anyone, anywhere. Are deathbed conversions valid? They are indeed, for here is one. But we quickly note:
   a. There is *one* deathbed conversion in the Bible, so no dying man will despair.
   b. There is *only* one, so no living man will presume. D. L. Moody once said: "Did ever the new birth take place in so strange a cradle?" Observe the contrast here:
      (1) In the morning the thief was nailed to a cross. In the evening he was wearing a crown.
      (2) In the morning he was an enemy of Caesar. In the evening he was a friend of God.
      (3) In the morning he was spurned by men. In the evening he was fellowshiping with angels.
      (4) In the morning he died as a criminal on earth. In the evening he lived as a citizen of heaven.
2. That salvation is by grace through faith alone. This conversion refutes:
   a. The doctrine of sacramentalism. He was saved apart from confirmation, sprinkling, Holy Communion, and church membership.
   b. The doctrine of baptismal regeneration.
   c. The doctrine of purgatory.
   d. The doctrine of universalism. Only *one* thief was saved.
3. That salvation will be rejected by some in spite of everything God can do. The other thief died, eternally lost. Here we see three men:
   a. One was dying *for* sin (the Savior).
   b. One was dying *from* sin (the repentant thief).
   c. One was dying *in* sin (the lost thief).

   All classes of humanity were represented at the cross. There were the indifferent ("the people stood beholding," Lk. 23:35); the religious ("the rulers derided him," Lk. 23:35); the materialistic ("the soldiers parted his raiment and cast lots," Lk. 23:34); and the earnest seeker ("Lord, remember me . . ." Lk. 23:42). The cross is indeed the judgment of this world. See John 12:31.

O. Jesus speaks to his mother and John.
   1. To Mary: "Woman, behold your Son."
   2. To John: "Behold your mother."
      a. Mary has stood by him at the cross along with Mary Magdalene, Salome (the mother of James and John), and other faithful women.
      b. John now takes Mary home to live with him.

P. Third cross utterance: "Woman, behold thy son! Behold thy mother!" (Jn. 19:26, 27).

Q. Fourth cross utterance: "My God, my God, why hast thou forsaken me?" (Mt. 27:46).
   Note: This prayer is deeper in its mystery and higher in its meaning than any other single prayer in the Bible. God forsaken by God! Who can understand that? The wisest and most profound Bible student feels utterly inadequate as he approaches it. It can never be mastered by the mortal mind, even though that mind has experienced new birth. Eternity alone will exegete it. Elizabeth Clephane has so well phrased it:

> "But none of the ransomed ever knew,
>   How deep were the waters crossed;
> Nor how dark was the night,
>   That the Lord passed through,
> Ere He found His sheep that was lost."

There are so many unexplained "whys" raised here.
1. Why did the Father turn his back upon the Son?
2. Why did not even the Son know the reason?
3. Why did innocent blood have to be shed for forgiveness of sin?

The first and third of these questions are partially answered in Hebrews 9:22; 1 Peter 2:24; 3:18; Isaiah 53. But what of the second question? Did not Christ know? According to Philippians 2:5-8, Christ voluntarily abstained from employing some of his divine attributes while upon this earth. Thus:
1. He abstained from using his omnipresence for a period (Jn. 11:15).
2. He abstained from using his omnipotence for a period (Jn. 5:19).
3. He abstained from using his omniscience for a period (Lk. 8:45; Mk. 13:32. See also Lk. 2:40).

R. Eighteenth prayer: Second prayer on the cross (Mt. 27:46).
1. A strange dark has obscured the sun from noon until 3:00 P.M.
2. Some of the crowd hear this prayer and think he is calling for Elijah (Mt. 27:45-47).
S. Fifth cross utterance: "I Thirst" (Jn. 19:28).
T. Old Testament Prophecy Fulfillment Number 32, That he would thirst. (Compare Ps. 22:15 with Jn. 19:28.)
1. Someone fills a sponge with sour wine and presses it to his mouth.
2. The bystanders wonder if Elijah will come and save him (Mt. 27:48, 49; Mk. 15:36; Jn. 19:28, 29).
U. Jesus receives the wine and cries out the victory (Mt. 27:50; Mk. 15:37; Jn. 19:30).
V. Sixth cross utterance: "It is finished" (Jn. 19:30).

Note: The sixth statement of Jesus is actually one word in the original Greek. It is *tetelestai*, meaning, "It was finished, and as a result it is forever done." This phrase was a farmer's word. When into his herd there was born an animal so beautiful and shapely that it seemed absolutely destitute of faults and defects, the farmer gazed upon the creature with proud, delighted eyes. *"Tetelestai!"* he said.

It was also an artist's word. When the painter or the sculptor had put the last finishing touches to the vivid landscape or the marble bust, he would stand back a few feet to admire his masterpiece, and, seeing in it nothing that called for correction or improvement, would murmur fondly, *"Tetelestai! Tetelestai!"*

Our Lord cries out, "It is finished!"

There are three important places where the Scriptures employ this word "finish." It is used in Genesis 2:1, referring to the creation of God's works. It is used here in John 19:30, referring to the salvation of his works. (See also Jn. 4:34; 5:36; 17:4.) It is used in Revelation 10:7 and 16:17, referring to the completion of his works.

With gladness we note that he did *not* say, "I am finished," for he was just beginning.

"Lifted up was He to die, 'It is finished,' was his cry;
Now in heav'n exalted high; Hallelujah! What a Savior!"

W. Seventh cross utterance: "Father, into thy hands I commend my spirit" (Lk. 23:46).
X. Nineteenth prayer: Third and final, on the cross (Lk. 23:46).
Y. Old Testament Prophecy Fulfillment Number 33, That he would commend his spirit to the Father. (Compare

Ps. 31:5 with Lk. 23:46.) It should be noted that Jesus left out the last part of Psalm 31:5, which said: "Thou hast redeemed me, O Lord God of truth."

Many awesome wonders follow the Savior's death (Mt. 27:51-56; Mk. 15:38-41; Lk. 23:45, 47-49).
1. A centurion who has watched him suffer and die cries out: "Truly this was a righteous man!"
2. The Temple veil is torn in two, from the top to the bottom.
3. The earth is shaken, some tombs are opened, and many dead saints arise.
4. These saints will later appear to many in Jerusalem after the resurrection.
5. The centurion cries out again in fear and awe: "Surely this man was the Son of God!"
6. The crowd at the cross is dispersed and the people return home beating their breasts.
7. The *Scofield Bible* has the following on these events: "The veil that was torn, or rent, divided the holy place from the holy of holies, into which only the high priest might enter on the Day of Atonement (see Ex. 26:31, note; Lev. 16:1-30). The tearing of that veil, which was a type of the human body of Christ (Heb. 10:20), signified that a 'new and living way' was opened for all believers into the very presence of God, with no other sacrifice or priesthood except Christ's (cf. Heb. 9:1-8; 10:19-22). Although the graves were opened at the time of Christ's death (vs. 50, 51), the bodies did not arise until 'after his resurrection' (v. 53). Christ is the firstborn from among the dead (Col. 1:18; Rev. 1:5) and 'the first fruits of them who slept' (1 Cor. 15:20). It is not said that these bodies returned to their graves. The wave sheaf (Lev. 23:10-12) typifies the resurrection of Christ, but it would appear from the symbol used that plurality is implied. It was a single 'corn of wheat' that fell into the ground in the crucifixion and entombment of Christ (Jn. 12:24); it was a sheaf which came forth in resurrection. The inference is that these saints went with the risen Christ into heaven."
Z. All four Gospel accounts record the death of Christ. But one wonders how such a thing could happen? Was not Christ God incarnate? Indeed he was! How, then, could God have actually died on the cross? To explain this, we must return briefly to the book of Genesis. Here we are told of Adam's creation and of his tragic sin. God had warned him that disobedience would result in death, and so it did. In fact, it brought down upon the head of mankind two kinds of death: physical and spiritual. Both kinds of death here can be defined by one word: separation. That is the biblical and theological meaning of the word death. Physical death is separation, the parting of the soul from one's body. Spiritual death is likewise separation, the parting of the unsaved person from God. This is sometimes called the second death (see Rev. 20:6, 14; 21:8).

So then, these two hellish enemies, physical and spiritual death, let loose by Adam, continued to curse and terrorize the human race for over forty centuries. Then, in the fulness of time, God sent his beloved Son to our world. The Father referred to his Son as the last Adam (among other names) in 1 Corinthians 15:45.

Why this title? Because he had come to undo what the first Adam had previously done; that is, he came to rid mankind of those two evil enemies, physical and spiritual death. This he did while on the cross, where he died spiritually, being separated from God; and died physically as he accomplished both tasks. Spiritual death was immediately given the death blow. Paul later assures us that *nothing* can now separate the believer from the love of God (Rom. 8:35–39). But what about physical death? Paul answers this question in 1 Corinthians 15:51–55:

> "Behold, I shew you a mystery; We shall not all sleep, but we shall all be changed. In a moment, in the twinkling of an eye, at the last trump: for the trumpet shall sound, and the dead shall be raised incorruptible, and we shall be changed. For this corruptible must put on incorruption, and this mortal must put on immortality. So when this corruptible shall have put on incorruption, and this mortal shall have put on immortality, then shall be brought to pass the saying that is written, Death is swallowed up in victory. O death, were is thy sting? O grave, where is thy victory?"

Step Sixty-one: From Calvary to Joseph's tomb

(Mt. 27:57–66; Mk. 15:42–47; Lk. 23:50–56; Jn. 19:31–42).

A. The Jews request that Pilate complete the execution of the thieves and Christ before the Sabbath begins (Jn. 19:31–37). The Jews had just viciously murdered a man but were now expressing their pious "concern" that the body be removed lest the Sabbath be polluted.
  1. The soldiers find the two thieves still alive and break their legs.
  2. The soldiers find the Savior already dead and pierce his side with a spear, gazing upon him as they do.
 B. Old Testament Prophecy Fulfillment Number 34, That his bones would not be broken. (Compare Ps. 34:20; Ex. 12:46; Num. 9:12 with Jn. 19:33–36.)
C. Old Testament Prophecy Fulfillment Number 35, That he would be stared at in death. (Compare Zech. 12:10 with Jn. 19:37; Mt. 27:36.)
D. Joseph of Arimathea boldly asks Pilate for the body of Jesus (Mt. 27:57; Mk. 15:43; Lk. 23:50–52; Jn. 19:38).
  1. Joseph was a rich but secret disciple of Jesus.
  2. He was a reputable member of the Sanhedrin, untainted by their wickedness.
  3. He was a good and righteous man, looking for the kingdom of God.
E. Pilate questions the centurion and learns that Jesus is indeed dead (Mk. 15:44).
F. Joseph is given the lifeless body of the Savior (Mt. 27:58, 59; Mk. 15:45, 46; Jn. 19:38–40).
  1. He gently takes the body down from the cross.
  2. He brings a roll of fine linen cloth.
  3. He is aided by Nicodemus, who comes with 100 pounds of myrrh and aloes.
  4. He and Nicodemus wrap Jesus' body in the clean linen cloths with the spices. The custom was to use about half as many pounds of spices as the weight of the body being prepared. Thus our Lord must have weighed around 190–200 pounds. The body would be prepared by rubbing it with myrrh and aloes, and then wrapping it with linen strips. The process would begin with a finger.

G. Jesus is laid in Joseph's rock-hewn sepulcher (Mt. 27:60, 61; Mk. 15:46, 47; Lk. 23:53–56; Jn. 19:41, 42).
  1. The two men roll a great stone against the door and depart.
  2. The two Marys (Magdalene and possibly Jesus' mother) linger near the tomb for awhile and depart.
H. Old Testament Prophecy Fulfillment Number 36, That he would be buried with the rich. (Compare Isa. 53:9 with Mt. 27:57–60.)

SATURDAY

I. The Pharisees meet with Pilate on the following day (Mt. 27:62–65).
  1. Their request:
    a. "Sir, we remember that that impostor while yet alive said, 'after three days I will arise!'"
    b. "Command therefore that the grave be made secure till the third day, lest his disciples come by night and steal him away, and say to the people, 'He has risen from the dead,' and the last deception be worse than the first."
  2. His answer: "You have a guard detachment; go and make it as secure as you can."
J. The Pharisees secure the sepulcher, seal the stone, and station their guard (Mt. 27:66). It is sad to note that the only group who remembered Christ's oft-repeated prophecies about his resurrection was his enemies.

Step Sixty-two: From Joseph's tomb to the heart of the earth

(1 Pet. 3:18–20).

SUNDAY

Step Sixty-three: From the heart of the earth to the resurrection garden

(Mt. 28:2–4; Mk. 16:9–11; Lk. 24:12; Jn. 20:1–18).

A. Jesus is resurrected physically from the dead. The last two chapters in Matthew (27–28) which speak of his death and resurrection could rightly be entitled, "The King is dead; long live the King!"
  1. There is a great earthquake.
  2. The angel of the Lord descends from heaven.
    a. His appearance is as lightning.
    b. His raiment is as snow.
    c. He rolls the stone away and sits upon it.
  3. The guards tremble, become as dead men, and finally flee in terror. Thus the very soldiers who were ordered to prevent the fulfillment of the prophecy of Christ's resurrection were the first witnesses of it.
B. Old Testament Prophecy Fulfillment Number 37, That he would be raised from the dead. (Compare Ps. 16:10 with Mt. 28:2–7.)
C. Mary Magdalene arrives at the garden to aid in the planned anointing of his body (Jn. 20:1, 2).
  1. She sees the stone has been removed.
  2. She runs and reports to Peter and John: "They took away the Lord from the sepulcher, and we know not where they laid him."

D. Peter and John arrive at the garden (Lk. 24:12; Jn. 20:3–10).
  1. John outruns Peter and, looking into the sepulcher, sees the linen cloths.
  2. Peter arrives and, entering into the sepulcher, sees the head napkin separated from the linen cloths. Thus, like a seed, Jesus came out of his tomb. The old shell (the outer wrappings) were left in the ground. (See Jn. 12:24.)

FIRST RESURRECTION APPEARANCE

E. Mary Magdalene returns to the garden alone (Jn. 20:11–18).
  1. She stands outside the sepulcher weeping.
  2. She looks into the sepulcher and sees two angels.
    a. The angels: "Woman, why are you weeping?"
    b. Mary: "Because they took away my Lord, and I know not where they laid him."
  3. She turns around and sees Jesus, but mistakes him for the gardener.
    a. Jesus: "Woman, why are you weeping; whom are you seeking?"
    b. Mary: "Sir, if you bore him away, tell me where you laid him, and I will take him away."
    c. Jesus: "Mary!"
    d. Mary: "Rabboni!" (Dear Teacher!)
    e. Jesus:
      (1) "Do not touch me, for I have not yet ascended to my Father."
      (2) "But go to my brethren and say to them, 'I am ascending to my Father and your Father, and to my God and your God!'" (Jn. 20:17).
          Note his phrase, "Go to my brethren." There is a progressive intimacy between Jesus and his disciples. He calls them servants (Jn. 13:13), friends (Jn. 15:15), and here, brethren.
  4. Mary runs and tells the disciples that she had seen and spoken to the living Lord, but they do not believe it (Mk. 16:9–11). It was a Samaritan woman to whom Christ first revealed his messiahship. (See Jn. 4:25, 26.) It is now to another woman, Mary Magdalene, that Christ first appears in his resurrection body. Both were formerly women of questionable moral backgrounds. (See Mk. 16:9.)

Step Sixty-four: From the resurrection garden to the Father
(Jn. 20:17).

SECOND RESURRECTION APPEARANCE

Step Sixty-five: From the Father to a road near Jerusalem
(Mt. 28:5–15; Mk. 16:2–8; Lk. 24:1–11).
A. The women who stood by him at the cross arrive at the garden.
  1. They come with spices and ointments to complete his burial.
  2. They anticipate a problem: "Who will roll us away the stone from the door of the sepulcher?"

3. They discover the stone has been moved.
4. They enter the sepulcher and are greeted by two angels.
  a. "Do not fear; do not be amazed. For I know that you seek Jesus of Nazareth, who was crucified."
  b. "Why seek the living among the dead? He is not here, for he has risen, as he said."
  c. "Remember how he spoke to you, while he was yet in Galilee, saying, 'The Son of man must be delivered into the hands of sinful men, and be crucified, and the third day rise again.'"
  d. "But go quickly and tell his disciples, and Peter, that he has risen from the dead. . . . '"
5. The women are filled with fear and joy and hasten to tell his disciples the glorious news.
6. Jesus appears to them en route.
  a. "Rejoice!"
  b. "Fear not; go tell my brethren to go into Galilee, and there shall they see me."
7. The women seize Jesus by the feet and worship him and continue their journey.
8. The disciples discount their unbelievable report as idle tales.
B. The sepulcher guards arrive at the Jerusalem Temple and report Jesus' resurrection.
C. The chief priests bribe them to lie about what really happened.
  1. They were to say: "His disciples came by night and stole him away while we slept."
  2. They are assured that no further punishment will be leveled at them.

THIRD RESURRECTION APPEARANCE

Step Sixty-six: From a road near Jerusalem to the Emmaus Road
(Mk. 16:12, 13; Lk. 24:13–35).
A. Jesus joins two of his followers, Cleopas and another person (his wife?) on the road to Emmaus, but is recognized by neither.
  1. He asks them what they were discussing and why they are so sad.
  2. They ask him where he has been during the recent days, not to have heard of the tremendous events which have taken place. They tell him:
    a. That there was a prophet, Jesus of Nazareth, who had been mighty in word and deed.
    b. That he had been condemned and crucified by their own rulers.
    c. That their personal hopes for Israel's redemption are now shattered.
    d. That his body was discovered missing and that there were unfounded rumors of his resurrection.
B. Jesus rebukes them for their unbelief and expounds the Old Testament Messianic passage to them, beginning with Moses.
C. Cleopas invites Jesus to lodge with them for the night.
D. The two followers recognize Jesus as he takes and blesses the bread at the supper table.
E. Jesus suddenly vanishes from their sight.

F. The couple share their heart experience with each other concerning their walk with the unrecognized stranger: "Did not our hearts burn within us, as he talked with us on the road and kept opening up to us the Scriptures?"

G. They thereupon return to Jerusalem and tell the disciples that Jesus has walked and talked with them.

H. They learn that Christ has also appeared to Peter. What a meeting this must have been. The last time he had seen Christ was when Peter was cursing the Lord!

FOURTH RESURRECTION APPEARANCE

Jesus appears to Simon Peter (Lk. 24:34; 1 Cor. 15:5).

FIFTH RESURRECTION APPEARANCE

Step Sixty-seven: From Emmaus to the upper room

(Lk. 24:36–43; Jn. 20:19–23).

A. Jesus walks through locked doors and appears to ten of his disciples late Sunday night. (Judas was dead and Thomas was absent.)

   1. Their reaction:
      a. By his words.
         (1) "Why are you troubled? And why do doubtings arise in your hearts?"
         (2) "Behold my hands and my feet, that it is I myself."
         (3) "Handle me, and see; for a spirit does not have flesh and bones as you see I have."

   This gives us valuable information concerning our own resurrection body, for we shall have a body like his (1 Jn. 3:2). Jesus had a body of flesh and bone, and so shall we. However, it was not limited by gravity or restricted by time, nor will our resurrected bodies be.

      b. By his deeds.
         (1) He shows them his pierced hands, feet, and side.
         (2) He eats a piece of broiled fish and some of a honeycomb.

B. Jesus breathes on them and imparts to them the Holy Spirit. As we have already noted, the disciples were terrified until they recognized Jesus.

   "And when he had so said, he showed unto them his hands and his side. Then were the disciples glad, when they saw the Lord" (Jn. 20:20).

   The last part of this verse may be compared to a statement made by some Greeks who once said to a disciple: "Sir, we would see Jesus" (Jn. 12:21).

   Early that morning Jesus had told Mary to, "touch me not; for I am not yet ascended to my Father: but go to my brethren, and say unto them, I ascend unto my Father, and your Father; and to my God, and your God" (Jn. 20:17). But here in the evening of that same day he invites the disciples to touch and handle him. Why the change? It is believed by many that he ascended that afternoon to present his blood to the Father for sprinkling upon the mercy seat in the heavenly tabernacle. The debt of sin had now been officially paid.

SIXTH RESURRECTION APPEARANCE

Step Sixty-eight: From the upper room back to the upper room (a week later)

(Jn. 20:24–29).

A. Thomas cannot believe the excited report of the other disciples.
   1. Their testimony: "We have seen the Lord."
   2. His unbelief: "Unless I see in his hands the imprint of the nails and press my finger into the mark of the nails, and my hand into his side, I will not at all believe."

B. Jesus again walks through locked doors and appears to the disciples, including Thomas.
   1. The Savior: "Bring here your finger and look at my hands, and bring your hand and press it into my side, and be not unbelieving but believing."
   2. The doubter: "My Lord and my God."
   3. The Savior: "Because you have seen me, Thomas, you have believed; blessed are they who have not seen, and yet have believed."

SEVENTH RESURRECTION APPEARANCE

Step Sixty-nine: From the upper room to the Sea of Tiberias

(Jn. 21:1–25).

A. Peter and six other disciples have spent an unsuccessful night fishing.

B. Thirty-sixth miracle: Catching a great number of fish (Jn. 21:6).
   1. Jesus calls out to them unrecognized from the shore at dawn: "Children, have ye any meat?" He was, of course, asking them if they had caught any fish! Someday, at the judgment seat of Christ, he will ask us this same question!
   2. The disciples answer in the negative and hear him say: "Cast out the net on the right side of the boat, and you will find some."
   3. The net is cast out and is immediately filled with 153 large fish.
   4. Peter recognizes Jesus and swims to meet him.

C. Jesus cooks breakfast for the seven disciples. He invites them to "come and dine" (Jn. 21:12). We must be fed by him before we can feed others.

D. Peter is closely questioned concerning his affection for Christ.
   1. Three times he is asked if he really loves the Savior.
   2. Three times he answers in the affirmative. In the Greek New Testament there are two different kinds of love. One is *phileo* love, which refers to that warm affection between two human beings. The other kind of love is an *agapao* love, which is a divine love—God's love for sinful man.

   This love is never found in the heart of any man prior to the ascension of Christ. In fact, Jesus asks Peter on three occasions (Jn. 21:15–19) if he really loves him. The first two times Jesus uses the second kind of love and asks the following question. "Peter, do you *agapao* me?" On both occasions Peter answers by choosing the first word. He says, "Lord, you know I *phileo* you." Finally, our Lord (condescendingly) uses the first word also. The reason for all this (as Peter would later find out) is explained in Romans 5:5 by Paul:

" . . . the love (agapao) of God is shed abroad in our hearts by the Holy Ghost which is given unto us."

Thus, the reason Peter answered the way he did was because the Holy Spirit had not yet come at Pentecost and it was therefore impossible for him to love Christ with this divine agapao love. Also to be noted here is Jesus' request that Peter feed his lambs (Jn. 21:15) and his sheep (21:16, 17). Again there is a play on the Greek here, for Christ uses two different words for feed. He says "be grazing my baby lambs," but discipline my older sheep. Today we have this truth in reverse. We discipline the young and feed the old!

E. Forty-sixth prediction: Peter's martyrdom (Jn. 21:18, 19).
1. "When you were younger, you girded yourself and walked where you desired."
2. "But when you are old, you will stretch out your hands and another will gird you and carry you where you would not go." (See 2 Pet. 1:14.)
F. Peter desires to know of the destiny reserved for John the apostle.
1. Peter: "But what of this man, Lord?"
2. Jesus: "If I desire that he remain till I come, what is it to you? Follow me!"
G. Jesus' answer later gives rise to the false rumor that John would never die.

EIGHTH RESURRECTION APPEARANCE

Step Seventy: From the Sea of Tiberias to Mount Tabor
(Mt. 28:16-20).
A. Jesus is worshiped on the mountain by the eleven in spite of some remaining unbelief.
B. He imparts to them a fact, a command, and a promise.
1. The fact: "All authority has been given unto me in heaven and upon earth."
2. The command: "Go therefore and disciple all the nations, baptizing them in the name of the Father and of the Son and of the Holy Spirit, teaching them to observe everything I commanded you."
3. The promise: "Lo, I am with you always, until the consummation of the ages."

NINTH RESURRECTION APPEARANCE

Step Seventy-one: From Mt. Tabor to the upper room
(Mk. 16:14-18; Lk. 24:44-49).
A. He gently rebukes the disciples for their initial unbelief concerning his resurrection.
B. He repeats his command for them to evangelize the world.
C. He expounds the law of Moses and the Psalms to them.
D. He tells them to wait in Jerusalem for the promise of the Father.

TENTH RESURRECTION APPEARANCE

Step Seventy-two: From the upper room to the Mount of Olives
(Mk. 16:19, 20; Lk. 24:50-53; Acts 1:4-11).
A. He blesses them and promises the baptism of the Spirit.
B. He orders them to witness for him:
1. in Jerusalem
2. in Judea
3. in Samaria
4. unto the uttermost part of the earth
C. He is received up into glory to the right hand of the Father.
D. Old Testament Prophecy Fulfillment Number 38, That he would ascend. (Compare Ps. 24:7-10 with Mk. 16:19; Lk. 24:51.) Did the resurrected Christ appear before any unsaved individuals? On the strength of Matthew 23:37-39 it would seem he did not.

"O Jerusalem, Jerusalem, thou that killest the prophets and stonest them which are sent unto thee, how often would I have gathered thy children together, even as a hen gathereth her chickens under her wings, and ye would not! Behold, your house is left unto you desolate. For I say unto you, ye shall not see me henceforth, till ye shall say, Blessed is he that cometh in the name of the Lord."

With these words we conclude our brief study of the greatest life ever lived. It should, however, be said that his glory story is not limited to the four Gospel accounts. In fact, each of the sixty-six biblical books presents a glimpse of this marvelous and mighty Messiah. Note the following "scriptural summary of the Savior."

Christ in Every Book
"Christ is the theme of the entire Revelation of God. He is promised in Genesis, revealed in the Law, prefigured in its history, praised in poetry, proclaimed in its prophecy, provided in its Gospels, proved in its Acts, preeminent in its Epistles and prevailing in Revelation.

He is seen in every book of the Bible. Take a journey through the Halls of Holy Writ and in every one of them you will see Christ. Starting with Genesis He is the Seed of the woman; in Exodus the Lamb for sinners slain; in Leviticus, our High Priest; in Numbers the Star of Jacob and the Brazen Serpent; in Deuteronomy the Prophet like unto Moses and the Great Rock; in Joshua the Captain of the Lord's Hosts; in Judges the Messenger of Jehovah; in Ruth our Kinsman-Redeemer and the Faithful Bridegroom; in 1 Samuel He is seen as the Great Judge; in 2 Samuel as the Princely King; in 1 Kings as David's Choice; in 2 Kings as the Holiest of All; in 1 Chronicles as King by birth; in 2 Chronicles as King by Judgment.

In Ezra He is seen as Lord of heaven and earth; in Nehemiah as the builder; in Esther our Mordecai; in Job our Daysman and our Risen, returning Redeemer; in Psalms the Son of God and the Good Shepherd; in Proverbs our Wisdom; in Ecclesiastes as the One above the sun; in Song of Solomon the great Church lover, the one Altogether Lovely and the Chiefest among ten thousand.

THE TEN RESURRECTION APPEARANCES OF CHRIST

FIRST DAY

1. **To Mary Magdalene in the garden**
   Mk. 16:9; Jn. 20:11-18

2. **To the women returning from the tomb**
   Mt. 28:9, 10

3. **To two disciples on the Emmaus Road**
   Lk. 24:13-32; Mk. 16:12, 13

4. **To Peter in Jerusalem**
   Lk. 24:34; 1 Cor. 15:5

5. **To ten of his apostles in the upper room**
   Lk. 24:36-43; Jn. 20:19-23

REMAINING 40 DAYS

6. **To the eleven in the upper room**
   Jn. 20:24-29

7. **To seven apostles by the Galilean Sea**
   Jn. 21:1-24

8. **To the eleven and 500 believers on Mt. Tabor**
   Mt. 28:16-20; 1 Cor. 15:6

9. **To the eleven and James, Jesus' half-brother, in Jerusalem**
   Mk. 16:14-18; Lk. 24:44-49; 1 Cor. 15:7

10. **To the eleven on the Mount of Olives**
    Lk. 24:50-53

In *Isaiah* He is the suffering and glorified Servant; in *Jeremiah* the Lord our Righteousness; in *Lamentations* the Man of Sorrows; in *Ezekiel* the glorious God; in *Daniel* the Smiting Stone and the Messiah. *Hosea* reveals Him as the risen Son of God; *Joel* as the outpourer of the Spirit; *Amos*, the Eternal Christ; *Obadiah*, the Forgiving Christ; *Jonah* as the Risen Prophet; *Micah* the Bethlehemite; in *Nahum* He is the Bringer of Good Tidings; in *Habakkuk*, the Lord in His Holy Temple; in *Zephaniah* the Merciful Christ; in *Haggai*, the Desire of all nations; in *Zechariah*, the Branch; and in *Malachi*, the Sun of Righteousness with healing in His wings.

Matthew shows Him as King of the Jews; *Mark* the Servant; *Luke* the Perfect Son of Man; *John* the Son of God; in *Acts*, He is the Ascended Lord, in *Romans* the Lord our Righteousness; in *1 Corinthians* our Resurrection; in *2 Corinthians* our Comforter; in *Galatians* the end of the Law; in *Ephesians* the head of the Church; in *Philippians* the Supplier of every need; in *Colossians* the Fullness of the Godhead; in *1 Thessalonians* He comes for His Church; in *2 Thessalonians* He comes with His Church; in *1 Timothy* He is the Mediator; in *2 Timothy* the Bestower of Crowns; in *Titus* Our Great God and Savior; in *Philemon* the Payer of our Debt; in *Hebrews* the rest of the Faith and the Fulfiller of Types; in *James*, the Lord drawing nigh; in *1 Peter* the Vicarious Sufferer; in *2 Peter* the Lord of Glory; in *1 John* the Way; *2 John* the Truth; *3 John* the Life; in *Jude*, He is Our Security; in *Revelation* the Lion of the Tribe of Judah, the Lamb of God, the Bright and Morning Star, the King of kings and Lord of lords." (Robert J. Wells, *Prophetic Messages for Modern Times*; Dallas; Texas Printing House, Inc., 1944; pp. 205, 206)

THE SUMMARIZATION FROM HIS LIFE

1. The thirty-six *miracles* of the Savior.
2. The thirty-eight *parables* of the Savior.
3. The nineteen *prayers* of the Savior.
4. The forty-five *predictions* of the Savior.
5. The sixteen *sermons* of the Savior.
6. The thirty-six *dialogues* of the Savior.
7. The sixteen *Old Testament references* of the Savior.
8. The twenty-two *Old Testament quotes* of the Savior.
9. The tenfold proof of the *deity* of the Savior.
10. The thirtyfold proof of the *humanity* of the Savior.
11. The thirty-seven *names and titles* of the Savior.
12. The thirty-seven *Old Testament prophecies fulfilled* by the Savior.
13. The twenty-seven *souls converted* by the Savior.
14. The fifteen *kinds of sufferings* experienced by the Savior.
15. The seven *last statements* of the Savior.
16. The ten *resurrection appearances* of the Savior.
17. The *political and religious parties* in the days of the Savior.
18. The *various places* visited by the Savior.
19. The many *individuals* who met the Savior.

THE MIRACLES OF THE SAVIOR

1. Changing of water into wine (Jn. 2:7-9).
2. Healing of the nobleman's son (Jn. 4:50).
3. Healing of the Capernaum demoniac (Mk. 1:25; Lk. 4:35).
4. Healing of Peter's mother-in-law (Mt. 8:15; Mk. 1:31; Lk. 4:39).
5. Catching a great number of fish (Lk. 5:5, 6).
6. Healing a leper (Mt. 8:3; Mk. 1:41).
7. Healing a paralytic (Mt. 9:2, 6, 7; Mk. 2:5, 10-12; Lk. 5:20, 24, 25).
8. Healing a withered hand (Mt. 12:13; Mk. 3:5; Lk. 6:10).
9. Healing a centurion's servant (Mt. 8:13; Lk. 7:10).
10. Raising a widow's son (Lk. 7:14).
11. Calming the stormy sea (Mt. 8:26; Mk. 4:39; Lk. 8:24).
12. Healing the Gadarene demoniac (Mt. 8:32; Mk. 5:8; Lk. 8:33).
13. Healing a woman with internal bleeding (Mt. 9:22; Mk. 5:29; Lk. 8:44).
14. Raising Jairus' daughter (Mt. 9:25; Mk. 5:41; Lk. 8:54).
15. Healing two blind men (Mt. 9:29).
16. Healing a dumb demoniac (Mt. 9:33).
17. Healing of a thirty-eight-year invalid (Jn. 5:8).
18. Feeding 5,000 men and their families (Mt. 14:19; Mk. 6:41; Lk. 9:16; Jn. 6:11).
19. Walking on the sea (Mt. 14:25; Mk. 6:48; Jn. 6:19).
20. Healing a demoniac girl (Mt. 15:28; Mk. 7:29).
21. Healing a deaf man with a speech impediment (Mk. 7:34, 35).

22. Feeding 4,000 men and their families (Mt. 15:36; Mk. 8:6).
23. Healing a blind man (Mk. 8:25).
24. Healing a man born blind (Jn. 9:7).
25. Healing a demoniac boy (Mt. 17:18; Mk. 9:25; Lk. 9:42).
26. Catching a fish with a coin in its mouth (Mt. 17:27).
27. Healing a blind and dumb demoniac (Mt. 12:22; Lk. 11:14).
28. Healing a woman with an eighteen-year infirmity (Lk. 13:10–17).
29. Healing a man with dropsy (Lk. 14:4).
30. Healing ten lepers (Lk. 17:11–19).
31. Raising of Lazarus (Jn. 11:43, 44).
32. Healing a blind man (Mt. 20:34; Lk. 18:42).
33. Healing a blind man (Mt. 20:34; Mk. 10:46, 52).
34. Destroying a fig tree (Mt. 21:19; Mk. 11:14).
35. Restoring (healing) a severed ear (Mt. 26:51; Mk. 14:47; Lk. 22:50, 51; Jn. 18:10).
36. Catching a great number of fish (Jn. 21:6).

A BRIEF SUMMARY OF HIS MIRACLES

Nature of the Miracles
1. Healing of individuals (seventeen in number)
   a. of fever (see 2, 4)
   b. of leprosy (see 6, 30)
   c. of paralysis (see 7, 9, 17)
   d. of a withered hand (see 8)
   e. of internal bleeding (see 13)
   f. of blindness (see 15, 23, 24, 32, 33)
   g. of deafness (see 21)
   h. of dropsy (see 29)
   i. of a severed ear (see 35)
2. Rebuking of demons (seven in number)
   a. concerning convulsions (see 3, 25)
   b. concerning insanity (see 12)
   c. concerning muteness (see 16)
   d. concerning an unknown affliction (see 20)
   e. concerning blindness and muteness (see 27)
   f. concerning paralysis (see 28)
3. Raising the dead (three in number)
   a. a little girl (see 14)

b. a young man (see 10)
c. Lazarus (see 31)
4. Protecting his disciples (two in number)
   a. while standing in a boat (see 11)
   b. while walking on the water (see 19)
5. Feeding the hungry (five in number)
   a. some wedding guests (see 1)
   b. 5000 men (see 18)
   c. 4000 men (see 22)
   d. four of his disciples (see 5)
   e. seven of his disciples (see 36)
6. Providing tax money (see 26)
7. Cursing a fig tree (see 34)

Comments on the Miracles
1. His miracles were performed anywhere and everywhere.
   a. at a wedding (see 1)
   b. at funerals (see 10, 31, 14)
   c. in graveyards (see 12)
   d. in synagogues (see 3, 8, 28)
   e. in homes (see 4, 7, 14, 20, 29)
   f. on seashores (see 36)
   g. in a garden (see 35)
   h. on a mountain (see 18, 22)
   i. by a pool (see 17)
   j. in boats (see 5, 11)
2. Our Lord touched the person during eleven of his miracles (see 4, 6, 14, 15, 19, 21, 23, 25, 28, 33, 35).
3. On one occasion he was touched (see 13).
4. On three occasions he spat while accomplishing the miracle (see 21, 23, 24).
5. Five of the miracles were performed on the Sabbath (see 8, 17, 24, 28, 29).
6. Jesus was filled with compassion as he performed six of his miracles (see 6, 10, 18, 22, 32, 33).
7. Jesus was filled with amazement during two of his miracles (see 9, 20).
8. Jesus groaned during one miracle (see 21).
9. Jesus wept during one miracle (see 31).
10. Four of his miracles had far-reaching results.
    a. The fifth resulted in the full-time call of Peter, Andrew, James, and John.

NOTEWORTHY MIRACLES

MIRACLE	WHY NOTEWORTHY	SCRIPTURE LOCATION
1. CHANGING WATER INTO WINE	First miracle	**Jn. 2**
2. WALKING ON THE SEA	Shows he is above natural law	**Jn. 6**
3. CALMING THE SEA	Shows he is in control of natural law	**Mt. 8**
4. FEEDING THE 5,000	Shows he cared for people and not just "souls"	**Jn. 6**
5. HEALING THE MANIAC OF GADARA	Most fearful case of demon possession on record	**Mk. 5**
6. RAISING LAZARUS	Greatest of all his miracles	**Jn. 11**
7. HEALING A MAN BORN BLIND	Explains the purpose for all his miracles	**Jn. 9**
8. THE FISH WITH A COIN IN ITS MOUTH	Illustrates his work as the second Adam	**Mt. 17**
9. CURSING THE FIG TREE	The saddest of all recorded miracles	**Mt. 24**
10. CATCHING A GREAT NUMBER OF FISH	Last miracle	**Jn. 21**

b. The thirty-first sealed his doom with the Pharisees.
c. The thirty-fourth signified the divine rejection of Israel.
d. The thirty-fifth doubtless saved Peter from instant death.

11. Some of his miracles revealed the characteristics of the human heart.
    a. its lack of faith (see 2, 11, 19)
    b. its wickedness (see 5, 16, 17, 27, 28)
    c. its ingratitude (see 30)

12. Sometimes he would ask a question as he performed the miracle.
    a. "Woman, what are you doing to me?" (see 1).
    b. "Which is easier to say, Your sins be forgiven you, or, Take up your bed and walk?" (see 7).
    c. "Is it lawful to do good on the Sabbath?" (see 8).
    d. "Where is your faith?" (see 11).
    e. "What is your name?" (see 12).
    f. "Who touched my clothing?" (see 13).
    g. "Do you believe that I can do this?" (see 15).
    h. "Do you wish to get well?" (see 17).
    i. "Where shall we buy loaves of bread?" (see 18).
    j. "What made you doubt?" (see 19).
    k. "How many loaves do you have?" (see 22).
    l. "Do you see anything?" (see 23).
    m. "From whom do the kings of the earth collect tribute?" (see 26).
    n. "If Satan is casting out Satan . . . how then shall his kingdom stand?" (see 27).
    o. "Where have you laid him?" (see 31).
    p. "What do you wish for me to do for you?" (see 32, 33).
    q. "Children, have you anything to eat?" (see 36).

13. Sometimes he issued a command as he performed the miracle.
    a. "Fill up the water jars with water" (see 1).
    b. "Launch out where it is deep and let down your nets for a catch" (see 5).
    c. "Stretch out your hand" (see 8).
    d. "Rise, take up your pallet and walk" (see 17, 7).
    e. "Have the men recline for eating in groups of fifty" (see 18).
    f. "Come!" (see 19).
    g. "Go and wash in the Pool of Siloam" (see 24).
    h. "Go to the sea and cast in a hook and take the first fish that comes up" (see 26).
    i. "Lazarus, come forth" (see 31).
    j. "Cast out the net on the right side of the boat and you will find some" (see 36).

14. The first and last miracles are recorded by John alone (see 1, 36).

15. Only two miracles are recorded by all four Gospel accounts (see 18, 35).

16. Sixteen of his miracles are mentioned by only one of the Gospels.
    a. Matthew alone records the following: 15, 16, 26 (Matthew's total miracle count is twenty-two).
    b. Mark alone records the following: 21, 23 (Mark's total miracle count is nineteen).
    c. Luke alone records the following: 5, 10, 28, 29, 30 (Luke's total miracle count is nineteen).
    d. John alone records the following: 1, 2, 17, 24, 31, 36 (John's total miracle count is nine).

17. During his first year, our Lord performed seven recorded miracles (see 1-7).

18. During his second year, our Lord performed twelve recorded miracles (see 8-19).

19. During his third year, our Lord performed five recorded miracles (see 20-24).

20. During his fourth year, our Lord performed twelve recorded miracles (see 25-36).

THE PARABLES OF THE SAVIOR
1. Two houses in a hurricane (Mt. 7:24-27; Lk. 6:47-49).
2. Forgiving the fifty and the five-hundred (Lk. 7:41, 42).
3. Subduing a strong man (Mk. 3:22-30).
4. The sower, the seed, and the soil (Mt. 13:1-9, 18-23; Mk. 4:1-20; Lk. 8:4-15).
5. Satan's tares in the Savior's field (Mt. 13:24-30, 36-43).
6. From scattering to sickling (Mk. 4:26-29).
7. The mighty mustard seed (Mt. 13:31, 32; Mk. 4:30-32; Lk. 13:18, 19).
8. The cook's leaven and the kingdom of heaven (Mt. 13:33; Lk. 13:20, 21).
9. Finding a fortune in a field (Mt. 13:44).
10. The price of a pearl (Mt. 13:45, 46).
11. Sorting out a sea catch (Mt. 13:47-50).
12. A trained man and his treasure (Mt. 13:52).
13. A rent cloth and a ruptured container (Mt. 9:16, 17; Mk. 2:21, 22; Lk. 5:36-39).
14. A generation of gripers (Mt. 11:16-19; Lk. 7:31-35).
15. The forgiven who wouldn't forgive (Mt. 18:23-35).
16. How to know your neighbor (Lk. 10:25-37).
17. Seven spirits and a swept house (Mt. 12:43-45; Lk. 11:24-26).
18. A fool in a fix (Lk. 12:16-21).
19. Keep the home fires burning (Lk. 12:32-40; Mt. 24:43, 44).
20. A sinning servant and a returning ruler (Mt. 24:45-51; Lk. 12:42-48).
21. A fruitless fig tree (Lk. 13:6-9).
22. Choosing the least at a wedding feast (Lk. 14:7-11).
23. Two fools and a henpecked husband (Lk. 14:15-24).
24. A missing sheep, the misplaced silver and a miserable son (Lk. 15:1-32).
25. The stewings of a steward (Lk. 16:1-13).
26. When Hades petitioned paradise (Lk. 16:19-31).
27. When our best is but the least (Lk. 17:7-10).
28. A widow and a weary judge (Lk. 18:1-8).
29. A haughty Pharisee and a humble Publican (Lk. 18:9-14).
30. When the last was first and the first was last (Mt. 20:1-16).
31. Three stewards and their silver (Lk. 19:11-27).
32. Two sons who changed their minds (Mt. 21:28-32).
33. The vicious vine keepers (Mt. 21:33-46; Mk. 12:1-12; Lk. 21:9-19).
34. A wedding guest with no wedding garment (Mt. 22:1-14).
35. The fig tree and the future (Mt. 24:32-35; Mk. 13:28-31; Lk. 21:29-33).
36. Five lamps that went out (Mt. 25:1-13).
37. Three stewards and their talents (Mt. 25:14-30).
38. Separating the sheep from the goats (Mt. 25:31-46).

A BRIEF SUMMARY OF HIS PARABLES
1. His parables covered the following subjects:
   a. correct foundations (see 1)
   b. forgiveness (see 2, 15)
   c. Satan (see 3, 5, 17)
   d. the human heart (see 4)
   e. the kingdom of heaven (see 4-13)
   f. the church (see 10)

NOTEWORTHY PARABLES

PARABLE	INTENDED LESSON	SCRIPTURE LOCATION
1. THE SOWER, SEED, AND SOIL	Explains the nature of the kingdom of heaven	**Mt. 13**
2. THE GOOD SAMARITAN	Shows me my duty to others. Demonstrates three possible human attitudes.*	**Lk. 10:30-37**
3. THE RICH FOOL	Preparedness—the uncertainty of this life	**Lk. 12:16-21**
4. THE LOST SHEEP, COIN, AND SON	The work of the Trinity in the salvation and restoration of sinners	**Lk. 15:3-32**
5. LAZARUS AND THE RICH MAN	The agony of hell	**Lk. 16: 19-31**
6. THE BUDDING OF THE FIG TREE	A great sign concerning Christ's return	**Mt. 24:32-35**
7. THE TEN VIRGINS	Future judgment and salvation of Israel	**Mt. 25:1-13**
8. SEPARATING OF THE SHEEP AND GOATS	Future judgment and salvation of the Gentiles	**Mt. 25:31-46**

*What is thine is mine (attitude of the thieves)
What is mine is mine (attitude of the Levite and Priest)
What is mine is thine (attitude of the Good Samaritan)

g. final judgment (see 5, 11, 38)
h. Israel (see 9, 14, 21, 33, 35)
i. compassion (see 16)
j. riches (see 18)
k. preparedness (see 19, 20, 36)
l. humility (see 22)
m. worldy attitudes (see 25)
n. hell (see 18, 26, 34)
o. stewardship (see 27, 31, 37)
p. prayer (see 28, 29)
q. repentance (see 32)
r. salvation (see 24)

2. He took his parables from various areas of life.
   a. farming (see 4, 5, 6, 7, 18, 21, 35)
   b. fishing (see 11)
   c. weddings (see 22, 23, 34, 36)
   d. shepherding (see 38, 24)
   e. the business world (see 25, 2, 30)

THE PRAYERS OF THE SAVIOR

1. At his baptism (Lk. 3:21).
2. Before his first preaching tour of Galilee (Mk. 1:35; Lk. 4:42).
3. After healing a leper (Lk. 5:16).
4. Before choosing his twelve disciples (Lk. 6:12).
5. After the feeding of the 5,000 (Mt. 14:23, Mk. 6:46; Jn. 6:15).
6. Before hearing Peter's great confession (Lk. 9:18).
7. During his transfiguration (Lk. 9:28, 29).
8. Upon hearing the report of the returning seventy (Mt. 11:25-27; Lk. 10:21, 22).
9. After visiting Mary and Martha (Lk. 11:1).
10. After receiving some small children (Mt. 19:13-15; Mk. 10:13-16; Lk. 18:15-17).
11. Before raising Lazarus (Jn. 11:41, 42).
12. When some Greeks desired to see him (Jn. 12:27, 28).
13. After leaving the upper room (Jn. 17:1-26).
14. In the garden (first prayer) (Mt. 26:39; Mk. 14:35, 36; Lk. 22:41, 42).
15. In the garden (second prayer) (Mt. 26:42; Mk. 14:39; Lk. 22:44).
16. In the garden (third prayer) (Mt. 26:44).
17. On the cross (first prayer) (Lk. 23:34).
18. On the cross (second prayer) (Mt. 27:46, 47; Mk. 15:34, 35).
19. On the cross (third prayer) (Lk. 23:46).

A SUMMARY OF HIS PRAYERS
1. What he prayed for:
   a. That the Father would bless his Galilean ministry (see 2).
   b. That the Father would guide him in selecting the twelve (see 4).
   c. That the Father would reveal the deity of the Son to Peter (see 6).
   d. Thanking the Father for revealing spiritual truths to the seventy (see 8).
   e. Thanking the Father for always hearing him (see 11).
   f. That the Father would be glorified (see 12).
   g. That the Father would glorify him (see 13).
   h. That the Father would keep, sanctify, unite, perfect, and gather to Christ all believers (see 13).
   i. That if possible, his hour of passion might pass from him (see 14, 15, 16).
   j. That his Father's will be done (see 14, 15, 16).
   k. That his enemies be forgiven (see 17).
   l. That he understand his sufferings (see 18).
   m. That the Father receive his spirit (see 19).
2. Those he prayed for:
   a. little children (see 10)
   b. his enemies (see 17)
   c. himself (see 12, 13, 14, 15, 16, 18, 19)
   d. all believers (see 13)
   e. the seventy disciples (see 8)
3. When he prayed:
   a. all night (see 4)
   b. shortly past midnight (see 13, 14, 15, 16)
   c. at dawn (see 2)

The Garden Prayers (Mt. 26:36-46) (Mk. 14:32-42) (Lk. 22:41-44)

FIRST PRAYER

- He crosses the Brook Kidron.
- He asks Peter, James, and John to pray.
- He prays concerning his cup and submits to the will of God.
- He awakens the sleeping apostles.

SECOND PRAYER

- He again prays and submits.
- He is strengthened by an angel.
- He again awakens the slumbering three disciples.

THIRD PRAYER

- He prays the same prayer.
- He awakens the three for the third time.
- He announces the coming of the soldiers.

The Calvary Prayers

FIRST PRAYER (Lk. 23:34)

"Father, forgive them; for they know not what they do."

SECOND PRAYER (Mt. 27:46) (Mk. 15:34)

"My God, my God, why hast thou forsaken me?"

THIRD PRAYER (Lk. 23:46)

"Father, into thy hands I commend my spirit."

---

    d. early morning (see 17)
    e. late afternoon (see 18, 19)
4. How he prayed:
    a. lifting up his eyes to heaven (see 11, 13)
    b. kneeling (see 14, 15)
    c. on his face (see 14, 15)
    d. hanging between earth and heaven (see 17, 18, 19)

THE PREDICTIONS OF THE SAVIOR
1. Concerning his ascension (Jn. 1:50, 51).
2. Concerning his death and resurrection (Jn. 2:19-22).
3. Concerning his death (Jn. 3:14).
4. Concerning the great white throne judgment (Mt. 7:21-23).
5. Concerning the future resurrection (Jn. 5:28, 29).
6. Concerning his betrayer (Jn. 6:70, 71).
7. Concerning his resurrection (Mt. 16:4).
8. Concerning his ascension (Jn. 7:33, 34).
9. Concerning Pentecost (Jn. 7:37-39).
10. Concerning his ascension (Jn. 8:14, 21).
11. Concerning his death (Jn. 8:28).
12. Concerning his death (Jn. 10:17, 18).
13. Concerning the church (Mt. 16:18, 19).
14. Concerning his resurrection (Mt. 16:21; Mk. 8:31; Lk. 9:22).
15. Concerning his Second Coming (Mt. 16:27; Mk. 8:38; Lk. 9:26).
16. Concerning his transfiguration (Mt. 16:28; Lk. 9:27).
17. Concerning his resurrection (Mt. 17:9; Mk. 9:9).
18. Concerning his sufferings (Mt. 17:12; Mk. 9:12).
19. Concerning his betrayal (Lk. 9:44; Mt. 17:22).
20. Concerning his resurrection (Mk. 9:31; Mt. 17:23).
21. Concerning his resurrection (Mt. 12:38-40; Lk. 11:29, 30).
22. Concerning the great white throne judgment (Mt. 12:41, 42; Lk. 11:31, 32).
23. Concerning the great white throne (Lk. 12:2, 3).
24. Concerning his sufferings (Lk. 17:25).
25. Concerning the last days (Lk. 17:26-30).
26. Concerning Armageddon (Lk. 17:34-37).
27. Concerning future rewards (Mt. 19:27-30; Mk. 10:28-31; Lk. 18:28-30).
28. Concerning his resurrection (Mt. 20:17-19; Mk. 10:32-34; Lk. 18:31-34).
29. Concerning the destruction of Jerusalem (Lk. 19:43, 44).
30. Concerning the setting aside of Israel (Mt. 21:43, 44).
31. Concerning his death (Jn. 12:20-26).
32. Concerning his death (Jn. 12:32).
33. Concerning the tribulation (Mt. 24:1-42).
34. Concerning his Second Coming (Mt. 24:29-41).
35. Concerning his death (Mt. 26:2).
36. Concerning his betrayal (Jn. 13:18-33; Mt. 26:21-25; Mk. 14:18-21; Lk. 22:21-23).
37. Concerning the death of Peter (Jn. 13:36).
38. Concerning Peter's first three denials (Jn. 13:38; Lk. 22:34).
39. Concerning his return (Jn. 14:2, 3).
40. Concerning being forsaken by his disciples (Mt. 26:31).
41. Concerning meeting his disciples in Galilee after his resurrection (Mt. 26:32; Mk. 14:28; 16:7).
42. Concerning Peter's second three denials (Mt. 26:33-35; Mk. 14:29-31).
43. Concerning his Second Coming (Mt. 26:64).
44. Concerning his Second Coming (Lk. 22:69).
45. Concerning the destruction of Jerusalem (Lk. 23:28-31).
46. Concerning Peter's martyrdom (Jn. 21:18, 19).

A BRIEF SUMMARY OF HIS PREDICTIONS

Concerning himself
1. That he would suffer, die, and rise again (see 2, 3, 7, 11, 12, 14, 17, 18, 19, 20, 21, 24, 28, 31, 32, 35).
2. That he would be transfigured (see 16).
3. That he would be betrayed (see 6, 19, 36).
4. That he would be denied (see 38, 42).
5. That he would be forsaken (see 40).

NOTEWORTHY PREDICTIONS

NATURE OF THE PROPHECY	LOCATION OF THE PROPHECY	
1. HIS SUFFERING, DEATH AND RESURRECTION	●JN. 2:19-22 ●JN. 3:14 ●JN. 10:11-18	●MT. 16:4, 21 ●MT. 17:22, 23 ●MT. 20:17-19
2. HIS TRANSFIGURATION	●MT. 16:28	
3. HIS BETRAYER	●JN. 6:70, 71	
4. THE DENIALS OF PETER	●JN. 13:38	●MK. 14:26-31
5. HIS APPEARANCE TO THEM IN GALILEE	●MT. 26:31,32	
6. HIS ASCENSION	●JN. 1:50, 51	
7. PENTECOST	●JN. 7:37-39	
8. THE CHURCH	●MT. 16:13-19	
9. THE RAPTURE	●JN. 14:2, 3	
10. THE SECOND COMING	●MT. 16:27	●MT. 26:24
11. THE GREAT WHITE THRONE JUDGMENT	●MT. 7:21-23	●MT. 12:41,42
12. THE FUTURE RESURRECTION	●JN. 5:28, 29	
13. THE LAST DAYS	●LK. 17:26-30	
14. ARMAGEDDON	●LK. 17:34-37	
15. FUTURE REWARDS	●MK. 10:28-31	
16. THE DEATH OF PETER	●JN. 21:18, 19	

6. That he would appear after his resurrection in Galilee (see 41).
7. That he would ascend (see 1, 8, 10).
8. That he would send the Holy Spirit (see 9).
9. That he would establish his church (see 13).
10. That he would temporarily set aside Israel (see 30).
11. That he would come again (see 15, 39, 43, 44).
12. That he would someday resurrect and judge all men (see 4, 5, 22, 23, 27).

Concerning other subjects
1. the last days (see 25)
2. Armageddon (see 26)
3. the destruction of Jerusalem (see 29, 45)
4. the tribulation (see 33)
5. the death of Peter (see 37, 46)

THE SERMONS OF THE SAVIOR
1. Preaching from Isaiah 61 in his hometown synagogue (Lk. 4:16-30).
2. Preaching on the characteristics of the kingdom of heaven (Sermon on the Mount) (Mt. 5-7; Lk. 6:20-49; 12:22-31, 57-59; 16:17).
3. Preaching on the nine examples of the kingdom of heaven (Mt. 13:1-52; Mk. 4:1-34; Lk. 8:4-18; 13:18-21).
4. Preaching on John the Baptist (Mt. 11:7-15; Lk. 7:24-30).
5. Preaching judgment and the resurrection (Jn. 5:19-47).

6. Preaching to the departing twelve (Mt. 10:5-16; 24-33; 37-42; Mk. 6:8-11; Lk. 9:3-5).
7. Preaching on the bread of life (Jn. 6:26-59).
8. Preaching on the source of defilement (Mt. 15:1-20; Mk. 7:1-23).
9. Preaching on the devil and his children (Jn. 10:1-18; 8:33-59).
10. Preaching on the Good Shepherd (Jn. 10:1-18).
11. Preaching on humility and hell (Mt. 18:1-20; Mk. 9:33—10:1; Lk. 9:46-50).
12. Preaching to the departing seventy (Mt. 11:20-24; Lk. 10:1-16).
13. Preaching against religious hypocrites (Mt. 23:1-36; Mk. 12:38-40; Lk. 20:45-47).
14. Preaching on the final tribulation (Mt. Olivet discourse) (Mt. 24:1-42; 10:17-23; 25:1-46; Mk. 13:1-37; Lk. 21:5-36; 12:11, 12).
15. Preaching on his Father's house (Jn. 14:1-31).
16. Preaching on the vine and the branches (Jn. 15:1—16:33).

A BRIEF SUMMARY OF HIS SERMONS
1. He was nearly killed after preaching one sermon (see 1).
2. He delivered one sermon sitting in a boat (see 3).
3. He preached his two longest sermons on two mountains (see 2, 14).
4. He preached several near the Temple in Jerusalem (see 5, 8, 9, 10, 13, 15, 16).

NOTEWORTHY SERMONS

SERMON	WHERE PREACHED	PURPOSE	SCRIPTURE LOCATION
1. Taken from Isaiah 61	*NAZARETH*	To identify himself as the Jewish Messiah.	**LK. 4**
2. Sermon on the Mount	*MT. TABOR (?)*	To *review* what believers should do today. To *preview* what the world will do in the millennium.	**MT. 5-7**
3. On judgment and resurrection	*IN THE JERUSALEM TEMPLE*	To equate himself with the Father as the *source* of life.	**JN. 5:19-47**
4. On Bread of life	*BY THE SEA OF GALILEE*	To equate himself with the Father as the *Bread* of life.	**JN. 6:22-71**
5. Feast of tabernacles sermon	*OUTSIDE THE JERUSALEM TEMPLE*	To invite people to the living Water.	**JN. 7:1-53**
6. Temple treasury sermon	*IN THE JERUSALEM TEMPLE*	To identify himself as the Light and the Life of the world.	**JN. 8:12-59**
7. Good Shepherd sermon	*IN JERUSALEM*	To fulfill Psalm 23 and Ezekiel 34.	**JN. 10:1-28**
8. Mt. Olivet discourse	*ON THE MT. OF OLIVES*	To act as a survival guide for believing Jews during the tribulation.	**MT. 24-25**
9. Sermons on the Father's house	*IN THE UPPER ROOM*	To prepare apostles for crucifixion and Pentecost.	**JN. 14**
10. Sermons on the vine and the Holy Spirit	*EN ROUTE TO GETHSEMANE*	To prepare believers for Christian service.	**JN. 15-16**

5. He delivered two sermons to preachers (see 6, 12).

6. He preached one sermon to defend himself (see 9).

7. He preached one sermon to defend his disciples (see 8).

8. He used a little child as an illustration during one sermon (see 11).

9. He preached one sermon in the upper room (see 15).

10. He preached one sermon in the moonlight (see 16).

11. During his first year he delivered one recorded sermon (see 1).

12. During his second year he delivered five recorded sermons (see 2-6).

13. During his third year he delivered four recorded sermons (see 7-10).

14. During his fourth year he delivered two recorded sermons (see 11, 12).

15. During his last week he delivered four recorded sermons (see 13-16).

THE PERSONAL DIALOGUES OF THE SAVIOR

1. With Nathanael, concerning his omniscience and ascension (Jn. 1:47-51).

2. With his mother, concerning his life's purpose (Jn. 2:3, 4).

3. With Nicodemus, concerning the new birth (Jn. 3:1-21).

4. With a Samaritan woman, concerning living waters (Jn. 4:6-26).

5. With a leper, concerning healing (Mt. 8:2-4).

6. With a centurion, concerning healing and faith (Mt. 8:6-13; Lk. 7:4-9).

7. With Simon the Pharisee, concerning love and forgiveness (Lk. 7:40-47).

8. With Jairus, concerning his daughter (Mk. 5:22, 23, 35, 36).

9. With an impotent man, concerning healing (Jn. 5:6-8, 14).

10. With a Syro-phoenician mother, concerning her daughter (Mt. 15:21-28).

11. With a blind man, concerning healing (Mk. 8:22-26).

12. With an adulterous woman, concerning her accusers (Jn. 8:10, 11).

13. With a man born blind, concerning his own deity (Jn. 9:7, 35-38).

14. With the father of a demoniac boy (Mk. 9:17-24).

15. With a lawyer, concerning one's neighbor (Lk. 10:25-37).

16. With three would-be disciples, concerning discipleship (Lk. 9:57-62).

17. With a man in a crowd, concerning covetousness (Lk. 12:13, 14).

18. With a leper, concerning gratitude (Lk. 17:13-19).

19. With a rich young ruler, concerning eternal life (Mt. 19:16-22).

20. With a blind man, concerning healing (Lk. 18:35-42).

21. With Zacchaeus, concerning salvation (Lk. 19:1-10).

22. With blind Bartimaeus, concerning healing (Mk. 10:46-52).

23. With a scribe, concerning the greatest of the commandments (Mk. 12:28-34).

24. With Judas (not Iscariot), concerning the abiding presence of the Trinity (Jn. 14:22, 23).

25. With Annas, concerning his teaching (Jn. 18:19-23).

26. With Caiaphas, concerning his own deity (Mt. 26:62-64).

27. With a dying thief, concerning paradise (Lk. 23:42, 43).

28. With Mary Magdalene, concerning his resurrection (Jn. 20:14-18).

29. With Cleopas, concerning his own resurrection (Lk. 24:17-27).
30. With Peter:
    a. Concerning soul-winning (Lk. 5:4-11).
    b. Concerning faith (Mt. 14:26-31).
    c. Concerning discipleship (Jn. 6:66-70).
    d. Concerning his deity (Mt. 16:15-19).
    e. Concerning his sufferings (Mt. 16:21-23).
    f. Concerning the paying of tribute (Mt. 17:25-27).
    g. Concerning forgiveness (Mt. 18:21, 22).
    h. Concerning humility (Jn. 13:6-11).
    i. Concerning his first denials (Jn. 13:36-38).
    j. Concerning his second denials (Mk. 14:29-31).
    k. Concerning his love for Christ (Jn. 21:15-22).
31. With Martha:
    a. Concerning the most important things (Lk. 10:38-42).
    b. Concerning the resurrection (Jn. 11:21-27, 39, 40).
32. With Judas:
    a. Concerning his betrayal in the upper room (Mt. 26:25; Jn. 13:27).
    b. Concerning his betrayal in the garden (Mt. 26:49, 50; Lk. 22:48).
33. With Pilate:
    a. Concerning his kingdom (Mt. 27:11-14; Mk. 15:1-5; Lk. 23:3; Jn. 18:33-38).
    b. Concerning his authority (Jn. 19:8-11).
34. With James and John:
    a. Concerning sectarianism (Mk. 9:38-42).
    b. Concerning revenge (Lk. 9:54-56).
    c. Concerning seating arrangements in the kingdom (Mt. 20:20-23; Mk. 10:35-40).
35. With Philip:
    a. Concerning the feeding of 5,000 men (Jn. 6:5-7).
    b. Concerning the Father (Jn. 14:8, 9).
36. With Thomas:
    a. Concerning the way of life (Jn. 14:5, 6).
    b. Concerning unbelief (Jn. 20:26-29).

OLD TESTAMENT EVENTS AND INDIVIDUALS MENTIONED BY THE SAVIOR
1. The creation of Adam and Eve (Gen. 1:27; 2:24; Mk. 10:6-8).
2. The murder of Abel (Gen. 4:10; Lk. 11:51).
3. The corruption of Noah's day and the flood (Gen. 6, 7; Lk. 17:26, 27).
4. The corruption of Lot's day and the fire (Gen. 19; Lk. 17:28, 29).
5. The worldliness of Lot's wife (Gen. 19:26; Lk. 17:32).
6. Moses and the burning bush (Ex. 3; Mk. 12:26).
7. Moses and the heavenly manna (Ex. 16:15; Jn. 6:31).
8. Moses and the brazen serpent (Num. 21:8; Jn. 3:14).
9. David and some shewbread (1 Sam. 21:6; Mt. 12:3, 4).
10. Solomon and the Queen of Sheba (1 Ki. 10:1; Mt. 12:42).
11. Elijah, a widow, and the famine (1 Ki. 17:1, 9; Lk. 4:25, 26).
12. Naaman and his leprosy (2 Ki. 5; Lk. 4:27).
13. The murder of Zechariah (2 Chron. 24:20, 21; Lk. 11:51).
14. Daniel and the abomination of desolation (Dan. 9:27; 11:31; 12:11; Mt. 24:15).
15. Jonah and the fish (Jonah 1:17; Mt. 12:40; 16:4).
16. Jonah and the repentance of the Ninevites (Jonah 3:4-10; Lk. 11:30; Mt. 12:41).

OLD TESTAMENT PASSAGES QUOTED BY THE SAVIOR
1. During his temptations
    a. The first temptation (in Mt.4:4; he quotes Deut. 8:3).
    b. The second temptation (in Mt. 4:7; he quotes Deut. 6:16).
    c. The third temptation (in Mt. 4:10; he quotes Deut. 6:13).
2. During his Sermon on the Mount
    a. In Matthew 5:21 (he quotes Ex. 20:13, sixth commandment).
    b. In Matthew 5:27 (he quotes Ex. 20:14, seventh commandment. Also compare Mt. 5:31 with Deut. 24;1). (Note: He later quotes some of the same commandments during his talk with a rich young ruler. See Mk. 10:19.)
3. During his hometown sermon: in Luke 4:18, 19 (he quotes Isa. 61:1, 2).
4. During various confrontations with Jewish rulers
    a. As he defended his associating with sinners (in Mt. 9:13; he quotes Hosea 6:6).
    b. As he expounds on marriage (in Mk. 10:7, 8; he quotes Gen. 2:24).
    c. As he is asked concerning the greatest of the commandments (in Mk. 12:29, 30; he quotes Deut. 6:4, 5).
    d. As he rebukes their vain traditions (in Mt. 15:7-9; he quotes Isa. 29:13).
    e. As the Pharisees question his authority (in Jn. 8:17; he quotes Deut. 17:6).
5. During his tribute to John the Baptist: In Lk. 7:27 (he quotes Mal. 3:1).
6. During his triumphal entry day: in Matthew 21:16 (he quotes Ps. 8:2).
7. During his cleansing of the Temple: in Lk. 19:46 (he quotes Isa. 56:7).
8. During a parable about Israel: in Matthew 21:42, 44 (he quotes Ps. 118:22, 23; Isa. 8:14, 15).
9. During a question session in the Temple: in Mk. 12:36 (he quotes Ps. 110:1).
10. During his last Passover night: predicting the world would hate the disciples as they hated him (in Jn. 15:25; he quotes Ps. 35:19; 69:4).
11. On the cross
    a. His fourth utterance (in Mt. 27:46; he quotes Ps. 22:1).
    b. His seventh utterance (in Lk. 23:46; he quotes Ps. 31:5).

THE DEITY OF THE SAVIOR
1. His deity was declared by angels.
    a. by Gabriel to Mary (Lk. 1:26-33)
    b. by Gabriel to Joseph (Mt. 1:20-23)
    c. by Gabriel (?) to some shepherds (Lk. 2:8-11)
    d. by Gabriel (?) to some women (Mt. 28:5, 6)
2. His deity was declared by the Father.
    a. at his baptism (Mt. 3:16, 17)
    b. at his transfiguration (Mt. 17:5)
    c. shortly before his passion (Jn. 12:27, 28)
3. His deity was declared by his mighty miracles (Jn. 20:30, 31; 21:25).
4. His deity was declared by his powerful sermons (Lk. 4:32; Jn. 7:46).
5. His deity was declared by his accurate prophecies (Mt. 26:32).

OLD TESTAMENT PASSAGES
QUOTED
BY CHRIST

NEW TESTAMENT QUOTE	OLD TESTAMENT PASSAGE	HISTORICAL OCCASION
1. MATTHEW 4:4 MATTHEW 4:7 MATTHEW 4:10	*DEUTERONOMY 8:3* *DEUTERONOMY 6:16* *DEUTERONOMY 6:13*	TEMPTATION
2. MATTHEW 5:21 MATTHEW 5:27	*EXODUS 20:13* *EXODUS 20:14*	SERMON ON THE MOUNT
3. LUKE 4:18, 19	*ISAIAH 61:1, 2*	HOMETOWN SERMON
4. MATTHEW 9:13 MARK 10:7, 8 MARK 12:29, 30 MATTHEW 15:7-9 JOHN 8:17	*HOSEA 6:6* *GENESIS 2:24* *DEUTERONOMY 6:4, 5* *ISAIAH 29:13* *DEUTERONOMY 17:6*	CONFRONTATIONS WITH THE JEWISH RULERS
5. LUKE 7:27	*MALACHI 3:1*	TRIBUTE TO JOHN
6. MATTHEW 21:16	*PSALM 8:2*	TRIUMPHAL ENTRY
7. LUKE 19:46	*ISAIAH 56:7*	TEMPLE CLEANSING
8. MATTHEW 21:42, 44	*PSALM 118:22, 23*	PARABLE ABOUT ISRAEL
9. MARK 12:36	*PSALM 110:1*	TEMPLE QUESTION SESSION
10. JOHN 15:25	*PSALMS 35:19; 69:4*	LAST PASSOVER
11. MATTHEW 27:46 LUKE 23:46	*PSALM 22:1* *PSALM 31:5*	ON THE CROSS

6. His deity was declared by his sinless life (Jn. 14:30).
   a. as attested by Pilate (Jn. 19:4)
   b. by Pilate's wife (Mt. 27:19)
   c. by Judas (Mt. 27:4)
   d. by the dying thief (Lk. 23:41)
   e. by the Roman centurion (Lk. 23:47)
7. His deity was declared by demons.
   a. as he healed a maniac (Mt. 8:28, 29)
   b. as he healed a man in Capernaum (Lk. 4:33, 34)
   c. as he healed many in Capernaum (Lk. 4:41; Mk. 3:11)

8. His deity was declared by those who worshiped him.
   a. the shepherds (Lk. 2:15)
   b. the wise men (Mt. 2:2, 11)
   c. a leper (Mt. 8:2)
   d. a ruler (Mt. 9:18)
   e. a Gentile mother (Mt. 15:25)
   f. a Hebrew mother (Mt. 20:20)
   g. a maniac (Mk. 5:6)
   h. a blind man (Jn. 9:38)
   i. an apostle (Thomas) (Jn. 20:28)
   j. all apostles (Mt. 14:33; 28:9)

9. His deity was declared by Satan (Mt. 4:3, 6).
10. His deity was declared by himself.
    a. He referred to himself as the Son of God (Jn. 9:35; 10:36; 11:4).
    b. He forgave sins (Mk. 2:5, 10).
    c. He is man's judge (Jn. 5:22, 27).
    d. He is the author of life (Jn. 5:24, 28, 29).
    e. He is to be honored like the Father (Jn. 5:23).
    f. He alone can save (Jn. 10:28; Lk. 19:10; Jn. 14:6).

THE HUMANITY OF THE SAVIOR
(He was as much man as if he had never been God.)
1. He had a human parentage (Lk. 1:31).
2. He had a human body (Mt. 26:12).
3. He had a human soul (Jn. 12:27).
4. He had a human spirit (Mk. 2:8; Lk. 23:46).
5. He increased in wisdom and stature (Lk. 2:52, 40).
6. He asked questions (Lk. 2:46; 8:45).
7. He learned obedience (Lk. 2:51).
8. He looked like a man.
    a. to the Samaritan woman (Jn. 4:9)
    b. to the Jews (Jn. 8:57; 10:33)
    c. to Mary Magdalene (Jn. 20:15)
9. He possessed flesh and blood (Jn. 6:51, 55).
10. He socialized (Jn. 2:1, 2).
11. He prayed (Lk. 11:1).
12. He was tempted (Mt. 4:1).
13. He hungered (Mt. 4:2; 21:18).
14. He thirsted (Jn. 4:7; 19:28).
15. He ate (Jn. 21:13-15; Lk. 24:41-43).
16. He became weary (Jn. 4:6).
17. He slept (Mt. 8:24).
18. He loved (Mk. 10:21).
19. He had compassion (Mt. 9:36; 14:14; 15:32; Lk. 7:13; Mk. 1:41; 9:22, 23; 5:19).
20. He was angered and grieved (Mk. 3:5).
21. He wept (Jn. 11:35; Lk. 19:41).
22. He experienced joy (Lk. 10:21).
23. He possessed zeal (Jn. 2:17).
24. He became sorrowful (Mt. 26:37; Mk. 14:34).
25. He sang (Mt. 26:30).
26. He sweat and agonized (Lk. 22:44).
27. He was troubled (Jn. 11:33; 12:27; 13:21; Mk. 14:33, 34).
28. He bled (Jn. 19:34).
29. He died (Mt. 27:50).
30. He was buried (Mt. 27:59, 60).

THE NAMES OF THE SAVIOR
(As mentioned in the four Gospels)
1. Babe: used by the angels (Lk. 2:12).
2. Bread of God: used by himself (Jn. 6:33).
3. Bridegroom:
    a. by himself (Mt. 9:15; 25:1, 5, 6, 10)
    b. by John the Baptist (Jn. 3:29)
4. Child:
    a. by Herod (Mt. 2:8, 9)
    b. by the angel of the Lord (Mt. 2:13, 20; also see Mt. 1:18, 23; 2:11, 14, 21; Lk. 2:17, 21, 27, 40)
5. Christ:
    a. by Herod (Mt. 2:4)
    b. by Peter (Mt. 16:16; Jn. 6:69)
    c. by himself (Mt. 22:42; 23:8, 10; 24:5, 23; Lk. 24:26, 46; Jn. 20:31)
    d. by Caiaphas (Mt. 26:63, 68)
    e. by Pilate (Mt. 27:17, 22)
    f. by the chief priests (Mk. 15:32)
    g. by the angels (Lk. 2:11)

h. by a dying thief (Lk. 23:39)
    i. by Andrew (Jn. 1:41)
    j. by a Samaritan woman (Jn. 4:25, 29)
    k. by a crowd (Jn. 7:41)
    l. by Martha (Jn. 11:27)
6. Consolation of Israel: by Simeon (Lk. 2:25)
7. Cornerstone: by himself (Mt. 21:42)
8. Carpenter: by the citizens of Nazareth (Mt. 13:55)
9. Dayspring from on high: by Zacharias (Lk. 1:78)
10. Door: by himself (Jn. 10:7, 9)
11. Emmanuel: by Isaiah (Mt. 1:23)
12. Friend of sinners: by an evil generation (Mt. 11:19)
13. God: by Thomas (Jn. 20:28)
14. Governor: by Micah (Mt. 2:6)
15. Gift of God: by himself (Jn. 4:10)
16. Holy One of God: by an unclean spirit (Mk. 1:24)
17. Heir: by some wicked citizens (Mt. 21:38)
18. Jesus:
    a. by Gabriel (Mt. 1:21; Mk. 16:6; Lk. 1:31)
    b. by Joseph (Mt. 1:25)
    c. by demons (Mt. 8:29; Mk. 1:24)
    d. by a Jerusalem crowd (Mt. 21:11)
    e. by Pilate (Mt. 27:17, 22, 37)
    f. by ten lepers (Lk. 17:13)
    g. by a cured blind man (Jn. 9:11)
    h. by some Greeks (Jn. 12:21)
    i. by some soldiers (Jn. 18:5, 7)
19. King (of the Jews and of Israel):
    a. by the wise men (Mt. 2:2)
    b. by himself (Mt. 21:5; 25:34, 40)
    c. by Pilate (Mt. 27:11, 37; Mk. 15:9, 12; Jn. 18:39; 19:14, 15, 19)
    d. by some Roman soldiers (Mt. 27:29; Jn. 19:3)
    e. by the chief priests (Mt. 27:42)
    f. by Nathanael (Jn. 1:49)
    g. by the triumphal entry crowd (Jn. 12:13, 15)
20. Lamb of God: by John the apostle (Jn. 1:29, 36)
21. Lord:
    a. by the unsaved (Mt. 7:22; 25:11, 44; Jn. 6:34)
    b. by a leper (Mt. 8:2)
    c. by the twelve (Mt. 8:25; 26:22; Lk. 9:54; 11:1; 22:49; 24:34; Jn. 11:12; 20:25)
    d. by himself (Mt. 12:8; 21:3; 24:42; Lk. 6:46; Jn. 13:14)
    e. by Peter (Mt. 14:28, 30; 16:22; 17:4; 18:21; Lk. 5:8; Jn. 6:68; 13:6, 36; 21:15, 16, 17, 21)
    f. by the mother of a demoniac daughter (Mt. 15:22)
    g. by the father of a demoniac son (Mt. 17:15)
    h. by two blind men (Mt. 20:30)
    i. by the faithful (Mt. 25:20, 22, 37)
    j. by the angel of the Lord (Lk. 2:11)
    k. by some would-be followers (Lk. 9:57, 59, 61)
    l. by Mary and Martha (Lk. 10:40; Jn. 11:3, 21, 27, 32, 39)
    m. by a dying thief (Lk. 23:42)
    n. by an immoral woman (Jn. 8:11)
    o. by a cured blind man (Jn. 9:36, 38)
    p. by John the apostle (Jn. 13:25; 21:7)
    q. by Thomas (Jn. 14:5; 20:28)
    r. by Philip (Jn. 14:8)
    s. by Mary Magdalene (Jn. 20:2)
22. Man:
    a. by John the Baptist (Jn. 1:30)
    b. by a cured blind man (Jn. 9:11)
23. Master:
    a. by himself (Mt. 10:24; 23:8)
    b. by his enemies (Mt. 12:38; 22:16, 24, 36; Mk. 12:19; Lk. 11:45; 19:39; Jn. 8:4)

c. by a rich young ruler (Mt. 19:16)
d. by Judas (Mt. 26:25, 49)
e. by the twelve (Mk. 4:38; 13:1; Jn. 4:31; 9:2; 11:8)
f. by the father of a demoniac son (Mk. 9:17)
g. by John the apostle (Mk. 9:38; 10:35)
h. by Peter (Mk. 11:21; Lk. 5:5; 8:45; 9:33)
i. by a sincere scribe (Mk. 12:32)
j. by a carnal listener (Lk. 12:13)
k. by Martha (Jn. 11:28)
l. by Mary Magdalene (Jn. 20:16)

24. Messiah:
a. by Andrew (Jn. 1:41)
b. by a Samaritan woman (Jn. 4:25)

25. Nazarene (Mt. 2:23)

26. Only begotten Son (Jn. 1:14, 18; 3:16, 18)

27. Prophet:
a. by himself (Mt. 13:57; Jn. 4:44)
b. by the triumphal entry crowd (Mt. 21:11)
c. by the Pharisees (Mt. 21:46)
d. by the citizens of Nain (Lk. 7:16)
e. by Cleopas (Lk. 24:19)
f. by a Samaritan woman (Jn. 4:19)
g. by the 5,000 he fed (Jn. 6:14)
h. by a Jerusalem crowd (Jn. 7:40)
i. by a cured blind man (Jn. 9:17)

28. Physician: by himself (Mt. 9:12; Lk. 4:23)

29. Rabbi:
a. by Andrew and John (Jn. 1:38)
b. by Nathanael (Jn. 1:49)
c. by Nicodemus (Jn. 3:2)
d. by a Capernaum crowd (Jn. 6:25)

30. Shepherd: by himself (Mt. 9:36; 25:32; 26:31; Jn. 10:2, 11, 14, 16)

31. Son of God:
a. by Satan (Mt. 4:3, 6)
b. by demons (Mt. 8:29; Mk. 3:11; Lk. 4:41)
c. by the twelve (Mt. 14:33)
d. by Peter (Mt. 16:16; Jn. 6:69)
e. by a centurion (Mt. 27:54)

f. by Mark (Mk. 1:1)
g. by Gabriel (Lk. 1:35)
h. by John the Baptist (Jn. 1:34)
i. by Nathanael (Jn. 1:49)
j. by himself (Jn. 9:35; 10:36; 11:4)
k. by Martha (Jn. 11:27)
l. by John the apostle (Jn. 20:31)

32. Son of man (Jesus' favorite name for himself). He said the Son of man:
a. Had nowhere to lay his head (Mt. 8:20).
b. Had power to forgive sins (Mt. 9:6).
c. Is Lord of the Sabbath (Mt. 12:8).
d. Would be in the heart of the earth for three days (Mt. 12:40).
e. Will someday send forth his angels (Mt. 13:41).
f. Shall come in great glory (Mt. 16:27; 24:30; 26:64).
g. Would rise again (Mk. 9:9; Mt. 17:9).
h. Would suffer (Mt. 17:12; Mk. 8:31).
i. Would be betrayed (Mt. 17:22; 26:2, 45; Mk. 9:31; 10:33).
j. Came to seek and save lost people (Mt. 18:11).
k. Shall someday sit upon his throne (Mt. 19:28).
l. Did not come to be ministered to but to help others (Mt. 20:28).
m. Will come again unexpectedly (Mt. 24:44; Lk. 12:40).
n. Shall confess believers before angels (Lk. 12:8).

33. Son of David:
a. by two Capernaum blind men (Mt. 9:27)
b. by a crowd of people (Mt. 12:23)
c. by a Syro-phoenician woman (Mt. 15:22)
d. by two Jericho blind men (Mt. 20:30; Mk. 10:47)
e. by the Palm Sunday crowd (Mt. 21:9)
f. by some small children (Mt. 21:15)

34. Son of Abraham (Mt. 1:1)

35. Son of Joseph. Wrongly used by:
a. the Nazareth citizens (Lk. 4:22)
b. Philip (Jn. 1:45)

36. Word (Jn. 1:1)

NAMES FOR CHRIST IN THE GOSPELS

B BABE
BREAD
BRIDEGROOM

C CHILD
CHRIST
CONSOLATION
CORNERSTONE

D DAYSPRING
DOOR

E EMMANUEL

F FRIEND
OF SINNERS

G GOD
GOVERNOR
GIFT

H HOLY ONE OF GOD
HEIR

I (I am the)
BREAD OF LIFE
LIGHT OF WORLD
DOOR
GOOD SHEPHERD
RESURRECTION
WAY-TRUTH
TRUE VINE

J JESUS

K KING OF JEWS
KING OF ISRAEL

L LAMB
LORD

M MAN
MASTER
MESSIAH

N NAZARENE

O ONLY BEGOTTEN

P PROPHET
PHYSICIAN

R RABBI

S SHEPHERD
SAVIOR
SON OF GOD
SON OF MAN
SON OF DAVID
SON OF ABRAHAM
SON OF JOSEPH

W WORD

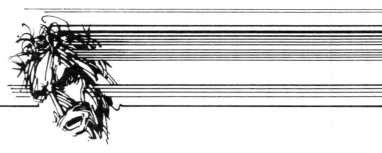

THE OLD TESTAMENT PROPHECIES FULFILLED BY CHRIST

OLD TESTAMENT PREDICTION	NATURE OF THE PROPHECY	NEW TESTAMENT FULFILLMENT
1. Isa. 7:14	BORN OF A VIRGIN	Mt. 1:22, 23
2. 2 Sam. 7:11, 12; Ps. 132:11; Isa. 9:6; 16:5; Jer. 23:5	GIVEN THE THRONE OF DAVID	Lk. 1:31, 32
3. Dan. 2:44; 7:14, 27; Micah 4:7	THIS THRONE TO BE AN ETERNAL THRONE	Lk. 1:33
4. Isa. 7:14	TO BE CALLED EMMANUEL	Mt. 1:23
5. Isa. 40:3-5; Mal. 3:1	TO HAVE A FORERUNNER	Lk. 1:76-78; 3:3-6; Mt. 3:1-3
6. Micah 5:2	TO BE BORN IN BETHLEHEM	Mt. 2:5, 6
7. Ps. 72:10; Isa. 60:3, 6, 9	TO BE WORSHIPED BY WISE MEN AND PRESENTED WITH GIFTS	Mt. 2:11
8. Num. 24:8; Hosea 11:1	TO BE IN EGYPT FOR A SEASON	Mt. 2:15
9. Jer. 31:15	BIRTHPLACE TO SUFFER A MASSACRE OF INFANTS	Mt. 2:17, 18
10. Isa. 11:1	TO BE CALLED A NAZARENE	Mt. 2:23
11. Ps. 69:9; 119:139	TO BE ZEALOUS FOR THE FATHER	Jn. 2:16, 17
12. Isa. 11:2; 61:1, 2; Ps. 45:7	TO BE FILLED WITH GOD'S SPIRIT	Lk. 4:18, 19
13. Isa. 53:4	TO HEAL MANY	Mt. 8:16, 17
14. Isa. 9:1, 2; 42:1-3	TO DEAL GENTLY WITH THE GENTILES	Mt. 12:17-21; 4:13-16
15. Isa. 6:9, 10	TO SPEAK IN PARABLES	Mt. 13:10-15
16. Isa. 53:3; Ps. 69:8	TO BE REJECTED BY HIS OWN	Jn. 1:11; 7:5
17. Zech. 9:9	TO MAKE A TRIUMPHAL ENTRY INTO JERUSALEM	Mt. 21:4, 5
18. Ps. 8:2	TO BE PRAISED BY LITTLE CHILDREN	Mt. 21:16

37. I am (used by Christ seven times in the Gospel of John):
    a. I am the Bread of Life (Jn. 6:35).
    b. I am the Light of the world (Jn. 9:5).
    c. I am the Door (Jn. 10:9).
    d. I am the Good Shepherd (Jn. 10:11).
    e. I am the resurrection (Jn. 11:25).
    f. I am the Way (Jn. 14:6).
    g. I am the true Vine (Jn. 15:1).

THE OLD TESTAMENT PROPHECIES FULFILLED BY THE SAVIOR

1. That he would be born of a virgin. (Compare Isa. 7:14 with Mt. 1:22, 23.)
2. That he would be given the throne of David. (Compare 2 Sam. 7:11, 12; Ps. 132:11; Isa. 9:6, 7; 16:5; Jer. 23:5 with Lk. 1:31, 32.)
3. That this throne would be an eternal throne. (Compare Dan. 2:44; 7:14, 27; Micah 4:7 with Lk. 1:33.)
4. That he would be called Emmanuel. (Compare Isa. 7:14 with Mt. 1:23.)
5. That he would have a forerunner. (Compare Isa. 40:3-5; Mal. 3:1 with Lk. 1:76-78; 3:3-6; Mt. 3:1-3.)
6. That he would be born in Bethlehem. (Compare Micah 5:2 with Lk. 2:4-6; Mt. 2:5, 6.)
7. That he would be worshiped by the wise men and presented with gifts. (Compare Ps. 72:10; Isa. 60:3, 6, 9 with Mt. 2:11.)
8. That he would be in Egypt for a season. (Compare Num. 24:8; Hos. 11:1 with Mt. 2:15.)
9. That his birthplace would suffer a massacre of infants. (Compare Jer. 31:15 with Mt. 2:17, 18.)
10. That he would be called a Nazarene. (Compare Isa. 11:1 with Mt. 2:23.)
11. That he would be zealous for the Father. (Compare Ps. 69:9; 119:139 with Jn. 2:13-17.)
12. That he would be filled with God's Spirit. (Compare Isa. 11:2; 61:1, 2; Ps. 45:7 with Lk. 4:18, 19.)
13. That he would heal many. (Compare Isa. 53:4 with Mt. 8:16, 17.)
14. That he would deal gently with the Gentiles. (Compare Isa. 9:1, 2; 42:1-3 with Mt. 12:17-21; 4:13-16.)

THE OLD TESTAMENT PROPHECIES FULFILLED BY CHRIST

OLD TESTAMENT PREDICTION	NATURE OF THE PROPHECY	NEW TESTAMENT FULFILLMENT
19. Ps. 118:22, 23	TO BE THE REJECTED CORNERSTONE	Mt. 21:42
20. Isa. 53:1	THAT HIS MIRACLES WOULD NOT BE BELIEVED	Jn. 12:37, 38
21. Ps. 41:9; 55:12-14	TO BE BETRAYED BY HIS FRIEND FOR THIRTY PIECES OF SILVER	Mt. 26:14-16, 21-25
22. Isa. 53:3	TO BE A MAN OF SORROWS	Mt. 26:37, 38
23. Zech. 13:7	TO BE FORSAKEN BY HIS DISC!PLES	Mt. 26:31, 56
24. Isa. 50:6	TO BE SCOURGED AND SPAT UPON	Mt. 26:67; 27:26
25. Zech. 11:12, 13; Jer. 18:1-4; 19:1-4	HIS PRICE MONEY TO BE USED TO BUY A POTTER'S FIELD	Mt. 27:9, 10
26. Isa. 53:12	TO BE CRUCIFIED BETWEEN TWO THIEVES	Mt. 27:38
27. Ps. 69:21	TO BE GIVEN VINEGAR TO DRINK	Mt. 27:34, 48; Jn. 19:28-30
28. Ps. 22:16; Zech. 12:10	TO SUFFER THE PIERCING OF HANDS AND FEET	Mk. 15:25; Jn. 19, 34, 37; 20:25-27
29. Ps. 22:18	HIS GARMENTS TO BE PARTED AND GAMBLED FOR	Lk. 23:34; Jn. 19:23, 24
30. Ps. 22: 7, 8	TO BE SURROUNDED AND RIDICULED BY HIS ENEMIES	Mt. 27:39-44; Mk. 15:29-32
31. Ps. 22:15	THAT HE WOULD THIRST	Jn. 19:28
32. Ps. 31:5	TO COMMEND HIS SPIRIT TO THE FATHER	Lk. 23:46
33. Ps. 34:20; Ex. 12:46; Num. 9:12	NO BONES TO BE BROKEN	Jn. 19:33-36
34. Zech. 12:10	TO BE STARED AT IN DEATH	Jn. 19:37; Mt. 27:36
35. Isa. 53:9	TO BE BURIED WITH THE RICH	Mt. 27:57-60
36. Ps. 16:10	TO BE RAISED FROM THE DEAD	Mt. 28:2-8
37. Ps. 24:7-10; Isa. 52:13	TO ASCEND	Mk. 16:19; Lk. 24:51

15. That he would speak in parables. (Compare Isa. 6:9, 10 with Mt. 13:10-15.)
16. That he would be rejected by his own. (Compare Isa. 53:3; Ps. 69:8 with Jn. 1:11; 7:5.)
17. That he would make a triumphal entry into Jerusalem. (Compare Zech. 9:9 with Mt. 21:4, 5.)
18. That he would be praised by little children. (Compare Ps. 8:2 with Mt. 21:16.)
19. That he would be the rejected cornerstone. (Compare Ps. 118:22, 23 with Mt. 21:42.)
20. That his miracles would not be believed. (Compare Isa. 53:1 with Jn. 12:37, 38.)
21. That his friend would betray him for thirty pieces of silver. (Compare Ps. 41:9; 55:12-14; Zech. 11:12, 13 with Mt. 26:14-16, 21-25.)
22. That he would be a man of sorrows. (Compare Isa. 53:3 with Mt. 26:37, 38.)
23. That he would be forsaken by his disciples. (Compare Zech. 13:7 with Mt. 26:31, 56.)
24. That he would be scourged and spat upon. (Compare Isa. 50:6 with Mt. 26:67; 27:26.)
25. That his price money would be used to buy a potter's field. (Compare Zech. 11:12, 13; Jer. 18:1-4; 19:1-4 with Mt. 27:9, 10.)
26. That he would be crucified between two thieves. (Compare Isa. 53:12 with Mt. 27:38; Mk. 15:27, 28; Lk. 22:37.)
27. That he would be given vinegar to drink. (Compare Ps. 69:21 with Mt. 27:34, 48; Jn. 19:28-30.)
28. That he would suffer the piercing of his hands and feet. (Compare Ps. 22:16; Zech. 12:10 with Mk. 15:25; Jn. 19:34, 37; 20:25-27.)
29. That his garments would be parted and gambled for. (Compare Ps. 22:18 with Lk. 23:34; Jn. 19:23, 24.)
30. That he would be surrounded and ridiculed by his enemies. (Compare Ps. 22:7, 8 with Mt. 27:39-44; Mk. 15:29-32.)
31. That he would thirst. (Compare Ps. 22:15 with Jn. 19:28.)
32. That he would commend his spirit to the Father. (Compare Ps. 31:5 with Lk. 23:46.)

33. That his bones would not be broken. (Compare Ps. 34:20; Ex. 12:46; Num. 9:12 with Jn. 19:33–36.)
34. That he would be stared at in death. (Compare Zech. 12:10 with Jn. 19:37; Mt. 27:36.)
35. That he would be buried with the rich. (Compare Isa. 53:9 with Mt. 27:57–60.)
36. That he would be raised from the dead. (Compare Ps. 16:10 with Mt. 28:2–7.)
37. That he would ascend. (Compare Ps. 24:7–10 with Mk. 16:19; Lk. 24:51.)

THE SOULS CONVERTED BY THE SAVIOR

1. Andrew (Jn. 1:40, 41)
   Circumstances: Saved when he left John the Baptist to follow the Lamb of God.
   Location: Near the Jordan River.
   Recorded testimony: "We have found the Messiah."
2. Peter (Jn. 1:41, 42)
   Circumstances: Saved when he was brought to Christ by his brother Andrew. Had his name changed by Jesus to Cephas (a stone).
   Recorded testimony: None recorded at this point. (For later testimony see Mt. 16:16.)
3. Philip (Jn. 1:43, 45)
   Circumstances: Saved as a result of a personal visit by Jesus in Bethsaida of Galilee. Answered the call of the Master to follow him.
   Recorded testimony: "We have found him, of whom Moses in the law, and the prophets did write, Jesus of Nazareth."
4. Nathanael (Jn. 1:45–51)
   Circumstances: Saved when he was brought to Christ by Philip. Was skeptical of Jesus at first.
   Recorded testimony: "Rabbi, thou art the Son of God; thou art the King of Israel."
5. Nicodemus (Jn. 3:1–21)
   Circumstances: Saved in Jerusalem during a night meeting with Jesus. He was a ruler of the Jews, a teacher, a good and sincere man, but was lost!
   Recorded testimony: None was given at this time. (See Jn. 7:51, given later.)
6. A Samaritan woman (Jn. 4:29)
   Circumstances: Saved at Jacob's well outside a city in Samaria. She immediately gave testimony of this fact to her friends in the city.
   Recorded testimony: "Come see a man, which told me all things that ever I did: is not this the Christ?"
7. A nobleman (Jn. 4:53)
   Circumstances: Saved in Capernaum after Jesus had healed his dying boy.
   Recorded testimony: None given.
8. An adulterous woman (Jn. 8:11)
   Circumstances: Saved in Jerusalem after being forgiven by Christ and rescued from a mob of self-righteous Pharisees.
   Recorded testimony: None given.
9. A blind man (Jn. 9:38)
   Circumstances: Saved in Jerusalem after receiving his sight. Witnessed boldly for Christ among the Pharisees and was thrown out of their synagogue for his testimony.
   Recorded testimony: "Lord, I believe."
10. Martha (Jn. 11:27)
    Circumstances: Saved outside Bethany shortly after the death of her brother Lazarus.
    Recorded testimony: "Yea, Lord: I believe that thou art the Christ, the Son of God which should come into the world."
11. A centurion (Mt. 8:5–13)
    Circumstances: Saved in Capernaum after requesting Jesus to heal his beloved servant. The Master was amazed at his tremendous faith.
    Recorded testimony: None given.
12. Matthew (Mt. 9:9)
    Circumstances: Saved at his place of business in Jerusalem. He leaves all and follows Christ.
    Recorded testimony: None given.
13. A Syro-phoenician woman (Mt. 15:28)
    Circumstances: Saved along the Mediterranean coastline as she requests Jesus to heal her demoniac daughter.
    Recorded testimony: None given.
14. A Gadara maniac (Mk. 5:15–20)
    Circumstances: Saved outside a cemetery on the eastern shoreline of the Galilean Sea. His salvation results in the death of 2,000 hogs!
    Recorded testimony: "And he departed, and began to publish in Decapolis how great things Jesus had done for him."
15. A woman with internal bleeding (Mk. 5:28, 34)
    Circumstances: Saved in a Capernaum crowd as she touched the hem of Jesus' garment by faith for healing.
    Recorded testimony: "If I may touch but his clothes, I shall be whole."
16. A Galilean leper (Mt. 8:2)
    Circumstances: Saved during Christ's first preaching tour of Galilee as he requests healing.
    Recorded testimony: "Lord, if thou wilt, thou canst make me clean."
17. The father of a demoniac son (Mk. 9:24)
    Circumstances: Saved as he meets Jesus at the base of the Mount of Transfiguration and begs for healing of his tormented son.
    Recorded testimony: "Lord, I believe; help thou mine unbelief."
18. Blind Bartimaeus (Mk. 10:46–52)
    Circumstances: Saved outside Jericho as he cried out for Christ to cure his blindness.
    Recorded testimony: None given.
19. A paralytic (Lk. 5:20)
    Circumstances: Saved in Capernaum as he was being lowered from the ceiling of a house.
    Recorded testimony: None given.
20. An immoral but heartbroken woman (Lk. 7:38, 47–50)
    Circumstances: Saved in the home of a Pharisee as she washed Jesus' feet with her tears and dried them with her hair.
    Recorded testimony: None given.
21. A Samaritan leper (Lk. 17:11–19)
    Circumstances: Saved on a country road as he returned to thank Jesus for healing him of leprosy.
    Recorded testimony: "With a loud voice [he] glorified God and fell down at his feet, giving him thanks."
22. A Publican (Lk. 18:13)
    Circumstances: Saved as he begged for mercy in the Temple of Jerusalem.
    Recorded testimony: None given. (Note: Even though Jesus refers to this in a parable, he very well could have had an actual case history in mind.)

23. Zacchaeus (Lk. 19:8, 9)
    Circumstances: Saved as he leaped from a sycamore tree in Jericho to meet Jesus.
    Recorded testimony: "Behold, Lord, the half of my goods I give to the poor; and if I have taken anything from any man by false accusation, I restore him fourfold."
24. A woman with an eighteen-year infirmity (Lk. 13:11-13)
    Circumstances: Saved in a Galilean synagogue as Jesus laid his hands on her for healing.
    Recorded testimony: She "glorified God."
25. Mary Magdalene (Mk. 16:9)
    Circumstances: Saved probably at the beginning of Christ's ministry when he cast seven demons from her. Referred to in this passage.
    Recorded testimony: None given.
26. A centurion at Calvary (Mt. 27:54)
    Circumstances: Saved while watching Jesus die on the cross.
    Recorded testimony: "Truly this was the Son of God."
27. A dying thief (Lk. 23:42)
    Circumstances: Saved while on a cross next to Jesus. He asks the Savior to remember him when he establishes his kingdom.
    Recorded testimony: None given.

THE SUFFERINGS OF THE SAVIOR

1. Rejected by:
    a. his nation (Jn. 1:11)
    b. his hometown (Lk. 4:28, 29)
    c. his friends (Mk. 3:21)
    d. his family (Jn. 7:5)
    e. the religious world (Jn. 7:1; 9:22)
2. Tempted by Satan (Lk. 4:1, 2, 13; 22:28)
3. Ridiculed because of:
    a. his hometown (Jn. 1:46; 7:52)
    b. his background (Jn. 8:41; 9:24, 29)
4. Threatened constantly:
    a. by Herod (Mt. 2:16)
    b. by his hometown (Lk. 4:29)
    c. by the Jews
        (1) because he healed on the Sabbath (Jn. 5:16; Lk. 6:10, 11)
        (2) because of his claims (Jn. 8:58, 59; 10:30-33)
        (3) because of his sermons (Jn. 8:40; Lk. 11:53, 54; Mk. 12:12; Mt. 26:1-4)
        (4) because of his miracles (Jn. 11:53; see also Jn. 12:10)
    d. by the devil (Mt. 26:37, 38; Mk. 14:33, 34; Lk. 22:44)
5. Homeless (Mt. 8:20)
6. Betrayed by a follower (Jn. 13:21)
7. Denied by a friend (Mt. 26:58, 69-75; Mk. 14:54, 66-72; Lk. 22:54-62; Jn. 18:15-18, 25-27)
8. Misunderstood by his disciples (Mt. 15:16; 16:6-11; Mk. 6:52; Jn. 10:6; 12:16)
9. Forsaken by all (Mt. 26:56)
10. Misquoted (Mt. 26:61)
11. Illegally tried seven times:
    a. first trial, before Annas (Jn. 18:12-14, 19-24)
    b. second trial, before Caiaphas (Mt. 26:57-68; Mk. 14:53-65)
    c. third trial, before the Sanhedrin (Mt. 27:1, 2; Mk. 15:1; Lk. 22:66—23:1)
    d. fourth trial, before Pilate (Jn. 18:28-38; Mt. 27:2, 11-14; Mk. 15:1-5; Lk. 23:1-6)
    e. fifth trial, before Herod (Lk. 23:7-12)
    f. sixth trial, before Pilate (Jn. 18:39—19:16; Mt. 27:15-26; Mk. 15:6-15; Lk. 23:13-25)
    g. seventh trial, before the Roman soldiers (Mt. 27:27-31; Mk. 15:16-20)
12. Indicted on false charges (Lk. 23:1, 2)
13. Mocked by:
    a. the Roman soldiers (Lk. 23:36, 37; Mk. 15:16-20)
    b. the watching crowd (Lk. 23:35)
    c. the chief priests (Mk. 15:31)
    d. the two thieves (Mk. 15:32; Mt. 27:44)
14. Tortured—our Lord was:
    a. slapped (Jn. 18:22)
    b. blindfolded (Lk. 22:64)
    c. spit upon (Mt. 26:67)
    d. buffeted (Mt. 26:67)
    e. scourged (Mt. 27:26)
    f. struck upon the head (Mt. 27:30)
    g. pierced with thorns (Mt. 27:29)
15. Crucified (Mt. 27; Mk. 15; Lk. 23; Jn. 19)

THE SEVEN LAST STATEMENTS OF THE SAVIOR

1. "Father, forgive them; for they know not what they do" (Lk. 23:34).
2. "Verily I say unto thee, today shalt thou be with me in paradise" (Lk. 23:43).
3. "Woman, behold thy son! Behold thy mother!" (Jn. 19:26, 27).
4. "My God, my God, why hast thou forsaken me?" (Mt. 27:46).
5. "I thirst" (Jn. 19:28).
6. "It is finished" (Jn. 19:30).
7. "Father, into thy hands I commend my spirit" (Lk. 23:46).

THE RESURRECTION APPEARANCES OF THE SAVIOR

1. To Mary Magdalene in the garden (Mk. 16:9; Jn. 20:11-18).
2. To the women returning from the tomb (Mt. 28:9, 10).
3. To two disciples on the Emmaus Road (Lk. 24:13-32; Mk. 16:12, 13).
4. To Peter in Jerusalem (Lk. 24:34; 1 Cor. 15:5).
5. To ten of his apostles in the upper room (Lk. 24:36-43; Jn. 20:19-23).
6. To eleven of his apostles in the upper room (Jn. 20:24-29).
7. To seven of his apostles by the Galilean Sea (Jn. 21:1-24).
8. To his apostles and 500 believers on Mt. Tabor (Mt. 28:16-20; 1 Cor. 15:6).
9. To eleven of his apostles and James, his half-brother, in Jerusalem (Mk. 16:14-18; Lk. 24:44-49; 1 Cor. 15:7).
10. To the eleven on the Mount of Olives (Lk. 24:50-53; Acts 1:3).

THE POLITICAL AND RELIGIOUS PARTIES IN THE SAVIOR'S TIME

I. Political and Religious Groups
    A. The Galileans:
        1. They were the political "extreme right" fanatics of their day.
        2. The group arose in Northern Palestine, headed up by one Judas of Galilee, who led a rebellion against all foreign elements. They advocated Galilee was for Galileans.

THE CRUCIFIXION OF CHRIST

9:00 A.M. TILL NOON

- Simon helps Christ bear his cross.
- Some women weep over Jesus.
- Christ is crucified between two thieves.
- The cross inscription is put in place.
- The soldiers cast lots for his garment.
- He is cruelly mocked by all.

"Father forgive them; for they know not what they do" **(Lk. 23:34).**

"Verily I say unto thee, today thou shalt be with me in paradise" **(Lk. 23:43).**

"Woman, behold thy son! Behold, thy mother!" **(Jn. 19:26, 27).**

NOON TILL 3:00 P.M.

"My God, my God, why hast thou forsaken me?" **(Mt. 27:46).**

"I thirst" **(Jn. 19:28).**

"It is finished" **(Jn. 19:30).**

"Father, into thy hands I commend my spirit" **(Lk. 23:46).**

- Darkness settles down in area.
- Christ accepts drugged vinegar.
- Temple veil rent in two.
- Earthquake opens some tombs.
- Testimony of the centurion.
- Confused crowd returns home.
- Soldier pierces Christ's side.
- Joseph and Nicodemus take his body from the cross.
- He is partially prepared for burial.
- He is laid in Joseph's tomb.
- Tomb is sealed with a great stone.

3. They came into violent collision with Pilate, who felt forced to slaughter a number of them on one occasion (Lk. 13:1).
4. Christ's enemies attempted to identify both him and the disciples with the Galileans (Mt. 26:69; Mk. 14:70; Lk. 23:6).

B. The Herodians:
   1. This was a political group from the family of Herod.
   2. They derived their authority from the Roman government, and favored Greek customs.
   3. They were committed to maintaining the status quo and were law-and-order advocates.
   4. They joined the efforts of the Pharisees to silence Christ.
      a. during his early ministry (Mk. 3:6)
      b. during the middle part (Mk. 12:13)
      c. during his final week (Mt. 22:16)
   5. They regarded him as a revolutionary fanatic.
   6. Christ soundly condemned the Herodians (Mk. 8:15; 12:13–17).

C. The Levites:
   1. They were the descendants of Levi, Jacob's third son (Gen. 29:34).
   2. They had charge of the Temple.
   3. The Jews sent some priests and Levites to check out the desert ministry of John the Baptist (Jn. 1:19).
   4. Jesus used a Levite (who didn't want to become involved) in his parable of the Good Samaritan (Lk. 10:32).

D. The Pharisees:
   1. This group arose during the time of the Maccabees under the reign of John Hyrcanus (135–104 B.C.).
   2. They were called the separatists in mockery by their enemies. This name was taken from the verb *parash*.
   3. They were the exponents and guardians of both written and oral law. In belief they were conservative, in distinction from the liberal Sadducees.
   4. They were the most bitter and hateful enemies of Christ.
      a. They condemned him for associating with sinners (Mt. 9:11; Lk. 7:39; 15:2).
      b. They condemned him for healing on the Sabbath (Lk. 6:7; 14:1).
      c. They condemned him for allowing his disciples to eat on the Sabbath (Mt. 12:1, 2).
      d. They accused him of casting out demons through Satan's power (Mt. 9:34).
      e. They sought to kill him early in his ministry (Mt. 12:14).
      f. They demanded that he perform signs for them (Mt. 12:38; 16:1).
      g. They despised him because he refused to always follow their vain traditions (Mt. 15:1, 2).
      h. They attempted to trap him on various theological issues.
         (1) concerning marriage (Mt. 19:3)
         (2) concerning tribute to Caesar (Mt. 22:15)
         (3) concerning the kingdom of God (Lk. 17:20)
         (4) concerning adultery (Jn. 8:3)
      i. They attempted to deny his miracles (Jn. 9:15).
      j. They cast doubt upon the legality of his birth (Jn. 8:41; 9:24).
      k. They accused him of outright lying (Jn. 8:13).
      l. They threatened retaliation upon all who would accept him (Jn. 9:22; 12:42).

m. They plotted his death (Jn. 11:47–53).

n. They ordered his arrest in Gethsemane (Jn. 18:3).

o. They demanded a guard be stationed at his tomb (Mt. 27:64).

5. The Pharisees were utterly denounced by John the Baptist (Mt. 3:7; Lk. 7:30).

6. The Pharisees were utterly denounced by Jesus (Mt. 5:20; 16:11; 23:1–36; Lk. 18:10).

7. The doctrine of the Pharisees would include:

a. an almost fatalistic concept of God's sovereignty

b. a belief in the resurrection of the just and the damnation of all wicked

c. the existence and ministry of angels

8. Nicodemus (Jn. 3:1) and Paul (Acts 23:6) were both Pharisees by birth and training.

9. The *Jewish Encyclopedia* lists seven types of Pharisees:

a. The "shoulder" Pharisee, who paraded his good deeds before men like a badge on the shoulder.

b. The "wait-a-little" Pharisee, who would ask someone to wait for him while he performed a good deed.

c. The "blind" Pharisee, who bruised himself by walking into a wall because he shut his eyes to avoid seeing a woman.

d. The "pestle" Pharisee, who walked with hanging head rather than observe alluring temptations.

e. The "ever-reckoning" Pharisee, who was always counting his good deeds to see if they offset his failures.

f. The "God-fearing Pharisee," who, like Job, was truly righteous.

g. The "God-loving" Pharisee, like Abraham.

10. The estimated number of Pharisees in Jesus' day was around 6,000.

E. The Sadducees:

1. This group came from Zadok, the high priest, during the reign of Solomon (1 Ki. 2:35).

2. They were the aristocratic and political party among the Jews and the rivals of the Pharisees.

3. The Sadducees were the modernists of the day. They denied the existence of spirits, the resurrection of the just, and the immortality of the soul. They were totally anti-supernatural.

4. They came into prominence about the same time the Pharisees did. Both parties briefly set aside their differences to accomplish their common goal of murdering Christ.

5. They attempted to ridicule Christ on the subject of the resurrection, but wound up being ridiculed themselves (Mk. 12:18; Lk. 20:27).

F. The Samaritans:

1. They were a mixed race living between the provinces of Judea and Galilee.

2. The race began in 722 B.C. when the Assyrian King Sargon II took the northern kingdom of Israel into captivity, leaving only the poorest and most uneducated Israelites behind. Later this group intermarried with the thousands of homesteaders who poured into the area from all over the world (2 Ki. 17:24–33).

3. The Samaritans later offered to help build the Jewish Temple in 535 B.C., but were refused (Ezra 4:1–3).

4. The Samaritan governor, Sanballat, attempted to frustrate the building of Jerusalem's walls during Nehemiah's time (Neh. 6:1–9).

5. A complete break between the Jews and Samaritans occurred when the grandson of Eliashib the high priest married Sanballat's daughter, contrary to the statute prohibiting mixed marriages (Neh. 13:23–28). Since he refused to annul the marriage, he was promptly expelled from the priesthood and exiled. He retired to Samaria, where Sanballat built a temple for him on Mt. Gerizim. This temple was destroyed by John Hyrcanus in 128 B.C. The reason was because the Samaritans had compromised with paganism under Antiochus Epiphanes IV by dedicating their temple to the Greek god Zeus.

6. By the time of the New Testament this hatred had reached its zenith (Jn. 4:9; 8:48).

7. Christ ordered his disciples not to enter Samaria during their first preaching tour (Mt. 10:5).

8. However, just prior to his ascension he commanded them to witness for him in that land (Acts 1:8).

9. Jesus himself did minister to the Samaritans during his earthly ministry (Jn. 4:1–42).

10. A Samaritan was the hero in one of his most famous parables (Lk. 10:33).

11. On one occasion he healed ten lepers. Only one returned to thank him, and he was a Samaritan (Lk. 17:16).

12. Jesus was rejected by the Samaritans during his final earthly ministry, because his face was set as though he would go to Jerusalem (Lk. 9:53).

G. The Sanhedrin:

1. This name comes from two Greek words: *sun* (together with), and *hedra* (a sitting place). It thus referred to a council board which sat in session.

2. The Sanhedrin was the religious and legal Jewish Supreme Court.

3. It may have come from the time of Moses (Num. 11:16, 17), or during the days of King Jehoshaphat (2 Chron. 19:8).

4. The council had seventy to seventy-two members and consisted of:

a. the high priest, who was president

b. the heads of the twenty-four priestly service divisions

c. the scribes and lawyers

d. the elders, who were the representatives of the laity

5. Here Christ stood during his third illegal trial (Mt. 26:65, 66; 27:1, 2). Here also he was blindfolded, spit upon, and beaten.

6. His trial before the Sanhedrin was a travesty of justice.
    a. They normally met in a semicircle with the prisoner standing in the midst, facing them. This was not done, for Jesus was blindfolded.
    b. Two clerks were appointed. One would record the votes for acquittal, the other for conviction. In Christ's case this was not done.
    c. The arguments for acquittal would be given first. This did not happen in Jesus' trial.
    d. If the vote was for acquittal, the prisoner was set free immediately. If the vote was for conviction, condemnation could not be pronounced until the following day. This procedure was not followed.
H. The scribes:
    1. They were the students, interpreters, and teachers of the Old Testament Scriptures, and the Savior's bitter enemies.
    2. He denounced them for making the Word of God of no effect by their traditions (Mt. 16:21; 21:15; 23:2; 26:3; Mk. 12:28-40).
    3. The scribes were also called lawyers (Mt. 22:35; Lk. 10:25; 11:45-52; 14:3).

THE VARIOUS PLACES VISITED BY THE SAVIOR

1. Bethabara: A few miles north of Jericho, on the eastern bank of the Jordan River where John baptized Jesus (Jn. 1:28; Mt. 3:13-17).
2. Bethany: Fifteen furlongs, or one and three-fourths miles from Jerusalem on the eastern slope of the Mount of Olives. It is on the road to Jericho. Bethany was the Judean headquarters of Jesus, as Capernaum was his Galilean headquarters.
    a. Here he raised Lazarus from the dead (Jn. 11).
    b. Mary and Martha entertained Christ here (Lk. 10:38-42).
    c. Mary anointed his feet here (Jn. 12:1-11).
    d. It was also the home of Simon the leper (Mk. 14:3).
    e. Here Christ blessed his disciples just prior to his ascension from the Mount of Olives (Lk. 24:50).
3. Bethlehem: Five miles south of Jerusalem.
    a. It was the birthplace of both Mary and Joseph (Lk. 2:1-4).
    b. It was here Christ was born (Micah 5:2; Jn. 7:42; Lk. 2).
4. Bethphage: On the slopes of Mount Olivet between Bethany and Jerusalem. Here the triumphal entry began (Mt. 21:1-11; Mk. 11:1-11; Lk. 19:29-40).
5. Bethsaida: Located at the place where the Jordan River enters the Sea of Galilee. It means "the place of catching."
    a. It was the home of Philip, Andrew, and Peter (Jn. 1:44).
    b. Jesus upbraided this city, along with others, for its unbelief (Lk. 10:11-14; Mt. 11:21).
    c. Here he also healed a blind man (Mk. 8:22-26).
6. Bireh: Located fifteen miles north of Jerusalem and the first stopping place for caravans going from Jerusalem to Galilee, Bireh is thought to be the place where Jesus was found to be missing during his visit to the Temple at age 12 (Lk. 2:41-45).
7. Caesarea Philippi: Situated at the base of Mount Hermon, northeast of the Galilean Sea. This was doubtless the farthest point north traveled by our Lord. Here he heard Simon Peter's great confession (Mt. 16:13-16).
8. Cana: Four miles northeast of Nazareth, on the road to Tiberias.
    a. It was the hometown of Nathanael (Jn. 21:2).
    b. Here Jesus performed his first miracle, that of turning water into wine (Jn. 2:1-11).
    c. Here he also worked his second miracle, the healing of the nobleman's son (Jn. 4:46-54).
9. Capernaum: Located along the northwest shore of Galilee, two-and-a-half miles from where the Jordan River enters the lake.
    a. This became the Galilean headquarters of his earthly ministry (Mt. 4:13; 9:1).
    b. Here he chose Matthew (Mt. 9:9).
    c. Here he delivered his great Bread of Life sermon (Jn. 6:24-71).
    d. Here he performed nine of his recorded miracles.
        (1) Healing of the centurion's servant (Mt. 8:5-13).
        (2) Healing of Peter's mother-in-law (Mt. 8:14, 15).
        (3) Healing of a demoniac (Mk. 1:21-27).
        (4) Healing of the palsied man who was lowered from the roof (Mk. 2:1-5).
        (5) Healing of the woman with a bloody issue (Mt. 9:22).
        (6) Healing of Jairus' daughter (Mt. 9:25).
        (7) Healing of two blind men (Mt. 9:29).
        (8) Healing of a dumb demoniac (Mt. 9:33).
        (9) The miracle of the tribute money (Mt. 17:24-27).
10. Chorazin: Two miles north of Capernaum. Christ pronounced judgment upon this city for its unbelief (Mt. 11:21-23).
11. Emmaus: About seven-and-a-half miles west of Jerusalem. Here Christ appeared to two disciples after his resurrection and revealed himself to them at the supper table (Lk. 24:13-31).
12. Gergesa: Located on the northeastern shore of Galilee, where Jesus healed the demon-filled maniac of Gadara (Mk. 5:1-21).
13. Gethsemane: Located across the Kidron valley from the golden gate of Jerusalem. It was the garden place where he prayed just prior to his betrayal and arrest (Mt. 26:36-56; Jn. 18:1-14).
14. Jenin: Twenty-four miles north of Samaria, where some believe Jesus healed the ten lepers (Lk. 17:11-19).
15. Jericho: Located seventeen miles northwest of Jerusalem near the Jordan River.
    a. Here Jesus healed a blind man named Bartimaeus (Lk. 18:35).
    b. Here Zacchaeus met Christ (Lk. 19:1-10).
    c. Jesus used this city to help illustrate his Good Samaritan parable (Lk. 10:30-37).
16. Jerusalem: The capital of God's world. It is situated on a rocky prominence about 2,500 feet above the Mediterranean and 3,800 feet above the Dead Sea. It is thirty-three miles east of the Mediterranean Sea and fourteen miles west of the Dead Sea.
    a. Jesus was dedicated here (Lk. 2:1-38).
    b. He attended the Passover at age twelve (Lk. 2:41-50).
    c. He cleansed the Temple (Jn. 2:13-17).
    d. He spoke to Nicodemus (Jn. 3:1-16).
    e. He healed a thirty-eight-year-old invalid (Jn. 5:8).

f. He preached on the Holy Spirit during the feast of the tabernacles (Jn. 7:10-39).

g. He forgave an adulterous woman (Jn. 8:1-11).

h. He preached on the devil and his children (Jn. 8:33-59).

i. He healed a man born blind (Jn. 9:7).

j. He preached a sermon on the Good Shepherd (Jn. 10:1-18).

k. He made his triumphal entry (Jn. 12:12-15).

l. He cursed the fig tree (Mt. 21:19).

m. He utterly condemned the wicked Pharisees (Mt. 23:1-36).

n. He preached the Mt. Olivet discourse (Mt. 24-25).

o. He wept over Jerusalem (Lk. 19:41; Mt. 23:37-39).

p. He conducted the service in the upper room (Jn. 13-14).

q. He preached on the vine and branches (Jn. 15-16).

r. He prayed his great high priestly prayer (Jn. 17).

s. He was arrested in Gethsemane (Mt. 26:47-56).

t. He restored a severed ear (Lk. 22:51).

u. He was condemned to death (Mt. 27:26).

v. He was crucified (Mt. 27:27-50).

w. He was buried (Mt. 27:57-60).

x. He rose from the dead (Mt. 28:1-10).

y. He visited the upper room for the first time after his resurrection (Lk. 24:36-43; Jn. 20:19-23).

z. He visited the upper room for the second time (Jn. 20:24-29).

aa. He visited the upper room for the third and final time (Mk. 16:14-18; Lk. 24:44-49).

bb. He ascended into heaven (Acts 1:4-11).

17. Jordan River: It begins at the base of Mount Hermon, about 1,700 feet above sea level. From there it goes to the waters of Merom, some twelve miles down course. From there it flows the five miles to the Sea of Galilee, some 682 feet below sea level. Finally, it proceeds the sixty-five miles to the Dead Sea, 1,300 feet below sea level. Thus, during its eighty-two-mile course, the Jordan River drops 3,000 feet. It was in the Jordan River that our Lord was baptized (Mt. 3:13-17).

18. Kidron: A valley, about two and three-fourths miles long, located immediately east of the wall of Jerusalem between the city and the Mount of Olives. Jesus crossed this valley en route to Gethsemane (Jn. 18:1).

19. Magdala: Located three miles north of Tiberias on the western shore of the Galilean Sea (Mt. 15:39). This was the home of Mary Magdalene (Lk. 8:2; Mk. 16:9).

20. Mount Hermon: Located some seventeen miles north of the Galilean Sea. It is by far the highest mountain in all Palestine, reaching 9,101 feet. Many believe this to be the "high mountain" of Matthew 17:1 where Christ was transfigured.

21. Mount of Olives: Located due east of Jerusalem, across from the Kidron Valley. Its height is 2,641 feet.

a. Here Christ wept over Jerusalem (Lk. 19:41-44).

b. Here he delivered his great sermon on prophecy (Mt. 25:24, 25).

c. Here he walked after the Passover in the upper room (Mt. 26:30; Mk. 14:26; Lk. 22:39).

d. From here he ascended into heaven (Lk. 24:50, 51; Acts 1:6-12).

22. Mount Tabor: Located five-and-a-half miles southeast of Nazareth. Its height is 1,843 feet above sea level. Some believe this was the mount of transfiguration instead of Mount Hermon. However, the text prefers the latter.

23. Mount Zion: The height which rises close to the southwest corner of the old walled city. Here was located the upper room (Mk. 14:12-16; Lk. 22:7-13; Jn. 13-14).

24. Nain: A city some ten miles southeast of Nazareth, where Jesus raised the dead son of a sorrowing widow (Lk. 7:11).

25. Nazareth: Located about midway between the Sea of Galilee and the Mediterranean Sea.

a. Both Joseph and Mary received the news from Gabriel concerning the virgin birth here (Lk. 1:26; Mt. 1:18-25).

b. Here Jesus grew into manhood (Lk. 2:39, 40, 51, 52).

c. Here he preached two sermons.

(1) After the first, on Isaiah 61, they attempted to kill him (Lk. 4:16-30).

(2) After the second, he was totally rejected by the citizens (Mt. 13:53-58; Mk. 6:1-6).

26. Sea of Galilee: This inland sea lake is thirteen miles long, seven-and-a-half miles wide, and thirty-two miles in circumference. It is 700 feet below sea level, and its greatest depth is 200 feet.

a. Beside this body of water, Jesus fed the 5,000 (Jn. 6:1-14).

b. On the Mount of Beatitudes, he gave the Sermon on the Mount (Mt. 5-7).

c. Here he calmed the wild stormy sea waters (Mt. 8:23-27).

d. Here he walked on the water (Jn. 6:15-21).

e. Here 2,000 hogs were drowned after he healed a maniac (Mk. 5:1-21).

f. Here he performed his last miracle (Mk. 14:28; 16:7; Jn. 21).

27. Sychar: Located some twenty-five miles due north of Jerusalem in Samaria. Here Jesus met the Samaritan woman at Jacob's well (Jn. 4).

28. Tyre: A city located on the Mediterranean Sea, some twenty miles due west of Caesarea Philippi. Jesus healed the Syro-phoenician woman's daughter in this area (Mk. 3:8; Lk. 6:17).

29. Wilderness of temptation: The exact spot is unknown. However, some feel it may have been southeast of Jerusalem in the Dead Sea area (Mt. 4:1).

THE MANY INDIVIDUALS WHO MET THE SAVIOR

I. Individuals mentioned in the Gospel accounts

A. The twelve apostles.

Simon Peter:

1. He was the most prominent and outspoken of the twelve.

2. He was a native of Bethsaida, a city on the Galilean sea (Jn. 1:44).

3. He was a brother of Andrew, and a partner with James and John in the fishing business (Lk. 5:7).

4. He was a married man (Mk. 1:30; 1 Cor. 9:5).

5. He was brought to Christ by his brother Andrew near the Jordan River (Jn. 1:41-43).

6. He was called full time later beside the Sea of Galilee (Lk. 5:3-11).

a. After fishing all night in vain, at Christ's command, he launched out into the deep and let his net down. Immediately a great catch of fish took place.

b. He then fell at Christ's feet and acknowledged his unworthiness.

7. He watched Christ heal his mother-in-law of a high fever (Mt. 8:14, 15).
8. He soon became the first of three which formed the inner circle of the apostles. The other two were James and John. These three alone:
    a. Were with Jesus at the raising of Jairus' daughter (Lk. 8:51).
    b. Accompanied him on the mount of transfiguration. Here Peter desired to build three tabernacles, one for Christ, one for Moses, and one for Elijah (Mt. 17:1-4).
    c. Were placed closest to Christ in Gethsemane by the Savior himself. All three were requested to pray. All three immediately fell asleep (Mt. 26:36-46).
9. Peter walked on the water (Mt. 14:28-31).
10. On one occasion Jesus watched a fickle crowd leave him and asked the apostles if they intended to also do this. Peter answered, "Lord, to whom shall we go? Thou hast the words of eternal life. And we believe and are sure that thou art the Christ, the Son of the living God" (Jn. 6:68, 69).
11. He declared his great confession concerning Christ's deity: "Thou art the Christ, the Son of the living God" (Mt. 16:16).
12. He was tempted by Satan to "straighten out" the Savior concerning his prophesied death and resurrection. For this he was severely rebuked by Jesus (Mt. 16:21-23).
13. He was commanded by Christ to go fishing in order that both he and the Savior might pay the Temple tribute: "Go thou to the sea, and cast an hook, and take up the fish that first cometh up; and when thou hast opened his mouth, thou shalt find a piece of money: that take, and give unto them for me and thee" (Mt. 17:27).
14. Jesus instructed him concerning forgiveness (Mt. 18:21, 22).
15. He was promised a future reward for having left all to follow Christ (Mt. 19:27-30).
16. Jesus sent Peter and John to prepare the Passover supper (Lk. 22:8).
17. Peter was present with Christ in the upper room.
18. Peter came to the Garden of Gethsemane with Christ. There in that quiet place:
    a. He immediately fell asleep (Mk. 14:37, 38).
    b. He cut off the ear of Malchus, the servant of the Jewish high priest (Jn. 18:10, 11).
19. He fled the garden in terror (along with the rest) and began to follow Christ afar off (Mk. 14:50, 54).
20. He denied his Lord three times beside an early morning fire in the outer court of the high priest (Jn. 18:15-18, 25-27).
21. His last denial was apparently overheard by the Savior: "And Peter said, Man, I know not what thou sayest. And immediately, while he yet spake, the cock crew. And the Lord turned, and looked upon Peter. And Peter remembered the word of the Lord, how he had said unto him, Before the cock crow, thou shalt deny me thrice" (Lk. 22:60, 61).

22. Peter hurriedly left the scene, weeping bitterly (Lk. 22:62).
23. Upon hearing Mary Magdalene's report concerning the empty tomb, Peter and John went there to investigate (Lk. 24:12; Jn. 20:2-10).
24. Jesus appeared to Simon Peter (Lk. 24:34; 1 Cor. 15:5).
25. Peter was among a group of seven apostles who gathered at the Galilean Sea. At this meeting:
    a. He aided in the miraculous catch of fish at Christ's command (Jn. 21:1-6).
    b. He jumped overboard and swam to shore in his eagerness to see Christ (Jn. 21:7).
    c. He was asked on three successive occasions if he loved the Savior (Jn. 21:15-17).
    d. His death by martyrdom was predicted by Christ (Jn. 21:18, 19).
    e. He asked Christ concerning his plans for John the apostle (Jn. 21:21).
26. He led the upper room ten-day prayer time and business meeting of the 120 apostles and disciples prior to Pentecost (Acts 1:15-26).
27. He preached his first recorded sermon at Pentecost (Acts 2:14-40).
28. He healed a lame man at the Temple gate and again preached a sermon (Acts 3:1-26).
29. He boldly addressed the Sanhedrin (Acts 4:8-12, 19, 20).
30. He passed divine judgment upon Ananias and Sapphira for lying to the Holy Spirit (Acts 5:1-11).
31. He healed many sick believers (Acts 5:15).
32. He again fearlessly answered the assembled Sadducees (Acts 5:29-32).
33. He was sent, along with John, to Samaria by the Jerusalem church. At this time, Peter:
    a. Ministered to the spiritual need of many Samaritans (Acts 8:14-17).
    b. Rebuked a greedy money-seeker named Simon (Acts 8:18-24).
34. He healed a man named Aeneas who had been bedridden for eight long years at Lydda (Acts 9:32-35). This led to a great revival.
35. He raised from the dead a believer named Dorcas at Joppa during her own funeral service (Acts 9:36-42). This also led to a revival.
36. He received his "sheet vision" at this time from God, instructing him that the gospel should be taken to Gentiles as well as Jews (Acts 10:9-16).
37. He was instructed by the Lord to go to Caesarea and minister to a Gentile-seeking sinner named Cornelius. This he did and led him and many others to Christ (Acts 10:17-48).
38. He then vindicated his actions among the Gentiles to the doubtful Jewish believers (Acts 11:1-18).
39. He was cast into prison and led to freedom by an angel from God during the night prior to his scheduled execution (Acts 12:1-11).
40. He immediately went to the home of John Mark's mother, where many believers had assembled to pray for his release (Acts 12:12-19).

41. He argued for Christian liberty during the Jerusalem council, which met to determine whether Gentile believers should submit to the Jewish rite of circumcision (Acts 15:7-11).
42. He met with Paul some three years after the apostle was saved en route to Damascus (Gal. 1:18).
43. He was on one occasion rebuked by Paul because of his compromise with the legalists of the day (Gal. 2:11-16).
44. He was the author of two New Testament epistles, 1 and 2 Peter.
45. Tradition teaches that he was crucified upside down at Rome.

Andrew:
1. He was a fisherman from Bethsaida in Galilee (Jn. 1:44).
2. He was an early disciple of John the Baptist, and, when introduced to Jesus, accepted him as the Messiah (Jn. 1:40).
3. He then immediately brought his brother Peter to Christ (Jn. 1:41, 42).
4. He was called by Christ to become a full-time disciple (Mt. 4:18, 19; 10:2).
5. He was present (along with three other disciples) at the healing of Peter's mother-in-law by Jesus (Mk. 1:29).
6. He was a prophecy student (Mk. 13:3, 4).
7. He gave a pessimistic report prior to the feeding of the 5,000 (Jn. 6:9).
8. He reported to Jesus concerning a request of some Greeks to see him (Jn. 12:22).
9. He was with ten other disciples in the upper room prior to Pentecost (Acts 1:13).

John, son of Zebedee:
1. He was the brother of James and perhaps the second most prominent disciple, next to Peter.
2. He was originally a disciple of John the Baptist (Jn. 1:35).
3. He was introduced to Christ by the Baptist himself (Jn. 1:36, 37).
4. He was called to follow Christ while fishing on the Galilean Sea (Mt. 4:18-22).
5. He was named an apostle, along with eleven others (Mt. 10:2-4; Lk. 6:14-16; Mk. 3:16-19).
6. He was one of the three key apostles who alone witnessed:
   a. the raising of Jairus' daughter (Lk. 8:41)
   b. the transfiguration (Mt. 17:1)
   c. the praying of Jesus in Gethsemane (Mt. 26:37)
7. He was gently rebuked by Christ on one occasion for his sectarianism. Luke 9:49, 50: "And John answered and said, Master, we saw one casting out devils in thy name; and we forbade him, because he followeth not with us. And Jesus said unto him, forbid him not: for he that is not against us is for us."
8. He desired Christ to judge a city which snubbed him by calling down fire from heaven (Lk. 9:54).
9. He asked for a special place of honor in the millennial kingdom of Christ (Mk. 10:35).
10. He was sent by Christ to aid Peter in making ready the final Passover supper (Lk. 22:8).

11. He asked Christ about the identity of his betrayer in the upper room (Jn. 13:25).
12. He forsook Christ in the garden and then followed him afar off (Jn. 18:15).
13. He was the only apostle at the cross (Jn. 19:26).
14. He assumed the responsibility of caring for Mary after the crucifixion of Christ (Jn. 19:27).
15. He visited the empty tomb with Peter (Jn. 20:2, 3).
16. He was the first to recognize Jesus at the postresurrection appearance beside the Galilean Sea (Jn. 21:7).
17. A rumor spread around concerning him that he would never die (Jn. 21:23).
18. He was with Peter when the healing of a lame man took place (Acts 3:1-11).
19. He was sent by the Jerusalem church to minister in Samaria (Acts 8:14, 15).
20. He was visited by Paul (Gal. 2:9).
21. He wrote five New Testament books: John, 1 John, 2 John, 3 John, and Revelation.
22. He was banished to the Isle of Patmos in the reign of Nero (or perhaps Domitian), received the vision of Revelation, was later liberated, and died a natural death while pastoring at Ephesus.

James, son of Zebedee:
1. He was apparently a rather well-to-do fisherman and elder brother of John the apostle (Mt. 4:21).
2. He was, at the time of his call by Christ, a fishing partner with Simon Peter (Lk. 5:10).
3. He was called by Christ to be one of his twelve apostles (Mt. 10:2).
4. He and his brother John were nicknamed "Sons of Thunder" by the Savior (Mk. 3:17).
5. He and John asked Christ for a special position in his future kingdom. For this the brothers invoked the displeasure of the remaining ten (Mk. 10:35, 36, 41).
6. On one occasion he wanted to call down fire from heaven to consume a Samaritan city which had rejected Christ. The Savior rebuked him for this attitude (Lk. 9:54, 55).
7. He was one of the inner circle trio with whom Christ spent much time. The other two were John and Peter. These three only:
   a. Accompanied Christ on the mount of transfiguration (Mt. 17:1).
   b. Were present when he healed Peter's mother-in-law (Mk. 1:29).
   c. Witnessed him raise Jairus' daughter from the dead (Mk. 5:37).
   d. Asked him privately about his Second Coming on the Mount of Olives (Mk. 13:3, 4).
   e. Were requested to pray for him in the Garden of Gethsemane (Mk. 14:33).
8. He was at the Sea of Galilee along with six other disciples after the resurrection when Christ forgave Peter (Jn. 21:1, 2).
9. He was present in the upper room at Pentecost (Acts 1:13).
10. He was imprisoned and martyred by King Herod (Acts 12:1, 2).

SIMON PETER

LK. 5:10	Brother of Andrew and fishing partner with James and John
MK. 1:30;	A married man
1 COR. 9:5	
JN. 1:41, 42	Brought to Christ by his brother Andrew
LK. 5:3-11	Later called into full-time service by Christ
MT. 8:14, 15	Watched Christ heal his mother-in-law
LK. 8:51; MT. 17:1-4	Became (along with James and John) one of the "key three"
MT. 26:36-40	
MT. 14:28-31	Walked on water
JN. 6:68, 69; MT. 16:16	Gave two great confessions concerning Christ's deity
MT. 16:21-23	Allowed Satan to influence him concerning Christ's death
MT. 17:27	Caught a fish with a coin in its mouth
MT. 18:21, 22	Was instructed by Christ concerning forgiveness
MT. 17:1-4	Saw the transfiguration of Christ
MT. 19:27	Was promised a reward for following Christ
LK. 22:8	Helped prepare for the final Passover
JN. 13:6, 24, 36	Was present with Christ in the upper room
JN. 18:10, 11	Cut off Malchus' ear in Gethsemane
MK. 14:50, 54	Followed Christ afar off
JN. 18:15-18, 25-27	Denied Christ on three occasions
LK. 22:62	Bitterly regretted these denials
LK. 24:12; JN. 20:2-10	Visited the empty tomb with John
LK. 24:34; 1 COR. 15:5	Was himself visited by the resurrected Christ
JN. 21:1-23	Was present at Christ's last miracle by the Galilean sea

ANDREW

JN. 1:44	Brother of Peter and a fisherman from Bethsaida in Galilee
JN. 1:40	An early disciple of John the Baptist
JN. 1:40	Accepted Christ and brought his brother to the Savior
JN. 6:12-22	Was tested by Christ during the feeding of the 5,000

JOHN

MT. 4:21	Brother of James and a fisherman
MT. 17:1-4	Was the most prominent apostle, a member of the "key three'
JN. 1:35	Was an original disciple of John the Baptist
LK. 9:49, 50	Was gently rebuked by Christ for his sectarianism on one occasion
MK. 10:35	Asked Christ for a special place of honor in the millennium
LK. 9:54	Demonstrated vindictiveness on one occasion
LK. 22:8	Helped prepare for the Last Supper
JN. 13:23	Leaned on the bosom of Christ during the Last Supper
JN. 19:26	Was the only apostle present at the cross
JN. 19:27	Assumed the responsibility of taking care of Mary
JN. 20:2, 3	Visited the empty tomb along with Peter
JN. 21:7, 23	Was present during the last miracle of Christ

JAMES

MT. 4:21	Brother of John, and fishing partner with Peter and Andrew
MK. 3:17	Was nicknamed "a son of thunder" by Christ
ACTS 12:1, 2	Was the first apostle to be martyred

PHILIP

JN. 1:43	Original disciple of John the Baptist
JN. 1:40-46	Brought Nathanael to Christ
JN. 6:5-7	Had his faith tested during the feeding of the 5,000
JN. 12:20-22	Was approached by some Greeks who desired to see Jesus
JN. 14:8, 9	Asked Christ to show him the Father

NATHANAEL
(also called *BARTHOLOMEW*)

THE TWELVE APOSTLES

JN. 1:45, 46	Was witnessed to under a fig tree by Philip
JN. 1:49	First to call Christ Son of God and King of Israel
JN. 1:51	Heard Christ's first prediction (the ascension)
JN. 21:2	Was present during Christ's final miracle

MATTHEW (also called *LEVI*)

LK. 5:27	Was a Publican tax collector
MT. 9:9	Responded to Christ after a simple "follow me" invitation
LK. 5:27-29	Hosted a large feast and shared his new faith

THADDAEUS (also called *JUDE*)

MK. 15:40	Brother of James the Less
JN. 14:22	Asked Christ how he would manifest himself

JAMES THE LESS

MK. 15:40	Title may refer to his size

SIMON THE ZEALOT

MT. 10:4; MK. 3:18	Member of a right-wing political party called the Zealots

THOMAS

JN. 11:16	Was a twin
JN. 11:16	Despaired at Christ's decision to raise Lazarus
JN. 14:5	Asked Christ where he was going in the upper room
JN. 20:24	Absent during the first resurrection appearance in the upper room
JN. 20:25	Felt he could not believe unless he saw and touched Christ
JN. 20:28	Fell at his feet after seeing Christ a week later
JN. 21:2	Was present during Christ's final miracle

JUDAS ISCARIOT

—	Thought to be the only apostle from Judea
JN. 12:6	Was a treasurer for the group
JN. 12:4-6	Was a heartless thief
JN. 6:70, 71	Given over to Satan even at beginning of ministry
MT. 26:15, 16	Agreed to betray Christ for thirty pieces of silver
LK. 22:3; JN. 13:27	Allowed Satan to actually enter into him
JN. 13:26-30	Dipped the sop with Christ in the upper room
JN. 18:2-4	Led soldiers to Gethsemane to arrest Christ
MT. 26:49	Betrayed the Savior with a kiss
MT. 27:3, 4	Returned his blood money in great remorse
MT. 27:5	Went out and hanged himself
JN. 17:12; 2 THESS. 2:3	Will possibly be the coming antichrist

Philip:
1. His home was in Bethsaida.
2. He was an early disciple of John the Baptist, and a close companion of John the apostle (Jn. 1:43).
3. He brought Nathanael to Christ immediately after his own conversion (Jn. 1:40–46).
4. Jesus once tested his faith by asking him how 5,000 hungry men could be fed. Philip flunked the test (Jn. 6:5–7).
5. During the triumphal entry he was approached by some Greeks who desired to see Jesus. This may indicate that Philip was easier for a stranger to converse with than the other eleven were (Jn. 12:20–22).
6. He asked Jesus to "shew us the Father, and it sufficeth us" in the upper room during the Last Supper (Jn. 14:8, 9).
7. Tradition tells he later went as a missionary to Phrygia and was martyred and buried at Hierapolis.

Bartholomew:
1. He is also called Nathanael (Jn. 1:45).
2. He was located under a fig tree by Philip (who may have been his brother) and persuaded to visit with Christ (Jn. 1:45, 46).
3. He was converted to Christ and became the first apostle to be told concerning the ascension (Jn. 1:50, 51). (Thus, the Savior predicted his own ascension even before his death and resurrection!)
4. Bartholomew (or Nathanael) was one of the seven apostles present at the fish breakfast prepared by the Savior on the Galilean shore (Jn. 21:2).
5. Legends say that later, in Armenia, he was flayed alive for his faith.

Matthew:
1. He was a Publican, a Roman tax collector, also called Levi (Lk. 5:27).
2. He was called by Christ by two simple words, "Follow me" (Mt. 9:9).
3. He prepared a great feast in his home before leaving and invited many of his sinner friends, doubtless to present Christ to them (Lk. 5:27–29).
4. A fifth-century church historian relates that he was martyred in Ethiopia where he had gone as a missionary.

Thomas:
1. He was a twin, for the word *didymus* (used in referring to him) means "twin." (See Jn. 11:16.)
2. He took a very dim view of Christ's decision to attend Lazarus' funeral. Upon hearing the announcement, this doubtful apostle sighed, "Let us go, that we may die with him" (Jn. 11:16).
3. He asked where Christ was going while they were in the upper room at the Last Supper (Jn. 14:5).
4. He was not present on that first Easter Sunday when Christ appeared to the apostles in the upper room (Jn. 20:24).
5. Because of his absence, he felt he could not believe their glad report. "Except I shall see

in his hands the print of the nails, and put my finger into the print of the nails, and thrust my hand into his side . . . " (Jn. 20:25).
6. He met the Savior eight days later and was invited to do just that. But Thomas rather fell at his feet and cried out, "My Lord and my God" (Jn. 20:28).
7. He was present with six other disciples when Jesus cooked breakfast on the Galilean shore (Jn. 21:2).
8. Tradition says he labored in Parthia, Persia, and India and that he suffered martyrdom near Madras, at Mount St. Thomas.

Jude:
1. He was the brother of James the Less (Mk. 15:40).
2. He was also called Thaddaeus (Mt. 10:3; Mk. 3:18).
3. He asked the Savior just how Christ would "manifest thyself unto us, and not unto the world?" (Jn. 14:22).
4. He gave his life for Christ in Persia, after preaching there and in Assyria also.

James the Less:
1. He was the brother of Jude, and may have been called "the less" because of his size (Mk. 15:40). (The word "less" is *mikros* in the Greek, and refers to something small in size.)
2. He preached in Palestine, and later in Egypt, where he was crucified.

Simon the Zealot:
1. He was a right-wing member of a political party called the Zealots (Mt. 10:4; Mk. 3:18).
2. Tradition says he was crucified.

Judas Iscariot:
1. He is thought to have lived near Hebron in Judah, and was thus the only non-Galilean among the twelve apostles.
2. He was the treasurer for the twelve (Jn. 12:6).
3. He was a heartless thief (Jn. 12:4–6).
4. He had committed himself to Satan at the beginning of Christ's ministry (Jn. 6:70, 71).
5. He made plans to betray Christ for thirty pieces of silver (Mt. 26:15, 16).
6. At this point Satan entered Judas and totally controlled him (Lk. 22:3; Jn. 13:27).
7. He received the sop from Jesus in the upper room, which marked him as the betrayer (Jn. 13:26, 27). The disciples, however, did not realize what Christ had done.
8. He led the band of soldiers to Gethsemane (Jn. 18:2–4).
9. He betrayed Christ with a kiss (Mt. 26:49).
10. In great remorse he returned the blood money and acknowledged to the indifferent Jewish priests his horrible sin (Mt. 27:3, 4).
11. He thereupon went out and hanged himself (Mt. 27:5).
12. He is thought by some to be the coming antichrist on the basis of Christ's statement in John 17:12, and Paul's words in 2 Thessalonians 2:3.

B. Those connected with Jesus' miracles.
1. The ruler of a wedding feast in Cana who favorably commented on the wine Jesus had secretly made (Jn. 2:9, 10).

2. The nobleman whose son Jesus healed (Jn. 4:50).
3. The Capernaum demoniac Jesus healed on the Sabbath in the local synagogue (Mk. 1:25).
4. Simon Peter's mother-in-law, whom Jesus healed of a raging fever (Mt. 8:15).
5. A leper Jesus touched and healed during his first preaching tour (Mk. 1:40, 41).
6. A paralytic healed by Christ after he was lowered from the roof of a house by his four friends (Mk. 2:5).
7. A man with a withered hand healed on the Sabbath in a synagogue (Mk. 3:5).
8. A centurion possessing great faith, whose servant Jesus healed (Mt. 8:5-13).
9. A widow from Nain whose dead son was raised at his own funeral (Lk. 7:14).
10. A Gerasene demoniac, living among the tombstones, from whom Jesus cast forth 6,000 (a legion) evil spirits into some nearby swine (Mk. 5:2-19).
11. A woman whose twelve-year issue of blood was immediately healed upon touching the hem of Christ's garment (Mk. 5:28).
12. Jairus' daughter, who was raised from the dead in her own bedroom (Mt. 9:25).
13. Two blind men who were healed after they had followed behind Christ, begging for mercy (Mt.9:27-29).
14. A mute man who spoke when Jesus cast out the demon causing his affliction (Mt. 9:32, 33).
15. An invalid of thirty-eight years who was healed by Jesus in Jerusalem near the Temple (Jn. 5:8).
16. The daughter of a Syro-phoenician woman who was healed of a demon-caused affliction after her mother demonstrated great faith in Christ (Mk. 7:29).
17. A deaf man with a speech impediment who was healed after Christ touched both his ears and his tongue (Mk. 7:31-37).
18. A blind man of Bethsaida who saw clearly after Christ touched his eyes twice (Mk. 8:22-25).
19. A man born blind in Jerusalem, healed after he followed Christ's command and washed in the pool of Siloam (Jn. 9:7).
20. A fearfully demon-afflicted boy who was healed after his father brought him to Christ at the base of the mount of transfiguration (Mt. 17:18).
21. A demoniac, deaf and mute, whose healing by Jesus was attributed to the devil by the wicked Pharisees (Mt. 12:22-29).
22. A woman suffering from a satanic-induced eighteen-year affliction, who was healed on the Sabbath (Lk. 13:10-17).
23. A man with dropsy healed on the Sabbath (Lk. 14:1-4).
24. Ten lepers who were healed by Jesus in Samaria en route to Jerusalem. Only one returned to thank him (Lk. 17:15).
25. A dead man of four days named Lazarus, who was raised from his grave outside Bethany (Jn. 11:43, 44).
26. An unnamed blind man healed by Jesus as he entered Jericho (Lk. 18:35-43).
27. A blind man named Bartimaeus healed by Jesus as he left Jericho (Mk. 10:46-52).
28. A servant of the high priest named Malchus whose severed ear (by the slashing sword of Simon Peter) was healed by Christ in Gethsemane (Jn. 18:10; Mt. 26:51).

C. Those connected with his parables.
   1. Two builders, one wise and one foolish (Mt. 7:24-27).
   2. A Pharisee named Simon whose critical attitude toward repentant sinners prompted a parable on forgiveness (Lk. 7:36-50).
   3. A servant, forgiven of much by his king, who refused to forgive a little from one of his own debtors (Mt. 18:23-35).
   4. The Good Samaritan and associates (Lk. 10:25-37).
   5. A materialistic fool who sold his immortal soul for silver (Lk. 12:13-21).
   6. A wicked servant who was caught red-handed by the unexpected return of his ruler (Lk. 12:45-48).
   7. Three wedding guests who refused an invitation to attend the king's marriage. Two were fools and one was henpecked (Lk. 14:15-24).
   8. A shepherd who sought for a sheep (Lk. 15:3-7).
   9. A woman who searched for a lost coin (Lk. 15:8-10).
   10. A father who forgave his younger prodigal son and lectured his older critical son (Lk. 15:11-32).
   11. A dishonest steward and his self-serving actions (Lk. 16:1-7).
   12. A saved beggar named Lazarus, a lost rich man, and a conversation with Abraham beyond the grave (Lk. 16:19-31).
   13. A persistent widow who received justice from a weary judge (Lk. 18:1-8).
   14. The prayer life of a haughty Pharisee and a humble Publican (Lk. 18:9-14).
   15. A vineyard owner who justified his unusual actions before his questioning workers (Mt. 20:1-16).
   16. A departing nobleman who entrusted ten pounds to his ten servants, one of which proved to be unfaithful (Lk. 19:11-27).
   17. Two sons who changed their minds. One said he would obey his father, but didn't. The other said he would not, but did (Mt. 21:28-32).
   18. A wedding guest who would pay dearly for refusing to wear the required wedding garment at the marriage of the king's son (Mt. 22:11-14).
   19. Ten wedding guests, five of whom were wise, five foolish (Mt. 25:1-13).
   20. Two faithful stewards and a foolish one (Mt. 25:14-30).

D. Various women in the Gospels.
   1. Mary (there are four women in the Gospel accounts with this name)
      a. Mary of Bethany. She was the sister of Lazarus and of Martha (Jn. 11:1). Christ commended her on one occasion for put-

ting first things first (Lk. 10:42). It was Mary who anointed Jesus' feet and head with expensive oil and wiped them with her hair (Mk. 14:3; Jn. 12:3; Mt. 26:6-13).

b. Mary, the mother of James and Joses. She may have been the wife of Cleopas (Lk. 24:18). Mary was at the cross (Mt. 27:56, 61), at his burial (Mk. 15:47), and came to the empty tomb (Mk. 16:1).

c. Mary Magdalene. Jesus cast seven demons from her (Mk. 16:9; Lk. 8:2). Mary was the first person to see the resurrected Christ (Jn. 20:1-18).

d. Mary, the earthly mother of Jesus. This sweet virgin presented Christ to the world (Lk. 1-2). Later she was present when he worked his first miracle (Jn. 2:1-11). She carefully followed his later ministry (Mt. 12:46), and was present at the cross (Jn. 19:25).

2. Salome (there are two Salomes referred to in the Gospel accounts)

a. Salome, the wife of Zebedee, and mother of James and John (Mt. 27:56; Mk. 15:40; 16:1). She helped him often in his ministry (Mk. 15:40, 41), and came to anoint his body on Easter morning (Mk. 16:1).

b. Salome, the daughter of Herodias and grandniece of Herod Antipas. Her sensuous dancing so stimulated Herod that as a reward she obtained the head of John the Baptist (Mt. 14:3-11; Mk. 6:17-28). Her name is not given in the Gospels.

3. Herodius. She was the wicked granddaughter of Herod the Great, who married her uncle Philip. Later she left him for his brother Herod Antipas. John the Baptist rebuked Herod for this immoral action (Lk. 3:19, 20). He was put in prison for this fearless preaching and later beheaded at her suggestion (Mt. 14:3-14; Mk. 6:14-29).

4. A poor widow. This woman was commended by the Savior when she dropped her only two mites into the Temple offering box (Lk. 21:1-4).

5. Elisabeth. She was the wife of Zacharias, and mother of John the Baptist (Lk. 1:5-57).

6. Anna. The daughter of Phanuel of Asher. Widowed after seven years of marriage, she became a prophetess, and at the age of eighty-four, when the infant Jesus was brought into the Temple to be dedicated, she recognized and proclaimed him as the Messiah (Lk. 2:36-38).

7. A weeping and repentant woman. This immoral woman showed her sorrow of repentance by washing his feet with her own tears and drying them with her hair in the home of a Pharisee named Simon (Lk. 7:36-38).

8. The Samaritan woman. She was converted at Jacob's well and, returning to her home, soon led the entire city population to meet Christ (Jn. 4:5-42).

9. Martha. She was the sister of Mary of Bethany and of Lazarus (Jn. 11:1). Christ gently reminded her on one occasion not to be overly bothered about material things, but to seek his fellowship first (Lk. 10:41).

10. A woman taken in the act of adultery. She was brought to Jesus by the Pharisees, who demanded her death. Christ freely forgave her (Jn. 8:1-11).

11. Two servant girls who accused Peter of being with Christ. This occurred during his trial before the Jewish Sanhedrin. Peter denied his Lord before both maidens (Mt. 26:69, 71).

E. Those connected with his birth.

1. The shepherds. These shepherds were the first to hear of his birth that night and were told by the angels themselves (Lk. 2:8-20).

2. Simeon. A righteous and devout man to whom the Holy Spirit had revealed that he would not die until he had seen the Messiah. When the infant Jesus was brought into the Temple, he took him into his arms and praised God (Lk. 2:25-34).

3. Anna. This elderly widow also praised Jesus at the Temple dedication (Lk. 2:36-38).

4. The wise men. These devout astronomers and religious leaders, perhaps from Persia, followed Jesus' star and, when they had found him, bowed in worship and presented their gifts (Mt. 2:1-16).

F. Those connected with his death and resurrection.

1. The Temple guard. These men arrested Christ in the Garden of Gethsemane (Mt. 26:47).

2. The Roman soldiers. They ridiculed him (Mt. 27:27, 28), crucified him, and cast lots for his garment (Mt. 27:35). Later a group was stationed at his tomb (Mt. 27:62-66).

3. Barabbas. He was a convicted criminal who was chosen over Christ to be set free by the Jewish mob (Mt. 27:16).

4. Simon of Cyrene. He was from the country of Cyrene (and the father of two boys, Alexander and Rufus), who were forced by the Romans to aid Christ in the carrying of his cross (Mk. 15:21).

5. Two false witnesses. These wretches attempted to twist the words of Christ concerning the Temple and his resurrection by taking them totally out of context. This occurred at Jesus' trial (Mt. 26:60, 61).

6. A petty official who slapped Jesus during his trial (Jn. 18:22).

7. Two dying thieves. One died saved, the other lost (Lk. 23:32, 39-43).

8. A centurion. A Roman commander at the cross who, after witnessing the fearful accompanying signs, acknowledged that Jesus was indeed the Son of God (Mt. 27:54).

9. Joseph of Arimathea. A rich and brave believer who obtained permission to carry the body of Christ from the cross to his own personal tomb (Mt. 27:57-60).

10. Cleopas. One of two disciples (the other was probably his wife, Mary) before whom the resurrected Savior appeared on the road to Emmaus (Lk. 24:13-18).

G. Priests

1. Zacharias—the husband of Elisabeth and father of John the Baptist (Lk. 1:5, 59, 60).

2. Annas—the corrupt high priest emeritus and father-in-law to the official high priest, Caiaphas. Jesus was first tried before this hateful old man (Jn. 18:13).

3. Caiaphas—Jesus was brought before him for the second illegal trial, the night preceding his crucifixion (Jn. 18:24).

H. Rulers

1. Nicodemus—a ruler of the Jews, converted by Christ himself (Jn. 3:1).

2. Augustus Caesar—the Roman ruler who issued the enrollment decree at the time of Christ's birth (Lk. 2:1).

3. Tiberius Caesar—the successor of Augustus who reigned during the ministry of Christ (Lk. 3:1).

4. Herod (there were three Herods in the Gospel accounts)

   a. Herod the Great (39 B.C. to 4 B.C.). He was an Edomite who, with Rome's approval, proclaimed himself king of Palestine in 39 B.C. It was this Herod who attempted to kill the child Jesus (Mt. 2:1-16).

   b. Herod Archelaus (4 B.C. to A.D. 6). Eldest son of Herod the Great who inherited Judea upon the death of his father (Mt. 2:22).

   c. Herod Antipas (4 B.C. to A.D. 39), younger son of Herod the Great, who took Galilee. He ruled for the most part during Jesus' earthly life. His adulterous marriage was condemned by John the Baptist (Mk. 6:18; Lk. 3:19, 20). Christ referred to him as "that fox" (Lk. 13:32). The Savior also stood before Herod during one of his unfair trials (Lk. 23:5-12).

5. Pilate. The Roman procurator of Judea from A.D. 26-36 (Mk. 15:1).

6. The family of Christ

   a. Mary (Mt. 1:8).

   b. Joseph (Mt. 1:19) was a gentle carpenter living in Nazareth.

   c. After Christ's supernatural birth, Mary and Joseph had natural children, raising at least four recorded sons. These were: James, Joses, Simon, and Judas (Mt. 13:55). They did not believe in Christ prior to the resurrection. (See Jn. 7:5.)

7. Some would-be-converts

   a. A certain scribe, who refused to follow Christ because of the hardships involved (Mt. 8:19, 20).

   b. Another disciple, who did not because of his parents (Mt. 8:21, 22).

   c. A rich young ruler, who failed due to his love for money (Mt. 19:16).

   d. A certain young man. This unknown man had apparently followed Christ for awhile, but fled in panic from the Garden of Gethsemane, leaving his coat in the hands of the arresting soldiers (Mk. 14:51, 52).

8. Associates of John the Baptist

   a. John himself. Jesus said there had never lived a greater man than this fearless and loyal prophet of God (Mt. 11:11).

   b. John's disciples. These disciples approached Christ on two occasions. The first concerned a question on his life style (Mt. 9:14), and the second on his deity (Mt. 11:2, 3).

9. Children

   a. Jesus ordered little children to be brought to him for blessing (Mk. 10:14).

   b. He used a child for an illustration of salvation (Mk. 9:36).

   c. He used the lunch of a little lad (Jn. 6).

   d. Children sang his praises in the Temple (Mt. 21:15).

10. Supernatural beings

    a. Satan (Mt. 4:1).

    b. demons (Mk. 1:23, 24; 3:11; 5:8, 9; Lk. 9:42).

    c. Gabriel, the archangel

       (1) His ministry to Mary (Lk. 1:28).

       (2) His ministry to Zacharias (Lk. 1:11).

       (3) His ministry to Joseph (Mt. 1:20, 24; 2:13, 19).

       (4) His ministry to the shepherds (Lk. 2:9).

    d. Other angels

       (1) Aiding at his birth (Lk. 2:13, 14).

       (2) Aiding during the temptation (Mk. 1:13).

       (3) Aiding during Gethsemane (Lk. 22:43).

       (4) Aiding during the resurrection (Mt. 28:2; Jn. 20:12).

11. The Trinity

    a. the Father (Mt. 3:17; Jn. 12:28; Mt. 17:5)

    b. the Holy Spirit (Mt. 3:16; 4:1)

12. General individuals

    a. Two lawyers. One tempted him concerning the Ten Commandments (Mt. 22:35), and the other on the subject of eternal life (Lk. 10:25).

    b. Simon the leper. A leper Jesus once healed who held a supper for the Savior just prior to his triumphal entry (Mt. 26:6).

    c. Some Greeks. This group desired to see him during the triumphal entry Sunday in Jerusalem (Jn. 12:20).

    d. The seventy. A special group Jesus sent out to do a house-to-house religious census of Palestine (Lk. 10:1).

    e. Theophilus. A friend of Luke's to whom he wrote both his Gospel account (Lk. 1:3), and the book of Acts (Acts 1:1).

    f. A sincere scribe. Jesus said this man was not far from the kingdom of God (Mk. 12:32).

THE EARLY CHURCH STAGE

INTRODUCING
THE EARLY CHURCH STAGE (Acts)

This stage covers a period of approximately thirty-eight years, from the miracle of Pentecost to the martyrdom of Paul. It is a wonderful story of Christian witness. The action centers around two great "crusades," the greater Jerusalem crusade (Acts 1-12), headed up by Peter, and the global crusade (Acts 13-28), led by Paul. The associates involved in their campaigns were John the apostle, Stephen, Philip, Barnabas, Silas, Timothy, and Luke.

The record tells us of the first deacons (Acts 6:1-5), martyrs (James and Stephen; see 7:60; 12:2), and missionaries (Acts 13:1-13). Believers are first called Christians during this time (11:26).

The account also relates the final two biblical resurrections of individuals: Dorcas (9:40, 41) and Eutychus (20:9-12). The preaching of the gospel is viciously attacked by the devil during this period. He attempts to bar it (4:18; 5:28), to buy it off (8:18), and finally, to blur it (16:16-18).

Both angels and demons are seen in action. An angel protects an apostle (Peter, Acts 12:7, 8) and plagues a king (Herod, Acts 12:23). Demons possess sorcerers (8:9;

13:6-10), damsels (16:16-18), and vagabonds (19:13-16). Both revivals (19:18-20) and riots (19:28-34) break out.

The Early Church Stage lists three significant conversions. The first is the eunuch (8:36-38), a descendant of Ham (Gen. 10:6-20); the second is Saul (Acts 9:1-6), a descendant of Shem (Gen. 10:21-31); and the third is Cornelius (Acts 10:44-48), a descendant of Japheth (Gen. 10:2-5).

The convert number jumps from 120 (1:15), to 3120 (2:41), to 8120 (4:4) to untold multitudes (5:14). Paul preaches before prisonkeepers (16:25-34), philosophers (17:16-31), Pharisees (23:6), and potentates (24:24, 25; 26:24-28).

Finally, the story that opens with an upper room prayer meeting (Acts 1:14) closes with a prison room praise meeting (2 Tim. 4:6-8, 18).

ACTS

  I. The Holy Land—Greater Jerusalem Crusade, Headed up by Peter, the Fisherman (1—12; 1:1—8:40; 9:32—11:18; 12:1-24)
    A. The activities of Peter:
      1. Peter and the 120 (1:1-26).
        a. Luke writes his second letter to Theophi-

ACTS of the Apostles

OPERATION HOLY LAND

CHAPTERS 1-12
The Greater Jerusalem Crusade
HEADED UP BY **PETER, THE FISHERMAN**

ASSISTED BY
JOHN, STEPHEN, and **PHILIP**

OPERATION WHOLE EARTH

CHAPTERS 13-28
The Global Crusade
HEADED UP BY **PAUL, THE TENTMAKER**

ASSISTED BY
**BARNABAS, SILAS, MARK
TIMOTHY,** and **LUKE**

Activities of the Holy Land Team

PETER

The 120 **1:1-26**

The Pentecostal crowd **2:1-47**

The lame man **3:1-11**

The high priest **4:1-35**

Ananias and Sapphira **5:1-16**

The lawyer Gamaliel **5:17-42**

Simon the sorcerer **8:14-25**

Aeneas the cripple **9:32-35**

Dorcas **9:36-43**

Cornelius the centurion **10:1-48**

The legalizers **11:1-18**

The angel of God **12:1-24**

STEPHEN

The complaint of the Greeks **6:1**

The conference of the twelve **6:2-4**

The choice of the seven **6:5-8**

The slander of the libertines **6:9-15**

The sermon of Stephen **7:1-53**

The stoning of Stephen **7:54-60**

PHILIP

The evangelist in the city of Samaria **(8:4-8)**

Philip, the soul-winner in the desert of Gaza **(8:26-39)**

"Then Philip opened his mouth, and began at the same scripture, and preached unto him Jesus.

And as they went on their way, they came unto a certain water: and the eunuch said, See, here is water; what doth hinder me to be baptized?

And Philip said, If thou believest with all thine heart, thou mayest. And he answered and said, I believe that Jesus Christ is the Son of God.

And he commanded the chariot to stand still: and they went down both into the water, both Philip and the eunuch; and he baptized him."

lus. His first one (the Gospel of Luke) was written to tell what Christ did while on earth through his physical body (see Lk. 1:1-4). His second letter (the book of Acts) was written to tell what Christ was doing while in heaven through his spiritual body, the church.

b. He begins by reminding Theophilus "of all that Jesus began both to do and to teach" (1:1). This, of course, was in stark contrast to the wicked Pharisees, who, according to the Savior, "say, and do not" (Mt. 23:3).

c. Luke speaks of the "many infallible proofs" which surrounded the resurrection ministry. During that time our Lord appeared at least ten different times to his followers.

d. Just prior to his ascension, Christ commanded his apostles that "they should not depart from Jerusalem, but wait for the promise of the Father" (1:4). Much ink has been used attempting to explain these five words, "the promise of the Father." Various passages of Scripture make it clear that this promise of the Father (Joel 2:28; Acts 2:16) and also of the Son (Jn. 14:16, 26; 15:26; 16:7) was a reference to the arrival of the Holy Spirit.

The Holy Spirit had, of course, already performed an Old Testament ministry, but now his work was to introduce three completely new elements.

(1) It was to be universal. Previous to this time the Holy Spirit had confined his work among humanity to the nation Israel. There is no record before the book of Acts where he fell upon the Greeks or Romans or Babylonians, etc. But now he was coming to bless all repenting sinners everywhere.

(2) It was to be permanent. Although the Holy Spirit did come upon certain Old Testament men, he often departed from them also.

(a) As illustrated by Samson. This Hebrew strong man enjoyed the presence of the Holy Spirit on various occasions (Jdg. 14:6, 19; 15:14). But then, because of sin and immorality, God's Spirit left Samson. One of the most tragic verses in the Bible records this event, when Samson awakes to hear Delilah say:

"The Philistines be upon thee, Samson. And he awoke out of his sleep, and said, I will go out as at other times before, and shake myself. And he wist not [literally, he knew not] that the Lord was departed from him" (Jdg. 16:20).

(b) As illustrated by Saul. As with Samson, the Holy Spirit came upon Saul, but later left him:

"And the Spirit of God came upon him" (1 Sam. 10:10).

"But the Spirit of the Lord departed from Saul" (1 Sam. 16:14).

(c) As illustrated by David. The Spirit of God came upon David when he was anointed by Samuel (1 Sam. 16:13) and, as far as it can be determined, remained with him until death. But David realized the Holy Spirit could depart and, on at least one occasion, pled with the Lord about this matter.

"Cast me not away from thy presence; and take not thy Holy Spirit from me" (Ps. 51:11).

No Christian today need ever (or should ever) pray this prayer. However, millions of believers could probably with profit pray the next phrase of David's Psalm of confession: "Restore unto me the joy of thy salvation" (Ps. 51:12). David offered this prayer after his great sin with Bath-sheba.

(3) It was to be perfecting. That is to say, the Spirit's new ministry would now be to make all repenting sinners grow in grace and be like Jesus. This was not the case in the Old Testament. There is no indication that the moral and spiritual nature of either Saul or Samson were advanced by the presence of the Holy Spirit. They apparently derived only his power and not his purity.

e. Jesus does not answer the apostles' question concerning the precise time when God would restore the kingdom to Israel, but does promise them something far more important just seconds prior to his ascension (Acts 1:8):

"But ye shall receive power, after that the Holy Ghost is come upon you: and ye shall be witnesses unto me both in Jerusalem, and in all Judaea, and in Samaria, and unto the uttermost part of the earth."

We note they were to be witnesses—not potentates, or psychologists, or promoters, but witnesses.

This verse is actually a table of contents and divine outline for the entire book of Acts. Note:

(1) witnessing in Jerusalem (Acts 1–7).
(2) witnessing in Judea and Samaria (Acts 8–12).
(3) witnessing unto the uttermost part of the earth (Acts 13–28).

f. When he had spoken these words, our Lord was taken up by God's Shekinah Glory cloud. This marks the seventh of at least nine appearances of this dazzling and divine cloud. Note that it appeared:

(1) To Israel en route to Palestine (Ex. 13:21; 14:19, 20).
(2) Over the tabernacle Holy of Holies (Lev. 16:2).
(3) Over the Temple Holy of Holies (2 Chron. 5:13, 14).
(4) In Ezekiel's time (Ezek. 10).
(5) At the birth of Christ (Lk. 2:9–11).

(6) At his transfiguration (Mt. 17:5).
(7) Here at his ascension (Acts 1:9).
(8) It will appear next at the rapture (1 Thess. 4:17).
(9) It will appear again during his Second Coming (Mt. 24:30).

g. As the disciples watched him ascend, two heavenly individuals appeared which said:

"Ye men of Galilee, why stand ye gazing up into heaven? This same Jesus, which is taken up from you into heaven, shall so come in like manner as ye have seen him go into heaven" (1:11).

These two individuals may have been heavenly men (like Moses and Elijah; see Mt. 17:3) or angels (see Lk. 24:4; Jn. 20:12). At any rate, we are told several things concerning his return:

(1) The going was personal, and so shall the return be (1 Thess. 4:16).
(2) The going was visible, and so shall the return be (Phil. 3:21).
(3) The going was from the Mount of Olives, and so shall the return be (Zech. 14:4).

h. The eleven apostles return to Jerusalem where they join an assembly of believers totaling 120 in a large upper room. This was probably the same upper room where the Last Supper was held (Lk. 22:12), and where Jesus appeared to them after his resurrection (Jn. 20:19, 26). It may have been the home of John Mark's mother. (See Acts 12:12.) We are not to believe, however, that the number of disciples was limited at that time to 120. (See 1 Cor. 15:6.)

i. We are told that "these [120] all continued with one accord in prayer and supplication" (1:14). The words "with one accord" come from a single Greek word, homothumadon, meaning "likemindedness." It is used twelve times in the Greek New Testament, and eleven instances are found in the book of Acts. This word was a favorite with both the people of God and the people of Satan.

(1) as used by God's people (2:1; 2:46; 4:24; 5:12; 15:25)
(2) as used by Satan's people (7:57; 12:20; 18:12; 19:29)

We note, then, that the early believers acted with one accord in matters of:

supplication (1:14)
expectation (2:1)
communication (2:46)
consecration (4:24)
separation (5:12)
cooperation (15:25)

j. Among the 120 were "the women, and Mary, the mother of Jesus, and . . . his brethren" (1:14). Note:

(1) The women: a reference to those godly women who had followed

Jesus from Galilee. These would include (among many others):

(a) Joanna, the wife of Herod's steward (Lk. 8:3)

(b) Mary and Martha (Jn. 11)

(c) Mary, the mother of James the less (Mk. 15:40)

(d) Mary Magdalene (Mk. 16:9)

(e) Salome (Mk. 15:40)

(f) Susanna (Lk. 8:3)

(2) Mary, the mother of Jesus. This is the final mention of Mary in the Bible.

(3) His brethren. These were Jesus' half-brothers (Mt. 13:55; Mk. 6:3), who had been unbelievers during his earthly ministry (Jn. 7:3-5) but were now believers. Two of these are thought to have written the New Testament epistles of James and Jude, which bore their names.

k. During the prayer meeting Simon Peter discusses the defection and death of Judas, which required the election of a new apostle to take his place (1:15-26).

(1) Peter quotes two Old Testament passages to show that the apostasy of Judas demands his replacement. Psalm 69:25 predicted his removal, and 109:8 his replacement. Jesus had already related Judas to Psalm 41:9 (Jn. 13:18, 19).

(2) It should be noted, however, that it was the defection of Judas and not his death that caused the replacement. No effort was made later to replace the martyred apostle James (see Acts 12:2).

(3) There were two requirements concerning the replacement.

(a) The man had to have been a follower of Christ throughout his ministry, and not a recent convert (see Jn. 15:27).

(b) He had to have been a witness to the resurrection.

l. At this point, two questions have been asked:

(1) Was the method of the election appropriate? We are told the disciples "gave forth their lots" (1:26). How was this carried out? Dr. Charles Ryrie writes:

"The two names were put on lots, placed in an urn, and then the one which first fell from the urn was taken to be the Lord's choice." (The Acts of the Apostles, p. 16)

This method was in perfect harmony with Old Testament practice. The high priest used this method to choose the scapegoat (Lev. 16:8) and, later, to divide the land of Palestine among the tribes (Num. 26:55).

(2) Was the election itself correct? There are those who would say it

was in error, that God apparently intended for Paul and not Matthias to become the twelfth apostle. However, there is no proof whatsoever of this. The title of apostle was not limited to the twelve, for Barnabas (Acts 14:14), James (Gal. 1:19; 1 Cor. 15:7), and Apollos (1 Cor. 4:6-9) were all called apostles also.

m. It may be furthermore noted that earnest prayer preceded the casting of lots.

"And they prayed, and said, Thou, Lord, which knowest the hearts of all men, show whether of these two thou hast chosen" (1:24).

At this point their thoughts may have gone back to the anointing of David by Samuel (1 Sam. 16:7). Apparently it will be Matthias who will be included in the fulfillment of such promises as Matthew 19:28 and Revelation 21:14.

2. Peter and the Pentecost crowd (2:1-47).

a. The chronology of Pentecost. Pentecost (a Greek word which simply means fifty) was the third of six great Israelite feasts mentioned in Leviticus 23:

(1) the Passover, unleavened bread feast (Lev. 23:4-8, a reference to Calvary)

(2) the sheaf of firstfruits (Lev. 23:9-14, a reference to the resurrection)

(3) the feast of seven weeks (Lev. 23:15-21, a prophetical reference to Pentecost)

(4) the feast of trumpets (Lev. 23:23-25, a reference to the rapture and Second Coming of Christ)

(5) the feast of atonement (Lev. 16; 23:26-32, a reference to the coming tribulation)

(6) the feast of tabernacles (Lev. 23:33-43, a reference to the millennium)

b. The comparison of Pentecost:

(1) New Testament Pentecost may be compared with Old Testament Pentecost:

Old Testament Pentecost occurred fifty days after Israel left Egypt. Note: the Passover lamb was slain on April 14, 1491 B.C., and Israel left Egypt the next night (Ex. 12:1, 2, 6, 12, 31). Exactly fifty days later they arrived at Mt. Sinai during the first week of June (Ex. 19:1).

New Testament Pentecost occurred fifty days after Christ rose from the dead. Note: Our Lord was, of course, crucified during the Passover week in April (Jn. 19:14). He then spent forty days with his disciples after the resurrection (Acts 1:3). Then, some ten days later (Acts 1:5; 2:1) New Testament Pentecost occurred.

Old Testament Pentecost celebrated a birthday, that of the nation Israel (Ex. 19:5).

New Testament Pentecost celebrated a birthday, that of the church (Acts 2:41-47).

Old Testament Pentecost witnessed the slaying of some 3,000 souls (Ex. 32:28).

New Testament Pentecost witnessed the saving of some 3,000 souls (Acts 2:41).

Old Testament Pentecost was introduced in a mighty way:

"And it came to pass on the third day in the morning, that there were thunders and lightnings, and a thick cloud upon the mount, and the voice of the trumpet exceedingly loud, so that all the people that were in the camp trembled. . . . And Mount Sinai was altogether in a smoke, because the Lord descended upon it in fire; and the smoke thereof ascended as the smoke of a furnace, and the whole mount quaked greatly" (Ex. 19:16, 18).

New Testament Pentecost was also introduced in a mighty way.

"And suddenly there came a sound from heaven as of a rushing mighty wind, and it filled all the house where they were sitting. And there appeared unto them cloven tongues like as of fire, and it sat upon each of them" (Acts 2:2, 3).

(2) New Testament Pentecost may be compared to Bethlehem:

At Bethlehem God the Father was preparing a body for his Son to work through.

"Wherefore, when he cometh into the world, he saith, Sacrifice and offering thou wouldest not, but a body has thou prepared me" (Heb. 10:5).

At Pentecost God the Father was preparing a body for his Spirit to work through.

"What? Know ye not that your body is the temple of the Holy Ghost who is in you, whom ye have of God, and ye are not your own?" (1 Cor. 6:19).

"And what agreement hath the temple of God with idols? For ye are the temple of the living God; as God hath said, I will dwell in them, and walk in them; and I will be their God, and they shall be my people" (2 Cor. 6:16).

(3) New Testament Pentecost may be compared to Old Testament Babel:

At Babel we see sinful men working for their own glory (Gen. 11:4).

At Pentecost we see saved men waiting for God's glory (Acts 1:14).

At Babel God confounded man's language (Gen. 11:9).

At Pentecost God clarified man's language (Acts 2:8).

At Babel God scattered men throughout the world (Gen. 11:9).

At Pentecost God gathered men within the church (Eph. 1:10).

c. The congregation at Pentecost. "And there were dwelling at Jerusalem Jews, devout men, out of every nation under heaven" (2:5). It was not long before the divine actions at Pentecost had drawn a huge crowd. All were amazed, because "we do hear them speak in our tongues the wonderful works of God" (2:11). However, some mocked, saying, "These men are full of new wine" (2:13). Peter quickly denies this. However, a comparison can be made between being filled with wine and being filled with the Holy Spirit. (See Eph. 5:18.)

Note:

(1) Both are the result of a crushing process (see Jn. 7:37-39).

(2) Both give a new boldness to the one under their control.

(3) Both produce a longing for more.

d. The clarification of Pentecost. The Apostle Peter preaches a message to explain just what is taking place and why.

(1) He begins by comparing what has just happened with Joel's Old Testament prophecy concerning the visitation of God's Spirit upon all flesh (Joel 2:28-32; cf. Acts 2:16-21). It should, however, be noted that the ultimate fulfillment of Joel's prophecy will occur during the tribulation (Acts 2:19, 20; cf. Isa. 13:10; Ezek. 32:7; Mt. 24:29; Rev. 6:12).

(2) Peter then offers a threefold proof that Christ is indeed the Messiah, because of:

(a) His works (2:22; Jn. 3:2; 12:42-45).

(b) His resurrection (2:24). Peter quotes Psalm 16:8-11 to show Israel that the Messiah's death and resurrection were also included in the will of God. He then points out to them that David (the author of Ps. 16) could not have been talking about himself.

(c) The ministry of the Holy Spirit at Pentecost (2:33). Peter finally interprets Psalm 110:1 as speaking of Christ. The Savior himself had done this while on earth (Mt. 22:41-45).

(3) Peter concludes by stating that Christ's resurrection was an absolute necessity, because:

(a) The power of death could not hold the Prince of life (2:24).

(b) God had promised David that from his seed would come an eternal King and kingdom (2:30).

(4) The message of Peter shook his audience to their very core.

"Now when they heard this, they were pricked in their heart, and said unto Peter and to the rest of the apostles, Men and brethren, what shall we do?" (2:37).

Here is the first instance of the convicting ministry of the Holy Spirit as promised by Jesus in John 16:8, 9. For other instances, see:

(a) the Samaritans (8:12)
(b) Saul (9:18; 22:16)
(c) Cornelius (10:47, 48)
(d) Lydia (16:15)
(e) the Philippian jailor (16:33)

(5) Peter answers: "Repent, and be baptized every one of you in the name of Jesus Christ for the remission of sins, and ye shall receive the gift of the Holy Spirit" (2:38). Perhaps no other single verse in all the Bible has been the object of so much controversy as has this one. Let us consider:

(a) It must be remembered that the book of Acts is a dispensational and therefore transitional book. This was a message to Israel concerning their national crime of murdering their own Messiah.

(b) The preposition *eis*, here translated "for," can also be rendered "because of," as it is in Luke 14:35; Matthew 3:11; 12:41.

(c) Whatever Peter meant here, it must be understood that nowhere do the Scriptures teach us that salvation is dependent upon water baptism (1 Cor. 1:17; cf. 15:1-4). Here Paul clearly states what the gospel is, and baptism is definitely not included. Thus, those who insist upon baptismal regeneration literally "rob Paul to pay Peter" (see also 2 Pet. 3:15, 16).

e. The communion at Pentecost (2:41-47).

(1) Then 3,000 Israelites respond to Peter's sermon and are baptized.

(2) They continue steadfastly in:
(a) doctrine
(b) fellowship
(c) the Lord's table
(d) prayer
(e) baptism
(f) praise and joy

(3) They enjoy all things in common (2:44). Note: This early system of mutual ownership (2:45) was common-ism, but definitely *not* communism. Observe the difference:

(a) Common-ism says, "What is mine is thine."
(b) Communism says, "What is thine is mine!"
It should be noted that:
(c) This system was temporary.
(d) It had its problems (Acts 5:1; 6:1).
(e) It soon failed (2 Thess. 3:7-10).

3. Peter and the lame man (3:1-11).
a. The miracle (3:1-11).

(1) Peter and John go to the Temple to pray. (The Jews observed three stated hours of prayer, probably based on Ps. 55:17 and Dan. 6:10. These were at the third hour—9:00 A.M.; the sixth hour—12:00 noon; and the ninth hour—3:00 P.M.)

(2) Upon entering, they are confronted by a crippled beggar who asks for alms. Peter answers:

"Silver and gold have I none; but such as I have give I thee: In the name of Jesus Christ of Nazareth rise up and walk" (3:6).

(3) The man is healed instantly and "entered with them into the temple, walking, and leaping, and praising God" (3:8). This verse is a reminder of Israel's future golden age, as described by Isaiah:

"Then shall the lame man leap as an hart, and the tongue of the dumb sing: for in the wilderness shall waters break out, and streams in the desert" (Isa. 35:6).

Note: In A.D. 1260, St. Thomas Aquinas visited the Roman Pope Innocent IV, who showed him all the fabulous wealth of the papacy. After the tour, Innocent said, "So you see, good Thomas, unlike the first pope, I cannot say, 'Silver and gold have I none.'" Aquinas nodded in quiet agreement, and then said softly: "And neither can you say, 'In the name of Jesus Christ of Nazareth, rise up and walk.'"

This marks the first of many apostolic miracles in the book of Acts. Note:

(a) Miracles of Peter. Healing many by his shadow in Jerusalem (5:15, 16).
Healing Aeneas at Lydda (9:32-35).
Raising Dorcas at Joppa (9:40-42).
(b) Miracles of Philip (8:6, 7, 13).
(c) Miracles of Stephen (6:8).
(d) Miracles of Paul: Blinding a sorcerer on Cyprus (13:11, 12).
Performing great signs and wonders at Iconium (14:3, 4).

Healing a cripple at Lystra (14:8–18).

Freeing a demoniac girl at Philippi (16:18).

Healing many at Ephesus (19:11, 12).

Raising a dead man at Troas (20:8–12).

Healing many on the Island of Melita (28:8, 9).

b. The message (3:12–26).

A huge crowd soon gathers at a place called Solomon's Porch as a result of this miracle. This place is mentioned again in Acts 5:12. It was an unofficial gathering place for the early Christians. Jesus had also taught on this spot (see Jn. 10:23). Peter uses this opportunity to preach on the cross.

(1) The promoters of the cross: The Jews.

(a) They had delivered Christ up to Pilate (3:13).

(b) They denied him when Pilate was determined to let him go. Peter himself, of course, had once done this (3:13).

(c) They preferred a murderer to their own Messiah (3:14).

(2) The Person of the cross: The Savior.

(a) He is the Son and Servant of God (3:13).

(b) He is Jesus (3:13).

(c) He is the Holy One (3:14).

(d) He is the Just (3:14).

(e) He is the Prince of life (3:15).

(f) He is the Christ (3:18).

(g) He is the Prophet of God (3:22).

(3) The prophecy of the cross: Many Old Testament prophets (Isa. 53) had predicted the sufferings of a Savior. Our Lord himself often spoke of this both before and after his death. (See Mt. 16:21 and Lk. 24:25–27.)

How Peter had changed—both the man and the message.

(a) The man: Here the same man who had once denied Christ before a little maiden (Lk. 22:56, 57) boldly proclaims him to the world.

(b) The message: Peter had formerly rebuked Christ concerning the Savior's statements about the cross (Mt. 16:22).

(4) The power of the cross:

(a) It was responsible for the healing of the lame man (3:16).

(b) It assured the blotting out of sins to all who repented (3:19, 26).

(5) The program of the cross:

(a) Christ would suffer and die (3:18).

(b) God would raise him up (3:15).

(c) He would then be taken up for awhile (3:21).

(d) He would someday return again (3:19, 20).

(6) The plea of the cross: "Repent ye therefore, and be converted, that your sins may be blotted out" (3:19).

4. Peter and the high priest (4:1–35).

a. The provocation (4:1–4).

(1) Peter and John are arrested and thrown in prison overnight for preaching Jesus (4:1–3).

(2) In spite of this, 5,000 new converts are added to the church (4:4; see also 2:41; 5:14; 6:7; 9:31; 12:24; 16:5; 19:20; 28:31).

b. The examination (4:4–22).

(1) Peter is required to explain what has happened before the high priest. The Sanhedrin was here (however impure the motives were), acting within its jurisdiction, for the Mosaic Law specified that whenever someone performed a miracle and used it for the basis of teaching, he was to be examined and, if the teaching was false, stoned (Deut. 13:1–5).

(2) Peter, filled with the Holy Spirit, tells the assembly the miracle was performed through the name of the Messiah, whom they had crucified. (Note: Peter's defense here was the first direct fulfillment of Jesus' promise in Mt. 10:16–20. See also Peter's later testimony and advice in 1 Pet. 3:15.)

(3) He then associates Jesus with the Old Testament prophecy by showing that Christ is the Cornerstone spoken of in Psalm 118:22. Jesus had previously applied this passage to himself (Mk. 12:10; 1 Pet. 2:4–8).

(4) He finally concludes with the reminder that:

"Neither is there salvation in any other: for there is none other name under heaven given among men, whereby we must be saved" (4:12).

(5) The Sanhedrin are amazed at the theological perception of these untrained apostles. Ordering them from the room, they ask themselves: "What shall we do to these men? For that indeed a notable miracle hath been done by them . . . and we cannot deny it" (4:16).

There is little doubt that they *would* have denied it if they could have (Mt. 28:11–15). Not only could they not deny the *miracle*; neither could they deny Peter's *message* concerning the resurrection of Christ. There is no record that here or at any other time the Sanhedrin ever attempted to deny the historical fact of Christ's resurrection. It may be said in passing that, concerning the healed cripple, there is no argument against the evidence of a transformed life.

(6) Peter and John are brought in and forbidden to preach or teach the name of Jesus. Both refuse, saying: "We cannot but speak the things which we have seen and heard" (4:20). (See also 1 Cor. 9:16; Jer. 20:9; Amos 3:8; Job 32:18-20.)

c. The exaltation (4:23-35).
(1) Upon being released, they join the other believers in a praise service to God. We note:
(a) They prayed with one accord (4:24).
(b) They acknowledged the sovereignty of God (4:24). The title "Lord" in this verse is *despotees*, meaning "absolute ruler." (See also Lk. 2:29 and Rev. 6:10.)
(c) They relied upon the truth of Scripture, including in their prayer the words of Psalm 2 (Acts 4:25, 26).
(d) They asked for specific things (4:29, 30).
(e) They sought only their Savior's glory (4:30).
This was indeed a prayer of faith, for in essence they were saying, "Lord, allow us to do more of that kind of thing which got us into hot water in the first place."
(2) As a result of this prayer and praise meeting:
(a) The building was shaken by the power of God (4:31).
(b) The believers were filled by the Spirit of God (4:31).
(c) The brotherhood was supplied by the grace of God (4:32-35).
"And the multitude of them that believed were of one heart and of one soul: neither said any of them that ought of the things which he possessed was his own; but they had all things common. And with great power gave the apostles witness of the resurrection of the Lord Jesus: and great grace was upon them all. Neither was there any among them that lacked: for as many as were possessors of lands or houses sold them, and brought the prices of the things that were sold. And laid them down at the apostles' feet: and distribution was made unto every man according as he had need."

5. Peter and Ananias and Sapphira (5:1-16).
a. The deception (5:1, 2). Ananias and Sapphira lied concerning the amount of a gift they presented to the Jerusalem church after selling some of their possessions. Their sin was in tempting God, that is, to see how far one can go in presuming upon God's goodness. (See Mt. 4:7; Ex. 17:2; Deut. 6:16.)
b. The discovery (5:3, 4). Ananias is exposed by Peter and executed by God for his sin of lying to the Holy Spirit. He thus becomes the first recorded believer to commit the sin unto death. (See 1 Cor. 11:30-32; 1 Jn. 5:16.)
c. The deaths (5:5-10).
(1) Some three hours after the death of Ananias, Sapphira is examined by Peter and, after relating the same lie, is judged in the same manner as was her husband.
(2) Satan had at first attacked the church from without, as a roaring lion. Now, he attacks it from within, as a serpent.

6. Peter and the lawyer Gamaliel (5:12-42).
a. Their deaths increased both the purity and the power of the Jerusalem church. Note:
"And by the hands of the apostles were many signs and wonders wrought among the people. . . . There came also a multitude out of the cities round about unto Jerusalem, bringing sick folks, and them which were vexed with unclean spirits: and they were healed every one" (5:12, 16).
b. The apostles are cast into prison for their testimony by the wicked Sadducees (5:17, 18).
c. The angel of God frees them during the first night and they continue preaching (5:19-26).
d. They are again apprehended and charged with civil disobedience by the high priest, who says:
"Did not we straitly command you that ye should not teach in this name? And, behold, ye have filled Jerusalem with your doctrine, and intend to bring this man's blood upon us" (5:28).
Note: The sudden sensitivity of the Jewish rulers was strange indeed, in the light of Matthew 27:20, 25.
e. Simon Peter speaks for the rest and declares: "We ought to obey God rather than men" (5:29).
Note: Peter believed in law and order (1 Pet. 2:13, 14), but had to submit to God's higher law (Acts 4:20).
f. He then again accuses them of their crime against Jesus, "whom ye slew and hanged upon a tree" (5:30). Note: the word "slew" here is an unusual verb, peculiar to Acts, and occurring again only

in 26:21. It means "to murder with one's own hands." Thus, Peter was saying in effect: "Yes, indeed, we do hold you guilty of the Savior's holy blood, for it was your wicked hands, and none other, which murdered him."

g. Upon hearing these words, the council is "cut to the heart," and takes counsel "to slay them" (5:33). The phrase "cut to the heart" is literally, "were sawn through," and occurs again only in 7:54. The Sanhedrin had repudiated the charge of being murderers of Christ, and yet were willing now to shed the blood of his disciples also.

h. At this time a Pharisee named Gamaliel, a highly respected Jewish doctor of the law, stands up and offers the following sound advice:

"Refrain from these men, and let them alone: for if this counsel or this work be of men, it will come to nought: But if it be of God, ye cannot overthrow it; lest haply ye be found even to fight against God" (5:38, 39).

A Persian wife once gave similar advice to her ungodly husband (Est. 6:13).

i. Gamaliel's words are heeded. The apostles are then beaten (their first physical suffering) and released, with a severe warning not to mention the name of Jesus again. Their reaction to this is both expected and exciting:

"And they departed from the presence of the council, rejoicing that they were counted worthy to suffer shame for his name. And daily in the temple, and in every house they ceased not to teach and preach Jesus Christ" (5:41, 42).

7. Peter and Simon the sorcerer (8:14-25).

a. Peter and John are sent by the Jerusalem church to aid in the new work which has begun in Samaria as a result of Philip's preaching.

b. Peter and John pray for them, "that they might receive the Holy Ghost" (8:15). Dr. Homer Kent writes:

"Why was the Spirit withheld until Peter and John arrived? Ritualists insist that an apostolic laying on of hands was required. Yet Saul of Tarsus received the Spirit through the imposition of the hands of Ananias, who was not an apostle (9:17). Others use this passage to show that reception of the Spirit is an event entirely separate from regeneration (a second blessing), and hold that a person can be born again but not necessarily possess the Holy Spirit, ignoring such passages as Romans 8:9.

The answer to this problem must not ignore the social and historical situation. The Samaritans needed to be shown the truth that salvation is of

the Jews (Jn. 4:22). The schism which had plagued the Jews and Samaritans would doubtless have been carried over into the church, unless some method should be devised to preserve the unity of the church. There could very easily have been Jewish Christians who would have no dealings with Samaritan Christians (cf. Jn. 4:9). By withholding the Spirit's coming until the apostles arrived, God insured that the work of Philip was united with that of the Jerusalem apostles. Peter used the keys committed to him (Mt. 16:18, 19) to open the door officially to the Samaritans, just as he did to 3,000 Jews at Pentecost, and would again a little later to the Gentiles at the house of Cornelius (chap. 10). It would be a great mistake, however, to treat this incident at Samaria as normative for all subsequent believers. A look at the Spirit's coming upon Saul (9:17) and Cornelius (10:44) will reveal considerable differences, so that the Samaritan experience was not the regular pattern in the book of Acts." (Jerusalem to Rome, pp. 79, 80)

It is thrilling to observe that it is John who aids Peter in this ministry to the Samaritans, for he and his brother James had once asked Jesus to call down fire from heaven upon that race of people (Lk. 9:54).

c. A religious charlatan named Simon attempts to purchase with money from Peter and John the power of the Holy Spirit. His action has given to the vocabulary of church history the word "Simony," which denotes the buying and selling of ecclesiastical rights and offices. He was not saved. Jesus himself had previously discounted this kind of false faith (Jn. 2:23-25; 6:26, 66).

8. Peter and Aeneas (9:32-35). Peter instantly heals a paralyzed man named Aeneas who has been bedridden for eight years at Lydda.

9. Peter and Dorcas (9:36-43). Peter resurrects a godly departed believer named Dorcas at her own funeral in Joppa.

10. Peter and Cornelius (10:1—11:18).

a. After raising Dorcas, Peter remains for awhile in Joppa at the house of a tanner named Simon. Apparently Peter's attitude toward the restrictions of Judaism was already widening (even though he would still need the sheet vision from God), for here he was, staying with a skin tanner. This was an unclean trade in the eyes of the Jews, for it involved the handling of dead bodies (9:43).

b. In Caesarea, some thirty miles up the coast, a Gentile Roman officer named Cornelius was seeking salvation. We are immediately told several things about this man.

(1) He was a centurion. This would make him commander of 100 Roman soldiers. The various centurions in the New Testament are usually pictured in a good light. (See Mt. 8:5-10; 27:54; Acts 22:25, 26; 27:1, 3, 42-44.)

(2) He was devout. He desired to know about God. Jesus had once said: "If any man will to do his will, he shall know of the doctrine . . . of God" (Jn. 7:17).

(3) He was nevertheless lost. (cf. Nicodemus, Jn. 3.)

c. An angel appears, telling Cornelius to send for Peter at Joppa. There are three factors necessary for the salvation of a sinner.

(1) the Spirit of God (Jn. 16:8)

(2) the Word of God (Rom. 10:17)

(3) the soul-winner of God (Rom. 10:14)

d. Cornelius sends two of his devout soldiers to fetch Peter. Unaware of all this, Peter is awaiting dinner at Simon's house when God sends him the sheet vision. From the skies there comes a great canvas filled with all sorts of animals. Peter is commanded by God to "kill and eat" (10:13).

e. Peter refuses, saying, "Not so, Lord" (10:14). His reply is in the form of a great contradiction. If he is Lord, one cannot say "Not so," and *if* one says, "Not so," he cannot be Lord.

f. God answers Peter: "What God hath cleansed, that call not thou common" (10:15). Jesus had already in effect taught this same truth (Mk. 7:14-23).

g. At this point the two soldiers arrive and Peter (realizing the purpose of the vision) goes with them to Cornelius. It is thrilling to note that God prepares both sinner and soul-winner, for whenever he is at work, he leads at both ends of the line. The Lord always prepares us *for* what he is preparing for *us* (10:17-21). We note this marks the second time in history God sends a Jewish missionary from Joppa to reach some Gentiles. (See also Jonah 1:3.)

h. Peter is warmly welcomed by Cornelius, who then attempts to worship him. Horrified, Peter cries out, "Stand up; I myself also am a man!" (10:26).

i. Peter preaches Christ to Cornelius (10:38-43). He tells:

"How God anointed Jesus of Nazareth with the Holy Ghost and with power: who went about doing good, and healing all that were oppressed of the devil; for God was with him. And we are witnesses of all things which he did both in the land of the Jews, and in Jerusalem; whom they slew and hanged on a tree: him God raised up the third day, and shewed him openly;

not to all the people, but unto witnesses chosen before of God, even to us, who did eat and drink with him after he rose from the dead. To him give all the prophets witness, that through his name whosoever believeth in him shall receive remission of sins."

j. Even as he spoke, God's Spirit fell upon the group (10:44). Dr. Homer Kent writes:

"This experience was the Gentile counterpart of the Pentecost, as 11:17 clearly shows, and included both the baptism of the Holy Spirit and the filling. The phenomenon of speaking in tongues was an evidence of the latter (as in 2:4), whether it took place in the form of a foreign language as at Pentecost (the household and military friends of Cornelius could have included persons from various places in the empire), or was of the variety known at Corinth which required a human interpreter is not certain. The former is perhaps more likely, inasmuch as no interpreters are indicated, and the similarity to Pentecost is especially noted." (*Jerusalem to Rome*, p. 95)

k. Cornelius and the converts of his household are baptized by Peter.

l. Peter returns to Jerusalem where he explains his Gentile preaching mission to the uneasy Jews who are eventually satisfied (11:1-18).

"When they heard these things, they held their peace, and glorified God, saying, Then hath God also to the Gentiles granted repentance unto life."

11. Peter and the angel of God (12:1-24).

a. King Herod Agrippa I, the murderer of John the Baptist and the ruler who questioned Jesus (Mt. 14:1-12; Lk. 23:6-12), suddenly and viciously orders the murder of James the apostle, and puts Peter on death row. James thus becomes the first apostle to die a martyr's death. His death is the only recorded one (with the exception of Judas) among the twelve. This execution was no doubt a fulfillment of Matthew 20:23; Mark 10:39. It is believed that James's brother, John, was the last of the twelve to die.

b. On the eve of his scheduled execution Peter is sound asleep in prison (12:6). He no doubt had full confidence in Jesus' promise that he would live to be an old man (Jn. 21:18).

c. During that same night, on the other side of town, "prayer was made without ceasing of the church unto God for him" (12:5).

d. Peter is supernaturally freed from prison by a mighty angel and hurriedly goes to the assembled prayer meeting to present

himself (12:7-12). The account which follows this is one of the most amusing (if not searching) accounts concerning prayer and faith in all the Bible. Note:
> "And when he had considered the thing, he came to the house of Mary the mother of John, whose surname was Mark; where many were gathered together praying. And as Peter knocked at the door of the gate, a damsel came to hearken, named Rhoda. And when she knew Peter's voice, she opened not the gate for gladness, but ran in, and told how Peter stood before the gate. And they said unto her, Thou art mad. But she constantly affirmed that it was even so. Then said they, It is his angel. But Peter continued knocking: and when they had opened the door, and saw him, they were astonished. But he, beckoning unto them with the hand to hold their peace, declared unto them how the Lord had brought him out of the prison. And he said, Go shew these things unto James, and to the brethren. And he departed, and went into another place."

It is tragic but true that often the most surprised people of all when God performs a miracle are the very ones who prayed the hardest for it.

  e. Herod orders the execution of the soldiers which were assigned to guard Peter (12:18, 19).

  f. Herod himself is fatally stricken with a judgment plague from God for allowing some citizens from Tyre and Sidon to worship him as a god (12:20-24).

B. The activities of Stephen (6:1—7:60).

 1. The complaint of some disciples (6:1).

  a. A problem had arisen due to the rapid growth of the early church. Those Jews who spoke only Greek complained that their widows were being discriminated against.

  b. They felt they were not being given as much food in the daily distribution as the Jewish widows who spoke Hebrew.

 2. The conference of the twelve (6:2-4).

  a. The apostles felt their first priority was to give themselves over continually to "prayer, and to the ministry of the word" (6:4).

  b. Therefore, it was not proper for them to "leave the word of God, and serve tables" (6:2). Note: The word for tables is *trapezai*, and often denotes banks, for moneylenders sat at tables to conduct their business (Mt. 21:12). Thus the stated need here was to find some qualified superintendents, and not just mere table waiters and cooks.

  c. Five requirements are listed for this new office.

   (1) They must be men.

   (2) They had to be saved.

   (3) They were to be reputable.

   (4) They had to be spiritual.

   (5) They were to possess wisdom.

   We note there existed no "double standard" between pastors and the deacons and trustees in the early church.

 3. The choice of the seven (6:5-8).

  a. All seven had Greek names and may have all come from the Grecian group. If so, this was a gracious gesture to the complainers.

  b. Upon being chosen, the seven were "set before the apostles: and when they had prayed, they laid their hands on them" (6:6). This was done in the Bible:

   (1) as an act of benediction (Mt. 19:13, 15; Gen. 48:14-20)

   (2) for the purpose of healing (Mk. 5:23; 6:5)

   (3) to impart the Holy Spirit (Acts 8:17, 19; 9:17)

   (4) for the purpose of ordination (Acts 6:6; 13:3; 1 Tim. 4:14; 2 Tim. 1:6; Num. 8:9, 10)

   (5) for identification (Num. 8:12)

  c. When this was done,
> "The word of God increased; and the number of the disciples multiplied in Jerusalem greatly; and a great number of the priests were obedient to the faith" (6:7).

Thus, when the complainings decreased, the conversions increased (Ps. 51:12, 13).

  d. Two of the original seven deacons were to do great things: one was Philip and the other was Stephen.

 4. The sermon of Stephen (6:9-15)

  a. The preaching ministry of Stephen had offended the synagogue of the Libertines, a group of former slaves who apparently had their own synagogue in Jerusalem (6:9).

  b. Being unable to "resist the wisdom and the spirit by which he spoke," they bring him before the Sanhedrin (6:10, 12). This blessed unanswerable wisdom was a fulfillment of Jesus' words in Luke 21:12-15.

  c. Stephen is indicted on three false charges of blasphemy:

   (1) against God (6:11)

   (2) against the Temple (6:13)

   (3) against the Mosaic Law (6:11, 13)

  d. Through all this, his face shines "as it had been the face of an angel" (6:15; see also Ex. 34:29-35; 1 Pet. 4:14).

  e. Stephen begins by briefly tracing the historical relationship which existed between:

   (1) God and Abraham (7:1-8)

   (2) God and Joseph (7:9-19)

   (3) God and Moses (7:20-44)

   (4) God and David (7:45-47)

  f. Stephen had apparently been teaching that the Jewish Temple was no longer necessary for the worship of the true

God. Christ, of course, had already said this (Jn. 4:20-24). To prove his assertion, Stephen points out the following facts:
   (1) That God had blessed Abraham and their fathers, even though they had not always lived in Palestine.
   (2) That during much of its history while in the land, Israel did not worship God in the Temple.
   (3) That even the possession of their Temple did not save Israel from being rebellious and disobedient.
g. The purpose then, of his speech seemed to be to show Israel from her own history that the possession of the Temple had been neither a necessity for, nor a guarantee of, the true worship of God.
h. Stephen closes his sermon with fierce denunciation of the wickedness which proceeded from Israel's leaders.
   "Ye stiffnecked and uncircumcised in heart and ears, ye do always resist the Holy Ghost: as your fathers did" (7:51).
   Here it may be observed that there are three murders in Israel's history that especially mark out her rejection of God's will.
   (1) The murder of John the Baptist, indicating the rejection of the Father.
   (2) The murder of Christ, showing the rejection of the Son.
   (3) The murder of Stephen, demonstrating the rejection of the Holy Spirit.
5. The stoning of Stephen (7:54-60).
a. His powerful sermon filled the crowd with hellish hatred.
   (1) They were cut to the heart (7:54).
   (2) They gnashed on him with their teeth (7:54).
   (3) They cried out with a loud voice (7:57).
   (4) They stopped their ears (7:57).
   (5) They ran upon him with one accord (7:57). This same word is used of the herd of demon-possessed swine which ran down to the sea (Mk. 5:13). Also, see its usage again in Acts 19:29.
b. All this, however, has no effect upon Stephen, who, "being full of the Holy Ghost":
   (1) Looks up steadfastly into heaven (7:55).
   (2) Sees the glory of God (7:55). We note that he began his sermon with the God of glory (7:2), and it was ended by the glory of God!
   (3) Beholds Jesus standing on the right hand of God (7:55). Stephen thus becomes the first of three men to see Jesus after his ascension. The other two are Paul (Acts 9:3-6) and John (Rev. 1:10, 12-16). Note: Stephen saw Jesus *standing* at God's right hand. This is the only refer-

ence to the Savior standing (after his ascension) until one reaches the book of Revelation. In all other descriptions he is said to be seated. (See Mt. 26:64; Acts 2:34; Col. 3:1; Eph. 1:20; Heb. 1:3, 13; 8:1; 10:12.) Perhaps our Lord rises to welcome his saints home.
c. Stephen is stoned by the bloodthirsty mob. This was not a legal trial but a lynching, for Jewish law at this time specified that capital cases must have a second trial at least one day later. Then, even after this, Roman permission had to be secured.
d. Stephen dies at the hands of wicked men, as once did his Master.
   (1) He calls upon God to "receive my spirit" (7:59), as once did Jesus (Lk. 23:46).
   (2) He prays for his enemies, "Lord, lay not this sin to their charge" (7:60), as once did Jesus (Lk. 23:34).
   We are told that, "when he had said this, he fell asleep" (7:60). This is God's description of a believer's death (Mt. 27:52; Jn. 11:11; Acts 13:36; 1 Cor. 15:18, 20, 51; 1 Thess. 4:13-15; 2 Pet. 3:4).
C. The activities of Philip (8:5-13, 26-40).
1. Shortly after his election as a deacon, Philip goes to Samaria and conducts a great evangelistic crusade.
2. Many are saved and miracles are performed, resulting in "great joy in that city" (8:8).
3. During the height of his ministry, Philip is instructed by God's angel to proceed toward "Gaza, which is desert" (8:26). This was an ancient Philistine city southwest of Jerusalem near the Mediterranean Sea.
4. Here he is led to an Ethiopian eunuch official who is returning from a religious pilgrimage to Jerusalem.
5. Philip joins his caravan and notes the eunuch is reading from Isaiah 53. Philip asks, "Understandest thou what thou readest?" (8:30).
6. The answer of the eunuch reflects the tragic condition of all lost sinners: "How can I, except some man should guide me?" (8:31; see Lk. 24:32, 45; Rom. 10:13-15, 17).
7. The action of Philip is likewise a beautiful summary description of the soul-winner's method of operation:
   "Then Philip opened his mouth, and began at the same scripture, and preached unto him Jesus" (8:35).
8. The eunuch believes and is baptized. At this point, "The Spirit of the Lord caught away Philip" (8:39). This may have been a miraculous removal as in the Old Testament instances of Ezekiel (3:12, 14; 8:3), and Elijah (1 Ki. 18:12; 2 Ki. 2:16). At any rate, Philip makes his way up the coast to Caesarea, where he settles. He next appears in the record some twenty years later, in Caesarea, when Paul visits him and his four daughters (Acts 21:8, 9). The eunuch returns to Ethiopia with great joy.

II. The Whole Earth Global Crusade, Headed up by Paul the Tentmaker (13—28; cf. 9:1–31; 11:19–30; 12:25).
  A. His background:
    1. Ancestry and youth (Acts 21:39; 22:3, 23:34; Rom. 11:1; Phil. 3:4, 5; 2 Cor. 11:22).
      a. He was born and raised in Tarsus in Cilicia (Acts 21:39).
      b. He was of the tribe of Benjamin (Rom. 11:1).
      c. He was a "Hebrew of the Hebrews" (Phil. 3:5).
    2. Education (Acts 22:3; 23:6; 26:4, 5; Gal. 1:13, 14; Phil. 3:5)
      a. He was taught by Gamaliel (Acts 22:3).
      b. He was a Pharisee and the son of a Pharisee (Acts 23:6).
    3. Character (Phil. 3:6; 1 Tim. 1:12, 13; 2 Tim. 1:3)
      a. To the best of his ability he had attempted to keep the law (Phil. 3:6).
      b. He performed everything he did with great zeal (Phil. 3:6).
      c. He persecuted the church in ignorance (1 Tim. 1:13).
  B. His war against the church:
    1. He "kept the raiment" of those that murdered Stephen, and consented to his death (Acts 7:57, 58; 8:1, 2; 22:20).
    2. He made havoc of the church (Acts 8:3). This word describes the act of a wild hog viciously uprooting a vineyard.
    3. He entered the homes of Christians and dragged them out to prison (Acts 8:3).
    4. He hounded Christians to their death in various cities (Acts 22:5).
    5. He beat believers (Acts 22:19).
    6. He voted to have them put to death (Acts 26:10).
    7. He attempted through torture to force them into cursing Christ (Acts 26:11).
    8. He persecuted the church beyond measure and "wasted it" (Gal. 1:13).
  C. His conversion (Acts 9:1–19; 22:5–16; 26:12–20; 1 Cor. 15:7–10; 1 Tim. 1:12–16)
    1. He is blinded by a heavenly light while on his way to persecute "those of this way" in Damascus (9:3). This is the first of many instances where believers are called by this name: 19:9, 23; 22:4; 24:14, 22.
    2. He falls to the ground and hears Christ say: "Saul, Saul, why persecutest thou me?" (9:4). He also sees Jesus at this time. (See 9:17, 27; 22:14; 26:16; 1 Cor. 9:1; 15:8.) This marks the first of at least seven instances when Paul saw the ascended Savior. Other occasions were:
      a. at Troas (16:9, 10)
      b. in Corinth (18:9, 10)
      c. in Jerusalem, during his first visit as a believer (22:17–21)
      d. in Jerusalem, during his final visit (23:11)
      e. en route to Rome (27:23, 24)
      f. when he was caught up into the third heaven (2 Cor. 12:1–4)
    We also note here in Acts 9:4 that to persecute Christians is in reality to persecute

Christ. Jesus thus identifies with his people (Mt. 25; 1 Cor. 12).
    3. Paul is gloriously saved and led blinded into Damascus where he remains alone without food or water for three days.
    4. God appears to a believer in Damascus named Ananias and gives him the first "prospect card" in church history.
      "And the Lord said unto him, Arise, and go into the street which is called Straight, and inquire in the house of Judas for one called Saul, of Tarsus: for, behold, he prayeth" (9:11).
    These three words, "Behold, he prayeth," are in themselves a summary of Paul's life. He here begins his ministry by prayer, and ends it in the same way. (See 2 Tim. 4:16.) Paul literally prayed anywhere and everywhere for anything and everything. He prayed for sinners and saints, for potentates and prison guards, for Jews and Gentiles, for leaders and laymen. (See the following references: Acts 16:25; 20:36; 21:5; 22:17; 28:8; Rom. 1:9; 10:1; Eph. 1:16; Phil. 1:4, 9; Col. 1:3, 9; 1 Thess. 1:2; 2 Tim. 1:3; Philemon 1:4.)
    Ananias is reluctant to aid Saul because of "how much evil he hath done to thy saints at Jerusalem" (9:13). His objections are overruled by God, who commands him:
      "Go thy way: for he is a chosen vessel unto me, to bear my name before the Gentiles, and kings, and the children of Israel: For I will show him how great things he must suffer for my name's sake" (9:15, 16).
    God predicts at this point that Paul will become:
      a. A chosen vessel. Later Paul described four kinds of vessels in his writings. They are:
        (1) a vessel of honor (Rom. 9:21)
        (2) a vessel of mercy (Rom. 9:23)
        (3) an earthen vessel (2 Cor. 4:7)
        (4) a sanctified and worthy vessel (2 Tim. 2:21)
      Paul himself became all four of these vessels.
      b. A Gentile missionary (Acts 13:47; 2 Tim. 1:11).
      c. A suffering servant. It is doubtful that any other human being ever suffered as much for Christ as did Paul.
        (1) He was plotted against:
          (a) in Damascus, after his salvation (Acts 9:23–25; 2 Cor. 11:32, 33)
          (b) in Jerusalem during his first visit as a believer (Acts 9:29)
          (c) in Macedonia, during his third missionary trip (Acts 20:3)
          (d) in Jerusalem, before a Jewish mob (Acts 21:30, 31)
          (e) in Jerusalem, before the Sanhedrin (Acts 23:10)
          (f) in Jerusalem, at the hands of forty men (Acts 23:12–22)
          (g) in Caesarea, at the hands of some Jews (Acts 25:3)

(2) He was at first mistrusted by believers (Acts 9:26).

(3) He was disliked by some believers (Phil. 1:14–18).

(4) His work was constantly opposed by his own countrymen and others, at:
  (a) Antioch (13:45, 50)
  (b) Iconium (14:2–5)
  (c) Thessalonica (17:5; 1 Thess. 2:2, 14–16)
  (d) Berea (17:13)
  (e) Corinth (18:6, 12)
  (f) Ephesus (19:26)

(5) He was stoned and left for dead (14:19).

(6) He was subjected to Satanic pressure (Acts 13:8, 16:16–18; 1 Thess. 2:18; 2 Cor. 12:7).

(7) He was beaten and jailed at Philippi (Acts 16:19–24).

(8) He was ridiculed
  (a) at Athens (17:18, 32)
  (b) at Caesarea (26:24)

(9) He was often falsely accused (24:5–9; 25:7).

(10) He endured a terrifying ocean storm (27:14–20).

Activities of the Whole Earth Team

PAUL: BEFORE HIS CONVERSION

HIS EARLY BACKGROUND

ANCESTRY AND YOUTH

Born and raised in Tarsus **(ACTS 21:39)**

Of the tribe of Benjamin **(ROM. 11:1)**

A Hebrew of the Hebrews **(PHIL. 3:5)**

EDUCATION

Taught by Gamaliel **(ACTS 22:3)**

A Pharisee and the son of a Pharisee **(ACTS 23:6)**

CHARACTER

Was an uninformed blasphemer **(1 TIM. 1:13)**

Displayed great zeal
1. In attempting to keep the law **(PHIL. 3:6)**
2. In attempting to destroy the church **(PHIL. 3:6)**

HIS WAR AGAINST THE CHURCH

Took part in Stephen's death **(ACTS 7:27-58; 8:1; 22:20)**   Beat Christians **(ACTS 22:19)**

Made havoc of the church **(ACTS 8:3)**

Voted to put them to death **(ACTS 26:10)**

Threw Christians in prison **(ACTS 8:3)**

Compelled them through torture to blaspheme **(ACTS 26:11)**

Hounded them to their death **(ACTS 22:4)**

Persecuted the church beyond measure and wasted it **(GAL. 1:13)**

PAUL: HIS CONVERSION

THE REFERENCES TO IT

ACTS 9:1-18   **ACTS 22:5-16**   **ACTS 26:12-20**   **1 COR. 15:8-10**   **1 TIM. 1:12-16**

THE DETAILS OF IT

En route to Damascus to persecute believers

Was knocked down and blinded by a heavenly light

Heard and accepted Christ as Lord and Savior

Was led to Damascus where he remained alone for three days

Was ministered to by a Damascus believer named Ananias

Received his sight and preached Christ in the synagogues

PAUL: HIS EARLY MINISTRY

Preached Christ in the synagogues in Damascus **ACTS 9:19-21**

Retired to the Arabian desert for a period of several years **GAL. 1:16, 17**

Returned to Damascus with greater knowledge and preaching power **GAL. 1:17, 18; ACTS 9:22-25**

Escaped from Damascus and visited Jerusalem for the first time since his conversion **ACTS 9:26-29; GAL. 1:18-20**

Was sent to Tarsus to escape a Jewish plot on his life **ACTS 9:30; GAL. 1:21**

Brought down to help out in Antioch by Barnabas **ACTS 11:24-26**

Visited Jerusalem a second time, bringing a love offering for the needy there **ACTS 11:30; GAL. 2:1-10**

Returned to Antioch to preach and teach the word **ACTS 12:25—13:3**

(11) He experienced the bite of a poisonous serpent (28:3, 4).

(12) He was imprisoned:
  (a) in Caesarea, for two long years (Acts 24:27)
  (b) in Rome (2 Tim. 1:8; 2:9; Eph. 6:20; Phil. 1:13; Philemon 1:9)

(13) He was forsaken by all (2 Tim. 4:10, 16; Paul's overall testimony concerning all his sufferings may be found in 2 Cor. 1:6; 4:8-10; 6:4-10; 7:5; 11:24-28; Phil. 3:7, 8, 10; Rom. 8:18).

5. God restores Saul's sight at the laying on of hands by Ananias. Saul is filled with the Holy Spirit and baptized (9:17, 18).

6. Saul begins his ministry in Damascus by proclaiming the deity of the Savior Jesus Christ. All who hear him are amazed. They simply cannot believe at first that the devil's vicious and bloodthirsty wolf has suddenly become one of God's most faithful and gentle sheep dogs (9:19-22).

D. His early ministry:

1. Paul retires to Arabia for a three-year spiritual retreat, probably to fully grasp the significance of the Old Testament Scriptures in the light of his newfound Savior (Gal. 1:17, 18).

2. After returning to Damascus he learns of a Jewish plot to kill him but escapes when his friends lower him in a basket from the city wall. He then makes the first of at least five trips to Jerusalem after his conversion.
  a. his first (Acts 9:23-30; Gal. 1:18, 19)
  b. his second (Acts 11:30)
  c. his third (Acts 15:1-30; Gal. 2:2-10)
  d. his fourth (Acts 18:21-23)
  e. his final (Acts 21:17—23:35)

3. Saul meets Peter and James and is vouched for (most disciples were still afraid of him) by Barnabas during a fifteen-day visit (Acts 9:26-28; Gal. 1:18, 19).

4. He then leaves Jerusalem to escape a plot on his life by the Grecians and returns to his hometown of Tarsus (Acts 9:29-31).

5. Some ten years later he is invited to join Barnabas, who has been sent to head up a newly established work in Antioch. It is in this city where the disciples are first called Christians (Acts 11:26; see also 26:28 and 1 Pet. 4:16 for the other two New Testament references to this title).

6. Barnabas and Saul again visit Jerusalem, bringing food supplies to the saints there who are suffering because of a famine. The prophet Agabus had warned of this. He appears again in 21:10 with a different kind of warning (11:27-30).

7. Upon finishing their errand of mercy, Barnabas and Saul return to Antioch, and bring back with them John Mark, a young nephew of Barnabas (12:25).

E. His first missionary journey (13–14).

1. Saul continues his work at Antioch along with the other prophets and teachers in that amazing church. Some of these early leaders are recorded for us.
  a. Simeon, called Niger: He may have been the Simon of Cyrene mentioned in Mark 15:21. "Niger" means black, indicating he may have been from North Africa.
  b. Manaen: The adjective describing Manaen means foster brother. Thus he and wicked King Herod the Great had apparently once been raised together in the royal court.

2. One day as these men were worshiping and fasting, the Holy Spirit commanded them, "Separate me Barnabas and Saul for the work whereunto I have called them" (13:2).

3. After a hand-laying dedication service, the Antioch church sends forth the world's first Christian foreign missionaries! We note here that the church at Antioch was totally independent of the Jerusalem church and recognized no ecclesiastical hierarchy whatsoever. A beautiful cooperation is seen here between a local church and the Holy Spirit (13:2-4).

4. At Paphos: Barnabas, Saul, and John Mark preach their way through Cyprus until they arrive at Paphos, located on the western shore of the island. Here the following events take place (13:5-13):
  a. Saul is called Paul for the first time (13:9).
  b. Paul works his first recorded miracle by temporarily blinding a false Jewish prophet and sorcerer named Bar-jesus, who actively opposed the gospel message. His name meant "Son of salvation," but Paul called him by his real name, "Thou child of the devil" (13:10). See also John 8:44. Both Peter and Paul performed similar miracles:
    (1) Both healed a lame man (3:1-8; cf. 14:8-12).
    (2) Both dealt with satanic pretenders (8:18-24; cf. 13:4-12).
    (3) Both were released from prison miraculously (12:5-10; cf. 16:25-29).
    (4) Both raised the dead (9:40; cf. 20:12).
  c. The governor at Paphos (Sergius Paulus) is converted (13:12).
  d. John Mark leaves the team and goes home (13:13).

5. At Antioch in Pisidia (13:14-50).
  a. Paul is invited to speak and preaches his first recorded message. It was similar to Stephen's in its historical retrospect, which sermon he may have heard. Paul stands to preach (the rabbi teacher would usually sit), thus gaining the attention of his Gentile listeners. He discusses the following:
    (1) the Exodus deliverance
    (2) the wilderness wanderings
    (3) the conquest of Canaan
    (4) the rule of Saul and David
    (5) the ministry of John the Baptist
    (6) the crucifixion and resurrection of David's Seed, the Lord Jesus Christ
  He then gave the invitation:

"Be it known unto you therefore, men and brethren, that through this man is preached unto you the forgiveness of sins: and by him all that believe are justified from all things, from which ye could not be justified by the law of Moses" (13:38, 39).

b. The Gentiles invite Paul to speak to them again on the following Sabbath. Paul's Gentile ministry is now in full swing. (See Acts 9:15; 22:21—as predicted by God—and Acts 13:47; 14:27; 15:3, 12; Gal. 2:2; Eph. 3:1, 6; Col. 1:27; 1 Tim. 3:16; 2 Tim. 1:11; 4:17.)

c. When he had preached to them the Gentiles "were glad, and glorified the word of the Lord" (13:48), but the Jews "were filled with envy, and spoke against those things" (13:45). This caused Paul to conclude sadly:

"It was necessary that the word of God should first have been spoken to you: but seeing ye put it from you, and judge yourselves unworthy of everlasting life, lo, we turn to the Gentiles" (13:46; see also 18:6; 28:28).

6. At Iconium (14:1-5).
   a. Many believed the gospel message here, but the unbelieving Jews stirred up trouble.
   b. Upon learning of a plot against their very lives, Paul and Barnabas left for Lystra.

7. At Lystra (14:6-25).
   a. Paul heals a man who had been born crippled and the amazed crowd looks upon the gospel team as gods, calling Barnabas "Jupiter," and Paul "Mercury." The Roman poet Ovid (43 B.C.) records the ancient myth concerning a visit of Zeus and Hermes (two Greek gods) to this area once, disguised as mortals. All turned them away except one old couple. Later a flood supposedly came in judgment and drowned all except this couple.
   b. Determining not to make the same mistake, the priest of Jupiter in Lystra prepares to worship the team by the sacrifice of animals and flowers.
   c. In horror, Paul rips his clothing and admonishes them:

"Sirs, why do ye these things? We also are men of like passions" (14:15).

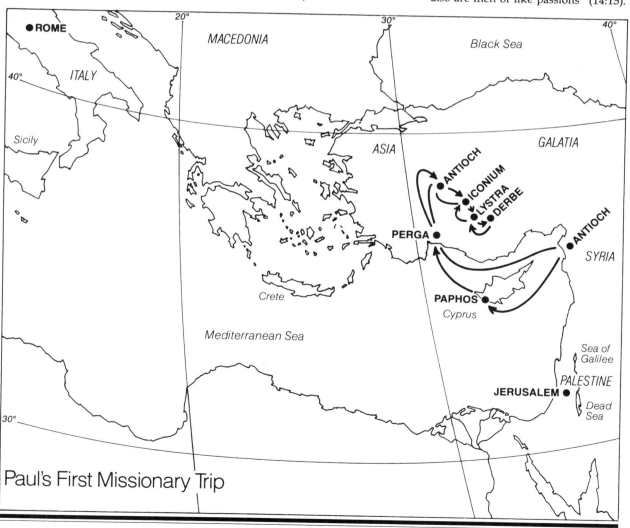

Paul's First Missionary Trip

All men are made of the same stuff (see Jas. 5:17; Acts 10:26; Rev. 22:9).

d. After preaching Christ, Paul is stoned and left for dead by the disappointed crowd which had been enraged by the troublemaking Jews (who had hounded Paul from Antioch and Iconium). Note: Some believe Paul actually died here and was then resurrected by God, experiencing at this time his heavenly visit spoken of in 2 Corinthians 12:1-9. However, there is a time problem here, for the stoning occurred in A.D. 47 or 48 and Paul wrote 2 Corinthians some seven years later in A.D. 55. But in 2 Corinthians he said the event occurred fourteen years prior. At any rate, this may have been where he received the scars he bore for Jesus' sake mentioned in Galatians 6:17. Whether he was dead or simply unconscious, a miracle is seen here, for we are told he immediately "rose up, and came into the city" (14:20).

e. The team proceed to Derbe and then return to Lystra, Iconium, and Antioch, revisiting and organizing new churches. This they accomplish through:
   (1) confirmation
   (2) exhortation
   (3) ordination
   (4) commendation (to God)
   Dr. Homer Kent writes:
   "In each church they visited the believers were organized by the choosing of elders. The word 'ordained' (14:23) translates a Greek term that originally meant to elect by a vote of raised hands. The word also developed the more general sense of 'choose' or 'appoint,' as the compound verb in Acts 10:41 indicates. Does 14:23 mean that Paul and Barnabas appointed the elders for each church, or does the more restricted meaning prevail with the sense that the missionaries established elders in the churches by arranging for congregational elections? Although there is no question but that the term is capable of either meaning, the following factors favor the interpretation of an election: (1) The choice of the verb *cheirotoneo* rather than one of the many general words for 'appoint' suggests that the special characteristics of this word should be understood. (2) The only other New Testament use of this exact verb is clearly with the sense of a congregational selection (2 Cor. 8:19). (3) Congregational selection was the apostolic practice in

the choice of the Seven (Acts 6:3).'' (*Jerusalem to Rome*, pp. 118, 119)

f. Paul and Barnabas then return to Antioch where they excitedly "rehearsed all that God had done with them, and how he had opened the door of faith unto the Gentiles" (14:27).
   Note: It is believed by some (M. Tenney, H. Kent, etc.) that Paul wrote the book of Galatians at this time. If so, this was his first New Testament epistle.

F. His role in the Jerusalem Council (Acts 15:1-35):
   1. A serious problem had arisen in the early church as to whether Gentile converts should submit to the Jewish rite of circumcision. Paul and Barnabas "had no small dissension and disputation" with these legalizers at Antioch (15:2). It would seem that at the first both Peter and James (the Lord's half-brother) had also taken this position (Gal. 2:11, 12). They would, however, soon reverse their convictions.
   2. A special conference was scheduled in Jerusalem to settle this dispute. The meeting apparently consisted of three sessions.
      a. the first public session (15:4, 5)
      b. a private session of the apostles and elders (15:6)
      c. the second public session (15:7-29)
   3. At this final session the delegates heard the reading of three special "committee reports" given by a leading apostle (Peter), two returning missionaries (Paul and Barnabas), and the pastor of the Jerusalem church (James, the Lord's half-brother, who was also moderator).
      a. Peter's report (15:7-11). He reminds them how God had ordered him to preach to the Gentiles in Cornelius's home and concludes by the admonishment:
         "Now therefore why tempt ye God, to put a yoke upon the neck of the disciples, which neither our fathers nor we were able to bear? But we believe that through the grace of the Lord Jesus Christ we shall be saved, even as they" (15:10, 11).
      b. Paul and Barnabas's report (15:12). They simply summarize the wonderful things God has allowed them to do during their first missionary journey.
      c. James' report (15:13-21).
         (1) He begins by summarizing God's stated present-day purpose in "visiting the Gentiles, to take out of them a people for his name" (15:14).
         (2) He then reminds them that when this was completed, God promised to return and "build again the tabernacle of David, which is fallen down" (15:16). This, of course, would usher in the glorious millennium.

Acts 13:2—14:28

PAUL: HIS FIRST MISSIONARY JOURNEY

STOP	EVENT	REFERENCE
Paphos in Cyprus	• Team consists of Paul, Barnabas, and John Mark. • Paul works his first recorded miracle—the blinding of Elymas. • Paul is first called by his Gentile name at this time. • Paul wins the deputy of Paphos to Christ.	ACTS 13:4-12
Antioch in Pisidia	• He preaches his first recorded message (six points and an invitation).	ACTS 13:13-50

THE POINTS

1. The Exodus deliverance
2. The wilderness wanderings
3. The conquest of Canaan

4. The rule of Saul and David
5. The ministry of John the Baptist
6. Crucifixion and resurrection of David's seed—Christ

THE INVITATION

"Be it known unto you therefore, men and brethren, that through this man is preached unto you the forgiveness of sins: and by him all that believe are justified from all things, from which ye could not be justified by the law of Moses" (ACTS 13:38, 39).

• Many Gentiles and some Jews receive his message.
• The Jewish leaders, however, reject it and run him out of town.
• He then states his intention to turn to the Gentiles (13:46).

STOP	EVENT	REFERENCE
Iconium	• Many also believe the gospel here. • But again the Jewish leaders stir up trouble.	ACTS 13:51—14:5
Lystra	• Paul heals a man crippled from birth. • An attempt is made by the crowd to worship Paul and Barnabas as the Greek gods Jupiter and Mercury. • Paul refuses their honor, is stoned and left for dead. • Upon being supernaturally raised, Paul continues preaching in Lystra and surrounding cities.	ACTS 14:6-25
Antioch in Syria	• The team returns to Antioch with history's first "foreign field report" by a returning missionary. • The possible writing of Galatians, Paul's first New Testament book, from Antioch.	ACTS 14:26-28

Acts 15:1-35

PAUL: HIS ROLE IN THE JERUSALEM COUNCIL

THE PROBLEM

• Should Gentile converts be forced to submit to the Jewish rite of circumcision?

THE SESSIONS

• First public session (15:4, 5)
• Private session consisting of the apostles and elders (15:6)
• Second public session (15:7-21)
  1. Peter's report (15:7-11)
  2. Paul and Barnabas' report (15:12)
  3. James' report (15:13-21)

THE DECISION

"Wherefore my judgment is, that we trouble not them, who from among the Gentiles are turned to God;
But that we write unto them, that they abstain from pollutions of idols, and from fornication, and from things strangled and from blood" (15:19, 20).

THE LETTERS

Formal letters were drafted and sent to all local churches informing them of the Jerusalem Council decision (15:22-35).

(3) James finally concludes by saying: "Wherefore my sentence is, that we trouble not them, which from among the Gentiles are turned to God: But that we write unto them, that they abstain from pollutions of idols, and from fornication, and from things strangled, and from blood" (15:19, 20).

We note that the final decision was made by James, the pastor of the Jerusalem church. This decision (directed by the Holy Spirit, see v. 28) showed great wisdom, in that it avoided undue and unnecessary offending of the unsaved Jew. (See also 1 Cor. 10:32, 33.)

4. This decision, supported fully by the delegates, was put into letter form and delivered to the various churches by four chosen men: Paul, Barnabas, Judas, and Silas (15:22, 23).

5. Paul and Barnabas return to Antioch (15:35).

G. His second missionary journey (15:36—18:22):
1. Paul and Barnabas—their argument (15:36-39).
   a. Paul proposes a second missionary trip to confirm the local churches organized during the first journey. Barnabas quickly agrees.
   b. Barnabas proposes to take John Mark with them again. Paul quickly disagrees.
   c. The "contention was so sharp between them that they departed asunder one from the other" (15:39).
      (1) Paul chooses Silas and heads toward Syria.
      (2) Barnabas takes John Mark and leaves for Cyprus. Happily, the New Testament records that Paul was later reconciled to both Barnabas (1 Cor. 9:6) and John Mark (Col. 4:10; Philemon 1:24; 2 Tim. 4:11). This is the last mention of Barnabas in the book of Acts.
2. Paul and Silas—their achievements (15:40—18:22).
   a. In Lystra (16:1-5).
      (1) Timothy joins the team.
      (2) He is circumcised by Paul because he was partly Jewish, so he would not give undue offense to the Jews. Later, Paul would refuse to circumcise Titus, a Gentile (Gal. 2:3). This was an application of Paul's stated principle in 1 Corinthians 9:20.
   b. In Troas (16:6-10).
      (1) Paul is forbidden by the Holy Spirit to preach in either Turkey or Bithynia.
      (2) We note that the need alone did not by itself constitute the call. It may be also said they did not attempt to second-guess God. They had just come from the east, they had been forbidden to go south or north, but

still they waited! God's perfect will is not always the easiest thing on earth to find, but once found, it becomes the most blessed. (See Mt. 7:7, 8; Lk. 11:9, 10.)
      (3) In a vision at Troas, Paul sees a man who pleads with him, saying: "Come over into Macedonia, and help us" (16:9).
      (4) The gospel team leaves immediately for Macedonia, now being joined by the beloved Greek physician, Luke. Acts 16:10 is the first of several "we" sections in this book. (See also 20:5, 6; 21:18; 27:1.)
   c. In Philippi (16:11-40). This famous chapter section records the conversion of a businesswoman, a demoniac girl, and a prison keeper.
      (1) The businesswoman (16:13-15). Paul preaches at a riverside prayer meeting and leads Lydia (a seller of purple cloth from Thyatira) to Christ. She is then baptized along with her household and opens her home to the gospel team.
      (2) The demoniac girl (16:16-18). Paul exorcises a demon from a slave girl and sets her free. She had previously followed them around, chanting, "These men are the servants of the most high God" (16:17). Just as a demon had recognized Jesus as the Holy One (Mk. 1:24), so this demon recognized the divine power in Paul and his companions.
      (3) The prison keeper (16:19-40).
         (a) The enraged owners of this ex-slave girl revenge themselves upon Paul by causing both him and Silas to be beaten and cast into prison as anarchists.
         (b) At midnight Paul and Silas pray and sing praises unto God: and the prisoners hear them (16:25). We thus have the first sacred concert ever held in Europe. They sang, as did Christ on the eve of his passion (Mt. 26:30; Mk. 14:26).
         (c) God sends a great earthquake which frees the prisoners. Upon seeing this, the jailor prepares to kill himself (fearing the terrible fate accorded all keepers who allow their prisoners to escape) but is reassured by Paul. He then asks the most important question a sinner can ever ask: "Sirs, what must I do to be saved?" (16:30).

Paul's answer is really the gospel in a nutshell: "Believe on the Lord Jesus Christ, and thou shalt be saved, and thy house" (16:31).

(d) The jailor and his household believe and are baptized that very night. His first Christian act of mercy is to wash the stripes of Paul and Silas.

(e) Paul, Silas, and Timothy leave Philippi, after receiving the apologies of some terrified city officials who have just learned that they shamelessly beat two Roman citizens. Luke apparently stays at Philippi to oversee the new work. The "we" is not mentioned again until 20:5, 6, when Paul returns to Philippi on his third journey.

d. In Thessalonica (17:1–9).
(1) Paul spends three weeks here in the home of Jason (possibly a kinsman, see Rom. 16:21), organizing a church from the Jewish converts, working all the while as a tentmaker that he might not be a burden to the believers. (See 1 Thess. 2:9; 2 Thess. 3:7–12.)
(2) The gospel is again opposed by some unbelieving Jews who drag Jason into court and unsuccessfully attempt to jail him.
(3) Paul, Timothy, and Silas leave by night for Berea.

e. In Berea (17:10–14).
(1) Paul finds the people here more open-minded than at Thessalonica, for they "received the word with all readiness of mind, and searched the scriptures daily, whether those things were so" (17:11).
(2) Paul is again forced to flee by night because of the Jewish troublemakers. Timothy and Silas remain in Berea.

f. In Athens (17:15–34).
(1) Paul preaches daily in both the synagogue and the open market while awaiting the arrival of Timothy and Silas.
(2) He is invited to explain his message at the open forum on Mars' Hill by the Epicurean and Stoic philosophers. This first group was named after their founder, Epicurus (341–270 B.C.). They believed that while God existed, he had no interest whatsoever in the welfare of men, and the chief end of life was pleasure. The second group was founded by Zeno (300 B.C.) and believed God was the world's soul which indwelt all things. They held life's goal was to rise above all things and show no emotion whatsoever to either pain or pleasure.
Both groups took a dim view of Paul's theology, referring to him as a "babbler" (17:18). This word in the

Greek is *spermologos,* used literally of birds making their nests.
(3) Paul preaches Christ to them. Note his tactful introduction:
"Then Paul stood in the midst of Mars' hill, and said, Ye men of Athens, I perceive that in all things ye are too superstitious [literally, "very religious"]. For as I passed by, and beheld your devotions, I found an altar with this inscription, TO THE UNKNOWN GOD. Whom therefore ye ignorantly worship, him declare I unto you" (17:22, 23).
Paul then presents four great truths about God.
(a) He is the Creator (17:24, 25).
(b) He is the Governor (17:26–29).
(c) He is the Savior (17:30).
(d) He is the Judge (17:31).
During the course of his sermon (17:28) Paul quotes from one of their own heathen poets (Arotus). See also Titus 1:12. He concludes the message, admonishing his listeners to repent.
"Because he hath appointed a day, in the which he will judge the world in righteousness by that man whom he hath ordained; whereof he hath given assurance unto all men, in that he hath raised him from the dead."
If this fact of the appointed judgment day was well known, Easter Sunday morning would become the most dreaded day of all the year for unsaved people (see Rev. 20:11–15).
(4) The reaction to the gospel message was mixed, as it always is.
(a) Some mocked. This, of course, would have included both the Epicureans, who disbelieved in a literal resurrection, and the Stoics, who ridiculed a personal resurrection.
(b) Some delayed. Note: "We will hear thee again of this matter" (17:32. Compare Felix's answer in 24:25).
(c) Some believed.

g. In Corinth (18:1–18).
(1) Here Paul meets a Christian Jew named Aquila and his wife Priscilla, who had recently been driven from Rome by the anti-Semitic activities of the empire at that time. To Paul's delight, they too are tentmakers. This remarkable couple is mentioned six times in the New Testament. There are inscriptions in the catacombs which hint that Priscilla was of a distinguished family of high standing in Rome. Later in Ephesus a church met in their home

(1 Cor. 16:19). In later years they apparently moved back to Rome (Rom. 16:3-5).

(2) Silas and Timothy catch up with Paul at this time. Note:

   (a) They had been left behind at Berea with instructions to meet Paul in Athens, but this had not worked out (17:14-16).

   (b) Silas had left Berea for Philippi to help Luke with the new church there (18:5).

   (c) Timothy, at Paul's request, had gone back to Thessalonica to oversee the work there (1 Thess. 3:1, 2).

   (d) Both men now greet Paul in Corinth. Silas brings a financial gift for Paul from the Philippian church for his missionary support (2 Cor. 11:8, 9; Phil. 4:15), and Timothy has a good report concerning the work in Thessalonica.

(3) Crispus, the chief ruler of the synagogue, is saved, along with many other Corinthians, all of whom are baptized.

(4) Paul is encouraged by God in a vision with the words:

> "Be not afraid, but speak, and hold not thy peace: For I am with thee, and no man shall set on thee to hurt thee: for I have much people in this city" (18:9, 10).

Every minister and missionary serving in God's perfect will can boldly claim this precious promise concerning their particular field of service. He remains here for eighteen months (18:11). During this period he writes both 1 and 2 Thessalonians.

(5) Once again the unbelieving Jews drag Paul into court before the governor named Gallio, accusing him of blasphemy. Gallio quickly dismisses this religious-centered case.

(6) Not to be denied, an unruly Greek mob (doubtless organized by the Jews to harm Paul) grab Sosthenes,

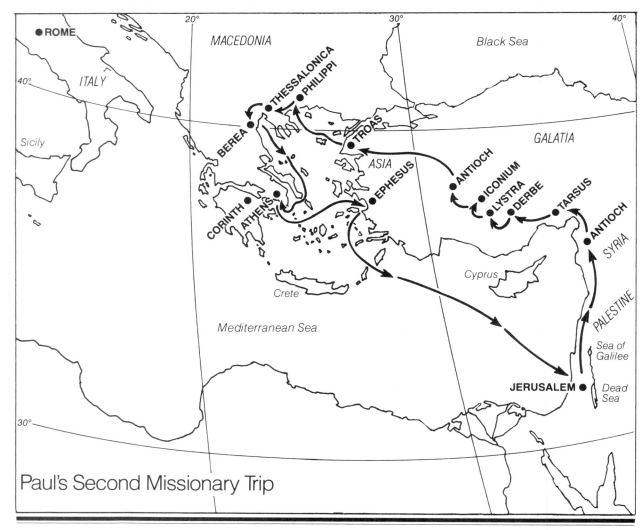

Paul's Second Missionary Trip

Acts 15:36—18:22

PAUL: HIS SECOND MISSIONARY JOURNEY

PAUL AND BARNABAS—THEIR ARGUMENT (15:36-39)

- Barnabas wants John Mark to accompany them on the second trip
- Paul refuses; Barnabas and John Mark leave for Cyprus

PAUL AND SILAS—THEIR ACCOMPLISHMENTS (15:40—18:22)

STOP	EVENT	REFERENCE
Lystra	• Timothy joins the team • He is circumcised by Paul	ACTS 16:1-5
Troas	• Paul is forbidden by the Holy Spirit to preach in either Turkey or Bithynia • He receives his Macedonian vision • Luke now joins the team	ACTS 16:6-10
Philippi	• Three thrilling salvation stories— *A BUSINESS WOMAN, A DEMONIAC GIRL, A PRISON-KEEPER*	ACTS 16:11-40
Thessa-lonica	• Paul spends three weeks in the home of Jason • The gospel is once again opposed by some unbelieving Jews	ACTS 17:1-9
Berea	• Here Paul finds a group of devout Bible lovers • He is again forced to flee because of Jewish troublemakers	ACTS 17:10-14
Athens	• Paul goes to Athens alone • Timothy and Silas are to join him later • He preaches his famous sermon on Mars' Hill **TITLE OF HIS MESSAGE:** *THE UNKNOWN GOD* **NATURE OF HIS MESSAGE:** *THREE POINTS* God is the Creator of all things **(17:24-29)** God is the Savior of all things **(17:30)** God is the Judge of all things **(17:31)** **RESULT OF HIS MESSAGE:** *THREEFOLD REACTION* Some mocked **(17:32)** Some delayed **(17:32)** Some believed **(17:34)**	ACTS 17:15-34
Corinth	• Paul meets Aquila and Priscilla, a Christian couple, also tentmakers • Silas and Timothy now rejoin him • He states for the second time his intention to go to the Gentiles **(18:6)** • Crispus, chief ruler of the synagogue, is saved • Paul is encouraged by the Lord in a vision • Sosthenes, the new synagogue ruler, attempts to have Paul arrested, but is himself beaten • Paul remains here for eighteen months • He writes 1 and 2 Thessalonians from here	ACTS 18:1-18
Ephesus	• He remains here but a short time • He is accompanied by Aquila and Priscilla, who remain at Ephesus	ACTS 18:19-21
Antioch	• He returns to his home church	ACTS 18:22

the successor of Crispus, and severely beat him. This experience apparently also leads to his conversion to Christ. (See 1 Cor. 1:1.)

(7) Paul leaves for Ephesus, accompanied by Aquila and Priscilla. At this time we are told he had "shorn his head . . . for he had a vow" (18:18). Much debate has occurred as to whether Paul was compromising his testimony by doing this Old Testament action.

h. In Ephesus (18:19-21). He abides here but a short while, declining their invitation to stay longer, saying:

"I must by all means keep this feast that cometh in Jerusalem: but I will return again unto you, if God will" (18:21).

Paul's last phrase here should condition all our plans (see 21:14; 1 Cor. 4:19; 16:7; Heb. 6:3; Jas. 4:15).

i. In Antioch and Jerusalem (18:22).

H. His third missionary journey (18:23—21:16):

1. Paul leaves for Turkey again, visiting and encouraging the believers there.

2. About this time an eloquent Bible teacher named Apollos (born in Alexandria, Egypt) arrives in Ephesus on a preaching tour. Apollos had learned of the ministry and message of John the Baptist while still in Egypt, but knew nothing from that point on. Armed with these limited facts, he had traveled afar, faithfully proclaiming what he knew.

3. In Ephesus he is heard by Aquila and Priscilla. They:

"Took him unto them, and expounded unto him the way of God more perfectly" (18:26).

4. After awhile, Apollos feels called to Corinth and leaves, carrying with him the written recommendations of fellow-believers in Ephesus. In Corinth he is greatly used of God, "for he mightily convinced the Jews, and that publicly, showing by the scripture that Jesus was Christ" (18:28). Apollos would later become pastor of the church at Corinth (1 Cor. 3:6).

5. Paul arrives in Ephesus. His two-year stay here is marked by three noteworthy events:

a. The disciples of John (19:1-12). He meets twelve followers of John the Baptist and asks them, "Have ye received the Holy Spirit *when* ye believed?" (literal translation of 19:2). Their honest answer is: "We have not so much as heard whether there be any Holy Spirit" (19:2).

Note: They were not unaware of the *existence* of the Holy Spirit, for John had clearly revealed this (Mt. 3:11, 16; Mk. 1:8, 10; Lk. 3:16, 22), but they simply had not heard of his blessed ministry at Pentecost. Paul brings them up to date and baptizes all twelve in the name of Jesus. The record also says:

"And when Paul had laid his hands upon them, the Holy Spirit came on them, and they spoke with tongues, and prophesied" (19:6).

For the next three months he continues his synagogue ministry and, upon being opposed there, rents a public hall and carries on the work. He probably taught from 11:00 A.M. to 4:00 P.M., and worked as a tentmaker both before and after this time slot. God performed great miracles through Paul at this time:

"So that from his body were brought unto the sick handkerchiefs or aprons, and the diseases departed from them, and the evil spirits went out of them" (19:12; cf. 5:15).

b. The divinations of Sceva (19:13-20). A family of vagabond Jews composed of Sceva, a chief priest, and his seven sons had been watching Paul do his mighty miracles and decided to attempt a little exorcism of their own. Seeing a demon-possessed man, they cried out, "We adjure you by Jesus whom Paul preacheth!" (19:13).

What followed would be amusing were it not so tragic:

"And the evil spirit answered and said, Jesus I know, and Paul I know; but who are ye? And the man in whom the evil spirit was leaped on them, and overcame them, and prevailed against them, so that they fled out of that house naked and wounded" (19:15, 16; cf. Mt. 7:21-23).

Exorcism is a dangerous thing unless the exorcist is anointed by the Holy Spirit. This story quickly spread throughout the city and resulted in a great revival, for many believers who had been practicing black magic confessed their deeds. Over $10,000 worth of occult books and magic charms were then burned at a public bonfire.

c. The defenders of Diana (19:21-41). Paul feels led to return to Jerusalem and plans to visit Greece on the route back. Timothy and Erastus are sent ahead to meet him in Greece.

About this time a riot is instigated by a silversmith named Demetrius, whose business of selling silver shrines of the Greek goddess Diana has been severely threatened through Paul's preaching. Soon the huge city amphitheater (capable of seating 25,000) is packed with a howling mob which chants almost hysterically for two uninterrupted hours, "Great is Diana of the Ephesians" (19:34). The temple of Diana (the Greek name was Artemis) was one of the seven wonders of the ancient world. The image within the temple was of a woman carved with many breasts to signify the fertility of nature. The original stone from which the image had been carved was reported to have fallen from heaven, leading some historians to believe it may have been a meteorite.

Paul determines to appear in the huge arena along with some believers who have been dragged there by the mob, but is persuaded not to at the last minute. After a session of logical reasoning, the city clerk of Ephesus convinces the mob to settle any grievances in the courts and the crowd finally disperses. At this period he writes 1 and 2 Corinthians.

6. Paul in Troas (20:1–12).

a. The apostle spends three months passing through Greece and is preparing to sail for Syria when he discovers a plot by the Jews against his life, so he decides to go north to Macedonia first. During this time he writes the book of Romans.

b. Timothy accompanies him on the first part of the trip and he picks up Luke at Philippi.

c. At Troas a young man named Eutychus accidentally plunges to his death from an upper balcony after falling asleep during a midnight sermon preached by Paul. To the great relief of all, Paul raises him from the dead and continues his sermon. At dawn he leaves for Jerusalem.

Note: Especially significant in this portion of Scripture is the phrase, "Upon the first day of the week" (20:7). The *New Scofield Bible* observes:

"Although Paul was in Troas seven days (v. 6), apparently neither he nor the local church met for the breaking of bread until the first day of the week (v. 7).

The fact that Paul and others sometimes attended Sabbath services in Jewish synagogues (17:1-3) does not prove that the apostolic Church kept the seventh day as a special day of worship. It only shows that the early missionaries took the Gospel message wherever and whenever they found people gathered together (5:19, 20; 13:5; 16:13; 25-33; 17:17, 19, 22; 18:7; 19:9; 25:6, 23). This witness was carried on daily (2:47; 17:17; 19:9) in every possible way (1 Cor. 9:19-22). The early churches were specifically warned against submitting themselves to the bondage of any legalistic observance of Sabbath days (Col. 2:16, cp. Gal. 4:9-11). On the other hand, in the exercise of their Christian liberty (Rom. 14:5, 6), these same churches voluntarily chose the first day of the week as an appropriate time for fellowship and worship (Acts 20:7; 1 Cor. 16:2), the day on which the Lord arose and repeatedly appeared to his disciples (Jn. 20:19-24, 25-29). It was a new day for a new people belonging to a new creation (2 Cor. 5:17), a day of commemoration and joy (Mt. 28:9

marg.), service (Mt. 28:10), and spiritual rest (Heb. 4:9, 10).

This observance of the first day of the week is corroborated by the early fathers: in the writings of Barnabas (c. A.D. 100), Ignatius (A.D. 107), Justin Martyr (A.D. 145-150), and Irenaeus (A.D. 155-202). The edict of Laocidea (fourth century A.D.) did not change the day of worship from the seventh to the first day of the week, as sometimes alleged, but rather put the stamp of official approval upon an observance already long established in the early churches." (*New Scofield Bible,* pp. 1194, 1195)

7. Paul in Miletus (20:13-38).

a. Here Paul sends for the Ephesian elders, who hurry to meet him at Miletus during a layover in his ship schedule. On this occasion the apostle delivers his third main recorded discourse.

(1) His first was addressed to the Jews in Pisidia (13:16-41).

(2) His second was to the Gentiles in Athens (17:22-31).

(3) His third, as seen here, was to the church (20:18-35).

b. Paul develops his message in a threefold manner here.

(1) Reviewing the past:

(a) With much tears and toil he had for three years served God in Ephesus (20:19, 31; also 2 Cor. 2:4).

(b) He had taught "publicly, and from house to house" the grace of God to sinners and saints alike (20:20, 21). It is significant that the world's most famous theologian was also a great soul-winner.

(c) He had declared unto them "all the counsel of God" (20:27).

(d) He had "coveted no man's silver, or gold, or apparel" (20:33). Note his testimony here:

"Yea, ye yourselves know, that these hands have ministered unto my necessities, and to them that were with me. I have showed you all things, how that so laboring ye ought to support the weak, and to remember the words of the Lord Jesus, how he said, It is more blessed to give than to receive" (20:34, 35).

Note: This statement is not found in the four Gospels account (although perhaps implied in Lk. 14:12). His own life, of course, perfectly exemplified it. (See 2 Cor. 8:9; Eph. 5:2; Phil. 2:5-8; also Jn. 21:25.)

(e) He could, therefore, with confidence say:

"I take you to record this day, that I am pure from the blood of all men" (20:26).

(2) Viewing the present:

(a) His situation:

"And now, behold, I go bound in the spirit unto Jerusalem, not knowing the things that shall befall me there" (20:22).

(b) Their situation:

"Take heed therefore unto yourselves, and to all the flock, over the which the Holy Ghost hath made you overseers, to feed the church of God, which he hath purchased with his own blood" (20:28).

(3) Previewing the future:

(a) Paul prays that he might finish his course with joy (20:24). This he would surely do (2 Tim. 4:7).

(b) He then warns them that,

"After my departing shall grievous wolves enter in among you, not sparing the flock. Also of your own selves shall men arise, speaking perverse things, to draw away disciples after them" (20:29, 30).

Paul later writes Timothy, who is in Ephesus, concerning the "grievous wolves" (1 Tim. 1:3–7). His prophecy concerning apostasy from "your own selves" was tragically fulfilled by men like Hymenaeus, Alexander, Philetus, and others. (See 1 Tim. 1:20; 2 Tim. 2:17.) Paul then commends them all to the grace of God, and the God of grace (20:32). After a tearful final prayer session, the apostle boards the ship and bids them goodbye.

8. Paul in Tyre (21:1–6). Here he spends seven days awaiting the ship to unload its cargo. At

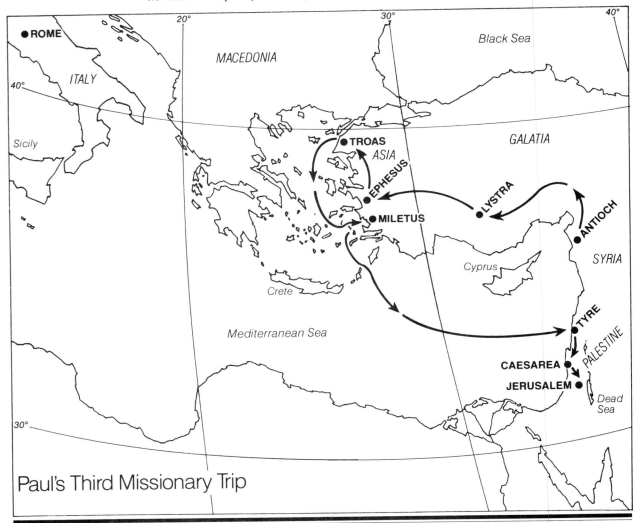

Paul's Third Missionary Trip

Acts 18:23—21:16

PAUL: HIS THIRD MISSIONARY JOURNEY

STOP	EVENT	REFERENCE
Ephesus	MINISTRY OF APOLLOS IN EPHESUS AND CORINTH (18:24-28)	
	He knew only the message of John the Baptist	
	He was more fully instructed by Aquila and Priscilla	
	He later became pastor of the church in Corinth	(1 Cor. 3:6)
	MINISTRY OF PAUL IN EPHESUS (19:1-41)	
	FIVE KEY EVENTS:	
	The disciples of John	(19:1-7)
	The divinations of Sceva	(19:13-17)
	The dedication of the converts	(19:18-20)
	The defenders of Diana	(19:23-41)
	The decision of Paul	(19:21)
Troas	HE RAISES EUTYCHUS FROM THE DEAD	(Acts 20:6-12)
Miletus	HE REVIEWS THE PAST	
	Had been with them two years	(20:19, 31)
	Had taught publicly and from house to house	(20:20, 21)
	Had declared the whole counsel of God	(20:27)
	Had coveted no man's silver	(20:33)
	Had exemplified Christ	(20:35)
	Was therefore pure from the blood of all men	(20:26)
	HE VIEWS THE PRESENT	
	His situation	(20:22)
	Their situation	(20:28)
	HE PREVIEWS THE FUTURE	
	His prayer	(20:24)
	His warning	(20:29, 30)
Tyre	HE IS WARNED BY THE HOLY SPIRIT NOT TO GO TO JERUSALEM	(21:4)
Caesarea	HE VISITS PHILIP AND HIS FOUR DAUGHTERS	(21:8, 9)
	HE IS WARNED BY AGABUS NOT TO GO TO JERUSALEM	(21:10, 11)

this time Paul is warned by the Holy Spirit "that he should not go up to Jerusalem" (21:4).

It would seem that the apostle missed God's will here. He had already been warned during the beginning of his ministry by the Lord to: "Make haste, and get thee quickly out of Jerusalem: for they will not receive thy testimony concerning me" (22:18).

Paul's motive for going to Jerusalem at this time seems to have been his great love for his people (Rom. 9:1–5) and his hope that the gifts of the Gentile churches, sent by him to the poor saints at Jerusalem (Rom. 15:25–28), would open the hearts of the law-bound Jewish believers to the gospel of God's grace. At any rate, it is very significant that his Jerusalem stop (even though brief) is one of the very few at which absolutely no fruit is recorded. After a meaningful prayer time, Paul leaves Tyre and sails for Caesarea.

9. Paul in Caesarea (21:7–14).
　a. He visits the home of Philip the evangelist and his four unmarried daughters, all of whom are prophetesses. These girls are the last mentioned in the Bible who had this gift. Others were:

(1) Miriam (Ex. 15:20)
(2) Deborah (Jdg. 4:4)
(3) Isaiah's wife (Isa. 8:3)
(4) Huldah (2 Ki. 22:14)
(5) Anna (Lk. 2:36)
　b. He is again warned by God concerning his Jerusalem trip, this time by the prophet Agabus, who demonstrates the treatment Paul will receive there by binding his hands and feet with the apostle's belt. Agabus is joined by other believers in begging Paul not to go.
　c. Fighting back tears, Paul answers:
　　"What mean ye to weep and to break mine heart? For I am ready not to be bound only, but also to die at Jerusalem for the name of the Lord Jesus" (21:13).
10. Paul in Jerusalem (21:15—23:30).
　a. James and the elders in Jerusalem rejoice as Paul relates how God has blessed his missionary trips to the Gentile world.
　b. Paul is then told of a rumor making its rounds among the Christian Jews in Jerusalem to the effect that he was teaching "all the Jews which are among the Gentiles to forsake Moses, saying that they ought not to circumcise their children,

neither to walk after the customs" (21:21).

c. To refute this rumor, he is advised to put himself under a Jewish vow of the shaven head and to sponsor four other young men who are doing the same (21:22-25).

d. Paul agrees, but is later set upon by a mob when some Jews from Turkey see him in the Temple and wrongly conclude he has brought a Gentile in with him (21:26-29).

e. He is saved from certain death by the commander of the Roman garrison stationed there, and taken to the armory (21:31-34).

f. After convincing the commander that he is not a certain Egyptian outlaw, Paul is allowed to address the Jewish mob (21:35-40). We note he makes his defense on the same Roman stairway where Pilate had condemned Christ to death some twenty-six years prior. In fact, the cries of the mob are similar (Lk. 23:18; cf. Acts 21:36).

g. He briefly relates his conversion to Christ on the Damascus Road.

h. The crowd retains a hostile silence (as Paul speaks in Hebrew) until he mentions his divine call to the Gentiles. Upon hearing that hated word they go berserk (22:21-23).

i. Paul is quickly brought inside the fort and ordered beaten to make him confess any crimes, but is spared of this when he informs the commander of his Roman citizenship (22:24-29).

j. Paul is brought before the Jewish Sanhedrin on the following day and defends himself. We now note:

(1) The reprisal against Paul (23:1, 2). At the order of Ananias the high priest, Paul is slapped on the mouth, as once was our Lord (Jn. 18:22).

(2) The retaliation of Paul (23:3).

"God shall smite thee, thou whited wall: for sittest thou to judge me after the law, and commandest me to be smitten contrary to the law?"

The phrase "whited wall" suggested a tottering wall whose precarious position had been disguised by a generous coat of whitewash. The meaning was that, although he held a high position, he would someday fall. In fact, he was assassinated some eight years later.

(3) The regret of Paul (23:4, 5). Paul apparently did not fully realize he was talking to the high priest, and he apologizes for speaking evil of a ruler.

(4) The ruse of Paul (23:6-10). Paul identifies himself as a Pharisee and a believer in the resurrection of the dead, thus causing an immediate split between the assembled Pharisees and the resurrection-denying Sadducees. The clamor becomes so intense that Paul is removed by the Roman commander.

Acts 21:17—23:30

PAUL: HIS FINAL VISIT TO JERUSALEM

STOP	EVENT	REFERENCE
Jerusalem	THE **RUMORS** AGAINST PAUL	
	• That he had degraded the Law of Moses	**21:21**
	• That he had desecrated the Temple of God	**21:28, 29**
	THE **WRONG ACTION** BY PAUL	
	• He places himself back under the law	**21:26**
	THE **RESCUE** OF PAUL	**21:31, 32**
	THE **REVIEW** BY PAUL	**22:1-30**
	• The apostle and the Jewish crowd	**22:1-23**
	• The apostle and the Roman centurion	**22:24-30**
	THE **REPRISAL** AGAINST PAUL	**23:1, 2**
	THE **RETALIATION** BY PAUL	**23:3**
	THE **REGRET** OF PAUL	**23:4, 5**
	THE **RUSE** BY PAUL	**23:6-10**
	THE **REVELATION** TO PAUL	**23:11**
	THE **RELATIVE** OF PAUL	**23:12-22**
	THE **REMOVAL** OF PAUL	**23:23-32**

(5) The revelation to Paul (23:11).

"And the night following, the Lord stood by him, and said, Be of good cheer, Paul: for as thou hast testified of me in Jerusalem, so must thou bear witness also at Rome."

Note: Paul had often hoped to get to Rome (Rom. 1:13). In Ephesus he had made definite plans to go, but at this point he was not sure he would get away from Jerusalem alive (Rom. 15:31, 32). But now, for the first time, God had said it.

(6) The rescue of Paul (23:12-30). Paul's nephew learns of a plot by forty fanatical Jews who had "bound themselves under a curse, saying that they would neither eat nor drink till they had killed Paul" (23:12). The Roman commander quickly removes Paul that very night to Caesarea, protected by 470 armed soldiers. He sends a letter on ahead to Felix in Caesarea, explaining why Paul is being sent to him.

11. Paul in Caesarea (23:31—26:32).

a. Before Felix (23:31—24:27). Both officially and personally, Felix was noted for his evil deeds. Tacitus, the Roman historian, writes: "Felix, indulging in every kind of barbarity and lust, exercised the power of a king in the spirit of a slave." Felix was later guilty of having the Jewish high priest Jonathan (Annas's son) assassinated.

(1) Paul is accused before Felix by a crafty Jewish lawyer from Jerusalem named Tertullus. The charges are threefold:

(a) Treason. He is accused of disturbing the peace and creating political dissension not only in Jerusalem, but throughout the world.

(b) Religious heresy.

(c) Temple desecration.

(2) Paul is allowed to answer these lying accusations.

(a) To the first charge he points out he has only been in Jerusalem twelve days, and could not possibly have created all the alleged trouble in that brief time.

(b) Concerning the second charge, he shows he is actually *more* orthodox than some members of the Sanhedrin who denied the Old Testament doctrine of the resurrection (see Dan. 12:2).

(c) In regard to the third charge he reminds the court that the Jews in Jerusalem itself could not make that indictment stick.

(3) Felix defers sentence until he receives the official testimony of Lysias, the arresting Roman commander.

(4) Shortly after this time, Paul has the opportunity to preach to both Felix and his wife, Drusilla. This girl, not yet twenty, is the youngest daughter of Herod Agrippa I (murderer of James, Acts 12:1, 2), and the sister of Agrippa II and Bernice, mentioned in 25:13. She had left a pagan Syrian king to marry Felix. (Drusilla died twenty-one years later in the eruption of Mt. Vesuvius.) Luke records this dramatic preaching session for us:

"And as he [Paul] reasoned of righteousness, temperance, and judgment to come, Felix trembled and answered, Go thy way for this time; when I have a convenient season, I will call for thee" (24:25).

b. Before Festus (25:1-12). In A.D. 58 there was a riot of pagans and Jews in Caesarea. Felix's soldiers put it down with such violence that the outraged Jews were able to force his recall. He was succeeded by Festus.

(1) Festus resists pressure from the Jews to return Paul back to Jerusalem (where they planned to kill him en route).

(2) Once again a wolf-band of Jewish lawyers come to Caesarea to make formal charges against the apostle.

(3) Sensing that Festus would give in to the Jews and send him to Jerusalem (which would have meant certain death), Paul appeals to Caesar (25:11). The Caesar to whom Paul appeals is Nero, who began his reign in A.D. 54. His early years were gentle in nature and gave no hint of the cruelties which would follow.

c. Before Agrippa (25:13—26:32). Agrippa II (son of Herod Agrippa) and Bernice come to Caesarea to visit Festus and Drusilla. Bernice was the sister of both Drusilla and Agrippa II.

(1) Upon hearing about Paul from Festus, Agrippa II requests an audience with the famous prisoner. Paul is brought into the palace court and, in chains, preaches Christ to his royal guests. Once again he begins by relating his personal testimony, which includes:

(a) His early religious training in Tarsus.

(b) His terrible persecution of Christians.

(c) His conversion on the Damascus Road.

(d) His call to the Gentiles. Paul then concludes with the following words (26:22, 23):

"Having therefore obtained help of God, I continue unto this day, witnessing both to small and great, saying none other things than those which the prophets and Moses did say should come: That Christ should suffer, and that he should be the first that should rise from the dead, and should show light unto the people, and to the Gentiles."

(2) At this point he is rudely interrupted by Festus, who "said with a loud voice, Paul, thou art beside thyself; much learning doth make thee mad" (26:24). Paul quickly brushes off this outburst and presses for a decision on the part of Agrippa. The embarrassed king answers: "Almost thou persuadest me to be a Christian" (26:28).

Note: It cannot be determined from this verse that Agrippa was at the point of accepting Christ. The Greek text reads: "In short, you are trying to persuade me to be a Christian." The king may have meant he could not be convinced in such a brief period of time.

(3) Paul is dismissed, and Agrippa turns to Festus, saying, "This man might have been set at liberty, if he had not appealed unto Caesar" (26:32). This, of course, was not true, for Festus had already indicated his plans to send Paul back to Jerusalem (25:9) which would have meant certain death.

(4) At this point a helpful comparison may be made between the Saul of the Old Testament and the New Testament Saul.

(a) The Old Testament Saul was tall and impressive, but the New Testament Saul was probably short and unimpressive (1 Sam. 9:2; compare Gal. 4:13, 14; 2 Cor. 10:10).

(b) Both were from the tribe of Benjamin (1 Sam. 9:1, 2; Phil. 3:5).

(c) The Old Testament Saul began as God's friend, but ended as his enemy. The New Testament Saul did the opposite (1 Sam. 10, 31; Acts 9; 2 Tim. 4).

Acts 23:31—26:32

PAUL, IN CAESAREA

STOP	EVENT	REFERENCE
Caesarea	**BEFORE FELIX**	**23:33—24:27**
	● The accusations of Tertullus	**24:1-9**
	● The answer of Paul	**24:10-21**
	● The apprehension of Felix	**24:24-26**
	BEFORE FESTUS	**25:1-12**
	● Festus threatens to send Paul to Jerusalem	
	● Paul appeals to be sent to Caesar	
	BEFORE AGRIPPA	**25:13—26:32**
	● Paul gives some information concerning himself	**26:1-23**
	● Paul gives an invitation concerning his Savior	**26:24-32**

Acts 27:1—28:31

PAUL: HIS TRIP TO AND TESTIMONY IN ROME

STOP	EVENT	REFERENCE
Mediterranean Sea	**EN ROUTE TO ROME**	**27:1—28:13**
	● The terrible Mediterranean storm	**27:1-44**
	● The treacherous Melita serpent	**28:1-10**
Rome	**IN ROME**	**28:14-31**
	● His meeting with the Jews	**28:17-29**
	● His ministry to all	**28:30, 31**
	HE WRITES EPHESIANS, COLOSSIANS, PHILIPPIANS, PHILEMON	

(d) In the hour of death the Old Testament Saul visited the witch of Endor, while the New Testament Saul called for the Word of God (1 Sam. 28:7; 2 Tim. 4:13).

(e) The Old Testament Saul took his own life in great fear, while the New Testament Saul gave his own life with great expectation (1 Sam. 31:4; 2 Tim. 4:6–8).

(f) The life of the Old Testament Saul was characterized by disobedience, while the New Testament Saul's was that of obedience (1 Sam. 13:13; 15:22, 23; Acts 26:19). "Whereupon, O King Agrippa, I was not disobedient unto the heavenly vision."

12. Paul en route to Rome (27–28).

a. Luke now joins Paul, who is placed aboard a ship sailing west with some other prisoners in the custody of Julius, a member of the imperial guard. This Roman official would later treat Paul with great kindness and respect (27:1–3).

b. After some difficult sailing, they arrive at Fair Havens on the southern side of the Isle Crete. At this time it is late autumn. Among the ancients the dangerous season for sailing was from September 14 to November 11. After this date all navigation on the open sea was discontinued. In spite of this knowledge, and over the protests of Paul (who had already been through at least three shipwrecks; see 2 Cor. 11:25), the boat officials set sail for Phoenix, planning to winter there.

c. Soon, however, they are caught up in the grasp of a vicious winter typhoon. One of the most vivid accounts of a storm in recorded history is now described for us by Luke (27:16–20).

(1) The ship is blown far out to sea, completely out of control.

(2) The terrified sailors band the ship with ropes to strengthen the hull.

(3) The following day as the seas grow higher they throw the cargo overboard.

(4) The next day all the tackle and loose objects are discarded.

(5) After fourteen frightful and desperate days, Luke writes:

"And when neither sun nor stars in many days appeared, and no small tempest lay on us, all hope that we should be saved was then taken away" (27:20).

d. Suddenly, the fearless apostle of God appears and, standing upon the pitching and water-soaked deck, announces:

"Sirs, ye should have hearkened unto me, and not have loosed from Crete, and to have gained this harm and loss.

And now I exhort you to be of good cheer: for there shall be no loss of any man's life among you, but of the ship. For there stood by me this night the angel of God, whose I am, and whom I serve, Saying, Fear not, Paul; thou must be brought before Caesar: and, lo, God hath given thee all them that sail with thee. Wherefore, sirs, be of good cheer: for I believe God, that it shall be even as it was told me."

e. He then warns everyone to stay on board (and not attempt to lower the emergency boat) and encourages all to eat by publicly saying grace over his bread. Soon the entire 276 souls on board begin to eat also (27:36).

f. At daybreak the ship hits a sandbar and runs aground. Julius denies the soldiers' request to kill the prisoners lest they escape, and orders all to swim for the nearby island of Melita. Soon every single person is safely ashore (27:44).

g. The people of Melita treat the shivering survivors with great kindness, building a bonfire on the beach to warm them.

h. Paul is suddenly bitten by a poisonous serpent which has hidden itself among the firewood he helped to gather. To the utter amazement of all, he suffers absolutely no discomfort whatsoever (28:6). This event was a direct fulfillment of Jesus' prophecy in Mark 16:18 and Luke 10:19.

i. During the three-month stay here, Paul heals many, including the feverish father of Publius, governor of the island.

j. In the early part of the spring, they board a new boat and sail for Rome. Paul is met by some Roman believers both at the Forum (forty-three miles from Rome) and then at the Three Taverns (thirty-five miles from Rome).

Note: The phrase in 28:15 "to meet us" is the same word found concerning the rapture of all believers in 1 Thessalonians 4:17, where we read, "to meet the Lord in the air." It is a term regularly used of the official welcome tendered by a delegation who went out to meet a visiting official and accompany him into the city.

k. Paul finally arrives in Rome and is granted great freedom, being guarded by only one soldier.

l. Soon after his arrival he assembles the local Jewish leaders to explain who he is and why he is in Rome appealing to Caesar. The Jews are curious to hear his strange message about Christ. After his sermon, some accept the Savior, but, of course, many do not.

This would be the last of seven recorded defenses of his ministry by the apostle. The others are:

(1) before the Jerusalem mob (22:1–23)

(2) before the chief captain (22:24–30)

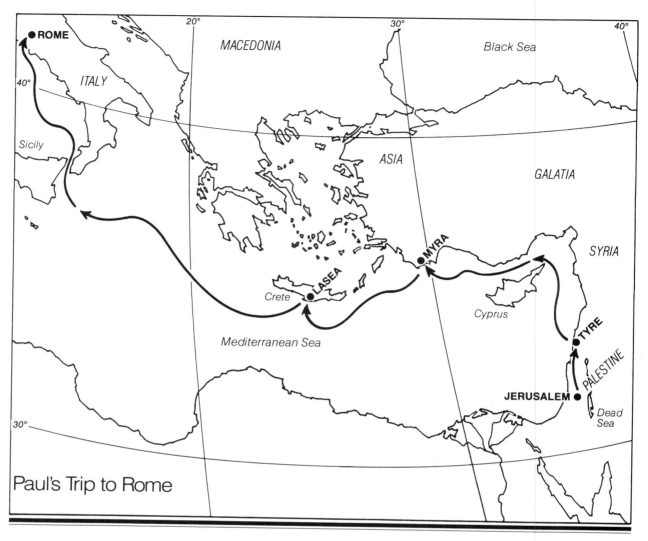

Paul's Trip to Rome

(3) before the Sanhedrin (23:1-10)
(4) before Felix (24:10-23)
(5) before Festus (25:8-12)
(6) before Agrippa (26:1-32)

m. To the unbelieving he quotes the words of Isaiah 6:9, 10, a quote used twice elsewhere in the New Testament by Jesus (Mt. 13:14, 15; Mk. 4:12; Lk. 8:10) and by John (Jn. 12:40, 41). Paul had already used it in his epistle to the Romans (Rom. 11:8).

n. Luke ends his remarkable account with the following words:

"And Paul dwelt two whole years in his own hired house, and received all that came in unto him, preaching the kingdom of God, and teaching those things which concern the Lord Jesus Christ, with all confidence, no man forbidding him."

During this time Paul writes Ephesians, Colossians, Philemon, and Philippians.

Note: Most Bible students feel he was released at this time and once more traveled around preaching Christ before his final arrest and martyrdom in Rome. It was probably during this time that he wrote 1 and 2 Timothy and Titus.

GALATIANS
INTRODUCTION:

1. At least thirteen New Testament epistles were written by Paul. For a number of years it was assumed that 1 Thessalonians was his first epistle. However, many conservative scholars now believe Galatians was his first.

2. One of the problems in dating the book concerns its destination. Was the letter written to the churches in northern Galatia (where Paul visited during his second and third missionary trips) or to the churches in southern Galatia (where he preached during his first trip)? If one accepts the southern theory, then Galatians was probably his first letter.

3. The Galatians themselves were an emotional and intense Celtic people. Caesar said: "They are fickle in their resolves, fond of change, and not to be trusted." This is demonstrated during Paul's first visit to them. In the morning they attempted to worship him, and in the afternoon to murder him (Acts 14). They were a branch of Gauls, originally from the north of the Baltic

Sea, who had split off from a main migration westward to France and had settled in Asia Minor during the third century, B.C.

4. Paul's work in Galatia had been highly successful. Great multitudes of people, mostly Gentiles, had accepted Christ. But after he left, the Judaizers from Jerusalem (a group of legalistic gospel-perverting Jews) had come to Galatia, teaching that Gentiles must put themselves back under the bondage of the law to be saved. The Galatians had thus received their message with the same zeal that they had accepted Paul's. There was then a general epidemic of circumcision among them.

5. They had not only attacked the message of Paul, but also his apostleship.

6. Galatians may have been the only book written personally by the apostle without the aid of a stenographer (see 6:11).

7. It is, next to 2 Corinthians, the most autobiographical of Paul's letters and the only epistle by Paul addressed to a group of local churches.

8. The key word is *liberty,* used eleven times in the letter. This is more than all his other epistles combined.

9. It has been said that Judaism was the cradle of Christianity and very nearly its grave. But God raised up Paul as the Moses of the Christian church to deliver believers from bondage.

10. Galatians finishes what Paul will begin in 2 Corinthians (concerning his apostleship), and begins what Paul will finish in Romans (concerning justification by faith).

11. There is a striking parallel between Galatians and Romans. At least nineteen passages may be favorably compared. Galatians is a rough sketch of which Romans is the finished picture.

12. A suggested chronology of the writing of Galatians:
    a. the events at Pentecost—A.D. 29 (Acts 2)
    b. Paul's conversion—A.D. 31 (Acts 9)
    c. his visit to Arabia—A.D. 31 (Gal. 1:17)
    d. the return to Damascus—A.D. 33
    e. his first visit as a saved man to Jerusalem—A.D. 33 (Gal. 1:18; Acts 9:26)
    f. his departure to Syria and Cilicia—A.D. 33 (Acts 9:30; Gal. 1:21)
    g. his early ministry in Antioch—A.D. 35 (Acts 11:25, 26)
    h. his second trip to Jerusalem—A.D. 46 (Acts 11:29, 30; Gal. 2:1-10)
    i. his first missionary trip from Antioch—A.D. 46 (Acts 13)
    j. his return to Antioch—A.D. 49 (Gal. 2:11; Acts 14:26)
    k. his confrontation with Simon Peter in Antioch (Gal. 2:11-14)
    l. his letter to the Galatians (attempting to correct their error by letter as he had done to Peter by the spoken word)
    m. the Jerusalem Council—A.D. 49 (Acts 15)

13. The nature of Galatians. J. Vernon McGee writes:
    a. "It is a stern, severe, and solemn message (Gal. 1:6-9; 3:1-5). It does not correct conduct, as the Corinthian letters do, but it is corrective—the Galatian believers were in grave peril. Because the foundations were being attacked, everything was threatened.

    The Epistle contains no word of commendation, praise, or thanksgiving. There is no request for prayer, and there is no mention of their standing in Christ. No one with him is mentioned by name (1:2). Compare this with the other epistles of Paul.

    b. The heart of Paul the apostle is laid bare, there is deep emotion and strong feeling. This is his fighting epistle—he has on his war paint. He has no toleration for legalism. Someone has said that Romans comes from the head of Paul while Galatians comes from the heart of Paul. 'Galatians takes up controversially what Romans puts systematically.'

    c. It is the declaration of emancipation from legalism of any type. This was Martin Luther's favorite Epistle, and it was on the masthead of the Reformation. It has been called the Magna Charta of the early church, the manifesto of Christian liberty, the impregnable citadel, and a veritable Gibraltar against any attack on the heart of the Gospel. 'Immortal victory is set upon its brow.'

    d. It is the strongest declaration and defense of the doctrine of justification by faith in or out of Scripture. It is God's polemic on behalf of the most vital truth of the Christian faith against any attack.

    Not only is a sinner saved by grace through faith, but the saved sinner lives by grace. Grace is a way to life and a way of life." (*Thru the Bible,* p. 108)

I. Vindication—a Defense (1-2). Paul defends his apostolic office.
   A. Paul's sorrow concerning their present troubles (1:1-9).
      "I marvel that ye are so soon removed from him that called you into the grace of Christ unto another gospel" (1:6).
      1. This "gospel" was really not an *allos* (Greek word meaning "another of the same kind"), but a *heteros* (Greek word meaning "another of a different kind").
      2. This "gospel" was not to be received, even though it came from an angel or from Paul himself.
      3. This "gospel," if received and believed, would result in divine judgment and damnation upon its recipients. The word "accuse" here is *anathema* in the Greek. (See also Acts 23:14; 1 Cor. 12:3; Rom. 9:3; 2 Thess. 1:9.)
   B. Paul's summary concerning his past travels (2:1-10). It has already been observed that the troublemaking Judaizers had attacked the authority and validity of Paul's apostleship. They apparently were accusing him of being a men-pleaser (a possible twisting of testimony in 1 Cor. 9:22) and of being under the thumb of the other apostles, and thus not being his own man. They were saying he was not one of the original twelve, but a Johnny-come-lately. Paul will now refute these charges.
      1. The source of his salvation and apostolic call.
         "For I neither received it of man, neither was I taught it, but by the revelation of Jesus Christ" (1:12).
         The Savior also revealed to Paul those facts concerning:
         a. The Last Supper (1 Cor. 11:23)
         b. The death and resurrection of Christ (1 Cor. 15:3, 4)

2. The need of his salvation and apostolic call (1:13-15). Here Paul gives his testimony and tells of the horrible life he lived prior to his conversion. The apostle loved to relate this testimony. (See Acts 22:1-16; 26:1-20; 1 Tim. 1:12-16.)

Paul now adds that his eventual call to Christian service actually began prior to his birth. "But . . . it pleased God, who separated me from my mother's womb, and called me by his grace" (1:15).

Two other unborn babies also experienced this early call.
   a. Jeremiah the prophet (Jer. 1:4-10)
   b. John the Baptist (Lk. 1:15-17)
3. The purpose of his salvation and apostolic call (1:16): "To reveal his son in me, that I might preach him among the heathen." Thus God revealed Christ *in* Paul so that he might reveal Christ *through* him.
4. The events following his salvation and apostolic call (1:17—2:21):
   a. He is converted en route to Damascus (Acts 9:1-22).
   b. He spends approximately three years in Arabia (Gal. 1:17).
   c. He returns to Damascus (Gal. 1:17; Acts 9:23-25; 2 Cor. 11:32, 33).
   d. He visits Jerusalem for the first time since his salvation (Gal. 1:18-20; Acts 9:26-29).

On this occasion he spends only fifteen days and meets with Peter and James, the Lord's brother.
   e. He leaves for Syria and Cilicia (Acts 9:30; Gal. 1:21; Acts 22:17-21).
   f. He ministers with Barnabas in Antioch (Acts 11:25, 26).
   g. He visits Jerusalem again along with Barnabas and Titus (Gal. 2:1-10; Acts 11:29, 30). It has now been fourteen years since his conversion. At this point in the record the Judaizers begin putting pressure upon Paul to mix their devilish legalism with God's pure grace, but they would run into a brick wall in this! James, Peter, and John encourage Paul to keep preaching God's grace to the Gentiles.
   h. He returns to Antioch along with Barnabas and John Mark (Acts 12:25).
   i. He departs for the first missionary journey with John Mark and Barnabas from Antioch (Acts 13).
   j. He returns to Antioch (Acts 14:26).
   k. He confronts Simon Peter in Antioch (Gal. 2:11-14). It is difficult to know just when this confrontation took place. Some would feel it happened at a later date, following the Jerusalem Council. At any rate, Peter had allowed the ever-present Judaizers to pressure him into with-

Galatians

PAUL'S SUMMARY CONCERNING HIS PAST TRAVELS (1:10)

The Source of His Salvation and Apostolic Call
"For I neither received it of man, neither was I taught it, but by the revelation of Jesus Christ" **(1:12).**

The Need of His Salvation and Apostolic Call (1:13-15)
(SEE ALSO ACTS 22:1-16; 26:1-20; 1 TIM. 1:12-16)
HIS TERRIBLE LIFE
"Beyond measure I persecuted the church of God, and wasted it" **(1:13).**

HIS WONDERFUL LORD
"It pleased God, who separated me from my mother's womb, and called me by his grace" **(1:15).**

The Purpose of His Salvation and Apostolic Call
"To reveal his Son in me, that I might preach him among the heathen" **(1:16).**

The Events Following His Salvation and Apostolic Call (1:17—2:21)
- He is converted en route to Damascus **(Acts 9:1-22)**
- He spends approximately three years in Arabia **(Gal. 1:17)**
- He returns to Damascus **(Gal. 1:7; Acts 9:23-25; 2 Cor. 11:32, 33)**
- He visits Jerusalem for the first time since his salvation **(Gal. 1:18-20; Acts 9:26-29)**
- He leaves for Syria and Cilicia **(Acts 9:30; 22:17-21; Gal. 1:21)**
- He ministers with Barnabas in Antioch **(Acts 11:25, 26)**
- He visits Jerusalem again **(Gal. 2:1-10; Acts 11:29, 30)**
- He returns to Antioch and Barnabas and John Mark **(Acts 12:25)**
- He departs on his first missionary journey **(Acts 13)**
- He returns to Antioch **(Acts 14:26)**
- He confronts Peter in Antioch. Reason: *Peter's legalism was denying:*
  a. The unity of the church **2:14**
  b. Justification by faith alone **2:15, 16**
  c. Freedom from the law **2:17, 18**
  d. The all-sufficiency of the indwelling Christ **2:19, 20**
  e. The grace of God **2:21**

"I am crucified with Christ: nevertheless I live; yet not I, but Christ liveth in me" **(2:20).**

drawing from all Gentile believers upon the arrival of some influential Jews from Jerusalem. Paul soundly rebukes Peter for this. By doing what he did, Peter was denying five major doctrines.
  (1) the unity of the church (2:14)
  (2) justification by faith alone (2:15, 16)
  (3) freedom from the law (2:17, 18)
  (4) the all-sufficiency of the indwelling Christ (2:19, 20)
  (5) the grace of God (2:21)

Peter's immediate reaction to this rebuke is not recorded. He very obviously did repent and bore Paul no ill will for it (see 2 Pet. 3:15). In 2:20 Paul pens one of the greatest statements in all the Bible:
"I am crucified with Christ: nevertheless I live; yet not I, but Christ liveth in me: and the life which I now live in the flesh I live by the faith of the Son of God, who loved me, and gave himself for me."

II. Denunciation—a disaster (3-4). Paul warns the Galatians concerning the bondage of works. He now employs three powerful illustrations to drive home the contrast between legalism and liberty.
A. A personal illustration. An example from their own experience (3:1-5). Here Paul says he has but two questions:
  1. How did you receive your new nature in the first place?
  "This only would I learn of you, received ye the Spirit by the works of the law, or by the hearing of faith?" (3:2)
  2. Can you add to your new nature?
  "Are you so foolish? Having begun in the Spirit, are ye now made perfect by the flesh?"

Warren Wiersbe writes:
"The illustration of human birth is appropriate here. Two human parents are required for a child to be conceived and born, and two spiritual parents are required for a child to be born into God's family: the Spirit of God and the Word of God (Jn. 3:1-8; 1 Pet. 1:22-25). When a normal child is born, he has all that he needs for life; nothing need be added. When the child of God is born into God's family, he has all that he needs spiritually; nothing need be added! All that is necessary is that the child have food, exercise, and cleansing that he might grow into maturity. It would be strange if the parents had to take the child to the doctor at one month to receive ears, at two months to receive toes, and so on." (Be Free, p. 57)
B. A legal illustration. A series of examples from the Mosaic Law (3:6—4:20):
  1. Abraham and the law.
    a. Abraham received his righteousness by faith in God long before the law was given (3:6, 17).
    b. God told Abraham (Gen. 12:3) that Gentiles would also receive their righteousness by faith (3:8, 9).

c. God not only pardons sinners by faith, but then preserves them by faith: "The just shall live by faith" (3:11). This all-important statement is taken from the Old Testament book of Habbakuk (2:4) and is used three times in the New Testament. (See Rom. 1:17 and Heb. 10:38.)
  2. Sinners and the law.
    "For as many as were of the works of the law are under the curse; for it is written, cursed is everyone that continueth not in all things which are written in the book of the law, to do them" (3:10; see Deut. 27:26).
    The New Testament author of the book of James had already written: "For whosoever shall keep the whole law, and yet offend in one point, he is guilty of all" (Jas. 2:10). Thus the Old Testament law may be likened to a long chain. To break this chain a person need only snap but a single link and the entire chain is broken!
  3. Israel and the law.
    a. It was given to Israel 430 years after the promise (justification by faith) was given. Warren Wiersbe writes:
    "The 430 years of verse 16 has puzzled Bible students for many years. From Abraham's call (Gen. 12) to Jacob's arrival in Egypt (Gen. 46) is 215 years. This may be computed as follows:
    (1) Abraham was 75 years old when God called him and 100 when Isaac was born (Gen. 12:4; 21:5). This gives us 25 years.
    (2) Isaac was 60 when Jacob was born (Gen. 25:26).
    (3) Jacob was 130 years old when he arrived in Egypt (Gen. 47:9). Thus, 25 + 60 + 130 = 215 years.
    (4) But Moses tells us that Israel sojourned in Egypt 430 years (Ex. 12:40); so the total number of the law is 645 years, not 430.
    (5) The length of stay in Egypt is recorded also in Genesis 15:13 and Acts 7:6, where the round number of 400 years is used. Several solutions have been offered to this puzzle, but perhaps the most satisfying is this: Paul is counting from the time Jacob went into Egypt, when God appeared to him and reaffirmed the Covenant (Gen. 46:1-4). The 430 years is the time from God's confirmation of His promise to Jacob until the giving of the law at Sinai." (Be Free, p. 77, 78)
    b. It was an insertion, given because of sin. "It was added because of transgression" (3:19).
    c. It was "ordained by angels in the hand of a mediator" (3:19). Note the following verses which attest to this fact of angelic activity on Mt. Sinai at the giving of the law.

"The Lord came from Sinai . . . and he came with ten thousands of saints. From his right hand went a fiery law for them" (Deut. 33:2).

"The chariots of God and twenty thousand, even thousands of angels; the Lord is among them, as in Sinai, in the holy place" (Ps. 68:17).

"Who [sinful Israel] have received the law by the disposition of angels, and have not kept it" (Acts 7:53).

"For the word spoken by angels [the law] was steadfast (Heb. 2:2).

d. It thus acted as Israel's "schoolmaster" (child-discipliner, from the Greek word *paidagogos)*: "Wherefore the law was our schoolmaster to bring us unto Christ" (3:24). J. Vernon McGee writes:

"The key word here is schoolmaster and has nothing to do with a school teacher in a present-day context. The term designated a slave or servant in a Roman home who had charge of any child born in the home. He fed, dressed, bathed, blew the nose of and paddled, the son born in the home. When the little fellow reached school age, he took him by the hand and led him to school. This is where he got the name of *paidagogos* (child leader). The law took mankind by the hand, led him to the cross of Christ and said, 'Little man, you need a Saviour.' The law turns us over to Christ. We are under Christ now and not under the law." (*Thru the Bible*, p. 110)

4. Christ and the law.
   a. He has redeemed us from its curse. "Christ hath redeemed us from the curse of the law, being made a curse for us: for it is written, cursed is every one that hangeth on a tree" (3:13; see Deut. 21:23). Again to quote from Dr. J. Vernon McGee:

   "This was a very strange law since the method of capital punishment under the law was by stoning. But if the crime was aggravated and atrocious, the body of the criminal was taken after death and hung up to display the seriousness of the crime." (*Ibid.,* p. 110)

   b. He did all this at God's appointed time through a human body.

   "But when the fulness of the time was come, God sent forth his Son, made of a woman, made under the law, to redeem them that were under the law" (4:4, 5).

   c. He unified all repenting sinners by joining them into his own body through Spirit baptism.

   "For ye are all the children of God by faith in Christ Jesus. For as many of you as have been baptized into Christ have put on Christ. There is neither Jew nor Greek, there is neither bond nor free, there is neither male nor female: for ye are all one in Christ Jesus. And if ye be Christ's, then are ye Abraham's seed, and heirs according to the promise" (3:26-29).

   There were three great divisions in the Roman world:
   (1) racial and religious—Jew and Greek
   (2) social and class—bond and free
   (3) man's world and woman's world
   But in Christ there is no *spiritual* distinction whatsoever.

   d. He thus guarantees our full adoption as sons of God.

   "Now I say, That the heir, as long as he is a child, differeth nothing from a servant, though he be lord of all; but is under tutors and governors until the time appointed of the father. Even so we, when we were children, were in bondage under the elements of the world: But when the fulness of the time was come, God sent forth his Son, made of a woman, made under the law, to redeem them that were under the law, that we might receive the adoption of sons. And because ye are sons, God hath sent forth the Spirit of his Son into your hearts, crying, Abba, Father. Wherefore thou art no more a servant, but a son; and if a son, then an heir of God through Christ" (4:1-7).

   Paul here of course does not mean that the law makes us children of God, while Christ makes us sons of God. But he does contrast the differences between a child and a son under the Roman legal system of the day.
   (1) *Childhood* refers to my condition in God's family, while *adoption* speaks of my position.
   (2) Through *regeneration* one enters into the family but by *adoption* he enjoys the family.
   (3) The circumstances leading to *childhood* are private, while those dealing with *adoption* are public.
   (4) A *child* is under guardians, while an *adopted adult* has full liberty.

   e. Paul also contrasts the differences between a son and a servant (4:7).
   (1) A *servant* retains his old nature, while a *son* enjoys that of his father.
   (2) A *servant* has a master, while a *son* has a father.
   (3) A *servant* obeys out of law and fear, but a *son* out of liberty and love.
   (4) A *servant* is promised no inheritance, while a *son* can legally expect to inherit all things.

5. The promise and the law.
   a. The law cannot change the promise (3:15-18).

b. The law is not greater than the promise (3:19, 20).

c. The law is not contrary to the promise (3:21-26).

d. The law cannot do what the promise can do (3:27-29).

6. The Galatians and the law (4:8-20). The apostle now returns to his readers. He wants to know:

a. After being released from spiritual slavery, why did they now desire to put back on their chains of bondage again (4:9, 10)? They were doing exactly this by observing *days* (Jewish holy days such as weekly sabbaths and special feast days), *months* (celebrations of new moons which began each month of the Jewish lunar calendar), *times* (seasons of week-long festivals such as the feast of tabernacles, unleavened bread, etc.), and *years* (Sabbatical and Jubilee years).

b. Where was that happy spirit once enjoyed between the apostle and the Galatians (4:11-15)? He reminds them of their past affection for him, which had made them willing (if it were possible) to pluck out their eyes for him! Some connect this statement in 4:15 with that in 2 Corinthians 12:7 concerning Paul's thorn in the flesh.

c. Why had they thus turned from him, viewing him, their real spiritual mother, as their enemy, and attached themselves to false legalizing teachers (4:16-20)? In perhaps no other single verse does the apostle display more of his agony and aspiration for all his converts than he does here in 4:19: "My little children, of whom I travail in birth again until Christ be formed in you."

d. An allegorical illustration—an example from Hagar and Sarah (4:21-31). It should be clearly stated that Paul is not denying the historical existence of these women in Genesis, or even attempting to teach a deeper and previously hidden "spiritual meaning." He is simply *using* the Old Testament doctrinal events to allegorize a point.

(1) The facts of Paul's allegory: Abraham had two sons and two wives. One son (Ishmael) was born naturally from his slave-wife Hagar. The other (Isaac) was born supernaturally from his freeborn wife Sarah. Isaac is ridiculed by Ishmael at his weaning ceremony. Therefore God orders Abraham to send away both Hagar and Ishmael.

(2) The applications of Paul's allegory:

(a) Hagar represents the law, while Sarah speaks of grace.

(b) Ishmael refers to the flesh and to those who would keep the law, thus remaining slave children.

A LEGAL ILLUSTRATION

Abraham and the Law
- Abraham received his righteousness by faith in God **(3:16, 17)**
- The Gentiles would receive their righteousness by faith **(3:8, 9)**
- God pardons and preserves sinners by faith *"The just shall live by faith"* **(3:11)**

Sinners and the Law
"For as many as are of the works of the law are under the curse" **(3:10)**

Israel and the Law
- It was given to Israel 430 years after the promise
- It was an insertion, given because of sin **(3:19)**
- It was "ordained by angels in the hand of a mediator" **(3:19)**
- It thus acted as Israel's "schoolmaster" **(3:24)**

Christ and the Law
- He has redeemed us from its curse **(3:13; see Deut. 21:23)**
- He did all this at God's appointed time through a human body **(4:4, 5)**
- He united all repenting sinners through Spirit baptism **(3:26-29)**
- He guarantees our full adoption as sons of God **(4:1-7)**

The Promise and the Law
- The law cannot change the promise **(3:15-18)**
- The law is not greater than the promise **(3:19, 20)**
- The law is not contrary to the promise **(3:21-26)**
- The law cannot do what the promise can do **(3:27-29)**

The Galatians and the Law
- Why did they now desire to put back on their chains of bondage? **(4:9, 10)**
- Where was that happy spirit once enjoyed? **(4:11-15)**
- Why had they turned from Paul to false teachers? **(4:16-20)**
- An allegorical illustration—an example from Hagar and Sarah **(4:21-31)**

(c) Isaac refers to the spirit and to those who would look to Jesus, thus becoming free sons.

(d) Hagar also represents Mount Sinai and the earthly city of Jerusalem, headquarters of legalism.

(e) Sarah also represents Mount Zion (inferred) and the heavenly city of Jerusalem, headquarters of liberty.

(f) For a believer to miss law and grace is to suffer persecution and ridicule as did Isaac from Ishmael.

III. Exhortation—a Desire (5, 6). Paul commends them to the liberty in Christ.
  A. This liberty and the legalism of the Jews (5:1-12). What does it mean to refuse this glorious liberty in Christ?
    1. It means to trade the blessed yoke of Christ for the burdensome yoke of the law (5:1). Note the contrast between these two yokes.
      a. The yoke of Christ:
        "Come unto me, all ye that labor and are heavy laden, and I will give you rest. Take my yoke upon you, and learn of me; for I am meek and lowly in heart: and ye shall find rest unto your souls. For my yoke is easy, and my burden is light" (Mt. 11:28-30).
      b. The yoke of the law:
        "Now therefore why tempt ye God, to put a yoke upon the neck of the disciples, which neither our fathers nor we were able to bear?" (Acts 15:10).
    2. It means to become debtor to the entire Mosaic Law (3:3; see also Deut. 27:26). Warren Wiersbe writes:
        "Imagine a motorist driving down a city street and either deliberately or unconsciously driving through a red light. He is pulled over by a policeman who asks to see his driver's license. Immediately the driver begins to defend himself. 'Officer, I know I ran that red light—but I have never robbed anybody. I've never committed adultery. I've never cheated on my income tax!'
        The policeman smiles as he writes out the ticket, because he knows that no amount of obedience can make up for one act of disobedience. It is one law, and the same law that protects the obedient man punishes the offender. To boast about keeping part of the law while at the same time breaking another part is to confess that I am worthy of punishment." (*Be Free*, pp. 118, 119)
    3. It means to fall from grace (5:4). This of course does not mean they had lost their salvation, for in the book of Galatians Paul refers to his readers as:
      a. brethren (nine times; see 1:2, 11; 3:15; 4:12, 31; 5:11, 13; 6:1, 18)
      b. children of God (3:26)
      c. sons of God (4:6)
      d. heirs of the promise (3:29)
        The Greek word here translated "fallen" is *ekpipto*, and is found in Acts 27:17, 26, 29, 32, where it refers to a ship not under control. This is the meaning here in Galatians. To put oneself back under the law means to deny the sweet and sure control of God's grace! Paul has already stated that it is tragically possible to frustrate (literally, to nullify, to make of none effect) the grace of God! (See Gal. 2:21.)
    4. It means to lose one's direction in the Christian race (5:7; see also Heb. 12:1, 2). It means, in short, to be reduced to a debtor, a slave,

and a misguided runner. Warren Wiersbe writes:
        "The believer who lives in the sphere of God's grace is free, rich, and running in the lane that leads to reward and fulfillment. The believer who abandons grace for law is a slave, a pauper, and a runner on a detour. In short, he is a loser. And the only way to become a winner is to 'purge out the leaven' (5:9), the false doctrine that mixes law and grace, and yield to the Spirit of God." (*Be Free*, p. 123)
  B. This liberty and the license of the libertines (5:13).
        "For, brethren, ye have been called unto liberty; only use not liberty for an occasion to the flesh, but by love serve one another."
    Paul now warns against the opposite of legalism, which is lawlessness.
  C. This liberty and the works of the flesh (5:15-21). In Romans 7 (as here in Gal. 5) Paul connects the commandments of God with the corruption of the flesh. This he does by pointing out the following:
    The law in itself is good (Rom. 7:7). The trouble came when sin used the law to make him feel guilty by arousing all kinds of evil and forbidden desires within him (7:8).
    He concludes by saying:
        "For I was alive without the law once: but when the commandment came, sin revived, and I died. And the commandment, which was ordained to life, I found to be unto death" (Rom. 7:9, 10).
    Here now in Galatians 5 he lists some seventeen works of the flesh, resulting from an illegal usage of the law. These are:
    1. adultery (sexual sins between married people)
    2. fornication (sexual sins between unmarried people)
    3. uncleanness (impurity)
    4. lasciviousness (sensuality)
    5. idolatry (worship of idols)
    6. witchcraft (Greek is *pharmakeia*, which can refer to sorcery and/or drugs)
    7. hatred (enmity)
    8. variances (Greek is *eris*, referring to the god of strife)
    9. emulations (rivalry, jealousy)
    10. wrath (temper, outburst of anger)
    11. strife (factions, cliques)
    12. seditions (divisions, dissensions)
    13. heresies (sects)
    14. envyings (coveting)
    15. murders (unlawful killing)
    16. drunkenness (rendered helpless by strong drink)
    17. revelings (carousings, orgies)
  D. This liberty and the fruit of the Spirit (5:22, 23). Warren Wiersbe writes:
        "The contrast between *works* and *fruit* is important. A machine in a factory *works*, and turns out a product, but it could never manufacture fruit. Fruit must grow out of life, and in the case of the believer, it is the life of the

Spirit. When you think of 'works' you think of effort, labor, strain, and toil; when you think of 'fruit' you think of beauty, quietness, the unfolding of life. The flesh produces 'dead works' (Heb. 9:14), but the Spirit produces living fruit . . . the New Testament speaks of several different kinds of fruit: people won to Christ (Rom. 1:13), holy living (Rom. 6:22), gifts brought to God (Rom. 15:16–18), good works (Col. 1:10), and praise (Heb. 13:15). The fruit of the Spirit listed in our passage has to do with character." (*Be Free*, pp. 133, 134)

Note now the various aspects of this Spirit-produced fruit.

1. love (divine concern for others)
2. joy (inward peace and sufficiency)
3. peace (a confidence and quietness of the soul)
4. longsuffering (patience, endurance without quitting)
5. gentleness (kindness)
6. goodness (love in action)
7. faith (dependability)
8. meekness (subdued strength)
9. temperance (self-control)

E. This liberty and the duty of the believer.

1. He is to love his neighbor as himself (5:14, 15).
2. He is to be led by the Spirit (5:18, 25).
3. He is to reckon himself crucified with Christ (5:24). The legalists, of course, would have none of this. They emphasized circumcision, *not* crucifixion.
4. He is to avoid boasting and envy (5:26).
5. He is to carefully and prayerfully restore the fallen (6:1).
6. He is to bear the burdens of others (6:2).
7. The legalists would do just the opposite by *adding* to the burdens of others (Acts 15:10; Mt. 23:4).
8. He is to avoid self-deception (6:13).
9. He is to bear his own burden (6:5).
10. He is to prove himself (6:4).
11. He is to communicate (financially give) to his spiritual leaders (6:6).
12. He is to properly sow the right habits of life (6:8).
13. He is not to be weary in well doing (6:9).
14. He is to do good to all (6:10).

F. This liberty and the marks of Paul (6:11–18).

"From henceforth let no man trouble me: for I bear in my body the marks of the Lord Jesus" (6:17).

J. Sidlow Baxter writes:

"This Galatian epistle was written to groups of believers scattered through a rural area, in which most of the people were agricultural workers of one sort or another. In keeping with the mentality and circumstances of the Galatians, Paul uses language and metaphors which are specially appropriate to them. There were four kinds of 'bearing' with which the Galatians were familiar above all else. These were: fruit-bearing, burden-bearing, seed-bearing, and brand-bearing (for as many of the agricultural labourers were slaves, they were branded to indicate whose property they were). See now how Paul makes use of these things in expounding the true liberty of the Spirit:

1. Fruit-bearing: 'The fruit of the Spirit is love, joy, peace, longsuffering,' etc. (5:22, 23).
2. Burden-bearing: 'Bear ye one another's burdens and so fulfill the law of Christ' (6:2).
3. Seed-bearing: 'Whatsoever a man soweth,' etc. (6:7). 'Let us not be weary in well doing, for . . . we shall reap' (6:9).
4. Brand-bearing: 'I bear in my body the marks [or brands] of the Lord Jesus' (6:17).

Liberty AND THE MARKS OF PAUL

FRUIT-BEARING
"The fruit of the Spirit is love, joy, peace, longsuffering . . ." **(5:22, 23).**

BURDEN-BEARING
"Bear ye one another's burdens, and so fulfill the law of Christ" **(6:2).**

SEED-BEARING
"Whatsoever a man soweth" **(6:7).**
"Let us not be weary in well doing, for . . . we shall reap" **(6:9).**

BRAND-BEARING
"I bear in my body the marks [or brands] of the Lord Jesus" **(6:17).**

There were five classes of persons who were branded, i.e., *slaves* (as a mark of ownership), *soldiers* (as a mark of allegiance), *devotees* (as a mark of consecration), *criminals* (as a mark of exposure), and the *abhorred* (as a mark of reproach). The marks of the Lord Jesus in the body of Paul were all these five in one!" (*Explore the Book*, Vol. 6. pp. 153, 154, 158. See 2 Cor. 11:23-28 for a history of some of these marks.)

1 THESSALONIANS

INTRODUCTION:

1. The church at Thessalonica was founded by Paul during his second missionary journey. (See Acts 17:1-10.) Of the many churches established by the apostle, only a few (six to be exact) would receive a New Testament epistle from Paul. Of the six, only the church at Corinth and the one in Thessalonica were blessed with two inspired letters.

2. He spends at least three weeks in Thessalonica in the home of Jason (possibly a kinsman, see Rom. 16:21) organizing the church, working all the while as a tentmaker, that he might not be a burden to the believers. (See 1 Thess. 2:9; 2 Thess. 3:7-12.)

3. His visit there is short-lived, for the gospel is opposed by some unbelieving Jews. Thus, under cover of night, Paul, Timothy, and Silas leave for Berea.

4. He soon is driven from Berea by the same vicious Jews and heads for Athens. Timothy and Silas remain in Berea.

5. While in Athens he sends word to Timothy requesting that his young helper go back and strengthen the work at Thessalonica, which command Timothy obeys (1 Thess. 3:1, 2).

6. From Athens, Paul goes to Corinth. Here at a later date both Silas and Timothy catch up with him. Timothy brings a good report concerning the work in Thessalonica. Paul is overjoyed and writes both 1 and 2 Thessalonians from Corinth at this time.

7. His first letter was written to encourage, establish, instruct, and inspire. The church was apparently composed of a great many Gentiles (Acts 17:4).

8. Henrietta Mears writes:

"Paul's success in Thessalonica has not been the usual experience of missionaries among the heathen. Carey in India, Judson in Burma, Morrison in China, and Moffat in Africa waited each seven years for his first convert. But here, the Holy Spirit allowed Paul to reap a sudden harvest." (*What the Bible Is All About*, p. 532)

I. The Reputation of the Church (chapter 1).
   A. It was an energetic church (1:1-3).
      "Remembering without ceasing your work of faith, and labour of love, and patience of hope . . ." (1:3).
   B. It was an elect church (1:4, 5).
      "Knowing, brethren beloved, your election of God" (1:4).
      Election is both individual and corporate. It covers both Christian and congregation. The latter is in view here. C. H. Spurgeon was once asked how he reconciled God's election with man's choice. He answered, "I never have to reconcile friends!"

Both these great theological truths are presented in the Bible. They are not contradictory, but complementary. The entire Trinity is directly involved in this election.
   1. In regard to the Father: we were saved before the foundation of the world (Eph. 1:4; 2 Tim. 1:9).
   2. In regard to the Son: we were saved at the cross (Gal. 2:20).
   3. In regard to the Holy Spirit: we were saved at the moment of our decision to accept Christ (1 Cor. 12:13; Titus 3:5).
   C. It was an exemplary church (1:7)
      "So that ye were ensamples to all that believe in Macedonia and Achaia."
   D. It was an enthusiastic church (1:8).
      "For from you sounded out the word of the Lord not only in Macedonia and Achaia, but also in every place your faith to God-ward is spread abroad . . ." (1:8).
   Dr. Charles Ryrie comments:
      "The word translated 'sounded out' is very picturesque. The Greek letters simply changed into English characters spell our word echo. Thus the picture is of the message of the gospel so stirring the strings of the Thessalonians' hearts that it reverberated in strong and clear tones to all Greece and everywhere." (*First and Second Thessalonians*, p. 27)
      Thus, while awaiting the trumpet *of* Christ to sound, these Thessalonians were sounding out the trumpet *for* Christ (see 1 Thess. 4:16; see also Rom. 1:8).
   E. It was an expectant church (1:9, 10).
      ". . . how ye turned to God from idols to serve the living and true God; and to wait for his Son from heaven, whom he raised from the dead, even Jesus, which delivered us from the wrath to come."
   Note the three tenses here in these verses.
   1. past tense; "ye turned"
   2. present tense; "to serve the living and true God"
   3. future tense; "to wait for his Son"
   All this may be tied in beautifully with Paul's statement concerning them in 1:3 where he writes of their "work of faith, and labour of love, and patience of hope. . . ." Thus we see:
   4. In the past, turning, and looking to the Father. This was their work of faith (see Jn. 6:28, 29; Acts 20:21).
   5. In the present, serving, and looking on the fields. This was their labor of love (see Jn. 4:35; 1 Cor. 15:58; Heb. 6:10).
   6. In the future, waiting, and looking for the Son. This was their patience of hope (see 2 Tim. 4:8).
   Dr. John Walvoord writes:
      "Paul was told how God had worked in the Thessalonians. It had resulted in their turning to God from idols to serve the living and the true God. This is a very accurate expression and one we should understand. It does not say that they turned *from* idols *to* God. Rather, they turned *to* God *from* idols to serve the living and true God. It was not reformation first and faith in Christ sec-

The Church of Thessalonica

1 Thessalonians

THE REPUTATION OF THE CHURCH

Energetic **1:1-3**

Elect **1:4, 5**

Exemplary **1:6, 7**

Enthusiastic **1:8**

Expectant **1:9, 10**

THE REVIEW OF THE CHURCH

Here Paul reviews those circumstances involved in the founding of their church.

The Activities of the **Shepherd** in Thessalonica

WHAT PAUL SAYS ABOUT HIMSELF

HE WAS . . .

A suffering traveler **2:1, 2**

A faithful steward **2:3-6**

As a gentle mother **2:7, 8**

A tireless laborer **2:9**

A consistent example **2:10**

As a concerned father **2:11, 12**

As a homesick brother **2:17**

An expectant soul-winner **2:19, 20**

A missionary superintendent **3:1-5**

A prayer warrior **2:13; 3:7-13**

The Activities of the **Sheep** in Thessalonica

WHAT PAUL SAYS ABOUT HIS CONVERTS **2:13, 14; 3:6**

The Activities of the **Serpent** in Thessalonica

WHAT PAUL SAYS ABOUT HIS ENEMIES—THE JUDAIZERS **2:14-16**

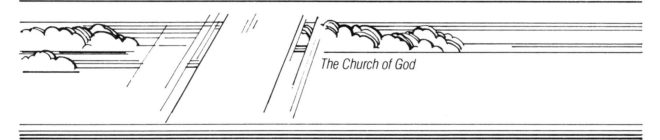

The Church of God

THE REMOVAL OF THE CHURCH

THE CHALLENGES OF THIS REMOVAL

KNOW GOD'S WILL

(What he wants me to do) **(4:3)**

KNOW GOD'S WAY

(How he wants me to do it)

a. *Concerning self*—Purity **(4:3-5)**

b. *Concerning saints*—Charity **(4:6-10)**

c. *Concerning sinners*—Honesty **(4:11, 12)**

THE CHRONOLOGY OF THIS REMOVAL

A REALIZATION **(4:13)**

A REPOSE **(4:14)**

A REVELATION **(4:15)**

A RETURN **(4:16)**

A RESURRECTION **(4:16)**

A RAPTURE **(4:17)**

A REUNION **(4:17)**

A REASSURANCE **(4:18)**

THE RESPONSIBILITY OF THE CHURCH

be watchful **(5:6)**

be respectful **(5:12, 13)**

be mindful **(5:14)**

be joyful **(5:16)**

be prayerful **(5:17)**

be faithful **(5:21)**

ond, but it was faith in Christ first with the result that idols were forsaken. The tense of the word *turned,* as it is found in the Greek New Testament, is in the aorist, which means that they turned once for all. It was a single, definite act." (*The Thessalonian Epistle,* p. 17)

II. The Review of the Church (2–3). In these chapters Paul reminds his readers of those circumstances involved in the founding of their church at Thessalonica, as recorded in Acts 17.

A. The activities of the shepherd in Thessalonica— what Paul says about himself (2:1-12, 17, 19, 20; 3:1-5, 7-13).

B. The activities of the sheep in Thessalonica— what Paul says about his converts (2:13, 14; 3:6).

C. The activities of the serpent in Thessalonica— what Paul says about his enemies, the Judaizers in Thessalonica (2:14-16, 18).

Let us now examine in some detail these three:

A. The activities of the shepherd in Thessalonica (2:1-12, 17, 19, 20; 3:1-5, 7-13). In these verses Paul offers a tenfold description of himself and his ministry.

1. The suffering traveler (2:1, 2).
   " . . . we had suffered before, and were shamefully entreated as ye know, at Philippi, we were bold in our God to speak unto you the gospel of God with much contention" (2:2).
   The Greek word here translated "contention" is *agonia,* from whence comes our English word *agony.*

2. The faithful steward (2:3-6).
   "For our exhortation was not a deceit, nor of uncleanness, nor in guile" (2:3).
   "For neither at any time used we flattering words . . ." (2:5).
   "Nor of men sought we glory . . ." (2:6).
   Here the apostle states that his message, motive, and method were all approved by God!

3. The gentle mother (2:7, 8).
   "But we were gentle among you, even as a nurse cherisheth her children" (2:7).
   Dr. Charles Ryrie comments:
   "The word cherish means 'to warm' and is used of the way a mother bird covers her young (Deut. 22:6); its only other occurrence in the New Testament is our Lord's relationship to his church (Eph. 5:29)." (*First and Second Thessalonians,* p. 37)
   How a mother feeds her child is almost as important as *what* she feeds it. This is also brought out in Ephesians 4:15: "But speaking the truth [the what] in love [the how] . . ."

4. The tireless laborer (2:9).
   "For ye remember, brethren, our labour and travail: for labouring night and day, because we would not be chargeable unto any of you, we preached unto you the gospel of God."
   Richard Wolff writes:
   "Paul had learned to cut out and stitch the coarse goats' hair cloth used for making tents, shoes, and mats. It was custom-

ary for a Rabbi to learn a trade." (*General Epistles of First and Second Thessalonians,* p. 19)

5. The consistent example (2:10).
   "Ye are witnesses, and God also, how holily and justly and unblameably we behaved ourselves among you that believe."
   Note his three key words here:
   a. holily—his testimony godward (spiritual)
   b. justly—his testimony manward (social)
   c. unblameable—his testimony selfward (personal)
   Thus, the upward, outward, and inward in Paul's life possessed that vital spiritual maturity a good leader simply must have.

6. The concerned father (2:11, 12).
   "As ye know how we exhorted and comforted and charged every one of you, as a father doth his children" (2:11).
   The apostle often pictures himself as a parent. (See 1 Cor. 4:14; 2 Cor. 6:13; Gal. 4:18, 19; Phil. 1:10.)

7. The homesick brother (2:17).
   "But we, brethren, being taken from you for a short time in presence, not in heart, endeavored the more abundantly to see your face with great desire."

8. The expectant soul-winner (2:19, 20).
   "For what is our hope, or joy, or crown of rejoicing? Are not even ye in the presence of our Lord Jesus Christ at his coming? For ye are our glory and joy."
   The Word of God mentions at least five possible rewards. These are:
   a. The incorruptible crown—given to those who master the old nature (1 Cor. 9:25-27).
   b. The crown of life—given to those who successfully endure temptation (Jas. 1:2, 3; Rev. 2:10).
   c. The crown of righteousness—given to those who especially love the doctrine of the rapture (2 Tim. 4:8).
   d. The crown of glory—given to those faithful preachers and teachers (1 Pet. 5:2-4).
   e. The crown of rejoicing—given to soul-winners (Prov. 11:30; 1 Thess. 2:19, 20).
   Note Paul's statement in 2:19, "at his coming." The Greek word here is *parousia,* and is a technical term for the arrival or visit of a king. The word appears in many key New Testament prophecy passages. (See: Mt. 24:3, 27, 37, 39; 2 Thess. 2:8; 1 Cor. 15:22, 23; 1 Thess. 4:13-18; Jas. 5:7, 8; 1 Jn. 2:28; 2 Pet. 1:16, 3:4.)

9. The mission superintendent (3:1-5). We have already seen how Paul was driven from Thessalonica and Berea by the unbelieving Jews. From Berea he went to Athens. While there he sent Timothy (who had remained in Berea) back to Thessalonica as a short-term missionary to strengthen the young church. In this passage he asks the Thessalonians not to pity him because of his manifold sufferings. The apostle states his trials had neither shaken nor surprised him, for, "we are ap-

pointed thereunto" (3:3; see also Jn. 16:2; 1 Cor. 4:9; 2 Tim. 3:12; Acts 9:16.)

William MacDonald has written:

"Paul reminds them that even when he was in Thessalonica, he used to tell them that Christians are appointed to afflictions. His predictions came true in their own lives; how well they knew it! Trials form a necessary discipline in our lives:

They prove the reality of our faith, and weed out those who are mere professors (1 Pet. 1:7).

They enable us to comfort and encourage others who are going through trials (2 Cor. 1:4).

They develop certain graces, such as patience, in our character (Rom. 5:3).

They make us more zealous in spreading the gospel (Acts 4:29; 5:27–29; 8:3, 4).

They help to remove the dross from our lives (Job 23:10)." (*Letters to the Thessalonians*, p. 44)

10. The prayer warrior (3:7–13). "Night and day praying exceedingly. . . ."

   a. What he thanked God for (3:7–9). Paul was so thankful for the comfort he received upon the good report from Timothy concerning the progress of the Thessalonian church.

      "Therefore, brethren, we were comforted over you in all our affliction and distress by your faith" (3:7).

   Charles Ryrie writes:

   "The word *comfort* means more than soothing; it means 'strengthening,' and it came to Paul at a time when he needed it, for he was in the midst of the pressure of affliction and distress. Both words imply trouble from without—'affliction' meaning 'choking, pressing care,' and 'distress' signifying the crushing kind of trouble. It is easy to see why he speaks of his situation in such terms, for he was at Athens alone and had just suffered four successive experiences of apparent defeat since he set foot in Europe. At Philippi he had been cast in jail and asked to leave the city. At Thessalonica he had been forced to leave and to guarantee that he would not return. At Berea he was pursued by the Jews and compelled to move on. At Athens he had had little success with the philosophers of the city. Surely he was in afflictions and distress and this news meant strength and life to him. It brought to him a revival of energy which was not a passing thing but a continual source of inspiration. . . ." (*First Thessalonians*, p. 48)

   b. What he asked God for (3:10–13):

      (1) That he might be allowed a return visit to Thessalonica.

      (2) That they would "increase and abound in love one toward another . . ." (3:12).

      (3) That God would establish their hearts "unblameable in holiness . . ." (3:13).

B. The activities of the sheep in Thessalonica (2:13, 14; 3:6).

   1. They had accepted God's word as truth in the midst of suffering (2:13, 14).

   2. They longed to see Paul again as much as he wanted to see them (3:6).

C. The activities of the serpent in Thessalonica. Paul's worst enemies in Thessalonica (as in other places) had been the vicious Judaizers. How Satan had used them!

   1. They had already "killed the Lord Jesus, and their own prophets" (2:15). See also Acts 2:23; 3:15; 5:30; 7:52.

   2. They had "persecuted us" (2:15).

   3. They "please not God, and are contrary to all men" (2:15).

   4. They had forbidden Paul to "speak to the Gentiles that they might be saved . . ." (2:16). See also Acts 13:50; 14:5, 19; 17:5; 18:12; 22:22.

   Paul has been accused of being antisemitic, but this is totally unfounded. The apostle himself, of course, was an Israelite and proud of his background. (See Phil. 3:4, 5.) Furthermore, his great heart literally bled for the conversion of his beloved nation. (See Rom. 9:1–3; 10:1.)

   Satan had not only worked through the Judaizers to oppose Paul but had apparently stepped into the picture himself!

   "Wherefore we would have come unto you, even I Paul, once and again; but Satan hindered us" (2:18).

III. The Removal of the Church (4).

A. The challenges of this removal (4:1–12).

   1. Because of this removal the Christian is to know God's will. (What does he want me to do?)

      "For this is the will of God, even your sanctification . . ." (4:3).

      God has but one will for sinners, and that is that they become saved! (See 1 Tim. 2:4; 2 Pet. 3:9.) In like manner he has only one will for saints and that is that they be sanctified! Here Paul, of course, refers to a daily growing in grace and maturing in the faith. The first step in sanctification is consecration. (See Rom. 12:1, 2.)

   2. Because of this removal, the Christian is to know God's way. (How does he want me to do it?)

      a. By abstaining from fornication (4:3). This is a reference to sexual sins in general.

      b. By not defrauding his brother (4:6).

      c. By loving his brother (4:9).

      d. By quietly working until and patiently awaiting the great day of God's removal (4:11, 12).

B. The chronology of this removal (4:13–18). In this great passage Paul answers a question that had bothered the Thessalonians. When he was among them (Acts 17) they had doubtless learned many precious truths about the glorious return of Christ to earth someday and the establishing of his kingdom. In fact, to some, this all seemed to be just around the corner. But since the apostle's departure, a number of believers had died. They obviously then would not be here on earth at the time of Christ's return. Did this mean they would miss everything? This then is the background to the great rapture passage before us here in chapter 4.

These next six verses (3–18) thus present for us:

1. A realization: "But I would not have you to be ignorant, brethren, concerning them which are asleep, that ye sorrow not, even as others which have no hope" (4:13). This is but one of four key areas about which Paul would not have us to be ignorant. The other three are:

   a. the events in the Old Testament (1 Cor. 10:1)

   b. the restoration of Israel (Rom. 11:25)

   c. the manifestation of spiritual gifts (1 Cor. 12:1)

2. A repose: "For if we believe that Jesus died and rose again, even so them also which sleep in Jesus will God bring with him" (4:14).

   The death of a believer is looked upon as a peaceful sleep. (See Mt. 27:52; Jn. 11:11; Acts 7:60; 13:36; 1 Cor. 15:6, 18, 20, 51; 2 Pet. 3:4.) However, it should be quickly stated that this verse in no way teaches soul sleep. That unscriptural doctrine is refuted by Matthew 17:3 and Revelation 6:9–11.

3. A revelation: "For this we say unto you by the word of the Lord, that we which are alive and remain unto the coming of the Lord shall not prevent [precede] them which are asleep" (4:15).

   Note Paul's usage of the pronoun "we." The apostle apparently hoped to be there when Christ came. He would later know otherwise. (See 2 Tim. 4:6.)

4. A return: "For the Lord himself shall descend from heaven with a shout, with the voice of the archangel, and with the trump of God" (4:16).

   It is often supposed that Michael will be this archangel on the basis of Daniel 12:1, 2. However, it is not unreasonable to suggest that Gabriel will be the angel involved at this time because of the vital part he played in those events surrounding the first coming of Christ. (See Lk. 1:19, 26; Mt. 1:20; 2:13.)

5. A resurrection. " . . . and the dead in Christ shall rise first" (4:16).

6. A rapture. "Then we which are alive and remain shall be caught up together with them in the clouds. . . . "

7. A reunion. " . . . to meet the Lord in the air: and so shall we ever be with the Lord" (4:17).

8. A reassurance. "Wherefore comfort one another with these words" (4:18).

IV. The Responsibility of the Church (5). This final section of Paul's epistle may be known as the "full" chapter.

   A. Be watchful (5:1–11).

      "Therefore let us not sleep as do others; but let us watch and be sober" (5:6).

      1. What we are to watch for—the glorious return of Christ!

      2. Why we are to watch for it.

         a. Because of who we are: "Ye are all the children of light, and the children of the day" (5:5).

            This is in contrast to the unsaved who are described as the children of darkness. Someday the Sun of Righteousness shall arise with healing in his wings (Mal. 4:2). It is therefore only logical that the children of light should await that glorious day!

         b. Because of what we shall escape. "For God hath not appointed us to wrath. . . . " This is a reference to both external wrath (Jn. 3:36; Col. 3:6) and tribulational wrath (Rev. 6:17; 15:1; 11:18). Paul begins and ends his epistle to the Thessalonian church with this precious promise. (Compare 1:9 with 5:9.) Note the apostle's conclusion here in 5:10:

            "Who died for us, that, whether we wake or sleep, we should live together with him."

      William MacDonald writes:

      "This verse emphasizes the tremendous price our Lord Jesus Christ paid to deliver us from wrath and insure our salvation. He died for us that whether awake or asleep we should live together with Him. There will be two classes of believers at His coming: (1.) Those who have died. (2.) Those who are living. The former are spoken of as being asleep, the latter as being awake. Whether we are among the living or the dead at the time of His return, we shall live with Him. Christians who die lose nothing. The Lord said the same thing, in effect, to Martha, 'I am the resurrection, and the life: he that believeth on me, though he die [i.e., a Christian who has died], yet shall he live [he will be raised at the rapture]; and whosoever liveth and believeth on me [a believer alive at the time of the rapture] shall never die (Jn. 11:25, 26)." (*Letters to the Thessalonians*, p. 68)

   B. Be respectful (5:12, 13).

      "And we beseech you, brethren, to know them which labour among you, and are over you in the Lord, and admonish you; and to esteem them very highly in love for their work's sake. And be at peace among yourselves."

      (See also 1 Pet. 5:1–5; Heb. 13:7–9, 14, 17.)

   C. Be mindful (5:14, 15).

      "Now we exhort you, brethren, warn them that are unruly, comfort the feebleminded, support the weak, be patient toward all men. See that none render evil for evil unto any man; but ever follow that which is good, both among yourselves, and to all men."

      1. What they were to do:

         a. Warn the unruly. The Greek word here is *ataktos*, which referred to soldiers who deserted their ranks.

         b. Comfort the feebleminded. A better word here would be fainthearted.

c. Support the weak, the immature. (See Rom. 14.)
   2. What they were not to do: "... render evil for evil. ..." (See also Rom. 12:17; 1 Pet. 3:9.)
D. Be joyful (5:16). "Rejoice evermore." This verse in the Greek is the shortest in the New Testament (and not Jn. 11:35). It is often however, one of the hardest to keep!
E. Be prayerful (5:17). "Pray without ceasing." Charles Ryrie writes:

"The Christian's joy puts him in the proper mood to pray without ceasing. Paul has already used the word *without ceasing* twice of his own remembrance of the Thessalonians (1:3; 2:13) and now he enjoins it on the believers. Outside the New Testament the word is used of a hacking cough and aptly illustrates what Paul has in mind here about prayer. Just as a person with a hacking cough is not always audibly coughing, though the tendency to cough is always there, so the Christian who prays without ceasing is not always praying audibly and yet prayer is always the attitude of his heart and life." (*First and Second Thessalonians*, p. 80)

F. Be thankful (5:18).
   "In every thing give thanks: for this is the will of God in Christ Jesus concerning you."
   (See also Eph. 5:20; Col. 3:17; Phil. 4:6.)
   The importance of this command cannot be overstated. The cure for pride in our lives is not to practice humility, lest we become proud of our piousness, but to be thankful! In Romans one, Paul describes the terrible final stages of Gentile world apostasy. The picture he paints is one of the most chilling in all the Bible. What horrible crime could possibly cause all this? Note his answer:
   "Because, when they knew God, they glorified him not as God, neither were thankful ..." (Rom. 1:21).
   Someone has offered the following little rule: Be careful for *nothing*, be prayerful in *everything*, and be *thankful* for anything.
G. Be faithful (5:19-28).
   1. "Quench not the Spirit" (5:19). The Holy Spirit is like a fire. (See Mt. 3:11; Lk. 3:16; Acts 2:3; Mk. 9:48; Heb. 11:34.) To quench the Spirit is one of two sins a believer can commit against this blessed third person of the Trinity who lives in our hearts. The other is to grieve him. (See Eph. 4:30.) To *quench* him is not to do what he wants us to do, while to *grieve* him is to do what he does not want us to do.
   2. "Despise not prophesyings" (5:20). The Thessalonian church had apparently gone to the one extreme on this subject while the Corinthian church would later go to the other. (See 1 Cor. 14.)
   3. "Prove all things ..." (5:21). Sniff out, but don't swallow everything.
   4. "Hold fast to that which is good" (5:21).
   5. "Abstain from all appearance of evil" (5:22).
   Note now his grand conclusion (5:23-28):

"And the very God of peace sanctify you wholly; and I pray God your whole spirit and soul and body be preserved blameless unto the coming of our Lord Jesus Christ. Faithful is he that calleth you, who also will do it. Brethren, pray for us. Greet all the brethren with an holy kiss. I charge you by the Lord that this epistle be read unto all the holy brethren. The grace of our Lord Jesus Christ be with you. Amen."

Verse 23 has been a main support for the doctrine of trichotomy, which teaches man is a threefold being, spirit, soul, and body. Whatever else may be involved in this verse, Paul is praying that God would sanctify the *total* believer. God is not involved in "saving souls," but in sanctifying individuals. Jesus strongly brings this out. (See Mt. 22:36-40.)

Note the final words in 5:23, "... unto the coming of our Lord Jesus Christ." Paul ends this chapter as he has done the previous four, with a reference to the second appearing of Christ. In the first chapter (1:10) he connects it with *salvation*; in the second (2:19, 20), with *service*; in the third (3:13) with *stability*; in the fourth (4:18) with *sorrow*, and here with *sanctification*.

This epistle, Paul commanded, was to "be read unto all the holy brethren" (5:27; see also Col. 4:16; 1 Tim. 4:13; Rev. 1:3).

2 THESSALONIANS

INTRODUCTION:
1. This little letter was written by Paul in the early fifties to the church in Thessalonica a few months after he had penned 1 Thessalonians. Both letters were written from the same place.
2. Paul wrote the first letter to tell them they had not missed the rapture! He now writes assuring them they were not enduring the great tribulation!
3. For its size, 2 Thessalonians has more about the antichrist than any other book in the Bible.
4. Merrill Tenney writes:

"Practically every major doctrine in the catalogue of faith is represented in these two small epistles. Although they were not written as doctrinal treatises, nor primarily to present the author's general theological views, they contain a well-rounded body of theological teaching. Paul and those who received his epistles believed in one living God (1, 1:9), the Father (2, 1:2), who has loved men and has chosen them to enjoy His salvation (2, 2:16; 1, 1:4). He has sent deliverance from wrath through Jesus Christ, His Son (1, 1:10), and has revealed this deliverance through the message of the gospel (1, 1:5; 2:9; 2, 2:14). This message has been confirmed and has been made real by the power of the Holy Spirit (1, 1:5; 4:8). The gospel concerns the Lord Jesus Christ, who was killed by the Jews (1, 2:15). He rose from the dead (1, 1:10; 4:14, 5:10). He is now in heaven (1, 1:10), but He will come again (1, 2:19; 4:15; 5:23; 2, 2:1). To Him is ascribed deity, for He is called Lord (1, 1:6), God's Son (1, 1:10), and the Lord Jesus Christ (1, 1:1; 3; 5:28; 2, 1:1). Believers (1) receiving the word of God (1, 1:6), (2) turn from idols, serve God and wait for the return of Christ (1, 1:9, 10). Their normal growth is in sanctification (1, 4:3, 7; 2,

Glorification, Tribulation, Consecration

2 Thessalonians

CHAPTER 1	**CHAPTER 2**	**CHAPTER 3**
The RAPTURE of the LORD	The WRATH of the LORD	The WILL of the LORD
A Pastoral Encouragement	A Prophetical Enlightenment	A Practical Exhortation
GLORIFICATION	*TRIBULATION*	*CONSECRATION*

2:13). In personal life they are to be clean (1, 4:4–6), industrious (1, 4:11, 12), prayerful (1, 5:17), and cheerful (1, 5:16). Theoretically and practically the Thessalonian letters embody all the essentials of Christian truth. (*New Testament Survey*, p. 283)

I. A Pastoral Encouragement (chapter 1). As has already been stated, the Thessalonian believers were undergoing severe persecutions for their faith in Christ. Paul now writes to assure them this is not the great tribulation and also to explain just why they are being allowed to suffer in the first place.

A. They could successfully endure the tribulation of *man*.

1. This tribulation had helped them grow in faith.

"We are bound to thank God always for you, brethren . . . because that your faith groweth exceedingly . . ." (1:3).

Dr. Charles Ryrie states that this verb "groweth exceedingly" is a very strong compound one, found only here in the New Testament, and indicates organic growth, as of a healthy plant.

2. This tribulation had helped them abound in love.

". . . the charity of every one of you all toward each other aboundeth" (1:3). (See also Rom. 5:3.)

3. This tribulation had helped them increase their steadfastness (patience).

"So that we ourselves glory in you in the churches of God for your patience and faith in all your persecutions and tribulations that ye endure" (1:4).

4. This tribulation had helped prepare them for God's kingdom.

". . . that ye may be counted worthy of the kingdom of God, for which ye also suffer" (1:5).

5. This tribulation would help bring glory to Christ.

"That the name of our Lord Jesus Christ may be glorified in you, and ye in him,

according to the grace of our God and the Lord Jesus Christ" (1:12).

Dr. John Walvoord writes:

"This is an expression often used but perhaps not always analyzed or understood as it should be. The Scriptures state: 'The heavens declare the glory of God; and the firmament sheweth his handiwork. Day unto day uttereth speech, and night unto night sheweth knowledge' (Ps. 19:1, 2). What does it mean when it is said that the heavens declare the glory of God? The heavens declare that God is perfect. The heavens manifest His wisdom, His power, and His intelligent end. The heavens are manifesting the glory of God in the sense that they reveal what God is and what He can do. But the heavens are not designed to reveal the love of God, the grace of God, nor the righteousness of God. That is where Christians come into the picture. We are designed to show 'the exceeding riches of his grace in his kindness toward us through Christ' (Eph. 2:7)." (*The Thessalonian Epistles*, p. 112)

B. They would successfully escape the tribulation of God.

1. The time of this tribulation:

". . . when the Lord Jesus shall be revealed from heaven with his mighty angels" (1:7). (See also Mt. 13:39, 41, 49; 16:27; 24:31; 25:31.)

2. The nature of this tribulation:

"In flaming fire taking vengeance . . ." (1:8).

3. The recipients of this tribulation (1:8):

a. "Them that know not God." These are probably those who may never have heard the spoken gospel, but did have both the witness of conscience and nature, and are therefore without excuse. (See especially Rom. 1:18–20; 2:12–16.)

b. "Them . . . that obey not the gospel of our Lord Jesus Christ." Here is doubtless a reference to those who actually heard but then refused the gospel invitation.

4. The results of this tribulation:

"Who shall be punished with everlasting destruction from the presence of the Lord, and from the glory of his power" (1:9). William MacDonald writes:

"Two classes are marked out for retribution:

a. Those who know not God—those who have rejected the knowledge of the true God as revealed in creation and in conscience (Rom. 1 and 2). They may never have heard the gospel.

b. Those who have not obeyed the gospel of our Lord Jesus Christ. These people have heard the gospel and have wilfully rejected it. The gospel is not simply a statement of facts to be believed but a Person to be obeyed. Belief in the New Testament sense involved obedience.

1:9 They shall suffer punishment. A god who doesn't punish sin is no god at all. The idea that a God of love must not punish sin overlooks the fact that God is also holy and must do what is morally right.

The nature of the punishment is here defined as eternal destruction. The word translated eternal (aionios) is used 70 times in the New Testament. Three times it may mean ages of limited duration (Rom. 16:25; Titus 1:2). The other times it means eternal or endless. It is used in Romans 16:26 to describe the unending existence of God.

Destruction never means annihilation. It means loss of well-being, or ruin as far as the purpose of existence is concerned. The wineskins which the Lord Jesus described in Luke 5:37 were destroyed (same word as used here). They did not cease to exist, but they were ruined as far as further usefulness was concerned.

The punishment of the wicked also includes banishment from the presence of the Lord and from the glory of His might. To perish without Him is to be without Him forever." (Letters to the Thessalonians, pp. 87, 88)

A final thought may prove helpful before leaving this chapter. In 1 Thessalonians Paul had dealt with the rapture of Christ. (See 1 Thess. 4:13-18.) But here in the opening chapter of 2 Thessalonians, he describes the revelation of Christ. These two great events are not one and the same and should not be confused. William MacDonald offers the following helpful distinction:

5. The rapture

a. Christ comes to the air (1 Thess. 4:16, 17).

b. He comes for his saints (1 Thess. 4:16, 17).

c. The rapture is a mystery, i.e., a truth unknown in Old Testament times (1 Cor. 15:51).

d. Christ's coming for his saints is never said to be preceded by signs in the heavens.

e. The rapture is identified with the day of Christ (1 Cor. 1:8; 2 Cor. 1:14; Phil. 1:6, 10).

f. The rapture is presented as a time of blessing (1 Thess. 4:18).

g. The rapture takes place in a moment, in the twinkling of an eye (1 Cor. 15:52). This strongly implies that it will not be witnessed by the world.

h. The rapture seems to involve the church primarily (Jn. 14:1-4; 1 Cor. 15:51-58; 1 Thess. 4:13-18).

i. Christ comes as the bright and morning star (Rev. 22:16). (Letters to the Thessalonians, p. 85)

6. The revelation

a. He comes to the earth (Zech. 14:4).

b. He comes with his saints (1 Thess. 3:13; Jude 14).

c. The revelation is not a mystery; it is the subject of many Old Testament prophecies (Ps. 72; Isa. 11; Zech. 14).

d. Christ's coming with his saints will be heralded by celestial portents (Mt. 24:29, 30).

e. The revelation is identified with the day of the Lord (2 Thess. 2:1-12, ASV).

f. The main emphasis of the revelation is on judgment (2 Thess. 2:8-12).

g. The revelation will be visible worldwide (Mt. 24:27; Rev. 1:7).

h. The revelation involves Israel primarily, then also the Gentile nations.

i. Christ comes as the sun of righteousness with healing in his wings (Mal. 4:2). (Letters to the Thessalonians, p. 85)

II. A Prophetical Enlightenment (chapter 2).

A. Facts concerning the day of the Lord (2:1-12).

1. The day of the Lord and the church (2:1-3). "That ye be not soon shaken in mind, or be troubled, neither by spirit, nor by word, nor by letter as from us, as that day of Christ is at hand. Let no man deceive you by any means: for that day shall not come, except there come a falling away first, and that man of sin be revealed, the son of perdition."

We begin this section by noting that the expression "day of Christ" should be translated "day of the Lord." A vast difference separates these two biblical days. The day of the Lord refers to the coming seven-year tribulation. (See especially Joel 1:15; 2:1, 2; Rev. 6:12-17.) The day of Christ points to that future millennium. (See 1 Cor. 1:8; 5:5; Phil. 1:6, 10; 2:16.) These believers had somehow been tricked by Satan into believing this dreadful day of the Lord had come. Paul admonishes them to allow nothing to shake their faith. He says:

a. "Neither by spirit." That is, don't believe any false prophet who might receive this "through the spirit."
b. "Nor by word." That is, don't listen to any false teacher who might teach this.
c. "Nor by letter or from us." That is, don't accept any letter supposedly coming from me which would teach this, for such a letter is false.

Note the expression, "a falling away first" (2:3). Some have translated this, "a catching away first," believing it to be a reference to the rapture. This is a theological possibility, but the Greek word is *apostasia*, from whence our English word apostasy comes. It thus would seem more likely to mean the world-wide religious apostasy which Paul would later write (in past) about. (See 1 Tim. 4:1-3; 2 Tim. 3:1-5; 4:3, 4.)

M.F. Unger writes:

"Before the day of the Lord bursts upon a Christ-rejecting world, there must first come the apostasy, or falling away. This is not simple departure from the faith often characterizing the church age (1 Tim. 4:1-5; 2 Tim. 3:1-8; Rev. 3:14-22), but the wholesale rebellion and thorough-going lapse into error and demonism of the period just preceding Christ's advent in glory (Lk. 18:8; Rev. 9:20, 21)." (*Unger's Bible Handbook*, p. 711)

What then is the relationship between the church and the day of the Lord? It is simply this: the tribulation cannot begin until the church is removed from the earth!

2. The day of the Lord and the Antichrist (2:3, 4, 5, 8, 9).
   a. His name: "that man of sin . . . the son of perdition" (2:3). His first name refers to his *character*, while the second speaks of his *origin*. Some believe that Judas Iscariot will be the antichrist, pointing out that the title, "son of perdition" is found but two times in the New Testament. Jesus himself had used it first in reference to Judas (see Jn. 17:12), and now Paul calls the antichrist by the same name. Such evidence is, of course, far from conclusive.
   b. His activities (2:4, 9):
      (1) He will oppose and exalt himself above God or any other object of worship (Dan. 11:36, 37; Rev. 13:15, 16).
      (2) He will occupy the Jewish Holy of Holies (Mt. 24:15).
      (3) He will actually claim to be God (Dan. 7:8, 20, 25).
      (4) He will be energized by Satan himself (Rev. 13:4).
      (5) He will work signs and false wonders (Rev. 13:13, 14).
   c. His judgment: ". . . . the Lord shall consume with the spirit of his mouth, and shall destroy with the brightness of his coming" (2:8). (See also Dan. 8:25; 11:45; Rev. 19:20.)

3. The day of the Lord and the restrainer (2:6, 7). "For the mystery of iniquity doth already work: only he who now letteth will let, until he be taken out of the way" (2:7).

Here Paul states that although the influence of the antichrist could be felt, even at that time, his full power and program were being held in check by a restrainer. (Note—the words "letteth" and "let" should be translated "hinder.")

Who or what is this powerful restrainer? There are several theories.
   a. It is human government. However, this is unlikely, for Satan already exercises strong influence upon the kingdoms of mankind. (See Mt. 4:8.)
   b. It is angels. This too is remote. (See Jude 1:9.)
   c. It is the Holy Spirit. This is by far the most logical conclusion. Dr. Charles Ryrie writes:

"The pretribulation argument is simply this. The restrainer is God, and the instrument of restraint is the God-indwelt church (cf. Eph. 4:6 for God indwelling; Gal. 2:20 for Christ indwelling; 1 Cor. 6:19 for the Spirit indwelling). It should be remembered that Christ said of the divinely indwelt and empowered church that 'the gates of hell shall not prevail against it' (Mt. 16:18), so we can say that this indwelt, empowered church is an adequate restraining instrument against the forces of darkness. The church will not go through any of the tribulation because the restrainer will be removed before the Man of Sin is revealed, which revelation (with the signing of the covenant with the Jews, Dan. 9:27) begins the tribulation period. Since the restrainer is ultimately God, and since God indwells all Christians, either He must be withdrawn from the hearts of believers while they are left on earth to go through the tribulation, or else when He is withdrawn all believers are taken with Him. Since it is impossible for a believer to be 'disindwelt' the only alternative is that believers too will be taken out of the way before the appearance of the Man of Sin, which signals the start of the tribulation." (*First and Second Thessalonians*, p. 112)

4. The day of the Lord and the unsaved (2:10, 11, 12).

"And for this cause God shall send them strong delusion, that they should believe a lie: That they all might be damned who believed not the truth, but had pleasure in unrighteousness" (2:11, 12).

Note it is *God* who sends these strong delusions. God's divine sovereignty is seen even in the activities of unsaved men and apostate angels. (See Ex. 4:21; Gen. 50:20; Josh. 11:20;

1 Sam. 16:14; 1 Ki. 22:19-23; Jdg. 9:23.) Dr. John Walvoord writes:

"Some understand from verse 11 that if a person in this present age of grace hears the gospel and does not receive Christ as Savior, then when Christ comes and takes His church home to glory these will find it impossible to be saved after the church is translated. It is unlikely that a person who rejects Christ in this day of grace will turn to Him in that awful period of tribulation. But the usual principle of Scripture is that while there is life there is hope. It is possible, though very improbable, that a person who has heard the gospel in this present age of grace will come to Christ after the rapture. The Scriptures definitely teach that God will send strong delusion to those who do not believe after the church is gone. God will judge their hearts, and if they deliberately turn away from the truth He will permit them to believe a lie. They will honor the man of sin as their god and as their king, instead of acknowledging the Lord Jesus Christ. The result will be 'That they all might be damned who believed not the truth, but had pleasure in unrighteousness' (v. 12)." (*The Thessalonian Epistles*, p. 129)

B. Facts concerning the beloved of the Lord (2:13-18).

"But we are bound to give thanks always to God for you, brethren, beloved of the Lord . . ." (2:13).

Paul has previously described the everlasting destruction of the unsaved (1:9). He now deals with the eternal salvation of the saved.

1. The source of this salvation: ". . . God hath from the beginning chosen you to salvation . . ." (2:13).
2. The method of this salvation: ". . . through sanctification of the Spirit . . ." (2:13).

   It has been said that had it not been for the Father and Son, there would have been no salvation feast, and were it not for the Spirit there would be no guests.
3. The means to this salvation: ". . . belief of the truth . . ." (2:13). This, of course, is the duty of the repenting sinner.
4. The goal of this salvation: ". . . to the obtaining of the glory of our Lord Jesus Christ" (2:14).
5. The responsibilities of this salvation: "Therefore, brethren, stand fast, and hold the traditions which ye have been taught, whether by word, or our epistle" (2:15).

III. A Practical Exhortation (3). In this final chapter to the Thessalonians Paul exhorts his readers through a request, a reassurance, a reprimand, and a review.

A. The request (3:1, 2):

"Finally, brethren, pray for us, that the word of the Lord may have free course, and be glorified, even as it is with you: And that we may be delivered from unreasonable and wicked men: for all men have not faith."

B. The reassurance (3:3-5):

"But the Lord is faithful, who shall stablish you, and keep you from evil. And we have confidence in the Lord touching you, that ye both do and will do the things which we command you. And the Lord direct your hearts into the love of God, and into the patient waitings for Christ."

C. The reprimand (3:6, 11-15):
   1. The recipients of this reprimand.
      a. the disorderly (unruly, undisciplined) (3:6, 11)
      b. the busybodies (gossipers) (3:11)
      c. the loafers (freeloaders) (3:10)
      d. the disobedient (those who refused Paul's instructions here) (3:14)
   2. The nature of this reprimand:
      a. They were to be identified and marked out (3:14).
      b. They were to be admonished for their failures (3:15).
      c. They were to be (if still unrepentant) excluded from Christian fellowship (3:6, 14).
      d. They were (nevertheless) to be treated as a brother and not as an enemy (3:15).

D. The review (3:7-10):

"For yourselves know how ye ought to follow us: for we behaved not ourselves disorderly among you; neither did we eat any man's bread for nought; but wrought with labour and travail night and day, that we might not be chargeable to any of you: Not because we have not power, but to make ourselves an ensample unto you to follow us. For even when we were with you, this we commanded you, that if any would not work, neither should he eat."

1 CORINTHIANS

INTRODUCTION:

1. The greatest human missionary of all times was the Apostle Paul. This ex-Pharisee, who had once hated and hounded Christians, made three great missionary trips, during which he established dozens of local New Testament churches. Thus the former vicious "wolf of the flock" became one of God's finest "sheep dogs."

2. The fact is that the New Testament is made up basically of some letters Paul wrote to some of these churches he started, and to their pastors. This list would contain:
   a. the Epistle to Rome (Romans)
   b. the Epistle to Ephesus (Ephesians)
   c. the Epistle to Colosse (Colossians)
   d. the Epistle to Philippi (Philippians)
   e. the Epistle to Galatia (Galatians)
   f. the two Epistles to Thessalonica (1 and 2 Thessalonians)
   g. the two Epistles to a pastor named Timothy (1 and 2 Timothy)
   h. the Epistle to a pastor named Titus (Titus)
   i. the two Epistles to Corinth (1 and 2 Corinthians)
   Here, then, we have an amazing fact: Out of the twenty-seven New Testament books, no less than twelve were written by Paul to his beloved mission churches.

3. Paul would have had little time, it would seem, for those modern "Christian movements" which bypass, downplay, and outright ignore the ministry and importance of local churches.
4. Of all his church letters, Romans is no doubt the most important, but 1 Corinthians is probably second in importance. This is so because of its great section of the resurrection of Christ and the believer (1 Cor. 15), and, if for no other reason, because of its sheer bulk, for 1 Corinthians is by far the longest epistle written by Paul.
5. There is almost no modern-day local church problem that is not covered in 1 Corinthians. The church was filled with theological and personal problems.
   a. They had perverted the doctrine of baptism (chapter 1).
   b. They were bragging about what little human wisdom they had (1).
   c. They were carnal to the core (3:1).
   d. They had deceived themselves (3:18).
   e. They had defiled their bodies (3:17).
   f. They were puffed up (4:18).
   g. They were tolerating horrible immorality (5:1).
   h. They were suing each other in heathen courts (6:1).
   i. They were confused about marriage (7:1).
   j. They had abused the doctrine of Christian liberty (8:9).
   k. They were not dressing properly in the house of God (11:6).
   l. They had made a mockery of the Lord's Supper (11:30).
   m. They had corrupted the gifts of the Spirit, especially tongues (14).
   n. They were confused on the subject of the resurrection (15).
   o. They had let down on their offerings (16).

   It has been said that if sins were horses, this church could have filled many stables.

Background to the Founding of the Church at Corinth

1. It was founded by Paul during his second missionary journey.
2. Acts chapter 18 relates the "groundbreaking" ceremonies.
   a. He leaves on his second trip with Silas (Acts 15:40).
   b. At Lystra they pick up Timothy (16:1).
   c. At Troas Paul receives his Macedonian vision (16:9).
   d. At Philippi a woman named Lydia, a demon-possessed girl, and a Roman jailer are all three saved (16:14-34).
   e. From Philippi Paul moves to Thessalonica (17:1).
   f. From there to Berea (17:10).
   g. From Berea to Athens (17:15).
   h. From Athens, finally to Corinth (18:1).
3. In Corinth Paul soon meets Aquila and Priscilla.
4. Crispus, the chief ruler of the synagogue, is saved (18:8).
5. God comforts Paul in a vision (18:9).
6. Paul stays at least eighteen months in Corinth before departing (18:11).
7. The Corinthian church was then pastored by a man called Apollos.

Background of Paul's First Letter to the Church at Corinth

1. During the summer of A.D. 53, Paul starts on his third missionary journey, apparently alone (Acts 18:23).
2. He arrives at Ephesus and spends three years there (18:10).
3. While at Ephesus he is visited by a delegation from Corinth with news concerning the tragic situation in their local church.
4. With a heavy heart, Paul sits down and writes 1 Corinthians.

1 Corinthians

SEVEN CORRUPTIONS (1-6)

1. **FOLLOWING HUMAN LEADERS, PAUL, APOLLOS, CEPHAS** 1:10-17
2. **FAVORING EARTHLY WISDOM** 1:18—2:13
3. **FLOUNDERING IN THE FLESH** 2:14—3:7
4. **FORGETTING FUTURE JUDGMENT** 3:8-23
5. **FLATTERING THEMSELVES** 4:1-21
6. **FAILING TO DISCIPLINE** 5:1-13
7. **FRAGMENTING THE BODY OF CHRIST** 6:1-20

SIX QUESTIONS (7-16)

"NOW CONCERNING THE THINGS ABOUT WHICH YE WROTE UNTO ME . . ." 7:1

WHAT ABOUT Marriage? Chapter 7

WHAT ABOUT Christian Liberty? Chapters 8-10

WHAT ABOUT Church Conduct? Chapter 11

WHAT ABOUT Spiritual Gifts? Chapters 12-14

WHAT ABOUT The Resurrection? Chapter 15

WHAT ABOUT The Collection? Chapter 16

An Analysis of 1 Corinthians

I. Preliminaries: The greetings of Paul (1:1-10).

A. Paul and Sosthenes send their regards. This Sosthenes may have been the same one referred to in Acts 18:17. He was the chief ruler of the synagogue in Ephesus who instigated a riot against Paul. It backfired, however, and he himself was beaten by some angry Greeks. This apparently led to his salvation.

B. Paul says (1:2), "with all that in every place call upon the name of Jesus." Thus, this epistle was written for *all* believers, as were his others (see 1 Thess. 5:27; Col. 4:16).

C. "The Lord Jesus Christ" (1:3). This great name is mentioned six times in the first ten verses of the epistle, doubtless because the church had not honored this grand title. Here is the reason why *any* local church has difficulties.

D. "Ye are enriched . . . in all utterance and . . . knowledge" (1:5). The Corinthian believers *knew* the truth and could *speak* the truth. They simply were not *practicing* the truth.

E. "Ye come behind in no gift." The Bible lists some eighteen gifts. The church at Corinth apparently had all of them.

F. Verse 8 is one of the greatest "security of the believer" statements in the entire Bible. Note the wording:

1. Confirm. This means to establish and make absolutely secure. The same verb is used in Romans 15:8, where Paul states that God confirmed in Christ the promises made in the Old Testament.

2. Blameless. A legal term meaning "not called into court, uncharged, unaccused." It does not mean *sinless*, but *chargeless*. (See also Col. 1:22; 1 Tim. 3:10.)

3. To the end . . . in the day. A reference to the rapture.

Conclusion: Paul is writing to one of the most backslidden, carnal, confused, and selfish churches on record. He thus could only predict their eventual salvation because of God's eternal security, in spite of their pitiful condition.

G. "God is faithful" (1:9). A brief summary of his faithfulness would include:

1. He is faithful in defending his people.

"I have found David my servant; with my holy oil have I anointed him . . . my faithfulness . . . shall be with him. The enemy shall not exact upon him; nor the son of wickedness afflict him" (Ps. 89:20, 22, 24).

2. He is faithful in times of temptation.

"There hath no temptation taken you, but such as is common to man; but God is faithful, who will not suffer you to be tempted above that ye are able; but will with the temptation also make a way of escape, that ye may be able to bear it" (1 Cor. 10:13).

3. He is faithful in keeping the Christian saved.

"But the Lord is faithful, who shall stablish you, and keep you from evil" (2 Thess. 3:3).

"I pray God your whole spirit and soul and body be preserved blameless unto the coming of our Lord Jesus Christ. Faithful is he that calleth you, who will also do it" (1 Thess. 5:23, 24).

4. He is faithful in chastening his children.

"I know, O Lord, that thy judgments are right, and that thou in faithfulness hast afflicted me" (Ps. 119:75).

"For whom the Lord loveth he chasteneth and scourgeth every son whom he receiveth" (Heb. 12:6).

5. He is faithful in forgiving confessed sin.

"If we confess our sins, he is faithful and just to forgive us our sins and to cleanse us from all unrighteousness" (1 Jn. 1:9).

6. He is faithful in hearing our prayers.

"Hear my prayer O Lord, give ear to my supplications; in thy faithfulness answer me" (Ps. 143:1).

Thus, their calling was through God, and since he is faithful, their salvation was sure. We note with sadness that Paul says nothing about their *present* condition (as in letters to other churches), but only mentions their *past* and *future*.

H. "The fellowship of his Son Jesus Christ" (1:9). Christians the world over love to talk and write and sing about this fellowship, and well they should; but it should be kept in mind that sometimes this fellowship involves suffering also. As Paul writes:

"That I may know him, and the power of his resurrection, and the fellowship of his sufferings, being made conformable unto his death" (Phil. 3:10).

Too often it would seem we want the first without the second. But there can be no power of the resurrection without the fellowship of his sufferings.

I. "No divisions among you" (1:10). Greek scholar W. E. Vine lists four distinct steps which may lead downward from harmony to a tragic break-up in a Christian unity. These are:

1. *Stasis*—a strong disagreement, a dissension (see Acts 15:2; 23:7, 10).

2. *Dichostasia*—a standing apart (see Gal. 5:20; Rom. 16:17).

3. *Schisma*—a severe rent, a tear (see 1 Cor. 11:18; Jn. 7:43; 9:16; 10:19).

4. *Hairesis*—a mature and established separation (see Acts 5:17; 24:5, 14; 26:5; 2 Pet. 2:1; Titus 3:10).

Here the third word is used by Paul, *schisma*, thus suggesting the Corinthian church was in danger of complete breakup.

J. "But that ye be perfectly joined together" (1:10). The phrase "perfectly joined together" in this verse comes from one Greek word. That word is *katartizo*. This word is used in three other important New Testament passages:

1. "Through faith we understand that the worlds were framed by the Word of God . . ." (Heb. 11:3). Here the word *katartizo* is translated "framed."

2. "Wherefore when he cometh into the world he saith, sacrifice and offering thou wouldst not, but a body hast thou prepared me" (Heb. 10:5). Here the word is translated "prepared."

3. "And going on from thence, he saw . . . James . . . and John his brother in a ship with Zebedee their father, mending their nets" (Mt. 4:21). In this final passage the word is translated "mending."

The point of all the above is simply this: God is desirous that church believers be joined together:

As perfectly as the sun, moon, and stars fit together (Heb. 11:3).

As perfectly as God formed the body for Jesus to use (Heb. 10:5).

As perfectly as a mended net is. Souls are not saved in a church plagued with problems simply because the net is broken and they get away.

II. The Report (1:11—6:20). Paul replies to a report made about the church in Corinth.

A. They were following human leaders (1:11-17). Paul begins by naming his source of information ("for it has been declared unto me . . . of Chloe." See 1:11). All too often unsigned critical letters are received by Christian leaders, finding fault with either the pastor or some other member in the church. How many times has vicious gossip from the mouths of nameless (and spineless) church members led to the destruction of their own church!

In verses 12 through 17 Paul writes to straighten out their first basic problem, that of baptism. How many churches have, since that time, been split right down the middle over the subject of baptism. Here the argument, however, was not over the mode or even the purpose, but concerning the different men who had baptized some of these Corinthian believers.

1. Paul had baptized some of them, of course (but very few in reality), when he established the church.

2. Apollos later pastored the church and also baptized some.

3. Peter (Cephas) had apparently baptized a few, although we know nothing as to when or where this might have taken place. Some believe it could have happened at Pentecost.

4. Christ is also mentioned in this list. As with Peter, we have no knowledge whatsoever as to where, when, and indeed *if* he ever did this.

At any rate, here is a local New Testament church hopelessly divided into four groups, with each group claiming superiority over the other three because of the man who had baptized them!

5. The Paulite group. The "claim to fame" of the first group was this: "We are of Paul and therefore better than you! Anyone knows Paul is a great *doctrinal* preacher, and that's the only kind to have."

6. The Apollosite group. The second group would probably retort, "We are of Apollos, and anyone with any sense at all will agree that Apollos is an *eloquent* preacher and can preach circles around Paul any day."

7. The Cephasite group. The third group might then answer, "We are of Cephas, and you can brag about doctrine and eloquence all you want to, but there's just nobody as down-to-earth and *practical* as Peter."

8. The Christite group. The fourth group could thereupon be pictured as looking down their long spiritual noses at the other three and piously saying, "We are of Christ, and therefore look to *no human preacher* to lead us and feed us."

"Was Paul crucified for you?" (1:13). We note Paul hits his own fan club first! It is easy to rebuke a group if they are wrong, especially if that group is against you anyway, but it is another thing to criticize sharply those who sing your praises the loudest. Paul was truly sold out for Jesus!

Dr. James Boyer writes the following concerning 1:16:

"Verse 16 introduces an interesting exception. Paul suddenly remembers that there was another whom he had baptized, Stephanas. From 16:15 and 17 we learn that Stephanas was among those who had just arrived from Corinth and was probably present at the time Paul was dictating this letter. It may well be that he prompted Paul, reminding him of the fact that he had baptized him also, when Paul mentions the others. Now, if Paul almost forgot Stephanas it might have been that he forgot others also, so the Apostle Paul includes the possibility of others as having been baptized by him. This does not argue against the doctrine of inspiration. Inspiration did not interfere with the personal style and characteristics of the individual writers, nor did inspiration produce omniscience. Inspiration guaranteed that what was written was what the Lord wanted written." (*For a World Like Ours*, p. 32)

"For Christ sent me not to baptize, but to preach the gospel" (1:17). This is probably the strongest verse in the Bible refuting the doctrine of baptismal regeneration (the unscriptural teaching which says one must be baptized to be saved).

We would note here that Paul did not say that Christ had forbidden him to baptize, for the apostle often did baptize his converts (see Acts 16:15, 33; 18:8; 19:5). What he is saying here is simply this: Water baptism is not a part of the gospel of Christ. Later in this same epistle, Paul defines the gospel:

"Moreover, brethren, I declare unto you the gospel . . . how that Christ died for our sins according to the scriptures; and that he was buried, and that he rose again the third day according to the scriptures" (1 Cor. 15:1, 3, 4). This, then, by itself, is the gospel.

B. They were favoring earthly wisdom (1:18—2:13). Paul points out to them the stupidity of this, for God had long since rejected man's wisdom.

"For it is written, I will destroy the wisdom of the wise, and will bring to nothing the understanding of the prudent" (1:19). (See also Job 5:12; Isa. 29:14.)

Note: In 3:19 Paul writes, "He taketh the wise in their own craftiness." For three classic New Testament examples of just this very thing, see Matthew 21:23-27 (concerning the baptism of

John); Matthew 22:15-22 (concerning the tribute to Caesar); and John 8:1-11 (concerning an adulterous woman). In his eternal wisdom, God chose instead the method of the cross to save men.

1. The reaction to God's plan.
   a. "It is the program of a fool!" (The conclusion of the unsaved; see 1:18.)
   b. "It is the power of God!" (The conclusion of the saved. See 1:18.)

   Note: In the original it states that the unbelievers are *perishing* and the believers *are being* saved. Both salvation and damnation are put in the *present* tense. (See Jn. 3:18, 26 in regard to the unsaved.) Concerning the saved, the New Testament describes their salvation in three tenses:
   (1) past tense—Romans 8:24 (justification)
   (2) present tense—1 Corinthians 1:18 (sanctification)
   (3) future tense—Romans 5:9 (glorification)

   Dr. Harry Ironside was once asked by a stranger if he was saved. The famous pastor replied, "Yes, I have been, I am being, and I shall be!"

2. The results of God's plan.
   a. To the Jew who required signs, it was a stumbling block (1:22, 23. See also Mt. 12:38; 16:1; Lk. 2:34).

   Note: Israel had rejected God's plan in spite of the fact that he had provided them with certain signs. (See Jn. 3:2; 20:30; Acts 2:19, 43; 5:12.)
   b. To the Greek, who required "wisdom," it was senseless (1:22, 23; see also Acts 17:21, 32).
   c. To all believers, who simply receive (and do not require) it is sanctification (1:30).

3. The reasons for God's plan (29).
   "But God hath chosen the foolish things of the world to confound the wise; and God hath chosen the weak things of the world to confound the things which are mighty; And base things of the world, and things which are despised, hath God chosen, yea, and things which are not, to bring to nought things that are: That no flesh should glory in his presence."

   Thus, in manifesting his own glory, God delighted in choosing:
   a. The foolish things of this world.
   (1) a bleeding lamb in Exodus 12
   (2) a smitten rock in Exodus 17
   (3) a brass snake in Numbers 21
   b. The weak things of this world.
   (1) a rod to defeat the Egyptians in Exodus 4
   (2) a sling to defeat a mighty giant in 1 Samuel 17
   (3) a bone to defeat the Philistines in Judges 15
   c. The base things of this world.
   (1) a harlot's son who became a mighty judge in Judges 11
   (2) a heathen girl who became David's great-grandmother in Ruth 4
   (3) an immoral woman who became a great soul-winner in John 4

   Note: Paul tactfully reminds the church that it was a good thing God did not choose the intellect and prestige of the world.

   "For ye see your calling, brethren, how that not many wise men after the flesh, not many mighty, not many noble, are called" (1:26).

   The great John Wesley was often helped during his ministry by a noble lady of high English society named Lady Huntington. This gracious woman who gave so much of her time, talent, and treasure to Christ would often testify as follows:

   "I am only going to heaven through the letter M. How thankful I am that Paul did not say that not *any* noble are called, but rather not *many* noble are called. Therefore, I am only going to heaven through the letter M!"

4. The review of God's plan (2:1-13). In these verses Paul reviews his own journey to Corinth during the third missionary trip, at which time he established the church there. He reminds them:
   a. That the message of the cross is not of the world (2:1-6).

   "And I, brethren, when I came to you, came not with excellency of speech or of wisdom, declaring unto you the testimony of God. For I determined not to know any thing among you, save Jesus Christ, and him crucified. And I was with you in weakness, and in fear, and in much trembling. And my speech and my preaching was not with enticing words of man's wisdom, but in demonstration of the Spirit and of power" (2:1-4).

   Prior to his visit in Corinth, Paul had spoken to the Greek philosophers on Mars' Hill in Athens (Acts 17:16-34). Here he delivered a powerful and eloquent message, using philosophy, poetry, and history along with great scriptural truths. The sermon, however, produced little fruit. Some (but not all) have therefore concluded that the apostle here in 1 Corinthians 2:1-4 is recording his determination to depend henceforth only and always upon the Holy Spirit and not to rely at all upon eloquence, philosophy, etc. Others have felt his condition as described in 2:3 was purely physical, perhaps due to nervous exhaustion. (See also 2 Cor. 7:5.)
   b. That the message of the cross had been ordained before this world (2:8).

   "Which none of the princes of this world knew; for had they known it, they would not have crucified the Lord of glory."
   c. That the message of the cross is reserved for the heirs of this world (2:9-13).

   "But as it is written, Eye hath not seen, nor ear heard, neither have entered into the heart of man, the things which God hath prepared for them that love him. But God hath revealed them unto us by his Spirit: for the Spirit searcheth all things, yea, the deep things of God" (2:9, 10).

C. They were floundering in the flesh (2:14—3:7). In those remarkable verses, Paul divides all men into three spiritual categories. These are:

1. The corpse (the natural man, 2:14): *psuchikos* man.

"But the natural man receiveth not the things of the Spirit of God: for they are foolishness unto him: neither can he know them, because they are spiritually discerned" (2:14).

Characteristics of the *psuchikos* man:

a. He may not be totally depraved (as evil as he could possibly be), but he is totally helpless to comprehend God's Word (see Acts 8:31).

b. He thus concludes the Scriptures are senseless (see Acts 17:18, 32; 26:24).

c. He is dead and must be resurrected, for he cannot be revived (see Rom. 5:12; Eph. 2:1).

2. The crybaby (the carnal man, 3:1-4): *sarkikos* man.

"And I, brethren, could not speak unto you as unto spiritual, but as unto carnal, even as unto babes in Christ" (3:1).

Characteristics of the *sarkikos* man:

a. He is helpless, as a newborn infant. The word "babes" used here is *nepios* in the original, and carries with it weakness without power of speech, immaturity and inexperience. This condition is also pictured in Ephesians 4:14.

"That we henceforth be no more children, tossed to and fro, and carried about with every wind of doctrine" (see also Gal. 4:3; 2 Pet. 1:9).

b. He is unable to receive anything but milk (3:2). This condition always suggests either infancy or infirmity. Milk is proper for awhile (1 Pet. 2:2) but "strong meat belongeth to them that are of full age, even those who by reason of use have their senses exercised to discern both good and evil" (Heb. 5:14; see also Heb. 5:11-13).

c. He walks and talks like an unsaved man. "Are ye not carnal and walk as men?" (3:3). All believers should consider this pointed question: "If you were arrested and charged with being a Christian, would there be enough evidence to convict you?" The Corinthians, it would seem, to a large extent would get off scot-free.

d. They compared spiritual leaders instead of spiritual truths. (See 2:13 as opposed to 3:4.) Paul answers this by saying: "I have planted, Apollos watered; but God gave the increase" (3:6). Only God can do this (see also 1 Ki. 18:30-38).

3. The conqueror (the spiritual man, 2:15): *pneumatikos* man.

"But he that is spiritual judgeth all things, yet he himself is judged of no man."

Characteristics of the *pneumatikos* man:

a. He is *not* sanctimonious.

b. He is *not* superior. (In matters of brains, strength, background, money, etc.)

c. He is *not* sensational.

d. He is *not* sugary sweet.

e. He is *not* straightlaced.

f. He is *not* segregated from society.

g. He is *not* superficial.

h. He is *not* spineless.

i. He *is* spiritual. To be spiritual is to be in harmony with God, as are his laws (Rom. 7:14). Thus, a spiritual man is simply one controlled and motivated by the Holy Spirit. (See 1 Cor. 15:46; Gal. 5:16, 25.)

Because of this, he can correctly judge "all things" (2:15). (See also 2 Tim. 2:15 as opposed to 2 Pet. 3:14-17.)

Paul states that, "We have the mind of Christ" (2:16). All believers enjoy this positionally (2 Cor. 5:17), but the spiritual man has it experientially (Phil. 2:5).

D. They were forgetting future judgment (3:8-23).

1. The meaning of the *bema* judgment. The Greek word *bema* (translated "judgment seat" in the KJV) was a familiar term to the people of Paul's day. Dr. Lehman Strauss writes:

"In the large Olympic arenas, there was an elevated seat on which the judge of the contest sat. After the contests were over, the successful competitors would assemble before the bema to receive their rewards or crowns. The bema was not a judicial bench where someone was condemned; it was a reward seat. Likewise, the Judgment Seat of Christ is not a judicial bench . . . the Christian life is a race, and the divine umpire is watching every contestant. After the church has run her course, He will gather every member before the bema for the purpose of examining each one and giving the proper reward to each." (*God's Plan for the Future*, p. 111)

2. The fact of the *bema* judgment. Many New Testament verses speak of this.

"But why dost thou judge thy brother? Or why dost thou set at nought thy brother? For we shall all stand before the judgment seat of Christ. For it is written, As I live, saith the Lord, every knee shall bow to me, and every tongue shall confess to God. So then every one of us shall give account of himself to God" (Rom. 14:10-12).

"Every man's work shall be made manifest, for the day shall declare it" (1 Cor. 3:13).

"For we must all appear before the judgment seat of Christ" (2 Cor. 5:10).

3. The purpose of the *bema* judgment.

a. Negative considerations.

(1) The purpose of the *bema* judgment is *not* to determine whether a particu-

lar individual enters heaven or not, for every man's eternal destiny is already determined before he leaves this life.

(2) The purpose of the *bema* judgment is *not* to punish believers for sins committed either before or after their salvation. The Scriptures are very clear that no child of God will have to answer for his sins after this life.

"He hath not dealt with us after our sins, nor rewarded us according to our iniquities. For as the heaven is high above the earth, so great is his mercy toward them that fear him. As far as the east is from the west, so far hath he removed our transgressions from us" (Ps. 103:10-12).

"Thou hast in love to my soul delivered it from the pit of corruption: for thou hast cast all my sins behind thy back" (Isa. 38:17).

"I have blotted out . . . thy transgressions and . . . thy sins" (Isa. 44:22).

"Thou wilt cast all their sins into the depths of the sea" (Micah 7:19).

"For I will be merciful . . . and their sins and their iniquities will I remember no more" (Heb. 8:12).

"The blood of Jesus Christ his Son cleanseth us from all sin" (1 Jn. 1:7).

b. Positive considerations. What, then, is the purpose of the *bema* judgment? In 1 Corinthians 4:2, Paul says that all Christians should conduct themselves as faithful stewards of God: "Moreover it is required in stewards, that a man be found faithful." The Apostle Peter later writes in a similar way: "Minister . . . as good stewards of the manifold grace of God" (1 Pet. 4:10).

In the New Testament world, a steward was the manager of a large household or estate. He was appointed by the owner and was entrusted to keep the estate running smoothly. He had the power to hire and fire and to spend and save, being answerable to the owner alone. His only concern was that periodic meeting with his master, at which time he was required to account for the condition of the estate up to that point. With this background in mind, it may be said that someday at the *bema* judgment all stewards will stand before their Lord and Master and be required to give an account of the way they have used their privileges and responsibilities from the moment of their conversion. In conclusion, it can be seen that:

(1) In the past, God dealt with us as sinners (Eph. 2:1-3; 1 Cor. 6:9-11; Rom. 5:6-8).

(2) In the present, God deals with us as sons (Rom. 8:14; Heb. 12:5-11; 1 Jn. 3:1, 2).

(3) In the future, God will deal with us (at the *bema*) as stewards.

4. The material to be tested at the *bema* judgment. In 1 Corinthians 3:11 the Apostle Paul explains the glorious fact that at the moment of salvation a repenting sinner is firmly placed on the foundation of the death, burial, and resurrection of Christ himself! His continuing instruction after his salvation is to rise up and build upon this foundation. Paul says,

"But let every man take heed how he buildeth thereupon. . . . Now if any man build upon this foundation gold, silver, precious stones, wood, hay, stubble; every man's work shall be made manifest: for the day shall declare it, because it shall be revealed by fire; and the fire shall try every man's work of what sort it is" (1 Cor. 3:10, 12, 13).

a. Negative considerations. It should be noted immediately that this passage does *not* teach the false doctrine known as purgatory, for it is the believer's *works* and not the believer *himself* that will be subjected to the fires.

b. Positive considerations. From these verses it is apparent that God classifies the works of believers into one of the following six areas: gold, silver, precious stones, wood, hay, stubble. There has been much speculation about the kinds of work down here that will constitute gold or silver up there. But it seems more appropriate to note that the six objects can be readily placed into two categories:

(1) Those indestructible and worthy objects which will survive and thrive in the fires. These are gold, silver, and precious stones.

(2) Those destructible and worthless objects which will be totally consumed in the fires. These are the wood, hay, and stubble.

c. Though it is difficult to know just what goes to make up a "golden work" or a "stubble work," we are nevertheless informed of certain general areas in which God is particularly interested.

(1) How we treat other believers.

"For God is not unrighteous to forget your work and labour of love, which ye have showed toward his name, in that ye have ministered to the saints, and do minister" (Heb. 6:10).

"He that receiveth a prophet in the name of a prophet shall receive a prophet's reward; and he that receiveth a righteous man in the name of a righteous man shall receive a righteous man's reward. And whosoever shall give to drink unto one of these little ones a cup of cold water only in the name of a disciple, verily I say unto you, he shall in no wise lose his reward" (Mt. 10:41, 42).

(2) How we exercise our authority over others.

"Obey them that have the rule over you, and submit yourselves: for they watch for your souls, as they that must give account, that they may do it with joy, and not with grief" (Heb. 13:17).

"Let not many of you become teachers, my brethren, knowing that as such we shall incur a stricter judgment" (Jas. 3:1, NASB).

(3) How we employ our God-given abilities.

"Wherefore I put thee in remembrance that thou stir up the gift of God which is in thee" (2 Tim. 1:6).

"Now there are varieties of gifts, but the same Spirit. . . . But one and the same Spirit works all these things, distributing to each one individually just as he wills" (1 Cor. 12:4, 11, NASB).

"As each one has received a special gift, employ it in serving one another, as good stewards of the manifold grace of God" (1 Pet. 4:10, NASB).

To these verses can be added the overall teaching of Jesus' parables of the ten pounds (Lk. 19:11-26) and the eight talents (Mt. 25:14-29).

(4) How we use our money.

"Charge them that are rich in this world that they be not high-minded, nor trust in uncertain riches, but in the living God, who giveth us richly all things to enjoy; that they do good, that they be rich in good works, ready to distribute, willing to communicate, laying up in store for themselves a good foundation against the time to come, that they may lay hold on eternal life" (1 Tim. 6:17-19).

"But this I say, He which soweth sparingly shall reap also sparingly; and he which soweth bountifully shall reap also bountifully. Every man according as he purposeth in his heart, so let him give; not grudgingly, or of necessity, for God loveth a cheerful giver" (2 Cor. 9:6, 7).

"Upon the first day of the week let every one of you lay by him in store, as God hath prospered him" (1 Cor. 16:2).

(5) How much we suffer for Jesus.

"Blessed are ye, when men shall revile you, and persecute you, and shall say all manner of evil against you falsely, for my sake. Rejoice, and be exceeding glad, for great is your reward in heaven" (Mt. 5:11, 12).

"Beloved, think it not strange concerning the fiery trial which is to try you, as though some strange thing happened unto you; but rejoice, inasmuch as ye are partakers of Christ's sufferings, that, when his glory shall be revealed, ye may be glad also with exceeding joy" (1 Pet. 4:12, 13).

"And Jesus answered and said, Verily I say unto you, There is no man that hath left house, or brethren, or sisters, or father or mother, or wife, or children, or lands, for my sake, and the gospel's, but he shall receive an hundredfold now in this time, houses, and brethren, and sisters, and mothers, and children and lands, with persecutions; and in the world to come eternal life" (Mk. 10:29, 30).

"For our light affliction, which is but for a moment, worketh for us a far more exceeding and eternal weight of glory" (2 Cor. 4:17).

"For I reckon that the sufferings of this present time are not worthy to be compared with the glory which shall be revealed in us" (Rom. 8:18).

(6) How we spend our time.

"Redeeming the time, because the days are evil" (Eph. 5:16).

"Walk in wisdom . . . redeeming the time" (Col. 4:5).

"And if ye call on the Father, who without respect of persons judgeth according to every man's work, pass the time of your sojourning here in fear" (1 Pet. 1:17).

(7) How we run that particular race which God has chosen for us.

"Know ye not that they which run in a race run all, but one receiveth the prize? So run, that ye may obtain" (1 Cor. 9:24).

"Brethren, I count not myself to have apprehended; but this one thing I do, forgetting those things which are behind, and reaching forth unto those things which are before, I press toward the mark for the prize of the high calling of God in Christ Jesus" (Phil. 3:13, 14).

"Let us lay aside every weight, and the sin which doth so easily beset us, and let us run with patience the race that is set before us" (Heb. 12:1).

"That I may rejoice in the day of Christ, that I have not run in vain" (Phil. 2:16).

(8) How effectively we control the old nature.

"And every man that striveth for the mastery is temperate in all things. Now they do it to obtain a corruptible crown, but we an incorruptible. I therefore so run, not as uncertainly; so fight I, not as one that beateth the air. But I keep under my body, and bring it into subjection, lest that by any means when I have preached to others, I myself should be a castaway" (1 Cor. 9:25-27).

(9) How many souls we witness to and win for Christ.

"The fruit of the righteous is a tree of life, and he that winneth souls is wise" (Prov. 11:30).

"For what is our hope, or joy, or crown of rejoicing? Are not even ye in the presence of our Lord Jesus Christ at his coming? For ye are our glory and joy" (1 Thess. 2:19, 20).

"And they that be wise shall shine as the brightness of the firmament, and they that turn many to righteousness as the stars for ever and ever" (Dan. 12:3).

(10) How we react to temptation.

"My brethren, count it all joy when ye fall into divers temptations, knowing this, that the trying of your faith worketh patience" (Jas. 1:2, 3).

"Behold, the devil shall cast some of you into prison, that ye may be tried; and ye shall have tribulation ten days; be thou faithful unto death, and I will give thee a crown of life" (Rev. 2:10).

(11) How much the doctrine of the rapture means to us.

"Henceforth there is laid up for me a crown of righteousness, which the Lord, the righteous judge, shall give me at that day; and not to me only, but unto all them also that love his appearing" (2 Tim. 4:8).

(12) How faithful we are to the Word of God and the flock of God.

"Feed the flock of God which is among you, taking the oversight thereof, not by constraint, but willingly; not for filthy lucre, but of a ready mind; neither as being lords over God's heritage, but being ensamples to the flock. And when the Chief Shepherd shall appear, ye shall receive a crown of glory that fadeth not away" (1 Pet. 5:2-4).

"I charge thee therefore before God and the Lord Jesus Christ, who shall judge the quick and the dead at his appearing and his kingdom, Preach the word" (2 Tim. 4:1, 2).

"Wherefore, I take you to record this day, that I am pure from the blood of all men. For I have not shunned to declare unto you all the counsel of God. Take heed therefore unto yourselves, and to all the flock over which the Holy Ghost hath made you overseers, to feed the church of God, which he hath purchased with his own blood" (Acts 20:26-28).

5. The results of the *bema* judgment seat of Christ.

a. Some will receive rewards.

"If any man's work abide which he hath built thereupon, he shall receive a reward" (1 Cor. 3:14).

The Bible mentions at least five possible rewards. They have already been described briefly under the last section. The rewards include:

(1) The incorruptible crown—given to those who master the old nature (1 Cor. 9:25-27).

(2) The crown of rejoicing—given to soul-winners (Prov. 11:30; 1 Thess. 2:19, 20; Dan. 12:3).

(3) The crown of life—given to those who successfully endure temptation (Jas. 1:2, 3; Rev. 2:10).

(4) The crown of righteousness—given to those who especially love the doctrine of the rapture (2 Tim. 4:8).

(5) The crown of glory—given to faithful preachers and teachers (1 Pet. 5:2-4; 2 Tim. 4:1, 2; Acts 20:26-28).

It has been suggested that these "crowns" will actually be talents and abilities with which to glorify Christ. Thus, the greater the reward, the greater the ability.

b. Some will suffer loss.

"If any man's work shall be burned, he shall suffer loss" (1 Cor. 3:15).

This word for "suffer" is *zemioo* in the Greek New Testament, and is used again by Paul in Philippians chapter 3, where he describes those things which were the greatest source of pride to him prior to salvation. He tells us,

"For I went through the Jewish initiation ceremony when I was eight days old, having been born into a pure-blooded Jewish home that was a branch of the old original Benjamin family. So I was a real Jew if there ever was one! What's more, I was a member of the Pharisees who demand the strictest obedience to every Jewish law and custom. And sincere? Yes, so much so that I greatly persecuted the church; and I tried to obey every Jewish rule and regulation right down to the very last point" (Phil. 3:5, 6, *TLB*).

But after his conversion, Paul writes, "For whom I have suffered the loss of all things . . . that I may win Christ" (Phil. 3:8). The point of all these teachings is simply this: at the *bema* judgment the carnal Christian will suffer the loss of many past achievements, even as Paul did, but with one important exception: Paul was richly compensated, since he suffered his loss to win Christ, while the carnal believer will receive nothing to replace his burned-up wood, hay, and stubble. Before leaving this section, the question may be asked, "Is it possible for someone who has earned certain rewards down here to lose them somehow through carnality?" Some believe this to be tragically possible on the basis of the following verses:

"Look to yourselves, that we lose not those things which we have wrought, but that we receive a full reward" (2 Jn. 8).

"Behold, I come quickly; hold that fast which thou hast, that no man take thy crown" (Rev. 3:11).

"Let no man beguile you of your reward" (Col. 2:18).

c. The passage in 3:14-17 actually lists three kinds of builders:
   (1) the wise builder (3:14)
   (2) the worldly builder (3:15)
   (3) the wicked builder (3:17)

   The wicked builder, of course, will *not* stand before the *bema*, but will be at the great white judgment throne (Rev. 20:11-15). The word "destroy" in 3:17 is *phtheiro* in the original and is often associated in the Greek New Testament with false doctrine and corrupt teachers. (See 1 Cor. 15:33; Eph. 4:22; 2 Pet. 2:12; Jude 10; Rev. 19:2.)

   It should also be observed that we shall account for not only what we *did,* but what we *could* have done if we would have (Rev. 3:1-3; Lk. 12:48; 1 Cor. 4:1), and what we *would* have done if we could have (Mt. 26:41; 1 Ki. 8:18).

6. The Old Testament foreshadowing of the *bema* judgment seat of Christ. Although the church is nowhere mentioned in the Old Testament, there is nevertheless a passage which can very easily be applied to the *bema* judgment. This can be found in the words of Boaz (a foreshadowing of Christ) to Ruth (a foreshadowing of the church), when he says, "It hath fully been showed me, all that thou hast done. . . . The Lord recompense thy work, and a full reward be given thee of the Lord God of Israel, under whose wings thou art come to trust" (Ruth 2:11, 12).

E. They were flattering themselves (4:1-21). The Corinthian leaders were apparently swollen with pride due to their authority in the local church. Paul attempts to correct this sinful attitude:

1. By six pictorial examples. In chapters 3 and 4 the apostle describes the work of a true minister of Christ.
   a. He is a husbandman (3:6). He is to cultivate.
   b. He is a builder (3:10). He is to construct.
   c. He is a steward (4:1). He is to control.
   d. He is a father (4:15). He is to counsel.
   e. He is a teacher (4:17). He is to communicate.
   f. He is a disciplinarian (4:21). He is to correct.

2. By two prophetical examples.
   a. Concerning the *bema* judgment (4:3-5). In their pride the Corinthians had felt perfect liberty to pass judgment upon Christian workers. However, Paul warns them against:
      (1) Judging others.
      (2) Judging even themselves. The reason, of course, is that they were to wait "until the Lord come, who both will bring to light the hidden things of darkness, and will make manifest the counsels of the hearts; and then shall every man have praise of God" (4:5).
   b. Concerning the millennium (4:8-10). Paul here employs one of the finest examples of divine sarcasm in all the Bible. He observes that the Corinthians must have convinced themselves they were actually ruling in the millennium, the way they were strutting around.

3. By one personal example—the life of Paul.
   a. His sufferings for the Savior.
      (1) He was buffeted (denotes a striking with clenched fists), despised, reviled, persecuted, and defamed. Note his reaction to all this, however:
         "Being reviled, we bless; being persecuted, we suffer; being defamed, we entreat" (4:12, 13).
      (2) He experienced hunger, thirst, nakedness, and had "no certain dwelling place."
      (3) He worked long hard hours, supporting himself. The word "labor" in 4:12 is *kopiao* in Greek, suggestive

of the labor which causes weariness. It was not simply a case of earning his living, but of working his fingers to the bone in doing it. (See also 1 Thess. 2:9; 2 Cor. 11:7.)

(4) He was looked upon as the filth of this world and the offscouring of all things.

(5) He was as a captured and condemned prisoner in the end of a victorious Roman parade, a spectacle to all.

It has been observed that the trouble with Christians in our country today is that no one is trying to kill them.

b. His concern for the saints.

"I write not these things to shame you, but as my beloved son, I warn you. For though ye have ten thousand instructors in Christ, yet have ye not many fathers: for in Christ Jesus I have begotten you through the gospel. Wherefore I beseech you, be ye followers of me" (4:14-16).

We note Paul admonishes them to "be ye followers of me." He repeats this request on at least three other occasions (see 1 Cor. 11:1; 2 Thess. 3:9; Phil. 3:17). In light of this it is unscriptural for a pastor or Christian leader (however sincere) to admonish his people, saying: "Don't look at my life, don't do as I do or say. Don't even look at men as your examples, look only to Christ!" See the words of Jesus on this in Matthew 5:13-16. Also to be noted are Paul's words "I have begotten you" (4:15), which may be compared with those found in Galatians 4:19 and 1 Thessalonians 2:11.

F. They were failing to discipline (5:1-13).

1. The need for discipline: "There is fornication among you" (5:1). The Greek word for fornication is *porneia* (root word of English pornography). Paul uses this word seventeen times in all his writings. Eleven of these are found in 1 Corinthians. Here the sin involved a man living with his stepmother in a sexual way. We note:

a. He was a church member. This is implied:

(1) Because his sinning partner is not rebuked. Paul is here only concerned with that sin committed by a member. The woman was apparently not a member.

(2) Because Paul orders him to be dismissed from the fellowship of the church.

b. He was guilty as charged. "It is reported commonly" (5:1).

c. He was unrepentant.

2. The failure to discipline. "Ye are puffed up, and have not rather mourned, that he that hath done this deed might be taken from among you" (5:2). They were puffed up, not because of the sin itself, but because of their tolerance and pride. At times tolerance can be downright treason.

Paul rebukes them for not mourning over this tragedy. How much better had the vain Corinthians heeded the advice of the following verses:

"Be afflicted and mourn and weep: let your laughter be turned to mourning and your joy to heaviness" (Jas. 4:9).

"The sacrifices of God are a broken spirit: a broken and a contrite heart, O God, thou wilt not despise" (Ps. 51:17).

But regardless of their brazen attitude, this church corruption had broken the tender heart of Paul, who would later write:

"For out of much affliction and anguish of heart I wrote unto you with many tears" (2 Cor. 2:4).

3. The authority to discipline. "In the name of our Lord Jesus Christ, when ye are gathered together" (5:4). Although the individual Christian is warned not to sit in judgment upon another Christian (1 Cor. 4:5), the assembled church does indeed have this right and responsibility. (See also Mt. 18:20.)

4. The procedure in discipline. The New Testament lays down various specific steps in exercising discipline.

a. First step—"Go and tell the person his fault between thee and him alone" (Mt. 18:15). At this initial stage the spirit of Galatians 6:1 should prevail:

"Brethren, if a man be overtaken in a fault, ye which are spiritual, restore such a one in the spirit of meekness; considering thyself, lest thou also be tempted."

b. Second step—"If he will not hear thee, then take with thee one or two more, that in the mouth of two or three witnesses every word may be established" (Mt. 18:16).

c. Third step—"If he shall neglect [literally, disregard] to hear them, tell it unto the church" (18:17).

d. Fourth step—"If he neglect to hear the church, let him be unto thee as a heathen man and a publican" (Mt. 18:17). "Yet count him not as an enemy, but admonish him as a brother" (2 Thess. 3:15).

5. The seriousness of discipline.

"To deliver such an one unto Satan for the destruction of the flesh, that the spirit may be saved in the day of the Lord Jesus" (5:5).

What does it mean to do this? The Greek word for *destruction* here is *olethros,* a reference to the act of spoiling or marring something. Apparently Paul was saying this, "If this fellow is having so much fun in his sin, then remove him entirely from your fellowship and let Satan kick him around a little. Let him taste what it's like to face a hostile world without the prayers and ministry of a local church!"

Thus, when a local Bible-believing church removes a person like this, it literally fulfills the divine command of Job 2:6:

"And the Lord said unto Satan, Behold, he is in thine hand; but save his life."

Paul was forced to take this drastic action against two other individuals at a later date.

"Holding faith, and a good conscience: which some having put away concerning faith have made shipwreck: of whom in Hymenaeus and Alexander; whom I have delivered unto Satan, that they may learn not to blaspheme" (1 Tim. 1:19, 20).

6. The reasons for discipline.
   a. To help the man find his way back to God. It worked, too, for the fellow did indeed repent (see 2 Cor. 2:6-8).
   b. To keep the sin from spreading throughout the church. "Know ye not that a little leaven leaveneth the whole lump?" (5:6.) Leaven is a type of evil in the Bible (see Mt. 16:6; Gal. 5:9).
   c. To maintain the standards of Christ to a watching world. (See Acts 5:1-13.) One reason why the church has so little influence in the world today is because the world has so much influence in the church.

7. The extent of discipline.
   a. Negative—the church is not to judge the outside world; that is, to nag and rebuke unbelievers for their smoking, card playing, etc., but rather to lead them to Christ.
   b. Positive—the New Testament lists at least three types of individuals to be dismissed from the fellowship of a local church.
      (1) A constant troublemaker (Prov. 6:19; 2 Thess. 3:6, 11, 14).
      (2) An immoral person (as seen here in 1 Cor. 5).
      (3) A heretic (one who denies the virgin birth, etc.; Titus 3:10; Rom. 16:17, 18).

G. They were fragmenting the body of Christ.
   "Dare any of you, having a matter against another, go to law before the unjust, and not before the saints?" (6:1).
   1. In God's sight, this action was improper (6:1-7).
      a. Because of whom they were judging at that time, namely other believers. Paul is not condemning the court system here as an institution, for he himself had used it (see Acts 25:10, 11). What he is saying is that feuding believers should use every means at their disposal to settle their legal difficulties and not drag each other before pagan courts.
      b. Because of whom they would judge at a future time, namely the world and angels! (See Dan. 7:18, 22; Mt. 19:28; 2 Pet. 2:4; Jdg. 6; Rev. 20:4.)
   2. In God's sight, this action was illegal (6:8). "Nay, ye do wrong, and defraud, and that your brethren." In other words, they not only refused to settle their petty problems out of court, but now planned to cheat one another in court!
   3. In God's sight, this action was intemperate (6:9-14).
      "All things are lawful unto me, but all things are not expedient; all things are lawful for me, but I will not be brought under the power of any" (6:12).
      By "all things" Paul, of course, refers to all moral things. The word "expedient" is sumphero in the Greek and literally means, "to bring together." (See Jn. 11:50 and 16:7 where the same word is used.)
      Verses 9 and 10 have bothered some Christians, but here the emphasis is not on the phrase "shall not inherit" in verse 9, but rather the phrase "and such were some of you" in verse 11. (See Eph. 2:1, 2; 5:5; Titus 3:3.)
   4. In God's sight, this action was immoral (6:15-20).
      a. Because our bodies are the members of the Savior. Paul asks:
         "Shall I then take the members of Christ, and make them the members of a harlot? God forbid" (6:15).
      The believer is thus forbidden to unscripturally involve himself in the systems of this present evil world. The child of God is to *flee* from unlawful involvements in sex (1 Cor. 6:18; 2 Tim. 2:22), silver (1 Tim. 6:10, 11) and society (1 Cor. 10:14).
      b. Because our bodies are the temples of the Spirit (6:19, 20). (See also 1 Pet. 1:18, 19.)

III. The Reply (7—16). Paul writes concerning a request made from the church in Corinth. In these remaining chapters Paul answers at least six of their questions. Question Number 1: What about marriage? (chapter 7).
   A. Various difficulties with this chapter. Of all Paul's epistles, containing some 100 chapters, no section has been more misunderstood than the one here in 1 Corinthians 7. Some have read these verses and erroneously concluded that:
      1. Paul hated marriage in general and women in particular. This is totally false. (See his statements in Heb. 13:4; Eph. 5:25-33; 1 Tim. 4:1-5; 5:14.)
      2. Paul taught that unmarried individuals could always serve God better than married ones. Again, this is simply not true! (See 1 Tim. 3:2, 11.)
      3. Paul admits to being uninspired in this chapter. The following four verses are offered as "proof" of this.
         a. "But I speak this by permission, and not of commandment" (v. 6).
         b. "But to the rest speak I, not the Lord" (v. 12).
         c. "Now concerning virgins I have no commandment of the Lord; yet I give my judgment" (v. 25).
         d. "But she is happier if she so abide, after my judgment: and I think also that I have the Spirit of God" (v. 40).

4. Let us now briefly examine each of these passages:
   a. The word "permission" is literally "a joint opinion" and may refer to the inspired "considered opinion" of both Paul and Sosthenes. At any rate, Paul was simply saying that this opinion was not a command but rather a divine suggestion. (For a comparable passage, see Rom. 12:1.)
   b. Verse 12 can be explained by comparing it with verse 10. In verse 10, Paul quotes a command uttered by the Lord Jesus himself while he was upon the earth (see Mt. 19:6). But here is a group situation (one partner saved, one unsaved) to whom Jesus issued no command while on earth, but now does so in heaven through Paul's inspired pen.
   c. The same answer given for verse 12 also applies here in verse 25.
   d. The word "think" here could also be translated "persuaded" (1 Cor. 7:40). (See Mt. 22:42; 1 Cor. 8:2 where the same Greek word is used. See also Paul's statements in 1 Tim. 3:16; 1 Cor. 2:4.)

B. Various solutions to this chapter. Chapter 7 of 1 Corinthians is, admittedly, a difficult one. However, several facts should be kept in mind.
   1. Chapters 7-16 contain Paul's *answers* to some questions asked him by the Corinthian church. We must therefore remember that *only* the answers are recorded here. It is entirely possible that a knowledge of the nature of their *questions* would shed much light on his answers! However, for some reason God did not choose to preserve this information for us.
   2. Certain verses in this chapter indicate that the apostle is here giving particular advice to govern a particular church at a particular time in history. Some of these verses apply to all Christians, but some do not. (See especially 7:7, 26, 29, 35.)

C. Various groups in this chapter. It is addressed to three classes of people.
   1. Those marriages in which both partners are saved (7:1-11).
      a. Both partners are to render "due benevolence" to each other (7:3). This phrase is translated "good will" in Ephesians 6:7.
      b. Neither partner is to "defraud" the other (7:5). The context shows this to be in regard to sexual rights. Paul reminds both that neither has "power" over his own body. This is to say that separate ownership of oneself does not exist in the marriage state. No partner may rightfully quote the words of Matthew 20:15 to the other partner: "Is it not lawful for me to do what I will with mine own?" Thus to defraud (deny) sexual rights one to the other is to invite being tempted by Satan. (See also 2 Cor. 2:11; 1 Pet. 5:8.)
   2. Those marriages in which one partner is unsaved (7:12-24). Paul has one basic admonishment here and it is that the believer should stay with the unbeliever if at all possible. This should be done:
      a. Because the very institution of marriage is ordained of God (7:14).
      b. Because the unbelieving partner is "sanctified" by the believing spouse (7:14). This is simply to say the Holy Spirit can work more easily in the life of an unsaved husband if there is in that home the example of a godly and faithful wife.
   3. Those unmarried individuals (7:25-40).
      a. There are times when it may be best to remain unmarried for awhile (7:27).
      b. There are times when an individual can do more for Christ single than married (7:32-34).
      c. At *all* times a believer should seek God's perfect will, concerning whether to marry or remain single. (See especially 7:23, 24.)

Question Number 2: What about Christian liberty? (8—10). As a child of God I have been liberated from the law of sin and of death. Does this imply I can now do any lawful thing I desire? Paul answers this by citing three examples.

A. A current example—the Corinthian believers (8:1-13).
   1. Their confusion: There were many pagan temples at Corinth upon which tons of animal meat was sacrificed daily. Some of this meat was consumed by the priests while the remainder was placed on sale in the various city meat markets. It probably sold cheaper, due to its previous usage. Some believers, spotting a bargain, were apparently buying this meat for their table. Other Christians were shocked at this. Here, then, was the question: Should saved people eat meat which had previously been sacrificed to idols?
   2. Paul's correction:
      "But meat commendeth us not to God: for neither, if we eat, are we the better; neither, if we eat not, are we the worse" (8:8). See also Mt. 15:11; Rom. 14:17).
      "As concerning therefore the eating of those things that are offered in sacrifice to idols, we know that an idol is nothing in the world, and that there is none other God but one" (8:4).
      "Howbeit there is not in every man that knowledge" (8:7).
   3. The conclusion:
      "Wherefore, if meat make my brother to offend, I will eat no flesh while the world standeth, lest I make my brother to offend" (8:13).
      Paul then admonishes the Corinthian believers:
      a. To attempt becoming a stepping stone (8:1). "Knowledge puffeth up, but charity edifieth." The Greek word for "edifieth" is *oikodomeo* and speaks of that action which builds a house (see Jn. 2:20; Mt. 7:24). The New Testament teaches that:
         (1) The believer is to build himself up (see Jude 1:20).

(2) He is to build up other Christians (see 1 Thess. 5:11; Rom. 14:19).

(3) He is to help build up the entire church (see 1 Cor. 14:12).

The word "puffeth up" is found but seven times in the Greek New Testament, six of which are used here in 1 Corinthians. (See 4:6, 18, 19; 5:2; 8:1; 13:4.) In every case it is associated with worldly knowledge. Note the following three quotes:

"And if any man think that he knoweth anything, he knoweth nothing yet as he ought to know" (1 Cor. 8:2).

"Knowledge is that act of passing from a state of unconscious ignorance to a state of conscious ignorance" (L.S. Chafer).

"I do not know what I may appear to the world; but to myself I seem to have been like a boy playing on the sea shore and diverting myself, now and then finding a smoother pebble or a prettier shell than ordinary, while the great ocean of truth lay all undiscovered before me" (Sir Isaac Newton).

b. To avoid becoming a stumbling stone.

"But take heed lest by any means this liberty of yours become a stumblingblock to them that are weak" (8:9).

The Scriptures declare that a Christian is responsible to at least five classes of people.

(1) the world in general (Mt. 5:16; 1 Tim. 3:7)

(2) his or her immediate family (Eph. 5 and 6)

(3) all believers in general (Eph. 4:32)

(4) weaker believers in particular (Rom. 14:1; 15:1) He is thus to be careful:

(a) Lest he cause a weaker brother to defile his conscience (1 Cor. 9:7, 10).

(b) Lest he cause a weaker brother to sin against Christ (8:12).

(5) the local church (1 Tim. 3:10; 1 Cor. 10:32)

c. How, though, can one decide upon that which is right or wrong? The Bible declares an action may be wrong on two counts.

(1) Because of an *inherent* sin factor. There are certain things that are always wrong because they go against the very grain of God's holiness. Such things would be murder, lying, adultery, stealing, idolatry, etc.

(2) Because of an *acquired* sin factor. There are certain things that, in and by themselves, are harmless, but through time and custom have acquired the taint of being evil. An example of this would be the wearing of cosmetics, once considered sinful

but now (if modestly applied) generally accepted among Christian women.

This first factor is *character* sin, and the second can be referred to as *reputation* sin. The child of God is to avoid both.

B. A personal example—the Apostle Paul (9:1-27). In those verses Paul points out that no one had more right to exercise Christian liberty than did he.

1. The basis of his rights.

a. He was an apostle and had seen Christ (9:1; see also Acts 9:17; 1 Cor. 15:8).

b. He had founded their own church there in Corinth (9:1, 2).

2. The extent of his rights.

a. To eat and drink any lawful thing (9:4).

b. To marry and enjoy a family life (9:5).

c. To expect those churches he founded to support him (9:6-11, 13, 14). This was both reasonable and proper because:

(1) A *soldier* is paid to fight, and he was a warrior for Christ.

(2) A *husbandman* enjoys the fruit of the grapes, and he had planted many vineyards.

(3) A *shepherd* partakes of the milk of his flock, and Paul had nurtured many lambs.

(4) A *priest* ministering in holy matters lived off the things in the Temple and Paul was God's special minister to the Gentiles. "Even so hath the Lord ordained that they which preach the gospel should live of the gospel" (9:14).

3. The employment of his rights.

"Nevertheless . . . we have not used this power; but suffer all things" (9:12).

Paul then explains why he chose not to employ all his rights:

"Lest we should hinder the gospel of Christ. . . . Lest any man should make my glorying void. . . . So that I may make the gospel of Christ without charge, that I abuse not my power in the gospel . . . . that I might gain the more . . . I am made all things to all men, that I might by all means save some" (9:12, 15, 18, 19, 22).

His life was a living testimony of these statements. Thus:

a. In ministering to the Jews (9:20). He circumcises Timothy in Lystra because the Jews in that area knew the young man's father was a Greek. He later preached in Hebrew before a mob of Jews in Jerusalem (see Acts 16 and 22).

b. In ministering to the Gentiles (9:21). He stands to preach, a practice of the Gentiles, while delivering a message in Antioch. He quotes from Greek literature when addressing some Greeks on Mars' Hill (see Acts 13 and 17).

c. In ministering to the weak believers (9:22). He refrains from eating meat and commands that weak Christians everywhere be received into full fellowship (see 1 Cor. 8:13; Rom. 14:1; 15:1).

    d. In ministering to himself:

"But I keep under my body, and bring it into subjection: lest that by any means when I have preached to others, I myself should be a castaway" (9:27).

Here the word "castaway" is *adokimos* in the Greek, meaning "disapproved." The same word is found in 2 Timothy 2:15.

C. An Old Testament example—the nation Israel (10:1-33).

  1. The narration (10:1-10). No other nation in the history of the world had enjoyed the liberty, freedom, and blessing of God as did Israel, yet she abused all this and was judged by God.

    a. The review of this freedom (10:1-4).

      (1) God guided them by his glory cloud (Ex. 13:21, 22).

      (2) He led them across the Red Sea (Ex. 14:22).

      (3) He sent them food and water (Ex. 16:15; 17:6).

    b. The rebellion against this freedom (10:5-10).

      (1) They were guilty of idolatry (Ex. 32:3, 4).

      (2) They were guilty of immorality (Ex. 32:6; Num. 25:1).

      (3) They were guilty of insubordination (Num. 21:5).

    c. The removal of this freedom.

      (1) Their idolatry was punished by the sword (Ex. 32:28).

      (2) Their immorality was punished by a sickness (Num. 25:9). Note: A contradiction has been imagined here, for Moses tells us 24,000 were killed in this plague (Num. 25:9), while Paul says 23,000 died (1 Cor. 10:8). However, the apostle limits his number to those who "fell in one day," while Moses gives the total death figure for the entire period.

      (3) Their insubordination was punished by serpents (Num. 21:6).

  2. The application (10:11-13). What was God's purpose in recording all these morbid events concerning Israel's failures? How do they apply to us today? The answer is clear and concise:

"Now all these things happened unto them for examples: and they are written for our admonition, upon whom the ends of the world are come" (10:11).

    a. They are recorded to admonish us concerning our weakness.

"Wherefore let him that thinketh he standeth take heed lest he fall" (10:12; see also 1 Cor. 9:27; Gal. 6:1).

Especially important here are Paul's two words, "Take heed." In the Bible God commands us to take heed concerning:

      (1) our speech (Ps. 39:1)

      (2) overconfidence (1 Cor. 10:12)

      (3) being deceived by others (Mt. 24:4)

      (4) our Christian liberty (1 Cor. 8:9)

      (5) our ministry to others (Acts 20:28; 1 Tim. 4:16; Col. 4:17)

    b. They are recorded to assure us concerning God's strength.

"There hath no temptation taken you but such as is common to man; but God is faithful, who will not suffer you to be tempted above that ye are able; but will with the temptation also make a way of escape, that ye may be able to bear it" (10:13).

It will prove helpful at this point to review the biblical doctrine of temptation.

      (1) The definition of temptation.

        (a) To entice to do evil. Satan tempted Christ and tempts Christians this way. (See Mt. 4:1; Heb. 2:18; 4:15; Jas. 1:13.)

        (b) To test or prove with the intent of making one stronger. God "tempts" his children this way. (See Gen. 22:1.)

        (c) To presume upon the goodness of God. Israel tempted God in this manner, as believers can today. (See Ps. 78:18; Acts 5:9; Mt. 4:7.)

      (2) The source of temptation.

        (a) The world. (See Mt. 13:22; Jn. 16:33; Titus 2:12; 2 Pet. 1:4; Gal. 1:4; 2 Tim. 4:10; 1 Jn. 2:15.)

        (b) The flesh. (See Mt. 26:41; Rom. 7:18; Gal. 5:19-21.)

        (c) The devil. (See 1 Chron. 21:1; Eph. 4:27; 6:11; 1 Tim. 3:6, 7; Jas. 4:7.)

      (3) The purpose of temptation. As we have already seen, God allows temptation to strengthen his children. It is therefore indeed *not* a sin to be tempted! (See Jas. 1:2, 12; 1 Pet. 1:6, 7.)

      (4) The victory over temptation. (See 1 Pet. 4:19; 2 Pet. 2:9.)

  3. The summation (10:14-33). After three pointed examples concerning Christian rights and responsibilities, the apostle concludes with the following in regard to eating meat sacrificial to idols.

    a. A believer is not to become a meat-market spy when buying his food in a worldly store (10:25).

    b. He is not to become a kitchen detective when eating his food in an unsaved home (10:27).

    c. He is, however, to refrain from eating idol meat if warned against by a weaker believer (10:28).

    d. He is always to remember that he shares the same body of Christ with all believers (10:16, 17).

    e. He is never to give offense "to the Jews, nor to the Gentiles, nor to the church of God" (10:32).

Question Number 3: What about church conduct? (11).

A. Rules concerning clothing (11:1-16). Nowhere in the Bible are we given the divine length for a woman's hemline or for that of a man's haircut. However, in this chapter Paul does list certain principles which should govern the personal appearance of believers, especially while in the house of God.

1. The man's appearance
   a. The man is to wear nothing on his head. This is to demonstrate:
      (1) His relationship to his Savior. "The head of every man is Christ" (11:3). "For a man indeed ought not to cover his head, forasmuch as he is the image and glory of God" (11:7).
      (2) His relationship to his spouse. "The head of the woman is the man" (11:3). "The woman is the glory of the man" (11:7).

      Thus, no male in a Christian service should wear a hat, as did the Roman priests and Jewish Rabbis, who wore a head covering called a tallis. The custom began due to a misinterpretation of Moses and his veil. (Compare Ex. 34:33 with 2 Cor. 3:13.)
   b. The man is to wear his hair shorter than that of the woman. Two factors may have led to this divine rule.
      (1) Because of the general implications. "Doth not even nature itself teach you, that, if a man have long hair, it is a shame unto him?" (11:14). In Paul's day long hair on a male was associated with being effeminate. Today it suggests (to some extent) rebellion against authority.
      (2) Because of a specific holy vow. This was the Old Testament Nazarite vow. (See Num. 6:1-22; Jdg. 13:4, 5; 1 Sam. 1:11; Lk. 1:15.)

2. The woman's appearance.
   a. She is to wear her hair long to demonstrate:
      (1) Her submission to her husband.
      (2) Her standards to the world. Harlots and slaves wore their hair short in Paul's time. A Christian woman was decidedly neither!
   b. She is to wear something upon her head, "because of the angels" (11:10). Some believe this passage suggests church members may share their pews with angels! (See Ps. 138:1; Eph. 3:10; 1 Tim. 5:21; Heb. 1:14; 1 Pet. 1:10, 12.)

B. Rules concerning communion (11:17-34).
   1. The person (11:23-25). From these verses we learn that:
      a. The most important fact involved in the table of the Lord is the Lord of the table. It is his table. He sanctioned it and suffered for it.
      b. Paul did not receive his information concerning the historical details of the Last Supper from any of the apostles who attended, but from Christ himself. This was also true concerning the details surrounding the preaching, death, and resurrection of the Savior. (See 1 Cor. 15:3; Acts 20:35; Gal. 1:11, 12.)
   2. The perversion (11:17-22). At their communion service the fickle and self-centered Corinthians had so involved themselves in the supper that they had totally ignored both other saints and the Savior. As a result some (the well-to-do) would stuff themselves with food and drink while others (the poor) would go away hungry. Many things happened on that momentous night in the upper room, but here in 11:23, Paul singles out Jesus' betrayal by Judas, which may have been a hint describing what the Corinthians were actually doing also.

      It should be noted that Paul does not teach here (11:22) against having fellowship banquets in a church basement. He does, however, seem to limit the communion service itself to that of bread and wine. The little phrase "in remembrance of me" (11:25) is important at this point, for it refutes two additional errors concerning the Lord's Supper.
      a. The bread and wine are memorials and not sacraments. The first (a memorial) takes place because one has already obtained grace, while the second (a sacrament) is performed to obtain grace.
      b. The bread and wine are symbolic in nature and not changed into anything. The Roman Catholic doctrine of transubstantiation teaches that the elements are actually changed by the priest on the altar into the body and blood of Christ.
   3. The purpose (11:26, 28). At the Lord's table we are told to:
      a. Look backward. "For as often as ye eat this bread, and drink this cup, ye do show the Lord's death."
      b. Look inward. "But let a man examine himself."
      c. Look forward. "Till he come."
   4. The partakers. What group is invited to this table? The Lord's Supper is only for believers, but it includes all believers. This would appear to be the case, whether they happened to be baptized members of a given local church or not.
   5. The prerequisites. Two kinds of individuals are forbidden to partake: the unsaved and the unclean. John the apostle (who attended the Lord's first table service) has given sound advice to aid both kinds of individuals here. To the unsaved, he offers John 3:16, and to the unclean (backslidden Christian), he extends 1 John 1:9.
   6. The penalty (11:29, 30).
      "For he that eateth and drinketh unworthily, eateth and drinketh damnation to himself, not discerning the Lord's body. For this cause many are weak and sickly among you, and many sleep."

Here several words deserve our consideration.

a. Unworthily. The word here is an adverb and not an adjective. Paul does not say, "If anyone who is not worthy partakes," but rather, "If anyone partakes in an unworthy manner."

b. Damnation. In the Greek this is the word *krima*, and should here be translated "judgment." (See Rom. 11:33; 1 Pet. 4:17 and Rev. 20:4 where the same word appears.) This judgment may be manifested in a twofold manner:

(1) Through physical sickness (11:30).

(2) Through physical death—"and many sleep." The Greek word for sleep here is *koimao* and refers to physical death. (See Jn. 11:11, 12; Acts 7:60; 1 Cor. 15:6, 18, 20, 51.)

7. The plea (11:31-34).

Question Number 4: What about spiritual gifts? (12—14).

A. The definition of a spiritual gift. It is a supernatural ability given by Christ through the Holy Spirit to the believer at the moment of his salvation. At this point two distinctions shall be made:

1. The distinction between the gift of the Spirit and the gifts from the Spirit. The *gift* occurred at Pentecost when the Spirit was sent by the Father as promised by Christ (Acts 1:4-8). The *gifts* are given today.

2. The distinction between spiritual gifts and human talents. Talent is a human and natural ability given at birth. A gift is supernatural and is received at one's second birth.

3. The distinction between a spiritual gift and an official office. Dr. Charles Ryrie has written the following:

"Many think of a spiritual gift as an office in the church which only a privileged few can ever occupy. Or else they consider gifts so out of reach of the ordinary believer that the best he can hope for is that someday he might happen to discover some little gift and be allowed to exercise it in some small way. Both of these conceptions are wrong. A spiritual gift is primarily an ability given to the individual. This means that the gift is not a place of service, for the gift is the ability, not where that ability is exercised. The gift of pastor, for instance, is usually associated with the office or position a person may occupy in the pastorate. But the gift is the ability to give shepherd-like care to people, regardless of where this is done. Of course, the man who occupies the office of a pastor should have and exercise the gift of pastor, but so should a dean of men in a Christian school. Indeed (though this may seem shocking at first), why shouldn't a Christian woman be given the gift of pastor to use among the children in her neighborhood or in her Sunday school class or as dean of women? Now I did not say that women should become pastors of churches to do the preaching and take the leadership of the people. I think that the office or position of the pastorate is reserved for men only; but this does not mean that the gift or the ability cannot be given to women." (*Balancing the Christian Life*, pp. 95, 96.)

B. The extent of spiritual gifts.

1. Each believer possesses at least one spiritual gift (see 1 Cor. 7:7; 12:7, 11; Eph. 4:7, 1 Pet. 4:10).

2. No believer possesses all the gifts (see 1 Cor. 12:29, 30).

C. The purpose of spiritual gifts. To glorify the Father (Rev. 4:11), and to edify both the believers and the church (Eph. 4:12, 13).

To illustrate these two purposes, Paul uses an analogy of the human body here in 1 Corinthians 12 and declares the following:

1. All believers are a part of Christ's body (12:12-14).

2. Not all believers (as the members of a human body) have the same working function within that body (12:14).

3. Each member is equally important to God (12:18).

4. Each member needs the other members. Thus:

a. The foot is not to say, "Because I am not the hand, I am not of the body" (12:15).

b. The ear is not to say, "Because I am not the eye, I am not of the body" (12:16). This attitude is one of envy.

c. The eye is not to say to the hand, "I have no need of thee" (12:21).

d. The head is not to say to the feet, "I have no need of thee" (12:21). This attitude is one of pride.

5. All members both suffer and rejoice with the other members (11:26).

D. The abuse of spiritual gifts.

1. Not using those gifts imparted to us (see 1 Tim. 4:14; 2 Tim. 1:6).

2. Attempting to use those gifts not imparted to us (see Num. 16:1-3; Acts 8:18-20).

E. The number of the spiritual gifts. In three main passages Paul lists some eighteen separate gifts. (These passages are: Rom. 12:6-8; 1 Cor. 12:4-10, 28; Eph. 4:7, 8.)

F. The time element of the spiritual gifts. There is scriptural evidence to indicate that God has placed his gifts into two time categories:

1. The sign gifts (given during the first century and then phased out). These are the gifts of apostleship, prophecy, healing, miracles, knowledge, tongues, and the interpretation of tongues. The sign gifts were given to meet a twofold need:

a. To validate the authority of the apostles and early Christians. (See 2 Cor. 12:12; Heb. 2:4; Rom. 15:19; Jn. 3:2; 20:30, 31; Mt. 10:5-8.) Those gifts used to accomplish this purpose would be healing and miracles. (See also Mt. 10:5-8; 11:4, 5.)

b. To disseminate new revelation and divine information. Those gifts used to accomplish this end would be prophecy, knowledge, and tongues.

However, with the completion of the canon in A.D. 95, the sign gifts became unnecessary. (See 2 Tim. 3:14-17; 2 Pet. 1:16-21.)

Note: From these two remarkable passages we learn that:

c. The written Word of God by itself can and does provide every conceivable need for the man of God in the work of God.

d. This written account is better fitted to accomplish God's work today than even that of Christ's miraculous transfiguration as witnessed by Simon Peter.

2. The stationary gifts (given on a permanent basis throughout church history). These are the gifts of wisdom, faith, discerning of spirits, helps, teaching, exhortation, giving, ruling, showing of mercy, evangelism, and that of the pastor-teacher.

G. The description of the spiritual gifts.

1. The gift of apostleship. (See Eph. 4:11; 1 Cor. 12:28.) A reference to certain men called by Christ himself (Jn. 15:16) and endowed with special authority to function as the official "charter members" of the early church.

a. The requirements. According to both Peter (Acts 1:22) and Paul (1 Cor. 9:1) one must have seen the resurrected Christ to qualify.

b. The number:
(1) the original twelve (Lk. 6:13)
(2) Matthias (Acts 1:26)
(3) Paul (Rom. 1:1)
(4) Barnabas (Acts 14:14; Gal. 2:9)
(5) James (1 Cor. 15:7; Gal. 1:19)

2. The gift of prophecy. (See Rom. 12:6; 1 Cor. 12:10; 14:1, 3-6; Eph. 4:11.) The supernatural ability to receive and transmit a revelation from God, especially that which concerns itself with future events. (See Mt. 13:14; 2 Pet. 1:20, 21; Rev. 1:3; Acts 11:27, 28; 21:10, 11.)

3. The gift of miracles (see 1 Cor. 12:28). A supernatural ability to perform those events outside and beyond the realm of nature. In the Bible there are three periods which witnessed a great outpouring of miracles.

a. During the time of Moses and Joshua
b. During the time of Elijah and Elisha
c. During the time of Christ and his apostles.

4. The gift of healing (see 1 Cor. 12:9, 28, 30). A supernatural ability to cure human ills, whether of physical, mental, or demonic origin. As has been previously stated, there is evidence that the sign gifts were phased out during the latter part of the first century at the completion of the scriptural canon. Paul decidedly possessed the gift of healing (Acts 14:10; 16:18; 19:12; 20:10; 28:8, 9), but for some reason did not employ it during the final months of his ministry. (See Phil. 2:26, 27; 1 Tim. 5:23; 2 Tim. 4:20.)

Here it should be emphasized that the removal of the sign gifts does *not* mean God cannot and will not supernaturally heal a believer today. I believe it does mean, however, that the *gift* of healing through an *individual* has ceased. God's present-day plan for healing is found in James 5:14-16.

5. The gift of knowledge (see 1 Cor. 12:8; 13:8). There is some uncertainty about the nature of this gift. It is mentioned but twice. Most likely it is connected with the gift of prophecy and may involve the ability to receive and record parts of God's Word.

6. The gift of tongues. There is perhaps no other single subject in the entire Bible which has generated more heat, hatred, confusion, and division than that of tongues. This sad situation existed in Corinth even as Paul wrote to them. Today the charismatic movement is literally sweeping the world of Christendom.

Views on tongues. There is no universal agreement in either the camp of the pro- or anti-tongues movement concerning the exact nature of New Testament tongue-speaking.

a. The unlearned human language view: This view says that all accounts of New Testament tongue-speaking refer to the same event, that is, the supernatural ability to suddenly speak in previously unlearned human languages. The following are arguments for this view.

(1) Because of the usage of the same vocabulary. Dr. John Walvoord writes: "The use of identical terms in reference to speaking with tongues in Acts and First Corinthians leaves no foundation for a distinction. In all passages, the same vocabulary is used: *laleo* and *glossa*, in various grammatical constructions. On the basis of the Greek and the statement of the text, no distinction is found." (*The Holy Spirit*, p. 183)

It is also pointed out that the word *glossa* is found fifty times in the Greek New Testament. Of these: sixteen times it refers to the physical organ (see Jas. 3:5); once it refers to flames of fires (Acts 2:3); thirty-three times it refers to human language.

(2) Because the word rendered "interpret" in 1 Corinthians 14:13 is *diermeneuo*, and literally means "to translate." Out of the twenty-one occasions where this word is found in the New Testament, eighteen definitely refer to translation. (See Acts 9:36.)

(3) Because of the description of the events at Pentecost (Acts 2:6-11). Also, Peter says (Acts 11:15) that the tongue-speaking he witnessed at Caesarea was identical to that at Pentecost.

(4) Because ecstatic gibberish could not be a sign to unbelievers (1 Cor. 14:22).

(5) Because Jesus warned against tongue-babbling. The Greek words *batta* and *logeo* in Matthew 6:7 refer to the act of babbling, or speaking without thinking.

(6) Because Paul offers no redefinition or clarification of Acts 2 when he writes 1 Corinthians 14.

(7) Because Paul quotes Isaiah 28:11, 12 in 1 Corinthians 14:21, which reference is definitely connected to human language. A brief background of Isaiah 28 is needed here.

   (a) In 721 the northern kingdom was destroyed.

   (b) Isaiah warns the southern kingdom (Judah) that the same thing will happen to them unless they repent.

   (c) He is ridiculed by a group of drunken priests and prophets who disbelieve the warning.

   (d) Isaiah responds by saying that since they would not listen when God spoke to them in *Hebrew*, they *would* when he spoke to them (through enemy soldiers) in the *Assyrian* language. (See also Moses' words in Deut. 28:15–68, especially v. 49.) (Concerning Titus's invasion in A.D. 70, see Jeremiah 5:15.) Thus, to be addressed in other tongues was a symbol of judgment to the Hebrew mind.

(8) Because of the advent of higher criticism in the eighteenth and nineteenth centuries. In other words, the critics of the Bible rejected the miracle of speaking unlearned human languages and advocated the ecstatic utterance view, thus identifying biblical tongues with other ancient mystery religions.

b. The nonhuman (angelic?) ecstatic utterance view: This position holds that the language spoken is decidedly nonearthly; rather, it is heavenly in its structure. Arguments supporting this view are:

(1) The tongue-speaking disciples at Pentecost are accused of drunkenness (Acts 2:13), a charge which would not be made if the language was of an earthly nature.

(2) Paul says tongues would cease (1 Cor. 13:8), a ridiculous statement if the gift is simply speaking unlearned human language.

(3) Because of Paul's words in 1 Corinthians 14:2, "For he that speaketh in an unknown tongue speaketh not unto men, but unto God: for no man understandeth him."

(4) Paul had the gift of tongues (1 Cor. 14:18), yet he could not understand the human speech of Lycaonia in Acts 14:11.

(5) Because of the distinction made between mind and spirit in 1 Corinthians 14:14, 15. Here it is claimed (by some) that God uses the *mind* to reveal certain revelation in human language and employs the *spirit* of man to reveal other information in nonhuman language.

(6) Because of the phrase "other tongues" in Acts 2:4. This is a translation of the Greek word *heteros*, which means, "another of a different kind." (See also Gal. 1:6, 7.)

(7) Because of the suggestion in 1 Corinthians 13:1, "Though I speak with the tongues of men and of angels." Note: Here it may be asked what kind of language do angels speak? While talking to men on earth they have been known to speak both Hebrew (Gen. 19) and Greek (Lk. 1). Even during their heavenly ministry they spoke languages which were understandable to men. (See Isa. 6; Rev. 4–5.)

c. The purpose of tongues.

  (1) Negative:

   (a) It was not for church edification (1 Cor. 14:4, 19).

   (b) It was not for personal edification. Here an objection may be raised, for does not Paul say, "He that speaketh in an unknown tongue edifieth himself"? He does indeed (1 Cor. 14:4). However, a problem is seen here. If tongues are for personal edification, and if the church house was filled with tongue-speaking (as the context definitely indicates—14:23), then how do we explain that, apart from the church at Laodicea (Rev. 3:14–18), this group at Corinth was the most carnal and confused church in the entire Bible? No gift was to be used for personal edification in a selfish way. Here Paul may actually be *rebuking* them for their unscriptural usage of this gift.

   (c) It was not to demonstrate Spirit baptism. (This erroneous concept is totally refuted in 1 Cor. 12:13; Rom. 6:3, 4; Col. 2:9–12; Eph. 4:5; Gal. 3:27, 28.)

  (2) Positive:

   (a) To validate the authority of the apostles and early Christians.

   (b) To demonstrate God's judgment upon unbelieving Israel.

   (c) To serve as a sign to seeking (but lost) individual Jews.

   (d) To impart new truths prior to the completion of the canon. When Paul wrote 1 Corinthians

14 there were but three New Testament books in existence (James, 1 and 2 Thessalonians). There was no written record available concerning such important issues as:

The doctrine of the church (later discussed in Ephesians and Colossians).

The doctrines of justification, sanctification, and glorification (later written about in Romans).

The doctrine of apostasy (Jude).

Christian forgiveness (Philemon).

The priesthood of Christ (Hebrews).

The life of Christ (the four Gospels).

Practical Christian service (1 and 2 Peter).

Christian love (as found in 1, 2, and 3 John).

Advice to pastors and deacons (as discussed in 1 and 2 Timothy and Titus).

In view of all this, no believer could quote or claim the blessed truth in 2 Timothy 3:16, 17, simply because it had not yet been written.

d. The regulation of tongues (1 Cor. 14).

(1) Speaking in tongues helps no Christian in the church (1 Cor. 14:3, 4).

(2) Speaking in a known tongue helps all (1 Cor. 14:3, 4).

(3) The tongue, like a musical instrument, is useless unless heard and distinctly understood (14:7).

(4) This distinction can sometimes mean the difference between life and death (14:8).

(5) Although Paul is said to have spoken in tongues (14:18), there is no stress on this whatsoever during any of his testimonies (as before Felix and Agrippa) or missionary trips. While he did not forbid the speaking in tongues, neither did he especially encourage it, for he realized that not all Christians, even during those days, had the gift. (See 1 Cor. 12:30; 14:39.)

(6) Paul taught that in the church, preaching (both foretelling and forthtelling) was 2,000 times to be preferred over tongues (14:19).

(7) Unanimous tongue-speaking was forbidden (14:23).

(8) Preaching, not tongues, is God's method for saving the lost (14:24, 25).

(9) Tongue-speaking was to be limited in number, with each to speak in turn (14:27).

(10) Women were absolutely forbidden to speak in tongues (14:34). In 1 Corinthians 11:3-10 Paul allowed a woman to speak in her natural and native tongue, but here he forbids her to use foreign tongues.

(11) All things in God's house are to be done decently and in order (14:40).

7. The gift of interpretation of tongues (see 1 Cor. 12:10). This was the supernatural ability to clarify and translate those messages spoken in tongues.

8. The gift of wisdom (see 1 Cor. 12:8). The supernatural ability to apply rightfully both human and divine knowledge.

9. The gift of spirit discernment (see 1 Cor. 12:10; 1 Jn. 4:1). The ability to distinguish between demonic, human, and divine works. Both Peter (Acts 8:23) and Paul (Acts 13:10; 16:16-18) possessed this gift.

10. The gift of giving (see Rom. 12:8). The ability to accumulate and give large sums of money to God's glory (see Acts 4:32-37; Gal. 4:15; Phil. 4:10-18; 2 Cor. 8:1-5. See also Lk. 21:1-4.)

11. The gift of exhortation (see Rom. 12:8). The ability to deliver challenging words (Prov. 25:11). Various New Testament people had this gift:

a. Barnabas (Acts 11:22, 24).

b. Judas (not Iscariot) and Silas (Acts 15:32).

c. "True yoke fellow" (Phil 4:3).

12. The gift of ministering (or of helps) (see Rom. 12:7; 1 Cor. 12:28; Eph. 4:12). The ability to render practical help in both physical and spiritual matters.

a. Dorcas had this gift (Acts 9:36-39).

b. Phoebe had this gift (Rom. 16:1, 2).

13. The gift of mercy-showing (see Rom. 12:8). The ability to minister to the sick and afflicted.

14. The gift of ruling (or administrating; see Rom. 12:8; 1 Cor. 12:28). The ability to organize, administer, and promote either people or projects. (See Titus 1:4, 5; see also the book of Nehemiah.)

15. The gift of faith. The Bible describes three kinds of basic faith:

a. Saving faith—given to all repenting sinners (Acts 16:31; Rom. 4:5; 5:1; 10:17).

b. Sanctifying faith—available to all believers (Gal. 2:20; 3:11; 5:22; Eph. 6:16; Rom. 1:17; Heb. 10:38).

c. Stewardship faith—given to some believers (Rom. 12:3; 1 Cor. 12:9). This is the *gift* kind of faith and is a supernatural ability to believe and expect great things from God.

16. The gift of teaching (see Rom. 12:7; 1 Cor. 12:28; Eph. 4:11). The ability to communicate and clarify the details of the Word of God.

a. Apollos had this gift (Acts 18:24, 25).

b. Aquila and Priscilla possessed it (Acts 18:26).

17. The gift of evangelism (see Eph. 4:11). The supernatural ability to point sinners to Christ

and to burden Christians about soul-winning. All believers, of course, are to witness for Christ, whether they have this special gift or not (2 Tim. 4:5). Philip, among others in the book of Acts, had this gift (Acts 8:5–12, 26–40).

18. The gift of pastor-teacher (see Eph. 4:11). The supernatural ability to preach and teach the Word of God and to feed and lead the flock of God (see 1 Pet. 5:1–4; Acts 20:28). This is the only "double-portion" gift of the eighteen gifts. Thus all teachers are not called to be pastors, but all pastors are to be teachers!

H. The indispensable ingredient in the spiritual gifts (13). The eighteen spiritual gifts may be thought of as God's divine bricks to be used in the construction of his holy and earthly temple. In the analogy, *charity* (love) serves as the "celestial cement" which holds the bricks together.

Paul ends the previous chapter with the words: "But covet earnestly the best gifts: and yet show I unto you a more excellent way" (12:31). Thus, chapter 13 is this more excellent way.

It should furthermore be noted that God used Paul, the mighty theologian, to write the greatest poem on love in the history of the world. Each Christmas season the National Safety Council issues the following admonition: "If you drink, don't drive, and if you drive, don't drink, because alcohol and gasoline don't mix." Some have erroneously concluded the same about theology and love. But God has commanded that they are *not* to be separated (see Rev. 2:1–4). Theology without love leads to dead orthodoxy. Love without theology leads to outright heresy.

1. The importance of love (13:1–3). Without love:
   a. The gift of tongues is as noisy brass and clanging cymbal.
   b. The gift of prophecy becomes nothing.
   c. Understanding all mysteries is of no avail.
   d. Possessing all knowledge is useless.
   e. Exercising mountain-moving faith is vanity.
   f. Giving away one's goals counts for naught.
   g. Sacrificing one's own body is totally without merit.
2. The impeccability of love (13:4–7).
   a. It suffereth long. Love is patient.
   b. It is kind. Love is not harsh or abrupt.
   c. It envieth not. Love is not jealous. It does not desire to deprive another of what he has.
   d. It vaunteth not itself. Love does not brag.
   e. It is not puffed up. Love is not arrogant.
   f. It does not behave itself unseemly. Love does not act unbecomingly.
   g. It seeketh not its own. Love is not self-centered.
   h. It is not provoked. Love is good-natured.
   i. It thinketh no evil. Love does not meditate upon evil inflicted by another, as if to avenge it.
   j. It rejoiceth not in iniquity. Love does not find joy in evil.
   k. It rejoiceth in the truth. Love finds its joy in goodness.
   l. It beareth all things. Love covers (literally) all things.
   m. It believeth all things. Love is not suspicious.
   n. It hopeth all things. Love is unconquerable.
3. The indestructibility of love (13:8–13).
   a. Contrasted with prophecy, tongues, and knowledge, love is continuous (13:8).
   b. Contrasted with faith and hope, love is supreme (13:13). Note: Paul does not say here that love is more durable than faith and hope, but simply is greater. In some divine manner we will continue using these three virtues even in heaven. Love is greater because:
      (1) It is the root of faith and hope.
      (2) It is for others, while faith and hope are largely personal.
      (3) It is the very essence of God himself.

Question Number 5: What about the resurrection? (15). Without doubt this chapter (along with Rom. 8) simply must be considered as one of the two greatest in the entire Word of God. Here we have the oldest written account of Christ's resurrection.

A. The prominence of the resurrection (15:1–4).
   1. The fact of Christ's resurrection: "He rose again" (15:4).
   2. The time element in Christ's resurrection: "the third day" (15:4). There are two main theories concerning this phrase.
      a. He was crucified on Friday. The well-known custom of the Jews was to count a part of a day as a whole day. Thus he would be in the tomb a portion of Friday (from 3:00 P.M. to 6:00 P.M.), all day Saturday, and a part of Sunday.
      b. He was crucified on Wednesday. If Matthew 12:40 is to be taken at face value, then Wednesday is the only day which would allow the necessary three full days and nights.
   3. The reason for the resurrection of Christ: "for our sins" (15:3). Christ was not a martyr dying for his faith, but a Savior dying for our sins. He did *not* say, "I am finished," but, "It is finished." All three persons in the Trinity were involved in his death and resurrection.
      a. The Father (Jn. 3:16; Acts 2:24).
      b. The Son (Jn. 10:11, 18).
      c. The Holy Spirit (Heb. 9:14; Rom. 1:4).
   4. The results of the resurrection of Christ: "By which also ye are saved" (15:2).

B. The proof of the resurrection (15:5–11). Paul refers to four here.
   1. The New Testament records ten main appearances of the resurrected Savior. They are to:
      a. Mary Magdalene (Jn. 20:11–18).
      b. The other woman (Mt. 28:9, 10).
      c. The two disciples (Lk. 24:13–32).
      d. Simon Peter (Lk. 24:33–35).

e. Ten apostles (Lk. 24:36-43). (Note: These five appearances were made on the first resurrection day.)

f. Eleven apostles (Jn. 20:26-31).

g. Seven apostles (Jn. 21:1-14).

h. Five hundred disciples (1 Cor. 15:6).

i. James, his half-brother (1 Cor. 15:7).

j. Eleven apostles on Mt. Olivet (Lk. 24:44-49; 1 Cor. 15:7). (These last five were made during the forty-day period.)

2. Paul then refers to his personal visit by the Savior. In fact, Jesus appeared to the apostle on at least five occasions.

a. On the road to Damascus (Acts 9:1-9; 22:6-11; 26:12-19).

b. In Corinth (Acts 18:9).

c. In Jerusalem (Acts 23:11).

d. On a sinking ship (Acts 27:23).

e. At an undesignated spot (perhaps Lystra; 2 Cor. 12:1-4).

C. The priority of the resurrection. (15:12-19, 29-32). In Paul's day, as in our own time, there were those who denied the subject of the resurrection in general. Today unbelievers advocate various theories to explain away his resurrection.

1. The fraud theory—that the disciples invented the whole thing.

2. The swoon theory—that Christ merely fainted on the cross and later revived in the coolness of the tomb.

3. The vision theory—that the disciples only imagined they saw him.

4. The spirit theory—that only his spirit arose. This is refuted by Luke 24:39.

5. The heart theory—that he was only resurrected in the hearts of his friends.

But in these verses Paul declares that if the doctrine of the resurrection is denied, then one is forced to nine horrible conclusions.

6. All gospel-preaching has been and will continue to be completely useless.

7. All gospel preachers become notorious liars and fools.

8. All living Christians are still in their sins.

9. All departed Christians are in hell.

10. All reason and purpose for life itself is destroyed.

11. The Savior himself is still rotting in some Middle-Eastern grave.

12. Christian service becomes a farce. Note verse 29:

"Else what shall they do which are baptized for the dead, if the dead rise not at all? Why are they then baptized for the dead?"

The verse has been somewhat of a problem.

a. Negative: Whatever its meaning, it does *not* support the totally unscriptural practice of the Mormon church of living people being baptized by proxy for dead people. To die lost is to forever remain lost. (See Lk. 16:19-31; Heb. 2:3; Rev. 22:11.)

b. Positive. Inasmuch as baptism refers to identification, Paul may be saying here that, if there be no resurrection of the dead, then what is the purpose of living believers picking up the standard left by departed believers?

13. Suffering for Christ is stupid and senseless (15:30, 32).

14. The sensual way is the only way. "Let us eat and drink; for tomorrow we die" (15:32).

D. The parade of the resurrection (15:20-28).

"But now is Christ risen from the dead, and become the first fruits of them that slept" (15:20).

In this verse Paul refers to the third of seven Jewish feasts mentioned in Leviticus 23. It was called the Feast of the First Fruits. Note:

1. On the first day, selected delegates marked out the spot in the grain field from which the sheaf would be cut.

2. On the second day the sheaf was cut and brought into the Temple.

3. On the third day it was presented to the Lord as a pledge sample.

Note now verses 23, 24:

"But every man in his own order: Christ, the firstfruits; afterward they that are Christ's at his coming. Then cometh the end, when he shall have delivered up the kingdom to God, even the Father; when he shall have put down all rule and all authority and power."

The Greek word for "order" here is *tagma*, a military term referring to troops in order of rank, as in a parade. Thus we see:

a. The resurrection of Christ (Mk. 16:2-8; Mt. 28:5-8; Lk. 24:1-8). His resurrection leads the parade, for it was the very first of its kind. The miracle Christ performed upon Lazarus (Jn. 11), for example, was not true resurrection, but simply the restoration of a dead mortal body to that of a living mortal body. Lazarus *died* again at a later date. But ultimate resurrection carries with it immortality.

b. The rapture resurrection. "Afterwards they that are Christ's at his coming" (15:23). These "troops" follow behind the head of the parade. (See 1 Cor. 15:53; 1 Thess. 4:16.)

c. The premillennial resurrection of Old Testament and tribulation saints. "Then cometh the end" (15:24; see Jn. 5:24; Dan. 12:2; Rev. 20:5, 6).

E. The plea of the resurrection (15:33, 34).

1. We are to "awake to righteousness, and sin not" (15:34).

2. We are to avoid those who deny the resurrection (15:33).

F. The pattern of the resurrection (15:35-38).

"But some men will say, How are the dead raised up? and with what body do they come?" (15:35).

Paul does not describe the method used by God in raising the dead, but instead gives a glorious example, a grain of wheat (15:37).

Several thrilling conclusions can be drawn from this illustration.

1. The old body, like a grain of wheat, has no power to change itself. Only God can grow wheat and raise the dead.
2. The old body, like a grain of wheat, must die to be changed.

   "Verily, verily I say unto you, except a corn of wheat fall into the ground and die, it abideth alone; but if it die, it bringeth forth much fruit" (Jn. 12:24).

   Thus death does not suppress the grain, but simply releases it.
3. The new body, like a grain of wheat, does not lose its identity. Both still retain a certain likeness of the former state (1 Cor. 13:12).

G. The perfection of the resurrection (15:39-49).
1. Attributes of the old sinful body:
   a. Sown in corruption (a perishable body) (15:42).
   b. Sown in dishonor (in a tinsel world) (15:43).
   c. Sown in weakness (subject to disease and infirmities) (15:43).
   d. Sown a natural body (bounded by the laws of nature) (15:44).
2. Attributes of the new sinless body:
   a. Raised in incorruption (an imperishable body) (15:42).
   b. Raised in glory (in a perfect world) (15:43).
   c. Raised in power (not subjected to disease and infirmities) (15:43).
   d. Raised a spiritual body (not bounded by the laws of nature) (15:44).

   In verse 44 Paul writes, "There is a natural body and there is a spiritual body." What is the difference? Consider a book with a sheet of plain white paper stuck inside it. In this illustration the book is man's body and the paper sheet is his spirit. Down here the book "bosses" the spirit. It has the final say. This is the natural body, governed by the physical laws of gravity and time.

   But now take the white sheet out of the book and wrap it around the book like a cover. Now the sheet (spirit) is on top. It has the final say. This is the spiritual body, which is unaffected by the physical laws of gravity or time, but enjoys the blessings of eternity.

   In verses 39-41 Paul suggests that the new spiritual body is as superior to the old natural body as:
   (1) The human body is to those of animals (15:39).
   (2) The heavens are to the earth (15:40).
   (3) The sun is to the moon (15:41).

H. The promise of the resurrection (15:50-53).
   "Behold, I shew you a mystery; we shall not all sleep, but we shall all be changed, in a moment, in the twinkling of an eye, at the last trump; for the trumpet shall sound, and the dead shall be raised incorruptible, and we shall be changed. For this corruptible must put on incorruption, and this mortal must put on immortality" (15:51-53).

We now note the following phrases:
1. "I shew you a mystery." What mystery? Let us suppose you began reading the Bible in Genesis chapter 1, and read through 1 Corinthians chapter 14. If you stopped your reading here, you would already have learned about many important facts, such as creation, man's sin, the flood, Bethlehem, Calvary, the resurrection, and the existence of heaven and hell.

   But you would be forced to conclude that a Christian could get to heaven only after physically dying. You would, of course, note the two exceptions of Enoch (Gen. 5:24) and Elijah (2 Ki. 2:11), but apart from these it would be clear that believers have to travel the path of the grave to reach the goal of glory.

   But now the secret is out, and here it is: Millions of Christians will someday reach heaven without dying. "Behold I show you a mystery; we shall not all sleep, but we shall all be changed" (1 Cor. 15:51). This, then, is the mystery of the rapture.
2. "We shall all be changed." Observe the word *all*. The Bible does not support a partial rapture theory.
3. "In the twinkling of an eye." This occurs as quickly as a gleam of light shines in the eye, about one fifth of a second.
4. "This corruptible must put on incorruption." This is a reference to the bodies of departed believers.
5. "This mortal must put on immortality." This is a reference to the bodies of living believers. (See also 1 Thess. 4:16, 17.)

I. The purpose of the resurrection (15:54).
   "So when this corruptible shall have put on incorruption and this mortal shall have put on immortality, then shall be brought to pass the saying that is written, Death is swallowed up in victory" (see Isa. 25:8; Hosea 13:14).

   The purpose of the resurrection should be clearly understood by Christians. It is a tragic fact that our world is indeed a materialistic one. Materialism has been defined as the art of knowing the *price* of everything, but the *value* of nothing. On occasion, however, in an attempt to avoid this philosophy, believers go to the other extreme and conclude God is *only* interested in non-physical matters. This sad error is sometimes seen in our churches in the separate deacon and trustee boards. Often this attitude imposes a higher moral standard upon deacons than trustees, for, after all, aren't the "spiritual" matters more important than the "physical" areas? The truth of the matter is that God is *very much* interested in physical things, especially in the bodies of Christians! (See 1 Cor. 6:19, 20; 2 Cor. 6:16; Eph. 5:28, 29; Rom. 12:1, 2.)

   What, then, is the purpose of the resurrection? Among other things, it is to destroy man's final enemy. Paul has already written: "The last enemy that shall be destroyed is death" (15:26). Mankind has five natural enemies:
1. The world (Gal. 1:4; 1 Jn. 2:15; Jas. 4:4).

2. The flesh (Rom. 7:18; 8:8; Gal. 5:17; 1 Jn. 2:16).
3. The devil (Mt. 13:39; Eph. 6:11).
4. Spiritual death (Jn. 5:24; 8:51; Rev. 2:11).
5. Physical death (Ps. 55:4; Heb. 2:15).

J. The power of the resurrection (15:55-58).

"O death, where is thy sting? O grave, where is thy victory? But thanks be to God, which giveth us the victory through our Lord Jesus Christ" (15:55, 57).

Here death is pictured as a venomous serpent and its poisonous fang is sin. But someday God will destroy both the rattler and its fang. Note also the twin phrases:

1. "O death, where is thy sting?" This may refer to living believers who will escape physical death at Christ's coming.
2. "O grave, where is thy victory?" This may refer to departed believers, whose bodies the graves will be forced to give up.

Paul ends this great, grand, and glorious chapter with the following:

"Therefore, my beloved brethren, be ye stedfast, unmoveable, always abounding in the work of the Lord, for as much as ye know that your labour is not in vain in the Lord" (15:58).

Question Number 6: What about the collection? (16)

A. The location of the offering: "the churches of Galatia" (16:1). The mention of "the churches of Galatia" is to be noted. The New Testament never speaks of the church in or of a country or province. The official "state church" institution in various countries today is totally foreign to the Bible.

B. The source of the offering: "Let everyone of you" (16:2). The local church is to be supported by its members. We note also it was to be done by everyone!

C. The time of the offering: "The first day of the week" (16:2). This is, of course, on Sunday. (See Mk. 16:2, 9; Lk. 24:1; Jn. 20:1, 19; Acts 20:7.)

D. The amount of the offering: "As God hath prospered" (16:2). Although no actual proportion is laid down, it is unthinkable that a believer would give less to God than that amount he tips a waitress in a restaurant.

E. The purpose for the offering: "For the saints" (16:1). This was a special collection to meet the immediate need of the poor in Jerusalem (see Rom. 15:26).

F. The custodians of the offering: "Whomsoever ye shall approve" (16:3). In all financial affairs of an assembly, the responsibility should be in the hands of more than one brother, to avoid the slightest suspicion of improper handling.

Paul concludes this epistle with some personal comments and a powerful challenge.

A. The comments:
1. He was planning to visit them again soon (16:5-9).
2. Timothy also might drop by (16:10, 11).
3. He had urged Apollos to come there, but God had willed otherwise for the time being (16:12).

4. He urges them to follow the spiritual advice of Stephanos, his first convert while in Greece (16:15, 16).
5. Various believers in Ephesus with Paul sent their welcome (16:17-20).

B. The challenge:

"Watch ye, stand fast in the faith, quit you like men, be strong. Let all things be done with charity" (16:13, 14).

"If any man love not the Lord Jesus Christ, let him be anathema. Maranatha!" (16:22).

1. The word "anathema" means "fitted for destruction." (See Rom. 9:3; Gal. 1:8, 9.)
2. The word "maranatha" means "the Lord comes." (See Phil 4:5; Jas. 5:7, 8; Rev. 1:7; 3:11.)

2 CORINTHIANS

INTRODUCTION:

1. Paul had organized the Corinthian church during his second missionary trip (Acts 18:1-18).
2. During his third missionary trip he visits the church (2 Cor. 12:14; 13:1).
3. He sends Titus to Corinth to organize a special love offering for the poverty-stricken saints in Jerusalem (1 Cor. 16:1; 2 Cor. 8:6, 10). Titus does this and returns to Paul.
4. He writes a letter (now lost) to the Corinthian church (1 Cor. 5:9). We must keep in mind that God did not choose to inspire *all* of the many letters written by Paul and the early church leaders, but *only* those which are found in the New Testament.
5. After a while, Paul writes another letter. This letter is the 1 Corinthians of the New Testament. There were two basic reasons why he wrote this epistle.
   a. To rebuke the church. Paul had heard about some tragic church factions from the household of Chloe, living there in Corinth (1 Cor. 1:11).
   b. To instruct the church. Paul was visited while in Ephesus by a three-man delegation from Corinth, who handed him a list of questions the church had for him (1 Cor. 16:17; 7:1; 8:1; 12:1).
6. He then sends Timothy to Corinth with this New Testament epistle (1 Cor. 4:17; 16:10, 11).
7. Timothy returns to Paul in Ephesus. This young preacher was apparently unable to straighten things out in Corinth (2 Cor. 1:1).
8. Paul desires to visit the church himself at this time, but is unable to (2 Cor. 1:15-17).
9. He soon hears that his work there is being undermined by some legalistic Judaizers who had just arrived from Jerusalem (2 Cor. 3:1; 10:12-18; 11:22, 23).
10. He now sends Titus back to Corinth with orders to straighten things out and meet him in Troas (2 Cor. 2:12, 13; 7:6, 7).
11. Paul comes to Troas, but does not find Titus. After a restless period, he departs to Macedonia (2 Cor. 2:12, 13).
12. Here he meets Titus, who gives him a favorable report concerning the work at Corinth.
13. With great relief Paul writes 2 Corinthians (2 Cor. 7:5-15).
14. Paul is finally able to visit Corinth at a later date for a period of three months. Here he writes the epistle of Romans (Acts 20:3; Rom. 15:22-29; Rom. 16:1, 23).

I. Consolation (1:1-7).
  A. The source of consolation and comfort:
   "The Father of our Lord Jesus Christ, the Father of mercies and the God of all comfort" (1:3).

   These two words "comfort" and "consolation" (both from the same Greek word) are found ten times in the first seven verses. Paul begins this epistle (1:3) and ends it (13:11) with the word *comfort*. Each member of the blessed Trinity is a Comforter.
   1. The Father (2 Cor. 1:3; Isa. 49:13).
   2. The Son (Jn. 14:1; Isa. 61:2; 2 Thess. 2:16).
   3. The Holy Spirit (Jn. 14:16, 26; 15:26; 16:7).

   The word for "comfort" comes from two Greek words, *para* (alongside) and *kaleo* (to call). Thus, to comfort a person is to answer his call and walk alongside him to cheer him, guide him, and, on occasion, to defend him. The Greek word was often used in a court of justice to denote a legal counsel for the defense, one who would plead another's cause. (See 1 Jn. 2:1.) Furthermore, it may be stated that God is the *only* source of real comfort. The prophetical prayer of Jesus on the cross as given in the Psalms (69:20) perfectly describes all human beings:
   "Reproach hath broken my heart; and I am full of heaviness: and I looked for some to take pity, but there was none; and for comforters, but I found none."
  B. The need for consolation and comfort:
   ". . . Our trouble, which came to us in Asia, that we were pressed out of measure, above strength, insomuch that we despaired even of life" (1:8).

   There are two types of people which need no comfort: the unborn and the dead (see Isa. 40:1, 2). C. H. Spurgeon said that the preacher who prepared his sermons for heartbroken people would never lack for an audience!
  C. The purpose for consolation and comfort:
   "Who comforteth us in all our tribulation, that we may be able to comfort them which are in any trouble, by the comfort wherewith we ourselves are comforted of God. For as the sufferings of Christ abound in us, so our consolation also aboundeth by Christ" (1:4, 5).

   There is a vast difference between *sympathy* and *empathy*. The first can only say, "I'm sorry for what you're going through," but the second may state, "I know exactly what you're going through." Thus, because our Lord Jesus suffered all things, he is able to offer all comfort. (See Heb. 2:14-18; 4:14-16.) The Savior not only comforts us, but suffers with us (Acts 9:4). The spiritual rule therefore in this: The more one suffers for Christ, the more comfort he receives from Christ, and the more ability he has to comfort other suffering people. Thus, he who has suffered much speaks many languages.

II. Explanation (1:8—2:13).
  A. Concerning his travail in Asia (1:8-14). Paul writes: "We were pressed out of measure, above strength, insomuch that we despaired even of life" (1:8). Just what he suffered here is not known. Some have connected this epistle with the account in Acts 19:23-41, but it would seem Paul himself did not suffer at that time. (See 1 Cor. 15:32 for a possible clue.) At any rate, it was so severe that he resigned himself to dying at that time.
   "But we had the sentence of death in ourselves, that we should not trust in ourselves, but in God which raiseth the dead" (1:9).

   Paul's faith here was like that of Isaac and Abraham in the Old Testament. (See Gen. 22:1-18; Heb. 11:17-19.)
   Note his testimony concerning God's threefold deliverance.
   1. "Who delivered us." This speaks of justification.
   2. "Who doth deliver." This speaks of sanctification.
   3. "Who will yet deliver." This speaks of glorification.
  B. Concerning his trip to Macedonia (1:15-24; 2:1, 12, 13).
   1. What he meant to do:
    "I intended at first to come to you, that you might twice receive a blessing; that is, to pass your way into Macedonia, and again from Macedonia to come to you, and by you to be helped on my journey to Judea" (1:15, 16, *NASB*).
   2. Why he did not do this:
    "But I determined this with myself, that I would not come again to you in heaviness" (2:1). (See also 1:23.)
    Paul realized he would be running into a hornet's nest if he visited them at this time, and thus felt led to come at a later date.
   3. Where he finally did go:
    "When I came to Troas to preach Christ's gospel, and a door was opened unto me of the Lord, I had no rest in my spirit, because I found not Titus my brother; but taking my leave of them, I went from thence into Macedonia" (2:12, 13).
  C. Concerning his tears in Ephesus (2:2-11).
   "For out of much affliction and anguish of heart I wrote unto you with many tears" (2:4).
   Here Paul apparently refers to the epistle of 1 Corinthians.
   1. He had wept over the fact that the church had once refused to rebuke the unrepentant man in 1 Corinthians 5.
   2. He now wept over the fact that the church refused to restore the repentant man.
    "Ye ought rather to forgive him and comfort him, lest perhaps such a one should be swallowed up with overmuch sorrow" (2:7).
    This restoration was to be forthcoming immediately:
    "Lest Satan should get an advantage of us: for we are not ignorant of his devices" (2:11).

III. Demonstration (of the Nature of the Ministry) (2:14—6:18).
  A. It is a triumphant one (2:14-16).
   "Now thanks be unto God, which always causeth us to triumph in Christ, and maketh

manifest the savour of his knowledge by us in every place" (2:14).

God has thus assured us of victory—total victory:

1. Regardless of when the problems arise (always).
2. Regardless of where the problems arise (every place).

To illustrate this promise, Paul likens the ministry to a victorious Roman parade during which the successful general (in this case, Jesus) would lead both *conquerors* (the saved) and *captives* (the unsaved) to their respective destinies.

From the marching parade there would ascend a sweet fragrance, caused by the burning of incense. Thus:

"To the one [captives] we are the savour of death unto death; and to the other [conquerors] the savour of life unto life" (2:16).

In the Old Testament, Joseph's presence was death for the baker (Gen. 40:16-19, 22) but life for the butler (Gen. 40:9, 13, 21).

Likewise, in the New Testament, Jesus' presence meant death for the unrepentant thief (Lk. 23:39), but life for the repentant thief (Lk. 23:40-43).

B. It is a sincere one.

"For we are not as many, which corrupt the word of God: but as of sincerity" (2:17). (See also 2 Pet. 3:14-16.)

The word "corrupt" means to peddle, or to huckster the Word of God. All false prophets are guilty of this horrible sin. (See Acts 8:18-23.)

C. It is an approved one (by God himself).

"Do we . . . need . . . or some others, epistles . . . or letters of commendation" (3:1-3).

The legalistic Judaizing teachers who plagued Paul's work carried formal and impressive letters of introduction from Jerusalem. Prior to his conversion, the apostle had done this also (Acts 9:2). But now all that had changed. Paul's letters were:

1. Personal ("Ye are our epistle").
2. Permanent ("written in our hearts").
3. Public ("known and read of all men").

D. It is a dependent one (3:4, 5).

"Not that we are sufficient [qualified] of ourselves . . . but our sufficiency is of God" (3:5; see also Phil. 4:13).

E. It is a superior one (3:6-18).

1. Its program is superior. Here Paul refers back to Exodus 34:29-35, when Moses came down from Mt. Sinai after receiving the Ten Commandments. On that occasion his face had so radiated God's glory that he wore a veil, lest he frighten the waiting Israelites below. But in 2 Corinthians 3:13 Paul explains that the real reason for the veil was to prevent Israel from viewing the glory which soon faded away.

But God's new program is superior to that of Moses, for its glory, as given by Christ, will never fade away. (See also Mt. 26:28; Heb. 8:8, 13.)

"For the letter [Old Testament law program] killeth, but the spirit [New Testament grace program] giveth life" (3:6).

2. Its power is superior.

"Now the Lord is that spirit; and where the spirit of the Lord is, there is liberty" (3:17).

3. Its purpose is superior. God's new ministry in Christ has a twofold purpose:
   a. Concerning Israel—to remove the veil of unbelief from their eyes (3:16).
   b. Concerning the church—to transform Christians into the very image of Christ (3:18).

F. It is an open one (4:1-4).

1. An open walk—"But have renounced the hidden things of dishonesty, not walking in craftiness."
2. An open talk—"Nor handling the word of God deceitfully; but by manifestation of the truth, commending ourselves to every man's conscience in the sight of God" (4:2).

This openness is vital, for sinners are already blinded by Satan and should not suffer additional harm by the lives of deceitful Christians.

G. It is a Christ-honoring one (4:5-7). Paul's message highlighted three points.

1. Who Christ is—he is the Lord.
2. What Christ has done.

"For God, who commanded the light to shine out of darkness [a reference to creation], hath shined in our hearts [a reference to redemption], to give the light of knowledge of the glory of God" (4:6).

3. Why Christ chose to use Paul.

"But we have this treasure in earthen vessels, that the excellency of the power may be of God, and not of us" (4:7).

H. It is a suffering one (4:8-18).

1. The nature of this suffering:
   a. troubled on every side
   b. perplexed
   c. persecuted
   d. struck down
   e. perishing outer man
2. The victory through this suffering:
   a. troubled, yet not distressed
   b. perplexed, but not in despair
   c. persecuted, but not forsaken
   d. struck down, but not destroyed
   e. renewed inner man
3. The results from this suffering. Immediate blessings:
   a. The privilege of bearing the marks of Christ (4:10, 11; see also Rom. 8:36; 1 Cor. 15:31; Gal. 6:17; Col. 1:24).
   b. The privilege of sharing the glory of God (4:15).
   Future blessings:
   c. resurrection (4:14)
   d. rewards (4:17, 18; see also Mk. 10:28-30)

I. It is a confident one (5:1-9).

1. That God will give to us (in the future) ". . . an house not made with hands, eternal in the heavens" (5:1).
2. That God has given to us (at the present ". . . the earnest [literally, the seal or pledge] of the Spirit" (5:5).

Note Paul's supreme confidence as a result of these facts: "Therefore we are *always* confident"

(5:6). The word "always" appears many times in Paul's writings.

concerning prayer (Rom. 1:9)
concerning praise (1 Cor. 1:4)
concerning work (1 Cor. 15:58)
concerning obedience (Phil. 2:12)

J. It is a compelling one (5:10-17). There were at least four compelling factors which prompted Paul to work day and night in the ministry.

1. The judgment of the saints (5:10). Note:
   a. The plan—we must
   b. The parties—all
   c. The presence—appear
   d. The place—before the judgment seat of Christ
   e. The purpose—that everyone may receive the things done in his body, according to that he hath done, whether it be good or bad.

   Note: Here the word "bad" should be rendered "worthless." (Compare with 1 Cor. 3:12.)

2. The need of sinners (5:14).
   "Because we thus judge, that if one died for all, then were all dead."

   Paul thus desired that his converts would be able to give a good accounting to Christ on that day.

3. The "terror of the Lord" (5:11). Here Paul refers to that reverential fear and respect which should characterize every believer. Paul's fear was that he might displease his glorious Master.

4. The love of Christ (5:14). "For the love of Christ constraineth us."

5. The power of the gospel (5:17).
   "Therefore if any man be in Christ, he is a new creature: old things are passed away; behold, all things are become new." This glorious gospel therefore assures us that:
   a. We might live *through* Christ (1 Jn. 4:9).
   b. We might live *with* Christ (1 Thess. 5:10).
   c. We might live *for* Christ (2 Cor. 5:15).

K. It is a representative one (5:18-21).
   "Now then we are ambassadors for Christ."
   1. An ambassador must be a citizen of the state he represents (Phil. 3:20; Col. 3:1, 2).
   2. He is chosen (Jn. 15:16).
   3. He is called home before war is declared (1 Thess. 1:10; 5:1-10).

L. It is a blameless one (6:1-8).
   "Giving no offence in anything, that the ministry be not blamed: But in all things approving ourselves as the ministers of God" (6:3, 4).
   The Bible has suffered much at the hands of its friends.

M. It is a paradoxical one (6:9, 10). A paradox is an apparent (but not real) contradiction. The Bible lists a number of paradoxes. Note:
   1. To find one's life, yet to eventually lose it (Jn. 12:25).
   2. Of losing one's life, yet to eventually find it.
   3. Of being unknown, yet to be well known (2 Cor. 6:9).
   4. Of dying, yet to possess life (2 Cor. 6:9).

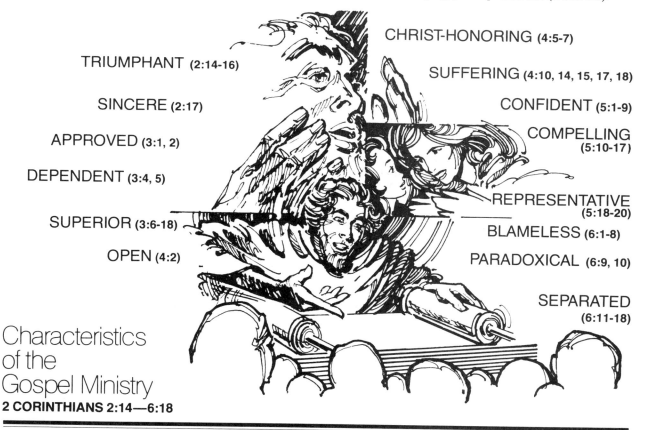

TRIUMPHANT (2:14-16)

SINCERE (2:17)

APPROVED (3:1, 2)

DEPENDENT (3:4, 5)

SUPERIOR (3:6-18)

OPEN (4:2)

CHRIST-HONORING (4:5-7)

SUFFERING (4:10, 14, 15, 17, 18)

CONFIDENT (5:1-9)

COMPELLING (5:10-17)

REPRESENTATIVE (5:18-20)

BLAMELESS (6:1-8)

PARADOXICAL (6:9, 10)

SEPARATED (6:11-18)

Characteristics
of the
Gospel Ministry
2 CORINTHIANS 2:14—6:18

5. Of being sorrowful, yet always rejoicing (2 Cor. 6:10).
6. Of dying, yet able to give life (Jn. 12:24).
7. Of being poor, yet making many rich (2 Cor. 6:10).
8. Of having nothing, yet possessing all things (2 Cor. 6:10).
9. Of hearing words that cannot be expressed (2 Cor. 12:4).
10. Of being strong when one is weak (2 Cor. 12:10).
11. Of knowing the love of Christ which surpasses knowledge (Eph. 3:19).
12. Of seeing the unseen (2 Cor. 4:18).

N. It may be concluded that the very life and ministry of our blessed Savior was itself a divine paradox.
1. He hungered, yet fed multitudes (Mt. 4:2; Jn. 6).
2. He thirsted, yet is the water of life (Jn. 19:28; 4:14).
3. He wearied, yet is our rest (Jn. 4:6; Mt. 11:29, 30).
4. He paid tribute, yet is the King of kings (Mt. 17:27; Rev. 19:16).
5. He prayed, yet hears our prayers (Mk. 14:32-42; Jn. 14:13, 14).
6. He wept, yet dries our tears (Jn. 11:35; Rev. 21:4).
7. He was sold for thirty pieces of silver, yet redeems the world (Mt. 26:15; 1 Pet. 1:18, 19).
8. He was led as a sheep to the slaughter, and yet is the Good Shepherd (Isa. 53:7; Jn. 10:11).
9. He was put to death, yet raises the dead (Jn. 19:33).

O. It is a separated one (6:11-18).
1. The nature of this separation.
"Be ye not unequally yoked together with unbelievers" (6:14).
This separation would no doubt cover such human ties as:
a. marriage
b. certain business partnerships
c. unsound ecclesiastical organizations
2. The logic of this separation. "What fellowship hath . . ."?
a. righteousness with lawlessness
b. light with darkness
c. Christ with Belial
d. believers with unbelievers
e. the temple of God with idols
3. The rewards of this separation (6:17, 18).
"Wherefore come out from among them, and be ye separate, saith the Lord, and touch not the unclean thing; and I will receive you, and will be a Father unto you, and ye shall be my sons and daughters, saith the Lord Almighty."

IV. Gratitude (7).
A. Paul's gratitude to God upon seeing Titus (7:1-6).
"For, when we were come into Macedonia, our flesh had no rest, but we were troubled on every side; without were fightings, within

were tears. Nevertheless God, that comforteth those that are cast down, comforted us by the coming of Titus."
B. Paul's gratification to God upon hearing Titus (7:7-16). Titus reported he had been well received by the Corinthian church and that Paul's previous letter had produced the desired twin goals of remorse and repentance over their various sins. One such sin was the case of a man living in sexual sin with his stepmother (1 Cor. 5). Paul exclaims:
"For godly sorrow worketh repentance to salvation not to be repented of: but the sorrow of the world worketh death" (7:10).

V. Solicitation (8, 9).
A. The examples of giving:
1. The Macedonians (8:1-5).
a. They gave by surrendering themselves to the Lord. "But first gave their own selves to the Lord" (8:5).
b. They gave by submitting themselves to the apostle. ". . . and unto us by the will of God" (8:5).
c. They gave by sharing their resources with the needy saints. "The fellowship of the ministering to the saints" (8:4).
2. The Son:
"For ye know the grace of our Lord Jesus Christ, that, though he was rich, yet for your sakes he became poor, that ye through his poverty might be rich" (8:9).
Thus, our Lord became what he was not (poor), that we might become what we were not (rich). The sinless Son of God became the Son of man that sinful sons of men might become the sons of God.
3. The Father: "Thanks be unto God for his unspeakable gift" (9:15).
B. The spirit of giving:
"For if there be first a willing mind, it is accepted according to that a man hath, and not according to that he hath not" (8:12).
"Every man according as he purposeth in his heart, so let him give; not grudgingly, or of necessity: for God loveth a cheerful giver" (9:7).
C. The grace of giving:
"Therefore, as ye abound in everything, in faith, and utterance, and knowledge, and in all diligence, and in your love to us, see that ye abound in this grace also" (8:7).
Jesus' words to the rich young ruler would apply here (Mk. 10:21).
D. The results of giving:
1. The facts.
a. Giving will bring blessing to the needy.
"For the administration of this service . . . supplieth the want of the saints" (9:12).
b. Giving will bring blessing to the giver.
(1) He will be provided for by the Lord.
"And God is able to make all grace abound toward you; that ye, always having all sufficiency in all things, may abound to every good work" (9:8).

"Now he that ministereth seed to the sower both minister bread for your food, and multiply your seed sown, and increase the fruits of your righteousness; being enriched in every thing to all bountifulness, which causeth through us thanksgiving to God" (9:10, 11).

    (2) He will be prayed for by the needy. "While they also, by prayer on your behalf, yearn for you because of the surpassing grace of God in you" (9:14, *ASV*).

c. Giving will bring blessing to God.

"For the ministry of this service is not only fully supplying the needs of the saints, but is also overflowing through many thanksgivings to God. Because of the proof given by this ministry they will glorify God" (9:12, 13, *NASB*).

2. The proof.

  a. Proof from the *world* of God:

"But this I say, He which soweth sparingly shall reap also sparingly; and he which soweth bountifully shall also reap bountifully" (9:6). (See also Prov. 22:9; Gal. 6:7, 9).

  b. Proof from the *Word* of God:

"As it is written, He that had gathered much had nothing over; and he that had gathered little had no lack" (8:15; see also Ex. 16:18).

"As it is written, He hath dispersed abroad; he hath given to the poor: his righteousness remaineth forever" (9:9; see also Ps. 112:9).

VI. Vindication (10:13). Paul pens these final chapters to defend his apostleship. Both his good name and ministry were being undermined by some jealous Judaizers who had probably come to Corinth from Jerusalem to stir up trouble. In his able defense he demonstrates that:

A. His methods were superior to those of his accusers.

1. He did not use carnal and fleshly weapons of war in fighting Satan (10:3-5).

"For the weapons of our warfare are not carnal, but mighty through God to the pulling down of strongholds" (10:4).

In defeating Satan one cannot fight fire with fire. He must use blood (see Rev. 12:11).

2. He did not employ a fake system of measurement (10:12, 17, 18).

"For we dare not . . . compare ourselves with some that commend themselves by themselves, and comparing themselves among themselves, are not wise" (10:12).

All too often both saved and unsaved people are guilty of this false measurement system.

  a. The unsaved man can usually find some poor miserable wretch who is worse than he is, thus relieving his own uneasy conscience and causing him to conclude his "superior morality" is sufficient, apart from Christ's righteousness.

  b. Sometimes Christian leaders fall victim to this snare also by comparing their own ministry to that of another believer's work. This can lead to envy (if his work is bigger than mine) or pride (if the opposite is true).

But Paul carefully avoided this trap. Note his words: "But he that glorieth, let him glory in the Lord. For not he that commendeth himself is approved, but whom the Lord commendeth" (10:17, 18).

3. He did not build upon other men's foundations (10:13-16). The apostle asked, "Do ye look on things after the outward appearance?" (10:7).

Apparently they had, for his enemies claimed that "his bodily presence is weak, and his speech contemptible" (10:10). Paul answered this by saying: "But though I be rude in speech, yet not in knowledge" (11:6). (See also 1 Cor. 2:1-4.)

A difficulty is seen here, for another passage seems to suggest that Paul was an eloquent and powerful speaker. (See Acts 14:9-18.) At any rate, Paul did not glory in whatever physical qualities he may have possessed. In this he was supported by both Old and New Testament teachings.

  a. 1 Samuel 16:6, 7:

"And it came to pass, when they were come, that he looked on Eliab, and said, Surely the Lord's anointed is before him. But the Lord said unto Samuel, Look not on his countenance, or on the height of his stature; because I have refused him: for the Lord seeth not as man seeth; for man looketh on the outward appearance, but the Lord looketh on the heart."

  b. John 7:24:

"Judge not according to the appearance, but judge righteous judgment."

B. His motives were superior to those of his accusers.

1. His jealousy over the church (11:1, 2).

"For I am jealous over you with godly jealousy: for I have espoused you to one husband, that I may present you as a chaste virgin to Christ" (11:2). (See also Col. 1:28.)

At this point let us distinguish between jealousy and envy.

  a. Jealousy. "The desire to possess one's own things." Contrary to popular opinion, this is a good and natural trait, if kept in proper bounds.

  b. Envy: "The desire to possess the things of another." This is always wrong.

2. His fear for the church (11:3-6).

"But I fear, lest by any means, as the serpent beguiled Eve through his subtilty, so your minds should be corrupted from the simplicity that is in Christ. For if he that cometh preacheth another Jesus whom we have not preached or if ye receive another spirit, which ye have not received, or another gospel, which ye have not accepted, ye might well bear with him" (11:3, 4). (See also Mt. 24:4, 5; Eph. 4:14; Gal. 1:6-8.)

3. His unselfish service to the church.

"Have I committed an offence in abasing myself that ye might be exalted, because I have preached to you the gospel of God freely? I robbed other churches, taking wages of them, to do you service. And when I was present with you, and wanted, I was chargeable to no man: for that which was lacking to me the brethren which came from Macedonia supplied: and in all things I have kept myself from being burdensome unto you, and so will I keep myself" (2 Cor. 11:7-9). (See also Phil. 4:15, 16.)

4. His warning to the church. Paul warns the Corinthian believers about the real nature of his enemies.

"For such are false apostles, deceitful workers, transforming themselves into the apostles of Christ. And no marvel; for Satan himself is transformed into an angel of light. Therefore it is no great thing if his ministers also be transformed as the ministers of righteousness; whose end shall be according to their works" (2 Cor. 11:13-15).

Paul then lists (11:20) at least five crimes committed by these false ministers upon true believers:

a. They made slaves of them.
b. They devoured them.
c. They took advantage of them.
d. They exalted themselves at the expense of others.
e. They (spiritually) struck them on the face.

5. His sufferings for the church.

"Of the Jews five times received I forty stripes save one. Thrice was I beaten with rods, once was I stoned, thrice I suffered shipwreck, a night and a day I have been in the deep; In journeyings often, in perils of waters, in perils of robbers, in perils by mine own countrymen, in perils by the heathen, in perils in the city, in perils in the wilderness, in perils in the sea, in perils among false brethren; in weariness and painfulness, in watchings often, in hunger and thirst, in fastings often, in cold and nakedness, beside those things that are without, that which cometh upon me daily, the care of all the churches.

Who is weak, and I am not weak? who is offended, and I burn not? If I must needs glory, I will glory of the things which concern mine infirmities. The God and Father of our Lord Jesus Christ, which is blessed forevermore, knoweth that I lie not. In Damascus the governor under Aretas the king kept the city of the Damascenes with a garrison, desirous to apprehend me: And through a window in a basket was I let down by the wall, and escaped his hands" (2 Cor. 11:24-33).

(Note the many other references to Paul's sufferings in this letter. See 1:3-11; 4:8-11; 6:4, 8-10; 7:5; 12:7-10.)

C. His miracles were superior to that of his accusers.

1. His supernatural sight (12:1-6).

"I knew a man in Christ above fourteen years ago, (whether in the body, I cannot tell; or whether out of the body, I cannot tell: God knoweth;) such an one caught up to the third heaven. And I knew such a man, (whether in the body, or out of the body, I cannot tell: God knoweth;) how that he was caught up into paradise, and heard unspeakable words, which it is not lawful for a man to utter" (2 Cor. 12:2-4).

Note: We cannot even speculate upon what Paul actually witnessed on this occasion. At a later date John the apostle apparently viewed a similar sight. (See Rev. 10:4.)

Some believe Paul actually died during his stoning at Lystra (Acts 14:19) and that during this time he experienced the vision here in 2 Corinthians 12, prior to being raised again from the dead by God.

2. His supernatural strength (12:7-10).

"And lest I should be exalted above measure through the abundance of the revelations, there was given to me a thorn in the flesh, the messenger of Satan to buffet me, lest I should be exalted above measure. For this thing I besought the Lord thrice, that it might depart from me. And he said unto me, My grace is sufficient for thee: for my strength is made perfect in weakness. Most gladly therefore will I rather glory in my infirmities, that the power of Christ may rest upon me. Therefore I take pleasure in infirmities, in reproaches, in necessities, in persecutions, in distresses for Christ's sake: for when I am weak, then am I strong (2 Cor. 12:7-10).

Note: This passage marks the fifth reference to Satan by Paul in 2 Corinthians. From these verses we learn:

a. His title: the god of this world (4:4).
b. His tactics:
    (1) To take advantage of believers (2:11).
    (2) To inflict suffering upon believers (12:7). See especially Job 1 and 2.
    (3) To blind unbelievers (4:4).
c. His treachery: disguising himself as an angel of light (11:14).
d. His trustees: false ministers (11:15).

What was the nature of this thorn in the flesh? There are various views. The main theory is that he suffered from chronic ophthalmia, a disease of the eyes, not extremely painful, but at times repulsive. It came upon Paul fourteen years prior to his writing this epistle, which was about the time of his entrance into Galatia. This was occasioned by some sort of physical infirmity. (See also Gal. 4:13–15; 6:11.)

It should also be remembered that he was blinded for awhile at his conversion (Acts 9:9). Satan thus may have exploited a natural infirmity.

3. His supernatural signs:

"Truly the signs of an apostle were wrought among you in all patience, in signs, and wonders, and mighty deeds" (12:12).

D. His mission was superior to that of his accusers. Paul was planning to make his third visit to them.

"This is the third time I am coming to you. In the mouth of two or three witnesses shall every word be established" (13:1). (See also Deut. 19:15.)

His proposed mission was based upon two principles:

1. He was a devoted parent.

"Behold, the third time I am ready to come to you; and I will not be burdensome to you: for I seek not yours, but you: for the children ought not to lay up for the parents, but the parents for the children" (12:14).

2. They were disobedient children.

"For I fear, lest, when I come, I shall not find you such as I would, and that I shall be found unto you such as ye would not: lest there be debates, envyings, wraths, strifes, backbitings, whisperings, swellings, tumults" (12:20).

E. His Messiah was superior to that of his accusers. Their master was either Satan (11:13–15) or self (10:12). But not Paul's.

"Since you are seeking for proof of the Christ who speaks in me, and who is not weak toward you, but mighty in you. For indeed he was crucified because of weakness, yet he lives because of the power of God. For we also are weak in him, yet we shall live with him because of the power of God directed toward you" (13:3, 4, *NASB*).

INTRODUCING THE EPISTLE STAGE
(Romans—Revelation)

During no other period in the entire history of the world has so much priceless literature appeared as during the years A.D. 45 to A.D. 100. These thrilling fifty-five years were literally packed with golden gems from God himself. They would take the form of twenty-two letters, commonly known as New Testament epistles. James, Jude, John, Peter, and Paul were thus chosen by God to complete his marvelous manuscript, the Bible, which had begun nearly fifteen centuries prior on the Moabite desert. By great and glorious flourishes of his pen, John, Scripture's final author (book of Revelation) brings to a climax the glory story introduced by Moses, Scripture's first author (book of Genesis).

The Bible is a Christ-centered book. The Old Testament is the preparation for his life, the Gospels a manifestation of his life, the book of Acts a propagation of his life, and the epistles an explanation of his life. The overriding theme of the epistles is Christ and his church. Most of these books are addressed to local congregations (Galatians, Romans, 1 and 2 Thessalonians, 1 and 2 Corinthians, Ephesians, Philippians, Colossians). Some are directed toward pastors of local churches (1 and 2 Timothy, Titus), while others are written to individual members in the local congregation (Philemon, 2 and 3 John).

At least one epistle is a beloved family letter (1 John), while another is painfully practical (James). Two have suffering Christians in mind (1 and 2 Peter), one warns about coming apostasy (Jude), and an unsigned letter (Hebrews) describes what Christ is now doing for his church in heaven. The final epistle wraps it all up, concluding with the marriage between heaven's Bridegroom and his Bride (Revelation).

ROMANS
INTRODUCTION

There are sixteen chapters, 433 verses, and 9,447 words in the King James translation of the book of Romans. If one would attempt to determine the worth of this book by its doctrine, history, and prophecy, and by the untold millions of saints and theologians its pages have produced during the last twenty centuries, then every one of these 9,447 words would be worth at least a billion dollars each! I have spent (literally) hundreds of happy hours studying and then summarizing Paul's magnificent epistle. No other study has so stirred my soul as has this one.

My earnest prayer is that God will be pleased to use these following pages (however insufficient they may be) to likewise inform, illuminate, and inspire many other believers concerning this grand and glorious epistle, which is really both the Constitution and Bill of Rights of the Christian faith.

The book of Romans can be likened to four buildings:

I. The Court House of Law—God's Wrath (Condemnation and Justification) (Rom. 1-5).
   A. The court reporter (1:1-17).
   B. The court record (1:18—4:25).
   C. The court review (5:1-21).

II. The Power Plant of Grace—God's Way (Sanctification and Preservation) (Rom. 6-8).
   A. The plan—first floor of sanctification (Rom. 6).
   B. The pain—second floor of frustration (Rom. 7).
   C. The prize—third floor of preservation (Rom. 8).

III. The Synagogue of Israel—God's Wisdom (Explanation and Vindication) (Rom. 9-11).
   A. The sovereignty of God and Israel's selection in the past (Rom. 9).

The EPISTLES of PAUL

1st MISSIONARY TRIP	FURLOUGH	2nd MISSIONARY TRIP	3rd MISSIONARY TRIP	FIRST IMPRISONMENT	RELEASE	FINAL IMPRISONMENT
	GALATIANS	1 THESSALONIANS	1 CORINTHIANS	EPHESIANS	1 TIMOTHY	2 TIMOTHY
		2 THESSALONIANS	2 CORINTHIANS	COLOSSIANS	TITUS	
			ROMANS	PHILEMON		
			HEBREWS (?)	PHILIPPIANS		

B. The righteousness of God and Israel's rejection at the present (Rom. 10).

C. The wisdom of God and Israel's restoration in the future (Rom. 11).

IV. The Temple of God—God's Will (Transformation and Exhortation) (Rom. 12-16).

    A. Public responsibilities for all the redeemed (12:1—15:6).

    B. Personal remarks for the Roman redeemed (15:14—16:27).

I. The Court House of Law—God's Wrath (Condemnation and Justification) (Rom. 1-5). In the first few chapters of Romans, Paul describes for us a legal case which could be entitled "The Supreme Creator of the Universe versus His Sinful Creatures."

    A. The court reporter (1:1-17).

        1. Paul's separation to the gospel (1:1).

            a. He was a servant (bondslave) of Christ.

            b. He was a called apostle. Two things were necessary for apostleship:

                (1) He had to have seen Jesus (1 Cor. 9:1; 15:8, 9).

                (2) His call must have come from God (Jn. 6:70; Acts 9:15). No man should enter the ministry unless God calls him. (See Jn. 15:16; Mt. 9:38; Heb. 5:14; Jer. 23:21; Ezek. 13:4-6, 10.)

            c. He was a separated saint. There are three specific separations which took place in Paul's life.

                (1) At his birth (Gal. 1:15).

                (2) On the Damascus Road (Acts 9:15, 16)—his conversion to Christ.

                (3) At Antioch (Acts 13:1, 2)—his call to service.

                Paul was separated as were Jeremiah (Jer. 1:5) and John (Lk. 1:15).

        2. Paul's explanation of the gospel (1:2-5).

            a. It is not new. Paul said the Old Testament prophets spoke of it. In Romans he quotes from the Old Testament no less than sixty-one times, from fourteen books. This totally refutes any claims of cults to have new and exotic truth concerning the gospel. It is rightly observed that "if something is new, it's probably not true, and if it's true, then it is not new!"

            b. It is about Jesus. The founder and finisher of the gospel is Christ.

            c. It was manifested through the incarnation. Paul speaks of the virgin birth and humanity of Christ in 1:3. Christ is the seed of David.

            d. It was declared through the resurrection. The Greek word "declared" in 1:4 is *horizo* (from which comes our word *"horizon"*), meaning "to mark out by sure signs." Thus, God's clear boundary between earth and heaven is Christ, the Son of God.

                (1) His humanity is spoken of, as seen by the following:

                    (a) He grew (Lk. 2:40, 52).

                    (b) He looked like a man (Jn. 4:9; 20:15).

                    (c) He became hungry (Mt. 4:2).

                    (d) He knew thirst (Jn. 19:28).

                    (e) He grew weary (Mk. 4:38; Jn. 4:6).

                    (f) He wept (Jn. 11:35; Lk. 19:41).

                    (g) He suffered, bled, and died (1 Pet. 2:21; Jn. 19:34; Mt. 27:50).

                (2) His deity is spoken of, as seen by the following:

                    (a) He is called God (Titus 2:13).

                    (b) He is eternal (Rev. 1:8, 18).

                    (c) He is unchanging (Heb. 13:8).

                    (d) He is all-powerful (Heb. 1:3).

                    (e) He is all-knowing (Col. 2:3).

                    (f) He is ever-present (Mt. 18:20).

              Both natures are spoken of in Isaiah 9:6; Galatians 4:4; and 1 Timothy 3:16. Note: The phrase "by the resurrection from the dead" (1:4) is literally "of the dead ones." Christ's resurrection is always referred to in the plural as it takes in all believers! (See Rom. 6:4; Jn. 5:21; 1 Cor. 15:22.)

            e. It bestows both salvation and service. Note Paul's testimony here: "By whom we have received grace and apostleship" (1:5). We note that grace precedes apostleship. A man must be saved before he can serve. Unsaved ministers are described in 2 Corinthians 11:13-15. Jesus must say, "Come unto me," before he says, "Go ye into all the world." John Wesley was a great example of this.

            f. It is received by faith (see also Rom. 5:1; Eph. 2:8, 9).

        3. Paul's thanksgiving for the gospel (1:6-15).

            a. Paul writes to all Roman believers, "Beloved of God, called . . . saints; grace to you and peace from God our Father, and the Lord Jesus Christ" (1:7).

              We note he calls them "saints." All believers are saints in God's sight.

              We note also here that grace precedes peace. There can be no peace apart from grace. (See Isa. 57:21; Jer. 6:14; Lk. 7:50; 8:48; Rom. 5:1, 1 Thess. 5:3.)

              Paul prefaces every single one of his thirteen epistles with these words, "Grace and peace." Peter (1 Pet. 1:2; 2 Pet. 1:2) and John (3 Jn. 3) do the same. Grace is "unmerited favor" and is first mentioned in Genesis 6:8. It is perhaps God's second greatest characteristic (after holiness) and may be spelled out and thought of as "God's righteousness at Christ's expense." (See Rom. 5:20; Eph. 2:8, 9; 1 Pet. 3:18; 1 Cor. 15:10.)

            b. Paul commends them for their universally known faith (1:8). We know that the Emperor Claudius had forced the Jews out of Rome because of one Chrestus, thought to be a misspelling for "Christ." (See also 1 Thess. 1:6-8.)

            c. He assured them of his constant prayers for them and also for himself that he "might have a prosperous journey by the will of God to some day visit them." God later answered this prayer, but not in the way Paul might have supposed (Acts 27–28). In Romans 16 Paul refers to 26 Roman saints by name.

d. He desired to come that he might both remit and receive a blessing (1:12). He had planned to come previously, but was hindered concerning his plans, once by Satan (1 Thess. 2:18) and once by God (Acts 16:6, 7). Thus, Paul's human plans were no more inspired than those of Christians today (see Rom. 15:22, 23). The spiritual gift mentioned in 1:11 was probably doctrine (1 Pet. 2:2).

e. He felt he owed a great gospel debt to every sinner (1:14; see also 2 Ki. 7:9). Because of this, Paul could say: "So, as much as in me is [literally, my side is ready], I am ready to preach the gospel to you that are at Rome also" (1:15). Paul preached at Jerusalem (the religious center of the world) and was mobbed (Acts 21:31; 22:22, 23). He preached at Athens (the intellectual center) and was mocked (Acts 17:32). He would later preach in Rome (the political center) where he would be martyred (2 Tim. 4:6).

4. Paul's confidence in the gospel (1:16, 17).

a. Paul lists his threefold philosophy concerning the gospel.
(1) I am debtor (1:14) to preach it.
(2) I am ready (1:15) to preach it.
(3) I am not ashamed (1:16) to preach it. Here he meant the gospel would never let him down, or put him to shame.

b. The gospel is God's power (1:16). There are two standards by which God's power is measured in the Bible. In the Old Testament it was according to that power by which God brought Israel out of Egypt. (See Ex. 14–15; Ps. 78.) In the New Testament the unit of measurement is the resurrection of Jesus (Eph. 1:20). The Greek word for "power" is *dunamis,* from which two words come: (1) dynamite—destructive power, and (2) dynamo—constructive power. The gospel of Christ is both. (See 2 Cor. 2:16.)

c. The gospel produces righteousness (1:17). This word, simply defined, means "right clothing." The Bible teaches that all sinners are naked before God (Gen. 3:10; Heb. 4:13; Rev. 3:17). Some sinners realize this and attempt to make their own suit of spiritual clothes, but God looks upon such clothes as filthy rags (Isa. 64:6). However, the gospel provides new clothes to all repenting sinners. (See 2 Cor. 6:7; Eph. 6:14; Rev. 19:7, 8.) This word may be used to summarize the book of Romans in a threefold manner:
(1) God is righteous.
(2) God demands righteousness.
(3) God provides righteousness.

d. The gospel says "the just shall live by faith" (1:17). These six words started the Protestant Reformation when Martin Luther experienced them. They are found in Habakkuk 2:4 and are quoted three times in the New Testament.
(1) Here in Romans 1:17, where the emphasis is "the just."
(2) In Galatians 3:11, where the emphasis is "shall live."
(3) In Hebrews 10:38, where the emphasis is "by faith."
Bishop Lightfoot has pointed out the following concerning these six words:
(4) The whole law was given to Moses in 613 precepts.
(5) David reduces them to eleven in Psalm 15.
(6) Isaiah brings it down to six.
(7) Micah limits it to three.
(8) Isaiah in another passage narrows it to two.
(9) But Habakkuk and Paul here summarize God's plan in a single statement!
Faith has been defined as "the hand of the heart."

B. The court record (1:18—4:25).
1. The defendants:
a. a heathen (the pagan man) (1:18–32)
b. a hypocrite (the moral man) (2:1–16)
c. a Hebrew (the religious man) (2:17—3:8)
2. The charge: High treason against the King of the universe (3:23).
3. The presiding Judge: The Lord Jesus Christ (Jn. 5:22; Acts 17:31).
4. The detailed indictment: God's fierce wrath is revealed against all ungodliness (sins against his Person) and unrighteousness (sins against his will). The first category is vertical while the second is horizontal in nature.
a. This wrath is manifested in a threefold way:
(1) In the biblical account itself (Jn. 3:36).
(2) In the cross of Calvary (Mt. 27:46; 1 Pet. 3:18).
(3) In the natural world (through tornadoes, earthquakes, famines, etc.).
b. The indictment of God against man is tenfold.
(1) They held down the truth (1:18; see also Lk. 4:42; 2 Thess. 2:6, 7).
(2) They knew God but did not honor him as God (1:21).
(3) They were unthankful (1:21). (Cf. Rom. 1:8; 1 Thess. 5:18.)
(4) They began foolish speculations— "became vain in their imaginations" (1:21).
(5) They allowed their hearts to become darkened (1:21).
(6) They thought themselves to be wise, but became fools (1:22). The Greek word for "become fools" here is *moraino,* a verb form of *moros,* from which we get our word "moron."

This was the beginning of human philosophy, a term ill-named, for it means "a lover of wisdom." (See Acts 17:18-21; 1 Cor. 1:18-21; 1 Tim. 6:3-5, 20; 2 Tim. 3:7; 4:4.)

(7) They preferred idols to the living God and *exchanged* (not changed, for no man, angel, or demon can do this) his glory for that of:

  (a) Man—the Greeks worshiped the human body, as does Hollywood today.

  (b) Birds—the Assyrians bowed down to birds.

  (c) Beasts—the Egyptians looked to cows and crocodiles.

  (d) Creeping things—the pagans worshiped snakes.

We note the vivid downward trend of man described here in 1:23. The Bible teaches devolution, not evolution.

(8) They gave their bodies over to sexual perversions (1:26, 27). The sin of homosexuality is usually the final stage in those civilizations which turn from God. It was for this crime that God burned Sodom off the map of the Middle East (Gen. 19) and later ordered the destruction of Jericho, along with other Old Testament cities (1 Ki. 14:24). In recent years the number of homosexuals in Western civilization has increased drastically.

(9) They were filled with unrighteous acts (1:29-32).

  (a) fornication—sexual sins in general.

  (b) wickedness (Mk. 7:22)

  (c) covetousness (Col. 3:5)

  (d) maliciousness—congealed anger

  (e) envy—discontent with another's possession or advantage

  (f) murder (Mt. 5:21, 22)

  (g) debate—contention and strife, a deliberate attempt to mislead

  (h) deceit—a bait or a snare

  (i) malignity—ill will, cruel ways

  (j) whisperers—secret slandering

  (k) backbiters—open slandering

  (l) God-haters

  (m) despiteful—insolent and insulting

  (n) proud—one who swaggers

  (o) boasters

  (p) evil inventors

  (q) disobedient to parents

  (r) without understanding (see Eph. 4:17-19)

  (s) covenant-breakers

  (t) without natural affection

  (u) implacable—unable to be satisfied

  (v) unmerciful

(10) They knew the seriousness of their crimes, but still continued and even encouraged others to join them (Mk. 14:10, 11; Rev. 11:10). For these crimes, God gave them over to a reprobate mind (a mind incapable of rational judgment) (Prov. 1:24-31; Rom. 1:24, 26, 28).

5. The jury:
  a. the law of God (2:12)
  b. the deeds of man (2:6)

6. The defense:
  a. The heathen (1:18-32)
    (1) The plea rendered: "I should be acquitted on the grounds of ignorance."
    (2) The plea refuted: "All men have both the witness of conscience (1:19) and that of nature" (1:20). (See Isa. 40:26; Ps. 8:3; 19:1-3; Acts 14:17; 17:29.) In other words, God does not reap wrath where he has not sown knowledge.

These twin witnesses are thus unmistakable and universal. As a result, all men are exposed both to them and by them.

  b. The hypocrite (2:1-16)
    (1) The plea rendered: "I should be acquitted on the grounds of comparison, that is, I'm not as bad as the pagan savage."
    (2) The plea refuted: "You do the same basic things, but in a more refined way." A classic example of one man judging another for the very thing he himself had committed was when David condemned a rich farmer who stole from a poor one (2 Sam. 11, 12).

Additional comments on the moral man:

    (3) Self-righteous people make one of two capital mistakes:
      (a) They misunderstand the height of God's law.
      (b) They underestimate the depth of their own moral conduct.
    (4) They desire the fruit of Christianity without the root!
    (5) They underestimate the awesome knowledge of God (2:1). But God knows all the facts.
      (a) He knows the number of the stars (Ps. 147:4).
      (b) He knows man's thoughts and words (Ps. 139:1, 2, 4, 23, 24).
      (c) He knows the number of hairs on man's head (Mt. 10:30).
      (d) He knows the past, present, and future (Acts 15:18).
      (e) He even knows what might have been (Mt. 11:23).
    (6) They despise his goodness and forbearance (2:4). To despise is to belittle, or to look down upon (Gen.

25:34; Heb. 12:2, 5). Thus, the moral man was despising:
  (a) God's forbearance; that is, his act of holding back his wrath.
  (b) God's goodness; that is, his act of holding forth his grace.
The moral man takes lightly both God's extended hand and his clenched fist.
(7) They assume their morality will excuse them from his judgment (2:3). It has been suggested that there are four possible ways a man might escape human punishment:
  (a) He might commit an undetected crime or remain an undetected criminal.
  (b) He might escape beyond the jurisdiction of the law.
  (c) He might hire a smart lawyer and "beat the rap."
  (d) He might escape, once put in prison.
  But with God there is no escape (Heb. 2:3). Man's only hope is to settle out of court.
  Without this settlement, all men will be judged concerning their *thoughts* (Rom. 2:16), *words* (Mt. 12:36), and *deeds* (Rev. 20:12). This will happen for "there is no respect of persons with God" (2:11). (See also Deut. 10:17; Acts 10:34; Jas. 2:1, 9; Eph. 6:9; Col. 3:25.)
(8) The self-righteous moral man, like the unrighteous pagan, will be judged by the twin witnesses of nature and conscience (Rom. 1:19, 20; 2:12-15). The Bible lists various kinds of conscience.
  (a) a good conscience (1 Tim. 1:5, 19)
  (b) a weak conscience (1 Cor. 8:12)
  (c) a convicting conscience (Jn. 8:9)
  (d) a defiled conscience (Titus 1:15)
  (e) a seared conscience (1 Tim. 4:2)
  It should be noted that man's conscience does not function legislatively, but only judicially. It is like an umpire that calls the strikes, but does not make the rules. Conscience, then, is a goad, but not a guide. Paul summarizes this section by saying: "For as many as have sinned without law shall also perish without law; and as many as have sinned in the law shall be judged by the law" (Rom. 2:12; see also Lk. 12:47, 48).
c. The Hebrew (2:17—3:8).
  (1) The plea rendered: "I should be acquitted on the grounds that I know the law of God and teach courses in religion."
  (2) The plea refuted: "You simply do not practice what you preach!"

Additional comments on the religious man:
  (3) His law could not save him (2:17-24). The Jew had defiled this law and his knowledge of God and had become a horrible testimony to the Gentiles (2:24; also Gen. 34:30; Ezek. 36:17, 20). It was performance of God's will, and not the possession of his law which averted judgment. Israel had simply not kept the law (Mt. 21:13; 23:4-36; Acts 15:10).
  (4) His circumcision could not save him (2:25-27). The Jews believed Abraham (the first to be circumcised—see Gen. 17:11) stood at the gate of hell to assure that no circumcised Jew would ever enter there. While circumcision was indeed the *seal* of God's promise, inward faith alone was the *source*. (See Deut. 10:12, 16; 30:6.) The rite of circumcision had already been set aside in Acts 15.
  (5) His birth could not save him (2:28, 29). Salvation comes not through place, face, or race, but by grace. (See Jn. 8:39, 44.)
Paul then quickly summarizes the case against Israel (3:1-8).
  (6) Even though the Jews had a national advantage over the Gentiles ("because that unto them were committed the oracles of God," Rom. 3:2), they had no spiritual advantage whatsoever.
  (7) Even though Israel had rejected Christ, God's promise would not fail (Rom. 3:3, 4; see also 2 Tim. 2:13).
  (8) Even though Israel's unrighteousness had simply "commended the righteousness of God" (that is, to show in a clearer light), he would still judge them along with the uncircumcised Gentiles. The end *never* justifies the means.
7. The verdict (Rom. 3:9-20): "Both Jews and Gentiles . . . are all under sin" (3:9). The verses describing the verdict are taken from various Old Testament passages: verses 10-12 come from Ecclesiastes 7:20; Psalms 14:2, 3; 53:2, 3. Verses 13-18 are from Psalms 5:9; 10:7; 36:1; 140:3; Isaiah 59:7, 8.
  a. Man is found to be depraved in character (3:10-12), a reference to what he is.
    (1) None are righteous. Even Mary needed a Savior (see Lk. 1:46, 47).
    (2) None sought for God. The Bible is not the record of man's search after God, but of God's search after man (see Gen. 3:9; Isa. 1:18; 55:1).
    (3) All had forsaken the right way (Isa. 53:6).
    (4) All had become unprofitable. This is a reference to something originally good which goes bad, like sour milk, rotten meat, and moldy bread (Isa.

1:6). Thus, men are unrighteous, unreasonable, unresponsive, and unrepentant.

b. Man is found to be depraved in conversation (3:13, 14), a reference to what he says. Man's words are like the sting of a serpent and the stench of a sepulcher.

c. Man is found to be depraved in conduct (3:15-18), a reference to what he does.

(1) He murders his brother.

(2) He mocks his God.

Paul has now proven his case, "that every mouth may be stopped, and all the world may become guilty before God" (3:19). He has exposed the perverted religion of the heathen, the pretended religion of the hypocrite, and the powerless religion of the Hebrew.

8. The sentence: Spiritual death, to be forever separated from God to suffer throughout all eternity in the lake of fire (Rom. 6:23; Rev. 20:11-15). The greatest crime of all can only be punished by the greatest penalty of all, if justice is to prevail.

9. The miracle (3:21-31): Up to this point the case of God against man has pretty well followed the format of earthly jurisprudence. But suddenly something totally different and unexpected takes place that would surely cause every earthly court reporter to gasp in utter amazement. After the Judge has carefully heard all the evidence and patiently listened to all the pleas, he finds no other choice but to invoke the supreme penalty, lest true justice be denied. But before the terrible sentence can be carried out, this same Judge quietly closes the case book, lays down the heavenly gavel, rises to his feet, takes off his judicial robes, and goes out to die for these three convicted defendants. This and this alone is justification.

The corrupt, doomed, and naked sinner may now be cleansed, delivered, and clothed in the very righteousness of Christ himself. Let us observe the facts concerning this righteousness.

a. The demonstration of this righteousness—Calvary. "Whom God hath set forth" (3:25).

b. The witnesses to this righteousness— "The law and the prophets" (3:21). The Mosaic law required two witnesses to attest to any fact (Deut. 19:15). This righteousness was often foreshadowed by the law through the Temple priesthood and offerings. This righteousness was often foretold by the prophets through their writings (Isa. 53; Lk. 24:25-27; Jn. 5:46; 1 Pet. 1:10, 11).

c. The cost of this righteousness—dearly purchased, but freely given. This excludes all boasting (Rom. 3:24, 27).

d. The results of this righteousness—"That he [God] might be just, and the justifier of him which believeth in Jesus" (3:26).

As the Old Testament closed, a great problem remained to be solved. It centered around the two words "remission" and "forbearance" (3:25).

The word remission refers to the act of letting something pass by—in this case, the sins of the Old Testament saints.

The word forbearance refers to the act of holding something back—in this case, the wrath of God upon those sins (Ps. 50:16-23; Acts 17:30).

How, then, could God possibly reconcile his holiness and righteousness to his mercy and grace? This problem was gloriously solved by Christ, who was,

"Set forth to be a propitiation . . . for the remission of sins that are past, through the forbearance of God" (3:25; see also Ps. 85:10).

The word "propitiation" means "satisfaction" and is a reference to the Old Testament Temple mercy seat. It was upon this golden seat that the priest sprinkled the blood of a lamb to separate God's wrath from man's sin. (See 1 Jn. 2:2; 4:10; Heb. 10:11, 12.) Why did Christ die? Among other things, to preserve and vindicate the justice of God.

e. The results of this righteousness—"redemption . . . in Christ Jesus" (3:24). The word "redemption" means to buy back in a slave market and to set free. (See Gal. 3:13; 4:5; Eph. 5:16; Col. 4:5; Lk. 24:21; Titus 2:14; 1 Pet. 1:18.)

f. The scope of this righteousness—"unto all" (3:22), unlimited in scope.

g. The bestowal of this righteousness—"upon all them that believe" (3:22), limited in bestowal!

h. The need of this righteousness—"for all have sinned, and come short of the glory of God" (3:23).

i. The requirement of this righteousness—"Therefore we conclude that a man is justified by faith without the deeds of the law" (3:28).

"Seeing it is one God, which shall justify . . . through faith" (3:30).

10. The two friends of the court (4:1-25). The Judge introduces two well-known faith experts who swear to the fact that they both anticipated and experienced the miracle of justification centuries ago.

a. The sworn testimony of Abraham, Israel's racial father (4:1-5, 9-25).

(1) Abraham and his righteousness (4:1-5, 9-12).

(a) How was Abraham saved? "For what saith the scripture? Abraham believed God, and it was counted unto him for righteousness" (4:3). (See Gen. 15:6.) This word "counted" could also be translated "imputed." To impute is to add something to someone's account. There are three major imputations in the Bible.

First, the imputation of Adam's sin to the human race (Rom. 3:23; 5:12; 1 Cor. 15:22).

Second, the imputation of the race's sin upon Christ (Isa. 53:5; Heb. 2:9; 1 Pet. 2:24; 2 Cor. 5:14).

Third, the imputation of God's righteousness to all believers (Phil. 3:9).

(b) When was Abraham saved? Was he saved before or after circumcision? In Genesis 15:6, Abraham is said to have been justified. At this time he was eighty-five years old (Gen. 16:16). In Genesis 17:24 we are told of his circumcision, at the age of ninety-nine. Thus, he was justified by faith and a child of God nearly fourteen years before he was circumcised!

(c) Why was Abraham saved? "... that he might be the father of all them that believe" (4:11). This includes both the uncircumcised (believing Gentiles) and the circumcision (believing Jews). Paul here once again points out that circumcision was merely the *seal* of Abraham's faith, while justification was the *source*. Dr. Allen Johnson writes:

"A good illustration of this is the old twenty-dollar gold piece. The seal of the United States was imprinted on the coin as a sign that it was U.S. currency, but the value of the coin remained the same even if it was melted down and the seal obliterated. Now the same seal can be impressed on an iron slug, but the presence of the sign doesn't alter the intrinsic worthlessness of the slug." (*The Freedom Letter*, p. 76)

(2) Abraham and his inheritance (4:13-15).

(a) What was Abraham promised? "... that he should be the heir of the world" (4:13). This is a reference to the Abrahamic Covenant, which guaranteed him he would father a great nation and that his seed would someday own Palestine forever. (See Gen. 12:2, 3, 7; 13:14-17; 15:5, 18; 17:8.)

(b) How was this promise given? "For the promise ... was not through the law, but through the righteousness of faith" (4:13).

In fact, the promise preceded the law by some 430 years.

(3) Abraham and his posterity (4:16-25).

(a) Who was Abraham's seed (4:16)? He had a threefold seed:

His earthly seed is Isaac (Gen. 21:3; Rom. 9:7).

His spiritual seed is all believers (Gal. 3:7).

His single seed is Christ (Gal. 3:16).

(b) How did Abraham receive his earthly seed? "He staggered not at the promise of God through unbelief; but was strong in faith, giving glory to God; and being fully persuaded, that what he had promised, he was able also to perform" (4:20, 21).

(c) How secure is Abraham's spiritual seed? "Therefore it is of faith, that it might be by grace; to the end the promise might be sure to all the seed" (4:16).

It is by faith, because this is the best way for a sinner to be saved. (See Num. 21; Jn. 3.) It is by grace, because this is the best way for God to be glorified. (See Eph. 2; Rev. 4 and 5.)

(d) How did Abraham's single seed accomplish all this? "Who was delivered for our offences, and was raised again for our justification" (4:25).

b. The sworn testimony of David, Israel's royal father (4:6-8)

(1) What great sins was David forgiven of? Adultery and murder (2 Sam. 11, 12).

(2) How was David forgiven? By the imputation of "righteousness without works" (4:6). David penned two Old Testament Psalms which dealt with his terrible sin.

(a) Psalm 32 is the record of the misery he experienced when he delayed (perhaps for a year) in confessing his sin. Paul quotes Psalm 32:1, 2, here in Romans 4:6-8.

(b) Psalm 51 is the actual prayer he uttered when he confessed this sin. We note that he says:

"For thou desirest not sacrifice; else would I give it: thou delightest not in burnt offering. The sacrifices of God are a broken spirit: a broken and a contrite heart, O God, thou wilt not despise" (51:16, 17).

Here David makes no effort to offer a sacrifice. The reason is that there was no offering in the

Levitical system which covered the sin of adultery and murder! By all rights, David should have been taken out and stoned. He therefore bypassed the law and threw himself completely upon the grace of God.

C. The court review.

1. A summary of justification (5:1-11).

a. Peace with God (5:1). The court battle is now over. The terms of the armistice have been signed.

b. Access to God (5:2). The believer can now approach God because of his new standing. In the Bible there is a distinction between our standing and our state.

Our standing refers to our position in heaven and never changes (1 Cor. 15:1; 2 Cor. 5:17).

Our state refers to our condition on earth and may change (for better or worse) daily (Phil. 2:19; Col. 4:7).

Our new standing now gives us that blessed privilege not experienced by either Jew or Gentile in the Old Testament. We now have access to God's throne itself. In the Old Testament there was very little of this. Consider:

(1) A Gentile was barred at the gates of the Temple.

(2) A Jewish woman was stopped at the woman's court.

(3) A non-Levite Hebrew could not enter the inner court.

(4) The high priest himself could only enter into the Holy of holies once a year. But on Calvary this veil separating God's glory from sinful man was rent in two by Christ. (See Mt. 27:51; Heb. 10:19.)

c. Assurance from God (5:3, 4). "Knowing that tribulation worketh":

(1) Patience (see Heb. 10:36; Jas. 1:3). This leads to . . .

(2) Experience (see Ps. 94:12; 2 Cor. 1:3-5; Gal. 4:19; Eph. 4:14, 15). This leads to . . .

(3) Hope. There are three requirements of an earthly hope:

(a) It must concern the future.

(b) It must concern something good in the future.

(c) It must concern something possible in the future.

This hope fulfills all three requirements (Eph. 1:17-22; 1 Pet. 1:3, 4; Titus 2:11). There are two kinds of hope, a verb and a noun.

(d) The verb "hope" says, "I hope to have" (earthly hope).

(e) The noun "hope" says, "I have a hope" (heavenly hope).

This assurance from God once prompted Andrew Murray to write:

"First, He brought me here, it is by His will I am in this strait place; in that fact I will rejoice. Next, He will keep me here in His love, and give me grace as His child. Then, He will make the trial a blessing, teaching me the lessons He intends for me to learn, and working in me the grace He meant to bestow. Last, in His good time He can bring me out again—how and when He knows. Thus: I am (1) here by God's appointment, (2) in His keeping, (3) under His training, and (4) for His time."

d. Indwelt by God (5:5). "The love of God is shed abroad in our hearts by the Holy Ghost which is given unto us."

There are three separate and distinct words for love in the Greek New Testament. In Romans Paul uses all three.

(1) *Storgos*—a natural, gravitational love; an instinctive concern for one's offspring; found in both animals and man. Only the negative form, *astorgos*, is used in Scripture (Rom. 1:31).

(2) *Philos*—a beautiful and friendly love. Paul describes this love in Romans 12:10.

(3) *Agapeo*—a divine love, found only in God. This love is not dependent upon the beauty of the object being loved. It is found 320 times in the Greek New Testament, but rarely in classical writings. (Homer used it ten times and Euripedes three times.)

This love is never found in the heart of any man prior to the ascension of Christ. In fact, Jesus asks Peter on three occasions (Jn. 21:15-19) if he really loves him. The first two times Jesus uses the third kind of love and asks the following question. "Peter, do you *agapeo* me?" On both occasions Peter answers by choosing the second word. He says, "Lord, you know I *phileo* you."

Finally, our Lord (condescendingly) uses the second word also. The reason for all this (as Peter would later find out) is explained in Romans 5:5 by Paul: "The love *(agapeo)* of God is shed abroad in our hearts by the Holy Ghost which is given unto us." Thus, the reason why Peter answered the way he did was because the Holy Spirit had not yet come at Pentecost and it was therefore impossible for him to love Christ with this divine *agapeo* love.

In John 11 we have a similar case in which we are told that Lazarus loved Jesus with a *phileo* love, but that Jesus loved Lazarus with an *agapeo* love (11:3, 5).

There are two beloved New Testament passages in which this *agapeo* love is in view.

Romans

THE VERDICT

"Both Jews and Gentiles . . . are all under sin" **(3:9)**.

"That every mouth may be stopped, and all the world may become guilty before God" **(3:19)**.

THE MIRACLE

JUSTIFICATION THROUGH THE RIGHTEOUSNESS OF CHRIST!

THE SUMMARY OF THE COURT

The blessing of justification (5:1-11)

1. Peace with God **5:1**
2. Access to God **5:2**
3. Assurance from God **5:3, 4**
4. Indwelled by God **5:5**
5. Preserved by God **5:6-11**

"For God so loved the world, that he gave his only begotten Son, that whosoever believeth in him should not perish, but have everlasting life" (Jn. 3:16).

"Husbands, love your wives, even as Christ also loved the church, and gave himself for it" (Eph. 5:25).

   e. Preserved in God (5:6-11).
     (1) Because of Christ's past work on Calvary's cross.
      (a) What did he do? "Christ died for the ungodly" (5:6).
      (b) When did he do this? "When we were yet without strength. . . . While we were yet sinners. . . . When we were enemies" (5:6, 8, 10; see also Eph. 2:1; 2:11, 12). Christ met the sinner on his own sinful level.
      (c) How did he do this? "By his blood" (5:9). The Bible has many clear statements about Christ's blood.
        It was innocent blood (Mt. 27:4, 19, 24).
        This was the testimony of Judas, Pilate's wife, and Pilate.
        It was shed blood (Mt. 26:28).
        It was precious blood (1 Pet. 1:18, 19).
        It was cleansing blood (1 Jn. 1:9).
        It was condemning blood (Mt. 27:25).
      (d) Why did he do this? To show forth God's love (5:8).
        To save men from God's wrath (5:9).

This includes present-day wrath (Jn. 3:36; Rom. 1:18).

This includes tribulational wrath (1 Thess. 1:10, 5:9).

This includes eternal wrath (Rev. 20:15).

     (2) Because of Christ's present work at God's right hand. "Much more . . . we shall be saved by his life" (5:10). This has been called the chapter of the "much mores." (See 5:9, 10, 15, 17, 20.)

My salvation was purchased by his bleeding and is preserved through his interceding. (See Heb. 1:3; 6:18-20; 7:25; 9:24.)

2. A summary of condemnation (5:12-21).
   a. The first head of state—Adam.
     (1) He brought sin into the world. At this point it may prove helpful to review both the origin and meaning of sin.
      (a) The origin of sin: In the universe, it was introduced by Satan. (See Ezek. 28:11-19; Isa. 14:12-15; Lk. 10:18; 1 Jn. 3:8; Rev. 12:3, 4.) In the world, it was introduced by Adam. (See Gen. 2:16, 17; Rom. 5:12; 1 Cor. 15:22; 1 Tim. 2:14.)
      (b) The meaning of sin: "To miss the mark" (Greek is *hamartia*). Here sin may be pictured as any attitude or act of man which does not hit the bull's-eye of God's glory target (Rom. 3:23). The secular use of its verbal form is illustrated in Judges 20:16.
        "To overstep the forbidden line" (Greek is *parabasis*). (See

THE CONTRAST BETWEEN ADAM AND CHRIST

Adam		Christ
• He brought sin and death into the world	**The nature of the act**	• He brought righteousness and life into the world
• In the Garden of Eden	**The place of the act**	• On the cross of Calvary
• Disobedience (Gen. 3:6)	**The reason for the act**	• Obedience (Lk. 22:42)
• Condemnation 1. Immediate judgment upon himself. 2. Imputed judgment upon his posterity. 3. Eternal judgment upon all.	**The results from the act**	• Justification 1. Immediate justification 2. Imputed righteousness 3. Eternal life
• The **law** served to demonstrate the **seriousness** of his act	**Relationship of the act to law and grace**	• **Grace** served to demonstrate the "**much more**" of his act (5:9, 10, 15, 17, 20)
• It abounded	**The scope of the act**	• It abounded much more

1 Jn. 3:4; Acts 1:25; Jas. 2:11.) Sin thus covers both man's inability to do right and his inclination to do wrong.

There are several theories about Adam's sin and its relationship to me.

The Pelagian view—this says that Adam's sin affected only himself, and merely resulted in a bad moral example.

Semi-Pelagian view—that Adam's sin merely weakened my will not to sin.

Federal (or Augustinian) view—that because of the unity of the human race, Adam's sin was imputed to posterity; Corrupt nature begets corrupt nature. This position is taken by Paul, both here in Romans 5 and in 3:23:

"For all have sinned [aorist tense, a once-for-all act in history] and come short [imperfect tense, repeatedly coming short] of the glory of God."

The Bible thus distinguishes between sin (the *root* of my problem, caused by Adam) and sins (the *fruit* of my problem, caused by myself). I am therefore not a sinner because I sin, but I sin because I am a sinner.

(2) He brought death into the world.
(a) This includes physical death (Gen. 3:19; 5:5; Ps. 90:10).

(b) This includes spiritual death (Mt. 7:23; 25:41; Rev. 2:11; 20:6, 14; 21:8).

Thus, through the disobedience of Adam, many were made sinners and condemned.

b. The second Head of state—Christ.
(1) He brought righteousness and life into the world.
(2) He brought the free and abundant gift of grace into the world. The word "abundance" is an old Latin word which means "to rise in waves."

We have already noted the "much mores" of this chapter. See especially verses 15, 17, 20:

"*Much more* the grace of God" (5:15)

"*Much more* . . . abundance of grace" (5:17)

'Where sin abounded, grace did *much more* abound" (5:20).

All this is simply to say that the repenting sinner receives *much more* in Christ than he lost to Adam.

II. The Power Plant of Grace—God's Way (Sanctification and Preservation—Rom. 6-8). Up to chapter 6 Paul does not discuss the sanctification of a saint. But from this point on, he does not discuss the justification of a sinner. It will prove helpful here to contrast these two words.

Justification is an act, while *sanctification* (which simply means "to set apart") is a work.

Justification is the means, while sanctification is the end.

The first removes the guilt and penalty of sin, while the second removes the growth and power of sin.

The former works for us, while the latter works in us.

The one declares us righteous, while the other makes us righteous.

Justification furnishes the track which leads to heaven, while sanctification furnishes the train.

We have already noted that sanctification simply means "to set apart." Thus, in the Bible:

1. Physical objects were said to be sanctified (Ex. 40:10, 11; 19:23).
2. People could sanctify themselves (Ex. 19:22).
3. One man could sanctify another (Ex. 13:2).
4. Evildoers could sanctify themselves to do iniquity (Isa. 66:17).
5. God sanctified Christ (Jn. 10:36).
6. Christ sanctified himself (Jn. 17:19).
7. A believer could sanctify an unbeliever (1 Cor. 7:14).
8. Carnal Christians are said to be sanctified (1 Cor. 1:1; 3:1, 2).
9. Believers are commanded to sanctify God (1 Pet. 3:15). Chapters 6-8 go to make up the second "building" in the book of Romans. There are three "floors" to this power plant of grace.

A. The plan—first floor of sanctification (Rom. 6)
   1. Know ye (6:1-10):
      a. That we have been "buried with him [Christ] by baptism into death" (6:4). Here Paul states not only that Christ died *for* me, but *as* me! The word "baptism" simply means "identification." This identification with Christ on Calvary is one of many "dry baptisms" in the Bible. Others would include:
         (1) The baptism of sin and suffering upon Christ (Mt. 20:22).
         (2) The baptism of the Holy Spirit upon believers at Pentecost (Acts 1:5).
         (3) The baptism of believers into the body of Christ (1 Cor. 12:13).
         (4) The baptism "for the dead" (1 Cor. 15:29). Note: This is thought to refer to that act of living believers identifying themselves with martyred believers by picking up their fallen banners.
         (5) The baptism "unto Moses" (1 Cor. 10:2).
         (6) The baptism of judgment during the tribulation (Mt. 3:11, 12).
      b. That we have been "planted together . . . in the likeness of his resurrection" (6:5). The believer has now been "transplanted" three times:
         (1) To the Garden of Eden where he sinned with Adam.
         (2) To the cross, where he died with Christ.
         (3) To the tomb, where he arose with Christ.
      c. That because of these two facts, the believer is:
         (1) "Dead to sin" (6:2).
         (2) "Freed from sin" (6:7).
         Death cancels all obligations. Sin here is personified as a cruel tyrant who taxes his subjects beyond all endurance. The

only way to beat the rap is to die! This, then, renders inactive (but does not remove) the body of sin and makes it powerless (see also Eph. 4:22-24; Col. 3:9, 10).
   2. Reckon ye (6:11, 12). This simply means that by *faith* we are to act upon these facts regardless of any personal *feelings.*
   3. Yield ye (6:13-15).
      a. We are to stop yielding (present tense) our body members as instruments of unrighteousness.
      b. We are to once for all (aorist tense) yield our body members as instruments of righteousness.
   4. Obey ye (6:16-23).
      a. Whom are we to obey?
         (1) The Christian is to obey his new Master and to ignore his old one (6:16). We can serve but one master at a time (Mt. 6:24).
         (2) The Christian is to obey that form of doctrine into which he has been delivered. (The Greek verb for delivered is the second person plural.) He was originally saved by being poured into the mold of salvation. He is now to obey the precepts of this mold and let it fashion and shape his new life.
      b. Why are we to obey?
         (1) Because we are "freed from sin" (6:22). This marks the sixth time Paul has stated this fact. (See 6:2, 6, 7, 14, 18.) There are three Latin theological terms which may help clarify this precious doctrine. These are:
            (a) *Non posse non pecare*—not able not to sin. This refers to believers before their salvation.
            (b) *Posse non pecare*—able not to sin. This describes them after their salvation. They now have the power to live victorious lives.
            (c) *Non posse pecare*—not able to sin. This describes existence after the rapture.
         (2) Because God desires the fruits of justification from believers which can only come through obedience (6:21, 22).

B. The pain—second floor of frustration (Rom. 7). Much speculation has centered around this chapter. Does Paul write here as a saved or an unsaved man? It has been suggested that no less than three spiritual conditions are described in this chapter which deals with the law. These are:
   1. The spiritual man and the law (7:1-6).
      a. A man was bound by the law as a wife was bound by her husband.
      b. Only death could set the unhappy married and bound wife free, in this case the death of her husband (7:3).
      c. Only death could set the unhappy and law-bound man free, in this case his own death (7:4, 6): "We are delivered from the law . . . being dead."

The Greek speaks of a violent death here, that of Calvary. In a sense it may be said it was necessary for both Christ and the believer to die in order to get together. Ponder the following:

(1) In the Old Testament, Christ was married to unfaithful Israel (see the book of Hosea).

(2) In the New Testament, sinners are bound by the power of sin and the chains of the law.

(3) Then, Christ died, freeing him of his Old Testament relationship of sinful Israel (during this dispensation of the church). At the same time the believer died, freeing him from the law and sin.

(4) This blessed relationship will be fully consummated at the marriage of the Lamb (see Rev. 19:7, 8).

d. The purpose of all this is "that we should bring forth fruit unto God" (7:4). The spiritual man is therefore delivered from the law.

2. The natural man and the law (7:7-13). A number believe that these verses describe Paul's life prior to salvation. However, there are some problems with this view. (See Phil. 3:6.)

a. The law was used by sin to slay Paul (7:9-11). This may have been a reference to his Bar Mitzvah (a religious ceremony observed by all thirteen-year Jewish lads) at which time he formally took upon him the solemn responsibilities of the law. His carefree days of childhood were then over. He was accountable to God for his actions.

b. The law was used by sin to work in him "all manner of concupiscence (forbidden and evil desires)" (7:8). In other words, the law both *revealed* and, as used by sin, *revived* Paul's sin nature. Sin thus used the law as its basis of operation in its war against Paul.

c. The law in itself is *not* evil, but rather is "holy, and just, and good" (7:12).

(1) It is holy because it came from God (7:14).

(2) It is just because it rightfully condemns the sinner.

(3) It is good because it prepared the sinner for Christ (Gal. 3:24).

d. The law was ineffective only because of the weakness of the flesh (7:18). Herein is the real problem. The finest and most experienced football coach in America would lose every single game if he had a team composed of crippled and blind players. The natural man is therefore doomed by the law.

3. The carnal man and the law (7:14-25).

a. Paul desired to do the good and avoid the bad: "For I delight in the law of God after the inward man" (7:22; see also 2 Cor. 4:16; Eph. 3:16).

b. He discovered, however (to his utter frustration), he was doing the bad and avoiding the good. Paul was long on desire but short on determination. The will was there, but not the way. He found "a law, that when I would do good, evil is present with me" (7:21). This is the third of the five biblical "laws" referred to here in Romans:

(1) the law of Moses (3:19)

(2) the law of faith (3:2)

(3) the law of sin (7:21, 23, 25)

(4) the law of the mind (7:16)

(5) the law of the spirit (8:2, 4)

c. In utter despair he cries out, "O wretched man that I am! Who shall deliver me from the body of this death?" (7:24). This may have been a spiritual comparison to the Roman act of punishing a murderer by binding to him the corpse of his victim, thus using its very rot and stench to execute the killer. Phillips writes:

"Suppose a biologist were to perform an experiment by grafting, at a given stage of development, a butterfly to a spider and do so in such a way that the two creatures were fused into one and thus grew to maturity. What a clash of instincts there would be in a monstrosity like this! One part of the creature's nature would long for the clear vault of heaven, while the other part would crave a web in a dark corner and a diet of blood. What could be done with such a creature? Nothing, except put it to death. There is a sense in which, in the Garden of Eden, Satan performed just such diabolical surgery on the human race." (*Exploring Romans*, p. 120)

Paul thus realizes that the believer cannot control, change, cleanse, conquer, command, correct, or crucify the flesh.

d. Paul ends chapter 6 with the statement that eternal life comes only through Jesus Christ (6:23). He ends chapter 7 by concluding that the victorious life can come only through Jesus Christ (7:25).

Note: Before leaving chapter 7 it may prove helpful to briefly summarize the purpose and ministry of the Old Testament law.

The law consisted of three sections.

(1) The Ten Commandments (Ex. 20:3-17; Deut. 5:7-21).

(2) The social regulations concerning the people (Ex. 21-23).

(3) The religious ordinances concerning the tabernacle (Ex. 24-40).

e. The law followed the Abrahamic Covenant by some five centuries, and therefore did not in any way abrogate God's previous promises (Gen. 12:1-3; Gal. 3:17, 18). It was a way *of* life, but not a way *to* life (see Gal. 2:15, 16; 3:21; 2 Cor. 3:7, 9).

f. Why did not Christ come during Abraham's time? Faith was then present (see Gen. 15; Rom. 4). The answer is that the chief meaning of the law lies in the developing of an expectation of the Redeemer by revealing human sinfulness.

g. It was therefore an addition because the covenant with Abraham lacked a sufficient emphasis on sin. God used the ministry of two men to fully develop the meaning of faith repentance which leads to salvation. Note these two men:

(1) Moses introduced the curse (Gal. 3:13).

(2) Abraham introduced the blessing (Gal. 3:9, 14).

(3) Moses pointed to the system of death (2 Cor. 3:6; Rom. 7:9, 10).

(4) Abraham pointed to the system of life (Rom. 4:17-25; Heb. 11:19).

(5) Moses led to the crucifixion (Gal. 2:19, 20; 3:13).

(6) Abraham led to the resurrection (Heb. 11:19; Rom. 4:17, 19, 23-25).

"But they both belong together, for the sinner is to be redeemed, and to this end renewal and new birth are needful. But the new birth has man's conversion as a presupposition, and conversion is twofold: a turning from and a turning to, a NO to oneself, and a YES to God, or, as the New Testament puts it, REPENTANCE and FAITH! Only here is revealed to us the true meaning of the Old Testament histories:

(a) Throughout centuries God spoke the word 'faith' into the history of salvation—this is the meaning of the Covenant with Abraham. Throughout 2000 years it was an education in faith.

(b) Throughout centuries God spoke the word 'repent' into the history of salvation—this is the meaning of the law of Moses. For some 1500 years it was an education in repentance." (Erich Sauer, *Dawn of World Redemption*, pp. 122, 123)

f. Then came Jesus "into Galilee, preaching the gospel of the kingdom of God, and saying, The time is fulfilled, and the kingdom of God is at hand: repent ye, and believe the gospel" (Mk. 1:14, 15).

Thus, in one statement, Jesus joins perfectly both the message of Moses and that of Abraham (see also Acts 20:21). We may therefore conclude that the law functioned as:

(1) A bridle, whereby God could control Israel from above.

(2) A hedge, which separated Israel from the nations of the world.

(3) A mirror, revealing the true condition of man.

(4) A stimulant, bringing to surface the hidden sin of man.

(5) A school teacher, preparing us for, and delivering us to, Christ (Gal. 3:19, 24; Rom. 3:20; 7:7).

C. The prize—third floor of preservation. Paul has thus far discussed:

1. Why does the sinner need to be saved? (Answer, condemnation.)

2. How is the sinner saved? (Answer, justification.)

3. What happens after the sinner gets saved? (Answer, sanctification.) He will now ask and answer.

4. Will the sinner remain saved? (Answer, preservation.)

It has been observed that if the Bible were likened to a beautiful ring set with jewels, the book of Romans would be the most beautiful jewel in the ring and the eighth chapter the most beautiful facet in the jewel. Romans 8 is in essence an amplification of John 5:24 and Revelation 21:5.

"Verily, Verily, I say unto you, He that heareth my word, and believeth on him that sent me, hath everlasting life, and shall not come into condemnation; but is passed from death unto life" (Jn. 5:24).

"And he that sat upon the throne said, Behold, I make all things new. And he said unto me, write: for these words are true and faithful" (Rev. 21:5).

Will the believing sinner remain saved? He will, because of seven new things:

a. Because of his new position. He is now placed in Christ (8:1-4).

(1) The believer and the law of sin and death—he is set free from it through Christ (8:2).

(2) The believer and the law of Moses—he can fulfill the righteousness of it, through Christ (8:4).

Note: We observe Paul does not say there is no fault, or sin, or imperfection, but *no condemnation*. We also observe the time element—it is *now* no condemnation.

b. Because of his new Guest. He is now indwelled by the Holy Spirit (8:5-13).

c. Because of his new adoption. He is now adopted by the Father (8:14-17).

(1) The theology of adoption: Defined—the word literally means "the placing of a son." Adoption logically follows regeneration. Regeneration gives one his nature as a child of God, whereas adoption gives him his position as a son of God (Rom. 8:15-23; Gal. 4:4-6; Eph. 1:5; 2 Cor. 6:18).

Contrasted—how spiritual adoption differs from civil adoption:

(a) We never adopt our own children, but God never adopts any other than his own.

(b) Civil adoption provides comfort for the childless, but God had a beloved Son (Mt. 3:17; 17:5) prior to adopting us!

(c) There are usually many pleasing characteristics in a civil-adopted child, but not in God's children prior to their adoption (Rom. 3:10-18).

(d) Civil adoption could never give a child the same nature of the Father, but God's adopted are given the very mind of Christ (1 Cor. 2:16).

(e) In some cases, civil adoption could be declared null and void, but God's adopted are absolutely secure.

Compared—how spiritual adoption compares with civil adoption:

(f) The Father must begin the action leading to adoption (Isa. 1:18; Jn. 3:16).

(g) Both adoptions give an inheritance to one who previously had none (Rom. 8:17; 1 Pet. 1:1-9).

(h) Both adoptions provide a new name (Rev. 2:17; Jn. 1:42).

(2) The Trinity in adoption:

(a) There is an intimacy toward the Father. "Whereby we cry, Abba, Father" (8:15). This is a very personal name for one's Father. Only Jesus himself had used this until now. (See Mk. 14:36; Mt.26:42.)

(b) There is an illumination by the Spirit. He both leads us (8:14) and assures us (8:16).

(c) There is an inheritance with the Son. "Joint heirs with Christ" (8:17; see also Heb. 2:11).

d. Because of his new expectation (8:18-25).

(1) The nature of this hope: the full and final redemption of all creation. This includes:

(a) The Christian himself. He will receive a new body.

It will be a body like Christ's body (1 Jn. 3:2).

It will be a body of flesh and bone (Lk. 24:39). Our Lord both spoke (Jn. 20:17) and ate and drank (Lk. 24:30, 41-43; Jn. 21:13) in his resurrected body.

It will be a recognizable body (1 Cor. 13:12). Jesus was recognized by all believers after his resurrection.

It will be a body in which the Spirit predominates (1 Cor. 15:44, 49).

It will be a body unlimited by time and space (Jn. 20:19).

(b) The creation itself. All creation "was made subject to vanity"

(8:20) as a result of man's rebellion in Eden (Gen. 3:17, 18; Isa. 24:5, 6). The word vanity is *maraios*, which means "to be idle, to have no purpose" (Eccles. 1:5-8). But someday creation "itself also shall be delivered from the bondage of corruption" (8:21).

e. Because of his new prayer Helper (8:26, 27). The Holy Spirit who already lives *in* us (8:9, 11), and witnesses *to* us (8:16), now is said to pray *for* us (8:26).

(1) The necessity for this new help. In the Greek, the word infirmities (8:26) is in the singular. Paul had but a single infirmity in mind here: our ignorance and inability in prayer. "For we know not what we should pray for as we ought" (8:26).

The word "helpeth" should not be overlooked at this point. It means "to aid in the completion of a task." The same word is used in Luke 10:40. All this simply means the Holy Spirit expects the believer to do his share of praying also.

(2) The intensity of this new help. "The Spirit himself maketh intercession for us with groanings which cannot be uttered" (8:26).This is the third "groan" mentioned in chapter 8.

(a) The groan of nature (8:22)

(b) The groan of the believer (8:23).

(c) The groan of the Holy Spirit (8:26).

f. Because of his new knowledge (8:28).

"And we know that all things work together for good to them that love God, to them who are the called according to his purpose" (8:28).

Here we should note two things this verse does *not* say:

(1) It does not say all things in and by themselves are good, but rather that they work together for good. A classic Old Testament example of this is Joseph's testimony to his brothers. (See Gen. 45:5-8; 50:20. See also Ps. 76:10.) Jacob (Joseph's father) did not always understand this principle, thus his troubled conclusion in Genesis 42:36.

(2) It does not say this is true for all people, but only for God-lovers. But for these, it is an all-inclusive statement. It covers the good and the bad, the bright and the dark, the sweet and the bitter, the easy and the hard, the happy and the sad. It may be depended upon in prosperity and poverty, in health and sickness, in the calm and in the storm, in life and in death.

g. Because of his new goal (8:29-39). "To be conformed to the image of his Son"

(8:29). God has one supreme purpose on this earth today, and that is to conform the largest number of people in the least amount of time into the image of his dear Son.

(1) The steps leading to this goal:
   (a) "He did foreknow" the believer (8:29).
   (b) "He . . . did predestinate" the believer (8:29).
   (c) "He . . . called" the believer (8:30).
   (d) "He . . . justified" the believer (8:30).
   (e) "He . . . glorified" the believer (8:30).
   These five words form a golden chain of God's grace and glory, linking up from eternity past to eternity future.

(2) The absolute guarantee of this goal.
   (a) Who would dare attempt to slander us to the Father? "Who shall lay anything to the charge of God's elect? It is God that justifieth" (8:33). Thus, the same Judge that once condemned the sinner (Rom. 3:19) has now justified him. Who would dare oppose this?

     "He that spared not his own Son, but delivered him up for us all, how shall he not with him also freely give us all things?" (8:32).

   (b) Who would dare attempt to separate us from the Son? "Who shall separate us from the love of Christ?" (8:35).
     Shall tribulation (outward pressure)? No!
     Shall distress (inward pressure)? No!
     Shall persecution? No!
     Shall famine? No!
     Shall nakedness? No!
     Shall peril? No!
     Shall sword? No!
     Note: These first seven things are a brief historical and prophetical autobiography on Paul's life.
     Shall death (physical dying)? No!
     Shall life (and all its temptations)? No!
     Shall angels (good angels)? No!
     Shall principalities (bad angels)? No!
     Shall powers (human rulers)? No!
     Shall things present (events of today)? No!
     Shall things to come (events of tomorrow)? No!

SEVEN CERTAINTIES

THE BELIEVER HAS A NEW Position (8:1-4).

THE BELIEVER HAS A NEW Guest (8:5-13).

THE BELIEVER HAS A NEW Adoption (8:14-17).

THE BELIEVER HAS A NEW Expectation (8:18-25).

THE BELIEVER HAS A NEW Prayer Helper (8:26, 27).

THE BELIEVER HAS A NEW Knowledge (8:28).

THE BELIEVER HAS A NEW Goal (8:29-39).

     Shall height? No!
     Shall depth? No!
     Shall any other creature (any conceivable thing in the universe)? No!

When the staunch believer John Chrysostom was brought before the Roman Emperor in the fifth century and threatened with banishment for his faith, he replied, "Thou canst not banish me, for this world is my Father's house." "But I will slay thee," said the Emperor. "Nay, thou canst not," said the noble champion of the faith, "for my life is hid with Christ in God." "I will take away thy treasures." "Nay, but thou canst not, for my treasure is in heaven and my heart is there." "But I will drive thee away from man and thou shalt have no friend left." "Nay, thou canst not, for I have a friend in heaven from whom thou canst not separate me! I defy thee; for there is nothing that thou canst do to hurt me!"

III. The Synagogue of Israel—God's Wisdom (Explanation and Vindication—Rom. 9-11). Introduction: Before proceeding any further, Paul felt it necessary to stop here and discuss two problems. One problem was that Israel had rejected Christ. Of this there could be no serious doubt. How, then, could the great Messianic Old Testament passages concerning the coming kingdom be fulfilled? Paul knew that the *unbelieving* Jew would conclude that he (Paul) was wrong in identifying Christ as Israel's Messiah in the first place. He also realized the believing Jew might conclude that God had simply failed in his Word somehow.

At first the problem had not appeared serious at all. Over 3,000 Jews were saved at Pentecost (Acts 2:41). Then the number jumped to 5,000, including a great company of priests in Jerusalem (Acts 4:4; 6:7). It seemed only a short time till all Israel would be saved. The day of the Lord surely was at hand (Acts 2:16-21). But suddenly opposition set in! Stephen the deacon was stoned to death (Acts 7:57-60). This tragedy was intensified by the slaying of James the apostle (Acts 12:2). The Jerusalem Christian leaders had often been jailed. This was the situation when Paul wrote Romans.

In passing, we may note here that had Paul felt the church had become Israel, there would have existed no problem in the first place! The second problem concerned the "power plant of grace," so gloriously described by the apostle in Romans 6-8. What would now happen? Would the tiny "workshop of Israel" be torn down during the "age of grace"? Paul clearly and concisely answers these questions in chapters 9-11.

A. The sovereignty of God and Israel's selection in the past (Rom. 9).
  1. The twofold confession of Paul (9:1-3).
    a. He had "great heaviness and continual sorrow" in his heart for Israel.
    b. He said he "could wish that myself were accursed from Christ for my own brethren." Paul shared the compassion of both Moses (Ex. 32:31, 32) and Christ (Mt. 23:37) over Israel's sinful condition (see also Gal. 1:8, 9).
  2. The ninefold advantage of Israel (9:4, 5).
    a. They were Israelites. They were a special nation (Deut. 7:6), one having power with God (Gen. 32:38).
    b. They enjoyed the adoption. The entire nation had been adopted by God (Ex. 4:22; Deut. 14:1; Jer. 31:9).
    c. They had the glory. A reference to the Shekinah cloud, that visible, luminous appearance of God's presence.
      (1) It led them across the wilderness (Ex. 13:21, 22; Num. 9:17-22).
      (2) It protected them at the Red Sea (Ex. 14:19, 20, 24).
      (3) It filled the tabernacle during Moses' dedication (Ex. 40:34-48).
      (4) It filled the Temple during Solomon's dedication (1 Ki. 8:10, 11; 2 Chron. 5:13, 14).
      (5) It was removed during Ezekiel's time (Ezek. 10).
    d. They had the covenants.
      (1) The Abrahamic Covenant—promising a mighty nation (Gen. 12:2, 3, 7; 13:14-17; 15:5, 18; 17:8).
      (2) The Palestinian Covenant—promising a land (Deut. 30:3).
      (3) The Davidic Covenant—promising an eternal kingdom (2 Sam. 7:12-16; 23:5; 2 Chron. 13:5).
      (4) The new covenant—promising new hearts (Jer. 31:31-34).
    e. They had the law (Ex. 20; Deut. 5).
    f. They had the services of God. It was Israel which ministered in both the tabernacles and the Temple.
    g. They had the promises. This included both Christ's birth and future reign (Isa. 9:6, 7).
    h. They had the fathers. Israel enjoyed a regenerate ancestry, which included such giants as Abraham, Moses, David, etc.
    i. They produced that line which led to the humanity of Christ (Mt. 1:1-16; Lk. 3:23-38).
  3. The fivefold example of history (9:6-29). Paul now proves God's sovereign and unmerited grace from Israel's own history.
    a. The example of Ishmael and Isaac (9:6-9). God's sovereignty is seen through the selection of Isaac (Abraham's younger son) over Ishmael (his older son). Only the descendants of Isaac would become citizens of God's chosen nation.
    b. The example of Esau and Jacob (9:10-13). Some have been troubled over Paul's statement here in verse 13: "As it is written, Jacob have I loved, but Esau have I hated." It should be noted that the statement obviously does *not* refer to the two boys, but to the nations they founded, namely, Israel and Edom! This Old Testament quote is not found in Genesis, but in Malachi 1:2-5. The Old Testament prophet Obadiah clearly tells us *why* God hated Edom. In each case here (9:6-13), God rejected men who had been first born into patriarchal families. In each case the parent wished to see the rejected one inherit the problem. Abraham pleaded for Ishmael (Gen. 17:18) and Isaac attempted to pass the blessing on to Esau (Gen. 27:1, 4, 30, 33).
    c. The example of Pharaoh (9:14-23).
      (1) The *facts* of God's dealings with Israel and Pharaoh.
        (a) God determined to pardon sinful Israel with undeserved grace. "I will have mercy on whom I will have mercy, and I will have compassion on whom I will have compassion" (9:15).
        (b) God determined to punish sinful Pharaoh with deserved judgment. "Even for this same purpose have I raised thee up, that I might shew my power in thee, and that my name might be declared throughout all the earth" (9:17).
      (2) The *fairness* of God's dealings with Israel and Pharaoh. Paul here answers two objections:
        (a) That God is not righteous. Some would claim that he was unfair in hardening Pharaoh's heart. It should be noted that on at least seven occasions in

the book of Exodus we are told that God hardened the heart of Pharaoh (4:21; 7:3; 9:12; 10:1, 20, 27; 11:10). How are we to understand this? A partial (and only partial) answer may be found in the following observation:

The manner in which a given object will react when confronted by an outside influence is wholly dependent upon the nature of that object. For example, imagine a winter scene. Yonder is a frozen river. On either side is a bank of yellow clay. Suddenly the sun comes from behind the clouds and shines brightly down upon the river and the banks. What happens next? The reaction is this: the ice will melt but the clay will harden. Thus we see in nature the same outside, heavenly influence softening one object but hardening the other.

Furthermore, it should be pointed out that on four occasions we are informed that Pharaoh hardened his own heart (Ex. 7:22; 8:15, 19; 9:35). The word "hardeneth" in 9:18 (kabed) is translated "heavy" in Exodus 17:12; 18:18; Psalm 38:4; Isaiah 1:4. Thus, God left his heart heavy with iniquities.

(b) Man is not responsible. "Thou wilt say then unto me, why doth he yet find fault? For who hath resisted his will?" (9:19). Paul spends little time on this objection, simply pointing out that the potter has power over the clay he works with in choosing the kind of vessel he makes. It should be noted here (9:21) that Paul does not say God *made* the clay as it was, but that he *worked* with it (see Jer. 18:1-6; Isa. 45:9; 64:6-8). Two kinds of vessels are described here: "The vessels of wrath fitted to destruction" (9:22). This is in the middle voice, meaning "to fit oneself."

"The vessels of mercy, which he had afore prepared unto glory" (9:23). The conclusion of the matter is that *hell* (destruction) is the deserved destination of the sinful man, while *heaven* (glory) is the undeserved destination of the saved man.

d. The example of Hosea (9:24-26). He predicted God would call out a "people which were not my people" (9:25; see also Hosea 1:10; 2:23). Here God's sovereignty is seen in reference to the saved Gentiles (1 Pet. 2:9, 10).

e. The example of Isaiah (9:27-29). He predicted, "though the number of the children of Israel be as the sand of the sea, a remnant shall be saved" (9:27; see also Isa. 1:9). Here God's sovereignty is seen in reference to the saved Israelite remnant.

4. The twofold conclusion of Paul (9:30-33).
   a. The Gentiles, through faith, had attained righteousness without ever seeking it.
   b. Israel, through the law, had not attained righteousness even after seeking it. They looked for a bold lion, but God sent them a bleeding lamb. They wanted a throne; they were offered a cross.

B. The righteousness of God and Israel's rejection at the present. Introduction: Romans 9 and 10 should always be read together. Chapter 9 shows why some Jews are saved, and chapter 10 explains why most are lost.

1. The source of righteousness (10:4, 5). "For Christ is the end of the law for righteousness to every one that believeth" (10:4). We might reword this verse to say that Christ is the end of the Old Testament law to the believer after the cross as George Washington was to the end of the British law to the American after the Revolutionary War. (See 2 Cor. 3:6-11; Heb. 7:11-19; Gal. 3:24; Eph. 2:15; Col. 2:14.)

2. The availability of righteousness (10:6-8). "The word is nigh thee, even in thy mouth, and in thy heart" (10:8). Because of this, we need not be concerned with:
   a. The incarnation—"Who shall ascend into heaven? (that is, to bring Christ down from above)" (10:6).
   b. The resurrection—"Who shall descend into the deep? (that is, to bring up Christ again from the dead)" (10:7).

3. The method of righteousness (10:9, 10). Some have made oral confession a condition of salvation on the basis of 10:10, "For with the heart man believeth unto salvation; and with the mouth confession is made unto salvation." (See also 10:9.)

The Bible, of course, does not impose this limitation. Paul evidently was stressing the same truth found in James 2:20, that is, a genuine possession of Christ in one's heart will surely lead to a confession of Christ with one's mouth. The fruit will prove the root. (See Mt. 10:32; Lk. 12:8; Jn. 12:42, 43; Mt. 12:34.) The method, then, of righteousness, is faith in Christ.

4. The scope of righteousness (10:11-13)—whosoever (see 10:11, 13). Paul had earlier shown that all men were lost. He now says that all can be saved. Compare the "whosoever" mentioned here with that in Revelation 20:15.

5. The presentation of righteousness (10:14, 15). These verses are a beautiful little discourse to demonstrate the necessity for taking the

THE RIGHTEOUSNESS OF GOD AND ISRAEL'S REJECTION AT THE PRESENT

Romans 10

1. THE **SOURCE**
OF GOD'S RIGHTEOUSNESS
(10:4, 5)

2. THE **AVAILABILITY**
OF GOD'S RIGHTEOUSNESS
(10:6-8)

3. THE **METHOD**
OF GOD'S RIGHTEOUSNESS
(10:9, 10)

4. THE **SCOPE**
OF GOD'S RIGHTEOUSNESS
(10:11-13)

5. THE **PRESENTATION**
OF GOD'S RIGHTEOUSNESS
(10:14, 15)

6. THE **REJECTION**
OF GOD'S RIGHTEOUSNESS
(10:16-21)

gospel which is intended *for* all, *to* all. In other words, world reconciliation demands world evangelization. Since salvation through Christ has been provided *for* all, it must now be proclaimed *to* all. Paul here summarizes God's program for world evangelism. It is in five steps.

a. In order to be saved, a sinner must call upon the Lord.

b. In order to call, he must believe.

c. In order to believe, he must hear.

d. In order to hear, there must be a preacher. (This may refer to any vehicle carrying the gospel message, be it a human agent, tract, radio broadcast, etc.)

e. In order to preach, they must be sent. This means by God himself. (See Isa. 6:8; Jn. 15:16; 20:21.) Paul then quotes from Isaiah 52:7, "How beautiful are the feet of them that preach the gospel of peace and bring glad tidings of good things!" The Greek word here translated beautiful means "full bloom, developed, mature." Paul may mean that witnessing for Christ produces a full-blooded, developed, and mature Christian.

6. The rejection of righteousness (10:1-3, 16-21).

a. Israel had zeal without knowledge. One may also, of course, suffer the opposite—knowledge without zeal. The first leads to hot fanaticism (Gal. 1:14; Acts 22:3). The second leads to cold formalism.

b. Paul's prayer was that God would give Israel this knowledge. He would have little in common with modern theology. Note the following statement by Reinhold Niebuhr: "Do not try to convert Jews. . . . Jews may find God more readily in their own faith than in Christianity."

c. Paul applies David's words about creation (Rom. 10:18; Ps. 19:4) to that of salvation to demonstrate that Israel's unbelief was not due to the fact that they had never heard, for this opportunity had been as wide as the star-studded heavens.

d. Both Moses (Deut. 32:21) and Isaiah (53:1; 65:1) had predicted this sad rejection (see Rom. 10:16, 19, 20).

e. God had been so patient with his rebellious nation. "All day long [for over fifteen centuries, the entire age of the law] I have stretched forth my hands unto a disobedient and gainsaying people" (Rom. 10:21; Isa. 65:2; see also Mt. 23:37-39). Israel had thus been guilty of:

(1) Disobedience of the Word of God.

(2) Disgruntlement with the God of the Word.

C. The wisdom of God, and Israel's restoration in the Future (Rom. 11). Paul has just discussed the rejection of Israel in chapter 10. He will now show that this rejection was neither *total* (1-25) nor *final* (26-33).

1. The rejection was not total (11:1-25).

a. The factions of Israel (11:1-10). This nation is now placed into two separate categories:

(1) The minority group: "Even so then at this present time also there is a remnant according to the election of grace" (11:5). Paul offers a twofold proof that God always has his faithful remnant.

(a) As seen through his own conversion (11:1).

(b) As seen in the time of Elijah (11:2-4). Elijah felt he was the only believer during his day and actually made "intercession to God against Israel" (11:2).

But God (who will *never* answer this kind of prayer, regardless of who prays it) quickly informed him that: "I have reserved to myself seven thousand men, who have not bowed the knee to the image of Baal" (Rom. 11:4; see also 1 Ki. 19:10, 14, 18).

(2) The majority group: "And the rest were blinded" (11:7). Present-day Israel is thus plagued with a threefold blindness:

(a) The blindness caused by the fall of Adam (Eph. 4:18).

(b) The blindness caused by Satan (2 Cor. 4:4).

(c) The blindness caused by God (Rom. 11:8).

This tragic spiritual blindness was predicted by both Isaiah (Isa. 29:10; Rom. 11:8) and David (Ps. 69:22, 23; Rom. 11:9, 10). The reason for this blindness is also predicted by David, namely, the Jews' treatment of Christ. Note the words in Psalm 69:21 which preceded this judgment prophecy of blindness: "They gave me also gall for my meat; and in my thirst gave me vinegar to drink." (See the fulfillment of this in Mt. 27:34, 48.)

b. The fullness of the Gentiles (11:11-25). This phrase (found in 11:25) should be distinguished from the times of the Gentiles mentioned by Christ in Luke 21:24.

(1) The "times" of the Gentiles is political in nature and refers to that period from the Babylonian captivity until the end of the Tribulation. (See Deut. 28:28-68; 2 Chron. 36:1-21; Dan. 9:24-27.)

(2) The *fullness* of the Gentiles is spiritual in nature, and refers to that period of time covering the completion of the body of Christ, made up of Jews and Gentiles, saved from Pentecost to the rapture. (See Acts 15:14; Eph. 4:11-13; 1 Cor. 12:12, 13.)

The details of this Gentile fullness period are as follows:

(3) Believing Gentiles are at the present time being placed into God's tree of salvation.

(4) They are taken from a wild olive tree (11:17).

(5) They are grafted into a good olive tree (11:24). This process is, as Paul rightly observes, "contrary to nature" (11:24). Normally, when the wild is grafted into the good, the good is conquered by the wild. However, when the good is grafted to the wild, just the opposite takes place.

(6) Gentiles are warned against boasting because of their new status, "For if God spared not the natural branches, take heed lest he also spare not thee" (11:21).

At this point, two thoughts must be kept in mind.

(7) Paul is *not* teaching that the church has replaced Israel. He has already asked and answered this question in 11:1, "I say then, Hath God cast away his people? God forbid."

(8) Paul is *not* teaching that a saved Gentile may be cut off from this tree and lose his salvation. He is simply saying that since God did not spare the nation Israel when they apostatized, he will likewise not spare an apostate church. Christendom is going in the same direction today as Israel once did, and God will reject and judge them for it. (See 1 Tim. 4:1-3; 2 Pet. 2:1-22; Rev. 3:14-22; 17:3-18.)

Paul offers these details concerning the fullness of the Gentiles, "For I would not, brethren, that ye should be ignorant of this mystery" (11:25). A mystery in the Bible is a previously hidden truth, not revealed in the Old Testament, but declared and, at times, explained in the New Testament.

(9) There are twelve such mysteries. Without amplification, these are:

(a) The mystery of the kingdom of heaven (Mt. 13:3-50; Mk. 4:1-25; Lk. 8:4-15).

(b) The mystery of the rapture (1 Cor. 15:51, 52; 1 Thess. 4:16).

(c) The mystery of the church as the body of Christ (Eph. 3:1-11; 6:19; Col. 4:3; Rom. 16:25).

(d) The mystery of the church as the bride of Christ (Eph. 5:28-32).

(e) The mystery of the indwelling Christ (Gal. 2:20; Col. 1:26, 27).

(f) The mystery of the incarnate Christ (Col. 2:2, 9; 1 Cor. 2:7).

(g) The mystery of godliness. (1 Tim. 3:16).

(h) The mystery of iniquity (2 Thess. 2:3-12; Mt. 13:33).

(i) The mystery of Israel's present blindness (Rom. 11:25).

(j) The mystery of the seven stars (Rev. 1:20).

(k) The mystery of Babylon the harlot (Rev. 17:5, 7).

(l) The mystery of God (Rev. 10:7; 11:15-19).

In Romans 11:25 the mystery is that "blindness in part is happened to Israel until the fullness of the Gentiles be come in."

2. The rejection was not permanent (11:26-36).

a. The Israel of God (11:26-32).

(1) They would be restored through the ratification of their promised covenant. "For this is my covenant unto them, when I shall take away their sins" (Rom. 11:27; see also Isa. 59:21; 27:9; Jer. 31:31-37; Heb. 8:8; 10:16; Zech. 13:1).

(2) They would be restored through the return of their promised Christ. "There shall come out of Sion the Deliverer, and shall turn away ungodliness from Jacob" (11:26; see Isa. 59:20).

b. The God of Israel (11:33-36).

"O the depth of the riches both of the wisdom and knowledge of God! how unsearchable are his judgments, and his ways past finding out! For who hath known the mind of the Lord? or who hath been his counsellor? Or who hath first given to him, and it shall be recompensed unto him again? For of him, and through him, and to him, are all things: to whom be glory for ever. Amen."

This is the first of five benedictions by Paul here in Romans. (See also 15:33; 16:20; 16:24; 16:25-27.)

IV. The Temple of God—God's Will (Transformation and Exhortation) (Rom. 12-16).

A. Public responsibilities for all the redeemed (12:1—15:13).

1. The believer and self (12:1-3). In chapter 6 Paul gives a detailed *explanation* of those steps leading to sanctification. In this chapter he now extends the *invitation*.

a. How is the invitation offered? "I beseech you." Paul does not issue a curt command, but rather a pleading request. Loving service simply cannot be commanded. This is the language of grace and the method of the apostle. (See also 1 Cor. 4:16; Eph. 4:1; 1 Tim. 2:1. Contrast this with Lk. 12:20.)

b. What is the believer invited to do? He is to present his body "a living sacrifice, holy, acceptable unto God." Note:

(1) It is to be his *body*. God is not primarily interested in our time, talents, or treasury. The only gift which satisfies the Redeemer Creator is the body of his redeemed creature! (See 1 Cor. 3:16; 6:19, 20; 2 Cor. 8:5.)

(2) It is to be his *living* body. Sometimes it is easier to die for the Lord than live for him.

(3) It is to be a *separated* (holy) living body.

c. Why is the believer invited to do this?

(1) Because he has already experienced God's mercy. All other faiths make sacrifice the root of mercy, but Christianity makes it the flower. (Contrast this with 1 Ki. 18:26-29; 2 Ki. 3:26, 27.)

(2) Because it is not only the proper and requested course of action, but also the practical and reasonable route. Note:

(a) To the *sinner*, God says, "Come now, and let us reason together, saith the Lord: Though your sins be as scarlet, they shall be as white as snow; though they be red like crimson, they shall be as wool" (Isa. 1:18). The proper and practical thing for the sinner to do is give God his heart.

(b) To the saint, God says, "Present your bodies . . . unto God, which is your reasonable service." The proper and practical thing for the saint to do is give God his body.

d. What are the results of obeying this invitation?

(1) The believer will not be conformed (molded) from without by the world.

(2) The believer will be transformed from within by the renewing of his mind. The word "transformed" is *metamorpheo* in the Greek, whence we get our word *metamorphosis*, that biological change whereby a caterpillar becomes a butterfly. The same word is used in the transfiguration of Jesus in Matthew 17:2. (See also 2 Cor. 3:18.) This transformation refers to that act of a believer arranging his outward *position* so that it agrees with his inward *condition*. (See 1 Pet. 1:14; 1 Jn. 2:15.) The renewing of the mind here in 12:2 is probably a reference to constant Bible study and prayer (Eph. 4:23; Col. 3:10). This daily renewing is the only safeguard against failure (1 Cor. 9:24-27).

(3) The believer will thus be able to discern and perform God's perfect will for his life.

(4) The believer will see himself as God sees him, and will not "think of himself more highly than he ought to think" (12:3).

2. The believer and service (12:4-21).

a. The tools of service (12:4-8) The Holy Spirit has provided the believer with various supernatural gifts with which he is to serve Christ. Seven of these tools of service are mentioned here:

(1) prophesying
(2) ministering
(3) teaching
(4) exhorting
(5) giving
(6) ruling
(7) showing of mercy

b. The techniques of service (12:9-21).

(1) We are to sincerely (without dissimulation) love all the saints (12:9, 10).

"To dwell above, with saints in love, that will indeed be glory; to dwell below with saints we know, well, that's a different story!"

(2) We are to "abhor that which is evil" (12:9; see Ps. 96:10; Heb. 1:9).

(3) We are to "cleave [like glue] to that which is good" (12:9; see Acts 8:29).

(4) We are to develop praise, patience, and prayer (12:12).

(5) We are to be fervent (at the boiling point) in our desire to please God (12:11). God hates indifference (Rev. 3:15, 16).

(6) We are to distribute to the needs of the saints (12:13; see 2 Cor. 9:1; Heb. 13:16; 1 Jn. 3:17).

(7) We are to eulogize (say nice things about) those who would persecute

us. The phrase "curse not" (12:14) is not a command against using profanity concerning our enemies, but rather of improper praying for them: "Lord, you know what he did to me and I hope you really chastise him for it." (See 1 Pet. 2:23; 3:9; 1 Cor. 4:12.)

(8) We are to "rejoice with them that do rejoice, and weep with them that weep" (12:15). Jesus did this (John 2, 11). (The theological reason for this is discussed in 1 Cor. 12:26.)

(9) We are to "mind not high things, but condescend to men of low estate" (12:16). Diotrephes was guilty of this (see 3 John 9).

(10) We are to destroy our enemies. The way we are to do this is make them our friends (12:18-21). Paul says: "Therefore if thine enemy hunger, feed him; if he thirst, give him drink: for in so doing thou shalt heap coals of fire on his head." The two classic Old Testament examples of this are found in David's treatment of King Saul (1 Sam. 24, 26) and Joseph's attitude toward his brothers (Gen. 45).

3. The believer and society (13:1-14); what he is to do (13:1-10).

a. His duties toward the rulers of the state (13:1-7).

(1) He is to be in subjection to the higher powers, for "the powers that be are ordained of God" (13:1). The Bible teaches that a child of God is not to love the *systems* of this world, or be conformed to its *patterns*, but nevertheless is to obey its *laws*. The Scriptures present both a separation from and a submission to the state on the part of the Christian (Titus 3:1; 1 Pet. 2:13).

The Jews of the Roman Empire were notoriously bad citizens. They refused to obey and used Deuteronomy 17:14, 15 as their proof text. However, Paul taught subjection to the state in spite of the shameful and shabby treatment he had often received at its hands (Acts 16:22-24, 37, 38; see Prov. 8:15, 16; Dan. 2:21; 4:17; Jn. 19:10, 11). Thus, human government is a divine institution given by God after the flood (Gen. 9) to assure order and prevent anarchy (see Jdg. 17:6).

(2) He is to know that "whosoever therefore resisteth the power, resisteth the ordinance of God" (13:2). It should be noted that Paul is here establishing general principles to guide the Christian living in a society governed by laws. He does not deal with what action the believer is to take when these laws are immoral or unscriptural. This question is answered in another passage (Acts 5:29).

(3) He is to render tribute (federal and local taxes), and custom (sales taxes) to the coffers of the state, and fear and honor to the keepers of that state (13:7). A man once stopped D. L. Moody in Chicago and asked him where he was going. The great evangelist replied, "To cast my vote in the forthcoming elections." Somewhat shocked, the man admonished him, "But, brother Moody, don't you realize you are a citizen of heaven and that this world is not your final home?" Moody smiled and said, "That's true, but in the meanwhile I pay my taxes in Cook County!"

b. His duties toward the rest of the state (13:8-10). "Owe no man anything but to love one another: for he that loveth another hath fulfilled the law" (13:8). This passage does not prohibit a Christian from buying a home or car on the installment plan. Taken in context, it simply says we are to pay our debts to society. Paul has already said, however, that *all* believers owe the gospel to the unsaved they come into contact with (Rom. 1:14).

Why he is to do these things (13:11-14).

"And that, knowing the time, that now it is high time to awake out of sleep: for now is our salvation nearer than when we believed. The night is far spent, the day is at hand: let us therefore cast off the works of darkness, and let us put on the armour of light."

Paul speaks of the night as almost over, while Jesus says it is yet to come (Jn. 9:4). Both are right. To the saint, the day breaks, but to the sinner, the night comes. This present world is the only hell the Christian will ever know, and it is the only heaven the unsaved will experience. This long night of sin has extended for thousands of years, beginning with Adam's rebellion. But the Morning Star has already appeared (Lk. 2). Soon the Sun of Righteousness will arise with healing in his wings. Every single New Testament epistle writer believed this. (See 1 Cor. 15:51; 1 Thess. 4:16, Paul; Jas. 5:8, 1 Pet. 4:7; 1 Jn. 2:18, 28; Jude 18.) Especially to be noted in Paul's phrase, "the day is at hand" in verse 12. This is the first of at least ten important "days" in the Bible, all future. These are:

(1) The day of the rapture (Rom. 13:12; Eph. 4:30; Phil. 1:6, 10; 2:16; Heb. 10:37; 2 Pet. 1:19). (May be regarded as a literal twenty-four-hour day.)

(2) The judgment seat of Christ day (1 Cor. 3:13; 5:5; 2 Tim. 1:18; 4:8; 1 Jn. 4:17). (May be regarded as a literal twenty-four-hour day and will include only Christians.)

(3) The day of the Lord (Joel 1:15; 2:1, 2, 11, 31; Acts 2:20; 2 Thess. 2:3; Rev. 6:17). (This "day" covers the entire tribulation, a period of seven years.)

(4) The day of Christ's Second Coming (Mt. 24:36; 26:29; 1 Thess. 5:2-4; 2 Thess. 1:10). (May be regarded as a literal twenty-four-hour day.)

(5) The day of Armageddon (Rev. 16:14). (May be regarded as a literal twenty-four-hour day.)

(6) The resurrection of the just day (Jn. 6:39, 40, 44, 54; 11:24). (May be regarded as a literal twenty-four-hour day and includes all Old Testament saints and tribulational believers.)

(7) The fallen angel judgment day (Jude 1:6). (May be regarded as a literal twenty-four-hour day).

(8) The day of Christ (1 Cor. 1:8; 2 Cor. 1:14; 2 Tim. 1:12). (This "day" covers the entire millennium, a period of one thousand years!)

(9) The great white throne judgment day (Mt. 7:22; 11:22; Jn. 12:48; Acts 17:31; Rom. 2:5, 16; 2 Pet. 2:9). (May be regarded as a literal twenty-four-hour day.)

(10) The new creation day (2 Pet. 3:7-13). (May be regarded as a literal twenty-four-hour day.)

Paul then exhorts the believer to "put on the armour of light" (13:12; see Eph. 6:10-17 for the specific pieces of this armor).

4. The believer and weaker saints (14:1-23).
   a. No believer is to be judged by another down here.
      (1) We are not to criticize his legalism (in matters of diet and days). "For the Kingdom of God is not meat and drink; but righteousness, and peace, and joy in the Holy Ghost" (14:17).
      (2) We are not to compromise our liberty.
         "That no man put a stumbling block or an occasion to fall in his brother's way." . . . "Let not then your good be evil spoken of." . . . "Let us therefore follow after the things which make for peace, and things wherewith one may edify another" (14:13, 16, 19).
   b. All believers will be judged by the Master up there.
      "For we shall all stand before the judgment seat of Christ. For it is written, as I live, saith the Lord, every knee shall bow to me, and every

tongue shall confess to God. So then every one of us shall give account of himself to God" (14:10-12).
There are some fourteen special categories of judgment in the Bible. In the book of Romans Paul refers to at least four of these.
   (1) The Garden of Eden judgment of Adam (Rom. 5:12).
   (2) The Calvary judgment of Christ (Rom. 4:25).
   (3) The judgment seat of Christ (Rom. 14:10).
   (4) The tribulational judgment of Satan (Rom. 16:20).

5. The believer and the Savior (15:1-13). The earthly ministry of our Lord is a pattern for the believer (1 Pet. 2:21-25).
   a. It was a sacrificial ministry: "For even Christ pleased not himself" (15:3).
   b. It was a suffering ministry: "As it is written, the reproaches of them that reproached thee fell upon me" (15:3).
   c. It was a scriptural ministry (15:4).
   d. It was a sharing ministry: "Wherefore receive ye one another, as Christ also received us, to the glory of God" (15:7).
   e. It was a sure ministry: "To confirm the promises made unto the fathers" (15:8).
   f. It was a spirited ministry: "For this cause I will confess to thee among the Gentiles, and sing unto thy name. And again he saith, Rejoice, ye Gentiles, with his people" (15:9, 10; see also Ps. 18:49; 117:1; Deut. 32:43; Isa. 11:10).

B. Personal remarks for the Roman redeemed (15:14—16:27).
   1. Paul gives a review of his past ministry (15:14-21).
      a. He mentions his specialized ministry: "The minister of Jesus Christ to the Gentiles" (15:16).
      b. He mentions his miracles, "Through mighty signs and wonders, by the power of the Spirit of God" (15:19). The book of Acts records many of Paul's miracles:
         (1) Striking a sorcerer with blindness in Paphos of Cyprus (13:11, 12).
         (2) Various miracles in Iconium (14:3, 4).
         (3) Healing a cripple in Lystra (14:8-18).
         (4) Curing a demoniac girl in Philippi (16:16-18).
         (5) Healing many of diseases and demons at Ephesus (19:11, 12).
         (6) Raising Eutychus at Troas (20:9, 10).
         (7) Restoring Publius's father of a fever and healing others on the Isle of Melita (28:8, 9).
      c. He mentions his mission field, "From Jerusalem, and round about unto Illyricum, I have fully preached the gospel of Christ" (Rom. 15:19).
      d. He mentions his methodology, "Yea, so have I strived to preach the gospel, not where Christ was named, lest I should

build upon another man's foundation" (Rom. 15:20).

e. He mentions his motivation, "To whom he was not spoken of, they shall see: and they that have not heard shall understand" (Rom. 15:21).

2. Paul gives a preview of his planned ministry (15:22—16:27).

a. He determines to visit them at a later time—as he goes to Spain (15:24, 28). The Pillars of Hercules beckoned to Paul, the westernmost reaches of mainland Europe, and the civilized world in his day. Did he later get to Spain? Just before his death he would write, "I have finished my course" (2 Tim. 4:7). Since Spain was on his itinerary we assume he did indeed get there.

b. He desires their prayers at the present time—as he goes to Rome (15:25-27, 30, 31). He was going there to deliver to the poor saints a financial offering which he had been collecting from all over the Empire. Paul had, no doubt, in his preconversion days, caused the poverty of many Christians in Rome. He asked prayer, "That I may be delivered from them that do not believe in Judea; and that my service which I have for Jerusalem may be accepted of the saints" (15:31). Note now:

(1) The commendation of the apostle: "I commend unto Phebe our sister" (16:1). Phebe carried the precious epistle to the Romans from Corinth.

(2) The salutations of the apostle. He now leaves the mountainpeaks of doctrine to come down to the pavements of Rome. He began his epistle by saying that "without ceasing I make mention of you always in my prayers" (1:9). At the end of his letter he mentions no less than twenty-eight of them by name:

Priscilla and Aquila: "Likewise greet the church that is in their house" (16:5). Local churches met in private homes at the very beginning. (See Acts 12:12; Col. 4:15; 1 Cor. 16:19; Philemon 2, 14, 15.) Paul had known this couple for some time (Acts 18:2, 18, 26; 1 Cor. 16:19).

Epaenetus: Paul's first convert in Achaia (16:5)

Mary: "Who bestoweth much labor on us" (16:6).

Note: Many of these faithful helpers of Paul are women. It was the women who also aided Christ in his hour of need when the men forsook him. He was aided by women:

(a) On the way to the cross (Lk. 2:27).

(b) At the cross (Jn. 19:25).

(c) At the burial (Mt. 27:61; Lk. 23:55).

(d) At the empty tomb (Jn. 20:11; Mk. 16:1).

Andronicus and Junia: a couple possibly related to Paul (16:7).

Amplias: "My beloved in the Lord" (16:8).

Urbane: "Our helper in Christ" (16:9).

Apelles: "Approved in Christ" (16:10). This man had apparently gone successfully through a test.

Stachys: "My beloved" (16:9).

Herodion: Grandson of Herod the Great? (16:11).

Aristobulus' household (16:10).

Narcissus' household (16:11).

Tryphena and Tryphosa: "Who labor in the Lord" (16:12).

Persis: "Which labored much in the Lord" (16:12).

Rufus and his mother: "Chosen in the Lord, and his mother and mine" (16:13). Note: Simon Cyrenian who carried the cross for Jesus was the father of Rufus (Mark 15:21).

Asyncritus (16:14).

Phlegon (16:14).

Hermas (16:14).

Patrobas (16:14).

Hermes (16:14).

Philologus (16:15).

Julia (16:15).

Nereus and his sister (16:15).

Olympas (16:15).

c. He detects a possible future problem.

"Now I beseech you, brethren, mark them which cause divisions and offences contrary to the doctrine which ye have learned; and avoid them. For they that are such serve not our Lord Jesus Christ, but their own belly; and by good words and fair speeches deceive the hearts of the simple."

The New Testament gives three reasons for dismissing a member from the fellowship of a local church.

(1) For troublemaking (Rom. 16:17; 2 Thess. 3:6; Prov. 6:19). Note: When Paul finally reached Rome, he found those troublemakers hard at work. (See Phil. 1:14-18; 3:18.)

(2) For immorality (1 Cor. 5).

(3) For heresy (Titus 3:10).

The procedure for dismissing such a person is described in 1 Corinthians 5:4 and Matthew 18:15-17. (See also 2 Thess. 3:14, 15.)

d. He declares the doom of Satan. "And the God of peace shall bruise Satan under your feet shortly." This prophecy will be fulfilled in a twofold manner:

(1) When he is cast into the bottomless pit for a thousand years during the millennium (Rev. 20:1-3).

(2) When he is cast into the lake of fire forever after the millennium (Rev. 20:10).

After sending greetings from seven of his companions who were with him at the time (Timothy, Lucius, Jason, Sosipater, Gaius, Erastus, Quartus, and Tertius, who wrote the letter and sends his own greetings), Paul ends the greatest letter in the history of the world with a glowing doxology:

"The grace of our Lord Jesus Christ be with you all. Amen. Now to him that is of power to stablish you according to my gospel, and the preaching of Jesus Christ, according to the revelation of the mystery, which was kept secret since the world began, but now is made manifest, and by the scriptures of the prophets, according to the commandment of the everlasting God, made known to all nations for the obedience of faith: To God only wise, be glory through Jesus Christ for ever. Amen" (16:24-27).

EPHESIANS

INTRODUCTION:

Dr. J. Vernon McGee has the following excellent introduction to this magnificent epistle. McGee writes:

"A quartet of men left Rome in the year A.D. 62, bound for the province of Asia, which was located in what is currently designated as Asia Minor. These men had on their persons four of the most sublime compositions of the Christian faith. These precious documents would be invaluable if they were in existence today. Rome did not comprehend the significance of the writings of an unknown prisoner. If she had, these men would have been apprehended and the documents seized.

When they bade farewell to the Apostle Paul, each was given an epistle to bear to his particular constituency. These four letters are designated 'The Prison Epistles of Paul' since he wrote them while imprisoned in Rome, awaiting a hearing before Nero, the Caesar at that time, to whom Paul, as a Roman citizen, had appealed his case.

This quartet of men and their respective places of abode can be identified:

1. Epaphroditus from Philippi (Phil. 4:18) had the Epistle to the Philippians.
2. Tychicus from Ephesus (Eph. 6:21) had the Epistle to the Ephesians.
3. Epaphras from Colosse (Col. 4:12) had the Epistle to the Colossians.
4. Onesimus, a slave from Colosse (Philemon 10) had the Epistle to Philemon (who was his master).

These epistles present a composite picture of Christ, the Church, the Christian life, and the inter-relationship and functioning of all. These different facets present the Christian life on the highest plane.

EPHESIANS presents 'the Church which is his body'—this is the invisible Church, of which Christ is the head.

COLOSSIANS presents Christ, 'the head of the body, the Church.' The emphasis is upon Christ, rather than on the Church.

PHILIPPIANS presents Christian living with Christ as the dynamic: 'I can do all things through Christ which strengtheneth me' (Phil. 4:13).

PHILEMON presents Christian living in action in a pagan society: 'If thou count me therefore a partner, receive him as myself. If he hath wronged thee, or oweth thee ought, put that on mine account' (Philemon 17, 18).

The gospel walked in shoe leather in the first century—it worked." (*Exploring Through Ephesians,* p. 3)

1. The Ephesian church was founded by Paul during his second missionary trip.
2. After spending eighteen months in Corinth (Acts 18:11), he visited Ephesus with Aquila and Priscilla (Acts 18:18).
3. Paul stayed there for only a short time but promised to return (Acts 18:19-21).
4. Aquila and Priscilla remained in Ephesus where God led them to instruct a powerful Bible preacher named Apollos in the details of the Word of God (Acts 18:24-26).
5. Paul returned during his third missionary trip and stayed three years (19:8-10; 20:31).
6. His stay in Ephesus is marked by three noteworthy events:
   a. The disciples of John episode (Acts 19:1-12).
   b. The divination of Sceva's sons episode (19:13-20).
   c. The defenders of Diana episode (19:21-41).
7. While in Ephesus he writes 1 and 2 Corinthians. (See 1 Cor. 16:8, 9.)
8. He also works many miracles (Acts 19:12).
9. He is later visited by the Ephesian elders during a layover at Miletus, en route to Jerusalem (Acts 20:16-38).
10. It is thought that this epistle may be the one referred to by Paul in Colossians 4:16.
11. Ephesus is the only New Testament church to receive a letter from more than one Bible writer. John the apostle also had a message for them (Rev. 2:1-7).
12. This church had more famous preachers than did any other church. This would include men such as Paul, Apollos, John, and Timothy.
13. Ephesians is the Joshua book of the New Testament.
14. Dr. Pierson calls it "Paul's third heaven epistle." It has been referred to as the Alps of the New Testament, the Mount Whitney of the High Sierras of all Scripture.

I. The Church Is Likened to a Body (chapter 1)
   A. The creating of this body (1:1-14).
      1. It was wrought and planned by the Father (1:1-6).
         He blessed us.
         He chose us.
         He predestinated us.
         He adopted us.
         He accepted us.

         This all happened before the foundation of the world! (See verse 4.) We now note the following things concerning these first six verses:

         a. Paul writes to those "at Ephesus, and to the faithful *in* Christ Jesus." Dr. J. Vernon McGee has written:

            "The little preposition in *(en)*, when it precedes Christ is the most important word of this epistle. Theologians have amassed an array of imposing theological words to define our salvation—such as redemption, atonement, justification, reconciliation, propitiation, and the vicarious substitutionary sacrifice of Christ. All of these are fine, and each presents one aspect of the

Ephesians

The Church of the Living God

LIKENED TO A BODY (1:23) CHAPTER ONE

LIKENED TO A TEMPLE (2:21) CHAPTER TWO

LIKENED TO A MYSTERY (3:4) CHAPTER THREE

LIKENED TO A SOLDIER (6:11) CHAPTER SIX

LIKENED TO A BRIDE (5:25) CHAPTER FIVE

LIKENED TO A NEW MAN (4:13, 24) CHAPTER FOUR

many facets of our salvation. None, however, seems entirely adequate. What does it mean to be saved? This is a question which is answered in utmost simplicity by the Bible term, 'in Christ.' To be saved means to be in Christ. A sinner who has trusted Christ for his salvation has as much right in heaven as has Christ—or he has no right there at all, for he is in Christ!" (*Exploring Through Ephesians*, p. 11)

b. Paul writes: "Blessed be the God and Father of our Lord Jesus Christ" (see v. 3). The word "blessed" is *eulogetos*, and means "to speak well of, to praise, to celebrate." This adjective is used only of God. (See Mk. 14:61; Lk. 1:68; Rom. 1:25; 9:5; 2 Cor. 1:3; 11:31; Eph. 1:3; 1 Pet. 1:3.) When the word "blessed" is used of man, the Greek term is *makarios*, and means "to pronounce happy." (See Mt. 5:3-11.) Thus, God desires for his children to bless him by saying nice things about him. Furthermore, God hears and records these things in his book of remembrance. (See Mal. 3:16.)

We note also that Paul carefully distinguishes the difference between Christ's relationship to the Father and our relationship to the Father. See also John 20:17 where Jesus does the same thing. (See also Jn. 1:14, 18; 3:16, 18; 1 Jn. 4:9; Rev. 1:5.)

2. It was bought and purchased by the Son (1:7-12).
   a. He redeemed us.
   b. He forgave us.
   c. He revealed God's will and way to us.
   d. He secured for us an inheritance.
   e. He gathers "all things . . . both which are in heaven, and which are on earth' (1:10).
   f. This all happened "in the dispensation of the fulness of times" (see 1:10).

Special note: The word translated "*dispensation*" here is *oikonomia* and is employed three times by the Greek text of Ephesians. The apostle writes concerning:
   (1) The dispensation of the fullness of time (1:10).
   (2) The dispensation of the grace of God (3:2).
   (3) The dispensation (translated by the word "fellowship" in the KJV) of the mystery (3:9).

It may prove helpful at this point to briefly define the concept of dispensationalism as developed by Paul.

The Greek word *oikonomia* is found some nineteen times in the New Testament. It is translated by the following English words:

steward (Lk. 12:42; 16:11; 3:8; 1 Cor. 4:1, 2; Titus 1:7; 1 Pet. 4:10)
stewardship (Lk. 16:2, 3, 4)
dispensation (1 Cor. 9:17; Eph. 1:10; 3:2; Col. 1:25)
fellowship (Eph. 3:9)
edifying (1 Tim. 1:4)

Note the following definitions of a dispensation.

"It is a period of time during which man is tested in respect of obedience to some specific revelation of the will of God" (from the *Scofield Bible*).

Thus the central idea in the word dispensation is that of managing or administrating the affairs of a household.

"As far as the use of the word in Scripture is concerned, a dispensation may be defined as a stewardship, administration, oversight or management of others' property. As we have seen, this involves responsibility, accountability, and faithfulness on the part of the steward. . . . A dispensation is primarily a stewardship arrangement and not a period of time (though obviously the arrangement will exist during a period of time . . . a dispensation is basically the arrangement involved, not the time involved; and a proper definition will take this into account. A concise definition of a dispensation is this: 'A dispensation is a distinguishable economy in the outworking of God's purpose.'" (Dr. Charles Ryrie, *Dispensationalism Today*, pp. 25, 29, 31)

To summarize: Dispensationalism views the world as a household run by God. In this household-world, God is dispensing or administering its affairs according to his own will and in various stages of revelation in the process of time. These various stages mark off the distinguishably different economies in the outworking of his total purpose, and these economies are the dispensations.

"A dispensation is a period of time expressing the divine viewpoint of human history. In other words, dispensations are the categories of human history, the divine outline of history, the divine interpretation of human history" (R. B. Thieme, *Dispensations*, p. 8)

The divisions of dispensationalism: Various numbers of dispensations have been listed. Some see four. Scofield offers seven. The following list suggests nine.

(4) The dispensation of innocence: from the creation of man to the fall of man (Gen. 1:26—3:6).
(5) The dispensation of conscience: from the fall of man to the flood (Gen. 3:7—6:7).
(6) The dispensation of civil government: from the flood to the dispersion of Babel (Gen. 6:8—11:9).
(7) The dispensation of promise, or, patriarchal rule: from Babel to Mt. Sinai (Gen. 11:10—Ex. 18:27).
(8) The dispensation of Mosaic Law: from Mt. Sinai to Pentecost (Ex. 19:1—Acts 1:26).
(9) The dispensation of the bride of the Lamb—the church: from Pentecost to the rapture (Acts 2:1—Rev. 5:14).
(10) The dispensation of the wrath of the Lamb—the tribulation: from the rapture to the Second Coming (Rev. 6:1—20:3).
(11) The dispensation of the rule of the Lamb—the millennium: from the Second Coming to the great white throne judgment (Rev. 20:4-15).
(12) The dispensation of the new creation of the Lamb—the world without end: from the great white throne judgment throughout all eternity (Rev. 21:1—22:21).

Keeping this outline in mind, one can see that in Ephesians 1:10; 3:2, 9, Paul is describing the sixth dispensation, that of the church.

3. It was taught and protected by the Spirit (1:13, 14).
   a. He seals us. This indicates the following:
      (1) ownership (1 Cor. 6:19, 20; 2 Tim. 2:19)
      (2) security (Eph. 4:30)
      (3) completed transaction (Jer. 32:9, 10; Jn. 17:4; 19:30)
   b. He becomes our earnest. An earnest is something of value (like money) given as a down payment for a purchased possession. This all happens at the time of salvation.
      Note: He is called "that Holy Spirit of promise" (1:13) because Jesus himself has promised he would come. (See Jn. 14:16, 17; 16:7, 13; Acts 1:4, 5.) Verse 14 is the third and final doxology in these first few verses. (See verses 6, 12, 14.)
B. The consecration of this body (1:15-23). Paul earnestly prays that the Ephesian church might know:
   1. The God of glory.
      "That the God of our Lord Jesus Christ, the Father of glory, may give unto you the spirit of wisdom and revelation in the knowledge of him" (v. 17).
   2. The glory of God.
      a. As it is seen in his saints. Paul has prayed that they might know the *person* of God, and now prays that they may know also the *program* and *power* of God.
         "The eyes of your understanding being enlightened; that ye may know what is the hope of his calling, and what the riches of the glory of his inheritance in the saints, and what is the exceeding greatness of his power to us-ward who believe, according to the working of his mighty power" (Eph. 1:18, 19).
      b. As it is seen in his Son.
         "Which he wrought in Christ, when he raised him from the dead, and set him at his own right hand in the heavenly places, far above all principality, and power, and might, and dominion, and every name that is named, not only in this world, but also in that which is to come" (1:20, 21). (See also Rom. 8:38; Eph. 3:10; 6:12; Col. 1:16; 1 Pet. 3:22.)
      c. As it is seen in his church.
         "And hath put all things under his feet, and gave him to be the head over all things to the church, which is his body, the fulness of him that filleth all in all" (Eph. 1:22, 23).
      Thus the believer is fighting *from* a victory and not *for* a victory. The divine "cards" have already been stacked; we have already won! (See also Mt. 28:18; Ps. 8:6; 110:1; 1 Cor. 15:25, 26.)

II. The Church Is Likened to a Temple (2).
  A. What we once were (2:1-3, 11, 12).
    1. We were dead in trespasses and sins.
    2. We were in obedience to Satan.
    3. We were the children of wrath (both by nature and choice).
    4. We were godless and unclean.
    5. We were separated from Christ.
    6. We were excluded from the commonwealth of Israel.
    7. We were strangers to the covenant of promise.
    8. We had no hope.
    9. We were without God in this present world.
  B. What God did (2:4-6).
    1. He loved us in mercy.
    2. He made us alive in Christ.
    3. He raised us up and seated us in heavenly places.
  C. Why God did it (2:7).
    "That in the ages to come he might shew the exceeding riches of his grace, in his kindness toward us, through Christ Jesus."
    Thus we who once so richly deserved his wrath will, throughout all eternity, display his grace.
  D. How God did it (2:8, 9, 13).
    1. By grace through faith.
    2. Totally apart from human merit.
    3. Through the blood of Christ.
  E. What we now are (2:10, 14-22).
    1. We are the workmanship of God. The Greek word for workmanship (2:10) is *poema*, from whence our English word "poem" comes. God has two treasured poems in this universe:
      a. The poem of creation (see Rom. 1:20; Rev. 4:11).
      b. The poem of salvation (see Eph. 2:10; Rev. 5:9). Thus, we are saved to be sure! This salvation is *apart from* works (2:8, 9) but *unto* works (2:10).
    2. We are (as Gentiles) united with Israel in Christ. That he might reconcile both unto God in one body (2:16). Chrysostom once wrote:
      "He does not mean that He has elevated us to that high dignity of theirs, but He has raised both of us and them to one still higher. I will give you an illustration. Let us imagine that there are two statues, one of silver and the other of lead, and then that both shall be melted down, and the two shall come out gold. So thus He has made the two one."
    3. We are assured of having access to the Father himself (2:18).
    4. We are placed "upon the foundation of the apostles and prophets, Jesus Christ himself being the chief corner stone" (2:20).
    5. We are a "building fitly framed together . . . unto a holy temple in the Lord . . . a habitation of God through the Spirit" (2:21, 22).
III. The Church Is Likened to a *Mystery* (3).
  A. His explanation of this mystery (3:1-13). Paul bares his heart.
    1. The when of this mystery:
      "Which in other ages was not made known unto the sons of men, as it is now revealed unto his holy apostles and prophets by the Spirit" (3:5).
      Whatever the mystery is, Paul here states no Old Testament saint knew of it.
    2. The what of this mystery.
      "That the Gentiles should be fellow heirs and of the same body, and partakers of his promise in Christ by the gospel" (3:6).
      In the Old Testament, Gentile salvation was known, but not without becoming Jews by proselytization (see Isa. 11:10; 42:6; 60:3; Zech. 2:11; Mal. 1:11). Compare these Old Testament verses with Ephesians 3:5, 6; Romans 16:25; Colossians 1:26.
    3. The who of this mystery.
      "Whereof I was made a minister, according to the gift of the grace of God given unto me by the effectual working of his power. Unto me, who am less than the least of all saints, is this grace given, that I should preach among the Gentiles the unsearchable riches of Christ (Eph. 3:7, 8).
      Paul here refers to himself as the least of all saints. (See also 1 Cor. 15:8, 9; 2 Cor. 12:11; 1 Tim. 1:15, 16.)
    4. The why of this mystery.
      "In order that the manifold wisdom of God might now be made known through the church to the rulers and the authorities in the heavenly places" (3:10, *NASB*).
      Thus this world becomes a university wherein both demons and angels might study the grace of God! (See also Eph. 1:21; 6:12; Col. 1:16; 2:15; 1 Pet. 1:12.)
  B. His supplication for this mystery (3:14-21). Paul bows his knee. There are two great prayers in this epistle.
    1. In 1:15-23, Paul prays for the eyes of the believer: "That . . . the eyes of your understanding being enlightened" (1:18). Here he wanted them to know the tremendous power of God.
    2. In 3:14-21 Paul prays for the hearts of the believer: "That Christ may dwell in your hearts" (3:17). Here he wanted them to know the tender love of Christ.
    Note briefly the elements of this love:
    3. The extent of God's love.
      a. It embraces the entire family throughout all time (3:15; see also Eph. 1:10; Heb. 12:23.).
      b. It embraces the individual member at this present time (3:16; see also 2 Cor. 4:16.).
    4. The nature of God's love.
      ". . . Which passeth knowledge" (3:19).
    5. The sufficiency of God's love.
      "Now unto him that is able to do exceeding abundantly above all that we ask or think, according to the power that worketh in us, unto him be glory in the church by Christ Jesus throughout all ages, world without end. Amen" (Eph. 3:20, 21).

IV. The Church Is Likened to a New Man (4).
   A. The new man and his position (4:4-16).
      1. The unity of his new position (4:4-6). Seven great stabilizers.
         a. One body (Christ's body—the church). (See 1 Cor. 12:12, 27; Eph. 5:30.)
         b. One Spirit (the Holy Spirit). (See 1 Cor. 12:4.)
         c. One hope. The Scriptures declare this hope to be:
            (1) good (2 Thess. 2:16)
            (2) better (Heb. 7:19)
            (3) blessed (Titus 2:13)
            (4) glorious (Col. 1:27)
            (5) lively (1 Pet. 1:3)
            (6) firm (Heb. 3:6; 6:11)
            (7) eternal (Titus 3:7)
         d. One Lord (the Savior) (1 Cor. 12:5).
         e. One faith (Jude 1:3; 1 Cor. 13:5; 16:13; Gal. 1:23; Phil. 1:27; 1 Tim. 1:2; 4:1; 5:8; 2 Tim. 4:7; Titus 1:4).
         f. One baptism (into Christ's body. Rom. 6:3, 4; 1 Cor. 12:13; Col. 2:9-12; Gal. 3:27, 28; 1 Pet. 3:21).
         g. One God (the Father) (Deut. 6:4; 1 Cor. 12:6).
      2. The unifier of his new position (4:7), one great Savior.
         a. His journey (4:7-10). Dr. Homer Kent writes the following concerning these verses:

            "Paul first issues a statement that God has bestowed gifts to believers to enable them to accomplish the goal of walking in unity (4:7). The previous paragraph has emphasized the fact of unity by pointing to the oneness of believers in various respects. Now Paul shows that each believer is an individual participant and recipient of the divine graces which he needs.

            Each person's grace is in proportion to what Christ in His sovereign wisdom has freely given. Not all receive the same gifts, or the same number of gifts, or the same amount of any one gift. Christ dispenses as He deems best.

            The scriptural proof (4:8-10) cited for the above assertion is drawn from Psalm 68:18. 'When he ascended up on high, he led captivity captive, and gave gifts unto men.' The historical circumstances of the psalm are uncertain. It depicts a victorious and triumphant return, probably of David to Mount Zion. If the psalm was intended to be Messianic (as this usage in Ephesians certainly suggests), then David is regarded as typical of his greater Son whose passion victory was followed by the ascension.

            The chief points in the quotation which were significant to the author were the victorious ascent and the dispensing of gifts to men. Certain other features, however, are also of special interest. 'He led captivity captive' is translated 'he captured prisoners' (Jerusalem Bible), 'he took many captives with him' (TEV), and 'he led a host of captives' (RSV). Messianically interpreted, this is usually referred to Christ's conquering of His enemies: Satan, sin, death, the curse. Others (a minority, but including many of the ancient Fathers) explain these 'captives' as friends, either the redeemed on earth, or Old Testament saints in hades (Heb., *sheol*).

            In support of this last interpretation, arguments such as the following are given:
            1. That which is led captive is taken to heaven. This is not true of Satan, sin, death, or the curse.
            2. The past tense (aorist) 'led captive' does not fit the regeneration of subsequent believers as well as some prior action.
            3. The interpretation that this refers to the descent of Christ to the realm of the dead at His death accords well with 1 Peter 3:19, 20.
            4. It fits Matthew 27:50-53, where the visible release of some Old Testament saints from hades may imply the spiritual release of all such.
            5. This harmonizes with the apparent change in location of paradise, which in the New Testament era is stated as being above, and equated with heaven (2 Cor. 12:2-4)." (*Ephesians, The Glory of the Church*, pp. 68, 69)
         b. His gifts (4:11).
            "And he gave some, apostles; and some, prophets; and some, evangelists; and some, pastors and teachers."
         c. His goal (4:12-16).
            "For the equipping of the saints for the work of service, to the building up of the body of Christ; until we all attain to the unity of the faith, and of the knowledge of the Son of God, to a mature man, to the measure of the stature which belongs to the fulness of Christ. As a result, we are no longer to be children, tossed here and there by waves, and carried about by every wind of doctrine, by the trickery of men, by craftiness in deceitful scheming. But speaking the truth in love, we are to grow up in all aspects into Him, who is the head, even Christ. From whom the whole body, being fitted and held together by that which every joint supplies, according to the proper working of each individual part, causes the growth of the body for the building up of itself in love" *(NASB).*

B. The new man and his disposition (4:1-3, 16-32).
  1. His walk (4:1-3, 17-19).
     a. Positive—adapted to the walk of the Savior (4:1-3).
        (1) In lowliness (Phil. 2:3; Mt. 11:29)
        (2) In meekness (2 Cor. 10:1)
        (3) In longsuffering (Gal. 5:22)
        (4) In forbearing (Col. 3:13)
        (5) In unity (Jn. 17:21; 1 Cor. 12:13)
     b. Negative—avoiding the walk of the sensual (4:17-19).
  2. His words (4:15, 29).
     "But speaking the truth in love . . . Let no corrupt communication proceed out of your mouth, but that which is good to the use of edifying, that it may minister grace unto the hearers."
  3. His works (4:20-28, 30-32).
     a. He is to *put off* the old man, "which is corrupt according to the deceitful lusts" (4:22).
     b. He is to *put on* the new man, "which after God is created in righteousness and true holiness" (4:24).
     c. He is to control his *tongue* (4:25).
        "Wherefore putting away lying, speak every man truth with his neighbour: for we are members one of another."
        Centuries ago, the great church father Chrysostom wrote concerning this verse:
        "Let not the eye lie to the foot, nor the foot to the eye. If there be a deep pit and its mouth covered with reeds shall present to the eye the appearance of solid ground, will not the eye use the foot to ascertain whether it is hollow underneath, or whether it is firm and resists? Will the foot tell a lie and not the truth as it is? And what, again, if the eye were to spy a serpent or a wild beast, will it lie to the foot?"
     d. He is to control his *temper* (4:26, 27).
        "Be ye angry, and sin not: let not the sun go down upon your wrath: neither give place to the devil."
        Moody once remarked that he wouldn't give a dime for a Christian without a temper, but he also wouldn't give a nickel for a believer who couldn't control that temper! There is, of course, righteous anger (see Mk. 3:5). However, Satan loves to use uncontrolled anger.
     e. He is to stop *stealing* (4:28). Dr. Homer Kent writes:
        "Paul's actual expression is 'the one stealing.' It is a present participle and can hardly be relegated to the one who 'stole' before he was converted. Rather, it seems to depict the continuing practice of pilfering that still characterized some of these Christians. We must recognize that many of the early Christians came from the ranks of slaves, where pilfering was a way of life. Conversion does not remove all such habits instantaneously, especially in matters where no great conscience has developed.
        Furthermore, let us recognize that stealing in the broad sense is not unknown among present-day Christians. Deans of students in any Christian school can elaborate on this problem at some length. Income tax returns, insurance claims, and examinations in school are only a few examples of situations where Christians are many times less than honest.
        The scriptural injunction is not merely that stealing cease, nor even that restitution be made. The Christian principle is laid down that each man should toil honestly at that which is good, not merely to meet his own needs and thus avoid temptation to thievery, but to be able to amass a surplus to help others in need. This is in stark contrast to the prevalent attitude which assumes that one is entitled to the supply of needs, whether or not he wishes to work. By working diligently, the individual removes some of the temptation to steal, and by assisting others in need, he helps remove the temptation from them also." (*Ephesians, the Glory of the Church,* p. 83)
     f. He is to stop *grieving* (4:30).
        "And grieve not the Holy Spirit of God, whereby ye are sealed unto the day of redemption."
     g. He is to *forgive* as he himself has been forgiven (4:32).
V. The Church Is Likened to a Bride (5).
  A. The bride—her duties as the church (5:1-21).
     1. To be separated (5:1-13).
        "But fornication, and all uncleanness or covetousness, let it not be once named among you, as becometh saints. . . . and have no fellowship with the unfruitful works of darkness, but rather reprove them" (5:3, 11).
     2. To be serving (5:14-16).
        "Redeeming the time, because the days are evil" (5:16).
     3. To be searching (5:17).
        "Wherefore be ye not unwise, but understanding what the will of the Lord is."
     4. To be Spirit-filled (5:18).
        "And be not drunk with wine wherein is excess; but be filled with the Spirit."
        Note: This verse does not encourage "moderate drinking," as some have supposed. The word translated "excess" is *asotia* in the Greek and refers to a riotous and unruly way of life.
     5. To be singing (5:19, 20).
        "Speaking to yourselves in psalms and hymns and spiritual songs, singing and making melody in your heart to the Lord; giving thanks always for all things unto God and the Father in the name of our Lord Jesus Christ."

B. The Bridegroom—his devotion to the church (5:22-33).
  1. His devotion illustrated—by marriage (5:22-24). The institution of human marriage was given to many by God to accomplish a twofold goal:
    a. For reasons of propagation (see Gen. 1:27, 28).
    b. For reasons of illustration (see Eph. 5:22-24). God chose this human relationship—the love of a man for his wife—to illustrate Christ's love for the church.
  2. His devotion demonstrated—on the cross (5:25). "Even as Christ loved the church, and gave himself for it." (See also Jn. 13:1.)
  3. His devotion consummated—at the rapture (5:26, 27).
    "That he might sanctify and cleanse it with the washing of water by the word, that he might present it to himself a glorious church, not having spot, or wrinkle, or any such thing; but that it should be holy and without blemish."
    a. The word "spot" refers to those imperfections from without, as caused by the world.
    b. The word "wrinkle" refers to those imperfections from within, caused by the flesh.

VI. The Church Is Likened to a Soldier (6).
A. Boot camp training (6:1-9).
  1. Children and parents:
    a. The child is to honor and obey his parents in the Lord. Here the word "obey" is different from that found in Ephesians 5:22. Both Samson and Absalom are sad warnings to those who would disobey this command. (See Jdg. 14:1-3; 2 Sam. 15:1-12; 2 Sam. 18:15.)
    b. The parent is to instruct and admonish his child in the Lord. (See Prov. 13:24; 19:18; 22:15; 23:13, 14; 29:15, 17; Deut. 6:6, 7.)
  2. Servants and masters (6:5-9).
    a. Servants are to serve their masters as they would serve Christ.
    b. Masters are to treat their servants as they would treat Christ. Both are to keep in mind that their "master also is in heaven; neither is there respect of person within him" (6:9).
B. Front line fighting (6:10-24).
  1. Our enemy—the devil.
    a. His cohorts: "For we wrestle not against flesh and blood, but against principalities, against powers, against the rulers of the darkness of this world, against spiritual wickedness in high places" (6:12).
     (1) Principalities. A possible reference to Satan's "generals" who have the oversight of entire nations (see Dan. 10).
     (2) Powers. May speak of his "privates" who possess human beings (see Mk. 5; Mt. 17).
     (3) World rulers. Those demons in charge of Satan's worldly business.
     (4) Spiritual wickedness. Those demons in charge of worldly religion.
    b. His tactics:
     (1) "The wiles of the devil" (6:11). Greek scholar K. Wuest writes: "Wiles is *methodeia* in the Greek, referring to 'cunning arts, deceit, craft, trickery.' It means to follow up, or investigate by method and settled plan, to follow craftily, frame devices, deceive" (*Ephesians and Colossians,* p. 141). (See also 1 Tim. 3:7; 2 Cor. 2:11.)
     (2) "The fiery darts of the wicked" (6:16). This is reference to arrows tipped with tow, pitch, or such material, then set on fire before they are discharged. (See also 1 Pet. 1:7; 4:12.)
  2. Our equipment—the armor of God (6:11, 13-17). Let us carefully note each piece of armor mentioned here. Paul very obviously takes those pieces of armor worn by the Roman soldier and makes spiritual application to each one.
    a. The girdle of truth. *Expositors' Commentary* says:
    "First in the list of these articles of equipment mentioned is the girdle. Appropriately so; for the soldier might be furnished with every other part of his equipment, and yet, wanting his girdle, would be neither fully clothed nor securely armed. His belt was no mere adornment of the soldier, but an essential part of his equipment. Passing round the loins and by the end of the breastplate (in later times supporting the sword), it was of special use in keeping other parts in place, and in securing the proper soldierly attitude and freedom of movement."
    Truth, as mentioned here, probably refers to truthfulness as found in a Christian. Thus a believer whose life is tainted with deceit and falsehood forfeits the very thing which holds other pieces of his armor together!
    b. The breastplate of righteousness. This speaks of right acts as practiced by the believer. The breastplate was to protect the heart of the soldier. Thus, unrighteous acts committed by a Christian rob him of this vital protection and expose his spiritual heart to Satan. (See Heb. 10:22; 13:9; Jas. 1:26; 4:8; 1 Jn. 3:19-22.)
    c. The sandals of the gospel. The Roman soldier wore sandals which were bound by thongs over the instep and around the ankle, and the soles were thickly studded with nails. This gave him a firm footing in time of attack. This may refer to the assurance and confidence which comes from knowing the great doctrinal truths associated with the gospel. (See 1 Pet. 3:15; Eph. 4:14.)

d. The shield of faith. K. Wuest writes: "The word *shield* used here designated the shield of the heavy infantry, a large, oblong one, four by two and one half feet, sometimes curved on the inner side." Hebrews 11 is a commentary on this piece of armor.

e. The helmet of salvation. The helmet, of course, protected the head and brain. This piece (like the sandals) may refer to the intake of Bible doctrine, lest one's eyes be blinded, his ears deafened, and his mind confused with the attacks from the world, the flesh, and the devil.

f. The sword of the Spirit. Here is the only *offensive* weapon listed among the various pieces of armor. The rest are *defensive* in nature. The sword of the Spirit is identified to be the Word of God. (See Heb. 4:12.) This, then, is the armor the Christian is commanded to wear. K. Wuest writes concerning the command in 6:13 ("Wherefore take unto you the whole armour of God"):

"Take unto you is *analambano*, meaning, 'to take up in order to use.' . . . The verb is aorist imperative, which construction issues a command given with military snap and curtness, a command to be obeyed at once and once for all. Thus, the Christian is to take up and put on all the armor of God as a once-for-all act and keep that armor on during the entire course of his life, not relaxing the discipline necessary for the constant use of such protection.

The historian Gibbon relates how the relaxation of discipline and disuse of exercise rendered soldiers less willing and less able to support the fatigue of service. They complained of the weight of armor, and obtained permission to lay aside much of it." (*Ephesians and Colossians*, p. 142)

3. Our exhortation—the trio of success.

a. We are to *stand*. No less than four times does Paul exhort us to do this (vs. 11, 13, 14). The believer is never told to attack the devil, but to withstand and resist him. (See 1 Pet. 5:8, 9.)

Thus, when tempted to do wrong, we should flee as did Joseph (Gen. 39:12), but when attacked by Satan for doing right, we should stand firm as did Daniel's three friends (Dan. 3). It has been observed that as pilgrims we walk, as witnesses we talk, as contenders we run, but as fighters we stand!

b. We are to *pray*. (See Mt. 17:21; Jude 1:20; 1 Tim. 2:8; 1 Thess. 5:17.)

c. We are to *watch*. (See 1 Cor. 16:13; 2 Cor. 6:5; 11:27; Mt. 24:43; Lk. 12:37-40; Acts 20:31; 1 Thess. 5:6; 1 Pet. 4:7; 2 Tim. 4:5; Rev. 3:2; 16:15.)

We may thus conclude that both watching and praying are the divine twin secrets for overcoming:

(1) The world (see Mk. 13:33).
(2) The flesh (see Mk. 14:38).
(3) The devil (see Eph. 6:18).

We should also do this for opportunities to serve Christ (see Col. 4:2, 3).

4. Our examples—the Apostle Paul and Tychicus (6:19-24).

a. Paul (6:21-24)

b. Tychicus (6:21-24) Dr. Homer Kent writes:

"In closing this letter, Paul explains that he will be sending it by his messenger Tychicus, who was also the bearer of the epistles to Philemon and to the Colossians (Col. 4:7). It is most probable that all three letters were carried on the same trip.

Tychicus was one of Paul's most trusted colleagues. He was from the province of Asia (Acts 20:4), and could have been from Ephesus, the capital. He had traveled with Paul on the third missionary journey and presumably accompanied him to Jerusalem with the collection. Now he was at Rome with the apostle, and would have the responsible task of delivering these important letters to their destinations, as well as conducting the runaway slave Onesimus safely to his master in Colosse.

Years later he would be sent by Paul to Ephesus once again (2 Tim. 4:12). To call him a 'beloved brother' was to emphasize Paul's personal attachment to him. To describe him as a 'faithful minister' points to his trustworthy performance of spiritual responsibilities. 'In the Lord' belongs to both expressions and denotes the spiritual realm in which Paul and Tychicus find the basis for their association." (*Ephesians, the Glory of the Church*, p. 125)

COLOSSIANS

INTRODUCTION:

1. Colossians is one of the epistles Paul wrote during his first Roman imprisonment. The others are Ephesians, Philippians, and Philemon.

2. The church at Colosse was probably started during Paul's third missionary journey. Although he personally never visited the city (see Col. 2:1) he did spend two years teaching the Word of God in Ephesus at the house of Tyrannus (see Acts 19:9, 10). Colosse was only ninety miles east of Ephesus. It is therefore suggested that one of his students during this time was a man from Colosse named Epaphras. After graduating from the two-year T.B.I. (Tyrannus Bible Institute), Epaphras may have gone back to evangelize the entire Lycus Valley. This valley, some ten miles long, contained three important cities: Laodicea, Hierapolis, and Colosse. Laodicea was only twelve miles from Colosse.

It is therefore possible that Paul's zealous young student started both the church in Colosse and the one in Laodicea! (See also Col. 4:16 and Rev. 3:14-22.)

3. The Colossian church was composed mainly of Gentile membership (see Col. 2:13).

4. Paul intended to visit it upon his release from prison (Philemon 1:22).

5. The church in Colosse may have met in the home of Philemon, for he lived at Colosse with one of his slaves, Onesimus (Col. 4:9 and the book of Philemon).

6. Some time after its beginning, the church at Colosse was infected by a deadly virus known as Judaistic Gnosticism. This represented the worst of both the Jewish and Greek world of thought. The "J-G virus" consisted of the following:
   a. Salvation could be obtained only through knowledge. This meant only those with superior intellects could hope to achieve salvation.
   b. Faith (belief without materialistic proof) was silly and useless.
   c. Matter itself was evil. The J-G virus taught that the world was created by a series of angelic emanations. In other words, God (the original source) created an angel who in turn created another angel, who created yet a third, etc., etc. Finally, the last of these angels created the world as we know it today. While this philosophy admitted to the *transcendence* of God (that he is above everything), it denied his *immanence* (that he is also in everything). This view immediately ruled out the incarnation of Christ, special divine creation, prayer, faith, miracles, the Second Coming, and the accuracy of the Bible.
   d. The goal of man was either morbid *asceticism* (avoiding all joys of life, and abusing the body for the spirit's sake) or that of unrestrained *licentiousness* (if it feels good, do it). The first was known as stoicism, and the last view Epicureanism. Scofield once observed: "Pure Christianity lives between two dangers ever present: the danger that it will evaporate into a philosophy . . . and the danger that it will freeze into a form."

   In conclusion, it may be said that the J-G virus error included dietary and Sabbath observations, circumcision rites, worship of angels, and the practice of asceticism. (See Col. 2:11, 16; 2:18; 2:21-23.)

7. Epaphras was apparently unable to deal properly with this vicious strain and thus makes the dangerous and wearisome 1000-mile trip from Colosse to Rome to seek Paul's advice.

8. When he left Colosse, Archippus assumed the pastorate (Col. 4:17). Archippus may have been the son of Philemon (Col. 1:2).

9. Upon reaching Rome and informing Paul, Epaphras was evidently also imprisoned (Philemon 1:23). This was doubtless because of bold preaching.

10. Paul writes the Colossian epistle to deal with the disease and sends it back by one of his trusted top lieutenants named Tychicus (Col. 4:7; cf. Acts 20:4; Eph. 6:21; 2 Tim. 4:12; Titus 3:12).

11. This epistle contains one of the greatest and most profound Christological passages to be found in any of Paul's writings. (See Col. 1:15-19.)

12. Colossians may be contrasted to other Pauline epistles. Thus:
   a. In Romans we are *justified* in Christ.
   b. In 1 Corinthians we are *enriched* in Christ.
   c. In 2 Corinthians we are *comforted* in Christ.
   d. In Galatians we are *free* in Christ.
   e. In Ephesians we are *quickened* in Christ.
   f. In Philippians we are *happy* in Christ.
   g. In Colossians we are *complete* in Christ.

13. This book thus presents the glorious culmination of it all. We are complete in Christ. This completeness is fourfold:
   a. Building downward: "Grounded and settled and . . . not moved away from the hope of the gospel" (1:23). This is the *deeper* life.
   b. Building upward: "Built up in him, and established in the faith" (2:7). This is the *higher* life.
   c. Building inward: "For ye are dead, and your life is hid with Christ in God" (3:3). This is the *inner* life.
   d. Building outward: "Walk with wisdom toward them that are without, redeeming the time" (4:5). This is *outer* life.

14. Colossians in a sense concludes that which Ephesians introduces. In Ephesians Paul dwells upon the body of the church, while in Colossians he writes of the head of that body. Because of this, both books are somewhat similar. For example, seventy-eight out of the ninety-five verses in Colossians are nearly identical to those in Ephesians.

15. It has been said that Colossians is to Ephesians what Galatians is to Romans.

I. The Deity and Preeminence of the Savior (1)
   A. The thanksgiving for this divine preeminence.
      1. It was the source of his praying (1:1-14). Colossians 1:9-14:
         "For this cause we also, since the day we heard it, do not cease to pray for you, and to desire that ye might be filled with the knowledge of his will in all wisdom and spiritual understanding; that ye might walk worthy of the Lord unto all pleasing, being fruitful in every good work, and increasing in the knowledge of God; strengthened with all might, according to his glorious power, unto all patience and longsuffering with joyfulness; giving thanks unto the Father, which hath made us meet to be partakers of the inheritance of the saints in light: Who hath delivered us from the power of darkness, and hath translated us into the kingdom of his dear Son: In whom we have redemption through his blood, even the forgiveness of sins."
      2. It was the source of his preaching (1:23-29). "The hope of the gospel . . . preached to every creature that is under heaven, of which I, Paul, am made a minister . . . according to the dispensation of God . . . to fulfil the word in God. . . . Whom we preach, warning . . . and teaching" (1:23, 25, 28).

      In these verses (1:23-29) Paul states that his preaching consisted of both the *sufferings* he endured, and the *secrets* he disclosed. Note:
         a. The sufferings: "Now I, Paul, rejoice in the midst of my sufferings for you, and I am filling up in my flesh that which is lacking of the afflictions of Christ for his

Colossians

●COLOSSE

The Deity and Preeminence of the Savior

CHAPTER ONE

THE THANKSGIVING FOR THIS DIVINE PREEMINENCE

It was the source of Paul's praying
"We give thanks to God and the Father of our Lord Jesus Christ, praying always for you" **(1:3).**

It was the source of Paul's preaching
"The hope of the gospel . . . whereof I Paul am made a minister" **(1:23).**

"Whom we preach, warning every man in all wisdom" **(1:28).**

THE THEOLOGY OF THIS DIVINE PREEMINENCE

Christ's relationship to the Father
"Who is the image of the invisible God, the firstborn of every creature" **(1:15).**

Christ's relationship to the universe
He was its past Creator **(1:16).**
He is its present sustainer **(1:17).**
He shall be its future reconciler **(1:20-22).**

Christ's relationship to the church
"And he is the head of the body, the church" **(1:18).**

The Danger and Perversion of the Serpent

CHAPTER TWO

THE NATURE OF THESE PERVERSIONS
- Enticing words **4**
- Philosophy **8**
- Traditions **8**
- Legalism **16, 17**
- Mysticism **18**
- Idolatry **18**
- Asceticism **20, 21**

THE ANSWER TO THESE PERVERSIONS
- Know who Jesus is **(2:3, 9)**
- Know what he has done for you **(2:13-15)**
- Know who you are **(2:10-12)**
- Know what you are to do for him **(2:6, 7)**

The Duty and Performance of the Saints

CHAPTERS THREE AND FOUR

- In relation to the Son of God **(3:1-4)**
- In relation to the Word of God **(3:16)**
- In relation to the work of God **(3:17)**
  1. What to put off **(3:5-9)**
  2. What to put on **(3:10-12, 14)**

- In relation to the peace of God **(3:15)**
- In relation to our talks with God **(4:2-4)**
- In relation to our testimony for God
  1. Before the unsaved **(4:5, 6)**
  2. In the home **(3:18-21)**
  3. On the job **(3:22-25)**
  4. In the church **(3:13)**
- In relation to the ministers of God **(4:7-18)**

---

body's sake, which is the church" (free translation of Col. 1:24 offered by J. V. McGee.) There are sufferings of Christ which of course we cannot share in, such as his suffering for the sins of the world. However, there are sufferings of Christ which we can indeed share. These would include suffering for righteousness' sake or enduring worldly persecutions for claiming his name.

b. The secrets:
"Even the mystery which hath been hidden from ages" (1:26).
"To whom God would make known . . . this mystery" (1:27).
"The mystery of God" (2:2).
"Praying also for us, that God would open unto us a door of utterance, to speak the mystery of Christ, for which I am also in bonds" (4:3). What are these "mysteries" Paul means? A biblical mystery is simply a sa-

cred secret previously kept from man in the Old Testament, but revealed in the New Testament. There are eleven such mysteries. Paul writes of eight of these; Matthew described one; and John the apostle lists two.

Out of the eight Pauline mysteries, no less than three are found here in Colossians. These are:
(1) The mystery that the body of Christ (the church) is to be composed of both saved Jews and Gentiles (Col. 4:3; see also Rom. 16:25; Eph. 3:1-12; 6:19).
(2) The mystery of the indwelling Christ (Col. 1:27; see also Gal. 2:20).
(3) The mystery of the incarnation of Christ (Col. 2:2, 9; see also 1 Cor. 2:7).
B. The theology of this divine preeminence.
1. Christ's relationship to the Father. "Who is the image of the invisible God, the firstborn

of all creation" (1:15). The word *image* here is used to express likeness, and refers to the visible manifestation of something invisible. Christ is not *similar* to God—he *is* God!

The word "firstborn" is *prototokos*, a reference to the highest priority of position. It does not speak of time, but of title. Christ is thus ascribed as Lord of all creation. (See Ps. 89:27.)

2. Christ's relationship to the universe. He was its past Creator (1:16). He is its present Sustainer (1:17). He shall be its future reconciler (1:20–22). Note:

   a. The nature of this reconciliation. Simply stated, it refers to the bringing about into a right relationship with the Father all those things within this sinful universe. This does not mean, of course, that all men (or any fallen angel) will be eventually saved. It does mean, however, that the glorious truth of Romans 8:28 will someday be totally realized.

   b. The time of this reconciliation. It began at the cross, but will be concluded with the sound of the seventh trumpet (see Rev. 11:15).

   c. The method of this reconciliation (Col. 1:14, 21, 22).

3. Christ's relationship to the church. "And he is the head of the body, the church, who is the beginning, the first-born from the dead, that in all things he might have the preeminence" (1:18).

   In summary, it may be said that, because of his preeminence, all things were made and are sustained by him, that they exist solely for him, and that someday they shall be delivered *to* him.

II. The Danger and Perversion of the Serpent (2).

A. The nature of these perversions:

1. Enticing words: "And this I say, lest any man should beguile you with enticing words" (2:4). This perversion would doubtless correspond favorably to the liberalism of the twentieth century, which has promised so much but produced so little.

2. Philosophy: "Beware lest any man spoil you through philosophy and vain deceit" (2:8). False philosophy is like a blind man looking in a dark room for a black cat that isn't there. It can also be described as that science of learning more and more about less and less until finally you know everything about nothing.

3. Traditions: "After the tradition of men . . . and not after Christ" (2:8). All traditions, of course, are not bad, but many are. Jesus soundly and severely denounced the wicked traditions of the godless Pharisees. (See Mt. 15:1–9.)

4. Legalism (2:16, 17): "Let no man therefore judge you in meat, or in drink, or in respect of an holyday, or of the new moon, or of the sabbath days: Which are a shadow of things to come; but the body is of Christ."

   Note especially verse 17 at this point. A believer who puts himself back under legal-

ism would be like a son admiring the photo of his father, but ignoring his father's actual presence.

5. Mysticism: "Let no man beguile you of your reward in [by] a voluntary [false] humility" (2:18). Mysticism stresses that inner light and ignores the true Light. It may confuse truth with personal experience.

6. Idolatry: "A worshipping of angels" (2:8).

7. Asceticism (Col. 2:20, 21): "Wherefore if ye be dead with Christ from the rudiments of the world, why, as though living in the world, are ye subject to ordinances, Touch not; taste not; handle not."

B. The answer to these perversions:

1. Know who Jesus is! "In whom are hidden all the treasures of wisdom and knowledge. . . . For in him dwelleth all the fulness of the Godhead bodily" (2:3, 9).

2. Know what he has done for you (Col. 2:13, 15): "And you, being dead in your sins and the uncircumcision of your flesh, hath he quickened together with him, having forgiven you all trespasses; blotting out the handwriting of ordinances that was against us, which was contrary to us, and took it out of the way, nailing it to his cross; and having spoiled principalities and powers, he made a shew of them openly, triumphing over them in it."

   Especially to be noted is verse 14. To expand the theological blessings of this verse, consider a statement found in Genesis 2:19: "Adam called every living creature . . . the name thereof." Adam must have had a tremendous vocabulary. Ernest Mayr, America's leading taxonomist, lists the species existing today—3500 mammals, 8600 birds, and 5500 reptiles and amphibians. In spite of all this, there were seven simple words unknown and unexperienced by Adam prior to his fall. These words were:

   a. death (Gen. 2:17)
   b. nakedness (3:7)
   c. cursed (3:14)
   d. sorrow (3:17)
   e. thorns (3:18)
   f. sweat (3:19)
   g. sword (3:24)

   After the fall, Adam soon added these bitter and bloody words to his vocabulary. The echo of these wicked words haunted Adam and mankind for over forty centuries. Then came the second Adam (a name for Jesus). The New Testament tells us how he met and dealt with each word.

   h. death (Jn. 11:25)
   i. nakedness (Jn. 19:23)
   j. cursed (Gal. 3:13)
   k. sorrow (Isa. 53:3)
   l. thorns (Jn. 19:5)
   m. sweat (Lk. 22:44)
   n. sword (Jn. 19:34)

   As a result of this, Paul literally shouts out the truth here in Colossians 2:14 that these terrible works of condemnation have forever been blotted out.

3. Know who you are (2:10, 12):
   "And ye are complete in him, which is the head of all principality and power: buried with him in baptism, wherein also ye are risen with him through the faith of the operation of God, who hath raised him from the dead."
4. Know what you are to do for him (2:6, 7):
   "As ye have therefore received Christ Jesus the Lord, so walk ye in him: Rooted and built up in him, and stablished in the faith, as ye have been taught, abounding therein with thanksgiving."

III. The Duty and Performance of the Saints (3-4).
   A. In relation to the Son of God (3:1-4):
      "If ye then be risen with Christ, seek those things which are above, where Christ sitteth on the right hand of God. Set your affection on things above, not on things on the earth. For ye are dead, and your life is hid with Christ in God. When Christ, who is our life, shall appear, then shall ye also appear with him in glory."
   B. In relation to the Word of God (3:16):
      "Let the word of Christ dwell in you richly in all wisdom; teaching and admonishing one another in psalms and hymns and spiritual songs, singing with grace in your hearts to the Lord."
   C. In relation to the work of God (3:17):
      "And whatsoever ye do in word or deed, do all in the name of the Lord Jesus, giving thanks to God and the Father by him."
   D. In relation to our personal life (3:5-12):
      "Mortify therefore your members which are upon the earth; fornication, uncleanness, inordinate affection, evil concupiscence, and covetousness, which is idolatry. . . . Put on therefore, as the elect of God, holy and beloved, bowels of mercies, kindness, humbleness of mind, meekness, longsuffering."
   E. In relation to our prayer life (4:2-4):
      "Continue in prayer, and watch in the same with thanksgiving; withal praying also for us, that God would open unto us a door of utterance, to speak the mystery of Christ, for which I am also in bonds: That I may make it manifest, as I ought to speak."
   F. In relation to our public life (4:5, 6):
      "Walk in wisdom toward them that are without, redeeming the time. Let your speech be alway with grace, seasoned with salt, that ye may know how ye ought to answer every man."
   G. In relation to the home (3:18-21):
      "Wives, submit yourselves unto your own husbands, as it is fit in the Lord. Husbands, love your wives, and be not bitter against them. Children, obey your parents in all things: for this is well pleasing unto the Lord. Fathers, provoke not your children to anger, lest they be discouraged."
   H. In relation to the job (3:22-25):
      "Servants, obey in all things your masters according to the flesh; not with eye-service, as menpleasers; but in singleness of heart, fearing God: And whatsoever ye do, do it heartily, as to the Lord, and not unto men; knowing that of the Lord ye shall receive the reward of the inheritance: for ye serve the Lord Christ. But he that doeth wrong shall receive for the wrong which he hath done: and there is no respect of persons."
   I. In relation to Christian lay people (3:13, 14):
      "Forbearing one another, and forgiving one another, if any man have a quarrel against any: even as Christ forgave you, so also do ye. And above all these things put on charity, which is the bond of perfectness."
   J. In relation to Christian leaders (4:7-18).
   In closing this powerful epistle, Paul lists key Christian leaders associated in some manner with his ministry at that time. They are:
      1. Tychicus—the carrier of the Colossian epistle
      2. Onesimus—the once runaway slave of Philemon
      3. Aristarchus—a fellow prisoner with Paul at this time
      4. John Mark—the author of Mark's Gospel
      5. Justus—nothing known about him except that he was a co-worker with Paul
      6. Epaphras—the imprisoned Colosse pastor
      7. Luke—Paul's beloved Greek physician and the author of Luke's Gospel and the book of Acts
      8. Demas—a co-worker who would eventually forsake Paul (2 Tim. 4:10)
      9. Archippus—the Colossian believer who assumed Epaphras' place as pastor during Paul's imprisonment

PHILEMON

INTRODUCTION:
1. This book, the shortest of all Paul's epistles, is one of the four letters written during the first Roman imprisonment. The other prison epistles are Philippians, Colossians, and Ephesians.
2. It is one of four personal letters to individuals penned by Paul. The others are 1 and 2 Timothy and Titus.
3. Dr. J. Vernon McGee writes:
   "The Epistles present a different style in revelation. God had used law, history, poetry, prophecy, and the Gospels heretofore, but in the Epistles He adopted a more personal and direct method. In this intimate way, He looks back to the cross and talks about the church. Someone has said that the Epistles are the love letters of Christ to us. Dr. Deissman divided them into two classifications: epistles and letters. The epistles are general, while the letters are more personal and individual. Under this division, the Epistle of Philemon would be classified as a letter, for it is individual and intimate. There is reason to believe that Paul did not expect its contents to be divulged (at other times he knew that he was writing Scripture). This does not detract from the inspiration and value of Philemon, but rather enhances its value and message. (*Thru the Bible*, p. 211)
4. The historical background of Philemon is as follows:
   a. Onesimus, a slave owned by Philemon (wealthy Colossian believer and long-time friend of Paul) had robbed his master and run away to Rome.

b. In some wonderful way Onesimus' path crosses that of Paul, resulting in his glorious conversion to Christ.

c. Upon hearing his testimony, Paul determines to send him back to Philemon.

d. To prepare the way (for what could be a very tense meeting), Paul pens this beautiful letter to Philemon. It is a masterpiece of Christian tact and ethics.

5. The letter provides us with one of the finest illustrations of that great theological truth of *imputation* (the act of reckoning something to another's account) as can be found anywhere in the Bible.

6. This epistle demonstrates that our letter-writing can be a ministry for God if we allow it to be so. Some who find it difficult to speak for God may well write for him.

I. The Appreciation for and Praise of Philemon (vs. 1-7).

A. Philemon's role as a friend to Paul.

"Our dearly beloved, and fellow worker" (v. 2).

Although Paul had never been to Colosse, he had in the past met Philemon. We may suppose this wealthy Colossian believer had prayed for and financially invested in the apostle's ministry.

B. Philemon's role as a family man.

"And to our beloved Apphia, and Archippus, our fellow soldiers, and to the church in thy house" (v. 2).

It is believed that Apphia was Philemon's wife and Archippus his son. In his Colossian letter (Col. 4:17) Paul seems to say that Archippus had assumed the role of the pastor there in Colosse when Epaphras (founder of the church) had departed for Rome to visit the imprisoned apostle. At any rate, Philemon seemed to have his family well in hand. He could loudly echo the final words of Joshua: "Choose you this day whom ye will serve . . . but as for me and my house, we will serve the Lord" (Josh. 24:15).

C. Philemon's role as a child of God.

"Hearing of thy love and faith, which thou hast toward the Lord Jesus" (v. 5).

No greater tribute can be paid to a believer than this. Paul speaks of Philemon's love for Jesus (because of who he is), and his faith in Jesus (because of what he is).

D. Philemon's role as a helper of saints.

"For we have great joy and consolation in thy love, because the hearts of the saints are refreshed by thee, brother" (v. 7).

Philemon's house was probably a free Holiday Inn to any and all believers journeying in that area. His life had also touched those saints in the Colosse church.

II. The Appeal and Plea for Onesimus (vs. 8-17).

A. The nature of this appeal: It was that Philemon would freely forgive Onesimus and restore him to his former position, keeping in mind that he was now not just Philemon's servant, but his brother in Christ.

B. The basis of this appeal: Philemon is asked to forgive and restore Onesimus for the sake of three individuals.

Paul's letter to PHILEMON

The A B C 's of Christian Forgiveness

A PHILEMON, The Christian Master

His role as a friend of Paul
"Our dearly beloved and fellowlabourer" **(v. 1).**

His role as a family man
"Our beloved Apphia, and Archippus our fellowsoldier, and to the church in thy house" **(v. 2).**

His role as a child of God
"Hearing of thy love and faith,
which thou hast toward all saints" **(v. 5).**

His role as a helper of saints
"For we have great joy and consolation in thy love, because the bowels of the saints are refreshed by thee, brother" **(v. 7).**

B ONESIMUS, The New Convert Slave

The nature of this appeal
To forgive and restore his new brother in Christ.

The basis of this appeal
To do this for the sake of three individuals:
For Onesimus' sake.
For Philemon's sake: "Which in time past was to thee unprofitable, but now profitable to thee and to me" **(v. 11).**
For Paul's sake: "If thou count me therefore a partner, receive him as myself. If he hath wronged thee, or oweth thee ought, put that on mine account" **(vs. 17, 18).**

C PAUL

Paul's appreciation for and praise of Philemon **(1:1-7).**
Paul's appeal and plea for Onesimus **(1:8-17).**

His assurance and pledge to Philemon (1:19-25)
"I Paul have written it with mine own hand, I will repay it: albeit I do not say to thee how thou owest unto me even thine own self besides" **(v. 19).**

His confidence in Philemon
"Having confidence in thy obedience I wrote unto thee, knowing that thou wilt also do more than I say" **(v. 21).**

His request to Philemon
"But withal prepare me also a lodging: for I trust that through your prayers I shall be given unto you" **(v. 22).**

1. For Onesimus' sake. This former dishonest slave had already learned so much in Rome and had proven to be such a help to the apostle. But his spiritual responsibility would demand that he now return and submit himself to Philemon. If he refused to do this, God's blessing upon him would be limited.

2. For Philemon's sake. The name *Onesimus* means "profitable." However, until his conversion, any resemblance between the name and his actions was purely accidental. But now Christ had made all things new. Therefore, if for no other reason (and indeed there were other good reasons), Philemon should restore Onesimus so that he might prove by his actions the meaning of his name.

3. For Paul's sake. One of the most beautiful examples of imputation is found in the following words: "If thou count me, therefore, a partner, receive him as myself. If he hath

wronged thee, or oweth thee anything, put that on mine account" (vs. 17, 18).

III. The Assurance and Pledge of Paul (1:19–25).

"I, Paul, am writing this with my own hand, I will repay it (lest I should mention to you that you owe to me even your own self as well)" (v. 19, NASB).

A. Paul has already reminded Philemon concerning his sufferings for Christ in that Roman prison (v. 9). This was in contrast, of course, to the "good life" Philemon was probably enjoying there in Colosse. The intended conclusion thus might be:

"If I, Paul, am willing to endure this persecution for Christ, cannot you forgive a fellow saint for Christ?"

B. The apostle then gently reminds Philemon that his very conversion experience could be traced back to Paul's ministry.

C. He closes this lovely letter expressing:

1. His confidence in Philemon:

"Having confidence in thy obedience I wrote unto thee, knowing that thou wilt also do more than I say" (v. 21).

2. His request to Philemon:

"At the same time prepare me also a lodging; for I trust that through your prayers I shall be given [released] unto you" (v. 22).

PHILIPPIANS

INTRODUCTION:

1. The church at Philippi was founded as a result of a supernatural vision experienced by Paul while at Troas during his second missionary trip (see Acts 16:8–10).

2. It was apparently Paul's favorite church. During his brief stay there he and Silas saw God work marvelously in the lives of at least three individuals:

a. An Asian businesswoman named Lydia whom God saved from Judaism (Acts 16:13–15).

b. A Greek soothsayer whom God saved from demonism (Acts 16:16–18).

c. A Roman jailor whom God saved from Emperiorism (the worship of Caesar) (Acts 16:19, 20).

3. Thus this church, conceived in a vision, would reach its apex in a prison. Strange and wonderful indeed are the ways of God.

4. The city of Philippi was founded by Philip of Macedon (father of Alexander the Great) in 357 B.C., and named after him. It was some 700 miles from Rome and enjoyed full Roman citizenship privileges. Dr. J. Dwight Pentecost writes:

"Rome in its conquest of the Middle East had been engaged in a war against Macedonia. History tells us the Roman army ran out of salt, and it was with salt that Roman soldiers were paid. (From this we get our expression that 'a man is not worth his salt.') The Roman legions threatened to defect and return home from the battle, which meant Macedonia would remain unconquered. The people of Philippi preferred to be ruled by the Romans rather than by the Macedonians, so they collected a great amount of salt and turned it over to the Roman army, and thus the soldiers were paid. They continued in their conquest and defeated the Macedonians, incorporating Macedonia into the Roman Empire. As a reward to the citizens of Philippi, the Roman emperor conferred upon them the status of a colony. This meant they had the same rights and privileges as Roman citizens as did the residents of the city of Rome. They were under the special, protective care of the emperor; they had all the privileges afforded by Roman law. Like residents of Rome, they were given privileges of freedom from taxation. They had been made Romans although they lived in Macedonia. As a consequence, many of the Roman soldiers chose to settle in Philippi instead of returning to Italy after they had completed their military service. Thus Philippi became a little Rome: Roman in its loyalties, Roman in its law, Roman in its philosophy and outlook. It was here the apostle came to begin to penetrate the continent of Europe with the Gospel of salvation by grace through faith." (The Joy of Living, pp. 12, 13)

5. Philippi thus became the first European city to receive the gospel and also to hear the first Christian concert, which featured a special duet at midnight.

6. In A.D. 57, at the end of his third missionary trip (some five years after his first visit), Paul seems to have paid two brief visits to Philippi (see 2 Cor. 1:16; Acts 19:21; 20:1–3).

7. A.D. 62 finds the apostle a prisoner in Rome. Acts 28:30, 31 indicates that he was confined to his own hired house, being chained to various Roman soldiers every six hours. Although he could not preach in public, he was allowed to write (Eph. 6:20; Phil. 1:7, 14, 16; Col. 4:18; Philemon 1:1, 10, 13).

8. It was therefore at this time, some ten years after his original visit to Philippi, that Paul wrote the epistle of Philippians to his favorite church.

9. This church, upon learning of his imprisonment in Rome, had sent a love offering to him by way of Epaphroditus. They had already sent him two other love gifts years back for his missionary endeavors in Thessalonica (Phil. 4:15, 16).

10. While in Rome, Epaphroditus had become very ill and nearly died. But God spared his life. Paul thus writes Philippians both to thank them for their gift and also to report the good news of Epaphroditus' recovery.

11. There are three bywords in this epistle. One is Christ (found in various forms some seventy times), another is the word joy (eighteen times), and the third is mind (mentioned twelve times).

I. Christ, the Purpose of Life (chapter 1). "For to me to live is Christ, and to die is gain" (1:21).

A. Causing Paul to rest in God's security (1:1–12).

1. His greetings to the saints at Philippi.

a. He writes to saints.

b. He also writes to bishops and deacons. Dr. John Walvoord writes:

"The mention of bishops and deacons indicates the advanced state of organization of the Church at Philippi now composed of mature and gifted believers from whom recognized leaders had come. As A. R. Fausset notes, 'This is the earliest epistle where bishops and deacons are mentioned, and the only one where they are separately addressed.' Of course, as early as Acts 6, men were appointed in the church to serve in a way similar to deacons. Although not called deacons, the prominence of this appointment

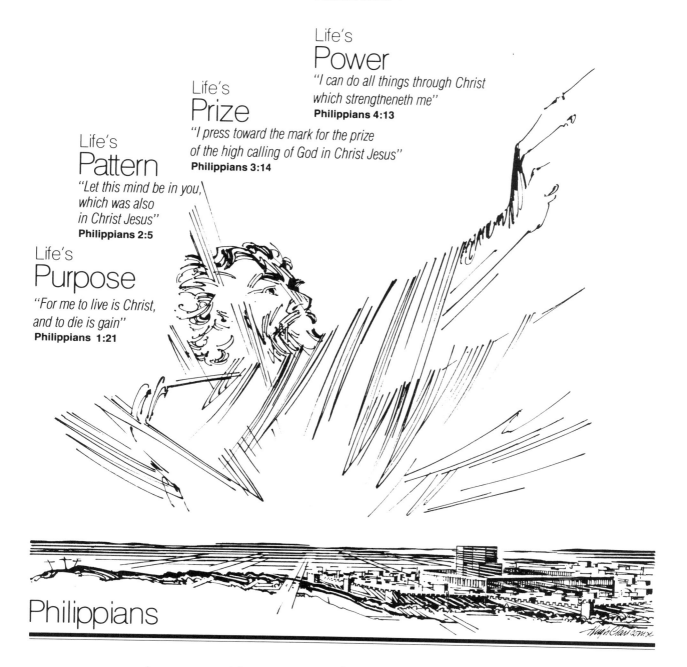

Life's
Power
"I can do all things through Christ
which strengtheneth me"
Philippians 4:13

Life's
Prize
"I press toward the mark for the prize
of the high calling of God in Christ Jesus"
Philippians 3:14

Life's
Pattern
"Let this mind be in you,
which was also
in Christ Jesus"
Philippians 2:5

Life's
Purpose
"For me to live is Christ,
and to die is gain"
Philippians 1:21

Philippians

of men to special service in Acts seems to recognize its significance. Elders were appointed in every church as early as Acts 14:23, and are mentioned in Acts 11:30; 20:27, 28; 1 Thessalonians 5:12, 13). (*Philippians, Triumph in Christ*, p. 24)

Greek scholar Kenneth Wuest writes in a similar manner:

"The word *bishop* is the translation of a Greek word used in secular pursuits of an overseer in any capacity, for instance, the official in charge of the repairing of a temple or an officer in an army. The word itself means 'to look upon.' Paul uses it as another name for an elder, the latter being the title

of the office so far as statutes in the church is concerned, the former being the title of that indicated the responsibility and activity of the office, that of overseeing the spiritual welfare of the local church. He brings the two names together as designating one individual in Acts 20:17, 28. The word *deacon* is the English spelling of a Greek word that was used as a general term to designate a servant. It covered both slaves and hired servants. It represented a servant, not in his relation to his master, but in his activity. The same word is translated 'minister' in 1 Corinthians 3:5; 2 Corinthians 3:6; Ephesians 3:7. Here it refers to a distinct class of officers in the apostolic church. The origin of the office is given us in Acts 6." (*Word Studies in Philippians*, p. 28)

As a final note here, consider the comments of J. Dwight Pentecost:

"The word 'deacon' comes from a compound Greek word that means 'to stir up the dust.' It presents the picture of one who is moving so rapidly through the dusty lanes of the villages of Palestine to discharge his duty that his feet kick up dust as he goes. There was so much for the deacons to do they could not loiter nor tarry. They went about their ministry with such diligence that they were stirring up the dust; thus those who were set apart to this ministry were called 'those who stir up the dust' or deacons." (*The Joy of Living*, p. 114)

2. His thanksgiving for the saints at Philippi (1:3-5).

"I thank my God upon every remembrance of you" (1:3).

3. His confidence in the saints at Philippi.

"Being confident of this very thing, that he which hath begun a good work in you will perform it until the day of Jesus Christ" (1:6).

Actually, of course, Paul's real confidence was in the *Savior* of these Philippian saints.

4. His prayer concerning the saints at Philippi.

"And this I pray, that your love may abound yet more and more in knowledge and in all judgment; that ye may approve things that are excellent; that ye may be sincere and without offence till the day of Christ" (Phil. 1:9, 10).

The word approve here means to place one's OK upon something after a period of testing. It was used by the Greeks to describe doctors who had passed their examinations. They were then certified physicians.

B. Causing Paul to rejoice in great suffering (1:12-20). The apostle could praise God for his prison experience. It had helped and not hindered the spread of the gospel. This was accomplished through three things:

1. The confinement of his fetters (1:13; 4:22). John Walvoord writes:

"Paul was guarded by imperial soldiers who were the cream of the Roman army, and the time of this writing was while he was in Rome, the center of the Roman government. Whether in Rome or elsewhere, however, according to the custom, the apostle was probably chained to a Roman soldier twenty-four hours a day, with a new guard every six hours. No doubt this was a most trying experience which subjected Paul to all the evil characteristics and whims of his guard even when he talked to his friends, when he prayed or when he attempted to write. Always there was this Roman guard. The

circumstances, however, also afforded him the priceless opportunity of witness, and each guard heard Paul's story. The claims of the grace of God and the transformation it afforded in his life subjected him to the scrutiny of each guard to see whether his testimony was genuine. The slightest deviation, impatience, or irritation would disqualify his testimony to the guard, and any lack of consistency in life would soon be communicated to others. The apostle's sincerity and his glowing account of God's grace manifested to him apparently were effective as guard after guard came to know Jesus Christ in an effective way.

Only God knows what went on in the rented room in which Paul was permitted to live. There the guards heard the conversation of Paul with his intimate friends and were able to ask questions about the strange words which they heard from their prisoner. In the lonely hours of the dark night, illuminated only by the moon, many a guard probably heard the testimony of Paul—his early career as a Pharisee, his antagonism and persecution of Christians, his remarkable conversion, and the causes of his imprisonment. No doubt all this was the subject of much conversation in the praetorian guard, and raised sympathy among the soldiers as they understood his unjust imprisonment. His chains had become an effective line of communication to the elite soldiers of the Roman Empire who, if converted, could carry the gospel to the ends of the earth as they were moved from place to place. It reminds us that every circumstance of life is a platform on which the transforming grace of God can be manifested in the life of the Lord's own." (*Triumph in Christ*, pp. 37, 38)

2. The courage of his friends (1:14). Paul's imprisonment had apparently jolted some of his timid believer friends into a bolder approach in presenting the gospel. One possibility for this may have been the conversion of several elite Roman soldiers. Thus their testimony would doubtless have given new courage to those regular church members in Rome.

3. The carnality of his foes (1:14-16).

"And many of the brethren in the Lord, waxing confident by my bonds, are much more bold to speak the word without fear. Some indeed preach Christ even of envy and strife; and some also of good will: The one preach Christ of contention, not sincerely, supposing to add affliction to my bonds."

The psalmist once wrote: "Surely the wrath of man shall praise thee" (Ps. 76:10).

In other words, in spite of the impure and insincere motives of his enemies in proclaiming the gospel, Paul nevertheless rejoiced, for, "whether in pretence, or in truth, Christ is preached; and I therein do rejoice, yea, and will rejoice" (1:18). The greatest problem of the world, then, as it is today, is not that the gospel is imperfectly preached, but that it is not preached at all.

4. The confidence in his future (1:19, 20). Paul is assured of two things:
   a. Through God's Spirit his needs would be supplied. Warren Wiersbe writes:

   "The word *supply* gives us our English word *chorus*. Whenever a Greek city was going to put on a special festival, someone had to pay for the singers and dancers. The donation called had to be a lavish one, and so this word came to mean 'to provide generously and lavishly.'

   Paul was not depending upon his own dwindling resources; he was depending on the generous resources of God, ministered by the Holy Spirit."
   (*Be Joyful*, p. 36)

   b. Through Paul's body the Savior would be magnified (1:20). How can this be done? It has been observed that through the telescope a distant object can be brought near, and through the microscope a small object can be made big. Thus, by rightly applying these instruments in a spiritual way, the believer can, through his body, cause Christ to become both big and near in the eyes of watching saints and sinners alike.

C. Causing Paul to remain in glad service (1:21-30).
   1. His desire was to depart and be with the Savior.

   "For to me to live is Christ, and to die is gain. . . . For I am in a strait betwixt two, having a desire to depart, and to be with Christ; which is far better" (1:21, 23; see also 2 Cor. 5:8).

   Note: Paul speaks of death as a departure (see also 2 Tim. 4:6). This word *depart* was used by:
   a. Soldiers, when they took down their tent and moved on.
   b. Politicians, when they set a prisoner free.
   c. Farmers, when they unyoked their oxen.

   2. His decision was to remain and minister to the saints.

   "Nevertheless to abide in the flesh is more needful to you" (1:24).
   a. This ministry involves striving. "Striving together for the faith of the gospel" (1:27). (See also Jude 1:3.)
   b. This ministry involves stability. "And in nothing terrified by your adversaries" (1:28). The word "terrified" here was used by the Greeks in referring to a horse shying away from battle (see also Isa. 41:10; Mt. 10:28; Heb. 13:5, 6).
   c. This ministry involves suffering. "For unto you it is given in the behalf of Christ, not only to believe on him, but also to suffer for his sake" (1:29).

II. Christ the Pattern of Life (chapter 2). Paul's subject in this chapter is that beautiful Christian virtue *unity*.
   A. The exhortation to unity (2:1-4).
      1. This unity is available (2:1). The word "if" in 2:1 should be translated "since." Thus:
         a. There *is* consolation and exhortation in the Son of God.
         b. There *is* encouragement and fellowship in the Spirit of God.
      2. This unity is attainable (2:2-4). It cannot be attained "through strife or vainglory; but in *lowliness* of mind let each esteem other better than themselves" (2:3).

      Plato defined "lowliness" as follows: "That state of mind which submits to the divine order of the universe, and does not impiously exalt itself." The word is used in a secular document of the Nile River at its low stage. How many tragic church splits would be avoided if only this principle were observed.
   B. The examples of unity (2:5-30).
      1. The example of Christ (2:5-8). Surely these verses rank among the greatest in all Scripture.

      "Let this mind be in you, which was also in Christ Jesus: Who, being in the form of God, thought it not robbery to be equal with God: But made himself of no reputation, and took upon him the form of a servant, and was made in the likeness of men: And being found in fashion as a man, he humbled himself, and became obedient unto death, even the death of the cross."

      We note from these verses just what Christ did to unite and unify the sinful creature with his holy Creator.
         a. He left heaven's glory (Jn. 17:5; 2 Cor. 8:9).
         b. He made himself of no reputation. The Greek word here in 2:7 is *kenoo* and means "to empty." Just what did Christ empty himself of?
            (1) Negative—he did *not* lay aside in any sense of the word his deity. He was, is, and ever shall be the total Son of God! (See Jn. 1:1; 17:5; 2 Cor. 4:4; Col. 1:15; 2:9; Heb. 1:3.)
            (2) Positive—he did, for awhile, hide his heavenly fame in an earthly frame. Even though he retained every single attribute of deity while on earth, he did, nevertheless, surrender to the Holy Spirit the independent exercise of those divine characteristics. (See Ps. 22:6; Isa. 53:3; Mk. 9:12; Rom. 15:3.) Two phrases need to be examined at this point. "The form of God": This does not mean that Christ had a physical shape prior to the incarnation. It refers to that inner, essential, and abiding nature of a person or thing. As an example, we might say, "The tennis player was in rare form today."

"Robbery to be equal with God": That is, he did not hold or consider the outer manifestation of his deity in heaven as a treasure to be grasped and retained at all costs. Christ in his incarnation did not concern himself with retaining all this.

c. He was made in the likeness of men (Jn. 1:14; Rom. 1:3; 8:3; Gal. 4:4; Heb. 2:14, 17). This simple but absolutely staggering fact cannot be even remotely grasped by human minds. The infinite holy Creator suddenly becomes in the likeness of his finite and sinful creatures (yet without sin).

Who can comprehend such unbelievable condescension? It is as if a mighty and magnificent earthly king would determine to lay aside for awhile his fantastic storehouse of wealth and, leaving behind an adoring and amazed court, take upon himself the body of a lowly ant. "The Son of man" was, by the way, our Lord's favorite name for himself while on earth.

d. He took upon himself the form of a servant. He did not come as a mighty human Caesar or some world-renowned human philosopher. Even this would have been a condescension of colossal proportions. He came, rather, as a lowly servant.

e. He humbled himself. That is, he submitted to authority (see 1 Pet. 2:21-24). He agreed to talk our language, to wear our clothes, to eat our food, to breathe our air, and to endure our vile and vicious treatment. Contrast his statement in the Garden with that of Lucifer's statement (Mt. 26:39; 42; Isa. 14:13, 14).

f. He became obedient unto death (Mt. 26:39; Jn. 10:18; Heb. 5:8; 12:2).

g. He died on a cursed cross. He did not just die, but suffered the worst kind of death both physically and judicially. (Gal. 3:13; Isa. 53; Ps. 22).

2. The example of the Father (2:9-11).

"Wherefore God also hath highly exalted him, and given him a name which is above every name: That at the name of Jesus every knee should bow, of things in heaven, and things in earth, and things under the earth; and that every tongue should confess that Jesus Christ is Lord, to the glory of God the Father" (Phil. 2:9-11).

We have examined the humiliation of Christ; now let us notice his exaltation.

a. He has been highly exalted by the Father himself (Isa. 52:13; Jn. 17:1; Acts 2:33; Heb. 2:9).

b. He has been given a name (position and place of authority) above all other names (Eph. 1:20; Heb. 1:4).

c. He will be universally acknowledged as Lord of all.

(1) The methods of this acknowledgment—by the bowing of the knee and the confession of the tongue.

(2) The creatures of this acknowledgment:

"Those in heaven": the world of angels.

"Those on earth": the world of saints and sinners.

"Those under the earth": the world of demons.

(See Rev. 5:13; 7:9-12; 14:6, 7; Isa. 45:23; Rom. 10:9, 10.)

Note: To confess him in this life as Lord means salvation, but to wait until the next life will result in damnation. Thus, the supreme question is not *when* a human being will do this, but rather where.

3. The example of Paul (2:12-18).

a. In matters of salvation—work it out.

"Work out your own salvation with fear and trembling" (2:12).

We note he did *not* say, "Work *for* your own salvation." The idea here is to complete something. The Greeks used this phrase in bringing a math problem to its logical conclusion and also to work a gold mine on a field.

"For it is God which worketh in you both to will and to do of his good pleasure" (2:13).

"It is thus not by imitation, but by incarnation" (Gal. 2:20). The Christian life is not to be a series of ups and downs, but rather of ins and outs. God works *in*; we are to work *out.*

b. In matters of illumination—hold it out.

"Whom ye shine as lights in the world; holding forth the word of life" (2:15, 16). Dr. J. Dwight Pentecost writes:

"The apostle uses an interesting word when he says 'holding forth.' It has the idea of two travelers going through the night, one with a light and one without a light. The one extends his light on the other who is following, that light might fall on his footsteps. . . . God has set you as a light. The word Paul translates 'light' is the word for *luminary.* It is the word for a light-giving heavenly body, a star if you please. This world is waiting for the sunrise of the Son of Righteousness, but until He slips over the horizon to bring His light to this world again, there is a star to cast its light that men might not fall. You are a star to hold forth the word of life; therefore, do all things without murmuring and complaining." (*The Joy of Living,* pp. 101, 102)

4. The example of Timothy (2:19-24). Timothy had a long and intimate contact with this church. (See Acts 16:3; 17:14; 15; 19:22; 20:3, 4; Phil. 2:19-23.)

a. Concerning the Philippian church, Timothy was a *shepherd.*

". . . who will naturally care for your state" (2:20).

b. Concerning the apostle, Timothy was a *son.*

". . . as a son with the father" (2:22).

c. Concerning the gospel, Timothy was a *servant.*

"He hath served with me in the gospel" (2:22).

Timothy is mentioned twenty-four times in Paul's letters.

5. The example of Epaphroditus (2:25–30). This man was a Gentile believer from Philippi. His name means "charming." He had been sent by the Philippian church to minister to Paul and bring him their offering.

a. His service:

(1) "My brother," indicating they were bound by a common love.

(2) "My companion in labour," indicating they were bound by a common work.

(3) "My fellowsoldier," indicating they were bound by a common danger.

b. His sickness: "For indeed he was sick nigh unto death: but God had mercy on him" (2:27).

c. His sorrow: "For he longed after you all, and was full of heaviness because that ye had heard that he had been sick" (2:26). Dr. J. Dwight Pentecost writes:

"The phrase 'full of heaviness' is a most graphic expression. It refers to that confused, restless, distracted state that is produced by some great physical stress, or mental or emotional stress. The burden of his homesickness is pressing so heavily upon Epaphroditus that he cannot give attention to that which normally would have occupied him. Such a state often accompanies illness, and one caring for someone recuperating from a physical illness must be prepared to cope with this distress that springs out of physical weakness. Such has been the weakness and physical state of Epaphroditus that he is to the point of distraction because of the care and concern that his illness caused." (*The Joy of Living,* pp. 119, 120)

d. His life: Dr. Warren Wiersbe aptly summarizes Epaphroditus' life by suggesting that he was:

(1) A balanced Christian (2:25).

"Epaphroditus was a balanced Christian! Balance is important in the Christian life. Some people emphasize 'fellowship' so much that they forget the *furtherance* of the Gospel. Others are so involved in defending the 'faith' of the Gospel that they neglect building *fellowship* with other be-

lievers. Epaphroditus did not fall into either of these traps. He was like Nehemiah, the man who rebuilt the walls of Jerusalem with his sword in one hand and his trowel in the other (Neh. 4:17). You cannot build with a sword nor battle with a trowel! It takes both to get the Lord's work accomplished. Dr. H. A. Ironside used to tell about a group of believers who thought only of 'fellowship.' They had little concern for reaching the lost or for defending the faith against its enemies. In front of their meeting place they hung a sign: 'JESUS ONLY.' But the wind blew away some of the letters, and the sign read 'US ONLY.' It was a perfect description of a group of people who were not balanced Christians." (*Be Joyful,* p. 76)

(2) A burdened Christian (2:26, 27).

(3) A blessed Christian (2:28–30).

III. Christ, the Prize of Life (chapter 3).

A. The corrupters of this prize (3:1–3, 18, 19). These verses are thought to refer to the Jewish Judaizers. Paul describes them and their actions in severe terms.

1. They were as dogs. They were always snapping at Paul's heels, and barking out their false doctrines.

2. They were evil workers. They performed their "good works" in the flesh (see Isa. 64:6; Mt. 23:15).

3. They were of the concision. This word is literally *mutilation* and is a pun on the word circumcision. They taught, of course, that circumcision was necessary for salvation. (See Acts 15:1; Gal. 6:12–18. God's real method of circumcision is found in Col. 2:11.)

4. They were the enemies of the cross of Christ.

5. Their belly was their God (Col. 2:20–23).

6. They were proud of what they should be ashamed of.

7. They were materialistic to the core.

B. The cost of this prize (3:4–6). Paul had gladly "counted as loss" his many earthly advantages after he had received Christ.

1. He had been circumcised on the eighth day. Paul had godly parents.

2. He was of the stock of Israel. He was not a proselyte, nor from Ishmael or Esau, but from the line of Isaac and Jacob.

3. He was of the tribe of Benjamin. This tribe was one of the most elite of the twelve. Israel's first king was from this tribe.

4. He was a Hebrew of the Hebrews. He spoke the right language. He had not become a Hellenizer (a Jew who adopted Greek culture). (See 2 Cor. 11:22; Acts 21:40; 22:2.) He had also studied under Gamaliel (Acts 22:3).

5. He was a Pharisee. Paul possessed the proper training.

6. He was known for his tremendous zeal in defending Judaism, and for his many good works (1 Cor. 15:9; Gal. 1:13, 14).
7. He had kept (as much as humanly possible) the Old Testament commandments.

C. The crown of this prize (3:7-17, 20, 21). Directly after his conversion, however, Paul laid aside all confidence in rite, race, religion, reputation, and human righteousness. He now possessed God's Redeemer. We have already seen what Paul set aside for Christ's sake. Now let us see what he gained in return.

1. He gained a new knowledge (3:7, 8).
   "But what things were gain to me, those I counted loss for Christ. Yea doubtless, and I count all things but loss for the excellency of the knowledge of Christ Jesus my Lord; for whom I have suffered the loss of all things, and do count them but dung, that I may win Christ" (3:7, 8).

   Martyred missionary Jim Elliot once wrote: "He is no fool who gives up what he cannot keep to gain what he cannot lose." (See also Jer. 9:23; 1 Cor. 2:2.)

2. He gained a new righteousness (3:9).
3. He gained a new power (3:10).
   "That I may know him and the power of his resurrection and the fellowship of his sufferings, being made conformable unto his death" (3:10).

   Far too many Christians are excited about the implications of the first half of this famous verse but show little interest in the last part. But it must be kept in mind that there is no power of the resurrection without the fellowship of the suffering. These go hand-in-hand! To know Christ in this manner has been the goal of all godly believers throughout history. See the following testimonies:
   a. Moses—Exodus 33:13
   b. David—Psalm 42:1, 2; 63:1, 2
   c. Philip—John 1:45 (See also Rom. 6:3-5; 8:17.)

4. He gained a new goal (3:11-17). John Walvoord writes:
   "He begins by saying, 'Not as though I had already attained, either were already perfect' (v. 12). The perfection he would have at the future resurrection was not yet attained, as he still had a sin nature, a sinful body, and was only too aware of the need for further spiritual progress. In stating that he was not already perfect, the apostle Paul used a Greek word, *teleioo*, meaning 'to reach a goal or fulfill a purpose.' The Greek word is the root of the English word *teleology* which refers to the design or purpose of the universe. The same word is found in Luke 13:32; John 17:23; 1 Cor. 2:6; 2 Cor. 12:9; Ephesians 4:12, and many other passages." (*Philippians, Triumph in Christ*, pp. 90, 91)

   Note especially Paul's statement in 3:13: "This one thing I do." For other biblical examples, see:
   a. Jesus and the rich young ruler (Mk. 10:21).

b. Martha and Jesus (Lk. 10:42).
c. An ex-blind man (Jn. 9:25).
d. The Psalmist (Ps. 27:4). (See also Jas. 1:8.)

Warren Wiersbe writes:
   "Consecration is the secret of power. If a river is allowed to overflow its banks, the area around it becomes a swamp. But if that river is dammed and controlled, it becomes a source of power." (*Be Joyful*, p. 97)

(Concerning Paul's phrase "reaching forth unto those things which are before," see 1 Cor. 9:24, 26; 2 Tim. 4:7, 8; Heb. 6:1; 12:1.)

5. He gained a new hope (3:20, 21).
   "For our conversation is in heaven, from whence also we look for the Saviour, the Lord Jesus Christ: Who shall change our vile body, that it may be fashioned like unto his glorious body, according to the working whereby he is able even to subdue all things unto himself."

   J. Vernon McGee writes:
   "Citizenship is *conversation* in the Authorized Version. An even better translation is that made by Mrs. Montgomery: 'For our city home is in heaven.' I like that. But the way I would prefer to translate it is this: 'We are a colony of heaven.' Now Paul also was a citizen of Rome, but what he is saying here is 'Our citizenship is in heaven.' Or 'We are a colony of heaven.' What does that mean? It means that the believer, since he is a citizen of heaven, is to take his orders from up there. He is to obey the laws from heaven. As someone has said, 'All the way to heaven is heaven.' A believer's life down here should mirror all the way to heaven. That is exactly what Paul is saying. This is the future." (*Probing Through Philippians*, p. 67)

   Thus, just as Philippi was a colony of Rome on foreign soil, the church is a colony of heaven on earthly, foreign soil.

IV. Christ, the Power of Life (chapter 4).
   A. This power can unify (4:1-3).
   B. This power can fortify (4:4-7).
      "Be careful for nothing; but in every thing by prayer and supplication with thanksgiving let your requests be made known unto God. And the peace of God, which passeth all understanding, shall keep your hearts and minds through Christ Jesus" (Phil. 4:6, 7).

   1. The two rules:
      a. "Be careful about nothing." The word "careful" here means "to be pulled in different directions." Paul is not talking about concern here, but about panic. (See Ps. 55:22; 1 Pet. 5:7.)
      b. Be prayerful about everything. Furthermore, our prayers should be both definite and devotional. It has been noted that there are but two areas over which the Christian is *not* to worry:
         (1) Those things which he himself can change. Here *perspiration* is the answer.

(2) Those things which he himself cannot change. Here *supplication* is the answer.

2. The two results (4:7).

"And the peace of God, which passeth all understanding, shall keep your hearts and minds through Christ Jesus."

The word *keep* here was often used to describe someone or something which was carefully guarded by the elite Roman soldiers of Caesar's palace. All Christians enjoy the peace *with* God mentioned in Romans 5:1, but only those who have successfully substituted care for prayer can enjoy the peace of God which truly passes understanding. Thus we see this peace guards:

a. Our hearts, protecting us from wrong feelings.

b. Our minds, protecting us from wrong thinking.

We should observe here that the familiar sign "Prayer changes things" is *not* always true. But prayer does change *us*, by protecting against those matters which were driving us to despair. (See Isa. 26:3; Ps. 119:165; 2 Cor. 10:5.) This, then, is God's marvelous method for keeping peace.

C. This power can purify (4:8, 9). These verses contain the briefest description of Christ in the entire Bible. The phrase "think on these things" may be literally translated "chew the cud."

D. This power can satisfy (4:10-12). Paul had learned in all of his circumstances "therewith to be content." It should be added, however, that contentment is *not* complacency; it is containment. The abiding Christ within Paul's body assured him of this satisfaction. Note the two kinds of Christians:

1. The thermometer believer. His satisfaction is totally dependent upon outside circumstances. He simply registers the prevailing spiritual temperature.

2. The thermostat believer. His satisfaction is totally independent of the outside circumstances. He is not only unaffected by it, but actually controls that area surrounding him.

E. This power can supply (4:13-23). "I can do all things through Christ which strengtheneth me" (4:13). The many little prepositions used by Paul are very important to summarize:

1. To be *in* Christ means salvation.

2. To work *through* Christ means sanctification.

3. To live *for* Christ means dedication.

4. To surrender *to* Christ means consecration.

5. To be *with* Christ means glorification.

Paul ends this lovely epistle of joy with the following glorious reminder:

"But my God shall supply all your need according to his riches in glory by Christ Jesus" (4:19).

1 TIMOTHY

INTRODUCTION:

1. This letter is one of the three New Testament books written especially to pastors of local churches. The other two are 2 Timothy and Titus.

2. This letter is the first New Testament book to discuss in detail those conditions which should prevail in a local church.

3. The letter was written by Paul to Timothy, who was pastoring the local church in Ephesus.

4. Paul composed the letter around A.D. 62-63 between his first and second imprisonment. The following arguments would seem to prove this theory.

a. Luke tells us that Paul spent two years in a Roman prison (Acts 28:30).

b. During this time he wrote Philippians, Colossians, Ephesians, and Philemon.

c. In these letters he expresses confidence that a release would be forthcoming (Phil. 1:23-25; 2:24; Philemon 1:22).

d. In Romans 15:24 Paul shared his plans to visit Spain. In 2 Timothy 4:7 he stated that he had "finished his course." However, at the time of his first imprisonment (Acts 28) he had not visited Spain. Thus he must have been released to make this trip.

5. Paul wrote both 1 Timothy and Titus during this interval.

6. On July 19, A.D. 64, Rome was burned (probably by Nero) and the Christians were blamed. Christianity then became an illegal religion and to evangelize was a crime punishable by death.

7. Paul was probably arrested again sometime after July of A.D. 64, and condemned to death.

8. During his second and final imprisonment he wrote 2 Timothy.

9. The New Testament has much to say concerning Timothy.

a. His name appears some twenty-four times.

b. He was from Lystra and probably was saved during Paul's first missionary trip (Acts 14:19, 20; 16:1, 2).

c. His mother (Eunice) and grandmother (Lois) were godly Jewish women, but his father was a pagan Greek (Acts 16:1; 2 Tim. 1:5).

d. He had been brought up on God's Word (2 Tim. 3:14, 15).

e. He is invited by Paul to "join the team" during the apostle's second trip (Acts 16:3). This team would consist of Silas, Paul, and Luke. Timothy may have been chosen to take John Mark's place. (See Acts 13:5.)

f. He is circumcised by Paul that he might have freedom to preach the gospel in the various Jewish synagogues (Acts 16:3; see also 1 Cor. 9:20).

g. Timothy is formally ordained by Paul and the presbytery (1 Tim. 4:14; 2 Tim. 1:6).

h. He also accompanies Paul during the third missionary trip (Acts 19:22; 20:4; 2 Cor. 1:1, 19).

i. He becomes Paul's close companion during the apostle's first imprisonment. (See Phil. 1:1; Col. 1:1; Philemon 1:1.)

j. Like Paul, Timothy also suffers imprisonment (see Heb. 13:23). He performs a ministry in at least five New Testament churches:

(1) Thessalonica (1 Thess. 3:2, 6)

(2) Corinth (1 Cor. 4:17; 16:10; 2 Cor. 1:19)

(3) Philippi (Phil. 2:19-23)

(4) Berea (Acts 17:14)

(5) Ephesus (1 Tim. 1:3)

k. Timothy may have been a somewhat reserved individual and one who did not always enjoy robust health. (1 Tim. 4:12, 14, 15, 16)

l. He was, nevertheless, a man of God. (See 1 Tim. 6:11.)

10. The key passage in 2 Timothy is 3:14, 15:

"But continue thou in the things which thou hast learned and hast been assured of knowing of whom thou hast learned them; and that from a child thou hast known the holy scriptures, which are able to make thee wise unto salvation through faith which is in Christ Jesus."

Keeping this in mind, the following six-point topical outline is suggested in dealing with this book.

a. The Savior and the family of God
b. The Apostle Paul and the family of God
c. The undershepherd (Timothy) and the family of God
d. The church officers and the family of God
e. The false teachers and the family of God
f. The various members and the family of God

I. The Savior and the Family of God. Paul touches on no less than ten great themes concerning the Person of our Lord Jesus Christ in 1 Timothy. These are:

A. His deity (1:17; 6:16).

"Now unto the King eternal, immortal, invisible, the only wise God, be honour and glory for ever and ever. Amen."

"Who only hath immortality, dwelling in the light which no man can approach unto; whom no man hath seen, nor can see: to whom be honour and power everlasting. Amen."

B. His purpose (1:15; 4:10).

"Christ Jesus came into the world to save sinners. . . . Who is the Saviour of all men" (1:15; 4:10).

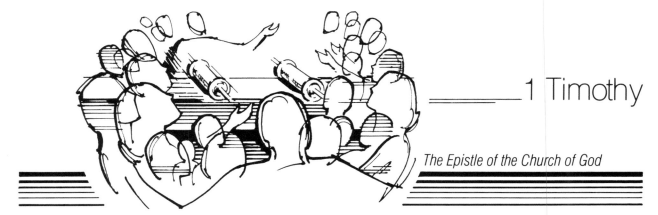

1 Timothy

The Epistle of the Church of God

The SAVIOR and the Church of God

His Deity (1:17)
His Purpose (4:10)
His Incarnation (3:16)
His Successful Ministry (3:16)
His Suffering and Death (6:13)

His Resurrection (3:16)
His Ascension (3:16)
His Mediatorship (2:5)
His Return (6:14)
His Millennial Reign (6:15)

PAUL and the Church of God

He was an apostle (1:1)

He was a former blasphemer and chief of sinners (1:13, 15)

He was a pattern and trophy (1:16)

He was a suffering servant (4:10)

He was a spiritual father (1:1)

He was an exhorter (6:13)

He was a preacher

His message—*the gospel (1:11)*
His mission field—*the Gentiles (2:7)*
His master—*The Savior (1:12)*

CHURCH OFFICERS and the Church of God

Seventeen qualifications for the office of a bishop (3:1-7)

INDIVIDUALS and the Church of God

ELDERS
(5:17, 19)

RICH MEMBERS
(6:17, 18)

WIDOWS
(5:3-6, 9, 11, 16)

SERVANTS
(6:1, 2)

C. His incarnation (3:16).
"God was manifest in the flesh" (3:16; see also Jn. 1:14; Dan. 2:11; Gal. 4:4; Isa. 7:14; 9:6).

Note: 1 Timothy 3:16 is one of the truly great verses in all the Bible, and may be viewed as an amplification of John 3:16. M.F. Unger writes:
"It refers to the basic body of divine revelation made known in Scripture and may well have constituted an early Christian hymn."

D. His successful ministry (3:16).
1. "Preached unto the Gentiles" (nations). This probably finds its ultimate fulfillment in the words of the Great Commission in Matthew 28:18-20.

Note the little phrase, "seen of angels" in 3:16. The earthly ministry of Christ was viewed by both elect and evil angels. (See Lk. 2:13; Mt. 4:11; Lk. 22:43—elect angels; and Mk. 1:23-26; 5:2-13—evil angels.)
2. "Believed on in the world." In spite of Israel's official rejection of him, our Lord left in his wake a powerful "minority group" of dedicated missionaries, numbering perhaps in the thousands (see 1 Cor. 15:6).

E. His suffering and death (6:13; 2:6). "Christ Jesus, who before Pontius Pilate witnessed a good confession" (6:13). "Who gave himself a ransom for all . . ." (2:6).

F. His resurrection (3:16). "Justified in the Spirit." This phrase seems to correspond with Romans 1:4, which verse is a definite reference to the resurrection of Christ.

G. His ascension (3:16).
"Received up into glory."

H. His mediatorship (2:5).
"For there is one God, and one mediator between God and men, the man Christ Jesus."

I. His return (6:14).
"The appearing of our Lord Jesus Christ."

J. His millennial reign (6:15).
"The blessed and only Potentate, the King of kings, and Lord of lords."

II. The Apostle Paul and the Family of God. Paul reveals several facts about himself in this letter to Timothy and the family of God at Ephesus.
A. He was an apostle by God's commandment (1:1; see Acts 9).
B. He was entrusted with God's glorious gospel (1:11).
C. He was thereupon strengthened by Christ himself for this ministry (1:12).
D. He had been a former blasphemer of Christ and a persecutor of Christians (1:13).
E. He nevertheless received mercy and grace, for he had done it ignorantly in unbelief (1:13, 14). Note: in verse 14 Paul lists the three motivating forces in his life:
1. Love. His love *for* Christ constrained him to labor (2 Cor. 5:14).
2. Faith. His faith *in* Christ empowered him to labor (Eph. 1:19).
3. Grace. His grace *from* Christ enabled him to labor (Heb. 12:28).
Thus, we are saved *by* grace (Eph. 2:8, 9), that we might serve *through* grace (Rom. 12:3-6).
F. His ministry was directed to the Gentiles (2:7).

G. To accomplish his divinely appointed goal he worked tirelessly and suffered reproach (4:10).
H. He thus became "a pattern to them which should hereafter believe on him [Jesus] to life everlasting" (1:16). Perhaps no other conversion has proven more profitable in soul-winning than has Paul's. He himself mentioned it often (see Gal. 1, 2; Phil. 3; Acts 22, 26).

III. The Undershepherd (Timothy) and the Family of God. Paul literally fills this epistle with admonitions to Timothy. The apostle not only spells out *what* he is to do, but also *why:*
"If thou put the brethren in remembrance of these things, thou shalt be a good minister of Jesus Christ, nourished up in the words of faith and of good doctrine, whereunto thou hast attained" (4:6).

Note these apostolic admonitions:
A. Remain in Ephesus (1:3). Paul here begs him thus, indicating that Timothy may have wanted to leave this difficult field.
B. Keep the church doctrinal standards pure (1:3).
C. Refuse to become bogged down with religious and worldly speculation (1:4; 4:7; 6:20).
D. Fight the good fight (1:18; 6:12). The Christian life is not a playground, but a battleground.
E. Maintain a good conscience (1:19). To go against a good conscience is to invite spiritual shipwreck.
F. Pray for all men (2:1). This is to be done because, if the church will not pray, then who else will? We note at the top of Paul's list is kings. At this time wicked Nero was upon the Roman throne.
1. The kinds of prayer:
a. supplications—asking for one's own needs
b. prayers—worship and adoration
c. intercessions—asking for another's needs
d. thanksgiving—appreciation for past grace and faith for future grace (see Phil. 4:6)
2. The attitudes in prayer:
a. Men
"I will therefore that men pray everywhere, lifting up holy hands [indicating a right relationship Godward], without wrath and doubting" [indicating a right relationship manward] (2:8).
b. Women
"In like manner also, that women adorn themselves in modest apparel" (2:9).
G. Do not allow congregational doctrine to be taught by a woman (2:12). Greek scholar Kenneth Wuest points out that here Paul uses the present infinitive tense instead of the aorist tense. Thus the command here should read, "I do not permit a woman to be a teacher." This of course does not prohibit her from teaching a ladies' Bible class, in Sunday school, etc. But the doctrinal teachers in the family of God are to be men (Acts 13:1; 1 Cor. 12:28, 29; Eph. 4:11). Paul now quickly gives Timothy two reasons for this.
1. Because of the original creation. "For Adam was first formed, then Eve" (2:13; see also Eph. 5:22; 1 Cor. 11:1-16).

2. Because of the original corruption. "And Adam was not deceived [*apatao*, to merely deceive], but the woman being deceived [*exapatao*, to totally deceive], was in the transgression" (2:14; see also 1 Cor. 11:8, 9).

3. The Word of God presents a divinely appointed threefold headship:
   a. the headship of Christ over his body (Col. 1:18)
   b. the headship of the pastor over his flock (Acts 20:28)
   c. the headship of the man over his wife (1 Cor. 11:1-16; 1 Tim. 2:12)

   Note: 1 Timothy 2:15 has been the object of much speculation: "Notwithstanding she shall be saved in childbearing, if they continue in faith and charity and holiness with sobriety." There are two basic interpretations offered to explain this verse.

   (1) That the salvation here refers to spiritual salvation. It is pointed out that the definite article precedes the word "childbearing" and should read "the childbearing," thus referring to the seed of the woman in Genesis 3:15, 16. Therefore, according to this view, Paul is saying that, while it was a woman which paved the way for the corruption in Eden, it was also a woman who paved the way for the incarnation at Bethlehem.

   (2) That the "salvation" here is from doctrinal error and warns against women teaching deceptions.

H. Warn against apostasy (4:6).
I. Discipline yourself (4:7).
J. Examine yourself (4:16).
K. Be an example (4:12). The pastor should not only exhort, but exemplify as well. He should be able to say: "Do as I *do*, as well as what I *say*." Here Paul lists five areas:
   1. in matters of speech
   2. in matters of conduct
   3. in matters of love
   4. in matters of faith
   5. in matters of purity
L. Give attention to "reading, to exhortation, to doctrine" (4:13). Paul has the Word of God in mind here. Thus, Timothy is to publicly:
   1. read it (reading)
   2. explain it (doctrine)
   3. exhort from it (exhortation)
M. Totally develop your spiritual gift (4:14, 15). What we don't *use*, we lose (see Heb. 2:1-3). The word "profiting" in 4:15 means "to cut forward, to blaze the way, to make a pioneer advance." A growing pastor means a growing church. A man cannot lead others where he has not been himself.
N. Be tactful and gentle (5:1, 2). Timothy was to be above reproach in dealing with people, especially the opposite sex.
O. Honor widows (5:3).
P. Be slow to judge elders (5:1, 19).
Q. Rebuke public sin publicly (5:20).

R. Show no bias or partiality (5:21).
S. Take care of yourself physically (5:23).
T. Avoid the love of money (6:10, 11).
U. Pursue righteousness, godliness, faith, love, perseverance, and gentleness (6:11).
V. Warn the rich about depending upon their riches (6:17).

IV. The Church Officers and the Family of God (3:1-13).
   A. The kinds of officers.
      1. Bishops (3:1-7; see also Titus 1:5-9). "If any man desire the office of a bishop, he desireth a good work" (3:1). The Greek word for "bishop" is *episkopos* and refers to an overseer. Here, of course, Paul had in mind the office of the pastor. Another name found in the New Testament which may refer to this same position is "elder" (*presbuteros* in the Greek). These two terms, bishop and elder, are often used interchangeably (Acts 20:17-28; Titus 1:5-7). The former term (bishop) speaks of his office responsibility, while the latter term (elder) refers to his spiritual maturity.
      2. Deacons (3:8-12). The exact nature and duties of this office are nowhere set forth in any systematic way in the New Testament. It seems almost certain that the office was created to solve the organizational problem of the early church, due in part to its rapid growth (Acts 6:1-8). The Greek word for "deacon" is *diakonos*. (See also Rom. 12:7, here translated "ministry," and Phil. 1:1.)
      3. Deaconess (3:11). Does this verse indicate the office of a deaconess? It is the view of some that it does.
   B. The qualifications for officers.
      1. Bishop (3:1-7).
         a. He must be a male.
         b. He must be blameless (without reproach).
         c. He must be the husband of one wife. Few New Testament statements have been the object of so much speculation as this little phrase in 3:2, "the husband of one wife." There are two main interpretations.
            (1) "The prohibition of polygamy" view. According to this theory, Paul is simply saying no church member who had several wives in his home could qualify as a bishop. However, this view has serious problems.
               (a) Paul had already forbidden this years ago (1 Cor. 7:2 and Rom. 7:1-3).
               (b) The Roman government had oulawed polygamy at this time.
               (c) There is no evidence that the early church ever had this problem.
               (d) This term literally says a "one woman man" and is found again in 5:9 (though here reversed) where it speaks of a widow as a "one man woman."
            (2) "The prohibition of divorce" view. According to this theory, a divorced

and remarried man is prohibited from occupying the office of the pastorate, regardless of the circumstances which may have surrounded the divorce. It must be kept in mind that Paul in this chapter is not discussing the *salvation* of a sinner, but the qualifications of an officer.

d. He must be vigilant (temperate).

e. He must be sober (serious-minded).

f. He must be of good behavior (orderly). This would be reflected in his sermons, clothes, and life manner.

g. He must be given to hospitality (a lover of strangers).

h. He must be "apt to teach" (having the ability and love for teaching; see Eph. 4:11).

i. He must not be given to wine.

j. He must not be a striker (not pugnacious).

k. He must not be greedy of money.

l. He must be patient (reasonable, gentle).

m. He must not be a brawler (not contentious).

n. He must not covet (desire something belonging to someone else).

o. He must rule his own house well.

p. He must not be a novice (a new convert).

q. He must maintain a good report from without (a good public testimony in his immediate community).

2. Deacon (3:8–13).

a. He must be grave (held in high respect).

b. He must not be double-tongued (two-faced, a talebearer).

c. He must not be given over to wine.

d. He must not be greedy of filthy lucre.

e. He must hold forth the mystery of the faith (to know, explain, and defend the great theological truths of the Bible).

f. He must maintain a pure conscience.

g. He must be tested and proven (his testimony within the church must be good).

h. He must be blameless (his testimony without the church must be good).

i. He must have a godly wife.

j. He must be the head of his family.

V. The False Teachers and the Family of God. In 1 Timothy, Paul not only warns against these tares among the wheat, but also describes them that they might be recognized by the family of God and dealt with.

A. They argue about fables and endless genealogies (1:4; 4:7).

B. They are guilty of vain jangling (empty chatter and aimless monologue—1:6).

C. They are ignorant of the very things they so dogmatically teach (1:7).

D. They go against their own conscience (1:19, 20; 4:2). Here Paul lists two men who had actually done this. They were Hymenaeus and Alexander (1:19, 20). These two would later deny the doctrine of the resurrection (2 Tim. 2:17; 4:14).

E. They shall increase in number and activity in the latter days (4:1). Note: The church at Ephesus had already been warned about this (Acts 20:29, 30) and would be warned once again (Rev. 2:2).

F. Their teachings would be energized by demons (4:1).

G. They would forbid meat-eating and marriage (4:3). God, of course, had already given both to man (Gen. 1:29; 9:3).

H. They are proud know-nothings, spiritually sick, showing a morbid interest in controversial questions (6:4).

I. They produce envy, strife, use abusive language, and harbor evil suspicions (6:4).

J. They cause constant friction (6:5).

K. They use the family of God as a means of gain (6:5).

L. They oppose the faith with pretended "facts" of science which are in reality empty chatter (6:20).

VI. The Various Members and the Family of God.

A. Widows: Some were to receive financial support from the church.

1. widows with no children (5:3, 5, 16)

2. widows with a family (5:4)

3. widows living in pleasure (5:6)

4. widows over sixty (5:9)

5. young widows (5:11)

B. Elders:

1. They were to receive double honor when they ruled well, especially in the duties of preaching and teaching (5:17).

2. They were to be assumed innocent of any accusation unless it came from two or three respected witnesses (5:19).

C. Servants:

1. They were to regard their masters as worthy of all honor (6:1).

2. This was to be done whether the master was lost (6:1) or saved (6:2).

D. Rich members:

1. They are not to be conceited or to fix their hopes on the uncertainty of their riches, but upon God (6:17).

2. They are to do good, that is, to be as rich in good works as in money (6:18).

3. They are to be generous and ready to share (6:18). Thus, rich people are to both *enjoy* and *employ* their riches.

TITUS

INTRODUCTION:

1. Titus, like Timothy, was one of Paul's "preacher boys."

2. Paul had assigned Titus to strengthen a previously established church work on the Isle of Crete. This island, southeast of Greece, was about 150 miles long and thirty-five miles wide, thus making it the largest of the Mediterranean islands. It was on the island of one hundred cities, consisting of mountains, but very fertile valleys. The highest mountain, Mt. Ida, was the traditional birthplace of the Greek god Zeus. The Cretans were relatives of the Philistines. They had a notorious reputation of being "always liars, evil beasts, and lazy gluttons" (Titus 1:12). This testimony came from one of their own poets and prophets. The origin of the church there is unknown, but may have been started by the same returning Cretans who were present at Pentecost (see Acts 2:11).

3. The epistle to Titus was written about the same time as 1 Timothy, during that period between Paul's first and second Roman imprisonment.
4. The three pastoral epistles may be favorably compared.
   a. In 1 and 2 Timothy Paul stresses *doctrine*.
   b. In Titus he emphasizes *duty*.
   c. The child of God is to *protect* the gospel in 1 Timothy.
   d. He is to *proclaim* it in 2 Timothy.
   e. He is to *practice* it in Titus.
5. A summary of the person and ministry of Titus would include:
   a. He was a Gentile (Greek; see Gal. 2:3).
   b. He was probably a convert of Paul (Titus 1:4).
   c. Some believe he may have been the brother of Luke.
   d. Titus first appears in the sacred account when he accompanied Paul and Barnabas to Jerusalem (Gal. 2:1).
   e. He is later sent by Paul to Corinth to straighten out certain disorders in the church there and to initiate an offering for the poor saints at Jerusalem (2 Cor. 8:6, 10).
   f. He then meets Paul in Macedonia and is sent back to Corinth carrying the epistle of 2 Corinthians to pave the way for Paul's coming and to complete their offering (2 Cor. 2:3, 12, 13; 7:5, 6, 13, 14; 8:16, 17, 23; 12:14, 18).
   g. He seems to have accompanied Paul during the third missionary trip.
   h. He is last mentioned in 2 Timothy 4:10, at which time Paul sends him from southern Greece to Dalmatia (Yugoslavia).
6. The epistle contains two outstanding doctrinal passages (see 2:11-14; 3:4-7).

I. Titus and the Apostle (1:1-4). In his introduction, Paul presents himself in a fourfold light.
   A. In regard to the Father, he was a bond slave (1:1).
   B. In regard to the Son, he was an apostle (1:1).
   C. In regard to the Word, he was a preacher.
      "But hath in due times manifested his word through preaching which is committed unto me . . ." (1:3).
      Thus, God's ordained method for communicating his Word is not through personal dialogue, but through pulpit delivery.
   D. In regard to Titus, he was a spiritual parent (1:4).
II. Titus and the Elders (1:5-16).
      "For this cause left I thee in Crete, that thou shouldest set in order the things that are wanting, and ordain elders in every city, as I had appointed thee" (1:5).
   A. Their qualifications (1:6-8): Paul now lists some fourteen characteristics to look for in potential elders.
      1. Blameless (literally, one not called into account).
      2. The husband of one wife (he could not be a divorced man).
      3. Having faithful children not accused of riot or unruly (he should have both believing and behaving children).
      4. Not self-willed (he must be self-motivated, but not self-willed). Note the contrast between the self-seeking of Lucifer in the Gar-

Paul's letter to Titus

Titus and the Apostle 1:1-4

PAUL PRESENTS HIMSELF IN A FOURFOLD LIGHT
In regard to the Father, he was a bondslave (1:1).
In regard to the Son, he was an apostle (1:1).
In regard to the Word, he was a preacher (1:3).
In regard to Titus, he was a spiritual parent (1:4).

Titus and the Elders 1:5-16

THEIR QUALIFICATIONS (1:6-8)

Blameless	The husband of one wife
Having faithful children	Not self-willed
Not soon angry	Not given to wine
No striker	Not given to filthy lucre
A lover of hospitality	A lover of good men
Sober	Just
Holy	Temperate

THEIR DUTIES (1:9-16)
To know the great truths in God's Word
To exhort (encourage) believers
To convince (refute) unbelievers

Titus and the Church 2:1—3:11

THE PEOPLE IN THE CHURCH

The older men	The older women
The younger women	The younger men
Servants	

THE SAVIOR OF THE CHURCH

His incarnation	His great example
His sacrificial death	His Second Coming

THE RESPONSIBILITIES OF THE CHURCH (3:1, 2, 8-10)

Titus and the Future 3:12-15

He would be relieved for awhile
He would meet Paul in southern Greece
He was to aid Zenas

den of Eden (Isa. 14:12-14; Ezek. 28:11-17) and the submission of Christ in the Garden of Gethsemane (Mt. 26:36-46).
      5. Not soon angry.
      6. Not given to wine.
      7. No striker (not violent).
      8. Not given to filthy lucre (he cannot be materialistic).
      9. A lover of hospitality.
      10. A lover of good men.
      11. Sober.
      12. Just.
      13. Holy (unpolluted).
      14. Temperate (self-controlled).
   B. Their duties (1:9-16):
      1. To know the great truths in God's Word.
      2. To exhort (encourage) believers.
      3. To convince (refute) unbelievers.
      By faithfully performing these three things, the elders could successfully silence the Cretan en-

emies of the gospel. Note Paul's scathing description of these false teachers:

    a. They were guilty of overturning (subverting) entire households.

    b. They were money-hungry opportunists, preying on religious people.

    c. They were lying, rude, cruel, and lazy gluttons.

    d. They possessed defiled minds.

        "Unto the pure all things are pure: but unto them that are defiled and unbelieving is nothing pure" (1:15).

        Paul is here, of course, talking about Mosaic dietary laws, and not morals in general (see Mt. 15:11; Rom. 14:14; Acts 10:15).

    e. "They profess that they know God; but in works they deny him, being abominable, and disobedient, and unto every good work reprobate" (1:16).

III. Titus and the Church (21:1—3:11).

  A. The people in the church (2:1-10). Paul now directs his attention to five key groups in a local church and urges Titus to develop certain Christian virtues in each group. These groups are:

    1. the older men (2:1, 2)

    2. the older women (2:3)

    3. the younger women (2:4, 5)

    4. the younger men (2:6-8)

    5. servants (2:9, 10)

  B. The Savior of the church (2:11-15; 3:4-7)

    1. His incarnation:

        "For the grace of God that bringeth salvation hath appeared to all men" (2:11).

        "But after that the kindness and love of God our Saviour toward man appeared" (3:4).

    2. His great example:

        "Teaching us that, denying ungodliness and worldly lusts, we should live soberly, righteously, and godly, in this present world" (2:12).

        We may observe three aspects in this verse:

    a. The *selfward* aspect—we are to live soberly.

    b. The *manward* aspect—we are to live righteously.

    c. The *godward* aspect—we are to live godly.

    3. His sacrificial death:

        "Who gave himself for us, that he might redeem us from all iniquity, and purify unto himself a peculiar people, zealous of good works" (2:14).

        Having thus been purchased and purified, God's people are now required to *perform*.

        "Not by works of righteousness which we have done, but according to his mercy he saved us, by the washing of regeneration, and renewing of the Holy Ghost, which he shed on us abundantly through Jesus Christ our Savior" (3:5, 6).

        God's mercy, *minus* man's righteousness, *plus* the Spirit's renewal equals *regeneration.*

    4. His Second Coming:

        "Looking for that blessed hope, and the glorious appearing of the great God and our Saviour Jesus Christ. . . . That being justified by his grace, we should be made heirs according to the hope of eternal life" (2:13; 3:7).

  C. The responsibilities of the church.

    1. To be subject to principalities and powers (3:1).

    2. To initiate good works (3:1).

    3. To maintain good works (3:8).

    4. To speak evil (slander) of no man.

    5. To demonstrate gentleness and meekness to all men (3:2).

    6. To avoid foolish questions, contentions, and legalistic arguments (3:9).

    7. To reject heresy and heretics (3:10).

IV. Titus and the Future (3:12-15).

  A. He would be relieved for awhile by either Artemas or Tychicus. Tychicus had already been sent by Paul on various missions to the churches at Ephesus (Eph. 6:21) and Colosse (Col. 4:7). He would later be sent to Ephesus again (see 2 Tim. 4:12).

  B. He was then to meet Paul in southern Greece (Nicopolis).

  C. He was to aid Zenas the lawyer and Apollos with their trip. We are not told the nature or route of this trip.

2 TIMOTHY

INTRODUCTION:

1. After being released from his first Roman imprisonment (Acts 28), Paul is once again arrested.

2. This arrest may have taken place suddenly in Troas, thus explaining why Paul left there without taking his cloak, parchments, or Old Testament scrolls (2 Tim. 4:13).

3. His second imprisonment was far different from the first.

    a. He was then a political prisoner awaiting trial. He is now a condemned criminal, awaiting death.

    b. Then he lived in his own hired house. Now he huddles in a cold, damp, dark dungeon.

    c. During his first imprisonment he was visited by many. Now he is forsaken by all.

4. This is his most personal letter; in Romans we see Paul the theologian; in 1 Corinthians, Paul the counselor; in 2 Corinthians, Paul the preacher; in Galatians, Paul the defender; in 1 Timothy and Titus, Paul the statesman; but here in 2 Timothy, Paul the *man.*

5. The letter is rich in personal allusions. Paul mentions twenty-three men, women, friends, and foes.

6. This epistle is his spiritual swan song, his dying shout of triumph.

7. Dr. J. Vernon McGee writes:

    "In Second Timothy Paul speaks of the ultimate outcome of gospel preaching. The final fruition will not be the total conversion of mankind, nor will it usher in the Millennium. On the contrary, there will come about an apostasy which will well-nigh blot out 'the faith' from the earth. This is in complete harmony with the startling word of Christ, 'When the Son of man cometh, shall he find faith on the earth?' This is not in keeping, of course, with a social gospel which expects to transform the world by tinkering with the social system. These vain optimists have no patience with the doleful

2 Timothy

PAUL

Preacher, Pattern, Prophet, Prisoner

Paul the PREACHER (CHAPTER 1)

*"Whereunto I am appointed a preacher,
and an apostle, and a teacher of the Gentiles"* **(1:11)**.

THE PREACHER AND HIS STUDENT *(TIMOTHY)*

● HIS CONCERN FOR TIMOTHY

He prayed for him **(1:3)**.
He knew his tears **(1:4)**.

● HIS CONFIDENCE IN TIMOTHY

● HIS COUNSEL TO TIMOTHY

Stir up your gift **(1:6)**.
Don't be ashamed of Christ's message or messenger **(1:8)**.
Hold fast to sound doctrine **(1:13)**.
Remain true to your ministry **(1:14)**.

THE PREACHER AND HIMSELF

● HE REVIEWS HIS PAST PERFORMANCE, MINISTERING AS:

AN APOSTLE **(1:1)**	A SERVANT **(1:3)**
A PRISONER **(1:8)**	A TEACHER **(1:11)**
A FATHER **(1:2)**	A SUFFERER **(1:12)**
A PREACHER **(1:11)**	

● HE RETAINS HIS PERMANENT HOPE

"For I know whom I have believed, and am persuaded that he is able to keep that which I have committed unto him against that day" **(1:12)**.

TWO VIEWS
A possible reference to his SALVATION, which Paul had deposited with Christ.
A possible reference to his SERVICE, which Christ had deposited with Paul.

● HE REGRETS THE ACTIONS OF SOME FALSE FRIENDS **(1:15)**.

● HE REJOICES CONCERNING THE ACTIONS OF A TRUE FRIEND **(1:16-18)**.

Paul the PATTERN (CHAPTER 2)

"And the things that thou hast heard of me among many witnesses, the same commit thou to faithful men, who shall be able to teach others also" **(2:2)**.

Paul the PROPHET (CHAPTER 3)

"This know also, that in the last days perilous times shall come" **(3:1)**.

Paul the PRISONER (CHAPTER 4)

"The time of my departure is at hand" **(4:6)**.

"I have finished my course" **(4:7)**.

---

words of 1 Timothy. Nevertheless, the cold and hard facts of history and the events of the present have demonstrated the accuracy of Paul." (*Second Timothy*, p. 196)

I. Paul the Preacher (chapter 1).
"Whereunto I am appointed a preacher, and an apostle, and a teacher of the Gentiles" (1:11).
  A. The preacher and his pupil (Timothy).
    1. Paul prayed for him day and night (1:3).
    2. He longed to see him (1:4).
    3. He was aware of his tears (1:4).
    4. He had full confidence in him (1:5).

5. He exhorted him to stir up his gift (1:6).
6. He is not to be ashamed of the message of Christ (1:8).
7. He is not to be ashamed of the messengers of Christ (1:8).
8. He is to hold fast to sound doctrine (1:13).
9. He is to remain true to his ministry (1:14).
  B. The preacher and himself.
    1. He reviews his past performance. The apostle gives a sevenfold description of himself in this chapter. He is:
      a. an apostle (1:1)

b. a father (1:2)

c. a faithful servant (1:3)

d. a prisoner (1:8)

e. a preacher (1:11)

f. a teacher (1:11)

g. a sufferer (1:12)

2. He retains his permanent hope.

"Nevertheless, I am not ashamed; for I know whom I have believed and am persuaded that he is able to keep that which I have committed unto him against that day" (1:12).

There are two views concerning the usage of "committed" in this verse.

a. Paul was here referring to his *salvation,* which he had deposited with Christ.

b. Paul was here referring to his *service,* which Christ had deposited with Paul.

3. He had been forsaken by many false friends while in prison.

4. He had been helped by one true friend while in prison—Onesiphorus (1:16-18).

II. Paul the Pattern (2).

"And the things that thou hast heard from me among many witnesses, the same commit thou to faithful men, who shall be able to teach others also" (2:2).

In this chapter Paul likens the life of the believer (especially a pastor) to eight earthly occupations:

A. A steward (2:2). A steward was the custodian and trustee of his master's estate in the New Testament world. The man of God is likewise expected to be faithful to his deposit, the glorious gospel of Christ. He is not only to keep this deposit, but to commit it to faithful men. The job of a local church is not to preserve the truth in a musty museum, but to proclaim it to the teeming masses.

B. A soldier (2:3, 4).

1. He is to endure the hardships of the war.

2. He is to avoid the entanglements of the world.

3. He is to please his Commander.

C. An athlete (2:5).

1. He is to contend for the reward.

2. He is to abide by the rules.

D. A farmer (2:6, 7).

1. He must perform in the area of sowing.

2. He will partake in the hour of reaping.

E. An instructor (2:11-14).

1. He is to remind his students that to die *with* Christ is to live *for* Christ (2:11).

2. He is to remind his students that to suffer *for* Christ is to reign *with* Christ.

F. A student (2:15).

1. As a student he is to study the Word of God.

a. That he might be approved before God.

b. That he might be assured before men.

2. As a student he is to shun the words of men.

G. A vessel (2:20, 21).

"But in a great house there are not only vessels of gold and of silver, but also of wood and of earth; and some to honor, and some to dishonor. If a man therefore purge himself from these, he shall be a vessel unto honor, sanctified, and meet for the master's use, and prepared unto every good work."

H. A servant (2:24).

"The servant of the Lord must not strive, but be gentle unto all men, apt to teach, patient, in meekness instructing those that oppose him."

III. Paul the Prophet (3). "This know also, that in the last days perilous times shall come" (3:1). The word "perilous" here is translated "exceeding fierce" in Matthew 8:28, describing the maniac of Gadara. Thus, in the last days Satan will attempt to turn this world into his own personal graveyard.

A. The symptoms of this "final days" disease (3:1-13). Men will be:

1. self-lovers

2. money-lovers

3. boasters

4. proud

5. blasphemers

6. disobedient to parents

7. unthankful

8. unholy (profane)

9. without natural affection

10. trucebreakers

11. false accusers

12. incontinent (without self-control)

13. fierce (savage)

14. despisers of good things

15. traitors (betrayers)

16. heady (reckless)

17. high-minded (drunk with pride)

18. pleasure-lovers

19. have religion without the Redeemer (3:5) ("Having a form of godliness, but denying the power of it.")

20. hold information without illumination (3:7) ("Ever learning, and never able to come to the knowledge of the truth.")

21. seducers (sorcerers)

22. deceiving and being deceived

B. The cure for this "final days" disease (3:14-17). "But continue thou in the things which thou hast learned and hast been assured of, knowing of whom thou hast learned them; and that from a child thou hast known the holy scriptures, which are able to make thee wise unto salvation through faith which is in Christ Jesus. All scripture is given by inspiration of God, and is profitable for doctrine, for reproof, for correction, for instruction in righteousness: That the man of God may be perfect, throughly furnished unto all good works."

In this remarkable passage Paul claims the Bible is profitable for:

1. Doctrine. The Bible may be used as the perfect textbook to present the systematic teachings of the great truths relating to God himself.

2. Reproof. The Bible is to be used to convict us of the wrong in our lives.

3. Correction. The Bible will then show us the right way.

4. Instruction in righteousness. The Bible provides all the necessary details which will allow a Christian to become fully equipped for every good work.

IV. Paul the Prisoner (4).
  A. His final charge (4:1, 2, 5).
    1. Preach the word.
    2. Be diligent at all times.
    3. Reprove, rebuke, and exhort whenever needed.
    4. Remain alert at all times.
    5. Bear up under persecutions.
    6. Evangelize your field.
    7. Utilize your ministry to the fullest.
  B. His final warning (4:3, 4).
    1. In the last days men will not tolerate healthy doctrine.
    2. They will be controlled by their own lusts.
    3. In their restlessness they will seek out many false teachers.
    4. Having refused the truth they will fall victim to fables.
  C. His final testimony (4:6, 7).
     "For I am now ready to be offered, and the time of my departure is at hand. I have fought a good fight, I have finished my course, I have kept the faith."
    1. The word translated "offered" is a liturgical word and signifies the pouring out of a religious drink offering (Num. 15:1-10). Paul had already regarded his ministry in winning the lost to Christ as an offering to God (Rom. 15:16; Phil. 2:17) and now his approaching death would complete the sacrifice.
    2. The word "departure" means "to take down a tent, to break camp, to pull in the anchor."
    3. His testimony in verse 7 should be contrasted with God's statement to wicked Belshazzar in Daniel 5:26.
  D. His final request (4:9, 11, 12, 13, 19, 21).
    1. Timothy was to come immediately.
    2. He was to bring John Mark with him. Years prior to this Mark had, of course, accompanied Paul and Barnabas on their first missionary trip, but had left the team and gone home. Due to this sign of immaturity, Paul had refused to include him in a second proposed trip. This action then prompted a break between Paul and Barnabas. (See Acts 13:3; 15:36-40.) But since that time John had so grown in God's grace that Paul desired to see him before his departure.
    3. He was to bring Paul's cloak he had left at Troas (4:13). The great sixteenth-century Bible translator William Tyndale would later make a similar request while confined to a damp prison cell:
       "I entreat your lordship, and that by the Lord Jesus, that if I must remain here for the winter, you would beg the Commissary to be so kind as to send me, from the things of mine which he has, a warmer cap, I feel the cold painfully in my head. Also a warmer cloak to patch my leggings. My overcoat is worn out, my shorts even are worn out. He has a woolen shirt of mine, if he will send it. But most of all I entreat and implore your kindness to do your best with the Commissary to be so good as to send me my Hebrew Bible, grammar, and vocabulary, that I may spend my time in that pursuit."
    4. Timothy was to bring Paul's study books.
    5. He was to bring the parchments—Paul's copies of the Old Testament. This statement is staggering in its implications. Here is a man who conducted the first three missionary trips ever attempted for Christ, who had personally seen the Savior on at least four occasions, who had written approximately half of the New Testament, and who had organized the first fifty or so Christian churches on this earth. Now in his hour of death he requests the Scriptures, for he evidently felt he could still learn from the precious pages.
       The child of God is in absolutely no danger whatsoever of learning too much about God's Word.
  E. His final sorrow (4:10, 14, 15, 16).
    1. Demas had forsaken him (Col. 4:10; Philemon 1:24).
    2. Alexander had persecuted him (1 Tim. 1:20; Acts 19:33).
    3. His friends at Rome had not helped him.
  F. His final confidence (4:8, 17, 18).
    1. God had stood by him during all past dangers (4:17).
    2. God would stand by him during any future dangers (4:18).
    3. Both past and future sufferings would be amply rewarded by that righteous Judge someday (4:8).
  G. His final prayer (4:22).
     "The Lord Jesus Christ be with thy spirit. Grace be with you. Amen."

1 PETER

INTRODUCTION:
1. Of the original twelve apostles, three were chosen to write inspired New Testament books or epistles. The three are Matthew, John, and Peter.
2. In his two epistles, Peter continues to fulfill Christ's commandment to him to feed his sheep and lambs. (See Jn. 21:15-17.)
3. Peter's name appears 210 times in the New Testament. Paul's name is found 162 times. The names of the remaining eleven apostles combined appear 142 times.
4. Peter has been called "the apostle of hope" (see 1:3, 13, 21; 3:15). Paul could thus be classified as the apostle of faith, and John the apostle of love.
5. A key word in this epistle is "suffering." It (or its equivalent) is used sixteen times. Six times it speaks of Christ's suffering and ten times that of believers. Another important word is "grace," which appears eight times.
6. The letter was probably written at the end of his life. It is thought that after this epistle he was arrested and tried. Between his trial and execution he wrote 2 Peter (2 Pet. 1:13-21).
   It must have been written around A.D. 64, on the eve of the outbreak of the persecution by Nero. Nero died in A.D. 68.
7. In 5:13 he identifies the place of writing as Babylon. There are two main theories concerning the location of Babylon.

a. It is literal Babylon on the Euphrates River. This would seem to be the natural interpretation of the passage. Furthermore, the list of countries in 1 Peter 1:1 is from East to West, which suggests that the writer was in the East at the time of writing. J. Vernon McGee writes:

"There was at this time a large colony of Jews in ancient Babylon who had fled Rome due to severe persecution under Claudius and at the time of writing bloody Nero was on the throne." (*Through the Bible*, p. 256)

In addition to this, the descendants of those Jews taken captive by Nebuchadnezzar were still living in and around Babylon.

b. It is Rome. Charles Ryrie writes:

"The place of the writing was Babylon (5:13), a symbolic name for Rome much used by writers who wished to avoid trouble with Roman authorities. . . . Peter was in Rome during the last decade of his life and wrote this epistle about A.D. 63, just before the outbreak of Nero's persecution in 64. Peter was martyred about 67." (*The Ryrie Study Bible*, p. 425)

Furthermore, it is argued that Peter states Mark (5:13) was with him at the time the epistle was written. However, just prior to this, Paul had written Timothy to bring Mark to Rome with him (2 Tim. 4:11).

8. The church apparently was affected by worldliness in the pews (2:11) and materialism in the pulpit (5:1-3).

9. Peter develops the doctrine of Christ in a remarkable way in the short epistle. He discusses:
   a. The incarnation of Christ (1:20).
   b. The names for Christ:
      (1) a spotless Lamb (1:19)
      (2) the Chief Cornerstone—his relationship to the Scriptures (2:6)
      (3) the precious Stone—his relationship to believers (2:7)
      (4) the stumbling Stone—his relationship to unbelievers (2:8)
      (5) the Bishop of our souls (2:25)
      (6) the chief Shepherd (5:4)
   c. his sinless life (1:19; 2:22)
   d. his suffering and death (1:11; 2:23, 24; 3:18; 4:1, 13; 5:1)
   e. his resurrection (3:21, 22)
   f. his ascension (3:22)
   g. his presence at God's right hand (3:22)
   h. his Second Coming (1:13, 17; 4:13; 5:1, 4)

10. Peter also offers a number of titles which describe believers. Perhaps in no other New Testament book are so many given. We are referred to as:
    a. obedient children (1:14)
    b. newborn babes (2:2)
    c. living stones (2:5)
    d. a holy priesthood (2:5)
    e. a royal priesthood (2:5)
    f. a holy nation (2:9)
    g. a peculiar people (2:9)
    h. strangers and pilgrims (2:11)
    i. Christians (4:16)
    j. the righteous (4:18)
    k. the elect of God (1:2)
    l. the people of God (2:10)
    m. the oracles of God (4:11)
    n. the flock of God (5:2)

11. It is generally considered that the Gospel of Mark reflects the teaching of Peter. Young John Mark had, no doubt, often heard Peter speak and preach.

12. Peter and John are the only two New Testament authors to refer to Christ as a Lamb (Jn. 1:29, 36; Rev. 5:6; 1 Pet. 1:19).

13. A careful reading of 1 Peter and Ephesians shows more than 100 parallels in teaching and wording. Note:

1 Peter	Ephesians
1:3	1:3
1:12	3:5, 10
4:11	3:6, 21
1:8	3:8
3:9	4:2
4:10	4:7, 11
2:2	4:13, 15

Peter was also familiar with the book of Romans, and perhaps other epistles from Paul (see 2 Pet. 3:15, 16).

I. God's Salvation: The Details of Sovereignty (1:1-25).
   A. The Source of our salvation—the entire Trinity (1:1, 2).
      1. The Father elected us. "Elect according to the foreknowledge of God" (v. 2). We are not told the basis of this election, it should be noted. However, God's election is based

God's Salvation   SIMON PETER

1 Peter

The details of sovereignty (1:1-25)

The duties of saints (2:1—3:13)

The discipline of suffering (3:14—4:19)

The delights of service (5:1-14)

squarely upon foreknowledge. Note: "For whom he did foreknow, he also did predestinate" (Rom. 8:29).

It should be quickly noted, though, that *both* man's responsibility (Jn. 3:16; Rom. 10:13; Rev. 22:17) and God's sovereignty (Eph. 1:4, 5) are clearly taught in the Bible.

In one single statement, our Lord combined both doctrines of election and free will. Note his words:

"All that the Father giveth me shall come to me [this is election]; and him that cometh to me I will in no wise cast out [this is free will]" (Jn. 6:37).

2. The Spirit sanctified us. "Through sanctification of the Spirit" (1:2). After we were elected, the Holy Spirit set us apart (the meaning of sanctification), convicted us of our sin (Jn. 16:8), and pointed us to Christ (Jn. 16:13, 14).

This is accomplished through the obedience of the believing sinner. It has been said that only he who believes obeys, and only he who obeys believes.

3. The Son redeemed us. "And sprinkling of the blood of Jesus Christ" (1:2).
Richard DeHaan writes:

"The basis for this statement is found in the Old Testament ceremonial system. In certain of the rituals, the blood of the sacrificial animals was sprinkled in special areas. This sprinkling had three different meanings.

1. First, it signified cleansing. The person who had been cured of leprosy, for example, went before the priest, and blood was sprinkled to indicate that he was now free from the disease and clean (Lev. 14:1-7).
2. Second, this act was used to symbolize the ratification of a covenant between God and man. Whenever Jehovah and His people entered into a covenant, it was sealed by the sprinkling of the blood of a sacrificial animal (see Ex. 24:3-8).
3. Third, the application of blood designated certain articles of the tabernacle or temple as set apart for worship. From that point on, the vessel was used exclusively for the service of the Lord (see Ex. 29:20-22)." (*Good News for Bad Times*, p. 15)

In light of all this, the triune God is to be blessed by the believer (v. 3). The Greek word for "blessed" is *eulogetos*, meaning "to speak well of." From this we get our word *eulogize*. Thus, the child of God is to speak well of the triune God. By doing this we "bless" God. Note his reaction to this.

"Then they that feared the Lord spoke often one to another; and the Lord hearkened, and heard it, and a book of remembrance was written before him for them that feared the Lord, and that thought upon his name" (Mal. 3:16).

B. The blessings of our salvation (1:3, 4).
1. A living hope. "His abundant mercy hath begotten us again unto a lively hope" (1:3). In his epistle Peter mentions three living things:
a. a living hope (1:3)
b. a living word (1:23)
c. a living stone (2:4)
2. A lasting home. "To an inheritance incorruptible, and undefiled, and that fadeth not away, reserved in heaven for you."
a. This home (inheritance) is *perfect* (incorruptible).
b. This home is *pure* (undefiled).
c. This home is *permanent* (it fadeth not away).
C. The trials in our salvation (1:5-9).
"Wherein ye greatly rejoice, though now for a season, if need be, ye are in heaviness through manifold temptations: That the trial of your faith, being much more precious than of gold that perisheth, though it be tried with fire, might be found unto praise and honour and glory at the appearing of Jesus Christ" (vs. 6, 7).

Peter speaks of how precious is the trial of our faith. In this epistle he also refers to precious *blood* (1:19), a *cornerstone* (2:4, 6, 7), and a humble *spirit* (3:4). All these, says Peter, are precious. In his second epistle he adds two more: "precious *faith*" (1:1) and "precious *promises*" (1:4).

Dr. Kenneth Wuest writes the following concerning verse 7.

"Peter tells us that this approval of our faith is much more precious than the approval of gold, even though that gold be approved through firetesting. . . .The picture here is of an ancient goldsmith who puts his crude gold ore in a crucible, subjects it to intense heat, and thus liquifies the mass. The impurities rise to the surface and are skimmed off. When the metal-worker is able to see the reflection of his face clearly mirrored in the surface of the liquid, he takes it off the fire, for he knows that the contents are pure gold. So it is with God and His child. He puts us in the crucible of Christian suffering, in which process sin is gradually put out of our lives, our faith is purified from the slag of unbelief that somehow mingles with it so often, and the result is the reflection of the face of Jesus Christ in the character of the Christian. This, above all, God the Father desires to see. Christlikeness is God's ideal for His child. Christian suffering is one of the most potent means to that end." (*First Peter in the Greek New Testament*, p. 27)

D. The Old Testament prophets and our salvation (1:10-12). These remarkable verses state the following:
1. The Old Testament prophets (like Isaiah) did not always understand their inspired prophecies about the future Messiah.
2. When they sought to know, they were told the predictions would be understood only at a later date (New Testament times). Our Lord once referred to this during his earthly ministry while speaking to his disciples.

"For verily I say unto you, that many prophets and righteous men have desired to see those things which ye see, and have not seen them; and to hear those things which ye hear, and have not heard them" (Mt. 13:17).

Especially to be noted is 1:11. All Bible prophecy concerning the Lord Jesus Christ (the author of our salvation) is summarized in this little sentence: "The sufferings of Christ, and the glory that shall follow."

Here Peter connects Christ's first coming (the sufferings) with his second coming (the glory). This, in a nutshell, is a panorama of the purpose, plan, and program of Almighty God. Note this beautiful outline as we trace it through the Word of God:

a. The sufferings—a Baby, wrapped in swaddling clothes (Lk. 2:12). The glory—a King, clothed in majestic apparel (Ps. 93:1).

b. The sufferings—he was the wearied traveler (Jn. 4:6). The glory—he will be the untiring God (Isa. 40:28, 29).

c. The sufferings—he had nowhere to lay his head (Lk. 9:58). The glory—he will become heir to all things (Heb. 1:2).

d. The sufferings—he was rejected by Israel (Jn. 1:11). The glory—he will be accepted by all the nations (Isa. 9:6).

e. The sufferings—wicked men took up stones to throw at him (Jn. 8:59). The glory—wicked men will cry for stones to fall upon them to hide them from him (Rev. 6:16).

f. The sufferings—a lowly Savior, acquainted with grief (Isa. 53:3). The glory—the mighty God, anointed with the oil of gladness (Heb. 1:9).

g. The sufferings—he was clothed with a scarlet robe in mockery (Lk. 23:11). The glory—he will be clothed with a vesture dipped in the blood of his enemies (Rev. 19:13).

h. The sufferings—he was smitten with a reed (Mt. 27:30). The glory—he will rule the nations with a rod of iron (Rev. 19:15).

i. The sufferings—wicked soldiers bowed their knee and mocked (Mk. 15:19). The glory—every knee shall bow and acknowledge him (Phil. 2:10).

j. The sufferings—he wore the crown of thorns (Jn. 19:5). The glory—he will wear the crown of gold (Rev. 14:14).

k. The sufferings—his hands were pierced with nails (Jn. 20:25). The glory—his hands will carry a sharp sickle (Rev. 14:14).

l. The sufferings—his feet were pierced with nails (Ps. 22:16). The glory—his feet will stand on the Mount of Olives (Zech. 14:4).

m. The sufferings—he had no form or comeliness (Isa. 53:2). The glory—he will be beautiful (Ps. 27:4).

n. The sufferings—he delivered up his spirit (Jn. 19:30). The glory—he is alive forevermore (Rev. 1:18).

o. The sufferings—he was laid in the tomb (Mt. 27:59, 60). The glory—he will sit on his throne (Heb. 8:1).

E. The holy angels and our salvation (1:12).

"Which things the angels desire to look into." One of the accomplishments of our salvation is to serve as an object lesson to heaven's elect angels. They do not experience our redemption but they are intensely interested in observing it! The following passages clearly bring this out:

"Then I Daniel looked and behold, there stood other two [angels] the one on this side of the bank of the river, and the other on that side of the bank of the river. And one said . . . How long shall it be to the end of these wonders?" (Dan. 12:5, 6).

"For I think that God hath set forth us the apostles last, as it were appointed to death: for we are made a spectacle unto the world, and to angels, and to men" (1 Cor. 4:9).

"To the intent that now unto the principalities and powers in the heavenly places might be known by the church the manifold wisdom of God" (Eph. 3:10).

F. The high calling of our salvation (1:13-17). In measuring up to this glorious salvation, the believer is exhorted by Peter to:

1. Gird up the loins of his mind. Peter will repeat this in his second epistle: "This second epistle, beloved, I now write unto you: in both which I stir up your pure minds by way of remembrance" (2 Pet. 3:1).

This girding calls to mind a patriarch of the Old Testament who wore a long flowing robe. Around that robe he had a big belt called a girdle. When the time came that he had to move swiftly, he pulled it up and lapped it over the belt. He girded up his loins and was ready for action.

2. Keep sober in spirit.

3. Fix his hope completely on God's grace.

4. Avoid returning to one's former life style.

5. Be holy (separated unto God) in all one's behavior.

6. Conduct himself in fear (a respectful awe and concern not to displease the Savior).

G. The awesome cost of our salvation (1:18-22).

"Forasmuch as ye know that ye were not redeemed with corruptible things, as silver and gold, from your vain conversation received by tradition from your fathers; but with the precious blood of Christ, as of a lamb without blemish and without spot" (vs. 18, 19).

H. The method of our salvation (1:23-25).

"Being born again, not of corruptible seed, but of incorruptible, by the word of God, which liveth and abideth for ever. For all flesh is as grass, and all the glory of man as the flower of grass. The grass withereth, and the flower thereof falleth away: But the word of the Lord endureth for ever. And this is the word which by the gospel is preached unto you" (vs. 23-25).

II. God's Salvation: The Duties of Saints (2:1—3:13).

A. Their duties concerning the Scriptures (2:1, 2). "As newborn babes, desire the sincere milk of the word, that ye may grow thereby" (2:2). The word "desire" speaks of an intense yearning. David had this desire for God's Word.

"The ordinances of the Lord are true and righteous altogether. More to be desired are they than gold, yea, than much fine gold, sweeter also than honey and the honeycomb" (Ps. 19:9, 10).

The nation Israel had shown no desire for the Word of God in the Old Testament. Thus, when the Son of God appeared they viewed him in the same manner.

"And when we shall see him, there is no beauty that we should desire him" (Isa. 53:2).

The word "sincere" is literally "unadulterated"—that is, nothing mixed with it. See Revelation 14:10 concerning a similar passage dealing with God's unadulterated wrath during the tribulation.

B. Their duties concerning the Savior (2:3-8). They are to view the Savior as God's precious Rock. The word "rock" or "stone" appears five times and the word "precious" is found three times in these verses. Note the various usages of this Redeemer-like rock as described in the Bible.

1. He is the smitten Rock to all who will drink (Ex. 17:6; 1 Cor. 10:4; Jn. 4:13, 14; 7:37-39).

2. He is the precious Stone to all who have drunk (1 Pet. 2:3, 7).

3. He is the chief Cornerstone to the church (Eph. 2:20).

4. He is the stumbling Stone to the Jews at his first coming (Rom. 9:32, 33; 1 Cor. 1:23).

5. He is the Headstone of the corner to the Jews at his Second Coming (Zech. 4:7).

6. He is the smiting Stone cut without hands to Gentile world powers at his Second Coming (Dan. 2:34).

7. He is the crushing Stone of judgment to all unbelievers (Mt. 21:44).

Peter says (2:4) this great Stone was "disallowed" by Israel. This word means "to put to a test and then repudiate." After examining Christ for thirty-four years, Israel "flunked" him. He simply was not what they were looking for in a Messiah!

Note, furthermore, the apostle's statement in 2:6: "Wherefore also it is contained in the Scripture, behold, I lay in Sion a chief cornerstone." Certainly here is the fulfillment of Christ's promise in Mt. 16:16, 18. Peter was *not* that foundation; Christ was. Finally (see 2:5), all believers are "lively stones, built up [into] a spiritual house, a holy priesthood, to offer up spiritual sacrifices, acceptable to God by Jesus Christ." (See also Rev. 1:6.)

C. Their duties concerning the body of Christ (2:9, 10).

1. To serve as priests of God. "But ye are a chosen generation, a royal priesthood, a holy nation, a peculiar [literally, encircled] people" (2:9).

Old Testament Israel *had* a priesthood, but the church *is* a priesthood. The *New Scofield*

Bible (p. 1334) offers the following excellent summary of the priesthood.

a. "Until the law was given, the head of each family was the family priest (Gen. 8:20; 26:25; 31:54).

b. When the law was proposed, the promise to perfect obedience was that Israel should be unto God 'a kingdom of priests' (Ex. 19:6); but Israel violated the law, and God shut up the priestly office to the Aaronic family, appointing the tribe of Levi to minister to Israel, thus constituting the typical priesthood. (Compare Ex. 13:2 and 19:6 with Num. 8:16. See also Ex. 28:1.)

c. In the church age, all Christians are unconditionally constituted 'a kingdom of priests' (v. 9; Rev. 1:6), the distinction which Israel failed to achieve by works. The priesthood of the Christian is, therefore, a birthright, just as every descendant of Aaron was born to the priesthood (Heb. 5:1).

d. The chief privilege of a priest is access to God. Under the law the high priest only could enter 'the holiest of all,' and that but once a year (Heb. 9:7); but when Christ died, the veil, a type of Christ's human body (Heb. 10:20), was rent, so that now the believer—priests, equally with Christ the High Priest—have access to God in the holiest (Heb. 10:19-22). The High Priest is corporeally there (Heb. 4:14-16; 9:24; 10:19-22)."

e. In the exercise of his office the New Testament believer-priest is:

(1) A sacrificer who offers a fourfold sacrifice:

(a) His own living body (Rom. 12:1; Phil. 2:17; 2 Tim. 4:6; Jas. 1:27; 1 Jn. 3:16).

(b) Praise to God, "the fruit of our lips giving thanks to his name," to be offered continually (Heb. 13:15; cf. Ex. 25:22: "I will commune with thee from above the mercy seat").

(c) His substance (Rom. 12:13; Gal. 6:6, 10; Titus 3:14; Heb. 13:2, 16; 3 Jn. 1:5-8).

(d) His service, i.e., "to do good" (Heb. 13:16).

(2) An Intercessor (Col. 4:12; 1 Tim. 2:1).

2. To shine as beacons of light.

"That ye should shew forth the praise of him who hath called you out of darkness into his marvellous light" (2:9).

D. Their duties concerning the government (2: 11-17).

1. To be above board. "Having your conversation honest among the Gentiles" (2:12).

2. To be obedient. "Submit yourselves to every ordinance of man for the Lord's sake" (2:13). Of course, this refers to those ordinances which do not contradict the Bible (Acts 5:29).

E. Their duties concerning their jobs (2:18-20).
"Servants, be subject to your masters with all fear; not only to the good and gentle, but also to the froward [the unfair, surly]" (2:18).

F. Their duties concerning sufferings (2:21-25).
"For even hereunto were ye called: because Christ also suffered for us, leaving us an example, that ye should follow his steps" (2:21).

"The word 'leaving' is literally 'leaving behind.' When Peter used the Greek word here translated 'example,' he went back to his boyhood days for an illustration. The word means literally 'writing under.' It was used of words given children to copy, both as a writing exercise and as a means of impressing a moral. Sometimes it was used with reference to the act of tracing over written letters . . . just as a child slowly, with painstaking effort and close application, follows the shape of the letters of his teacher and thus learns to write, so saints should, with like painstaking effort and by close application, endeavor to be like the Lord Jesus in their own personal lives." (*First Peter in the Greek New Testament*, p. 67)

Thus, the great example for the suffering Savior. Our Lord suffered blamelessly, graciously, and trustfully. When he was reviled, he reviled not again. When he suffered, he threatened not. What, then, did he do? He "committed himself to him [the Father] that judgeth righteously" (2:23).

Note especially Peter's statement, "by whose stripes ye were healed" (2:24). Is there physical healing in the atonement? According to Matthew 8:16, 17, this was indeed predicted by Isaiah (53:4) and was fulfilled during the earthly ministry of Christ. But in 1 Peter 2 the apostle definitely links up Christ's stripes to the healing of our souls and *not* our bodies.

Kenneth Wuest writes:

"The word 'stripes' in the Greek presents a picture of our Lord's lacerated back after the scourging He endured at the hands of the Roman soldiers. The Romans used a scourge of cords or thongs to which latter were attached pieces of lead or brass, on small, sharp-pointed bones. Criminals condemned to crucifixion were ordinarily scourged before being executed. The victim was stripped to the waist and bound in a stooping position, with the hands behind the back, to a post or pillar. The suffering under the lash was intense. The body was frightfully lacerated. The Christian martyrs at Smyrna about A.D. 155 were so torn by the scourges that their veins were laid bare, and the inner muscles and sinews and even the intestines were exposed. . . . Peter remembered the body of our Lord after the scourging, the flesh so dreadfully mangled that the disfigured form appeared in his eyes as one single bruise." (*First Peter in the Greek New Testament*, p. 69)

G. Their duties concerning the home (3:1-7).
   1. The believing wife (3:1-6) is:
      a. to be in subjection to her husband
      b. to be chaste
      c. to be beautiful inside

"Whose adorning, let it not be that outward adorning of plaiting the hair, and wearing of gold, or putting on of apparel" (3:3).

It should be quickly noted that this verse does *not* forbid a Christian woman to visit a beauty shop or a jewelry store. Those who would insist it does have a problem here, for Peter also refers to the wearing of clothes! What the passage *does* teach is that believing women are not to dress in a gaudy manner. History tells us the Roman women of that day went to ridiculous lengths in the adornment of the hair. The hair was arranged layer upon layer and interlaced with golden combs and nets. After the styling ordeal was completed many would stay up all night lest they spoil their coiffures for the next day's festivities. This godless external display had already been soundly condemned by the prophet Isaiah centuries ago (Isa. 3:16-26). Where then is their beauty to come from?

"Let it be the hidden [woman] of the heart, in that which is not corruptible, even the ornament of a meek and quiet spirit, which is in the sight of God of great price" (3:4).

By displaying this inner beauty (as well as keeping a neat and attractive outward appearance) the Christian wife has a far greater opportunity of winning her unsaved husband to Christ (3:1).

Peter now points to an Old Testament wife who exhibited these womanly virtues. She was Sarah, Abraham's beloved wife.

   2. The believing husband (3:7).
"Likewise, ye husbands, dwell with them according to knowledge, giving honour unto the wife, as unto the weaker vessel, and as being heirs together of the grace of life; that your prayers be not hindered" (3:7).

Here the Christian husband is to do two things in regard to his wife:

a. He is to "dwell with them according to knowledge." That is, he must have an intelligent recognition of the marriage relationship. He simply must understand that:
   (1) His wife is a weaker vessel. This weakness is limited to the physical realm, however. She is *not* weaker intellectually or spiritually.
   (2) His wife is his fellow-heir. She shares the same spiritual equality before God as he does. Thus, the arrogant husband who lightly dismisses his wife to "the kitchen and the bedroom," insults not only her, but God himself.

b. He is to give "honour unto the wife." That is, he is to assign her a special place in his heart. If these principles are not followed, then every prayer coming from that household will be hindered.

H. Their duties concerning the local church (3:8-13).
1. Be of one mind (maintain the spirit of harmony).
2. Love each other.
3. Show compassion ("have a heart").
4. Do not return evil for evil, "but contrariwise blessing" (3:9). To return evil for good is *unnatural.* To return evil for evil is *natural.* To return good for evil is *supernatural.*

III. God's Salvation: The Discipline of Suffering (3:14—4:19).
A. Suffering justifies the sinner.

"For Christ also hath once suffered for sins, the just for the unjust, that he might bring us to God" (3:18).

Note the *route* and *results* of his suffering.

1. He went and "preached unto the spirits in prison" (3:19). What is involved in these words? Who were these spirits? In his book *Good News for Bad Times,* Richard DeHaan lists four main theories which have been offered to explain these questions:

"By whom also he went and preached unto the spirits in prison, who at one time were disobedient . . . while the ark was preparing" (1 Pet. 3:19, 20).

"Just who were these spirits? Your answer determines your interpretation of this perplexing passage, and dictates the answer to a second question, 'What message was preached?' The word 'preached' means 'to herald' or 'to proclaim,' and can refer either to communicating the Gospel or giving an announcement. Four main views are held regarding the identification of these 'spirits in prison.'

a. They were the souls of the people to whom Christ preached by the Holy Spirit through Noah during the 120 years the ark was being built. Many good scholars hold this view, but it is not without problems. The antithesis expressed in the words, 'being put to death in the flesh but made alive by the spirit' (v. 18), some claim, would more naturally refer to our Lord's human body and spirit than to the Holy Spirit. Furthermore, they object, to apply the term 'spirits' to people is questionable. The Bible sometimes speaks of human beings as 'souls,' and mentions 'the spirits of just men made perfect' (Heb. 12:23), but the Word of God never calls human beings 'spirits.' This term seems to be reserved for supernatural and nonhuman beings.

b. The 'spirits in prison' were the mongrel offspring of a union between fallen angels (the 'sons of God' of Genesis 6:1, 2) and women. Those who take this position contend that when Jesus died, He descended immediately into hades and announced to these imprisoned spirits that He had paid the price for sin. Objections to this view are that the purpose for this declaration is not given, and that one must accept the theory that fallen angels

were actually able to live in the marriage relationship with human women and produce offspring.

c. These spirits were wicked angels of Noah's day who engaged in some kind of monstrous evil, but who probably did not actually marry women. The people who hold this view consider the 'sons of God' of Genesis 6 to be fallen angels who entered into or possessed the bodies of violent men. These men in turn fathered children with even more lawless traits. The term *nephilum,* translated 'giants' in Genesis 6:4, thus would denote men who 'fall upon' or attack others rather than 'fallen ones' or 'giants.' Scholars who give this explanation of the 'spirits in prison' see the sinning angels of Genesis as the same ones to whom Peter referred as 'delivered . . . into chains of darkness' (2 Peter 2:4). They say the purpose of Christ's entrance into hades was to tell this special group of wicked angels that their doom was certain. He had paid the price for sin and would soon demonstrate that He was indeed their Master by rising from the dead. This interpretation is possible only for those who feel that the 'sons of God' of Genesis 6 were fallen angels, and that they possessed men's bodies and personalities for the purpose of leading the human race away from God.

d. The 'spirits in prison' are wicked beings and Old Testament believers. Those who hold this view say that Christ descended into hades between His death and resurrection to make an announcement to all wicked spirits, and to release the Old Testament saints being kept there in a special compartment. Paul declares that Jesus 'descended first into the lower parts of the earth' and 'led captivity captive' (Eph. 4:8-10). Some Bible scholars see a dual purpose for our Lord's descent into hades. They say He first announced to fallen angels that He had conquered sin and paid its penalty. Then, contending that the believers of the ages before Calvary were not fully forgiven until Christ had presented His sacrifice, they maintain that He went to them immediately after His death to take them to heaven. This view can be held only if one is convicted that the 'compartment' theory of hades is biblical, and that Old Testament saints were not permitted to enter heaven until Jesus had died on the cross.

An exact identification of the 'spirits in prison' is not possible. Because a reference is made to Noah however, very likely they are either supernatural spirit creatures connected with the terrible conditions that led to the deluge, or the people to whom Noah preached while preparing the ark" (pp. 103, 104).

2. He is "gone into heaven, and is on the right hand of God; angels and authorities and powers being made subject unto him" (3:22).

Note: Another difficult section of Scripture occurs at this point in Peter's first epistle. Again, Richard DeHaan writes the following helpful words:

"Peter wrote, 'Who at one time were disobedient, when once the longsuffering of God waited in the days of Noah, while the ark was preparing, in which few, that is, eight souls, were saved by water, the like figure unto which even baptism doth also now save us (not putting away of the filth of the flesh, but the answer of a good conscience toward God), by the resurrection of Jesus Christ' (1 Pet. 3:20, 21).

The best way to approach these verses is to examine the thoughts one by one as Peter expressed them.

a. Noah and his family were 'saved by water.' A little reflection makes it immediately clear that the water would have destroyed Noah and his family, not saved them if they had not been in the ark. The flood, which killed the rest of mankind, became the intermediary means of deliverance when it lifted the ark. If it had not, of course, the ark and its inhabitants would have been submerged, as were all of the highest mountains and tallest buildings.

b. The scene of safety in the midst of judgment is portrayed by baptism. Peter wrote, 'The like figure unto which even baptism doth also now save us' (1 Pet. 3:21).

The Greek term translated 'figure' is *antitupon*, and our word 'antitype' is a transliteration of it. The water of baptism, therefore, is an antitype of the water of the flood. It therefore 'saves' us in the same way the deluge 'saved' Noah and his family. The water, representing judgment and death, buoyed up the ark so that its occupants were not drowned. Similarly, when we enter the water of baptism, symbol of judgment and death, we declare that we have found deliverance from the divine wrath because we are safe in the Ark; that is, in Christ. In His death on the cross He bore God's judgment against sin, and by faith in Him we have been brought into safety. When a believer is baptized, he signifies that through union with Christ he is rescued from condemnation and death.

c. The water of baptism is not a cleansing agent. The verse says, 'not the putting away of the filth of the flesh' (v. 21). Baptism, rather than being the agent for cleansing, is 'the answer of a good conscience toward God.' The Greek word translated 'answer' is *eperotema*, which means 'question,' 'appeal' or 'pledge.'

The latter fits this passage best, for baptism is a declaration by the Christian of his intention to 'walk in newness of life' (see Rom. 6:4). This pledge issues from his clear conscience as a foreign sinner, freed from guilt through his 'by-faith union' with Jesus Christ" (pp. 104, 105).

B. Suffering purifies the saint.

1. It gives him spiritual prosperity.

"But and if ye suffer for righteousness' sake, happy [prosperous] are ye" (3:14).

The apostle says that in view of the fact that they are being reproached, they are happy. The word "happy" is the translation of a Greek word which means "prosperous." It is used in Matthew 5:3-11, where it is translated "blessed." It refers in these contexts to a spiritually prosperous state or condition of the believer. That is, if the world persecutes a Christian, that is an indication of the spiritual prosperity of his life. The world does not persecute a worldly Christian, only a spiritual one. It is spirituality that rubs its fur the wrong way.

"But not only is the fact of persecution an indication of a spiritually prosperous life, but also of the fact that the Holy Spirit is resting upon the Christian. The words 'rest upon' (see 4:14) are the translation of a Greek word used in a manuscript of 103 B.C. as a technical term in agriculture. The writer speaks of a farmer resting his land by sowing light crops upon it. He relieved the land of the necessity of producing heavy crops, and thus gave it an opportunity to recuperate its strength. The word is used in Matthew 11:28 where our Lord says, 'Come unto me, all ye that labor and are heavy laden, and I will give you rest,' literally, 'and I will rest you.' Here our Lord causes the sinner who comes to Him to cease from his own efforts at carrying his load of guilt and suffering, taking it upon Himself, allowing the believer in his new life powers to function as a child of God. In our First Peter passage, the Holy Spirit rests and refreshes the believer in the sense that He takes over the saint's battle with sin and the heretofore futile effort at living a life pleasing to God, by giving him victory over the evil nature whose power was broken the moment God saved him, and by producing in his life His own fruit. The Spirit of the Glory, even the Spirit of God, is resting with refreshing power upon the child of God, causing him to live a life which pleases God and toward which the world hurls its venom and hate." (K. Wuest, *First Peter*, p. 120)

2. It gives him scriptural answers.

"But sanctify the Lord God in your hearts: and be ready always to give an answer to every man that asketh you a reason of the hope that is in you, with meekness and fear" (3:15).

A general rule of thumb is that suffering saints search the Scriptures more than others, if for no other reason than to find comfort in and answers for their pain! Dr. Kenneth Wuest writes:

"Not only were these Christian Jews to find a refuge in Christ Jesus as they set Him apart as Lord of their lives, but they were to be ready to give an answer to these persecutors who attacked them and the Word of God which they believed. The words 'give an answer' are the translation of a Greek word used as a legal term in the courts. It means literally 'to talk off from,' and was used of an attorney who talked his client off from a charge preferred against him. He presented a verbal defense. The exhortation is to Christians to talk the Bible off from the charges preferred against it, thus presenting for it a verbal defense." (*Ibid.*, p. 89)

  3. It gives him victory over his old nature (4:1-3).
C. Suffering unifies the church (4:7-11).

"As every man hath received the gift, even so minister the same one to another, as good stewards of the manifold grace of God. If any man speak, let him speak as the oracles of God; if any man minister, let him do it as of the ability which God giveth: that God in all things may be glorified through Jesus Christ, to whom be praise and dominion for ever and ever. Amen" (vs. 10, 11).

Here in these verses Peter exhorts believers to:
  1. Be accurate in speaking the Word of God.
  2. Be accurate in performing the will of God.
D. Suffering glorifies the Savior (4:12-19).

"Beloved, think it not strange concerning the fiery trial which is to try you, as though some strange thing happened unto you: But rejoice, inasmuch as ye are partakers of Christ's suffering that, when his glory shall be revealed, ye may be glad also with exceeding joy" (vs. 12, 13).

Note: In his epistle (4:16) Peter refers to a believer as a *Christian*. This title is used but two other times in the entire Bible (Acts 11:26 and 26:28). What Peter is saying in these verses is that suffering glorifies the Savior *if* one suffers as a Christian, that is, for his faith. But if he suffers as an evildoer, the Lord is not glorified. We are to suffer because of our position, and not our disposition. The grand conclusion concerning the entire subject of suffering is given in 4:19:

"Wherefore, let them that suffer according to the will of God commit the keeping of their souls to him in well doing, as unto a faithful Creator."
IV. God's Salvation: The Delights of Service (5:1-14).
  A. Serving as a shepherd (5:1-4).

"The elders which are among you I exhort, who am also an elder, and a witness of the sufferings of Christ, and also a partaker of the glory that shall be revealed: Feed the flock of God which is among you, taking the oversight thereof, not by constraint, but willingly; not for filthy lucre, but of a ready mind; neither as being lords over God's heritage, but being ensamples to the flock. And when the chief Shepherd shall appear, ye shall receive a crown of glory that fadeth not away."

In his epistle Peter refers to himself as an *apostle* (1:1), an *elder*, a *witness*, and a *partaker* (5:1). Here again, as we have already seen (1:11) he links together "the sufferings of Christ and . . . the glory that shall be revealed" (5:1).
  1. The responsibilities of the shepherd (5:1-3).
    a. To feed the flock of God (see Acts 20:28). This responsibility would also include tending, guiding, and guarding the sheep.
    b. To do this willingly and not by constraint.
    c. To do this humbly, and not in a high-handed manner.
    d. To be a pattern for God's flock.
  2. The rewards of the shepherd (5:4).

"And when the chief Shepherd shall appear, ye shall receive a crown of glory that fadeth not away."

This is one of at least five possible rewards a believer may earn. These are:
    a. The incorruptible crown—given to those who master the old nature (1 Cor. 9:25-27).
    b. The crown of rejoicing—given to soul-winners (Prov. 11:30; 1 Thess. 2:19, 20; Dan. 12:3).
    c. The crown of life—given to those who successfully endure temptation (Jas. 1:12; Rev. 2:10).
    d. The crown of righteousness—given to those who especially love the doctrine of the rapture (2 Tim. 4:8).
    e. The crown of glory—given to faithful preachers and teachers (1 Pet. 5:2-4; 2 Tim. 4:1, 2; Acts 20:26-28).

It has been suggested that these "crowns" will actually be talents and abilities with which to glorify Christ. Thus, the greater the reward, the greater the ability.
B. Serving as a saint (5:5-7).

"Likewise, ye younger, submit yourselves unto the elder. Yea, all of you be subject one to another, and be clothed with humility: for God resisteth the proud, and giveth grace to the humble. Humble yourselves therefore under the mighty hand of God, that he may exalt you in due time: Casting all your care upon him; for he careth for you."
C. Serving as a soldier (5:8-14).

"Be sober, be vigilant; because your adversary the devil, as a roaring lion, walketh about, seeking whom he may devour: Whom resist stedfast in the faith, knowing that the same afflictions are accomplished in your brethren that are in the world" (vs. 8, 9).

Peter now ends this magnificent epistle by once again reminding his readers of the ministry of suffering.

"But the God of all grace, who hath called us unto his eternal glory by Christ Jesus, after that ye have suffered a while, make you perfect, stablish, strengthen, settle you" (5:10).

Especially to be noted are the words "the God of all grace." This is the story of the Christian life. The believer is to go from grace to grace! (See Jn. 1:16.) James says, "He giveth more grace" (Jas. 4:6). The Scriptures speak of:

1. saving grace (Eph. 2:8, 9)
2. serving grace (1 Cor. 15:9, 10)
3. sanctifying grace (Rom. 5:17; 6:17)
4. sacrificing grace (2 Cor. 8:1-9)
5. singing grace (Col. 3:16)
6. speaking grace (Col. 4:6)
7. strengthening grace (2 Tim. 2:1)
8. suffering grace (1 Pet. 5:10; 2 Cor. 12:9)

In closing, Peter refers to Silvanus, "a faithful brother" (5:12). He was the messenger of this epistle and Peter's secretary. Silvanus is the lengthened form of Silas and doubtless this was the same individual who was Paul's traveling companion. (See Acts 15:40; 2 Cor. 1:19; 1 Thess. 1:1; 2 Thess. 1:1.)

2 PETER
INTRODUCTION:

1. This is Peter's second and final epistle.
2. The early church was at first somewhat reluctant to accept this epistle as canonical. There were two basic reasons for this:
   a. Supposed differences in style between 1 Peter and 2 Peter.
   b. The difference in the vocabulary of the two epistles.
3. However a careful study of this epistle shows that it indeed came from the hand of Simon Peter.
   a. It claims to have been written by Peter (1:1).
   b. The writer was at the transfiguration of Christ (1:16-18; see also Mt. 17:1-13).
   c. He was told by the Savior concerning his death (1:13-15; see also Jn. 21:18, 19).
   d. He had already written his readers another epistle (3:1; see also 1 Pet. 1:1).
4. This epistle contains the only interconnective reference from one apostolic epistle to another. In other words, Peter refers to Paul's writings (3:15, 16).
5. It is very similar to the book of Jude. Out of twenty-five verses in Jude, no less than nineteen are reiterated in some fashion in 2 Peter.
6. The theme of 1 Peter is suffering, while that of 2 Peter is full knowledge. It appears some sixteen times with cognate words.
7. Thus 2 Peter may be favorably compared to 2 Timothy.
   a. Both books are the last written by their authors.
   b. Both contain a key passage on the subject of inspiration (2 Pet. 1:20, 21; 2 Tim. 3:16).
   c. Both warn against false teachers (2 Tim. 3 and 2 Pet. 2).
   d. Both men knew they would die a martyr's death for Christ (2 Tim. 4:6; cf. 2 Pet. 1:13-15).
8. The summary statement of this epistle is 3:18:
   "But grow in grace and in the knowledge of our Lord and Savior Jesus Christ. To him be glory both now and forever. Amen."

The Fullness of God's Plan

SIMON PETER

2 Peter

The MULTIPLICATION of the power of God (1:1-4)

The ADDITIONS by the child of God (1:5-9)

The EXAMINATION of the calling of God (1:10-12)

The REVELATION to the apostle of God (1:13-15)

The TRANSFIGURATION of the Son of God (1:16-18)

The INSPIRATION of the Word of God (1:19-21)

The DEVIATION by the enemies of God (2:1—3:4)

The CONDEMNATION of the former world of God (3:5, 6)

The ANNIHILATION of the present world of God (3:7-12)

The NEW CREATION of the future world of God (3:13-18)

I. The Multiplication of the Power of God (1:1-4).

"Grace and peace be multiplied unto you through the knowledge of God, and of Jesus our Lord, according as his divine power hath given unto us all things that pertain unto life and godliness, through the knowledge of him that hath called us to glory and virtue" (1:2, 3).

Notice especially that tremendous phrase in 1:3, "according as his divine power hath given unto us all things that pertain unto life and godliness." Henrietta Mears has offered the following illustration concerning this glorious statement:

"Look at a criminal condemned to be hanged. Suppose a messenger comes to him and says: 'The governor has taken your case into consideration, and I have brought you a purse of a thousand dollars.' The criminal will say, 'What good will it do me? I am to be hanged tomorrow.' 'Well, I have another message. He has considered your case and sent you the deed to a million-dollar estate.' The condemned man despairingly shakes his head and says, 'What can I do with that? I must be hanged tomorrow.' But the messenger goes on. 'Stop! I have another offer to make. I have brought you the governor's own inauguration robe for you to wear with special favor.' The condemned man bursts into tears, as he says, 'Do you intend to mock me? How would I appear ascending the steps of the gallows, wearing the governor's own robe?' Then the messenger says, 'Wait, I have one more message. The governor has sent you a pardon. What do you say to that?' The poor man looks at him and says he doesn't believe it. But the messenger hands the pardon, signed by the governor, with the official stamp upon it. Then the man leaps for joy, while tears of gratitude run down his face. Then the messenger says, 'I am not through yet. I have brought you the pardon, the purse of gold, the deed, and the royal robe which are yours in addition.' These are the 'all things' God has given us in Christ, His Son. With these, nothing can defeat the young Christian. The way I can escape the awful sins in this world every day and all the day is by partaking of His nature and letting Him live through me. Lay hold of the great and precious promises: that by these ye might be partakers of the divine nature." (*What the Bible is All About*, pp. 622-633)

Just what are these "exceeding great and precious promises"? They consist totally of the glorious doctrinal facts presented in the Word of God. Peter speaks of all this being "multiplied unto you through the knowledge of God." This knowledge is a knowledge of God's Word. Shallow knowledge makes superficial Christians.

II. The Additions by the Child of God (1:5-9).

"And besides this, giving all diligence, add to your faith . . ." (1:5).

Peter now lists seven qualities the believer is to expand and develop. These are:

A. Virtue. This quality has been described as "excellence with energy." It also includes the praise of God by the child of God (1 Pet. 2:9).

B. Knowledge. A reference to moral discernment. This discernment, of course, comes from a study of the Bible.

C. Temperance—self-control (Prov. 16:32; 25:28).

D. Patience—godly (and gracious) endurance.

E. Godliness—the right worship and devotion to God.

F. Kindness—acts of goodness.

G. Charity—a love for saints, sinners, the Scriptures, and the Savior. By encouraging his readers to supply themselves with these Christian elements, Peter is literally fulfilling Jesus' prophecy concerning himself in Luke 22:31, 32:

"And the Lord said, Simon, Simon, behold, Satan hath desired to have you, that he may sift you as wheat. But I have prayed for thee, that thy faith fail not. And when thou art converted [literally, turned about. Here Jesus refers to that spiritual maturity that would come at Pentecost], strengthen thy brethren."

Note the results of all this:

"For if these things be in you, and abound, they make you that ye shall neither be barren nor unfruitful" (1:8).

This chapter has been called the "math chapter."

1. Multiplication: "Grace and peace be multiplied unto you" (1:2).

2. Addition: "Add to your faith" (1:5).

3. Subtraction: "He was purged from his old sins" (1:9).

III. The Examination of the Calling of God (1:10-12).

"Wherefore the rather, brethren, give diligence to make your calling and election sure: for if ye do these things, ye shall never fall" (1:10).

Peter is saying here that we are to possess that necessary confidence concerning both our *salvation* from God, and our *service* for God. No child of God is effective if he has doubts concerning either of these.

IV. The Revelation to the Apostle of God (1:13-15).

"Yea, I think it meet, as long as I am in this tabernacle, to stir you up by putting you in remembrance; knowing that shortly I must put off this my tabernacle, even as our Lord Jesus Christ hath shewed me. Moreover I will endeavor that ye may be able after my decease to have these things always in remembrance."

Peter knew of his approaching death (Jn. 21:18), as did *Moses* (Deut. 4:22; 31:14), and *Paul* (2 Tim. 4:6). He speaks of his death as "my decease" (1:15). The word here is actually "my exodus," and is also used to describe the death of Jesus (Lk. 9:31).

V. The Transfiguration of the Son of God (1:16-18).

"For we . . . were eyewitnesses of his majesty" (1:16).

Here Peter reviews that glorious moment when he had once, along with James and John, viewed the breathtaking, eye-blinding, and mind-boggling transfiguration of the Lord Jesus Christ.

VI. The Inspiration of the Word of God (1:19-21).

"We have also a more sure word of prophecy; whereunto ye do well that ye take heed, as unto a light that shineth in a dark place, until the day dawn, and the day star arise in your hearts: Knowing this first, that no prophecy of the scripture is of any private interpretation. For the prophecy came not in old time by the will of man: but holy men of God spake as they were moved by the Holy Ghost."

These three verses certainly contain some of the most profound statements concerning the importance, interpretation, and impartation of the Word of God.

A. The importance of God's Word (1:19). Peter says we have "a more sure word of prophecy." It should be noted that he had just described the mighty transfiguration, but now declares that the written Word (the Scriptures) become a surer confirmation for the believer than even Peter's eyewitness account on that mountain. This of course does not contradict Christian experience, but it does say that Christian experience should be confirmed by the Word of God. Note Peter's beautiful description of Christ here: "Until the day dawn, and the day star arise in your hearts." To the *church*, he is the day star (see Rev. 22:16), but to *Israel*, he becomes the Sun of righteousness (Mal. 4:2).

B. The interpretation of God's Word (1:20). This verse is saying that no single verse in the Bible should be interpreted in and of itself, apart from the remaining 31,172 verses. For example:
   1. Proxy baptism is not taught in 1 Corinthians 15:29 (whatever else it may teach), for no other verse in the Bible confirms this.
   2. Baptismal regeneration cannot be concluded from Acts 2:38, for many other verses clearly refute it. It is still true that a *text* taken out of *context* is a *pretext!*

C. The impartation of God's Word (1:21). Here we are told that the authors of the Bible were carried along by the Spirit of God as (it may be said) a sailboat is carried along by the wind. They did *not* go into a coma or trance, but were fully aware of what was happening (see also 2 Tim. 3:16; Lk. 1:70; Acts 3:18). One final thought here. The same Holy Spirit, who originally gave the Word, now desires to teach it both to and through men of God today. (See 1 Cor. 2:9-16; Jn. 14:26; 16:13, 14.)

VII. The Deviation of the Enemies of God (2:1—3:4).
   A. The identity of these enemies.
      1. In the former days:
         a. Wicked angels (2:4). All angels who sided in with Lucifer during his great revolt (Isa. 14:12-15; Ezek. 28:11-19; Rev. 12:3, 4) will, of course, along with Satan, someday be judged by God. However, it is believed by many that in this passage Peter has in mind a special group of fallen angels who added to their original iniquity by the sin described in Genesis 6:1-5. As a result, these evil spirits are already "delivered . . . into chains [literally, pits] of darkness, to be reserved [kept, confined] unto judgment" (see also Jude 1:6).
         b. Those citizens during Noah's day (2:5). "And spared not the old world . . . bringing in the flood upon the world of the ungodly." The Greek word for "flood" here is *kataklusmos,* which means "to overwhelm with water." Our English word "cataclysmic" comes from this.
         c. Those citizens during Lot's day (2:6-9). "And turning the cities of Sodom and Gomorrha into ashes condemned them with an overthrow" (2:6). Here the Greek word for "overthrow" is *katastrepho,* referring to the act of turning over and under, "to throw down." Our English word "catastrophe" comes from this. (See Gen. 19; Jude 7.)

In these verses (2:6-9) we are given some additional facts about Lot not recorded in the Genesis 19 account.
   (1) Facts about his *salvation*. He is referred to as just and righteous. It would have been difficult to deduct this at times from the Old Testament account, "Nevertheless, the foundation of God standeth sure, having this seal, the Lord knoweth them that are his" (2 Tim 2:19).
   (2) Facts about his *soul*. We are told he "vexed his righteous soul from day to day with their unlawful deeds" (2:8). Also note the phrase, "And delivered just Lot, vexed with the filthy conversation [conduct] of the wicked" (2:7). The verb "vexed" is found twice in these verses. Each comes from a different Greek word. In 2:7 the word is *kataphoneo,* which means "to wear down with toil, to exhaust with labor, to oppress." The second word is *basanizo,* meaning "to torture, to torment." Thus, through compromise, Lot subjected his righteous soul to exhausting labor and cruel torment.
   (3) Facts about his *Savior*. "The Lord knoweth how to deliver the godly out of temptation" (2:9; see Gen. 19:15, 17, 22; Ps. 34:15, 17, 19; 1 Cor. 10:13).

During his earthly ministry our Lord used the historical account of both Noah and Lot to illustrate those conditions which will prevail just prior to the final judgment.

"And as it was in the days of Noah, so shall it be also in the days of the Son of man. They did eat, they drank, they married wives, they were given in marriage, until the day that Noah entered into the ark, and the flood came, and destroyed them all. Likewise also as it was in the days of Lot; they did eat, they drank, they bought, they sold, they planted, they builded; but the same day that Lot went out of Sodom it rained fire and brimstone from heaven, and destroyed them all. Even thus shall it be in the day when the Son of man is revealed" (Lk. 17:26-30).

In passing it may be said here that Lot is a type of the church, which will be taken out *prior to* judgment, while Noah is a foreshadow of Israel, which nation will be preserved *during* judgment.

   d. False prophets. "But there were false prophets also among the people. . . . Who have forsaken the right way, and are gone astray, following the way of Balaam . . . who loved the wages of unrighteousness" (2:1, 15). See Numbers 22–24 for the background of Balaam. He was a typical hireling prophet, anxious to market his gift for money. He is also referred to in Jude 1:11 and Revelation 2:14.

  2. In the latter days:
    a. False teachers. "Even as there shall be false teachers among you" (2:1).
    b. Scoffers. "Knowing this first, that there shall come in the last days scoffers, walking after their own lusts" (3:3).

B. The iniquity of these enemies. How can these foes be recognized? What are their marks, and what is their message? The apostle lists no less than twenty-six characteristics of these cursed creatures:

  1. They bring in destructive heresies. These heresies are introduced along with and alongside the truth. A tiny portion of deadly poison placed in a gallon of wholesome milk is far more dangerous than a bottle of marked poison, for the fatal milk is often unrecognized until it is too late (2:1).

  2. They deny the Lord who bought them. This little phrase completely refutes the doctrine of the limited atonement (2:1).

  3. They speak evil of the way of truth (2:2). In doing this they gather to themselves many disciples. "And many shall follow their pernicious [lustful] ways." False followers will go after false teachers. The passage in 1 Corinthians 11:19 explains why God permits the cults of the day.

  4. They will exploit (if possible) the very elect of God. "And through covetousness shall they with feigned words make merchandise of you" (2:3). The phrase translated "feigned works" is *plastos* in the Greek. We get our word "plastic" from this. Peter is saying that their work may be stretched or shortened to fit any and all theological systems. However, the heretics will be punished, for "their damnation slumbereth not" (see also Deut. 32:35).

  5. They "walk after the flesh in the lust of uncleanness" (2:10).

  6. They despise (look upon with utter contempt) all forms of government (2:10).

  7. They are presumptuous, self-willed, and possess no regard or respect for either men or angels (2:10).

  8. They possess the nature of brute wild animals (2:12).

  9. They condemn without even understanding what they are rejecting (2:12).

  10. They are committed to the perverted hedonist philosophy (2:13): "They that count it pleasure to riot in the daytime." The word for "riot" in the Greek is *truphee*, meaning "softness, effeminacy, luxurious living." They do not work for a living. (See also Acts 17:21; Titus 1:12; Phil. 3:19; 1 Thess. 5:7.)

  11. They are spots and blemishes in their own society (2:13).

  12. They pretend to have roots in historic Christianity. "Sporting [revealing] themselves with their own deceivings while they feast with you." This is thought to have referred to that love feast held in the early church before the Lord's Supper (1 Cor. 11:17–34).

  13. Their hearts are eaten up with adultery (2:14). They cannot look at an attractive woman without mentally undressing her.

  14. They entice the unstable (2:14).

  15. They are materialistic to the core (2:14).

  16. They are children of cursing (2:14).

  17. They have totally forsaken the right way (2:15).

  18. They are wells (springs) without water (2:17).

  19. They are empty "clouds that are carried with a tempest; to whom the mist of darkness is reserved for ever" (2:17).

    Dr. K. Wuest writes:

    "Tempest is *lailaps* in the Greek, referring to a whirlwind, a tempestuous wind, a squall, violent wind. It is never a single gust, nor a steadily blowing wind, however violent, but a storm breaking from black thunder clouds in furious gusts . . . throwing everything topsy-turvy." (*In These Last Days,* p. 59)

  20. They speak "great swelling words of vanity" (2:18).

  21. They play upon the sensual nature of man (2:18). "They allure through the lusts of the flesh . . . those that were clean escaped from them who live in error." In other words, they drag down to destruction those who might have otherwise escaped.

  22. They are the blind leading the blind (2:19). "While they promise them liberty, they themselves are the servants of corruption." On at least two occasions our Lord referred to this characteristic while he was on earth.

    "Let them alone; they are blind leaders of the blind. And if the blind lead the blind, both shall fall into the ditch" (Mt. 15:14).

    "Woe unto you, scribes and Pharisees, hypocrites! For ye compass sea and land to make one proselyte, and when he is made, ye make him twofold more the child of hell than yourselves" (Mt. 23:15).

  23. Their "latter end is worse with them than the beginning" (2:20). One of our Lord's most frightening accounts on demonic activity vividly illustrates the twenty-third characteristic of the enemies of the faith. He said:

    "When the unclean spirit is gone out of a man, he walketh through dry places, seeking rest, and findeth none. Then he saith, I will return into my house from whence I came out; and when he is come, he findeth it empty, swept, and garnished. Then goeth he, and taketh with himself seven other spirits more wicked than himself, and they enter in and dwell there: and the last state of that man is worse than the first. Even so shall it be also unto this wicked generation" (Mt. 12:43–45).

Here is a case of reformation without regeneration! Peter then concludes:

"For it had been better for them [false teachers] not to have known the way of righteousness, than, after they have known it, to turn from the holy commandment delivered unto them" (2:21).

Again it should be observed that Christ had previously spoken concerning this subject.

"And that servant, which knew his lord's will, and prepared not himself, neither did according to his will, shall be beaten with many stripes. But he that knew not, and did commit things worthy of stripes, shall be beaten with few stripes. For unto whomsoever much is given, of him shall be much required: and to whom men have committed much, of him they will ask the more" (Lk. 12:47, 48).

24. They are as filthy hogs and dogs (2:22). "The dog is turned to his own vomit again; and, the sow that was washed [in the Greek tense it is literally the sow that washed itself] to her wallowing in the mire." Is Peter teaching here that a Christian can lose his salvation? He is not: See his statements on eternal security in 1 Peter 1:3–5. Nowhere in the Bible does God call a believer a hog or a dog. These are false teachers!

25. They ridicule the Second Coming and reject any thought of coming judgment. "Where is the promise of his coming? For since the fathers fell asleep, all things continue as they were from the beginning of the creation" (3:4).

26. They utterly and eternally close their minds to those truths revealed in both God's world and in his Word. "For this they willingly are ignorant of" (3:5). An agnostic is therefore not a person who says "I can't believe," but rather, "I won't believe!" They are without excuse. (See Rom. 1:18–20.)

VIII. The Condemnation of the Former World of God (3:5, 6). "The heavens were of old, and the earth standing out of the water and in the water: whereby the world that then was, being overflowed with water perished." The phrase "the earth standing out of the water and in the water," may be a reference to the statement in Genesis 1:7:

"And God made the firmament [space], and divided the waters which were under the firmament from the waters which were above the firmament."

A number of Bible students have advocated a canopy theory which teaches that prior to the great Flood much of the ocean's present water volume was suspended in the upper atmosphere in the form of invisible water vapor. Thus, as early as the second day of creation, God had already prepared for the watery judgment he would employ in Noah's day. These atmospheric oceans then came pouring down as recorded in Genesis 7:11. The word "overflowed" in the Greek is *katakluzo*, from whence our English word "cataclysm" comes.

IX. The Annihilation of the Present World of God (3:7–12). Probably few men in America today are as qualified to write concerning these verses as is Dr. Henry Morris. Morris is the Director of the Institute for Creation Research. He writes the following:

"Question: 'Will the world eventually be destroyed in a nuclear holocaust?' Answer: The over-forty generation still remembers the unbelievable headlines of August, 1945, describing the awful destruction in Hiroshima, when the first atomic bomb was unveiled and the world entered the nuclear age. Bible-believing Christians recall how they thought immediately of the great prophecy in 2 Peter 3:10: 'The day of the Lord will come as a thief in the night; in the which the heavens shall pass away with a great noise, and the elements shall melt with fervent heat, the earth also and the works that are therein shall be burned up.'

Yes, the earth will eventually undergo a cataclysmic destruction, which may well consist of actual atomic disintegration. The Greek word translated 'elements' in the above passage actually means the basic subdivisions of matter, corresponding quite closely to the modern scientific concept of the chemical elements. The word translated 'melt' means 'break apart.' The phrase 'pass away' does not mean 'be annihilated' but, rather 'pass out of sight.' The 'heavens' are not the stars, but the 'sky' or 'air.' Finally, 'great noise' and 'fervent heat' are intrinsically associated with atomic explosions.

Peter's prophecy may well describe, therefore, a final cataclysm when the earth itself, with its atmosphere, will experience a vast nuclear chain reaction and perish in a tremendous atomic holocaust. Although it is conceivable that man's activities may lead to this final conflagration, it seems likely that God Himself will bring it about.

The very existence of such a remarkable prophecy in the Bible is evidence of inspiration. The scientific discovery that matter can be converted into energy is one of the greatest triumphs of twentieth-century science, and yet this plain forecast of atomic disintegration into 'fervent heat' has been in the Bible for 1,900 years."

There are, in fact, numerous other references in the Bible indicating the fundamental equivalence of matter and energy, and also the even more remarkable fact that the structural integrity of "matter" is maintained by something which is non-material, the mysterious "binding energy" of the atom.

Peter, for example, says that the heavens and the earth which are now, are kept in store (that is, "preserved" or "conserved") by the same Word (2 Pet. 3:7)—by the same omnipotent Word which first created them. Similarly, in Hebrews 1:3, the Scriptures say that the Creator, the Lord Jesus Christ, is now "upholding all things by the Word of his

But the day of the Lord will come as a thief in the night; in the which the heavens shall pass away with a great noise, and the elements shall melt with fervent heat, the earth also and the works that are therein shall be burned up.
2 Peter 3:10

power." Note—"things" are held together by "power," or energy. Likewise, Paul says "in Christ all things consist" (literally, "cohere") (Col. 1:17).

Finally the Bible tells us that "the worlds" (that is, the "spacetime cosmos") were framed by the Word of God, so that "things which are seen were not made of things which do appear" (Heb. 11:3). These are only a few of the scores of examples of the scientific insights of the Bible, not, of course, couched in the technical jargon of modern textbooks, but expressing clearly the basic truths behind the jargon.

Furthermore, not only is the basic fact of the essential non-mechanical nature of matter stated in the cited references, but also the actual identity and source of the nuclear forces and binding energies which hold the atomic nucleus together. That source of power is nothing less than Christ Himself! He is the omnipotent Creator and Sustainer of the universe!

"No wonder that Paul says: 'For in him we live and move and have our being, so that he is not far from every one of us' (Acts 17:27, 28). The very atoms of our bodies are preserved from instant disintegration by the Lord Jesus Christ. The very brain cells which men employ to devise their vain

speculations about their origin and destiny, denying the Word which created them, are held together by the One whom they continually blaspheme by their unbelief. If He were to withdraw His gracious sustaining power for only an instant, the whole world would collapse into chaos.

And, in fact, that is exactly what is going to happen some day! From the face of His wrath and His outraged grace and mercy, 'the earth and the heaven fled away; and there was found no place for them' (Rev. 20:11). In the fires of atomic dissolution, all the age-long effects of the Curse that have filled the earth with the scars of physical convulsions, disorders, decay, and death will be purged out forever. And that which brought on the Curse—rebellion and sin, in the persons of the devil and his angels and of all those men who have rejected or neglected God's Word and His great salvation in Jesus Christ—will be separated forever from the presence of God and the redeemed (Rev. 20:10-15; 2 Thess. 1:9).

But then the earth, with its heavens, will be made new again! 'We according to his promise, look for new heavens and a new earth, wherein

Nevertheless we, according to his promise, look for new heavens and a new earth, wherein dwelleth righteousness. **2 Peter 3:13**

dwelleth righteousness' (2 Pet. 3:13). 'Behold,' says the Lord Jesus, 'I make all things new' (Rev. 21:5). The primeval creative power of the divine Word will be exercised once more and the 'times of restitution of all things' (Acts 3:21) will come. God will answer the prayers of the faithful through the ages, when they pray: 'Thy kingdom come; thy will be done, in earth, as it is in heaven' (Mt. 6:10).

How utterly, fantastically foolish it is today for anyone to dare to question God's Word and to neglect His gracious gift of forgiveness and salvation. 'Heaven and earth shall pass away,' said Jesus, 'but my words shall not pass away' (Mt. 24:35). 'The world passeth away, and the lust thereof, but he that doeth the will of God abideth forever'' (1 Jn. 2:17). (*The Bible Has the Answer*, pp. 344-346)

    X. The New Creation (3:13-18).

JAMES

INTRODUCTION:

1. James was the oldest half-brother of Jesus (Mk. 6:3; Mt. 13:55). He was the full brother of Jude, who wrote the book of Jude.

2. James was an unbeliever prior to the resurrection (Jn. 7:3-10).

3. Christ then appeared to him (1 Cor. 15:7). He later appears in the upper room awaiting Pentecost (Acts 1:14).

4. He became the first pastor of the Jerusalem church (Acts 12:17; 15:13; Gal. 2:1, 9, 10, 12).

5. His epistle is perhaps the earliest in the New Testament, dated around A.D. 45. The synagogue rather than the church is mentioned as the place of meeting (see 2:2). It was thus written when the church was still in the circle of Judaism.

6. It is the most Jewish book in the New Testament. M. F. Unger writes:

   "If the several passages referring to Christ were eliminated, the whole epistle would be as proper in the canon of the Old Testament as it is in the New Testament. In fact, the epistle could be described as an interpretation of the Old Testament law and the Sermon on the Mount in the light of the gospel of Christ." (*Unger's Bible Handbook*, p. 783)

   It may be considered the Proverbs of the New Testament.

7. "He was known as an unusually good man, and was surnamed 'the Just' by his countrymen. It is said that he spent so much time on his knees in prayer that they became hard and callous like a camel's knees. He is thought to have been married" (1 Cor. 9:5). (*Halley's Bible Handbook*, p. 657)

8. Like Jude, James does not "pull his rank" by pointing out the physical relationship between himself and Christ. He simply refers to himself as "a servant of God and of the Lord Jesus Christ" (1:1).

9. The Greek language of James is of the highest quality.

10. There are only four Old Testament direct quotes, but at least fifty-three Old Testament references in the epistle of James.

11. James, like Jesus, loved to use Old Testament characters and the realm of nature as illustrations. Note:

    Old Testament Characters:
    a. Abraham (2:21)
    b. Isaac (2:21)
    c. Rahab (2:25)
    d. Job (5:11)
    e. Elijah (5:17)
      Realm of Nature:
    f. Wind-tossed waves of the sea (1:6)
    g. Withering grass and fading flowers (1:10, 11)
    h. Fire (3:5)
    i. Fountains of water (3:11)
    j. Figs and olives (3:12)
    k. Sowing and harvesting (3:18)
    l. Early and latter rains (5:7)
    m. Drought (5:17)

12. Some have imagined a contradiction between James and Paul. Martin Luther believed this, and referred to the book as "a right strawy epistle!" Note:

    James—"Ye see, then, that by works a man is justified, and not by faith only" (2:24).

    Paul—"For by grace are ye saved through faith; and that not of yourselves, it is the gift of God—not of works, lest any man should boast" (Eph. 2:8, 9).

    Luther and others were, of course, wrong on this conclusion. There is no contradiction here. Note:

    Paul speaks of justification before God.

    James describes justification before man.

    We are justified *by* faith, says Paul.

    We are justified *for* works, says James.

    Paul is interested in the *root* of justification.

    James is concerned about the *fruit* of justification.

    It was John Calvin who said: "Faith alone saves, but the faith that saves is not alone!"

    Furthermore, on occasion Paul stresses *works* (1 Tim. 6:18; Titus 3:8; Eph. 2:10), while James emphasizes *faith* (Jas. 2:5).

13. James meets Paul during his (Paul's) first trip to Jerusalem after his Damascus Road conversion (Gal. 1:18, 19).

14. He also conferred with Paul during the apostle's last trip to Jerusalem (Acts 21:18-25).

15. Tradition says that shortly before Jerusalem was destroyed, when many Jews were accepting Christ, Annas the high priest assembled the Sanhedrin and commanded James publicly to renounce Christ as Israel's Messiah. Upon his refusal, he was thrown from the pinnacle of the Temple and stoned to death as he lay dying from the fall.

16. The word "perfect" is found a number of times in the book of James. It is from the Greek word *teleios*, meaning "mature." This word will be used in developing the outline of James' epistle.

  I. Suffering Makes a Mature Man (1:1-20).
    A. The sources of suffering:

      "My brethren, count it all joy when ye fall into various trials" (1:2).

        "Blessed is the man that endureth temptation" (1:12).

      These verses speak of two kinds of sufferings:

      1. Trial sufferings. These come from God and are sent to bring out the best in us! Note the following:

        "And it came to pass after these things, that God did test Abraham . . . and he said, take now thy son, thine only son Isaac, whom thou lovest, and get thee into the land of Moriah; and offer him there for a burnt offering upon one of the

Characteristics of the Mature Man  JAMES

James

Suffering
MAKES A MATURE MAN (1:1-20)

"My brethren, count it all joy when ye fall into divers temptations." **1:2**

Scripture Study
MAKES A MATURE MAN (1:13-17, 19, 20, 22-25)

"Receive with meekness the engrafted word, which is able to save your souls." **1:21**

Sincerity
MAKES A MATURE MAN (2:1-13)

"For whosoever shall keep the whole law, and yet offend in one point, he is guilty of all." **2:10**

Christian Service
MAKES A MATURE MAN (2:14-26)

"For as the body without the spirit is dead, so faith without works is dead also." **2:26**

Sound Speech
MAKES A MATURE MAN (3:1-18; 1:26, 27)

"For we all stumble in many ways. If any one does not stumble in what he says, he is a perfect man, able to bridle the whole body as well." **(3:2, New American Standard Bible)**

Submission to God
MAKES A MATURE MAN (4:1-17)

"Submit yourselves therefore to God." **4:7**

Self-Sacrifice
MAKES A MATURE MAN (5:1-6)

Steadfastness
MAKES A MATURE MAN (5:7-11)

Supplication
MAKES A MATURE MAN (5:12-18)

Soul-Winning
MAKES A MATURE MAN (5:19, 20)

---

mountains which I will tell thee of" (Gen. 22:1, 2; see also Heb. 11:17).

"And thou shalt remember all the way which the Lord thy God led thee these forty years in the wilderness, to humble thee, and to test thee, to know what was in thine heart, whether thou wouldest keep his commandments, or not" (Deut. 8:2; see also 8:3).

"And Moses said unto the people, fear not; for God is come to test you, and that his fear may be before your faces, that ye sin not" (Ex. 20:20).

"Ye are they [Christ to his disciples] who have continued with me in my trials" (Lk. 22:28).

"In this ye greatly rejoice, though now for a season, if need be, ye are in heaviness through manifold trials" (1 Pet. 1:6).

2. Temptation sufferings. These come from the devil (using the world and the flesh) and are sent to bring out the worst in us.

"Let no man say when he is tempted, I am tempted of God: for God cannot be tempted with evil, neither tempteth he any man: But every man is tempted, when he is drawn away of his own lust, and enticed" (Jas. 1:13, 14; see also Gen. 3:1-6; Mt. 4:1; 2 Cor. 11:3, 4).

In conclusion, it may be said that both trials and temptations are often opposite sides of the same coin. This is to say that both God and Satan may be working in the life of a believer through the same event, one to purify him, the other to pervert him. (See Job 1, 2.)

B. The characteristics of suffering:
1. They are often sudden: "When ye fall . . ." (1:2).
2. They are certain: James says *when* ye fall, not, *if* ye fall!
3. They are sorted: "into divers [various] trials." These are financial, physical, spiritual, mental, and social trials.

C. The purpose of suffering: As we have already noted, God either causes or allows all sufferings to fall into our lives. Why does he do this?
1. Because suffering produces endurance down here.
   "Knowing this, that the trying of your faith worketh patience. But let patience have her perfect work, that ye may be perfect and entire, wanting nothing" (1:3, 4).
2. Because suffering promises rewards up there.
   "Blessed is the man that endureth temptation: for when he is tried, he shall re-

ceive the crown of life, which the Lord hath promised to them that love him" (1:12).

D. The attitude in suffering: How is the believer to respond to trials and tribulations?

"My brethren, count it all joy when ye fall into divers temptations" (1:2; see also Mt. 5:12; 1 Pet. 1:6; 4:12-14).

II. Scripture Study Makes a Mature Man (1:17, 18, 21-25). These verses bring out four precious truths.

A. The Father has given us the old Book.

"Every good gift and every perfect gift is from above, and cometh down from the Father of lights, with whom is no variableness, neither shadow of turning" (1:17).

B. The old Book has given us the new birth.

"Of his own will begat he us with the word of truth, that we should be a kind of firstfruits of his creatures . . . . Wherefore lay apart all filthiness and superfluity of naughtiness, and receive with meekness the engrafted word, which is able to save your souls" (1:18, 21).

C. The believer is therefore to read it carefully.

"But whoso looketh into the perfect law of liberty, and continueth therein, he being not a forgetful hearer, but a doer of the work, this man shall be blessed in his deed" (1:25).

D. The believer is therefore to heed it carefully.

"But be ye doers of the word, and not hearers only, deceiving your own selves" (1:22).

III. Sincerity Makes a Mature Man (2:1-13).

A. The root of insincerity (2:1-8). The basis of this is partiality to the rich.

"For if there come unto your assembly a man with a gold ring, in goodly apparel, and there come in also a poor man in vile raiment; and ye have respect to him that weareth the gay clothing, and say unto him, Sit thou here in a good place; and say to the poor, Stand thou there, or sit here under my footstool: Are ye not then partial in yourselves, and are become judges of evil thoughts?" (2:2-4).

B. The fruit of insincerity (2:9-13).

"But if ye have respect to persons, ye commit sin, and are convinced of the law as transgressors. For whosoever shall keep the whole law, and yet offend in one point, he is guilty of all."

IV. Christian Service Makes a Mature Man (2:14-26).

A. The problem: These verses, as has already been pointed out in the Introduction, have caused some undue concern among many Christians. Does James really contradict Paul here in matters of justification? Is this his goal? It would be difficult for him to do this, for at the time James wrote, Paul had yet to finish the first line of his many epistles!

B. The proof:

"What doth it profit, my brethren, though a man say he hath faith, and have not works? can faith save him? . . . . Even so faith, if it hath not works, is dead, being alone. Yea, a man may say, Thou hast faith, and I have works: shew me thy faith without thy works, and I will shew thee my faith by my works. Thou believest that there is one God; thou

doest well: the devils also believe and tremble. But wilt thou know, O vain man, that faith without works is dead? . . . Ye see then how that by works a man is justified, and not by faith only" (2:14, 17-20, 24).

These verses are not meant to be *saving* texts, but *sign* texts. The proof of the pudding is still in the eating. The *only* test of a man's salvation is through his works. A silent believer may be indeed considered a saint before God, but he remains a sinner before man until he walks the walk and talks the talk of Christian service.

C. The pattern: James names two Old Testament people to illustrate his point here.

1. Abraham:

"Was not Abraham our father justified by works, when he had offered Isaac his son upon the altar?" (2:21).

The chronology of Abraham's life is important to note here. He was justified before God at the age of 85 (Gen. 15:6; 16:16). He was justified before man at the age of (approximately) 137 (Gen. 22:1-14; 23:1).

2. Rahab:

"Likewise also was not Rahab the harlot justified by works, when she had received the messengers, and had sent them out another way?" (2:25).

Rahab's *salvation* is recorded in Joshua 2:1-14, and the *service* in 2:15, 16. Dr. Charles Ryrie writes:

"Unproductive faith cannot save, because it is not genuine faith. Faith and works are like a two-coupon ticket to heaven. The coupon of works is not good for passage, and the coupon of faith is not valid if detached from works." (*Ryrie Study Bible*, p. 421)

V. Sound Speech Makes a Mature Man (3:1-18; 1:26, 27).

A. The importance of the tongue:

"For we all stumble in many ways. If any one does not stumble in what he says, he is a perfect man, able to bridle the whole body as well" (3:2, *NASB*).

Taken in proper context, this is one of the most profound and far-reaching statements in the entire Bible.

B. The illustrations of the tongue:

1. Our tongues direct us as a horse is guided by the bit in its mouth.
2. Our tongues direct us as a ship is guided by a small rudder.

It has been suggested that the body is the congregation and the tongue is its teacher.

C. The iniquity of the tongue:

"So also the tongue is a small part of the body, and yet it boasts of great things. Behold, how great a forest is set aflame by such a small fire! And the tongue is a fire, the very world of iniquity; the tongue . . . defiles the entire body, and sets on fire the course of our lives, and is set on fire by hell" (3:5, 6, *NASB*).

A fire usually has a small beginning. Here we are told that the tremendous destructive power of the tongue comes from hell itself. (See also 3:14-16.)

D. The incorrigibility of the tongue:
"For every species of beasts and birds, of reptiles and creatures of the sea, is tamed, and
has been tamed by the human race. But no
one can tame the tongue; it is restless evil and
full of deadly poison" (3:7, 8, *NASB*).
Humanly speaking, the tongue simply cannot
be changed (3:7, 8; cf. Rom. 3:13, 14). Only eternity will reveal the frustration and agony caused
by careless and hateful words.

E. The inconsistency of the tongue:
"Therewith bless we God, even the Father;
and therewith curse we men, which are made
after the similitude of God. Out of the same
mouth proceedeth blessing and cursing. My
brethren, these things ought not so to be.
Doth a fountain send forth at the same place
sweet water and bitter?" (3:9-12).
An Egyptian king named Amasis once sent a
sacrifice to his god and requested the priest to
send back the best and worst part of the animal.
The priest sent back the tongue, which organ
said he, represented both demands. It has been
said that the Christian should so live that he
would not hesitate to sell his talking parrot to the
town gossip!

F. The instruction for the tongue:
"Who is a wise man and endued with knowledge among you? let him shew out of a good
conversation his works with meekness of wisdom. . . . But the wisdom that is from above is
first pure, then peaceable, gentle, and easy to
be entreated, full of mercy and good fruits,
without partiality, and without hypocrisy.
And the fruit of righteousness is sown in
peace of them that make peace" (3:13, 17, 18).

VI. Submission to God Makes a Mature Man (4:1-17).
"Submit yourselves, therefore, to God" (4:7).
A. We are to do this that we might escape:
1. the flesh (4:1-3)
2. the world (4:4, 5)
3. the devil (4:6, 7)
B. We are to do this that we might enjoy:
1. God's grace.
"But he giveth more grace. Wherefore he
saith, God resisteth the proud, but giveth
grace unto the humble" (4:6).
2. God's guidance.
"Go to now, ye that say, Today or to-mor-
row we will go into such a city, and continue there a year, and buy and sell, and
get gain. Whereas ye know not what shall
be on the morrow. For what is your life? It
is even a vapour, that appeareth for a little
time, and then vanisheth away. For that
ye ought to say, If the Lord will, we shall
live, and do this, or that" (4:13-15).
3. God's goodness.
"Humble yourselves in the sight of the
Lord, and he shall lift you up" (4:10).

VII. Self-Sacrifice Makes a Mature Man (5:1-6).
VIII. Steadfastness Makes a Mature Man (5:7-11).
A. An example from the past:
"Take, my brethren, the prophets, who have
spoken in the name of the Lord, for an example of suffering affliction, and of patience. Behold, we count them happy which endure. Ye
have heard of the patience of Job, and have
seen the end of the Lord; that the Lord is very
pitiful, and of tender mercy" (5:10, 11).
B. An example from the present:
"Be patient therefore, brethren, unto the coming of the Lord, Behold, the husbandman
waiteth for the precious fruit of the earth, and
hath long patience for it, until he receive the
early and latter rain" (5:7).
C. An example from the future:
"Be ye also patient; stablish your hearts: for
the coming of the Lord draweth nigh. Grudge
not one against another, brethren, lest ye be
condemned: behold, the judge standeth before the door" (5:8, 9).

IX. Supplication (Prayer) Makes a Mature Man (5:12-18).
"Is any sick among you? let him call for the elders
of the church; and let them pray over him, anointing him with oil in the name of the Lord: And the
prayer of faith shall save the sick, and the Lord
shall raise him up; and if he have committed sins,
they shall be forgiven him. Confess your faults
one to another, and pray one for another; that ye
may be healed. The effectual fervent prayer of a
righteous man availeth much" (5:14-16).
These verses have been the object of much speculation.
A. What is meant by the anointing of a sick person
with oil?
1. Negative:
a. This is not a reference to extreme unction, a Roman Catholic dogma which
prepares a dying person for death. The
practice in these verses is to restore the
sick, not bury them!
b. This does not give sanction to faith healers. We note instead that several elders
of the church are to be involved here.
2. Positive:
a. The men involved. "The elders of the
church" (5:14). As we have already
stated, these were the spiritual leaders of
the church.
b. The medicine involved. "Anointing him
with oil" (5:14). The Greek word here is a
reference to olive oil, used as a common
medicinal remedy in the ancient East (see
Isa. 1:6; Lk. 10:34). In his book *The Game
of Life*, author Roy Roberts gives the following helpful words as taken from professor James E. Rosscup:
"In brief, oil did have therapeutic
value in ancient times as well as today, but it is best to understand it
here as a symbol of God's miraculous
work in healing. That it had good medicinal effects is clear. It possessed
soothing and curative value for animals, like sheep (Ps. 23:5), and men
(Isa. 1:6). The good Samaritan in
Christ's parable applied oil to the
wounds of the man he helped (Lk.
10:34). But, it is not the meaning of
James for various reasons. Though it
was therapeutic in some cases, it

would not be a cure in all sicknesses in general. Further, James does not say in v. 15 that the oil will cure the sick or even that the oil plus the prayer will make him well. Specifically, he does say that 'the prayer of faith shall save the sick,' and makes no claim for the oil. It is not the oil, but the Lord who 'shall raise him up.' It is more adequate to say that the anointing is for the purpose of symbolizing tangibly the setting apart of the man to the miraculous healing work of God. It would be an aid to his faith by prompting a sense of expectancy. Christ Himself applied saliva to men at times evidently to symbolize, by physical contact, the healing that God would effect (Mk. 7:33; 8:23). There is Old Testament support for the idea that the anointing could signify the setting apart of the man to God for His will and operation. There are numerous applications of oil, not to cure but to set apart or identify things or persons with God in some sense. Jacob anointed the stone at Bethel to identify it as symbolizing the 'house of God' in which he had been a guest (Gen. 28:18; 31:13). When he poured oil upon it, it was not to make it well! It was a ceremonial custom later to anoint priests (Ex. 29:7; Lev. 8:12), prophets (1 Ki. 19:16), and kings (1 Sam. 10:1; 1 Ki. 19:15). This was to symbolize that they were set apart to and identified with God for His will. When Jesus sent out the twelve disciples, they 'anointed with oil many that were sick, and healed them.' " (Mk. 6:13) (pp. 171, 172)

B. Will all sick people be automatically healed by this action? To rephrase the question: Is it ever God's will for believers to experience prolonged illness? It is sometimes not God's will to heal sick Christians! Suffering, if rightly understood and endured by the believer, can bring about the glory of God. (See Ex. 4:11; 1 Tim. 5:23; 2 Tim. 4:20; 2 Cor. 12:1-10; Jn. 9:1-3.) Sometimes, of course, sickness *is* a penalty for sin (see Jn. 5:14).

C. What is involved in the confession of 5:16? James says we are to confess our faults *one to another!* As we have already noted, there are times when unconfessed sin does bring suffering. James may have reference to this very thing here at this point. *If* a sick believer had wronged another Christian in the church, he was now encouraged to confess this, that God might be able to bless him both spiritually and physically.

James then says: "The effectual fervent prayer of a righteous man availeth much" (5:16). The "righteous man" spoken of here may refer either to the elder who prays for the sick believer, or the believer himself who, having been restored to fellowship through confession, can now pray

effectively. James mentions Elijah as an Old Testament example of effective prayer (5:17; cf. 1 Ki. 17-18).

X. Soul-winning Makes a Mature Man.
"Brethren, if any of you do err from the truth, and one convert him; let him know, that he which converteth the sinner from the error of his way, shall save a soul from death, and shall hide a multitude of sins" (5:19, 20).

HEBREWS
INTRODUCTION:
1. Let us imagine a conversation between a Hindu and a Christian. The Hindu listens intently as the Christian briefly summarizes the earthly ministry of Jesus Christ. At the conclusion of the message four basic questions might quickly come to his mind.
  a. Question: Why did Jesus have to be born? Answer: "No man hath seen God at any time; the only begotten Son, which is in the bosom of the Father, he hath declared him" (Jn. 1:18).
  b. Question: Why did Jesus have to die? Answer: "Who gave himself for our sins, that he might deliver us from this present evil world, according to the will of God and our Father" (Gal. 1:4).
  c. Question: Why did Jesus have to be resurrected? Answer: "And if Christ be not risen, then is our preaching vain, and your faith is also vain" (1 Cor. 15:14).
  d. Question: Why did Jesus have to ascend? Answer: The book of Hebrews!
2. The book of Hebrews presents the only full discussion in the New Testament of Christ as the believer's High Priest. It answers the question, "Whatever happened to Jesus?"
3. The author: unknown. There are three suggested authors.
  a. Paul.
    (1) Because the early church believed he was the author.
    (2) Because of the characteristic closing of the epistle (13:25; cf. 2 Thess. 3:17, 18).
    (3) Because of the expression "the just shall live by faith." This expression is an Old Testament quote (Hab. 2:4) which is used three times in the New Testament (Rom. 1:17; Gal. 3:11; Heb. 10:38). The argument here is that inasmuch as Paul used the expression the first two times, he probably used it on the third occasion here in Hebrews.
    (4) Because of Peter's statement in 2 Peter 3:15, 16. Here Peter states that Paul had written to the same people he was addressing, the Jews of the dispersion (1 Pet. 1:1; 2 Pet. 3:1). Peter then refers to Paul's letter as Scripture. The book of Hebrews is the only New Testament book which fits this description.
    (5) Because it was written from Italy (13:24) by a friend of Timothy (13:23) who was in prison at the time (10:34). This would tie in with Paul's imprisonment as recorded in Acts 28.
  b. Barnabas.
    (1) Because he was a Levite and the book of Hebrews seems to have been written by a Levite.
    (2) Because of the comparison between Acts 4:36 and Hebrews 13:22.

c. Apollos.
  (1) Because of the eloquent Greek style of Hebrews.
  (2) Because the Old Testament quotes in Hebrews are taken from the Septuagint, while Paul usually quoted from the Hebrew Old Testament.
4. The destination of the letter. Several theories:
  a. Jerusalem. However, this would seem doubtful:
    (1) Because of Hebrews 2:3.
    (2) Because of Hebrews 6:10; 10:34. The readers of this epistle were apparently able to minister to others, but the Jerusalem church was poverty-stricken (Acts 11:27-30).
    (3) Because of Hebrews 12:4. But the Jerusalem church had suffered martyrdom (Acts 7:59, 60; 12:2).
    (4) Because there is no mention of the Temple.
  b. Rome.
  c. Ephesus.
5. The book of Hebrews has been called the fifth Gospel. The first four describe what Christ once did on earth, while Hebrews describes what he is now doing in heaven.
6. Hebrews 10:11 reveals that the book was written before the destruction of the Temple by Titus in A.D. 70.
7. Hebrews may be compared to Romans.
  a. Romans reveals the *necessity* of the Christian faith.
  b. Hebrews reveals the *superiority* of the Christian faith.
8. There are six key words in this book. They are:
  a. perfect (used fourteen times)
  b. eternal, forever (used fifteen times)
  c. better (thirteen times)
  d. partakers (nine times)
  e. heaven (seventeen times)
  f. priest, high priest (thirty-two times)
9. There are at least eighty-six direct references to the Old Testament in Hebrews, taken from one hundred passages.
  I. The Superior Person—Christ (1:1—5:10).
    A. He is better than the prophets (1:1-3).
      1. Because of the Father's declaration to him. In the past God had given his word to the prophets in many installments and by various methods. But only Jesus could declare the full message of the invisible God.
      2. Because of the Father's description of him.
        a. He was appointed by God as heir of all things (Ps. 2:8; Jn. 3:35).
        b. He was the One through whom God made the ages (Jn. 1:3).
        c. He is the absolute expression of the collective attributes of deity (Jn. 1:18; Rom. 9:5).
        d. He is the "brightness of his glory."
        e. He is the upholder of all things (Col. 1:17).
        f. He is the purifier of sins.
        g. He is now at God's right hand.
        These verses (2, 3) give us the first few great names and titles of Christ in the book of Hebrews.
        Note:
          Author (12:2)
          The Apostle (3:1)
          Captain (2:10; 12:2)

Christ (3:6)
Finisher (12:2)
Firstborn (1:6)
Forerunner (6:20)
God (1:8)
Heir (1:2)
High Priest (2:17)
Lord (2:3)
Mediator (8:6)
Shepherd (13:20)
Son (1:2)
Surety (7:22)

B. He is better than the angels (1:4—2:18).
  1. Because of his rank. "He hath by inheritance obtained a more excellent name than they" (1:4).
  2. Because of his relationship. "I will be to him a Father, and he shall be to me a Son" (1:5). Because of this, God commanded heaven's angels to worship him (1:6). John Bunyan once wrote: "If Jesus be not God, then heaven will be filled with idolators."
  3. Because of his reign. "Thy throne, O God, is forever and ever" (1:8).
  4. Because of his righteousness. "A sceptre of righteousness is the sceptre of thy kingdom" (1:8).
First Warning—about disregarding God's Word (2:1-4).
  Hebrews contains five key warnings. This is the first. Here is the argument. If Israel in Old Testament times was punished for disobeying the word of angels, how much greater would be punishment for disobeying God's Word as spoken by his own Son! (Gen. 19; Deut. 33:2; Ps. 68:17; Acts 7:54; Gal. 3:19; cf. Lk. 4:18-21; 19:10; Mt. 16:21; 20:28.)
  5. Because of his redemptive ministry (2:5-18).
    a. The necessity for his redemptive ministry. Why did Jesus find it necessary to take upon himself a body of flesh?
      (1) In order to recapture our lost destiny (2:5-9)
        (a) Man was originally created to rule over all things.
        (b) He was put on probation (made a little lower than the angels) for awhile.
        (c) Due to his sin, he has not yet been able to rule over all things.
        (d) Jesus came to complete man's original purpose for him.
        Author Ray C. Stedman writes the following:
          "The writer insists that when David says 'all things,' he means all things, everything. For he adds, *Now in putting everything in subjection to him, he left nothing outside his control.* Here is man's intended destiny, his authorized dominion. Man was made to be king over all God's universe. Surely this passage includes far more than the earth. It envisions the created universe of God as far as man

has ever been able to discover it, in all the illimitable reaches of space and whatever lies beyond that. All this is to be put under man's dominion. It is a vast and tremendous vision.

But man's authority was derived authority. Man himself was to be subject to the God who indwelt him. He was to be the means by which the invisible God became visible to His creatures. He was to be the manifestation of God's own life which dwelt in the royal residence of his human spirit. As long as man was subject to the dominion of God within him, he would be able to exercise dominion over all the universe around. Only when man accepted dominion could he exercise dominion.

The writer further points out that man was made lower than the angels for a limited time to learn what the exercise of that dominion meant. He was given a limited domain: this earth, this tiny planet whirling its way through the great galaxy to which we belong, amid all the billions of galaxies of space! And he was also given a limited physical body so that within that limited area man should learn the principles by which his dominion could be exercised throughout the universe. This limitation is described as being *lower than the angels.*

But the passage goes on to describe man's present state of futility. *As it is we do not yet see everything in subjection to him.* There is the whole story of human history in a nutshell. How visibly true this is: we do not yet see everything in subjection to him. Man attempts to exercise his dominion but he no longer can do so adequately. He has never forgotten the position God gave him, for throughout the history of the race there is a continual restatement of the dreams of man for dominion over the earth and the universe. This is why we cannot keep off the highest mountain. We have to get up there, though we have not lost a thing up there and we know when we get there we will only see what the bear saw: the other side of the mountain. But we have to be there. We have to explore the depths of the sea. We

have to get out into space. Why? Because it is there.

Man consistently manifests a remarkable racial memory, a vestigial recollection of what God told him to do. The trouble is that when he tries to accomplish this now he creates a highly explosive and dangerous situation, for his ability to exercise dominion is no longer there. Things get out of balance. This is why we are confronted with an increasingly serious situation in our day when our attempt to control insects by pesticides and other poisons creates an imbalance that threatens serious results. The history of man is one of continually precipitating a crisis by attempting to exercise dominion.

If we go back into recorded history to the earliest writings of men, the most ancient of history, we find that men were wrestling with the same moral problems then that we are wrestling with today. We have made wonderful advances in technology, but have made absolutely zero progress when it comes to moral relationships. Somewhere man has lost his relationship with God.

The fall of man is the only adequate explanation of this. Since then the universe is stamped with futility. Everything man does is a dead-end to a successful conclusion. Even in the individual life this is true. How many have realized the dreams and ideals they began with? Who can say, 'I have done all that I wanted to do; I have been all that I wanted to be'? Paul in Romans puts it, *'The creation was subjected to futility'* (Rom. 8:20).

But the writer of Hebrews says, *We see Jesus!* This is man's one hope. With the eye of faith we see Jesus already crowned and reigning over the universe, the man Jesus fulfilling man's lost destiny." (*What More Can God Say?* pp. 20–22)

What a fantastic contrast between the two phrases in 2:8, 9: "But now we see not . . ." and "But we see Jesus. . . ."

Thus, what the first Adam lost in the Garden, the second Adam regained upon Golgotha.

(2) In order to recover our lost unity (2:10–13). As a result of his sufferings, Christ now unites us to the Father and becomes our elder Brother.

(3) In order to reassure our lost confidence (2:14-18).

"Forasmuch then as the children are partakers of flesh and blood, he also himself likewise took part of the same; that through death he might destroy him that had the power of death, that is, the devil; and deliver them who through fear of death were all their lifetime subject to bondage."

C. He is better than Moses (3:1-19). Reason: Moses was a servant in God's house, while Christ is the beloved Son (3:1-6).

Second warning—about doubting God's Word (3:7-19; see also 4:11).

1. An example:

"Harden not your hearts, as in the provocation, in the day of temptation in the wilderness: When your fathers tempted me, proved me, and saw my works forty years. Wherefore I was grieved with that generation, and said, They do alway err in their heart; and they have not known my ways. So I sware in my wrath, They shall not enter into my rest" (3:8-11).

2. An exhortation:

"Take heed, brethren, lest there be in any of you an evil heart of unbelief, in departing from the living God. But exhort one another daily, while it is called To-day; lest any of you be hardened through the deceitfulness of sin."

Note: The word "exhort" here in verse 13 is *parakaleo*, which means to urge someone to pursue some course of conduct.

D. He is better than Joshua (4:1-16).

"For if Jesus had given them rest, then would he not afterward have spoken of another day. There remaineth therefore a rest to the people of God" (4:8, 9).

The word "Jesus" here should be translated "Joshua." Jesus is better than Joshua because the rest he gives is eternal, whereas Joshua's rest lasted a bare 25-40 years.

1. The admonishments in God's Word. This chapter records the first of thirteen "Let us" admonitions to be found in Hebrews. Note:
   a. "Let us therefore fear" (4:1).
   b. "Let us labour therefore to enter into that rest" (4:11).
   c. "Let us hold fast our profession" (4:14).
   d. "Let us therefore come boldly unto the throne of grace" (4:16).
   e. "Let us go on unto perfection" (6:1).
   f. "Let us draw near with a true heart in full assurance of faith" (10:22).
   g. "Let us hold fast the profession of our faith without wavering" (10:23).
   h. "Let us consider one another to provoke unto love and to good works" (10:24).
   i. "Let us lay aside every weight" (12:1).
   j. "Let us run with patience the race that is set before us" (12:1).
   k. "Let us have grace" (12:28).

   l. "Let us go forth therefore unto him without the camp" (13:13).
   m. "Let us offer the sacrifice of praise to God continually" (13:15).

   Note especially item *d* (4:16) here. Luther, Zwingli, and Calvin nailed to the masthead of their movement three great principles taken from Hebrews:
   No sacrifice but Calvary.
   No priest but Christ.
   No confessional but the throne of grace.

2. The "rests" in God's Word. We have described three great biblical rests.
   a. The rest of creation (4:4).
   b. The rest of salvation (4:10).
   c. The rest of consecration (4:11).

3. The power of God's Word.

   "For the word of God is quick, and powerful, and sharper than any two-edged sword, piercing even to the dividing asunder of soul and spirit, and of the joints and marrow, and is a discerner of the thoughts and intents of the heart. Neither is there any creature that is not manifest in his sight: but all things are naked and opened unto the eyes of him with whom we have to do" (4:12, 13).

E. He is better than Aaron (5:1-10).
   1. He possesses perfectly that which Aaron possessed in part.
      a. Like Aaron, he was taken from among men (5:1).
      b. Like Aaron, he was chosen by God (5:4).
      c. Like Aaron, he had compassion (5:2).
      d. Like Aaron, he learned obedience (5:8; see also Heb. 2:10). Note: Christ was always perfect in his Person, but while on earth also became perfect in his work.
      e. Like Aaron, he prayed (5:7).
      f. Like Aaron, he suffered (5:8; see also Phil. 2:8).
   2. He possesses perfectly that which Aaron lacked completely.
      a. Unlike Aaron, he is God's unique Son (5:5).
      b. Unlike Aaron, he is a Priest after Melchizedek (5:6).
      c. Unlike Aaron, he becomes the author of eternal salvation (5:9).

II. The Superior Purpose—Perfection (5:11—6:20).

"Therefore leaving the principles of the doctrine of Christ, let us go on unto perfection" (6:1).

Third warning—about departing from God's Word (5:11—6:20).

A. The particulars of this danger.
   1. The symptoms:
      a. Apathy (5:11).
         "Of whom we have many things to say, and hard to be uttered, seeing ye are dull of hearing."
      b. Ambiguity (5:12).
         "For when for the time ye ought to be teachers, ye have need that one teach you again which be the first principles of the oracles of God; and are become such as have need of milk, and not of strong meat."

Author Ray Stedman writes:

"I read of a principal in a high school who had an administrative post to fill. He promoted one of his teachers with ten years of teaching experience to the job. When the announcement was made, another teacher in this school came to him terribly upset. She said, 'Why did you put that teacher in this position? He has only had ten years of experience and I've had twenty-five years, yet you passed me over in favor of him.' And the principal said, 'I'm sorry; you're wrong. You haven't had twenty-five years of experience. You have had one year's experience twenty-five times.'" (What More Can God Say?)

The reason for this uncertainty and immaturity is explained in 5:13, 14; cf. 1 Corinthians 3:1, 2; 1 Peter 2:1, 2. See also Joshua 5:12, where we are told that the manna ceased *after* Israel entered the Promised Land.

  c. Apostasy (6:4-6).

2. The theories. Perhaps no other single biblical passage has been the subject of more speculation and interpretation than these words in Hebrews 6:4-6. Various theories hold that these verses describe one of the following kinds of people.

  a. Saved people who lose their salvation through some horrible sin. Of course, if this be true, then the same passage also teaches that they could never be saved again!

  b. Professed believers who have only "tasted" the things of God and never really "swallowed" them. However, this is entirely unsupportable, for the same Greek word is used also in Hebrews 2:9 concerning Jesus who, "by the grace of God should taste death for every man."

  c. Jewish professed believers living while the Temple was still standing. The *Scofield Bible* presents this view:

"Hebrews 6:4-8 presents the case of Jewish professed believers who halt short of faith in Christ after advancing to the very threshold of salvation, even 'going along with' the Holy Spirit in His work of enlightenment and conviction (Jn. 16:8-10). It is not said that they had faith. This supposed person is like the spies at Kadesh-barnea (Deut. 1:19-26) who saw the land and had the very fruit of it in their hands, and yet turned back." (p. 1295)

  d. A hypothetical case of what could not happen.

"'If one could fall away' (v. 6) it would be impossible to renew him again to repentance; for, in such an instance, it would be necessary for Christ to be crucified a second time.

Obviously, this will not occur (Heb. 10:12, 14); thus to fall away is impossible." (*The New Scofield Bible,* p. 1315)

  e. Backsliders who are in danger of committing the sin unto death (see 1 Cor. 11:30; Acts 5:1-11; 1 Jn. 5:16, 17). None of these views is without its problems. It seems, however (in the mind of the author) that the final view would more closely describe this apostasy and define these people.

3. The example (6:7, 8). It should be noted that here it is *not* the field which is destroyed, but the fruit. (See also 1 Cor. 3:15; Jn. 15:6; Heb. 10:30.)

B. The protections from this danger (6:1-3, 8-20. *If this sin can be committed by believers, is there sufficient protection against it to those who desire it? There is indeed.*

1. The performance of the believer (6:1-3, 8-12).

  a. He is to "go on unto perfection [maturity]" (6:1). That is, he is to leave the foundation for the walls, and the ABC's for the Ph.D.

  b. He is to minister to the saints (6:10).

  c. He is to show love for Jesus' name (6:10).

  d. He is to be diligent (6:11).

  e. He is to imitate those "who through faith and patience inherit the promises" (6:12).

Thus, while good works will not save a sinner from hell, they will spare a saint from judgment. (See 1 Cor. 11:31.)

2. The promise of the Father (6:13-18).

  a. The fact of this promise:

    (1) It was available to Abraham.

    (2) It is available to us.

  b. The nature of this promise. "We may have strong encouragement, we who have fled for refuge in laying hold of the hope set before us" (6:18, *NASB*).

  c. The security of this promise (6:17, 18). It is based on two unchangeable things:

    (1) God's eternal character (what God is).

    (2) God's written Word (what God has said).

3. The priesthood of Christ (6:19, 20). Jesus is described here as our forerunner. This word has been associated with a small boat called a forerunner. In the ancient world large ocean vessels often experienced difficulty when approaching the shallow Greek harbors. To counteract this, a small forerunner boat would often be sent out to help secure the vessel's anchor within the harbor itself. Dr. Kenneth Wuest writes:

"The anchor of the believer is, therefore, fastened within the veil of the Holy of Holies of heaven. We have some rich figures here. This present life is the sea; the soul, a ship . . . the soul of the believer, as a tempest-tossed ship, is held by the anchor within the veil, fastened by faith to the blessed reality within the veil." (*Hebrews in the Greek New Testament,* p. 125)

III. The Superior Priesthood—Melchizedek (7-10). It has already been stated that Christ is a priest after the order of Melchizedek and not after Aaron. This immediately offers a fourfold advantage.

A. It offers a better source (chapter 7). From Aaron to Melchizedek.

1. Christ was given a royal priesthood. Melchizedek was a king as well as a Priest (Gen. 14:18).

2. Christ was given an authoritative priesthood. Melchizedek received the tithes of Abraham (Gen. 14:20).

Here in Hebrews 7:4-10 the author points out that inasmuch as Levi (founder of the Levitical priesthood from which Aaron the first high priest came) was in the loins of Abraham (he would become his great grandson) that he (Levi) in reality tithed to Melchizedek through Abraham. The conclusion is that under the law the Levitical priests received tithes from the people, but back in Genesis 14 the Levitical priests paid tithes to Melchizedek.

3. Christ was given a timeless priesthood. Melchizedek was "without descent, having neither beginning of days, nor end of life" (7:3), but Aaron died (Heb. 7:8; cf. Num. 20:23-29).

Note: This does *not* necessarily mean that Melchizedek was actually Christ (although he may have been) but that inasmuch as we have no record of his birth or death he *does* become a type of Christ not only in his *office*, but also in his *origin*.

4. Christ was given an independent priesthood. Melchizedek was ordained by an oath from God and not by the tribe of Levi. In the Old Testament no one could serve as a priest unless he was descended from Aaron (Ezra 2:61, 62). However, neither Melchizedek nor Christ came from this tribe (Heb. 7:14, 22-24).

5. Christ was given an everlasting priesthood (Heb. 7:17; Ps. 110:4).

6. Christ was given an immutable (changeless) priesthood (7:24).

7. Christ was given an all-inclusive priesthood. Under this arrangement Christ was not *presented* an offering but actually *became* one (7:27). Author Ray Stedman writes the following concerning verse 27:

"As a priest, Jesus Christ could find no unblemished sacrifice that He could offer except Himself, so He offered Himself as a sacrifice; there was found no other priest worthy of offering such a sacrifice, so Christ became both Priest and Victim." (*What More Can God Say?* p. 115)

This dual arrangement can be seen by listening to his seven final sentences while on the cross. The first three demonstrate his priestly ministry while the final four speak of his sacrificial role.

8. Christ was given a holy priesthood (7:26).

"For such an high priest became us, who is holy, harmless, undefiled, separate from sinners, and made higher than the heavens" (7:26).

This is in contrast to the Levitical priesthood, whose representatives often allowed corruption and idolatry to control their lives (see Ex. 32:1-6, 21-25; 1 Sam. 2:12-17; 8:1-3).

9. Christ was given a perfecting priesthood (7:19, 25).

"Wherefore he is able also to save them to the uttermost that come unto God by Him, seeing he ever liveth to make intercession [intervention] for them" (7:25).

This verse is usually applied to the salvation of the lost (from "the uttermost to the uttermost"), but in its context it refers to the *preservation* of the saved. Thus, Christ *died* down here on Calvary to bring us salvation, and now *lives* up there in glory to keep us saved. (See also Rom. 8:34; Rev. 1:18.)

B. It offers a better script (8). From the old covenant to the new. The Old Testament Hebrew word for "covenant" was *berit*, meaning "to cut or divide." (See Gen. 15:10; Jer. 34:18, 19.) This cutting was in reference to the cutting of sacrificial animals. Between these bloody pieces of flesh the two parties of the *berit* would walk. However, in the Genesis 15 account, God put Abraham to sleep and walked through alone, thus signifying that particular *berit* to be unconditional. This ceremony was also known as a blood covenant. This Old Testament concept is brought out in the New Testament by the Greek word *diatheke*. A *diatheke* is a treaty between two parties, but binding only on one, according to the terms fixed by the other. This important word appears no less than twenty-two times in the book of Hebrews. It is always translated by the English words "covenant" and (or) "testament." (See also Lk. 22:20; 1 Cor. 11:25; 2 Cor. 3:6.)

Another Greek word, *suntheke,* although it is the regular term employed for a treaty, is used but four times and always in a bad light (see Jn. 9:22; Lk. 22:5; Acts 23:20; 24:9).

In Hebrews 8 the author contrasts the new covenant with a certain Old Testament covenant (not the one, however, made with Abraham).

1. The old covenant.
   a. It was mediated by Moses (Ex. 19; Jn. 1:17; Gal. 3:19).
   b. It was conditional (see Deut. 28).
   c. It could not produce the necessary righteousness (8:8).
   d. It was written on dead stones (Ex. 32:15).

2. The new covenant.
   a. It is mediated by Christ (9:15; Jn. 1:17).
   b. It is unconditional (8:9).
   c. It can produce the necessary righteousness (8:11).
   d. It is written on living hearts (8:10).

There are at least four theories concerning the recipients of this new covenant. These are:

1. The church has replaced Israel as the participant in the new covenant. This is totally refuted by Paul in Romans 9—11.

2. The new covenant is with the nation Israel only. However, this seems to be out of context with Hebrews 8.

The Better Things

Christ: the SUPERIOR PERSON **1:1—5:10**
Perfection: the SUPERIOR PURPOSE **5:11—6:20**
Melchizedek: the SUPERIOR PRIESTHOOD **7:1—10:39**
Faith: the SUPERIOR PRINCIPLE **11:1—13:25**

The Better Nots

DON'T DISREGARD his Word **2:1-4**
DON'T DOUBT his Word **3:12, 13; 4:11**
DON'T DEPART from his Word **6:4-6**
DON'T DESPISE his Word **10:26-29**
DON'T DISAGREE with his Word **12:25**

The Superior Person *(Christ)*

Better than the Prophets **1:1-3**
Better than the Angels **1:4—2:8**
Better than Moses **3:1—4:7**
Better than Joshua **4:8-16**
Better than Aaron **5:1-10**

The Superior Purpose **5:11—6:20**
(Perfection)

The Superior Priesthood **7-10**
(Melchizedek)

It offers a better source **(chapter 7)**

It offers a better sanctuary **(chapter 9)**

The Superior Principle *(Faith)*
The people of faith **(Chapter 11)**
The pattern of faith **(Chapter 12)**

"For Christ is not entered into the holy places made with hands, which are figures of the true; but into heaven itself, now to appear in the presence of God for us" **(Heb. 9:24).**

Hebrews *... The "Better" Book*

3. There are two new covenants in this chapter. One refers to Israel, and the other to the church.

4. There is but one new covenant which will be fulfilled eschatologically with Israel, but participated in soteriologically by the church today. Of these four views it would seem that while the third is possible, the fourth is *probable.*

C. It offers a better sanctuary (9). From the earthly to the heavenly.

1. The earthly sanctuary. Its inferiority:
   a. It was of this world (9:1).
   b. It was a temporary one (9:8; see also 8:13).
   c. It was a copy (shadow, type) of the real one (9:9).
   d. It was (to most) totally inaccessible (9:7).
   e. It was associated with God's first work of creation (9:11). Here the word "building" is better rendered "creation."
   f. It was made by human hands (9:24).
   g. It featured the blood of animals (9:13).
   h. It was ineffective in matters of eternal salvation (9:9).
   i. It had no abiding hope (9:10).

2. The heavenly sanctuary. Its superiority:
   a. It is of heaven.
   b. It is continuous.
   c. It is the real thing.
   d. It is totally accessible to all (4:16; 10:19).
   e. It is associated with God's second work of redemption.
   f. It was made without human hands (9:24).
   g. It features the blood of Christ (9:12).
   h. It is totally effective in matters of eternal salvation (9:12).
   i. It has an abiding hope. Note these three little phrases in 9:24, 26, 28:

      "He appeared" (9:26)—his former work as a *Prophet.*

      "Now to appear" (9:24)—his present work as a *Priest.*

      "Shall he appear" (9:28)—his future work as a *King.*

      At this point the author of Hebrews has described for us the full sevenfold ministry of our Lord.

      (1) his incarnation (1:2; 2:16, 17)
      (2) his ministration (5:7-9)
      (3) his crucifixion (6:6; 7:27; 2:9)
      (4) his resurrection (13:20)
      (5) his ascension (4:4; 6:20)
      (6) his intercession (7:25; 8:1; 9:12, 24)
      (7) his revelation (9:28)

D. It offers a better sacrifice (10). From animal lambs to God's Lamb.

1. The necessity for God's Lamb:

   "For it is not possible that the blood of bulls and of goats should take away sins" (10:4).

   These sacrifices could (for awhile) *cover* sin, but these sacrifices could not *cleanse* it. (See also 10:6, 11; Isa. 1:11; Jer. 6:20; Hos. 6:6; Amos 5:21, 22.)

2. The obedience of God's Lamb.

   "Wherefore, when he cometh into the world, he saith, Sacrifice and offering thou wouldest not, but a body hast thou prepared me: . . . Then said I, Lo, I come . . . to do thy will, O God" (10:5, 7).

   These may be considered as our Lord's first recorded words in reference to his earthly ministry, uttered perhaps as he left the Ivory Palaces of glory to join himself to that tiny mass of human flesh within Mary's womb.

3. The accomplishments effected by God's Lamb:
   a. a completed redemption
   b. a current sanctification
   c. a coming glorification

   "And every priest standeth daily ministering and offering oftentimes the same sacrifices, which can never take away sins: But this man, after he had offered one sacrifice for sins for ever, sat down on the right hand of God; from henceforth expecting till his enemies be made his footstool. For by one offering he hath perfected for ever them that are sanctified."

4. The exhortations from God's Lamb:
   a. Confidence concerning sins:

      "And their sins and iniquities will I remember no more. . . . Having therefore, brethren, boldness to enter into the holiest by the blood of Jesus. . . . Let us draw near with a true heart in full assurance of faith. . ." (10:17, 19, 22; see also 10:35-37).

   b. Consciousness concerning saints: Is the believer responsible for the welfare of other Christians? He is indeed. Note:

      "And let us consider one another to provoke unto love and to good works: Not forsaking the assembling of ourselves together, as the manner of some is; but exhorting one another: and so much the more, as ye see the day approaching" (10:24, 25; see also 10:34).

Fourth warning—about despising God's Word (10:26-31).

Do these fearful verses refer to saved or unsaved people? While one cannot be absolutely dogmatic here, it would seem from the phrase in verse 30, "The Lord shall judge his people" that the author had believers in mind. If this be correct, then the sin unto death may be in mind here. Thus (if true) this passage can be tied into Hebrews 6:4-6.

IV. The Superior Principle—Faith (11-13).

A. The people of faith (11). The author of Hebrews has just ended chapter 10 with a summary statement concerning the believer and his great High Priest. The statement is: "Now the just shall live by faith" (10:39).

   Having come this far in the epistle, some of the readers might be wondering: Exactly what is this faith like? Has anyone really lived like this before? The author now answers these questions. This chapter has been called the divine Hall of Fame and the *Westminster Abbey of Scripture.*

1. Faith described (11:1-3):

   "Now faith is the substance of things hoped for, the evidence of things not seen. For by it the elders obtained a good report. Through faith we understand that the worlds were framed by the word of God, so that things which are seen were not made of things which do appear" (11:1-3).

   a. Faith is the confident assurance of things hoped for, the proof of things not seen (loose paraphrase of 11:1).

   b. "Faith enables the believing soul to treat the future as present, and the invisible as seen" (J. Oswald Sanders).

   c. According to verse 3, faith is vital if we are to go beyond the very first verse in Genesis 1. (See also 11:6.)

   d. Faith is trust in the unseen, but not the unknown. (See also 11:27.)

   e. "Faith is the title-deed of things hoped for" (Moulton and Milligan).

2. Faith demonstrated (4-40). The author now calls to memory many Old Testament people to illustrate the amazing accomplishments wrought through faith in God. Note the heroes and the home runs in heaven's divine league:

   a. The heroes:
      (1) Abel
      (2) Enoch
      (3) Noah
      (4) Abraham
      (5) Sarah
      (6) Isaac
      (7) Jacob
      (8) Joseph
      (9) Moses
      (10) Moses' parents
      (11) Joshua
      (12) Gideon
      (13) Rahab
      (14) Barak
      (15) Samson
      (16) Jephthah
      (17) David
      (18) Samuel
      (19) others

   b. The home runs
      (1) By faith the proper sacrifice was offered (Abel—v. 4).
      (2) By faith a rapture took place (Enoch—v. 5).
      (3) By faith eight escaped the flood waters (Noah—v. 7).
      (4) By faith difficult commands were obeyed (Abraham):
         (a) To give up his native land (11:8-10).
         (b) To offer up his beloved son (11:17-19).

      Note: Concerning verse 19 it should be stated that Abraham believed God at this point before there was any precedent for physical resurrection either by promise or example.

      It has been observed that by faith Abraham obeyed God when he did not know *where* (11:8-10), when he did not know *how* (11:11, 12), when he did not know *when* (11:13-16), and when he did not know *why* (11:17-19).

      (5) By faith a barren womb gave forth birth (Sarah—vs. 11, 12).
      (6) By faith great predictions were made:
         (a) Concerning the marriage and family of Jacob (Isaac—v. 20; see also Gen. 28:1-4).
         (b) Concerning the Messiah's tribal line (Jacob—v. 21; see also Gen. 49:10).
         (c) Concerning the Exodus (Joseph—v. 22; see also Gen. 50:24, 25).
      (7) By faith a babe was hidden for three months (by Moses' parents—v. 23).
      (8) By faith a nation was delivered from slavery (Moses—vs. 24-29).
         (a) The determination of Moses to deliver Israel (11:24).
         (b) The reasons for this determination (11:25-27).
         (c) The results of this determination (11:28, 29).
      (9) By faith a city was shouted down (Joshua—v. 30).
      (10) By faith a harlot was saved (Rahab—v. 31).
      (11) By faith military reformers delivered Israel (Gideon, Barak, Samson, and Jephthah—v. 32).
      (12) By faith a shepherd boy was anointed king (Samuel—v. 32; see also 1 Sam. 16).
      (13) By faith kingdoms were subdued (David—vs. 32, 33; also 2 Sam. 8).
      (14) By faith righteous acts were wrought (v. 33). Many Old Testament prophets, priests, and kings did this.
      (15) By faith promises were obtained (v. 33). Many Old Testament examples of this also.
      (16) By faith the mouths of lions were shut (v. 33; see Jdg. 14:5, 6; 1 Sam. 17:34-37; Dan. 6:22).
      (17) By faith the violence of fire was quenched (v. 34; see Dan. 3:25).
      (18) By faith believers escaped the edge of the sword (v. 34; see 2 Ki. 6:14-17).
      (19) By faith weakness became strength (v. 34).

(20) By faith many waxed valiant in fight (v. 34).

(21) By faith many turned to flight the armies of aliens (v. 34).

(22) By faith women received their dead (v. 35; see 1 Ki. 17:24; 2 Ki. 4:35).

(23) By faith many endured torture (v. 35).

(24) By faith many endured imprisonment (v. 36; see 2 Chron. 16:10).

(25) By faith some endured temptation (v. 37; see Gen. 39:12).

(26) By faith some endured death by the sword, stoning, and by being sawn asunder (v. 36, 37); (see 2 Chron. 24:20-22; Mt. 23:35).

3. Faith deposited (11:13-16, 38-40). After reading all this one may well ask what possible goal could have sustained the faith of these suffering saints? The answer is given in the above verses. They deposited their faith in the vaults of that celestial city "which hath foundations, whose builder and maker is God" (11:10).

B. The pattern of faith (12).
  1. Look to the Son of God (12:1-3).
    a. We have already stated our convictions that Paul was the author of Hebrews. This amazing apostle was many things. He was a missionary, a soul-winner, a pastor, a great theologian, a tentmaker, etc. But in his spare time he also seemed to be a sports lover. Often in his writings, Paul uses sports as an analogy to get his point across. For example:
      (1) Wrestling: "For we wrestle not against flesh and blood, but against principalities, against powers, against the rulers of the darkness of this world, against spiritual wickedness in high places" (Eph. 6:12).
      (2) Boxing: "I have fought a good fight. . ." (2 Tim. 4:7). "So fight I, not as one that beateth the air" (1 Cor. 9:26).
      (3) Racing: "Know ye not that they which run in a race run all, but one receiveth the prize? So run that ye may obtain. . . . I therefore so run. . ." (1 Cor. 9:24, 26).
    b. Here in Hebrews 12 Paul chooses the third analogy—that of a footrace.
    c. "We also are compassed about with so great a cloud of witnesses" (12:1).
      (1) Great. We often feel (wrongly so) that we are all alone, as Elijah once did (1 Ki. 19:10, 14, 18).
      (2) Cloud. This underlines the word "great." The Greek here is not *nephele*, which refers to a detached and sharply outlined cloud, but *nephos*, speaking of a huge mass of clouds, covering the entire visible space of the heavens.
      (3) Witnesses. Who are these witnesses? They are not angels, for the Greek word is *marturos*, referring to

one who has both seen, heard, and performed something, usually while suffering at the time. It speaks of a well-qualified expert. The context strongly suggests that these witnesses are the faith heroes mentioned in chapter 11.

  d. "Let us lay aside every weight" (12:1). Here the word is *onkos* and refers to a bulk or mass. The concern of the Greek runner was not simply whether something was immoral or moral, but rather how it would affect his race. Thus, the enemy of the best is often not the worst, but the good.

  e. "And the sin which doth so easily beset us" (12:1). The word "beset" means "to surround, to cleverly encircle, to ambush." It speaks of a loosely-fitting robe. Paul may have had in mind the sin of unbelief here, but it also refers to any sin the believer allows to upset him.

  f. "Let us run with patience the race that is set before us" (12:1). Note the implications of this statement.
    (1) Every believer has been entered in this race by God himself. It is not just for pastors and missionaries. Note: The usual word for race *(dromos)* is not used here, but rather the Greek word *agon*, from which we get our English word "agony." This is a serious race.
    (2) The pace of each runner is set by God.
    (3) The object of the race is to please God and win rewards. Its goal is *not* heaven!
    (4) Every runner is expected to win.

  g. "Looking unto Jesus" (12:2). The phrase here speaks of a steadfast, intent, and continuous gaze. How easy it is to get our eyes off him and look to the left or right.

    Perhaps to our left we see another runner behind us. It may be that a runner is far ahead of us on the right. This then can produce *pride* (as we view the left runner) and *envy* (as we see the runner on the right). Both are sin and cause us to slow down! We are instead to keep looking at Jesus.
    (1) If you would be disappointed, look to others.
    (2) If you would be discouraged, look to yourself.
    (3) If you would be delighted, look at Jesus.

  h. "The author and finisher of our faith" (12:2). Christ is both Founder and Finisher of the Christian faith. Confucius, Buddha, and Mohammed founded three worldwide religious movements, but death finished Confucius, Buddha, and Mohammed.

  i. "For the joy that was set before him endured the cross" (12:2). The nature of this joy is explained in Jude 1:24:

"Now unto him [Jesus] that is able to keep you from falling, and to present you faultless before the presence of his glory with exceeding joy" (see also Jn. 17:6-12, 26).

j. "Despising the shame, and is set down at the right hand . . . of God" (12:2; see Phil. 2:5-11).

k. "For consider him . . ." (12:3). Time and again we are driven back to the Gospel accounts by the writers of the epistles.

2. Submit to the discipline of God (12:4-11).

a. Reasons for discipline:

(1) To make us think about God and his Word. "And ye have forgotten the exhortation which speaketh unto you as unto children" (12:5). This is often our problem—we forget! David admonished: "Bless the Lord, O my soul, and forget not all his benefits" (Ps. 103:2). The exhortation here in Hebrews 12:5, 6 is taken from Proverbs 3:11, 12.

(2) To prove that God loves us (12:6). "For whom the Lord loveth he chasteneth, and scourgeth every son whom he receiveth." The word "chasten" here refers to that instruction in right behavior. The word "scourge" speaks of that correction in wrong behavior.

(3) To prove we really belong to God (12:7, 8). "If ye endure chastening, God dealeth with you as with sons; for what son is he whom the father chasteneth not? But if ye be without chastisement, whereof all are partakers, then are ye bastards, and not sons" (12:7, 8).

(4) To make us more like Jesus (12:10). "That we might be partakers of his holiness."

b. Reactions to discipline (12:5, 11):

(1) The believer can despise it, that is, treat it too lightly (as Esau did his birthright).

(2) The believer can faint under it, that is, treat it too seriously.

(3) The believer can be exercised by it. The real question is not simply how many mistakes a Christian makes, but how much he learns through those mistakes! The Psalms speak concerning this:

"Blessed is the man whom thou chastenest, O Lord, and teachest him out of thy law" (94:12).

"Before I was afflicted I went astray: but now have I kept thy word" (119:67).

"It is a good thing for me that I have been afflicted: that I might learn thy statutes" (119:71).

"I know, O Lord, that thy judgments are right and that thou in faithfulness hast afflicted me" (119:75).

c. Results of discipline (12:11):

"Now no chastening for the present seemeth to be joyous, but grievous: nevertheless afterward it yieldeth the peaceable fruit of righteousness unto them which are exercised thereby" (12:11).

Fifth warning—about disagreeing with God's Word (12:25).

3. Prepare for the kingdom of God (12:12-29).

a. Lift up your drooping hands. Begin working for Christ (12:12).

b. Strengthen your weak knees. Begin praying (12:12).

c. Make straight paths for your feet. Homer Kent writes:

"If one's feet are lame, special care must be taken that the path on which they walk has no dangerous obstacles. Spiritually speaking, the one whose faith is weak must not venture into areas where his spiritual strength is insufficient. Otherwise the . . . lame believer may aggravate his lameness into a dislocation of the limbs." (Epistle to the Hebrews, p. 265)

C. The performance of faith (13).

1. Its duties:

a. Continue to love the brethren (13:1).

b. Continue to show hospitality to strangers (13:2). The "entertaining of angels" of this verse may refer to Genesis 18.

c. Remember the prisoners and the ill-treated (13:3). These prisoners may be those in bonds (like Paul himself) for their testimony.

d. Let marriage be held in honor among all. The seventh commandment has been, is, and will continue to be required by God for man (saved and unsaved alike) to obey—"Thou shalt not commit adultery."

e. Let your way of life be free from the love of money (13:5).

f. Remember those who lead you and teach you God's Word (13:7).

g. Don't be carried away by varied and strange teachings (13:9).

h. Continue offering up a sacrifice of praise to God (13:15; see also 1 Pet. 2:5, 9). In addition to this, the believer is commanded to offer up the sacrifice of his own body (Rom. 12:1) and that of good works (Heb. 13:16).

i. Obey your teachers and submit to them (13:17). The reason is that someday God will hold those leaders accountable.

j. Pray for Christian leaders, especially the author of the book of Hebrews.

2. Its delights: Our most holy faith brings with it many precious blessings. Note:

a. ". . . for he [God] hath said, I will never leave thee, nor forsake thee" (13:5).

b. "So that we may boldly say, The Lord is my helper, and I will not fear what man shall do unto me" (13:6).

c. "Jesus Christ, the same yesterday, and to-day, and for ever" (13:8).

d. "We have an altar, whereof they [the Temple priests] have no right to eat which serve the tabernacle" (13:10).

e. "For here have we no continuing city, but we seek one to come" (13:14).

f. "Now the God of peace, that brought again from the dead our Lord Jesus, that great shepherd of the sheep, through the blood of the everlasting covenant, make you perfect in every good work to do his will, working in you that which is well-pleasing in his sight, through Jesus Christ; to whom be glory for ever and ever. Amen" (13:20, 21).

JUDE

INTRODUCTION:

1. Jude was the brother of James (author of the book of James and first pastor of the Jerusalem church in Acts 15) and half-brother of Jesus. (See Mk. 6:3.)

2. Along with his brothers, Jude did not believe in the ministry of Jesus until after the resurrection (Jn. 7:3-8). But sometime between the resurrection and ascension both boys were gloriously saved. They were present (along with their mother Mary) in the upper room just prior to Pentecost (Acts 1:13).

3. Jude was apparently married and was accompanied by his wife as he performed missionary work (1 Cor. 9:5).

4. "The beginning of the age of the Church is described in the Acts of the Apostles. The end of the Church Age is set forth in the Epistle of Jude, which might well be called the Acts of the Apostates.

Jude is the only book in all God's Word entirely devoted to the great apostasy which is to come upon Christendom before the Lord Jesus Christ returns. This brief message of twenty-five verses is the vestibule to the Revelation. . . . Without Jude, the prophetic picture which begins with the teachings of Christ in the Gospels and develops throughout the epistle would be incomplete. See Luke 18:8; 2 Thessalonians 2:3; 1 Timothy 4:1; 2 Timothy 4:3; 2 Peter 2:1; 3:3. Jude

brings the teachings of the entire Bible about apostasy to a tremendous climax. He takes us back to the very dawn of human history. We are reminded of apostasy at the gate of Eden and within God's ancient people Israel. Our thoughts are turned to princes and prophets, to saints and sinners, to eternal fire and everlasting darkness, to the sea and to the stars, to past judgments and future glory." (Dr. S. Maxwell Coder, *Jude, the Acts of the Apostles*, pp. 3, 4)

5. Jude has been called the Judges of the New Testament.

6. It is very similar to 2 Peter. Peter placed the ministry of false teachers in the future (2 Pet. 2:1), whereas Jude saw them as already present (1:4).

7. Jude refers to two noncanonical books. They are:
   a. *The Assumption of Moses* (Jude 1:9)
   b. *The Book of Enoch* (1:14, 15)
   Paul had previously also done this. (See Acts 17:28; 2 Tim. 3:8.)

8. "Jude was intending to write an epistle regarding 'our common salvation' (1:3), when the Spirit detoured him to write concerning the apostasy. It is a graphic and striking description of the apostasy. What was a little cloud the size of a man's hand in Jude's day is, in our day, a storm of hurricane proportions—because we are in the apostasy of which he foretold. It is a question now of how much worse it can become before genuine believers are taken out by the rapture." (*Thru the Bible*, p. 293, J. Vernon McGee)

I. The Problem of Apostasy (1:1-4).
   A. The author of this epistle. "Jude, the servant of Jesus Christ, and brother of James" (1:1). We note Jude does not "pull rank" here by reminding us that he was an actual half-brother of Jesus.
   B. The recipients of this epistle. "To them that are sanctified by God the Father, and preserved in Jesus Christ, and called" (v. 1).

   The phrase "preserved in Jesus Christ," should be translated "kept *for* Jesus Christ." It is used of Peter's and Paul's imprisonments in Acts 12:5 and 25:4, 21. (See also 1 Pet. 1:4.)

   Even before Jude warns about the terrible apostasy which had already settled down upon the world of his day and would grow progres-

The Arrogant Apostate

JUDE

Jude

The Problem of Apostasy
JUDE 1:1-4

The Description of Apostasy
JUDE 1:4, 8, 10, 16, 19

Historical Examples and Causes of Apostasy
JUDE 1:5-7, 9, 11

The Metaphors of Apostasy
JUDE 1:12, 13

The Judgment upon Apostasy
JUDE 1:14, 15

The Safeguards Against Apostasy
JUDE 1:20-25

sively worse, he reassures the believers that they are kept for Christ! Here he supplies us with the inspired answer to the prayer of Christ: "Holy Father, keep through thine own name those whom thou hast given me" (Jn. 17:11). (See also 1 Thess. 5:23.)

Jude continues with: "Mercy unto you, and peace, and love, be multiplied" (v. 2). S. Maxwell Coder writes:

"There is an *upward* look in the word *mercy*, an *inward* look in the word *peace*, and an *outward* look in the word *love*. These three related us properly to *God*, to our *own inner being*, and to our *brethren* around us. When they are multiplied, and only then, will we be able to cope with the great apostasy." (*Jude, the Acts of the Apostates*, p. 13)

C. The purpose of this epistle (vs. 3, 4).

"Beloved, when I gave all diligence to write unto you of the common salvation, it was needful for me to write unto you, and exhort you that ye should earnestly contend for the faith which was once delivered unto the saints. For there are certain men crept in unawares, who were before of old ordained to this condemnation, ungodly men, turning the grace of our God into lasciviousness, and denying the only Lord God, and our Lord Jesus Christ."

We note:

1. Jude's compulsion: "It was needful for me" (3). The meaning of the word *needful* is "to bear down upon, to compress." God literally pressured Jude to write this (see also 1 Cor. 9:16).

2. Jude's command: "That ye should earnestly contend for the faith which was once delivered unto the saints" (3).

He said we are to contend, but not be contentious. For the latter, see Titus 3:9. To *contend* involves both defense and offense. An excellent Old Testament example of this is found in Nehemiah 4:17, 18.

Note also what we are to contend for. It is *the faith*, that is, the entire Word of God. Furthermore, this faith (in the Greek language) was once for all delivered unto the saints! John would later warn all not to *add to* or *take from* this faith (see Rev. 22:18, 19).

3. Jude's concern. "For there are certain men crept in unawares . . ." (4). The word "unawares" is literally "having settled down alongside" (see also 2 Pet. 2:1).

II. The Description of Apostasy. In no less than sixteen tense and terrible terms, Jude describes the filthy fruit of apostasy. Before listing these, let us define what an apostate really is. S. Maxwell Coder writes: "An apostate has received light, but not life. He may have received, in some degree, the written Word; but he has not received the living Word, the Son of God" (*Jude, the Acts of the Apostates*, p. 21).

(See also 2 Thess. 2:10; Acts 8:13-23.)

Now let us consider their doctrine.

A. They are ungodly men (4). This means they are destitute of reverential awe toward God (2 Tim. 3:5).

B. They twist God's grace into licentiousness (4). This is what the cults of the day do.

C. They deny and say harsh things about the Person and work of Christ (4, 15). This is what the heretics of the day do (Titus 1:16).

D. They are given over to sensuous dreams (8).

E. They defile the flesh (theirs and others') (8).

F. They reject both divine and human authority (8).

G. They ridicule the existence of angels (8).

H. They mock and curse at anything they do not understand (10).

I. They "do their thing" like dumb and unreasoning animals (10).

J. They are grumblers and fault-finders (16).

K. They follow after their own lusts (16).

L. They are arrogant (16).

M. They flatter people, using flowery language for the sake of gaining an advantage (16).

N. They are divisive (19).

O. They are worldly-minded (19).

P. They are devoid of the Spirit (19).

III. The Historical Examples of Apostasy (5, 6, 7, 9, 11). In the above verses Jude describes seven individuals or groups of individuals who fell into apostasy.

A. Israel:

"I will therefore put you in remembrance, though ye once knew this, how that the Lord, having saved the people out of the land of Egypt, afterward destroyed them that believed not" (5).

1. Question: When and where did this take place? It began at Kadesh-barnea shortly after Israel had left Egypt for Palestine. Here at Kadesh they were influenced by the "mixed multitude" (an unsaved group of Egyptians and non-Hebrews) who had left Egypt with them, causing them to rebel against God's Word.

2. Question: Does this mean that all the children of Israel became apostates, and, upon dying, went into eternal hell?

It does not, for God *never* sends his people to hell. (See Ex. 3:7; 5:1; Deut. 33:29.) What it does mean is that it is tragically possible for even believers to become ensnared into the trap of apostasy and suffer for it without actually becoming apostates themselves. (See also 1 Cor. 10:1-12; Heb. 3:12, 18, 19; 4:1.) The word *apollumi*, translated "destroyed" in this verse, is used elsewhere as "physical death" (Lk. 15:17).

B. The angels.

"And the angels which kept not their first estate, but left their own habitation, he hath reserved in everlasting chains under darkness unto the judgment of the great day" (6).

We shall deal with this group of apostates after discussing the sin and destruction of Sodom and Gomorrah.

C. The citizens of Sodom and Gomorrah:

"Even as Sodom and Gomorrah, and the cities about them in like manner, giving themselves over to fornication, and going after strange flesh, are set forth for an example, suffering the vengeance of external fire" (7).

Some of the most depraved sexual perverts of ancient times lived in Sodom. God destroyed this cesspool of sin in Genesis 19.

Let us now go back to the wicked angels of verse 6, for a similarity may exist between their sin and that of Sodom. Here we must consider two things:

1. The fact of their sin. The Scriptures are explicit that there exist two kinds of fallen angels—the unchained and those chained. The unchained at present have access to high places and to the bodies of unsaved men (Eph. 6:12; Lk. 8:27; Mk. 1:23). These unchained angels will, of course, someday be judged by God. Their one main sin was that of following Satan in his foul rebellion against God (1 Cor. 6:3; Isa. 14:12-17; Ezek. 28:12-19). The chained are at present already incarcerated, as stated by both Peter (2 Pet. 2:4) and Jude. It was apparently to this place that certain unchained fallen angels on two separate occasions begged Christ not to send them "before their time" (Mk. 1:24; Lk. 8:31; Mt. 8:28).

2. The nature of their sin. It is believed that the sin which led to this premature punishment of a limited number of fallen angels can be directly linked to Genesis 6. It will be remembered that in this chapter we read of the "sons of God" marrying the "daughters of men." Many believe this to be a reference to fallen angels (sons of God) actually mating with earthly women (daughters of men). Dr. Kenneth Wuest, Greek scholar, brings out the fact that the words in Jude "in like manner" are an adverbial accusative, referring back to the phrase "giving themselves over to fornication." In other words, the comparison is made between the sin of Sodom and the sin of these angels. What was sin of Sodom? The answer of course was the sexual perversion. Wuest writes:

> "The word 'strange' is the translation of the Greek word *heteras* which means 'another of a different kind.' In committing this sin of fornication, the angels transgressed the limits of their own kind, and invaded the realm of another order of being. The sin of Sodom was the transgressing of the male beyond the limitations imposed by God." (*Word Studies in First Peter*, p. 103)

3. One final thought concerning this passage and this subject. Jude is admonishing his readers to remember three well-known Old Testament examples of apostasy. These were:

    a. The historical example of Israel's unbelief.

    b. The historical example of those angels who kept not their first estate.

    c. The historical example of Sodom's destruction.

    Concerning the first example, the minds of Jude's readers would immediately go back to Numbers 14, the account of Israel's great rebellion at Kadesh-barnea. As they read the third example, they would at once remember the frightful passage recorded in Genesis 19, the fiery destruction of Sodom on the plains. But what other chapter would come to mind concerning the second historical example if Genesis 6 is ruled out? Note: At this point we have described for us representatives of each of the three great classes of God's creatures mentioned in Scripture: saved men, angels, and unsaved men.

D. The devil.

"Yet Michael the archangel, when contending with the devil he disputed about the body of Moses, durst not bring against him a railing accusation, but said, The Lord rebuke thee" (9).

In this passage Satan is indirectly brought in as an apostate.

1. The source of this statement: It appears to have been quoted from a first-century book entitled *The Assumption of Moses*. A copy of this was found in 1861. This, of course, does not mean that the entire book was inspired simply because Jude takes one little part from it. Paul quoted from Titus 1:2. He also mentions the name of two of the magicians in Egypt, although their names are not mentioned in the Old Testament (2 Tim. 3:8). James also tells us that Elijah's prayer caused a three-and-a-half-year drought, a fact not recorded in the Old Testament account (Jas. 5:17; cf. 1 Ki. 17:1; 18:1).

2. The theology of this statement: Why did Satan desire Moses' body? *The Assumption of Moses* gives two reasons why Moses should not have a decent burial.

    a. Because Moses had formerly murdered an Egyptian.

    b. Because he (Satan) was king of death and had a right to all dead bodies.

    Two other reasons have been offered by church theologians to explain this, both of which seem more reasonable than the above two.

    c. Because Satan wanted the body to be found by Israel and worshiped as a sacred relic. We do know that the nation would later worship the serpent of brass he had once made (2 Ki. 18:4).

    d. Because Satan desired to keep Moses from appearing with Elijah on the Mount of Transfiguration (Mt. 17).

3. The hero of this statement. In Deuteronomy 34:5, 6 we read, "So Moses, the servant of the Lord, died there in the land of Moab, according to the word of the Lord. And he buried him in a valley in the land of Moab . . . but no man knoweth of his sepulcher unto this day." Apparently the "he" in this verse is a reference to the archangel Michael, the hero of this statement. He is mentioned three times in the Old Testament (Dan. 10:13, 21; 12:1) and again in the New Testament, in addition to the reference in Jude (Rev. 12:7-9).

E. Cain. "Woe unto them! for they have gone in the way of Cain" (11). The way (apostasy) of Cain is described in Genesis 4:1-7. He brought a bloodless sacrifice to God. That is the way of the apostate liberals of our day. They look to culture instead of Calvary. (See 1 Jn. 3:11, 12.)

F. Balaam. "And ran greedily after the error of Balaam for reward" (11). Balaam was a false money-grabbing prophet mentioned in Numbers 22-25. Thus the error of Balaam was making merchandise of the gospel ministry. Many modern apostates do this.

G. Korah. "And perished in the gainsaying of Korah" (1:11). In Numbers 16 Korah led a rebellion against Moses, the official spokesman for God. For this great sin he was sent down into the pit, the earth opening up its bowels and swallowing him. Present-day apostates speak evil against pastors, missionaries, Bible teachers, and other God-appointed men.

In summarizing this section, note the words of S. Maxwell Coder:

"Cain was a tiller of the soil; Balaam was a prophet, Korah was a prince in Israel. One reason for this selection of three men may be to demonstrate that apostasy is not confined to one class of persons. This evil is not peculiar to religious leaders. It touches prophets, princes, and people alike. There are apostates in pulpit, palace, and poorhouse." (*Jude, the Acts of the Apostates*, p. 66)

IV. The Metaphors of Apostasy.

"These men are those who are hidden reefs in your love-feasts when they feast with you without fear, caring for themselves; clouds without water, carried along by winds; autumn trees without fruit, doubly dead, uprooted; wild waves of the sea, casting up their own shame like foam; wandering stars, for whom the black darkness has been reserved forever" (vs. 12, 13, *New American Standard Bible*).

Once again, to quote from S. Maxwell Coder:

"The more minutely we examine this great epistle, the most impressive becomes its delineation of the doctrine of apostasy. Jude has now covered the whole creation, from angels to men and brute beasts. There yet remains the realm of nature, and in five flashing inspired word-pictures he brings before us the earth, the air, the trees, the sea, and the starry heavens, to complete the panorama needed to provide the church with a magnificent final summary of conditions as they are to be in Christendom just before the scenes of Revelation are unveiled." (*Jude, the Acts of the Apostates*, p. 75)

A. Hidden rocks. Describing the unseen dangers of apostasy. We note that these rocks are hidden in the Christian love-feasts, a reference to the Lord's Table in the early days of the church. How are we to understand this? Paul explains it in 1 Corinthians 11:17-30. The first-century church had a full meal in connection with Holy Communion. But some of these apostates (or perhaps believers influenced by apostasy) had joined themselves at these gatherings. As a result, some practiced gluttony and drunkenness, while others were actually going hungry. Divine judgment had taken many in death due to this.

B. Waterless clouds. Describing the false promises of apostasy. (See also Prov. 25:14.) These clouds are said to be carried along by the winds. Doubtless the "winds" here are demonic activity. Apostates are the captives of Satan. For a refreshing contrast, see 2 Peter 1:21.

C. Autumn trees. Describing the barren profession of apostasy. The Greek phrase here is literally "late autumn trees," suggesting the fact that the great apostasy is to come as the autumn of the Church Age is waning and the winter of judgment is nigh. (See also Mt. 13:30; 15:30; Prov. 2:22.)

D. Wild waves. Describing the wasted effort of apostasy. The sea is often a symbol for evil in the Bible (Isa. 57:20, 21). The apostasy of the last days will be characterized by much learning (2 Tim. 3:7) and mighty works (Mt. 7:22), but neither to any avail.

E. Wandering stars. This describes the aimless purpose of apostasy—perhaps the most frightening characteristic of apostasy.

A quote from S. Maxwell Coder is appropriate here:

"By way of contrast, true believers enjoy a lifelong love-feast. They are borne along by the Holy Spirit, unmoved by winds of false doctrine. After a life of fruitfulness, they go home to be with Christ, in glory and honor. Forever afterward they dwell in light unutterable. Instead of being lifeless, dangerous rocks, they are living stones (1 Pet. 2:5). Rather than waterless clouds they are sources of living water (Jn. 7:38). Far from being dead trees, they are called 'trees of righteousness, the planting of the Lord' (Isa. 61:3). In contrast with raging waves, their peace is like a river and their righteousness as the waves of the sea (Isa. 48:18). Whereas wandering stars have reserved for them the blackness of darkness forever, true believers shall shine as the stars forever and ever" (Dan. 12:3). (*Jude, the Acts of the Apostates*, pp. 82, 83)

V. The Judgment of Apostasy.

"And Enoch also, the seventh from Adam, prophesied of these, saying, Behold, the Lord cometh with ten thousands of his saints, to execute judgment upon all, and to convince all that are ungodly among them of all their ungodly deeds which they have ungodly committed, and of all their hard speeches which ungodly sinners have spoken against him" (1:14, 15).

A. The source of this statement. Around 100 B.C., a non-canonical book entitled *The Book of Enoch* was written. It contained 108 chapters. In 1773 a copy of this work was discovered. The apostle Jude was inspired by God to take the words which are found here in verses 14, 15 from this book.

B. The speaker of this statement. The book, of course, was not written by Enoch, but the statement here was apparently taken from his text. Both Enoch and Noah were fearless preachers of prophecy and righteousness. (See also 2 Pet. 2:5.)

The amazing faith of this pre-Flood prophet may be seen in that he predicted the Second Coming of Christ centuries before our Lord came the *first* time! Enoch thus predicts his coming in Genesis, while John proclaims it in Revelation (see Rev. 19:11-14). Both men refer to the same event.

    1. He comes with his saints (Col. 3:4; 1 Thess. 3:13).

    2. He comes to judge (Heb. 9:26-28; 2 Pet. 3:7).

VI. The Safeguards Against Apostasy (vs. 20-25).

  A. We are to build. "But ye, beloved, building up yourselves on your most holy faith" (20). This is accomplished through the Word of God. (See 2 Pet. 1:5-7; Acts 20:32; Rom. 10:17; 1 Pet. 2:2; 1 Jn. 2:5.)

  B. We are to pray. "Praying in the Holy Ghost" (v. 20). See Ephesians 6:18.

  C. We are to keep ourselves in God's love. In verse 1 we are kept for Jesus, but here we are to keep in God's love. How is this done? While the believer cannot escape the *boundary* of God's love (Ps. 139:7-12), he can withdraw himself from the full *blessings* of this love (Jn. 15:9).

  D. We are to anticipate the rapture.

    "Looking for the mercy of our Lord Jesus Christ unto eternal life" (21; see also Lk. 12:37; Titus 2:13).

  E. We are to win the lost (22, 23).

    "And of some have compassion, making a difference: And others save with fear, pulling them out of the fire; hating even the garment spotted by the flesh."

  S. Maxwell Coder writes:

    "In a brief manual for personal work, three groups of people are set before us:

      1. Those who need compassionate tenderness, because sincere doubts trouble them.

      2. Those requiring urgent boldness if they are to be snatched from an eternity of fiery judgment.

      3. Those who must be dealt with in cautious compassion lest the soulwinner himself be contaminated by their sins."

    (*Jude, The Acts of the Apostates*, p. 113)

    The following examples are suggested to represent each of these three groups:

    First group: Those individuals troubled by alcohol and drugs.

    Second group: Unsaved persons being strongly influenced to join one of the perverted cults of Christianity such as the Mormons.

    Third group: A beautiful woman concerning immorality in her life.

    In closing, we note Jude's great and grand and glorious benediction. "Now unto him that is able to keep you from falling, and to present you faultless before the presence of his glory with exceeding joy, To the only wise God our Saviour, be glory and majesty, dominion and power, both now and ever. Amen" (24, 25).

1 JOHN

INTRODUCTION:

1. The Spirit of God directed John the apostle to pen five of the New Testament epistles. Apart from Paul, no other author would write as much sacred Scripture in the New Testament as he did. His five books are: The Gospel of John, three epistles, the Revelation. The following distinction between these books is offered:

    Gospel of John
  Speaks of salvation
  The past
  Christ the Prophet
  The cross
    Epistles of John
  Speak of sanctification
  The present
  Christ the Priest
  The *koinonia* (fellowship)
    Revelation of John
  Speaks of glorification
  The future
  Christ the King
  The crown

2. John wrote his Gospel account to prove the *deity* of Christ. He now writes his epistles to prove the *humanity* of Christ. Heretical emphasis on both points existed during his time.

3. The *New Scofield Bible* suggests:

    "It [1 John] is a family letter from the Father to His 'little children' who are in the world. With the possible exception of the Song of Solomon, it is the most intimate of the inspired writings. The sin of a Christian is treated as a child's offense against his Father, and is dealt with as a family matter (1:9; 2:1)." (p. 1342)

4. In the Gospel, John describes us as sheep in God's fold, in the epistle as members in his family, and in the Revelation as priests in his kingdom (Jn. 10; 1 Jn. 2; Rev. 1).

5. It is believed by some that John directed his epistles to the same readers who would later receive the book of Revelation—that is, the seven churches in Asia Minor.

    This first epistle is somewhat difficult to outline in a chapter-by-chapter fashion. The following, therefore, is a tenfold subject-matter outline, all ten areas describing the key theme of 1 John, which is *fellowship*.

I. The Source of This Fellowship (1:1, 2; 3:5, 8, 16; 4:9, 10, 14, 19; 5:20). The source of this fellowship is the *incarnation* and *crucifixion* of our Lord Jesus Christ.

  A. "That which was from the beginning, which we have heard, which we have seen with our eyes, which we have looked upon, and our hands have handled, of the Word of life; (For the life was manifested, and we have seen it, and bear witness, and shew unto you that eternal life, which was with the Father, and was manifested unto us)" (1:1, 2).

  B. "And ye know that he was manifested to take away our sins; and in him is no sin. . . . He that committeth sin is of the devil; for the devil sinneth from the beginning. For this purpose the Son of God was manifested, that he might destroy the works of the devil" (3:5, 8).

  C. "Hereby perceive we the love of God, because he laid down his life for us: and we ought to lay down our lives for the brethren" (3:16).

  D. "In this was manifested the love of God toward us, because that God sent his only begotten Son into the world, that we might live through him. Herein is love, not that we loved God, but that he loved us, and sent his Son to be the propitiation for our sins" (4:9, 10).

The Fellowship Epistle

JOHN

1 John

The SOURCE
of this fellowship
JESUS CHRIST
His incarnation **1:1, 2; 3:5, 8**
His crucifixion **3:16; 4:9, 10, 14**

The PURPOSE
of this fellowship
That we might know and love God and his people
(see also 1:4; 2:26; 3:13, 22; 5:13-15)

The REQUIREMENTS
for this fellowship
WALK in the light **(1:7)**
RECOGNIZE our sins **(1:8)**
CONFESS our sins **(1:9)**
KEEP his commandments **(2:3-8; 5:2, 3)**
ABIDE in Christ **(2:28)**
KEEP unspotted from the world **(2:3; 5:21)**
MINISTER to the brethren in need **(3:17)**

The TESTS
of this fellowship
A quick quiz to determine one's fellowship
Do I conduct my life down here in view of the rapture? **(3:3)**
      YES ☐   NO ☐
Do I continually dwell in sin? **(3:6, 9; 5:18)**
      YES ☐   NO ☐
Do I hate my spiritual brother? **(4:20)**
      YES ☐   NO ☐
Do I desire to help my brother? **(3:17)**
      YES ☐   NO ☐
Do I really love my brother? **(4:7, 21)**
      YES ☐   NO ☐
Do I really love God? **(5:2)**
      YES ☐   NO ☐
Do I enjoy a rapport with other servants of God? **(4:6)**
      YES ☐   NO ☐
Am I plagued with constant fear? **(4:18)**
      YES ☐   NO ☐
Am I able to overcome the world? **(5:4)**
      YES ☐   NO ☐
Can I recognize false doctrine when it comes my way? **(4:1-3)**
      YES ☐   NO ☐
Am I straight on the deity of Christ? **(4:15; 5:1)**
      YES ☐   NO ☐
Am I straight on the work of Christ? **(5:13, 20)**
      YES ☐   NO ☐

The MAINTENANCE
of this fellowship
of the SON of GOD **(2:1, 2)**
by the SPIRIT of GOD **(2:20, 27)**
from the SAINT of GOD **(1:8, 9)**

The FAMILY MEMBERS
of this fellowship
Little children **(2:13)**
Young men **(2:14)**
Fathers **(2:14)**

The ENEMIES
of this fellowship
"Love not the world, neither the things that are in the world . . . for all that is in the world . . . is not of the Father" **(2:15, 16)**

The EVIL SYSTEMS in the world
ACTS 17:24; JN. 3:16; 1 JN. 5:19; JAS. 4:4; JAS. 1:27 ROM. 12:2; 1 COR. 11:32; 2:17
The EVIL SEDUCERS in the world
2:22; 2:26
The EVIL SPIRITS in the world 4:1-3

The PROMISES
of this fellowship
● Promise of eternal life **2:25**
● Confidence at the rapture **2:28**
● A new body like his **3:2**
● Confidence at the judgment **4:17**
● Boldness in service **4:18**

The WITNESSES
to this fellowship
IN HEAVEN   ON EARTH
   THE FATHER   WATER (baptism)
   THE SON   BLOOD (communion)
   THE HOLY SPIRIT

SEPARATION
from this fellowship
Fellowship with **God** will keep one from **sin** or **sin** will keep one from fellowship with **God.**

E. "And we have seen and do testify that the Father sent the Son to be the Saviour of the world" (4:14).

F. "If a man say, I love God, and hateth his brother, he is a liar: for he that loveth not his brother whom he hath seen, how can he love God whom he hath not seen?" (4:20).

It can be readily seen by the above verses that Jesus Christ did not come into this world simply to preach the gospel, but that he came so there might be a gospel to preach.

II. The Purpose of This Fellowship.

A. That we might know more about the Father:
1. He is light (1:5).
2. He is righteous (3:7).
3. He is omniscient (3:20).
4. He is love (4:8, 16).
5. He is invisible (4:12).
6. He is life (5:11).

B. That we might love the Father (4:19).

C. That we might understand the Father's love (3:16).

D. That we might allow the Father's love to be perfected in us (2:5; 4:12).

E. That we might love the family of God (3:11, 23; 4:7, 11).

F. That we might experience the fullness of joy (1:4).

G. That we might receive assurance concerning our salvation (5:13).

H. That we might receive assurance concerning our prayers (3:22; 5:14, 15).

I. That we might not be seduced by the world (2:26).

J. That we might not be surprised in tribulation (3:13).

III. The Requirements for This Fellowship.

A. We must walk in the light (1:7).
"But if we walk in the light, as he is in the light, we have fellowship one with another."

B. We must recognize our sins (1:8).
"If we say that we have no sin, we deceive ourselves, and the truth is not in us."

C. We must confess our sins (1:9).
"If we confess our sins, he is faithful and just to forgive us our sins, and to cleanse us from all unrighteousness."

The word "confess" here is the Greek word *homologeo,* which means "to agree with." Thus, when the Holy Spirit points out a sin in our life we are immediately to agree with him. While the blood of Christ will cleanse us from every sin, it will not cleanse us of even one excuse.

D. We must keep his commandments (2:3-8; 5:2, 3). Some have imagined a contradiction in these verses. Note:

"Brethren, I write no new commandment unto you, but an old commandment which ye had from the beginning . . . Again a new commandment I write unto you" (2:7, 8).

However, upon close inspection, this is a glorious *addition* rather than a *contradiction*.

1. The old commandment:
"Thou shalt not avenge, nor bear any grudge against the children of thy people,

but thou shalt love thy neighbor as thyself: I am the Lord" (Lev. 19:18).

"But the stranger who dwelleth with you shall be unto you as one born among you, and thou shalt love him as thyself; for ye were sojourners in the land of Egypt: I am the Lord your God" (Lev. 19:34; see also Deut. 10:19).

Thus, the Old Testament command required love as a basis of fellowship. But Jesus added to the intensity of this love while he was upon the earth. Observe his words:

2. The new commandment:
"A new commandment I give unto you, that ye love one another; as I have loved you, that ye also love one another (Jn. 13:34; see also Jn. 15:12).

This new command was given during the Last Supper in the upper room. John would never forget that sacred occasion.

E. We must abide in Christ (2:28).
"And now, little children, abide in him . . ." (See also Jn. 15.)

F. We must keep ourselves unspotted from the world. This includes both immorality (3:3) and idolatry (5:21).

G. We must minister to our brethren in need (3:17).
"But whosoever hath this world's good, and seeth his brother have need, and shutteth up his bowels of compassion from him, how dwelleth the love of God in him?"

IV. The Tests of This Fellowship. How can we really know that he has indeed saved us and that we are daily walking with him in fellowship? John proposes a list of test questions to help us in determining both our sonship and fellowship.

A. Do I conduct my life down here in view of the rapture?
"And every man that hath this hope in him purifieth himself even as he is pure" (3:3).

B. Do I continually dwell in sin?
"Whosoever abideth in him sinneth not; whosoever sinneth hath not seen him, neither known him. . . . Whosoever is born of God doth not commit sin; for his seed remaineth in him, and he cannot sin, because he is born of God" (3:6, 9).

"We know that whosoever is born of God sinneth not, but he that is begotten of God keepeth himself, and that wicked one toucheth him not" (5:18).

These verses, of course, do not teach sinless perfection. The Greek verbs are all in the present tense referring to the *constant* practices of sin. Thus, while we may not be *sinless,* John nevertheless states we should *sin less.*

C. Do I hate my spiritual brother?
"If a man says, I love God, and hateth his brother, he is a liar; for he that loveth not his brother, whom he hath seen, how can he love God, whom he hath not seen?" (4:20).

D. Do I desire to help my brother? (3:17).

E. Do I really love my brother? (4:7, 21). Here, of course, John is referring to *real* love! Biblical love may be defined as "unselfish concern for the welfare of another."

F. Do I really love God?

"By this we know that we love the children of God, when we love God, and keep his commandments" (5:2).

G. Do I enjoy a rapport with other servants of God?

"We are of God. He that knoweth God heareth us; he that is not of God heareth not us. By this know we the spirit of truth, and the spirit of error" (4:6).

H. Am I plagued with constant fear?

"There is no fear in love, but perfect love casteth out fear, because fear hath punishment. He that feareth is not made perfect in love" (4:18).

I. Am I able to overcome the world?

"For whatsoever is born of God overcometh the world; and this is the victory that overcometh the world, even our faith" (5:4).

J. Can I recognize false doctrine when it comes my way?

"Beloved, believe not every spirit, but try the spirits whether they are of God: because many false prophets are gone out into the world. Hereby know ye the Spirit of God: Every spirit that confesseth that Jesus Christ is come in the flesh is of God: And every spirit that confesseth not that Jesus Christ is come in the flesh is not of God: and this is that spirit of antichrist, whereof ye have heard that it should come; and even now already is it in the world" (4:1-3).

K. Am I straight on the deity of Christ?

"Whosoever shall confess that Jesus is the Son of God, God dwelleth in him, and he in God" (4:15).

"Whosoever believeth that Jesus is the Christ is born of God: and every one that loveth him that begat loveth him also that is begotten of him" (5:1).

L. Am I straight on the work of Christ? (5:13, 20). This, then, is the twelve-question test given by John. If one fails the test, he should conclude:

1. I am not saved (or, more likely)
2. I need to get into the Word, pray, and grow in grace by serving the Master.

V. The Maintenance of This Fellowship. What assurance do we have that the sweet communion enjoyed today will be with us when we awaken tomorrow? This fellowship is kept:

A. Through the occupation of the Son of God. Whatever happened to Jesus? Where is he and what is he doing? John answers these questions for us. He is with the Father and functions for the believer as:

1. Our Advocate.

"My little children, these things write I unto you, that ye sin not. And if any man sin, we have an advocate with the Father, Jesus Christ the righteous" (2:1).

The word "advocate" here is the Greek word *parakletos,* meaning "to call alongside of." The *New Scofield Bible* defines this office as follows:

"Advocacy is that work of Jesus Christ for sinning believers which He carries on with the Father, whereby, because of the

eternal efficacy of Christ's sacrifice, He restores them to fellowship." (p. 1343)

2. Our Propitiation.

"And he is the propitiation for our sins, and not for ours only, but also for the sins of the whole world" (2:2).

The root Greek word here translated "propitiation" is rendered "mercy seat" in Hebrews 9:5. The mercy seat was a part of that sacred Ark of the Covenant which rested in the Holy of Holies. Upon this golden mercy seat, every day of atonement, was sprinkled the blood of an animal (Lev. 16:14). This meant that the righteous sentence of the law had been executed, changing a judgment seat into a mercy seat (Heb. 9:11-15). It signified that man had thus been reconciled to God. The work of Christ thus served as a propitiation, whereby God's righteousness was forever satisfied. (See also 4:10.)

B. Through the habitation of the Spirit of God.

"But ye have an unction from the Holy One, and ye know all things. . . . But the anointing which ye have received of him abideth in you, and ye need not that any man teach you; but as the same anointing teacheth you of all things, and is truth, and is no lie, and even as it hath taught you, ye shall abide in him" (2:20, 27).

This verse does *not,* of course, deny the office of a human teacher (see Eph. 4:11, 12). What it does say is that we are to test any system of teaching by the Word of God.

C. Through the cooperation of the saint of God. How is the believer expected to help maintain his fellowship with heaven?

1. By recognizing his sins (1:8).
2. By confessing his sins (1:9).

VI. The Family Members of This Fellowship (2:13, 14). John here seems to classify God's family into three groups, according to their spiritual maturity.

A. Little children: "I write unto you, little children, because you have known the Father" (2:13). Here the Greek word is *paidia,* referring to a babe in Christ.

B. Young men: "I write unto you, young men, because ye have overcome the wicked one" (2:13). "I have written unto you, young men, because ye are strong, and the word of God abideth in you, and ye have overcome the wicked one" (2:14).

C. Fathers: "I write unto you, fathers, because ye have known him that is from the beginning, because ye have overcome the wicked one" (2:13). "I have written unto you, fathers, because ye have known him that is from the beginning" (2:14).

VII. The Enemies of This Fellowship. John lists at least three terrible forces which the believer must be on guard against lest his walk with Jesus be marred.

A. The systems of this world.

"Love not the world, neither the things that are in the world. If any man love the world, the love of the Father is not in him. For all that is in the world, the lust of the flesh, and the lust of the eyes, and the pride of life, is not of the Father, but is of the world. And the world passeth away, and the lust thereof: but he that doeth the will of God abideth for ever" (2:15-17).

1. A definition of this world. In the Bible there are several kinds of worlds.
   a. The physical world (Acts 17:24).
   b. The human world (Jn. 3:16).
   c. The evil world (1 Jn. 5:19; Jn. 12:31; 15:18).

   Obviously John had this third "world" in mind here. A believer *lives* on the first world, is a *member* of the second, but must *avoid* the third.

2. The divisions within this world:
   a. The lust of the flesh.
   b. The lust of the eyes.
   c. The pride of life.

   As John penned these words his thoughts may well have gone back to a beautiful garden and a terrible wilderness where two individuals were subjected to these satanic temptations by the devil himself!
   Eve and the beautiful garden (Gen. 3:6):
   "The woman saw that the tree was good for food" (the lust of the flesh).
   "And that it was pleasant to the eyes" (the lust of the eyes).
   "And a tree . . . to make one wise" (the pride of life).
   Christ and the terrible wilderness (Mt. 4:3, 8, 6):
   "Command that these stones be made bread" (the lust of the flesh).
   "He [Satan] showeth him [Jesus] all the kingdoms of the world" (the lust of the eyes).
   "Cast thyself down [from the pinnacle of the Temple] . . . for he shall give his angels charge concerning thee . . ." (the pride of life).

3. The deceitfulness of this world. Dr. Warren Wiersbe writes:
   "The world appeals to a Christian through the lust of the flesh, the lust of the eyes, and the pride of life. And once the world takes over in one of these areas, a Christian will soon realize it. He will lose his enjoyment of the Father's love and his desire to do the Father's will. The Bible will become boring and prayer a difficult chore. Even Christian fellowship may seem empty and disappointing. It is not that there is something wrong with others, however—what's wrong is the Christian's worldly heart." (*Be Real*, p. 74)

4. The destruction of this world. "And the world passeth away" (see also 2 Pet. 3:10-12).

B. The seducers of this world.
   "Little children, it is the last time: and as ye have heard that antichrist shall come, even now are there many antichrists; whereby we know that it is the last time" (2:18).
   "They went out from us, but they were not of us; for if they had been of us, they would no doubt have continued with us: but they went out, that they might be made manifest that they were not all of us" (2:19).

"Who is a liar but he that denieth that Jesus is the Christ? He is an antichrist, that denieth the Father and the Son" (2:22).
"These things have I written unto you concerning them that seduce you" (2:26).

C. The spirits of this world.
   "Hereby know we that we dwell in him, and he in us, because he hath given us of his Spirit" (4:13).

VIII. The Promises of This Fellowship.
A. Everlasting life with Christ.
   "And this is the promise that he hath promised us, even eternal life" (2:25).
B. Confidence at the rapture (2:28).
C. Receiving a new body like his resurrected body (3:2).
D. Confidence at the judgment seat (4:17).
E. Boldness in service down here (4:18).

IX. The Witnesses to This Fellowship.
   "This is he that came by water and blood, even Jesus Christ; not by water only, but by water and blood. And it is the Spirit that beareth witness, because the Spirit is truth. For there are three that bear record in heaven, the Father, the Word, and the Holy Ghost: and these three are one. And there are three that bear witness in earth, the Spirit, and the water, and the blood: and these three agree in one" (5:6-8).

   These verses are not among the easiest to interpret. Let us begin by observing that the last part of verse 7 is not listed in most ancient manuscripts. Thus, the first part of the verse should read, "Because there *are* three that bear record. . . ." This apparently refers to the three witnesses already mentioned in verse 6 and amplified in verse 8. What are these witnesses?
   A. The identity of the witnesses:
      1. the water
      2. the blood
      3. the Spirit
   B. The interpretation of the witnesses:
      1. The water and blood. There are at least four theories here.
         a. the baptism and death of Christ
         b. the water and blood that flowed from his side
         c. a symbolic reference to purification and redemption
         d. a symbolic reference to the ordinances of baptism and the Lord's Supper
         Most conservative theologians prefer the first of these, the baptism and death of Christ (Mt. 3:13-17; Heb. 9:12).
      2. The Spirit. There is no doubt that the Holy Spirit is in mind here.
   C. The implications of these witnesses. A twofold witness is all that is necessary for men (Deut. 19:15; Mt. 18:16; Jn. 8:17), but God has given us *three!*

X. The Separation from This Fellowship (5:16, 17).
   "There is a sin unto death" (5:16). The Bible teaches that my *union* with Christ is so strong that nothing can break it; but my *communion* with him is so fragile that the slightest sin shatters it. M. F. Unger writes:
   "Prayer and the Problem of Serious Sin, 16-17. It is possible for a true believer to fall into sin, 16a. If and when this happens, a fellow believer is to

pray for him, 16b. As a result God will give the sinning Christian preservation of physical life (not eternal life, for this life is eternal and unforfeitable). However, this intercession is effective only in the case of sin not unto physical death, 16c.

'There is a sin unto death,' 16d. This is persistent, willful sinning in a believer in which 'the flesh is destroyed' (physical death) so 'that the spirit might be saved' (1 Cor. 5:1-5; Acts 5:1-11; 1 Cor. 11:30). Both Saul and Samson are types of this very severe chastening in the Old Testament. This sin is not to be prayed for because it involved the execution of an immutable law of God unaltered by prayer, 16e. Sin has different degrees of seriousness, 16. 'All unrighteousness is sin, but there is a sin which is not unto [physical] death' (involving lesser chastisements, cf. 1 Cor. 11:30)." (*Unger's Bible Handbook*, p. 829)

2 JOHN

INTRODUCTION:
1. This is the only book in the Bible addressed to a woman.
2. It holds the same place in John's writings that Philemon holds in Paul's epistles.
3. It is the shortest book in the entire Bible.
4. John does not mention his own name or the name of this woman. This may have been done to prevent persecution from the Roman authorities of the time, who viewed Christianity as an unlawful religion.

I. This Lady Is Commended by the Apostle (vs. 1-4). "I rejoiced greatly that I found of thy children walking in truth." Here it perhaps should be noted that some Bible students believe the "elect lady" of this epistle was actually a local church. If this be the case, then the children here are church members. However, it is the view of this author that it is written to an actual woman and these are her children.

II. This Lady Is Commanded by the Apostle (vs. 5, 6). The commandment is actually twofold.
A. That she walk in truth.

B. That she walk in love. See also verse 3. How important it is not to separate these two. To practice truth without love leads to *legalism*. To employ love without truth leads to *liberalism*. Paul likewise combines these two: "But, speaking the truth in love, may grow up into him in all things, who is the head, even Christ" (Eph. 4:15).

III. This Lady Is Cautioned by the Apostle (vs. 7-13).
A. Look out for Satan (vs. 7, 9, 10, 11).

"For many deceivers are entered into the world, who confess not that Jesus Christ is come in the flesh. This is a deceiver and an antichrist. . . . Whosoever transgresseth, and abideth not in the doctrine of Christ, hath not God. He that abideth in the doctrine of Christ, he hath both the Father and the Son. If there come any unto you, and bring not this doctrine, receive him not into your house, neither bid him God speed: For he that biddeth him God speed is partaker of his evil deeds."

B. Look out for self (v. 8).

"Look to yourselves, that we lose not those things which we have wrought, but that we receive a full reward."

John wanted this beloved lady to receive a full reward for faithful service at the judgment seat of Christ (see 1 Cor. 3:5-17).

3 JOHN

INTRODUCTION:
1. J. Vernon McGee says:

"This is a letter similar to John's second epistle, in that it is personal in character, and it carries the same theme of truth. However, this letter deals with principalities. In his second epistle, John says that truth is worth *standing for;* and in the third epistle that truth is worth *working for!*" (*Third John*, p. 291)
2. In his second epistle John dealt with the problem of welcoming *deceivers* (which should not have been

The Elect Lady

2 John

Commended by the Apostle 1:1-4
"I rejoiced greatly that I found of thy children walking in truth, as we have received a commandment from the Father" **(1:4).**

Commanded by the Apostle 1:5, 6
● That she walk in love
● That she walk in truth

Cautioned by the Apostle 1:7-13
● Look out for Satan

"For many deceivers are entered into the world, who confess not that Jesus Christ is come in the flesh. This is a deceiver and an antichrist" **(1:7).**

"If there come any unto you, and bring not this doctrine, receive him not into your house, neither bid him God speed" **(1:10).**
● Look out for self

"Look to yourselves, that we lose not those things which we have wrought, but that we receive a full reward" **(1:8).**

GAIUS

DIOTREPHES

DEMETRIUS

3 John

The Exhorter
1:1-8

GAIUS

His prosperity

JOHN'S PRAYER FOR HIM

"Beloved, I wish above all things that thou mayest prosper and be in health, even as thy soul prospereth" (1:2).

JOHN'S PRAISE OF HIM

He had walked in truth.

He had ministered to missionaries.

The Egotist
1:9-11

DIOTREPHES

His pride

GUILTY ON FIVE CHARGES

1. Had attempted to occupy the leading place
2. Had refused to receive John the apostle
3. Had slandered the apostles
4. Had refused to entertain missionaries
5. Had attempted to excommunicate believers

The Example
1:12-14

DEMETRIUS

His praise

"Demetrius hath good report of all men, and of the truth itself: yea, and we also bear record; and ye know that our record is true" (1:12).

---

done); in this epistle he discusses the error of not receiving *believers* (which should have been done).

3. This is the second shortest book in the Bible.

4. This epistle gives an excellent (though brief) glimpse of church life at the close of the first century.

I. The Prosperity of Gaius (vs. 1-8). There were at least three New Testament people by this name. One was from Corinth (Rom. 16:23), one from Macedonia (Acts 19:29), and one from Derbe (Acts 20:4, 5). However, it is impossible to identify the Gaius here with one of these three. Whoever he was, John the apostle loved him dearly.

   A. John's prayer for him:

   "Beloved, I wish above all things that thou mayest prosper and be in health, even as thy soul prospereth" (v. 2).

   The Greek word here translated "prosper" is *euodoumai*, meaning "to have a good journey."

   B. John's praise of him (1:3-8).

      1. Gaius had extended Christian hospitality to some traveling missionaries and Bible teachers.

      2. They had reported that Gaius was living by the standards of the gospel and keeping his life clean and true.

II. The Pride of Diotrephes (vs. 9-11). J. Vernon McGee writes:

   "The missionaries of the early church were itinerants. They went from place to place. Since the local inn was a wretched and dirty place, and there were no Holiday Inns or Howard Johnson Motels, these missionaries were entertained in the homes of believers. Gaius opened his home, for which John congratulates him. Diotrephes opposed this practice, and John censors him for it. His 'hang-up' was that he loved to have recognition and attention, and be the center of attraction. He had to rule or ruin. There is generally one like him in every church who wants to control the church and

the preacher. He was guilty on 5 charges: (1) must occupy the leading place; (2) actually refused to receive John; (3) made malicious statements against the apostles; (4) refused to entertain the missionaries (he apparently wanted to do the teaching); (5) excommunicated those who did entertain the missionaries (he tried to be the first Pope). He was Diotrephes, the dictator." (*Through the Bible*, p. 292)

III. The Praise of Demetrius (1:12-14).

   "Demetrius hath good report of all men, and of the truth itself: yea, and we also bear record; and ye know that our record is true."

REVELATION

INTRODUCTION:

Revelation is the only prophetical book in the New Testament (in contrast to seventeen books in the Old Testament).

   Revelation is the only book in all the Bible which begins by promising a special blessing on those who study it, and ends by promising a special curse on those who add or take away from it.

   It was written by John the apostle, who had already written four other New Testament books. They are: The Gospel of John, 1 John, 2 John, and 3 John. The author had previously reached farther back into eternity than any other Bible writer (see Jn. 1:1-3). In Revelation he reaches farther on into eternity than any other writer (see Rev. 21, 22).

A. Revelation may be compared to the book of Daniel.

   1. Concerning the indestructible Jewish nation (Dan. 3, 6; cf. Rev. 12).

   2. Concerning the ministry of the antichrist (Dan. 3:1-7; 7:7, 8, 24, 25; 8:9-12, 23, 24, 25; 9:27; 11:36-45; cf. Rev. 13).

   3. Concerning the length of the tribulation (Dan. 9:24-27; cf. Rev. 11:2; 12:6, 14; 13:5).

Note, however, that Daniel was a sealed book (Dan. 12:9), whereas Revelation is not (Rev. 22:10).

B. Revelation may be compared to the book of Genesis. In Genesis we are told, "And the gathering of the waters called he seas" (1:10). In Revelation we are told: "And there was no more sea" (21:1).

In Genesis is described the first Adam with his wife Eve in the Garden of Eden, reigning over the earth (1:27, 28). In Revelation is described the last Adam with his wife, the Church, in the City of God, reigning over all the universe (21:9).

In Genesis God created the sun and moon, the day and the night (1:5, 16). In Revelation we are told, "There shall be no night there" (22:5). "And the city had no need of the sun, neither of the moon, to shine in it: for the glory of God did lighten it, and the Lamb is the light thereof" (21:23).

In Genesis the tree of life is denied to sinful man (3:22). In Revelation the tree of life "yielded her fruit every month: and the leaves of the tree were for the healing of the nations" (22:2).

In Genesis man hears God say, "Cursed is the ground for thy sake" (3:17). In Revelation man will hear God say: "And there shall be no more curse" (22:3). In Genesis Satan appears to torment man for awhile (3:1). In Revelation Satan disappears, himself to be tormented forever (20:10).

In Genesis the old earth was punished through a flood (7:12). In Revelation the new earth shall be purified through a fire (2 Pet. 3:6-12; Rev. 21:1). In Genesis, man's early home was beside a river (2:10). In Revelation, man's eternal home will be beside a river: "And he shewed me a pure river of water of life, clear as crystal, proceeding out of the throne of God and of the Lamb" (22:1). In Genesis the Patriarch Abraham goes to weep for Sarah (23:2). In Revelation the children of Abraham will have God himself wipe away all tears from their eyes (21:4).

In Genesis God destroys an earthly city, wicked Sodom, from the sands (Gen. 19). In Revelation God presents a heavenly city, new Jerusalem, from the skies (Rev. 21:1).

Genesis ends with a believer in Egypt, lying in a coffin (50:1-3). Revelation ends with all believers in eternity, reigning forever (21:4).

J. Vernon McGee writes:

"This book is like a great union station where the great trunk lines of prophecy come in from other portions of Scripture. Revelation does not originate, but consummates. It is imperative to a right understanding of the book to be able to trace each great subject of prophecy from the first reference to the terminal." (*Reveling Through Revelation*, p. 4)

C. Some of the great subjects of prophecy which find their consummation here are:

1. the Lord Jesus Christ (Gen. 3:15; cf. Rev. 1:13; 12:5).
2. the church (Mt. 16:18; cf. Rev. 19:7-9).
3. the resurrection of saints (Dan. 12:2, 3; 1 Thess. 4:13-18; 1 Cor. 15:51, 52; Rev. 20:4-6).
4. the great tribulation (Deut. 4:30, 31; Isa. 24; cf. Rev. 6-18).
5. Satan (Isa. 14:12-15; Ezek. 28:11-19; cf. Rev. 20:1-10).
6. the man of sin (2 Thess. 2:1-12; cf. Rev. 19:19-21).
7. false religion (Gen. 11:1-9; Mt. 13; cf. Rev. 17).
8. the times of the Gentiles (Dan. 2:37; Lk. 21:24; cf. Rev. 18).
9. the Second Coming of Christ (Jude 1:14, 15; cf. Rev. 19:11-16).

D. There are at least four main interpretations to this last book in the Bible.

1. It is pure fiction. This is the view of the agnostics.
2. It is allegorical. This says no part of the book may be taken literally. It is simply a symbolic account of the age-long struggle between good and evil. This is the view of most liberals.
3. It is historical. Here two kinds of history are in mind:

   a. Past history. This is often called the preterist theory. "Preterist" is from a Latin word which means "past." Dr. Charles Ryrie writes:

   "Thus, the preterist interpreters are those who see Revelation as having already been fulfilled in the early history of the church. Chapters 5—11 are said to record the church's victory over Judaism; chapters 12—19 her victory over pagan Rome; and 20—22 her glory because of these victories. The persecutions described are those of Nero and Domitian, and the entire book was fulfilled by the time of Constantine (A.D. 312)." (*Revelation*, p. 8)

   b. Continuous history. Again to quote Ryrie:

   "This interpretative viewpoint states that in Revelation there is a panorama of the history of the church from the days of John to the end of the age. It holds that the book has been in the process of being fulfilled throughout the whole Christian era. Those who hold this view see in the symbols the rise of papacy, the corruption of the church and the various wars throughout church history. Most of the reformers interpreted the book in this manner." (*Revelation*, pp. 8, 9)

4. It is prophetical. This view sees those events from chapter 4 onward as yet to be fulfilled. This view alone does justice to the book. Revelation, like all other books in the Bible, is to be taken in the plain, normal sense of the word. To do otherwise is to dishonor Christ, the divine Author. Dr. David L. Cooper once suggested: "When the plain sense of Scripture makes common sense, seek no other sense."

E. This book lists more titles for the Savior than does any other book in the Bible. Note but some of them:

1. Jesus Christ (1:1)
2. the faithful Witness (1:5)
3. the first Begotten of the dead (1:5)
4. the Prince of kings of the earth (1:5)
5. the Alpha and Omega (1:8)
6. the First and the Last (1:17)
7. the Son of man (1:13)
8. the Son of God (2:18)
9. the Keeper of David's keys (3:7)
10. the Keeper of the keys of hell and death (1:18)
11. the Lion of the tribe of Judah (5:5)
12. the root of David (5:5)
13. the slain Lamb (5:6)
14. the angry Lamb (6:16, 17)

15. the tender Lamb (7:17)
16. our Lord (11:8)
17. the man Child (12:5)
18. the King of saints (15:3)
19. the Faithful and True (19:11)
20. the Word of God (19:13)
21. the King of kings (19:16)
22. the Lord of lords (19:16)
23. the Beginning and the End (22:13)
24. the Bright and Morning Star (22:16)

F. The Numbers 7 and 12 are predominant in the book of Revelation.
   1. The number 7:
      a. seven spirits (1:4)
      b. seven stars (1:16)
      c. seven lamps (4:5)
      d. seven seals (5:1)
      e. seven horns (5:6)
      f. seven eyes (5:6)
      g. seven angels (8:2)
      h. seven trumpets (8:2)
      i. seven thunders (10:3)
      j. seven heads (12:3)
      k. seven crowns (12:3)
      l. seven plagues (15:1)
      m. seven vials (17:1)
      n. seven mountains (17:9)
      o. seven kings (17:10)
   2. The number 12:
      a. 12,000 from each of the twelve tribes (7:4-8)
      b. a crown of twelve stars (12:1)
      c. twelve gates (21:12)
      d. twelve angels (21:12)
      e. twelve foundations (21:14)
      f. twelve apostles (21:14)
      g. 12,000 furlongs (21:16)

G. There are more Old Testament quotations and allusions in the book of Revelation than in any other New Testament book.
   1. thirteen in Genesis
   2. twenty-seven in Exodus
   3. four in Leviticus
   4. three in Numbers
   5. ten in Deuteronomy
   6. one in Joshua
   7. one in Judges
   8. one in 2 Samuel
   9. six in 2 Kings
   10. one in 1 Chronicles
   11. one in Nehemiah
   12. forty-three in Psalms
   13. two in Proverbs
   14. seventy-nine in Isaiah
   15. twenty-two in Jeremiah
   16. forty-three in Ezekiel
   17. fifty-three in Daniel
   18. two in Hosea
   19. eight in Joel
   20. nine in Amos
   21. one in Habakkuk
   22. two in Zephaniah
   23. fifteen in Zechariah
   24. one in Malachi

H. Revelation is totally a book about God's Lamb. The book can thus be outlined as follows:
   The Witnesses of the Lamb Instructed (1-3)
   The Worship of the Lamb Invited (4-5)
   The Wrath of the Lamb Invoked (6-19)
   The Reign of the Lamb Instituted (20)
   The Wife of the Lamb Introduced (21-22)

Part One:

The Witnesses of the Lamb Instructed (1-3)
   I. The Servant of God (1:1-10). John, the beloved apostle, receives and transmits a special message.
      A. The source of the message (1:1).
         1. given by the Father to the Son
         2. given by the Son to an angel (possibly Gabriel or Michael)
         3. given by the angel to the apostle
      B. The promise of the message (1:3).
         "Blessed is he that readeth, and they that hear the words of this prophecy, and keep those things which are written therein."
         This is the first of seven beatitudes in Revelation. See also:
         1. 14:13—"Blessed are the dead which die in the Lord."
         2. 16:15—"Blessed is he that watcheth."
         3. 19:9—"Blessed are they which are called unto the marriage supper of the Lamb."
         4. 20:6—"Blessed . . . is he that hath part in the first resurrection."
         5. 22:7—"Blessed is he that keepeth the sayings . . . of this book."
         6. 22:14—"Blessed are they that do his commandments."
      C. The reason for the message (1:3).
         "For the time is at hand."
         Here the word is not *chronos* (regular word for clock-time) but *kairos,* referring to a fixed season. This "fixed season" is that described by Daniel in 9:24-27. Someday a group of Jews will be able to rightly conclude by comparing both Daniel and Revelation, that this "fixed, determined season" is indeed at their very doorsteps.
         In addition to this, God is desirous to "shew unto his servants things which must shortly come to pass" (as God records time). See 2 Peter 3:9; Romans 16:20 (1:1).
         The word "shortly" can also mean rapidly. Note the following verses which reveal God's desire to lift back the curtain of the future for his saints.
         1. "Surely the Lord God will do nothing but he revealeth his secret unto his servants" (Amos 3:7).
         2. "But there is a God in heaven that revealeth his secrets" (Dan. 2:28).
         3. "I thank thee, O Father, Lord of heaven and earth, because thou hast hid these things from the wise and prudent, and hath revealed them unto babes" (Mt. 11:25).
         4. "Unto you it is given to know the mysteries of the kingdom of God" (Lk. 8:10).
      D. The recipients of the message (1:4).
         "To the seven churches which are in Asia."
      E. The theme of the message. The person and work of Jesus Christ.
         1. His past work—redemption. "Unto him that loved us [literally, 'keeps on loving us'], and washed us [literally, 'once-for-all washed us'] from our sins in his own blood" (1:5).

2. His present work—sanctification. "And hath made us kings and priests unto God and his Father" (1:6).

3. His future work—glorification. "Behold, he cometh with clouds; and every eye shall see him, and they also which pierced him: and all kindreds of the earth shall wail because of him" (1:7; see also Dan. 7:13, 14; Mt. 24:30; Acts 1:9).

F. The doxology of the message (1:6).
"To him be glory and dominion forever and ever, Amen."

This is the first of four grand doxologies in Revelation. John presents these in chronological order, from the simple to the sublime. These are:

1. 4:11—"Glory and honour and power."
2. 5:13—"Blessing and honour and glory and power."
3. 7:12—"Blessing and glory and wisdom and thanksgiving, and honour, and power, and might."

G. The location of the message (1:9).
"I John, who also am your brother, and companion in tribulation, and in the kingdom and patience of Jesus Christ, was in the isle that is called Patmos, for the word of God, and for the testimony of Jesus Christ."

John now explains why he was on this isle. He was exiled there from about A.D. 86 to 96. Patmos was a rugged, volcanic island off the coast of Asia Minor. It was about ten miles long and six miles wide. He was probably put there by the Roman Emperor Domitian. Domitian was the brother of Titus (who destroyed the city of Jerusalem). Thus God allowed one pagan to destroy his earthly city, but would use his brother to allow the heavenly new Jerusalem to first be described to man. Marvelous and mysterious indeed are the workings of grace!

John speaks of being in tribulation. There were at least four reasons why Rome persecuted Christians:

1. For political purposes. The Christian took no part in the pantheon (worship of many gods). In fact, Christians were regarded as atheists, for they worshiped no visible God.

2. For economic purposes. No money or sacrifices were forthcoming from believers to Roman idols.

3. For "moral" purposes. Christians were often looked upon as cannibals, for did they not secretly "eat the flesh and drink the blood" of their religious founder?

4. For scapegoat purposes. Nero attempted to blame various state problems upon the Christians living in Rome.

H. The time of the message (1:10).
"I was in the Spirit on the Lord's day" (see also 4:2; 17:3; 21:10).

This doubtless was on a Sunday (see Mt. 28:1; Acts 20:7; 1 Cor. 16:1, 2).

I. The mode of the message (1:10).
"And heard behind me a great voice, as of a trumpet."

The trumpet call is heard many more times in this book (see 4:1; 8:2, 7, 8, 10, 12; 9:1, 13; 11:15).

II. The Son of God (1:11-20).
A. His declaration (1:11):
"Saying I am Alpha and Omega, the first and the last: and, What thou seest, write in a book, and send it unto the seven churches which are in Asia; unto Ephesus and unto Smyrna, and unto Pergamos, and unto Thyatira, and unto Sardis, and unto Philadelphia, and unto Laodicea."

B. His description (1:12-16):
1. He was holding seven stars and seven golden lampstands.
2. He was clothed in a full-length robe.
3. His chest was circled with a golden band.
4. His head and hair were as white as wool or snow.
5. His eyes were as flames of fire (Heb. 4:13).
6. His feet gleamed like burnished bronze.
7. His voice was as the sound of many waters (Ps. 29:3-9).
8. He held a sharp double-edged sword in his mouth (Heb. 4:12).
9. His face was as the sun shining in its full strength (Mt. 17:2).

C. His deliverance (1:17, 18):
"And when I saw him, I fell at his feet as dead. And he laid his right hand upon me, saying unto me, Fear not; I am the first and the last: I am he that liveth, and was dead; and, behold, I am alive for evermore. Amen; and have the keys of hell and of death."

The effect of this dazzling sight upon John was nothing less than paralyzing. John had once walked with Christ for three years. He had witnessed his miracles and heard his sermons. He had leaned upon his breast in the upper room and watched him die on the cross. Finally he had rejoiced in his resurrection and viewed his ascension. But that had all happened some sixty years before. Now, he sees the resplendent Redeemer in all his blinding brightness and drops at his feet as a dead dog. John became as an insect in the fiery furnace of the sun. But John's loving Lord quickly performed that tender task the apostle had so often seen him do. He reached out and touched the one in need. Compare Revelation 1:17 with the following Gospel accounts:

1. Matthew 8:14, 15: "And when Jesus was come into Peter's house, he saw his wife's mother laid, and sick of a fever. And he touched her hand, and the fever left her."

2. Matthew 9:27-29: "Two blind men followed him saying and crying, Thou Son of David, have mercy on us . . . then touched he their eyes . . . and their eyes were opened."

3. Matthew 17:7: "And Jesus came and touched them [Peter, James, and John, who became terrified after watching his transfiguration on a mountain] and said, Arise, and be not afraid."

4. John 9:6: "He spat on the ground and anointed the eyes of the blind man."

5. Luke 5:12, 13: "And it came to pass when he was in a certain city, behold a man full of leprosy: who seeing Jesus fell on his face and besought him saying, Lord, if thou wilt, thou

canst make me clean. And he put forth his hand and touched him."

6. Luke 7:14: "And he came and touched the bier [of the widow's dead son in Nain] . . . and said, Young man, I say unto thee, arise."

7. Luke 22:51: "And he touched his ear [of one of his enemies whom Peter had wounded in the garden] and healed him."

Jesus assures John that *"I am alive!"* The real symbol of Christianity is *not* the cross, but the empty tomb. History relates the account of Julian the apostate, a nephew of the Roman Caesar Constantine. Julian was reared in a Christian home. But in his youth he renounced his faith and embraced paganism. When he became Emperor in A.D. 361, he sought to blot out Christianity. In the days of his cruel reign, one of his cronies said to a humble Christian, "And your Jesus—what is your carpenter of Nazareth doing now?"

The Spirit-filled believer quietly replied, "He is building a coffin for your emperor!" In 363, after he had reigned but two years, Julian died on the battlefield, facing a Persian army. One of the most famous incidents of history then followed. As they carried the Emperor off the field and as he lay dying, he lifted up his dimming eyes to heaven and, with a bloody gasp, cried out, "O Galilean, thou hast conquered at last!"

Jesus furthermore assures John that, "I have the keys of hell and of death." There are five keys mentioned in the New Testament and our Lord carries them all. The other four are:

the keys to the kingdom (Mt. 16:19)
the key of knowledge (Lk. 11:52)
the key to the throne of David (Rev. 3:7)
the key to the bottomless pit (Rev. 9:1; 20:1)

D. His definition (1:19, 20): Jesus now interprets to John the meaning of the seven stars and lampstands the apostle sees him holding.

1. The seven stars were the angels of the seven churches. J. Vernon McGee writes:

"Angels can be either human or divine—the word here is *messenger*. It could refer to a member of the angelic host of heaven; it could refer to a ruler or teacher of the congregation. Personally, I think that it refers to the local pastors. It is good to hear a pastor being called an angel—sometimes we are called other things!" (*Reveling Through Revelation,* p. 17)

2. The seven lampstands were seven specific churches. Upon hearing this, John could understand why he saw Christ dressed the way he was. He is now appearing as our great High Priest. The golden lampstands speak of his present work in heaven in maintaining the lights. Aaron lighted the lamps in the tabernacle, put them out with snuffers, filled them with oil, and trimmed the wicks. Christ now does this with his present lights, which are the local churches.

III. The Churches of God (2-3). At the time Revelation was written (around A.D. 95-100) there may have existed well over 100 separate and independent local churches in the world. Paul had, of course, personally planted dozens of churches by himself. Other apostles would doubtless have done the same thing. But out of the many, Christ chose seven representative churches and addressed himself to these. It has been suggested that the listing of these seven appears in the sacred record to accomplish at least the following purposes:

A. The contemporary purpose: That Christ had a direct message to seven literal churches existing at that time.

B. The composite purpose: That these messages are meant to be applied by all churches existing in all ages.

C. The chronological purpose: That the characteristics of these churches serve as a prophetical preview of the seven great periods in Christendom from Pentecost to the rapture. A suggested out-

The book of Revelation

PART ONE

Witnesses
of the Lamb Instructed (Rev. 1-3)

The Servant of God (Rev. 1:1-10)
John receives a special message on the Isle of Patmos
THE SOURCE OF THE MESSAGE **(1:1)**
THE PROMISE OF THE MESSAGE **(1:3)**
THE REASON FOR THE MESSAGE **(1:3)**
THE RECIPIENTS OF THE MESSAGE **(1:4)**
THE THEME OF THE MESSAGE **(1:5)**
THE DOXOLOGY OF THE MESSAGE **(1:6)**
THE LOCATION OF THE MESSAGE **(1:9)**
THE TIME OF THE MESSAGE **(1:10)**
THE MODE OF THE MESSAGE **(1:10)**

The Son of God (Rev. 1:11-20)
● *HIS DECLARATION* **(1:11)**
● *HIS DESCRIPTION* **(1:12-16)**
● *HIS DELIVERANCE* **(1:17, 18)**
● *HIS DEFINITION* **(1:19, 20)**

The Churches of God (Rev. 2:1—3:22)
EPHESUS **(2:1-7)**   SARDIS **(3:1-6)**
SMYRNA **(2:8-11)**   PHILADELPHIA **(3:7-13)**
PERGAMOS **(2:12-17)**   LAODICEA **(3:14-22)**
THYATIRA **(2:18-29)**

line of this predictive panorama may be seen as follows:

1. Ephesus (A.D. 30-300)—name means "desirable." The Apostolic Church.
2. Smyrna (100-313)—name means "myrrh." The Martyr Church.
3. Pergamos (314-590)—name means "marriage." The Compromising Church.
4. Thyatira (590-1517)—name means "continual sacrifice." The Roman Catholic Church.
5. Sardis (1517-1700)—name means "remnant." The Reformation Church.
6. Philadelphia (1700-1900)—name means "brotherly love." The Revival Church.
7. Laodicea (1900—rapture)—name means "people's rights." The Worldly Church.

In Revelation 2 and 3, the Savior speaks his mind to his churches. It is therefore in these chapters (and not in Mt. 28 or Acts 1) that the final words of Christ to the church are recorded. We now consider each of the seven.

1. The church at Ephesus (2:1-7).
   a. The City. J. Vernon McGee describes Ephesus for us:

   "Ephesus was the chief city of the province of Asia. It was called 'the Vanity Fair of Asia.' It was both the religious and commercial center of that entire area which influenced both east and west—Europe and Asia.

   The temple of Diana was there, which was one of the seven wonders of the ancient world, being the largest Greek temple ever constructed (418 feet by 240 feet). There were over 100 external columns about 56 feet in height, of which 36 were hand-carved. It was built over a marsh on an artificial foundation of skins and charcoal so that it was not affected by earthquakes. The doors were of cypress wood; columns and walls were of Parian marble; the staircase was carved out of one vine from Cyprus. The temple served as the bank of Asia and was the depository of vast sums of money. It was an art gallery displaying the masterpieces. . . . Behind a purple curtain was the lewd and crude image of Diana, the goddess of fertility. She was many-breasted, carried a club in one hand and a trident in the other" (Reveling Through Revelation, p. 19)

   Ephesus was a large city with a population of 225,000 and possessed a huge harbor.

   b. The Counselor (what Jesus says about himself).
   c. The commendation (the good things about the church): He begins by making a statement that will be repeated to every one of the seven churches. The statement is, "I know thy works" (2:2, 9, 13, 19; 3:1, 8, 15).

      (1) It was an evangelistic church.

      (2) It was a patient church (unlike the Christians Peter wrote to; see 2 Pet. 1:6).
      (3) It was a separated church (unlike the Corinthian church (see 1 Cor. 5).
      (4) It was an orthodox church.
      (5) It was a persecuted but persistent church (unlike the Christians in the book of Hebrews; see Heb. 12:1-15).
      (6) It was a democratic church. "Thou hatest the deeds of the Nicolaitans, which I also hate" (2:6). This word comes from two Greek words, nikao, meaning "to conquer" and laos, meaning "people." Many believe John was speaking here to the growing distinction between clergy and laity.

   d. The condemnation: "Nevertheless I have somewhat against thee, because thou hast left thy first love" (2:4).

      It is tragically possible to be so busy working for Christ that one neglects Christ. God did not create Adam to evangelize the world with the gospel, or to build the largest Sunday school in Eden (as important as these may be), but to fellowship with his Creator.

   e. The counsel: They were to do three things.
      (1) Remember. Their heads were to be given over to Christ.
      (2) Repent. Their hearts were to be given over to Christ.
      (3) Repeat. Their hands were to be given over to Christ. Unless this was done, fearful results would transpire. "I will come unto thee quickly, and will remove thy candlestick out of his place" (2:5).

      The child of God need never pray the words of Psalm 51:11, "Cast me not away from thy presence, and take not thy holy spirit from me." However, every Bible-believing local church should often repeat these words. There is absolutely no eternal security for any local church presented in the Bible. A believer can never fall from grace, but his church can. History records the sad fact that Christ did indeed later remove the lampstand of the church in Ephesus. It has been gone for centuries, smothered by the Moslems. There is today no local church within miles of Ephesus.

   f. The challenge: Just as he began by a statement he would repeat to the remaining churches, our Lord ends in similar fashion. Here two statements are made.
      "He that hath an ear, let him hear what the Spirit saith unto the churches" (2:7, 11, 17, 29; 3:6, 13, 22).
      To Ephesus, the challenge is:

"To him that overcometh will I give to eat of the tree of life, which is in the midst of the paradise of God" (2:7).

This tree, once given to Adam, disappears after his sin (Gen. 3:24). Here (Rev. 2:7) it is mentioned again for the first time. (See also Rev. 22:2, 14.)

The definition and method of overcoming is given in 1 John 5:4, 5.

    g. The church period (A.D. 30-100). This period saw the writing of the entire New Testament and an attempt to evangelize the known Roman world. The heroes of this period would include the apostles Paul, Jude, James, Luke, etc.

2. The church at Smyrna (2:8-11).

    a. The city

      (1) It was some forty miles north of Ephesus.

      (2) It was a splendid city of rare beauty on a fine bay.

      (3) It was on a direct trade route from India and Persia to Rome.

      (4) It was celebrated for its schools of science and medicine, for its handsome buildings, and wide paved streets.

      (5) The temple of Bacchus, god of wine, was there.

      (6) Many apostate Jews lived here.

      (7) It was the traditional birthplace of Homer.

    b. The Counselor: "These things saith the first and the last, which was dead and is alive" (2:8).

    c. The commendation:

      (1) They had suffered poverty for Christ (but God saw them as rich). Many believers doubtless belonged to the various city labor guilds of that day prior to their conversion. But because of their newfound faith they apparently had lost the right to guilds. Many may have gone bankrupt. (See also Mt. 6:20; 2 Cor. 6:10.)

      (2) They had suffered persecution for Christ (but God promised them a reward). Dr. Charles Ryrie writes:

        "The instigators of the persecution were apostate Jews who were in reality instruments of Satan. At the martyrdom of Polycarp (disciple of John the Apostle) in 168, these Jews eagerly assisted by gathering *on the Sabbath* wood and fagots for the fire in which he was burned" (*Revelation*, p. 23). (See also Rom. 2:28, 29; Jn. 8:44; Rev. 3:9.)

Jesus warns his church that they would have "tribulation ten days" (2:10). He may have referred to an actual ten-day period of fearful blood-letting. Or he might have meant the ten intensive periods of persecution by ten Roman Emper-

ors. These periods will be listed under letter g. It has been estimated that at least five million saints were martyred during this period. This would be over one hundred million, in proportion to today's world population.

    d. The condemnation: None given.

    e. The counsel:

      (1) Be fearless.

      (2) Be faithful.

    f. The challenge—twofold:

      (1) "I will give thee a crown of life" (2:10; see also Jas. 1:12).

      (2) "He . . . shall not be hurt of the second death" (2:11).

    g. The church period (100-313).

      (1) The ten Roman persecutions during this era:

        (a) Nero (64-68)—killed Peter and Paul.

        (b) Domitian (81-96)—thought Christianity was atheistic. Killed thousands of believers. Banished John to Patmos.

        (c) Trajan (98-117)—was the first to pass laws against Christianity. Burned Ignatius at stake.

        (d) Pius (137-161)—killed Polycarp, disciple of John.

        (e) Marcus Aurelius (161-180)—thought Christianity an absurd superstition. Beheaded the great writer and defender of the faith, Justin Martyr.

        (f) Severus (193-211)—killed Origen's father.

        (g) Thracian (235-238)—brutal barbarian. Commanded all Christian leaders to die.

        (h) Decius (249-251)—determined to exterminate Christianity.

        (i) Valerian (253-260)—killed Cyprian, Bishop of Carthage.

        (j) Diocletian (284-305)—last and most severe persecution. For ten years believers were hunted in caves and forests. They were burned, thrown to wild beasts, and put to death by every torture cruelty could devise. But Diocletian's own wife and daughter accepted Christ.

      (2) Some champions during this period would include:

        (a) Justin Martyr (100-167), early defender of Christianity. He died for Christ at Rome.

        (b) Irenaeus (130-200), a pupil of Polycarp (John's disciple).

        (c) Tertullian (160-220), Bishop of Carthage and defender of Christianity.

        (d) Eusebius (264-340), the founder of church history.

3. The church at Pergamos (2:12-17).

    a. The city.

(1) It was the political capital city of Asia, some seventy-five miles north of Ephesus.

(2) It boasted one of the finest libraries of antiquity which contained some 200,000 volumes. This library was later given by Mark Antony to Cleopatra.

(3) It was in this city that parchment was first used.

b. The Counselor: "These things saith he which hath the sharp sword with the two edges" (2:12).

c. The commendation: They had kept the faith, even though living in the very city Satan had chosen as his temporary headquarters. For centuries the devil had carried on his empire from Babylon. (See Gen. 11:1-9; Dan. 5.) But when that nation fell he apparently transferred it (at least for awhile) to Pergamos. The city worshiped, among other objects, a living serpent. Satan will later move his capital back to Babylon (Rev. 17, 18).

Many in Pergamos had been martyred for their faith. One is mentioned here, Antipas by name. His name never appears in any other historical record. But God knew all about this anonymous humble believer who lived and died for Christ some twenty centuries ago. (See Jn. 10:3; 2 Tim. 2:19.)

d. The condemnation: "But I have a few things against thee" (2:14).

(1) Some were practicing the doctrine of Balaam. Balaam was a false Old Testament prophet who attempted to put a curse on the nation Israel (Num. 22:1—25:9). The New Testament refers to his doctrine, his error and his way.

(a) His way (2 Pet. 2:15)—his way was his covetousness. Balaam's services could be readily bought.

(b) His error (Jude 1:11)—he wrongly supposed a holy God would be forced to curse sinful Israel.

(c) His doctrine (Rev. 2:14)—he rightly concluded that if you can't curse them, then corrupt them through immorality and idolatry.

(2) Some were practicing the doctrine of the Nicolaitans (2:15). This philosophy had already been condemned by Christ in the church at Ephesus (2:6). However, we see that what was once *deeds* in the first church had now become hardened into *doctrine.*

e. The counsel: "Repent; or else I will come unto thee quickly and will fight against them with the sword of my mouth" (2:16).

f. The challenge: "To him that overcometh will I give. . . ."

(1) Hidden manna to eat. This speaks of special fellowship with Christ. (See Jn. 6:32-35; Heb. 9:4.)

(2) A white stone with a new name written within. Charles Ryrie writes: "The meaning of the white stone with the new name written is derived from either one or both of two customs of the day. The first was that of judges who determined a verdict by placing in an urn a white and black pebble. If the white one came out it meant acquittal; thus the white stone would mean the assurance that there is no condemnation to those who are in Christ Jesus. The other custom was the wearing of amulets, a good luck charm worn around the neck. If this is the reference, then the stone is the Lord's way of reminding the people that they had Him and needed no other thing." (*Revelation*, p. 25)

g. The church period (315-590).

(1) One of the key individuals during this period was a soldier named Constantine. He was made Emperor in 306 by his dying father and the Roman troops. Upon coming to power in the East, he was immediately faced with destruction by the Western Emperor named Maxentius. Constantine realized his uneasy troops must be strengthened, and thus claimed to have seen in a dream the image of the cross and to have heard a voice saying, "By this sign, conquer!" Thus inspired, he led his men to victory, defeating his enemy at the famous battle of Milvian Bridge, just outside Rome.

In 313 he signed the Edict of Toleration, which granted freedom to Christians. It then became fashionable to join the church. He promised gold pieces and white robes to all converts. Soon pagans had joined the church by the thousands, taking with them their heathen practices. The church then became so worldly and the world so churchy that no difference could be seen. Loraine Boettner lists the following unscriptural doctrines which were introduced during this general time period:

(a) making prayers for the dead (300)

(b) making the sign of the cross (300)

(c) the worship of saints and angels (375)

(d) institution of the mass (394)

(e) worship of Mary (431)

(f) doctrine of extreme unction (526)

(g) doctrine of purgatory (593)

(2) Some champions during this time would include:

(a) John Chrysostom (347-407), the greatest preacher of his day.

(b) Jerome (340-420), the scholar who translated the Bible into Latin.

(c) Augustine (354-430), one of the greatest theologians of all time.

4. The church at Thyatira (2:18-29).

a. The city

(1) It was thirty-five miles southeast of Pergamos.

(2) The city may have been founded by Alexander the Great around 300 B.C.

(3) It was a union city, and headquarters for the trade guilds, such as tanners, potters, weavers, dyers, and robe-makers.

(4) Lydia, the first convert of Paul in Europe (Acts 16:14), was a native of this city. Today it has a population of 25,000.

b. The Counselor: "These things saith the Son of God, who hath his eyes like unto a flame of fire, and his feet are like fine brass" (2:18).

c. The commendation: Fivefold.

(1) goods works (the last was better than the first)

(2) love

(3) service (faithfulness)

(4) faith

(5) patience

d. The condemnation: "Notwithstanding I have a few things against thee" (2:20). God's main objection with this church centered in the fact that they were allowing the ministry of a false prophetess aptly named Jezebel.

(1) Her Old Testament counterpart. This Jezebel was the pagan murderous wife of King Ahab (1 Ki. 16:28—19:21; 21:1-29; 2 Ki. 9:22-37).

(2) Her sin in the church:

(a) She was teaching men, which is forbidden (see 1 Tim. 2:12-14).

(b) She was teaching immorality and idolatry.

(c) She was totally unrepentant.

(3) Her punishment:

(a) Her followers will go through the great tribulation and become false churches in Revelation 17.

(b) Her children (followers) will suffer the second death at the great white throne judgment (Rev. 20:11-15).

(c) She would serve as an example to other churches concerning the wrath of God. (See also Acts 5:11-13; 1 Tim. 5:22.)

e. The counsel: "But unto you I say, and unto the rest in Thyatira, as many as have not this doctrine, and which have not known the depths of Satan, as they speak; I will put upon you none other burden. But that which ye have already hold fast till I come" (2:24, 25). We note the phrase, "the depths of Satan." The devil, like the Lord, has his systematic doctrinal textbooks. (See 1 Tim. 4:1.)

f. The challenge: "And he that overcometh, and keepeth my works unto the end, to him will I give power over the nations: And he shall rule them with a rod of iron; as the vessels of a potter shall they be broken to shivers: even as I received of my Father. And I will give him the morning star" (2:26-28). (See also Ps. 2:9; Rev. 22:16.)

g. The church period (590-1517). As we have previously noted, the name "Thyatira" means "continual sacrifice," and may refer in general to the Roman Catholic Church. Note the following items:

(1) A study of the papacy: The word "pope" means "father." At first it was applied to all Western bishops. About A.D. 500, it began to be restricted to the bishop of Rome. The idea that the Roman bishop should have authority over all the church was a slow growth, bitterly contested at every step. Power was evenly distributed in five main areas for the first four centuries: Rome, Constantinople, Antioch, Jerusalem, and Alexandria.

Leo I (440-461). He was the forerunner of future popes, and bishop of Rome. He gained great popularity by twice saving the city, once from Atilla the Hun, and later from Genseric the Vandal.

Gregory I (590-694). He was the first real pope. He consolidated Christendom after the fall of Rome in 476, and was basically a good man.

(2) Some evil popes:

(a) Sergius III (904-911). He lived with a notorious harlot, Marozia, and they raised their illegitimate children to become popes and cardinals.

(b) Benedict IX (1033-1045). He was made pope as a boy of twelve. He committed murders and adulteries in broad daylight and robbed graves. Finally the enraged people of Rome drove him out of the city.

(c) Gregory VI (1046). He was one of three rivals for the throne at this time. Benedict IX and Sylvester III both laid claim to it with him. Rome swarmed with hired assassins, as each pope was trying to cut the throat of the other. Finally, Emperor Henry III stepped in, kicked all three out, and appointed his own pope, Clement II.

(d) Innocent III (1198–1216). He was the most powerful of all popes. He condemned England's Magna Carta, and forbade Bible reading.

(5) Some champions during this period would include:

(a) John Wycliffe (1320–1384). He was the first to translate the entire Bible into English.

(b) John Huss (1369–1415), a fearless preacher who honored the Bible above the church. He was burned at the stake by the pope.

(c) William Tyndale (1484–1536). In 1525 he printed (Wycliffe had written) the first copy of the New Testament in English ever produced.

(d) Erasmus (1466–1536). Great student of the Greek New Testament.

5. The church at Sardis (3:1–6).

a. The city:

(1) It was thirty miles south of Thyatira and the capital of Lydia.

(2) The city was thought to be impregnable, but Cyrus the Great captured it by following a secret path up the cliff.

(3) Coins were first minted here.

(4) It was noted for its great wealth, the chief of which was its flourishing carpet industry.

b. The Counselor: "These things saith he that hath the seven spirits of God, and the seven stars" (3:1).

c. The commendation: "Thou hast a few names even in Sardis which have not defiled their garments: and they shall walk with me in white: for they are worthy" (3:4).

God always has his remnant in every church and church age (see 1 Ki. 19:10, 18; Rom. 11:5).

d. The condemnation: "Thou hast a name that thou livest, and art dead" (3:1). J. Vernon McGee writes:

"This is a picture of Protestantism. The great truths which were recovered in the Reformation have been surrendered by a compromising church. Although the great denominations and churches still repeat by rote the creeds of the church; in mind, heart and life they have repudiated them. Imposing programs, elaborate rituals, and multiplication of organizations have been substituted for the Word of God and real spiritual life. There is activity, but no actions, motion without movement, promotion without progress, and program without power. Although the outward form remains, the living creature has vacated the shell." (*Reveling Through Revelation*, p. 28)

The word to Sardis proves that the Reformation was not a restoration to the New Testament ideal church.

e. The counsel: "Be watchful, and strengthen the things which remain, that are ready to die: for I have not found thy works perfect before God. Remember therefore how thou hast received and heard, and hold fast, and repent. If therefore thou shalt not watch, I will come on thee as a thief, and thou shalt not know what hour I will come upon thee" (3:2, 3).

f. The challenge: Here the challenge is twofold to all overcomers:

(1) His name would remain in the Book of Life. Often this book is referred to in both Old and New Testament (Ex. 32:32; Dan. 12:1; Ps. 69:28; Lk. 10:20; Phil. 4:3; Heb. 12:23; Rev. 3:5; 13:8; 17:8; 20:12, 15; 21:27; 22:19). Whatever else may be involved here, these verses do *not* teach that a saved person can ever be lost! In fact, quite the opposite, for many prove one cannot be lost because each saved person's name is written in this book. (See especially Dan. 12:1; Lk. 10:20; Rev. 13:8; 17:8; 21:27.)

(2) His name would be confessed by Jesus before the Father (Lk. 12:8, 9).

g. The church period (1517–1700). Some champions during this period would include:

(1) Martin Luther (1483–1546)—one of the greatest men of all time, founder of Protestantism. He received a law degree, then decided to enter priesthood. After three miserable years, he finally found the peace of mind he had been looking for in Romans 1:17: "The just shall live by *faith*." In 1508 he became a teacher in the University of Wittenberg. It was in this city, on October 31, 1517, that Luther posted his ninety-five theses on the church door, attacking the sale of indulgences. Printed copies were eagerly awaited all over Germany. It proved to be the spark that set Europe aflame. At the Diet of Worms in 1521, Luther refused to be bullied into recanting, uttering

his famous sentence, "Here I stand; I can do naught else, so help me God!" Luther's three grand gifts to us are:

    (a) The universal priesthood of believers.

    (b) The Bible is the sole authority for the Christian faith.

    (c) Justification is by faith alone, and not by works.

(2) Zwingli (1484-1531)—the great co-laborer with Luther.

(3) John Calvin (1509-1564)—one of the greatest theologians of the Christian faith. His five points of doctrine (TULIP) are:

    (a) Total depravity of man.

    (b) Unconditional election of man by God.

    (c) Limited atonement (Christ died only for believers).

    (d) Irresistible grace.

    (e) Perseverance of the saints (eternal security). Many Christians, of course, do not accept all five of these points of theology.

(4) John Knox (1515-1572)—he single-handedly swept Romanism out of Scotland.

(5) Roger Williams (1604-1684). He came to the Massachusetts Bay Colony in 1631. After being banished he went to Providence, Rhode Island. There he founded the first Baptist church in America.

6. The church at Philadelphia (3:7-13).

  a. The city

    (1) It was built as a center of Greek culture around 200 B.C.

    (2) It is located some thirty miles southeast of Sardis.

    (3) Philadelphia was celebrated for its excellent wine.

    (4) The city had a heavy Jewish population.

    (5) It was destroyed by an earthquake in A.D. 17, but soon rebuilt by Tiberius Caesar.

  b. The Counselor: "I know thy works: behold, I have set before thee an open door, and no man can shut it: for thou hast a little strength and hast kept my word, and hast not denied my name" (3:8).

    J. Vernon McGee writes the following concerning Christ's description here: "Christ reminds them that He is holy—holy at His birth (Lk. 1:35), holy at His death (Acts 2:27), and holy in His present priestly office (Heb. 7:26). He is likewise true (Jn. 1:9; 14:6; 15:1). 'True' means genuine with an added note of perfection and completeness. Moses did not give the true bread. See John 6:32-35. He also has the Key of David (see Isa. 22:22). This is different from the keys of hades and death (1:18). This speaks of His regal claims as the Ruler of this universe (Lk. 1:32). He will sit on the throne of David in the Millennium, but today He is sovereign." (*Reveling Through Revelation*, p. 31)

  c. The commendation: The church at Philadelphia hears two of the most blessed and precious things which could ever be said about a local church.

    (1) You openly confess to the inspiration of the Word of God.

    (2) You openly confess to the incarnation of the Son of God.

  d. The condemnation: None given.

  e. The counsel: "Behold, I come quickly: hold that fast which thou hast, that no man take thy crown" (3:11).

  f. The challenge:

    (1) "I have set before thee an open door, and no man can shut it" (3:8). This is the first of four special doors in Revelation. These are:

      (a) The door of service (3:8). (See also Acts 14:27; 1 Cor. 16:9; 2 Cor. 2:12; Col. 4:3.)

      (b) The door of the human hearts (Rev. 3:20).

      (c) The door of rapture (4:1).

      (d) The door of the Second Coming (19:11).

    (2) I will subdue your enemies (3:9; see also Phil. 2:10, 11).

    (3) I will keep you from the hour of temptation (3:10).

    (4) I will make you a pillar in the temple of my God (3:12).

  g. The church period (1700-1900). Champions of this period would include:

    (1) Jonathan Edwards (1703-1758), one of America's greatest preachers and theologians. His sermon "Sinners in the Hands of an Angry God" is a masterpiece.

    (2) John Wesley (1703-1791), the founder of the Methodist Church and one of England's greatest sons of all time.

    (3) George Whitefield (1714-1770), looked upon as perhaps the greatest public preacher since Simon Peter. He helped to organize the Presbyterian church.

    (4) William Carey (1761-1834), great missionary to Burma.

    (5) Adoniram Judson (1788-1850), missionary to China.

    (6) David Livingstone (1813-1873), missionary to Africa.

    (7) D. L. Moody (1837-1899), world-famous evangelist.

7. The church at Laodicea (3:14-22).

  a. The city:

    (1) "These seven churches lie within a great arc beginning with Ephesus, swinging upward and eastward

through Smyrna and Pergamum and back down to Laodicea. Thus, this last city is about ninety miles due east of Ephesus and about forty-five miles southeast of Philadelphia. The name of the town means 'judgment of the people.' " (*Revelation*, C. Ryrie, p. 31)

(2) This city was founded by Antiochus II and named after his wife. It was a very common name for women.

(3) It was a banking center and possessed immense wealth.

(4) It was graced with resplendent temples and theaters.

(5) An excellent and well-known medical school was built there.

(6) The city was famous for its eye salve called cellyrium.

(7) It was noted for the manufacture of rich garments of black glossy wool.

(8) Several mineral streams were located nearby.

b. The Counselor: "These things saith the Amen, the faithful and true witness, the beginning of the creation of God" (3:14). Here Christ describes himself as:

(1) The faithful and true witness (a reference to what he is).

(2) The beginning of the creation of God (a reference to what he does). John Phillips writes:

"He introduces Himself to Laodicea as 'the beginning of the creation of God,' or as the margin of the American Standard Version puts it, 'the origin of the creation of God.' He it was who flung the stars into space, plowed out the basins of the sea, reared against the skyline of the world the mighty Himalayan range. Not a blade of grass grows without His permission; not a speck of dust moves. He is the origin of the creation of God, the all-controlling one of the dynamic Christ." (*Exploring Revelation*, p. 89)

c. The commendation: This church may be contrasted with the church at Philadelphia. Concerning that one, Christ had no bad statement, but here at Laodicea he can find nothing good to say!

d. The condemnation:

(1) What they thought they were: "I am rich and increased with goods, and have need of nothing" (3:17; see also Lk. 12:16-20).

(2) What God said they were:

(a) They were lukewarm in works. "I know thy works, that thou art neither cold nor hot: I would thou wert cold or hot. So then because thou art lukewarm. . . . I will spew [Greek is *emeo*, 'to vomit'] thee out of my mouth" (3:15, 16).

Charles Ryrie writes:
"Near Laodicea were hot mineral springs whose water could be drunk only if very hot. When lukewarm it became nauseating." (*Revelation*, p. 31)

According to his words here, Christ apparently has more respect for fiery hot fanaticism or for icy cold formalism than for lifeless and lame lukewarmness.

(b) They were lacking in everything else.

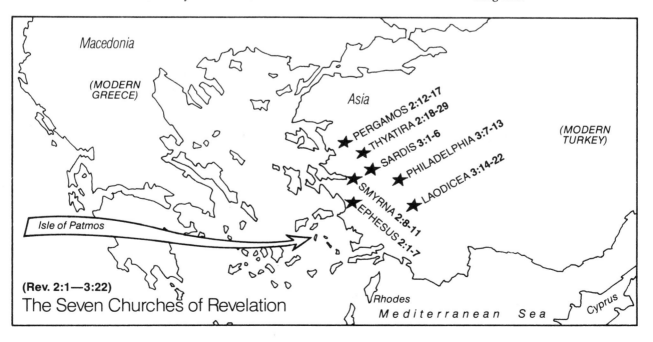

(Rev. 2:1—3:22)
The Seven Churches of Revelation

[1] They were wretched.

[2] They were miserable.

[3] They were poor.

[4] They were blind (see 2 Pet. 1:9).

[5] They were naked.

e. The counsel: They are to obtain from God three things so desperately needed:

(1) Gold (faith) that they might be rich.

(2) White raiment (works blessed by God), that they might be clothed.

(3) Eye salve (forgiveness), that they might see.

f. The challenge:

(1) "As many as I love, I rebuke and chasten" (3:19; see Heb. 12:5-8).

(2) "Behold, I stand at the door, and knock: if any man hear my voice and open the door, I will come in to him, and will sup with him, and he with me" (3:20).

J. Vernon McGee writes:

"His invitation is to the evening meal, the last call for dinner. It is an invitation to come to Him before the night of the Great tribulation." (*Reveling Through Revelation*, p. 36)

Millions of Christians have doubtless viewed Holman Hunt's famous picture of Christ as the Light of the World. Here the artist has depicted Jesus wearing a crown of thorns and standing outside a door which represents the human heart. This painting now hangs in Saint Paul's Cathedral in London. Phillips writes:

"When it was first displayed, critics came to comment on the work. One of them turned to the painter and said, 'Mr. Hunt, you have painted a masterpiece, but you have made one very serious mistake. You have painted a door without a handle.' 'That is no mistake,' replied the artist. 'The handle is on the inside.'" (*Exploring Revelation*, p. 93)

(3) "To him that overcometh will I grant to sit with me in my throne, even as I also overcame, and am set down with my Father in his throne" (3:21).

g. The church age. Little comment is needed to describe the sad state of Christendom as it exists today. Many groups which brazenly carry the name of Christian seem to prefer Communism to democracy, encourage immorality, support anarchy, downplay every important biblical doctrine, ridicule Bible believers and, in general, literally fulfill Paul's prediction when he wrote: "Having a form of godliness, but denying the power thereof" (2 Tim. 3:5). However, it must be quickly added that a small (but powerful) and growing minority of individuals in local churches and schools are demonstrating a love for the Scriptures, the Savior, and the souls of men rarely seen in church history. These schools and churches are filled with people who have heard him knock and have gladly opened wide their doors.

Part Two:

The Worship of the Lamb Invited (4-5)

I. Introduction. John begins this new section with the words "after this" (4:1). The Greek phrase is *meta tauta*, "after these things." What things? The context would suggest that he refers to the rapture which occurs between chapters 3 and 4. The *meta tauta* phrase both opens and closes this verse in the original language. The church has been referred to some nineteen times in the first three chapters. It now completely drops from the pages of the book until the end of the tribulation in Revelation 19. The only godly group Satan can find to torment during the tribulation is the nation Israel. Only two conclusions may be reached from these facts.

A. The church has been wiped out, through persecution by Satan. This concept is, of course, totally unscriptural (see Mt. 16:18).

B. The church has been taken out, through the rapture, by Christ. Various New Testament passages would strongly support this (see 1 Cor. 15:51; 1 Thess. 4:16). John now:

1. Sees a door (Jn. 10:9).

2. Hears a trumpet (1 Thess. 4:16).

II. The Seven-Sealed Book. We now take you by way of the rapture into heaven itself to witness the crisis of a seven-sealed book.

A. The initiation. John now becomes the second of two recorded human beings who are allowed a glimpse of that dazzling kingdom in the sky called heaven.

1. He sees the glory of the Father upon the throne (4:2, 3). Revelation is a *throne* book, the word being used forty-five times, as compared with only fifteen other occurrences of the word in the entire New Testament.

John could distinguish no form or give no description of the awesome One upon this throne, save to say, "He that sat was to look upon like a jasper and a sardine stone" (4:3). Here the jasper, a white stone, and the sardine, a fiery red stone, may refer to God's two basic characteristics, his glory and his grace. These were also the first and last stones among the twelve that the Old Testament high priest bore upon his breastplate. These stones represented the twelve tribes of Israel, arranged according to the births of the twelve sons of Jacob (Ex. 28). Reuben was the first tribe, which name meant "Behold a son," and Benjamin was the last, meaning, "Son of my right hand." This may be God's way of reminding all creatures throughout all eternity of:

PART TWO

Worship
of the Lamb Invited (Rev. 4-5)

The initiation (Rev. 4:1-11)
John sees the Father (4:1-3)
John sees the twenty-four elders (4:4, 5)
John sees the four living creatures (4:6-11)

The proclamation (Rev. 5:1, 2)
"Who is worthy to open the book, and to loose the seals thereof?"

The investigation (Rev. 5:3)
"No man in heaven, nor in earth, neither under the earth was able. . . ."

The lamentation (Rev. 5:4)
"And I wept much . . . ."

The manifestation (Rev. 5:5-7)
The sovereign Lion (and bleeding Lamb) is able

The adoration (Rev. 5:8-14)
"Worthy is the lamb!" (5:12)

---

a. The incarnation of Christ (his humanity) via the jasper stone, Reuben ("Behold a son").

b. The exaltation of Christ (his deity) via the sardine stone, Benjamin ("Son of my right hand").

2. He sees a beautiful green rainbow around the throne (4:3).

3. He sees twenty-four elders with golden crowns (4:4). These twenty-four may consist of a special representative body of both Old Testament and New Testament saints (1 Chron. 24:3-5, 18; Lk. 1:5-9; Rev. 21:12-14). The Greek tells us they are all wearing *stephanos* crowns (martyr crowns) rather than *diadems* (monarch crowns). Thus they must be human beings rather than angels. Daniel saw these thrones being set up (not, "cast down"; see Dan. 7:9), but they were empty in his day. John sees them occupied now.

4. He hears lightnings and thunderings, which means that the awful storm of the great tribulation is about to unleash its fury (4:5). In the Old Testament at Mt. Sinai God thundered when he gave men his law. Now he does the same when he prepares to judge men for breaking that law.

5. He sees "seven lamps of fire burning before the throne, which are the seven spirits of God" (4:5). Several suggestions have been offered to explain this verse:

a. It refers to the earthly ministry of Christ as prophesied in Isaiah 11:1-3.

b. It refers to the sevenfold ministry of the Holy Spirit (restraining, convicting, regenerating, sealing, baptizing, indwelling, filling).

c. It refers to the seven angels of judgment later spoken of in Revelation 8:1-6.

6. He sees a crystal sea of glass (Rev. 4:6). Dr. Donald Barnhouse has written concerning this sea:

"Before the throne there was a glassy sea, like crystal. The concordance immediately takes us to the temple built by Solomon after the model of the tabernacle. 'And he made a molten sea, ten cubits from one brim to the other; it was round all about, and its height was five cubits' (1 Ki. 7:23). This great basin, fifteen feet in diameter, was supported on the backs of twelve oxen of brass, facing outward. Here the priests came for their cleansing. Each time before they entered the holy place they stopped for the cleansing ceremony. But thank God the laver will be turned to crystal. The day will come when none of the saints will ever need confession!

One of the greatest joys in the anticipation of Heaven is that the laver is of crystal. I shall never have to go to the Heavenly Father again to tell Him I have sinned. I shall never have to meet that gaze of Christ that caused Peter to go out and weep bitterly. The laver is of crystal only because I and all the saints of the ages will have been made like unto the Lord Jesus Christ." (*Revelation, an Expository Commentary*, p. 94)

7. He sees and hears the testimony of four special angelic creatures (4:6-8). The Greek for "wild beast" is *therion*. But here the word used is *zoa* (root word for zoology), meaning "living creatures."

a. Who are these four living creatures? J. Vernon McGee writes:

"These creatures, of the highest intelligence, are in God's presence. They resemble the Cherubim of Ezekiel 1:5-10; 10:20 and the seraphim of Isaiah 6:2, 3. Are they a new order of creatures in heaven that have not been revealed before in Scripture?" (*Reveling Through Revelation*, p. 43)

b. What is their purpose? Perhaps to remind all creatures throughout all eternity of the blessed earthly and heavenly ministry of Christ. This is suggested by their appearance:

(1) The first was like a lion. He communicates the office of Christ as King—as seen in the Gospel of Matthew.

(2) The second was like a calf. He communicates the office of Christ as a servant—as seen in the Gospel of Mark.

(3) The third was like a man. He communicates the humanity of Christ—as seen in the Gospel of Luke.

(4) The fourth was like an eagle. He communicates the deity of Christ—as seen in the Gospel of John.

B. The proclamation. John sees these seven things and they fill him with awe and wonder. But now he witnesses an eighth event, which causes despair to flood his soul. The crisis of the seven-sealed book is about to begin.

"And I saw in the right hand of him that sat on the throne a book written within and on the backside, sealed with seven seals. And I saw a strong angel proclaiming with a loud voice, Who is worthy to open the book, and to loose the seals thereof?" (5:1, 2).

What is this book (really a rolled-up scroll), sealed so securely with seven seals? Whatever it contained, the scroll was extremely important, for history informs us that under Roman law all legal documents pertaining to life and death were to be sealed seven times. A number of theologians believe that this is actually the legal title deed to the earth. Thus the angel's proclamation was, in effect, "Who is worthy to reclaim the earth's title deed? Who is able to pour out the seven-sealed judgment to purify this planet, and to usher in the long-awaited golden-age millennium?" Who indeed was worthy? (See also Jer. 32:6-16.)

C. The investigation.

"And no man in heaven, nor in earth, neither under the earth, was able to open the book, neither to look thereon" (5:3).

Let us follow the angel as he begins his threefold search.

1. The search in heaven. Was there any among the redeemed worthy to claim the earth's title deed? There was not.

a. Adam originally possessed this title deed (Gen. 1:28, 29), but was cheated out of it by the devil (Gen. 3:1-19).

b. Noah, the hero of the flood, subsequently became the drunkard of the vineyard, thus disqualifying himself (Gen. 6-9).

c. Abraham, the father of Israel, backslid and went to Egypt temporarily (Gen. 12).

d. David, the man after God's own heart (1 Sam. 16:7), later broke God's heart through lust and murder (2 Sam. 11).

e. John the Baptist, the forerunner of Christ, in a moment of weakness doubted that same Messiah (Mt. 11:3).

f. Peter, the "rock," denied his Lord in the hour of need (Mt. 26:70).

g. Paul, perhaps the greatest Christian who ever lived, compromised his testimony (Acts 21).

2. The search on earth. Who could accomplish in the sinful environment of earth what no man could achieve even in the sinless environment of heaven? Preachers and priests might minister to the earth, and kings rule over sections of it, but claim it they could not!

3. The search under the earth (in Hades). If no saint or angel *could* purify this earth, then certainly no sinner or demon *would*, even if this were possible.

D. The lamentation.

"And I wept much, because no man was found worthy to open and to read the book, neither to look thereon" (5:4).

Why did John weep? Perhaps because (among other things) he realized that the ultimate resurrection and glorification of his own body was directly connected with the removal of the curse placed upon this earth. (See Rom. 8:17-23.)

This passage marks the final instance of a believer weeping. Sorrow, sufferings, and death have combined to carve out an ocean of human tears since Adam's tragic rebellion against God.

1. Abraham wept over Sarah's body (Gen. 23:2).

2. Israel weeps over slavery conditions in Egypt (Ex. 2:23; 3:7).

3. Moses weeps over Miriam's sin (Num. 12:13).

4. Joshua weeps over the defeat of Israel (Josh. 7:6-9).

5. Naomi weeps as she leaves Moab (Ruth 1:9).

6. Hannah weeps over her barrenness (1 Sam. 1:10).

7. Samuel weeps over the failure of Saul (1 Sam. 15:35).

8. David weeps over his great sin (Ps. 32:4; 51:17).

9. Tamar weeps after being ravished by Amnon (2 Sam. 13:19).

10. David weeps over the death of his rebellious son (2 Sam. 18:33).

11. Hezekiah weeps over the threat to Jerusalem (2 Chron. 32:20).

12. The Jewish captives weep en route to Babylon (Ps. 137:1).

13. Daniel weeps over Israel's sin (Dan. 10:2).

14. Nehemiah weeps over Jerusalem's broken walls (Neh. 1:4).

15. Mordecai weeps over Haman's murderous plot (Est. 4:1).

16. A mother weeps over her sick child (Mt. 15:22).

17. A father weeps over his demoniac son (Mk. 9:24).

18. A widow weeps over her dead son (Lk. 7:13).

19. Two sisters weep over their dead brother (Jn. 11:33).

20. The Savior weeps over Lazarus (Jn. 11:35) and Jerusalem (Lk. 19:41).

But all this weeping will soon end when the rightful Ruler of this universe comes forth!

E. The manifestation.

"And one of the elders saith unto me, Weep not: behold, the Lion of the tribe of Juda, the Root of David, hath prevailed to open the book, and to loose the seven seals thereof. And I beheld, and, lo, in the midst of the throne and of the four beasts, and in the midst of the elders, stood a Lamb as it had been slain, having seven horns and seven eyes, which are the seven Spirits of God sent forth into all the earth. And he came and took the book out of the right hand of him that sat upon the throne" (Rev. 5:5-7).

Phillips writes:

"John turned to behold a Lion. But instead of a shaggy mane and gaping jaws and dreadful teeth, he saw—a Lamb! Was there ever a more dramatic moment in the history of the universe? The Lion was none other than the Lamb!" (*Exploring Revelation,* John Phillips, p. 106)

Who is this heavenly Hero who so boldly removes the scroll from the Father's right hand? We need not speculate for one second about his identity, for he is the Lord Jesus Christ himself. The proof is overwhelming.

1. He has the characteristics of a lamb. Our Lord is referred to as a Lamb twenty-nine times in the New Testament. In all but one instance (1 Pet. 1:19) it is the Apostle John who employs this title. Furthermore,

   a. It is a pet lamb. There are two words for "lamb" in the Greek New Testament. One is *amnos* (a lamb in general) and the other is *arnion* (a special household pet lamb). Here in Revelation 5:6 the second Greek word is used. (For a related Old Testament passage, see 2 Sam. 12:1-4.)

   b. It is a slain lamb. Here the Greek word for slain is *sphatto,* and refers to a violent death of some sort. The same word is found in the following passage: "We should love one another. Not as Cain, who was of that wicked one, and slew his brother" (1 Jn. 3:11, 12).

      The word *sphatto* is found only seven times in the New Testament, and four of these usages refer to the death of Christ (Rev. 5:6, 9, 12; 13:8).

   c. It is an all-powerful lamb. The lamb is pictured as possessing seven horns, which in biblical symbolic language refers to power and authority.

   d. It is an all-knowing lamb. The lamb is pictured as possessing seven eyes, referring to perfect knowledge and wisdom.

2. He has the characteristics of a lion. John calls him "The Lion of the tribe of Juda, the Root of David," and so he is. Three key Bible chapters explain this title.

   a. In Genesis 49 the dying Jacob predicted that Judah, his fourth son, would be like a lion, and that the later kings of Israel, including Christ himself, would come from his tribe (Gen. 49:8-10).

   b. In 2 Samuel 7 God told David (who was of the tribe of Judah) that his kingdom would be eternal and that his household would rule forever (2 Sam. 7:8-17).

   c. In Luke 1 the angel Gabriel explained to Mary (who was of the house of David)

that her virgin-born son would inherit all the Old Testament promises as found in Genesis 49 and 2 Samuel 7 (Lk. 1:30-33). Thus John sees Christ as a Lamb, since he once came to redeem his people. This was his *past* work. John also sees him as a lion, for he shall come again to reign over his people. This will be his *future* work. The source of his claim to the earth's scepter is therefore related to his slain Lamb characteristics while the strength of his claim is due to his mighty Lion characteristics.

F. The adoration.

"And when he had taken the book, the four beasts and four and twenty elders fell down before the Lamb, having every one of them harps, and golden vials full of odours, which are the prayers of saints. And they sung a new song, saying, Thou art worthy to take the book and to open the seals thereof: for thou wast slain, and hast redeemed us to God by thy blood out of every kindred, and tongue, and people, and nation; and hast made us unto our God kings and priests: and we shall reign on the earth.

And I beheld, and I heard the voice of many angels round about the throne and the beasts and the elders: and the number of them was ten thousand times ten thousand, and thousands of thousands; saying with a loud voice, Worthy is the Lamb that was slain to receive power, and riches, and wisdom, and strength, and honour, and glory, and blessing.

And every creature which is in heaven, and on the earth, and under the earth, and such as are in the sea, and all that are in them, heard I saying, Blessing, and honour, and glory, and power be unto him that sitteth upon the throne, and unto the Lamb for ever and ever. And the four beasts said, Amen. And the four and twenty elders fell down and worshipped him that liveth for ever and ever" (5:8-14).

1. The source of this worship. It comes from all directions and includes every creature.

   a. the twenty-four elders

   b. the four living creatures

   c. uncounted angels

   d. all upon the earth

   e. all under the earth

At this point it should be noted that John carefully separates the *singing* he heard from the *saying* (chanting). Of all the various groups involved, only the redeemed are described as singing.

W. A. Criswell writes:

"Always the redeemed sing. God's blood-washed sing. God's children sing, but angels do not sing. Here is my conclusion. Music is made up of major chords and minor chords. The minor chords speak of the wretchedness, death and sorrow of this fallen creation. Most of nature moans and groans in a plaintive and minor key. The sound of the wind through the forest, the sound of the storm, the sound of the wind around the house, is always in a minor key. It wails. The sound of the ocean moans in its restlessness, in its speechless travail. Even the nightingale's, the sweetest song, is the saddest. Most of the sounds of nature are in a minor key. It reflects the wretchedness, the despair, the hurt, the agony, the travail of this fallen creation. But an angel knows nothing of this. An angel knows nothing of the wretchedness, nothing of the despair, nothing of the fall of our lost race." (*Expository Sermons on Revelation*, pp. 204, 205)

2. The subject of this worship: "Worthy is the Lamb."
  a. What he once did: "For thou wast slain, and hast redeemed us to God by thy blood" (5:9).
    Note:
    (1) Isaac once asked, "*Where* is the Lamb?" (Gen. 22:7).
    (2) John the Baptist then answered "*Behold* the Lamb!" (Jn. 1:29).
    (3) All creation now says, "*Worthy* is the Lamb!" (Rev. 5:12).
      J. Vernon McGee writes:
        "They sing of His blood in heaven. Down here many denominational churches are taking from their hymn books all songs about the Blood of Christ, but the Blood is not being taken out of the hymn books in heaven—they sing about the Blood up there!"
      We are told that this singing is a new song (5:9).
    (4) The *old* song is that of creation. (See Job 38:7; Rev. 4:11.)
    (5) The *new* song is that of redemption.
  b. What he now receives: "Power, riches, wisdom, strength, honor, glory, and blessing" (Rev. 5:12).

Part Three:

The Wrath of the Lamb Invoked (5-19).
  "For two breathtaking, soul-inspiring chapters, we have been in heaven. The scroll has changed hands, and the right to judge and rule the world has been placed upon Jesus. Now we must come down from the mount and out of the ivory palaces. Down here, on the rebel planet of earth, the tempo is increasing, passions are rising. Evil men and seducers are waxing worse and worse. Disobedience to parents has grown up into brawling maturity, defying all authority. Men have become inventors of evil things, and their fearful inventions have become Frankenstein monsters, threatening to destroy the globe. The time has come for God to intervene in human affairs, so judgment is given to the Son." (John Phillips, *Exploring Revelation*, p. 110)

At the beginning of chapter 4, John took us up from earth to heaven by means of the rapture of Christ. Here in chapter 6 we abruptly return to earth to view the wrath of Christ. The wrath of Jesus is invoked along the following seven avenues, through:
  I. The Seal Judgments.
  II. The Reign of the Devil.
  III. The Vial Judgments.
  IV. The Destruction of the World's Religious System.
  V. The Destruction of the World's Economic System.
  VI. The Bloodbath at Armageddon.
  VII. The Destruction of the Antichrist and the False Prophet.

We shall now examine each of these seven terrible judgments.

  I. The Seal Judgments (Rev. 6:1-17; 8:1—9:21; see also Mt. 24:4-8).
    A. The first seal (Rev. 6:2).
      "And I saw, and behold, a white horse; and he that sat on him had a bow; and a crown was given unto him; and he went forth conquering and to conquer."
    This is doubtless a symbolic picture of the antichrist as he subdues to himself the ten nations of the revived Roman Empire. This may be thought of as the "cold war" period. We note he carries no arrow, which may indicate conquest by diplomacy rather than a shooting war.
    B. The second seal (Rev. 6:3, 4).
      "And when he had opened the second seal, I heard the second beast say, Come and see. And there went out another horse that was red; and power was given to him that sat thereon to take peace from the earth, and that they should kill one another; and there was given unto him a great sword."
    The uneasy peace which the rider on the white horse brings to earth is temporary and counterfeit. The antichrist promises peace, but only God can actually produce it.
    As Isaiah would write, "But the wicked are like the troubled sea, when it cannot rest, whose waters cast up mire and dirt. There is no peace, saith my God, to the wicked" (Isa. 57:20, 21). Now open and bloody hostility breaks out among some of the nations.
    C. The third seal (Rev. 6:5, 6).
      "And when he had opened the third seal, I heard the third beast say, Come and see. And I beheld, and lo a black horse; and he that sat on him had a pair of balances in his hand. And I heard a voice in the midst of the four beasts say, A measure of wheat for a penny, and three measures of barley for a penny; and see thou hurt not the oil and the wine."
    Dr. Charles Ryrie writes the following concerning this seal:
      "The third judgment brings famine to the world. The black horse forebodes death, and the pair of balances bespeaks a careful rationing of food. Normally, a 'penny' (a Roman denarius, a day's wages in Palestine in Jesus' day, Mt. 20:2) would buy eight measures of wheat or twenty-four of barley.
        Under these famine conditions the same wage will buy only one measure of wheat or three of barley. In other words, there will be one-eighth of the normal supply of food. The phrase 'see thou hurt not the oil and the wine' is an ironic twist in this terrible situation. Apparently luxury food items will not be in short supply, but of course most people will not be able to afford them. This situation will only

PART THREE

Wrath
of the Lamb Invoked (Rev. 5-19)

1. He pours out the seven seal judgments **(6:1-17; 8:1—9:21)**
2. He allows the devil to reign **(12-13)**
3. He pours out the seven vial judgments **(14-16)**
4. He destroys the world's religious systems **(17)**
5. He destroys the world's political and economic systems **(18)**
6. He defeats sinners and Satan at Armageddon **(19:1-19, 21)**
7. He condemns the antichrist and false prophet into hell **(19:20)**

FIRST DIVINE PUNISHMENT

**THE LAMB POURS OUT
THE SEVEN SEALS
OF JUDGMENT**
Rev. 6:1-17; 8:1—9:21 SEE ALSO Mt. 24:4-8.

1st seal—*WHITE HORSE*
COLD WAR **(6:2)**

2nd seal—*RED HORSE*
HOT WAR **(6:3, 4)**

3rd seal—*BLACK HORSE*
FAMINE **(6:5, 6)**

4th seal—*PALE HORSE*
WIDESPREAD DEATH BY WAR, STARVATION, AND WILD BEASTS **(6:7, 8)**

5th seal
THE CRY OF THE MARTYRED **(6:9-11)**

6th seal
EARTH'S GREATEST EARTHQUAKE, EARTH'S GREATEST COSMIC DISTURBANCE, EARTH'S GREATEST PRAYER MEETING **(6:12-17)**

INTERLUDE
A short period between the sixth and seventh seals **(7:1-17)**
THE CONVERSION AND CALL OF THE 144,000 **(7:1-8)**
THE CONVERSION OF A GREAT MULTITUDE **(7:9-17)**

7th seal

COMPOSED OF
SEVEN TRUMPETS **(8:1—11:19)**

FIRST TRUMPET **(8:7)**
One third of vegetation destroyed

SECOND TRUMPET **(8:8, 9)**
One third of ocean life and ships destroyed

THIRD TRUMPET **(8:10, 11)**
One third of fresh water poisoned

FOURTH TRUMPET **(8:12)**
One third of sun, moon, and stars darkened

FIFTH TRUMPET **(9:1-12)**
their location **(9:1)**   their duration **(9:5, 6)**
their leader **(9:1, 11)**   their description **(9:7-10)**
their torment **(9:3, 4)**
FIRST HELLISH INVASION OF DEMONS UPON THIS EARTH

SIXTH TRUMPET **(9:13-21)**
leaders **(9:14)**   damage **(9:15, 18)**
source **(9:14)**   description **(9:17-19)**
number **(9:16)**   results **(9:20, 21)**
duration **(9:15, 18)**
SECOND HELLISH INVASION OF DEMONS UPON THIS EARTH

INTERLUDE **(10:1—11:14)**
THE MESSAGE OF THE ANGEL OF GOD **(10:1-11)**
THE MEASURING OF THE TEMPLE OF GOD **(11:1, 2)**
THE MINISTRY OF THE WITNESSES OF GOD **(11:3-14)**

SEVENTH TRUMPET **(11:15-19)**
"THE KING IS COMING!"

---

serve to taunt the populace in their impoverished state." (*Revelation*, p. 45, 46)

Will the food problem really be as bad as all this during the tribulation?

Dean Stanley has written a graphic description of the destruction of Jerusalem by Nebuchadnezzar in 586 B.C., and the terrible famine which followed. His words serve as a faint hint of the horrible conditions which prevail during the third seal. Stanley writes:

"Famine and its accompanying visitation of pestilence ravaged the crowded population within the walls. It was only by a special favour of the king that a daily supply of bread was sent to Jeremiah, in his prison, from the bakers' quarters, and at last even this failed. The nobles, who had prided themselves on their beautiful complexions, purer than snow, whiter than milk, ruddy as rubies, polished as sapphires (Lam. 4.7), had become ghastly and black with starvation. Their wasted skeleton forms could hardly be recognized in the streets. The ladies of Jerusalem, in their magnificent crimson robes, might be seen sitting in despair on the dunghills. From these foul heaps were gathered morsels to eke out the failing supply of food (Lam. 4:5). There was something specially piteous in the sight of the little children, with their parched tongues, fainting in the streets, asking for bread, crying to their mothers for corn and wine (Lam. 2:11, 12, 19). There was something still more terrible in the hardening feeling with which the parents turned away from them. The Hebrew mothers seemed to have lost even the instincts of the brute creation, to have sunk to the level of the unnatural ostriches that leave their nests in the wilderness (Lam. 4:3). Fathers devoured the flesh of their own sons and their own daughters (Ezek. 5:10; Baruch 2:3). The hands even of compassionate mothers have sodden their own children, the mere infants just born (Lam. 2:20; 4:10)." (*The Unfolding Drama of Redemption,* p. 363, quoted by W. G. Scroggie)

D. The fourth seal (Rev. 6:7, 8).

"And when he had opened the fourth seal, I heard the voice of the fourth beast say, Come and see. And I looked, and behold a pale horse: and his name that sat on him was Death, and Hell followed with him. And power was given unto them over the fourth part of the earth, to kill with sword, and with hunger, and with death, and with the beasts of the earth."

1. The identity of these riders. John calls them "Death" and "Hell," apparently referring to physical and spiritual death. Thus the devil will destroy the bodies and damn the souls of multitudes of unbelievers during this third-seal plague.

2. The damage done by these riders. One-fourth of all humanity perishes during this plague. It is estimated that during the Second World War one out of forty persons lost their lives, but this seal judgment alone will claim one out of four persons—nearly one billion human beings! We note the phrase, "with the beasts of the earth." Here John Phillips has written:

"The beasts are closely linked with the pestilence, and this might be a clue. The most destructive creature on earth as far as mankind is concerned, is not the lion or the bear, but the rat. The rat is clever, adaptable, and destructive. If ninety-five percent of the rat population is exterminated in a given area, the rat population will replace itself within a year. It has killed more people than all the wars in history, and makes its home wherever man is found. Rats carry as many as thirty-five diseases. Their fleas carry bubonic plague, which killed a third of the population of Europe in the fourteenth century. Their fleas also carry typhus, which in four centuries has killed an estimated two hundred million people. Beasts, in this passage, are linked not only with pestilence, but with famine. Rats menace human food supplies, which they both devour and contaminate, especially in the more underdeveloped countries which can least afford to suffer loss." (*Exploring Revelation,* p. 116)

Also to be noted are the words of Dr. Frank Holtman, head of the University of Tennessee bacteriological department.

"While the greater part of a city's population could be destroyed by an atomic bomb, the bacteria method might easily wipe out the entire population within a week. The virus causing parrot fever, one of the most deadly of human diseases, is appraised by scientists as being the most preferable for this purpose. While the cost of producing psittacosis bombs is comparatively cheap, its lethal potency is extremely high. According to Thomas R. Henry, science editor, less than one cubic centimeter of this virus is required to infect 20 million human beings when released in the air as an infinitesimal spray."

E. The fifth seal (Rev. 6:9–11).

"And when he had opened the fifth seal, I saw under the altar the souls of them that were slain for the word of God, and for the testimony which they held; and they cried with a loud voice, saying, How long, O Lord, holy and true, dost thou not judge and avenge our blood on them that dwell on the earth? And white robes were given unto every one of them; and it was said unto them that they should rest yet for a little season, until their fellow-servants also and their brethren, that should be killed as they were, should be fulfilled."

Here is religious persecution as never before! These three verses are loaded with theological implications.

1. They refute the damnable doctrine of soul-sleep.

2. They correct the error of one general resurrection. It is evident that these martyred souls did not receive their glorified bodies at the rapture, as did the church-age saints. Therefore it can be concluded that these are Old Testament saints who will experience the glorious bodily resurrection after the tribulation (see Rev. 20:4-6).

3. They suggest the possibilities of an intermediate body. (See also 2 Cor. 5:1-3.) Dr. John Walvoord writes:

"These martyred dead here pictured have not been raised from the dead and have not received their resurrection bodies. Yet it is declared that they are given robes. The fact that they are given robes would almost demand that they have a body of some sort. A robe could not hang upon an immaterial soul or spirit. It is not the kind of body that Christians now have, that is, the body of earth; nor is it the resurrection body of flesh and bones of which Christ spoke after His own resurrection. It is a temporary body suited for their presence in heaven but replaced in turn by their everlasting resurrection body given at the time of Christ's return." (*The Revelation of Jesus Christ,* p. 134)

F. The sixth seal (6:12-17).

"And I beheld when he had opened the sixth seal, and lo, there was a great earthquake; and the sun became black as sackcloth of hair, and the moon became as blood; and the stars of heaven fell unto the earth, even as a fig tree casteth her untimely figs, when she is shaken of a mighty wind. And the heaven departed as a scroll when it is rolled together; and every mountain and island were moved out of their places. And the kings of the earth, and the great men, and the rich men, and the chief captains and the mighty men, and every bondman, and every free man, hid themselves in the dens and in the rocks of the mountains; and said to the mountains and rocks, Fall on us, and hide us from the face of him that sitteth on the throne, and from the wrath of the Lamb: For the great day of his wrath is come; and who shall be able to stand?"

As it can be seen, this fearful judgment ushers in:

1. The greatest earthquake in history. There have, of course, been hundreds of severe earthquakes in man's history.
   a. The earliest recorded was in July of 365 in the Middle East.
   b. The most destructive was in January of 1556 in China. Nearly one million lost their lives.
   c. The worst in the United States:
      (1) The San Francisco earthquake, April 18, 1906. Killed 700 people. Cost $500 million.
      (2) The Anchorage, Alaska, earthquake, March 27, 1964. Killed 114. Cost $750 million. But at the *end* of the tribulation there will be one even worse than the one occurring in the sixth seal. (See Rev. 16:18.)
2. The greatest cosmic disturbances in history. These may be a result of nuclear war. Hal Lindsey writes:

   "Do you know what happens in a nuclear explosion? The atmosphere rolls back on itself! It's this tremendous rush of air back into the vacuum that causes much of the destruction of a nuclear explosion. John's words in this verse are a perfect picture of an all-out nuclear exchange. When this happens, John continues, every mountain and island will be jarred from its present position. The whole world will be literally shaken apart!" (*There's a New World Coming*, p. 110)
3. The greatest prayer meeting in history. But they prayed for the wrong thing. The only object to protect the sinner from the *wrath* of the Lamb is the *righteousness* of the Lamb.

G. Interlude (7:1-17). Between the sixth and seventh seal judgments, God calls a divine time-out. During this pause, two significant events take place.
1. The conversion and call of the 144,000 (Rev. 7:1-8).

   "And after these things I saw four angels standing on the four corners of the earth, holding the four winds of the earth, that the wind should not blow on the earth, nor on the sea, nor on any tree. And I saw another angel ascending from the east, having the seal of the living God: and he cried with a loud voice to the four angels, to whom it was given to hurt the earth and the sea, saying, Hurt not the earth, neither the sea, nor the trees, till we have sealed the servants of our God in their foreheads. And I heard the number of them which were sealed: and there were sealed an hundred and forty and four thousand of all the tribes of the children of Israel."

This passage does not mean that God will save only Jews during the tribulation, for in Revelation 7:9-17, the Bible declares that a great multitude from every nation will be saved. What this chapter does teach, however, is that God will send out 144,000 "Hebrew Billy Sundays" to evangelize the world. This will be a massive number indeed, especially when we consider that there are less than 35,000 missionaries of all persuasions in the world today! Our Lord doubtless had the ministry of the 144,000 in mind when he said, "And this gospel of the kingdom shall be preached in all the world for a witness unto all nations; and then shall the end come" (Mt. 24:14).

Judah heads up this list, and not Reuben, the firstborn. Both Dan and Ephraim are missing. Both tribes were guilty of going into idolatry (Jdg. 18; 1 Ki. 11:26; Hosea 4). The tribes of Levi and Manasseh here take their place. However, both are listed in Ezekiel's millennial temple (Ezek. 48), so they simply forfeit their chance to preach during the tribulation. Some have concluded on the basis of Genesis 49:17 and Jeremiah 8:16 that the antichrist will come from the tribe of Dan.

Dr. J. Dwight Pentecost offers the following interesting words concerning the conversion of the 144,000:

"In 1 Corinthians 15:8 is a clue concerning the way God will work after the church's rapture. After the apostle had listed those to whom the resurrected Christ appeared, so as to authenticate His resurrection, he says, 'And last of all he was seen of me also, as of one born out of due time.' This phrase, 'born out of due time,' means a premature birth. That is exactly what the apostle Paul is saying—'I was one that was born prematurely.' What did he mean? Comparing Revelation 7 with Paul's statement in 1 Corinthians 15, we conclude that after the rapture of the church, God will perform the same miracle He performed in Saul of Tarsus on the Damascus Road 144,000 times over." (*Will Man Survive?* p. 148)
2. The conversion of "a great multitude" (7:9-17)
   a. Their number: countless (7:9).

b. Their praise: "Salvation to our God which sitteth upon the throne, and unto the Lamb" (7:10).
c. Their background: "These are they which came out of great tribulation, and have washed their robes, and made them white in the blood of the Lamb" (7:14).
d. Their service: serving God continuously (7:15).
e. Their reward: to be both fed and led by the Lamb (7:17).

H. The seventh seal (8:1—11:19).

"And when he had opened the seventh seal, there was silence in heaven about the space of half an hour" (8:1).

This marks the only occasion in recorded history that heaven is silent. There is not the slightest sound or movement.

1. The purpose of the silence. During the sixth seal, mankind seemed to weaken for the first time during the tribulation. A merciful and patient God now awaits further repentance, but all to no avail. God takes no pleasure in the death of the wicked (Ezek. 33:11).

2. The duration of the silence. It lasted for thirty minutes. The number thirty in the Bible is often associated with mourning. Israel mourned for thirty days over the death of both Aaron (Num. 20:29) and Moses (Deut. 34:8).

3. We now examine the contents of the seventh seal, which consists of seven trumpet judgments.

a. The first trumpet (8:7).

"The first angel sounded, and there followed hail and fire mingled with blood, and they were cast upon the earth; and the third part of trees was burnt up, and all green grass was burnt up" (Rev. 8:7).

It has been observed that plant life was the first to be created, and it is the first to be destroyed (Gen. 1:11, 12). John Phillips writes:

"Looked upon as a literal occurrence, an ecological disaster without parallel in historic times is described. The planet is denuded of a third of its trees and all of its grass. The consequences of this are bound to be terrible. The United States, for example, has already proceeded with deforestation to such an extent that the country contains only enough vegetation to produce sixty percent of the oxygen it consumes." (*Exploring Revelation*, p. 129)

b. The second trumpet (8:8, 9).

"And the second angel sounded, and as it were a great mountain burning with fire was cast into the sea; and the third part of the sea became blood; and the third part of the creatures which were in the sea, and had life, died; and the third part of the ships were destroyed."

Dr. Herman A. Hoyt writes:

"Here we read of a great mountain burning with fire. This may refer to a meteoric mass from the sky falling headlong into the sea, perhaps the Mediterranean Sea. The result is to turn a third part of the sea a blood-red color and bring about the death of a third part of the life in the sea. Death may be caused by the chemical reaction in the water, such as radioactivity following atomic explosion. The third part of ships may be destroyed by the violence of the waters produced by the falling of the mass." (*Revelation*, p. 49)

c. The third trumpet (8:10, 11).

"And the third angel sounded, and there fell a great star from heaven, burning as it were a lamp, and it fell upon the third part of the rivers, and upon the fountains of waters; and the name of the star is called Wormwood; and the third part of the waters became wormwood; and many men died of the waters, because they were made bitter."

This star could refer to a meteor containing stifling and bitter gases, which fall on the Alps or some other freshwater source. During the second trumpet a third of the salt water was contaminated. Now a third of earth's fresh water suffers a similar fate. Many species of wormwood grow in Palestine. All species have a strong, bitter taste.

d. The fourth trumpet (8:12).

"And the fourth angel sounded, and the third part of the sun was smitten, and the third part of the moon, and the third part of the stars; so as the third part of them was darkened, and the day shone not for a third part of it, and the night likewise" (Rev. 8:12).

Our Lord may have had this trumpet judgment in mind when he spoke the following words:

"And except those days should be shortened, there should no flesh be saved; but for the elect's sake those days shall be shortened" (Mt. 24:22).

"And there shall be signs in the sun, and in the moon, and in the stars" (Lk. 21:25).

The Old Testament prophecy of Amos is also significant here:

"And it shall come to pass in that day, saith the Lord God, that I will cause the sun to go down at noon, and I will darken the earth in the clear day" (Amos 8:9).

It was on the fourth day that God created the sun, moon, and stars (Gen. 1:14-16). They were to be for "signs, and for seasons, and for days, and for years." After the flood, God promised not to alter this divine arrangement (Gen. 8:22). But in the tribulation, during the fourth trumpet, earth's very light will be limited by judgment. Between the fourth and fifth trumpets, John reports:

"And I beheld, and heard an angel flying through the midst of heaven, saying with a loud voice, Woe, woe, woe, to the inhabiters of the earth by reason of the other voices of the trumpet of the three angels, which are yet to sound" (8:13).

The word "angel" here should be translated "eagle." An eagle is sometimes pictured as God's method of judgment (Deut. 28:49; Hosea 8:1). Thus, even the brute creation will be used by God during the tribulation. This marks the last of three occasions on which a creature speaks in the Bible. (For the other two, see Gen. 3:1-5—a serpent; and Num. 22:28-30—an ass.)

e. The fifth trumpet (9:1-12). J. Vernon McGee writes:

"The last three trumpets are marked off from the other four by identification with the three woes (8:13; 9:12; 11:14). These woes mark the deepest darkness and most painful intensity of the Great Tribulation. This is generally associated with the last part (3½ years), the blackest days in human history." (Reveling Through Revelation, p. 73)

The ninth chapter of Revelation, which contains both fifth and sixth trumpet judgments, may be the most revealing section in all the Bible concerning the subject of demonology. Prior to this, God has already made it known that there are two kinds of unfallen angels. These are the Cherubim (Gen. 3:24; Ex. 25:8; Ezek. 10:1-20), and the Seraphim (Isa. 6:1-8). Here he may be describing for us the two kinds of fallen angels. We now note the first type as revealed by the fifth trumpet judgment.

(1) The location of these demons—the bottomless pit (9:1). Literally this phrase is "shaft of the abyss." The word "shaft" here indicates that there is an entrance from the surface of the earth to the heart of our planet. In this chapter we learn for the first time of a place called the bottomless pit. God mentions it no less than seven times in the book of Revelation (9:1, 2, 11; 11:7; 17:8; 20:1-3).

(2) The identity of these demons. Some have identified these with the sons of God in Genesis 6:1, 2. Here the theory is that these demons attempted sexual relations with women, resulting in immediate confinement in the bottomless pit. We

do know that some demons are already chained and others at present have access to the bodies of men.

(a) Unchained demons (Lk. 4:34; Mt. 8:29; Lk. 8:27-31).

(b) Chained demons (Jude 1:6, 7; 2 Pet. 2:4; 1 Pet. 3:18-20). Thus another name for this bottomless pit may be the *tartarus* mentioned in the Greek text of 2 Peter 2:4. Here Satan will be later confined during the millennium (Rev. 20:3).

(3) The one who releases these demons. This "fallen star" mentioned in 9:1 seems to be Satan himself. (See also Isa. 14:12; Lk. 10:18; 2 Cor. 11:14.) Prior to this time, Christ has held the key to the pit (Rev. 1:18), but now allows the devil to use it for a specific purpose.

(4) The torment of these demons (9:3, 4).

"And there came out of the smoke locusts upon the earth: and unto them was given power, as the scorpions of the earth have power. And it was commanded them that they should not hurt the grass of the earth, neither any green thing, neither any tree; but only those men which have not the seal of God in their foreheads."

J.A. Seiss writes:

"The pain from the sting of a scorpion, though not generally fatal, is, perhaps, the most intense that any animal can inflict upon the human body. The insect itself is the most . . . malignant that lives, and its poison is like itself. Of a boy stung in the foot by a scorpion (it was related that) . . . he rolled on the ground, grinding his teeth, and foaming at the mouth. It was a long time before his complainings moderated, and even then he could make no use of his foot, which was greatly inflamed. And such is the nature of the torment which these locusts from the pit inflict. They are also difficult to be guarded against, if they can be warded off at all, because they fly where they please, dart through the air, and dwell in darkness." (The Apocalypse, p. 83)

(5) The duration of these demons. Charles Ryrie writes:

"Horrible as the torment will be, God will place certain limitations on the activity of these demons. They will be limited as to what they may strike and as to how far they may go and as to how long they may do what they will do. They will not attack the vegetation of the earth (as common locusts do); they may only attack certain men, that is, those who have not the seal of God in their foreheads (the 144,000; cf. 7:3). The wicked will persecute God's servants, the 144,000; but in turn they will be tormented by this plague which God allows. The demon-locusts will also be limited in that they may not kill men, just torment them.

Further, the duration of this plague will be five months. The effect of this torment is to drive men to suicide, but they will not be able to die. Although men will prefer death to the agony of living, death will not be possible. Bodies will not sink and drown; poisons and pills will have no effect; and somehow even bullets and knives will not do their intended job." (*Revelation*, p. 62)

The reason men cannot die is probably because Satan has the key to the shaft and will not allow his followers to leave the earth scene where the battle of light and darkness is being fought.

(6) The description of these demons (9:7-10). The shapes of these creatures are absolutely hideous. They are like horses prepared for battle. Crowns of gold seem to be upon their heads. Their faces are like men, their hair like women, their teeth like lions. They have on breastplates as of iron. Their tails are like those of a scorpion. The sound of their wings is like that of many chariots rushing toward battle.

The king of these demons (9:11). His name is Apollyon, which means "destroyer." Here is Satan's hellish "Michael the Archangel."

(7) The horrible reality of these demons. John Phillips writes:

"Modern man professes not to believe in demons, but they exist just the same. Moreover, they are clever with a diabolical cunning. Man's attitude toward the demon world may well be likened to man's attitude in the dark ages toward bacteria. If we could be transported back to London in the year 1666, we would find ourselves in a nightmare world. The great bubonic plague is at its height. The sights and sounds of the city are like the terrible climax of a horror movie. It is generally believed that fresh air is the culprit. The College of Physicians recommends the frequent firing of guns to blow away the deadly air. People seal themselves into their rooms and burn foul-smelling messes to ward off the fresh air. Chimneys are sealed, rooms are gray with smoke, and people choke in the suffocating stench. Outside, palls of black smoke hang over the city. People sit in the tightly sealed chambers, grimly determined to endure the smarting smoke, convinced they are thus immune to the plague. We tell them they are wrong, that the plague is not caused by the fresh air but by germs, microscopic organisms spread by fleas—and they laugh us to scorn.

Modern man has adopted a similar attitude toward the demon world. We tell them that the world is in the grip of Satan and that he has countless hosts of invisible demons to aid him in his dark designs against mankind. We say that these unseen beings are intelligent, and that before long, they are to be joined by countless more of their kind, worse even than themselves. People look at us with pitying scorn and suggest we peddle our theories to the publishers of science fiction. But it is true all the same. Once the pit is opened, the world of men will be invaded by a virus far more dreadful than the bubonic plague, a virus all the more deadly because it is able to think and because it directs its attack against the soul rather than the body." (*Exploring Revelation*, p. 137)

f. The sixth trumpet (9:13-21). As we have already noted, it would seem John describes two kinds of demons which will invade earth during the tribulation. The sixth trumpet now ushers in the second invasion.

(1) The leaders of this invasion. Four special satanic angels. These may function to Satan as the four living creatures do to God (Rev. 4:6-8).

(2) The armies of this invasion.

(a) They number two hundred million. By normal standards, this mighty army would occupy a territory one mile wide and eighty-seven miles long.

(b) The description. These demons, unlike the first invasion, seem to be mounted upon some type of hellish horse. The horses' heads looked much like lions', with smoke, fire, and flaming sulphur billowing from their mouths. The riders wear fiery-red breastplates.

(3) The source of this invasion. The Euphrates River. This is where evil began on earth (Zech. 5:8-11; Gen. 3), where false religion began (Gen. 4:3; 10:9, 10; 11:4), and where it will come to its end (Rev. 17-18).

(4) The duration of this invasion. Thirteen months.

(5) The damage wrought by this invasion. One third of humanity is killed through fire, smoke, and brimstone. One fourth had already been slain by the fourth seal (6:8). This would be approximately one billion. Now one third is killed, meaning another billion die. This invasion is therefore the opposite of the fifth trumpet judgment during which no man was able to die.

(6) The results of this invasion (9:20, 21).

"And the rest of the men which were not killed by these plagues yet repented not of the works of their hands that they should not worship devils, and idols of gold, and silver, and brass, and stone, and of wood: which neither can see, nor hear, nor walk: Neither repented they of their murders, nor of their sorceries, nor of their fornication, nor of their thefts."

At this point over one half of the world's population has been wiped out. And what is the response of the survivors? Total unrepentance and intensified rebellion. That very year the F.B.I reports will probably show a thousand percent increase in idolatry, murder, drug-related crimes (the word "sorceries" is the Greek *pharmakeion*, from which we get our "pharmacy." It is the Greek word for drugs), sex, felonies, and robbery.

g. Interlude (Rev. 10:1—11:14). We have already noted a previous time-out period between the sixth and seventh seal judgments. At this time a similar interlude occurs between the sixth and seventh trumpet judgments. During this pause three significant events take place.

(1) The message of the angel of God (10:1-11).

(a) Who is he? He apparently is not Jesus, for he "sware by him that liveth for ever and ever" (10:6). If this were Christ, he would have sworn by himself. (See Heb. 6:13.) He may well be Michael the Archangel (see Dan. 12:1). He is probably the same angel referred to in 5:2; 7:2; 8:3; and 18:2.

(b) What does he have? A little open book. This is probably the seven-sealed book of Revelation 5:1.

(c) What does he say? He announces no further delay would transpire before earth felt the total and terrifying hammer of God's angry judgment. He also orders John to consume his little black book, predicting that it would be sweet in his mouth, but bitter in his stomach. Up to this point John had seen the first part of the tribulation and it had been sweet indeed to witness ungodly Gentiles receiving their just punishment. But now he will be allowed to preview the last three and a half years of the tribulation, which period would begin with the wholesale slaughter of Israel's people by the antichrist. This was indeed bitter medicine to him.

It should be noted that this passage (10:4) contains the only *sealed* part of the book of Revelation.

(2) The measuring of the temple of God (11:1, 2). Here John is put to work with a nine-foot ruler (see Ezek. 40:5), measuring the tribulation temple. He is also to record the identity of its worshipers. God is always interested in those who worship him. However, the outer court was to be left out, "for it is given unto the Gentiles: and the holy city shall they tread under foot forty and two months" (11:2).

See also Luke 21:24, where Jesus predicted this. The forty-two-month final tribulational period is referred to in Daniel 7:25; 12:7; Revelation 12:6, 14; 13:5.

(3) The ministry of the witnesses of God (11:3-14).

(a) Their identity:

"And I will give power unto my two witnesses, and they shall prophesy a thousand two hundred and threescore days, clothed in sackcloth" (Rev. 11:3).

Who are these witnesses?

Some hold that they are Elijah and Enoch. Hebrews 9:27 states that all men are appointed to die, and since these two men did not experience physical death, they will be sent back to witness and eventually to die a martyr's death.

Some hold that they are Elijah and Moses.

Elijah: Because of Malachi 4:5, 6, which predicts that God will send Elijah during that great and dreadful day of the Lord. (See also Mt. 17:11.) Because Elijah appeared with Moses on the Mount of Transfiguration to talk with Jesus (Mt. 17:3).

Because Elijah's Old Testament ministry of preventing rain for some three years will be repeated by one of the witnesses during the tribulation (1 Ki. 17:1; cf. Rev. 11:6).

Moses: Because of Jude 9, where we are informed that after the death of Moses, Satan attempted to acquire his dead body, so that God would not be able to use him against the antichrist during the tribulation.

Because Moses' Old Testament ministry of turning water into blood will be repeated by one of the witnesses during the tribulation (Ex. 7:19; cf. Rev. 11:6). Because Moses appeared with Elijah on the Mount of Transfiguration (Mt. 17:3).

(b) Their ministry.

To prophesy in sackcloth before men as God's anointed lampstands.

To destroy their enemies in the same manner that their enemies would attempt to destroy them.

To prevent rain for three and a half years.

To turn waters into blood.

To smite the earth with every kind of plague.

(c) Their death. The antichrist is finally allowed to kill them. The word "beast" is first mentioned here in 11:7. There are thirty-five other references to him in Revelation. It should also be noted that he could not kill the witnesses until "they shall have finished their testimonies." Satan cannot touch one hair on the head of the most humble saint until God gives him specific permission (see Job 1:12; 2:6).

These two, like Paul, finished their testimonies (2 Tim. 4:7). Contrast this with Belshazzar's sad death (Dan. 5:26).

To show his contempt for them, he refuses to permit their dead bodies to be buried, but leaves them to rot in the streets of Jerusalem.

All the earth celebrates their deaths through a hellish Christmas; men actually send gifts to each other. This is the only reference to the word *rejoice* in the entire tribulation.

The dead bodies of these two prophets are viewed by all the nations of the world in a three-and-a-half-day period.

Their bodies will be on display in Jerusalem (11:8). It is called Sodom because of its immorality, and Egypt because of its worldliness.

(d) Their resurrection (here the word "great" appears three times).

A great voice calls them up to heaven (Rev. 11:12).

A great fear falls upon those who witness this (Rev. 11:11).

A great earthquake levels one-tenth of Jerusalem and kills 7000 prominent men (Rev. 11:13).

John Phillips writes:

"Death cannot hold them, and they arise from the grave. John tells us that they have a triumphant resurrection. He says, 'And after three days and a half the Spirit of life from God entered into them and they stood upon their feet; and great fear fell upon them which saw them.' Picture the scene—the sun-drenched streets of Jerusalem, the holiday crowds flown in from the ends of the earth for a firsthand look at the corpses of these detested men, the troops in the beast's uniform, the temple police. There they are: devilish men from every kingdom under heaven, come to dance and feast at the triumph of the beast. And then it happens! As the crowds strain at the police cordon to peer curiously at the two dead bodies, there comes a sudden change.

Their color changes from cadaverous hue to the blooming, rosy glow of youth. Those stiff, stark limbs—they bend, they move! Oh, what a sight! They rise! The crowds fall back, break, and form again.

They also have a triumphant rapture. John says, 'And they heard a great voice from heaven saying unto them, Come up hither. And they ascended up to heaven in a cloud; and their enemies beheld them.' But will these evil men repent when faced with this, the greatest of all miracles? Not a bit of it! 'Father Abraham!' cried the rich man from the flames of a lost eternity. 'Father Abraham . . . if one went unto them from the dead, they will repent.' Back came the solemn reply, 'If they hear not Moses and the prophets, neither will they be persuaded though one rose from the dead' (Lk. 16:30, 31). And here not just one, but two arise, and repentance is the farthest thing from the minds of men." (*Exploring Revelation*, p. 158)

h. The seventh trumpet (11:15-19).

"And the seventh angel sounded; and there were great voices in heaven, saying, The kingdoms of this world are become the kingdoms of our Lord, and of his Christ; and he shall reign for ever and ever" (11:15).

This seventh angel proclaims the glorious news that very soon now the Lord Jesus Christ will take over the nations of this world as their rightful ruler. The announcement produces a twofold reaction:

(1) The citizens of heaven rejoice.
(2) The nations of the earth become angry.

The seventh angel prepares us not only for the consummation of the ages, but also for the explanation for all things.

"But in the days of the voice of the seventh angel, when he shall begin to sound, the mystery of God should be finished" (10:7).

Dr. W.A. Criswell writes:

"The mystery of God is the long delay of our Lord in taking the kingdom unto Himself and in establishing righteousness in the earth. The mystery of God is seen in these thousands of years in which sin . . . and death run riot.

The enemies of righteousness and the enemies of all that we hold dear rise, increase in power and spread blood and darkness over the face of the earth, and we wonder where God is. Our missionaries are slain, our churches are burned to the ground, people in this earth by uncounted millions and millions are oppressed, living in despair, and God just looks. He seemingly does not intervene; He does not say anything, and He does not move. Sin just develops. It goes on and on. Oh, the mystery of the delay of the Lord God! But somewhere beyond the starry sky there stands a herald angel with a trumpet in his hand, and by the decree of the Lord God Almighty, there is a day, there is an hour, there is a moment, there is an elected time when the angel shall sound and the kingdoms of this world shall become the kingdoms of our God and of His Christ." (*Sermons on Revelation*, pp. 199, 200)

Note: At the sounding of this trumpet, "the temple of God was opened in heaven, and there was seen in this temple the ark of his testament" (11:19). It would appear an actual tabernacle exists in heaven from this and other verses. (See Isa. 6:1-8; Ex. 25:9, 20; Heb. 8:2, 5; 9:24; Rev. 14:15, 17; 15:5, 6, 8; 16:1, 17.)

II. The Reign of the Devil (12-13). The Devil and the Jews (12).

A. His hatred of Israel in the past (12:1-5).

1. A woman with twelve stars (12:1, 2). The woman, of course, represents the nation Israel (Gen. 37:9, 10). Here is the first of four symbolic women in Revelation:

a. a suffering woman—Israel (Rev. 12)
b. a bloody harlot—the world's religious systems (Rev. 17)
c. an arrogant queen—the world's economic system (Rev. 18)
d. a pure bride—the true church (Rev. 19)

We note she cries aloud in her agony (12:2). Dr. Herman A. Hoyt writes:

"The activity of the woman from the time of Abraham to the birth of Christ is described in verse 2. The present

SECOND DIVINE PUNISHMENT

**THE LAMB ALLOWS
THE DEVIL TO REIGN
REV. 12-13**

THE DEVIL AND THE JEWS
His hatred for Israel in the past **(12:1-5)**
A woman with twelve stars
A dragon with seven heads
His hatred for Israel in the future **(12:6-17)**
His war against Michael **(12:7-12)**
His wrath against Israel **(12:6, 13-17)**

THE DEVIL AND THE WORLD
His cohort, the antichrist **(13:1-10)**
His cohort, the false prophet **(13:1-18)**

tense of the verses provides a dramatic setting. The woman is continuously with child. She is continually crying . . . in the pain of travail. She is continuously experiencing labor to be delivered . . . Herein, then, are pictured the experiences of Israel as a nation from the moment she was brought into existence with the call of Abraham until the day Christ was born in Bethlehem. The entire message of the Old Testament from Genesis to Malachi describes what is here set forth in one verse." (*Revelation*, p. 61)

2. A dragon with seven heads (12:3-5). There is no question concerning the identity of this vicious creature. He is given at least seven titles and subtitles in Revelation 12 alone.
   a. The great red dragon (12:3).
      (1) Great, because of his vast power (see Mt. 4:8, 9).
      (2) Red, because he was the first murderer (see Jn. 8:44).
      (3) Dragon, because of his viciousness (see 2 Cor. 6:15).
   b. The old serpent (12:9).
      (1) Old, which takes us back to the Garden of Eden (Gen. 3).
      (2) Serpent, which reminds us of the first body he used (Gen. 3).
   c. The devil (12:9), one who slanders (see 12:10; also Job 1, 2; Zech. 3:1-7; Lk. 22:31).
   d. Satan (12:9), the adversary (see 1 Pet. 5:8).
   e. The deceiver of the world (12:9). Note: He not only deceives men, but angels as well! In 12:4 we are told that his tail *"drew* [literally, 'pulled down,' or 'to drag'; see Acts 14:19 where the same word is used] the third part of the stars of heaven. . . ." This is apparently a reference to the number of angels Satan persuaded to join him in his original revolt against God (Isa. 14:12-15; Ezek. 28:11-19).
   f. The persecutor of the woman (12:4).
   g. The hater of Christ (12:5). This verse tells us three things about Jesus.
      (1) His incarnation "the man child" (see Gal. 4:4, 5).
      (2) His ascension "caught up unto God."
      (3) His future reign "to rule all nations with a rod of iron" (Ps. 2:6-9).
B. His hatred for Israel in the future (12:6-17).
   1. His war against Michael (12:7). Satan loses this war and is cast down to the earth. No longer can he now accuse the saints before God in heaven. He is now overcome by the blood of the Lamb (12:11).
   2. His wrath against Israel (12:13, 15, 17). This marks the last and most severe anti-Semitic movement in history. A.W. Kac writes:
      "Next to the survival of the Jews, the most baffling historical phenomenon is the ha-

tred which he has repeatedly encountered among the nations of the earth. This hostility to the Jews, which goes under the name of antisemitism, is as old as Jewish existence. It is endemic; i.e., like many contagious diseases it is always with us to some degree. But under certain circumstances it assumes epidemic proportions and characteristics. It is prevalent wherever Jews reside in sufficiently large numbers to make their neighbors aware of their presence. 'The growth of antisemitism,' Chaim Weizman declares, 'is proportionate to the number of Jews per square kilometre. We carry the germs of antisemitism in our knapsack on our backs.' " (*Rebirth of the State of Israel*, p. 306)
   a. Throughout the long history, Satan has made every attempt to exterminate Israel. This he has done by resorting to:
      (1) enslaving (Ex. 2)
      (2) drowning (Ex. 14)
      (3) starving (Ex. 16)
      (4) tempting (Ex. 32; Num. 14)
      (5) cursing (Num. 23)
      (6) capturing (2 Ki. 17, 24)
      (7) swallowing (Jonah 2)
      (8) burning (Dan. 3)
      (9) devouring (Dan. 6)
      (10) hanging (Est. 3)
      Of course, to all this could be added the gas ovens of Adolf Hitler. But the most vicious attack is yet to come.
   b. But God himself will step in and preserve a "remnant of her seed" (12:17). John tells us:
      "And to the woman were given two wings of a great eagle, that she might fly into the wilderness, into her place, where she is nourished for a time, and times, and half a time, from the face of the serpent" (Rev. 12:14).
      "And I will bring the third part through the fire, and will refine them as silver is refined, and will try them as gold is tried; they shall call on my name, and I will hear them: I will say, It is my people; and they shall say, The Lord is my God" (Zech. 13:9).
      Thus it would seem that at least one-third of Israel will remain true to God and be allowed by him to escape into a special hiding place for the duration of the tribulation. We shall now consider the location of this hiding place. While it is not actually specified in Scripture, many Bible students believe that this place will be Petra. This is based on the following three passages:
      (1) Zechariah 14:5: "And ye shall flee to the valley of the mountains, for the valley of the mountains shall reach unto Azal; yea, ye shall flee . . . and the Lord my God shall come, and all the saints with thee."
      (The "Azal" mentioned here is thought to be connected with Petra.)

(2) Isaiah 63:1: "Who is this that cometh from Edom, with dyed garments from Bozrah?" The first few verses of Isaiah 63 deal with the Second Coming of Christ. He comes to Edom (of which Petra is capital) and Bozrah (a city in Edom) for some reason, many believe to receive his Hebrew remnant who are hiding there.

(3) Daniel 11:41: "He shall enter also into the glorious land, and many countries shall be overthrown; but these shall escape out of his hand, even Edom."

Thus for some reason the land of Edom will not be allowed to fall into the hands of the antichrist. It is assumed by some that the reason is to protect the remnant.

Many years ago the noted Bible scholar W. E. Blackstone, on the basis of these verses, hid thousands of copies of the New Testament in and around the caves and rocks of Petra. He felt that someday the terrified survivors of the antichrist's bloodbath will welcome the opportunity to read God's Word, preferring it even over the Dow-Jones stock average and the *Wall Street Journal.* On October 14, 1974, I had the opportunity to visit Petra. Before leaving America my students were asked to sign their names, along with their favorite Scripture verse, in the front pages of a large Bible. I then included the following letter:

"Attention to all of Hebrew background: This Bible has been placed here on October 14, 1974, by the students and Dean of the Thomas Road Bible Institute in Lynchburg, Va., U.S.A. We respectfully urge its finder to prayerfully and publicly read the following Bible chapters. They are: Daniel 7 and 11; Matthew 24; 2 Thessalonians 2; Revelation 12 and 13."

We then wrapped the Bible in heavy plastic and placed it in one of the remote caves among the thousands in Petra.

Petra has been called "the rainbow city," and once had 267,000 inhabitants. It was a large market center at the junction of a great caravan route. The city is inaccessible except through the gorge or canyon in the mountains, which is wide enough for only two horses abreast. The perpendicular walls of the gorge are from 400 to 700 feet high and are brilliant in splendor, displaying every color of the rainbow.

The old buildings, cut from the solid rock of the mountain, still stand. A clear spring bubbles over rose-red rocks. Wild figs grow on the banks. Everything awaits Israel.

The Devil and the World (13).

C. His cohort, the antichrist (13:1–10).

"And he shall speak great words against the most High, and shall wear out the saints of the most High" (Dan. 7:25).

"And the king shall do according to his will; and he shall exalt himself, above every god, and shall speak . . . things against the God of gods" (Dan. 11:36).

"That man of sin . . . the son of perdition, who opposeth and exalteth himself above all that is called God or that is worshipped, so that he as God sitteth in the temple of God, shewing himself that he is God. . . . Even him whose coming is after the working of Satan, with all power and signs and lying wonders" (2 Thess. 2:3, 4, 9).

"Who is a liar but he that denieth that Jesus is the Christ? He is antichrist that denieth the Father and the Son" (1 Jn. 2:22).

"And I saw, and behold a white horse; and he that sat on him had a bow, and a crown was given unto him; and he went forth conquering and to conquer" (Rev. 6:2).

"And I stood upon the sand of the sea and saw a beast rise up out of the sea. . . . And the beast which I saw was like unto a leopard, and his feet were as the feet of a bear, and his mouth as the mouth of a lion; and the dragon gave him his power . . . and great authority. . . . And he opened his mouth in blasphemy against God" (Rev. 13:1, 2, 6).

These passages describe for us the most powerful and perverted person who will ever walk the paths of this earth. We shall briefly examine this vile and vicious man along the following lines:

1. His personal characteristics:
   a. He will be an intellectual genius (Dan. 8:23).
   b. He will be an oratorical genius (Dan. 11:36).
   c. He will be a political genius (Rev. 17:11, 12).
   d. He will be a commercial genius (Rev. 13:16, 17; Dan. 11:43).
   e. He will be a military genius (Rev. 6:2; 13:2).
   f. He will be a religious genius (Rev. 13:8; 2 Thess. 2:4). J. Vernon McGee writes:
      "He will achieve the goal of present-day religionists: one religion for the whole world. Have you noticed today the tremendous move to bring together the religions of the world? A startling comment comes from a Jewish rabbi: 'Whether Messiah is a person or an assembly is of minor importance,' said Chief Rabbi Marcus Melchoir of Denmark. 'I believe Messianic times would come if the United Nations were made Messiah.'
      If this rabbi would be willing to accept the UN as Messiah, do you think he would not recognize as Messiah a

man who is able to do what the UN apparently cannot do—put Europe back together and bring about world peace?" (*Reveling Through Revelation*, p. 19)

Thus, to use various American presidents as an analogy, here is a world leader possessing:

(1) the leadership of a Washington and Lincoln

(2) the eloquence of a Franklin Roosevelt

(3) the charm of a Teddy Roosevelt

(4) the charisma of a Kennedy

(5) the popularity of an Ike

(6) the political savvy of a Johnson

(7) the intellect of a Jefferson

2. His various names and titles (in addition to that of the antichrist):

a. The man of sin (2 Thess. 2:3).

b. The son of perdition (2 Thess. 2:8).

c. The wicked one (2 Thess. 2:8).

d. The willful king (Dan. 11:36).

e. The beast (Rev. 11:7; this title is found thirty-six times in the book of Revelation).

f. The little horn (Dan. 7:8).

3. His Old Testament forerunners. Just as there are many Old Testament characters which depict the person and work of the Lord Jesus (such as Melchizedek in Genesis 14 and Isaac in Genesis 22), there are a number of Old Testament men who describe for us the coming ministry of the antichrist:

a. Cain—by his murder of the chosen seed (Gen. 4:5-14; Jude 11; 1 Jn. 3:12).

b. Nimrod—by his creation of Babylon and the tower of Babel (Gen. 10, 11).

c. Pharaoh—by his oppression of God's people (Ex. 1:8-22).

d. Korah—by his rebellion (Num. 16:1-3; Jude 11).

e. Balaam—by his attempt to curse Israel (Num. 23, 24; 2 Pet. 2:15; Jude 11; Rev. 2:14).

f. Saul—by his intrusion into the office of the priesthood (1 Sam. 13:9-13).

g. Goliath—by his proud boasting (1 Sam. 17).

h. Absalom—by his attempt to steal the throne of David (2 Sam. 15:1-6).

i. Jeroboam—by his substitute religion (1 Ki. 12:25-31).

j. Sennacherib—by his efforts to destroy Jerusalem (2 Ki. 18:17).

k. Nebuchadnezzar—by his golden statue (Dan. 3:1-7).

l. Haman—by his plot to exterminate the Jews (Est. 3).

m. Antiochus Epiphanes—by his defilement of the Temple (Dan. 11:21-35).

4. His identity.

a. Some believe the antichrist will be a Gentile, since he comes from the sea (Rev. 13:1), which is often a symbol for Gentile and heathen nations.

Tim LaHaye writes on the nationality of the antichrist:

"One of the most frequently asked questions about the Antichrist concerns his nationality. Revelation 13:1 indicates that he 'rises up out of the sea,' meaning the sea of peoples around the Mediterranean. From this we gather that he will be a Gentile. Daniel 8:8, 9 suggests that he is the 'little horn' that came out of the four Grecian horns, signaling that he will be part Greek. Daniel 9:26 refers to him as the prince of the people that shall come, meaning that he will be of the royal lineage of the race that destroyed Jerusalem. Historically this was the Roman Empire; therefore he will be predominantly Roman. Daniel 11:36, 37 tells us that he regards not 'the God of his fathers' (KJV). Taken in context, this suggests he will be a Jew. In all probability the antichrist will appear to be a Gentile and, like Adolph Hitler and others who feared to reveal Jewish blood, will keep his Jewish ancestry a secret. It may be known only to God, but the Bible teaches that he will be a Roman-Grecian Jew, a composite man representing the peoples of the earth. This technically qualifies him to be the embodiment of all evil men." (*Revelation*, p. 172)

b. Some believe he will be a resurrected individual, on the basis of Revelation 13:3 and 17:8.

c. Some believe he will be Judas Iscariot, on the basis of the following verses:

(1) John 6:70, 71. Here Jesus refers to Judas as the devil.

(2) Luke 22:3; John 13:27. Here Satan actually enters Judas. This is never said of any other individual in the Bible.

(3) John 17:12; 2 Thessalonians 2:3. The title "son of perdition" is only found twice in the New Testament. In the first instance Jesus used it to refer to Judas. In the second instance Paul used it to refer to the antichrist.

(4) Acts 1:25. Here Peter says that Judas after his death went "to his own place." Some have seen in this a reference to the bottomless pit, and believe that Satan has retained Judas here for the past 2000 years in preparation for his future role of the antichrist.

5. His rise to power.

a. Through the power of Satan (Rev. 13:2; 2 Thess. 2:3, 9-12).

b. Through the permission of the Holy Spirit. His present-day manifestation is being hindered by the Holy Spirit until the Rapture of the church. God is in control of all situations down here and will continue to be. (See Job 1 and 2; 2 Thess. 2:6, 7.)

c. Through the formation of a ten-nation organization. He will proceed from a ten-dictatorship confederation which will come into existence during the tribulation. These dictators are referred to as "ten horns" in Daniel 7:7; Revelation 12:3; 13:1; 17:7, 12. In his rise to power he will defeat three of these dictators (Dan. 7:8, 24). This ten-horned confederation is the revived Roman Empire. This is derived from the fact that the most important prophetic details concerning the old Roman Empire in Daniel 2:40–44 are still unfulfilled.

The revived Roman Empire is the last of the seven Gentile world powers to plague the nation Israel. These powers are referred to as seven heads in Revelation 12:3; 13:1; 17:7. They are:

Egypt, which enslaved Israel for 400 years (Ex. 1–12).

Assyria, which captured the northern kingdom of Israel (2 Ki. 17).

Babylon, which captured the southern kingdom of Israel (2 Ki. 24).

Persia, which produced wicked Haman (Est. 3).

Greece, which produced, indirectly, Antiochus Epiphanes (Dan. 11).

Rome, which destroyed Jerusalem in A.D. 70 (see Lk. 21) and which will hound Israel in the revived empire as never before in all history (Rev. 12).

d. Through the cooperation of the false religious system (Rev. 17).

e. Through his personal charisma and ability.

f. Through a false (or real?) resurrection (Rev. 13:3)

g. Through a false peace program, probably in the Middle East (Dan. 8:25).

h. Through a master plan of deception and trickery (Mt. 24:24; 2 Thess. 2:9; Rev. 13:14). Out of the ninety-one occurrences in the New Testament of the words meaning "to deceive," or "to go astray," twenty-two of them belong definitely to passages dealing with the antichrist and the tribulation. (See 2 Thess. 2:3, 9, 10, 11; Mt. 24:4, 5, 11, 24; 2 Tim. 3:13; Rev. 12:9; 18:23; 19:20; 20:3, 8, 10.)

Three reasons explain this fearful deception.

(1) Universal ignorance of God's Word (see Mt. 22:29).

(2) Fierce demonic activity (see 1 Tim. 4:1).

(3) The empty soul (see Lk. 11:24–26).

6. His activities.

a. He begins by controlling the Western power block (Rev. 17:12).

b. He makes a seven-year covenant with Israel but breaks it after three and a half years (Dan. 9:27).

There is ample scriptural evidence to show that the antichrist will allow (and perhaps even encourage) the building of the temple and the rendering of its sacrifices during the tribulation. (See Dan. 9:27; Mt. 24:15; 2 Thess. 2:4; Rev. 13:14, 15; 11:2.)

In his book *Will Man Survive?* Dr. J. D. Pentecost quotes from a Jewish ad that appeared in the *Washington Post* during May, 1967.

"A project to rebuild the temple of God in Israel is now being started. With divine help and guidance the temple will be completed. It will signal a new era in Judaism. Jews will be inspired to conduct themselves in such a moral way that our Maker will see fit to pay us a visit here on the earth. Imagine the warm feelings that will be ours when this happy event takes place."

c. He gains absolute control over the Middle East after the Russian invasion (Ezek. 38, 39).

d. He attempts to destroy all of Israel (Rev. 12).

e. He destroys the false religious system, so that he may rule unhindered (Rev. 17:16, 17).

f. He thereupon sets himself up as God (Dan. 11:36; 2 Thess. 2:4–11; Rev. 13:5).

g. He briefly rules over all nations (Ps. 2; Dan. 11:36; Rev. 13:16).

h. He is utterly crushed by the Lord Jesus Christ at the battle of Armageddon (Rev. 19).

i. He is the first creature to be thrown into the lake of fire (Rev. 19:20).

The July, 1965, *Reader's Digest* book section condenses the book *A Gift of Prophecy*, written by that famous (but equally false) prophetess, Jeane Dixon. The article concludes with the following words:

"A child born in the Middle East on February 5, 1962, will revolutionize the world and eventually unite all warring creeds and sects into one all-embracing faith. This person, who has been the subject of some of Jeane Dixon's strongest, clearest visions, was born of humble peasant origin. Mankind, she says, will begin to feel the great force of this man about 1980, and his power will grow mightily until 1999, at which time there will be peace on earth to all men of good will."

As we read this we are reminded of the Savior's words to a group of wicked and unbelieving Pharisees: "I am come in my Father's name, and ye receive me not; if another shall come in his own name, him ye will receive" (Jn. 5:43).

7. His amazing ability to imitate. The antichrist would surely have been a tremendously successful mimic on any late-night TV talk show! Note the following areas in which he

will attempt to imitate the person and the work of Christ.

   a. The antichrist comes in the very image of Satan, as Christ came in the image of God (Rev. 13:4; 2 Thess. 2:9; cf. Col. 1:15 and Heb. 1:3).

   b. The antichrist is the second person in the hellish trinity, as Christ is in the heavenly Trinity (Rev. 16:13; cf. Mt. 28:19).

   c. The antichrist comes up from the abyss while Christ comes down from heaven (Rev. 11:7; 17:8; cf. Jn. 6:38).

   d. The antichrist is a savage beast while Christ is a sacrificial Lamb (Rev. 13:2; cf. Rev. 5:6-9).

   e. The antichrist receives his power from Satan, as Christ received his power from his Father (Rev. 13:2; cf. Mt. 28:18).

   f. The antichrist will experience a resurrection (perhaps a fake one), just as Christ experienced a true one (Rev. 13:3; 12; cf. Rom. 1:4).

   g. The antichrist will receive the worship of all unbelievers, as Christ did of all believers (Rev. 13:3, 4, 8; Jn. 5:43; cf. Mt. 2:11; Lk. 24:52; Jn. 20:28; Phil. 2:10, 11).

   h. The antichrist will deliver mighty speeches, as did Christ (Dan. 7:8; Rev. 13:5; cf. Jn. 7:46). Satan will doubtless give to the antichrist his vast knowledge of philosophy, science, and human wisdom accumulated through the centuries (Ezek. 28:12).

   i. The greater part of the antichrist's ministry will last some three and a half years, about the time span of Christ's ministry (Rev. 13:5; 12:6, 14; cf. Jn. 2:13; 6:4; 11:55).

   j. The antichrist will attempt (unsuccessfully) to combine the three Old Testament offices of prophet, priest, and king, as someday Christ will successfully do.

   k. The antichrist's symbolic number is six, while the symbolic number of Christ is seven (Rev. 13:18; cf. Rev. 5:6, 12).

   l. The antichrist will someday kill his harlot wife, while Christ will someday glorify his holy bride (Rev. 17:16; 17; cf. Rev. 21:1, 2).

D. His cohort, the false prophet (13:11-18).

"And I beheld another beast coming up out of the earth" (Rev. 13:11).

1. His identity. Who is this second beast of Revelation 13 who is also called on three later occasions "the false prophet" (Rev. 16:13; 19:20; 20:10)? Some believe he will be a Jew (while the antichrist will be a Gentile), and that he will head up the apostate church.

2. His activities. It has already been pointed out that the antichrist will attempt to mimic Christ; it would appear that the false prophet will try to copy the work of the Holy Spirit. Thus the following analogy has been suggested between the Spirit of God and the second beast.

   a. The Holy Spirit is the third person of the heavenly Trinity (Mt. 28:19), while the false prophet is the third person of the hellish trinity (Rev. 16:13).

   b. The Holy Spirit leads men into all truth (Jn. 16:13), while the false prophet seduces men into all error (Rev. 13:11, 14).

   c. The Holy Spirit glorifies Christ (Jn. 16:13, 14), while the false prophet glorifies the antichrist (Rev. 13:12).

   d. The Holy Spirit made fire to come down from heaven at Pentecost (Acts 2:3), while the false prophet will do likewise on earth in view of men (Rev. 13:13).

   e. The Holy Spirit gives life (Rom. 8:2) while the false prophet kills (Rev. 13:15).

   f. The Holy Spirit marks with a seal all those who belong to God (Eph. 1:13), while the false prophet marks those who worship Satan (Rev. 13:16, 17).

3. His mark.

"And he causeth all, both small and great, rich and poor, free and bond, to receive a mark in their right hand, or in their foreheads; that no man might buy or sell, save he that had the mark, or the name of the beast, or the number of his name. Here is wisdom. Let him that hath understanding count the number of the beast: for it is the number of a man; and his number is six hundred threescore and six" (Rev. 13:16-18).

Perhaps no other single passage in the Word of God has been the object of more silly and serious speculation than this one. How are we to understand the number 666? In concluding this section, we shall quote from two well-known authors:

"In Greek (as in Hebrew and in Latin) the letters of the alphabet serve likewise as signs for the figures. *Alpha* signifies one; *beta*, two, etc. For any name it is, therefore, possible to add together the numerical value of each letter and to arrive at a total which forms 'the number of a man.' The name of the antichrist will give the total of 666. Men have sought to apply this method with reference to all the persons in history who have seemed to be the antichrist. By more or less arranging the letters of the titles of these persons they have arrived at the number 666 for the names of Nero, Mohammed, the Pope, Napoleon, and even Hitler, not to speak of many others. In our opinion the proof that these interpretations are still premature is that they are all contradictory. We are convinced that when the last and great antichrist appears, the true believers of the entire world will recognize him. The Holy Spirit will give to them enough light to calculate unanimously the number of his name." (Rene Pache, *The Return of Jesus Christ*, p. 183)

"Probably the simplest explanation here is the best, that the triple six is the number of a man, each digit falling short of the perfect number seven. Six in the

Scripture is man's number. He was to work six days and rest the seventh. The image of Nebuchadnezzar was sixty cubits high and six cubits broad. Whatever may be the deeper meaning of the number, it implies that this title, referring to the first beast, Satan's masterpiece, limits him to man's level, which is far short of the deity of Jesus Christ." (Dr. John Walvoord, *The Revelation of Jesus Christ*, p. 210)

Whatever is involved in this hellish mark, it is apparently very important, for it is referred to again no less than six times (see Rev. 14:9, 11; 15:2; 16:2; 19:20; 20:4).

III. The Vial Judgments (14-16).

A. Those events preceding the vial judgments (14-15). We have already seen that two chapters (4, 5) are given over to describing some heavenly action just prior to the fearful seal judgments which began in Revelation 6. Here John introduces the vial judgments in a similar way. Chapters 14-15 record some heavenly action before the vial judgments in 16.

1. The song of the 144,000 (14:1-5). Here we note:

a. This group is the same as mentioned in chapter 7. There they are redeemed. Here they are raptured. And note—not one is missing. J. Vernon McGee writes:

"It is clear from Chapter 13 that this is the darkest day and the most horrible hour in history. It is truly hell's holiday. Every thoughtful mind must inevitably ask the question—How did God's people fare during this period? Could they make it through to the end with overwhelming odds against them? The Shepherd who began with 144,000 sheep is now identified with them as a Lamb with 144,000. He did not lose one." (*Reveling Through Revelation*, p. 21)

b. This group makes up the greatest numbered choir of all time.

c. They sing a new song, accompanied by heavenly harps (Ps. 57).

d. They are undefiled with women (14:4; cf. 9:21).

e. There is no guile in their mouth (14:5; cf. 2 Thess. 2:9-12).

2. The messages from three special angels (14:6-12).

a. The first message:

"And I saw another angel fly in the midst of heaven, having the everlasting gospel to preach unto them that dwell on the earth, and to every nation, and kindred, and tongue, and people, saying with a loud voice, Fear God, and give glory to him; for the hour of his judgment is come; and worship him that made heaven, and earth, and the sea, and the fountains of waters" (Rev. 14:6, 7).

We see in this verse something absolutely unique—an angel of God preach-

THIRD DIVINE PUNISHMENT

THE LAMB POURS OUT THE SEVEN VIAL JUDGMENTS (Rev. 14-16)

THOSE EVENTS PRECEDING THE VIAL JUDGMENTS (14-15)

The song of the 144,000 **(14:1-5)**

The messages from three special angels

- The first message **(14:6, 7)**
- The second message **(14:8)**
- The third message **(14:9-12)**

The voice of the Holy Spirit **(14:13)**

The first announcement of Armageddon **(14:14-20)**

The sights and sounds of the temple in heaven **(15:2-4)**

THOSE EVENTS ACCOMPANYING THE VIAL JUDGMENTS **(Rev. 16:1-21)**

FIRST VIAL JUDGMENT **(16:2)**

Terrible sores upon the followers of antichrist

SECOND VIAL JUDGMENT **(16:3)**

Total poisoning of all salt water

THIRD VIAL JUDGMENT **(16:4-7)**

Total poisoning of all fresh water

FOURTH VIAL JUDGMENT **(16:8, 9)**

Fearful and blistering heat from the sun

FIFTH VIAL JUDGMENT **(16:10, 11)**

Darkness upon the capital of the antichrist

SIXTH VIAL JUDGMENT **(16:12-16)**

THE RESULTS: The drying up of the River Euphrates

THE REASON: To prepare for Armageddon

THE REBELS: Three unclean spirits

SEVENTH VIAL JUDGMENT **(16:17-21)**

The world's greatest earthquake

The world's greatest hailstorm

ing the gospel to sinners. Up to this point God has used only men to reach other men (Acts 1:8; 2 Pet. 1:21; 2 Cor. 4:7). But now, due to the severity of the tribulation, angels will be used.

b. The second message:

"And there followed another angel, saying, Babylon is fallen, is fallen, that great city, because she made all nations drink of the wine of the wrath of her fornication" (Rev. 14:8).

This second message is to announce the imminent destruction of the political and economic Babylon (see Rev. 18).

c. The third message:

"And the third angel followed them, saying with a loud voice, If any man worship the beast and his image, and receive his mark in his forehead, or in his hand, the same shall drink of the wine of the wrath of God, which is poured out without mixture into the cup of his indignation; and he shall be tormented with fire and brimstone in the presence of the holy angels, and in the presence of the Lamb; and the smoke of their torment ascendeth up forever and ever: and they have no rest day nor night, who worship the beast and his image, and whosoever receiveth the mark of his name" (Rev. 14:9-11).

Here is the last hellfire-and-brimstone message that will ever be preached to the unsaved, and it is delivered not by a Jonathan Edwards or a Billy Sunday, but by an angel! Apparently no one responds to the invitation. Here God will pour out his undiluted wrath, something he has done once before upon Christ at Calvary. How tragic that Christ once drank this same cup for the very unrepentant sinners who are now forced to drink it again.

3. The message from the Holy Spirit (14:13).
"And I heard a voice from heaven saying unto me, Write, Blessed are the dead which die in the Lord from henceforth: Yea, saith the Spirit, that they may rest from their labours; and their works do follow them." Up to this point in history the general rule is, Blessed are the *living.* (See Eccl. 9:4; Phil. 1:23, 24.) But now it is better for believers to die. John Phillips writes:

"In happy contrast with the doom of those who deify the beast is the destiny of those who defy the beast. Two things are said of these as well. They will resist. John says, 'Here is the patience of the saints: here are they that keep the commandments of God, and the faith of Jesus. And I heard a voice from heaven saying unto me, Write, Blessed are the dead which die in the Lord from henceforth: Yea, saith the Spirit, that they may rest from their labours; and their works do follow them.' Except for the hundred and forty-four thousand, those who defy the beast can anticipate death in a thousand fiendish ways, but it is death instantly transformed by God into blessing! 'I'll make you suffer!' screams the beast. 'You'll make us saints!' reply the overcomers. 'I'll persecute you to the grave,' roars the beast! 'You'll promote us to glory!' reply the overcomers. 'I'll blast you!' snarls the beast. 'You'll bless us!' reply the overcomers. The beast's rage against these noble martyrs will all be in vain. He will utterly fail at last. They will be rewarded. 'Yea, saith the Spirit, that they may rest from their labours; and their works do follow them.' Their troubles will be over. They will enter into reward on the shining banks of the crystal sea." (*Exploring Revelation,* p. 193)

It has been rightly observed that this world is the only *heaven* the unsaved will ever know, and the only *hell* the saved will ever experience.

4. The first announcement of Armageddon (14:14-20):

"And I looked, and behold a white cloud, and upon the cloud one sat like unto the Son of man, having on his head a golden crown, and in his hand a sharp sickle. And another angel came out of the temple, crying with a loud voice to him that sat on the cloud, Thrust in thy sickle, and reap: for the time is come for thee to reap; for the harvest of the earth is ripe. And he that sat on the cloud thrust in his sickle on the earth; and the earth was reaped.

And another angel came out of the temple which is in heaven, he also having a sharp sickle. And another angel came out from the altar, which had power over fire; and cried with a loud cry to him that had the sharp sickle, saying, Thrust in thy sharp sickle, and gather the clusters of the vine of the earth; for her grapes are fully ripe. And the angel thrust in his sickle into the earth, and gathered the vine of the earth, and cast it into the great winepress of the wrath of God. And the winepress was trodden without the city, and blood came out of the winepress, even into the horse bridles, by the space of a thousand and six hundred furlongs."

The full implications of these verses will be more fully discussed in Revelation 19.

5. The sights and sounds of the temple in heaven (15:2-4).
   a. John hears the songs of the triumphal (15:2-4).
      (1) What they sing. They sing the song of Moses and the song of the Lamb (15:3). Note the contrast between these songs:

The song of Moses was sung beside the Red Sea (Ex. 15); the song of the Lamb will be sung beside the crystal sea. The song of Moses was sung over Egypt; the song of the Lamb will be sung over Babylon. The song of Moses described how God brought his people out; the Song of the Lamb will describe how God brings his people in. The song of Moses was Scripture's first song; the Song of the Lamb will be Scripture's last song.

      (2) Why they sing. ". . . For thou only art holy . . . for thy judgments are made manifest" (15:4).
   b. John sees the smoke of the Temple (15:5-8; see also Isa. 6:1-8; Ex. 25:9, 40; Heb. 8:2, 5; 9:24; Rev. 14:15, 17; 16:1, 17).

"And one of the four beasts gave unto the seven angels seven golden vials full of the wrath of God, who liveth for ever and ever. And the temple was filled with smoke from the glory of God, and from his power; and no man was able to enter into the temple, till the seven plagues of the seven angels were fulfilled" (15:7, 8).

John Phillips writes:

"Since Calvary, the way into the holiest in heaven has been opened to all, because the blood of Christ has blazed a highway to the heart of God. But now, for a brief spell, that royal road is barred. God's wrath, once poured out upon His Son on man's behalf, is to be out-poured again. The world which crucified the Lamb and which now has crowned its rebellions with the worship of the beast, is to be judged to the full. So bright glory burns within the temple, filling it with smoke and standing guard at the door. The way into the holiest is barred again for a while." (*Exploring Revelation*, p. 198)

B. Those events accompanying the vial judgments (Rev. 16).

1. The first vial judgment:

"And the first went, and poured out his vial upon the earth; and there fell a noisome and grievous sore upon the men which had the mark of the beast, and upon them which worshipped his image" (16:2).

J. Vernon McGee writes:

"God is engaged in germ warfare upon the followers of antichrist . . . These putrefying sores are worse than leprosy or cancer. This compares to the sixth plague in Egypt, and is the same type of sore or boil" (Ex. 9:8-12). (*Reveling Through Revelation*, p. 36)

2. The second vial judgment:

"And the second angel poured out his vial upon the sea; and it became as the blood of a dead man; and every living soul died in the sea" (16:3).

Dr. Charles Ryrie writes the following concerning this plague:

"The second bowl is poured on the sea, with the result that the waters became blood and every living thing in the sea dies. The 'as' is misplaced in the Authorized Version, the correct reading being 'became blood as of a dead man.' The vivid image is of a dead person wallowing in his own blood. The seas will wallow in blood. Under the second trumpet, one-third of the sea creatures died (8:9); now the destruction is complete. The stench and disease that this will cause along the shores of the seas of the earth are unimaginable" (*Revelation*, p. 97).

3. The third vial judgment:

"And the third angel poured out his vial upon the rivers and fountains of waters; and they became blood. And I heard the angel of the waters say, Thou art righteous, O Lord, which art and wast and shall be, because thou has judged thus. For they have shed the blood of saints and prophets, and thou hast given them blood to drink; for they are worthy. And I heard

another out of the altar say, Even so, Lord God Almighty, true and righteous are thy judgments" (Rev. 16:4-7).

Two significant things may be noted in these verses:

a. This third vial judgment is, among other things, an answer to the cry of the martyrs under the altar at the beginning of the tribulation. Their prayer at that time was, "How long, O Lord, holy and true, dost thou not judge and avenge our blood on them that dwell on the earth?" (Rev. 6:10).

b. These verses indicate that God has assigned a special angel as superintendent on earth's waterworks. When we compare this with Revelation 7:1, where we are told that four other angels control the world's winds, we realize that even during the hellishness of the tribulation, this world is still controlled by God.

4. The fourth vial judgment:

"And the fourth angel poured out his vial upon the sun; and power was given unto him to scorch men with fire. And men were scorched with great heat, and blasphemed the name of God, which hath power over these plagues; and they repented not to give him glory" (Rev. 8, 9; see also Deut. 32:24; Isa. 24:6; 42:25; Mal. 4:1; Lk. 21:25).

Perhaps the two most illuminating passages in Scripture about man's total depravity can be found in Revelation 9:20, 21, and 16:9. Both sections deal with the world's attitude toward God during the tribulation.

a. "And the rest of the men which were not killed by these plagues yet repented not of the works of their hands, that they should not worship devils, and idols of gold, and silver, and brass, and stone, and of wood, which neither can see, nor hear, nor walk; neither repented they of their murders, nor of their sorceries, nor of their fornication, nor of their thefts" (Rev. 9:20, 21).

b. ". . . and they repented not to give him glory" (Rev. 16:9).

What do these verses prove? They prove that in spite of horrible wars, of terrible famines, of darkened skies, of raging fires, of bloody seas, of stinging locusts, of demonic persecutions of mighty earthquakes, of falling stars, and of cancerous sores, sinful mankind still will not repent.

5. The fifth vial judgment:

"And the fifth angel poured out his vial upon the seat of the beast; and his kingdom was full of darkness; and they gnawed their tongues for pain, and blasphemed the God of heaven because of their pains and their sores, and repented not of their deeds" (Rev. 16:10, 11; see also Isa. 60:2; Joel 2:1, 2, 31; Nahum 1:6, 8; Amos 5:18; Zeph. 1:15).

This plague, poured out upon "the seat of the beast" (literally, his "throne"), will apparently concentrate itself upon the ten nations of the revived Roman Empire. Again we read those tragic words "and repented not of their deeds."

6. The sixth vial judgment:

"And the sixth angel poured out his vial upon the great river Euphrates; and the water thereof was dried up, that the way of the kings of the east might be prepared. And I saw three unclean spirits like frogs come out of the mouth of the dragon and out of the mouth of the beast, and out of the mouth of the false prophet. For they are the spirits of devils, working miracles, which go forth unto the kings of the earth and of the whole world, to gather them to the battle of that great day of God Almighty" (Rev. 16:12-14).

Here the God of heaven employs psychological warfare upon his enemies, conditioning them to gather themselves together in the near future at Armageddon.

The Euphrates River is 1800 miles long and in some places 3600 feet wide. It is thirty feet deep. This river has been the dividing line between western and eastern civilization since the dawn of history. It served as the eastern border of the Old Roman Empire. Thus, the Euphrates becomes both the cradle and grave of man's civilization. Here the first godless city (Enoch, built by Cain; see Gen. 4:16, 17) went up, and here the last rebellious city will be constructed (Babylon, built by the antichrist; see Rev. 18).

7. The seventh vial judgment:

"And the seventh angel poured out his vial into the air; and there came a great voice out of the temple of heaven, from the throne, saying, It is done. And there were voices, and thunders, and lightnings; and there was a great earthquake, such as was not since men were upon the earth, so mighty an earthquake, and so great. And the great city was divided into three parts, and the cities of the nations fell; and great Babylon came in remembrance before God, to give unto her the cup of wine of the fierceness of his wrath. And every island fled away, and the mountains were not found. And there fell upon men a great hail out of heaven, every stone about the weight of a talent and men blasphemed God because of the plague of the hail, for the plague thereof was exceeding great" (16:17-21).

Thus end the seal, trumpet, and vial judgments. Three items in this last vial are worthy of observation:

a. The statement, "It is done," is the second of three biblical occurrences in which this phrase is connected with some great event. The first event was Calvary and the last will be the threshold of eternity.

"When Jesus therefore had received the vinegar, he said, It is finished; and he bowed his head, and gave up the ghost" (Jn. 19:30).

"And he said unto me, It is done. I am Alpha and Omega, the beginning and the end. I will give unto him that is athirst of the fountain of the water of life freely" (Rev. 21:6).

b. The world's greatest earthquake takes place. The intensity of an earthquake is measured on an instrument called a Richter scale. The greatest magnitude ever recorded so far has been 8.9. The greatest loss of life due to an earthquake occurred on January 23, 1556, in Shensi Province, China, and killed some 830,000 people. However, that earthquake will be but a mild tremor compared to the tribulation earthquake, which, we are told, will level all the great cities of the world.

c. The world's greatest shower of hailstones comes crashing down on mankind. These gigantic icy chunks will weigh up to 125 pounds apiece.

IV. The Destruction of the World's Religious System (Rev. 17).

"And there came one of the seven angels which had the seven vials, and talked with me, saying unto me, come hither; I will shew unto thee the judgment of the great whore that sitteth upon many waters" (17:1).

This brutal, bloody, and blasphemous harlot is none other than the universal false church, the wicked wife of Satan. God had no sooner begun his blessed work in preparing for himself a people than the devil did likewise. In fact, the first baby to be born on this earth later became Satan's original convert. (See Gen. 4:8; 1 Jn. 3:12.) We shall now consider the historical, current, and future activities of this perverted prostitute.

A. The harlot viewed historically.

1. Satan's church began officially at the Tower of Babel in Genesis 11:1-9, nearly twenty-four centuries B.C. Here, in the fertile plain of Shinar, probably very close to the original Garden of Eden, the first spade of dirt was turned for the purpose of devil-worship.

2. The first full-time minister of Satan was Nimrod, Noah's wicked and apostate grandson (Gen. 10:8-10).

3. Secular history and tradition tell us that Nimrod married a woman who was as evil

FOURTH DIVINE PUNISHMENT

THE LAMB DESTROYS THE WORLD'S RELIGIOUS SYSTEMS (Rev. 17:1-18)

THE HISTORY OF THIS RELIGIOUS HARLOT (17:1-6)

Drunk with the blood of saints
Covered with the filth of hell
Decked with the wealth of the world

THE FUTURE OF THIS RELIGIOUS SYSTEM (17:7-18)

Teams up at first with the antichrist
Is destroyed at last by the antichrist

and demonic as himself. Her name was Semerimus. Knowing God's promise of a future Savior (Gen. 3:15), Semerimus brazenly claimed that Tammuz, her first son, fulfilled this prophecy.

4. Semerimus thereupon instituted a religious system which made both her and her son the objects of divine worship. She herself became the first high priestess. Thus began the mother-child cult which later spread all over the world. The city of Babylon was the seat of Satan worship until it fell, in 539 B.C., to the Persians.

   a. From Babylon it spread to Phoenicia under the name of Ashteroth and Tammuz.

   b. From Phoenicia it traveled to Pergamos in Asia Minor. This is the reason for John's admonition to the church at Pergamos in the book of Revelation: "I know thy works, and where thou dwellest, even where Satan's seat is" (Rev. 2:13).

   c. In Egypt the mother-child cult was known as Isia and Horus.

   d. In Greece it became Aphrodite and Eros.

   e. In Rome this pair was worshiped as Venus and Cupid.

   f. In China it became known as Mother Shing Moo and her child.

   Dr. J. Dwight Pentecost writes:

   "Several years ago I visited an archeological museum in Mexico City. A recent find had just been put on display which Mexican archeologists had authenticated as belonging to the period about 200 years before Christ. The object was the center of religious worship among some of the early Indians in Mexico. To my amazement, it was an image of a mother with a child in her arms. This Babylonian religion spread abroad to become the religion of the world." (*Prophecy for Today*, p. 133)

5. What was the teaching of Semerimus' satanic church?

   a. That Semerimus herself was the way to God. She actually adopted the title "Queen of Heaven."

   b. That she alone could administer salvation to the sinner through various sacraments, such as the sprinkling of holy water.

   c. That her son Tammuz was tragically slain by a wild boar during a hunting trip.

   d. That he was, however, resurrected from the dead forty days later. Thus, each year afterward, the temple virgins of this cult would enter a forty-day fast as a memorial to Tammuz' death and resurrection.

   e. After the forty-day fast, a joyful feast called Ishtar took place. At this feast colored eggs were exchanged and eaten as a symbol of the resurrection. An evergreen tree was displayed and a yule log was burned. Finally, hot cakes marked with the letter T (to remind everybody of Tammuz) were baked and eaten.

6. About 2000 B.C., God called Abraham away from all this (see Josh. 24:2, 3) and led him into the Promised Land. But by the ninth century B.C., Israel had returned to this devil worship under the influence of wicked Jezebel (1 Ki. 16:30–33). At this time the cult was worshiped under the name of Baal.

7. Both Ezekiel and Jeremiah warned against this hellish thing.

   "Then he brought me to the door of the gate of the Lord's house which was toward the north; and behold, there sat women weeping for Tammuz" (Ezek. 8:14).

   "The children gather wood, and the fathers kindle the fire, and the women knead their dough, to make cakes to the queen of heaven . . . to burn incense to the queen of heaven, and to pour out drink offerings unto her" (Jer. 7:18; 44:25).

8. By the time of Christ, this cult had so influenced Roman life that the Caesars were not only crowned as emperors of Rome, but also bore the title *Pontifex Maximus*, meaning, "high priest." They were high priests of the Babylonian satanic church.

9. During A.D. 306, a Roman emperor named Constantine was threatened by a very powerful enemy army. Realizing that his uneasy troops needed confidence, Constantine claimed to have seen a vision on the eve of battle. He saw a large blue flag with a red cross on it and heard a mighty voice which said, *In hoc signo vinces*—"In this sign conquer." He thereupon marched his troops into a shallow river, claimed them to be officially baptized, and ordered the sign of the cross painted on all his weapons. Thus inspired, he led his troops to victory and subsequently made Christianity the state religion of Rome.

   The Roman priests of Tammuz soon discovered that they could easily make the transition into Christianity (with certain changes) and thereupon carried their traditions forward without interruption by promoting the Madonna-Child worship concept, the holy water sacrament, etc.

   Thus for nearly 300 years the devil had desperately attempted to destroy the church from outside by his terrible persecutions. But with the advent of Constantine he changed his tactics, walking the aisle to work from within. The corrupted church was already flourishing in Christ's day, and the Savior delivered a scathing attack against some of its very deacons and elders (Mt. 23).

B. The harlot viewed currently. Is mystery Babylon at work today? She is indeed—stronger and more sinful than ever. At least three New Testament writers describe her latter-day activities and characteristics:

   1. Paul.

      "This know also, that in the last days perilous times shall come. For men shall be lovers of their own selves, covetous, boasters, proud, blasphemers, disobedient to parents, unthankful, unholy, without natural affection, trucebreakers, false accusers, incontinent, fierce, despisers of those who are good, traitors, heady, highminded, lovers of pleasures more than lovers of God, having a form of godliness but denying the power thereof" (2 Tim. 3:1-5).

"For the time will come when they will not endure sound doctrine but after their own lusts shall they heap to themselves teachers, having itching ears; and they shall turn away their ears from the truth, and shall be turned unto fables" (2 Tim. 4:3, 4).

2. Peter.
"But there were false prophets also among the people, even as there shall be false teachers among you, who privily shall bring in damnable heresies, even denying the Lord that bought them" (2 Pet. 2:1).

3. John.
"I know thy works, that thou art neither cold nor hot; I would thou wert cold or hot. So then because thou art lukewarm, and neither cold nor hot, I will spue thee out of my mouth. Because thou sayest, I am rich and increased with goods, and have need of nothing, and knowest not that thou art wretched, and miserable, and poor, and blind, and naked" (Rev. 3:15-17).

This harlot church will probably be composed of apostate masses from Protestantism, Catholicism, Judaism, and every other major world religion. It is entirely possible that the World Council of Churches will spearhead this latter-day ungodly union.

C. The harlot viewed prophetically. What will the future hold for this vile and vicious woman? According to Revelation 17, the false church lends all her evil strength to elevate the antichrist during the first part of the tribulation. For awhile she flourishes, luxuriating in surpassing wealth and opulence. But suddenly things change drastically. John describes this for us:

"The scarlet animal and his ten horns [which represent ten kings who will reign with him] all hate the woman, and will attack her and leave her naked and ravaged by fire" (17:16).

The probable reason for all this is that after she has put the antichrist into power, the harlot then attempts to control him. History gives us many examples of the Roman Catholic Church (and indeed other religious systems) attempting to control kings and rulers. Note the edict of Pope Gregory VII in the eleventh century:

"It is laid down that the Roman Pontiff is universal bishop, that his name is the only one of its kind in the world. To him alone it belongs to dispose or reconcile bishops. . . . He alone may use the ensigns of empire; all princes are bound to kiss his feet; he has the right to de-

pose emperors, and to absolve subjects from their allegiance. He holds in his hands the supreme mediation in questions of war and peace, and he alone may adjudge contested succession to kingdoms—all kingdoms are held in feifs under Peter . . . the Roman church has never erred, . . . the Pope is above all judgment." (*Short Paper on Church History*, p. 355)

But the antichrist won't bow. He will turn on her, destroy her buildings, burn her holy books, and murder her priests. One of the most ironical turn of events in all history will be the destruction of the false church. For this evil organization will meet its doom not at the hands of Gabriel, or the Father, or the Son, or the Spirit, but the antichrist.

It has been suggested that he will begin by detesting the harlot, then despoiling her, then disgracing her, then devouring her, and finally destroying her.

This hatred is based both on providential and practical reasons. To summarize the future activities of this horrible harlot, we note:

1. Her influence will be worldwide (17:1).
2. This influence will be used to corrupt the entire earth (17:2).
3. She will possess vast and unlimited wealth (17:4).
4. She is drunken with the blood of God's saints (17:6). Only eternity will reveal how many tens of millions of believers have been cruelly murdered in the name of religion.
5. She teams up (for awhile) with the beast (antichrist) (17:3, 7).
6. She has her name written on her forehead (17:5). In the time of John it was common for prostitutes to wear their name in jewelry upon their forehead, thus advertising their trade.
7. She may have her headquarters in Rome (17:9). Rome sits upon seven mountains.

V. The Destruction of the World's Economic System (Rev. 18).
"And after these things I saw another angel come down from heaven, having great power; and the earth was lightened with his glory. And he cried mightily with a strong voice, saying, Babylon the great is fallen, is fallen, and is become the habitation of devils, and the hold of every foul spirit, and a cage of every unclean and hateful bird."

In his excellent commentary on the book of Revelation, Dr. J. Vernon McGee writes:

"In chapters 17 and 18 two Babylons are brought before us. The Babylon of chapter 17 is ecclesiastical. The Babylon of chapter 18 is economic. The first is religious—the apostate church. The second is political and commercial. The apostate church is hated by the kings of the earth (Rev. 17:16); the commercial center is loved by the kings of the earth (Rev. 18:9). The apostate church is destroyed by the kings of the earth; political Babylon is destroyed by the judgment of God (verses 5, 8). Obviously, mystery Babylon is destroyed first—in the midst of the Great Tribulation; while commercial Babylon is destroyed at the Second Coming of

FIFTH DIVINE PUNISHMENT

THE LAMB DESTROYS THE WORLD'S POLITICAL AND ECONOMIC SYSTEMS
(Rev. 18:1-24)

THE HEADQUARTERS OF THESE SYSTEMS WILL BE IN A CITY

The location of the city:
Perhaps the rebuilt city of Babylon

THE DESCRIPTION OF THE CITY

- Hotbed of demons and false doctrine **(18:2)**
- Capital of godless materialism **(18:3, 11-17)**
- Filled with both iniquity and arrogance **(18:5-7)**
- Center of drug activities and bloodshedding **(18:23, 24)**

THE DESTRUCTION OF THE CITY

- The source of its destruction: God himself **(18:8, 20)**.
- The means of destruction: Perhaps via nuclear energy. **(See 18:9, 10, 15, 17, 19.)**
- The reaction to its destruction:
Despair on earth **(18:19)**
Delight in heaven **(18:20)**

Christ. These two Babylons are not one and the same city." (*Reveling Through Revelation*, p. 58)

We shall now trace economic and political Babylon through a twofold outline.

A. The location of the city. Is this city a literal one? Of that there seems to be no doubt. It is an actual literal city which will outshine all other cities during the tribulation and doubtless also serve as headquarters for the antichrist. Will ancient Babylon actually be rebuilt on the Euphrates, as in Daniel's time? Some believe it will, for the following reasons:

1. Ancient Babylon was never suddenly destroyed, as prophesied in Isaiah 13:19.
2. The description of literal Babylon by Jeremiah in chapter 51 is very similar to the one given by John in Revelation 18.
3. Babylon is said to be destroyed during the day of the Lord, which is an Old Testament term referring to the tribulation (Isa. 13:6).
4. According to Isaiah 14, Israel will enter into God's rest after Babylon is destroyed. Since this has not yet happened, the event must be yet in the future.
5. Archaeological discoveries have shown that bricks and stones from ancient Babylon have been re-used for building purposes, contrary to the prophecy of Jeremiah 51:26.
6. Jeremiah predicts that Babylon will drink of the cup of the wrath of God last among all the kingdoms of the earth.
7. The vision of the woman in the ephah (Zech. 5:5-11) indicates a return of wickedness and commerce to Babylon.
8. The description in Revelation 18 is best understood if taken literally.

This list is derived from *Bible Prophecy Notes,* by R. Ludwigson. Dr. Charles Ryrie writes:

"Whether the city will be rebuilt once again on the Euphrates is a matter of debate. Nevertheless, the name is used for more than a city

in these chapters (17–18); it also stands for a system. This is much the same as the way Americans speak of Wall Street or Madison Avenue. They are actual streets, but they also stand for the financial or advertising enterprises." (*Revelation*, p. 100)

B. The description of the city.
1. It had become the habitation of demons and false doctrines (Rev. 18:2).
2. Both rulers and merchants had worshiped at her shrine of silver (Rev. 18:3).
3. Her sins had reached into the heavens (Rev. 18:5).
4. She had lived in sinful pleasure and luxury (Rev. 18:7).
5. Her prosperity had blinded her to the judgment of God (Rev. 18:7). There is in this chapter a list (Rev. 18:11-17) of no less than twenty-five of the world's most expensive luxury items.
6. She had deceived all nations with her sorceries (Rev. 18:23).
7. She was covered with the blood of many of God's saints (Rev. 18:24).

C. The destruction of the city.
"And there followed another angel, saying, Babylon is fallen, is fallen, that great city, because she made all nations drink of the wine of the wrath of her fornication" (Rev. 14:8).

". . . and great Babylon came in remembrance before God, to give unto her the cup of the wine of the fierceness of his wrath" (Rev. 16:19).

"And after these things I saw another angel come down from heaven, having great power; and the earth was lightened with his glory. And he cried mightily with a strong voice, saying, Babylon the great is fallen, is fallen" (Rev. 18:1, 2).

It is the opinion of this study that Babylon will literally be rebuilt during the tribulation. The Old Testament city of Babylon is mentioned more times in the Bible than any other city with the exception of Jerusalem. It is mentioned no less than 260 times. What will this restored "City of Satan" be like? Dr. Lehman Strauss has given us an excellent description of ancient Babylon:

"Babylon was founded by Nimrod, the great-grandson of Noah (Gen. 10:8-10). Surviving a series of conflicts, it became one of the most magnificent and luxurious cities in the known world. Superbly constructed, it spread over an area of fifteen square miles, the Euphrates River flowing diagonally across the city. The famous historian Herodotus said the city was surrounded by a wall 350 feet high and 87 feet thick—wide enough for six chariots to drive abreast. Around the top of the wall were 250 watchtowers placed in strategic locations. Outside the huge wall was a large ditch, or moat, which surrounded the city and was kept filled with water from the Euphrates River. The large ditch was meant to serve as an additional protection against attacking enemies, for any attacking enemy would have to cross this body of water first before approaching the great wall.

The cost of constructing this military defense was estimated to be in excess of one billion dollars. When we consider the value of a billion dollars, in those days, plus the fact that it was all built with slave labor, one can imagine something of the wonder and magnificence of this famous city. But in addition to being a bastion for protection, Babylon was a place of beauty. The famous hanging gardens of Babylon are on record yet today as one of the seven wonders of the world. Arranged in an area 400 feet square, and raised in perfectly-cut terraces one above the other, they soared to a height of 350 feet. Viewers could make their way to the top by means of stairways, which were 10 feet wide. Each terrace was covered with a large stone slab topped with a thick layer of asphalt, two courses of brick cemented together, and, finally, plates of lead to prevent any leakage of water. On top of all this was an abundance of rich, fertile earth planted with vines, flowers, shrubs, and trees. From a distance these hanging gardens gave the appearance of a beautiful mountainside, when viewed from the level plains of the valley. The estimated cost to build this thing of beauty ran into hundreds of millions of dollars.

The tower of Babel with its temples of worship presented an imposing sight. The tower itself sat on a base 300 feet in breadth and rose to a height of 300 feet. The one chapel on the top contained an image alone reported to be worth $17,500,000 and sacred vessels, used in worshipping Babylonian gods, estimated at a value of $200,000,000. In addition to this wealth and grandeur the temple contained the most elaborate and expensive furniture ever to adorn any place of worship." (*The Prophecies of Daniel,* pp. 147, 148)

This, then, is what ancient Babylon looked like. And who can doubt that the revived Babylon will outshine the glories of the old? As Dr. J. Vernon McGee suggests:

"In this day Babylon will dominate and rule the world; she will have the first dictatorship. The stock market will be read from Babylon; Babylon will set the styles for the world; a play to be successful will have to be a success in Babylon. And everything in the city is in rebellion against Almighty God and centers in Antichrist. No one dreamed that this great city would be judged. Yet by the time the sun went down, Babylon was nothing but smoldering ruins. When the news goes out the world is stunned, and then begins the wail. The whole world will howl when Babylon goes down." (*Reveling Through Revelation,* p. 6)

We shall now note several features involved in the destruction of Babylon.

1. The source of her destruction—God himself. (See Rev. 18:8, 20.)
2. The means of her destruction. It would almost seem that atomic power of some sort is used to accomplish this. This is strongly suggested by the swiftness of the judgment, the raging fires, and the distance kept by those who watched her burn—possibly due to fear of radioactive fallout. (See Rev. 18:9, 10, 15, 17, 19.)
3. The reaction to her destruction.
   a. By those on earth.
      "And they cast dust on their heads, and cried, weeping and wailing, saying, Alas, alas, that great city, wherein were made rich all that had ships in the sea by reason of her costliness! For in one hour is she made desolate" (Rev. 18:19).
      There are three classes of people who weep over Babylon. They are the monarchs (18:9), the merchants (18:11) and the mariners (18:17).
   b. By those in heaven.
      "Rejoice over her, thou heaven, and ye holy apostles and prophets; for God hath avenged you on her" (Rev. 18:20).
      There are three events in the tribulation which cause all of heaven to rejoice.
      (1) When Satan is cast out (Rev. 12:12).
      (2) When Babylon is destroyed (Rev. 18:20).
      (3) When the Lamb is married to the church (Rev. 19:7).
4. The reasons for her destruction.
   a. The city will become the headquarters of all demonic activity during the tribulation (Rev. 18:2).
   b. Her devilish pride (Rev. 18:7).
   c. Her gross materialism. This wicked city will import and export twenty-eight principal items of merchandise, beginning with gold and ending with the bodies of men (Rev. 18:12, 13).
   d. Her drug activities (Rev. 18:23).
   e. Her bloodshedding (Rev. 18:24).
5. The Old Testament foreshadows her destruction. On a night in 539 B.C., the Babylon of the Old Testament was captured by the Medes and Persians. Just prior to this, Daniel the prophet had read the fearful words of God to a frightened Belshazzar: "God hath numbered thy kingdom, and finished it. . . . Thou art weighed in the balances, and art found wanting. . . . Thy kingdom is divided" (Dan. 5:26-28). Someday God himself will once again write these fearsome words across the skies of Babylon.

VI. The Bloodbath at Armageddon (Rev. 19:1-19, 21).

A. The glory feast in heaven—introducing a bride (19:1-10). This glorious event is celebrated by the usage of heaven's greatest praise word. That word is *Alleluia* (Hallelujah)! Nowhere else in the New Testament can it be found. The Holy Spirit has reserved it for this occasion. (In the Old Testament it appears some twenty-four times in the Psalms.) Heaven now celebrates the Lamb's victory over the harlot, and his marriage to the bride. We are told that "to her was granted that she should be arrayed in fine linen, clean and white: for the fine linen is the righteousness of saints" (19:8). Dr. Charles Ryrie writes:

SIXTH DIVINE PUNISHMENT

THE LAMB DEFEATS BOTH SINNERS AND SATAN AT ARMAGEDDON
(Rev. 19:1-19, 21)

THE GLORY FEAST IN HEAVEN
Introducing a bride **(19:1-10)**

THE GLORY FEAST ON EARTH
Introducing a battle **(19:11-21)**
- The location of the battle
- The reasons for the battle
- The chronology of the battle
- The results of the battle

"The bride's array, fine linen, which is explained as 'the righteousness,' requires the translation 'righteous deeds.' In other words, the wedding garment of the bride will be made up of the righteous deeds done in life. The bride is the bride because of the righteousness of Christ; the bride is clothed for the wedding because of her acts." (*Revelation*, p. 111)

Dr. Lehman Strauss writes: "Has it ever occurred to you . . . that at the marriage of the Bride to the Lamb, each of us will be wearing the wedding garment of our own making?"

B. The gory feast on earth—introducing a battle (Rev. 19:11–21). The Holy Spirit of God has chosen five capable authors to describe for us in clear and chilling language that most famous of all battles—Armageddon. These five authors include David, Isaiah, Joel, Zechariah, and John.

"Why do the heathen rage, and the people imagine a vain thing? The kings of the earth set themselves, and the rulers take counsel together, against the Lord, and against his anointed, saying, Let us break their bands asunder, and cast away their cords from us. He who sitteth in the heavens shall laugh: the Lord shall have them in derision. Then shall he speak unto them in his wrath, and vex them in his great displeasure. Thou shalt break them with a rod of iron; thou shalt dash them in pieces like a potter's vessel" (Ps. 2:1-5, 9).

"Come near, ye nations, to hear; and hearken, ye people: let the earth hear, and all that is therein; the world, and all things that come forth from it. For the indignation of the Lord is upon all nations, and his fury upon all their armies: he hath utterly destroyed them, he hath delivered them to the slaughter. Their slain also shall be cast out, and their stench shall come up out of their carcasses, and the mountains shall be melted with their blood. And all the host of heaven shall be dissolved, and the heavens shall be rolled together as a scroll: and all their host shall fall down, as the leaf falleth off from the vine, and as a falling fig from the fig tree. For my sword shall be bathed in heaven: behold, it shall come down upon Edom, and upon the people of my curse,

to judgment. The sword of the Lord is filled with blood: it is made fat with fatness, and with the blood of lambs and goats, with the fat of the kidneys of rams: for the Lord hath a sacrifice in Bozrah, and a great slaughter in the land of Edom" (Isa. 34:1-6).

"I have trodden the winepress alone; and of the people there was none with me; for I will tread them in mine anger, and trample them in my fury; and their blood shall be sprinkled upon my garments, and I will stain all my raiment. For the day of vengeance is in mine heart, and the year of my redeemed is come. And I will tread down the people in mine anger, and make them drunk in my fury, and I will bring down their strength to the earth" (Isa. 63:3, 4, 6).

"I will also gather all nations, and will bring them down into the valley of Jehoshaphat, and will plead with them there for my people and for my heritage Israel, whom they have scattered among the nations, and parted my land . . . Proclaim ye this among the Gentiles; Prepare war, wake up the mighty men, let all the men of war draw near; let them come up; beat your plowshares into swords, and your pruninghooks into spears: let the weak say, I am strong. Assemble yourselves, and come, all ye heathen, and gather yourselves together round about: there cause thy mighty ones to come down, O Lord. Let the heathen be wakened, and come up to the valley of Jehoshaphat; for there will I sit to judge all the nations round about. Put in the sickle, for the harvest is ripe: come, get you down; for the press is full, the vats overflow; for their wickedness is great. Multitudes, multitudes in the valley of decision: for the day of the Lord is near in the valley of decision. The sun and the moon shall be darkened, and the stars shall withdraw their shining. The Lord also shall roar out of Zion, and utter his voice from Jerusalem; and the heavens and the earth shall shake: but the Lord will be the hope of his people, and the strength of the children of Israel" (Joel 3:2, 9–16).

"Behold I will make Jerusalem a cup of trembling unto all the people round about, when they shall be in the siege both against Judah and against Jerusalem" (Zech. 12:2).

"For I will gather all nations against Jerusalem to battle; and the city shall be taken, and the houses rifled, and the women ravished; and half of the city shall go forth into captivity, and the residue of the people shall not be cut off from the city. Then shall the Lord go forth, and fight against those nations, as when he fought in the day of battle. . . . And this shall be the plague with which the Lord will smite all the people that have fought against Jerusalem; their flesh shall consume away while they stand upon their feet, and their eyes shall consume away in their holes, and their tongue shall consume away in their mouth" (Zech. 14:2, 3, 12).

"And I looked, and behold, a white cloud, and upon the cloud one sat like unto the Son of man, having on his head a golden crown, and in his hand a sharp sickle. And another angel came out of the temple, crying with a loud voice to him that sat on the cloud, Thrust in thy sickle, and reap: for the time is come for thee to reap; for the harvest of the earth is ripe. And he that sat on the cloud thrust in his sickle on the earth, and the earth was reaped. And another angel came out of the temple which is in heaven, he also having a sharp sickle. And another angel came out from the altar, which had power over fire; and cried with a loud cry to him that had the sharp sickle, saying, Thrust in thy sharp sickle, and gather the clusters of the vine of the earth, for her grapes are fully ripe. And the angel thrust his sickle into the earth, and gathered the vine of the earth, and cast it into the great winepress of the wrath of God. And the winepress was trodden without the city, and blood came out of the winepress, even unto the horse bridles, by the space of a thousand and six hundred furlongs" (Rev. 14:14-20).

"And he gathered them together into a place called in the Hebrew tongue Armageddon" (Rev. 16:16).

"And I saw heaven opened and behold, a white horse; and he that sat upon him was called Faithful and True, and in righteousness he doth judge and make war. His eyes were as a flame of fire, and on his head were many crowns, and he had a name written that no man knew but he himself. And he was clothed with a vesture dipped in blood; and his name is called The Word of God. And the armies which were in heaven followed him upon white horses, clothed in fine linen, white and clean.

And out of his mouth goeth a sharp sword, that with it he should smite the nations; and he shall rule them with a rod of iron; and he treadeth the winepress of the fierceness and wrath of Almighty God. And he hath on his vesture and on his thigh a name written, KING OF KINGS AND LORD OF LORDS.

And I saw an angel standing in the sun; and he cried with a loud voice, saying to all the fowls that fly in the midst of heaven, Come and gather yourselves together unto the supper of the great God; that ye may eat the flesh of kings, and the flesh of captains, and the flesh of mighty men, and the flesh of horses, and of them that sit on them, and the flesh of all men, both free and bond, both small and great.

And I saw the beast, and the kings of the earth, and their armies, gathered together to make war against him that sat on the horse, and against his army. And the beast was taken, and with him the false prophet that wrought miracles before him, with which he deceived them that had received the mark of the beast, and them that worshipped his image. These both were cast alive into a lake of fire burning with brimstone.

And the remnant were slain with the sword of him that sat upon the horse, which sword proceeded out of his mouth: and all the fowls were filled with their flesh" (Rev. 19:11-21).

In his booklet entitled *Profiles of Prophecy,* Dr. S. Franklin Logsdon writes:

"A former president of the Norwegian Academy of Sciences, helped by historians from Britain, Egypt, Germany and India, and using an electronic computer, has found that since 3600 B.C. the world has known only 292 years of peace. In this period of more than 55 centuries there have been 14,531 wars, large and small, in which more than 3.6 billion people were killed. Since 650 B.C. there have been 1,656 arms races, all except 16 ending in war, and those 16 ended in economic collapse for the countries concerned" (p. 54).

But this coming war of Armageddon will be by far the biggest, boldest, bloodiest, most brazen, and most blasphemous of all. We shall now consider the negative and positive elements of this war.

Negative:

1. Armageddon is not the same as the Russian invasion of Ezekiel 38. Note the differences:
   a. Russia invades from the north, but at Armageddon the nations come from all directions.
   b. Russia invades to capture Israel's wealth, but this invasion is to destroy the Lamb and his people.
   c. Gog leads the Russian invasion, but the antichrist leads this one.

2. Armageddon is not the final war in the Bible—the final war occurs after the millennium (Rev. 20:7-9). Armageddon takes place at the end of the tribulation.

Positive:

3. The location of the battle. Dr. Herman A. Hoyt aptly describes the location:

   "The staggering dimensions of this conflict can scarcely be conceived by man. The battlefield will stretch from Megiddo on the north (Zech. 12:11; Rev. 16:16) to Edom on the south (Isa. 34:5, 6; 63:1), a distance of sixteen hundred furlongs—approximately two hundred miles. It will reach from the Mediterranean Sea on the west to the hills of Moab on the east, a distance of almost one hundred miles. It will include the Valley of Jehoshaphat (Joel 3:2, 12) and the Plains of Esdraelon. At the center of the entire area will be the city of Jerusalem (Zech. 14:1, 2).

   Into this area the multiplied millions of men, doubtless approaching 400 million, will be crowded for the final holocaust of humanity. The kings with their armies will come from the north and the south, from the east and from the west. . . . In the most dramatic sense this will be the 'Valley of decision' for humanity (Joel 3:14) and the great winepress into which will be poured the fierceness of the wrath of Almighty God" (Rev. 19:15). (*The End Times,* p. 163)

a. Thus there would seem to be at least four important names involved in the battle of Armageddon:

(1) The Valley of Jehoshaphat—a valley just east of Jerusalem, between the Holy City and the Mount of Olives (Joel 3:2, 12).

(2) The Valley of Esdraelon—a valley twenty miles long and fourteen miles wide, north and west of Jerusalem between the Holy City and the Mediterranean Sea.

(3) Megiddo—a flat plain in the Valley of Esdraelon (Zech. 12:11).

(4) Bozrah—a city in Edom, east of the Jordan River and near Petra, the capital city of Edom. These two cities will play an important role during the Second Coming of our Lord (Isa. 34:6 and 63:1).

Marvin Vincent writes concerning Armageddon and its location:

"Megiddo was in the plain of Esdraelon, which has been the chosen place for encampment in every contest carried on in Palestine from the days of . . . Assyria unto the disastrous march of Napoleon Bonaparte from Egypt into Syria. Jews, Gentiles, Saracens, Christian Crusaders, and anti-Christian Frenchmen; Egyptians, Persians, Druses, Turks, and Arabs, warriors of every nation that is under heaven, have pitched their tents on the plains of Esdraelon, and have beheld the banners of their nation wet with the dews of Mt. Tabor and Mt. Hermon." (*Word Studies in the New Testament*, p. 542)

b. In addition to church history, a number of battles took place in this area, as reported by the Old Testament:

(1) Deborah and Barak defeated the Canaanites (Jdg. 4, 5).

(2) Gideon defeated the Midianites (Jdg. 7).

(3) The Philistines defeated and killed Saul (1 Sam. 31).

(4) David defeated Goliath (1 Sam. 17).

(5) An Egyptian king killed Josiah (2 Ki. 23).

Two authors aptly describe this battle for us:

"Palestine is to be given a blood bath of unprecedented proportions which will flow from Armageddon at the north down through the Valley of Jehoshaphat, will cover the land of Edom, and will wash over all Judea and the city of Jerusalem. John looks at this scene of carnage and he describes it as blood flowing to the depths of the horses' bridles. It is beyond human imagination to see a lake that size that has been drained from the veins of those who have followed the purpose of Satan to try to exterminate God's chosen people in order to prevent Jesus Christ from coming to reign." (J. D. Pentecost, *Prophecy for Today*, p. 118)

"The Battle of Armageddon will result in wholesale carnage among the legions of the beast. The brilliance of Christ's appearing will produce a trembling and demoralization in the soldiers (Zech. 12:2; 14:13). The result of this demoralization and trembling will be the desertion from the antichrist and the rendering of him inoperative (2 Thess. 2:8). This tremendous light from heaven will produce astonishment and blindness in animals and madness in men (Zech. 12:4). A plague will sweep through the armies from this light and men will rot right where they stand (Zech. 14:12, 15). The blood of animals and men will form a lake two hundred miles long and bridle deep (Rev. 14:19, 20). The stench of this rotting mass of flesh and blood will fill the entire region (Isa. 34:1–3). The mangled forms of men and the rotting flesh of men and beasts will provide a feast for the carrion birds. (Rev. 19:17, 18, 21). The beast and the false prophet will then be cast alive into the lake of fire forever" (Rev. 19:20). (*The End Times*, H. Hoyt, p. 165)

4. The reasons for the battle. What will draw all the nations of the world into the area of Armageddon? They will gather themselves there for perhaps various reasons. It would seem that the following are three of the more important reasons:

a. Because of the sovereignty of God. In at least five distinct passages we are told that God himself will gather the nations here:

(1) "He hath delivered them to the slaughter" (Isa. 34:2).

(2) "I will also gather all nations, and will bring them down into the valley of Jehoshaphat" (Joel 3:2).

(3) "For I will gather all nations against Jerusalem to battle" (Zech. 14:2).

(4) "For my determination is to gather the nations . . . to pour upon them mine indignation, even all my fierce anger" (Zeph. 3:8).

(5) "And he gathered them together into a place called in the Hebrew tongue Armageddon" (Rev. 16:16).

b. Because of the deception of Satan (Rev. 16:13, 14). In this passage we are told that three special unclean spirits will trick the nations into gathering at Armageddon.

c. Because of the hatred of the nations for Christ.

(1) A number of passages tell us of this devilish hatred (Ps. 2:1–3; Rev. 11:18).

(2) The nations, led by the antichrist, will doubtless realize the imminent return of Christ (Rev. 11:15; 12:12).

(3) They will also be aware of his touching down on the Mount of Olives (Zech. 14:4; Acts 1:9-12).

(4) Thus it is not unreasonable to assume they will gather in that area to destroy him at the moment of his return to earth.

5. The chronology of the battle.

a. The drying up of the Euphrates River (Rev. 16:12). Dr. Donald Barnhouse quotes Seiss in describing this:

"From time immemorial the Euphrates with its tributaries has been a great and formidable boundary between the peoples east of it and west of it. It runs a distance of 1800 miles, and is scarcely fordable anywhere or any time. It is from three to twelve hundred yards wide, and from ten to thirty feet in depth; and most of the time it is still deeper and wider. It was the boundary of the dominion of Solomon, and is repeatedly spoken of as the northeast limit of the lands promised to Israel. . . . History frequently refers to the great hindrance the Euphrates has been to military movements; and it has always been a line of separation between the peoples living east of it and those living west of it." (*Revelation*, p. 301)

Thus when this watery barrier is removed, tens of millions of soldiers from China, India, and other Asian powers will march straight for Armageddon and destruction.

b. The destruction of Jerusalem. Perhaps the saddest event during the tribulation will be the siege and destruction of the Holy City. This will be the forty-seventh and last takeover of the beloved city of David. The following passages bear this out:

"Behold, I will make Jerusalem a cup of trembling unto all people around about, when they shall be in the siege" (Zech. 12:2).

"For I will gather all nations against Jerusalem to battle; and the city shall be taken, and the houses rifled, and the women ravished; and half the city shall go forth into captivity" (Zech. 14:2).

"And when we shall see Jerusalem compassed with armies, then know that the desolation thereof is nigh" (Lk. 21:20).

When these two events transpire, both the angels in paradise and the demons in perdition will surely hold their breath.

John Phillips writes the following, describing the events mentioned in 19:17-21.

"In a few graphic sentences we are told how Satan's rickety empire collapses like a house of cards when the Lord appears. We are told how Satan's forces are to be doomed at Armageddon. John says, 'And I saw an angel standing in the sun; and he cried with a loud voice saying to all the fowls that fly in the midst of heaven, Come and gather yourselves together unto the supper of the great God; that ye may eat the flesh of kings, and the flesh of captains, and the flesh of mighty men, and the flesh of horses, and of them that sit on them, and the flesh of all men, both free and bond, both small and great.' As the armies, assembled at the cockpit of the earth, stare in amazement at the appearing of the King of glory, their gaze is momentarily directed to the sun. There, standing in its glare, is an angel; at his summons, enormous flocks of birds appear, circling and wheeling around the armies of earth, croaking to one another in anticipation of the coming feast, dipping low over the horrified troops, and climbing again to the skies. The battle has not yet been fought, but the omens are dreadful. With each passing moment, the sky grows darker with these birds of prey. There cannot be a vulture, an eagle, a raven, left on earth that has not obeyed the summons and come to the supper of God. Satan's armies are doomed; the fierce fowls know it and have come to bury the dead in the name of the living God.

We are next told how Satan's forces are to be drawn to Armageddon. John says, 'And I saw the beast, and the kings of the earth, and their armies gathered together to make war against him that sat on the horse and against his army.' Thus, tersely, is the mobilization of the world described. Whatever may have been their original motives in converging on Armageddon, all animosities are forgotten, and the men are united by the challenge from on high.

In recent times, science fiction writers have made much of imagined plots against our planet. They have told of invasions from Venus and Mars and from the deep recesses of space. They have depicted a terrified world suddenly united in a common cause in the face of a threat from the far reaches of the sky. This is what happens here, but this is no fantasy of fiction; this is the real thing. The planet is invaded at last from outer space, not by horrible insect-like monsters, but by the Lord Himself and His glorious hosts. The devil knows his hour has come but, careless of human life, he fights to the bitter end. What the beast will say to his armies, his allies, and his antagonists can well be imagined:

'Gentlemen, we are at war and have been at war one with another. The time has come for us to unite in a common cause. The things which unite us now are far more important than the things which divide us. It is no longer a question of which of us will rule the world; it is a question of common survival. The time has come for us to take final counsel together against the Lord and against His anointed. He has put Himself in our power. He has dared to appear on earth. The last time He came, we crucified Him; this time we shall cast His bands asunder and cast away His cords from us forever. We have tried uniting for peace; it has not proved a durable bond. Now let us unite for war. Let us deal with this invasion of our planet once and for all. Let us deal with this invasion of white-robed psalm singers. Let us show them how men, freed of all religious opiates, can fight. Let us hurl our defiance in their teeth. Time and again I have given you proofs of my mighty and supernatural powers. That dread lord of darkness whom we serve has defied these heavenly hosts for countless ages and is more than a match for them all. Come, let us rid the world and its atmosphere forever of these unwanted chanters of hymns.'

The nations unite, as Psalm 2 foretells. Yet, as the great conference of kings disbands and the heralds proclaim the new resolutions, peal after peal of mocking laughter sound down from the sky for 'He that sitteth in the heavens shall laugh; the Lord shall have them in derision' (Ps. 2:4).

It is the same old story. The nations in their folly were united against Christ at His first advent. The early church proclaimed it so: 'Lord, thou art God, which hast made heaven, and earth, and the sea, and all that in them is: Who by the mouth of thy servant David hast said, Why did the heathen rage, and the people imagine vain things? The kings of the earth stood up, and the rulers were gathered together against the Lord, and against his Christ. For of a truth against thy holy child Jesus, whom thou hast anointed, both Herod, and Pontius Pilate, with the Gentiles, and the people of Israel, were gathered together, for to do whatsoever thy hand and thy

counsel determined before to be done. And now, Lord, behold their threatenings' (Acts 4:24-29). The nations united against Christ at His first coming, and they will do so again. They did their worst when they crucified Him but only succeeded in accomplishing God's will. They will do the same when they unite against the Lord to oppose His return. The nations will imagine that they are working out their own schemes and plans as they march toward Esdraelon, but they are simply marching in step with God's will. They are drawn to Armageddon.

Finally, we are told how Satan's forces are to be destroyed at Armageddon. We read, 'And the beast was taken, and with him the false prophet that wrought miracles before him, with which he deceived them that had received the mark of the beast, and them that worshipped his image. These both were cast alive into the lake of fire burning with brimstone. And the remnant were slain with the sword of him that sat upon the horse, which sword proceeded out of his mouth: and all the fowls were filled with their flesh.' With what panoply and pomp the armies march across the plains of Galilee, file through the passes and deploy on the fertile fields of Megiddo! What masses of military equipment are stockpiled in the hills! What fleets ride at anchor in the Red Sea, the Persian Gulf, and along the shorelines of the eastern Mediterranean! What stirring strains of martial music are heard. The ground shakes to the beat of marching feet; the skies darken with aircraft drawn from the ends of the earth. Amazing new weapons, given to men by the beast, are brought into place. Miracles are wrought by the false prophet to encourage the troops. The final commands are given.

Then suddenly it will all be over. In fact, there will be no war at all, in the sense that we think of war. There will be just a word spoken from Him who sits astride the great white horse. Once He spoke a word to a fig tree, and it withered away. Once He spoke a word to howling winds and heaving waves, and the storm clouds vanished and the waves fell still. Once He spoke to a legion of demons bursting at the seams of a poor man's soul, and instantly they fled. Now He speaks a word, and the war is over. The blasphemous, loud-mouthed beast is stricken where he stands. The false prophet, the miracle-working wind-

SEVENTH DIVINE PUNISHMENT

THE LAMB CONDEMNS THE ANTICHRIST AND FALSE PROPHET INTO HELL
(Rev. 19:20)

bag from the pit is punctured and still. The pair of them are bundled up and hurled head-long into the everlasting flames. Another word, and the panic-stricken armies reel and stagger and fall down dead. Field marshals and generals, admirals and air commanders, soldiers and sailors, rank and file, one and all—they fall. And the vultures descend and cover the scene. Thus ends the battle of Armageddon! For a thousand years there will be peace on earth after that. Men will beat their swords into plowshares and their spears into pruning hooks, their tanks into tractors and their missiles into silos for grain. The ages will roll by, and the words for war in human speech will become archaic fragments of a language dead to mankind." (*Exploring Revelation*, pp. 247-250)

VII. The Destruction of the Antichrist and False Prophet. "And the beast was taken, and with him the false prophet that wrought miracles before him, with which he deceived them that had received the mark of the beast, and them that worshipped his image. These both were cast alive into a lake of fire burning with brimstone" (19:20).

Part Four:

The Reign of the Lamb Instituted (20)

I. The great chain (20:1-3).
"And I saw an angel come down from heaven, having the key of the bottomless pit and a great chain in his hands. And he laid hold on the dragon, that old serpent, which is the Devil, and Satan, and bound him a thousand years, and cast him into the bottomless pit, and shut him up, and set a seal upon him, that he should deceive the nations no more, till the thousand years should be fulfilled: and after that he must be loosed a little season."

II. The great resurrection (20:6).
"Blessed and holy is he that hath part in the first resurrection: on such the second death hath no power, but they shall be priests of God and of Christ, and shall reign with him a thousand years."
A. The resurrection of Christ (1 Cor. 15:23).
B. The resurrection of believers at the rapture (1 Thess. 4:16; 1 Cor. 15:51-53).
C. The resurrection of Old Testament and tribulational saints (Rev. 20:6). Many Old and New Testament passages speak of this third resurrection. (See Job 19:25, 26; Ps. 49:15; Isa. 25:8; 26:19; Dan. 12:2; Hosea 13:14; Jn. 5:28, 29; Heb. 11:35.)
D. The resurrection of the unsaved (Rev. 20:5, 11-14).

III. The Great Reign (20:4, 6). Some 250 years ago, Isaac Watts wrote a hymn based on the truths found in Psalm 98. The name of this world-famous hymn is "Joy to the World." At Christmas it is sung all across the world by millions of Christians and non-Christians alike. But a close study of the words of this hymn reveals that Watts did not have in mind the Bethlehem coming of Christ, but rather the millennial coming of our Lord. Observe his words:

"Joy to the World! The Lord is come!
Let earth receive her King.
Let every heart prepare him room,
And heaven and nature sing.

No more let sins and sorrows grow,
Nor thorns infest the ground;
He comes to make his blessings flow,
Far as the curse is found.

He rules the world with truth and grace
And makes the nations prove
The glories of his righteousness,
And wonders of his love."

A. The fact of the millennium. The word itself is a Latin term which signifies "one thousand years." "And they lived and reigned with Christ a thousand years" (Rev. 20:4). In the first seven verses of Revelation 20, John mentions the thousand-year period no less than six times. In spite of this some have argued that, since this number is found in only one New Testament passage, one cannot insist that the thousand-year period will really come to pass. To emphasize their point, reference is made to 2 Peter 3:8—"One day is with the Lord as a thousand years, and a thousand years as one day."

It is interesting (and perhaps revealing) to note that the same group which attempts to shorten the thousand-year period of Revelation to one day (and thus do away entirely with the millennium) also attempts to expand the six days of creation in Genesis to thousands of years. One is tempted to ask, "Why can't God mean exactly what he says?"

Dr. Rene Pache writes the following helpful words:

"Let us notice again this fact: the teaching of the Old Testament concerning the millennium is so complete that the Jews in the Talmud succeeded in developing it entirely themselves, without possessing the gifts furnished by the New Testament later. For example, they had indeed affirmed before the Apocalypse that the messianic kingdom would last one thousand years. One should not, therefore, claim (as some have done) that without the famous passage of Revelation 20:1-10 the doctrine of the millennium would not exist." (*The Return of Christ*, p. 380)

B. During the history of the Christian church men have held three major views about the millennium.
1. Postmillennialism. This theory says that through the preaching of the gospel the world will eventually embrace Christianity and become a universal "society of saints."

PART FOUR

Reign
of the Lamb Instituted (Rev. 20:1-15)

1. The Great Chain (20:1-3)

2. The Great Resurrection (20:6)

3. The Great Reign (20:4, 6)

4. The Great Revolt (20:7-10)

5. The Great Throne (20:11-15)
- •THE FACT OF THIS THRONE
- •THE JUDGE OF THIS THRONE
- •THE JURY AT THIS THRONE
  1. Book of conscience
  2. Book of words
  3. Book of secret works
  4. Book of public works
  5. Book of life
- •THE JUDGED AT THIS THRONE
- •THE JUDGMENT AT THIS THRONE

At this point Christ will be invited to assume command and reign over man's peaceful planet. Thus, though postmillennialists believe in a literal thousand-year reign, their position is false, for the Bible clearly teaches that the world situation will become worse and worse, not better and better, prior to Christ's Second Coming (see 1 Tim. 4:1; 2 Tim. 3:1-5). This position was popularized by a Unitarian minister named Daniel Whitby (1638-1726), and it flourished until the early part of the twentieth century. Then came World War I, and men began to wonder. Finally the postmillennial theory was quietly laid to rest amid Hitler's gas ovens during the Second World War. Today a postmillennialist is harder to find than a 1940 Wendell Willkie button.

2. Amillennialism. This view teaches that there will be no thousand-year reign at all, and that the New Testament church inherits all the spiritual promises and prophecies of Old Testament Israel. In this view Isaiah's beautiful prophecy of the bear and the cow lying together and the lion eating straw like the ox (Isa. 11:7) simply doesn't mean what it says at all! However, if the eleventh chapter of Isaiah cannot be taken literally, what proof do we have that the magnificent fifty-third chapter should not likewise be allegorized away?

3. Premillennialism. This teaches that Christ will return just prior to the millennium and will personally rule during this glorious thousand-year reign. This position alone is the scriptural one, and is the oldest of these three views. From the apostolic period on, the premillennial position was held by the early church fathers.

IV. The great revolt (20:7-10).

"And when the thousand years are expired, Satan shall be loosed out of his prison, and shall go out to deceive the nations which are in the four quarters of the earth, Gog and Magog, to gather them together to battle: the number of whom is as the sand of the sea. And they went up on the breadth of the earth, and compassed the camp of the saints about, and the beloved city: and fire came down from God out of heaven, and devoured them. And the devil that deceived them was cast into the lake of fire and brimstone where the beast and the false prophet are, and shall be tormented day and night forever and ever."

The eternal lake of fire will thus be the devil's final destination. Satan has been, is now, or shall be in one of the following locations:

A. In heaven, God's anointed angel (past location—Ezek. 28:14).

B. In heaven, as God's chief (present location—Job 1, 2).

C. On earth, as the antichrist's spiritual guide (future location, during the tribulation—Rev. 12:12).

D. In the bottomless pit (future, during the millennium—Rev. 20:1-3).

E. On earth again (future, after the millennium—Rev. 20:8, 9).

F. In the lake of fire (future and forever—Rev. 20:10).

"And when the thousand years are expired, Satan shall be loosed out of his prison, and shall go out to deceive the nations which are in the four quarters of the earth, Gog and Magog, to gather them together to battle, the number of whom is as the sand of the sea. And they went up on the breadth of the earth, and compassed the camp of the saints about, and the beloved city" (Rev. 20:7-9).

Dr. J. Vernon McGee writes the following words concerning these verses:

"When the late Dr. Chafer (founder of Dallas Theological Seminary) was once asked why God loosed Satan after he once had him bound, he replied, 'If you will tell me why God let him loose in the first place, I will tell you why God lets him loose the second time.' Apparently Satan is released at the end of the Millennium to reveal that the ideal conditions of the kingdom, under the personal reign of Christ, do not change the human heart. This reveals the enormity of the enmity of man against God. Scripture is accurate when it describes the heart as 'desperately wicked' and incurably so. Man is totally depraved. The loosing of Satan at the end of the 1000 years proves it." (*Reveling Through Revelation*, p. 74)

We have already discussed the purposes accomplished by the sacrifices during the millennium. Apparently millions of maturing children will view these sacrifices and hear the tender salvation plea of the priests, but will stubbornly harden their sinful hearts. The fact that earth's mighty King at Jerusalem once bled as a lowly Lamb at Calvary will mean absolutely nothing to them! Outwardly they will conform, but inwardly they will despise. Finally, at the end of the millennium, the world will be offered for the first time in ten centuries "a choice, and not an echo." Millions will make a foolish and fatal choice.

Dr. J. Dwight Pentecost quotes F. C. Jennings, who writes:

"Has human nature changed, at least apart from sovereign grace? Is the carnal mind at last at friendship with God? Have a thousand years of absolute power and absolute benevolence, both in unchecked activity, done away with all war forever and forever?

These questions must be marked by a practical test. Let Satan be loosed once more from his prison. Let him range once more earth's smiling fields that he knew of old. He saw them last soaked with blood and flooded with tears, the evidence and accompaniments of his own reign; he sees them now 'laughing with abundance' . . . But as he pursues his way further from Jerusalem, the center of this blessedness, these tokens become fainter, until, in the faroff 'corner of the earth,' they cease altogether, for he finds myriads who have instinctively shrunk from close contact with that holy center, and are not unprepared once more to be deceived." (*Things to Come*, p. 549)

However, this insane and immoral insurrection is doomed to utter and complete failure. As a war correspondent, the Apostle John duly records this final battle:

"And fire came down from God out of heaven, and devoured them. And the devil that deceived them was cast into the lake of fire and brimstone, where the beast and the false prophet are, and shall be tormented day and night for ever and ever" (Rev. 20:9, 10).

Obviously this battle, referred to as Gog and Magog, is not the same as the one in Ezekiel 38 and 39.

Dr. J. Vernon McGee writes concerning this:
"Because the rebellion is labeled 'Gog and Magog,' many Bible students identify it with Gog and Magog of Ezekiel 38 and 39. This, of course, is not possible, for the conflicts described are not parallel as to time, place, or participants—only the name is the same.

The invasion from the north by Gog and Magog of Ezekiel 38 and 39 breaks the false peace of the Antichrist and causes him to show his hand in the midst of the Great Tribulation. That rebellion of the godless forces from the north will have made such an impression on mankind that after 1000 years the last rebellion of man bears the same label. We have passed through a similar situation in this century. World War I was so devastating that when war broke out again in Europe, it was labeled again 'World War' but differentiated by the number 2. Now World War III is being predicted. Likewise the war in Ezekiel 38 and 39 is Gog and Magog I, while this reference in verse 8 is to Gog and Magog II." (*Reveling Through Revelation*, p. 77)

V. The Great Throne (20:11-15).
"And I saw a great white throne, and him that sat on it, from whose face the earth and the heaven fled away; and there was found no place for them. And I saw the dead, small and great, stand before God; and the books were opened: and another book was opened, which is the book of life: and the dead were judged out of those things which were written in the books, according to their works. And the sea gave up the dead which were in it; and death and hell delivered up the dead which were in them: and they were judged every man according to their works. And death and hell were cast into the lake of fire. This is the second death. And whosoever was not found written in the book of life was cast into the lake of fire."

A. The fact of this throne (Heb. 9:27). See Revelation 20:11-15, above.
"I beheld till the thrones were cast down, and the Ancient of Days did sit, whose garment was white as snow, and the hair of his head like the pure wool; his throne was like the fiery flame, and his wheels as burning fire. A fiery stream issued and came forth from before him; thousand thousands ministered unto him, and ten thousand times ten thousand stood before him; the judgment was set, and the books were opened" (Dan. 7:9, 10).

B. The Judge on this throne—Christ himself.
"For the Father judgeth no man, but hath committed all judgment unto the Son . . . and hath given him authority to execute judgment also, because he is the Son of man" (Jn. 5:22, 27).

"Him God raised up the third day, and showed him openly . . . And he commanded us to preach unto the people, and to testify that it is he which was ordained of God to be the Judge of quick and dead" (Acts 10:40, 42).

"I charge thee therefore before God, and the Lord Jesus Christ, who shall judge the quick and the dead at his appearing and his kingdom" (2 Tim. 4:1).

C. The jury at this throne—five sets of books.
1. The book of conscience (Rom. 2:15). Although man's conscience is not an infallible guide, he will nevertheless be condemned by those occasions when he deliberately violated it.
2. The book of words (Mt. 12:36, 37).
"But I say unto you that every idle word that men shall speak, they shall give account thereof in the day of judgment. For

PART FIVE

Wife
of the Lamb Introduced (Rev. 21-22)

"And there came unto me one of the seven angels . . . saying, Come hither, I will show thee the bride, the Lamb's wife" (21:9).

Her Habitation—The Fabulous City (21:1—22:5)

ITS OCCUPANTS	ITS LOCATION
ITS SIZE	ITS SHAPE
ITS WALLS	ITS GATES
ITS FOUNDATIONS	ITS STREETS
ITS THRONE	ITS RIVER
ITS TREE OF LIFE	ITS WORSHIP CENTER
ITS LIGHT SOURCE	ITS ACTIVITIES
ITS DURATION	• A place of learning
	• A place of singing
	• A place of service
	• A place of fellowship

Her Husband—The Faithful Savior (22:6-21)

HIS PROMISE **(22:6, 7, 12, 20)**

HIS COMMAND **(22:10)**

HIS SELF-DESCRIPTION **(22:13, 16)**

HIS INVITATION **(22:17)**

HIS WARNING **(22:18, 19)**
1. Don't add to God's Word
2. Don't take from God's Word

---

by thy words thou shalt be justified, and by thy words thou shalt be condemned."
3. The book of secret words.
"God shall judge the secrets of men by Jesus Christ" (Rom. 2:16).
"For God shall bring every work into judgment, with every secret thing, whether it be good, or whether it be evil" (Eccl. 12:14).
4. The book of public works.
"Whose end shall be according to their works" (2 Cor. 11:15).
"For the Son of man shall come in the glory of his Father with his angels; and then he shall reward every man according to his works" (Mt. 16:27).
5. The book of life (Ex. 32:32, 33; Ps. 69:28; Dan. 12:1; Phil. 4:3; Rev. 3:5; 13:8; 17:8; 20:12, 15; 21:27; 22:19).
D. The judged at this throne. As has previously been discussed (see notes under "The judgment seat of Christ"), only unsaved people will stand before this throne. "The wicked shall be turned into hell, and all the nations that forget God" (Ps. 9:17).
E. The judgment at this throne—the eternal lake of fire (Rev. 20:14, 15; Mt. 25:41, 46).

Part Five:

The Wife of the Lamb Introduced (21-22)
"And there came unto me one of the seven angels . . . saying, Come hither, I will show thee the bride, the Lamb's wife" (21:9).
I. Her Habitation—the Fabulous City (21:1—22:5).
A. The descent of this city (21:1, 2).
"And I saw a new heaven and a new earth: for the first heaven and the first earth were passed away; and there was no more sea" (21:1).
John here sees a new heaven and earth. Thus, between Revelation 20 and 21 the old heaven and earth is apparently destroyed. We note:

1. The fact of this destruction.
"Heaven and earth shall pass away, but my words shall not pass away" (Mt. 24:35).
"Thou, Lord, in the beginning hast laid the foundation of the earth, and the heavens are the works of thine hands; they shall perish but thou remainest; and they shall all wax old as doth a garment, and as a vesture shalt thou fold them up, and they shall be changed; but thou art the same, and thy years shall not fail" (Heb. 1:10-12).
"But the day of the Lord will come as a thief in the night, in the which the heavens shall pass away with a great noise, and the elements shall melt with a fervent heat; the earth also and the works that are therein shall be burned up" (2 Pet. 3:10, 11).
2. The reason for this destruction. At this stage in the Bible, the final rebellion has been put down, the false prophet, the antichrist, and the devil himself are all in the lake of fire forever, and the wicked dead have been judged. In light of this, why the necessity for this awesome destruction? It is part of the purifying process.
God will someday do to creation what he did to his beloved Israel in the Old Testament: "Behold, I have refined thee . . . I have chosen thee in the furnace of affliction" (Isa. 48:10).
B. The description of this city (21:3—22:5).
1. The occupants. Who will dwell in this shining city of the stars?
a. The Father (Rev. 4:2, 3; 5:1-7).
b. The Son (Rev. 5:6).
c. The Holy Spirit (Rev. 14:13; 22:17).
d. The holy and elect angels (Heb. 12:22; Rev. 5:11). These angels would include:
(1) The seraphim (Isa. 6:1-7).

(2) The cherubim (Ps. 80:1; 99:1; Rev. 4:6-8).

(3) Gabriel (Dan. 8:16; 9:21; Lk. 1:11, 19, 26, 27; Mt. 1:20; 2:13, 19).

(4) Michael (Dan. 10:13, 21; 12:1; Jude 1:9; Rev. 12:7).

e. The twenty-four elders (Rev. 4:4, 10, 11).

f. Saved Israel (Heb. 11:16; Mt. 25:10, 23; Rev. 14:1-3; 15:1-3).

g. The church (Heb. 12:22, 23; Rev. 19:1, 7, 8; 21:1, 9-11).

h. All the redeemed that ever lived (Rev. 5:9; 7:9, 10). In contrast to the above, note who will be *excluded* from this dazzling city.

(1) the fearful
(2) the unbelieving
(3) the abominable
(4) the murderers
(5) the whoremongers
(6) the sorcerers
(7) the idolaters
(8) the liars (Rev. 21:8) "And there shall in no wise enter into it any thing that defileth" (21:27; see also 22:15).

2. The location. The New Jerusalem is pictured as a stationary city floating above the earth in space. The new earth will thus become a satellite planet encircling this starry capital, from which earth will receive its light (Rev. 21:24, 26).

3. The size. In 21:26 the city is measured and found to be 12,000 furlongs long, 12,000 furlongs wide, and 12,000 furlongs high. According to our present-day measurements, this city would be roughly 1500 miles long, wide, and high. If placed in America, it would reach from New York City to Denver, Colorado, and from Canada to Florida.

4. The shape. Some have seen it as a cube, and others view it as a vast pyramid.

5. The walls. They measure some 216 feet high and are made of jasper (21:12, 17, 18).

6. The gates. There are twelve gates—three on the north, three on the south, three on the east, and three on the west. On each gate is the name of one of the tribes of Israel. Each gate is guarded by an angel. Each gate is composed of a beautiful solid white pearl stone. These gates will never be closed (Rev. 21:12, 13, 21, 25). Again McGee writes:

"The names of the twelve tribes may be inscribed on the twelve gates, but the important feature is the material of construction. Each is a perfect pearl. This is the one jewel that sets forth the Church.

'Again, the Kingdom of heaven is like unto a merchant man, seeking goodly pearls: who, when he had found one pearl of great price, went and sold all that he had, and bought it' (Mt. 13:45, 46). The Church is the pearl of great price. The comparison of the church to the formation of a pearl is striking and suggestive. The pearl is different from all other precious gems, for instead of coming from the earth, the pearl comes from the sea. Other stones are mined from the earth, found in rock and ore. They are taken out, cut, and polished to reveal their beauty. But the pearl comes out of the sea, and it comes from a living organism. A little grain of sand or some other particle begins to cut into the side of a living organism. To protect itself, the organism sends out a fluid to coat the object. Layer upon layer coats it until a beautiful pearl is formed.

The New Jerusalem is the home of the Church, and the gates of pearl are there to remind us throughout eternity that we were a little grain of sharp, dirty sand that was a hurt in the side of Christ. We were not attractive: we were in rebellion against God, walking according to the course of this world. But Christ took that ugly thing—which was you—and covered it with His righteousness. You and I are covered with Him. The beauty is not in the grain of sand, but in what the organism puts around it. God sees us in Christ, and He is lovely. The pearl was lightly esteemed by Israel, but was precious to the Gentiles. We have no value in ourselves, yet we are the pearl of great price. The price that is put upon a thing gives it its value. The price that He paid gives us value. Christ gave His life to get us, and to Him we are precious." (*Reveling Through Revelation*, pp. 101, 102)

7. The foundations. The city rests upon twelve layers of foundation stones with each layer being inlaid with a different precious gem. These are:

a. First foundation—inlaid with jasper, a crystal clear diamond, as bright as a transparent icicle in the sunshine.

b. Second foundation—inlaid with sapphire, a blue opaque stone with gold specks.

c. Third foundation—inlaid with chalcedony, a sky-blue stone with stripes of other colors running through it.

d. Fourth foundation—inlaid with emerald, a bright green stone.

e. Fifth foundation—inlaid with sardonyx, a white stone with layers of red.

f. Sixth foundation—inlaid with sardius, a fiery red stone.

g. Seventh foundation—inlaid with chrysolyte, a transparent golden yellow stone.

h. Eighth foundation—inlaid with beryl, a sea-green stone.

i. Ninth foundation—inlaid with topaz, a transparent golden green stone.

j. Tenth foundation—inlaid with chrysoprasus, a blue-green stone.

k. Eleventh foundation—inlaid with jacinth, a violet stone.

l. Twelfth foundation—inlaid with amethyst, a flashing purple stone. These twelve foundations were not only inlaid with costly gems, but each foundational layer carried the name of one of the twelve apostles in the New Testament (Rev. 21:14, 19, 20).

8. The streets. The central boulevard of the New Jerusalem is composed of pure, transparent gold. The buildings themselves also seem to be made of gold (Rev. 21:18, 21).

9. The throne (Rev. 4:2, 3, 6; 22:3).

10. The river (Ps. 46:4; Rev. 22:1).

11. The tree of life (Rev. 22:2). When God created man and placed him in the Garden of Eden, he put at Adam's disposal the tree of life. But when man sinned, he was driven from Eden and from this tree (see Gen. 2:9; 3:24). At this point in human history the tree of life disappears, but here in the New Jerusalem it reappears, to bloom and blossom as never before.

12. The worship center (21:3, 22).

"And I heard a great voice out of heaven saying, Behold, the tabernacle of God is with men, and he will dwell with them, and they shall be his people, and God himself shall be with them, and be their God. . . . And I saw no temple therein: for the Lord God Almighty and the Lamb are the temple of it."

13. The light source (21:23; 22:5).

"And the city had no need of the sun, neither of the moon, to shine in it: for the glory of God did lighten it, and the Lamb is the light thereof. And there shall be no night there; and they need no candle, neither light of the sun; for the Lord God giveth them light: and they shall reign for ever and ever." Because of this, there will be no night there.

14. The activities.

a. Heaven will be a place of learning:

"For we know in part and we prophesy in part. But when that which is perfect is come, then that which is in part shall be done away" (1 Cor. 13:9, 10).

"Wherefore I also, after I heard of your faith in the Lord Jesus, and love unto all the saints, cease not to give thanks for you, making mention of you in my prayers; that the God of our Lord Jesus Christ, the Father of glory, may give unto you the spirit of wisdom and revelation in the knowledge of him: The eyes of your understanding being enlightened; that ye may know what is the hope of his calling, and what the riches of the glory of his inheritance in the saints. And what is the exceeding greatness of his power to us-ward who believe, according to the working of his mighty power, which he wrought in Christ, when he raised him from the dead, and set him at his own right hand in the heavenly places, far above all principality, and power, and might, and dominion, and every name that is named, not only in this world, but also in that which is to come" (Eph. 1:15–21).

It is evident as one ponders the theology of Paul's prayer here that all these glorious spiritual truths cannot possibly be learned in their fullest sense by the believer down here. These precious principles must surely find their consummation in eternity. This is also true concerning his later prayer in the same epistle:

"For this cause I bow my knees unto the Father of our Lord Jesus Christ, . . . that Christ may dwell in your hearts by faith; that ye, being rooted and grounded in love, may also be able to comprehend with all saints what is the breadth, and length, and depth, and height; and to know the love of Christ, which passeth knowledge, that ye might be filled with all the fulness of God" (Eph. 3:14, 17, 18, 19).

b. Heaven will be a place of singing.

"Sing, O ye heavens; for the Lord hath done it: shout, ye lower parts of the earth: break forth into singing, ye mountains, O forest and every tree therein: for the Lord hath redeemed Jacob and glorified himself in Israel" (Isa. 44:23).

"But we see Jesus. . . . Saying, I will declare thy name unto my brethren, in the midst of the church will I sing praises unto thee" (Heb. 2:9, 12).

"And they sung a new song, saying, Thou art worthy . . . for thou wast slain, and hast redeemed us to God by thy blood out of every kindred, and tongue and people and nation" (Rev. 5:9).

"And they sung as it were a new song before the throne . . . and no man could learn that song but the hundred and forty and four thousand, which were redeemed from the earth" (Rev. 14:3).

"And they sing the song of Moses the servant of God, and the song of the Lamb, saying, Great and marvelous are thy works, Lord God Almighty; just and true are thy ways, thou King of saints" (Rev. 15:3).

c. Heaven will be a place of service.

"And his servants shall serve him" (Rev. 22:3).

"Therefore are they before the throne of God, and serve him day and night in his temple" (Rev. 7:15).

While we cannot be sure of the exact nature of this service, we do know from the following passages that a portion of our labor for the Lamb will be that of exercising authority and judgment over men and angels:

"If we suffer, we shall also reign with Him . . ." (2 Tim. 2:12).

. . . Come hither, I will shew thee the bride, the Lamb's wife **(Rev. 21:9).**

After this I beheld, and, lo, a great multitude, which no man could number, of all nations, and kindreds, and people, and tongues, stood before the throne, and before the Lamb, clothed with white robes, and palms in their hands;
And cried with a loud voice, saying, Salvation to our God which sitteth upon the throne, and unto the Lamb **(Rev. 7:9, 10).**

And one of the elders answered, saying unto me, What are these which are arrayed in white robes? and whence came they?
And I said unto him, Sir, thou knowest. And he said to me, These are they which came out of great tribulation, and have washed their robes, and made them white in the blood of the Lamb **(Rev. 7:13, 14).**

"Do ye not know that the saints shall judge the world? Know ye not that we shall judge angels?" (1 Cor. 6:2, 3).

"And they shall reign for ever and ever" (Rev. 22:5).

d. Heaven will be a place of fellowship. The question is often asked, "Will we know and recognize each other in heaven?" To this the Scripture answers an emphatic yes! During his transfiguration, our Lord spoke freely with Moses and Elijah (Mt. 17:3), centuries after both these Old Testament heroes had departed from this earth; yet they are still recognized as Moses and Elijah. In addition to this, the Apostle John, during his vision of the Revelation, sees and recognizes the differences between elders, angels, and various redeemed peoples from all the nations of the earth. Perhaps the apex of this beautiful truth is found in Paul's love chapter:

"For now we see through a glass darkly; but then face to face: now I know in part; but then shall I know even as also I am known" (1 Cor. 13:12).

Not only will believers enjoy blessed fellowship with other believers, but even more important, we shall know and be known by the Savior in a far more intimate way than ever possible here on earth.

15. The duration.
"And they shall reign for ever and ever" (22:5).

II. Her Husband—the Faithful Savior (22:6-21).
   A. His promise:
      1. To come surely (22:6): "The things which must shortly be done."
      2. To come quickly (22:7): "Behold, I come quickly." See also verses 12 and 20.
      3. To reward the faithful: "My reward is with me, to give every man according as his work shall be."
   B. His command:
      "Seal not the sayings of the prophecy of this book: for the time is at hand" (22:10).
   C. His self-description:
      1. "I am Alpha and Omega, the beginning and the end, the first and the last" (22:13).
      2. "I am the root and the offspring of David, and the bright and morning star" (22:16).
   D. His invitation (22:17):
      "And the Spirit and the bride say, Come. And let him that is athirst come. And whosoever will, let him take the water of life freely."
   E. His warning (22:18, 19):
      "For I testify unto every man that heareth the words of the prophecy of this book, If any man shall add unto these things, God shall add unto him the plagues that are written in this book: And if any man shall take away from the words of the book of this prophecy, God shall take away his part out of the book of life, and out of the holy city, and from the things which are written in this book."

The Theological Method

Perhaps no other single word has been so successfully twisted by the devil today as has the biblical word "doctrine." In the minds of millions, doctrine involves the following concepts:

1. Doctrine is that silly and useless practice of arguing (in the spirit and tradition of medieval monks) such things as: "How many angels can dance on the head of a pin?" "Could God create a stone so heavy that he couldn't lift it?" "Could he plant an immovable post in the ground and then throw an unstoppable rock at it?"
2. Doctrine divides, whereas love unites.
3. One cannot mix doctrine with soul-winning.
4. Doctrine is dull and impractical.
5. Doctrine is over the heads of most people.
6. Why learn a lot of doctrine when we don't live up to the light we already have?
7. The key goal is to let the Bible master us, and not spend our energies in mastering the Bible.

In answering these charges, one could say that they are as far removed from the truth as the Babe in Bethlehem is from Rudolph the Red-Nosed Reindeer! Each argument needs but a brief refutation.

1. True biblical doctrine has nothing whatsoever to do with dancing angels, massive rocks, sturdy posts, and speeding stones! The word doctrine, as found in the Bible, refers to the systematic (and often simple) gathering and presentation of the facts concerning any great body of truth.
2. True doctrine does indeed divide. It divides light from darkness, right from wrong, and life from death. But it also unites, for God's love cannot be known or appropriated by sinful men without the involvement of doctrine.
3. These two not only *can* be mixed, they *must* be mixed if God's commands are to be followed. It is thrilling to note that the greatest soul-winner of all time and the greatest theologian who ever lived were one and the same—the Apostle Paul! The same man who went door to door, pleading with tears for men to accept Christ (Acts 20:20, 21, 26), also wrote some 50 percent of the New Testament, including that most profound of all doctrinal books, the epistle to the Romans.
4. To the contrary, doctrine will put both a fire and a song in the hearts of those who read and heed its tremendous truths.

    "And they said one to another, Did not our heart burn within us, while he talked with us by the way, and while he opened to us the scriptures?" (Lk. 24:32).

    "Speaking to yourselves in psalms and hymns and spiritual songs, singing and making melody in your heart to the Lord" (Eph. 5:19).

    "Blessed is he that readeth, and they that hear the words of this prophecy, and keep those things which are written therein: for the time is at hand" (Rev. 1:3).

    "Behold, I come quickly: blessed is he that keepeth the sayings of the prophecy of this book" (Rev. 22:7).
5. This is simply not true, as refuted by Christ himself.

    "At that time Jesus answered and said, I thank thee, O Father, Lord of heaven and earth, because thou hast hid these things from the wise and prudent, and hast revealed them unto babes. Come unto me, all ye that labour and are heavy laden, and I will give you rest. Take my yoke upon you, and learn of me; for I am meek and lowly in heart; and ye shall find rest unto your souls. For my yoke is easy, and my burden is light" (Mt. 11:25, 28-30).
6. To follow this twisted logic would mean never to go beyond the first commandment (Ex. 20:3), which says we are to have no gods or interests placed before the true God. But who has not on occasion been guilty of this? Should we therefore conclude that the sixth and seventh commandments ("Thou shalt not kill; thou shalt not commit adultery," Ex. 20:13, 14) should not be kept simply because we do not always obey the first commandment?

7. This statement is pious nonsense, for one cannot possibly be even remotely influenced, let alone mastered, by that which he or she knows nothing about. It is true that the goal of Bible study is to become Spirit controlled. But the *fruit* of the Spirit can never come apart from the *root* of personal study.

Having listed and answered those objections to studying doctrine, let us now give some important advantages for doing it.

1. Doctrine will help save us from theological food poisoning.

"Till I come, give attendance to reading, to exhortation, to doctrine. Neglect not the gift that is in thee, which was given thee by prophecy, with the laying on of the hands of the presbytery. Meditate upon these things; give thyself wholly to them; that thy profiting may appear to all. Take heed unto thyself, and unto the doctrine; continue in them; for in doing this thou shalt both save thyself, and them that hear thee" (1 Tim. 4:13-16).

"Now the Spirit speaketh expressly, that in the latter times some shall depart from the faith, giving heed to seducing spirits, and doctrines of devils" (1 Tim. 4:1).

"I charge thee therefore before God, and the Lord Jesus Christ, who shall judge the quick and the dead at his appearing and his kingdom; preach the word; be instant in season, out of season; reprove, rebuke, exhort with all longsuffering and doctrine. For the time will come when they will not endure sound doctrine; but after their own lusts shall they heap to themselves teachers, having itching ears; and they shall turn away their ears from the truth, and shall be turned unto fables" (2 Tim. 4:1-4).

2. Doctrine will help settle us.

"That we henceforth be no more children, tossed to and fro, and carried about with every wind of doctrine, by the sleight of men, and cunning craftiness, whereby they lie in wait to deceive" (Eph. 4:14).

3. Doctrine will acquaint us with the details of God's eternal plan.

a. Concerning the history of Israel.

"Moreover, brethren, I would not that ye should be ignorant, how that all our fathers were under the cloud, and all passed through the sea" (1 Cor. 10:1).

b. Concerning the restoration of Israel.

"For I would not, brethren, that ye should be ignorant of this mystery, lest ye should be wise in your own conceits; that blindness in part is happened to Israel, until the fulness of the Gentiles be come in" (Rom. 11:25).

c. Concerning spiritual gifts.

"Now concerning spiritual gifts, brethren, I would not have you ignorant" (1 Cor. 12:1).

d. Concerning the rapture.

"But I would not have you to be ignorant, brethren, concerning them which are asleep, that ye sorrow not, even as others which have no hope" (1 Thess. 4:13).

e. Concerning the destruction of this earth.

"But, beloved, be not ignorant of this one thing, that one day is with the Lord as a thousand years, and a thousand years as one day. But the day of the Lord will come as a thief in the night; in the which the heavens shall pass away with a great noise, and the elements shall melt with fervent heat, the earth also and the works that are therein shall be burned up" (2 Pet. 3:8, 10).

4. Doctrine helps us edify God.

"Study to shew thyself approved unto God, a workman that needeth not to be ashamed, rightly dividing the word of truth" (2 Tim. 2:15).

5. Doctrine helps us equip ourselves.

"But evil men and seducers shall wax worse and worse, deceiving, and being deceived. But continue thou in the things which thou hast learned and hast been assured of, knowing of whom thou hast learned them; and that from a child thou hast known the holy scriptures, which are able to make thee wise unto salvation through faith which is in Christ Jesus. All scripture is given by inspiration of God, and is profitable for doctrine, for reproof, for correction, for instruction in righteousness; that the man of God may be perfect, throughly furnished unto all good works" (2 Tim. 3:13-17).

"Finally, my brethren, be strong in the Lord, and in the power of his might. Put on the whole armour of God, that ye may be able to stand against the wiles of the devil. For we wrestle not against flesh and blood, but against principalities, against powers, against the rulers of the darkness of this world, against spiritual wickedness in high places. Wherefore take unto you the whole armour of God, that ye may be able to withstand in the evil day, and having done all, to stand. Stand therefore, having your loins girt about with truth, and having on the breastplate of righteousness; and your feet shod with the preparation of the gospel of peace; above all, taking the shield of faith, wherewith ye shall be able to quench all the fiery darts of the wicked. And take the helmet of salvation, and the sword of the Spirit, which is the word of God" (Eph. 6:10-17).

THE DOCTRINE OF THE TRINITY

THE DOCTRINE OF THE TRINITY

I. The Existence of God. The greatest and most profound idea the human mind can ever conceivably entertain concerns the possibility of the existence of a personal God. The sheer importance of man's response to this idea cannot be exaggerated, for it will not only govern his life down here but also determine his ultimate destiny. Unless one satisfactorily answers the *who* question, he cannot possibly solve the how, why, when, and where problems of his own existence.

A. Some philosophical arguments for the existence of God.

1. The universal belief argument: All mankind has some idea of a supreme Being. This argument has often been challenged but never refuted. While the concepts of God found among many cultures and civilizations differ greatly on the number, name, and nature of this supreme Being, nevertheless the idea remains. A classic example of this is the amazing story of Helen Keller (1880–1968). From the age of two, Miss Keller was blind, deaf, and without the sense of smell. After months of agonizing and fruitless attempts on the part of her teacher to communicate with this young girl, a miracle occurred. One day Helen suddenly understood the concept and meaning of running water! From this humble foundation Miss Keller built a lofty tower of thought, including the ability to use her voice in speaking. She became an educated and articulate human being. Sometime after she had progressed to the point that she could engage in conversation, she was told of God and his love in sending Christ to die on the cross. She is said to have responded with joy, "I always knew he was there, but I didn't know his name!"

2. The cosmological argument: Every effect must have an adequate cause. Robert Culver writes:

"One of the great names of British science, mathematics, and philosophy is Sir Isaac Newton (1642–1727). Sir Isaac had a miniature model of the solar system made. A large golden ball representing the sun was at its center and around it revolved smaller spheres, representing the planets—Mercury, Venus, Earth, Mars, Jupiter, and the others. They were each kept in an orbit relatively the same as in the real solar system. By means of rods, cogwheels, and belts they all moved around the center gold ball in exact precision. A friend called on the noted man one day while he was studying the model. The friend was not a believer in the biblical doctrine of divine creation. According to reports, their conversation went as follows:

Friend: 'My, Newton, what an exquisite thing! Who made it for you?'

Newton: 'Nobody.'

Friend: 'Nobody?'

Newton: 'That's right! I said nobody! All of these balls and cogs and belts and gears just happened to come together, and wonder of wonders, by chance they began revolving in their set orbits with perfect timing!'

Of course, the visitor understood the unexpressed argument: 'In the beginning, God created the heaven and the earth.'" (*The Living God*, pp. 29, 30)

3. The ontological argument: "Man has an idea of a Most Perfect Being. This idea includes the idea of existence, since a being, otherwise perfect, who did not exist would not be as perfect as a perfect being who did exist. Therefore, since the idea of existence is contained in the idea of the Most Perfect Being, the Most Perfect Being must exist." (C. C. Ryrie)

4. The anthropological argument: The conscience and moral nature of man demands a self-conscious and moral Maker. This built-in barometer supplies no information, and the information on which it passes judgment may be incorrect. But nevertheless, conscience tells us we *ought* to do what is right regarding the information we have. Robert Culver writes:

"This sense of duty may be weak (1 Cor. 8:12), good (1 Pet. 3:16), defiled (1 Cor. 8:7), seared (1 Tim. 4:2), strong or pure (1 Cor. 8:7, 9). But it is never absent. The only adequate explanation is that the great Moral Being, who created us all, planted the moral sense in us. No other explanation is adequate." (*The Living God*, p. 31)

B. Scriptural arguments for the existence of God. None. The Bible simply assumes existence of God.

Psalm 14:1: "The fool hath said in his heart, There is no God. They are corrupt, they have done abominable works, there is none that doeth good."

Hebrews 11:6: "But without faith it is impossible to please him; for he that cometh to God must believe that he is, and that he is a rewarder of them that diligently seek him." Clark Pinnock aptly summarizes all this when he writes:

"For the Scripture then, the existence of God is both a historical truth (God acted into history), and an existential truth (God reveals himself to every soul). His existence is both objectively and subjectively evident. It is necessary *logically* because our assumption of order, design, and rationality rests upon it. It is necessary *morally* because there is no explanation for the shape of morality apart from it. It is necessary *personally* because the exhaustion of all material possibilities still cannot give satisfaction to the heart. The deepest proof for God's existence apart from history is just life itself. God has created man in his image, and man cannot elude the implications of this fact. Everywhere their identity pursues them." (*Set Forth Your Case*, p. 77)

II. The Definition of God.

"There is but one only living and true God, who is infinite in being and perfection, a most pure spirit, invisible, without body, parts, or passions, immutable, immense, eternal, incomprehensible, almighty, most wise, most holy, most free, most absolute, working all things according to the counsel of his own immutable and most righteous will, for his own glory; most loving, gracious, merciful, long-suffering, abundant in goodness and truth, forgiving iniquity, transgression, and sin; the rewarder of them that diligently seek him; and withal most just and terrible in his judgments; hating all sin, and who will by no means clear the guilty." (Westminster Catechism)

III. The Names of God.

A. Elohim: Used 2,570 times, it refers to God's power and might.

Genesis 1:1: "In the beginning God created the heaven and the earth."

Psalm 19:1: "The heavens declare the glory of God; and the firmament sheweth his handiwork."

B. El: Four compounds of his name. There are two significant places where this name was used in the Old Testament. One came from the lips of Jerusalem's first sovereign, and the other from history's first sinner.

1. Elyon: The strongest strong One.

a. Jerusalem's first sovereign (Melchizedek)

Genesis 14:17-20: "And the king of Sodom went out to meet him after his return from the slaughter of Chedorlaomer, and of the kings that were with him, at the valley Shaveh, which is the king's dale. And Melchizedek king of Salem brought forth bread and wine: and he was the priest of the most high God. And he blessed him, and said, Blessed be Abram of the most high God, possessor of heaven and earth: And blessed be the most high God, which hath delivered thine enemies into thy hand. And he gave him tithes of all."

b. History's first sinner (Satan)

Isaiah 14:13, 14: "For thou hast said in thine heart, I will ascend into heaven, I will exalt my throne above the stars of God: I will sit also upon the mount of the congregation, in the sides of the north: I will ascend above the heights of the clouds; I will be like the most High."

2. Roi: The strong One who sees. In Genesis 16 an angered and barren Sarai had cast into the wilderness her pregnant and arrogant handmaiden Hagar. When all hope for survival had fled, this pagan Egyptian girl was visited and ministered to by El Roi himself—the strong God who sees.

Genesis 16:13: "And she called the name of the Lord that spake unto her, Thou God seest me: for she said, Have I also here looked after him that seeth me?"

3. Shaddai: The breasted One. Used forty-eight times in Old Testament. The Hebrew word *shad* is often used to designate the bosom of a nursing mother.

Genesis 17:1: "And when Abram was ninety years old and nine, the Lord appeared to Abram, and said unto him, I am the Almighty God; walk before me, and be thou perfect."

This revelation of God came to Abraham at a much needed time in his life. His sin in marrying Hagar (Gen. 16) had doubtless prevented that full and unhindered fellowship which had previously flowed between him and God. In addition, he now was an old man, nearly 100, humanly unable to father the long-anticipated heir.

Psalm 91:1: "He that dwelleth in the secret place of the most High shall abide under the shadow of the Almighty."

4. Olam: The everlasting God. Isaiah 40 is usually regarded as one of the greatest Old Testament chapters. The prophet begins by predicting both the first and second advent of Christ. He then contrasts the awesome power of the true God with the miserable impotence of all idols. But carnal Israel had trouble accepting all this, wondering just how these wonderful events could transpire to answer their doubts. Isaiah declares:

Isaiah 40:28-31: "Hast thou not known? hast thou not heard, that the everlasting God, the Lord, the Creator of the ends of the earth, fainteth not, neither is weary? there is no searching of his understanding. He giveth power to the faint; and to them that have no might he increaseth strength. Even the youths shall faint and be weary, and the young men shall utterly fall: But they that wait upon the Lord shall renew their strength; they shall mount up with wings as eagles; they shall run, and not be weary; and they shall walk, and not faint."

C. Adonai: Master, Lord. God owns all his creation. Malachi 1:6: "A son honoureth his father, and a servant his master: if then I be a father, where is mine honour? and if I be a master, where is my fear? saith the Lord of hosts unto you, O priests, that despise my name. And ye say, Wherein have we despised thy name?" The Hebrew Old Testament name *Adonai* and its Greek New Testament counterpart *Kurios* describe the relationship between master and slave. *Adonai* thus carries with it a twofold implication.

1. The master has a right to expect obedience. Robert Lightner writes:

> "In Old Testament times the slave was the absolute possession of his master, having no rights of his own. His chief business was to carry out the wishes of his master. The slave had a relationship and responsibility different from that of the hired servant. The hired servant could quit if he did not like the orders of his master. But not so with the slave; he could do nothing but obey (cf. Gen. 24:1–12). (*The God of the Bible*, p. 116)

2. The slave may expect provision. Again, to quote Lightner:

> "The slave had no worry of his own. It was the master's business to provide food, shelter, and the necessities of life. Since the slave is the possession of the master, his needs become the master's. Obedience is the only condition for this provision. This truth is marvelously displayed in Paul, who was himself a bond slave, when he assured the Philippians that God would supply all their needs (Phil. 4:19). Only the obedient slave can expect this from his master." (*Ibid.* p. 117)

D. Jehovah. God's most common name. It occurs 6,823 times. The self-existent One, the God of the covenant (Gen. 2:4). Nine compound names of Jehovah are:

1. Jireh: The Lord will provide.
   Genesis 22:13, 14: "And Abraham lifted up his eyes, and looked, and behold behind him a ram caught in a thicket by his horns: and Abraham went and took the ram, and offered him up for a burnt offering in the stead of his son. And Abraham called the name of that place Jehovah-jireh: as it is said to this day, In the mount of the Lord it shall be seen."

2. Nissi: The Lord, my Banner.
   Exodus 17:15: "And Moses built an altar, and called the name of it Jehovah-nissi."
   This passage is significant, for it marks the first battle and subsequent victory of Israel on its march after leaving Egypt. The great lawgiver Moses mounted a hill and with outstretched arms prayed for the Israelite armies, headed up by Joshua, in their pitched battle against the fierce Amalekites.

3. Shalom: The Lord is Peace.
   Judges 6:24: "Then Gideon built an altar there unto the Lord, and called it Jehovah-shalom: unto this day it is yet in Ophrah of the Abiezrites."
   As one studies the thrilling account of Gideon he reads how Jehovah-shalom did indeed bring peace to Israel over the Midianites through this warrior and his 300 trumpet-blowing soldiers.

4. Sabaoth: The Lord of hosts. *Sabaoth* is derived from the Hebrew word *tsaba,* meaning "host." The Lord of hosts is a reference to the captain of heaven's armies. These armies are said to be composed of angels. (See Ps. 68:17; 104:4; 148:2; Mt. 26:53.) Christ himself is their leader. (See Josh. 5:14.) The great prophet Isaiah describes his vision during which he was allowed to see Jehovah of hosts (Isa. 6:3).
   Isaiah 6:1–3: "In the year that King Uzziah died I saw also the Lord sitting upon a throne, high and lifted up, and his train filled the temple. Above it stood the seraphims: each one had six wings; with twain he covered his face, and with twain he covered his feet and with twain he did fly. And one cried unto another, and said, Holy, holy, holy, is the Lord of hosts: the whole earth is full of his glory."

5. Maccaddeschcem: The Lord thy Sanctifier.
   Exodus 31:13: "Speak thou also unto the children of Israel, saying, Verily my sabbaths ye shall keep: for it is a sign between me and you throughout your generations; that ye may know that I am the Lord that doth sanctify you."
   This great name for God, first mentioned in Exodus, appears many times in the following book, Leviticus. To be sanctified is to be set apart, and that is what God desired to do for his people—to set them apart for special service.

6. Rohi (Raah): The Lord my Shepherd.
   Psalm 23:1: "The Lord is my shepherd; I shall not want."
   Of all the compound names of Jehovah, this is at once the most easily understood title—that good, and great, and chief Shepherd God.

7. Tsidkenu: The Lord our Righteousness.
   Jeremiah 23:6: "In his days Judah shall be saved, and Israel shall dwell safely: and this is his name whereby he shall be called, THE LORD OUR RIGHTEOUSNESS."
   According to Jeremiah the official name for the Messiah during the future millennium will be Jehovah-Tsidkenu.

8. Shammah: The Lord who is present.
   Ezekiel 48:35: "It was round about eighteen thousand measures: and the name of the city from that day shall be, The Lord is there."
   In this passage Ezekiel describes for us the dimensions of the millennial temple and

then gives us the new name for Jerusalem during earth's golden age: Jehovah-shammah.

9. Rapha: The Lord our Healer.

Exodus 15:26: "And said, If thou wilt diligently hearken to the voice of the Lord thy God, and wilt do that which is right in his sight, and wilt give ear to his commandments, and keep all his statutes, I will put none of these diseases upon thee, which I have brought upon the Egyptians: for I am the Lord that healeth thee."

By this new name God introduced to Israel the terms of his heavenly "medicare" health plan while they were on their way to Canaan. If only they had accepted this gracious policy.

IV. The Nature of God.

A. God is Spirit. Emory Bancroft has written:

"God as Spirit is incorporeal, invisible, without material substance, without physical parts or passions and therefore free from all temporal limitations." (*Elemental Theory*, p. 23)

Jesus made this clear when he told the Samaritan woman: "God is a Spirit; and they that worship him must worship him in Spirit and in truth" (Jn. 4:24). Some have been disturbed, however, as they compare this statement with certain Old Testament expressions which speak of God's arms (Deut. 33:27), his eyes (Ps. 33:18), ears (2 Ki. 19:16), and mouth (Isa. 58:14). However, these terms are simply anthropomorphic expressions. An anthropomorphic expression is a term which is used to explain some function or characteristic of God by using words descriptive of human elements. Robert Lightner writes: "Such expressions do not mean that God possesses these physical parts. He is Spirit (Jn. 4:24). Rather, they mean since God is spirit and eternal, He is capable of doing precisely the functions which are performed by these physical properties in man." (*The God of the Bible*, p. 67)

B. God is a Person. Again, to quote from Robert Lightner:

"Personality involves existence with the power of self-consciousness and self-determination. To be self-conscious means to be able to be aware of one's self among others. It is more than mere consciousness. Even animals possess something which makes them aware of things around them. The brute, however, is not able to objectify himself. Man, in contrast to the brute, possesses both consciousness and self-consciousness. Self-determination has to do with the ability to look to the future and prepare an intelligent course of action. It also involves the power of choice. The brute also has determination, but he does not have self-determination—the power to act from his own free will and to thus determine his acts. It is usually admitted that there are three elements of personality—intellect, emotion, and will." (*Ibid.*, p. 65)

Thus, as a Person, God exhibits all those elements involved in personality.

1. He creates.

Genesis 1:1: "In the beginning God created the heaven and the earth."

2. He destroys.

Genesis 18:20; 19:24, 25: "And the Lord said, Because the cry of Sodom and Gomorrah is great, and because their sin is very grievous. . . . Then the Lord rained upon Sodom and upon Gomorrah brimstone and fire from the Lord out of heaven. And he overthrew those cities, and all the plain, and all the inhabitants of the cities, and that which grew upon the ground."

3. He provides.

Psalm 104:27-30: "These wait all upon thee; that thou mayest give them their meat in due season. That thou givest them they gather: thou openest thine hand, they are filled with good. Thou hidest thy face, they are troubled: thou takest away their breath, they die, and return to their dust. Thou sendest forth thy spirit, they are created: and thou renewest the face of the earth."

4. He promotes.

Psalm 75:6, 7: "For promotion cometh neither from the east, nor from the west, nor from the south. But God is the judge: he putteth down one, and setteth up another."

5. He cares.

1 Peter 5:6, 7: "Humble yourselves therefore under the mighty hand of God, that he may exalt you in due time: Casting all your care upon him; for he careth for you."

6. He hears.

Psalm 94:9, 10: "He that planted the ear, shall he not hear? He that formed the eye, shall he not see? He that chastiseth the heathen, shall not he correct? He that teacheth man knowledge, shall not he know?"

7. He hates.

Proverbs 6:16: "These six things doth the Lord hate: yea, seven are an abomination unto him."

8. He grieves.

Genesis 6:6: "And it repented the Lord that he had made man on the earth, and it grieved him at his heart."

9. He loves.

John 3:16: "For God so loved the world, that he gave his only begotten Son, that whosoever believeth in him should not perish, but have everlasting life."

C. God is One.

Deuteronomy 6:4, 5: "Hear, O Israel: The Lord our God is one Lord: And thou shalt love the Lord thy God with all thine heart, and with all thy soul, and with all thy might."

1 Kings 8:60: "That all the people of the earth may know that the Lord is God, and that there is none else."

Isaiah 44:6–8: "Thus saith the Lord the King of Israel, and his Redeemer the Lord of hosts; I am the first, and I am the last; and beside me there is no God. And who, as I, shall call, and shall declare it, and set it in order for me, since I appointed the ancient people? and the things that are coming, and shall come, let them show unto them. Fear ye not, neither be afraid: have not I told thee from that time, and have declared it? ye are even my witnesses. Is there a God beside me? yea, there is no God; I know not any."

Isaiah 45:5, 6: "I am the Lord, and there is none else, there is no God beside me: I girded thee, though thou hast not known me: That they may know from the rising of the sun, and from the west, that there is none beside me. I am the Lord, and there is none else."

Isaiah 46:9: "Remember the former things of old: for I am God, and there is none else; I am God, and there is none like me."

Ephesians 4:4–6: "There is one body, and one Spirit, even as ye are called in one hope of your calling; one Lord, one faith, one baptism, one God and Father of all, who is above all, and through all, and in you all."

1 Timothy 2:5: "For there is one God, and one mediator between God and men, the man Christ Jesus."

D. God is a Trinity. C. C. Ryrie writes:

"There is only one God, but in the unity of the Godhead there are three eternal and co-equal Persons, the same in substance, but distinct in subsistence."

Robert Culver writes:

"Two expressions have been traditionally employed to designate certain inner relations between the Father and the Son, and the Father and the Son with the Spirit. These two expressions are the eternal generation of the Son by the Father and the eternal spiration (or procession) of the Spirit from the Father and the Son. They began to be employed about the time of the council of Nicea (A.D. 325). They expressed in scriptural language the idea that the Son and the Spirit were eternally with the Godhead. John 1:14 refers to our Lord as the 'only begotten' of the Father. And John 14:16, 26 and 15:26 speak of the Spirit as 'proceeding from the Father and the Son.'" (The Living God, p. 96)

1. False views concerning the Trinity. There are two serious errors about the doctrine of the Trinity.
   a. The error of tri-theism. This says that the Trinity consists of three separate (but cooperating) Gods.
   b. The error of modalism. According to this view there is but one God who simply reveals himself through three different modes, or roles. For example, a particular man could be considered a *husband* to his wife, a *father* to his children, and an *employee* to his boss.

2. Proposed illustration demonstrating the Trinity. Throughout church history various illustrations have been offered to demonstrate the Trinity. Seven such examples are as follows. The first four are totally unscriptural, while the final three possess some limited possibilities.
   a. a three-leaf clover
   b. the three states of water (liquid, vapor, and solid)
   c. the threefold nature of man (body, soul, spirit)
   d. the three parts of an egg (shell, white, yolk)
   e. the nature of light, consisting of three kinds of rays
      (1) chemical rays—rays that are invisible, and can neither be felt nor seen
      (2) light rays—rays that are seen, but cannot be felt
      (3) heat rays—rays that are felt, but never seen
   f. The dimensional example: A book has height, width, and length. These three cannot be separated, yet they are not the same.
   g. a triangle

3. Old Testament passages regarding the Trinity.
   a. The first name used for God: Elohim (Gen. 1:1). This name is plural in form but is joined to a singular verb.
   b. The creation of man.
      Genesis 1:26: "And God said, Let us make man in our image, after our likeness: and let them have dominion over the fish of the sea, and over the fowl of the air, and over the cattle, and over all the earth, and over every creeping thing that creepeth upon the earth."
   c. The explusion from Eden.
      Genesis 3:22: "And the Lord God said, Behold, the man is become as one of us, to know good and evil: and now, lest he put forth his hand, and take also of the tree of life, and eat, and live forever.
   d. The confusion at Babel.
      Genesis 11:7: "Go to, let us go down, and there confound their language, that they may not understand one another's speech."
   e. The usage of the same word, *echad*, in Genesis 2:24 and in Deuteronomy 6:4. *Echad* is Hebrew for "one." These passages teach that God is one, as husband and wife are one.
   f. The teachings of King Agur.
      Proverbs 30:4: "Who hath ascended up into heaven, or descended? who hath gathered the wind in his fists? who hath bound the waters in a garment? who hath established all the ends of the earth? what is his name, and what is his son's name, if thou canst tell?"

g. The plural forms used in Ecclesiastes 12:1 and Isaiah 54:5.

   (1) "Remember now thy Creator in the days of thy youth . . ." (Eccl. 12:1). In the original this is literally "thy creators."

   (2) "For thy Maker is thine husband. . ." (Isa. 54:5). Here "maker" should be translated "makers."

h. The triune conversations in Isaiah.

Isaiah 6:8: "Also I heard the voice of the Lord, saying, Whom shall I send, and who will go for us? Then said I, Here am I; send me."

Isaiah 48:16: "Come ye near unto me, hear ye this; I have not spoken in secret from the beginning; from the time that it was, there am I: and now the Lord God, and his Spirit, hath sent me."

Isaiah 63:9, 10: "In all their affliction he was afflicted, and the angel of his presence saved them: in his love and in his pity he redeemed them; and he bare them, and carried them all the days of old. But they rebelled, and vexed his holy Spirit: therefore he was turned to be their enemy, and he fought against them."

i. The conversation between the Father and Son in the Psalms.

Psalm 2:1-7: "Why do the heathen rage and the people imagine a vain thing? The kings of the earth set themselves, and the rulers take counsel together, against the Lord, and against his Anointed, saying, Let us break their bands asunder, and cast away their cords from us. He that sitteth in the heavens shall laugh: the Lord shall have them in derision. Then shall he speak unto them in his wrath, and vex them in his sore displeasure. Yet have I set my King upon my holy hill of Zion. I will declare the decree: the Lord hath said unto me, Thou art my Son; this day have I begotten thee."

Psalm 45:6-8: "Thy throne, O God, is for ever and ever: the scepter of thy kingdom is a right scepter. Thou lovest righteousness, and hatest wickedness: therefore God, thy God, hath anointed thee with the oil of gladness above thy fellows. All thy garments smell of myrrh, and aloes, and cassia, out of the ivory palaces, whereby they have made thee glad."

Psalm 110:1-5: "The Lord said unto my Lord, Sit thou at my right hand, until I make thine enemies thy footstool. The Lord shall send the rod of thy strength out of Zion: rule thou in the midst of thine enemies. Thy people shall be willing in the day of thy power, in the beauties of holiness from the womb of the morning: thou hast the dew of thy youth. The Lord hath sworn, and will not repent, Thou art a priest for ever after the order of Melchizedek. The Lord at thy right hand shall strike through kings in the day of his wrath."

4. New Testament passages regarding the Trinity.

a. The baptism of Christ.

Matthew 3:16, 17: "And Jesus, when he was baptized, went up straightway out of the water: and, lo, the heavens were opened unto him, and he saw the Spirit of God descending like a dove, and lighting upon him: And lo a voice from heaven, saying, This is my beloved Son, in whom I am well pleased."

b. The temptation of Christ.

Matthew 4:1: "Then was Jesus led up of the Spirit into the wilderness to be tempted of the devil."

c. The teachings of Jesus.

John 14:16: "And I will pray the Father, and he shall give you another Comforter, that he may abide with you for ever."

The Greek word here translated "another" is *allos,* meaning another of the same kind. *Heteros* is the Greek word for another of a different kind. It is never used in referring to the Trinity.

John 14:26: "But the Comforter, which is the Holy Ghost, whom the Father will send in my name, he shall teach you all things, and bring all things to your remembrance, whatsoever I have said unto you."

d. The baptismal formula.

Matthew 28:19, 20: "Go ye therefore, and teach all nations, baptizing them in the name of the Father, and of the Son, and of the Holy Ghost: Teaching them to observe all things whatsoever I have commanded you: and, lo, I am with you alway, even unto the end of the world. Amen."

e. The apostolic benediction.

2 Corinthians 13:14: "The grace of the Lord Jesus Christ, and the love of God, and the communion of the Holy Ghost, be with you all. Amen."

5. A scriptural summary of the Trinity.

a. The Father is God (Jn. 6:44-46; Rom. 1:7; 1 Pet. 1:2).

b. The Son is God (Isa. 9:6; Jn. 1:1; 20:28; 1 Tim. 3:16; Titus 2:13; Heb. 1:8).

c. The Spirit is God (Acts 5:3, 4; Heb. 9:14).

V. The Attributes of God. Reduced to its simplest definition, an attribute of God is whatever God has in any way revealed as being true of himself. Some theologians prefer the word "perfection" to that of attribute. A. W. Tozer has written:

"If an attribute is something true of God, it is also something that we can conceive as being true of him. God, being infinite, must possess attributes about which we can know nothing." (*The Knowledge of the Holy*, p. 19)

"In the awful abyss of the divine being may lie attributes of which we know nothing and which can have no meaning for us, just as the attributes of mercy and grace can have no personal meaning for seraphim or cherubim. These holy beings may know of these qualities in God but be unable to feel them sympathetically for the reason that they have not sinned and so do not call forth God's mercy and grace. So there may be, and I believe there surely are, other aspects of God's essential being which He has not revealed even to His ransomed and Spirit-illuminated children." (*Ibid*, p. 52)

Finally, it must be concluded that there are hidden facets of God's nature wholly unknown (and perhaps unknowable) by any created being, even angels. They are known only by Jehovah God himself. We now consider some twenty-one attributes or perfections of God.

A. God is self-existent.

> Exodus 3:13, 14: "And Moses said unto God, Behold, when I come unto the children of Israel, and shall say unto them, The God of your fathers hath sent me, What is his name? what shall I say unto them? And God said unto Moses, I AM THAT I AM: and he said, Thus shalt thou say unto the children of Israel, I AM hath sent me unto you."

We have already discussed in a previous study the existence of God, but one of his attributes is self-existence. This is simply to say (with staggering implications) that God exists because he exists. He is not dependent upon anything or anyone for his thoughts (Rom. 11:33, 34), his will (Rom. 9:19; Eph. 1:5), his power (Ps. 115:3), or his counsel (Ps. 33:10, 11).

B. God is self-sufficient.

> Psalm 50:10–12: "For every beast of the forest is mine, and the cattle upon a thousand hills. I know all the fowls of the mountains: and the wild beasts of the field are mine. If I were hungry, I would not tell thee: for the world is mine, and the fullness thereof."

This attribute is closely connected to the attribute of self-existence, but carries it a step further. This means God has never had in eternity past, nor can ever have in the ages to come, a single need for which his own divine nature has not already provided.

C. God is eternal. Simply defined, this means God is absolutely free from the tyranny of time. In him there is no past or future, but one always and never-ending present. He is neither conditioned nor confined by time.

> Deuteronomy 33:27: "The eternal God is thy refuge, and underneath are the everlasting arms: and he shall thrust out the enemy from before thee: and shall say, Destroy them."

> Psalm 102:11, 12: "My days are like a shadow that declineth; and I am withered like grass. But thou, O Lord, shalt endure for ever; and thy remembrance unto all generations."

During one of his dialogues with the wicked Pharisees, the Son of God made reference to his attribute of eternity. Note his declaration:

> John 8:56, 57: "Your father Abraham rejoiced to see my day: and he saw it, and was glad. Then said the Jews unto him, Thou art not yet fifty years old, and hast thou seen Abraham?"

It should be observed that he did not say, "before Abraham was, I was," but "before Abraham was, I am" (Jn. 8:58).

> Psalm 90:2: "Before the mountains were brought forth, or ever thou hadst formed the earth and the world, even from everlasting to everlasting, thou art God."

D. God is infinite. God has no limitations. He is bounded only by his own nature and will.

> 1 Kings 8:22, 23, 27: "And Solomon stood before the altar of the Lord in the presence of all the congregation of Israel, and spread forth his hands toward heaven: And he said, Lord God of Israel, there is no God like thee, in heaven above, or on earth beneath, who keepest covenant and mercy with thy servants that walk before thee with all their heart. But will God indeed dwell on the earth? behold, the heaven and heaven of heavens cannot contain thee; how much less this house that I have builded?"

> Jeremiah 23:24: "Can any hide himself in secret places that I shall not see him? saith the Lord. Do not I fill heaven and earth? saith the Lord."

E. God is omnipresent. The great theologian A. H. Strong defines this attribute as follows:

> "God, in the totality of His essence, without diffusion or expansion, multiplication or division, penetrates and fills the universe in all its parts." (*Systematic Theology*, p. 279)

The omnipresence of God thus means he is present everywhere with his whole being at the same time. The great danger to avoid in rightly understanding this attribute is the grievous error of pantheism, which says that God is everywhere, and everything is God. This is totally false. Two aspects should be kept in mind as one studies the omnipresence of God.

1. God's immanence. This speaks of God being in the world, acting within and through his creation.

2. God's transcendence. This affirms that God is above and beyond his creation.

> Psalm 139:7–12: "Whither shall I go from thy spirit? or whither shall I flee from thy presence? If I ascend up into heaven, thou art there: if I make my bed in hell, behold, thou art there. If I take the wings of the morning, and dwell in the uttermost parts of the sea; even there shall thy hand lead me, and thy right hand shall hold me. If I say, Surely the darkness shall cover me; even the night shall be light about me. Yea, the darkness hideth not from thee; but the night shineth as the day: the darkness and the light are both alike to thee."

> Matthew 18:20: "For where two or three are gathered together in my name, there am I in the midst of them."

F. God is omnipotent (all-powerful).

Genesis 18:14: "Is any thing too hard for the Lord? At the time appointed I will return unto thee, according to the time of life, and Sarah shall have a son."

Revelation 19:6: "And I heard as it were the voice of a great multitude, and as the voice of many waters, and as the voice of mighty thunderings, saying, Alleluia: for the Lord God omnipotent reigneth."

This means God can do anything if it can be done and if it does not contradict his own nature. To illustrate these two things: God *cannot* create a rock so heavy that he couldn't lift it, because the very nature of this act would be impossible to perform. God *cannot* lie, or steal, for these things would contradict his own nature. Here are some areas in which God's omnipotence is clearly seen.

1. Over nature.
   a. He separates light from darkness (Gen. 1:4).
   b. He separates the waters by the firmament (space) (Gen. 1:7).
   c. He separates the seas from the dry land (Gen. 1:10).
   d. He measures oceans in his hands (Isa. 40:12).
   e. He weighs mountains in his scale (Isa. 40:12).
   f. He regards nations as a drop in the bucket (Isa. 40:15).
   g. He looks upon the islands as small particles of dirt (Isa. 40:15).
2. Over men.
   Daniel 4:30–32: "The king spake, and said, Is not this great Babylon, that I have built for the house of the kingdom by the might of my power, and for the honour of my majesty? While the word was in the king's mouth, there fell a voice from heaven, saying, O king Nebuchadnezzar, to thee it is spoken; the kingdom is departed from thee. And they shall drive thee from men, and thy dwelling shall be with the beasts of the field: they shall make thee to eat grass as oxen, and seven times shall pass over thee, until thou know that the most High ruleth in the kingdom of men, and giveth it to whomsoever he will."
3. Over angels.
   Psalm 103:20: "Blessed the Lord, ye his angels, that excel in strength, that do his commandments, hearkening unto the voice of his word."
4. Over Satan (Job 1:12; 2:6). The first two chapters of Job deal with Satan's accusations against the patriarch before God. The devil then subjects Job to various fierce and fiery trials, but not before being granted the needed specific permission from the omnipotent God himself.
5. Over death.
   Hebrews 2:14, 15: "Forasmuch then as the children are partakers of flesh and blood, he also himself likewise took part of the same; that through death he might destroy him that had the power of death, that is, the devil; and deliver them who through fear of death were all their lifetime subject to bondage."
G. God is omniscient (all-knowing). God possesses (without prior discovery of facts) complete and universal knowledge of all things past, present, and future. This includes not only the actual, but also the possible. This total and immediate knowledge is based on his eternity (he has always, and will always exist), and his omnipresence (he has been, is, and will always be everywhere at the same time).

Psalm 147:5: "Great is our Lord, and of great power: his understanding is infinite."

Isaiah 40:13, 14: "Who hath directed the Spirit of the Lord, or being his counselor hath taught him? With whom took he counsel, and who instructed him, and taught him in the path of judgment, and taught him knowledge, and showed to him the way of understanding?"

Hebrews 4:13: "Neither is there any creature that is not manifest in his sight: but all things are naked and opened unto the eyes of him with whom we have to do."

Psalm 104:24: "O Lord, how manifold are thy works! In wisdom hast thou made them all: the earth is full of thy riches."

1. He sees all things.
   Proverbs 15:3: "The eyes of the Lord are in every place, beholding the evil and the good."
2. He knows all things (the big and small of his universe).
   Psalm 147:4: "He telleth the number of the stars; he calleth them all by their names."
   Matthew 10:29, 30: "Are not two sparrows sold for a farthing? and one of them shall not fall on the ground without your Father. But the very hairs of your head are all numbered."
3. He knows mankind.
   a. Our thoughts.
      Psalm 139:2b: "Thou understandest my thought afar off."
      Psalm 44:21: "Shall not God search this out? For he knoweth the secrets of the heart."
   b. Our words.
      Psalm 139:4: "For there is not a word in my tongue, but, lo, O Lord, thou knowest it altogether."
   c. Our deeds (Ps. 139:3; Rev. 2:2, 9, 13, 19; 3:1, 8, 15).
      Psalm 139:2a: "Thou knowest my downsitting and mine uprising."
   d. Our sorrows.
      Exodus 3:7: "And the Lord said, I have surely seen the affliction of my people which are in Egypt, and have heard their cry by reason of their taskmasters; for I know their sorrows."

e. Our needs.

Matthew 6:32: "(For after all these things do the Gentiles seek:) for your heavenly Father knoweth that ye have need of all these things."

f. Our devotion.

Genesis 18:17-19: "And the Lord said, Shall I hide from Abraham that thing which I do; Seeing that Abraham shall surely become a great and mighty nation, and all the nations of the earth shall be blessed in him? For I know him, that he will command his children and his household after him, and they shall keep the way of the Lord, to do justice and judgement; that the Lord may bring upon Abraham that which he hath spoken of him."

Genesis 22:11, 12: "And the angel of the Lord called unto him out of heaven, and said, Abraham, Abraham: and he said, Here am I. And he said, Lay not thine hand upon the lad, neither do thou any thing unto him: for now I know that thou fearest God, seeing thou hast not withheld thy son, thine only son from me."

2 Chronicles 16:9: "For the eyes of the Lord run to and fro throughout the whole earth, to shew himself strong in the behalf of them whose heart is perfect toward him. Herein thou hast done foolishly: Therefore from henceforth thou shalt have wars."

g. Our frailties.

Psalm 103:14: "For he knoweth our frame; he remembereth that we are dust."

h. Our foolishness.

Psalm 69:5: "O God, thou knowest my foolishness; and my sins are not hid from thee."

i. He knows his own.

John 10:14: "I am the good shepherd, and know my sheep, and am known of mine."

2 Timothy 2:19: "Nevertheless the foundation of God standeth sure, having this seal, The Lord knoweth them that are his. And, Let every one that nameth the name of Christ depart from iniquity."

4. He knows the past, present, and future.

Acts 15:18: "Known unto God are all his works from the beginning of the world."

5. He knows what might or could have been.

Matthew 11:23: "And thou, Capernaum, which art exalted unto heaven, shalt be brought down to hell: for if the mighty works, which have been done in thee, had been done in Sodom, it would have remained until this day."

A. W. Tozer has written:

"God perfectly knows Himself and, being the source and author of all things, it fol- lows that He knows all that can be known. And this He knows instantly and with a fullness of perfection that includes every possible item of knowledge con- cerning everything that exists or could have existed anywhere in the universe at any time in the past or that may exist in the centuries or ages yet unborn. God knows instantly and effortlessly all matter and all matters, all mind and every mind, all spirit and all spirits, all beings and ev- ery being, all creaturehood, and all crea- tures, every plurality and all pluralities, all law and every law, all relations, all causes, all thoughts, all mysteries, all enigmas, all feeling, all desires, every unuttered secret, all thrones and dominions, all personal- ities, all things visible and invisible in heaven and in earth, motion, space, time, life, death, good, evil, heaven, and hell." (*The Knowledge of the Holy,* p. 62)

H. God is wise. We have already noted God's omni- science is based upon his eternity and omnipres- ence. We may now suggest his wisdom is grounded upon his omniscience. Robert Lightner writes:

"Though very closely related, knowledge and wisdom are not the same. Nor do they always accompany each other. No doubt we have all known those who had acquired a great deal of facts but who lacked the ability to use them wisely. Both knowledge and wisdom are im- perfect in man but perfect and perfectly re- lated to each other in God. Only He knows how to use His infinite knowledge to the best possible end. Through His wisdom God ap- plies His knowledge to the fulfillment of His own purposes in ways which will bring the most glory to Him." (*The God of the Bible,* p. 99)

Following are but a few of the passages which declare the wisdom of God.

Psalm 136:5: "To him that by wisdom made the heavens: for his mercy endureth for ever."

Proverbs 3:19: "The Lord by wisdom hath founded the earth; by understanding hath he established the heavens."

1 Corinthians 2:7: "But we speak the wis- dom of God in a mystery, even the hidden wisdom, which God ordained before the world unto our glory."

1 Timothy 1:17: "Now unto the King eter- nal, immortal, invisible, the only wise God, be honour and glory for ever and ever. Amen."

Jude 1:25: "To the only wise God our Sav- iour, be glory and majesty, dominion and power, both now and ever. Amen."

I. God is immutable. In a sentence, this says that God never differs from himself. He may on occa- sion alter his dealings with men in a dispensa- tional sense, but his divine character remains constant. This is a vital attribute of God, without which he could not be God. For example, a per- son may only change in two directions. He may go from better to worse or from worse to better. But it is unthinkable that God could travel down either of these roads.

Hebrews 1:10-12: "And, Thou, Lord, in the beginning hast laid the foundation of the earth; and the heavens are the works of thine hands: They shall perish; but thou remainest; and they all shall wax old as doth a garment; and as a vesture shalt thou fold them up, and they shall be changed: but thou art the same, and thy years shall not fail."

James 1:17: "Every good gift and every perfect gift is from above, and cometh down from the Father of lights, with whom is no variableness, neither shadow of turning."

Acts 1:11: "Which also said, Ye men of Galilee, why stand ye gazing up into heaven? this same Jesus, which is taken up from you into heaven, shall so come in like manner as ye have seen him go into heaven."

Hebrews 13:8: "Jesus Christ the same yesterday, and to day, and for ever."

J. God is sovereign. This means that God is the absolute and sole ruler in the universe. To be truly sovereign demands that one have the total freedom, power, knowledge, wisdom, and determination to carry out a predetermined course of action. God possesses all these in infinite measure and is thus sovereign.

Two ancient problems usually surface during any discussion of the sovereignty of God.

1. If God is sovereign, how do we explain the presence of sin and evil? A. W. Tozer writes:
"The Zend-Avesta, sacred book of Zoroastrianism, loftiest of the great non-biblical religions, got around this difficulty neatly enough by postulating a theological dualism. There were two gods, Ormazd and Ahriman, and these between them created the world. The good Ormazd made all good things and the evil Ahriman made the rest. It was quite simple. Ormazd had no sovereignty to worry about, and apparently did not mind sharing his prerogatives with another." (*The Knowledge of the Holy*, p. 117)
This explanation is of course totally unscriptural. The only positive statement in our present ignorance is that the sovereign God has indeed allowed for (but not arranged for) sin to enter this universe, that through it all he might receive the most glory (Rev. 4:11) and that the elect (Rom. 8:28) might receive the most good.

2. If God is sovereign, how do we reconcile the responsibility and freedom of man? Again, to quote from A. W. Tozer:
"Here is my view: God sovereignly decreed that man should be free to exercise moral choice, and man from the beginning has fulfilled that decree by making his choice between good and evil. When he chooses to do evil, he does not thereby countervail the sovereign will of God but fulfills it. Inasmuch as the eternal decree decided not which choice the man should make but that he should be free to make it." (*Ibid*, p. 118)

Psalm 135:6: "Whatsoever the Lord pleased, that did he in heaven, and in earth, in the seas, and all deep places."

Isaiah 46:9-11: "Remember the former things of old: for I am God, and there is none else; I am God, and there is none like me, declaring the end from the beginning, and from ancient times the things that are not yet done, saying, My counsel shall stand, and I will do all my pleasure: calling a ravenous bird from the east, the man that executeth my counsel from a far country: yes, I have spoken it, I will also bring it to pass; I have purposed it, I will also do it."

K. God is incomprehensible. By this it is stated that no one except God himself can even remotely understand and comprehend God.

Job 5:7-9: "Yet man is born unto trouble, as the sparks fly upward. I would seek unto God, and unto God would I commit my cause: Which doeth great things and unsearchable; marvellous things without number."

Job 11:7-9: "Canst thou by searching find out God? canst thou find out the Almighty unto perfection? It is as high as heaven; what canst thou do? deeper than hell; what canst thou know? The measure thereof is longer than the earth, and broader than the sea."

Psalm 36:5, 6: "Thy mercy, O Lord, is in the heavens; and thy faithfulness reacheth unto the clouds. Thy righteousness is like the great mountains; thy judgments are a great deep: O Lord, thou preservest man and beast."

Romans 11:33: "O the depth of the riches both of the wisdom and knowledge of God! how unsearchable are his judgments, and his ways past finding out!"

To illustrate this attribute, consider the following: Let us suppose in heaven we are able to double our learning each year concerning the person and attributes of God. This is not at all an unreasonable assumption, for the Christian will possess a sinless and glorified body, along with a holy and tireless desire to know more about Jesus. So here is a believer who begins eternity with X amount of knowledge about God. At the beginning of his second year he has doubled this, the third year he learns four times as much, the fourth year, eight times as much, etc. By the end of his eleventh year he will have increased his knowledge concerning God 1000-fold. At the conclusion of year number twenty-one the figure jumps to one million. At the end of the thirty-first year the number leaps to one billion. Following the forty-first year it reaches one trillion! As he finishes his first century in eternity his knowledge of God (doubling each year) would reach 10^{30} (one followed by 30 zeros)! This figure is thousands of times more than the combined total of all the grains of sand on all the seashores of the earth. But this number simply marks his first one hundred years. How much knowledge-doubling will he have experienced at the end of his first one million years? This staggering figure cannot even be comprehended by the mortal mind, but whatever it is, and however many zeros it represents, it will double itself the very next year!

The point of all the above is simply this: Throughout the untold and unnumbered trillions and trillions of years in timeless eternity, each child of God can double his or her learning about the Creator each year and yet never even remotely exhaust the awesome height, depth, or length to be known of the person of God.

L. God is inscrutable.

"How unsearchable are his judgments, and his ways past finding out" (Rom. 11:33).

This attribute refers to the inexplicable and mysterious ways of God. It raises the most painful question of all: Why does a loving and wise God allow certain terrible tragedies to occur? As an example, here is a young, spirit-filled pastor. He has spent a number of years diligently preparing for the ministry. His wife has sacrificed to help put him through school. But now all this is paying off. His church is experiencing an amazing growth. Souls are saved weekly. New converts are baptized each Sunday. Additional Sunday school buses are purchased and a new building is planned. A skeptical community slowly finds itself being profoundly influenced by this vibrant and exciting pastor and his people. Suddenly, without any warning, the minister is killed in a freak accident. Shortly after the funeral the still confused and stunned congregation extends a call to another man. But the new minister shows little compassion and less leadership ability. Soon the flock is scattered and the once thrilling testimony of a growing and glowing work is all but stilled.

How many times since Abel's martyrdom at the dawn of human history have similar tragedies taken place? One need only change the names, places, and rearrange some of the details. But the searing and searching question remains: Why does God permit such terrible things? A clue (and only a clue) to this question is seen in Revelation 10:7: "But in the days of the voice of the seventh angel, when he shall begin to sound, the mystery of God should be finished, as he hath declared to his servants the prophets."

But until the sound of that blessed trumpet, the perplexed child of God can arrive at no better conclusion than once offered by Abraham: "Shall not the Judge of all the earth do right?" (Gen. 18:25).

This sublime statement is amplified on at least three other biblical occasions.

1. By Moses:

"He is the Rock, his work is perfect; for all his ways are justice; a God of truth and without iniquity, just and right is he" (Deut. 32:4).

2. By Job:

"Naked came I out of my mother's womb, and naked shall I return thither. The Lord gave and the Lord hath taken away; blessed be the name of the Lord" (1:21). "Though he slay me, yet will I trust in him" (13:15).

3. By a Galilean crowd in Jesus' day:

"He hath done all things well . . ." (Mk. 7:37).

M. God is holy. Without a doubt the most prominent attribute of God as presented by both Old and New Testament Scriptures is his holiness. This one single perfection would perhaps come closer to describing the eternal Creator than any other characteristic he possesses. It has been suggested that his holiness is the union of all other attributes, as pure white light is the union of all the colored rays of the spectrum. Note but a few biblical references:

Leviticus 19:2: "Speak unto all the congregation of the children of Israel, and say unto them, Ye shall be holy: for I the Lord your God am holy."

Psalm 99:9: "Exalt the Lord our God, and worship at his holy hill; for the Lord our God is holy."

1 Peter 1:15: "But as he which hath called you is holy, so be ye holy in all manner of conversation."

A. W. Tozer writes:

"Holy is the way God is. To be holy He does not conform to a standard. He is that standard. He is absolutely holy with an infinite, incomprehensible fullness of purity that is incapable of being other than it is. Because He is holy, all His attributes are holy; that is, whatever we think of as belonging to God must be thought of as holy.

God is holy and He has made holiness the moral condition necessary to the health of His universe. Sin's temporary presence in the world only accents this. Whatever is holy is healthy; evil is a moral sickness that must end ultimately in death. The formation of the language itself suggests this, the English word holy deriving from the Anglo-Saxon *halig, hal*, meaning 'well, whole.'

Since God's first concern for His universe is its moral health, that is, its holiness, whatever is contrary to this is necessarily under His eternal displeasure. To preserve His creation God must destroy whatever would destroy it. When He arises to put down iniquity and save the world from inseparable moral collapse, He is said to be angry. Every wrathful judgement in the history of the world has been a holy act of preservation. The holiness of God, the wrath of God, and the health of the creation are inseparably united. God's wrath is His utter intolerance of whatever degrades and destroys. He hates iniquity as a mother hates the polio that would take the life of her child." (*The Knowledge of the Holy*, p. 113)

In the Bible God underlines his holiness by direct commands, objects, personal visions, and individual judgments.

1. The direct commandments.

a. the moral law (Ten Commandments) (Ex. 10:10-25; 20:1-17)

b. the spiritual law (feasts and offerings) (Ex. 35-40; Lev. 1-7, 23)

c. the ceremonial law (diet, sanitation, etc.) (Lev. 11-15)

2. The objects. The main object was the tabernacle itself.
3. Personal visions.
   a. Moses' vision.

      Exodus 33:18-23: "And he said, I beseech thee, shew me thy glory. And he said, I will make all my goodness pass before thee, and I will proclaim the name of the Lord before thee; and will be gracious to whom I will be gracious, and will shew mercy on whom I will shew mercy. And he said, Thou canst not see my face: for there shall no man see me, and live. And the Lord said, Behold, there is a place by me, and thou shalt stand upon a rock: And it shall come to pass, while my glory passeth by, that I will put thee in a clift of the rock, and will cover thee with my hand while I pass by: And I will take away mine hand, and thou shalt see my back parts: but my face shall not be seen."

   b. Isaiah's vision.

      Isaiah 6:1-5: "In the year that king Uzziah died I saw also the Lord sitting upon a throne, high and lifted up, and his train filled the temple. Above it stood the seraphim: each one had six wings; with twain he covered his face, and with twain he covered his feet, and with twain he did fly. And one cried unto another, and said, Holy, holy, holy, is the Lord of hosts: the whole earth is full of his glory. And the posts of the door moved at the voice of him that cried, and the house was filled with smoke. Then said I, Woe is me! for I am undone; because I am a man of unclean lips, and I dwell in the midst of a people of unclean lips: for mine eyes have seen the King, the Lord of hosts."

   c. Daniel's vision.

      Daniel 7:9-14: "I beheld till the thrones were cast down, and the Ancient of days did sit, whose garment was white as snow, and the hair of his head like the pure wool: his throne was like the fiery flame, and his wheels as burning fire. A fiery stream issued and came forth from before him: thousand thousands ministered unto him, and ten thousand times ten thousand stood before him: the judgment was set, and the books were opened. I beheld then because of the voice of the great words which the horn spake: I beheld even till the beast was slain, and his body destroyed, and given to the burning flame. As concerning the rest of the beasts, they had their dominion taken away: yet their lives were prolonged for a season and time. I saw in the night visions, and, behold, one like the Son of man came with the clouds of heaven, and came to the Ancient of days, and they brought him near before him. And there was given him dominion, and glory, and a kingdom, that all people, nations, and languages, should serve him: his dominion is an everlasting dominion, which shall not pass away, and his kingdom that which shall not be destroyed."

   d. John's vision.

      Revelation 4:8-11: "And the four beasts had each of them six wings about him; and they were full of eyes within: and they rest not day and night, saying, Holy, holy, holy, Lord God Almighty, which was, and is, and is to come. And when those beasts give glory and honour and thanks to him that sat on the throne, who liveth for ever and ever, the four and twenty elders fall down before him that sat on the throne, and worship him that liveth for ever and ever, and cast their crowns before the throne, saying, Thou art worthy, O Lord, to receive glory and honour and power: for thou hast created all things, and for thy pleasure they are and were created."

4. Individual judgments.
   a. Upon Nadab and Abihu, for offering strange fire (Lev. 10:1-3).
   b. Upon Korah, for rebellion (Num. 16:4-12, 31-33).
   c. Upon Uzziah, for intruding into the office of the priest (2 Chron. 26:16-21).
   d. Upon Herod, for blasphemy (Acts 12:20-23).
   e. Upon Christ, for the sins of the world (Isa. 53:1-10; Ps. 22:1; Heb. 2:7; 1 Pet. 2:21-25; 3:18).

N. God is righteous and just. Righteousness can be defined as moral equity. Justice is the illustration of this moral equity. In righteousness God reveals his love for holiness. In justice God reveals his hatred for sin. The Scriptures present this twin attribute in a threefold light.

1. The intrinsic righteousness and justice of God.

   Exodus 9:27: "And Pharaoh sent, and called for Moses and Aaron, and said unto them, I have sinned this time: the Lord is righteous, and I and my people are wicked."

   Ezra 9:15: "O Lord God of Israel, thou art righteous:-for we remain yet escaped, as it is this day: behold, we are before thee in our trespasses: for we cannot stand before thee because of this."

   Nehemiah 9:8: "And foundest his heart faithful before thee, and madest a covenant with him to give the land of the Canaanites, the Hittites, the Amorites, the Perizzites, and the Jebusites, and the Girgashites, to give it, I say, to his seed, and hast performed thy words; for thou art righteous."

Daniel 9:14: "Therefore hath the Lord watched upon the evil, and brought it upon us: for the Lord our God is righteous in all his works which he doeth: for we obeyed not his voice."

2. The legislative righteousness and justice of God.

Psalm 67:4: "O let the nations be glad and sing for joy: for thou shalt judge the people righteously, and govern the nations upon earth. Selah."

Psalm 7:9: "Oh let the wickedness of the wicked come to an end; but establish the just: for the righteous God trieth the hearts and reins."

Psalm 96:10: "Say among the heathen that the Lord reigneth: the world also shall be established that it shall not be moved: he shall judge the people righteously."

Psalm 119:137: "Righteous art thou, O Lord, and upright are thy judgments."

a. Rewarding the good.

2 Timothy 4:8: "Henceforth there is laid up for me a crown of righteousness, which the Lord, the righteous judge, shall give me at that day: and not to me only, but unto all them also that love his appearing."

It should be pointed out, however, that while God's righteousness guarantees rewards, it does not bestow them. A. W. Strong writes:

"Neither justice or righteousness bestows reward. This follows from the fact that obedience is due to God, instead of being optional or a gratuity. No creature can claim anything for his obedience. If God rewards, He rewards in virtue of His goodness and faithfulness, but not in virtue of His justice or His righteousness." (*Systematic Theology*, p. 293)

b. Punishing the evil.

2 Timothy 4:14: "Alexander the coppersmith did me much evil: the Lord reward him according to his works."

Revelation 16:5-7: "And I heard the angel of the waters say, Thou art righteous, O Lord, which art, and wast, and shalt be, because thou hast judged thus. For they have shed the blood of saints and prophets, and thou hast given them blood to drink; for they are worthy. And I heard another out of the altar say, Even so, Lord God Almighty, true and righteous are thy judgments."

3. The imputed righteousness of God.

Romans 4:3: "For what saith the scripture? Abraham believed God, and it was counted unto him for righteousness."

Romans 4:6-8: "Even as David also describeth the blessedness of the man, unto whom God imputeth righteousness without works, Saying, Blessed are they whose iniquities are forgiven, and whose sins are covered. Blessed is the man to whom the Lord will not impute sin."

Philippians 3:7-9: "But what things were gain to me, those I counted loss for Christ. Yea doubtless, and I count all things but loss for the excellency of the knowledge of Christ Jesus my Lord: for whom I have suffered the loss of all things, and do count them but dung, that I may win Christ, and be found in him, not having mine own righteousness, which is of the law, but that which is through the faith of Christ, the righteousness which is of God by faith."

1 Peter 2:24: "Who his own self bare our sins in his own body on the tree, that we, being dead to sins, should live unto righteousness: by whose stripes ye were healed."

O. God is true.

Titus 1:1, 2: "Paul, a servant of God, and an apostle of Jesus Christ, according to the faith of God's elect, and the acknowledging of the truth which is after godliness; in hope of eternal life, which God, that cannot lie, promised before the world began."

John 17:3: "And this is life eternal, that they might know thee the only true God, and Jesus Christ, whom thou hast sent."

1 Thessalonians 1:9: "For they themselves show of us what manner of entering in we had unto you, and how ye turned to God from idols to serve the living and true God."

Romans 3:4: "God forbid: yea, let God be true, but every man a liar; as it is written, That thou mightest be justified in thy sayings, and mightest overcome when thou art judged."

"By truth we mean that attribute of the divine nature in virtue of which God's being and God's knowledge eternally conform to each other." (A. W. Strong, *Systematic Theology*, p. 260)

Truth is therefore anything factual about God. The child of God may well say, "I speak (or serve) the truth," but only the Son of God can say, "I am the truth!" (Jn. 14:6). Again to quote from A. W. Strong:

"Since Christ is the truth of God, we are successful in our search for truth only as we recognize Him. Whether all roads lead to Rome depends upon which way your face is turned. Follow a point of land out into the sea, and you find only ocean. With the back turned upon Jesus Christ all following after truth leads only into mist and darkness." (*Ibid*, p. 262)

God is the ultimate and only source and standard of truth. This is why the Bible describes the "God that cannot lie" (Titus 1:2), and concludes that it is utterly "impossible for God to lie" (Heb. 6:18).

This may be taken a step farther and stated that he not only cannot lie, but that he *need not* lie. A lie is almost always resorted to by human beings to get out of a tight spot, to impress someone, to gain an advantage, etc. But almighty God never finds himself in any of these situations. In the Psalms he speaks to us concerning this.

Psalm 50:10-12; "For every beast of the forest is mine, and the cattle upon a thousand hills. I know all the fowls of the mountains: and the wild beasts of the field are mine. If I were hungry, I would not tell thee: for the world is mine, and the fullness thereof."

P. God is faithful.

Deuteronomy 7:9: "Know therefore that the Lord thy God, he is God, the faithful God, which keepeth covenant and mercy with them that love him and keep his commandments to a thousand generations."

Psalm 36:5: "Thy mercy, O Lord, is in the heavens; and thy faithfulness reacheth unto the clouds."

Psalm 89:1, 2: "I will sing of the mercies of the Lord for ever: with my mouth will I make known thy faithfulness to all generations. For I have said, Mercy shall be built up for ever: thy faithfulness shalt thou establish in the very heavens."

Lamentations 3:22, 23: "It is of the Lord's mercies that we are not consumed, because his compassions fail not. They are new every morning: great is thy faithfulness."

God's faithfulness refers to his self-loyalty and to that of his entire creation. He will not (indeed, cannot) change his character nor fail to perform all he has promised. God's faithfulness is seen in many areas.

1. In nature.

Psalm 119:90: "Thy faithfulness is unto all generations: thou hast established the earth, and it abideth."

Genesis 8:22: "While the earth remaineth, seedtime and harvest, and cold and heat, and summer and winter, and day and night shall not cease."

Colossians 1:17: "And he is before all things, and by him all things consist."

2. In keeping his promises to his friends.

a. Adam.

Galatians 4:4: "But when the fulness of the time was come, God sent forth his Son, made of a woman, made under the law."

b. Abraham.

Genesis 15:4: "And, behold, the word of the Lord came unto him, saying, This shall not be thine heir; but he that shall come forth out of thine own bowels shall be thine heir."

Genesis 18:14: "Is any thing too hard for the Lord? At the time appointed I will return unto thee, according to the time of life, and Sarah shall have a son."

Genesis 21:1, 2: "And the Lord visited Sarah as he had said, and the Lord did unto Sarah as he had spoken. For Sarah conceived, and bare Abraham a son in his old age, at the set time of which God had spoken to him."

c. Moses.

Exodus 3:21: "And I will give this people favour in the sight of the Egyptians: and it shall come to pass, that, when ye go, ye shall not go empty."

Exodus 12:35, 36: "And the children of Israel did according to the word of Moses; and they borrowed of the Egyptians jewels of silver, and jewels of gold, and raiment: and the Lord gave the people favour in the sight of the Egyptians, so that they lent unto them such things as they required. And they spoiled the Egyptians."

d. Joshua.

Joshua 1:1-5: "Now after the death of Moses the servant of the Lord it came to pass, that the Lord spake unto Joshua the son of Nun, Moses' minister saying, Moses my servant is dead; now therefore arise, go over this Jordan, thou, and all this people, unto the land which I do give to them, even to the children of Israel. Every place that the sole of your foot shall tread upon, that have I given unto you, as I said unto Moses. From the wilderness and this Lebanon even unto the great river, the river Euphrates, all the land of the Hittites, and unto the great sea toward the going down of the sun, shall be your coast. There shall not any man be able to stand before thee all the days of thy life: as I was with Moses, so I will be with thee: I will not fail thee, nor forsake thee."

Joshua 23:14: "And, behold, this day I am going the way of all the earth: and ye know in all your hearts and in all your souls, that not one thing hath failed of all the good things which the Lord your God spake concerning you; all are come to pass unto you, and not one thing hath failed thereof."

e. David.

2 Samuel 7:12, 13: "And when thy days be fulfilled, and thou shalt sleep with thy fathers, I will set up thy seed after thee, which shall proceed out of thy bowels, and I will establish his kingdom. He shall build an house for my name, and I will stablish the throne of his kingdom for ever."

Luke 1:31-33: "And, behold, thou shalt conceive in thy womb, and bring forth a son, and shalt call his name JESUS. He shall be great, and shall be called the Son of the Highest: and the Lord God shall give unto him the throne of his father David: And he shall reign over the house of Jacob for ever; and of his kingdom there shall be no end."

f. Hezekiah.

2 Kings 19:32-34: "Therefore thus saith the Lord concerning the king of Assyria, He shall not come into this city, nor shoot an arrow there, nor come before it with shield, nor cast a bank against it. By the way that he came, by the same shall he return, and shall not come into this city, saith the Lord. For I will defend this city, to save it, for mine own sake, and for my servant David's sake."

3. In keeping his promises to his enemies.

a. Ahab.

1 Kings 21:17-19: "And the word of the Lord came to Elijah the Tishbite, saying, Arise, go down to meet Ahab king of Israel, which is in Samaria: behold, he is in the vineyard of Naboth, whither he is gone down to possess it. And thou shalt speak unto him, saying, Thus saith the Lord, Hast thou killed, and also taken possession? And thou shalt speak unto him, saying, Thus saith the Lord, In the place where dogs licked the blood of Naboth shall dogs lick thy blood, even thine."

1 Kings 22:34-38: "And a certain man drew a bow at a venture, and smote the king of Israel between the joints of the harness: wherefore he said unto the driver of his chariot, Turn thine hand, and carry me out of the host; for I am wounded. And the battle increased that day: and the king was stayed up in his chariot against the Syrians, and died at even: and the blood ran out of the wound into the midst of the chariot. And there went a proclamation throughout the host about the going down of the sun, saying, Every man to his city, and every man to his own country. So the king died, and was brought to Samaria; and they buried the king in Samaria. And one washed the chariot in the pool of Samaria; and the dogs licked up his blood; and they washed his armour; according unto the word of the Lord which he spake."

b. Jezebel.

1 Kings 21:23: "And of Jezebel also spake the Lord, saying, The dogs shall eat Jezebel by the wall of Jezreel."

2 Kings 9:30: "And when Jehu was come to Jezreel, Jezebel heard of it; and she painted her face, and tired her head, and looked out at a window."

2 Kings 9:35-37: "And they went to bury her: but they found no more of her than the skull, and the feet, and the palms of her hands. Wherefore they came again, and told him. And he said, This is the word of the Lord, which he spake by his servant Elijah the Tishbite, saying, In the portion of Jezreel shall dogs eat the flesh of Jezebel: And the carcase of Jezebel shall be as dung upon the face of the field in the portion of Jezreel; so that they shall not say, This is Jezebel."

4. In times of temptation.

1 Corinthians 10:13: "There hath no temptation taken you but such as is common to man: but God is faithful, who will not suffer you to be tempted above that ye are able; but will with the temptation also make a way to escape, that ye may be able to bear it."

5. In chastening his children.

Psalm 119:75: "I know, O Lord, that thy judgments are right, and that thou in faithfulness hast afflicted me."

Hebrews 12:6: "For whom the Lord loveth he chasteneth, and scourgeth every son whom he receiveth."

6. In forgiving our sins.

1 John 1:9: "If we confess our sins, he is faithful and just to forgive us our sins, and to cleanse us from all unrighteousness."

7. In answering our prayers.

Psalm 143:1: "Hear my prayer, O Lord, give ear to my supplications: in thy faithfulness answer me, and in thy righteousness."

8. In keeping the saved *saved.*

1 Corinthians 1:8, 9: "Who shall also confirm you unto the end, that ye may be blameless in the day of our Lord Jesus Christ. God is faithful, by whom ye were called unto the fellowship of his Son Jesus Christ our Lord."

1 Thessalonians 5:23, 24: "And the very God of peace sanctify you wholly; and I pray God your whole spirit and soul and body be preserved blameless unto the coming of our Lord Jesus Christ. Faithful is he that calleth you, who also will do it."

2 Thessalonians 3:3: "But the Lord is faithful, who shall stablish you, and keep you from evil."

9. In defending his people.

Psalm 89:20: "I have found David my servant; with my holy oil have I anointed him."

Psalm 89:24: "But my faithfulness and my mercy shall be with him: and in my name shall his horn be exalted."

1 Samuel 12:22: "For the Lord will not forsake his people for his great name's sake: because it hath pleased the Lord to make you his people."

2 Timothy 2:13: "If we believe not, yet he abideth faithful: he cannot deny himself."

Q. God is Light. He is both the source and strength of all illumination. This refers not only to those golden beams of energy radiating from the sun and stars, but also to moral, mental, and spiritual rays of information and inspiration.

1 Peter 2:9: "But ye are a chosen generation, a royal priesthood, an holy nation, a peculiar people; that ye should shew forth the praises of him who hath called you out of darkness into his marvellous light."

1 John 1:7: "But if we walk in the light, as he is in the light, we have fellowship one with another, and the blood of Jesus Christ his Son cleanseth us from all sin."

2 Corinthians 4:6: "For God, who commanded the light to shine out of darkness, hath shined in our hearts, to give the light of the knowledge of the glory of God in the face of Jesus Christ."

1 Timothy 6:16: "Who only hath immortality, dwelling in the light which no man can approach unto; whom no man hath seen, nor can see: to whom be honour and power everlasting. Amen."

James 1:17: "Every good gift and every perfect gift is from above, and cometh down from the Father of lights, with whom is no variableness, neither shadow of turning."

1 John 1:5: "This then is the message which we have heard of him, and declare unto you, that God is light, and in him is no darkness at all."

R. God is good. A. W. Strong defines goodness as follows:

"Goodness is the eternal principle of God's nature which leads Him to communicate of His own life and blessedness to those who are like Him in moral character." (*Systematic Theology*, p. 289)

A. W. Tozer writes in similar fashion:

"The goodness of God is that which disposes Him to be kind, cordial, benevolent, and full of good will toward men. He is tenderhearted and of quick sympathy, and His unfailing attitude toward all moral beings is open, frank, and friendly. By His nature He is inclined to bestow blessedness and He takes holy pleasure in the happiness of His people." (*The Knowledge of the Holy*, p. 88)

Psalm 107:8: "Oh that men would praise the Lord for his goodness, and for his wonderful works to the children of men!"

Psalm 23:6: "Surely goodness and mercy shall follow me all the days of my life: and I will dwell in the house of the Lord for ever."

Romans 2:4: "Or despisest thou the riches of his goodness and forbearance and long-suffering; not knowing that the goodness of God leadeth thee to repentance?"

S. God is merciful.

"Mercy is that eternal principle of God's nature which leads Him to seek the temporal good and eternal salvation of those who have opposed themselves to His will, even at the cost of infinite self-sacrifice." (A. W. Strong, *Systematic Theology*, p. 289)

Gods' mercy is optional, in that he is in no way obligated to save sinners as he is to punish sinners. But he chooses to do so.

The Old Testament speaks four times as much about the mercy of God as does the New Testament. It is mentioned twenty-six times in Psalm 136 alone. Mercy then, among other things, is not getting what we deserve, namely, hell.

1. The example of David (Ps. 51). This is the confessional Psalm prayed by David after his shameful sin with Bathsheba, which included both adultery and murder. He begins by pleading for mercy and ends by acknowledging that no animal sacrifice could cleanse his sin. He then bypasses the Levitical offerings and throws himself completely upon the mercy of God.

2. The example of Israel.

Psalm 103:8-17: "The Lord is merciful and gracious, slow to anger, and plenteous in mercy. He will not always chide: neither will he keep his anger for ever. He hath not dealt with us after our sins; nor rewarded us according to our iniquities. For as the heaven is high above the earth, so great is his mercy toward them that fear him. As far as the east is from the west, so far hath he removed our transgressions from us. Like as a father pitieth his children, so the Lord pitieth them that fear him. For he knoweth our frame; he remembereth that we are dust. As for man, his days are as grass; as a flower of the field, so he flourisheth. For the wind passeth over it, and it is gone; and the place thereof shall know it no more. But the mercy of the Lord is from everlasting to everlasting upon them that fear him, and his righteousness unto children's children."

Hebrews 8:8, 12: "For finding fault with them, he saith, Behold, the days come, saith the Lord, when I will make a new covenant with the house of Israel and with the house of Judah. For I will be merciful to their unrighteousness, and their sins and their iniquities will I remember no more."

3. The example of Jonah.

Jonah 4:2: "And he prayed unto the Lord, and said, I pray thee, O Lord, was not this my saying, when I was yet in my country: Therefore I fled before unto Tarshish: for I knew that thou art a gracious God, and merciful, slow to anger, and of great kindness, and repentest thee of the evil."

4. The example of Paul.

1 Timothy 1:13, 16: "Who was before a blasphemer, and a persecutor, and injurious: but I obtained mercy, because I did it ignorantly in unbelief. Howbeit for this cause I obtained mercy, that in me first Jesus Christ might shew forth all longsuffering, for a pattern to them which should hereafter believe on him to life everlasting."

T. God is gracious. The very simplest definition of this beautiful attribute is unmerited favor. It is helpful at this point to contrast mercy with grace. God's *mercy* allows him to withhold *merited* punishment. God's *grace* allows him to freely bestow *unmerited* favor. *Mercy* is not getting what we deserve, namely, hell. *Grace* is getting what we do not deserve, namely, heaven.

Psalm 111:4: "He hath made his wonderful works to be remembered: the Lord is gracious and full of compassion."

Psalm 116:5: "Gracious is the Lord, and righteous; yea, our God is merciful."

1 Peter 2:3: "If so be ye have tasted that the Lord is gracious."

1 Peter 5:10: "But the God of all grace, who hath called us unto his eternal glory by Christ Jesus, after that ye have suffered a while, make you perfect, stablish, strengthen, settle you."

1. God's grace is seen through all dispensations in history. It is first mentioned on the eve of the first universal world destruction (Gen. 6:8) and the last reference occurs in Scripture's final verse (Rev. 22:21).

2. God's grace is always a free gift.

Romans 3:24: "Being justified freely by his grace through the redemption that is in Christ Jesus."

Ephesians 2:8, 9: "For by grace are ye saved through faith; and that not of yourselves: it is the gift of God: Not of works, lest any man should boast."

3. God's grace always precedes his peace.

Romans 1:7: "To all that be in Rome, beloved of God, called to be saints: Grace to you and peace from God our Father, and the Lord Jesus Christ."

This little phrase, "Grace to you and peace," a common salutation in that day, is found many times in the New Testament, but always in this order—never, "peace and grace." It is also spiritually true that one cannot experience God's peace until he has first appropriated his grace.

4. God's grace was incarnate in Christ (Jn. 1:17).

John 1:14: "And the Word was made flesh, and dwelt among us, (and we beheld his glory, the glory as of the only begotten of the Father,) full of grace and truth."

Titus 2:11: "For the grace of God that bringeth salvation hath appeared to all men."

5. God's grace is greater than man's sin.

Romans 5:20: "Moreover the law entered, that the offence might abound. But where sin abounded, grace did much more abound."

6. God's grace was displayed at Calvary.

Hebrews 2:9: "But we see Jesus, who was made a little lower than the angels for the suffering of death, crowned with glory and honour; that he by the grace of God should taste death for every man."

7. God's grace makes the sinner what he is (2 Cor. 12:9).

1 Corinthians 15:10: "But by the grace of God I am what I am: and his grace which was bestowed upon me was not in vain;

but I laboured more abundantly than they all: yet not I, but the grace of God which was with me."

Hebrews 4:16: "Let us therefore come boldly unto the throne of grace, that we may obtain mercy, and find grace to help in time of need."

8. God's grace was perhaps the attribute which prompted him to create the world in the first place (see Eph. 2).

U. God is Love. This is at once the most universally known and universally misunderstood attribute of all. Millions have simply equated love with God, thus weakening or totally denying his other perfections. A man and woman may have an affair hidden from their spouses and justify their adulterous relationship by their great "love" for each other. But God's love cannot be separated or isolated from his holiness and hatred for sin. Having said all this, however, it must be admitted that of all his attributes, God's love is probably more quickly seized upon by seeking sinners than any other perfection. The smallest child can sing with great understanding: "Jesus loves me, this I know, for the Bible tells me so!"

Two definitions of love may be offered at this point:

1. Love is unselfish concern about another's welfare.

2. Love is that act of one person seeking the highest good for another person.

Of all the twenty-one attributes presented during this study, the final three (mercy, grace, love) will probably be the most difficult to explain to angels who have never experienced them. It would be like attempting to explain the breathtaking majesty of the Grand Canynon during a magnificent sunset and the glorious sound coming from a nearby symphony orchestra to a friend who had been born blind and deaf. Following are a few objects of God's love.

1. God loves Israel.

Deuteronomy 7:7, 8: "The Lord did not set his love upon you, nor choose you, because ye were more in number than any people; for ye were the fewest of all people. But because the Lord loved you, and because he would keep the oath which he had sworn unto your fathers, hath the Lord brought you out with a mighty hand, and redeemed you out of the house of bondmen, from the hand of Pharaoh king of Egypt."

Isaiah 49:15: "Can a woman forget her sucking child, that she should not have compassion on the son of her womb? yea, they may forget, yet will I not forget thee."

Jeremiah 31:3: "The Lord hath appeared of old unto me, saying, Yea, I have loved thee with an everlasting love: therefore with lovingkindness have I drawn thee."

Hosea 11:1: "When Israel was a child, then I loved him, and called my son out of Egypt."

Malachi 1:2: "I have loved you, saith the Lord. Yet ye say, Wherein hast thou loved us? Was not Esau Jacob's brother? saith the Lord: yet I loved Jacob."

2. God loves the world.

John 3:16: "For God so loved the world, that he gave his only begotten Son, that whosoever believeth in him should not perish, but have everlasting life."

1 Timothy 2:3, 4: "For this is good and acceptable in the sight of God our Saviour; who will have all men to be saved, and to come unto the knowledge of the truth."

2 Peter 3:9: "The Lord is not slack concerning his promise, as some men count slackness; but is longsuffering to usward, not willing that any should perish, but that all should come to repentance."

3. God loves the church.

Ephesians 5:25-32: "Husbands, love your wives, even as Christ also loved the church, and gave himself for it; that he might sanctify and cleanse it with the washing of water by the word, that he might present it to himself a glorious church, not having spot, or wrinkle, or any such thing; but that it should be holy and without blemish. So ought men to love their wives as their own bodies. He that loveth his wife loveth himself. For no man ever yet hated his own flesh; but nourisheth and cherisheth it, even as the Lord the church; for we are members of his body, of his flesh, and of his bones. For this cause shall a man leave his father and mother, and shall be joined unto his wife, and they two shall be one flesh. This is a great mystery: but I speak concerning Christ and the church."

4. God loves the sinner.

Romans 5:8: "But God commendeth his love toward us, in that, while we were yet sinners, Christ died for us."

5. God loves the spiritual Christian.

Galatians 2:20: "I am crucified with Christ: nevertheless I live; yet not I, but Christ liveth in me: and the life which I now live in the flesh I live by the faith of the Son of God, who loved me, and gave himself for me."

6. God loves the carnal Christian (Lk. 15:12-24).

7. God loves his Son.

John 3:35: "The Father loveth the Son, and hath given all things into his hand."

John 10:17: "Therefore doth my Father love me, because I lay down my life, that I might take it again."

John 15:9: "As the Father hath loved me, so have I loved you: continue ye in my love."

John 17:23, 24: "I in them, and thou in me, that they may be made perfect in one; and that the world may know that thou hast sent me, and hast loved them, as thou hast loved me. Father, I will that they also, whom thou hast given me, be with me where I am; that they may behold my glory, which thou hast given me: for thou lovedst me before the foundation of the world."

Matthew 3:17: "And lo a voice from heaven, saying, This is my beloved Son, in whom I am well pleased."

Matthew 17:5: "While he yet spake, behold, a bright cloud overshadowed them: and behold a voice out of the cloud, which said, This is my beloved Son, in whom I am well pleased; hear ye him."

8. God loves the cheerful giver.

2 Corinthians 9:7: "Every man according as he purposeth in his heart, so let him give; not grudgingly, or of necessity: for God loveth a cheerful giver."

THE DOCTRINE OF THE SON

THE DOCTRINE OF THE SON

I. Introduction. It has been estimated that some forty billion individuals have lived upon this earth since Adam. What a contrast can be seen in this vast multitude of humanity. It includes black men, white men, brown, and yellow men. These men have explored and settled every corner of their earth. They speak dozens of languages, practice multitudes of religions, and have formulated numerous cultures.

But every single human being shares one vital thing. His purpose of life down here and his eternal destiny afterward depends completely upon his personal relationship with the subject of this study, the Lord Jesus Christ. It is, therefore, absolutely impossible to overemphasize the importance of his life. The key question of the universe continues to be: "What think ye of Christ?" (Mt. 22:42).

Note the following:

To the artist he is the One altogether lovely (Song of Sol. 5:16).

To the architect he is the chief Cornerstone (1 Pet. 2:6).

To the astronomer he is the Sun of righteousness (Mal. 4:2).

To the baker he is the Bread of life (Jn. 6:35).

To the banker he is the hidden treasure (Mt. 13:44).

To the builder he is the sure foundation (Isa. 28:16).

To the carpenter he is the door (Jn. 10:7).

To the doctor he is the great Physician (Jer. 8:22).

To the educator he is the new and living way (Heb. 10:20).

To the farmer he is the sower and the Lord of harvest (Lk. 10:2).

II. The Preexistence of Jesus Christ as God. It is possible (as some have done) to hold to Jesus' preexistence without believing in his deity. For example, the Jehovah's Witnesses cult brazenly declares that Christ preexisted as Michael the archangel prior to Bethlehem. But the Bible dogmatically declares both his preexistence *and* his deity.

A. The fact of his divine existence.

1. As taught by John the Baptist.

"John bare witness of him, and cried, saying, This was he of whom I spake, He that cometh after me is preferred before me: for he was before me" (Jn. 1:15). (See also Jn. 1:27, 30.)

According to Luke 1:36, John's birth occurred six months prior to Christ's birth, but John declares that "he was before me," a reference to Jesus' preexistence.

2. As taught by the Apostle John.

"In the beginning was the Word, and the Word was with God, and the Word was God" (Jn. 1:1).

"(For the life was manifested, and we have seen it, and bear witness, and shew unto you that eternal life, which was with the Father, and was manifested unto us)" (1 Jn. 1:2).

Here the Apostle John connects Jesus' preexistence to his deity.

3. As taught by the Apostle Paul.

"Who, being in the form of God, thought it not robbery to be equal with God: but made himself of no reputation, and took upon him the form of a servant, and was made in the likeness of men: and being found in fashion as a man, he humbled himself, and became obedient unto death, even the death of the cross" (Phil. 2:6–8).

4. As taught by the Apostle Peter.

"Who verily was foreordained before the foundation of the world, but was manifest in these last times for you" (1 Pet. 1:20).

5. As taught by Christ himself.

"For I came down from heaven, not to do mine own will, but the will of him that sent me" (Jn. 6:38).

"I am the living bread which came down from heaven: if any man eat of this bread, he shall live for ever: and the bread that I will give is my flesh, which I will give for the life of the world. When Jesus knew in himself that his disciples murmured at it, he said unto them, Doth this offend you? What and if ye shall see the Son of man ascend up where he was before?" (Jn. 6:51, 61, 62).

"Jesus said unto them, Verily, verily I say unto you, Before Abraham was, I am" (Jn. 8:58).

"And now, O Father, glorify thou me with thine own self with the glory which I had with thee before the world was" (Jn. 17:5).

Here Christ requests that the Father share his glory with the Son. But note the Father's previous statement about his glory in Isaiah:

"I am the LORD: that is my name; and my glory will I not give to another . . ." (Isa. 42:8).

One is thus forced to conclude that either Christ was God indeed and had rightful claim to this glory, or he was an arrogant imposter demanding something the Father would never give him!

B. The activities of the divine preexistent Christ. What was the Savior doing prior to his Bethlehem appearance? The Scriptures make it plain that he was busy indeed.

1. He was creating the universe.
"All things were made by him; and without him was not any thing made that was made" (Jn. 1:3).
"For by him were all things created, that are in heaven, and that are in earth, visible and invisible, whether they be thrones, or dominions, or principalities, or powers: all things were created by him, and for him" (Col. 1:16).
"Hath in these last days spoken unto us by his Son, whom he hath appointed heir of all things, by whom also he made the world. . . . And, thou, Lord, in the beginning hast laid the foundation of the earth; and the heavens are the works of thine hands" (Heb. 1:2, 10).
This creation included everything, from electrons to galaxies, and from angels to Adam.

2. He was controlling this created universe.
"Who being the brightness of his glory, and the express image of his person, and upholding all things by the word of his power, when he had by himself purged our sins, sat down on the right hand of the Majesty on high" (Heb. 1:3).
"And he is before all things, and by him all things consist" (Col. 1:17).
Our Lord Jesus not only put all things together, but he continues to keep all things together.

3. He was communing with the Father.
"I in them, and thou in me, that they may be made perfect in one; and that the world may know that thou hast loved me" (Jn. 17:23).
"Father, I will that they also, whom thou hast given me, be with me where I am; that they may behold my glory, which thou hast given me: for thou lovedst me before the foundation of the world" (Jn. 17:24).

III. The Old Testament Ministry of Jesus Christ. The Old Testament records a number of theophanies. A theophany is a pre-Bethlehem appearance of Christ. Most Bible theologians hold that the recurring angel of the Lord episode in the Old Testament is to be identified with Christ himself. This theological position is strongly suggested by two key passages.

The first is found in Genesis 48:16 where the dying patriarch, Jacob, is blessing his two grandchildren. The old founder of Israel prays:
"The angel who redeemed me from all evil, bless these lads . . ." (Gen. 48:16).

As no regular angel can redeem men, it is assumed the angel here is actually Christ.

The second passage is found in Judges 13 where a barren couple has just learned from the angel of the Lord about the future birth of Samson. In gratitude, Manoah (the father), requests the name of the angel that he might call the babe after him. Note the answer, however:
"And the angel of the Lord said unto him, why askest thou thus after my name, seeing it is secret?" (Jdg. 13:18).

This word, "secret," is from the same Hebrew root word found in Isaiah 9:6, where it is translated "wonderful."
"For unto us a child is born, unto us a son is given: and the government shall be upon his shoulder: and his name shall be called Wonderful, Counsellor, The mighty God, The everlasting Father, The Prince of Peace" (Isa. 9:6).

Inasmuch as we know the "wonderful" in this verse refers to Christ, it is highly probable that Judges 13:18 does as well.

Let us now examine some of these Old Testament theophanies.

A. He appeared to Hagar, Abraham's Egyptian wife (Gen. 16:7-14). The first biblical reference to the angel of the Lord occurs here as he tenderly ministers to a pagan and pregnant Egyptian girl.

B. He appeared to Abraham (Gen. 18:1; 22:11-13). These two appearances came at critical times in Abraham's life. One (Gen. 18) concerned itself with the destruction of Sodom, and the other (Gen. 22) with the last-minute salvation of Isaac.

C. He appeared to Jacob (Gen. 28:13; 32:24-32; 48:16). It will be remembered that Christ not only appeared to Jacob, but actually wrestled with him. (See Gen. 32.) This was doubtless that same divine One he had seen standing atop a ladder some twenty years before. (See Gen. 28.)

D. He appeared to Moses (Ex. 3:2; 23:20; 33:18-23). These three occasions were all connected with Mt. Sinai.
The first was *near* the mountain.
"And when the Lord saw that he turned aside to see, God called unto him out of the midst of the bush, and said, Moses, Moses. And he said, Here am I. And he said, Draw not near here: put off thy shoes from off thy feet, for the place whereon thou standest is holy ground" (Ex. 3:4, 5).
The second occasion was *on* the mountain.
"Behold, I send an angel before thee, to keep thee in the way, and to bring thee into the place which I have prepared" (Ex. 23:20).
The final occasion was *in* the mountain.
"And it shall come to pass, while my glory passeth by, that I will put thee in a clift of the rock, and will cover thee with my hand while I pass by" (Ex. 33:22).

E. He appeared to Joshua (Josh. 5:13-15). He appears to Joshua on the eve of the battle against Jericho and introduces himself as the captain of the Lord's host.

F. He appeared to Gideon (Jdg. 6:11-24). The angel of the Lord finds a very discouraged Gideon threshing wheat beside a wine press to hide it from the oppressing Midianites.

G. He appeared to Samson's parents (Jdg. 13).

H. He appeared to Isaiah (Isa. 6:1-13). Isaiah is allowed to see more of the glory of the preincarnate Christ than any other Old Testament prophet.

I. He appeared to three young Hebrews in the fiery furnace (Dan. 3:25). How thrilling are the astonished words of pagan king Nebuchadnezzar which accompanied this appearance:

"Then Nebuchadnezzar the king was astonished, and rose up in haste, and spake, and said unto his counselors, Did not we cast three men bound into the midst of the fire? They answered and said unto the king, True, O king. He answered and said, Lo, I see four men loose, walking in the midst of the fire, and they have no hurt; and the form of the fourth is like the Son of God" (Dan. 3:21, 22).

J. He appeared to Daniel (Dan. 6:22; 7:9-14). The first of these appearances was in a lion's den.

"Then said Daniel unto the king, O king, live forever. My God hath sent his angel, and hath shut the lion's mouth, that they have not hurt me . . ." (Dan. 6:21, 22).

The second appearance was in a vision.

"I beheld till the thrones were cast down, and the Ancient of days did sit, whose garment was white as snow, and the hair of his head like the pure wool: his throne was like the fiery flame, and his wheels as burning fire. A fiery stream issued and came forth from before him: thousand thousands ministered unto him, and ten thousand times ten thousand stood before him: the judgment was set, and the books were opened. I beheld then because of the voice of the great words which the horn spake: I beheld even till the beast was slain, and his body destroyed, and given to the burning flame. As concerning the rest of the beasts, they had their dominion taken away: yet their lives were prolonged for a season and time. I saw in the night visions, and, behold, one like the Son of man came with the clouds of heaven, and came to the Ancient of days, and they brought him near before him. And there was given him dominion, and glory, and a kingdom, that all people, nations, and languages, should serve him: his dominion is an everlasting dominion, which shall not pass away, and his kingdom that which shall not be destroyed" (Dan. 7:9-14).

K. He appeared to Zechariah (Zech. 1:8-13; 2:8-11; 3:10; 6:12-15). In this book, Zechariah describes Christ as protecting Jerusalem (1:8-13), measuring Jerusalem (2:8-11), cleansing Jerusalem (3:10), and building Jerusalem (6:12-15).

IV. The Virgin Birth Incarnation of Jesus Christ.

A. False views concerning the incarnation.

1. The Ebionites. They denied the reality of Jesus' divine nature. The Ebionite error is refuted by John the Apostle in the first verse of his Gospel account.

"In the beginning was the Word, and the Word was with God, and the Word was God" (Jn. 1:1).

2. The Gnostics. They denied the reality of Jesus' human nature. The Gnostic error is refuted by John the apostle in the first verse of his first epistle.

"That which was from the beginning, which we have heard, which we have seen with our eyes, which we have looked upon, and our hands have handled, of the Word of life" (1 Jn. 1:1).

3. The Arians. They affirmed Jesus' preexistence, but denied his deity.

This is the position of the present-day Jehovah's Witnesses.

4. The Nestorians. They believed two persons actually indwelt the body of Christ, the human person and the divine.

5. The Eutychians. They went to the opposite extreme and said both natures (the human and the divine) mingled to make up a third and totally different nature from the original two natures.

B. The true view of the incarnation.

"In the one person, Jesus Christ, there are two natures, a human nature and a divine nature, each in its completeness and integrity, and these two natures are organically and indissolubly united, yet so that no third nature is formed thereby." (A. H. Strong, *Systematic Theology*, p. 673)

"He always says, I, me, mine. He is always addressed as thou, thee, thine. He is always spoken of as He, His, Him. It was the same person to whom it was said, 'Thou Lord, in the beginning hast laid the foundations of the earth, and the heavens are the works of thine hands.'" (Charles Hodge, as quoted by Charles Baker, *A Dispensational Theology*, p. 300)

Thus, in the Old Testament we have man made in the image of God and in the New Testament we see God made in the image of man.

C. The miracles involved in the incarnation.

1. That God the Son could take upon himself the full nature of man and yet retain the full nature of God.

The Bible declares that he was as much God as if he had never been man, and as much man as if he had never been God. This is known as the hypostatic union. There is no earthly analogy that can be used even to remotely illustrate this. The following examples have been unsuccessfully offered:

a. the relationship between man's body and soul

b. that between the Father and the Son

c. that between husband and wife

d. that between the believer and the Holy Spirit

e. that between a Dr. Jekyll and Mr. Hyde

f. that between oxygen and hydrogen which produces water

2. That a human body could be conceived within a mother's womb without an earthly father.

The miracle of the virgin birth was not the actual birth, but the conception of Christ's earthly body.

Furthermore, this conception was not only supernatural, but unique also, for God had already performed supernatural births for Sarah, Hannah, Elisabeth, and others.

D. The perpetuity of the incarnation. When the Son of God joined himself to a body at Bethlehem it was an eternal arrangement. He will continue to manifest himself in this body (in its resurrected state, of course) throughout the ages.

E. The prophecies concerning the incarnation. Old Testament.

1. By Isaiah the prophet.

"Therefore the Lord himself shall give you a sign; Behold a virgin shall conceive, and bear a son, and shall call his name Immanuel" (Isa. 7:14).

"For unto us a child is born, unto us a son is given: and the government shall be upon' his shoulder: and his name shall be called Wonderful, Counsellor, The mighty God, The everlasting Father, The Prince of Peace. Of the increase of his government and peace there shall be no end, upon the throne of David, and upon his kingdom, to order it, and to establish it with judgment and with justice henceforth even for ever. The zeal of the Lord of hosts will perform this" (Isa. 9:6, 7).

2. By Micah the prophet.

"But thou, Bethlehem Ephratah, though thou be little among the thousands of Judah, yet out of thee shall he come forth unto me that is to be ruler in Israel; whose goings forth have been from of old, from everlasting" (Micah 5:2).

New Testament. Heavenly announcements were given to at least eight individuals or groups concerning the incarnation in the New Testament.

3. To Zacharias.

"And he shall go before him in the spirit and power of Elijah, to turn the hearts of the fathers to the children, and the disobedient to the wisdom of the just; to make ready a people prepared for the Lord. And thou, child, shalt be called the prophet of the Highest: for thou shalt go before the face of the Lord to prepare his ways" (Lk. 1:17, 76).

4. To Mary.

"And, behold, thou shalt conceive in thy womb, and bring forth a son, and shalt call his name Jesus. And the angel answered and said unto her, The Holy Ghost shall come upon thee, and the power of the Highest shall overshadow thee: therefore also that holy thing which shall be born of thee shall be called the Son of God" (Lk. 1:31, 35).

5. To Elisabeth.

"And she spake out with a loud voice, and said, Blessed art thou among women, and blessed is the fruit of thy womb" (Lk. 1:42).

6. To Joseph.

"But while he thought on these things, behold, the angel of the Lord appeared unto him in a dream, saying, Joseph, thou son of David, fear not to take unto thee Mary thy wife: for that which is conceived in her is of the Holy Ghost. And she shall bring forth a son, and thou shalt call his name Jesus: for he shall save his people from their sins" (Mt. 1:20, 21).

7. To the shepherds.

"And the angel said unto them, Fear not: for, behold, I bring you good tidings of great joy, which shall be to all people. For unto you is born this day in the city of David, a Saviour, which is Christ the Lord. And this shall be a sign unto you; Ye shall find the babe wrapped in swaddling clothes, lying in a manger" (Lk. 2:10-12).

8. To the wise men.

"Now when Jesus was born in Bethlehem of Judaea in the days of Herod the king, behold, there came wise men from the east to Jerusalem, Saying, Where is he that is born King of the Jews? for we have seen his star in the east, and are come to worship him" (Mt. 2:1, 2).

9. To Simeon.

"And, behold, there was a man in Jerusalem, whose name was Simeon; and the same man was just and devout, waiting for the consolation of Israel: and the Holy Ghost was upon him. And it was revealed unto him by the Holy Ghost, that he should not see death, before he had seen the Lord's Christ. And he came by the Spirit into the temple: and when the parents brought in the child Jesus, to do for him after the custom of the law. Then took he him up in his arms, and blessed God, and said, Lord, now lettest thou thy servant depart in peace, according to thy word: for mine eyes have seen thy salvation, which thou hast prepared before the face of all people; a light to lighten the Gentiles, and the glory of thy people Israel" (Lk. 2:25-32).

10. To Anna.

"And she coming in that instant gave thanks likewise unto the Lord, and spake of him to all them that looked for redemption in Jerusalem" (Lk. 2:38).

F. The reasons for the incarnation. Why the virgin birth incarnation? God never does anything without a good reason, and in this case, there were some fourteen excellent reasons for the incarnation.

1. To reveal the invisible God.

   "No man hath seen God at any time; the only begotten Son, which is in the bosom of the Father, he hath declared him. Jesus saith unto him, Have I been so long time with you, and yet hast thou not known me, Philip? he that hath seen me hath seen the Father; and how sayest thou then, Shew us the Father?" (Jn. 1:18; 14:9).

2. To fulfill prophecy.

   "And I will put enmity between thee and the woman, and between thy seed and her seed; it shall bruise thy head, and thou shalt bruise his heel" (Gen. 3:15).

3. To guarantee the Davidic covenant. The Davidic covenant assured David that someday an heir from his own seed would rule over Israel on his throne forever.

   "Now therefore so shalt thou say unto my servant David, Thus saith the Lord of hosts, I took thee from the sheepcote, from following the sheep, to be ruler over my people, over Israel: and I was with thee whithersoever thou wentest, and have cut off all thine enemies out of thy sight, and have made thee a great name, like unto the name of the great men that are in the earth. Moreover I will appoint a place for my people Israel, and will plant them, that they may dwell in a place of their own, and move no more; neither shall the children of wickedness afflict them any more, as beforetime, and as since the time that I commanded judges to be over my people Israel, and have caused thee to rest from all thine enemies. Also the Lord telleth thee that he will make thee a house. And when thy days be fulfilled, and thou shalt sleep with thy fathers, I will set up thy seed after thee, which shall proceed out of thy bowels, and I will establish his kingdom. He shall build an house for my name, and I will stablish the throne of his kingdom for ever. I will be his father and he shall be my son. If he commit iniquity, I will chasten him with the rod of men, and with the stripes of the children of men: but my mercy shall not depart away from him, as I took it from Saul, whom I put away before thee. And thine house and thy kingdom shall be established for ever before thee: thy throne shall be established for ever. According to all these words, and according to all this vision, so did Nathan speak unto David" (2 Sam. 7:8–17).

   "And, behold, thou shalt conceive in thy womb, and bring forth a son, and shalt call his name JESUS. He shall be great, and shall be called the Son of the Highest: and the Lord God shall give unto him the throne of his father David: And he shall reign over the house of Jacob for ever; and of his kingdom there shall be no end' (Lk. 1:31–33).

4. To make a sacrifice for our sins.

   "But we see Jesus, who was made a little lower than the angels for the suffering of death, crowned with glory and honour; that he by the grace of God should taste death for every man" (Heb. 2:9).

   "For it is not possible that the blood of bulls and of goats should take away sins. Wherefore when he cometh into the world, he saith, Sacrifice and offering thou wouldest not, but a body hast thou prepared me: By the which will we are sanctified through the offering of the body of Jesus Christ once for all. But this man, after he had offered one sacrifice for sins for ever, sat down on the right hand of God" (Heb. 10:4, 5, 10, 12).

   "And ye know that he was manifested to take away our sins; and in him is no sin" (1 Jn. 3:5).

   "For even the Son of man came not to be ministered unto, but to minister, and to give his life a ransom for many" (Mk. 10:45).

5. To reconcile man to God.

   "To wit, that God was in Christ, reconciling the world unto himself, not imputing their trespasses unto them; and hath committed unto us the word of reconciliation" (2 Cor. 5:19).

   "Wherefore in all things it behoved him to be made like unto his brethren, that he might be a merciful and faithful high priest in things pertaining to God, to make reconciliation for the sins of the people" (Heb. 2:17).

   "For there is one God, and one mediator between God and men, the man Christ Jesus; who gave himself a ransom for all, to be testified in due time" (1 Tim. 2:5, 6).

6. To provide an example for believers.

   "For even hereunto were ye called: because Christ also suffered for us, leaving us an example, that ye should follow his steps" (1 Pet. 2:21).

   "He that saith he abideth in him ought himself also so to walk, even as he walked" (1 Jn. 2:6).

7. To provide the believer with a high priest.

   "Wherefore in all things it behoved him to be made like unto his brethren, that he might be a merciful and faithful high priest in things pertaining to God, to make reconciliation for the sins of the people" (Heb. 2:17).

   "Wherefore, holy brethren, partakers of the heavenly calling, consider the Apostle and High Priest of our profession, Christ Jesus" (Heb. 3:1).

8. To destroy the devil and his works.

   "Forasmuch then as the children are partakers of flesh and blood, he also himself likewise took part of the same; that through death he might destroy him that had the power of death, that is the devil" (Heb. 2:14).

"He that committeth sin is of the devil; for the devil sinneth from the beginning. For this purpose the Son of God was manifested, that he might destroy the works of the devil" (1 Jn. 3:8).

9. To escape the historical curse.
   a. Upon Adam's seed.
      "Wherefore as by one man sin entered into the world, and death by sin; and so death passed upon all men, for that all have sinned" (Rom. 5:12).
   b. Upon King Jehoiakim and his son, Jehoiachin. Both these wicked rulers, Jehoiakim (Jer. 36:30) and Jehoiachin (Jer. 22:30) were judged by God and warned that their physical seed would never prosper upon the throne of David.

10. To heal the brokenhearted.
   "The Spirit of the Lord is upon me, because he hath anointed me to preach the gospel to the poor; he hath sent me to heal the brokenhearted, to preach deliverance to the captives, and recovering of sight to the blind, to set at liberty them that are bruised" (Lk. 4:18).

11. To set at liberty the bruised (Lk. 4:18).

12. To proclaim the acceptable year of the Lord (Lk. 4:18).

13. To give life—abundant life.
   "He that believeth on the Son hath everlasting life: and he that believeth not the Son shall not see life; but the wrath of God abideth on him" (Jn. 3:36).
   "The thief cometh not, but for to steal, and to kill, and to destroy: I am come that they might have life, and that they might have it more abundantly" (Jn. 10:10).

14. To glorify the Father (Jn. 13:31; 14:13; 17:4).
   "Therefore, when he was gone out, Jesus said, Now is the Son of man glorified, and God is glorified in him" (Jn. 13:31).
   "And whatsoever ye shall ask in my name, that will I do, that the Father may be glorified in the Son" (Jn. 14:13).
   "I have glorified thee on the earth: I have finished the work which thou gavest me to do" (Jn. 17:4).

V. The Biblical Names and Titles of Jesus Christ. It may be true that a rose by any other name would smell as sweet. But not so concerning Bible names, which often give keen insight into the lives of those who bear the titles. This is especially true concerning Christ. A wealth of information concerning his person and work can be obtained from studying the names and titles ascribed to him. Note some of these:

Adam (1 Cor. 15:45)
Advocate (1 Jn. 2:1)
Almighty (Rev. 1:8)

Amen (Rev. 3:14)
Angel of the Lord (Gen. 16:9-14; Jdg. 6:11-14)
Anointed (Ps. 2:2)
Apostle (Heb. 3:1)
Author (Heb. 12:2)
Alpha (Rev. 1:8; 21:6)
Babe (Lk. 2:16)
Beginning of creation (Rev. 3:14)
Begotten of Father (Jn. 1:14)
Beloved (Eph. 1:6)
Bishop (1 Pet. 2:25)
Blessed (1 Tim. 6:15)
Branch (Zech. 3:8)
Brazen Serpent (Jn. 3:14)
Bridegroom (Mt. 9:15)
Bright Morning Star (Rev. 22:16)
Captain (Josh. 5: 4)
Carpenter (Mt. 13:55; Mk. 6:3)
Child (Isa. 9:6)
Christ (Mt. 1:16; 2:4)
Commander (Isa. 55:4)
Consolation of Israel (Lk. 2:25)
Cornerstone (Eph. 2:20)
Dayspring from on high (Lk. 1:78)
Day Star (2 Pet. 1:19)
Deliverer (Rom. 11:26)
Desire of nations (Hag. 2:7)
Door of the sheepfold (Jn. 10:7)
Emmanuel (Mt. 1:23)
Express image of God (Heb. 1:3)
Faithful witness (Rev. 1:5; 3:14; 19:11)
Father of eternity (Isa. 9:6)
First Fruits (1 Cor. 15:23)
Foundation (Isa. 28:16)
Fountain (Zech. 13:1)
Forerunner (Heb. 6:20)
Friend of sinners (Mt. 11:19)
Gift of God (2 Cor. 9:15)
Glory of God (Isa. 60:1)
God (Jn. 1:1; Rom. 9:5; 1 Tim. 3:16)
Governor (Mt. 2:6)
Guide (Ps. 48:14)
Head of Church (Col. 1:18)
Heir of all things (Heb. 1:2)
High Priest (Heb. 3:1; 7:1)
Holy Child (Acts 4:30)
Holy One of God (Mk. 1:24)
Holy One of Israel (Isa. 41:14)
Horn of salvation (Ps. 18:2)
I AM: He calls himself this name seven times in John's Gospel:
   I am the Bread of Life (6:35).
   I am the Light of the World (9:5).
   I am the Good Shepherd (10:11).
   I am the Door (10:9).
   I am the Resurrection (11:25).
   I am the true Vine (15:1).
   I am the Way (14:6).
Jehovah (Isa. 26:4; 40:3)
Jesus (Mt. 1:21)
Judge (Micah 5:1; Acts 10:42)
King:
   King of Israel (Mt. 27:42; Jn. 1:49)
   King of kings (Rev. 17:14; 19:16)
Lamb of God (Jn. 1:29, 36)
Lawgiver (Isa. 33:22)

Lion of the tribe of Judah (Rev. 5:5)
Lord of lords (Rev. 19:16)
Man (Acts 17:31; 1 Tim. 2:5)
Master (Mt. 8:19)
Mediator (1 Tim. 2:5)
Messiah (Dan. 9:25; Jn. 1:41)
Mighty God (Isa. 9:6; 63:1)
Minister (Heb. 8:2)
Nazarene (Mk. 1:24)
Only begotten Son (Jn. 1:18)
Passover (1 Cor. 5:7)
Physician (Mt. 9:12)
Potentate (1 Tim. 6:15)
Prince (Acts 3:15; 5:31)
Prophet (Acts 3:22)
Propitiation (1 Jn. 2:2; 4:10)
Power of God (1 Cor. 1:24)
Purifier (Mal. 3:3)
Priest (Heb. 4:14)
Rabbi—On three well-known occasions he was
    called by this name:
    by Nicodemus (Jn. 3:2)
    by Judas (Mt. 26:25)
    by Mary Magdalene (Jn. 20:16).
Ransom (1 Tim. 2:6)
Reaper (Rev. 14:15)
Redeemer (Isa. 59:20; 60:16)
Refiner (Mal. 3:3)
Refuge (Isa. 25:4)
Righteousness (Jer. 23:6; 33:16)
Rock (Deut. 32:15)
Rod (Isa. 11:1)
Root of David (Rev. 22:16)
Rose of Sharon (Song of Sol. 2:1)
Sacrifice (Eph. 5:2)
Samaritan (Good) (Lk. 10:33)
Savior—he was called Savior by:
    his mother (Lk. 1:47)
    the angels (Lk. 2:11)
    the men of Samaria (Jn. 4:42)
Second Man (1 Cor. 15:47)
Seed of Abraham (Gal. 3:16, 19)
Seed of David (2 Tim. 2:8)
Seed of the woman (Gen. 3:15)
Servant (Isa. 42:1; 49:5-7)
Shepherd:
    The Chief Shepherd (1 Pet. 5:4)
    The Good Shepherd (Jn. 10:11, 14)
    The Great Shepherd (Heb. 13:20)
    My Shepherd (Ps. 23:1)
Shiloh (Gen. 49:10)
Son of David—he was called by this name by the
    following:
    two blind men in Capernaum (Mt. 9:27)
    the Syro-Phoenician woman (Mt. 15:22)
    two blind men in Jericho (one named Bartimaeus;
        Mt. 20:30; Mk. 10:46, 47)
    the Palm Sunday crowd (Mt. 21:9)
Son of God—Christ refers to himself by this name
    on only two occasions: John 9:35; 10:36. But
    many in the Gospels call him this:
    Satan (Mt. 4:3, 6)
    Gabriel (Lk. 1:35)
    a demon (Mt. 8:29; Lk. 4:41)
    a disciple (Mt. 14:33)
    Peter (Mt. 16:16)

Martha (Jn. 11:27)
Nathanael (Jn. 1:49)
a centurion (Mt. 27:54)
Son of man: his favorite name for himself.
    According to his own testimony, the Son of man:
    Came not to be ministered to (Mt. 20:28).
    Came to seek and save that which was lost (Mt.
        18:11).
    Can alone forgive sin (Mt. 9:6).
    Had not where to lay his head (Mt. 8:20).
    Is Lord of the Sabbath (Lk. 6:5).
    Would be betrayed (Mt. 17:22).
    Should suffer (Mt. 17:12).
    Would be lifted up (Jn. 3:14).
    Would be three days in the heart of the earth
        (Mt. 12:40).
    Would be raised from the dead (Mt. 17:9).
    Will come again in the glory of his Father (Mt.
        16:27; 24:30).
    Will send forth his angels (Mt. 13:41).
    Shall sit upon the throne of his glory (Mt. 19:28).
Son of Mary (Mk. 6:3).
Son of the Most High (Lk. 1:32)
Stone (Mt. 21:42; Mk. 12:10; Acts 4:11; Rom. 9:32,
    33; Eph. 2:20; 1 Pet. 2:6, 7)
Sun of Righteousness (Mal. 4:2)
Teacher (Master) (Mt. 26:18; Jn. 3:2; 11:28)
Wonderful (Isa. 9:6)
Word—the Apostle John's favorite name for Christ
    (Jn. 1:1; Rev. 19:13)
VI. The Humanity of Jesus Christ.
    A. He had a human parentage (Lk. 1:31; Gal. 4:4).
    B. He had a human body, soul, and spirit.
        1. Body.
            "For in that she hath poured this oint-
            ment on my body, she did it for my
            burial" (Mt. 26:12).
        2. Soul.
            "Now is my soul troubled; and what
            shall I say? Father, save me from this
            hour: but for this cause came I unto this
            hour" (Jn. 12:27).
            "Then said he unto them, My soul is
            exceeding sorrowful, even unto death:
            tarry ye here, and watch with me" (Mt.
            26:38).
        3. Spirit.
            "And immediately when Jesus perceived
            in his spirit that they so reasoned within
            themselves, he said unto them, Why
            reason ye these things in your hearts?"
            (Mk. 2:8).
            "And when Jesus had cried with a
            loud voice, he said, Father, into thy
            hands I commend my spirit: and having
            said thus, he gave up the ghost" (Lk.
            23:46).
    C. He looked like a man.
        1. To a Samaritan woman.
            "Then saith the woman of Samaria unto
            him, How is it that thou, being a Jew,
            askest drink of me, which am a woman
            of Samaria? for the Jews have no deal-
            ings with the Samaritans" (Jn. 4:9).

2. To the Jews.

"Then said the Jews unto him, Thou art not yet fifty years old, and hast thou seen Abraham?" (Jn. 8:57).

3. To Mary.

"Jesus saith unto her, Woman, why weepest thou? whom seekest thou? She, supposing him to be the gardener, saith unto him, Sir, if thou have borne him hence, tell me where thou hast laid him, and I will take him away" (Jn. 20:15).

4. He possessed flesh and blood (Heb. 2:14).

5. He grew (Lk. 2:40).

6. He asked questions (Lk. 2:46).

7. He increased in wisdom (Lk. 2:52).

8. He was limited in knowledge. Here it should be pointed out that this limitation was self-imposed. According to Philippians 2:5–8 (a passage we will examine in great detail in a later part of the study), Christ voluntarily abstained from using (yet always retained) certain divine attributes while here on earth, that he might totally depend upon the power and wisdom of the Holy Spirit. This fact helps explain the following passages:

"And Jesus, immediately knowing in himself that virtue had gone out of him, turned him about in the press, and said, Who touched my clothes?" (Mk. 5:30).

"And said, Where have ye laid him? They said unto him, Lord, come and see" (Jn. 11:34).

"And seeing a fig tree afar off having leaves, he came, if haply he might find any thing thereon: and when he came to it, he found nothing but leaves; for the time of figs was not yet" (Mk. 11:13).

"But of that day and that hour knoweth no man, no, not the angels which are in heaven, neither the Son, but the Father" (Mk. 13:32).

9. He prayed (Mk. 1:35; Lk. 11:1).

10. He was tempted (Mt. 4:1; Heb. 2:18; 4:15).

11. He learned obedience (Heb. 5:8).

12. He hungered.

"And when he had fasted forty days and forty nights, he was afterward ahungered" (Mt. 4:2).

"Now in the morning as he returned into the city, he hungered" (Mt. 21:18).

13. He thirsted.

"There cometh a woman of Samaria to draw water: Jesus saith unto her, Give me to drink" (Jn. 4:7).

"After this, Jesus knowing that all things were now accomplished, that the scripture might be fulfilled, saith, I thirst" (Jn. 19:28).

14. He was weary (Jn. 4:6).

15. He slept.

"And, behold, there arose a great tempest in the sea, insomuch that the ship was covered with the waves: but he was asleep" (Mt. 8:24).

16. He loved.

"Then Jesus beholding him loved him, and said unto him, One thing thou lackest: go thy way, sell whatsover thou hast, and give to the poor, and thou shalt have treasure in heaven: and come, take up the cross, and follow me" (Mk. 10:21).

17. He had compassion.

"But when he saw the multitudes, he was moved with compassion on them, because they fainted, and were scattered abroad, as sheep having no shepherd" (Mt. 9:36).

18. He was angered and grieved.

"And when he had looked round about on them with anger, being grieved for the hardness of their hearts, he saith unto the man, Stretch forth thine hand. And he stretched it out: and his hand was restored whole as the other" (Mk. 3:5).

19. He wept.

"Jesus wept" (Jn. 11:35).

"And when he was come near, he beheld the city, and wept over it" (Lk. 19:41).

20. He experienced joy.

"Looking unto Jesus the author and finisher of our faith; who for the joy that was set before him endured the cross, despising the shame, and is set down at the right hand of the throne of God" (Heb. 12:2).

"In that hour Jesus rejoiced in spirit, and said, I thank thee, O Father, Lord of heaven and earth, that thou hast hid these things from the wise and prudent, and hast revealed them unto babes: even so, Father; for so it seemed good in thy sight" (Lk. 10:21).

21. He was troubled.

"When Jesus therefore saw her weeping, and the Jews also weeping which came with her, he groaned in the spirit, and was troubled" (Jn. 11:33).

"Now is my soul troubled; and what shall I say? Father, save me from this hour: but for this cause came I unto this hour" (Jn. 12:27).

"When Jesus had thus said, he was troubled in spirit, and testified, and said, Verily, verily, I say unto you, that one of you shall betray me" (Jn. 13:21).

"And he taketh with him Peter and James and John, and began to be sore amazed, and to be very heavy; and saith unto them, My soul is exceeding sorrowful unto death: tarry ye here and watch" (Mk. 14:33, 34).

22. He sweat drops as of blood (Lk. 22:44).

23. He suffered (1 Pet. 4:1).

24. He bled (Jn. 19:34).

25. He died (Mt. 27:50; 1 Cor. 15:3).

26. He was buried (Mt. 27:59, 60).

VII. The Deity of Jesus Christ.

A. Shown by the Old Testament.

1. The witness of David.

    "Thy throne, O God, is for ever and ever: the scepter of thy kingdom is a right scepter. Thou lovest righteousness, and hatest wickedness: therefore God, thy God, hath anointed thee with the oil of gladness above thy fellows" (Ps. 45:6, 7).

    "The Lord said unto my Lord, Sit thou at my right hand, until I make thine enemies thy footstool" (Ps. 110:1).

2. The witness of Isaiah.

    "For unto us a child is born, unto us a son is given: and the government shall be upon his shoulder: and his name shall be called Wonderful, Counsellor, The mighty God, The everlasting Father, The Prince of Peace" (Isa. 9:6).

3. The witness of Daniel.

    "I saw in the night visions, and, behold, one like the Son of man came with the clouds of heaven, and came to the Ancient of days, and they brought him near before him. And there was given him dominion, and glory, and a kingdom, that all people, nations, and languages, should serve him: his dominion is an everlasting dominion, which shall not pass away, and his kingdom that which shall not be destroyed" (Dan. 7:13, 14).

B. Shown by the Gospels.

1. He is omnipotent (Mt. 28:18).
    a. over disease (Mt. 8:1–4; Lk. 4:39)
    b. over demons (Mt. 8:16, 17; 28–32; Lk. 4:35)
    c. over men (Mt. 9:9; Jn. 17:2)
    d. over nature (Mt. 8:26)
    e. over sin (Mt. 9:1–8)
    f. over traditions (Mt. 9:10–17)
    g. over death (Lk. 7:14, 15; 8:54, 56; Jn. 11:4)

2. He is omniscient (Jn. 2:24; 16:30).
    a. He knew the whereabouts of Nathanael (Jn. 1:48).
    b. He knew the plot of Judas (Jn. 6:70; 13:11).
    c. He knew the hearts of the Pharisees (Mt. 12:25; Lk. 5:22; 6:8; 7:39, 40).
    d. He knew the thoughts of the scribes (Mt. 9:3, 4).
    e. He knew the sincerity of one scribe (Mk. 12:34).
    f. He knew the history of the Samaritan woman (Jn. 4:29).
    g. He knew the problems of his disciples (Lk. 9:46, 47). If rightly understood, there is no contradiction here between his omniscience and his being limited in knowledge (as we have already discussed). He retained every whit of his deity while on earth (thus his omniscience) but voluntarily abstained from using it, that he might be totally dependent upon the Holy Spirit (thus his limited knowledge in certain areas).

3. He is omnipresent (Mt. 18:20; 28:20; Jn. 3:13; 14:20).

4. He is worshiped as God (cf. Mt. 4:9, 10).
    a. by the angels (Heb. 1:6).
    b. by the shepherds (Lk. 2:15)
    c. by the wise men (Mt. 2:2, 11)
    d. by a leper (Mt. 8:2)
    e. by a ruler (Mt. 9:18)
    f. by a Syro-Phoenician woman (Mt. 15:25)
    g. by a mother (Mt. 20:20)
    h. by a maniac (Mk. 5:6)
    i. by a man born blind (Jn. 9:38)
    j. by Thomas (Jn. 20:28)
    k. by some Greeks (Jn. 12:20, 21)
    l. by his apostles (Mt. 14:33; 28:9)

5. He forgives sins (Mk. 2:5, 10, 11).

6. He judges.

    "For the Father judgeth no man, but hath committed all judgment unto the Son" (Jn. 5:22).

7. He saves (Mt. 18:11; Jn. 10:28).

C. Shown by the Acts.

1. The testimony of Stephen.

    "And they stoned Stephen, calling upon God, and saying, Lord Jesus, receive my spirit" (Acts 7:59).

2. The testimony of a eunuch.

    "And Philip said, If thou believest with all thine heart, thou mayest. And he answered and said, I believe that Jesus Christ is the Son of God" (Acts 8:37).

D. Shown by the epistles.

1. In the writings of Paul. Note the language of just a few of these great Pauline verses on the deity of Christ.

    "I am crucified with Christ: nevertheless I live; yet not I, but Christ liveth in me: and the life which I now live in the flesh I live by the faith of the Son of God, who loved me, and gave himself for me" (Gal. 2:20).

    "Who is the image of the invisible God, the first-born of every creature: For by him were all things created, that are in heaven, and that are in earth, visible and invisible, whether they be thrones, or dominions, or principalities, or powers: all things were created by him, and for him: And he is before all things, and by him all things consist" (Col. 1:15–17).

    "For in him dwelleth all the fullness of the Godhead bodily" (Col. 2:9).

    "And without controversy great is the mystery of godliness: God was manifest in the flesh, justified in the Spirit, seen of angels, preached unto the Gentiles, believed on in the world, received up into glory" (1 Tim. 3:16).

    "Looking for that blessed hope, and the glorious appearing of the great God and our Savior Jesus Christ" (Titus 2:13).

2. In the writings of Peter. Consider also a sampling of Peter's testimony concerning Christ's deity.

    "Who is gone into heaven, and is on the right hand of God; angels and authorities and powers being made subject unto him" (1 Pet. 3:22).

"For he received from God the Father honor and glory, when there came such a voice to him from the excellent glory, This is my beloved Son, in whom I am well pleased" (2 Pet. 1:17).

3. In the writings of Jude.

"To the only wise God our Savior, be glory and majesty, dominion and power, both now and ever. Amen" (Jude 1:25).

4. In the writings of James.

"My brethren, have not the faith of our Lord Jesus Christ, the Lord of glory, with respect of persons" (Jas. 2:1).

5. In the writings of John.

"And we know that the Son of God is come, and hath given us an understanding, that we may know him that is true, and we are in him that is true, even in his Son Jesus Christ. This is the true God, and eternal life" (1 Jn. 5:20).

"I am he that liveth, and was dead; and, behold, I am alive for evermore, Amen; and have the keys of hell and of death" (Rev. 1:18).

"And he hath on his vesture and on his thigh a name written, KING OF KINGS, AND LORD OF LORDS" (Rev. 19:16).

Dr. John Walvoord quotes the following from Charles Hodge:

"All divine names and titles are applied to Him. He is called God, the mighty God, the great God, God over all; Jehovah; Lord; the Lord of lords and King of kings. All divine attributes are ascribed to Him. He is declared to be omnipresent, omniscient, almighty, and immutable, the same yesterday, today, and forever. He is set forth as the creator and upholder and ruler of the universe. All things were created by Him and for Him; and by Him all things consist. He is the object of worship to all intelligent creatures, even the highest; all the angels (i.e., all creatures between man and God) are commanded to prostrate themselves before Him. He is the object of all the religious sentiments; of reverence, love, faith, and devotion. To Him men and angels are responsible for their character and conduct. He required that man should honour Him as they honoured the Father; that they should exercise the same faith in Him that they do in God. He declares that He and the Father are one, that those who had seen Him had seen the Father also. He calls all men unto him; promises to forgive their sins; to send them the Holy Spirit; to give them rest and peace; to raise them up at the last day; and to give them eternal life. God is not more, and cannot promise more, or do more than Christ is said to be, to promise, and to do. He has, therefore, been the Christian's God from the beginning, in all ages and in all places." (*Jesus Christ, Our Lord*, p. 31)

VIII. The Impeccability of Jesus Christ. This subject deals with sinlessness. Here two facts should be stated:

A. Christ did not sin. We are informed that:

1. He knew no sin.

"For he hath made him to be sin for us, who knew no sin; that we might be made the righteousness of God in him" (2 Cor. 5:21).

2. He did no sin.

"Who did no sin, neither was guile found in his mouth" (1 Pet. 2:22).

"For we have not an high priest which cannot be touched with the feeling of our infirmities; but was in all points tempted like as we are, yet without sin" (Heb. 4:15).

3. He had no sin.

"And ye know that he was manifested to take away our sins; and in him is no sin" (1 Jn. 3:5).

"Hereafter I will not talk much with you: for the prince of this world cometh, and hath nothing in me" (Jn. 14:30).

B. These facts concerning the sinlessness of Christ while upon the earth are attested by many individuals, some of which were his enemies:

1. Pilate.

"Pilate therefore went forth again, and saith unto them, Behold, I bring him forth to you, that ye may know that I find no fault in him" (Jn. 19:4).

2. Pilate's wife.

"When he was set down on the judgment seat, his wife sent unto him, saying, Have thou nothing to do with that just man: for I have suffered many things this day in a dream because of him" (Mt. 27:19).

3. Judas.

"Saying, I have sinned in that I have betrayed the innocent blood. And they said, What is that to us? see thou to that" (Mt. 27:4).

4. The dying thief.

"And we indeed justly; for we receive the due reward of our deeds: but this man hath done nothing amiss" (Lk. 23:41).

5. The Roman centurion.

"Now when the centurion saw what was done, he glorified God, saying, Certainly this was a righteous man" (Lk. 23:47).

C. Christ could not sin. There is no question concerning the fact that Jesus did not sin while on this earth, but *could* he have done so? Author W. E. Best writes:

"The point of view that Christ could sin is designated by the idea of peccability, and the fact that He could not sin is expressed by the term impeccability. To suggest the capability or possibility of sinning would disqualify Christ as Saviour, for a peccable Christ would mean a peccable God. Holiness is far more than the absence of sin; it is positive virtue. The advocates of peccability say,

'Christ could have sinned, but He did not.' To say that He could have sinned is to deny positive holiness. To deny positive holiness, therefore, is to deny the holy character of God. Holiness is positive virtue which has neither room for nor interest in sin. The Lord Jesus could not sin because the days of His flesh meant only addition of experience, not variation of character. Holy humanity was united to Deity in one indivisible person, the impeccable Christ. Jesus Christ cannot have more holiness because He is perfectly holy; He cannot have less holiness because He is unchangingly holy." (*Studies in the Person and Work of Jesus Christ*, p. 3)

The question is asked, however: If Christ could not have sinned, then what was the purpose of the temptations in the wilderness? Here it should be observed that these trials were not to see if Christ would sin, but to *prove* he would not.

IX. The Earthly Ministry of Jesus Christ.
  A. It has been rightly said that the first three Gospel accounts (Matthew, Mark, Luke) offer the *presentation* of Christ's earthly ministry, while the fourth account (John) gives us the *interpretation* of that life.
  B. The following is but a brief outline of the most important events in his life down here.
    1. his birth (Lk. 2:7)
    2. his circumcision (Lk. 2:21)
    3. the trip to Egypt (Mt. 2:14)
    4. early life in Nazareth (Lk. 2:39)
    5. the visit to the Temple when he was twelve (Lk. 2:42)
    6. the baptism (Mt. 3:16)
    7. the temptation (Mt. 4:1)
    8. his first miracle in Cana (Jn. 2:7-9)
    9. the first Temple cleansing (Jn. 2:15)
    10. conversation with Nicodemus (Jn. 3:1-21)
    11. conversation with the Samaritan woman (Jn. 4:1-42)
    12. his sermon on Isaiah 61 in Nazareth (Lk. 4:16-30)
    13. the choosing of the twelve (Mt. 10:2-4)
    14. Sermon on the Mount (Mt. 5-7)
    15. parable of the sower (Mt. 13)
    16. feeding the 5,000 (Jn. 6:1-18)
    17. walking on the water (Jn. 6:19)
    18. forgiving an adulterous woman (Jn. 8:1-11)
    19. healing a man born blind (Jn. 9:1-38)
    20. sermon on the Good Shepherd (Jn. 10:1-18)
    21. hearing Peter's confession (Mt. 16:16)
    22. transfiguration (Mt. 17:1-23)
    23. parable of the Good Samaritan (Lk. 10:25-37)
    24. parable of the rich fool (Lk. 12:16-21)
    25. parable of the prodigal son (Lk. 15:1-32)
    27. raising of Lazarus (Jn. 11:1-44)
    28. speaking to the rich young ruler (Mt. 19:16-26)
    29. conversion of Zacchaeus (Lk. 19:1-10)
    30. anointing by Mary of Bethany (Jn. 12:1-8)
    31. his triumphal entry (Mt. 21:9-11)
    32. the cursing of the fig tree (Mt. 21:19)
    33. indicting Israel's leaders (Mt. 23)
    34. weeping over Jerusalem (Mt. 23:37-39; Lk. 19:41)
    35. Mount Olivet discourse (Mt. 24-25)
    36. the Last Supper (Jn. 13-14)
    37. Gethsemane (Jn. 18:1-11)
    38. trial and condemnation by Pilate (Jn. 19:1-16)
    39. crucifixion (Jn. 19:17-37)
    40. conversion of the dying thief (Lk. 23:39-43)
    41. his glorious resurrection (Mt. 28; Mk.16; Lk. 24; Jn. 20)
    42. appearance to Mary Magdalene (Jn. 20:1-18)
    43. appearance on the Emmaus Road (Lk. 24:13-32)
    44. appearance to his disciples (Lk. 24:33-48)
    45. restoration of Peter (Jn. 21)
    46. ascension (Lk. 24:51)

X. The Character of Jesus Christ. What kind of man was our Lord? What were some of his characteristics? Consider:
  A. His zeal (Jn. 2:17).
    1. His zeal forced him to remain behind in Jerusalem as a boy (Lk. 2:49).
    2. His zeal led him to become the first circuit preacher (Lk. 4:42-44; 8:1).
    3. His zeal caused his friends to think him mad.
        "And when his friends heard of it, they went out to lay hold on him: for they said, He is beside himself" (Mk. 3:21). The words "He is beside himself" may be paraphrased, "He has gone crazy over religion."
    4. His zeal prompted him to risk his life in purifying the Temple (Jn. 2:15-17).
    5. His zeal gave him no rest until he accomplished his mission.
        "I am come to send fire on the earth; and what will I, if it be already kindled? But I have a baptism to be baptized with; and how am I straitened till it be accomplished" (Lk. 12:49, 50).
  B. His compassion (Heb. 5:2).
    1. Upon the shepherdless multitudes.
        "But when he saw the multitudes, he was moved with compassion on them, because they fainted, and were scattered abroad, as sheep having no shepherd" (Mt. 9:36).
    2. Upon the sick multitudes.
        "And Jesus went forth, and saw a great multitude, and was moved with compassion toward them, and he healed their sick" (Mt. 14:14).
    3. Upon the hungry multitudes.
        "Then Jesus called his disciples unto him, and said, I have compassion on the multitude, because they continue with me now three days, and have nothing to eat: and I will not send them away fasting, lest they faint in the way" (Mt. 15:32).
    4. Upon a widow (Lk. 7:13).
    5. Upon a leper (Mk. 1:41).
    6. Upon a father (Mk. 9:22, 23).
    7. Upon a demoniac (Mk. 5:19).

C. His meekness and gentleness (2 Cor. 10:1; 1 Pet. 2:21, 22).

1. In dealing with our infirmities.

"Behold my servant, whom I have chosen; my beloved, in whom my soul is well pleased: I will put my Spirit upon him, and he shall show judgment to the Gentiles. He shall not strive, nor cry; neither shall any man hear his voice in the streets. A bruised reed shall he not break, and smoking flax shall he not quench, till he send forth judgment unto victory. And in his name shall the Gentiles trust" (Mt. 12:18-21).

2. In washing the feet of the disciples (Jn. 13:4, 5).

3. In his own words.

"Come unto me, all ye that labor and are heavy laden, and I will give you rest. Take my yoke upon you, and learn of me; for I am meek and lowly in heart: and ye shall find rest unto your souls. For my yoke is easy, and my burden is light" (Mt. 11:28-30).

4. In his sufferings and death.

"He was oppressed, and he was afflicted, yet he opened not his mouth: he is brought as a lamb to the slaughter, and as a sheep before her shearers is dumb, so he openeth not his mouth" (Isa. 53:7).

D. His courage.

1. As seen in his hometown proclamation (Lk. 4:16-30). During this, his first recorded sermon in Nazareth, he boldly pointed out Israel's historical unbelief which prompted God even back in Old Testament times to bypass, on occasion, the chosen people and bless believing Gentiles instead. A murderous attempt was made on his life at the end of the message.

2. As seen in his two cleansings of the Temple (Jn. 2:13-17; Mt. 21:12-16). The first of these took place at the beginning of his ministry and the second during the final week. Both took great personal courage.

3. As seen in his fearless ministry to a madman (Mk. 5:1-9). No coward would have dared confront (as did our Lord) this raging lunatic who doubtless possessed superhuman and satanic strength.

4. As seen in risking his life to raise Lazarus (Jn. 11:7, 8, 16, 53). He was fully aware (as were his frightened disciples) that a trip to Bethany at this time would simply invite the enraged Jews to attempt to stone him again. (See Jn. 11:8.) But he went anyway.

5. As seen in denouncing the wicked Pharisees (Mt. 23). Never in written history was a group of religious hypocrites so soundly and severely rebuked as were the wicked Pharisees by the Savior here in Matthew 23. Furthermore, he condemned this powerful and perverted group to their face.

6. As seen in his approach to Calvary.

"And they were in the way going up to Jerusalem; and Jesus went before them: and they were amazed; and as they followed, they were afraid. And he took again the twelve, and began to tell them what things should happen unto him, saying, Behold, we go up to Jerusalem; and the Son of man shall be delivered unto the chief priests, and unto the scribes; and they shall condemn him to death, and shall deliver him to the Gentiles: And they shall mock him, and shall scourge him, and shall spit upon him, and shall kill him: and the third day he shall rise again" (Mk. 10:32-34).

"And it came to pass, when the time was come that he should be received up, he steadfastly set his face to go to Jerusalem" (Lk. 9:51).

E. His love (Jn. 15:13). As a member of the Trinity, Christ naturally loves that which his Father loves. However, while he was on earth, he especially loved:

1. his Father (Jn. 14:31; 15:10)
2. his disciples (Jn. 13:34; 17:2, 9, 12; 19:25-27)
3. little children (Mk. 10:13-16)
4. certain close friends (Jn. 11:1-3; 13:23)
5. the city of Jerusalem (Mt. 23:37; Lk. 19:41)

XI. The Biographers of Jesus Christ. There were, of course, four human authors used by the Holy Spirit to describe Jesus' ministry. Each pictures him in a different light. Note:

Matthew: the prophesied King; lionlike; prohetic; written to the Jew; the Davidic King; David's righteous Branch.

Mark: the obedient Servant; oxlike; practical; written to the Roman; the Servant of the Lord; my Servant, the Branch.

Luke: the perfect Man; manlike; historical; written to the Greek; the Son of man; the Man, the Branch.

John: the mighty God; eaglelike; spiritual; written to all the world; the Word of God; the Branch of the Lord (see Isa. 4:2; Jer. 23:5, 6; Zech. 3:8; 6:12).

XII. The Kenosis (divine emptying) of Jesus Christ. Perhaps the most profound theological passage in the entire Bible is found in Philippians 2:5-11.

"Let this mind be in you, which was also in Christ Jesus: Who, being in the form of God, thought it not robbery to be equal with God: But made himself of no reputation, and took upon him the form of a servant, and was made in the likeness of men: And being found in fashion as a man, he humbled himself, and became obedient unto death, even the death of the cross. Wherefore God also hath highly exalted him, and given him a name which is above every name: That at the name of Jesus every knee should bow, of things in heaven, and things in earth, and things under the earth; And that every tongue should confess that Jesus Christ is Lord, to the glory of God the Father" (Phil. 2:5-11).

These verses impart the following information:

A. He left heaven's glory (Jn. 17:5; 2 Cor. 8:9).

B. He made himself of no reputation. The Greek word here in Philippians 2:7 is *kenoo* and means "to empty." Just what did Christ empty himself of?

1. Negative—he did *not* lay aside, in any sense of the word, his deity. He was, is, and ever shall be the total Son of God. (See Jn. 1:1; 2 Cor. 4:4; Col. 1:15; 2:9; Heb. 1:3).
2. Positive—he did, for awhile, hide his heavenly fame in an earthly frame. Even though he retained every single attribute of deity while on earth, he did, nevertheless, surrender the independent exercise of those divine characteristics.

There is a common false view of the *kenosis* which teaches that he emptied himself of his *relative* attributes (omniscience, omnipotence, omnipresence), while retaining his *immanent* attributes (his holiness, love, and truth). But this is in error. He did, it is true, abstain for awhile from using some of these relative attributes, but he *never* gave them up.

a. He abstained from his omnipresence for a period.
"Then said Jesus unto them plainly, Lazarus is dead. And I am glad for your sakes that I was not there, to the intent ye may believe; nevertheless let us go unto him" (Jn. 11:14, 15).

b. He abstained from his omniscience for a period.
"And Jesus said, Who touched me? When all denied, Peter and they that were with him said, Master, the multitude throng thee and press thee, and sayest thou, Who touched me? And Jesus said, Somebody hath touched me: for I perceive that virtue is gone out of me" (Lk. 8:45, 46).
"But of that day and that hour knoweth no man, no, not the angels which are in heaven, neither the Son, but the Father" (Mk. 13:32).

c. He abstained from his omnipotence for a period.
"Then answered Jesus and said unto them, Verily, verily, I say unto you, The Son can do nothing of himself, but what he seeth the Father do: for what things soever he doeth, these also doeth the Son likewise. For the Father loveth the Son, and showeth him all things that himself doeth: and he will show him greater works than these, that ye may marvel" (Jn. 5:19, 20).

Two phrases found in Philippians 2 need to be examined at this point.

The form of God: This does not mean that Christ had a physical shape prior to the incarnation. It refers to that inner, essential, and abiding nature of a person or thing. As an example, we might say, "The tennis player was in rare form today."

Robbery to be equal with God: That is, he did not hold or consider the outer manifestation of his deity in heaven as a treasure to be grasped and retained at all costs. Christ in his incarnation did not concern himself with retaining all this.

C. He was made in the likeness of men (See Jn. 1:14; Rom. 1:3; Gal. 4:4; Heb. 2:14, 17). This simple but absolutely staggering fact cannot be even remotely grasped by human minds. The infinite holy Creator suddenly becomes in the likeness of his finite and sinful creatures (yet without sin). It is as if a mighty and magnificent earthly king would determine to lay aside for awhile his storehouse of wealth, and, leaving behind an adoring and amazed court, take upon himself the body of a lowly ant. The "Son of man" was, by the way, our Lord's favorite name for himself while on earth. He took upon himself the form of a servant. He did not come as a mighty human Caesar or some world-renowned human philosopher. Even this would have been a condescension of colossal proportions. He came, rather, as a lowly servant. J. Vernon McGee writes:

"He could have been born in the palace in Rome. He could have been born a Caesar. But God had already promised He would be in the line of David. . . . Have you ever noticed what Isaiah said concerning Him:

'And there shall come forth a rod out of the stem of Jesse, and a Branch shall grow out of his roots' (Isa. 11:1).

For years that bothered me. I felt like saying, 'Isaiah, you should have said out of the stem of David.' I think if Isaiah could have spoken to me, he would have said, 'Oh, how you fellows miss it. The stem comes out of Jesse!' When Jesus was born, Israel was under the heel of Rome; the royal line of David was no longer on the throne, but had returned to peasantry. You see, Jesse, the father of King David, was a peasant, a farmer in Bethlehem. And when Jesus was born, the royal line was again in the peasant class. Jesus was born into a poor family. Though He was the Son of David, the stem came out of Jesse. He took upon Himself the form of a servant" (*Probing Through Philippians*, p. 36).

D. He humbled himself. That is, he submitted to authority.
"For even hereunto were ye called: because Christ also suffered for us, leaving us an example, that ye should follow his steps: Who did no sin, neither was guile found in his mouth: Who, when he was reviled, reviled not again; when he suffered, he threatened not; but committed himself to him that judgeth righteously: Who his own self bare our sins in his own body on the tree, that we, being dead to sins, should live unto righteousness: by whose stripes ye were healed" (1 Pet. 2:21–24).

He agreed to talk our language, to wear our clothes, to eat our food, to breathe our air, and to endure our vile and vicious treatment. Contrast his statement in the garden with Lucifer's statement.

"And he went a little farther, and fell on his face, and prayed, saying, O my Father, if it be possible, let this cup pass from me: nevertheless not as I will, but as thou wilt. He went away the second time, and prayed, saying, O my Father, if this cup may not pass away from me, except I drink it, thy will be done" (Mt. 26:39, 42).

"For thou hast said in thine heart, I will ascend into heaven, I will exalt my throne above the stars of God: I will sit also upon the mount of the congregation, in the sides of the north: I will ascend above the heights of the clouds; I will be like the most High" (Isa. 14:13, 14).

E. He became obedient unto death (see Mt. 26:39; Jn. 10:18; Heb. 5:8; 12:2).

F. He died on a cross. He did not just die, but suffered the worst kind of death both physically and judicially. (See Ps. 22; Isa. 53; Gal. 3:13.)

We have examined the humiliation of Christ, and now lets us notice his exaltation.

G. He has been highly exalted by the Father himself.

"Behold, my servant shall deal prudently, he shall be exalted and extolled, and be very high" (Isa. 52:13).

"These words spake Jesus, and lifted up his eyes to heaven, and said, Father, the hour is come; glorify thy Son, that thy Son also may glorify thee" (Jn. 17:1).

"Therefore being by the right hand of God exalted, and having received of the Father the promise of the Holy Ghost, he hath shed forth this which ye now see and hear" (Acts 2:33).

"But we see Jesus, who was made a little lower than the angels for the suffering of death, crowned with glory and honor; that he by the grace of God should taste death for every man" (Heb. 2:9).

H. He has been given a name (position and place of authority) above all other names (Eph. 1:20, 21; Heb. 1:4).

I. He will be universally acknowledged as Lord of all.

1. The methods of this acknowledgment: By the bowing of the knee and the confession of the tongue.

2. The creatures of this acknowledgment:
   a. Those in heaven: the world of angels.
   b. Those on earth: the world of saints and sinners.
   c. Those under the earth: the world of demons. (See Isa. 45:23; Rom. 10:9, 10; Rev. 5:13; 7:9-12; 14:6, 7).

      Note: To confess him in this life as Lord means salvation, but to wait until the next life will result in damnation. Thus, the supreme question is not *when* a human being will do this, but rather *where*.

XIII. The Office of Jesus Christ. In the Old Testament three great offices were created by God to meet the spiritual and material needs of his chosen people. These offices are:

A. The prophet, an individual who represented God before man. A prophet thus exercised:

1. Hindsight. He knew the secrets of the past. Moses wrote of man's creation, his fall, the universal flood, and other early events which transpired centuries before he himself was born in Egypt.

2. Insight. He knew the problems and needs of the present. Prophets like Isaiah, Amos, Joel, Jeremiah, and others thundered out God's wrath against the sin and decay of their times.

3. Foresight. He knew the secrets of the future. Daniel writes of the coming tribulation, and Ezekiel describes the glorious millennium.

B. The priest, an individual who represented man before God.

1. Qualifications for the priesthood:
   a. He must be taken from among men, a man with compassion for other men (see Heb. 5:1, 2).
   b. He must be chosen by God (Num. 16:5; Heb. 5:4).
   c. He must be consecrated to God (Lev. 21:6, 7).

C. The king, an individual who ruled for God.

1. He was to come from the tribe of Judah (Gen. 49:10).
2. He was to come from the seed of David (2 Sam. 7:8-17; Ps. 89:3, 4).

As fulfilled by Christ in the New Testament:

D. He fulfilled the office of the prophet.

1. This office was predicted for him by Moses in Deuteronomy 18: 18, 19 (cf. Jn. 1:21).
2. It began at the River Jordan and ended at Calvary.
3. He was recognized as being a prophet. See Jn. 4:19 (Samaritan woman), Luke 7:16 (people of Galilee), Matthew 21:11, John 7:40 (people of Jerusalem), Luke 22:64 (his enemies), Luke 24:19 (disciples on Emmaus Road).

   This is his *past* ministry.

E. He fulfills the office of the priest.

1. This began at the cross and will end at the Second Coming.
2. He met the qualifications for the priest's office.
   a. He was taken from among men (Heb. 2:16; 4:15).
   b. He was chosen by God (Heb. 5:4-6; Mt. 3:16, 17; 17:5).
   c. He was consecrated to God (Lk. 1:35; Heb. 7:26).
3. He performed the responsibilities of the priest's office.
   a. He offered himself upon Calvary (Heb. 2:9).
   b. He prayed (and prays) for his people (Jn. 17; Rom. 8:34; Heb. 7:25).
   c. He blesses his people (Eph. 1:3; 2:11-22).

      This is his *present* ministry.

F. He will fulfill the office of the king.

1. He comes from the tribe of Judah.
2. He comes from the seed of David.

   "And one of the elders saith unto me, Weep not; behold, the Lion of the tribe of Judah, the Root of David, hath prevailed to open the book, and to loose the seven seals thereof" (Rev. 5:5).

XIV. The Death of Jesus Christ.

A. The awesomeness of it—the murder of Israel's Messiah, the killing of the Creator.

1. As pondered by the Old Testament prophets.

"Of which salvation the prophets have enquired and searched diligently, who prophesied of the grace that should come unto you: searching what, or what manner of time the Spirit of Christ which was in them did signify, when it testified beforehand the sufferings of Christ, and the glory that should follow" (1 Pet. 1:10, 11).

"Then he said unto them, O fools, and slow of heart to believe all that the prophets have spoken: Ought not Christ to have suffered these things, and to enter into his glory? And beginning at Moses and all the prophets, he expounded unto them in all the scriptures the things concerning himself" (Lk. 24:25-27).

"I gave my back to the smiters, and my cheeks to them that plucked off the hair: I hid not my face from shame and spitting" (Isa. 50:6).

"Surely he hath borne our griefs, and carried our sorrows: yet we did esteem him stricken, smitten of God, and afflicted. But he was wounded for our transgressions, he was bruised for our iniquities: the chastisement of our peace was upon him; and with his stripes we are healed. All we like sheep have gone astray; we have turned every one to his own way; and the Lord hath laid on him the iniquity of us all. He was oppressed, and he was afflicted, yet he opened not his mouth: he is brought as a lamb to the slaughter, and as a sheep before her shearers is dumb, so he openeth not his mouth" (Isa. 53:4-7).

"My God, my God, why hast thou forsaken me? why art thou so far from helping me, and from the words of my roaring?" (Ps. 22:1).

"But I am a worm, and no man; a reproach of men, and despised of the people. All they that see me laugh me to scorn: they shoot out the lip, they shake the head, saying, He trusted on the Lord that he would deliver him: let him deliver him, seeing he delighted in him" (Ps. 22:6-8).

"For dogs have compassed me: the assembly of the wicked have inclosed me: they pierced my hands and my feet. I may tell all my bones: they look and stare upon me. They part my garments among them, and cast lots upon my vesture" (Ps. 22:16-18).

"They gave me also gall for my meat; and in my thirst they gave me vinegar to drink" (Ps. 69:21).

"And after threescore and two weeks shall Messiah be cut off" (Dan. 9:26).

"Awake, O sword, against my shepherd, and against the man who is my fellow [equal], saith the Lord of hosts; smite the shepherd, and the sheep shall be scattered" (Zech. 13:7).

2. As pondered by the New Testament apostles.

"And while they abode in Galilee, Jesus said unto them, The Son of man shall be betrayed into the hands of men: and they shall kill him, and the third day he shall be raised again. And they were exceeding sorry" (Mt. 17:22, 23).

"A little while, and ye shall not see me: and again, a little while, and ye shall see me, because I go to the Father. Then said some of his disciples among themselves, What is this that he saith unto us, A little while, and ye shall not see me: and again a little while, and ye shall see me: and, Because I go to the Father?" (Jn. 16:16, 17).

3. As pondered by the heavenly angels (1 Pet. 1:12; Eph. 3:10).

We are told that angels desire to look into the things of salvation (1 Pet. 1:12). Surely some of these accompanying things which transpired during the earthly life of our Lord must have filled them with joy and pride. They marveled at his birth. They were inspired by his sermons and thrilled by his miracles. But how did those holy heavenly creatures react when they watched their beloved celestial Creator being systematically slaughtered by brutal mortal sinners? We cannot tell, but surely astonishment and outrage must have flooded their beings.

B. The scope of it. For whom did Christ die? In general, it may be said that he died for the world, for the elect, and for each man.

1. His death for the world.

"For God so loved the world, that he gave his only begotten Son, that whosoever believeth in him should not perish, but have everlasting life" (Jn. 3:16).

"The next day John seeth Jesus coming unto him, and saith, Behold the Lamb of God, which taketh away the sin of the world" (Jn. 1:29).

"And he is the propitiation for our sins: and not for ours only, but also for the sins of the whole world" (1 Jn. 2:2).

"For the grace of God that bringeth salvation hath appeared to all men" (Titus 2:11).

"But there were false prophets also among the people, even as there shall be false teachers among you, who privily shall bring in damnable heresies, even denying the Lord that brought them, and bring upon themselves swift destruction" (2 Pet. 2:1).

"The Lord is not slack concerning his promise, as some men count slackness; but is long-suffering to us-ward, not willing that any should perish, but that all should come to repentance" (2 Pet. 3:9).

"Who gave himself a ransom for all, to be testified in due time" (1 Tim. 2:6).

"For therefore we both labor and suffer reproach, because we trust in the living God, who is the Savior of all men, specially of those that believe" (1 Tim. 4:10).

2. His death for the elect.

"But ye believe not, because ye are not of my sheep, as I said unto you. My sheep hear my voice, and I know them, and they follow me: and I give unto them eternal life; and they shall never perish, neither shall any man pluck them out of my Father's hand" (Jn. 10:26-28).

"I pray for them: I pray not for the world, but for them which thou hast given me, for they are thine" (Jn. 17:9).

"And she shall bring forth a son, and thou shalt call his name Jesus: for he shall save his people from their sins" (Mt. 1:21).

"Take heed therefore unto yourselves, and to all the flock, over the which the Holy Ghost hath made you overseers, to feed the church of God, which he hath purchased with his own blood" (Acts 20:28).

"Who hath saved us, and called us with an holy calling, not according to our works, but according to his own purpose and grace, which was given us in Christ Jesus before the world began, but is now made manifest by the appearing of our Savior Jesus Christ, who hath abolished death, and hath brought life and immortality to light through the gospel" (2 Tim. 1:9, 10).

"According as he hath chosen us in him before the foundation of the world, that we should be holy and without blame before him in love" (Eph. 1:4)

"Husbands, love your wives, even as Christ also loved the church, and gave himself for it" (Eph. 5:25).

"And all that dwell upon the earth shall worship him, whose names are not written in the book of life of the Lamb slain from the foundation of the world" (Rev. 13:8).

3. His death for each man.

"But we see Jesus, who was made a little lower than the angels for the suffering of death, crowned with glory and honor; that he by the grace of God should taste death for every man" (Heb. 2:9).

C. Old Testament examples of it. During that first Easter Sunday afternoon the resurrected Christ appeared unrecognized to two disciples on their way to Emmaus. After listening to their despair over the recent crucifixion of Israel's Messiah, our Lord admonished them as follows:

"Then he said unto them, O fools, and slow of heart to believe all that the prophets have spoken: Ought not Christ to have suffered these things, and to enter into his glory? And beginning at Moses and all the prophets, he expounded unto them in all the scriptures the things concerning himself" (Lk. 24:25-27).

The following Old Testament events which speak of Jesus' death were no doubt referred to by our Lord to those disciples during that afternoon conversation.

1. the coats of skin (Gen. 3:21)
2. the Passover lamb (Ex. 12)
3. the Levitical offerings (Lev. 1-5)
4. the ordinance of the red heifer (Num. 19)
5. the sacrifice on the day of atonement (Lev. 16)
6. the ark (1 Pet. 3:18-22)
7. the passage through the Red Sea (1 Cor. 10:1, 2)
8. the two memorials (Josh. 3-4)
9. the branch cast into the waters of Marah (Ex. 15:23-26)
10. the smitten rock (1 Cor. 10:4)
11. the brazen serpent (Jn. 3:14)

D. The importance of it. Henry Thiessen writes: "The death of Christ has a prominent place in the New Testament. The last three days of our Lord's earthly life occupy about one-fifth of the narratives in the four Gospels. If all the three and a half years of His public ministry had been written out as fully as the last three days, we would have a 'Life of Christ' of some 8400 pages! . . . Torrey claims that the death of Christ is mentioned directly in the New Testament more than 175 times. Since there are 7,959 verses in the New Testament, this would mean that one out of every 53 verses refers to this theme." (Lectures in Systematic Theology, p. 313)

Thiessen also writes:

"The death of Christ is the essential thing in Christianity. Other religions base their claim to recognition on the teaching of their founders; Christianity is distinguished from all of them by the importance it assigns to the death of its Founder. Take away the death of Christ as interpreted by the Scriptures, and you reduce Christianity to the level of the ethnic religions. Though we would still have a higher system of ethics, were we to take away the cross of Christ, we would have no more salvation than these other religions. Napoleon said when banished to St. Helena, that Alexander, Caesar, Charlemagne, and he had founded mighty kingdoms on force, but that Jesus Christ had founded His on love. This is true, if we mean love expressed in His substitutionary death.

It is of Supreme Interest in Heaven. The death of Christ is the subject of supreme interest in heaven. We may expect those who have gone to heaven to have a fuller and truer conception of life's values than those who are still limited in their vision by their existence in the body. We are told that when Moses and Elijah appeared on the Mount of Transfiguration, they conversed with Christ 'about the decease which he was about to accomplish at Jerusalem' (Lk. 9:30, 31). We also find that the four living creatures and the twenty-four elders sang the song of redemption through the death of Christ (Rev. 5:8-10). Even the multitude of angels around the throne, though not in need of redemption themselves, joined in the song of the Lamb that was slain (Rev. 5:11, 12). Since those who have the veil of human limitations completely removed from their eyes—those who have entered into the fuller fruits of redemption through the blood of Christ—extol Christ's death above everything else, we mortals ought to study into the true meaning of that death." (*Lectures in Systematic Theology*, pp. 313, 314)

In fact, our Lord himself spoke of his death often. See the following:

"Jesus answered and said unto them, Destroy this temple, and in three days I will raise it up" (Jn. 2:19).

"And as Moses lifted up the serpent in the wilderness, even so must the Son of man be lifted up" (Jn. 3:14).

"Saying, the Son of man must suffer many things, and be rejected of the elders, and chief priests and scribes, and be slain, and be raised the third day" (Lk. 9:22).

"And while they abode in Galilee, Jesus said unto them, The Son of man shall be betrayed into the hands of men: and they shall kill him, and the third day he shall be raised again. And they were exceeding sorry" (Mt. 17:22, 23).

"Therefore doth my Father love me, because I lay down my life, that I might take it again" (Jn. 10:17).

"Saying, Behold, we go up to Jerusalem; and the Son of man shall be delivered unto the chief priests, and unto the scribes; and they shall condemn him to death, and shall deliver him to the Gentiles: and they shall mock him, and shall scourge him, and shall spit upon him, and shall kill him: and the third day he shall rise again" (Mk. 10:33, 34).

"She hath done what she could: she is come aforehand to anoint my body to the burying" (Mk. 14:8).

"And I, if I be lifted up from the earth, will draw all men unto me" (Jn. 12:32).

"Then saith Jesus unto them, All ye shall be offended because of me this night: for it is written, I will smite the shepherd, and the sheep of the flock shall be scattered abroad" (Mt. 26:31).

"Rise, let us be going: behold, he is at hand that doth betray me" (Mt. 26:46).

"Nevertheless I tell you the truth; It is expedient for you that I go away: for if I go not away, the Comforter will not come unto you; but if I depart, I will send him unto you" (Jn. 16:7).

E. The false theories concerning it.
1. The payment-to-Satan theory. This says man had sold his immortal soul to Satan through sin and that Christ's death was the devil's "pound of flesh" ransom note. This is wholly untrue, for Christ's death assured the final and eternal damnation of the devil. The only thing God owes Satan is a place in Gehenna hell forever.
2. The moral influence theory. Here we are told God allowed Christ to die to show that he can enter into man's sufferings. By this act God thus may stimulate man's sympathy for Christ. This too is false, for (among other reasons) the very ones who put him to death continued to hate him and his followers the most. Furthermore, God's eternal plan is not to "share man's sufferings with him," but rather to save him, that man might someday share the riches of Christ.
3. The example theory. Christ's death simply showed how one man can give his life for others. But what would this single act accomplish? Soldiers, law officers, mothers, and other individuals had done this very thing thousands of times prior to and following Christ's death. What could Calvary add to all this?
4. The satisfaction theory. This teaches that Jesus died to appease God's offended honor. It acted somewhat like a pistol duel at dawn where an insulated man takes revenge for prior insult and injury. While this theory is closer to the truth than the former ones, it still smacks of error. There was absolutely no revenge involved in the death of Christ.
F. The substitutional (and orthodox) theory. This alone is the correct view. Dr. John Walvoord writes:

"Christ in His death fully satisfied the demands of a righteous God for judgment upon sinners and, as their infinite sacrifice, provided a ground not only for the believer's forgiveness, but for his justification and sanctification." (*Jesus Christ Our Lord*, p. 162)
G. The need for it. Henry Thiessen writes:

"At first God and man stood face to face with each other. In sinning, Adam turned his back upon God. Then God turned His back upon Adam. Christ's death has satisfied the demands of God and now God has again turned His face toward man. It remains for man to turn round about and face God. Since God has been reconciled by the death of His Son, man is now entreated to be reconciled to God." (Lecture 2, *Systematic Theology*, pp. 327, 328)

The need, therefore, for Christ's death was twofold:
1. It was necessary because of God's holiness (Lev. 11:44; Prov. 15:9).
2. It was necessary because of man's sinfulness (Rom. 3:10-20).

H. The results from it.

1. In relation to sinners—redemption.

"In whom we have redemption through his blood, the forgiveness of sins, according to the riches of his grace" (Eph. 1:7).

"Christ hath redeemed us from the curse of the law, being made a curse for us: for it is written, Cursed is every one that hangeth on a tree" (Gal. 3:13).

"And when he had taken the book, the four beasts and four and twenty elders fell down before the Lamb, having every one of them harps, and golden vials full of odors, which are the prayers of saints. And they sung a new song, saying, Thou art worthy to take the book, and to open the seals thereof: for thou wast slain, and hast redeemed us to God by thy blood out of every kindred, and tongue, and people, and nation; and hast made us unto our God kings and priests: and we shall reign on the earth. And I beheld, and I heard the voice of many angels round about the throne and the beasts and the elders: and the number of them was ten thousand times ten thousand, and thousands of thousands; saying with a loud voice, Worthy is the Lamb that was slain to receive power, and riches, and wisdom, and strength, and honor, and glory, and blessing" (Rev. 5:8-12).

2. In relation to saints—sanctification.

"Who gave himself for our sins, that he might deliver us from this present evil world, according to the will of God and our Father" (Gal. 1:4).

"By the which will we are sanctified through the offering of the body of Jesus Christ once for all" (Heb. 10:10).

"Having therefore, brethren, boldness to enter into the holiest by the blood of Jesus, by a new and living way, which he hath consecrated for us, through the veil, that is to say, his flesh" (Heb. 10:19, 20).

3. In relation to Satan—destruction.

"Forasmuch then as the children are partakers of flesh and blood, he also himself likewise took part of the same; that through death he might destroy him that had the power of death, that is, the devil" (Heb. 2:14).

"And having spoiled principalities and powers, he made a show of them openly, triumphing over them in it" (Col. 2:15).

"He that committeth sin is of the devil; for the devil sinneth from the beginning. For this purpose the Son of God was manifested, that he might destroy the works of the devil" (1 Jn. 3:8).

"And the great dragon was cast out, that old serpent, called the Devil, and Satan, which deceiveth the whole world: he was cast out into the earth, and his angels were cast out with him. And I heard a loud voice saying in heaven, Now is come salvation, and strength, and the kingdom of our God, and the power of his Christ: for the accuser of our brethren is cast down, which accused them before our God day and night. And they overcame him by the blood of the Lamb, and by the word of their testimony; and they loved not their lives unto the death" (Rev. 12:9-11).

XV. The Heart of the Earth Descent of Jesus Christ.

"For as Jonas was three days and three nights in the whale's belly; so shall the Son of man be three days and three nights in the heart of the earth" (Mt. 12:40).

"For Christ also hath once suffered for sins, the just for the unjust, that he might bring us to God, being put to death in the flesh, but quickened by the Spirit: By which also he went and preached unto the spirits in prison; which sometime were disobedient, when once the longsuffering of God waited in the days of Noah, while the ark was a preparing, wherein few, that is, eight souls were saved by water" (1 Pet. 3:18-20).

"Now that he ascended, what is it but that he also descended first into the lower parts of the earth?" (Eph. 4:9).

On the strength of these verses, the following events are suggested. Between his death and resurrection, our Lord descended into the lower parts of this earth to perform a twofold ministry:

A. To depopulate the "saved" compartment of Hades (Lk. 16:19-31). The final debt on the salvation of these believers was now paid, thus allowing them to enter the third heaven (2 Cor. 12:2).

B. To preach judgment upon the fallen angels who had attempted to corrupt human flesh and thus prevent the promised incarnation of Christ. (See Gen. 3:15; 6:1-4.) The theme of Christ's message therefore was, "It didn't work!" (See also 2 Pet. 2:4; Jude 1:6.)

XVI. The Resurrection of Jesus Christ.

A. The resurrection—denied by some. There is surely no other single doctrine in all the Bible so hated by Satan as the resurrection of Christ. He has attempted (always unsuccessfully) to ridicule it, downplay it, deny it, or simply explain it away. Here are but a few theories the devil has inspired his children (ungoldly men) to promote concerning this precious doctrine.

1. The fraud theory. This says that either Jesus or his disciples (or both) simply invented the entire thing. It would have us believe that Christ was simply a clever crook who read the prophecies regarding the Messiah in the Old Testament and set about arranging for them to be fulfilled by himself. However, it would have been somewhat difficult for an imposter to arrange the place where he was to be born (it had to be Bethlehem), or for some Roman soldiers to cooperate by not breaking his bones on the cross.

2. The swoon theory. We are informed here that Christ merely fainted on the cross and was later revived by the cool, dark air of the tomb. But how did he get out of that tomb? What bright light did he use to blind and terrify the Roman soldiers who stood guard outside?

3. The vision theory. This would advocate that the early disciples were guilty of using some kind of primitive LSD. If this be true, then the practice was certainly widespread, for on one occasion alone over 500 claimed to have seen him. There is not one speck of biblical or secular evidence to support such an empty theory.

4. The spirit theory. This holds that only Jesus' spirit arose. But Jesus is said to have eaten while in his resurrected body. The very nailprints were still there. This view, like the above, cannot for one second stand the logic of reason.

5. The heart theory. Here we are to believe that he was only resurrected in the heart of his friends. The trouble here, however, is that none of those friends actually believed he would literally rise from the dead until they saw him with their own eyes, and heard his words with their ears.

B. The resurrection—declared by many.
1. David predicted it.
"For thou wilt not leave my soul in hell; neither wilt thou suffer thine Holy One to see corruption" (Ps. 16:10).

2. Isaiah predicted it.
"And he made his grave with the wicked, and with the rich in his death; because he had done no violence, neither was any deceit in his mouth. Yet it pleased the Lord to bruise him; he hath put him to grief: when thou shalt make his soul an offering for sin, he shall see his seed, he shall prolong his days, and the pleasure of the Lord shall prosper in his hand. He shall see of the travail of his soul, and shall be satisfied: by his knowledge shall my righteous servant justify many; for he shall bear their iniquities. Therefore will I divide him a portion with the great, and he shall divide the spoil with the strong; because he hath poured out his soul unto death: and he was numbered with the transgressors; and he bare the sin of many, and made intercession for the transgressors" (Isa. 53:9-12).

3. Jesus himself predicted it many times.
"Then certain of the scribes, and of the Pharisees answered, saying, Master, we would see a sign from thee. But he answered and said unto them, An evil and adulterous generation seeketh after a sign; and there shall no sign be given to it, but the sign of the prophet Jonas: For as Jonas was three days and three nights in the whale's belly; so shall the Son of man be three days and three nights in the heart of the earth" (Mt. 12:38-40).

"From that time forth began Jesus to shew unto his disciples, how that he must go unto Jerusalem, and suffer many things of the elders and chief priests and scribes, and be killed, and be raised again the third day" (Mt. 16:21).

"Then came the disciples to Jesus apart, and said, Why could not we cast him out? And while they abode in Galilee, Jesus said unto them, The Son of man shall be betrayed into the hands of men: and they shall kill him, and the third day he shall be raised again. And they were exceeding sorry" (Mt. 17:19, 22, 23).

"Behold, we go up to Jerusalem; and the Son of man shall be betrayed unto the chief priests and unto the scribes, and they shall condemn him to death, and shall deliver him to the Gentiles to mock, and to scourge, and to crucify him: and the third day he shall rise again" (Mt. 20:18, 19).

"But after I am risen again, I will go before you into Galilee" (Mt. 26:32).

"Saying, The Son of man must suffer many things, and be rejected of the elders and chief priests and scribes, and be slain, and be raised the third day" (Lk. 9:22).

"Then answered the Jews and said unto him, What sign showest thou unto us, seeing that thou doest these things? Jesus answered and said unto them, Destroy this temple, and in three days I will raise it up. Then said the Jews, Forty and six years was this temple in building, and wilt thou rear it up in three days? But he spake of the temple of his body. When therefore he was risen from the dead, his disciples remembered that he had said this unto them; and they believed the scripture, and the word which Jesus had said" (Jn. 2:18-22).

C. The resurrection—doubted by most. It is ironic and sad that the predicted resurrection of Christ was remembered only by his enemies, the Pharisees, and not by his friends.

"Now the next day, that followed the day of the preparation, the chief priests and Pharisees came together unto Pilate, saying, Sir, we remember that that deceiver said, while he was yet alive, After three days I will rise again. Command therefore that the sepulchre be made sure until the third day, lest his disciples come by night, and steal him away, and say unto the people, He is risen from the dead: so the last error shall be worse than the first" (Mt. 27:62-64).

So much for his enemies. But what about his friends?

1. The women did not remember (Mk. 16:1-3).

2. Mary Magdalene did not remember (Jn. 20:13).

3. Peter and John did not remember (Lk. 24:12; Jn. 20:9).

4. The apostles did not remember (Lk. 24:9-11).
5. The two disciples on the Emmaus Road did not remember (Lk. 24:13-31).
6. Thomas did not remember (Jn. 20:24-29).

D. The resurrection—described by one (Paul; see 1 Cor. 15).

1. The proofs of the resurrection.
   a. The empty tomb.
   b. The tremendous change in the lives of the disciples.
   c. The silence from both the Romans and Pharisees. Not once did either of these enemy groups ever attempt to deny Christ's resurrection. They hated it and tried to suppress it, but could not refute it.
   d. The change from Saturday to Sunday as the main day of worship. As ingrained as the Sabbath was in the hearts and history of the apostles, it would have taken some fantastic event to change their thinking here.
   e. The existence of the church. In the less than fifty years after Christ's death, the Christian church had become a mighty power, causing the Roman government to view with growing concern its influence upon men and women. Legends and religions simply do not develop this quickly.

2. The appearances after the resurrection. Our Lord appeared no less than seventeen times after his resurrection. Five of these occurred during the first Easter Sunday, and six more took place between that time and his ascension. The remaining six happened between Pentecost and the completion of the Bible. Dr. John Walvoord in his book *Jesus Christ Our Lord* (pp. 193-195) describes these appearances:
   a. The first appearance of Christ was to Mary Magdalene as she remained at the site of the tomb after Peter and John had left. Here she saw Christ and first mistook him for the gardener, but immediately recognized him when he spoke to her (Jn. 20:11-17; cf. Mk. 16:9-11). After she had seen the risen Lord, Mary Magdalene returned to report the appearance of Christ to her friends (Mk. 16:10-11; Jn. 20:18).
   b. The second appearance of Christ was to the other women who were also returning to the tomb and saw Christ on the way (Mt. 28:9-10). The best texts seem to indicate that the phrase "as they went to tell his disciples" is an interpolation, and they were actually returning after telling the disciples.
   The record of the guards concerning the angel's rolling away the stone is another testimony to the resurrection of Christ from unwilling witnesses (Mt. 28:11-15).
   c. The third appearance was to Peter in the afternoon of the resurrection day.

Concerning this there are no details, but it is most significant that Christ first sought Peter, the denier, of all the twelve (Lk. 24:34; 1 Cor. 15:5).
   d. The fourth appearance of Christ was to the disciples as they walked on the road to Emmaus. By supernatural delay of recognition, Christ was able to expound to them the Old Testament Scriptures concerning his death and resurrection. His identity was not known to them until he broke bread (Mk. 16:12, 13; Lk. 24:13-35).
   e. The fifth appearance of the resurrected Christ was to the ten disciples (Mk. 16:14; Lk. 24:36-43; Jn. 20:19-23). Mark's account refers to them as the eleven, but it is obvious from the context that only ten were there, as Thomas was absent. After the departure of Judas, the remaining disciples were often referred to as the "eleven," even if all were not actually present. In a similar way, Paul refers to the "twelve" as witnesses of the resurrection (1 Cor. 15:5), but actually, Judas Iscariot was already dead.
   f. The sixth appearance was to the eleven disciples a week after his resurrection. At this time Thomas was present (Jn. 20:26-29).
   g. The seventh appearance was to seven disciples by the Sea of Galilee (Jn. 21:1-23). On this occasion he talked significantly to Simon Peter following the miraculous catch of fish.
   h. The eighth appearance was to five hundred and is recited by Paul as an outstanding proof of his resurrection (1 Cor. 15:6).
   i. The ninth appearance was to James, the Lord's brother (1 Cor. 15:7). There is some evidence that James was not a believer prior to the resurrection (Jn. 7:3-5), but immediately after the resurrection he is numbered among the believers (Acts 1:14; Gal. 1:19). He later became one of the outstanding leaders in the apostolic church.
   j. The tenth appearance was to eleven disciples on the mountain in Galilee. On that occasion he gave them the Great Commission to preach the gospel (Mt. 28:16-20). A similar commission is given in Mark 16:15-18, which may have been the same instance or an earlier appearance.
   k. The eleventh appearance occurred at the time of his ascension from the Mount of Olives (Lk. 24:44-53; Acts 1:3-9). This is the last appearance of Christ to his disciples prior to his glorification in heaven.
   l. The twelfth appearance of the resurrected Christ was to Stephen just prior to his martyrdom (Acts 7:55, 56). Subse-

quent appearances, while different in character, confirm the fact of his resurrection.

m. The thirteenth appearance of Christ was to Paul on the road to Damascus as he was about to continue his work of persecuting Christians (Acts 9:3-6; cf. 22:6-11; 26:13-18). On this occasion Paul was converted.

n. The fourteenth appearance seems to have been to Paul in Arabia (Acts 26:17; Gal. 1:12, 17). The appearance is not clearly stated but may be inferred from Galatians 1:12. Some believe that the instructions to Paul, which he mentions in Acts 26:17, were given to him in Arabia, not at the original appearance on the road to Damascus. There is no record of the precise revelation given to Paul in Acts 9 or Acts 22. In Acts 22:10 he is promised a later revelation which would give him the necessary instruction.

o. The fifteenth appearance of Christ was to Paul in the Temple when Paul was warned concerning the persecution which was to come (Acts 22:17-21; cf. 9:26-30; Gal. 1:18).

p. The sixteenth appearance of Christ was to Paul while he was in prison in Caesarea, when it is recorded that "the Lord stood by him" and told him that he would bear witness in Rome (Acts 23:11).

q. The seventeenth appearance of Christ was to the Apostle John at the beginning of the revelation given to him (Rev. 1:12-20).

Taken as a whole, the appearances are of such various character and to so many people under so many different circumstances that the proof of the resurrection of Christ is as solid as any historical fact that could be cited in the first century.

3. The importance of the resurrection (see 1 Cor. 15:12-19). The resurrection of Christ is the Constitution, Bill of Rights, and Declaration of Independence of the Christian faith. The sign of Christianity is really not the cross, but an empty tomb. If one denies the resurrection, he is forced to six horrible conclusions:

a. All gospel preaching has been, is now, and always will be, utterly and completely useless.

b. All past, present, and future faith is futile.

c. All preachers become notorious liars.

d. All living Christians are still in their sins.

e. All departed Christians are in hell.

f. All reason and purpose for life itself is destroyed.

4. The order of the resurrection (1 Cor. 15:20-24). The resurrection of Christ is represented here as being the first of its kind, thus indicating that previous miracles, such as the raising of Lazarus, were more on the order of restoring a dead mortal body to a living mortal body. True resurrection carries with it *glorification*. There are three such resurrections:

a. The resurrection of Christ (Mt. 28:5-8; Mk. 16:2-8; Lk. 24:1-8).

b. The rapture resurrection.

"For this corruptible must put on incorruption, and this mortal must put on immortality" (1 Cor. 15:53).

"For the Lord himself shall descend from heaven with a shout, with the voice of the archangel, and with the trump of God: and the dead in Christ shall rise first" (1 Thess. 4:16).

c. The premillennial resurrection of Old Testament and tribulation saints.

"Verily, verily, I say unto you, He that heareth my word, and believeth on him that sent me, hath everlasting life, and shall not come into condemnation; but is passed from death unto life" (Jn. 5:24).

"And many of them that sleep in the dust of the earth shall awake, some to everlasting life, and some to shame and everlasting contempt" (Dan. 12:2).

"But the rest of the dead lived not again until the thousand years were finished. This is the first resurrection. Blessed and holy is he that hath part in the first resurrection: on such the second death hath no power, but they shall be priests of God and of Christ, and shall reign with him a thousand years" (Rev. 20:5, 6).

5. The nature of the resurrection.

What kind of body did Jesus have after his resurrection? This is of great importance to the believer, for we someday will have a similar body. (See 1 Jn. 3:1-3.)

a. His new body had flesh and bone.

"Behold my hands and my feet, that it is I myself: handle me, and see; for a spirit hath not flesh and bones, as ye see me have. And when he had thus spoken, he showed them his hands and his feet" (Lk. 24:39, 40).

b. He ate food in this new body (see Lk. 24:41-43; Jn. 21:12, 13).

c. His new body still bore the marks of his crucifixion.

"Then saith he to Thomas, Reach hither thy finger, and behold my hands; and reach hither thy hand, and thrust it into my side: and be not faithless, but believing" (Jn. 20:27).

"And when he had thus spoke, he showed them his hands and his feet" (Lk. 24:40).

"And I beheld, and, lo, in the midst of the throne and of the four beasts, and in the midst of the elders, stood a Lamb as it had been slain, having seven horns and seven eyes, which are the seven Spirits of God sent forth into all the earth" (Rev. 5:6).

d. His new body was not subjected to material laws.

"Then the same day at evening, being the first day of the week, when the doors were shut where the disciples were assembled for fear of the Jews, came Jesus and stood in the midst, and saith unto them, Peace be unto you" (Jn. 20:19).

"And their eyes were opened, and they knew him; and he vanished out of their sight. And as they thus spake, Jesus himself stood in the midst of them, and saith unto them, Peace be unto you" (Lk. 24:31, 36).

6. The example of the resurrection: a grain of wheat (Jn. 12:24; 1 Cor. 15:35-38).

7. The superiority of the resurrection (1 Cor. 15:39-41).

The new body is as superior to the old body as:

a. Man is to beast.

b. Heaven is to the earth.

c. The sun is to the moon.

8. The results of the resurrection (1 Cor. 15:42-58).

a. In relation to the believer: *immediate blessings.*

(1) A guarantee of our justification.

"Who was delivered for our offenses, and was raised again for our justification" (Rom. 4:25).

(2) A guarantee of present-day power and strength (Eph. 1:18—2:10).

(3) A guarantee of fruitful labor.

"Therefore, my beloved brethren, be ye steadfast, unmovable, always abounding in the work of the Lord, forasmuch as ye know that your labour is not in vain in the Lord (1 Cor. 15:58).

(4) A guarantee of our own resurrection.

"Knowing that he which raised up the Lord Jesus shall raise up us also by Jesus, and shall present us with you" (2 Cor. 4:14).

Future blessings.

(5) Exchanging corruption for incorruption (1 Cor. 15:42).

(6) Exchanging dishonor for glory (1 Cor. 15:43).

(7) Exchanging weakness for power (1 Cor. 15:43).

(8) Exchanging a material body for a spiritual body (1 Cor. 15:44).

b. In relation to the Savior:

(1) It is the mark of his deity.

"And declared to be the Son of God with power, according to the spirit of holiness, by the resurrection from the dead" (Rom. 1:4).

"Him God raised up the third day, and showed him openly" (Acts 10:40).

(2) It is the springboard of his exaltation.

"The God of our fathers raised up Jesus, whom ye slew and hanged on a tree. Him hath God exalted with his right hand to be a Prince and a Saviour, for to give repentence to Israel, and forgiveness of sins" (Acts 5:30, 31).

"Wherefore God also hath highly exalted him, and given him a name which is above every name: that at the name of Jesus every knee should bow, of things in heaven, and things in earth, and things under the earth; and that every tongue should confess that Jesus Christ is Lord, to the glory of God the Father" (Phil. 2:9-11).

(3) It marks the beginning of his headship over the church.

"And what is the exceeding greatness of his power to usward who believe, according to the working of his mighty power, which he wrought in Christ, when he raised him from the dead, and set him at his own right hand in the heavenly places, far above all principality, and power, and might, and dominion, and every name that is named, not only in this world, but also in that which is to come: And hath put all things under his feet, and gave him to be the head over all things to the church, which is his body, the fullness of him that filleth all in all" (Eph. 1:19-23).

c. In relation to the sinner: It warns him of a coming judgment day.

"Because he hath appointed a day, in the which he will judge the world in righteousness by that man whom he hath ordained; whereof he hath given assurance unto all men in that he hath raised him from the dead" (Acts 17:31).

d. In relation to the devil: It seals his doom forever (Heb. 2:14; Rev. 20:10).

e. In relationship to the Sabbath: It transfers the worship day from Saturday to Sunday (Acts 20:7; 1 Cor. 16:2; Heb. 7:12).

f. The symbol of the resurrection: Baptism (Rom. 6:3-11; Col. 2:11-13).

XVII. The Ascension and Present Ministry of Jesus Christ.
  A. The fact of this ascension and ministry.
    1. Scripture regarding his ascension.
       "So then after the Lord had spoken unto them, he was received up into heaven, and sat on the right hand of God" (Mk. 16:19).
       "And it came to pass, while he blessed them, he was parted from them, and carried up into heaven" (Lk. 24:51).
       "And when he had spoken these things, while they beheld, he was taken up; and a cloud received him out of their sight" (Acts 1:9).
    2. Scripture regarding his present ministry.
       "Who is he that condemneth? It is Christ, that died, yea rather, that is risen again, who is even at the right hand of God who also maketh intercession for us" (Rom. 8:34).
       "If ye then be risen with Christ, seek those things which are above, where Christ sitteth on the right hand of God" (Col. 3:1).
       "Who being the brightness of his glory, and the express image of his person, and upholding all things by the word of his power, when he had by himself purged our sins, sat down on the right hand of the Majesty on high" (Heb. 1:3).
       "Now of the things which we have spoken this is the sum: We have such a high priest, who is set on the right hand of the throne of the Majesty in the heavens" (Heb. 8:1).
       "But this man, after he had offered one sacrifice for sins for ever, sat down on the right hand of God; from henceforth expecting till his enemies be made his footstool" (Heb. 10:12, 13).
       "Looking unto Jesus the author and finisher of our faith; who for the joy that was set before him endured the cross, despising the shame, and is set down at the right hand of the throne of God" (Heb. 12:2).
       "Who is gone into heaven, and is on the right hand of God; angels and authorities and powers being made subject unto him" (1 Pet. 3:22).
  B. The purpose of this ascension and ministry.
    1. To be our Forerunner.
       "Which hope we have as an anchor of the soul, both sure and steadfast, and which entereth into that within the veil; whither the forerunner is for us entered, even Jesus, made a high priest for ever after the order of Melchizedek" (Heb. 6:19, 20).
    2. To prepare a place for us.
       "In my Father's house are many mansions: if it were not so, I would have told you. I go to prepare a place for you" (Jn. 14:2).
    3. To give spiritual gifts to his followers (Eph. 4:10-14).
    4. To offer encouragement to his followers.
       "Seeing then that we have a great high priest, that is passed into the heavens, Jesus the Son of God, let us hold fast our profession. For we have not an high priest which cannot be touched with the feeling of our infirmities; but was in all points tempted like as we are, yet without sin. Let us therefore come boldly unto the throne of grace, that we may obtain mercy, and find grace to help in time of need" (Heb 4:14-16).
       "Wherefore seeing we also are compassed about with so great a cloud of witnesses, let us lay aside every weight, and the sin which doth so easily beset us, and let us run with patience the race that is set before us, looking unto Jesus the author and finisher of our faith; who for the joy that was set before him endured the cross, despising the shame, and is set down at the right hand of the throne of God. For consider him that endured such contradiction of sinners against himself, lest ye be wearied and faint in your minds" (Heb. 12:1-3).
    5. To make high priestly prayers for us (Rom. 8:34; Heb. 4:14-16; 7:25-27; 8:1; 9:24).
       Here he functions in a twofold manner:
       a. Acting as our *Intercessor* (due to the weakness and frailties of the believer).
          While on earth, our Lord once told Peter:
          "Simon, Simon, behold, Satan hath desired to have you, that he may sift you as wheat: But I have prayed for thee, that thy faith fail not . . . " (Lk. 22:31, 32).
          According to many New Testament passages, the Savior continues to peform this blessed ministry for his people from heaven.
          "Wherefore he is able to save them to the uttermost that come unto God by him, seeing he ever liveth to make intercession for them" (Heb. 7:25).
       b. Acting as our *Advocate* (due to the sins of the believer).
          "If we confess our sins, he is faithful and just to forgive us our sins, and to cleanse us from all unrighteousness" (1 Jn. 1:9).
          "My little children, these things write I unto you, that ye sin not. And if any man sin, we have an advocate with the Father, Jesus Christ the righteous" (1 Jn. 2:1).
          "For Christ is not entered into the holy places made with hands, which are the figures of the true; but into heaven itself, now to appear in the presence of God for us" (Heb. 9:24).
          "And I heard a loud voice saying in heaven, Now is come salvation, and strength, and the kingdom of

our God, and the power of his Christ: for the accuser of our brethren is cast down, which accused them before our God day and night" (Rev. 12:10).

6. To send the promise of the Father (Holy Spirit) (Jn. 16; Acts 1:4; 2:33).

7. To care for his churches (Rev. 1:10—3:22). In this amazing passage, the Apostle John, on the Isle of Patmos, sees the resurrected and glorified Christ standing among seven golden lampstands, dressed in the garb of a high priest. He is told that the lampstands symbolize local churches on earth.

8. To work through his people.

"Verily, verily, I say unto you, He that believeth on me, the works that I do shall he do also; and greater works than these shall he do; because I go unto my Father" (Jn. 14:12).

9. To wait until his enemies become his footstool (Heb. 10:12, 13).

XVIII. The Twofold Future Coming of Jesus Christ.

A. At the rapture—for his people.

"But I would not have you to be ignorant, brethren, concerning them which are asleep, that ye sorrow not, even as others which have no hope. For if we believe that Jesus died and rose again, even so them also which sleep in Jesus will God bring with him. For this we say unto you by the word of the Lord, that we which are alive and remain unto the coming of the Lord shall not prevent them which are asleep. For the Lord himself shall descend from heaven with a shout, with the voice of the archangel, and with the trump of God: and the dead in Christ shall rise first: Then we which are alive and remain shall be caught up together with them in the clouds, to meet the Lord in the air: and so shall we ever be with the Lord. Wherefore comfort one another with these words" (1 Thess. 4:13-18).

"Behold, I show you a mystery; We shall not all sleep, but we shall all be changed, In a moment, in the twinkling of an eye, at the last trump: for the trumpet shall sound, and the dead shall be raised incorruptible, and we shall be changed. For this corruptible must put on incorruption, and this mortal must put on immortality. So when this corruptible shall have put on incorruption, and this mortal shall have put on immortality, then shall be brought to pass the saying that is written, Death is swallowed up in victory. O death, where is thy sting? O grave, where is thy victory? The sting of death is sin; and the strength of sin is the law. But thanks be to God, which giveth us the victory through our Lord Jesus Christ" (1 Cor. 15:51-57).

B. After the tribulation—with his people.

"Immediately after the tribulation of those days shall the sun be darkened, and the moon shall not give her light, and the stars shall fall from heaven, and the powers of the heavens shall be shaken: And then shall appear the sign of the Son of man in heaven: and then shall all the tribes of the earth mourn, and they shall see the Son of man coming in the clouds of heaven with power and great glory. And he shall send his angels with a great sound of a trumpet, and they shall gather together his elect from the four winds, from one end of heaven to the other" (Mt. 24:29-31).

"And Enoch also, the seventh from Adam, prophesied of these, saying, Behold, the Lord cometh with ten thousands of his saints" (Jude 14).

"Behold, he cometh with clouds; and every eye shall see him, and they also which pierced him: and all kindreds of the earth shall wail because of him. Even so, Amen" (Rev. 1:7).

"And I saw heaven opened, and behold a white horse; and he that sat upon him was called Faithful and True, and in righteousness he doth judge and make war. His eyes were as a flame of fire, and on his head were many crowns; and he had a name written, that no man knew, but he himself. And he was clothed with a vesture dipped in blood: and his name is called The Word of God. And the armies which were in heaven followed him upon white horses, clothed in fine linen, white and clean. And out of his mouth goeth a sharp sword, that with it he should smite the nations: and he shall rule them with a rod of iron: and he treadeth the winepress of the fierceness and wrath of Almighty God. And he hath on his vesture and on his thigh a name written, KING OF KINGS, AND LORD OF LORDS. And I saw an angel standing in the sun; and he cried with a loud voice, saying to all the fowls that fly in the midst of heaven, Come and gather yourselves together unto the supper of the great God; that ye may eat the flesh of kings, and the flesh of captains, and the flesh of mighty men, and the flesh of horses, and of them that sit on them, and the flesh of all men, both free and bond, both small and great. And I saw the beast, and the kings of the earth, and their armies, gathered together to make war against him that sat on the horse, and against his army. And the beast was taken, and with him the false prophet that wrought miracles before him, with which he deceived them that had received the mark of the beast, and them that worshipped his image. These both were cast alive into a lake of fire burning with brimstone. And the remnant were slain with the sword of him that sat upon the horse, which sword proceeded out of his mouth: and all the fowls were filled with their flesh" (Rev. 19:11-21).

XIX. The Millennial Reign of Jesus Christ.

"For unto us a child is born, unto us a son is given: and the government shall be upon his shoulder: and his name shall be called Wonderful, Counsellor, The mighty God, The everlasting Father, The Prince of Peace. Of the increase of his government and peace there shall be no end, upon the throne of David, and upon his kingdom, to order it, and to establish it with judgment and with justice from henceforth even for ever. The zeal of the Lord of hosts will perform this" (Isa. 9:6, 7).

"Behold, the days come, saith the Lord, that I will raise unto David a righteous Branch, and a King shall reign and prosper, and shall execute judgment and justice in the earth. In his days Judah shall be saved, and Israel shall dwell safely: and this is his name whereby he shall be called, THE LORD OUR RIGHTEOUSNESS" (Jer. 23:5, 6).

"He shall be great, and shall be called the Son of the Highest: and the Lord God shall give unto him the throne of his father David: And he shall reign over the house of Jacob for ever; and of his kingdom there shall be no end" (Lk. 1:32, 33).

"Pilate therefore said unto him, Art thou a king then? Jesus answered, Thou sayest that I am a king. To this end was I born, and for this cause came I into the world, that I should bear witness unto the truth. Every one that is of the truth heareth my voice" (Jn. 18:37).

XX. The Old Testament Witnesses of Jesus Christ. The Bible is a Christ-centered book. Jesus himself said the Old Testament spoke of him (Jn. 5:39). Following is a brief panorama of his story in history, as demonstrated by some Old Testament men and women. Events in their lives remind us of some aspect in the Savior's New Testament ministry.

A. Adam: his headship over a new creation (Gen. 1:28; Rom. 5:17-19; 1 Cor. 15:22, 45, 47; Heb. 2:7-9).

B. Moses: his prophetical ministry (Deut. 18:15-18; Heb. 3:5, 6).

C. Melchizedek: his priestly ministry (Gen. 14:18-20; Ps. 110:4; Heb. 5-8).

D. David: his kingly ministry (2 Sam. 7:1-17; Mk. 11:10; Rev. 5:5; 22:16).

E. Jeremiah: his sorrows (Jer. 3:20; 5:1-5; 8:20-22; 9:1; 10:19; 11:19).

F. Joseph: his sufferings (the most perfect type of Christ in the Old Testament).

   1. Hated without a cause (Gen. 37:4, 8; Jn. 15:25).

   2. Ridiculed (Gen. 37:19; Lk. 22:63).

   3. Plotted against (Gen. 37:20; Jn. 11:53).

   4. Stripped of his robe (Gen. 37:23; Jn. 19:23, 24).

   5. Sold for silver (Gen. 37:28; Mt. 26:14-16).

   6. Lied about (Gen. 39:14; Mt. 26:61).

   7. Placed in captivity with two guilty men (Gen. 40:1-3; Lk. 23:32, 33).

   8. Unrecognized by his own (Gen. 42:8; Jn. 1:11).

G. Isaac: his death (Gen. 22:2, 8, 10; Mt. 26:36, 42, 43).

H. Jonah: his resurrection (Jonah 1:17; Mt. 12:40; 16:4; Lk. 11:29).

I. Joshua: his victorious life (Josh. 1:3, 5, 6, 8, 9; Jn. 10:17, 18; 19:30).

J. Noah: his saving life (Gen. 6:13, 14, 17, 18; 1 Pet. 3:18-22).

K. Abraham: his father (Gen. 22:7, 8; Mt. 26:36, 42, 43).

L. Daniel: his acceptance by the Father (Dan. 9:23; 10:11, 19; Mt. 3:17; 17:5).

M. Elijah: his forerunner (Isa. 40:3, 4; Mt. 17:11, 12).

N. Elisha: his miracles: Elisha performs fourteen miracles, nearly double those of any other Old Testament man, except Moses (2 Ki. 2:9; Jn. 3:2).

O. Ezekiel: his parables. There are sixty-nine parables in the Old Testament; twenty-three are to be found in Ezekiel's book alone (Ezek. 17:2; 20:49; Mt. 13:3).

P. Ruth: his church (Ruth 2-4; 2 Cor. 11:2).

Q. Boaz: his love for the church (Ruth 2-4; Eph. 5:25-27).

R. Ezra: his zeal for the Scriptures (Neh. 8; Mt. 21:42; 22:29; Mk. 12:10, 24; Lk. 4:21; 24:27; Jn. 10:35).

S. Nehemiah: his zeal for the Holy City (Neh. 1-2; Mt. 23:37-39; Lk. 19:41).

T. Absalom: his opposition:

   1. From Judas. Absalom was a betrayer and member of David's inner circle, as was Judas of Jesus' inner circle (2 Sam. 15; Mt. 26:14).

   2. From the coming antichrist. Absalom plotted against the Davidic throne, as will the antichrist (2 Sam. 15; Rev. 13).

U. Solomon: his wisdom (1 Ki. 3:11-13; Lk. 4:22; Jn. 7:46).

V. Lot: his backslidden followers (Gen. 19; 2 Pet. 2:7).

The SON of God in the WORD of God

GENESIS 3:15; 49:10	Seed of the woman and Shiloh
EXODUS 12:3	Passover Lamb
LEVITICUS 8:7-9	Anointed high Priest
NUMBERS 21:8; 24:17	Star of Jacob and brazen serpent
DEUTERONOMY 18:15; 32:4	Prophet like Moses and great Rock
JOSHUA 5:14	Captain of the Lord's host
JUDGES 2:1	Messenger of Jehovah
RUTH 2:1	Kinsman-Redeemer
1 SAMUEL 2:10	Great Judge
2 SAMUEL 7:13	Seed of David
1 KINGS 8:15, 26	Lord God of Israel
2 KINGS 19:15	God of the cherubim
1 CHRONICLES 16:35	God of our salvation
2 CHRONICLES 20:6	God of our fathers
EZRA 1:2	Lord of heaven and earth
NEHEMIAH 1:5	Covenant-keeping God
ESTHER	The God of providence
JOB 19:25	Risen and returning Redeemer
PSALMS 2:1, 7, 12; 16:10; 23:1; 24:7-10	The anointed Son, the Holy One, The Good Shepherd, and the King of Glory
PROVERBS Chapter 8	The wisdom of God
ECCLESIASTES	The one above the sun
SONG OF SOLOMON 5:10; 16	Chiefest among 10,000 and altogether lovely
ISAIAH 7:14; 9:6; 52:13; 53:3	Virgin-born Immanuel; Child and Son; Wonderful, Counselor, Mighty God, Everlasting Father, Prince of Peace; Righteous Servant, and Man of Sorrows
JEREMIAH: 23:6; 33:16	The Lord our righteousness
LAMENTATIONS 3:22, 23, 31-33	The faithful and compassionate God
EZEKIEL	The Lord is there
DANIEL 2:34; 3:25; 7:13	Smiting Stone, Son of God, Son of man
HOSEA 13:9, 14	King of the resurrection
JOEL 2:28-32; 2:11; 3:2, 9-17	God of the battle and giver of the Spirit
AMOS 4:13; 7:9	God of hosts and of the plumbline
OBADIAH 1:8, 15	Destroyer of the proud
JONAH 2:10; 3:1; 4:9-11	The risen Prophet, God of second choice, The long-suffering one
MICAH 4:1-5; 5:2; 7:18, 19	God of Jacob, the Bethlehemite, and the pardoning God
NAHUM 1:2, 15	The avenging God and bringer of good tidings
HABAKKUK 1:12, 13; 2:14; 3:13	The everlasting pure, glorious, and anointed one
ZEPHANIAH 3:15	The King of Israel

The SON of God in the WORD of God

HAGGAI 2:7	Desire of all nations
ZECHARIAH 3:8; 6:12; 6:13; 9:9; 12:10; 14:9	Branch, builder of Temple, King of Triumphal entry, pierced one, King of the earth
MALACHI 3:16	Lord of remembrance
MATTHEW 2:2; 27:37	King of the Jews
MARK 9:35; 10:43, 44	Servant
LUKE 2:40, 52; 9:22, 56, 58; 22:48	Perfect man
JOHN 1:1-5; 20:28, 31	Eternal God
ACTS 1:9	Ascended Lord
ROMANS 10:4	The Lord our righteousnes
1 CORINTHIANS Chapter 15	Our resurrection
2 CORINTHIANS 1:3	God of all comfort
GALATIANS 4:4, 5	Redeemer from the law
EPHESIANS 1:22; 2:20; 5:23; 4:7, 8	Head of the church and giver of gifts
PHILIPPIANS 1:19; 4:19; 2:5-8	Supplier of every need and obedient Servant
COLOSSIANS 1:19; 2:9	Fullness of the Godhead
1 THESSALONIANS 4:13-18; 5:2, 23	The coming Christ
2 THESSALONIANS 2:8	The consuming Christ
1 TIMOTHY 2:15; 3:16; 1:15	Mediator and Savior of sinners
2 TIMOTHY 4:8; 3:16, 17	Righteous and rewarding Judge and author of Scripture
TITUS 1:3; 2:10, 13; 3:4	Our great God and Savior
PHILEMON	Payer of our debt
HEBREWS 1:2 **1:4; 3:3** **2:10; 5:9; 12:2** **2:17; 3:1, 4:14** **7:25-27; 9:24** **12:24** **13:20**	Appointed Heir of all things One better than the prophets and angels Captain of our salvation Merciful and faithful High Priest Great Intercessor Mediator of new covenant Great Shepherd of the sheep
JAMES 4:6-8; 5:15; 5:7, 8	Ever-present God, Great Physician, and the coming one
1 PETER 1:19; 2:21-24; 5:4; 3:22	Unblemished Lamb, great example, Chief Shepherd, Lord of Glory
2 PETER 1:17	The beloved Son
1 JOHN 1:1; 2:1; 2:2; 3:8; 4:15; 5:5	Word of life, advocate, propitiation, and Son of God
2 JOHN 1:3	Son of the Father
3 JOHN 1:4, 8	The Truth
JUDE 1:1, 25	Preserver and only wise God
REVELATION 1:8; 5:5 **5:7; 6:17** **19:16** **22:16**	The Alpha and Omega, Lion of Judah, The slain and angry Lamb, The King of kings The bright and morning Star

THE DOCTRINE OF THE FATHER

THE DOCTRINE OF THE FATHER

Imagine yourself among a group of Christians who have been given a biblical test with but three essay questions on it. Here are the questions.

Number 1

Put down everything you know about the Person and work of Jesus Christ, the second Person in the Trinity. (Probably most of the group could fill several pages of material about the Savior in a reasonable amount of time. So far, so good!)

Number 2

Put down everything you know about the Person and work of the Holy Spirit, the third Person in the Trinity. (Now the pens do not move as rapidly or as confidently as before. There are long pauses between sentences. At the end of the given time period the average believer has probably written at least one-half page or more.)

Number 3

Put down everything you know about the Person and work of God the Father, first Person in the Trinity. (Oh, how silent the room now becomes! Finally, one statement is written: "He is the Father of Jesus Christ." But what can be added to this? It is my opinion that precious few in that group of Christians would be able to write even one-half dozen lines about the Father.)

This all but universal ignorance about the Father is inexcusable, for he is mentioned by the Savior alone well over 200 times during his earthly ministry. Our Lord taught the following about him:

    A. He is spirit (Jn. 4:24).
    B. He is omnipotent (Mt. 19:26).
    C. He is omniscient (Mt. 10:29).
    D. He is holy (Jn. 17:11).
    E. He is righteous (Jn. 17:25).
    F. He is loving (Jn. 3:16; 17:23).
    G. He is good (Mt. 6:26, 28–30; 10:29, 30).

    W. Graham Scroggie writes:
      "But the outstanding truth which Christ taught about God is that He is *Father*. This term, applied to Him, occurs 189 times—in Matthew, 44; in Mark 4; in Luke, 17; and in John, 124." (*A Guide to the Gospels,* p. 560)

I. He is the Father of all life.
    "For with thee is the fountain of life: in thy light shall we see light" (Ps. 36:9).
    "For as the Father hath life in himself; so hath he given to the Son to have life in himself" (Jn. 5:26).
    "God that made the world and all things therein . . . he giveth to all life, and breath, and all things" (Acts 17:24, 25).

"This I say therefore, and testify in the Lord, that ye henceforth walk not as other Gentiles walk, in the vanity of their mind, having the understanding darkened, being alienated from the life of God through the ignorance that is in them, because of the blindness of their heart" (Eph. 4:17, 18).

"The heavens declare the glory of God; and the firmament sheweth his handiwork" (Ps. 19:1).

"Praise ye him, all his angels: praise ye him, all his hosts. Praise ye him, sun and moon: praise him, all ye stars of light. Praise him, ye heavens of heavens, and ye waters that be above the heavens. Let them praise the name of the Lord: for he commanded, and they were created" (Ps. 148:2–5).

See also Colossians 1:16.

A. He tends and cares for vegetation.
    "He causeth the grass to grow for the cattle, and herb for the service of man: that he may bring forth food out of the earth. . . . The trees of the Lord are full of sap; the cedars of Lebanon, which he hath planted" (Ps. 104:14, 16).
    "And why take ye thought for raiment? Consider the lilies of the field, how they grow; they toil not, neither do they spin: And yet I say unto you, That even Solomon in all his glory was not arrayed like one of these. Wherefore, if God so clothe the grass of the field, which today is, and tomorrow is cast into the oven, shall he not much more clothe you, O ye of little faith?" (Mt. 6:28–30).

B. He tends and cares for brute nature.
    "He causeth the grass to grow for the cattle, and herb for the service of man: that he may bring forth food out of the earth. . . . The trees of the Lord are full of sap; the cedars of Lebanon, which he hath planted; where the birds make their nests: as for the stork, the fir trees are her house. The high hills are a refuge for the wild goats; and the rocks for the conies. . . . Thou makest darkness, and it is night: wherein all the beasts of the forest do creep forth. The young lions roar after their prey, and seek their meat from God. . . . These wait all upon thee; that thou mayest give them their meat in due season" (Ps. 104:14, 16, 18, 20, 21, 27).
    "Behold the fowls of the air: for they sow not, neither do they reap, nor gather into barns; yet your heavenly Father feedeth them. Are ye not much better than they? . . . Are not two sparrows sold for a farthing? and one of them shall not fall on the ground without your Father" (Mt. 6:26; 10:29).

C. He tends and cares for the weather.

"Whatsoever the Lord pleased, that did he in heaven, and in earth, in the seas, and all deep places. He causeth the vapours to ascend from the ends of the earth; he maketh lightnings for the rain; he bringeth the wind out of his treasuries" (Ps. 135:6, 7).

"Who covereth the heaven with clouds, who prepareth rain for the earth, who maketh grass to grow upon the mountains. . . . He giveth snow like wool: he scattereth the hoarfrost like ashes. He casteth forth his ice like morsels: who can stand before his cold? He sendeth out his word, and melteth them: he causeth his wind to blow, and the waters flow" (Ps. 147:8, 16, 18).

"Fire, and hail; snow, and vapours; stormy wind fulfilling his word" (Ps. 148:8).

D. He tends and cares for the seasons.

"While the earth remaineth, seedtime and harvest, and cold and heat, and summer and winter, and day and night shall not cease" (Gen. 8:22).

"Nevertheless he left not himself without witness, in that he did good, and gave us rain from heaven, and fruitful seasons, filling our hearts with food and gladness" (Acts 14:17).

II. He Is the Father of Our Lord Jesus Christ. During his earthly ministry Jesus spoke more about the Father than any other subject.

A. The Father sent his Son.

"Then said Jesus to them again, peace be unto you: as my Father hath sent me, even so send I you" (Jn. 20:21).

"As the living Father hath sent me, and I live by the Father" (Jn. 6:57).

"The Father that sent me beareth witness of me" (Jn. 8:18).

"But when the fulness of the time was come, God sent forth his Son, made of a woman" (Gal. 4:4).

"And we have seen and do testify that the Father sent the Son to be the Saviour of the world" (1 Jn. 4:14; see also Jn. 3:16; 8:16; 12:49).

B. The Father commanded the angels to worship his Son.

"And . . . when he bringeth in the first begotten into the world, he saith, And let all the angels of God worship him" (Heb. 1:6; see also Lk. 2:8–15).

C. He sealed his Son.

"Labour not for the meat which perisheth, but for that meat which endureth unto everlasting life, which the Son of man shall give unto you: for him hath God the Father sealed" (Jn. 6:27).

D. He honored (and honors) his Son.

"Jesus answered, If I honour myself, my hour is nothing: it is my Father that honoureth me; of whom ye say, that he is your God" (Jn. 8:54).

E. He bore witness to his Son (Jn. 8:18).

F. He loved (and loves) his Son.

"Therefore doth my Father love me, because I lay down my life, that I might take it again" (Jn. 10:17).

G. He glorified his Son.

"Now is my soul troubled; and what shall I say? Father, save me from this hour: but for this cause came I unto this hour. Father, glorify thy name. Then came there a voice from heaven, saying, I have both glorified it, and will glorify it again" (Jn. 12:27, 28).

"These words spake Jesus, and lifted up his eyes to heaven, and said, Father, the hour is come; glorify thy Son, that thy Son also may glorify thee. . . . And now, O Father, glorify thou me with thine own self with the glory which I had with thee before the world was" (Jn. 17:1, 5).

H. He taught his Son.

"Then said Jesus unto them, When ye have lifted up the Son of man, then shall ye know that I am he, and that I do nothing of myself; but as my Father hath taught me, I speak these things" (Jn. 8:28).

I. He anointed his Son.

"And he came to Nazareth, where he had been brought up: and, as his custom was, he went into the synagogue on the sabbath day, and stood up for to read. And there was delivered unto him the book of the prophet Esaias. And when he had opened the book, he found the place where it was written, The Spirit of the Lord is upon me, because he hath anointed me to preach the gospel to the poor; he hath sent me to heal the brokenhearted, to preach deliverance to the captives, and recovering of sight to the blind, to set at liberty them that are bruised, To preach the acceptable year of the Lord. And he closed the book, and he gave it again to the minister, and sat down. And the eyes of all them that were in the synagogue were fastened on him. And he began to say unto them, This day is this scripture fulfilled in your ears" (Lk. 4:16-21).

"For he whom God hath sent speaketh the words of God: for God giveth not the Spirit by measure unto him" (Jn. 3:34).

J. He delighted in his Son.

"Behold my servant, whom I uphold; mine elect, in whom my soul delighteth; I have put my spirit upon him: he shall bring forth judgment to the Gentiles" (Isa. 42:1).

"And lo a voice from heaven, saying, This is my beloved Son, in whom I am well pleased" (Mt. 3:17).

"While he yet spake, behold, a bright cloud overshadowed them: and behold a voice out of the cloud, which said, This is my beloved Son, in whom I am well pleased; hear ye him" (Mt. 17:5).

"For he received from God the Father honour and glory, when there came such a voice to him from the excellent glory, This is my beloved Son, in whom I am well pleased" (2 Pet. 1:17).

K. He listened to his Son.

"Then they took away the stone from the place where the dead was laid. And Jesus lifted up his eyes, and said, Father, I thank thee that thou hast heard me. And I knew that thou hearest me always: but because of the people which stand by I said it, that they may believe that thou hast sent me" (Jn. 11:41, 42).

"Now is my soul troubled; and what shall I say? Father, save me from this hour: but for this cause came I unto this hour. Father, glorify thy name. Then came there a voice from heaven, saying, I have both glorified it, and will glorify it again" (Jn. 12:27, 28).

"Then said Jesus unto him, Put up again thy sword into his place: for all they that take the sword shall perish with the sword. Thinkest thou that I cannot now pray to my Father, and he shall presently give me more than twelve legions of angels?" (Mt. 26:52, 53).

L. He offered his Son.

"Then said Jesus unto Peter, Put up thy sword into the sheath: the cup which my Father hath given me, shall I not drink it?" (Jn. 18:11).

"He that spared not his own Son, but delivered him up for us all, how shall he not with him also freely give us all things?" (Rom. 8:32).

"In this was manifested the love of God toward us, because that God sent his only begotten Son into the world, that we might live through him. Herein is love, not that we loved God, but that he loved us, and sent his Son to be the propitiation for our sins" (1 Jn. 4:9, 10).

M. He was totally satisfied by his Son.

"And he that sent me is with me: the Father hath not left me alone; for I do always those things that please him" (Jn. 8:29).

N. He raised his Son.

"Paul, an apostle, (not of men, neither by man, but by Jesus Christ, and God the Father, who raised him from the dead)" (Gal. 1:1).

"Which he wrought in Christ, when he raised him from the dead, and set him at his own right hand in the heavenly places" (Eph. 1:20).

O. He exalts his Son.

"Wherefore God also hath highly exalted him, and given him a name which is above every name: That at the name of Jesus every knee should bow, of things in heaven, and things in earth, and things under the earth; and that every tongue should confess that Jesus Christ is Lord, to the glory of God the Father" (Phil. 2:9-11).

"Far above all principality, and power, and might, and dominion, and every name that is named, not only in this world, but also in that which is to come" (Eph. 1:21).

P. He makes his Son head of the church.

"And hath put all things under his feet, and gave him to be the head over all things to the church" (Eph. 1:22).

Q. He commits judgment unto his Son.

"The Father loveth the Son, and hath given all things into his hand" (Jn. 3:35).

"For the Father judgeth no man, but hath committed all judgment unto the Son. . . . And hath given him authority to execute judgment also, because he is the Son of man" (Jn. 5:22, 27).

Lewis Chafer writes the following concerning the relationship between the Father and the Son.

"The relationship of the second person to the first person has from all eternity been that of a Son, and, like all else, related to the Godhead, is not only eternal but is unchangeable. He did not become a Son of the Father, as some say that He did, by His incarnation, or by His resurrection, nor is He a Son by mere title, nor is He temporarily assuming such a relationship that He may execute His part in the covenant of Redemption.

He was the only begotten of the Father from all eternity, having no other relation to time and creation than that He is the Creator of them. It is evident that the Father and Son relationship sets forth only the features of emanation and manifestation and does not include the usual conception of derivation, inferiority, or distinction as to the time of beginning.

It is probable that the terms Father and Son, as applied to the first and second persons in the Godhead, are somewhat anthropomorphic in character. That sublime and eternal relationship which existed between these two persons is best expressed to human understanding in the terms of Father and Son, but wholly without implication that the two Persons, on the divine side, are not equal in every particular." (*Systematic Theology,* Vol. I, pp. 313-315)

III. He Is the Father of All Believers. While God is the *Creator* of all men (Gen. 1:27; Eccl. 12:1; Acts 17:24-26), he is the *Father* only of believers.

"Behold, what manner of love the Father hath bestowed upon us, that we should be called the sons of God: therefore the world knoweth us not, because it knew him not" (1 Jn. 3:1).

A. He foreknew the believer (Rom. 8:29; 1 Pet. 1:2).

B. He predestinated the believer.

"For whom he did foreknow, he also did predestinate to be conformed to the image of his Son, that he might be the firstborn among many brethren" (Rom. 8:29).

"In whom also we have obtained an inheritance, being predestinated according to the purpose of him who worketh all things after the counsel of his own will" (Eph. 1:11).

"And when the Gentiles heard this, they were glad, and glorified the word of the Lord: and as many as were ordained to eternal life believed" (Acts 13:48).

C. He elected the believer.

"According as he hath chosen us in him before the foundation of the world, that we should be holy and without blame before him in love" (Eph. 1:4).

"But we are bound to give thanks always to God for you, brethren beloved of the Lord, because God hath from the beginning chosen you to salvation through sanctification of the Spirit and belief of the truth" (2 Thess. 2:13).

"Peter, an apostle of Jesus Christ, to the strangers scattered throughout Pontus, Galatia, Cappadocia, Asia, and Bithynia, elect according to the foreknowledge of God the Father, through sanctification of the Spirit, unto obedience and sprinkling of the blood of Jesus Christ: Grace unto you, and peace, be multiplied" (1 Pet. 1:1, 2).

"Receiving the end of your faith, even the salvation of your souls" (1 Pet. 2:9).

D. He gave all the elected believers to Christ.

"All that the Father giveth me shall come to me; and him that cometh to me I will in no wise cast out" (Jn. 6:37).

"No man can come to me, except the Father which hath sent me draw him: and I will raise him up at the last day" (Jn. 6:44).

"My Father, which gave them me, is greater than all; and no man is able to pluck them out of my Father's hand" (Jn. 10:29).

"Jesus knowing that the Father had given all things into his hands, and that he was come from God, and went to God" (Jn. 13:3).

E. He called the believer (Rom. 8:30).

F. He conforms the believer to the image of Christ (Rom. 8:29).

G. He redeemed the believer.

"In whom we have redemption through his blood, the forgiveness of sins, according to the riches of his grace" (Eph. 1:7).

H. He justified the believer (Rom. 8:33).

I. He indwells the believer.

"Jesus answered and said unto him, If a man love me, he will keep my words: and my Father will love him, and we will come unto him, and make our abode with him" (Jn. 14:23).

J. He sealed the believer with the Holy Spirit.

"In whom ye also trusted, after that ye heard the word of truth, the gospel of your salvation: in whom also after that ye believed, ye were sealed with that holy Spirit of promise" (Eph. 1:13).

"And grieve not the holy Spirit of God, whereby ye are sealed unto the day of redemption" (Eph. 4:30).

It was, of course, the Father who sent the Holy Spirit at the request of Christ to the believer in the first place. See John 14:16, 26; 15:26.

K. He keeps the believer.

"My Father, which gave them me, is greater than all; and no man is able to pluck them out of my Father's hand" (Jn. 10:29).

"And now I am no more in the world, but these are in the world, and I come to thee. Holy Father, keep through thine own name those whom thou hast given me, that they may be one, as we are" (Jn. 17:11).

L. He honors the believer.

"If any man serve me, let him follow me; and where I am, there shall also my servant be: if any man serve me, him will my Father honour" (Jn. 12:26).

M. He blesses the believer.

"Blessed be the God and Father of our Lord Jesus Christ, who hath blessed us with all spiritual blessings in heavenly places in Christ" (Eph. 1:3).

N. He loves the believer.

"Now our Lord Jesus Christ himself, and God, even our Father, which hath loved us, and hath given us everlasting consolation and good hope through grace" (2 Thess. 2:16).

"He that hath my commandments, and keepeth them, he it is that loveth me: and he that loveth me shall be loved of my Father, and I will love him, and will manifest myself to him" (Jn. 14:21).

"And ye also shall bear witness, because ye have been with me from the beginning" (Jn. 15:27).

O. He comforts the believer.

"Blessed be God, even the Father of our Lord Jesus Christ, the Father of mercies, and the God of all comfort" (2 Cor. 1:3).

"And God shall wipe away all tears from their eyes; and there shall be no more death, neither sorrow, nor crying, neither shall there be any more pain: for the former things are passed away" (Rev. 21:4).

"Now our Lord Jesus Christ himself, and God, even our Father, which hath loved us, and hath given us everlasting consolation and good hope through grace" (2 Thess. 2:16).

P. He sanctifies the believer.

"Jude, the servant of Jesus Christ, and brother of James, to them that are sanctified by God the Father, and preserved in Jesus Christ, and called" (Jude 1).

"Sanctify them through thy truth: thy word is truth." (Jn. 17:17).

Q. He bestows peace upon the believer. (See Rom. 1:7; 1 Cor. 1:3; Gal. 1:3; Eph. 1:2; Phil. 1:2; Col. 1:2; 1 Thess. 1:1; 2 Thess. 1:2; Titus 1:4.)

R. He is glorified when the believer bears fruit.

"Herein is my Father glorified, that ye bear much fruit; so shall ye be my disciples" (Jn. 15:8).

S. He reveals truth to the believer.

"At that time Jesus answered and said, I thank thee, O Father, Lord of heaven and earth, because thou hast hid these things from the wise and prudent, and hast revealed them unto babes" (Mt. 11:25).

"And Jesus answered and said unto him, Blessed are thou, Simon Barjona: for flesh and blood hath not revealed it unto thee, but my Father which is in heaven" (Mt. 16:17).

"In that hour Jesus rejoiced in spirit, and said, I thank thee, O Father, Lord of heaven and earth, that thou hast hid these things from the wise and prudent, and hast revealed them unto babes: even so, Father; for so it seemed good in thy sight" (Lk. 10:21).

"That the God of our Lord Jesus Christ, the Father of glory, may give unto you the spirit of wisdom and revelation in the knowledge of him" (Eph. 1:17).

T. He supplies the needs of believers.

"(For after all these things do the Gentiles seek:) for your heavenly Father knoweth that ye have need of all these things. But seek ye first the kingdom of God, and his righteousness; and all these things shall be added unto you" (Mt. 6:32, 33).

"Who being past feeling have given themselves over unto lasciviousness, to work all uncleanness with greediness" (Phil. 4:19).

U. He seeks the worship of believers.

"But the hour cometh, and now is, when the true worshippers shall worship the Father in spirit and in truth: for the Father seeketh such to worship him" (Jn. 4:23).

V. He chastens believers.

"And ye have forgotten the exhortation which speaketh unto you as unto children, My son, despise not thou the chastening of the Lord, nor faint when thou art rebuked of him: For whom the Lord loveth he chasteneth, and scourgeth every son whom he receiveth. If ye endure chastening, God dealeth with you as with sons; for what son is he whom the father chasteneth not? But if ye be without chastisement, whereof all are partakers, then are ye bastards, and not sons. Furthermore we have had fathers of our flesh which corrected us, and we gave them reverence: shall we not much rather be in subjection unto the Father of spirits, and live? For they verily for a few days chastened us after their own pleasure; but he for our profit, that we might be partakers of his holiness" (Heb. 12:5–10).

W. He restores the believer.

"He restoreth my soul: he leadeth me in the paths of righteousness for his name's sake" (Ps. 23:3).

"Restore unto me the joy of thy salvation; and uphold me with thy free spirit" (Ps. 51:12).

"And the son said unto him, Father, I have sinned against heaven, and in thy sight, and am no more worthy to be called thy son. But the father said to his servants, Bring forth the best robe, and put it on him; and put a ring on his hand, and shoes on his feet: And bring hither the fatted calf, and kill it; and let us eat, and be merry: For this my son was dead, and is alive again; he was lost, and is found. And they began to be merry" (Lk. 15:21–24).

X. He will someday gather all believers in Christ.

"That in the dispensation of the fulness of times he might gather together in one all things in Christ, both which are in heaven, and which are on earth; even in him" (Eph. 1:10).

Y. He will someday reward all believers.

"Take heed that ye do not your alms before men, to be seen of them: otherwise ye have no reward of your Father which is in heaven" (Mt. 6:1).

"But without faith it is impossible to please him; for he that cometh to God must believe that he is, and that he is a rewarder of them that diligently seek him" (Heb. 11:6).

"Henceforth there is laid up for me a crown of righteousness, which the Lord, the righteous judge, shall give me at that day: and not to me only, but unto all them also that love his appearing" (2 Tim. 4:8).

Z. He will someday glorify all believers.

"Moreover whom he did predestinate, them he also called: and whom he called, them he also justified: and whom he justified, them he also glorified" (Rom. 8:30).

THE DOCTRINE OF THE HOLY SPIRIT

THE DOCTRINE OF THE HOLY SPIRIT

During one of his missionary trips, the Apostle Paul questioned a group of Ephesian "church members" (actually, they were disciples of John the Baptist) about the doctrine of the Holy Spirit. Their answer must have shocked him somewhat, for they replied, ". . . We have not so much as heard whether there be any Holy Ghost" (Acts 19:2).

If Paul was shocked, surely the Father and Son were saddened as they viewed yet another example of the almost universal ignorance concerning the ministry of the blessed third Person in the Trinity. This statement by these Ephesian disciples, perhaps as no other in the Bible, illustrates the sorry and shameful treatment often given him. His very existence has been ignored and his ministry misunderstood. May the prayer of song writer Andrew Reed be our prayer as we approach our study of the Holy Spirit:

"Holy Ghost, with light divine, Shine upon this heart of mine; Chase the shades of night away, Turn my darkness into day."

I. The Personality of the Holy Spirit. The Holy Spirit of God is a Person, as much as the Father and Son are Persons, and therefore experiences all the sinless elements involved within a divine personality.
    A. He has a mind.
        "And he that searcheth the hearts knoweth what is the mind of the Spirit, because he maketh intercession for the saints according to the will of God" (Rom. 8:27).
        The first "he" in this verse is a reference to the Son of God, as seen in verse 34 of Romans 8, while the second "he" refers to the Holy Spirit himself. What a fantastic truth is seen here, for the believer enjoys the intercessory ministry of both the Son and Holy Spirit.
    B. He searches out the human mind.
        "But God hath revealed them unto us by his Spirit: for the Spirit searcheth all things, yea, the deep things of God" (1 Cor. 2:10).
        In the verse just prior to this (2:9) Paul paraphrases from Isaiah 64:4 and writes:
        "But as it is written, eye hath not seen, nor ear heard, neither have entered into the heart of man, the things which God hath prepared for them that love him."
        Because of this, some have erroneously concluded that it is impossible for even the redeemed to know anything concerning heaven.
        But here in 2:10 we are told that the Holy Spirit reveals such things to us.
    C. He has a will.
        "But all these worketh that one and the self-same Spirit, dividing to every man severally as he will" (1 Cor. 12:11).
        This is a reference to the various spiritual gifts which the Holy Spirit imparts to believers as he determines.
    D. He forbids.
        "Now when they had gone throughout Phrygia and the region of Galatia, and were forbidden of the Holy Ghost to preach the word in Asia, after they were come to Mysia, they assayed to go into Bithynia: but the Spirit suffered them not" (Acts 16:6, 7).
        Here Paul, Silas, and Timothy were prohibited from going to two possible mission fields by the Spirit.
    E. He permits.
        "And after he had seen the vision, immediately we endeavored to go into Macedonia, assuredly gathering that the Lord had called us for to preach the gospel unto them" (Acts 16:10).
        This explains the reason for the previous prohibition.
    F. He speaks. Note to whom he speaks:
        1. To Philip in a desert.
            "Then the Spirit said unto Philip, Go near, and join thyself to this chariot" (Acts 8:29).
        2. To Peter on a housetop.
            "While Peter thought on the vision, the Spirit said unto him, Behold, three men seek thee" (Acts 10:19).
        3. To some elders in Antioch.
            "As they ministered to the Lord, and fasted, the Holy Ghost said, Separate me Barnabas and Saul for the work whereunto I have called them" (Acts 13:2).
        4. To seven churches in Asia Minor (Rev. 2–3). On no less than seven occasions (one to each church) do we read the words:
            "He that hath an ear, let him hear what the Spirit saith unto the churches" (see Rev. 2:7, 11, 17, 29; 3:6, 13, 22).
    G. He loves.
        "Now I beseech you, brethren, for the Lord Jesus Christ's sake, and for the love of the Spirit, that ye strive together with me in your prayers to God for me" (Rom. 15:30).
        It is wonderful to know that each believer is loved by the Father (Jn. 14:21; 16:27; 2 Cor. 9:7;

Eph. 2:4; 2 Thess. 2:16; Heb. 12:6), Son (Gal. 2:20; Eph. 3:19; Rev. 1:5; 3:19), *and* Holy Spirit.

H. He grieves.

"And grieve not the Holy Spirit of God, whereby ye are sealed unto the day of redemption" (Eph. 4:30).

The command here is, literally, "stop grieving the Holy Spirit of God." They were already doing this. (For further details concerning the nature of this grievance, see Rev. 2:4.) This grieving attribute of the Holy Spirit is really an extension of his love, for while one may be angered by his enemies, he can only be grieved by those he loves.

I. He prays.

"Likewise the Spirit also helpeth our infirmities: for we know not what we should pray for as we ought: but the Spirit itself maketh intercession for us with groanings which cannot be uttered" (Rom. 8:26).

In the difficult moments of our lives, how comforting it is to know we are being prayed for, perhaps by family members or some godly pastor, but how much more blessed to realize that the Holy Spirit of God offers up fervent and effective prayer for us.

In the New Testament alone there are some 261 passages which refer to the Holy Spirit. He is mentioned fifty-six times in the Gospels, fifty-seven times in the book of Acts, 112 times in the Pauline epistles, and thirty-six times in the remaining New Testament.

II. The Deity of the Holy Spirit.

A. He is omnipresent.

"Whither shall I go from thy Spirit? or whither shall I flee from thy presence?" (Ps. 139:7).

In this Psalm, David concludes it was impossible for him to escape God's Spirit. This was true even if he ascended to the heights, descended into the depths, traveled across the sea, or surrounded himself with darkness.

B. He is omniscient.

"But God hath revealed them unto us by his Spirit: for the Spirit searcheth all things, yea, the deep things of God. For what man knoweth the things of a man, save the spirit of man which is in him? even so the things of God knoweth no man, but the Spirit of God" (1 Cor. 2:10, 11).

C. He is omnipotent.

"And the earth was without form, and void; and darkness was upon the face of the deep. And the Spirit of God moved upon the face of the waters" (Gen. 1:2).

D. He is eternal.

"How much more shall the blood of Christ, who through the eternal Spirit offered himself without spot to God, purge your conscience from dead works to serve the living God?" (Heb. 9:14).

E. He is called God.

"But Peter said, Ananias, why hath Satan filled thine heart to lie to the Holy Ghost, and to keep back part of the price of the land? While it remained, was it not thine own? and after it was sold, was it not in thine own power? why hast thou conceived this thing in thine heart? thou hast not lied unto men, but unto God" (Acts 5:3, 4).

F. He is made equal with the Father and the Son. While the Holy Spirit does indeed occupy a place of submission in the Trinity, he is nevertheless not one whit behind the Father or Son in all their divine attributes. His perfect equality with the Father and Son is demonstrated through the following New Testament examples:

1. As seen in the baptismal experience of Christ.

"And Jesus, when he was baptized, went up straightway out of the water: and, lo, the heavens were opened unto him, and he saw the Spirit of God descending like a dove, and lighting upon him: And lo a voice from heaven, saying, This is my beloved Son, in whom I am well pleased" (Mt. 3:16, 17).

2. As seen in the temptation of Christ.

"Then was Jesus led up of the Spirit into the wilderness to be tempted of the devil. And when he had fasted forty days and forty nights, he was afterward ahungered. And when the tempter came to him, he said, If thou be the Son of God, command that these stones be made bread. But he answered and said, It is written, Man shall not live by bread alone, but by every word that proceedeth out of the mouth of God. Then the devil taketh him up into the holy city, and setteth him on a pinnacle of the temple, and saith unto him, If thou be the Son of God, cast thyself down: for it is written, He shall give his angels charge concerning thee: and in their hands they shall bear thee up, lest at any time thou dash thy foot against a stone. Jesus said unto him, It is written again, Thou shalt not tempt the Lord thy God" (Mt. 4:1-7).

3. As declared by Jesus in the upper room.

"And I will pray the Father, and he shall give you another Comforter, that he may abide with you for ever" (Jn. 14:16).

"But the Comforter, which is the Holy Ghost, whom the Father will send in my name, he shall teach you all things, and bring all things to your remembrance, whatsoever I have said unto you" (Jn. 14:26).

"But when the Comforter is come, whom I will send unto you from the Father, even the Spirit of truth, which proceedeth from the Father, he shall testify of me" (Jn. 15:26).

4. As declared by Paul.

"For through him we both have access by one Spirit unto the Father" (Eph. 2:18).

"The grace of the Lord Jesus Christ, and the love of God, and the communion of the Holy Ghost, be with you all. Amen" (2 Cor. 13:14).

"For the law of the Spirit of life in Christ Jesus hath made me free from the law of sin and death. For what the law could not do, in that it was weak through the flesh, God sending his own Son in the likeness of sinful flesh, and for sin, condemned sin in the flesh" (Rom. 8:2, 3).

5. As declared by Peter.
"Elect according to the foreknowledge of God the Father, through sanctification of the Spirit, unto obedience and sprinkling of the blood of Jesus Christ: Grace unto you, and peace, be multiplied" (1 Pet. 1:2).
"If ye be reproached for the name of Christ, happy are ye; for the Spirit of glory and of God resteth upon you: on their part he is evil spoken of, but on your part he is glorified" (1 Pet. 4:14).

6. As declared in the book of Acts.
"Therefore being by the right hand of God exalted, and having received of the Father the promise of the Holy Ghost, he hath shed forth this, which ye now see and hear" (Acts 2:33).

7. As declared by Jesus on the Mount of Olives.
"Go ye therefore, and teach all nations, baptizing them in the name of the Father, and of the Son, and of the Holy Ghost: Teaching them to observe all things whatsoever I have commanded you: and, lo, I am with you alway, even unto the end of the world. Amen" (Mt. 28:19, 20).

III. The Names and Titles of the Holy Spirit. Often in the Scripture one may learn much about someone simply by studying the names and titles given to that person. So it is with the Holy Spirit. The thirteen titles ascribed to him provide much insight into his true nature. He is called:

A. The Spirit of God.
"Know ye not that ye are the temple of God, and that the Spirit of God dwelleth in you?" (1 Cor. 3:16).

B. The Spirit of Christ.
"But ye are not in the flesh, but in the Spirit, if so be that the Spirit of God dwell in you. Now if any man have not the Spirit of Christ, he is none of his" (Rom. 8:9).

C. The eternal Spirit.
"How much more shall the blood of Christ, who through the eternal Spirit offered himself without spot to God, purge your conscience from dead works to serve the living God?" (Heb. 9:14).

D. The Spirit of truth.
"Howbeit when he, the Spirit of truth, is come, he will guide you into all truth: for he shall not speak of himself; but whatsoever he shall hear, that shall he speak: and he will show you things to come" (Jn. 16:13).

E. The Spirit of grace.
"Of how much sorer punishment, suppose ye, shall he be thought worthy, who hath trodden under foot the Son of God, and hath counted the blood of the covenant, wherewith he was sanctified, an unholy thing, and hath done despite unto the Spirit of grace?" (Heb. 10:29).

F. The Spirit of glory.
"If ye be reproached for the name of Christ, happy are ye: for the Spirit of glory and of

God resteth upon you: on their part he is evil spoken of, but on your part he is glorified" (1 Pet. 4:14).

G. The Spirit of life.
"For the law of the Spirit of life in Christ Jesus hath made me free from the law of sin and death" (Rom. 8:2).

H. The Spirit of wisdom and revelation.
"That the God of our Lord Jesus Christ, the Father of glory, may give unto you the spirit of wisdom and revelation in the knowledge of him" (Eph. 1:17).

I. The Comforter.
"But the Comforter, which is the Holy Ghost, whom the Father will send in my name, he shall teach you all things, and bring all things to your remembrance, whatsoever I have said unto you" (Jn. 14:26).

J. The Spirit of promise.
"And, being assembled together with them, commanded them that they should not depart from Jerusalem, but wait for the promise of the Father, which, saith he, ye have heard of me. For John truly baptized with water; but ye shall be baptized with the Holy Ghost not many days hence" (Acts 1:4, 5).

K. The Spirit of adoption.
"For ye have not received the spirit of bondage again to fear; but ye have received the Spirit of adoption, whereby we cry, Abba, Father" (Rom. 8:15).

L. The Spirit of holiness.
"And declared to be the Son of God with power, according to the Spirit of holiness, by the resurrection from the dead" (Rom. 1:4).

M. The Spirit of faith.
"We having the same spirit of faith, according as it is written, I believed, and therefore have I spoken; we also believe, and therefore speak" (2 Cor. 4:13).

IV. The Emblems of the Holy Spirit. Like the thirteen names and titles, his six designated emblems throw light upon both his nature and mission.

A. The Dove: indicating purity, peace, and modesty.
"And John bare record, saying, I saw the Spirit descending from heaven like a dove, and it abode upon him" (Jn. 1:32).
"My dove, my undefiled, is but one; she is the only one of her mother, she is the choice one of her that bare her. The daughters saw her, and blessed her; yea, the queens and the concubines, and they praised her" (Song of Sol. 6:9).
"And I said, Oh that I had wings like a dove! for then would I fly away, and be at rest" (Ps. 55:6).
"O my dove, that art in the clefts of the rock, in the secret places of the stairs, let me see thy countenance, let me hear thy voice; for sweet is thy voice, and thy countenance is comely" (Song of Sol. 2:14).

B. Water: indicating life and cleansing.
"For I will pour water upon him that is thirsty, and floods upon the dry ground: I will pour my Spirit upon thy seed, and my blessing upon thine offspring" (Isa. 44:3).

"In the last day, that great day of the feast, Jesus stood and cried, saying, If any man thirst, let him come unto me, and drink. He that believeth on me, as the Scripture hath said, out of his belly shall flow rivers of living water. (But this spake he of the Spirit, which they that believe on him should receive: for the Holy Ghost was not yet given; because that Jesus was not yet glorified)" (Jn. 7:37-39).

C. Oil: indicating light, healing, and anointing for service.

"The Spirit of the Lord is upon me, because he hath anointed me to preach the gospel to the poor; he hath sent me to heal the broken-hearted, to preach deliverance to the captives, and recovering of sight to the blind, to set at liberty them that are bruised" (Lk. 4:18).

"How God anointed Jesus of Nazareth with the Holy Ghost and with power: who went about doing good, and healing all that were oppressed of the devil; for God was with him" (Acts 10:38).

"Thou hast loved righteousness, and hated iniquity; therefore God, even thy God, hath anointed thee with the oil of gladness above thy fellows" (Heb. 1:9).

"But ye have an unction from the Holy One, and ye know all things" (1 Jn. 2:20).

D. A Seal: indicating ownership, finished transaction, identification, security, genuineness, value, authority.

"In whom ye also trusted, after that ye heard the word of truth, the gospel of your salvation: in whom also, after that ye believed, ye were sealed with that Holy Spirit of promise" (Eph. 1:13).

"And grieve not the Holy Spirit of God, whereby ye are sealed unto the day of redemption" (Eph. 4:30).

"Who hath also sealed us, and given the earnest of the Spirit in our hearts" (2 Cor. 1:22).

There are three important occasions in the Bible when a seal is used:

1. As used by Darius to place Daniel in the lion's den.

"Then the king commanded, and they brought Daniel, and cast him into the den of lions. Now the king spake and said unto Daniel, Thy God whom thou servest continually, he will deliver thee. And a stone was brought, and laid upon the mouth of the den; and the king sealed it with his own signet, and with the signet of his lords; that the purpose might not be changed concerning Daniel" (Dan. 6:16, 17).

2. As used by Ahasuerus (upon the advice of wicked Haman) to plot the wholesale murder of the Persian Jews.

"And Haman said unto king Ahasuerus, There is a certain people scattered abroad and dispersed among the people in all the provinces of thy kingdom; and their laws are diverse from all people; neither keep they the king's laws: therefore it is not for the king's profit to suffer them. If it please the king, let it be written that they may be destroyed: and I will pay ten thousand talents of silver to the hands of those that have the charge of the business, to bring it into the king's treasuries. And the king took his ring from his hand, and gave it unto Haman the son of Hammedatha the Agagite, the Jews' enemy. And the king said unto Haman, The silver is given to thee, the people also, to do with them as it seemeth good to thee. Then were the king's scribes called on the thirteenth day of the first month, and there was written according to all that Haman had commanded unto the king's lieutenants, and to the governors that were over every province, and to the rulers of every people of every province according to the writing thereof, and to every people after their language; in the name of king Ahasuerus was it written, and sealed with the king's ring" (Est. 3:8-12).

3. As used by Pilate to seal the tomb of Jesus. "So they went, and made the sepulchre sure, sealing the stone, and setting a watch" (Mt. 27:66).

E. Wind: indicating unseen power.

"The wind bloweth where it listeth, and thou hearest the sound thereof, but canst not tell whence it cometh, and whither it goeth: so is every one that is born of the Spirit" (Jn. 3:8).

"And when the day of Pentecost was fully come, they were all with one accord in one place. And suddenly there came a sound from heaven as of a rushing mighty wind, and it filled all the house where they were sitting" (Acts 2:1, 2).

F. Fire: indicating presence, approval, protection, purifying, gift, judgment.

1. The presence of the Lord.

"And the angel of the Lord appeared unto him in a flame of fire out of the midst of a bush: and he looked, and, behold, the bush burned with fire, and the bush was not consumed" (Ex. 3:2).

2. The approval of the Lord.

"And there came a fire out from before the Lord, and consumed upon the altar the burnt offering and the fat: which when all the people saw, they shouted, and fell on their faces" (Lev. 9:24).

3. The protection of the Lord.

"And the Lord went before them by day in a pillar of a cloud, to lead them the way; and by night in a pillar of fire, to give them light; to go by day and night" (Ex. 13:21).

4. The purifying from the Lord.

"In the year that king Uzziah died I saw also the Lord sitting upon a throne, high and lifted up, and his train filled the temple. Above it stood the seraphim: each one had six wings; with twain he covered his face, and with twain he did fly. And one cried unto another, and said, Holy,

holy, holy, is the Lord of hosts: the whole earth is full of his glory. And the posts of the door moved at the voice of him that cried, and the house was filled with smoke. Then said I, Woe is me! for I am undone; because I am a man of unclean lips, and I dwell in the midst of a people of unclean lips: for mine eyes have seen the King, the Lord of hosts. Then flew one of the seraphim unto me, having a live coal in his hand, which he had taken with the tongs from off the altar: And he laid it upon my mouth, and said, Lo, this hath touched thy lips; and thine iniquity is taken away, and thy sin purged. Also, I heard the voice of the Lord, saying, Whom shall I send, and who will go for us? Then said I, Here am I; send me" (Isa. 6:1–8).

    5. The gift of the Lord.
        "And there appeared unto them cloven tongues like as of fire, and it sat upon each of them" (Acts 2:3).
    6. The judgment of the Lord.
        "For our God is a consuming fire" (Heb. 12:29).
G. An earnest: indicating first-fruits, down-payment, a pledge, an assurance of the eventual complete payment.
    "Who hath also sealed us, and given the earnest of the Spirit in our hearts" (2 Cor. 1:22).
    "Now he that hath wrought us for the selfsame thing is God, who also hath given unto us the earnest of the Spirit" (2 Cor. 5:5).
    "Which is the earnest of our inheritance until the redemption of the purchased possession, unto the praise of his glory" (Eph. 1:14).

V. The Various Ministries of the Holy Spirit. Many erroneously believe the Holy Spirit first came to earth at Pentecost in Acts 2. This is not true. The Word of God assigns no less than eleven mighty ministries of the Spirit, and the first three were performed in Old Testament times. These eleven ministries are:
    One: His ministry concerning the universe
    Two: His ministry concerning the Scriptures
    Three: His ministry concerning the nation Israel
    Four: His ministry concerning the devil
    Five: His ministry concerning the Savior
    Six: His ministry concerning the sinner
    Seven: His ministry concerning the church
    Eight: His ministry concerning the day of Pentecost
    Nine: His ministry concerning the believer
    Ten: His ministry concerning the spiritual gifts
    Eleven: His ministry concerning the fruit of Christ
We shall now briefly consider these separately.
A. His ministry concerning the universe. According to David, the Father created all things.
    "The heavens declare the glory of God; and the firmament showeth his handiwork" (Ps. 19:1).
    However, John declares the Son did it.
    "All things were made by him; and without him was not any thing made that was made. In him was life; and the life was the light of men" (Jn. 1:3, 4).
    Finally, in other passages, the Holy Spirit is said to have performed the initial act of creation.

What are we to believe? The answer is, of course, that all three persons in the Trinity had a part. As an illustration let us consider an important executive who determines to build a spacious and expensive home. He thus employs an architect to design the necessary plans for this home. The architect thereupon secures a competent contractor to follow his blueprints. In this illustration the executive is the Father, the architect the Son, and the contractor is the Holy Spirit. The following verses then refer to the work of this divine Contractor.
    "Thou sendest forth thy spirit, they are created: and thou renewest the face of the earth" (Ps. 104:30).
    "By his Spirit he hath garnished the heavens; his hand hath formed the crooked serpent" (Job 26:13).
    "The Spirit of God hath made me, and the breath of the Almighty hath given me life" (Job 33:4).
    "And the earth was without form, and void; and darkness was upon the face of the deep. And the Spirit of God moved upon the face of the waters" (Gen. 1:2).
It has been suggested that the Hebrew word (here translated "moved") has reference to the gentle motion of a dove as she quietly hovers over her nest, imparting her body heat upon the eggs until they are hatched.
B. His ministry concerning the Scriptures. In a word, the Holy Spirit is the author of the Word of God. He has furthermore chosen three basic methods in the preparation and reception of his divine manuscript, the Bible. These "steps of the Spirit" are:
    Revelation: that process whereby the Holy Spirit spoke to the forty human writers of the Bible the message he wanted them to transmit.
    Inspiration: that process whereby the Holy Spirit guided the very pen of these forty writers so that the spoken message would be accurately written.
    Illumination: that process whereby the Holy Spirit takes the written word when it is preached and read and enlightens those human ears who will hear it. The following passages bear all this out.
    1. The Holy Spirit is the Author of the Old Testament.
        a. According to David.
            "The Spirit of the Lord spake by me, and his word was in my tongue" (2 Sam. 23:2).
        b. According to Isaiah.
            "As for me, this is my covenant with them, said the Lord; My Spirit that is upon thee, and my words which I have put in thy mouth, shall not depart out of thy mouth, nor out of the mouth of thy seed, nor out of the mouth of thy seed's seed, saith the Lord, from henceforth and for ever" (Isa. 59:21).
        c. According to Jeremiah.
            "Then the Lord put forth his hand, and touched my mouth. And the Lord

said unto me, Behold, I have put my words in thy mouth" (Jer. 1:9).

d. According to Jesus.

"For verily I say unto you, Till heaven and earth pass, one jot or one tittle shall in no wise pass from the law, till all be fulfilled" (Mt. 5:18).

"If he called them gods, unto whom the word of God came, and the Scripture cannot be broken" (Jn. 10:35).

e. According to Peter.

"For the prophecy came not in old time by the will of man: but holy men of God spake as they were moved by the Holy Ghost" (2 Pet. 1:21).

f. According to Paul.

"And that from a child thou hast known the Holy Scriptures, which are able to make thee wise unto salvation through faith which is in Christ Jesus. All Scripture is given by inspiration of God, and is profitable for doctrine, for reproof, for correction, for instruction in righteousness: That the man of God may be perfect, throughly furnished unto all good works" (2 Tim. 3:15-17).

2. The Holy Spirit is the Author of the New Testament.

a. According to Jesus.

"These things have I spoken unto you, being yet present with you. But the Comforter, which is the Holy Ghost, whom the Father will send in my name, he shall teach you all things, and bring all things to your remembrance, whatsoever I have said unto you" (Jn. 14:25, 26).

b. According to Paul.

"If any man think himself to be a prophet, or spiritual, let him acknowledge that the things that I write unto you are the commandments of the Lord" (1 Cor. 14:37).

"Which things also we speak, not in the words which man's wisdom teacheth, but which the Holy Ghost teacheth; comparing spiritual things with spiritual" (1 Cor. 2:13).

"For this we say unto you by the word of the Lord, that we which are alive and remain unto the coming of the Lord shall not prevent them which are asleep" (1 Thess. 4:15).

c. According to Peter.

"Wherefore, beloved, seeing that ye look for such things, be diligent that ye may be found of him in peace, without spot, and blameless. And account that the long-suffering of our Lord is salvation; even as our beloved brother Paul also according to the wisdom given unto him hath written unto you; as also in all his epistles, speaking in them of these things; in which are some things hard to be understood, which they that are un-

learned and unstable wrest, as they do also the other Scriptures, unto their own destruction" (2 Pet. 3:14-16).

d. According to John.

"I was in the Spirit on the Lord's day, and heard behind me a great voice, as of a trumpet, saying, I am Alpha and Omega, the first and the last: and, What thou seest, write in a book, and send it unto the seven churches which are in Asia: unto Ephesus, and unto Smyrna, and unto Pergamos, and unto Thyatira, and unto Sardis, and unto Philadelphia, and unto Laodicea" (Rev. 1:10, 11).

"He that hath an ear, let him hear what the Spirit saith unto the churches: To him that overcometh will I give to eat of the tree of life, which is in the midst of the paradise of God" (Rev. 2:7).

C. His ministry concerning Israel.

1. He came upon Israel's leaders. No less than sixteen Old Testament individuals are said to have experienced the anointing of the Holy Spirit.

a. Upon Joseph.

"And Pharaoh said unto his servants, Can we find such a one as this is, a man in whom the Spirit of God is?" (Gen. 41:38).

b. Upon Moses.

"And I will come down and talk with thee there: and I will take of the spirit which is upon thee, and will put it upon them; and they shall bear the burden of the people with thee, that thou bear it not thyself alone" (Num. 11:17).

c. Upon Joshua.

"And the Lord said unto Moses, Take thee Joshua the son of Nun, a man in whom is the spirit, and lay thine hand upon him" (Num. 27:18).

d. Upon Othniel.

"And the Spirit of the Lord came upon him, and he judged Israel, and went out to war: and the Lord delivered Chushan-rishathaim king of Mesopotamia into his hand; and his hand prevailed against Chushan-rishathaim" (Jdg. 3:10).

e. Upon Gideon.

"But the Spirit of the Lord came upon Gideon, and he blew a trumpet; and Abiezer was gathered after him" (Jdg. 6:34).

f. Upon Jephthah.

"Then the Spirit of the Lord came upon Jephthah, and he passed over Gilead, and Manasseh, and passed over Mizpeh of Gilead, and from Mizpeh of Gilead he passed over unto the children of Ammon" (Jdg. 11:29).

g. Upon Samson. At least three times we read of the Holy Spirit coming upon this Hebrew strong man.

"And the Spirit of the Lord came mightily upon him, and he rent him as he would have rent a kid, and he had nothing in his hand: but he told not his father or his mother what he had done" (Jdg. 14:6).

"And the Spirit of the Lord came upon him, and he went down to Ashkelon, and slew thirty men of them, and took their spoil, and gave change of garments unto them which expounded the riddle. And his anger was kindled, and he went up to his father's house" (Jdg. 14:19).

"And when he came unto Lehi, the Philistines shouted against him: and the Spirit of the Lord came mightily upon him, and the cords that were upon his arms became as flax that was burnt with fire, and his bands loosed from off his hands. And he found a new jawbone of an ass, and put forth his hand, and took it, and slew a thousand men therewith" (Jdg. 15:14, 15).
h. Upon Saul.
  (1) After he was anointed king by Samuel.
      "And when they came thither to the hill, behold, a company of prophets met him; and the Spirit of God came upon him, and he prophesied among them" (1 Sam. 10:10).
  (2) Just before his victory at Jabesh-gilead.
      "And the Spirit of God came upon Saul when he heard those tidings, and his anger was kindled greatly" (1 Sam. 11:6).
i. Upon David. Unlike Saul's case, we are never told that the Holy Spirit departed from David. However, on one occasion David was afraid he might indeed withdraw himself. (See Ps. 51:11.)
      "Then Samuel took the horn of oil, and anointed him in the midst of his brethren: and the Spirit of the Lord came upon David from that day forward. So Samuel rose up, and went to Ramah" (1 Sam. 16:13).
j. Upon Elijah.
  (1) As testified to by Obadiah.
      "And it shall come to pass, as soon as I am gone from thee, that the Spirit of the Lord shall carry thee whither I know not; and so when I come and tell Ahab, and he cannot find thee, he shall slay me: but I thy servant fear the Lord from my youth" (1 Ki. 18:12).
  (2) As testified to by some prophets at Jericho.
      "And they said unto him, Behold now, there be with thy servants fifty strong men; let them go, we

pray thee, and seek thy master: lest peradventure the Spirit of the Lord hath taken him up, and cast him upon some mountain, or into some valley. And he said, Ye shall not send" (2 Ki. 2:16).
k. Upon Elisha.
      "And when the sons of the prophets who were to view at Jericho saw him, they said, The spirit of Elijah doth rest on Elisha. And they came to meet him, and bowed themselves to the ground before him" (2 Ki. 2:15).
l. Upon Ezekiel.
      "And the spirit entered into me when he spake unto me, and set me upon my feet, that I heard him that spake unto me" (Ezek. 2:2).
m. Upon Daniel.
  (1) As testified to by King Nebuchadnezzar.
      "O Belteshazzar, master of the magicians, because I know that the spirit of the holy gods is in thee, and no secret troubleth thee, tell me the visions of my dream that I have seen, and the interpretation thereof" (Dan. 4:9).
  (2) As testified by a frightened queen.
      "There is a man in thy kingdom, in whom is the spirit of the holy gods; and in the days of thy father light and understanding and wisdom, like the wisdom of the gods, was found in him; whom the king Nebuchadnezzar thy father, the king, I say, thy father, made master of the magicians, astrologers, Chaldeans, and soothsayers" (Dan. 5:11).
  (3) As testified by King Darius.
      "Then this Daniel was preferred above the presidents and princes, because an excellent spirit was in him; and the king thought to set him over the whole realm" (Dan. 6:3).
n. Upon Micah.
      "But truly I am full of power by the Spirit of the Lord, and of judgment, and of might, to declare unto Jacob his transgression, and to Israel his sin" (Micah 3:8).
o. Upon Azariah the prophet.
      "And the Spirit of God came upon Azariah the son of Oded" (2 Chron. 15:1).
p. Upon Zechariah the high priest.
      "And the Spirit of God came upon Zechariah the son of Jehoiada the priest, which stood above the people, and said unto them, Thus saith God, Why transgress ye the commandments of the Lord, that ye cannot

prosper? because ye have forsaken the Lord, he hath also forsaken you" (2 Chron. 24:20).

2. He came upon Israel's elders.

"And the Lord came down in a cloud, and spake unto him, and took of the spirit that was upon him, and gave it unto the seventy elders: and it came to pass, that, when the spirit rested upon them, they prophesied, and did not cease" (Num. 11:25).

3. He came upon Israel's tabernacle.

"Then a cloud covered the tent of the congregation, and the glory of the Lord filled the tabernacle" (Ex. 40:34).

4. He came upon Israel's Temple.

"And it came to pass, when the priests were come out of the holy place, that the cloud filled the house of the Lord" (1 Ki. 8:10).

5. He led Israel through the desert.

"Thou gavest also thy good Spirit to instruct them, and withheldest not thy manna from their mouth, and gavest them water for their thirst" (Neh. 9:20).

In spite of his goodness to them, Israel grieved the blessed Holy Spirit.

"But they rebelled, and vexed his Holy Spirit: therefore he was turned to be their enemy, and he fought against them" (Isa. 63:10).

6. He will come upon Israel during the tribulation.

"And I saw another angel ascending from the east, having the seal of the living God: and he cried with a loud voice to the four angels, to whom it was given to hurt the earth and the sea. saying, Hurt not the earth, neither the sea, nor the trees, till we have sealed the servants of our God in their foreheads. And I heard the number of them which were sealed: and there were sealed a hundred and forty and four thousand of all the tribes of the children of Israel" (Rev. 7:2-4).

"And it shall come to pass afterward, that I will pour out my Spirit upon all flesh; and your sons and your daughters shall prophesy, your old men shall dream dreams, your young men shall see visions: And also upon the servants and upon the handmaids in those days will I pour out my Spirit. And I will show wonders in the heavens and in the earth, blood, and fire, and pillars of smoke. The sun shall be turned into darkness, and the moon into blood, before the great and the terrible day of the Lord come. And it shall come to pass, that whosoever shall call on the name of the Lord shall be delivered: for in mount Zion and in Jerusalem shall be deliverance, as the Lord hath said, and in the remnant whom the Lord shall call" (Joel 2:28-32).

7. He will come upon Israel during the millennium.

"And I will pour upon the house of David, and upon the inhabitants of Jerusalem, the spirit of grace and of supplications: and they shall look upon me whom they have pierced, and they shall mourn for him, as one mourneth for his only son, and shall be in bitterness for him, as one that is in bitterness for his firstborn" (Zech. 12:10).

"And ye shall know that I am the Lord, when I have opened your graves, O my people, and brought you up out of your graves. And shall put my Spirit in you, and ye shall live, and I shall place you in your own land: then shall ye know that I the Lord have spoken it, and performed it, saith the Lord" (Ezek. 37:13, 14).

"Neither will I hide my face any more from them: for I have poured out my Spirit upon the house of Israel, saith the Lord God" (Ezek. 39:29).

D. His ministry concerning the devil. The Holy Spirit now acts as a divine dam, holding back and limiting the full power of Satan and of sin.

1. As stated by Isaiah.

"So shall they fear the name of the Lord from the west, and his glory from the rising of the sun. When the enemy shall come in like a flood, the Spirit of the Lord shall lift up a standard against him" (Isa. 59:19).

2. As stated by Paul.

"For the mystery of iniquity doth already work: only he who now letteth will let, until he be taken out of the way. And then shall that Wicked be revealed, whom the Lord shall consume with the spirit of his mouth, and shall destroy with the brightness of his coming: Even him, whose coming is after the working of Satan with all power and signs and lying wonders, And with all deceivableness of unrighteousness in them that perish; because they received not the love of the truth, that they might be saved. And for this cause God shall send them strong delusion, that they should believe a lie: That they all might be damned who believed not the truth, but had pleasure in unrighteousness. But we are bound to give thanks always to God for you, brethren, beloved of the Lord, because God hath from the beginning chosen you to salvation through sanctification of the Spirit and belief of the truth: Whereunto he called you by our gospel, to the obtaining of the glory of our Lord Jesus Christ" (2 Thess. 2:7-14).

Here Paul states that at the beginning of the tribulation the restraining power of the Holy Spirit will be somewhat removed, thus allowing Satan and his hateful antichrist to briefly reign over the earth for a seven-year period.

E. His ministry concerning the Savior. From his bodily conception to his final ascension, the Lord Jesus Christ was led by the Holy Spirit.

1. The Savior was begotten by the Holy Spirit. "And the angel answered and said unto her, The Holy Ghost shall come upon thee, and the power of the Highest shall overshadow thee: therefore also that holy thing which shall be born of thee shall be called the Son of God" (Lk. 1:35).

   "Now the birth of Jesus Christ was on this wise: When as his mother Mary was espoused to Joseph, before they came together, she was found with child of the Holy Ghost. Then Joseph her husband, being a just man, and not willing to make her a public example, was minded to put her away privily. But while he thought on these things, behold, the angel of the Lord appeared unto him in a dream, saying, Joseph, thou son of David, fear not to take unto thee Mary thy wife: for that which is conceived in her is of the Holy Ghost" (Mt. 1:18-20).

   Thus the real Father of Christ's body was the Holy Spirit, and the real miracle was not in the Savior's birth, but in his supernatural conception.

2. The Savior was anointed by the Holy Spirit. "And Jesus, when he was baptized, went up straightway out of the water: and, lo, the heavens were opened unto him, and he saw the Spirit of God descending like a dove, and lighting upon him" (Mt. 3:16).

   "The Spirit of the Lord is upon me, because he hath anointed me to preach the gospel to the poor: he hath sent me to heal the broken-hearted, to preach deliverance to the captives, and recovering of sight to the blind, to set at liberty them that are bruised" (Lk. 4:18).

   "How God anointed Jesus of Nazareth with the Holy Ghost and with power: who went about doing good, and healing all that were oppressed of the devil; for God was with him" (Acts 10:38).

   "Thou hast loved righteousness, and hated iniquity; therefore God, even thy God, hath anointed thee with the oil of gladness above thy fellows" (Heb. 1:9).

3. The Savior was sealed by the Holy Spirit. "Labor not for the meat which perisheth, but for that meat which endureth unto everlasting life, which the Son of man shall give unto you: for him hath God the Father sealed" (Jn. 6:27).

   The seal here demonstrated the Son's identification with both Father and Spirit. It also spoke of his genuineness, value, and authority.

4. The Savior was led by the Holy Spirit. "Then was Jesus led up of the Spirit into the wilderness to be tempted of the devil" (Mt. 4:1).

5. The Savior was empowered by the Holy Spirit. "But if I cast out devils by the Spirit of God, then the kingdom of God is come unto you" (Mt. 12:28).

According to Philippians 2:5-8, Christ abstained from using, in an independent way, his divine attributes (his omnipresence, omniscience, etc.) while on earth, but chose rather to depend completely upon the Holy Spirit for strength and guidance.

6. The Savior was filled by the Holy Spirit. "For he whom God hath sent speaketh the words of God: for God giveth not the Spirit by measure unto him" (Jn. 3:34).

   "And Jesus being full of the Holy Ghost returned from Jordan, and was led by the Spirit into the wilderness" (Lk. 4:1).

   The words "filled" and "full" refer simply to control. Thus, the Savior was totally controlled by the Holy Spirit while on this earth.

7. The Savior sorrowed in the Holy Spirit. "When Jesus therefore saw her weeping, and the Jews also weeping which came with her, he groaned in the spirit, and was troubled" (Jn. 11:33).

8. The Savior rejoiced in the Holy Spirit. "In that hour Jesus rejoiced in spirit, and he said, I thank thee, O Father, Lord of heaven and earth, that thou hast hid these things from the wise and prudent, and hast revealed them unto babes: even so, Father; for so it seemed good in thy sight" (Lk. 10:21).

9. The Savior offered himself at Calvary through the Holy Spirit. "How much more shall the blood of Christ, who through the eternal Spirit offered himself without spot to God, purge your conscience from dead works to serve the living God?" (Heb. 9:14).

10. The Savior was raised from the dead by the Holy Spirit. "And declared to be the Son of God with power, according to the Spirit of holiness, by the resurrection from the dead" (Rom. 1:4).

    "For Christ also hath once suffered for sins, the just for the unjust, that he might bring us to God, being put to death in the flesh, but quickened by the Spirit" (1 Pet. 3:18).

11. The Savior commanded his disciples after his resurrection through the Holy Spirit. "Until the day in which he was taken up, after that he through the Holy Ghost had given commandments unto the apostles whom he had chosen" (Acts 1:2).

12. The Savior will someday return and raise the dead in Christ through the Holy Spirit. "But if the Spirit of him that raised up Jesus from the dead dwell in you, he that raised up Christ from the dead shall also quicken your mortal bodies by his Spirit that dwelleth in you" (Rom. 8:11).

    The point of this particular section of our study should be painfully obvious. If the sinless Son of God found it necessary to depend totally upon the Holy Spirit to form every word and guide every step, how much more is this absolutely vital for *us*.

F. His ministry concerning the sinner. During his midnight discourse, just prior to entering Gethsemane, our Lord spoke the following words to his sorrowing disciples about the Holy Spirit:

"Nevertheless I tell you the truth; It is expedient for you that I go away: for if I go not away, the Comforter will not come unto you; but if I depart, I will send him unto you. And when he is come, he will reprove the world of sin, and of righteousness, and of judgment: Of sin, because they believe not on me; Of righteousness, because I go to my Father, and ye see me no more; Of judgment, because the prince of this world is judged" (Jn. 16:7-11).

The key word in this passage is the word "reprove." In the Greek it is *elegcho* which is elsewhere translated as follows:

To convince.

"Which of you convinceth me of sin? And if I say the truth, why do ye not believe me?" (Jn. 8:46).

To convict.

"And they which heard it, being convicted by their own conscience, went out one by one, beginning at the eldest, even unto the last: and Jesus was left alone, and the woman standing in the midst" (Jn. 8:9).

To tell someone his fault.

"Moreover if thy brother shall trespass against thee, go and tell him his fault between thee and him alone: if he shall hear thee, thou hast gained thy brother" (Mt. 18:15).

Thus the holy Hound of Heaven, as he has been called, will track down the sinner, and, upon "catching" him, will (1) convince him; (2) convict him; and (3) tell him his faults.

1. He convicts man:
   a. Of sin. Here the sin is not sex, smoking, or swearing, but rejecting Christ's sacrifice on Calvary. This is, of course, the one ultimate sin which will damn a man's soul in hell forever.

   "He that believeth on him is not condemned: but he that believeth not is condemned already, because he hath not believed in the name of the only begotten Son of God" (Jn. 3:18).

   It is important to fully understand this fact. Often the seeking sinner is left confused and uncertain. How many sins must he be expected to repent of to be saved? What about those sins he may have forgotten? Not only is this concept confusing to the particularly immoral unsaved man, but it is equally so to the moral unsaved man. After all, he does not drink, gamble, smoke, or even fudge on his income tax report. Thus, he concludes he has no need of salvation. But, in fact, he too, like the drunkard, is guilty of rejecting Christ's sacrifice on the cross and, therefore, is in deperate need of repentance and salvation.

   b. Of Christ's righteousness. Later the Holy Spirit directed the Apostle Paul to write an entire epistle on this one word "right-

eousness." In this epistle (the book of Romans) Paul stresses three things:
   (1) God *is* righteousness.
   (2) God *demands* righteousness.
   (3) God *provides* righteousness.

   c. Of future judgment. In this area, the Holy Spirit would point out to the sinner that:
   (1) All unsaved people belong to Satan.
       "Ye are of your father the devil, and the lusts of your father ye will do: he was a murderer from the beginning, and abode not in the truth, because there is no truth in him. When he speaketh a lie, he speaketh of his own: for he is a liar, and the father of it" (Jn. 8:44).

   d. Satan's doom is already in the making.
   "And the God of peace shall bruise Satan under your feet shortly. The grace of our Lord Jesus Christ be with you. Amen" (Rom. 16:20).

   e. Therefore all sinners will someday share his doom.
   "Then shall he say also unto them on the left hand, Depart from me, ye cursed, into everlasting fire, prepared for the devil and his angels" (Mt. 25:41).

2. There are seven classic and clear examples of this convicting ministry of the blessed Holy Spirit in the book of Acts.
   a. The crowd at Pentecost.
   "Ye men of Israel, hear these words; Jesus of Nazareth, a man approved of God among you by miracles and wonders and signs, which God did by him in the midst of you, as ye yourselves also know: Him, being delivered by the determinate counsel and foreknowledge of God, ye have taken, and by wicked hands have crucified and slain" (Acts 2:22, 23).

   "Now when they heard this, they were pricked in their heart, and said unto Peter and to the rest of the apostles, Men and brethren, what shall we do?" (Acts 2:37).

   b. The Ethiopian eunuch.
   "Then the Spirit said unto Philip, Go near, and join thyself to this chariot. And Philip ran thither to him, and heard him read the prophet Esaias, and said, Understandeth thou what thou readest? And he said, How can I, except some man should guide me? And he desired Philip that he would come up and sit with him. The place of the Scripture which he read was this, He was led as a sheep to the slaughter; and like a lamb dumb before his shearer, so opened he not his mouth: In his humiliation his judgment was taken away: and who shall declare his generation? for his life is taken from the earth. And the eunuch

answered Philip, and said, I pray thee, of whom speaketh the prophet this? of himself, or of some other man? Then Philip opened his mouth, and began at the same Scripture, and preached unto him Jesus. And as they went on their way, they came unto a certain water: and the eunuch said, See, here is water; what doth hinder me to be baptized? And Philip said, If thou believest with all thine heart, thou mayest. And he answered and said, I believe that Jesus Christ is the Son of God. And he commanded the chariot to stand still: and they went down both into the water, both Philip and the eunuch; and he baptized him" (Acts 8:29-38).

c. Saul of Tarsus.

"And Saul, yet breathing out threatenings and slaughter against the disciples of the Lord, went unto the high priest, and desired of him letters to Damascus to the synagogues, that if he found any of this way, whether they were men or women, he might bring them bound unto Jerusalem. And as he journeyed, he came near Damascus: and suddenly there shined round about him a light from heaven: And he fell to the earth, and heard a voice saying unto him, Saul, Saul, why persecutest thou me? And he said, Who art thou Lord? And the Lord said, I am Jesus whom thou persecutest; it is hard for thee to kick against the pricks. And he trembling and astonished said, Lord, what wilt thou have me to do? And the Lord said unto him, Arise, and go into the city, and it shall be told thee what thou must do" (Acts 9:1-6).

d. A centurion named Cornelius.

"While Peter yet spake these words, the Holy Ghost fell on all them which heard the word" (Acts 10:44).

e. The Philippian jailor.

"And at midnight Paul and Silas prayed, and sang praises unto God: and the prisoners heard them. And suddenly there was a great earthquake, so that the foundations of the prison were shaken: and immediately all the doors were opened, and every one's bands were loosed. And the keeper of the prison awaking out of his sleep, and seeing the prison doors open, he drew out his sword, and would have killed himself, supposing that the prisoners had been fled. But Paul cried with a loud voice, saying, Do thyself no harm: for we are all here. Then he called for a light, and sprang in, and came trembling, and fell down before Paul and Silas, and brought them out, and said, Sirs, what must I do to be saved? And they said,

Believe on the Lord Jesus Christ, and thou shalt be saved, and thy house. And they spake unto him the word of the Lord, and to all that were in his house. And he took them the same hour of the night, and washed their stripes; and was baptized, he and all his, straightway. And when he had brought them into his house, he set meat before them, and rejoiced, believing in God with all his house" (Acts 16:25-34).

f. A governor named Felix.

"And after certain days, when Felix came with his wife, Drusilla, which was a Jewess, he sent for Paul, and heard him concerning the faith in Christ. And as he reasoned of righteousness, temperance, and judgment to come, Felix trembled, and answered, Go thy way for this time; when I have a convenient season, I will call for thee" (Acts 24: 24, 25).

g. A king named Agrippa.

"Then Agrippa said unto Paul, Thou art permitted to speak for thyself. Then Paul stretched forth the hand, and answered for himself" (Acts 26:1).

"That Christ should suffer, and that he should be the first that should rise from the dead, and should show light unto the people, and to the Gentiles. And as he thus spake for himself, Festus said with a loud voice, Paul, thou art beside thyself; much learning doth make thee mad. But he said, I am not mad, most noble Festus; but speak forth the words of truth and soberness. For the king knoweth of these things, before whom also I speak freely: for I am persuaded that none of these things are hidden from him; for this thing was not done in a corner. King Agrippa, believest thou the prophets? I know that thou believest. Then Agrippa said unto Paul, Almost thou persuadest me to be a Christian" (Acts 26:23-28).

In conclusion it may be stated that the chief ministry performed by the Holy Spirit to the sinner is that of old-fashioned, pulse pounding, blood racing conviction.

G. His ministry concerning the church. Of the three basic institutions in the Bible (marriage, human government, and the church), none is more important to the Holy Spirit than the church. It was to aid the growth of the church that he formally came at Pentecost.

1. The Holy Spirit and the universal church. He formed it.

"Now therefore ye are no more strangers and foreigners, but fellow citizens with the saints, and of the household of God; and are built upon the foundation of the apostles and prophets, Jesus Christ himself being the chief cornerstone; in whom all the building fitly framed together groweth unto a holy temple in the Lord: in whom ye also are builded together for a habitation of God through the Spirit" (Eph. 2:19-22).

2. The Holy Spirit and the local church.

a. He desires to inspire its worship service. "For we are the circumcision, which worship God in the spirit, and rejoice in Christ Jesus, and have no confidence in the flesh" (Phil. 3:3).

If allowed by pastor and people, the Spirit of God can guarantee both the presence and power of God at each church meeting.

b. He desires to direct its missionary work. "Then the Spirit said unto Philip, Go near, and join thyself to this chariot" (Acts 8:29).

"As they ministered to the Lord, and fasted, the Holy Ghost said, Separate me Barnabas and Saul for the work whereunto I have called them. So they, being sent forth by the Holy Ghost, departed unto Seleucia; and from thence they sailed to Cyprus" (Acts 13:2, 4).

"Now when they had gone throughout Phrygia and the region of Galatia, and were forbidden of the Holy Ghost to preach the word in Asia, after they were come to Mysia, they assayed to go into Bithynia: but the Spirit suffered them not. And after he had seen the vision, immediately we endeavored to go into Macedonia, assuredly gathering that the Lord had called us for to preach the gospel unto them" (Acts 16:6, 7, 10).

c. He desires to aid in its singing services. "And be not drunk with wine, wherein is excess; but be filled with the Spirit; speaking to yourselves in psalms and hymns and spiritual songs, singing and making melody in your heart to the Lord" (Eph. 5:18, 19).

Many times a visiting speaker in a church has discovered to his delight that the music director has unknowingly chosen those songs and special music which correspond perfectly to the message. Obviously, both speaker and song leader were sensitive to the ministry of the Spirit.

d. He desires to appoint its preachers. "Take heed therefore unto yourselves, and to all the flock, over the which the Holy Ghost hath made you overseers, to feed the church of God, which he hath purchased with his own blood" (Acts 20:28).

e. He desires to anoint its preachers. "And my speech and my preaching was not with enticing words of man's wisdom, but in demonstration of the Spirit and of power" (1 Cor. 2:4).

Here we see the divine order of service. He first appoints and then anoints his servants. The appointing is a once-for-all event, but the anointing must be sought daily.

f. He desires to warn its members. "Now the Spirit speaketh expressly, that in the latter times some shall depart from the faith, giving heed to seducing spirits, and doctrines of devils" (1 Tim. 4:1).

g. He desires to determine its decisions. "For it seemed good to the Holy Ghost, and to us, to lay upon you no greater burden than these necessary things" (Acts 15:28).

This all-important decision made at the Jerusalem Council concerning circumcision is a beautiful example of the teamwork between a local church and the Holy Spirit. Those assemblies governed by congregational vote often pride themselves on their democratic policies. But the real goal can only be achieved through a democratic-theocratic combined team effort.

h. He desires to condemn or bless its efforts as needed. "He that hath an ear, let him hear what the Spirit saith unto the churches; To him that overcometh will I give to eat of the tree of life, which is in the midst of the paradise of God" (Rev. 2:7).

"He that hath an ear, let him hear what the Spirit saith unto the churches; He that overcometh shall not be hurt of the second death" (Rev. 2:11).

"He that hath an ear, let him hear what the Spirit saith unto the churches; To him that overcometh will I give to eat of the hidden manna, and will give him a white stone, and in the stone a new name written, which no man knoweth saving he that receiveth it" (Rev. 2:17).

"He that hath an ear, let him hear what the Spirit saith unto the churches" (Rev. 2:29). (Cf. 3:6, 13, 22.)

Churches are often overly concerned about improving their image in the eyes of the younger generation, society, the business world, academic circles, etc. But the real concern should be directed toward that One who alone is properly qualified to improve and correct—namely, the Holy Spirit.

i. He desires to head up its visitation and evangelistic programs. "And the Spirit and the bride say, Come. And let him that heareth say, Come. And let him that is athirst come. And whosoever will, let him take the water of life freely" (Rev. 22:17).

In this, the Scripture's final invitation, we see the Holy Spirit speaking through the church urging the unsaved to come to Christ.

H. His ministry concerning the day of Pentecost. Of all the important days in history, the day of Pentecost must surely be ranked near the top. At this time, the Holy Spirit performed one of his greatest and most far-reaching works.

"And when the day of Pentecost was fully come, they were all with one accord in one place. And suddenly there came a sound from heaven as of a rushing mighty wind, and it filled all the house where they were sitting. And there appeared unto them cloven tongues, like as of fire, and it sat upon each of them. And they were all filled with the Holy Ghost, and began to speak with other tongues, as the Spirit gave them utterance" (Acts 2:1–4).

1. The background of Pentecost. Just minutes before his dramatic ascension, our resurrected Lord commanded his disciples:

"And being assembled together with them, commanded them that they should not depart from Jerusalem, but wait for the promise of the Father, which, saith he, ye have heard of me" (Acts 1:4).

Much ink has been used attempting to explain these five words, "the promise of the Father." What was this promise of the Father? Various passages of Scripture make it clear that this promise of the Father, and also of the Son, was a reference to the arrival of the Holy Spirit.

"And it shall come to pass afterward, that I will pour out my Spirit upon all flesh; and your sons and your daughters shall prophesy, your old men shall dream dreams, your young men shall see visions" (Joel 2:28).

"Men and brethren, this scripture must needs have been fulfilled, which the Holy Ghost by the mouth of David spake before concerning Judas, which was guide to them that took Jesus" (Acts 1:16).

"And I will pray the Father, and he shall give you another Comforter, that he may abide with you for ever" (Jn. 14:16).

"But the Comforter, which is the Holy Ghost, whom the Father will send in my name, he shall teach you all things, and bring all things to your remembrance, whatsoever I have said unto you" (Jn. 14:26).

"But when the Comforter is come, whom I will send unto you from the Father, even the Spirit of truth, which proceedeth from the Father, he shall testify of me" (Jn. 15:26).

"Nevertheless I tell you the truth; It is expedient for you that I go away: for if I go not away, the Comforter will not come unto you; but if I depart, I will send him unto you" (Jn. 16:7).

The Holy Spirit had, of course (as we have seen) already performed an Old Testament ministry, but now his work was to introduce three completely new elements.

a. His new ministry was to be universal. Previously the Holy Spirit had confined his work among humanity to the nation Israel. There is no record before the book of Acts that he fell upon the Greeks, or Romans, or Babylonians, etc. But here in Acts he came to bless all repenting sinners everywhere.

b. It was to be permanent. Although the Holy Spirit did come upon certain Old Testament men, he often departed from them also.

(1) As illustrated by Samson. This Hebrew strong man enjoyed the presence of the Holy Spirit on various occasions.

"And the Spirit of the Lord came mightily upon him, and he rent him as he would have rent a kid, and he had nothing in his hand: but he told not his father or his mother what he had done" (Jdg. 14:6).

"And the Spirit of the Lord came upon him, and he went down to Ashkelon, and slew thirty men of them, and took their spoil, and gave change of garments unto them which expounded the riddle. And his anger was kindled and he went up to his father's house" (Jdg. 14:19).

"And he found a new jawbone of an ass, and put forth his hand, and took it, and slew a thousand men therewith" (Jdg. 15:15).

But then, because of sin and immorality, God's Spirit left Samson. One of the most tragic verses in the Bible records this event, when Samson awakes to hear Delilah say:

"The Philistines be upon thee, Samson. And he awoke out of his sleep, and said, I will go out as at other times before, and shake myself. And he wist not that the Lord was departed from him" (Jdg. 16:20).

(2) As illustrated by Saul. As with Samson, the Holy Spirit came upon Saul, but later left him, as demonstrated by the following:

"And when they came thither to the hill, behold a company of prophets met him; and the Spirit of God came upon him, and he prophesied among them" (1 Sam. 10:10).

"But the Spirit of the Lord departed from Saul, and an evil spirit from the Lord troubled him" (1 Sam. 16:14).

(3) As illustrated by David. The Spirit of God came upon David when he was anointed by Samuel:

"Then Samuel took the horn of oil, and anointed him in the midst of his brethren: and the Spirit of the Lord came upon David from that day forward. So Samuel rose up, and went to Ramah" (1 Sam. 16:13).

So far as it can be determined, the Holy Spirit remained with him until death. But David realized the Holy Spirit could depart, and on at least one occasion, pleaded with the Lord about this matter.

"Cast me not away from thy presence; and take not thy Holy Spirit from me" (Ps. 51:11).

c. It was to be perfecting. That is to say, his new ministry would now be to make all repenting sinners grow in grace and be like Jesus. This was not the case in the Old Testament. There is no indication that the moral and spiritual nature of either Saul or Samson was advanced by the presence of the Holy Spirit. They apparently derived only his power, and not his purity.

2. The chronology of Pentecost. Pentecost (from a Greek word which simply means fifty) is the third of six great Israelite feasts mentioned in Leviticus 23. These feasts actually summarize the entire future work of the Trinity in the New Testament. Consider:
a. The Passover, unleavened bread feast (a reference to Calvary). See verses 4-8.
b. The Sheaf of First Fruits (a reference to the resurrection). See verses 9-14.
c. The Feast of Seven Weeks (a prophetical reference to Pentecost). See verses 15-21.
d. The Feast of Trumpets (a reference to the rapture and Second Coming of Christ). See verses 23-25.
e. The Feast of Atonement (a reference to the coming tribulation). See verses 26-32.
f. The Feast of Tabernacles (a reference to the millennium). See verses 33-43.

3. The comparisons of Pentecost.
a. New Testament Pentecost may be compared with Old Testament Pentecost. Old Testament Pentecost occurred fifty days after Israel left Egypt.

"And the Lord spake unto Moses and Aaron in the land of Egypt, saying, This month shall be unto you the beginning of months: it shall be the first month of the year to you" (Ex. 12:1, 2).

"And ye shall keep it up until the fourteenth day of the same month: and the whole assembly of the congregation of Israel shall kill it in the evening" (Ex. 12:6).

"For I will pass through the land of Egypt this night, and will smite all the firstborn in the land of Egypt, both man and beast; and against all the gods of Egypt I will execute judgment: I am the Lord" (Ex. 12:12).

"And he called for Moses and Aaron by night, and said, Rise up, and get you forth from among my people, both ye and the children of Israel; and go, serve the Lord, as ye have said" (Ex. 12:31).

Fifty days later they arrived at Mt. Sinai.

"In the third month, when the children of Israel were gone forth out of the land of Egypt, the same day came they into the wilderness of Sinai" (Ex. 19:1).

New Testament Pentecost occurred fifty days after Christ rose from the dead. Note: Our Lord was, of course, crucified during the Passover week in April.

"And it was the preparation of the passover, and about the sixth hour: and he saith unto the Jews, Behold your King" (Jn. 19:14).

He then spent forty days with his disciples after the resurrection.

"To whom also he showed himself alive after his passion by many infallible proofs, being seen of them forty days, and speaking of the things pertaining to the kingdom of God" (Acts 1:3).

Then, some ten days later, New Testament Pentecost occurred.

"For John truly baptized with water; but ye shall be baptized with the Holy Ghost not many days hence" (Acts 1:5).

"And when the day of Pentecost was fully come, they were all with one accord in one place" (Acts 2:1).

Old Testament Pentecost celebrated a birthday—that of the nation Israel.

"Now therefore, if ye will obey my voice indeed, and keep my covenant, then ye shall be a peculiar treasure unto me above all people: for all the earth is mine" (Ex. 19:5).

The Scriptures tell us that angels were involved in the giving of the law at Mt. Sinai. See Acts 7:53; Galatians 3:19.

New Testament Pentecost celebrated a birthday—that of the church.

"Then they that gladly received his word were baptized: and the same day there were added unto them about three thousand souls. And they continued steadfastly in the apostles' doctrine and fellowship, and in breaking of bread, and in prayers. And fear came upon every soul: and many wonders and signs were done by the apostles. And all that believed were together, and had all things common; and sold their possessions and goods, and parted them to all men, as every man had need. And they, continuing daily with one accord in the temple, and breaking bread from house to house, did eat their meat with gladness and singleness of heart, praising God, and having favor with all the people. And the Lord added to the church daily such as should be saved" (Acts 2:41-47).

Old Testament Pentecost witnessed the slaying of some 3,000 souls.

"And the children of Levi did according to the word of Moses: and there fell of the people that day about three thousand men" (Ex. 32:28).

Israel's worship of the golden calf, while encamped at the base of Mt. Sinai, was a tragic episode in its history.

New Testament Pentecost witnessed the saving of some 3,000 souls.

"Then they that gladly received his word were baptized: and the same day there were added unto them about three thousand souls" (Acts 2:41).

What an amazing contrast is seen here between these two Pentecosts. In fact, the difference is so important that Paul takes an entire chapter in one of his epistles to discuss it. Note but two verses in this chapter:

"Not that we are sufficient of ourselves to think anything as of ourselves; but our sufficiency is of God; who also hath made us able ministers of the New Testament; not of the letter, but of the spirit; for the letter killeth, but the spirit giveth life" (2 Cor. 3:5, 6).

Old Testament Pentecost was introduced in a mighty way.

"And it came to pass on the third day in the morning, that there were thunders and lightnings, and a thick cloud upon the mount, and the voice of the trumpet exceeding loud; so that all the people that was in the camp trembled" (Ex. 19:16).

"And mount Sinai was altogether on a smoke, because the Lord descended upon it in fire: and the smoke thereof ascended as the smoke of a furnace, and the whole mount quaked greatly" (Ex. 19:18).

New Testament Pentecost was introduced in a mighty way.

"And suddenly there came a sound from heaven as of a rushing mighty wind, and it filled all the house where they were sitting. And there appeared unto them cloven tongues like as of fire, and it sat upon each of them" (Acts 2:2, 3).

b. New Testament Pentecost may be compared to Bethlehem. At Bethlehem God the Father was preparing a body for his Son to work through.

"Wherefore, when he cometh into the world, he saith, Sacrifice and offering thou wouldest not, but a body hast thou prepared me" (Heb. 10:5).

At Pentecost God the Father was preparing a body for his Spirit to work through.

"What! know ye not that your body is the temple of the Holy Ghost which is in you, which ye have of God, and ye are not your own?" (1 Cor. 6:19).

"And what agreement hath the temple of God with idols? for ye are the temple of the living God; as God hath said, I will dwell in them, and walk in them; and I will be their God, and they shall be my people" (2 Cor. 6:16).

Because of this, Pentecost can never be repeated in the same sense that Bethlehem can never again happen. It is therefore as unscriptural to have a "tarrying meeting" to pray down another Pentecost as it would be to have a meeting and plead for the shepherds and wise men to reappear. The events occurring in Luke 2 and Acts 2 are forever in the past.

c. New Testament Pentecost may be compared to Old Testament Babel. At Babel we see sinful men working for their own glory.

"And they said, Go to, let us build us a city, and a tower, whose top may reach unto heaven; and let us make us a name, lest we be scattered abroad upon the face of the whole earth" (Gen. 11:4).

At Pentecost we see saved men waiting for God's glory.

"These all continued with one accord in prayer and supplication, with the women, and Mary the mother of Jesus, and with his brethren" (Acts 1:14).

At Babel God confounded man's language.

"Therefore is the name of it called Babel; because the Lord did there confound the language of all the earth: and from thence did the Lord scatter them abroad upon the face of all the earth" (Gen. 11:9).

At Pentecost God clarified man's language.

"And how hear we every man in our own tongue, wherein we were born?" (Acts 2:8).

At Babel God scattered men throughout the world.

"Therefore is the name of it called Babel; because the Lord did there confound the language of all the earth: and from thence did the Lord scatter them abroad upon the face of all the earth" (Gen. 11:9).

At Pentecost God gathered men within the church.

"That in the dispensation of the fulness of time he might gather together in one all things in Christ, both which are in heaven, and which are on earth; even in him" (Eph. 1:10).

I. His ministry concerning the Christian. Thus far we have discussed the ministry of the Holy Spirit in regard to the universe, the Scriptures, Israel, Satan, Christ, sinners, the church, and Pentecost. But what ministry does he perform for that special group of New Testament people called Christians? The instant an unsaved person prays, "God be merciful to me, a sinner," the Holy Spirit immediately effects a five- fold work in him.

1. The Holy Spirit regenerates the believing sinner. He literally recreates him and gives him the nature of God. The Holy Spirit thus functions as a divine "midwife" to the repenting sinner as he ushers him into the kingdom of God. This is accomplished by the instrument of "water," which is symbolic language for the Word of God. The following passages bear this out:

"Not by works of righteousness which we have done, but according to his mercy he saved us, by the washing of regeneration, and renewing of the Holy Ghost" (Titus 3:5).

"Jesus answered and said unto him, Verily, verily, I say unto thee, Except a man be born again, he cannot see the kingdom of God. Nicodemus saith unto him, How can a man be born when he is old? can he enter the second time into his mother's womb, and be born? Jesus answered, Verily, verily, I say unto thee, Except a man be born of water and of the Spirit, he cannot enter into the kingdom of God. That which is born of the flesh is flesh; and that which is born of the Spirit is spirit. Marvel not that I said unto thee, Ye must be born again" (Jn. 3:3-7).

"Being born again, not of corruptible seed, but of incorruptible, by the word of God, which liveth and abideth for ever" (1 Pet. 1:23).

"Of his own will begat he us with the word of truth, that we should be a kind of first-fruits of his creatures" (Jas. 1:18).

2. The Holy Spirit baptizes the believing sinner.

"Know ye not, that so many of us as were baptized into Jesus Christ were baptized into his death? Therefore we are buried with him by baptism into death: that like as Christ was raised up from the dead by the glory of the Father, even so we also should walk in newness of life" (Rom. 6:3, 4).

"For by one Spirit are we all baptized into one body, whether we be Jews or Gentiles, whether we be bond or free; and have been all made to drink into one Spirit" (1 Cor. 12:13).

"For as many of you as have been baptized into Christ have put on Christ" (Gal. 3:27).

"There is one body, and one Spirit, even as ye are called in one hope of your calling; One Lord, one faith, one baptism" (Eph. 4:4, 5).

"Buried with him in baptism, wherein also ye are risen with him through the faith of the operation of God, who hath raised him from the dead" (Col. 2:12).

The question is often asked: Does a person have to be baptized to be saved? The answer is an emphatic yes—*but not by water baptism.* The purpose of the Holy Spirit's placing the believer into the body of Christ is twofold:

a. He does it to answer Christ's prayer for Christian unity.

"That they all may be one; as thou, Father, art in me, and I in thee, that they also may be one in us: that the world may believe that thou hast sent me" (Jn. 17:21).

b. He does it to prepare a bride for Christ, composed of all believers saved from Pentecost until the rapture.

"So we, being many, are one body in Christ, and every one members one of another" (Rom. 12:5).

"For we being many are one bread, and one body: for we are all partakers of that one bread" (1 Cor. 10:17).

"For by one Spirit are we all baptized into one body, whether we be Jews or Gentiles, whether we be bond or free; and have been all made to drink into one Spirit" (1 Cor. 12:13).

"Now ye are the body of Christ, and members in particular" (1 Cor. 12:27).

"And hath put all things under his feet, and gave him to be the head over all things to the church, which is his body, the fulness of him that filleth all in all" (Eph. 1:22, 23).

"There is one body, and one Spirit, even as ye are called in one hope of your calling" (Eph. 4:4).

"For the perfecting of the saints, for the work of the ministry, for the edifying of the body of Christ" (Eph. 4:12).

"For the husband is the head of the wife, even as Christ is the head of the church: and he is the saviour of the body" (Eph. 5:23).

"For we are members of his body, of his flesh, and of his bones" (Eph. 5:30).

"And let the peace of God rule in your hearts, to the which also ye are called in one body: and be ye thankful" (Col. 3:15).

"For I am jealous over you with godly jealousy: for I have espoused you to one husband, that I may present you as a chaste virgin to Christ" (2 Cor. 11:2).

"And I heard as it were the voice of a great multitude, and as the voice of many waters, and as the voice of mighty thunderings, saying, Alleluia: for the Lord God omnipotent reigneth. Let us be glad and rejoice, and give honor to him: for the marriage of the Lamb is come, and his wife hath made herself ready. And to her was granted that she should be arrayed in fine linen, clean and white: for the fine linen is the righteousness of saints. And he saith unto me, Write, Blessed are they which are called unto the marriage supper of the Lamb. And he saith unto me, These are the true sayings of God" (Rev. 19:6-9).

3. The Holy Spirit indwells the believing sinner. In other words, he not only joins us to the Savior (through the baptism), but he joins himself to us. Jesus, prior to his crucifixion, predicted both of these ministries. He said:

"At that day ye shall know that I am in my Father, and ye in me [the baptizing], and I in you [the indwelling]" (Jn. 14:20).

"Now we have received, not the spirit of the world, but the Spirit which is of God; that we might know the things that are freely given to us of God" (1 Cor. 2:12).

"Know ye not that ye are the temple of God, and that the Spirit of God dwelleth in you?" (1 Cor. 3:16).

"And I will pray the Father, and he shall give you another Comforter, that he may abide with you for ever" (Jn. 14:16).

"In the last day, that great day of the feast, Jesus stood and cried, saying, If any man thirst, let him come unto me, and drink. He that believeth on me, as the Scripture hath said, out of his belly shall flow rivers of living water. (But this spake he of the Spirit, which they that believe on him should receive: for the Holy Ghost was not yet given; because that Jesus was not yet glorified)" (Jn. 7:37-39).

"But ye are not in the flesh, but in the Spirit, if so be that the Spirit of God dwell in you. Now if any man have not the Spirit of Christ, he is none of his" (Rom. 8:9).

"And he that keepeth his commandments dwelleth in him, and he in him. And hereby we know that he abideth in us, by the Spirit which he hath given us" (1 Jn. 3:24).

The purpose of this indwelling ministry is to control the newly created nature.

"Therefore if any man be in Christ, he is a new creature: old things are passed away; behold all things are become new" (2 Cor. 5:17).

"This I say then, Walk in the Spirit, and ye shall not fulfill the lust of the flesh. For the flesh lusteth against the Spirit, and the Spirit against the flesh: and these are contrary the one to the other; so that

ye cannot do the things that ye would. But if ye be led of the Spirit, ye are not under the law" (Gal. 5:16-18).

"That he would grant you, according to the riches of his glory, to be strengthened with might by his Spirit in the inner man" (Eph. 3:16).

4. The Holy Spirit seals the believing sinner.

"Who hath also sealed us, and given the earnest of the Spirit in our hearts" (2 Cor. 1:22).

"In whom ye also trusted, after that ye heard the word of truth, the gospel of your salvation: in whom also after that ye believed, ye were sealed with that holy Spirit of promise" (Eph. 1:13).

"And grieve not the holy Spirit of God, whereby ye are sealed unto the day of redemption" (Eph. 4:30).

The presence of the Holy Spirit himself seems to be the seal here, who is given by the Father to assure the believer of his eternal salvation. This seal is also referred to as an earnest.

"Who hath also sealed us, and given the earnest of the Spirit in our hearts" (2 Cor. 1:22).

"Now he that hath wrought us for the self-same thing is God, who also hath given unto us the earnest of the Spirit" (2 Cor. 5:5).

"Which is the earnest of our inheritance until the redemption of the purchased possession, unto the praise of his glory" (Eph. 1:14).

5. The Holy Spirit fills the believing sinner.

"And they were all filled with the Holy Ghost, and began to speak with other tongues, as the Spirit gave them utterance" (Acts 2:4).

A great deal of controversy and misunderstanding throughout church history has come into existence concerning this ministry of the Holy Spirit. For example, what is the difference between the indwelling and the filling of the Holy Spirit? To aid in understanding this vital distinction, consider the following illustration.

A guest is invited into a home. But upon entering that home he is immediately confined to a small room somewhere near the front door. For awhile, he may even be forgotten by his host. Finally, however, the owner of the house is convicted concerning his shabby treatment of the house guest. He thereupon gives his guest free access to every room in the house.

In this illustration the Holy Spirit is, of course, the invited guest. The host is the believing sinner, and the house stands for his life. The difference then between the indwelling and the filling is the difference between being confined in a small room somewhere and being given free access to all the rooms.

The filling, therefore, does not mean the believer gets more of the Holy Spirit, but rather the Holy Spirit gets more of the believer.

In the light of these five ministries we may observe that:

6. All five of these ministries happen instantaneously to the believing sinner. They all occur by faith and are not in the least dependent upon one's personal emotional feelings at the time.

7. The first four ministries can never be lost, and therefore need not be and should not be asked for again. Nowhere in the Bible are we commanded to ask God to baptize us by his Spirit, or to seal us with his Spirit, or to regenerate and indwell us. If a man has accepted Christ, he has for all eternity been regenerated, indwelled, baptized, and sealed by the Holy Spirit.

8. The fifth ministry, however, can be lost, and therefore should be asked for as many times as needed. The following passages bring this out:

"And be not drunk with wine, wherein is excess; but be filled with the Spirit" (Eph. 5:18).

"This I say then, Walk in the Spirit, and ye shall not fulfill the lust of the flesh" (Gal. 5:16).

Believers in the book of Acts experienced the filling of the Holy Spirit often in their lives.

"And they were all filled with the Holy Ghost, and began to speak with other tongues, as the Spirit gave them utterance" (Acts 2:4).

"Then Peter, filled with the Holy Ghost, said unto them, Ye rulers of the people, and elders of Israel" (Acts 4:8).

"Wherefore, brethren, look ye out among you seven men of honest report, full of the Holy Ghost and wisdom, whom we may appoint over this business" (Acts 6:3).

"But he, being full of the Holy Ghost, looked up steadfastly into heaven, and saw the glory of God, and Jesus standing on the right hand of God" (Acts 7:55).

"And Ananias went his way, and entered into the house; and putting his hands on him said, Brother Saul, the Lord, even Jesus, that appeared unto thee in the way as thou camest, hath sent me, that thou mightest receive thy sight, and be filled with the Holy Ghost" (Acts 9:17).

"For he was a good man, and full of the Holy Ghost and of faith: and much people was added unto the Lord" (Acts 11:24).

"Then Saul, (who also is called Paul,) filled with the Holy Ghost, set his eyes on him" (Acts 13:9).

"And the disciples were filled with joy, and with the Holy Ghost" (Acts 13:52).

9. The first four ministries give us peace *with* God.

"Therefore being justified by faith, we have peace with God through our Lord Jesus Christ" (Rom. 5:1).

But the fifth ministry assures us the peace *of* God.

"And the peace of God, which passeth all understanding, shall keep your hearts and minds through Christ Jesus" (Phil. 4:7).

Thus, all Christians, regardless of how backslidden they might be, enjoy peace with God, but only Spirit-controlled believers can know that blessed peace of God.

10. In Acts 2:13 and in Ephesians 5:18 a comparison is made between being filled with the Spirit and being filled with wine.

"Others mocking said, These men are full of new wine" (Acts 2:13).

"And be not drunk with wine, wherein is excess; but be filled with the Spirit" (Eph. 5:18).

In all fairness, a comparison can be made between these two:

a. Both control the user and give him a new boldness, one in the good sense and the other in the bad sense of the word.

b. Both produce a desire for more.

11. The fifth ministry is lost whenever disobedience is found in the life of the believer. This disobedience may manifest itself in either (or both) of the following ways:

a. The sin of *quenching* the Holy Spirit.

"Quench not the Spirit" (1 Thess. 5:19).

This sin involves not doing that which the Holy Spirit would have us do. It is negative in nature. The same word is used elsewhere in reference to the putting out of a fire.

"A bruised reed shall he not break, and smoking flax shall he not quench, till he send forth judgment into victory" (Mt. 12:20).

"Above all, taking the shield of faith, wherewith ye shall be able to quench all the fiery darts of the wicked" (Eph. 6:16).

"Quenched the violence of fire, escaped the edge of the sword, out of weakness were made strong, waxed valiant in fight, turned to flight the armies of the aliens" (Heb. 11:34).

b. The sin of *grieving* the Holy Spirit.

"And grieve not the Holy Spirit of God, whereby ye are sealed unto the day of redemption" (Eph. 4:30).

This sin involves doing that which the Holy Spirit would not have us do. It is positive in nature.

To illustrate: A believer boards a plane in Chicago for Los Angeles and finds himself seated next to an unsaved man. In flight the Holy Spirit attempts to witness to the unsaved man through the testimony of the Christian, but he remains silent and fails to witness. At this point, the believer has *quenched* the Holy Spirit. He has not done that which the Spirit of God wanted him to do.

As the flight continues, however, the two men introduce themselves and begin talking, but not about spiritual things. In fact, to the shame of the Christian, several off-color stories are passed between the two men. Now the saved man has gone the second step and *grieved* the Holy Spirit—he has done that which the Holy Spirit did not want him to do.

These two sins, if left unchecked for a long period of time, can eventually lead to that "sin unto death" as described in the following passages:

"To deliver such a one unto Satan for the destruction of the flesh, that the spirit may be saved in the day of the Lord Jesus" (1 Cor. 5:5).

The sin unto death in this case was immorality on the part of a totally carnal believer in Corinth.

"For this cause many are weak and sickly among you, and many sleep" (1 Cor. 11:30).

In the case of Ananias and Sapphira, gross dishonesty and blatant hypocrisy led to the sin unto death (Acts 5:1-11). That Ananias was indeed a believer is proven by the question Peter asked him:

"Why hath Satan filled thine heart to lie to the Holy Ghost . . . ?" (Acts 5:3).

The sin unto death does not mean one loses salvation, but it does imply the possibility that God will remove him from the scene down here earlier than originally planned. This seemed to have been in the thoughts of Paul when he wrote:

"I therefore so run, not as uncertainly; so fight I, not as one that beateth the air: But I keep under my body, and bring it into subjection: lest that by any means, when I have preached to others, I myself should be a castaway" (1 Cor. 9:26, 27).

12. The fifth ministry may (and should be) instantly regained. This can be accomplished:
a. By knowing God's means of forgiveness and cleansing—the blood of Christ.

"But if we walk in the light, as he is in the light, we have fellowship one with another, and the blood of Jesus Christ his Son cleanseth us from all sin" (1 Jn. 1:7).

b. By knowing God's method of forgiveness and cleansing—the confession of the Christian.

"If we confess our sins, he is faithful and just to forgive us our sins, and to cleanse us from all unrighteousness" (1 Jn. 1:9).

This confession is absolutely vital, for while Christ's blood will cleanse us from all sins, it will not cleanse us from a single *excuse.*

God does not demand golden vessels, nor does he require silver ones, but he must have clean ones. Thus the union with the Spirit is so strong that nothing can break it, but the communion with the Spirit is so fragile that the smallest sin can shatter it.

Consider another illustration: A family leaves California to visit friends in New York. The first half of their trip is rather uneventful, but while they are in the Chicago area, their automobile breaks down. After some difficulty, the services of a mechanic are secured and the car is repaired. What action does the family take now? Does the driver head back for California and take another run for New York? All would agree that this, of course, would be sheer stupidity. What does this family do? They simply continue on from the spot where they first broke down.

This little travel story has a direct application to the Spirit-filled life. When God saves a man, he puts him on the road to heaven. For a while the trip may go smoothly for the new convert. But there will come a time when he will break down somewhere along the line. Perhaps the spiritual motor trouble will be caused by some angry words, or a wicked deed, or some careless act. The Spirit has been quenched and grieved and all forward progress ceases immediately. There the man sits.

What should he do? He should immediately secure the services of that divine mechanic, the Holy Spirit. If he confesses his sins and depends upon Christ's blood, his broken testimony will once again be restored. *Then* what should the believer do? The answer is obvious, of course; but there is a false concept among Christians today that once a child of God sins (particularly if it is a serious sin) he automatically loses all previous progress and must start all over. This simply is not the case! The secret of the Spirit-filled life is the knowledge that broken fellowship can be instantly restored by confession and by Christ's blood.

13. The fifth ministry assures the believer of the following blessings:
a. The Holy Spirit will pray for him.

"Likewise the Spirit also helpeth our infirmities: for we know not what we should pray for as we ought: but the Spirit itself maketh intercession for us with groanings which cannot be uttered" (Rom 8:26).

In the original text, the word "infirmities" is in the singular. Thus the one infirmity in mind here is our inability to pray as we ought to pray. It is for this reason that the Spirit comes to our aid. However, it should be kept in mind that the Bible says he "helpeth" us, which simply means he desires the Christian to do his part also. Therefore, to be effectively prayed for, we ourselves must pray.

"But ye, beloved, building up yourselves on your most holy faith, praying in the Holy Ghost" (Jude 20).

"For through him we both have access by one Spirit unto the Father" (Eph. 2:18).

"Praying always with all prayer and supplication in the Spirit, and watching thereunto with all perseverance and supplication for all saints" (Eph. 6:18).

b. The Holy Spirit will guide him.

"Howbeit when he, the Spirit of truth, is come, he will guide you into all truth: for he shall not speak of himself; but whatsoever he shall hear, that shall he speak: and he will show you things to come" (Jn. 16:13).

"For as many as are led by the Spirit of God, they are the sons of God" (Rom. 8:14).

c. The Holy Spirit will teach him.

"But the anointing which ye have received of him abideth in you, and ye need not that any man teach you: but as the same anointing teacheth you of all things, and is truth, and is no lie, and even as it hath taught you, ye shall abide in him" (1 Jn. 2:27).

d. The Holy Spirit will empower him for witnessing.

"But ye shall receive power, after that the Holy Ghost is come upon you: and ye shall be witnesses unto me both in Jerusalem, and in all Judea, and in Samaria, and unto the uttermost part of the earth" (Acts 1:8).

e. The Holy Spirit will impart the love of Christ to him and through him.

"And hope maketh not ashamed; because the love of God is shed abroad in our hearts by the Holy Ghost which is given unto us" (Rom. 5:5).

f. The Holy Spirit will conform him to the image of Christ.

"But we all, with open face beholding as in a glass the glory of the Lord, are changed into the same image from glory to glory, even as by the Spirit of the Lord" (2 Cor. 3:18).

The ultimate goal and stated intention of the Father is to conform the believer throughout eternity into the image of Christ. This is made clear in such passages as Philippians 3:21 and 1 John 3:2. But God the Spirit desires to start this glorious work in each child of God at the moment of salvation. (See Phil. 3:10.)

g. The Holy Spirit will strengthen his new nature.

"That he would grant you, according to the riches of his glory, to be strengthened with might by his Spirit in the inner man" (Eph. 3:16).

This he does through Bible study (1 Pet. 2:2) and prayer (Jude 1:20).

h. The Holy Spirit will reveal biblical truth to him.

"But God hath revealed them unto us by his Spirit: for the Spirit searcheth all things, yea, the deep things of God" (1 Cor. 2:10).

i. The Holy Spirit will assure him concerning salvation and service.

"The Spirit itself beareth witness with our spirit, that we are the children of God" (Rom. 8:16).

"And he that keepeth his commandments dwelleth in him, and he in him. And hereby we know that he abideth in us, by the Spirit which he hath given us" (1 Jn. 3:24).

j. The Holy Spirit will give him liberty.

"For the law of the Spirit of life in Christ Jesus hath made me free from the law of sin and death" (Rom. 8:2).

"Now the Lord is that Spirit: and where the Spirit of the Lord is, there is liberty" (2 Cor. 3:17).

k. The Holy Spirit will fill his mouth with appropriate things.

"But when they shall lead you, and deliver you up, take no thought beforehand what ye shall speak, neither do ye premeditate: but whatsoever shall be given you in that hour, that speak ye: for it is not ye that speak, but the Holy Ghost" (Mk. 13:11).

Several instances come to mind in the book of Acts where this blessed prophecy was fulfilled. See Acts 4:8-22; 5:29-33; 7:55.

J. His ministry concerning the gifts of Christ.

"There is one body, and one Spirit, even as ye are called in one hope of your calling; one Lord, one faith, one baptism, one God and Father of all, who is above all, and through all, and in you all. But unto every one of us is given grace according to the measure of the gift of Christ. Wherefore he saith, When he ascended up on high, he led captivity captive, and gave gifts unto men" (Eph. 4:4-8).

In the Bible the entire Trinity is often described in the act of giving. God loves to give. It was the Father who gave his dearly beloved Son.

"For God so loved the world, that he gave his only begotten Son, that whosoever believeth in him should not perish, but have everlasting life" (Jn. 3:16).

It was the Son who freely gave his precious blood.

"And he took bread, and gave thanks, and brake it, and gave unto them, saying, This is my body which is given for you: this do in remembrance of me" (Lk. 22:19).

Finally, after his arrival at Pentecost, the Holy Spirit began his ministry of gift-giving to the church, and will continue it until the rapture.

1. The definition of a spiritual gift.

A spiritual gift is a supernatural ability given by Christ through the Holy Spirit to the believer at the moment of his salvation. At this point two distinctives should be made.

a. The distinction between the gift of the Spirit and the gifts of the Spirit. The gift occurred at Pentecost when the Holy Spirit came in answer to the promise of Christ. The gifts occur today.

b. The distinction between gifts and talents. A talent is a human and natural ability given at birth. It may be in the area of music, speech, organization, etc. But no natural talent, however great it might be, can be used by its owner to glorify God until it is sanctioned by the Holy Spirit. When this occurs, the talent then may become a gift.

To illustrate this, let's consider an individual who is a brilliant and talented musician. His ability is acclaimed by millions. But the performer is not a Christian and thus his talent can never be used by the Holy Spirit for the glory of God. But let us assume the man hears the gospel and accepts Christ as Savior. Now the Holy Spirit may determine to transform the man's natural talent into a supernatural gift. As there is no specific gift of music as such, the musician's new efforts for Christ would probably fall under that of exhortation, which is a listed gift.

2. The extent of the spiritual gifts.
a. Each believer possesses at least one spiritual gift.
"As every man hath received the gift, even so minister the same one to another, as good stewards of the manifold grace of God" (1 Pet. 4:10).

"But unto every one of us is given grace according to the measure of the gift of Christ" (Eph. 4:7).

"For I would that all men were even as I myself. But every man hath his proper gift of God, one after this manner, and another after that" (1 Cor. 7:7).

"But the manifestation of the Spirit is given to every man to profit withal" (1 Cor. 12:7).

"But all these worketh that one and the selfsame Spirit, dividing to every man severally as he will" (1 Cor. 12:11).

b. No believer possesses all the gifts.
"Are all apostles? are all prophets? are all teachers? are all workers of miracles? Have all the gifts of healing? do all speak with tongues? do all interpret?" (1 Cor. 12:29, 30).

3. The purpose of the spiritual gifts.
a. To glorify the Father.
"Thou art worthy, O Lord, to receive glory and honor and power: for thou hast created all things, and for thy pleasure they are and were created" (Rev. 4:11).

b. To edify the church.
"For the perfecting of the saints, for the work of the ministry, for the edi-

fying of the body of Christ: Till we all come in the unity of the faith, and of the knowledge of the Son of God, unto a perfect man, unto the measure of the stature of the fulness of Christ" (Eph. 4:13).

4. The abuse of the spiritual gifts.
a. Not using those gifts imparted to us.
"Wherefore I put thee in remembrance, that thou stir up the gift of God, which is in thee by the putting on of my hands" (2 Tim. 1:6).

"Neglect not the gift that is in thee, which was given thee by prophecy, with the laying on of the hands of the presbytery" (1 Tim. 4:14).

b. Attempting to use those gifts not imparted to us.
c. Not using the gifts in love.
"Though I speak with the tongues of men and of angels, and have not charity, I am become as sounding brass, or a tinkling cymbal" (1 Cor. 13:1).

How often are those blessed gifts abused. Only eternity will reveal the number of men in the ministry who should never have been there. On the other hand (and just as tragic) there has doubtless been a great company of men who were called into God's service, but never answered it. But perhaps the greatest abuse of all is the use of gifts without love.

If one rightly comprehends the material given thus far on gifts, he can understand why God sometimes seems to use a carnal Christian in a great way in spite of the glaring (or often secret) sins in his life. However, in such cases God is only blessing the gift and not the man personally. At the judgment seat of Christ (see 1 Cor. 3) there will doubtless be many surprises as perhaps a number of world-famous Christian leaders receive so little actual personal reward from Christ because of their sins and carnality.

5. The number of the spiritual gifts. In three main passages, the Apostle Paul lists eighteen separate spiritual gifts for us. These passages are: Romans 12:6-8; 1 Corinthians 12:4-7; Ephesians 4:11.

6. The nature of the spiritual gifts. It would seem that these eighteen gifts can be placed into two basic categories, the permanent stationary gifts and the temporary sign gifts.

7. The description of the spiritual gifts.
a. The seven temporary sign gifts. These would include the gifts of apostleship, prophecy, miracles, healing, tongues, interpretation of tongues, and knowledge.

At this point it is relevant to ask by what right do we designate the sign gifts as temporary in duration. The answer is found in the miraculous nature of the gift itself. Imagine yourself to be a spokesman sent from God some twenty centuries ago, before most of the New Testament was written. You have a message from the Lord. But how can your listeners be sure you are not one more false prophet among the many of the day? One dramatic indication of your genuineness would be the ability to perform miraculous signs. Note the following verses which bring this out:

"The same came to Jesus by night, and said unto him, Rabbi, we know that thou art a teacher come from God: for no man can do these miracles that thou doest, except God be with him" (Jn. 3:2).

"And many other signs truly did Jesus in the presence of his disciples, which are not written in this book" (Jn. 20:30).

"For I will not dare to speak of any of those things which Christ hath not wrought by me, to make the Gentiles obedient, by word and deed" (Rom. 15:18).

"Truly the signs of an apostle were wrought among you in all patience, in signs, and wonders, and mighty deeds" (2 Cor. 12:12).

"God also bearing them witness, both with signs and wonders, and with divers miracles, and gifts of the Holy Ghost, according to his own will?" (Heb. 2:4).

The sign gifts were given primarily to validate the authority of the Savior and his apostles prior to the writing of the New Testament. Afterward, this miraculous proof was no longer needed, for the Scriptures themselves reveal the true from the false.

(1) The gift of apostleship. A reference to certain men called by Christ himself and endued with special power to function as the official "charter members" of the newly organized church.

"And he gave some, apostles; and some, prophets; and some, evangelists; and some, pastors and teachers" (Eph. 4:11).

"And God hath set some in the church, first apostles, secondarily prophets, thirdly teachers, after that miracles, then gifts of healings, helps, governments, diversities of tongues" (1 Cor. 12:28).

(a) Apostolic requirements. One must have seen the resurrected Christ.

"Beginning from the baptism of John, unto that same day that he was taken up from us, must one be ordained to be a witness with us of his resurrection" (Acts 1:22).

"Am I not an apostle? am I not free? have I not seen Jesus Christ our Lord? are not ye my work in the Lord?" (1 Cor. 9:1).

(b) Apostolic number. The total number of the early apostles was not limited to twelve. (See Lk. 6:13; Acts 1:26; 14:14; Rom. 1:1; 11:13; Gal. 1:19; 1 Cor. 9:1; 15:7; 2 Cor. 11:5; 12:12.)

(2) The gift of prophecy.

"Having then gifts differing according to the grace that is given to us, whether prophecy, let us prophesy according to the proportion of faith" (Rom. 12:6).

"To another the working of miracles; to another prophecy; to another discerning of spirits; to another divers kinds of tongues; to another the interpretation of tongues" (1 Cor. 12:10).

(See also 1 Cor. 14:1, 3–6; Eph. 4:11.)

Prophecy is the supernatural ability to see into the future. The Bible itself was written in this manner. (See Mt. 13:14; 2 Pet. 1:20, 21.)

"Blessed is he that readeth, and they that hear the words of this prophecy, and keep those things which are written therein: for the time is at hand" (Rev. 1:3).

"And in these days came prophets from Jerusalem unto Antioch. And there stood up one of them named Agabus, and signified by the Spirit that there should be great dearth throughout all the world: which came to pass in the days of Claudius Caesar" (Acts 11:27, 28).

"And as we tarried there many days, there came down from Judea a certain prophet, named Agabus. And when he was come unto us, he took Paul's girdle, and bound his own hands and feet, and said, Thus saith the Holy Ghost, So shall the Jews at Jerusalem bind the man that owneth this girdle, and shall deliver him into the hands of the Gentiles" (Acts 21:10, 11).

(3) The gift of miracles. A supernatural ability to perform those events outside and beyond the realm of nature; the ability to set aside for a time the regular laws of nature.

"And God hath set some in the church, first apostles, secondarily prophets, thirdly teachers, after that miracles, then gifts of healings, helps, governments, diversities of tongues" (1 Cor. 12:28).

(4) The gift of healing. A supernatural ability to cure human ills, whether of physical, mental, or demonic origin.

"To another faith by the same Spirit; to another the gifts of healing by the same Spirit; and God hath set some in the church, first apostles, secondarily prophets, thirdly teachers, after that miracles, then gifts of healing, helps, governments, diversities of tongues. Have all the gifts of healing? do all speak with tongues? do all interpret?" (1 Cor. 12:9, 28, 30).

(a) The purpose of the gift of healing. As in the case of miracles, this gift was apparently given to attest to the authority and power of the one doing the healing.

(b) The limitation of the gift of healing. Christ did not heal all those he encountered. (See Lk. 4:25-27; Jn 5:3-9.)

Paul was limited in his healing abilities as seen in his own affliction (2 Cor. 12:7-10).

As seen in the case of Epaphroditus (Phil. 2:26, 27).

As seen in the case of Timothy (1 Tim. 5:23).

As seen in the case of Trophimus (2 Tim. 4:20).

(5) The gift of tongues.

"To another the working of miracles; to another prophecy; to another discerning of spirits; to another divers kinds of tongues: to another the interpretation of tongues" (1 Cor. 12:10).

Until the completion of the New Testament God used the gift of tongues to act as a sign to the unbeliever (both Jew and Gentile) and as a means to edify the believer.

"He that speaketh in an unknown tongue edifieth himself: but he that prophesieth edifieth the church. Wherefore tongues are for a sign, not to them that believe, but to them that believe not: but prophesying serveth not for them that believe not, but for them which believe" (1 Cor. 14:4, 22).

(6) The gift of the interpretation of tongues (1 Cor. 12:10). This is the supernatural ability to clarify and interpret those messages uttered in an unknown language.

(7) The gift of knowledge. The supernatural ability to receive by revelation and transmit by inspiration, a portion of the Word of God.

"For to one is given by the Spirit the word of wisdom; to another the word of knowledge by the same Spirit" (1 Cor. 12:8).

These, then, are the seven temporary sign gifts.

b. The eleven permanent gifts.

(1) The gift of wisdom (1 Cor. 12:8). If the definition of the gift of knowledge is correct, then the gift of wisdom would refer to that supernatural ability to rightfully *apply* and spiritually *employ* that information gathered through the gift of knowledge.

(2) The gift of the discerning of spirits.

"To another the working of miracles; to another prophecy; to another discerning of spirits; to another divers kinds of tongues; to another the interpretation of tongues" (1 Cor. 12:10).

(See also 1 Jn. 4:1.)

This gift is the supernatural ability to distinguish between demonic, human, and divine spirits in another person. Both Peter and Paul possessed this gift.

(3) The gift of giving.

"Or he that exhorteth, on exhortation: he that giveth, let him do it with simplicity; he that ruleth, with diligence; he that showeth mercy, with cheerfulness" (Rom. 12:8).

This is the supernatural ability to accumulate and give large amounts of one's finances to the glory of God. In the book of Acts members of three local churches apparently possessed this gift.

(a) The Jerusalem church (Acts 4:32-37).

(b) The Galatian church (Gal. 4:15).

(c) The Philippian church (Phil. 4:10-18).

A pre-Pentecost foreshadowing of this gift is seen in the account of the widow's mite (Lk. 21:1-4).

(4) The gift of exhortation (Rom. 12:8; see also Prov. 25:11).

Several New Testament individuals had this gift:

(a) Barnabas (Acts 11:22-24).

(b) Judas (not Iscariot) and Silas (Acts 15:32).

(c) A believer referred to as "yokefellow" (Phil. 4:3).

(d) Paul.

"Therefore I thought it necessary to exhort the brethren, that they would go before unto you, and make up beforehand your bounty, whereof ye had notice before, that the same might be ready, as a matter of bounty, and not as of covetousness" (2 Cor. 9:5).

(See also Acts 14:22; 1 Thess. 2:11; 4:1; 5:14).

(e) Peter.

"The elders which are among you I exhort, who am also an elder, and a witness of the sufferings of Christ, and also a partaker of the glory that shall be revealed" (1 Pet. 5:1).

(f) Jude (Jude 3).

(5) The gift of ministering. The supernatural ability to render practical help in both physical and spiritual matters.

"Or ministry, let us wait on our ministering; or he that teacheth, on teaching" (Rom. 12:7).

"And God hath set some in the church, first apostles, secondarily prophets, thirdly teachers, after that miracles, then gifts of healings, helps, governments, diversities of tongues" (1 Cor. 12:28).

This gift is called the gift of helps in 1 Corinthians 12:28. How sorely needed is the gift of helps in local churches today. There seems to be an abundance of eloquent pastors and colorful evangelists, but where are the helpers?

(a) Dorcas had this gift (Acts 9:36–39).

(b) Phoebe had this gift (Rom. 16:1, 2).

(6) The gift of the showing of mercy.

"Or he that exhorteth, on exhortation: he that giveth, let him do it with simplicity; he that ruleth, with diligence; he that showeth mercy, with cheerfulness" (Rom. 12:8).

Often untrained laypeople possess this supernatural ability to minister to those sick and afflicted.

(7) The gift of ruling, or administration (see Rom. 12:8). This is the supernatural ability to organize, administer, and promote the various affairs of a local church (Titus 1:4, 5). A local church will not grow beyond a certain point unless it employs the ministry of those individuals empowered with this gift.

(8) The gift of faith. The Bible describes three kinds of faith:

(a) Saving faith: given to all repenting sinners.

"And they said, Believe on the Lord Jesus Christ, and thou shalt be saved, and thy house" (Acts 16:31).

(See also Rom. 4:5; 5:1; 10:17.)

(b) Sanctifying faith: available to all believers.

"I am crucified with Christ: nevertheless I live; yet not I, but Christ liveth in me: and the life which I now live in the flesh I live by the faith of the Son of God, who loved me, and gave himself for me" (Gal. 2:20).

(See also Gal. 3:11; 5:22; Eph. 6:16; Rom. 1:17; Heb. 10:38.)

(c) Stewardship faith: given to some believers.

"For I say, through the grace given unto me, to every man that is among you, not to think of himself more highly than he ought to think; but to think soberly according as God hath dealt to every man the measure of faith" (Rom. 12:3).

(See 1 Cor. 12:9.)

This is the *gift* kind of faith, and is a supernatural ability to believe and expect great things from God.

(9) The gift of teaching. The supernatural ability to communicate and clarify the details of the Word of God.

"Or ministry, let us wait on our ministering; or he that teacheth, on teaching" (Rom. 12:7).

This gift was given to:

(a) Paul.

"For I have not shunned to declare unto you all the counsel of God" (Acts 20:27).

(b) Apollos (Acts 18:24, 25).

(c) Aquila and Priscilla (Acts 18:26).

While no one can present a better gospel than that in the Bible, there are those who can teach that gospel better. This is the gift of teaching.

(10) The gift of evangelism. The supernatural ability to point sinners to Christ and to burden Christians about soul-winning. All believers are to witness for Christ whether they have this special gift or not. Timothy, for example, was not an evangelist, but he was a soul-winner.

"But watch thou in all things, endure afflictions, do the work of an evangelist, make full proof of thy ministry" (2 Tim. 4:5).

There are others, however, who were given this gift. Philip, among others in the book of Acts, possessed it (Acts 8:26–40; 21:8).

(11) The gift of pastor-teacher. The supernatural ability to preach and teach the Word of God and to feed and lead the flock of God.

"The elders which are among you I exhort, who am also an elder, and a witness of the sufferings of Christ, and also a partaker of the glory that shall be revealed: Feed the flock of God which is among you, taking the oversight thereof, not by constraint, but willingly; not for filthy lucre, but of a ready mind; neither as being lord over God's heritage, but being ensamples to the flock. And when the chief Shepherd shall appear, ye shall receive a crown of glory that fadeth not away" (1 Pet. 5:1-4).

(See also Acts 20:28.)

This is the only "double-portion" gift of the eighteen gifts. Thus, all teachers are not called to be pastors, but all pastors are to be teachers.

K. His ministry concerning the fruit of the Spirit. We now come to the eleventh and final recorded ministry performed by the Holy Spirit of God. In a very real sense it best demonstrates his ultimate goal here on earth, namely, to bear fruit for Christ through believers.

"But now being made free from sin, and become servants to God, ye have your fruit unto holiness, and the end everlasting life" (Rom. 6:22).

"Wherefore, my brethren, ye also are become dead to the law by the body of Christ; that ye should be married to another, even to him who is raised from the dead, that we should bring forth fruit unto God" (Rom. 7:4).

"That ye might walk worthy of the Lord unto all pleasing, being fruitful in every good work, and increasing in the knowledge of God" (Col. 1:10).

1. The commands to bear fruit.
   a. God desires his new creation to do the same as he ordered his old creation to do.
      "And God blessed them, and God said unto them, Be fruitful, and multiply, and replenish the earth, and subdue it: and have dominion over the fish of the sea, and over the fowl of the air, and over every living thing that moveth upon the earth" (Gen. 1:28).
   b. God desires the believer to fulfill the prophecy concerning Joseph.
      "Joseph is a fruitful bough, even a fruitful bough by a well; whose branches run over the wall" (Gen. 49:22).
   c. God desires his children to experience the blessings of Psalm 1.
      "And he shall be like a tree planted by the rivers of water, that bringeth forth his fruit in his season; his leaf also shall not wither; and whatsoever he doeth shall prosper" (Ps. 1:3).

d. God desires his children of light to function *today* as his tree of life will function in eternity. (See Rev. 22:1, 2.)

2. The prerequisites for bearing fruit.
   a. One must die to this world.
      "Verily, verily, I say unto you, Except a corn of wheat fall into the ground and die, it abideth alone: but if it die, it bringeth forth much fruit" (Jn. 12:24).
   b. One must abide in the savior. (See Jn. 15:1-5; 16.)
      In the Old Testament the nation Israel was God's chosen vine vessel.
      "Thou hast brought a vine out of Egypt: thou hast cast out the heathen, and planted it" (Ps. 80:8).
      But Israel refused to bear fruit.
      "Israel is an empty vine, he bringeth forth fruit unto himself: according to the multitude of his fruit he hath increased the altars; according to the goodness of his land they have made goodly images" (Hosea 10:1).
      Thus, that nation was eventually set aside by Jesus.
      "Therefore say I unto you, The kingdom of God shall be taken from you, and given to a nation bringing forth the fruits thereof" (Mt. 21:43).
      In the Gospels, Christ was God's chosen vine vessel while he was on this earth.
      "I am the true vine, and my Father is the husbandman" (Jn. 15:1).
      (See also Isa. 11:1; 53:2.)
      Jesus told his disciples they were to be branches. The only useful function of a branch is to bear fruit. A branch does not produce fruit, it simply bears it.

3. The two kinds of fruit.
   a. Outer fruit: soul-winning.
      "Say not ye, There are yet four months, and then cometh harvest? behold, I say unto you, Lift up your eyes, and look on the fields; for they are white already to harvest. And he that reapeth receiveth wages, and gathereth fruit unto life eternal: that both he that soweth and he that reapeth may rejoice together" (Jn. 4:35, 36).
      (See also Rom. 1:13; Prov. 11:30.)
   b. Inner fruit: Christlikeness.
      "But the fruit of the Spirit is love, joy, peace, long-suffering, gentleness, goodness, faith, meekness, temperance: against such there is no law" (Gal. 5:22, 23). (Cf. Eph. 5:9.)
      It should be noted that the word fruit in both of these passages is in the singular. Paul does not say "the fruits of the Spirit are," but rather, "the fruit of the Spirit is." The reason is this: all the fruit of the Spirit, unlike all the gifts of the Spirit, are to be possessed by every believer.

4. The eleven fruits of the Spirit.

a. Love.

"And above all these things put on charity, which is the bond of perfectness" (Col. 3:14).

b. Joy.

"But the fruit of the Spirit is love, joy, peace, long-suffering, gentleness, goodness, faith" (Gal. 5:22).

"For the kingdom of God is not meat and drink; but righteousness, and peace, and joy in the Holy Ghost" (Rom. 14:17).

c. Peace. There are two kinds of peace:

(1) The peace *with* God.

"Therefore being justified by faith, we have peace, with God through our Lord Jesus Christ" (Rom. 5:1).

This peace is *positional* peace and includes all believers at the moment of their salvation.

(2) The peace *of* God.

"And the peace of God, which passeth all understanding, shall keep your hearts and minds through Christ Jesus" (Phil. 4:7).

This peace is *experienced,* and includes only those believers who are filled with God's Spirit. It can be defined as reassurance in tribulation.

d. Longsuffering: the ability to cheerfully bear an unbearable situation and to patiently endure the unendurable.

"By pureness, by knowledge, by longsuffering, by kindness by the Holy Ghost, by love unfeigned" (2 Cor. 6:6).

"Or despisest thou the riches of his goodness and forbearance and longsuffering; not knowing that the goodness of God leadeth thee to repentance?" (Rom. 2:4).

e. Gentleness: a quiet and respectful kindness.

"To speak evil of no man, to be no brawlers, but gentle, shewing all meekness unto all men" (Titus 3:2).

"And the servant of the Lord must not strive; but be gentle unto all men, apt to teach, patient . . ." (2 Tim. 2:24).

f. Faith.

"I am crucified with Christ: nevertheless I live; yet not I, but Christ liveth in me: and the life which I now live in the flesh I live by the faith of the Son of God, who loved me, and gave himself for me" (Gal. 2:20).

"But that no man is justified by the law in the sight of God, it is evident: for, The just shall live by faith" (Gal. 3:11).

g. Righteousness: right acts; going the appointed mile.

"Being filled with the fruits of righteousness, which are by Jesus Christ, unto the glory and praise of God" (Phil. 1:11).

"Now no chastening for the present seemeth to be joyous, but grievous: nevertheless, afterward it yieldeth the peaceable fruit of righteousness unto them which are exercised thereby" (Heb. 12:11).

h. Goodness: wholesome acts; going the extra mile.

"And whosoever shall compel thee to go a mile, go with him twain" (Mt. 5:41).

i. Meekness: subdued strength.

(1) Paul used this method in dealing with the Corinthian church.

"What will ye? shall I come unto you with a rod, or in love, and in the spirit of meekness?" (1 Cor. 4:21).

(2) This is the method to be used by spiritual people in restoring a backslider.

"Put on therefore, as the elect of God, holy and beloved, bowels of mercies, kindness, humbleness of mind, meekness, longsuffering; forbearing one another, and forgiving one another, if any man have a quarrel against any: even as Christ forgave you, so also do ye" (Col. 3:12, 13). (Cf. Gal. 6:1.)

(3) It is to be used in keeping unity within a church.

"With all lowliness and meekness with longsuffering, forbearing one another in love; endeavouring to keep the unity of the Spirit in the bond of peace" (Eph. 4:2, 3).

(4) It is the method to be used in dealing with all men.

"And the servant of the Lord must not strive; but be gentle unto all men, apt to teach, patient; in meekness instructing those that oppose themselves; if God peradventure will give them repentance to the acknowledging of the truth" (2 Tim. 2:24, 25). (Cf. Titus 3:2.)

j. Temperance: self-control. The great New Testament example of this is the Apostle Paul. Observe his testimony:

"For though I be free from all men, yet have I made myself servant unto all, that I might gain the more. And unto the Jews I became as a Jew, that I might gain the Jews; to them that are under the law, as under the law, that I might gain them that are under the law; to them that are without law, as without law, (being not without law to God, but under the law to Christ,) that I might gain them that are without law. To the weak became I as weak, that I might gain the weak: I am made all things to all men, that I might by all means save some. And this I do for the gospel's sake, that I might be partaker thereof with you. Know ye not that they which run in a race run all, but one receiveth the prize? So run, that ye may obtain. And every man that striveth for the mastery is temperate in all things. Now they do it to obtain a corruptible crown; but we an incorruptible. I therefore so run, not as uncertainly; so fight I, not as one that beateth the air: But I keep under my body, and bring it into subjection: lest that by any means, when I have preached to others, I myself should be a castaway" (1 Cor. 9:19-27).

k. Truth: living an open life, without guile and hypocrisy.

"Therefore, seeing we have this ministry, as we have received mercy, we faint not; but have renounced the hidden things of dishonesty, not walking in craftiness, nor handling the word of God deceitfully; but, by manifestation of the truth, commending ourselves to every man's conscience in the sight of God" (2 Cor. 4:1, 2).

THE DOCTRINE OF MAN

THE DOCTRINE OF MAN

We shall approach this study of man in the following manner:

I. His Origin.
II. His Nature.
III. His Original Duties and Responsibilities.
IV. His Tragic Sin and Fall.
V. His Present-Day Condition.
VI. His Destiny.

I. His Origin. Three theories have been propounded to explain man's origin:

A. Atheistic evolution. This theory holds that man is the accidental and random product of a blind and nonpersonal series of chemical and biological events. Simply defined, evolution is that process by which all living organisms have developed from the simple to the more complex forms. This theory would have us believe that our world and all it contains came into being through evolving mud in time past. We are assured that if we but allow a little mud enough time it will, of and by itself, produce the music of a Beethoven, the paintings of a Raphael, the writings of a Shakespeare, and the teachings of a Christ. Needless to say, this theory is not only unscriptural, but nonsensical as well.

B. Theistic evolution. This teaches that there is one God, the Creator of matter, who chose the method of evolution to bring all things including man into their present state of existence. However, evolution as a method is clearly, strongly, and completely refuted by the Bible.

1. Genesis teaches that life began on dry land, while evolution says it began on some remote sea bottom.

   "And God said, Let the earth bring forth grass, the herb yielding seed, and the fruit tree yielding fruit after his kind, whose seed is in itself, upon the earth: and it was so. And the earth brought forth grass, and herb yielding seed after his kind, and the tree yielding fruit, whose seed was in itself, after his kind: and God saw that it was good" (Gen. 1:11, 12).

2. Genesis declares that birds existed before insects, while evolution reverses this order.

   "And God said, Let the waters bring forth abundantly the moving creature that hath life, and fowl that may fly above the earth in the open firmament of heaven. And God said, Let the earth bring forth the living creature after his kind, cattle, and creeping thing, and beast of the earth after his kind: and it was so" (Gen. 1:20, 24).

3. Genesis states that birds and fishes were created at the same time, but evolution says fishes evolved hundreds of millions of years before birds developed.

   "And God created great whales, and every living creature that moveth, which the waters brought forth abundantly, after their kind, and every winged fowl after his kind: and God saw that it was good" (Gen. 1:21).

4. Genesis stresses (ten times) that the entities created were to reproduce "after their kinds," while evolution postulates the slow ascent of all organisms from a common ancestor.

5. Genesis says that Adam was made from the dust of the ground into the image of God, while evolution claims Adam descended from a sub-ape creature.

6. Genesis records woman's coming from man's side, while evolution teaches both man and woman developed simultaneously.

7. Genesis tells us that man was originally a vegetarian while evolution teaches us he was probably a head-hunting cannibal.

   "And God said, Behold, I have given you every herb bearing seed, which is upon the face of all the earth, and every tree, in the which is the fruit of a tree yielding seed; to you it shall be for meat" (Gen. 1:29).

C. Special creation. This is the view that man is a direct product from the hand of God and that the statements in Genesis 1 and 2 are to be taken at face value. In addition to this, a number of Bible students see in these first two chapters a clear case for believing in a special twenty-four-hour, six-day creation week. This, it is believed, can be seen:

1. As indicated by the Hebrew language. If the days were really long periods of time, the Hebrew word *olam* (meaning a long, indefinite time) would doubtless have been used, rather than the Hebrew word *yom* (which means day).

   "The use of a numerical adjective with the word *day* in Genesis 1 limits it to a normal day . . . in historical narratives the numerical adjective always limits the word to a twenty-four-hour period (cf. Numbers 7 for a remarkable parallel)." (Dr. John C. Whitcomb, Jr., *Creation According to God's Word*, p. 4)

2. As indicated by the genealogies found in Genesis 5 and 11. If evolution is correct and man is really a million years old, then we would be forced to allow a fifty-thousand-year gap between each name in these two chapters. Furthermore, if life itself is nearly one billion years old, then each day in Genesis 1 would have to stand for approximately 125 million years.

3. As indicated by Moses at Mt. Sinai.

"Six days shalt thou labor, and do all thy work: But the seventh day is the sabbath of the Lord thy God: in it thou shalt not do any work, thou, nor thy son, nor thy daughter, thy manservant, nor thy maidservant, nor thy cattle, nor thy stranger that is within thy gates: For in six days the Lord made heaven and earth, the sea, and all that in them is, and rested the seventh day: wherefore the Lord blessed the sabbath day, and hallowed it" (Ex. 20:9-11).

"Wherefore the children of Israel shall keep the sabbath, to observe the sabbath throughout their generations, for a perpetual covenant. It is a sign between me and the children of Israel for ever: for in six days the Lord made heaven and earth, and on the seventh day he rested, and was refreshed" (Ex. 31:16, 17).

4. As indicated by David.

"By the word of the Lord were the heavens made; and all the host of them by the breath of his mouth. He gathereth the waters of the sea together as a heap: he layeth up the depth in storehouses. For he spake, and it was done; he commanded, and it stood fast" (Ps. 33:6, 7, 9).

5. As indicated by Jesus. The Savior evidently accepted literally the first three chapters of Genesis.

"Which was the son of Enos, which was the son of Seth, which was the son of Adam, which was the son of God" (Lk. 3:38).

"And he answered and said unto them, Have ye not read, that he which made them at the beginning made them male and female" (Mt. 19:4).

"If I have told you earthly things, and ye believe not, how shall ye believe, if I tell you of heavenly things?" (Jn. 3:12).

"For had ye believed Moses, ye would have believed me: for he wrote of me. But if ye believe not his writings, how shall ye believe my words?" (Jn. 5:46, 47).

6. As indicated by Paul.

"Wherefore, as by one man sin entered into the world, and death by sin; and so death passed upon all men, for that all have sinned: Nevertheless death reigned from Adam to Moses, even over them that had not sinned after the similitude of Adam's transgression, who is the figure of him that was to come. For if by one man's offense death reigned by one; much more they which receive abundance of grace and of the gift of righteousness shall reign in life by one, Jesus Christ. For as by one man's disobedience many were made sinners, so by the obedience of one shall many be made righteous" (Rom. 5:12, 14, 17, 19).

"For the earnest expectation of the creature waiteth for the manifestation of the sons of God. For the creature was made subject to vanity, not willingly, but by reason of him, who hath subjected the same in hope; because the creature itself also shall be delivered from the bondage of corruption into the glorious liberty of the children of God. For we know that the whole creation groaneth and travaileth in pain together until now" (Rom. 8:19-22).

"For the man is not of the woman; but the woman of the man. Neither was the man created for the woman; but the woman for the man. For as the woman is of the man, even so is the man also by the woman; but all things of God" (1 Cor. 11:8, 9, 12).

"All flesh is not the same flesh: but there is one kind of flesh of men, another flesh of beasts, another of fishes, and another of birds. It is sown a natural body, it is raised a spiritual body. There is a natural body, and there is a spiritual body. And so it is written, The first man Adam was made a living soul; the last Adam was made a quickening spirit. Howbeit that was not first which is spiritual, but that which is natural; and afterward that which is spiritual. The first man is of the earth, earthy: the second man is the Lord from heaven. As is the earthy, such are they also that are earthy: and as is the heavenly, such are they also that are heavenly, And as we have borne the image of the earthy, we shall also bear the image of the heavenly" (1 Cor. 15:39, 44-49).

"But I fear, lest by any means, as the serpent beguiled Eve through his subtilty, so your minds should be corrupted from the simplicity that is in Christ" (2 Cor. 11:3).

"For Adam was first formed, then Eve. And Adam was not deceived, but the woman being deceived was in the transgression" (1 Tim. 2:13, 14).

7. As indicated by Benjamin Warfield (one of the greatest orthodox theologians of modern time). Although Warfield admitted the possibility of man existing for over 100 thousand years, he personally believed man's creation date to be no earlier than 5,000 to 10,000 B.C. (p. 248 in *Biblical and Theological Studies*).

8. As indicated by Edward Young (outstanding Hebrew scholar).

"The six days are to be understood in a chronological sense, that is one day following another in succession. This fact is emphasized in that the days are designated one, two, three, etc." (*Westminster Theological Journal*, May 1963, p. 169)

9. As indicated by the *Interpreter's Bible* (Vol. I, p. 417).

"There can be no question but that by 'day' the author means just what we mean—the time required for one revolution of the earth on its axis. Had he meant an aeon he would certainly, in view of his fondness for numbers, have stated the number of millenniums each period embraces."

Note: Even though the *Interpreter's Bible* (a very liberal work) would doubtless consider the first eleven chapters of Genesis as pure myth, it nevertheless holds that the Genesis writer believed in a literal six-day creation account.

In concluding this first section it is important to remind ourselves of the absolute necessity of believing God's Word concerning our origin, for if we allow Satan to water this down for us, we may permit the same doubt concerning our present mission as ambassadors for Christ and our future destiny.

It is here proper to remember the words of Jesus to Nicodemus:

"If I have told you earthly things, and ye believe not, how shall ye believe, if I tell you of heavenly things?" (Jn. 3:12).

II. His Nature. In dealing with man's nature, we will ask and attempt to answer five basic questions.

A. How is man made in the image and likeness of God?

"And God said, Let us make man in our image, after our likeness; and let them have dominion over the fish of the sea, and the fowl of the air, and over the cattle, and over all the earth, and over every creeping thing that creepeth upon the earth. So God created man in his own image, in the image of God created he him; male and female created he them" (Gen. 1:26, 27).

How are we to understand these words? Throughout the history of the Christian church various theories have been propounded.

1. That this likeness is a reference to the trinity of man. In other words, as God is triune in nature (Father, Son, and Holy Spirit), he created man a triune creature consisting of spirit, soul, and body. Advocates of this theory point to the following verses to support their claims:

"For the word of God is quick, and powerful, and sharper than any twoedged sword, piercing even to the dividing asunder of soul and spirit, and of the joints and marrow, and is a discerner of the thoughts and intents of the heart" (Heb. 4:12).

"And the very God of peace sanctify you wholly; and I pray God your whole spirit and soul and body be preserved blameless unto the coming of our Lord Jesus Christ" (1 Thess. 5:23).

2. That man is created in the image of God in that his Creator gave him self-consciousness, God-consciousness, and a sense of morality. Simply stated, this means man can identify himself, know his God, look back to his birth, and plan for his death.

3. That when God spoke these words he was thinking of the future incarnation of Christ, the God-man, and his present-day work in making the Christian like himself. Note the following verses:

"For our conversation is in heaven; from whence also we look for the Saviour, the Lord Jesus Christ: Who shall change our vile body, that it may be fashioned like unto his glorious body, according to the working whereby he is able even to subdue all things unto himself" (Phil. 3:20, 21).

"For whom he did foreknow, he also did predestinate to be conformed to the image of his Son, that he might be the firstborn among many brethren" (Rom. 8:29).

"Beloved, now are we the sons of God, and it doth not yet appear what we shall be: but we know that, when he shall appear, we shall be like him; for we shall see him as he is" (1 Jn. 3:2).

4. At any rate, there seems to be an image of God in all men which cannot be lost, and an image which *can* be lost.

a. That image which cannot be lost.

"For a man indeed ought not to cover his head, forasmuch as he is the image and glory of God: but the woman is the glory of the man" (1 Cor. 11:7).

"But the tongue can no man tame; it is an unruly evil, full of deadly poison. Therewith bless we God, even the Father; and therewith curse we men, which are made after the similitude of God" (Jas. 3:8, 9).

In the following verse God institutes capital punishment and justifies it on the grounds that a murderer should die for taking the life of another creature made in the image of God.

"Whoso sheddeth man's blood, by man shall his blood be shed: for in the image of God made he man" (Gen. 9:6).

The Bible therefore indicates that all unsaved men still display certain traces of the original image of God's creation.

b. That image which can be lost.

"Lie not one to another, seeing that ye have put off the old man with his deeds; and have put on the new man, which is renewed in knowledge after the image of him that created him" (Col. 3:9, 10).

"And that ye put on the new man, which after God is created in righteousness and true holiness" (Eph. 4:24).

Thus it would seem that there is a part of God's image which was lost after Adam sinned and must now be restored by the Holy Spirit at the moment of salvation. This lost image would seem to be the ability to know God and the desire to love him.

B. Is man a dichotomous (two-part) being, or is he a trichotomous (three-part) being? That is, does he consist of body and soul, or does he possess body, soul, and spirit?

1. The following two arguments support dichotomy.

   a. Man is a dichotomous being not just because of the plan of God, but because of the very nature of the universe, which only recognizes material and nonmaterial. In other words, man's body belongs to the material and his soul to the nonmaterial. What else is left? Therefore as man's spirit is decidedly nonmaterial, it must be placed into the camp of the nonmaterial and thus becomes identical with the soul.

   b. Often in the Bible the terms *soul* and *spirit* are used interchangeably. The virgin Mary seems to do this very thing during her hymn of praise to God.

      "And Mary said, My soul doth magnify the Lord, and my spirit hath rejoiced in God my Saviour" (Lk. 1:46, 47). (Cf. 2 Cor. 7:1; Jas. 5:20; 1 Pet. 2:11.)

2. Basic evidences for trichotomy would include:

   a. The fact that some passages use both terms interchangeably does not mean that there is no distinction whatsoever. For example, the phrases "Kingdom of God" and "Kingdom of heaven" are on occasion used interchangeably, yet most Bible students would recognize a general and decided difference between them.

   b. In at least two essential passages the New Testament carefully distinguishes between body and soul.

      "And the very God of peace sanctify you wholly; and I pray God your whole spirit and soul and body be preserved blameless unto the coming of our Lord Jesus Christ" (1 Thess. 5:23).

      "For the word of God is quick, and powerful, and sharper than any twoedged sword, piercing even to the dividing asunder of soul and spirit, and of the joints and marrow, and is a discerner of the thoughts and intents of the heart" (Heb. 4:12).

   c. The Hebrew word *nephesh* is translated by the word "soul" 428 times in the Old Testament. But on two occasions it is rendered "beast" and in nine other passages we find the word "creature" being used.

      "And he that killeth a beast shall make it good; beast for beast" (Lev. 24:18).

      "And the Lord God formed man of the dust of the ground, and breathed into his nostrils the breath of life; and man became a living soul" (Gen. 2:7).

      "And out of the ground the Lord God formed every beast of the field, and every fowl of the air; and brought them unto Adam to see what he would call them: and whatsoever Adam called every living creature, that was the name thereof" (Gen. 2:19).

      The point of the above is simply this: The Bible on occasion pictures animals as possessing souls. Therefore, as man is different from animals, he must have something higher, and that higher thing is the spirit. Nowhere in the Scriptures do we read of an animal possessing a spirit.

   d. Trichotomy is the best theory to explain the three levels of consciousness in all men, that of self-consciousness (through the soul), world-consciousness (through the body), and God-consciousness (through the spirit).

   Hebrew scholar Dr. Merrill F. Unger has written the following concerning this question:

      "The two terms are often used interchangeably . . . however, soul and spirit as synonymous terms are not always employed interchangeably. The soul is said to be lost, for example, but not the spirit. When no technical distinctions are set forth, the Bible is dichotomous, but otherwise it is trichotomous. Theologians have pored over these distinctions ceaselessly." (*Unger's Bible Dictionary*, p. 1043)

C. Where and how does man receive his soul?"

1. First view: All men have known other existences prior to this earthly life in heaven or somewhere in time past and therefore receive their original soul from previous existence into their earthly bodies. This is known as the preexistence theory, and, needless to say, has absolutely no scriptural support to back it up.

   Leslie B. Flynn writes:

      "Preexistentialism was held by Origen, the early Christian leader in Alexandria, to justify the wide disparity of conditions in which people enter our world. The same view was espoused by Philo the Jewish philosopher, to explain the soul's imprisonment in the body. Four centuries before Christ, Plato taught the preexistence of the soul to account for the existence of ideas not derived from the sense." (*Man, Ruined and Restored*, p. 45)

2. Second view: Each human soul is an immediate and special creation by God and enters the developing fetus at an early stage. This is called the creationist theory. The following verses are offered to support this view:

"Then shall the dust return to the earth as it was: and the spirit shall return unto God who gave it" (Eccl. 12:7).

"The burden of the word of the Lord for Israel, saith the Lord, which stretcheth forth the heavens, and layeth the foundation of the earth, and formeth the spirit of man within him" (Zech. 12:1).

"For I will not contend for ever, neither will I be always wroth: for the spirit should fail before me, and the souls which I have made" (Isa. 57:16).

"Furthermore, we have had fathers of our flesh which corrected us, and we gave them reverence: shall we not much rather be in subjection unto the Father of spirits, and live?" (Heb. 12:9).

One basic objection, however, has been leveled at the creation theory. If God creates each soul in heaven separately and sends it down into the developing body, then why are all men sinners? It is wrong, furthermore, to say the soul is thereupon corrupted by the body, for nowhere does the Scripture teach that the source of sin in man stems from his body of flesh and blood and bones. Quite the contrary, for sin is said to come from man's stubborn and rebellious will, and his will is an aspect of his soul. In other words, does God create a sinful soul in the first place? If he does, he then becomes the author of sin. But if, instead, he creates a pure and innocent soul, then why and how and when does man become a sinner? Would not one of the more than sixty billion individuals who have lived, or are living on this earth, have decided to keep his pure soul unspotted and sinless?

3. Third view: That both body and soul are passed on through natural generations. This is called the traducian theory and is the view of most theologians (with notable exceptions such as Charles Hodge). Passages that would tend to support this view are as follows:

"Behold, I was shapen in iniquity; and in sin did my mother conceive me" (Ps. 51:5).

"Who can bring a clean thing out of an unclean? not one" (Job 14:4).

"The wicked are estranged from the womb: they go astray as soon as they be born, speaking lies" (Ps. 58:3).

"That which is born of the flesh is flesh; and that which is born of the Spirit is spirit" (Jn. 3:6).

"Among whom also we all had our conversation in times past in the lusts of our flesh, fulfilling the desires of the flesh and of the mind; and were by nature the children of wrath, even as others" (Eph. 2:3).

However, as in the case of the theory of creationism, a serious charge is likewise leveled at the traducian view. The problem is this: If the child receives his soul from his parents, then how did Jesus escape the sin-tainted nature of Mary and remain the pure and perfect Savior that he was? But it would seem that this argument overlooks one basic but absolutely vital fact: the personality of the Lord Jesus Christ did not come into existence at Bethlehem through either the creation or traducian method. The indisputable scriptural fact is that as God he always existed. Thus, while he could pray ". . . a body hast thou prepared for me" (Heb. 10:5), he also would pray later:

"And now, O Father, glorify thou me with thine own self with the glory which I had with thee before the world was" (Jn. 17:5).

D. What is the soul? The nature of man's soul, is, like the doctrine of the Trinity, a mystery which simply cannot be grasped by mortal mind. Only a fool would attempt a dogmatic answer to this question. The following statements are therefore but suggestions and not absolute answers. In the opinion of this writer it would seem the Bible indicates not so much that I *have* a soul, but rather I *am* a soul. I *have* a body and I *have* a spirit, but the soul is *me*. But again, who can be dogmatic here?

"Behold, I show you a mystery; we shall not all sleep, but we shall be changed, in a moment, in the twinkling of an eye, at the last trump: for the trumpet shall sound, and the dead shall be raised incorruptible, and we shall be changed. For this corruptible must put on incorruption, and this mortal must put on immortality. So when this corruptible shall have put on incorruption, and this mortal shall have put on immortality, then shall be brought to pass the saying that is written, Death is swallowed up in victory" (1 Cor. 15:51-54).

E. What are the basic characteristics of the soul? As one consults various theological works on the makeup of man, he discovers that the discussion usually centers around four basic words. These are: intellect, sensibility, conscience, and will. Here again, let it be emphasized that no absolute and all-inclusive definition is possible, but the following statements are offered as guidelines.

1. Intellect—that aspect of the soul which tells me whether a given issue is right or wrong.

2. Sensibility—that aspect which tells me what I would *like* to do about the issue.

3. Conscience—that aspect which tells me what I *should* do about the issue.

The Bible lists several kinds of conscience:

a. An evil conscience.

"Let us draw near with a true heart in full assurance of faith, having our hearts sprinkled from an evil conscience, and our bodies washed with pure water" (Heb. 10:22).

b. A defiled conscience.

"Unto the pure all things are pure: but unto them that are defiled and unbelieving is nothing pure; but even their mind and conscience is defiled" (Titus 1:15).

c. A weak conscience.

"Howbeit there is not in every man that knowledge: for some with conscience of the idol unto this hour eat it as a thing offered unto an idol; and their conscience being weak is defiled. But when ye sin so against the brethren, and wound their weak conscience, ye sin against Christ" (1 Cor. 8:7, 12).

d. A good conscience.

"And Paul, earnestly beholding the council, said, Men and brethren, I have lived in all good conscience before God until this day" (Acts 23:1).

"Now the end of the commandment is charity out of a pure heart, and of a good conscience, and of faith unfeigned: Holding faith, and a good conscience; which some having put away, concerning faith have made shipwreck" (1 Tim. 1:5, 19).

"Pray for us: for we trust we have a good conscience, in all things willing to live honestly" (Heb. 13:18).

"Having a good conscience; that, whereas they speak evil of you, as of evildoers, they may be ashamed that falsely accuse your good conversation in Christ. The like figure whereunto even baptism doth also now save us, (not the putting away of the filth of the flesh, but the answer of a good conscience toward God) by the resurrection of Jesus Christ" (1 Pet. 3:16, 21).

e. A pure conscience.

"Holding the mystery of the faith in a pure conscience" (1 Tim. 3:9).

f. A seared conscience.

"Speaking lies in hypocrisy; having their conscience seared with a hot iron" (1 Tim. 4:2).

4. Will—that aspect which tells me what I *shall* do about the issue.

III. His Original Duties and Responsibilities. Why did God create man? Before giving the various reasons, it should be strongly stated that God *did not* make man because he was lonely! Long before he created angels or man, the Father was having blessed fellowship with his beloved Son.

"And now, O Father, glorify thou me with thine own self with the glory which I had with thee before the world was. Father, I will that they also, whom thou hast given me, be with me where I am; that they may behold my glory, which thou hast given me: for thou lovedst me before the foundation of the world" (Jn. 17:5, 24).

"The Lord possessed me in the beginning of his way, before his works of old. I was set up from everlasting, from the beginning, or ever the earth was. When there were no depths, I was brought forth; when there were no fountains abounding

with water. Before the mountains were settled, before the hills was I brought forth: while as yet he had not made the earth, nor the fields, nor the highest part of the dust of the world. When he prepared the heavens, I was there: when he set a compass upon the face of the depth: when he established the clouds above: when he strengthened the fountains of the deep: when he gave to the sea his decree, that the waters should not pass his commandment: when he appointed the foundations of the earth: Then I was by him, as one brought up with him: and I was daily his delight, rejoicing always before him" (Prov. 8:22-30).

But why, then, did he create man? According to a passage in Revelation:

"Thou art worthy, O Lord, to receive glory and honor and power: for thou hast created all things, and for thy pleasure they are and were created" (Rev. 4:11).

Man, then, was created to demonstrate the glory of God and to fellowship with the God of glory. Upon his creation he is given the following duties and responsibilities:

A. Man was to assume the headship over all nature.

"And God said, Let us make man in our image, after our likeness: and let them have dominion over the fish of the sea, and over the fowl of the air, and over the cattle, and over all the earth, and over every creeping thing that creepeth upon the earth" (Gen. 1:26).

The New Testament makes it clear that man was made to eventually assume headship over the entire universe (Heb. 2:5-8).

B. Man was to make his headquarters in Eden and especially to care for this beautiful garden paradise.

"And the Lord God took the man, and put him into the garden of Eden to dress it and to keep it" (Gen. 2:15).

C. Man was to provide names for every living creature.

"And out of the ground the Lord God formed every beast of the field, and every fowl of the air; and brought them unto Adam to see what he would call them: and whatsoever Adam called every living creature, that was the name thereof. And Adam gave names to all cattle, and to the fowl of the air, and to every beast of the field; but for Adam there was not found a help meet for him" (Gen. 2:19, 20).

D. Man was to love and protect his wife.

"Therefore shall a man leave his father and his mother, and shall cleave unto his wife: and they shall be one flesh" (Gen. 2:24).

E. Man was to reproduce himself and populate the earth with his kind.

"And God blessed them, and God said unto them, Be fruitful, and multiply, and replenish the earth, and subdue it: and have dominion over the fish of the sea, and over the fowl of the air, and over every living thing that moveth upon the earth" (Gen. 1:28).

F. Man was to enjoy all the fruits of the various trees (except one).

"And the Lord God commanded the man, saying, Of every tree of the garden thou mayest freely eat" (Gen. 2:16).

G. Man was forbidden to partake of the fruit of the tree of the knowledge of good and evil.

"But of the tree of the knowledge of good and evil, thou shalt not eat of it: for in the day that thou eatest thereof thou shalt surely die" (Gen. 2:17).

IV. His Tragic Sin and Fall.

A. The temptation that led to the fall. According to Genesis 3:1 Satan, working through the serpent, enticed Eve to disobey God and partake of the forbidden fruit.

"Now the serpent was more subtile than any beast of the field which the Lord God had made. And he said unto the woman, Yea, hath God said, Ye shall not eat of every tree of the garden?" (Gen. 3:1).

We here note Satan's approach to Eve. He begins by slyly *doubting* God's Word, but soon is brazenly *denying* the Word of God.

"And the serpent said unto the woman, Ye shall not surely die" (Gen. 3:4).

B. The transgression that caused the fall.

"And the woman said unto the serpent, We may eat of the fruit of the trees of the garden: But of the fruit of the tree which is in the midst of the garden, God hath said, Ye shall not eat of it, neither shall ye touch it, lest ye die" (Gen. 3:2, 3).

In these verses Eve commits two fatal mistakes. She *adds* to God's Word (God did not say, "Neither shall ye touch it"), and then she *takes from* God's Word (she omitted the original command, "Thou shalt surely die").

"But of the tree of knowledge of good and evil, thou shalt not eat of it: for in the day that thou eatest thereof thou shalt surely die" (Gen. 2:17).

"For I testify unto every man that heareth the words of the prophecy of this book, If any man shall add unto these things, God shall add unto him the plagues that are written in this book: And if any man shall take away from the words of the book of this prophecy, God shall take away his part out of the book of life, and out of the holy city, and from the things which are written in this book" (Rev. 22:18, 19).

"Every word of God is pure: he is a shield unto them that put their trust in him. Add thou not unto his words, lest he reprove thee, and thou be found a liar" (Prov. 30:5, 6).

"And when the woman saw that the tree was good for food, and that it was pleasant to the eyes, and a tree to be desired to make one wise, she took of the fruit thereof, and did eat, and gave also unto her husband with her; and he did eat" (Gen. 3:6).

C. The trial that followed the fall. Adam the sinner, after a brief and futile attempt to hide, now confesses to his crime. At this point the righteous Judge sets up his court in Eden and the trial begins. A threefold sentence is soon passed down:

1. Upon the serpent.

"And the Lord God said unto the serpent, Because thou hast done this, thou art cursed above all cattle, and above every beast of the field; upon thy belly shalt thou go, and dust shalt thou eat all the days of thy life" (Gen. 3:14).

Isaiah indicates that this judgment will continue to be binding upon the serpent even during the millennium.

"The wolf and the lamb shall feed together, and the lion shall eat straw like the bullock: and dust shall be the serpent's meat. They shall not hurt nor destroy in all my holy mountain, saith the Lord" (Isa. 65:25).

2. Upon Satan.

"And I will put enmity between thee and the woman, and between thy seed and her seed; it shall bruise thy head, and thou shalt bruise his heel" (Gen. 3:15).

At first glance this verse would merely seem to predict the natural hatred of man for snakes. But for centuries devout Bible students have seen a far more precious and profound truth underlying these words. For in this verse they claim to see no less than a thrilling prediction of the cross and the resurrection, of the Savior's great victory over Satan. Theologically, then, verse 15 may be translated as follows: "And there will be an intense hatred between Satan and Christ. Eventually Christ shall crush the head of Satan, while suffering a heel wound in the process." See also:

"And the God of peace shall bruise Satan under your feet shortly. The grace of our Lord Jesus Christ be with you. Amen" (Rom. 16:20).

"But he was wounded for our transgressions, he was bruised for our iniquities; the chastisement of our peace was upon him; and with his stripes we are healed" (Isa. 53:5).

3. Upon Adam. Adam and Eve would experience a sevenfold sentence because of their sin.

a. Shame.

"And the eyes of them both were opened, and they knew that they were naked; and they sewed fig leaves together, and made themselves aprons" (Gen. 3:7).

b. Fear.

"And they heard the voice of the Lord God walking in the garden in the cool of the day: and Adam and his wife hid themselves from the presence of the Lord God amongst the trees of the garden. And the Lord God called unto Adam, and said unto him, Where art thou? And he said, I heard thy voice in the garden, and I was afraid, because I was naked; and I hid myself" (Gen. 3:8–10).

c. Discord.

"And the man said, The woman whom thou gavest to be with me, she gave me of the tree, and I did eat. And the Lord God said unto the woman, What is this that thou hast done? And the woman said, The serpent beguiled me, and I did eat" (Gen. 3:12, 13).

This is the first historical example of passing the buck.

d. Death.

(1) Physical death.

"And all the days that Adam lived were nine hundred and thirty years: and he died" (Gen. 5:5).

"The days of our years are threescore years and ten; and if by reason of strength they be fourscore years, yet is their strength labour and sorrow; for it is soon cut off, and we fly away" (Ps. 90:10).

(2) Spiritual death.

"And then will I profess unto them, I never knew you: depart from me, ye that work iniquity" (Mt. 7:23).

"Then shall he say also unto them on the left hand, Depart from me, ye cursed, into everlasting fire, prepared for the devil and his angels" (Mt. 25:41).

"He that hath an ear, let him hear what the Spirit saith unto the churches; He that overcometh shall not be hurt of the second death" (Rev. 2:11).

"Blessed and holy is he that hath part in the first resurrection; on such the second death hath no power, but they shall be priests of God and of Christ, and shall reign with him a thousand years" (Rev. 20:6).

"And death and hell were cast into the lake of fire. This is the second death" (Rom. 20:14).

"But the fearful, and unbelieving, and the abominable, and murderers, and whoremongers, and sorcerers, and idolaters, and all liars, shall have their part in the lake which burneth with fire and brimstone: which is the second death" (Rev. 21:8).

e. Suffering.

"Unto the woman he said, I will greatly multiply thy sorrow and thy conception; in sorrow thou shalt bring forth children; and thy desire shall be to thy husband, and he shall rule over thee" (Gen. 3:16).

f. Weariness of labor.

"And unto Adam he said, Because thou hast hearkened unto the voice of thy wife, and hast eaten of the tree, of which I commanded thee, saying, Thou shalt not eat of it; cursed is the ground for thy sake; in sorrow shalt thou eat of it all the days of thy life; thorns also and thistles shall it bring forth to thee; and thou shalt eat the herb of the field; In the sweat of thy face shalt thou eat bread, till thou return unto the ground; for out of it wast thou taken; for dust thou art, and unto dust shalt thou return" (Gen. 3:17–19).

g. Separation.

"And the Lord God said, Behold, the man is become as one of us, to know good and evil: and now, lest he put forth his hand, and take also of the tree of life, and eat, and live for ever: therefore the Lord God sent him forth from the garden of Eden, to till the ground from whence he was taken. So he drove out the man; and he placed at the east of the garden of Eden Cherubims and a flaming sword which turned every way, to keep the way of the tree of life" (Gen. 3:22–24).

D. The theories that explain the fall. Were the effects of Adam's fall merely confined to himself, or do they continue somehow to make themselves known in the lives of twentieth century men?

1. The liberal position: As the entire story is simply a Hebrew legend, there can, of course, be no effect whatsoever.

2. The Pelagian position: Palagius was a fifth-century British monk who taught that Adam's sin affected only himself, for God imputes to men only those sins which they personally and consciously perform. Pelagius said the only effect of Adam's sin on posterity was that of a bad example. The doctrine of Pelagianism was condemned by the council of Carthage in A.D. 418.

3. The Arminian position: Arminius (1560–1609) was a professor who lived and taught in Holland. This theory teaches that while Adam's sin definitely weakened the will of his posterity to remain sinless, it did not destroy the possibility.

4. The Augustinian position: Augustine was one of the greatest of the early church fathers. He taught that because of the unity of the human race in Adam, man's sin is imputed to his posterity. Thus, corrupted nature begets corrupted nature. This final view is the only position which is amply supported by the Scriptures.

"Wherefore, as by one man sin entered into the world, and death by sin; and so death passed upon all men, for that all have sinned" (Rom. 5:12).

"Therefore as by the offence of one judgment came upon all men to condemnation; even so by the righteousness of one the free gift came upon all men unto justification of life. For as by one man's disobedience many were made sinners, so by the obedience of one shall many be made righteous" (Rom. 5:18, 19).

"For as in Adam all die, even so in Christ shall all be made alive" (1 Cor. 15:22).

At this point it should be said that in the New Testament the Apostle Paul often distinguishes between "sin" and "sins." According to Paul:

Sin—the root of my problem and a reference to my corrupted nature which I received from Adam.

Sins—the fruit of my problem and a reference to those actions resulting from my corrupted nature.

It is vital to understand this distinction, for God will not deal with us favorably concerning our sins until we allow him to treat our sin nature. I sin (commit individual transgressions) because I am a sinner, and therefore do not become a sinner because I sin! Thus modernism is content to treat the boils on the skin of mankind (sins) but the real disease is in the bloodstream (sin nature). Paul summarizes all this in a single verse, which should be literally translated:

"For all have sinned [past tense, in Adam] and are [present time, in daily experience] falling short of God's glory" (Rom. 3:23).

From all this we therefore conclude that Adam's individual transgression resulted in a sin nature for him, but with us it is the other way around—our sin nature results in individual transgressions.

V. His Present-Day Condition.
  A. The fallacies.
    1. Man is *dirt* and therefore cannot be saved. According to this position, the only real difference between a mushroom, a man, and a mountain is simply in the accidental arrangement of the atoms.
    2. Man is *divine*, and therefore need not be saved. Thus, as Christian witnesses we are told that our primary ministry to the poor, lost, helpless drunkard is to simply inform him that he is made in God's image and carries the divine spark of divinity within him. He therefore need only to fan that small flame and begin living that victorious life God wants him to live.
  B. The facts. In his first epistle to the church at Corinth, Paul places all living men into three spiritual categories:
    1. The natural man.
      "But the natural man receiveth not the things of the Spirit of God: for they are foolishness unto him: neither can he know them, because they are spiritually discerned" (1 Cor. 2:14).

The Bible describes all unsaved men (the natural man) as being spiritually depraved.
      a. Negative aspects of depravity.
        (1) Depravity does not mean that all unsaved men are as depraved as they can possibly become. Most American men, for example, do not run around murdering little children or robbing banks. But some do. Also, few housewives suddenly abandon their families and become professional harlots.
        (2) Depravity does not hold that a sinner has no sense of God, nor of good and evil. Often, to the shame of the Christian, unsaved men and women demonstrate a higher morality than shown by their professing neighbors and family members.
        (3) Depravity does not teach that an unsaved man cannot admire the noble, or even perform noble and heroic acts. Many battle accounts record the bravery of unsaved soldiers who pay the supreme sacrifice to save the lives of their endangered buddies. On other occasions unsaved firemen and policemen have laid down their lives to protect individuals they may not even know.
      b. Positive aspects of depravity.
        (1) Depravity means that all sinners are capable of all wicked things. This means that a freedom-loving Winston Churchill still possessed within his nature all the potential cruelty of an Adolf Hitler.
        (2) Depravity teaches that no sinner has the power to please God.

The following Scriptures aptly describe the natural man:

"But I know you, that ye have not the love of God in you" (Jn. 5:42).

"For I know that in me (that is, in my flesh,) dwelleth no good thing: for to will is present with me; but how to perform that which is good I find not" (Rom. 7:18).

"Because the carnal mind is enmity against God: for it is not subject to the law of God, neither indeed can be. So then they that are in the flesh cannot please God" (Rom. 8:7, 8).

"That at that time ye were without Christ, being aliens from the commonwealth of Israel, and strangers from the covenants of promise, having no hope, and without God in the world" (Eph. 2:12).

"As it is written, There is none righteous, no, not one: There is none that understandeth, there is none that seeketh after God. They are all gone out of the way, they are together become unprofitable; there is none that doeth good, no, not one" (Rom. 3:10-12).
    2. The carnal man.
      "And I, brethren, could not speak unto you as unto spiritual, but as unto carnal, even as unto babes in Christ. I have fed you with milk, and not with meat: for hitherto ye were not able to bear it, neither yet now are ye able. For ye are yet

carnal: for whereas there is among you envying, and strife, and divisions, are ye not carnal, and walk as men?" (1 Cor. 3:1-3).

Here Paul sadly describes a Christian who is indwelt by the Holy Spirit, but who still allows himself to be controlled by the passions of the flesh. Paul calls him a baby, for he has never learned to grow.

    3. The Spirit-controlled man.

"But he that is spiritual judgeth all things, yet he himself is judged of no man" (1 Cor. 2:15).

VI. His Destiny. In the throes of despair, the suffering patriarch Job once cried out:

"Man that is born of a woman is of few days, and full of trouble. He cometh forth like a flower, and is cut down: he fleeth also as a shadow, and continueth not" (Job 14:1, 2).

Later during the same dialogue Job would sign and ask:

"If a man die, shall he live again? all the days of my appointed time will I wait, till my change come" (Job 14:14).

Finally, in chapter 19, Job reaffirms his own personal faith in God and in the destiny of man. Job exclaims:

"For I know that my Redeemer liveth, and that he shall stand at the latter day upon the earth: And though after my skin worms destroy this body, yet in my flesh shall I see God" (Job 19:25, 26).

It has been said that the three largest questions of mankind are as follows:

Where did I come from?

Why am I here?

Where am I going?

Thus far in this study, questions one and two have been answered. This final section will answer the third question.

A. False views concerning the destiny of man.

    1. *Nirvana:* An oriental Hindu philosophy (which at certain periods in history has wormed its way into Christian thought) which teaches that at death a man ceases all personal existence and is absorbed by some great life-giving principle in the universe. According to this thought, a man, while he lives, can be pictured as a small wave ripple, skimming the top of a mighty ocean. But when the wind stops (the moment of death), the wave is then received back into the ocean from whence it came, and forever loses its previous identity. This is refuted by:

"And behold, there appeared unto them Moses and Elias talking with him" (Mt. 17:3).

Here we see Moses (who had died 2,000 years earlier) and Elijah (who had departed over seven centuries back) both reappearing on the Mount of Transfiguration to Peter, James, and John. This, of course, proves that absence from this earth does not mean the termination of personality or personhood.

"Now if Christ be preached that he rose from the dead, how say some among you that there is no resurrection of the dead?

But if there be no resurrection of the dead, then is Christ not risen: And if Christ be not risen, then is our preaching vain, and your faith is also vain. Yea, and we are found false witnesses of God; because we have testified of God that he raised up Christ: whom he raised not up, if so be that the dead rise not. For if the dead rise not, then is not Christ raised: And if Christ be not raised, your faith is vain; ye are yet in your sins. Then they also which are fallen asleep in Christ are perished. If in this life only we have hope in Christ, we are of all men most miserable. But now is Christ risen from the dead, and become the firstfruits of them that slept" (1 Cor. 15:12-20).

"So also is the resurrection of the dead. It is sown in corruption; it is raised in incorruption: it is sown in dishonor; it is raised in glory: it is sown in weakness; it is raised in power: it is sown a natural body; it is raised a spiritual body. There is a natural body, and there is a spiritual body. And so it is written, The first man Adam was made a living soul; the last Adam was made a quickening spirit. Howbeit that was not first which is spiritual, but that which is natural; and afterward that which is spiritual. The first man is of the earth, earthy: the second man is the Lord from heaven. As is the earthy, such are they also that are earthy: and as is the heavenly, such are they also that are heavenly. And as we have borne the image of the earthy, we shall also bear the image of the heavenly" (1 Cor. 15:42-49).

    2. *Restorationism:* The belief that in a future life all men will be given a second chance to make the choice for God that they did not make during this life. This is refuted by:

"He, that being often reproved hardeneth his neck, shall suddenly be destroyed, and that without remedy" (Prov. 29:1).

"Jesus answered and said unto him, Verily, verily, I say unto thee, Except a man be born again, he cannot see the kingdom of God" (Jn. 3:3).

"For God so loved the world, that he gave his only begotten Son, that whosoever believeth in him should not perish, but have everlasting life. For God sent not his Son into the world to condemn the world; but that the world through him might be saved. He that believeth on him is not condemned: but he that believeth not is condemned already, because he hath not believed in the name of the only begotten Son of God" (Jn. 3:16-18).

"There was a certain rich man, which was clothed in purple and fine linen, and fared sumptuously every day: And there was a certain beggar named Lazarus, which was laid at his gate, full of sores, and desiring to be fed with the crumbs which fell from the rich man's table:

moreover the dogs came and licked his sores. And it came to pass, that the beggar died, and was carried by the angels into Abraham's bosom: the rich man also died, and was buried; and in hell he lifted up his eyes, being in torments, and seeth Abraham afar off, and Lazarus in his bosom. And he cried and said, Father Abraham, have mercy on me, and send Lazarus, that he may dip the tip of his finger in water, and cool my tongue; for I am tormented in this flame. But Abraham said, Son, remember that thou in thy lifetime receivedst thy good things, and likewise Lazarus evil things: but now he is comforted, and thou art tormented. And beside all this, between us and you there is a great gulf fixed: so that they which would pass from hence to you cannot; neither can they pass to us, that would come from thence. Then he said, I pray thee therefore, father, that thou wouldest send him to my father's house: For I have five brethren; that he may testify unto them, lest they also come into this place of torment. Abraham saith unto him, They have Moses and the prophets; let them hear them. And he said, Nay, father Abraham: but if one went unto them from the dead, they will repent. And he said unto him, If they hear not Moses and the prophets, neither will they be persuaded, though one rose from the dead" (Lk. 16:19-31).

If these verses teach anything, they strongly and sternly declare that at the moment of death there exists absolutely no chance for the salvation of an unsaved person. We may be tempted to argue with God concerning the *why* of the matter, but not the *what* of the matter. Origen (second-century church father) was one of the earliest proponents of restorationism. He even taught the possibility of Satan himself being restored to the faith he once rebelled against. Restorationists use the following Scripture verses for "proof" of their position.

"And he shall send Jesus Christ, which before was preached unto you: whom the heaven must receive until the times of restitution of all things, which God hath spoken by the mouth of all his holy prophets since the world began" (Acts 3:20, 21).

"For as in Adam all die, even so in Christ shall all be made alive" (1 Cor. 15:22).

"That in the dispensation of the fulness of times he might gather together in one all things in Christ, both which are in heaven, and which are on earth; even in him" (Eph. 1:10).

"For this is good and acceptable in the sight of God our Saviour; who will have all men to be saved, and to come unto the knowledge of the truth" (1 Tim. 2:3, 4).

"For therefore we both labour and suffer reproach, because we trust in the living God, who is the Saviour of all men, specially of those that believe" (1 Tim. 4:10).

"For Christ also hath once suffered for sins, the just for the unjust, that he might bring us to God, being put to death in the flesh, but quickened by the Spirit; by which also he went and preached unto the spirits in prison" (1 Pet. 3:18, 19).

However, a quick glance at the context of the above verses show that all the "restored" here are those who have accepted Christ as Savior. The passage in 1 Peter has been the subject of some controversy, but whatever else, it does not teach restorationism. The verb "preached" in verse 19 in the original Greek does not refer to gospel preaching.

3. *Materialism:* Atheistic belief that man, upon death, forever ceases to be and quietly rots into nothingness. This philosophy has been aptly described on an ancient tombstone: "I was not, I became, I am not, I care not." This is refuted by:

"Now this I say, brethren, that flesh and blood cannot inherit the kingdom of God; neither doth corruption inherit incorruption. Behold, I show you a mystery; we shall not all sleep, but we shall all be changed, in a moment, in the twinkling of an eye, at the last trump: for the trumpet shall sound, and the dead shall be raised incorruptible, and we shall be changed. For this corruptible must put on incorruption, and this mortal must put on immortality. So when this corruptible shall have put on incorruption, and this mortal shall have put on immortality, then shall be brought to pass the saying that is written, Death is swallowed up in victory. O death, where is thy sting? O grave, where is thy victory? The sting of death is sin; and the strength of sin is the law. But thanks be to God, which giveth us the victory through our Lord Jesus Christ" (1 Cor. 15:50-57).

Materialism may be correctly defined as that clever worldly art of knowing the *price* of everything, but the *value* of nothing.

4. *Annihilationism:* This theory, espoused by the Jehovah's Witnesses, along with various other groups, teaches that all the ungodly will someday literally be "uncreated," or annihilated by God. It is refuted by:

"And these shall go away into everlasting punishment: but the righteous into life eternal" (Mt. 25:46).

"And the third angel followed them, saying with a loud voice, If any man worship the beast and his image, and receive his mark in his forehead, or in his hand, the same shall drink of the wine of the wrath of God, which is poured out without mixture into the cup of his indignation; and he shall be tormented with fire and brimstone in the presence of the holy angels, and in the presence of the Lamb: And the smoke of their torment ascendeth up for ever and ever: and they have no rest day nor night, who worship the beast and his image, and whosoever receiveth the mark of his name" (Rev. 14:9–11).

Those believing in annihilationism attempt to undergird their claims by quoting certain Scripture verses in the Psalms:

"For evildoers shall be cut off: but those that wait upon the Lord, they shall inherit the earth" (Ps. 37:9).

"The Lord preserveth all them that love him: but all the wicked will he destroy" (Ps. 145:20).

Refute: The same Hebrew word *karath,* translated "cut off" in Psalm 37:9 is also used in reference to the crucifixion of the Messiah as prophesied in Daniel 9:26. Christ was certainly not annihilated at Calvary.

In Psalm 145:20 the identical Hebrew word here rendered "destroy" is found describing the punishment of both Egypt (Ex. 10:7) and Israel (Hosea 13:9), neither of which nation has yet to suffer annihilation.

5. *Soul sleep:* The view that the soul sleeps between death and the resurrection. It is refuted by:

"Therefore we are always confident, knowing that, whilst we are at home in the body, we are absent from the Lord: (For we walk by faith, not by sight:) We are confident, I say, and willing rather to be absent from the body, and to be present with the Lord. Wherefore we labor, that, whether present or absent, we may be accepted of him" (2 Cor. 5:6–9).

"For I am in a strait betwixt two, having a desire to depart, and to be with Christ; which is far better: Nevertheless to abide in the flesh is more needful for you" (Phil. 1:23, 24).

"And when he had opened the fifth seal, I saw under the altar the souls of them that were slain for the word of God, and for the testimony which they held: And they cried with a loud voice, saying, How long, O Lord, holy and true, dost thou not judge and avenge our blood on them that dwell on the earth? And white robes were given unto every one of them; and it was said unto them, that they should rest yet for a little season, until their fellow servants also and their brethren, that should be killed as they were, should be fulfilled. And I beheld when he had opened the sixth seal, and, lo, there was a great earthquake; and the sun became black as sackcloth of hair, and the moon became as blood" (Rev. 6:9–12).

This passage in Revelation not only refutes soul sleep, but, to the contrary, teaches that departed believers can both ask questions and receive answers in heaven. It also seems to suggest the possibilities of a temporary body given them prior to their future resurrected bodies.

6. *Purgatory:* The belief of Roman Catholics that all those who die at peace with the church but are not perfect must undergo penal and purifying sufferings. However, this is only for those who die in venial (lesser) sin, for all dying in mortal sin are forever condemned to hell. Roman doctrine teaches that a person's stay in purgatory may be shortened by the gifts or services rendered by living people in behalf of the beloved dead one through the Roman Catholic Church. This is refuted by:

"But Christ being come an high priest of good things to come, by a greater and more perfect tabernacle, not made with hands, that is to say, not of this building; neither by the blood of goats and calves, but by his own blood he entered in once into the holy place, having obtained eternal redemption for us. For if the blood of bulls and of goats, and the ashes of a heifer sprinkling the unclean, sanctifieth to the purifying of the flesh; how much more shall the blood of Christ, who through the eternal Spirit offered himself without spot to God, purge your conscience from dead works to serve the living God?" (Heb. 9:11–14).

"For Christ is not entered into the holy places made with hands, which are the figures of the true; but into heaven itself, now to appear in the presence of God for us: nor yet that he should offer himself often, as the high priest entereth into the holy place every year with blood of others; for then must he often have suffered since the foundation of the world: but now once in the end of the world hath he appeared to put away sin by the sacrifice of himself. And as it is appointed unto men once to die, but after this the judgment: So Christ was once offered to bear the sins of many; and unto them that look for him shall he appear the second time without sin unto salvation" (Heb. 9:24–28).

"But this man, after he had offered one sacrifice for sins for ever, sat down on the right hand of God; this is the covenant that I will make with them after those days, saith the Lord; I will put my laws into their hearts, and in their minds will I write them; and their sins and iniquities will I remember no more" (Heb. 10:12, 16, 17).

7. *Limbo:* Another aspect of Roman Catholic theology which teaches that all unbaptized children and the mentally incompetent, upon death, proceed to a permanent place of "natural happiness," but not heaven. This is refuted by:

"At the same time came the disciples unto Jesus, saying, Who is the greatest in the kingdom of heaven? And Jesus called a little child unto him, and set him in the midst of them, and said, Verily I say unto you, Except ye be converted, and become as little children, ye shall not enter into the kingdom of heaven. Whosoever therefore shall humble himself as this little child, the same is greatest in the kingdom of heaven. And whoso shall receive one such little child in my name receiveth me. But whoso shall offend one of these little ones which believe in me, it were better for him that a millstone were hanged about his neck, and that he were drowned in the depth of the sea. Woe unto the world because of offenses! for it must needs be that offenses come; but woe to that man by whom the offense cometh! Wherefore if thy hand or thy foot offend thee, cut them off, and cast them from thee: it is better for thee to enter into life halt or maimed, rather than having two hands or two feet to be cast into everlasting fire. And if thine eye offend thee, pluck it out, and cast it from thee: it is better for thee to enter into life with one eye, rather than having two eyes to be cast into hell fire. Take heed that ye despise not one of these little ones; for I say unto you, that in heaven their angels do always behold the face of my Father which is in heaven" (Mt. 18:1-10).

8. *Reincarnation:* The belief in the transmigration or rebirth of the soul which has been fundamental to most religions and philosophies of India. As one sows in the present life, so one shall reap in the next, good deeds resulting in a good state of rebirth, bad deeds in a bad state of rebirth. Thus a man's state of life is seen not as something fortuitous or meaningless, but as the working out, for good or ill, of the effects of a previous existence and the predetermining of a future state. This theory, like the previous seven, is totally without scriptural support.

B. Scriptural considerations concerning the destiny of man.

1. Before the cross. Where was the abode of the dead prior to Calvary? It is held by a number of Bible students that before Jesus died, the souls of all men descended into an abode located somewhere in the earth known as Hades in the New Testament and Sheol in the Old Testament. Originally, there were two sections of Hades, one for saved and one for the lost. The saved section is sometimes called "Paradise," and is at other times referred to as "Abraham's bosom."

"And Jesus said unto him, Verily I say unto thee, Today shalt thou be with me in paradise" (Lk. 23:43).

"And it came to pass, that the beggar died, and was carried by the angels into Abraham's bosom: the rich man also died, and was buried" (Lk. 16:22).

There is no name given for the unsaved section apart from the general designation of Hades. In Luke 16:19-31 the Savior relates the account of a poor believer who died and went to the saved part of Hades and of a rich unbeliever who died and went to the unsaved section. (See VI A 2, Restorationism.)

A number of extremely interesting conclusions may be derived from this historical account as related by Christ.

a. The activities of angels in carrying believers to their reward.

b. The possibilities of an intermediate, pre-resurrection body for the lost as well as the saved.

c. The irony of an occupant in hell desiring to become a soul-winner.

d. The nature of the rich man's request to send Lazarus to testify to his five lost brothers, reasoning that "if one went unto them from the dead, they will repent." This pathetic request was of course denied, simply because it would not have worked. The fact of the matter is that Christ did actually raise a man with the same name as Lazarus a few months later. What were the results of this? Did it cause the unbelieving Jews to come to the Savior? Hardly. In fact, just the opposite occurred, for the wicked Pharisees not only decided to kill Jesus for his action (Jn. 11:53), but actually planned (if necessary) to murder the resurrected Lazarus also (Jn. 12:10, 11).

However, many believe that all this changed after Christ had made full payment for the believer's sins on Calvary. The *Scofield Bible* suggests that during the time of his death and resurrection, our Lord descended into Hades, depopulated Paradise, and led a spiritual triumphal entry into the heavenlies with all the saved up to that time. The following is offered as proof of this:

"Wherefore he saith, When he ascended up on high, he led captivity captive, and gave gifts unto men. (Now that he ascended, what is it but that he also descended first into the lower parts of the earth? He that descended is the same also that ascended up far above all heavens, that he might fill all things)" (Eph. 4:8-10).

In his book *Revelation*, the late Dr. Donald Barnhouse writes:

"When He ascended on High He emptied Hell of Paradise and took it straight to the presence of God. Captivity was taken captive. . . . From that moment onward there was to be no separation whatsoever for those who believe in Christ. The gates of Hell would never more prevail against any believer."

"And I say also unto thee, That thou art Peter, and upon this rock I will build my church; and the gates of hell shall not prevail against it" (Mt. 16:18).

2. After the cross. The state of the unsaved dead remained (and remains) unchanged af-

ter the cross. They remain in Hades awaiting the final great white throne judgment.

"And I saw a great white throne, and him that sat on it, from whose face the earth and the heaven fled away; and there was found no place for them. And I saw the dead, small and great, stand before God; and the books were opened: and another book was opened, which is the book of life: and the dead were judged out of those things which were written in the books, according to their works. And the sea gave up the dead which were in it; and death and hell delivered up the dead which were in them: and they were judged every man according to their works. And death and hell were cast into the lake of fire. This is the second death. And whosoever was not found written in the book of life was cast into the lake of fire" (Rev. 20:11-15).

This means the lost rich man is still in Hades, there having since been joined by Judas, Herod, Nero, Hitler, etc., and will remain until after the millennium and the resurrection of the unjust.

"But the rest of the dead lived not again until the thousand years were finished . . ." (Rev. 20:5).

But a glorious change has occurred concerning the state of those who fall asleep in Jesus. Note the following Scriptures:

"But he, being full of the Holy Ghost, looked up steadfastly into heaven, and saw the glory of God, and Jesus standing on the right hand of God, and they stoned Stephen, calling upon God, and saying, Lord Jesus, receive my spirit. And he kneeled down, and cried with a loud voice, Lord, lay not this sin to their charge. And when he had said this, he fell asleep" (Acts 7:55, 59, 60).

"For to me to live is Christ, and to die is gain. For I am in a strait betwixt two, having a desire to depart, and to be with Christ; which is far better" (Phil. 1:21, 23).

"We are confident, I say, and willing rather to be absent from the body, and to be present with the Lord" (2 Cor. 5:8).

Thus, according to these verses, both Stephen and Paul, along with all other departed believers, are now in the heavenlies with Christ. In the following Scripture Paul refers to this place as "the third heaven."

"It is not expedient for me doubtless to glory. I will come to visions and revelations of the Lord. I knew a man in Christ above fourteen years ago, (whether in the body, I cannot tell; or whether out of the body, I cannot tell: God knoweth;) such a one caught up to the third heaven. And I knew such a man, (whether in the body, or out of the body, I cannot tell: God knoweth;) how that he was caught up into paradise, and heard unspeakable words, which it is not lawful for a man to utter" (2 Cor. 12:1-4).

A SCRIPTURAL SUMMARY OF HELL

I. Denying the Doctrine

Of all the many doctrines in the Bible, undoubtedly the very first that the unbeliever will deny and the weak believer will question is the doctrine of hell. Satan has successfully accomplished this coveted goal through the following three methods:

A. *Rationalism:* "There is no God, and therefore there can be no hell." This rationalism often disguises itself in the garb of "science." Harold Bryson writes:

"Other people deny the existence of hell on the basis of modern thinking. Some assume that many scientific discoveries of the twentieth century render belief in a future life impossible. Using scientific study of the dissolution of the chemical elements of the body, they deny any possibility of a bodily resurrection. Also, the theory of organic evolution tries to demonstrate man's common origin with lower life forms. Evolution destroys the basis for believing that man has a higher destiny than any other creature. Some naively insist that the penetration of space leaves no place for the biblical teachings on heaven and hell. It has been assumed that if man finds no evidence of heaven in space then there is likewise no hell located in the opposite direction." (*Yes, Virginia, There Is a Hell,* p. 12)

Charles Darwin rejected the doctrine of hell.

"Disbelief crept over me at a very slow rate, but was at last complete. I can hardly see how anyone ought to wish Christianity to be true; for, if so, the plain language of the text seems to show that the men who do not believe—and this would include my father, brother, and almost all my best friends—will be everlastingly punished. And this is a damnable doctrine." (*The Christian Agnostic.* London, Hodder & Stoughton, 1965, p. 164)

The English agnostic clergyman John A. T. Robinson, bishop of Woolwich writes:

"There are still a few who would like to bring back hell, as some want to bring back . . . hanging. They are usually the same types who wish to purge Britain of . . . sex and violence." (*But That I Can't Believe.* New York, The New American Library, 1967, p. 69).

B. *Ridicule:* "There may be a God, but it is silly to speculate about multitudes of disembodied spirits frying in some literal lake of fire somewhere."

One of America's most famous atheists was Robert G. Ingersoll who ridiculed the idea of hell whenever and wherever he could. When asked to coin a slogan to help promote a cigar which bore his name, he quipped, "Smoke in this world, and not in the one to come!" Ingersoll loved the writings of the great poet Robert Burns. He often stated that one page of Burns had more literary merit than an entire book by Moses! Upon Ingersoll's death some wag suggested that an appropriate epitaph for his tombstone would be to simply print the name of his favorite author: "Robert Burns"!

On this subject, Ingersoll said:

"The idea of hell was born of revenge and brutality on the one side, and cowardice on the other . . . I have no respect for any man who preaches it . . . I dislike this doctrine, I hate it, I despise it, I defy this doctrine!"

The famous news editor Horace Greeley is said to have refused to make a contribution to a religious group who solicited funds to be used in "keeping people out of hell." His reason was that, in his opinion, there were not nearly enough people going to hell at that present time!

C. *Religion:* "There is a God, but he is a God of Love, and therefore would not and could not send anyone to hell!" This, of course, is the position of liberalism. Recent theologians like Karl Barth, Emil Brunner, Paul Tillich, and others either denied or downplayed the doctrine of hell. The cults of Christianity have at least one common ground, and that is, there is no hell!

The Christian Science church defines hell as error of mortal mind.

The Jehovah's Witnesses teach that the wicked will simply be annihilated.

The Mormons believe in hell, but not as an endless existence. They teach that life after death involves three levels: celestial, terrestrial, and telestial. The celestial level includes Mormons in an intermediate state, who will eventually become gods. The terrestrial level includes Christians and other persons who rejected the Mormon message. The telestial level is reserved for those currently in hell who await a final resurrection. Mormons teach that these will ultimately be saved and not suffer punishment forever.

The Seventh-Day Adventists claim that God will someday blot out all sin and sinners and establish a clean universe again.

The late Bishop James Pike wrote:

"A Heaven of infinite bliss and a Hell of infinite torment is an impossible contradiction. The kind of people who would qualify for heaven would not be in bliss knowing that there were a lot of people in suffering with no chance whatever for change—the have-nots, the underprivileged. Those suitable for Heaven would want to go to Hell to be alongside them in their needs. Jesus, as shown by the reports of his ministry on earth, would be there alongside them too. God in his heaven would find himself lonely and might well join everybody there—or change the whole scheme." (*Protestant Power and the Coming Revolution,* p. 173)

Regardless of the doubts and denials of men, the Bible dogmatically declares the existence and reality of hell. Here the devout believer would agree with the Apostle Paul: "God forbid: yea, let God be true, but every man a liar; as it is written, That thou mightest be justified in thy sayings, and mightest overcome when thou art judged" (Rom. 3:4).

II. The Doctrine of Hell.

A. The background of Gehenna hell.

We have already seen that, following the tribulation, all the unsaved dead will be resurrected from Hades in the heart of the earth to appear before the great white judgment throne. (This is clearly stated in Rev. 20:11-15.) They will then be cast into Gehenna hell forever. Gehenna is a New Testament word with an Old Testament background. It is found twelve times in the Greek New Testament, eleven of those instances coming from the mouth of the Savior himself (Mt. 5:22, 29, 30; 10:28; 18:9; 25:15, 33; Mk. 9:43, 45; 9:47; Lk. 12:5; Jas. 3:6). A brief etymology of the word "Gehenna" will be helpful here. In the Old Testament, a wicked Israelite king named Ahaz forsook the worship of Jehovah and followed the devil-god Molech. In his insane and immoral attempt to please Molech, the king actually sacrificed his own children in the fires as burnt offerings to his abominable idol.

"Ahaz was twenty years old when he began to reign, and he reigned sixteen years in Jerusalem: but he did not that which was right in the sight of the Lord, like David his father: For he walked in the ways of the kings of Israel, and made also molten images for Baalim. Moreover he burnt incense in the valley of the son of Hinnom, and burnt his children in the fire, after the abominations of the heathen whom the Lord had cast out before the children of Israel. He sacrificed also and burnt incense in the high places, and on the hills, and under every green tree" (2 Chron. 28:1-4).

"And he defiled Topheth, which is in the valley of the children of Hinnom, that no man might make his son or his daughter to pass through the fire to Molech" (2 Ki. 23:10).

This all took place in a deep and narrow valley to the south of Jerusalem called the Valley of Hinnom. It was called by this name because of its owners, the sons of Hinnom. Jeremiah the prophet also writes about both the Valley of Hinnom and Topheth.

"And they have built the high places of Tophet, which is in the valley of the son of Hinnom, to burn their sons and their daughters in the fire; which I commanded them not, neither came it into my heart. Therefore, behold, the days come, saith the Lord, that it shall no more be called Tophet, nor the valley of the son of Hinnom, but the valley of slaughter: for they shall bury in Tophet, till there be no place. And the carcases of this people shall be meat for the fowls of the heaven, and for the beasts of the earth; and none shall fray them away" (Jer. 7:31-33).

Walter Price writes:

"Topheth was probably the point south of Jerusalem where three valleys met. The Tyropoeon Valley which runs through the old city and down by the Western Wall of the temple mount, intersects here with the Valley of Hinnom. The Valley of the Sons of Hinnom sweeps around the western side of the city and turns east below the Ophel to meet the Valley of Kidron. All three of these valleys converge at the spot where ancient Israel offered sacrifices to the Ammonite god Molech (2 Chron. 28:3; 33:6). Here also the field of Akeldama is located (Mt. 27:7, 8; Acts 1:18, 19). The Talmud places the mouth of hell in this place. The Arabs also call this lower end of the Hinnom Valley, where it meets Kidron, at Topheth, the Valley of Hell. In Jesus' day the city garbage dump was located there. The fighting between Jews and Romans ended here in A.D. 70. As many as 600,000 bodies of dead Jews, slain in the defense of Jerusalem against the Romans, were carried out through the Dung Gate to be buried in Topheth." (*The Coming Antichrist,* pp. 202, 203).

As one therefore combines both Old Testament and New Testament meanings, he has described for him a place of filth and sorrow, of smoke and pain, of fire and death. This, then, is the word the Holy Spirit chose to employ in describing the final destiny for the unsaved.

B. The location of hell.

Where is hell located? The Bible definitely indicates that Hades is somewhere down in the heart of the earth.

"And the earth opened her mouth, and swallowed them up, and their houses, and all the men that appertained unto Korah, and all their goods. They, and all that appertained to them, went down alive into the pit, and the earth closed upon them: and they perished from among the congregation" (Num. 16:32, 33).

It teaches, however, the following about Gehenna.

"But the children of the kingdom shall be cast out into outer darkness: there shall be weeping and gnashing of teeth" (Mt. 8:12).

"Then said the king to the servants, Bind him hand and foot, and take him away, and cast him into outer darkness; there shall be weeping and gnashing of teeth" (Mt. 22:13).

"And cast ye the unprofitable servant into outer darkness: there shall be weeping and gnashing of teeth" (Mt. 25:30).

"There are wells without water, clouds that are carried with a tempest; to whom the mist of darkness is reserved for ever" (2 Pet. 2:17).

"Raging waves of the sea, foaming out their own shame; wandering stars, to whom is reserved the blackness of darkness for ever" (Jude 1:13).

From these five verses it becomes immediately clear that Gehenna hell is located away from this earth, a place of outer darkness, to be found, perhaps, in some remote spot near the edge of God's universe.

C. The nature and characteristics of hell.

What will Gehenna really be like? Consider:

1. Hell is a place of unquenchable fire.

"Whose fan is in his hand, and he will thoroughly purge his floor, and gather his wheat into the garner; but he will burn up the chaff with unquenchable fire" (Mt. 3:12).

"The Son of man shall send forth his angels, and they shall gather out of his kingdom all things that offend, and them

which do iniquity; and shall cast them into a furnace of fire: there shall be wailing and gnashing of teeth" (Mt. 13:41, 42).

"And if thy hand offend thee, cut it off: it is better for thee to enter into life maimed, than having two hands to go into hell, into the fire that never shall be quenched" (Mk. 9:43).

Opposing positions have been taken concerning whether the fire here is literal fire. It has been suggested that the fire is not real fire but something far worse. However, the Greek language would indicate otherwise. The same Greek word for fire (*pur*) used in Matthew 13:42 is also found in Matthew 17:15 and Luke 17:29.

"And shall cast them into a furnace of fire: there shall be wailing and gnashing of teeth" (Mt. 13:42).

"Lord, have mercy on my son: for he is lunatick, and sore vexed: for ofttimes he falleth into the fire, and oft into the water" (Mt. 17:15).

"But the same day that Lot went out of Sodom it rained fire and brimstone from heaven, and destroyed them all" (Lk. 17:29).

2. Hell is a place of memory and remorse.

In Luke 16:19–31 the unsaved rich man experienced memory and remorse over his lost condition in Hades. Surely these experiences will not be lessened in Gehenna.

3. Hell is a place of thirst.

It would seem difficult indeed to accept this account literally unless the fire in hell is literal. But what of Lazarus' finger and the rich man's tongue? Can this be interpreted literally? It has been speculated that on the basis of this passage and also the one in 2 Corinthians 5 that temporary bodies of some sort are given to both unsaved and saved until the final resurrection of all.

4. Hell is a place of misery and pain.

"The same shall drink of the wine of the wrath of God, which is poured out without mixture into the cup of his indignation; and he shall be tormented with fire and brimstone in the presence of the holy angels, and in the presence of the Lamb: And the smoke of their torment ascendeth up for ever and ever: and they have no rest day nor night, who worship the beast and his image, and whosoever receiveth the mark of his name" (Rev. 14:10, 11).

5. Hell is a place of frustration and anger.

"And shall cast them into a furnace of fire; there shall be wailing and gnashing of teeth" (Mt. 13:42).

"And shall cut him asunder, and appoint him his portion with the hypocrites: there shall be weeping and gnashing of teeth" (Mt. 24:51).

6. Hell is a place of separation.

Often the unsaved man jokes about hell in the following manner: "Well, if I do go to hell, I won't be lonely, for all my friends will be there too." But quite the opposite is true! In at least four separate passages Gehenna hell is called "the second death."

"He that hath an ear, let him hear what the Spirit saith unto the churches; he that overcometh shall not be hurt of the second death" (Rev. 2:11).

"Blessed and holy is he that hath part in the first resurrection: on such the second death hath no power, but they shall be priests of God and of Christ, and shall reign with him a thousand years. And whosoever was not found written in the book of life was cast into the lake of fire" (Rev. 20:6, 15).

As we have already noted, "death" in the Bible refers to separation. Thus hell is literally the second death, for the sinner will be forever separated from God, and, inasmuch as Gehenna is a place of darkness, this separation will doubtless isolate him from the companionship of unsaved friends as well.

Thus, the worst thing about hell is closely connected to the best thing about heaven, and that is, the first is a place where Jesus Christ will be conspicuously absent, while the second location is a place where he will be conspicuously present!

7. Hell is a place of undiluted divine wrath.

Man has already experienced some of God's wrath on this earth, but not in its pure state. After the flood there has been the rainbow, for up to this point God has always heard and answered the prophet Habakkuk's prayer,

"O Lord, I have heard thy speech, and was afraid: O Lord, revive thy work in the midst of the years, in the midst of the years make known; in wrath remember mercy" (Hab. 3:2).

But no more! All living unsaved men should carefully ponder over the following frightful words:

"The same shall drink of the wine of the wrath of God, which is poured out without mixture into the cup of his indignation; and he shall be tormented with fire and brimstone in the presence of the holy angels, and in the presence of the Lamb" (Rev. 14:10).

8. Hell is a place originally prepared for Satan and his hosts.

Perhaps the saddest fact about hell is that unsaved man goes there as an uninvited guest, so to speak. Note Jesus' words:

"Then shall he say also unto them on the left hand, Depart from me, ye cursed, into everlasting fire, prepared for the devil and his angels" (Mt. 25:41).

How tragic, therefore, that the sinner will refuse heaven, the place prepared for all repenting men, only to eventually descend into hell, a place originally not created for him!

"In my Father's house are many mansions: if it were not so, I would have told you. I go to prepare a place for you" (Jn. 14:2).

9. Hell is a place created for all eternity.

The Greek word for "everlasting" is *aionios*, and is found seventy-one times in the New Testament. Sixty-four of these instances are in reference to God, such as his eternal power, Spirit, kingdom, covenant, etc. The remaining seven instances are directly related to the duration of hell. In other words, hell will continue as long as God's works continue, which is forever! Many passages bring this truth out:

"And many of them that sleep in the dust of the earth shall awake, some to everlasting life, and some to shame and everlasting contempt" (Dan. 12:2).

"And these shall go away into everlasting punishment: but the righteous into life eternal" (Mt. 25:46).

"Even as Sodom and Gomorrah, and the cities about them in like manner, giving themselves over to fornication, and going after strange flesh, are set forth for an example, suffering the vengeance of eternal fire" (Jude 1:7).

Without doubt the most difficult truth to accept, even for Christians, is the duration of hell. One might understand a sixty-five-year old sinner going to hell for sixty-five years, or 650, or 6500, or even 65 million years. But why the endless ages? How can a just God rightfully punish forever those sins which were committed in a brief period of time on earth?

A full answer to this exists only in the mind of God. However, hell does vividly demonstrate the heinousness of sin and the holiness of God. Thus, sins against God's eternal holiness can only be punished by God's eternal justice.

Finally, the following should be noted: As there is no injustice or partiality with God (Rom. 2:6, 11), it naturally follows that the degrees of suffering in hell will vary greatly, being in direct relationship to the sinner's life on earth. Various Scriptures bear this out.

"Then began he to upbraid the cities wherein most of his mighty works were done, because they repented not: Woe unto thee, Chorazin! woe unto thee, Bethsaida! for if the mighty works, which were done in you, had been done in Tyre and Sidon, they would have repented long ago in sackcloth and ashes. But I say unto you, It shall be more tolerable for Tyre and Sidon at the day of judgment, than for you. And thou, Capernaum, which art exalted unto heaven, shalt be brought down to hell: for if the mighty works, which have been done in thee, had been done in Sodom, it would have remained until this day. But I say unto you, That it shall be more tolerable for the land of Sodom in the day of judgment, than for thee" (Mt. 11:20-24).

"And that servant, which knew his lord's will, and prepared not himself, neither did according to his will, shall be beaten with many stripes. But he that knew not, and did commit things worthy of stripes, shall be beaten with few stripes. For unto whomsoever much is given, of him shall be much required: and to whom men have committed much, of him they will ask the more" (Lk. 12:47, 48).

"Then in the audience of all the people he said unto his disciples, Beware of the scribes, which desire to walk in long robes, and love greetings in the markets, and the highest seats in the synagogues, and the chief rooms at feasts: Which devour widows' houses, and for a shew make long prayers: the same shall receive greater damnation" (Lk. 20:45–47).

"Then saith Pilate unto him, Speakest thou not unto me? knowest thou that I have power to crucify thee, and have power to release thee? Jesus answered, Thou couldest have no power at all against me, except it were given thee from above: therefore he that delivered me unto thee hath the greater sin" (Jn. 19:10, 11).

D. The occupants of hell.
Who shall be someday confined to Gehenna forever?
1. Satan.
"And the God of peace shall bruise Satan under your feet shortly. The grace of our Lord Jesus Christ be with you. Amen" (Rom. 16:20).

"And the devil that deceived them was cast into the lake of fire and brimstone, where the beast and the false prophet are, and shall be tormented day and night for ever and ever" (Rev. 20:10).
2. The antichrist.
"And then shall that Wicked be revealed, whom the Lord shall consume with the spirit of his mouth, and shall destroy with the brightness of his coming" (2 Thess. 2:8).
3. The false prophet.
"And the beast was taken, and with him the false prophet that wrought miracles before him, with which he deceived them that had received the mark of the beast, and them that worshipped his image. These both were cast alive into a lake of fire burning with brimstone" (Rev. 19:20).
As this judgment takes place prior to the millennium, these two foul criminals thus become the first and second unsaved creatures to enter the lake of fire.
4. Fallen angels.
"God spared not the angels that sinned, but cast them down to hell, and delivered them into chains of darkness, to be reserved unto judgment" (2 Pet. 2:4).
The word translated "hell" is *tartaros* in the Greek New Testament and is found only here. It is possible that *tartaros* is a special place in Gehenna.

"And the angels which kept not their first estate, but left their own habitation, he hath reserved in everlasting chains under darkness unto the judgment of the great day" (Jude 1:6).
According to Paul, the believer will take part in the passing of judgment upon fallen angels. (See 1 Cor. 6:3.)
5. Judas Iscariot.
The betrayer of Jesus Christ is singled out here in particular because there are those (notably the late Kenneth S. Wuest of the Moody Bible Institute faculty) who believe Judas will be consigned to a special place in Gehenna on the basis of Peter's words concerning him in the upper room just prior to Pentecost:
"That he may take part of this ministry and apostleship, from which Judas by transgression fell, that he might go to his own place" (Acts 1:25).
6. All unsaved people.
In Revelation 21:8 John classified all sinners into eight general categories:
"But the fearful, and unbelieving, and the abominable, and murderers, and whoremongers, and sorcerers, and idolaters, and all liars, shall have their part in the lake which burneth with fire and brimstone: which is the second death" (Rev. 21:8).

A SCRIPTURAL SUMMARY OF HEAVEN

Both heaven and hell are either ignored, ridiculed, or denied by the world today. In his book *The Biblical Doctrine of Heaven*, Dr. Wilbur Smith lists two significant quotes from a world-famous theologian and a scientist about heaven:
"It is unwise for Christians to claim any knowledge of either the furniture of heaven or the temperature of hell" (Dr. Reinhold Niebuhr).
"As for the Christian theology, can you imagine anything more appallingly idiotic than the Christian idea of heaven?" (Dr. Alfred Whitehead).

A common approach of the liberal clergyman is that he does indeed believe in a literal heaven and hell, but limits them both to this earth! In other words, life's good experiences are "heaven," and its bad moments "hell." Without him probably being at all aware of it, his Bible-denying philosophy does contain a very potent truth. The facts are that this world is indeed the only hell the believer will ever experience, and the only heaven the unbeliever will ever know!

Sometimes a "pious" objection is raised concerning the very study of heaven. The protest goes: "But don't you think we can become so heavenly minded that we're no earthly good?" This may be, but for every one like this, there are probably ten believers who are so *earthly* minded that they are no *heavenly* good! (See Col. 3:1–3).

In reality, we are told a surprising number of things in the Word of God about our future home. Contrary to popular opinion, heaven is discussed far more than hell in the Scriptures!

I. The Capital of Heaven.
In the Bible we read of three heavens. Briefly, these are:

A. The First Heaven—home of the birds and clouds.

"I beheld, and, lo, there was no man, and all the birds of the heavens were fled" (Jer. 4:25).

"The leaves thereof were fair, and the fruit thereof much, and in it was meat for all: the beasts of the field had shadow under it, and the fowls of the heaven dwelt in the boughs thereof, and all flesh was fed of it" (Dan. 4:12).

"Behold the fowls of the air: for they sow not, neither do they reap, nor gather into barns; yet your heavenly Father feedeth them. Are ye not much better than they?" (Mt. 6:26).

"And Jesus saith unto him, The foxes have holes, and the birds of the air have nests; but the Son of man hath not where to lay his head" (Mt. 8:20).

It can be readily seen that as beautiful as this heaven may be on occasion, it is not the eternal home of the redeemed.

B. The Second Heaven—home of the sun, moon, and stars.

"That in blessing I will bless thee, and in multiplying I will multiply thy seed as the stars of the heaven, and as the sand which is upon the sea shore; and thy seed shall possess the gate of his enemies" (Gen. 22:17).

"The heavens declare the glory of God; and the firmament sheweth his handiwork" (Ps. 19:1).

In the sixties (beginning with the Russian orbit in 1961 and climaxing with the U.S. moon landing in 1969) man for the first time in history succeeded in developing a space craft that would transport him out of the first heaven into the second heaven! But as wide and wonderful as it is, the second heaven (like the first) cannot be confused with the heaven of salvation.

C. The Third Heaven—home of God.

"I knew a man in Christ above fourteen years ago, (whether in the body, I cannot tell; or whether out of the body, I cannot tell: God knoweth;) such an one caught up to the third heaven" (2 Cor. 12:2).

"But will God indeed dwell on the earth? behold, the heaven and heaven of heavens cannot contain thee; how much less this house that I have builded? And hearken thou to the supplication of thy servant, and of thy people Israel, when they shall pray toward this place: and hear thou in heaven thy dwelling place; and when thou hearest, forgive" (1 Ki. 8:27, 30).

This and this alone is the true third heaven! It has already been noted how man's brain power recently transported him from the first to the second heaven. But no space vehicle can ever be devised which will take him from the second to the third heaven! This journey can only be effected by blood, and not by brain! In fact, Jesus once told Nicodemus a man could not even see this heaven, let alone enter it, apart from the new birth. (See Jn. 3:3.)

In Matthew 6:9 our Lord taught his disciples to pray:

"After this manner therefore pray ye: Our Father which art in heaven, Hallowed be thy name" (Mt. 6:9).

Here of course, he was referring to the third heaven, the abode of God. However, the Bible teaches that within this heavenly abode there exists a dazzling, high, and holy city called the New Jerusalem. This beautiful and blessed city is therefore not only the center of God's presence, but will be the permanent home for all the redeemed throughout eternity. Both Old and New Testament believers looked and longed for this celestial city.

"There is a river, the streams whereof shall make glad the city of God, the holy place of the tabernacles of the Most High" (Ps. 46:4).

"Glorious things are spoken of thee, O city of God. Selah" (Ps. 87:3).

"For he looked for a city which hath foundations, whose builder and maker is God. But now they desire a better country, that is, a heavenly: wherefore God is not ashamed to be called their God" (Heb. 11:10, 16).

"But ye are come unto mount Sion, and unto the city of the living God, the heavenly Jerusalem, and to an innumerable company of angels" (Heb. 12:22).

"In my Father's house are many mansions: if it were not so, I would have told you. I go to prepare a place for you. And if I go and prepare a place for you, I will come again, and receive you unto myself; that where I am, there ye may be also" (Jn. 14:2, 3).

"And I John saw the holy city, new Jerusalem, coming down from God out of heaven, prepared as a bride adorned for her husband" (Rev. 21:2).

II. The Characteristics of Heaven (facts about the New Jerusalem).

A. The shape of this city.

"And the city lieth four-square, and the length is as large as the breadth . . . the length and the breadth and the height of it are equal" (Rev. 21:16). This description allows for two possibilities, namely that the New Jerusalem is either in the shape of a cube or of a vast pyramid.

B. The size of this city.

". . . and he measured the city with the reed, twelve thousand furlongs" (Rev. 21:16).

According to our present-day measurements this city would be roughly 1400 miles long, high, and wide. If placed in America, it would reach from New York City to Denver, Colorado, and from Canada to Florida!

How big is a city this size? Our earth has approximately 120 million square miles of water surface and 60 million square miles of land surface. If one multiplies 1400 by 1400 by 1400 (the dimensions of the New Jerusalem), he arrives at the total cubic miles of the city, a staggering figure of 2 billion, 700 million. This is some fifteen times the combined surface of the entire earth, including both land and water area!

It has been estimated that approximately 40 billion people have lived on our planet since the creation of Adam. Of this number, over 4 billion are living today. Density studies of city populations assure us that every single one of these 40 billion could easily be accommodated upon just the first "foundational floor" of this marvelous 1400-layered metropolis.

C. The inhabitants of this city.

Who will dwell in that shining city of the stars?

1. The holy and elect angels.

"But ye are come unto mount Sion, and unto the city of the living God, the heavenly Jerusalem, and to an innumerable company of angels" (Heb. 12:22).

"And I beheld, and I heard the voice of many angels round about the throne, and the beasts, and the elders: and the number of them was ten thousand times ten thousand, and thousands of thousands" (Rev. 5:11).

God of course knows their number, but they are presented to men as uncountable. There may be as many angels as there are stars in the heavens, for angels are often associated with the stars (Job 38:7; Ps. 148:1-3; Rev. 9:1, 2; 12:3, 4, 7-9). If this be so, there exist untold trillions of these heavenly beings! (See Ps. 68:17; Mt. 26:53; Dan. 7:9, 10.)

2. The 24 elders (Rev. 4:4).

3. The Church.

As the following passages indicate, the New Jerusalem is in reality the Bridegroom's wedding ring to his beloved bride!

"But ye are come unto mount Sion, and unto the city of the living God, the heavenly Jerusalem, and to an innumerable company of angels, to the general assembly and church of the firstborn, which are written in heaven, and the God the Judge of all, and to the spirits of just men made perfect" (Heb. 12:22, 23).

"And after these things I heard a great voice of much people in heaven, saying, Alleluia; Salvation, and glory, and honour, and power, unto the Lord our God: Let us be glad and rejoice, and give honour to him: for the marriage of the Lamb is come, and his wife hath made herself ready. And to her was granted that she should be arrayed in fine linen, clean and white; for the fine linen is the righteousness of saints" (Rev. 19:1, 7, 8).

"And I saw a new heaven and a new earth: for the first heaven and the first earth were passed away; and there was no more sea. And there came unto me one of the seven angels which had the seven vials full of the seven last plagues, and talked with me, saying, Come hither, I will show thee the bride, the Lamb's wife. And he carried me away in the spirit to a great and high mountain, and showed me that great city, the holy Jerusalem, descending out of heaven from God, having the glory of God: and her light was like unto a stone most precious, even like a jasper stone, clear as crystal" (Rev. 21:1, 9-11).

4. Saved Israel.

Although the New Jerusalem is basically a wedding present from the Bridegroom (Christ) to the Bride (the Church), Israel nevertheless is also invited to dwell within these jasper walls.

Several passages bear this out:

"But now they desire a better country, that is, a heavenly: wherefore God is not ashamed to be called their God: for he hath prepared for them a city" (Heb. 11:16).

"And while they went to buy, the bridegroom came; and they that were ready went in with him to the marriage: and the door was shut. His lord said unto him, Well done, good and faithful servant; thou hast been faithful over a few things, I will make thee ruler over many things: enter thou into the joy of thy lord" (Mt. 25:10, 23).

Our Lord quotes these words during his Mt. Olivet discourse. In relating two parables he likens saved Israel to some prepared wedding guests (parable of the ten virgins), and later as two faithful servants (parable of the talents). He thus pictures saved Israel as joining the bride and Bridegroom.

5. The Father.

"And immediately I was in the spirit; and, behold, a throne was set in heaven, and one sat on the throne. And he that sat was to look upon like a jasper and a sardine stone: and there was a rainbow round about the throne, in sight like unto an emerald" (Rev. 4:2, 3).

There seems no doubt that the One John sees sitting upon this throne is the Father himself.

The only other description of the Father in the Bible is found in Daniel 7:9:

"I beheld till the thrones were cast down, and the Ancient of days did sit, whose garment was white as snow, and the hair of his head like pure wool: his throne was like the fiery flame, and his wheels as burning fire."

6. The Son.

"And I beheld, and, lo, in the midst of the throne and of the four beasts, and in the midst of the elders, stood a Lamb as it had been slain, having seven horns and seven eyes, which are the seven Spirits of God sent forth into all the earth" (Rev. 5:6).

Here we learn that not only is the Lamb of God an occupant of heaven, but the very source and strength and center of heaven, without which there could be no heaven! Thus we see:

The light of heaven is the face of Jesus.

The joy of heaven is the presence of Jesus.

The song of heaven is the name of Jesus.

The theme of heaven is the work of Jesus.

The employment of heaven is the work of Jesus.

The fullness of heaven is the Person of Jesus.

7. The Holy Spirit.

Although the Spirit of God is not as prominent as the Father or Son, he is unquestionably an occupant of the New Jerusalem as attested by the following passages:

"And I heard a voice from heaven saying unto me, Write, Blessed are the dead which die in the Lord from henceforth: Yea, saith the Spirit, that they may rest from their labours: and their works do follow them" (Rev. 14:13).

"And the Spirit and the bride say, Come. And let him that heareth say, Come. And let him that is athirst come. And whosoever will, let him take the water of life freely" (Rev. 22:17).

D. The Foundation of this city.

The city rests upon twelve layers of foundation stones with each layer being inlaid with a different precious gem. These are:

First foundation—inlaid with jasper, a crystal-clear diamond, as bright as a transparent icicle in the sunshine.

Second foundation—inlaid with sapphire, a blue opaque stone with gold specks.

Third foundation—inlaid with chalcedony, a sky-blue stone with stripes of other colors running through it.

Fourth foundation—inlaid with emerald, a bright green stone.

Fifth foundation—inlaid with sardonyx, a white stone with layers of red.

Sixth foundation—inlaid with sardius, a fiery red stone.

Seventh foundation—inlaid with chrysolyte, a transparent golden yellow stone.

Eighth foundation—inlaid with beryl, a sea-green stone.

Ninth foundation—inlaid with topaz, a transparent golden-green stone.

Tenth foundation—inlaid with chrysoprasus, a blue-green stone.

Eleventh foundation—inlaid with jacinth, a violet stone.

Twelfth foundation—inlaid with amethyst, a flashing purple stone.

These twelve foundations were not only inlaid with costly gems, but each foundational layer carried the name of one of the twelve apostles in the New Testament.

"And the wall of the city had twelve foundations, and in them the names of the twelve apostles of the Lamb" (Rev. 21:14).

E. The walls of this city.

The walls of the New Jerusalem are some 216 feet high and are made of jasper.

"And he measured the wall thereof, an hundred and forty and four cubits, according to the measure of a man, that is, of the angel. And the building of the wall of it was of jasper: and the city was pure gold, like unto clear glass" (Rev. 21:17, 18).

The wall is obviously not for protection, but for design and beauty only. In comparison to size, a 216-foot wall around a 1400-mile high city would be like a one-inch curb around the Empire State Building!

F. The gates of this city.

There are twelve gates to this city, three gates on each side. On each gate is the name of one of the tribes of Israel. Each gate is composed of a beautiful solid white pearl.

"And had a wall great and high, and had twelve gates, and at the gates twelve angels, and names written thereon, which are the names of the twelve tribes of the children of Israel: On the east three gates; on the north three gates; on the south three gates; and on the west three gates. And the twelve gates were twelve pearls; every several gate was of one pearl" (Rev. 21:12, 13, 21a).

G. The main street of this city.

The central boulevard of the New Jerusalem is composed of pure transparent gold.

". . . and the street of the city was pure gold, as it were transparent glass" (Rev. 21:21b).

When one considers the price of gold (nearly $600 an ounce at the beginning of the eighties), the total worth of this city becomes incomprehensible!

H. The throne within this city.

"And immediately I was in the spirit; and behold, a throne was set in heaven, and one sat on the throne. And he that sat was to look upon like a jasper and a sardine stone: and there was a rainbow round about the throne, in sight like unto an emerald. And before the throne there was a sea of glass like unto crystal: and in the midst of the throne, and round about the throne, were four beasts full of eyes before and behind" (Rev. 4:2, 3, 6).

I. The river of life in this city.

"And he showed me a pure river of water of life, clear as crystal, proceeding out of the throne of God and of the Lamb" (Rev. 22:1).

The Holy Spirit doubtless meant to make at least some reference to this river when he inspired David to write:

"And he shall be like a tree planted by the rivers of water, that bringeth forth his fruit in his season; his leaf also shall not wither; and whatsoever he doeth shall prosper" (Ps. 1:3).

"There is a river, the streams whereof shall make glad the city of God, the holy place of the tabernacles of the Most High" (Ps. 46:4).

J. The tree of life in this city.

"In the midst of the street of it, and on either side of the river, was there the tree of life, which bare twelve manner of fruits, and yielded her fruit every month: and the leaves of the tree were for the healing of the nations" (Rev. 22:2).

When God created man and placed him in the Garden of Eden he placed at Adam's disposal (among many other things) the tree of life. But when man sinned, he was driven from Eden and from this tree.

"And out of the ground made the Lord God to grow every tree that is pleasant to the sight, and good for food; the tree of life also in the midst of the garden, and the tree of knowledge of good and evil" (Gen. 2:9).

"So he drove out the man; and he placed at the east of the garden of Eden cherubim, and a flaming sword which turned every way, to keep the way of the tree of life" (Gen. 3:24).

At that point in human history the tree of life disappears, but here in the New Jerusalem it will blossom and bloom as never before! In his book *Reveling Through Revelation,* Dr. J. Vernon McGee writes the following words concerning this river and this tree:

"Up to this chapter, the New Jerusalem seems to be all mineral and no vegetable. Its appearance is as the dazzling display of a fabulous jewelry store, but there is no soft grass to sit upon, no green trees to enjoy, and no water to drink or food to eat. However, here introduced are the elements which add a rich softness to this city of elaborate beauty."

Paul Lee Tan writes:

"Because of the location of the tree of life 'on either side of the river,' theologians have understood the 'tree' to be not a single tree, but a single kind of tree . . . a row of trees on either side of the river. Others, however, see one tree planted at the middle of the river, with branches extending to both banks. The tree is large enough to span the river, so that the river is in the midst of the street, and the tree is on both sides of the river." (*The New Jerusalem,* p. 28)

K. The relationship between this city and earthly Jerusalem.

We have already seen there will be two fabulous cities of God in the future. One is located on the earth. It will be known as Jehovah Tsidkenu, meaning, "the Lord our righteousness" (Jer. 23:6; 33:16), and Jehovah Shammah, meaning "the Lord is there" (Ezek. 48:35). The other city is suspended in space and is called the New Jerusalem (Rev. 21:2). This one of course is thousands of times the size of the earthly city and will endure forever.

L. The nature of the resurrected bodies in this city.

To summarize, all resurrected bodies shall reside in the heavenly city, but will reign upon the earthly city. Having now examined our future location, what do we know about our transformation and (finally) our vocation? In other words, what will be the nature of these resurrected bodies and what activities will we carry on through them?

In 1 Corinthians 15, Paul answers questions concerning this transformation. In verses 39–41 Paul suggests that the new spiritual body is as superior to the old natural body as:

The human body is to those of animals (15:39).

The heavens are to the earth (15:40).

The sun is to the moon (15:41).

Such then, will be the nature of our transformed bodies:

1. These bodies will be like his glorious body (Phil. 3:21; 1 Jn. 3:1–3).
2. They will consist of flesh and bone (Lk. 24:39, 40).
3. Christ ate in his glorified body (Lk. 24:41–43; Jn. 21:12–15).
4. These bodies will not be subjected to laws of gravity and time (Jn. 20:19; Lk. 24:31, 36).

5. They will be recognizable bodies (Mt. 8:11; Lk. 16:23; 1 Cor. 13:12).
6. They will be eternal bodies (2 Cor. 5:1).
7. They will be (as we have already seen) bodies in which the spirit predominates (1 Cor. 15:44, 49).

M. The activities of the redeemed in this city.

A popular but totally perverted concept of heaven would describe that future life in the skies in terms of some disembodied spirits piously perched on fleecy clouds and strumming their golden harps. This may be heaven according to Walt Disney, but New Testament it is not! The Scripture would indicate that:

1. Heaven will be a place of singing.

"Sing, O ye heavens; for the Lord hath done it: shout, ye lower parts of the earth: break forth into singing, ye mountains, O forest, and every tree therein: for the Lord hath redeemed Jacob, and glorified himself in Israel" (Isa. 44:23).

"Saying, I will declare thy name unto my brethren, in the midst of the church will I sing praise unto thee" (Heb. 2:12).

"And they sung as it were a new song before the throne, and before the four beasts, and the elders: and no man could learn that song but the hundred and forty and four thousand, which were redeemed from the earth" (Rev. 14:3).

"And they sing the song of Moses the servant of God, and the song of the Lamb, saying, Great and marvellous are thy works, Lord God Almighty; just and true are thy ways, thou King of saints" (Rev. 15:3).

2. Heaven will be a place of fellowship.

One of the most beloved gospel songs is entitled, "Leaning On the Everlasting Arms." The first stanza begins: "What a fellowship, what a joy divine. . . ." Sometimes, however, as one observes the petty squabbling which goes on in local churches, this verse might be rephrased to read: "What? A fellowship? What? A joy divine?" But in heaven real and eternal fellowship will prevail.

Not only will believers enjoy blessed fellowship with other believers, but, even more important, we shall know and be known by the Savior in a far more intimate way than ever possible here on earth.

3. Heaven will be a place of serving.

"Therefore are they before the throne of God, and serve him day and night in his temple: and he that sitteth on the throne shall dwell among them" (Rev. 7:15).

"And there shall be no more curse: but the throne of God and of the Lamb shall be in it; and his servants shall serve him" (Rev. 22:3).

While we cannot be dogmatic on the exact nature of this service, we do know from the following passages that a portion of our labor for the Lamb will be that of exercising authority and judgment over men and angels:

"Do ye not know that the saints shall judge the world? and if the world shall be judged by you, are ye unworthy to judge the smallest matters? Know ye not that we shall judge angels? how much more things that pertain to this life?" (1 Cor. 6:2, 3).

"If we suffer, we shall also reign with him: if we deny him, he also will deny us" (2 Tim. 2:12).

"And there shall be no night there; and they need no candle, neither light of the sun; for the Lord God giveth them light: and they shall reign for ever and ever" (Rev. 22:5).

4. Heaven will be a place of learning.

"For we know in part, and we prophesy in part. But when that which is perfect is come, then that which is in part shall be done away" (1 Cor. 13:9, 10).

What will we learn about in heaven?

a. We will learn concerning the *person* of God.

b. We will learn concerning the *plan* of God. One of the most painful questions asked here on earth by Christians is why a loving and wise God allows certain terrible tragedies to occur. As an example, here is a young, spirit-filled pastor. He has spent a number of years diligently preparing for the ministry. His wife has sacrificed to help put him through school. Now all this is paying off. His church is experiencing amazing growth. Souls are saved weekly. New converts are baptized each Sunday. Additional Sunday school busses are purchased and a new building is planned. A skeptical community slowly finds itself being profoundly influenced by this vibrant and exciting pastor and his people. Suddenly, without any warn-ing, the minister is killed in a freak accident. Shortly after the funeral the still confused and stunned congregation extends a call to another man. But the new minister shows little compassion and less leadership ability. Soon the flock is scattered and the once thrilling testimony of a growing and glowing work is all but stilled!

How many times since Abel's martyrdom at the dawn of human history have similar tragedies like this taken place? But the searing and searching question remains: Why does God permit such terrible things?

We may rest assured that in heaven God will take each of us aside and explain fully the reason for all our sufferings and trials. We then will say the words once stated by a Galilean crowd in Jesus' day: "He hath done all things well . . ." (Mk. 7:37).

c. We will learn concerning the *power* of God.

"In the beginning God created the heaven and the earth" (Gen. 1:1).

Just how vast is our universe? It is so huge that it takes a beam of light (which travels some 700 million miles per hour) over ten billion years to cross the known universe! Within this universe are untold trillions of stars, planets, and other heavenly bodies. God made them all to instruct man concerning his power and glory (Ps. 19:1; 147:4; Isa. 40:26). We shall someday therefore visit each star and explore every corner of our Father's universe!

THE DOCTRINE OF THE CHURCH

THE DOCTRINE OF THE CHURCH

In the book of Ephesians the Apostle Paul warned his readers against "the wiles of the devil," and the "fiery darts of the wicked" (Eph. 6:11, 16). Satan has always, of course, bitterly opposed both the work and workers of God. His battle with Jesus began in the Garden of Eden (Gen. 3:15) and continued without pause throughout the Old Testament, but with the advent of the incarnation, life, crucifixion, resurrection, and ascension of Christ, the intensity of the struggle increased a thousandfold. During the first few centuries of church history, the devil attacked the doctrine of the deity of Christ. Then (after a terrible defeat in A.D. 325) he moved against the doctrine of justification by faith. But he had not counted on the actions of one Martin Luther. Again, turning in another direction, he lashed out against the inspiration of the Scriptures. This reached its high point during the final years of the nineteenth century and early years of the twentieth century, about the time God was raising up great schools of the Scripture, such as the Moody Bible Institute in Chicago, and other Bible centers to counteract this satanic attack.

Finally, in a desperate effort to corrupt and confuse the work of God (before the coming of the Son of God), Satan has boldly and brazenly declared all-out war upon the very bride of Christ, the church itself. Today one need only scan the horizon of Christendom to discover just how successful Satan has been along these lines. There is a desperate need for the study of and subsequent return to the scriptural teachings of the church. This must be, "Lest Satan should get an advantage of us; for we are not ignorant of his devices" (2 Cor. 2:11).

I. The Meaning of the Word "Church." The Greek word in the New Testament for our English word "church" is *ekklesia*. It is derived from the verb *ekkaleo*. The compound *ek* means "out," and *kaleo* means "to call or summon." Thus, the literal meaning is "to call out."

A. Its connection with the Hebrew world of the Old Testament. The New Testament Greek word *ekklesia* has a loose connection with the Hebrew word *qahal*, which is found some 100 times in the Old Testament. It is translated by the English words "congregation, assembly, company." *Qahal* may refer to those assemblies gathered together for purposes of:

1. Evil counsel (Gen. 49:6; Ps. 26:5). In the Genesis passage Jacob is lamenting a past evil deed of Simeon and Levi, two of his sons, who plotted and carried out the cold-blooded murder of several pagans. (See also Gen. 34.)

2. Civil affairs (1 Ki. 12:3; Prov. 5:14). In 1 Kings 12:3, Israel's elders had gathered together at Shechem to discuss a very important civil affair, the coronation of Rehoboam, Solomon's son, as their next king.

3. War (Num. 22:4; Jdg. 20:2). The first passage here records the war council of Moab against Israel, while the second relates the sad meeting of Israel's eleven tribes who had gathered to go to war against the twelfth tribe, Benjamin.

4. Religious worship of God (2 Chron. 20:5). The word can also describe the assembly of angels (Ps. 89:5).

B. Its connection with the secular Greek world. In secular Greek, *ekklesia* referred only to an assembly or meeting and never to the people which composed that assembly. Even a wild and ignorant lynch mob could be referred to as an *ekklesia* (Acts 19:32). When the people left the meeting they were not considered as composing an *ekklesia*. Thus, the Greek mind would never see in this word a religious connection.

C. Its connection to the theological world of the New Testament. The New Testament reveals a development of the word *ekklesia* from the simple nontechnical meaning of "assembly" to the full-blown technical and theological designation for "the people of God." Of its 114 occurrences in the New Testament, with but five exceptions (Acts 7:38; 19:32, 39, 41; Heb. 2:12), the *ekklesia* church is presented in this light. One of these five passages (Acts 7:38) deals with Stephen's address before the Sanhedrin during which he described the nation Israel at Mt. Sinai as "the church in the wilderness." The next three times occur in reference to the wild Greek mob at Ephesus (Acts 19:32, 39, 41), while the final passage (Heb. 2:12) apparently describes Christ's song of praise to the Father concerning all the elect, both Old Testament and New Testament saints.

II. The Origin of the Church. When and where did the church actually begin? Here we are confronted with several different views.

A. It began with Adam in Genesis 3. In a discussion of this question, Dr. Earl Radmacher quotes R. B. Kuiper who says:

"And if we assume, as undoubtedly we may, that Adam and Eve believed the promise of God that the seed of the serpent would indeed bruise the heel of the woman, but that the woman's seed would bruise the serpent's head . . . then it may be asserted that they constituted the first Christian church." (*The Nature of the Church*, pp. 193, 194)

B. It began with Abraham in Genesis 12. This is the position of most covenant theologians. The logic behind this view is the belief that as Israel once functioned as God's church in the Old Testament, so the church now functions as God's Israel in the New Testament.

C. It began with John the Baptist in Matthew 3.

Here the argument is that John was Scripture's first baptizer, and inasmuch as Christ later commanded his church to practice this worldwide (Mt. 28:19), the conclusion is that the church began with John.

D. It began with Christ. Here four different time periods are advocated by those who believe it began with the Savior.

1. At the call of the twelve apostles in Matthew 10. Thomas P. Simmons holds this view. He writes:

"In locating the founding of the church we must find a time when something that answers to the description of the church came into existence. This rule points us to the time when, after a night of prayer, Christ selected the twelve disciples. With this selection, these twelve men, for the first time, became a body. They had a head—Christ. They had a treasurer—Judas. They were supposed to be baptized believers. They were banded together to carry out Christ's will. What more than this did they become . . . ?" (*A Systematic Study of Bible Doctrine*, p. 354)

2. With Peter's confession in Matthew 16. Advocates of this position place the church at this point for the simple reason that it is first mentioned by Christ here. (See Mt. 16:18.)

3. With the Last Supper in Matthew 26; Mark 14; Luke 22; John 13. Those who defend this view point out that it was at this time that Christ instituted the ordinance of the Lord's Supper, indicating the church now existed.

4. On the first Easter Sunday night after Jesus' resurrection in John 20.

"Then said Jesus to them again, Peace be unto you: as my Father hath sent me, even so send I you. And when he had said this, he breathed on them, and saith unto them, Receive ye the Holy Ghost" (20:21, 22).

Here it is argued that the final element necessary for the completion of the promised church is now given, namely, the Person and power of the Holy Spirit.

E. With Paul. Here, as in the case of Christ, several time periods are offered.

1. At the time of his conversion in Acts 9. Proponents of this position remind us that the church could hardly have begun until the conversion of its most famous theologian and epistle writer, the Apostle Paul.

2. At the time of his first missionary trip in Acts 13. Some are convinced that the assembly at Jerusalem, even though referred to as a church, was in reality not one, but rather a group of mainly Jewish believers operating under a modified Old Testament economy. However, in Acts 13 Paul begins his lifelong ministry of establishing 100 percent Christian local churches.

3. At the time of his Roman imprisonment in Acts 28. During this (his first) Roman imprisonment, Paul wrote Philippians, Philemon, Colossians, and Ephesians. Disciples of this last view feel these four New Testament church epistles alone (later to include Paul's three letters to Timothy and Titus) compose God's message to local churches, thus their Acts 28 church origin position.

F. Here, then, are the theories. Which are we to believe? Godly and able men may be cited to support each view, but the bulk of Bible students hold the position that the church began at Pentecost. This view has been amply defended by both Dr. Lewis Sperry Chafer and Dr. Charles C. Ryrie. These men write:

"Apparently for want of due consideration of all that enters into the case, some theologians have sustained the idea that those things which characterize the Old Testament revelation are carried forward without change into the New Testament. The necessity of observing dispensational distinctions arises in connection with the abrupt abandonment of existing features and the introduction of new features which mark the transition from one dispensation to the next. This line of demarcation is especially clear between the present age and that which preceded it, and between the present age and that which is to follow. Certain events which serve to produce these changes are properly styled age-transforming. Things cannot be the same in this age as they were in the past age, after the death of Christ has taken place, His resurrection, His ascension, and the advent of the Spirit on Pentecost. In like manner, things cannot be the same in the coming age as they are in this age, after there is brought about the second advent of Christ to reign on the earth, the binding of Satan, the removal of the Church, and the restoration of Israel. Those who see no force in this declaration have hardly considered the measureless meaning of these age-transforming occurrences. In the light of these determining issues, it may be seen (a) that there could be no Church in the world—constituted as she is and distinctive in all her features—until Christ's death; for her relation to that death is not a mere anticipation, but is based wholly on His finished work and she must be purified by His precious blood. (b) There could be no Church until Christ arose from the dead to provide her with resurrection life. (c) There could be no Church until He had ascended up on high to become her Head; for she is a New Creation with a new federal headship in the resurrected Christ. He is, likewise, to her as the head is to the body. Nor could the Church survive for a moment were it not for His intercession and advocacy in heaven. (d) There could be no Church on earth until the advent of the Holy Spirit; for the most basic and fundamental reality respecting the Church is that she is a temple for the habitation of God through the Spirit. She is regenerated, baptized, and sealed by the Spirit." (Lewis Chafer, *Systematic Theology,* Vol. IV, p. 45)

That the day of Pentecost marked the beginning of the church seems evident for the following reasons:

1. "The Lord spoke of the church as being future in Matthew 16:18. This apparently means that the church did not exist in Old Testament times.

2. The resurrection and ascension of Christ are essential to the functioning of the church. It is built on the resurrection (Eph. 1:19, 20), and the giving of gifts is required for its operation, which giving of gifts in turn is dependent on Christ's being ascended (Eph. 4:7–12). If by some stretch of imaginative theology the body of Christ could be said to have been in existence before the ascension of Christ, then it will have to be concluded that it was an ungifted and inoperative body. The church's being built on the resurrection and ascension of Christ makes it distinctive to this age.

3. But the principal evidence that the church began on the day of Pentecost concerns the baptizing work of the Holy Spirit. The Lord declared that this particular and distinctive ministry of the Spirit was still future just before his ascension (Acts 1:5). On the day of Pentecost it first occurred (the record does not say so in Acts 2 but it does in Acts 11:15, 16). Now, what is it that Spirit baptism does? The answer to this is found in 1 Corinthians 12:13; it places the believer in the body of Christ. Since this is the only way to enter the body (i.e., by the baptizing work of the Spirit), and since this work of the Spirit first occurred on the day of Pentecost, then the conclusion seems obvious that the church, the body of Christ, began on the day of Pentecost." (Charles Ryrie, *A Survey of Bible Doctrine,* pp. 157, 158)

III. The Nature of the Church. Before attempting to determine what it *is,* let us consider some things the church is *not.*

  A. The church considered from a negative viewpoint.

    1. It is not a new name for Israel.
Covenant theologians teach that the church has become God's elect people, as Israel once was. But this is not the case, as seen by the following arguments.

      a. The promises are different.
        (1) The promises and provisions concerning Israel were basically earthly in scope (see Ex. 15:26; Deut. 28).
        (2) The promises concerning the church are basically heavenly in scope (see Eph. 1:3; Col. 3:1–3).
      b. The seed is different.
        (1) Abraham's physical seed refers to Israel (Rom. 9:7).
        (2) Abraham's spiritual seed refers to the church (Gal. 3:7).
      c. The births are different.
        (1) Israel celebrated its birthday at the base of Mt. Sinai (Ex. 19–20).
        (2) The church celebrated its birthday at Pentecost (Acts 2). The author of Hebrews brings out the great contrast between these two entities (12:18–24).
        (3) Israelites became what they were by physical birth.
        (4) Believers become what they are by spiritual birth.
      d. The nationality is different.
        (1) Israel belonged to this earth and to the world system.
        (2) The church is composed of all nations and has no citizenship down here, but its members are strangers and pilgrims (1 Pet. 2:11).
      e. The relationship with the Father is different.
        (1) God is never presented as the Father of individual Israelites in the Old Testament.
        (2) God is presented as the Father of all New Testament believers (Rom. 8:15; 1 Jn. 3:1).
        (3) Israel is now under God's judgment (Rom. 10:21; 11:8).
        (4) The church is free from all present judgment (Col. 2:13–15).
        (5) Israel was God's servant (Isa. 41:8).
        (6) The church—each believer—is God's son (Jn. 1:12; 1 Jn. 3:1).
      f. The relationship with the Son is different.
        (1) Israel is pictured as an unfaithful wife (Isa. 54:1–17; Jer. 3:1, 14, 20; Ezek. 16:1–59; Hosea 2:1–23).
        (2) The church is pictured as a chaste virgin bride yet to be married in heaven (2 Cor. 11:2; Rev. 19:7–9).
        (3) Christ was a stumbling stone to Israel (1 Cor. 1:23; 1 Pet. 2:8).
        (4) Christ is the Foundation and chief Cornerstone of the church (Eph. 2:20–22; 1 Pet. 2:4, 5).
        (5) Christ is Israel's Messiah and King (Jn. 1:49).
        (6) Christ is the church's Savior, Bridegroom, and Head (Eph. 5:23).
      g. The relationship with the Holy Spirit is different.

(1) The Holy Spirit rarely came upon individual Old Testament Israelites.

(2) The Holy Spirit actually lives inside each New Testament believer (see 1 Cor. 6:19).

h. The temple is different.

(1) Israel *had* a Temple (Ex. 25:8).

(2) The church *is* a temple (Eph. 2:21).

The above contrasts should make it clear that the church is not Israel. Paul carefully distinguished these two separate entities when he wrote:

"Give none offense, neither to the Jews, nor to the Gentiles, nor to the church of God" (1 Cor. 10:32).

2. It is not the kingdom.

The church is to be built up during this present time (Eph. 4:12), while the kingdom will be set up at a future time (Acts 15:16; Rev. 11:15).

3. It is not a building structure composed of wood, bricks, nails, and mortar.

4. It is not a state or national organization. Earl Radmacher writes:

"It is common today, especially in European countries, to witness a close connection between the state and the church so that one particular church is governed and supported by the state. It is interesting to note that all of the leading reformers, who so heroically freed the church from the Roman Catholic Church and the Pope, fastened a state church upon the people wherever they went and the churches which stood for absolute religious liberty were persecuted by these state churches." (*The Nature of the Church*, p. 149)

5. It is not a denominational organization. Again, Radmacher writes:

"People often speak of the various denominations or churches, as, for instance, the Episcopal Church, the Lutheran Church, the Presbyterian Church; but this use of *ekklesia* is never found in the Scriptures." (*Ibid.*, p. 150)

6. It is not what the Roman Catholic theologians say it is.

"It has been seen that the Roman Catholic doctrine of the church falls into two divisions, namely, the mystical body of Christ and the church on earth. These do not refer to two different churches, for the constituency of each one is the same; but they refer to two aspects of the church. Because of the identification of the mystical body with the visible church, their conclusion is that there is no salvation outside of the visible church. Although there are numerous books on the Protestant-Catholic dialogue and their ecumenical interests, it has been noted that any 'return' of Protestants to Rome must involve the recog-

nition of the Pope as the vicegerent of Christ." (*The Nature of the Church*, p. 368)

7. It is not what the liberal theologians say it is.

"Liberalism, being strongly influenced by the social gospel, saw little need for the local churches, which simply impeded the progress of the transformation of society by feverishly clinging to their ecclesiastical dogmas and traditions. The church was regarded as being extraneous to the Christian faith, and a strictly human, mundane organization." (*Ibid.*, p. 369)

8. It is not what the neo-liberal theologians say it is.

"Neo-liberalism, reacting against the worldly, human organization of the liberals, brought in a new sense of the importance of the church. They have come to believe that there is a church over and beyond the split denominations. It is a living society, begun in the work of Jesus and continuing that work through the ages. Thus, it is not simply a social organization; it is a divine institution, founded by God. This institution is often referred to by neo-liberals as the *koinonia*, the spiritual fellowship of all those who have committed themselves to the reign of God. One must not be deceived by the seeming orthodoxy, for in reality it is a subtle form of existentialism in which the church is simply a subjective state of being as regards the I-Thou encounter. Neo-liberalism denies that the organized church was in the plan of Christ." (*Ibid.*, p. 369)

9. It is not what the neo-orthodox theologians say it is.

"Neo-orthodoxy has some striking similarities to neo-liberalism as regards the doctrine of the church, especially concerning the fluid nature of it. The church is an 'event,' that is, 'The Church is not constituted once for all, but that it is continually being recreated by renewed divine activity.' There are striking differences, however. Not only does Barth give much greater place to the Holy Spirit as the Creator of the church, but, whereas neo-liberalism tends to think of the organized church as a necessary evil, Barth feels that it is *the church.* Finally, he believes that the one, holy, universal church exists in each of the local congregations." (*Ibid.*, p. 369)

10. It is not what the neo-evangelical theologians say it is.

"Neo-evangelicalism finds one of its most serious differences with fundamentalism in its doctrine of the church. Neo-evangelicalism tends to sacrifice the purity of the church for the peace and unity of the church. It is their opinion that heretics and unbelievers within the church do not affect the nature of the church. Thus, they are willing to sacrifice purity for unity and opportunity. The job of separating the wheat from the tares, they say, will be Christ's at the second advent. Little attention is given to the New Testament passages demanding definite discipline and purgation in the church. Because the neo-evangelicalist believes that rapprochement can be effected with liberalism and neo-orthodoxy, he is willing to subordinate doctrinal particularity." (*Ibid.*, p. 369)

B. The church considered from a positive viewpoint. We have briefly examined ten things that the church is *not*. Now the question: What *is* the church? Here three distinct positions may be distinguished.

1. The *ekklesia* of the New Testament refers only to those geographical groups of baptized believers who regularly assemble, led by pastors and deacons, for the purpose of worship, instruction, fellowship, and evangelism. This position, of course, would categorically deny the existence of a universal and invisible church. Thomas P. Simmons holds this view. He writes:

"Now the imaginary universal, invisible church never functions collectively. It holds no services, observes no ordinances, sends out and supports no missionaries. It is simply a colossal nonentity, without function, purpose, or reason for existence. It is the local church that functions for Christ. And it is the local church alone that can rightly be called the body of Christ." (*A Systematic Study of Bible Doctrine*, p. 353)

The extreme of this view is the bride-of-Christ position which says only a select group will compose the Savior's bride.

2. The *ekklesia* of the New Testament refers primarily (if not only) to that invisible body of Christ, composed of all believers, saved from the day of Pentecost to the rapture.

The extreme of this view is to downplay, if not actually deny the worth of local church assemblies, substituting instead swimming pool baptismal parties, coffeehouse evangelism, and ecumenical religious dialogues and buzz sessions.

3. The *ekklesia* of the New Testament embraces both the total body of Christ (including living and departed believers) and individual local assemblies, with the main emphasis being placed on the latter meaning. This position is held by most Bible students. The total body seems in view in 1 Corinthians 15:9; Galatians 1:13; Ephesians 5:25–32; Hebrews 12:23; Revelation 19:6–9, while the bulk of the remaining *ekklesia* references describe local church assemblies.

IV. The Purpose of the Church.

A. Its purpose considered from a negative viewpoint.

1. The purpose of the church is not to save the world.

The leaven of Matthew 13:33 is certainly not a picture of the gospel permeating and purifying society, thus turning it into the golden age of the millennium. To the contrary, world events will sour and become much worse before they get better (2 Tim. 3:1–7; 2 Pet. 3:1–5).

2. The purpose of the church is not to serve the world.

Nowhere in the New Testament is the church told to lobby for stronger pollution laws, or march for civil rights, or stage "pray-ins" for unpopular wars. This is not, of course, to say that individual believers cannot be involved in social action.

3. The purpose of the church is not to attempt to rule the world, as it did during Europe's Dark Ages.

4. The purpose of the church is not to fight the world.

All too often Bible believers fall victim to this error. Although there are those special occasions when local churches simply must stand up and thunder out against immorality and sin, the church's job is not to expend all its energies and resources fighting communism and alcoholism.

5. The purpose of the church is not to imitate the world.

It has been sadly observed that today the church is so worldly and (on occasion) the world so churchy that angels themselves could not separate the two.

6. The purpose of the church is not to isolate itself from the world.

This is the opposite error from that of imitation. About the time of Constantine there arose a new religious movement known as "monasticism." The philosophy of monasticism was that one could escape the perversions of the world by removing himself from the peoples of this world. But the job of the church is not to spend its life in silent contemplation.

B. Its purpose considered from a positive viewpoint. One of the great Bible teachers of this century was C.I. Scofield, author of the Scofield Reference Edition of the Bible. But many cannot agree with him concerning the purpose of the church. Scofield writes:

"Much is said concerning the 'mission of the church.' The 'church which is his body' has for its mission to build itself up until the body is complete (Eph. 4:11–16; Col. 2:19), but the visible church, as such, is charged with no mission. The commission to evangelize the world is personal, and not corporate. So far as the Scripture story goes, the work of evangelization was done by individuals called directly of the Spirit to that work. Churches and individuals helped the work of these men, but there is no trace of any corporate responsibility attaching to 'the church' as such." (*Bible Correspondence Course*, III, p. 431)

It is almost inconceivable to read these words from the pen of such a scriptural giant. Surely Paul would not have agreed with him. The driving force behind his evil actions prior to conversion was to destroy every single local church (Acts 8:3). The burning purpose after his salvation was to start local churches (Acts 14:23). The sole reason for his second missionary trip was to establish those churches (Acts 15:36, 41; 16:5). One of his heaviest burdens was for the welfare of those local churches (2 Cor. 11:28). Of his thirteen known New Testament epistles, nine are directly written to local churches, and three to pastors of local churches. In these epistles he gives detailed instruction concerning the worship services (1 Cor. 11:1-16), communion (1 Cor. 11:17-34), gifts (1 Cor. 12), and officer responsibilities (1 Tim. 3; Titus 1) for local churches.

In view of the above, it is difficult indeed to conclude that Paul looked upon the church as an institution without program, plan, or purpose. The facts are that Christ has literally loaded down his church with many and manifold responsibilities and tasks.

1. It is to love God.

   "Nevertheless I have somewhat against thee, because thou hast left thy first love" (Rev. 2:4).

2. It is to glorify God (Eph. 1:5, 6, 11, 12, 14; 3:21; 2 Thess. 1:12). How do we glorify God?

   a. Through our praise and prayer (Ps. 50:23; Jn. 14:13; Heb. 13:15).

   b. Through our fruitbearing (Jn. 15:8).

   c. Through our giving (Phil. 4:18; Heb. 13:16).

   d. Through our preaching and ministry (1 Pet. 4:11).

   e. Through our loving (Rom. 15:5, 6).

   f. Through our acknowledging of God's Son (Phil. 2:9-11).

   g. Through our believing of God's Word (Rom. 4:20).

   h. Through our suffering (Jn. 21:18, 19; 1 Pet. 4:14, 16).

   i. Through our witnessing (2 Thess. 3:1).

3. It is to display God's grace. (Eph. 2:7; 3:6, 10; 1 Pet. 2:9).

4. It is to evangelize the world (Mt. 28:19, 20; Mk. 16:15; Lk. 24:47; Jn. 20:21; Acts 1:8). Gordon G. Johnson writes:

   "One day Dr. Wilfred Grenfell, medical missionary to Labrador, was guest at dinner in London, together with a number of socially prominent British men and women. During the course of the dinner the lady seated next to him turned and said, 'Is it true, Dr. Grenfell, that you are a Missionary?' Dr. Grenfell looked at her for a moment before replying. Then he said, 'Is it true, madam, that you are not?' " (My Church, p. 88)

5. It is to baptize believers (Mt. 28:19).

6. It is to instruct believers (Mt. 28:19; Phil. 4:8, 9; 1 Tim. 4:6; 5:17; 2 Tim. 2:2, 24, 25).

7. It is to edify believers (1 Cor. 14:26; Eph. 4:11, 12, 16; 1 Thess. 5:11; 2 Pet. 3:18; Jude 20).

8. It is to discipline believers.

   There are three kinds of New Testament discipline.

   a. Self-discipline (1 Cor. 11:31; 2 Cor. 7:1; 1 Jn. 3:3).

   b. Sovereign discipline (Jn. 15:2; Acts 5:5, 10; 1 Cor. 11:32; Heb. 12:9, 10; 1 Pet. 4:17).

   c. Church discipline (Mt. 18:17; Rom. 16:17; 1 Cor. 5:1-13; Gal. 6:1; 2 Thess. 3:6, 14; Titus 3:10, 11; 2 Jn. 1:10).

   The nature of this judgment discipline will be discussed at a later point in our study.

9. It is to provide fellowship for believers (Acts 2:42; 1 Cor. 1:9; 2 Cor. 8:4; 13:14; Gal. 2:9; Phil. 1:5; 2:1; 1 Jn. 1:3, 6, 7).

   John MacArthur, Jr., writes:

   "The New Testament word for fellowship is koinonia. It means communion or fellowship—intimate communication. God designed men for fellowship. In Genesis 2:18, God says, 'It is not good that the man should be alone.' Man was not made to be isolated; being alone is not the will of God. People were made for fellowship. And the church, the body of Christ, is the epitome of fellowship—a body for fellowship! The church is a fellowship. The church was never intended to be only a building—a place where lonely people walk in, listen, and walk out still alone—but a place of fellowship.

   Bruce Larson says, 'The neighborhood bar is possibly the best counterfeit there is to the fellowship Christ wants to give His Church. It's an imitation dispensing liquor instead of grace, escape rather than reality. But it is a permissive, accepting, and inclusive fellowship. It is unshockable, it is democratic. You can tell people secrets and they usually don't tell others, or want to. The bar flourishes, not because most people are alcoholics, but because God has put into the human heart the desire to know and be known, to love, and be loved, and so many seek a counterfeit at the price of a few beers.'

   This need for fellowship is the genius of the church." (John MacArthur, Jr., The Church, The Body of Christ, p. 169)

   MacArthur goes on to discuss the basis, nature, dangers, and responsibilities involved within this blessed fellowship.

   a. The basis of Christian fellowship—the Person of Christ (1 Jn. 1:3).

   b. The nature of Christian fellowship—sharing (Acts 2:44-47; 4:32, 34, 35).

   c. The dangers of losing Christian fellowship—sin (1 Cor. 10:16, 21).

   d. The responsibilities of Christian fellowship:

(1) Confess our faults (Jas. 5:16).

(2) Rebuke sin in each other (Eph. 5:11; 1 Tim. 5:20).

(3) Forgive one another (2 Cor. 2:6, 8; Eph. 4:32; Col. 3:13).

(4) Bear one another's burdens (Gal. 6:2).

(5) Gently restore one another (Gal. 6:1).

(6) Prefer the weaker brother (Rom. 14:13; 15:1).

(7) Comfort and exhort each other (1 Thess. 4:18; 5:11).

(8) Pray one for another (Jas. 5:16).

(9) Edify one another (Rom. 14:19; Heb. 10:24).

(10) Admonish one another (Rom. 15:14; Col. 3:16).

10. It is to care for its own in time of need. (2 Cor. 8, 9; 1 Tim. 5:1–16; Jas. 1:27).

11. It is to provoke Israel to jealousy.

Robert L. Saucy writes:

"The extension of the blessings of salvation to those outside Israel during the age of the church when Israel is judicially blinded is designed by God to effect the final salvation of Israel and the fulfillment of her covenant promises. This in turn will bring the full Messianic blessing upon all nations (Rom. 11:11–15). The apostle explains this intent of God when he says of Israel, 'They did not stumble so as to fall, did they? May it never be! But by their transgression salvation has come to the Gentiles, to make them jealous' (v. 11, NASB: cf. 10:10). The apostle magnified his ministry as an apostle to the Gentiles according to his testimony that 'somehow I might move to jealousy my fellowcountrymen and save some of them' (11:13, 14, NASB).

Through the grafting in of the Gentiles into the root of the Abrahamic blessing which initially belonged to Israel, God purposes by the church to bring a jealousy upon Israel which will cause her to desire to return to the place of blessing through repentance and the acknowledgment of Christ as her true Messiah." (The Church in God's Program, p. 89)

12. It is to prepare rulers for the millennial kingdom (Rom. 8:17; 2 Tim. 2:12).

13. It is to act as a restraining and enlightening force in this present world (Mt. 5:13–16; 2 Thess. 2:6, 7; cf. Gen. 18:22, 23; 19:12–25).

14. It is to promote all that is good (Gal. 6:10). Henry Thiessen writes:

"While the believer is to separate from all worldly alliances (2 Cor. 6:14–18), he is yet to support all causes that seek to promote the social, economic, political, and educational welfare of the community. Paul says: 'So then, as we have op-portunity, let us work that which is good toward all men, and especially toward them that are of the household of the faith' (Gal. 6:10).

Here we note that we have a primary duty toward fellow-believers, but that we also have a duty toward the rest of the world. In this day of social service it is necessary to be clear as to the place of this ministry toward the world. Jesus' practice is the best example to follow. He always subordinated physical and other material help to the spiritual. He went about doing good and healing all that were oppressed of the devil, though His principal mission was never lost sight of (Acts 10:38–43). We should devote ourselves to social service on the same principle on which a man picks up sharp nails that he finds in the street on the way to his work. It is one thing for him to devote his entire time to ridding the streets of nails, and another to remove such nails as he can without interfering with his main task. That is, the work of reformation must be definitely subordinated to the work of evangelization. So also in the case of philanthropy. The Christian should make all his benevolences bear testimony to Christ. Jesus may have fed the five thousand as a humanitarian act; but He certainly did it primarily as a testimony to His own power and deity. Clearly, He went to dinners and suppers in order to testify to the truth. It appears that He healed the man born blind in order to win his soul (Jn. 9:35–38). In other words, the Christian must make all his good works testify to Christ." (Lectures in Systematic Theology, p. 436)

In summary, it may be said that the job of a local church is to make as many people as much like Jesus in the shortest time possible. God the Father is so much in love with his beloved Son that he desires to populate the entire universe throughout eternity with those individuals which resemble Jesus Christ (1 Jn. 3:2). But he desires to start the work in repenting sinners down here right now.

V. The Founding of the Church. Of all recorded statements our Lord made while upon this earth, perhaps no two have been more misunderstood, misinterpreted, and maligned than the ones in Matthew 16:18, 19:

"And I say also unto thee, That thou art Peter, and upon this rock I will build my church; and the gates of hell shall not prevail against it. And I will give unto thee the keys of the kingdom of heaven: and whatsoever thou shalt bind on earth shall be bound in heaven: and whatsoever thou shalt loose on earth shall be loosed in heaven."

Does this really teach that Jesus actually predicted his church would be built upon a man, and that that man was Simon Peter?

Henry C. Thiessen writes in detail concerning these verses and the claims of the Roman Catholic church.

"In the first place, note that we have here the word *petra* not *petros*. The former Greek word occurs sixteen times in the New Testament: eleven times it means a ledge of rock, and five times it is used metaphorically and refers to Christ (Mt. 16:18; Rom. 9:33; 1 Cor. 10:4 *bis*; 1 Pet. 2:8). Could Matthew 16:18 be an exception? In 1 Corinthians 10:4 the 'rock' (*petra*) is said to be Christ. Note that Peter himself used that term of Christ (1 Pet. 2:8, comp. vs. 4–8). In the second place, Jesus' parable of the two builders and the two foundations teaches the same thing. The house that was built upon the 'rock' (*ten petran*) stood the test of the rains, the floods, and the winds (Mt. 7:24–27). Surely the reference is to Himself. To the same effect, also, is Paul's teaching that Christ is the foundation of the building of God (1 Cor. 3:11) and the chief corner stone (Eph. 2:20–22). *Petra* is a ledge, whereas *petros* is a single rock. He says the distinction is nowhere confounded in literature. To the claim that Jesus spoke Aramaic and that we cannot tell whether the distinction of terms was made in the Aramaic, he replied that we have too little Aramaic from that time to prove or disprove the point. Besides, it is not certain that Jesus said this in Aramaic." (W. Hersey Davis, *Unpublished Seminar Notes*)

"To the objection that this view makes Jesus speak of Himself in the third person in Matthew 16:18 (*kai epi taute te petra*) we reply that He clearly does this in John 2:19, where He speaks of Himself as a temple. Those who heard Him say this, either did not understand His meaning or did not want to understand it, for they misquoted Him before Caiaphas (Mt. 26:61). Nor does the granting of the 'keys' to Peter present any difficulty. We must observe that Christ gave him the 'keys of the kingdom of heaven,' not of the Church (Mt. 16:19). If our interpretation of this term is correct, then Christ merely gave him the 'keys' to Christendom. Peter did open the door to the Jews and proselytes on the day of Pentecost (Acts 2), and to the Gentiles in the house of Cornelius later on (Acts 10). These two times in which Peter took the initiative would seem to fulfill the conditions of this promise. As for the authority to bind and loose (Mt. 16:19), it should be noted that Jesus later gave the same authority to declare people saved and forgiven on the basis of the fulfilled conditions to these blessings, that is, whenever an individual has fulfilled them." (*Ibid.*, pages 412, 413)

VI. The History, Growth, and Character of the Various New Testament Churches. In 1 Corinthians 10:11 Paul writes:

"Now all these things happened unto them for ensamples: and they are written for our admonition, upon whom the ends of the world are come."

Here, he refers to those Old Testament events. But we may with scriptural justification apply these same words to the events recorded for us in the New Testament. Present-day church leaders will profit greatly by examining the joys, sorrows, sins, and strong points of these early local churches. The following is a brief summary of twenty-three such New Testament churches.

A. The church in Jerusalem:
  1. Began at Pentecost (Acts 2:47) with at least 3120 (Acts 2:41).
  2. Was pastored by James, the half-brother of Christ (Acts 15:13).
  3. Performed many wonders and signs (Acts 2:43; 5:12–16).
  4. Had all things in common (Acts 2:44, 45; 4:32–35).
  5. Was in one accord (Acts 2:46).
  6. Spent a good deal of time in prayer (Acts 2:42; 3:1; 4:24; 12:5–17).
  7. Witnessed at every opportunity (Acts 3:12; 4:5; 5:42; 4:33).
  8. Radiated Jesus (Acts 4:13; 6:15).
  9. Was kept pure by God (had standards) (Acts 5:1–11; 8:18–24).
  10. Grew constantly (Acts 2:47; 5:14; 4:4; 12:24).
  11. Endured persecution (Acts 4:1–3; 4:21; 5:17–41; 7:54–60; 8:1–3; 12:1–4).
  12. Appointed deacons (Acts 6:1–7).
  13. Practiced baptism and the Lord's Supper (Acts 2:41, 46).
  14. Sent forth missionaries (Acts 8:5, 14; 11:22; 13:1–3; 15:22).
  15. Held the important meeting on circumcision (Acts 15).
  16. Was Spirit-led (Acts 2:1–18; 4:31; 13:2–4; 15:28).
  17. Preached the word (Acts 2:16–36; 3:13–26; 5:42; 6:4; 7:1–53).
  18. Contended for the faith (Acts 15:1–21).
  19. Apparently later compromised with the Judaizers (Acts 21:18–25).

B. The church in Antioch of Syria:
  1. Was founded during that persecution period which followed the martyrdom of Stephen (Acts 11:19).
  2. Experienced a great ingathering of souls (Acts 11:21).
  3. The Jerusalem church sent Barnabas to "check it out" (Acts 11:22).
  4. He became the first pastor (Acts 11:23).
  5. Added many to the church at this time (Acts 11:24).
  6. Barnabas then called Saul as associate pastor (Acts 11:25).
  7. Here both would work for a year (Acts 11:26).
  8. Was where believers were first called Christians (Acts 11:26).
  9. Took up a large love offering for the needy believers in Jerusalem (Acts 11:30).
  10. Was the home church of the first two Christian missionaries (Paul and Barnabas) (Acts 13:1–3; 14:26).
  11. Later became their headquarters, both after their first missionary trip (Acts 14:26) and following the Jerusalem Council (Acts 15:35).

12. Silas was from this church (Acts 15:34).
13. Was where Paul set Peter straight on matters of legalism (Gal. 2:11).

C. The church in Antioch of Pisidia:
1. Was begun by Paul during his first missionary trip (Acts 13:14).
2. Was where he preached his first recorded sermon (Acts 13:16).
3. Was formed from the converts coming out of this meeting (Acts 13:43).
4. Paul turned from the Jews (Acts 13:46).
5. Paul relates his heavenly calling as a light to the Gentiles (Acts 13:47).

D. The church in Lystra:
1. Was organized during Paul's first missionary trip (Acts 14:6).
2. Was where he healed the impotent man (Acts 14:10).
3. This led to his being almost worshiped (Acts 14:11).
4. Paul was stoned (Acts 14:19; 2 Tim. 3:11).
5. Was where Paul picked up Timothy during his second missionary trip (Acts 16:1-3).

E. The church in Derbe (Acts 14:21, 22).

F. The church in Iconium:
1. Paul led many to Christ here during his first trip (Acts 14:2).
2. He also worked great signs and wonders (Acts 14:3).
3. He was driven out by the unbelieving Jews (Acts 14:5).

G. The church in Philippi:
1. Paul organized a church in the home of a woman convert named Lydia (Acts 16:15, 40).
2. A demon-possessed girl was his next convert (Acts 16:18).
3. She was followed by the Philippian jailor (Acts 16:33).
4. Paul later wrote a letter to this church (Phil. 1:1).
5. Timothy ministered to this church (Phil. 2:19).
6. Had sent Epaphroditus to minister to Paul while the apostle was in prison (Phil. 2:25).
7. Was in danger of legalism (Phil. 3:1-3).
8. Paul writes and asks "true yokefellow" to help two quarreling church women named Euodias and Syntyche (Phil. 4:1-3).
9. Helped to supply the material needs of Paul (Phil. 4:15, 18).

H. The church in Thessalonica:
1. Was founded during Paul's second missionary trip (Acts 17:1).
2. Witnessed a great harvest of souls (Acts 17:4).
3. Paul is accused of turning the world upside down (Acts 17:6).
4. In spite of their zeal, they were not good Bible students (Acts 17:3).
5. Later Paul wrote two letters to this church (1 Thess. 1:1; 2 Thess. 1:1).
6. The believers had a reputation for witnessing (1 Thess. 1:8).
7. They were persecuted by the unbelieving Jews because of their faith (1 Thess. 2:14).

8. Timothy ministered to this church (1 Thess. 3:1, 2).
9. Had some lazy members (2 Thess. 3:10).
10. Had some busybodies (2 Thess. 3:11).
11. Had some disobedient members (2 Thess. 3:14, 15).

I. The church in Berea:
This church was commended for its knowledge of and love for the Word of God (Acts 17:11).

J. The church in Athens:
It is not certain whether a local assembly came into being after Paul's sermon on Mars Hill, but if so, a convert named Dionysius probably led it (Acts 17:34).

K. The church in Corinth:
1. Was founded during Paul's second trip (Acts 18:1).
2. Aquila and Priscilla aided in this (Acts 18:2).
3. The chief ruler of the Jewish synagogue, a man named Crispus, was one of Paul's first converts (Acts 18:8).
4. His successor, Sosthenes, was also later evidently saved (compare Acts 18:17 with 1 Cor. 1:1).
5. Paul stayed eighteen months (Acts 18:11).
6. Paul wrote several letters to this church (1 Cor. 5:9; 2 Cor. 10:9, 10), two of which are included in the New Testament canon (1 Cor. 1:2; 2 Cor. 1:1).
7. Experienced almost total confusion in matters relating to:
   a. Baptism (1 Cor. 1:12-17).
   b. Earthly wisdom (1 Cor. 1:26).
   c. Carnality and strife (1 Cor. 3:1-3).
   d. Judging others unfairly (1 Cor. 4:7).
   e. Immorality (1 Cor. 5:1).
   f. Taking other believers to court (1 Cor. 6:1-4).
   g. Marriage (1 Cor. 7:1).
   h. Christian liberty (1 Cor. 8-9).
   i. The Lord's Table (1 Cor. 11:17-34).
   j. Spiritual gifts (1 Cor. 12-14).
   k. The doctrine of the resurrection (1 Cor. 15).
   l. Tithing (1 Cor. 16).
8. Was later pastored by Apollos (1 Cor. 3:6).

L. The church in Ephesus:
1. Was founded during Paul's second trip (Acts 18:19).
2. May have been pastored by Apollos, Timothy, and the Apostle John.
3. Paul wrought many miracles there and saw much fruit (Acts 19:11-41).
   a. Wicked books are burned.
   b. The false goddess Diana is challenged.
4. Paul went soul-winning door-to-door (Acts 20:17-21).
5. Was the only Christian church ever to receive letters from two New Testament writers. Paul wrote Ephesians to them (Eph. 1:1), and John the apostle would later direct a portion of Revelation to them (Rev. 2:1-7). According to John's letter, this church:

a. Worked hard and possessed patience.

b. Had high church standards.

c. Suffered for Christ.

d. Had left their first love.

e. Needed to remember, repent, and return to Christ, else their candlestick be removed.

f. Hated the deeds of the licentious Nicolaitans.

M. The church in Troas:

Here Paul raised up Eutychus, a believer who had gone asleep during Paul's sermon and had fallen down from the third loft of the building (Acts 20:7-12).

N. The church in Rome:

1. The origin and founder of this church is unknown.

2. Priscilla and Aquila labored there and a local church met in their home (Rom. 16:3-5).

3. Had a ringing testimony throughout all the land (Rom. 1:8).

4. Paul mentions more personal friends here than in any other New Testament book he wrote. The names of some twenty-six individuals may be counted in Romans 16.

O. The church in Galatia:

1. Various local churches in Galatia were organized by Paul during his first trip.

2. Had all apparently fallen victim to the legalistic Judaizers, who would continually plague Paul's gospel of grace (Gal. 1:6-9).

3. The New Testament epistle Galatians was written to these churches (Gal. 3:1).

P. The church in Colosse:

1. Was founded by Epaphras during Paul's third trip (Col. 2:1; 1:7, 12, 13).

2. Philemon and Onesimus attended this church (Col. 4:9; Philemon 1:1, 2).

3. Paul commanded the Colossian epistle to be read to the Laodicean church and the one he wrote them to be read to the Colossian church (Col. 4:16).

Q. The church in Babylon (1 Pet. 5:13):

1. Was filled with suffering believers (1 Pet. 1:6).

2. Some of this suffering was due to sin (1 Pet. 4:15-17).

R. The church in Smyrna (Rev. 2:8-11):

1. Had suffered much for Christ.

2. Had been slandered by those from the synagogue of Satan.

3. Satan had imprisoned some of them.

S. The church in Pergamos (Rev. 2:12-17):

1. Was located in the very center of satanic worship.

2. Had nevertheless remained loyal to Christ in spite of martyrdom.

3. Members were, however, tolerating some in the church who were guilty of sexual sins.

4. They were also tolerating those who held the doctrine of the Nicolaitans.

T. The church in Thyatira (Rev. 2:18-29):

1. Had performed many good deeds.

2. But they permitted a false prophetess named Jezebel to teach that sexual sin was not a serious matter.

U. The church in Sardis (Rev. 3:1-6).

1. Had a reputation, but was dead.

2. Was to strengthen what little good remained.

V. The church in Philadelphia (Rev. 3:7-13):

1. Was not strong, even though it had obeyed God's Word.

2. This they had done during persecution.

W. The church in Laodicea (Rev. 3:14-20):

1. Was the worst church mentioned in the New Testament.

2. Believers were neither hot nor cold.

3. Bragged about their wealth, claiming they had need of nothing, but in reality were wretched, miserable, poor, blind, and naked.

4. God admonished them to totally repent and allow him to reenter and once again fellowship with them.

Clarence Benson offers the following appraisal of the growth, character, and organization of the early church.

"There were daily additions to the number of believers, and only a short time after the day of Pentecost the number reached five thousand. At the end of the first century, Pliny told the Emperor Trojan that 'so many believe in Christ that the temples of pagan worship are deserted.' At the end of the third century there were no less than five million adherents, for 'the Church lifted empires off their hinges and turned the stream of the centuries out of its channel.' By the tenth century there were fifty million members, and despite the long night of popery and the chill of formalism which followed, at the opening of the nineteenth century professing Christendom numbered two hundred million.

The classic history of ancient Rome is given by Gibbon in *Decline and Fall of the Roman Empire*, written in the eighteenth century by a scholar who was distinctly antagonistic to Christianity. But even Gibbon named four distinct reasons why Christianity grew so rapidly in the ancient world:

A. The inflexible zeal and enthusiasm of the Christians.

They took the teachings of Jesus at their face value. They refused to compromise with any pagan religion or secular code. As a later historian comments, 'They were absolutely happy, always getting into trouble.'

B. The Christian doctrine of the future life. Even among the most brilliant of the Greek and Roman writers, ignorance, hesitancy, and professed insincerity about immorality are found.

C. The miraculous power ascribed to the early Church.

'With great power gave the apostles witness' (Acts 4:33). Marvelous miracles were wrought by the disciples to demonstrate the truth of their assertion. Some of these are recorded in the New Testament, but there were many more.

D. The pure, austere morals of the Christians.
They would not compromise with pagan immoralities. They abandoned sins when they became Christians, lived exemplary lives and exhibited a standard of virtue unknown to the ancient world. The virtuous way of life was beyond the understanding of men. They had been used to 'mystery' religions imported from the Orient, and were dependent upon secret rites for their appeal. But the ancient Christians exhibited what the apostle calls, 'the mystery of godliness.' The first Christian aim in those days was to be Christlike in life.

The character of the local church is the sum-total of the character of its members. Today there is a vast difference in the character of the various members of the average church—in every local assembly there may be 'tares' and 'wheat' growing together, that is, both saved and unsaved members. The apostolic Church was perhaps the nearest approach to the true Church. The early Christians were:

1. United (Acts 2:44; 4:32; Eph. 4:1-7).
'All that believed were together, and had all things common.' The apostolic organization was more than a Christian church. It was a Christian family. Bound by ties more solemn and sacred than ties of blood, they lived each day in mutual help and apart from the world. Its members were entirely agreed on all the weightier matters of the church, for they were all taught by the same Spirit. They were of one mind concerning God, Christ, the Holy Spirit, the depravity of sin, the necessity of holiness, the inspiration of the Scriptures, and the importance of prayer. The mighty operations of the Spirit of God were evidenced as the result of their unity.

2. Steadfast (Acts 2:42; Eph. 4:14-16).
a. Steadfast in doctrine.
No turning aside from facts to fables, no heaping up teachers with itching ears, no wavering like the waves of the sea, tossing about from doubt in despair! They were steadfast in their belief in God's Word.
b. Steadfast in fellowship.
If the members had stopped to criticize, no doubt they would have found faults in their church, but they felt that the society of Jerusalem composed the true Church, so they remained steadfast. They were quick to see their own failures, but slow to criticize others' faults.
c. Steadfast in the ordinances.
Christ was the substance of sermons and the center of worship. The institution of the Lord's Supper and of Baptism represented the work of grace in the hearts of the early believers (Rom. 6:3, 4; 1 Cor. 11:23-26).

d. Steadfast in prayer.
They prayed 'in one accord' and received such a wonderful answer that they continued steadfast in prayer. The true Church is composed of praying Christians (Acts 1:3, 4, 12-14).

3. Charitable (Acts 2:45; 4:34, 35; Eph. 4:28-32).
They 'sold their possessions and goods, and parted them to all men, as every man had need.' The members gave spontaneously. Their love for perishing souls was so great that they sold out their businesses and disposed of their lands, laying the money at the disciples' feet. They gladly gave up the care of their possessions for the care of priceless, immortal souls. The people who engaged in this sharing responded as the result of spontaneous expression of Christian affection and faith, not by legislated direction or force. Their charity was a wonderful testimony of the love of Christ in their lives. Those who looked on the scene could well comment, 'See how those Christians love.'

4. Joyful (Acts 2:46, 47; Eph. 5:18-21).
They continued daily with one accord in the temple with gladness and singleness of heart. It was this singleness of heart that made them happy. They were not divided between Christ and the world, but being wholly the Lord's, they rejoiced in the Lord. Their communion with Christ was not clouded with the things of time and sense. All things were to them full of God, and since they rejoiced in God, they were full of His joy.

5. Successful (Acts 2:41, 47; 5:14; 6:7; 13:44; 16:5; 18:8).
Never was a church so richly blessed as the apostolic organization. It grew by leaps and bounds. For the first two centuries the Church ran along the ground like wild-fire, and out of nothing assumed such vast proportions that the whole world was 'turned upside down.'
a. They had favor with God.
The early members were added to the Lord (Acts 5:14) and by the Lord (2:47b). These members were real additions. Frequently today only the names of members are added to churches. These names increase the numbers, but they do not augment the churches' strength. These members adulterate the churches, weaken and defile them, and bring upon them much grief and dishonor. It is quite evident that the devil adds continually to churches such as are not saved. When the Lord adds to the church it is quite a different matter. These members are united, steadfast, charitable, joyful; it is their

presence that makes the churches successful.

b. They had favor with men.

It is a most remarkable thing that in spite of opposition and persecution from rulers and governments, the early Church was exceedingly popular—far more than the average church today. The sincerity and joy of these first Christians could not fail to impress the men of the world who were looking for life and happiness. These men believed in the reality of what they saw, and when they realized that the members of the church were united, steadfast, charitable, joyful, and downright earnest, they were greatly moved."

VII. The Symbols of the Church. There are six main symbols depicting Christ and his Church in the New Testament. These are:

A. The Head and body.

"For as we have many members in one body, and all members have not the same office: so we, being many, are one body in Christ, and every one members one of another" (Rom. 12:4, 5).

"Know ye not that your bodies are the members of Christ?" (1 Cor. 6:15).

"For as the body is one, and hath many members, and all the members of that one body, being many, are one body: so also is Christ. For by one Spirit are we all baptized into one body" (1 Cor. 12:12, 13).

"Now ye are the body of Christ, and members in particular" (1 Cor. 12:27).

"There is one body, and one Spirit" (Eph. 4:4).

"For we are members of his body, of his flesh, and of his bone" (Eph. 5:30).

"And he is the head of the body, the church" (Col. 1:18; see also 1 Cor. 10:16, 17; Eph. 1:23; 2:16; 4:12, 16; 5:23; Col. 3:15).

In light of these verses, the church, his body, is to:

1. Be in subjection *to* the Head.
2. Experience unity *with* the Head.
3. Work in glad service *for* the Head.
4. Take direction *from* the Head.

B. The Bridegroom and the bride.

"For I am jealous over you with godly jealousy: for I have espoused you to one husband, that I may present you as a chaste virgin to Christ" (2 Cor. 11:2).

"Husbands, love your wives, even as Christ also loved the church and gave himself for it; that he might sanctify and cleanse it with the washing of water by the word, that he might present it to himself a glorious church, not having spot, or wrinkle, or any such thing; but that it should be holy and without blemish. So ought men to love their wives as their own bodies. He that loveth his wife loveth himself. For no man ever yet hated his own flesh; but nourisheth and cherisheth it, even as the Lord the church:

For we are members of his body, of his flesh, and of his bones. For this cause shall a man leave his father and mother, and shall be joined unto his wife, and they two shall be one flesh. This is a great mystery; but I speak concerning Christ and the church" (Eph. 5:25-32).

"Come hither, I will show thee the bride, the Lamb's wife" (Rev. 21:9; see also Eph. 5:2; 3:14-21).

From these verses we learn that Christ's love for his Church is:

1. Unconditional.
2. Unbounded.
3. Unknowable.
4. Unmerited and undeserved.
5. Unequaled and unparalleled.

C. The Vine and the branches.

"I am the true vine, and my Father is the husbandman. Every branch in me that beareth not fruit he taketh away; and every branch that beareth fruit, he purgeth it, that it may bring forth more fruit. Now ye are clean through the word which I have spoken unto you. Abide in me, and I in you. As the branch cannot bear fruit of itself, except it abide in the vine; no more can ye, except ye abide in me. I am the vine, ye are the branches: He that abideth in me, and I in him, the same bringeth forth much fruit: for without me ye can do nothing" (Jn. 15:1-5).

This beautiful passage relates the responsibilities of the branch.

1. It is to abide in the vine.
2. It is to bear (not produce) fruit from and for the vine.
3. It is only to bear fruit. A branch is useless for anything else. Its wood cannot be used for furniture, firewood, or building purposes.
4. It is to bear much fruit. This is in stark contrast to Israel, God's fruitless Old Testament vine (Jdg. 9:7-15; Ps. 80:8; Isa. 5:1-7; Ezek. 15:2; Hosea 10:1).
5. It is to be submitted to pruning.

D. The Shepherd and the sheep.

"I am the good shepherd; the good shepherd giveth his life for the sheep" (Jn. 10:11).

"Now the God of peace, that brought again from the dead our Lord Jesus, that great shepherd of the sheep, through the blood of the everlasting covenant" (Heb. 13:20).

"And when the chief Shepherd shall appear, ye shall receive a crown of glory that fadeth not away" (1 Pet. 5:4).

Thus, to his Church, Christ is the Good Shepherd (because of what he has accomplished in the past, namely justification—see Ps. 22), the Great Shepherd (because of what he accomplishes in the present, namely, sanctification—see Ps. 23), and the Chief Shepherd (because of what he shall accomplish in the future, namely, glorification—see Ps. 24).

E. The High Priest and a kingdom of priests.

"But ye are a chosen generation, a royal priesthood, an holy nation, a peculiar people; that ye should show forth the praises of him who hath called you out of darkness into his marvelous light" (1 Pet. 2:9).

"And hath made us kings and priests unto God and his father" (Rev. 1:6).

"And hast made us unto our God kings and priests: and we shall reign on the earth" (Rev. 5:10).

"But they shall be priests of God and of Christ, and shall reign with him a thousand years" (Rev. 20:6).

The Old Testament priest was to offer up an animal sacrifice. The New Testament priest is to offer up sacrifices also, but of a different kind. He is to offer up:

1. The sacrifice of his body as a living offering (Rom. 12:1).
2. The sacrifice of praise (1 Pet. 2:5, 9; Heb. 13:15).
3. The sacrifice of doing good (Heb. 13:16).
4. The sacrifice of substance (Heb. 13:16).

F. The Cornerstone and the living stones.

"Now therefore ye are no more strangers and foreigners, but fellow-citizens with the saints, and of the household of God; and are built upon the foundation of the apostles and prophets, Jesus Christ himself being the chief corner stone; in whom all the building fitly framed together groweth unto an holy temple in the Lord: In whom ye also are builded together for an habitation of God through the Spirit" (Eph. 2:19-22).

"To whom coming, as unto a living stone, disallowed indeed of men, but chosen of God, and precious, ye also, as lively stones, are built up a spiritual house, an holy priesthood, to offer up spiritual sacrifices, acceptable to God by Jesus Christ" (1 Pet. 2:4, 5).

Note: There are two Greek words translated by the one English word "temple."

1. *Naos,* referring to the holy place and the Holy of Holies.
2. *Hieron,* having in mind the entire temple structure, outer courts, porches, porticoes, etc.

The Temple mentioned in Ephesians 2:21 is *naos.* While upon earth Christ never entered the *naos* area, which was restricted to the Levitical priests alone. He drove the moneychangers from the *hieron* temple, not the *naos* temple. But now, his church has actually *become* that which he could not *enter* during his earthly ministry.

Dr. Earl Radmacher writes the following concerning the role of Christ as cornerstone.

"In Christ, Jew and Gentile have been united in one as the cornerstone by which the two partitions of the building are united. In Christ the building has coherence and stability in its structure. In Christ, the rest of the building finds its inner harmony, oneness, correspondence, and design." (*The Nature of the Church,* p. 262)

VIII. The Old Testament Foreshadows of the Church. The institution of the church, of course, was not revealed in the Old Testament. Paul makes this clear in Ephesians 3:1-12. However, there are two special brides mentioned in the Old Testament whose lives beautifully lend themselves as a remarkable foreshadow of the coming New Testament church. These two women are Eve and Rebekah.

A. The bride Eve.
   1. Eve proceeded from Adam's side as the church came from Christ's side (Gen. 2:21, 22; cf. Jn. 19:34).
   2. Eve thus became espoused to the first head of creation while the church would be joined to the final Head of creation (Gen. 1:28; cf. Rev. 11:15).
   3. Eve became bone of his bone and flesh of his flesh, while the church did the same with Christ (Gen. 2:23; cf. Eph. 5:30).

B. The bride Rebekah. Genesis 24 is the greatest single typical chapter in the entire Old Testament. The four key individuals involved in this chapter are Abraham, Isaac, the servant, and Rebekah.
   1. Abraham sends his trusted servant to a distant land to fetch a bride for Isaac his son. He becomes a type of the Father who has done the same for his Son (Gen. 24:4; Mt. 22:2, 3).
   2. Isaac, having been previously offered up on Mt. Moriah, is content to await the arrival of his bride. He becomes a type of the Son who now awaits the arrival of his bride in heaven (Gen. 24:63; Heb. 10:12-14).
   3. The servant arrives in that distant land for the sole purpose of taking a bride. He becomes a foreshadow of the Holy Spirit.
      a. He was sent by the Father (Jn. 14:16).
      b. He came at Pentecost to take a bride (1 Cor. 12:13).
      c. He elevates Christ as the servant did Isaac (Gen. 24:36; Jn. 16:13, 14).
   4. Rebekah, upon hearing about Isaac, agrees to go with the servant. She becomes a foreshadow of the church.
      a. Like the church and Christ, she loved her bridegroom even before seeing him (1 Pet. 1:8).
      b. Like the church and Christ, she received an earnest from the riches of Isaac (Gen. 24:53; 2 Cor. 1:22; Eph. 1:14).
      c. Like the church and Christ, she begins her long pilgrimage to meet her bridegroom (Gen. 24:59; 1 Pet. 2:11).
      d. Like the church and Christ, she is prayed for by her bridegroom (Gen. 24:63; Rom. 8:34).
      e. Like the church and Christ, she is received into the home of her father-in-law (Gen. 24:67; Jn. 14:2).

IX. The Organization of the Church. Henry Thiessen writes:

"There have been individuals and groups of believers who have taught that the Scriptures give no warrant for our present-day organized churches. It is held that believers should get together, observe the Lord's Supper, study God's Word, and cooperate in Christian service without anything resembling a formal organization. But that this is an extreme view of the matter is clear. There are indications that very early in Jerusalem the Church must have had at least a loose kind of organization, and there is conclusive evidence that soon thereafter local churches were definitely organized.

That there must have been a simple organization even in the Church in Jerusalem is evident from a number of things. The believers adhered to a definite doctrinal standard (Acts 2:42; cf. Eph. 20); they met for spiritual fellowship (ibia); they united in prayer (Acts 2:42; Mt. 18:19, 20); they practiced baptism (Acts 2:41) and observed the Lord's Supper (Acts 2:42, 46); they kept account of the membership (Acts 2:14, 41; 4:4); they met for public worship (Acts 2:46); and they provided material help for the needy of their number (Acts 2:44, 45). The Apostles were the ministers in this Church, but they soon added the seven men of Acts 6:1-7 to take care of the ministration to the poor. On the day of Pentecost they were assembled in 'the upper room' (Acts 1:13; 2:1), wherever that may have been; but more usually they seem to have met in some home of a Christian (Acts 2:46), though for some services apparently they still visited the temple (Acts 2:46; 3:1), as we have just seen. All these factors indicate the beginnings of organization in the Jerusalem Church.

A. They had church officers. There are, besides the example of this first Church, many other indications that the Scriptures teach the propriety and necessity of organizing local groups of believers into churches. Paul, when retracing his steps from Derbe on his first journey, 'appointed for them elders in every church' (Acts 14:23). The original indicates that this was done by a show of hands and not by apostolic authority. He definitely asks Titus to 'appoint elders' (Titus 1:5). We have already seen that the Jerusalem Church appointed stewards to look after the need of the poor (Acts 6:1-7). There must have been a way of ascertaining the sentiment of the people, and a regulation that stated who was entitled to vote on the question (Acts 6:2-6). In the Church at Ephesus there were 'elders' (Acts 20:17), in the Church at Antioch, 'prophets and teachers' (Acts 13:1), and in the Church at Philippi, 'bishops and deacons' (Phil. 1:1).

B. They had stated times of meeting. We are informed that the disciples met on the 'first day of the week,' immediately following Christ's resurrection (Jn. 20:19, 26). In his first letter to the Corinthians Paul instructs the readers to lay by them in store as the Lord has prospered them on the first day of the week (1 Cor. 16:2). That is, on that day the collection was to be taken. On Paul's last journey to Jerusalem he stops at Troas and meets with the disciples there on the first day of the week (Acts 20:7). And in the Revelation John tells us that he was in the Spirit on the 'Lord's Day' (1:10). We have already referred to Canright's work, in which he proves that Sunday observance originated with the apostles. There must have been an action taken with regard to the day to be observed and business transactions presuppose an organization.

C. They regulated church decorum (1 Cor. 14:34) and exercised church discipline. Jesus had given instructions that in the case of a believer who refused to bow to private admonition, the dispute was to be referred to the church for discipline (Mt. 18:17). Paul requests the Corinthians most definitely to exercise church discipline (1 Cor. 5:13). He gives similar instructions to the Church at Rome (Rom. 16:17). In 3 John 10 we are told that Diotrephes acted high-handedly in church discipline. Here again organization is presupposed; for it is necessary to draw the line in such matters.

D. They raised money for the Lord's Work. Writing to the Corinthian Church from Ephesus, Paul says that he has already given orders to the churches of Galatia, and then gives them instructions to contribute to the collection for the saints (1 Cor. 16:1, 2). They are to give systematically (on the first day of the week), proportionately (as each may prosper), and purposefully (for the saints). In his Second Epistle to the Corinthians he urges them to give liberally (2 Cor. 8:7-9; 9:6) and cheerfully (2 Cor. 9:7). He commends the Macedonian churches for their great liberality in this connection (2 Cor. 8:1-5) and urges the Corinthian Church to follow their example (2 Cor. 8:6—9:5). In his Epistle to the Romans he tells of the offering which he is taking to Jerusalem (Rom. 15:25-28). Before Felix, Paul refers to this offering which he had brought to his nation (Acts 24:17). It is clear that he thinks of this contribution as coming from the 'churches of Galatia' and the 'churches of Macedonia.' The same thing is implied when Paul says that the Corinthians began a year ago (2 Cor. 8:10; 9:2). They did this as individuals composing the Church; and yet he addresses them as a group. Organized effort seems to be implied in his exhortation to carry out their earlier intention (2 Cor. 8:11; 9:3-5).

E. They sent letters of commendation to the other churches. This was done when Apollos left Ephesus and went to Corinth (Acts 18:24-28). It is also implied in Paul's sarcastic question, whether he will have to bring letters of commendation when he returns to Corinth (2 Cor. 3:1). Romans 16:1, 2 is probably a sample of such a letter with regard to Phoebe. Insofar as this practice grew, it must have become necessary to ascertain the mind of the church as to who was worthy of such a letter. Organization is to be presupposed in such a procedure. The Council at Jerusalem rendered a decision with reference to the conditions on which Gentiles might be admitted into fellowship (Acts 15:22-29). This, too, presupposes an organization of some sort or other." (*Lectures in Systematic Theology*, pp. 415-417)

X. The Government of the Church. Within the confines of organized Christianity today three separate church systems of government exist. These are:

A. The monarchial, hierarchial form. This is also known as the Episcopal system, taken from the Greek word *episkopos*, translated in the New Testament by the two English words "overseer" (Acts 20:28) and "bishop" (Phil 1:2; 1 Tim. 3:2; Titus 1:7; 1 Pet. 2:25).

The Roman Catholic, Episcopal, Methodist, and Greek Catholic churches have all adopted (with various modifications) this basic form of church government. It is a government by bishops, aided by priests and deacons. The essential concept is that the right to consecrate other bishops and ordain both priests and deacons belongs only to the bishops themselves. This provides a succession of bishops and their rulership over the two subordinate ministries.

This system of government arose during the second century A.D. and is not to be found in the New Testament.

B. The federal, representative form. This is also known as the Presbyterian system, taken from the Greek word *presbuteros*. This word, found sixty-two times (in its noun form) is always translated by the English word "elder." Its system of government is best illustrated by the Presbyterian and Reformed churches of today.

The federal system operates somewhat similarly to that of the U.S. government. Each local church duly elects ruling elders to represent them. This group forms the church session. A distinction is usually made in this session between those ruling elders who govern but do not teach, preach, or administer the ordinances, and those elders (the chief being the pastor) who do (1 Tim. 5:17).

The next high-ranking body in this system is the presbytery, which includes all ordained ministers or teaching elders and one ruling elder from each local congregation in a given district. Although pastors are elected by their own congregations, they must be approved by the presbytery.

Above the presbytery is the synod (from a Greek word meaning "company"), and over the synod is the general assembly, the Supreme Court of its kind. Charles Ryrie writes the following:

"Arguments in support of the federal type include the fact that elders were appointed by the apostles (Acts 14:23; Titus 1:5), there were obviously rulers over the churches besides the apostles (Heb. 13:7, 17), in matters of discipline the leaders gave instructions as to what to do (1 Cor. 5; 1 Tim. 5:20), and ordination passages imply the federal system." (*A Survey of Bible Doctrine*, p. 146)

W. L. Lingle suggests that the Jerusalem Council in Acts 15 illustrates this form of government. He writes:

"If the church at Antioch had been entirely independent it could have settled this question for itself, and with such men as Paul and Barnabas present it was abundantly able to do so. As a matter of fact the Church at Antioch referred this question to a church council at Jerusalem. . . . Note well that it was composed of apostles and elders. It must have looked a good deal like a Presbyterian Synod or General Assembly. Note also that this council composed of apostles and elders, after full deliberations, settled the question authoritatively, and that the Church at Antioch and other churches accepted its decisions." (*Presbyterians: Their Ministry and Beliefs*, p. 16)

C. The congregational, democratic form. This type of government is clearly seen in Baptist, Congregational, Evangelical Free, Disciples of Christ, and Independent Bible churches. Followers of this form believe no outside man or group of men should exercise authority over a local assembly. Therefore, the government should be in the hands of the members themselves. The pastor is considered to be the single elder in the church. He is called and elected by the church congregation. Deacons are then chosen to assist him in shepherding the flock.

Again, to quote from Charles Ryrie:

"Arguments in favor of this form of government include the many passages that speak of the responsibilities of the entire church (1 Cor. 1:10; Phil. 1:27), the passages which seem to commit the ordinances of the church to the entire group, not just leaders (Mt. 28:19, 20; 1 Cor. 11:2, 20), the apparent involvement of the whole church in choosing leaders (Acts 6:3, 5; 15:2, 30; 2 Cor. 8:19), and the fact that the whole church was involved in exercising discipline (Mt. 18:17; 1 Cor. 5; 2 Thess. 3:14ff.).

Under the congregational system, the pastor is usually considered to be the single elder in the church. This is supported by the fact that the seven churches of Revelation 2 and 3 apparently had a single leader (called the 'angel' but referring to a human leader), and by the fact that in 1 Timothy 3 the first part of the passage speaks of *the* bishop (elder) while the latter part (vs. 8-13) mentions the deacons. This would seem to indicate that there was only one elder in each church although there were several deacons." (*A Survey of Bible Doctrine*, p. 147)

XI. The Officers of the Church.

A. The kinds of officers.

1. Bishops (1 Tim. 3:1-7; see also Titus 1:5-9).

"This is a true saying. If a man desire the office of a bishop, he desireth a good work" (3:1).

The Greek word for "bishop" is *episkopos* and refers to an overseer. Here, of course, Paul had in mind the office of the pastor.

Another name found in the New Testament which may refer to this same position is "elder" (*presbuteros* in the Greek). These two terms, bishop and elder, are often used interchangeably (Acts 20:17-28; Titus 1:5-7). The former term (bishop) speaks of his office responsibility, while the latter term (elder) refers to his spiritual maturity.

2. Deacons (1 Tim. 3:8-12). The exact nature and duties of this office are nowhere set forth in any systematic way in the New Testament. It seems almost certain that the office was created to solve the organizational problem of the early church, due in part to its rapid growth (Acts 6:1-8). The Greek word for "deacon" is *diakonos*. (See also Rom. 12:7, here translated "ministry," and Phil. 1:1.)

3. Deaconess (1 Tim. 3:11). Does this verse indicate the office of a deaconess? It is the view of some (Dr. Homer Kent, Grace Theological Seminary; Dr. Kenneth Wuest, former Greek instructor, Moody Bible Institute; etc.) that it does.

B. The qualifications for officers.
   1. Bishop (1 Tim. 3:1-7).
      a. He must be a male.
      b. He must be blameless (without reproach).
      c. He must be the husband of one wife. Few New Testament statements have been the object of so much speculation as verse 2: "the husband of one wife." There are two main interpretations to the verse.
         (1) "The prohibition of polygamy" view. According to this theory, Paul is simply saying no church member who had several wives in his home could qualify as a bishop. However, this view has serious problems.
            (a) Paul had already forbidden this years ago (Rom. 7:1-3; 1 Cor. 7:2).
            (b) The Roman government had outlawed polygamy at this time.
            (c) There is no evidence that the early church ever had this problem.
            (d) This term literally says a "one-woman man" and is found again in 5:9 (though here reversed) where it speaks of a widow as a "one-man woman."
         (2) "The prohibition of divorce" view. According to this theory a divorced and remarried man is prohibited from occupying the office of the pastorate, regardless of the circumstances which may have surrounded the divorce.
      d. He must be vigilant (temperate).
      e. He must be sober (serious-minded).
      f. He must be of good behavior (orderly). This would be reflected in his sermons, clothes, and life manner.
      g. He must be given to hospitality (a lover of strangers).
      h. He must be "apt to teach" (having the ability and love for teaching; see Eph. 4:11).
      i. He must not be given to wine.
      j. He must not be a striker (not pugnacious).
      k. He must not be greedy for money.
      l. He must be patient (reasonable, gentle).
      m. He must not be a brawler (not contentious).
      n. He must not covet (desire something belonging to someone else).
      o. He must rule his own house well.
      p. He must not be a novice (a new convert).
      q. He must maintain a good report from without (a good public testimony in his immediate community).
   2. Deacon (1 Tim. 3:8-13).
      a. He must be grave (held in high respect).
      b. He must not be double-tongued (two-faced, a talebearer).
      c. He must not be given over to wine.
      d. He must not be greedy.
      e. He must hold forth the mystery of the faith (know, explain, and defend the great theological truths of the Bible).
      f. He must maintain a pure conscience.
      g. He must be tested and proven (his testimony within the church must be good).
      h. He must be blameless (his testimony without the church must be good).

C. The responsibilities of the officers. In Philippians 1:1, Paul writes to "all the saints in Jesus Christ which are at Philippi, with the bishops and deacons."

Three well-known authors write concerning these officers and their duties. The first is Dr. John Walvoord.

"The mention of bishops and deacons indicates the advanced state of organization of the Church at Philippi now composed of mature and gifted believers from whom recognized leaders had come. As A. R. Fausset notes, 'This is the earliest epistle where bishops and deacons are mentioned, and the only one where they are separately addressed.' Of course, as early as Acts 6, men were appointed in the church to serve in a way similar to deacons. Although not called deacons, the prominence of this appointment of men to special service in Acts seems to recognize its significance. Elders were appointed in every church as early as Acts 14:23, and are mentioned in Acts 11:30; 20:27, 28; 1 Thessalonians 5:12, 13." (*Philippians, Triumph in Christ*, p. 24)

Greek scholar Kenneth Wuest writes:

"The word bishop is the translation of a

Greek word used in secular pursuits of an overseer in any capacity, for instance, the official in charge of the repairing of a temple or an officer in an army. The word itself means 'to look upon.' Paul uses it as another name for an elder, the latter being the title of the office so far as statutes in the church is concerned, the former being the title that indicated the responsibility and activity of the office, that of overseeing the spiritual welfare of the local church. He brings the two names together as designating one individual in Acts 20:17, 28.

The word deacon is the English spelling of a Greek word that was used as a general term to designate a servant. It covered both slaves and hired servants. It represented a servant, not in his relation to his master, but in his activity. The same word is translated 'minister' in 1 Corinthians 3:5; 2 Corinthians 3:6; Ephesians 3:7. Here it refers to a distinct class of officers in the apostolic church. The origin of the office is given us in Acts 6." (*Word Studies in Philippians*, p. 28)

As a final note here, consider the comments of J. Dwight Pentecost:

"The word 'deacon' comes from a compound Greek word that means 'to stir up the dust.' It presents the picture of one who is moving so rapidly through the dusty lanes of the villages of Palestine to discharge his duty that his feet kick up dust as he goes. There was so much for the deacons to do they could not loiter nor tarry. They went about their ministry with such diligence that they were stirring up the dust; thus those who were set apart to this ministry were called 'those who stir up the dust' or deacons." (*The Joy of Living*, p. 114)

Of these two offices, the most important is that of the bishop (pastor). In general it may be said that his responsibilities are as follows:

1. He is to administer the ordinances (Mt. 28:19, 20).
2. He is to be a man of prayer (1 Tim. 2:1).
3. He is to warn his flock (1 Tim. 4:1, 6).
4. He is to study the Word (2 Tim. 2:15).
5. He is to preach the Word (2 Tim. 4:2; Acts 6:2–4).
6. He is to exhort and rebuke (1 Thess. 5:12; Titus 2:15).
7. He is to watch over souls.
   a. His own (Acts 20:28; Col. 4:17; 1 Tim. 4:16; 6:11).
   b. Those of others (Acts 20:28–31; Heb. 13:17).
8. He is to feed and lead his flock (Acts 20:28; 1 Pet. 5:2).
9. He is to be an example to all (1 Cor. 11:1; 4:16; Phil. 3:17; 2 Thess. 3:9; 1 Tim. 4:12; Heb. 13:7; 1 Pet. 5:3).

Pastor John MacArthur, Jr., writes concerning Paul's fourfold perspective of pastoral priorities in Acts 20:19-22 (page 15 in *Leadership, God's Priority for the Church*):

"1. A right perspective toward *God*. 'Serving the Lord with all humility of mind, and with many tears, and trials, which befell me by the lying in wait of the Jews.'
2. A right perspective toward the *church*. 'And how I kept back nothing that was profitable unto you, but have shown you, and have taught you publicly.'
3. A right perspective toward the *lost*. 'And from house to house, testifying both to the Jews and also to the Greeks, repentance toward God, and faith toward our Lord Jesus Christ.'
4. A right perspective toward *himself*. 'And now, behold, I go bound in the spirit unto Jerusalem, not knowing the things that shall befall me there.' "

To this list MacArthur then adds five more priorities as found in Acts 20:28-35.

"1. To keep right with God. 'Take heed, therefore, unto yourselves.'
2. To feed and lead the flock of God. 'And to all the flock, over which the Holy Spirit hath made you overseers, to feed the church of God, which he hath purchased with his own blood.'
3. To warn and watch . . . to protect the flock (from false teachers and other emissaries of Satan). 'For I know this, that after my departing shall grievous wolves enter in among you, not sparing the flock. Also, of your own selves shall men arise, speaking perverse things, to draw away disciples after them. Therefore, watch and remember, that for the space of three years I ceased not to warn everyone night and day with tears.'
4. To pray and study. 'And now, brethren, I commend you to God, and to the word of his grace, which is able to build you up, and to give you an inheritance among all them who are sanctified.'
5. To be free from self-interest. 'I have coveted no man's silver, or gold, or apparel. Yea, ye yourselves know that these hands have ministered unto my necessities, and to them that were with me. I have shown you all things, how that so laboring ye ought to support the weak, and to remember the words of the Lord Jesus, how he said, It is more blessed to give than to receive.' " (*Leadership*, p. 41)

Before leaving this section, what about the responsibilities of women in a local church? Again, to quote from MacArthur:

"In Romans 16:1, a woman, Phoebe, is referred to as a *diakonon*, thus indicating that both men and women may serve in this office.

The Scripture does have much to say regarding the woman's role in the church.

Immediately after Christ's ascension, women gathered with the apostles and disciples in the upper room in Jerusalem. In the early church beginnings, women were a vital part (Acts 5:14). One of the early converts, Mary, the mother of John Mark, donated her house as a meeting place for believers in Jerusalem. Lydia did the same in Philippi (Acts 16:14, 15). In the last chapter of Romans, eight women are named out of the twenty-six whom Paul singles out for significant service to Christ. The daughters of Philip were used of God to prophesy (Acts 21:8, 9). Aquila and Priscilla were used to instruct Apollos (Acts 18:24-26).

In addition to the historical precedent, the Scriptures give clear instruction for women's ministry: Women have a vital place in evangelism. Psalm 68:11 (RV): 'The Lord giveth the Word; the women that publish the tidings are a great host.'

Paul perhaps paid the highest compliment to women when he said, 'The woman is man's glory' (1 Cor. 11:7).

In addition to these positive areas of ministry for women, the Scripture indicates some areas where women are NOT to serve: 1 Timothy 2:11, 12 is the most important statement in the area of leadership roles in the church. Along with 1 Corinthians 14:33-35 it indicates a universal spiritual principle, that the divine order for women is subordination (not inferiority) to men. This principle is based on the facts that woman was created last (1 Tim. 2:13) and was first to sin (1 Tim. 2:14). Since the emphasis in both passages seems most easily applicable to public worship, women are not to be in positions of authority over men.

Nowhere in the New Testament is a woman ever commended to serve as an elder. In fact, it's obvious that 1 Timothy 3:1-7 and Titus 1:5-9, which list qualifications for elders, can refer only to a man.

At first 1 Timothy 2:12 may appear negative and unfriendly toward women, but the words are in fact, '. . . expressive of a feeling of sympathy and basic understanding. They mean: let a woman not enter a sphere of activity for which by dent of her very creation she is not suited.' (Wm. Hendriksen, *1 & 2 Timothy & Titus*, p. 108)

Placing women in responsibilities meant for men misuses their Godgiven calling and forfeits their areas of greatest ministry." (*Leadership*, pp. 38-40)

A final quote from Charles Ryrie is helpful here:

"There are many times on both the home and foreign fields where there are simply no men to do the work. In such instances this writer feels that we need to remember that Paul not only commanded that things be done decently and in order, but also that they be done. In such cases, then, one feels that it is better to do the work with capable women, even though this is not ideal, than to do nothing. However, women must be cautioned against continuing in such work

after there are trained men available for the job. . . . To know the scriptural pattern is absolutely essential. To aim our labors toward attaining the ideal is the only practical way to serve the present-day situation." (*The Role of Women in the Church*, pp. 80, 81)

XII. **The Ordinances of the Church.** The meaning of an ordinance: An ordinance is an outward and visible symbolic rite commanded in the Bible to be practiced by the church which sets forth a central truth of the Christian faith. It is a memorial or reminder of some precious historical event of great significance.

The distinction between an ordinance and a sacrament: "A sacrament is something presented to the senses, which has the power, by divine institution, not only signifying, but also of efficiently conveying grace" (as defined by the Roman Catholic Council of Trent in 1551). An ordinance therefore differs from a sacrament in that it is performed not to obtain grace, but because the one observing it has already obtained that grace.

The number of the ordinances: The Roman Catholic Church teaches that there are seven sacraments. These are: ordination, confirmation, matrimony, extreme unction, penance, baptism, the eucharist (communion). Of these seven, the New Testament lists but two, and (as we have already seen) regards them as memorial ordinances and not sacraments. These two are the Lord's Supper and baptism.

A. The Lord's Supper.
1. The Scriptures describing the Lord's Supper. Matthew 26:26-30; Mark 14:22-26; Luke 22:17-20; 1 Corinthians 11:23-34. The actual details of the supper are not mentioned in John's Gospel. However, some believe Jesus had this in mind in John 6:51, 53-56.
2. The names for the Lord's Supper.
   a. The *eucharist* (Greek word for the "giving of thanks"). Taken from 1 Corinthians 11:24.
   b. The *eulogia* (Greek word for "blessing"). Taken from 1 Corinthians 10:16, "the cup of blessing."
   c. The *prosphora* (Greek word for "offering"). This name came into being because gifts or offerings for the poor were made at the celebration of the supper.
   d. Communion. This name derives from 1 Corinthians 10:16, "the communion of the blood of Christ."
   e. The breaking of bread. This expression is found in Acts 2:42 and is thought by some to refer to the Lord's Supper.
3. The views concerning the Lord's Supper.
   a. Transubstantiation: The Roman Catholic doctrine which teaches that the bread and wine actually become the body and blood of Christ when consecrated by the priest during mass, even though they still look and taste the

same. Thus the one partaking literally eats Christ's flesh and drinks his blood. Needless to say, this is without scriptural support. In fact, it is totally refuted by the book of Hebrews (7:24-27; 9:12, 24, 25, 28; 10:11, 12).

b. Consubstantiation: The Lutheran doctrine which teaches that, while the bread and wine remain the same, the presence of the body of Christ is nevertheless "in, with, and under" both elements. While this error is not as severe as the above, it too is totally unscriptural.

c. Memorialization: The doctrine which teaches that the bread and wine are mere symbols to remind and aid the believer in observing both the first and second comings of our Lord. This precitce is both scriptural and sensible (1 Cor. 11:24-26).

4. The Old Testament type of the Lord's Supper. A beautiful type is seen in the Passover Lamb, the sprinkled blood of which saved the Israelite from the death plague in Egypt prior to the Exodus.

"For I will pass through the land of Egypt this night, and will smite all the firstborn in the land of Egypt, both man and beast; and against all the gods of Egypt I will execute judgment: I am the Lord. And the blood shall be to you for a token upon the houses where ye are: and when I see the blood, I will pass over you, and the plague shall not be upon you to destroy you, when I smite the land of Egypt" (Ex. 12:12, 13).

"Then Moses called for all the elders of Israel, and said unto them, Draw out and take you a lamb according to your families, and kill the passover. And ye shall take a bunch of hyssop, and dip it in the blood that is in the bason, and strike the lintel and the two side posts with the blood that is in the bason, and none of you shall go out at the door of his house until the morning" (Ex. 12:21, 22).

"And it shall come to pass, when your children shall say unto you, What mean ye by this service? That ye shall say, It is the sacrifice of the Lord's passover, who passed over the houses of the children of Israel in Egypt, when he smote the Egyptians, and delivered our houses. And the people bowed the head and worshipped" (Ex. 12:26, 27).

In the New Testament Paul connects the Passover Lamb with that of the Lord's Table. Note:

"Purge out therefore the old leaven, that ye may be a new lump, as ye are unleavened. For even Christ our passover is sacrificed for us: Therefore let us keep the feast, not with old leaven, neither with the leaven of malice and wicked-

ness; but with the unleavened bread of sincerity and truth" (1 Cor. 5:7, 8).

5. The purpose of the Lord's Supper. The Lord's table involves a threefold look.
   a. We are to look backward. "For as often as ye eat this bread, and drink this cup, ye do show the Lord's death" (1 Cor. 11:26).
   b. We are to look inward. "But let a man examine himself, and so let him eat of that bread, and drink of that cup" (1 Cor. 11:28).
   c. We are to look forward. "Till he come" (1 Cor. 11:26).

The Lord's Supper is therefore historical, personal, and prophetical. It speaks of the cross, the conscience, and the crown.

6. The partakers of the Lord's Supper. What group is invited to this table? The Lord's Supper is only for believers, but it includes all believers. This would appear to be the case, whether they happened to be members of a given local church or not.

7. The prerequisites of the Lord's Supper. Individuals who are forbidden to partake: the unsaved and the unclean. John the apostle (who attended the first Lord's Supper) has given sound advice to aid both kinds of individuals here. To the unsaved, he offers John 3:16, and to the unclean (backslidden Christian), he extends 1 John 1:9.

8. The penalty of the Lord's Supper.

"For he that eateth and drinketh unworthily, eateth and drinketh damnation to himself, not discerning the Lord's body. For this cause many are weak and sickly among you, and many sleep" (1 Cor. 11:29, 30).

Here several words deserve our consideration.

Unworthily. The word here is an adverb and not an adjective. Paul does not say, "If anyone who is not worthy partakes," but rather, "If anyone partakes in an unworthy manner."

Damnation. In the Greek this is the word *krima,* and should here be translated "judgment." (See Rom. 11:33; 1 Pet. 4:17 and Rev. 20:4, where the same word appears.) This judgment may be manifested in a twofold manner: through physical sickness (11:30) and through physical death—"and many sleep." The Greek word for sleep here is *koimao* and refers to physical death (Jn. 11:11, 12; Acts 7:60; 1 Cor. 15:6, 18, 20, 51).

At this communion service the fickle and self-centered Corinthians had so involved themselves in the supper that they had totally ignored other saints and the Savior. As a result some (the well-to-do) would stuff themselves with food and drink while others (the poor) would go away hungry.

Many things happened on that momentous night in the upper room, but here in 1 Corinthians 11:23 Paul singles out his betrayal by Judas, which may have been a hint describing what the Corinthians were actually doing also.

It should be noted that Paul does not teach here (1 Cor. 11:22) against having fellowship banquets in a church basement. He does, however, seem to limit the communion service itself to that of bread and wine.

9. The frequency of the Lord's Supper. Dr. Charles Ryrie writes:

"How often should the Lord's Supper be observed? Some churches do it every three months and usually precede it by a preparation service sometime during the week before the Sunday it will be observed. Others do it once every month, while some feel it should be observed every Sunday. Actually the Scriptures do not clearly specify the exact frequency of taking the Lord's Supper. Although the first believers apparently did it daily immediately following Pentecost, this does not mean that it was observed in every house gathering every day but only daily somewhere in the city of Jerusalem (Acts 2:46). At Troas (Acts 20:7) it was observed on Sunday, but the text does not explicitly state that it was done every Sunday, though such a conclusion would be easily inferred from the passage. But however frequently it is done, it might be well to observe it sometimes in the evening service—not only because it was a supper, but also because this allows those who may be prevented from coming to a morning observance to participate on a regular basis. Since it is one of the most important things a church does, it should always be given ample time and never 'tacked on' and rushed through."
(*A Survey of Bible Doctrine,* p. 150)

B. Baptism.

"Go ye, therefore, and teach all nations, baptizing them in the name of the Father, and of the Son, and of the Holy Ghost" (Mt. 28:19).

1. The meaning of the word baptism. Dr. Gordon G. Johnson writes:

"What do Greek authorities say about the meaning of the word? Let us consider three of the more well-known lexicons. The classical Greek lexicon was written by Liddell and Scott, Church of England men. The New Testament Greek lexicon was compiled by Thayer, a scholar of the Congregational Church. The lexicon of theological terms was written by a German Lutheran named Cremer. All these men agree that the word in its origin means to dip, immerse, submerge or overwhelm.

Dr. Thomas J. Conant in his *Meaning and Use of Baptizein* sums up a study of the use of the word throughout the his-

tory of Greek literature with these words, 'In all the word has retained its ground meaning without change. From the earliest age of Greek literature down to its close, a period of about 2000 years, not an example has been found in which the word has any other meaning.'

The words sprinkling or pouring are never used in the New Testament for the rite of baptism. This has compelled scholars of all denominational groups to admit that in the original meaning and in the New Testament use baptism meant immersion. Luther said: 'The term baptism is a Greek word. It may be rendered a dipping, when we dip something in water, that it may be entirely covered with water.' Calvin says: 'The word baptize signifies to immerse; and the rite of immersion was observed by the ancient church.' Brenner, a Roman Catholic says, 'For 1300 years was baptism generally and regularly an immersion of the person under water, and only in extraordinary cases, a sprinkling or pouring with water. The latter was moreover disputed as a mode of baptism, nay even forbidden.' Other men may be mentioned, but this is sufficient to show us the universal acceptance of the meaning of the word 'baptism.'

We might then rightly ask, 'How and when did sprinkling become the mode of baptism?' This mode arose because people came to feel there was something magical about baptism and that it brought salvation to the recipient. This conception cannot be supported by Scripture. But if it were true, a person dying without baptism would be lost. A sick or injured person could not be immersed because of his physical condition, but he might die. If baptism were necessary to salvation, he would be lost. Thus, sprinkling began to be practiced.

The first record of the use of sprinkling was about A.D. 250 when Novatian lay sick in bed and thought he was to die. He had water poured all over him on the bed as an act of baptism. It wasn't until A.D. 1311 that the Roman Catholic Church at the Council of Ravenna made sprinkling or immersion allowables as modes of baptism. Not until 1644 did the Church of England adopt sprinkling by vote of Parliament. The year before it was voted upon and recommended to Parliament by the Assembly of Divines. The vote was 25 to 24 in favor of sprinkling. A New Testament Church cannot make such accommodations to human whim." (*My Church,* pp. 41, 42)

2. The kinds of baptism. It has already been demonstrated that the basic theological meaning of the word baptism is "identifica-

tion." Following is a list of eight different kinds of baptism in the New Testament. Each may be correctly defined by this word "identification."

a. The baptism of sin upon Christ at Calvary (Lk. 12:50).

b. The baptism of the Holy Spirit upon believers at Pentecost (Mt. 3:11; Acts 1:5; 2:1–4).

c. The baptism of all Christians by the Holy Spirit into the body of Christ" (1 Cor. 12:13).

d. The baptism of Israel unto Moses (1 Cor. 10:2).

e. The baptism of John the Baptist (national baptism of repentance) (Mk. 1:4; Acts 13:24).

f. The baptism of Jesus.
   (1) With water by John (Mt. 3:15).
   (2) With the Holy Spirit by the Father (Mt. 3:16).

g. The baptism for the dead (1 Cor. 15:29).

h. The water baptism of new converts in the book of Acts.
   (1) At Pentecost. Here 3,000 were baptized by Peter and the apostles (Acts 2:41).
   (2) At Samaria. Here many were baptized by Philip the evangelist (Acts 8:12).
   (3) At Gaza. Here the Ethiopian eunuch was baptized by Philip (Acts 8:38).
   (4) At Damascus. Here Paul is baptized by Ananias (Acts 9:18).
   (5) At Caesarea. Here Peter baptized Cornelius and his friends (Acts 11:48).
   (6) At Philippi. Here Paul baptized Lydia and the Philippian jailor (Acts 16:15, 33).
   (7) At Corinth. Here Paul baptized Crispus, Gaius, Stephanas, and others (Acts 18:8; 1 Cor. 1:14, 16).
   (8) At Ephesus. Here Paul baptized some followers of John the Baptist (Acts 19:3–5).

3. The false views on baptism.

a. That it is necessary for salvation. This is totally erroneous. Dozens of key passages, such as Romans 4:1–6; Ephesians 2:8, 9; Titus 3:5, and many others make it clear that salvation is by grace through faith plus nothing.

The strongest refutation of baptismal regeneration is found in 1 Corinthians 1:17: "For Christ sent me not to baptize, but to preach the gospel." In 1 Corinthians 15:1–4 Paul explains what the gospel is, and baptism is definitely not a part of it (see also 1 Cor. 4:15).

An oft-repeated "proof-text" for baptismal regeneration is Acts 2:38: "Then Peter said unto them, repent, and be baptized every one of you in the name of Jesus Christ for the remission of sins." The Greek preposition *eis* (here translated "for") can also be rendered, "because of," as it is in Matthew 12:41.

In addition, the question asked in the preceding verse (Acts 2:37) is not the restricted "What must I do to be saved?" of Acts 16:30, but the broader: "What shall we do?" Hence, it is not strange that we have here a broader answer than in Acts 16:30.

b. That it replaces circumcision. This cannot be, however, for several reasons.
   (1) Circumcision was performed upon male babies only, but in the New Testament we have the baptism of women mentioned (Acts 8:12; 16:14, 15).
   (2) Circumcision had nothing to do with the faith of the baby. Only his nationality was in mind.
   (3) Baptism has nothing to do with the nationality of the believer. Only his faith is in mind.
   (4) Circumcision continued to be practiced among Jewish believers even after the institution of baptism (Acts 16:3).

4. The scriptural view on baptism.

a. That *all* believers be baptized. F.F. Bruce writes: "The idea of an unbaptized Christian is simply not entertained in the New Testament" (*The Book of the Acts,* p. 77). Baptism is therefore not a personal choice, but a divine command.

b. That *only* believers be baptized. The two words *belief* and *baptism* are inseparably linked together in the New Testament. Belief is always assumed to be the *root* of which baptism becomes the *fruit.* Note:

"Then they that gladly received his word were baptized" (Acts 2:41).

"But when they believed Philip preaching the things concerning the kingdom of God, and the name of Jesus Christ, they were baptized, both men and women" (Acts 8:12).

"And as they went on their way, they came unto a certain water: and the eunuch said, See, here is water; what doth hinder me to be baptized? And Philip said, If thou believest with all thine heart, thou mayest. And he answered and said, I believe that Jesus Christ is the Son of God. And he commanded the chariot to stand still: and they went down both into the water, both Philip and the eunuch: and he baptized him" (Acts 8:36–38).

"And a certain woman named Lydia, a seller of purple, of the city of Thyatira, which worshipped God, heard us: whose heart the Lord opened, that she attended unto the things which were spoken of Paul.

And when she was baptized, and her household, she besought us, saying, If ye have judged me to be faithful to the Lord, come into my house, and abide there. And she constrained us" (Acts 16:14, 15).

"And brought them out, and said, Sirs, what must I do to be saved? And they said, Believe on the Lord Jesus Christ, and thou shalt be saved, and thy house. And they spake unto him the word of the Lord, and to all that were in his house. And he took them the same hour of the night, and washed their stripes; and was baptized, he and all his, straightway" (Acts 16:30–33).

"And Crispus, the chief ruler of the synagogue, believed on the Lord with all his house; and many of the Corinthians hearing believed, and were baptized" (Acts 18:8).

"Then said Paul, John verily baptized with the baptism of repentance, saying unto the people, that they should believe on him which should come after him, that is, on Christ Jesus. When they heard this, they were baptized in the name of the Lord Jesus" (Acts 19:4, 5).

In the light of the Scriptures the practice of baptizing infants must be completely ruled out.

5. The symbolism of baptism. What exactly does baptism symbolize? One's interpretation of this will determine his view on the *mode* of baptism also. Here are two views concerning the symbolism of baptism.
   a. The view of the affusionist. He is one who sprinkles or pours the baptismal water. The affusionist believes the object lying behind baptism is to represent the coming of the Holy Spirit upon the believer. He reasons that inasmuch as Calvary is represented by one ordinance (the Lord's Supper) then there would be no need of a second ordinance representing the same event.
   b. The view of the immersionist. He is one who requires the complete submerging of the believer in water. The immersionist relates baptism to Christ's death, burial, and resurrection on the grounds that the believer is said to have been baptized into his death, burial, and resurrection, according to Romans 6:1–10 and Colossians 2:11–13.

   While it is true that there is a similarity here to the Lord's Supper, there are also important differences. Note:
   (1) The Lord's Supper speaks primarily of Christ's death.
   (2) Baptism speaks primarily of the believer's death.
   (3) The return of Christ is seen in the Lord's Supper.
   (4) The resurrection of Christ is seen in baptism.
   (5) Justification (the cross) and glorification (the crown) are in view in the Lord's Supper.
   (6) Sanctification is seen in baptism.
      "Therefore, we are buried with him by baptism into death, that as Christ was raised up from the dead by the glory of the Father, even so we also should walk in newness of life" (Rom. 6:4).
6. The purpose of baptism. Robert L. Saucy suggests a twofold purpose.
   a. Identification with the Savior.
      "Baptism is, therefore, first and foremost, identification with Jesus Christ. By this act the initiate indicated that he was entering the realm of Christ's lordship and power. But not only was the name of Christ pronounced over the baptized, but the baptized also called upon the name of the Lord (Acts 22:16). In doing so, he openly confessed in penitence and faith his submission to the lordship of Jesus (cf. Rom. 10:9). It is, as Beasley-Murray aptly notes, the time when one who has been an enemy of Christ makes 'his final surrender.' Baptism is therefore the sign of the working of the gospel in which God unites the believer to Himself through Christ, and the believer testifies to the subjective reality of that union in his life.

      Identification with Christ is also identification with His great saving acts. The waters of baptism are thus related to washing or cleansing from the defilement of sin (Acts 22:16; 1 Cor. 6:11; Heb. 10:22; cf. Acts 2:38). Even more often, however, in Scripture the baptismal act signifies the believer's death to the old life and his resurrection as a new creature in union with Christ. The apostle bases his appeal to a holy life on the fact that 'we are buried with him by baptism into death: that like as Christ was raised up from the dead by the glory of the Father, even so we also should walk in newness of life' (Rom. 6:4). Similarly, to the Colossians he writes, 'having been buried with Him in baptism, in which you were also raised up with Him through faith in the working of God, who raised Him from the dead' (Col. 2:12, *NASB*). Peter sees an analogy to baptism in the flood waters of judgment and death through which Noah was borne by the ark to a new life (1 Pet. 3:20 ff.). While cleansing from sin is the result of this participation with Christ, the salvation experience is, at its heart, the death of the old life and the resurrection to a new life in union with Christ. The importance of this understanding and its significance in understanding baptism is emphasized by Moule when he notes that 'as soon as baptism is treated chiefly as a cleansing, the tendency is to interpret it as a cleansing from past sins, with the corollary that thereafter the baptized must keep himself clean. But as long as membership in Christ is treated as a new life . . . the supernatural, wholly divine agency is more prominent.' "

b. Identification with the church.

"Identification with Christ is at the same time identification with His body, the church. Death and resurrection with Christ refer not only to union with Christ but to a unity of Christ composed of many members. 'For as the body is one, and hath many members, and all the members of that one body, being many, are one body: so also is Christ' (1 Cor. 12:12; cf. Rom. 12:4, 5). One is not united to the Head without at the same time being united with the body. So Paul writes that all believers in Christ are made into 'one new man' (Eph. 2:15).

Since baptism signifies the inward reality of the participation into His body, it was the normal initiatory rite into the visible body. In this act the new converts were identified outwardly with the fellowship of believers (Acts 2:41). Not only is the individual transition from the old life to new life made public in baptism, but the transition from union with the world to that of the community of believers is proclaimed as well. In the rite of baptism the believer took his stand with the disciples of Christ." (*The Church in God's Program*, pp. 194, 195)

XIII. The Worship of the Church.

"Give unto the Lord the glory due unto his name: worship the Lord in the beauty of holiness" (Ps. 29:2).

"But the hour cometh, and now is when the true worshippers shall worship the Father in spirit and in truth: for the Father seeketh such to worship him. God is a Spirit: and they that worship him must worship him in spirit and in truth" (Jn. 4:23, 24).

A. The definition of worship. There are three Greek verbs translated by the one English word "worship." These words are:

1. *Proskuneo:* "to bow or prostrate oneself in submissive lowliness and deep reverence."
2. *Sebomai:* "to look upon with awe."
3. *Latreuo:* "to render service for."

Andrew W. Blackwood has defined it thus: "Worship is man's response to God's revelation of Himself." To worship God is therefore to ascribe to him the supreme homage of which he alone is worthy.

B. The importance of worship. The difference between Adam and all other creatures in the Garden was not in his size or strength, but in his ability (and command) to worship the Creator.

C. The reasons for worship.

1. We are to worship God for his work in creation.

"O come, let us worship and bow down: let us kneel before the Lord our Maker" (Ps. 95:6).

"The four and twenty elders fall down before him that sat on the throne, and worship him that liveth for ever and ever, and cast their crowns before the throne, saying, Thou art worthy, O Lord, to receive glory and honour and power: for thou hast created all things, and for thy pleasure they are and were created" (Rev. 4:10, 11; see also Ps. 8).

2. We are to worship God for his work in redemption.

"And they sung a new song, saying, Thou art worthy to take the book, and to open the seals thereof: for thou wast slain, and hast redeemed us to God by the blood out of every kindred, and tongue, and people, and nation" (Rev. 5:9).

D. The elements in worship. How are New Testament church members to worship God? What characteristics should be seen in their personal lives and in their local assemblies? How can true worship best be effected in the church?

1. Through the ministering of God's Word.

a. It should be *studied* (Acts 6:2; 2 Tim. 2:15; 3:15).

b. It should be *read* (Col. 4:16; 1 Thess. 5:27; 1 Tim. 4:13; Rev. 1:3).

c. It should be *taught* (Acts 2:42; 6:7; 12:24; 18:28; 19:20; 1 Tim. 4:6; 2 Tim. 1:13; 2:2).

d. It should be *preached* (2 Tim. 4:2).

2. Through the keeping of the ordinances.

a. The ordinance of baptism.

b. The ordinance of the Lord's Supper.

3. Through the singing of psalms, hymns, and spiritual songs. (See Eph. 5:19; Col. 3:16; Jas. 5:13). Robert Saucy writes: "The many doxologies extolling the 'blessedness' (Rom. 1:25; 9:5; 2 Cor. 11:31; Eph. 1:3) and 'glory' of God (Rom. 11:36; Gal. 1:5; Phil. 4:20; 2 Tim. 4:18), which occur at the beginning as well as within and at the end of the New Testament epistles are expressive of what took place in the worship services." (*The Church in God's Program*, p. 184)

4. Through the lifting up of prayers, intercessions, supplications, and thanksgivings. (See Acts 2:42, 46; 3:1; 4:31; Eph. 6:18; Phil. 4:6; Col. 4:2; 1 Thess. 5:17; 1 Tim. 2:1, 2, 8.)

5. Through the offering up of sacrifices. According to 1 Peter 2:5-9 and Revelation 1:6,

every New Testament believer is a priest unto God. The main function of the Old Testament priest was to sacrifice. So it is with the New Testament priests. Their priestly service toward God is fourfold.

   a. The sacrifice of our bodies (Rom. 12:1).

   b. The sacrifice of our praise (Heb. 13:15).

   c. The sacrifice of our good works (Heb. 13:16).

   d. The sacrifice of our substance (Phil. 4:18).

XIV. The Stewardship of the Church.

"Let a man so account of us, as of the ministers of Christ, and stewards of the mysteries of God. Moreover it is required in stewards, that a man be found faithful" (1 Cor. 4:1, 2).

". . . as good stewards of the manifold grace of God" (1 Pet. 4:10).

In the New Testament world a steward was the manager of a household or estate. He was appointed by the owner and entrusted to keep the estate running smoothly. Both Paul and Peter write with this background in view, reminding us we are God's stewards. The estate responsibilities entrusted to us are threefold.

  A. How we use our time. Pastor David Jeremiah writes:

"There is a gift which comes to us from a royal source each day of our lives, bright and sparkling, absolutely untouched, unspoiled. What is this gift? The priceless gift of time. Each day we receive a fresh, new supply—24 hours, 1,440 minutes, 86,400 seconds. Twenty-four hours we have never lived before—twenty-four hours we shall never live again." (*Biblical Stewardship*, p. 9)

  B. How we use our talents (see Mt. 25:14-30; Lk. 12:37; 1 Cor. 4:7; 7:7).

Pastor Jeremiah points out the following:

   1. God has wisely given each individual a talent or talents to use for His glory.

   2. What we do with what we have will be the basis of our judgment.

   3. If we do not use our talent for God we will lose it.

  C. How we use our money.

"In the New Testament there are thirty-eight parables. Twelve of these are about money. One out of every six verses in Matthew, Mark and Luke has to do with money. Because 100% of what we have comes from God, we are responsible to use it all wisely and in accordance with God's will. Like every other area of stewardship, God is interested in the whole picture, not just a percentage. What we do with all our treasure is important to Him!" (*Biblical Stewardship*, p. 23)

How do I feel about money?

   1. I must recognize that money comes from God (Deut. 8:18; 1 Chron. 29:11, 12; Jas. 1:17).

   2. I must recognize that money in itself cannot satisfy (Isa. 55:1, 2).

It has been said that there are two kinds of unhappy people on this earth. The first group is unhappy because they didn't get those things they wanted, while the second group is sad because they did.

   3. I must refuse to substitute silver for the Savior (see Lk. 16:13; 1 Tim. 6:10, 17).

   4. I must believe that God will graciously supply all my needs that I cannot honestly provide for myself (Mt. 6:31, 32; Phil 4:19).

   5. The pattern of giving.

     a. The example of the Macedonians (2 Cor. 8:1-3).

     b. The example of the Father (2 Cor. 9:15).

     c. The example of the Son (2 Cor. 8:9).

   6. The plan of giving. Our giving should be systematic (1 Cor. 16:2).

   7. The paradox of giving. A paradox is an apparent (but not real) contradiction. Here is the paradox. If I have $100 and give God $15 I should wind up with $85. But somehow that $85 will, in the long run, pay more bills and buy more necessities than the original $100 could possibly have done. The classic example of this is the two small fishes and five barley loaves given to Christ by a little boy (Jn. 6:9-13; see also Prov. 11:24, 25).

   8. The purpose of giving.

     a. That God's work might be supported (1 Tim. 5:17, 18).

     b. That our lives might be blessed (Prov. 3:9, 10; 28:20; Mal. 3:10; Lk. 6:38; 2 Cor. 9:6).

     c. That other Christians might be challenged (2 Cor. 9:2). Paul encourages the Corinthian church to continue to collect their love offering for the needy saints, pointing out that in doing this their "zeal hath provoked very many" (2 Cor. 9:2).

     d. That the Father might be glorified (2 Cor. 9:12).

     e. That needy saints may be provided for (Acts 11:29; 1 Jn. 3:17).

   9. The privilege of giving. Whether we realize it or not, God does not need our money. (See Ps. 50:12-15.) But he has graciously allowed us to give back to him—and actually get credit for it—that which is already his!

   10. The pleasure of giving. "Every man according as he purposeth in his heart, so let him give; not grudgingly, or of necessity: for God loveth a cheerful giver" (2 Cor. 9:7; see also 2 Cor. 8:11, 12).

XV. The Discipline of the Church.

  A. The definition of discipline. To discipline is to penalize an individual for breaking the laws of a unit of society to which he belongs with the view of restoring him back to those laws.

  B. The basis of discipline. The basis of discipline of a local church is the holiness of God.

"Thy testimonies are very sure; holiness becometh thine house, O Lord, forever" (Ps. 93:5).

"Because it is written, be ye holy; for I am holy" (1 Pet. 1:16).

To take this holiness lightly is to invite discipline (Heb. 10:30; 1 Pet. 4:17).

C. The authority of discipline. The ultimate authority resides in Christ, who authorizes his church to exercise it when needed (Mt. 16:19; 18:17-20; 1 Cor. 5:4).

D. The recipients of discipline. Who demands church discipline?

1. Troublemakers and those who sow discord (Prov. 6:16, 19; Rom. 16:17).
2. The unruly, disorderly, and undisciplined (1 Thess. 5:14; 2 Thess. 3:6, 11).
3. Those who disobey the great doctrines of the faith (2 Thess. 3:14).
4. Those who deny the great doctrines of the faith (1 Tim. 6:3, 5; 2 Tim. 2:16-18; Titus 3:10; 2 Jn. 1:10, 11; Rev. 2:14).
5. The immoral (1 Cor. 5:1-5).

E. The procedures in discipline. Church discipline is to be handled prayerfully, carefully, and justly.

1. First step: Note and mark those who are in need of discipline (Rom. 16:17; 2 Thess. 3:14).
2. Second step: Arrange a private meeting with the offender (Mt. 18:15).
3. Third step: If this fails, set up a second meeting, this time with several others present (Mt. 18:16). During these preliminary private and semiprivate meetings the individual should be repeatedly admonished (Titus 3:10), rebuked (2 Tim. 4:2), and warned (1 Thess. 5:14).
4. Fourth step: As a final resort, the unrepentant one is to be brought before the entire church (Mt. 18:17; 1 Tim. 5:20).
5. Fifth step: Upon refusal to submit to church discipline the guilty party is to be spiritually excommunicated. This constitutes two fearful things, a *denial* and a *deliverance.*

   a. He is to be denied Christian fellowship.
      (1) "Avoid them" (Rom. 17:17).
      (2) "Withdraw yourselves from" (2 Thess. 3:6).
      (3) "From such withdraw thyself" (1 Tim. 6:3, 5).
      (4) "Reject" (Titus 3:10).
      (5) "Have no company with him" (2 Thess. 3:14).
   b. He is to be *delivered* over to Satan.
      "To deliver such an one unto Satan for the destruction of the flesh, that the spirit may be saved in the day of the Lord Jesus" (1 Cor. 5:5).
      "Of whom is Hymeneus and Alexander: whom I have delivered unto Satan, that they may learn not to blaspheme" (1 Tim. 1:20).
      What does it mean to do this? The Greek word for destruction in 1 Corinthians 5:5 is *olethros,* a reference to the act of spoiling or marring something.
      Apparently Paul was here saying, "If this fellow (the church member living in adultery) is having so much fun in his sin, then remove him entirely from your fellowship and let Satan kick him

around a little! Let him taste what it's like to face a hostile world without the prayers and ministry of a local church."
Thus, when a local Bible-believing church removes a person like this, it literally fulfills the divine command of Job 2:6, "And the Lord said unto Satan, behold, he is in thine hand; but save his life."

F. The heart attitude in discipline.

1. We are to avoid both vengeance and arrogance.
   "Brethren, if a man be overtaken in a fault, ye which are spiritual, restore such an one in the spirit of meekness, considering thyself, lest thou also be tempted" (Gal. 6:1).
2. We are to view the individual as an erring brother and not a bitter enemy.
   "Yet count him not as an enemy, but admonish him as a brother" (2 Thess. 3:15).
3. We are to approach him with sorrow and not sarcasm (see 1 Cor. 5:2; 2 Cor. 2:4).
4. We are to be ready to forgive him when repentance occurs (2 Cor. 2:7; 7:10, 11). This last attitude is of supreme importance for two reasons.
   a. Lest perhaps such a one should be swallowed up with overmuch sorrow (2 Cor. 2:7).
   b. Lest Satan should get an advantage of us: for we are not ignorant of his devices. (2 Cor. 2:11).

G. The purpose of discipline.

1. It is to maintain the standards of the church to a watching world (Mt. 5:13-16; Acts 5:1-16; Rom. 2:24).
2. It is to keep sin from spreading throughout the church (Josh. 7:3; 1 Cor. 5:6, 7).
3. It is to help the guilty person find his way back to God. (2 Cor. 2:6-8).
4. It is to escape God's twofold judgment upon habitually sinning saints.
   a. Sickness (1 Cor. 11:30).
   b. Physical death (1 Cor. 11:30).
   "For if we would judge ourselves, we should not be judged" (1 Cor. 11:31).

H. The scope of discipline. The church is called upon to discipline (if needed) *all* believers, but *only* believers. It has no authority to judge individual worldly unbelievers for their smoking, swearing, sexual activities, etc. Its only duty to an unsaved person is to lead him or her to Jesus Christ.

I. The reaction to discipline. How is the guilty person to react when disciplined by either God himself or by a local church?

1. He can despise it, that is, treat it too lightly (as did Esau concerning his birthright; Heb. 12:5).
2. He can faint under it, that is, treat it too seriously (Heb. 12:5).
3. He can be exercised by it (Heb. 12:10, 11). The real question is not so much what I

have done wrong (though this, of course, is important), but what is my attitude about it.

XVI. The Warfare of the Church.
A. Our enemy—the devil (Eph. 5:10-18).
1. His cohorts:
"For we wrestle not against flesh and blood, but against principalities, against powers, against the rulers of the darkness of this world, against spiritual wickedness in high places" (Eph. 6:12).
a. Principalities. A possible reference to Satan's "generals" who have the oversight of entire nations (see Dan. 10).
b. Powers. May speak of his "privates" who possess human beings (see Mt. 17; Mk. 5).
c. World rulers. Those demons in charge of Satan's worldly business.
d. Spiritual wickedness. Those demons in charge of worldly religion.
2. His tactics:
a. "The wiles of the devil" (Eph. 6:11). Greek scholar K. Wuest writes:
"Wiles is *methodeia* in the Greek, referring to 'cunning arts, deceit, craft, trickery.' It means to follow up, or investigate by method and settled plan, to follow craftily, frame devices, deceive." (*Ephesians and Colossians*, p. 141)
(See also 2 Cor. 2:11; 1 Tim. 3:7.)
b. "The fiery darts of the wicked" (6:16). This has reference to arrows tipped with tar, pitch, or such material, then set on fire before they were discharged (see also 1 Pet. 1:7; 4:12).
B. Our equipment—the armor of God (Eph. 6:11, 13-17). Let us carefully note each piece of armor mentioned here. Paul very obviously takes those pieces of armor worn by the Roman soldier and makes spiritual application to each one.
1. The girdle of truth. *Expositor's Commentary* says:
"First in the list of these articles of equipment mentioned is the girdle. Appropriately so; for the soldier might be furnished with every other part of his equipment, and yet, wanting his girdle, would be neither fully clothed nor securely armed.
His belt was no mere adornment of the soldier, but an essential part of his equipment. Passing round the loins and by the end of the breastplate (in later times supporting the sword), it was of special use in keeping other parts in place, and in securing the proper soldierly attitude and freedom of movement."
Truth, as mentioned here, probably refers to truthfulness as found in a Christian. Thus a believer whose life is tainted with deceit and falsehood forfeits the very thing which holds other pieces of his armor together.

2. The breastplate of righteousness. This speaks of right acts as practiced by the believer. The breastplate was to protect the heart of the soldier. Thus, unrighteous acts committed by a Christian rob him of this vital protection and expose his spiritual heart to Satan. (See Heb. 10:22; 13:9; Jas. 1:26; 4:8; 1 Jn. 3:19-22).

3. The sandals of the gospel. The Roman soldier wore sandals which were bound by thongs over the instep and around the ankle, and the soles were thickly studded with nails. This gave him a firm footing in time of attack. This may refer to the assurance and confidence which come from knowing the great doctrinal truths associated with the gospel. (See Eph. 4:14; 1 Pet. 3:15.)

4. The shield of faith. K. Wuest writes:
"The word shield used here designated the shield of the heavy infantry, a large, oblong one, four by two and one half feet, sometimes curved on the inner side."
Hebrews 11 is a commentary on this piece of armor.

5. The helmet of salvation. The helmet, of course, protected the head and brain. This piece (like the sandals) may refer to the intake of Bible doctrine, lest one's eyes be blinded, his ears deafened, and his mind confused with the attacks from the world, the flesh, and the devil.

6. The sword of the spirit. Here is the only offensive weapon listed among the various pieces of armor. The rest are defensive in nature. The sword of the Spirit is identified as the Word of God (see Heb. 4:12). This, then, is the armor the Christian is commanded to wear.
K. Wuest writes concerning the command in Ephesians 6:13; "Wherefore take unto you the whole armour of God":
"Take unto you is *analambano*, meaning, 'to take up in order to use' . . . . The verb is aorist imperative, which construction issues a command given with military snap and curtness, a command to be obeyed at once and once for all. Thus, the Christian is to take up and put on all the armor of God as a once-for-all act and keep the armor on during the entire course of his life, not relaxing the discipline necessary for the constant use of such protection. The historian Gibbon relates how the relaxation of discipline and disuse of exercise rendered soldiers less willing and less able to support the fatigue of service. They complained of the weight of armor, and obtained permission to lay aside much of it." (*Ephesians and Colossians*, p. 142)
C. Our exhortation—the trio of success.
1. We are to stand. No less than four times does Paul exhort us to do this (vs. 11, 13, 14). The believer is never told to attack the devil, but to withstand and resist him (see

1 Pet. 5:8, 9). Thus, when tempted to do wrong, we should flee as did Joseph (Gen. 39:12), but when attacked by Satan for doing right, we should stand firm as did Daniel's three friends (Dan. 3).

2. We are to pray. (See Mt. 17:21; 1 Thess. 5:17; 1 Tim. 2:8; Jude 20.)

3. We are to watch. (See Mt. 24:43; Lk. 12:37-40; Acts 20:31; 1 Cor. 16:13; 2 Cor. 6:5; 11:27; 1 Thess. 5:6; 2 Tim. 4:5; 1 Pet. 4:7; Rev. 3:2; 16:15.) We may thus conclude that both watching and praying are the divine twin secrets for overcoming:

    a. The world (Mk. 13:33).

    b. The flesh (Mk. 14:38).

    c. The devil (Eph. 6:18).

XVII. The Destiny of the Church. Everyone likes a story that has a happy ending. The story of the church has such a happy ending. The Bridegroom gets the bride and together they live happily ever after! The glorious destiny of the church is as follows:

A. To be caught up by the Bridegroom at the rapture (1 Cor. 15:51-53; 1 Thess. 4:15-17; Rev. 4:1).

B. To be examined and rewarded at the judgment seat of Christ (Rom. 14:10-12; 1 Cor. 3:13; 2 Cor. 5:10).

C. To be united with Christ at the marriage *service* of the Lamb (2 Cor. 11:2; Eph. 5:22-32; Rev. 19:7, 8).

D. To be seated with Christ at the marriage *supper* of the Lamb (Rev. 19:9).

E. To reign with Christ during the millennium (Rev. 1:6; 3:21; 20:6).

F. To share the New Jerusalem with Christ throughout all eternity (Rev. 21:1, 2, 9-27).

G. To illustrate the glory of Christ throughout all eternity (Eph. 1:6, 12; 2:1-7; 3:10).

THE DOCTRINE OF SIN

THE DOCTRINE OF SIN

The word "sin" is found hundreds of times in the Bible in both Old and New Testaments. Its first mention is in Genesis 4:7, where it is said to have been lurking at the door of the world's first murderer, Cain.

The second reference is found in Genesis 18:20, where it causes the fiery and fearsome destruction of Sodom. The final mention is in Revelation 18:5, where it brings down the full wrath of an angry God upon the political and economic systems of this entire world.

What is this deadly and damnable thing that is so hated by God and so harmful to man? The very word carries with it the hissing sound of a vicious viper.

Some twenty centuries ago the angel Gabriel appeared to a troubled carpenter named Joseph to reassure him of the purity of Mary.

"Joseph, thou son of David, fear not to take unto thee Mary, thy wife, for that which is conceived in her is of the Holy Spirit. And she shall bring forth a son, and thou shalt call his name Jesus; for he shall save his people from their sins" (Mt. 1:20, 21).

Approximately thirty years after this angelic announcement, this babe, who had now grown into strong manhood, was publicly introduced by John the Baptist in the following manner:

"Behold, the Lamb of God, who taketh away the sin of the world" (Jn. 1:29).

From these verses we are told that the basic reason for the incarnation of God's Son was to deal with this terrible thing called sin.

I. The Definition and Meaning of Sin. There are two words in the Greek New Testament which perhaps most closely define sin:
   A. *Hamartema*—"to miss a mark." Here sin may be pictured as any attitude or act of man which does not hit the bull's eye of God's glory target. This meaning is strongly brought out by Paul in Romans 3:23, "For all have sinned and come short of the glory of God." The secular use of its verbal form is illustrated in Judges 20:16, where it is stated that the tribe of Benjamin had a corps of left-handed warriors who "could sling stones at a hair-breadth and not miss."
   B. *Parabasis*—"to overstep a forbidden line." According to this definition, sin occurs when man deliberately (or accidentally) steps over the line of the law of God. The following passages bring this out:
      "Whosoever committeth sin transgresseth also the law: for sin is the transgression of the law" (1 Jn. 3:4).

"Which Judas, by transgression fell" (Acts 1:25).

"If thou kill, thou art become a transgressor of the law" (Jas. 2:11).

This emphasizes the positive aspect of sin. Various theological definitions of sin would include:

"Sin is lack of conformity to the moral law of God, either in act, disposition, or state" (A. H. Strong).

"Sin is a transgression of, or want of conformity to the divine law" (Charles Hodge).

"Sin may be defined ultimately as anything in the creature which does not express, or which is contrary to, the holy character of the Creator" (James Oliver Buswell, Jr.).

"Sin is a restless unwillingness on the part of the creature to abide in the sphere and limitation in which the Creator, guided by infinite wisdom, had placed him" (L. S. Chafer).

II. The Origin of Sin.
   A. The origin of sin into the universe. According to five key biblical passages of Scripture, a powerful angelic creature named Lucifer once (perhaps before the creation of the earth) led a wicked revolt against Jehovah God himself in an insane attempt to dethrone the rightful King, the Lord Jesus Christ. While this treachery proved unsuccessful, it did, nevertheless, introduce into the universe a new evil element hitherto unknown. This perverted principle was sin. Lucifer degenerated into the devil and became, therefore, the source and strength of sin. The five biblical passages previously mentioned are: Ezekiel 28:11-19; Isaiah 14:12-15; Luke 10:18; 1 John 3:8; Revelation 12:3, 4.
   B. The origin of sin into the world. While an angel introduced sin into the universe, it was a man who invited it into the world. In the Old Testament Moses describes the act historically, and in the New Testament Paul describes it theologically.
      "And the Lord God commanded the man saying, Of every tree of the garden thou mayest freely eat: But of the tree of the knowledge of good and evil thou shalt not eat of it: for in the day that thou eatest thereof thou shalt surely die" (Gen. 2:16, 17).
      "And when the woman saw that the tree was good for food and that it was pleasant to the eyes, and a tree to be desired to make one wise, she took of the fruit thereof, and did eat, and gave also unto her husband with her; and he did eat" (Gen. 3:6).

"Wherefore, as by one man sin entered into the world, and death by sin; and so death passed upon all men, for that all have sinned" (Rom. 5:12).

"For as in Adam all die" (1 Cor. 15:22).

Lewis Chafer writes:

"The essential fact, which cannot be restated too often, is that, in his temptation, Satan proposed to the first parents that they adopt the precise course he had himself espoused and pursued, which was to assume independence of God by departing from His will and purpose. Short-sighted ambition doubly blinded by unholy pride was willing to exchange the perfection of estate and destiny which the infinite love, wisdom, and power of the Creator has designed, for the wretched warfare of a self-centered life with its eternal agonizing experience in death. Evidently the whole truth was not displayed before these human beings. They were told that they would be like *Elohim* (Gen. 3:5), but only in one respect—their eyes would be open and they would know good and evil. they were, as created, experiencing the good; as fallen they would experience the evil. They had nothing to gain but rather everything to lose. The creature, whether angel or human, is by creation not only the property of the Creator by rights more vital than any other, but, as created, the creature is wholly dependent on the Creator. This relationship was blessed indeed before the fall and engendered no offense. By repudiating God through disobedience, Adam and Eve embarked upon a tempest-tossed, shoreless sea without compass, rudder, or helm. Such a course could only lead to ignominious failure and to the final judgments of the One whom they had rejected and abjured. The truth that sin is insanity is thus fully demonstrated.

In the last analysis, there are but two philosophies of life. One is to be conformed to the will of God which is the original divine arrangement, the other is to forsake the Creator and renounce His authority and purpose. In respect to the latter philosophy, it may be said that there is probably no pride so despicable as that which resents the authority of the Creator and which presumes to devise a program of life and achievement which is a substitute for the original plan and purpose of God. One philosophy is satanic, and this hideous fact is not changed even though the whole human race has embraced the satanic ideal. Appearing in the Garden, Satan brought no great volume elucidating his philosophy. Having led up to his ignoble proposition with such strategy as only Satan can command—he appealed to natural desires, he belittled sin, he attacked the character of God by intimating that God is untrustworthy and unloving—he proposed a likeness to *Elohim*. The translation 'Be as gods' is most misleading. The original text says, 'Be as *Elohim*.' The satanic philosophy is expressed perfectly in these brief words and it leads on, regardless of a moment of satisfaction of self and pride, to the lake of fire, and the same end is announced for all, angels or human beings, who adopt and pursue this course to its bitter end.

Satan's purpose did not consist merely in rejecting God; he was designing a vast cosmos world system in which he proposed to utilize and misappropriate the elements which belong to God's creation, which, in themselves, are good. Satan creates nothing. No step in the satanic cosmos project was more essential than that he should secure the allegiance of humanity. The issues at stake in the Garden of Eden were, in respect to Satan's career, such as would determine his realization of his whole undertaking. He must gain supremacy over man or fail completely. Little did Adam and Eve realize that, so far from attaining independence, they were becoming bondslaves to sin and Satan." (*Systematic Theology*, Vol. II, pp. 249, 250)

Berkhof suggests the following along this line: "The fall of man was occasioned by the temptation of the serpent, who sowed in man's mind the seeds of distrust and unbelief. Though it was undoubtedly the intention of the tempter to cause Adam, the head of the covenant, to fall, yet he addressed himself to Eve, probably because (a) she was not the head of the covenant and therefore would not have the same sense of responsibility; (b) she had not received the command of God directly but only indirectly, and would consequently be more susceptible to argumentation and doubt; and (c) she would undoubtedly prove to be the most effective agent in reaching the heart of Adam.

The course followed by the tempter is quite clear. In the first place he sows the seeds of doubt by calling the good intention of God in question and suggesting that His command was really an infringement of man's liberty and rights. When he notices from the response of Eve that the seed has taken root, he adds the seeds of unbelief and pride, denying that transgression will result in death, and clearly intimating that the command was prompted by the selfish purpose of keeping man in subjection. He asserts that by eating from the tree man would become like God. The high expectations thus engendered induced Eve to look intently at the tree, and the longer she looked, the better the fruit seemed to her. Finally, desire got the upper hand, and she ate and also gave unto her husband, and he ate." (*Systematic Theology*, p. 223)

III. The Nature of Sin.

A. Sin is not eternal. In the third century a Persian philosopher named Manes developed a school of thought called Manichaeism. This taught in essence that there are two dual eternal and impersonal principles which exist side by side in this universe. One is the principle of good, and the other the principle of evil.

B. Sin is not merely the absence of good. Some teach that as darkness is merely the absence of light, sin is simply the nonpresence of goodness. This is unscriptural, for sin is as real and positive to the soul of man as cancer and leprosy are to his physical body.

C. Sin is not simply the weakness or frailty of the human flesh. This false view would see sin as mere frailties of the flesh such as hunger, thirst, and weariness.

D. Sin has no standard of its own. Sin must derive its measurements from that which is positive or good. One may assume good apart from evil (which indeed was true historically), but evil cannot exist apart from good. By its very nature sin (and evil) must oppose and pervert something its opposite. Every sin is, in reality, a perversion of some good principle.

E. Sin and evil cannot really manifest themselves as such, but must (to some extent) be disguised as good.

For example, Hitler's stated reason for the systematic slaughter of untold Jews and East Europeans was for the "protection and good" of his own people, Germany.

A rebel feels free to rape and burn in order to "awaken the conscience" of a careless society unconcerned about the "plight" of his particular minority group.

A hijacker threatens and terrifies an entire passenger plane to "correct" the wrongs a certain government may have done in holding some "innocent" political prisoners.

Thus, even in a sin-cursed world, evil dare not expose itself in the raw, as the vicious and vile wolf it really is, but is forced to assume in some form the garb of a sheep.

F. Sin must not only disguise itself *as* the good, but must also actually connect itself *to* the good.

In itself it has no unifying power. Here sin may be likened to a virus, and the good to a healthy cell.

Much research is now going on concerning the nature and makeup of a virus. Some believe it is a bridge between the living and non-living. A virus contains DNA (deoxyribonucleic acid), that necessary genetic code of all living organisms, but it has no sugar or fat molecules, nor does it possess nucleotides or amino acids. It can play dead like a crystal for long duration. Upon being revived, it fastens to the wall of a living cell like a mosquito, driving a tubular shaft in and injecting its own DNA genes. These genes take over the total function of the cell, gathering free-floating nucleotides and produce copies of the original virus. The virus even secretes an enzyme which breaks down existing cell DNA and uses this for itself.

When several hundred virus DNAs have been assembled, the cell is milked dry. Then the original virus (outside the cell wall) secretes a final enzyme which dissolves the cell wall. An army of virus particles march forth, each seeking new cells to invade, leaving behind the empty broken husk of what had been, an hour before, a healthy, living cell. The operation is simple, ruthless, and effective.

Therefore (as we have already said) sin must disguise itself *as* and connect itself *to* the good. But not so with the good, which has no connection whatsoever with evil, and cannot disguise itself but must be manifested by its true nature.

G. A feature of evil not usually considered is that it must often strive against itself.

For example, a miser is at variance with a spendthrift. A proud stoic will view with contempt a glutton. A promiscuous heterosexual is sickened at the sexual perversions of a homosexual.

But this is not so with the good, where all its elements and attributes complement and do not contradict each other. Love, grace, truth, wisdom, righteousness, and justice are all the closest of friends. Thus, good has only one enemy, the evil, but any given evil has two enemies, the good and another conflicting evil. A classic example of this was seen during World War II when the two most wicked men on earth hated each other with a passion seldom seen. These two bitter enemies were Adolf Hitler and Joseph Stalin.

H. Even though we have used sin and evil interchangeably thus far, the terms are sometimes to be distinguished from each other.

For example, sin is not always the exact same thing as evil. We often refer to cyclones, floods, fires, earthquakes, and such as evil, and well they may be. But these cannot be called sin. This fact should be understood, as many Christians have been troubled and confused over the words of God in Isaiah 45:7, where we read:

"I form the light, and create darkness: I make peace and create evil. I the Lord do all these things."

Here the Hebrew word *ra* is used, which can also be translated "calamity." Thus, while we read of God creating evil, the Scriptures assure us he does not create sin. (See 2 Cor. 5:21; Titus 1:2; Heb. 4:15; 6:18; Jas. 1:13; 1 Pet. 2:22; 1 Jn. 3:5.)

IV. The Universality of Sin. The indisputable fact that all men are sinners is attested to by the following five sources:

A. The testimony of history. It has been estimated that some forty billion human beings have lived (or are living) upon this earth since Adam. It would not be unreasonable to suggest that perhaps one third of these forty billion people lost their lives at the hand of another human being. Hundreds of millions of living flesh-and-blood creatures have been stabbed, stoned, strangled, shot, gassed, bombed, burned, buried alive, hung, and drowned by other living flesh-and-blood creatures.

B. The testimony of conscience. How often has man's built-in "sin gauge" smote him to despair and even to suicide over his sinful actions. This club of conscience strikes all men, regardless of their brains, brawn, bloodstream, or banking powers. Thus, while the voice of conscience can be defiled, it cannot be denied.

C. The testimony of religions. Louis Berkhof writes the following:

"The history of religions and of philosophy testify to it. The history of religions testifies to the universality of sin. The question of Job, 'How shall a man be just with God?' is a question that was asked not merely in the realm of special revelation, but also outside of it in the Gentile world. The heathen religions testify to a universal consciousness of sin and of the need of reconciliation with a Supreme Being. There is a general feeling that the gods are offended and must be propitiated in some way. There is a universal voice of conscience, testifying to the fact that man falls short of the ideal and stands condemned in the sight of some higher Power. Altars reeking with the blood of sacrifices, often the sacrifices of dear children, repeated confessions of wrong-doing, and prayers for deliverance from evil— all point to the consciousness of sin. Missionaries find this wherever they go. The history of philosophy is indicative of the same fact. Early Greek philosophers were already wrestling with the problem of moral evil, and since their day no philosopher of name was able to ignore it. They were all constrained to admit the universality of it, and that in spite of the fact they were not able to explain the phenomenon. There was, it is true, a superficial optimism in the eighteenth century, which dreamt of the inherent goodness of man, but in its stupidity flew in the face of the facts and was sharply rebuked by Kant. Many liberal theologians were induced to believe and to preach this inherent goodness of man as gospel truth, but today many of them qualify it as one of the most pernicious errors of the past. Surely the facts of life do not warrant such optimism." (*Systematic Theology*, pp. 239, 240)

D. The testimony of the Scriptures.
   1. General statements concerning the sinfulness of man.
      "For there is no man that sinneth not" (1 Ki. 8:46).
      "Who can say, I have made my heart clean, I am pure from my sin?" (Prov. 20:9).
      "The heart is deceitful above all things, and desperately wicked" (Jer. 17:9).
      "For there is not a just man upon earth, that doeth good and sinneth not" (Eccl. 7:20).
      "All we like sheep have gone astray" (Isa. 53:6).
      "But we are all as an unclean thing, and all our righteousnesses are as filthy rags; and we all do fade as a leaf, and our iniquities like the wind, have taken us away" (Isa. 64:6).
      "For all have sinned and come short of the glory of God" (Rom. 3:23).
      "But the scripture hath concluded all under sin" (Gal. 3:22).
      "For in many things we offend all" (Jas. 3:2).
      "If we say that we have no sin, we deceive ourselves and the truth is not in us" (1 Jn. 1:8).
      "If we say that we have not sinned, we make him a liar, and his word is not in us" (1 Jn. 1:10).
   2. Personal statements concerning the sinfulness of man.
      On at least eight separate occasions in the Bible an individual is forced to utter those three tragic but true words, "I have sinned."
      a. Pharaoh (Ex. 9:27; 10:16)
      b. Balaam (Num. 22:34)
      c. Achan (Josh. 7:20)
      d. Saul (1 Sam. 26:21)
      e. David (2 Sam. 12:13; 24:10)
      f. Job (7:20; see 27:6; 40:3, 4; 42:6)
      g. the prodigal son (Lk. 15:21)
      h. Judas (Mt. 27:4)
      A double tragedy is seen here, for out of these eight confessions, it would seem only three really were sincere and experienced the forgiveness of a gracious God.
   E. The testimony of our children. The good must be taught to our children. The bad they know already. Sharing is not natural, but selfishness is.
V. The Exceeding Sinfulness of Sin. There are two unfathomable areas which even the most spiritual believer can but penetrate slightly. One is the lofty heights of the Creator's holiness. The other is the fearful depths of the creature's sinfulness. Scripture offers three major proofs and illustrations of the exceeding sinfulness of sin.
   A. The angelic proof. Consider a kindly and highly experienced craftsman creating a magnificent figure from out of nothing. Upon its creation this figure is given life, covered with dazzling precious gems, and equipped with a beautiful musical system. The craftsman then places his newly created being over all the universe, to rule (under him) and to enjoy. Millions of other created beings look to this creature for guidance. His only responsibility is to faithfully serve his wise and wonderful Creator. But one dark day, for absolutely no reason whatsoever, this privileged being who had received so much from the craftsman, viciously lashes out against his benevolent benefactor and leads a wicked rebellion to drive him from the very universe he originally created.
   What base and perverted ingratitude all this would display. And yet, such was the case when Lucifer rebelled against his mighty Creator, Jehovah God. The depths and depravity of this sin, in light of its background, can never be comprehended by any creature, angelic or human (Isa. 14:12–15; Ezek. 28:11–19).
   B. The human proof. L. S. Chafer writes:
      "One individual, the first of the human creation, committed one sin and that sin being apparently so innocuous men are prone to ridicule the thought that God would notice it at all; yet that one sin is, according to divine estimation, sufficiently evil to cause the degeneracy and depravity of the unfallen person who committed the sin, and to cause uncounted millions of his posterity to suffer in the flesh and die, and the vast majority of them to spend eternity in the realms of woe." (*Systematic Theology*, Vol. II, p. 252)

C. The divine proof.

"The Son of God suffered to an infinite degree and died on the cross because of sin. There was no other way whereby redemption could be secured. However, had there never been but one sin committed in this world, the same depths of suffering and death by the Son of God would have been required as a righteous ground for divine forgiveness of that one sin and the justification of that sinner." (*Ibid.*, p. 252)

VI. The Consequences of Sin.

A. Upon Lucifer. As Lucifer was the first sinner, he naturally experienced the first terrible results of sin.

1. Immediate consequences: Lucifer lost his coveted position as heaven's anointed cherub (Ezek. 28:14) and became earth's depraved dragon (Rev. 12:7).
2. Future consequences: The devil will someday be forever cast into the lake of fire, a place God himself prepared for the universe's first sinner (Mt. 25:41; Rev. 20:10).

B. Upon man. When Adam opened the door for sin, two vicious criminals also rushed in and immediately began tormenting the human race. The names of these two terrible gangsters are physical death and spiritual death. In the Bible the theological meaning for death is "separation."

1. Physical death: God created Adam with the possibilities of living forever (Gen. 2:9) but Adam sinned (Gen. 3:19) and therefore had to later experience physical death, that is, the separation of his body and soul (Gen. 5:5; Ps. 90:10; Jn. 19:30).
2. Spiritual death: Because of sin, all unsaved people will someday be forever separated from God in the lake of fire. This is referred to as the second death (Mt. 7:23; 25:41; Rev. 2:11; 20:6, 14; 21:8). It should be furthermore stated that, although the second death as mentioned above is still future for the sinner, the Bible nevertheless teaches that all unsaved people right now are considered by God to be dead in trespasses and sins and separated even at this present time from his fellowship (Eph. 2:1-12). Both physical and spiritual death seem to be in the mind of God when he warned Adam about the consequences of sin. The Hebrew of Genesis 2:17 may be translated, "For in the day that thou eatest thereof, in dying thou shalt surely die."

   In summary it may be said then that sin:
   a. Dulls man's ears (Acts 28:27).
   b. Darkens his eyes (Eph. 4:18).
   c. Diverts his feet (Isa. 53:6).
   d. Defiles his tongue (Rom. 3:13, 14).
   e. Deceives his heart (Jer. 17:9).
   f. Devours his intellect (1 Cor. 2:14).
   g. Dooms his soul (Ezek. 18:4).

C. Upon nature. After sin, man's paradise became a wilderness. The roses contained thorns and the docile tiger suddenly became a hungry meat-eater. This will continue to be the case until the curse is lifted during the millennium. In the New Testament Paul writes about the consequences of sin upon nature:

"For all creation is waiting patiently and hopefully for that future day when God will resurrect His children. For on that day, thorns and thistles, sin, death, and decay—the things that overcame the world against its will at God's command—will all disappear, and the world around us will share in the glorious freedom from sin which God's children enjoy. For we know that even the things of nature, like animals and plants, suffer in sickness and death as they await this great event" (Rom. 8:19-22, *The Living Bible*).

D. Upon the holy angels. Man's sin apparently became an object lesson for angels as their Creator allowed them to enter into his blessed work of redeeming mankind. The following passages seem to bear this out:

"For we are made a spectacle unto . . . angels" (1 Cor. 4:9).

"I charge thee before God, and the Lord Jesus Christ, and the elect angels" (1 Tim. 5:21).

"And it [the Law] was ordained by angels" (Gal. 3:19).

"Which things [matters concerning salvation] the angels desire to look into" (1 Pet. 1:12).

"Are they [angels] not all ministering spirits, sent forth to minister for them who shall be heirs of salvation?" (Heb. 1:14).

E. Upon God himself. What effect did man's sin have upon God? It meant that he could no longer rest as he had done when creation was completed (Gen. 2:2). It meant that he began his second (and greatest) work, that of redemption. To this very day, God continues to work in matters of redemption.

"But Jesus answered them, My Father worketh hitherto, and I work" (Jn. 5:17).

"I must work the works of him that sent me" (Jn. 9:4).

"He which hath begun a good work in you will perform it until the day of Jesus Christ" (Phil. 1:6).

VII. The Imputation of Sin. Were the effects of Adam's fall merely confined to himself, or do they continue somehow to make themselves known in the lives of twentieth-century men?

A. The liberal position. The entire story is simply a Hebrew legend.

B. The Pelagian position. Pelagius was a British monk who taught that Adam's sin affected only himself, for God imputes to men only those sins which they personally and consciously perform. Pelagius said the only effect of Adam's sin on posterity was that of a bad example. The doctrine of Pelagianism was condemned by the Council of Carthage in A.D. 418.

C. The Arminian position. Arminius (1560-1609) was a professor who lived and taught in Holland. This theory teaches that, while Adam's sin definitely weakened the will of his posterity to remain sinless, it did not, however, destroy the possibility.

D. The Augustinian position. Augustine was one of the greatest of the early church fathers. He taught that, because of the unity of the human race in Adam, his sin therefore is imputed to his posterity. Thus, corrupted nature begets corrupted nature. This final view is the only position which is amply supported by the Scriptures.

"Wherefore, as by one man sin entered into the world, and death by sin; and so death passed upon all men, for that all have sinned" (Rom. 5:12).

"Therefore, as by the offense of one judgment came upon all men to condemnation; even so by the righteousness of one the free gift came upon all men unto justification of life" (Rom. 5:18).

At this point it will be helpful to read the summaries offered by two well-known theologians.

"The origin of sin in the human race. With respect to the origin of sin in the history of mankind, the Bible teaches that it began with the transgression of Adam in paradise, and therefore with a perfectly voluntary act on the part of man. The tempter came from the spirit world with the suggestion that man, by placing himself in opposition to God, might become like God. Adam yielded to the temptation and committed the first sin by eating of the forbidden fruit. But the matter did not stop there, for by that first sin Adam became the bond-servant of sin. That sin carried permanent pollution with it, and a pollution which, because of the solidarity of the human race, would affect not only Adam but all his descendants as well. As a result of the fall the father of the race could only pass on a depraved human nature to his offspring. From that unholy source sin flows on as an impure stream to all the generations of men, polluting everyone and everything with which it comes in contact. It is exactly this state of things that made the question of Job so pertinent, 'Who can bring a clean thing out of an unclean? not one.' (Job 14:14). But even this is not all. Adam sinned not only as the father of the human race, but also as the representative head of all his descendants; and therefore the guilt of his sin is placed to their account, so that they are all liable to the punishment of death. It is primarily in that sense that Adam's sin is the sin of all. That is what Paul teaches us in Romans 5:12: 'Through one man sin entered into the world, and death through sin; and so death passed unto all men, for that all sinned.' The last words can only mean that they all sinned in Adam, and sinned in such a way as to make them all liable to the punishment of death. It is not sin considered merely as pollution, but sin as guilt that carries punishment with it. God adjudges all men to be guilty sinners in Adam, just as He adjudges all believers to be righteous in Jesus Christ. That is what Paul means, when he says: 'So then as through one act of righteousness the free gift came unto all men to justification of life. For as through the one man's disobedience the

many were made sinners, even so through the obedience of the one shall the many be made righteous' (Rom. 5:18, 19)." (L. Berkhof, *Systematic Theology*, pp. 221, 222)

"As a matter of fact the representative principle runs through the entire range of human life. Representative action is a sociological fact everywhere and is recognized in all orderly legal systems. For example, it may properly be said, I signed the Declaration of Independence as of the Fourth of July, 1776. I was not there, but my representatives acted as my representatives, and I am implicated in all the consequences of their action. Further, I declared war and entered World War II with the whole nation as of December 7, 1941. I was not present when the action was taken. I was only listening over the radio. I might have been an unborn child. Nevertheless, my representatives acted for me and as representing me, therefore it was my action, and I am implicated and involved in all the consequences of that action.

Just so, I became a wicked, guilty sinner in the Garden of Eden. I turned my back upon fellowship with my holy God. I deliberately corrupted the character of godly holiness which God imparted to His creation. I willfully began to spread corruption through the creation over which God had intended me to rule. I was not there. No, but my representative was there, and he acted as such in my place and I was driven out from the garden and excluded from the the tree of life." (J. Oliver Buswell, *A Systematic Theology of the Christian Religion*, p. 295)

VIII. The Kinds of Sin. Are some sins worse than other sins? While it is true that the Bible teaches in a general sense that to be guilty of one is to be guilty of all sins (Jas. 2:10), it also indicates there are sins of greater degree and sins of lesser degree. We note the following words of Jesus:

"And that servant which knew his lord's will, and prepared not himself, neither did according to his will, shall be beaten with many stripes. But he that knew not, and did commit things worthy of stripes, shall be beaten with few stripes. For unto whomsoever much is given, of him shall be much required: and to whom men have committed much, of him they will ask the more" (Lk. 12:47, 48).

Let us consider some of the various kinds of sins as indicated in the Word of God:

A. Sins of ignorance.

"Then said Jesus, Father, forgive them; for they know not what they do" (Lk. 23:34).

"Jesus answered [Pilate] . . . he that delivered me unto thee [the wicked Jew] hath the greater sin" (Jn. 19:11).

"For as many as have sinned without law shall also perish without law: and as many as have sinned in the law shall be judged by the law" (Rom. 2:12).

"And I thank Christ Jesus our Lord, who hath enabled me, for that he counted me faithful, putting me into the ministry; who was before a blasphemer, and a persecutor, and injurious; but I obtained mercy because I did it ignorantly in unbelief" (1 Tim. 1:12, 13).

B. Sins of infirmity.

"Who can understand his errors? Cleanse thou me from secret faults" (Ps. 19:12).

"He hath not dealt with us after our sins; nor rewarded us according to our iniquities. . . . For he knoweth our frame; he remembereth that we are dust" (Ps. 103:10, 14).

"Likewise the Spirit also helpeth our infirmities: for we know not what we should pray for as we ought: but the Spirit itself maketh intercession for us with groanings which cannot be uttered" (Rom. 8:26).

"For whatsoever is not of faith is sin" (Rom. 14:23).

"We then that are strong ought to bear the infirmities of the weak . . ." (Rom. 15:1).

"Watch and pray, that ye enter not into temptation: the spirit indeed is willing, but the flesh is weak" (Mt. 26:41).

C. Sins of carelessness.

"I said, I will take heed to my ways, that I sin not with my tongue" (Ps. 39:1).

"Take heed to yourselves, that your hearts be not deceived" (Deut. 11:16).

"But take heed lest by any means this liberty of yours become a stumblingblock to them that are weak" (1 Cor. 8:9).

"Wherefore let him that thinketh he standeth take heed lest he fall" (1 Cor. 10:12).

"Therefore we ought to give the more earnest heed to the things which we have heard, lest at any time we should let them slip" (Heb. 2:1).

D. Sins of presumption.

"Keep back thy servant also from presumptuous sins" (Ps. 19:13).

"Them that walk after the flesh in the lust of uncleanness, and despise government. Presumptuous are they, self-willed" (2 Pet. 2:10).

"Who, knowing the judgment of God, that they which commit such things are worthy of death, not only do the same, but have pleasure in them that do them" (Rom. 1:32).

E. The unpardonable sin.

"Wherefore I say unto you, all manner of sin and blasphemy shall be forgiven unto men: but the blasphemy against the Holy Ghost shall not be forgiven unto men. And whosoever speaketh a word against the Son of man, it shall be forgiven him: but whosoever speaketh against the Holy Ghost, it shall not be forgiven him, neither in this world, neither in the world to come" (Mt. 12:31, 32).

Much ink has been spilled over these words. What is this unforgivable and unpardonable sin? Who can commit it? Can it be done today? Two main views have been offered to explain this sin.

1. That the sin can be committed by any unbeliever today and occurs when a sinner rejects the convicting voice of the Holy Spirit once too often. At this point, the Holy Spirit forever ceases to deal with the sinner and he is hopelessly condemned, with no chance of salvation, however he may later desire it. Genesis 6:3 is sometimes offered in support of this theory. However, an examination of the passage shows this meaning is taken completely out of its context. In reality there is no scriptural basis for the first theory.

2. That the sin was dispensational in nature, that it was the sin of ascribing to Satan the earthly miracles peformed by our Savior and therefore cannot be committed today. This theory is generally held by the majority of Bible students and the passage context would seem to support its accuracy. (See Mt. 12:22–24.)

F. The sin unto death.

"For this cause many are weak and sickly among you, and many sleep" (1 Cor. 11:30).

"There is a sin unto death" (1 Jn. 5:16).

As in the case of the unpardonable sin, the sin unto death has been the object of some controversy. The commonly accepted view is that the sin can only be committed by a child of God, and happens when the believer lives such a wretched life that the Father finally reaches down and takes him home to heaven earlier than he normally would have. In other words, just as there is a premature birth, there is a premature death. Evidence of this theory is thought by some to be seen in Acts 5:1-11; 1 Corinthians 5:1-5 (here, though, the Corinthian believer apparently repented—see 2 Cor. 2:6-11). Some who hold this theory use it as a theological basis for interpreting such difficult passages as Hebrews 6:4-10; 10:26-30.

IX. The Metaphors of Sin.

A. Sin is *poisonous,* like a viper (Ps. 140:3; Mt. 23:33).

B. Sin is *stubborn,* like a mule (Job 11:12).

C. Sin is *cruel,* like a bear (Dan. 7:5).

D. Sin is *destructive,* like a canker worm (Joel 2:25).

E. Sin is *unclean,* like a wild dog (Prov. 26:11).

F. Sin is *cunning,* like a fox (Lk. 13:32).

G. Sin is *fierce,* like a wolf (Jn. 10:12).

H. Sin *devours,* like a lion (Ps. 22:13; Dan. 7:4).

I. Sin is *filthy,* like a swine (2 Pet. 2:22).

X. The Christian's Sin. One of the truly great and far-reaching blessings of salvation is God's dealings with the subject of our sin. The repenting sinner is immediately and eternally saved from the *penalty* of sin (in the past), provided with victory over the *power* of sin (in the present), and guaranteed final removal from the *presence* of sin (in the future). But what happens when the Christian fails to use the available power and falls into sin? How does God view sin in the life of his child? Is it indeed possible (as some have claimed) to remain sinless from the cross to the crown?

A. The fact of sin. Charles Ryrie writes:

"Being a Christian does not free one from sinning. Of course there are some who teach eradication of the sin nature in this life, but the picture and doctrine of the New Testament seem to teach otherwise. In fact, John mentions three false claims which people in his day made in this regard in 1 John 1:8-10.

1. Verse 8 speaks of denying the *presence* of the principle of sin.

2. Verse 9 of the denial of *particular* sins.

3. Verse 10 of the denial of *personally* sinning." (*A Survey of Bible Doctrine*, p. 112)

B. The effect of sin. The child of God immediately loses the following six things upon sinning. A seventh may be lost.

  1. The loss of light (1 Jn. 1:6).

  2. The loss of joy (Ps. 51:12; Jn. 15:11; Gal. 5:22; 1 Jn. 1:4).

  3. The loss of peace (1 Jn. 3:4–10).

  4. The loss of love (1 Jn. 2:5, 15–17; 4:12).

  5. The loss of fellowship (1 Jn. 1:3, 6, 7).

  6. The loss of confidence (1 Jn. 3:19–22).

  7. The possible loss of health and even physical life (1 Cor. 5:17; 11:30).

C. The preventives against sin.

  1. The Word of God (Ps. 119:11; Jn. 15:7; 17:17; 2 Tim. 3:16, 17). It has been often observed that the Bible will keep one from sinning, or sin will keep one from the Bible.

  2. The intercession of the Son of God (Lk. 22:32; Jn. 17:15; Rom. 8:34; Heb. 7:23–25).

  3. The ministry of the Spirit of God (Zech. 4:6; Jn. 7:37–39).

D. The remedy for sin. Dr. L. S. Chafer writes:

"The responsibility resting upon the unregenerate man who would avail himself of the forgiveness of *all* trespasses and be saved is expressed in the one all-inclusive word—*believe,* while the responsibility resting upon the regenerate man who would be forgiven and restored to right relations with God is expressed in the one word—*confess.* These two words are each specifically adapted to the situation, relationships, and circumstances with which they are associated. Untold confusion follows when unregenerate men are told to confess as a condition of forgiveness and salvation, which confusion is equalled when a regenerate man is told to believe as a condition of securing a renewal of right relations to God. Hymnology is sometimes misleading at this point. By such hymns, words are put into the lips of the unsaved which encourage them to conceive of themselves as wanderers who are returning to God. As a matter of fact, the unregenerate man has never before been in any favorable relation to God. When, as a part of his salvation, he is forgiven, it is unto a hitherto unexperienced *union* with God which abides forever; but when the Christian is forgiven it is unto the restoration of *communion* with God which may be broken again all too soon. The saints of all the ages have returned to the blessings of their covenant relation to God by the confession of their sin. This, however, is far removed from those terms upon which they entered the covenant at the beginning. The loss of the blessing within the covenant is different, indeed, from the loss of the covenant relation itself. In the case of a believer related to God by the New Covenant made in His blood, restoration to communion, as always, is by confession of sin to God. We read in 1 John 1:9, 'If we confess our sins, he is faithful and just to forgive us our sins, and to

cleanse us from all unrighteousness.' Similarly, in 1 Corinthians 11:31, 32 it is stated that 'if we would judge ourselves, we should not be judged. But when we are judged, we are chastened of the Lord, that we should not be condemned with the world.' Since confession and self-judgment refer to the same action on the part of the believer, these passages emphasize the same important truth. Confession and self-judgment are the outward expression of heart-repentance; and repentance, which is a change of mind or purpose, brings the sin-burdened Christian back into agreement with God. While practicing sin, he was opposed to the will and character of God; by repentance, expressed to God in the confession of sin and self-judgment, he returns to agreement with God. 'Two cannot walk together, except they be agreed,' nor can the Christian have fellowship with God who is Light and at the same time be walking in darkness (1 Jn. 1:6). To walk in the light is not to become the light, which would mean attainment to infinite holiness. God alone is Light. Nor does walking in the light mean that one never does wrong. It is rather that when the searchlight, which God is, penetrates the heart and life and discloses that which is contrary to His will, the wrong thus disclosed is by a true heart-repentance at once confessed and judged before God. Assurance is given to the believer that when thus adjusted to the light (which is 'walking in the light'), the sin is forgiven and its pollution cleansed by the blood of Christ. Both 1 John 1:8 and 10 are in the nature of parenthesis. The word of assurance presented in 1:7 is continued in 1:9 which states that, 'If we confess our sins (which is adjustment to God who is the Light), he is faithful and just to forgive us our sins, and to cleanse us from all unrighteousness.' Confession of sin, it should be observed, is first and always to God and is to be extended to others only as they have been directly injured by the sin. So, likewise, this divine forgiveness and cleansing are not said to be acts of divine mercy and kindness, being wrought rather on the basis of absolute righteousness which is made possible through the fact that the penalty which the sin merits has fallen upon the Substitute—God's provided Lamb. Since the Substitute has endured the penalty, God is seen to be just rather than merciful when He justifies the unsaved who do no more than to 'believe in Jesus' (Rom. 3:26), and just rather than merciful when He forgives the Christian who has sinned, on no other condition than that he 'confess' his sin (1 Jn. 1:9). In forgiving the Christian who confesses his sin, God is 'faithful' to His eternal character and purpose and is 'just' in so doing because of the penalty which Christ has endured. The basis for this provision whereby the Christian may be forgiven and cleansed in the faithfulness and justice of God is found in the declaration which consummates this context (1 Jn. 2:2), where it is said that 'he is the propitiation for our sins.' Since this context is concerned only with the sins of Christians, the great aspect of propitiation for a lost world is mentioned here only incidentally. Too much emphasis cannot be placed on the fact that Christ is the propitiation for our sins. By His death He has rendered God propitious and free to forgive and cleanse the Christian who confesses his sin.

It is evident that the divine forgiveness of the believer is household in its character. It contemplates, not the once-for-all forgiveness which is a part of salvation (Col. 2:13), but the forgiveness of the one who already and permanently is a member of the household and family of God. Vital union with God, which is secured by Christ for the believer, has not been and cannot be broken (Rom. 8:1, RV). This renewal is unto fellowship and communion with God. At no point in Christian doctrine is the specific and unique character of the present grace-relationship to God more clearly seen than in household forgiveness." (*Systematic Theology*, Vol. II, pp. 336-338)

XI. The Reasons for Sin. We have already observed the biblical teachings that God is nowhere pictured as the Author of sin. But why did he allow it? Could he not have prevented it? The answer is of course that he could have, but chose not to. Why? Several suggestions have been offered along this line.

A. God created both angels and men as intelligent creatures possessing moral natures which could determine and choose between right and wrong. Had God stopped Lucifer and Adam one second before their sin, he would, in effect, have violated their moral natures and reduced them to mere walking robots.

B. God allowed man to sin so that he might display his grace. Thus, prior to Adam, God was already exhibiting his omnipresence (in being everywhere at once), his omnipotence (in setting the galaxies into motion), and his omniscience (in creating the angels). But there was one attribute, one characteristic perhaps closer to his heart than any other, and that was his grace. Where there is no sin there is no need of grace.

As Paul would later write: "But where sin abounded, grace did much more abound" (Rom. 5:20). Why then did God allow Adam to sin? No man knows. But it does not seem unreasonable to believe that part of the answer lies in the above suggestion, that is for God to display his marvelous grace. Again, in the words of Paul:

"Even when we were dead in sins, [He] hath quickened us together with Christ [by grace are ye saved:] . . . that in the ages to come he might shew the exceeding riches of his grace in his kindness toward us through Jesus Christ" (Eph. 2:5, 7).

XII. The Ultimate and Final Victory over Sin. In four key passages, New Testament writers Paul, Peter, and John describe for us this thrilling victory. Note:

"For he must reign, till he hath put all enemies under his feet. The last enemy that shall be destroyed is death. For he hath put all things under his feet. But when he saith all things are put under him it is manifest that he is excepted, which did put all things under him. And when all things shall be subdued unto him, then shall the Son also himself be subject unto him that put all things under him, that God may be all in all" (1 Cor. 15:25-28).

(See also Heb. 12:22-24; 2 Pet. 3:7-13; Rev. 20:11-15.)

THE DOCTRINE OF SALVATION

THE DOCTRINE OF SALVATION

It has been observed that among the many thousands of English words, the three most *difficult* are "I was wrong," and the two most *delightful* are "check enclosed." Be that as it may, it can be safely concluded that the most *dynamic* single word in our language is the word *salvation*.

I. The Meaning of Salvation. Salvation means to effect successfully the full delivery of someone or something from impending danger. The very word carries with it a twofold implication:
   A. That someone or something needs to be saved.
      1. Only a sick person needs a doctor. Man is desperately ill. (See Isa.1:6; Mt. 9:12.)
      2. Only an accused person needs a lawyer. Man stands condemned in God's court of law (Rom. 3:10-19).
      3. Only a drowning person needs a lifeguard. Man finds himself flooded by the waters of sin (Ps. 69:1, 2).
      4. In his excellent book, *Salvation Is Forever*, Robert Gromacki lists the following reasons why men are lost.
         a. They are lost because of their rejection of biblical revelation (Ps. 19:1; Acts 14:17; Rom. 1:19, 20).
         b. They are lost because of disobeying their own conscience (Rom. 2:14-16).
         c. They are lost because of their relationship to the world (Eph. 2:2; Jas. 4:4; 1 Jn. 2:15-17).
         d. They are lost because of their relationship to Satan (Mt. 4:8, 9; Jn. 8:42-44; 12:31; 2 Cor. 4:4; Col. 1:13; 1 Jn. 3:10; 5:19).
         e. They are lost because of their relationship to sin (Gen. 2:17; 8:21; Job 14:4; Eccl. 7:20; Jer. 17:19; Mk. 7:20-23; Rom. 5:12; 7:14; Eph. 4:18).

            A sinner may not be as *bad* as he can be (like an Adolf Hitler) but he is nevertheless as *bad off* as he can be. Man is both dead (spiritually) and dying (physically). (See Gen. 2:17.) This can be likened to a condemned criminal in death row awaiting the electric chair and suffering from terminal cancer.
         f. They are lost because of their relationship to God (Jn. 3:36; Eph. 2:12; 1 Jn. 5:12; Jude 1:19).
   B. That someone is able and willing to save. Such a Savior must fulfill both requirements.
      1. He must be able to save. It is possible for a person to have the desire but not the ability to save another individual. Many a physician has stood in utter frustration beside the bed of his dying patient, wanting so much to give aid, but totally helpless to do so.
      2. He must be willing to save. It is possible for a person to have the ability but not the desire to save another individual. In 1978 a man in the United States, in desperate need of a rare blood transfusion, died. The tragedy of the story was that he suffered and died needlessly, for one of his own relatives possessed that rare type of blood and could have easily donated some, but stubbornly refused. Perhaps the greatest ability after all is *availability*.

II. The Source of Salvation. Jesus Christ is the source of salvation. He meets both requirements.
      1. He is able to save.

         "For in that he himself hath suffered being tempted, he is able to help them that are tempted" (Heb. 2:18).

         "Now unto him who is able to do exceeding abundantly above all that we ask or think, according to the power that worketh in us" (Eph. 3:20).

         "For I know whom I have believed and am persuaded that he is able to keep that which I have committed unto him against that day" (2 Tim. 1:12).

         "Wherefore, he is able also to save them to the uttermost that come unto God by him, seeing he ever liveth to make intercession for them" (Heb. 7:25).

         "Now unto him that is able to keep you from falling, and to present you faultless before the presence of his glory with exceeding joy" (Jude 24).
      2. He is willing to save.

         "And behold, there came a leper and worshipped him, saying, Lord, if thou wilt, thou canst make me clean. And Jesus put forth his hand, and touched him, saying, I will; be thou clean. And immediately his leprosy was cleansed" (Mt. 8:2, 3).

         "God our Saviour, who will have all men to be saved, and to come unto the knowledge of the truth" (1 Tim. 2:3, 4).

         "The Lord is not slack concerning his promise . . . but is longsuffering to usward, not willing that any should perish, but that all should come to repentance" (2 Pet. 3:9).

III. The False Hopes of Salvation.

"There is a way which seemeth right unto a man, but the end thereof are the ways of death" (Prov. 14:12).

A. Education. On two separate occasions Paul warns Timothy about the folly of depending on education (1 Tim. 6:20; 2 Tim. 3:7).

B. Church membership.

C. Good works (Eph. 2:8, 9).

D. Baptism (1 Cor. 1:17).

E. Proper environment.

F. Keeping the law (Gal. 2:16).

G. Confirmation. Religious confirmation is as far removed from redemption's transformation as a lump of coal from a glittering diamond.

H. Living by the Golden Rule.

I. Sincerity.

J. Lodge membership.

K. Tithing.

L. Secular organizations (the Peace Corps, United Nations, etc.; see Ps. 2; Rev. 18). During the coming great tribulation the combined secular organizations of this world will turn against the Father and attempt to dethrone his Son, only to be themselves utterly destroyed by the brightness of his coming.

M. Religious organizations (the World Council of Churches, etc.; see Rev. 17). The unified religious movement will likewise suffer destruction during the tribulation.

IV. The Threefold Method of Salvation. While God has indeed dealt with his creatures under different dispensations (the pre-law stages, the age of the law, the post-law stage, etc.), he *saves* them all by the identical threefold method:

A. Salvation is always by blood (Heb. 9:22). Furthermore, this blood must be innocent, shed, and applied.

B. Salvation is always through a person (Jonah 2:9; Acts 4:12; 1 Thess. 5:9; Heb. 5:9).

C. Salvation is always by grace (Eph. 2:8, 9; Titus 2:11).

1. This grace is preceded by the sinner's faith (Rom. 5:1; Heb. 11:6).

2. This grace is followed by the Savior's peace (Rom. 1:7; 1 Cor.1:3; Gal. 1:3).

V. The Work of the Trinity in Salvation. Stephen D. Swihart offers the following helpful information: "The relationship of the Father to the Son, and the Son to the Holy Spirit in the plan of salvation is unique. A careful study of the following outline will make this association plain."

A. The Father's work: Design the plan in eternity.

1. Foreknow (Rom. 8:29; 11:2; 1 Pet. 1:2, 20).

2. Predestinate (Acts 4:28; Rom. 8:29, 30; 1 Cor. 2:7; Eph. 1:5, 11).

3. Choose/elect (Mt. 20:16; 22:14; 24:22, 24, 31; Mk. 13:20, 22, 27; Lk. 18:7; Acts 9:15; 22:14; 26:16; Rom. 8:33; 9:11; 11:5, 7, 28; 16:13; Eph. 1:4; Col. 3:12; 1 Thess. 1:4; 2 Thess. 2:13; 2 Tim. 2:10; 1 Pet. 1:2; 2:4, 6, 9; 2 Pet. 1:10; Rev. 17:14).

4. Call (Mt. 20:16; 22:14; Acts 2:39; Rom. 1:6, 7; 8:29, 30; 9:7, 11, 24; 11:29; 1 Cor. 1:2, 9, 24, 26; Gal. 1:6, 15; 5:8, 13; Eph. 1:18; 4:1, 4; Phil. 3:14; Col. 3:15; 1 Thess. 2:12; 5:24; 2 Thess.

1:11; 2:14; 1 Tim. 6:12; 2 Tim. 1:9; Heb. 3:1; 9:15; 11:18; 1 Pet. 1:15; 2:9, 21; 3:1; 5:10; 2 Pet. 1:3, 10; Jude 1; Rev. 17:14).

B. The Son's work: Discharge the plan in fullness of time.

1. God's eternal covenant with Christ: real.

a. Matthew 26:54; Mark 14:21; Luke 22:22 with Luke 24:25-27, 46; Acts 2:23; 4:25-28; 13:27, 28; 26:22, 23; 1 Corinthians 15:3, 4; 1 Peter 1:11, 20.

b. 2 Corinthians 1:20; Galatians 3:17; cf. Luke 1:68-79; Hebrews 11:13, 17-19, 39, 40.

c. Romans 8:28-30; Ephesians 3:11; cf. Ephesians 1:3-14; 2 Timothy 1:9.

d. Philippians 2:6-8; Hebrews 10:5-9; cf. John 4:34; 5:30; 6:38; 17:14; 18:11.

e. Isaiah 42:6; cf. Malachi 3:1.

f. Hebrews 7:22; cf. Hebrews 9:15, 16; 12:24; 13:20.

2. God's eternal covenant with Christ: revealed.

a. That Christ should be the second federal Head of the human race (1 Cor. 15:45-47).

b. That Christ would partake of flesh and bones (Heb. 10:5-9).

c. That Christ would function in a Son and Servant relationship to God (Isa. 43:10; 49:3-6; 52:13; Mt. 12:8-20; Jn. 10:17; 12:49; 14:28, 31; Acts 3:26; Phil. 2:7).

d. That Christ would die for the sins of the world (Mt. 1:21; 18:11; Jn. 1:29; 12:23, 47; 17:1-5; Acts 3:26; Rom. 5:6; 1 Tim. 1:15; Heb. 2:14, 15; 10:5-10; 1 Jn. 3:5, 8; 4:9, 10).

e. That Christ would receive as his inheritance the nations, along with all power and authority (Ps. 2:6-8; 8:5-8; 22:27; 110:1-7; Dan. 7:13, 14; Mt. 11:27; 28:18; Jn. 3:35; Eph. 1:20-23; Rev. 1:5).

C. The Spirit's work: Declare the plan daily.

1. Propagation (Lk. 8:5-15; Rom. 1:16; 10:14-17; 15:18-21; 1 Cor. 1:18-24; Col. 1:4-6; 1 Thess. 1:5, 6; 2:13; 2 Thess. 2:13, 14; Heb. 4:12; Jas. 1:18, 21; 1 Pet. 1:23-25).

2. Conviction (Zech. 12:10; Jn. 16:7-11; 1 Cor. 14:24).

3. Regeneration (Jn. 3:3-7; Titus 3:5, 6).

4. Sanctification (Rom. 15:16; 2 Thess. 2:13; 1 Pet. 1:2). (*The Victor Bible Source Book*, pp. 120, 121)

VI. The Costliness of Salvation.

A. According to David and Moses, *creation* was effected by God's fingers, and came about through his spoken word. Note:

"And God said, Let there be light: and there was light" (Gen. 1:3; see also 1:6, 9, 11, 14, 20, 24, 26).

"When I consider thy heavens, the work of thy fingers, the moon and the stars, which thou hast ordained, what is man, that thou art mindful of him?" (Ps. 8:3, 4).

"By the word of the Lord were the heavens made, and all the host of them by the breath of his mouth . . . for he spoke, and it was done; he commanded, and it stood fast" (Ps. 33:6, 9).

B. According to Isaiah and Peter, *salvation* was effected by God's arms, and came about through his shed blood. Note:

"Who hath believed our report? and to whom is the arm of the Lord revealed?" (Isa. 53:1).

"Surely he hath borne our griefs, and carried our sorrows: yet we did esteem him stricken, smitten of God, and afflicted. But he was wounded for our transgressions, he was bruised for our iniquities: the chastisement of our peace was upon him; and with his stripes we are healed. All we like sheep have gone astray; we have turned everyone to his own way; and the Lord hath laid on him the iniquity of us all" (Isa. 53:4-6).

"Forasmuch as ye know that ye were not redeemed with corruptible things, as silver and gold, from your vain conversation received by tradition from your fathers; but with the precious blood of Christ, as of a lamb without blemish and without spot" (1 Pet. 1:18, 19).

In the book of Revelation John records all of heaven praising Christ for his work in *creation* (4:11) and *salvation* (5:9).

VII. The Old Testament Types of Salvation.

A. Adam and Eve, illustrating that salvation clothes us (Gen. 3:21; Zech. 3:1-5; Rev. 3:5, 18; 19:7, 8). The first terrible result of sin upon Adam and Eve was the realization of their shame and nakedness before God (Gen. 3:7). But the gracious Creator then forgave and clothed his two sinful citizens in Eden (3:21).

B. Cain and Abel, illustrating that salvation guarantees us acceptance. It also demonstrates (in Cain's example) the wrong way to be accepted (Gen. 4:4; Eph. 1:6). Abel made the first recorded "public profession of Christ" on earth when he offered the blood sacrifice while Cain became the first religious rebel by offering a bloodless sacrifice.

C. The Ark and the Passover, illustrating that salvation protects us from God's wrath (Gen. 7:1; Ex. 12:23; see also Rom. 1:18; Col. 3:6; 1 Thess. 1:10; Rev. 6:17). The unprotected will be subjected to a future world judgment wrath (the message of the Ark) and to a personal great white throne judgment (the lesson from the Passover).

D. Abraham and Isaac, illustrating that salvation provides for us an acceptable substitute (Gen. 22:12-14; see also Isa. 53:4-6; 1 Pet. 3:18). Some twenty centuries after Abraham offered up Isaac, another Father lifted up his only Son on that same spot, but this time there was no last-minute reprieve.

E. The Manna and the smitten Rock, illustrating that salvation satisfies us (Ex. 16:14; 17:6; see also Ps. 103:5; 107:9). Bread from the sky and water from a rock. Oh, the total and tender satisfaction of God's salvation.

F. The brazen serpent, illustrating that salvation cures us (Num. 21:9; Jn. 3:14). In the New Testament Christ applied this Old Testament event to himself and led Nicodemus to salvation.

G. Naaman, illustrating that salvation cleanses us (1 Ki. 5:1-14; Ps. 51:7). This Syrian pagan was the only man in the entire Old Testament to be cleansed from the dreadful scourge of leprosy.

H. The tabernacle, illustrating that salvation restores lost fellowship (Ex. 25:22; Ps. 23:3). One of Israel's most tragic moments in the Old Testament was the worship of a devilish Egyptian golden calf god. (See Ex. 32.) Both idolatry and immorality were involved in that sordid affair. But the newly constructed tabernacle was able to once again assure Israel's fellowship with God.

VIII. The Vocabulary of Salvation. There are fifteen key words in the vocabulary of salvation. These are:

conversion	redemption	justification
substitution	regeneration	sanctification
reconciliation	imputation	glorification
propitiation	adoption	preservation
remission	supplication	origination

We shall now examine each of these important terms.

A. Conversion.

"The law of the Lord is perfect, converting the soul" (Ps. 19:7).

"Restore unto me the joy of thy salvation, and uphold me with a willing spirit. Then will I teach transgressors thy ways and sinners shall be converted unto thee" (Ps. 51:13; see also Mt. 18:3; Acts 3:19; 15:3; Jas. 5:20).

The Greek word translated "conversion" has reference to a twofold turning on the part of an individual. One has to do with *repentance* (a turning from), and the other with *faith* (a turning to).

1. Repentance (Greek, *metanoia*).

a. What repentance is not:

(1) It is not reformation, that act of turning over a new leaf.

(2) It is not remorse, that act of regretting the *fruit* of one's crime, but not the *root*. Here we have two biblical examples.

Esau: "He found no place of repentance, though he sought it carefully with tears" (Heb. 12:17; for the full background of this, read Gen. 27).

Judas: "Then Judas, who had betrayed him, when he saw that he was condemned, repented, and brought again the thirty pieces of silver to the chief priests and elders" (Mt. 27:3). That this was only remorse and not true repentance is shown in verse 5 of Matthew 27 where we are told: "And he cast down the pieces of silver in the temple, and departed, and went and hanged himself."

(3) It is *not* penitence, that act of attempting to make up for one's sins through good works.

b. What repentance is: It is a voluntary and sincere change in the mind of the sinner, causing him to turn from his sin. It should be noted here that we said *sin* and not *sins*. True repentance involves the turning from one specific sin, the previous rejection of Christ. Jesus spelled this out very clearly for us.

"Nevertheless I tell you the truth; It is expedient for you that I go away; for if

I go not away, the Comforter will not come unto you; but if I depart, I will send him unto you. And when he is come, he will reprove the world of sin, and of righteousness, and of judgment: of sin, because they believe not on me; of righteousness, because I go to my Father, and ye see me no more. Of judgment because the prince of this world is judged" (Jn. 16:7-11).

God is not primarily interested in convincing a sinner to give up smoking, swearing, drinking, and illicit sex, as bad as these may be, for this will never save him. His great sin which will eventually condemn him forever is the rejection of Jesus Christ. Repentance therefore deals with a turning from this horrible crime of spurning Calvary.

In the ministry of John:
"Repent ye: for the kingdom of heaven is at hand" (Mt. 3:2).

"Bring forth therefore fruits meet for repentance" (Mt. 3:8).

In the ministry of Jesus:
". . . for I am not come to call the righteous, but sinners to repentance" (Mt. 9:13).

"I tell you, nay; but, except ye repent, ye shall all likewise perish" (Lk. 13:5).

"I say unto you, that likewise joy shall be in heaven over one sinner that repenteth, more than over ninety and nine just persons, which need no repentance" (Lk. 15:7).

"And [he] said unto them . . . that repentance and remission of sins should be preached in his name among all nations, beginning at Jerusalem" (Lk. 24:47).

In the ministry of Peter:
"Then said Peter unto them, repent and be baptized" (Acts 2:38).

"Repent ye therefore and be converted" (Acts 3:19).

In the ministry of Paul:
"But [I] showed first unto them of Damascus, and at Jerusalem, and throughout all the coasts of Judea, and then to the Gentiles, that they should repent" (Acts 26:20).

"And the times [prior to the cross] of their ignorance God winked at [overlooked]; but now commandeth all men everywhere to repent" (Acts 17:30).

2. Faith.
   a. What it is not.
      (1) It is not a "blind leap into the dark."
      (2) It is not supposition.
      (3) It is not speculation.
      (4) It is not opinion or hypothesis.
   b. What it is. It is a voluntary and sincere change in the mind of the sinner, causing him to turn to the Savior.

   We have now seen both sides of the coin of conversion. Repentance is a turning *from* sin, and faith is a turning *to*

Christ. Paul includes both concepts during his farewell message to the Ephesian elders.

"Testifying both to the Jews, and also to the Greeks, repentance toward God, and faith toward our Lord Jesus Christ" (Acts 20:21).
   c. How it is produced.
      "So, then, faith cometh by hearing and hearing by the word of God" (Rom. 10:17).

      Here Paul is saying that faith comes from hearing the message, and the message comes through preaching Christ.
   d. Why it is so necessary.
      "But without faith it is impossible to please him; for he that cometh to God must believe that he is, and that he is a rewarder of them that diligently seek him" (Heb. 11:6).
      (1) The sinner is saved by faith (Rom. 5:1; Eph. 2:8, 9).
      (2) The saint is sanctified (grows in grace) by faith. Thus, by faith:
         We live (Rom. 1:17).
         We stand (2 Cor. 1:24).
         We walk (2 Cor. 5:7).
         We fight (1 Tim. 6:12).
         We overcome (1 Jn. 5:4).

B. Substitution.
   "For Christ also hath once suffered for sins, the just for the unjust, that he might bring us to God" (1 Pet. 3:18).
   1. Temporary substitution. In Old Testament times, prior to Calvary, the sheep died for the shepherd.
      "And Abraham stretched forth his hand, and took the knife to slay his son. And the angel of the Lord called unto him out of heaven, and said, Abraham, Abraham: and he said, Here am I. And he said, Lay not thine hand upon the lad, neither do thou any thing unto him: for now I know that thou fearest God, seeing thou hast not withheld thy son, thine only son from me. And Abraham lifted up his eyes, and looked, and behold behind him a ram caught in a thicket by his horns: and Abraham went and took the ram, and offered him up for a burnt offering in the stead of his son" Gen. 22:10-13).
      "Speak ye unto all the congregation of Israel, saying, In the tenth day of this month they shall take to them every man a lamb, according to the house of their fathers, a lamb for an house: And if the household be too little for the lamb, let him and his neighbor next unto his house take it according to the number of souls; every man according to his eating shall make your count for the lamb. Your lamb shall be without blemish, a male of the first year: ye shall take it out from the sheep, or from the goats: And ye shall keep it up until the fourteenth day of the same month: and the whole congregation

of Israel shall kill it in the evening. And they shall take of the blood and strike it on the two side posts and on the upper door post of the houses, wherein they shall eat it" (Ex. 12:3-7).

"For I will pass through the land of Egypt this night, and will smite all the firstborn in the land of Egypt, both man and beast; and against all the gods of Egypt I will execute judgment: I am the Lord. And the blood shall be to you a token upon the houses where ye are: and when I see the blood, I will pass over you, and the plague shall not be upon you to destroy you, when I smite the land of Egypt" (Ex. 12:12, 13).

2. Permanent substitution.

"For it is not possible that the blood of bulls and of goats should take away sins" (Heb. 10:4).

In New Testament times, after Calvary, the Shepherd died for the sheep.

"I am the good shepherd: the good shepherd giveth his life for the sheep" (Jn. 10:11).

Thus, Christ became on the cross what he was not—namely, sin—that we might become what we were not—namely, righteous. The Son of God became the Son of man that sons of men might become the sons of God. (See 2 Cor. 5:21. Read carefully Isa. 53.)

C. Reconciliation.

"God was in Christ, reconciling the world unto himself" (2 Cor. 5:19).

1. The meaning of reconciliation.

a. The Old Testament meaning: The Hebrew word *kaphar*, which means to cover something, is found some eighty-three times in the Old Testament. Of these, it is translated "atonement" seventy-six times and "reconciliation" seven times.

b. New Testament meaning. The Greek word *allasso* means to change from that of enmity to that of friendship. (See especially Eph. 2:16; Col. 1:20-22; also Mt. 5:24; Rom. 5:10, 11; 11:15; 1 Cor. 7:11; 2 Cor. 5:18-20.)

2. The implications of reconciliation.

a. That a previous animosity once existed.

b. That the offended party (or parties) now views things differently.

3. The two phases of reconciliation.

a. God has reconciled himself to the world through Christ.

"And all things are of God, who hath reconciled us to himself by Jesus Christ, and hath given to us the ministry of reconciliation; to wit, that God was in Christ, reconciling the world unto himself, not imputing their trespasses unto them; and hath committed unto us the word of reconciliation" (2 Cor. 5:18, 19).

b. Man is now to reconcile himself to God through Christ.

"Now then we are ambassadors for Christ, as though God did beseech you by us: we pray you in Christ's stead, be ye reconciled to God" (2 Cor. 5:20).

4. The chronology of reconciliation.

a. In Eden God and man faced each other in fellowship.

b. After the fall, God and man turned from each other.

c. At Calvary God turned his face toward man.

d. At conversion (through repentance and faith) man turns his face toward God.

D. Propitiation.

"And he is the propitiation for our sins: and not for ours only, but also for the sins of the whole world" (1 Jn. 2:2).

"Herein is love, not that we loved God, but that he loved us, and sent his Son to be the propitiation for our sins" (1 Jn. 4:10).

1. The meaning of propitiation. The Greek word *hilasmos* means "to render favorable, to satisfy, to appease."

2. The method of propitiation.

"Being justified freely by his grace through the redemption that is in Christ Jesus: Whom God hath set forth to be a propitiation through faith in his blood" (Rom. 3:25).

"But now in Christ Jesus ye who sometimes were far off are made nigh by the blood of Christ" (Eph. 2:13).

3. The necessity for propitiation. It was necessary because of God's wrath (that stern reaction of the divine nature to evil in man).

"He that believeth on the Son hath everlasting life: and he that believeth not the Son shall not see life; but the wrath of God abideth on him" (Jn. 3:36).

"For the wrath of God is revealed from heaven against all ungodliness and unrighteousness of men, who hold the truth in unrighteousness" (Rom. 1:18).

"Let no man deceive you with vain words: for because of these things cometh the wrath of God upon the children of disobedience" (Eph. 5:6).

"For which things' sake the wrath of God cometh on the children of disobedience" (Col. 3:6).

"And said to the mountains and rocks, Fall on us, and hide us from the face of him that sitteth on the throne, and from the wrath of the Lamb" (Rev. 6:16).

"And the nations were angry, and thy wrath is come, and the time of the dead, that they should be judged, and that thou shouldest give reward unto thy servants the prophets, and to the saints, and them that fear thy name, small and great; and shouldest destroy them which destroy the earth" (Rev. 11:18).

"The same shall drink of the wine of the wrath of God, which is poured out without mixture into the cup of his indignation; and he shall be tormented with fire and brimstone in the presence of the holy angels, and in the presence of the Lamb" (Rev. 14:10).

"And out of his mouth goeth a sharp sword, that with it he should smite the nations: and he shall rule them with a rod of iron: and he treadeth the winepress of the fierceness and wrath of Almighty God" (Rev. 19:15).

4. The place of propitiation.
   a. The Old Testament temporary place—the mercy seat in the tabernacle (typically).

   "And there I will meet with thee, and I will commune with thee from above the mercy seat, from between the two cherubims which are upon the ark of the testimony, of all things which I will give thee in commandment unto the children of Israel" (Ex. 25:22).

   "And over it the cherubims and glory shadowing the mercy seat; of which we cannot now speak particularly. Now when these things were thus ordained, the priests went always into the first tabernacle accomplishing the service of God" (Heb. 9:5-7).

   b. The New Testament permanent place—the center cross on Golgotha (actually).
   "For if, when we were enemies we were reconciled to God by the death of his Son, much more, being reconciled, we shall be saved by his life" (Rom. 5:10).

   "And, having made peace through the blood of his cross, by him, to reconcile all things unto himself; by him, I say, whether they be things in earth, or things in heaven" (Col. 1:20).

5. The results of propitiation.
   a. God is justified in forgiving sin.
   b. God is justified in bestowing righteousness.

   "Whom God hath set forth to be a propitiation through faith in his blood, to declare his righteousness for the remission of sins that are past, through the forbearance of God; to declare, I say, at this time his righteousness that he might be just, and the justifier of him which believeth in Jesus" (Rom. 3:25, 26).

E. Remission.
   "To him [Jesus] gave all the prophets witness, that through his name whosoever believeth in him shall receive remission of sins" (Acts 10:43; see also Mt. 26:28; Lk. 24:47; Heb. 9:22).
   1. The meaning of remission. This concept is practically synonymous with the word *forgiveness*. It refers to a sending back, a putting away.
      a. In Matthew 1:19; 5:31; and Hebrews 9:26 it is translated "put away."
      b. In Luke 6:37; Ephesians 4:32; and Colossians 2:13 it is translated "forgive."
   2. The Old Testament example of remission. A classic illustration is found in Leviticus 16

where the high priest brought two goats to the tabernacle during the great day of atonement. One goat was killed and its blood sprinkled upon the mercy seat. Concerning the other goat we read:

   "And Aaron shall lay both his hands upon the head of the live goat and confess over him all the iniquities of the children of Israel, and all their transgressions in all their sins, putting them upon the head of the goat, and shall send him away by the hand of a fit man into the wilderness: And the goat shall bear upon him all their iniquities into a land not inhabited: and he shall let go the goat in the wilderness" (Lev. 16:21, 22).

   In light of this, carefully note Paul's words in Hebrews 13:12, 13:

   "Wherefore Jesus also, that he might sanctify the people with his own blood, suffered without the gate. Let us go forth therefore unto him without the camp, bearing his reproach" (Heb. 13:12, 13).

3. The problem of remission.
   "Whom God hath set forth to be a propitiation through faith in his blood, to declare his righteousness for the remission of sins that are past, through the forbearance of God" (Rom. 3:25).

   As the Old Testament closed, a great problem remained to be solved. It centered around the two words *remission* and *forbearance*.
   a. The word *remission* (as we have already seen) refers to the act of letting something pass by, in this case the sins of the Old Testament saints.
   b. The word *forbearance* refers to the act of holding something back, in this case, the wrath of God upon those sins (Ps. 50:16-22; Acts 14:16; 17:30).

   How, then, could God possibly reconcile his *holiness* and *righteousness* to his *mercy* and *grace?* This problem was of course gloriously solved by Christ who was "set forth to be a propitiation" (Rom. 3:25). This then became the grand fulfillment of the prediction: "Mercy and truth are met together; righteousness and peace have kissed each other" (Ps. 85:10). Thus Paul could write with absolute confidence:

   "To declare, I say, at this time his righteousness: that he might be just, and the justifier of him which believeth in Jesus" (Rom. 3:26).

4. The uniqueness of remission. Of the fifteen key words in the vocabulary of salvation, remission alone has to do with *subtraction*, whereas all other terms speak of glorious *addition*.

F. Redemption.
   "Blessed be the Lord God of Israel; for he hath visited and redeemed his people" (Lk. 1:68).

   "Christ hath redeemed us from the curse of the law ' (Gal. 3:13).

"And they sung a new song, saying, Thou art worthy to take the book, and to open the seals thereof; for thou wast slain, and hast redeemed us to God by thy blood out of every kindred, and tongue, and people, and nation" (Rev. 5:9).

1. The threefold meaning of redemption.
   a. To pay a ransom price for something or someone.
      "Neither by the blood of goats and calves, but by his own blood he entered in once into the holy place, having obtained eternal redemption for us" (Heb. 9:12).
   b. To remove from a slave marketplace.
      "Christ hath redeemed us from the curse of the law, being made a curse for us: for it is written, cursed is every one that hangeth on a tree" (Gal. 3:13).
   c. To effect a full release.
      "For we know that the whole creation groaneth and travaileth in pain together until now. And not only they, but ourselves also, which have the firstfruits of the Spirit even we ourselves groan within ourselves, waiting for the adoption, to wit, the redemption of our body" (Rom. 8:22, 23; see also Rom. 3:24; 1 Cor. 1:30; Eph. 1:7, 14; 4:30; Col. 1:14).

2. The Old Testament example of redemption. One of the most important Old Testament offices was that of a *goel*, or kinsman-redeemer. *Baker's Dictionary of Theology* describes this office as follows:
   "It is used in the regaining possession of a property which had been sold for debt (Lev. 25:25). It is used in the restoring or preserving of the name of one who had died without offspring: his brother is then to take his wife (Levirate marriage), and raise up seed to him, that his name be not forgotten in Israel (Deut. 25:5). Boaz is the most familiar example of this" (Ruth 3:4; p. 252).
   There were three requirements a *goel* had to fulfill.
   a. He must be a near kinsman (Lev. 25:48, 49; Ruth 3:12, 13).
   b. He must be able to redeem (Jer. 50:34).
   c. He must be willing to redeem.
   Jesus Christ, of course, successfully fulfilled all three of these requirements.
   He became a near kinsman (Heb. 2:14-16; 4:15).
   He was able to redeem (Jn. 10:11, 18).
   He was willing to redeem (Heb. 10:4-10).

3. The costliness of redemption.
   "Forasmuch as ye know that ye were not redeemed with corruptible things as silver and gold, from your vain conversation received by tradition from your fathers; but with the precious blood of Christ, as of a lamb without blemish and without spot" (1 Pet. 1:18, 19).

G. Regeneration.
   "Not by works of righteousness which we have done, but according to his mercy he saved us, by the washing of regeneration, and renewing of the Holy Ghost" (Titus 3:5).
   1. The definition of regeneration. It is that process whereby God through a second birth imparts to the believing sinner a new nature.
      "Jesus answered and said unto him [Nicodemus], Verily, verily, I say unto thee, except a man be born again, he cannot see the Kingdom of God" (Jn. 3:3).
      "But as many as received him, to them gave he power to become the sons of God, even to them that believe on his name: which were born, not of blood, nor of the will of the flesh, nor of the will of man, but of God" (Jn. 1:12, 13).
      "Whosoever believeth that Jesus is the Christ is born of God" (1 Jn. 5:1).
   2. The necessity for regeneration. It is necessary because of the corruptness of human nature.
      "Can the Ethiopian change his skin, or the leopard his spots? Then may ye also do good, that are accustomed to do evil" (Jer. 13:23; see also Rom. 3:10-18; 7:18; 8:7; Gal. 5:19-21).
      By nature all men are:
      a. Dead to God (Eph. 2:1).
      b. Children of wrath (Eph. 2:3).
      c. Sons of disobedience (Eph. 2:2).
      d. Cursed with Adam's sin nature (Rom. 5:12; 1 Cor. 15:47).
   3. The extent of regeneration.
      a. Individual (Titus 3:5).
      b. Universal. By universal is meant the redemption of nature itself. This will transpire during the millennium. (See Mt. 19:28; Rom. 8:19-23.)
   4. The means of regeneration. Three factors are vital for a sinner to experience redemption.
      a. The Word of God (Jn. 3:5; Eph. 5:26; Titus 3:5; Jas. 1:18; 1 Pet. 1:23).
      b. The man of God (Rom. 10:13-15; 1 Cor. 4:15; 2 Cor. 5:18-20; Gal. 4:19; Phil. 1:10).
      c. The Spirit of God (Jn. 3:5, 6; 1 Cor. 2:14; Titus 3:5).
      These three factors should not be lightly passed over. They teach that no sinner has ever been saved since Adam apart from them. Some may deny the necessity of the second factor, however (the man of God), pointing out that people often came to Christ while alone, after reading a gospel tract. But just how was that tract written, printed, and distributed in the first place? Obviously saved human beings were involved. If the above is true, then it is not unreasonable to conclude that as the Holy Spirit looks for a human instrument (mothers) to bring living souls into this world, he likewise seeks out human instruments (soul-winners) to usher sinners into the kingdom of God.
   5. The biblical illustrations of regeneration. Among the many conversions in the Bible

the two which perhaps most vividly demonstrate the life-changing process effected by regeneration are those of Manasseh in the Old Testament and Saul of Tarsus in the New Testament.

a. Manasseh (2 Ki. 21:1-18; 2 Chron. 33:1-20).

(1) The fourteenth ruler of Judea was, without doubt, the most unique king ever to sit upon either the northern or southern throne. Note the following:

(a) He was king longer than any other of either kingdom (fifty-five years).

(b) He had the godliest father of all Judean kings up to that time (Hezekiah).

(c) His grandson Josiah was the finest king of all.

(d) He was the only wicked king to genuinely repent prior to his death.

(e) He was the most wicked of all kings prior to his salvation.

(2) The preconversion reign (as recorded in 2 Ki. 21:1-18; 2 Chron. 33:1-20) of Manasseh would probably have surpassed that of Stalin and Hitler in terms of sheer wickedness. Consider the following information:

(a) He rebuilt all pagan Baalite altars his father had destroyed (2 Chron. 33:3).

(b) He set up a Zodiac center for the heathen worship of the sun, moon, and stars in every house of God (2 Chron. 33:4, 5).

(c) He sacrificed his own children to satanic gods in the Valley of Hinnon as his grandfather Ahaz had done (33:6).

(d) He consulted spirit-mediums and fortunetellers (33:6).

(e) Tradition says he murdered Isaiah by having him sawn asunder (Heb. 11:37).

(f) God said he was more wicked than heathen nations which had once occupied Palestine (2 Ki. 21:22).

(g) He shed innocent blood from one end of Jerusalem to another (2 Ki. 21:16).

(h) He totally ignored repeated warnings of God in all this (2 Chron. 33:10).

(i) He was imprisoned temporarily by the king of Assyria.

(j) He repented while in prison and was forgiven by God.

(k) He was later allowed to return as king of Judah.

b. Saul of Tarsus. His war against the church:

(1) He "kept the raiment" of those that murdered Stephen, and consented to his death (Acts 7:57, 58; 8:1, 2; 22:20).

(2) He made havoc of the church (Acts 8:3). This word describes the act of a wild hog viciously uprooting a vineyard.

(3) He entered the homes of Christians and dragged them out to prison (Acts 8:3).

(4) He hounded Christians to their death in various cities (Acts 22:5).

(5) He beat believers (Acts 22:19).

(6) He voted to have them put to death (Acts 26:10).

(7) He attempted through torture to force them into cursing Christ (Acts 26:11).

(8) He persecuted the church beyond measure and "wasted it" (Gal. 1:13).

His conversion (Acts 9:1-19; 22:5-16; 26:12-20; 1 Cor. 15:7-10; 1 Tim. 1:12-16):

(9) He was blinded by a heavenly light en route to persecute "those of this way" in Damascus (Acts 9:2).

(10) He fell to the ground and heard Christ say: "Saul, Saul, why persecutest thou me?" (Acts 9:4). He also *saw* Jesus at this time.

(11) Paul was gloriously saved and led blinded into Damascus where he remained alone without food or water for three days.

6. The fruits of regeneration. The twice-born person now loves the following:

a. Other Christians (1 Jn. 3:14).

b. Jesus (1 Jn. 5:1, 2).

c. The separated life (1 Jn. 2:15, 16; 5:4).

d. His enemies (Mt. 5:43-45).

e. The Word of God (Ps. 119:24, 40, 47, 48, 72, 97, 103, 111, 113, 127, 129, 140, 143, 159, 162, 165, 168; 1 Pet. 2:2).

f. The souls of men (Rom. 9:1-3; 10:1; 2 Cor. 5:14).

g. Prayer (Eph. 5:19, 20).

H. Imputation

"Blessed is the man to whom the Lord will not impute sin" (Rom. 4:8).

1. Definition of imputation: To impute is the act of one person adding something good or bad to the account of another person.

2. Kinds of imputation: In the Bible there are three main theological imputations:

a. The imputation of Adam's sin upon the human race.

"Wherefore, as by one man sin entered into the world, and death by sin; and so death passed upon all men, for that all have sinned" (Rom. 5:12).

"For as in Adam all die" (1 Cor. 15:22; see also Rom. 3:23).

This first imputation seems at first to be totally unjust. Why should Adam's sin be imputed to me when it happened in a remote part of this world thousands of years before I was even born? If the story ended here it might be unjust, but it doesn't. Read on.

b. The imputation of the race's sin upon Christ.

"But he was wounded for our transgressions, he was bruised for our iniquities; the chastisement of our peace was upon him, and with his stripes we are healed" (Isa. 53:5).

"My righteous servant [shall] justify many; for he shall bear their iniquities" (Isa. 53:11).

"That he, by the grace of God, should taste death for every man" (Heb. 2:9).

"Who his own self bore our sins in his own body on the tree, that we, being dead to sins, should live unto righteousness; by whose stripes ye were healed" (1 Pet. 2:24; see also 2 Cor. 5:14-21).

The first imputation was an unwilling one (for no human would voluntarily accept Adam's guilt), but the second imputation was effected upon a totally willing volunteer.

"I am the good shepherd; the good shepherd giveth his life for the sheep" (Jn. 10:11).

"No man taketh it from me, but I lay it down of myself . . ." (Jn. 10:18).

c. The imputation of God's righteousness upon the believing sinner.

"But what things were gain to me, those I counted loss for Christ. Yea doubtless, and I count all things but loss for the excellency of the knowledge of Christ Jesus my Lord; for whom I have suffered the loss of all things and do count them but dung, that I may win Christ, and be found in him, not having mine own righteousness which is of the law, but that which is through the faith of Christ, the righteousness which is of God by faith" (Phil. 3:7-9).

This imputation, like the second, must be voluntary. God forces the righteousness of Christ upon no one.

3. Biblical examples of imputation.

a. Abraham.

"And the scripture was fulfilled which saith, Abraham believed God, and it was imputed unto him for righteousness: and he was called the friend of God" (Jas. 2:23; see also Gen. 15:6; Rom. 4:3).

b. David.

"Even as David also describeth the blessedness of the man unto whom God imputeth righteousness without works, saying, Blessed are they whose iniquities are forgiven, and whose sins are covered. Blessed is the man to whom the Lord will not impute sin" (Rom. 4:6-8; see also Ps. 32:1, 2).

c. Onesimus. Dr. J. Dwight Pentecost writes:

"Paul's prison cell in Rome became a pulpit from which the gospel went out to multitudes in the capital city of the Roman Empire. Among those to whom the gospel came in transforming power was a runaway slave, Onesimus, who had stolen from his master and made his way from the city of Colosse in Asia Minor over to Rome. While Paul could have used this newfound son in the faith to minister to his needs as a prisoner, he purposed to send Onesimus back to Philemon, his master. Paul wrote the letter to Philemon to exhort him to forgive and restore his runaway slave, and to count him as a brother in Christ. Paul recognized that before such a restoration could be made, the debt which Onesimus had incurred must be paid. Onesimus had nothing with which he could discharge that debt, and so in penning his epistle the Apostle says (vs. 17, 18), 'If thou count me therefore a partner, receive him as myself. If he hath wronged thee, or oweth thee ought, put that on mine account; I Paul have written it with mine own hand, I will repay it.' And in those words the Apostle was giving a classic example of the great Christian doctrine of imputation." (*Things Which Become Sound Doctrine,* p. 40)

d. Stephen.

"And they stoned Stephen, calling upon God, and saying, Lord Jesus, receive my spirit. And he kneeled down, and cried with a loud voice, Lord, lay not this sin to their charge. And when he had said this, he fell asleep" (Acts 7:59, 60).

e. Paul.

"At my first answer no man stood with me, but all men forsook me: I pray God that it may not be laid to their charge" (2 Tim. 4:16).

I. Adoption.

"But when the fulness of the time was come, God sent forth his Son made of a woman, made under the law, to redeem them that were under the law, that we might receive the adoption of sons" (Gal. 4:4, 5).

1. The theology of adoption.

a. Adoption defined. The word literally means the placing of a son. Adoption logically follows regeneration. Regeneration gives one his nature as a child of God, whereas adoption gives him his position as a son of God (Rom. 8:15-23; 2 Cor. 6:18; Gal 4:4-6; Eph. 1:5).

b. How spiritual adoption differs from civil adoption.

(1) We never adopt our own children, but God never adopts any other.

(2) Civil adoption provides comfort for the childless, but God had a beloved Son (Mt. 3:17; 17:5) prior to adopting us.

(3) There are usually many pleasing characteristics in a civil adopted child, but not in God's children prior to their adoption (Rom. 3:10-18).

(4) Civil adoption could never give the child the nature of the father, but God's adopted are given the very mind of Christ (1 Cor. 2:16).

(5) In some cases, civil adoption could be declared null and void, but God's adopted are absolutely secure.

c. How spiritual adoption compares with civil adoption.

(1) The Father must begin the action leading to adoption (Isa. 1:18; Jn. 3:16).

(2) Both adoptions give an inheritance to one who previously had none (Rom. 8:17; 1 Pet. 1:1-9).

(3) Both adoptions provide a new name (Jn. 1:42; Rev. 2:17).

2. The Trinity in adoption.

a. There is an intimacy toward the Father. "Whereby we cry, Abba, Father" (Rom. 8:15). This is a very personal name for one's Father. Only Jesus himself had used this until now (Mt. 26:42; Mk. 14:36).

b. There is an illumination by the Spirit. He both leads us (Rom. 8:14) and assures us (8:16).

c. There is an inheritance with the Son. "Joint heirs with Christ" (Rom. 8:17; see also Heb. 2:11).

J. Supplication (prayer).

"I exhort therefore, that, first of all, supplications, prayers, intercessions, and giving of thanks be made for all men" (1 Tim. 2:1).

"Praying always with all prayer and supplication in the Spirit" (Eph. 6:18).

"Be careful for nothing; but in everything by prayer and supplication with thanksgiving let your requests be made known unto God" (Phil. 4:6).

It may be said that no sinner is saved without prayer and no believer is sanctified (to grow in grace) apart from prayer. The prayer may be like Solomon's prayer (one of the longest in the Bible, with thirty verses, see 1 Ki. 8:23-53) or like Peter's prayer (one of the shortest, with one verse containing three words, see Mt. 14:30), but in any case, prayer must be exercised.

1. Definition of prayer. Prayer may be best defined as "having fellowship with God." It is more than simply talking *to* God, but rather talking *with* God. It implies a two-way give and take.

2. Elements in prayer. According to the model prayer of Jesus which was given to us at the request of the disciples (see Lk. 11:1; Mt. 6:9-13), prayer includes the following ten elements:

a. A personal relationship with God: "Our Father." The word *our* signifies the believer's brotherly relationship between himself and all other Christians. While the Bible nowhere presents the universal fatherhood of God, it does declare the universal brotherhood of believers. The word *Father* signifies the relationship between God and the believer.

b. Faith: "which art in heaven." Paul declares that without this element our prayers are useless. (See Heb. 11:6.)

c. Worship: "Hallowed be thy name." David felt this part of prayer to be so important that he appointed a select group of men who did nothing else in the Temple but praise and worship God. (See 1 Chron. 23:5; 25:1, 7.) In the book of Revelation, John sees four special angels who exist solely to worship God and who "rest not day and night, saying, Holy, holy, holy, Lord God Almighty, which was, and is, and is to come" (Rev. 4:8). See also Christ's statement to the Samaritan woman (Jn. 4:23, 24).

d. Expectation: "Thy kingdom come." This kingdom is that blessed millennial kingdom spoken of so much in the Old Testament (see Isa. 2:2-4; 25:8; 35:1, 8, 10; 65:20, 25) and later previewed by John in the New Testament (Rev. 20:1-6).

e. Submission: "Thy will be done in earth, as it is in heaven." Jesus would later give the finest example of this element in Gethsemane (Mt. 26:39).

f. Petition: "Give us this day our daily bread." This suggests that our praying should be as our eating—daily.

g. Confession: "And forgive us our debts." The blood of Christ will forgive us of every sin, but not one excuse. Only confessed sin can be forgiven (see 1 Jn. 1:9).

h. Compassion: "as we forgive our debtors." (See Mt. 18:21-35 and 1 Jn. 4:20.)

i. Dependence: "And lead us not into temptation, but deliver us from evil." It should be understood that while God has never promised to keep us *from* temptation, he has promised to preserve us *in* and *through* temptation (1 Cor. 10:13).

j. Acknowledgment: "For thine is the kingdom, and the power, and the glory forever." (See David's great prayer in 1 Chron. 29:10-19, where he actually anticipates the final part of Jesus' model prayer.)

3. Reasons for prayer. Why should we pray?

a. Because of the repeated command of God (1 Sam. 12:23; Rom. 12:12; Col. 4:2; 1 Thess. 5:17; 1 Tim. 2:8).

b. Because of the example of Christ (Heb. 5:7; 1 Pet. 2:21-23).

c. Because of the example of the early church (Acts 1:14; 2:42; 6:4; 12:5).

d. Because prayer is God's chosen method for the following:

(1) Defeating the devil (Lk. 22:32; 1 Pet. 4:7).

(2) Saving the sinner (Lk. 18:13).

(3) Restoring the backslider (Jas. 5:16).

(4) Strengthening the saint (Jude 20).

(5) Sending forth laborers (Mt. 9:38; Acts 13:2, 3).

(6) Curing the sick (Jas. 5:13–15).

(7) Glorifying God's name (Rev. 5:8; 8:2–4).

(8) Accomplishing the impossible (Mt. 21:22; Mk. 9:29; Acts 12:5–7; Jas. 5:17, 18).

(9) Giving good things (Ps. 102:17; Mt. 7:7–11).

(10) Imparting wisdom (Jas. 1:5).

(11) Bestowing peace (Phil. 4:5–7).

(12) Keeping one from sin (Mt. 26:41).

(13) Revealing the will of God (Lk. 11:9, 10).

e. Because of the example of the greatest Christian of all time—Paul (Acts 9:10, 11; 16:25; 20:36; 21:5; Rom. 1:9; 10:1; Eph. 1:16; Phil. 1:4; Col. 1:3; 1 Thess. 1:2; 2 Thess. 1:11; 1 Tim. 2:8; 2 Tim. 1:3; Philemon 1:4).

4. Direction of prayer: To whom should we pray? To the Father? Son? Spirit? The basic New Testament rule is this: Prayer should be made *to* the Father, *through* the Spirit, *in the name of* Jesus (Rom. 8:15, 16, 26, 27).

5. Objects of prayer: For whom should we pray?

a. For ourselves. In the Scriptures, Abraham's servant (Gen. 24:12), Peter (Mt. 14:30), and the dying thief (Lk. 23:42) all prayed for themselves. The first prayer was for guidance, the second for survival from drowning, and the third for salvation.

b. For one another (Jas. 5:16; Rom. 1:9).

c. For pastors. The Apostle Paul requested prayer for himself from both Ephesian and Colossian believers.

"And for me, that utterance may be given unto me, that I may open my mouth boldly, to make known the mystery of the gospel, for which I am an ambassador in bonds: that therein I may speak boldly, as I ought to speak" (Eph. 6:19, 20).

"Withal praying also for us, that God would open unto us a door of utterance, to speak the mystery of Christ, for which I am also in bonds" (Col. 4:3).

d. For sick believers (Jas. 5:14, 15).

e. For rulers.

"I exhort therefore, that, first of all, supplications, prayers, intercessions, and giving of thanks, be made for all men; for kings, and for all that are in authority; that we may lead a quiet and peaceable life in all godliness and honesty. For this is good and acceptable in the sight of God our Savior" (1 Tim. 2:1–3).

How easy it is (and how sinful) to criticize our leaders but never remember to pray for them.

f. For our enemies (Mt. 5:44; Acts 7:59, 60).

g. For Israel (Ps. 122:6; Isa. 62:6, 7).

h. For all men (1 Tim. 2:1).

6. Positions of prayers. No specific position. It is the heart that counts. Note the various positions as described in the Bible.

a. Standing (Mk. 11:25) (suggested by Jesus).

b. Sitting (1 Chron. 17:16–27) (done by David).

c. Bowing (Ex. 34:8) (Moses).

d. Lying (Ps. 6:6) (David).

e. Prostrated (Ps. 28:2) (David).

f. On one's face (Mt. 26:39) (Jesus).

g. On one's knees (1 Ki. 8:54; Dan. 6:10; Lk. 22:41; Acts 20:36) (Solomon, Daniel, Jesus, Paul).

h. With the face between the knees (1 Ki. 18:4) (Elijah).

7. Time of prayer: Anytime.

a. Early in the morning (Mk. 1:35).

b. At noon (Ps. 55:17).

c. Late in the afternoon (Acts 3:1).

d. In the evening (Ps. 141:2).

e. At midnight (Acts 16:25).

8. Hindrances to prayer.

a. Known sin (Ps. 66:18).

b. Insincerity (Mt. 6:5).

c. Carnal motives (Jas. 4:3).

d. Unbelief (Jas. 1:5, 6).

e. Satanic activity (Dan. 10:10–13). On certain occasions the sovereign God for a short period of time may allow satanic interference to block the prayer line of the believer. This is usually for the purpose of testing and purifying his child, as the book of Job and the tenth chapter of Daniel so vividly illustrate.

f. Domestic problems (1 Pet. 3:7).

g. Pride (Lk. 18:10–14).

h. Robbing God (Mal. 3:8–10).

i. Refusing to help the needy (Prov. 21: 3; 1 Jn. 3:16, 17).

j. Refusing to submit to biblical teaching (Prov. 1:24–28; 28:9; Zech. 7:11–14).

k. Refusing to forgive or to be forgiven (Mt. 5:23, 24; 6:12, 14).

9. Qualifications of prayer. What are the ground rules of prayer? The following points absolutely must be met:

a. Prayer should be humble (Ps. 10:17; Lk. 18:13).

b. Prayer should be bold (1 Jn. 5:13–15).

c. Prayer should be in faith (Heb. 11:6).

d. Prayer should be sincere (Ps. 145:18).

e. Prayer should be simple (Mt. 6:7).

f. Prayer should be persistent (Lk. 18:7; Col. 4:2).

g. Prayer should be definite (Ps. 27:4; Acts 12:5). All too often our prayers are so vague and indefinite as to render them totally meaningless. Petitions like, "Lord, save that soul nearest hell," or, "heal all the sick and comfort all the lonely," simply provide no basis for divine action.

h. Prayers should be in accord with Scripture (1 Jn. 5:14). They must be grounded in and bounded by the word of God if we are to find his will for our lives.

K. Justification. This is the eleventh great word in the vocabulary of salvation.

"How then can man be justified with God? or how can he be clean that is born of a woman?" (Job 25:4).

"Therefore being justified by faith, we have peace with God through our Lord Jesus Christ" (Rom. 5:1).

1. The need for justification. In his epistle to the Romans, the Apostle Paul presents sinful man in a courtroom on trial for his very life. The *charge* is high treason against the King of the universe (Rom. 3:23). The presiding *Judge* is the Lord Jesus Christ himself (Jn. 5:22; Acts 17:13). The *jury* is made up of the Law of God and the deeds of man (Rom. 2:6, 12). After proper deliberation a just and fair *verdict* of "guilty" is returned (Rom. 3:9-20). A terrifying *sentence* is then imposed—spiritual death, meaning to be forever separated from God to suffer throughout all eternity in the lake of fire (Rom. 6:23; Rev. 20:11-15).

In light of all this it can be readily seen that a desperate need for justification existed.

2. The definition of justification.

a. Negative considerations (what it is *not*):

(1) It does not mean to be acquitted, that is, to successfully defend oneself against all charges (Rom. 3:19).

(2) It does not mean to be pardoned, that is, to be found guilty, but given a second chance.

(3) It does not mean to be paroled, that is, to be guilty and set free with certain restrictions.

b. Positive considerations (what it *is*): The great theologian, A. Strong, has defined justification in the following way:

"By justification we mean that judicial act of God which, on account of Christ, to whom the sinner is united by faith, He declares that sinner to be no longer exposed to the penalty of the law, but restored to His favor." (*Systematic Theology*, p. 849)

Justification is thus that legal act whereby man's status before God is changed for the good.

3. The method of justification.

"Therefore it is of faith that it might be by grace" (Rom. 4:16).

a. It is of faith (Rom. 5:1), as this is the best way for the sinner to be saved (Num. 21:5-9; cf. Jn. 3:14-16). One of the great Old Testament examples of salvation can be found in Numbers 21 (and referred to in Jn. 3). At that time many sinning Israelites had suffered fatal wounds by poisonous snakes. But God offered a cure, requiring only that, by faith, the stricken victim gaze upon a brass serpent atop a pole.

b. It is of grace (Rom. 3:24; Titus 3:7), as this is the best way for God to be glorified (Eph. 2:1-10).

4. The two great examples of justification.

a. Abraham. He was justified apart from circumcision (Gen. 15:6). In Genesis 16:16 we are informed that he was eighty-six at the time of his conversion. In 17:24 we are told he was ninety-nine when circumcision took place (see especially Rom. 4:1-5, 9-25).

Note: Some have imagined a contradiction between Paul (Rom. 4:4, 5) and James (Jas. 2:24) concerning the justification of Abraham. There exists no such contradiction. Let us note what these two men say about justification. Paul says that through *faith* a man is justified before God. James says that through *works* a man is justified before men. Paul says faith is the *root* of justification. James says works is the *fruit* of justification.

The teaching of the Reformation was: "Good works make not a good man, but a good man doeth good works!"

b. David. He was justified apart from the Levitical offerings (Ps. 32:1, 2; 51:16, 17; Rom. 4:6-8).

5. The results of justification.

a. The remission of sin's penalty (Acts 13:38, 39; Rom. 4:7; 6:23; 8:1, 33, 34; 2 Cor. 5:21; Eph. 1:7; 4:32; Col. 2:13).

b. The restoration to divine favor (Rom. 5:1-11).

c. The imputation of Christ's righteousness (Mt. 22:11; Lk. 15:22-24; Rom. 4:11; 1 Cor. 1:30; 2 Cor. 5:21).

In conclusion, man justifies only the innocent, but God only the guilty. Man justifies on the basis of self-merit, but God on the basis of the Savior's merit.

L. Sanctification.

"And for their sakes I sanctify myself, that they also might be sanctified through the truth" (Jn. 17:19).

"Husbands, love your wives, even as Christ also loved the church, and gave himself for it; that he might sanctify and cleanse it" (Eph. 5:25, 26).

"For this is the will of God, even your sanctification" (1 Thess. 4:3).

"And the very God of peace sanctify you wholly" (1 Thess. 5:23).

1. Sanctification defined.

a. Negative considerations (what it is *not*):

(1) It is *not* the eradication of the sinful nature. In fact, those who boast of the eradication of their sinful natures actually claim that which Paul, James, and John admit they had not attained.

"Not as though I had already attained, either were already perfect: but I follow after, if that I may apprehend that for which also I am apprehended of Christ Jesus" (Phil. 3:12–14; cf. Jas. 3:2; 1 Jn. 1:8, 9; 2:1).

Note: The opposite (and equally erroneous) position of eradicationism is *antinomianism*, which means literally "against the law." This was the theory that a Christian was under no moral obligation whatsoever to observe the commandments. Thus, the first view was an attempt to *eliminate* sin, while the second simply *enjoyed* it.

Both sinless perfection and sinful imperfections are unscriptural doctrines. Although the Christian cannot be sinless, he can, nevertheless, through sanctification, *sin less.*

(2) It is not the "second blessing." In 2 Corinthians 1:15 Paul writes: "And in this confidence I was minded to come unto you before, that ye might have a second benefit." Some have taken their theology of the second blessing from this verse. However, Paul describes the Corinthian believers in his first epistle as already being sanctified (1:2; 6:11).

(3) It is *not* the baptism by the Holy Spirit. In 1 Corinthians 12:13 Paul says *all* believers have been baptized by the Holy Spirit, regardless of their personal spiritual condition. Compare this with 1 Corinthians 3:1–4.

b. Positive considerations (what it *is*): Sanctification occurs in various forms some 300 times in the New Testament and 760 times in the Old Testament for a total of 1060 in the Bible. The basic meaning in all these instances is "to set apart." Thus:

(1) Days and seasons were sanctified (Gen. 2:3; Deut. 5:12; Neh. 13:19–22; Joel 1:14; 2:15).

(2) Physical objects were sanctified. These included:
Mt. Sinai (Ex. 19:23).
The Levitical offerings (Ex. 29:27).
The fields (Lev. 27:22).
The tabernacle (Ex. 29:44).
The city gates (Neh. 3:1).
Houses (Lev. 27:14).

(3) People were to sanctify themselves (Lev. 11:44).

(4) One man could sanctify another (Ex. 13:1, 2).

(5) Evildoers sanctified themselves (Isa. 66:17).

(6) Moses was punished for not sanctifying God (Deut. 32:51).

(7) God sanctified Christ (Jn. 10:36).

(8) Christ sanctified himself (Jn. 17:19).

(9) A believing married partner can sanctify the unbelieving partner (1 Cor. 7:14).

(10) Carnal Christians are said to be sanctified (1 Cor. 1:2; cf. 3:3).

(11) Believers are to sanctify God (1 Pet. 3:15).

2. Sanctification contrasted. At this point it may help to contrast sanctification with justification.

a. Justification deals with our *standing*, while sanctification deals with our *state.*

b. Justification is that which God does *for* us, while sanctification is that which God does *in* us.

c. Justification is an *act*, while sanctification is a *work.*

d. Justification is the *means*, while sanctification is the *end.*

e. Justification makes us *safe*, while sanctification makes us *sound.*

f. Justification *declares* us good, while sanctification *makes* us good.

g. Justification removes the *guilt and penalty* of sin, while sanctification checks the *growth and power* of sin.

h. Justification furnishes the *track* which leads to heaven, while sanctification furnishes the *train.*

3. Sanctification achieved. In Romans 6 Paul clearly lays out the program leading to that lifelong process of growing in grace and spiritual maturity, which is sanctification. The plan involves four simple commands.

a. "Know ye!" (Rom. 6:1–10).

(1) That we have been "buried with him [Christ] by baptism into death" (6:4). Here Paul says Christ not only died *for* me, but *as* me! The word "baptism" simply means "identification." This identification with Christ on Calvary is one of many "dry baptisms" in the Bible. Others would include:

(a) The baptism of sin and suffering upon Christ (Mt. 20:22).

(b) The baptism of the Holy Spirit upon believers at Pentecost (Acts 1:5).

(c) The baptism of believers into the body of Christ (1 Cor. 12:13).

(d) The baptism "for the dead" (1 Cor. 15:29).
Note: This is thought to refer to the act of living believers identifying themselves with martyred believers by picking up their fallen banners.

(e) The baptism "unto Moses" (1 Cor. 10:2).

(f) The baptism of judgment during the tribulation (Mt. 3:11, 12).

(2) That we have been "planted together . . . in the likeness of his resurrection" (6:5). The believer has now been "transplanted" three times:

(a) To the Garden of Eden, where he sinned with Adam.

(b) To the cross, where he died with Christ.

(c) To the tomb, where he arose with Christ.

(3) That because of these two facts, the believer is:

(a) "Dead to sin" (6:2).

(b) "Freed from sin" (6:7).

Death cancels all obligations. Sin here is personified as a cruel tyrant who taxes his subjects beyond all endurance. The only way to beat the rap is to die! This then renders inactive (but does not remove) the body of sin and makes it powerless. (See also Eph. 4:22-24; Col. 3:9, 10.)

b. "Reckon ye" (Rom. 6:11, 12). This simply means that by faith we are to act upon these facts regardless of any personal feelings.

c. "Yield ye" (Rom. 6:16-23).

(1) We are to stop yielding (present tense) our body members as instruments of unrighteousness.

(2) We are to once for all (aorist tense) yield our body members as instruments of righteousness.

d. "Obey ye."

(1) Whom are we to obey?

(a) The Christian is to obey his new Master and to ignore his old one (Rom. 6:16). We can serve but one master at a time (Mt. 6:24).

(b) The Christian is to obey that form of doctrine into which he has been delivered. (The Greek verb "delivered" is the second person plural.) He was originally saved by being poured into the mold of salvation. He is now to obey the precepts of this mold and let it fashion and shape his new life.

(2) Why are we to obey?

(a) Because we are "freed from sin" (6:22). There are three Latin theological terms which may clarify this precious doctrine. These are:

Non posse non pecare—not able not to sin. This refers to believers before their salvation.

Posse non pecare—able not to sin. This describes them after their salvation. They now have the power to live victorious lives.

Non posse pecare—not able to sin. This describes their existence after the rapture.

(b) Because God desires the fruits of justification from believers which can only come through obedience (6:21, 22).

M. Glorification.

"Moreover, whom he did predestinate, them he also called; and whom he called, them he also justified; and whom he justified, them he also glorified" (Rom. 8:30).

"By whom also we have access by faith into this grace in which we stand, and rejoice in hope of the glory of God" (Rom. 5:2).

"For I reckon that the sufferings of this present time are not worthy to be compared with the glory which shall be revealed in us" (Rom. 8:18).

"It [the human body] is sown in dishonor; it is raised in glory" (1 Cor. 15:43).

"When Christ, who is our life, shall appear, then shall ye also appear with him in glory" (Col. 3:4).

"The elders who are among you I exhort, who am also an elder, and a witness of the sufferings of Christ, and also a partaker of the glory that shall be revealed" (1 Pet. 5:1).

1. The meaning of glorification. It refers to the ultimate and absolute physical, mental, and spiritual perfections of all believers (Rom. 8:22, 23; 1 Cor. 15:41-44, 51-55; 2 Cor. 4:14-18; 5:1-4; Jude 1:24, 25).

2. The time of glorification. It will begin at the rapture and continue throughout all eternity (1 Cor. 15:51-53; 1 Thess. 4:13-18).

3. The purpose of glorification. Glorification is both the logical and necessary final side of the great salvation triangle. It completes justification and sanctification. Note:

a. In the past, Christ the Prophet saved us from the penalty of sin through justification.

b. In the present, Christ the Priest saves us from the power of sin through sanctification.

c. In the future, Christ the King shall save us from the presence of sin through glorification.

4. The results of glorification. What kind of body will the believer possess?

a. It will be a body like Christ's body (Phil. 3:21; 1 Jn. 3:2).

b. It will be a body of flesh and bone (Lk. 24:39).

c. It will be a recognizable body (1 Cor. 13:12).

d. It will be a body in which the Spirit predominates (1 Cor. 15:44, 49).

"It is sown a natural body; it is raised a spiritual body. There is a natural body, and there is a spiritual body" (1 Cor. 15:44).

"And as we have borne the image of the earthy, we shall also bear the image of the heavenly" (1 Cor. 15:49).

This situation is of course reversed today, as Mark 14:38 brings out: "Watch ye and pray, lest ye enter into temptation. The spirit truly is ready, but the flesh is weak" (Mk. 14:38).

e. It will be a body unlimited by time, gravity, or space. On at least three occasions during the early days following his resurrection, our Lord defied all natural laws by suddenly appearing in and out of locked rooms to comfort his disciples.

First occasion: He disappears from the home of two disciples in Emmaus.

"And their eyes were opened, and they knew him; and he vanished out of their sight" (Lk. 24:31).

Second occasion: He appears to the apostles in Jerusalem.

"Then the same day at evening, being the first day of the week, when the doors were shut where the disciples were assembled for fear of the Jews, came Jesus and stood in the midst, and saith unto them, Peace be unto you" (Jn. 20:19).

Third occasion: He appears (eight days later) to eleven apostles in Jerusalem.

"And after eight days again his disciples were within, and Thomas with them: then came Jesus, the doors being shut, and stood in the midst, and said, Peace be unto you" (Jn. 20:26).

f. It will be an eternal body (2 Cor. 5:1).

g. It will be a glorious body (Rom. 8:18; 1 Cor. 15:43).

The Hebrew word for "glory" is *kabod,* which means literally "to be heavy," lending itself to that one laden down with riches (Gen. 31:1), power (Isa. 8:7), and position (Gen. 45:13). It can also refer to moral beauty (Ex. 33:18-23).

The Greek word for glory is *doxa,* which means literally "to manifest an honorable opinion."

Both words often suggest the brightness and brilliance of supernatural light. Putting all these meanings together it may be suggested that the believer's glorified body will be supernaturally enriched and empowered to serve God in an appointed position by radiating the brightness of grace to angels and the universe.

N. Preservation.

"And the very God of peace sanctify you wholly: and I pray God your whole spirit and soul and body be preserved blameless unto the coming of our Lord Jesus Christ. Faithful is he that calleth you, who also will do it" (1 Thess. 5:23, 24).

"Jude, the servant of Jesus Christ, and brother of James, to them that are sanctified by God the Father, and preserved in Jesus Christ, and called" (Jude 1).

O. Origination.

"Wherefore David blessed the Lord before all the congregation: and David said, Blessed be thou, Lord God of Israel our father, for ever and ever. Thine, O Lord, is the greatness, and the power, and the glory, and the victory, and the majesty: for all that is in the heaven and the earth is thine, O Lord, and thou art exalted as head above all. Both riches and honour come of thee, and thou reignest over all; and in thine hand is power and might; and in thine hand is it to make great, and to give strength unto all. Now therefore, our God, we thank thee, and praise thy glorious name. But who am I, and what is my people, that we should be able to offer so willingly after this sort? for all things come of thee, and of thine own have we given thee" (1 Chron. 29:10-14).

We now briefly (and bravely) discuss the final word concept in the vocabulary of salvation. It deals with what is, without doubt, the most profound (and often perverted) subject in the entire Word of God. Throughout church history (especially from the sixteenth century onward) no other single theme has stirred such thunder and turmoil as has this subject. Some detest it, while others delight in it, but no honest Bible student can ignore it. By what means and for what reasons was the plan of salvation originated? Why are not all men saved? Can indeed all men be saved?

1. The terms included within the subject of salvation origination: eight words here must be considered: decree, ordain, foreknowledge, election, counsel, predestination, purpose, and called.

a. Decree.

"For by him were all things created, that are in heaven, and that are in earth, visible and invisible, whether they be thrones, or dominions, or principalities, or powers; all things were created by him, and for him" (Col. 1:16).

"Thou art worthy, O Lord, to receive glory and honor and power: for thou hast created all things, and for thy pleasure they are and were created" (Rev. 4:11).

The decree of God is defined by the Westminster *Shorter Catechism* as follows: "The decree of God is His eternal purpose according to the counsel of His will, whereby, for His own glory, He hath foreordained whatsoever comes to pass."

In his book *Systematic Theology,* L. Berkhof lists seven characteristics involved in this decree.

(1) It is founded in divine wisdom.

"And to make all men see what is the fellowship of the mystery, which from the beginning of the world hath been hid in God, who created all things by Jesus Christ: to the intent that now unto the principalities and powers in heavenly places might be known by the church the manifold wisdom of God, according to the eternal purpose which he purposed in Christ Jesus our Lord" (Eph. 3:9-11).

"O Lord, how manifold are thy works! In wisdom hast thou made them all: the earth is full of thy riches" (Ps. 104:24).

"The Lord by wisdom hath founded the earth; by understanding hath he established the heavens" (Prov. 3:19).

(2) It is eternal.

"The divine decree is eternal in the sense that it lies entirely in eternity. In a certain sense it can be said that all acts of God are eternal, since there is no succession of moments in the Divine Being. But some of them terminate in time, as, for instance, creation and justification. Hence we do not call them eternal but temporal acts of God. The decree, however, while it relates to things outside of God, remains in itself an act within the Divine Being, and is therefore eternal in the strictest sense of the word." (*Systematic Theology*, p. 104)

"Known unto God are all his works, from the beginning of the world" (Acts 15:18; see also Eph. 1:4; 2 Tim. 1:9).

(3) It is efficacious (effective).

"This does not mean that God has determined to bring to pass Himself by a direct application of His power all things which are included in His decree, but only that what He has decreed will certainly come to pass; that nothing can thwart His purpose." (*Ibid.*, p. 104)

"The counsel of the Lord standeth for ever" (Ps. 33:11).

"There are many devices in a man's heart; nevertheless, the counsel of the Lord, that shall stand" (Prov. 19:21).

"Remember the former things of old: for I am God, and there is none else; I am God, and there is none like me, declaring the end from the beginning, and from ancient times the things that are not yet done, saying, My counsel shall stand, and I will do all my pleasure" (Isa. 46:9, 10; see also Isa. 14:24).

(4) It is immutable.

"Man may and often does alter his plans for various reasons. It may be that in making his plans he lacked seriousness of purpose, that he did not fully realize what the plan involved or that he is wanting the power to carry it out. But in God nothing of the kind is conceivable. He is not deficient in knowledge, veracity, or power. Therefore He need not change His decree because of a mistake of ignorance, nor because of in-ability to carry it out. And He will not change it, because He is the immutable God, and because He is faithful and true." (*Ibid.*, p. 105)

"Ye men of Israel, hear these words; Jesus of Nazareth, a man approved of God among you by miracles and wonders and signs which God did by him in the midst of you, as ye yourselves also know; him being delivered by the determinate counsel and foreknowledge of God, ye have taken, and by wicked hands have crucified and slain: whom God hath raised up, having loosed the pains of death: because it was not possible that he should be holden of it" (Acts 2:22-24).

(5) It is unconditional or absolute. This means it is not dependent upon the weather, the goodness or badness of men, the stock market, etc. (See Dan. 4:25-37.)

(6) It is universal or all-comprehensive.

"The decree includes whatsoever comes to pass in the world, whether it be in the physical or in the moral realm, whether it be good or evil (Eph. 1:11). It includes: (a) the good actions of men, Ephesians 2:10; (b) their wicked acts, Proverbs 16:4; Acts 2:23; 4:27, 28; (c) contingent events, Genesis 45:8; 50:20; Proverbs 16:33; (d) the means as well as the end, Psalm 119:89-91; 2 Thessalonians 2:13; Ephesians 1:4; (e) the duration of man's life, Job 14:5; Psalm 39:4, and the place of his habitation, Acts 17:26." (*Ibid*, p. 105)

(7) It is, with reference to sin, permissive.

"It is customary to speak of the decree of God respecting moral evil as permissive. By His decree God rendered the sinful actions of man infallibly certain without deciding to effectuate them by acting immediately upon and in the finite will. This means that God does not positively work in man 'both to will and to do' when man goes contrary to His revealed will . . . It is a decree which renders the future sinful act absolutely certain, but in which God determines (a) not to hinder the sinful self-determination of the finite will; and (b) to regulate and control the result of this sinful self-determination" (Ps. 78:29; 106:15; Acts 14:16; 17:30).

b. Ordain (Greek, *tasso*) also translated "appoint." To ordain means "to place or put in order, to arrange." In the New Testament we have three nontheological examples of this.

"Then the eleven disciples went away into Galilee, into a mountain where Jesus had appointed them" (Mt. 28:16).

"For I also am a man set under authority, having under me soldiers, and I say unto one, Go, and he goeth; and to another, Come, and he cometh; and to my servant, Do this, and he doeth it" (Lk. 7:8).

"Let every soul be subject unto the higher powers. For there is no power but of God: the powers that be are ordained of God" (Rom. 13:1).

In the theological usage of the word, note:

"And when the Gentiles heard this, they were glad, and glorified the word of the Lord: and as many as were ordained to eternal life believed" (Acts 13:48).

"Forasmuch as ye know that ye were not redeemed with corruptible things, as silver and gold, from your vain conversation received by tradition from your fathers; but with the precious blood of Christ, as of a lamb without blemish and without spot: Who verily was foreordained before the foundation of the world, but was manifest in these last times for you" (1 Pet. 1:18–20).

c. Foreknowledge (Greek, *proginosko*). This means "to know experientially, to know beforehand." This prior knowledge is seen operating in the following areas:

(1) The realm of creation itself.

"Known unto God are all his works from the beginning of the world" (Acts 15:18).

(2) The nation Israel.

"Hear this word that the Lord hath spoken against you, O children of Israel, against the whole family which I brought up from the land of Egypt, saying, You only have I known of all the families of the earth: therefore I will punish you for all your iniquities" (Amos 3:1, 2).

"I say then, Hath God cast away his people? God forbid . . . God hath not cast away his people which he foreknew" (Rom. 11:1, 2).

(3) The crucifixion and resurrection of Christ.

"And truly the Son of man goeth, as it was determined: but woe unto that man by whom he is betrayed" (Lk. 22:22).

"Him being delivered by the determinate counsel and foreknowledge of God, ye have taken, and by wicked hands have crucified and slain: Whom God hath raised up, having loosed the pains of death: because it was not possible that he should be holden of it" (Acts 2:23, 24).

"Who [Christ] verily was foreordained before the foundation of the world" (1 Pet. 1:20).

"And all that dwell upon the earth shall worship him, whose names are not written in the book of life of the Lamb slain from the foundation of the world" (Rev. 13:8).

(4) The believer.

(a) His physical condition (Ps. 139).

(b) His spiritual condition.

"For whom he did foreknow, he also did predestinate" (Rom. 8:29).

"Elect according to the foreknowledge of God the Father" (1 Pet. 1:2).

d. Election (Greek, *eklektos*). To elect is "to pick or choose from a number." It means to select for an appointed task.

(1) Christ was God's elect.

"A living stone, disallowed indeed of men, but chosen of God, and precious" (1 Pet. 2:4; see also Isa. 42:1; 49:5; Lk. 23:35; 1 Pet. 2:6).

(2) A certain group of angels have been elected.

"I charge thee before God, and the Lord Jesus Christ, and the elect angels" (1 Tim. 5:21).

(3) Old Testament Israel was an elect nation.

"The God of this people of Israel, chose our fathers" (Acts 13:17; see also Deut. 4:37; 7:6–8; 1 Ki. 3:8; Isa. 44:1, 2; Mt. 24:22, 24, 31; Rom. 9:25–27).

(4) Believing Jews today are an elect group.

"Even so, then, at this present time also there is a remnant according to the election of grace" (Rom. 11:5).

(5) Certain men were elected to perform important tasks in God's ministry:

(a) Jeremiah (Jer. 1:5)

(b) David (1 Sam. 16:12; 2 Sam. 7:8; Ps. 78:70–72)

(c) Abraham (Gen. 12:1–3)

(d) John the Baptist (Lk. 1:13–17)

(e) Paul (Acts 9:15)

(f) Isaac (Rom. 9:7)

(g) Jacob (Rom. 9:11)

(6) The twelve apostles were elected by God.

"And when he had called unto him his twelve disciples" (Mt. 10:1).

"Ye have not chosen me, but I have chosen you, and ordained you" (Jn. 15:16; see also Jn. 6:70; Acts 1:2, 24; 10:41).

(7) The plan of salvation was chosen by God.

"But God hath chosen the foolish things of the world to confound the wise; and God hath chosen the weak things of the world to confound the things which are mighty; and base things of the world, and things which are despised hath God chosen, yea and things which are not, to bring to nought things that are" (1 Cor. 1:27, 28).

(8) The people of salvation were chosen by God.

"Who shall lay anything to the charge of God's elect?" (Rom. 8:33).

"According as he hath chosen us in him before the foundation of the world" (Eph. 1:4).

"But we are bound to give thanks always to God for you, brethren beloved of the Lord, because God hath from the beginning chosen you to salvation" (2 Thess. 2:13).

"Therefore, I endure all things for the elect's sake, that they also may obtain the salvation which is in Christ Jesus with eternal glory" (2 Tim. 2:10).

"Paul, a servant of God, and an apostle of Jesus Christ, according to the faith of God's elect, and the acknowledging of the truth which is after godliness; in hope of eternal life, which God, that cannot lie, promised before the world began" (Titus 1:1, 2).

"Hearken, my beloved brethren, Hath not God chosen the poor of this world rich in faith, and heirs of the kingdom which he hath promised to them that love him?" (Jas. 2:5).

"Peter, an apostle of Jesus Christ, to the strangers scattered throughout Pontus, Galatia, Cappadocia, Asia, Bithynia, elect according to the foreknowledge of God the Father, through sanctification of the Spirit, unto obedience and sprinkling of the blood of Jesus Christ: Grace unto you, and peace be multipled" (1 Pet. 1:1, 2).

"But ye are a chosen generation, a royal priesthood, an holy nation, a peculiar people; that ye should shew forth the praises of him who hath called you out of darkness into his marvellous light" (1 Pet. 2:9).

"These shall make war with the Lamb, and the Lamb shall overcome them: for he is Lord of lords, and King of kings: and they that are with him are called, and chosen, and faithful" (Rev. 17:14).

e. Counsel (Greek, *boulema*). This word refers to "deliberate and willful intention." Biblical examples are:

(1) The intention of the Pharisees to kill Christ (Jn. 11:53).

(2) The intention of the Pharisees to kill Peter and John (Acts 5:33).

(3) The intention of the centurion to save Paul (Acts 27:43).

(4) The intention of God to offer up Christ (Acts 2:23; 4:26–28).

(5) The intention of God to save the elect.

"In whom also we have obtained an inheritance, being predestinated according to the purpose of him who worketh all things after the counsel of his own will" (Eph. 1:11).

"Wherein God, willing more abundantly to show unto the heirs of promise the immutability of his counsel, confirmed it by an oath" (Heb. 6:17).

(6) The intention of God to control all things.

"The counsel of the Lord standeth forever, the thoughts of his heart to all generations" (Ps. 33:11).

"There are many devices in a man's heart; nevertheless, the counsel of the Lord, that shall stand" (Prov. 19:21).

"O Lord, thou art my God. I will exalt thee, I will praise thy name; for thou hast done wonderful things; thy counsels of old are faithfulness and truth" (Isa. 25:1).

"Declaring the end from the beginning, and from ancient times the things that are not yet done, saying, My counsel shall stand, and I will do all my pleasure" (Isa. 46:10).

f. Predestination (Greek, *proorizo, horizo*). To predestinate is "to mark out beforehand, to determine a boundary." The English word "horizon" comes from *horizo*. It is our horizon, of course, which marks out the earth from the sky. The Greek word is also translated by the words "determination" and "declaration." This word is used in reference to:

(1) The declaration of the deity of Christ (Rom. 1:4). While He was on earth, God the Father marked off the true identity and nature of his beloved Son, Jesus Christ.

(2) The predetermining of the death of Christ at the hands of wicked men (Lk. 22:22; Acts 2:23; 4:27, 28).

(3) The predetermining of national boundaries.

"God that made the world and all things therein, seeing that he is Lord of heaven and earth, dwelleth not in temples made with hands; neither is worshipped with men's hands, as though he needed anything, seeing he giveth to all life, and breath, and all things; and hath made of one blood all nations of men for to dwell on all the face of the earth, and hath determined the times before appointed, and the bounds of their habitation" (Acts 17:24-26).

(4) The predetermining of believers to be conformed to Christ.

"For whom he did foreknow, he also did predestinate to be conformed to the image of his Son, that he might be the firstborn among many brethren. Moreover, whom he did predestinate, them he also called: and whom he called, them he also justified; and whom he justified, them he also glorified" (Rom. 8:29, 30).

"Having made known unto us the mystery of his will, according to his good pleasure which he hath purposed in himself: That in the dispensation of the fulness of times he might gather together in one all things in Christ, both which are in heaven, and which are on earth; even in him. In whom also we have obtained an inheritance, being predestinated according to the purpose of him who worketh all things after the counsel of his own will" (Eph. 1:9-12).

The Westminster Confession of Faith states this act of God as follows:

"God from all eternity did by the most wise and holy counsel of His own Will, freely and unchangeably ordain whatsoever to pass: yet so as thereby neither is God the author of sin, nor is violence offered to the Will of the creatures, nor is the liberty of contingency of second causes taken away, but rather established."

g. Purpose (Greek *prothesis*). This literally means a "setting forth."

(1) The setting forth of the shewbread in the tabernacle (Lk. 6:4; Heb. 9:2).

(2) The setting forth of nations for judgment.

(a) Assyria (Isa. 14:26)

(b) Tyre (Isa. 23:9)

(c) Babylon (Isa. 46:11)

(d) Israel (Jer. 4:28; 51:29)

(3) The setting forth of Pharaoh as an object of God's judgment (Rom. 9:17).

(4) The setting forth of the divine plan to work through Isaac (instead of Ishmael) and Jacob (instead of Esau) (Rom. 9:6-13).

h. Called (Greek, *kaleo, klesis*). The word here means "to officially summon."

(1) As used in reference to Jesus' parables:

(a) The parable of the Lord of the vineyard (Mt. 20:8).

(b) The parable of the departing Master (Mt. 25:14).

(2) As used in reference to the call of the elect.

"Moreover whom he did predestinate, them he also called: and whom he called them he also justified: and whom he justified, them he also glorified" (Rom. 8:30).

"God is faithful, by whom ye were called unto the fellowship of his Son Jesus Christ our Lord" (1 Cor. 1:9).

"I therefore, the prisoner of the Lord, beseech you that ye walk worthy of the vocation wherewith ye are called" (Eph. 4:1).

"That ye would walk worthy of God, who hath called you unto his kingdom and glory" (1 Thess. 2:12).

"Wherefore also we pray always for you, that our God would count you worthy of this calling, and fulfill all the good pleasure of his goodness, and the work of faith with power" (2 Thess. 1:11).

"Who hath saved us, and called us with an holy calling, not according to our works, but according to his own purpose and grace, which was given us in Christ Jesus before the world began" (2 Tim. 1:9).

"Nor yet that he should offer himself often, as the high priest entereth into the holy place every year with blood of others" (Heb. 9:25).

"Wherefore, holy brethren, partakers of the heavenly calling, consider the Apostle and High Priest of our profession, Christ Jesus" (Heb. 3:1).

"Wherefore the rather, brethren, give diligence to make your calling and election sure: for if ye do these things ye shall never fall" (2 Pet. 1:10).

These then, are the eight key words which must be considered in the study of salvation's origination. Again by way of review, these eight words are: decree, ordain, foreknowledge, election, counsel, predestination, purpose, and called.

2. The two basic positions concerning the subject of salvation's origination. Why are some people saved and others lost? Does man have *any* say in his salvation? Does he have *all* say? No serious Bible student denies the *fact* of God's election. However, good men do disagree concerning the *nature* of this election.

a. Position number one (summarized by Dr. John R. Rice).

(1) Defined.

"The only people that God predestinates to be saved are those whom He did foreknow, that is, those who, in His infinite knowledge, God knows will, when given the opportunity, come to trust in Christ to be saved. It is not that predestination *causes* people to trust Christ and be saved. No, they are only predestinated to be saved because God knows that they will put their trust in Christ. Predestination is based wholly on God's foreknowledge." (*Predestinated for Hell? No!*, p. 90)

Perhaps one of the most qualified theologians to hold this position is Henry C. Thiessen. He writes:

"Furthermore, He chose those who He foreknew would accept Christ. The Scriptures definitely base God's election on His foreknowledge: 'Whom He foreknew, He also foreordained, . . . and whom He foreordained, them He also called' (Rom. 8:29, 30); 'to the elect . . . according to the foreknowledge of God the Father' (1 Pet. 1:1, 2). Although we are nowhere told what it is in the foreknowledge of God that determines His choice, the repeated teaching of Scripture that man is responsible for accepting or rejecting salvation necessitates our postulating that it is man's reaction to the revelation God has made of Himself that is the basis of His election. May we repeat: Since mankind is hopelessly dead in trespasses and sins and can do nothing to obtain salvation, God graciously restores to all men sufficient ability to make a choice in the matter of submission to Him. This is the salvation-bringing grace of God that has appeared to all men. In His foreknowledge He perceives what each one will do with this restored ability, and elects men to salvation in harmony with His knowledge of their choice of Him. There is no merit in this transaction." (*Systematic Theology*, pp. 344, 345)

(2) Defended. A number of scriptural principles are offered to support this first position. Some areas follow:

(a) Because Christ is said to have died for all men. (See Jn. 1:4, 7; 12:32, 33, 47; Rom. 5:18; 8:32; 1 Tim. 2:6; 4:10; Heb. 2:9; 2 Pet. 2:1; 3:9; 1 Jn. 2:2.)

(b) Because of the justice of God. Henry Thiessen writes:

"It is admitted that God is under no obligation to provide salvation for anyone, since all are responsible for their present lost condition. It is also admitted that God is not obliged actually to save anyone, even though Christ has provided salvation for men. But it is difficult to see how God can choose some from the mass of guilty and condemned men, provide salvation for them and efficiently secure their salvation, and do nothing about all the others, if, as we read, righteousness is the foundation of His throne. God would not be partial if He permitted all men to go to their deserved doom; but how can He be other than partial if He selects some from this multitude of men and does things for them and in them that He refuses to do for the others, if there is not something about the two classes that makes the difference? We hold that common grace is extended to all, and that everyone has the ability restored to him to 'will to do His will.' The salvation-bearing grace of God has appeared to all men; but some receive the grace of God in vain. It seems to us that only if God makes the same provisions for all and makes the same offers to all, is He truly just." (*Systematic Theology*, pp. 346, 347)

(c) Because he (Christ) bore all our iniquities (Isa. 53:6).

(d) Because of the command for all men to repent (Acts 17:30).

(e) Because of the universal "whosoever will" invitation (Jn. 3:16; Rom. 10:13; Rev. 22:17).

b. Position number two.

(1) Defined. Augustus H. Strong explains this view:

"Election is that eternal act of God, by which in His sovereign pleasure, and on account of no foreseen merit in them, he chooses certain out of the number of sinful men to be the recipients of the special grace of His Spirit, and so to be made voluntary partakers of Christ's salvation." (*Systematic Theology*, p. 779)

Years before Strong, church father Augustine had written in similar fashion: "He chooses us, not because we believe but that we may believe; lest we should say that we first chose Him."

(2) Defended. Charles F. Baker writes the following in defense of the second position:

"In approaching the doctrine of Election, we must keep certain scriptural facts in mind. The first is that God is absolutely righteous. As Paul introduces the subject of Election in Romans 9 he asks the question which comes to the mind of everyone who has ever seriously considered the doctrine: 'What shall we say then? Is there unrighteousness with God?' (vs. 14). And he immediately answers: 'Perish the thought.' The second fact we need to consider is the estate of man under sin. Man is a responsible being who is fully accountable to God. He is responsible for his apostasy from God and his lost condition. He merits only the judgment of God. The third thing which Scripture presents is that no man of himself seeks after God. In other words, Scripture teaches that, even though God provided a salvation for the whole world, not one would accept it and be saved unless God first of all took the initiative by Himself seeking after man." (*Dispensationed Theology*, p. 389)

3. The objections leveled against these views of salvation's origination.

a. First position.

(1) It leaves salvation wholly in the hands of man. Thus:

(a) The soul-winner has 100 percent power to decide who will get a chance to go to heaven.

(b) The sinner (upon hearing the message) has 100 percent power to decide whether he will go to heaven.

(2) It does violence to the word "election." If God merely knew who would accept him, he would be thus limited to crystal-ball gazing and not electing or choosing in any sense of the word whatsoever. It would be like "electing" all those who will be born in the U.S.A. next year to become Americans.

(3) It limits God's purpose and his glory to the actions of men.

b. Second position.

(1) It makes God a respector of persons.

(2) It forces salvation upon the elect.

(3) It denies the freedom of men.

(4) It views election as an arbitrary act of God.

(5) It discourages evangelism and missionary activity.

(6) It generates pride in the mind of the elect.

(7) It does violence to the word "whosoever."

(8) It leads to the doctrine of reprobation, the decree that certain ones should be lost.

4. Some conclusions on salvation's origination. In light of all we have just discussed, what position is the correct one? What are we to believe and teach?

a. The Bible clearly presents in the strongest language *both* the sovereignty of God *and* the responsibility of man. Furthermore, these two simply cannot be totally reconciled in the mind of man. To do so would be like attempting to pour the Atlantic Ocean into a small bucket. Consider the following illustration. Here is a mighty river flowing from eternity past to eternity future. Its ultimate destination is the glory of God and the good of the elect. On either side of the river is a clay bankside. One side is called the Sovereignty of God Bank, and the other side is the Responsibility of Man Bank. Some of the elect can be seen standing on both banks discussing (and on occasion perhaps denouncing) the theology of the opposite bank dwellers. But in doing this the great and glorious River of Grace flowing at their very feet is overlooked. The perfect Will of God would direct both sides to embark upon that river and experience all its bountiful blessings. It takes two bank sides to make a river.

As a final thought here, what happens to a river if one of its supporting banks is removed? This of course has happened to earthly rivers through earthquakes or enemy bombs. When this occurs, the once life-giving waters cease flowing and the river becomes an ill-smelling, insect-ridden swamp.

To overemphasize one aspect of election and ignore or deny the other side is to turn salvation's river of redemption into a theological and sectarian swamp.

b. We do not possess all the facts about anything (1 Cor. 8:2). God has indeed told us everything he wants *us* to know, but certainly not everything *he* knows. (See also 1 Cor. 13:9, 12.) Following a discussion concerning the sovereignty of God, Paul freely confesses his ignorance and breaks into singing over the marvelous and matchless wisdom of God:

"O the depth of the riches both of the wisdom and knowledge of God! how unsearchable are his judgments, and his ways past finding out! For who hath known the mind of the Lord? or who hath been his counsellor? Or who hath first given to him, and it shall be recompensed unto him again? For of him, and through him, and to him, are all things: to whom be glory for ever. Amen" (Rom. 11:33-36).

c. God cannot do *anything* which is either unfair or unreasonable. It is not simply that he *wouldn't* but that he *couldn't* (Heb. 6:18). We must therefore interpret anything God *does* by what he *is*.

"Shall not the Judge of all the earth do right?" (Gen. 18:25).

"He is the rock, his work is perfect; for all his ways are justice; a God of truth and without iniquity, just and right is he" (Deut. 32:4).

"And straightway his ears were opened, and the string of his tongue was loosed, and he spake plain. And he charged them that they should tell no man: but the more he charged them, so much the more a great deal they published it; and were beyond measure astonished, saying, He hath done all things well: he maketh both the deaf to hear, and the dumb to speak" (Mk. 7:35-37).

The words penned by King Solomon some thirty centuries ago are appropriate as we bring this section to a close.

"The preacher sought to find out acceptable words: and that which was written was upright, even words of truth. The words of the wise are as goads, and as nails fastened by the masters of assemblies, which are given from one shepherd. And further by these, my son, be admonished: of making many books there is no end; and much study is a weariness of the flesh. Let us hear the conclusion of the whole matter: Fear God, and keep his commandments: for this is the whole duty of man" (Eccl. 12:10-13).

IX. The Completeness of Salvation. A modern proverb runs: "Youth is such a wonderful thing, but it's a shame to waste it all upon teenagers!" Be that as it may, one can rephrase the proverb in the area of salvation to read: "Salvation is such a wonderful thing, but it's a shame to waste it all upon the soul!"

The truth of the matter is that when we speak of winning souls to Christ we imply that salvation is limited to this area. However, God's salvation fully embraces man's soul, spirit, and body.

A. Salvation in regard to man's body.

"It is sown a natural body; it is raised a spiritual body. There is a natural body, and there is a spiritual body" (1 Cor. 15:44).

"Who shall change our vile body, that it may be fashioned like unto his glorious body, according to the working whereby he is able even to subdue all things unto himself" (Phil. 3:21).

"And not only they, but ourselves also, which have the firstfruits of the Spirit, even we ourselves groan within ourselves, waiting for the adoption, to wit, the redemption of our body" (Rom. 8:23).

B. Salvation in regard to man's soul.

"Which hope we have as an anchor of the soul, both sure and steadfast, and which entereth into that within the vail" (Heb. 6:19).

"Wherefore lay apart all filthiness and superfluity of naughtiness, and receive with meekness the engrafted word, which is able to save your souls" (Jas. 1:21).

"Receiving the end of your faith, even the salvation of your souls" (1 Pet. 1:9).

"Wherefore let them that suffer according to the will of God commit the keeping of their souls to him in well doing, as unto a faithful Creator" (1 Pet. 4:19).

C. Salvation in regard to man's spirit.

"The Spirit itself beareth witness with our spirit, that we are the children of God" (Rom. 8:16).

"The Lord Jesus Christ be with thy spirit. Grace be with you. Amen" (2 Tim. 4:22).

"To the general assembly and church of the firstborn, which are written in heaven, and to God the Judge of all, and to the spirits of just men made perfect" (Heb. 12:23).

X. The Security of Salvation. Does the Bible present a *whole* (unconditional and permanent) salvation, or does it offer a *holey* (conditional and temporary) salvation?

A. The problems of eternal security. Dr. John F. Walvoord writes:

"While most believers in Christ accept the doctrine that they can have assurance of salvation at any given moment in their experience, the question is often raised, "Can a person once saved become lost again?" Since the fear of losing salvation could seriously affect a believer's peace of mind, and because his future is so vital, this question is a most important aspect of the doctrine of salvation.

The claim that one who is once saved may be lost again is based on certain biblical passages which seem to raise questions concerning the continuance of salvation. In the history of the church, there have been opposing systems of interpretation known as Calvinism, in support of eternal security, and Arminianism, in opposition to eternal security (each named after its foremost apologist, John Calvin or Jacob Arminius)." (*Major Bible Themes*, p. 220)

Those holding the Arminian position confidently assure us that their view is amply supported by some 100 biblical passages. It will prove helpful to all at this point to examine the more important of these verses. They can be arranged under the following topical headings:

1. These passages deal with false teachers: Matthew 7:15-23; 24:11, 24; 2 Corinthians 11:13-15; 1 Timothy 4:1; 2 Peter 2:1-22; 3:16, 17; 1 John 2:19; 2 John 1:7; Jude 1:4, 10-16; Revelation 22:18, 19.

   The men described in the above verses are apostates. An apostate is one who has received light but not life. He knows something of the Word of God, but nothing about the God of the Word. He then refuses to give even mental assent to the great truths of the Bible. His description and deeds are as follows:

   a. He is a grievous and ravening wolf dressed in sheep's clothing (Mt. 7:15; Acts 20:29).
   b. He hates real sheep (Acts 20:29).
   c. He will deceive many through great signs and wonders (Mt. 24:11, 24).
   d. He is a perverse empire-builder (Acts 20:30).
   e. He is divisive and materialistic (Rom. 16:17, 18).
   f. He gives impressive speeches, using flowery language (Rom. 16:18).
   g. He deceives by allowing Satan to disguise him as an angel of light, rather than a demon of darkness (2 Cor. 11:13, 15).
   h. His nature and message are demon-controlled (1 Tim. 4:1-3).
   i. He perverts the doctrine of the Son of God (2 Pet. 2:1; 2 Jn. 1:7; Jude 4).
   j. He perverts the doctrine of the Word of God (2 Pet. 3:16; Rev. 22:18, 19).
   k. He perverts the doctrine of the grace of God (Jude 4).
   l. He can be (eventually) identified by his fruits (Mt. 7:16-20; Jas. 3:11, 12; 1 Jn. 2:19).

2. These passages deal with the act of conversion itself: Matthew 10:32, 33; John 8:51; 1 Corinthians 15:1, 2; 2 Corinthians 13:5; Colossians 1:23; Hebrews 2:1-4; 12:25, 29; James 2:14-26; 1 John 3:6, 8, 9; 5:18; 2 John 1:9. Note a few of these passages:

   a. "Verily, verily, I say unto you, If a man keep my saying, he shall never see death" (Jn. 8:51). Just what "saying" (teaching, commandment) is Jesus referring to here? In a previous conversation (Jn. 6:28) a crowd had asked him: "What shall we do, that we might work the

works of God?" Our Lord answered: "This is the work of God, that ye believe on him [Christ] whom he [the Father] hath sent" (Jn. 6:29).

   b. "Moreover, brethren, I declare unto you the gospel which I preached unto you, which also ye have received, and wherein ye stand; by which also ye are saved, if ye keep in memory what I preached unto you, unless ye have believed in vain" (1 Cor. 15:1, 2).

      The key phrase here is "unless ye have believed in vain." What does this mean? Paul explains it in 15:12. There were apparently in Corinth some professing believers who denied the resurrection of Christ. The apostle thus says they were not saved in the first place and their faith was in vain since it is impossible for a denier of Christ's resurrection to experience the new birth.

      The little word "if" in 15:2 has also bothered some. But here in the Greek New Testament it is in the first-class condition and should be rendered "since." This is also true concerning the *if* in Colossians 1:23.

   c. "Whosoever is born of God doth not commit sin: for his seed remaineth in him: and he cannot sin, because he is born of God" (1 Jn. 3:9).

      Greek scholar Kenenth Wuest writes: "The infinitive in the present tense in Greek always speaks of continuous, habitual action, never the mere fact of the action. . . . the translation therefore is, 'He is not able to habitually sin.' The Greek text here holds no warrant for the erroneous teaching of sinless perfection." (*In the Last Days*, p. 150)

      The same Greek construction also holds true for 1 John 3:6; 5:18.

   d. "But whosoever therefore shall confess me before men, him will I confess also before my Father which is in heaven. But whosoever shall deny me before men, him will I also deny before my Father which is in heaven" (Mt. 10:32, 33).

      At the beginning of this chapter Jesus is instructing his apostles before sending them out to preach for the first time. In the above-quoted verses he reminds them of the seriousness of their task. They are to warn their hearers that to personally reject the Messiah here on earth would someday mean his rejection of them in heaven.

3. These passages deal with Christian rewards: 1 Corinthians 3:11-15; 2 Corinthians 5:9, 10; Galatians 6:9; Colossians 3:24, 25; 2 Timothy 2:12; James 1:12; 2 John 1:18; Revelation 2:7, 11, 17, 26; 3:5, 12, 21.

   a. "If we suffer, we shall also reign with him: if we deny him, he also will deny us" (2 Tim. 2:12). The *deny* here can be tied into 1 Corinthians 3:15: "If any man's work shall be burned, he shall suffer loss: but he himself shall be saved; yet so as by fire." Thus the denial here is that of rewards.

b. "Knowing that of the Lord ye shall receive the reward of the inheritance: for ye serve the Lord Christ. But he that doeth wrong shall receive for the wrong which he hath done: and there is no respect of persons" (Col. 3:24, 25).

4. These passages deal with missing God's best: 1 Corinthians 9:27; 10:5; Hebrews 3:11-19; 4:1-16; 12:14, 15.

a. "But I keep under my body, and bring it into subjection, lest that by any means, when I have preached to others, I myself should be a castaway" (1 Cor. 9:27). The word "castaway" here is *adokimos*, which means "disapproved." Paul was not in the least concerned about his *salvation* from God (2 Tim. 1:12), but he was very concerned about his *service* for God. He did not want to be set on a spiritual shelf somewhere.

b. "But with many of them God was not well pleased; for they were overthrown in the wilderness" (1 Cor. 10:5). Also, "So I swore in my wrath, they shall not enter into my rest" (Heb. 3:11).

These verses review the tragic Old Testament account of Israel's unbelief at Kadesh-barnea in Numbers 14, where they refused to enter Palestine. Because of this, God would not allow anyone under twenty (Joshua and Caleb excepted) to enter. Even Moses (because of a later sin) was refused passage. However, all this had nothing whatever to do with spiritual damnation, but rather with physical destruction. It simply (and sadly) meant that most of that generation would never get out of the hot desert into a land flowing with milk and honey. In the Psalms we are told of God's reaction to Israel's terrible sin in the wilderness. Note:

"For their heart was not right with him, neither were they stedfast in his covenant. But he, being full of compassion, forgave their iniquity, and destroyed them not: yea, many a time turned he his anger away, and did not stir up all his wrath" (Ps. 78:37, 38).

"Many times did he deliver them; but they provoked him with their counsel, and were brought low for their iniquity. Nevertheless he regarded their affliction, when he heard their cry" (Ps. 106:43, 44).

Moses' eventual salvation certainly cannot be questioned even though he was not allowed to enter the land. However, he is mentioned in the New Testament (Mt. 17:1-4).

The point of all the above is simply this: the author of Hebrews uses this historical example to exhort believers to press on in their Christian lives and enter into God's perfect will.

"Let us therefore, fear, lest, a promise being left us of entering into his rest, any of you should seem to come short of it. . . . Let us labor, therefore, to enter into that rest, lest any man fall after the same manner of unbelief" (Heb. 4:1, 11).

5. These passages deal with God's discipline:

a. "And he that doubteth is damned if he eat, because he eateth not of faith; for whatsoever is not of faith is sin" (Rom. 14:23).

b. "For he that eateth and drinketh unworthily, eateth and drinketh damnation to himself, not discerning the Lord's body" (1 Cor. 11:29).

c. "Having damnation, because they have cast off their first faith" (1 Tim. 5:12).

The problem word found in each of these three verses is the word "damnation." In each case the Greek word could be better rendered by the word "judgment." In the first passage Paul refers to a believer eating certain foods he was not sure God wanted him to eat. In the second passage the apostle speaks of believers partaking of the Lord's table with known sin in their lives. In the third passage he describes young believing widows who had displayed a worldly attitude toward sex and marriage. While *none* of these parties involved faced damnation, they all would, however, be judged by God. Peter summarizes all this and uses the same Greek word.

"For the time is come that judgment must begin at the house of God: and if it first begin at us, what shall the end be of them that obey not the gospel of God?" (1 Pet. 4:17; see also Heb. 12:5-11).

6. These passages deal with fruit-bearing, testimony, and Christian maturity: Matthew 5:13; John 8:31; 15:1-6; Acts 13:43; 14:22; James 1:26; 2 Peter 1:9-11; 1 John 2:24.

a. "As he spake these words, many believed on him. Then said Jesus to those Jews which believed on him, If ye continue in my word, then are ye my disciples indeed; and ye shall know the truth, and the truth shall make you free" (Jn. 8:30-32). Our Lord would later amplify this statement: "I am come that they might have life, and that they might have it more abundantly" (Jn. 10:10). While all Christians have *life*, only fruitbearing Christians enjoy *abundant* life.

b. "If a man abide not in me, he is cast forth as a branch, and is withered; and men gather them, and cast them into the fire, and they are burned" (Jn. 15:6). We note that it is *men* here who gather these fruitless branches and burn them, and *not God.* A similar example is given by Christ during the Sermon on the Mount.

"Ye are the salt of the earth: but if the salt have lost his savor, wherewith shall it be salted? it is thenceforth good for nothing, but to be cast out and to be trodden under foot of men" (Mt. 5:13).

These verses thus describe useless testimony before men, and not lost salvation before God.

7. These passages deal with a believer being influenced by false doctrines: 2 Corinthians 11:2-4; Galatians 5:4; Colossians 2:4, 8, 18; 1 Thessalonians 3:5; 1 Timothy 1:6, 19, 20; 6:20, 21; 2 Timothy 2:18, 26.

One of the reasons a Christian is to mature in the faith is:

"That we henceforth be no more children, tossed to and fro, and carried about with every wind of doctrine, by the sleight of men, and cunning craftiness, by which they lie in wait to deceive" (Eph. 4:14).

Here Paul sadly admits it is tragically possible for a true believer to become entangled with false doctrine.

a. The false doctrine of legalism.

"Christ is become of no effect unto you, whosoever of you are justified by the law; ye are fallen from grace" (Gal. 5:4).

This verse is probably the favorite proof-text of Arminian theology, especially the phrase "ye are fallen from grace." But it must be asked just what had caused them to fall? It was a frantic (and fruitless) effort to fulfill the Mosaic law. Does this then mean that a Christian who does his very best to perform good works will lose his salvation? It does not! Paul faults the Galatians *not* because of their *evil* against the law, but because of their *effort* to keep the law. Thus, to fall from grace is the act of allowing the legalism of law to prevent one from enjoying the full liberty of love. It is possible that both Peter (Gal. 2:11-14) and James (Acts 21:18-26) "fell from grace" for awhile over this matter. (See also 1 Tim. 1:6, 7.)

b. The false doctrine of worldly wisdom and philosophy.

"Beware lest any man spoil you through philosophy and vain deceit, after the tradition of men, after the rudiments of the world, and not after Christ" (Col. 2:8; see also 1 Tim. 6:20, 21).

c. The false doctrine of angel worship (Col. 2:18).

d. The false doctrine of a past resurrection theory (see 1 Tim. 1:19, 20; 2 Tim. 2:18).

8. These passages deal with the sin unto death: Acts 5:1-11; Romans 6:16; 8:13; 1 Corinthi-

ans 5:5; 11:30; Hebrews 6:4-20; 10:26; James 1:13-15; 5:19, 20; 1 John 5:16. The sin unto death is a sin which only a believer can commit. It refers not to his eternal soul, but to his earthly service. It is committed when he allows his life to become so carnal and unproductive that God simply takes him home early via physical death. This sin (or perhaps sins) can vary among Christians.

a. Ananias and Sapphira committed this sin (Acts 5:1-11).

b. Some of the Corinthian believers had committed it (1 Cor. 11:30).

c. The man in 1 Corinthians 5 was in danger of committing it (vs. 1-5).

d. Hymenaeus and Alexander were in danger of committing it (1 Tim. 1:20).

e. Some to whom the book of Hebrews was addressed were in danger of committing it (Heb. 5:1—6:8; 10:26).

9. This passage deals with the unpardonable sin.

"Wherefore I say unto you, All manner of sin and blasphemy shall be forgiven unto men: but the blasphemy against the Holy Ghost shall not be forgiven unto men. And whosoever speaketh a word against the Son of Man, it shall be forgiven him: but whosoever speaketh against the Holy Ghost, it shall not be forgiven him, neither in this world, neither in the world to come" (Mt. 12:31, 32).

These verses have bothered many Christians and unsaved alike. Two basic questions must be asked here.

a. To whom did Jesus speak these words? They were directed toward the wicked Pharisees (Mt. 12:24, 25).

b. What grievous sin had they committed? For many months they had had the priceless privilege of hearing the Savior's sermons and viewing his mighty miracles. But instead of believing, they degraded the Son of God, accusing him of performing miracles through satanic energy. By doing this they committed the unpardonable sin. What else could God himself possibly do to convince them? It was not, of course, that they *couldn't* believe, but that they *wouldn't* believe.

In light of the above, the unpardonable sin cannot be committed today, as Jesus is not walking about in his earthly body performing miracles.

10. These passages deal with the nation Israel and the tribulation: Matthew 22:1-13; 24:13, 45-51; 25:1-30; Luke 13:23-30.

a. Each of these passages deals with those unsaved Israeli individuals who survive the tribulation, but find themselves spiritually unprepared to meet their returning Messiah. Jesus uses the parabolic method to relate this sad truth in each of the five passages.

(1) The parable of the wedding guest without a wedding garment (Mt. 22:1-13).

(2) The parable of the unfaithful servant (Mt. 24:45-51).

(3) The parable of the ten virgins (Mt. 25:1-13).

(4) The parable of the eight talents (Mt. 25:14-30).

(5) The parable of the shut door (Lk. 13:23-30).

b. One passage deals with sheer physical survival during the tribulation. Note: "But he that shall endure unto the end, the same shall be saved" (Mt. 25:13). What "end" is he referring to here? According to verses 3, 6, and 14 it is clear that it is the end of the tribulation.

11. This passage deals with Gentile nations: Romans 11:13-24. Especially to be noted are verses 21 and 22.

"For if God spared not the natural branches, take heed lest he also spare not thee. Behold therefore the goodness and severity of God: on them which fell, severity; but toward thee, goodness, if thou continue in his goodness: otherwise thou also shalt be cut off."

In dealing with this entire passage, let us consider four questions.

a. To whom is Paul talking? Gentile people (11:13).

b. What is he talking about? He tells about the opportunity of Gentiles to share in the spiritual blessings of Abraham (see especially Rom. 4:23-25).

c. Who are the broken-off branches mentioned in 11:17? They represent the nation Israel which had just rejected its own Messiah (Mt. 21:42, 43).

d. Who are the grafted branches here? They represent Gentile people.

The conclusion is that this passage has nothing whatsoever to do with individuals losing their salvation, but rather with the Gentiles receiving (during the church age) those blessings forfeited by Israel.

12. These passages deal with the testimony of local churches: Revelation 2-3.

"Nevertheless I have somewhat against thee, because thou hast left thy first love. Remember therefore from whence thou art fallen, and repent, and do the first works; or else I will come unto thee quickly, and will remove thy candlestick out of his place, except thou repent" (Rev. 2:4, 5).

"Be watchful and strengthen the things which remain, that are ready to die: for I have not found thy works perfect before God. Remember therefore how thou hast received and heard, and hold fast, and repent. If therefore thou shalt not watch, I will come on thee as a thief, and thou shalt not know what hour I will come upon thee" (Rev. 3:2, 3).

"I know thy works, that thou art neither cold nor hot: I would thou wert cold or hot. So then because thou art lukewarm, and neither cold nor hot, I will spue thee out of my mouth" (Rev. 3:15, 16).

The last verse in chapter 1 makes it perfectly clear that Jesus speaks these words to local churches and the issue in question concerns itself with the personal testimony of each local church, and not the individual members within the church.

13. These passages deal with head assent instead of heart acceptance: Matthew 13:1-8, 18-23; Luke 11:24-28, John 6:66.

a. The seed and the four soils (Mt. 13:1-8, 18-23). Some have mistakenly concluded that all four individuals here (as represented by different kinds of soil) were originally saved, but only one retained this salvation. However, a little logic will show the error of this position. Does the Bible teach that every person who hears the gospel will be saved? It does not. Furthermore, the Scripture teaches that a person cannot be saved without eventually showing *some* kind of fruit, however small. Thus, the only born-again individual here was the fourth, as proven by his fruit.

b. The man and the unclean spirits (Lk. 11:24-28). Here is clearly a case of moral reformation without regeneration. A demon (let alone eight) cannot dwell in the heart of a saved man (see 1 Jn. 4:1-6).

c. The defecting disciples (Jn. 6:66). The word "disciple" simply means "one who learns." Many of those who followed Christ were simply bandwagon, fair-weather friends. When the sun grew hot and the road bumpy, they just drifted away. For a while they may have *professed* salvation, but they never *possessed* it. (See also Jn. 2:23-25; 12:42, 43.)

14. These passages deal with the destruction of Jerusalem by Nebuchadnezzar: Ezekiel 3:18-21; 33:8.

One of the most important rules in rightly understanding any passage in the Bible is to put it into its proper context. Ezekiel wrote these words around 597 B.C. from Babylon (where he had been taken captive by Nebuchadnezzar) prior to the final destruction of Jerusalem, which occurred in 586 B.C. While Ezekiel was in exile, God had commissioned him to be a "watchman unto the house of Israel" (3:17; 33:7). He was to warn those still living in Jerusalem that, unless they repented immediately, a similar fate awaited them. In other words, those arrogant Jerusalem citizens felt that inasmuch as they had already escaped Nebuchadnezzar's first (605 B.C.) and second (597 B.C.) siege, they had nothing to fear and need not repent.

15. This passage deals with certain issues, such as Christian forgiveness: Matthew 18:23-35.

One of the basic rules in interpreting a parable is not to make it "walk on all fours," that is, one should avoid imagining a great spiritual meaning in each tiny detail of the parable. For example, are we to infer from verse 25 that a man's wife and children will be sent to hell by God because of the husband's sin debt? This nonsense is soundly refuted by Ezekiel 18:20 and a host of other biblical passages. Actually the key to the parable is found in Matthew 18:21, where Peter asks Christ concerning how often a Christian should forgive someone.

16. These passages deal with the Book of Life: Exodus 32:32, 33; Psalm 69:28; Daniel 12:1; Philippians 4:3; Revelation 3:5; 13:8; 17:8; 20:12, 15; 21:27; 22:19. Also see Luke 10:20; Romans 9:3. Here two separate books apparently are in mind.

   a. The book of physical life.

      "And it came to pass on the morrow, that Moses said unto the people, Ye have sinned a great sin: and now I will go up unto the Lord; peradventure I shall make an atonement for your sin. And Moses returned unto the Lord, and said, Oh, this people have sinned a great sin, and have made them gods of gold. Yet now, if thou wilt forgive their sin—and if not, blot me, I pray thee, out of thy book which thou hast written" (Ex. 32:30–32).

      Moses here may have been offering himself as a physical substitute for the nation Israel, which had just grieved and angered God through the sin of golden calf worship.

      "Let them be blotted out of the book of the living and not be written with the righteous" (Ps. 69:28).

      Here David obviously refers to the physical death of his enemies.

   b. The book of eternal life.

      "Notwithstanding in this rejoice not, that the spirits are subject unto you; but rather rejoice, because your names are written in heaven" (Lk. 10:20).

17. These passages deal with certain individuals:

   a. Esau (Heb. 12:16, 17). The account here has reference to events recorded in Genesis 25:27–34 and 27:1–46. They concern themselves with the birthright and blessing of the eldest son, and have nothing to do with the doctrine of salvation. There is not the slightest evidence that Esau was ever a saved man.

   b. Balaam (Num. 22–24). Balaam was a typical hireling prophet, seeking only to make a market of his gift. He was, to King Balak (his employer), the best prophet that money could buy! Three New Testament passages make it clear that he was never a saved man (2 Pet. 2:15; Jude 1:11; Rev. 2:14).

   c. Saul. Was the first king of Israel a saved man? Some have advocated that he was, on the basis of the following verses:

1 Samuel 10:6–12; 11:6, 13–15; 12:13; 14:35; 15:30, 31. However, the bulk of Bible students have held that he was not. A great number of passages would seem to bear this out: 1 Samuel 13:13, 14; 14:37, 44; 15:22, 23, 35; 16:14; 18:10–12; 20:30–33; 22:17; 28:6, 16.

   d. Judas. Was the world's most notorious traitor ever saved? The Scriptures answer with a resounding *no!* See Luke 22:3, 22; John 6:70, 71; 12:4–6; 13:27.

      Dr. Robert Gromacki has written:

      "The *repentance* of Judas has caused some perplexity. Matthew wrote, 'Then Judas, which had betrayed him, when he saw that he was condemned, repented himself and brought again the thirty pieces of silver to the chief priest and elders, Saying, I have sinned in that I have betrayed the innocent blood. And they said, What is that to us? see thou to that. And he cast down the pieces of silver in the temple, and departed, and went and hanged himself' (Mt. 27:3–5).

      What kind of repentance was this? This particular Greek word indicates an emotional regret *(metamelomai)*, not a repentance of moral and spiritual guilt *(metanoeo)*. Judas was sorry over what had happened to Jesus because he did not realize that it would go that far. After being with Jesus three years he knew that Jesus was not worthy of death. He tried to reverse the trial action by returning the money, but it was too late. In remorse, he hanged himself. If this had been genuine repentance, he would have sought out Jesus or the eleven apostles. When the disciples prayed about the appointment of the twelfth apostle, they said, 'Thou, Lord, which knowest the hearts of all men, shew whether of these two thou hast chosen, That he may take part of this ministry and apostleship, from which Judas by transgression fell, that he might go to his own place' (Acts 1:24, 25).

      Judas did not fall from salvation; he fell from the apostleship. There is a vast difference. Judas is a perfect example of those unsaved Christian workers mentioned by Jesus in the conclusion of the Sermon on the Mount: 'Not every one that saith unto me, Lord, Lord, shall enter into the kingdom of heaven; but he that doeth the will of my Father which is in heaven. Many will say to me in that day, Lord, Lord, have we not prophesied in thy name? and in thy name have cast out devils? and in thy name done many wonderful works? And then will I profess unto them, I never knew you: depart from me, ye that work iniquity'" (Mt. 7:21–23).

Judas had done all of these things (Mt. 10; Lk. 10). He had performed a ministry for Christ, but he did not know Christ as his Savior from sin. He was a totally unsaved man, from the beginning to the end." (*Salvation Is Forever*, pp. 166, 167)

e. Simon (Acts 8:5-25). In John 2:23-25 it is recorded that a number of bandwagon jumpers believed in Jesus, "when they saw the miracles which he did." But, we are told, Jesus "did not commit himself unto them, because he knew all men." These fickle men were interested in his *miracles*, but were deaf concerning his *message*. The passage in Acts 8 records a similar thing. Even though Simon "believed" (probably based on the miracles performed by Philip—see 8:6), and was actually baptized (8:13), there is no indication he was ever saved. (See especially vs. 20-23.)

f. The prodigal son (Luke 15:11-32). What was Jesus' purpose in relating this parable? It was to emphasize the joy in heaven over men repenting here on earth. This is clearly indicated in verses 7, 10, and 32. Is the repentance in this story that of a lost man being saved or of a saved man being restored to fellowship? The latter is true. This son did not lose his salvation and then regain it, for in the depths of sin and despair he could still say, "I will arise and go to *my father.*" No unsaved man can ever refer to God in such a manner.

g. Demas. "For Demas hath forsaken me, having loved this present world, and is departed unto Thessalonica" (2 Tim. 4:10). Whatever else one may conclude here, this is a sad commentary on one of Paul's companions. We had previously read of him fellowshiping with both the apostle and Luke (Col. 4:12). The truth of the matter is that, as John Mark had once done (Acts 13:13), Demas failed Paul in an hour of great need. The John Mark story had a happy ending, however (2 Tim. 4:11). Perhaps the Demas story had a better ending also if we were told all the facts.

B. The proofs of eternal security. We have discussed at some length the problems concerning eternal security. Now what are the proofs of this precious biblical doctrine? Does the Bible indeed teach once saved always saved? It surely does. In fact, the work of the entire Trinity guarantees it.

1. The work of the Father:
   a. Because of his plan and program (Rom. 8:28-30; Eph. 1:3-11; 2:7). Note the features of this plan.
      (1) To predestinate all those he foreknew to be conformed to the image of Christ (Rom. 8:29).
      (2) To accept all those in Christ (Eph. 1:6; Col. 3:3). This means that the believer has as much right to be in heaven as Christ does, for he is in Christ.
      (3) To call, justify, and glorify all those accepted in Christ (Rom. 8:30). Note especially the last phrase of this verse, "them he also glorified." Glorification, of course, will not take place until the rapture (1 Cor. 15:51-54). But here in Romans 8:30 Paul puts the word in the past tense. In other words, in God's sight the believer is *already* glorified in heaven with Christ. This is the strongest verse in the Bible on eternal security.
      (4) To gather them all in Christ in the fullness of time (Eph. 1:10).
      (5) To display those he has gathered in Christ as trophies of his grace throughout eternity (Eph. 2:7).
   b. Because of his power (Jn. 10:29; Rom. 4:21; 8:31-39; 14:4; 1 Cor. 1:8, 9; Eph. 3:20; Phil. 1:6; 2 Tim. 1:12; 4:18; Heb. 7:25; 1 Pet. 1:5; Jude 24).
   c. Because of his love (Rom. 5:7-11; 8:31-33).
   d. Because of his faithfulness in chastening his own (Heb. 12:1-11).

2. The work of the Son:
   a. Because of his promises (Jn. 5:24; 6:37; 10:27, 28).
   b. Because of his prayer (Jn. 17:9-12, 15, 20).
   c. Because of his death (Isa. 53:5, 11; Mt. 26:28; Jn. 19:30).
      Here the law of double jeopardy is seen. This law states that a man cannot be tried or punished twice for the same crime. Through his death Christ was punished for my sin. By accepting him as Savior I agreed to allow him to pay my sin debt. But if I must eventually pay for my own sin in hell (because I fell from grace prior to death) then the righteous Judge of the universe becomes guilty of breaking the law of double jeopardy.
   d. Because of his resurrection (Rom. 6:3-10; Col. 2:12-15).
   e. Because of his present ministry.
      (1) His work as our *advocate* in heaven assures our eternal security (Rom. 8:34; Heb. 9:24; 1 Jn. 2:1).
      (2) His work as our *intercessor* in heaven assures our eternal security (Jn. 17:1-26; Rom. 8:34; Heb. 7:23-25).
         Dr. John Walvoord writes:
         "The present ministry of Christ in glory has to do with the eternal security of those on earth who are saved. Christ both intercedes and serves as our advocate. As intercessor, He has in view the weakness, ignorance, and immaturity of the believer—things concerning which there is no guilt. In this ministry Christ not

only prays for His own who are in the world and at every point of their need (Lk. 22:31, 32; Jn. 17:9, 15, 20; Rom. 8:34), but on the grounds of His own sufficiency in His unchanging priesthood, He guarantees that they will be kept saved forever (Jn. 14:19; Rom. 5:10; Heb. 7:25)." (*Major Bible Themes*, p. 226)

The summary statement of all the above is Romans 5:10: "For if, when we were enemies, we were reconciled to God by the death of his Son, much more, being reconciled, we shall be saved by his life." The glorious truth Paul is literally shouting about here is this: Jesus Christ died to get me saved, but he now lives to keep me saved. This is why he is said in Hebrews 5:9 to be the author of *eternal* salvation.

3. The work of the Holy Spirit:

a. He regenerates the believer (Jn. 3:3-7; Titus 3:5; Jas. 1:18; 1 Pet. 1:23). This means the Christian has a new nature that wants to do the things of God.

b. He baptizes the believer into the body of Christ (Rom. 6:3, 4; 1 Cor. 12:13; Gal. 3:27; Eph. 4:4, 5; Col. 2:12). The believer thus becomes bone of his bone and flesh of his flesh.

c. He indwells the believer (Jn. 7:37-39; 14:16; Rom. 8:9; 1 Cor. 2:12; 3:16; 6:19; 1 Jn. 3:24). Note especially John 14:16:

"And I will pray the Father, and he shall give you another Comforter, that he may abide with you *forever*."

d. He seals the believer (2 Cor. 1:22; 5:5; Eph. 1:13, 14; 4:30). It has already been noted that Romans 8:30 is probably the strongest verse in the Bible concerning eternal security. The second strongest would doubtless be Ephesians 4:30:

"And grieve not [literally, stop grieving] the Holy Spirit of God, whereby ye are sealed unto the day of redemption."

What is this day of redemption? According to Romans 8:23 it is a reference to the rapture. In other words, the child of God is sealed by the Spirit of God until the day of the rapture itself.

e. He strengthens the believer (Eph. 3:16).

f. He prays for the believer (Rom. 8:26).

XI. The Assurances of Salvation.

"These things have I written unto you that believe on the name of the Son of God; that ye may know that ye have eternal life and that ye may believe on the name of the Son of God" (1 Jn. 5:13).

"Examine yourselves, whether ye be in the faith; prove your own selves" (2 Cor. 13:5).

In his excellent book on salvation, Dr. Robert Gromacki lists twelve things by which one may test his salvation experience. They are:

A. First, have you enjoyed spiritual fellowship with God, with Christ, and with fellow believers? (1 Jn. 1:3, 4)

B. Second, do you have a sensitivity to sin? (1 Jn. 1:5-10)

C. Third, are you basically obedient to the commandments of Scripture? (1 Jn. 2:3-5)

D. Fourth, what is your attitude toward the world and its values? (1 Jn. 2:15)

E. Fifth, do you love Jesus Christ and look forward to his coming? (2 Tim. 4:8; 1 Jn. 3:2, 3)

F. Sixth, do you practice sin less now that you have professed faith in Christ? (1 Jn. 3:5, 6)

G. Seventh, do you love other believers? (1 Jn. 3:14)

H. Eighth, have you experienced answered prayer? (1 Jn. 3:22; 5:14, 15)

I. Ninth, do you have the inner witness of the Holy Spirit? (Rom. 8:15, 16; 1 Jn., 4:13)

J. Tenth, do you have the ability to discern between spiritual truth and error? (Jn. 10:3-5, 27; 1 Jn. 4:1-6)

K. Eleventh, do you believe the basic doctrines of the faith? (1 Jn. 5:1)

L. Twelfth, have you experienced persecution for your Christian position? (Jn. 15:18-20; Phil. 1:28) (*Salvation Is Forever*, pp. 177-182)

THE DOCTRINE OF SATAN

THE DOCTRINE OF SATAN

There is scarcely a culture, tribe, or society to be found in this world which does not have some concept or fear of an invisible evil power. This has been attested to by Christian missionaries and secular anthropologists alike. Witch doctors, shrunken heads, voodoo dolls, and totem poles all give dramatic evidence of this universal fear. One may well ask where this fear came from and toward whom is it directed? Let us now consider:

I. The Existence of Satan.
   A. His existence is doubted by the world.
      1. As shown by the typical cartoon concept. Most of the world today pictures the devil as a medieval and mythical two-horned, fork-tailed impish creature, dressed in red flannel underwear, busily pitching coal into the furnaces of hell. Stand-up TV comic Flip Wilson has made a fortune causing millions to laugh with his famous "the devil made me do it" line.
      2. As shown by the denial from liberal pulpits. Christ-denying liberals have of course long since thrown out such "outdated" concepts as the *old devil* and the *new birth*. Liberal theologian Dr. Reinhold Niebuhr once wrote: "It is unwise for Christians to claim any knowledge of either the furniture of heaven or the temperature of hell." The late Bishop Pike said that as a young seminary student he had totally rejected an angelic sky-high heaven, or a devilish red-hot hell. In the fifties a national secular magazine took a poll of some 5000 American clergymen and discovered that a full 73 percent ridiculed the concept of a personal devil of any sort.
      3. As shown by the silence from conservative pulpits. Even Bible-believing pastors and lay-people are, it would seem, extremely reluctant to "give the devil his due." Some time ago an article was published entitled, "If I Were the Devil." Let me briefly quote from it.
         "If I were the devil, the first thing I would do is to deny my own existence! This strange approach is, of course, the absolute opposite of that used by God Who desires, perhaps above all else, to be fully believed in! (See Heb. 11:6.) But this is not so with Satan. This disciple of doubt seems to thrive best when he is either underestimated, ignored or denied.
         Suppose there is a Bible-believing church which is going through a spiritual crisis. For some months no soul has walked its aisles. The attendance and offerings are down and the members are becoming restless. Finally, in desperation, a special committee is appointed by the congregation to discover the source of this coldness and lifelessness. After considerable prayer and probing, the committee submits its report. What are its findings? I believe it may be safely assumed that the average committee would lay the blame on one or more of the following: (1) the pastor; (2) certain officials; (3) a cold congregation; or (4) a difficult neighborhood.
         But what fact-finding group would return the following indictment? 'We believe the main source of our heartaches for the past few months is Satanic! We believe the reason no souls have been saved recently is due to an all-out attack on our church by the devil! We close our report with a strong recommendation that the congregation call a special meeting, rebuke Satan, plead the blood of Christ and claim the victory!'
         'If I were the devil I would deny my existence in the world and downplay it in the local church, thus freeing me to go about my business unheeded, unhindered and unchecked!'" (*The Baptist Bulletin*, Dec., 1971, p. 13)
   B. His existence is declared by the Bible. We have seen how Satan's existence is doubted, denied, or downplayed in the world of men. But quite the opposite is true in the Word of God.
      1. The devil is mentioned in seven Old Testament books: Genesis, 1 Chronicles, Job (twelve times), Psalms, Isaiah, Ezekiel, and Zechariah.
      2. He is to be found in nineteen New Testament books, and is referred to by every New Testament writer.
         a. Matthew refers to him.
            "Then was Jesus led up of the Spirit into the wilderness to be tempted of the devil" (Mt. 4:1).
         b. Mark refers to him.
            "And they come to Jesus, and see him that was possessed with the devil, and had the legion, sitting, and clothed, and in his right mind: and they were afraid" (Mk. 5:15).

c. Luke refers to him.

"Then entered Satan into Judas surnamed Iscariot, being of the number of the twelve" (Lk. 22:3).

d. John refers to him.

"He that committeth sin is of the devil; for the devil sinneth from the beginning. For this purpose the Son of God was manifested, that he might destroy the works of the devil" (1 Jn. 3:8).

e. Paul refers to him.

"And the God of peace shall bruise Satan under your feet shortly. The grace of our Lord Jesus Christ be with you. Amen" (Rom. 16:20).

f. Peter refers to him.

"Be sober, be vigilant; because your adversary the devil, as a roaring lion, walketh about, seeking whom he may devour" (1 Pet. 5:8).

g. James refers to him.

"Submit yourselves therefore to God. Resist the devil, and he will flee from you" (Jas. 4:7).

h. Jude refers to him.

"Yet Michael the archangel, when contending with the devil he disputed about the body of Moses, durst not bring against him a railing accusation, but said, The Lord rebuke thee" (Jude 9).

3. He is mentioned by the Lord Jesus Christ some fifteen times. Note but a few of these:

"Then saith Jesus unto him, Get thee hence Satan; for it is written, Thou shalt worship the Lord thy God, and him only shalt thou serve" (Mt. 4:10).

"But he turned, and said unto Peter, Get thee behind me, Satan: thou art an offence unto me: for thou savourest not the things that be of God, but those that be of men" (Mt. 16:23).

"Then shall he say also unto them on the left hand, Depart from me, ye cursed, into everlasting fire, prepared for the devil and his angels" (Mt. 25:41).

"And he said unto them, I beheld Satan as lightning fall from heaven" (Lk. 10:18).

"Ye are of your father the devil, and the lusts of your father ye will do. He was a murderer from the beginning, and abode not in the truth, because there is no truth in him. When he speaketh a lie, he speaketh of his own: for he is a liar, and the father of it" (Jn. 8:44).

"Jesus answered them, Have not I chosen you twelve, and one of you is a devil?" (Jn. 6:70).

"And the Lord said, Simon, Simon, behold, Satan hath desired to have you, that he may sift you as wheat" (Lk. 22:31).

Thus to deny the personality of Satan, is to deny both the statements of the Scriptures and the testimony of the Savior himself.

II. The Origin of Satan. Often a twofold accusation is hurled at the Christian by the cynic. "All right, if your God is so wise and good, then why did he create the devil, and if he is so powerful, why doesn't he destroy the devil?" A simple scriptural answer to these two questions is, "He didn't, but he will."

There are two important passages in the Word of God concerning the origin and fall of the devil.

A. His origin and fall as related by Ezekiel. In his book, Ezekiel predicts coming judgment upon the city of Tyre in chapters 26, 27 and the first part of chapter 28. This has already been fulfilled, for the city was sacked by Nebuchadnezzar in 573 B.C., and later destroyed by Alexander in 332 B.C. But during the second half of chapter 28, the prophet goes beyond the earthly scene, and describes for us the creation and judgment of a vile and vicious nonhuman creature. Let us consider it first of all from the King James Version and then from a well-known paraphrase.

King James Version

"Son of man, take up a lamentation upon the king of Tyrus, and say unto him, Thus saith the Lord God; Thou sealest up the sum, full of wisdom, and perfect in beauty. Thou hast been in Eden the garden of God; every precious stone was thy covering, the sardius, topaz, and the diamond, the beryl, the onyx, and the jasper, the sapphire, the emerald, and the carbuncle, and gold: the workmanship of thy tabrets and of thy pipes was prepared in thee in the day that thou wast created. Thou art the anointed cherub that covereth; and I have set thee so; thou wast upon the holy mountain of God; thou hast walked up and down in the midst of the stones of fire, thou wast perfect in thy ways from the day that thou wast created, till iniquity was found in thee. By the multitude of thy merchandise they have filled the midst of thee with violence, and thou hast sinned: therefore I will cast thee as profane out of the mountain of God: and I will destroy thee, O covering cherub, from the midst of the stones of fire. Thine heart was lifted up because of thy beauty, thou hast corrupted thy wisdom by reason of thy brightness: I will cast thee to the ground, I will lay thee before kings, that they may behold thee. Thou hast defiled thy sanctuaries by the multitude of thine iniquities, by the iniquity of thy traffick; therefore will I bring forth a fire from the midst of thee, it shall devour thee, and I will bring thee to ashes upon the earth in the sight of all them that behold thee. All they that know thee among the people shall be astonished at thee: thou shalt be a terror, and never shalt thou be any more" (Ezek. 28:12–19).

Paraphrase Version

"Son of dust, weep for the king of Tyre. Tell him, the Lord God says: You were the perfection of wisdom and beauty. You were in Eden, the garden of God; your clothing was bejeweled with every precious stone—ruby, topaz, diamond, chrysolite, onyx, jasper, sapphire, carbuncle, and emerald—all in beautiful settings of finest gold. They were given to you on the day you were created. I appointed you to be the anointed guardian cherub. You had access to the holy mountain of God. You walked among the stones of fire. You were perfect in all you did from the day you were created until that time when wrong was found in you. Your great wealth filled you with internal turmoil and you sinned. Therefore, I cast you out of the mountain of God like a common sinner. I destroyed you, O overshadowing cherub, from the midst of the stones of fire. Your heart was filled with pride because of all your beauty; you corrupted your wisdom for the sake of your splendor. Therefore I have cast you down to the ground and exposed you helpless before the curious gaze of kings. You defiled your holiness with lust for gain: therefore I brought forth fire from your own actions and let it burn you to ashes upon the earth in the sight of all those watching you. All who know you are appalled at your fate; you are an example of horror; you are destroyed forever" (Ezek. 28:12-19, *The Living Bible*).

Let us now observe some key words in this passage:

1. "Thou . . . [art] full of wisdom, and perfect in beauty" (v. 12). No human being is ever described in these terms, but rather the contrary. Note the following Scriptures:

    "For there is no man that sinneth not" (1 Ki. 8:46).

    "Who can say, I have made my heart clean, I am pure from my sin?" (Prov. 20:9).

    "The heart is deceitful above all things, and desperately wicked" (Jer. 17:9).

    "For there is not a just man upon earth, that doeth good and sinneth not" (Eccl. 7:20).

    "All we like sheep have gone astray" (Isa. 53:6).

    "But we are all as an unclean thing, and all our righteousnesses are as filthy rags; and we all do fade as a leaf, and our iniquities like the wind, have taken us away" (Isa. 64:6).

    "For all have sinned and come short of the glory of God" (Rom. 3:23).

    "But the scripture hath concluded all under sin" (Gal. 3:22).

    "For in many things we offend all" (Jas. 3:2).

    "If we say that we have no sin, we deceive ourselves and the truth is not in us" (1 Jn. 1:8).

    "If we say that we have not sinned, we make him a liar, and his word is not in us" (1 Jn. 1:10).

    So we see that this verse in Ezekiel cannot possibly refer to any human being.

2. "Thou hast been in Eden, the garden of God" (v. 13). Some have speculated that Ezekiel had Adam in mind here, but the Genesis account nowhere speaks of Adam's clothing being "bejeweled with every precious stone," and then fitted in "beautiful settings of finest gold."

3. "The workmanship of thy tabrets and of thy pipes" (v. 13). Here Dr. J. Dwight Pentecost writes:

    "Musical instruments were originally designed to be means of praising and worshipping God. It was not necessary for Lucifer to learn to play a musical instrument in order to praise God. If you please, he had a built-in pipe organ, or, he was an organ. That's what the prophet meant when he said, 'the workmanship of thy tabrets and of thy pipes. . . .' Lucifer, because of his beauty, did what a musical instrument would do in the hands of a skilled musician, bring forth a psalm of praise to the glory of God. Lucifer didn't have to look for someone to play the organ so that he could sing the doxology—he was a doxology." (*Your Adversary, the Devil*, p. 16)

4. "The anointed cherub that covereth" (v. 14).

    a. He was anointed. In the Old Testament, there were three anointed offices, that of the prophet, priest, and king. Here is a suggestion that Lucifer may have originally been created to function (under Christ) as heaven's prophet, priest, and king. But he failed. This may be the reason why God separated these offices. We note this definite separation of the offices of priest and king in two specific Old Testament passages.

        (1) The example of King Saul. In 1 Samuel 13, Saul attempts to intrude into the office of the priesthood by offering a sacrifice. Let us read the details of this:

            "And Saul said, Bring hither a burnt offering to me, and peace offerings. And he offered the burnt offering. And it came to pass, that as soon as he had made an end of offering the burnt offering, behold, Samuel came; and Saul went out to meet him, that he might salute him. And Samuel said, What hast thou done? And Saul said, Because I saw that the people were scattered from me, and that thou camest not within the days appointed, and that the Philistines gathered themselves together at Michmash; therefore said I, The Philistines will come down now upon me to Gilgal, and I have not made supplication unto the Lord: I forced myself therefore, and offered a burnt offering. And Samuel said to Saul, Thou hast done foolishly: thou hast not kept the commandment of the Lord thy God, which he commanded thee: for now would the Lord have established thy kingdom upon Israel for ever. But now thy kingdom shall not continue: the Lord hath sought him a man after his own heart, and the Lord hath commanded him to be captain over his people, because thou hast not kept that which the Lord commanded thee" (1 Sam. 13:9-14).

(2) The example of King Uzziah. This Judean ruler was for the most part a wise and good king. However, like Lucifer, he allowed his heart to become power-crazy. Listen to the sad results:

"But when he was strong, his heart was lifted up to his destruction: for he transgressed against the Lord his God, and went into the temple of the Lord to burn incense upon the altar of incense. And Azariah the priest went in after him, and with him fourscore priests of the Lord, that were valiant men: And they withstood Uzziah the king, and said unto him, It appertaineth not unto thee, Uzziah, to burn incense unto the Lord, but to the priests the sons of Aaron, that are consecrated to burn incense: go out of the sanctuary; for thou hast trespassed; neither shall it be for thine honour from the Lord God. Then Uzziah was wroth, and had a censer in his hand to burn incense: and while he was wroth with the priests, the leprosy even rose up in his forehead before the priests in the house of the Lord, from beside the incense altar. And Azariah the chief priest, and all the priests, looked upon him, and, behold, he was leprous in his forehead, and they thrust him out from thence; yea, himself hasted also to go out, because the Lord had smitten him. And Uzziah the king was a leper unto the day of his death, and dwelt in a several house, being a leper; for he was cut off from the house of the Lord: and Jotham his son was over the king's house, judging the people of the land" (2 Chron. 26:16-21).

b. He was a guardian cherub. A cherub was a special kind of angelic being whose purpose was to protect God's holiness (see Gen. 3; Ex. 25; 1 Ki. 6; Ezek. 1; Rev. 4). Both archaeological and biblical evidences suggest they bore the likeness of a lion, calf, eagle, and man. Apparently Lucifer was created (among other purposes) to demonstrate the earthly work of Christ, as pictured by the four gospel writers:

Matthew presents Christ as the lion-like king.

Mark presents him as the calf-like servant.

Luke presents him as the perfect man.

John presents him as the eagle-like God.

In fact, some Bible scholars suggest that these four living creatures described in Revelation 4 exist to carry on the work that God had once assigned to Lucifer. The reason there are four may be that God determined never to entrust this much power to one angel again. John describes for us the location and activities of these living cherubim.

"And before the throne there was a sea of glass like unto crystal: and in the midst of the throne, and round about the throne, were four beasts full of eyes before and behind. And the first beast was like a lion, and the second beast like a calf, and the third beast had a face as a man, and the fourth beast was like a flying eagle. And the four beasts had each of them six wings about him; and they were full of eyes within: and they rest not day and night, saying, Holy, holy, holy, Lord God Almighty, which was, and is, and is to come" (Rev. 4:6-8).

5. "Thine heart was lifted up because of thy beauty" (v. 17). Here is the first sin, and the self-creation of the first sinner in all the universe. In the New Testament the Apostle Paul refers to this tragic historical account, using it as a warning against the ordination of an immature pastoral candidate.

"This is a true saying, If a man desire the office of a bishop, he desireth a good work. A bishop then must be blameless, the husband of one wife, vigilant, sober, of good behaviour, given to hospitality, apt to teach; not given to wine, no striker, not greedy of filthy lucre; but patient, not a brawler, not covetous; One that ruleth well his own house, having his children in subjection with all gravity; (For if a man know not how to rule his own house, how shall he take care of the church of God?) Not a novice, lest being lifted up with pride he fall into the condemnation of the devil. Moreover he must have a good report of them which are without; lest he fall into reproach and the snare of the devil" (1 Tim. 3:1-7).

B. His origin and fall as related by Isaiah.

"How art thou fallen from heaven, O Lucifer, son of the morning! how art thou cut down to the ground, which didst weaken the nations! For thou hast said in thine heart, I will ascend into heaven, I will exalt my throne above the stars of God: I will sit also upon the mount of the congregation, in the sides of the north: I will ascend above the heights of the clouds; I will be like the most High" (Isa. 14:12-14).

Note these five foolish and fatal "I wills" of the devil:

1. *I will* ascend into heaven. Obviously Satan had the third heaven in mind here, the very abode of God. (See 2 Cor. 12:2.)
2. *I will* exalt my throne above the stars of God. This is probably a reference to angels. Satan desired the worship of angels.
3. *I will* sit also upon the mount of the congregation, in the sides of the north. Lucifer now seeks to enter God's "executive office" somewhere in the north and sit at his very desk. He would attempt to control not only the angels, but the size and number of the starry galaxies also.
4. *I will* ascend above the heights of the clouds. This may well refer to that special Shekinah glory cloud of God found so frequently in the Bible.
5. *I will* be like the most High. It is revealing to note the name for God that Satan uses here. He wanted to be like El-Elyon, the most High. This name literally means, "the strongest strong one." The devil could have picked other names for God. He could have used El-Shaddai, which means, "the breasted one, the one who feeds his children," but he didn't. He might have selected Jehovah-Rohi, which means, "the shepherd God," but he avoided this title also. The reason is obvious. Satan coveted God's strength, but was not interested in his feeding and leading attributes.

At this point a great contrast can be seen between Lucifer's attitude in the garden of God, and the Savior's attitude centuries later in the Garden of Gethsemane. In the first Garden, the devil viciously fought for his own will, but in the second garden, on three occasions, we hear our meek Messiah pray, *"Not my will."* Let's look at Matthew's account of this midnight episode:

"Then cometh Jesus with them unto a place called Gethsemane, and saith unto the disciples, Sit ye here, while I go and pray yonder. And he took with him Peter and the two sons of Zebedee, and began to be sorrowful and very heavy. Then saith he unto them, My soul is exceeding sorrowful, even unto death: tarry ye here, and watch with me. And he went a little farther, and fell on his face, and prayed, saying, O my Father, if it be possible, let this cup pass from me: nevertheless not as I will, but as thou wilt. And he cometh unto the disciples, and findeth them asleep, and saith unto Peter, What, could ye not watch with me one hour? Watch and pray, that ye enter not into temptation: the spirit indeed is willing, but the flesh is weak. He went away again the second time, and prayed, saying, O my Father, if this cup may not pass away from me, except I drink it, thy will be done. And he came and found them asleep again: for their eyes were heavy.

And he left them, and went away again, and prayed the third time, saying the same words" (Mt. 26:36-44).

We have thus far looked at the existence and origin of Satan. Now, what about his personality?

III. The Personality of Satan.
    A. He is a real person. In 1 Corinthians 15 the Apostle Paul distinguishes between heavenly bodies and earthly bodies. He writes:

    "All flesh is not the same flesh: but there is one kind of flesh of men, another flesh of beasts, another of fishes, and another of birds. There are also celestial bodies, and bodies terrestrial; but the glory of the celestial is one, and the glory of the terrestrial is another" (1 Cor. 15:39, 40).

    In view of the fact that Satan is a fallen angel from the celestial world, it is not, some believe, unreasonable to suggest that he too possesses a body—not a flesh-and-blood, terrestrial body, of course, but perhaps a body of some substance, nevertheless.

    B. He possesses intelligence.
    "Lest Satan should get an advantage of us: for we are not ignorant of his devices" (2 Cor. 2:11).
    "But I fear, lest by any means, as the serpent beguiled Eve through his subtilty, so your minds should be corrupted from the simplicity that is in Christ" (2 Cor. 11:3).

    C. He possesses memory. One of the most amazing episodes in the earthly ministry of Christ was the temptation experience at the hands of Satan.

    "Then was Jesus led up of the Spirit into the wilderness to be tempted of the devil. And when he had fasted forty days and forty nights, he was afterward an hungered. And when the tempter came to him, he said, If thou be the Son of God, command that these stones be made bread. But he answered and said, It is written, Man shall not live by bread alone, but by every word that proceedeth out of the mouth of God. Then the devil taketh him up into the holy city, and setteth him on a pinnacle of the temple, and saith unto him, If thou be the Son of God, cast thyself down: for it is written, He shall give his angels charge concerning thee: and in their hands they shall bear thee up, lest at any time thou dash thy foot against a stone. Jesus said unto him, It is written again, Thou shalt not tempt the Lord thy God. Again, the devil taketh him up into an exceeding high mountain, and sheweth him all the kingdoms of the world, and the glory of them; and said unto him, All these things will I give thee, if thou wilt fall down and worship me. Then said Jesus unto him, Get thee hence, Satan: for it is written, Thou shalt worship the Lord thy God, and him only shalt thou serve. Then the devil leaveth him, and, behold, angels came and ministered unto him" (Mt. 4:1-11).

    We often are reminded of how Jesus quoted Scripture to refute the devil, and so he did, quoting three times from the book of Deuteronomy.

But it is sometimes overlooked that here in this same Matthew 4 passage, the devil also quoted Scripture to Christ. Note again the reference:

"And saith unto him, If thou be the Son of God, cast thyself down: for it is written, He shall give his angels charge concerning thee: and in their hands they shall bear thee up, lest at any time thou dash thy foot against a stone" (Mt. 4:6).

This quote was taken from Psalm 91:11, 12. To be sure, he took it completely out of context and twisted it, but Shakespeare was right, "the devil doth quote scripture." Now the question may be asked: How was Satan able to do this? Well, apparently he had *memorized* Psalm 91. Many Christians have never even *read* that Psalm, but, Satan, it would seem, has committed it to memory. Another example of this "Scripture-spouting serpent" is found in Revelation 12:12:

"Therefore rejoice, ye heavens, and ye that dwell in them. Woe to the inhabiters of the earth and of the sea! for the devil is come down unto you, having great wrath, because he knoweth that he hath but a short time."

Satan will be thrown out of heaven during the middle of the tribulation and will come down to earth, "having great wrath, because he knoweth that he hath but a short time." How does he know this? The apparent answer is that he has carefully read the ninth chapter of Daniel. If I were the devil, I'd read the Bible. I could then twist and turn the Scriptures in such a way as to mislead saints and sinners alike.

D. He possesses a will. Paul instructs Timothy in dealing with backslidden Christians. He says to be gentle but firm, that "they may recover themselves out of the snare of the devil, who are taken captive by him at his will" (2 Tim. 2:26).

E. He possesses emotions.

1. Desire.

"And the Lord said, Simon, Simon, behold, Satan hath desired to have you, that he may sift you as wheat" (Lk. 22:31).

2. Pride. In describing the qualifications of a deacon, Paul lists the following restriction:

"Not a novice, lest being lifted up with pride he fall into condemnation of the devil" (1 Tim. 3:6).

3. Wrath.

"Therefore rejoice, ye heavens, and ye that dwell in them. Woe to the inhabiters of the earth and of the sea! for the devil is come down unto you, having great wrath, because he knoweth that he hath but a short time" (Rev. 12:12).

F. He possesses great organizational ability. The Bible speaks of Satan's synagogues, doctrines, and deep things.

"Now the Spirit speaketh expressly, that in the latter times some shall depart from the faith, giving heed to seducing spirits, and doctrines of devils" (1 Tim. 4:1).

"I know thy works, and tribulation, and poverty, (but thou art rich) and I know the blasphemy of them which say they are Jews, and are not, but are the synagogue of Satan" (Rev. 2:9).

"But unto you I say, and unto the rest in Thyatira, as many as have not this doctrine, and which have not known the depths of Satan, as they speak; I will put upon you none other burden" (Rev. 2:24).

1. It was the devil that organized and led the first rebellion against God. Revelation 12:4 indicates that he persuaded one-third of heaven's angels to march with him.

"And his tail drew the third part of the stars of heaven, and did cast them to the earth: and the dragon stood before the woman which was ready to be delivered, for to devour her child as soon as it was born" (Rev. 12:4).

2. It will be the devil who will organize and lead the last rebellion against God.

"And when the thousand years are expired, Satan shall be loosed out of his prison, and shall go out to deceive the nations which are in the four quarters of the earth, Gog and Magog, to gather them together to battle: the number of whom is as the sand of the sea. And they went up on the breadth of the earth, and compassed the camp of the saints about, and the beloved city: and fire came down from God out of heaven and devoured them" (Rev. 20:7–9).

The organizational abilities of the devil, as demonstrated by these two episodes, one a historical account and the other a future event, are simply staggering to contemplate. To illustrate this ability, consider the following: During the Civil War, without a doubt, the most beloved and respected southern general was Robert E. Lee. Lee was kind and considerate to his troops, brilliant in battle, and fearless to a fault. During some of the lesser battles the Confederate troops on occasion would refuse to fight until their vaunted leader would retire to the rear, lest he be killed over an unimportant piece of ground. "Better a thousand should die than Lee," became the concern and cry of Johnny Reb. In light of this near worship of Lee, what chance would a disgruntled soldier have in his clumsy attempts to destroy the brave General and assume full command himself? Furthermore, what are the odds that he could persuade fully one-third of Lee's officers and boot soldiers to willingly join ranks with him? And yet this is precisely what Lucifer did as seen in Revelation 12:4. Not only has he once performed this unbelievable trick during earth's earliest days, but he will someday pull it off again, this time following the glorious millennium.

3. It was the devil who systematically subjected the Old Testament patriarch Job to fiery trials in an attempt to break him. (See Job 1–2.) Paul warns about the devil and his wicked (but highly organized) cohorts:

"Put on the whole armour of God, that ye may be able to stand against the wiles of the devil. For we wrestle not against flesh and blood, but against principalities, against powers, against the rulers of the darkness of this world, against spiritual wickedness in high places" (Eph. 6:11, 12).

IV. The Names of Satan. There are no less than twenty-two names and titles of this perverted ex-prince of paradise, which study by itself gives much insight into his evil character.

A. Satan (adversary): his most common name, used some fifty-two times.

B. The devil (slanderer): used thirty-five times.

C. The prince of the power of the air.

"Wherein in time past ye walked according to the course of this world, according to the prince of the power of the air, the spirit that now worketh in the children of disobedience" (Eph. 2:2).

D. The god of this age.

"In whom the god of this world hath blinded the minds of them which believe not, lest the light of the glorious gospel of Christ, who is the image of God, should shine unto them" (2 Cor. 4:4).

E. The king of death.

"Forasmuch then as the children are partakers of flesh and blood, he also himself likewise took part of the same; that through death he might destroy him that had the power of death, that is the devil" (Heb. 2:14).

F. The prince of this world.

"Now is the judgment of this world: now shall the prince of this world be cast out" (Jn. 12:31).

G. The ruler of darkness.

"For we wrestle not against flesh and blood, but against principalities, against powers, against the rulers of the darkness of this world, against spiritual wickedness in high places" (Eph. 6:12).

H. Leviathan (one who dwells in the sea of humanity).

"In that day the Lord with his sore and great and strong sword shall punish leviathan the piercing serpent, even leviathan that crooked serpent; and he shall slay the dragon that is in the sea" (Isa. 27:1).

Here Satan is likened to a powerful water dinosaur that swam the waters in the beginning of earth's history. Job describes these fearful sea serpents:

"Canst thou draw out leviathan with an hook? or his tongue with a cord which thou lettest down? Canst thou put an hook into his nose? or bore his jaw through with a thorn?" (Job 41:1, 2).

"Who can open the doors of his face? his teeth are terrible round about. His scales are his pride, shut up together as with a close seal. One is so near to another, that no air can come between them. They are joined one to another, they stick together, that they cannot be sundered. By his neesings a light doth shine, and his eyes are like the eyelids of the morning. Out of his mouth go burning lamps, and sparks of fire leap out. Out of his nostrils goeth smoke, as out of a seething pot or cal-

dron. His breath kindleth coals, and a flame goeth out of his mouth. In his neck remaineth strength, and sorrow is turned into joy before him. The flakes of his flesh are joined together: they are firm in themselves; they cannot be moved. His heart is as firm as a stone; yea, as hard as a piece of the nether millstone. When he raiseth up himself, the mighty are afraid: by reason of breakings they purify themselves. The sword of him that layeth at him cannot hold: the spear, the dart, nor the habergeon. He esteemeth iron as straw, and brass as rotten wood. The arrow cannot make him flee: slingstones are turned with him into stubble. Darts are counted as stubble: he laugheth at the shaking of a spear. Sharp stones are under him: he spreadeth sharp pointed things upon the mire. He maketh the deep to boil like a pot: he maketh the sea like a pot of ointment. He maketh a path to shine after him; one would think the deep to be hoary. Upon earth there is not his like, who is made without fear. He beholdeth all high things: he is a king over all the children of pride" (Job 41:14-34).

I. Lucifer (lightbearer, shining one).

"How art thou fallen from heaven, O Lucifer, son of the morning! how art thou cut down to the ground, which didst weaken the nations" (Isa. 14:12).

He was called Lucifer, for he once functioned as "the son of the morning." But with the advent of Christ, the true "sun of righteousness has arisen with healing in his wings" (Mal. 4:2).

J. The dragon.

"And there was war in heaven: Michael and his angels fought against the dragon; and the dragon fought and his angels" (Rev. 12:7).

K. The deceiver.

"And the devil that deceived them was cast into the lake of fire and brimstone, where the beast and the false prophet are, and shall be tormented day and night for ever and ever" (Rev. 20:10).

Satan is not only a deceiver, but self-deceived as well. This is the worst deception. He once thought and still believes he can defeat Jehovah God and his Christ.

L. Apollyon (destroyer).

"And they had a king over them, which is the angel of the bottomless pit, whose name in the Hebrew tongue is Abaddon, but in the Greek tongue hath his name Apollyon" (Rev. 9:11).

Man's unbelievable brutality and cruelty to fellowmen can often only be explained by the evil energy and sometimes even possession by this deadly destroyer.

M. Beelzebub (prince of demons).

"But when the Pharisees heard it, they said, This fellow doth not cast out devils, but by Beelzebub the prince of the devils" (Mt. 12:24).

Our blessed Lord was once compared to the devil by the wicked Pharisees.

N. Belial (vileness, ruthlessness).

"And what concord hath Christ with Belial? or what part hath he that believeth with an infidel?" (2 Cor. 6:15).

Vileness and ruthlessness often go hand in hand, as seen by the rise of vicious rape and senseless murder cases.

O. The wicked one.

"The field is the world; the good seed are the children of the kingdom; but the tares are the children of the wicked one" (Mt. 13:38).

In this extended parable our Lord describes Satan as that wicked one who sowed bad seed (tares) in God's wheat field.

"And we know that we are of God, and the whole world lieth in wickedness" (1 Jn. 5:19).

P. The tempter.

"For this cause, when I could no longer forbear, I sent to know your faith, lest by some means the tempter have tempted you, and our labour be in vain" (1 Thess. 3:5).

He is called the tempter, of course, because of his first crime against humanity in enticing Eve to disobey God. (See Gen. 3.)

Q. The accuser of the brethren.

"And I heard a loud voice saying in heaven, Now is come salvation, and strength, and the kingdom of our God, and the power of his Christ: for the accuser of our brethren is cast down, which accused them before our God day and night" (Rev. 12:10).

This title describes one of the most malicious and misunderstood present-day activities of the devil. We shall consider this in detail in a later part of our study.

R. An angel of light.

"And no marvel; for Satan himself is transformed into an angel of light. Therefore it is no great thing if his ministers also be transformed as the ministers of righteousness; whose end shall be according to their works" (2 Cor. 11:14, 15).

These verses and this title by itself explains the rise of the many false cults of today. How polished and popular his ministers often become. How cleverly they can distort and twist the Word of God.

S. A liar.

"Ye are of your father the devil, and the lusts of your father ye will do. He was a murderer from the beginning, and abode not in the truth, because there is no truth in him. When he speaketh a lie, he speaketh of his own: for he is a liar, and the father of it" (Jn. 8:44).

He is a liar because of his words in Genesis 3:4, 5.

"And the serpent said unto the woman, Ye shall not surely die: For God doth know that in the day ye eat thereof, then your eyes shall be opened, and ye shall be as gods, knowing good and evil" (Gen. 3:4, 5).

T. A murderer.

"Ye are of your father the devil, and the lusts of your father ye will do. He was a murderer from the beginning, and abode not in the truth, because there is no truth in him. When he speaketh a lie, he speaketh of his own: for he is a liar, and the father of it" (Jn. 8:44).

It was Satan who inspired Cain to slaughter his godly brother, Abel, thus earning his title as a murderer.

U. The enemy.

"The enemy that sowed them is the devil; the harvest is the end of the world; and the reapers are the angels" (Mt. 13:39).

V. A roaring lion.

"Be sober, be vigilant; because your adversary the devil, as a roaring lion, walketh about, seeking whom he may devour" (1 Pet. 5:8).

As the lion is king of beasts, so is Satan, king over demons. Both are powerful and ruthless concerning their victims.

V. The Activities of Satan. Thus far we have considered the *existence, origin, personality,* and *names* of Satan. Now let us examine his *activities.* Just what does this ex-prince of paradise do? We shall see that whatever else he may be accused of, Satan can never be charged with laziness.

A. He imitates God.

Imitation may well be the most sincere form of flattery. While the devil hates God, on the one hand, he nevertheless possesses an obsession to be like God. How ironic that God offers freely to all repenting sinners that priceless privilege which Satan desperately and unsuccessfully has long sought, namely, to be like God. The Apostle John describes this truth for us:

"Behold, what manner of love the Father hath bestowed upon us, that we should be called the sons of God: therefore the world knoweth us not, because it knew him not. Beloved, now are we the sons of God, and it doth not yet appear what we shall be: but we know that, when he shall appear, we shall be like him; for we shall see him as he is" (1 Jn. 3:1, 2).

How does Satan imitate God? Consider:

1. He has a false trinity.

"And the beast which I saw was like unto a leopard, and his feet were as the feet of a bear, and his mouth as the mouth of a lion; and the dragon gave him his power, and his seat, and great authority" (Rev. 13:2).

"And I saw three unclean spirits like frogs come out of the mouth of the dragon, and out of the mouth of the beast, and out of the mouth of the false prophet" (Rev. 16:13).

The true Trinity consists, of course, in the Father, the Son, and the Holy Spirit. But Satan mimics this heavenly trio with his own hellish threesome. In this terrible trinity, he assumes the part of the Father; the antichrist is likened to the Son; and the false prophet is assigned the role of the Holy Spirit.

2. He has his synagogues.

"I know thy works, and tribulation, and poverty, (but thou art rich) and I know the blasphemy of them which say they are Jews, and are not, but are the synagogue of Satan" (Rev. 2:9).

It is tragic but true that there are today literally thousands of churches in America alone in which the Book, blood, and blessed hope are never even remotely referred to! Dr. Donald Barnhouse used to say that when searching for the devil one should not forget to check behind the pulpit.

3. He has his doctrines.

"Now the Spirit speaketh expressly, that in the latter times some shall depart from the faith, giving heed to seducing spirits, and doctrines of devils" (1 Tim. 4:1).

Some of these doctrines taught in Satan's school of systematic theology would be: free love, abortion on demand, homosexuality, salvation by good works, evolution, and many other Christ-dishonoring creeds of our day.

4. He has his mysteries.

"But unto you I say, and unto the rest in Thyatira, as many as have not this doctrine, and which have not known the depths of Satan, as they speak; I will put upon you none other burden" (Rev. 2:24).

"For the mystery of iniquity doth already work: only he who now letteth will let, until he be taken out of the way" (2 Thess. 2:7).

5. He has his throne.

"I know thy works, and where thou dwellest, even where Satan's seat is: and thou holdest fast my name, and hast not denied my faith, even in those days wherein Antipas was my faithful martyr, who was slain among you, where Satan dwelleth" (Rev. 2:13).

"And the beast which I saw was like unto a leopard, and his feet were as the feet of a bear, and his mouth as the mouth of a lion; and the dragon gave him his power, and his seat, and great authority" (Rev. 13:2).

Note especially the phrase "where Satan's seat is." This seems to indicate that Satan has transferred his headquarters from Babylon (see Gen. 11:1-9) to Pergamos in Turkey during John's day. However, the Apostle John later hints (see Rev. 18) that the devil's capital will once again be transferred back to Babylon during the tribulation.

6. He has his kingdom.

"And the devil said unto him, All this power will I give thee, and the glory of them: for that is delivered unto me; and to whomsoever I will give it" (Lk. 4:6).

Often the question is asked whether Satan really had the right to offer the Savior the kingdoms of this earth. In a very real sense, he did. Note the testimony of John the apostle:

"Hereafter I will not talk much with you: for the prince of this world cometh, and hath nothing in me" (Jn. 14:30).

"And we know that we are of God, and the whole world lieth in wickedness" (1 Jn. 5:19).

7. He has his worshipers.

"And they worshipped the dragon which gave power unto the beast: and they wor-

shipped the beast, saying, Who is like unto the beast? who is able to make war with him?" (Rev. 13:4).

8. He has his angels.

"And there was war in heaven: Michael and his angels fought against the dragon; and the dragon fought and his angels" (Rev. 12:7).

In a previous verse (Rev. 12:4) John seems to indicate that Satan may have persuaded a full one-third of heaven's angels to join with him in his foul revolt against Jehovah God.

9. He has his ministers.

"Therefore it is no great thing if his ministers also be transformed as the ministers of righteousness; whose end shall be according to their works" (2 Cor. 11:15).

It is sobering to contemplate that the "God is dead" movement of several decades ago was not started by a communist or atheist, but was the product of a Methodist professor teaching in a church-related college. By the way, that movement itself is now dead while God is still very much alive.

10. He has his miracles.

"Even him, whose coming is after the working of Satan with all power and signs and lying wonders" (2 Thess. 2:9).

Certain false religious leaders have deceived multitudes of people because of their apparent ability to perform genuine miracles. But the Scriptures declare that the devil also possesses this power. Hear the warning of Jesus on this matter.

"Not every one that saith unto me, Lord, Lord, shall enter into the kingdom of heaven; but he that doeth the will of my Father which is in heaven. Many will say to me in that day, Lord, Lord, have we not prophesied in thy name? and in thy name have cast out devils? and in thy name done many wonderful works? And then will I profess unto them, I never knew you: depart from me, ye that work iniquity" (Mt. 7:21-23).

11. He has his sacrifices.

"But I say, that the things which the Gentiles sacrifice, they sacrifice to devils, and not to God: and I would not that ye should have fellowship with devils" (1 Cor. 10:20).

12. He has his fellowship (1 Cor. 10:20).

13. He has his armies.

"And it shall come to pass in that day, that the LORD shall punish the host of the high ones that are on high, and the kings of the earth upon the earth" (Isa. 24:21).

These infernal armies will someday be soundly defeated by Almighty God at Armageddon.

"And I looked, and behold a white cloud, and upon the cloud one sat like unto the Son of man, having on his head a golden crown, and in his hand a sharp sickle. And another angel came out of the temple, crying with a loud voice to him that sat on the cloud, Thrust in thy sickle, and reap: for the time is come for thee to reap; for the harvest of the earth is ripe. And another angel came out of the temple which is in heaven, he also having a sharp sickle" (Rev. 14:14-17).

"And he gathered them together into a place called in the Hebrew tongue Armageddon" (Rev. 16:16).

"And I saw heaven opened, and behold a white horse; and he that sat upon him was called Faithful and True, and in righteousness he doth judge and make war. His eyes were as a flame of fire, and on his head were many crowns; and he had a name written, that no man knew, but he himself. And he was clothed with a vesture dipped in blood: and his name is called The Word of God. And the armies which were in heaven followed him upon white horses, clothed in fine linen, white and clean. And out of his mouth goeth a sharp sword, that with it he should smite the nations: and he shall rule them with a rod of iron: and he treadeth the winepress of the fierceness and wrath of Almighty God. And he hath on his vesture and on his thigh a name written, KING OF KINGS, AND LORD OF LORDS" (Rev. 19:11-16).

Thus we see through these thirteen examples just how Satan imitates God. But what other activity does this apostate angel indulge in?

B. He sows tares among God's wheat. Our Lord described this activity in his most extended parable.

"Another parable put he forth unto them, saying, The kingdom of heaven is likened unto a man which sowed good seed in his field: But while men slept, his enemy came and sowed tares among the wheat, and went his way. But when the blade was sprung up, and brought forth fruit, then appeared the tares also. So the servants of the householder came and said unto him, Sir, didst not thou sow good seed in thy field? from whence then hath it tares? He said unto them, An enemy hath done this. The servants said unto him, Wilt thou then that we go and gather them up? But he said, Nay; lest while ye gather up the tares, ye root up also the wheat with them. Let both grow together until the harvest: and in the time of harvest I will say to the reapers, Gather ye together first the tares, and bind them in bundles to burn them: but gather the wheat into my barn" (Mt. 13:24-30).

"Then Jesus sent the multitude away, and went into the house: and his disciples came unto him, saying, Declare unto us the parable of the tares of the field. He answered and said unto them, He that soweth the good seed is the Son of man; the field is the world; the good seed are the children of the kingdom; but the tares are the children of the wicked one; the enemy that sowed them is the devil; the harvest is the end of the world; and the reapers are the angels. As therefore the tares are gathered and burned in the fire; so shall it be in the end of this world. The Son of man shall send forth his angels, and they shall gather out of his kingdom all things that offend, and them which do iniquity; and shall cast them into a furnace of fire: there shall be wailing and gnashing of teeth. Then shall the righteous shine forth as the sun in the kingdom of their Father. Who hath ears to hear, let him hear" (Mt. 13:36-43).

C. He instigates false doctrine.

"Now the spirit speaketh expressly, that in the latter times some shall depart from the faith, giving heed to seducing spirits, and doctrines of devils; speaking lies in hypocrisy; having their conscience seared with a hot iron; forbidding to marry, and commanding to abstain from meats, which God hath created to be received with thanksgiving of them which believe and know the truth" (1 Tim. 4:1-3).

D. He perverts the Word of God. This he does by:
 1. Taking it out of context.

"And saith unto him, If thou be the Son of God, cast thyself down: for it is written, He shall give his angels charge concerning thee: and in their hands they shall bear thee up, lest at any time thou dash thy foot against a stone" (Mt. 4:6).

"Now the serpent was more subtle than any beast of the field which the LORD GOD had made. And he said unto the woman, Yea, hath God said, Ye shall not eat of every tree of the garden? And the woman said unto the serpent, We may eat of the fruit of the trees of the garden: but of the fruit of the tree which is in the midst of the garden, God hath said, Ye shall not eat of it, neither shall ye touch it, lest ye die. And the serpent said unto the woman, Ye shall not surely die" (Gen. 3:1-4).

 2. Causing it to be misinterpreted. How much anguish, frustration, and confusion has the devil wrought simply by causing Christians and non-Christians alike to misinterpret God's Word.

 3. Overstressing one side of a doctrine and ignoring the other side. A classic example of this, of course, would be the doctrine of predestination and free will. An untold number of believers (including preachers) have gone off the deep end by overstressing one side of this two-sided coin.

 4. Understressing certain doctrines. Perhaps the one great biblical truth downplayed today is that vital doctrine of the local church. To quote once more from the article, "If I Were the Devil":

"Then I would turn to that most despised and deadly institution of all—the local church! I would continue to attack it from the outside (just to keep in practice), but would concentrate the bulk of my evil efforts from within. 'The church is dead' would become my creed and cry. If I were the devil I would do my utmost to convince professing Christians that the local church is finished! Not weak, not ineffective; but dead and decaying! I would encourage them to dig a hole, carve an epitaph, and bury it as quietly and quickly as possible. Christianity could then proceed to new glories where cell groups would replace Sunday nights and sermons would be set aside for buzz sessions."

Let it be said in conclusion at this point that, contrary to popular opinion, Satan is *not* afraid of the Word of God. In fact, he delights to use it—*if* he can misinterpret or mangle it in some fashion. This can be aptly demonstrated by the various false cults whose followers often spout Scripture verses by the dozens to "prove" their false doctrines, all taken out of context, of course.

E. He hinders the works of God's servants.

"Wherefore we would have come unto you, even I Paul, once again; but Satan hindered us" (1 Thess. 2:18).

He cannot do this, of course, except by the direct permission of God who sometimes allows hindrances to teach the believer spiritual lessons.

F. He resists the prayers of God's servants.

"Then said he unto me, Fear not, Daniel: for from the first day that thou didst set thine heart to understand, and to chasten thyself before thy God, thy words were heard, and I am come for thy words. But the prince of the kingdom of Persia withstood me one and twenty days: but lo, Michael, one of the chief princes, came to help me; and I remained there with the kings of Persia" (Dan. 10:12, 13).

Again, as in the former point, it should be noted that Satan cannot do this without God's approval. Thus, sometimes our prayer life is made difficult not because of personal sin, or unwillingness on God's part, but due solely to satanic interference.

G. He blinds men to the truth.

"In whom the god of this world hath blinded the minds of them which believe not, lest the light of the glorious gospel of Christ, who is the image of God, should shine unto them" (2 Cor. 4:4).

H. He steals the Word of God from human hearts.

"When any one heareth the word of the kingdom, and understandeth it not, then cometh the wicked one, and catcheth away that which was sown in his heart. This is he which received seed by the way side" (Mt. 13:19).

I. He accuses Christians before God.

"And the LORD said unto Satan, Whence comest thou? Then Satan answered the LORD, and said, From going to and fro in the earth, and from walking up and down in it. And the LORD said unto Satan, Hast thou considered my servant Job, that there is none like him in the earth, a perfect and an upright man, one that feareth God, and escheweth evil? Then Satan answered the LORD, and said, Doth Job fear God for nought? Hast not thou made an hedge about him, and about his house, and about all that he hath on every side? thou hast blessed the work of his hands, and his substance is increased in the land. But put forth thine hand now, and touch all that he hath, and he will curse thee to thy face. And the LORD said unto Satan, Behold, all that he hath is in thy power; only upon himself put not forth thine hand. So Satan went forth from the presence of the LORD" (Job 1:7-12).

"And the LORD said unto Satan, Hast thou considered my servant Job, that there is none like him in the earth, a perfect and an upright man, one that feareth God, and escheweth evil? and still he holdeth fast his integrity, although thou movest me against him, to destroy him without cause. And Satan answered the LORD, and said, Skin for skin, yea, all that a man hath will he give for his life. But put forth thine hand now, and touch his bone and his flesh, and he will curse thee to thy face. And the LORD said unto Satan, Behold, he is in thine hand; but save his life" (Job 2:3-6).

"And he shewed me Joshua the high priest standing before the angel of the Lord, and Satan standing at his right hand to resist him. And the Lord said unto Satan, The Lord rebuke thee, O Satan; even the Lord that hath chosen Jerusalem rebuke thee: is not this a brand plucked out of the fire? Now Joshua was clothed with filthy garments, and stood before the angel. And he answered and spake unto those that stood before him, saying, Take away the filthy garments from him. And unto him he said, Behold, I have caused thine iniquity to pass from thee, and I will clothe thee with change of raiment" (Zech. 3:1-4).

"And the great dragon was cast out, that old serpent, called the Devil, and Satan, which deceiveth the whole world: he was cast out into the earth, and his angels were cast out with him. And I heard a loud voice saying in heaven, Now is come salvation, and strength, and the kingdom of our God, and the power of his Christ: for the accuser of our brethren is cast down, which accused them before our God day and night" (Rev. 12:9, 10).

These verses inform us concerning one of Satan's most treacherous hatchet jobs, that of bad-mouthing believers. In fact, this was one of several key reasons why the crucified and resurrected Christ had to ascend back to heaven that he might function as our divine defense lawyer.

The following passages speak of this ministry: "And the Lord said, Simon, Simon, behold, Satan hath desired to have you, that he may sift you as wheat: but I have prayed for thee, that thy faith fail not: and when thou art converted, strengthen thy brethren" (Lk. 22:31, 32).

"Wherefore he is able also to save them to the uttermost that come unto God by him, seeing he ever liveth to make intercession for them" (Heb. 7:25).

"Who shall lay any thing to the charge of God's elect? It is God that justifieth. Who is he that condemneth? It is Christ that died, yea, rather, that is risen again, who is even at the right hand of God, who also maketh intercession for us" (Rom. 8:33, 34).

J. He lays snares for men.

"And that they may recover themselves out of the snare of the devil, who are taken captive by him at his will" (2 Tim. 2:26).

"Moreover he must have a good report of them which are without; lest he fall into reproach and the snare of the devil" (1 Tim. 3:7).

An old song reads: "When the danger least thou fearest, then the devil's snare is nearest."

K. He tempts.

"Then was Jesus led up of the Spirit into the wilderness to be tempted of the devil" (Mt. 4:1).

"Put on the whole armour of God, that ye may be able to stand against the wiles of the devil" (Eph. 6:11).

The word "tempt" can refer to two things:

1. To test, to prove with the idea of making better, as seen in Genesis 22:1.

"And it came to pass after these things, that God did tempt Abraham . . ."

2. To entice to do evil, as seen in Matthew 4:1.

L. He afflicts.

"So went Satan forth from the presence of the LORD, and smote Job with sore boils from the sole of his foot unto his crown" (Job 2:7).

"And ought not this woman, being a daughter of Abraham, whom Satan hath bound, lo, these eighteen years, be loosed from this bond on the sabbath day?" (Lk. 13:16).

"And lest I should be exalted above measure through the abundance of the revelations, there was given to me a thorn in the flesh, the messenger of Satan to buffet me, lest I should be exalted above measure" (2 Cor. 12:7).

"How God anointed Jesus of Nazareth with the Holy Ghost and with power: who went about doing good, and healing all that were oppressed of the devil; for God was with him" (Acts 10:38).

The sobering fact to be kept in mind here is that his victims in these verses are believers. While Satan cannot possibly *possess* a Christian, he can, nevertheless (as allowed by God, of course) *oppress* a child of God, both in the mental and physical realm. Sometimes God allows this to happen to purify his child (as in the case of Job), and at other times to punish a believer for his sin. Paul writes of this second case.

"It is reported commonly that there is fornication among you, and such fornication as is not so much as named among the Gentiles, that one should have his father's wife. And ye are puffed up, and have not rather mourned, that he that hath done this deed might be taken away from among you. For I verily, as absent in body, but present in spirit, have judged already, as though I were present, concerning him that hath so done this deed, in the name of our Lord Jesus Christ, when ye are gathered together, and my spirit, with the power of our Lord Jesus Christ, to deliver such an one unto Satan for the destruction of the flesh, that the spirit may be saved in the day of the Lord Jesus" (1 Cor. 5:1-5).

M. He deceives.

"And the great dragon was cast out, that old serpent, called the Devil, and Satan, which deceiveth the whole world: he was cast out into the earth, and his angels were cast out with him" (Rev. 12:9).

"And shall go out to deceive the nations which are in the four quarters of the earth, Gog and Magog, to gather them together to battle: the number of whom is as the sand of the sea" (Rev. 20:8).

"And the devil that deceived them was cast into the lake of fire and brimstone, where the beast and the false prophet are, and shall be tormented day and night for ever and ever" (Rev. 20:10).

An old proverb says: The worst deception is self-deception. This may be true, but certainly in the area of faith, the most *common* deception is satanic deception. Probably his greatest deception of all time is the false but almost universally believed concept that one may work his or her way into heaven.

N. He undermines the sanctity of the home.

"Let the husband render unto the wife due benevolence: and likewise also the wife unto the husband. The wife hath not power of her own body, but the husband: and likewise also the husband hath not power of his own body, but the wife. Defraud ye not one the other, except it be with consent for a time, that ye may give yourselves to fasting and prayer; and come together again, that Satan tempt you not for your incontinency" (1 Cor. 7:3-5).

Now read a paraphrase of this same passage: "The man should give his wife all that is her right as a married woman, and the wife should do the same for her husband: for a girl who marries no longer has full right to her own body, for her husband then has his rights to it, too; and in the same way the husband no longer has full right to his own body, for it belongs also to his wife. So do not refuse these rights to each other. The only exception to this rule would be the agreement of both husband and wife to refrain from the rights of marriage for a limited time, so that they can give themselves more completely to prayer. Afterwards, they should come together again so that Satan won't be able to tempt them because of their lack of self-control" (1 Cor. 7:3-5, TLB).

Very few marriage counselors ever take satanic activity into consideration when advising couples having marital problems. Sometimes the real fault lies not with the husband or wife, but squarely with Satan. The devil despises the very institution of marriage because it was originated and given by God himself. (See Gen. 2:20-25.)

O. He prompts both saints and sinners to transgress against the holiness of God.

1. It was Satan who caused David to disobey God.

"And Satan stood up against Israel, and provoked David to number Israel" (1 Chron. 21:1).

2. It was Satan who caused Judas to betray Christ.

"And supper being ended, the devil having now put into the heart of Judas Iscariot, Simon's son, to betray him" (Jn. 13:2).

3. It was Satan who caused Peter to rebuke Christ, and later to deny him.

"Then Peter took him, and began to rebuke him, saying, Be it far from thee, Lord: this shall not be unto thee. But he turned, and said unto Peter, Get thee behind me, Satan: thou art an offence unto me: for thou savourest not the things that be of God, but those that be of men" (Mt. 16:22, 23).

"Jesus answered him, Wilt thou lay down thy life for my sake? Verily, verily, I say unto you, The cock shall not crow, till thou hast denied me thrice" (Jn. 13:38).

4. It was Satan who caused Ananias to lie to the Holy Spirit.

"But Peter said, Ananias, why hath Satan filled thine heart to lie to the Holy Ghost, and to keep back part of the price of the land?" (Acts 5:3).

VI. The Various Geographical and Spiritual Locations of Satan. We have already demonstrated the common error today which pictures Satan as a medieval and mythical two-horned, fork-tailed creature. Now the question: What of his past, present, and future locations? The devil is like a check forger in that he moves around constantly. Satan has been to, is in, or will occupy the following six locations:

A. In the heavenlies, as God's choir leader. This was his past location, prior to his fall. See Ezekiel 8.

B. In the heavenlies, as God's chief enemy. This is his present location.

"Now there was a day when the sons of God came to present themselves before the Lord, and Satan came also among them. And the Lord said unto Satan, Whence comest thou? Then Satan answered the Lord, and said, From going to and fro in the earth, and from walking up and down in it" (Job 1:6, 7).

"And he showed me Joshua the high priest standing before the angel of the LORD, and Satan standing at his right hand to resist him. And the LORD said unto Satan, The LORD rebuke thee, O Satan; even the LORD that hath chosen Jerusalem rebuke thee: is not this a brand plucked out of the fire?" (Zech. 3:1, 2).

C. On earth only. This will be his first future location. During the final half of the coming tribulation, Satan will be cast out of heaven, and his sphere of activities will be limited to this earth. See Rev. 12: 7-12.

Some believe that this passage refers to his original fall in Genesis, but this cannot be, as proven by the two phrases, "the accuser of our brethren," and "by the blood of the lamb." In other words, at the time of his first fall there were no "brethren" to accuse, and the blood of God's perfect lamb had not yet been spilled.

Also to be noted in this passage is the phrase, "for the devil is come down unto you, having great wrath, because he knoweth that he hath but a short time." How will the devil know this? From reading the book of Daniel. When he came to chapter 9 and read about the seventy weeks, he then understood the length of the tribulation to be seven years.

D. In the bottomless pit. This will be his second future location. Immediately after Christ's great victory at Armageddon, we read the following words:

"And I saw an angel come down from heaven, having the key of the bottomless pit and a great chain in his hand. And he laid hold on the dragon, that old serpent, which is the Devil, and Satan, and bound him a thousand years, and cast him into the bottomless pit, and shut him up, and set a seal upon him, that he should deceive the nations no more, till the thousand years should be fulfilled: and after that he must be loosed a little season" (Rev. 20:1-3).

E. On earth for the last time after the millennium. This will be his third future location.

"And when the thousand years are expired, Satan shall be loosed out of his prison, and shall go out to deceive the nations which are in the four quarters of the earth, Gog and Magog, to gather them together to battle: the number of whom is as the sand of the sea. And they went up on the breadth of the earth, and compassed the camp of the saints about, and the beloved city: and fire came down from God out of heaven and devoured them" (Rev. 20:7-9).

Where will Satan get this mighty army? They will consist of many of the millions born during the millennium of saved parents who survived the great tribulation and entered earth's golden age. Yet many of these "kingdom kids" will refuse to accept Christ, in spite of their perfect environment, giving King Jesus lip service to be sure, but retaining unregenerate hearts all the while. Thus, when Satan is released, they will eagerly join his revolt against God's anointed.

F. In the lake of fire forever. This will be the devil's final future location.

"And the devil that deceived them was cast into the lake of fire and brimstone, where the beast and the false prophet are, and shall be tormented day and night for ever and ever" (Rev. 20:10).

VII. The Limitations of Satan. As one compiles and analyzes the many biblical passages on the devil, it becomes evident that he is the most powerful creature in all God's universe. This depraved and deadly dragon possesses more strength and "savvy" than any archangel or saint. But in spite of all this, he is still a creature and not the Creator. Because of this blessed truth, his power and knowledge are limited. We shall now consider the restrictions of this red dragon.

A. He is not omnipresent. The devil cannot be in China, Chicago, and Cuba at the same instant. However, this is not by any means to say that believers in those areas cannot be tempted at the same instant, for Satan has literally millions of fallen angels to do his bidding, thus extending his ministry universally.

B. He is not omnipotent. While he is still the strongest creature in the universe, his power compared to God's is like an ant pitted against a mighty elephant.

C. He is not omniscient. The devil has, admittedly, acquired an immense amount of knowledge by simply being around during the last 6,000 years, but he is totally ignorant of many things known by the most humble and uneducated believer. He knows nothing of God's love, his mercy, his grace, and his forgiveness. The devil does not know the future, nor all the secrets of the past. The question is often asked concerning Satan's reported wisdom and Bible-reading habits. If he has indeed read the Word of God, then doesn't he know his doom is sealed, and that the lake of fire will be his eternal imprisonment? He is indeed aware of these prophecies, but it must be kept in mind that according to Ezekiel 28:17, sin has corrupted the wisdom of Satan to the point where he still thinks he can defeat God. Sometimes the most clever criminal is a psychopathic killer.

VIII. The Christian's Victory Over Satan. The word *nikao* is found twenty-eight times in the Greek New Testament, and is almost always translated by the word "overcome." There are three important verses in which this word is used:

"These things I have spoken unto you, that in me ye might have peace. In the world ye shall have tribulation: but be of good cheer; I have overcome the world" (Jn. 16:33).

"Ye are of God, little children, and have overcome them: because greater is he that is in you, than he that is in the world" (1 Jn. 4:4).

"He that overcometh shall inherit all things; and I will be his God, and he shall be my son" (Rev. 21:7).

If language means anything at all, these verses promise the child of God total victory over his enemy, the devil. But how does the Christian experience this promised victory? He does it by keeping the same fundamental facts in mind that any would-be victor would, whether in the secular or spiritual battlefield. Here then are four fundamental facts:

A. He must know his own weaknesses.
B. He must know his own strength.
C. He must know the weakness of his enemy.
D. He must know the strength of his enemy.

To either overestimate or underestimate in any of these four areas could prove to be a fatal error.

In one of his parables, our Lord warns of this very thing:

"For which of you, intending to build a tower, sitteth not down first, and counteth the cost, whether he have sufficient to finish it? Lest haply, after he hath laid the foundation, and is not able to finish it, all that behold it begin to mock him, saying, This man began to build, and was not able to finish. Or what king, going to make war against another king, sitteth not down first, and consulteth whether he be able with ten thousand to meet him that cometh against him with twenty thousand? Or else, while the other is yet a great way off, he sendeth an ambassage, and desireth conditions of peace" (Lk. 14:28-32).

Let us now examine these four facts the victor must be aware of:

A. The weakness of the Christian.

"I am the vine, ye are the branches: He that abideth in me, and I in him, the same bringeth forth much fruit: for without me ye can do nothing. If a man abide not in me, he is cast forth as a branch, and is withered; and men gather them, and cast them into the fire, and they are burned" (Jn. 15:5, 6).

When I was first saved, I felt the Christian life was a 50/50 proposition. That is to say, I would carry my 50 percent of the load, and God would assume the remaining half. But to my dismay I kept dropping my end of the load. I then suggested to God that we alter the proportions whereby he would carry 60 percent and I would be responsible for the remaining 40 percent. But alas, this also proved too heavy. So, I reasoned, a 70/30 agreement would surely work. But again, failure. Finally, after many years in the work of the Lord, I sometimes think I have things down to a 98/2 arrangement. But I still am tempted to feel that I surely, by *now*, must be able to carry on at least 2 percent of the Master's work by myself. There simply has to be something I can perform in the flesh for God. But Jesus said, "for without me ye can do nothing."

In Romans 7:18, Paul refers to this very thing:
"For I know that in me (that is, in my flesh) dwelleth no good thing: for to will is present with me; but how to perform that which is good I find not" (Rom. 7:18).

So then, the first basic fact a Christian must be aware of to assure victory over Satan is his own weakness.

B. The strength of the Christian. This is the second vital principle to be observed in guaranteeing spiritual success. What, though, is our chief strength? The answer is:

"I am crucified with Christ: nevertheless I live; yet not I, but Christ liveth in me: and the life which I now live in the flesh I live by the faith of the Son of God, who loved me, and gave himself for me" (Gal. 2:20).

"I can do all things through Christ which strengtheneth me" (Phil. 4:13).

C. The weakness of Satan. Third, we must fully understand the weakness of our enemy. According to the Scriptures, the devil is powerless in the following areas:

1. He cannot tempt a believer except by God's permission. This is brought out vividly in Job 1:8-12.

"And the Lord said unto Satan, Hast thou considered my servant Job, that there is none like him in the earth, a perfect and an upright man, one that feareth God, and escheweth evil? Then Satan answered the Lord, and said, Doth Job fear God for nought? Hast not thou made an hedge about him, and about his house, and about all that he hath on every side? thou hast blessed the work of his hands, and his substance is increased in the land. But put forth thine hand now, and touch all that he hath, and he will curse thee to thy face. And the Lord said unto Satan, Behold, all that he hath is in thy power; only upon himself put not forth thine hand. So Satan went forth from the presence of the Lord" (Job 1:8–12).

It should be noted here that in verse 10 Satan told the exact truth, for God had indeed made a hedge about Job. Thus, when a child of God is being subjected to some fiery temptation or trial, he should keep the following thrilling truths in mind.

First, God knows exactly how much his child can bear.

"For he knoweth our frame; he remembereth that we are dust" (Ps. 103:14).

Second, he will not allow Satan to go beyond this breaking point.

"There hath no temptation taken you but such as is common to man: but God is faithful, who will not suffer you to be tempted above that ye are able; but will with the temptation also make a way to escape, that ye may be able to bear it" (1 Cor. 10:13).

Third, he only allows the temptation in the first place to strengthen and purify us. In Genesis 50, Joseph reviewed with his brothers their former act of treachery in selling him into Egyptian slavery. He concluded:

"But as for you, ye thought evil against me; but God meant it unto good, to bring to pass, as it is this day, to save much people alive" (Gen. 50:20).

James and Peter also affirm this third principle.

"James, a servant of God and of the Lord Jesus Christ, to the twelve tribes which are scattered abroad, greeting. My brethren, count it all joy when ye fall into divers temptations; knowing this, that the trying of your faith worketh patience. But let patience have her perfect work, that ye may be perfect and entire, wanting nothing" (Jas. 1:1-4).

"Blessed is the man that endureth temptation: for when he is tried, he shall receive the crown of life, which the Lord hath promised to them that love him" (Jas. 1:12).

"Wherein ye greatly rejoice, though now for a season, if need be, ye are in heaviness through manifold temptations: That the trial of your faith, being much more precious than of gold that perisheth, though it be tried with fire, might be found unto praise and honour and glory at the appearing of Jesus Christ" (1 Pet. 1:6, 7).

2. He cannot stand to be resisted.

"Submit yourselves therefore to God. Resist the devil, and he will flee from you" (Jas. 4:7).

But how does one go about resisting the devil? James answers this—by submitting first to God.

"Neither give place to the devil" (Eph. 4:27).

Satan enjoys a lively debate (like the one he carried on with Eve in Genesis 3), but he cannot tolerate being resisted. The Christian can successfully resist the devil if he does the following:

First, he must know how the devil attacks. Paul warns of this.

"Lest Satan should get an advantage of us: for we are not ignorant of his devices" (2 Cor. 2:11).

But what are his devices? During the final section of our study we will briefly consider the sixteen deadly devices of the devil.

Second, he must stand guard waiting for Satan to attack.

"Be sober, be vigilant; because your adversary the devil, as a roaring lion, walketh about, seeking whom he may devour" (1 Pet. 5:8).

Third, he must have on the proper protection when Satan attacks.

"Finally, my brethren, be strong in the Lord, and in the power of his might. Put on the whole armour of God, that ye may be able to stand against the wiles of the devil. For we wrestle not against flesh and blood, but against principalities, against powers, against the rulers of the darkness of this world, against spiritual wickedness in high places. Wherefore take unto you the whole armour of God, that ye may be able to withstand in the evil day, and having done all, to stand. Stand therefore, having your loins girt about with truth, and having on the breastplate of righteousness: and your feet shod with the preparation of the gospel of peace; above all, taking the shield of faith, wherewith ye shall be able to quench all the fiery darts of the wicked. And take the helmet of salvation, and the sword of the Spirit, which is the word of God" (Eph. 6:10-17).

The Apostle Paul, of course, spent the last part of his ministry in a Roman prison (Acts 28). Doubtless he had many opportunities to watch his Roman guards put on their full battle armor. As the book of Ephesians was written during this time, it seems very probable that the Holy Spirit led Paul to take each piece of armor and apply it to the Christian fight against Satan. It has often been observed that Paul lists no armor protection piece for the back parts. The reason is obvious, of course. The Roman soldier was never expected to turn his back to the enemy.

3. He cannot stand the blood of Christ, nor the positive testimony of the Christian.

> "And they overcame him by the blood of the Lamb, and by the word of their testimony; and they loved not their lives unto the death" (Rev. 12:11).

D. The strength of Satan. This is the fourth and final principle one must grasp to assure victory—the strong points of his enemy. The following list could well be called "The Sixteen Deadly Ds of the Devil."

1. Disappointment. Who has not experienced this emotion literally hundreds of times? But to the knowledgeable Christian *all* disappointments are *his* (God's) appointments, and must be viewed as such, lest Satan gain the advantage. To be disappointed is to forget Romans 8:28:

> "And we know that all things work together for good to them that love God, to them who are the called according to his purpose."

2. Discouragement. Discouragement is the second stage of disappointment. All discouragement is of the devil. An event from church history is reported concerning the great reformer, Martin Luther. For days he had been in the valley of discouragement. The pope was trying to kill him. Some of his friends had shunned him. Suddenly he noticed his godly wife coming downstairs dressed in black as if in mourning.

"Woman, where are you going?" he asked.

"To a funeral, husband," she replied.

"Oh, but who died?" he said.

"God did," she softly answered.

With that the great reformer exploded with righteous indignation. It wasn't enough that the pope was trying to kill him, but now he must deal with blasphemy in his own household.

"Woman, who told you such a thing?" he demanded.

Looking him straight in the eye (as only a wife can do) she said: "You did, Martin! The way you've been acting the past few weeks, I was sure you had somehow found out that God was dead!" At that point Luther knelt and asked both God and his wife to forgive him for his discouragement.

To be discouraged is to forget 1 Samuel 30:6:

> "And David was greatly distressed; for the people spake of stoning him, because the soul of all the people was grieved, every man for his sons and for his daughters: but David encouraged himself in the LORD his God."

3. Despair. Despair is the third and final stage of disappointment and discouragement. Unless checked it can prove fatal to the Christian life. To despair is to forget 2 Corinthians 4:8:

> "We are troubled on every side, yet not distressed; we are perplexed, but not in despair."

4. Doubt. Satan used this deadly *D* for the first time in the Garden of Eden. He began his attack upon Eve by doubting the Word of God.

> "And he said unto the woman, Yea, hath God said, Ye shall not eat of every tree of the garden?" (Gen. 3:1).

To doubt is to forget 1 Timothy 2:8:

> "I will therefore that men pray every where, lifting up holy hands, without wrath and doubting."

5. Disbelief. Disbelief is but the final form of doubt. This was vividly demonstrated in Eden. As we have already noted, Satan began by doubting God's Word in Genesis 3:1. He then finished (when he realized he had Eve's ear) by denying the command of the Lord.

> "And the serpent said unto the woman, Ye shall not surely die: for God doth know that in the day ye eat thereof, then your eyes shall be opened, and ye shall be as gods, knowing good and evil" (Gen. 3:4, 5).

To disbelieve is to forget Hebrews 3:12:

> "Take heed, brethren, lest there be in any of you an evil heart of unbelief, in departing from the living God."

6. Distraction. This *D* of the devil can be a very subtle one, for often the distractions are not in themselves bad. In fact, they may be good and wholesome. For example, it is so easy to be distracted from God's perfect will by one's own family or employment. It has been rightly said that often the real enemy of the *best* is not the *worst*, but the *good*.

To be distracted is to forget Matthew 14:30:

> "But when he saw the wind boisterous, he was afraid; and beginning to sink, he cried, saying, Lord, save me."

7. Doublemindedness. How many believers have been affected by this *D*-virus! The Scriptures are replete with examples. Consider but a few:

> "No man can serve two masters: for either he will hate the one, and love the other; or else he will hold to the one, and despise the other. Ye cannot serve God and mammon" (Mt. 6:24).

> "That we henceforth be no more children, tossed to and fro, and carried about with every wind of doctrine, by the sleight of men, and cunning craftiness, whereby they lie in wait to deceive" (Eph. 4:14).

> "Love not the world, neither the things that are in the world. If any man love the world, the love of the Father is not in him. For all that is in the world, the lust of the flesh, and the lust of the eyes, and the pride of life, is not of the Father, but is of the world. And the world passeth away, and the lust thereof: but he that doeth the will of God abideth for ever" (1 Jn. 2:15–17).

The New Testament word which describes a double-minded man in the Greek literally means "a two-souled man." He is like a cork, floating on a wave, now carried to the shore, now away from it. The ancient writer of myths, Aesop, described a double-minded person when he wrote about a time when the beasts and the fowls were engaged in war. The bat tried to belong to both parties. When the birds were victorious, he would wing around telling everyone that he was a bird; when the beasts won a fight, he would walk around assuring everyone that he was a beast. But soon his hypocrisy was discovered by both the beasts and the birds. He had to hide himself, and now he can appear openly only by night.

A more modern story comes to us from our American Civil War concerning a neutral observer attempting to escape after being accidentally trapped in a furious battle. Hoping to continue neutral, he put on a pair of Confederate pants and a Yankee coat and dashed across no-man's land, only to be immediately shot down by both sides. Both pants and coat were literally riddled with bullets.

To be double-minded is to forget James 1:8 and 4:8:

"A double minded man is unstable in all his ways."

"Draw nigh to God, and he will draw nigh to you. Cleanse your hands, ye sinners; and purify your hearts, ye double minded."

8. Dishonesty. The ways Satan can inflict this deadly *D* upon Christians are almost without number. The child of God need not simply lie or steal to be dishonest. To hold back certain facts in a given situation may be dishonest. To owe God tithes and offerings is dishonest. To be less than we should be as pastors, parents, or workers is to cheat our people and children and thus become dishonest. It is estimated that over one-half *billion* dollars each year is raised by false "faith healers" (who cannot do what they claim) and smooth-talking liberals (who do not believe what they say).

To be dishonest is to forget 2 Corinthians 4:2:

"But have renounced the hidden things of dishonesty, not walking in craftiness, nor handling the word of God deceitfully; but by manifestation of the truth commending ourselves to every man's conscience in the sight of God."

9. Deceit. The word deceit is found many times in the New Testament. As one considers them, it is amazing just how many occur in those passages dealing either with the Word of God or the last days, or both. Note but a few of these:

"And then shall that Wicked be revealed, whom the Lord shall consume with the spirit of his mouth, and shall destroy with the brightness of his coming: Even him, whose coming is after the working of Satan with all power and signs and lying

wonders, and with all deceivableness of unrighteousness in them that perish; because they received not the love of the truth, that they might be saved. And for this cause God shall send them strong delusion, that they should believe a lie: That they all might be damned who believed not the truth, but had pleasure in unrighteousness" (2 Thess. 2:8-12).

"For we are not as many, which corrupt the word of God: but as of sincerity, but as of God, in the sight of God speak we in Christ" (2 Cor. 2:17).

"Therefore seeing we have this ministry, as we have received mercy, we faint not; but have renounced the hidden things of dishonesty, not walking in craftiness, nor handling the word of God deceitfully; but by manifestation of the truth commending ourselves to every man's conscience in the sight of God" (2 Cor. 4:1, 2).

"For such are false apostles, deceitful workers, transforming themselves into the apostles of Christ" (2 Cor. 11:13).

"For many deceivers are entered into the world, who confess not that Jesus Christ is come in the flesh. This is a deceiver and an antichrist" (2 Jn. 1:7).

In other words, the devil's big *D* in the last days is deceit. On the one hand, the weird cults of our day deceive people by attempting to *add* to God's Word, while the liberals practice deception by taking *away* from the Scriptures. Jesus himself apparently warns against both deceiving groups in his last spoken message.

"I Jesus have sent mine angel to testify unto you these things in the churches. I am the root and the offspring of David, and the bright and morning star. And the Spirit and the bride say, Come. And let him that heareth say, Come. And let him that is athirst come. And whosoever will, let him take the water of life freely. For I testify unto every man that heareth the words of the prophecy of this book, If any man shall add unto these things, God shall add unto him the plagues that are written in this book: And if any man shall take away from the words of the book of this prophecy, God shall take away his part out of the book of life, and out of the holy city, and from the things which are written in this book" (Rev. 22:16-19).

To be deceitful is to forget Jeremiah 17:9:
"The heart is deceitful above all things, and desperately wicked: who can know it?"

10. Dullness. There may be some disagreement concerning the author of the book of Hebrews, or even questions concerning the location of the recipients. But there is no doubt about the spiritual condition of the readers. In a word, they suffered from dullness. The author reminded them of the need among their group for sound Bible teachers to stem

the tide of iniquity and apostasy prevalent even in that day. But, the author concluded, they simply could not be used. He sadly states why:

"For when for the time ye ought to be teachers, ye have need that one teach you again which be the first principles of the oracles of God; and are become such as have need of milk, and not of strong meat. For every one that useth milk is unskilful in the word of righteousness: for he is a babe. But strong meat belongeth to them that are of full age, even those who by reason of use have their senses exercised to discern both good and evil" (Heb. 5:12–14).

This dullness was also infecting the church at Corinth. Listen to Paul's stern admonition to them:

"And I, brethren, could not speak unto you as unto spiritual, but as unto carnal, even as unto babes in Christ. I have fed you with milk, and not with meat: for hitherto ye were not able to bear it, neither yet now are ye able. For ye are yet carnal: for whereas there is among you envying, and strife, and divisions, are ye not carnal, and walk as men?" (1 Cor. 3:1–3).

To suffer dullness is to forget Heb. 5:11:
"Of whom we have many things to say, and hard to be uttered, seeing ye are dull of hearing."

11. Deadness. Deadness is simply unchecked dullness. A summary of God's overall plan concerning sin and the sinner is as follows: Whereas we were once dead *in* sin, after God's marvelous grace, we now are to be dead *to* sin. Note:

"And you hath he quickened, who were dead in trespasses and sins; even when we were dead in sins, hath quickened us together with Christ, (by grace ye are saved)" (Eph. 2:1, 5).

"What shall we say then? Shall we continue in sin, that grace may abound? God forbid. How shall we, that are dead to sin, live any longer therein? Likewise reckon ye also yourselves to be dead indeed unto sin, but alive unto God through Jesus Christ our Lord" (Rom. 6:1, 2, 11).

Thus, we are to be *dead* to sin, but *alive* unto righteousness. But many believers have allowed Satan to twist these two facts, whereby they become dead to righteousness, and alive to sin.

"Even so faith, if it hath not works, is dead, being alone. For as the body without the spirit is dead, so faith without works is dead also" (Jas. 2:17, 26).

To suffer deadness is to forget Revelation 3:1:

"And unto the angel of the church in Sardis write; These things saith he that hath the seven Spirits of God, and the seven stars; I know thy works, that thou hast a name that thou livest, and art dead."

12. Delay. At the great white judgment throne it may be revealed that this deadly *D* of the devil has been used to damn more souls to hell than any other. It has been remarked that many a man is in hell today who meant to get saved at the eleventh hour, but who died at ten-thirty. It should be made clear to all sinners the terrible danger of procrastination, for God has never promised to save anyone tomorrow. Both James and the author of Hebrews warn of this danger.

"Again, he limiteth a certain day, saying in David, To day, after so long a time; as it is said, To day if ye will hear his voice, harden not your hearts. For if Jesus had given them rest, then would he not afterward have spoken of another day" (Heb. 4:7, 8).

"Go to now, ye that say, To day or to morrow we will go into such a city, and continue there a year, and buy and sell, and get gain: Whereas ye know not what shall be on the morrow. For what is your life? It is even a vapour, that appeareth for a little time, and then vanisheth away. For that ye ought to say, If the Lord will, we shall live, and do this, or that" (Jas. 4:13–15).

To delay is to forget Proverbs 27:1:
"Boast not thyself of tomorrow; for thou knowest not what a day may bring forth."

13. Discord. It has been rightly observed that far more Bible-believing churches have been split over *disposition* than *position*. This is to say the tragic cause of a split is usually discord rather than doctrine. Some troublemaker begins his or her deadly gossip in a local church, raising questions and doubts in the minds of people, doubts that otherwise would have never been entertained. How effectively Satan uses this tool, and how painful it will be at the *bema* judgment seat of Christ for the carnal sowers of discord. To sow discord is to forget Proverbs 6:16–19:

"These six things doth the Lord hate: yea, seven are an abomination unto him: A proud look, a lying tongue, and hands that shed innocent blood, an heart that deviseth wicked imaginations, feet that be swift in running to mischief, a false witness that speaketh lies, and he that soweth discord among brethren."

14. Defilement. Several hundred young people once stood at the altar of the famed Moody Memorial Church in Chicago to answer the call for full-time Christian service. The speaker, Dr. Vance Havner, looked down at this group and uttered a rather strange statement. He said: "Young people, God is pleased that you have come to this prayer altar. But do *not* pray, 'Lord, use me.'" Havner then went on to explain his statement. "You need not ask Him to use you. He'll do that all right! In fact, He'll wear you out, for there's not enough of you to go around as it is! What you should pray, therefore, is 'Lord, make me usable.'"

God does not require golden vessels, nor silver containers, but he insists upon clean ones. A believer who defiles himself with the things of this world can never be used by God, regardless of his education, ability, energy, or experience.

To become defiled is to forget 1 Corinthians 3:16, 17.

"Know ye not that ye are the temple of God, and that the Spirit of God dwelleth in you? If any man defile the temple of God, him shall God destroy; for the temple of God is holy, which temple ye are."

15. Defame. How often are Christians guilty of criticizing or belittling other believers. In fact, some of the most cutting remarks a child of God may receive are at the hands of another child of God. We should be very careful in guarding against this satanic D, for all believers will gain or suffer rewards at the *bema* judgment on account of it.

"For God is not unrighteous to forget your work and labour of love, which ye have shewed toward his name, in that ye have ministered to the saints, and do minister" (Heb. 6:10).

"He that receiveth a prophet in the name of a prophet shall receive a prophet's reward; and he that receiveth a righteous man in the name of a righteous man shall receive a righteous man's reward. And whosoever shall give to drink unto one of these little ones a cup of cold water only in the name of a disciple, verily I say unto you, he shall in no wise lose his reward" (Mt. 10:41, 42).

To defame someone is to forget Psalm 101:5:

"Whoso privily slandereth his neighbour, him will I cut off: him that hath an high look and a proud heart will not I suffer."

16. Disobedience. There are two famous men by the name of Saul in the Bible—one in the Old Testament and one in the New Testament. A very profitable study can be made by comparing and contrasting these two men. Both were from the tribe of Benjamin (1 Sam. 9:2; Phil. 3:5). One was tall and impressive, the other short and unimpressive (1 Sam. 9:2; 2 Cor. 10:10; Gal. 4:13, 14). The first began as God's friend but ended up as his enemy, while the second started as his enemy but wound up as God's friend (1 Sam. 9:16; 10:6, 7; 28:6; Acts 9:1; 2 Tim. 4:18). One went to the witch of Endor in the hour of his death, while the other turned to the Word of God (1 Sam. 28:7; 2 Tim. 4:13). What really

made the difference between these two me The answer is tragically simple—one w s disobedient, the other was obedient.

"And Samuel said, Hath the Lord as great delight in burnt offerings and sacrifices, as in obeying the voice of the Lord? Behold, to obey is better than sacrifice, and to hearken than the fat of rams. For rebellion is as the sin of witchcraft, and stubbornness is as iniquity and idolatry. Because thou hast rejected the word of the Lord, he hath also rejected thee from being king" (1 Sam. 15:22, 23).

"Whereupon as I went to Damascus with authority and commission from the chief priests, at midday, O king, I saw in the way a light from heaven, above the brightness of the sun, shining round about me and them which journeyed with me. And when we were all fallen to the earth, I heard a voice speaking unto me, and saying in the Hebrew tongue, Saul, Saul, why persecutest thou me? it is hard for thee to kick against the pricks. And I said, Who art thou, Lord? And he said, I am Jesus whom thou persecutest. But rise, and stand upon thy feet: for I have appeared unto thee for this purpose, to make thee a minister and a witness both of these things which thou hast seen, and of those things in the which I will appear unto thee; delivering thee from the people, and from the Gentiles, unto whom now I send thee, to open their eyes, and to turn them from darkness to light, and from the power of Satan unto God, that they may receive forgiveness of sins, and inheritance among them which are sanctified by faith that is in me. Whereupon, O king Agrippa, I was not disobedient unto the heavenly vision" (Acts 26:12-19).

To disobey is to forget Romans 6:14-18: "For sin shall not have dominion over you: for ye are not under the law, but under grace. What then? shall we sin, because we are not under the law, but under grace? God forbid. Know ye not, that to whom ye yield yourselves servants to obey, his servants ye are to whom ye obey; whether of sin unto death, or of obedience unto righteousness? But God be thanked, that ye were the servants of sin, but ye have obeyed from the heart that form of doctrine which was delivered you. Being then made free from sin, ye became the servants of righteousness" (Rom. 6:14-18).

THE DOCTRINE OF ANGELS

THE DOCTRINE OF ANGELS

Throughout his long history, man has often wondered whether he is indeed the only intelligent being in his universe, and whether life as we know it is confined to the earth alone. One of the most recent scientific attempts is the search for extraterrestrial life. Coded messages are now being transmitted into the distant recesses of outer space by means of radio telescopes. The scientist then anxiously awaits the results of his bold probe. Will his signals be picked up by nonearthly ears? If life is out there, will it prove friend or foe?

In light of all this, it seems tragic that man does not turn to the Word of God in his search, for the Bible clearly answers this question, as it does all other questions which confront humanity.

Is there intelligent life in the universe? Are there other living and rational creatures "out there" besides man? There are indeed. Are they friend or foe? They are both. Is their "civilization" older than ours? It is. Will we ever learn to communicate with them? We not only *will*, but a number of human beings *already have* met and talked with them.

Who are these cosmic creatures? They are called *angels*.

Belief in angels is found in the history of all nations. The ancient Egyptians, Phoenicians, Greeks, and others all expressed their belief in angels. A. S. Joppie writes:

"The Mohammedans believe in angels. They believe that two angels are assigned to each person. The angel on the right hand records all your good deeds. The angel on your left records all your evil deeds.

The Hebrews taught there were four great angels: (1) Gabriel, who reveals the secrets of God to men. (2) Michael, who fights and avenges God's foes. (3) Raphael, who receives the departing spirits of the dead. (4) Uriel, who will summon everybody to judgment." (*All about Angels*, p. 43)

In the apocryphal book of Tobit is an account of an angel by the name of Raphael. The young man whom the angel accompanied was in danger of being devoured by a big fish. The angel saved him. Then he told the young man to use the heart and liver of the fish against demon influence, and the gall against eye diseases, etc.

According to Moslem legend, when Mohammed was transported to heaven, he saw an angel there with "70,000 heads, each head had 70,000 faces, each face had 70,000 mouths, each mouth had 70,000 tongues, and each tongue spoke 70,000 languages." This would make more than 31,000 *trillion* languages, and nearly five billion mouths!

The earliest archaeological evidence of angels to date appears on the stela of Ur-Nammus (2250 B.C.), and shows angels flying over the head of this king while he is in prayer.

But enough of tradition and history. What does the Bible say about angels?

I. The Existence of Angels. Angels are mentioned in thirty-four books of the Bible for a total of some 273 times (108 times in the Old Testament and 165 in the New Testament).

"The chariots of God are twenty thousand, even thousands of angels" (Ps. 68:17).

"But ye are come unto Mount Zion, and unto the city of the living God, the heavenly Jerusalem, and to an innumerable company of angels" (Heb. 12:22).

"Who maketh his angels spirits, his ministers a flaming fire" (Ps. 104:4).

"Praise ye him, all his angels, praise ye him, all his hosts" (Ps. 148:2).

II. The Origin of Angels.

A. The source of their origin.

Angels, like everything else in this universe, were made by God the Father through Jesus Christ in the energy of the Holy Spirit. See Genesis 1:1, 2; 2:1; Nehemiah 9:6; John 1:1-3; Ephesians 3:9; Colossians 1:16.

B. The method of their origin. Angels, like man, were created by a special act of God. They did not evolve into being.

"Praise ye him, all his angels: praise ye him, all his hosts. Let them praise the name of the Lord: for he commanded, and they were created" (Ps. 148:2, 5).

Each angel is therefore a direct creation from God. This is perhaps why they are referred to as sons of God (Gen. 6:2, 4; Job 1:6; 2:1). The word "son" seems to indicate a direct creation of God, as Adam is called the "son of God" (see Lk. 3:38). Believers are also called this, as they are recreated in Christ individually as sons of God (Jn. 3:3; Gal. 3:26; Eph. 2:8-10; 4:24; 1 Jn. 3:1, 2).

Their number, once completed at creation, was forever fixed. This is assumed because we never read of God creating more of them and Jesus said they do not reproduce themselves (Mt. 22:30). Furthermore, since we are told they cannot die (Lk. 20:36) we conclude the original number of angels will never increase or decrease in size. For these reasons they must be considered a *company* of beings, and not a *race*.

C. The time of their origin.

"Then the Lord answered Job out of the whirlwind, and said. . . . Where wast thou when I laid the foundations of the earth? Declare, if thou hast understanding when the morning stars sang together, and all the sons of God shouted for joy?" (Job 38:1, 4, 7).

In these verses God declares that creation of angels took place prior to the creation of the earth.

D. The purpose of their origin. Angels were created to glorify Jesus Christ.

"For by him were all things created, that are in heaven, and that are in earth, visible and invisible, whether they be thrones, or dominions, or principalities, or powers: all things were created by him, and for him" (Col. 1:16).

"And again, when he bringeth in the first begotten into the world, he saith, And let all the angels of God worship him" (Heb. 1:6).

"Thou art worthy, O Lord, to receive glory and honour and power: for thou hast created all things, and for thy pleasure they are and were created" (Rev. 4:11).

III. The Nature of Angels.

A. They are spirit beings. (See Ps. 104:4; Heb. 1:7, 14.)

While we are informed by Christ himself that spiritual beings do not possess flesh and bone (Lk. 24:39), does this prove angels do not have any kind of body? It apparently does not, for devout and able theologians have taken both sides of this issue in centuries past. One therefore cannot be dogmatic concerning this. Some have pointed to 1 Corinthians 15:40 as an indication that they *do* possess bodies:

"There are also celestial bodies, and bodies terrestrial: but the glory of the celestial is one, and the glory of the terrestrial is another."

At any rate, on two specific occasions angels are described as partaking of physical food (Gen. 18:1-8; 19:1-3), and on one occasion as applying physical force (Acts 12:7).

B. They are invisible beings. While on occasion they do manifest themselves, their normal practice is to remain invisible. Certainly one basic reason for this is to prevent both unsaved and saved men from worshiping them. (See Rom. 1:18-32; Col. 2:18; Rev. 19:10; 22:9.)

C. They are innumerable. God, of course, knows their number, but they are presented to men as uncountable. There may be as many angels as there are stars in the heavens, for angels are associated with the stars (Job 38:7; Ps. 148:1-3; Rev. 9:1, 2; 12:3, 4, 7-9). If this be so, there would exist untold *trillions* of these heavenly beings. A hint of their huge number can be seen in Mark 5:9 where Satan could afford to give over 6,000 of his fallen angels to torment one poor lunatic. See also: "The Lord came from Sinai . . . with ten thousand of saints" (Deut. 33:2). The "saints" here are doubtless angels.

"I beheld till the thrones were cast down, and the Ancient of days did sit, whose garment was white as snow, and the hair of his head like the pure wool: his throne was like the fiery flame, and his wheels as burning fire. A fiery stream issued and came forth from before him: thousand thousands ministered unto him, and ten thousand times ten thousand stood before him: the judgment was set, and the books were opened" (Dan. 7:9, 10).

"The chariots of God are twenty thousand, even thousands of angels" (Ps. 68:17).

"Thinkest thou that I cannot now pray to my Father, and he shall presently give me more than twelve legions of angels?" (Mt. 26:53).

"But ye are come unto Mount Zion, and unto the city of the living God, the heavenly Jerusalem, and to an innumerable company of angels" (Heb. 12:22).

"And I beheld, and I heard the voice of many angels round about the throne . . . and the number of them was ten thousand times ten thousand, and thousands of thousands" (Rev. 5:11).

One of the reasons (perhaps the main reason) for the dispensation of the grace of God to all repenting sinners is stated by Paul in the book of Ephesians: "that in the ages to come he might shew the exceeding riches of his grace in his kindness toward us through Christ Jesus" (Eph. 2:7). There is little doubt that much of this display of grace will be for the benefit of angels. Thus, if their number is indeed as large as it appears, then each redeemed sinner will have a vast congregation of *billions* of angels to preach and testify to.

D. They possess separate and individual personalities, probably no two alike.

They have the three necessary features required of personality:

1. Intelligence (Dan. 9:21, 22; 10:14; Rev. 19:10; 22:8, 9).

2. Will (Isa. 14:12-15; Jude 1:6).

3. Emotion. They display *joy* (Job 38:7; Lk. 2:13) and *desire* (1 Pet. 1:12).

E. They are (because of Adam's fall) superior to men. (See Ps. 8:4, 5; Heb. 2:6-11.)

1. They are stronger than men.

"Bless the Lord, ye his angels, that excel in strength, that do his commandments hearkening unto the voice of his word" (Ps. 103:20).

". . . the Lord Jesus shall be revealed from heaven with his mighty angels" (2 Thess. 1:7).

"Whereas angels, which are greater in power and might . . ." (2 Pet. 2:11).

2. They are smarter than men (Dan. 9:21, 22; 10:14).

3. They are swifter than men.

"Yea, while I was speaking in prayer . . . Gabriel . . . being caused to fly swiftly, touched me" (Dan. 9:21).

"And I saw another angel fly in the midst of heaven . . ." (Rev. 14:6).

Their superiority in these areas seems to stem from two things.

a. Being unhindered by a fallen nature.

b. Being unbounded by the laws of gravity and time.

F. They are, however, inferior to God.

1. They are not omnipresent (Dan. 10:12). The angel here in Daniel 10 was in heaven at the time of Daniel's prayer and was sent by God to aid him.

2. They are not omnipotent (Dan. 10:13; Jude 9). This same angel was experiencing satanic pressure, which hindered him for a full three weeks.

3. They are not omniscient.
"But of that day and hour knoweth no man, no, not the angels of heaven, but my Father only" (Mt. 24:36).

G. They, like man, may have been made in the image of God. How was man made in God's image? It has been suggested that this image consisted of two things, personality and holiness.

1. *Personality* gives the basic *capacity* to have fellowship with the person of God, for only real persons, of course, can have fellowship.

2. *Holiness* provides the basic *requirement* to enjoy that fellowship, for two cannot experience fellowship unless they are morally agreed (Heb. 12:14).

If the above definition is correct, then angels can be said to have been made in the image of God also.

IV. The Moral Classification of Angels. It is believed that all angels were originally created without fault and, like Adam in the Garden, placed on a probation of some sort. They were theologically, during this time, *posse non pecarre* (able not to sin). But the probation period ended when heaven's chief angel, Lucifer by name, instigated a great revolt against Jehovah God himself. (See Isa. 14:12-15; Ezek. 28:11-19.) It is suggested by Revelation 12:3, 4 that he was able to persuade one third of heaven's angels to side with him in this terrible rebellion. The ones who did so thus became *non posse non pecarre* (not able not to sin), while the remaining two thirds were pronounced *non posse pecarre* (not able to sin).

From that point on the *faithful* angels are referred to as holy and elect angels (Mk. 8:38; 1 Tim. 5:21), while the *fallen* angels are known as the devil's angels (Mt. 25:41; Rev. 12:9).

V. The Characteristics of the Faithful Angels.
A. Their rank.
1. The archangels.
a. Michael. His name means "Who is like God." This should be contrasted to Satan's evil desire to "be like the most High" (Isa. 14:14). Michael is mentioned by name on four separate occasions in the Bible.
(1) He helps a lesser-ranked angel get through to answer Daniel's prayer (Dan. 10:13, 21).
(2) He will stand up for Israel during the tribulation (Dan. 12:1).
(3) He disputes with Satan concerning the dead body of Moses (Jude 9).
(4) He fights against Satan in the heavenlies (Rev. 12:7).
b. Gabriel. His name means "The mighty one of God."
(1) He explains the vision of the Ram and Goat battle to Daniel (Dan. 8:16).
(2) He explains the seventy weeks to Daniel (Dan. 9:21).
(3) He predicts the birth of John the Baptist to Zacharias (Lk. 1:19).

(4) He predicts the birth of Jesus to Mary (Lk. 1:26).
(5) He assures Joseph concerning the purity of Mary (Mt. 1:20).
(6) He warns Joseph about the plot of Herod (Mt. 2:13).
(7) He tells Joseph about the death of Herod (Mt. 2:19).
Note: Some Bible students have identified Gabriel with the various appearances of the Angel of the Lord in the remaining pages of the New Testament. If this is true, then Gabriel can be seen in the following ten occasions.
(8) He announces the birth of Christ to the shepherds (Lk. 2:9).
(9) He strengthens Christ in the Garden of Gethsemane (Lk. 22:43).
(10) He rolls the stone back at Christ's resurrection (Mt. 28:2).
(11) He frees the apostles from prison (Acts 5:19).
(12) He sends Philip to the desert of Gaza to meet the eunuch (Acts 8:26).
(13) He instructs Cornelius to send for Peter (Acts 10:3).
(14) He frees Peter from prison (Acts 12:7).
(15) He executes wicked Herod for blasphemy (Acts 12:23).
(16) He assures Paul on the deck of a sinking ship (Acts 27:23).
(17) He will sound the trumpet at the rapture (1 Thess. 4:16).
2. The cherubim (Gen. 3:24; Ex. 25:18-20; Ezek. 1:4-28; 10:1-22).
a. The description of the cherubim:
(1) Each has four faces.
(a) The face in front is as a man.
(b) The face on the right is as a lion.
(c) The face on the left is as an ox.
(d) The face in back is as an eagle.
(2) Each has two pairs of wings.
(a) One pair spreads out from the middle of the back.
(b) The other pair is used to cover the body.
These wings make a noise like waves crashing upon the seashore.
(3) They have the legs of men, but their feet are cloven like calves' feet, which shine like burnished brass.
(4) They have four human hands, with one located under each wing.
(5) They apparently travel in groups of four. The outstretched wings of each cherubim touches those of the remaining three companions, so that they form a square. When they move, they move as a group without turning their bodies.
b. The duties of the cherubim:
(1) They kept Adam from the Tree of Life after the fall, lest he eat of it

and live forever in his sin (Gen. 3:24).

Note: There is an interesting analogy between the cherubim as guarding the entrance to paradise and the winged bulls and lions of Babylon and Assyria, colossal figures with human faces standing guard at the entrances of temples and palaces. Inasmuch as both these nations occupied the very spot where the original Garden of Eden may have been located, it is not unreasonable to suggest that these idols were perverted statue copies of the real cherubim.

(2) Two golden cherubim were constructed at God's command and placed at either end on top of the ark lid in the tabernacle Holy of Holies (Ex. 25:18-20; Heb. 9:5).

(3) They appeared to Ezekiel (Ezek. 1, 10).

(4) Prior to his fall, Satan (then known as Lucifer) was the chief cherub angel (Isa. 14:12; Ezek. 28:14).

3. The seraphim (Isa. 6:1-7). The Hebrew word for *seraphim* means "burning ones," and probably speaks of the burning devotion to God on the part of these angelic beings. These beings are mentioned only once in the Bible. Their description and duties are as follows:

a. They have six wings. Two are used to cover their face, two to cover their feet, and two are used to fly.

b. They proclaim in a great chorus the majesty of God, crying out: "Holy, holy, holy, is the Lord of hosts; the whole earth is full of his glory" (Isa. 6:3).

c. The awesome sound of their mighty praises shakes the foundation of the heavenly temple.

d. Isaiah, the great prophet, views all this in a vision. He is immediately convicted concerning both his sin and the sin of the nation Israel.

e. He is ministered to by one of the seraphim, who flew over to the heavenly altar and, with a pair of tongs, picked out a burning coal. He then touched Isaiah's lips with it and said: "Lo, this hath touched thy lips, and thine iniquity is taken away, and thy sin purged" (Isa. 6:7).

4. Living creatures (Rev. 4:6-9; 5:8; 6:1, 3, 5, 7). These special heavenly beings are in some ways similar to both the cherubim and the seraphim, but seem to be in a separate class by themselves. Their number appears to be limited to four. It has been suggested that they now hold those privileges and responsibilities once assigned to Lucifer, before he became the devil.

a. John the apostle sees these four standing before the shining crystal sea in heaven surrounding God's throne.

b. They are covered with eyes, both in front and behind.

c. Each of the four has a different face.
   (1) One has the face of a lion.
   (2) One has the face of an ox.
   (3) One has the face of a man.
   (4) One has the face of an eagle.

d. Each creature has six wings.

Note: As it has been observed, there are similarities here between the cherubim and the living creatures. But differences may also be seen. The cherubim each have four faces, while the living creatures have but one. The cherubim possess four wings, whereas the living creatures have six.

e. Without ceasing day or night, they proclaim God's praise, saying: "Holy, holy, holy, Lord God Almighty, who was, and is, and is to come" (Rev. 4:8).

f. Each of the four living creatures will announce one of the first four great tribulational judgments of the seven-sealed book (Rev. 6:1, 3, 5, 7).

g. It has been suggested that the faces of both the cherubim and the living creatures are to remind the elect throughout all eternity of the earthly ministry performed by our blessed Lord. These faces correspond directly to the fourfold gospel presentation of Christ.
   (1) Matthew presents him as the lion of the tribe of Judah.
   (2) Mark presents him as the lowly ox.
   (3) Luke presents him as the perfect man.
   (4) John presents him as the mighty Godlike eagle.

5. Ruling angels (Eph. 1:21; 3:10; Col. 1:16; 2:10; 1 Pet. 3:22). In the above passages the following organizational features are mentioned.
   a. principalities
   b. powers
   c. thrones
   d. authorities
   e. dominions
   f. might

While it is impossible to distinguish clearly among these six, it is nevertheless evident that they describe various levels of ruling positions assigned to angels, ranging perhaps (to use an earthly analogy) from generals to privates.

6. Guardian angels.

"Take heed that ye despise not one of these little ones; for I say unto you, that in heaven their angels do always behold the face of my Father which is in heaven" (Mt. 18:10).

"Are they not all ministering spirits, sent forth to minister for them who shall be heirs of salvation?" (Heb. 1:14).

The Bible does not state whether each believer has a specific guardian angel, or whether various angels on occasion simply protect and aid the heirs of salvation. Both are logical possibilities.

7. Angels associated with horses and chariots.

"And it came to pass, as they still went on, and talked, that, behold, there appeared a chariot of fire, and horses of fire, and separated them, and Elijah went up by a whirlwind into heaven" (2 Ki. 2:11).

"And Elisha prayed, and said, Lord, I pray thee, open his eyes, that he may see. And the Lord opened the eyes of the young man, and he saw; and behold, the mountain was full of horses and chariots of fire round about Elisha" (2 Ki. 6:17).

"The chariots of God are twenty thousand, even thousands of angels" (Ps. 68:17).

"I saw at night, and behold, a man was riding on a red horse, and he was standing among the myrtle trees which were in the ravine, with red, sorrel, and white horses behind him. Then I said, 'My lord, what are these?' And the angel who was speaking with me said to me, 'I will show you what these are.' And the man who was standing among the myrtle trees answered and said, 'These are those whom the Lord has sent to patrol the earth.' So they answered the angel of the Lord who was standing among the myrtle trees, and said, 'We have patrolled the earth, and behold, all the earth is peaceful and quiet' " (Zech. 1:8-11, *NASV*).

"And the armies which were in heaven followed him upon white horses, clothed in fine linen, white and clean" (Rev. 19:14).

If these verses are to be taken in a literal sense, then one must conclude (whatever problems may be involved) that certain angels work closely with creatures of the animal kingdom in performing their ministry.

B. Their appearance. A detailed description of the cherubim and seraphim has already been considered in our study. But what about the general appearance of angels? The Scriptures offer the following description.

"And entering into the sepulchre, they saw a young man sitting on the right side, clothed in a long white garment; and they were amazed" (Mk. 16:5).

"His countenance was like lightning, and his raiment white as snow" (Mt. 28:3).

"And it came to pass, as they were much perplexed about this, behold, two men stood by them, in shining garments" (Lk. 24:4).

"And I saw another mighty angel come down from heaven, clothed with a cloud; and a rainbow was upon his head, and his face was as though it were the sun, and his feet like pillars of fire" (Rev. 10:1).

"And the seven angels came out of the temple, having the seven plagues, clothed in pure and white linen, and having their breasts girded with golden girdles" (Rev. 15:6).

"And after these things I saw another angel come down from heaven, having great power, and the earth was made bright with his glory" (Rev. 18:1).

In view of their dazzling splendor and great glory it is not difficult to understand why both unsaved (Col. 2:18) and saved men (Rev. 19:10; 22:8, 9) have attempted to worship angels.

C. Their names and titles.
1. Ministers (Ps. 103:20, 21; 104:4). This signifies their religious duties and spiritual service.
2. Host (Gen. 32:1, 2; Josh. 5:14; 1 Sam. 17:45; Ps. 89:8). This name speaks of their military service.
3. Chariots (2 Ki. 6:16, 17; Ps. 68:17; Zech. 6:5). This may refer to their swiftness.
4. Watchers (Dan. 4:13, 17). This speaks of their duties as supervisors and agents.
5. Sons of the mighty (Ps. 29:1; 89:6). This title may refer to their awesome strength and power.
6. Sons of God (Gen. 6:2, 4; Job 1:6; 2:1; 38:7). Dr. L. S. Chafer writes:

"In Old Testament terminology, sometimes angels are called sons of God while men are called servants of God. In the New Testament this is reversed. Angels are servants and Christians are the sons of God. This particular order may be due to the fact that, in the Old Testament men are seen as related to this sphere over which angels are superior; while in the New Testament, saints are seen as related to their final exaltation into the likeness of Christ, compared to which the angels are inferior." (*Systematic Theology*, Vol. II, p. 23)

7. Holy Ones, saints (Ps. 89:7; Dan. 8:13; Zech. 14:5). This refers to their total separation to the will of God.
8. Stars (Job 38:7; Ps. 148:2, 3; Rev. 12:3, 4). This may indicate both their number and their brightness.

D. Their work and ministry.
1. Their activities in heaven.
   a. They worship the Person of God (1 Ki. 22:19; Ps. 29:1, 2; Isa. 6:3; Rev. 4:8; 19:4).
   b. They observe the people of God (Lk. 12:8, 9; 15:10; 1 Cor. 4:9; 11:10; Eph. 3:10; 1 Tim. 5:21; 1 Pet. 1:12).

   "For I think that God hath set forth us the apostles last, as it were appointed to death: for we are made a spectacle unto the world, and to angels, and to men" (1 Cor. 4:9).

   "For this cause ought the woman to have power on her head because of the angels" (1 Cor. 11:10).

   "The gospel . . . sent down from heaven; which things the angels desire to look into" (1 Pet. 1:12).
   c. They inquire into the prophetical plan of God (Dan. 12:5, 6).
   d. They rejoice in the works of God.
      (1) His work of creation (Job 38:7; Rev. 4:11).
      (2) His work of redemption (1 Tim. 3:16; Rev. 5:11, 12).

e. They perform the will of God (Gen. 28:12; Ps. 103:29; 104:4; Dan. 7:10).

f. They witness the wrath of God (Rev. 14:10).

2. Their activities on earth.

a. Concerning the saved (see especially Heb. 1:14; Rev. 22:16).

(1) They inform, instruct, and interpret concerning both the will and Word of God. Note the following individuals who received that kind of ministry from angels.

(a) Daniel (Dan. 7:16; 10:5, 11)

(b) Zechariah (Zech. 1:9, 13, 14, 19; 2:3; 5:5-10; 6:4, 5)

(c) Zacharias (Lk. 1:11-17)

(d) Mary (Lk. 1:26-33)

(e) Joseph (Mt. 1:20; 2:13, 19)

(f) The shepherds (Lk. 2:9-12)

(g) The women at the tomb (Lk. 24:4-7)

(h) The apostles (Acts 1:10, 11)

(i) Philip (Acts 8:26)

(j) Cornelius (Acts 10:3-6)

(k) John (Rev. 17:1; 21:9)

(2) They protect.

"The angel of the Lord encampeth round about them that fear him, and delivereth them" (Ps. 34:7).

"For he shall give his angels charge over thee, to keep thee in all thy ways" (Ps. 91:11).

Dr. Billy Graham relates the following account:

"The Reverend John G. Paton, a missionary in the New Hebrides Islands, tells a thrilling story involving the protective care of angels. Hostile natives surrounded his mission headquarters one night, intent on burning the Patons out and killing them. John Paton and his wife prayed all during that terror-filled night that God would deliver them. When daylight came they were amazed to see the attackers unaccountably leave. They thanked God for delivering them.

A year later, the chief of the tribe was converted to Jesus Christ, and Mr. Paton, remembering what had happened, asked the chief what had kept him and his men from burning down the house and killing them. The chief replied in surprise, 'Who were all those men you had with you there?' The missionary answered, 'There were no men there; just my wife and I.' The chief argued that they had seen many men standing guard—hundreds of big men in shining garments with drawn swords in their hands. They seemed to circle the mission station so that the natives were afraid to attack. Only then did Mr. Paton realize that God had sent His angels to protect them. The chief agreed that there was no other explanation. Could it be that God had sent a legion of angels to protect His servants, whose lives were being endangered?" (*Angels: God's Special Agents*, p. 3)

(a) Angels protected Lot from the Sodomites (Gen. 19:10, 11).

(b) Angels protected Elisha from the Syrians (2 Ki. 6:15-17).

(3) They comfort.

"And as he [Elijah] lay and slept under a juniper tree, behold, an angel touched him, and said unto him, Arise and eat" (1 Ki. 19:5).

"For there stood by me [Paul] this night an angel of God, whose I am, and whom I serve, saying, Fear not, Paul" (Acts 27:23-24).

(4) They deliver.

"But an angel of the Lord by night opened the prison doors, and brought them [the apostles] forth" (Acts 5:19).

"And, behold, an angel of the Lord came upon him, and a light shone in the prison; and he smote Peter on the side, and raised him up, saying, Arise quickly. And his chains fell off from his hands" (Acts 12:7).

(5) They minister to the believer at the moment of death.

"And it came to pass that the beggar died, and was carried by the angels into Abraham's bosom" (Lk. 16:22).

b. Concerning the unsaved.

(1) They judged the Egyptians (Ex. 12:13, 23).

(2) They judged the Sodomites (Gen. 19:13).

(3) They judged the Assyrians (2 Ki. 19:35).

(4) They judged Herod (Acts 12:23).

(5) They will judge the earth during the tribulation.

(a) They hold back the four winds of heaven (Rev. 7:1).

(b) They pronounce the seven trumpet judgments (Rev. 8:2).

(c) They cast Satan and his angels out of heaven (Rev. 12:7, 8).

(d) They announce the eternal hell awaiting all unbelievers (Rev. 14:10).

(e) They predict the fall of Babylon (Rev. 14:8).

(f) They announce the fall of Babylon (Rev. 18:1, 2).

(g) They pour out the seven vial judgments (Rev. 15:1).

(h) They announce Armageddon (Rev. 19:17).

(i) They accompany Christ at his Second Coming (2 Thess. 1:7, 8).

(j) They gather the unsaved for eternal hell (Mt. 13:39-43).

(k) They bind Satan in the bottomless pit (Rev. 20:1).

c. Concerning Israel.

(1) Angels fought for Israel (Jdg. 5:20).

(2) They gave the law to Israel (Deut. 33:2; Acts 7:53; Gal. 3:19; Heb. 2:2).

(3) They seal the 144,000 Israelites (Rev. 7:1-3).

(4) They will regather faithful Israel (Mt. 24:31).

d. Concerning the Savior.

(1) They worship him (Heb. 1:6).

(2) They were made by him and for him (Col. 1:17).

(3) They predicted his birth (Mt. 1:20, 21; Lk. 1:31).

(4) They announced his birth (Lk. 2:9-13).

(5) They helped protect him (Ps. 91:11; Mt. 2:13).

(6) They ministered to him in the wilderness (Mt. 4:11).

(7) They ministered to him in the garden (Lk. 22:43).

(8) They rolled away the tombstone (Mt. 28:2).

(9) They announced his resurrection (Mt. 28:6).

(10) They predicted his Second Coming (Acts 1:10, 11).

(11) They will accompany him at the Second Coming (2 Thess. 1:7, 8).

(12) They are in total subjection to him (1 Pet. 3:22).

Dr. Lewis Sperry Chafer quotes Dr. Cooke:

"How constant their attendance on the Incarnate Saviour during his mysterious life amongst men! At his birth they are his heralds, and with songs exultant announce the glad tidings to mankind. In his temptation they minister to him; in his agonies they succour him; on his resurrection they are the first to proclaim his triumph; on his ascension they come to escort him to the mediatorial throne; in his glorified state they render him supreme homage as their Lord; and when he returns to judge the world they will form his retinue! What sublime thoughts would be suggested, what emotions of wonder and joy would be excited, by the scenes they witnessed on earth and still witness in heaven, in reference to Christ, his twofold nature, and his great redeeming work.

God incarnate! This was new to them. They had seen the Son in his deity; but never till now enshrined in humanity. What amazing condescension! Obeying his own law as if he were a mere creature, and in the attitude of a servant! This was new. They had seen him as the governor of the universe; but never till now as a subject! Encountering Satan in conflict and prolonged temptation! This was new. They had seen him frown the arch-rebel from his presence and hurl him to perdition; but never till now submitting to be tempted by him whose subtlety and power had seduced myriads to eternal ruin. Suffering the scorn and reproach of sinful men! This was new. They had seen myriads of happy spirits worship, adore, and love him, but never till now had they seen him personally insulted, reproached, and maltreated by his creatures. Groaning in Gethsemane, and crucified between two thieves, and dying as a sacrificial victim! This was new. They had seen him supremely happy and glorious; but to see him agonize, to hear that dying wail, and to behold him a bloody corpse, and all this to save the world which had revolted from him! What mysterious love! To see him, after all this, enthroned and glorified in human nature. This was a new fact in the moral history of the universe. The whole scenes were full of interest, wonder, and mystery; a gradation of wonders rising in succession, until they culminated in the permanent presence of the God-man, resplendent with a glory that fills the heaven of heavens. Here were chapters of instruction for angelic minds to ponder; here were developments of hidden truths; here were discoveries of the Divine perfections, never known before, and still unfolding in brighter effulgence as ages roll on!" (*Systematic Theology*, Vol. II, p. 22)

E. Their destiny.

1. To spend eternity in the New Jerusalem along with the elect (Heb. 12:22, 23; Rev. 22:10-12).

2. To learn throughout eternity of God's grace as exhibited by the elect (Eph. 2:4-7; 3:10, 11).

VI. The Characteristics of Evil Angels.

A. The names for fallen angels.

1. *Shedim.* "They [Israel] sacrificed unto devils, not to God" (Deut. 32:17). The Hebrew word here translated "devils" is *shedim.* "Yea, they sacrificed their sons and their daughters unto devils" (Ps. 106:37; see also 1 Cor. 10:20).

2. *Seirim, sair, satyr.* "And they shall no more offer their sacrifices unto devils" (Lev. 17:7).

"But wild beasts of the desert shall lie there; and their houses shall be full of doleful creatures, and ostriches shall dwell there, and he-goats shall dance there" (Isa. 13:21). The word "he-goat" is *satyr* in the Hebrew, and is thought to be tied in to demon creatures of some sort. Dr. Fred Dickason writes:

"The Hebrews were to sacrifice at the altar of the Tabernacle and not to sacrifice in the desert to 'he-goats.' Jeroboam I appointed worship for the *Seirim* (2 Chron. 11:15), and Josiah 'brake down the high places of the gates' which is to be read *Seirim* (2 Ki. 23:8)." (*Angels, Elect and Evil*, p. 152)

3. *Elilim.* "For all the gods of the nations are idols; but the Lord made the heavens" (Ps. 96:5).
4. *Gad.* "But ye are they that forsake the Lord, that forget my holy mountain, that prepare a table for that troop." The *New American Standard Bible* translates the word "troop" here (*gad* in the Hebrew) by the word "fortune."
5. *Qeter.* "Thou shalt not be afraid for the terror by night, nor for the arrow that flieth by day. Nor for the pestilence that walketh in darkness, nor for the destruction that wasteth at noonday" (Ps. 91:5, 6). The phrase "destruction that wasteth at noonday" may refer to demonic activity.
6. The devil's angels (Mt. 25:41; Rev. 12:9).
7. The angels which kept not their first estate (2 Pet. 2:4; Jude 6).
8. Familiar spirits (Deut. 18:11; Isa. 8:10; 19:3).
9. Unclean spirits (Mt. 10:1; Mk. 1:27; 3:11; 5:13; Acts 5:16; 8:7; Rev. 16:13).
10. Evil spirits (Lk. 7:21; Acts 19:12, 13).
11. Seducing spirits (1 Tim. 4:1).
12. Wicked spirits (Lk. 11:26).
13. Demons. The word *daimon* is found more than seventy-five times in the Greek New Testament. In each case it is translated (incorrectly) by the word *devil* in the King James Version. There are a number of theories concerning the origin of demons. Among these are the following:
    a. They are spirits of deceased wicked men. However, this cannot be, for the Bible declares the unsaved dead are in Hades and not roaming the earth (Ps. 9:17; Lk. 16:23; Rev. 20:13).
    b. They are spirits of a pre-Adamic race. But there is no scriptural support whatsoever for this view. The Bible declares that Adam was the first man (1 Cor. 15:45).
    c. They are the spirits from the unnatural union between angels and women in Genesis 6. However, this view, like the previous two, is without the slightest biblical support.

The most logical conclusion is that the word "demon" is simply another title or name for fallen angels. The following verses describe the activities of demons: Matthew 4:24; 7:22; 8:16; 9:32; 10:8; 12:22; 15:22; 17:18; Mark 1:32, 34, 39; 3:13; 6:13; 9:38; 16:9, 17; Luke 4:33, 41; 8:2; 11:14; John 7:20; 8:48; 1 Corinthians 10:20, 21; 1 Timothy 4:1; James 2:19; Revelation 9:20.

B. The location of fallen angels.
   1. Unchained angels, having a certain amount of freedom at the present time (Ps. 78:49; Eph. 6:12; Rev. 12:7-9)
   2. Chained angels, having no freedom at the present time.
      a. The angels in tartarus (2 Pet. 2:4; Jude 6).
      b. The angels in the bottomless pit (the abyss) (Lk. 8:31; Rev. 9:1, 2, 11; 11:7; 17:8; 20:1-3).
      c. The angels bound in the Euphrates River (Rev. 9:14).
C. The sin of the bound angels. It has already been observed that one third of heaven's angels joined Lucifer in his rebellion against God. These, of course, are the fallen angels of the Bible. Someday they will be judged by God and thrown into Gehenna hell. But why have some of their number suffered imprisonment already? Many Bible students believe the answer to this question is found in Genesis 6:1, 2, 4:

"And it came to pass, when men began to multiply on the face of the earth, and daughters were born unto them, that the sons of God saw the daughters of men that they were fair; and they took them wives of all which they chose. . . . There were giants in the earth in those days; and also after that, when the sons of God came in unto the daughters of men, and they bare children to them, the same became mighty men which were of old, men of renown."

Much controversy has surrounded these verses. Who were the "sons of God" who married the daughters of men? There are two basic approaches to this. The simple interpretation is that the sons of God were those individuals belonging to the line of Seth while the daughters of men were the unsaved girls who belonged to the line of Cain. The second and more involved interpretation holds that the sons of God were wicked and fallen angelic beings of some kind who committed immoral and unnatural physical acts with women in general.

1. Basic arguments for the first view.
   a. This is the most natural way to interpret the passage.
   b. The statement of Jesus in Matthew 22:30: "For in the resurrection they [saved human beings in heaven] neither marry, nor are given in marriage, but are as the angels of God in heaven."
   c. The law of biogenesis—life begets similar life. Note the statement "after its kind" in Genesis 1:11, 12, 21, 24, 25.
   d. Paul's statement in 1 Corinthians 15:38-40: "There are also celestial bodies, and bodies terrestrial." This would indicate these two can never co-join.
   e. Moses did not use the regular Hebrew word for angels (*malak*) which he later employs at least twenty-eight times in the Pentateuch.

f. "Mighty men" (supposed offspring of angels and women) is the Hebrew word *gibbor* (Gen. 6:4) which is used dozens of times in the Old Testament and always refers to human men (Jdg. 6:12).

2. Basic arguments for the second view.

   a. The Hebrew language seems to favor it.

      (1) The Hebrew phrase *bne-elohim* (sons of God) always refers to angels in the Old Testament (Job 1:6; 2:1; 38:7; Dan. 3:25).

      (2) The Hebrew word *nephilim* (translated "giants" in Gen. 6:4) actually should be rendered "fallen ones." The normal word for a huge man is *rapha*. Thus, men like Og and Goliath were described by the word *rapha* (Deut. 3:11; 1 Chron. 20:6).

   b. Ancient pagan legends. There is almost always a basis for commonly held ancient legends, however weird and distorted they might have become. In 6:4 we read concerning the "men of renown," which some believe is the historical basis for the legends of Hercules and other children of the gods of mythology. This later corresponds to such Babylonian figures as Gilgamesh, the supposed son of a goddess and a mortal. He was called "two-thirds god and one-third man."

   c. The common opinion of Jewish scholars. Josephus, a great Jewish historian, brings this out in his writings. The Septuagint (the Greek translation of the Hebrew Old Testament and the Bible used by Jews) translates Genesis 6:2 as the "angels of God."

   d. The interpretation of the early church. It was not until the fourth century that another view opposed to the angels of God theory was offered. The late Dr. James M. Gray (past president of Moody Bible Institute) writes, "There is reason to believe this view would not have changed . . . had it not been for certain erroneous opinions and practices of Christendom" (*Spiritism and the Fallen Angels*). Gray suggests two such reasons:

      (1) Angel worship. The church sometime after the fourth century began worshiping angels, so the natural thing would be to deny any angel could do such vile things with humanity.

      (2) Celibacy. If indeed these sons of God were human men, then the monks would have scriptural justification for indulging in sexual acts in spite of their official vows of celibacy.

   e. Various New Testament passages.

      "For Christ also hath once suffered for sins, the just for the unjust, that he might bring us to God, being put to death in the flesh but quickened by the Spirit: By which also he went and preached unto the spirits in prison; which sometime were disobedient, when once the long-suffering of God waited in the days of Noah, while the ark was a preparing wherein few, that is, eight souls were saved by water" (1 Pet. 3:18-20).

      It is thought by some that these spirits were these sons of God in Genesis 6. The reason for their iniquity was a satanic attempt to corrupt human flesh and thus prevent the promised incarnation (Gen. 3:15) from taking place. But here Peter describes Christ as telling them their foul plan didn't work. For another suggested passage along this line, see Jude 5-7.

   f. The fact that there are two kinds of fallen angels, the unchained and those already chained. The *unchained* now have access to high places and to the bodies of unsaved men (Mk. 1:23; Lk. 8:27; Eph. 6:12). The *chained* are at present already incarcerated (2 Pet. 2:4; Jude 5-7). The thought is that these are chained because of their involvement in Genesis 6.

      In conclusion it should be noted that a *third* view has been recently advocated which says the sons of God were indeed fallen angels who totally controlled and possessed all the evil men living before the flood. These demons may have even attempted to change (by genetic engineering, as we see today) the DNA code of future babies like some deadly virus.

D. The organization and rank of fallen angels.

   "For we wrestle not against flesh and blood, but against principalities, against powers, against the rulers of the darkness of this world, against spiritual wickedness in high places" (Eph. 6:12; see also Mt. 12:24-30).

   These verses indicate that Satan's kingdom of evil angels is as organized as God's elect angelic group.

   1. There are evil angels who rule over the nations of this world (Dan. 10:13).

   2. A wicked angel named Legion headed up a large group of fallen spirits that had possessed the maniac of Gadara (Mk. 5:9).

   3. The bottomless pit is under the control of an angel called Abaddon (in the Hebrew) and Apollyon (in the Greek; Rev. 9:11).

   4. Four military angels will lead a hellish army 200 million strong during the latter part of the tribulation (Rev. 9:15).

   5. Three angels organize those events which lead to the battle of Armageddon (Rev. 16:13, 14).

E. The appearance of fallen angels. Fallen angels, like good angels, are invisible spiritual beings. However, on occasion they do manifest themselves. There are three New Testament passages which offer some description of these corrupted creatures.

   1. Revelation 9:7-10. The shapes of these creatures are absolutely hideous. They are like horses prepared for battle. Crowns of gold

783

seem to be upon their heads. Their faces are like men, their hair like women, their teeth like lions. They have on breastplates as of iron. Their tails are like those of a scorpion. The sound of their wings is like that of many chariots rushing toward battle.

2. Revelation 9:13-21. These demons are mounted upon some type of hellish horse. The horses' heads look much like lions' heads, with smoke, fire, and flaming sulphur billowing from their mouths. The riders wear fiery-red breastplates.

3. Revelation 16:13.

"And I saw three unclean spirits like frogs come out of the mouth of the dragon, and out of the mouth of the beast, and out of the mouth of the false prophet."

F. The personalities of fallen angels. Author John Phillips writes:

"Modern man professes not to believe in demons, but they exist just the same. Moreover, they are clever with a diabolical cunning. Man's attitude toward the demon world may well be likened to man's attitude in the dark ages toward bacteria. If we could be transported back to London in the year 1666, we would find ourselves in a nightmare world. The great bubonic plague is at its height. The sights and sounds of the city are like the terrible climax of a horror movie. It is generally believed that fresh air is the culprit. The College of Physicians recommends the frequent firing of guns to blow away the deadly air. People seal themselves into their rooms and burn foul-smelling messes to ward off the fresh air. Chimneys are sealed, rooms are gray with smoke, and people choke in the suffocating stench. Outside, palls of black smoke hang over the city. People sit in the tightly sealed chambers, grimly determined to endure the smarting smoke, convinced they are thus immune to the plague. We tell them they are wrong, that the plague is not caused by fresh air but by germs, microscopic organisms spread by fleas—and they laugh us to scorn.

Modern man has adopted a similar attitude toward the demon world. We tell them that he (Satan) has countless hosts of invisible demons to aid him in his dark designs against mankind. We say that these unseen beings are intelligent, and that before long, they are to be joined by countless more of their kind worse even than themselves. People look at us with pitying scorn and suggest we peddle our theories to the publishers of science fiction. But it is true all the same. Once the pit is opened, the world of men will be invaded by a virus far more dreadful than the bubonic plague, a virus all the more deadly because it is able to think and because it directs its attack against the soul rather than the body."
(*Exploring Revelation*, p. 137)

1. Fallen angels have names (Lk. 8:30; Rev. 9:11).

2. They speak.

"Let us alone; what have we to do with thee, thou Jesus of Nazareth? Art thou come to destroy us? I know thee, who thou art: the Holy One of God . . . Thou art Christ, the Son of God" (Lk. 4:34, 41).

"What have I to do with thee, Jesus, thou Son of God most high? I beseech thee, torment me not" (Lk. 8:28).

"Art thou come here to torment us before the time?" (Mt. 8:29).

"Send us into the swine, that we may enter into them" (Mk. 5:12).

"Jesus I know, and Paul I know; but who are ye?" (Acts 19:15).

"Thou art the Son of God" (Mk. 3:11).

3. They possess intelligence.
   a. They know who Jesus is (Lk. 4:34).
   b. They know of future damnation (Mt. 8:29).
   c. They know the saved from the unsaved (Acts 16:15; Rev. 9:4).
   d. They are able to formulate a Satan-centered systematic theology (1 Tim. 4:1).

4. They experience emotion.
   a. Fear (Lk. 8:28; Jas. 2:19).
   b. Disdain (Acts 16:15).

5. They possess great strength (Ex. 8:7; 7:11, 12; Dan. 10:13; Mk. 5:2-4; 9:17-26; Acts 19:16; 2 Cor. 10:4, 5; Rev. 9:15-19).

G. The activities of fallen angels.

1. They oppose God's purpose (Dan. 10:10-14; Eph. 6:12).

2. They execute Satan's program (1 Tim. 4:1; Rev. 9; 16:12-14).

3. They disseminate false doctrine (2 Thess. 2:2; 1 Tim. 4:1).

4. They afflict human beings.
   a. Some cause insanity (Mt. 8:28; 17:15, 18; Mk. 5:15; Lk. 8:27-29).
   b. Some cause muteness of speech (Mt. 9:33).
   c. Some cause immorality (Mt. 10:1; Mk. 1:23-26; 3:11; Lk. 4:36; Acts 5:16; 8:7; Rev. 16:13).
   d. Some cause deafness (Mk. 9:25).
   e. Some cause epilepsy (Mt. 17:15-18).
   f. Some cause blindness (Mt. 12:22).
   g. Some cause suicidal mania (Mk. 9:22).
   h. Some cause personal injuries (Mk. 9:18).
   i. Some cause physical defects (Lk. 13:11).

5. They can possess human beings. In the Bible there are at least twelve major examples of individuals possessed by fallen angels.
   a. Saul, Israel's first king, was often troubled by an evil spirit (1 Sam. 16:14; 18:10; 19:9). He became insanely jealous of David (1 Sam. 18:8), and attempted often to kill him:
      (1) By piercing him with a javelin (1 Sam. 18:11; 19:10).
      (2) By trickery (1 Sam. 18:25).
      (3) By hunting him down like a wild animal in the Judean wilderness for some thirteen years (1 Sam. 24:1, 2, 11; 24:11; 26:1, 2).
   He attempted to kill his own son Jonathan for befriending David (1 Sam. 20:33). He murdered eighty-five priests of God for helping David (1 Sam. 22:17). He

was forsaken by God (1 Sam. 28:6). He visited the witch of Endor in the hour of his death (1 Sam. 28:7).

b. Those seven demon-possessed persons delivered by Jesus.
  (1) A Capernaum demoniac (Mk. 1:25; Lk. 4:35).
  (2) A Geresene demoniac (Mt. 8:32; Mk. 5:8; Lk. 8:33).
  (3) A dumb demoniac (Mt. 9:33).
  (4) A demoniac girl (Mt. 15:28; Mk. 7:29).
  (5) A demoniac boy (Mt. 17:18; Mk. 9:25; Lk. 9:42).
  (6) A blind and deaf demoniac (Mt. 12:22; Lk. 11:14).
  (7) A woman with an eighteen-year infirmity (Lk. 13·10–17).

Note especially the fearful results of being demon-possessed as described in the two case studies of the Geresene demoniac and the demon-possessed boy.

c. The maniac.
  (1) He was exceedingly fierce, so that no man could control him.
  (2) He had broken all the chains put upon him.
  (3) He was living among the tombs.
  (4) He constantly screamed out and cut himself with stones.
  (5) He was naked and controlled by 6000 demons.
  (6) He had been possessed for a long time.

d. The boy.
  (1) He had been possessed since childhood.
  (2) The demon would bruise him and rip at him.
  (3) He would be thrown into water and fire.
  (4) He suffered severe convulsions.
  (5) Often he was thrown violently to the ground and caused to roll around, foaming at the mouth.
  (6) He was rendered unconscious and feared dead upon the removal of the demon by Jesus.

e. Mary Magdalene (Mk. 16:9; Lk. 8:2). Mary had seven demons living in her prior to her conversion.

f. Simon (Acts 8:18–24). A demon possessed Simon to twist the gospel message into a perverted profit system.

g. Elymas (Acts 13:8–11). This demon-possessed sorcerer attempted to frustrate Paul's efforts to win the governor of Cyprus to Christ.

h. A slave girl (Acts 16:16–18). In this amazing account a demon (through a possessed girl) tried to identify itself with the work of Paul, so that the message of Christ might be confused in the minds of those in Philippi.

To this list could be added the many unnamed possessed people who were de- livered by the apostles. (See Acts 5:16; 8:7; 19:12.)

6. Demons will inflict grievous torture upon unsaved mankind during the great tribulation.

The ninth chapter of Revelation, which contains both fifth and sixth trumpet judgments, may be the most revealing section in all the Bible concerning demonology.

a. The torment of these demons.

"And there came out of the smoke locusts upon the earth: and unto them was given power, as the scorpions of the earth have the power. And it was commanded them that they should not hurt the grass of the earth, neither any green thing, neither any tree; but only those men which have not the seal of God in their foreheads" (Rev. 9:3, 4).

J. A. Seiss writes:

"The pain from the sting of a scorpion, though not generally fatal, is, perhaps, the most intense that any animal can inflict upon the human body. The insect itself is the most . . . malignant that lives, and its poison is like itself. Of a boy stung in the foot by a scorpion (it was related that) . . . he rolled on the ground, grinding his teeth, and foaming at the mouth. It was a long time before his complainings moderated, and even then he could make no use of his foot, which was greatly inflamed. And such is the nature of the torment which these locusts from the pit inflict. They are also difficult to be guarded against, if they can be warded off at all, because they fly where they please, dart through the air, and dwell in darkness." (*The Apocalypse*, p. 83)

b. The duration of these demons. Charles Ryrie writes:

"Horrible as the torment will be, God will place certain limitations on the activity of these demons. They will be limited as to what they may strike and as to how far they may go and as to how long they may do what they will do. They will not attack the vegetation of the earth (as common locusts do); they may only attack certain men, that is, those who have not the seal of God in their foreheads (the 144,000, cf. 7:3). The wicked will persecute God's servants, the 144,000; but in turn they will be tormented by this plague which God allows. The demon-locusts will also be limited in that they may not kill men, just torment them. Further, the duration of this plague will be five months. The effect of this torment is to drive men to suicide, but they will not be able to die. Although men will prefer death to the agony of living, death will not be possible. Bodies will not sink and drown; poisons and pills will have no effect; and somehow even bullets and knives will not do their intended job." (*Revelation*, p. 62)

The reason men cannot die is probably because Satan has the key to the shaft and will not allow his followers to leave the earth scene where the battle of light and darkness is being fought.

c. The description of these demons (Rev. 9:7-10). It would seem that the Apostle John describes two kinds of demons which will invade earth during the tribulation. The sixth trumpet now ushers in the second invasion.

(1) The leaders of this invasion. Four special satanic angels. These may function to Satan as the four living creatures do to God (Rev. 4:6-8).

(2) The armies of this invasion. The number—two hundred million. By normal standards this mighty army would occupy a territory one mile wide and eighty-seven miles long.

The description. These demons, unlike those of the first invasion, seem to be mounted upon some type of hellish horse. The horses' heads look much like lions', with smoke, fire, and flaming sulphur billowing from their mouths. The riders wear fiery-red breastplates.

(3) The source of this invasion: the Euphrates River. This is where evil began on earth (Gen. 3; Zech. 5:8-11), where false religion began (Gen. 4:3; 10:9, 10; 11:4), and where it will come to its end (Rev. 17-18).

(4) The duration of this invasion: thirteen months.

(5) The damage wrought by this invasion. One third of humanity is killed through fire, smoke, and brimstone. One fourth has already been slain by the fourth seal (Rev. 6:8). This would be approximately one billion. Now one third is killed, meaning another billion die. This invasion is therefore the opposite of the fifth trumpet judgment, during which no man was able to die.

(6) The results of this invasion.
"And the rest of the men which were not killed by these plagues yet repented not of the works of their hands, that they should not worship devils, and idols of gold, and silver, and brass, and stone, and of wood: which neither can see, nor hear, nor walk: Neither repented they of their murders, nor of their sorceries, nor of their fornication, nor of their thefts" (Rev. 9:20, 21).

At this point over one half of the world's population has been wiped out. And what is the response of the survivors? Total unrepentance and intensified rebellion. That very year the FBI reports will probably show a 1000 percent increase in idolatry, murder, drug-related crimes (the word "sorceries" is the Greek *pharmakeion*, from which we get our word "pharmacy"; it is the Greek word for drugs), sex, felonies, and robbery.

d. The king of these demons (9:11). His name is Apollyon, which means "destroyer." Here is Satan's hellish Michael the archangel.

7. Demons are, however, on occasion, actually used by God to fulfill his divine purpose.

a. A demon was used to punish wicked king Abimelech (Jdg. 9:23).

b. A demon was used to prepare for the execution of King Ahab in battle (1 Ki. 22:19-23).

c. A demon brought out the true nature of unsaved King Saul (1 Sam. 16:14).

d. Demons were used to punish rebellious Israel during the time of wandering.
"He cast upon them the fierceness of his anger, wrath, and indignation, and trouble, by sending evil angels among them" (Ps. 78:49).

e. Demons will be used to bring ungodly nations to Armageddon for slaughtering at the end of the tribulation (Rev. 16:13-16).

H. The destiny of unsaved angels.

1. To be judged by Christ and his church (1 Cor. 6:3).

2. To be cast into the lake of fire forever (Mt. 25:41; 2 Pet. 2:4; Jude 6).

Is there any chance whatsoever for the salvation of a fallen angel? Dr. Fred Dickason writes:

"Furthermore, we may deduce that evil angels are nonredeemable. Those that followed Satan in his sin, fell decisively and are permanently left in their evil state without recourse or even the possibility of redemption. They are irrevocably consigned to the lake of fire (Mt. 25:41).

What evidence is there for such a position? First, there is no record of any angel ever being delivered from sin. True, this is an argument from silence, which is never too strong; but if Christ's redemption extended to angels, we could rightly expect some mention of it in God's revelation of the grace of His Son's work. We read of many other accomplishments of the death of Christ besides the redemption of man, but nothing of the salvation of angels. We read of His cross as their judgment (Jn. 16:11; Col. 2:14, 15), but it is never presented as their blessing in any sense.

Second, there is the definite statement that Christ did not take hold of angels to save them, but only of believing man (Heb. 2:16). He passed by angels to help man.

Third, it is implied in Hebrews 2:14-17 and is evident from the very nature of angels, that Christ did not and could not take upon Himself the nature of angels. Hebrews tells us that Christ saves those who are His 'brethren' (2:11). He had to be made like them, in fact one of them, to save them; so He took upon Himself 'flesh and blood' (2:14). This means that He entered into the race of men by the virgin birth, retaining His deity in essence (though not always its expression) and adding to His person sinless but genuine humanity. As the God-man He is a genuine representative of the race because He is truly human, as well as divine. On the cross, Christ was the effective Mediator between God and men because He was the God-man, representing both God and man in the settlement of our debt of sin. For man He suffered the penalty as a genuine substitute, since He genuinely participated in our humanity.

Christ could not lay hold on angels in like fashion to represent and to redeem them. Their very nature forbids it. Angels are not a race to which genuine additions may enter. They are individually separate creations of God, and they do not procreate (Mt. 22:28-30). Christ could not become their Kinsman-Redeemer by birth or creation and so represent angels as a class before God.

But since Christ did become the last Adam, the Head of a new race of men reborn by faith in Christ, we have a song no angel can sing—of Jesus the God-man and His saving grace (Jn. 1:12, 13; Heb. 2:9-12).

We must reject any teaching of universal restoration of all men, or even of Satan, to God. Only humans can be saved, and only those who trust Christ in this life will be saved. So taught Christ who died and rose again (Mt. 25:41; Jn. 5:29; 8:24). The lake of fire is an eternal torment for wicked men and angels (Rev. 14:10, 11; 19:20; 20:11-15)." (*Angels, Elect and Evil,* pp. 40-42)

THE DOCTRINE OF THE BIBLE

THE DOCTRINE OF THE BIBLE

Part One: How the Bible Came into Being

Everybody knows the Bible has been and continues to be the world's best seller, but not everybody knows just how this amazing book came down to us today. It *could* have happened this way: At some early ecumenical "Scripture session," a group of prophets and priests got together in Jerusalem to write a religious best seller. A committee was soon formed which assigned the books, appointed the authors, and arranged for all other details. Upon completion, the publicity chairman commissioned the Palestinian Press to print up the first one million copies.

We said it *could* have happened that way. But of course it didn't. God used three wonderful methods as he carefully carved out that most blessed of all books, the Bible. These three "tools of the Trinity" are referred to as *revelation, inspiration,* and *illumination.* Let us use an earthly story to illustrate this.

Over fifty years ago a famous German scientist named Albert Einstein developed a very important mathematical concept of the nature of our universe. Let us picture the scene. He suddenly summons you into his home for a secret conference. He invites you to be seated and immediately explains why you have been asked to come. He begins: "I have just completed one of the most comprehensive scientific theories since the days of Sir Isaac Newton. I want you to write this all down on paper and send it to the news media of the world. Here is my astonishing theory—energy equals mass times the speed of light squared $(E = mc_2)$!"

He then goes on to explain how mass and energy are equivalent, and that the property called mass is simply concentrated energy. You are awed as he continues with his amazing grasp of the universe. Finally he stops and says: "Now I want you to write this all down in your own words, but in order to make sure you get everything right, I want to help you in choosing those words."

So the next few hours are spent in this manner. Dr. Einstein gently but firmly guides you in the selection of the verbs and nouns from your own vocabulary. At long last you have it all down, the exact and complete revelation of truth from Albert Einstein described perfectly in your own handwriting and from your personal reservoir of words.

Before you leave, the aged scientist speaks once again: "One final thing that will encourage you: I plan to call every important newspaper and television editor, telling them that the message they will receive from you is true and they should both believe it and publish it!"

Here we have an example (however weak) of God's three tools and how they function. *Revelation* occurred when Dr. Einstein called you in and imparted to you his great truth. *Inspiration* took place when he guided you as

you wrote it down. *Illumination* happened when he encouraged the news editor to accept his report as given by you.

How then did we receive our Bible? Well, around 1400 B.C. God began to quietly call some forty men and women into his presence. Oh, he didn't call them in all at once, mind you. In fact, it took him nearly fifteen centuries to complete the job. He spoke the burden of his great heart in simple but sublime language to those chosen forty. With a holy hush they heard him tell of creation and corruption, of condemnation, justification, sanctification, and glorification. Weighty words, indeed. When he had finished, the first tool in carving out the Bible was set aside. *Revelation* had occurred.

Now we see this almighty Author as he quickly but carefully guides each chosen human vessel in his assigned writing task. Each of the forty is dealt with individually. Job, a rich farmer, will write differently than will Amos, a poor farmer. The words of the educated Paul will be more complicated on occasion than those of the uneducated John or Peter. But all will carry with them the divine approval of heaven itself.

Finally, the last scribe lays down his (or her) pen. The angels watch as their Creator lays aside the second tool in the making of his manuscript. *Inspiration* has taken place.

Soon many thousands of men and women join the ranks of those original forty and begin their assigned task of taking God's glory story to the uttermost parts of the earth. As they do, untold multitudes are stopped in their tracks, convinced in their hearts, and saved from their sins. By what secret power did all this take place? The answer is simple: the Author of the Bible is using the third and final tool. *Illumination* continues to take place.

And so the Scriptures are shaped. To summarize thus far, think of the three tools as follows:

Revelation: From God to man (man hears that which God wants written).

Inspiration: From man to paper (man writes that which God wants written).

Illumination: From paper to heart (man receives the light of that which God has written).

Now that we have observed the purpose of these three tools, let us turn our thoughts to the nature of each weapon. We have examined the fruit of the tools, but what of the root? How did God make the weapon itself? We first consider:

I. Revelation. We know God spoke to man, but how did he speak? Hebrews 1:1 informs us he spoke to the fathers and prophets in many ways. A careful examination of the Bible reveals at least eight different modes of communication. These are:
   A. He often spoke to men through angels. Consider:
      1. Angels reassured Abraham of the birth of

Isaac and informed him of God's decision to destroy Sodom (Gen. 18).

2. Angels warned Lot to flee Sodom before the awful destruction took place (Gen. 19).

3. The angel Gabriel explained the nature of the tribulation to Daniel (Dan. 9:21-27).

4. Gabriel informed Zacharias he would have a son who would become the forerunner of Christ (Lk. 1:11-20).

5. Gabriel informed Mary that God had chosen her as his vessel for Christ's birth (Lk. 1:26-37).

6. Angels announced the birth of Christ to the shepherds (Lk. 2:8-14).

7. An angel announced the resurrection of Christ to some women (Mt. 28:5-7).

8. An angel directed Philip to the seeking eunuch (Acts 8:26).

9. An angel directed Peter out of a Roman prison (Acts 12:7-10).

B. He spoke to men through a loud voice.

1. He spoke directly to Adam (Gen. 3:9-19).

2. He spoke directly to Noah (Gen. 6:13-21).

3. He spoke directly to Abraham (Gen. 12:1-3).

4. He spoke directly to Moses (Ex. 20:1-17).

5. He spoke directly to Joshua (Josh. 1:1-9).

6. He spoke directly to Samuel (1 Sam. 3:1-14).

7. He spoke directly to Nathan, about David (2 Sam. 7:4-16).

8. He spoke directly to Elijah (1 Ki. 17:2-4).

9. He spoke directly to Jeremiah (Jer. 1:4, 5).

C. He spoke to men through a still, small voice (1 Ki. 19:11, 12; Ps. 32:8).

D. He spoke to men through nature (Ps. 19:1-3; Acts 14:15-17; Rom. 1:18-20).

E. He spoke to one man through the mouth of an ass (Num. 22:28). This has to be one of the funniest moments in the Bible!

F. He spoke to men through dreams. On a number of occasions God chose this method.

1. Jacob received the confirmation of the Abrahamic Covenant in a dream (Gen. 28:12).

2. Solomon received both wisdom and a warning in a dream (1 Ki. 3:5; 9:2).

3. Joseph in the New Testament received three messages in three dreams.

 a. Assuring him of Mary's purity (Mt. 1:20).

 b. Commanding him to flee to Egypt (Mt. 2:13).

 c. Ordering him to return to Palestine (Mt. 2:19-22).

4. The wise men were warned of Herod's evil intentions in a dream (Mt. 2:12).

G. He spoke to men through visions. *Unger's Bible Dictionary* defines a vision as: "A supernatural presentation of certain scenery or circumstances to the mind of a person while awake." It may be noted that many great truths in the Scriptures were related to men through this unique method.

1. Jacob was instructed in a vision to go to Egypt (Gen. 46:2).

2. David was warned of judgment in a vision (1 Chron. 21:16).

3. Isaiah saw God's holiness in a vision (Isa. 6:1-8).

4. Daniel saw the great Gentile powers in a vision (Dan. 7, 8).

5. Daniel saw the glories of Christ in a vision (Dan. 10:5-9).

6. Daniel saw the rise and fall of Alexander the Great in a vision (Dan. 8).

7. Ezekiel saw the regathering of Israel in a vision (Ezek. 37).

8. Ananias was ordered to minister to Saul in a vision (Acts 9:10).

9. Cornelius was instructed to send for Peter in a vision (Acts 10:3-6).

10. Peter was ordered to minister to Cornelius in a vision (Acts 10:10-16).

11. Paul was ordered to Macedonia in a vision (Acts 16:9).

12. Paul was comforted at Corinth in a vision (Acts 19:9).

13. Paul was comforted at Jerusalem in a vision (Acts 23:11).

14. Paul viewed the glories of the third heaven in a vision (2 Cor. 12:1-4).

15. The Apostle John received the book of Revelation in a vision.

H. He spoke to men through Christophanies. A Christophany is a pre-Bethlehem appearance of Christ. Some theologians have seen a number of these appearances in the Old Testament, believing that the term "the Angel of the Lord," is actually another name of Christ. If this is true, the following examples of Christophany communication could be submitted.

1. The Angel of the Lord wrestled with Jacob (Gen. 32:24-30).

2. The Angel of the Lord redeemed Jacob from all evil (Gen. 48:16).

3. The Angel of the Lord spoke to Moses from the burning bush (Ex. 3:2).

4. The Angel of the Lord protected Israel at the Red Sea (Ex. 14:19).

5. The Angel of the Lord prepared Israel for the Promised Land (Ex. 23:20-23; Ps. 34:7; Isa. 63:9; 1 Cor. 10:1-4).

6. The Angel of the Lord commissioned Gideon (Jdg. 6:11).

7. The Angel of the Lord ministered to Elijah (1 Ki. 19:7).

8. The Angel of the Lord reassured Joshua (Josh. 5:13-15).

9. The Angel of the Lord saved Jerusalem (Isa. 37:36).

10. The Angel of the Lord preserved three godly Hebrew men (Dan. 3:25).

How then did God communicate his revelation to the forty human authors? To be truthful, we simply do not know. He could have used any one or a combination of these eight modes of communication as have been described above.

II. Inspiration. We have discussed various possibilities and ways God may have employed in the giving of his revelation to the human authors. Now let us consider the next major step, that of inspiration. The ears have heard the message, but how will the fingers react? What is involved in transferring the voice of God into the vocabulary of man? We shall now examine five areas along this particular line. But before we do this, let us define the word itself. The term "inspiration" is found but once in the New Testament. This occurs in 2 Timothy 3:16. Here Paul says, "All scripture is given by inspiration of God . . ." The Greek word is *theopneustos,* and literally means, "God-breathed."

A. Various theories of inspiration.

1. The natural theory. This says the Bible writers were inspired in the same sense that William Shakespeare was inspired. In other words, that spark of divine inspiration that supposedly is in all men simply burned a little brighter in the hearts of the Bible writers. This theory is totally rejected by the Apostle Peter.

    "Knowing this first, that no prophecy of the scripture is of any private interpretation" (2 Pet. 1:20).

2. The mechanical theory—that God coldly and woodenly dictated the Bible to his writers as an office manager would dictate an impersonal letter to his secretary. It should be noted here that the Bible is the story of divine love, and God is anything but mechanical or cold concerning this subject. The Holy Spirit therefore never transgressed the limits of the writer's vocabulary. Thus, the educated Paul uses many of the "85¢" words, while the less educated John employs more of the "25¢" words. But both writings are equally inspired by God. (See 2 Tim. 3:16.) Here Dr. Charles Hodge has well written:

    "The Church has never held what has been stigmatized as the mechanical theory of inspiration. The sacred writers were not machines. Their self-consciousness was not suspended; nor were their intellectual powers superseded. Holy men spoke as they were moved by the Holy Ghost. It was men not machines; not unconscious instruments, but living, thinking, willing minds, whom the Spirit used as His organs . . . The sacred writers impressed their peculiarities on their several productions as plainly as though they were the subjects of no extraordinary influence." (*Systematic Theology,* Vol. I, p. 157)

3. The content (or concept) theory—that only the main thought of a paragraph or chapter is inspired. This theory is immediately refuted by many biblical passages.

    "For verily I say unto you, Till heaven and earth pass, one jot or one tittle shall in no wise pass from the law, till all be fulfilled" (Mt. 5:18).

    "Now these be the last words of David. David the son of Jesse said, and the man who was raised up on high, the anointed of the God of Jacob, and the sweet psalmist of Israel said, The Spirit of the Lord spake by me, and his word was in my tongue" (2 Sam. 23:1, 2).

4. The partial theory—that only certain parts of the Bible are inspired. This of course is the position of the liberal theologian who would cheerfully accept those portions of the Bible which deal with love and brotherhood, but quickly reject the passages dealing with sin, righteousness, and future judgment. But let it be said that heaven and hell are like up and down—you can't have one without the other. Paul refutes the partial theory in 2 Timothy 3:16.

    In his textbook, *A Dispensational Theology,* Dr. Charles F. Baker writes:

    "A certain bishop is purported to have said that he believed the Bible to have been inspired in spots. When asked for his authority for such a statement, he quoted Hebrews 1:1, stating that this meant that God spoke at various times in varying degrees. Thus, some spots were fully inspired, others were only partially inspired, and still others were not inspired at all. The bishop was embarrassed when a layman asked: 'How do you know that Hebrews 1:1, the one scripture upon which you base your argument, is one of those fully inspired spots?' " (p. 38)

5. The spiritual-rule-only theory. This says the Bible may be regarded as our infallible rule of faith and practice in all matters of religious, ethical, and spiritual value, but not in other matters such as historical and scientific statements. This is pious nonsense. Consider the following: Here is a pastor greatly beloved by his congregation. How would this man of God feel if only his "moral" and "spiritual" statements made in the pulpit were accepted by his members? How would he react when the members would smile and take lightly any scientific or historical statements he might make? The fallacy of the spiritual-rule-only theory is that any book or man whose scientific or historical statements are open to question can certainly not be trusted in matters of moral and spiritual pronouncements! This theory is soundly refuted by Jesus himself in John 3:12.

    "If I have told you earthly things, and ye believe not, how shall ye believe, if I tell you of heavenly things?"

6. The plenary-verbal theory—that all (plenary) the very words (verbal) of the Bible are inspired by God. This view alone is the correct one.

    "But he answered and said, It is written, Man shall not live by bread alone, but by every word that proceedeth out of the mouth of God" (Mt. 4:4).

    "All scripture is given by inspiration of God, and is profitable for doctrine, for reproof, for correction, for instruction in righteousness: That the man of God may be perfect, throughly furnished unto all good works" (2 Tim. 3:16, 17).

    "Which things also we speak, not in the words which man's wisdom teacheth, but which the Holy Ghost teacheth; comparing spiritual things with spiritual" (1 Cor. 2:13).

"For I have given unto them the words which thou gavest me; and they have received them, and have known surely that I came out from thee and they have believed that thou didst send me" (Jn. 17:8).

"It is the spirit that quickeneth; the flesh profiteth nothing: the words that I speak unto you, they are spirit, and they are life" (Jn. 6:63).

3. Scripture texts on inspiration.

The Bible, of course, strongly claims its writings are from God. Compiling a few choice texts, we discover that:

1. No Old Testament Scripture was thought up by the prophet himself (2 Pet. 1:20).

2. All Old Testament Scriptures were given by the Holy Spirit as he moved upon men (2 Pet. 1:21).

3. This Spirit-breathed inspiration was given in many ways (Heb. 1:1).

4. Once it was given, this inspired writing:
   a. Could not be broken or shaken down (Jn. 10:35).
   b. Is exact in all details, down to the smallest stroke and letter (Mt. 5:18).
   c. Would abide forever (Mt. 5:18; 1 Pet. 1:25).

5. The Old Testament writers did not always understand the nature of everything they wrote about (Lk. 10:23, 24; 1 Pet. 1:10-12).
   a. They did not completely understand the details of Christ's suffering.
   b. They did understand that the mysteries would be clearer to a generation other than theirs.

6. The four Gospels were given by inspiration of God (Heb. 1:1; 2 Pet. 3:2).

7. Paul believed his writings were inspired by God (1 Cor. 2:4; 15:3; 1 Thess. 2:13; 4:15).

Note: Some have felt that Paul claimed no inspiration when he wrote certain passages in 1 Corinthians 7. Consider the following:

"But I speak this by permission, and not of commandment" (v. 6).

"But to the rest speak I, not the Lord" . . . (v. 12).

"Now concerning virgins I have no commandment of the Lord: yet I give my judgment . . ." (v. 25).

"But she is happier if she so abide, after my judgment: and I think also that I have the Spirit of God" (v. 40).

Let us now briefly examine each of these passages:

a. In verse 6 the word "permission" is literally "a joint opinion," and may refer to the inspired "considered opinion" of both Paul and Sosthenes. At any rate, Paul was simply saying this opinion was not a command but rather a divine suggestion. For a comparable passage, see Romans 12:1.

b. Verse 12 can be explained by comparing it with verse 10. There, Paul quotes a command uttered by the Lord Jesus himself while he was upon the earth (Mt.

19:6). But here is a group situation (one partner saved, one unsaved) to which Jesus issued no command while on earth, but now does so in heaven through Paul's inspired pen.

c. The same answer given for verse 12 also applies here in verse 25.

d. The word "think" in verse 40 could also be translated "persuaded." See Matthew 22:42; 1 Corinthians 8:2 where the same Greek word is used.

8. Paul used the Holy Spirit's words to explain the Holy Spirit's facts (1 Cor. 2:13).

9. Paul's writings were received through a special revelation from Christ (Gal. 1:11, 12).

10. Paul's writings were to be read by all (Col. 4:6; 1 Thess. 5:27).

11. Peter believed his writings were inspired by God (2 Pet. 3:2).

12. Peter believed Paul's writings were inspired (2 Pet. 3:15, 16).

13. John believed his writings were inspired (Rev. 22:18, 19). John warned:
    a. That if anyone added to his words, God would add horrible plagues to him.
    b. That if anyone subtracted from his words, God would remove his name from the Holy City.

C. Implications of inspiration.

As one carefully considers the subject of inspiration, he is led to the following nine conclusions:

1. Plenary-verbal inspiration does not teach that all parts of the Bible are equally important, but only that they are equally inspired. For example, Judges 3:16 is obviously not as important as John 3:16, but both these verses were inspired by God.

"But Ehud made him a dagger which had two edges, of a cubit length; and he did gird it under his raiment upon his right thigh" (Jdg. 3:16).

"For God so loved the world, that he gave his only begotten Son, that whosoever believeth in him should not perish, but have everlasting life" (Jn. 3:16).

2. Plenary-verbal inspiration does not guarantee the inspiration of any modern or ancient translation of the Bible, but deals only with the original Hebrew and Greek languages.

3. Plenary-verbal inspiration does not allow for any false teaching, but it does on occasion record the lie of someone. For example, Satan distorts the truth and lies to Eve (Gen. 3:4). Therefore we have an accurate record of the devil's words. As one reads the Bible, he must carefully distinguish between what God records and what he sanctions. Thus, while lying, murder, adultery, and polygamy are to be found in the Word of God, they are never approved by the God of the Word.

4. Plenary-verbal inspiration does not permit any historical, scientific, or prophetical error whatsoever. While it is admitted that the Bible is not a textbook on science, it is nevertheless held that every scientific statement in the Scriptures is absolutely true.

5. Plenary-verbal inspiration does not prohibit personal research. The New Testament writer Luke begins his Gospel account with the following words:
"Inasmuch as many have undertaken to compile an account of the things accomplished among us, just as those who from the beginning were eyewitnesses and servants of the Word have handed them down to us, it seemed fitting for me as well, having investigated everything carefully from the beginning, to write it out . . ." (Lk. 1:1-3, *NASB*).
6. Plenary-verbal inspiration does not deny the use of extra-biblical sources. Here several examples come to mind.
   a. On at least two occasions, Paul quotes from heathen authors (Acts 17:28; Titus 1:12).
   b. Jude quotes from an ancient Hebrew book, one not included in the Bible (Jude 14, 15).
7. Plenary-verbal inspiration does not overwhelm the personality of the human author. The Bible writers experienced no coma-like trances as do some mediums during a séance, but on the contrary, always retained their physical, mental, and emotional powers. Various passages testify to this. See Isaiah 6:1-11; Daniel 12.
8. Plenary-verbal inspiration does not exclude the usage of pictorial and symbolic language. This is to say the Holy Spirit does not demand we accept every word in the Bible in a wooden and legalistic way. For example, a case could not be made that God has feathers like a bird, by referring to Psalm 91:4. Here the thought is simply that the persecuted believer can flee to his heavenly Father for protection and warmth.
9. Plenary-verbal inspiration does not mean uniformity in all details given in describing the same event. Here an Old Testament and a New Testament example come to mind.
   a. Old Testament example: The wicked reign of King Manasseh is vividly described for us in two separate chapters. These are 2 Kings 21:1-18 and 2 Chronicles 33:1-20. In 2 Kings we read only of his sinful ways, but in 2 Chronicles we are told of his eventual prayers of forgiveness and subsequent salvation. The reason for this may be that God allowed the author of 2 Kings to describe the reign of Manasseh from an earthly standpoint (even though he inspired the pen of the author), while he guided the pen of the author of 2 Chronicles to record Manasseh's reign from a heavenly viewpoint. God alone, of course, knows true repentance when he sees it coming from the human heart.
   b. New Testament example: There are four different accounts concerning the superscription on the cross at Calvary.
      (1) Matthew says—"This is Jesus the King of the Jews" (Mt. 27:37).
      (2) Mark says—"The King of the Jews" (Mk. 15:26).
      (3) Luke says—"This is the King of the Jews" (Lk. 23:38).
      (4) John says—"Jesus of Nazareth the King of the Jews" (Jn. 19:19).
      The entire title probably read, "This is Jesus of Nazareth, the King of the Jews."
10. Plenary-verbal inspiration assures us that God included all the necessary things he wanted us to know, and excluded everything else (2 Tim. 3:15-17).
D. Importance of inspiration.
   Of the three tools involved in the making of our Bible, inspiration is the most important. This is true because:
   1. One may have inspiration without revelation. We have already seen how Luke carefully checked out certain facts concerning the life of Christ and was then led to write them on paper (Lk. 1:1-4; 1 Jn. 1:1-4).
   2. One may have inspiration without illumination. Peter tells us the Old Testament prophets did not always understand everything they wrote about (1 Pet. 1:11). But without inspiration, the Bible falls.
E. Completion of inspiration.
   Is inspiration still going on today? Has God inspired the writing (or will he someday) of a sixty-seventh book of the Bible? For nearly twenty centuries now, evangelical Christians everywhere have held to the belief that when John the apostle wrote Revelation 22:21 and wiped his pen, inspiration stopped. Furthermore, it is generally believed his warning not to add to or subtract from his book included not only the book of Revelation, but the entire Bible. (See Rev. 22:18, 19.) It is of utmost importance that this is clearly understood, else the following tragic conclusions take place. If inspiration is still going on today, then one is forced to admit that:
   1. God could have inspired the weird and wicked writings of a Joseph Smith, or a Mary Baker Eddy, or a Charles Russell, or a Herbert W. Armstrong.
   2. Perhaps we still do not possess all the details concerning the plan of salvation, details vital to escape hell and enter heaven.
   3. God has allowed millions of devoted and faithful Christians to believe a horrible lie for some 2000 years.
III. Illumination. We have already stated that, without inspiration, no Scripture ever would have been written. We may now claim that without illumination, no sinner ever would have been saved! Illumination, then, is that method used by the Holy Spirit to shed divine light upon all seeking men as they look into the Word of God. Illumination is from the written word to the human heart.
   A. Reasons for illumination.
      Why is this third step necessary? Why cannot sinful man simply read and heed the biblical message without divine aid?
      1. It is necessary because of natural blindness. Paul writes of this:

"But the natural man receiveth not the things of the Spirit of God: for they are foolishness unto him: neither can he know them, because they are spiritually discerned" (1 Cor. 2:14).

Our Lord also commented on this during his earthly ministry:

"And Simon Peter answered and said, Thou art the Christ, the Son of the living God. And Jesus answered and said unto him, Blessed art thou, Simon Bar-jona: for flesh and blood hath not revealed it unto thee, but my Father which is in heaven" (Mt. 16:16, 17).

2. It is necessary because of satanic blindness. Again we note the sober words of Paul:

"But if our gospel be hid, it is hid to them that are lost: In whom the god of this world hath blinded the minds of them which believe not . . ." (2 Cor. 4:3, 4).

3. It is necessary because of carnal blindness (1 Cor. 3; Heb. 5:12-14; 2 Pet. 1).

B. Results of illumination.
  1. Sinners are saved.

"The Lord openeth the eyes of the blind . . ." (Ps. 146:8).

"The entrance of thy words giveth light . . ." (Ps. 119:130).

  2. Christians are strengthened.

"As newborn babes, desire the sincere milk of the word, that ye may grow thereby" (1 Pet. 2:2).

"But God hath revealed them unto us by his Spirit . . ." (1 Cor. 2:10).

"For God, who commanded the light to shine out of darkness, hath shined in our hearts, to give the light of knowledge . . ." (2 Cor. 4:6).

"Thy word is a lamp unto my feet, and a light unto my path" (Ps. 119:105).

C. Implications of illumination.
  1. The Holy Spirit looks for a certain amount of sincerity before he illuminates any human heart. We are quick to point out sincerity is not enough to save anyone. However, it should also be noted that it is equally impossible for an insincere person to be saved. This first implication is brought out in several passages.

"But without faith it is impossible to please him: for he that cometh to God must believe that he is, and that he is a rewarder of them that diligently seek him" (Heb. 11:6).

"God is a Spirit: and they that worship him must worship him in spirit and in truth" (Jn. 4:24).

Furthermore, it should be stated here that no Christian should ever look upon illumination as automatic. That is to say, God has never promised to reveal precious and profound biblical truths to any believer who will not search the Scriptures for himself.

Note the following admonitions:

"Man shall not live by bread alone, but by every word that proceedeth out of the mouth of God" (Mt. 4:4).

"But these are written that ye might believe that Jesus is the Christ, the Son of God . . ." (Jn. 20:31).

"These were more noble than those in Thessalonica, in that they received the word with all readiness of mind, and searched the scriptures daily . . ." (Acts 17:11).

"Study to shew thyself approved unto God, a workman that needeth not to be ashamed, rightly dividing the word of truth" (2 Tim. 2:15).

"As newborn babes, desire the sincere milk of the word, that ye might grow thereby" (1 Pet. 2:2).

2. The Holy Spirit often seeks out the aid of a believer in performing his task of illuminating the hearts of others. This is seen:
  a. In the ministry of Philip to the Ethiopian eunuch.

"And Philip ran hither to him, and heard him read the prophet Esaias, and said, Understandest thou what thou readest? And he said, How can I, except some man should guide me. . . . Then Philip opened his mouth, and began at the same scripture, and preached unto him Jesus" (Acts 8:30, 31, 35).

  b. In the ministry of Paul to the Jews at Thessalonica.

"And Paul, as his manner was, went in unto them, and three sabbath days reasoned with them out of the scriptures" (Acts 17:2).

  c. In the ministry of Aquila and Priscilla to Apollos.

"And he began to speak boldly in the synagogue: whom when Aquila and Priscilla had heard, they took him unto them, and expounded unto him the way of God more perfectly" (Acts 18:26).

  d. In the ministry of Apollos to the Jews at Corinth.

"For he mightily convinced the Jews, and that publicly, shewing by the scriptures that Jesus was Christ" (Acts 18:28).

Part Two: Views on the Bible

I. The Position of Israel. In spite of her sin and sorrows, Old Testament Israel held steadfast in the belief that her thirty-nine holy books were indeed the very Word of God. Even though one of her kings would attempt to burn it (Jer. 36), the nation as a whole would continue to believe it. The following words of Moses beautifully summarize Israel's position concerning the Word of God:

"Hear, O Israel: The Lord our God is one Lord: And thou shalt love the Lord thy God with all thine heart, and with all thy soul, and with all thy might. And these words, which I command thee this day, shall be in thine heart: And thou shalt teach them diligently unto thy children, and shalt talk of them when thou sittest in thine house, and when thou walkest by the way, and when thou liest down, and when thou risest up. And thou shalt bind them for a sign upon thine hand, and they shall be as frontlets between thine eyes. And thou shalt write them upon the posts of thy house, and on thy gates" (Deut. 6:4-9).

II. The Position of the Early Church. During the third, fourth, and fifth centuries the church held no less than 184 councils, not to deal with civil rights, ecology problems, or political ills, but to deal with any and all heresy that would dare tamper with the pure Word of God.

III. The Position of Agnosticism. In the book, *A Guide to the Religions of America,* Dr. Bertrand Russell makes the following statement:

"An agnostic regards the Bible exactly as enlightened clerics regard it. He does not think that it is divinely inspired; he thinks its early history legendary, and no more exactly true than that in Homer; he thinks its moral teaching sometimes good, but sometimes very bad. For example: Samuel ordered Saul, in a war, to kill not only every man, woman, and child of the enemy, but also all the sheep and cattle. Saul, however, let the sheep and cattle live, and for this we are told to condemn him. I have never been able to admire Elisha for cursing the children who laughed at him, or to believe (what the Bible asserts) that a benevolent Deity would send two she-bears to kill the children."

IV. The Position of Liberalism. Probably the most famous liberal of the twentieth century was the late Harry Emerson Fosdick. He has written the following words which typify the liberal attitude:

"When one moves back to the Scriptures with a mind accustomed to work in modern ways he finds himself in a strange world. . . . Knowing modern astronomy he turns to the Bible to find the sun and the moon standing still on the shadow retreating on a sundial. Knowing modern biology he hears that when Elisha had been so long dead that only his bones were left, another dead body, thrown into the cave where he was buried, touched his skeleton and sprang to life again, or that after our Lord's resurrection many of the saints long deceased arose and appeared in Jerusalem. Knowing modern physics he turns to the Bible to read that light was created three days before the sun and that an axe-head floated when Elisha threw a stick into the water. Knowing modern medicine he finds in the Scripture many familiar ailments, epilepsy, deafness, dumbness, blindness, insanity, ascribed to the visitation of demons. . . . We live in a new world. We have not kept the forms of thought and categories of explanation in astronomy, geology, biology, which the Bible contains. We have definitely and irrevocably gotten new ones. . . ."

V. The Position of the Cults. In general it may be said that the major cults and sects of Christianity give lip service to the Bible; nevertheless they look upon the writings of their various founders as equal if not superior to the Scriptures. For example:

A. Christian Scientist (founded by Mary Baker Eddy; 1821-1910). George Channing, an international Christian Science lecturer and practitioner, writes the following:

"Each person, of any religion, can find what is satisfying to him as the spiritual meaning in the Bible. But Christian Scientists feel that Mrs. Mary Baker Eddy's Book, *Science and Health with Key to the Scriptures,* offers the complete spiritual meaning of the Bible. They believe that this full meaning would not have been available to them without Mrs. Eddy's discovery."

B. Jehovah's Witnesses (founded by Charles Taze Russell; 1851-1916). Mr. Russell calmly announces in the opening pages of his *Studies in the Scriptures* that it would be far better to leave the Bible unread but read his comments on it than to omit his writings and read the Bible.

C. Mormonism (founded by Joseph Smith; 1805-1844). This cult teaches that the *Book of Mormon,* first printed in 1830, must be regarded on an equal basis with the Bible.

VI. The Position of Romanism. Rome believes that the church is the divinely appointed custodian of the Bible and has the final word on what is meant in any specific passage. It accepts the apocryphal books as a part of the inspired Scriptures. Rome's position on the Bible could be diagrammed as a triangle, with the Pope at the top, and the Bible and church tradition at the bottom.

VII. The Position of Mysticism. Those holding this view lean heavily upon that divine "inner light" to reveal and guide them into all truth. Thus the personal experiences, feelings, etc., of an individual are looked upon as vital to discovering divine truth along with the Word of God itself.

VIII. The Position of Neo-Orthodoxy (popularized by Karl Barth in his *Epistle to the Romans,* first published in 1918). This position holds that the Bible may well contain the Word of God, but that, until it becomes such, it is as dead and uninspired as any other ancient or modern historical book might be. Thus the Bible is not to be viewed as objective, but subjective in nature. It is only the Word of God as it *becomes* the Word of God to me. Neo-orthodoxy would thus view the first eleven chapters as "religious myths." This term is defined as a "conveyer of theological truth in a historical garb, but which theological truth is not dependent upon the historicity of the garb itself for its validity."

IX. The Position of Neo-Evangelicalism. In the latter part of 1957, one of the leaders of this position wrote the following:

"The New Evangelicalism in the latest dress of orthodoxy or Neo-orthodoxy is the latest expression of theological liberalism. The New Evangelicalism differs from Fundamentalism in its willingness to handle the social problems which Fundamentalism evaded. There need be no dichotomy between the personal gospel and the social gospel. . . . The New Evangelicalism has changed its strategy from one of separation to one of infiltration. . . . The evangelical believes that Christianity is intellectually defensible but the Christian cannot be obscurantist in scientific questions pertaining to the Creation, the age of man, the Universality of the flood and other moot biblical questions."

X. The Position of Orthodoxy. This view holds that the Bible alone is the illuminated, inspired revelation of God and is therefore the sole ground of authority for believers. Orthodoxy claims the Bible is objective in nature and proclaims not a social gospel, but a sinner gospel. According to this view, whenever there is a clear contradiction between the Bible and any assumed "fact" of history or science, it is that "fact" which must give way to the Bible, and not the reverse.

A. This was the view of the Old Testament writers concerning the Old Testament.
1. Moses (Ex. 4:10-12)
2. Samuel (1 Sam. 8:10)
3. Joshua (Josh. 23:14)
4. David (2 Sam. 23:2, 3)
5. Isaiah (Isa. 1:10)
6. Jeremiah (Jer. 1:6-9)
7. Ezekiel (Ezek. 3:10-12)
8. Daniel (Dan. 10:9-12)
9. Joel (Joel 1:1)
10. Amos (Amos 3:1)
11. Obadiah (Obad. 1:1)
12. Jonah (Jonah 1:1)
13. Micah (Micah 1:1)
14. Nahum (Nahum 1:1)
15. Habakkuk (Hab. 2:2)
16. Zephaniah (Zeph. 1:1)
17. Haggai (Hag. 1:1)
18. Zechariah (Zech. 1:1)
19. Malachi (Mal. 1:1)

Here it should be kept in mind that the Old Testament refers to itself as the Word of God some 3,808 times.

B. This was the view of the New Testament writers concerning the Old Testament. The New Testament writers refer to at least 161 Old Testament events and quote from over 246 Old Testament passages. Some of these events and passages are as follows:
1. Old Testament events referred to in the New Testament (from the 161 events, twenty-two of the more important ones are listed here):
   a. creation (Gen. 1:1; Heb. 11:3)
   b. man made in God's image (Gen. 1:26; 1 Cor. 11:7)
   c. God resting (Gen. 2:2, 3; Heb. 4:4)
   d. the institution of marriage (Gen. 2:24; Mt. 19:4-6)
   e. the fall (Gen. 3:6-8; Rom. 5:12-19)
   f. the murder of Abel (Gen. 4:8; 1 Jn. 3:12)
   g. Enoch's translation (Gen. 5:21-24; Heb. 11:5)
   h. the ark of Noah (Gen. 6:14-16; 7:1-12; Lk. 17:26, 27; 2 Pet. 3:6)
   i. the call of Abraham (Gen. 12:1; Heb. 11:8)
   j. the meeting of Abraham and Melchizedek (Gen. 14:18-20; Heb. 7:1-4)
   k. the destruction of Sodom (Gen. 19; Mt. 11:24; Lk. 17:32)
   l. Isaac's birth (Gen. 19:26; Gal. 4:23)
   m. the offering up of Isaac (Gen. 22:10; Heb. 11:17-19)
   n. the burning bush (Ex. 3:2; Lk. 20:37; Acts 7:30)
   o. the Exodus (Ex. 12-14; Acts 7:36; Heb. 11:29; 1 Cor. 10:1)
   p. the giving of manna (Ex. 16:15; Jn. 6:31)
   q. the giving of the law (Ex. 20; Gal. 3:19)
   r. the serpent of brass (Num. 21:8, 9; Jn. 3:14)
   s. Elijah and the drought (1 Ki. 17; Lk. 4:25; Jas. 5:17)
   t. the healing of Naaman (2 Ki. 5:14; Lk. 4:27)
   u. Daniel in the lion's den (Dan. 6:22; Heb. 11:33)
   v. Jonah in the belly of the fish (Jonah 1:17; Mt. 12:40; 16:4)
2. Old Testament passages referred to in the New Testament:
   a. Be ye holy, for I am holy (Lev. 11:44; 1 Pet. 1:16).
   b. I will never leave thee nor forsake thee (Josh. 1:5; Heb. 13:5).
   c. Be ye angry and sin not (Ps. 4:4; Eph. 4:26).
   d. There is none righteous, no not one (Ps. 14:1; Rom. 3:10).
   e. Whom the Lord loveth he chasteneth (Prov. 3:12; Heb. 12:6).
   f. God shall wipe away all tears from their eyes (Isa. 25:8; Rev. 21:4).
   g. Death is swallowed up in victory (Hosea 13:14; 1 Cor. 15:54).
   h. I will pour out my spirit upon all flesh (Joel 2:28; Acts 2:17).
   i. Whosoever shall call on the name of the Lord shall be saved (Joel 2:32; Rom. 10:13).
   j. The earth is the Lord's and the fulness thereof (Ps. 24:1; 1 Cor. 10:26).
   k. My son, despise not the chastening of the Lord (Prov. 3:11; Heb. 12:5).
   l. Blessed is he that cometh in the name of the Lord (Ps. 118:26; Mt. 21:9).
   m. Charity covereth a multitude of sins (Prov. 10:12; 1 Pet. 4:8).
   n. How beautiful are the feet of them that preach the gospel (Isa. 52:7; Rom. 10:15).

C. This was the view of the New Testament writers concerning the New Testament.
1. Peter's testimony (2 Pet. 3:2).
2. Paul's testimony (1 Cor. 2:4, 13; 15:3; 1 Thess. 2:13; 4:15).
3. John's testimony (Rev. 22:18, 19).
4. James' testimony (Jas. 1:21; 4:5).
5. Jude's testimony (Jude 3).

D. This was the view of the Lord Jesus Christ concerning the entire Bible.
1. Our Lord began his ministry by quoting from the Old Testament. Compare Matthew 4:4, 7, 10 with Deuteronomy 8:3; 6:13, 16.
2. Our Lord ended his ministry by quoting from the Old Testament. Five of his last seven statements on the cross were lifted from the pages of the Old Testament. Compare:
   a. Luke 23:34 with Isaiah 53:12
   b. Luke 23:43 with Isaiah 53:10, 11
   c. Matthew 27:46 with Psalms 22:1

d. John 19:28 with Psalms 69:21
e. Luke 23:46 with Psalms 31:5

3. Our Lord preached one of his first public messages from an Old Testament text. Compare Luke 4:16–19 with Isaiah 61:1, 2.
4. Our Lord informed the Pharisees they erred, "not knowing the scriptures" (Mt. 22:29).
5. Our Lord justified his own actions by referring to the Old Testament:
   a. when he ate on the Sabbath (Mt. 12:1–8).
   b. when he healed on the Sabbath (Mt. 12:10–21).
   c. when he cleansed the Temple (Mt. 21:13).
   d. when he accepted the praise of the crowds at his triumphal entry (Mt. 21:16).
6. Our Lord believed in the history of the Old Testament. He referred to—
   a. creation (Mk. 10:6).
   b. Noah's ark (Mt. 24:38).
   c. Lot's wife (Lk. 17:32).
   d. destruction of Sodom (Lk. 17:29).
   e. Jonah and the fish (Mt. 12:40).
   f. the Queen of Sheba and Solomon (Mt. 12:42).
   g. the repentance of Nineveh (Mt. 12:41).
   h. Naaman the leper (Lk. 4:27).
   i. Elijah and the widow (Lk. 4:25, 26).
   j. Moses and the serpent (Jn. 3:14).
   k. the first marriage (Mt. 19:5–7).
   l. the blood of Abel (Lk. 11:51).
   m. Abraham, Isaac, and Jacob (Mt. 22:31, 32).
   n. the burning bush (Lk. 20:37).
   o. the wilderness manna (Jn. 6:31).
   p. the murder of Zacharias (Mt. 23:35).
7. Our Lord said the law would be fulfilled (Mt. 5:18) and the Scriptures could not be broken (Jn. 10:35).

It has been estimated that over one tenth of Jesus' recorded New Testament words were taken from the Old Testament. In the four Gospels, 180 of the 1,800 verses which report his discourses are either Old Testament quotes or Old Testament allusions.

In concluding this section it may be said that every single Old Testament book is either directly or indirectly referred to in the New Testament (with the possible exception of the Song of Solomon). About half the great sermons in the book of Acts are composed of verses taken from the Old Testament. Peter's twenty-three-verse sermon at Pentecost takes twelve of these verses from the Old Testament (Acts 2:14–36). Stephen's forty-eight-verse message is completely Old Testament in nature (Acts 7:2–50). Paul's first recorded sermon occurring in Acts 13:16–41 is twenty-six verses long and, of these, fifteen are from the Old Testament.

Part Three: What Great Personalities Have Said about the Bible

I. United States Presidents.
   A. George Washington (First): "It is impossible to rightly govern the world without the Bible."
   B. John Adams (Second): "The Bible is the best book in the world. It contains more . . . than all the libraries I have seen."
   C. Thomas Jefferson (Third): "The Bible makes the best people in the world."
   D. John Quincy Adams (Sixth): "It is an invaluable and inexhaustible mine of knowledge and virtue."
   E. Andrew Jackson (Seventh): "That book, sir, is the rock on which our Republic rests."
   F. Zachary Taylor (Twelfth): "It was for the love of the truths of this great book that our fathers abandoned their native shore for the wilderness."
   G. Abraham Lincoln (Sixteenth): "But for this Book we could not know right from wrong. I believe the Bible is the best gift God has ever given to man."
   H. Ulysses S. Grant (Eighteenth): "The Bible is the Anchor of our liberties."
   I. Rutherford B. Hayes (Nineteenth): "The best religion the world has ever known is the religion of the Bible. It builds up all that is good."
   J. Benjamin Harrison (Twenty-third): "It is out of the Word of God that a system has come to make life sweet."
   K. William McKinley (Twenty-fifth): "The more profoundly we study this wonderful Book . . . the better citizens we will become."
   L. Theodore Roosevelt (Twenty-sixth): "No educated man can afford to be ignorant of the Bible."
   M. Woodrow Wilson (Twenty-eighth): "The Bible is the one supreme source of revelation of the meaning of life."
   N. Herbert Hoover (Thirty-first): "The whole of the inspirations of our civilization springs from the teachings of Christ . . . to read the Bible . . . is a necessity of American life."
   O. Franklin D. Roosevelt (Thirty-second): "It is a fountain of strength. . . . I feel that a comprehensive study of the Bible is a liberal education for anyone."
   P. Dwight D. Eisenhower (Thirty-fourth): "In the highest sense the Bible is to us the unique repository of eternal spiritual truths."
II. World Leaders.
   A. William Gladstone: "I have known ninety-five great men of the world in my time, and of these, eighty-seven were followers of the Bible."
   B. Winston Churchill: "We rest with assurance upon the impregnable rock of Holy Scripture."
   C. Chiang Kai-Shek: "The Bible is the voice of the Holy Spirit."
   D. Haile Selassie: "The Bible is not only a great book of historical reference, but it also is a guide for daily life, and for this reason I respect it and I love it."
   E. Syngman Rhee: "Fellow prisoners held the Bible and turned the pages for me because my fingers were so crushed that I could not use them. I read the Bible, and I have read it the rest of my life."
III. Generals.
   A. Douglas MacArthur: "Believe me, sir, never a night goes by, be I ever so tired, but I read the Word of God before I go to bed."
   B. William K. Harrison: "The Bible is the Word of

God, given by His inspiration for our use and benefit."

C. Robert E. Lee: "The Bible is a book in comparison with which all others in my eyes are of minor importance, and in which in all my perplexities and distresses has never failed to give me light and strength."

D. Stonewall Jackson: "God's promises change not . . . let us endeavor to adorn the doctrine of Christ in all things."

E. Oliver Cromwell (upon hearing Phil. 4:11-13 read as he lay dying): "He that was Paul's Christ is my Christ too."

IV. Scientists.

A. Sir Isaac Newton: "We account the Scriptures of God to be the most sublime philosophy. I find more sure marks of authenticity in the Bible than in any profane history whatsoever."

B. Sir Francis Bacon: "The volume of Scriptures. . . . reveal the will of God."

C. Sir John Herschel: "All human discoveries seem to be made only for the purpose of confirming more and more strongly the truths come from on high and contained in the sacred writings. . . ."

D. Michael Faraday: "Why will people go astray when they have this blessed Book to guide them?"

E. James Dwight Dana: "Young men, as you go forth, remember that I, an old man, who has known only science all his life, say unto you that there are no truer facts than the facts found within the Holy Scriptures."

V. Historians.

A. Arnold J. Toynbee: "It pierces through the Intellect and plays directly upon the heart."

B. H. G. Wells: "The Bible has been the Book that held together the fabric of Western civilization. . . . The civilization we possess could not come into existence and could not have been sustained without it."

C. Thomas Carlyle: "A Noble book! All men's book! . . . grand in its sincerity, in its simplicity, and in its epic melody."

VI. Physicians.

A. Mark Hopkins: "Thus we have every conceivable species of historical proof, both external and internal. Thus do the very stones cry out."

B. Charles W. Mayo: "In sickness or in health, one can find comfort and constructive advice in the Bible."

VII. Lawyers.

A. Daniel Webster: "I believe the Scriptures of the Old and New Testament to be the will and the Word of God."

B. Benjamin Franklin: "Young men, my advice to you is that you cultivate an acquaintance with, and a firm belief in, the Holy Scriptures."

C. Patrick Henry: "This is a Book worth more than all the others that were ever printed."

VIII. Educators.

A. Timothy Dwight: "The Bible is a window in this prison-world through which we may look into eternity."

B. William Lyon Phelps: "Everyone who has a thorough knowledge of the Bible may truly be called educated. . . . I believe knowledge of the Bible

without a college course is more valuable than a college course without the Bible."

C. Henry Van Dyke: "No other book in the world has had such a strange vitality, such an outgoing power of influence and inspiration. . . . No man is poor or desolate who has this treasure for his own."

IX. Philosophers and Writers.

A. Charles Dana: "Of all the books, the most indispensable and the most useful, the one whose knowledge is the most effective, is the Bible."

B. Horace Greeley: "It is impossible to mentally or socially enslave a Bible-reading people."

C. Immanuel Kant: "The existence of the Bible as a book for the people is the greatest benefit which the human race has ever experienced."

D. John Locke: "It has God for its Author, salvation for its end, and truth, without any mixture of error, for its matter: it is all pure, sincere, nothing too much, nothing wanting."

E. Count Leo Tolstoy: "Without the Bible the education of a child in the present state of society is impossible."

F. John Ruskin: "All I have taught in art, everything I have written, whatever greatness there has been in any thought of mine, whatever I have done in my life, has simply been due to the fact that, when I was a child, my mother daily read with me a part of the Bible, and daily made me learn a part of it by heart."

G. John Milton: "There are no songs like the songs of the Scriptures, no orations like the orations of the prophets."

H. William Cowper: "A Glory gilds the sacred page, Majestic like the sun: it gives a light to every age—it gives, but borrows none. . . ."

I. John Dryden: "It speaks no less than God in every line; Commanding words whose force is still the same. . . ."

J. Sir Walter Scott: "Within this awful volume lies the Mystery of mysteries."

K. Charles Dickens: "It is the best Book that ever was or ever will be in the world. . . ."

X. People from Various Fields.

A. J. Edgar Hoover: "The Bible is the unfailing guide which points the way for men to the perfect life."

B. Bernard Baruch: "I have always placed the Bible as number one among the four books I think everyone should read and study. Therein one will find all the problems that beset mankind."

C. Helen Keller: "In the Bible I find a confidence mightier than the utmost evil. . . ."

D. Lowell Thomas: "The Bible is of vital importance in teaching freedom. . . ."

E. King George V: "The English Bible is . . . the most valuable thing that this world affords."

XI. The Church Fathers.

A. Augustine: "Let us give in and yield our assent to the authority of Holy Scripture, which knows not how either to be deceived or to deceive. . . ."

B. John Chrysostom: "It is a great thing, this reading of the Scriptures! For it is not possible, I say, not possible ever to exhaust the minds of the Scriptures. It is a well which has no bottom."

C. Athanasius: "They were spoken and written by God through men who spoke of God. . . . Let no man add to these, neither let him take aught from these."

D. Origen: "For my part, I believe that not one jot or tittle of the divine instruction is in vain. We are never to say that there is anything impertinent or superfluous in the Scriptures of the Holy Spirit. . . ."

E. Jerome: "Give ear for a moment that I may tell you how you are to walk in the Holy Scriptures. All that we read in the Divine Book, while glistening and shining without, is yet far sweeter within."

F. Luther: "It cannot be otherwise, for the Scriptures are Divine; in them God speaks, and they are His Word. To hear or to read the Scriptures is nothing else than to hear God."

G. Calvin: "The Scriptures is the school of the Holy Spirit, in which, as nothing necessary and useful to be known is omitted, so nothing is taught which is not beneficial to know."

In concluding this section it may be necessary to stop here and consider some anticipated objections about all these "pious commercials" for the Bible. Some have felt the statements made by political persons, such as U.S. presidents, were made solely for election purposes, for, it is claimed, no atheist could ever be voted into the White House. But to say this is to deny the integrity of almost every American president. It should also be pointed out that many of these statements were made at a time when either the man was not a candidate for reelection, or had already moved out of the White House.

Furthermore, while history shows many famous "Bible haters" who later became "Bible lovers," it never records the opposite. To take this a step further, it can be shown that no evil and murderous dictator or tyrant in history was ever a friend of the Bible and that no good and wise leader was ever an enemy of God's Word. Thus to deny the authority of the Bible is to set oneself against practically every great leader in Western civilization. While it is true that this in itself constitutes no absolute proof of the Scriptures, it does, nevertheless, lend itself to Abraham Lincoln's famous proverb:

"You can fool some of the people all of the time, and all of the people some of the time, but you can't fool all of the people all of the time!"

Part Four: Symbols for the Bible

I. A Mirror.
"For if a person just listens and doesn't obey, he is like a man looking at his face in a mirror; as soon as he walks away, he can't see himself anymore or remember what he looks like. But if anyone keeps looking steadily into God's law for free men, he will not only remember it but he will do what it says, and God will greatly bless him in everything he does" (Jas. 1:23-25, TLB).
It is called a mirror because it reflects the mind of God and the true condition of man.

II. A Seed.
"Being born again, not of corruptible seed, but of incorruptible, by the word of God, which liveth and abideth for ever" (1 Pet. 1:23).
"Of his own will begat he us with the Word of Truth, that we should be a kind of firstfruits of his creatures" (Jas. 1:18).
"Hear ye therefore the parable of the sower. When any one heareth the word of the kingdom, and understandeth it not, then cometh the wicked one, and catcheth away that which was sown in his heart. This is he which received seed by the way side. But he that received the seed into stony places, the same is he that heareth the word, and anon with joy receiveth it; yet hath he not root in himself, but dureth for a while: for when tribulation or persecution ariseth because of the word, by and by he is offended. He also that received seed among the thorns is he that heareth the word; and the care of this world, and the deceitfulness of riches, choke the word, and he becometh unfruitful. But he that received seed into the good ground is he that heareth the word, and understandeth it; which also beareth fruit, and bringeth forth, some an hundredfold, some sixty, some thirty" (Mt. 13:18-23).
It is called a seed because, once properly planted, it brings forth life, growth, and fruit.

III. Water.
"Husbands, love your wives, even as Christ also loved the church, and gave himself for it; that he might sanctify and cleanse it with the washing of water by the word, that he might present it to himself a glorious church, not having spot, or wrinkle, or any such thing; but that it should be holy and without blemish" (Eph. 5:25-27).
It is called water because of its cleansing, quenching, and refreshing qualities. (See Ps. 42:1; 119:9; Prov. 25:25; Isa. 55:10; Heb. 10:22; Rev. 22:17.)

IV. A Lamp.
"Thy word is a lamp unto my feet, and a light unto my path" (Ps. 119:105).
"For the commandment is a lamp; and the law is light; and reproofs of instruction are the way of life" (Prov. 6:23).
"We have also a more sure word of prophecy; whereunto ye do well that ye take heed, as unto a light that shineth in a dark place, until the day dawn, and the day star arise in your hearts" (2 Pet. 1:19).
It is called a lamp because it shows us where we are now, it guides us in the next step, and it keeps us from falling.

V. A Sword.
"For the word of God is quick, and powerful, and sharper than any two-edged sword, piercing even to the dividing asunder of soul and spirit, and of the joints and marrow, and is a discerner of the thoughts and intents of the heart" (Heb. 4:12).
"And take the helmet of salvation, and the sword of the Spirit, which is the word of God" (Eph. 6:17).
It is called a sword because of its piercing ability, operating with equal effectiveness upon sinners, saints, and Satan. Of the various armor pieces mentioned in Ephesians 6:11-17, all to be worn by the believer, the only offensive piece is the "sword of the Spirit, which is the word of God."

VI. Precious Metals.
A. Gold (Ps. 19:10; 119:127).
B. Silver (Ps. 12:6).

"Therefore I love thy commandments above gold; yea above fine gold" (Ps. 119:127).

"The words of the Lord are pure words: as silver tried in a furnace of earth, purified seven times" (Ps. 12:6).

It is referred to as precious metals because of its desirability, its preciousness, its beauty, and its value.

VII. Nourishing Food.

A. Milk.

"As newborn babes, desire the sincere milk of the word, that ye may grow thereby" (1 Pet. 2:2).

B. Meat.

"For when for the time ye ought to be teachers, ye have need that one teach you again which be the first principles of the oracles of God; and are become such as have need of milk, and not of strong meat. For every one that useth milk is unskilful in the word of righteousness; for he is a babe. But strong meat belongeth to them that are of full age, even those who by reason of use have their senses exercised to discern both good and evil" (Heb. 5:12-14).

C. Bread.

"I am the living bread which came down from heaven: if any man eat of this bread, he shall live for ever: and the bread that I will give is my flesh, which I will give for the life of the world" (Jn. 6:51).

D. Honey.

"More to be desired are they than gold, yea, than much fine gold: sweeter also than honey and the honeycomb" (Ps. 19:10).

It is referred to as nourishing food because of the strength it imparts.

VIII. A Hammer.

"Is not my word like as a fire? saith the Lord; and like a hammer that breaketh the rock in pieces?" (Jer. 23:29).

It is referred to as a hammer because of its ability to both tear down and build up. (See Acts 9:4; Jude 20.)

IX. A Fire.

"Then I said, I will not make mention of him, nor speak any more in his name. But his word was in mine heart as a burning fire shut up in my bones, and I was weary with forbearing, and I could not stay" (Jer. 20:9).

"And they said one to another, Did not our heart burn within us, while he talked with us by the way, and while he opened to us the scriptures?" (Lk. 24:32).

It is called a fire because of its judging, purifying, and consuming abilities.

Part Five: The Supreme Authority of the Bible

Perhaps the grandest and most conclusive description of the Bible was penned by the Apostle Paul in a letter to a young pastor. He wrote:

"And that from a child thou hast known the holy scriptures, which are able to make thee wise unto salvation through faith which is in Christ Jesus. All scripture is given by inspiration of God, and is profitable for doctrine, for reproof, for correction, for instruction in righteousness: That the man of God may be perfect, throughly furnished unto all good works" (2 Tim. 3:15-17).

In this remarkable passage Paul claims that the Bible is profitable—

1. For doctrine—that is, it may be used as the perfect textbook to present the systematic teachings of the great truths relating to God himself.
2. For reproof—that is, the Bible is to be used to convict us of the wrong in our lives.
3. For correction—that is, it will then show us the right way.
4. For instruction in righteousness—that is, God's Word provides all the necessary details which will allow a Christian to become fully equipped for every good work.

Because of all this, the Bible rightly demands absolute and sole authority over any other source in the life of the child of God. This authority would exceed that of the following:

I. Human Reason. God gave us our minds and desires that we should use them! This is seen in two classic passages, one directed to the unsaved, the other to the saved.

"Come now, and let us reason together, saith the Lord; though your sins be as scarlet, they shall be as white as snow; though they be red like crimson, they shall be as wool" (Isa. 1:18).

"I beseech you therefore, brethren, by the mercies of God, that ye present your bodies a living sacrifice, holy, acceptable unto God, which is your reasonable service. And be not conformed to this world: but be ye transformed by the renewing of your mind, that ye may prove what is that good, and acceptable, and perfect, will of God" (Rom. 12:1, 2).

However, there are times when God desires us to submit our human reasoning to him. Note the following admonition:

"Trust in the Lord with all thine heart; and lean not unto thine own understanding. In all thy ways acknowledge him, and he shall direct thy paths. Be not wise in thine own eyes: fear the Lord, and depart from evil" (Prov. 3:5-7).

Often our reasoning is as the thinking of Naaman, who when asked to take a sevenfold bath in Jordan's muddy waters, angrily replied:

"Behold, I thought, He will surely come out to me, and stand, and call on the name of the Lord his God, and strike his hand over the place, and recover the leper" (2 Ki. 5:11).

But Elisha did not do so. Often God's ways are different from our ways.

"For my thoughts are not your thoughts, neither are your ways my ways, saith the Lord. For as the heavens are higher than the earth, so are my ways higher than your ways, and my thoughts than your thoughts" (Isa. 55:8, 9).

II. The Church. The New Testament abounds with passages which declare Christ the Head of the Church. (See Eph. 1:22; 2:19, 20; 4:15, 16; 5:23-30; Col. 1:18; 2:9.) The Savior, it must be remembered, gave birth to the Church, and not the other way around. (See Mt. 16:18.) Thus the Christian must look to the Bible and not to any earthly church for final instruction. Sometimes even those local churches mentioned in the Bible itself were grievously wrong. Note the following description of New Testament churches, some of which were started by Paul himself.

A. The church at Ephesus.

"Nevertheless I have somewhat against thee, because thou hast left thy first love. Remember therefore from whence thou art fallen, and repent, and do the first works; or else I will come unto thee quickly, and will remove thy candlestick out of his place, except thou repent" (Rev. 2:4, 5).

B. The church at Pergamos.

"But I have a few things against thee, because thou hast there them that hold the doctrine of Balaam, who taught Balac to cast a stumblingblock before the children of Israel, to eat things sacrificed unto idols, and to commit fornication. So hast thou also them that hold the doctrine of the Nicolaitanes, which thing I hate. Repent; or else I will come unto thee quickly, and will fight against them with the sword of my mouth" (Rev. 2:14-16).

C. The church at Thyatira.

"Notwithstanding I have a few things against thee, because thou sufferest that woman Jezebel, which calleth herself a prophetess, to teach and to seduce my servants to commit fornication, and to eat things sacrificed unto idols" (Rev. 2:20).

D. The church at Sardis.

"And unto the angel of the church in Sardis write: These things saith he that hath the seven Spirits of God, and the seven stars; I know thy works, that thou hast a name that thou livest, and art dead. Be watchful, and strengthen the things which remain, that are ready to die: For I have not found thy works perfect before God. Remember therefore how thou hast received and heard, and hold fast, and repent. If therefore thou shalt not watch, I will come on thee as a thief, and thou shalt not know what hour I will come upon thee" (Rev. 3:1-3).

E. The church at Laodicea.

"I know thy works, that thou art neither cold nor hot. I would thou wert cold or hot. So then because thou art lukewarm, and neither cold nor hot, I will spue thee out of my mouth. Because thou sayest, I am rich, and increased with goods, and have need of nothing; and knowest not that thou art wretched, and miserable, and poor, and blind, and naked: I counsel thee to buy of me gold tried in the fire, that thou mayest be rich; and white raiment, that thou mayest be clothed, and that the shame of thy nakedness do not appear; and anoint thine eyes with eyesalve, that thou mayest see. As many as I love, I rebuke and chasten: be zealous therefore and repent" (Rev. 3:15-19).

III. Tradition. In this atomic and space age where change occurs at rocket speed, many have come to appreciate some of our beautiful traditions of the past. And rightly so! But traditions, like changes, can be wrong. If a thing was in error when it began, it is still in error regardless of the centuries that separate it from us today. Often in the past, hurtful "traditions of the fathers" had crept into the church of the living God. Our Savior himself was grieved over some harmful Jewish traditions. Note his words:

"And honour not his father or his mother, he shall be free. Thus have ye made the commandment of God of none effect by your tradition" (Mt. 15:6). Later Paul would warn also of this.

"Beware lest any man spoil you through philosophy and vain deceit, after the tradition of men, after the rudiments of the world, and not after Christ" (Col. 2:8).

IV. Popes and Preachers. Even the most godly pastors are, after all, only finite men fully capable (apart from God's grace) of the vilest sins. This is true of popes as well.

V. Feelings and Experiences. At times Christians fall into error because they "feel led" to do or say certain things. However, we must learn that at times our feelings can be treacherous and totally untrustworthy. The psalmist often spoke of this:

"I had fainted, unless I had believed to see the goodness of the Lord in the land of the living" (Ps. 27:13).

"Why art thou cast down, O my soul? and why art thou disquieted in me? hope thou in God: for I shall yet praise him for the help of his countenance" (Ps. 42:5).

"I cried unto God with my voice, even unto God with my voice; and he gave ear unto me. In the day of my trouble I sought the Lord: my sore ran in the night, and ceased not: my soul refused to be comforted. I remembered God, and was troubled: I complained, and my spirit was overwhelmed. Thou holdest mine eyes waking: I am so troubled that I cannot speak. I have considered the days of old, the years of ancient times. I call to remembrance my song in the night: I commune with mine own heart: and my spirit made diligent search. Will the Lord cast off for ever? and will he be favourable no more? Is his mercy clean gone for ever? doth his promise fail for evermore? Hath God forgotten to be gracious? hath he in anger shut up his tender mercies? And I said, This is my infirmity: but I will remember the years of the right hand of the most High" (Ps. 77:1-10).

"I said in my haste, All men are liars" (Ps. 116-11).

This is not only the case with our feelings, but also our experiences. One of Job's three "friends," Eliphaz, based all his advice to the suffering Job on experience (Job 4:12-16). He is later severely rebuked by God himself for doing this (Job 42:7).

Thus, as valuable as personal experience may be, it is no substitute for the revealed Word of God.

Listed below are the various functions of this authoritative book called the Bible.

A. It upholds (Ps. 119:116).

B. It orders steps (Ps. 119:133).

C. It produces joy (Ps. 119:162).

D. It strengthens (Ps. 119:28; 1 Jn. 2:14).

E. It gives hope (Ps. 119:74, 81).

F. It gives light (Ps. 119:105, 130).

G. It gives understanding (Ps. 119:169).

H. It shows God's will (Isa. 55:11).

I. It builds up (Acts 20:32).

J. It produces fruit (Jn. 15:7).

K. It convicts of sin (Heb. 4:12).

L. It converts the soul (Jas. 1:18; 1 Pet. 1:23).
M. It cleanses the conscience (Jn. 15:3).
N. It consecrates life (Jn. 17:17).
O. It corrects the wrong (2 Tim. 3:16).
P. It confirms the right (Jn. 8:31).
Q. It comforts the heart (Ps. 119:50, 54).

Because of this, the child of God is to respond to this authoritative book in the following ways:

Read it (Deut. 31:11; Isa. 34:16; Lk. 4:16; Eph. 3:4; Col. 3:16; 4:1; 1 Thess. 5:27; 2 Tim. 4:13; Rev. 1:3).
Heed it (Ps. 119:9; 1 Tim. 4:16).
Seed it (Mt. 28:19, 20).
Desire it (1 Pet. 2:2).
Preach it (2 Tim. 4:2).
Rightly divide it (2 Tim. 2:15).
Live by it (Mt. 4:4).
Use it (Eph. 6:17).
Suffer for it, and if need be, die for it (Rev. 1:9; 6:9; 20:4).

The child of God is to *know* it in his head, *stow* it in his heart, *show* it in his life, and *sow* it in the world.

See also the following Scripture verses: Deuteronomy 4:1-10; 12:32; Joshua 1:8; Psalm 33:6; Proverbs 30:5, 6; Mark 4:24; Luke 8:12; John 12:48–50; Romans 8:7; 1 Corinthians 2:14; Hebrews 1:1-3; 2:1–4; Revelation 1:1–3; 20:12; 22:18, 19.

Part Six: How the Sixty-Six Books of the Bible Were Collected and Preserved

I. The Writing Materials of the Bible. The Spirit of God moved upon the authors of the Bible to record their precious messages upon whatever object was in current use at the time of the writing. Thus once again we see the marvelous condescension of God. These writing materials would include:
A. Clay (Jer. 17:13; Ezek. 4:1).
B. Stone (Ex. 24:12; 13:18; 32:15, 16; 34:1, 28; Deut. 5:22; 27:2, 3; Josh. 8:31, 32).
C. Papyrus (made by pressing and gluing two layers of split papyrus reeds together in order to form a sheet) (2 Jn. 12; Rev. 5:1).
D. Vellum (calf skin), parchment (lamb skin), leather (cowhide) (2 Tim. 4:13).
E. Metal (Ex. 28:36; Job 19:24; Mt. 22:19, 20).
II. The Original Language of the Bible.
A. The Old Testament was written in Hebrew, with the following exceptions appearing in Aramaic: Ezra 4:8—6:18; 7:12-26; Jeremiah 10:11; Daniel 2:4—7:28. Why did God choose Hebrew? In their book *A General Introduction to the Bible,* authors Geisler and Nix note the following:

"It is a pictorial language, speaking with vivid, bold metaphors which challenge and dramatize the story. The Hebrew language possesses a facility to present 'pictures' of the events narrated. 'The Hebrew thought in pictures, and consequently his nouns are concrete and vivid. There is no such thing as neuter gender; for the Semite everything is alive. Compound words are lacking. . . . There is no wealth of adjectives. . . .' The language shows 'vast powers of association and, therefore, of imagination.' Some of this is lost in the English translation, but even so, 'much of the vivid, concrete, and forthright character of our English Old Testament is really a carrying over into English of something of the genius of the Hebrew tongue.' As a pictorial language, Hebrew presents a vivid picture of the acts of God among a people who became examples or illustrations for future generations (cf. 1 Cor. 10:11). The Old Testament was intended to be presented graphically in a 'picture-language.'

Further, Hebrew is a personal language. It addresses itself to the heart and emotions rather than merely to the mind or reason. Sometimes even nations are given personalities (cf. Mal. 1:2, 3). Always the appeal is to the person in the concrete realities of life and not to the abstract or theoretical. Hebrew is a language through which the message is felt rather than thought. As such, the language was highly qualified to convey to the individual believer as well as to the worshiping community the personal relation of the living God in the events of the Jewish nation. It was much more qualified to record the realization of revelation in the life of a nation than to propositionalize that revelation for the propagation among all nations." (pp. 219, 220)

B. The entire New Testament was written in Greek. Again, to quote from Geisler and Nix:

"Greek was an intellectual language. It was more a language of the mind than of the heart, a fact to which the great Greek philosophers gave abundant evidence. Greek was more suited to codifying a communication or reflection on a revelation of God in order to put it into simple communicable form. It was a language that could more easily render the credible into the intelligible than could Hebrew. It was for this reason that New Testament Greek was a most useful medium for expressing the propositional truth of the New Testament, as Hebrew was for expressing the biographical truth of the Old Testament. Since Greek possessed a technical precision not found in Hebrew, the theological truths which were more generally expressed in the Hebrew of the Old Testament were more precisely formulated in the Greek of the New Testament.

Furthermore, Greek was a nearly universal language. The truth of God in the Old Testament, which was initially revealed to one nation (Israel), was appropriately recorded in the language of the nation (Hebrew). But the fuller revelation given by God in the New Testament was not restricted in that way. In the words of Luke's gospel, the message of Christ was to 'be preached in his name to all nations' (Lk. 24:47). The language most appropriate for the propagation of this message was naturally the one that was most widely spoken throughout the world. Such was the common (Koine) Greek, a thoroughly international language of the first century Mediterranean world.

It may be concluded, then, that God chose the very languages to communicate His truth which had, in His providence, been prepared to express most effectively the kind of truth He desired at that particular time, in the unfolding of His overall plan. Hebrew, with its pictorial and personal vividness, expressed well the biographical truth of the Old Testament. Greek, with its intellectual and universal potentialities, served well for the doctrinal and evangelistic demands of the New Testament." (p. 221)

III. The Reason for the Writing of the Bible. Perhaps the one supreme difference between man and all other creatures (apart from his immortal soul, of course), is his God-given ability to express his thoughts on paper. It has been observed that while it was no doubt desirable to speak *to* the prophets "in divers manners" in time past, the best way to communicate with *all* men of *all* ages is through the written record. The advantages of the written method are many, of course.

A. Precision—one's thoughts must be somewhat precise to be written.

B. Propagation—the most accurate way to communicate a message is usually through writing.

C. Preservation—men die, and memories fail, but the written record remains. It may be said that the New Testament especially was written for the following reasons:

  1. Because of the demands of the early church (1 Thess. 5:27; 1 Tim. 4:13; 2 Tim. 3:16, 17).

  2. Because of false doctrines (to counteract them).

  3. Because of missionary endeavors (to propagate them).

  4. Because of persecution and politics.

IV. The Old Testament.

A. The order of the books in the Hebrew Old Testament. The thirty-nine books in our English Old Testament appear somewhat differently in a present-day Hebrew Bible. They cover the identical material but number twenty-four and are arranged in a threefold division:

  1. The Law (Torah).
     a. Genesis
     b. Exodus
     c. Leviticus
     d. Numbers
     e. Deuteronomy

  2. The Prophets (Nebhiim).
     a. Former Prophets—four books:
        (1) Joshua
        (2) Judges
        (3) Samuel
        (4) Kings
     b. Latter Prophets (major and minor):
        Major Section
        (1) Isaiah
        (2) Jeremiah
        (3) Ezekiel
        Minor Section
        (1) Hosea
        (2) Joel
        (3) Amos
        (4) Obadiah
        (5) Jonah
        (6) Micah
        (7) Nahum
        (8) Habakkuk
        (9) Zephaniah
        (10) Haggai
        (11) Zechariah
        (12) Malachi

  3. The Writings.
     a. The poetical books (3)
        (1) Psalms
        (2) Proverbs
        (3) Job
     b. The Scrolls (5)
        (1) Song of Solomon
        (2) Ruth
        (3) Lamentations
        (4) Ecclesiastes
        (5) Esther
     c. Prophetic—historical (3)
        (1) Daniel
        (2) Ezra—Nehemiah
        (3) Chronicles

B. The suggested order of the writings. Many believe the book of Job to be the oldest in the Word of God. It may well have been written as early as 2000 B.C. One of the earliest written parts was that section found in Exodus 17. This recording occurred on Israel's route to Palestine. Joshua had just won a tremendous victory over a fierce desert tribe called the Amalekites. After the battle was over we read:

"And the Lord said unto Moses, Write this for a memorial in a book, and release it in the ears of Joshua: for I will utterly put out the remembrance of Amalek from under heaven" (Ex. 17:14).

Other early sections of the Word of God would of course include the Law of Moses. (See Deut. 31:24-26.) The following is a mere suggestion of the time of the writing of the Old Testament books:

  1. Job—2150 B.C.
  2. Pentateuch—1402 B.C.
  3. Joshua—before 1350 B.C.
  4. Judges and Ruth—before 1050 B.C.
  5. Psalms—before 965 B.C.
  6. Proverbs, Ecclesiastes, Song of Solomon—before 926 B.C.
  7. 1 and 2 Samuel—before 926 B.C.
  8. 1 Kings and 1 Chronicles—before 848 B.C.
  9. Obadiah—848 B.C.
  10. Joel—835 B.C.
  11. Jonah—780 B.C.
  12. Amos—765 B.C.
  13. Hosea—755 B.C.
  14. Isaiah—750 B.C.
  15. Micah—740 B.C.
  16. Jeremiah and Lamentations—640 B.C.
  17. Nahum—630 B.C.
  18. Habakkuk and Zephaniah—625 B.C.
  19. Ezekiel—593 B.C.
  20. 2 Kings and 2 Chronicles—before 539 B.C.
  21. Daniel—before 538 B.C.
  22. Haggai and Zechariah—520 B.C.

23. Esther—after 476 B.C.
24. Ezra—after 458 B.C.
25. Nehemiah—after 445 B.C.
26. Malachi—432 B.C.

C. The location of the Old Testament books.

1. Before the Babylonian captivity. Prior to this period (606 B.C.) the Old Testament books were apparently laid beside the Ark of the Covenant in the Temple. This is indicated in the following passages:

"And Moses came and told the people all the words of the Lord, and all the judgments; and all the people answered with one voice, and said, All the words which the Lord hath said will we do. And Moses wrote all the words of the Lord, and rose up early in the morning, and builded an altar under the hill, and twelve pillars, according to the twelve tribes of Israel. . . . And he took the book of the covenant, and read in the audience of the people: and they said, All that the Lord hath said will we do, and be obedient" (Ex. 24:3, 4, 7).

"And it came to pass, when Moses had made an end of writing the words of this law in a book, until they were finished, that Moses commanded the Levites, which bare the ark of the covenant of the Lord, saying, Take this book of the law, and put it in the side of the ark of the covenant of the Lord your God, that it may be there for a witness against thee" (Deut. 31:24-26).

"And Hilkiah the high priest said unto Shaphan the scribe, I have found the book of the law in the house of the Lord. And Hilkiah gave the book to Shaphan, and he read it. And Shaphan the scribe came to the king, and brought the king word again, and said, Thy servants have gathered the money that was found in the house, and have delivered it into the hand of them that do the work, that have the oversight of the house of the Lord. And Shaphan the scribe shewed the king, saying Hilkiah the priest hath delivered me a book. And Shaphan read it before the king" (2 Ki. 22:8-10).

"So Joshua made a covenant with the people that day, and set them a statute and an ordinance in Shechem. And Joshua wrote these words in the book of the law of God, and took a great stone, and set it up there under an oak, that was by the sanctuary of the Lord" (Josh. 24:25, 26).

"Then Samuel told the people the manner of the kingdom, and wrote it in a book, and laid it up before the Lord. And Samuel sent all the people away, every man to his house" (1 Sam. 10:25).

2. During the Babylonian captivity. The books were probably carried to Babylon and later collected by Daniel. In 9:2 of his book, the prophet Daniel writes:

"In the first year of his reign I Daniel understood by books the number of the years, whereof the word of the Lord came to Jeremiah the prophet that he would accomplish seventy years in the desolations of Jerusalem."

Here Daniel specifically states he was reading Jeremiah and "the books," a reference no doubt to the other Old Testament books written up to that time.

3. After the Babylonian captivity. These books may have been taken back to Jerusalem by Ezra the prophet and kept in the newly completed Temple. (See Ezra 3:10, 11; 6:15-18; Neh. 8:1-8.)

V. The New Testament. The New Testament was written over a period of about fifty years (approximately A.D. 50-100), by eight separate human authors.

A. A suggested chronological order and possible dating of the New Testament books.

1. James—A.D. 49 (written from Jerusalem)
2. 1 and 2 Thessalonians—A.D. 52 (written from Corinth)
3. 1 Corinthians—A.D. 55 (written from Macedonia)
4. 2 Corinthians—A.D. 56 (written from Macedonia)
5. Galatians—A.D. 57 (written from Ephesus)
6. Romans—A.D. 58 (written from Corinth)
7. Luke—A.D. 59 (written from Caesarea)
8. Acts—A.D. 60 (written from Rome)
9. Philippians, Colossians, Ephesians, Philemon—A.D. 61, 62 (written from Rome)
10. Matthew—A.D. 63 (written from Judea)
11. Mark—A.D. 63 (written from Rome)
12. Hebrews—A.D. 64 (written from Jerusalem)
13. 1 Timothy—A.D. 65 (written from Macedonia)
14. 1 Peter—A.D. 65 (written from Babylon)
15. 2 Peter—A.D. 66 (unknown)
16. Titus—A.D. 66 (written from Greece)
17. Jude—A.D. 67 (unknown)
18. 2 Timothy—A.D. 67 (written from Rome)
19. John—A.D. 85-90 (written from Ephesus)
20. 1 John—A.D. 90-95 (written from Judea)
21. 2 and 3 John—A.D. 90-95 (written from Ephesus)
22. Revelation—A.D. 90-95 (written from the Isle of Patmos)

B. The human writers.

1. Matthew—author of Matthew
2. Mark—author of Mark
3. Luke—author of Luke and Acts
4. John—author of John, 1, 2, 3 John, and Revelation
5. James—author of James
6. Jude—author of Jude
7. Peter—author of 1 and 2 Peter
8. Paul—author of the fourteen remaining New Testament epistles

VI. The Determination of the Canon.

A. The tests given to the biblical books. Various books of the Bible, especially those of the New Testament, were submitted to certain rigid tests by the early church. These tests included:

1. Authorship—who wrote the book or the epistle?
2. Local church acceptance—had it been read by the various churches? What was their opinion?
3. Church fathers' recognition—had the pupils of the disciples quoted from the book? As an example, a man named Polycarp was a disciple of John the apostle. Therefore one test of a book might be, "What did Polycarp think of it?"
4. Book subject matter (content)—what did the book teach? Did it contradict other recognized books?
5. Personal edification—did the book have the ability to inspire, convict, and edify local congregations and individual believers?

In closing this section it should be stated that it was a combination of these five steps which helped determine whether a book was inspired or not. Canonicity was *not* determined at all by either the age or the language of a given book. For example, there were many ancient books mentioned in the Old Testament (see Num. 21:14; Josh. 10:3) which were not in the Old Testament canon. Also, some of the apocryphal books (such as Tobit) were written in Hebrew but were not included in the Old Testament, while some books (like portions of Daniel) written in Aramaic were included in the canon.

B. The writings that were unacceptable. After the Old Testament canon was recognized by the Jews as officially closed, and prior to the New Testament period, there arose a body of literature called the Apocrypha. This word literally means "that which is hidden" and consists of fourteen books.

1. The contents of the Old Testament Apocrypha.
   a. 1 Esdras covers much of the material found in Ezra, Nehemiah, and 2 Chronicles. But it also includes a fanciful story concerning three Jewish servants in Persia. They were all asked a question by King Darius concerning what was the greatest thing in the world. One said wine, another replied women, while the third claimed it was truth. He won, and when offered a reward, suggested the king allow the Jews to rebuild the Temple in Jerusalem.
   b. 2 Esdras contains certain visions given to Ezra dealing with God's government of the world and the restoration of certain lost Scriptures.
   c. Tobit is the story of a pious Jew (Tobit) who is accidentally blinded (by sparrow dung) and is later healed by an angel named Raphael, who applies a concoction of fish heart, liver, and gall to his eye.
   d. Judith is the story of a beautiful and devout Jewish princess who saves Jerusalem from being destroyed by Nebuchadnezzar's invading armies. This she does by beguiling the enemy general through her beauty, then returning to Jerusalem with his head in her handbag!
   e. The remainder of Esther. There are additional inserts to this book to show the hand of God in the narrative by putting the word "God" in the text. The word God does not appear in the Old Testament book of Esther.
   f. The Wisdom of Solomon has been called "The Gem of the Apocrypha," and is one of the loftier books of the Apocrypha.
   g. Ecclesiasticus, also called "the Wisdom of Jesus, the Son of Sirach," resembles the book of Proverbs, and gives rules for personal conduct in all details of civil, religious, and domestic life.
   h. 1 Maccabees, an historical account on the Maccabean period, relates events of the Jews' heroic struggle for liberty (175–135 B.C.).
   i. 2 Maccabees covers in part the same period as 1 Maccabees but is somewhat inferior content-wise.
   j. Baruch was supposedly written by Jeremiah's secretary, Baruch. It contains prayers and confessions of the Jews in exile, with promises of restoration.
   k. The Song of the Three Children, inserted in the book of Daniel, right after the fiery furnace episode (Dan. 3:23), contains an eloquent prayer of Azariah, one of the three Hebrew men thrown into the fire.
   l. The story of Susanna is a story relating how the godly wife of a wealthy Jew in Babylon, falsely accused of adultery, was cleared by the wisdom of Daniel.
   m. Bel and the Dragon is also added to the book of Daniel. The book contains two stories:
      (1) The first concerns how Daniel proves to the king that his great god Bel is a dead idol, and that the Bel priests are religious crooks.
      (2) *Unger's Handbook* describes the second story in the following words:
          "The other legend concerns a dragon worshiped in Babylon. Daniel, summoned to do it homage, feeds it a mixture of pitch, hair, and fat, which causes it to explode. The enraged populace compels the King to throw Daniel in the den of lions where he is fed on the sixth day by the prophet Habakkuk, who is angelically transported to Babylon by the hair of his head while carrying food and drink to the reapers in Judea. On the seventh day the King rescues Daniel and throws his would-be destroyers to the hungry lions." (p. 459)
   n. The Prayer of Manasses is the supposed confessional prayer of wicked King Manasseh of Judah, after he was carried

away prisoner to Babylon by the Assyrians.

2. Reasons for rejecting the Apocrypha. "Why don't you Protestants have all the books of the Bible in your King James Version?" Often Christians and Bible lovers are confronted with this question by those who have accepted the Apocrypha into their translations of the Bible. Why indeed do we *not* include these fourteen books? There are many sound scriptural reasons.

   a. The Apocrypha was never included in the Old Testament canon by such recognized authorities as the Pharisees, Ezra the prophet, etc.

   b. It was never quoted by the Jews, by Jesus, or by any other New Testament writers.

   c. The great Jewish historian Josephus excluded it.

   d. The well-known Jewish philosopher Philo did not recognize it.

   e. The early church fathers excluded it.

   f. The Bible translator Jerome did not accept the books as inspired, although he was forced by the Pope to include them in the Latin Vulgate Bible.

   g. None of the fourteen books claim divine inspiration; in fact, some actually disclaim it.

   h. Some books contain historical and geographical errors.

   i. Some books teach false doctrine, such as praying for the dead.

   j. No Apocryphal book can be found in any catalogue list of canonical books composed during the first four centuries A.D. In fact, it was not until 1596 at the Council of Trent that the Roman Catholic Church officially recognized these books, basically in an attempt to strengthen their position, which had been grievously weakened by the great reformer Martin Luther.

C. Some canonical books were at first doubted but later fully accepted. During the first few years of early church history there were some twelve biblical books which were temporarily objected to for various reasons.

1. Old Testament books.

   a. The Song of Solomon—because it seemed to some to be a mere poem on human love.

   b. Ecclesiastes—because some felt it taught atheism. (See 9:5.)

   c. Esther—because it did not mention the word "God" in the entire book.

   d. Ezekiel—because it seemed to contradict the Mosaic Law.

   e. Proverbs—because it seemed to contradict itself. (See 26:4, 5.)

2. New Testament books.

   a. Hebrews—because of the uncertainty about the book's authorship.

   b. James—because it seemed to contradict the teachings of Paul. (Compare Jas. 2:20 with Eph. 2:8, 9.)

   c. 2 and 3 John—because they seemed to be simply two personal letters.

   d. Jude—because the author refers to an uncanonical Old Testament book, the book of Enoch.

   e. Revelation—because of the uncertainty about the book's authorship and because of its many mysterious symbols.

VII. The Finalization of the Canon.

A. The Old Testament. By the year 300 B.C. (at the latest) all Old Testament books had been written, collected, revered, and recognized as official, canonical books. Many believe Ezra the prophet led the first recognition council.

B. The New Testament. During the Third Council of Carthage, held in A.D. 397, the twenty-seven New Testament books were declared to be canonical. However, it absolutely must be understood that the Bible is *not* an authorized collection of books, but rather a collection of authorized books. In other words, the twenty-seven New Testament books were not inspired because the Carthage Council proclaimed them to be, but rather the Council proclaimed them to be such because they were already inspired.

Part Seven:
Important Historical Translations of the Bible

Perhaps the most thrilling story in mankind's history is the true account of the earnest (and sometimes agonizing) efforts to translate God's precious Word into the language of a particular day. Literally billions of intensive man-hours have been spent doing this. We shall now briefly examine some of the better-known fruits of all this study.

I. Publications Up to the Time of Jesus.

A. The Dead Sea Scrolls. During 1947, in a series of caves near the Dead Sea, a discovery was made that would soon excite the entire religious world: the Dead Sea Scrolls. Dr. William F. Albright states this find was "the most important discovery ever made concerning the Old Testament manuscripts." These scrolls were probably hidden there sometime during the second century B.C. by a Jewish group called the Essenes. They included fragments of every Old Testament book in the Hebrew Bible with the exception of the book of Esther.

Especially exciting was a complete scroll on the book of Isaiah. The reason this discovery was so important was that until this event, the earliest copy we had of Isaiah's writings was made during the twelfth century A.D. Now scholars could move back over a thousand years closer to the time when the prophet actually wrote (around 700 B.C.). When a comparison was made between the Dead Sea copy and the twelfth century A.D. copy, they were found to be almost identical, once again reassuring us that our copy of God's Word today is indeed accurate and reliable.

B. The Greek Septuagint. The Greek Septuagint is a translation of the Old Testament Hebrew into the Greek language. This was done around 280 B.C. at the request of some Jewish leaders. The reason was because many Jews had moved into Egypt and other places outside of Palestine, and as a result, were unable to read or speak Hebrew. So a translation was prepared in the common Greek language of the day. It was called the "Septuagint" (the Greek word for seventy) because, according to tradition, it was supposedly translated by seventy Jewish scholars in seventy days. The Septuagint was the Bible in Jesus' day.

II. Publications up to the Seventh Century A.D.

A. The Papyri. This consisted of hundreds of sheets found in central Egypt in 1895. Some were stuffed in mummy cases and embalmed crocodile bodies. Among the various sheets was a $3^1/_2 \times 2^1/_2$-inch fragment containing John 18:31-38. Carbon-14 dating has shown this to have been written around A.D. 125. Thus the fragment is the oldest known Bible manuscript.

B. The Latin Vulgate. During the fourth century A.D. it was felt a new translation of the Bible was needed in Latin, which was then the common language in the Western world. Thus, in A.D. 382 the great scholar Jerome was appointed by Damascus, the Bishop of Rome, to begin doing this. For the next twenty-five years Jerome worked on this, going right to the Hebrew and Greek. The term "vulgate" comes from the Latin word which means "common." Thus, until the King James Version in 1611, the Latin Vulgate became the recognized Bible for nearly 1200 years. In 1228 the Vulgate was divided into chapters by Stephen Langton, Archbishop of Canterbury. It was divided into verses by Robert Stephens in 1551, and these verses were numbered by Montanus around A.D. 1571. The Vulgate was also the first Bible to be printed by John Gutenburg in 1455. One of these printed copies now resides in the U.S. Library of Congress and is valued at $350,000.

C. Codex Sinaiticus. This was an ancient manuscript of the Greek Septuagint, written approximately A.D. 330. It was discovered by the German Bible scholar Tischendorf in the monastery of St. Catherine on Mount Sinai in 1844. He noticed in a wastebasket, waiting to be burned, vellum pages with Greek writings on them. The codex Sinaiticus contained 199 leaves of the Old Testament. On December 24, 1933, this codex which came so close to being burned was sold to the British government by the Russians for $510,000, making it the most expensive book purchase of all time.

D. Codex Vaticanus. Also written around A.D. 330, it has been in the Vatican Library in Rome since 1481. Roman Catholic popes had constantly refused to allow competent Bible scholars to study it until the nineteenth century. It is thought that both this codex and the Mt. Sinai copy are two of the original fifty copies ordered by Emperor Constantine shortly after he assumed power over the Roman Empire in A.D. 312. It is, however, incomplete, omitting the pastoral epistles, Philemon, Revelation, and the last few chapters of Hebrews.

E. Codex Alexandrinus. This is dated around A.D. 450 and was written in Egypt. In 1708 it was given to the Patriarch of Alexandria (where it got its name). In 1757 it was transferred to the British museum.

F. The Coptic Version. During the second century a new kind of language came into being which was sort of a cross between Greek and Egyptian. It became known as Coptic. Several translations of God's Word were made at this time (around A.D. 350) from the Greek into Coptic.

G. The Ethiopic Version. Ethiopia was the land south of Egypt in Africa. The Ethiopian eunuch of Acts 8:26-39 probably introduced Christianity there. This translation was a good verbal rendering of the Greek. It was fluent, readable, and helpful, and dates around A.D. 350.

H. The Gothic Version. The land of the Goths was located north of the Danube River and west of the Black Sea. The Goths were an extremely warlike people. During one of their raids in Asia Minor they captured a young man named Ulfilos. Ulfilos was a Christian and a scholar who later translated the Scriptures into Gothic—with the exception of 1 and 2 Samuel and 1 and 2 Kings. The reason for this was due to the many wars recorded in these four Old Testament books. Ulfilos did not want to encourage the Goths along this line. The Gothic Version, dated about A.D. 350, thus became the first translation of the Bible into a barbarian language. One of Ulfilos' versions still exists. It is called the Codex Argentus, and was written in gold and silver letters upon purple vellum. It now resides in the University Library at Upsala, Sweden.

I. The Armenian Version. Armenia is north of Mesopotamia. About A.D. 406 a great missionary and writer named Mesrob began translating the Bible into Armenian after reducing the language to an alphabet. The Armenian Version has been called "the most beautiful and accurate of all ancient versions—the Queen of Versions."

III. Publications in English from the Seventh Century to the Present. Historians have classified the English language into three main periods.

A. Old English Period—from A.D. 450 to 1100.

B. Middle English Period—from A.D. 1100 to 1500.

C. Modern English Period—from A.D. 1500 to date.

Keeping this outline in mind we shall now consider some major attempts to publish the Bible in English.

A. Old English Period—A.D. 450 to 1100. There were at least ten known translators of the Bible during this period. The list would include a servant, two bishops, two monks, a king, two priests, an archbishop, and a hermit. Of these ten, we will examine the following three:

1. Caedmon (died in 680). This stable worker at a monastery in North England did not translate the Bible on paper but rather memorized great portions of it and sang it with his harp in short lines of beautiful Celtic-Saxon verse wherever he traveled. He sang the story of Genesis, Exodus, a part of Daniel, the doctrines of the resurrection, ascension, and the Second Coming of Christ, and of heaven and hell.

2. Bede (674-735). This godly monk, scholar, historian, and theologian is often called today by the title of "the Father of English History." In his textbook, *General Biblical*

Introduction, author H.S. Miller writes the following about Bede:

"His important work is the translation of the Gospel of John, which he finished just as he was breathing his last. All the day before Ascension Day, 735, the good old monk . . . had been dictating his translations, for he said, 'I do not want my boys to read a lie, or to work to no purpose after I am gone.'

The next day he was very weak, and suffered much. His scribe said, 'Dear master, there is yet one chapter to do, but it seems very hard for you to speak.' Bede replied, 'Nay, it is easy, take up thy pen and write quickly.' In blinding tears the scribe wrote on. 'And now father, there is just one sentence more.' Bede dictated it and said, 'Write quickly.' The scribe said, 'It is finished, master.' 'Ay, it is finished!' echoed the dying saint, and with the Gloria chant upon his lips he passed to the great Master whom he had loved and served so long." (p. 320)

3. Alfred (king of England, 871-901). Here Miller writes:

"Alfred loved . . . the Bible. He was King, lawgiver, teacher, writer, translator. His wish was 'that all the freeborn youth of his kingdom should employ themselves on nothing till they could first read well the English scriptures.' He translated the ten commandments and other Old Testament laws, placing them at the head of his laws for England. He also translated the Psalms and the Gospels. . . ." (p. 321)

B. Middle English Period—A.D. 1100 to 1500. Here we will examine but one name—that of John Wycliffe.

John Wycliffe (1320-1384) has often been called "The Morning Star of Reformation." He was a great Oxford University teacher, preacher, reformer, and translator. Wycliffe was the first man to completely translate the entire Bible into the English language. By placing God's Word in the common language he thus did for England what Martin Luther would later do for Germany. His was the only English Bible for 145 years. As a sample of his English, note the following translation of the Lord's prayer:

"Our Fadir that art in hevenes, halewid be thi name; Thi kingdom comme to, Be thi wille done in heven so in erthe; Gyve to us this dai oure breed over other substance, and forgive to us oure dettis as we forgyven to oure detouris; and leede us not into tempacioun, but delyvere us fro yvel."

C. Modern English Period—A.D. 1500 to date.

1. *Tyndale's Version* (1525). Perhaps no other single man in history did as much in translating the Word of God for the people of God as did William Tyndale. Tyndale worked in constant danger, for under Catholic Emperor Charles V, it was a crime punishable by horrible torture, burning at the stake, or actual burial alive, for anyone to read, purchase, or possess any New Testament book. But prior to his martyrdom, it is estimated that some 50,000 copies of the New Testament were circulated by this fearless and faithful servant of God. Early in 1526, Tyndale's New Testaments began pouring into England concealed in cases of merchandise, barrels, bales of cloths, sacks of flour and corn, and every other secret way which could be found. For every testament the devil burned, God would allow Tyndale to publish three more to take its place!

It is thought that Tyndale's New Testament was based on the printed Greek New Testament text of the great scholar Erasmus (first printed on March 1, 1516), and that his Old Testament text was taken in part from the 1488 Hebrew publication. He also consulted the Latin Vulgate and Martin Luther's translation.

2. *The Coverdale Version* (A.D. 1535). Miles Coverdale was born in 1488. He was converted to Christ and developed a strong love for Scripture. He was a friend of Tyndale and later finished his Old Testament translation and revised his New Testament. It was a secondary translation; that is, it was based on previous translations of the Bible into Latin, German, and English. The reason for this is that Coverdale was not familiar with the Greek or Hebrew. The first edition came off the press on October 4, 1535. This was indeed a milestone for God's Word, as it marked the first whole Bible printed in English.

3. *Matthew's Version* (1537). This version was prepared by John Rogers, who used the pseudonym Thomas Matthew. The reason for this was that Rogers, known friend of Tyndale, felt his work would be more acceptable to various authorities if this relationship was not known. Rogers would later be burned to death during the reign of Mary Tudor in 1555. Matthew's Version was the first revision of the Tyndale Bible. It was approved by King Henry VIII, who had hated Tyndale and his work. A divine irony is seen here.

4. *The Great Bible Version* (1539). The notes and prefaces of Tyndale's and Coverdale's translations aroused so much argument that Henry VIII authorized a new version which would include no controversial footnote material. It was called the Great Bible because of its size. Due to its extreme value it was usually chained to a "reading post" within a church. In 1538 the King issued an injunction to all churches to purchase a copy of the Great Bible. This was to be paid for by the parson and parishioners. The importance of the Great Bible is that it became the first official English Bible "appointed to be read in all the churches." The King James Bible is basically a revision of the Great Bible.

5. *The Geneva Version* (1557). During the vicious Protestant persecution under Mary Tudor,

many reformers fled to Geneva, Switzerland, and enjoyed the protection of Geneva's great leader, John Calvin. It was here that Calvin's brother-in-law, William Whittingham, translated the Scriptures into the Geneva Version. This Bible became important for the following reasons:

  a. It was the first version to divide the text into verses.
  b. It was the first to omit the Apocrypha.
  c. It was kissed by Queen Elizabeth (daughter of Henry VIII) at her coronation, a policy which is still followed by English kings and queens.
  d. It was the most-loved Bible of the common people up to that time and went through more than 160 editions.
  e. It was the Bible of Shakespeare and John Bunyan.
  f. It was the Bible the pilgrims brought with them on the Mayflower in 1620 to America.

The text of the Geneva Bible was based on that of the Great Bible.

6. *The Bishop's Bible* (1568). This version was translated because of the following reasons:

  a. The Church of England did not like the notes in the Geneva Version.
  b. The Geneva Version was undermining the authority of the Great Bible and that of the bishops.

It was translated by Matthew Parker, Archbishop of Canterbury, aided by nine other bishops; thus its name, the Bishop's Bible. The Bishop's Bible was the second "Authorized Version" of the church, but was never accepted by the common people. In fact, Queen Elizabeth simply ignored it. The Bishop's Bible has gone down in history as the most unsatisfactory and useless of all the old translations.

7. *The Rheims—Douai Bible* (1582). This version was an attempt by the Pope to win England back to the Roman fold, but he utterly failed. It was headed by William Allen and Gregory Martin, two Protestant turncoats from Oxford University. The name comes from the two places where the Old Testament and New Testament were produced. The Douai Version was therefore the first Catholic English Bible and was taken almost literally from the Latin Vulgate. The footnotes in this version strongly attacked all Protestant "heresies," and defended all Roman Catholic doctrine and practices.

8. *The King James Version* (1611). One of the first tasks which King James I faced upon mounting his throne at the beginning of the seventeenth century was the reconciliation of various religious parties within his kingdom. The King James Version began with a request by Puritan spokesman Dr. Reynolds of Oxford concerning the feasibility of a new Bible translation. James agreed almost at once. He had disliked the popular Geneva Bible because of its footnotes. He also real-

ized that neither the Geneva, nor the Great, nor the Bishop's version could be held up by him as a rallying point for Christians.

The following quote is from H.S. Miller— "On July 22, 1604, the King announced that he had appointed 54 men as translators. The only indispensable qualification was that they should have proven efficiency as Biblical scholars. . . . A list of 47 revisers has been preserved; the other seven may have died or resigned before the work had really begun.

The revisers were organized into six groups, two meeting at Westminster, two at Cambridge, two at Oxford. One group at Westminster had Genesis to 2 Kings, the other had Romans to Jude: one group at Cambridge had 1 Chronicles to Ecclesiastes, the other had the Apocrypha; one group at Oxford had Isaiah to Malachi, the other had Matthew to Acts and Revelation. These men were the great Hebrew and Greek scholars of this day.

Each reviser first made his own translation, then passed it on to be reviewed by each member of his group; then when each group had completed a book, a copy of it was sent to each of the other five groups for their independent criticism. Thus each book went through the hands of the entire body of revisers. Then the entire version, thus amended, came before a select committee of six, two from each of the three companies, and they ironed out ultimate differences of opinion, put the finishing touches . . . and prepared it for the printer.

The revisers were governed by 15 rules, the gist of a few of them being: (1) The Bishop's Bible shall be followed and as little altered as the truth of the original will permit; (2) The old ecclesiastical words shall be retained; (3) The chapter divisions shall not be changed, unless very necessary; (4) No marginal notes at all, except explanation of Hebrew and Greek words which cannot be briefly and fitly expressed in the text; (5) Whenever the Tyndale, Matthew, Coverdale, the Great Bible, or the Geneva agrees better with the text than the Bishop's Bible, they are to be used." (*General Biblical Introduction*, pp. 363, 364)

The King James Version also doubtless made use of the four available printed Hebrew Old Testament Bibles at that time, and Erasmus' fifth edition of the Greek New Testament.

The King James Version is remarkable for many reasons. It was, first of all, undoubtedly the most beautiful, beloved, and popular translation of all time. It was also probably the only translation in which no parties involved had an axe to grind. In other words, it was a national undertaking in which no one had any interest at heart save that of producing the best possible version of the Scriptures.

It must be said, however, that the King James Version was not immediately accepted by the general public. The Roman Catholics claimed it favored Protestantism. The Arminians said it leaned toward Calvinism. The Puritans disliked certain words like "bishop," "ordain," and "Easter." But after some forty years it overtook the popular Geneva Bible and has retained its tremendous lead ever since.

9. *The English* (1881–1885) and *American* (1901) *Revision.* By the latter part of the nineteenth century, the Church of England felt a new revision of the King James Version was needed for the following reasons:

The change in the meaning of some of the English words.

The discovery of new manuscripts since 1611.

The improved science of biblical criticism. A better knowledge of the Greek and Hebrew.

Thus, on May 3, 1870, the initial formalities began. The Canterbury Convocation adopted five resolutions.

a. "We do not contemplate any new translation of the Bible, or any alteration of the language, except when in the judgment of the most competent scholars such change is necessary."

b. It offered a uniformity of renderings— that is, it translated the same Hebrew and Greek word by the same English word. The King James Version did not do this, but used a great variety of English words to translate a single Greek word. (For example, the Greek word *meno*, which means "to remain," is translated by ten different words in the King James Version. The Greek word *dunamis*, meaning "power," is translated by thirteen different English words.)

c. It translated the Greek tenses more accurately, especially the aorist and the imperfect tenses.

d. It translated the Greek definite article more accurately.

e. It translated the Greek preposition more accurately.

The English revised New Testament was published in England on May 17, 1881, and sale in the United States began on May 20. The excitement in this country about receiving a new version of the Bible was at an unbelievable high. For example, the people of Chicago wanted the New Testament about the same time New York would have it, and they could not wait until a fast train could bring it, so two Chicago dailies (the *Tribune* and the *Times*) had the first six books (Matthew to Romans, about 118,000 words) telegraphed from New York to Chicago (978 miles), by far the largest message ever sent over the wire. These papers then published all this on May 22, 1881.

But to the great disappointment of its friends, the English Version of 1881–1885 whose popularity had risen so high so fast almost immediately cooled off. People soon realized how much they would miss the familiar and loved words, phrases, grace, ease, poetry, and rhythm of the King James Version.

In 1901 the *American Standard Version* was published. Although it enjoyed better permanent reception than the English one, it still has not seriously cut into the lead of the King James Version.

10. *The Revised Standard Version* (1952). This work has been one of the most controversial versions of the Bible ever published. The Revised Standard Version was authorized by the National Council of Churches of Christ in the U.S.A. and is the "official" version of this group. Hebrew scholar Dr. Merrill F. Unger summarizes the Revised Standard Version in the following way:

"Although this version has many excellencies, it is weak and obscure in its translation of certain key Old Testament messianic passages."

11. *The Amplified Bible* (1954). This is a literal translation with multiple expressions using associated words to convey the original thought. The New Testament uses the Greek text of Westcott and Hort plus twenty-seven translations and revisions. The Old Testament is similarly extensive. The version is intended to supplement other translations authentically, concisely, and in convenient form.

12. *Good News for Modern Man* (1966). This translation of the New Testament by Dr. Robert G. Bratcher (plus a distinguished review committee) is a paraphrase which gained enormous popularity in a short period of time. It was intended to communicate the Scriptures to the masses of English-speaking people around the world and has been much used as an instrument of evangelism for persons outside the church. It has since become available as a complete Bible called *The Good News Bible.*

13. *The Jerusalem Bible* (1966). This is a translation from the Hebrew Masoretic, Greek Septuagint, Dead Sea Scrolls, and accepted Greek and Aramaic New Testament texts—all compared with the French Version. It was produced by twenty-eight principal collaborators in translation and literary revision under Alexander Jones, general editor.

14. *The New American Bible* (1970). This is a Catholic translation that is a highlight of Bible publishing in the present century. All basic texts were consulted, and the work was twenty-six years in the making. Over fifty recognized biblical scholars, the majority of them college professors, labored to produce this outstanding version. Scholars were

Catholic, Protestant, and Jewish. The purpose was to produce a more accurate translation from the older manuscripts, and this was made possible by the Pope in 1943. Prior to this version, Catholics had been required to use the later Vulgate as the basis for translation.

15. *The Living Bible* (1971). An extremely popular version, this paraphrase is the work of Kenneth L. Taylor. The initial source was the *American Standard Version* of 1901, but Dr. Taylor and the Greek and Hebrew specialists he consulted for accuracy also used the most respected texts available.

16. *The New American Standard Bible* (1971). This Bible was translated by an editorial board of fifty-four Greek and Hebrew scholars and required nearly eleven years to complete.

Other new translations and versions appear frequently.

Part Eight:
Proofs That the Bible is the Word of God

I. First Supernatural Element—Its Amazing Unity. That the Bible is a unity is a fact no honest reader can deny. In the preface of most Bibles, the thirty-nine Old Testament and twenty-seven New Testament books are listed in two parallel columns down the page. But a more accurate way would be to place the entire sixty-six collection in a clock-like circle, with Genesis occupying the first minute past twelve, Exodus the second, Leviticus the third, and so on. Finally, the book of Revelation would be placed on the number twelve, right next to Genesis. It is simply thrilling how these two books, Genesis the first and Revelation the last, perfectly dovetail together in a unity only God could create. For example:

In Genesis we read: "In the beginning God created the heaven and the earth" (1:1).
In Revelation we read: "I saw a new heaven and a new earth" (21:1).

In Genesis we see described the first Adam and his wife Eve in the Garden of Eden, reigning over the earth (1:27, 28).
In Revelation we see described the last Adam and his wife, the Church, in the City of God, reigning over all the universe (21:9).

In Genesis, we are told: "and the gathering of the waters called the seas" (1:10).
In Revelation we are told: "and there was no more sea" (21:1).

In Genesis God created the day and the night, the sun and moon (1:5, 16).
In Revelation "there shall be no night there" (22:5). "And the city had no need of the sun, neither of the moon, to shine in it: for the glory of God did lighten it, and the Lamb is the light thereof" (21:23).

In Genesis the tree of life is denied to sinful man (3:22).
In Revelation the tree of life "yielded her fruit every month: and the leaves of the tree were for the healing of the nations" (22:2).

In Genesis man hears God say: "Cursed is the ground for thy sake" (3:17).
In Revelation man will hear God say: "and there shall be no more curse" (22:3).

In Genesis Satan appears to torment man (3:1).
In Revelation Satan disappears, himself to be tormented forever (20:10).

In Genesis the old earth was punished through a flood (7:12).
In Revelation the new earth shall be purified through a fire (2 Pet. 3:6–12; Rev. 21:1).

In Genesis, man's early home was beside a river (2:10).
In Revelation, man's eternal home will be beside a river—"and he shewed me a pure river of water of life, clear as crystal, proceeding out of the throne of God and of the Lamb" (22:1).

In Genesis the patriarch Abraham weeps for Sarah (23:2).
In Revelation the children of Abraham will have God himself wipe away all tears from their eyes (21:4).

In Genesis God destroys an earthly city, wicked Sodom, from the sands (ch. 19).
In Revelation God presents a heavenly city, new Jerusalem, from the skies (21:1).

Genesis ends with a believer in Egypt, lying in a coffin (50:1–3).
Revelation ends with all believers in eternity, reigning forever (21:4).

A. This unity is achieved in spite of the long period of time involved in its writing.
   1. More than fifteen centuries elapsed between the writing of Genesis and Revelation.
   2. Nearly 400 years elapsed between the writing of Malachi and Matthew.
B. This unity is achieved in spite of the many authors (some forty) and their various occupations (approximately nineteen).
   "The Lord gave the Word: great was the company of those who published it" (Ps. 68:11).
   1. Moses was an Egyptian prince.
   2. Joshua was a soldier.
   3. Samuel was a priest.
   4. David was a king.
   5. Esther was a queen.
   6. Ruth was a housewife.
   7. Job was a rich farmer.
   8. Amos was a poor farmer.
   9. Ezra was a scribe.
   10. Isaiah was a prophet.
   11. Daniel was a prime minister.
   12. Nehemiah was a cupbearer.
   13. Matthew was a tax collector.
   14. Mark was an evangelist.
   15. Luke was a physician.
   16. John was a wealthy fisherman.
   17. Peter was a poor fisherman.
   18. Jude and James probably were carpenters.
   19. Paul was a tentmaker.
C. This unity is achieved in spite of the different geographical places where the Bible was written.
   1. In the desert (Ex. 17).
   2. On Mt. Sinai (Ex. 20).

3. In Palestine (most).
4. In Egypt (Jeremiah?).
5. On the Isle of Patmos (Revelation).
6. In Babylon (Daniel).
7. In Persia (Esther).
8. In Corinth (1 and 2 Thessalonians).
9. In Ephesus (Galatians?).
10. In Caesarea (Luke?).
11. From Rome (2 Timothy).

D. This unity is achieved in spite of the many different styles of its writing.
1. As history.
2. As prophecy.
3. As biography.
4. As autobiography.
5. As poetry.
6. As law.
7. In letter form.
8. In symbolic form.
9. In proverb form.
10. In doctrinal form.

Let us imagine a religious novel of sixty-six chapters which was begun by a single writer around the sixth century A.D. After the author has completed but five chapters, he suddenly dies. But during the next 1000 years, up to the sixteenth century, around thirty amateur "free-lance" writers feel constrained to contribute to this unfinished religious novel. Few of these authors share anything in common. They speak different languages, live at different times in different countries, have totally different backgrounds and occupations, and write in different styles.

Let us furthermore imagine that at the completion of the thirty-ninth chapter, the writing for some reason suddenly stops. Not one word is therefore added from the sixteenth until the twentieth century. After this long delay it begins once again when eight new authors add the final twenty-seven chapters.

With all this in mind, what would be the chances of this religious novel becoming a moral, scientific, prophetic, and historical unity? The answer is obvious—not one in a million. And yet this is the story of the Bible.

II. Second Supernatural Element—Its Indestructibility. The story is told of a visitor who toured a blacksmith shop. Viewing heaps of discarded hammers but only one huge anvil, he asked: "How often do you replace your anvil?" With a smile the owner replied, "Never! It is the anvil that wears out the hammers, you know!"

So it is with the Word of God. The hammers of persecution, ridicule, higher criticism, liberalism, and atheism have for centuries pounded out their vicious blows upon the divine anvil, but all to no avail. There they lie, in rusting piles, while the mighty anvil of the Scriptures stands unbroken, unshaken, and unchipped.

A. Its indestructibility in spite of political persecutions (from the Roman Emperors).

In A.D. 303, Emperor Diocletian thought he had destroyed every hated Bible. After many tireless years of ruthless slaughter and destruction, he erected a column of victory over the embers of a burned Bible. The title on the column read: "Extinct is the Name of Christian." Twenty years later, the new Emperor Constantine offered a reward for any remaining Bibles. Within twenty-four hours no less than fifty copies were brought out of hiding and presented to the king.

B. Its indestructibility in spite of religious persecutions.

1. As seen through the persecutions by Roman Catholic popes.

Almost without exception, the early popes opposed the reading and translating of the Bible. In 1199, Pope Innocent III ordered the burning of all Bibles.

2. As seen through the persecutions leveled against John Wycliffe and William Tyndale.

Of all the heroes in church history, no two other names are so closely associated with the Word of God as the names of Wycliffe and Tyndale. The very mention of these two men was no doubt sufficient to turn the devil livid with rage. It is therefore no surprise to read of the vicious attacks leveled against them.

a. John Wycliffe. Wycliffe lived at a time (the early part of the fourteenth century) when the burning question was: Who shall rule England, the king or the pope? Wycliffe believed the best way to break the grievous yoke of Romanism would be to place the Bible into the hands of the common people. This he did by translating (for the first time in history) the complete Bible into English. He then organized and sent forth a group of preachers (called the Lollards) to teach the Word of God all across England.

On December 28, 1384, while conducting a service in the Lutterworth Church, he was suddenly stricken with paralysis and died three days later. After his death, those who hated his Bible translation activities said the following things about Wycliffe:

" 'John Wycliffe, the organ of the devil, the enemy of the Church, the confusion of the common people, the idol of heretics, the looking glass of hypocrites, the encourager of schism, the sower of hatred, the storehouse of lies, the sink of flattery, was suddenly struck by the judgment of God . . . that mouth which was to speak huge things against God and against His Saints or holy church, was miserably drawn aside . . . showing plainly that the curse which God had thundered forth against Cain was also inflicted upon him.' [From the mouth of a Monk]

'That pestilent wretch John Wycliffe, the son of the old serpent, the forerunner of Antichrist, who had completed his iniquity by inverting a new translation of the Scriptures.' " (H. S. Miller, *Biblical Introduction*, p. 329)

One would almost conclude the Savior had this in mind when he spoke the following words:

"These things have I spoken unto you, that ye should not be offended. They shall put you out of the synagogues: yea, the time cometh, that whosoever killeth you will think that he doeth God service. And these things will they do unto you, because they have not known the Father, nor me" (Jn. 16:1-3).

One final quotation from Miller's book seems appropriate here:

"In 1415, the Council of Constance which consigned John Hus and Jerome of Prague to a cruel death, demanded that the bones of the notorious heretic Wycliffe . . . be taken out of the consecrated ground and scattered at a distance from the sepulchre. Thirteen years later (1428), 44 years after his death, Pope Clement VIII, ordered no further delay; the grave was torn up, the coffin and skeleton borne down to the bank of the River Swift, a fire was kindled, the bones were burned, and the ashes thrown into the river. In the words of Thomas Fuller, so often quoted: 'The Swift conveyed them into the Avon, the Avon into the Severn, the Severn into the narrow seas; they into the main ocean; and thus the ashes of Wycliffe are the emblem of his doctrine, which is now dispersed all the world over.' " (pp. 329, 330)

b. William Tyndale (1484-1536). Tyndale was one of the greatest translators of God's Word who ever lived. He was born in England, and so skilled in seven languages (Hebrew, Greek, Latin, Italian, Spanish, English, and Dutch), that whichever he might be speaking one would believe that language was his native tongue. Our own King James Version is practically a fifth revision of Tyndale's, and it retains many of the words and much of the character, form, and style of his version. In 1525, he printed the first copy ever produced of the New Testament in English. His overall goal in life was perhaps best expressed through a statement he made in 1521:

"I defy the Pope and all his laws; if God spares my life, ere many years I will cause a boy that driveth the plough shall know . . . the Scripture."

"In 1529, an amusing and thrilling event happened in England and Europe concerning the Word of God. Tyndale had been driven from England and had fled to Germany, but had continued producing New Testaments and slipping them back into England. One day, the Bishop of London (Bishop Tunstall) mentioned to a British merchant, a man named Packington and a secret friend of Tyndale, his desire to buy up all copies of the New Testament.

Said Packington, 'My Lord, if it be your pleasure, I can buy them, for I know where they are sold, if it be in your Lord's pleasure to pay for them. I will then assure you to have every book of them that is imprinted.'

Said the Bishop, 'Gentle master Packington, do your diligence and get them; and with all my heart I will pay for them whatsoever they cost you, for the books are erroneous . . . and I intend to destroy them all, and burn them at St. Paul's Cross.'

Packington then came to Tyndale and said, 'William, I know that thou art a poor man, and hast a heap of New Testaments and books by thee, by the which thou hast endangered thy friends and beggared thyself; and I have now gotten thee a merchant, which with ready money shall dispatch thee of all that thou hast, if you think it so profitable to thyself.'

'Who is the merchant?' asked Tyndale.

'The Bishop of London,' answered Packington.

'Oh, that is because he will burn them.'

'Yes, marry, but what of that? The Bishop will burn them anyhow, and it is best that you should have the money for enabling you to imprint others instead.'

'I shall do this,' said Tyndale, 'for these two benefits shall come thereof: First, I shall get money to bring myself out of debt, and the whole world will cry out against the burning of God's Word; and Second, the overplus of the money that shall remain to me shall make me more studious to correct the said New Testament, and so newly to imprint the same once again, and I trust the second will be much better than ever was the first.' So the bargain was made. The bishop had the books, Packington had the thanks, and Tyndale had the money. Later, a man named Constantine was being tried as a heretic, and the judge promised him favor if he would tell how Tyndale received so much help in printing so many Testaments.

He replied, 'My Lord, I will tell you truly: It is the Bishop of London that hath helped, for he hath bestowed among us a great deal of money upon the New Testaments to burn them, and that hath been, and yet is, our chief help and comfort.' " (*Biblical Introduction*, p. 334)

Again, to quote from Miller's textbook:

"On Friday, October 6, 1536, Tyndale was executed. By the Emperor's laws, only Anabaptists were burned alive, so he escaped that fate. He was led out and permitted to engage in a few moments of prayer. With fervent zeal and a loud voice he cried, 'Lord, open the King of England's eyes!' Then his feet were bound to the stake, the iron chain was fastened around his neck, with a hemp rope loosely tied in a noose, and fagots and straw were heaped around him. At a given signal the rope was tightened, and Tyndale was strangled to death. Then the torch was applied, and the body was quickly consumed." (pp. 338, 339)

C. Its indestructibility in spite of philosophical persecution. Here several cases come to mind:

1. Voltaire. He once said, "Another century and there will be not a Bible on the earth." The century is gone, and the circulation of the Bible is one of the marvels of the age. After he died, his old printing press and the very house where he lived was purchased by the Geneva Bible Society and made a depot for Bibles.

   On December 24, 1933, the British Government bought the valuable Codex Sinaiticus from the Russians for half a million dollars. On that same day, a first edition of Voltaire's work sold for eleven cents in Paris bookshops.

2. Thomas Paine. He once said, "I have gone through the Bible as a man would go through a forest with an axe to fell trees. I have cut down tree after tree; here they lie. They will never grow again." Tom Paine thought he had demolished the Bible, but since he crawled into a drunkard's grave in 1809, the Bible has leaped forward as never before.

3. Joseph Stalin. This bloody butcher took over all of Russia at the death of Lenin in the late twenties. From this point on until his death in the fifties, Stalin instituted a "ban the Bible" purge from the U.S.S.R. such as had never been witnessed before. This miserable man literally attempted to wipe the Word of God and the God of the Word from the Russian minds. Did he succeed? A recent poll taken in Russia shows that today more people than ever believe in God and his Word.

III. Third Supernatural Element—Its Historical Accuracy. Less than a century ago, the agnostic took great glee in sneeringly referring to the "hundreds of historical mistakes" in the Bible. But then came the science of archaeology and with each shovel full of dirt the sneers have become less visible, until today they scarcely can be seen. When one thinks of historical scholarship and the Bible, three brilliant scholars come to mind. These three are:

A. Sir William Ramsey. For many years Ramsey was professor of humanity at the University of Aberdeen, Scotland. He was, in his time, the world's most eminent authority on the geography and history of ancient Asia Minor (Turkey today). In his zeal to study every available early document concerning that period and area, he undertook an intensive research of the New Testament book of Acts and also the Gospel of Luke. This study, however, was approached with much skepticism. At that time he penned the following description of the book of Acts: ". . . a highly imaginative and carefully colored account of primitive Christianity."

But after many years of intensive study, this scholar, who began an unbeliever, became a staunch defender of the Word of God. The absolute historical accuracy of Luke's writings, even in the most minute details, captured first his brain and then his heart. Ramsey authored many books, but one of his better known is entitled: *The Bearing of Recent Discovery on the Trustworthiness of the New Testament.* Ramsey's overall opinion of the Bible is perhaps best seen in the following quote:

"I take the view that Luke's history is unsurpassed in regard to its trustworthiness . . . you may press the words of Luke in a degree beyond any other historian's and they stand the keenest scrutiny and the hardest treatment."

B. William F. Albright. One of the greatest and most respected oriental scholars who ever lived was William F. Albright. He writes the following concerning the Bible and his historical findings:

"The reader may rest assured: nothing has been found to disturb a reasonable faith, and nothing has been discovered which can disprove a single theological doctrine. . . . We no longer trouble ourselves with attempts to 'harmonize' religion and science, or to 'prove' the Bible. The Bible can stand for itself." (Robert Young, *Young's Analytical Concordance to the Bible,* p. 51)

C. Robert Dick Wilson. Probably the most qualified Old Testament linguist of all time was Robert Dick Wilson. He was born in 1856 and took his undergraduate work at Princeton University, graduating in 1876. He then completed both the M.A. and the Ph.D. After this, he spent two years at the University of Berlin in further postgraduate studies. Wilson taught Old Testament courses at Western Theological Seminary in Pittsburgh and returned to Princeton where he received international fame as a Hebrew scholar without peer. He was perfectly at home in over forty ancient Semitic languages. Dr. Wilson writes the following about himself:

"If a man is called an expert, the first thing to be done is to establish the fact that he is such. One expert may be worth more than a million other witnesses that are not experts. Before a man has the right to speak about the history and the language . . . of the Old Testament, the Christian Church has the right to demand that a man should establish his ability to do so. For forty-five years continuously, since I left college, I have devoted myself to the one great study of the Old Testament, in all its languages, in all its archaeology, in all its translations, and as far as possible in everything bearing upon its text and history. I tell you this so that you may see why I can and do speak as an expert. I may add that the result of my forty-five years of study of the Bible has led me all the time to a firmer faith that in the Old Testament we have a true historical account of the history of the Israelite people; and I have a right to commend this to some of those bright men and women who think that they can laugh at the old-time Christian and believer in the Word of God. . . . I have claimed to be an expert. Have I the right to do so? Well, when I was in the Seminary I used to read my New Testament in nine different languages. I learned my Hebrew by heart, so that I could recite it without the intermission of a syllable . . . as soon as I graduated from the Seminary, I became a teacher of Hebrew for a year and then I went to Germany. When I got to Heidelburg, I made a decision. I decided—and did it with prayer—to consecrate my life to the study of the Old Testament. I was twenty-five then; and I judged from the life of my ancestors that I should live to be seventy; so that I should have forty-five years to work. I divided the period into three parts. The first fifteen years I would devote to the study of the languages necessary. For the second fifteen I was going to devote myself to the study of the text of the Old Testament; and I reserved the last fifteen years for the work of writing the results of my previous studies and investigations, so as to give them to the world. And the Lord has enabled me to carry out that plan almost to a year." (David Otis Fuller, *Which Bible?* pp. 40, 41)

D. Authenticated by archaeology. *Halley's Bible Handbook* lists some 112 examples. *Unger's Bible Handbook* lists 96. A summary of both these lists would include the following, all given to prove the historical accuracy of the Bible.

1. The Garden of Eden (Gen. 2:8-14). Archaeology has long established that the lower Tigris-Euphrates Valley in Mesopotamia (where Eden was located) was the cradle of civilization.

2. The Fall of man (Gen. 3:1-24). Many non-Hebrew cultures record this event. It is found in the Babylonian tablet called the Temptation Seal, in the Assyrian Archives, referred to as the Adam and Eve Seal, and in the Egyptian Library of Amen-hotep III.

3. The longevity of early mankind (Gen. 5:1-32). The oldest known outline of world history is the Weld-Blumdell Prism, written around 2170 B.C. This outline includes a list of eight pre-flood rulers. The shortest reign was said to have been 18,600 years, while the longest covered a period of 43,200 years. Of course this was gross exaggeration, but the point is that the historical root for all this may be found in the Genesis account which does accurately state that Methuselah did indeed live to be 969 years of age. A common

objection to this and other so-called legends would claim that early mankind simply invented myths of their ancestors doing things they wished they could have done. But the fallacy of this argument may be demonstrated by the fact that there is no ancient legend of a nation or tribe of flying men, in spite of the fact that all men everywhere have always longed to soar into the skies.

4. The universal flood (Gen. 6:1—9:29). There is so much evidence concerning the flood in Noah's day that one scarcely knows where to start. It can be demonstrated that, without exception, every major human culture has a flood tradition. Especially is this true in the ancient Babylonian civilization, as seen by their Epic of Gilgamesh. If the author may be allowed a personal illustration here, I am acquainted with a New Tribes missionary named Rod Wallin. Some years ago Rod began his work among a primitive people in the highlands of New Guinea. He was the first white man ever to set foot in that area. Many years were spent learning their difficult language. He then discovered to his astonishment that these natives had a detailed flood tradition.

5. The Tower of Babel (Gen. 11:1-9). Over two dozen ancient temple towers in Mesopotamia called ziggurats have been excavated.

6. Abraham's birthplace (Gen. 11:27-31). World-famous archaeologist C.L. Wooley's excavation in 1922-34 in Mesopotamia has made Ur of the Chaldees one of the best-known ancient sites of all times. When Abraham left Ur in 2000 B.C. the city was at the height of its splendor as a commercial and religious center. (See also Josh. 24:2.)

7. Abraham's visit to Egypt (Gen. 12:10-20). Due to space problems, many of the following Old Testament events which have been authenticated by archaeology will simply be alluded to and not expanded upon.

8. Abraham's battle with the kings in Genesis 14.

9. The destruction of Sodom and Gomorrah (Gen. 18-19). William Albright found at the Southeast corner of the Dead Sea great quantities of relics of a period dating between 2500 and 2000 B.C., with evidence of a dense population which for some reason ceased abruptly around 2000 B.C. The evidence indicated an earthquake and an explosion.

10. Joseph and Potiphar's wife (Gen. 39). There is an Egyptian story entitled "A Tale of Two Brothers" which may have for its foundation the events related in Genesis 39.

11. The Seven-year famine (Gen. 41:46-57).

12. Israel's entrance into Egypt (Ex. 1:1-6).

13. The episode of the bricks without straw (Ex. 1:11; 5:7-19).

14. Moses' birth (Ex. 2:10).

15. The death of Pharaoh's firstborn (Ex. 12:29).

16. The Exodus (Ex. 12:1—14:31).

17. The fact of Rahab's house located on Jericho's wall (Josh. 2:15).
18. The fall of Jericho (Josh. 6:1-27). The archaeologist Garstang found evidence that Jericho was destroyed about 1400 B.C. (about the date given to Joshua) and that the walls had fallen flat, outward, and down the hillside. This was extremely unusual, for had the city been captured the usual way, its walls would have been pushed inward by the ramming weapons of that day. He also found the layer of ashes left by Joshua's fire. (See Josh. 6:24.)
19. Deborah's victory of the Canaanites (Jdg. 4:23, 24; 5:19).
20. Saul's reign (1 Sam. 9:1—31:13).
21. David's conquests (2 Sam. 1:1—24:25).
22. Solomon's gold (1 Ki. 14:25, 26).
23. Solomon's stables (1 Ki. 9:19; 10:26-29). The Oriental Institute has found the ruins of his stables with their stone hitching-poles and mangers.
24. Solomon's copper furnaces (1 Ki. 7).
25. Solomon's navy (1 Ki. 9).
26. Jeroboam's calves (1 Ki. 12:25-33).
27. Shishak's invasion (1 Ki. 14:25-28).
28. The building of Samaria by Omri (1 Ki. 16:24).
29. The rebuilding of Jericho (1 Ki. 16:34).
30. Ahab's house of ivory (1 Ki. 22:39).
31. Jezebel's cosmetic box (2 Ki. 9:30). The actual saucers in which she mixed her cosmetics have been found in Samaria among the ruins of Ahab's ivory house.
32. The Assyrian captivity of northern Israel (2 Ki. 15:29).
33. The tunnel of Hezekiah (2 Ki. 20:20; 2 Chron. 32:3, 4).
34. Manasseh's reign (2 Ki. 21:1-15).
35. Esther's palace (Est. 1:2).
36. The Babylonian captivity of Judah (2 Ki. 25).
37. The reign of Belshazzar (Dan. 5).
38. The fall of Babylon (Dan. 5).
39. The edict of Cyrus (Ezra 1:2, 3; 2 Chron. 36:22, 23).
40. The repentance of Nineveh in Jonah's day (Jonah 4). History has shown that during the reign of Shalmaneser II (the King of Nineveh in Jonah's time), there was a sudden religious movement which resulted in a change from the worship of many gods to that of one God whom they called Nebo. Nebo was probably the Assyrian name for the Hebrew *Elohim* (Gen. 1:1). It would seem that in earlier days he had been worshiped as the supreme and only God. To the worship of this God the nation now returned.

IV. Fourth Supernatural Element—Its Scientific Accuracy. It has previously been discussed in this study that although the Bible is primarily a spiritual message from God and not specifically a scientific textbook, all scientific statements found in the Scriptures must nevertheless be taken literally and at face value. Actually the Bible contains far more specific scientific statements than one might realize. Some of these precepts would include:

A. The fact that the earth is spherical. Some seven centuries B.C. the Hebrew prophet Isaiah wrote: "It is he that sitteth upon the circle of the earth . . ." (Isa. 40:22).
   While it is true that a few Greek philosophers did postulate this as early as 540 B.C., the common man held the earth to be flat until the introduction of the compass and the fifteenth-century voyages of Columbus and Magellan.

B. The fact that the earth is suspended in space. The book of Job is thought to be one of the oldest in the Bible, written perhaps earlier than 1500 B.C. At this time one of the most advanced "scientific" theories concerning the earth was that our planet was flat and rested securely upon the back of a gigantic turtle who was slowly plodding through a cosmic sea of some sort. But note the refreshing (and accurate) words of Job:
   "He stretcheth out the north over the empty place, and hangeth the earth upon nothing" (Job 26:7).
   All this was not known by the scientists of the world until the writings of Sir Isaac Newton in A.D. 1687.

C. The fact that the stars are innumerable. Nearly twenty centuries B.C., God spoke to Abraham one night and said:
   "Look now toward heaven, and tell the stars, if thou be able to number them: and he said unto him, So shall thy seed be" (Gen. 15:5).
   Abraham must have at first wondered about this. God was promising him to be the founder of a nation whose descendants would be as uncountable as the stars. But Abraham could count the stars. There they were—a little under 1200 visible to the naked eye. Was his future nation to be limited to this number? Although we are not told so, he must have reasoned that perhaps there were "a few more" up there that he couldn't see. And he would not be disappointed, for today scientists tell us there are probably as many stars in the heavens as there are grains of sand on all the sea shores of the world. In fact, in a previous conversation with Abraham, God used this very comparison:
   "And I will make thy seed as the dust of the earth: so that if a man can number the dust of the earth, then shall thy seed also be numbered" (Gen. 13:16).
   Thus does the Bible describe the heavens. (See also Jer. 33:22; Heb. 11:12.) But what about the scientific opinion of that day? As late as A.D. 150 the famous astronomer Ptolemy dogmatically declared the number of the stars to be exactly 1056.

D. The fact that there are mountains and canyons in the sea. As recently as a century or so ago, the ocean's volume and size was viewed as a watery bowl, which sloped from the coastline gently downward toward the middle, where it was deepest. It then was thought to proceed upward to the other side. Of course we now know this to be totally untrue. Some of the highest mountains and deepest canyons are located on the floor of the Pacific Ocean. In fact, the deepest hole yet found is the Marianas Trench, just off the Philippines; it is over seven miles deep.

But long before ocean science discovered this, the Bible graphically described it. During one of his songs of deliverance, David spoke of the canyons of the sea (2 Sam. 22:16), and a backslidden prophet described the submerged mountains during the world's first submarine trip. (See Jonah 2:6.)

E. The fact that there are springs and fountains in the sea. Shortly after World War II, research ships discovered many underwater volcanoes. The number is estimated today to be at least 10,000. Further research by Dr. William W. Rubey of the U.S. Geological Survey has shown the present rate of water increase from underwater volcanic outlets to be 430 million tons each year. The earth's heat drives the entrapped water from underground molten rock and forces it out through one of these natural openings.

This interesting fact is vividly described in at least three Old Testament passages. (See Gen. 7:11; 8:2; Prov. 8:28.)

F. The fact that there are watery paths (ocean currents) in the sea. In his booklet *Has God Spoken?* author A. O. Schnabel writes the following:

"David said in Psalms 8:8 that God had subjected all things to men, including: 'Whatsoever passeth through the paths of the sea.' The Hebrew word 'paths' carries the literal meaning of 'customary roads.'

Matthew Fountaine Maury is called 'The Pathfinder of the Seas.' This American is the father of today's oceanography and responsible for the establishment of Annapolis Academy. A statue of Maury stands in Richmond, Virginia—charts of the sea in one hand, and Bible in the other. Until Maury's efforts there were no charts or sailing lanes. One day during a temporary illness, his eldest son was reading to him from the Bible, and read Psalms 8:8. Maury stopped him and said, 'Read that again.' After hearing it again, he exclaimed, 'It is enough—if the Word of God says there are paths in the sea, they must be there, and I am going to find them.' Within a few years he had charted the sea lanes and currents. His *Physical Geography of the Sea* was the first textbook of modern oceanography." (p. 38)

G. The fact of the hydrologic cycle. This would include precipitation, evaporation, cloud construction, movements of moisture by wind circuits, etc. (See Job 26:8; 36:27, 28; 37:16; 38:25-27; Ps. 135:7; Eccles. 1:6, 7.)

H. The fact that all living things are reproduced after their own kind.

"And God created great whales, and every living creature that moveth, which the waters brought forth abundantly, after their kind, and every winged fowl after his kind: and God saw that it was good" (Gen. 1:21).

"And of every living thing of all flesh, two of every sort shalt thou bring into the ark, to keep them alive with thee; they shall be male and female" (Gen. 6:19).

For hundreds of years scientists followed the spontaneous generation theory of Aristotle (350 B.C.). They believed eggs of all lower animals (insects, etc.) were formed out of rotting substance. Frogs and other small sea life, they thought, had their origin in slime pools. In fact, it was not until 1862 that Louis Pasteur proved once for all that there was no such thing as spontaneous generation. Then, in 1865, a monk named Johann Mendel demonstrated even more forcibly the rigid laws of heredity. But one could learn all this in the first few chapters of the Bible.

I. The facts involved in health and sanitation. The great law was given in the Bible by Moses, of course, who established hundreds of rules to govern health and sanitation. Moses grew up in the court of Pharaoh, spending the first forty years of his life there. About this time a famous ancient medical book called *The Papyrus Ebers* was being written in Egypt. Because of Egypt's role in the world at that time, this work soon achieved fame as the official standard for its day. Actually it was filled with quack cures, old wives' tales, and practically every false superstition of its day. In his book *None of These Diseases*, author S. McMillen writes:

"Several hundred remedies for diseases are advised in the Papyrus Ebers. The drugs include 'lizard's blood, swine's teeth, putrid meat, stinking fat, moisture from pig's ears, milk goose grease, asses' hoofs, animal fats from various sources, excreta from animals, including human beings, donkeys, antelopes, dogs, cats, and even flies.'" (p. 11)

The point of all the above is simply this—Moses was well acquainted with all the medical knowledge of his day. Yet in all his writings and proven remedies concerning health and sanitation, he never once even indirectly refers to the false "cures" found in the Papyrus Ebers. Let us now examine what he did prescribe for the health of marching Israel:

1. Concerning sickness. Moses gave comprehensive laws concerning sickness. These included laws for those having leprosy or cases with open sores. He thus laid down rules for the recognition of infected individuals, for quarantine or isolation, and concerning the uncleanness of anything touched by these people. In other words, Moses recorded laws comparable to modern health and sanitation practice in most civilized countries today.

Again, to quote from *None of These Diseases*:

"For many hundreds of years the dreaded disease leprosy had killed countless millions of people in Europe. The extent of the horrible malady among Europeans is given by Dr. George Rosen, Columbia University professor of Public Health: 'Leprosy cast the greatest blight that threw its shadow over the daily life of medieval humanity. Not even the Black Death in the fourteenth century . . . produced a similar state of fright. . . .'

What did the physicians offer to stop the ever-increasing ravages of leprosy? Some taught that it was brought on by eating hot food, pepper, garlic and the meat of diseased hogs. Other physicians said it was caused by malign conjunctions of the planets. Naturally, their suggestions for prevention were utterly worthless. . . . What [finally] brought the major plagues of the Dark Ages under control? George Rosen gives us the answer: 'Leadership was taken by the church, as the physicians had nothing to offer. The church took as its guiding principle the concept of contagion as embodied in the Old Testament. . . . This idea and its practical consequences are defined with great clarity in the book of Leviticus . . . once the condition of leprosy had been established, the patient was to be segregated and excluded from the community. Following the precepts laid down in Leviticus the church undertook the task of combatting leprosy. . . . It accomplished the first great feat . . . in methodical eradication of disease.' " (p. 13)

2. Concerning sanitation. Two quotes from Dr. McMillen are helpful here:

"Up to the close of the eighteenth century, hygenic provisions, even in the great capitals, were quite primitive. It was the rule for excrement to be dumped into the streets which were unpaved and filthy. Powerful stenches gripped villages and cities. It was a heyday for flies as they bred in the filth and spread intestinal disease that killed millions.

Such waste of human lives that could have been saved if people had only taken seriously God's provision for freeing man of diseases! With one sentence the Book of books pointed the way to deliverance from the deadly epidemics of typhoid, cholera, and dysentery: 'You shall set off a place outside the camp and, when you go out to use it, you must carry a spade among your gear and dig a hole, have easement, and turn to cover the excrement' (Deut. 23:12, 13, *Berkeley*)." (p. 15)

Dr. McMillen goes on to say that until the beginning of this century there was a frightful mortality rate in the hospitals of the world due to infection caused by doctors not washing their hands. In the maternity ward alone of the world-famous Vienna Medical Center Hospital, one out of every six women died due to infection. McMillen then writes:

"Such mortality would not have occurred if surgeons had only followed the method God gave to Moses regarding the meticulous method of hand washing and changing of clothes after contact with infectious diseases. . . . The Scriptural method specified not merely washing in a basin, but repeated washings in running water, with time intervals allowed for drying and exposure to sun to kill bacteria not washed off." (pp. 17, 18)

3. Concerning circumcision. Some final thoughts from McMillen are extremely appropriate here. In the third chapter of his book he discusses the astonishing scarcity of cervical cancer among Jewish women. Medical science has now attributed this blessing to the rite of circumcision practiced by Jewish males. This simple operation prevents the growth of cancer-producing Smegma bacillus which during physical relations can be transferred from the uncircumcised male to the female. McMillen then writes:

"There is one final but remarkably unique fact about the matter of circumcision. In November, 1946, an article in *The Journal of the American Medical Association* listed the reasons why circumcision of the newborn male is advisable. Three months later a letter from another specialist appeared in the same journal. He agreed heartily with the writer of the article on the advantages of circumcision, but he criticized him for failing to mention the safest time to perform the operation. This is a point well taken. L. Emmett Holt and Rustin McIntosh report that a newborn infant has a peculiar susceptibility to bleeding between the second and fifth days of life. . . . It is felt that the tendency to hemorrhage is due to the fact that the important blood-clotting element, Vitamin K, is not formed until the fifth to the seventh day. . . . A second element which is also necessary for the normal clotting of blood is prothrombin. . . . It appears (based on data from the science of Pediatrics) that an eight-day old baby has more available prothrombin than on any other day in its entire life. Thus one observes that from a consideration of Vitamin K and prothrombin determinations the perfect day to perform a circumcision is the eighth day." (pp. 21–23)

Keeping all this in mind, one simply marvels at the accuracy of the Book when the following passage is read:

"And God said unto Abraham, Thou shalt keep my covenant therefore, thou, and thy seed after thee in their generations. This is my covenant, which ye shall keep, between me and you and thy seed after thee; Every man child among you shall be circumcised. And ye shall circumcise the flesh of your foreskin; and it shall be a token of the covenant betwixt me and you. And he that is eight days old shall be circumcised among you, every man child in your generations, he that is born in the house, or bought with money of any stranger, which is not of thy seed" (Gen. 17:9–12).

J. The facts concerning the human bloodstream. The Bible is also an accurate commentator on human blood. In Leviticus 17:11, God lays down one of his key statements concerning this subject. Here he declares:

"For the life of the flesh is in the blood."

One searches in vain to read in this ancient Book any reference whatsoever to that false medical practice known as bloodletting which plagued mankind from the fourth century B.C. until the nineteenth century A.D. Only eternity will reveal how many sick individuals were actually killed through this "cure." No other nonbiblical writer understood the nature of the blood. In fact, many scientists (Herophilos, for example, a physician in the medical museum at Alexandria, Egypt) believed blood to be a carrier of *disease* instead of life. The death of our own George Washington is thought to have been due in part to excessive bloodletting.

K. The facts involved in the two laws of thermodynamics. Apart from gravity itself, two of the most solid and immutable laws in all physics are the first and second laws of thermodynamics. Albert Einstein himself testified that in all the known universe there is no time or place where the two do not apply.

The First Law of Thermodynamics—that of energy conservation. This law states that although energy can change forms, it cannot be either created or destroyed and therefore the sum total remains constant. Thus no energy is now being created or destroyed anywhere in the known universe.

The Second Law of Thermodynamics—that of energy deterioration. This law states that when energy is being transformed from one state to another, some of it is turned into heat energy which cannot be converted back into useful forms. In other words, this universe may be looked upon as a wound-up clock that is slowly running down.

These two absolute laws were not fully realized or established by scientists until around A.D. 1850. Yet there are literally dozens of specific references to these laws in the Word of God.

1. Passages describing the First Law.

"Thus the heavens and the earth were finished, and all the host of them. And on the seventh day God ended his work which he had made; and he rested on the seventh day from all his work which he had made. And God blessed the seventh day, and sanctified it: because that in it he had rested from all his work which God created and made" (Gen. 2:1-3).

"By the word of the Lord were the heavens made; and all the host of them by the breath of his mouth. He gathereth the waters of the sea together as an heap: He layeth up the depth in storehouses. Let all the earth fear the Lord: let all the inhabitants of the world stand in awe of him. For he spake, and it was done; he commanded, and it stood fast" (Ps. 33:6-9).

"Of old hast thou laid the foundation of the earth: and the heavens are the work of thy hand" (Ps. 102:25).

"For we which have believed do enter into rest, as he said, As I have sworn in my wrath, if they shall enter into my rest: although the works were finished from the foundation of the world. . . . For he that is entered into his rest, he also hath ceased from his own works, as God did from his" (Heb. 4:3, 10).

2. Passages describing the Second Law.

"They shall perish, but thou shalt endure: yea, all of them shall wax old like a garment: as a vesture shalt thou change them, and they shall be changed" (Ps. 102:26).

"For I reckon that the sufferings of this present time are not worthy to be compared with the glory which shall be revealed in us. For the earnest expectation of the creature waiteth for the manifestation of the sons of God. For the creature was made subject to vanity, not willingly, but by reason of him who hath subjected the same in hope. Because the creature itself also shall be delivered from the bondage of corruption into the glorious liberty of the children of God. For we know that the whole creation groaneth and travaileth in pain together until now. And not only they, but ourselves also, which have the firstfruits of the Spirits, even we ourselves groan within ourselves, waiting for the adoption, to wit, the redemption of our body" (Rom. 8:18-23).

"And, Thou, Lord, in the beginning hast laid the foundation of the earth; and the heavens are the works of thine hands: They shall perish; but thou remainest; and they all shall wax old as doth a garment; and as a vesture shalt thou fold them up, and they shall be changed: but thou art the same, and thy years shall not fail" (Heb. 1:10-12).

God brought the First Law into being after the original creation (see Gen. 1:31) and instituted the Second Law after man's fall (Gen. 3:17). Finally, it may be assumed that both laws will be rescinded after the great white throne judgment.

"For, behold, I create new heavens and a new earth: and the former shall not be remembered, nor come into mind" (Isa. 65:17).

"For as the new heavens and the new earth, which I will make, shall remain before me, saith the Lord, so shall your seed and your name remain" (Isa. 66:22).

"Nevertheless we, according to his promise, look for new heavens and a new earth, wherein dwelleth righteousness" (2 Pet. 3:13).

"And I saw a new heaven and a new earth: for the first heaven and the first earth were passed away; and there was no more sea. And I John saw the holy city, new Jerusalem, coming down from God out of heaven, prepared as a bride adorned for her husband. And I heard a great voice out of heaven saying, Behold, the tabernacle of God is with men, and he will dwell with them, and they shall be his people, and God himself shall be with them, and be their God. And God shall wipe away all tears from their eyes; and there shall be no more death, neither sorrow, nor crying, neither shall there be any more pain: for the former things are passed away. And he that sat upon the throne said, Behold, I make all things new. And he said unto me, Write: for these words are true and faithful" (Rev. 21:1-5).

Here then are at least twelve scientific principles accurately described in the Bible, some of them centuries before man discovered them. Not only does the Word of God include that which is scientifically correct, but it also totally avoids the "scientific" nonsense that is found in all other ancient religious writings.

The Egyptians believed the world was hatched from a great cosmic egg. The egg had wings and flew. This resulted in mitosis. They also believed the sun was a reflection of earth's light, and that man sprang from little white worms they found in the slime which oozes after the overflow of the Nile. In the sacred Vedas of India we read:

"The moon is 50,000 leagues higher than the sun, and shines by its own light; night is caused by the sun's setting behind a huge mountain, several thousand feet high, located in the center of the earth; that this world, flat and triangular is composed of seven states— one of honey, another of sugar, a third of butter, and still another of wine, and the whole mass is borne on the heads of countless elephants which in shaking produce earthquakes."

In the Library of the Louvre in Paris there are three and a half miles of obsolete science books. In 1861 the French Academy of Science published a brochure of fifty-one "scientific facts" which supposedly contradicted the Bible. These were used by the atheists of that day in ridiculing Christians. Today all fifty-one of those "facts" are *unacceptable* to modern scientists.

Surely the devout Christian can utter a hearty amen with Dr. James Dwight Dana of Yale University, probably the most eminent geologist in American history, who once addressed a graduating class in these words:

"Young men! As you go out into the world to face scientific problems, remember that I, an old man who has known only science all his life long, say to you, that there is nothing truer in all the universe than the scientific statements contained in the Word of God!"

V. Fifth Supernatural Element—Its Prophetical Accuracy. One of the acid tests of any religion is its ability to predict the future. In this area (as in all other areas) the Bible reigns supreme. One searches in vain through the pages of other sacred writings to find even a single line of accurate prophecy. Some seven centuries B.C. the Hebrew prophet Isaiah wrote:

"Let them . . . shew us what shall happen . . . or declare us things for to come. Shew the things that are to come hereafter, that we may know that ye are gods . . ." (Isa. 41:22, 23).

So be it! We now consider the amazingly accurate prophecies under the following categories:

A. Prophecies dealing with the nation Israel.
   1. Israel would become a great nation (Gen. 12:1-3).
   2. Her kings would come out of the tribes of Judah (Gen. 49:10).
   3. She would spend 400 years in Egypt (Gen. 15:13).
   4. The nation would suffer a civil war (1 Ki. 11:31).
   5. The nation would spend seventy years in Babylon (Jer. 25:11; 29:10).
   6. She would return (in part) to Jerusalem after the seventy years (Dan. 9:1, 2).
   7. Israel would eventually be scattered among the nations of the world (Deut. 28:25, 64; Lev. 26:33).
   8. Israel would become a byword among these nations (Deut. 28:37).
   9. Israel would loan to many nations, but borrow from none (Deut. 28:12).
   10. She would be hounded and persecuted (Deut. 28:65-67).
   11. Israel would nevertheless retain her identity (Lev. 26:44; Jer. 46:28).
   12. She would remain alone and aloof among the nations (Num. 23:9).
   13. Israel would reject her Messiah (Isa. 53).
   14. Because of this, her enemies would dwell in her land (Lev. 26:32; Lk. 21:24).
   15. Jerusalem would be destroyed (Lk. 19:41-44; 21:20).
   16. Israel would, in spite of all these things, endure forever (Gen. 17:7; Isa. 66:22; Jer. 31:35, 36; Mt. 24:34).
   17. Israel would return to Palestine in the latter days prior to the Second Coming of Christ (Deut. 30:3; Ezek. 36:24; 37:1-14; 38:1—39:29).

B. Prophecies dealing with various Gentile nations.
   1. Edom. Esau, Jacob's brother, was the founder of the nation Edom (see Gen. 36). Years after his death, Edom refused to help Israel, the nation founded by Jacob (see Num. 20) and actually delighted in persecuting God's people. Because of this, God pronounced doom upon Edom. According to various biblical prophecies:
      a. Their commerce was to cease.
      b. Their race was to become extinct.
      c. Their land was to be desolate (Jer. 49:17, 18; Ezek. 35:3-7; Obadiah; Mal. 1:4).

      All this has taken place in spite of her unbelievably strong fortified capital, Petra. In A.D. 636 Petra was captured by Mohammed, and shortly after this Petra and Edom drop from the pages of history.
   2. Babylon. Babylon was the first of four world powers mentioned in Daniel 2:31-43 and 7:1-8. Daniel prophesied the demise of mighty Babylon, as did Isaiah (13:17-19) and

Jeremiah (51:11). This literally happened on the night of October 13, 539 B.C., when Darius the Median captured the city by diverting the course of the Euphrates River which had flowed under the walls of the city. (See Dan. 5.)

3. Media-Persia. One of the most remarkable passages on prophecy is found in Daniel 8:1-7, 20, 21, written beside a river in 551 B.C. In a vision Daniel is told of a series of battles that would not take place until some 217 years later. Here the prophet describes for us the crushing defeats of Darius III (here pictured as a ram) by the Greek Alexander the Great (symbolized as a he-goat). This took place in three decisive battles—Granicus, in 334 B.C.; Issus, in 333 B.C.; and Gaugamela, in 331 B.C.

4. Greece. In this same chapter, Daniel predicts the dissolution of the Greek empire (upon the death of Alexander) into four smaller and separate powers, each ruled over by one of his generals (Dan. 7:6; 8:8, 20, 21). This happened in exact detail in 301 B.C. after Alexander died of a raging fever at the age of thirty-three in Babylon.

5. Rome. In Daniel 2:40, 41 we read:

"And the fourth kingdom shall be as strong as iron: forasmuch as iron breaketh all these, shall it break in pieces and bruise. And whereas thou sawest the feet and toes, part of potter's clay, and part of iron, the kingdom shall be divided. . . ."

Here Daniel rightly predicted that Rome, the fourth kingdom (which would come into power between the times of Nebuchadnezzar and Christ) should be "as strong as iron."

And so Rome was. By 300 B.C. Rome had become a major power in the Mediterranean world. By 200 B.C., she had conquered Carthage, her archenemy. In 63 B.C., the Roman general Pompey entered Jerusalem. Daniel noted in his prophecy, however, that, "The kingdom shall be divided." This, of course, happened in A.D. 364.

6. Egypt. Some 600 years before Christ, the prophet Ezekiel wrote:

". . . The word of the Lord came unto me, saying . . . set thy face against Pharaoh king of Egypt, and prophesy against him, and against all Egypt. It shall be the basest of the kingdoms; neither shall it exalt itself any more above the nations: for I will diminish them, that they shall no more rule over the nations" (Ezek. 29:1, 2, 15).

The history of Egypt is, of course, one of the oldest in recorded Western civilization. The country was united into a single kingdom about 3200 B.C. and was ruled by a succession of dynasties down to the time of Alexander the Great, who conquered Egypt in 332 B.C. We note that Ezekiel does not predict the disappearance of Egypt, as he did concerning Edom (35:3-7), but simply the demise of Egypt. The prophecy was that Egypt would be cut short and never again become a world power. This prophecy has been fulfilled to the last letter.

7. Russia. See Ezekiel 38:39. (Russia will be treated under that section dealing with prophecies concerning last-day conditions.)

C. Prophecies dealing with specific cities.

1. Tyre. Ezekiel's prophecy in chapter 26 concerning the city of Tyre is surely one of the greatest in the entire Bible. Tyre was actually two cities, one on the coastline, some sixty miles northwest from Jerusalem, and the other on an island, a half mile out in the Mediterranean Sea. In this prophecy, Ezekiel predicts:

a. The Babylonian king, Nebuchadnezzar, was to capture the city.

b. Other nations would later participate in Tyre's destruction.

c. The city was to be scrapped and made flat, like the top of a rock.

d. It was to become a place for the spreading of nets.

e. Its stones and timber were to be laid in the sea (Zech. 9:3, 4).

f. The city was never to be rebuilt.

Has all this taken place? Consider the following historical facts:

Ezekiel wrote all this around 590 B.C. Some four years later, 586 B.C., Nebuchadnezzar surrounded the city of Tyre. The siege lasted thirteen years and in 573 B.C. the coastal city was destroyed. But he could not capture the island city. During the next 241 years the island city of Tyre dwelt in safety and would have doubtless ridiculed Ezekiel's prophecy concerning total destruction.

But in 332 B.C. Alexander the Great arrived upon the scene and the island city was doomed. Alexander built a bridge leading from the coastline to the island by throwing the debris of the old city into the water. In doing this he literally scraped the coastline clean. (Some years ago an American archaeologist named Edward Robinson discovered forty or fifty marble columns beneath the water along the shores of ancient Tyre.)

After a seven-month siege, Alexander took the island city and destroyed it. From this point on, the surrounding coastal area has been used by local fishermen to spread and dry their nets.

Tyre has never been rebuilt in spite of the well-known nearby freshwater springs of Roselain, which yield some 10,000 gallons of water daily.

2. Jericho. In the sixth chapter of Joshua we see described the fall of Jericho's walls and the subsequent destruction of the city. Immediately after this, Joshua makes an amazing threefold prophecy about this fallen city:

a. That Jericho would be rebuilt again by one man.

b. That the builder's oldest son would die when the work on the city had begun.

c. That the builder's youngest son would

die when the work was completed. (See Josh. 6:26.)

Joshua uttered those words around 1450 B.C. Did all this happen? Some five centuries after this, in 930 B.C., we are told:

That a man named Hiel from Bethel rebuilt Jericho.

That as he laid the foundations, his oldest son, Abiram, died.

That when he completed the gates, his youngest son, Segub, died. (See 1 Ki. 16:34.)

3. Nineveh (Nahum 1-3). During the time of Jonah, God had spared the wicked city of Nineveh by using that Hebrew prophet (after an unpleasant submarine trip) to preach repentance. But the city had soon returned to its evil ways. So around 650 B.C., another prophet, Nahum, predicted the complete overthrow of Nineveh.

At the time of this prophecy, Nineveh appeared to be impregnable; her walls were one hundred feet high and broad enough for chariots to drive upon. The city had a circumference of sixty miles and was adorned by more than 1,200 strong towers.

In spite of all this, the city fell, less than forty years after Nahum's prophecy. An alliance of Medes and Babylonians broke through her walls during August of 612 B.C., after a two-month siege. The victory was due in part to the releasing of the city's water supply by traitors within. The destruction was so total that Alexander the Great marched his troops over the desolate ground which had once given support to her mighty buildings, and never knew there had once been a city there.

4. Jerusalem (Mt. 24:1, 2; Lk. 19:41-44; 21:20-24). These sad words were uttered by Jesus himself. He predicted Jerusalem would be destroyed, her citizens would be slaughtered, and her Temple would be completely wrecked, with not one stone left upon another.

This all literally happened less than forty years later. In February of A.D. 70, the Roman general Titus surrounded Jerusalem with 80,000 men to crush a revolt that had begun some five years back. In April of that year he began the siege in earnest. Conditions soon became desperate within the city walls. Women ate their own children, and grown men fought to the death over a piece of bird's dung for food! Finally, in September of the same year, the walls were battered down and the slaughter began. When the smoke had cleared, over a half-million Jews lay dead. A number of these had been crucified by Titus. Eventually the Temple was leveled and the ground under it plowed up, just as our Lord had predicted.

D. Prophecies dealing with particular individuals.

1. Josiah. The following incident concerns a wicked Israelite king named Jeroboam:

"As Jeroboam approached the altar to burn incense to the golden calf-idol, a prophet of the Lord from Judah walked up to him. Then, at the Lord's command, the prophet shouted, 'O altar, the Lord says that a child named Josiah shall be born into the family line of David, and he shall sacrifice upon you the priests from the shrines on the hills who come here to burn incense; and men's bones shall be burned upon you'" (1 Ki. 13:1, 2, *TLB*).

This all took place in 975 B.C. Some 350 years went by; then in 624 B.C., we are told of the actions of a new king of Israel:

"He also tore down the altar and shrine at Bethel which Jeroboam I had made when he led Israel into sin. He crushed the stones to dust and burned the shameful idol of Asherah. As Josiah was looking around, he noticed several graves in the side of the mountain. He ordered his men to bring out the bones in them and to burn them there upon the altar at Bethel to defile it, just as the Lord's prophet had declared would happen to Jeroboam's altar" (2 Ki. 23:15, 16, *TLB*).

2. Cyrus. Perhaps the greatest Old Testament prophet was Isaiah. For some sixty-two years this eloquent and godly man wrote and preached. But even though Jerusalem was at rest when he ministered, Isaiah predicted her captivity (as did also Jeremiah; see Jer. 25:12; 29:10) and subsequent restoration.

"That saith of Cyrus, He is my shepherd, and shall perform all my pleasure: even saying to Jerusalem, Thou shalt be built; and to the temple, Thy foundation shall be laid" (Isa. 44:28).

Isaiah penned these words around 712 B.C. By 606 B.C., Nebuchadnezzar, the Babylonian king, had captured Jerusalem and had led many captive Jews (see Ps. 137) into his capital. For seventy long years they remained here. This was all predicted, of course, by Jeremiah (Jer. 25:12; 29:10). Then, in 536 B.C., the miracle happened. The prophet Ezra tells us:

". . . that the Word of the Lord . . . might be fulfilled, the Lord stirred up the spirit of Cyrus . . . that he made a proclamation throughout all his kingdom, and put it also in writing, saying, Thus saith Cyrus . . . The Lord God of heaven hath . . . charged me to build an house at Jerusalem, which is in Judah" (Ezra 1:1, 2).

So then, Isaiah rightly predicted that Cyrus would allow the Jews to return and rebuild their Temple in Jerusalem 176 years before it happened.

3. Alexander the Great. Although Daniel does not refer to him by name, there seems little doubt that Alexander is the "he-goat" mentioned in Daniel 8:3-8.

Alexander was the first real world conqueror. He crossed the Hellespont in the spring of 334 B.C. and soon met and crushed the Persian troops at the battle of Issus in 333 B.C. Josephus, the Jewish historian, tells us that when Alexander approached Jerusalem, he was met at the gates by the high priest, who thereupon proceeded to show him that his victories over the Persians had all been prophesied by Daniel in 553, some 220 years in advance. The Greek warrior was reportedly so impressed at all this that he worshiped the high priest and spared Jerusalem.

4. Antiochus Epiphanes. Like Alexander, Antiochus is not mentioned by name, but is surely referred to in Daniel 8:9-14. Antiochus was a bloodthirsty, Jew-hating Syrian general who conquered Palestine in 167 B.C. He then entered the Temple Holy of Holies and horribly desecrated it by slaughtering a hog on the altar! Daniel foresaw this terrible event some 386 years before it happened.

5. John the Baptist. In Isaiah 40:3-5, the prophet correctly describes the future message of John the Baptist 700 years in advance. (See also Mt. 3:1-3.)

E. Prophecies fulfilled by our Lord during his earthly ministry. In the Old Testament there are some thirty-seven basic prophecies concerning the earthly ministry of the anticipated Savior. While upon this earth, Jesus Christ fulfilled every single prediction. Consider the following texts:

1. He would be born of a virgin (cf. Isa. 7:14 with Mt. 1:22, 23).
2. He would be given the throne of David (cf. 2 Sam. 7:12, 13 with Lk. 1:31).
3. He would be called Emmanuel (cf. Isa. 7:14 with Mt. 1:23).
4. He would be rejected by his own (cf. Isa. 53:3 with Jn. 1:11; 7:5).
5. He would have a forerunner (cf. Isa. 40:3-5; Mal. 3:1 with Mt. 3:1-3; Lk. 1:76-78; 3:3-6).
6. He would be born in Bethlehem (cf. Micah 5:2, 3 with Mt. 2:5, 6).
7. He would be visited by the magi and presented with gifts (cf. Isa. 60:3, 6, 9 with Mt. 2:11).
8. He would be in Egypt for a season (cf. Hosea 11:1 with Mt. 2:15).
9. His birthplace would suffer a massacre of infants (cf. Jer. 31:5 with Mt. 2:17, 18).
10. He would be called a Nazarene (cf. Isa. 11:1 with Mt. 2:23).
11. He would be zealous for his father (cf. Ps. 69:9 with Jn. 2:13-17).
12. He would be filled with God's Spirit (cf. Isa. 61:1-3; 11:2 with Lk. 4:18, 19).
13. He would be a light to the Gentiles (cf. Isa. 42:1-3, 6, 7 with Mt. 4:13-16; 12:18-21).
14. He would heal many (cf. Isa. 53:4 with Mt. 8:16, 17).
15. He would deal gently with the Gentiles (cf. Isa. 9:1, 2; 42:1-3 with Mt. 12:17-21).
16. He would speak in parables (cf. Isa. 6:9, 10 with Mt. 13:10-15).
17. He would make a triumphal entry into Jerusalem (cf. Zech. 9:9 with Mt. 21:4, 5).
18. He would be praised by little children (cf. Ps. 8:2 with Mt. 21:16).
19. He would be the rejected cornerstone (cf. Ps. 118:22, 23 with Mt. 21:42).
20. His miracles would not be believed (cf. Isa. 53:1 with Jn. 12:37, 38).
21. His friend would betray him for thirty pieces of silver (cf. Ps. 41:9; 55:12-14; Zech. 11:12, 13 with Mt. 26:14-16, 21-25).
22. He would be a man of sorrows (cf. Isa. 53:3 with Mt. 26:37, 38).
23. He would be forsaken by his disciples (cf. Zech. 13:7 with Mt. 26:31, 56).
24. He would be scourged and spat upon (cf. Isa. 50:6 with Mt. 26:67; 27:26).
25. His price money would be used to buy a potter's field (cf. Jer. 18:1-4; 19:1-3; Zech. 11:12, 13 with Mt. 27:9, 10).
26. He would be crucified between two thieves (cf. Isa. 53:12 with Mt. 27:38; Mk. 15:27, 28; Lk. 22:37).
27. He would be given vinegar to drink (cf. Ps. 69:21 with Mt. 27:34, 48).
28. He would suffer the piercing of his hands and feet (cf. Ps. 22:16; Zech. 12:10 with Mk. 15:25; Jn. 19:34, 37; 20:25-27).
29. His garments would be parted and gambled for (cf. Ps. 22:18 with Lk. 23:34; Jn. 19:23, 24).
30. He would be surrounded and ridiculed by his enemies (cf. Ps. 22:7, 8 with Mt. 27:39-44; Mk. 15:29-32).
31. He would thirst (cf. Ps. 22:15 with Jn. 19:28).
32. He would commend his spirit to the Father (cf. Ps. 31:5 with Lk. 23:46).
33. His bones would not be broken (cf. Ex. 12:46; Num. 9:12; Ps. 34:20 with Jn. 19:33-36).
34. He would be stared at in death (cf. Zech. 12:10 with Mt. 27:36; Jn. 19:37).
35. He would be buried with the rich (cf. Isa. 59:9 with Mt. 27:57-60).
36. He would be raised from the dead (cf. Ps. 16:10 with Mt. 28:2-7).
37. He would ascend (cf. Ps. 24:7-10 with Mk. 16:19; Lk. 24:50).

VI. Sixth Supernatural Element—Its Universal Influence Upon Civilization.
A. Western civilization is founded directly upon the Bible and its teachings. Its very manner of life had its origin in Acts 16:9, when Paul, obedient to his heavenly vision, directed his second missionary journey toward Europe instead of Asia and the East.
B. The world's calendar and most of its holidays stem from the Bible.
C. It was the Bible which elevated the blood-drinking savages of the British Isles to decency.
D. The Bible has influenced, if not directed, the advancement of all fine arts.
1. Literature. Ruskin quotes over 5,000 scriptural references in his writings. Milton's greatest works are rooted in the Word of God, as are Shakespeare's and those of others such as Coleridge, Scott, Pope, Bryant, Longfellow, Kipling, Carlyle, Macaulay, Hawthorne, Irving, and Thoreau, to name a few.
2. Art. Many world-famous paintings depicting well-known scenes in the Bible are preserved

today. These paintings can be found in every important museum on earth. They have been done by the greatest and most talented artists of all time. These would include Leonardo da Vinci, Rembrandt, Raphael, Michelangelo, and others.

Music. The Bible has produced more inspiring music than all other combined books in the world.

Bach—History has concluded that Johann Sebastian Bach "anticipated every important [musical] idea that has been born since his day. He is the inspiration of the pianist, the organist, and the composer." Bach was a zealous Lutheran who devoted most of his genius to church-centered music. Also consider

Mendelssohn—author of "St. Paul, Elijah"
Brahms—"Requiem"
Beethoven—"Mt. of Olives," "Samson and Delilah"
Handel—"Messiah" (he quotes from fifteen books of the Bible)
Haydn—"The Creation"

E. The Bible has produced the law of the Western world. Early attempts of governing forms such as the English common law, the Bill of Rights, the Magna Carta, and our own Constitution are all rooted in God's gift to Moses on Mt. Sinai, the Ten Commandments.

VII. Seventh Supernatural Element—Its Care and Copy.

A. No book in history has been copied as many times with as much care as has been the Word of God. The Talmud lists the following rules for copying the Old Testament:

1. The parchment had to be made from the skin of a clean animal, prepared by a Jew only, and was to be fastened by strings from clean animals.

2. Each column must have no less than forty-eight or more than sixty lines.

3. The ink must be of no other color than black, and had to be prepared according to a special recipe.

4. No word nor letter could be written from memory; the scribe must have an authentic copy before him, and he had to read and pronounce aloud each word before writing it.

5. He had to reverently wipe his pen each time before writing the Word of God, and had to wash his whole body before writing the sacred name Jehovah.

6. One mistake on a sheet condemned the sheet; if three mistakes were found on any page, the entire manuscript was condemned.

7. Every word and every letter was counted, and if a letter were omitted, an extra letter inserted, or if one letter touched another, the manuscript was condemned and destroyed at once.

The old rabbi gave the solemn warning to each young scribe: "Take heed how thou dost do thy work, for thy work is the work of heaven; lest thou drop or add a letter of a manuscript and so become a destroyer of the world!"

The scribe was also told that while he was writing if even a king would enter the room and speak with him, the scribe was to ignore him until he finished the page he was working on, lest he make a mistake. In fact, some texts were actually annotated—that is, each letter was individually counted. Thus in copying the Old Testament they would note that the letter *aleph* (first letter in the Hebrew alphabet) occurred 42,377 times, and so on.

According to Westcott and Hort, the points in which we cannot be sure of the original words are insignificant in proportion to the bulk of the whole, some 1/1000. Thus only one letter out of 1,580 in the Old Testament is open to question, and none of these uncertainties would change in the slightest any doctrinal teaching.

B. Today there are almost 5,000 ancient Greek manuscripts of the New Testament. This perhaps does not seem like many, until one considers that:

1. Fifteen hundred years after Herodotus wrote his history there was only one copy in the entire world.

2. Twelve hundred years after Plato wrote his classic, there was only one manuscript.

3. Today there exist but a few manuscripts of Sophocles, Euripedes, Virgil, and Cicero.

VIII. Eighth Supernatural Element—Its Amazing Circulation. When David Hume said, "I see the twilight of Christianity and the Bible," he was much confused, for he could not tell the sunrise from the sunset!

A. Only one-half of one percent of all books published survive seven years. Eighty percent of all books are forgotten in one year. For example, let us imagine that during this year, 200 new books are published in America. Statistics show that by next year only forty of these 200 will remain. At the end of the seventh year, of the original 200, only one lonely book will survive.

What other ancient religious book can even remotely be compared to the Bible? Where could one go today to purchase a copy of Zen Vedas, or the Egyptian Book of the Dead? In fact, dozens of religions which once flourished have simply disappeared from the face of the earth without leaving the slightest trace. But the smallest child can walk into almost any bookstore in America and pick up a copy of the Word of God.

IX. Ninth Supernatural Element—Its Absolute Honesty. Perhaps no other single statement so completely summarizes the Bible as does the following: "The Bible is not a book that man *could* write if he would, or *would* write if he could." Let us analyze this one section at a time.

"Man could not write the Bible if he would." Even if a man had all the necessary spirituality he could not know the facts involved in the historical, scientific, and prophetical statements we have previously seen in the Bible. Thus, without God's direction the Bible is not a book that man could write if he would.

"Man would not write the Bible if he could." Suppose God would give sinful man all the necessary facts and abilities to write the Bible. What then? Man still *would* not write it correctly if he *could*. Note the following reasons:

A. Because of the bad things God writes about some of his friends. Here five men immediately come to mind. Most of these individuals are mentioned in the Faith Hall of Fame (Hebrews 11).

1. Noah—indeed a man of God. He walked with God, he was a just man (Gen. 6:9), and he obeyed God (Heb. 11:7). Yet after the flood this great hero of the faith gets dead drunk and exposes his nakedness and shame to his entire family (Gen. 9:20-24). Surely a mere human author would not have written all this.

2. Moses—the meekest man in all the earth during his time (Num. 12:3), and a leader who single-handedly led an entire nation of enslaved Hebrews out of captivity in Egypt. But en route to Palestine we read of his anger and direct disobedience to the clearly revealed Word of God. (See Num. 20:7-12.) Surely man would have eliminated this part of Moses' record.

3. David—without exception the grandest human king who ever sat upon a throne. God himself would testify that here was a man after his own heart. (See 1 Sam. 13:14; 16:7, 12, 13.) David's fearlessness (1 Sam. 17:34-36, 49), love for God (Ps. 18, 103, etc.), and kindness (1 Sam. 24:6, 7) were universally known. But in 2 Samuel 11 this same king is accurately accused of lust, adultery, lying, and cold-blooded murder. Who but God would write in such a manner?

4. Elijah—few other Old Testament prophets are as colorful and exciting as Elijah the Tishbite. In 1 Kings 18, he champions the cause of God against 450 priests of Satan, but in the very next chapter he is pictured as running for his very life from a mere woman.

5. Peter—self-appointed spokesman for Christ who so confidently assured the Savior that, "Though all men shall be offended because of thee, yet will I never be offended" (Mt. 26:33). But in the hour of Jesus' great need we read of Peter: "Then began he to curse and to swear, saying, I know not the man" (Mt. 26:74).

B. Because of the good things God writes about some of his enemies. As we have already seen, on many occasions God records bad things about his friends, and he often mentions good things about his enemies. This can be seen in the accounts of Esau (Gen. 33); Artaxerxes (Neh. 2); Darius (Dan. 6); Gamaliel (Acts 5:34-39); Julius (Acts 27:1-3); etc.

The point of all the above is simply this—the Bible is *not* an edited book. God literally "tells it like it is."

Human authors, however sincere, simply do not consistently write this way.

C. Because of certain doctrines repugnant to the natural mind. Many examples could be listed here, but the following three will demonstrate this:

1. The doctrine of eternal hell. (See Rev. 14:10, 11.)

2. The doctrine of man's total helplessness. (See Rom. 7:18; Eph. 2:8, 9.)

3. The doctrine of final judgment upon saved and unsaved. (See 1 Cor. 3:9-15; Rev. 20:11-15.)

X. Tenth Supernatural Element—Its Life-Transforming Power. According to an ancient proverb—"The proof of the pudding is in the eating." So it is. Undoubtedly the greatest proof of all that the Bible is indeed God's Word is its amazing ability to change corrupt humanity.

The Bible is a beautiful palace built of sixty-six blocks of solid marble—the sixty-six books. In the first chapter of Genesis we enter the vestibule, filled with the mighty acts of creation.

The vestibule gives access to the law courts—the five books of Moses—passing through which we come to the picture gallery of the historical books. Here we find hung upon the walls scenes of battlefields, representations of heroic deeds, and portraits of eminent men belonging to the early days of the world's history.

Beyond the picture gallery we find the philosopher's chamber—the book of Job—passing through which we enter the music room—the book of Psalms—where we listen to the grandest strains that ever fell on human ears.

Then we come to the business office—the book of Proverbs—where right in the center of the room, stands facing us the motto, "Righteousness exalteth a nation, but sin is a reproach to any people."

From the business office we pass into the chapel—Ecclesiastes, or the Song of Solomon with the rose of sharon and the lily of the valley, and all manner of fine perfume and fruit and flowers and singing birds.

Finally we reach the observatory—the prophets, with their telescopes fixed on near and distant stars, and all directed toward "the Bright and Morning Star," that was soon to arise.

Crossing the court we come to the audience chamber of the King—the Gospels—where we find four vivid lifelike portraits of the King himself. Next we enter the workroom of the Holy Spirit—the Acts of the Apostles—and beyond that the correspondence room—the epistles—where we see Paul and Peter and James and John and Jude busy at their desks.

Before leaving we stand a moment in the outside gallery—the Revelation—where we look upon some striking pictures of the judgments to come, and the glories to be revealed, concluding with an awe-inspiring picture of the throne room of the King.

THE DOCTRINE OF PROPHECY

THE DOCTRINE OF PROPHECY

I. The Rapture of the Church.
  A. The meaning of the word "rapture." The term is derived from the Latin verb *rapere,* which means "to transport from one place to another." Thus the next great scheduled event predicted by the Bible will take place when the Lord Jesus comes in the air to catch up his own. Several key passages bring this out:

  > "For this we say to you by the word of the Lord, that we who are alive, and remain until the coming of the Lord, shall not precede those who have fallen asleep. For the Lord Himself will descend from heaven with a shout, with the voice of the archangel, and with the trumpet of God; and the dead in Christ shall rise first. Then we who are alive and remain shall be caught up together with them in the clouds to meet the Lord in the air, and thus we shall always be with the Lord" (1 Thess. 4:15–17, *NASB*).

  > "Behold, I shew you a mystery; We shall not all sleep, but we shall all be changed, in a moment, in the twinkling of an eye, at the last trump: for the trumpet shall sound, and the dead shall be raised incorruptible, and we shall be changed. For this corruptible must put on incorruption, and this mortal must put on immortality" (1 Cor. 15:51–53).

  B. The participants of the rapture. For whom will Jesus come? It is the view of this theological summary that Christ will come again for his church, which is composed of all saved people from Pentecost up to the rapture itself. The actual participants of the rapture include:
    1. The Lord Jesus himself.
    2. The archangel (perhaps Michael; see Dan. 10:13, 21; 12:1; Jude 9; Rev. 12:7).
    3. The bodies of dead believers: "for this corruptible must put on incorruption."
    4. The translated bodies of living believers: "and this mortal must put on immortality."
  C. The false views of the rapture.
    1. That the rapture is the same as the Second Coming of Christ. False. At the rapture Jesus comes for his church in the air, while at the Second Coming he comes with his people to the earth. See Jude 14, 15; Revelation 19:11–16.
    2. That the rapture will include only "spiritual" Christians, and that carnal Christians will be left behind to endure the tribulation. This theory is refuted by one little word in 1 Corinthians 15:51, where Paul says that "we shall *all* be changed." This false view is often called the "partial rapture" theory.
    3. That the rapture will not occur until the middle of the tribulation, thus forcing the entire church to go through the first three and a half years of God's wrath. This theory is called mid-tribulationism, and is refuted by Paul in 1 Thessalonians 5:9, where he says, "For God hath not appointed us to wrath. . . ."
    4. That the rapture will not occur until the end of the tribulation. This is known as post-tribulationism, and is refuted by 1 Thessalonians 5:9 and Revelation 3:10.

  The New Testament pictures the Church as the body and bride of Christ. If the mid-tribulation or post-tribulation view were correct, then a part of this body would suffer amputation, and a section of the bride would be left behind. In addition to this, one would be forced to conclude that all bodies of carnal departed Christians would likewise be left in the grave. This simply is not the clear teaching of the Word of God.

  The Bible teaches that the rapture is pre-tribulational in nature and includes all believers. See Romans 5:9 and 1 Thessalonians 1:10. Perhaps the strongest proof of this statement is the fact that up to chapter 6 of Revelation the church is mentioned many times, but from chapter 6 to chapter 19 (the period of the tribulation) there is no mention whatsoever of the church on earth. In fact, the only godly group which Satan can find to persecute is the nation Israel! See Revelation chapter 12.

  In Revelation 4:1 John declares, "After this I looked, and, behold, a door was opened in heaven: and the first voice which I heard was as it were of a trumpet talking with me; which said, Come up hither. . . ." We are told that Christians are God's ambassadors on earth (2 Cor. 5:20) and that he will someday declare war on this earth. The first thing a king or president does after he declares war on another country is to call his ambassadors home! Thus we conclude that the church will escape the tribulation.
  D. The purpose of the rapture.
    1. To judge and reward the church of God.
      > "For we must all appear before the judgment seat of Christ; that everyone may receive the things done in his body . . . whether it be good or bad" (2 Cor. 5:10).

2. To remove the Spirit of God.

"For the mystery of lawlessness is already at work; only he who now restrains will do so until he is taken out of the way" (2 Thess. 2:7, *NASB*).

Many theologians believe the "he" in this verse is a reference to the Holy Spirit. Thus the Spirit of God has been acting as a divine dam, faithfully holding back the waters of sin. But at the rapture his blessed influence will be removed to a large extent in order to prepare the way for the tribulation.

E. The mystery of the rapture. In 1 Corinthians 15:51 Paul declares, "Behold, I show you a mystery. . . ." What is this secret of the Savior? Let us suppose you began reading the Bible in Genesis chapter 1, and read through 1 Corinthians chapter 14. If you stopped your reading here, you would already have learned about many important facts, such as creation, man's sin, the flood, Bethlehem, Calvary, the resurrection, and of the existence of heaven and hell.

But you would be forced to conclude that a Christian could get to heaven only after physically dying. You would of course note the two exceptions of Enoch (Gen. 5:24) and Elijah (2 Ki. 2:11), but apart from these it would be clear that believers have to travel the path of the grave to reach the goal of glory.

But now the secret is out, and here it is: millions of Christians will someday reach heaven without dying. "Behold, I show you a mystery; we shall not all sleep, but we shall all be changed" (1 Cor. 15:51). This, then, is the mystery of the rapture.

F. The trumpet of the rapture. In at least three biblical passages concerning the rapture, a trumpet is mentioned (1 Cor. 15:52; 1 Thess. 4:16; Rev. 4:1). How are we to understand this? Dr. J. Dwight Pentecost writes, "The phrase 'the trump of God' is significant, for in the Old Testament the trumpet was used for two things—to summon to battle and to summon to worship." (J. Dwight Pentecost, *Prophecy for Today*, p. 30)

Which of the two meanings, however, is involved at the rapture? Dr. Pentecost suggests that *both* meanings are in mind, one directed toward angels and the other to believers.

1. To angels the trumpet blast will mean "Prepare for battle!" According to various New Testament passages (Jn. 14:30; Eph. 6:12; 1 Jn. 5:19) this present world lies in the hands of the evil one, the devil, and the very atmosphere is filled with his wicked power and presence. Satan will obviously resist believers being caught up through his domain and becoming freed from his wicked worldly system. Therefore, the trumpet commands the angels, "Prepare for battle! Clear the way for the catching up of those resurrected bodies and those living believers!"

2. To all believers the trumpet blast will mean "Prepare to worship!" In Numbers 10:1-3 we read,

"And the Lord spake unto Moses, saying, 'Make thee two trumpets of silver . . . that thou mayest use them for the calling of the assembly . . . and when they shall blow with them, all the assembly shall assemble themselves to thee at the door of the tabernacle. . . .'"

Regarding the rapture trumpet, Numbers 10:4 seems to be especially significant:

"If they blow but with one trumpet, then the princes, which are heads of the thousands of Israel, shall gather themselves unto thee."

At the rapture only one trumpet is sounded, suggesting that in God's sight *all* believers occupy a place of utmost importance. We are all "head princes" in the mind of God.

G. The Old Testament foreshadowing of the rapture.

1. Seen in Enoch, who was taken from the world *before* the Flood judgment (Gen. 5:24).

2. Seen in Lot, who was removed from Sodom *before* the fire judgment (Gen. 19:22-24).

H. The challenge of the rapture. Because of this glorious coming event, the child of God is instructed to do many things.

1. He is to attend the services of the Lord regularly.

". . . not forsaking the assembling of ourselves together, as the manner of some is; but exhorting one another; and so much the more, as ye see the day approaching" (Heb. 10:25).

2. He is to observe the Lord's Supper with the rapture in mind.

"For as often as ye eat this bread, and drink this cup, ye do show the Lord's death till he come" (1 Cor. 11:26).

3. He is to love believers and all men.

"And the Lord make you to increase and abound in love one toward another, and toward all men . . . to the end he may stablish your hearts . . . at the coming of our Lord Jesus Christ with all his saints" (1 Thess. 3:12, 13).

4. He is to be patient.

"Be ye also patient; stablish your hearts; for the coming of the Lord draweth nigh" (Jas. 5:8).

5. He is to live a separated life.

". . . we know that, when he shall appear, we shall be like him, for we shall see him as he is. And every man that hath this hope in him purifieth himself . . ." (1 Jn. 3:2, 3).

". . . denying ungodliness and worldly lusts, we should live soberly, righteously, and godly, in this present world; looking for that blessed hope, and the glorious appearing of the great God and our Saviour Jesus Christ" (Titus 2:12, 13).

"And now, little children, abide in him, that, when he shall appear, we may have confidence, and not be ashamed before him at his coming" (1 Jn. 2:28).

6. He is to refrain from judging others.

"Therefore judge nothing before the time, until the Lord come, who both will bring to light the hidden things of darkness, and will make manifest the counsels of the hearts; and then shall every man have praise of God" (1 Cor. 4:5).

7. He is to preach the Word.

"I charge thee therefore before God, and the Lord Jesus Christ, who shall judge the quick and the dead at his appearing and his kingdom; preach the word . . ." (2 Tim. 4:1, 2).

"Feed the flock of God . . . and when the chief Shepherd shall appear, ye shall receive a crown of glory that fadeth not away" (1 Pet. 5:2, 4).

8. He is to comfort the bereaved.

"For the Lord himself shall descend from heaven . . . wherefore comfort one another with these words" (1 Thess. 4:16, 18).

9. He is to win souls.

"Keep yourselves in the love of God, looking for the mercy of our Lord Jesus Christ unto eternal life. And of some have compassion, making a difference: and others save with fear, pulling them out of the fire . . ." (Jude 21-23).

10. He is to be concerned with heaven.

"If ye then be risen with Christ, seek those things which are above, where Christ sitteth on the right hand of God. Set your affection on things above, not on things on the earth. For ye are dead, and your life is hid with Christ in God. When Christ, who is our life, shall appear, then shall ye also appear with him in glory" (Col. 3:1-4).

I. The effect of the rapture. What will be the reaction of a sin-sick society when millions of people suddenly disappear? Certainly the believers will be missed. It is evident from the Bible that the sudden disappearance of both Enoch and Elijah (two Old Testament types of the rapture) caused considerable confusion and alarm among their friends. How much more confusion and alarm will come from the sudden and mysterious disappearance of literally millions of men and women, boys and girls!

II. The *Bema*—The Judgment Seat of Christ.

A. The meaning of the *bema* judgment. The Greek word *bema* (translated "judgment seat" in the King James Version) was a familiar term to the people of Paul's day. Dr. Lehman Strauss writes:

"In the large olympic arenas, there was an elevated seat on which the judge of the contest sat. After the contests were over, the successful competitors would assemble before the *bema* to receive their rewards or crowns. The *bema* was not a judicial bench where someone was condemned; it was a reward seat. Likewise, the Judgment Seat of Christ is not a judicial bench . . . the Christian life is a race, and the divine umpire is watching every contestant. After the church has run her course, He will gather every member before the *bema* for the purpose of examining each one and giving the proper reward to each." (*God's Plan for the Future*, p. 111)

B. The fact of the *bema* judgment. Many New Testament verses speak of this.

"But why dost thou judge thy brother? Or why dost thou set at nought thy brother? For we shall all stand before the judgment seat of Christ. For it is written, As I live, saith the Lord, every knee shall bow to me, and every tongue shall confess to God. So then every one of us shall give account of himself to God" (Rom. 14:10-12).

"Every man's work shall be made manifest, for the day shall declare it . . ." (1 Cor. 3:13).

"For we must all appear before the judgment seat of Christ . . ." (2 Cor. 5:10)

C. The purpose of the *bema* judgment.

1. Negative considerations.

a. The purpose of the *bema* judgment is *not* to determine whether a particular individual enters heaven or not, for every man's eternal destiny is already determined before he leaves this life.

b. The purpose of the *bema* judgment is *not* to punish believers for sins committed either before or after their salvation. The Scriptures are very clear that no child of God will have to answer for his sins after this life.

"Thou hast in love to my soul delivered it from the pit of corruption: for thou hast cast all my sins behind thy back" (Isa. 38:17).

"I have blotted out . . . thy transgressions and . . . thy sins" (Isa. 44:22).

". . . the blood of Jesus Christ his Son cleanseth us from all sin" (1 Jn. 1:7).

2. Positive considerations. What then is the purpose of the *bema* judgment? In 1 Corinthians 4:2 Paul says that all Christians should conduct themselves as faithful stewards of God:

"Moreover it is required in stewards, that a man be found faithful."

The Apostle Peter later writes in a similar way:

"Minister . . . as good stewards of the manifold grace of God" (1 Pet. 4:10).

In the New Testament world, a steward was the manager of a large household or estate. He was appointed by the owner and was entrusted to keep the estate running smoothly. He had the power to hire and fire and to spend and save, being answerable to the owner alone. His only concern was that periodic meeting with his master, at which time he was required to account for the condition of the estate up to that point.

With this background in mind, it may be said that someday at the *bema* judgment all stewards will stand before their Lord and Master and be required to give an account of the way they have used their privileges and responsibilities from the moment of their conversion.

In conclusion, it can be seen that:

a. In the past, God dealt with us as sinners (Rom. 5:6-8; 1 Cor. 6:9-11; Eph. 2:1-3).

b. In the present, God deals with us as sons (Rom. 8:14; Heb. 12:5-11; 1 Jn. 3:1, 2).

c. In the future, God will deal with us (at the *bema*) as stewards.

D. The materials to be tested at the *bema* judgment. In 1 Corinthians 3:11 the Apostle Paul explains the glorious fact that at the moment of salvation a repenting sinner is firmly placed on the foundation of the death, burial, and resurrection of Christ himself. His continuing instruction after his salvation is to rise up and build upon this foundation. Paul says,

"But let every man take heed how he buildeth thereupon. . . . Now if any man build upon this foundation gold, silver, precious stones, wood, hay, stubble; every man's work shall be made manifest: for the day shall declare it, because it shall be revealed by fire; and the fire shall try every man's work of what sort it is" (1 Cor. 3:10b, 12, 13).

Negative considerations. It should be noted immediately that this passage does *not* teach the false doctrine known as purgatory, for it is the believer's *works* and not the believer *himself* that will be subjected to the fires.

Positive considerations. From these verses it is apparent that God classifies the works of believers into one of the following six areas: gold, silver, precious stones, wood, hay, stubble. There has been much speculation about the kinds of work down here that will constitute gold or silver up there. But it seems more appropriate to note that the six objects can be readily placed into two categories:

Those indestructible and worthy objects which will survive and thrive in the fires. These are the gold, silver, and precious stones.

Those destructible and worthless objects which will be totally consumed in the fires. These are the wood, hay, and stubble.

Though it is difficult to know just what goes to make up a "golden work" or a "stubble work," we are nevertheless informed of certain general areas in which God is particularly interested.

1. How we treat other believers.

"For God is not unrighteous to forget your work and labour of love, which ye have showed toward his name, in that ye have ministered to the saints, and do minister" (Heb. 6:10).

"He that receiveth a prophet in the name of a prophet shall receive a prophet's reward; and he that receiveth a righteous man in the name of a righteous man shall receive a righteous man's reward. And whosoever shall give to drink unto one of these little ones a cup of cold water only in the name of a disciple, verily I say unto you, he shall in no wise lose his reward" (Mt. 10:41, 42).

2. How we exercise our authority over others.

"Obey them that have the rule over you, and submit yourselves: for they watch for your souls, as they that must give account, that they may do it with joy, and not with grief . . ." (Heb. 13:17).

"Let not many of you become teachers, my brethren, knowing that as such we shall incur a stricter judgment" (Jas. 3:1, NASB).

3. How we employ our God-given abilities.

"Wherefore I put thee in remembrance that thou stir up the gift of God which is in thee . . ." (2 Tim. 1:6).

"Now there are varieties of gifts, but the same Spirit. . . . But one and the same Spirit works all these things, distributing to each one individually just as He wills" (1 Cor. 12:4, 11, NASB).

"As each one has received a special gift, employ it in serving one another, as good stewards of the manifold grace of God" (1 Pet. 4:10, NASB).

To these verses can be added the overall teaching of Jesus' parables of the ten pounds (Lk. 19:11-26) and the eight talents (Mt. 25:14-29).

4. How we use our money.

"Charge them that are rich in this world that they be not highminded; nor trust in uncertain riches, but in the living God, who giveth us richly all things to enjoy; that they do good, that they be rich in good works, ready to distribute, willing to communicate; laying up in store for themselves a good foundation against the time to come, that they may lay hold on eternal life" (1 Tim. 6:17-19).

"But this I say, He which soweth sparingly shall reap also sparingly; and he which soweth bountifully shall reap also bountifully. Every man according as he purposeth in his heart, so let him give; not grudgingly, or of necessity: for God loveth a cheerful giver" (2 Cor. 9:6, 7).

"Upon the first day of the week let every one of you lay by him in store, as God hath prospered him . . ." (1 Cor. 16:2).

5. How much we suffer for Jesus.

"Blessed are ye, when men shall revile you, and persecute you, and shall say all manner of evil against you falsely, for my sake. Rejoice, and be exceeding glad, for great is your reward in heaven . . ." (Mt. 5:11, 12).

"Beloved, think it not strange concerning the fiery trial which is to try you, as though some strange thing happened unto you; but rejoice, inasmuch as ye are partakers of Christ's sufferings, that, when his glory shall be revealed, ye may be glad also with exceeding joy" (1 Pet. 4:12, 13).

"And Jesus answered and said, Verily I say unto you, there is no man that hath left house, or brethren, or sisters, or father, or mother, or wife, or children, or lands, for my sake, and the gospel's, but he shall receive an hundredfold now in this time, houses, and brethren, and sisters, and mothers, and children, and lands, with persecutions; and in the world to come eternal life" (Mk. 10:29, 30).

"For our light affliction, which is but for a moment, worketh for us a far more exceeding and eternal weight of glory" (2 Cor. 4:17).

"For I reckon that the sufferings of this present time are not worthy to be compared with the glory which shall be revealed in us" (Rom. 8:18).

6. How we spend our time.

". . . redeeming the time, because the days are evil" (Eph. 5:16).

"And if ye call on the Father, who without respect of persons judgeth according to every man's work, pass the time of your sojourning here in fear" (1 Pet. 1:17).

"So teach us to number our days, that we may apply our hearts unto wisdom" (Ps. 90:12).

7. How we run that particular race which God has chosen for us.

"Know ye not that they which run in a race run all, but one receiveth the prize? So run, that ye may obtain" (1 Cor. 9:24).

"Brethren, I count not myself to have apprehended; but this one thing I do, forgetting those things which are behind, and reaching forth unto those things which are before, I press toward the mark for the prize of the high calling of God in Christ Jesus" (Phil. 3:13, 14).

"Let us lay aside every weight, and the sin which doth so easily beset us, and let us run with patience the race that is set before us" (Heb. 12:1).

8. How effectively we control the old nature.

"And every man that striveth for the mastery is temperate in all things. Now they do it to obtain a corruptible crown, but we an incorruptible. I therefore so run, not as uncertainly; so fight I, not as one that beateth the air. But I keep under my body, and bring it into subjection, lest that by any means when I have preached to others, I myself should be a castaway" (1 Cor. 9:25-27).

9. How many souls we witness to and win to Christ.

"For what is our hope, or joy, or crown of rejoicing? Are not even ye in the presence of our Lord Jesus Christ at his coming? For ye are our glory and joy" (1 Thess. 2:19, 20).

"And they that be wise shall shine as the brightness of the firmament, and they that turn many to righteousness as the stars for ever and ever" (Dan. 12:3).

10. How we react to temptation.

"My brethren, count it all joy when ye fall into divers temptations, knowing this, that the trying of your faith worketh patience" (Jas. 1:2, 3).

"Behold, the devil shall cast some of you into prison, that ye may be tried; and ye shall have tribulation ten days; be thou faithful unto death, and I will give thee a crown of life" (Rev. 2:10).

11. How much the doctrine of the rapture means to us.

"Henceforth there is laid up for me a crown of righteousness, which the Lord, the righteous judge, shall give me at that day; and not to me only, but unto all them also that love his appearing" (2 Tim. 4:8).

12. How faithful we are to the Word of God and the flock of God.

"Feed the flock of God which is among you, taking the oversight thereof, not by constraint, but willingly; not for filthy lucre, but of a ready mind; neither as being lords over God's heritage, but being ensamples to the flock. And when the Chief Shepherd shall appear, ye shall receive a crown of glory that fadeth not away" (1 Pet. 5:2-4).

"I charge thee therefore before God and the Lord Jesus Christ, who shall judge the quick and the dead at his appearing and his kingdom, Preach the word . . ." (2 Tim. 4:1, 2).

E. The results of the *bema* judgment seat of Christ.

1. Some will receive rewards.

"If any man's work abide which he hath built thereupon, he shall receive a reward" (1 Cor. 3:14).

The Bible mentions at least five possible rewards. These have already been described briefly under the last section. The rewards include:

a. The incorruptible crown—given to those who master the old nature (1 Cor. 9:25-27).

b. The crown of rejoicing—given to soul-winners (Prov. 11:30; Dan. 12:3; 1 Thess. 2:19, 20).

c. The crown of life—given to those who successfully endure temptation (Jas. 1:2, 3; Rev. 2:10).

d. The crown of righteousness—given to those who especially love the doctrine of the rapture (2 Tim. 4:8).

e. The crown of glory—given to faithful preachers and teachers (Acts 20:26-28; 2 Tim. 4:1, 2; 1 Pet. 5:2-4).

It has been suggested that these "crowns" will actually be talents and abilities with which to glorify Christ. Thus, the greater the reward, the greater the ability!

2. Some will suffer loss.

"If any man's work shall be burned, he shall suffer loss . . ." (1 Cor. 3:15).

F. The Old Testament foreshadowing of the *bema* judgment seat of Christ. Although the church is nowhere mentioned in the Old Testament, there is nevertheless a passage which can very easily be applied to the *bema* judgment. This can be found in the words of Boaz (a foreshadowing of Christ) to Ruth (a foreshadowing of the church):

"It hath fully been showed me, all that thou hast done. . . . The Lord recompense thy work, and a full reward be given thee of the Lord God of Israel, under whose wings thou art come to trust" (Ruth 2:11, 12).

III. The Marriage of the Lamb.

A. The fact of the marriage. Many passages in the Word of God teach that the most fantastic and wonderful wedding of all time is yet to take place in this universe.

1. This marriage is described through the parables of Jesus.

"The kingdom of heaven is like unto a certain king, which made a marriage for his son" (Mt. 22:2).

"Then shall the kingdom of heaven be likened unto ten virgins, which took their lamps, and went forth to meet the bridegroom" (Mt. 25:1).

"Let your loins be girded about, and your lights burning, and ye yourselves like unto men that wait for their lord, when he will return from the wedding" (Lk. 12:35, 36).

2. This marriage is described through the vision of John.

"Let us be glad and rejoice, and give honour to him; for the marriage of the Lamb is come, and his wife hath made herself ready" (Rev. 19:7).

B. The host of the marriage. The New Testament very clearly presents the Father as the divine Host who gives this marriage. He is pictured as preparing it, then sending his servants out to invite the selected guests (Lk. 14:16-23).

C. The Bridegroom of the marriage. The Father's beloved Son (Mt. 3:17; 17:5), the Lord Jesus Christ, is the Bridegroom.

1. As stated by John the Baptist.

"John answered and said, A man can receive nothing except it be given him from heaven. Ye yourselves bear me witness that I said, I am not the Christ, but that I am sent before him. He that hath the bride is the bridegroom; but the friend of the bridegroom, which standeth and heareth him, rejoiceth greatly because of the bridegroom's voice: this my joy therefore is fulfilled. He must increase, but I must decrease" (Jn. 3:27-30).

2. As stated by the Lord Jesus Christ.

"I came not to call the righteous, but sinners to repentance. And they said unto him, Why do the disciples of John fast often, and make prayers . . . but thine eat and drink? And he said unto them, Can ye make the children of the bridechamber fast while the bridegroom is with them? But the days will come when the bridegroom shall be taken away from them, and then shall they fast in those days" (Lk. 5:32-35).

D. The bride of the marriage. In two key passages the Apostle Paul makes crystal clear the identity of the bride:

"Wives, submit yourselves unto your own husbands, as unto the Lord. For the husband is the head of the wife, even as Christ is the head of the church; and he is the Saviour of the body. Therefore, as the church is subject unto Christ, so let the wives be to their own husbands in everything. Husbands, love your wives, even as Christ also loved the church, and gave himself for it, that he might sanctify and cleanse it with the washing of water by the Word, that he might present it to himself a glorious church, not having spot, or wrinkle, or any such thing; but that it should be holy and without blemish. So ought men to love their wives as their own bodies. He that loveth his wife loveth himself. For no man ever yet hated his own flesh, but nourisheth and cherisheth it, even as the Lord the church. For we are members of his body, of his flesh, and of his bones. For this cause shall a man leave his father and mother, and shall be joined unto his wife, and they two shall be one flesh. This is a great mystery; but I speak concerning Christ and the church" (Eph. 5:22-32).

"For I am jealous over you with godly jealousy, for I have espoused you to one husband, that I may present you as a chaste virgin to Christ" (2 Cor. 11:2).

E. The guests of the marriage.

"And he saith unto me, Write, Blessed are they which are called unto the marriage supper of the Lamb . . ." (Rev. 19:9).

Who are these invited guests of the Lamb's marriage to the Church?

1. In general. A group which would include all believing Gentiles who were converted prior to Pentecost or after the rapture.

2. In particular. A group which would include all saved Israelites everywhere. The ten virgins mentioned in Matthew 25 are Israelites. The five wise represent saved Israelites and the five foolish represent unsaved ones. They cannot represent the Church, for the Church is the *bride*, inside with the Bridegroom. The virgins are guests who have been invited to the wedding. Note that a bride is never invited to her own wedding. If she refuses to come, there is no wedding.

F. The service schedule of the marriage. The marriage of Christ to the Church will follow the oriental pattern of marriage as described for us in the New Testament. It consisted of three separate stages:

1. The betrothal stage. New Testament marriages were often begun when the couple was very young (sometimes even prior to birth) by the groom's father. He would sign a legal enactment before the proper judge, pledging his son to a chosen girl. The father would then offer the proper dowry payment. Thus, even though the bride had never seen the groom, she was nevertheless betrothed or espoused to him. A New Testament example of this first step was that of Mary and Joseph.

"Now the birth of Jesus Christ was on this wise: when as his mother Mary was espoused to Joseph, before they came together, she was found with child of the Holy Ghost" (Mt. 1:18).

Both Mary and Joseph had come from Bethlehem and had perhaps been betrothed, or promised to each other, since childhood. But now Mary was found to be with child before the marriage could be consummated, and of course Joseph could arrive at only one conclusion—she had been untrue to him. Then the angel of the Lord explained to Joseph the glories of the virgin birth.

Thus the betrothal stage consisted of two steps: The selection of the bride and the payment of the dowry.

With this in mind we can state that the marriage of the Lamb is still in its betrothal stage:

a. The bride has been selected.

"Blessed be the God and Father of our Lord Jesus Christ, who hath blessed us with all spiritual blessings in heavenly places in Christ, according as he hath chosen us in him before the foundation of the world, that we should be holy and without blame before him in love" (Eph. 1:3, 4).

b. The dowry has been paid.

"What? Know ye not that your body is the temple of the Holy Ghost which is in you, which ye have of God, and ye are not your own? For ye are bought with a price. Therefore, glorify God in your body and in your spirit, which are God's" (1 Cor. 6:19, 20).

"Forasmuch as ye know that ye were not redeemed with corruptible things, as silver and gold . . . but with the precious blood of Christ, as of a lamb without blemish and without spot" (1 Pet. 1:18, 19).

2. The presentation stage. At the proper time the father would send his servants to the house of the bride so that they could carry out the proper legal contract. The bride would then be led to the home of the groom's father.

When all was ready, the father of the bride would place her hand in the hand of the groom's father. He would then place her hand in that of his son.

Applying this background to the marriage of the Lamb, the Church still awaits this second phase, the presentation stage, which we know as the rapture. The following verses speak of this stage:

". . . Christ also loved the church and gave himself for it . . . that he might present it to himself a glorious church, not having spot or wrinkle or any such thing, but that it should be holy and without blemish" (Eph. 5:25, 27).

"Now unto him that is able to keep you from falling, and to present you faultless before the presence of his glory with exceeding joy . . ." (Jude 24).

"Let us be glad and rejoice, and give honour to him, for the marriage of the Lamb is come, and his wife hath made herself ready. And to her was granted that she should be arrayed in fine linen, clean and white; for the fine linen is the righteousness of saints" (Rev. 19:7, 8).

Then follow the events which comprise the second stage:

a. The Heavenly Father will send for the bride.

"After this I looked, and behold, a door was opened in heaven; and the first voice which I heard was as it were of a trumpet talking with me, which said, Come up hither . . ." (Rev. 4:1).

b. The proper legal papers of marriage will be shown.

"Nevertheless the foundation of God standeth sure, having this seal, the Lord knoweth them that are his . . ." (2 Tim. 2:19).

c. The bride will be taken to the Father's home.

"In my Father's house are many mansions; if it were not so I would have told you. I go to prepare a place for you. And if I go and prepare a place for you, I will come again and receive you unto myself, that where I am, there ye may be also" (Jn. 14:2, 3).

3. The celebration stage. After the private marriage service was completed the public marriage supper would begin. To this many guests would be invited. It was during such a celebration that our Lord performed his first miracle, that of changing water into wine (see Jn. 2:1-11). Jesus later made reference to this third step when he spoke the following words:

"Let your loins be girded about and your lights burning, and ye yourselves like unto men that wait for their lord, when he will return from the wedding. . . . Blessed are those servants whom the lord, when he cometh, shall find watching. Verily I say unto you, that he shall gird himself, and make them to sit down to meat, and will come forth and serve them" (Lk. 12:35-37).

G. The time of the marriage. When does the wedding transpire? In view of what has already been said, it would seem that the wedding *service* (the presentation stage) will be privately conducted in heaven, perhaps shortly after the *bema* judgment seat of Christ. The wedding *supper* (the celebration stage) will be publicly conducted on earth shortly after the Second Coming of Christ.

It is no accident that the Bible describes the millennium as occurring right after the celebration supper has begun. (The supper is described in Revelation 19 while the millennium is described in Revelation 20.) In New Testament times the length and cost of this supper were determined by the wealth of the father. Therefore, when his beloved Son is married, the Father of all grace (whose wealth is unlimited) will rise to the occasion by giving his Son and the bride a hallelujah celebration which will last for a thousand years.

H. The certainty of the marriage. Earthly marriages may be prevented because of various unexpected problems.

1. In an earthly wedding there can be a last-minute refusal on the part of either the bride or groom. But not with the heavenly marriage.

   a. The Bridegroom has already expressed his great love for his bride (Eph. 5:25), and he never changes.

      "This same Jesus, which is taken up from you into heaven, shall so come in like manner as ye have seen him go into heaven" (Acts 1:11).

      ". . . Jesus Christ, the same yesterday, and today, and forever" (Heb. 13:8).

   b. The bride has already been glorified and is sinless, and therefore cannot be tempted into changing her mind or losing her love for the Bridegroom.

      ". . . a glorious church, not having spot, or wrinkle . . . but . . . holy and without blemish" (Eph. 5:27).

      "For by one offering he hath perfected forever them that are sanctified" (Heb. 10:14).

2. In an earthly wedding a serious legal problem might arise, such as lack of age, or even that of a previous marriage—but not in the heavenly wedding. (See Rom. 8:33-39.)

3. In an earthly wedding the tragedy of death might intervene—but not in the heavenly wedding.

   a. The bride will never die.

      "And whosoever liveth and believeth in me shall never die" (Jn. 11:26).

   b. The Bridegroom will never die.

      "I am he that liveth, and was dead; and behold, I am alive forever more, Amen" (Rev. 1:18).

IV. The Crisis of a Seven-sealed Book.

A. The proclamation.

   "And I saw in the right hand of him that sat on the throne a book written within and on the backside, sealed with seven seals. And I saw a strong angel proclaiming with a loud voice, Who is worthy to open the book, and to loose the seals thereof?" (Rev. 5:1, 2).

   The circumstances surrounding this crisis occur shortly after the rapture of the church. John has been caught up into heaven (Rev. 4:1), where he writes about the marvelous things he sees and hears.

   1. He sees the glory of the Father upon the throne (Rev. 4:2, 3).

   2. He sees a beautiful green rainbow around this throne (Rev. 4:3).

   3. He sees twenty-four elders with golden crowns (Rev. 4:4). (These twenty-four may consist of a special representative body of both Old Testament and New Testament saints. The Greek text tells us they are all wearing *stephanos* crowns, or martyrs' crowns, rather than diadems, or monarchs' crowns. Thus they must be humans rather than angels.)

   4. He hears lightnings and thunderings, which means that the awful storm of the great tribulation is about to unlash its fury (Rev. 4:5).

   3. He sees a crystal sea of glass (Rev. 4:6).

      Dr. Donald Barnhouse has written concerning this sea:

      "Before the throne there was a glassy sea, like crystal. The concordance immediately takes us to the temple built by Solomon after the model of the tabernacle. 'And he made a molten sea, ten cubits from the one brim to the other; it was round all about, and its height was five cubits' (1 Ki. 7:23). This great basin, fifteen feet in diameter, was supported on the backs of twelve oxen of brass, facing outward. Here the priests came for their cleansing. Each time before they entered the holy place they stopped for the cleansing ceremony. But thank God the laver will be turned to crystal. The day will come when none of the saints will ever need confession! One of the greatest joys in the anticipation of Heaven is that the laver is of crystal. I shall never have to go to the Heavenly Father again to tell Him I have sinned. I shall never have to meet that gaze of Christ that caused Peter to go out and weep bitterly. The laver is of crystal only because I and all the saints of all the ages will have been made like unto the Lord Jesus Christ." (Donald G. Barnhouse, *Revelation: An Expository Commentary*, p. 94)

   6. He sees and hears the testimony of four special angelic creatures (Rev. 4:6-8).

      The first of these creatures had the characteristics of a lion, the second of a calf, the third of a man, and the fourth of an eagle. These six things John sees and writes about, for they fill him with delight. But he now witnesses a seventh event, which causes despair to flood his soul. The crisis of a seven-sealed book is about to begin. What is this book (really a rolled-up scroll), sealed so securely with seven seals? Whatever it contained, the scroll was extremely important, for history informs us that under Roman law all legal documents pertaining to life and death were to be sealed seven times. A number of theologians believe that this is actually the legal title deed to the earth. Thus the angels' proclamation was, in effect: "Who is worthy to reclaim the earth's title deed? Who is able to pour out the seven-sealed judgment, to purify this planet, and to usher in the long-awaited golden-age millennium?" Who indeed *was* worthy?

B. The investigation.

   "And no man in heaven, nor in earth, neither under the earth, was able to open the book, neither to look thereon" (Rev. 5:3).

   Let us follow the angel as he begins his three-fold search.

   1. The search in heaven. Was there any among the redeemed worthy to claim the earth's title deed? There was not.

a. Adam originally possessed this title deed (Gen. 1:28, 29), but was cheated out of it by the devil (Gen. 3:1-19).

b. Noah, the hero of the flood, subsequently became the drunkard of the vineyard, thus disqualifying himself (Gen. 6-9).

c. Abraham, the father of Israel, backslid and went to Egypt temporarily (Gen. 12).

d. David, the man after God's own heart, (1 Sam. 16:7), later broke God's heart through lust and murder (2 Sam. 11).

e. John the Baptist, the forerunner of Christ, in a moment of weakness doubted that same Messiah (Mt. 11:3).

f. Peter, the "rock," denied his Lord in the hour of need (Mt. 26:70).

g. Paul, perhaps the greatest Christian who ever lived, compromised his testimony (Acts 21).

2. The search on earth. Who could accomplish in the sinful environment of earth what no man could achieve even in the sinless environment of heaven? Preachers and priests might minister to the earth, and kings rule over sections of it, but *claim* it they could not.

3. The search under the earth (in hades). If no saint or angel *could* purify this earth, then certainly no sinner or demon *would*.

C. The lamentation.

"And I wept much, because no man was found worthy to open and to read the book, neither to look thereon" (Rev. 5:4).

Why did John weep? Perhaps because (among other things) he realized that the ultimate resurrection and glorification of his own body were directly connected with the removal of the curse placed upon this earth. (See Rom. 8:17-23.)

D. The manifestation.

"And one of the elders saith unto me, Weep not: behold, the Lion of the tribe of Juda, the Root of David, hath prevailed to open the book, and to loose the seven seals thereof. And I beheld, and, lo, in the midst of the throne and of the four beasts, and in the midst of the elders, stood a Lamb as it had been slain, having seven horns and seven eyes, which are the seven Spirits of God sent forth into all the earth. And he came and took the book out of the right hand of him that sat upon the throne" (Rev. 5:5-7).

Who is this heavenly Hero who so boldly removes the scroll from the Father's right hand? We need not speculate for one second about his identity, for he is the Lord Jesus Christ himself. The proof is overwhelming.

1. He has the characteristics of a lamb. Our Lord is referred to as a lamb twenty-nine times in the New Testament. In all but one instance (1 Pet. 1:19) it is the Apostle John who employs this title. Furthermore:

a. It is a pet lamb. There are two words for "lamb" in the Greek New Testament. One is *amnos* (a lamb in general) and the other is *arnion* (a special household pet lamb). Here in Revelation 5:6 the second Greek word is used. For a related Old Testament passage, see 2 Samuel 12:1-4.

b. It is a slain lamb. Here the Greek word for slain is *sphatto,* and refers to a violent death of some sort. The same word is found in the following passage: ". . . we should love one another. Not as Cain, who was of that wicked one, and slew his brother" (1 Jn. 3:11, 12).

The word *sphatto* is found only seven times in the New Testament, and four of these usages refer to the death of Christ (Rev. 5:6, 9, 12; 13:8).

c. It is an all-powerful lamb. The lamb is pictured as possessing seven horns, which in biblical symbolic language refer to power and authority.

d. It is an all-knowing lamb. The lamb is pictured as possessing seven eyes, referring to perfect knowledge and wisdom.

2. He has the characteristics of a lion. John calls him "The Lion of the tribe of Juda, the Root of David," and so he is. Three key Bible chapters explain this title.

a. In Genesis 49 the dying Jacob predicted that Judah, his fourth son, would be like a lion, and that the later kings of Israel, including Christ himself, would come from his tribe (Gen. 49:8-10).

b. In 2 Samuel 7 God told David (who was of the tribe of Judah) that his kingdom would be eternal and that his household would rule forever (2 Sam. 7:8-17).

c. In Luke 1 the angel Gabriel explained to Mary (who was of the house of David) that her virgin-born son would inherit all the Old Testament promises as found in Genesis 49 and 2 Samuel 7 (Lk. 1:30-33).

John sees Christ as a Lamb, since he once came to redeem his people. This was his past work. John also sees him as a lion, for he shall come again to reign over his people. This will be his future work. The *source* of his claim to the earth's scepter is therefore related to his slain lamb characteristics, while the *strength* of his claim is due to his mighty lion characteristics.

E. The adoration. (See Rev. 5:9-14.)

V. The Tribulation. A discouraged and despondent Job once exclaimed in despair:

"Man that is born of a woman is of few days, and full of trouble. He cometh forth like a flower, and is cut down; he fleeth also as a shadow, and continueth not" (Job 14:1, 2).

Job's pessimistic description is tragically true for the unsaved man, apart from the grace of God. Throughout his tortured and sinful history he has been subjected to calamities, disasters, and plagues, which have tracked him as a wolf would a rabbit.

But according to the Bible there is coming a calamity unlike any which this weary world has ever seen. Although this future period will be relatively short, it will nevertheless destroy more of this earth's population than all previous disasters combined. In fact, nearly one billion people will be struck down during the *beginning* of this terrible coming disaster.

A. The names for this period. No less than twelve titles for this blood-chilling period can be found in the Bible.

1. The day of the Lord. This title is used more frequently than any other. See, for example, Isaiah 2:12; 13:6, 9; Ezekiel 13:5; 30:3; Joel 1:15; 2:1, 11, 31; 3:14; Amos 5:18, 20; Obadiah 15; Zephaniah 1:7, 14; Zechariah 14:1; Malachi 4:5; Acts 2:20; 1 Thessalonians 5:2; 2 Thessalonians 2:2; 2 Peter 3:10.

    A distinction should be made between the day of the Lord and the day of Christ. The day of Christ is a reference to the millennium. See 1 Corinthians 1:8; 5:5; 2 Corinthians 1:14; Philippians 1:6, 10; 2:16.

2. The day of God's vengeance (Isa. 34:8; 63:1-6).

3. The time of Jacob's trouble (Jer. 30:7).

4. The seventieth week (Dan. 9:24-27).

5. The time of the end (Dan. 12:9).

6. The great day of his wrath (Rev. 6:17).

7. The hour of his judgment (Rev. 14:7).

8. The end of this world (Mt. 13:40, 49).

9. The indignation (Isa. 26:20; 34:2).

10. The overspreading of abominations (Dan. 9:27).

11. The time of trouble such as never was (Dan. 12:1).

12. The tribulation (Mt. 24:21, 29).

The word "tribulation" is derived from the Latin *tribulum,* which was an agricultural tool used for separating the husks from the corn. As found in the Bible, the theological implications would include such concepts as a pressing together, an affliction, a burdening with anguish and trouble, a binding with oppression.

Keeping this in mind, it would seem that of all the twelve names for the coming calamity the last one would most accurately describe this period. Therefore from this point on, the term tribulation will be employed.

B. The nature of the tribulation. The following passages aptly describe this future and fearful time.

"Howl ye, for the day of the Lord is at hand. . . . Therefore shall all hands be faint, and every man's heart shall melt. . . . For the stars of heaven and the constellations thereof shall not give their light; the sun shall be darkened in his going forth, and the moon shall not cause her light to shine. . . . And I will punish the world for their evil . . ." (Isa. 13:6, 7, 10, 11).

"For the indignation of the Lord is upon all nations, and his fury upon all their armies. . . . Their slain also shall be cast out, and their stink shall come up out of their carcasses, and the mountains shall be melted with their blood. And all the host of heaven shall be dissolved, and the heavens shall be rolled together as a scroll . . ." (Isa. 34:2-4).

"I have trodden the winepress alone . . . for I will tread them in mine anger, and trample them in my fury; and their blood shall be sprinkled upon my garments, and I will stain all my raiment. For the day of vengeance is in mine heart. . . . And I will tread down the

people in mine anger, and make them drunk in my fury . . ." (Isa. 63:3, 4, 6).

"For nation shall rise against nation, and kingdom against kingdom; and there shall be famines and pestilences and earthquakes in divers places. . . . And many false prophets shall rise, and shall deceive many. And because iniquity shall abound, the love of many shall wax cold. . . . For then shall be great tribulation, such as was not since the beginning of the world to this time, no, nor ever shall be. And except those days should be shortened, there should no flesh be saved . . ." (Mt. 24:7, 11, 12, 21, 22).

"And there shall be signs in the sun and in the moon and in the stars, and upon the earth distress of nations, with perplexity, the sea and the waves roaring, men's hearts failing them for fear . . . for the powers of heaven shall be shaken" (Lk. 21:25, 26).

". . . the day of the Lord so cometh as a thief in the night. For when they shall say, Peace and safety, then sudden destruction cometh upon them, as travail upon a woman with child; and they shall not escape" (1 Thess. 5:2, 3).

". . . and, lo, there was a great earthquake; and the sun became black as sackcloth of hair, and the moon became as blood; and the stars of heaven fell unto the earth, even as a fig tree casteth her untimely figs, when she is shaken of a mighty wind. And the heaven departed as a scroll when it is rolled together; and every mountain and island were moved out of their places. And the kings of the earth, and the great men, and the rich men, and the chief captains, and the mighty men, and every bondman, and every free man, hid themselves in the dens and in the rocks of the mountains, and said to the mountains and rocks, Fall on us, and hide us from the face of him that sitteth on the throne, and from the wrath of the Lamb, for the great day of his wrath is come; and who shall be able to stand?" (Rev. 6:12-17).

C. The length of the tribulation. To establish this time-span we must now briefly consider the most important, the most amazing, and the most profound single prophecy in the entire Word of God. It is often referred to as the prophecy of the seventy weeks, and was written by Daniel, who was living in Babylon around 550 B.C. Daniel, a former Jewish captive, had been reading Jeremiah's prophecy, which predicted that after a seventy-year captivity period, God would permit the Jews to return to Jerusalem (Jer. 25:11; 29:10). As Daniel studied those words he began to pray, confessing both his sins and the sins of Israel. During this powerful and tearful prayer, the angel Gabriel appeared to Daniel and related to him the prophecy of the seventy weeks, which reads as follows:

"Seventy weeks are determined upon thy people and upon thy holy city, to finish the transgression, and to make an end of sins, and to make reconciliation for iniquity, and to bring in everlasting righteousness, and to seal up the vision and prophecy, and to anoint the most holy. Know therefore and understand, that from the going forth of the commandment to restore and to build Jerusalem unto the Messiah the Prince shall be seven weeks, and threescore and two weeks; the street shall be built again, and the wall, even in troublous times. And after threescore and two weeks shall Messiah be cut off, but not for himself; and the people of the prince that shall come shall destroy the city and the sanctuary; and the end thereof shall be with a flood, and unto the end of the war desolations are determined. And he shall confirm the covenant with many for one week: and in the midst of the week he shall cause the sacrifice and the oblation to cease, and for the overspreading of abominations he shall make it desolate, even until the consummation, and that determined shall be poured upon the desolate" (Dan. 9:24-27).

1. To whom does this prophecy refer? It refers to Israel.
2. What is meant by the term "seventy weeks"? In his correspondence course on the book of Daniel, Dr. Alfred Martin of Moody Bible Institute writes the following helpful words:
   "The expression translated 'seventy weeks' is literally 'seventy sevens.' Apart from the context one would not know what the 'sevens' were. One would have to inquire, 'seven of what?' This expression in Hebrew would be as ambiguous as if one were to say in English, 'I went to the store and bought a dozen.' A dozen of what? One of the basic principles of interpretation is that one must always interpret in the light of the context, that is, in the light of the passage in which a given statement occurs. As one searches this context, remembering that the vision was given in answer to the prayer, one notes that Daniel had been reading in Jeremiah that God would 'accomplish seventy years in the desolations of Jerusalem' (Dan. 9:2). This is the clue. Daniel is told in effect, 'Yes, God will accomplish seventy years in the captivity; but now He is showing you that the whole history of the people of Israel will be consummated in a period of seventy sevens of years.'" (Alfred Martin, *Daniel, the Framework of Prophecy*, pp. 85, 86)

   To further clarify the meaning of the seventy weeks, it should be noted that Israel had in its calendar not only a week of seven days (as in Ex. 23:12), but also a "week" of seven years (Gen. 29:27, 28; Lev. 25:3, 4, 8-10). In other words, God is here telling Daniel that he would continue to deal with Israel for another 490 years before bringing in everlasting righteousness.
3. When was the seventy-week period to begin? It was to begin with the command to rebuild Jerusalem's walls. The first two chap-

ters of Nehemiah inform us that this command was issued during the twentieth year of Artaxerxes' accession. The *Encyclopaedia Britannica* sets this date on March 14, 445 B.C.

4. What are the four distinct time periods mentioned within the seventy-week prophecy and what was to happen during each period?
   a. First period. Seven weeks (forty-nine years), from 445 B.C. to 396 B.C. The key event during this time was the building of the streets and walls of Jerusalem "even in troublous times." This literally took place. See Nehemiah 2-6.
   b. Second period. Sixty-two weeks (434 years), from 396 B.C. to A.D. 30. At the end of this second period the Messiah was crucified. See Matthew 27, Mark 15, Luke 23, and John 19.

   The brilliant British scholar and Bible student, Sir Robert Anderson, has reduced the first two periods into their exact number of days. This he has done by multiplying 483 (the combined years of the first two periods) by 360 (the days in a biblical year, as pointed out in Genesis 7:11, 24; 8:3, 4).

   The total number of days in the first sixty-nine weeks (or 483 years) is 173,880. Anderson then points out that if one begins counting on March 14, 445 B.C., and goes forward in history, these days would run out on April 6, A.D. 32.

   It was on this very day that Jesus made his triumphal entry into the city of Jerusalem! Surely our Lord must have had Daniel's prophecy in mind when he said, "If thou hadst known, even thou, at least in this thy day, the things which belong to thy peace! But now they are hid from thine eyes" (Lk. 19:42).

   Of course, it was also on this same day that the Pharisees plotted to murder Christ (Lk. 19:47). Thus Daniel, writing some five-and-one-half centuries earlier, correctly predicted the very day of Christ's presentation and rejection!
   c. Third period. One-half week (three-and-one-half years), the first half of the tribulation. At the beginning of this period the antichrist will make a seven-year pact with Israel.
   d. Fourth period. One-half week (three-and-one-half years), the last half of the tribulation. At the beginning of this period the antichrist will break his pact with Israel and will begin his terrible bloodbath. At the end of the last week (and of the entire seventy-week period), the true Messiah will come and establish his perfect millennium.
5. Do the seventy weeks run continuously? That is to say, is there a gap somewhere between these 490 years, or do they run without pause until they are completed?

   Dispensational theology teaches that these "weeks" do not run continuously, but that there has been a gap or parenthesis of nearly

2000 years between the sixty-ninth and seventieth week.

The chronology may be likened to a seventy-minute basketball game. For sixty-nine minutes the game has been played at a furious and continuous pace. Then the referee for some reason calls time out with the clock in the red and showing one final minute of play. No one knows for sure when the action will start again, but at some point the referee will step in and blow his whistle. At that time the teams will gather to play out the last minute of the game.

God has stepped in and stopped the clock of prophecy at Calvary. This divine "time out" has already lasted some twenty centuries, but soon now the Redeemer will blow his trumpet and the final "week" of action will be played upon this earth.

6. Does the Bible offer any other examples of time gaps in divine programs? It does indeed. At least three instances come to mind in which gaps of many centuries can be found in a single short paragraph.
   a. Isaiah 9:6, 7. In the first part of verse 6 a gap of at least twenty centuries is separated by a colon. The phrase "unto us a son is given" refers to Bethlehem, while the words "and the government shall be upon his shoulder" look forward to the millennium.
   b. Zechariah 9:9, 10. Verse 9 is a clear reference to the triumphal entry of our Lord, but verse 10 looks ahead to the millennium.
   c. Isaiah 61:1, 2. In verse 2 of this passage Christ's earthly ministry (to "proclaim the acceptable year of the Lord") and the tribulation (the "day of vengeance of our God") are separated by only a comma. It is extremely important to note that when Jesus read this passage during his sermon in Nazareth, he ended the reading at this comma, for "the day of vengeance" was not the purpose of his first coming. See Luke 4:18, 19.

D. The purpose of the tribulation. Why this terrible period? At least six scriptural reasons are forthcoming:
   1. To harvest the crop that has been sown throughout the ages by God, Satan, and mankind. This aspect is so important that our Lord took an entire sermon to discuss it. (See Mt. 13:3-8, 18-30, 37-43.)
   2. To prove the falseness of the devil's claim. Since his fall (Isa. 14:12-14), Satan has been attempting to convince a skeptical universe that he rather than Christ is the logical and rightful ruler of creation. Therefore, during the tribulation the sovereign God will give him a free and unhindered hand to make good his boast. Needless to say, Satan will fail miserably.
   3. To prepare a great martyred multitude for heaven.
      "After this I beheld, and, lo, a great multitude, which no man could number, of all nations and kindreds and people and tongues, stood before the throne. . . . These are they which came out of great tribulation, and have washed their robes, and made them white in the blood of the lamb" (Rev. 7:9, 14).
   4. To prepare a great living multitude for the millennium.
      "And before him shall be gathered all nations; and he shall separate them one from another, as a shepherd divideth his sheep from the goats; and he shall set the sheep on his right hand, but the goats on the left. Then shall the king say unto them on his right hand, Come, ye blessed of my Father, inherit the kingdom prepared for you from the foundation of the world" (Mt. 25:32-34).
   5. To punish the Gentiles.
      "For the wrath of God is revealed from heaven against all ungodliness and unrighteousness of men . . ." (Rom. 1:18).
      "And for this cause God shall send them strong delusion, that they should believe a lie, that they all might be damned who believe not the truth, but had pleasure in unrighteousness" (2 Thess. 2:11, 12).
   6. To purge Israel.
      "And I will cause you to pass under the rod . . . and I will purge out from among you the rebels . . ." (Ezek. 20:37, 38).
      "And he shall sit as a refiner and purifier of silver; and he shall purify the sons of Levi, and purge them as gold and silver, that they may offer unto the Lord an offering in righteousness" (Mal. 3:3).

E. The personalities of the tribulation. As in a Shakespearean play, a number of actors will render their parts and say their lines during the earth's most sobering drama, the tribulation.
   1. The Holy Spirit. Contrary to some, the Holy Spirit will *not* be removed when the church is raptured. He will instead (it would seem) perform a ministry similar to his work in the Old Testament. At any rate, his presence will be felt in the tribulation, as indicated by the prophet Joel. (See Joel 2:28, 30-32.)
   2. The devil.
      "Woe to the inhabiters of the earth and of the sea! For the devil is come down unto you, having great wrath, because he knoweth that he hath but a short time" (Rev. 12:12).
   3. Two special (Old Testament?) witnesses.
      "And I will give power unto my two witnesses, and they shall prophesy a thousand two hundred and threescore days, clothed in sackcloth" (Rev. 11:3).
   4. The antichrist.
      "And he shall speak great words against the most High, and shall wear out the saints of the most High . . ." (Dan. 7:25).
      "And the king shall do according to his will; and he shall exalt himself, and magnify himself above every god, and shall

speak . . . things against the God of gods . . ." (Dan. 11:36).

"And I stood upon the sand of the sea and saw a beast rise up out of the sea. . . . And the beast which I saw was like unto a leopard, and his feet were as the feet of a bear, and his mouth as the mouth of a lion; and the dragon gave him his power . . . and great authority. . . . And he opened his mouth in blasphemy against God . . ." (Rev. 13:1, 2, 6).

5. The false prophet.

"And I beheld another beast coming up out of the earth . . ." (Rev. 13:11).

6. A multitude of specialized angels. Angels have been employed throughout the Bible to perform God's work, but at no other time will they be as busy as during the tribulation. The book of Revelation describes the following for us:

   a. Seven angels with seven trumpets (Rev. 8, 9, 11).
   b. Seven angels with seven vials of wrath (Rev. 16).
   c. An angel with the seal of the living God (Rev. 7:2).
   d. An angel with a golden censer (Rev. 8:3).
   e. An angel with a little book and a measuring reed (Rev. 10:1, 2; 11:1).
   f. An angel with the everlasting gospel (Rev. 14:6).
   g. An angel with a harvest sickle (Rev. 14:19).
   h. An angel with a message of doom (Rev. 18:1, 21).
   i. An angel with a strange invitation (Rev. 19:17).
   j. An angel with a key and a great chain (Rev. 20:1).

   In the Old Testament the prophet Daniel informs us that one of these angels will be Michael the archangel himself (Dan. 12:1).

7. One-hundred-forty-four thousand Israelite preachers.

   The Bible clearly teaches that the 144,000 will consist of 12,000 saved and commissioned preachers from each of the twelve tribes of Israel (Rev. 7). It is interesting to compare the various listings of Israel's twelve tribes in the Bible. For example, here in Revelation 7 the two tribes of Dan and Ephraim are omitted and are replaced by Joseph (Ephraim's father) and Levi (Dan's priestly brother).

   We are not told the reason for this omission. Some believe that Dan is left out because of the hint that the antichrist will come from this tribe (Gen. 49:17; Jer. 8:16). Ephraim's absence may possibly be accounted for due to their sad tendency to apostatize (Hosea 6:4, 10).

   Whatever the reason for their omission here, the glorious fact remains that both Dan and Ephraim take their rightful place in the land of Israel during the millennium. Both are mentioned by Ezekiel (Ezek. 48:2, 5) as he describes the location of the twelve tribes during Christ's thousand-year reign.

   Dr. J. Dwight Pentecost offers the following interesting words concerning the conversion of the 144,000:

   "In 1 Corinthians 15:8 is a clue concerning the way God will work after the church's rapture. After the apostle has listed those to whom the resurrected Christ appeared, so as to authenticate His resurrection, he says, 'And last of all he was seen of me also, as of one born out of due time.' This phrase, 'born out of due time,' means a premature birth. That is exactly what the apostle Paul is saying—'I was one that was born prematurely.' What did he mean? Comparing Revelation 7 with Paul's statement in 1 Corinthians 15, we conclude that after the rapture of the church, God will perform the same miracle He performed in Saul of Tarsus on the Damascus Road 144,000 times over."(J. Dwight Pentecost, *Will Man Survive?* p. 148)

8. An army of locust-like demons from the bottomless pit (Rev. 9:1–12).

   a. The description of these demons.

      "The locusts looked like horses armored for battle. They had what looked like golden crowns on their heads, and their faces looked like men's. Their hair was long like women's, and their teeth were those of lions. They wore breastplates that seemed to be of iron, and their wings roared like an army of chariots rushing into battle. They had stinging tails like scorpions, and their power to hurt, given to them for five months, was in their tails" (Rev. 9:7-10, *TLB*).

   b. The destruction by these demons.

      "They were told not to hurt the grass or plants or trees, but to attack those people who did not have the mark of God on their foreheads. They were not to kill them, but to torture them for five months with agony like the pain of scorpion stings. In those days men will try to kill themselves, but won't be able to—death will not come. They will long to die—but death will flee away!" (Rev. 9:4-6, *TLB*).

      In this chapter we learn for the first time of a place called the bottomless pit. God mentions it no less than seven times in the book of Revelation. See Revelation 9:1, 2, 11; 11:7; 17:8; 20:1, 3. It is possible that this is the same place referred to by both Peter and Jude in their writings. See 2 Peter 2:4; Jude 6.

9. An army of horse-and-rider demons from the Euphrates River (Rev. 9:13–21).

   a. Their appearance and actions.

      "I saw their horses spread out before me in my vision; their riders wore fiery-red breastplates, though some were sky-blue and others yellow. The horses' heads looked much like lions', and smoke and fire and flaming sulphur billowed from their mouths, killing one-third of all mankind. Their power of death was not only in their mouths, but in their tails as well, for their tails were similar to serpents' heads that struck and bit with fatal wounds" (Rev. 9:17-19, *TLB*).

b. Their number. This hellish demonic army will number 200 million strong (Rev. 9:16).

c. Their leaders.

" 'Release the four mighty demons held bound at the great River Euphrates.' They had been kept in readiness for that year and month and day and hour, and now they were turned loose to kill a third of all mankind" (Rev. 9:14, 15, *TLB*).

Thus this fantastic army of 200 million is led into battle by these four demons.

10. Three evil spirits.

"And I saw three evil spirits disguised as frogs leap from the mouth of the Dragon, the Creature, and his False Prophet. These miracle-working demons conferred with all the rulers of the world to gather them for battle against the Lord on that great coming Judgment Day of God Almighty" (Rev. 16:13, 14, *TLB*).

11. A cruel, power-mad ruler from the north. Some 2600 years ago a Hebrew prophet named Ezekiel prophesied that a wicked and God-hating nation north of Palestine would rise up and invade Israel just prior to the Second Coming of Christ. He predicts this in Ezekiel 38 and 39, where we learn the following information:

a. That the name of this nation will be Rosh (Ezek. 38:2, *NASB*). In this same verse Ezekiel specifies two cities of Rosh, Meshech and Tubal. These names are remarkably similar to those of Moscow and Tobalek, the two ruling city capitals of Russia today.

b. That the name of the leader of this nation will be Gog (Ezek. 38:3).

c. That Russia (Rosh) will invade Israel in the latter days (Ezek. 38:8).

d. That this invasion will be aided by various allies of Rosh (Ezek. 38:5, 6), such as
(1) Iran (Persia);
(2) South Africa (Ethiopia);
(3) North Africa (Libya);
(4) Eastern Europe (Gomer);
(5) Southern Russia (Togarmah).

In Ezekiel 38:15 the prophet describes the major part that horses will play during this invasion. It is a well-known fact that the cossacks of southern Russia have always owned and bred the largest herd of horses in history.

12. A persecuted woman.

"And there appeared a great wonder in heaven: a woman clothed with the sun, and the moon under her feet, and upon her head a crown of twelve stars" (Rev. 12:1).

These words are unquestionably symbolic, but to whom do they refer?

a. Her identity.

(1) She is not Mary. Mary never spent three and a half years in the wilderness, as does this woman (Rev. 12:6, 14). Neither was Mary personally hated, chased, and persecuted, as we see here (Rev. 12:13, 17). While Mary did give birth to that One who will someday "rule all nations with a rod of iron" (Rev. 12:5), the language in this chapter has a wider reference than to Mary.

(2) She is not the church. The church did not bring the manchild into existence, as does this woman (Rev. 12:5), but rather the opposite. See Matthew 16:18.

(3) She is Israel. A Jewish Christian who reads Revelation 12:1 will undoubtedly think back to the Old Testament passage in which Joseph describes a strange dream to his father and eleven brothers:

"Behold, I have dreamed a dream . . . the sun and the moon and eleven stars made obeisance to me" (Gen. 37:9).

This was of course fulfilled when Joseph's eleven brothers bowed down to him in Egypt (Gen. 43:28). The point of all the above is that the language of Revelation 12:1 describes Israel and nothing else.

b. Her activities.

(1) This woman (Israel) is hated by Satan because of:

(a) Her historical work of bringing Christ into the world (Micah 5:2; Rev. 12:5, 13).

(b) Her future work of spreading the gospel to the world (Mt. 24:14; Rev. 7:1-8; 12:17).

(2) This woman is hidden by God for three and a half years (Rev. 12:6, 14). Some believe on the basis of Zechariah 13:9 that approximately one third of the Israelites living during the awful tribulation will escape the wrath of Satan by fleeing to the ancient city of Petra.

13. A vile harlot.

"One of the seven angels who had poured out the plagues came over and talked with me. 'Come with me,' he said, 'and I will show you what is going to happen to the Notorious Prostitute, who sits upon the many waters of the world. The kings of the world have had immoral relations with her, and the people of the earth have been made drunk by the wine of her immorality.' So the angel took me in spirit into the wilderness. There I saw a woman sitting on a scarlet animal that had seven heads and ten horns, written all over with blasphemies against God. The woman wore purple and scarlet clothing and beautiful jewelry made of gold and precious gems and pearls, and held in her hand a golden goblet full of obscenities. A mysterious caption was written on her forehead: 'Babylon the Great, Mother of Prostitutes and Idol Worship Everywhere around the World.' I could see that she was drunk—drunk with the blood of the martyrs of Jesus she had killed. I stared at her in horror" (Rev. 17:1-6, *TLB*).

14. An arrogant queen.

"After all this I saw another angel come down from heaven with great authority, and the earth grew bright with his splendor. He gave a mighty shout, 'Babylon the Great is fallen, is fallen; she has become a den of demons, a haunt of devils and every kind of evil spirit. For all the nations have drunk the fatal wine of her intense immorality. The rulers of earth have enjoyed themselves with her, and businessmen throughout the world have grown rich from all her luxurious living.' Then I heard another voice calling from heaven, 'Come away from her, my people; do not take part in her sins, or you will be punished with her. For her sins are piled as high as heaven and God is ready to judge her for her crimes. Do to her as she has done to you, and more—give double penalty for all her evil deeds. She brewed many a cup of woe for others—give twice as much to her. She has lived in luxury and pleasure—matching it now with torments and with sorrows. She boasts, "I am queen upon my throne. I am no helpless widow. I will not experience sorrow" ' " (Rev. 18:1-7, *TLB*).

15. A pure bride.

"Let us be glad and rejoice, and give honour to him, for the marriage of the Lamb is come, and his wife hath made herself ready. And to her was granted that she should be arrayed in fine linen, clean and white; for the fine linen is the righteousness of saints" (Rev. 19:7, 8).

This is, of course, a description of the church, which is composed of all believers saved from Pentecost to the rapture. See 2 Corinthians 11:2; Ephesians 5:23-32.

16. A mighty warrior from heaven.

"And I saw heaven opened, and behold, a white horse; and he that sat upon him was called Faithful and True, and in righteousness he doth judge and make war. His eyes were as a flame of fire, and on his head were many crowns; and he had a name written that no man knew, but he himself. And he was clothed with a vesture dipped in blood: and his name is called The Word of God. And the armies which were in heaven followed him upon white horses, clothed in fine linen, white and clean. And out of his mouth goeth a sharp sword, that with it he should smite the nations: and he shall rule them with a rod of iron: and he treadeth the winepress of the fierceness and wrath of Almighty God. And he hath on his vesture and on his thigh a name written, KING OF KINGS, AND LORD OF LORDS" (Rev. 19:11-16).

a. His identity. There is absolutely no doubt whatsoever as to whom these words refer. No angel in heaven, no soldier on earth, no demon in hell could even remotely fill this description. This heavenly warrior is the Lord Jesus Christ himself.

b. His names and titles.
   (1) Faithful and True.
   (2) The Word of God.
   (3) The King of kings.
   (4) The Lord of lords.
   (5) A name known only to himself.

c. His purpose for coming.
   (1) To smite the nations.
   (2) To judge the nations.
   (3) To rule the nations.

One other passage in Revelation describes this breathtaking event:

"And the seventh angel sounded; and there were great voices in heaven, saying, The kingdoms of this world are become the kingdoms of our Lord, and of his Christ; and he shall reign forever and ever. And the four and twenty elders which sat before God on their seats fell upon their faces and worshiped God, saying, We give thee thanks, O Lord God Almighty, which art, and wast, and art to come; because thou hast taken to thee thy great power, and hast reigned. And the nations were angry, and thy wrath is come, and the time of the dead, that they should be judged, and that thou shouldest give reward unto thy servants the prophets, and to the saints, and them that fear thy name, small and great; and shouldest destroy them which destroy the earth" (Rev. 11:15-18).

F. The chronology of the tribulation. We have examined very briefly the sixteen main *actors* of the tribulation; now we turn our attention to the *action* of this seven-year period. *The first half of the tribulation* (three-and-one-half years):

1. The formal organization of the super harlot church (Rev. 17).

2. The appearance of the antichrist and his false prophet. We have already observed a number of things about this perverted pair from the pit. See Daniel 7:19-25; 11:36-45; 2 Thes-

salonians 2:1–12; Revelation 13. It is entirely possible that the antichrist will come from the United Nations, while the false prophet may well proceed from the World Council of Churches.

It is also entirely feasible that both personages are alive and active in this world right now, and are waiting for the rapture to remove the final barrier, thus allowing them to begin their deadly and damnable work.

3. The revival of the Roman Empire (Dan. 2:41; 7:7, 8; Rev. 13:1; 17:12). During his Olivet discourse our Lord uttered the following sober sentence concerning Jerusalem. It was both historical and prophetical in its scope.

> ". . . and Jerusalem shall be trodden down of the Gentiles, until the times of the Gentiles be fulfilled" (Lk. 21:24).

Concerning this, Scofield observes,

> "The 'times of the Gentiles' began with the captivity of Judah under Nebuchadnezzar (2 Chron. 36:1–21), since which time Jerusalem has been under Gentile overlordship." (*Scofield Bible,* p. 1106)

Both the history and the prophecy of Christ's statement are taken from two chapters in the book of Daniel. In chapter 2 God reveals these "times of the Gentiles" to a Babylonian king, and in chapter 7 he reveals his great secret to Daniel himself.

From these two extended passages and from secular history we learn that:

a. Four major powers (or kingdoms) will rule over Palestine.
b. These powers are viewed by mankind as gold, silver, brass, iron, and clay.
c. These powers are viewed by God as four wild animals: a winged lion, a bear, a winged leopard, and an indescribably brutal and vicious animal.
d. These four powers stand for
   (1) Babylon—from 625 B.C. to 539 B.C.
   (2) Medo-Persia—from 539 B.C. to 331 B.C.
   (3) Greece—from 331 B.C. to 323 B.C.
   (4) Rome—three periods are to be noted here:
     (a) The first period—the original empire—from 300 B.C. to A.D. 476.
     (b) The second period—the intervening influence—from A.D. 476 to the present. We are amazed at Rome's continuing world influence centuries after the official collapse of its empire. As Erich Sauer observes,

> "The Roman *administration* lives on in the Church of Rome. The ecclesiastical provinces coincided with the State provinces; and Rome, the chief city of the world empire, became the chief city of the world church, the seat of the Papacy.

> The Roman *tongue* lives on in the Latin of the Church, and is still in use in the international technical language of law, medicine, and natural science.

> The Roman *law* lives on in legislation. The Corpus Juris Romanum (body of Roman law) of the Eastern Roman Emperor Justinian (A.D. 527–565) became the foundation of jurisprudence among the Latin and Germanic peoples throughout the Middle Ages and far into Modern times.

> The Roman *army* lives on in military systems. It became the model for armaments and western defence. We still use Latin words such as captain, major, general, battalion, regiment, army, infantry, artillery, and cavalry." (Erich Sauer, *The Triumph of the Crucified,* p. 132)

     (c) The third period—the revived empire—from the rapture to Armageddon.

e. This revived Roman Empire will consist of ten nations.
f. The antichrist will personally unite these western nations.

One has only to consult his newspaper in order to follow the rapid present-day fulfillment of this revived Roman Empire prophecy. Students of history will readily agree that the unity of any empire of nations depends upon four factors. These are the military, the economic, the political, and the religious.

4. The antichrist's seven-year covenant with Israel.

> "And your covenant with death shall be disannulled, and your agreement with hell shall not stand" (Isa. 28:18).

> "And he shall confirm the covenant with many for one week . . ." (Dan. 9:27).

a. The background of the covenant. From June 4 through June 8, 1967, the world-famous six-day war between Israel and Egypt took place. When the smoke had cleared, Israel had won a stunning and fantastic victory. Her land area had increased from 7,992 square miles to over 26,000 square miles. With less than 50,000 troops she had all but annihilated Nasser's 90,000 soldiers. During that fateful week Egypt suffered 30,000 casualties, 197 planes, 700 tanks, and watched two billion dollars go up in smoke. Israel, on the other hand, lost 61 tanks, 275 dead, and 800 wounded. But in spite of all this, Israel's position in Palestine today is anything but secure. She continues to find herself surrounded by powerful enemies who have sworn by their gods to drive her into the sea. In addition to this her northern neighbor, Soviet Russia, views her land with growing interest.

The Word of God indicates that this already intolerable situation will worsen. Then (shortly after the rapture), to her astonishment and relief, a powerful Western leader (the antichrist) will pretend to befriend Israel. In fact, he will propose a special seven-year security treaty, guaranteeing to maintain the status quo in the Middle East. Israel will swallow this poisoned bait, hook, line, and sinker.

   b. The betrayal of the covenant.

"This king will make a seven-year treaty with the people, but after half that time, he will break his pledge and stop the Jews from all their sacrifices and their offerings; then, as a climax to all his terrible deeds, the Enemy shall utterly defile the sanctuary of God . . ." (Dan. 9:27, *TLB*).

5. The pouring out of the first six seals (Mt. 24:4–8; Rev. 6:1–17).

"And I saw in the right hand of him that sat on the throne a book written within and on the backside, sealed with seven seals" (Rev. 5:1).

"And I saw when the Lamb opened one of the seals, and I heard as it were the noise of thunder . . ." (Rev. 6:1).

   a. The first seal (Rev. 6:2).
   b. The second seal (Rev. 6:3, 4).
   c. The third seal (Rev. 6:5, 6).
   d. The fourth seal (Rev. 6:7, 8).
   e. The fifth seal (Rev. 6:9–11).
   f. The sixth seal (Rev. 6:12–17).

6. The mass return of the Jews to Palestine. One of the most remarkable chapters in all the Bible concerns itself with the latter-day return of the Jews to Palestine (Ezek. 37:1–14).

Even today we see the beginning of this future Israelite ingathering.

In 1882 there were approximately 25,000 Jews in Palestine.
In 1900 there were 50,000.
In 1922 there were 84,000.
In 1931 there were 175,000.
In 1948 there were 650,000.
In 1952 there were 1,421,000.
Today there are approximately 3,000,000 Jews in Palestine.

Thus the number of Jews has increased nearly 120 times in less than 95 years! They have been gathered from over one hundred countries.

7. The conversion and call of the 144,000.

"And after these things I saw four angels standing on the four corners of the earth, holding the four winds of the earth, that the wind should not blow on the earth, nor on the sea, nor on any tree. And I saw another angel ascending from the east, having the seal of the living God; and he cried with a loud voice to the four angels, to whom it was given to hurt the earth and the sea, saying, Hurt not the earth, neither the sea, nor the trees, till we have sealed the servants of our God in their foreheads. And I heard the number of them which were sealed: and there were sealed an hundred and forty and four thousand of all the tribes of the children of Israel" (Rev. 7:1–4).

This passage does not mean that God will save only Jews during the tribulation, for in Revelation 7:9–17 the Bible declares that a great multitude from every nation will be saved. What this chapter does teach, however, is that God will send out 144,000 "Hebrew Billy Sundays" to evangelize the world. This will be a massive number indeed, especially when we consider that there are less than 35,000 missionaries of all persuasions in the world today.

Our Lord doubtless had the ministry of the 144,000 in mind when he said,

"And this gospel of the kingdom shall be preached in all the world for a witness unto all nations; and then shall the end come" (Mt. 24:14).

8. The rebuilding of the Jewish Temple. There is ample scriptural evidence to show that the antichrist will allow (and perhaps even encourage) the building of the Temple and the rendering of its sacrifices during the tribulation. See Daniel 9:27; 12:11; Matthew 24:15; 2 Thessalonians 2:4; Revelation 13:14, 15; 11:2.

9. The ministry of the two witnesses (Rev. 11:3–13).

   a. Their identity. A number of scholars believe these two are Moses and Elijah.
   b. Their ministry.
     (1) To prophesy in sackcloth before men as God's anointed lampstands.
     (2) To destroy their enemies in the same manner that their enemies would attempt to destroy them.
     (3) To prevent rain for three and a half years.
     (4) To turn waters into blood.
     (5) To smite the earth with every kind of plague.
   c. Their death.
     (1) The antichrist is finally allowed to kill them.
     (2) To show his contempt for them, he refuses to permit their dead bodies to be buried, but leaves them to rot in the streets of Jerusalem.
     (3) All the earth celebrates their deaths through a hellish Christmas; men actually send gifts to each other!
     (4) The dead bodies of these two prophets are viewed by all the nations of the world in a three-and-a-half day period.

d. Their resurrection (here the word "great" appears three times).
  (1) A great voice calls them up to heaven (Rev. 11:12).
  (2) A great fear falls upon those who witness this (Rev. 11:11).
  (3) A great earthquake levels one-tenth of Jerusalem and kills 7000 prominent men (Rev. 11:13).

G. *The middle segment of the tribulation* (a brief undetermined period). We have already suggested that the seven-year tribulation may be broken up into three sections. The first part is three-and-one-half years, the middle perhaps just a few days, and the last again three-and-one-half years. We shall now observe six important events which may, with some degree of certainty, be placed in this brief middle period.
  1. The Gog and Magog invasion into Palestine (Ezek. 38, 39).
    "Son of man, set thy face toward Gog, of the land of Magog, the prince of Rosh, Meshech, and Tubal, and prophesy against him, and say, Thus saith the Lord Jehovah: Behold, I am against thee, O Gog, prince of Rosh, Meshech, and Tubal . . ." (Ezek. 38:2, 3, *ASV*, 1901).
    a. The identity of the invaders. Where is the land of Magog? It seems almost certain that these verses in Ezekiel refer to none other than that Communist bear, the U.S.S.R. Note the following threefold proof of this.
      (1) Geographical proof. Ezekiel tells us in three distinct passages (38:6, 15; 39:2) that this invading nation will come from the "uttermost parts of the north" (as the original Hebrew renders it). A quick glance at any world map will show that only Russia can fulfill this description.
      (2) Historical proof. The ancient Jewish historian Josephus (first century A.D.) assures us that the descendants of Magog (who was Japheth's son and Noah's grandson) migrated to an area north of Palestine. But even prior to Josephus, the famous Greek historian Herodotus (fifth century B.C.) writes that Meshech's descendants settled north of Palestine.
      (3) Linguistic proof. Dr. John Walvoord writes concerning this,
        "In Ezekiel 38, Gog is described as 'the prince of Rosh' *(ASV)*. The Authorized Version expresses it as the 'chief prince.' The translation 'the prince of Rosh' is a more literal rendering of the Hebrew. 'Rosh' may be the root of the modern term 'Russia.' In the study of how ancient words come into modern language, it is quite common for the consonants to remain the same and the vowels to be changed. In the word 'Rosh,' if the vowel 'O' is changed to 'U' it becomes the root of the modern word 'Russia' with the suffix added. In other words, the word itself seems to be an early form of the word from which the modern word 'Russia' comes. Genesius, the famous lexicographer, gives the assurance that this is a proper identification, that is, that Rosh is an early form of the word from which we get Russia. The two terms 'Mesheck' and 'Tubal' also correspond to some prominent words in Russia. The term 'Mesheck' is similar to the modern name 'Moscow' and 'Tubal' is obviously similar to the name of one of the prominent Asiatic provinces of Russia, the province of Tobolsk. When this evidence is put together, it points to the conclusion that these terms are early references to portions of Russia; therefore the geographic argument is reinforced by the linguistic argument and supports the idea that this invading force comes from Russia." (*The Nations in Prophecy,* pp. 107, 108)
    b. The allies in the invasion. Ezekiel lists five nations who will join Russia during her invasion. These are Persia, Ethiopia, Libya, Gomar, and Togarmah. These may (although there is some uncertainty) refer to the following present-day nations:

    Persia—modern Iran
    Ethiopia—Black African nations (South Africa)
    Libya—Arabic African nations (North Africa)
    Gomer—East Germany
    Togarmah—Southern Russia and the Cossacks, or perhaps Turkey

    c. The reasons for the invasion.
      (1) To cash in on the riches of Palestine (Ezek. 38:11, 12).
      (2) To control the Middle East. Ancient conquerors have always known that he who would control Europe, Asia, and Africa must first control that Middle East bridge which leads to these three continents.
      (3) To challenge the authority of the antichrist (Dan. 11:40–44).
    d. The chronology of the invasion. Here it is utterly impossible to be dogmatic. The following is therefore only a suggested possibility, based on Ezekiel 38 and Daniel 11:40–44.
      (1) Following a preconceived plan, Egypt attacks Palestine from the south (Dan. 11:40a).
      (2) Russia thereupon invades Israel from the north by both an amphibious and a land attack (Dan. 11:40b).

(3) Russia does not stop in Israel, but continues southward and double-crosses her ally by occupying Egypt also (Dan. 11:42, 43).

(4) While in Egypt, Russia hears some disturbing news coming from the east and north and hurriedly returns to Palestine. We are not told what the content of this news is. Several theories have been offered:

   (a) That it contains the electrifying news that the antichrist has been assassinated, but has risen from the dead. See Revelation 13:3.

   (b) That it concerns itself with the impending counterattack of the Western leader (the antichrist).

   (c) That it warns of a confrontation with China and India ("Kings of the East"), who may be mobilizing their troops.

e. The destruction of the invaders. Upon her return, Russia is soundly defeated upon the mountains of Israel. This smashing defeat is effected by the following events, caused by God himself:

(1) A mighty earthquake (Ezek. 38:19, 20).

(2) Mutiny among the Russian troops (Ezek. 38:21).

(3) A plague among the troops (Ezek. 38:21).

(4) Floods, great hailstones, fire and brimstone (Ezek. 38:22; 39:6).

f. The results of the invasion.

(1) Five sixths (83 percent) of the Russian soldiers are destroyed (Ezek. 39:2).

(2) The first grisly feast of God begins (Ezek. 39:4, 17, 18, 19, 20). A similar feast would seem to take place later, after the battle of Armageddon (Mt. 24:28; Rev. 19:17, 18).

(3) The Communist threat will cease forever.

(4) Seven months will be spent in burying the dead (Ezek. 39:11-15).

(5) Seven years will be spent in burning the weapons of war (Ezek. 39:9, 10).

Dr. John Walvoord writes the following concerning this seven-year period:

"There are some . . . problems in the passage which merit study. A reference is made to bows and arrows, to shields and chariots, and to swords. These, of course, are antiquated weapons from the standpoint of modern warfare. The large use of horses is understandable, as Russia today uses horses a great deal in connection with their army. But why should they use armor, spears, bows and arrows? This certainly poses a problem. There have been two or more answers given. *One* of them is that Ezekiel is using language with which he was familiar—the weapons that were common in his day—to anticipate modern weapons. What he is saying is that when this army comes, it will be fully equipped with the weapons of war. Such an interpretation, too, has problems. We are told in the passage that they used the wooden shafts of the spears and the bows and arrows for kindling wood. If these are symbols, it would be difficult to burn symbols. However, even in modern warfare there is a good deal of wood used. . . .

A second solution is that the battle is preceded by a disarmament agreement between nations. If this were the case, it would be necessary to resort to primitive weapons easily and secretly made if a surprise attack were to be achieved. This would allow a literal interpretation of the passage.

A third solution has also been suggested based on the premise that modern missile warfare will have developed in that day to a point where missiles will seek out any considerable amount of metal. Under these circumstances, it would be necessary to abandon the large use of metal weapons and substitute wood such as is indicated in the primitive weapons." (*The Nations in Prophecy,* pp. 115, 116)

2. The martyrdom of the two witnesses (Rev. 11:7). There is a hint in Revelation 11:8 that the two witnesses will be crucified by the antichrist.

3. The martyrdom of the 144,000 Hebrew evangelists (Rev. 14:1-5).

4. The casting out of heaven's monster (Rev. 12:3-15).

a. The identity of this monster. There is no doubt whatever concerning the identity of this "creature from the clouds." He is pinned down by no less than four titles.

(1) The great red dragon (Rev. 12:3).

(2) That old serpent (Rev. 12:9).

(3) The devil (Rev. 12:9).

(4) Satan (Rev. 12:9).

b. The location of this monster. Satan has been, is now, or shall be in one of the following locations:

(1) In heaven, as God's anointed angel (past location—Ezek. 28:14).

(2) In heaven, as God's chief enemy (present location—Job 1-2).

(3) On earth, as the antichrist's spiritual guide (future location, during the tribulation—Rev. 12:12).

(4) In the bottomless pit (future, during the millennium—Rev. 20:1-3).

(5) On earth again (future, after the millennium—Rev. 20:8, 9).

(6) In the lake of fire (future and forever—Rev. 20:10).

c. The activities of this monster.

(1) He deceives all living unbelievers (Rev. 12:9).

(2) He accuses all departed believers (Rev. 12:10).

(3) He persecutes the nation Israel (Rev. 12:13).

5. The destruction of the false church (Rev. 17:16). One of the most ironic turn of events in all history will be the destruction of the false church. This evil organization will meet its doom, not at the hands of Gabriel, or the Father, or the Son, or the Spirit, but the antichrist.

We have already seen how the false church elevates the antichrist into power. But then she apparently attempts to control him. He will have none of it, however, and will destroy her buildings, burn her holy books, and murder her priests.

H. *The last half of the tribulation* (three-and-one-half years).

1. The full manifestation of the antichrist. After the judgment of Russia, the destruction of the false church, and the murder of most of God's preachers (the 144,000 and the two witnesses), an unbelievable vacuum will undoubtedly settle down upon the world. The antichrist will immediately exploit this. The following is but a suggestion of the chronology of events which may take place at this critical time.

a. The antichrist and his false prophet make their headquarters in Jerusalem after God destroys Russia.

b. Here in the holy city, perhaps during a television speech, the antichrist is suddenly assassinated, as millions of astonished viewers watch (Rev. 13:3, 14).

c. Before his burial—perhaps during the state funeral—he suddenly rises from the dead. The world is electrified!

d. The antichrist is immediately worshiped by the world as God.

e. The false prophet thereupon makes a statue of the antichrist, causes it to speak, and places it in the Holy of Holies (Dan. 9:27; 12:11; Mt. 24:15; 2 Thess. 2:4).

f. A law is passed which stipulates that no one can buy, sell, work, or obtain any necessity of life unless he carries a special mark on his right hand or his forehead to identify him as a worshiper of the beast (Rev. 13:16, 17).

g. The number of this mark is 666 (Rev. 13:18).

2. The worldwide persecution of Israel.

"And at that time shall Michael stand up, the great prince which standeth for the children of thy people; and there shall be a time of trouble, such as never was since there was a nation even to that same time . . ." (Dan. 12:1).

When the Israelites see the statue of the antichrist standing in their Holy of Holies, the words of Christ will come to their minds. He had warned them of this very thing many centuries earlier (Mt. 24:15-20).

"And when the dragon saw that he was cast unto the earth, he persecuted the woman which brought forth the man-child" (Rev. 12:13).

At this point the Jews of the world will travel down one of three roads:

a. Many Israelites will be killed by the antichrist.

"And it shall come to pass that in all the land, saith the Lord, two parts therein shall be cut off and die; but the third shall be left therein" (Zech. 13:8).

b. Some Israelites will follow the antichrist.

"And then shall many be offended, and shall betray one another, and shall hate one another. And many false prophets shall rise, and shall deceive many. And because iniquity shall abound, the love of many shall wax cold" (Mt. 24:10-12).

". . . I know the blasphemy of them which say they are Jews, and are not, but are the synagogue of Satan" (Rev. 2:9).

"Behold, I will make them of the synagogue of Satan which say they are Jews, and are not, but do lie; behold, I will make them to come and worship before thy feet, and to know that I have loved thee" (Rev. 3:9).

c. A remnant of Israel will be saved.

"And to the woman were given two wings of a great eagle, that she might fly into the wilderness, into her place, where she is nourished for a time, and times, and half a time, from the face of the serpent" (Rev. 12:14).

"And I will bring the third part through the fire, and will refine them as silver is refined, and will try them as gold is tried; they shall call on my name, and I will hear them: I will say, It is my people; and they shall say, The Lord is my God" (Zech. 13:9).

Thus it would seem that at least one third of Israel will remain true to God and be allowed by him to escape into a special hiding place for the duration of the tribulation. We shall now consider the location of this hiding place. While it is not actually specified in Scripture, many Bible students believe that this place will be Petra. This is based on the following three passages:

(1) Zechariah 14:5: "And ye shall flee to the valley of the mountains, for the

valley of the mountains shall reach unto Azal; yea, ye shall flee . . . and the Lord my God shall come, and all the saints with thee." (The "Azal" mentioned here is thought to be connected with Petra.)

   (2) Isaiah 63:1: "Who is this that cometh from Edom, with dyed garments from Bozrah?" The first few verses of Isaiah 63 deal with the Second Coming of Christ. He comes to Edom (of which Petra is capital) and Bozrah (a city in Edom) for some reason, and many believe that reason is to receive his Hebrew remnant who are hiding there.

   (3) Daniel 11:41: "He shall enter also into the glorious land, and many countries shall be overthrown; but these shall escape out of his hand, even Edom. . . ."

Thus for some reason the land of Edom will not be allowed to fall into the hands of the antichrist. It is assumed by some that the reason is to protect the remnant.

3. The pouring out of the last seal judgment (Rev. 8, 9; 11:15-19). This final seal judgment consists of seven trumpet plagues.
  a. The sounding of the first trumpet (Rev. 8:7).
  b. The sounding of the second trumpet (Rev. 8:8, 9).
  c. The sounding of the third trumpet (Rev. 8:10, 11).
  d. The sounding of the fourth trumpet (Rev. 8:12).
  e. The sounding of the fifth trumpet (Rev. 9:1).
  f. The sounding of the sixth trumpet (Rev. 9:13).
  g. The sounding of the seventh trumpet (Rev. 11:15).

4. The messages of three special angels (Rev. 14:6-12).
  a. The first message (Rev. 14:6, 7).
  b. The second message (Rev. 14:8).
  c. The third message (Rev. 14:9-11).

5. The pouring out of the seven bowls ("vials") of judgment (Rev. 16).
  "And I heard a great voice out of the temple saying to the seven angels, Go your ways, and pour out the vials of the wrath of God upon the earth" (Rev. 16:1).
  a. The first vial judgment (Rev. 16:2).
  b. The second vial judgment (Rev. 16:3).
  c. The third vial judgment (Rev. 16:4-7).
  d. The fourth vial judgment (Rev. 16:8, 9).
  e. The fifth vial judgment (Rev. 16:10, 11).
  f. The sixth vial judgment (Rev. 16:12-14).
  g. The seventh vial judgment (Rev. 16:17-21).

6. The sudden destruction of economic and political Babylon (Rev. 18).
  "And there followed another angel, saying, Babylon is fallen, is fallen, that great city, because she made all nations drink of the wine of the wrath of her fornication" (Rev. 14:8).
  ". . . and great Babylon came in remembrance before God, to give unto her the cup of the wine of the fierceness of his wrath" (Rev. 16:19).
  "And after these things I saw another angel come down from heaven, having great power; and the earth was lightened with his glory. And he cried mightily with a strong voice, saying, Babylon the great is fallen, is fallen . . ." (Rev. 18:1, 2).
  It is likely that literal Babylon will be rebuilt during the tribulation. The Old Testament city of Babylon is mentioned more times in the Bible than any other city with the exception of Jerusalem. It is mentioned no less than 260 times.

7. The battle of Armageddon (Rev. 16:16). The Holy Spirit of God has chosen five capable authors to describe for us in clear and chilling language that most famous of all battles—Armageddon. These five authors include David, Isaiah, Joel, Zechariah, and John. (See Isa. 34:1-6; 63:3, 4, 6; Joel 3:2, 9-16; Zech. 12:2; 14:2, 3, 12; Rev. 16:16; 19:11-21.)
  In his little booklet entitled *Profiles of Prophecy,* Dr. S. Franklin Logsdon writes:
  "A former president of the Norwegian Academy of Sciences, helped by historians from Britain, Egypt, Germany and India, and using an electronic computer, has found that since 3600 B.C. the world has known only 292 years of peace. In this period of more than 55 centuries there have been 14,531 wars, large and small, in which more than 3.6 billion people were killed. Since 650 B.C., there have been 1,656 arms races, all except 16 ending in war, and those 16 ended in economic collapse for the countries concerned."
  But this coming War of Armageddon will be by far the biggest, boldest, bloodiest, most brazen, and most blasphemous of all times. We shall now consider the negative and positive elements of this war.
  a. *Negative*
    (1) Armageddon is not the same as the Russian invasion of Ezekiel 38. Note the differences:
      (a) Russia invades from the north, but at Armageddon the nations come from all directions.
      (b) Russia invades to capture Israel's wealth, but this invasion is to destroy the Lamb and his people.
      (c) Gog leads the Russian invasion, but the antichrist leads this one.
    (2) Armageddon is not the final war in the Bible—the final war occurs after the millennium (Rev. 20:7-9). Armageddon takes place at the end of the tribulation.

b. *Positive*

(1) The location of the battle. Dr. Herman A. Hoyt aptly describes the location:

"The staggering dimensions of this conflict can scarcely be conceived by man. The battlefield will stretch from Megiddo on the north (Zech. 12:11; Rev. 16:16) to Edom on the south (Isa. 34:5, 6; 63:1), a distance of sixteen hundred furlongs—approximately two hundred miles. It will reach from the Mediterranean Sea on the west to the hills of Moab on the east, a distance of almost one hundred miles. It will include the Valley of Jehoshaphat (Joel 3:2, 12) and the Plains of Esdraelon. At the center of the entire area will be the city of Jerusalem (Zech. 14:1, 2). Into this area the multiplied millions of men, doubtless approaching 400 million, will be crowded for the final holocaust of humanity. The kings with their armies will come from the north and the south, from the east and from the west. . . . In the most dramatic sense this will be the 'Valley of decision' for humanity (Joel 3:14) and the great winepress into which will be poured the fierceness of the wrath of Almighty God (Rev. 19:15)." (*The End Time,* p. 163)

Thus there would seem to be at least four important names involved in the battle of Armageddon:

(a) The Valley of Jehoshaphat—a valley situated just east of Jerusalem, between the Holy City and the Mount of Olives. See Joel 3:2, 12.

(b) The Valley of Esdraelon—a valley twenty miles long and fourteen miles wide, situated north and west of Jerusalem between the Holy City and the Mediterranean Sea.

(c) Megiddo—a flat plain located in the Valley of Esdraelon (Zech. 12:11).

(d) Bozrah—a city in Edom, east of the Jordan River and near Petra, the capital of Edom. These two cities will play an important role during the Second Coming of our Lord. See Isaiah 34:6 and 63:1.

Marvin Vincent writes concerning Armageddon and its location:

"Megiddo was in the plain of Esdraelon, which has been a chosen place for encampment in every contest carried on in Palestine from the days of . . . Assyria unto the disastrous march of Napoleon Bonaparte from Egypt into Syria. Jews, Gentiles, Saracens, Christian Crusaders, and anti-Christian Frenchmen; Egyptians, Persians, Druses, Turks, and Arabs, warriors of every nation that is under heaven, have pitched their tents on the plains of Esdraelon, and have beheld the banners of their nation wet with the dews of Mt. Tabor and Mt. Hermon." (*Word Studies in the New Testament,* pp. 542, 543; quoted by Pentecost, *Things to Come,* p. 341)

In addition to church history, a number of battles took place in this area, as reported by the Old Testament:

(e) It was here that Deborah and Barak defeated the Canaanites (Jdg. 4–5).

(f) It was here that Gideon defeated the Midianites (Jdg. 7).

(g) It was here that the Philistines defeated and killed Saul (1 Sam. 31).

(h) It was here that David defeated Goliath (1 Sam. 17).

(i) It was here that an Egyptian king killed Josiah (2 Ki. 23).

(2) The reasons for the battle. What will draw all the nations of the world into the area of Armageddon? They will gather themselves there for perhaps various reasons. It would seem that the following are three of the more important reasons:

(a) Because of the sovereignty of God. In at least five distinct passages we are told that God himself will gather the nations here:

". . . he hath delivered them to the slaughter" (Isa. 34:2).

"I will also gather all nations, and will bring them down into the valley of Jehoshaphat . . ." (Joel 3:2).

"For I will gather all nations against Jerusalem to battle . . ." (Zech. 14:2).

"And he gathered them together into a place called in the Hebrew tongue Armageddon" (Rev. 16:16).

(b) Because of the deception of Satan (Rev. 16:13, 14). In this passage we are told that three special unclean spirits will trick the nations into gathering at Armageddon.

(c) Because of the hatred of the nations for Christ. A number of passages tell us of this devilish hatred (Ps. 2:1-3; Rev. 11:18). The nations, led by the anti-christ, will doubtless realize the imminent return of Christ (Rev. 11:15; 12:12). They will also be aware of his touching down on the Mount of Olives (Zech. 14:4; Acts 1:9–12). Thus it is not unreasonable to assume they will gather in that area to destroy him at the moment of his return to earth.

(3) The chronology of the battle.

(a) The drying up of the Euphrates River (Rev. 16:12). Dr. Donald Barnhouse quotes Seiss in describing this:

> "From time immemorial the Euphrates with its tributaries has been a great and formidable boundary between the peoples east of it and those west of it. It runs a distance of 1800 miles, and is scarcely fordable anywhere or at any time. It is from three to twelve hundred yards wide, and from ten to thirty feet in depth; and most of the time it is still deeper and wider. It was the boundary of the dominion of Solomon, and is repeatedly spoken of as the northeast limit of the lands promised to Israel. . . . History frequently refers to the great hindrance the Euphrates has been to military movements; and it has always been a line of separation between the peoples living east of it and those living west of it." (*Revelation*, p. 301)

Thus, when this watery barrier is removed, tens of millions of soldiers from China, India, and other Asian powers will march straight for Armageddon and destruction.

(b) The destruction of Jerusalem. Perhaps the saddest event during the tribulation will be the siege and destruction of the Holy City. This will be the forty-seventh and last takeover of the beloved city of David. The following passages bear this out:

> "For I will gather all nations against Jerusalem to battle; and the city shall be taken, and the houses rifled, and the women ravished; and half the city shall go forth into captivity . . ." (Zech. 14:2).

> "And when ye shall see Jerusalem compassed with armies, then know that the desolation thereof is nigh" (Lk. 21:20).

When these two events transpire, both the angels in paradise and the demons in perdition will surely hold their breath. The reason for their suspense will be discussed in the next major section.

VI. The Second Coming of Christ. Surely John the apostle must have penned the following words with great awe.

> "And the seventh angel sounded; and there were great voices in heaven, saying, The kingdoms of this world are become the kingdoms of our Lord, and of his Christ; and he shall reign forever and ever" (Rev. 11:15).

> "And I saw heaven opened, and behold, a white horse; and he that sat upon him was called Faithful and True, and in righteousness he doth judge and make war. His eyes were as a flame of fire, and on his head were many crowns; and he had a name written, that no man knew, but he himself. And he was clothed with a vesture dipped in blood: and his name is called The Word of God. And the armies which were in heaven followed him upon white horses, clothed in fine linen, white and clean. And out of his mouth goeth a sharp sword, that with it he should smite the nations: and he shall rule them with a rod of iron: and he treadeth the winepress of the fierceness and wrath of Almighty God. And he hath on his vesture and on his thigh a name written, KING OF KINGS AND LORD OF LORDS" (Rev. 19:11–16).

A. The chronology of the Second Coming of Christ.

1. It begins with fearful manifestations in the skies.

> "Immediately after the tribulation of those days shall the sun be darkened, and the moon shall not give her light, and the stars shall fall from heaven, and the powers of the heavens shall be shaken" (Mt. 24:29).

> "And there shall be signs in the sun, and in the moon, and in the stars; and upon the earth distress of nations, with perplexity, the sea and the waves roaring, men's hearts failing them for fear . . . for the powers of heaven shall be shaken" (Lk. 21:25, 26).

2. In the midst of this, the heavens open and Jesus comes forth.

> "And then shall appear the sign of the Son of man in heaven; and then shall all the tribes of the earth mourn, and they shall see the Son of man coming in the clouds of heaven with power and great glory" (Mt. 24:30).

> "Behold, he cometh with clouds; and every eye shall see him . . ." (Rev. 1:7).

> "And I saw heaven opened, and behold, a white horse; and he that sat upon

him was called Faithful and True . . ." (Rev. 19:11).

3. The returning Savior touches down upon the Mount of Olives, causing a great earthquake (Zech. 14:4, 8). Dr. J. Dwight Pentecost writes the following concerning this earthquake:

"A news magazine reported some time ago that a large hotel chain has sent a crew of engineers and geologists to Jerusalem to explore the possibility of building a hotel on the top of the Mount of Olives. After their exploration they reported that the site was a poor place to build because the Mount of Olives is the center of a geological fault, and an earthquake in that area might divide the Mount and a hotel would certainly be destroyed. So they decided against building there and found another piece of property in another area. Subsequently another hotel was erected on the Mount of Olives which provides a breathtaking view of the old city of Jerusalem." (Will Man Survive? p. 162)

4. After touching down on the Mount of Olives, Christ proceeds to Petra and Bozrah, two chief cities in Edom. It would seem that he goes to Edom to gather the hiding Israelite remnant. Accompanied by the holy angels, the church, and the remnant, Christ marches toward Armageddon (Isa. 34:6; 63:1).

B. The purpose of the Second Coming of Christ.

1. To defeat the antichrist and the world's nations assembled at Armageddon. Two authors aptly describe this battle for us:

"Palestine is to be given a blood bath of unprecedented proportions, which will flow from Armageddon at the north down through the Valley of Jehoshaphat, will cover the land of Edom, and will wash over all Judea and the city of Jerusalem. John looks at this scene of carnage and he describes it as blood flowing to the depths of the horses' bridles. It is beyond human imagination to see a lake that size that has been drained from the veins of those who have followed the purpose of Satan to try to exterminate God's chosen people in order to prevent Jesus Christ from coming to reign." (Pentecost, Prophecy for Today, pp. 118, 119)

"The Battle of Armageddon will result in wholesale carnage among the legions of the beast. The brilliance of Christ's appearing will produce a trembling and demoralization in the soldiers (Zech. 12:2; 14:13). The result of this demoralization and trembling will be the desertion from the antichrist and the rendering of him inoperative (2 Thess. 2:8). This tremendous light from heaven will produce astonishment and blindness in animals and madness in men (Zech. 12:4). A plague will sweep through the armies from this light and men will rot right where they stand (Zech. 14:12, 15). The blood of ani-

mals and men will form a lake two hundred miles long and bridle deep (Rev. 14:19, 20). The stench of this rotting mass of flesh and blood will fill the entire region (Isa. 34:1-3). The mangled forms of men and the rotting flesh of men and beasts will provide a feast for the carrion birds (Rev. 19:17, 18, 21). The beast and the false prophet will then be cast alive into the lake of fire forever (Rev. 19:20)." (Hoyt, The End Times, p. 165)

2. To regather, regenerate, and restore faithful Israel. Perhaps the most frequent promise in all the Old Testament concerns God's eventual restoration of Israel. The prophets repeat this so often that it becomes a refrain—a chorus of confidence.

Note the following:

"Fear not, for I am with thee; I will bring thy seed from the east, and gather thee from the west; I will say to the north, Give up; and to the south, Keep not back: bring my sons from far, and my daughters from the ends of the earth" (Isa. 43:5, 6).

"For I will set mine eyes upon them for good, and I will bring them again to this land; and I will build them, and not pull them down . . ." (Jer. 24:6).

". . . Thus saith the Lord God, I will even gather you from the people, and assemble you out of the countries where ye have been scattered, and I will give you the land of Israel" (Ezek. 11:17).

Perhaps the most sublime song of praise concerning Israel's restoration is sung by the prophet Micah:

"Who is a God like unto thee, that pardoneth iniquity, and passeth by the transgression of the remnant of his heritage? He retaineth not his anger for ever, because he delighteth in mercy. He will turn again; he will have compassion upon us; he will subdue our iniquities; and thou wilt cast all their sins into the depths of the sea" (Micah 7:18, 19).

In the New Testament our Lord also speaks about this during one of his last sermons:

"And he shall send his angels with a great sound of a trumpet, and they shall gather together his elect from the four winds, from one end of heaven to the other" (Mt. 24:31).

Thus will our Lord gather Israel when he comes again and, as we have already observed, he will begin by appearing to the remnant hiding in Edom. Here we note:

a. Their temporary sorrow.

"And I will pour upon the house of David, and upon the inhabitants of Jerusalem, the spirit of grace and of supplications; and they shall look upon me whom they have pierced, and they shall mourn for him, as one mourneth for his only son, and shall be in bitterness for him, as one that is in bitterness for his firstborn. In that day shall there be a great mourning in Jerusalem . . . in the valley of Megiddon. And the land shall mourn, every family apart; the family of the house of David apart, and their wives apart . . ." (Zech. 12:10-12).

"And one shall say unto him, What are these wounds in thine hands? Then he shall answer, Those with which I was wounded in the house of my friends" (Zech. 13:6).

"Behold, he cometh with clouds; and every eye shall see him, and they also which pierced him; and all kindreds of the earth shall wail because of him" (Rev. 1:7).

b. Their ultimate joy.

"He will swallow up death in victory; and the Lord God will wipe away tears from off all faces; and the rebuke of his people shall he take away from off all the earth; for the Lord hath spoken it. And it shall be said in that day, Lo, this is our God; we have waited for him, and he will save us. This is the Lord . . . we will be glad and rejoice in his salvation" (Isa. 25:8, 9).

"I, even I, am he that blotteth out thy transgressions for mine own sake, and will not remember thy sins" (Isa. 43:25).

"For the Lord shall comfort Zion; he will comfort all her waste places, and will make her wilderness like Eden, and her desert like the garden of the Lord; joy and gladness shall be found therein; thanksgiving, and the voice of melody" (Isa. 51:3).

"For ye shall go out with joy, and be led forth with peace: the mountains and the hills shall break forth before you into singing, and all the trees of the field shall clap their hands" (Isa. 55:12).

3. To judge and punish faithless Israel. In the book of Romans the great Apostle Paul makes two significant statements concerning his beloved nation Israel. He writes,

"And so all Israel shall be saved; as it is written, There shall come out of Sion the Deliverer, and shall turn away ungodliness from Jacob" (Rom. 11:26).

"For they are not all Israel which are of Israel" (Rom. 9:6).

By the first statement Paul of course meant that all *faithful* Israel would be saved. As we have previously seen, this blessed event will occur during the tribulation.

By the second statement Paul writes concerning *faithless* Israel. In other words, all that glitters is not gold. From the very moment God began working through Abraham (the first Hebrew), Satan also began working through members of that same race. Thus, as

the Bible has been advanced by faithful Israel throughout history, it has likewise been opposed by faithless Israel.

Therefore, when the matter of all Israel returns, he will be especially gracious to *true* Israel but especially harsh with *false* Israel. Note the tragic record of false Israel.

a. Her sins against the Father.
   (1) Rebelling (Num. 14:22, 23).
   (2) Rejecting (1 Sam. 8:7).
   (3) Robbing (Mal. 3:2-5).
b. Her sins against the Son.
   (1) She refused him (Jn. 1:11).
   (2) She crucified him (Acts 2:22, 23; 3:14, 15; 4:10; 5:30; 1 Thess. 2:14-16).
c. Her sins against the Holy Spirit—stubborn resistance. (See Acts 7:51.)
d. Her sins against the kingdom.
   (1) She refused to use her God-given abilities to promote it (Mt. 25:24-30; Lk. 19:20-24).
   (2) She made light of the marriage feast (Mt. 22:5).
   (3) She refused to wear the proper wedding garments (Mt. 22:11-13).
e. Her sins against her own people.
   (1) She stole from widows (Mt. 23:14).
   (2) She killed her own prophets (Mt. 23:31, 34, 35; Acts 7:58).
f. Her sins against the world.
   (1) She led others into her own wretched blindness (Mt. 23:16, 24).
   (2) She was filled with hypocrisy (Mt. 16:6, 12; Rom. 2:17-23).
   (3) She had blasphemed the name of God among the Gentiles (Rom. 2:24).
g. Her sins against the gospel.
   (1) She opposed it in Jerusalem (Acts 4:2; 5:28; 9:29; 21:28; 23:2, 12).
   (2) She opposed it in Damascus (Acts 9:22-25).
   (3) She opposed it in Antioch of Pisidia (Acts 13:45, 50).
   (4) She opposed it in Iconium (Acts 14:2).
   (5) She opposed it in Lystra (Acts 14:19).
   (6) She opposed it in Thessalonica (Acts 17:5).
   (7) She opposed it in Berea (Acts 17:13).
   (8) She opposed it in Corinth (Acts 18:6, 12).
   (9) She opposed it in Caesarea (Acts 25:6, 7).

The Apostle Paul dearly loved his nation, and doubtless wrote the following description of faithless Israel and her future judgment with a heavy and weeping heart:

"Who both killed the Lord Jesus, and their own prophets, and have persecuted us; and they please not God, and are contrary to all men, forbidding us to speak to the Gentiles that they might be saved, to fill up their sins alway: for the wrath is come upon them to the uttermost" (1 Thess. 2:15, 16).

Thus the tragic prophecy of Ezekiel will someday be fulfilled upon faithless Israel:

"But as for them whose heart walketh after the heart of their detestable things and their abominations, I will recompense their way upon their own heads, saith the Lord God" (Ezek. 11:21).

"And I will purge out from among you the rebels, and them that transgress against me . . ." (Ezek. 20:38).

4. To separate the sheep from the goats (Mt. 25:31-46).
   a. The false views of this judgment.
      (1) That this "sheep and goat" judgment is the same as the great white throne judgment of Revelation 20:11-15. They are not the same, for one takes place at the end of the tribulation while the other occurs at the end of the millennium.
      (2) That the sheep and goat judgment deals only with entire nations. Some have imagined the nations of the world lined up before God. At his command, Russia steps forward and is judged—then America, then Cuba, etc. This is not the case. The word translated "nations" in Matthew 25:32 should be rendered "Gentiles."
   b. The basis of this judgment. The test in this judgment is how those Gentiles who survive the tribulation have treated faithful Israel (here referred to by Christ as "my brethren").

   In Nazi Germany, during the Second World War, escaping Jews were on a number of occasions befriended and protected by various German families who, in spite of their nationality, did not agree with Adolf Hitler. Apparently the same thing will happen during the tribulation. Gentiles from all nations will hear the message of faithful Israel and believe it and, at the risk of their own lives, will protect the messengers.

5. To bind Satan.

   "And the God of peace shall bruise Satan under your feet shortly . . ." (Rom. 16:20).

   "And I saw an angel come down from heaven, having the key of the bottomless pit and a great chain in his hand. And he laid hold on the dragon, that old serpent, which is the Devil, and Satan, and bound him a thousand years, and cast him into the bottomless pit, and shut him up, and set a seal upon him, that he should deceive the nations no more till the thousand years should be fulfilled . . ." (Rev. 20:1-3).

6. To resurrect Old Testament and tribulational saints. It is the view of this study guide that at the rapture of the church God will raise only those believers who have been saved from Pentecost till the rapture. According to

this view, all other believers will be resurrected just prior to the millennium.
   a. The fact of this resurrection. At least nine passages bring out this resurrection.
      (1) Job 19:25, 26.
      (2) Psalm 49:15.
      (3) Isaiah 25:8.
      (4) Isaiah 26:19.
      (5) Daniel 12:2.
      (6) Hosea 13:14.
      (7) John 5:28, 29.
      (8) Hebrews 11:35.
      (9) Revelation 20:4, 5.
   b. The order of this resurrection. This is the third of four major biblical resurrections. These are:
      (1) The resurrection of Christ (1 Cor. 15:23).
      (2) The resurrection of believers at the rapture (1 Thess. 4:16; 1 Cor. 15:51-53).
      (3) The resurrection of Old Testament and tribulational saints.
      (4) The resurrection of the unsaved (Rev. 20:5, 11-14).

   Thus one of the reasons for the Second Coming will be to resurrect those non-church-related saints. For many long centuries Father Abraham has been patiently awaiting that city "which hath foundations, whose builder and maker is God" (Heb. 11:10); God will not let him down.

7. To judge fallen angels.

   "Know ye not that we shall judge angels?" (1 Cor. 6:3).

   All fallen angels are of course included in this judgment. But some believe that they fall into two main categories—chained and unchained.
   a. Unchained fallen angels.

      "And Jesus asked him, saying, What is thy name? And he said, Legion, because many devils were entered into him. And they besought him that he would not command them to go out into the deep" (Lk. 8:30, 31).

      "For we wrestle not against flesh and blood, but against principalities, against powers, against the rulers of the darkness of this world, against spiritual wickedness in high places" (Eph. 6:12).

      The point of these passages is simply this—there is a group of fallen angels (demons) who have freedom of movement, and can therefore possess the bodies of both men and animals. Their one sin was that of following Satan in his foul rebellion against God. See Isaiah 14:12-17; Ezekiel 28:12-19.
   b. Chained fallen angels.

      "Christ also suffered. He died once for the sins of all us guilty sinners, although he himself was innocent of any sin at any time, that he might bring us safely home to God. But though his body died, his spirit lived on, and it was in the spirit that he visited the spirits in prison, and preached to them—spirits of those who, long before in the days of Noah, had refused to listen to God, though he waited patiently for them while Noah was building the ark. Yet only eight persons were saved from drowning in that terrible flood" (1 Pet. 3:18-20, TLB). (See also 2 Pet. 2:4; Jude 6.)

According to the above passages these fallen angels do not have the freedom the previous angels do, but are right now in "solitary confinement" awaiting their judgment at the end of the tribulation. Why the difference? Many Bible scholars believe that this group of angels was guilty of two grievous sins—not only did they join Satan's revolt, but they also committed sexual perversion with "the daughters of men" before the flood. See Genesis 6:2.

C. The time-element involved in the Second Coming of Christ. According to Daniel 12:11, 12, there will be a period of seventy-five days between the Second Coming of Christ and the millennial reign. Dr. S. Franklin Logsdon has written,

"We in the United States have a national analogy. The President is elected in the early part of November, but he is not inaugurated until January 20th. There is an interim of 70-plus days. During this time, he concerns himself with the appointment of Cabinet members, foreign envoys and others who will comprise his government. In the period of 75 days between the termination of the Great Tribulation and the Coronation, the King of glory likewise will attend to certain matters." (Profiles of Prophecy, p. 81)

It would therefore appear that the seventy-five days will be spent in accomplishing seven basic things already mentioned under "Purposes of the Second Coming."

VII. The Millennium—the Thousand-year Reign of Christ.

A. The fact of the millennium. The word itself is a Latin term which signifies "one thousand years."

". . . and they lived and reigned with Christ a thousand years" (Rev. 20:4).

In the first seven verses of Revelation 20, John mentions the thousand-year period no less than six times. In spite of this some have argued that, since this number is found in only one New Testament passage, one cannot insist that the thousand-year period will really come to pass. To emphasize their point, reference is made to 2 Peter 3:8:

". . . One day is with the Lord as a thousand years, and a thousand years as one day."

It is interesting (and perhaps revealing) to note that the same group which attempts to shorten the thousand-year period of Revelation to one day (and thus do away entirely with the millennium) also attempts to expand the six days of creation in Genesis to thousands of years. One is

tempted to ask, "Why can't God mean exactly what he says?"

Dr. Rene Pache writes the following helpful words:

"Let us notice again this fact: the teaching of the Old Testament concerning the millennium is so complete that the Jews in the Talmud succeeded in developing it entirely themselves, without possessing the gifts furnished later by the New Testament. For example, they had indeed affirmed before the Apocalypse that the messianic kingdom would last one thousand years. One should not, therefore, claim (as some have done) that without the famous passage of Revelation 20:1-10 the doctrine of the millennium would not exist." (The Return of Jesus Christ, p. 380)

During the history of the Christian church men have held three major views about the millennium.

1. Postmillennialism. This theory says that through the preaching of the gospel the world will eventually embrace Christianity and become a universal "society of saints." At this point Christ will be invited to assume command and reign over man's peaceful planet. Thus, though postmillennialists believe in a literal thousand-year reign, their position is false, for the Bible clearly teaches that the world situation will become worse and worse prior to Christ's Second Coming—not better and better. See 1 Timothy 4:1; 2 Timothy 3:1-5. This position was popularized by a Unitarian minister named Daniel Whitby (1638-1726), and it flourished until the early part of the twentieth century. Then came World War I, and men began to wonder. Finally the postmillennial theory was quietly laid to rest amid Hitler's gas ovens during the Second World War. Today a postmillennialist is harder to find than a 1940 Wendell Willkie button.

2. Amillennialism. This view teaches that there will be no thousand-year reign at all, and that the New Testament church inherits all the spiritual promises and prophecies of Old Testament Israel. In this view Isaiah's beautiful prophecy of the bear and the cow lying together and the lion eating straw like the ox (Isa. 11:7) simply doesn't mean what it says. However, if the eleventh chapter of Isaiah cannot be taken literally, what proof do we have that the magnificent fifty-third chapter should not likewise be allegorized away?

3. Premillennialism. This view teaches that Christ will return just prior to the millennium and will personally rule during this glorious thousand-year reign. This position alone is the scriptural one, and is the oldest of these three views. From the apostolic period on, the premillennial position was held by the early church fathers.

a. Theologians who held it during the first century A.D.

(1) Clement of Rome—40 to 100.

(2) Ignatius—50-115.

(3) Polycarp—70-167.

b. Theologians who held it during the second century A.D.
   (1) Justin Martyr—100-168.
   (2) Irenaeus—140-202.
   (3) Tertullian—150-220.
c. Theologians who held it during the third century A.D.
   (1) Cyprian—200-258.
   (2) Commodianus—250.

Beginning in the fourth century, however, the Roman Catholic Church began to grow and premillennialism began to wither, for Rome viewed herself as God's instrument to usher in the promised kingdom of glory. For centuries the precious doctrine of premillennialism was lost except to a few groups.

But in the past few hundred years God has graciously revived premillennialism and restored it to its proper place, using men like Alford, Seiss, Darby, and C. I. Scofield.

B. The purpose of the millennium.
   1. To reward the saints of God.
      "Verily there is a reward for the righteous . . ." (Ps. 58:11).
      ". . . to him that soweth righteousness shall be a sure reward" (Prov. 11:18).
      "Rejoice, and be exceeding glad, for great is your reward in heaven . . ." (Mt. 5:12).
      "For the Son of man shall come in the glory of his Father with his angels; and then he shall reward every man according to his works" (Mt. 16:27).
      "Then shall the King say . . . Come, ye blessed of my Father, inherit the kingdom prepared for you from the foundation of the world" (Mt. 25:34).
   2. To answer the oft-prayed model prayer. In Luke 11:1-4 and Matthew 6:9-13 our Lord, at the request of his disciples, suggested a pattern prayer to aid all believers in their praying. One of the guidelines was this: "Thy kingdom come." Here the Savior was inviting his followers to pray for the millennium. Someday he will return to fulfill the untold millions of times these three little words have wafted their way to heaven by Christians—"Thy kingdom come."
   3. To redeem creation. In Genesis 3 God cursed nature because of Adam's sin. From that point on, man's paradise became a wilderness. The roses suddenly contained thorns, and the docile tiger became a hungry meat-eater. But during the millennium all this will change. Paul describes the transformation for us in his epistle to the Romans:
      "For all creation is waiting patiently and hopefully for that future day when God will resurrect his children. For on that day thorns and thistles, sin, death, and decay—the things that overcame the world against its will at God's command—will all disappear, and the world around us will share in the glorious freedom from sin which God's children enjoy. "For we know that even the things of nature, like animals and plants, suffer in sickness and death as they await this great event" (Rom. 8:19-22, *TLB*).
   4. To fulfill three important Old Testament covenants.
      a. The Abrahamic Covenant. God promised Abraham two basic things:
         (1) That his seed (Israel) would become a mighty nation (Gen. 12:1-3; 13:16; 15:5; 17:7; 22:17, 18).
         (2) That his seed (Israel) would someday own Palestine forever (Gen. 12:7; 13:14, 15, 17; 15:7, 18-21; 17:8).
      b. The Davidic Covenant (2 Chron. 13:5; 2 Sam. 7:12-16; 23:5). Here the promise was threefold:
         (1) That from David would come an everlasting throne.
         (2) That from David would come an everlasting kingdom.
         (3) That from David would come an everlasting King.
      c. The new covenant (Isa. 42:6; Jer. 31:31-34; Heb. 8:7-12). This promise was also threefold:
         (1) That he would forgive their iniquity and forget their sin.
         (2) That he would give them new hearts.
         (3) That he would use Israel to reach and teach the Gentiles.
   5. To prove a point. This is the point: Regardless of his environment or heredity, mankind apart from God's grace will inevitably fail. For example:
      a. The age of *innocence* ended with willful disobedience (Gen. 3).
      b. The age of *conscience* ended with universal corruption (Gen. 6).
      c. The age of *human government* ended with devil-worshiping at the Tower of Babel (Gen. 11).
      d. The age of *promise* ended with God's people out of the Promised Land and enslaved in Egypt (Ex. 1).
      e. The age of the *law* ended with the creatures killing their Creator (Mt. 27).
      f. The age of the *church* will end with worldwide apostasy (1 Tim. 4).
      g. The age of the *tribulation* will end with the battle of Armageddon (Rev. 19).
      h. The age of the *millennium* will end with an attempt to destroy God himself (Rev. 20). (Note: Just where and how Satan will gather this unsaved human army at the end of the millennium will be discussed later.)
   6. To fulfill the main burden of biblical prophecy. All Bible prophecy concerning the Lord Jesus Christ is summarized in one tiny verse by the Apostle Peter:
      ". . . the sufferings of Christ, and the glory that should follow" (1 Pet. 1:11).
      Here Peter connects Christ's first coming (the sufferings) with his Second Coming (the glory).

In this verse is the "suffering-glory story" of the Savior. Furthermore, when a sinner repents and becomes a part of the body of Christ, he too shares in this destiny. Note the following:

"For I reckon that the sufferings of this present time are not worthy to be compared with the glory which shall be revealed in us" (Rom. 8:18).

"And our hope of you is steadfast, knowing that as ye are partakers of the sufferings, so shall ye be also of the consolation" (2 Cor. 1:7).

"If we suffer, we shall also reign with him . . ." (2 Tim. 2:12).

"Beloved, think it not strange concerning the fiery trial which is to try you, as though some strange thing happened unto you; but rejoice, inasmuch as ye are partakers of Christ's sufferings; that when his glory shall be revealed, ye may be glad also with exceeding joy" (1 Pet. 4:12, 13).

"The elders which are among you I exhort, who am also an elder, and a witness of the sufferings of Christ, and also a partaker of the glory that shall be revealed" (1 Pet. 5:1).

C. The titles of the millennium.
1. The world to come (Heb. 2:5).
2. The kingdom of heaven (Mt. 5:10).
3. The kingdom of God (Mk. 1:14).
4. The last day (Jn. 6:40).
5. The regeneration (Mt. 19:28).

"And Jesus said unto them, Verily I say unto you that ye which have followed me, in the regeneration when the Son of Man shall sit in the throne of his glory, ye also shall sit upon twelve thrones judging the twelve tribes of Israel" (Mt. 19:28).

The word "regeneration" is found only twice in the English Bible, here and in Titus 3:5, where Paul is speaking of the believer's new birth. The word literally means "re-creation." Thus the millennium will be to the earth what salvation is to the sinner.

6. The times of refreshing (Acts 3:19).
7. The restitution of all things (Acts 3:21).
8. The day of Christ. This is by far the most common biblical name for the millennium. See 1 Corinthians 1:8; 5:5; 2 Corinthians 1:14; Philippians 1:6; 2:16.

D. Old Testament examples of the millennium.
1. The Sabbath. This word literally means "rest." In Old Testament times God wisely set aside a sabbath or rest time after a period of activity. A rest was to be observed:
   a. After six workdays (Ex. 20:8-11; Lev. 23:3).
   b. After six work weeks (Lev. 23:15, 16).
   c. After six work months (Lev. 23:24, 25, 27, 34).
   d. After six work years (Lev. 25:2-5).
2. The jubilee year (Lev. 25:10-12).
3. The tabernacle—because God's glory dwelt in the Holy of Holies (Ex. 25:8; 29:42-46; 40:34).

4. The feast of tabernacles (Lev. 23:34-42).
5. The Promised Land (Deut. 6:3; Heb. 4:8-10).
6. The reign of Solomon.
   a. Because of the vastness of his kingdom (1 Ki. 4:21).
   b. Because of its security (1 Ki. 4:25).
   c. Because of his great wisdom (1 Ki. 4:29, 34).
   d. Because of the fame of his kingdom (1 Ki. 10:7).
   e. Because of the riches of his kingdom (1 Ki. 10:27).

E. The nature of the millennium. What will the thousand-year reign of Christ be like? Dr. J. Dwight Pentecost has compiled the following extended and impressive facts:

A. Peace. The cessation of war through the unification of the kingdoms of the world under the reign of Christ, together with the resultant economic prosperity (since nations need not devote vast proportions of their expenditure on munitions) is a major theme of the prophets. National and individual peace is the fruit of Messiah's reign (Isa. 2:4; 9:4-7; 11:6-9; 32:17, 18; 33:5, 6; 54:13; 55:12; 60:18; 65:25; 66:12; Ezek. 28:26; 34:25, 28; Hosea 2:18; Micah 4:2, 3; Zech. 9:10).

B. Joy. The fullness of joy will be a distinctive mark of the age (Isa. 9:3, 4; 12:3-6; 14:7, 8; 25:8, 9; 30:29; 42:1, 10-12; 52:9; 60:15; 61:7, 10; 65:18, 19; 66:10-14; Jer. 30:18, 19; 31:13, 14; Zeph. 3:14-17; Zech. 8:18, 19; 10:6, 7).

C. Holiness. The theocratic kingdom will be a holy kingdom, in which holiness is manifested through the King and the King's subjects. The land will be holy, the city holy, the temple holy, and the subjects holy unto the Lord (Isa. 1:26, 27; 4:3, 4; 29:18-23; 31:6, 7; 35:8, 9; 52:1; 60:21; 61:10; Jer. 31:23; Ezek. 36:24-31; 37:23, 24; 43:7-12; 45:1; Joel 3:21; Zeph. 3:11, 13; Zech. 8:3; 13:1, 2; 14:20, 21).

D. Glory. The kingdom will be a glorious kingdom, in which the glory of God will find full manifestation (Isa. 4:2; 24:23; 35:2; 40:5; 60:1-9).

E. Comfort. The King will personally minister to every need, so that there will be the fullness of comfort in that day (Isa. 12:1, 2; 29:22, 23; 30:26; 40:1, 2; 49:13; 51:3; 61:3-7; 66:13, 14; Jer. 31:23-25; Zeph. 3:18-20; Zech. 9:11, 12; Rev. 21:4).

F. Justice. There will be the administration of perfect justice to every individual (Isa. 9:7; 11:5; 32:16; 42:1-4; 65:21-23; Jer. 23:5; 31:23, 29, 30).

G. Full knowledge. The ministry of the King will bring the subjects of his kingdom into full knowledge. Doubtless there will be an unparalleled teaching ministry of the Holy Spirit (Isa. 11:1, 2, 9; 41:19, 20; 54:13; Hab. 2:14).

H. Instruction. This knowledge will come about through the instruction that issues from the King (Isa. 2:2, 3; 12:3-6; 25:9; 29:17-24; 30:20, 21; 32:3, 4; 49:10; 52:8; Jer. 3:14, 15; 23:1-4; Micah 4:2).

I. The removal of the curse. The original curse placed upon creation (Gen. 3:17-19) will be removed, so that there will be abundant productivity to the earth. Animal creation will be changed so as to lose its venom and ferocity (Isa. 11:6-9; 35:9; 65:25).

J. Sickness removed. The ministry of the King as a healer will be seen throughout the age, so that sickness and even death, except as a penal measure in dealing with overt sin, will be removed (Isa. 33:24; Jer. 30:17; Ezek. 34:16).

K. Healing of the deformed. Accompanying this ministry will be the healing of all deformity at the inception of the millennium (Isa. 29:17-19; 35:3-6; 61:1, 2; Jer. 31:8; Micah 4:6, 7; Zeph. 3:19).

L. Protection. There will be a supernatural work of preservation of life in the millennial age through the King (Isa. 41:8-14; 62:8, 9; Jer. 32:27; 23:6; Ezek. 34:27; Joel 3:16, 17; Amos 9:15; Zech. 8:14, 15; 9:8; 14:10, 11).

M. Freedom from oppression. There will be no social, political or religious oppression in that day (Isa. 14:3-6; 42:6, 7; 49:8, 9; Zech. 9:11, 12).

N. No immaturity. The suggestion seems to be that there will not be the tragedies of feeble-mindedness nor of dwarfed bodies in that day (Isa. 65:20). Longevity will be restored.

O. Reproduction by the living peoples. The living saints who go into the millennium in their natural bodies will beget children throughout the age. The earth's population will soar. These born in the age will not be born without a sin nature, so salvation will be required (Jer. 30:20; 31:29; Ezek. 47:22; Zech. 10:8).

P. Labor. The period will not be characterized by idleness, but there will be a perfect economic system, in which the needs of men are abundantly provided for by labor in that system, under the guidance of the King. There will be a fully developed industrialized society, providing for the needs of the King's subjects (Isa. 62:8, 9; 65:21-23; Jer. 31:5; Ezek. 48:18, 19). Agriculture as well as manufacturing will provide employment.

Q. Economic prosperity. The perfect labor situation will produce economic abundance, so that there will be no want (Isa. 4:1; 30:23-25; 35:1, 2, 7; 62:8, 9; 65:21-23; Jer. 31:5, 12; Ezek. 34:26; 36:29, 30; Joel 2:21-27; Amos 9:13, 14; Micah 4:1, 4; Zech. 8:11, 12; 9:16, 17).

R. Increase of light. There will be an increase of solar and lunar light in the age. This increased light probably is a major cause in the increased productivity of the earth (Isa. 4:5; 30:26; 60:19, 20; Zech. 2:5).

S. Unified language. The language barriers will be removed so that there can be free social interchange (Zeph. 3:9).

T. Unified Worship. All the world will unite in the worship of God and God's Messiah (Isa. 45:23; 52:1, 7-10; 66:17-23; Zeph. 3:9; Zech. 8:23; 9:7; 13:2; 14:16; Mal. 1:11; Rev. 5:9-14).

U. The manifest presence of God. God's presence will be fully recognized and fellowship with God will be experienced to an unprecedented degree (Ezek. 37:27, 28; Zech. 2:2, 10-13; Rev. 21:3).

V. The fullness of the Spirit. Divine presence and enablement will be the experience of all who are in subjection to the authority of the King (Isa. 32:13-15; 41:1; 44:3; 59:19, 21; 61:1; Ezek. 11:19, 20; 36:26, 27; 37:14; 39:29; Joel 2:28, 29).

W. The perpetuity of the millennial state. That which characterizes the millennial age is not viewed as temporary, but eternal (Isa. 51:6-8; 55:3, 13; 56:5; 60:19, 20; 61:8; Jer. 32:40; Ezek. 16:60; 37:26-28; 43:7-9; Dan. 9:24; Hosea 2:19-23; Joel 3:20; Amos 9:15)." (*Things to Come*, pp. 487-490)

F. The citizens of the millennium.

1. Considered negatively. No unsaved persons will enter the millennium (Isa. 35; Jer. 31:33, 34; Ezek. 20:37, 38; Zech. 13:9; Mt. 18:3; 25:30, 46; Jn. 3:3). However, millions of babies will evidently be reared in the millennium. They will be born of saved but mortal Israelite and Gentile parents who survived the tribulation and entered the millennium in that state of mortality (thus the possible reason for the Tree of Life in Rev. 22:2). As they mature, some of these babies will refuse to submit their hearts to the new birth, though their outward acts will be subjected to existing authority. Thus Christ will rule with a rod of iron (Zech. 14:17-19; Rev. 2:27; 12:5; 19:15). Dr. Rene Pache writes concerning this:

   "As beautiful as the Millennium is, it will not be heaven. . . . Sin will still be possible during the thousand years (Isa. 11:4; 65:20). Certain families and certain nations will refuse to go up to Jerusalem to worship the Lord (Zech. 14:17-19). Such deeds will be all the more inexcusable because the tempter will be absent and because the revelations of the Lord will be greater. . . . Those who have been thus smitten will serve as examples to all those who would be tempted to imitate them (Isa. 66:24)." (*The Return of Jesus Christ*, pp. 428, 429)

2. Considered positively.

   a. Saved Israel.

      (1) Israel will once again be related to God by marriage (Isa. 54:1-17; 62:2-5; Hosea 2:14-23).

      (2) Israel will be exalted above the Gentiles (Isa. 14:1, 2; 49:22, 23; 60:14-17; 61:6, 7).

(3) Israel will become God's witness during the millennium (Isa. 44:8; 61:6; 66:21; Jer. 16:19-21; Micah 5:7; Zeph. 3:20; Zech. 4:1-7; 8:3).

b. Saved Old Testament and tribulation Gentiles (Isa. 2:4; 11:12; Rev. 5:9, 10).

c. The church (1 Cor. 6:2; 2 Tim. 2:12; Rev. 1:6; 2:26, 27; 3:21).

d. The elect angels (Heb. 12:22).

G. The King of the millennium. The Lord Jesus Christ will of course be King supreme, but there are passages which suggest that he will graciously choose to rule through a vice-regent, and that vice-regent will be David. Note the following Scripture:

"But they shall serve the Lord their God, and David their king, whom I will raise up unto them" (Jer. 30:9).

Jeremiah wrote these words some 400 years after the death of David, so he could not have been referring to his earthly reign here.

"And I will set up one shepherd over them, and he shall feed them, even my servant David; he shall feed them, and he shall be their shepherd" (Ezek. 34:23). (See also Ezekiel 37:24.)

"Afterward shall the children of Israel return, and seek the Lord their God, and David their king, and shall fear the Lord and his goodness in the latter days" (Hosea 3:5).

If we can take these passages literally, David will once again sit upon the throne of Israel. He will thus be aided in his rule by:

1. The church (1 Cor. 6:3).
2. The apostles (Mt. 19:28).
3. Nobles (Jer. 30:21).
4. Princes (Isa. 32:1; Ezek. 45:8, 9).
5. Judges (Zech. 3:7; Isa. 1:26).

H. The geography of the millennium.
1. Palestine.
   a. To be greatly enlarged and changed (Isa. 26:15; Obad. 1:17-21). For the first time Israel will possess all the land promised to Abraham in Genesis 15:18-21.
   b. A great fertile plain to replace the mountainous terrain.
   c. A river to flow east-west from the Mount of Olives into both the Mediterranean and the Dead Seas. The following passages from *The Living Bible* bear this out:
   ". . . The Mount of Olives will split apart, making a very wide valley running from east to west, for half the mountain will move toward the north and half toward the south. . . . Life-giving waters will flow out from Jerusalem, half toward the Dead Sea and half toward the Mediterranean, flowing continuously both in winter and in summer. . . . All the land from Geba (the northern border of Judah) to Rimmon (the southern border) will become one vast plain . . ." (Zech. 14:4, 8, 10).
   "Sweet wine will drip from the mountains, and the hills shall flow

with milk. Water will fill the dry stream beds of Judah, and a fountain will burst forth from the Temple of the Lord to water Acacia Valley" (Joel 3:18).

"He told me: 'This river flows east through the desert and the Jordan Valley to the Dead Sea, where it will heal the salty waters and make them fresh and pure. Everything touching the water of this river shall live. Fish will abound in the Dead Sea, for its waters will be healed. . . . All kinds of fruit trees will grow along the river banks. The leaves will never turn brown and fall, and there will always be fruit. There will be a new crop every month—without fail! For they are watered by the river flowing from the Temple. The fruit will be for food and the leaves for medicine' " (Ezek. 47:8, 9, 12).

2. Jerusalem.
   a. The city will become the worship center of the world.
   "But in the last days Mount Zion will be the most renowned of all the mountains of the world, praised by all nations; people from all over the world will make pilgrimages there" (Micah 4:1, *TLB*).
   "In the last days Jerusalem and the Temple of the Lord will become the world's greatest attraction, and people from many lands will flow there to worship the Lord. 'Come,' everyone will say, 'let us go up the mountain of the Lord, to the Temple of the God of Israel; there he will teach us his laws, and we will obey them.' For in those days the world will be ruled from Jerusalem" (Isa. 2:2, 3, *TLB*).
   b. The city will occupy an elevated site (Zech. 14:10).
   c. The city will be six miles in circumference (Ezek. 48:35). (In the time of Christ the city was about four miles.)
   d. The city will be named "Jehovah-Shammah," meaning "the Lord is there" (Ezek. 48:35).

I. The temple in the millennium.
1. Its biblical order. The millennial temple is the last of seven great scriptural temples. These are:
   a. The tabernacle of Moses—Exodus 40 (1500-1000 B.C.).
   b. The Temple of Solomon—1 Kings 8 (1000-586 B.C.).
   c. The Temple of Zerubbabel (rebuilt later by Herod)—Ezra 6; John 2 (516 B.C. to A.D. 70).
   d. The temple of the body of Jesus—John 2:21 (4 B.C. to A.D. 30).
   e. The spiritual temple, the church—Acts 2; 1 Thess. 4 (from Pentecost till the rapture).
   (1) The whole church (Eph. 2:21).

(2) The local church (1 Cor. 3:16, 17).

(3) The individual Christian (1 Cor. 6:19).

f. The tribulational temple—Revelation 11 (from the rapture till Armageddon).

g. The millennial temple—Isaiah 2:3; 60:13; Ezekiel 40-48; Daniel 9:24; Joel 3:18; Haggai 2:7, 9.

2. Its holy oblation. Palestine will be redistributed among the twelve tribes of Israel during the millennium. The land itself will be divided into three areas. Seven tribes will occupy the northern area and five the southern ground. Between these two areas there is a section called "the holy oblation," that is, that portion of ground which is set apart for the Lord. Dr. J. Dwight Pentecost quotes Merrill F. Unger on this:

"The holy oblation would be a spacious square, thirty-four miles each way, containing about 1160 square miles. This area would be the center of all the interests of the divine government and worship as set up in the Millennial earth. . . . The temple itself would be located in the middle of this square (the holy oblation) and not in the City of Jerusalem, upon a very high mountain, which will be miraculously made ready for that purpose when the temple is to be erected (see Isa. 2:4; Ezek. 37:26; Micah 4:1-4)." (*Things to Come*, pp. 510, 514)

3. Its priesthood. On four specific occasions we are told that the sons of Zadok will be assigned the priestly duties (Ezek. 40:46; 43:19; 44:15; 48:11).

Zadok was a high priest in David's time (the eleventh in descent from Aaron). His loyalty to the king was unwavering. Because of this, he was promised that his seed would have this glorious opportunity (1 Sam. 2:35; 1 Ki. 2:27, 35).

4. Its prince. In his description of the temple, Ezekiel refers to a mysterious "prince" some seventeen times. Whoever he is, he occupies a very important role in the temple itself, apparently holding an intermediary place between the people and the priesthood. We are sure that he is not Christ, since he prepares a sin offering for himself (Ezek. 45:22), and is married and has sons (Ezek. 46:16). Some suggest that the prince is from the seed of King David, and that he will be to David what the false prophet was to the antichrist.

5. Its negative aspects. Several articles and objects present in the temples of Moses, Solomon, and Herod will be absent from the millennial temple.

a. There will be no veil. This was torn in two from top to bottom (Mt. 27:51) and will not reappear in this temple. Thus there will be no barrier to keep man from the glory of God.

b. There will be no table of showbread. This will not be needed, for the living Bread himself will be present.

c. There will be no lampstands. These will not be needed either, since the Light of the world himself will personally shine forth.

d. There will be no Ark of the Covenant. This will also be unnecessary, since the Shekinah glory himself will hover over all the world, as the glory cloud once did over the ark.

e. The east gate will be closed. Observe the words of Ezekiel:

"This gate shall be shut, and no man shall enter in by it; because the Lord, the God of Israel, hath entered in by it; therefore it shall be shut" (Ezek. 44:2).

This gate, it has been suggested, will remain closed for the following reasons:

(1) This will be the gate by which the Lord Jesus Christ enters the temple. As a mark of honor to an eastern king, no person could enter the gate by which he entered.

(2) It was from the eastern gate that the glory of God departed for the last time in the Old Testament (Ezek. 10:18, 19). By sealing the gate, God reminds all those within that his glory will never again depart from his people.

6. Its sacrifices. As we have already seen, several pieces of furniture in the Old Testament temple will be missing in the millennial edifice. However, the brazen altar of sacrifice will again be present. There are at least four Old Testament prophecies which speak of animal sacrifices in the millennial temple: Isaiah 56:6, 7; 60:7; Jeremiah 33:18; Zechariah 14:16-21. But why the need of these animal blood sacrifices during the golden age of the millennium?

To answer this, one must attempt to project himself into this fabulous future period. Here is an age of no sin, sorrow, sufferings, sickness, Satan, or separation.

During the millennium millions of children will be born and reared by saved Israelite and Gentile parents who survived the tribulation. In spite of their perfect environment, however, these "kingdom kids" will need the new birth. As sons and daughters of Adam they, too, as all others, will require eternal salvation (Jn. 3:3; Rom. 3:23). But how can these children be reached? What object lessons can be used? Here is a generation which will grow up without knowing fear, experiencing pain, witnessing hatred, taking dope, or seeing a jail.

This is one reason that the sacrificial system will be reinstituted during the millennium. These sacrifices will function as:

a. A reminder to all of the necessity of the new birth.

b. An object lesson of the costliness of salvation.

c. An example of the awfulness of sin.

d. An illustration of the holiness of God.

VIII. The Final Revolt of Satan.

"And when the thousand years are expired, Satan shall be loosed out of his prison, and shall go out to deceive the nations which are in the four quarters of the earth, Gog and Magog, to gather them together to battle, the number of whom is as the sand of the sea. And they went up on the breadth of the earth, and compassed the camp of the saints about, and the beloved city . . ." (Rev. 20:7-9).

Dr. J. Vernon McGee writes the following words concerning these verses:

"When the late Dr. Chafer (founder of Dallas Theological Seminary) was once asked why God loosed Satan after he once had him bound, he replied, 'If you will tell me why God let him loose in the first place, I will tell you why God lets him loose the second time.' Apparently Satan is released at the end of the Millennium to reveal that the ideal conditions of the kingdom, under the personal reign of Christ, do not change the human heart. This reveals the enormity of the enmity of man against God. Scripture is accurate when it describes the heart as 'desperately wicked' and incurably so. Man is totally depraved. The loosing of Satan at the end of the 1000 years proves it." (*Reveling Through Revelation*, pp. 74, 75)

We have already discussed the purposes accomplished by the sacrifices during the millennium. Apparently millions of maturing children will view these sacrifices and hear the tender salvation plea of the priests, but will stubbornly harden their sinful hearts. The fact that earth's mighty King at Jerusalem once bled as a lowly Lamb at Calvary will mean absolutely nothing to them. Outwardly they will conform, but inwardly they will despise.

Finally, at the end of the millennium, the world will be offered for the first time in ten centuries "a choice, and not an echo." Millions will make a foolish and fatal choice. Dr. J. Dwight Pentecost quotes F. C. Jennings, who writes:

"Has human nature changed, at least apart from sovereign grace? Is the carnal mind at last friendship with God? Have a thousand years of absolute power and absolute benevolence, both in unchecked activity, done away with all war forever and forever? These questions must be marked by a practical test. Let Satan be loosed once more from his prison. Let him range once more earth's smiling fields that he knew of old. He saw them last soaked with blood and flooded with tears, the evidence and accompaniments of his own reign; he sees them now 'laughing with abundance'. . . . But as he pursues his way further from Jerusalem, the center of this blessedness, these tokens become fainter, until, in the faroff 'corner of the earth,' they cease altogether, for he finds myriads who have instinctively shrunk from close contact with that holy center, and are not unprepared once more to be deceived." (Pentecost, *Things to Come*, p. 549)

However, this insane and immoral insurrection is doomed to utter and complete failure. As a war correspondent, the Apostle John duly records this final battle:

". . . and fire came down from God out of heaven, and devoured them. And the devil that deceived them was cast into the lake of fire and brimstone, where the beast and the false prophet are, and shall be tormented day and night for ever and ever" (Rev. 20:9, 10).

Obviously this battle, referred to as Gog and Magog, is not the same as the one in Ezekiel 38 and 39.

IX. The Great White Throne Judgment.

A. The fact of this throne (Heb. 9:27).

"And I saw a great white throne, and him that sat on it, from whose face the earth and the heaven fled away; and there was found no place for them. And I saw the dead, small and great, stand before God; and the books were opened; and another book was opened, which is the book of life; and the dead were judged out of those things which were written in the books, according to their works. And the sea gave up the dead which were in it; and death and hell delivered up the dead which were in them; and they were judged every man according to their works. And death and hell were cast into the lake of fire. This is the second death. And whosoever was not found written in the book of life was cast into the lake of fire" (Rev. 20:11-15).

"I beheld till the thrones were cast down, and the Ancient of Days did sit, whose garment was white as snow, and the hair of his head like the pure wool; his throne was like the fiery flame, and his wheels as burning fire. A fiery stream issued and came forth from before him; thousand thousands ministered unto him, and ten thousand times ten thousand stood before him; the judgment was set, and the books were opened" (Dan. 7:9, 10).

B. The judge of this throne—Christ himself.

"For the Father judgeth no man, but hath committed all judgment unto the Son . . . and hath given him authority to execute judgment also, because he is the Son of man" (Jn. 5:22, 27).

"Him God raised up the third day, and showed him openly. . . . And he commanded us to preach unto the people, and to testify that it is he which was ordained of God to be the Judge of quick and dead" (Acts 10:40, 42).

"I charge thee therefore before God, and the Lord Jesus Christ, who shall judge the quick and the dead at his appearing and his kingdom . . ." (2 Tim. 4:1).

C. The jury at this throne—five sets of books.

1. The book of conscience (Rom. 2:15). Although man's conscience is not an infallible guide, he will nevertheless be condemned by those occasions when he deliberately violated it.

2. The book of words.

"But I say unto you that every idle word that men shall speak, they shall give account thereof in the day of judgment. For by thy words thou shalt be justified, and by thy words thou shalt be condemned" (Mt. 12:36, 37).

3. The book of secret words.

"God shall judge the secrets of men by Jesus Christ" (Rom. 2:16).

"For God shall bring every work into judgment, with every secret thing, whether it be good, or whether it be evil" (Eccl. 12:14).

4. The book of public works.

". . . whose end shall be according to their works" (2 Cor. 11:15).

"For the Son of man shall come in the glory of his Father with his angels; and then he shall reward every man according to his works" (Mt. 16:27).

5. The book of life (Ex. 32:32, 33; Ps. 69:28; Dan. 12:1; Phil. 4:3; Rev. 3:5; 13:8; 17:8; 20:12, 15; 21:27; 22:19).

D. The judged at this throne. As has previously been discussed (see notes under "The judgment seat of Christ"), only unsaved people will stand before this throne.

"The wicked shall be turned into hell, and all the nations that forget God" (Ps. 9:17).

E. The judgment at this throne—the eternal Lake of Fire (Mt. 25:41, 46; Rev. 20:14, 15).

X. The Destruction of this Present Earth and Surrounding Heavens.

A. The fact of this destruction.

"Heaven and earth shall pass away, but my words shall not pass away" (Mt. 24:35).

"Thou, Lord, in the beginning hast laid the foundation of the earth, and the heavens are the works of thine hands; they shall perish, but thou remainest; and they shall all wax old as doth a garment, and as a vesture shalt thou fold them up, and they shall be changed; but thou art the same, and thy years shall not fail" (Heb. 1:10-12).

"But the day of the Lord will come as a thief in the night, in the which the heavens shall pass away with a great noise, and the elements shall melt with fervent heat; the earth also and the works that are therein shall be burned up" (2 Pet. 3:10, 11).

B. The reason for this destruction. At this stage in the Bible the final rebellion has been put down, the false prophet, the antichrist, and the devil himself are all in the lake of fire forever, and the wicked dead have been judged. In light of this, why the necessity for this awesome destruction?

Suppose a vandal were to pour crankcase oil on stacks of gold and silver. In this illustration, the vandal would represent the devil, the crankcase oil would stand for sin, and the gold and silver for God's perfect creation. God will someday arrest the devil, of course, and forever confine him to prison. But what about the oily sinstains that remain on his gold and silver creation? To solve the problem, God does what the Fort Knox authorities might consider doing in such a case—he purges the stains in a fiery wash. And it works. For the hotter the flame, the more rapidly the oil evaporates, and the brighter the gold becomes.

God will someday do to creation what he did to his beloved Israel in the Old Testament:

"Behold, I have refined thee . . . I have chosen thee in the furnace of affliction" (Isa. 48:10).

XI. The New Creation of Heaven and Earth.

"For, behold, I create new heavens and a new earth; and the former shall not be remembered, nor come into mind" (Isa. 65:17).

"For as the new heavens and the new earth, which I shall make, shall remain before me, saith the Lord, so shall your seed and your name remain" (Isa. 66:22).

"Nevertheless we, according to his promise, look for new heavens and a new earth, wherein dwelleth righteousness" (2 Pet. 3:13).

"And I saw a new heaven and a new earth; for the first heaven and the first earth were passed away; and there was no more sea" (Rev. 21:1).

Some see this new world as the last of six worlds. These would include:

A. The original world (Gen. 1:1).

B. The pre-flood world (Gen. 3:6—7:10).

C. The present world (Gen. 9:1-17; Rom. 8:19-22).

D. The tribulational world (Isa. 24; Rev. 6-19).

E. The millennial world (Isa. 35).

F. The new world (Rev. 21-22).

A Topical Summary of the Bible

This method of study offers helpful fingertip facts concerning approximately 135 important biblical topics. Under each topic the student will find the scriptural locations relating to that topic.

For example, let us suppose a Sunday school teacher is preparing a lesson on the resurrection of Lazarus. This, of course, was one of Christ's most well known miracles. If the teacher should desire more background material on the *number* and *nature* of biblical miracles, along with the *names* of those performing them, he or she need only turn to the topic of miracles. There he will find listed all the recorded miracles in the Bible. It will be discovered for example, that Christ performed thirty-six such miracles while on earth, and that the raising of Lazarus was number thirty-one of these thirty-six. In addition, the total number of Old Testament and New Testament miracles exceeds 200. Finally, the miracles were performed by over twenty-five individuals or groups of individuals, such as Satan, angels, demons, Moses, Joshua, Elijah, Elisha, Peter, Paul, etc. By this arrangement it can be quickly observed that Elisha, for example, accomplished fourteen miracles, which was twice the number done by Elijah. Thus, God literally fulfilled Elisha's request that a double portion of Elijah's spirit would fall upon him (2 Ki. 2:9). The topical study method therefore provides both quick and concise factual information about each of the 135 biblical subjects.

A TOPICAL SUMMARY OF THE BIBLE

Abominations

1. The froward is an abomination to God (Prov. 3:32; 11:20).
2. A false balance is an abomination to God (Prov. 11:1).
3. The sacrifices of the wicked are abominations to God (Prov. 15:8; 21:27).
4. The thoughts of the wicked are an abomination to God (Prov. 15:26).
5. The justification of the wicked and the condemnation of the just are an abomination to God (Prov. 17:15).
6. A proud look is an abomination to God (Prov. 6:17).
7. A lying tongue is an abomination to God (Prov. 6:17; 12:22).
8. Hands that shed innocent blood are an abomination to God (Prov. 6:17).
9. A heart that deviseth wicked imaginations is an abomination to God (Prov. 6:18).
10. Feet that are swift in running to mischief are an abomination to God (Prov. 6:18).
11. A false witness is an abomination to God (Prov. 6:19).
12. One who sows discord among brethren is an abomination to God (Prov. 6:19).

Accusations

1. As made against three godly Hebrew men (Dan. 3:8).
2. As made against Daniel (Dan. 6:24).
3. As made against Jesus.
    a. For his healing on the Sabbath (Mt. 12:10).
    b. For supposed perversion and anarchy (Lk. 22:2).
    c. For his claim to be Israel's Messiah (Mt. 27:37).
4. As made against Paul.
    a. Because of his belief in the resurrection (Acts 26:6-8).
    b. For supposedly inciting riots and desecrating the Temple (Acts 24:2-8).
5. Against Satan—only God can do this (Jude 1:9).
6. Against believers—by Satan (Rev. 12:10).

Agricultural Operations

1. Binding sheaves (Gen. 37:7).
2. Churning of milk (Prov. 30:33).
3. Fertilizing (Lk. 13:6-9).
4. Gleaning (Ruth 2).
5. Grafting (Rom. 11:17-24).
6. Harrowing (Job 39:10).
7. Harvesting.
    a. As done by Reuben (Gen. 30:14).
    b. As done by Joshua the Beth-shemite (1 Sam. 6:13, 14).
    c. As done by angels (Mt. 13:39; Rev. 14:15).
8. Irrigating (Deut. 11:10).
9. Mowing (Amos 7:1).
10. Planting.
    a. As done by God (Gen. 2:8).
    b. As done by Noah (Gen. 9:20).
    c. As done by Abraham (Gen. 21:33).
    d. As done by a certain householder (Mt. 21:33).
11. Plowing.
    a. As done by Elisha (1 Ki. 19:19).
    b. As done by Job's servants (Job 1:14).
12. Pruning (Lev. 25:3, 4).
13. Sowing.
    a. As done by Isaac (Gen. 26:12).
    b. As done by a sower (Mt. 13).
14. Treading (1 Cor. 9:9; 1 Tim. 5:18).
15. Threshing.
    a. As done by Gideon (Jdg. 6:11).
    b. As done by Ornan (1 Chron. 21:20).
16. Winnowing (Ruth 3:2).

Allegories (An allegory is a prolonged metaphor.)

1. The Shepherd Psalm (Ps. 23).
2. The Grape Vine (Ps. 80:8-14).
3. God's Vineyard (Isa. 5:1-7).
4. The Great Eagle (Ezek. 17:1-10).
5. The Lioness (Ezek. 19:1-9).
6. The Bread of Life (Jn. 6:26-51).
7. The Sheepfold and Shepherd (Jn. 10).
8. The Vine (Jn. 15:1-7).
9. The Christian Foundation (1 Cor. 3:10-15).
10. The Whole Armor of God (Eph. 6:10-17).
11. Hagar and Sarah (Gal. 4:21-31).

Altars

1. As built by Noah (Gen. 8:20).
2. As built by Abraham.
    a. In Shechem (Gen. 12:7, 8).
    b. In Hebron (Gen. 13:18).
    c. In Moriah (Gen. 22:2, 9).
3. As built by Isaac (Gen. 26:25).
4. As built by Jacob.
    a. At Shechem (Gen. 33:20).
    b. At Bethel (Gen. 35:1-7).
5. As built by Moses (Ex. 17:15).
6. As built by Balak (Num. 23:1, 4, 14).
7. As built by Joshua (Josh. 8:30).
8. As built by the tribes living east of Jordan (Josh. 22:10).
9. As built by Gideon (Jdg. 6:24).
10. As built by Manoah (Jdg. 13:20).
11. As built by Israel (Jdg. 21:4).
12. As built by Samuel (1 Sam. 7:15, 17).
13. As built by Saul (1 Sam. 14:35).

14. As built by David (2 Sam. 24:25).
15. As built by Jeroboam (1 Ki. 12:32, 33).
16. As built by Ahab (1 Ki. 16:32).
17. As built by Elijah (1 Ki. 18:31, 32).
18. As built by Urijah (2 Ki. 16:11).
19. As built by Manasseh (2 Ki. 21:3).
20. As built by Zerubbabel (Ezra 3:2).

(Note: There were four basic kinds of altars: (1) earthen, (2) stone, (3) wood covered by brass, and (4) wood covered by gold.

Animal Kingdom

1. Adder (Prov. 23:32).
2. Ant (Prov. 6:6; 30:25).
3. Antelope (Isa. 51:20) (here translated "wild bull").
4. Ape (1 Ki. 10:22).
5. Asp (Isa. 11:8).
6. Ass (Jn. 12:14).
7. Badger (also translated "coney") (Ex. 25:5; Lev. 11:5).
8. Bat (Isa. 2:20).
9. Bear (1 Sam. 17:34-37; Isa. 11:7; Dan. 7:5; Rev. 13:2; 2 Ki. 2:24).
10. Bees (Jdg. 14:8).
11. Behemoth (Job 40:15).
12. Camel (Gen. 24:10; Mt. 3:4; 19:24; 23:24).
13. Chameleon (Lev. 11:30).
14. Chamois (mountain sheep) (Deut. 14:5).
15. Cock (Mt. 26:34).
16. Cockatrice (Isa. 11:8).
17. Cormorant (a large black bird) (Lev. 11:17).
18. Crane (Isa. 38:14).
19. Cricket (translated "beetle") (Lev. 11:22).
20. Crocodile (translated in various ways) (Ezek. 29:3; 32:2; Ps. 74:14).
21. Cuckow (seagull) (Lev. 11:16).
22. Dog (Jdg. 7:5; 1 Ki. 21:23, 24; Eccles. 9:4; Mt. 15:26, 27; 7:6; Lk. 16:21; 2 Pet. 2:22; Rev. 22:15).
23. Dove (Gen. 8:8; Mt. 3:16; 10:16; 2 Ki. 6:25; Jn. 2:16).
24. Eagle (Ex. 19:4; Isa. 40:31; Ezek. 1:10; Dan. 7:4; Rev. 4:7; 12:14).
25. Elephant (1 Ki. 10:22).
26. Falcon (kite) (Lev. 11:14).
27. Fish (Jonah 1:17; Ex. 7:18; Mt. 14:17, 17:27; Lk. 24:42; Jn. 21:9).
28. Flea (1 Sam. 24:14; 26:20).
29. Fly (Eccles. 10:1; also see Ex. 8:16-19).
30. Fox (Jdg. 15:4; Neh. 4:3; Mt. 8:20; Lk. 13:32).
31. Frog (Ex. 8:2; Rev. 16:13).
32. Gazelle (often translated "roe" and "roebuck") (Deut. 12:15).
33. Gecko (lizard) (Lev. 11:30).
34. Gnat (Mt. 23:24).
35. Goat (Gen. 15:9; 37:31; Dan. 8:5; Lev. 16; Mt. 25:33).
36. Hare (a rodent) (Lev. 11:6).
37. Hart (Deut. 14:5).
38. Hawk (Job 39:26).
39. Heron (stork) (Deut. 14:18).
40. Hoopoe (lapwing) (Lev. 11:19).
41. Hornet (Ex. 23:28; Deut. 7:20; Josh. 24:12).
42. Horse (1 Ki. 4:26; 2 Ki. 2:11; Rev. 6:2-8; 19:14).
43. Horseleech (Prov. 30:15).
44. Hyena (translated "beast") (Eccles. 3:18, 19).
45. Kite (a bird of prey) (Lev. 11:14).
46. Leopard (Isa. 11:6; Jer. 13:23; Dan. 7:6; Rev. 13:2).
47. Leviathan (Job 41:1).
48. Lice (Ex. 8:16).
49. Lion (Jdg. 14:8; 1 Ki. 13:24; Isa. 65:25; Dan. 6:7; 1 Pet. 5:8; Rev. 4:7; 13:2).
50. Lizard (Lev. 11:30).
51. Locust (Ex. 10:4; Joel 1:4; Mt. 3:4; Rev. 9:3).
52. Mole (a burrowing rat) (Isa. 2:20).
53. Moth (Mt. 6:19; Isa. 50:9; 51:8).
54. Mule (2 Sam. 18:9; 1 Ki. 1:38).
55. Osprey (a fish bird) (Lev. 11:13).
56. Ossifrage (largest of the vultures) (Lev. 11:13).
57. Ostrich (Lam. 4:3).
58. Owl (sometimes translated "swan") (Isa. 34:14).
59. Ox (bullock) (1 Sam. 11:7; 15:14; 2 Sam. 6:6; 1 Ki. 19:20, 21; Isa. 1:3; Dan. 4:25, 32; Lk. 14:5, 19).
60. Partridge (1 Sam. 26:20).
61. Peacock (1 Ki. 10:22).
62. Pelican (Ps. 102:6).
63. Pygarg (a desert animal) (Deut. 14:5).
64. Quail (Ex. 16:13; Num. 11:31).
65. Raven (Gen. 8:7; 1 Ki. 17:4).
66. Scorpion (1 Ki. 12:11, 14; Lk. 10:19; Rev. 9:3, 5, 10).
67. Serpent (Gen. 3:1; Ex. 4:3; Num. 21:9; Rev. 12:9).
68. Sheep (Ex. 12:5; Gen. 4:2; Lk. 15:4; Jn. 10:7).
69. Snail (Ps. 58:8).
70. Sparrow (Mt. 10:31).
71. Spider (Isa. 59:5).
72. Swallow (Isa. 38:14).
73. Swine (Mt. 7:6; 8:32; Lk. 15:15, 16).
74. Tortoise (Lev. 11:29).
75. Turtledove (Gen. 15:9; Lk. 2:24).
76. Unicorn (wild ox) (Num. 23:22).
77. Viper (Isa. 30:6).
78. Weasel (Lev. 11:29).
79. Whale (Gen. 1:21).
80. Wolf (Isa. 11:6; Mt. 7:15).
81. Worm (Job 7:5; 17:14; 21:26; Isa. 14:11; 66:24; Mk. 9:43-48; Jonah 4:7).

Anointings

1. Of a stone by Jacob (Gen. 28:18; 31:13).
2. Of the high priest by Moses (Ex. 28:41; 29:7).
3. Of the tabernacle by Moses (Ex. 40:9).
4. Of Saul by Samuel (1 Sam. 9:16; 10:1).
5. Of David
   a. By Samuel (1 Sam. 16:12; Ps. 89:20).
   b. By the men of Judah (2 Sam. 2:4, 7).
   c. By all of Israel (2 Sam. 5:3).
6. Of Solomon by Zadok (1 Ki. 1:39).
7. Of Christ.
   a. By the Father (Ps. 2:2; 45:7; Lk. 4:18; Acts 4:27; 10:38; Heb. 1:9).
   b. By the Holy Spirit (Mt. 3:16).
   c. By an immoral woman (Lk. 7:38).
   d. By Mary of Bethany (Jn. 11:2).
8. Of all believers by the Holy Spirit (2 Cor. 1:21).
9. Of Lucifer by God (prior to his fall) (Ezek. 28:14).
10. Of sick believers by church elders (Jas. 5:14).
    Note: There are four basic kinds of anointings: (1) oil (Ex. 40:9), (2) blood (Lev. 8:23, 24; 9:9, 3), (3) water (Lev. 8:6), (4) spiritual (2 Cor. 1:21).

Arrows

1. As shot by Jonathan to warn David (1 Sam. 20:20).
2. As shot by Joash the king at Elisha's request (2 Ki. 13:15-19).
3. As shot by an unknown Syrian archer (1 Ki. 22:34).

4. As shot by Jehu (2 Ki. 9:24).
5. As shot by a Philistine archer at Saul (1 Sam. 31:3).

Assassinations

1. Cain kills Abel (Gen. 4:8) (reason: envy).
2. Lamech kills a young man (Gen. 4:23) (reason: pride and revenge).
3. Simon and Levi kill Hamor and Shechem (Gen. 34:26) (reason: revenge).
4. Moses kills an Egyptian (Ex. 2:12) (reason: to help an Israelite slave).
5. Ehud kills Eglon (Jdg. 3:21) (reason: to strike a blow for freedom).
6. Jael kills Sisera (Jdg. 4:17-21) (reason: same as 5).
7. Joab kills Abner (2 Sam. 3:27) (reason: to eliminate competition).
8. Rechab and Baanah kill Ish-bosheth (2 Sam. 4:6) (reason: to get in David's good grace).
9. David kills Uriah (2 Sam. 12:9) (reason: to conceal a terrible crime).
10. Absalom kills Amnon (2 Sam. 13:28, 29) (reason: revenge for Amnon's raping his sister).
11. Joab kills Absalom (2 Sam. 18:14) (reason: revenge).
12. Joab kills Amasa (2 Sam. 20:10) (reason: to be rid of a troublemaker).
13. Zimri kills Elah (1 Ki. 16:10) (reason: to steal his throne).
14. Jezebel kills Naboth (1 Ki. 21:13) (reason: envy).
15. Hazael kills Ben-hadad (2 Ki. 8:7, 15) (reason: to steal his throne).
16. Jehu kills Jehoram (2 Ki. 9:24) (reason: to fulfill a prophecy).
17. Jehu kills Ahaziah (2 Ki. 9:27) (reason: because he was with Jehoram).
18. Jehu kills Jezebel (2 Ki. 9:30-37) (reason: to fulfill a prophecy).
19. Some servants kill Joash (2 Ki. 12:20, 21) (reason: his cruel ways).
20. Shallum kills Zechariah (2 Ki. 15:10) (reason: to take his throne).
21. Menahem kills Shallum (2 Ki. 15:14) (reason: to take his throne).
22. Pekah kills Pekahiah (2 Ki. 15:25) (reason: to take his throne).
23. Hoshea kills Pekah (2 Ki. 15:30) (reason: to take his throne).
24. Some servants kill Amon (2 Ki. 21:23) (reason: because of his cruelty).
25. Ishmael kills Gedaliah (2 Ki. 25:25) (reason: an act of anarchy).
26. Israel kills Zechariah the high priest (2 Chron. 24:20, 21) (reason: because of his fearless preaching against sin).
27. Nebuchadnezzar kills Zedekiah's sons (Jer. 39:6) (reason: to punish him for his rebellion).
28. Herod kills some Bethlehem babies (Mt. 2:16) (reason: an attempt to kill Christ).
29. Herodias kills John the Baptist (Mk. 6:25, 27) (reason: because of his preaching against adultery).
30. The Savior of the world is killed. Who killed Jesus?
    a. The Jews did (Acts 5:30; 1 Thess. 2:15).
    b. Judas did (Mk. 14:10, 11).
    c. Pilate did (Mt. 27:24-26).
    d. The Roman soldiers did (Mt. 27:27-31).
    e. The sinner did (Isa. 53:4-9).
    f. The Father did (Isa. 53:10).
31. The Jewish elders kill Stephen (Acts 7:58, 59).

32. Herod kills James (Acts 12:2) (reason: because of his preaching).
33. Sinners in Pergamos kill Antipas (Rev. 2:13) (reason: because of his testimony).
34. The antichrist will kill the two witnesses (Rev. 11:7) and the leaders of the false church (Rev. 17) (reasons: (1) because of their testimony, (2) because of the church's attempt to control him).

Banquets (suppers, feasts)

1. Abraham's feast for some angels (Gen. 18:1-8).
2. Lot's feast for some angels (Gen. 19:3).
3. Abraham's feast for Isaac (Gen. 21:8).
4. Laban's feast for Jacob (Gen. 29:22).
5. Joseph's feast for his brethren (Gen. 43:16-34).
6. Samson's wedding feast (Jdg. 14:10-18).
7. David's feast for Abner (2 Sam. 3:20).
8. Israel's feast for David (1 Chron. 12:39).
9. Solomon's thanksgiving feast (1 Ki. 3:15).
10. Solomon's dedication feast (1 Ki. 8:65).
11. Elisha's ordination feast (1 Ki. 19:21).
12. Ahasuerus' feast for his nobles (Est. 1:3-12).
13. Ahasuerus' feast for Esther (Est. 2:17, 18).
14. Esther's feast for Haman (Est. 7:1-10).
15. Job's feast for his children (Job 1:13).
16. Belshazzar's feast for his nobles (Dan. 5).
17. Herod's feast for his nobles (Mk. 6:21).
18. Jesus' feast for 5,000 men (Mt. 14:15-21).
19. Jesus' feast for 4,000 men (Mt. 15:32-39).
20. A certain king's feast for his son (Mt. 22:1-14; Lk. 14:16-24).
21. Simon's feast for Jesus (Mk. 14:3; Jn. 12:1, 2).
22. The wedding feast in Cana (Jn. 2:1-12).
23. A Pharisee's feast for Jesus (Lk. 7:36-50).
24. Matthew's feast for Jesus (Lk. 5:29).
25. A father's feast for his repentant son (Lk. 15:23).
26. The upper room Passover feast (Jn. 13).
27. The Emmaus feast (Lk. 24:30).
28. The upper room post-Calvary feast (Lk. 24:42, 43).
29. Jesus' feast for seven of his disciples (Jn. 21:12, 13).
30. The feast at Armageddon (Rev. 19:17, 18).
31. The marriage feast of the Lamb (Rev. 19:9).
32. The Levitical Old Testament feasts.
    a. The weekly Sabbath feast (Ex. 20:8-11; Lev. 23:1-3).
    b. The seventh-year Sabbath feast (Ex. 23:10, 11; Lev. 25:2-7).
    c. The fiftieth-year (Jubilee) Sabbath feast (Lev. 25:8-16). (Note: These three speak of God's creation, as they come in cycles of seven, just as God rested on the seventh day from his creative acts. The next six feasts continue to explain and unfold God's perfect work among mankind.)
    d. The Passover feast (Lev. 23:4-8). This speaks of Calvary (1 Cor. 5:7).
    e. The feast of the first fruits (Lev. 23:9-14). This speaks of the resurrection (1 Cor. 15:23).
    f. The feast of Pentecost (Lev. 23:15-22). This speaks of the coming of the Holy Spirit at Pentecost (Acts 2).
    g. The feast of trumpets (Lev. 23:23-25). This speaks of Jesus' Second Coming (1 Thess. 4:13-18).
    h. The day of atonement feast (Lev. 23:26-32). This speaks of the tribulation (Rev. 6-19).
    i. The feast of tabernacles (Lev. 23:33-44). This speaks of the millennium (Rev. 20:1-6).

33. The post-Levitical feasts.
    a. The feast of Purim (Est. 9). This was to be a yearly feast to celebrate the deliverance of the Jews in Persia from Haman.
    b. The feast of dedication (Jn. 10:22). This was to celebrate the restoration of the Temple from Antiochus Epiphanes.

Baptisms
1. The baptism of sin upon Christ at Calvary (Lk. 12:50; Mt. 20:20–23).
2. The baptism of the Holy Spirit upon believers at Pentecost (Acts 1:5; 2:1–4; Mt. 3:11).
3. The baptism of God's wrath upon this world during the tribulation (Mt. 3:12; 13:30; Rev. 6:16, 17).
4. The baptism of all Christians by the Holy Spirit into the body of Christ (1 Cor. 12:13).
5. The baptism of Israel unto Moses (1 Cor. 10:2).
6. The baptism of John the Baptist (national baptism of repentance) (Mk. 1:4; Acts 13:24).
7. The baptism of Jesus.
    a. With water by John (Mt. 3:15).
    b. With the Holy Spirit by the Father (Mt. 3:16).
8. The baptism for the dead (1 Cor. 15:29). (Note: It is suggested that the student check with several reliable commentaries for possible explanations of this baptism and of Moses' baptism also, as listed in number 5 above.)
9. The water baptism of new converts in the book of Acts.
    a. At Pentecost. Here 3,000 were baptized by Peter and the apostles (Acts 2:41).
    b. At Samaria. Here many were baptized by Philip the evangelist (Acts 8:12).
    c. At Gaza. Here the Ethiopian eunuch was baptized by Philip (Acts 8:38).
    d. At Damascus. Here Paul was baptized by Ananias (Acts 9:18).
    e. At Caesarea. Here Peter baptized Cornelius and his friends (Acts 11:48).
    f. At Philippi. Here Paul baptized Lydia and the Philippian jailor (Acts 16:15, 33).
    g. At Corinth. Here Paul baptized Crispus, Gaius, Stephanas, and others (Acts 18:8; 1 Cor. 1:14, 16).
    h. At Ephesus. Here Paul baptized some followers of John the Baptist (Acts 19:3–5).

Basins
1. A basin which contained Passover blood (Ex. 12:22).
2. A basin which contained Passover water (Jn. 13:5).

Baskets
1. The baskets that contained seventy human heads (2 Ki. 10:7).
2. A basket that contained some good figs (Jer. 24:1, 2).
3. A basket that contained some bad figs (Jer. 24:1, 2).
4. A basket of summer fruits (Amos 8:1).
5. Three white baskets filled with food (Gen. 40:16, 17).
6. Twelve baskets of fish (Mt. 14:20).
7. Seven baskets of fish (Mt. 15:37).
8. A basket containing an apostle (Acts 9:25; 2 Cor. 11:33).

Beds
1. Jacob's bed. On his deathbed the old patriarch blessed the founders of the twelve tribes of Israel and predicted the future of each tribe (Gen. 47:31; 48:1; 49:33; especially note 49:10).
2. Michal's bed. In 1 Samuel 19 David escapes from murderous Saul when David's wife, Michal, helps him through a window and disguises her bed to make it appear to Saul that David is still there.
3. Elijah's bed. In 1 Kings 17 Elijah lays the dead son of a widow upon his bed and raises him up.
4. Elisha's bed. In 2 Kings 4, Elisha does the same thing for the parents of a boy in Shunem.
5. The palsied man's bed. Jesus heals a man with palsy in Capernaum and orders him to pick up his bed and walk away (Mt. 9:1–7).
6. The bed that was lowered from a roof. Some friends of a palsied man employed this unique way to bring their patient to Jesus (Lk. 5:18).
7. The impotent man's bed. Jesus heals a crippled invalid of thirty-eight years (Jn. 5:8).
8. Aeneas' bed. Peter heals a palsied man who had been bedridden for some eight years (Acts 9:33, 34).

Benedictions
1. As given by Aaron (Num. 6:24–26).
2. As given by David (1 Chron. 29:10–19).
3. As given by Solomon (1 Ki. 8:54–61).
4. As given by Paul (Rom. 15:13; 2 Cor. 13:14; Eph. 3:20, 21; 2 Thess. 2:16, 17).
5. As given by the author of Hebrews (Heb. 13:20, 21).
6. As given by Jude (Jude 1:24, 25).
7. As given by angels and the redeemed in heaven (Rev. 4:8–11; 5:9–14; 7:11, 12; 11:15–18; 19:1–6).

Bereavements (or tears)
1. Hagar weeps for Ishmael in the desert (Gen. 21:16).
2. Abraham weeps at the funeral of Sarah (Gen. 23:2).
3. Esau weeps upon hearing of Jacob's treachery (Gen. 27:34; Heb. 12:17).
4. Jacob weeps for joy upon finding Rachel (Gen. 29:11).
5. Esau and Jacob both weep at their reunion (Gen. 33:4).
6. Jacob weeps over the apparent death of Joseph (Gen. 37:35).
7. Joseph weeps at the reunion of his brothers (Gen. 45:14).
8. Joseph weeps at the funeral of his father Jacob (Gen. 50:1).
9. Israel weeps for freedom in Egypt (Ex. 2:23; 3:7).
10. The Egyptians weep over the death of their firstborn (Ex. 12:30).
11. Israel weeps because of their sins (Num. 11:4, 10; 14:1; Jdg. 2:4; 3:9, 15; 4:3; 6:6, 7; 10:10).
12. Moses weeps over Miriam's sin (Num. 12:13).
13. Israel weeps at the funeral of Aaron (Num. 20:29).
14. Israel weeps at the death of Moses (Deut. 34:8).
15. Joshua weeps over the defeat of Israel (Josh. 7:6–9).
16. Sisera's mother weeps at his death (Jdg. 5:28).
17. Samson's wife weeps to secure a favor (Jdg. 14:16).
18. Naomi weeps as she leaves Moab (Ruth 1:9).
19. Hannah weeps over her barrenness (1 Sam. 1:10).
20. Samuel weeps over fickle Israel (1 Sam. 7:9).
21. Israel weeps over the threatened city of Jabesh-gilead (1 Sam. 11:4).
22. Samuel weeps over the failure of Saul (1 Sam. 15:35).
23. David and Jonathan weep over Saul (1 Sam. 20:41).
24. Saul weeps over his own stupidity (1 Sam. 24:16).
25. Israel weeps at the death of Samuel (1 Sam. 25:1).
26. David weeps at the destruction of Ziklag (1 Sam. 30:4).

27. David weeps at the death of Saul and Jonathan (2 Sam. 1:17).
28. David weeps at the murder of Abner (2 Sam. 3:32).
29. David weeps over his great sin (Ps. 32:4; 51:17).
30. David weeps at the death of his infant child (2 Sam. 12:15-23).
31. Tamar weeps upon being wronged by Amnon (2 Sam. 13:19).
32. David weeps at the murder of Amnon (2 Sam. 15:23).
33. David weeps at the death of Absalom (2 Sam. 18:33).
34. Israel weeps at the death of Jeroboam's son (1 Ki. 14:18).
35. Elisha weeps over the future cruelty of King Hazael (2 Ki. 8:11, 12).
36. Joash weeps at the death of Elisha (2 Ki. 13:14).
37. Hezekiah weeps at the announcement of his impending death (2 Ki. 20:2, 3).
38. Hezekiah and Isaiah weep over the threat to Jerusalem (2 Chron. 32:20).
39. The Jewish captives weep en route to Babylon (Ps. 137:1).
40. Jeremiah weeps over the sins of Jerusalem (Jer. 9:1).
41. Some old Jews weep at the dedication of Zerubbabel's Temple (Ezra 3:12, 13; Hag. 2:3-9).
42. Daniel weeps over Israel's sin (Dan. 10:2).
43. Ezra weeps over Jerusalem's sin (Ezra 10:1).
44. Nehemiah weeps over Jerusalem's broken walls (Neh. 1:4).
45. Mordecai weeps over the wicked plot of Haman (Est. 4:1).
46. Esther weeps as she pleads for her people (Est. 8:3).
47. Job weeps for his sons (Job 1:18-22).
48. Job's friends weep for Job (Job 2:12).
49. Some Bethlehem parents weep for their children (Mt. 2:18).
50. Mary and Joseph weep over the missing Jesus (Lk. 2:48).
51. A maniac in Gadara weeps at the sight of Jesus (Mk. 5:7).
52. A Syro-phoenician mother weeps over her child (Mt. 15:22).
53. Jairus' household weeps over his little girl (Mk. 5:39).
54. A father weeps over his demoniac son (Mk. 9:24).
55. A widow weeps over her dead son (Lk. 7:13).
56. An immoral woman weeps over her sin (Lk. 7:38).
57. A rich man weeps in hell (Lk. 16:24).
58. Mary and Martha weep over Lazarus (Jn. 11:33).
59. Jesus weeps over Lazarus (Jn. 11:35).
60. Jesus weeps over Jerusalem (Lk. 19:41).
61. Some Jerusalem women weep for Jesus (Lk. 23:28).
62. Jesus weeps in the Garden (Mk. 14:32-42; Heb. 5:7).
63. Mary Magdalene weeps over Jesus (Jn. 20:11).
64. The disciples weep over the departure and death of Christ (Jn. 16:6; Mk. 16:10).
65. Peter weeps over his sin (Mt. 26:75).
66. Dorcas' friends weep at her funeral (Acts 9:39).
67. Paul weeps over the Ephesian church (Acts 20:36, 37).
68. Paul weeps over the Corinthian church (2 Cor. 2:4).
69. Paul weeps over Israel (Rom. 9:2).
70. The Ephesian elders weep over Paul (Acts 20:37).
71. The Christians at Caesarea weep over Paul (Acts 21:13).
72. Timothy weeps over his ministry (2 Tim. 1:4).
73. John weeps over a seven-sealed book (Rev. 5:5).
74. The faithful martyrs weep during the tribulation (Rev. 7:17).
75. Israel will weep at the Second Coming of Christ (Zech. 12:10, 12).
76. The nations will weep at the Second Coming of Christ (Mt. 24:30).
77. The world's merchants will weep over fallen Babylon (Rev. 18:18).

Bible Statistics
(according to *Unger's Bible Handbook*, p. 895)

OLD TESTAMENT STATISTICS
1. thirty-nine books
2. nine hundred twenty-nine chapters
3. 23,214 verses
4. 593,493 words
5. longest book—Psalms
6. shortest book—Obadiah
7. seventeen historical books
8. five poetical books
9. seventeen prophetical books

NEW TESTAMENT STATISTICS
1. twenty-seven books
2. two hundred sixty chapters
3. 7,959 verses
4. 181,253 words
5. longest book—Acts
6. shortest book—2 John
7. four Gospels
8. one historical
9. twenty-two epistles

It was not until A.D. 1250 that the Bible was divided into chapters. At that time Cardinal Hugo incorporated chapter divisions into the Latin Bible. His divisions, although for convenience, were not always accurate; however, essentially those same chapter divisions have persisted to this day. In 1551 Robert Stephens introduced a Greek New Testament with the inclusion of verse divisions. He did not fix verses for the Old Testament. The first entire English Bible to have verse divisions was the Geneva Bible (1560).

Boats (ships)
1. Noah's ark. This ship, the most important ever built, was used to save humanity during the universal flood (Gen. 7:1).
2. Moses' ark. At the tender age of three months, Moses was placed in a tiny boat to escape death (Ex. 2:3).
3. Jonah's boat. Jonah boarded a ship to go to Tarshish but God had other plans (Jonah 1:3).
4. The boats of the disciples.
   a. James and John were in their boat when Christ called them to follow him (Mt. 4:21, 22).
   b. Jesus used Peter's boat to preach from and then called him also (Lk. 5:3).
   c. Jesus used the bow of a boat to preach his sermon on the sower and the seed (Mt. 13:2).
   d. Jesus rebuked the angry sea from a boat (Mt. 8:24).
   e. Jesus entered a boat after walking on the sea (Jn. 6:21).
5. Paul's boat. This boat was shipwrecked en route to Rome (Acts 27:41).

Books

The Bible of course is itself a collection of sixty-six inspired books. But in the Bible other books are referred to:

1. The book of Wars (Num. 21:14).
2. The book of Jasher (Josh. 10:13).
3. The Chronicles of David (1 Chron. 27:24).
4. The book of Gad (1 Chron. 29:29).
5. The book of the Prophet Iddo (2 Chron. 13:22).
6. The book of Nathan (1 Chron. 29:29).
7. The book of Jehu (2 Chron. 20:34).
8. The record book of Ahasuerus (Est. 2:23; 6:1). This book indirectly helped save the Jews in Persia.
9. The book of Remembrance (Mal. 3:16).
10. The book of Life (Dan. 12:1; Phil. 4:3; Rev. 20:12; 22:19).
11. The book of Judgment (Dan. 7:10; Rev. 20:12).
12. The seven-sealed book (Rev. 5:1).
13. An angel's book (Rev. 10:2).

Brooks

1. Jabbok. Here Jacob wrestled with God (Gen. 32:22).
2. Eshcol. Here the twelve spies of Israel cut down a sample of the marvelous fruit of the Promised Land (Num. 13:23).
3. Sinai. Into this stream at the base of the mountain Moses disposed of the golden calf Israel had made (Deut. 9:21).
4. Besor. Here David and his mighty men camped briefly en route to do battle with the Amalekites (1 Sam. 30:9).
5. Cherith. Here Elijah was fed by some ravens (1 Ki. 17:3, 4).
6. Kishon. Here Deborah and Barak defeated Sisera (Jdg. 4:13).
7. Kidron. The Savior crossed this brook en route to Gethsemane (Jn. 18:1).

Calendar (Jewish)

1. Abib (also called Nisan). This was the first month of the Jewish sacred calendar and corresponds roughly to our April. Important festivals occurring during Abib are:
   a. First day—fast for Nadab and Abihu (Lev. 10:1, 2).
   b. Tenth day—selection of Passover Lamb (Ex. 12:3); fast for Miriam (Num. 20:1).
   c. Fourteenth day—Passover lamb killed in the evening (Ex. 12:6).
   d. Fifteenth day—first day of unleavened bread (Num. 28:17).
   e. Sixteenth day—offering of first fruits (Lev. 23:10); also beginning of harvest, with fifty days to Pentecost (Lev. 23:15).
   f. Twenty-first day—close of Passover, and end of unleavened bread (Lev. 23:6).
   g. Twenty-sixth day—fast for the death of Joshua (Josh. 24:29).
2. Zif (May).
   a. Tenth day—fast for the death of Eli and capture of the Ark (1 Sam. 4:11).
   b. Twenty-eighth day—fast for the death of Samuel (1 Sam. 25:1).
3. Sivan (June).
   a. Second day—feast of Pentecost (Lev. 23:15-21).
   b. Twenty-second day—fast for Jeroboam's wicked reign (1 Ki. 12:27).
4. Tammuz (July)—seventeenth day—fast in memory of the broken law at Mt. Sinai (Ex. 32:19); also the capture of Jerusalem by Titus in A.D. 70.

5. Ab (August).
   a. First day—fast for the death of Aaron (Num. 20:28).
   b. Ninth day—fast for Kadesh-barnea tragedy (Num. 14:29-31).
6. Elul (September).
   a. Seventh day—feast for dedication of Jerusalem's walls by Nehemiah (Neh. 12:27).
   b. Seventeenth day—fast for the evil report of the ten spies (Num. 13:26).
7. Ethanim (October).
   a. First day—feast of trumpets (Lev. 23:24; Num. 29:1, 2).
   b. Seventh day—fast over golden calf tragedy (Ex. 32).
   c. Tenth day—great day of atonement (Acts 27:9).
   d. Fifteenth day—beginning of feast of tabernacles (Lev. 23).
   e. Twenty-third day—dedication of Solomon's Temple (1 Ki. 8).
8. Bul (November) seventh day—fast for the end of the southern kingdom and the blinding of Zedekiah, Judah's last king (2 Ki. 25:7).
9. Chisleu (December) sixth day—fast in memory of God's Word being burned by Jehudi (Jer. 36:23).
10. Tebeth (January).
11. Shebat (February).
    a. Twenty-third day—fast for the tragic war of the ten tribes against Benjamin (Jdg. 20).
    b. Twenty-ninth day—memorial of the death of Antiochus Epiphanes, the great Old Testament enemy of the Jews.
12. Adar (March).
    a. Seventh day—fast for Moses' death (Deut. 34:5).
    b. Fifteenth day—great feast of Purim, instituted when Esther saved all the Jews living in Persia (Est. 9:26).
    c. Twenty-third day—feast for the dedication of Zerubbabel's Temple (Ezra 6:16).

Calls (to special service)

1. Noah (Gen. 6:14)—to build a ship.
2. Abraham (Gen. 12:1, 2)—to leave his home for a strange land.
3. Isaac (Gen. 26:1-5)—to stay in Palestine and carry on his father's faith.
4. Jacob (Gen. 28:12-15)—to be true to his grandfather's faith.
5. Joseph (Gen. 37:5-9)—to exercise spiritual authority over his brothers.
6. Moses (Ex. 3:1-12)—to free Israel from Egyptian bondage.
7. Aaron (Lev. 8:2)—to become Israel's first high priest.
8. Eleazar (Num. 3:32; 20:28; 34:17)—to assume responsibility over the tabernacle and to bcome Israel's high priest.
9. Phinehas (Num. 25:10-13)—to receive God's covenant of peace for his family.
10. Joshua (Josh. 1:1-9)—to lead Israel into Canaan.
11. Othniel (Jdg. 3:9, 10)—to defeat the Mesopotamians.
12. Ehud (Jdg. 3:15)—to defeat the Moabites.
13. Deborah and Barak (Jdg. 4:4-9)—to defeat the Canaanites.
14. Gideon (Jdg. 6:11-16)—to defeat the Midianites.
15. Jephthah (Jdg. 11:29)—to defeat the Ammonites.
16. Samson (Jdg. 13:24, 25)—to defeat the Philistines.
17. Samuel (1 Sam. 3:1-14)—to replace Eli.

18. Saul (1 Sam. 9)—to be Israel's first king.
19. David (1 Sam. 16)—to be Israel's finest king.
20. Solomon (1 Ki. 3:1-14)—to serve God as did his father.
21. Jeroboam (1 Ki. 11:26-40)—to head up ten tribes of Israel.
22. Elijah (1 Ki. 17:1-4)—to preach judgment against sin.
23. Elisha (2 Ki. 2:1-13)—to replace (and surpass) the ministry of Elijah.
24. Jehu (2 Ki. 9:1-6)—to rule over the ten tribes of Israel.
25. Ezra (Ezra 7:6-10)—to teach the Word of God to the returning Jews.
26. Nehemiah (Neh. 2:18)—to build the wall around Jerusalem.
27. Esther (Est. 4:13-16)—to save her people from death.
28. Isaiah (Isa. 6:1-13)—to become God's greatest prophet.
29. Jeremiah (Jer. 1:4-10)—to be a prophet to the nations.
30. Ezekiel (Ezek. 3:10-27)—to be Israel's watchman on the wall.
31. Daniel (Dan. 2:19-23)—to interpret dreams.
32. Hosea (Hosea 1:1, 2)—to marry a harlot.
33. Amos (Amos 1:1ff)—to preach against the sins of the ten tribes.
34. Jonah (Jonah 1:1, 2)—to warn Nineveh about coming judgment unless they repented.
35. John the Baptist (Lk. 1:76-80)—to prepare the way for Christ.
36. Peter and Andrew (Mt. 4:18-20)—to follow Christ.
37. James and John (Mt. 4:21, 22)—to follow Christ.
38. Philip (Jn. 1:43)—to follow Christ.
39. Nathanael (Jn. 1:44-51)—to follow Christ.
40. Matthew (Mt. 9:9)—to follow Christ.
41. The rich young ruler (Mt. 19:16-21)—to sell his goods and follow Christ.
42. Matthias (Acts 1:23-26)—to take the place of Judas.
43. Stephen (Acts 6:5, 8-15)—to function as a deacon and evangelist.
44. Philip (Acts 6:5; 8:5-8)—to function as a deacon and evangelist.
45. Saul (Acts 9:15, 16; 13:1, 2)—to become the church's first missionary-evangelist-pastor.
46. Barnabas (Acts 11:22-30)—to help Paul.
47. John Mark (Acts 13:5; 15:39)—to help Paul.
48. Silas (Acts 15:40)—to help Paul.
49. Timothy (Acts 16:1-3)—to help Paul and later pastor a church.
50. Apollos (Acts 18:24-26)—to be an evangelist and pastor.
51. Jude (Jude 1:3)—to write the book of Jude.

Caves

1. Where Lot fled to after Sodom's destruction (Gen. 19:30).
2. Where Sarah, Abraham, Isaac, Rebekah, Leah, and Jacob were buried (Gen. 23:19; 25:9; 35:29; 49:30, 31). The name of this cave was Machpelah.
3. Where five wicked kings hid (Josh. 10:16, 17). The name of this cave was Makkedah.
4. Where David escaped from Saul (1 Sam. 22:1). The name of this cave was Adullam.
5. Where David spared Saul (1 Sam. 24:1-8). The name of this cave was Engedi.
6. Where Obadiah hid 100 prophets of God (1 Ki. 18:4).
7. Where God spoke to Elijah (1 Ki. 19:9-18).
8. Where God spoke to Moses (Ex. 33:21-23).
9. Where Lazarus was buried (Jn. 11:38).
10. Where our Lord was laid (Mt. 27:59, 60).

Chains

1. Those of Samson (Jdg. 16:11, 12).
2. Those of a maniac (Lk. 8:29).
3. Those of Paul (Acts 28:20; 2 Tim. 1:16).
4. Those of Peter (Acts 12:6, 7).

Chapters
(the 101 most important chapters in the Bible)

OLD TESTAMENT:

The Old Testament has 929 chapters. The following forty-eight have been selected because of their historical, prophetical, theological, or practical significance.

Genesis
   1—creation of all things
   3—Fall of man
   6—the universal flood
   11—the Tower of Babel
   12—the call of Abraham
   15—the confirmation of the Abrahamic Covenant

Exodus
   3—the call of Moses
   12—the Passover
   14—the Red Sea crossing
   16—the giving of the Sabbath
   20—the giving of the Law
   40—the completion of the tabernacle

Leviticus
   8—the anointing of Aaron as Israel's first high priest
   23—the feasts of Israel

Numbers
   14—the rebellion at Kadesh-barnea
   21—the serpent of brass

Deuteronomy
   28—Israel's future predicted by Moses

Joshua
   4—Israel enters the Promised Land

Ruth
   4—the marriage of Boaz and Ruth

1 Samuel
   9—the anointing of Saul as Israel's first king
   16—the anointing of David

2 Samuel
   6—Jerusalem becomes the capital of Israel
   7—the giving of the Davidic Covenant

1 Kings
   8—the dedication of the Temple by Solomon
   12—the divided kingdom of Israel

2 Kings
   17—the capture of the northern kingdom by Assyria
   19—the saving of Jerusalem by the death angel
   24—the capture of the southern kingdom by Babylon

Ezra
   1—the decree of Cyrus and the return to Jerusalem

Job
1—the confrontations between God and Satan (see also Job 2)

Psalms
22—the Psalm of Calvary
23—the Psalm of the Good Shepherd
51—the great confession of sin chapter
119—the Psalm of the Word of God

Isaiah
7—the prophecy of the virgin birth
14—the fall of Satan
35—the millennium
53—the sufferings of Christ

Jeremiah
31—the promise of the new covenant to Israel

Ezekiel
10—the departure of the glory cloud from Israel
28—the prehistorical life of Satan
37—the dry bone vision of Israel's restoration
38—the future Russian invasion into Palestine (see also Ezek. 39)
40—the future millennial temple

Daniel
2—the dream of the future Gentile world powers (see also Daniel 7)
9—the vision of the seventy weeks

Jonah
2—the great fish and Jonah

Zechariah
14—the Second Coming of Christ

NEW TESTAMENT

The New Testament has 260 chapters. The following fifty-three have been selected because of their historical, prophetical, theological, or practical significance.

Matthew
3—the baptism of Jesus
4—the temptation of Jesus
5—the Sermon on the Mount
6—the Lord's Prayer
13—the parable of the sower
16—the promise of the Church
17—the transfiguration of Jesus
21—the rejection of Israel by Jesus
27—the crucifixion of Jesus
28—the resurrection of Jesus

Luke
1—the birth of John the Baptist
2—the birth of Jesus

John
2—the first miracle of Jesus
3—Jesus and Nicodemus
11—the resurrection of Lazarus
13—the Lord's Supper
14—the Father's House sermon
15—the abiding chapter
17—the prayer of Jesus

Acts
1—the ascension of Jesus
2—Pentecost
9—the conversion of Saul
13—the call of Saul and Barnabas
15—the Jerusalem Council
16—the Macedonian vision

Romans
5—the justification chapter
6—the sanctification chapter
8—the glorification chapter
11—the dispensation chapter
12—the consecration chapter

1 Corinthians
3—the judgment seat of Christ
7—the marriage chapter
11—teachings on the Lord's Supper
12—the gifts of the Spirit
13—the love chapter
14—the tongues chapter
15—the resurrection chapter

Galatians
5—the fruit of the Spirit

Ephesians
5—the love of Christ for his Church
6—the protection of the believer

Philippians
2—the kenosis (emptying) of Christ

1 Thessalonians
4—the rapture

1 Timothy
5—duties of pastors and deacons

Hebrews
11—faith chapter
12—chastisement chapter

James
3—gossip chapter

1 John
1—fellowship chapter

Jude
1—apostasy chapter

Revelation
6—beginning of tribulation
13—the ministry of the antichrist
19—Second Coming of Christ
20—great white throne judgment
21—new heaven and new earth

Chariots

1. Joseph's chariot (Gen. 41:43; 46:29)
2. Pharaoh's chariot (Ex. 14:6)
3. Sisera's chariot (Jdg. 4:15)
4. Absalom's chariot (2 Sam. 15:1)
5. Rehoboam's chariot (1 Ki. 12:18)
6. Ahab's chariot (1 Ki. 22:34-38)

7. Elijah's chariot (2 Ki. 2:11)
8. Jehu's chariot (2 Ki. 9:16)
9. Naaman's chariot (2 Ki. 5:9)
10. the eunuch's chariot (Acts 8:28)

Churches

1. The church in Jerusalem (Acts).
   a. Began at Pentecost (2:47) with at least 3120 (2:41). Was pastored by James, the half-brother of Christ (15:13).
   b. Performed many wonders and signs (2:43; 5:12-16).
   c. Had all things in common (2:44, 45; 4:32-35).
   d. Were in one accord (2:46).
   e. Spent a good deal of time in prayer (2:42; 3:1; 4:24; 12:5-17).
   f. Witnessed at every opportunity (3:12; 5:42; 4:33).
   g. Radiated Jesus (4:13; 6:15).
   h. Was kept pure by God (had standards) (5:1-11; 8:18-24).
   i. Grew constantly (2:47; 5:14; 4:4; 12:24).
   j. Endured persecution (4:1-3; 4:14-21; 5:17-41; 7:54-60; 8:1-3; 12:1-4).
   k. Appointed deacons (6:1-7).
   l. Practiced baptism and Lord's Supper (2:41, 46).
   m. Sent forth missionaries (8:5, 14; 11:22; 13:1-3; 15:22, 27).
   n. It was here the important meeting on circumcision was held (Acts 15).
   o. Were spirit-led (2:1-18; 4:31; 13:2-4; 15:28).
   p. Preached the word (2:16-36; 3:13-26; 7:1-53; 6:4; 5:42).
   q. Contended for the faith (15:1-21).
   r. Apparently later compromised with the Judaizers (21:18-25).
2. The church in Antioch of Syria.
   a. It was founded during that persecution period which followed the martyrdom of Stephen (Acts 11:19).
   b. It experienced a great ingathering of souls (11:21).
   c. The Jerusalem church sent Barnabas to "check it out" (11:22).
   d. He became the first pastor (11:23).
   e. Many were added to the church at this time (11:24).
   f. Barnabas then called Saul as associate pastor (11:25).
   g. Here both would work for a year (11:26).
   h. It was here believers were first called Christians (11:26).
   i. The Antioch church took up a large love offering for the needy believers in Jerusalem (11:30).
   j. Antioch was the home church of the first two Christian missionaries (Paul and Barnabas) (13:1-3; 14:26).
   k. It later became their headquarters both after their first missionary trip (14:26) and following the Jerusalem Council (15:35).
   l. Silas was from this church (15:34).
   m. It was at Antioch where Paul set Peter straight on matters of legalism (Gal. 2:11).
3. The church in Antioch of Pisidia.
   a. This church was begun by Paul during his first missionary trip (13:14).
   b. Here he preached his first recorded sermon (13:16).
   c. The church was formed from the converts coming out of this meeting (13:43).

d. At Antioch of Pisidia Paul turned from the Jews (13:46).
   e. At Antioch of Pisidia Paul relates his heavenly calling as a light to the Gentiles (13:47).
4. The church in Lystra.
   a. It was organized during Paul's first missionary trip (14:6).
   b. Here he healed the impotent man (14:10).
   c. This led to his being almost worshiped (14:11).
   d. Here Paul was stoned (14:19; 2 Tim. 3:11).
   e. It was at Lystra that Paul picked up Timothy during his second missionary trip (16:1-3).
5. The church in Derbe (14:20-22).
6. The church in Iconium:
   a. Paul led many to Christ here during his first trip (14:2).
   b. He also worked great signs and wonders here (14:3).
   c. He was driven from Iconium by the unbelieving Jews (14:5).
7. The church in Philippi.
   a. Paul organized a church in the home of a woman convert named Lydia (16:15, 40).
   b. A demon-possessed girl was his next convert (16:18).
   c. She was followed by the Philippian jailor (16:33).
   d. Paul later wrote a letter to this church (Phil. 1:1).
   e. Timothy ministered to this church (Phil. 2:19).
   f. The church had sent Epaphroditus to minister to Paul while the apostle was in prison (Phil. 2:25).
   g. The church was in danger of legalism (Phil. 3:1-3).
   h. Paul writes and asks "true yokefellow" to help two quarreling church women named Euodias and Syntyche (Phil. 4:1-3).
   i. The church at Philippi helped to supply the material needs of Paul (Phil. 4:15, 18).
8. The church in Thessalonica.
   a. Founded during Paul's second missionary trip (Acts 17:1).
   b. Witnessed a great harvest of souls (17:4).
   c. Paul is accused here of turning the world upside down (17:6).
   d. In spite of their zeal, they were not good Bible students (17:11).
   e. Later Paul wrote two letters to this church (1 Thess. 1:1; 2 Thess. 1:1).
   f. The believers there had a reputation for witnessing (1 Thess. 1:8).
   g. They were persecuted by the unbelieving Jews for their faith (1 Thess. 2:14).
   h. Timothy ministered to this church (1 Thess. 3:1, 2).
   i. There were some lazy members in this church (2 Thess. 3:10).
   j. There were some busybodies there (2 Thess. 3:11).
   k. There were some disobedient members there (2 Thess. 3:14, 15).
9. The church in Berea. This church was commended for its knowledge of and love for the Word of God (Acts 17:11).
10. The church in Athens. It is not certain whether a local assembly came into being after Paul's sermon on Mars Hill, but if so, a convert named Dionysius probably led it (Acts 17:34).
11. The church in Corinth.
   a. Founded during Paul's second trip (Acts 18:1).
   b. Aided in this by Aquila and Priscilla (Acts 18:2).

c. The chief ruler of the Jewish synagogue, a man named Crispus, was one of Paul's first converts (18:8).

d. His successor, Sosthenes, later was also evidently saved. (Compare Acts 18:17 with 1 Cor. 1:1.)

e. Paul stayed here eighteen months (Acts 18:11).

f. To this church Paul wrote several letters (1 Cor. 5:9; 2 Cor. 10:9, 10), two of which are included in the New Testament canon (1 Cor. 1:2; 2 Cor. 1:1).

g. The church at Corinth experienced almost total confusion:
   (1) In matters relating to baptism (1 Cor. 1:12).
   (2) Earthly wisdom (1:26).
   (3) Carnality and strife (3:1-3).
   (4) Judging others unfairly (4:7).
   (5) Immorality (5:1).
   (6) Taking other believers to court (6:1-4).
   (7) Marriage (7:1).
   (8) Christian liberty (8-9).
   (9) The Lord's Table (11:17-34).
   (10) Spiritual gifts (12-14).
   (11) The doctrine of the resurrection (ch. 15).
   (12) Tithing (ch. 16).

h. Later pastored by Apollos (1 Cor. 3:6).

12. The church in Ephesus.
   a. Founded during Paul's second trip (Acts 18:19).
   b. May have been pastored by Apollos, Timothy, and the Apostle John.
   c. Paul wrought many miracles there and saw much fruit (Acts 19:11-41).
      (1) Wicked books were burned.
      (2) The false goddess Diana was challenged.
   d. Paul went soul-winning door-to-door there (Acts 20:17-21).
   e. The church at Ephesus was the only Christian church ever to receive letters from two New Testament writers. Paul wrote Ephesians to them (Eph. 1:1), and John the apostle would later direct a portion of his book Revelation to them (Rev. 2:1-7). According to John's letter, this church:
      (1) Worked hard and possessed patience.
      (2) Had high church standards.
      (3) Suffered for Christ.
      (4) Had left their first love, however.
      (5) Needed to remember, repent, and return to Christ, else their candlestick be removed.
      (6) Hated the deeds of the licentious Nicolaitans.

13. The church in Troas. Here Paul raised up Eutychus, a believer who had gone asleep during Paul's sermon and had fallen down from the third loft of the building (Acts 20:7-12).

14. The church in Rome.
   a. The origin and founder of this church is unknown.
   b. Priscilla and Aquila labored there and a local church met in their home (Rom. 16:3-5).
   c. The church had a ringing testimony throughout all the land (Rom. 1:8).
   d. Paul mentions having more personal friends in this book than in any other New Testament book. The names of some twenty-six individuals may be counted in Roman 16.

15. The church in Galatia.
   a. The various local churches in Galatia were organized by Paul during his first trip.

b. They had all apparently fallen victim to the legalistic Judaizers, who would continually plague Paul's gospel of grace (Gal. 1:6-9).

c. The New Testament epistle Galatians was written to these churches (Gal. 3:1).

16. The church in Colosse.
   a. It was founded during Paul's third trip by Epaphras (Col. 2:1; 1:7, 12, 13).
   b. Philemon and Onesimus (Col. 4:9; Philemon 1:1, 2).
   c. Paul commanded the Colossian epistle to be read to the Laodicean church, and ordered the one he wrote them be read to the Colossian church (Col. 4:16).

17. The church in Babylon (1 Pet. 5:13).
   a. Wherever this church was located, it was filled with suffering believers (1 Pet. 1:6).
   b. Some of this suffering was due to sin (1 Pet. 4:15-17).

18. The church in Smyrna (Rev. 2:8-11).
   a. They had suffered much for Christ.
   b. They had been slandered by those from the synagogue of Satan.
   c. Satan had imprisoned some of them.

19. The church in Pergamos (Rev. 2:12-17).
   a. They were located in the very center of satanic worship.
   b. They had nevertheless remained loyal to Christ in spite of martyrdom.
   c. They were, however, tolerating some in the church who were guilty of sexual sins.
   d. They were also tolerating those who held the doctrine of the Nicolaitans.

20. The church in Thyatira (Rev. 2:18-29).
   a. They had performed many good deeds.
   b. But they permitted a false prophetess named Jezebel to teach that sexual sin was not a serious matter.

21. The church in Sardis (Rev. 3:1-6).
   a. This church had a reputation, but was dead.
   b. They were to strengthen what little good remained.

22. The church in Philadelphia (Rev. 3:7-13).
   a. Even though this church was not strong, it had obeyed God's Word.
   b. This they had done during persecution.

23. The church in Laodicea (Rev. 3:14-22).
   a. This was the worst church mentioned in the New Testament.
   b. They were neither hot nor cold.
   c. They bragged about their wealth, claiming they had need of nothing, but in reality they were wretched, miserable, poor, blind, and naked.
   d. God admonished them to totally repent and allow him to reenter fellowship with them.

Circumcisions

1. That of Ishmael (Gen. 17:23).
2. That of Abraham (Gen. 17:24).
3. That of Isaac (Gen. 21:4).
4. That of every male of Shechem's camp (Gen. 34:24).
5. That of Moses' son (Ex. 4:25).
6. That of every male of Israel's camp (Josh. 5:2-9).
7. That of John the Baptist (Lk. 1:59).
8. That of Jesus (Lk. 2:21).
9. That of Timothy (Acts 16:1, 3).
10. That of Paul (Phil. 3:4, 5).

Cities

ACRE (PTOLEMAIS)
1. Paul stopped here on his final trip to Jerusalem (Acts 21:7).
2. Acre is important because of its excellent harbor and ease of access to the plain of Esdraelon.

ALEXANDRA
The home of Apollos (Acts 18:24-26).

ANATHOTH
The home of Jeremiah (Jer. 1:1).

ANTIOCH OF PISIDIA
Paul preached his first recorded sermon here during the first missionary trip (Acts 13:14-52).

ANTIOCH OF SYRIA
1. The disciples were first called Christians here (Acts 11:19-26).
2. The first missionaries were sent forth from here (Acts 13:1-3).

ANTIPATRIS
The soldiers who took Paul captive from Jerusalem to Caesarea stopped here for the night (Acts 23:31).

ARAD
The men of this city took some of the children of Israel prisoners. Israel vowed to destroy them for this. (Compare Num. 21:1, 2 with 33:40; Josh. 12:14; Jdg. 1:16).

ARIMATHAEA
Home of Joseph, who, along with Nicodemus, claimed the body of our Lord (Mt. 27:57-60).

ASHDOD
One of the five main Philistine cities. Here the Ark of the Covenant soundly defeated the pagan god Dagon (1 Sam. 5:1-8).

ASHKELON
1. Another key Philistine city (1 Sam. 6:17).
2. The birthplace of Herod the Great.
3. Here Samson slew thirty men (Jdg. 14:19).

ASHTAROTH
Home of a number of giants (Deut. 1:4; Josh. 9:10).

ATHENS
Capital city of Greece, where Paul preached his Mars Hill sermon (Acts 17:15-34).

BABYLON
1. Capital city of the Babylonian Empire.
2. Home of the Tower of Babel and original headquarters of all false religions (Rev. 17).
3. The place where Daniel and Ezekiel lived and wrote their Old Testament books.

BEER-SHEBA
The southern limit of Israel (Jdg. 20:1). This city was really a cluster of wells in the open desert. Abraham made a covenant with Abimelech here (Gen. 21:31), and it was in this area that Hagar fled (Gen. 21:14).

BEREA
A place of Bible-loving believers, visited by Paul during his first missionary trip (Acts 17:10-12).

BETHANY
1. Where Lazarus was raised from the dead (Jn. 11).
2. Where Mary anointed the feet of Jesus (Jn. 12:1-11).
3. Where the Lord blessed his disciples just prior to his ascension (Lk. 24:50).

BETHEL
1. Where Abraham worshiped God when he came to Palestine (Gen. 12:8; 13:3, 4).
2. Where Jacob dreamed his "ladder dream" (Gen. 28:11-19).
3. Where Jacob was commanded to return (Gen. 35:1, 8, 15).
4. Where Jeroboam set up a golden calf religion (1 Ki. 12:26-29).
5. Where Elisha was mocked by some wild youths (2 Ki. 2:1-3; 2:23, 24).

BETHLEHEM
1. The burial place of Rachel (Gen. 35:15-18).
2. The home of Boaz and Ruth (Ruth).
3. The birthplace of David and the site of his anointing (1 Sam. 16:4-13).
4. The birthplace of Jesus (Micah 5:2; Jn. 7:42; Lk. 2).
5. Birthplace of Mary and Joseph (Lk. 2:1-4).

BETH-PEOR
Site of the last sermon and burial place of Moses (Deut. 4:44-46; 34:1-6).

BETHPHAGE
Jesus here mounted the donkey he rode into Jerusalem (Mt. 21:1).

BETHSAIDA
1. The home of Philip, Andrew, and Peter (Jn. 1:44).
2. One of the cities upbraided by Jesus (Lk. 10:11-14).
3. Where Jesus healed a blind man (Mk. 8:22-26).

BETH-SHAN
Where the bodies of Saul and Jonathan were nailed to the wall (1 Sam. 31:8-13).

BETH-SHEMESH
1. The birthplace of Samson (Jdg. 13:2-25).
2. Where a number of men were slain for looking into the ark of God (1 Sam. 6:19-21).

CAESAREA
1. The home of Cornelius (Acts 10:1-18).
2. Where God struck down Herod Agrippa I (Acts 12:19-23).
3. The home of Philip the evangelist and his daughters (Acts 21:10-13).
4. Where Paul witnessed to Felix (Acts 24:25).
5. Where Paul witnessed to Agrippa (Acts 26:28).

CAESAREA-PHILIPPI
Where Jesus heard Peter's great confession (Mt. 16:13).

CANA
1. Home of Nathanael (Jn. 21:2).
2. Place where Jesus performed his first miracle, that of turning water into wine (Jn. 2:1–11).
3. Place where Jesus performed his second miracle, that of healing the nobleman's son (Jn. 4:46–54).

CAPERNAUM
1. Main headquarters of Jesus' earthly ministry (Mt. 4:13; 9:1).
2. Where Jesus chose Matthew (Mt. 9:9).
3. Where Jesus delivered his great Bread of Life sermon (Jn. 6:24–71).
4. Where Jesus performed at least nine of his thirty-six recorded miracles:
   a. Healing of the Centurion's servant (Mt. 8:5–13).
   b. Healing of Peter's mother-in-law (Mt. 8:14, 15).
   c. Healing of a demoniac (Mk. 1:21–27).
   d. Healing of palsied man who was lowered from the roof (Mk. 2:1–5).
   e. Healing of the woman with a bloody issue (Mt. 9:22).
   f. Healing of Jairus' daughter (Mt. 9:25).
   g. Healing of two blind men (Mt. 9:29).
   h. Healing of a dumb demoniac (Mt. 9:33).
   i. The miracle of the tribute money (Mt. 17:24–27).

COLOSSE
1. A city which received a New Testament letter from Paul (Colossians).
2. Home of Philemon and Onesimus (Col. 4:9).

CORINTH
1. Home of Aquila and Priscilla (Acts 18:1, 2).
2. Where God appeared to Paul in a vision (Acts 18:9, 10).
3. Paul visited here on his second trip and spent eighteen months in the city (Acts 18:11).
4. This city would receive two of Paul's New Testament epistles (1 and 2 Cor.).

CYRENE
Home of Simon, who carried Jesus' cross (Mt. 27:32).

DAMASCUS
1. The home of Abraham's faithful servant (Gen. 15:2).
2. Where Elisha visited a sick king (2 Ki. 8:7).
3. Israel's King Ahaz built a pagan altar in Jerusalem after seeing a similar one in Damascus (2 Ki. 16:10).
4. The city connected with Paul's conversion (Acts 9:1–18).

DAN
1. A city marking the northern limit of Israel (1 Sam. 3:20).
2. One of two cities where Jeroboam set up his golden calves (1 Ki. 12:29).

DERBE
A stopping point during Paul's first missionary trip (Acts 16:1).

DOTHAN
1. The place from which Joseph was sold into slavery (Gen. 37:17).
2. Where Elisha struck some Syrian soldiers with blindness (2 Ki. 6:13).

EKRON
One of the five main Philistine cities whose leaders hurriedly rid themselves of the troublesome ark of God (1 Sam. 10–12).

EMMAUS
Where Jesus appeared to two disciples after his resurrection (Lk. 24:13–31).

ENDOR
Where Saul visited the witch (1 Sam. 28:7–14).

EN-GEDI
Near where David hid from Saul in a cave (1 Sam. 24:1–22).

EPHESUS
1. Visited by Paul during his second missionary trip (Acts 18:19).
2. City where Apollos was instructed by Aquila and Priscilla (Acts 18:24–26).
3. Where Paul met some of John the Baptist's disciples (Acts 19:1–7).
4. Where the gospel led to a book-burning ceremony and a confrontation with the pagan goddess Diana (Acts 19:18–41).

EZION-GEBER
Home of Solomon's navy (1 Ki. 9:26; 22:48).

GATH
Philistine city, hometown of Goliath (1 Sam. 17:4).

GAZA
1. Philistine city whose main gate was ripped up and carried away by Samson (Jdg. 16:1–3).
2. Where Samson was imprisoned after his betrayal by Delilah (Jdg. 16:21).
3. Area where Philip met the eunuch (Acts 8:26).

GERAR
1. Where Abraham lied the second time about Sarah (Gen. 20).
2. Where Isaac lied about Rebekah (Gen. 26).

GIBEAH
Hometown of the Old Testament king, Saul (1 Sam. 10:26).

GIBEON
1. A city that tricked Joshua into sparing it (Josh. 9:1–27).
2. Where the sun stood still (Josh. 10:12, 13).
3. Where God appeared to Solomon and granted him wisdom (1 Ki. 3:4–15).

GILGAL
1. The first stop of Israel after they crossed the River Jordan west (Josh. 4:19).
2. Where Joshua heard Caleb's testimony (Josh. 14:6–15).
3. Where Saul was publicly proclaimed king (1 Sam. 11:14, 15).
4. Where Saul intruded into the office of the priesthood (1 Sam. 13:4–14).
5. Where Saul lied to Samuel about killing the enemy (1 Sam. 15:12–23).
6. Where Elisha cured a pot of poisonous stew (2 Ki. 4:38–41).

GOMORRAH

A city near Sodom which was destroyed along with it (Gen. 19:24, 25).

HARAN

1. City where Abraham got bogged down for awhile after his call to Canaan (Gen. 11:31; 12:4).
2. The home of Rebekah (Gen. 24:10). Home of Jacob for twenty years. Here all his sons except Benjamin were born (Gen. 28-29).

HAZOR

Headquarters of Israel's enemy Sisera (Jdg. 4:1, 2).

HEBRON

1. Where Abraham built an altar to God (Gen. 13:18).
2. The burial place of Sarah (Gen. 23:2, 19), of Abraham (25:9), of Isaac (35:27-29), and of Jacob (Gen. 50:13).
3. Where David was anointed king over Judah (2 Sam. 2:1-3).
4. Where (seven years later), David was anointed king over all Israel (2 Sam. 5:1-5).
5. Where Joab killed Abner (2 Sam. 3:27).
6. The headquarters of Absalom during his brief rebellion (2 Sam. 15:7-10).
7. One of the six cities of refuge (Josh. 20:7).

ICONIUM

A stop during Paul's first missionary trip (Acts 13:51).

JABESH-GILEAD

A city saved from a cruel fate by King Saul (1 Sam. 11).

JERICHO

1. Home of Rahab the harlot (Josh. 2).
2. City shouted down by Israel (Josh. 6).
3. Location of an Old Testament school of the prophets (2 Ki. 2:5, 15).
4. City from which Elijah departed into heaven (2 Ki. 2:1-5).
5. Where Jesus healed a blind man named Bartimaeus (Lk. 18:35).
6. Where Jesus met Zacchaeus (Lk. 19:1-10).
7. The city Jesus used to illustrate his Good Samaritan parable (Lk. 10:30-37).

JERUSALEM

1. First mentioned in Genesis 14:18 when Abraham fellowshiped with its mysterious King-Priest Melchizedek around 2000 B.C.
2. Joshua later defeated its wicked king (Adonizedek) during Israel's southern campaign invasion of Palestine around 1450 B.C. (Josh. 10:1).
3. It was taken temporarily by the tribe of Judah around 1425 B.C. (Jdg. 1:8).
4. It was the location of a vile sexual crime committed by the perverted Jebusites who controlled it around 1405 B.C. (Jdg. 19:22-30).
5. It was captured by David around 1050 B.C. (2 Sam. 5:6-12) and made the capital of his kingdom (2 Sam. 6:1-19).
6. It was temporarily taken by Absalom around 1020 B.C. (2 Sam. 16:15).
7. David returned to Jerusalem (2 Sam. 19:15-25).
8. Solomon built the Temple around 1005 B.C. (1 Ki. 6).
9. It was plundered by Shishak, King of Egypt, during Rehoboam's reign, around 925 B.C. (1 Ki. 14:25-28; 2 Chron. 12:2-12).
10. The city was plundered by the Philistines and the Arabians during Jehoram's reign, around 890 B.C. (2 Chron. 21:16, 17).
11. It was plundered by the Syrians during the reign of Joash around 850 B.C. (2 Chron. 24:23, 24).
12. It was plundered by northern Israel during Amaziah's reign around 800 B.C. (2 Chron. 25:23).
13. It was surrounded by the Assyrian king, Sennacherib, during Hezekiah's reign, around 710 B.C. (2 Chron. 32).
14. Manasseh, its wicked king, was briefly captured by the Assyrians around 690 B.C. (2 Chron. 33).
15. It was taken briefly by Pharaoh-Necho after King Josiah's death, around 630 B.C. (2 Ki. 23:28-37).
16. It was besieged by Nebuchadnezzar during the reign of Jehoiachin, around 598 B.C. (2 Ki. 24:10-16).
17. It was destroyed and the Temple burned by Nebuchadnezzar during the reign of Zedekiah, Judah's last king, around 588 B.C. (2 Ki. 25).
18. The city began to be reconstructed after the decree of Cyrus by some returning Jews, around 536 B.C. (Ezra 1).
19. The Temple was dedicated by Zerubbabel, around 516 B.C. (Ezra 3:8-13).
20. The walls of the city were completed under Nehemiah, around 445 B.C. (Neh. 6:15).
21. Alexander the Great visited the city in 332 B.C.
22. Jerusalem was captured by Ptolemy Soter in 320 B.C.
23. It was annexed to Egypt in 302.
24. The walls were destroyed and its Temple desecrated by Antiochus Epiphanes in 170 B.C.
25. The Temple was cleansed and rededicated by Mattathias of the House of Hasmon in 167-164 B.C.
26. Jerusalem was captured by the Roman general Pompey in 63 B.C.
27. The walls were rebuilt by Antipater (Herod the Great's Father) in 44 B.C.
28. In 20 B.C., Herod the Great began his world-famous project of enlarging and rebuilding the Temple begun by Zerubbabel. It was built of large blocks of white stone and its facade was plated with gold, so that at a distance it resembled a mountain covered with snow. It cost many millions and took forty-six years to complete. (See Jn. 2:20.)
29. Jesus was dedicated (Lk. 2:1-38).
30. He attended the Passover when he was twelve (Lk. 2:41-50).
31. He cleansed the Temple (Jn. 2:13-17).
32. He spoke to Nicodemus (Jn. 3:1-16).
33. He healed a thirty-eight-year-old invalid (Jn. 5:8).
34. He preached during the feast of the tabernacles on the Holy Spirit (Jn. 7:10-39).
35. He forgave an adulterous woman (Jn. 8:1-11).
36. He preached on the devil and his children (Jn. 8:33-59).
37. He healed a man born blind (Jn. 9:7).
38. He preached a sermon on the Good Shepherd (Jn. 10:1-18).
39. He made his triumphal entry (Jn. 12:12-15).
40. He cursed the fig tree (Mt. 21:19).
41. He utterly condemned the wicked Pharisees (Mt. 23:1-36).
42. He preached the Mt. Olivet discourse (Mt. 24-25).
43. He wept over Jerusalem (Lk. 19:41; Mt. 23:37-39).
44. He conducted the service in the upper room (Jn. 13-14).
45. He preached on the vine and branches (Jn. 15-16).

46. He prayed his great high priestly prayer (Jn. 17).
47. He was arrested in Gethsemane (Mt. 26:47–56).
48. He restored a severed ear (Mt. 26:51).
49. He was condemned to death (Mt. 27:26).
50. He was crucified (Mt. 27:27–50).
51. He was buried (Mt. 27:57–60).
52. He rose from the dead (Mt. 28:1–10).
53. He visited the upper room for the first time after his resurrection (Lk. 24:36–43; Jn. 20:19–23).
54. He visited the upper room for the second time (Jn. 20:24–29).
55. He visited the upper room for the third and final time (Mk. 16:14–18; Lk. 24:44–49).
56. He ascended into heaven (Acts 1:4–11).
57. The disciples conducted a prayer meeting in the upper room (Acts 1:12–26).
58. The day of Pentecost came (Acts 2:1–13).
59. Peter preached his first sermon (Acts 2:14–41).
60. The lame man was healed (Acts 3:1–11).
61. Peter preached his second sermon (Acts 3:12–26).
62. The disciples experienced their first persecution (Acts 4:1–3).
63. Peter preached his third sermon (Acts 4:5–12).
64. The disciples conducted a mighty prayer meeting (Acts 4:23–31).
65. Ananias and Sapphira were judged (Acts 5:1–11).
66. The disciples experienced their second persecution (Acts 5:17–28, 40–42).
67. The first deacons were chosen (Acts 6:1–7).
68. Stephen became the first martyr for Jesus after the ascension; the disciples' third persecution (Acts 6:8—7:60).
69. The disciples experienced their fourth persecution (Acts 8:1–3).
70. Saul returned to Jerusalem after his mighty conversion and was vouched for by Barnabas (Acts 9:26–28).
71. A famine hit the city (Acts 11:27–30).
72. The disciples experienced their fifth persecution (Acts 12:1–19).
73. The council on circumcision was held (Acts 15).
74. Paul was arrested (Acts 21:17—23:22).
75. The Temple and city of Jerusalem were destroyed by Titus the Roman general on September 8, A.D. 70 (Mt. 24:2).
76. In A.D. 132 the Jewish rebel Bar-Kochba recaptured Jerusalem from the Romans.
77. In 135 the revolt was utterly crushed by Emperor Hadrian, who destroyed the city and changed its name to Aelia Capitalina. He built a temple dedicated to Jupiter on the old Jewish Temple site.
78. In 325 Constantine the Great declared Jerusalem a "Christian city."
79. In 614 the Persians conquered the city.
80. In 629 it was taken by the Byzantines.
81. In 638 the Caliph Omar entered Jerusalem.
82. In 691 the famous Dome of the Rock was completed.
83. In 1099 the European crusaders captured Jerusalem.
84. In 1187 Saladin (an Armenian Moslem) took it from the crusaders.
85. In 1229 the crusaders retook it again.
86. In 1244 an army of nomad Turks from central Asia massacred and sacked the city.
87. In 1249 the Mamelukes (Turks from Russia) took the city.
88. In 1517 a Turkish dynasty founded by the Sultan Osman I captured Jerusalem. It would remain in the hands of the Ottoman dynasty until 1917.

89. On Tuesday, December 11, 1917, the British general Allenby entered Jerusalem on foot by way of the Jaffa Gates, thus putting an end to the 400-year reign of the "Abominable Turk."
90. On May 14, 1947, the British government, acting upon the recommendation of the United Nations Commission for the Partition of Palestine among the Arabs, hauled down the Union Jack flag and left Jerusalem.
91. On May 14, 1948, at 4:00 P.M., the Jewish National Council met at Tel Aviv and read the Declaration of Independence.
92. On May 28, 1948, the old city section of Jerusalem fell to Jordan.
93. In December 1948, David Ben-Gurion, Israel's first Prime Minister, moved to New Jerusalem.
94. In April 1949, the Israel-Transjordan Armistice Agreement was signed, whereby Jerusalem was divided between the two countries.
95. On December 13, 1949, the New City of Jerusalem was declared the capital of the State of Israel.
96. On June 5, 1967, the world-famous six-day war began.
97. On June 7, 1967, Israeli troops captured the Old City and reunited all Jerusalem.

JEZREEL
1. The home of Naboth (1 Ki. 21:1–29).
2. The place of Jezebel's death (2 Ki. 9:10, 30–37).
3. Where Jehu killed two kings, Joram of the north, and Ahaziah of the south (2 Ki. 8:29; 9:24, 27).

JOPPA
1. Where Jonah attempted to flee from God's command (Jonah 1:3).
2. Where Peter raised Dorcas from the dead (Acts 9:36–41).
3. Where Peter received his "sheet" vision concerning the Gentiles (Acts 9:43).

KERIOTH
The birthplace of Judas Iscariot.

KIRJATH-JEARIM
Where the Ark of the Covenant was kept for twenty years (1 Sam. 6:21; 7:1, 2).

LAODICEA
Home of one of the seven churches mentioned in Revelation 3:14.

LYDDA
Where Peter cured Aeneas (Acts 9:32–35).

LYSTRA
1. Home of Timothy (Acts 16:1–4).
2. Where Paul was stoned (Acts 14:19; 2 Tim. 3:11).

MAGDALA
Home of Mary Magdalene (Lk. 8:2; Mk. 16:9).

MASADA
1. Where David hid from Saul (1 Sam. 24:22; 1 Chron. 12:8).
2. King Herod's winter headquarters.
3. The site of the Jews' last stand during the A.D. 66–73 revolt against the Romans. The 960 besieged Jews killed themselves rather than surrender.

MICHMASH

The site of Israel's great victory over the Philistines as led by Jonathan (1 Sam. 14:1-23).

MILETUS

A seaport town where Paul met with some Ephesian elders (Acts 20:15-38).

MIZPAH

1. Where Jacob and Laban parted (Gen. 31:49).
2. The hometown of Jephthah (Jdg. 11:34).
3. Where eleven tribes declared war on Benjamin (Jdg. 21:1-8).
4. Where Samuel gathered Israel for prayer and rededication (1 Sam. 7:5-7).
5. Where Saul was introduced to Israel as their first king (1 Sam. 10:17-24).

   Note: Saul was anointed at Ramah by Samuel (1 Sam. 9:15, 16; 10:1), introduced at Mizpah, and publicly crowned at Gilgal (1 Sam. 11:15).

MYRA

Where Paul changed ships as a prisoner en route to Rome (Acts 27:5, 6).

NAIN

Where Jesus raised a widow's son from the dead (Lk. 7:11-18).

NAZARETH

1. Where the angels announced the birth of Jesus to both Mary and Joseph (Lk. 1:26; Mt. 1:19, 20).
2. Where Jesus grew into manhood (Lk. 2:39, 40).
3. Where he preached his Isaiah 61 sermon (Lk. 4:16-30).
4. Where he was set at naught by the townspeople, because "a prophet is not without honor, save in his own country" (Mt. 13:53-58; Mk. 6:1-6).

NINEVEH

1. The ancient captial of Assyria. Jonah was to preach there (Jonah 1).
2. Referred to by Jesus as an Old Testament example (Mt. 12:41).

NOB

1. Where David took refuge during his flight from Saul (1 Sam. 21:1).
2. Where Saul murdered eighty-five priests of the Lord (1 Sam. 22:18).

PAPHOS

A city in southwest Cyprus where Paul worked his first recorded miracle (Acts 13:6-12).

PERGA

Where John Mark left Paul and Barnabas to return home (Acts 13:13).

PERGAMOS

A church in this city is numbered among the seven churches in Revelation (Rev. 2:12).

PETRA

1. The home of Esau (Gen. 36:1).
2. Home of some proud and treacherous Edomites (Obadiah).

3. The possible refuge of saved Israel during the tribulation (Rev. 12:14; Zech. 14:5; Isa. 63:1).

PHILADELPHIA

A church in this city is also numbered in Revelation (Rev. 3:7-13).

PHILIPPI

1. Paul wrote a letter to the church in this city (Philippians).
2. Paul led three to Christ here. These conversion stories are well known:
   a. A Hebrew woman, Lydia (Acts 16:14, 15).
   b. A demon-possessed Greek girl (Acts 16:16-19).
   c. A Roman, the Philippian jailor (Acts 16:25-34).

RABBAH-AMMON

Where Uriah was murdered (2 Sam. 11:2-17).

RAMAH

1. Home of Hannah, Samuel's mother (1 Sam. 1:19).
2. One of Samuel's three circuit stops (the other two were Gilgal and Mizpah (1 Sam. 7:16).
3. Where Israel gathered to demand a king (1 Sam. 8:4, 5).
4. Permanent headquarters of Samuel (1 Sam. 15:34; 16:13).
5. Where Samuel was buried (1 Sam. 25:1).

ROME

1. A church in this city received the greatest theological epistle ever written, the book of Romans.
2. Paul was martyred in Rome (2 Tim. 4).

SALAMIS

A city in southeast Cyprus where Paul preached during his first missionary trip (Acts 13:4, 5).

SAMARIA

1. The capital city of the northern kingdom (1 Ki. 16:24; 2 Ki. 3:1).
2. Where Ahab built his beautiful ivory palace (1 Ki. 16:31-33).
3. Where Elijah confronted Ahab about the murder of Naboth (1 Ki. 21:18).
4. Where Ahab, mortally wounded, died beside a pool (1 Ki. 22:37, 38).
5. Where Elisha led some blinded Syrian soldiers (2 Ki. 6:19).
6. The city saved by four lepers (2 Ki. 7:1-20).
7. Where Naaman was healed (2 Ki. 5:3-14).
8. Where Jehu killed all the Baalite priests (2 Ki. 10:17-28).
9. Where Philip the evangelist led a great revival (Acts 8:5-25).

SHECHEM

1. Where Jacob buried his household's false gods (Gen. 35:4).
2. Where Simeon and Levi tricked their enemies (Gen. 34).
3. Where Joseph's bones were buried (Josh. 24:32).
4. One of the six cities of refuge (Josh. 20:7, 8).
5. The headquarters of Abimelech's evil doings (Jdg. 9).
6. Where Rehoboam was crowned king (1 Ki. 12:1).
7. Where Joshua gave his farewell address (Josh. 24:1).

SHILOH
1. Home of the tabernacle after Israel conquered Palestine (Josh. 18:1).
2. Where Joshua divided up the land (Josh. 18:2–10; 19:51; 21:1–3).
3. Where the remaining Benjaminite warriors found wives (Jdg. 21:16–23).
4. Where Hannah prayed for a son (1 Sam. 1).
5. Where God appeared to Samuel (1 Sam. 3:21).
6. Where Jeroboam's wife attempted to trick Ahijah the prophet (1 Ki. 14:1–18).

SHUNEM
Home of the Shunammite woman whose son Elisha raised (2 Ki. 4:8).

SIDON
1. Home of Jezebel (1 Ki. 16:31–33).
2. Home of the Syro-phoenician woman whose daughter Jesus healed (Mt. 15:21–28).

SMYRNA
A church in this city is listed as one of the seven in Revelation (2:8–11).

SODOM
1. Abraham refused to enter into a pact with the wicked king of this perverted city (Gen. 14:21–24).
2. God destroyed Sodom (Gen. 19).

SUCCOTH
1. Jacob's home for a while after meeting up with Esau (Gen. 33:17).
2. A city punished by Gideon because of their refusal to feed his hungry troops (Jdg. 8:5–16).

SYCHAR
Home of the Samaritan woman who talked with Jesus at the well (Jn. 4:7–26).

TARSUS
Birthplace of Paul (Acts 9:11; 21:39; 22:3).

TEKOA
1. Home of Amos the prophet (Amos 1:1).
2. Home of a woman who attempted to reconcile David and Absalom (2 Sam. 14:2–4).

THESSALONICA
1. Paul established a church here during his second missionary trip (Acts 17:1–9).
2. He later wrote two New Testament epistles to this church (1 and 2 Thess.).

THYATIRA
1. Home of Lydia (Acts 16:14).
2. Location of one of the seven churches in Revelation 2:18–24.

TIBERIAS
The town at the mouth of the Jordan River and the Sea of Galilee (Jn. 6:1; 21:1).

TROAS
1. Where Paul received his Macedonian vision (Acts 16:11).

2. Where Paul revived Eutychus (Acts 20:6–12).
3. Where Paul left his cloak (2 Tim. 4:13).

TYRE
1. Home of Hiram, the supplier for Solomon's Temple (1 Ki. 5:1–11; 9:11–14).
2. The city of Ezekiel's great prophecy (Ezek. 26).
3. Where God struck down Herod with a plague (Acts 12:20).
4. Where Paul knelt down by the seashore and prayed (Acts 21:2–6).

UR
Birthplace of Abraham (Gen. 11:27, 28; 15:7; Neh. 9:7).

ZAREPHATH
Home of a widow with whom Elijah stayed (1 Ki. 17:9–24; Lk. 4:26).

ZOAR
Near the cave where Lot and his daughters stayed after Sodom's destruction (Gen. 19:30).

Clouds
1. The rainbow cloud of Noah (Gen. 9:13).
2. The little cloud of Elijah (1 Ki. 18:44).
3. The glory cloud of God:
   a. It led Israel across the wilderness (Ex. 13:21, 22; Num. 9:17–22).
   b. It protected Israel at the Red Sea (Ex. 14:19, 20, 24).
   c. It appeared when Israel murmured in the Zin wilderness (Ex. 16:10).
   d. It appeared when God spoke to Moses on Mt. Sinai (Ex. 19:9, 16; 24:15, 16, 18; 34:5).
   e. It filled the tabernacle during Moses' dedication (Ex. 40:34–38).
   f. It stood above the mercy seat in the Holy of Holies (Lev. 16:2).
   g. It appeared when God appointed the seventy (Num. 11:25).
   h. It appeared when Miriam spoke against Moses' wife (Num. 12:5).
   i. It appeared as Moses pled for Israel (Num. 14:14).
   j. It appeared during Korah's rebellion (Num. 16:42).
   k. It filled the Temple during Solomon's dedication (1 Ki. 8:10, 11; 2 Chron. 5:13, 14).
   l. It was seen by Ezekiel (Ezek. 1:28; 8:11; 10:3, 4).
   m. It appeared to the shepherds at Christ's birth (Lk. 2:8, 9).
   n. It was present at Christ's baptism (Mt. 3:16).
   o. It was present at Christ's transfiguration (Mt. 17:5).
   p. It was present at Christ's death (Mt. 27:45).
   q. It was present at Christ's ascension (Acts 1:9).
   r. It will appear at the rapture (1 Thess. 4:17).
   s. It will appear during the tribulation at the funeral of God's two witnesses (Rev. 11:12).
   t. It will appear during the Second Coming (Dan. 7:13; Mt. 24:30, 64; Rev. 1:7; 14:14).

Colors
1. Black—Leviticus 13:31, 37; Esther 1:6; Job 30:30; Lamentations 4:8.
2. White—Leviticus 13:38; Daniel 7:9; Matthew 17:2; Ecclesiastes 9:8.
3. Scarlet—Isaiah 1:18; Revelation 17:3, 4.

4. Purple—Exodus 28:5.
5. Red—Matthew 16:2, 3.
6. Blue—Exodus 26:31.
7. Yellow—Leviticus 13:30, 32.
8. Green—Revelation 9:4.

Commands
TO ADAM
1. Be fruitful, and multiply, and replenish the earth, and subdue it (Gen. 1:28).
2. But of the tree of the knowledge of good and evil, you shall not eat (Gen. 2:17).

TO NOAH
1. Make an ark of gopher wood (Gen. 6:14).
2. And of every living thing of all flesh, two of every sort you shall bring into the ark (Gen. 6:19).
3. Come with all your house into the ark (Gen. 7:1).
4. Go forth from the ark (Gen. 8:16).
5. Be fruitful, and multiply, and replenish the earth (Gen. 9:1).

TO ABRAHAM
1. Go out from your country unto a land I will show you (Gen. 12:1).
2. This shall not be your heir (Gen. 15:4).
3. Take an heifer (Gen. 15:9).
4. And you shall circumcise the flesh of your foreskin (Gen. 17:11).
5. Your name shall be Abraham (Gen. 17:5).
6. You shall not call her name Sarai, but Sarah (Gen. 17:15).
7. Take your son and offer him for a burnt offering (Gen. 22:2).

TO ISAAC
Do not go down into Egypt (Gen. 26:2).

TO JACOB
1. Your name shall no longer be called Jacob, but Israel (Gen. 32:28).
2. Arise, go up to Bethel, and dwell there (Gen. 35:1).
3. Fear not to go down into Egypt (Gen. 46:3).

TO MOSES
1. Take off your shoes (Ex. 3:5).
2. You shall say to the children of Israel, I AM hath sent me to you (Ex. 3:14).
3. Cast your rod on the ground (Ex. 4:3).
4. Put your hand into your bosom (Ex. 4:6).
5. Go, and I will be with your mouth (Ex. 4:12).
6. Take your rod, and stretch out your hand upon the waters of Egypt (Ex. 7:19).
7. Each man take a lamb (Ex. 12:3).
8. Lift up your rod over the sea and divide it (Ex. 14:16).
9. Smite the rock (Ex. 17:6).
10. Write this for a memorial in a book (Ex. 17:14).
11. Let them make me a sanctuary (Ex. 25:8).
12. Go, get down; for your people have corrupted themselves (Ex. 32:7).
13. Behold, there is a place by me, and you shall stand upon a rock (Ex. 33:21).
14. Take Aaron and the anointing oil (Lev. 8:2).
15. Gather seventy men of the elders of Israel (Num. 11:16).
16. Send men, that they may search the land of Canaan (Num. 13:2).
17. Speak unto the rock (Num. 20:8).
18. Make a fiery serpent and set it upon a pole (Num. 21:8).
19. Strip Aaron of his garments, and put them upon Eleazar his son (Num. 20:26).
20. Take Joshua and lay hands upon him (Num. 27:18).
21. Get up unto Mount Nebo (Deut. 32:49). Note: Some forty years prior to this, God had commanded him to climb another mountain, Mt. Sinai (see Ex. 19:20).

TO ISRAEL
1. You shall have no other gods before me.
2. You shall not make any graven image.
3. You shall not take the name of the Lord your God in vain.
4. Remember the Sabbath day, to keep it holy.
5. Honor your father and mother.
6. You shall not kill.
7. You shall not commit adultery.
8. You shall not steal.
9. You shall not bear false witness.
10. You shall not covet (Ex. 20:3–17).
11. You shall love the Lord your God with all your heart, and with all your soul, and with all your might (Deut. 6:5). (See also 10:12.)
12. These words which I command you shall be in your heart (Deut. 6:6). (See also 11:18-20.)
13. You shall teach (God's words) diligently unto your children (Deut. 6:7).
14. You shall fear the Lord your God, and serve him (Deut. 6:13).
15. Circumcise the foreskin of your heart, and be no longer stiffnecked (Deut. 10:16).
16. Whatever I command you, observe and do it. You shall not add to or subtract from it (Deut. 12:32).

TO JOSHUA
1. Moses my servant is dead; now arise, go over Jordan. (Josh. 1:2).
2. Have I not commanded you? Be strong and courageous; do not be afraid, or dismayed (Josh. 1:9).
3. Circumcise again the children of Israel (Josh. 5:2).
4. Go around the city once. Do this for six days and the seventh day you shall circle the city seven times (Josh. 6:3, 4).
5. Get up; why do you lie upon your face? (Josh. 7:10).

TO GIDEON
1. Proclaim in the ears of the people, saying, Whoever is fearful and afraid, let him return and depart (Jdg. 7:3).
2. The people are still too many; bring them down to the water, and I will try them there (Jdg. 7:4).

TO SAMUEL
1. I will send you a man out of the land of Benjamin, and you shall anoint him to be captain over my people Israel (1 Sam. 9:16).
2. Look not on his appearance, for the Lord looks on the heart. Arise, anoint him: for this is he (1 Sam. 16:7, 12).

TO DAVID
1. And the Lord said, Go up to Hebron. (2 Sam. 2:1).
2. You shall not build me a house to dwell in (1 Chron. 17:4).

TO ELIJAH

1. Go and hide yourself by the brook Cherith (1 Ki. 17:3).
2. Get thee to Zarephath (1 Ki. 17:9).
3. Go, show yourself to Ahab (1 Ki. 18:1).
4. Rise up and eat, because the journey is too great for you (1 Ki. 19:7).

TO BELIEVERS

1. Abstain from all appearances of evil (1 Thess. 5:22).
2. Abstain from all fleshly lusts (1 Pet. 2:11).
3. Avoid troublemakers (Rom. 16:17).
4. Avoid profane and vain babblings (1 Tim. 6:20).
5. Avoid false science (1 Tim. 6:20).
6. Avoid foolish questions (Titus 3:9).
7. Avoid arguments about the law (Titus 3:9).
8. Be reconciled to a brother (Mt. 5:24).
9. Be wise as serpents (Mt. 10:16).
10. Be harmless as doves (Mt. 10:16).
11. Be thankful (Col. 3:15).
12. Be patient toward all men (1 Thess. 5:14; 2 Tim. 2:24).
13. Be ready to give an answer of the hope that is in you (1 Pet. 3:15).
14. Be transformed (Rom. 12:2).
15. Be patient in tribulation (Rom. 12:12).
16. Be children in (avoiding) malice (1 Cor. 14:20).
17. Be men in understanding (1 Cor. 14:20).
18. Be steadfast (1 Cor. 15:58).
19. Be unmovable (1 Cor. 15:58).
20. Be always abounding in God's work (1 Cor. 15:58).
21. Be of one mind (Rom. 12:16).
22. Be separate from the unclean (2 Cor. 6:17).
23. Be angry and sin not (Eph. 4:26).
24. Be filled with the Spirit (Eph. 5:18).
25. Be anxious for nothing (Phil. 4:6).
26. Be an example to other believers (1 Tim. 4:12).
27. Be gentle to all men (2 Tim. 2:24).
28. Be ready to teach (2 Tim. 2:24).
29. Be content with what you have (Heb. 13:5).
30. Be vigilant (1 Pet. 5:8).
31. Do not be like the hypocrites in prayer (Mt. 6:5).
32. Do not be afraid of men (Lk. 12:4).
33. Do not be conformed to this world (Rom. 12:2).
34. Do not be children in understanding (1 Cor. 14:20).
35. Do not be deceived by evil companions (1 Cor. 15:33).
36. Do not be unequally yoked with unbelievers (2 Cor. 6:14–18).
37. Do not be drunk with wine (Eph. 5:18).
38. Do not be weary in well-doing (2 Thess. 3:13).
39. Do not be slothful (Heb. 6:12).
40. Do not be influenced by strange doctrines (Heb. 13:9).
41. Beware of false prophets (Mt. 7:15; Phil. 3:2).
42. Beware of (evil) men (Mt. 10:17).
43. Beware of covetousness (Lk. 12:15).
44. Beware of backsliding (2 Pet. 3:17).
45. Do not bid false teachers Godspeed (2 Jn. 10, 11).
46. Bring up children in the Lord (Eph. 6:4).
47. Cast your cares upon God (1 Pet. 5:7).
48. Have confidence in God (Heb. 10:35).
49. Come out from among the world (2 Cor. 6:17).
50. Count it joy when you are tempted (Jas. 1:2).
51. Treat others as you expect to be treated (Mt. 7:12).
52. Desire the milk of the Word (1 Pet. 2:2).
53. Do all to God's glory (1 Cor. 10:31; Col. 3:17, 23).
54. Do all things without murmuring or disputing (Phil. 2:14).

55. Earnestly contend for the faith (Jude 3).
56. Give no place to Satan (Eph. 4:27).
57. Give thanks (Eph. 5:20; Phil. 4:6).
58. Give time to reading (1 Tim. 4:13).
59. Give no offense (1 Cor. 10:32).
60. Give freely (2 Cor. 9:6, 7).
61. Give as God has prospered (1 Cor. 16:2).
62. Give willingly (2 Cor. 8:12).
63. Give purposely (2 Cor. 9:7).
64. Do not grieve the Holy Spirit (Eph. 4:30).
65. Grow in grace (2 Pet. 3:18).
66. Have no fellowship with darkness (Eph. 5:11).
67. Have compassion (Jude 23).
68. Have a good conscience (1 Pet. 3:16).
69. Hold forth the Word of life (Phil. 2:16).
70. Hold fast sound words (2 Tim. 1:13).
71. Honor fathers (Eph. 6:2).
72. Honor mothers (Mt. 19:19).
73. Honor widows (1 Tim. 5:3).
74. Honor rulers (1 Pet. 2:17).
75. Lay aside all envy (1 Pet. 2:1).
76. Lay aside all evil speaking (1 Pet. 2:1).
77. Do not lay up treasures on earth (Mt. 6:19).
78. Let your light shine (Mt. 5:16).
79. Let everyone deny himself (Mt. 16:24).
80. Let him share with the needy (Lk. 3:11).
81. Let everyone obey civil laws (Rom. 13:1).
82. Let no man deceive himself (1 Cor. 3:18).
83. Let everyone examine himself at communion (1 Cor. 11:28).
84. Let your requests be made known to God (Phil. 4:6).
85. Let your speech be with grace (Col. 4:6).
86. Do all things in decent order (1 Cor. 14:40).
87. Let those who are taught support the teacher (Gal. 6:6).
88. Let wives be subject to their husbands (Eph. 5:22; Col. 3:18).
89. Let husbands love their wives (Eph. 5:25).
90. Let wives reverence their husbands (Eph. 5:33).
91. Let everyone be swift to hear, slow to speak, slow to wrath (Jas. 1:19).
92. Let the afflicted pray (Jas. 5:13).
93. Let the adorning of women be more inward than outward (1 Pet. 3:3, 4).
94. Don't let the left hand know what the right hand is doing (Mt. 6:3).
95. Do not let sin reign in the body (Rom. 6:12).
96. Do not let the sun go down on your wrath (Eph. 4:26).
97. Follow things that edify (Rom. 14:19).
98. Walk in the Spirit (Gal. 5:25).
99. Do not provoke one another (Gal. 5:26).
100. Do not be weary in well-doing (Gal. 6:9).
101. Come boldly to the throne of grace (Heb. 4:16; 10:19–23).
102. Do not forsake assembling together in worship (Heb. 10:25).
103. Exhort one another (Heb. 10:25).
104. Lay aside every weight (Heb. 12:1).
105. Run with patience the race before us (Heb. 12:1).
106. Look to Jesus (Heb. 12:2).
107. Offer the sacrifice of praise to God continually (Heb. 13:15).
108. Do not judge one another in doubtful things (Rom. 14:1).
109. Do not cause others to stumble (Rom. 14:13).
110. Mark troublemakers (Rom. 16:17; Phil. 3:17).

111. Pray for your persecutors (Mt. 5:44; Lk. 6:28).
112. Pray for laborers (Mt. 9:38; Lk. 10:2).
113. Present your body to God (Rom. 12:1).
114. Put on the new man (Eph. 4:24; Col. 3:10).
115. Put on the whole armor of God (Eph. 6:11, 13).
116. Do not quench the Spirit (1 Thess. 5:19).
117. Consider yourself dead to sin (Rom. 6:11).
118. Redeem the time (Eph. 5:16).
119. Resist the devil (Jas. 4:7; 1 Pet. 5:9).
120. Restore backsliders in meekness (Gal. 6:1).
121. Strengthen feeble knees (Heb. 12:12).
122. Study to show yourself approved to God (2 Tim. 2:15).
123. Take no anxious thought of tomorrow (Mt. 6:34).
124. Take the Lord's Supper (1 Cor. 11:24–26).
125. Be careful not to despise little ones (Mt. 18:10).
126. Be aware of yourself and your doctrine (1 Tim. 4:16).
127. Withdraw from disorderly people (2 Thess. 3:6, 14).

Confessions of Sin

1. Judah, concerning the sin of immorality (Gen. 38:26).
2. Pharaoh, concerning his persecution of Israel (Ex. 10:16).
   Note: Not all confessions in the Bible were genuine!
3. Balaam, concerning his disobedience to God's Word (Num 22:34).
4. Achan, concerning his goods stolen from Jericho (Josh. 7:20).
5. Saul, concerning (1) his sparing of the spoils of war, and (2) concerning his murderous intents toward David. (1 Sam. 15:24, 30; 26:21).
6. David, concerning (1) his sin with Bath-sheba, and (2) his sin in numbering Israel (2 Sam. 12:13; Ps. 51:4; and 2 Sam. 24:10, 17).
7. Job, concerning his self-righteousness (Job 42:6).
8. Shimei, concerning his sin of cursing David (2 Sam. 19:20).
9. Manasseh, concerning his evil reign on Judah's throne (2 Chron. 33:11–13).
10. Daniel, concerning his personal sins and those of Israel (Dan. 9:20).
11. Moses, concerning Israel's golden calf sin (Ex. 32:30–32).
12. Isaiah, concerning his personal sins, and those of Israel (Isa. 6:5; 59:12).
13. Jeremiah, concerning his personal sins, and those of Israel (Jer. 3:25).
14. Ezra, concerning his personal sins, and those of Judah (Ezra 10:1).
15. Nehemiah, concerning his personal sins, and those of Judah (Neh. 1:6).
16. The prodigal son, concerning his riotous living (Lk. 15:18).
17. Peter, concerning his denial of Christ (Mt. 26:75).
18. Judas, concerning his remorse in betraying Christ (Mt. 27:4).
19. A Corinthian believer, concerning his immorality (1 Cor. 5:1–13; 2 Cor. 2:1–11; 7:9, 10).

Conversions
OLD TESTAMENT CONVERSIONS
1. Abel (Gen. 4:4).
2. Abraham (Gen. 12:1–3; 15:6).
3. Jacob (Gen. 28:19–22).
4. Rahab (Josh. 2:9).
5. Ruth (Ruth 1:16).
6. Samuel (1 Sam. 3:1–10).
7. David (1 Sam. 16:13).
8. Widow of Zarephath (1 Ki. 17:24).
9. Shunammite woman (2 Ki. 4:30).
10. Naaman (2 Ki. 5:14, 15).
11. Manasseh (2 Chron. 33:10–13, 18, 19).
12. Cyrus (Ezra 1:2–4; Isa. 44:28).
13. Nebuchadnezzar (Dan. 3:28, 29; 4:1, 2, 34, 35, 37).
14. Darius (Dan. 6:25–27).
15. King of Nineveh (Jonah 3:5–9).

NEW TESTAMENT CONVERSIONS
1. Peter (Jn. 1:42).
2. Andrew (Jn. 1:40).
3. Philip (Jn. 1:43).
4. Nathanael (Jn. 1:49).
5. Nicodemus (Jn. 3).
6. Samaritan woman (Jn. 4:29).
7. Nobleman (Jn. 4:53).
8. Adulterous woman (Jn. 8:11).
9. A blind man (Jn. 9:38).
10. Martha (Jn. 11:27).
11. A centurion (Mt. 8:10, 13).
12. Matthew (Mt. 9:9).
13. A Syro-phoenician woman (Mt. 15:28).
14. Another centurion (Mt. 27:54).
15. The Gadara maniac (Mk. 5:15).
16. A woman with internal bleeding (Mk. 5:34).
17. The father of a demoniac son (Mk. 9:24).
18. Bartimaeus (Mk. 10:52).
19. A scribe (Mk. 12:34).
20. A paralytic (Lk. 5:20).
21. An immoral woman (Lk. 7:38).
22. A leper (Lk. 17:12–19).
23. A publican (Lk. 18:13, 14).
24. Zacchaeus (Lk. 19:8).
25. A woman with an eighteen-year infirmity (Lk. 13:12, 13).
26. Mary Magdalene (Mk. 16:9).
27. A dying thief (Lk. 23:42).
28. A lame man (Acts 3:8).
29. The Ethiopian eunuch (Acts 8:37).
30. Saul (Acts 9:6).
31. Cornelius (Acts 10:44).
32. Sergius Paulus (Acts 13:12).
33. Lydia (Acts 16:14, 15).
34. A demoniac girl (Acts 16:18).
35. The Philippian jailor (Acts 16:32, 34).
36. Crispus (Acts 18:8).
37. Apollos (Acts 18:24, 25).

Counterfeits

1. False christs (Mt. 24:4, 5, 24).
2. False ministers (2 Cor. 11:14, 15).
3. False Christians (Gal. 2:3, 4).
4. False apostles (2 Cor. 11:13).
5. False religious teachers (2 Pet. 2:1).
6. False prophets (1 Jn. 4:1).
7. False gospel (Gal. 1:6–12).
8. False doctrines (Heb. 13:9).
9. False commandments (Titus 1:13, 14).
10. False miracle workers (2 Thess. 2:7–12).
11. False science (1 Tim. 6:20).
12. False religion (Jas. 1:26).
13. False worship (Mt. 15:8, 9).
14. False prayer (Jas. 4:3).

Covenants

A covenant (*berith,* in the Old Testament Hebrew; *diatheke* in the New Testament Greek) is a promise or an agreement between God and man. A covenant may be conditional or unconditional. There are eight important covenants in the Bible:

1. The covenant with all repenting sinners to save them through Christ. (See Titus 1:1, 2; Heb. 13:20.) This covenant is unconditional (has no strings attached).
2. The covenant with Adam (Gen. 1:28; 2:15, 16; 3:15-19).
   a. Before the Fall—that he could remain in Eden as long as he obeyed. This was conditional.
   b. After the Fall—that God would someday send a Savior. This was unconditional.
3. The covenant with Noah (Gen. 8:21, 22).
   a. That the earth would not be destroyed by water again.
   b. That the seasons would continue until the end. This was unconditional.
4. The covenant with Abraham (Gen. 12:2, 3, 7; 13:14-17; 15:5, 18; 17:8).
   a. That God would make Abraham the founder of a great nation.
   b. That God would someday give Palestine forever to Abraham's seed. This was an unconditional covenant.
5. The covenant with Moses and Israel (Ex. 19:3-8; Lev. 26; Deut. 28).
   a. That Israel could have the land at that time to enjoy if she obeyed.
   b. That Israel would forfeit all God's blessings if she disobeyed. This was a conditional covenant.
6. The covenant with David (2 Chron. 13:5; 2 Sam. 7:12-16; 23:5).
   a. That from David would come an everlasting throne.
   b. That from David would come an everlasting kingdom.
   c. That from David would come an everlasting King. This was an unconditional covenant.
7. The covenant with the church (Mt. 16:18; 26:28; Lk. 22:20; Heb. 13:20, 21).
   a. That Christ would build his church with his own blood.
   b. That all the fury of hell would not destroy it.
   c. That he would perfect all the members of his church. This was an unconditional covenant.
8. The new covenant with Israel (Jer. 31:31-34; Isa. 42:6; 43:1-6; Deut. 1:1-9; Heb. 8:7-12).
   a. That God would eventually bring Israel back to himself.
   b. That he would forgive their iniquity and forget their sin.
   c. That he would use them to reach and teach Gentiles.
   d. That he would establish them in Palestine forever. This was an unconditional covenant.

Crowns

1. The crown of the high priest (Ex. 29:6; 39:30).
2. The crown of thorns (Mt. 27:29).
3. The crown of a soul-winner (Phil. 4:1; 1 Thess. 2:19).
4. The crown of righteousness (2 Tim. 4:8).
5. The crown of life (Jas. 1:12; Rev. 2:10; 3:11).
6. The crown of heaven's King of kings (Rev. 14:14; 19:12).
7. The crown of incorruption (1 Cor. 9:25).
8. The crown of glory (1 Pet. 5:4).
9. The crown of demons (Rev. 9:7).
10. The crown of Satan (Rev. 12:3).
11. The crown of the antichrist (Rev. 6:2; 13:1).

Cruses

1. The one David took from Saul (1 Sam. 26:12).
2. The one God filled for a widow at Elijah's command (1 Ki. 17:12).

Cups

1. A silver cup (Gen. 44:2, 12).
2. A cup of suffering (Mt. 26:39).
3. A wine cup (Mt. 26:27).
4. A cup of wrath (Isa. 51:17; Rev. 16:19).
5. The cup of filthiness (Rev. 17:4).
6. The cup of salvation (Ps. 116:13).

Curses

1. Upon the serpent (Gen. 3:14, 15).
2. Upon the ground (Gen. 3:17, 18; 5:29; 8:21).
3. Upon nature (Rom. 8:19-22).
4. Upon Cain (Gen. 4:11).
5. Upon Canaan (Gen. 9:25).
6. Upon disobedient Israel (Deut. 28:15).
7. Upon the enemies of Israel (Gen. 12:3).
8. Upon a fruitless fig tree (Mk. 11:21).
9. Upon all unbelievers (Mt. 25:41).
10. Upon false preachers (Gal. 1:8).
11. Upon Jehoiakim (Jer. 22:18, 19; 36:30).
12. Upon all who attempt to remain under the law (Gal. 3:10).
13. Upon Christ, for our sin (Gal. 3:13).

Days

Introduction: There are at least ten important "days," all yet in the future, that this world will experience. Some of these days refer to a twenty-four-hour period, while others stand for a much longer period of time.

1. The day of the rapture (Rom. 13:12; Eph. 4:30; Phil. 1:6, 10; 2:16; 2 Pet. 1:19; may be regarded as a literal twenty-four-hour day).
2. The judgment seat of Christ day (1 Cor. 3:13; 5:5; 2 Tim. 1:18; 4:8; 1 Jn. 4:17; may be regarded as a literal twenty-four-hour day and will include only Christians).
3. The day of the Lord (Joel 1:15; 2:1, 2, 11, 31; Acts 2:20; 2 Thess. 2:3; Rev. 6:17; this "day" covers the entire tribulation, a period of seven years).
4. The day of Christ's Second Coming (Mt. 24:36; 26:29; 1 Thess. 5:2-4; 2 Thess. 1:10; may be regarded as a literal twenty-four-hour day).
5. The day of Armageddon (Rev. 16:14; may be regarded as a literal twenty-four-hour day).
6. The resurrection of the just day (Jn. 6:39, 40, 44, 54; 11:24; may be regarded as a literal twenty-four-hour day and includes all Old Testament saints and tribulational believers).
7. The fallen angel judgment day (Jude 1:6; may be regarded as a literal twenty-four-hour day).
8. The day of Christ (1 Cor. 1:8; 2 Cor. 1:14; 2 Tim. 1:12; this "day" covers the entire millennium, a period of one thousand years).

9. The great white throne judgment day (Mt. 7:22; 11:22; Jn. 12:48; Acts 17:31; Rom. 2:5, 16: 2 Pet. 2:9; may be regarded as a literal twenty-four-hour day).
10. The new creation day (2 Pet. 3:7-12; may be regarded as a literal twenty-four-hour day).

Deserts
1. Arabia, where Paul went after his conversion (Gal. 1:17).
2. Midian, where Moses spent the second forty years of his life (Ex. 2:15, 21; 3:1; Acts 7:29).
3. Paran, where David hid from Saul (1 Sam. 25:1).
4. Shur, where God spoke to Hagar (Gen. 16:9-14).
5. Sin, where Israel marched through en route to Sinai (Ex. 16:1).
6. Temptation wilderness, where Jesus was tempted (Mt. 4:1).

Diseases and Infirmities
1. Barrenness, as suffered by Sarah, Hannah, and Elisabeth (Gen. 16:1; 1 Sam. 1:6; Lk. 1:7).
2. Blains and boils, as suffered by the Egyptians during the sixth plague, by King Hezekiah, and by Job (Ex. 9:9, 10; 2 Ki. 20:7; Job 2:7).
3. Blindness, as suffered by the following New Testament individuals:
   a. Two Capernaum blind men (Mt. 9:29).
   b. A Bethsaida blind man (Mk. 8:25).
   c. A Jerusalem man born blind (Jn. 9:7).
   d. A blind beggar near Jericho named Bartimaeus (Mk. 10:46).
   e. A blind beggar near Jericho (unnamed) (Lk. 18:42).
4. Botch (may have been syphilis), as suffered by the Egyptians (Deut. 28:27; 28:35).
5. Bloody flux (dysentery), as suffered by the father of Publius (Acts 28:8).
6. Broken bones (Lev. 21:19).
7. Crooked back (Lev. 21:20).
8. Canker (cancer) (2 Tim. 2:17).
9. Dropsy, as suffered by the man in Luke 14:2.
10. Dwarfism (Lev. 21:20).
11. Deafness, as suffered by the man in Mark 7:34, 35.
12. Dumbness, as suffered by the man in Matthew 9:33.
13. Demon possession, as suffered by:
   a. Saul (1 Sam. 16:14).
   b. A Capernaum demoniac (Mk. 1:25; Lk. 4:35).
   c. A Geresene demoniac (Mt. 8:32; Mk. 5:8; Lk. 8:33).
   d. A dumb demoniac (Mt. 9:33).
   e. A demoniac girl (Mt. 15:28; Mk. 7:29).
   f. A demoniac boy (Mt. 17:18; Mk. 9:25; Lk. 9:42).
   g. A blind and dumb demoniac (Mt. 12:22; Lk. 11:14).
   h. Mary Magdalene (Mk. 16:9).
   i. Simon of Samaria (Acts 8:9-23).
   j. A sorcerer named Elymas (Acts 13:8).
   k. A greek girl (Acts 16:16-18).
   l. Seven sons of Sceva (Acts 19:14-16).
14. Emerods (tumors), as suffered by the Philistines who captured the ark of God (1 Sam. 5:6).
15. Fever, as suffered by:
   a. Peter's mother-in-law (Mt. 8:14, 15).
   b. A little boy (Jn. 4:52).
16. Issue (an unnatural flow of blood), as suffered by a Capernaum woman for twelve years (Mt. 9:20).
17. Itch (eczema), as mentioned by Moses in Deuteronomy 28:27.
18. Lameness, as suffered by:
   a. Mephibosheth, the son of Jonathan (2 Sam. 4:4; 9:13).
   b. A man in Jerusalem who dwelt near the pool of Bethesda (Jn. 5:5).
   c. A man in Jerusalem who dwelt near the gate called Beautiful (Acts 3:2).
   d. A man in Lystra (Acts 14:8).
19. Leprosy, as suffered by:
   a. Miriam (Num. 12:10).
   b. Naaman (2 Ki. 5:1).
   c. Four Samaritan beggars (2 Ki. 7:3).
   d. Azariah (2 Ki. 15:5).
   e. A Galilean man (Mk. 1:40).
   f. Simon (Mt. 26:6).
   g. A Samaritan and his nine unthankful friends (Lk. 17:12).
20. Palsy (paralysis), as suffered by:
   a. A Capernaum man (Lk. 5:18).
   b. A centurion's servant (Mt. 8:6).
   c. Aeneas (Acts 9:33).
21. Sores (ulcerated openings) as suffered by:
   a. Old Testament Israel (Isa. 1:6).
   b. Lazarus the beggar (Lk. 16:20).
   c. The ungodly in the tribulation (Rev. 16:2).
22. Sunstroke, as perhaps suffered by the Shunammite woman's son (2 Ki. 4:19).
23. Worms (a possible reference to intestinal roundworm infection), as suffered by Herod (Acts 12:21-23).

Dispensations
1. The dispensation of innocence (from the creation of man to the Fall of man (Gen. 1:28—3:6).
2. The dispensation of conscience (from the Fall to the flood (Gen. 4:1-8:14).
3. The dispensation of civil government (from the flood to the dispersion at Babel) (Gen. 8:15—11:9).
4. The dispensation of promise or patriarchal rule (from Babel to Mount Sinai) (Gen. 11:10; Ex. 18:27).
5. The dispensation of the Mosaic Law (from Mount Sinai to the upper room) (Ex. 19; Acts 1:26).
6. The dispensation of the bride of the Lamb, the Church (from the upper Room to the rapture) (Acts 2:1; Rev. 3:22).
7. The dispensation of the wrath of the Lamb—the tribulation (from the rapture to the Second Coming) (Rev. 6:1—20:3).
8. The dispensation of the rule of the Lamb—the millennium (from the Second Coming through the great white throne judgment) (Rev. 20:4-15).
9. The dispensation of the new creation of the Lamb—the world without end (from the great white throne judgment throughout all eternity) (Rev. 21-22).

Doors
1. Literal doors
   a. The door to the ark (Gen. 6:16; 7:16).
   b. The Passover door (Ex. 12:7, 23).
   c. The tabernacle door (Ex. 29:11).
   d. Christ's resurrection door (Mt. 27:60; 28:2).
2. Symbolic doors
   a. The door of prayer (Mt. 6:6).
   b. The door of service (1 Cor. 16:9; 2 Cor. 2:12; Col. 4:3; Rev. 3:8).
   c. The door of the human heart (Rev. 3:20).
   d. The door of salvation (Jn. 10:7).

e. The door of faith (Acts 14:27).
f. The door of the rapture (Rev. 4:1).
g. The door of the Second Coming (Mt. 24:33).

Dreams and Visions

DREAMS

1. Jacob received the confirmation of the Abrahamic covenant in a dream (Gen. 28:12).
2. Solomon received both wisdom and a warning in a dream (1 Ki. 3:5; 9:2).
3. Joseph in the New Testament received three messages in three dreams.
   a. Assuring him of Mary's purity (Mt. 1:20).
   b. Commanding him to flee to Egypt (Mt. 2:13).
   c. Ordering him to go back to Palestine (Mt. 2:19–22).
4. The wise men were warned of Herod's evil intentions in a dream (Mt. 2:12).

VISIONS

1. Jacob was instructed to go to Egypt in a vision (Gen. 46:2, 3).
2. David was warned of judgment in a vision (1 Chron. 21:16).
3. Isaiah saw God's holiness in a vision (Isa. 6:1–8).
4. Daniel saw the great Gentile powers in a vision (Dan. 7–8).
5. Daniel saw the glories of Christ in a vision (Dan. 10:5–9).
6. Daniel saw the rise and fall of Alexander the Great in a vision (Dan. 8).
7. Ezekiel saw the regathering of Israel in a vision (Ezek. 37).
8. Ananias was ordered to minister to Saul in a vision (Acts 9:10).
9. Cornelius was instructed to send for Peter in a vision (Acts 10:3–6).
10. Peter was ordered to minister to Cornelius in a vision (Acts 10:10–16).
11. Paul was ordered to Macedonia in a vision (Acts 16:9).
12. Paul was comforted at Corinth in a vision (Acts 18:9).
13. Paul was comforted at Jerusalem in a vision (Acts 23:11).
14. Paul viewed the glories of the third heaven in a vision (2 Cor. 12:1–4).
15. John the apostle received the book of the Revelation in a vision.

Earthquakes

1. As experienced by Israel at the giving of the Law from Mt. Sinai (Ex. 19:18).
2. As experienced by Elijah in a cave (1 Ki. 19:11).
3. As experienced in the days of Uzziah (Zech. 14:5; Amos 1:1).
4. As experienced by a centurion at the crucifixion (Mt. 27:54).
5. As experienced by the Roman tomb guard at the resurrection (Mt. 28:2–4).
6. As experienced by the Philippian jailor at midnight (Acts 16:26).
7. As will be experienced by this world during the tribulation:
   a. At the opening of the sixth seal (Rev. 6:12).
   b. At the opening of the seventh seal (Rev. 8:5).
   c. At the raising of the two witnesses (Rev. 11:13).
   d. At the pouring out of the seventh vial at Armageddon (Zech. 14:4, 5; Rev. 16:16–21).

Escapes

1. A captive of Chedorlaomer escaped and told Abraham about the imprisonment of Lot (Gen. 14:12, 13).
2. Lot escaped the judgment upon Sodom (Gen. 19:17–20).
3. Ehud escaped after killing Eglon (Jdg. 3:26).
4. Sisera escaped from Barak and Deborah, only to be killed by a girl named Jael (Jdg. 4:17).
5. A servant of Job escaped and told his master some terrible news (Job 1:15–19).
6. David escaped on many occasions:
   a. From Saul in the palace room (1 Sam. 19:10).
   b. From Saul by being let down from a bedroom window (1 Sam. 19:12).
   c. From the king of Gath (1 Sam. 22:1).
   d. From the city of Keilah, whose citizens would have handed him over to Saul (1 Sam. 23:13).
7. A young man claimed to have escaped from a Philistine victory over Israel with news of how Saul met his death (2 Sam. 1:3).
8. The Savior escaped the murderous intent of the wicked Pharisees:
   a. After preaching in Nazareth (Lk. 4:28–30).
   b. After preaching in Jerusalem (Jn. 10:39).
9. Peter escaped from a Roman prison (Acts 12:7).
10. Paul escaped the waiting Jews by being lowered from a Jerusalem city wall in a basket (Acts 9:25; 2 Cor. 11:33).
11. All believers can escape present-day temptation (1 Cor. 10:13).
12. All believers will escape a future wrath (1 Thess. 5:9).

Excuses

1. As offered by Adam for disobeying God: "The woman whom thou gavest me to be with me, she gave me of the tree, and I did eat" (Gen. 3:12).
2. As offered by Eve for disobeying God: "The serpent beguiled me, and I did eat" (Gen. 3:13).
3. As offered by Lot for wanting to stay in doomed Sodom: "I cannot escape to the mountain, lest some evil take me, and I die" (Gen. 19:19).
4. As offered by Moses for not wanting to go into Egypt.
   a. First excuse: "Who am I, that I should go unto Pharaoh, and that I should bring forth the children of Israel out of Egypt?" (Ex. 3:11).
   b. Second excuse: "But behold, they will not believe me, nor hearken unto my voice: for they will say, the Lord hath not appeared unto thee" (Ex. 4:1).
   c. Third excuse: "O my Lord, I am not eloquent, neither heretofore, nor since thou hast spoken unto thy servant: but I am slow of speech, and of a slow tongue" (Ex. 4:10).
5. As offered by Aaron for constructing the golden calf. "And Aaron said, Let not the anger of my Lord wax hot: thou knowest the people, that they are set on mischief. For they said unto me, Make us gods, which shall go before us: for as for this Moses, the man that brought us up out of the land of Egypt, we wot not what is become of him. And I said unto them, Whosoever hath any gold, let them break it off. So they gave it me: then I cast it into the fire, and there came out this calf" (Ex. 32:22–24).
6. As offered by ten spies for not entering the Promised Land:
   "But the men that went up with him said, We be not able to go up against the people; for they are

stronger than we. And they brought up an evil report of the land which they had searched unto the children of Israel saying, The land, through which we have gone to search it, is a land that eateth up the inhabitants thereof; and all the people that we saw in it are men of a great stature. And there we saw the giants, the sons of Anak, which come of the giants: and we were in our own sight as grasshoppers, and so we were in their sight" (Num. 13:31-33).

7. As offered by Israel for wanting a king: "Behold, thou art old, and thy sons walk not in thy ways: now make us a king to judge us like all the nations" (1 Sam. 8:5).

8. As offered by Saul.
   a. For assuming priestly duties:
   "And Samuel said, What hast thou done? And Saul said, Because I saw that the people were scattered from me, and that thou camest not within the days appointed, and that the Philistines gathered themselves together at Michmash; therefore said I, The Philistines will come down now upon me to Gilgal, and I have not made supplication unto the Lord: I forced myself therefore, and offered a burnt offering" (1 Sam. 13:11, 12).
   b. For sparing an enemy God told him to destroy.
   "But the people took of the spoil, sheep and oxen, the chief of the things which should have been utterly destroyed, to sacrifice unto the Lord thy God in Gilgal" (1 Sam. 15:21).

9. As offered by Elijah for hiding in a cave: "I have been very jealous for the Lord God of hosts: for the children of Israel have forsaken thy covenant, thrown down thine altars, and slain thy prophets with the sword: and I, even I only, am left: and they seek my life, to take it away" (1 Ki. 19:10).

10. As offered by three invited guests for not attending a wedding.
    a. The excuse of the first guest: "I have bought a piece of ground, and I must needs go and see it: I pray thee have me excused" (Lk. 14:18).
    b. The excuse of the second guest: "I have bought five yoke of oxen, and I go to prove them: I pray thee have me excused" (Lk. 14:19).
    c. The excuse of the third guest: "I have married a wife, and therefore I cannot come" (Lk. 14:20).

11. As offered by an unfaithful servant for fruitless labor: "Then he which had received the one talent came and said, Lord, I knew thee that thou art an hard man, reaping where thou hast not sown, and gathering where thou hast not strawed: And I was afraid, and went and hid thy talent in the earth: lo, there thou hast that is thine" (Mt. 25:24, 25).

12. As offered by Felix for not accepting Christ: "Go thy way for this time; when I have a convenient season, I will call for thee" (Acts 24:25).

Fables

1. The fable of the bramble tree—related by Jotham to ridicule the mad dog ruler Abimelech (Jdg. 9:7-15).
2. The fable of the thistle bush—related by Jehoash, King of Israel, to Amaziah, King of Judah to ridicule him (2 Ki. 14:8, 9).

Famines

1. The famine in Palestine, causing Abraham to go into Egypt (Gen. 12:10).
2. The famine in Palestine causing Isaac to go into Philistia (Gen. 26:1).
3. The famine in Palestine, causing Jacob's eleven sons to go into Egypt (Gen. 41:54-57).
4. The famine in Palestine, causing Naomi to go into Moab (Ruth 1:1).
5. The famine in David's day, caused by Saul's bloodstained house (2 Sam. 21:1).
6. The famine in Elijah's day, caused by the sins of Ahab and Israel (1 Ki. 17:1).
7. The famines in Elisha's day.
   a. First famine: resulting in Elisha working a miracle of purifying some poisonous stew (2 Ki. 4:38).
   b. Second famine: resulting in the salvation of a city through four lepers (2 Ki. 6:25).
   c. Third famine: resulting in a woman, a servant, and a king knowing that there was still a prophet of God in Israel (2 Ki. 8:1-6).
8. The famine in Jerusalem, caused by Nebuchadnezzar's siege (2 Ki. 25:2; Jer. 14).
9. The famine in Nehemiah's day, resulting in a sermon being preached by Nehemiah, and an ensuing revival of the people (Neh. 5:3-13).
10. The famine in Paul's day, resulting in help being sent by outside Christians to the believers in Judea (Acts 11:28).
11. The famine in the tribulation, which will contribute to the death of millions (Rev. 6:5-8).

Fasts

1. That of Moses, which lasted for forty days, as he prayed concerning Israel's sin (Deut. 9:9, 18, 25-29; 10:10).
2. That of David:
   a. As he lamented over Saul's death (2 Sam. 1:12).
   b. As he lamented over Abner's death (2 Sam. 3:35).
   c. As he lamented over his child's sickness (2 Sam. 12:16).
3. That of Elijah, which lasted for forty days, as he fled from Jezebel (1 Ki. 19:7-18).
4. That of Ahab, as he humbled himself before God (1 Ki. 21:27-29).
5. That of Darius, as he worried over Daniel's fate (Dan. 6:18-24).
6. That of Daniel:
   a. As he read Jeremiah's prophecy and prayed for Judah's sins (Dan. 9:1-19).
   b. As he prayed over a mysterious vision God had given him. This fast lasted for twenty-one days (Dan. 10:3-13).
7. That of Esther, as she sorrowed over Haman's wicked plot to destroy her people. This fast lasted for three days (Est. 4:13-16).
8. That of Ezra, as he wept over the sins of the returning remnant (Ezra 10:6-17).
9. That of Nehemiah, as he wept over the broken-down wells of Jerusalem (Neh. 1:4--2:10).
10. That of the Ninevites, as they heard the preaching of Jonah (Jonah 3).
11. That of Anna, as she awaited the baby Messiah (Lk. 2:37).
12. That of Jesus, as he was tempted by the devil. This fast lasted for forty days (Mt. 4:1-11).
13. That of John's disciples (Mt. 9:14, 15).
14. That of the elders in Antioch, prior to the sending out of Paul and Barnabas (Acts 13:1-5).

15. That of Cornelius, as he sought out God's plan of salvation (Acts 10:30).
16. That of Paul:
    a. After his salvation on the Damascus Road. This fast lasted for three days (Acts 9:9).
    b. While on a sinking ship. This lasted for fourteen days (Acts 27:33, 34).
    c. All throughout his ministry (2 Cor. 6:5; 11:27).

Fields

1. Isaac was in a field in Hebron when he saw Rebekah (Gen. 24:63).
2. Jacob worshiped God in a field in Shechem after his meeting with Esau (Gen. 33:19).
3. Balaam attempted to curse Israel in the field of Zophim, atop Mt. Pisgah (Num. 23:14).
4. The mother of Samson was in a field of Dan when God spoke to her about Samson's birth (Jdg. 13:9).
5. Samson used some foxes to burn up a Philistine cornfield (Jdg. 15:4, 5).
6. Boaz met Ruth in his Bethlehem field (Ruth 2:3).
7. Some citizens of Israel were killed by God in a field in Bethshemesh for looking into the Ark of the Covenant (1 Sam. 6:14-19).
8. Jonathan warned David of Saul's murderous intents in a field near Ramah (1 Sam. 20:5, 11, 35).
9. Jeremiah was ordered by God to purchase a field near Jerusalem (Jer. 32:6-15).
10. The longest and most comprehensive of Jesus' parables concerned itself with a sower and a field. (Mt. 13).
11. The prodigal's elder brother was in a field when he heard the celebration which accompanied the brother's return (Lk. 15:25).
12. The betrayal money of Christ, returned by Judas, was used to purchase a potter's field (Mt. 27:8; Acts 1:18).

Fires

1. The fire of God from heaven which destroyed Sodom (Gen. 19:24).
2. The fire Abraham built to sacrifice Isaac (Gen. 22:7).
3. The burning bush Fire from which Moses received his call (Ex. 3:2).
4. The fire of the seventh Egyptian plague (Ex. 9:24).
5. The guiding pillar fire that led Israel by night (Ex. 13:21).
6. The fire which appeared at the giving of the law (Ex. 19:8).
7. The fire ordered by Moses to destroy the golden calf (Ex. 39:20).
8. The fire God sent to consume Aaron's offerings (Lev. 9:24).
9. The strange fire of Nadab and Abihu (Lev. 10:1).
10. The judgment fire of God at Taberah to punish Israel (Num. 11:1).
11. The judgment fire of God which consumed Korah and 250 of his followers (Num. 16:35).
12. The fire ordered by Joshua to destroy Jericho (Josh. 6:24).
13. The fire ordered by Joshua to consume Achan (Josh. 7:15, 25).
14. The fire made by Samson to burn the cornfields of the Philistines (Jdg. 15:5).
15. The Mount Carmel fire, which consumed Elijah's offering (1 Ki. 18:38).
16. The fire that God was not in, as witnessed by Elijah in a cave (1 Ki. 19:12).
17. The fire which destroyed a hundred soldiers and protected Elijah (2 Ki. 1:7-11).
18. The fire used to transport Elijah home to glory (2 Ki. 2:11).
19. The fire and chariots which surrounded and protected Elisha (2 Ki. 6:17).
20. The fire of Manasseh in Hinnon, used to burn up his own children (2 Ki. 21:6).
21. The fire of Nebuchadnezzar which would not burn three Hebrew believers (Dan. 3:25).
22. The fire at which Simon Peter warmed his hands when he denied the Savior (Jn. 18:18).
23. The fire where Paul shook off a snake (Acts 28:5).
24. The fire at the judgment seat of Christ (1 Cor. 3:13).
25. The all-consuming judgment fire of God, to be used in destroying his enemies (2 Thess. 1:8; Heb. 12:29; Rev. 20:15).
26. The fire God will use in purifying this earth (2 Pet. 3:7).

Foods

1. Spices
   a. cumin (Isa. 28:25; Mt. 23:23)
   b. anise (Mt. 23:23)
   c. coriander (Ex. 16:31; Num. 11:7)
   d. mint (Mt. 23:23)
   e. rue (Lk. 11:42)
   f. mustard (Mt. 13:31; 17:20)
   g. salt (Job 6:6)
2. Vegetables
   a. beans (2 Sam. 17:28; Ezek. 4:9)
   b. lentils (Gen. 25:34)
   c. cucumbers (Num. 11:5; Isa. 1:8)
   d. melons (Num. 11:5)
   e. garlic (Num. 11:5)
   f. leeks (Num. 11:5)
   g. onions (Num. 11:5)
   h. millet (Ezek. 4:9)
   i. gourds (2 Ki. 4:39)
3. Fruits
   a. olives (Deut. 8:8)
   b. figs (Jer. 24:1-3)
   c. grapes (Deut. 23:24)
   d. pomegranates (Num. 13:23)
   e. sycamore fruit (Amos 7:14)
   f. nuts (Gen. 43:11)
   g. almonds (Gen. 43:11)
4. Grains
   a. barley (Ruth 3:17)
   b. wheat (Rev. 6:6; 1 Sam. 6:13)
   c. corn (Gen. 41:35)
5. Fish (Jn. 6, 21)
6. Fowl
   a. pigeon (Gen. 15:9; Lev. 1:14)
   b. turtledove (Lev. 12:8)
   c. partridge (1 Sam. 26:20; Jer. 17:11)
   d. quail (Ex. 16:13; Num. 11:31, 32; Ps. 105:40)
   e. sparrow (Lk. 12:6)
7. Locusts (Lev. 11:22; Mt. 3:4)
8. Meat animals
   a. venison (Gen. 27:7)
   b. calf (Lk. 15:23)
   c. lamb (2 Sam. 12:4)
   d. goat (Gen. 27:9)
   e. sheep (2 Sam. 17:29)
   f. oxen (1 Ki. 19:21)

9. Various foods and drinks
   a. eggs (Lk. 11:12)
   b. cheese (1 Sam. 17:18)
   c. butter (Jdg. 5:25; Isa. 7:15)
   d. milk (Gen. 18:8; Isa. 55:1)
   e. honey (1 Sam. 14:25; 1 Ki. 14:3; Mt. 3:4)
   f. wine (Jn. 2)

Funerals

1. Sarah's funeral. Abraham bought a cave from a pagan, and wept over the body of his beloved wife (Gen. 23:1-20). Sarah was 127 years old.
2. Abraham's funeral. Isaac and Ishmael attended and buried him alongside Sarah in the cave of Machpelah (Gen. 25:7-11). Abraham was 175 years old.
3. Deborah's funeral. Jacob buried his mother's old nurse under an oak tree in Bethel (Gen. 35:8, 9).
4. Rachel's funeral. Jacob buried her just outside the city of Bethlehem, and set a pillar upon her grave (Gen. 35:16-20).
5. Isaac's funeral. Esau and Jacob met and buried their father next to Abraham in Hebron (Gen. 35:27-29). Isaac was 180 years old.
6. Jacob's funeral. Joseph and his brothers carried their father out of Egypt back into Canaan and buried him at Hebron (Gen. 50:1-13). Jacob was 147 years old.
7. Joseph's funeral. At his command, Joseph was buried by his sons in Egypt, but predicted that his bones would someday be carried back to Palestine (Gen. 50:22-26). Joseph was 110 years old.
8. Nadab and Abihu's funeral. There was to be no weeping at this funeral (Lev. 10:1-7).
9. Miriam's funeral. Moses and Aaron buried their sister at Kadesh (Num. 20:1).
10. Aaron's funeral. Moses and Aaron's son, Eleazar, buried the first high priest of Israel on Mt. Hor. Israel then mourned him for thirty days (Num. 20:23-29).
11. Moses' funeral. God himself attended Moses' funeral and buried him on Mt. Pisgah. Apparently Michael the archangel and Satan were at this funeral (Deut. 34; Jude 1:9). Moses was 120 years old.
12. Joshua's funeral. Israel's great warrior was buried on a hill belonging to the tribe of Ephraim (Josh. 24:29, 30). Joshua was 110 years old.
13. Samuel's funeral. All Israel gathered at Ramah to bury their beloved prophet-priest. Both Saul and David may have attended but not at the same time (1 Sam. 25:1).
14. David's funeral. Solomon buried his great father in the city of David after hearing his dying words of admonition (1 Ki. 2:1-11). David was seventy years of age.
15. The widow of Zarephath's son's funeral. This marked the first biblical resurrection from the dead. Elijah performed it (1 Ki. 17:17-24).
16. The Shunammite's son's funeral. This marked the second biblical resurrection (2 Ki. 4:18-37).
17. A nameless man's funeral in Elisha's day. This funeral doubtless caused the pallbearers to run for their lives from the graveyard (2 Ki. 13:20, 21). This is the third Old Testament resurrection.
18. The daughter of Jairus' funeral (Mk. 5:35-43; Lk. 8:41, 42, 49-56; Mt. 9:18-26).
    a. Peter, James and John attended.
    b. Flute players played.
    c. A large crowd beat their breasts and wept in their sorrow.
    d. The Savior was ridiculed.

This was the first New Testament resurrection of an individual from the dead.
19. The widow of Nain's son (Lk. 7:11-18).
    a. Many people attended.
    b. Our Lord told the mother to cease crying.
    c. The coffin was touched by Jesus.
    d. The corpse sat up and began to speak.
    This was the second New Testament resurrection from the dead.
20. Lazarus' funeral (Jn. 11:1-46).
    a. Many people attended.
    b. The sorrowing went on for at least four days.
    c. Jesus comforted both Mary and Martha.
    d. Jesus himself wept.
    e. Jesus offered a public prayer.
    f. Jesus raised Lazarus, calling him by name, and ordered him to be loosed from the grave clothes.
    This was the third New Testament resurrection from the dead.
21. Dorcas' funeral (Acts 9:36-42).
    a. The corpse was laid in an upper chamber.
    b. Many rose to their feet and gave public testimony concerning the good works of Dorcas.
    c. Peter moved everyone aside, knelt down, prayed, and raised her from the dead.
    This was the fourth New Testament resurrection from the dead. Note: Some may object to this, claiming that the resurrection of Christ should be counted as the fourth New Testament example. But this is not true, for Christ's resurrection is the first (1 Cor. 15:20), as he never died afterward. (See Rev. 1:18.)

Gardens

1. The garden of God (Ezek. 28:11-17).
   a. Was the home of Lucifer before he became Satan.
   b. Had stones of fire.
   c. Was headquarters for God's holy mountain.
   d. Witnessed sin enter the universe.
2. The Garden of Eden (Gen. 2:8—3:24).
   a. Was the home of the first man.
   b. Was located in Mesopotamia to the east.
   c. Had all sorts of beautiful trees, including
      (1) The tree of life.
      (2) The tree of the knowledge of good and evil.
   d. Was watered by four rivers.
   e. Witnessed sin enter the human race.
3. The Garden of Gethsemane (Mt. 26:36; Jn. 18:1).
   a. Witnessed the three prayers of Jesus.
   b. Witnessed his kiss of betrayal and arrest.
4. The garden of the resurrection (Jn. 19:41—20:18; Mt. 28:2-4; Mk. 16:9-11; Lk. 24:12), where:
   a. Jesus was laid in a tomb cave.
   b. A great earthquake occurred.
   c. The Roman soldiers were blinded.
   d. Jesus appeared to Mary Magdalene.
   e. Peter and John saw the empty tomb.

Garments

Introduction: There are a number of garments in the Bible worn by various individuals which carry either a historical or a theological significance.
1. The leafy garments with which Adam and Eve attempted to clothe themselves (Gen. 3:7).
2. The animal garments with which God later clothed them (Gen. 3:21).
3. The many-colored coat of Joseph (Gen. 37:3, 31, 32).

4. The torn coat of Joseph (in Egypt) (Gen. 39:12).
5. The garments of the high priest of Israel (Ex. 28:4–43; 39:1–31; Lev. 8:7–9; 16:4).
6. The garments taken from Aaron and put upon Eleazar (Num. 20:28).
7. The "goodly Babylonish garment" stolen by Achan (Josh. 7:21).
8. The garment with which Boaz covered Ruth (Ruth 3:9).
9. The little coat that Hannah brought for Samuel in the Temple at Shiloh (1 Sam. 2:19).
10. The robe given to David by Jonathan to seal their friendship covenant (1 Sam. 18:4).
11. The beautiful linen robe David wore when he carried the ark of God to Jerusalem (1 Chron. 15:27).
12. Tamar's many-colored garment which she tore after being attacked by Ammon (2 Sam. 13:18, 19).
13. Saul's robe which David cut during the wicked king's sleep (1 Sam. 24:11).
14. Jeroboam's torn garment. This was ripped into twelve pieces by the prophet Ahijah to symbolize the coming fragmentation of the kingdom of Israel (1 Ki. 11:29–31).
15. The robe of Ahab's which Jehoshaphat foolishly wore (2 Chron. 18:29).
16. The "filthy garments" of Joshua the high priest as he stood before God (Zech. 3:3).
17. The garments of John the Baptist (Mt. 3:4).
18. The robe given to the returning prodigal son by his father (Lk. 15:22).
19. The unused wedding garment (Mt. 22:11).
20. The linen cloth discarded by a young man at Gethsemane (Mk. 14:51).
21. The fisherman's coat of Simon Peter (Jn. 21:7).
22. The garments worn by the Savior.
    a. At Bethlehem, swaddling clothes (Lk. 2:7, 12).
    b. During his earthly ministry (Mt. 9:21; 14:36; 17:2; Jn. 13:4).
    c. At Calvary.
       (1) The soldiers placed a scarlet robe on him in mockery (Mt. 27:28; Jn. 19:2, 5).
       (2) Herod placed a "gorgeous robe" upon him in mockery (Lk. 23:11).
       (3) The soldiers gambled for his seamless garment at the foot of the cross (Mt. 27:35).
       (4) Nicodemus and Joseph of Arimathaea wrapped him in linen clothes (Jn. 19:40).
    d. His present-day garments (Rev. 1:13).
    e. His Second Coming garments (Dan. 7:9; Rev. 19:13; Isa. 63:1–3).
23. The cloak of Paul's that he requested while in a Roman prison (2 Tim. 4:13).
24. The robe of the righteous (Rev. 19:7, 8, 14).
25. The robe of the unrighteous (Isa. 64:6).
26. The white robes of those martyred during the tribulation (Rev. 6:11; 7:9).

Gates

1. The gate at Sodom—where Lot met the two angels (Gen. 19:1).
2. The gate at Bethlehem—where Boaz arranged to marry Ruth (Ruth 4:1).
3. The gate at Shalem—where Shechem agreed to be circumcised, as requested by Jacob's two sons (Gen. 34:20).
4. The gate of Jericho—this gate was sealed to keep all Israelite soldiers out. But two spies had already entered (Josh. 2:5, 7).

5. The gate at Gaza. Samson ripped this gate from its foundations and carried it away (Jdg. 16:2, 3).
6. The gate at Shiloh. Here the aged Eli fell and died upon hearing the news concerning Israel's defeat and the capture of the ark of God by the Philistines (1 Sam. 4:18).
7. The gate of Gath. David scrabbled on this gate and pretended to be insane (1 Sam. 21:13).
8. The gate of Samaria—here four lepers made a decision that would later save the starving city (2 Ki. 7:3).
9. The palace gate in Persia. Here Mordecai overheard a plot against the king's life which later would be used by God in saving all the Jews in Persia (Est. 2:21–23).
10. The gate of the rich man—where Lazarus begged for bread (Lk. 16:20).
11. The Temple gate Beautiful—where Peter healed a cripple (Acts 3:2).
12. Gates in the old city of Jerusalem:
    a. The sheep gate (speaks of salvation) (Neh. 3:1).
    b. The fish gate (speaks of soul-winning) (Neh. 3:3).
    c. The valley gate (speaks of humility) (Neh. 3:13).
    d. The dung gate (speaks of unclean habits) (Neh. 3:14).
    e. The fountain gate (speaks of the Holy Spirit) (Neh. 3:15).
    f. The water gate (speaks of the Word of God) (Neh. 3:26).
    g. The horse gate (speaks of the believers' warfare) (Neh. 3:28).
    h. The east gate (speaks of the rapture and Second Coming) (Neh. 3:29).
    i. The Miphkad gate (speaks of the judgment seat of Christ) (Neh. 3:31).
13. Gates in the new city of Jerusalem (Rev. 21:12, 13).
    a. There are twelve gates in the New Jerusalem, three on the north, three on the south, three on the east, and three on the west.
    b. Each gate is guarded by an angel.
    c. On each gate is the name of one of the twelve founders of the tribes of Israel.
14. Symbolic gates in the Bible.
    a. The gate of salvation (Mt. 7:13).
    b. The gate of damnation (Mt. 7:13).
    c. The gate of death (Job 38:17; Isa. 38:10; Ps. 9:13; 107:18).
    d. The gate of heaven (Ps. 24:7, 9; Gen. 28:17).
    e. The gate of hell (Mt. 16:18).

Genealogies

1. The genealogy of Cain (Gen. 4:16–24).
2. The genealogy of Adam (Gen. 5:1–32).
3. The genealogy of Japheth (Gen. 10:1–5; 1 Chron. 1:5–7).
4. The genealogy of Ham (Gen. 10:6–20; 1 Chron. 1:8–16).
5. The genealogy of Shem (Gen. 10:22–31; 11:10–30; 1 Chron. 1:17–27).
6. The genealogy of Abraham (Gen. 25:1–4, 12–18; 1 Chron. 1:28–34).
7. The genealogy of Isaac (Gen. 25:19–23).
8. The genealogy of Jacob (Gen. 49:1–27; 1 Chron. 2:1, 2).
9. The genealogy of Esau (Gen. 36:1–43; 1 Chron. 1:35–42).
10. The genealogy of Judah (1 Chron. 2:3–12; 4:1–4).
11. The genealogy of Simeon (1 Chron. 4:24–38).
12. The genealogy of Reuben (1 Chron. 5:1–8).

13. The genealogy of Levi (1 Chron. 6:1–53).
14. The genealogy of Issachar (1 Chron. 7:1–5).
15. The genealogy of Benjamin (1 Chron. 7:6–12).
16. The genealogy of Naphtali (1 Chron. 7:13).
17. The genealogy of Asher (1 Chron. 7:30–40).
18. The genealogy of Jesse (1 Chron. 2:13–17).
19. The genealogy of Caleb (1 Chron. 2:18–20, 42–55).
20. The genealogy of David (1 Chron. 3:1–24).
21. The genealogy of Ephraim (1 Chron. 7:20–27).
22. The genealogy of Pharez (Ruth 4:18–22).
23. The genealogy of the Lord Jesus Christ.
    a. The biological line through Mary (Lk. 3:23–38).
    b. The legal line through Joseph (Mt. 1:1–17).

Giants

1. Og (Deut. 3:11). This giant who was king of Bashan had an iron bed which measured thirteen and a half feet long and was six feet wide.
2. Sippai (1 Chron. 20:4).
3. Lahmi (1 Chron. 20:5). The brother of Goliath.
4. An unnamed giant (1 Chron. 20:6). He had six fingers on each hand and six toes on each foot. He was slain by Jonathan (David's nephew).
5. Goliath (1 Sam. 17:4). He was nearly ten feet tall. Note: The tallest man in recorded human history was Robert Wadlow, of Alton, Illinois. He was eight feet eleven and a half inches tall, and weighed 491 pounds.
6. Ishbi-benob (2 Sam. 21:16).
7. Saph (2 Sam. 21:18).

Gifts

1. The gift of Abraham to Melchizedek (Gen. 14:20).
   a. Nature of the gift—Abraham's tithes.
   b. Purpose of the gift—to show honor to the first ruler of Jerusalem.
2. The gift of Jacob to Esau (Gen. 32:13–15).
   a. Nature of the gift—400 goats, 200 ewes, 20 rams, 30 milk camels, 40 cows, 10 bulls, 30 donkeys.
   b. Purpose of the gift—to make up for cheating Esau out of his blessing.
3. The gifts of Israel's twelve tribal leaders to the tabernacle (Num. 7:12–89).
   a. Nature of the gifts—each brought a silver platter, a silver bowl, a tiny gold box of incense, a young bull, six yearlings, two oxen, six rams, six goats.
   b. Purpose of the gifts—to please God.
4. The gifts of the queen of Sheba to Solomon (1 Ki. 10:1, 2, 10).
   a. Nature of the gift—spices, jewels, and $3,500,000 in gold.
   b. Purpose of the gift—to assure good relations between Israel and Sheba.
5. The gift of Belshazzar to Daniel (which gift he refused) (Dan. 5:16, 17).
   a. Nature of the gift—the office of third ruler in the kingdom.
   b. Purpose of the gift—to have the handwriting on the wall interpreted.
6. The gifts of the Syrian king to an Israelite king (2 Ki. 5:4–6).
   a. Nature of the gift—$20,000 in silver, $60,000 in gold, and ten suits of clothing.
   b. Purpose of the gift—to secure the healing of Naaman the leper.

7. The gifts of the wise men to Christ (Mt. 2:11).
   a. Nature of the gifts—gold, frankincense, and myrrh.
   b. Purpose of the gifts—to offer honor and praise to heaven's King.
8. The gift of Mary of Bethany to Christ (Jn. 12:2–8; Mt. 26:7–13).
   a. Nature of the gift—a jar of costly perfume.
   b. Purpose of the gift—to show her adoration and to anoint the Savior.
9. The gift of an immoral woman to Christ (Lk. 7:37, 38).
   a. Nature of the gift—an exquisite flask filled with expensive perfume.
   b. Purpose of the gift—to seek his forgiveness.
10. The gifts of wicked unbelievers to each other during the tribulation (Rev. 11:10).
    a. Nature of the gifts—probably alcohol, drugs, pornographic literature, etc.
    b. Purpose of the gifts—to celebrate the death of God's two witnesses.
11. The gift of the believer to the Lord (Rom. 12:1–3).
    a. Nature of the gift—his body, as a living sacrifice.
    b. Purpose of the gift—that the believer might prove God's perfect will for his life.
12. The gift of the Father to the world (Jn. 3:16; 2 Cor. 9:15).
    a. Nature of the gift—Christ.
    b. Purpose of the gift—"That whosoever believeth in him should not perish, but have everlasting life."
13. The gift of the Son to the sheep (Jn. 10:11; 14:3).
    a. Nature of the gift—"The Good Shepherd giveth his life for the sheep."
    b. Purpose of the gift—"That where I am, there ye may be also."
14. The gifts of the Holy Spirit to the believer (Rom. 12:6–8; 1 Cor. 12:4–31; Eph. 4:7–16).
    a. Nature of the gifts—some eighteen in number, which include:
       (1) apostleship
       (2) prophecy
       (3) miracles
       (4) healing
       (5) tongues
       (6) interpretation of tongues
       (7) knowledge
       (8) wisdom
       (9) discerning of spirits
       (10) giving
       (11) exhortation
       (12) ministering
       (13) showing of mercy
       (14) ruling
       (15) faith
       (16) teaching
       (17) evangelism
       (18) pastor-teacher
    b. Purpose of the gifts:
       (1) To glorify the Father.
       (2) To edify both the believer and the church.

Hills

1. The hill near Rephidim, where Israel won its first battle en route to the Promised Land (Ex. 17:8, 9).
2. The hill at Moab, where Joshua circumcised the new male Israelite generation (Josh. 5:3).
3. The hill at Hachilah, where David spared Saul's life (1 Sam. 26:1).

4. The hill at Samaria, where King Omri purchased and built his new capital, calling it by the same name (1 Ki. 16:24).
5. The hill near Samaria, where Elijah called down fire upon some soldiers sent to arrest him (2 Ki. 1:9).
6. The hill at Nazareth, where a furious mob from Jesus' hometown attempted to murder him by casting him down (Lk. 4:29).
7. The hill of Golgotha, a hill resembling a skull where the Savior was crucified (Mt. 27:33).
8. The hill of Areopagus, a hill in Athens where Paul preached his Mars Hill sermon (Acts 17:18-33).

Hymns and Songs

1. The songs of Moses.
   a. After he had led Israel through the Red Sea (Ex. 15:1-19).
   b. Just prior to his death (Deut. 32:1-4). (See also Rev. 15:3, 4.)
2. The song of Israel as they dug some wells en route to the Promised Land (Num. 21:17, 18).
3. The song of Deborah and Barak, after their victory over Sisera (Jdg. 5:1-31).
4. The song of Hannah at the dedication of her son Samuel (1 Sam. 2:1-10).
5. The song sung by the Israelite women to celebrate David's victory over Goliath (1 Sam. 18:6, 7).
6. The song of the Levitical choir who sang at the Temple dedication (2 Chron. 5:12-14).
7. The song of Jehoshaphat's marching choir which led his soldiers into battle against Judah's enemies (2 Chron. 20:20-23).
8. The song of this Levitical choir during the great restoration of the Temple during Hezekiah's reign (2 Chron. 29:25-28).
9. The song of Mary, after learning of the future virgin birth. Her song is known as the "Magnificat" (Lk. 1:46-55).
10. The song of Zacharias, at the circumcision of his son John the Baptist. This is known as the "Benedictus" (Lk. 1:68-79).
11. The song sung by the disciples in the upper room (Mt. 26:30).
12. The song of Paul and Silas while in a Philippian jail at midnight (Acts 16:25).
13. The songs of praise God desires believers to sing (Eph. 5:19; Col. 3:16).
14. The new song sung by all believers to glorify Christ in heaven (Rev. 5:9, 10).
15. The song of the 144,000 (Rev. 14:1-3).
16. The song of the tribulational overcomers (Rev. 15:2-4).

Idols and False Gods

1. Asherah—The chief goddess of Tyre, referred to as the lady of the sea. Gideon destroyed a statue of this lover goddess of Baal, which had been worshiped by his own father (Jdg. 6:24-32).
2. Ashtoreth—A Canaanite goddess, another lover of Baal. The prophet Samuel led Israel in a great revival which resulted in the people giving up the sexual practices associated with the worship of Ashtoreth (1 Sam. 7:3, 4).
3. Baal—the chief male deity of the Canaanite pantheon. The struggle between Baal and Jehovah came to a dramatic head on Mt. Carmel under Elijah (1 Ki.

18:17-40). Jehu later dealt a severe blow to Baalism (2 Ki. 11:18).
4. Baal-zebub—the prince of the demons, according to Jesus (Mt. 10:25; 12:24). The name literally means "lord of the flies."
5. Dagon—the chief Philistine agriculture god and father of Baal. The Ark of the Covenant destroyed an idol of Dagon in its own temple (1 Sam. 5:1-7). Later, Samson would destroy the very temple of Dagon (Jdg. 16:23-30).
6. Diana—a grotesque many-breasted Asiatic goddess, who was believed to be the nursing mother of other gods, men, animals, and even plants. Paul encountered Diana while in Ephesus (Acts 19:27, 35).
7. Jupiter—the chief Roman god of heaven (another name for the Greek god Zeus). The people of Lystra called Barnabas "Jupiter," perhaps because of his impressive appearance (Acts 14:12, 13).
8. Mercury—the Roman god of commerce, speed, and eloquence. He was the son of Jupiter. As a messenger of the gods he had wings on his feet. Paul was mistaken for Mercury at Lystra because of his speaking abilities (Acts 14:12).
9. Merodach (also called Marduk)—he was the head god of the Babylonian pantheon and Nebuchadnezzar's favorite god.
10. Molech—the most horrible idol in the Scriptures. He was a detestable Semitic deity honored by the sacrifice of children who were cruelly burned alive. Solomon actually built an altar for this vicious monster at Tophet in the Valley of Hinnon (1 Ki. 11:7). Later both King Ahaz and his godless grandson Manasseh sacrificed their children to this fiendish blood-demanding idol (2 Chron. 28:1-4; 33:6).
11. Nanna—the moon god of Ur, once worshiped by Abraham before his salvation (Josh. 24:2).
12. Nebo—the Babylonian god of wisdom and literature (Isa. 46:1).
13. Nishroch—the Assyrian god of Sennacherib. The king was murdered in the temple of his idol after returning from the death angel defeat at Jerusalem (2 Ki. 19:37).
14. Rimmon—the Syrian god of Namaan the leper (2 Ki. 5:15-19).
15. Satyr—a shaggy, goat-like idol worshiped by the ancient world, made in the actual likeness of the demons it represented (Isa. 13:21; 34:14; Lev. 17:7; 2 Chron. 11:15).
16. Tammuz—a Babylonian idol given over to the memory of Tammuz, who was the son of Nimrod and Semerimus. His wicked mother instituted a religious system which featured the mother-child cult which later spread all over the world (Ezek. 8;14; Jer. 7:18; 44:25).
17. Nameless idols:
    a. Rachel's household gods (Gen. 31:19).
    b. The golden calf at Sinai (Ex. 32). (See also 1 Ki. 12:28.)
    c. The golden image in the plain of Dura (Dan. 2).
    d. The unknown god on Mars Hill (Acts 17).
    e. The statue of the beast (Rev. 13:14).

Inns

1. The Midian Inn, where Moses nearly committed the sin unto death (Ex. 4:24).
2. The Bethlehem Inn, where Joseph and Mary were refused lodging (Lk. 2:7).
3. The Jericho Inn, where a good Samaritan took his wounded friend (Lk. 10:34).

Invitations

1. To enter the ark of safety (Gen. 7:1).
2. To consider the benefits of being saved (Isa. 1:18).
3. To satisfy one's hunger and thirst (Isa. 55:1-3).
4. To test the claims of Jesus (Jn. 1:48; 4:29).
5. To rest upon Christ (Mt. 11:28-30).
6. To follow the Savior (Mt. 19:21; Mk. 10:21).
7. To attend a great supper (Lk. 14:16).
8. To attend a great wedding (Mt. 22:4).
9. To enter the kingdom (Mt. 25:34).
10. To drink of that living water (Jn. 4:10; Rev. 22:17).

Islands

1. The Isle of Cyprus, the home of Barnabas, which was evangelized by Paul and Barnabas during the first missionary journey (Acts 13:4-13).
2. The Isle of Crete, where Paul assigned Titus as pastor (Titus 1:4, 5, 10-12).
3. The Isle of Melita, where Paul supernaturally survived the bite of a deadly serpent (Acts 27:39—28:11). Here he also healed the father of Publius, governor of the island.
4. The Isle of Patmos, where the exiled John was given the book of Revelation vision (Rev. 1:9).

Journeys

1. Noah's descendants, from Mt. Ararat to Babel (Gen. 11:1-9).
2. Abraham, from Ur of the Chaldees to Canaan (Gen. 12:1-9).
3. Abraham, from Canaan to Egypt (Gen. 12:10-20).
4. Abraham, from Hebron to Mt. Moriah (Gen. 22).
5. Rebekah, from Haran to Canaan (Gen. 24).
6. Jacob, from Hebron to Bethel to Haran (Gen. 28-29).
7. Jacob, from Haran to Bethel (Gen. 32-35).
8. Joseph, from Canaan to Egypt (Gen. 37).
9. Jacob and his family, from Canaan to Egypt (Gen. 42-46).
10. Moses, from Egypt to Midian (Ex. 2:15).
11. Moses, from Midian back to Egypt (Ex. 3-4).
12. Israel, from Egypt to Canaan (Ex. through Josh.).
13. Ruth, from Moab to Bethlehem (Ruth 1).
14. Saul, from Gibeah to Ramah. (1 Sam. 9).
15. Samuel, from Ramah to Bethlehem (1 Sam. 16).
16. David, from Philistia to Hebron (2 Sam. 2:1).
17. David, from Hebron to Jerusalem (2 Sam. 5:7).
18. David, from Jerusalem to the eastern wilderness (2 Sam. 15:23).
19. Solomon, from Jerusalem to Gibeon (1 Ki. 3:4, 5).
20. The queen of Sheba, from North Africa to Jerusalem (1 Ki. 10).
21. Rehoboam, from Jerusalem to Shechem (1 Ki. 12:1).
22. Elijah, from the brook at Cherith to Mt. Carmel (1 Ki. 17-18).
23. Elijah, from Mt. Carmel to Mt. Horeb (1 Ki. 19).
24. Naaman, from Syria to Samaria (2 Ki. 5).
25. The captives of Judah, from Palestine to Babylon (2 Ki. 24-25; Ps. 137; Dan. 1).
26. The captives of Judah, from Babylon to Jerusalem (Ezra 1; Ps. 126).
27. Nehemiah, from Babylon to Jerusalem (Neh. 1-2).
28. Joseph and Mary, from Nazareth to Bethlehem (Lk. 2:4).
29. Jesus, from the glory of heaven to this sinful earth (Lk. 2:7; Phil. 2:5-8; Gal. 4:4).
30. Jesus, from this sinful earth to the glory of heaven (Acts 1).
31. The wise men, from Persia to Bethlehem (Mt. 2:1-12).
32. Joseph, from Bethlehem to Egypt (Mt. 2:13, 14).
33. Joseph, from Egypt to Nazareth (Mt. 2:23).
34. Philip, from Jerusalem to Samaria (Acts 8:5).
35. Philip, from Samaria to the Gaza Desert (Acts 8:26).
36. Paul, from Jerusalem to Damascus (Acts 9).
37. Peter, from Joppa to Caesarea (Acts 10).
38. Barnabas, from Jerusalem to Antioch (Acts 11:19-26).
39. Paul and Barnabas, from Antioch to their first missionary trip (Acts 13-14).
40. Paul and Silas, from Antioch to the second trip (Acts 15:36—18:22).
41. Paul, from Antioch to his third trip (Acts 18:23—21:15).
42. Paul, from Jerusalem to Rome (Acts 21:16—28:31).

Judgments

1. Past judgments.
   a. The Garden of Eden judgment (Gen. 3:14-19; Rom. 5:12; 1 Cor. 15:22).
   b. The Flood judgment (Gen. 6:5-7; 2 Pet. 3:1-6).
   c. The Calvary judgment (Mt. 27:33-37; Isa. 53:1-10; Ps. 22:1; Heb. 2:9; 1 Pet. 2:21-25; 3:18).
   d. The Israelite judgments.
      (1) At the hands of the Assyrians (2 Ki. 17).
      (2) At the hands of the Babylonians (2 Ki. 24-25).
      (3) At the hands of the Romans (Mt. 24:2; Lk. 19:41-44).
      (4) At the hands of Christ himself (Mt. 21:17-19, 33-46).
2. Present-day judgments.
   a. Upon local churches by the Savior (Rev. 2-3).
   b. Upon individual believers.
      (1) When the believer judges himself (1 Cor. 11:31; 1 Jn. 1:9).
      (2) When the Father has to step in and judge (Heb. 12:3-13; 1 Cor. 11:30; 1 Pet. 4:17; 1 Jn. 5:16; Acts 5:1-11).
3. Future judgments.
   a. The (bema) judgment seat of Christ (1 Cor. 3:9-15; 2 Cor. 5:10; Rom. 14:10; Rev. 22:12).
   b. The tribulational judgment (Rev. 6-19).
      (1) Upon man's religious systems (Rev. 17).
      (2) Upon man's economic and political systems (Rev. 18).
      (3) Upon man's military systems (Rev. 19:11-21).
      (4) Upon man himself (Rev. 6, 8, 9, 16).
   c. The lamp and talent judgment. This refers to Israel (Mt. 24:45-51; 25:1-30; Ezek. 20:33-38).
   d. The sheep and goat judgment. This refers to the Gentiles (Mt. 25:31-46).
   e. The judgment upon the antichrist and false prophet (Rev. 19:20).
   f. The judgment upon Satan.
      (1) In the bottomless pit for one thousand years (Rev. 20:1-3).
      (2) In the lake of fire forever (Rev. 20:10).
   g. The fallen angel judgment (1 Cor. 6:3; 2 Pet. 2:4; Jude 1:6).
   h. The great white throne judgment (Rev. 20:11-15).

Keys

1. The key to the kingdom of heaven (Mt. 16:19).
2. The key of knowledge (Lk. 11:52).

3. The key of the Davidic throne (Isa. 22:22; Rev. 3:7).
4. The keys of hell and death (Rev. 1:18).
5. The key to the bottomless pit (Rev. 9:1; 20:1).

Kisses

1. The kiss of deceit, by Jacob upon Isaac (Gen. 27:26, 27).
2. The kiss of introduction, by Jacob upon Rachel (Gen. 29:11).
3. The kiss of reconciliation, by Esau upon Jacob (Gen. 33:4).
4. The kiss of forgiveness, by Joseph upon his brothers (Gen. 45:14, 15).
5. The kiss of farewell, by Jacob upon his two grandchildren (Gen. 48:10).
6. The kiss of two brothers by Aaron upon Moses (Ex. 4:27).
7. The kiss of return, by Moses upon Jethro (Ex. 18:7).
8. The kiss of sorrow, by Naomi upon Ruth and Orpah (Ruth 1:9).
9. The kiss of coronation, by Samuel upon Saul (1 Sam. 10:1).
10. The kiss of friendship, by David upon Jonathan (1 Sam. 20:41).
11. The kiss of a subdued welcome, by David upon Absalom (2 Sam. 14:33).
12. The kiss of politics, by Absalom upon the citizens of Israel (2 Sam. 15:5).
13. The kiss of murder, by Joab upon Amasa (2 Sam. 20:9).
14. The kiss of salvation, by the believer upon Christ (Ps. 2:12).
15. The kiss of righteousness and peace (Ps. 85:10).
16. The kiss of lovers (Song of Sol. 1:2).
17. The kiss of repentance, by a harlot upon the feet of Christ (Lk. 7:45).
18. The kiss of restoration, by a father upon his prodigal son (Lk. 15:20).
19. The kiss of betrayal, by Judas upon Christ (Mt. 26:49).
20. The kiss of church leaders, by the Ephesian elders upon Paul (Acts 20:37).

Lamps (lights and torches)

1. The burning lamp of the Abrahamic Covenant (Gen. 15:17).
2. The golden lamp of the tabernacle (Ex. 25:37).
3. The lamps of Gideon (Jdg. 7:16).
4. The lamp of Samuel and Eli (1 Sam. 3:3).
5. The golden lamp of the Temple (1 Ki. 7:49).
6. The lamps of the ten virgins (Mt. 25:1).

Last Words

1. As spoken by Jacob (Gen. 49:10).
2. As spoken by Joseph (Gen. 50:24).
3. As spoken by Moses (Deut. 33:27-29).
4. As spoken by Caleb (Josh. 14:7-12).
5. As spoken by Joshua (Josh. 23:14; 24:15).
6. As spoken by Samson (Jdg. 16:28).
7. As spoken by Eli (1 Sam. 4:15-18).
8. As spoken by Saul (1 Sam. 31:4).
9. As spoken by David (2 Sam. 23:1-4; 1 Ki. 2:1-9).
10. As spoken by Elijah (2 Ki. 2:8-11).
11. As spoken by Elisha (2 Ki. 13:14-19).
12. As spoken by Belshazzar (Dan. 5:13-16).
13. As spoken by Daniel (Dan. 12:8).
14. As spoken by Simeon (Lk. 2:25-35).
15. As spoken by Jesus (Mt. 28:18-20; Acts 1:8).

16. As spoken by Stephen (Acts 7:59, 60).
17. As spoken by Paul (2 Tim. 4:6-8).
18. As spoken by James (Jas. 5:19, 20).
19. As spoken by Peter (2 Pet. 3:13-18).
20. As spoken by Jude (Jude 1:24, 25).
21. As spoken by John (Rev. 22:18-21).

Letters

1. David wrote to Joab concerning Uriah (2 Sam. 11:14, 15).
2. The king of Syria wrote to the king of Israel concerning Naaman (2 Ki. 5:5-7).
3. Jezebel wrote to the rulers of Jezreel concerning Naboth (1 Ki. 21:8).
4. Jehu wrote to the rulers of Jezreel concerning Ahab's seventy sons (2 Ki. 10:1, 2).
5. Sennacherib wrote to Hezekiah concerning surrender (2 Ki. 19:14).
6. Hezekiah wrote to the Israelite leaders concerning the Passover (2 Chron. 30:1).
7. Elijah wrote to King Jehoram predicting judgment upon his sinful reign (2 Chron. 21:12).
8. The enemies of Zerubbabel wrote letters to the Persian king attempting to smear him (Ezra 4:6-16).
9. The Persian king thereupon wrote a letter to Judah's enemies, giving them permission to stop the work of the Temple by the remnant (Ezra 4:17-22).
10. Darius wrote a letter granting permission to continue the Temple construction (Ezra 6:6-12).
11. Artaxerxes wrote a letter to the manager of the royal forest, ordering him to provide Nehemiah with building material for Jerusalem's walls (Neh. 2:8).
12. Mordecai wrote to the Jews concerning the new Feast of Purim (Est. 9:20).
13. Nehemiah's enemy, Sanballat, wrote to him, attempting to discourage him (Neh. 6:5).
14. The Jewish high priest wrote to the religious leaders in Damascus concerning the Christian problem (Acts 9:2).
15. James wrote to the Christian churches concerning the Jerusalem Council decision on circumcision (Acts 15:23).
16. The believers in Ephesus wrote a letter of recommendation to the Corinthian believers concerning Apollos (Acts 18:27).
17. Claudius Lysias wrote to Felix concerning the Apostle Paul (Acts 23:25).
18. Paul wrote Philemon concerning Onesimus (Philemon).
19. Jesus wrote to his seven churches in Turkey concerning their spiritual condition (Rev. 1-3).

Lies

1. Satan lied to Eve (Gen. 3:4).
2. Abraham lied to Pharaoh (Gen. 12:13).
3. Abraham lied to Abimelech (Gen. 20:2).
4. Sarah lied to God (Gen. 18:15).
5. Jacob lied to Isaac (Gen. 27:19).
6. Isaac lied to Abimelech (Gen. 26:7).
7. Laban lied to Jacob (Gen. 29:18-24).
8. Jacob's sons lied to Jacob (Gen. 37:32).
9. Potiphar's wife lied to her husband (Gen. 39:17).
10. Pharaoh lied to Moses (Ex. 8:8).
11. An Amalekite soldier lied to David (2 Sam. 1:2-10).
12. David lied to Abimelech and Achish (1 Sam. 21:12).
13. Rahab lied to the Jericho searching party (Josh. 2:4).

14. Michal lied to her father Saul (1 Sam. 19:13-17).
15. Saul lied to David (1 Sam. 18:17).
16. Ananias and Sapphira lied to Peter (Acts 5:1).

Literature Styles of the Bible
1. Historical (many Old Testament books, and a few New Testament books).
2. Prophetical (the books of Daniel, Revelation, etc.).
3. Poetical (Psalms, Proverbs, etc.).
4. Legal (parts of Exodus, Deuteronomy, Hebrews, etc.).
5. Biographical (Matthew, Mark, Luke, John, etc.).
6. Autobiographical (Nehemiah, parts of Daniel, etc.).
7. Doctrinal (Romans, Ephesians, etc.).
8. Fables (see under proper heading).
9. Similes (see under proper heading).
10. Metaphors (see under proper heading).
11. Allegories (see under proper heading).
12. Parables (see under proper heading).
13. Types and foreshadows (see under proper heading).
14. Symbols and emblems (see under proper heading).
15. Paradoxes (see under proper heading).

Longevities
1. Adam lived to be 930 (Gen. 5:5).
2. Seth, 912 (5:8).
3. Enos, 905 (5:11).
4. Cainan, 910 (5:14).
5. Mahalaleel, 895 (5:17).
6. Jared, 962 (5:20).
7. Enoch, 365 (5:23).
8. Methuselah, 969 (5:27).
9. Lamech, 777 (5:31).
10. Noah, 950 (9:29).
11. Shem, 600 (11:10, 11).
12. Arphaxad, Shem's son, 438 (11:12, 13).
13. Salah, 433 (11:14, 15).
14. Eber, 464 (11:16, 17).
15. Peleg, 239 (11:18, 19).
16. Reu, 239 (11:20, 21).
17. Serug, 230 (11:22, 23).
18. Nahor, 148 (11:24, 25).
19. Terah, 205 (11:32).
20. Sarah, 127 (23:1).
21. Abraham, 175 (25:7).
22. Ishmael, 137 (25:17).
23. Isaac, 180 (35:28).
24. Jacob, 147 (47:28).
25. Joseph, 110 (50:26).
26. Moses, 120 (Deut. 34:7).
27. Joshua, 110 (Josh. 24:29).

Lots (the casting of)
1. To determine which sacrificial animal would be the scapegoat in the tabernacle (Lev. 16:8).
2. To determine the land area for Israel's twelve tribes (Num. 26:55; Josh. 18:10).
3. To determine the Levitical work load and responsibility in the Temple during Nehemiah's time (Neh. 10:34).
4. To determine who would live in Jerusalem during Nehemiah's time (Neh. 11:1).
5. To determine who should be thrown overboard in a storm (Jonah 1:7).
6. To determine who would receive the Savior's seamless coat (Mt. 27:35).
7. To determine who would replace Judas (Acts 1:26).

Marriages
1. Adam to Eve (Gen. 2:21-25).
2. Lamech to Adah and Zillah (Gen. 4:19).
3. Isaac to Rebekah (Gen. 24:63-67).
4. Esau to Judith (Gen. 26:34, 35).
5. Abraham to Keturah (Gen. 25:1).
6. Jacob to Leah and Rachel (Gen. 29:18-23).
7. Joseph to Asenath (Gen. 41:45).
8. Moses to Zipporah (Ex. 2:21).
9. Samson to a Philistine girl (Jdg. 14).
10. Boaz to Ruth (Ruth 4:13).
11. David to Michal (1 Sam. 18:20, 28).
12. David to Abigail (1 Sam. 25:39).
13. David to Bath-sheba (2 Sam. 11:27).
14. Solomon to Pharaoh's daughter (1 Ki. 3:1).
15. Ahab to Jezebel (1 Ki. 16:31).
16. Ahasuerus to Esther (Est. 2:17).
17. Hosea to Gomer (Hosea 1:2, 3).
18. Joseph to Mary (Mt. 1:24).
19. Herod to Herodias (Mt. 14:3, 4).
20. A Cana couple (Jn. 2).
21. Christ to the Church (Rev. 19:7, 8).

Memorials
1. The rainbow (Gen. 9:13-16)—reminder: that God would never again destroy the world by a flood.
2. The Passover (Ex. 12:11-14)—reminder: that the blood of a lamb saved sinners from judgment.
3. Some brazen censors (Num. 16:39, 40)—reminder: that no one except Aaron's seed must attempt to offer incense.
4. The Sabbath (Deut. 5:15)—reminder: of a completed creation.
5. Twelve stones (Josh. 4:7)—reminder: of God's mighty power in bringing Israel across the Jordan into Palestine.
6. The manna in the Ark of the Covenant (Ex. 16:32)—reminder: of God's supernatural provision in the desert.
7. The feast of Purim (Est. 9:28)—reminder: of salvation from wicked Haman.
8. The feast of tabernacles (Lev. 23:39-43)—reminder: of Israel's deliverance from Egypt.
9. The anointing of Jesus' head and feet by Mary, the sister of Lazarus (Mt. 26:6-13; Jn. 12:1-7)—reminder: of Mary's devotion to Christ.
10. The Lord's Supper (Lk. 22:19)—reminder: of the broken body and shed blood of Christ.

Metaphors (figures of speech in which the subject is described by identification with something else)
1. Judah is a lion's whelp (Gen. 49:9).
2. Dan shall be a serpent (Gen. 49:17).
3. Go and tell that fox (Lk. 13:31, 32).
4. This is my body . . . this is my blood (Mt. 26:26-28; Mk. 14:22-24).
5. I am the bread of life (Jn. 6:35).
6. I am the true Vine (Jn. 15:1).
7. You are the salt of the earth (Mt. 5:13).
8. I am the Light of the world (Jn. 8:12).
9. I am the Door (Jn. 10:9).
10. I am the Good Shepherd (Jn. 10:14).

Metrology (the science of weights, measurements, and money)

1. Bath—6 gallons (1 Ki. 7:26).
2. Bekah—¼ ounce (Ex. 38:26).
3. Bushel—1 peck (Mt. 5:15; Mk. 4:21; Lk. 11:33).
4. Cab—2 quarts (2 Ki. 6:25).
5. Cubit—18 inches (Gen. 6:15; 1 Sam. 17:4; Est. 5:14; Dan. 3:1).
6. Cor—6½ bushels of dry measure, or 61 gallons of liquid (Ezek. 45:14).
7. Daric (dram)—$5.00 (Neh. 7:70; Ezra 2:69).
8. Day's Journey—around 20 miles (Lk. 2:44).
9. Denarius (penny)—a day's wages (Mt. 20:2; 22:19; Lk. 10:35).
10. Didrachmon (didrachma)—32¢ (Mt. 17:24). Also equivalent to a Jewish half-shekel of silver.
11. Drachme (Drachma)—16¢ (Lk. 15:8, 9).
12. Ephah—1 bushel, or 6 gallons of grain (Ruth 2:17; 1 Sam. 17:17).
13. Farthing—¼ cent (Mt. 10:29; Mk. 12:42).
14. Fathom—6 feet (Acts 27:28).
15. Finger span (digit)—¾ inch (Jer. 52:21).
16. Firkin (metretes)—9 gallons (Jn. 2:6).
17. Furlong—⅛ mile (Lk. 24:13; Jn. 6:19; Rev. 14:20; 21:16).
18. Gerah—1/40 ounce (Ex. 30:13).
19. Handbreadth—3 inches (1 Ki. 7:26; Ps. 39:5).
20. Hin—6 quarts (Ex. 29:40).
21. Homer—90 gallons, or 11 bushels (Num. 11:32; Hosea 3:2).
22. Log—1 pint (Lev. 14:10).
23. Measure—1 peck (Gen. 18:6; Mt. 13:33).
24. Maneh—2 pounds (Ezek. 45:12).
25. Mile—4,880 feet (Mt. 5:41).
26. Mina (translated pound in 1 Ki. 10:17)—$16.00.
27. Mite—⅛ cent (Mk. 12:42).
28. Omer—7 pints (Ex. 16:22).
29. Pace—1 yard (2 Sam. 6:13).
30. Pound
    a. In Luke 19:13 it was $16.00 (where the Greek word for pound is mina).
    b. In Nehemiah 7:71 the pound was silver and was worth around $40.00.
    c. In 1 Kings 10:17 the pound was gold and worth $600.00.
31. Quadrans—¼ cent (Mt. 5:26; Mk. 12:42).
32. Reed—11 feet (Ezek. 42:16; Rev. 21:15).
33. Sabbath day's journey—½ mile (Acts 1:12).
34. Seah—a gallon and 5 pints (Gen. 18:6; 1 Sam. 25:18).
35. Shekel
    a. Of weight—½ ounce (1 Sam. 17:5, 7).
    b. Of silver—64 cents (Josh. 7:21; 2 Ki. 7:1; Jer. 32:9).
36. Span—9 inches (Ex. 28:16).
37. Stater (tetradrachma)—64 cents (Mt. 17:27).
38. Talent
    a. In Matthew 18:24; 25:15 it is worth $1000.
    b. In 2 Kings 5:5; in Esther 3:9 it is silver and worth $2500.
    c. In 1 Kings 10:10, 14 it is gold and worth $30,000.

Minerals

NON-PRECIOUS MINERALS

1. Asphalt—a mixture of hydrocarbons which form crude mineral oils and petroleums. When exposed to air, asphalt hardens (Gen. 11:3).

2. Brimstone—a highly combustible sulphur substance.
    a. God used burning brimstone to destroy Sodom (Gen. 19:24; Deut. 29:23; Lk. 17:29).
    b. He will use it during the tribulation (Rev. 9:17, 18).
    c. He will use it to destroy Russia (Ezek. 38:22).
    d. He will use it during the battle of Armageddon (Isa. 34:9).
    e. He will use it upon all sinners in the lake of fire (Ps. 11:6; Isa. 34:9; Rev. 14:10; 19:20; 20:10; 21:8).
3. Brass—a reference to bronze or copper. This mineral was mined in the ancient world by the Phoenicians.
    a. Some of the tabernacle furniture was made of brass (Ex. 38).
    b. Some of the Temple furniture was made of brass (1 Ki. 7).
    c. The serpent in the wilderness was made of brass (Num. 21:9; Jn. 3:14).
    d. Part of the statue in Nebuchadnezzar's dream was made of brass (Dan. 2:32).
    e. Samson was bound with fetters of brass (Jdg. 16:21).
    f. Goliath's armor was made of brass (1 Sam. 17).
4. Chalkstone—or limestone (Isa. 27:9).
5. Clay—a compound arising from the decomposition of certain rocks.
    a. Man is viewed as clay by God (Isa. 45:9; 64:8; Rom. 9:21).
    b. Israel is described as a broken clay vessel (Jer. 18:4-6).
    c. Part of the statue in Nebuchadnezzar's dream was made of clay (Dan. 2:33).
    d. The sinner is pictured as being in a pit of miry clay (Ps. 40:2).
    e. Jesus used clay and spittle to anoint the eyes of a blind man (Jn. 9:6).
6. Coral (Job 28:18; Ezek. 27:16).
7. Flint—a reference to any very hard compact rock (Ex. 4:25; Deut. 8:15; Josh. 5:2, 3; Isa. 50:7).
8. Iron
    a. A giant named Og had a huge bed made of iron (Deut. 3:11).
    b. The Canaanite chariots were made of iron (Josh. 17:16; Jdg. 1:19; 4:3).
    c. Goliath's spearhead was made of iron (1 Sam. 17:7).
    d. Elisha caused an iron axe-head to float (2 Ki. 6:6).
    e. Joseph was bound with iron in Egypt (Ps. 105:18).
    f. Part of the statue in Nebuchadnezzar's dream was made of iron (Dan. 2:33).
9. Lead (Ezek. 2:18).
10. Marble (Est. 1:6; 1 Chron. 29:2). Marble is recrystallized limestone.
11. Salt
    a. Lot's wife became a pillar of salt (Gen. 19:26).
    b. The Levitical offerings were to be seasoned with salt (Lev. 2:13; Mk. 9:49).
    c. A special covenant was performed by using salt (Num. 18:19; 2 Chron. 13:5).
    d. Abimelech destroyed a city and sowed it with salt (Jdg. 9:45).
    e. Elisha purified some polluted waters by using salt (2 Ki. 2:20, 21).

PRECIOUS MINERALS (and stones)

1. Amethyst—a purple form of quartz, the ninth stone in the breastplate of the high priest and the twelfth in the

foundation of the New Jerusalem (Ex. 28:19; 39:12; Rev. 21:20).

2. Bdellium—a milky quartz, spotted with gold flecks (Num. 11:7; Gen. 2:12).

3. Beryl—a blue-green silicate, the tenth stone in the breastplate and eighth in the Holy City (Ex. 28:20; 39:13; Ezek. 1:16; 10:9; Dan. 10:6; Rev. 21:20).

4. Carbuncle—a red silicate, the third stone in the breastplate (Isa. 54:12; Ezek. 28:13).

5. Chalcedony—the third stone in the new city (Rev. 21:19).

6. Chrysolyte—yellow-green, the seventh stone in the Holy City (Rev. 21:20).

7. Coral (Job 28:18; Ezek. 27:16).

8. Chrysoprasus—apple green, the tenth stone in the Holy City (Rev. 21:20).

9. Crystal—transparent, colorless, beautifully shaped, and remarkably brilliant (Rev. 21:11; Job 28:17).

10. Diamond—the sixth stone of the breastplate (Ex. 28:18; 39:11; Jer. 17:1; Ezek. 28:13).

11. Emerald—deep green, the fourth stone in the breastplate and also the fourth in the new city (Ex. 28:18; 39:11; Ezek. 27:16; 28:13; Rev. 4:3; 21:19).

12. Jacinth—the seventh stone in the breastplate and eleventh in the Holy City (Rev. 9:17; 21:20).

13. Jasper—the twelfth stone of the breastplate and the first of the Holy City (Ex. 28:20; 39:13; Ezek. 28:13; Rev. 4:3; 21:11, 18, 19). John described the Father by using the jasper and sardine stones. The walls of the New Jerusalem are of jasper.

14. Onyx—the eleventh stone of the breastplate (Gen. 2:12; Ex. 25:7; 28:20; 39:13; Job 28:16; Ezek. 28:13).

15. Pearl—the gates of the Holy City (Job 28:18; Mt. 7:6; 13:45, 46; 1 Tim. 2:9; Rev. 17:4; 18:12; 21:21).

16. Ruby—a fiery red, associated with wisdom and virtue (Job 28:18; Prov. 3:15; 8:11; 20:15; 31:10; Lam. 4:7).

17. Sapphire—a brilliant blue, the second stone in the Holy City (Ex. 24:10; 28:18; 39:11; Job 28:6, 16; Lam. 4:7; Isa. 54:11; Ezek. 1:26; 10:10; 28:13; Rev. 21:19).

18. Sardius—first stone of breastplate and sixth of Holy City (Ex. 28:17; 39:10; Ezek. 28:13; Rev. 4:3; 21:20).

19. Sardonyx—the fifth stone in the new city (Rev. 21:20).

20. Topaz—yellow, the ninth stone in the new city (Ex. 28:17; 39:10; Job 28:19; Ezek. 28:13; Rev. 21:20).

21. Gold
   a. The tabernacle and Temple vessels were made of gold (Ex. 25; 1 Ki. 6).
   b. Part of the statue in Nebuchadnezzar's dream was gold (Dan. 2:32).
   c. Nebuchadnezzar made an entire statue of gold (Dan. 3:1).
   d. Israel made a golden calf idol (Ex. 32).
   e. The Philistines made some golden mice (1 Sam. 6:4).
   f. Jeroboam made two golden calves (2 Ki. 10:29).
   g. The wise men presented Christ with gifts of gold (Mt. 2:11).
   h. The twenty-four elders wore crowns of gold (Rev. 4:4).
   i. The apparel of the ascended Christ was golden (Dan. 10:4; Rev. 1:13; 14:14).
   j. The street of the New Jerusalem will be a transparent gold (Rev. 21:18, 21).

22. Silver:
   a. Abraham purchased the cave of Machpelah for 400 pieces of silver (Gen. 23:15).
   b. Joseph was sold for twenty pieces of silver (Gen. 37:28).
   c. Moses made two silver trumpets (Num. 10:2).
   d. Delilah betrayed Samson for 1100 pieces of silver (Jdg. 16:5).
   e. David purchased a threshingfloor for fifty shekels of silver (2 Sam. 24:24).
   f. Achan stole 200 shekels of silver (Josh. 7:21).
   g. Haman offered a Persian king 10,000 talents of silver to destroy the Jews (Est. 3:9).
   h. Hosea bought his wife out of slavery for fifteen pieces of silver (Hosea 3:2).
   i. Part of the statue in Nebuchadnezzar's dream was silver (Dan. 2:32).
   j. Jesus was sold out by Judas for thirty pieces of silver (Mt. 26:15; 27:3-9).

Miracles
MIRACLES PERFORMED BY THE TRINITY
(forty-nine or more)

1. Creation (Gen. 1, 2; Heb. 11:3; Prov. 8; Ps. 104).
2. Enoch's translation (Gen. 5:19-24; Heb. 11:5; Jude 14, 15).
3. The flood (Gen. 6-8; Mt. 24:37-39; Heb.11:7; 1 Pet. 3:20; 2 Pet. 2:5).
4. Confusion at Babel (Gen. 11; Isa. 13:1).
5. Plaguing of Pharaoh (Gen. 12:10-20).
6. The burning lamp and smoking furnace (Gen. 15:17, 18).
7. Sarah's conception (Gen. 17:15-19; 18:10-14; 21:1-8).
8. Destruction of Sodom (Gen. 19; Mt. 10:15; 2 Pet. 2:6; Jude 7).
9. Lot's wife (Gen. 19:24-28; Lk. 17:28, 32).
10. Plaguing Abimelech (Gen. 20:1-7, 17, 18).
11. Hagar's well (Gen. 21:14-21).
12. The burning bush (Ex. 3:1-14; Deut. 33:16; Mk. 12:26; Lk. 20:37; Acts 7:30, 31).
13. Moses' rod (Ex. 4:1-5; 7:8-13; 2 Tim. 3:8).
14. Moses' leprous hand (Ex. 4:6-12).
15. The Exodus journey (Deut. 8:4; 29:5; Neh. 9:21).
16. Balaam's speaking donkey (Num. 22:20-35; 2 Pet. 2:15; Jude 11).
17. The death of Moses (Deut. 32).
18. The fall of Dagon (1 Sam. 5:1-5).
19. The Philistines' emerods (1 Sam. 5:6-12; 6:17, 18; Deut. 28:27; Ps. 78:66).
20. Judgment on the men of Bethshemesh (1 Sam. 6:19).
21. Judgment upon Uzzah (2 Sam. 6:7).
22. Judgment upon Israel for David's sin (1 Sam. 24:10-16).
23. Judgment upon the disobedient man of God (1 Ki. 13:24).
24. Judgment upon Jeroboam (2 Chron. 13:20).
25. Feeding Elijah (1 Ki. 17:2-6).
26. Speaking through nature to Elijah (1 Ki. 19:9-18).
27. Taking Elijah to heaven (2 Ki. 2:9-11).
28. Reviving a dead man through Elisha's bones (2 Ki. 13:21).
29. Judging Uzziah with leprosy (2 Chron. 26:15-21; 2 Ki. 15:1-8).
30. Healing Hezekiah (2 Ki. 20:1-11; 2 Chron. 32:24; Isa. 38).
31. The handwriting on the wall (Dan. 5:5, 25).
32. Sending a storm (Jonah 1:1-16).
33. Preparing a fish (Jonah 1:17—2:10).
34. Preparing a gourd (Jonah 4:6).

35. Preparing a worm (Jonah 4:7).
36. Preparing an east wind (Jonah 4:8–10).
37. Allowing Elisabeth to bear a son (Lk. 1:6–13, 57).
38. The virgin birth (Mt. 1:18–24; Lk. 1:26–37; 2:6, 7).
39. The star in the east (Mt. 2:1–10).
40. The transfiguration (Mt. 17:1–13; Mk. 9:1–13; Lk. 9:28–36; 2 Pet. 1:16–18).
41. The Calvary miracles
    a. Darkness (Mt. 27:45; Lk. 23:44).
    b. Earthquake (Mt. 27:51).
    c. Rent veil (Mt. 27:51; Mk. 15:38; Lk. 23:45).
    d. Restoration of bodies (Mt. 27:52, 53).
42. The resurrection (Mt. 28; Mk. 16; Lk. 24; Jn. 20).
43. The ascension (Mk. 16:19, 20; Lk. 24:50–52; Acts 1:4–11).
44. Pentecost (Acts 2:1–4).
45. Shaking of the place after the prayer meeting (Acts 4:31).
46. Judgment upon Ananias and Sapphira (Acts 5:1–11).
47. Allowing Stephen to view the third heaven (Acts 7:55, 56).
48. Blinding Saul (Acts 9:8).
49. Coming upon the Gentiles (Acts 10:44–46).
50. Raising Paul (from the dead?) (Acts 14:19–28; see also 2 Cor. 12:1–5).
51. Freeing Paul and Silas (Acts 16:19–40).

MIRACLES PERFORMED BY SATAN (unnumbered)
1. Plaguing Job with sorrows (Job 1–2).
2. Tempting Christ (Mt. 4:1–11; Lk. 4:1–13).

MIRACLES PERFORMED BY CHRIST
(thirty-six specific miracles)
1. Changing of water into wine (Jn. 2:7, 8).
2. Healing of the nobleman's son (Jn. 4:50).
3. Healing of the Capernaum demoniac (Mk. 1:25; Lk. 4:35).
4. Healing of Peter's mother-in-law (Mt. 8:15; Mk. 1:31; Lk. 4:39).
5. Catching a great number of fish (Lk. 5:5, 6).
6. Healing a leper (Mt. 8:3; Mk. 1:41).
7. Healing a paralytic (Mt. 9:2; Mk. 2:5; Lk. 5:20).
8. Healing a withered hand (Mt. 12:13; Mk. 3:5; Lk. 6:10).
9. Healing a centurion's servant (Mt. 8:13; Lk. 7:10).
10. Raising a widow's son (Lk. 7:14).
11. Calming the stormy sea (Mt. 8:26; Mk. 4:39; Lk. 8:24).
12. Healing the Gadarene demoniac (Mt. 8:32; Mk. 5:8; Lk. 8:33).
13. Healing a woman with internal bleeding (Mt. 9:22; Mk. 5:29; Lk. 8:44).
14. Raising Jairus' daughter (Mt. 9:25; Mk. 5:41; Lk. 8:54).
15. Healing two blind men (Mt. 9:29).
16. Healing a dumb demoniac (Mt. 9:33).
17. Healing of an invalid (Jn. 5:8).
18. Feeding 5,000 men and their families (Mt. 14:19; Mk. 6:41; Lk. 9:16; Jn. 6:11).
19. Walking on the sea (Mt. 14:25; Mk. 6:48; Jn. 6:19).
20. Healing a demoniac girl (Mt. 15:28; Mk. 7:29).
21. Healing a deaf man (with a speech impediment) (Mk. 7:34, 35).
22. Feeding 4,000 men and their families (Mt. 15:36; Mk. 8:6).
23. Healing a blind man (Mk. 8:25).
24. Healing a man born blind (Jn. 9:7).
25. Healing a demoniac boy (Mt. 17:18; Mk. 9:25; Lk. 9:42).

26. Catching a fish with a coin in its mouth (Mt. 17:27).
27. Healing a blind and dumb demoniac (Mt. 12:22; Lk. 11:14).
28. Healing a woman with an eighteen-year infirmity (Lk. 13:10–17).
29. Healing a man with dropsy (Lk. 14:4).
30. Healing ten lepers (Lk. 17:11–19).
31. Raising of Lazarus (Jn. 11:43, 44).
32. Healing a blind man (Mt. 20:34; Lk. 18:42).
33. Healing a blind man (Mt. 20:34; Mk. 10:46).
34. Destroying a fig tree (Mt. 21:19; Mk. 11:14).
35. Restoring (healing) a severed ear (Mt. 26:51; Mk. 14:47; Lk. 22:50, 51; Jn. 18:10).
36. Catching a great number of fish (Jn. 21:6).

MIRACLES PERFORMED BY THE ANTICHRIST AND THE FALSE PROPHET (unnumbered: 2 Thessalonians 2:9; Revelation 13:15).

MIRACLES PERFORMED BY THE ANGELS
1. Blinding the Sodomites (Gen. 19:9–11).
2. The rock-fire miracle (Jdg. 6:19–24).
3. Feeding of Elijah (1 Ki. 19:5–7).
4. Judging the Assyrian army (2 Ki. 19:35).
5. Preserving three Hebrew men in a fire (Dan. 3:25).
6. Preserving Daniel in a den of lions (Dan. 6:1–24).
7. Giving of the law (Acts 7:53; Gal. 3:19; Heb. 2:2).
8. Future regathering of Israel (Mt. 24:31).
9. Rescuing Moses' dead body from Satan (Jude 1:9).
10. Death punishment of Herod (Acts 12:23).
11. Freeing of Peter from prison (Acts 12:1–17).
12. Opening prison doors for disciples (Acts 5:19–23).
13. Rolling away the stone at Christ's resurrection (Mt. 28:2).
14. Pouring out of the wrath of God (Rev. 6–19).

MIRACLES PERFORMED BY DEMONS
1. Affecting Abimelech and the men of Shechem (Jdg. 9:23).
2. Affecting Saul (1 Sam. 16:14; 19:9).
3. The prophets of Ahab (1 Ki. 22:23).
4. The nation Israel (Hosea 4:12; Zech. 13:2; Mt. 10:1).
5. Mary Magdalene (Lk. 8:2).
6. A man in Capernaum (Mk. 1:21–28).
7. A man in Capernaum (Mt. 12:22).
8. Two men, east of the Sea of Galilee (Mt. 8:28–34).
9. A man in Capernaum (Mt. 9:32–34).
10. A little girl (Mt. 15:21–28).
11. A little boy (Mt. 17:14–21).
12. Various people in and around Jerusalem (Acts 5:16).
13. Various people in and around Samaria (Acts 8:7).
14. A Philippian slave girl (Acts 16:16–18).
15. Various people in and around Ephesus (Acts 19:12).
16. Sceva and his seven sons (Acts 19:14–16).
17. All unsaved people (Eph. 2:2; 1 Tim. 4:1).
18. The kings of the earth (Rev. 16:13).

MIRACLES PERFORMED BY JOSEPH
1. Interpreting the dreams of two jail mates (Gen. 40:1–23).
2. Interpreting the dream of Pharaoh (Gen. 41:14–32).

MIRACLES PERFORMED BY MOSES AND AARON
1. Turning the Nile into blood (Ex. 4:9; 7:14–24; Ps. 78:44; 105:29).
2. The plague of frogs (Ex. 8:1–6; Ps. 78:45; 105:30).

3. The plague of lice (Ex. 8:16-19; Ps. 105:31).
4. The plague of flies (Ex. 8:20-31; Ps. 78:45; 105:31).
5. The plague of murrain upon the beasts (Ex. 9:1-7).
6. The plague of boils (Ex. 9:8-11).
7. The plague of hail (Ex. 9:13-25; Ps. 78:47, 48; 105:32, 33).
8. The plague of locusts (Ex. 10:1-20; Ps. 78:46; 105:34, 35).
9. The plague of darkness (Ex. 10:21-29; Ps. 105:28).
10. The plague of the death of the firstborn (Ex. 11, 12; Ps. 78:51; 105:36; 135:8; 136:10).
11. The cloud and the fire (Ex. 13:21, 22; 40:34-38; Ps. 78:14; 105:39; Neh. 9:12, 19; 1 Cor. 10:1, 2, 6, 11).
12. The Red Sea parting (Ex. 14:21-31; Ps. 78:53; 106:9, 11, 22; Heb. 11:29).
13. The healing of Marah's bitter waters (Ex. 15:22-27; Num. 33:8).
14. The giving of manna (Ex. 15:6-15; Num. 11:1-9; Josh. 5:11, 12; Neh. 9:15; 20; Ps. 78:20; 105:40; see also Jn. 6:22-59.).
15. The giving of quails (Ex. 16:8, 11-15; Num. 11:31-34; Ps. 78:26-30; 105:39-42).
16. The smitten rock (Ex. 17:1-9; Ps. 78:16, 17; 105:41).
17. The victory over the Amalekites (Ex. 17:8-16; Num. 13:29; 14:25; Deut. 25:17-19; Ps. 83:7).
18. The miracles at Sinai (Ex. 19:16-25; Deut. 4:5; 5:7-22; 9:8-11; Ps. 68:8; Heb. 12:18-21).
19. The punishment of Nadab and Abihu (Lev. 10:1-7; Num. 3:1-4; 26:61; 1 Chron. 24:2).
20. The fire at Taberah (Num. 11:1-3; Deut. 9:22; Ps. 78:21).
21. Miriam's leprosy (Num. 12; 20:1; Lev. 13:46; Deut. 24:8, 9).
22. Judgment upon Korah (Num. 16; 26:9-11; Ps. 106:17).
23. The budding of Aaron's rod (Num. 17; Heb. 9:4).
24. The brazen serpent (Num. 21:4-9; 2 Ki. 18:4; Jn. 3:14; 1 Cor. 10:9).
25. The miracle water (Num. 21:13-18).

MIRACLES PERFORMED BY THE EGYPTIAN MAGICIANS (see also 2 Tim. 3:8)
1. Turning water into blood (Ex. 7:22).
2. Bringing up frogs (Ex. 8:7).

MIRACLES PERFORMED BY JOSHUA
1. The parting of Jordan (Josh. 3:7-17; Ps. 114:3).
2. The shouting down of Jericho (Josh. 6).
3. The victory at Gibeon (Josh. 10:12-15; Isa. 28:21).

MIRACLES PERFORMED BY GIDEON
1. The fleece (Jdg. 6:25-40).
2. The Midian victory (Jdg. 7).

MIRACLES PERFORMED BY SAMSON
1. The slain lion (Jdg. 14:5-10).
2. The foxes (Jdg. 15:1-6).
3. The hip and thigh slaughter (Jdg. 15:7, 8).
4. Escaping from bonds (Jdg. 15:9-14).
5. Slaying of 1000 Philistines (Jdg. 15:15-20).
6. The uprooting of doors (Jdg. 16:1-3).
7. The miracles of his own hair (Jdg. 16:4-22).
8. The destruction of Dagon's temple (Jdg. 16:23-31).

MIRACLE PERFORMED BY WITCH OF ENDOR
(1 Sam. 28).

MIRACLES PERFORMED BY DAVID
1. Overcoming a lion and a bear (1 Sam. 17:34-37).
2. Defeating Goliath (1 Sam. 17).

MIRACLE PERFORMED BY SOLOMON
Praying down fire from heaven (2 Chron. 7:1).

MIRACLE PERFORMED BY A NAMELESS MAN OF GOD
Withering the hand of Jeroboam (1 Ki. 13:4).

MIRACLE PERFORMED BY AHIJAH
Recognizing Jeroboam's disguised wife (1 Ki. 14:1-6).

MIRACLES PERFORMED BY ELIJAH
1. The three-year drought (1 Ki. 17:1; Jas. 5:17).
2. The unfailing barrel and cruse (1 Ki. 17:13-16; Lk. 4:25, 26).
3. Raising of the widow's son (1 Ki. 17:17-24).
4. Praying down fire on Mt. Carmel (1 Ki. 18:1-39).
5. Causing it to rain (1 Ki. 18:1, 2, 41-46).
6. Destruction of King Ahaziah's soldiers (2 Ki. 1:1-16).
7. Dividing the waters at Jordan (2 Ki. 2:8).

MIRACLES PERFORMED BY ELISHA
1. Parting of Jordan River (2 Ki. 2:14).
2. Solving Jericho's water problem (2 Ki. 2:19-22).
3. Judgment of young hecklers from Bethel (2 Ki. 2:23, 24).
4. Flooding ditches for the Israelite army in Edom (2 Ki. 3:16-20).
5. Creating oil for a widow (2 Ki. 4:1-7).
6. Raising of the Shunammites' son (2 Ki. 4:32-37).
7. Healing of the poisonous stew (2 Ki. 4:38-41).
8. Multiplying food (2 Ki. 4:42-44).
9. Healing Naaman (2 Ki. 5:1-19).
10. Judgment upon Gehazi (2 Ki. 5:26, 27).
11. Causing an axehead to float (2 Ki. 6:1-7).
12. Allowing his servant to see protecting angels (2 Ki. 6:17).
13. Judging Syrians with blindness (2 Ki. 6:18).
14. Delivering starving Samaria (2 Ki. 7).

MIRACLES PERFORMED BY DANIEL
1. Interpreting Nebuchadnezzar's dreams (Dan. 2:19-45; 4:4-27).
2. Interpreting the handwriting on the wall (Dan. 5:13-28).

MIRACLES PERFORMED BY THE APOSTLES
(unnumbered: Mk. 3:15; 6:7; 16:17-20; Lk. 9:1, 2; 10:9, 17, 19; Acts 5:12).

MIRACLES PERFORMED BY PETER
1. Healing of a lame man (Acts 3:6-8).
2. Healing many (Acts 5:15).
3. Healing Aeneas (Acts 9:32-34).
4. Raising Dorcas from the dead (Acts 9:36-41).

MIRACLES PERFORMED BY PAUL.
1. The blinding of Elymas (Acts 13:10, 11).
2. Healing of a cripple (Acts14:8-10).
3. Miracles in Ephesus (Acts 19:11, 12).
4. Raising Eutychus (Acts 20:1-12).
5. Miracles at Melita (Acts 28:1-10).

MIRACLES PERFORMED BY STEPHEN (unnumbered: Acts 6:8).

MIRACLES PERFORMED BY PHILIP (unnumbered: Acts 8:5-8, 13, 17).

MIRACLES PERFORMED BY SIMON THE SORCERER (Acts 8:9-11).

MIRACLES PERFORMED BY SEVEN FALSE EXORCISTS (Acts 19:13-20).

MIRACLES PERFORMED BY A FEMALE SOOTHSAYER (Acts 16:16-24).

Mountains

1. Ararat—where the ark of Noah landed in Turkey (Gen. 8:4).
2. Carmel—where Elijah challenged the priests of Baal. It is straight west of the Sea of Galilee, and overlooking the Mediterranean Sea (1 Ki. 18:19).
3. Ebal—where the curses of Israel (if the people disobeyed) were pronounced. Located in Samaria (Deut. 11:29; 27:9-13).
4. Gerizim—where the blessings of Israel (for obedience) were pronounced. Located opposite Mt. Ebal (Deut. 11:29). Also the place where the Samaritans later built their temple (Jn. 4:20, 21).
5. Gilboa—where Saul was defeated by the Philistines and killed, along with Jonathan, his son. Located on the eastern side of the Plain of Esdraelon (1 Sam. 31:1-6).
6. Gilead—where Jacob and Laban made their covenant. Located southeast of the Galilean Sea (Gen. 31:20-49).
7. Harmon—where Jesus was transfigured. Located southwest of Nazareth (Mt. 17).
8. Hor—where Aaron died. Located northeast of Kadeshbarnea (Num. 20:25-29).
9. Horeb—the sacred mountain chain of which Sinai was the summit. Located in the peninsula between the Gulf of Aqabah and the Suez.
   a. Here Moses received his commission at the burning bush (Ex. 3:1).
   b. Here he brought water out of the rock (Ex. 17:6).
   c. Here Elijah fled from Jezebel (1 Ki. 19:8).
   d. Here the people waited as Moses spent forty days on Mt. Sinai (Ex. 32-33).
10. Lebanon—where the wood for Solomon's Temple was taken (1 Ki. 5:6-14). Lebanon is a snowclad mountain range extending in a northeasterly direction for 100 miles along the Syrian coast.
11. Moriah—where Abraham offered up Isaac, and where Solomon built the Temple (Gen. 22:2; 2 Chron. 3:1).
12. Nebo—the summit point of Mt. Pisgah where Moses viewed the Promised Land. It was located east of the Jordan River (Deut. 3:27; 34:1-4).
13. Olives—just east of Jerusalem.
   a. David crossed this during his flight from Absalom (2 Sam. 15:30).
   b. Here Jesus wept over Jerusalem (Lk. 19:41).
   c. Here he preached his final discourse (Mt. 24-25).
14. Pisgah—where Balaam attempted to curse Israel, and where Moses was buried. Located east of the Jordan River (Num. 22-24; Deut. 34:5, 6).
15. Sinai—the summit of Mt. Horeb where Moses received the ten commandments (Ex. 20:1-17).
16. Tabor—where Deborah and Barak descended to defeat Sisera. Located in Galilee, east of Nazareth (Jdg. 4:6-15).

Musical Instruments

1. Castanets—the name comes from the word which means chestnut. In ancient times two chestnuts were attached to the fingers and beat together to make music (Ps. 150:5).
2. Cornet—a hollow, curved horn, originally made from an animal's horn, and later from metal (Ps. 98:6; Dan. 3:5, 7, 10, 15).
3. Cymbal—two concave plates of brass which were clanged together or beat (2 Sam. 6:5; Ps. 150:5; 1 Cor. 13:1).
4. Drum (also referred to as a timbrel, tabret, and tambourine). It was a wooden hoop with skins pulled across the frame (Ex. 15:20; Jdg. 11:34; Ps. 68:25; 81:2; 1 Chron. 13:8).
5. Dulcimer—a resonance box with strings stretched across it, played with small hammers. Note: the word dulcimer in Daniel 3:5, 10, 15 probably does not refer to this stringed-box instrument, but rather to the bagpipe.
6. Flute—a straight pipe with holes (Dan. 3:5; Jdg. 5:16).
7. Harp—the first musical instrument mentioned in the Bible (Gen. 4:21). It was made of wood and had ten strings (1 Sam. 16:16).
8. Lyre—an instrument with five or more strings stretched across a rectangular frame. The strings were made from the small intestines of sheep. It was similar to the harp (1 Sam. 16:23, *RSV*).
9. Organ—a simple reed instrument, made of wood, ivory, or bone, perhaps to be identified with the oboe (Gen. 4:21; Job 21:12; Ps. 150:4).
10. Psaltery—similar to, but not the same as the harp. The psaltery was thought by some to have been a bottle-shaped string instrument (1 Sam. 10:5; 2 Chron. 5:12; Ps. 71:22).
11. Sackbut—a portable, harplike instrument which was tied to the player's waist and held upright as he walked and played. It was considered a luxury in oriental musical instruments (Dan. 3:5, 7, 10, 15).
12. Trumpet—usually made from the horn of a ram or goat, but on one occasion, from silver. (See Num. 10:1-10; Jdg. 7:16-23; Mt. 24:31; 1 Cor. 15:52; 1 Thess. 4:16; Rev. 8:2).
13. Zither (psaltery)—ten-stringed instrument, similar to the harp (Ps. 33:2; 144:9).

Mysteries

Introduction: A mystery in the Bible is a previously hidden truth, not revealed in the Old Testament, but declared, and, at times explained, in the New Testament.

1. The mystery of the kingdom of heaven (Mt. 13:3-50; Mk. 4:1-25; Lk. 8:4-15). These verses, according to the *New Scofield Bible,* "Describe the result of the presence of the Gospel in the world during the present age, that is, the time of seed-sowing which began with our Lord's personal ministry and will end with 'the harvest.' The result is the mingled tares and wheat, good fish and bad, in the sphere of Christian profession. It is Christendom" (p. 1013). Note the eightfold development of this mystery:

a. The sower, the seed, and the soil (Mt. 13:1-9, 18-23). This deals with the purpose of Christ, his methods, and the nature of men's hearts.

b. Satanic tares in the Savior's field (Mt. 13:24-30, 36-43). Satan will oppose God's work. The wheat and tares will not be completely separated until harvesttime.

c. From scattering to sickling (Mk. 4:26-29). The kingdom of heaven will have a gradual development.

d. The mighty mustard seed (Mt. 13:31, 32; Mk. 4:30-32; Lk. 13:18, 19). The kingdom of heaven will have a humble start, and will consist of both saved and unsaved until the harvest.

e. The cook's leaven and the kingdom of heaven (Mt. 13:33; Lk. 13:20, 21). This does not teach that the leaven here will convert the world, but rather that it would influence it.

f. Finding a fortune in a field (Mt. 13:44). This may speak of the Jewish remnant.

g. The price of a pearl (Mt. 13:45, 46). This may be the first reference to the church in the Bible.

h. Sorting out a sea catch (Mt. 13:47-50). This indicates the fairness and completeness of the final judgment.

"Such, then, is the mystery form of the Kingdom. It is the sphere of Christian profession during this age. It is a mingled body of true and false, wheat and tares, good and bad. It is defiled by formalism, doubt, and worldliness. But within it Christ sees the true children of the true Kingdom who, at the end, are to 'shine forth as the sun.' In the great field, the world, He sees His treasure that He redeems for His own through His Cross. Thus, in this aspect of the Kingdom, He sees the Church, His Body and Bride composed of believing Israelites and Gentiles, and for joy sells all that He has (2 Cor. 8:9) and buys the field, the treasure, and the pearl." (New Scofield Bible, p. 1017)

2. The mystery of the rapture (1 Cor. 15:51, 52; 1 Thess. 4:16). The mystery revealed here is that those believers living at the time of Christ's appearance will be glorified and caught up without seeing death.

3. The mystery of the Church as the body of Christ, composed of saved Jews and Gentiles of this age (Rom. 16:25; Eph. 3:1-11; 6:19; Col. 4:3). Paul explains this mystery in Ephesians 3:6: "That the Gentiles should be fellow heirs, and of the same body, and partakers of his promise in Christ by the gospel."

4. The mystery of the Church as the bride of Christ (Eph. 5:28-32). The mystery here is that Christ is to the Church what a loving husband is to his wife.

5. The mystery of the indwelling Christ (Gal. 2:20; Col. 1:26, 27). Not only are saved Gentiles made a part of the body and bride of Christ, but are actually themselves indwelled by the living Savior.

6. The mystery of the incarnate Christ (Col. 2:2, 9; 1 Cor. 2:7). Jesus Christ, possessor of all knowledge, became full man, yet retained his total deity while in human flesh.

7. The mystery of Christ's work in restoring a sinner to godliness (1 Tim. 3:16). Nicodemus finally understood the simplicity of this beautiful mystery.

8. The mystery of iniquity (Mt. 13:33; 2 Thess. 2:3-12). This refers to:

a. The identity of the antichrist—unknown until the tribulation.

b. The appearance of the antichrist—after the rapture.

c. The work of the antichrist—powerful but totally perverted works.

d. The power source of the antichrist—Satan himself.

9. The mystery of Israel's present-day blindness (Rom. 11:25). This declares that Israel as a nation will remain blind and deaf to the gospel until the "fullness of the Gentiles" is come in. This period is from Pentecost until the rapture.

10. The mystery of the seven stars (Rev. 1:20). Jesus himself explains this mystery:

"The mystery of the seven stars which thou sawest in my right hand, and the seven golden lampstands. The seven stars are the angels of the seven churches; and the seven lampstands which thou sawest are the seven churches" (Rev. 1:20).

11. The mystery of Babylon, the harlot (Rev. 17:5, 7). Here the mystery refers to the development (Gen. 11), degradation (Mt. 23), and eventual destruction (Rev. 17:16, 17) of Satan's harlot church.

12. The mystery of God (Rev. 10:7; 11:15-19). This is no doubt the most profound and perplexing mystery of all. The mystery is this: Why has God allowed so much sin, suffering, sorrow, and Satanic activity to go on for these thousands of years? Why has he (up till this very hour) delayed his stated purpose which will someday take place? That day when . . ."the kingdoms of this world are become the kingdoms of our Lord, and of his Christ; and he shall reign for ever and ever" (Rev. 11:15).

Nations, Peoples, and Countries

1. Akkadians—lived in the northern part of Mesopotamia (Gen. 10:10).
2. Ammonites—lived east of the Dead Sea (Jdg. 11:5).
3. Amorites—lived in the central part of Mesopotamia (1 Sam. 7:14).
4. Arabians—lived in the northern part of the Arabian peninsula (2 Chron. 17:11; 21:16; Gal. 1:17).
5. Assyrians—lived in northern part of Mesopotamia (2 Ki. 18:9).
6. Babylonians—lived in the southern part of Mesopotamia (2 Ki. 25:1).
7. Canaanites—lived in Palestine and southern Syria (Gen. 12:6).
8. Chaldeans—lived in southern Mesopotamia (Dan. 3:8).
9. Cilicians—lived near Tarsus (Paul's native city). Called the Kue people in the Old Testament (1 Ki. 10:28, 29).
10. Cretans—lived on the island of Crete (Acts 2:11; Titus 1:12).
11. Cypriotes—lived on the Island of Cyprus (Acts 13:4).
12. Edomites—lived south of the Dead Sea (Num. 20:14).
13. Egyptians—lived in Egypt (Gen. 12:10).
14. Elamites—lived east of Babylon (Acts 2:9).
15. Ethiopians—lived south of Egypt (Acts 8:27).
16. Greeks—lived on the Greek islands (Jn. 12:20).
17. Hittites—lived in central Asia Minor (Gen. 15:20).
18. Hurrians—lived in northern Asia Minor. Also known as the Horites and the Hivites (Ex. 34:11; Josh. 9:1).
19. Lydians—lived in western Asia Minor. Also called Ludims (Jer. 46:9).
20. Medes—lived in northwest Persia (Dan. 5:28-31).

21. Midianites—lived in the central part of the Sinai Peninsula (Ex. 3:1).
22. Moabites—lived northeast of the Dead Sea (Ruth 1:1).
23. Persians—lived east of Mesopotamia (Neh. 1:1).
24. Philistines—lived on the southern coast of Palestine (Jdg. 13:1).
25. Phoenicians—lived on the northern coasts of Palestine (Acts 11:19).
26. Sumerians—lived in the southern part of Babylon (Gen. 11:1).
27. Syrians—lived east of the Sea of Galilee (2 Ki. 5:1).

Numbers

1. *One.* The primary number. Signifies absolute singleness (Ex. 4:4-6; Deut. 6:4; Eph. 4:4-6).
2. *Two.* The number of witness and support.
   a. Two great lights of creation (Gen. 1:16).
   b. Two angels at Sodom (Gen. 19:1).
   c. Two cherubim on the ark (Ex. 25:22).
   d. The commandments were written on two stones (Ex. 31:18).
   e. Two witnesses to establish a truth (Deut. 17:6; Mt. 26:60).
   f. The good report of the two spies at Kadesh (Num. 14:6).
   g. Two spies at Jericho (Josh. 2:1).
   h. Two are better than one (Eccl. 4:9).
   i. Jesus sent out disciples two by two (Lk. 10:1).
   j. He sends Peter and John into Jerusalem (Mk. 14:13).
   k. Two angels attend the resurrection (Lk. 24:4).
   l. Two angels are present at the ascension (Acts 1:10).
   m. God's two immutable things (Heb. 6:18).
   n. The two tribulational witnesses (Rev. 11:3).
3. *Three.* Number of unity, accomplishment, and of the universe.
   a. Concerning the universe: space, matter, time.
   b. Concerning space: three dimensional, height, breadth, length.
   c. Concerning matter: energy, motion, phenomena.
   d. Concerning time: past, present, future.
   e. The unity of the human race can be traced to Noah's three sons (Gen. 6:10).
   f. Three days were involved in the crossing of the Jordan (Josh. 1:11).
   g. Israel's national life involved three yearly feasts (Ex. 23:14, 17).
   h. Gideon accomplished a mighty victory through three bands of soldiers (Jdg. 7:22).
   i. Three days of preparation led to a revival in Ezra's time (Ezra 10:9).
   j. Three days were involved in the decision to build the walls of Jerusalem in Nehemiah's time (Neh. 2:11).
   k. Esther prepared her heart for three days before meeting with the king (Est. 4:16).
   l. God prepared Jonah in the fish's belly for three days (Jonah 1:17).
   m. Christ was in the heart of the earth for three days (Jn. 2:19).
   n. His earthly ministry lasted some three years (Lk. 13:7).
   o. Concerning the Trinity: Father, Son, Holy Spirit.
   p. Concerning man (his nature): body, soul, spirit.
   q. Concerning man (his enemies): the world, the flesh, the devil.
   r. Concerning the tabernacle and the Temple: outer court, inner court, Holy of Holies.
   s. Concerning the offices of Christ: Prophet, Priest, King.
   t. Concerning salvation: justification, sanctification, glorification.
4. *Four.* An earth-related number.
   a. Four directions: north, south, east, west.
   b. Four seasons: summer, winter, fall, spring (Gen. 8:22).
   c. Four great earthly kingdoms (Dan. 7:3).
   d. Four kinds of spiritual soil (Mt. 13).
   e. Four horsemen of the tribulation (Rev. 6).
   f. Fourfold earthly ministry of Christ.
      Matthew describes him as a King.
      Mark as a Servant.
      Luke as the perfect Man.
      John as the mighty God.
5. *Five.* The number of grace.
   a. There were five Levitical offerings (Lev. 1-5).
   b. God's grace would allow five Israelites to chase one hundred of their enemies (Lev. 26:8).
   c. There were five wise virgins (Mt. 25:2).
   d. Jesus used five barley loaves to feed 5,000 (Mt. 14:17).
6. *Six.* This is the number of man.
   a. God created man's world in six days (Gen. 1:31).
   b. There were six cities of refuge (Num. 35:6).
   c. Israel marched around Jericho six times (Josh. 6:3).
   d. Goliath was six cubits high (1 Sam. 17:4).
   e. The number of the antichrist is 666 (Rev. 13:18).
   f. Nebuchadnezzar's statue was sixty cubits by six (Dan. 3:1).
7. *Seven.* The number of God, or divine perfection.
   a. God rested on the seventh day (Gen. 2:2).
   b. His word is as silver purified by fire seven times (Ps. 12:6).
   c. Seventy weeks (or years) are determined upon Israel (Dan. 9:24).
   d. Jesus taught Peter to forgive seventy times seven (Mt. 18:22).
   e. There are seven miracles in the Gospel of John.
   f. There were seven sayings on the cross.
   g. John wrote to seven churches (Rev. 1:4).
   h. He saw seven golden candlesticks (Rev. 1:12).
   i. There are seven stars in Christ's hand (Rev. 1:16).
   j. The Father holds a seven-sealed book (Rev. 5:1).
   k. Seven angels pronounce judgment in the tribulation (Rev. 8:2).
8. *Eight.* The new beginning number.
   a. Eight are saved from the flood (Gen. 7:13, 23).
   b. Circumcision was to be performed on the eighth day (Gen. 17:12).
   c. Thomas saw Jesus eight days after the resurrection (Jn. 20:26).
9. *Nine.* The fullness of blessing number.
   a. The fruit of the Spirit is ninefold (Gal. 5:22, 23).
   b. Sarah was ninety at the birth of Isaac (Gen. 17:17).
   c. There are eighteen gifts of the Spirit (Rom. 12; 1 Cor. 12; Eph. 4).
10. *Ten.* The human government number.
    a. The revived Roman Empire will consist of ten nations (Dan. 7:24; Rev. 17:12).
    b. The northern kingdom had ten tribes (1 Ki. 11:31-35).
    c. A local government of ten men decided the fate of Ruth (Ruth 4:2).

11. *Twelve.* The divine government number.
    a. There were twelve tribes of Israel (Rev. 7).
    b. There were twelve apostles (Mt. 10).
    c. There will be twelve gates and foundations in the New Jerusalem (Rev. 21).
12. *Thirty.* Associated with sorrow, mourning.
    a. Israel mourned after Aaron's death for thirty days (Num. 20:29).
    b. Israel mourned for Moses thirty days (Deut. 34:8).
13. *Forty.* The number of testing, trial.
    a. It rained forty days during the flood (Gen. 7:4).
    b. Moses spent forty years in the desert (Ex. 3).
    c. Israel spied out the land for forty days (Num. 13:25).
    d. Moses spent forty days on Mt. Sinai (Ex. 24:18).
    e. Israel wandered forty years in the desert (Num. 14:33).
    f. Goliath taunted Israel for forty days (1 Sam. 17:16).
    g. Jonah preached repentance to Nineveh for forty days (Jonah 3:4).
    h. Jesus spent forty days in the wilderness before being tempted (Mt. 4:2).
    i. Forty days elapsed between the resurrection and ascension of Christ (Acts 1:3).
14. *Fifty.* Associated with celebration and ceremony.
    a. The feast of weeks was fifty days after the Passover (Lev. 23:15, 16).
    b. The fiftieth year was to be a jubilee to Israel (Lev. 25:10).
    c. Pentecost occurred fifty days after Christ's resurrection (Acts 1–2).
    d. Absalom appointed fifty men to run before him (2 Sam. 15:1).
    e. Adonijah did the same (1 Ki. 1:5).
15. *Seventy.* Associated with human committees and judgment.
    a. Moses appointed seventy elders (Num. 11:16).
    b. Jesus appointed seventy disciples (Lk. 10:1).
    c. The Sanhedrin was made up of seventy men.
    d. Tyre was to be judged for seventy years (Isa. 23:15).
    e. Israel spent seventy years in Babylon (Jer. 29:10).
    f. God would accomplish his total plan upon Israel in seventy times seven years (Dan. 9:24).

Occupations
1. Bakers (Gen. 40:1).
2. Butlers (Gen. 40:2).
3. Barbers (Ezek. 5:1).
4. Boat builders (1 Ki. 9:26).
5. Braziers (Gen. 4:22).
6. Brickmakers (Gen. 11:3).
7. Caulkers (Ezek. 27:9).
8. Carpenters (2 Sam. 5:11).
9. Confectioners (1 Sam. 8:13).
10. Cooks (1 Sam. 8:13).
11. Coppersmiths (2 Tim. 4:14).
12. Draftsmen (Ezek. 4:1).
13. Druggists (Ex. 30:25, 35).
14. Dyers (Ex. 25:5).
15. Embalmers (Gen. 50:3).
16. Embroiderers (Ex. 28:39).
17. Engravers (Ex. 28:11).
18. Fishermen (Mt. 4:18).
19. Fullers (2 Ki. 18:17).
20. Gardeners (Jer. 29:5).
21. Goldsmiths (2 Chron. 2:7).
22. Jewelers (Ex. 28:17-21).
23. Masons (2 Ki. 12:12).
24. Molders (Ex. 32:4).
25. Military men (Acts 10:1).
26. Musicians (2 Sam. 6:5).
27. Needleworkers (Ex. 26:36).
28. Painters (Jer. 22:14).
29. Porters (2 Sam. 18:26).
30. Potters (Isa. 64:8).
31. Refiners (Mal. 3:3).
32. Seamstresses (Ezek. 13:18).
33. Silversmiths (Acts 19:24).
34. Smelters (Job 28:1, 2).
35. Smiths (1 Sam. 13:19).
36. Spinners (Ex. 35:25).
37. Stonecutters (Ex. 31:5).
38. Tailors (Ex. 39:1).
39. Tanners (Acts 9:43).
40. Tax collectors (Mt. 9:9).
41. Tentmakers (Acts 18:3).
42. Weavers (Ex. 28:32).
43. Workers in metals (Ex. 31:3, 4).

Offerings
1. Burnt (Ex. 29:18).
2. Drink (Lev. 23:13).
3. Heave (Lev. 7:14).
4. Meal (Lev. 2:1).
5. Peace (Lev. 7:11).
6. Sin (Lev. 4:3).
7. Trespass (Lev. 5:6).
8. Wave (Lev. 7:30).

Palaces
1. The palace of Artaxerxes (Neh. 1:1; 2:1).
2. Of Solomon (1 Ki. 7:1).
3. Of Ahasuerus (Est. 1:2).
4. Of Belshazzar (Dan. 5:5).
5. Of Darius (Dan. 6:18).
6. Of the high priest (Mt. 26:3, 58, 69).
7. Of Caesar (Phil. 1:13).

Parables

A parable is a placing beside or comparison of earthly truths with heavenly truths. It is an earthly story (often historical in nature, but not necessarily so) with a heavenly meaning. It is something placed "by the side of" in order to explain.

OLD TESTAMENT PARABLES
1. The parable of Mt. Moriah (Gen. 22; Heb. 11:17-19).
2. The parable of the tabernacle (Ex. 25-31; Heb. 9:1-10).
3. The parable of the trees (Jdg. 9:7-15).
4. The parable of the ewe lamb (2 Sam. 12:1-4).
5. The parable of the two sons (2 Sam. 14:1-24).
6. The parable of the wounded prophet (1 Ki. 20:35-43).
7. The parable of the shepherdless flock (1 Ki. 22:13-28).
8. The parable of the thistle and the cedar (2 Ki. 14:8-14).
9. The parable of the nature of wisdom (Job 28).
10. The parable of the vine out of Egypt (Ps. 80).
11. The parable of the little city (Eccl. 9:14-18).
12. The parable of the master's crib (Isa. 1:2-9).
13. The parable of the Lord's vineyard (Isa. 5:1-7).

14. The parable of the almond rod and the boiling pot (Jer. 1:11–19).
15. The parable of the marred girdle (Jer. 13:1–11).
16. The parable of the wine bottle (Jer. 13:12–14).
17. The parable of the potter and the clay (Jer. 18:1–10).
18. The parable of the broken bottle (Jer. 19:1–13).
19. The parable of the two baskets of figs (Jer. 24:1–10).
20. The parable of the cup of fury (Jer. 25:15–38).
21. The parable of the bonds and yokes (Jer. 27, 28).
22. The parable of the hidden stones (Jer. 43:8–13).
23. The parable of the living creatures (Ezek. 1:1–28).
24. The parable of the eaten scroll (Ezek. 2, 3).
25. The parable of the tile (Ezek. 4:1–17).
26. The parable of the shaved head and beard (Ezek. 5:1–17).
27. The parable of the Temple wickedness (Ezek. 8:1–18).
28. The parable of the writer's inkhorn (Ezek. 9, 10).
29. The parable of the cauldron and the flesh (Ezek. 11:1–25).
30. The parable of the great escape (Ezek. 12:1–28).
31. The parable of the vine branch (Ezek. 15:1–8).
32. The parable of the harlot wife (Ezek. 16:1–63).
33. The parable of the great eagle (Ezek. 17:1–24).
34. The parable of the lioness and her whelps (Ezek. 19:1–9).
35. The parable of the plucked up vine (Ezek. 19:10–14).
36. The parable of the two sisters (Ezek. 23:1–49).
37. The parable of the boiling cauldron (Ezek. 24:1–4).
38. The parable of the prophet's dead wife (Ezek. 24:15–24).
39. The parable of the cedar in Lebanon (Ezek. 31:1–18).
40. The parable of the unfaithful shepherds (Ezek. 34:1–31).
41. The parable of the valley of dry bones (Ezek. 37:1–14).
42. The parable of the two sticks (Ezek. 37:15–28).
43. The parable of the rising waters (Ezek. 47:1–12).
44. The parable of the great image (Dan. 2:31–45).
45. The parable of the great tree (Dan. 4:1–37).
46. The parable of the four beasts (Dan. 7:1–28).
47. The parable of the ram and the goat (Dan. 8:1–25).
48. The parable of the harlot wife (Hosea 1–3).
49. The parable of the horse and myrtle trees (Zech. 1:8–17).
50. The parable of the horns and smiths (Zech. 1:18–21).
51. The parable of the measuring line (Zech. 2:1–13).
52. The parable of Joshua the priest (Zech. 3:1–10).
53. The parable of the golden candlestick (Zech. 4:1–6).
54. The parable of the flying scroll (Zech. 5:1–4).
55. The parable of the woman and the basket (Zech. 5:5–11).
56. The parable of the four war chariots (Zech. 6:1–8).
57. The parable of the crowns (Zech. 6:9–15).
58. The parable of beauty and bands (Zech. 11:1–17).

CHRIST'S PARABLES
1. Two houses in a hurricane (Mt. 7:24–27; Lk. 6:47–49).
2. Forgiving the fifty and the five hundred (Lk. 7:41, 42).
3. Subduing a strong man (Mk. 3:22–30).
4. The sower, the seed, and the soil (Mt. 13:1–9; 18–23; Mk. 4:1–20; Lk. 8:4–15).
5. Satan's tares in the Savior's field (Mt. 13:24–30, 36–43).
6. From scattering to sickling (Mk. 4:26–29).
7. The mighty mustard seed (Mt. 13:31, 32; Mk. 4:30–32; Lk. 13:18, 19).
8. The cook's leaven and the kingdom of heaven (Lk. 13:20, 21).
9. Finding a fortune in a field (Mt. 13:44).

10. The price of a pearl (Mt. 13:45, 46).
11. Sorting out a sea catch (Mt. 13:47–50).
12. A trained man and his treasure (Mt. 13:52).
13. A rent cloth and a ruptured container (Mt. 9:16, 17; Mk. 2:21, 22; Lk. 5:36–39).
14. A generation of gripers (Mt. 11:16–19; Lk. 7:31–35).
15. The forgiven who wouldn't forgive (Mt. 18:23–35).
16. How to know your neighbor (Lk. 10:25–37).
17. Seven spirits and a swept house (Mt. 12:43–45; Lk. 11:24–26).
18. A fool in a fix (Lk. 12:16–21).
19. Keep the home fires burning (Lk. 12:35-40; Mt. 24:43, 44).
20. A sinning servant and a returning ruler (Mt. 24:45–51; Lk. 12:42–48).
21. A fruitless fig tree (Lk. 13:6–9).
22. Choosing the least at a wedding feast (Lk. 14:7–11).
23. Two fools and a henpecked husband (Lk. 14:15–24).
24. A missing sheep, misplaced silver, and a miserable son (Lk. 15:1–32).
25. The stewings of a steward (Lk. 16:1–13).
26. When hades petitioned paradise (Lk. 16:19–31).
27. When our best is but the least (Lk. 17:7–10).
28. A widow and a weary judge (Lk. 18:1–8).
29. A haughty Pharisee and a humble Publican (Lk. 18:9–14).
30. When the last was first and the first was last (Mt. 20:1–16).
31. Three stewards and their silver (Lk. 19:11–27).
32. Two sons who changed their minds (Mt. 21:28–32).
33. The vicious vinekeepers (Mt. 21:33–46; Mk. 12:1–12; Lk. 20:9–19).
34. A wedding guest with no wedding garment (Mt. 22:1–14).
35. The fig tree and the future (Mt. 24:32–35; Mk. 13:28–31; Lk. 21:29–33).
36. Five lamps that went out (Mt. 25:1–13).
37. Three stewards and their talents (Mt. 25:14–30).
38. Separating the sheep from the goats (Mt. 25:31–46).

REMAINING NEW TESTAMENT PARABLES
1. The great sheet parable (Acts 10:9–22).
2. The parable of rewards (1 Cor. 3:12–15).
3. The olive tree parable (Rom. 11:13–25).
4. The parable of the two women, sons, and mountains (Gal. 4:19–31).
5. The whole armor of God parable (Eph. 6:11–17).
6. The rest of God (Promised Land) parable (Heb. 3:7—4:16).
7. The parable of the two mountains (Heb. 12:18–24).
8. The parable of the tongue (Jas. 3).
9. The parable of the sevenfold lampstand (Rev. 1:9—3:22).
10. The parable of a seven-sealed book (Rev. 5:1–14).
11. The parable of the four horsemen (Rev. 6:1–8).
12. The parable of the persecuted woman (Rev. 12:1–17).
13. The parable of the seven-headed, ten-horned dragon (Rev. 12:3, 4; 13:1).
14. The bloody harlot parable (Rev. 17).
15. The arrogant queen parable (Rev. 18).
16. The pure bride parable (Rev. 19:1–10).

Paradoxes
1. Of finding one's life, yet eventually losing it (Mt. 10:39; Jn. 12:25).

2. Of losing one's life, yet eventually finding it (Mt. 10:39).
3. Of being unknown, yet being well known (2 Cor. 6:9).
4. Of dying, yet possessing life (2 Cor. 6:9).
5. Of dying, yet being able to give life (Jn. 12:24).
6. Of being sorrowful, yet always rejoicing (2 Cor. 6:10).
7. Of being poor, yet making many rich (2 Cor. 6:10).
8. Of having nothing, yet possessing all things (2 Cor. 6:10).
9. Of hearing words that cannot be expressed (2 Cor. 12:4).
10. Of being strong when one is weak (2 Cor. 12:10).
11. Of knowing the love of Christ which surpasses knowledge (Eph. 3:19).
12. Of seeing the unseen (2 Cor. 4:18).

It may be concluded that the very life and ministry of our blessed Savior was itself a divine paradox.
1. He hungered, yet fed multitudes (Mt. 4:2; Jn. 6).
2. He thirsted, yet is the Water of life (Jn. 19:28; 4:14).
3. He wearied, yet is our rest (Jn. 4:6; Mt. 11:29, 30).
4. He paid tribute, yet is the King of kings (Mt. 17:27; Rev. 19:16).
5. He prayed, yet hears our prayers (Mk. 14:32–42; Jn. 14:13, 14).
6. He wept, yet dries our tears (Jn. 11:35; Rev. 21:4).
7. He was sold for thirty pieces of silver, yet redeems the world (Mt. 26:15; 1 Pet. 1:18, 19).
8. He was led as a sheep to the slaughter, and yet is the Good Shepherd (Isa. 53:7; Jn. 10:11).
9. He was put to death, yet raises the dead (Jn. 5:25; 19:33).

Passovers
1. The death angel Passover in Egypt (Ex. 12:21).
2. The first Passover in the Promised Land (Josh. 5:10).
3. The Passover in Hezekiah's time (2 Chron. 30:2).
4. The Passover in Josiah's time (2 Ki. 23:22).
5. The first Passover by the returning remnant (Ezra 6:19).
6. The Passover attended by Jesus at age twelve (Lk. 2:41, 42).
7. The cleansing of the Temple Passover (Jn. 2:13).
8. The feeding of the 5,000 Passover (Jn. 6:4).
9. The raising of Lazarus Passover (Jn. 11:55).
10. The upper room Passover (Mt. 26:19).
11. The Passover associated with the death of James and the freedom of Peter (Acts 12:4).
12. The future Passover in the millennium (Ezek. 45:21).

Plagues
UPON NATIONS
1. Egypt
   a. Waters turn to blood (Ex. 7:20).
   b. Plague of frogs (Ex. 8:6).
   c. Lice (Ex. 8:17).
   d. Beetles, flies (8:24).
   e. Cattle disease (9:3).
   f. Boils (9:10).
   g. Hail (9:24).
   h. Locusts (10:13).
   i. Darkness (10:22).
   j. Death of the firstborn (12:29).
2. Israel
   a. Death by the sword, due to idolatry (Ex. 32:27), 3000 die.
   b. Death by fire, due to complaining (Num. 11:1).
   c. Death by an unnamed plague, due to lust (Num. 11:31–35).
   d. Death for unbelief (Num. 14:37).
   e. Death by an earthquake for rebellion (Num. 16:32), 250 die.
   f. Death by poisonous serpents for rebellion (Num. 21:6).
   g. Death for immorality (Num. 25:9), 24,000 die.
   h. Death for looking into the ark of God (1 Sam. 6:19), 50,070 die.
   i. Death due to David's census (2 Sam. 24:15), 70,000 die.
3. Philistia
   a. Death by thunder and lightning due to attacking Israel (1 Sam. 7:10).
   b. Suffering by emerods, for capturing the ark of God (1 Sam. 5:8, 9).
4. Syria—a plague of blindness for attacking Israel (2 Ki. 6:18).
5. Russia—death by pestilence for attacking Israel (Ezek. 38:21, 22).
6. All nations during the tribulation
   a. White horse plague of cold war (Rev. 6:2), first seal.
   b. Red horse plague of hot war (Rev. 6:3, 4), second seal.
   c. Black horse plague of famine (Rev. 6:5, 6), third seal.
   d. Pale horse plague of death (Rev. 6:7, 8), fourth seal.
   e. Sixth seal plague of earthquake (Rev. 6:12).
   f. First trumpet plague (Rev. 8:7), one third of vegetation destroyed.
   g. Second trumpet plague (Rev. 8:8), one third of salt waters become blood.
   h. Third trumpet plague (Rev. 8:10, 11), one third of fresh waters become bitter.
   i. Fourth trumpet plague (Rev. 8:12), one third of moon, sun, stars darkened.
   j. Fifth trumpet plague (Rev. 9:12), men plagued with scorpion stings for five months.
   k. Sixth trumpet plague (Rev. 9:14), one third of earth's population slain.
   l. First vial plague (Rev. 16:2), sores upon men.
   m. Second vial plague (Rev. 16:3), all sea life destroyed.
   n. Third vial plague (Rev. 16:4), all rivers become blood.
   o. Fourth vial plague (Rev. 16:8, 9), men scorched by the sun.
   p. Fifth vial plague (Rev. 16:10), darkness upon the empire of the antichrist.
   q. Sixth vial plague (Rev. 16:12), drying up of the Euphrates River.
   r. Seventh vial plague (Rev. 16:17–21; 18), destruction of political and economic Babylon.

UPON INDIVIDUALS
1. Upon Pharoah for attempting to marry Sarah (Gen. 12:17).
2. Upon Abimelech for attempting to marry Sarah (Gen. 20:18).
3. Upon Moses, to show him God's power (Ex. 4:6, 7).
4. Upon Nadab and Abihu for offering strange fire (Lev. 10:1, 2).
5. Upon Miriam, for criticizing Moses (Num. 12:1–10).
6. Upon Saul, for his disobedience (1 Sam. 16:14).
7. Upon Nabal, for his hatred of David (1 Sam. 25:38).

8. Upon Jeroboam, for his false religion (1 Ki. 13:4).
9. Upon Gehazi, for lying (2 Ki. 5:20–27).
10. Upon Uzziah, for attempting to assume priestly duties (2 Chron. 26:16–21).
11. Upon Herod, for receiving worship from men (Acts 12:20–25).
12. Upon Bar-Jesus, for opposing Paul (Acts 13:6–11).

Plains

1. The plains of Moreh, where Abraham built his first altar (Gen. 12:6).
2. Of Mamre, where God appeared to him (Gen. 18:1).
3. Of Shinar, where the Tower of Babel was built (Gen. 11:2).
4. Of Jordan, where Sodom was located (Gen. 13:11).
5. Of Moab, where final preparations were made to cross the Jordan (Num. 26:3, 63; 31:12; Deut. 34:1, 8).
6. Of Jericho, where Joshua met Christ and prepared to conquer the land (Josh. 5:10). Also where Judah's last king, Zedekiah, was captured by Nebuchadnezzar (2 Ki. 25:5).
7. Of Dura, where Nebuchadnezzar built his golden statue (Dan. 3:1).

Plants

1. Aloe (Ps. 45:8; Prov. 7:17; Jn. 19:38–40). A succulent plant with thick, fleshy leaves and a tall stem with many bell-shaped flowers. Used for purifying the bodies of the dead.
2. Anise (Mt. 23:23).
3. Balm (Gen. 37:25; Jer. 8:22). An evergreen shrub with white blossoms and apple-like fruit. Gum resin from its bark was used for medicinal purposes.
4. Barley (Ruth 1:22; 2 Ki. 7:1, 16, 18; Jn. 6:1–13). A staple cereal.
5. Briar (Jdg. 8:7, 16).
6. Bulrush (Ex. 2:3). A tall plant whose stems were used for paper making.
7. Calamus (Song of Sol. 4:14; Ezek. 27:19). It comes from the reed and cane family. Strong-smelling oil was taken from its root.
8. Coriander (Ex. 16:31; Num. 11:6–9). It has leaves like parsley, white or pinkish flowers, and a rounded gray seed which contains a valuable oil used for flavoring or perfume.
9. Cumin (Isa. 28:27; Mt. 23:23). A small delicate plant, used for medicinal purposes and spice for food.
10. Flax (Ex. 9:31; 26:1; 28:6; Josh. 2:6; Prov. 31:13). A plant used to make linen.
11. Gall (Ps. 69:21; Mt. 27:34). It is thought this may have been a plant related to the opium poppy.
12. Garlic (Num. 11:5). Used as food flavoring.
13. Gourd (2 Ki. 4:39; Jonah 4:6–10). A large (eight to ten foot high) bush with rich green or bronze leaves, with bright red fruit. Its oil was used for fuel for lamps.
14. Grass (Ps. 103:15).
15. Henna (Song of Sol. 1:14; 4:13, *RSV*). A shrub which produces white scented flowers, used to color the hair or fingernails in reddish and yellowish hues.
16. Hyssop
    a. Old Testament hyssop (Ex. 12:22; Lev. 14:4; Ps. 51:7). This was a plant of the mint family, with small leaves and bunches of golden flowers. It was used for sprinkling blood, for cleansing lepers, and for other rites of purification.
    b. New Testament hyssop (Jn. 19:29). A tall, yellow-green plant with strong stems and ribbon-like leaves.
17. Leeks (Num. 11:5). A favorite onion-resembling vegetable in Palestine, also used for medicinal purposes.
18. Lentils (Gen. 25:34; 2 Sam. 17:28; 23:11; Ezek. 4:9). It has the appearance of a pea and is used as a cereal or for making bread.
19. Lilies (Mt. 6:28). A beautiful purple flower.
20. Mandrake (Gen. 30:14–16).
21. Mint (Mt. 23:23). A small leaf plant used for medicinal, flavoring, and perfume purposes.
22. Mustard (Mt. 13:13–32; 17:20). A yellow-flowered plant whose leaves were used as a vegetable.
23. Myrrh (Mt. 2:11). The resin, or drippings of a thorny bush, with thin bark.
24. Pomegranate (Ex. 28:31–34). A wild shrub with dark green, shiny leaves, and bright red, wax-like flowers. The fruit is dark red in color, about the size of an orange. It was used as a medicine and for food.
25. Reed (Ezek. 40:3; Isa. 18:2). A tall plant with purple blossoms, used as a measuring device, and to make pens for writing purposes.
26. Rose (Isa. 35:1; Song of Sol. 2:1). The famous Rose of Sharon was a beautiful tulip-like flower with bright red blossoms.
27. Rue (Lk. 11:42). A five foot tall plant with clusters of bright yellow flowers, used as a disinfectant, as flavoring, and for medicinal remedies.
28. Rush (Job 8:11; Isa. 35:7). A flowery plant used to make baskets, wicker chair seats, etc.
29. Scarlet (Lev. 14:51). A large evergreen shrub, the shoots of which are the breeding ground of an insect from which a scarlet dye is taken. The bark of the tree yields a black dye.
30. Spikenard (Song of Sol. 1:12; 4:14; Mk. 14:3–6). A small plant with hairy stems from which the costly, sweet-smelling ointment which bears its name is taken.
31. Tares (Job 31:40; Mt. 13:24–30, 36–43). One of the most destructive weeds of the Holy Land. The seeds often contain a poisonous fungus which when eaten produces dizziness, nausea, and sometimes even death.
32. Thistle (Gen. 3:18; Hosea 10:8; Mt. 7:16; Heb. 6:8). A tall weed with yellow flowers and a spiny stem.
33. Thorns (Mt. 7:16).
34. Vine (Isa. 5:2–7; Jn. 15:1–8).
35. Wheat (Gen. 41:1–7).

Plots

1. That of Cain against Abel (Gen. 4:8), to lure him in a field that he might kill him. Reason: envy.
2. Of Jacob and Rachel against Esau and Isaac (Gen. 27), to deceive Isaac into believing that Jacob was Esau. Reason: to secure the blessing.
3. Of Simeon and Levi against Shechem (Gen. 34), to trick Shechem and his tribe to circumcize themselves. Reason: to murder them in revenge for seducing their sister.
4. Of Joseph's brothers against Joseph (Gen. 37:18), to sell him into Egyptian slavery and then tell their father a wild animal had eaten him. Reason: jealousy.
5. Of Tamar against Judah (Gen. 38), to disguise herself as a common harlot and then lure Judah into her tent for sexual purposes. Reason: possible reason to have a child.

6. Of Potiphar's wife against Joseph (Gen. 39:13-19), to accuse Joseph of rape. Reason: to obtain revenge for Joseph's prior refusal to sexually defile himself.
7. Of Pharaoh against the male Hebrew babies (Ex. 1), to kill all male babies. Reason: to prevent Israel from growing any more and becoming a threat to him.
8. Of Korah against Moses (Num. 16:1-3), to demand an equal (if not superior) place of leadership to that of Moses. Reason: probably jealousy, envy, and power hunger.
9. Of the Gibeonites against Joshua (Josh. 9), to deceive Joshua (by dressing in old and ragged clothes) into believing they had come as citizens from a far-off country. Reason: so that Joshua would enter into an agreement with them and thus their people would be saved from a war of destruction.
10. Of Delilah against Samson (Jdg. 16:4-20), demanding he prove his love to her by telling her the secret of his great strength. Reason: to earn the blood money promised her by the Philistines.
11. Of Saul against David (1 Sam. 18). Saul offered the hand of his daughter Michal in marriage to David if he would singlehandedly kill 100 Philistines. Reason: he thought David would himself be killed in attempting this.
12. Of Absalom against David (2 Sam. 15). Under the pretense of fulfilling a vow to God, Absalom received permission to visit Hebron. Reason: he actually went there to organize and announce his rebellion.
13. Of Adonijah against Solomon (1 Ki. 1). He invited some leading Israelites (including a general and chief priest) to a feast. Reason: he would use this occasion to stage his rebellion against his brother Solomon.
14. Of Jezebel against Naboth (1 Ki. 21). A letter was sent ordering Naboth to be murdered under the pretense of the crime of blasphemy. Reason: so that Ahab could obtain his vineyard.
15. Of certain Chaldeans against three Hebrew young men (Dan. 3). Their good names and loyalty were slandered before King Nebuchadnezzar. Reason: jealousy.
16. Of certain Chaldeans against Daniel (Dan. 6). They caused a law to be made whereby no one could pray for awhile to any other god except King Darius. Reason: to kill Daniel.
17. Of Sanballat against Nehemiah (Neh. 4, 6). Sanballat opposed Nehemiah's work by ridiculing it and finally by threatening it. Reason: to keep the wall of Jerusalem from going up.
18. Of Haman against the Persian Jews (Est. 3), that all Jews be put to death by royal decree on a given date. Reason: because of Haman's hatred for one Jew, Mordecai.
19. Of Satan against Job (Job 1, 2), to take away Job's family, wealth, and health. Reason: that he might blaspheme God.
20. Of Herod against Christ (Mt. 2), to kill the infant Christ by the sword. Reason: to rid the country of a king that might threaten Herod's rule.
21. Of Satan against Christ (Mt. 4), to turn stones into bread, to defy gravity, and to worship Satan. Reason: to cause Christ to sin.
22. Of Herodias against John (Mt. 14), an immoral dance which prompted Herod to grant Herodias' request for the head of John the Baptist. Reason: to avenge herself upon John for his fearless preaching against her wickedness.

23. Of the Jewish leaders against Christ (Jn. 11:47-57), to kill Christ as soon as possible. Reason: to silence his message.
24. Of the Jewish leaders against Lazarus (Jn. 12:10, 11), to kill Lazarus. Reason: to dispose of the greatest of Christ's miracles—the raising of a dead man four days in the grave.
25. Of the Jewish leaders against all believers (Jn. 9:22; 12:42), a law imposing excommunication from the Temple to all who would accept Christ. Reason: to prevent people from following the Savior.
26. Of Judas against Christ (Mt. 26:14-16), to betray the Son of God with a kiss. Reason: to earn the thirty pieces of silver.
27. Of the synagogue leaders against Stephen (Acts 6:8-15), to stone him. Reason: so that his message of judgment might be silenced.
28. Of Saul against believers (Acts 8:3; 9:1, 2), to imprison them. Reason: that their gospel message might be silenced.
29. Of the Damascus Jews against Paul (Acts 9:22-25), to kill him as he left Damascus through the city gate. Reason: that this turncoat Pharisee might be silenced.
30. Of the Jerusalem Jews against Paul.
   a. First occasion (Acts 9:26-29; 22:17-21).
   b. Second occasion (Acts 21:31).
   c. Third occasion (Acts 23:6-10).
   d. Fourth occasion (Acts 23:12-14).
   e. Fifth occasion (Acts 24:1).
   f. Sixth occasion (Acts 25:1-3).
31. Of Herod against believers (Acts 12). He placed James and Peter on death row. Reason: to please the unbelieving Jews.
32. Of Asian Jews against Paul.
   a. At Antioch in Pisidia (Acts 13:14, 45, 50).
   b. At Iconium (Acts 14:1, 2).
   c. At Lystra (Acts 14:6, 7, 19).
33. Of Greek Jews against Paul.
   a. At Thessalonica (Acts 17:1, 5).
   b. At Berea (Acts 17:13).
   c. At Corinth (Acts 18:1, 12).
   d. At Macedonia (Acts 20:3).
34. Of Demetrius against Paul (Acts 19:24-27). He (rightly) accused Paul of blasphemy against the goddess Diana. Reason: the merchants of the Diana movement were losing money.
35. Of Alexander the coppersmith against Paul (2 Tim. 4:14). He did Paul great harm. Reason: his hatred of the gospel.

Political and Religous Groups

1. The diaspora. The Jews scattered abroad, due to the Assyrian and Babylonian captivities (Acts 2:5, 9-11).
2. Epicurianism. A first-century hedonistic philosophy developed by Epicurius (341-270 b.c.). See Acts 17:18.
3. The Galileans. Jewish followers of a rebel named Judas of Galilee. They were the right wingers of the day (Lk. 13:1).
4. The Hellenists. Greek-speaking Jews (Acts 6:1).
5. The Herodians. A political dynasty from the family of Herod. They derived their authority from the Roman government (Mk. 3:6; 8:15; 12:13-17).
6. The Levites. The descendants of Levi who had charge of the Temple (Jn. 1:19; Lk. 10:32).
7. The Libertines. A group of ex-slaves who apparently had their own synagogues in Jerusalem (Acts 6:9).

8. The Nazarites. Those individuals taking a special religious vow as prescribed in Numbers 6. (See Jdg. 13:3-7; Lk. 1:15.)
9. The Pharisees. The separatists, legalists, and guardians of both the written and oral law (Mt. 12:1, 2; 23).
10. The Proselytes. Gentile converts to Judaism (Mt. 23:15; Acts 2:10; 13:43).
11. The Publicans. The state-appointed tax collectors of Roman revenue (Lk. 3:13; 19:8; Mt. 9:9).
12. The Sadducees. The liberal resurrection-denying left wing members of the Sanhedrin (Mk. 12:18; Lk. 20:27).
13. The Samaritans. A race of half Jew and Gentile living between the provinces of Judea and Galilee (Jn. 4:9; 8:48; Mt. 10:5; Lk. 10:33; 17:16).
14. The Sanhedrin. The religious and legal Jewish Supreme Court (Mt. 26:65, 66; 27:1, 2).
15. The Scribes. The students, interpreters, and teachers of the Old Testament law (Mt. 16:21; 21:15; 23:2; 26:3). They were also called lawyers (Lk. 10:25).
16. The Stoics. A group founded by Zeno (300 B.C.) who believed life's goal was to rise above all things and to show no emotion to either pain or pleasure (Acts 17:18).
17. The Zelotes. A group of Jewish patriots, fanatical defenders of theocracy (Lk. 6:15; Acts 1:13).

Pools

1. The pool of Gibeon, where Joab and Abner's servants fought a bloody battle (2 Sam. 2:13).
2. The pool of Hebron, where Saul's son, Ish-bosheth, was executed (2 Sam. 4:12).
3. The pool of Hezekiah, which aided in the defense of Jerusalem (2 Ki. 20:20).
4. The pool of Samaria, where Ahab's bloody chariot was washed (1 Ki. 22:38).
5. The pool of Bethesda, where Jesus healed a man of a thirty-eight-year infirmity (Jn. 5:2).
6. The pool of Siloam, where Jesus instructed a blind man to wash and receive his sight (Jn. 9:7).

Porches

This word, as used in the Scriptures, refers to an area with a roof supported by columns.
1. The royal porch at Jericho. Ehud used this porch in his escape after killing Eglon the Moabite king (Jdg. 3:23).
2. Solomon's porch of judgment (1 Ki. 7:7). This porch is mentioned several times in the New Testament.
   a. Jesus preached here and was almost stoned (Jn. 10:22-39).
   b. Many sick folk lay here, praying to be healed (Jn. 5:2).
   c. Peter preached from here after healing a cripple (Acts 3:11).
   d. It served as an early meeting place for believers (Acts 5:12).
3. The porch of the high priest, where Peter denied Christ and heard the cock crow (Mt. 26:71; Mk. 14:68).
4. The prince's porch in the millennial temple (Ezek. 44:3; 46:2, 8).

Prayers
PRAYERS OF PETITION
1. For an heir
   a. Prayer of Abraham for Isaac (Gen. 15:2, 3).
   b. Prayer of Isaac for Jacob and Esau (Gen. 25:21-23).
   c. Prayer of Hannah for Samuel (1 Sam. 1:9-13).
   d. Prayer of Zacharias for John (Lk. 1:13).
2. For a city
   a. Sodom—prayed for by Abraham (Gen. 18:23-33).
   b. Jerusalem—prayed for by Hezekiah (2 Ki. 19:14-19).
   c. Nineveh—prayed for by her own citizens (Jonah 3).
3. For a bride—the prayer of Abraham's servant for a bride for Isaac (Gen. 24:12-14).
4. For deliverance from danger
   a. Jacob—that God would save him from Esau (Gen. 32:9-12).
   b. David—that God would save him from Saul (Ps. 31, 57, 142).
   c. Disciples—that Christ would save them from drowning (Mt. 8:24, 25).
   d. Peter—that Christ would save him from drowning (Mt. 14:28-31).
   e. Jerusalem church—that God would deliver Peter from prison (Acts 12:5).
   f. Heathen sailors, that God would spare their lives (Jonah 1:14).
5. Moses, for ten plagues to fall upon Egypt (Ex. 8-12).
6. Moses, for the Red Sea to part its waters (Ex. 14:21).
7. Joshua, for the Jordan River to part its waters (Josh. 4:15-18).
8. Moses, for a glimpse of God's glory (Ex. 33:18).
9. Moses, for a new leader (Num. 27:15-17).
10. For a new apostle to take Judas' place—prayer of the disciples (Acts 1:24, 25).
11. Moses, for a visit to Canaan (Deut. 3:23-25).
12. Moses, for Aaron, after his sin in making the golden calf (Deut. 9:20).
13. Joshua, for extra sunlight (Josh. 10:12).
14. For a sign—a prayer by Gideon (Jdg. 6:36-40).
15. For strength—a prayer by Samson (Jdg. 16:28-31).
16. For one's household
    a. For an unborn child—prayer by Manoah, Samson's father (Jdg. 13:12).
    b. For a son—prayer of David for Solomon (1 Chron. 29:19; Ps. 72).
    c. For two sons—request of the mother of James and John for her sons (Mt. 20:20, 21).
17. For forgiveness and confession
    a. David—to be forgiven for
       (1) Numbering the people (2 Sam. 24:10).
       (2) Immorality with Bathsheba (Ps. 32, 51).
    b. Manasseh to be forgiven and reinstated as king (2 Chron. 33:11-13).
    c. Job—to be forgiven for pride (Job 40:3, 4; 42:6). (Compare with 27:6.)
    d. Prodigal son—to be forgiven for backsliding (Lk. 15:17-19).
18. For wisdom—prayer by Solomon (1 Ki. 3:5-9). (Also see Jas. 1:5-8.)
19. For rain and fire
    a. Elijah, for fire (1 Ki. 18:36, 37).
    b. Elijah, for rain (1 Ki. 18:42, 43).
    c. David, for fire (1 Chron. 21:26).
    d. Joel, for rain (Joel 1:19, 20).
20. For spiritual vision—prayer by Elisha for his servant (2 Ki. 6:17).
21. For a lengthened life—prayer by Hezekiah for himself (2 Ki. 20:1-3).
22. For prosperity in one's work—prayer by Jabez for himself (1 Chron. 4:10).

23. For false friends
    a. Job—for his false friends (Job 42:7-10).
    b. Paul—for his false friends (2 Tim. 4:16).
24. For personal guidance in war matters—prayer by David for himself (1 Sam. 17:45; 30:8; 2 Sam. 2:1; 5:19).
25. For interpretation of a dream—prayer by Daniel and his three friends (Dan. 2:18).
26. For new birth information (Acts 10:1-6).
27. For relief in hell—prayer by the rich man for himself (Lk. 16:22-31).
28. For boldness in witnessing—prayer by the disciples for themselves (Acts 4:24-30).
29. For one's enemies—prayer by Stephen for his murderers (Acts 7:59, 60).
30. For the ministry of the Holy Spirit
    a. Upon the Samaritans—prayer by the disciples (Acts 8:14, 15).
    b. Upon the Greeks—prayer by Peter (Acts 11:5).
    c. Upon the Ephesians—prayer by Paul (Acts 19:6).
31. For the personal will of God—prayer by Paul for himself (Acts 9:5, 6).
32. For outgoing missionaries—prayer by Antioch elders for Paul and Silas (Acts 13:3).
33. For a prosperous journey—prayer by Paul for himself (Rom. 1:9-11).
34. For the removal of a handicap—prayer by Paul for himself (2 Cor. 12:7-10).
35. For justice to be meted out—prayer by martyred souls (Rev. 6:10).
36. For a successful ministry—prayer by Paul for Timothy (2 Tim. 1:3-6).
37. For rocks and mountains to fall upon them—prayer by wicked men (Rev. 6:16, 17).
38. For Christ's return—prayer by John (Rev. 22:20).
39. For healing (Jas. 5:13-18).
    a. Abraham for Abimelech (Gen. 20:17, 18).
    b. David, for his sick child (2 Sam. 12:16).
    c. A man of God, for Jeroboam (1 Ki. 13:6).
    d. A leper, for himself (Mt. 8:2).
    e. A centurion, for his servant (Mt. 8:5-9).
    f. A maniac, for himself (Mk. 5:6).
    g. Jairus, for his daughter (Mt. 9:18).
    h. A diseased woman, for herself (Mt. 9:20, 21).
    i. Two blind men (Mt. 9:27).
    j. A Syro-phoenician mother for her daughter (Mt. 15:21-28).
    k. A father, for his son (Mt. 17:14-16).
    l. Bartimaeus, for himself (Mk. 10:46, 47).
    m. A deaf and dumb man, for himself (Mk. 7:32-34).
    n. Ten lepers, for themselves (Lk. 17:12-16).
    o. A nobleman, for his son (Jn. 4:46-50).
    p. Mary and Martha, for their sick brother (Jn. 11:30).
    q. Paul, for Publius' father (Acts 28:8).
40. For resurrection
    a. Elijah, for a dead son (1 Ki. 17:20, 21).
    b. Elisha, for a dead son (2 Ki. 4:33-35).
    c. Peter, for Dorcas (Acts 9:36-43).
41. For the welfare of Israel
    a. That God would bless the twelve tribes—by Jacob (Gen. 48, 49). (Also by Aaron—Num. 6:24.)
    b. That God would deliver her from Egypt—by Israel herself (Ex. 2:23).
    c. That God would give her victory—by Moses (Ex. 17:10-12).
    d. That God would spare her—by Moses (Ex. 32:31, 32; Num. 11:1, 2; 21:7-9) and by Jehoshaphat (2 Chron. 20:5-12).

    e. That God would protect her—by Moses (Num. 10:35, 36).
    f. That God would lead her—by Israel herself (Jdg. 1:1).
    g. That God would forgive her
       (1) By Israel herself (Jdg. 10:10).
       (2) By Moses (Num. 14:13-19).
       (3) By David (Ps. 85).
       (4) By Jeremiah (Jer. 14:20-22).
       (5) By Daniel (Dan. 9).
       (6) By Ezra (Ezra 9:5; 10:4).
       (7) By Nehemiah (Neh. 1:4-11).
       (8) By Habakkuk (Hab. 3).
    h. That God would sanctify her tabernacle (1 Ki. 8:22-54).
    i. That God would save her—Paul (Rom. 10:1).
42. For the welfare of the church
    a. Rome (Rom. 1:8-10).
    b. Ephesus (Eph. 1:15-20; 3:13-21).
    c. Philippi (Phil. 1:2-7).
    d. Colosse (Col. 1:1-14).
    e. Thessalonica (1 Thess. 1:2, 3; 3:9-13; 2 Thess. 1:3, 11, 12; 2:13, 16, 17).
    f. Jerusalem (Heb. 13:20, 21).
    g. Pontus, Galatia, Cappadocia, Asia, Bithynia (1 Pet. 5:10, 11).

PRAYERS OF PRAISE

1. Thanking God for his goodness—by David (Ps. 100, 103, 106, 107).
2. Thanking God for the Red Sea deliverance—by Israel (Ex. 15).
3. Thanking God for the birth of Samuel—by Hannah (1 Sam. 2:1-10).
4. Thanking God for his Word—by David (Ps. 119).
5. Thanking God for the deliverance from Babylon—by David and Ezra (Ps. 126; Ezra 7:27).
6. Thanking God for being the handmaiden of Christ—by Mary (Lk. 1:46-55).
7. Thanking God for the birth of Christ—by the angels (Lk. 2:25-38).
8. Thanking God for the Christ child—by Simeon and Anna (Lk. 2:25-38).
9. Thanking God for his wisdom—by Paul and David (Rom. 11:33-36; Ps. 139).
10. Thanking God for being allowed to suffer for him—by disciples, Paul, and Silas (Acts 5:41; 16:25).
11. Thanking God for his great mercy—by David (Ps. 136).
12. Thanking God for his mighty creation
    a. By David (Ps. 8, 19).
    b. By the twenty-four elders in heaven (Rev. 4:10, 11; 15:3, 4).
13. Thanking God for his wonderful redemption—by the hosts of heaven (Rev. 5:8-14; 7:9-12).
14. Thanking God for finally taking matters in hand (Rev. 11:16-18).
15. Thanking God for judging the great harlot (Rev. 19:1-10).

PRAYERS OF COMPLAINT

1. By Moses (Ex. 3-5; Num. 11:11-15). Reason for complaint:
   a. Moses did not want to go back to Egypt.
   b. Moses felt the burden of leading Israel into Canaan was too great.
2. By Joshua (Josh. 7:6-9), because Israel had just suffered defeat at the hands of Ai.

3. By Elijah (1 Ki. 19:4), because Jezebel was trying to kill him.
4. By Job (Job 3:3-12; 10:18-22), because of his terrible suffering.
5. By Jeremiah (Jer. 4:10; 20:7-13), because he thought God had deceived him.
6. By Jonah (Jonah 4), because God had spared Nineveh.
7. By Habakkuk (Hab. 1), because he could not understand the affliction of the godly and the apparent prosperity of the wicked.
8. By David (Ps. 42; 43; 102:1-11), because of his persecution from Saul.

Prisons

1. Where Joseph was placed (Gen. 39:20-23—Egypt).
2. Where Joseph's brethren were placed (Gen. 42:17—Egypt).
3. Where the Sabbath-breaker was placed (Num. 15:34—wilderness).
4. Where Samson was placed (Jdg. 16:21—Gaza).
5. Where Micaiah was placed (1 Ki. 22:27—Samaria).
6. Where Jeremiah was placed (Jer. 32:2; 37:4-21; 38:13—Jerusalem).
7. Where John the Baptist was placed (Mt. 4:12—near the Dead Sea).
8. Where the apostles were placed (Acts 5:18—Jerusalem).
9. Where Peter was placed (Acts 12:4—Jerusalem).
10. Where Paul and Silas were placed (Acts 16:19-35—Philippi).
11. Where Paul was placed (Acts 21:33; 23:10—Jerusalem).
12. Where Paul was placed (Acts 23:35; 24:27—Herod's judgment hall in Caesarea).
13. Where Paul was placed (Phil. 1:13; Philemon 1:1—Rome).

Promises (to the believer)

1. Abundant life (Jn. 10:10).
2. A crown of life (Rev. 2:10).
3. A heavenly home (Jn. 14:1-3).
4. A new name (Isa. 62:1, 2).
5. Answers to prayer (1 Jn. 5:14).
6. Assurance (2 Tim. 1:12).
7. Cleansing (Jn. 15:3).
8. Clothing (Zech. 3:4).
9. Comfort (Isa. 51:3).
10. Companionship (Jn. 15:15).
11. Deliverance (2 Tim. 4:18).
12. Divine sonship (1 Jn. 3:1, 2).
13. Everlasting life (Jn. 3:16).
14. Fellowship of Christ (Mt. 18:19).
15. Fruitfulness (Jn. 15:4, 5).
16. Gifts of the Spirit (1 Cor. 12).
17. Glory after death (Mt. 13:43).
18. God's protecting care (1 Pet. 5:6, 7).
19. Growth (Eph. 4:11-15).
20. Guidance (Isa. 42:16).
21. Hope (Heb. 6:18, 19).
22. Inheritance (1 Pet. 1:3, 4).
23. Joy (Isa. 35:10).
24. Knowledge (Jer. 24:7).
25. Liberty (Rom. 8:2).
26. Peace (Jn. 14:27).
27. Power for service (Jn. 14:12).
28. Renewal (Titus 3:5).

29. Rest (Heb. 4:9, 11).
30. Restoration (Isa. 57:18; 1 Jn. 1:9).
31. Resurrection (Rom. 8:11).
32. Rich rewards (Mt. 10:42).
33. Spiritual fullness (Jn. 6:35).
34. Spiritual healing (Hosea 6:1).
35. Spiritual light (Jn. 12:46).
36. Spiritual treasures (Mt. 6:19, 20).
37. Strength (Phil. 4:13).
38. Temporal blessings (Mt. 6:25-33).
39. Understanding (Ps. 119:104).
40. Victory (1 Jn. 5:4).
41. Wisdom (Jas. 1:5).

Prophecies

PROPHECIES MADE BY CHRIST

1. Concerning his ascension (Jn. 1:50, 51).
2. Concerning his death and resurrection (Jn. 2:19-22).
3. Concerning his death (Jn. 3:14).
4. Concerning the great white throne judgment (Mt. 7:21-23).
5. Concerning the future resurrection (Jn. 5:28, 29).
6. Concerning his betrayer (Jn. 6:70, 71).
7. Concerning his resurrection (Mt. 16:4).
8. Concerning his ascension (Jn. 7:33, 34).
9. Concerning Pentecost (Jn. 7:37-39).
10. Concerning his ascension (Jn. 8:14, 15).
11. Concerning his death (Jn. 8:28).
12. Concerning his death (Jn. 10:17, 18).
13. Concerning the church (Mt. 16:18, 19).
14. Concerning his resurrection (Mt. 16:21; Mk. 8:31; Lk. 9:22).
15. Concerning his Second Coming (Mt. 16:27; Mk. 8:38; Lk. 9:26).
16. Concerning his transfiguration (Mt. 16:28; Lk. 9:27).
17. Concerning his resurrection (Mt. 17:9; Mk. 9:9).
18. Concerning his sufferings (Mt. 17:12; Mk. 9:12).
19. Concerning his betrayal (Mt. 17:22; Lk. 9:44).
20. Concerning his resurrection (Mt. 17:23; Mk. 9:31).
21. Concerning his resurrection (Mt. 12:28-40; Lk. 11:29, 30).
22. Concerning the great white throne judgment (Mt. 12:41, 42; Lk. 11:31, 32).
23. Concerning the great white throne (Lk. 12:2, 3).
24. Concerning his sufferings (Lk. 17:25).
25. Concerning the last days (Lk. 17:26-30).
26. Concerning Armageddon (Lk. 23:28-31).
27. Concerning future rewards (Mt. 19:27-30; Mk. 10:28-31; Lk. 18:28-30).
28. Concerning his resurrection (Mt. 20:17-19; Mk. 10:32-34; Lk. 18:31-34).
29. Concerning the destruction of Jerusalem (Lk. 19:43, 44).
30. Concerning the setting aside of Israel (Mt. 21:43, 44).
31. Concerning his death (Jn. 12:20-26).
32. Concerning his death (Jn. 12:32).
33. Concerning the tribulation (Mt. 24:1-42).
34. Concerning his second coming (Mt. 25:29-31).
35. Concerning his death (Mt. 26:2).
36. Concerning his betrayal (Mt. 26:21-25; Mk. 14:18-21; Lk. 22:21, 22; Jn. 13:18-33).
37. Concerning the death of Peter (Jn. 13:36).
38. Concerning Peter's first three denials (Lk. 22:34; Jn. 13:38).
39. Concerning his return (Jn. 14:2, 3).
40. Concerning being forsaken by his disciples (Mt. 26:31).

41. Concerning meeting his disciples in Galilee after his resurrection (Mt. 26:32; Mk. 14:28; 16:7).
42. Concerning Peter's second three denials (Mt. 26:33–35; Mk. 14:29–31).
43. Concerning his Second Coming (Mt. 26:64).
44. Concerning his Second Coming (Lk. 22:69).
45. Concerning the destruction of Jerusalem (Lk. 23:28–31).
46. Concerning Peter's martyrdom (Jn. 21:18, 19).

PROPHECIES FULFILLED BY CHRIST

1. That he would be born of a woman (Gen. 3:15; cf. Gal. 4:4).
2. That he would be from the line of Abraham (Gen. 12:3, 7; 17:7; Rom. 9:5; cf. Gal. 3:16).
3. That he would be from the tribe of Judah (Gen. 49:10; cf. Heb. 7:14; Rev. 5:5).
4. That he would be from the house of David (2 Sam. 7:12, 13; Lk. 1:31–33; cf. Rom. 1:3).
5. That he would be born of a virgin (Isa. 7:14; cf. Mt. 1:22, 23).
6. That he would be given the throne of David (2 Sam. 7:11, 12; Ps. 132:11; Isa. 9:6, 7; 16:5; Jer. 23:5; cf. Lk. 1:31, 32).
7. That this throne would be an eternal throne (Dan. 2:44; 7:14, 27; Micah 4:7; cf. Lk. 1:33).
8. That he would be called Emmanuel (Isa. 7:14; cf. Mt. 1:23).
9. That he would have a forerunner (Isa. 40:3–5; Mal. 3:1; Mt. 3:1–3; cf. Lk. 1:76–78; 3:3–6).
10. That he would be born in Bethlehem (Micah 5:2; Mt. 2:5, 6; cf. Lk. 2:4–6).
11. That he would be worshiped by wise men and presented with gifts (Ps. 72:10; Isa. 60:3, 6, 9; cf. Mt. 2:11).
12. That he would be in Egypt for a season (Num. 24:8; Hosea 11:1; cf. Mt. 2:15).
13. That his birthplace would suffer a massacre of infants (Jer. 31:15; cf. Mt. 2:17, 18).
14. That he would be called a Nazarene (Isa. 11:1; cf. Mt. 2:23).
15. That he would be zealous for the Father (Ps. 69:9; 119:139; cf. Jn. 6:37–40).
16. That he would be filled with God's Spirit (Ps. 45:7; Isa. 11:2; 61:1, 2; cf. Lk. 4:18, 19).
17. That he would heal many (Isa. 53:4; cf. Mt. 8:16, 17).
18. That he would deal gently with the Gentiles (Isa. 9:1, 2; 42:1–3; cf. Mt. 4:13–16; 12:17–21).
19. That he would speak in parables (Isa. 6:9, 10; cf. Mt. 13:10–15).
20. That he would be rejected by his own (Ps. 69:8; Isa. 53:3; cf. Jn. 1:11; 7:5).
21. That he would make a triumphal entry into Jerusalem (Zech. 9:9; cf. Mt. 21:4, 5).
22. That he would be praised by little children (Ps. 8:2; cf. Mt. 21:16).
23. That he would be the rejected cornerstone (Ps. 118:22, 23; cf. Mt. 21:42).
24. That his miracles would not be believed (Isa. 53:1; cf. Jn. 12:37, 38).
25. That his friend would betray him for thirty pieces of silver (Ps. 41:9; 55:12–14; Zech. 11:12, 13; cf. Mt. 26:14–16, 21–25).
26. That he would be a man of sorrows (Isa. 53:3; cf. Mt. 26:37, 38).
27. That he would be forsaken by his disciples (Zech. 13:7; cf. Mt. 26:31, 56).
28. That he would be scourged and spat upon (Isa. 50:6; cf. Mt. 26:67; 27:26).
29. That his price money would be used to buy a potter's field (Jer. 18:1–4; 19:1–4; Zech. 11:12, 13; cf. Mt. 27:9, 10).
30. That he would be crucified between two thieves (Isa. 53:12; cf. Mt. 27:38; Mk. 15:27, 28; Lk. 22:37).
31. That he would be given vinegar to drink (Ps. 69:21; cf. Mt. 27:34, 48; Jn. 19:28–30).
32. That he would suffer the piercing of his hands and feet (Ps. 22:16; Zech. 12:10; cf. Mk. 15:25; Jn. 19:34, 37; 20:25–27).
33. That his garments would be parted and gambled for (Ps. 22:18; cf. Lk. 23:34; Jn. 19:23, 24).
34. That he would be surrounded and ridiculed by his enemies (Ps. 22:7, 8; cf. Mt. 27:39–44; Mk. 15:29–32).
35. That he would thirst (Ps. 22:15; cf. Jn. 19:28).
36. That he would commend his spirit to the Father (Ps. 31:5; cf. Lk. 23:46).
37. That his bones would not be broken (Ex. 12:46; Num. 9:12; Ps. 34:20; cf. Jn. 19:33–36).
38. That he would be stared at in death (Zech. 12:10; Mt. 27:36; cf. Jn. 19:37).
39. That he would be buried with the rich (Isa. 53:9; cf. Mt. 27:57–60).
40. That he would be raised from the dead (Ps. 16:10; cf. Mt. 28:2–7).
41. That he would ascend (Ps. 24:7–10; cf. Mk. 16:19; Lk. 24:51).
42. That he would then become a greater high priest than Aaron (Ps. 110:4; cf. Heb. 5:4, 5, 6, 10; 7:11–28).
43. That he would be seated at God's right hand (Ps. 110:1; cf. Mt. 22:44; Heb. 10:12, 13).
44. That he would become a smiting scepter (Num. 24:17; Dan. 2:44, 45; cf. Rev. 19:15).
45. That he would rule the heathen (Ps. 2:8; cf. Rev. 2:27).

PROPHECIES CONCERNING BIRTHS

1. Isaac's birth (Gen. 15:4; 17:19, 21; 18:10, 14). Fulfillment: Genesis 21:1–3.
2. Jacob and Esau's births (Gen. 25:19–23). Fulfillment: Genesis 25:24–26.
3. Samson's birth (Jdg. 13:2–5). Fulfillment: Judges 13:24.
4. Samuel's birth (1 Sam. 1:17, 18). Fulfillment: 1 Samuel 1:20.
5. Birth of Shunammite woman's son (2 Ki. 4:16). Fulfillment: 2 Kings 4:17.
6. John the Baptist's birth (Lk. 1:13–17). Fulfillment: Luke 1:57–64.
7. Christ's birth (Lk. 1:26–33). Fulfillment: Luke 2:4–7.

PROPHECIES CONCERNING CITIES

1. Tyre
   a. The coastal city to be captured by Nebuchadnezzar (Ezek. 26:7).
   b. The island city to later be scrapped and made flat, like the top of a rock (Ezek. 26:4, 14; 28:1–10).
   c. Both cities to become a place for the spreading of nets (Ezek. 26:14).
   d. Both to have their stones and timbers thrown into the sea (Zech. 9:3, 4).
   e. Neither to be rebuilt (Ezek. 26:14).
2. Jericho (Josh. 6:26).
   a. To fall on the seventh day at the hands of Joshua (Josh. 6:1–5). Fulfillment: Joshua 6:20.
   b. The city to be rebuilt later by one man (Hiel).

c. The builder's oldest son (Abiram) to die when work on the city began.

d. The builder's youngest son (Segub) to die when the work was completed. Fulfillment: 1 Kings 16:34.

3. Nineveh
   a. The city to be totally destroyed (Nahum 1:3, 6).
   b. This destruction to be effected (in part) by a mighty overflowing of the Tigris River (Nahum 1:8).
   c. The attackers of the city to wear red (Nahum 2:3). Fulfillment: Testimony of history. In 612 B.C. the Medes and Babylonians (who were especially fond of the color red) destroyed Nineveh.

4. Jerusalem
   a. To become God's chosen place (Deut. 12:5, 6, 11; 26:2; Josh. 9:27; 10:1; 1 Ki. 8:29; 11:36; 15:4; 2 Ki. 21:4, 7; 2 Chron. 7:12; Ps. 78:68).
   b. To be spared from invasion by Israel (ten northern tribes) and Syria (Isa. 7:1-7).
   c. To be spared from invasion by the Assyrians (Isa. 37:33-35). Fulfillment: Isaiah 37:36, 37.
   d. To be destroyed by the Babylonians (Isa. 3:8; Jer. 11:9; 26:18; Micah 3:12).
   e. The Temple of Solomon to suffer destruction (1 Ki. 9:7-9; Ps. 79:1; Jer. 7:11-14; 26:18; Ezek. 7:21, 22; 24:21; Micah 3:12). Fulfillment: Lamentations 2:7; 2 Chronicles 36:19.
   f. The Temple vessels to be carried to Babylon and later returned to Jerusalem (Jer. 28:3). Fulfillment: 2 Kings 25:14, 15; 2 Chronicles 36:18; Ezra 1:7-11. See also Daniel 5:1-4.
   g. To be rebuilt by the Jews after spending seventy years in Babylonian captivity (Isa. 44:28; Jer. 25:11, 12; 29:10). Fulfillment: Ezra 1:1-4.
   h. To have its streets and walls rebuilt during a period of trouble (Dan. 9:25). Fulfillment: Ezra 4, 5; Nehemiah 2—6.
   i. The walls to be rebuilt 483 years prior to the crucifixion of Christ (Dan. 9:26). Fulfillment: testimony of history. From March 14, 445 B.C. (date of rebuilding of walls) until April 6 (crucifixion of Christ) equals 483 years, or 173,880 days.
   j. To be destroyed by the Romans (Lk. 19:41-44).
   k. The Temple of Herod also to be burned at this time (Mt. 24:1, 2). Fulfillment: testimony of history. Accomplished by Titus in A.D. 70.
   l. To be trodden down by Gentiles until the Second Coming (Lk. 21:24). Fulfillment: testimony of history.
   m. To be occupied by the antichrist during the tribulation (Zech. 12:2; 14:2).
   n. To become the worship center of the world during the millennium (Isa. 2:2, 3; Micah 4:1).

PROPHECIES CONCERNING INDIVIDUALS

Old Testament

1. Joshua and Caleb to enter Canaan after a period of forty years (Num. 14:24, 30). Fulfillment: Joshua 3:7, 17; 14:6-12.
2. Sisera to be defeated by a woman (Jdg. 4:9). Fulfillment: Judges 4:21.
3. Hophni and Phinehas to die on the same day (1 Sam. 2:34). Fulfillment: 1 Samuel 4:11.
4. The priesthood to be removed from the line of Eli (1 Sam. 2:27-36; 3:11-14). Fulfillment: 1 Kings 2:26, 27.

5. Saul to become Israel's first king and to save them from the Philistines (1 Sam. 9:15, 16). Fulfillment: 1 Samuel 11, 14.
6. Saul's kingdom not to continue (1 Sam. 13:14; 15:28; 24:20). Fulfillment: 2 Samuel 3:1; 5:1-3.
7. Saul to die in battle on a certain day (1 Sam. 28:19). Fulfillment: 1 Samuel 31:1-6.
8. Solomon to build the Temple, not David (1 Chron. 17:1-12). Fulfillment: 1 Kings 7:51.
9. The sword not to depart from David's house because of sin (2 Sam. 12:10-12). Fulfillment: 2 Samuel 13:28, 29; 16:21, 22.
10. Jeroboam's house (dynasty) to be destroyed (1 Ki. 14:10, 11, 13, 14). Fulfillment: 1 Kings 15:27, 28.
11. Ahab to be victorious over the Syrians (1 Ki. 20:28). Fulfillment: 1 Kings 20:29, 30.
12. Ahab to die in battle for killing Naboth (1 Ki. 21:19; 22:17). Fulfillment: 1 Kings 22:37.
13. The dogs would then lick his blood from his chariot (1 Ki. 21:19). Fulfillment: 1 Kings 22:38.
14. Jezebel to be eaten by some wild dogs (1 Ki. 21:23; 2 Ki. 9:10). Fulfillment: 2 Kings 9:35.
15. Elisha to receive a double portion of Elijah's spirit (2 Ki. 2:10). Fulfillment: testimony of history. He performed twice the miracles of Elijah.
16. Naaman to recover from his leprosy (2 Ki. 5:3, 8, 10). Fulfillment: 2 Kings 5:14.
17. The starving citizens of Samaria to enjoy an abundance of food in twenty-four hours (2 Ki. 7:1). Fulfillment: 2 Kings 7:16, 17.
18. An arrogant aid of the king to see this miracle, but not eat of the food (2 Ki. 7:2, 19). Fulfillment: 2 Kings 7:17, 20.
19. A Syrian king (Hazael) not to recover of his sickness (2 Ki. 8:10). Fulfillment: 2 Kings 8:15.
20. Jehu to have four generations upon the throne of Israel (2 Ki. 10:30). Fulfillment: 2 Kings 15:12.
21. Jehu's dynasty to then be destroyed (Hosea 1:4). Fulfillment: 2 Kings 15:8-12.
22. Joash to defeat the Syrians on three occasions (2 Ki. 13:18, 19). Fulfillment: 2 Kings 13:25.
23. Jehoram to suffer with an intestinal disease because of his sin (2 Chron. 21:15). Fulfillment: 2 Chronicles 21:18, 19.
24. Amaziah to die for his idolatry (2 Chron. 25:16). Fulfillment: 2 Chronicles 25:20, 22, 27.
25. Sennacherib not to invade Jerusalem (Isa. 37:33-35). Fulfillment: Isaiah 37:36, 37.
26. Sennacherib to fall by the sword in his own land (Isa. 37:7). Fulfillment: Isaiah 37:37, 38.
27. Hezekiah to be healed of a fatal disease (Isa. 38:5). Fulfillment: Isaiah 38:9.
28. Jehoahaz to never return to Judah, but to die in his Egyptian captivity (Jer. 22:10-12). Fulfillment: 2 Kings 23:33, 34.
29. Josiah to burn the decayed bones of Jeroboam's pagan priests upon the false altar Jeroboam had constructed (1 Ki. 13:1-3). Fulfillment: 2 Kings 23:4-6.
30. Jehoiachin to be captured by Nebuchadnezzar (Jer. 22:25). Fulfillment: 2 Kings 24:15.
31. A false prophet named Hananiah to die within a year (Jer. 28:15, 16). Fulfillment: Jeremiah 28:17.
32. Zedekiah to be captured by Nebuchadnezzar (Jer. 21:7). Fulfillment: Jeremiah 52:8, 9.
33. Zedekiah to be blinded (Ezek. 12:13). Fulfillment: Jeremiah 52:11.

34. Nebuchadnezzar to win over the Egyptians at Carchemish (Jer. 46). Fulfillment: testimony of history.
35. Nebuchadnezzar to invade Egypt (Jer. 43:9-13; 46:26; Ezek. 29:19, 20). Fulfillment: testimony of history.
36. Nebuchadnezzar to be reduced to an animal for his pride (Dan. 4:19-27). Fulfillment: Daniel 4:28-37.
37. Belshazzar to have his kingdom removed from him (Dan. 5:5, 25-28). Fulfillment: Daniel 5:30.
38. Cyrus to allow the Jews to go back and rebuild Jerusalem (Isa. 44:28). Fulfillment: Ezra 1:1, 2.
39. Alexander the Great to conquer Greece and establish a world empire (Dan. 2:32, 39; 7:6; 8:5-8, 21; 11:3). Fulfillment: testimony of history.
40. Alexander to defeat the Persians (Dan. 8:5-8). Fulfillment: testimony of history.
41. Alexander to die suddenly and his kingdom to be divided into four parts (Dan. 8:8, 22; 11:4). Fulfillment: testimony of history.
42. Antiochus Epiphanes to persecute the Jews and profane their Temple (Dan. 8:11, 25). Fulfillment: testimony of history.

New Testament
1. Zacharias to be mute until the birth of his son (Lk. 1:20). Fulfillment: Luke 1:57-64.
2. John the Baptist to be Christ's forerunner (Isa. 40:3-5; Mal. 3:1; Lk. 1:76, 77). Fulfillment: Matthew 3:1-11; Luke 3:2-6).
3. Simeon to live until he had seen the Messiah (Lk. 2:25, 26). Fulfillment: Luke 2:28-32.
4. Peter to deny Christ (Jn. 13:38). Fulfillment: John 18:24-27.
5. Peter to suffer martyrdom for Christ (Jn. 21:18, 19; 2 Pet. 1:12-14). Fulfillment: testimony of history.
6. Judas to give himself over to Satan (Jn. 6:70). Fulfillment: Luke 22:3; John 13:27.
7. Judas to betray Christ (Jn. 6:71; 13:21). Fulfillment: Matthew 26:47-50; Luke 22:47, 48; John 18:2-5).
8. Paul
   a. To suffer much for Christ (Acts 9:16). Fulfillment: 2 Corinthians 11:23-28; 12:7-10; Galatians 6:17; Philippians 1:29, 30.
   b. To be a minister to the Gentiles (Acts 9:15). Fulfillment: Acts 13:46; 18:6; 22:21; 26:17; 28:28; Romans 11:13; Ephesians 3:1; 1 Timothy 2:7; 2 Timothy 1:11.
   c. To preach before kings (Acts 9:15). Fulfillment: Acts 24—26.
   d. To go to Rome (Acts 23:11). Fulfillment: Acts 28:16.

PROPHECIES CONCERNING ISRAEL
1. The people of Shem to be especially blessed of God (Gen. 9:26). Fulfillment: Matthew 1:1; John 4:22.
2. A great nation to come from Abraham (Gen. 12:2). Fulfillment: Numbers 23:10.
3. This nation to exist forever (Jer. 31:35-37). Fulfillment: testimony of history.
4. Israel's kings to come from the tribe of Judah (Gen. 49:10). Fulfillment: 1 Samuel 16:1, 2; 1 Chronicles 28:4; Luke 1:26, 27.
5. Canaan to be given to Israel forever (Gen. 13:15). Partial fulfillment: Joshua 21:43-45. Future fulfillment: Isaiah 60:21; Ezekiel 37:25.
6. Israel to sojourn in another land (Egypt) for 400 years, there to serve and be afflicted (Gen. 15:13). Fulfillment: Exodus 12:40.
7. God would judge this oppressive nation (Egypt) for

this oppression (Gen. 15:14). Fulfillment: Exodus 7:14—12:29.
8. Israel to leave Egypt with great substance (Gen. 15:14). Fulfillment: Exodus 12:35, 36.
9. Israel to return to Canaan from Egypt in the fourth generation (Gen. 15:16). Fulfillment: Joshua 3:16, 17.
10. Israel to conquer Canaan gradually (Ex. 23:29, 30). Fulfillment: Judges 1:19-36.
11. Those (over twenty) who sinned at Kadesh-barnea would not see the Promised Land, but wander forty years in the wilderness (Num. 14:32-34). Fulfillment: Numbers 26:63-65.
12. Israel to set a king over them (Deut. 17:14-20). Fulfillment: 1 Samuel 10:24.
13. Israel to suffer a tragic civil war after the death of Solomon (1 Ki. 11:11, 31). Fulfillment: 1 Kings 12:16, 17, 19, 20.
14. The northern kingdom to be carried away into Assyrian captivity (1 Ki. 14:15, 16; Hosea 1:5; 10:1, 6). Fulfillment: 2 Kings 17:6, 7, 22, 23.
15. This would happen sixty-five years after the Isaiah and Ahaz meeting (Isa. 7:8). Fulfillment: 2 Kings 17:24.
16. The southern kingdom to be carried away into Babylonian captivity (Jer. 13:19; 20:4, 5; 21:10; Micah 4:10). Fulfillment: 2 Kings 24:10, 14.
17. The Temple to be destroyed (1 Ki. 9:7; 2 Chron. 7:20, 21; Jer. 7:14). Fulfillment: 2 Kings 25:9.
18. The length of the Babylonian captivity would be seventy years (Jer. 25:11; 29:10). Fulfillment: Daniel 9:2.
19. Israel to then return to the land (Jer. 29:10). Fulfillment: Ezra 1.
20. The Temple vessels once carried into Babylon to be brought back to the land (2 Ki. 25:14, 15; Jer. 28:3; Dan. 5:1-4). Fulfillment: Ezra 1:7-11.
21. Israel eventually to be scattered among the nations of the world (Lev. 26:33; Deut. 4:27, 28; 28:25, 64-67; Hosea 9:17).
22. Israel to "abide many days" without the following:
   a. a king
   b. an heir apparent
   c. the Levitical offerings
   d. the Temple
   e. the Levitical priesthood (Hosea 3:4). Fulfillment: testimony of history.
23. Israel also to be free from idolatry during this terrible time (Hosea 3:4). Fulfillment: testimony of history.
24. Israel to become a byword among the nations (Deut. 28:37). Fulfillment: testimony of history.
25. Israel to loan to many nations, but borrow from none (Deut. 28:12). Fulfillment: testimony of history.
26. Israel to be hounded and persecuted (Deut. 28:65-67). Fulfillment: testimony of history.
27. Israel nevertheless to retain her identity (Lev. 26:44; Jer. 46:28). Fulfillment: testimony of history.
28. Israel to remain alone and aloof among the nations (Num. 23:9). Fulfillment: testimony of history.
29. Israel to reject her Messiah (Isa. 53:1-9). Fulfillment: Luke 23:13-25.
30. Israel to return to Palestine in the latter days prior to the Second Coming of Christ (Deut. 30:3; Ezek. 36:24; 37:1-14). Fulfillment: historical testimony (since 1948).

PROPHECIES CONCERNING THE LAST DAYS

"And as it was in the days of Noah, so shall it be also in the days of the Son of man. . . . Also as it was in the days of Lot . . ." (Lk. 17:26, 28).

From these verses and other New Testament passages we glean the following "signs of the times."

1. Increase of wars and rumors of war (Joel 3:9, 10; Mt. 24:6, 7).
2. Extreme materialism (2 Tim. 3:1, 2; Rev. 3:14-19).
3. Lawlessness (Ps. 78:8; Prov. 30:11-14; 2 Tim. 3:2, 3).
4. Population explosion (Gen. 6:1).
5. Increase in speed and knowledge (Dan. 12:4).
6. Departure from the Christian faith (2 Thess. 2:3; 1 Tim. 4:1, 3, 4; 2 Tim. 3:5; 4:3, 4; 2 Pet. 3:3, 4).
7. Intense demonic activity (Gen. 6:1-4; 1 Tim. 4:1-3).
8. Unification of the world's religious, political, and economic systems (Rev. 13:4-8, 16, 17; 17:1-18; 18:1-24).
9. The rise of Russia as a world power (Ezek. 38, 39).
10. The absence of gifted leadership among the nations (thus making it easy for the antichrist to take over).
11. Rock music (a possible catalyst for the necessary unification of certain world systems).
12. Universal drug usage (Rev. 9:21) (the word "sorceries" here can also refer to drugs).
13. Abnormal sexual activity (Rom. 1:17-32; 2 Pet. 2:10, 14; 3:3; Jude 1:18).
14. Mass slaughter of innocents by unconcerned mothers (abortion). The phrase "without natural affection" occurs twice in the New Testament (Rom. 1:31; 2 Tim. 3:3). The last occurrence is definitely tied to the end times.
15. Widespread violence (Gen. 6:11, 13; Rev. 9:21).
16. Rejection of God's Word (2 Tim. 4:3, 4; 2 Pet. 3:3, 4, 16).
17. Rejection of God himself (Ps. 2:1-3).
18. Blasphemy (2 Tim. 3:2; 2 Pet. 3:3; Jude 1:18).
19. Self and pleasure lovers (2 Tim. 3:2, 4).
20. Men minus a conscience (1 Tim. 4:2).
21. Religious hucksters (2 Pet. 2:3).
22. Outright devil worshipers (Rev. 9:20; 13:11-14).
23. Rise of false prophets and antichrists (Mt. 24:5, 11; 2 Pet. 2:1, 2).
24. False claims of peace (1 Thess. 5:1-3).
25. Rapid advances in technology (Gen. 4:22).
26. Great political and religious upheavals in the Holy Land (Mt. 24:32-34).

PROPHECIES CONCERNING NATIONS

1. Egypt
   a. To experience seven years of plenty and seven years of famine (Gen. 41:1-7, 17-24; 45:6, 11). Fulfillment: Genesis 41:47, 48, 53-57; 47:13, 20.
   b. To host Israel for 400 years and afflict them (Gen. 15:13). Fulfillment: Exodus 12:40; Acts 7:6.
   c. To be judged for this by the ten plagues (Gen. 15:14; Ex. 3:20; 6:1; 7:5). Fulfillment: Exodus 7:14—12:29.
   d. To pursue Israel but fail and perish (Ex. 14:3, 4). Fulfillment: Exodus 14:5-9, 23-28, 30, 31.
   e. To defeat Israel at Megiddo (Jer. 2:16, 17, 19, 36, 37). Fulfillment: 2 Kings 23:29-35.
   f. To stumble and fall before Babylon at Carchemish (Jer. 46:5, 6, 10-12). Fulfillment: testimony of history.
   g. To be invaded by Nebuchadnezzar (Jer. 43:7-13; 46:13-26). Fulfillment: testimony of history.
   h. To decline from its exalted position and become a base nation (Ezek. 29:1, 2, 15). Fulfillment: testimony of history.
   i. To suffer (perhaps to be double-crossed) at the

hand of the antichrist during the tribulation (Dan. 11:40-43; Joel 3:19).
   j. To be restored and blessed by God along with Assyria and Israel during the millenium (Isa. 19:21-25).

2. Babylon
   a. To expand under Nebuchadnezzar (Hab. 1:5-10). Fulfillment: testimony of history.
   b. To defeat the Egyptians at Carchemish (Jer. 46). Fulfillment: testimony of history.
   c. To defeat the Assyrians (Nahum). Fulfillment: testimony of history.
   d. To be defeated by the Medes and Persians (Isa. 13:17; Jer. 51:11). Fulfillment: Daniel 5.

3. Three world powers to follow Babylon (Persia, Greece, Rome) (Dan. 2, 7). Fulfillment: testimony of history.

4. Persia
   a. To consist of an alliance between two peoples (the Medes and Persians) (Dan. 8:1-4, 20). Fulfillment: testimony of history.
   b. To defeat the Babylonians (Dan. 2:39; 7:5). Fulfillment: Daniel 5.
   c. To be defeated by the Greeks (Dan. 8:5-8, 21, 22). Fulfillment: testimony of history.

5. Greece
   a. To be invaded by Persia (Dan. 11:2). Fulfillment: testimony of history.
   b. Alexander the Great to conquer Greece and establish a world empire (Dan. 2:32, 39; 7:6; 8:5-8, 21; 11:3). Fulfillment: testimony of history.
   c. To defeat the Persians (Dan. 8:5-8). Fulfillment: testimony of history.
   d. To be divided into four parts after Alexander's death (Dan. 8:8, 22; 11:4). Fulfillment: testimony of history.

6. Rome
   a. To defeat the Greeks (Dan. 2:40; 7:7; 11:18, 19). Fulfillment: testimony of history.
   b. To destroy Jerusalem (Mt. 23:37-39). Fulfillment: testimony of history—A.D. 70, by Titus.
   c. To be revived during the tribulation (Dan. 2:41; 7:7, 8; Rev. 13:1; 17:12).
   d. To be destroyed by Christ at the Second Coming (Dan. 2:34, 35, 44; 7:9, 14, 27).

7. Russia
   a. To invade Israel during the tribulation (Ezek. 28:8-11, 16).
   b. To be joined by various allies (Ezek. 38:4-7).
   c. To come down for a "spoil" (Ezek. 38:12).
   d. To suffer a disastrous defeat at the hand of God, losing some 83 percent of its troops (Ezek. 39:2).

PROPHECIES CONCERNING THE TRIBULATION

A. The nature of the tribulation
   1. Unbelievably bloody wars (Mt. 24:6, 7; Rev. 6:2-4; 14:20).
   2. Drunkenness (Mt. 24:38; Lk. 17:27).
   3. Illicit sex (Mt. 24:38; Lk. 17:27; Rev. 9:21).
   4. Gross materialism (Lk. 17:28; Rev. 18:12-14).
   5. Rise of false messiahs and prophets (Mt. 24:5, 11, 24).
   6. Horrible religious persecution of believers (Mt. 24:10; Rev. 16:6; 17:6).
   7. Men to hide in the caves of the rocks in fear of God (Isa. 2:19-21; Rev. 6:15-17).
   8. The pangs and sorrows of death to seize men, similar to those of women in labor (Isa. 13:8; Jer. 30:6).

9. Terrible worldwide famines (Rev. 6:5, 6, 8).
10. Humans to be slaughtered by predatory wild beasts (Rev. 6:8).
11. Disastrous earthquakes (Rev. 6:12; 11:13; 16:18).
12. Fearful heavenly signs and disturbances (Lk. 21:25; Rev. 6:12–14; 8:12).
13. Universal tidal waves and ocean disasters (Lk. 21:25; Rev. 8:8, 9; 16:3).
14. The stars, moon, and sun to be darkened (Isa. 13:10; Joel 2:30, 31; 3:15).
15. The moon to be turned into blood (Joel 2:31; Rev. 6:12).
16. The heavens to be rolled together like a scroll (Isa. 34:4; Joel 2:10; Rev. 6:14).
17. Massive hailstones composed of fire and blood to fall upon the earth (Rev. 8:7; 16:21).
18. Huge meteorites to fall upon the earth (Rev. 8:8–11).
19. Stars of the heavens to fall upon the earth (Rev. 6:13).
20. Both salt waters and fresh waters to become totally polluted (Rev. 8:8–11; 11:6; 16:3, 4).
21. Universal disaster of land ecology (Rev. 8:7).
22. Events to steadily go from bad to worse. "As if a man did flee from a lion, and a bear met him; or went into the house, and leaned his hand on the wall, and a serpent bit him" (Amos 5:19).
23. A time of thick darkness and utter depression (Joel 2:2).
24. No period in history to even compare to it (Jer. 30:7; Dan. 12:1; Mt. 24:21, 22).
25. A time of famine of the very word of God itself. "Behold, the days come, saith the Lord God, that I will send a famine in the land, not a famine of bread, nor a thirst for water, but of hearing the words of the Lord. And they shall wander from sea to sea, and from the north even to the east, they shall run to and fro to seek the word of the Lord, and shall not find it" (Amos 8:11, 12).
26. A time of absolutely no escape from God's fierce judgment. "Though they dig into hell, thence shall mine hand take them; though they climb up to heaven, thence will I bring them down. And though they hide themselves in the top of Carmel, I will search and take them out thence; and though they be hid from my sight in the bottom of the sea, thence will I command the serpent, and he shall bite them" (Amos 9:2, 3).
27. Worldwide drug usage (Rev. 9:21).
28. Universal idolatry and devil worship (Rev. 9:20; 13:11–17).
29. Murderous demonic invasions (Rev. 9:3–20).
30. Subterranean eruptions (Rev. 9:1, 2).
31. Scorching solar heat (Rev. 16:8, 9).
32. Terrifying periods of total darkness (Rev. 16:10).
33. Unchecked city-wide fires (Rev. 18:8, 9, 18).
34. A plague of putrid cancerous sores (Rev. 16:2).
35. The total destruction of the earth's religious, political, and economic systems (Rev. 17, 18).
36. A universal dictatorial rule by the antichrist (Rev. 13).
37. An all-out, no-holds-barred attempt to destroy Israel (Rev. 12:1–17).
38. Survivors of this period to be more rare than gold (Isa. 13:12).
39. Men's blood to be poured out like dust and their flesh like dung (Zeph. 1:17).
40. The slain to remain unburied and the mountains to be covered with their blood (Isa. 34:3; 66:24).
41. The earth to be removed out of its orbit (Isa. 13:13).
42. The earth to be turned upside down (Isa. 24:1, 19).
43. The earth to reel to and fro like a drunkard (Isa. 24:20).
44. The most frightful physical plague in all history. "And this shall be the plague wherewith the Lord will smite all the people that have fought against Jerusalem; their flesh shall consume away while they stand upon their feet, and their eyes shall consume away in their holes, and their tongue shall consume away in their mouth" (Zech. 14:12).
45. A 200-mile river of human blood to flow (Rev. 14:20).
46. Scavenger birds to eat the rotted flesh of entire armies of men (Mt. 24:28; Rev. 19:17–19).

B. The events occurring with the tribulation.
The first three and one-half years
1. Formal organization of the harlot church (1 Tim. 4:1–3; 2 Tim. 3:1–5; Rev. 17).
2. Appearance of the antichrist and his false prophet (Rev. 13).
3. Revival of the Roman Empire (Dan. 2:41; 7:7; Rev. 13:1; 17:12).
4. The antichrist's seven-year covenant with Israel (Isa. 28:18; Dan. 9:27).
5. Pouring out of the first six seals (Mt. 24:4–8; Rev. 6:1–17).
6. Mass return of the Jews to Palestine (Isa. 43:5, 6; Ezek. 34:11–13; 36:24; 37:1–14).
7. Conversion and call of the 144,000 (Mt. 24:14; Rev. 7:1–4).
8. Abomination of desolation (Dan. 9:27; 12:11; Mt. 24:15; 2 Thess. 2:4; 11:2).
9. Ministry of the two witnesses (Rev. 11:3–13).
Middle part (brief undetermined period)
10. The Gog and Magog invasion into Palestine (Ezek. 38, 39).
11. The martydom of the two witnesses (Rev. 11:7).
12. The martyrdom of the 144,000 (Rev. 14:1–5).
13. The casting out of Satan from heaven (Rev. 12:3–15.)
14. The destruction of the false church (Rev. 17:16).
Last three and one-half years
15. The full manifestation of the antichrist (Rev. 13:16–18).
16. The worldwide persecution of Israel (Dan. 12:1; Zech. 11:16; Mt. 24:21; Rev. 12:13).
17. The pouring out of the last seal judgment (Rev. 8, 9; 11:15–19).
18. The messages of three special angels (Rev. 14:6–12).
19. The pouring out of the seven vials of judgment (Rev. 16).
20. The sudden destruction of economic and political Babylon (Rev. 18).
21. The battle of Armageddon (Ps. 2:1–5, 9; Isa. 34:1–6; 63:3, 4, 6; Joel 3:2, 9–16; Zech. 12:2; 14:2, 3, 12; Rev. 14:14–20; 16:16; 19:11–21).

FUTURE PROPHECIES (A Basic Overview)

Prophecies concerning the rapture. (1 Cor. 15:51–53; 1 Thess. 4:14–18; Heb. 9:24–28; Rev. 4:1).

Prophecies concerning the judgment seat of Christ (1 Cor. 3:9–15; 2 Cor. 5:10; Rom. 14:10).

Prophecies concerning a seven-sealed book (Rev. 5–11).

Prophecies concerning the marriage service of the Lamb (Mt. 22:2; 25:1; Lk. 12:35, 36; Jn. 3:27–30; 2 Cor. 11:2; Eph. 5:22–32; Jude 1:24).

Prophecies concerning the Second Coming (Zech. 14:4, 8; Mt. 24:29, 30; 2 Thess. 1:7; Rev. 1:7; 11:15; 19:11–16).

Prophecies concerning the binding of Satan (Rom. 16:20; Rev. 20:1–3).

Prophecies concerning the resurrection of Old Testament and tribulational saints (Job 19:25, 26; Ps. 49:15; Isa. 25:8; 26:19; Dan. 12:2; Hosea 13:14; Jn. 5:28, 29; Heb. 11:35; Rev. 20:4, 5).

Prophecies concerning the judgment of Israel (parable of the ten virgins and the seven talents) (Mt. 25:1-30).

Prophecies concerning the judgment of Gentiles (parable of the sheep and goats) (Mt. 25:31-46).

Prophecies concerning the marriage supper of the Lamb (Lk. 12:35-37; 14:16, 17; Rev. 19:7-9).

Prophecies concerning the millennium (see detailed notes).

Prophecies concerning the final revolt and defeat of Satan (Rev. 20:7-10).

Prophecies concerning the judgment of fallen angels (Mt. 8:28, 29; Mk. 1:23, 24; 1 Cor. 6:3; 2 Pet. 2:4; Jude 1:6).

Prophecies concerning the great white throne judgment (Ps. 9:17; Eccl. 12:14; Dan. 7:9, 10; Mt. 12:36, 37; Heb. 9:27; Rev. 20:11-15).

Prophecies concerning the destruction of this present earth and heaven (Mt. 24:35; Heb. 1:10-12; 2 Pet. 3:3-12).

Prophecies concerning the creation of a new heaven and earth (Isa. 65:17; 66:22; 2 Pet. 3:13, 14; Rev. 21:1).

GENERAL PROPHECIES
1. The eating of the forbidden fruit to bring physical and spiritual death (Gen. 2:17). Fulfillment: Genesis 3:7, 8; 5:5.
2. The flood to occur in 120 years (Gen. 6:3). Fulfillment: Genesis 7:10.
3. The flood never to be repeated (Gen. 9:15). Fulfillment: testimony of history.
4. Canaan to be a servant to his brothers (Gen. 9:25). Fulfillment: Joshua 9:21, 23, 27; Judges 1:28.
5. The people of Shem to be especially blessed by God (Gen. 9:26). Fulfillment: John 4:22; Romans 3:1, 2; 9:4, 5.
6. The people of Japheth to share in Shem's blessing (Gen. 9:27). Fulfillment: Romans 9:30; 11:11, 12, 25.
7. The firstborn of all unprotected homes in Egypt to die in one night (Ex. 12:12, 13). Fulfillment: Exodus 12:29, 30.
8. The Red Sea to part (Ex. 14:13-18). Fulfillment: Exodus 14:26-31.
9. The Jordan River to part (Josh. 3:13). Fulfillment: Joshua 3:14-17.
10. Jericho to fall on the seventh day (Josh. 6:1-5). Fulfillment: Joshua 6:20.

MILLENNIAL PROPHECIES
1. The Temple to be rebuilt (Isa. 2:2; Ezek. 40-48; Joel 3:18; Hag. 2:7-9; Zech. 6:12, 13).
2. Israel to be regathered (Isa. 43:5, 6; Jer. 24:6; 29:14; 31:8-10; Ezek. 11:17; 36:24, 25, 28; Amos 9:14, 15; Zech. 8:6-8; Mt. 24:31).
3. Israel to recognize her Messiah (Isa. 8:17; 25:9; 26:8; Zech. 12:10-12; Rev. 1:7).
4. Israel to be cleansed (Jer. 33:8; Zech. 13:1).
5. Israel to be regenerated (Jer. 31:31-34; 32:39; Ezek. 11:19, 20; 36:26).
6. Israel to once again be related to God by marriage (Isa. 54:1-17; 62:2-5; Hosea 2:14-23).
7. Israel to be exalted above the Gentiles (Isa. 14:1, 2; 49:22, 23; 60:14-17; 61:6, 7).
8. Israel to become God's witnesses (Isa. 44:8; 61:6; 66:21; Ezek. 3:17; Micah 5:7; Zeph. 3:20; Zech. 8:3).

9. Christ to rule from Jerusalem with a rod of iron (Ps. 2:6-8, 11; Isa. 2:3; 11:4).
10. David to aid in this rule as vice-regent (Isa. 55:3, 4; Jer. 30:9; Ezek. 34:23; 37:24; Hosea 3:5).
11. All sickness to be removed (Isa. 33:24; Jer. 30:17; Ezek. 34:16).
12. The original curse (Gen. 3:17-19) upon creation to be neutralized (Isa. 11:6-9; 35:9; 65:25; Joel 3:18; Amos 9:13-15).
13. The wolf, lamb, calf, and lion to lie down together in peace (Isa. 11:6, 7; 65:25).
14. A little child to safely play with once poisonous serpents and spiders (Isa. 11:8).
15. Physical death to be swallowed up in victory (Isa. 25:8).
16. All tears to be dried (Isa. 25:8; 30:19).
17. The deaf to hear, the blind to see, and the lame to walk (Isa. 29:18; 35:5, 6; 61:1, 2; Jer. 31:8).
18. Man's knowledge about God to be vastly increased (Isa. 41:19, 20; 54:13; Hab. 2:14).
19. No social, political or religious oppression (Isa. 14:3-6; 49:8, 9; Zech. 9:11, 12).
20. Full ministry of the Holy Spirit (Isa. 32:15; 45:3; 59:21; Ezek. 36:27; 37:14; Joel 2:28, 29).
21. Christ himself to be the good, great, and chief Shepherd (Isa. 40:11; 49:10; 58:11; Ezek. 34:11-16).
22. A time of universal singing (Isa. 35:6; 52:9; 54:1; 55:12; Jer. 33:11).
23. A time of universal praying (Isa. 56:7; 65:24; Zech. 8:22).
24. A unified language (Zeph. 3:9).
25. The wilderness and deserts to bloom (Isa. 35:1, 2).
26. God's glory to be seen by all nations (Isa. 60:1-3; Ezek. 39:21; Micah 4:1-5; Hab. 2:14).
27. Longevity of man to be restored (Isa. 65:20).
28. Universal peace (Isa. 2:4; 32:18).
29. Universal holiness (Zech. 13:20, 21).
30. Solar and lunar light to increase (Isa. 4:5; 30:26; 60:19, 20; Zech. 2:5).
31. Palestine to become greatly enlarged and changed (Isa. 26:15; Obad. 1:17-21).
32. A river to flow east-west from the Mount of Olives into both the Mediterranean and Dead Seas (Ezek. 47:8, 9, 12; Joel 3:18; Zech. 14:4, 8, 10).
33. Jerusalem to become known as Jehovah Isidkenu (the Lord, our righteousness), and Jehovah Shammah (the Lord is there) (Jer. 33:16; Ezek. 48:35).
34. Jerusalem to become the worship center of the world (Isa. 2:2, 3; Micah 4:1).
35. Jerusalem's streets to be filled with happy boys and girls playing (Zech. 8:5).
36. The city to occupy an elevated site (Zech. 14:10).
37. The earthly city to be six miles in circumference (Ezek. 48:35).
38. The heavenly, suspended city (New Jerusalem) to be 1500 by 1500 by 1500 miles (Rev. 21:10, 16).

Punishments
1. By banishment (Ezra 7:26; Rev. 1:9).
2. By imprisonment (Gen. 39:20-23).
3. By confiscation (Ezra 7:26).
4. By beating (Deut. 25:1-3; 2 Cor. 11:24).
5. By scourging (Mt. 27:26).
6. By enforced labor (Jdg. 16:21).
7. By burning (Lev. 20:14; Dan. 3:6).
8. By hanging (Gen. 40:22; Est. 7:10).
9. By stoning (Lev. 24:14; 2 Chron. 24:21; Acts 7:59).

10. By beheading (2 Ki. 6:30–33; 2 Tim. 4:6).
11. By maiming (Deut. 25:11, 12).
12. By crucifixion (Mt. 27:31).

Questions

1. Serpent to Eve: "Hath God said, Ye shall not eat of every tree of the garden?" (Gen. 3:1).
2. God to Adam: "Where art thou?" (Gen. 3:9).
3. God to Cain: "Where is Abel thy brother?" (Gen. 4:9).
4. Cain to God: "Am I my brother's keeper?" (Gen. 4:9).
5. Abraham to God: "What wilt thou give me, seeing I go childless?" (Gen. 15:2).
   "Wilt thou also destroy the righteous with the wicked?" (Gen. 18:23).
6. Isaac to Abraham: "Where is the lamb for a burnt offering?" (Gen. 22:7).
7. Isaac to Jacob: "Art thou my very son Esau?" (Gen. 27:24).
8. Jacob to Laban: "What is this thou hast done unto me? Did not I serve with thee for Rachel?" (Gen. 29:25).
9. A heavenly guest to Jacob: "What is thy name?" (Gen. 32:27).
10. Jacob to Joseph: "What is this dream that thou hast dreamed?" (Gen. 37:10).
11. Joseph to Potiphar's wife: "How . . . can I do this great wickedness, and sin against God?" (Gen. 39:9).
12. God to Moses: "What is that in thine hand?" (Ex. 4:2).
13. Pharaoh to Moses: "Who is the Lord, that I should obey his voice to let Israel go?" (Ex. 5:2).
14. Israel to Moses: "What shall we drink?" (Ex. 15:24).
15. Moses to God: "What shall I do unto this people? they be almost ready to stone me" (Ex. 17:4).
16. Korah to Moses: "Ye take too much upon you, seeing all the congregation are holy, every one of them, and the Lord is among them: wherefore then lift ye up yourselves above the congregation of the Lord?" (Num. 16:3).
17. Moses to Israel: "Hear now, ye rebels; must we fetch you water out of this rock?" (Num. 20:10).
18. Balaam to Balak: "How shall I curse, whom God hath not cursed?" (Num. 23:8).
19. Joshua to Lord's captain: "Art thou for us, or for our adversaries?" (Josh. 5:13).
20. Gideon to God: "If the Lord be with us, why then is all this befallen us?" (Jdg. 6:13).
21. Delilah to Samson: "Tell me, I pray thee, wherein thy great strength lieth" (Jdg. 16:6).
22. Boaz to his reapers: "Whose damsel is this?" (Ruth 2:5).
23. Saul to Samuel: "Am not I a Benjamite, of the smallest of the tribes of Israel?" (1 Sam. 9:21).
24. Samuel to Saul: "What hast thou done?" (1 Sam. 13:11).
    "Hath the Lord as great delight in burnt offerings and sacrifices, as in obeying the voice of the Lord?" (1 Sam. 15:22).
25. Samuel to Jesse: "Are here all thy children?" (1 Sam. 16:11).
26. David to Israel's army: "Who is this uncircumcised Philistine, that he should defy the armies of the living God?" (1 Sam. 17:26).
27. Elijah to Israel: "How long halt ye between two opinions?" (1 Ki. 18:21).
28. Naaman to his servants: "Are not Abana and Pharpar, rivers of Damascus, better than all the waters of Israel? may I not wash in them, and be clean?" (2 Ki. 5:12).
29. Artaxerxes to Nehemiah: "Why is thy countenance sad, seeing thou art not sick?" (Neh. 2:2).
30. The king of Persia to Haman: "What shall be done unto the man whom the king delighteth to honour?" (Est. 6:6).
31. Satan to God: "Doth Job fear God for nought?" (Job 1:9).
32. Job's wife to Job: "Dost thou still retain thine integrity?" (Job 2:9).
33. Job to three friends: "If a man die, shall he live again?" (Job 14:14).
34. Bildad to Job: "How then can man be justified with God?" (Job 25:4).
35. God to Job: "Where wast thou when I laid the foundations of the earth?" (Job 38:4).
36. David to God: "What is man, that thou art mindful of him?" (Ps. 8:4).
    "Who shall abide in thy tabernacle? Who shall dwell in thy holy hill?" (Ps. 15:1).
    "Who is this King of glory?" (Ps. 24:8, 10).
    "Why art thou cast down, O my soul?" (Ps. 42:5, 11; 43:5).
    "Whom have I in heaven but thee?" (Ps. 73:25).
    "Wherewithal shall a young man cleanse his way?" (Ps. 119:9).
    "Whither shall I go from thy spirit?" (Ps. 139:7).
37. Captured Israel to Babylonian soldiers: "How shall we sing the Lord's song in a strange land?" (Ps. 137:4).
38. Solomon to his son: "Who can say, I have made my heart clean, I am pure from my sin?" (Prov. 20:9).
    "Who can find a virtuous woman?" (Prov. 31:10).
39. God to Isaiah: "Whom shall I send, and who will go for us?" (Isa. 6:8).
40. God to Israel: "Hast thou not known? hast thou not heard, that the everlasting God, the Lord, the Creator of the ends of the earth, fainteth not, neither is weary?" (Isa. 40:28).
41. Isaiah to Israel: "Who hath believed our report? And to whom is the arm of the Lord revealed?" (Isa. 53:1).
42. Jeremiah to God: "Is there no balm in Gilead; is there no physician there?" (Jer. 8:22).
43. God to Israel: "Can the Ethiopian change his skin, or the leopard his spots?" (Jer. 13:23).
    "Will a man rob God?" (Mal. 3:8).
44. God to Jeremiah: "Behold, I am the Lord, the God of all flesh: is there any thing too hard for me?" (Jer. 32:27).
45. God to Ezekiel: "Son of man, can these bones live?" (Ezek. 37:3).
46. Nebuchadnezzar to his counselors: "Did not we cast three men bound into the midst of the fire?" (Dan. 3:24).
47. Darius to Daniel: "Is thy God, whom thou servest continually, able to deliver thee from the lions?" (Dan. 6:20).
48. Amos to Israel: "Can two walk together, except they be agreed?" (Amos 3:3).
49. Micah to God: "Who is a God like unto thee, that pardoneth iniquity?" (Micah 7:18).
50. Israelite remnant to returning Messiah: "What are these wounds in thine hands?" (Zech. 13:6).
51. Magi to Herod: "Where is he that is born King of the Jews?" (Mt. 2:2).
52. Zacharias to the angel: "Whereby shall I know this? for I am an old man and my wife well stricken in years" (Lk. 1:18).

53. Mary to Gabriel: "How shall this be, seeing I know not a man?" (Lk. 1:34).
54. Mary to Jesus: "Son, why hast thou thus dealt with us?" (Lk. 2:48).
55. Jesus to Mary: "Wist ye not that I must be about my Father's business?" (Lk. 2:49).
56. John to Jesus: "I have need to be baptized of thee, and comest thou to me?" (Mt. 3:14).
57. Nathanael to Philip: "Can there any good thing come out of Nazareth?" (Jn. 1:46).
58. Jesus to crowd: "But if the salt have lost its savour, wherewith shall it be salted?" (Mt. 5:13).
59. Nicodemus to Jesus: "How can a man be born when he is old?" (Jn. 3:4).
60. Samaritan woman to Jesus: "How is it that thou, being a Jew, askest drink of me, which am a woman of Samaria?" (Jn. 4:9).
61. Jesus to impotent man: "Wilt thou be made whole?" (Jn. 5:6).
62. Demons to Jesus: "Art thou come to destroy us?" (Lk. 4:34).
63. Jesus to Pharisees: "If Satan cast out Satan, he is divided against himself; how shall then his kingdom stand?" (Mt. 12:26).
64. John the Baptist to Jesus: "Art thou he that should come? or look we for another?" (Lk. 7:19).
65. A lawyer to Jesus: "And who is my neighbour?" (Lk. 10:29).
66. Rich man to himself: "What shall I do, because I have no room where to bestow my fruits?" (Lk. 12:17).
67. Jesus to Pharisees: "Can ye not discern the signs of the times?" (Mt. 16:3).
68. Jesus to disciples: "Whom say ye that I am?" (Mt. 16:15).
   "What is a man profited, if he shall gain the whole world, and lose his own soul?" (Mt. 16:26).
69. Peter to Jesus: "How oft shall my brother sin against me, and I forgive him?" (Mt. 18:21).
70. Pharisees to Jesus: "Is it lawful for a man to put away his wife?" (Mt. 19:3).
   "Art thou greater than our father Abraham?" (Jn. 8:53).
71. Rich young ruler to Jesus: "What good thing shall I do, that I may have eternal life?" (Mt. 19:16).
72. Herodians to Jesus: "Is it lawful to give tribute unto Caesar?" (Mt. 22:17).
73. Sadducees to Jesus: "In the resurrection whose wife shall she be?" (Mt. 22:28).
74. A lawyer to Jesus: "Which is the great commandment in the law?" (Mt. 22:36).
75. Disciples to themselves: "What manner of man is this, that even the wind and sea obey him?" (Mk. 4:41).
76. Jesus to disciples: "Who touched my clothes?" (Mk. 5:30).
   "Will ye also go away?" (Jn. 6:67).
   "Children, have ye any meat?" (Jn. 21:5).
77. Nazareth Jews to themselves: "Is not this Joseph's son?" (Lk. 4:22).
78. Jesus to disciple: "How many loaves have ye?" (Mk. 6:38).
79. Disciple to Jesus: "Why could we not cast him out?" (Mk. 9:28).
   "What shall be the sign of thy coming, and of the end of the world?" (Mt. 24:3).
80. Jesus to Jewish rulers: "The baptism of John, was it from heaven, or of men?" (Mk. 11:30).

81. Peter to Jesus: "Lord, to whom shall we go?" (Jn. 6:68).
82. Jesus to Judas: "Have not I chosen you twelve, and one of you is a devil?" (Jn. 6:70).
83. Nicodemus to Pharisees: "Doth our law judge any man, before it hear him?" (Jn. 7:51).
84. Chief priests to officers: "Why have ye not brought him?" (Jn. 7:45).
85. Jesus to an immoral woman: "Woman, where are those thine accusers?" (Jn. 8:10).
86. Disciples to Jesus: "Who did sin, this man, or his parents?" (Jn. 9:2).
   "Wilt thou at this time restore again the kingdom to Israel?" (Acts 1:6).
87. Jesus to Martha: "Whosoever liveth and believeth in me shall never die. Believeth thou this?" (Jn. 11:26).
88. Jesus to Mary and Martha: "Where have ye laid him?" (Jn. 11:34).
89. Jesus to Philip: "Have I been so long time with you, and yet hast thou not known me?" (Jn. 14:9).
90. Judas to Jewish rulers: "What will ye give me, and I will deliver him unto you?" (Mt. 26:15).
91. Judas to Jesus: "Master, is it I?" (Mt. 26:25).
92. Jesus to Peter: "Simon, sleepest thou?" (Mk. 14:37).
   "Lovest thou me?" (Jn. 21:17).
93. Jesus to Peter, James, and John: "Could ye not watch with me one hour?" (Mt. 26:40).
94. Jesus to Judas: "Betrayest thou the Son of man with a kiss?" (Lk. 22:48).
95. Jesus to soldiers: "Whom seek ye?" (Jn. 18:4).
96. Chief priests to Jesus: "Art thou the Christ?" (Lk. 22:67).
97. Pilate to Jesus: "Art thou the King of the Jews?" (Mt. 27:11).
98. A servant of the high priest to Peter: "Did not I see thee in the garden with him?" (Jn. 18:26).
99. Pilate to Jesus: "What is truth?" (Jn. 18:38).
100. Pilate to rulers: "Whom will ye that I release unto you?" (Mt. 27:17).
101. Jesus to the Father: "My God, my God, why hast thou forsaken me?" (Mt. 27:46).
102. Women among themselves: "Who shall roll us away the stone from the door of the sepulchre?" (Mk. 16:3).
103. Angels to women: "Why seek ye the living among the dead?" (Lk. 24:5).
104. Jesus to Mary Magdalene: "Woman, why weepest thou?" (Jn. 20:15).
105. Emmaus disciples to each other: "Did not our heart burn within us, while he talked with us by the way, and while he opened to us the scriptures?" (Lk. 24:32).
106. Angels to the disciples: "Ye men of Galilee, why stand ye gazing up into heaven?" (Acts 1:11).
107. Various Jews to themselves: "How hear we every man in our own tongue, wherein we were born?" (Acts 2:8).
108. Jews to themselves: "Men and brethren, what shall we do?" (Acts 2:37).
109. Peter to Ananias: "Why hath Satan filled thine heart to lie to the Holy Ghost?" (Acts 5:3).
110. Philip to the eunuch: "Understandest thou what thou readest?" (Acts 8:30).
111. Eunuch to Philip: "How can I, except some man should guide me?" (Acts 8:31).
112. Jesus to Saul: "Why persecutest thou me?" (Acts 9:4).
113. Saul to Jesus: "Lord, what wilt thou have me to do?" (Acts 9:6).

114. Peter to Jerusalem Council: "Why tempt ye God, to put a yoke upon the neck of the disciples, which neither our fathers nor we were able to bear?" (Acts 15:10).

115. Philippian jailor to Paul and Silas: "Sirs, what must I do to be saved?" (Acts 16:30).

116. Greek philosopher to Paul: "What will this babbler say?" (Acts 17:18).

117. Paul to Ephesian seekers: "Have ye received the Holy Ghost since ye believed?" (Acts 19:2).

118. Paul to Israel: "Thou therefore which teachest another, teachest thou not thyself?" (Rom. 2:21).
"What advantage then hath the Jew?" (Rom. 3:1).
"Shall we continue in sin, that grace may abound?" (Rom. 6:1).
"Who shall lay any thing to the charge of God's elect?" (Rom. 8:33).
"Who shall separate us from the love of Christ?" (Rom. 8:35).
"How then shall they call on him in whom they have not believed? and how shall they believe in him of whom they have not heard? and how shall they hear without a preacher?" (Rom. 10:14).
"Hath God cast away his people?" (Rom. 11:1).

119. Paul to Corinthian believers: "Is Christ divided?" (1 Cor. 1:13).
"Are ye not carnal, and walk as men?" (1 Cor. 3:3).
"Do ye not know that the saints shall judge the world?" (1 Cor. 6:2).
"Know ye not that your body is the temple of the Holy Ghost?" (1 Cor. 6:19).
"For if the trumpet give an uncertain sound, who shall prepare himself to the battle?" (1 Cor. 14:8).
"How say some among you that there is no resurrection of the dead?" (1 Cor. 15:12).
"O death,, where is thy sting? O grave, where is thy victory?" (1 Cor. 15:55).
"What fellowship hath righteousness with unrighteousness? and what communion hath light with darkness?" (2 Cor. 6:14).

120. Paul to Galatians: "Received ye the Spirit by the works of the law, or by the hearing of faith?" (Gal. 3:2).
"Wherefore then serveth the law?" (Gal. 3:19).

121. Paul to Timothy: "If a man know not how to rule his own house, how shall he take care of the church of God?" (1 Tim. 3:5).

122. Paul to Hebrews: "For unto which of the angels said he at any time, Thou art my son?" (Heb. 1:5).
"How shall we escape, if we neglect so great salvation?" (Heb. 2:3).
"What son is he whom the father chasteneth not?" (Heb. 12:7).

123. James to believers: "What doth it profit, my brethren, though a man say he hath faith, and have not works?" (Jas. 2:14).
"Doth a fountain send forth at the same place sweet water and bitter?" (Jas. 3:11).
"From whence come wars and fightings among you?" (Jas. 4:1).
"Know ye not that the friendship of the world is enmity with God?" (Jas. 4:4).
"For what is your life?" (Jas. 4:14).

124. Peter to believers: "Where is the promise of his coming?" (2 Pet. 3:4).

125. John to believers: "Who is he that overcometh the world?" (1 Jn. 5:5).

"Who is worthy to open the book, and to loose the seals thereof?" (Rev. 5:2).
"How long, O Lord, holy and true, dost thou not judge and avenge our blood on them that dwell on the earth?" (Rev. 6:10).
"For the great day of his wrath is come; and who shall be able to stand?" (Rev. 6:17).
"Who is like unto the beast? who is able to make war with him?" (Rev. 13:4).

Rainbows
1. As seen by Noah (Gen. 9:13).
2. As seen by Ezekiel (Ezek. 1:27, 28).
3. As seen by John (Rev. 4:3; 10:1).

Revivals and Reforms
1. Under Jacob (Gen. 35:1-4). Background: On the return to Bethel, Jacob ordered his entire household to put away their false gods, and to wash and change their garments. This they did as Jacob built an altar to the true God. The false gods were then buried under an oak in Shechem.
2. Under Samuel (1 Sam. 7:3-6). Background: At the exhorting of Samuel the people put away their false gods and prepared their hearts to serve the only true God.
3. Under Moses (Ex. 14:31—15:21). Background: This occurred when complaining Israel saw the mighty hand of God in the parting of the Red Sea. On the safe (eastern) side of the sea, Moses led the people in a song of praise, while Miriam and the women furnished the special music.
4. Under David (1 Chron. 15:25-28; 16:1-43; 29:10-25). Background: There were two occasions during which David led the people in a revival.
   a. When the Ark of the Covenant was brought into Jerusalem for the first time (1 Chron. 15-16).
   b. At the dedication of the materials to be used in building the future Temple (1 Chron. 29).
5. Under Solomon (2 Chron. 7:1-3). Background: At the actual dedication of the constructed Temple.
6. Under Elijah (1 Ki. 18:21-40). Background: During the contest with the prophets of Baal on Mt. Carmel.
7. Under Asa (1 Ki. 15:11-15). Background: Asa removed the Sodomites and all false idols out of the land. He even deposed his own grandmother because of her idolatry.
8. Under Jehu (2 Ki. 10:15-28). Background: Jehu exterminated all Baal worshipers and their temples.
9. Under Jehoiada (2 Ki. 11:17-20). Background: This godly high priest led the people in a covenant whereby they forsook their idols and worshiped God.
10. Under Josiah (2 Ki. 22-23). Background: This revival really began when the book of Moses (Genesis through Deuteronomy) was accidentally discovered during a Temple cleanup event. The public reading of God's Word had a profound effect upon both King Josiah and his people.
11. Under Jehoshaphat (2 Chron. 19). Background: King Jehoshaphat led a revival when he ordered the cleansing of the Temple and the sanctification of the Levitical priests.
12. Under Hezekiah (2 Chron. 29-31). Background: Like Jehoshaphat, King Hezekiah experienced revival when he cleansed the Temple of God.
13. Under Manasseh (2 Chron. 33:11-20). Background: When wicked King Manasseh became converted, he

led his people in a revival by ordering the destruction of all idols.

14. Under Ezra (Ezra 9-10). Background: Through Ezra's preaching on separation, the Jewish remnant ceased their ungodly marriage alliances with the heathen of the land.
15. Under Nehemiah (Neh. 13). Background: After Nehemiah had built the wall around Jerusalem, Ezra stood by its gates and publicly read and taught from God's Word, causing a great revival.
16. Under Jonah (Jonah 3). Background: The Ninevites, through Jonah's preaching, repented and stayed the destructive hand of God.
17. Under Esther (Est. 9:17-22). Background: This time of repentance and rejoicing followed the salvation of the Jews from the plot of wicked Haman.
18. Under John the Baptist (Lk. 3:2-18). Background: John preached the imminent appearance of Israel's Messiah, warning them to repent and submit to water baptism.
19. Under the Savior (Jn. 4:28-42). Background: The conversion of a sinful Samaritan woman instigated this revival.
20. Under Philip (Acts 8:5-12). Background: The strong preaching of Philip the evangelist concerning the kingdom of God produced a great revival in Samaria.
21. Under Peter (Acts 2:1-47; 9:32-35). Background: Peter saw revival on at least two occasions.
    a. At Pentecost, after his great sermon (Acts 2).
    b. At Lydda, after he had healed Aeneas (Acts 9).
22. Under Paul (Acts 19:11-20). Background: One of the greatest biblical revivals occurred in Ephesus during Paul's third missionary journey. This account should be carefully read.

Rivers

1. Pison—one of four rivers in the Garden of Eden (Gen. 2:11).
2. Gihon—another river in Eden (Gen. 2:13).
3. Hiddekel—a third river in Eden (also called Tigris—Gen. 2:14). Also where Daniel received his vision of the glory of God (Dan. 10:4).
4. Euphrates—the fourth river in the Garden of Eden (Gen. 2:14). Crossed by Jacob during his flight from Laban (Gen. 31:20, 21). Referred to by Joshua as the dividing point in Abraham's life (Josh. 24:2, 3). Constituted the northeast boundary of Solomon's empire (1 Ki. 4:21). It is now a prisonhouse for four hellish angels (Rev. 9:13-15), and will be dried up during the tribulation (Rev. 16:12).
5. Nile—southern land boundary of the Abrahamic Covenant (Gen. 15:18). This river was seen by Pharaoh in his dream (Gen. 41:1-18); turned to blood by Moses (Ex. 7:17-25).
6. Arnon—boundary river between Israel and Moab (Num. 21:13; Josh. 12:1; Jdg. 11:22).
7. Jabbok—brook-like river where Jacob wrestled with God (Gen. 32:22-32).
8. Kanah—river that served as a boundary between the tribes of Ephraim and Manasseh (Josh. 16:8; 17:9).
9. Kishon—located near the town of Megiddo where Deborah and Barak defeated Sisera (Jdg. 5:21), near where Elijah defeated the priests of Baal (1 Ki. 18:40).
10. Ahava—river at which the returning Babylonian Jews gathered before going back to Jerusalem (Ezra 8:21).
11. Chebar—where Ezekiel saw some of his visions (Ezek. 1:1; 3:15, 23; 10:15-22; 43:3).
12. Abana and Pharpar—two of the Damascus rivers mentioned by Naaman (2 Ki. 5:12).
13. Jordan—the principal river in Palestine and most famous river in the Bible. Joshua parted the Jordan as Israel marched into the Promised Land (Josh. 3:13-17). Elijah parted the river for himself and Elisha (2 Ki. 2:7, 8). Elisha did likewise to test the power of God (2 Ki. 2:13, 14). Naaman washed his leprosy away there (2 Ki. 5:10-14). John baptized Jesus there (Mt. 3:13-17).
14. Millennial river (Ezek. 47:1-12; Zech. 14:8).
15. Eternal river (Rev. 22:1, 2).

Roads and Highways

1. The highway leading through Edom (Num. 20:19). This was blocked by the Edomites, thus forcing the weary Israelites to go around another way.
2. The highway from Bethel to Shechem (Jdg. 21:19). The continuation of the tribe of Benjamin was settled through a celebration which took place alongside this road.
3. The highway from Ekron (a city in Philistia) to the Israelite city of Beth-shemesh (1 Sam. 6:12). Two cows carrying the Ark of the Covenant in a cart made their way along this road.
4. The Jerusalem to Jericho road (Lk. 10:30). This road played an important part in Jesus' parable of the Good Samaritan.
5. The Bethphage to Jerusalem road (Mt. 21:1-9). Here Jesus mounted the foal of an ass and rode into Jerusalem on Palm Sunday.
6. The Jerusalem to Emmaus road (Lk. 24:13). Christ appeared to two of his disciples on the first Easter Sunday.
7. The Jerusalem to Antioch road (Acts 9:3). The Apostle Paul met Christ on this road.
8. The millennial highway (Isa. 19:23; 35:8). This will stretch from Egypt to Assyria, and will be used by many nations coming to worship in Jerusalem.

Rocks and Stones

1. The rocks struck by Moses.
    a. At Rephidim (Ex. 17:1-6), at which time he obeyed God.
    b. In the desert of Zin (Num. 20:1-12), at which time he disobeyed God.
2. The two stones God gave to Moses (Ex. 24:12) which contained the commandments.
3. The stone Jacob used as a pillow, which he anointed after his vision (Gen. 28:11, 18, 22).
4. The stone Jacob moved from the well at Haran (Gen. 29:10).
5. The stone used as a pillar memorial between Jacob and Laban (Gen. 31:45).
6. The stone Jacob anointed with oil upon his return to Bethel (Gen. 35:14).
7. The twelve memorial stones taken from the River Jordan (Josh. 4:5).
8. The great stone used by Joshua as a memorial reminder to Israel (Josh. 24:26).
9. The stone used by the citizens of Beth-shemesh in sacrificing to celebrate the return of the Ark of God (1 Sam. 6:14).
10. The stone named Eben-ezer by Samuel (1 Sam. 7:12).
11. The five smooth stones picked by David when he met Goliath (1 Sam. 17:40).
12. The stones thrown at David by Shimei (2 Sam. 16:13).

13. The huge fifteen-foot-high stones in the foundation of the Temple (1 Ki. 7:10).
14. The twelve stones used by Elijah in building an altar on Mt. Carmel (1 Ki. 18:31).
15. The stones used in the slaying of Zechariah, Israel's fearless high priest (2 Chron. 24:21).
16. The stones used in an attempt to kill Christ (Jn. 8:59; 10:31).
17. The stone which sealed the tomb of Christ (Mt. 27:60).
18. The stones used to slay Stephen (Acts 7:59).

Seals

1. The seal of Darius over the den of lions where Daniel was placed (Dan. 6:17)
2. The seal of Ahasuerus which sentenced the Jews in Persia to death (Est. 3:12).
3. The seal of Ahasuerus which allowed the Jews to defend themselves (Est. 8:8, 10).
4. The seal of Jezebel which doomed Naboth (1 Ki. 21:8).
5. The seal of Jeremiah's purchased field (Jer. 32:10).
6. The seal upon the tomb of Christ (Mt. 27:66).
7. The seal of Abraham's righteousness (Rom. 4:11).
8. The seven seals of Revelation (Rev. 5:1).
9. The seal upon the foreheads of the 144,000 (Rev. 7:3, 4).
10. The seal of the Holy Spirit (2 Cor. 1:22; Eph. 1:13; 4:30; 2 Tim. 2:19).

Seas

1. The Mediterranean Sea (Acts 10:6; 27:40). Also called the Great Sea (see Josh. 1:4).
2. The Dead Sea. Also called the Salt Sea (Josh. 18:19).
3. The Red Sea (Ex. 14:21).
4. The Galilean Sea (Mt. 4:18).

Sermons

1. Aaron, to the Hebrew elders in Egypt (Ex. 4:29-31).
2. Moses, to the Hebrew elders at Sinai (Ex. 19:7, 8).
3. Moses, to all Israel in the Moab desert:
    a. First sermon (Deut. 1—4).
    b. Second sermon (Deut. 5—26).
    c. Third sermon (Deut. 27—30).
4. Joshua, to all Israel (Josh. 23, 24).
5. Samuel
    a. To Israel at Ramah (1 Sam. 8:10-18).
    b. To Israel at Gilgal (1 Sam. 12:1-25).
6. David, to Israel in Zion (1 Chron. 29:1-5, 10-20).
7. Solomon, to Israel at the Temple dedication (1 Ki. 8:12-21, 54-61).
8. Rehoboam, to the ten tribes at Shechem (1 Ki. 12:12-14).
9. Elijah, to the ten tribes on Mt. Carmel (1 Ki. 18:21).
10. Josiah, to Israel (2 Ki. 23:2; 2 Chron. 35:3-6).
11. Hezekiah, to Israel's leaders (2 Chron. 29:3-11).
12. Jonah, to Nineveh (Jonah 3:4).
13. John the Baptist, near the Jordan River, to Israel (Mt. 3:1-3, 7-12; Lk. 3:4-18; Jn. 1:15-34; 3:27-36).
14. Jesus. His three most famous sermons.
    a. On an unknown mountain (Mt. 5—7).
    b. By the seaside (Mt. 13).
    c. On the Mt. of Olives (Mt. 24, 25).
15. Peter
    a. To the Jews at Pentecost (Acts 2:14-40).
    b. To the Jews at the beautiful gate (Acts 3:12-26).
    c. To the Sanhedrin (Acts 4:5-12).
    d. To Cornelius at Caesarea (Acts 10:34-43).
    e. To the Jerusalem Council at Jerusalem (Acts 15:7-11).
16. Stephen, to the Jewish leaders at Jerusalem (Acts 7:1-53).
17. James, to the Jerusalem Council at Jerusalem (Acts 15:13-21).
18. Paul
    a. To the assembled synagogue at Antioch in Pisidia (Acts 13:16-41).
    b. To philosophers in Athens (Acts 17:22-31).
    c. To Ephesian elders in Miletus (Acts 20:18-35).
    d. To a Jerusalem mob at Jerusalem (Acts 22:1-21).
    e. To Felix and his court at Caesarea (Acts 24:10-21, 25).
    f. To Agrippa and his court at Caesarea (Acts 26:2-29).
    g. To terrified shipmates on the high seas (Acts 27:21-26).
    h. To curious Jews in Rome (Acts 28:17-20, 25-28).

Shoes and Sandals

1. The shoes Moses took off at the burning bush (Ex. 3:5).
2. The shoes Joshua removed outside the city of Jericho (Josh. 5:15).
3. The old shoes used by the Gibeonites to trick Joshua (Josh. 9:5, 13).
4. The sandal of Boaz removed to publicly validate the purchase of land from Naomi (Ruth 4:7, 8).
5. The shoes ordered placed on the prodigal son by his father (Lk. 15:22).
6. The shoes of Peter in a Jerusalem prison (Acts 12:8).

Signs

1. A rainbow, as a sign that the world would never again be destroyed by water (Gen. 9:13-17).
2. The ten plagues in Egypt, of the power of God (Ex. 10:2).
3. Unleavened bread, of the deliverance from Egypt (Ex. 13:7-9).
4. The Sabbath, of completion and rest (Ex. 31:13).
5. Twelve stones, of the parting of Jordan (Josh. 4:6).
6. A fleece, of answered prayer and God's approval (Jdg. 6:17).
7. Two censers, of invoked punishment at the unlawful offering of incense (Num. 16:36-40).
8. A "slow" sundial, of Hezekiah's recovery (2 Ki. 20:8-11).
9. The virgin birth, of God incarnate (Isa. 7:14).
10. A torn altar, of the destruction of a false religion (1 Ki. 13:5).
11. A fire, of the impending Babylonian invasion (Jer. 6:1).
12. The prophet Jonah, of the resurrection of Christ (Mt. 16:4).
13. Swaddling clothes, of the birth of Christ (Lk. 2:12).
14. Tongues, of God's power to unbelievers (1 Cor. 14:22).

Similes

1. "I have likened the daughter of Zion to a comely and delicate woman" (Jer. 6:2).
2. "They sank into the bottom as a stone" (Ex. 15:5).
3. "For they came up . . . as grasshoppers" (Jdg. 6:5).
4. "All we like sheep have gone astray" (Isa. 53:6).
5. "I will liken him unto a wise man" (Mt. 7:24).
6. ". . . shall be likened unto a foolish man" (Mt. 7:26).
7. "The Spirit of God descending like a dove" (Mt. 3:16).

8. "Then shall the righteous shine forth as the sun" (Mt. 13:43).
9. "This generation . . . like unto children sitting in the market" (Mt. 11:16).
10. "His face did shine as the sun" (Mt. 17:2).
11. "The kingdom of heaven is likened unto a man" (Mt. 13:24).
12. "The kingdom of heaven is likened unto a certain king" (Mt. 18:23).
13. "Except ye be converted and become as little children" (Mt. 18:3).
14. "They . . . are as the angels of God in heaven" (Mt. 22:30).
15. "Ye are like unto whited sepulchres" (Mt. 23:27).
16. "I send you forth as lambs among wolves" (Lk. 10:3).
17. "I beheld Satan as lightning fall from heaven" (Lk. 10:18).
18. "His sweat was as it were great drops of blood falling to the ground" (Lk. 22:44).
19. "He was led as a sheep to the slaughter" (Acts 8:32).
20. "There fell from his eyes as it had been scales" (Acts 9:18).
21. "We are made as the filth of the world" (1 Cor. 4:13).
22. "As a vesture shalt thou fold them up" (Heb. 1:12).
23. "All flesh is as grass" (1 Pet. 1:24).
24. "Ye also, as lively stones, are built up a spiritual house" (1 Pet. 2:5).
25. "But these . . . as brute beasts" (Jude 1:10).
26. "A great voice as of a trumpet" (Rev. 1:10).
27. "His hairs were white like wool" (Rev. 1:14).
28. "His eyes were as a flame of fire" (Rev. 1:14).
29. "His feet like unto fine brass" (Rev. 1:15).
30. "His voice as the sound of many waters" (Rev. 1:15).
31. "I will come on thee as a thief" (Rev. 3:3).
32. "The first beast was like a lion" (Rev. 4:7).
33. "The second beast like a calf" (Rev. 4:7).
34. "The third beast had a face as a man" (Rev. 4:7).
35. "The fourth beast was like a flying eagle" (Rev. 4:7).
36. "The sun became black as sackcloth of hair" (Rev. 6:12).
37. "The moon became as blood" (Rev. 6:12).
38. "The heaven departed as a scroll" (Rev. 6:14).
39. "Their torment was as the torment of a scorpion" (Rev. 9:5).
40. "It shall be in thy mouth sweet as honey" (Rev. 10:9).
41. "The beast . . . was like unto a leopard" (Rev. 13:2).
42. "His feet were as the feet of a bear" (Rev. 13:2).
43. "His mouth as the mouth of a lion" (Rev. 13:2).
44. "The sea . . . became as the blood of a dead man" (Rev. 16:3).
45. "The number . . . as the sand of the sea" (Rev. 20:8).
46. "A pure river of water . . . clear as crystal" (Rev. 22:1).

Sins

1. Disobedience (Gen. 3:6).
2. Drunkenness (Gen. 9:21).
3. Self-worship (Gen. 11:1-9).
4. Sodomy (Gen. 19; Rom. 1:24-32).
5. Hatred (Gen. 27:41).
6. Deceit (Gen. 27:11-15).
7. Incest (Gen. 19:33-38).
8. Lying (Gen. 26:7, 8).
9. Jealousy (1 Sam. 18:8-12).
10. Rape (2 Sam. 13:14).
11. Plotting murder (Gen. 37:18-22; 4:8).
12. Mockery (2 Ki. 2:23, 24).
13. Adultery (2 Sam. 11:4, 27).

14. Murmuring (Num. 14:29).
15. Rebellion (Num. 16).
16. Idolatry (Ex. 32).
17. Blasphemy (Acts 12:20-23).
18. Breaking the Sabbath (Num. 15:32-36).
19. Covetousness (Josh. 7).
20. Compromise (Jdg. 2:1-3).
21. Taking bribes (1 Sam. 8:3).
22. Eating blood (1 Sam. 14:33).
23. Practicing witchcraft (1 Sam. 28:7-18).
24. Intruding into the priests' office (1 Sam. 2:17).
25. Causing division among God's people (2 Sam. 15:4).
26. Despising a husband (2 Sam. 6:16-23).
27. Offering human sacrifices (2 Ki. 17:17).
28. Pride (1 Sam. 14:12-14).
29. Self-will (Ezek. 28:17).
30. Despising God's Word (2 Chron. 36:16).
31. Attributing to Satan the work of the Holy Spirit (Mt. 12:24-32).
32. Prayerlessness (Hosea 7:7).
33. Polluting the house of God (Jn. 2:14-16).
34. Scattering the sheep (Jer. 23:1).
35. Teaching false doctrine (Mt. 16:6).
36. Lack of mercy (Mt. 18:23-35).
37. Hypocrisy (Mt. 23).
38. Denying Christ (Mt. 26:69-75).
39. Crucifying Christ (Acts 2:23).
40. Being stiff-necked (Acts 7:51).
41. Unthankfulness (Rom. 1:21).
42. Boasting (Rom. 1:30).
43. Disobeying parents (Rom. 1:30).
44. Without natural affection (Rom. 1:31).
45. Living in the flesh (Gal. 3:3).

Spears and Swords

1. The sword of the cherubim (Gen. 3:24).
2. Those used by Simeon and Levi (Gen. 34:25, 26).
3. The one held by an angel against Balaam (Num. 22:23).
4. Joshua's victorious sword against Ai (Josh. 8:18).
5. The sword of the captain of the Lord's host (Josh. 5:13).
6. The one used by Goliath (1 Sam. 17:45).
7. Saul's swords and spears:
   a. The ones he used in attempting to kill David (1 Sam. 18:11; 19:9).
   b. The one used in attempting to kill Jonathan (1 Sam. 20:33).
   c. The one David took from him while he slept (1 Sam. 26:12).
   d. The one he fell upon (1 Sam. 31:4).
8. The sword used to kill wicked Athaliah (2 Ki. 11:20).
9. The sword Peter used to strike the servant of the high priest (Mt. 26:51).
10. The one used to pierce the side of Christ (Jn. 19:34).
11. The one used by Herod to kill James (Acts 12:1, 2).
12. The one used by Herod to kill John the Baptist (Mt. 14:10).
13. The one almost used by the Philippian jailor to kill himself (Acts 16:27).
14. The (symbolic) one carried by the antichrist (Rev. 6:4).
15. The (symbolic) one carried by the returning true Christ (Rev. 19:15).

Staffs, Sticks, and Rods

1. As used by Jacob
   a. The rods used in an attempt to control the birth of animals (Gen. 30:37).

b. The staff he carried over Jordan (Gen. 32:10).

c. The staff he used upon his deathbed (Heb. 11:21).

2. The staff Judah unknowingly gave to his daughter-in-law (Gen. 38:18).

3. As used by Moses
   a. Seeing it turn into a serpent (Ex. 4:2).
   b. Using it to bring down the ten plagues upon Egypt (Ex. 7:19).
   c. Parting the Red Sea with it (Ex. 14:16).
   d. Standing with it on a hill praying for Israel (Ex. 17:9).
   e. Striking a rock with it:
      (1) At Rephidim (Ex. 17:6, 7).
      (2) In the wilderness of Zin (Num. 20:8–11).

4. As used by Aaron
   a. To swallow up the rods-turned-snakes of the magicians in Egypt (Ex. 7:12).
   b. To demonstrate God's blessings upon him as his rod blossomed (Num. 17:8).

5. The staff used by Balaam to beat his donkey (Num. 22:27).

6. The staff used by the twelve spies to carry fruit found in the Promised Land (Num. 13:23).

7. The staff used by an angel to consume Gideon's offering (Jdg. 6:21).

8. The rod used by Jonathan to secure honey from a hive (1 Sam. 14:27).

9. The stick used by Elisha which caused an axehead to float (2 Ki. 6:6).

10. The two sticks used by Ezekiel to predict the eventual union and millennial blessings of Israel's twelve tribes (Ezek. 37:16–28).

11. The staff Zechariah broke to predict coming judgment upon Gentile nations (Zech. 11:10).

12. The rod given John by an angel to measure the tribulational temple (Rev. 11:1).

13. The (metaphorical) rod Christ will use to rule all nations in the millennium (Rev. 2:27; 12:5; 19:15).

14. The rod and staff of the Good Shepherd (Ps. 23:4).

Suicides

1. Saul (1 Sam. 31:4).
2. Saul's armorbearer (1 Sam. 31:5).
3. Ahithophel (2 Sam. 17:23).
4. Zimri (1 Ki. 16:18).
5. Judas (Mt. 27:3–5).

Symbols and Emblems

A symbol may be defined as a visible object used to represent someone or something.

1. Symbols of Christ
   a. Alpha and Omega (Rev. 1:11).
   b. An anchor (Heb. 6:19).
   c. Bread, manna (Jn. 6:31–35).
   d. An eagle (Ex. 19:4; Rev. 4:7).
   e. The firstfruits of a crop (1 Cor. 15:20).
   f. A hen (Mt. 23:37).
   g. A lamb (Jn. 1:29; Rev. 5:6).
   h. Light (Jn. 1:9).
   i. A lily (Song of Sol. 2:1).
   j. A lion (Ezek. 1:10; Rev. 4:7; 5:5).
   k. An ox or calf (Ezek. 1:10; Rev. 4:7).
   l. A rock (Mt. 16:18; 1 Pet. 2:8).
   m. A rose (Song of Sol. 2:1).
   n. A root (Isa. 11:1; Rev. 5:5; 22:16).
   o. A serpent (Jn. 3:14).

p. A star (Rev. 22:16).

q. A stone
   (1) Living stone (1 Pet. 2:4).
   (2) A cornerstone (1 Pet. 2:6).
   (3) A precious stone (1 Pet. 2:7).
   (4) A stumbling stone (Rom. 9:33; 1 Pet. 2:8.)
   (5) A rejected stone (Mt. 21:42; Acts 4:11).
   (6) A crushing stone (Dan. 2:34).

r. The sun (Rev. 22:5).

s. A temple (Jn. 2:19).

t. A vine (Jn. 15:1).

u. A worm (Ps. 22:6).

2. Symbols for the Church and Believers:
   a. An athlete (1 Cor. 9:24–27; 2 Tim. 2:5; Heb. 12:1).
   b. A body (1 Cor. 12:27; Eph. 3:6; 4:4; Col. 1:18).
   c. Branches (Jn. 15:1).
   d. A bride (2 Cor. 11:2; Rev. 21:2).
   e. A building (1 Cor. 3:9).
   f. Candlesticks, lampstands (Rev. 1:20).
   g. A family (Eph. 3:15).
   h. A farmer (2 Tim. 2:6).
   i. Lights (Mt. 5:14; Jn. 12:36; Eph. 5:8; Phil. 2:15; 1 Thess. 5:5).
   j. Priests (1 Pet. 2:9; Rev. 1:6; 5:10; 20:6).
   k. Pearls (Mt. 13:45, 46).
   l. Salt (Mt. 5:13).
   m. Sheep, lambs (Lk. 10:3; Jn. 10:11; 21:15–17).
   n. Soldiers (2 Tim. 2:3).
   o. Stewards (1 Cor. 4:2; 1 Pet. 4:10).
   p. Stones (Eph. 2:19–22; 1 Pet. 2:5).
   q. A temple (2 Cor. 6:16; 2 Pet. 2:5).
   r. A vessel (2 Cor. 4:7; 2 Tim. 2:21).
   s. A wife (Rev. 21:9).
   t. Wheat (Mt. 13:29, 30).

3. Symbols for Israel
   a. A linen girdle (Jer. 13:10).
   b. A marred clay vessel (Jer. 18:4).
   c. Two baskets of figs (Jer. 24:1).
   d. Three bunches of hair (Ezek. 5:1, 2).
   e. Dross in a furnace (Ezek. 22:18).
   f. A valley of dry bones (Ezek. 37:1, 2).
   g. Two sticks (Ezek. 37:16, 17).
   h. A barren fig tree (Mt. 21:19; Lk. 13:6).
   i. An empty vine (Hosea 10:1).
   j. An unturned, half-baked cake (Hosea 7:8).
   k. A backslidden heifer (Hosea 10:11).
   l. A silly dove (Hosea 7:11).
   m. A wild ass (Hosea 8:9).
   n. Dust (Gen. 13:16).
   o. Sand (Gen. 22:17).
   p. Sheep (Ps. 100:3).
   q. Stars (Gen. 22:17; Dan. 12:3).
   r. Three servants (Mt. 25:14, 15).
   s. Ten servants (Lk. 19:12, 13).
   t. Ten virgins (Mt. 25:1).
   u. A harlot wife (Hosea 4:15).
   v. Three wedding guests (Lk. 14:16–24).
   w. A hidden treasure (Mt. 13:44).
   x. A persecuted woman (Rev. 12:13).
   y. Precious jewels (Mal. 3:17).
   z. Trees of righteousness (Isa. 61:3).

4. Symbols for Satan
   a. A dragon (Rev. 12:3, 7).
   b. A serpent (Rev. 20:2).
   c. A roaring lion (1 Pet. 5:8).
   d. A sower (Mt. 13:39).

e. An angel of light (2 Cor. 11:14).

f. A prince (Jn. 12:31).

5. Symbols for apostates

a. Waterless clouds (Jude 1:12).

b. Fruitless trees (Jude 1:12).

c. Raging, wild waves (Isa. 57:20; Jude 1:13).

d. Wandering stars (Jude 1:13).

e. Dogs (2 Pet. 2:22).

f. Hogs (2 Pet. 2:22).

g. Brute beasts (Jude 1:10).

h. Goats (Mt. 25:33).

i. Tares (Mt. 13:30).

6. Symbols for sinners

a. Wayside ground (Mt. 13:4).

b. Stony ground (Mt. 13:5).

c. Thorny ground (Mt. 13:7).

d. Unclean sea creatures (Mt. 13:47, 48).

e. A bruised reed (Mt. 12:20).

f. A smoking flax (Mt. 12:20).

g. Sheep without a shepherd (Mt. 9:36).

7. Symbols for the Bible

a. A mirror (Jas. 1:23-25).

b. A seed (Mt. 13:18-23; Jas. 1:18; 1 Pet. 1:23).

c. Water (Eph. 5:25-27).

d. A lamp (Ps. 119:105; Prov. 6:23; 2 Pet. 1:19).

e. A sword (Heb. 4:12; Eph. 6:17).

f. Precious metals

(1) Gold (Ps. 19:10; 119:127).

(2) Silver (Ps. 12:6).

g. Nourishing food

(1) Milk (1 Pet. 2:2).

(2) Meat (Heb. 5:12-14).

(3) Bread (Jn. 6:51).

(4) Honey (Ps. 19:10).

h. A hammer (Jer. 23:29).

i. A fire (Jer. 20:9; Lk. 24:32).

8. Symbols for the Holy Spirit

a. A dove (Jn. 1:32).

b. Water (Isa. 44:3; Jn. 7:37-39).

c. Oil (Lk. 4:18; Acts 10:38; Heb. 1:9; 1 Jn. 2:27).

d. A seal (2 Cor. 1:22; Eph. 1:13; 4:30).

e. Wind (Jn. 3:8; Acts 2:1, 2).

f. Fire (Acts 2:3).

g. An earnest (2 Cor. 1:22; 5:5; Eph. 1:14).

9. Symbols for the kingdom of heaven

a. A field (Mt. 13:3-30).

b. A tree (Mt. 13:31, 32).

c. The sea (Mt. 13:47, 48).

d. The marriage feast (Mt. 22:2).

10. Symbols for coming judgment

a. A sickle (Rev. 14:14).

b. A dragnet (Mt. 13:47).

c. A wine press (Isa. 63:3).

d. A falling stone (Dan. 2:34).

e. Four horses (Rev. 6:2-8).

f. A white throne (Rev. 20:11).

11. Symbols for wickedness, uncleanness

a. Leaven (Mt. 16:6).

b. Leprosy (Lev. 13:44).

c. An ephah (Zech. 5:6).

12. Symbols of the antichrist

a. A little horn (Dan. 7:8).

b. A seven-headed, ten-horned beast from the sea (Rev. 13:1).

13. Symbols for sorrow

a. Ashes (Est. 4:1; Job 2:8; Dan. 9:3; Jonah 3:6).

b. Sackcloth (Est. 4:1; Jonah 3:6).

c. Torn clothing (1 Sam. 4:12; 2 Sam. 13:31; Ezra 9:3; Job 1:20; 2:12; Mt. 26:65).

14. Symbol for the false prophet—a two-horned lamb (Rev. 13:11).

15. Symbol for faith—hyssop (Ex. 12:22).

16. Symbols for the death and resurrection of Christ

a. The great fish in Jonah 1-2.

b. Baptism (Rom. 6:2-10).

17. Symbol for the body and blood of Christ

a. Bread (Mt. 26:26; 1 Cor. 11:24).

b. Wine (Mt. 26:28; 1 Cor. 11:25).

18. Symbol for prayer—the altar of incense (Ex. 30:1; Lk. 1:10; Rev. 5:8; 8:3, 4).

19. Symbols for Christianity

a. The cross (Gal. 6:14; Eph. 2:16; Col. 1:20).

b. The empty tomb (Mt. 28:1-8; 1 Cor. 15:14).

20. Symbols for religion and rebellion

a. A bloodless fruit of the ground offering (Gen. 4:3, 5).

b. Fig leaves (Gen. 3:7).

c. The Tower of Babel (Gen. 11:1-9).

d. A golden statue (Dan. 3).

e. A bloody harlot (Rev. 17:1-6).

f. The antichrist's statue (Rev. 13:14, 15).

g. A numerical mark (Rev. 13:16-18).

21. Symbol for rewards

a. Crowns (Rev. 4:4).

b. A white stone (Rev. 2:17).

c. Hidden manna (Rev. 2:17).

d. A morning star (Rev. 2:28).

e. White raiment (Rev. 3:18; 19:8).

22. Symbol for human righteousness—filthy rags (Isa. 64:6).

23. Symbols for human life

a. As grass (Ps. 90:5, 6; Jas. 1:10; 1 Pet. 1:24).

b. A vapor (Jas. 4:14).

c. A breath (Job 7:7).

d. Vanishing smoke (Ps. 102:3).

24. Symbols for soul-winning

a. Fish (Mt. 4:18, 19; Lk. 5:1-10).

b. Harvest grain (Jn. 4:35-38).

25. Symbol of the curse—thorns (Gen. 3:17, 18).

26. Symbols for good works (1 Cor. 3:12)—gold, silver, precious stones.

27. Symbols for worthless works (1 Cor. 3:12)—wood, hay, stubble.

28. Symbols for Gentile world powers

a. Babylon

(1) The golden head of a great statue (Dan. 2:32, 37).

(2) A lion and eagle-like beast (Ezek. 17:3; Dan. 7:4).

b. Medo-Persia

(1) The silver chest and arms of a great statue (Dan. 2:32, 39).

(2) A flesh-eating, bear-like beast (Dan. 7:5).

(3) A two-horned ram (Dan. 8:3, 4).

c. Greece

(1) The bronze stomach and thigh of a great statue (Dan. 2:32, 39).

(2) A leopard bird-like beast (Dan. 7:6).

(3) A one-horned male goat (Dan. 8:5-8, 20-22).

d. Rome

(1) The iron and clay legs and feet of a great statue (Dan. 2:33, 40-43).

(2) A dreadful beast with iron teeth (Dan. 7:7).

e. The revived Roman Empire—a seven-headed, ten-horned beast (Rev. 12:3; 17:12-16).

29. Symbols for various individuals
    a. Nebuchadnezzar, a tree (Dan. 4:10, 20-22).
    b. Antiochus Epiphanes, a little horn (Dan. 8:9).
    c. Alexander the Great, a male goat (Dan. 8:5).
    d. Joshua and Zerubbabel, two olive trees (Zech. 4:1-6).

30. Symbol for the earth's title deed—a seven-sealed book (Rev. 5:1).

31. Symbol for the world's godless religious systems—a great bloody harlot (Rev. 17:1-6).

32. Symbol for the world's godless political and economic systems—an arrogant queen (Rev. 18).

33. Symbol for God's finished work of creation—the Sabbath (Gen. 2:1-3; Ex. 20:8-11).

34. Symbol for God's finished work of redemption—the first day (Mt. 28:1).

Temples

1. The temple (tabernacle) of Moses (Ex. 40).
2. The Temple of Solomon (1 Ki. 6).
3. The Temple of Zerubbabel (Ezra 3).
4. The Temple of Herod (Jn. 2:20).
5. The temple of Christ's body (Jn. 2:21).
6. The temple of the believer's body (1 Cor. 6:19; 2 Cor. 6:16).
7. The temple of collective believers (Eph. 2:20-22; 1 Pet. 2:5).
8. The tribulational temple (Mt. 24:15; Rev. 11:1).
9. The millennial temple (Ezek. 40; Acts 15:16).
10. The heavenly temple (Rev. 11:19; 14:15; 15:5, 6, 8; 16:1, 17).

Thrones

1. The throne of God (Ps. 45:6; 103:19; Isa. 6:1; Rev. 4:2).
2. The throne of David
    a. During his lifetime (2 Sam. 2:4; 5:3).
    b. During the millennium (Jer. 30:9; 33:17; Hosea 3:5).
3. The twelve thrones for the apostles (Mt. 19:28).
4. The throne of Christ (2 Cor. 5:10) for believers.
5. The throne of Satan (Rev. 2:13).
6. The twenty-four thrones for the elders (Rev. 4:4).
7. The great white throne (Rev. 20:11) for unbelievers.

Towers

1. The tower of Babel (Gen. 11:4).
2. The tower of Shechem (Jdg. 9:51, 52).
3. The tower of Jezreel (2 Ki. 9:17).

Trees

1. Acacia (Ex. 25:5, 10; 26:26).
2. Algum (2 Chron. 2:8).
3. Almond (Num. 17:8).
4. Almug (1 Ki. 10:11, 12).
5. Apple (Prov. 25:11; Song of Sol. 2:3, 5; 7:8; Joel 1:12).
6. Box (Isa. 41:19; 60:13).
7. Bramble (Jdg. 9:14, 15).
8. Cassia (Ex. 30:24).
9. Cedar (1 Ki. 6:15).
10. Chestnut, plane (Gen. 30:37; Ezek. 31:8).
11. Cinnamon (Ex. 30:23; Prov. 7:17; Rev. 18:13).
12. Cypress (1 Ki. 6:15-35; Isa. 55:13; 60:13, *RSV*).
13. Fig (Jdg. 9:10, 11; Isa. 38:21; Mt. 21:19).
14. Fir, Pine (1 Ki. 5:10; Isa. 37:24).

15. Frankincense (Mt. 2:11).
16. Mulberry (2 Sam. 5:23, 24).
17. Myrtle (Isa. 41:19; 55:13).
18. Oak (Gen. 35:4; Ezek. 27:6; Zech. 11:2).
19. Olive (Gen. 8:11; Deut. 24:20; Ps. 52:8; Isa. 17:6; 24:13; Hosea 14:6).
20. Palm (Num. 33:9; 2 Chron. 28:15; Jn. 12:13; Rev. 7:9).
21. Pistachio (Gen. 43:11, RSV).
22. Poplar (Gen. 30:37; Hosea 4:13).
23. Sycamine (Lk. 17:6).
24. Sycamore (Amos 7:14; Lk. 19:4).
25. Tamarisk (Gen. 21:33; 1 Sam. 22:6; 31:13, *RSV*).
26. Terebinth (oak) (2 Sam. 18:9, 10).
27. Thyine (Rev. 18:12).
28. Willow (Ps. 137:1-5; Isa. 44:4).
29. Wormwood (Deut. 29:18; Jer. 23:15; Rev. 8:10, 11).

Trumpets

1. Moses' two silver trumpets (Num. 10:2).
2. Joshua's seven rams' trumpets (Josh. 6:4).
3. Ehud's trumpet (Jdg. 3:12-30).
4. Gideon's 300 trumpets (Jdg. 7).
5. David's trumpet (2 Sam. 6:15).
6. Zadok's trumpet (1 Ki. 1:39).
7. Solomon's trumpets (2 Chron. 5:13).
8. Ezra's trumpets (Ezra 3:10).
9. The rapture of the church trumpet (1 Cor. 15:52; 1 Thess. 4:16).
10. The seven judgment trumpets (Rev. 8:2).
11. The regathering of Israel trumpet (Mt. 24:31).

Types, Foreshadows

A type is a shadow cast on the pages of the Old Testament describing a truth, the fulfillment of which is found in the New Testament. It can be an event, person, or thing. It must be historical and christocentric.

1. Types of Christ
    Individuals
    a. Adam: his headship over a new creation (Gen. 1:28; Rom. 5:17-19; 1 Cor. 15:22, 45, 47; Heb. 2:7-9).
    b. Moses: his prophetical ministry (Deut. 18:15-18; Heb. 3:5, 6).
    c. Melchizedek: his priestly ministry (Gen. 14:18-20; Ps. 110:4; Heb. 5-8).
    d. David: his kingly ministry (2 Sam. 7:1-17; Mk. 11:10; Rev. 5:5; 22:16).
    e. Jeremiah: his sorrows (Jer. 3:20; 5:1-5; 8:20-22; 9:1; 10:19; 11:19).
    f. Joseph: his sufferings (most perfect type of Christ in Old Testament).
        (1) Hated without a cause (Gen. 37:4, 8; Jn. 15:25).
        (2) Ridiculed (Gen. 37:19; Lk. 22:63).
        (3) Plotted against (Gen. 37:20; Jn. 11:53).
        (4) Stripped of his robe (Gen. 37:23; Jn. 19:23, 24).
        (5) Sold for silver (Gen. 37:28; Mt. 26:14-16).
        (6) Lied about (Gen. 39:14; Mt. 26:61).
        (7) Placed in captivity with two guilty men (Gen. 40:1-3; Lk. 23:32, 33).
        (8) Unrecognized by his own (Gen. 42:8; Jn. 1:11).
    g. Isaac: his death (Gen. 22:2, 8, 10; Mt. 26:36, 42, 43).
    h. Jonah: his resurrection (Jonah 1:17; Mt. 12:40; 16:4; Lk. 11:29).
    i. Joshua: his victorious life (Josh. 1:3, 5, 6, 8, 9; Jn. 10:17, 18; 19:30).
    j. Noah: his saving life (Gen. 6:13, 14, 17, 18; 1 Pet. 3:18-22).

k. Abraham: his father (Gen. 22:7, 8; Mt. 26:36, 42, 43).
l. Daniel: his acceptance by the Father (Dan. 9:23; 10:11, 19; Mt. 3:17; 17:5).
m. Elijah: his forerunner (Isa. 40:3, 4; Mt. 17:11, 12).
n. Elisha: his miracles: Elisha performed fourteen miracles, nearly double those of any other Old Testament man except Moses (2 Ki. 2:9; Jn. 3:2).
o. Ezekiel: his parables. There are sixty-nine parables in the Old Testament; twenty-three are to be found in Ezekiel's book alone (Ezek. 17:2; 20:49; Mt. 13:3).
p. Ruth: his church (Ruth 2, 3, 4; 2 Cor. 11:2).
q. Boaz: his love for the church (Ruth 2, 3, 4; Eph. 5:25-27).
r. Ezra: his zeal for the Scriptures (Neh. 8; Mt. 21:42; 22:29; Mk. 12:10, 24; Lk. 4:21; 24:27; Jn. 10:35).
s. Nehemiah: his zeal for the Holy City (Neh. 1, 2; Mt. 23:37-39; Lk. 19:41).
t. Solomon: his wisdom (1 Ki. 3:11-13; Lk. 4:22; Jn. 7:46).
u. Lot: his backslidden followers (Gen. 19; 2 Pet. 2:7).
v. Absalom: his opposition
   (1) From Judas. Absalom was a betrayer and member of David's inner circle, as was Judas of Jesus' inner circle (2 Sam. 15; Mt. 26:14).
   (2) From the coming antichrist. Absalom plotted against the Davidic throne, as will the antichrist (2 Sam. 15; Rev. 13).

Brute Creatures
a. Lamb (Ex. 29:38; Jn. 1:29).
b. Dove (Lev. 5:11; Lk. 2:24).
c. Eagle (Ex. 19:4; Mt. 23:37).
d. Lion (Hosea 11:10; Rev. 5:5).
e. Sheep (Lev. 1:10; Isa. 53:7).
f. Heifer (Gen. 15:9; Num. 19).
g. Scapegoat (Lev. 16).
h. Ram (Gen. 22:13).
i. Pigeon (Gen. 15:9; Lev. 5:11).
j. Ox (Num. 7:87).
k. Bullock (Ex. 29:11).
l. Serpent (Num. 21:8, 9; Jn. 3:14).

Events
a. The coats of skin (Gen. 3:21).
b. The Passover (Ex. 12; 1 Cor. 5:7, 8).
c. The sacrifice on the day of atonement (Lev. 16).
d. The giving of manna (Ex. 16:14-22; Jn. 6).
e. The ark and the flood (Gen. 6—8; 1 Pet. 3:18-22).
f. The striking of the rock (Ex. 17:5-7; 1 Cor. 10:4).
g. The passage through the Red Sea (Ex. 14; 1 Cor. 10:1, 2).
h. The two memorials (Josh. 4).
i. The branch cast into the waters at Marah (Ex. 15:23-26).

Feasts
a. The Passover feast. Speaks of Calvary (Lev. 23:4-8; 1 Cor. 5:7).
b. The feast of firstfruits. Speaks of the resurrection (Lev. 23:9-14; 1 Cor. 15:23).
c. The feast of Pentecost. Speaks of the coming of the Holy Spirit (Lev. 23:15-22; Acts 2:1-4).
d. The feast of trumpets. Speaks of the rapture and Second Coming (Lev. 23:23-25; 1 Thess. 4:13-18).
e. The day of atonement feast. Speaks of the tribulation (Lev. 23:26-32; Rev. 6—19).
f. The feast of tabernacles. Speaks of the millennium (Lev. 23:33-44; Rev. 20:1-6).

The Offerings
a. The burnt offering (Lev. 1). Speaks of Christ's willingly offering himself.
b. The meal offering (Lev. 2). Speaks of his purity and sinlessness.
c. The peace offering (Lev. 3). Speaks of his accomplishments on the cross.
d. The sin offering (Lev. 4). Speaks of his dealing with sin's guilt.
e. The trespass offering (Lev. 5). Speaks of his dealing with sin's injury.

The Buildings
a. The tabernacle (Ex. 40).
b. The Temple (1 Ki. 8).

2. Types of antichrist
   a. Cain, by his murder of the chosen seed (Gen. 4:5-14; 1 Jn. 3:12).
   b. Nimrod, by his creation of Babylon and the Tower of Babel (Gen. 10, 11; Rev. 17, 18).
   c. Pharaoh, by his oppression of God's people (Ex. 1:8-22; Rev. 12).
   d. Korah, by his rebellion (Num. 16:1-3; Rev. 13:6).
   e. Balaam, by his attempt to curse Israel (Num. 23, 24; Dan. 7:25).
   f. Saul, by his intrusion into the office of the priesthood (1 Sam. 13:9-13; Mt. 24:15; Rev. 13:15-18).
   g. Goliath, by his proud boasting (1 Sam. 17; Dan. 11:36).
   h. Absalom, by his attempt to steal the throne of David (2 Sam. 15:1-6; 2 Thess. 2:3, 4, 9).
   i. Jeroboam, by his substitute religion (1 Ki. 12:25-31; Rev. 13:15).
   j. Sennacherib, by his efforts to destroy Jerusalem (2 Ki. 18:17; Zech. 14:2).
   k. Nebuchadnezzar, by his golden statue (Dan. 3:1-7; Rev. 13:15).
   l. Haman, by his plot to exterminate the Jews (Est. 3; Rev. 12:13-17).
   m. Antiochus Epiphanes, by his defilement of the Temple (Dan. 11:21-35; Mt. 24:15).
3. Types of the church
   a. Eve, Adam's wife (Gen. 2:23-25; 3:20).
   b. Rebekah, Isaac's wife (Gen. 24).
   c. Ruth, Boaz's wife (Ruth 4).
4. Types of Israel
   Concerning her immorality (book of Hosea)
   a. Gomer, the wife of Hosea.
   b. Jezreel, Loruhamah, and Loammi, children of Hosea.
   Concerning her immorality
   a. Jonah in the fish (Jonah 2). The Jews can't be swallowed!
   b. Three Hebrew men in the fire (Dan. 3). They can't be burned!
   c. Daniel in the lion's den (Dan. 6). They can't be eaten!
   d. Moses in the water (Ex. 14). They can't be drowned!
   e. Esther in Persia (Est. 3-7). They can't be hanged!
5. Types of the Father
   a. Abraham (Gen. 22).
   b. Jacob (Gen. 37:3).
   c. David (2 Sam. 9).
   d. Hosea (Hosea 1-3).
6. Type of the Holy Spirit—Abraham's servant (Gen. 24).
7. Types of backslidden believers
   a. Lot (Gen. 13:10, 11; 19:1; 2 Pet. 2:7).

b. Obadiah (1 Ki. 18:3-16).

c. Two and a half Israelite tribes (Num. 32).

8. Type of all unsaved—Esau (Gen. 25; Heb. 12:16, 17).

9. Type of wickedness—Babylon (Jer. 50-52; Zech. 5).

10. Type of worldliness—Egypt (Gen. 12:10; Num. 11:5; 14:3; Isa. 31:1).

11. Type of victory—Canaan (Ex. 3:8, 17; 13:5; Heb. 3-4).

12. Types of false religion
    a. Adam's fig leaves (Gen. 3:7).
    b. Cain's ground offering (Gen. 4:3).
    c. Nimrod's tower (Gen. 11:1-9).
    d. Aaron's golden calf (Ex. 32).
    e. Jezebel's teachings (1 Ki. 18:19; 2 Ki. 9:22; Rev. 2:20).
    f. Nebuchadnezzar's statue (Dan. 3).

13. Types of the rapture
    a. Lot, a type of the church which will escape from the tribulation (Gen. 19:22; 1 Thess. 1:10; 5:9).
    b. Noah, a type of Israel which will endure through the tribulation (Gen. 6-8; Mt. 24:3; Rev. 12).

14. Types of the coming great tribulation
    a. The universal flood, foreshadowing the scope of it (Gen. 6-8; 2 Pet. 3:1-9).
    b. The destruction of Sodom, foreshadowing the nature of it (Gen. 19; 2 Pet. 3:10-13).
    c. The ten plagues upon Egypt, foreshadowing the intensity of it (Ex. 7-12; Rev. 6-19).

15. Type of Armageddon—the locust plague in Joel's day (Joel 2:1-11; Rev. 14:14-20).

16. Types of the millennium
    a. The Sabbath (Ex. 20:8-11; Lev. 23:3).
    b. The jubilee year (Lev. 25:10-12).
    c. The tabernacle (Ex. 25:8; 29:42-46; 40:34).
    d. The feast of tabernacles (Lev. 23:34-42).
    e. The Promised Land (Deut. 6:3; Heb. 4:8-10).
    f. The reign of Solomon
        (1) The vastness of his kingdom (1 Ki. 4:21).
        (2) The security of it (1 Ki. 4:25).
        (3) His great wisdom (1 Ki. 4:29, 34).
        (4) His great fame (1 Ki. 10:7).
        (5) His great riches (1 Ki. 10:27).

17. Old Testament individuals who foreshadow New Testament individuals
    a. Elijah, foreshadowing John the Baptist (1 Ki. 17:1; 18:21; Mt. 17:10-13; Mk. 6:14-20).
    b. Abel, foreshadowing Stephen (Gen. 4:8; Acts 7:57, 58).
    c. Joshua and Zerubbabel, foreshadowing the two witnesses in the tribulation (Zech. 4; Rev. 11).

Valleys

1. Shaveh, south of Jerusalem, where Abraham met Melchizedek (Gen. 14:17, 18).

2. Gerar, where Isaac lived and dug his wells (Gen. 26:17, 18).

3. Eschol, where the twelve spies visited while checking out the land of Palestine (Num. 32:9).

4. Achor, near Jericho, where Achan was stoned (Josh. 7:24-26).

5. Aijalon, where Joshua worked his miracle with the sun (Josh. 10:12).

6. Hinnon, south of Jerusalem, where Ahaz and Manasseh offered up their own children to devil gods. God named the eternal lake of fire after this valley—Gehenna (2 Chron. 28:3; 33:6).

7. Jezreel, where the Midianite army, later defeated by Gideon, was encamped (Jdg. 6:33).

8. Sorek, where Delilah lived (Jdg. 16:4).

9. Elah, where David fought Goliath (1 Sam. 17:2; 21:9).

10. Rephaim, where David fought and defeated the Philistines (2 Sam. 5:22-25).

11. Salt, where Amaziah slew 10,000 Edomites (2 Ki. 14:7).

12. Berachah, where Jehoshaphat held a praise service (2 Chron. 20:26).

13. Megiddo
    a. Where Barak defeated Sisera (Jdg. 4:15; 5:19, 20).
    b. Where Jehu slew Ahaziah (2 Ki. 9:27).
    c. Where Josiah was killed (2 Ki. 23:29, 30).

14. Jehoshaphat, where the battle of Armageddon will be decided. This valley is known as the Kidron Valley in the New Testament (Joel 3:2, 12, 14).

15. Hamon-gog, where the defeated Russian troops will be buried (Ezek. 39:11).

Vessels, Pitchers, and Waterpots

1. Rebekah filled up a pitcher for Abraham's servant (Gen. 24:16).

2. Gideon used 300 pitchers to defeat the Midianites (Jdg. 7:16).

3. Peter and John followed a young man carrying a pitcher of water (Mk. 14:13).

4. Jesus filled some waterpots with wine at Cana (Jn. 2:6).

5. Jesus met a woman carrying a waterpot in Samaria (Jn. 4:28).

6. A widow saw God supernaturally create oil in her empty vessels (2 Ki. 4:3-7).

7. The vessels in the house of God
    a. In the tabernacle (Ex. 40:9; Heb. 9:21).
    b. In the Temple (2 Chron. 4:19).
    c. Taken by Nebuchadnezzar (Dan. 1:2; 2 Chron. 36:7).
    d. Desecrated by Belshazzar (Dan. 5:2, 3).
    e. Returned by Zerubbabel (Ezra 1:7-11).

8. The vessels carried by the ten virgins (Mt. 25:4).

9. The vessel that Peter saw in a vision (Acts 10:11).

10. The vessel belonging to the widow of Zarephath (1 Ki. 17:10).

11. The vessel made as Jeremiah watched (Jer. 18:4, 5).

12. The vessel Ezekiel used (Ezek. 4:9).

13. The vessel that Jeremiah broke (Jer. 19:10).

14. The vessel carried by Hagar (Gen. 21:14).

15. The old vessels carried by the Gibeonites (Josh. 9:13).

16. The vessel of milk given Sisera by Jael (Jdg. 4:19).

17. The vessel of wine used in the dedication of Samuel (1 Sam. 1:24).

18. The vessel of oil used in anointing Saul (1 Sam. 10:1).

19. The vessel of wine David carried to his brothers doing battle with the Philistines (1 Sam. 16:20).

20. Two vessels of wine sent to David by Abigail (1 Sam. 25:18).

21. Symbolic vessels
    a. Earthen vessels—the bodies of believers (2 Cor. 4:7).
    b. Weaker vessel—the believer's wife (1 Pet. 3:7).
    c. Vessels of honor—the saved. Also called vessels of mercy, of gold, and of silver (Rom. 9:21, 23; 2 Tim. 2:20, 21).
    d. Vessels of dishonor—the unsaved. Also called vessels of destruction, of wood, and of earth (Rom. 9:21, 22; 2 Tim. 2:20).

Vineyards

1. The vineyard planted by Noah (Gen. 9:20).
2. The vineyard of Naboth (1 Ki. 21:1).
3. The vineyard of Timnah where Samson killed a lion (Jdg. 14:5).
4. The vineyards of Shiloh, where the remaining 400 Benjaminite soldiers found wives (Jdg. 21:20).
5. Parabolic vineyards (Isa. 5:1-7; Mt. 20:1-16; 21:28-32, 33-41; Lk. 13:6-9).

Vows

1. The vow of Jacob at Bethel (Gen. 28:20).
2. The vow of the Nazarite (Num. 6:2, 21).
3. The vow of Jephthah concerning the offering of a sacrifice (Jdg. 11:30).
4. The vow of Hannah concerning a yet unborn child (1 Sam. 1:11).
5. The vow of Absalom, used to deceive David (2 Sam. 15:7).
6. The vow of Jezebel to kill Elijah (1 Ki. 19:1, 2).
7. The vow of Jonah inside the fish (Jonah 2:9).
8. The vow of Paul (Acts 18:18).
9. The vow of four men and Paul (Acts 21:23-26).
10. The vow of certain Jews to kill Paul (Acts 23:12).

Walls

1. The wall where the angel of the Lord trapped Balaam (Num. 22:24).
2. The walls of Jericho that fell (Josh. 6:20; Heb. 11:30).
3. The wall in Saul's palace where an attempt was made to kill David (1 Sam. 19:10).
4. The wall of Beth-shan where the Philistines fastened the body of Saul (1 Sam. 31:10).
5. The walls of Rabbah, where Uriah was killed by an enemy arrow (2 Sam. 11:24).
6. The wall of Abel, over which the head of Sheba was thrown (2 Sam. 20:21, 22).
7. The walls of Jerusalem
   a. Built by Solomon (1 Ki. 9:15).
   b. Destroyed by Nebuchadnezzar (2 Ki. 25:10).
   c. Rebuilt by Nehemiah (Neh. 2:17; 6:15).
8. A wall in Moab where the Moabite king sacrificed his own son (2 Ki. 3:27).
9. A wall in Samaria, where an Israelite king heard a horrible story (2 Ki. 6:26).
10. The wall in Damascus over which Paul escaped from a plot on his life (Acts 9:25; 2 Cor. 11:33).
11. The wall in the millennial temple (Ezek. 42:20).
12. The wall surrounding the new Jerusalem (Rev. 21:14-19).

Wars and Battles

1. Wars in Genesis—Abraham fought against a Mesopotamian king to rescue his nephew Lot (Gen. 14:1-16).
2. Wars of Israel en route to Canaan
   a. Victory over the Amalekites (Ex. 17:8-16).
   b. Defeat by the Amalekites (Num. 14:39-45).
   c. Victory over the southern Canaanites (Num. 21:1-4).
   d. Victory over the Amorites (Num. 21:21-31).
   e. Victory over the king of Bashan (Num. 21:33-35).
   f. Victory over the Midianites (Num. 31:6-12).
3. Wars of Israel in conquering Palestine
   a. Victory over Jericho (Josh. 6:1-27).
   b. Defeat by Ai (Josh. 7:1-5).
   c. Victory over Ai (Josh. 8:1-29).
   d. Victory over the king of Jerusalem and his four allies (Josh. 10:8-26).
   (These above victories made up the central campaign.)
   e. Victory over Libnah (Josh. 10:29, 30).
   f. Victory over Lachish (Josh. 10:31, 32).
   g. Victory over Gezer (Josh. 10:33).
   h. Victory over Eglon (Josh. 10:34, 35).
   i. Victory over Hebron (Josh. 10:36, 37).
   j. Victory over Debir (Josh. 10:38, 39).
   (The above victories were won during the southern campaign.)
   k. Victory over Jabin, king of Hazor and his allies, by the waters of Merom, north of the Galilean Sea (Josh. 11:1-15). (This victory made up the northern campaign.)
4. Wars during the period of the judges
   a. Othniel defeated the Mesopotamians (Jdg. 3:10).
   b. Ehud, over the Moabites (Jdg. 3:26-29).
   c. Shamgar, over the Philistines (Jdg. 3:31).
   d. Deborah and Barak, over the northern Canaanites (Jdg. 4:1-16).
   e. Gideon, over the Midianites (Jdg. 7:9-25).
   f. Abimelech, defeated by the citizens of Shechem (Jdg. 9:43-57).
   g. Jephthah, over the Ammonites (Jdg. 11:32, 33).
   h. Jephthah, over the tribe of Ephraim (Jdg. 12:1-6).
   i. Samson, over the Philistines (Jdg. 15:9-15).
   j. The tribe of Dan, over the city of Laish (Jdg. 18:27-29).
   k. Eleven tribes, over Benjamin (Jdg. 20:18-48).
   l. Israel, defeated by the Philistines (1 Sam. 4:1-22).
   m. Israel, over the Philistines (1 Sam. 5:7-14).
5. Wars during the United Kingdom period
   a. Saul, over the Ammonites (1 Sam. 11:1-11).
   b. Jonathan, over the Philistines (1 Sam. 13:5; 14:31).
   c. Saul, over the Amalekites (1 Sam. 15:7-9).
   d. David, over Goliath (1 Sam. 17).
   e. David, over the Philistines (1 Sam. 18:27).
   f. David and his 400 soldiers, over the Philistines (1 Sam. 18:27).
   g. David and his 600 men, over the Amalekites (1 Sam. 27:8; 30:1-20).
   h. Saul, defeated and killed by the Philistines (1 Sam. 31).
   i. The house of David, over the house of Saul (2 Sam. 3:1).
   j. David, over the Jebusites (2 Sam. 5:6-9).
   k. David, over the Philistines (2 Sam. 5:17-20).
   l. David, over the Philistines (2 Sam. 5:22-25).
   m. David, over Moab (2 Sam. 8:2).
   n. David, over Zobah (2 Sam. 8:3, 4).
   o. David, over Syria (2 Sam. 8:5, 6).
   p. David, over Ammon-Rabbah (2 Sam. 11:1; 12:26-31).
   q. David, over Absalom (2 Sam. 18:1-8).
   r. David, over Sheba (2 Sam. 20:1, 2, 14-22).
   s. David, over the Philistines (2 Sam. 21:15-22).
6. Wars during the Chaotic Kingdom period
   a. The civil wars between Israel's tribes.
      (1) The original revolt (1 Ki. 12:1-21).
      (2) Fighting between Rehoboam (southern king) and Jeroboam (northern king). See 1 Kings 15:6.
      (3) Fighting between Asa (southern king) and Baasha (northern king). See 1 Kings 15:16.

(4) Fighting between Amaziah (southern king) and Jehoash (northern king). See 2 Kings 14:8-14.

(5) Fighting between Ahaz (southern king) and Pekah (northern king). See 2 Kings 16:5; Isaiah 7:1-14.

b. Wars allowed by God to punish Judah's unfaithful rulers.

(1) Egypt, against Jerusalem in Rehoboam's reign (1 Ki. 14:25-28).

(2) The Philistines, against Joram (2 Chron. 21:16, 17).

(3) The Syrians, against Joash (2 Chron. 24:23, 24).

(4) Edom, against Ahaz (2 Chron. 27:16-19).

(5) Assyria, against Manasseh (2 Chron. 33:11).

c. Amaziah, over Edom (2 Chron. 25:5-13).

d. Uzziah, over the Philistines (2 Chron. 26:6, 7).

e. Ahab and Syria.

(1) First war—victory (1 Ki. 20:13-21).

(2) Second war—victory (1 Ki. 20:22-30).

(3) Third war—defeat and death of Ahab (1 Ki. 22:29-38).

f. Jehoshaphat and Jehoram, over Moab—with Elisha's help (2 Ki. 3:16-27).

g. Jehoram, over Syria—with Elisha's help (2 Ki. 6:8-23).

h. Four lepers, over the Syrian army (2 Ki. 6:24, 25; 7:3-11).

i. The war between Edom and Judah (2 Ki. 8:20-22).

j. The allied war of Ahaziah (southern king) and Joram (northern king) against Syria (2 Ki. 8:28, 29).

k. Syria, against Israel's eastern two-and-a-half tribes (2 Ki. 10:32, 33).

l. Assyria, against the northern kingdom (2 Ki. 15:29; 17:5, 6).

m. Assyria, against Damascus (2 Ki. 16:7-9).

n. God, against Assyria (2 Ki. 19:35).

o. Babylon, against Assyria (Nahum 2, 3).

p. Asa, against Ethiopia (2 Chron. 14:6-15).

q. Jehoshaphat, against the Ammonites and Moabites (2 Chron. 20:1-30).

r. Josiah, against the Egyptians (2 Ki. 23:29, 30).

s. Babylon, against the southern kingdom (2 Ki. 25:1-3).

7. Wars during the Babylonian captivity period

a. The battle of Carchemish, between Egypt and Babylon (Jer. 46:1-8). Babylon was victorious.

b. The battle between the Medo-Persians and Babylon (Dan. 5). Persia was victorious.

c. The battle between the Greeks and the Persians (Dan. 8). Greece was victorious. Note: This war was predicted by Daniel during the Babylonian captivity period, but would not take place historically until around 331 B.C.

8. Wars during the return period. The Persian Jews against their enemies (Est. 9).

9. Wars between Satan and God

a. The historical fall of Satan (Isa. 14:12-15; Ezek. 28:11-19).

b. The future casting of Satan out of heaven (Rev. 12:7-12).

c. The final revolt of Satan (Rev. 20:7-10).

10. Wars during the tribulation

a. The Russian invasion into Palestine (Ezek. 38, 39).

b. The battle of Armageddon (Rev. 14:14-20; 16:16; 19:11-21).

Weapons

1. Battering rams (Ezek. 4:2; 21:22; 26:9).
2. Battle ax, mace (Ps. 2:9; 35:3; Prov. 25:18; Ezek. 26:9).
3. Bows, arrows (Gen. 27:3; 2 Sam. 22:35).
4. Breastplate, coat of mail (1 Sam. 17:5, 38; Isa. 59:17; Eph. 6:14).
5. Girdle, belt (2 Sam. 20:8).
6. Greaves, leg protection (1 Sam. 17:6).
7. Helmet (1 Sam. 17:5; Isa. 59:17; Eph. 6:17).
8. Rock-throwing engines (2 Chron. 26:14, 15).
9. Sling (1 Sam. 17:40).
10. Shield (1 Sam. 17:7, 41; Eph. 6:16).
11. Spear, lance, javelin, dart (Josh. 8:18; Jdg. 5:8; 1 Sam. 18:11).
12. Sword (Gen. 27:40; Eph. 6:17).

Wells

1. In the Kadesh wilderness, where God spoke to Hagar (Gen. 16:14).
2. In the Paran wilderness, where he met her the second time (Gen. 21:19).
3. In Beer-sheba, where Abraham made a covenant with Abimelech (Gen. 21:30).
4. In the city of Nahor, where Abraham's servant discovered Rebekah (Gen. 24:11-20).
5. In the Valley of Gerar, as dug by Isaac (Gen. 26:17-22, 32).
6. In Haran, where Jacob met Rachel (Gen. 29:1-12).
7. In Midian, where Moses met Zipporah (Ex. 2:15-21).
8. In the wilderness, as dug by the Israelites (Num. 21:16-18).
9. In the village of Bahurim, where two of David's spies hid out from Absalom (2 Sam. 17:18, 19).
10. In Ramah, where Saul sought after David (1 Sam. 19:18-24).
11. In Sirah, where Joab met Abner (2 Sam. 3:26).
12. In Bethlehem, where David longed to drink (2 Sam. 23:15).
13. In Elim, where Israel drank from twelve wells en route to Mt. Sinai (Ex. 15:27).
14. In Samaria, where Jesus met the Samaritan woman (Jn. 4:6).

Windows

1. The window in the ark (Gen. 8:6).
2. The window through which Abimelech saw Isaac and Rebekah (Gen. 26:8).
3. The window of Rahab the harlot (Josh. 2:15, 18, 21).
4. The window of Michal in Gibeah, from which David escaped the wrath of Saul (1 Sam. 19:12).
5. The window of Michal in Jerusalem through which she viewed a celebration led by her husband David and later criticized him for it (2 Sam. 6:16).
6. The window in Jezreel from which Jezebel was thrown to her death (2 Ki. 9:30, 32).
7. Solomon's window, where he viewed a young man enticed by a harlot (Prov. 7:6).
8. Elisha's window, where he ordered a king to shoot an arrow (2 Ki. 13:17).
9. The eastern window of Daniel, which he opened during his prayer time as he knelt toward Jerusalem (Dan. 6:10).
10. The window in Troas by which Eutychus sat before he fell during Paul's message (Acts 20:9).
11. The window (opening) in the wall of Antioch through

which Paul escaped the plot of some Jews (2 Cor. 11:33).
12. Symbolic windows:
 a. The flood windows of heaven (Gen. 7:11; 8:2).
 b. The blessing windows of heaven (Mal. 3:10).

Windstorms

1. During Noah's flood (Gen. 8:1).
2. During the locust plague in Egypt (Ex. 10:13, 19).
3. During the Red Sea crossing (Ex. 14:21).
4. During the quail plague in the wilderness (Num. 11:31).
5. During the Mt. Carmel contest (1 Ki. 18:45).
6. During God's meeting with Elijah on Mt. Horeb (1 Ki. 19:11).
7. During the translation of Elijah (2 Ki. 2:11).
8. During Daniel's vision of the four beasts (Dan. 7:2).
9. During Jonah's sea trip (Jonah 1:4).
10. During Jonah's visit to Nineveh (Jonah 4:8).
11. As God talked with Job (Job 38:1).
12. As the disciples crossed the Sea of Galilee from west to east (Mt. 8:26).
13. As the disciples crossed the Sea of Galilee from east to west (Mt. 14:24).
14. During Pentecost (Acts 2:2).
15. During Paul's trip to Rome (Acts 27:14, 15).

THE SECOND COMING OF CHRIST (REV. 19)
One

THE RAPTURE OF THE CHURCH (1 THESS. 4)
Two

THE ASCENSION OF CHRIST (ACTS 2)
Three

THE RESURRECTION OF CHRIST (MT. 28)
Four

THE DEATH OF CHRIST (MT. 27)
Five

THE BIRTH OF CHRIST (LK. 2)
Six

THE COMPLETION OF THE NEW TESTAMENT (REV. 22)
Seven

THE COMPLETION OF THE OLD TESTAMENT (MAL. 4)
Eight

THE BIRTH OF THE CHURCH (ACTS 2)
Nine

THE BIRTH OF ISRAEL (GEN. 12)
Ten

THE CREATION OF MAN (GEN. 1, 2)
Eleven

THE CREATION OF THE WORLD (GEN. 1)
Twelve

The Twelve Greatest Days in History

Historical Study Summaries

Introduction to Nine Old Testament and New Testament Nations

Prior to the great flood there seemed to be no distinct and separate community of nations as we see today. But following the rebellion at Babel they came into existence, each with its own language and (perhaps at a later date) its unique cultural and racial peculiarities.

Of the many dozens of nations, nine have played (or will play) an important part in the historical and spiritual development of God's chosen nation, the people of Israel.

These nine are: The Canaanites, Sumerians, Philistines, Egyptians, Assyrians, Babylonians, Persians, Greeks, and Romans.

The first eight of this group have already played a historical role. The ninth (Rome) will assume a prophetical part (in addition to the historical role it has previously assumed), for its ancient empire will be revived and ruled over by the fearful antichrist.

Nine Old Testament and New Testament Nations

THE CANAANITES

I. Introduction.
 A. The word Canaanite is a general term for those people living in the Promised Land at the time of Israel's entrance led by Joshua. They would include the Phoenicians, Philistines, Ammonites, Hittites, Jebusites, Amorites, and Hivites.
 B. Many of these people were the descendants of Canaan, Ham's fourth son. (See Gen. 9:22-27; 10:6, 15-20.) The name Canaanite may well have come from him. However, some believe the land was called Canaan by the Phoenicians, who traveled there to secure a purple dye from the Murex shellfish. This trade became so well known that the Greeks referred to the entire area as Canaan, a Greek word meaning blood-red.
 C. Some of the early cities founded by the Canaanites were Gezer, Megiddo, Jericho, Sodom, Gomorrah, and Jerusalem.
 D. The abundance of the land can be seen through the testimony of an Egyptian refugee named Sinuhe who fled to Canaan around 1950 B.C. He writes:
 "It is a good land . . . figs and grapes are in it; it has more wine than water, it has much honey and olive oil in plenty; all fruits are upon its trees; limitless barley is there, and all kinds of herds and flocks."
 This statement should be compared with Exodus 3:8 and Deuteronomy 8:8.

 E. The Canaanites probably invented the alphabet. Theirs consisted of thirty-one alphabetic signs.
 F. The first recorded war in biblical history took place between four Mesopotamian kings and five Canaanite kings. (See Gen. 14.)
II. The Religion of the Canaanites.
 A. It may be stated without exaggeration that the Canaanite religion was the most sexually perverted, morally depraved, and bloodthirsty of all ancient history. It was for this reason that God ordered Joshua to exterminate their very culture, citizens, and cities. (See Deut. 7:1-5; 20:10-15; Josh. 9:24.)
 B. There are three primary sources proving the disgusting debauchery of the Canaanites.
 1. The Word of God. (See Gen. 13:13; 15:16; 18:20; 19:1-11; Num. 25:1-3; Jdg. 19:14-25; 1 Ki. 14:24; 15:12; 22:46; 2 Ki. 23:7.) These verses refer primarily to their sexual sins.
 2. The testimony of Philo of Byblos, a Phoenician scholar, who wrote around 100 B.C. He collected ancient religious materials from his homeland.
 3. The Ras Shamra literature of ancient Ugarit, found in A.D. 1929.
 C. The head god of the Canaanite religion was El. His wife was Asherah. He also married his three sisters, one of whom was Astarte. (See Jdg. 10:6.) El had seventy children, the most famous being Baal. El not only killed his brother, but also some of his own sons. He then cut off his daughter's head, castrated his father, castrated himself, and compelled his confederates to do the same.
 D. The sister of Baal (and daughter of El) was Anat. She became the vile and vicious goddess of passion, war, and violence. She fought Baal's enemies. The Baal-epic of Ugarit depicts her as follows:
 "With her might she mowed down the dwellers of the cities, she struck down the people of the sea-coasts, she destroyed the men of the east. She drove men into her temple and closed the doors so that no one could escape. She hurled chairs at the youths, tables at the warriors, footstools at the mighty men. She waded up to the knees, up to the neck in blood. Human heads lay at her feet, human hands flew over her like locusts. She tied the heads of her victims as ornaments upon her back, their hands she tied upon her belt. Her liver was swollen with laughing, her heart was full of joy. When she was satisfied she washed her hands in streams of human blood before turning again to other things."

E. The national god of the Canaanite Ammonites was Molech. (See 1 Ki. 11:5, 7.) An important rite in the worship of Molech was the sacrificial burning of children. Two Judean kings, Ahaz and Manasseh, abandoned the worship of Israel's true God and actually sacrificed their own children to this murderous Molech. (See 2 Ki. 16:3; 21:6.) Thus, the slaughtering of little ones became a common practice of the Canaanite religion. (See Ezek. 16:20, 21; 23:37.) In excavations at Gezer, an archaeologist named Macalister (1904-1909) found the ruins of a Canaanite temple. Inside he discovered hundreds of urns containing the bones of children from four to twelve years old who had been burned alive. Another horrible practice along this line was called "foundation sacrifice." This called for the slaughter of a child upon the construction of a house. Its body would then be stuffed into a wall to assume "good luck" to the remaining family.

F. Some reference has already been made to the sexual perversions of the Canaanites. Its priests were usually notorious homosexuals, and the priestesses common prostitutes. Cult figures, figurines, and other objects have been dug up, some of which are carved idols of human sex organs.

THE SUMERIANS

I. Rise of the Mesopotamian Cities and Peoples.

A. It is speculated that sometime prior to 3000 B.C., the events in Genesis 11 took place. Nimrod, Ham's grandson, led a rebellion against God by constructing the Tower of Babel.

B. After the language dispersion, various groups settled all over the Middle East.

C. By the year 3000 B.C., two groups of people had settled in Mesopotamia, a word meaning, "the land between the two rivers." These rivers are the Tigris and the Euphrates, both of which flow south into the Persian Gulf.

D. One group, called the Akkadians, lived in the upper valleys, and the other group, known as the Sumerians, occupied the lower valleys. This was known as the land of Sumer.

II. Political History of the Valleys.

A. Some of the more important cities of the southern area where the Sumerians lived were Eridu, Kish, Lagash, Larsa, Nippur, Umma, Ur, and Urak.

B. Between 2500-2300 B.C., the kings of Ur had made their city the ruling one over all of Sumer. They then invaded the Akkadians in the north.

C. Shortly after 2300 B.C., the story changed and the Sumerians were conquered by a powerful Akkadian ruler named Sargon.

D. According to tradition, as a baby Sargon was left to die in a basket on the Euphrates River. He was found by a gardener who raised him to become a soldier.

E. Sargon was a superb military leader, organizer, and administrator. He established the first recorded empire in history and united all of Mesopotamia.

F. His headquarters were in the city of Babylon. He ruled for fifty-six years. Sargon was a great lawgiver.

G. After his death, however, his children were unable to continue his strong rule. Sumer was then invaded and conquered by a group of barbarian mountain men from the north called the Gutians. They ruled for approximately 100 years (2170-2070 B.C.).

H. At this time the Sumerians rallied and drove out the Gutians. The new capital became the thriving seaport of Ur on the Persian Gulf. The greatest ruler of this era was a man called Dungi. He was an able administrator and compiled the Law Code of Dungi, which predated the Code of Hammurabi by some three centuries.

I. The Sumerian state ended around 2000 B.C. when some wandering eastern people called the Elamites invaded and conquered Sumer.

III. The Accomplishments of the Mesopotamians.

A. The Sumerians were excellent architects and builders. The city of Ur, for example, had a massive royal palace with huge staircases, large columns, and paneled walls. On these walls were beautiful paintings of humans and animals. The aristocrats lived in homes two stories high, which were built around a courtyard. They also knew how to construct a vault, arch, and a dome. One architectural form (later copied by the Egyptians for their pyramids) was the ziggurat. This was a temple tower with a platform built upon another platform, each one a little smaller than the last. It was probably patterned after the Tower of Babel.

B. They used gold and silver and possessed a knowledge of alloys, casting, and setting, which resulted in excellent metal work and jewelry.

C. Astronomy, mathematics, astrology, mapmaking, and surgery were taught in schools.

D. There were numerous songs, legends, and ballads written by the Sumerians. Among the most famous were *The Creation* and *The Epic of Gilgamesh.*

E. The Sumerians made great strides in mathematics, inventing a numerical system based on the unit of six. They multiplied, divided, and worked in fractions. They had a lunar calendar, with a year of 354 days.

F. The kings of ancient Sumeria made use of chariots and their troops were well organized, marching in compact units. They were armed with copper helmets and spears.

G. They were also very skillful in agriculture, raising great crops of grain, vegetables, and dates. They kept such domestic animals as cows, sheep, and goats. For plowing they made use of oxen while the donkeys pulled their carts and chariots. They also had a flourishing dairy industry.

H. The Sumerians were the earliest recorded people to write. They employed pictographic symbols, but later changed these symbols into conventional signs, writing them upon soft clay tablets with a stylus. The stylus had a triangular tip and made the strokes in the shape of a wedge. This writing later became known as cuneiform, that is, "wedge-shaped."

IV. The Religion of the Mesopotamians.

A. Religion dominated the lives of the people, as in other civilizations of ancient times.

B. There were gods for each city and town, and for each characteristic, or phase of nature. A complicated mythology was developed.
   1. Ishtar, the mother-goddess, was the goddess of love and fertility.
   2. Tammuz, the favorite son deity, was the god of spring, flowers, and grain; he also was god of the hereafter, where he lived half of the year, returning to earth each spring.
   3. During the Babylonian dynasty, Tammuz was replaced by a similar god, Marduk of the Amorites.
C. The Babylonians also worshiped heavenly bodies, which led to a study of astronomy and a strong belief in astrology.
D. There were sacrifices of all kinds, including human.
E. There were temples, altars, and schools run by the priests.
F. Omens, oracles, and magic played an important part in religion.
   1. Dreams were deemed important and were interpreted.
   2. The future was often foretold by reading the lines on the liver of a sheep bought for sacrificial purposes.

THE PHILISTINES
I. Introduction.
   A. These sea people settled in Palestine around 1200 B.C., having traveled from the Isle of Crete (Caphtor). (See Deut. 2:23; Jer. 47:4; Amos 9:7. They came from the line of Ham, through his second son Mizraim (1 Chron. 1:12). Because of this they were distantly related to the Egyptians.
   B. It is thought that, en route to Palestine, they may have destroyed the Hittites and the great ancient Syrian city of Ugarit. In 1190 B.C. they attempted to invade Egypt but were repulsed by Egyptian Pharaoh Ramses III. After this they settled on the upper coastline and gave Palestine its name.
   C. The Philistines formed a five-city league called the Pentapolis. This consisted of Gaza, Ashdod, Askelon, Ekron, and Gath. Each city was ruled by a lord.
   D. The Philistines were very religious, worshiping Dagon (the grain god), Ashtaroth (god of propagation), and Baal-zebub (god of habitation). (See 1 Sam. 5:4; 31:10; 2 Ki. 1:2.) Baal-zebub later became known as Beelzebub, meaning "the prince of demons" (Mt. 12:24). The Philistines celebrated their victories in the house of their idols (1 Sam. 31:9) and often carried their gods into battle (2 Sam. 5:21).
   E. The main reason for their early victories over Israel was their possession of the "atomic bomb" of the day, iron smelting. This they probably learned from the Hittites, who were the first to rediscover this method after the great flood. (See 1 Sam. 13:5, 19-22.)
   F. The Philistines were the "boozers" of their day, consuming great quantities of barley beer.
II. The Bible and the Philistines.
   A. Shamgar and Samson fought with them (Jdg. 3:31; 13:1; 15:20).
   B. Jonathan, Saul's son, defeated them (1 Sam. 14:1-47).
   C. They were eventually driven back to the coast by Samuel (1 Sam. 7:12-14).
   D. Saul lost to them and was killed in the battle (1 Sam. 31).
   E. David fought with them (1 Sam. 17; 2 Sam. 5).
   F. They were totally subjected by the time of Solomon (1 Ki. 4:21).

THE EGYPTIANS
I. Introduction.
   A. Egypt, like Mesopotamia, saw the rise of the earliest record of man (apart from the Bible). Egypt was protected on all sides by natural barriers. The sea on the north and deserts on the south, east, and west had to be crossed by any would-be enemy.
   B. Egyptian civilization is really a gift from the Nile River. The longest river in the world (4037 miles), it starts at Lake Victoria in North Africa and flows north, ending in the Mediterranean Sea.
   C. The Nile winds make two-way navigation on the river easy. Ships going north would simply drift downstream, while those vessels headed south would raise their sails and be pushed against the up-river current.
   D. Because of the lay of the land, upper Egypt is really in the south (being higher) and lower Egypt is located north at the delta, where the river parts into seven currents and pours into the sea.
   E. The rulers of upper Egypt (south) wore a white crown, while those of lower Egypt (north) wore a red crown.
II. The Dynasties of Egypt. The period from 3300 B.C. to the reign of Alexander the Great (330 B.C.) was divided politically into thirty dynasties by Manetho, a historian of the third century B.C.
III. A Basic Outline of Egypt's History.
   A. Early dynastic period—3000-2700 B.C. Dynasty 1 and 2. Capital at Memphis—biblical Noph (Isa. 19:13; Jer. 2:16; 46:14, 19; Ezek. 30:13, 16). Note: A ruler named Menes was the first king of the thirty dynasties. It is thought that he was the Mizraim of Genesis 10:6. Mizraim was the second son of Ham.
   B. Old kingdom—2700-2200 B.C. Dynasty 3 to 6. During this time the great pyramids were constructed.
   C. First intermediary period—2200-2000 B.C. Dynasty 7 to 10.
   D. Middle kingdom—2000-1800 B.C. Dynasty 11 and 12. Capital moved to Thebes (biblical No) (Jer. 46:25; Ezek. 30:14-16; Nahum 3:8). This was the time of the artistic decorations of the tombs.
   E. Second intermediary period—1800-1600 B.C. Dynasty 13 to 17. The Hyksos, Asian overlords, ruled from 1674-1567 B.C., during the fifteenth to seventeenth dynasties.
   F. New kingdom—1600-1100 B.C. Dynasty 18 to 20. The age of Egypt's supreme power and wealth. During this time the children of Israel were in Egypt and the Exodus took place.
   G. Post-empire period—1100-300 B.C. Dynasty 21 to 30. During dynasty twenty-two Shishak ruled (1 Ki. 11:40; 14:25-27; 2 Chron. 12:2-12). During

dynasty twenty-six, Pharaoh Necho ruled (2 Ki. 23:28-30, 33-35; 2 Chron. 35:20-24; 36:4; Jer. 46:2). Persian rule—525-332 B.C. Ptolemaic period—300-30 B.C. Alexander the Great—332-323 B.C. Ptolemy I-XII—304-51 B.C. Cleopatra—51-30 B.C. Of these seven periods, the most important events transpired during the old, middle, and new kingdoms.

IV. A Brief History of Important Events.

  A. The old kingdom (2700-2200 B.C.). Includes dynasties 3-6.

    1. The first pyramid was built by Pharaoh Zoser. It was probably copied and improvised upon from the ziggurats of Mesopotamia. Zoser was of the third dynasty.

    2. Pharaoh Khufu (also called Cheops) of the fourth dynasty ordered the construction of the great pyramid. The Greeks considered this pyramid one of the seven wonders of the ancient world. It took some 100,000 men over twenty years to complete it. The base of the pyramid is 755 feet; limestone blocks, each weighing two-and-a-half tons, were used.

    3. The great Sphinx was built for Pharaoh Khafre (son of Khufu), also of the fourth dynasty. It had a lion's body and a Pharaoh's head. The body is 240 feet long and 66 feet high. Its face is thirteen feet wide.

    4. Pepi II, of the sixth dynasty, was the final and most powerful king of the old kingdom. He ruled for more than ninety years. Shortly after his death, the old kingdom came to an end.

      For the next 200 years (2200-2000 B.C.) there was political chaos in Egypt as one invader after another crossed the deserts and disrupted life. Irrigation and building projects fell into ruin and civil war raged as three ambitious families tried to set up their own government. This is sometimes called the feudal age, and consisted of dynasties 7-10. The patriarch Abraham visited Egypt during this period (Gen. 12:10-20) around 2085 B.C.

  B. The middle kingdom (2000-1800 B.C.). Includes dynasties 11, 12.

    1. Pharaoh Amenhotep I, of the eleventh dynasty, reunited Egypt. He and his successors began rebuilding the country and developing world trade.

    2. It was during the final part of the middle kingdom period, around 1897 B.C., that Joseph was sold into Egyptian slavery (Gen. 37) and Jacob, his father, moved to Egypt (Gen. 46) in 1875 B.C.

      Similar conditions of turmoil and warfare which had marked the last years of the old kingdom prevailed during the final period of the middle kingdom. Shortly after 1700 B.C., a group of invaders called the Hyksos (shepherd kings) moved into the Delta from Syria and Asia and conquered northern (lower) Egypt.

      The Hyksos had war chariots pulled by horses. They used two-edged daggers and swords. The bows were of a powerful double-curved nature and shot bronze-tipped arrows. The Egyptians, untrained and almost unarmed, were no match for them. The Hyksos stopped all work on the pyramids, introduced new gods, and attempted to simplify the Egyptian language.

      The total time period of this second intermediary period would be from 1800-1600 B.C., covering dynasties 13-17. It is thought by some (but not all) that the Hebrew oppression in Egypt began at this time (Ex. 1) around 1730 B.C. In 1580 a rebellion led by Egyptian soldier Ahmose I successfully drove out the hated Hyksos invaders.

  C. The new kingdom (1600-1100 B.C.). Includes dynasties 18-20.

    1. Ahmose I and his successors spent much of their time rebuilding Egypt. An intense spirit of nationalism prevailed. Many believe it was during this time and for these reasons (need for cheap labor and suspicion of all foreigners) that the Hebrew oppression in Egypt began. Thus, all the Pharaohs mentioned in the book of Exodus would come from the famous eighteenth dynasty. Consider:

      a. The "new king" who "knew not Joseph" of Exodus 1:8, would be Thutmose I (1539-1520 B.C.). Moses was born in 1525 B.C.

      b. The "daughter of Pharaoh" of Exodus 2:5 was Hatshepsut, who raised Moses and took over the throne of Egypt when her husband Thutmose II died.

      c. The pharaoh who sought to kill Moses of Exodus 2:15 was Thutmose III, step-son of Hatshepsut, who bitterly hated the queen and deposed her. Upon his coming to power, Moses, a friend of Hatshepsut, would naturally suffer Thutmose III's wrath also.

      d. The pharaoh during the ten plagues of Exodus 5:1 was Amenhotep II. This pharaoh's tomb was never finished. This may be explained in Exodus 14:8-31 where we are told Pharaoh and his armies perished in the Red Sea crossing attempt. Furthermore, his son never ruled over Egypt. Again, Exodus 12:29 may account for this, as we are told the pharaoh lost a child in the Passover death plague.

    2. The more important rulers during this period belonged to the famous eighteenth dynasty. Some have already been mentioned. A few from the new kingdom period are:

      a. Ahmose I. The first ruler of the eighteenth dynasty, and one who helped drive out the Hyskos, thus reuniting Egypt.

      b. Hatshepsut. The one who raised Moses and first queen to assume the godship with the kingship of Egypt. She wore a double crown and false beard.

      c. Thutmose III. The step-son of Hatshepsut who hated her with a passion and was finally able to depose her. Thutmose III was one of the greatest of all Egyptian pharaohs. He is called the Alexander the

Great and Napoleon of Egypt. His empire stretched from the Sudan to northern Syria. He was pharaoh when Moses fled Egypt at age forty. He left Egypt so secure that it remained the greatest power of its time for many decades.

d. Amenhotep II. The pharaoh of the ten plagues.

e. Amenhotep III. The Egyptian empire reached its zenith during his reign. He was called Amenhotep III the Magnificent.

f. Amenhotep IV. He is better known as Akhnaton, and attempted to change the polytheistic religion of Egypt to worship of the sun god, Aton. He may have been influenced by the power of the true God which was demonstrated during the ten plagues.

Amenhotep IV married a beautiful woman named Nefertiti. Many paintings and statues have been found of this couple. It is interesting to note that ancient records have been unearthed (the El-Amarna tablets found in A.D. 1880) which include urgent messages from certain Canaanite kings in Palestine to Amenhotep IV for Egyptian help in repulsing a group of invading people called the Hapirus. It is thought by some (but many would disagree) that the Hapirus were in reality the Hebrews as led by Joshua.

g. Tutankhaton. He was the son-in-law of Amenhotep IV. In A.D. 1922 his tomb was discovered by Howard Carter. The tomb contained over $100,000 in gold alone. Tutankhaton's mummy had been placed inside three golden cases and put in a stone sarcophagus. The coffin was then enclosed in four gilded wooden outer cases. He began ruling at age ten in 1361 B.C. and died at nineteen.

h. Ramses II. He was the last powerful Pharaoh and one of the most boastful, ruling for some sixty-seven years. He signed the first recorded treaty in history (around 1250 B.C.) with the Hittites.

i. Ramses III. He is remembered for defeating the Philistines in a pitched sea battle in 1190 B.C.

From this point on it was downhill all the way for Egypt. The only other important Pharaoh in biblical history was Necho II of the twenty-sixth dynasty. He killed the godly Judean king, Josiah (2 Ki. 23:29), and was soundly defeated by the Babylonians at the battle of Carchemish in 605 B.C. (Jer. 46:2).

THE BABYLONIANS

I. Introduction.

A. Between the years 2000–1800 B.C., Mesopotamia was controlled by an eastern group of people called the Elamites. (See Gen. 10:22; 14:1, 9.) They are commonly known to us today as the Persians.

B. In 1760 B.C. the Elamites were driven out of Mesopotamia by a people living west of the Eu-

phrates, called the Amorites. The victorious Amorite general who led this invasion was named Hammurabi. With him began the old Babylonian kingdom. After his death it would almost immediately disintegrate, and remain in pieces for nearly 1000 years until the coming of a Chaldean soldier named Nebuchadnezzar, who would establish the new (and second) Babylonian kingdom.

II. The Old Babylonian Kingdom.

A. In 1760 Hammurabi conquered the Tigris-Euphrates Valley and made the city of Babylon on the Euphrates his capital.

B. The chief Babylonian god was Marduk. Hammurabi claimed he was Marduk's representative on earth, thus establishing the divine right of kings to rule.

C. He is known not only as the founder of the Babylonian Empire, but also for the Code of Hammurabi. This included a set of laws, some 300 in number, which controlled the social, political, and economic aspects of Babylonian life. Hammurabi did not invent these laws, but simply codified and summarized what had already been given by a former Sumerian lawgiver named Dungi, some 300 years previous.

D. The old Babylonian empire prospered all during his reign. Finally, after ruling for forty-two years, he died. Shortly after his death in 1708 B.C., a group of warriors from Asia Minor called the Hittites conquered Mesopotamia and the old Babylonian kingdom was no more. The Hittites were the descendants of Heth. (See Gen. 10:15; 23:3–20; 27:46.)

E. For approximately 170 years the Hittites controlled the Babylonian kingdom area. Finally, in 1530 B.C., they were subdued by the Kassites, a people living in northern Mesopotamia. (See Gen. 2:13; 10:8.) They controlled the area for nearly 400 years, being themselves finally driven out by the Assyrians and the Elamites.

III. The New Babylonian Kingdom.

A. Around 620 B.C. a group of people known as the Chaldeans rebuilt the city of Babylon, which had been burned to the ground by the Assyrians in 721 B.C. After the citizens had attempted a revolt, the Chaldeans came from the southern end of Mesopotamia, and were led by a man named Nabopolassar. He then became governor of the city of Babylon. Shortly after this he arranged for his son to be married to the daughter of the king of Media, who ruled a power structure north of Mesopotamia. In 612 B.C. Nabopolassar's famous son, Nebuchadnezzar, led an allied attack of Babylonians and Medes against Nineveh, the capital city of Assyria.

B. The revolt was successful, thus giving birth to the new Babylonian kingdom.

C. In 606 B.C. Nebuchadnezzar defeated the remaining challenger, Egypt, at the famous battle of Carchemish. Nebuchadnezzar pursued the fleeing Egyptians as far west as Jerusalem. His first visit to Jerusalem was short, for he hurried home on August 15, 605 B.C., because of the sudden death of his father. But before he finished, he would lay siege to the Holy City on at least three occasions and ultimately burn it to the ground. These occasions were:

1. 605 B.C. He occupied the city, allowed Jehoiakim (Josiah's son) to rule as his puppet king, took some of the Temple treasures and key royal descendants to Babylon. Among this group of teenagers were Daniel and his three friends (2 Chron. 36:6, 7; Dan. 1:1-3).

2. 597 B.C. He came again and took the rest of the treasures to Babylon along with Ezekiel the prophet, King Jehoiachin (Jehoiakim's son), and 10,000 princes, officers, and chief men (2 Ki. 24:14-16). This occurred on March 16, 597.

3. 586 B.C. He returned once more to punish the rebellion led by Zedekiah, Judah's last king. This time the walls were broken, the Temple destroyed, and the city burned. Zedekiah's sons were killed and he himself was blinded and carried into Babylon where he would die. He then began the extensive improvement of the city of Babylon. (See Dan. 4.) It became the capital of his kingdom. The walls around the city were 300 feet high, and eighty-five feet thick. They were built as a square, with each side nine miles long. The area inside occupied some 200 square miles—about the size of New York City today.

Babylon was founded by Nimrod, the great-grandson of Noah (Gen. 10:8-10). Surviving a series of conflicts, it became one of the most magnificent and luxurious cities in the known world. Superbly constructed, it spread over an area of fifteen square miles, the Euphrates River flowing diagonally across the city. The famous historian Herodotus said the city was surrounded by a wall 350 feet high and eighty-seven feet thick—extending thirty-five feet below the ground to prevent tunneling, and wide enough for six chariots to drive abreast. Around the top of the wall were 250 watchtowers placed in strategic locations. Outside the huge wall was a large ditch, or moat, which surrounded the city and was kept filled with water from the Euphrates River. The large ditch was meant to serve as an additional protection against attacking enemies, for any attacking enemy would have to cross this body of water before approaching the great wall. Within this wall were one hundred gates of brass.

But in addition to being a bastion for protection, Babylon was a place of beauty. The famous hanging gardens of Babylon are still on record today as one of the seven wonders of the world. Arranged in an area 400 feet square, and raised in perfectly cut terraces one above the other, they soared to a height of 350 feet. Viewers could make their way to the top by means of stairways which were ten feet wide. From a distance these hanging gardens presented an imposing sight. The tower itself sat on a base 300 feet in breadth and rose to a height of 300 feet. The great temple of Marduk, adjoining the Tower of Babel, was the most renowned sanctuary in all the Euphrates Valley. It contained a golden image of Bel and a golden table which together weighed not less than 50,000 pounds. At the top were golden images of Bel and Ishtar, two golden lions, a golden table forty feet long and fifteen feet wide, and a human figure of solid gold, eighteen feet high. Babylon was literally a city of gold. (See Isa. 14:4.) The city had fifty-three temples and 180 altars to Ishtar.

D. Nebuchadnezzar died in 562 B.C.

E. After several brief reigns by weak men, Nebuchadnezzar was succeeded by Nabonidus, who had married Nebuchadnezzar's daughter. He ruled from 556-539 B.C. After becoming weary of the crown, he left the city of Babylon in control of his son, Belshazzar, and retired to the east, to become the first archaeologist recorded in history.

F. On October 13, 539 B.C., the city of Babylon was taken by the allied forces of the Medes and Persians. Belshazzar was slain and the new Babylonian kingdom was no more. (See Dan. 5.)

G. The Babylonians excelled in astronomy (a scientific study of the stars and planets) and astrology (a religious interpretation of that study). They also were great builders. Nebuchadnezzar built the famous hanging gardens to satisfy his homesick wife, Ametis, who often longed for the mountains of her native land, Media. His own palace covered seven acres. The banquet hall alone was 171 feet long by sixty-five feet wide—over 11,000 square feet.

THE ASSYRIANS

I. Introduction.

A. Without doubt the cruelest people in ancient history, and among the cruelest that ever lived, were the Assyrians. They conquered and ruled by sheer brute terror. They took over Mesopotamia around 1200 B.C.

B. They instituted the method of depopulating a subdued enemy nation. The citizens of a defeated country would thus be carried from their homeland to Assyria as slaves. Their land would then become available for homesteading to those foreigners who desired to live there.

C. The Assyrians developed the science of siege warfare, whereby battering rams and other equipment were used in destroying enemy walls and fortifications.

D. They also were the founders of the "pony express" system. Through this ancient "postal system" the king was kept in close touch with his governors.

E. They built temples and palaces with massive gateways, stairs, towers, and arches. Huge palaces were constructed for their kings. The home of Sargon II at Khorsabad occupied twenty-five acres, with over 200 large rooms, and housed 80,000 guests.

F. The capital and most important city of Assyria was Nineveh. Nineveh lay on the eastern side of the Tigris, and was one of the greatest—if not the greatest—of the cities of antiquity. It had

1,200 towers, each 200 feet high, and its wall was 100 feet high, and of such breadth that three chariots could drive on it abreast. It was sixty miles in circumference, and could, within its walls, grow corn enough for its population of 600,000. Zenophon says the basement of its wall was of polished stone, and its width fifty feet. In the city was a magnificent palace, with courts and walls covering more than 100 acres. The roofs were supported by beams of cedar, resting on columns of cypress, inlaid and strengthened by bands of sculptured silver and iron; its gates were guarded by huge lions and bulls sculptured in stone; its doors were of ebony and cypress encrusted with iron, silver, and ivory, and paneling the rooms were sculptured slabs of alabaster, and cylinders and bricks with cuneiform inscriptions. Hanging gardens were filled with rich plants and rare animals, and served with other temples and palaces, libraries and arsenals, to adorn and enrich the city; and all was built by the labor of foreign slaves.

II. Important Assyrian Kings.
   A. Tiglath-pileser I (1114–1076 B.C.). He was one of the earliest powerful kings. He called himself ruler of the earth and claimed to have personally killed four huge buffalo, ten elephants, and 120 lions.
   B. Ashur-nasir-pal (883–859). The great foreign expansion invasions began with this king.
   C. Shalmaneser III (858–824). He is not known in the Bible, but his records tell us that King Ahab was involved in a war with him. He was the son of Ashur-nasirpal.
   D. Tiglath-pileser III (746–728). This Assyrian general usurped the throne and revived the empire which had degenerated for some eighty years after the death of Shalmaneser III. He is often referred to in the Bible (2 Ki. 15:29; 16:7, 10). At a time of dispute between Israel and Judah, the king of Judah foolishly called on him for help. Soon after, Tiglath-pileser invaded Israel and carried off many of the citizens of the two-and-a-half tribes living east of Jordan (2 Ki. 15:29, 30). This Assyrian king really developed the army into a world-famous fighting machine.
   E. Shalmaneser V (727–722). He captured and imprisoned Hoshea, the last northern king of Israel (2 Ki. 17:1–6), and died while laying siege to Samaria.
   F. Sargon II (721–705). He was Shalmaneser's general who finished the sacking of Samaria. He is mentioned in Isaiah 20:1. Sargon was later assassinated.
   G. Sennacherib (705–681). He was the able son of Sargon II. At the time of his father's death, Sennacherib was governor of the city of Babylon. He later destroyed Babylon for their attempt to rebel. Sargon II surrounded Jerusalem in 701 B.C. and demanded that King Hezekiah surrender. But God saved the city by sending his death angel, who slew 185,000 Assyrian troops (2 Ki. 18–19; 2 Chron. 32; Isa. 36–37. Sennacherib was later himself murdered by one of his own sons.
   H. Esarhaddon (681–669). He rebuilt Babylon, which had been destroyed by Sennacherib his father. Esarhaddon was a great king and may have been the one who imprisoned the Judean king, Manasseh, in Babylon for awhile (2 Chron. 33).
   I. Ashurbanipal (668–626). He allowed various foreigners to move into the depopulated northern kingdom territory and homestead the land. This was the beginning of the Samaritan race (2 Ki. 17:24). He was the last powerful Assyrian king. The empire survived only fifteen years after his death. The capital city of Nineveh fell in 612 B.C. History tells us that Nabopolassar, king of the Babylonian invasion forces, besieged the city for three years, leading three massive attacks against it, and failing each time. Because of this, the Assyrians inside Nineveh rejoiced and began holding drunken parties. But suddenly the Tigris River overflowed its banks and sent its wildly churning waters against the walls of the city. Soon it had washed a hole, into which rushed Babylonians, and the proud city was destroyed.

The destruction of Nineveh was so great that Alexander the Great marched his troops over the same desolate ground which had once given support to her mighty buildings and did not even know there had once been a city there. The city itself was not excavated until as recently as A.D. 1845.

THE PERSIANS
   I. Introduction.
      A. For some 220 years (550 to 330 B.C.) the Persians ruled what was at that time the most extensive empire in history.
      B. They established one of the best systems of government and developed the largest political systems known until the Roman Empire. Their kingdom was divided into twenty-one provinces called satrapies. The superior justice of their code of law was also seen, in that even kings were subjected to it.
      C. Their two main capitals were Susa and Persepolis.
      D. Like the Assyrians before them, the Persians made great usage of the "pony express" system, stationing horses each fourteen miles. In this manner important news could reach the king from the outposts of the empire in less than ten days.
      E. Many believe the Persian palaces were the most beautiful ever built.
      F. The main Persian teacher was Zoroaster, born around 600 B.C. He developed a system of dualism, consisting of good (demonstrated by light) and evil (illustrated by darkness). Zoroaster taught (in crude form) the bliss of heaven for the righteous, and the sufferings of hell for the wicked. He also taught future judgment. Although a pagan, and much in error, Zoroaster was apparently the first unsaved man after the great flood to found a world religion which included these biblical concepts.
      The Persians were also remarkably tolerant in allowing those peoples conquered by them to continue their various religious worship systems.
      G. The Persians were great lovers of dogs. In no other ancient civilization has this noble animal fared so well. It was believed a stare from a dog

could frighten off a demon. To strike a dog was a crime and to neglect a puppy was as serious as neglecting a human baby.

II. A Brief Chronological History of Persia.

A. By 550 B.C. a Persian general had subdued the Medes and united them into a top fighting force with the Persians. Prior to this time they had been dominated by that nation.

B. The name of this Persian was Cyrus the Great, one of the most important men ever to live. In 547 B.C. he conquered Croesus, the fabulously rich king of Lydia (that land between the Mediterranean and the Black Sea). Cyrus used camel troops to accomplish this.

C. After this he conquered all those territories as far east as the Indian borders. He finally turned to Babylon. In 536 B.C. he took the city of Babylon and had Belshazzar executed. (See Dan. 5.)

D. Cyrus then allowed the Jewish remnant to return to Jerusalem a few years later. (See Ezra 1.) He died in battle in 529 B.C. Cyrus is mentioned often in the Bible. (See Ezra 1-5; Isa. 44:28; 45:1; Dan. 1:21; 6:28; 10:1.)

E. He was succeeded by his son Cambyses II (529-522) who conquered Egypt. The Temple rebuilding in Jerusalem was stopped for awhile by royal order during his reign. (See Ezra 4:7, 11.) Cambyses committed suicide while learning of a revolt against him.

F. Darius the Great (522-486) took over and saved the crumbling empire by restoring law and order. Darius was very cruel. When the city of Babylon attempted a revolt, he crucified 3000 of its leading citizens. He did, however, allow the temple work (that Cambyses had stopped) to continue (see Ezra 6:1-12).

In 490 B.C., Darius the Great led a huge fleet of 600 ships carrying some 60,000 Persian crack cavalry and foot soldiers to capture Athens and subdue the Greek civilization. But he was soundly defeated on a small plain called Marathon by the brilliant Greek general, Miltiades. In spite of the vastly numerical superiority of the Persians, the Greeks outcircled their foes and cut them down like overripe wheat. The battle of Marathon is listed as number six in the book, *History's 100 Greatest Events*, by William A. De-Witt.

G. Xerxes (486-465), the son of Darius, then reigned. He was the King Ahasuerus of the book of Esther. In the spring of 480 B.C., Xerxes crossed the Dardanelles with over 100,00 men and hundreds of ships. History tells us Xerxes wept while watching the dazzling display of his smartly marching armies, all carrying their brightly colored flags and banners. When asked why he wept, the king replied, "Because I know all this military glory is but for a moment and will soon fade away forever. Because in much less than one hundred years from now every man present here today will have died, myself included." Disaster struck soon after, for he lost 400 ships in a severe spring storm at sea. In blind frustration and anger, Xerxes beat upon the stormy waters with his belt.

Upon landing in Greece, his proud Persian troops were stopped for an entire day at the mountainous pass called Thermopylae. Here, a Greek captain named Leonidas and his 300 brave Spartan soldiers held back the entire invading army for twenty-four hours, inflicting great losses on them, and allowing the much smaller Greek army to carry out an orderly retreat to safety. Xerxes eventually broke through and burned Athens to the ground. But most of its citizens had escaped to the island of Salamis. The king then set sail for Salamis, confident of victory, for he outnumbered his enemy at least three to one. But the smaller and swifter Greek fighting boats had mastered the art of ramming. Soon, before his horrified eyes, Xerxes viewed the slaughter of his proud navy.

He left for Persia a defeated man. The remaining troops were put under the command of General Nardonius. One year later, Nardonius was defeated and killed in a pitched battle at Plataea in 479 B.C. The Persian Empire was then dealt the final death blow. J. F. C. Fuller's well-known book, *The Decisive Battles of the Western World*, lists the battles at Salamis and Plataea among the most important in recorded history.

H. Artaxerxes (465-423), was the son of Xerxes I and the king in the time of both Ezra (Ezra 7:1) and Nehemiah (Neh. 2:1).

I. Darius III (335-331 B.C.). The Persian Empire was destroyed during his short reign, by Alexander the Great.

THE GREEKS

I. Background.

A. From 546-479 B.C. the Greek states were constantly threatened by Persian invasions. But this all ended after the victorious battles of Salamis and Plataea.

B. Shortly after these battles, Greece entered its Golden Age, led by an Athenian democratic leader named Pericles (461-429 B.C.). A number of its citizens would become some of the most famous who ever lived.

1. Herodotus (485-425), the father of history.
2. Hippocrates (460-370), the father of modern medicine.
3. Socrates (469-399), philosopher.
4. Plato (427-347), philosopher.
5. Aristotle (384-322), philosopher.
6. Demosthenes (385-322), one of history's greatest composers of oration.

C. However, the Golden Era was short-lived, for two of the leading Greek city states, Sparta and Athens, began fighting among themselves. Their three armed conflicts are known as the Peloponnesian wars (from 459-404 B.C.). Sparta came out ahead after these wars.

II. The Rise of Alexander the Great.

A. In 338 B.C., a man from Macedonia conquered Greece. He was assassinated two years later, in 336 B.C. His name was Philip of Macedon (380-336 B.C.).

B. Philip was succeeded by his son, Alexander the Great, who would soon become one of the world's most famous conquerors. He was twenty at the time. He immediately prepared to carry out his father's orders to invade Persia.

C. In 334 B.C. he crossed the Hellespont (which separated Asia Minor from the Middle East).
   1. He defeated the Persians at Granicus in 334 B.C.
   2. He routed them again at Issus in 333 B.C.
   3. He destroyed Tyre, spared Jerusalem, and was welcomed by Egypt. Here he founded the city of Alexandria.
   4. He forever crushed the Persians at Arbela in 331 B.C.
D. In 327 he invaded India. At this time he also laid plans to rebuild the city of Babylon to its former glory. But in India he died in 323 B.C. at the age of thirty-two.
E. His mighty empire was soon divided by his four generals.
   1. Ptolemy—who ruled Egypt. Cleopatra came from this line.
   2. Seleucus—who took Syria. From Syria came the notorious Antiochus Epiphanes IV (176-163 B.C.).
   3. Cassander—who took Greece and Macedonia.
   4. Lysimachus—who ruled Asia Minor.

THE ROMANS
I. The Making of the Roman Empire.
   A. The traditional date for the founding of Rome is April 21, 753 B.C. Cicero says the name came from its founder, Romulus. He ruled for thirty-nine years and then mysteriously disappeared, having supposedly been taken up into heaven.
   B. By the year 338 B.C., Rome controlled central Italy.
   C. Then came the historic Punic Wars between Rome and Carthage, with the latter being destroyed in 146 B.C.
      1. First war (264-241 B.C.).
      2. Second war (218-202 B.C.). Hannibal appeared during this war. He terrified the Romans when he marched a herd of elephants over the Alps in 218 B.C. and defeated two large Roman armies. He also routed his enemy at Cannae in 216 B.C. Finally a Roman general named Scipio defeated Hannibal at Zama in 202 B.C. Rome then became the mistress of the Mediterranean.
      3. Third war (149-146). The city of Carthage was taken and burned.
   D. Pompey, the famous Roman general, conquered Palestine in 63 B.C. This was followed by a period of civil wars and uncertainty.
   E. The empire was then saved and consolidated by Julius Caesar during his famous Gallic wars (58-51 B.C.). On the Ides of March 44, B.C., Caesar was assassinated in Rome.
II. History from New Testament Times to the End of the Roman Empire.
   A. The empire was then taken over by Octavius (also known as Augustus) Caesar. He defeated Brutus and Cassius (two of the rebels who murdered Julius Caesar) at Philippi in 42 B.C. In 31 B.C. Octavius defeated the forces of Anthony and Cleopatra at Actium, and made Egypt into a Roman province. The Roman Empire now entered its zenith of power and glory. It was during Octa-

vius' rule that our Lord was born (Lk. 2:1). Octavius ruled from 31 B.C. to A.D. 14.
   B. Octavius was succeeded by Tiberius Caesar (A.D. 14-37). The ministries of both John the Baptist and the Savior took place at this time.
   C. Caligula (A.D. 37-41), also known as Little Boots. He became a ruthless maniac and was assassinated. Caligula was in power during the early part of the book of Acts.
   D. Claudius (41-54). He was poisoned by his own wife. Paul conducted his great missionary trips during his reign.
   E. Nero (54-68). After a normal eight-year reign, Nero degenerated into an insane monster. He had Rome burned and murdered many Christians by falsely blaming them for the fire. Peter and Paul were martyred during his reign. In A.D. 68 Nero committed suicide.
   F. The Roman general Vespasian (68-79) became ruler. He ordered his son Titus to destroy Jerusalem. This was done in A.D. 70.
   G. Upon his death, Titus took the throne. He ruled from A.D. 79-81. During his rule, Pompeii was destroyed by Mt. Vesuvius.
   H. In A.D. 81, Domitian ascended to power. He banished John the apostle to the Isle of Patmos (Rev. 1:9).
   I. The ten or more Roman emperors had one thing in common—they all hated Christians!
   J. Finally, in A.D. 284, Diocletian came into power. His reign is known as the last one to persecute believers, but also the most ruthless. Diocletian separated the Eastern empire from the West and appointed a man named Maximian to rule the eastern part. In 305 he resigned.
   K. When Diocletian left the throne, two men immediately began contending for it. One was the son of Maximian, and the other was Constantine. The issue as to who would rule Rome was settled in A.D. 312, just outside the city, at a place called Milvian Bridge. Here Constantine soundly defeated his rival to power.
   L. In 313 Constantine issued the famous Edict of Toleration, which in effect made Christianity his state religion. He also presided over the Council of Nicaea in 325.
   M. Julian the apostate, the nephew of Constantine, became ruler after the death of his uncle. He attempted to replace Christianity but failed. His dying words on a battlefield in 363 were: "Oh Galilean, thou hast conquered at last!"
   N. Theodosius the Great (378-395), a champion of Christianity, once more divided the empire into Eastern and Western sections, as Diocletian had previously done.
   O. During the years 450-455, Attila the Hun and the vandals plundered Italy and Rome.
   P. In 476 Romulus Augustulus, the last Roman emperor, was dethroned.

Introduction to Old Testament Commands

Some years ago, while shopping in a Jerusalem bookstore, I saw a book which contained in paragraph form the 613 Old Testament laws as interpreted by Judaism. I have modified the original format by placing each law in actual one-sentence commands. To do this required the writing in long hand of each statement. Only after struggling through this tedious process does one fully comprehend the bondage of the Law of Moses and appreciate the blessing of grace! Upon completion of this section, the words of both Peter and Paul took on new significance.

"Now therefore why tempt ye God, to put a yoke upon the neck of the disciples, which neither our fathers nor we were able to bear?" (Acts 15:10).

"For as many as are of the works of the law are under the curse: for it is written, Cursed is every one that continueth not in all things which are written in the book of the law to do them. But that no man is justified by the law in the sight of God, it is evident: for, The just shall live by faith" (Gal. 3:10, 11).

"Stand fast therefore in the liberty wherewith Christ hath made us free, and be not entangled again with the yoke of bondage" (Gal. 5:1).

Finally, it should be noted that the reader may not always agree with the interpretation placed on some of the Scripture references by the rabbis. To my mind, a number of their theological conclusions seemed entirely unrelated to the verse itself. In spite of this, I still felt it helpful if one could view the Old Testament Scriptures through the eyes of Judaism.

The 613 Old Testament Commandments

The total number of the biblical commandments (precepts and prohibitions) is given in rabbinic tradition as 613. It is held that all 613 were revealed to Moses at Mt. Sinai, and that they fall into two classifications.

1. Mandatory laws—248 in number, corresponding to the limbs of the human body (divided into eighteen sections).
2. Prohibition laws—365 in number, equal to the solar days in a year (divided into thirteen sections).

THE MANDATORY COMMANDMENTS

God
1. One must believe that God exists (Ex. 20:2).
2. Acknowledge his unity (Deut. 6:4).
3. Love God (Deut. 6:5).
4. Fear God (Deut. 6:13).
5. Serve God (Ex. 23:25; Deut. 11:13).
6. Cleave to God (Deut. 10:20).
7. Swear only by his name (Deut. 10:20).
8. Imitate God (Deut. 28:9).
9. Sanctify God's name (Lev. 22:32).

Torah
10. The shema must be recited each morning and evening (Deut. 6:7).
11. Study the Torah and teach it to others (Deut. 6:7).
12. The Tefillin must be bound on one's head (Deut. 6:8).
13. It should be also bound on one's arm (Deut. 6:8).
14. A zizit is to be made for the garments (Num. 15:38).
15. A mezuzah is to be fixed on the door (Deut. 6:9).
16. The people are to assemble every seventh month to hear the Torah read (Deut. 31:12).
17. The king must write a special copy of the Torah for himself (Deut. 17:18).
18. Each Jew should have a Torah scroll for himself (Deut. 31:19).
19. God is to be praised after meals (Deut. 8:10).

Temple and the Priest
20. The Jews should build a Temple (Ex. 25:8).
21. They should respect it (Lev. 19:30).
22. It must be guarded at all times (Num. 18:4).
23. The Levites should perform their special duties in it (Num. 18:23).
24. Before entering the Temple or participating in its service, the priests must wash their hands and feet (Ex. 30:19).
25. The priests must light the candelabrum daily (Ex. 27:20, 21).
26. The priests must bless Israel (Num. 6:23).
27. They must set the shewbread and frankincense before the altar (Ex. 25:30).
28. The incense must be burned twice daily on the golden altar (Ex. 30:7).
29. Fire shall be kept burning on the altar continually (Lev. 6:13).
30. The ashes are to be removed daily (Lev. 6:10, 11).
31. Ritually unclean persons must be kept out of the Temple (Num. 5:2).
32. Israel is to honor its priests (Lev. 21:8).
33. The priests must be dressed in special priestly raiment (Ex. 28:2).
34. The ark is to be carried on the shoulders of the priests (Num. 7:9).
35. The oil used in anointing must be prepared according to a special formula (Ex. 30:31).
36. The priestly families should officiate in rotation (Deut. 18:6-8).
37. In honor of certain dead close relatives, the priests should make themselves ritually unclean (Lev. 21:2, 3).
38. The high priest may marry only a virgin (Lev. 21:13).

Sacrifices
39. The tamid sacrifice must be offered twice daily (Num. 28:3).
40. The high priest must also offer a meal offering twice daily (Lev. 6:13).
41. An additional sacrifice (musaf) should be offered every Sabbath (Num. 28:9).
42. One shall also be offered on the first of every month (Num. 28:11).
43. A musaf is to be offered on each of the seven days of Passover (Lev. 23:36).
44. On the second day of Passover a meal offering of the first barley must also be brought (Lev. 23:10).
45. On Shavuot a musaf must be offered (Num. 28:26, 27).
46. Two loaves of bread must be offered as a wave offering (Lev. 23:17).
47. An additional sacrifice must be made on Rosh Ha-Shanah (Num. 29:1, 2).
48. Another offering must be made on the day of atonement (Num. 29:7, 8).
49. On this day the avodah must also be performed (Lev. 16).
50. On every day of the festival of Sukkot a musaf must be brought (Num. 29:13).
51. It is to be brought also on the eighth day thereof (Num. 29:36).
52. Every male Jew should make pilgrimage to the Temple three times a year (Ex. 23:14).
53. He must appear there during the three pilgrim festivals (Ex. 34:23; Deut. 16:16).
54. One should rejoice on the festivals (Deut. 16:14).
55. On the fourteenth of Nisan one should slaughter the paschal lamb (Ex. 12:6).

56. The lamb is then to be roasted and eaten on the night of the fifteenth (Ex. 12:8).
57. Those who were ritually impure in Nisan should slaughter the paschal lamb on the fourteenth of Iyyar (Num. 9:11).
58. It should then be eaten with mazzah and bitter herbs (Ex. 12:8; Num. 9:11).
59. Trumpets should be sounded when the festive sacrifices are brought, and also in times of tribulation (Num. 10:10).
60. Cattle to be sacrificed must be at least eight days old (Lev. 22:27).
61. They must also be without blemish (Lev. 22:21).
62. All offerings must be salted (Lev. 2:13).
63. It is a mitzvah to perform the ritual of the burnt offering (Lev. 1:2).
64. This is also true with the sin offering (Lev. 6:18).
65. This is also true with the guilt offering (Lev. 7:1).
66. This is also true with the peace offering (Lev. 3:1).
67. This is also true with the meal offering (Lev. 2:1; 6:7).
68. Should the Sanhedrin err in a decision, its members must bring a sin offering (Lev. 4:13).
69. This offering must also be brought by a person who has unwittingly transgressed a karet (Lev. 4:27).
70. When in doubt as to whether one has transgressed such a prohibition, a "suspensive" guilt offering must be brought (Lev. 5:17, 18).
71. For stealing or swearing falsely and for other sins of like nature, a guilt offering must be brought (Lev. 5:15; 19:20, 21; 21-25).
72. In special circumstances the sin offering can be according to one's means (Lev. 5:1-11).
73. One must confess one's sins before God and repent for them (Num. 5:6, 7).
74. A man who has a seminal issue must bring a sacrifice (Lev. 15:13-15).
75. A woman who has an issue must bring a sacrifice (Lev. 15:28, 29).
76. A woman must also bring a sacrifice after childbirth (Lev. 12:6).
77. A leper must bring a sacrifice after he has been cleansed (Lev. 14:10).
78. One must tithe one's cattle (Lev. 27:32).
79. The firstborn of clean (permitted) cattle are holy and must be sacrificed (Ex. 13:2).
80. The firstborn of man must be redeemed (Ex. 22:28; Num. 18:15).
81. The firstling of the ass must be redeemed (Ex. 34:20).
82. If not, its neck is to be broken (Ex. 13:13).
83. Animals set aside as offerings must be brought to Jerusalem without delay (Deut. 12:5, 6).
84. They may be sacrificed only in the Temple (Deut. 12:14).
85. Offerings from outside the land of Israel may also be brought to the Temple (Deut. 12:26).
86. Sanctified animals which have become blemished must be redeemed (Deut. 12:15).
87. A beast exchanged for an offering is also holy (Lev. 27:33).
88. The priests should eat the remainder of the meal offering (Lev. 6:9).
89. They also are to eat of the flesh of sin and guilt offerings (Ex. 29:33).
90. But consecrated flesh which has become ritually unclean must be burned (Lev. 7:19).
91. Also, that flesh not eaten within its appointed time must be burned (Lev. 7:17).

Vows
92. A Nazarite must let his hair grow during the period of his separation (Num. 6:5).
93. When that period is over he must shave his head and bring his sacrifice (Num. 6:18).
94. A man must honor his vows and his oaths (Deut. 23:21).
95. These can only be annulled in accordance with the law (Num. 30:3).

Ritual Purity
96. Anyone who touches a carcass becomes ritually unclean (Lev. 11:8, 24).
97. Anyone who touches one of the eight species of reptiles becomes ritually unclean (Lev. 11:29-31).
98. Food becomes unclean by coming into contact with a ritually unclean object (Lev. 11:34).
99. Menstruous women are ritually impure (Lev. 15:19).
100. After childbirth women are ritually impure for seven days (Lev. 12:2).
101. A leper is ritually unclean (Lev. 13:3).
102. A leprous garment is ritually unclean (Lev. 13:51).
103. A leprous house is unclean (Lev. 14:44).
104. A man having a running issue is unclean (Lev. 15:2).
105. Semen is unclean (Lev. 15:16).
106. A woman suffering from a running issue is unclean (Lev. 15:19).
107. A human corpse is unclean (Num. 19:14).
108. The purification water purifies the unclean, but it makes the clean ritually impure (Num. 19:13, 21).
109. It is a mitzvah to become ritually clean by ritual immersion (Lev. 15:16).
110. To become cleansed of leprosy one must follow the specified procedures (Lev. 14:2).
111. He must shave off all of his hair (Lev. 14:9).
112. Until cleansed, the leper must be bareheaded with clothing in disarray so as to be easily distinguishable (Lev. 13:45).
113. The ashes of the red heifer are to be used in the process of ritual purification (Num. 19:2-9).

Donations to the Temple
114. If a person undertakes to give his own value to the Temple he must do so (Lev. 27:2-8).
115. If a man declares an unclean beast as a donation to the Temple he must give the animal's value in money as fixed by the priest (Lev. 27:11, 12).
116. This is true concerning a house (Lev. 27:14).
117. This is true concerning a field (Lev. 27:16, 22, 23).
118. If one unwittingly derives benefits from Temple property, full restitution plus a fifth must be made (Lev. 5:16).
119. The fruit of the fourth year's growth of trees is holy and may be eaten only in Jerusalem (Lev. 19:24).
120. In reaping a field one must leave the corners for the poor (Lev. 19:9).
121. The gleanings also must be left (Lev. 19:9).
122. The forgotten sheaves must also be left (Deut. 24:19).
123. The misformed bunches of grapes must also be left (Lev. 19:10).
124. The gleanings of the grapes must also be left (Lev. 19:10).
125. The firstfruits must be separated and brought to the Temple (Ex. 23:19).
126. The great heave offering (terumah) must be separated and given to the priest (Deut. 18:4).

127. One must give one tenth of his produce to the Levites (Lev. 27:30; Num. 18:24).
128. A second tithe is to be separated and eaten only in Jerusalem (Deut. 14:22).
129. The Levites must give a tenth of their tithe to the priests (Num. 18:26).
130. In the third and sixth years of the seven-year cycle one was to separate a tithe for the poor instead of the second tithe (Deut. 14:28).
131. A declaration was to be recited when separating the various tithes (Deut. 26:13).
132. This was also required when bringing the firstfruits to the Temple (Deut. 26:5).
133. The first portion of the dough must be given to the priest (Num. 15:20).

The Sabbatical Year
134. In the seventh year everything that grows is owner-less and available to all (Ex. 23:11).
135. The fields were to be fallow and the ground was not to be tilled (Ex. 34:21).
136. The jubilee year (fiftieth) was to be sanctified (Lev. 25:10).
137. On the day of atonement the shafar was to be sounded and all Hebrew slaves set free (Lev. 25:9).
138. In the jubilee year all land was to be returned to its ancestral owners (Lev. 25:24).
139. In a walled city the seller had the right to buy back a house within a year of the sale (Lev. 25:29, 30).
140. Starting from entry into the land of Israel, the years of the jubilee must be counted and announced yearly and septennially (Lev. 25:8).
141. In the seventh year all debts are annulled (Deut. 15:3).
142. However, one could collect upon a debt owed by a stranger (Deut. 15:3).

Concerning Animals for Consumption
143. A priest must receive his share of a slaughtered animal (Deut. 18:3).
144. He also is to receive the first of the fleece (Deut. 18:4).
145. A herem (special vow) must distinguish between that which belongs to the Temple and that which goes to the priests (Lev. 27:21, 28).
146. To be fit for consumption, beast and fowl must be slaughtered according to the law (Deut. 12:21).
147. If they are not of a domesticated species, their blood must be covered with earth after slaughter (Lev. 17:13).
148. The parent bird was to be set free when taking the nest (Deut. 22:7).
149. Beasts to be examined to see if they were permitted for consumption (Lev. 11:2).
150. The same was true for fowls (Deut. 14:11).
151. The same was true for locusts (Lev. 11:21).
152. The same was true for fish (Lev. 11:9).
153. The Sanhedrin was to sanctify the first day of every month and reckon the years and the seasons (Ex. 12:2; Deut. 16:1).

Festivals
154. One was to rest on the Sabbath (Ex. 23:12).
155. This day was to be delcared holy at its onset and termination (Ex. 20:8).
156. On the fourteenth of Nisan all leaven was to be removed from each household (Ex. 12:15).

157. On the fifteenth of Nisan the Exodus account must be related (Ex. 13:8).
158. During the fifteenth the mazzah is to be eaten (Ex. 12:18).
159. On the first day of Passover one must rest (Ex. 12:16).
160. On the seventh day of Passover one must also rest (Ex. 12:16).
161. Starting from the day of the first sheaf (sixteenth of Nisan) one shall count forty-nine days (Lev. 23:35).
162. One was to rest on the Shavvot (Lev. 23).
163. One was to rest on Rosh Ha-Shanah (Lev. 23:24).
164. On the day of atonement one must fast (Lev. 16:29).
165. On the day of atonement one must rest (Lev. 16:29, 31).
166. One must rest on the first day of Sukkot (Lev. 23:35).
167. One must rest on the eighth day of Sukkot (Lev. 23:36).
168. During the festival of Sukkot, Israel was to dwell in booths (Lev. 23:42).
169. Four kinds of trees were to be included in the booth construction (Lev. 23:40).
170. On Rosh Ha-Shanah the shofar was to be sounded (Num. 29:1).

Community
171. Every male was to give half a shekel to the Temple annually (Ex. 30:12, 13).
172. A prophet was to be obeyed (Deut. 18:15).
173. A king was to be appointed (Deut. 17:15).
174. The Sanhedrin was to be obeyed (Deut. 17:11).
175. In case of division, the majority opinion would prevail (Ex. 23:2).
176. Judges and officials shall be appointed in every town (Deut. 16:18).
177. They shall judge the people impartially (Lev. 19:15).
178. Whoever is aware of evidence must come to the court to testify (Lev. 5:1).
179. Witnesses shall be examined thoroughly (Deut. 13:15).
180. False witnesses shall have done to them what they intended to do to the accused (Deut. 19:19).
181. Each unsolved murder requires the sacrifice of a red heifer (Deut. 21:4).
182. Six cities of refuge should be established (Deut. 19:3).
183. The Levites shall be given cities to live in (Num. 35:2).
184. A fence should be built around one's roof to protect others from potential hazards (Deut. 22:8).

Idolatry
185. Idolatry and its appurtenances must be destroyed (Deut. 7:5; 12:2).
186. A city which has been perverted must be treated according to the law (Deut. 13:17).
187. The seven Canaanite nations were to be destroyed (Deut. 20:17).
188. The memory of Amalek was to be blotted out (Deut. 25:19).
189. The deeds of Amalek were to be blotted out (Deut. 25:17).

War
190. All regulations concerning war were to be observed (Deut. 20:11, 12).
191. A priest was to be appointed for special duties in times of war (Deut. 20:2).
192. The military camp was to be kept in a sanitary condition (Deut. 23:14, 15).

193. Each soldier was to be equipped with the necessary implements to assure this (Deut. 23:14).

Social
194. Stolen property must be restored to its owners (Lev. 5:23).
195. Give charity to the poor (Lev. 25:35, 36; Deut. 15:8).
196. When a Hebrew slave goes free, the owner must give him gifts (Deut. 15:14).
197. The poor were to receive loans without interest (Ex. 22:24).
198. A loan with interest was permitted to foreigners (Deut. 23:21).
199. Restore a pledge to its owner if he needs it (Ex. 22:25; Deut. 24:13).
200. Pay the worker his wages on time (Deut. 24:15).
201. He is also to be permitted to eat of the produce with which he is working (Deut. 23:25, 26).
202. Help must be given to unload an animal when necessary (Ex. 23:5).
203. Help must be given to load man or beast when necessary (Deut. 22:4).
204. Lost property must be restored to its owner (Ex. 23:4; Deut. 22:1).
205. It is required to reprove the sinner (Lev. 19:17).
206. It is required to love one's neighbor as oneself (Lev. 19:18).
207. One must also love the proselyte (Deut. 10:19).
208. Weights and measures must be accurate (Lev. 19:36).

Family
209. Respect the wise (Lev. 19:32).
210. Honor one's parents (Ex. 20:12).
211. Fear one's parents (Lev. 19:3).
212. One should marry to perpetuate the human race (Gen. 1:28).
213. Marriage is to be governed by the law (Deut. 24:1).
214. A bridegroom is to rejoice with his bride for one year (Deut. 24:5).
215. Male children must be circumcised (Gen. 17:10; Lev. 12:3).
216. If a man dies childless his brother should marry his widow (Deut. 25:5).
217. If not, he must then release her (halizah) (Deut. 25:9).
218. He who violates a virgin must marry her and may never divorce her (Deut. 22:29).
219. If a man unjustly accuses his wife of premarital promiscuity he shall be flogged, and may never divorce her (Deut. 22:18, 19).
220. The seducer must be punished according to the law (Ex. 22:15-23).
221. The female captive must be treated in accordance with her special regulations (Deut. 21:11).
222. Divorce could be executed only by means of a written document (Deut. 24:1).
223. A woman suspected of adultery had to submit to the required test (Num. 5:15-27).

Judicial
224. As required by the law, the punishment of flogging must be administered (Deut. 25:2).
225. The one guilty of unwitting homicide must be exiled (Num. 35:25).
226. Capital punishment may be by the sword (Ex. 21:20).
227. It may also be by strangulation (Ex. 21:16).
228. It may also be by fire (Lev. 20:14).
229. It may also be by stoning (Deut. 22:24).

230. In some cases the body of the executed shall be hanged (Deut. 21:22).
231. In this case the body must be buried on the same day (Deut. 21:23).

Slaves
232. Hebrew slaves must be treated according to the special laws for them (Ex. 21:2).
233. The master should marry his Hebrew maidservant (Ex. 21:8).
234. If not, he must redeem her (Ex. 21:8).
235. The alien slave must be treated according to the regulations applying to him (Lev. 25:46).

Torts
236. The applicable law must be administered in the case of injury caused by a person (Ex. 21:18).
237. This is true if injury is caused by an animal (Ex. 21:28).
238. This is true if injury is caused by a pit (Ex. 21:33, 34).
239. Thieves must be punished (Ex. 21:37—22:3).
240. Judgment must be rendered in cases of trespass by cattle (Ex. 22:4).
241. This is true also in cases of arson (Ex. 22:5).
242. This is true also in cases of embezzlement by an unpaid guardian (Ex. 22:6-8).
243. This is also true in claims against a paid guardian (Ex. 22:9-12).
244. This is also true in claims against a hirer or a borrower (Ex. 22:13).
245. This is also true in disputes arising out of sales (Lev. 25:14).
246. This is also true concerning inheritance disputes (Ex. 22:8).
247. This is true in all other matters (Deut. 25:12).
248. The persecuted are to be rescued even if it means killing the oppressor (Num. 27:8).

THE PROHIBITION COMMANDMENTS

Idolatry and Related Practices
1. One must not believe in any but the one true God (Ex. 20:3).
2. Do not make images for yourself (Ex. 20:4).
3. Do not make images for others to worship (Lev. 19:4).
4. Do not make images for any purpose (Ex. 20:20).
5. Do not bow down to any image (Ex. 20:5).
6. Do not serve any image (Ex. 20:5).
7. Do not sacrifice children to Molech (Lev. 18:21).
8. Do not practice necromancy (Lev. 19:31).
9. Do not resort to familiar spirits (Lev. 19:31).
10. Do not take the mythology of idolatry seriously (Lev. 19:4).
11. Do not construct a pillar even for the worship of God (Deut. 16:22).
12. Do not construct a dais for the same purpose (Lev. 20:1).
13. Do not plant trees in the Temple (Deut. 16:21).
14. Do not swear by idols or instigate an idolater to do so (Ex. 23:13).
15. Do not encourage idol worship even by non-Jews (Ex. 23:13).
16. Do not encourage Jews to worship idols (Deut. 13:12).
17. Do not listen to anyone who disseminates idolatry (Deut. 13:8).
18. Do not withhold from hating him (Deut. 13:9).
19. Do not pity such a person (Deut. 13:9).
20. Do not defend such a person (Deut. 13:9).

21. Do not attempt to conceal his crime (Deut. 13:9).
22. It is forbidden to derive any benefit from the ornaments of idols (Deut. 7:25).
23. Do not rebuild destroyed idols (Deut. 13:17).
24. Do not enjoy any benefit from its wealth (Deut. 13:18).
25. Do not use anything connected with idols or idolatry (Deut. 7:26).
26. It is forbidden to prophesy in the name of idols (Deut. 18:20).
27. It is forbidden to prophesy falsely in the name of God (Deut. 18:20).
28. Do not listen to the one who prophesies for idols (Deut. 13:3, 4).
29. Do not fear the false prophet nor hinder his execution by death (Deut. 18:22).
30. Do not imitate the ways of idolaters or practice their customs (Lev. 20:23).
31. Do not practice their customs (Lev. 19:26).
32. Do not practice their soothsaying (Deut. 18:10).
33. Do not practice their enchanting (Deut. 18:10, 11).
34. Do not practice their sorcery (Deut. 18:10, 11).
35. Do not practice their charming (Deut. 18:10, 11).
36. Do not imitate their consulting of ghosts (Deut. 18:10, 11).
37. Do not imitate their speaking to familiar spirits (Deut. 18:10, 11).
38. Do not imitate their necromancy (Deut. 18:10, 11).
39. Women are not to wear male clothing (Deut. 22:5).
40. Men are not to wear female clothing (Deut. 22:5).
41. Do not tattoo yourself in the manner of the idolaters (Lev. 19:28).
42. Do not wear garments made of both wool and linen (Deut. 22:11).
43. Do not shave the sides of your head (Lev. 19:27).
44. Do not shave your beard (Lev. 19:27).
45. Do not lacerate yourself over your dead (Lev. 19:28; Deut. 14:1; 16:1).

Prohibitions Resulting from Historical Events
46. It is forbidden to return to Egypt and dwell there permanently (Deut. 17:16).
47. Do not indulge in impure thoughts or sights (Num. 15:39).
48. Do not make a pact with the seven Canaanite nations (Ex. 23:32).
49. Do not save the life of any of them (Deut. 20:16).
50. Do not show mercy to idolaters (Deut. 7:2).
51. Do not permit them to dwell in Israel (Ex. 23:33).
52. Do not intermarry with them (Deut. 7:3).
53. A Jewess may not marry an Ammonite or Moabite even if he converts to Judaism (Deut. 23:4).
54. One should not hate a descendant of Esau because of his genealogy (Deut. 23:8).
55. One should not hate an Egyptian because of his genealogy (Deut. 23:8).
56. Do not make peace with the Ammonite or Moabite nations (Deut. 23:7).
57. Fruit trees are forbidden to be destroyed even in times of war (Deut. 20:19).
58. Do not fear your enemy (Deut. 7:21).
59. Do not forget the evil done by Amalek (Deut. 25:19).

Blasphemy
60. Do not blaspheme the holy name (Lev. 24:16).
61. Do not break an oath made by his holy name (Lev. 19:12).

62. Do not take God's name in vain (Ex. 20:7).
63. Do not profane it (Lev. 22:32).
64. Do not try the Lord God (Deut. 6:16).
65. Do not erase God's name from the holy texts or destroy institutions devoted to his worship (Deut. 12:4).
66. Do not allow the body of one hanged to remain so overnight (Deut. 21:23).

Temple
67. Be not lax in guarding the Temple. (Num. 18:5).
68. The high priest must not enter the Temple indiscriminately (Lev. 16:2).
69. A priest with a physical blemish may not enter there at all (Lev. 21:23).
70. He cannot serve there even if the blemish is of a temporary nature (Lev. 21:17).
71. He may not participate in the service there until it has passed (21:18).
72. The Levites and the priests must not interchange in their functions (Num. 18:3).
73. Intoxicated persons may not enter the sanctuary or teach the law (Lev. 10:9-11).
74. It is forbidden for non-priests to serve in the Temple (Num. 18:4).
75. This is also true for unclean priests (Lev. 22:2).
76. This is also true for priests who have performed the necessary ablution but are still within the time limit of their uncleanness (Lev. 21:6).
77. No unclean person may enter the Temple (Num. 5:3).
78. No unclean person may enter the Temple mount (Deut. 23:11).
79. The altar must not be made of hewn stones (Ex. 20:25).
80. The ascent leading to it must not be by steps (Ex. 20:26).
81. The fire on it may not be extinguished (Lev. 6:6).
82. Nothing but the specified incense may be burned on the golden altar (Ex. 30:9).
83. Regular oil cannot be manufactured with the same ingredients as that of anointing oil (Ex. 30:32).
84. Anointing oil cannot be misused (Ex. 30:32).
85. Regular incense cannot be used on the golden altar (Ex. 30:37).
86. Do not remove the staves from the ark (Ex. 25:15).
87. Do not remove the breastplate from the ephod (Ex. 28:28).
88. Do not make any incision in the upper garment of the high priest (Ex. 28:32).

Sacrifices
89. Do not offer sacrifices outside the Temple (Deut. 12:13).
90. Do not slaughter consecrated animals outside the Temple (Lev. 17:3, 4).
91. Do not sanctify a blemished animal (Lev. 22:20).
92. Do not slaughter a blemished animal (Lev. 22:22).
93. Do not sprinkle the blood of a blemished animal (Lev. 22:24).
94. Do not burn the inner parts of a blemished animal (Lev. 22:22).
95. Do not do any of the above even if the blemish is of a temporary nature (Deut. 17:1).
96. Do not even allow a Gentile to offer such an animal (Lev. 22:25).
97. Do not inflict a blemish on an animal consecrated for sacrifice (Lev. 22:21).

98. Leaven or honey may not be offered on the altar (Lev. 2:11).
99. Nothing unsalted may be offered on the altar (Lev. 2:13).
100. An animal received as the hire of a harlot or as the price of a dog may not be offered (Deut. 23:19).
101. Do not kill an animal and its young on the same day (Lev. 22:28).
102. It is forbidden to use olive oil in the sin offering (Lev. 5:11).
103. The same is true with frankincense (Lev. 5:11).
104. Do not use olive oil in the jealousy offering (Num. 5:15).
105. Do not use frankincense in the jealousy offering (Num. 5:15).
106. Do not substitute sacrifices (Lev. 27:10).
107. Do not take from one category and give to the other (Lev. 27:26).
108. Do not redeem the firstborn of permitted animals (Num. 18:17).
109. Do not sell the tithe of the herd (Lev. 27:33).
110. Do not sell a field consecrated by the herem vow (Lev. 27:28).
111. Do not redeem a field consecrated by the herem vow (Lev. 27:28).
112. In slaughtering a bird for a sin offering, do not split its head (Lev. 5:8).
113. Do not work with a consecrated animal (Deut. 15:19).
114. Do not shear a consecrated animal (Deut. 15:19).
115. Do not slaughter the paschal lamb while there is still leaven about (Ex. 34:25).
116. Do not leave overnight those parts that are to be offered up (Ex. 23:10).
117. Do not leave overnight those parts that are to be eaten (Ex. 12:10).
118. Do not leave any part of the festive offering until the third day (Deut. 16:4).
119. Do not leave any part of the second paschal lamb (Num. 9:13).
120. Do not leave the thanksgiving offering until the morning (Lev. 22:30).
121. Do not break a bone of the first paschal lamb (Ex. 12:46).
122. Do not break a bone of the second lamb (Num. 9:12).
123. Do not carry their flesh out of the house where it is being eaten (Ex. 12:46).
124. Do not allow the remains of the meal offering to become leaven (Lev. 6:10).
125. Do not eat the paschal lamb raw or sodden (Ex. 12:9).
126. Do not allow an alien resident to eat of it (Ex. 12:45).
127. Do not allow an uncircumcised person to eat of it (Ex. 12:48).
128. Do not allow an apostate to eat of it (Ex. 12:43).
129. A ritually unclean person must not eat of holy things (Lev. 12:4).
130. Holy things which have become unclean must not be eaten (Lev. 7:19).
131. Sacrificial meat which is left after the time-limit cannot be eaten (Lev. 19:6-8).
132. Meat slaughtered with the wrong intentions cannot be eaten (Lev. 7:18).
133. The heave offering cannot be eaten by a non-priest (Lev. 22:10).
134. Neither can a priest's sojourner or hired worker eat it (Lev. 22:10).
135. Neither can an uncircumcised person eat it (Lev. 22:10).
136. Neither can an unclean priest eat it (Lev. 22:4).
137. The daughter of a priest who is married to a non-priest may not eat of holy things (Lev. 22:12).
138. The meal offering of the priest must not be eaten (Lev. 6:16).
139. The flesh of the sin offering sacrificed within the sanctuary may not be eaten (Lev. 6:23).
140. Consecrated animals which have become blemished cannot be eaten (Deut. 14:3).
141. Do not eat the second tithe of corn (Deut 12:17).
142. Do not drink the second tithe of wine (Deut. 12:17).
143. Do not eat the second tithe of oil (Deut. 12:17).
144. Do not eat unblemished firstlings outside Jerusalem (Deut. 12:17).
145. The priests may not eat the sin-offerings or the trespass-offerings outside the Temple courts (Deut. 12:17).
146. Do not eat the flesh of the burnt offerings at all (Deut. 12:17).
147. The lighter sacrifices may not be eaten before the blood has been sprinkled (Deut. 12:17).
148. A non-priest may not eat of the holiest sacrifices (Deut. 12:17).
149. A priest may not eat the firstfruits outside the Temple courts (Ex. 29:33).
150. One may not eat the second tithe while in the state of impurity (Deut. 26:14).
151. One may also not do this if in the state of mourning. (Deut. 26:14).
152. Its redemption money may not be used for anything other than food and drink (Deut. 26:14).
153. Do not eat untithed produce (Lev. 22:15).
154. Do not change the order of separating the various tithes (Ex. 22:28).
155. Do not delay payment of offerings, either freewill or obligatory (Deut. 23:22).
156. Do not come to the Temple on the pilgrim festivals without an offering (Ex. 23:15).
157. Do not break your word (Num. 30:3).

Priests
158. A priest may not marry a harlot (Lev. 21:7).
159. He may not marry a profane woman (Lev. 21:7).
160. He may not marry a divorcée (Lev. 21:7).
161. The high priest cannot marry a widow (Lev. 21:14).
162. He cannot take a concubine (Lev. 21:15).
163. Priests cannot enter the sanctuary with overgrown hair of the head (Lev. 10:6).
164. They must not enter the sanctuary with torn clothing (Lev. 10:6).
165. They must not leave the courtyard during the Temple service (Lev. 10:7).
166. An ordinary priest may not render himself ritually impure except for those relatives specified (Lev. 21:1).
167. The high priest cannot become impure for anybody (Lev. 21:11).
168. He cannot become impure for any reason (Lev. 21:11).
169. The tribe of Levi shall have no part in the division of the land of Israel (Deut. 18:1).
170. The tribe of Levi shall not partake of the spoils of war (Deut. 18:1).
171. It is forbidden to make oneself bald as a sign of mourning for one's dead (Deut. 14:1).

Dietary Laws
172. A Jew may not eat unclean cattle (Deut. 14:7).
173. He may not eat unclean fish (Lev. 11:11).

174. He may not eat unclean fowl (Lev. 11:13).
175. He may not eat creeping things that fly (Deut. 14:19).
176. He may not eat creatures that creep upon the ground (Lev. 11:41).
177. He may not eat reptiles (Lev. 11:44).
178. He may not eat worms found in fruit or produce (Lev. 11:42).
179. He may not eat any detestable creature (Lev. 11:43).
180. He cannot eat an animal that has died naturally (Deut. 14:21).
181. He cannot eat a torn or mauled animal (Ex. 22:30).
182. He cannot eat any limb taken from a living animal (Deut. 12:23).
183. He cannot eat the sinew of the thigh (Gen. 22:33).
184. He cannot eat blood (Lev. 7:26).
185. He cannot eat a certain type of fat (Lev. 7:23).
186. It is forbidden to cook meat together with milk (Ex. 23:19).
187. It is forbidden to eat of such a mixture (Ex. 34:26).
188. One cannot eat an ox condemned to stoning (Ex. 21:28).
189. One may not eat bread made of new corn itself before the omer offering has been brought on the sixteenth of Nisan (Lev. 23:14).
190. One may not eat of roasted corn until the omer has been offered (Lev. 23:14).
191. One may not eat of green corn (Lev. 23:14).
192. One may not eat orlah (Lev. 19:23).
193. One may not eat the growth of mixed planting in the vineyard (Deut. 22:9).
194. Any use of wine libations to idols is prohibited (Deut. 32:38).
195. Gluttony and drunkenness is prohibited (Lev. 19:26; Deut. 21:20).
196. It is forbidden to eat anything on the day of atonement (Lev. 23:29).
197. One may not eat leaven (hamez) during the Passover (Ex. 13:3).
198. One may not eat anything containing an admixture of such during the Passover (Ex. 13:20).
199. One may not eat leaven the day before the Passover (Deut. 16:3).
200. During the Passover no leaven may be seen in one's possession (Ex. 13:7).
201. During the Passover no leaven may be found in one's possession (Ex. 12:19).

Nazarites
202. A Nazarite may not drink wine or any beverage made from grapes (Num. 6:3).
203. He may not eat fresh grapes (Num. 6:3).
204. He may not eat dried grapes (Num. 6:3).
205. He may not eat grape seeds (Num. 6:4).
206. He may not eat grape peel (Num. 6:4).
207. He may not render himself ritually impure for his dead (Num. 6:7).
208. He may not enter a tent in which there is a corpse (Lev. 21:11).
209. He must not shave his hair (Num. 6:5).

Agriculture
210. One cannot reap the whole of a field without leaving the corners for the poor (Lev. 23:22).
211. Do not gather up the ears of corn that fall during reaping or during harvest (Lev. 19:9).
212. Do not gather the misformed clusters of grapes (Lev. 19:10).
213. Do not gather the grapes that fall (Lev. 19:10).
214. Do not return to take a forgotten sheaf (Deut. 24:19).
215. Do not sow different species of seed together (Lev. 19:19).
216. Do not sow corn in a vineyard (Deut. 22:9).
217. Do not crossbreed different species of animals (Lev. 19:19).
218. Do not work with two different species yoked together (Deut. 22:10).
219. Do not muzzle an animal working in a field to prevent it from eating (Deut. 25:4).
220. Do not till the earth in the seventh year (Lev. 25:4).
221. Do not prune trees in the seventh year (Lev. 25:4).
222. Do not reap (in the usual manner) produce in the seventh year (Lev. 25:5).
223. Do not reap fruit in the seventh year (Lev. 25:5).
224. Do not till the earth or prune trees in the jubilee year (Lev. 25:11).
225. Do not harvest produce in the jubilee year (Lev. 25:11).
226. Do not harvest fruit in the jubilee year (Lev. 25:11).
227. One may not sell one's landed inheritance in the land of Israel permanently (Lev. 25:23).
228. One may not change the lands of the Levites (Lev. 25:33).
229. One may not leave the Levites without support (Deut. 12:19).

Loans, Business, and the Treatment of Slaves
230. One cannot demand repayment of a loan after the seventh year (Deut. 15:2).
231. One may however refuse to lend to the poor because that year is approaching (Deut. 15:9).
232. Do not deny charity to the poor (Deut. 15:7).
233. Do not send a Hebrew slave away empty-handed when he finishes his period of service (Deut. 15:13).
234. Do not dun a debtor when you know he cannot pay (Ex. 22:24).
235. Do not lend to another Jew at interest (Lev. 25:37).
236. Do not borrow from another Jew at interest (Deut. 23:20).
237. Do not participate in an agreement involving interest either as a guarantor, witness, or writer of the contract (Ex. 22:24).
238. Do not delay payment of wages (Lev. 19:13).
239. Do not take a pledge from a debtor by violence (Deut. 24:10).
240. Do not keep a poor man's pledge when he needs it (Deut. 24:12).
241. Do not take any pledge from a widow (Deut. 24:17).
242. Do not take a pledge from any debtor if he earns his living with it (Deut. 24:6).
243. Kidnaping a Jew is forbidden (Ex. 20:13).
244. Do not steal (Lev. 19:11).
245. Do not rob by violence (Lev. 19:13).
246. Do not remove a landmark (Deut. 19:14).
247. Do not defraud (Lev. 19:13).
248. Do not deny receipt of a loan or a deposit (Lev. 19:11).
249. Do not swear falsely regarding another man's property (Lev. 19:11).
250. Do not deceive anybody in business (Lev. 25:14).
251. Do not mislead a man even verbally (Lev. 25:17).
252. Do not harm a stranger verbally (Ex. 22:20).
253. Do not do him injury in trade (Ex. 22:20).
254. Do not return a runaway slave who has fled to the land of Israel to his master (Deut. 23:16).

255. Do not take any advantage of such a slave (Deut. 23:17).
256. Do not afflict the widow or the orphan (Ex. 22:21).
257. Do not misuse a Hebrew slave (Lev. 25:39).
258. Do not sell a Hebrew slave (Lev. 25:42).
259. Do not treat him cruelly (Lev. 25:43).
260. Do not allow a heathen to mistreat him (Lev. 25:53).
261. Do not sell your Hebrew maidservant (Ex. 21:8).
262. If you marry her, do not withhold food, clothing, and conjugal rights from her (Ex. 21:10).
263. Do not sell a female captive (Deut. 21:14).
264. Do not treat her as a slave (Deut. 21:14).
265. Do not covet another man's possessions (Ex. 20:17).
266. Even the desire alone is forbidden (Deut. 5:18).
267. A worker must not cut down standing corn during his work (Deut. 23:25).
268. He must not take more fruit than he can eat (Deut. 23:25).
269. One must not keep a lost article he has found (Deut. 22:3).
270. One cannot refuse to help a man or an animal which is collapsing under its burden (Ex. 23:5).
271. It is forbidden to defraud with weights and measures (Lev. 19:35).
272. It is forbidden to possess inaccurate weights (Deut. 25:13).

Justice
273. A judge must not perpetrate injustice (Lev. 19:15).
274. He must not accept bribes (Ex. 23:8).
275. He must not be partial (Lev. 19:15).
276. He must not be afraid (Deut.1:17).
277. He may not favor the poor (Ex. 23:3; Lev. 19:15).
278. He may not discriminate against the wicked (Ex. 23:6).
279. He shall not pity the condemned (Deut. 19:13).
280. He shall not pervert the judgment of strangers or orphans (Deut. 24:17).
281. It is forbidden to hear one litigant without the other being present (Ex. 23:1).
282. A capital case cannot be decided by a majority of one (Ex. 23:2).
283. A judge should not accept another judge's opinion unless he is convinced of its correctness (Ex. 23:2).
284. One ignorant of the law cannot be appointed as a judge (Deut. 1:17).
285. Do not give false testimony (Ex. 20:16).
286. Do not accept testimony from a wicked person (Ex. 23:1).
287. Do not accept testimony from relatives of a person involved in the case (Deut. 24:16).
288. Do not pronounce judgment on the basis of the testimony of one witness (Deut. 19:15).
289. Do not murder (Ex. 20:13).
290. Do not convict on circumstantial evidence alone (Ex. 23:7).
291. A witness must not sit as a judge in capital cases (Num. 35:30).
292. Do not execute anybody without proper trial and conviction (Num. 35:12).
293. Do not pity or spare the pursuer (Deut. 25:12).
294. Punishment is not to be inflicted for an act committed under duress (Deut. 22:26).
295. Do not accept ransom for a murderer (Num. 35:31).
296. Do not accept ransom for a manslayer (Num. 35:32).
297. Do not hesitate to save another person from danger (Lev. 19:16).

298. Do not leave a stumblingblock in the way (Deut. 22:8).
299. Do not mislead another person by giving wrong advice (Lev. 19:14).
300. It is forbidden to administer more than the assigned number of lashes to the guilty (Deut. 25:2, 3).
301. Do not tell tales (Lev. 19:16).
302. Do not bear hatred in your heart (Lev. 19:17).
303. Do not shame a Jew (Lev. 19:17).
304. Do not bear a grudge (Lev. 19:18).
305. Do not take revenge (Lev. 19:18).
306. Do not take the dam when you take the young birds (Deut. 22:6).
307. Do not shave a leprous scall (Lev. 13:33).
308. Do not remove other signs of that affliction (Deut. 24:8).
309. Do not cultivate a valley in which a slain body was found (Deut. 21:4).
310. Do not suffer a witch to live (Ex. 22:17).
311. Do not force a bridegroom to perform military service during the first year of his marriage (Deut. 24:5).
312. Do not rebel against the transmitters of the tradition of the law (Deut. 17:11).
313. Do not add to the precepts of the law (Deut. 13:1).
314. Do not subtract from the precepts of the law (Deut. 13:1).
315. Do not curse a judge (Ex. 22:27).
316. Do not curse a ruler (Ex. 22:27).
317. Do not curse any Jew (Lev. 19:14).
318. Do not curse a parent (Ex. 21:17).
319. Do not strike a parent (Ex. 21:15).
320. Do not work on the Sabbath (Ex. 20:10).
321. Do not walk further than the permitted limits (Ex. 16:29).
322. Do not inflict punishment on the Sabbath (Ex. 35:3).
323. Do not work on the first day of the Passover (Ex. 12:16).
324. Do not work on the seventh day of the Passover (Ex. 12:16).
325. Do not work on the Shavuot (Lev. 23:21).
326. Do not work on Rosh Ha-Shanah (Lev. 23:25).
327. Do not work on the first day of Sukkot (Lev. 23:35).
328. Do not work on the eighth day of Sukkot (Lev. 23:36).
329. Do not work on the day of atonement (Lev. 23:28).

Incest and Other Forbidden Relationships
330. It is forbidden to have sexual relations with one's mother (Lev. 18:7).
331. This is true also with one's step-mother (Lev. 18:8).
332. This is true with one's sister (Lev. 18:9).
333. This is true with one's step-sister (Lev. 18:11).
334. This is true with a daughter-in-law (Lev. 18:10).
335. This is true with a granddaughter (Lev. 18:10).
336. This is true with a daughter (Lev. 18:10).
337. This is also forbidden between mother and daughter (Lev. 18:17).
338. It is forbidden between a mother and her daughter-in-law (Lev. 18:17).
339. It is forbidden between a grandmother and her granddaughter (Lev. 18:17).
340. It is forbidden between nephew and aunt (Lev. 18:12).
341. It is forbidden between niece and aunt (Lev. 18:13).
342. It is forbidden with one's paternal uncle's wife (Lev. 18:14).
343. It is forbidden with one's daughter-in-law (Lev. 18:15).
344. It is forbidden with one's brother's wife (Lev. 18:16).

345. It is forbidden with one's wife's sister (Lev. 18:18).
346. It is forbidden to have sexual relations with a menstruous woman (Lev. 18:19).
347. Do not commit adultery (Lev. 18:20).
348. A man shall not have sexual relations with an animal (Lev. 18:23).
349. A woman shall not have sexual relations with an animal (Lev. 18:23).
350. Homosexuality is forbidden (Lev. 18:22).
351. Homosexuality is forbidden with one's father (Lev. 18:7).
352. Homosexuality is forbidden with one's uncle (Lev. 18:14).
353. It is forbidden to have any intimate physical contact with anyone except one's own wife (Lev. 18:6).
354. A mamzer may not marry a Jewess (Deut. 23:3).
355. Harlotry is forbidden (Deut. 23:18).
356. A divorcée may not be remarried to her first husband if, in the meanwhile, she has married another (Deut. 24:4).
357. A childless widow may not marry anybody other than her late husband's brother (Deut. 25:5).
358. A man may not divorce a wife whom he married after having raped her (Deut. 22:29).
359. This is also true if he has slandered her (Deut. 22:19).
360. An eunuch may not marry a Jewess (Deut. 23:2).
361. Castration is forbidden (Lev. 22:24).

The Monarchy
362. An elected king must be of the seed of Israel (Deut. 17:15).
363. He must not accumulate an excess number of horses (Deut. 17:16).
364. He must not multiply unto himself many wives (Deut. 17:17).
365. He must not multiply unto himself much wealth (Deut. 17:17).

Introduction to Archaeology

The Christian religion is of course based on that principle called faith (Heb. 11:6). This simply means a scientist or philosopher cannot sit in a study or lab and, through sheer human logic, arrive at the correct spiritual facts about God and the universe. These truths are only brought out in the holy Scriptures, which must be accepted by childlike faith.

However, it should be quickly pointed out that while this faith is on many occasions and in many areas above human reasoning, it is *never* unreasonable! Furthermore, it can be stated that the Creator has left strong hints and signs throughout his great creation which indicate to the honest seeker both the reality of his existence and the reliability of his Word!

The great Apostle Paul brings this out in his first recorded sermon:

"Who in times past suffered all nations to walk in their own ways. Nevertheless he left not himself without witness, in that he did good, and gave us rain from heaven, and fruitful seasons, filling our hearts with food and gladness" (Acts 14:16, 17).

Among the various external witnesses mentioned by Paul here which affirm God and his Word would certainly be the science of archaeology. The dedicated spade has done much to authenticate the accuracy of the Word of God.

This section thus presents some eighty-three "sanctified spades" or discoveries which bring out the historical dependability of the Scriptures.

The Bible and Archaeology

1. Creation (Gen. 1:1).
2. Original monotheism (Gen. 1:1).
3. The Garden of Eden (Gen. 2:8-17).
4. The fall of man (Gen. 3:1-24).
5. Earliest civilization (Gen. 4:1-26).
6. Pre-flood longevity (Gen. 5:1-32).
7. The universal flood (Gen. 6-9).
8. The table of nations (Gen. 10:1-32).
9. The Tower of Babel (Gen. 11:1-9).
10. Ur of the Chaldeans (Gen. 11:31; 12:1).
11. The existence of Haran (Gen. 11:31; 12:5).
12. The battle route of Chedorlaomer (Gen. 14:1-12).
13. The Hittite empire (Gen. 15:20).
14. The existence of Nahor (Gen. 24:10).
15. The employment of camels in patriarchal times (Gen. 24:11).
16. The cities of Sodom and Gomorrah (Gen. 19).
17. The abundance of food in Gerar in time of famine (Gen. 26:1).
18. The concern of Laban (Gen. 31:14-35).
19. Joseph and Potiphar's wife (Gen. 39).
20. The bricks without straw (Ex. 1:11; 5:7-19).
21. The death of the firstborn in Egypt (Ex. 12).
22. The destruction of Pharaoh and his armies in the Red Sea (Ex. 14).
23. The parting of the Jordan River (Josh. 3).
24. The destruction of Jericho (Josh. 6).
25. The wealth of Gibeon (Josh. 10:2).
26. The springs of Kirjath-sepher (Josh. 15:13-19).
27. The use of the hornet in conquering Palestine (Josh. 24:12).
28. The burial of Joshua (Josh. 24:30).
29. Cities in the book of Judges (Jdg. 1:21-29).
30. The Philistines and iron weapons (Jdg. 1:19).
31. The Deborah and Barak battle account (Jdg. 4).
32. Gideon's hidden grain pit (Jdg. 6:11-18).
33. The tower temple of the false god Berith (Jdg. 9).
34. The destruction of Gibeah (Jdg. 20).
35. The destruction of Shiloh (1 Sam. 4).
36. Saul's house in Gibeah (1 Sam. 10:26).
37. Jonathan's victory over the Philistines (1 Sam. 14).
38. The music of David (1 Sam. 16:18, 23; 1 Chron. 15:16).
39. The death of Saul (1 Sam. 31).
40. The pool of Gibeon (2 Sam. 2).
41. The capture of Jerusalem (2 Sam. 5:6-10).
42. The wealth of Solomon (1 Ki. 4:26; 9:26; 10:22).
43. The invasion into Judah by Shishak, King of Egypt (1 Ki. 14:25-28; 2 Chron. 12:2-4).
44. The reign of northern king Omri (1 Ki. 16:23, 24).
45. The rebuilding of Jericho (Josh. 6:26; 1 Ki. 16:34).
46. The victory of Elijah on Mt. Carmel (1 Ki. 18).
47. Ahab's house of ivory (1 Ki. 22:39).
48. The pool of Samaria (1 Ki. 22:37, 38).
49. The war between Israel and Moab (2 Ki. 3).
50. The man "on whose hand the king leaned" (2 Ki. 7).
51. The punishment of King Jehu (2 Ki. 10:29-33).
52. The official seal of the servant of Jeroboam II (2 Ki. 14:23-29).
53. Repentance of Nineveh (Jonah 3).
54. The tribute of money Menaham paid to Assyrian king Pul (2 Ki. 15:16-20).
55. The accomplishments and judgment of King Uzziah (2 Chron. 26).
56. The capture of Israel by Assyrian kings Pul, Shalmaneser, and Sargon (2 Ki. 15, 17).

57. Ahaz's money tribute to King Tiglath-pileser (2 Ki. 16:5-9).
58. The historicity of Sargon (Isa. 20:1).
59. The seal and tomb of Shebna, Hezekiah's scribe (Isa. 22:15, 16; 36:2).
60. The destruction of Lachish by Sennacherib (2 Chron. 32:9; Isa. 10:29).
61. Sennacherib's failure to capture Jerusalem (2 Ki. 18-19; 2 Chron. 32; Isa. 36-37).
62. The murder of Sennacherib by his own sons (Isa. 37:37, 38).
63. The imprisonment of Manasseh by the Assyrians (2 Chron. 33:11).
64. The discovery of the book of the law in the Temple during Josiah's reign (2 Chron. 34:8-32).
65. Hezekiah's water tunnel (2 Ki. 20:20; 2 Chron. 32:30).
66. Hezekiah's wall repairs (2 Chron. 32:5).
67. The destruction of Lachish by Nebuchadnezzar (Jer. 34:7).
68. The captivity of Jehoiachin and the appointment of Zedekiah (2 Ki. 24:10-19; 25:27-30).
69. The futile hope of Zedekiah in looking to Egypt to aid against Babylon (Jer. 37:1, 5-11).
70. The treachery of Ishmael against Gedaliah and his officials (Jer. 41:1-15).
71. The great stones buried by Jeremiah in Tahpanhes, Egypt (Jer. 43:8-13).
72. Jewish life in the Babylonian exile (Jer. 29:4-7).
73. The great statue and fiery furnace of Nebuchadnezzar (Dan. 3).
74. The pride of Nebuchadnezzar and the greatness of Babylon (Dan. 4).
75. The insanity of Nebuchadnezzar (Dan. 4).
76. The historicity of Belshazzar (Dan. 5).
77. The capture of Babylon and execution of Belshazzar (Dan. 5).
78. Daniel and the lion's den (Dan. 6).
79. The book of Esther and Ahasuerus the Persian king (Est.).
80. The edict of King Cyrus (Ezra 1:1-4).
81. The historicity of Darius the Great (Ezra 6:1-15).
82. The wall constructed by Nehemiah (Neh. 1-6).
83. The enemies of Nehemiah (Neh. 2, 4, 6).

The Bible and Archaeology

1. Creation (Gen. 1:1).

   "In the beginning God created the heaven and the earth" (Gen. 1:1).

   Between the years 1848-1876 the tablets with the first extrabiblical account of creation were discovered from the library of Assyrian emperor Ashurbanipal (669-626 B.C.), doubtless dating before 2000 B.C. This Babylonian-Sumerian epic of creation is called the "Enuma elish" and consisted of seven cantos, written on seven tablets. Although grossly perverted in some areas, they do bear striking resemblances to the true Genesis creation account. For example:
   a. Both accounts speak of an original chaos and darkness.
   b. Both accounts have a similar order of events: light, firmament, dry land, luminaries, man, and God (or gods) resting.

2. Original monotheism (Gen. 1:1). The two earliest recorded civilizations are the Egyptians and the Sumerians. Both at the beginning were monotheistic.
   a. Egyptian: Sir Flinders Petrie, outstanding archaeologist, gave testimony to this.

   b. Sumerian:
      "According to many present authorities, the Sumerians were originally monotheistic in their belief, for the most ancient written records state clearly that they believed in only one God. This is a very important fact to note, because until very recently a large number of historians believed that mankind originally was polytheistic and that gradually, as human beings became civilized, they formed a higher conception of the deity." (Albert Hyma, Professor of History, University of Michigan, *College Outline Series, Ancient History,* p. 10)

3. The Garden of Eden (Gen. 2:8-17).

   "And the Lord God planted a garden eastward in Eden; and there he put the man whom he had formed. And out of the ground made the Lord God to grow every tree that is pleasant to the sight, and good for food; the tree of life also in the midst of the garden, and the tree of knowledge of good and evil" (Gen. 2:8, 9).

   Many ancient peoples record a beautiful pain-free land. One Middle East account is called the Epic of Emmerkar, and speaks glowingly of a land known as Dilmun. Archaeologist Clifford Wilson writes:

   "We are told that birth in that land was without distress until Enki ate certain plants that involved a deadly curse. The Epic tells us that the land was a clear and pure place, that the lion did not kill, and the lamb and the lion lived together peacefully. There was no sickness and mankind had only one speech by which he addressed the gods." (*Rocks, Relics and Biblical Reliability,* p. 21)

4. The fall of man (Gen. 3:1-24).

   "And when the woman saw that the tree was good for food, and that it was pleasant to the eyes, and a tree to be desired to make one wise, she took of the fruit thereof, and did eat, and gave also unto her husband with her; and he did eat" (3:6).
   a. The myth of Adapa, an ancient account of the fall, was found in the archives of both Assyrian (Ashurbanipal, seventh century), and Egyptian (Amenhotep III, fourteenth century B.C.) kings. Adapa was apparently the Babylonian Adam.
   b. In 1932, E. Speiser of the University of Pennsylvania discovered a similar temptation seal, showing a fruitbearing tree. On the right are a man and woman. She is picking fruit from the tree. Behind her is a serpent.
   c. There is also a strong resemblance existing between the cherubim (present at the fall, see Gen. 3:24) as described by Ezekiel (Ezek. 1), and the winged lion statues which guarded the ancient religious temples of Mesopotamia. The Sphinx in Egypt may also owe its design to the appearance of the cherubim.
   d. Worldwide traditions of the fall are found among Chinese, Hindu, Greek, Persian, and other peoples.

5. Earliest civilization (Gen. 4:1-26).

   "And Abel was a keeper of sheep, but Cain was a tiller of the ground" (Gen. 4:2).

   "And Adah bore Jabal: he was the father of such as dwell in tents and of such as have cattle. And his brother's name was Jubal: he was the father of all such as handle the harp and pipe. And Zidal, she also bore Tubal-cain, an instructor of every craftsman in bronze and iron . . . "(Gen. 4:20-22).

Farming and cattle-raising are shown by archaeology to be the beginning of man's civilization. Arts, crafts, music, and the rise of urban life are illustrated at many Mesopotamian mounds.

6. Pre-flood longevity (Gen. 5:1-32).

"And all the days of Methuselah were nine hundred sixty and nine years: and he died" (5:27).

The Weld-Blundell Prism preserves a very ancient list of Sumerian kings. It contains eight pre-flood rulers said to have reigned a total of 241,200 years over certain cities in southern Mesopotamia. The shortest reign was 18,600 and the longest was 43,200 years.

7. The universal flood (Gen. 6-9).

"And God said unto Noah, the end of all flesh is come before me; for the earth is filled with violence through them; and, behold, I will destroy them with the earth. Make thee an ark of gopher wood; rooms shalt thou make in the ark, and shalt pitch it within and without with pitch" (Gen. 6:13, 14).

a. In 1853, H. Rassman unearthed some Babylonian flood tablets in Nineveh, taken from the Assyrian king Ashurbanipal's library (669-626 B.C.). The eleventh book in this discovery was the Epic of Gilgamesh. Gilgamesh was a legendary Mesopotamian king who set out on a journey to find his ancestor Utnapishtim, from whom he hoped to discover the secret of eternal life. He finally found him. Utnapishtim told Gilgamesh he had once lived in a land called Shuruppak and had been a worshiper of the tree god Ea. He then related the story of the flood and his escape from it. His story may be summarized as follows:

"The assembly of the gods decided to send a deluge. They said, 'on the sinner let his sin rest. O man of Shuruppak, build a ship, save your life. Construct it with six stories, each with seven parts. Smear it with bitumen inside and outside. Launch it upon the ocean. Take into the ship seed of life of every kind.' So I built it. With all that I had I loaded it, with silver, gold, and all living things that I had. I embarked upon the ship with my family and kindred. I closed the door. The appointed time arrived. I observed the appearance of the day. It was terrible. All light was turned to darkness. The rains poured down. The storm raged like a battle charge on mankind. The boat trembled. The gods wept. I looked out upon the sea. All mankind was turned to clay, like logs floating about. The tempest ceased. The flood was over. The ship grounded on Mt. Zazir. On the seventh day, I sent out a dove; it returned. I sent out a swallow; it returned. I sent out a raven; it alighted; it waded about; it croaked; it did not return. I disembarked. I appointed a sacrifice. The gods smelled the sweet savor. They said, 'Let it be done no more.'" (Suggested by Halley's Handbook, p. 76)

b. The Gilgamesh Epic belongs to the heritage of all great nations of the ancient Middle East. The Hittites and Egyptians translated it into their own tongues.

c. The early Aborigines of nearly every country of the world have preserved records of the universal flood. Anthropologist Dr. Richard Andree has collected forty-six flood legends from North and South America, twenty from Asia, five from Europe, seven from Africa, and ten from the South Sea Islands and Australia.

8. The table of nations (Gen. 10:1-32).

"Now these are the generations of the sons of Noah: Shem, Ham, and Japheth; and unto them were sons born after the flood" (10:1).

"These are the families of the sons of Noah, after their generations, in their nations: and by these were the nations divided in the earth after the flood" (10:32).

M. F. Unger writes:

"This table stands unique in ancient literature, without a remote parallel even among the Greeks, for their framework in the mythological and the peoples are only Greek or Aegean tribes. W. F. Albright calls the Table of Nations, 'an astonishingly accurate document.'" (Unger's Bible Handbook, p. 52) Albright goes on to say:

"It shows such a remarkably modern understanding of the ethnic and linguistic situation in the ancient world, in spite of all its complexity, that scholars never fail to be impressed with the author's knowledge of the subject." (Old Testament Commentary, p. 138)

9. The Tower of Babel (Gen. 11:1-9).

"And they said one to another, Come, let us make brick, and burn them thoroughly. And they had brick for stone, and slime had they for mortar" (11:3). "And they said, Come, let us build us a city and a tower, whose top may reach unto heaven; and let us make us a name, lest we be scattered abroad upon the face of the whole earth" (11:4).

There are more than two dozen ancient temple towers called ziggurats which have been excavated in southern Mesopotamia.

Note especially the language in 11:4. This passage does not teach that early mankind stupidly attempted to build a tower which would reach into outer space. The phrase "whose top may reach unto heaven," should be literally translated "whose top is heaven," since the two words "may reach" are not found in the original language. Archaeological evidence suggests that the Tower of Babel was in reality a building given over to astrology, or the heathen worship of the heavens. Among the ruins of ancient Babylon is a building 153 feet high with a 400-foot base. It was constructed of dried bricks in seven stages, to correspond with the known planets to which they were dedicated. The lowermost was black, the color of Saturn, the next orange, for Jupiter, the third red, for Mars, and so on. These stages were surmounted by a lofty tower, on the summit of which were the signs of the Zodiac. Dr. Donald Barnhouse writes:

"It was an open, defiant turning to Satan and the beginning of devil worship. This is why the Bible everywhere pronounces a curse on those who consult the sun, the moon, and the stars of heaven."

10. Ur of the Chaldeans (Gen. 11:31; 12:1).

"And Terah took Abram, his son, and Lot, the son of Haran, his son's son, and Sarai, his daughter-in-law, his son Abram's wife; and they went forth with them from Ur of the Chaldeans, to go into the land of Canaan . . ." (11:31).

"And he (Stephen) said, Men, brethren, and fathers, hearken: the God of glory appeared unto our father Abraham, where he was in Mesopotamia, before he dwelt in Haran" (Acts 7:2).

Abraham was born and raised in the city of Ur of the Chaldees. Ur was a seaport on the Persian Gulf, at the mouth of the Euphrates River, some twelve miles from the traditional site of the Garden of Eden. But preceding the time of Abraham, it was the most magnificent city in all the world; a center of manufacturing, farming, and shipping, in a land of fabulous fertility and wealth, with caravans going in every direction to distant lands, and ships sailing from the docks of Ur down the Persian Gulf with cargoes of copper and hard stone.

For years the skeptic ridiculed the actual existence of Ur. But during the years of 1922–1934, C. T. Wooley of the British museum thoroughly explored the secrets of these ruins.

The most conspicuous building of the city in Abraham's day was the ziggurat, or the temple tower, which was probably patterned after the Tower of Babel. This tower was square, terraced, and built of solid brick. Each successive terrace was planted with trees and shrubbery. The city had two main temples, one dedicated to Nannar, the Moon-god, and the other to his wife, Ningal.

These temples had an inner court surrounded by a series of rooms. The old foundations were still standing, with long water troughs coated with bitumen. Deep grooves made with knives on the great brick tables showed where the sacrificial animals had been dissected. They were cooked on the hearths of the temple kitchens. Even the ovens for baking bread were there. "After 3800 years," noted Wooley in his diary, "we were able to light the fire again and put into commission once more the oldest kitchen in the world."

"Oils, cereals, fruit, wool and cattle made their way into vast warehouses, perishable articles went to the temple shops. Many goods were manufactured in factories owned by the temple, for example in the spinning-mills which the priests managed. One workshop produced twelve different kinds of fashionable clothing. Tablets found in this place gave the names of the mill-girls and their quota of rations. . . . Ur of the Chaldees was a powerful, prosperous, colorful and busy capital city. . . ." (*The Bible As History,* Werner Keller, p. 42)

Wooley wandered through those alleyways, past the great temples, and exclaimed in his diary:

"We must radically alter our view of the Hebrew patriarch when we see that his earlier years were passed in such sophisticated surrounding. He was the citizen of a great city and inherited the traditions of an old and highly organized civilization. The houses themselves reveal comfort and even luxury. We found copies of the hymns which were used in the services of the temple and together with them, mathematical tables."

11. The existence of Haran (Gen. 11:31; 12:5).

". . . and they came unto Haran, and dwelt there" (11:31).

". . . and Terah died in Haran" (11:32).

"And Abram was seventy and five years old when he departed out of Haran" (12:4).

Various archaeological sources confirm the existence of Haran during the time of Abraham. The Assyrian documents describe it as a thriving city on the great east-west trade route between Nineveh and Damascus.

12. The battle route of Chedorlaomer (Gen. 14:1–12).

"Twelve years they served Chedorlaomer, and in the thirteenth year they rebelled. And in the fourteenth year came Chedorlaomer, and the kings that were with him, and smote [them] . . ." (14:4, 5).

This, the first recorded war in the Bible, occurred when four Mesopotamian kings attacked (and defeated) five Canaanite kings, falling upon them by an eastern route.

"The places, named in verses 5, 6, by way of which the four Eastern kings came against Sodom, were so far east of the ordinary trade route, that W. F. Albright said that he once considered it an indication of the legendary character of the fourteenth chapter of Genesis; but, in 1929, he discovered a line of great mounds . . . along the east border of Gilead and Moab, of cities that flourished about 2000 B.C., and indicating that it was a well-settled country, on the trade route between Damascus and the gold and copper regions of Edom and Sinai." (*Halley's Bible Handbook,* p. 97)

13. The Hittite empire (Gen. 15:20).

"And I have said, I will bring you up out of the affliction of Egypt unto the land of the Canaanites, and the Hittites . . ." (Ex. 3:17).

a. The Hittites are mentioned forty-seven times in the Old Testament. Esau married a Hittite wife (Gen. 26:34, 35; 36:2), and one of David's followers (Uriah) was a Hittite (2 Sam. 11:3).

b. However, prior to the nineteenth century the only mention of the Hittites was in the biblical record. This caused the liberal critics to ridicule and sneer at the "historical fables" of the Scriptures.

c. But in 1906 all this changed. German archaeologist Hugo Winkler discovered in Asia Minor the city of Boghaz-Keul, an ancient Hittite capital. Over 10,000 tablets were excavated from that area. This confirms Joshua's description of the entire western fertile crescent as the "land of the Hittites" (Josh. 1:4).

Many scholars now consider the Hittites one of the three most influential peoples of ancient history. They were the first to discover the secret of iron-smelting after the universal flood. In 1925, scholar A. H. Sayce wrote a book entitled, *The Hittites, The Story of a Forgotten Empire.*

The Hittites occupied much of Mesopotamia for awhile, and nearly defeated the Egyptians, forcing Ramses II into a peace treaty after the battle of Kadesh in the twelfth century B.C. Their empire was later destroyed by the Assyrians in 717 B.C.

14. The existence of Nahor (Gen. 24:10).

"And the servant took ten camels of the camels of his master, and departed . . . and he arose, and went to Mesopotamia, unto the city of Nahor" (Gen. 24:10).

In 1933, Andre Parrot excavated a Mesopotamian city located on the Euphrates River called Mari. Some 20,000 clay tablets were dug up at that site. Many confirm the existence of Nahor.

15. The employment of camels in patriarchal times (Gen. 24:11).

"And he made his camels to kneel down outside the city . . ." (Gen. 24:11).

For years the critic had pointed to early references of camels in Genesis as historical inaccuracies, asserting that camels were not known in either Egypt or Canaan until long after the time of Abraham. However, archaeologist J. P. Free has demonstrated evidence proving camels did indeed make their appearance even prior to Abraham. Statuettes, figurines, plaques bearing representations of camels, rock carvings, and drawings, camel bones, a camel skull and a camel's-hair rope have been found, which date as far back as 3000 B.C.

16. The cities of Sodom and Gomorrah (Gen. 19).
">. . . and Lot . . . pitched his tent toward Sodom" (Gen. 13:12).
". . . the cry of Sodom and Gomorrah is great, and . . . their sin is very grievous" (Gen. 18:20).
"And there came two angels to Sodom at evening; and Lot sat in the gate of Sodom . . ." (Gen. 19:1).
We shall consider this well-known account in Genesis 19 in three phases.

a. The existence of these cities. Prior to 1968 there existed no extrabiblical reference to the cities of Sodom or Gomorrah. But at that time a young graduate in Near Eastern studies from Rome University changed all this, with his breathtaking discovery of the capital of a buried and forgotten civilization. His name is Giovanni Pettinato. The name of this ancient city was Ebla. The find consisted of thousands of tablets. Among the many ancient towns mentioned in the tablets are those of Sodom and Gomorrah. But this is not all. There were actually five sister "cities of the Plain" (Gen. 14:2). These were: Sodom, Gomorrah, Admah, Zeboiim, and Zoar. We are told in that same verse that an earlier name for Zoar was Bela. These tablets from Ebla refer, very precisely, by name, to these five cities. One of the tablets records a business receipt for some grain shipped between Ebla and Sodom.

b. The fertile area which once surrounded Sodom.
"And Lot lifted up his eyes, and beheld all the plain of Jordan, that it was well watered every where, before the Lord destroyed Sodom and Gomorrah, even as the garden of the Lord . . ." (Gen. 13:10).
In 1924 Dr. W. F. Albright and Dr. M. G. Kyle, directing a joint expedition of the American Schools and Xenia Seminary, found, at the southeast corner of the Dead Sea, five oases, made by fresh water streams and, centrally located to them, on a plain 500 feet above the level of the Dead Sea, at a place called Bab-ed-Dra, the remains of a great fortified enclosure, evidently a "high place" for religious festivals. There were great quantities of potsherds, flints, and other remains of a period dating between 2500 B.C. and 2000 B.C., and evidence that the population ended abruptly about 2000 B.C. This evidence that the region was densely populated and prosperous indicates that it must have been very fertile, "like the garden of God." That the population ceased abruptly, and that it has been a region of unmixed desolation ever since, seems to indicate that the district was destroyed by some great cataclysm which changed the soil and climate.
The opinion of Albright and Kyle, and most archaeologists, is that Sodom and Gomorrah were located on these oases, further down the streams, and that the site is now covered by the Dead Sea.

c. The destruction of these cities. The destruction of Sodom was effected by a rain of "brimstone and fire." In examining the meaning of this expression, scholars have ruled out volcanic actions on the basis of negative geological indications. Many believe that it refers to an earthquake resulting in an enormous explosion. Several factors are pointed out by Leon Wood as favoring this view. The idea of brimstone and fire suggests incendiary materials raining upon the city as the result of an explosion. Another descriptive word used is "overthrew" (Gen. 19:29), and this fits the thought of an earthquake. That Abraham saw smoke rising in the direction of the city indicates that there was fire. Inflammable asphalt has long been known in the area. Records from ancient writers speak of strong sulphuric odors which suggest that quantities of sulphur were there in past time. Further, the whole Jordan Valley constitutes an enormous fault in the earth's surface, given to earthquake conditions. It is possible, then, that God did see fit miraculously to time an earthquake at this precise moment, which could have released great quantities of gas-mixed sulphur with various salts found in abundance, and measurably increased the flow of asphalt seepage. Lightning could have ignited all and the entire country been consumed as indicated. The Bible is clear that God does use natural means to accomplish his purpose when and to the extent that they are available. He may have done so here.

American scholar Jack Finegan writes:
"A careful examination of the literary, geological and archaeological evidence leads to the conclusion that the corrupt 'cities of the plain' (Gen. 19:29) lay in the area which is now submerged beneath the slowly rising waters of the southern section of the Dead Sea, and that their destruction came about through a great earthquake which was probably accompanied by explosions, lightning, issue of natural gas and general conflagration."
The subsidence released volcanic forces that had been lying dormant deep down along the whole length of the fracture. In the upper valley of the Jordan near Bashan there are still the towering craters of extinct volcanoes; great stretches of lava and deep layers of basalt have been deposited on the limestone surface. From time immemorial the area around this depression has been subject to earthquakes. There is repeated evidence of them and the Bible itself records them. As if in confirmation of the geological explanation of the disappearance of Sodom and Gomorrah, Sanchuniathon, the Phoenician priest, uses these words in his "Ancient History," which has now been rediscovered: "The Vale of Sidimus sank and became a lake, always steaming and containing no fish, a symbol of vengeance and of death for the transgressor."
"If we take a rowing boat across the 'Salt Sea' to the southernmost point we shall see, if the sun is shining in the right direction, something quite fantastic: some distance from the shore, and clearly visible under the surface of the water, stretch the outlines of forests which extraordi-

narily high salt content of the Dead Sea has kept in preservation. The trunks and roots in the shimmering green must be very ancient indeed. Once upon a time, when they were in blossom and green foliage covered their twigs and branches, perhaps the flocks of Lot grazed under their shadow." (Werner Keller, *The Bible As History*, pp. 94, 98)

17. The abundance of food in Gerar in time of famine (Gen. 26:1).

"And there was a famine in the land, beside the first famine that was in the days of Abraham. And Isaac went unto . . . Gerar" (Gen. 26:1). (See also 20:1.)

In 1927, archaeologist W. F. Petrie excavated the Philistine city of Gerar. He discovered ancient pottery that showed Gerar was a great grain center around the year 2000 B.C., the actual time of Abraham and Isaac.

18. The concern of Laban (Gen. 31:14–35).

"And Laban went to shear his sheep: and Rachel had stolen the images that were her father's. And Jacob stole away unawares to Laban. . . . And it was told Laban on the third day that Jacob was fled. And he took his brethren with him, and pursued after him seven days' journey; and they overtook him in the Mount Gilead" (Gen. 31:19, 20, 22, 23).

"This incident has long been a puzzle. Why was Laban so greatly concerned about recovering these images which Rachel had stolen? Attempting to recapture them he conducted a long (275 miles) and expensive expedition. Excavations at Nuzi in northern Mesopotamia, in the region in which Laban lived, show that the possession of the household gods of a father-in-law by a son-in-law was legally acceptable as proof of the designation of that son-in-law as principal heir . . . . It is no wonder that Jacob was angry that he should be accused of such a deed, and that the two men set up a boundary and promised not to cross it to injure one another. Jacob never made evil use of these images which Rachel had stolen, but ordered that they should be buried at Shechem" (Gen. 35:2–4). (*New Scofield Bible*, p. 46)

These Nuzi tablets help explain not only Laban's concern here, but also throw much light on other Bible events such as:

a. Abraham's attempts to make Eliezer his heir (Gen. 15:2).

b. A slave girl given to a new bride (Gen. 29:24, 29).

c. A barren wife bearing legal children through her concubine (Gen. 16:2).

d. The giving of a sandal to seal an agreement (Ruth 4:7).

19. Joseph and Potiphar's wife (Gen. 39).

"And it came to pass after these things, that his master's wife cast her eyes upon Joseph; and she said, Lie with me" (Gen. 39:7).

Several centuries after the events in Genesis 39, a story entitled, "A Tale of Two Brothers" became very popular in Egypt. A copy of it can be seen today in the British museum. The editor of the English edition of Brugsch's *History of Egypt* surmises that this story had its roots from that incident. In the Egyptian account a married man sends his younger brother, who was unmarried, and to whom he had entrusted everything to his home, to bring some seed corn. The wife tempts him. He refuses. She, angered, reports to her husband that the brother made several advances. The husband plans to kill him. The brother then flees, but later becomes king of Egypt.

20. The bricks without straw (Ex. 1:11; 5:7–19).

"And Pharaoh commanded the same day the taskmasters of the people, and their officers, saying, Ye shall no more give the people straw to make brick, as heretofore: let them go and gather straw for themselves" (Ex. 5:6,7).

a. Some years ago, world-famous Egyptologist Eric Peet stated the account in Exodus 5 was in error, showing the ignorance of Moses (or whoever wrote the book of Exodus), for straw was totally unnecessary in making bricks because of the nature of the Nile mud.

b. But in 1883 another archaeologist named Naville succeeded in unearthing what was believed to be some storepits at Tell el Maskhuta on the edge of Goshen. He identified the place as Pithom, one of Pharaoh's treasure cities (Ex. 1:11), where the Israelites made bricks. He found the walls of those structures were made with bricks, some of which had straw and some did not.

c. After this, in another area, an ancient Egyptian document called the Papyrus Anastasi was unearthed. It contained the lament of an officer who had to erect buildings on the northern frontier of Egypt. The inscription read: "I am without equipment. There are no people to make bricks and there is no straw in the district." (Quoted by archaeologist J. P. Free in *Archaeology and the Bible*, p. 91)

21. The death of the firstborn in Egypt (Ex. 12).

"And it came to pass, that at midnight the Lord smote all the firstborn in the land of Egypt, from the firstborn of Pharaoh who sat on his throne unto the firstborn of the captive who was in the dungeon; and all the firstborn of cattle" (12:29).

Most believe that the Pharaoh of the ten plagues was Amenhotep II. For some reason his son did not succeed him after his death. This is probably explained by the above verse.

22. The destruction of Pharaoh and his armies in the Red Sea (Ex. 14).

". . . and the Lord overthrew the Egyptians in the midst of the sea. And the waters returned and covered the chariots, and the horsemen, and all the host of Pharaoh that came into the sea after them; there remained not so much as one of them" (14:27, 28).

The tomb of Amenhotep II was never finished. Some believe the answer for this is found in the above verses.

23. The parting of the Jordan River (Josh. 3).

"And it shall come to pass, as soon as the soles of the feet of the priests who bear the ark of the Lord . . . shall rest in the waters of the Jordan, that the waters . . . shall be cut off . . . and they shall stand in one heap" (3:13).

". . . the waters which came down from above stood and rose up in one heap very far from the city Adam . . ." (3:16).

We read that the waters of Jordan were blocked from Adam (the modern Damieh), about sixteen miles north of Jericho. Three times in relatively modern history (1266, 1906, 1927) a landslide has blocked the Jordan's flow. In 1927 the river was stopped for over twenty-one hours. On occasion, the miracles of the Bible are miracles of synchronization or timing.

24. The destruction of Jericho (Josh. 6).

"So the people shouted when the priests blew with the trumpets: and it came to pass, when the people heard the sound of the trumpet, and the people shouted with a great shout, that the wall fell down flat, so that the people went up into the city, every man, straight before him, and they took the city" (6:20).

a. It has been shown that the walls of Jericho have fallen down some seventeen times, often due to earthquake activity. The city was destroyed and apparently rebuilt around 1500 B.C. It was protected by a double wall of brick, the outer wall being six feet thick and thirty feet high. The space between the walls was fifteen feet. This city was extremely crowded, which probably explains why houses like Rahab's (Josh. 2:15) were erected over the space between the walls. These walls display evidence of violent destruction; the outer wall had tumbled forward down the slope. Ashes, charred timbers, reddened masses of stone and brick show that a fire accompanied the fall of the city. (See Josh. 6:24.)

b. John Garstang, a British archaeologist who excavated Jericho, found under the ashes and fallen walls, in the ruins of storehouses, an abundance of food stuffs, wheat, barley, dates, lentils, and such, turned to charcoal by intense heat.

c. The question may be asked why the conquerors did not appropriate these spoils of war. This is readily answered by Joshua 6:18, where Israel is forbidden to take anything (except the gold and silver to be used in the Temple).

Note: At this point an interesting archaeological discovery found in 1896 should be considered. During that year some 350 clay tablets were excavated at the Egyptian court in Amarna. These are thus referred to as the Amarna Tablets. They comprise a group of letters written by the various Palestinian and Syrian cities to the two kings of Egypt who lived around 1400 B.C. They wrote the Egyptians asking their help to repulse a group of invading Habiru people. Some scholars have identified the Habiru conquests with the Hebrews during Joshua's time. The name Joshua actually appears on one of the tablets. However, this theory is not accepted by many scholars.

25. The wealth of Gibeon.

". . . Gibeon was a great city, as one of the royal cities . . ." (Josh. 10:2).

It is now clear that the source of Gibeon's prosperity was a flourishing and well-organized wine trade. Excavations led by J. B. Prichard of Columbia University in 1959–1960 led to the discovery of extensive wine cellars. Some of these cellars had obviously been used as wine presses for trampling out the grapes; other cavities, protected by a waterproof cover, could be identified as fermentation vats. The total storage capacity so far discovered approaches 50,000 gallons. It should be remembered also that those men from Gibeon who deceived Joshua were carrying wine vessels with them. (See Josh. 9:4.)

26. The springs of Kirjath-sepher (Josh. 15:13–19).

". . . give me also springs of water. And he gave her the upper springs, and the lower springs" (15:19).

a. In this passage Caleb promises the hand of his daughter in marriage to the man who could capture the Canaanite city of Kirjath-sepher. Othniel, Caleb's own nephew, accomplished this. The old warrior then gives the two nearby springs of the city as a wedding present at the request of his daughter.

b. Archaeology has discovered the presence of an upper well and a lower well near the site. Grooves worn in the remains of the old well curbs show usage from ancient times.

c. The excavators also found clear evidence of immediate occupation of the city after its conquest. There was no period of decay or neglect. There was no neutral stratum lying between the old Canaanite city and the Israelite city.

27. The use of the hornet in conquering Palestine.

"And I sent the hornet before you, which drove them out from before you, even the two kings of the Amorites; but not with thy sword, nor with thy bow" (Josh. 24:12).

a. This statement is made three times in the Old Testament. The first two times it is stated as a prophecy (Ex. 23:28; Deut. 7:20), and here in Joshua as a fulfillment.

b. There is no scriptural record concerning this event or just how God actually carried it out. We do know that while Moses was in Midian for forty years, a powerful Egyptian Pharaoh named Thutmose III commenced a series of military invasions of Canaan, overcoming the defenses of the Amorites and other nations of the land. Little, of course, did he know that by his conquests he was actually helping prepare the way for Israel's conquests under Joshua by weakening those nations.

c. The interesting story here is that archaeologists have discovered that the personal coat of arms badge worn by Thutmose himself was the image of a hornet. God may well have had this in mind in those three passages.

28. The burial of Joshua.

"And they buried him in the border of his inheritance . . . which is in Mount Ephraim . . ." (Josh. 24:30).

a. The Greek text (the Septuagint) adds a significant remark at this point. It reads: "There they put with him into the tomb in which they buried him, the knives of stone with which he circumcised the children of Israel in Gilgal." (See Josh. 5:5.)

b. Ten miles northwest of Bethel lies Kefr Ishula, the "village of Joshua." In the neighboring hillside are some rock tombs. In 1870 a number of stone knives were found in one of these sepulchers.

29. Cities in the book of Judges (Jdg. 1:21–29). Joseph P. Free writes:

"We find the indication in Judges 1:21 that at the time of the Conquest of Canaan . . . the Israelites did not drive out the inhabitants of Jerusalem. The fact that Israel did not take Jerusalem is confirmed by the Amarna Tablets, which show that the King of Jerusalem remained loyal to the Pharaoh of Egypt. According to the Bible, Bethel was destroyed during the early period of the judges (1:23–25), and excavations there in 1924 showed that the town was completely destroyed during that period. The Bible indicates, on the other hand, that during this same period Bethshan, Megiddo, and Gezer were thriving towns but not subject to the Israelites. The excavations at these latter sites show the correctness of this indication that they were not held by Israel at the time of the judges." (*Archaeology and Bible History*, pp. 141, 142)

30. The Philistines and iron weapons.

"And the Lord was with Judah; and he drove out the inhabitants of the mountain, but could not drive out the inhabitants of the valley, because they had chariots of iron" (Jdg. 1:19).

"Now there was no blacksmith found throughout all the land of Israel; for the Philistines said, Lest the Hebrews make themselves swords or spears; But all the Israelites went down to the Philistines, to sharpen every man his plow share, and his . . . axe, and his sickle" (1 Sam. 13:19, 20).

Archaeological evidence has demonstrated that the Philistines were the first inhabitants of Palestine to possess iron weapons, having learned the secret of iron smelting from the Hittites. According to the Bible, Israel does not have iron weapons until the time of David, some two centuries after the arrival of the Philistines (2 Sam. 12:31; 1 Chron. 29:7). Excavations have revealed many iron relics of 1100 B.C., in Philistia, but none in the hill country of Palestine previous to David's time.

In 1927 archaeologist Petrie excavated the Philistine mound of Tell Jemmeh, eight miles south of Gaza. Here he discovered a sword-furnace of the Philistines. The furnace was a receptacle containing a flue, and it gave evidence of great heat.

31. The Deborah and Barak battle account (Jdg. 4).

"And the children of Israel again did evil in the sight of the Lord . . . And the Lord sold them into the hand of Jabin, king of Canaan . . ." (4:1, 2).

"And the Lord routed Sisera [Jabin's commander] and all his chariots . . ." (4:15).

The Oriental Institute, excavating in 1937 at Megiddo (one of the capital cities of the Canaanites), found in the stratum of twelfth century B.C., indications of a tremendous fire. Underneath the floor of the palace of that city they recovered 200 pieces of beautifully carved ivory and gold ornaments. One shows a group of captives presenting tribute presents to a Canaanite king. These could well be Israelites prior to the great victory at the base of Mt. Tabor.

32. Gideon's hidden grain pit (Jdg. 6:11-18).

". . . Gideon thrashed wheat by the wine-press to hide it from the Midianites" (6:11).

In excavations in and around Gideon's area done by Kyle and Albright (1926-1928) in the stratum belonging to the time of the judges, many hidden grain pits were found.

33. The tower temple of the false god Berith (Jdg. 9).

"The son of Gideon, Abimelech, sought to gain power in Israel, but soon found himself opposed by the men of Shechem. When Abimelech and his followers attacked the town of Shechem, the Shechemites shut themselves in an inner fortress, called the 'hold of the house of the god Berith' (Jdg. 9:46). In order to gain this stronghold, Abimelech and his men gathered wood, piled it about the structure,

and set fire to the wood pile (9:49). Archaeological confirmation of such a burning was found in 1926 in the excavations of the German archaeologist, Sellin. He found a building from this period which he identified with the House of Berith. The pottery evidence showed that it had been built about 1300 B. C. and was finally destroyed by burning about 1150 B.C." (*Archaeology and Bible History*, p. 143)

34. The destruction of Gibeah (Jdg.20).

"And the children of Israel rose up in the morning, and encamped against Gibeah" (20:19).

". . . the Benjamites looked behind them, and behold, the flame of the city ascended up to heaven" (20:40).

In the twelfth century B.C. a tragic intertribal war broke out in Israel, pitting eleven tribes against the tribe of Benjamin. The eleven tribes won and burned Gibeah, the stronghold city of Benjamin.

W. F. Albright found the ruins of Gibeah during excavation work in 1922. The strata dating back to that time showed ample evidence that the city had indeed suffered a severe fiery destruction.

35. The destruction of Shiloh (1 Sam. 4).

"So the people sent to Shiloh, that they might bring from there the Ark of the Covenant of the Lord of hosts . . ." (4:4).

"And the messenger answered and said, Israel is fled before the Philistines and there hath been also a great slaughter among the people . . . and the Ark of God is taken" (4:17).

a. When Israel entered Canaan, the tabernacle of Moses was set up at Shiloh, a city eight miles north of Bethel. (See Josh. 18:1; 19:51; Jdg. 18:31; 1 Sam. 1:9; 3:3; 4:4.)

b. The city of Shiloh was apparently destroyed by the Philistines along with the tabernacle when they captured the Ark of the Covenant. God allowed this because of their sin. The destruction must have been total and terrible. (See Ps. 78:60; Jer. 7:12, 14; 26:6.) It must have occurred in 1 Samuel 4.

c. When the ark was later recovered, the men of Israel brought it to the city of Kirjath-jearim (1 Sam. 7:1) and not to Shiloh. Finally, in the days of David it was taken to Jerusalem. (See 2 Sam. 6.)

d. For years the very existence of Shiloh was questioned by liberal critics of the Bible. But between the years 1926-1928 a Danish expedition dug at Shiloh. Pottery evidence confirmed not only the existence of the city, but its importance also. The conclusions were that Shiloh had been inhabited from the thirteenth to the eleventh centuries B.C., but had been uninhabited from about 1050 to 300 B.C. W. F. Albright confirmed this find.

36. Saul's house in Gibeah.

"And Saul also went home to Gibeah . . ." (1 Sam. 10:26).

A few miles north of Jerusalem, near an ancient road which leads to Samaria, lies Tell el-Ful, which means, literally, "the hill of beans." This is Gibeah, the capital and home of Saul's kingdom. In 1922-1923 W. F. Albright excavated the ruins of his fortress castle. It was a two-storied building with an open forty by thirty yard courtyard. The tell contained a variety of pottery, a number of large cooking pots, and an iron plow, indicating that some sort of agriculture was carried on there. Note Saul's activities as described in 1 Samuel

11:5. Albright also found a large double wall, perhaps the very one Israel's first king used to sit by. (See 1 Sam. 20:25.)

37. Jonathan's victory over the Philistines (1 Sam. 14).

"Now it came to pass . . . that Jonathan the son of Saul said unto the young man that bare his armour, Come, and let us go over to the Philistines' garrison, that is on the other side . . ." (1 Sam. 14:1).

"And between the passages, by which Jonathan sought to go over unto the Philistines' garrison, there was a sharp rock on the one side, and a sharp rock on the other side: and the name of the one was Bozez, and the name of the other Seneh" (14:4).

The one craig was situated northward over toward Mishmash, and the other, southward over toward Gibeah (v. 5).

"And that first slaughter, which Jonathan and his armourbearer made, was about twenty men, within as it were an half acre of land, which a yoke of oxen might plow" (14:14).

Major Vivian Gilbright, a British army officer, relates an amazing story regarding this passage in his reminiscences about World War I. He writes:

"In the first world war a brigade major in Allenby's army in Palestine was on one occasion searching his Bible, with the light of a candle, looking for a certain name. His brigade had received orders to take a village that stood on a rocky prominence on the other side of a deep valley. It was called Michmash and the name seemed somehow familiar. Eventually he found it here in First Samuel. The brigade major reflected that there must still be this narrow passage through the rocks, between the two spurs, and at the end of it the 'half acre of land.' He woke the commander and they read the passage through together once more. Patrols were sent out. They found the pass, which was thinly held by the Turks, and which led past two jagged rocks—obviously Bozez and Seneh. Up on top, beside Michmash, they could see by the light of the moon a small flat field. The brigadier altered his plan of attack. Instead of deploying the whole brigade, he sent one company through the pass under cover of darkness. The few Turks whom they met were overpowered without a sound, the cliffs were scaled, and shortly before daybreak the company had taken up a position on 'the half acre of land.' The Turks woke up and took to their heels in disorder since they thought that they were being surrounded by Allenby's army. They were all killed or taken prisoner. 'And so' (concludes Major Gilbright) 'after thousands of years British troops successfully copied the tactics of Saul and Jonathan.' "

38. The music of David (1 Sam. 16:18, 23; 1 Chron. 15:16).

"Then answered one of the servants, and said, Behold, I have seen a son of Jesse the Bethlehemite, that is cunning in playing . . ." (16:18).

"And it came to pass, when the evil spirit from God was upon Saul, that David took an harp, and played with his hand . . ." (16:23).

"And David spake to the chief of the Levites to appoint their brethren to be the singers with instruments of music, psalteries and harps and cymbals, sounding, by lifting up the voice with joy" (1 Chron. 15:16). (See also Ps. 137:1–6.)

Archaeologist J. A. Thompson writes:

"One of the clearest pictures we have of David in the Biblical record is that of a musician and an organizer of the temple music (1 Chron. 25). It is now clear that Palestine was well known around the East for many centuries as a land where music was widely enjoyed. As early as 1900 b.c. Egyptian artists painted Palestinian nomads who visited their land with donkeys and goods for trade. Among the people pictured were some who carried stringed instruments like harps. Egyptian monuments of the New Empire from about 1550 onwards refer to a variety of examples of music from the land of Canaan." (*The Bible and Archaeology*, p. 98)

39. The death of Saul (1 Sam. 31).

"And they cut off his head, and stripped off his armour . . . . And they put his armour in the house of Ashtaroth; and they fastened his body to the wall of Beth-shan" (31:9, 10).

Beth-shan is just east of Mt. Gilboa at the junction of the Jezreel and Jordan valleys. In 1921 C. S. Fisher and other archaeologists from the University Museum of Pennsylvania began excavating in this area. They soon uncovered in the stratum of 1000 b.c. the ruins of a temple of Ashtaroth and also a temple to Dagon.

40. The pool of Gibeon (2 Sam. 2).

"And Abner . . . and Joab . . . went out, and met together by the pool of Gibeon: and they sat down, the one on the one side of the pool, and the other on the other side of the pool" (2:12, 13).

In 1956, beneath a field of tomatoes in el-Jib (modern name for Gibeon) Professor J. B. Pritchard of Columbia University discovered the Pool of Gibeon, apparently a well-known spot in its day. He found a circular shaft over thirty feet in diameter and thirty feet deep, which had been driven vertically into bedrock. A spiral path led down a ramp cut into the inside wall. Below that a winding staircase, with two openings for light and air, descended for a further forty-five feet to the reservoir itself, chiseled out of solid limestone. When the rubble which covered the whole layout had been cleared away, the great cistern slowly began to fill with water again from the fissures in the rock as it had done 3,000 years ago.

41. The capture of Jerusalem (2 Sam. 5:6–10).

"Nevertheless, David took the stronghold of Zion: the same is the city of David. And David said on that day, Whosoever getteth up to the gutter, and smiteth the Jebusites . . . he shall be chief and captain . . ." (5:7, 8).

a. Controversy has surrounded this word "gutter." Some believe the word should be translated "hook." Thus, the account would tell us, David took the city by scaling its walls with hooks. However, the majority of archaeologists believe "gutter" refers to a secret watercourse, found by David, thus allowing him entrance into the city. If this is the case, the watercourse was rediscovered in 1867 by a British captain named Warren.

b. Werner Keller writes of this:

"On the east side of Jerusalem where the rock slopes down into the Kidron Valley lies the 'Ain Sitti Maryam,' the 'Fountain of the Virgin Mary.' In the Old Testament it is called 'Gihon,' 'bubbler,' and it has always been the main water supply for the inhabitants of the city. The road to it goes past the remains of a small mosque and into a vault. Thirty steps lead down to a little basin in which the pure water from the heart of the rock is gathered.

In 1867 Captain Warren, in company with a crowd of pilgrims, visited the famous spring, which, according to the legend, is the place where Mary washed the swaddling clothes of her little Son. Despite the semi-darkness Warren noticed on this visit a dark cavity in the roof, a few yards above the spot where the water flowed out of the rock. Apparently no one had ever noticed this before because when Warren asked about it nobody could tell him anything.

Filled with curiosity, he went back to the Virgin Fountain next day equipped with a ladder and a long rope. He had no idea that an adventurous and somewhat perilous quest lay ahead of him.

Behind the spring a narrow shaft led off at first horizontally and then straight up into the rock. Warren was an alpine expert and well acquainted with this type of chimney climbing. Carefully, hand over hand, he made his way upwards. After about 40 feet the shaft suddenly came to an end. Feeling his way in the darkness, Warren eventually found a narrow passage. Crawling on all fours, he followed it. A number of steps had been cut in the rock. After some time he saw ahead of him a glimmering of light. He reached a vaulted chamber which contained nothing but old jars and glass bottles covered in dust. He forced himself through a chink in the rock and found himself in broad daylight in the middle of the city, with the Fountain of the Virgin lying far below him.

Closer investigation by Parker, who in 1910 went from the United Kingdom under the auspices of the Palestine Exploration Fund, showed that this remarkable arrangement dated from the second millennium B.C. The inhabitants of old Jerusalem had been at pains to cut a corridor through the rock in order that in time of siege they could reach in safety the spring that meant life or death to them.

Warren's curiosity had discovered the way which 3,000 years earlier David had used to take the fortress of Jerusalem by surprise." (The Bible As History, p. 190)

42. The wealth of Solomon (1 Ki. 4:26; 9:19; 9:26; 10:23).
"... Solomon had ... cities for his chariots, and cities for his horsemen ... which Solomon desired to build in Jerusalem, and in Lebanon, and in all the land of his dominion" (1 Ki. 9:19).
"And King Solomon made a navy of ships in Ezion-geber, which is beside Eloth, on the shore of the Red Sea, in the land of Edom" (1 Ki. 9:26).
"So King Solomon exceeded all the kings of the earth in riches and for wisdom" (1 Ki. 10:23).
Archaeological discoveries relating to Solomon's time are quite remarkable. Professor Albright has observed that the age of Solomon was one of the most flourishing periods in the history of Palestine. Evidence of vast storehouses of wealth have been found in the excavated cities of Hazor, Megiddo, Beth Shemesh, and other trading centers of the day.

It is evident from the Bible (1 Ki. 7:46) that Solomon must have had considerable sources of copper. Many tons would have been required for all the brass items used in the Temple. There is little doubt about the existence of mines and metal-working furnaces in the Jordan area of Palestine. Archaeologist Nelson Glueck writes:
"I found fragments of slag on some of the tells north of Admah and especially upon the site of ancient Succoth. In Solomon's time this entire district in the Jordan Valley hummed with industrial activity devoted to the turning out of finished metal articles for the adornment of the new temple." (The River Jordan, p. 146)
J. A. Thompson writes:
"It is interesting to learn from the Bible that Solomon had a port on the Red Sea . . . that a port existed here is born out by the excavations at Ezion Geber. The town produced various pieces of evidence which pointed to the existence of a port there. In the first place, there were many items which may very easily be reconciled with sea activity, such as copper and iron nails, pieces of rope of various kinds and pieces of tar. Further there were items found here which came from other lands. Some were of Egyptian origin and yet others came from southern Arabia. All of this points to a center of trade in which the sea played a great part." (The Bible and Archaeology, p. 106)

43. The invasion into Judah by Shishak, King of Egypt (1 Ki. 14:25–28; 2 Chron. 12:2–4).
"And it came to pass, that in the fifth year of king Rehoboam, Shishak king of Egypt came up against Jerusalem, because they had transgressed against the Lord . . . And he took the fenced cities which pertained to Judah, and came to Jerusalem" (2 Chron. 12:2, 4).
Archaeological findings show Shishak was the founder of the twenty-second dynasty. His gold-masked body was discovered at Tanis in 1938–1939. His victory inscriptions found at Thebes list the towns taken in Judah and Israel.

44. The reign of northern king Omri (1 Ki. 16:23, 24).
"In the thirty and first year of Asa . . . began Omri to reign over Israel, twelve years: six years reigned he in Tirzah. And he bought the hill of Samaria . . . and built on the hill, and called the name of the city which he built, after the name of Shemer, owner of the hill, Samaria" (1 Ki. 16:23, 24).
Harvard University archaeologists have excavated Samaria and discovered the foundations of Omri's palace, but nothing older than Omri, evidence that he was the founder of the city. His name is also mentioned on the famous Moabite Stone. Omri's fame in the world of his day is also attested to by the Assyrians' reference to him on the Black Obelisk of Shalmaneser III over a century later. In fact, after Omri, Israel was known to her enemies as Bit-Humri, "the house of Omri."

45. The rebuilding of Jericho (Josh. 6:26; 1 Ki. 16:34).
"And Joshua adjured them at that time, saying, Cursed be the man before the Lord, that riseth up and buildeth this city Jericho: he shall lay the foundation thereof in his firstborn, and in his youngest son shall he set up the gates of it" (Josh. 6:26).
"In his [Ahab's] days did Hiel the Bethelite build Jericho: he laid the foundation thereof in Abiram

his firstborn, and set up the gates thereof in his youngest son Segub, according to the word of the Lord, which he spake by Joshua the son of Nun" (1 Ki. 16:34).

M. F. Unger writes:

"The rebuilding of Jericho is confirmed by archaeological diggings. Recent excavations trace the city's occupation from dim antiquity. Despite confusion in interpreting the evidence . . . the Bible stands confirmed on this point, with no occupational levels from Joshua's time to Ahab's era, when small ruins from the century point to Hiel's rebuilding the site." (*Unger's Bible Handbook*, p. 220)

46. The victory of Elijah on Mt. Carmel (1 Ki. 18).

"Now therefore send, and gather to me all Israel unto mount Carmel, and the prophets of Baal four hundred and fifty, and the prophets of the groves four hundred, which eat at Jezebel's table" (18:19).

Archaeologist J. A. Thompson discusses this event:

"The story of the conflict of Ahab with Elijah gains much from modern discovery. It was a time of severe drought. This drought is attested in the writings of Josephus who quoted from the Greek writer Meander, who had drawn on some Phoenician sources. Of greater interest, however, is the fact that the god Baal, who features so much in this story, is now depicted for us in very great detail as a result of the tablet discoveries from Ras Shamra, the former Ugarit, a great Canaanite town and the site of several temples. Baal was peculiarly the god of fertility. He controlled the seasons and was responsible for the storm and the rain. If a drought was upon the land, it was due to Baal's working. The devotee would appeal to him for a relief of these conditions. With scorn, Elijah, on Mount Carmel, exposed the emptiness of this belief (1 Ki. 18). If Baal failed, the God of Israel would not. At the word of Elijah, and in answer to his prayer, the rain came.

There is another feature of this story. In the Hebrew text there are in fact two gods referred to in 1 Kings 18:19. These are Baal and Asherah (translated in the Authorized Version as 'the groves'). The documents excavated at Ugarit show us that Asherah was a female goddess, the consort of Baal, a sensuous, lustful creature. She, like Baal, had her prophets in Israel, four hundred of them (1 Ki. 18:19). The Authorized Version of the Bible needs to be revised here to read: 'the prophets of Baal four hundred and fifty, and the prophets of Asherah four hundred.' " (*The Bible and Archaeology*, pp. 124, 125)

47. Ahab's house of ivory (1 Ki. 22:39).

"Now the rest of the acts of Ahab, and all that he did, and the ivory house which he made, and all the cities that he built, are they not written in the book of the chronicles of the kings of Israel?" (1 Ki. 22:39).

A Harvard University expedition in 1908–1910 found, in Samaria, the ruins of this house. Its walls had been faced with ivory. There were thousands of pieces of the most exquisitely carved and inlaid panels, plaques, cabinets, and couches.

48. The pool of Samaria (1 Ki. 22:37, 38).

"So the king died, and was brought to Samaria; and they buried the king in Samaria."

Archaeologists have excavated a pool of water at the northern end of one of Samaria's palace courtyards. Its dimensions are thirty-three feet by seventeen feet. The location would indicate it was used for watering horses, and, no doubt, for washing chariots.

49. The war between Israel and Moab (2 Ki. 3).

"But it came to pass, when Ahab was dead, that the king of Moab rebelled against the king of Israel" (3:5).

This chapter relates the account of the revolt of Mesha, king of Moab, against Israel. He lost this war, thanks to Elisha's supernatural help, and in utter frustration, before the horrified eyes of the victorious Israeli troops, offered up his eldest son to the devilish Moabite god Chemosh.

In 1868 the famous Moabite Stone was discovered by F. A. Klein, a German missionary at Dibon, some twenty miles east of the Dead Sea. This stone three-and-a-half feet high, by two-and-a-half feet wide by one foot thick was erected by King Mesha and gives his account of this battle in 2 Kings 3. However, as could be expected, he tells an entirely different story. He correctly relates his rebellion against Israel, but changes the results of the battle, making himself the glorious winner.

50. The man "on whose hand the king leaned" (2 Ki. 7).

Fred H. Wright writes:

"In 2 Kings 7:2 an officer of the king is referred to as being 'a lord on whose hand the king leaned.' Verses 17 and 19 mention the same man. The American Standard Revised Version (A.S.V.) translates captain instead of lord. There has been in the past much question as to what was the nature of this officer's task. The word in the Hebrew means literally 'the third.' Some have argued that the man was a third ranking officer. But now pictures on Assyrian monuments have explained this Hebrew word. There an Assyrian war chariot is represented as having three men in its crew: the driver, the man who did the fighting, and the third man who grasped the two straps that were attached to the back of the chariot and thus made a living back for the vehicle. Standing at the back of the chariot, he would prevent the driver or fighter from being thrown from the chariot as it traveled over bumpy ground. To be 'the third man' in the king's chariot was a responsible position, and such a man would be assigned to important tasks when the king was at home and not away fighting. This man was then in very truth 'the third man on whose hand the king leaned.' " (*Highlights of Archaeology in Bible Lands*, pp. 49, 50)

51. The punishment of King Jehu (2 Ki. 10:29–33).

"But Jehu took no heed to walk in the law of the Lord God of Israel with all his heart . . ." (10:31).

"In those days the Lord began to cut Israel short . . ." (10:32).

The Black Obelisk of Shalmaneser III found in 1845 shows a figure with marked Jewish features kneeling at the feet of the king and above it this inscription: "The tribute of Jehu, son [successor] of Omri, silver, gold, bowls of gold, chalices of gold, cups of gold, vases of gold, lead, sceptre for the king and spear-shafts I have received."

52. The official seal of the servant of Jeroboam II (2 Ki. 14:23–29).

". . . Jeroboam the son of Joash king of Israel began to reign in Samaria, and reigned forty and one years" (14:23).

Jeroboam's beautiful palace in Samaria has been excavated. The jasper seal of "shema, servant of Jeroboam" was also discovered, with its magnificently executed lion.

53. Repentance of Nineveh (Jonah 3).

"So the people of Nineveh believed God, and proclaimed a fast, and put on sackcloth, from the greatest of them even to the least of them" (3:5).

This chapter describes the greatest revival in all recorded history. No other physical miracle in this book (or any other Old Testament book) compares with the marvel and extent of this spiritual miracle. In the New Testament Jesus later warned that his entire generation (in general) would someday be drastically affected because:

"The men of Nineveh shall rise in judgment with his generation and shall condemn it: because they repented at the preaching of Jonah; and behold, a greater than Jonah is here" (Mt. 12:41).

The critic, however, always anxious to knock the Bible, has gleefully pointed out that secular history records no such revival in Nineveh, as described here. However, secular history may indeed hint at this sacred revival recorded in Jonah, after all. It is known that about this time there was a religious movement in Nineveh, which resulted in a change from the worship of many gods to that of one God whom they called Nebo. Nebo was the son in the Babylonian trinity. His name meant, "The proclaimer, the prophet."

He was the proclaimer of the mind and will of the trinity head. Nebo was the god of wisdom, the creator, the angelic overseer. Some believe Nebo had been worshiped in earlier days as the only supreme God. It is known that the Ninevite ruler Adal-Nirari III (810–783) had advocated a monotheistic worship system of some kind. If the revival took place at this time as a result of Jonah's preaching, then the use of their national name for the Son of God is what we might possibly expect. Jonah did not preach repentance to the Ninevites in the name of Yahweh (the Hebrew God of the covenant), but in the name of Elohim (the triune Creator of the universe; Gen. 1:1).

54. The tribute of money Menahem paid to Assyrian king Pul (2 Ki. 15:16–20).

"And Pul . . . came against the land: and Menahem gave Pul a thousand talents of silver. . . . And Menahem exacted the money of Israel, even of all the mighty men of wealth, of each man fifty shekels of silver, to give to the king of Assyria. So the king of Assyria turned back, and stayed not there in the land" (15:19, 20).

Menahem was one of Israel's last kings. During his reign the Assyrian threat became serious. When Pul (the Tiglath-Pileser of history) made a move toward Israel, Menahem was able to buy him off. In the excavated annals of Tiglath-Pileser we read:

"As for Menahem, I overwhelmed him like a snowstorm and he fled like a bird alone, and bowed to my feet. I returned him to his place and imposed tribute upon him."

The figure of fifty shekels referred to in 2 Kings 15:20 is now known to be the average price for a slave. Menahem was required to assess his men at the price of a slave and thus buy their freedom. His annals also mention Uzziah, Ahaz, Pekah, and Hoshea. These are two southern and two northern kings often mentioned in the Bible.

55. The accomplishments and judgment of King Uzziah (2 Chron. 26).

"Also he built towers in the desert, and digged many wells: for he had much cattle, both in the low country, and in the plains . . ." (26:10).

"But when he was strong, his heart was lifted up to his destruction: for he transgressed against the Lord his God, and went into the temple of the Lord to burn incense upon the altar of incense" (26:16).

"And Uzziah the king was a leper unto the day of his death, and dwelt in a [separate] house, being a leper; for he was cut off from the house of the Lord. . ." (26:21).

In 1958 Professor Michael Evenari, Vice President of the Hebrew University, discovered traces of several Judean forms equipped with cisterns, irrigation systems, and fortifications, all dating back to the days of Uzziah.

In 1959 Professor Aharoni of Hebrew University discovered a Judean Palace two miles south of Jerusalem, on Rachel's hill on the road to Bethlehem. It was 250 feet by 150 feet square, surrounded by a casemated wall like that of King Ahab in Samaria, and had a triple gate in the style of Solomon's day. Three sides of the courtyard were surrounded by buildings, two sides residential and the third for stores. There was no doubt about the occupant of this magnificent but lonely outpost. They had excavated the palace of Uzziah the leper.

56. The capture of Israel by Assyrian kings Pul, Shalmaneser, and Sargon (2 Ki. 15, 17).

"In the days of Pekah king of Israel, came Tiglath-pileser king of Assyria . . . and carried them captive to Assyria. And Hoshea . . . made a conspiracy against Pekah . . . and smote him, and slew him, and reigned in his stead . . ." (15:29, 30).

"Against him [Hoshea] came up Shalmaneser . . . and Hoshea became his servant and gave him presents" (17:3).

"And the king of Assyria brought men from Babylon, . . . and placed them in the cities of Samaria instead of the children of Israel: and they possessed Samaria, and dwelt in the cities thereof" (17:24).

From the hand of these Assyrian kings we read the following excavated inscriptions:

"The House of Omri and all its people together with their goods I carried off to Assyria. Pekah their king they deposed and I placed Hoshea over them as king. From him I received 10 talents of gold and 1000 talents of silver." (Pul)

"In my first year I captured Samaria. I took captive 27,290 people. People of other lands, who never paid tribute, I settled in Samaria." (Sargon)

57. Ahaz's money tribute to King Tiglath-pileser (2 Ki. 16:5–9).

"So Ahaz sent messengers to Tiglath-pileser, king of Assyria, saying, I am thy servant and thy son. . . . And Ahaz took the silver and gold that was found in the house of the Lord, and in the treasures of the king's house, and sent it for a present to the king of Assyria. And the king of Assyria . . . went up against Damascus, and took it, and carried the people of it captive to Kir, and slew Rezin" (16:7-9).

An excavated inscription of Tiglath-pileser reads:

"The tribute of Ahaz the Judean I received, gold, silver, lead, tin, and linen. Damascus I destroyed. Rezin I took. His officers I impaled alive on stakes. . . ."

58. The historicity of Sargon (Isa. 20:1).

"In the year that Tartan came unto Ashdod (when Sargon, the king of Assyria, sent him,) and fought against Ashdod, and took it" (Isa. 20:1).

Until the advent of modern archaeology the name Sargon never appeared in ancient literature apart from references in Isaiah. Critics were, as usual, quick to point out another "historical blunder" in the Bible. But in 1843 their sneers suddenly disappeared, for archaeologist Paul Emil Botta excavated a huge palace at Khorsabad, on the northern edge of Nineveh. The building turned out to be the empire headquarters of Sargon himself. Other finds since this have confirmed that Sargon was one of the greatest (if not greatest) of all Assyrian kings. In one of his records we are told:

"Azuri, King of Ashdod, had schemed not to deliver tribute any more. . . . In a sudden rage I marched quickly in my state chariot and with my cavalry . . . against Ashdod . . . and I besieged and conquered . . . Ashdod . . . and they bore my yoke. . . ."

59. The seal and tomb of Shebna, Hezekiah's scribe (Isa. 22:15, 16; 36:2).

"Thus saith the Lord God of hosts, Go, get thee unto this treasurer, even unto Shebna, which is over the house, and say, What hast thou here? And whom hast thou here, that thou hast hewed thee out a sepulchre here, as he that heweth him out a sepulchre on high, and that graveth an habitation for himself in a rock?" (22:15, 16).

"Then came forth unto him [Hezekiah] . . . Shebna the scribe . . ." (36:3).

In 1935 J. L. Starkey excavated at Lachish and found a stone seal, having on it the name Shebna, apparently coming from the age of King Hezekiah. Also, in the British Museum is a limestone lintel of a tomb of a certain Shebna, dating back to the time of Hezekiah. It is inscribed with archaic Hebrew.

60. The destruction of Lachish by Sennacherib (2 Chron. 32:9; Isa. 10:29).

"After this did Sennacherib king of Assyria . . . himself [lay] siege against Lachish, and all his power with him . . ." (2 Chron. 32:9).

Historian Werner Keller writes:

"Anyone who wishes to re-live the frightful battle of Lachish, vividly and dramatically to the smallest detail, must pay a visit to the British Museum. It is here that the massive reliefs, which eyewitnesses created on the orders of Sennacherib 2,650 years ago, have found a resting place. Sir Henry Layard salvaged this precious object from the ruins of Nineveh.

On the turrets and breastwork of the stronghold of Lachish with its stout high walls the Judahite defenders fought with clenched teeth. They showered a hail of arrows on the attackers, hurled stones down upon them, threw burning torches—the fire-bombs of the ancient world—among the enemy. The faces, curly hair, and short beards are easily recognisable. Only a few wear any protection for head or body.

At the foot of the wall the Assyrians are attacking with the utmost violence and with every type of weapon. Sennacherib had deployed the whole range of approved assault-tactics. Every Assyrian is armed to the teeth: each one wears shield and helmet. Their engineers have built sloping ramps of earth, stones and felled trees. Siege-engines, the first tanks in history, push forward up the ramps against the walls. They are equipped in front with a battering ram which sticks out like the barrel of a cannon. The crew consists of three men. The archer shoots his arrows from behind a sheltering canopy. A warrior guides the ram, and under its violent blows stones and bricks crash down from the walls. The third man douses the tanks with ladlefuls of water extinguishing the smouldering fire-bombs. Several tanks are attacking at the same time. Tunnels are being driven into the rock beneath the foundations of the walls. Behind the tanks come the infantry, bowmen, some of them kneeling, some stooping, protected by a shieldbearer. The first captives, men and women, are being led off. Lifeless bodies are hanging on pointed stakes—impaled. James Lesley Starkey, a British archaeologist, dug up the ruins of the walls of the fortress of Lachish. The holes and breaches made by the Assyrian tanks can be seen to this day." *The Bible As History*, pp. 258, 259)

61. Sennacherib's failure to capture Jerusalem (2 Ki. 18-19; 2 Chron. 32; Isa. 36-37).

"Therefore thus saith the Lord concerning the king of Assyria, He shall not come into this city, nor shoot an arrow there, nor come before it with shields, nor cast a bank against it. By the way that he came, by the same shall he return, and shall not come into this city, saith the Lord. For I will defend this city to save it for mine own sake, and for my servant David's sake" (Isa. 37:33-35).

"Then the angel of the Lord went forth, and smote in the camp of the Assyrians a hundred and fourscore and five thousand: and when they arose early in the morning, behold, they were all dead corpses" (37:36).

Thus reads the biblical account of Sennacherib's Judean invasion. The following is taken from Sennacherib's own record of this time.

"As to Hezekiah the Jew, he did not submit to my yoke. I laid siege to forty-six of his strong cities, walled forts and to countless small villages in the vicinity and conquered them by means of well-stamped earth-ramps and battering rams brought thus near to the walls. . . . Himself I made a prisoner in Jerusalem, his royal residence, like a bird in a cage."

62. The murder of Sennacherib by his own sons.

"So Sennacherib king of Assyria departed, and went and returned, and dwelt at Nineveh. And it came to pass as he was worshipping in the house of Nisroch his god, that Adrammelech and Sharezer his sons smote him with the sword; and they escaped . . . and Esar-haddon his son reigned in his stead" (Isa. 37:37, 38).

Esar-haddon, his son and successor relates this very event in an inscription: "A firm determination fell upon my brothers. They forsook the gods and turned to their deeds of violence, plotting evil. To gain the kingship they slew Sennacherib their father."

63. The imprisonment of Manasseh by the Assyrians.
   "Wherefore the Lord brought upon them the captains of the host of the king of Assyria, which took Manasseh [in chains], and bound him with fetters, and carried him to Babylon" (2 Chron. 33:11).
   Archaeologist Fred Wright writes:
   "At first thought some might question the Bible story because it says Manasseh was taken to Babylon, whereas Nineveh was the capital city of Assyria. Furthermore, Esar-haddon's father, Sennacherib, had cruelly destroyed the city of Babylon and left it in ruins. But archaeology furnishes what would otherwise be a missing link in the story. It records the fact that Esar-haddon rebuilt Babylon. In his record he says that he rebuilt it, and that he made it a magnificent city. He mentions Manasseh in one of his inscriptions: 'I summoned the Kings of Syria . . . Manasseh, King of Judah . . . I gave them their orders.' " (Highlights of Archaeology in Bible Lands, p. 49)

64. The discovery of the book of the law in the Temple during Josiah's reign (2 Chron. 34:8–32).
   "Now in the eighteenth year of his reign, . . . he sent Shaphan . . . and Maaseiah . . . and Joah . . . to repair the house of the Lord his God" (34:8).
   ". . . Hilkiah the priest found a book of the law of the Lord given by Moses" (34:14).
   M. F. Unger writes:
   ". . . archaeology throws interesting light on the possible reason for the repairmen's finding this document in their work on the temple. The discovery is closely linked with the activity of the stonemasons and carpenters, and it is entirely possible this copy of the Pentateuch had been placed in the cornerstone of the temple when it was erected by Solomon (c. 966 B.C.). Doubtless the masonry documents come to light. Archaeology has demonstrated that it was customary in ancient times to place documents in the foundations of buildings, as it is done even to the present day.
   Nabonidus, a Babylonian king of the sixth century B.C., for example, delighted to dig into foundations of buildings ancient in his day to recover documents deposited there centuries earlier. This he did at the temple of Shamash at Sippar in lower Mesopotamia." (Archaeology and the Old Testament, p. 281)

65. Hezekiah's water tunnel (2 Ki. 20:20; 2 Chron. 32:30).
   "And . . . Hezekiah . . . made a pool, and a conduit, and brought water into the city . . ." (2 Ki. 20:20).
   "This same Hezekiah also stopped the upper watercourse of Gihon, and brought it straight down to the west side of the city of David . . ." (2 Chron. 32:30).
   The most important source of water in ancient Jerusalem was the spring of Gihon situated just east of the temple area in the Kidron Valley. Accordingly, it was exposed to an attacking enemy. To counteract this, Hezekiah had constructed a great conduit leading from the Gihon spring outside the city to a special reservoir inside the city called the Pool of Siloam. This conduit, 1777 feet long and hewn out of the solid rock, is one of the most amazing devices for water supply in all the biblical period. Workmen, employing hand picks, operating in zigzag fashion from opposite sides and finally meeting in the middle, excavated a conduit that averages six feet in height. The Pool of Siloam reservoir measures about thirty by twenty feet.
   Archaeologically the most interesting thing about Hezekiah's tunnel is the six-line inscription in classical Hebrew beautifully cut at the wall of the conduit about nineteen feet from the Siloam end of the aqueduct. In 1180 two small Arab boys were playing in that area when one of them discovered it. The inscription reads:
   "The boring through is completed. Now this is the story of the boring through. While the workmen were still lifting pick to pick, each toward his neighbor, and while three cubits remained to be cut through, each heard the voice of the other. . . ."
   The inscription was subsequently chiseled out of the rock and taken by the Turkish government to the archaeological museum of Istanbul.

66. Hezekiah's wall repairs.
   "Also he strengthened himself, and built up all the wall that was broken, and raised it up to the towers, and another wall [outside it] . . ." (2 Chron. 32:5).
   "Hezekiah's repairs in the wall, hurriedly done, under pressure of the Assyrian siege, are distinctly indicated in the walls as they stand today. Foundations of the outer wall have been discovered, running parallel to David's wall, 30 feet apart." (Halley's Bible Handbook, p. 225)

67. The destruction of Lachish by Nebuchadnezzar.
   ". . . the king of Babylon's army fought against . . . Lachish . . . and against Azekah: for these [fortified] cities remained of the cities of Judah" (34:7).
   One of the most important finds of the early twentieth century was the Lachish Ostraca. These consist of twenty-one letters written in biblical Hebrew, all written by a man named Hoshiah (who was stationed at some military outpost) to Jaosh, the high commanding officer at Lachish. Lachish was located thirty miles southwest of Jerusalem, on the main route from central Palestine to Egypt. The ruins of this city and these potsherd documents were excavated by J. L. Starkey in 1935. The letters give us an independent view of conditions in Judah before the fall of Jerusalem.
   Letter number three concerns the movement of Jewish troops. Letter number four reads:
   "We are watching for the signal stations of Lachish, according to all the signals you are giving, because we cannot see the signals of Azekah."
   These letters also refer to and mention by name certain persons whose names appear in the biblical narrative: "Gemariah," an officer of King Zedekiah (Jer. 29:3). "Jaazaniah," a military captain of Nebuchadnezzar (2 Ki. 25:23), "Mattaniah," original name of King Zedekiah (2 Ki. 24:17), and others are mentioned. The father of Baruch, Jeremiah's scribe is also referred to. His name was Neriah (Jer. 43:3). This message, of course, told Jaosh that Azekah had fallen. Nebuchadnezzar could now withdraw his engineers for the attack on the last fortress at Lachish.
   We have already seen how the storm troops of Sennacherib had rushed the walls of Lachish in 701 B.C. But this was nothing compared to the destruction the Babylonians would now effect. British archaeologists with the Welcome-Marston expedition obtained information about the terrible end of Lachish in 1938 after six strenuous seasons of excavating. A sad note to this story, however, was the tragic murder of J. L. Starkey,

one of the excavators of Lachish in 1938, at the age of forty-three. He was shot to death by the Arabs near Hebron.

Werner Keller writes:

"Investigation of the stratum which marked the Babylonian work of destruction produced, to Starkey's astonishment, ashes. Ashes in incredible quantities. Many of the layers are several yards thick and are still—after 2,500 years—higher than the remains of the solid walls of the fortress. Nebuchadnezzar's engineers were specialists in the art of incendiarism, past masters at starting conflagrations.

Whatever wood they could lay hands on they dragged to the spot, stripped the whole area around Lachish of its forests and thickets, cleared the hills of timber for miles around, piled the firewood as high as a house outside the walls and set it alight. Countless olive groves were hacked down for this purpose: the layer of ashes contains masses of charred olive stones. Day and night sheets of flame leapt sky high, a ring of fire licked the walls from top to bottom. The besieging force piled on more and more wood until the white-hot stones burst and the walls caved in." (*The Bible As History*, p. 283)

68. The captivity of Jehoiachin and the appointment of Zedekiah (2 Ki. 24:10-19; 25:27-30).

"At that time . . . Nebuchadnezzar king of Babylon came up against Jerusalem, and the city was besieged" (24:10).

"And he carried away Jehoiachin to Babylon . . ." (24:15).

"And the king of Babylon made Mattaniah . . . king in his stead, and changed his name to Zedekiah" (24:17).

"And it came to pass in the seven and thirtieth year of the captivity of Jehoiachin king of Judah . . . that Evil-merodach king of Babylon in the year that he began to reign did [liberate] Jehoiachin . . . out of prison" (25:27).

"And his allowance was a continual allowance given him by the king . . ." (25:30).

In 1955 archaeologist D. J. Wiseman was deciphering some Babylonian tablets in the British Museum when he discovered the following message on one of them:

"In the seventh year . . . the king [Nebuchadnezzar] . . . encamped over against the city of Judaeans [Jerusalem] and conquered it on the second day of Adar [March 597]. He took the king [Jehoiachin] prisoner, and appointed in his stead a king after his own heart [Zedekiah]. He exacted heavy tribute and had it brought to Babylon."

Even prior to this, in 1934, E. F. Weider was translating some similar Babylonian tablets which had been excavated in 1899 by Professor Robert Koldeway. On four different receipts for allotted food stuffs, among them the best quality sesame oil, he came across a familiar name, "Jehoiachin, the king of the land of Judah."

69. The futile hope of Zedekiah in looking to Egypt to aid against Babylon (Jer. 37:1, 5-11).

"Then Pharaoh's army was come forth out of Egypt: and when the Chaldeans that besieged Jerusalem heard tidings of them, they departed from Jerusalem" (37:5).

"Thus, saith the Lord . . . Behold, Pharaoh's army, which is come forth to help you, shall return to Egypt into their own land" (37:7).

Archaeological evidence shows that an army did in fact at that time, come up from the Nile under Pharaoh Apries, as Herodotus, the Greek historian also mentions. Its destination, however, was not Jerusalem. Apries was making an attack by land and sea against the Phoenician ports. Evidence on fragments of Egyptian monuments of Pharaoh's presence in Tyre and Sidon at that time have been found.

70. The treachery of Ishmael against Gedaliah and his Officials (Jer. 41:1-15).

"Then arose Ishmael . . . and smote Gedaliah . . . with the sword, and slew him, whom the king of Babylon had made governor over the land" (41:2).

"And it came to pass the second day after he had slain Gedaliah, and no man knew it, that there came certain men [to Mizpah] . . . with offerings and incense in their hand, to bring them to the house of the Lord" (41:4, 5).

"And it was so, when they came into the [center] of the city, that Ishmael . . . slew them, and cast them into the midst of the pit . . ." (41:7).

The site of ancient Mizpah where Gedaliah once governed has been excavated by the Pacific School of Religion of Berkeley, California, under the direction of F. W. Bade. In the rock stratum belonging to this period he found a deep cistern containing a large number of skeletons.

71. The great stones buried by Jeremiah in Tahpanhes, Egypt (Jer. 43:8-13).

"Then came the word of the Lord unto Jeremiah in Tahpanhes, saying, Take great stones in thine hand and hide them in the clay in the brickkiln, which is at the entry of Pharaoh's house in Tahpanhes, in the sight of the men of Judah; and say unto them, Thus saith the Lord of hosts, the God of Israel; Behold, I will send and take Nebuchadnezzar the king of Babylon, my servant, and will set his throne upon these stones that I have hid; and he shall spread his royal pavilion over them. And when he cometh, he shall smite the land of Egypt . . ." (43:8-11).

In 1886 Sir Flinders Petrie unearthed both this pavement and palace of the Egyptian Pharaoh. He found a platform of brick work, which was located outside the door of the house, looking very much as if it was the actual platform to which Jeremiah refers in his message, where Nebuchadnezzar was to spread his pavilion. In fact, great stones were actually found embedded under this area.

Shortly after 1886 three cylinders were discovered near this site and sold to the Cairo museum. They contain an inscription telling about Nebuchadnezzar's great building activities at Babylon. It would seem they were placed at this spot to commemorate the visit of King Nebuchadnezzar to Egypt.

72. Jewish life in the Babylonian exile (Jer. 29:4-7).

"Thus saith the Lord of hosts, the God of Israel, unto all that are carried away captives, whom I have caused to be carried away from Jerusalem unto Babylon; Build ye houses, and dwell in them; and plant gardens, and eat the fruit of them; take ye wives, and beget sons and daughters; and take wives for your sons, and give your daughters to husbands, that they may bear sons and daughters; that ye may be increased there, and not diminished. And seek the peace of the city whither I have caused you to be carried away captives, and pray unto the Lord for it: for in the peace thereof shall ye have peace" (Jer. 29:4-7).

Werner Keller comments on this:

"So wrote the prophet Jeremiah from Jerusalem to the elders, priests, prophets and to the whole nation that at Nebuchadnezzar's bidding had been carried off to Babylon. Following his well-considered advice, they sought and found 'the peace of the city,' and did not fare at all badly. The Exile in Babylon was not to be compared with the harsh existence of the children of Israel on the Nile, in Pithom and Raamses in the days of Moses. Apart from a few exceptions (Isa. 47:6) there was no heavy forced labour. Nowhere is there any mention of their having to make bricks by the Euphrates. Yet Babylon ran what was probably the greatest brick-making industry in the world at that time. For never was there so much building going on in Mesopotamia as under Nebuchadnezzar.

Anyone who took Jeremiah's advice as his guide got on well, some indeed very well. One family which had made the grade has left to posterity its dust-covered business documents on clay. 'Murashu and Sons'—International Bank—Insurance, Conveyancing, Loans—Personal and real estate—Head office: Nippur—Branches everywhere—a firm with a reputation throughout the world, the 'Lloyds' of Mesopotamia.

The Murashus—displaced persons from Jerusalem—had done well for themselves in Nippur since 587 B.C. They were an old established office. Their firm still stood for something in Mesopotamia even in the Persian era. The 'books' of 'Murashu and Sons' are full of detailed information about the life of the exiles, such as their names, their occupations, their property.

Scholars from the University of Pennsylvania discovered some of the Jewish firm's deeds stored in its former business premises in Nippur. They were in great clay jars, which, in accordance wtih security precautions in those days, had been carefully sealed with asphalt. It was not only Assyriologists who read the translations of these documents with delight.

The offices of Murashu and Sons were a hive of activity. For 150 years they enjoyed the confidence of their clients, whether it was a matter of conveyance of large estates and sections of the canals or of slaves. Anyone who could not write, when he came eventually to add his signature, put, instead of his name, the print of his fingernail on the documents. It corresponded to putting a cross, in the presence of witnesses, as in the case of illiterates today.

The rate of interest was 20 percent, not introduced by Murashu, let it be said. That was the normal rate in those days.

'Murashu and Sons' may serve as an example of the profession, which since the days of the Exile has been associated with the children of Israel. It became for them the profession par excellence and has remained so until now: that of merchant and trader. In their homeland they had only been peasants, settlers, cattle breeders and tradesmen. The law of Israel had made no provision for commerce: it was an alien occupation. The word 'Canaanite' was for them synonymous with 'shopkeeper,' 'merchant,' people whom the prophets had vigorously castigated for their sins. 'He is a merchant, the balances of deceit are in his hand: he loveth to oppress' (Hosea 12:7; Amos 8:5, 6).

The switch over to this hitherto forbidden profession was extremely clever—a fact that is seldom properly understood. For it proved to be in the last resort, when added to a tenacious attachment to their old faith, the best guarantee of the continuance of Israel as a people. As farmers and settlers scattered throughout a foreign land they would have intermarried and interbred with people of other races and in a few generations would have been absorbed and disappeared. This new profession demanded that their houses should be in more or less large societies, within which they could build themselves into a community and devote themselves to their religious practices. It gave them cohesion and continuity.

The Israelites could have chosen no better training college." (*The Bible As History,* pp. 287, 289)

73. The great statue and fiery furnace of Nebuchadnezzar (Dan. 3).

"Nebuchadnezzar . . . made an image of gold . . . and . . . set it up in the plain of Dura, in the province of Babylon. Then Nebuchadnezzar . . . sent to gather . . . all the rulers of the provinces, to come to the dedication of the image . . ." (3:1,2).

"Then an herald cried aloud . . . fall down and worship the golden image. . . . And whoso falleth not down and worshippeth, shall the same hour be cast into the midst of a burning fiery furnace" (3:4-6).

Fred H. Wright writes:

"The Image of Nebuchadnezzar. Archaeology has discovered that the king's demand for public worship of his image, as related in the third chapter of Daniel, was part of a general policy he adopted in various places of his empire. Sir Leonard Wooley found an example of this new policy in his excavations at Ur of the Chaldees. It seems that when Nebuchadnezzar restored the temple worship at Ur by making over the building, he changed the old order of having the rites secret in the sanctuary, and made it so that great crowds could watch the priest as he made his offerings on an open-air altar, and even the image of the god could be seen through an open door behind him. Thus, when the Bible says that this same king set up an image in a public place and demanded that everybody worship it, the king was carrying out the same policy as he did at Ur. What had previously been secret now became public. Other kings had set up images, but the new thing that Nebuchadnezzar did was to command general and public worship by everybody. The three Hebrew children of the Book of Daniel refused to obey and so were thrown into the fiery furnace.

Babylonian fiery furnaces. Daniel's account of the three Hebrew children being cast into the fiery furnace has been called folklore by some Bible critics. They have implied that no such thing could have actually happened in those days. But the archaeologists have discovered actual proof that men had such experiences in the long ago. The early excavators at Babylon uncovered a peculiarly shaped building that at first seemed like a brick kiln. An inscription was found that specified the purpose of this building, and this is what it said: 'This is the place of burning where men who blasphemed the gods of Chaldea died by fire.'

That this method of punishment was in common use in earlier times is seen from an inscription of the Assyrian King Ashurbanipal. It reads: 'Saulmagina my rebellious brother, who made war with me, they threw into a burning fiery furnace, and destroyed his life.'

Furthermore, a letter has come to light which indicates that a king of Larsa, a contemporary of King Hammurabi, gave sentence for a slave to be thrown into a furnace." (*Highlights of Archaeology in Bible Lands*, pp. 64, 65)

74. The pride of Nebuchadnezzar and the greatness of Babylon (Dan. 4).

"The king spake, and said, Is not this great Babylon, that I have built for the house of the kingdom by the might of my power, and for the honour of my majesty?" (4:30).

Archaeologist J. A. Thompson writes the following: "And Nebuchadnezzar was proud indeed as the inscriptions show. Among the ruins of the city Koldewey found a good deal of inscribed materials, partly on bricks and stones and partly on baked clay tablets. Many of the written records indicate the pride and confidence of Nebuchadnezzar, as a selection of these inscriptions will show:

'A great wall which like a mountain cannot be moved I made of mortar and bricks. . . . Its foundation upon the bosom of the abyss I placed down deeply . . . its top I raised mountain high. I triplicated the city wall in order to strengthen it, I caused a great protecting wall to run at the foot of the wall of burnt brick. . . .

When Marduk the great lord named me the legitimate son and to direct the affairs of the land . . . Babylon his mighty city . . . its great gates strong bulls of bronze, and terrible serpents ready to strike, I placed. That which no king had done my father did in that he enclosed the city with two moat-walls of mortar and brick. As for me, a third great moat wall, one against the second, I built with mortar and brick, and with the moat-wall of my father joined and closely united it. Its foundation upon the bosom of the abyss I laid down deeply, its top I raised mountain high. . . .

The produce of the lands, the products of the mountains, the bountiful wealth of the sea, within her I gathered . . . great quantities of grain beyond measure I stored up in her. At that time the palace, my royal abode . . . I rebuilt in Babylon . . . great cedars I brought from Lebanon, the beautiful forest to roof it. . . .'

Concerning one of the temples, Nebuchadnezzar spoke in the following terms:

'Huge cedars from Lebanon, their forest with my clean hands I cut down. With radiant gold I overlaid them, with jewels I adorned them . . . the side chapels of the shrine of Hebo, the cedar beams of their

roofs I adorned with lustrous silver. Giant bulls I made of bronze work and clothed them with white marble. I adorned them with jewels and placed them upon the threshold of the gate of the shrine. . . .' " (*The Bible and Archaeology*, pp. 160, 161)

75. The insanity of Nebuchadnezzar (Dan. 4).

"The same hour was the thing fulfilled upon Nebuchadnezzar; and he was driven from men, and did eat grass as oxen, and his body was wet with the dew of heaven, till his hairs were grown like eagles' feathers, and his nails like birds' claws" (4:33).

The king's insanity is corroborated by history. Josephus quotes from a Babylonian historian named Berasus who mentions a strange malady suffered by Nebuchadnezzar. There is also the testimony of Abydenus, the Greek historian of 268 B.C.

It is possible that Nebuchadnezzar himself gives testimony concerning this. Archaeologist Sir Henry Rawlinson has translated an excavated inscription of the king. It reads:

"For four years the seat of my kingdom in the city . . . did not rejoice my heart. In all my dominions I did not build a high place of power; the precious treasures of my kingdom I did not lay out in the worship of Merodach, my lord, the joy of my heart. In Babylon the city of my sovereignty and the seat of my empire I did not sing his praises, and I did not furnish his altars: nor did I clear out the canals."

76. The historicity of Belshazzar (Dan. 5).

"Belshazzar the king made a great feast to a thousand of his lords, and drank wine before the thousand" (5:1).

Henry Halley writes:

"Until 1853 no mention of Belshazzar was found in Babylonian records, and Nabonidas (555-538 B.C.), was known to have been the last king of Babylon. To the critics this was one of the evidences that the Book of Daniel was not historical. But in 1853 an inscription was found in a cornerstone of a temple built by Nabonidas in Ur to a god, which reads: 'May I, Nabonidas, king of Babylon, not sin against thee. And may reverence for thee dwell in the heart of Belshazzar, my first-born, a favorite son.'

From other inscriptions it has been learned that Nabonidas, much of the time, was in retirement outside of Babylon, and that Belshazzar was in control of the army and the government, co-regent with his father, and that it was he who surrendered to Cyrus. This explains how Daniel could be 'third ruler' in the kingdom" (5:16, 29). (*Halley's Bible Handbook*, p. 344)

77. The capture of Babylon and execution of Belshazzar (Dan. 5).

"In the same hour came forth fingers of a man's hand, and wrote over against the [lampstand] upon the plaster of the wall of the king's palace . . ." (5:5).

" . . . thy kingdom is divided, and given to the Medes and Persians" (5:28).

"In that night was Belshazzar the king of the Chaldeans slain. And Darius the Median took the kingdom . . ." (5:30, 31).

Old Testament Hebrew scholar Leon Wood writes: "The word for 'plaster' is used also in the Hebrew, meaning, 'chalk' or 'lime' (e.g., Isa. 27:9). The surface on which the writing appeared was apparently of lime plaster. The archaeologist Koldeway, who excavated Babylon, says that the largest room he found in the palace complex was 55 feet wide by 169 feet long, and had plastered walls. He tells also of a niche in one of the long walls, opposite the entrance, in which he suggests the king may have been seated during such time of feasting. Against a white plastered surface, any dark object would have stood out distinctly." (*A Commentary on Daniel*, p. 136)

Concerning the actual capture of the city, the Greek historian Herodotus tells us that the Babylonian armies at first moved north to challenge the advancing Persian troops, but were soon driven back behind the walls of Babylon. Cyrus then proceeded to divert the Euphrates River from its normal bed, under the walls of the city, channeling the waters to a near-by reservoir he had dug. Another Greek historian, Xenophon, states that entrance was made into the city at a time when the Babylonians were feasting at a drunken orgy.

78. Daniel and the lion's den (Dan. 6).
> "Then the king commanded, and they brought Daniel, and cast him into the den of lions . . ." (6:16).

Archaeology has now determined this was a common method of state execution (along with burning) in the Assyrian and Babylonian empires.

The excavator Diculafoy was working one day among the ruins of Babylon when he fell into what looked like a well. He was rescued by his fellow workmen, and then it became their purpose to determine what the place was. On the curb was an inscription which said: "The Place of execution, where men who angered the king died torn by wild animals."

When the palace at Shushan was being excavated, a record was discovered that gave a list of 484 men of high rank who had died in a lion's den. An inscription of the Assyrian king Ashurbanipal indicates that the same custom was common in his day. He records: "The rest of the people who had rebelled they threw alive among bulls and lions, as Sennacherib my grandfather used to do. Lo, again following his footsteps those men I threw into the midst of them."

79. The book of Esther and Ahasuerus the Persian king (Est.).
> "Now it came to pass in the days of Ahasuerus, (this is Ahasuerus which reigned, from India even unto Ethiopia, over an hundred and seven and twenty provinces:) that in those days, when the king Ahasuerus sat on the throne of his kingdom, which was in Shushan the palace . . ." (Est. 1:1, 2).

J. A. Thompson writes:
"The chief characters of the book, Vashti, Haman, and Mordecai are unknown in non- Biblical history. Excavations, however, as well as general historical evidence make it clear that there is much in the book that shows the writer to have been correctly informed on many of the background details of the story.

Xerxes (Ahasuerus) was a historical person. The picture given in the Book of Esther of a king who was a despot and thoroughly sensuous in character corresponds with the account given by the Greek historian Herodotus. He greatly enlarged his harem at Persepolis, as excavation shows, and became involved in a shameful affair with his brother's wife and later with the daughter as well.

The description of the ornate palace with its bright curtains is quite in the manner of the gaudy palaces of the Persians. Excavations at Susa (biblical Shushan) have yielded abundant evidence of the rich ornamentation of the walls of the palace and of the richly colored glazed bricks used there. This palace, commenced by Darius, was described in glowing terms. It was built of special timbers and adorned with gold, lapis lazuli, turquoise, silver, and ebony, and was erected by men who came from all over the empire.

The story of Esther could well fit into the time of Xerxes, for he reigned for twenty years, and the events of this book do not go beyond the twelfth or possibly the thirteenth year (Est. 3:7, 12). The banquet in the third year may coincide with the great council that Xerxes held before the invasion of Greece, and the four years that intervened before Esther became queen may well fit into the time that the king was absent in Greece (Est. 1:3; 2:16). The standard commentaries on the Book of Esther point out that many of the customs referred to in the story are quite in keeping with Persian practice. Thus the arrangements for the banquet (1:6-8), obeisance before the king and his favorites (3:2), belief in lucky and unlucky days (3:7), exclusion of mourning garb from the palace (4:2), hanging as the death penalty (5:14), dressing a royal benefactor in the king's robes (6:8), dispatching couriers with royal messages (3:13; 8:10) are all customs that are now well-known from the written records that have come to light. There are, moreover, a good number of Persian words in the book, largely from the language of government and trade." (*The Bible and Archaeology*, pp. 194, 195)

80. The edict of King Cyrus (Ezra 1:1-4).
> "Now in the first year of Cyrus . . . he made a proclamation throughout all his kingdom, and put it also in writing, saying . . . The Lord God of heaven . . . hath charged me to build him an house at Jerusalem, which is in Judah. Who is there among you of all his people? his God be with him, and let him go up to Jerusalem . . . and build the house of the Lord God of Israel . . ." (1:1-3).

The findings of archaeology have fully documented this edict. Excavations including the Nabonidus Chronicle, the Cyrus Cylinder, and other written documents show us Cyrus was a master of propaganda and knew how to exploit every occasion to the best advantage for himself. He had a well-known policy of returning the gods to their own homes. A part of the Cyrus Cylinder testifies to this practice: "I also gathered all the former inhabitants and returned them to their former habitations . . . may all the gods whom I have resettled in their sacred cities daily ask Bel and Nebo for a long life for me. . . ."

81. The historicity of Darius the Great (Ezra 6:1-15).
> "And this house [Jewish Temple] was finished on the third day of the month Adar, which was in the sixth year of the reign of Darius the king" (6:15).

Here it should be clearly stated that there exists ample proof of Darius' existence apart from the biblical record. The main reason for referring to him is that his name is connected to a very important archaeological discovery. This find is known as the Behistun Inscription.

© Hugh Claycombe 1981

The Tabernacle

**From the Wilderness of
Sinai until the building of
Solomon's Temple in 950 B.C.**

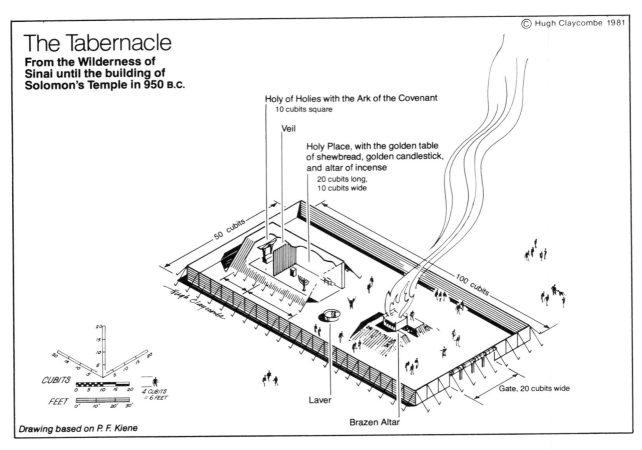

Holy of Holies with the Ark of the Covenant
10 cubits square

Veil

Holy Place, with the golden table
of shewbread, golden candlestick,
and altar of incense

20 cubits long,
10 cubits wide

50 cubits

100 cubits

Gate, 20 cubits wide

Laver

Brazen Altar

CUBITS

FEET

4 CUBITS
= 6 FEET

Drawing based on P. F. Kiene

© Hugh Claycombe 1981

Solomon's Temple

950 B.C.—586 B.C.

A permanent resting place for the
Ark of the Covenant. Similar to the
tabernacle, but the Holy Place and the
Holy of Holies were doubled in size.
Known in the ancient world for its
breathtaking beauty and
craftsmanship. It stood for four
hundred years until destroyed by
the Babylonians.

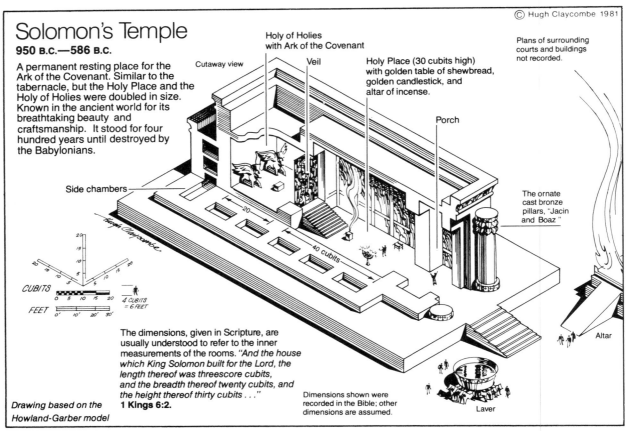

Holy of Holies
with Ark of the Covenant

Cutaway view

Veil

Holy Place (30 cubits high)
with golden table of shewbread,
golden candlestick, and
altar of incense.

Plans of surrounding
courts and buildings
not recorded.

Porch

Side chambers

The ornate
cast bronze
pillars, "Jacin
and Boaz"

20

40 cubits

Altar

CUBITS

FEET

4 CUBITS
= 6 FEET

The dimensions, given in Scripture, are
usually understood to refer to the inner
measurements of the rooms. *"And the house
which King Solomon built for the Lord, the
length thereof was threescore cubits,
and the breadth thereof twenty cubits, and
the height thereof thirty cubits . . ."*
1 Kings 6:2.

*Drawing based on the
Howland-Garber model*

Dimensions shown were
recorded in the Bible; other
dimensions are assumed.

Laver

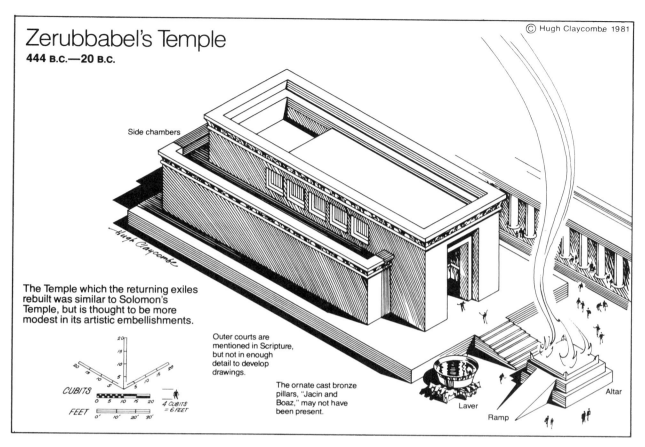

Zerubbabel's Temple
444 B.C.—20 B.C.

© Hugh Claycombe 1981

Side chambers

The Temple which the returning exiles rebuilt was similar to Solomon's Temple, but is thought to be more modest in its artistic embellishments.

CUBITS

FEET

Outer courts are mentioned in Scripture, but not in enough detail to develop drawings.

The ornate cast bronze pillars, "Jacin and Boaz," may not have been present.

Laver

Ramp

Altar

4 CUBITS = 6 FEET

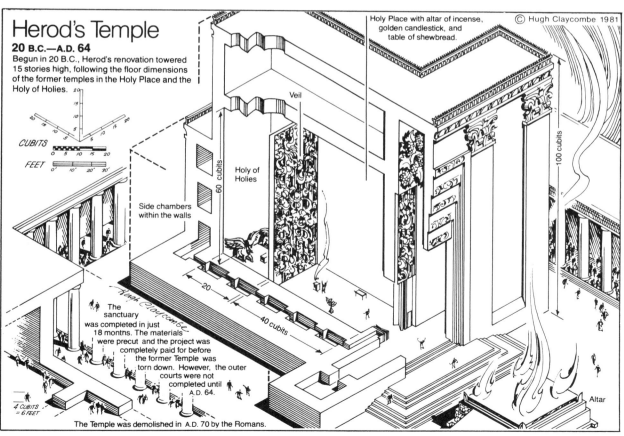

Herod's Temple
20 B.C.—A.D. 64

Begun in 20 B.C., Herod's renovation towered 15 stories high, following the floor dimensions of the former temples in the Holy Place and the Holy of Holies.

© Hugh Claycombe 1981

Holy Place with altar of incense, golden candlestick, and table of shewbread.

Veil

CUBITS

FEET

Holy of Holies

60 cubits

100 cubits

Side chambers within the walls

20

40 cubits

The sanctuary was completed in just 18 montns. The materials were precut and the project was completely paid for before the former Temple was torn down. However, the outer courts were not completed until A.D. 64.

4 CUBITS = 6 FEET

Altar

The Temple was demolished in A.D. 70 by the Romans.

In 1835 Henry C. Rawlinson discovered, on the Behistun mountain, 200 miles N.E. of Babylon, a great isolated rock, rising 1700 feet out of the plain, and on the face of this rock, on a perpendicular cliff, 400 feet above the road, a smoothed surface with carvings. Rawlinson made the dangerous climb and obtained plaster of Paris impressions from it. It took him ten years to read it. The inscription, some 1200 lines, was written in wedge-shaped characters of ancient Assyria and Babylon. It was carved in three languages, Persian, Elamite, and Akkadian. The message told of how Darius the Great (522-486 B.C.) received tribute from some conquered rebels. The importance of the Behistun Inscription is that it became the gateway to the understanding of both Assyrian and Babylonian antiquity.

82. The wall constructed by Nehemiah (Neh. 1-6).

"Then said I unto them, Ye see the distress that we are in, how Jerusalem lieth waste, and its gates thereof are burned with fire: come, and let us build up the wall of Jerusalem, that we be no more a reproach. . . . And they said, Let us rise up and build . . .'" (2:17, 18).

"So the wall was finished . . . in fifty and two days" (6:15).

British archaeologist Kathleen Kenyon has excavated a part of Nehemiah's famous wall. This remained the wall of Jerusalem in that area until the destruction of Jerusalem by Titus in A.D. 70.

83. The enemies of Nehemiah (Neh. 2, 4, 6).

"But when Sanballat . . . and Geshem the Arabian, heard it, they laughed us to scorn, and despised us, and said, What is this thing that ye do? will ye rebel against the king?" (2:19).

"But it came to pass, that when Sanballat heard that we builded the wall, he was [angry] . . .'" (4:1).

"And conspired all of them together to come and to fight against Jerusalem, and to hinder it" (4:8).

"That Sanballat and Geshem sent unto me, saying, Come, let us meet together in some one of the villages. . . . But they thought to do me mischief" (6:2).

The name Sanballat appears on one of the Elephantine papyri. These documents were found in 1903 on the island of Elephantine, located at the first cataract of the Nile in Egypt. They were written by a Jewish military colony which had been settled at that place. The letters were penned in Aramaic, the diplomatic and trade language of the day. They tell about the Jewish Temple at Elephantine being sacked by an anti-Jewish persecution around 411 B.C.

In these documents Sanballat is referred to as governor of Samaria. The name Geshem is now also known to us from the sources, one being a contemporary inscription found at Hegra in Arabia, and the other found in a temple on the borders of Egypt. In this temple was found a bowl dedicated to a goddess by a son of Geshem.

INTRODUCTION TO THE HISTORY OF ISRAEL

It is generally known that the nation Israel began with the call of Abraham in Genesis 12, that Moses led its people out of Egyptian captivity, and that Joshua brought them into Canaan. After this the nation *floundered* under the Judges, *flourished* under David and Solomon, and became *fragmented* under wicked King Rehoboam. It finally suffered

exile at the hands of Assyria and Babylon, only to be returned and restored to the land by God during the days of Zerubbabel, Ezra, and Nehemiah.

In Jesus' time mighty Rome ruled over the Holy Land and, four decades after his ascension, destroyed Israel's Temple in A.D. 70.

It is also common knowledge that after wandering and wondering for nearly nineteen long centuries, Israel was once again established in her beloved land. But what had happened during that great interval? This study will attempt to briefly trace those events transpiring between the first and twentieth centuries. It is a tragic, turbulent, thrilling, and finally triumphant tale!

Heroes such as *Bar Cochba*, *Ben Yehouda*, and *Theodor Herzl* make their appearance. This period speaks of the *Balfour Declaration*, the *Peel Commission*, and the hated *White Paper*. *Masada* (a Jewish fortress) falls, and the *Haganah* (Jewish liberation army) arises. Jerusalem is violated by some bloody crusaders, visited by a British general, and vindicated by a Burma Road!

The History of Israel from A.D. 70 to A.D. 1973

Introduction. On September 8, A.D. 70, by God's judgment, the Jewish Temple in Israel was burned and destroyed by Titus, the Roman general. On October 6, A.D. 1973, by God's grace, the Jewish state of Israel was saved from destruction from the Egyptians and Syrians.

The following is but the briefest summary of those swift-moving, often sorrowful, and always eventful years between these two important dates. These nineteen centuries can be historically divided into ten main periods:

I. The Roman Period (A.D. 70-325).
II. The Byzantine Period (325-614).
III. The Persian Period (614-634).
IV. The Arab Period (634-1072).
V. The Seljuk Period (1072-1099).
VI. The Crusaders Period (1099-1291).
VII. The Mameluke Period (1291-1517).
VIII. The Turkish (Ottoman) Period (1517-1917).
IX. The British Period (1917-1948).
X. The Independent Period (1948—present day).

I. The Roman Period (A.D. 70-325).

A. In A.D. 36 Pilate sent a force of cavalry and infantry into Samaria to crush an imagined revolt against his rule. Many innocent people were slaughtered, resulting in the Samaritans sending a delegation to the Roman officials, complaining about Pilate's cruelty and demanding his removal. Pilate was relieved of his office and ordered to Rome. He was later exiled to Gaul and subsequently committed suicide.

B. Soon after his removal, Judea and the other territories formerly governed by Pilate and Herod the Great were given to Herod's grandson, Herod Agrippa. He was killed by God for an act of blasphemy. (See Acts 12:20-23.) Agrippa was eventually succeeded by both Felix (Acts 24) and Festus (Acts 25-26). Finally, a Roman governor named Florus was appointed. He was so cruel and crude that the Jews revolted in A.D. 65 against their Roman rulers. They captured the strong fortress of Masada on the borders of the Dead Sea and put the Roman garrison there to death.

In Jerusalem the captain of the Temple guard, a man named Eleazer, formed a revolutionary group called the Zealots. They attacked and captured the Jerusalem castle of Antonia and executed the Roman guard. This rebellion quickly spread to various Judean cities.

C. Rome thereupon ordered a general stationed in Syria, named Cestius, to enter Palestine and crush this revolt. He invaded the land with 23,000 troops in A.D. 66. The Jews drew back inside the walls of Jerusalem. After a siege of six months, for some unknown reason Cestius suddenly drew back and retreated. The Jews thereupon rushed out and killed 6,000 of the retreating Roman soldiers, and confiscated the huge quantity of war booty left by the enemy troops. They now became confident of any future Roman encounters.

D. The Christians inside Jerusalem (perhaps being warned by God) for some reason at this time left the city and settled in the area of Perea across the Jordan River. When Nero the Roman Emperor heard of Cestius' strange retreat, he sent Vespasian, one of his ablest generals, to restore order. Vespasian, now joined by his famous son, Titus, invaded northern Galilee with 60,000 Roman troops. Many Jewish cities were destroyed. It was during this campaign that Josephus, the Jewish historian, was captured.

E. During the winter of A.D. 68, trouble broke out in Rome, leading to the suicide of Nero. After one year of turmoil, Vespasian was able to become the new emperor. He then sent Titus to subdue Jerusalem, that hotbed of Jewish anarchy. Titus arrived at Jerusalem in February of A.D. 70 with 80,000 Roman troops, plus thousands of battering rams and siege engines.

F. In the city itself a tragic situation had developed. No less than three bitter factions were actually fighting each other over control of Jerusalem. One group held upper Jerusalem, another lower Jerusalem, and the third controlled the Temple area. Riots and assassinations were frequent, while the most powerful legions in the world waited at the gates. The city was terribly overcrowded, for tens of thousands of pilgrims had rushed there to protect themselves against the advancing Roman army.

G. Titus' appeal to surrender was ridiculed. The siege officially began during the Passover. It would prove to be perhaps the most bitter in all history, with neither side expecting or giving the slightest mercy. The Jews threw massive stones and poured boiling oil down upon the heads of their enemies. The Romans responded by crucifying hundreds of Jewish prisoners each day in full view of the city walls.

Famine soon stalked the city. On July 17 the daily sacrifices ceased because of the scarcity of animals. Women were reduced to eating their own dead children and grown men fought to the death over a few ounces of bird dung for food.

H. The Romans eventually broke down a section of the wall, only to discover that the desperate Jews had built an inner wall in the meantime. Finally, on September 8, the Romans smashed into the city, burned the Temple, and leveled the walls. Some one million Jews were murdered by sword, fire, and crucifixion.

I. An amazing prophecy was now fulfilled, which had been uttered by Christ some thirty-five years previous.

Note his words: "And Jesus went out, and departed from the temple: and his disciples came to him for to show him the buildings of the temple. And Jesus said unto them, See ye not all these things? verily I say unto you, There shall not be left here one stone upon another, that shall not be thrown down" (Mt. 24:1, 2).

A secular historical source informs us that there was a widely circulated (but unconfirmed) rumor among the Roman troops during the siege to the effect that the Jews had hidden vast quantities of gold and silver between the stones of their Temple. This then accounted for the Romans' action in removing every stone in an attempt to locate this gold.

J. Titus took many captives to Rome, where they were forced to work in dangerous mines or thrown to wild animals in the arena. Tens of thousands were sold into the slave markets of the world. In fact, the mass of Jewish captives so glutted the slave market that their captors were forced to sell them at incredibly low prices. To commemorate the occasion, Titus struck a coin, representing Israel as a sorrowing woman in chains sitting under a palm tree.

K. As has been already stated, in A.D. 65 the stronghold of Masada had been taken by the Jews. After the destruction of Jerusalem, several hundred families somehow escaped that burning city and made their way to Masada, making the total number on its lofty top 967 men, women, boys, and girls. Masada is a boat-shaped upper plateau rock, abruptly rising some 1400 feet, almost perpendicularly above its surroundings. It covered an area of twenty acres, with a circumference of nearly a mile. Masada had been strongly fortified in 35 B.C. by King Herod the Great himself. Josephus said he did this for two reasons:

   1. As a place of refuge if the Jews in Judea turned against his rule.
   2. For fear of Cleopatra, lest she persuade the Roman general Mark Antony to kill Herod and give her rule over Judea.

L. Whatever his reasons, Herod spared no expense or trouble in fortifying and developing Masada. He ordered the construction of two magnificent palaces, great storerooms, rooms for taking hot baths, and almost everything else a rich king could afford in those days. An ingenious reservoir was carved out which held over seven million gallons of water. It was filled regularly each year in January by the rains which only fell during a few days at that time. Josephus tells us the walls around the plateau were eighteen feet high and twelve feet wide, on which had been erected thirty-seven towers some seventy-five feet high. When the escaping Jewish families made their way to the top they found vast quantities of foodstuffs such as wine, oil, grains, and dates which had been stored there by Herod one hundred years before. Because of the dry atmosphere, the food was as good as the day it was placed there. In addition, the families discovered great amounts of iron, bronze, lead, and enough weapons to supply 10,000 men.

It was but a short time until the Romans discovered the whereabouts of these escaping Jews. In the spring of A.D. 72, the Roman general Silva was ordered to surround Masada with 15,000 men and subdue it, lest the empire lose face.

M. For two years the Jews held out. During this time, Silva constructed an earthen incline (using slave labor taken from Jerusalem) leading up to the western side, which was the lowest point from the top to the desert floor. He then broke through the wall, only to find (as had Titus previously) that the Jews had built another inside wall. The battering rams were useless against this wall, for it was made of logs and dirt. Thus any pounding simply packed the dirt even more. He then attempted to burn the massive logs in the wall. Josephus writes of this:

"Just as the fire broke out a gust of wind from the north alarmed the Romans: it blew back the flame from above and drove it in their faces, and as their engines seemed on the point of being consumed in the blaze they were plunged into despair. Then all of a sudden as if by divine providence the wind swung to the south, and blowing strongly in the reverse direction carried and flung the flames against the wall, turning it into one solid blazing mass." (*The Jewish War*, p. 384)

N. The Jewish leader Eleazer ben Yair realized the Romans would successfully break through on the following day. This meant the Jews' wives would be raped, their children enslaved, and the men murdered. Thus, on the final night he urged all to commit suicide.

O. So eloquent was his speech that, in an unprecedented action, the men moved toward their wives and children with broken hearts, but determined wills. After tearful farewells, each man quickly slew his own family! Again we note the words of Josephus:

"Unable to endure any longer the horror of what they had done, and thinking they would be wronging the dead if they outlived them a moment longer, they quickly made one heap of all they possessed and set it on fire; and when ten of them had been chosen by lots to be the executioners of the rest, every man lay down beside his wife and children where they lay, flung his arms round them, and exposed his throat to those who must perform the painful office. These unflinchingly slaughtered them all, then agreed on the same rule for each other, so that the one who drew the lot should kill the nine and last of all himself: such perfect confidence they all had in each other that neither in doing nor in suffering would one differ from another. So finally the nine presented their throats, and the one man left till last, first surveyed the ranks of the dead in case amidst all the slaughter someone was still left in need of his hand; then finding

that all had been dispatched set the palace blazing fiercely, and summoning all his strength, drove his sword right through his body and fell dead by the side of his family. Thus, these men died supposing that they had left no living soul to fall into the hands of the Romans; but an old woman escaped, along with another who was related to Eleazer . . . and five little children." (*Ibid.*, p. 391)

P. In the year A.D. 130 the Roman Emperor, Hadrian, made plans to rebuild Jerusalem. He constructed a temple to Jupiter on the former Temple of Solomon site. This horrified the Jews. In A.D. 132 a daring young Jewish warrior named Bar Cochba (son of the star) arose and claimed to be the fulfillment of Balaam's prophecy:

"I shall see him, but not now: I shall behold him, but not [near]: there shall come a Star out of Jacob, and a Scepter shall rise out of Israel, and shall smite . . . his enemies; and Israel shall do valiantly. Out of Jacob shall come he that shall have dominion . . ." (Num. 24:17–19).

The most influential Jewish priest of the time, Rabbi Akiba, accepted Bar Cochba as Israel's true Messiah. To join the revolt one had to have a finger hacked off as a pledge of his allegiance.

Q. Over 200,000 enlisted. Soon they had captured fifty strong places and over 1000 villages from the Romans. Bar Cochba was finally subdued by the Roman general, Julius Severus, in A.D. 135. He was slain and Rabbi Akiba was flayed alive, repeating: "Hear, O Israel: the Lord our God is one Lord" (Deut. 6:4).

R. Over 500,000 Jewish people were killed during this the last attempt to take their native land until May of 1948. Meanwhile in Jerusalem, Hadrian completed the reconstruction of Jerusalem, but renamed it Aelia Capitolina. Most of the "civilized" world now turned against the Jews. A little group settled at Tiberas, which became the center for Judaism.

II. The Byzantine Period (325–614).
A. Constantinople, or Byzantium, as it was called, was made capital of the eastern half of the Roman Empire. Christianity spread rapidly after the "conversion" of Constantine. Churches were built and Palestine flourished.

B. With the advent of Constantine the Great (A.D. 325) the Jews were even persecuted by professing Christians. The only brief reprieve came at the hand of Emperor Julian the Apostate. This man hated Christ and promised to rebuild the Jewish Temple to disprove the Savior's prophecy (Mt. 23:37–39; 24:1, 2). But the workmen were driven from Mt. Moriah by strange fire bursting from the foundation area. The probable reason for this was that the numerous subterranean passages had become heavy with inflammable gas and took fire from the workmen's torches. At any rate, the project was quickly abandoned. Julian died on a battlefield after reigning for only eighteen months in A.D. 363.

C. During much of the Byzantine period the Jews were not allowed to visit Jerusalem except on September 8, the anniversary of the destruction of their Temple.

III. The Persian Period (614–634).

    A. On May 20, 614, Jerusalem was conquered along with Palestine by the Persian warrior Chosroes II. Nearly 34,000 people were slain and almost every Christian church destroyed. The Jews supported this invasion, being promised some relief when the masters of the Holy Land took over. But these promises were never kept. Chosroes then carried off the "true cross" which Queen Helena (mother of Constantine) had reportedly found during her pilgrimage to Palestine.

    B. In A.D. 629 the Byzantines rallied under Emperor Heraclius and drove out the Persians. The "true cross" was recovered and brought back to Jerusalem.

IV. The Arab Period (634–1072).

    A. The great founder of the Moslem faith, Mohammed, was born in Mecca in A.D. 570. He was raised by his uncle, Abu-Taleb. Mohammed later worked for and married a rich widow named Khadija. In A.D. 611, at the age of forty, he received his famous vision dream which told him the purpose of his mission: "There is no god but Allah, and Mohammed is his prophet."

    His immediate goal thus became to unite the Arab people under the banner of Allah. But the citizens of Mecca rejected this monotheistic approach. For years they had worshiped a great black stone (possibly a meteorite), around which were 360 idols.

    B. Escaping for his life, Mohammed fled to a rival city called Medina. This is known as the Hegira (the flight). It took place in June of A.D. 622. Moslems date their era from this time.

    C. The citizens of Medina accepted him and his following quickly grew. He returned to Mecca in 630. Little by little the Arabs submitted to him. Mohammed died in 632 at Medina. His successors developed a simple rule in dealing with their enemies—the Koran, tribute, or the sword. This meant one could accept the Koran (the Moslem holy book), pay tribute, or be slaughtered by the sword. They captured Syria in July of 634. In 637 the Arab general Omar surrounded Jerusalem. He made the following announcement: "Health and happiness to everyone that follows the right way. We require of you to testify that there is but one God, and that Mohammed is his Apostle. If you refuse this, consent to pay tribute, and be under us forthwith. Otherwise I shall bring men against you who love death better than you do the drinking of wine. . . ."

    D. The victorious Moslems were finally stopped in their westward advances by Charles Martel at the Battle of Tours in A.D. 732.

    E. In A.D. 1009 the Moslems ordered the destruction of the Church of the Holy Sepulchre. Some 30,000 Christian buildings are said to have been destroyed at this time.

V. The Seljuk Period (1072–1099).

    A. The Seljuks were a Turkish dynasty which overran the Middle East for around twenty-five years. They were driven out by the Egyptians shortly before the arrival of the crusaders. The Seljuks occupied Jerusalem in 1076.

    B. The Seljuks came from near the borders of China. They had been converted to Islam. They persecuted both Jews and Christians.

VI. The Crusaders Period (1099–1291). This period was not only the most turbulent, but in many ways the most tragic post-Calvary era of the history of Palestine. It was turbulent because of the hundreds of thousands of European troops marching across the land to fight with equally massive Arab armies. It was tragic because much of the butchery and bloodletting was done in the name of Jesus, by professing Christian warriors.

    There were eight main crusades during this time to free Jerusalem from the pagan Arabs. Between the fourth and fifth crusades were launched two children's crusades, perhaps the saddest of all attempts.

    A. The first crusade (Nov. 18, 1095).

        1. This crusade really began around 1087 when a European named Peter the Hermit visited the Holy Land. Peter was deformed in stature but possessed the heart of a lion, and the voice of a god. While there, he visited the Christian bishop of Jerusalem, who had been imprisoned by the Moslem Seljuks. The bishop sent a letter by Peter to the Roman Pope Urban II, asking him to raise an army to deliver Jerusalem.

        2. Urban welcomed this plea, seeing in it an opportunity to strengthen his weak rule by creating a unifying holy cause—the salvation of the Holy City from the pagans.

        3. On November 18, 1095, a special meeting was held in Clermont, France. This was attended by the Pope, Peter the Hermit, thirteen archbishops, 225 bishops, 390 abbots, great numbers of priests and monks, thousands of knights, and innumerable multitudes of people. The Pope introduced Peter who made a fiery speech:

            "From the borders of Jerusalem . . . evil tidings have come. An accursed race, estranged from God, has invaded the lands of the Christians . . . and have depopulated them by fire, steel, and ravage. They have led away many into captivity, they have torn down the churches of Christ, or used them for their own rites. In some they stable their horses, and befoul the altars with the filth from their own bodies.

            Even now they are torturing Christians, binding them and filling them with arrows, or making them kneel, bending their heads to try if their swords can cut through their necks with a single blow. They are ravishing Christian women. Pilgrims from our lands have been forced to pay toll at the gates of cities and at the entrance of churches. Those who had no money were searched, even the callouses on their bare heels were cut to see if they carried money there. They were given poison to drink, until they vomited, but findings no coins in the vomit, their bowels have been cut open with a sword so that if any treasure was hidden there it might be disclosed. Who can relate this without being deeply grieved? For they are your blood brothers—children of the same Christ and sons of the same church!"

4. At this point the speaker was interrupted, as thousands literally rushed forward to offer their lives in reclaiming the Holy City.

5. The first crusade was headed up by Godfrey of Bouillon. After unbelievable hardships en route, they reached Palestine, only to be stopped by the strong fortress at Antioch. At this time a young monk named Peter Bartholomew claimed to have had a dream in which Saint Andrew came to him and said: "Arise! Go and dig in a spot which I will show thee in the Church of St. Peter, and thou shalt find a spear wherewith the soldier pierced the side of the Lord. Take the sacred weapon and carry it at the head of the army and the infidels shall flee before it."

This was done and the spear was found. On July 1, 1098, following a communion service, the city of Antioch was taken by the crusaders. On May 9, 1099, they arrived at Jerusalem. Again things seemed hopeless until they were advised by a hermit living on Mt. Olivet to march around the city seven times.

6. Shortly after this, Jerusalem was taken, the crusaders beating down their enemies indiscriminately, without mercy. On July 23, 1099, Godfrey was elected as governor and defender of Jerusalem. The first crusade had ended.

B. The second crusade (A.D. 1146).
1. It was instituted by Pope Eugenius III, and aided greatly by the powerful preaching of St. Bernard of Clairvaux. The king of France and emperor of Germany headed it up. It was a total disaster, costing the lives of over 250,000 Englishmen and Germans.

2. A terrible new threat now arose between the second and third crusades in the person of Saladin, the greatest Arab military genius of all time. On July 15, 1187, this brilliant Moslem leader totally defeated the crusaders at the Horn of Hattin, the traditional site of Christ's Sermon on the Mount, near the Galilean Sea. Continuing his conquests, Saladin took the city of Jerusalem on Friday, October 12, 1187.

C. The third crusade (1189–1192). Richard the Lion Heart, king of England led this attempt. He captured some of the Christian strongholds previously taken by Saladin, but failed to recover Jerusalem.

D. The fourth crusade (1202–1204). Pope Innocent III instigated this return. It was led by Count Baldwin of Flanders. It did not even reach Palestine but became bogged down in the city of Constantinople.

Between the fourth and fifth crusades, there occurred two attempts on the part of children to recover the Holy Land.
1. Led by Stephen, a French shepherd boy. In June of 1212, a twelve-year-old French shep-

herd boy claimed to have had a vision in which Christ told him that the previous crusades had failed due to unclean hearts and hands. But innocent boys and virgin girls could wrest control of Jerusalem from the Arabs. In July of that year, over 30,000 young people, from eight to eighteen, began marching toward Palestine. Whenever they came to the walls of any city they inquired, in their ignorance, if it were the Holy Jerusalem. After a month's journey they had lost 10,000 by death or dropout. When the ocean came into view they ran down, fully expecting the waters to part for them. When they did not, the number soon dwindled to six thousand. Wicked slave dealers then promised to take them by ship to Palestine. Instead they were sold into slavery in Africa and Egypt.

2. Led by Nicholas, a German lad. The group led by this ten-year-old boy suffered a similar fate.

E. The fifth crusade (1218–1221). This expedition was led by King Andrew of Hungary, and Emperor Frederick II of Germany. They landed at Egypt and occupied it. The Moslems were so concerned that they offered to cede all Palestine to them if they would withdraw from Egypt. Such an offer had never been and never would again be made to Christians. But the greedy crusaders were so taken with the prospects of capturing the treasure houses of Egypt that they refused the offer, and thereby lost one of the greatest opportunities of all time.

F. The sixth crusade (1228–1229). This crusade was different from most. First, it succeeded. Second, it was cursed by Pope Gregory IX, who hated its leader Frederick II. Frederick effected a treaty with the Moslems, which released Bethlehem and Jerusalem to the crusaders. On February 18, 1229, he entered the Holy City and proclaimed himself king.

G. The seventh crusade (1248). In 1244 Jerusalem again fell to the Moslems, prompting the seventh attempt. It was led by the French king, Louis IX, but accomplished little. The king himself was captured for awhile and held for ransom money.

H. The eighth crusade (1267). This final crusade was co-led by King Louis of France and Prince Edward of England. It accomplished nothing. Dr. G. Frederick Owen writes:

"The fate of the Crusader Kingdom in Palestine was sealed with the final fall of Acre. Only Athlit, a small but strong fortress south of Mount Carmel was yet untaken. Here the Christians gathered waiting for they hardly knew what; clinging to the last foothold until they saw all was lost; then on that last sad night they gathered in a large assembly room within the church, had prayer, then passed to their ships, hoisted sails, and the last of the Crusaders turned their backs upon Palestine and sailed away to Cyprus. Thus ended the drama which had lasted for one hundred and ninety-two years. The crescent had triumphed over the cross, and the Crusaders left behind only the ruins of their castles, their blood that coursed through the veins of the natives with whom they had intermarried and the memory of wars which they had waged and a kingdom which they had founded and lost." (*Abraham to the Middle East Crisis*, p. 246)

VII. The Mameluke Period (1291-1517).

A. The word mameluke means "slave." The Mamelukes were Turkish slaves in Egypt which served as royal bodyguards. Then these valiant cavalrymen revolted against their Egyptian masters and took over the throne of Egypt. After this they overran Palestine, driving out the Crusaders in A.D. 1291. The Mamelukes placed heavy and grievous restrictions upon both Palestinian Jews and Christians. By law, Jews had to wear yellow turbans and Christians blue turbans to distinguish them from the first-class Moslem citizens.

B. In the Mameluke era the Holy Land suffered one of the most severe and prolonged droughts on record. After awhile, food simply disappeared. People ate cats, dogs, vermin, and on occasion, even little children.

VIII. The Ottoman (Turkish) Period (1517-1917).

A. In 1517 Selim I (the Grim) of Turkey defeated the Mamelukes and took over Palestine. Even prior to this the Ottoman Turks (named after the Sultan Osman I) had taken over Constantinople in 1453. From there they ruled Palestine. The son of Selim I was Selyman (also called Subeiman) the magnificent. He ruled from 1520-1566 and was the greatest monarch during the 400-year Turkish occupation of Palestine. Among other achievements, he rebuilt the walls of Jerusalem, which stand today as a monument to his greatness. Soon after his death the land was ruled by a number of pashas (provincial governors of Turkish birth). They paid the head sultan of the Turkish government in Constantinople huge bribes to rule over certain parts of the Middle East. This really began the era of the "Abominable Turk." With few exceptions, Palestine was now ruled over by a group of greedy, dense, and cruel tax collectors, who raped both people and land. Jews, Arabs, and Christians suffered under their disgraceful rule.

B. In 1798 Napoleon Bonaparte entered the Middle East. During that year he captured Egypt with 30,000 troops and a large fleet of ships. He then announced his intention to conquer Palestine and restore to the Jews this fatherland. Because of this, many Jews looked upon him as their true Messiah, an honor they had last paid some 665 years prior to Bar-Cochba.

C. Napoleon then marched north along the Maritime plain and conquered Gaza, Jaffa, and Caesarea. At this time he demonstrated some of his cruelty, murdering over 3,000 prisoners of war at Jaffa on the beach, claiming he could find no other way to dispose of them. A Turkish army attempted to repulse him in the Jezreel Valley, but he defeated them at the foot of Mt. Tabor.

D. But Napoleon could not take the strong central city of Acre. This coastal metropolis was defended by both the Turks and the British. Had he captured Acre, history would doubtless have been changed. The famous French emperor then set sail for home, never to return.

E. In 1838 the British Consulate opened in Jerusalem, the first of its kind. In 1843 France, Prussia, Austria, and Spain had done the same. The great European powers now became very interested in Palestine. Protestants, Catholics, and Jews also founded missions during this time. The Jewish population began slowly to rise. In 1839 there were 12,000 Jews, in 1880, 35,000, in 1900, 70,000, and by 1914, there were 90,000.

F. The Crimean War of 1853 was fought over the rights to Palestine. It began when Russia invaded Turkey to wrest some control from the Ottoman Empire at Constantinople concerning the Holy Land. Turkey turned to France and England for help. Russia lost that war.

In this same year, a Jew in Europe who would later become world-famous wrote of his longing for the Holy Land. He wrote: "You ask me what I wish: my answer is a national existence, which we have not. You ask me what I wish: my answer is the Land of Promise. You ask me what I wish: my answer is, the temple, all we have forfeited, all we have yearned after, all for which we have fought, our beauteous country, our holy creed, our simple manners, and our ancient customs." This statement was made by Benjamin Disraeli, Prime Minister of Great Britain in 1868, 1874-80, and creator of the modern British Conservative Party.

G. In 1878 a Jew sleeping in a barn outside Paris, France, had what he believed to be a vision from God. Whatever the source, his dream would later play a vital part in the unification of the New State of Israel. The Jew's name was Eliezer Ben Yehouda. His vision concerned a command from God to reintroduce the Hebrew language in Palestine. At the time of his dream there were some twelve million Jews scattered throughout all the world speaking in almost every known language except Hebrew. Returning to his homeland in Russia, Ben Yehouda married a Jewess named Deborah. The following year they set sail for Palestine.

En route, Ben Yehouda solemnly pledged to his new bride that henceforth he would only speak to her in Hebrew. They landed at Jaffa and made their way to Jerusalem. There, at the wailing (western) wall the couple witnessed over 20,000 Jews praying, most of whom could not understand each other. Ben Yehouda suddenly began speaking to the entire crowd in Hebrew. He was nearly stoned at first by the shocked Jews, who felt what little Hebrew they knew should be limited to prayer use. But he remained steadfast. After suffering much from his own countrymen because of his holy burden, his wife died. Her last request was that her younger sister come from Russia and take her place in marriage, that Ben Yehouda's work could continue. Upon her tombstone he wrote: "To Deborah, the first mother of the newly-reborn Jewish people."

Ben Yehouda's own people continued to hate him and actually arranged to have him arrested by their cruel masters, the Turks. But suddenly an internationally famous Jew named Theodor Herzl became interested in his dream. Soon things began to change. The hearts of the Jewish people softened. They now looked upon Ben Yehouda as a hero, and agreed on the importance of what he was trying to do. The German Jews of Palestine were the first to inaugurate Hebrew in their schools. Other groups followed. Ben Yehouda edited a Hebrew dictionary of eight volumes. In it he listed not only the Hebrew words of the Bible and the Talmud, but coined many new words also. He thus accomplished what had previously been absolutely unheard of—the revival and resurrection of a dead language. Never in world history had this happened.

H. The most significant event of the 400-year Turkish rule, and indeed in Holy Land history since Bar-Cochba's A.D. 132 revolt, occurred in 1897. It was during that year that Theodor Herzl, an Austrian Jew, launched a political movement in Basel, Switzerland, known as Zionism. Two-hundred-four delegates from Europe, Africa, America, and Palestine attended this momentous meeting which began on August 29. From this day there emerged the world Zionist organization, having for its goal a legally secured publicly recognized home for Jewish people in Palestine.

Herzl cried out: "There is a land without a people! There is a people without a land! Give the land without a people to the people without a land!" This conference accomplished three far-reaching things:

1. It gave the Jews a living and not latent hope for reunion with their land.

2. It gave birth to the Jewish flag, featuring broad stripes of blue and white with a star of David in the center.

3. It produced the Jewish national anthem, "Hatikvah," meaning, "the hope." Note its wording:

> "So long as still within our breasts
> the Jewish heart beats true.
> So long as still towards the East,
> to Zion, looks the Jew.
> So long our hopes are not yet lost—
> two thousand years we cherished them—
> to live in freedom in the land,
> of Zion and Jerusalem!"

Herzl at that time predicted that within fifty years the proposed Jewish state would become a fact. History shows he missed it by but nine months. Fifteen of the original 204 delegates were present to see this amazing prophecy come true in May of 1948. There was a sad note, however, amidst the excitement of this conference—the fading of the Messianic hope. Max Nordau addressed the conference:

> "The New Zionism, which has been called political, differs from the old, religious, messianic variety in that it disavows all mysticism, no longer identifies itself with messianism, and does not expect the return to Palestine to be brought about by a miracle, but desires to prepare the way by its own efforts."

I. Immediately after the conference, Herzl launched into a program of ceaseless diplomatic efforts and negotiations with governmental leaders throughout Europe and western Asia. He visited Russia, Great Britain, Italy, Germany, and talked with the Pope. He then went to Constantinople to see the Turkish Sultan himself, who controlled Palestine.

G. Frederick Owen describes this amazing meeting:

> "For months he sought the privilege of a personal interview with this grand ruler. Then one day while Herzl sat waiting in the outer office, one of Sultan's many slaves entered and beckoned the distinguished-looking man to follow him. They walked through the long and spacious corridors and finally arrived at the throne room. The room was decorated with many precious gems, and the Sultan's throne was of pure gold. Tall, dignified, handsome Theodor Herzl made a low, respectful bow and began to speak as only Herzl could speak.
>
> The Jews, he said, were persecuted everywhere in Europe, and could not seem to find a home anywhere but in America, which could not take them all. Would the Sultan consider letting them return to Palestine, their ancient homeland? While the small, round, gorgeously clothed Sultan sat on the soft pillows on his golden throne and listened, he was sufficiently impressed with his tall, handsome, eloquent visitor that he decorated him for his personal heroism and offered to permit the Jews to return to Palestine for twenty million dollars!"

J. Humanly speaking, this was the greatest opportunity afforded the Jews in thirty centuries, since the days of Solomon, when they owned and controlled the Holy Land. But it was not to be. Herzl could persuade neither rich Jew nor Gentile to commit even a fraction of this human sales price. The golden opportunity soon faded forever. On July 3, 1904, Theodor Herzl died of a heart attack.

K. He had, however, created a mighty wave of determination out on the stormy sea of Judaism which would increase in intensity, not to be stopped until it crashed heavily upon the shores of the Promised Land.

Forty-five years later a touching and meaningful ceremony look place in Israel. Walter K. Price writes of this:

> "It was near two o'clock on the afternoon of August 16, 1949, when an airplane, flown by an American pilot, appeared over the Mediterranean coast of Israel. Immediately it was joined by four fighter planes from the Israeli air force. That day this plane had flown from Austria. It carried the remains of a Jew who had died forty-five years before and whose body had slept quietly, all these years, wrapped in a blue and white flag of Zion, in a cemetery in Vienna. The grave in which it had been interred was an ordinary grave like many others there. A tall stone, surrounded by a wrought iron railing, over which ivy had crept through the passing years, made it indistinguishable, until one noted something else. Above, below, and on all sides of the stone

and the railing, there was handwriting in Hebrew, Russian, and German. These writings were not desecrations. Rather, they were expressions of reverence felt by thousands of Jews who had visited that grave since 1904. The writings contained requests, hopes, prayers, proverbs, and blessings. Coming from all parts of the world, Jews had expressed in many different languages their longing for a national home in Israel and their appreciation to the man whose body lay there for his leadership in the ultimate fulfillment of this divinely implanted aspiration.

And now, in 1949, only one year after the new State of Israel had been formed, the body of that man was being brought to Israel, where it would lie in the sacred soil of Givat Herzl outside Jerusalem. As the plane landed at Lydda airport, it was surrounded by an honor guard of Israeli soldiers, sailors, and air force men, holding aloft unsheathed sabers. The metal coffin, encased in a wooden box and covered with a prayer shawl, was lifted reverently from the plane and placed upon a black bier. Minutes later it lay in state upon a catafalque on the Mediterranean Promenade of Tel Aviv. Thousands of Jews quietly passed that coffin in solemn procession. At dawn a vast caravan of cars wound its way up through the hill country of Judea to place the coffin on a little ridge outside Jerusalem. In groups of ten, farmers, businessmen, workers, old settlers, and new immigrants walked by emptying the soil from three hundred Jewish settlements in the Holy Land into that grave to cover the coffin. A rabbi read the Kaddish, the prayer for the dead. Drums sounded. The great crowd, estimated at over one hundred thousand, sang 'Hatikvah,' the Zionist anthem. On that occasion, Prime Minister David Ben-Gurion said, 'This is the second most important return of a dead hero to Israel in Jewish history. The first occurred over 3,300 years ago when the body of Joseph was returned in a coffin from Egypt.'

Laid to rest in the soil of his beloved fatherland was the founder of modern political Zionism, Theodor Herzl." (*Next Year in Jerusalem*, pp. 11, 12)

L. In 1898, just one year after the Jewish Conference in Switzerland, another event occurred in Palestine itself which had both historical and prophetical overtones. It happened when the German Emperor Kaiser Wilhelm II rode through the Jaffa Gate on a white charger into the Holy City. He was clothed in white garments and wearing a crown of gold. This pompous display was an attempt by Germany to gain a foothold in the Middle East. Although it failed, it did serve to remind Bible students of a former ride by a gentle conqueror on the foal of an ass (Mt. 21:1-9; Jn. 12:12-15) and of a future ride by a victorious dictator on a white horse (Rev. 6:1, 2; 13:1-18).

M. By the end of the nineteenth century, hostility against the abominable Turk was growing in Palestine. Especially did the Arabs dislike the Turks.

In 1912 a discontented Turkish element organized a revolt called the Young Turk revolution. The Arabs supported this, hoping for a better rule, but soon found their new masters were as corrupt as the old ones were.

N. In the summer of 1914 an event took place which would forever change the political and geographical situation in the Middle East. It occurred on June 28 in Serbia when the Archduke Ferdinand (nephew and heir of the Austrian Emperor) was shot and killed. Austria and Germany almost immediately declared war on Serbia. Russia came to help Serbia, along with Britain, France, and Italy.

O. Turkey sided in with Germany on November 5, 1914. But on June 9, 1916, the Arabs revolted against the Turks. They were aided in this by Thomas E. Lawrence, a former British archaeologist, who would later gain world fame as Lawrence of Arabia. He helped raise an army of 200,000 Arabs to fight on the side of Great Britain.

IX. The British Period (1917-1948).
A. On April 6, 1917, America entered World War I. In July of that year, British General Sir Edmund Allenby was appointed Commander of the allied armies in Palestine. On November 16, the strong coastal city of Jaffa was taken, leaving Jerusalem open for attack. On December 8, British troops arrived at Jerusalem. This was the day of the Jewish Feast of Hanukkah, which commemorated the delivery of Jerusalem by the Maccabees in the year 165 B.C. Early Sunday morning, December 9, the Turks began fleeing the city, without firing a shot.

B. On December 11, General Allenby made his official entry, walking into Jerusalem by the Jaffa Gate. It was through this same gate in A.D. 637 that the Caliph Omar had entered Jerusalem after taking it from the western (Roman) world. Now a descendant from that world was restoring it to the people. G. Frederick Owen writes:

"The name Allenby fell upon the ears of the inhabitants of Jerusalem with singular force. To them it sounded like the blending of the Arabic words Allah (God) and Neby (prophet)—the prophet of God! To the people he was the twentieth-century prophet of God sent to deliver them from the Turkish yoke. Jewish and Arab joy knew no bounds." (*Jerusalem*, p. 118)

C. What would now happen to the Jews in their liberated land? A series of events which had already occurred in England would determine all this. During the war there was a serious shortage of acetone, a chemical needed for the explosive used in artillery shells. The First Lord of the Admiralty (Winston Churchill) turned to a brilliant Jewish chemist for help. This man, Dr. Chaim Weizmann, soon discovered a method of producing acetone in the laboratory by fermenting maize. This proved vital to Britain's war effort. A grateful government then sought to reward Weizman. He asked nothing for himself, only that Palestine be made a homeland for his people, the Jews. Later, a grateful Jewish people would bestow upon this quiet chemist their highest honor by electing him Israel's first president. He received this news in New York on May 17, 1948, just three days after the birth of the nation.

D. After much discussion, the British Government on November 2, 1917, issued the famous Balfour Declaration, in the form of a letter from the Foreign Secretary, Arthur Balfour, to the English Jewish leader, Lord Rothschild. The letter read: "His Majesty's Government views with favour the establishment in Palestine of a National Home for the Jewish people, and will use their best endeavors to facilitate the achievement of this objective, it being clearly understood that nothing shall be done that shall prejudice the civil and religious rights of existing non-Jewish communities in Palestine, or the rights and political status enjoyed by Jews in any other country."

E. This was approved by various allied leaders, including U. S. President Woodrow Wilson.

F. On June 30, 1920, the first British High Commissioner, Sir Herbert Samuel, a Jew, arrived in Jerusalem to assume his duties. He was dressed in white from head to foot, even wearing a white helmet. Samuel thus became the first Jew to exercise any real political authority over the Holy Land in more than 2500 years, the last one being King Zedekiah in 587 B.C.

G. At the first, the British, Arabs, and Jews experienced no real difficulty in living together. In fact, in a letter dated March 3, 1919, Emir Feisal, Arab spokesman of the day, wrote the following words to the American Zionist leader Felix Frankfurter: "The Arabs, especially the educated among us, look with deepest sympathy on the Zionist Movement. Our deputation here in Paris is fully acquainted with the proposals submitted yesterday by the Zionist Organization to the Peace Conference and we regard them as moderate and proper. We will do our best insofar as we are concerned to help their attainment; we will offer the Jews a hearty welcome home . . . I think that neither can be a real success without the other."

H. But trouble soon broke out. The British had made promises to both Jews and Arabs that they simply could not keep. In 1929 many Jews were killed by the Arabs at the wailing (western) wall in Jerusalem. A rumor had it that the Jews were plotting to destroy the Dome of the Rock and the Mosque of Aksa in order to construct their own temple. In addition to religious problems, there existed economic and social fears. Arab state rulers and land owners were disturbed over Jewish farmers paying Palestinian Arab laborers higher wages than were being paid elsewhere in the Middle East.

I. In 1936, another outburst took place, led by the Arab leader of Jerusalem. During that year, Britain sent a Royal Commission headed by Lord Peel to study the Holy Land problem. The Peel Commission thus recommended the partition of Palestine between Jew and Arab. The Jews accepted their findings, but the Arabs would not hear of it. Finally, on May 17, 1939, Great Britain issued a White Paper to appease the Arabs (who represented the vast majority of Middle East peoples). The storm clouds of World War II were quickly gathering over Europe, and England did not want to fight both Nazis and Moslems.

J. The White Paper promised that Palestine would become an Arab state with a Jewish minority limited to 30 percent of the population. Jewish immigration would be cut down and the right of Jews to own land in Palestine would be restricted to a few areas. To the Jews, this was a bitter betrayal of the Balfour Declaration. Especially were they opposed to the immigration restrictions in light of the growing danger of anti-Semitism in Hitler's Germany.

K. During this time the famous Haganah (Jewish People's Defense Army) was organized. In September of 1939, German troops invaded Poland and World War II began.

L. In spite of their conflict with Britain, the Palestinian Jews determined to side in with the allies against the axis. At this time David Ben-Gurion declared: "We shall fight the White Paper as if there were no war; we shall fight the war as if there were no White Paper." And so they did. Over 130,000 Israelis enlisted in the army. Many Jews served as spies behind enemy lines for Great Britain. Moshe Dayan, who would become world-famous during the Six Day War of June, 1967, lost his eye during British war activities against Syria in the forties. But the Arab leadership, which had been favored by the White Paper, for awhile sided in with Hitler. Their Jerusalem leaders actually went to Germany to collaborate with the Nazis.

M. After the war, Ben-Gurion visited the Nazi death camps at Auschwitz and Belsen. He came back to Palestine more determined than ever to establish a national homeland for all Jews.

N. Tensions between the Arabs, Jews, and British intensified after the war. In July of 1947, an incident of international scope occurred which helped formulate the British decision to leave Palestine in 1948. It is known as the Exodus Event. It began when a refuge ship purchased in America and renamed Exodus 1947 headed toward Europe during the month of July. Arriving at the Coast of France, this 4,000-ton wooden river boat picked up 4,554 Jewish refugees and began the journey to Palestine. British ships soon spotted it and attempted to sink it for violating the White Paper law. But the ship was able to make it to the Haifa harbor. Here 4,554 refugees were arrested by the British, put on three prison ships, and herded out to sea again, dropping anchor back at a French harbor. But this time the Jews refused to leave the ship and went on a hunger strike. This tragedy made world news. In desperation, Great Britain scrapped their White Paper policy and asked the U. N. to partition Palestine between Arab and Jew. This also marked the sixth and final *aliyah* returns, all which prepared for the new State of Israel. The Hebrew word, *aliyah*, means "to go up." It can refer to one being called forward to read from the Torah in a synagogue service, or may be used as a term

for those returning to Palestine. The six Palestine *aliyahs* are:
1. 1882-1903
2. 1903-1914
3. 1919-1925
4. 1925-1932
5. 1933-1939
6. 1940-1948

O. The U. N. Special Committee on Palestine then retired to Geneva and recommended that the British mandate be ended. The committee advocated the partition of Palestine and the creation of statehood for Israel. On November 29, 1947, by a thirty-three to thirteen vote (ten abstentions) the United Nations General Assembly passed this resolution. The next day Arab hostilities broke out against the Jews.

Early during 1948, Britain announced its intention to yield up the mandate and evacuate Palestine at midnight on May 14. Immediately both Arab and Jewish underground war activities were speeded up.

At sunrise on May 14, Great Britain's flag, the Union Jack, was hauled down from its staff over the Government House in Jerusalem. The presiding British High Commissioner, Sir Allen Gorden Cunningham, then left the Holy Land for the last time amidst a seventeen-gun salute. The thirty-year British rule was over.

P. Shortly before 4:00 P.M. that same day, David Ben-Gurion drove down Rothschild Boulevard in Tel Aviv and entered a white, modern, two-story art museum. Attending this meeting were some 400 individuals. This number included Jewish religious and political leaders plus many representatives of the local and worldwide press. At exactly 4:00 P.M., Ben-Gurion called the meeting to order. The assembly arose and sang the Jewish National Anthem, while in an adjoining room the Palestine symphony orchestra played.

Q. In Jerusalem, over 100,000 Jews listened by radio to the Tel Aviv ceremonies, unable to attend, being cut off and surrounded by Arab armies. The music had hardly ceased when Ben-Gurion rose, and in firm, strong, and emphatic voice read in Hebrew the Declaration of Independence of the new State of Israel. Israel's first Prime Minister stood under a portrait of Theodor Herzl and read the historic 697-word document in seventeen minutes. Some of the key paragraphs in this proclamation of freedom read as follows:

"In the Land of Israel the Jewish people came into being. In this land was shaped their spiritual, religious and national character. Here they lived in sovereign independence. Here they created a culture of national and universal import, and gave to the world the eternal Book of Books.

Exiled by force, still the Jewish people kept faith with their land in all the countries of their dispersion, steadfast in their prayer and hope to return and here revive their political freedom.

Fired by this attachment of history and tradition, the Jews in every generation strove to renew their roots in the ancient Homeland and in recent generations they came home in their multitudes. . . .

It is the natural right of the Jewish people, like any other people, to control their own destiny in their sovereign State.

Accordingly we, the members of the National Council, representing the Jewish people in the Land of Israel and the Zionist Movement, have assembled on the day of the termination of the British mandate for Palestine, and, by virtue of our natural and historic right and of the resolution of the General Assembly of the United Nations, do hereby proclaim the establishment of a Jewish State in the Land of Israel—the State of Israel. . . .

The State of Israel will be open to Jewish immigration and the ingathering of exiles. It will devote itself to developing the land for the good of all its inhabitants.

It will rest upon the foundations of liberty, justice and peace as envisioned by the prophets of Israel. . . .

We call upon the Jewish people throughout the Diaspora to join forces with us in immigration and construction, and to be at our right hand in the great endeavor to fulfill the age-old longing for the redemption of Israel.

We trust in the Rock of Israel, we set our hands in witness to this proclamation, at this session of the Provisional Council of State, on the soil of the Homeland, in the city of Tel Aviv, this Sabbath eve, the fifth day of Iyar, 5708, the fourteenth day of May, nineteen hundred and forty-eight."

R. At 5:00 P.M. on that same day in New York, a special emergency meeting of the U. N. General Assembly was held to consider the war clouds of the Middle East which would certainly unleash their fury at 6:00 New York time (midnight in Palestine). They had one hour to do something. Suddenly an amazing and totally and unexpected news bulletin from Washington, D. C., was received at the U. N. President Harry Truman had just recognized the new Jewish State. The time was 6:11 P.M. in New York, but six hours later in Jerusalem. Truman thus recognized the Israeli State just eleven minutes after it had come into existence! His message read as follows:

"This Government has been informed that a Jewish State has been proclaimed in Palestine, and recognition has been requested by the Provisional Government thereof. The United States Government recognizes the Provisional Government as the 'de facto' authority of the New State of Israel."

Three days later, on May 18, Russia recognized Israel. Thus, for the first time since September 8, A.D. 70, the Holy Land by official Gentile action belonged to the Jews.

X. The Independent Period (1948—present day). Between May 14, 1948, and October 6, 1973, no less than four major wars have been waged in the Middle East between the Jews and Arabs.

A. The War of Independence began on November 29, 1947, and continued (with some interruption) until February 24, 1949.

1. On May 15, 1948, Israel was invaded by Egypt, Jordan, Iraq, Syria, and Lebanon. This pitted some forty-five million Arabs against 64,000 Jews. They closed in from the north, south, and east, while Israel's back was to the Mediterranean Sea in the west.

2. The Arabs in soldiers outnumbered the Jews forty to one, in population, 100 to one, in equipment, 1,000 to one, and in area, 5,000 to one. Just prior to the war, British Field Marshal Montgomery visited Palestine and sadly predicted it would take the Arabs but eight days to drive the Jews into the sea. Their land was awkward and difficult to protect, being long and narrow with 600 miles of land frontiers, all bordering on hostile Arab states.

3. The plan of the allied Arab attack was simple: From the *south*, Egypt would send two 5000-man brigades to sweep up the Negev, one making for Tel Aviv, the other for Jerusalem. From the *north*, Lebanese, Syrian, and Iraqi armies would smash through Galilee, sweep into Haifa, and head for Tel Aviv. From the *east*, Jordan would send 10,000 men to occupy the West Bank, capture the Old City of Jerusalem, and lay siege to the New City.

4. Against this massive and well-armed invasion, Israel had but 10,000 rifles, each with fifty rounds of ammunition, four ancient artillery pieces, and 3,600 sub-machine guns.

5. The situation seemed absolutely hopeless for Israel. But the different attitudes of the opposing armies and not the size or strength would determine the outcome. To the Arabs the name of the game was expansion and revenge, but to the desperate Jews it was sheer survival. It is a known fact that human beings will fight harder to save their lives than to enlarge their lands. This alone would make the difference. Dr. G. F. Owens writes:

   "Four exceedingly important goals lay before the Jewish military leaders: *first*, to defend to the utmost every Jewish settlement in the path of the invading armies; *second*, to create a navy to lift the blockade and bring in men, munitions, and immigrants by way of the sea; *third*, to lift the siege of Jerusalem; and, *fourth*, to take the offensive and save Israel." (*Abraham to the Middle East Crisis*, p. 325)

   As the war continued, they were successful in accomplishing all four goals.

   a. They defended their farm and small town settlements.
   b. They created a navy (of sorts). Five dismantled former refuge ships were located. To these were added an icebreaker and a fishing trawler. These seven ships constituted Israel's navy. On May 27, four Egyptian ships appeared off the coast of Tel Aviv. The only Israeli ship available for any kind of battle was the Elath, equipped with two actual twenty-millimeter guns and two dummy six-inch guns designed in cardboard to deceive the enemy. This fooled and frightened the enemy ships into a hasty retreat. Later, during a naval engagement on October 21, *The King Farouk*, flagship of the Egyptian Navy was sunk by Israel.
   c. They lifted the siege of Jerusalem. The main roads leading to Jerusalem were controlled by the Arabs. In an amazing display of ingenuity and energy, several thousand Israeli citizens carved a secret "Burma Road" out of the limestone hills of Judea which surrounded Jerusalem. Across this one-track goat path route were carried the desperately needed food and weapons for the 100,000 Jews inside Jerusalem. Banners were stretched across the jeeps used in the rescue which contained the words of Psalm 137:5, "If I forget thee, O Jerusalem, let my right hand forget her cunning."
   d. They later launched a counter offensive.

6. After intense fighting from May 15 to June 11, a four-week truce was effected by the United Nations. During this lull, Israel secretly purchased huge amounts of war weapons from Czechoslovakia. When fighting again broke out on July 9, Israel simply stomped the Arabs. On July 18, hostilities again ceased. On September 17, U. N. mediator Count Bernadotte was brutally murdered by a Jewish terrorist group known as the Stern Gang. Needless to say, this did nothing for Israel's image. Ben-Gurion offered a twenty-thousand dollar reward for their capture.

7. On October 15, the final phase of the war began, this time centering in the Sinai. As before, the newly supplied Israeli troops simply ran over their Egyptian enemies. On February 24, 1949, the War of Independence ended.

8. The tiny nation had not only survived, but found herself much strengthened. But a costly price was attached to the victory—the lives of 6,000 Jews, approximately 1 percent of the total population. (To experience such a loss, America would have to lose over two million soldiers in an eight-month battle.) As a result of her War of Independence, Israel gained 23 percent more territory than had been allotted to her by the 1947 partition plan. In retrospect, the Arabs should have accepted that partition.

9. William F. Albright, professor of Semitic languages at Johns Hopkins Univeristy, expressed his wonder at such accomplishments. He wrote:

   "No other phenomenon in history is quite so extraordinary as the unique event represented by the Restoration of Israel. . . . At no other time in world history, so far as it is known, has a people been destroyed, and then come back after a lapse of time and reestablished itself. It is utterly out of the question to seek a parallel for the recurrence of Israel's restoration after 2500 years of former history." (*Israel: Its Role in Civilization,* p. 31)

Between the first and second Middle East wars a number of significant events took place. Israel was admitted to United Nations membership on May 11, 1949. On July 5, 1950, the Law of Return was enacted, confirming the right of every Jew in the world to live in Israel. But unrest and tension continued. During 1949-1956, Israel lost nearly 1,200 servicemen. By 1952, the population of Israel was doubled by Jewish immigrants. They eventually came from 110 countries, speaking 80 different languages.

One of the most romantic immigrations was known as "Operation Magic Carpet." It involved a Moslem land located in the southwest part of the Arabian Peninsula called Yemen. In this land lived 50,000 Jews. Their community dated back to biblical times. For many centuries they had been poor and segregated in ghettos. The Arabs did not allow them to ride a camel or horse. They were forced to dismount from even a donkey if a Moslem passed by. But they remained true to the Jewish religion, believing someday they would return to Jerusalem. Every boy received some religious schooling in Hebrew, and since there was never more than one copy of the Scriptures to a class, learned to read it upside down or side-wise as easily as the correct way. But then news about the great events transpiring in the Holy Land began to reach those Yemenite Jews. Slowly they crossed hot burning desert areas to reach refugee camps. When Israeli leaders heard of this, converted bombers were sent to pick them up. Some of the flight crews were concerned. Most of these backward people had never even seen an automobile, let alone ridden in an airplane. What if they should suddenly panic in mid-flight? But the anxiety was unfounded. The Yemenites just smiled and explained that God was literally fulfilling his promise in Isaiah 40:31, which they quoted from memory with ease:

"But they that wait upon the Lord shall renew their strength; they shall mount up with wings like eagles; they shall run, and not be weary; and they shall walk, and not faint."

In a very short time every single Jew in Yemen was airlifted to Israel.

Another spectacular airlift was named "Operation Ali Baba," which brought over 120,000 Jews to Israel from Baghdad. These were the descendants of those Jews taken to Babylon by Nebuchadnezzar. For awhile after the 1948 war, Israel prospered. But trouble soon began, caused by growing Russian attempts to get a foothold in the Middle East and because of the ambitions of an Egyptian colonel named General Abdel Nasser. In 1952, he took control of the army and deposed fat and foolish King Farouk from the throne. His first accomplishment was to persuade Great Britain to evacuate the Suez Canal Zone. He then began construction of the billion dollar dam at Aswan. Nasser now saw himself as the spokesman for the Arab world. To enhance his position he called for the destruction of Israel over the powerful Voice of the Arabs radio station, a burning desire he knew was shared by all Arabs.

To finance his own part in this, Nasser committed 50 percent of Egypt's cotton crop for five years ahead to pay for some $200,000,000 worth of Soviet-supplied jet planes, tanks, guns, ammunition, and other war material. On September 27, 1955, he announced his deal to purchase these arms from Russia.

Because of his dealings with Russia, the United States withdrew its previous offer of a $64,000,000 loan to help build the Aswan Dam. In anger, Nasser nationalized the Suez Canal Company on July 26, 1956. Tiny Israel suddenly found herself in a desperate situation once again. Both the Suez Canal and the Gulf of Eilat on the Red Sea were barred to her ships. Egypt was developing military bases in Sinai in the shadow of her frontiers. On May 14, Nasser ordered the U. N. troops out of Sinai.

B. The Sinai War began on Monday, October 29, 1956, and ended on November 5, 1956.

1. Unlike the 1948 war, Israel did not sit by and await the Arab onslaught, but launched her own lightning attack at 5:00 P.M. on October 29. G. F. Owen summarized the following action:

"Within one week the fast-moving, hard-hitting Israeli forces had overrun and cleared the entire Sinai Peninsula, destroyed or dispersed about one-quarter to one-third of the Egyptian army, and captured vast stores of supplies and Russian-built equipment. They had taken about 5,600 prisoners, and had killed from 2,000 to 3,000 men at a cost of 171 dead, 600 wounded and 4 prisoners. It was so unusual a military campaign that the New York Times styled it one of the most remarkable operations in world history!" (*Abraham to the Middle East Crisis,* p. 386)

2. At this time Great Britain and France invaded Egypt to protest Nasser's nationalization of the Suez Canal. Egypt reacted by sinking ships and barges all along the canal to make it useless to the European powers. Russia threatened to come to Nasser's aid. The U. S. quickly promised to back Britain if this happened. Armageddon seemed just around the corner.

However, by December of that year, the U. N. troops had control of the canal and the Middle East crisis was, for the present, over. After controlling the Sinai for over four months, Israel, pressured by U. S. Secretary of State John Foster Dulles, pulled their forces out of that area, a decision they would later deeply regret.

3. The period between 1957-1966 was one of relative peace. Few border incidents took place. Israel used this time to greatly strengthen her military might.

But things began to worsen as the Soviet Union stepped up its activities in the Middle East. In February of 1966, a regime sympathetic to Russia came to power in Syria. The border raid incidents once more began. Nasser was persuaded by Russia to raise his sagging prestige by once again threatening to destroy Israel. On May 14, 1967, Nasser ordered his country to mobilize and began gathering troops on the Sinai border. The U. N. was then ordered out of that area.

On May 30, he mended some broken fences with Jordanian King Hussein. An agreement was reached which placed Jordanian troops under Egyptian command for the coming attack upon Israel.

We now summarize the events of the third Middle East war.

C. The Six Day War began on June 5, 1967, and ended on June 10, 1967. Walter Price describes this war.

"The situation became intolerable. The United States, busy with the war in Vietnam and threatened with student and racial anarchy at home, was unable to bring pressure to bear in order to relieve the situation. On June 5, 1967, Israel struck at her enemies and, in one of the most brilliant campaigns in the annals of war, completely defeated them in less than a week. In the first day of the war, Israel gained complete control of the air by virtually destroying the entire air force of Egypt, Jordan and Syria. In rapid thrusts, Israeli troops then overran the entire Sinai Peninsula, including Sharm al-Sheikh, and drove to the eastern bank of the Suez Canal. The Gaza strip was also taken along with Jordanian-occupied Jerusalem. All the rest of Jordan's holdings on the west bank of the Jordan river were taken, including the major cities of Bethlehem, Hebron, Jericho, Nablus, Ramallah, and Jenin. From Galilee, Israeli forces drove into Syria until her armor stood before the gates of Damascus.

Israel secured the Golan Heights, from which Israeli fishing on the Sea of Galilee and border villages had been shelled by the Syrians during nearly twenty years of Israel's existence. Egypt suffered the most. Seven divisions totaling 80,000 to 100,000 men were completely routed or destroyed. The entire armored force which Egypt had in Sinai, composed of 600 to 700 Soviet supplied tanks, was destroyed. More than 100 undamaged tanks fell into Israeli hands. Huge quantities of Soviet supplied equipment were taken from Egypt, including 400 field guns, 50 self-propelled guns, and literally thousands of vehicles, along with large caches of ammunition and provisions of all kinds. Four hundred forty-four Arab planes were destroyed on the ground when Israel attacked airfields in Egypt, Jordan, Syria, and Iraq.

The major air thrust was against Egypt. Israeli planes, up from fields near Tel Aviv and flying 150 feet above the Mediterranean in order to avoid radar detection, swept into Egypt from the sea and devastated Egyptian air bases from Cairo to Suez and to the Red Sea coast. Soviet-supplied MiG-21s and MiG-19s were lined up neatly in rows: all of them were obliterated by Israeli jets. Sixteen Egyptian air fields were put out of commission during the first hours of the war. Twenty-six Egyptian radar screens were destroyed. During the raids only two MiG-21s got off the ground and they were soon shot down—but only after they had managed to down two Israeli planes. It is believed that 100 out of Egypt's 350 pilots were killed on the ground during this first Israeli air strike. Russia had supplied Egypt with several billion dollar's worth of military equipment since 1955—most of which was lost to Israel in a matter of hours. When the cease-fire came, Israel had gained the Gaza Strip; the whole of the Sinai Peninsula; all of Jordan's west bank territory, including the Old City of Jerusalem; and the Golan Heights. The Arab states had been delivered a crippling blow, and Soviet Russia received a major setback in the Middle East." (*Next Year in Jerusalem*, pp. 92, 93)

Israel had now increased her territory from 8,000 square miles to 26,500. This had cost her 679 killed and 2,563 wounded. After the Six Day War, Israel displayed an air of confidence which almost bordered on cockiness. The tiny David-like nation had slain (for the present at least) all of her Goliath-like enemies. Peace might just be possible this time.

But the unquenchable anger in the heart of the Arab continued to seethe, this time not just for victory, but for revenge. Then, in June 1973, disturbing reports began filtering into Jerusalem concerning troop movements in both Syria and Egypt. But they were not taken seriously for several reasons.

One, Israel regarded Egypt's new President, Anwar Sadat, as a weak sister. Second, the June warning was actually the fifth received during the previous two years. For example, on April 28, Golda Meir had issued a general mobilization which had cost Israel $9,600,000 per day and tore over a third of the manpower out of the economy. But nothing had happened after all.

So now General Moshe Dayan, along with Meir and the Israeli cabinet, thought that these troop movements were just a war of nerves, a bluff to produce another mobilization with the accompanying paralysis of the economy and tremendous financial drain. During the final week of September, the U. S. issued three warnings to Israel, but these were also discounted. Israel would pay a fearful price for this carelessness.

D. The Yom Kippur War began on Saturday, October 6, and ended on October 25.

1. At exactly 2:00 P.M. on that fateful Saturday, Israel was attacked simultaneously by Egypt in the south and Syria in the north. Most of the Jews had been fasting during the previ-

ous twenty-four hours, for October 6 was the most sacred time of their entire year—the day of atonement.

2. The attack had originally been set for 6:00 P.M., but two Russian Orbital Sputniks had relayed information that Israel had finally taken invasion threats seriously and had begun mobilization.

3. The raw power and massive troop movements were simply staggering. In fact, before it ended, this would be the largest conventional war, in terms of armored forces, since the end of World War II in 1945.

   Some 5,000 tanks alone were employed, more than Hitler used when he invaded Russia, and more than the combined total owned by Britain and France in 1973. Over one million men would fight, of which 838,000 were Arabs, pitted against 275,000 Jews. Abba Eban, foreign minister of Israel, in his statement to the United Nations on October 8, 1973, said: "Egypt attacked us with 3,000 tanks, 2,000 heavy guns, 1,000 aircraft, and 600,000 men."

4. By any conventional measurement, the Yom Kippur War should have been the annihilation of the State of Israel. She was caught off guard and hopelessly outnumbered both man and machine-wise. Indeed, for awhile it looked just this way. Golda Meir would later confess: "For the first time in our twenty-five-year history, we thought we might have lost."

   At one point in the war, only seven battered tanks stood in the way of the Syrians in the north and less than ninety separated the Egyptians in the south. But for some unexplained reasons, both enemies suddenly stopped their advances for a full forty-eight hours. This gave the hard-pressed nation the priceless time so desperately needed to complete mobilization.

   On Friday, October 19, the greatest tank battle in world history was fought in the Sinai desert. Thousands of these armored war machines slugged it out. When the battle smoke had cleared, Israel had won a decisive battle.

5. Another miracle of the Yom Kippur War was the unprecedented decision of King Hussein to remain out of the fighting. His country had taken part in the previous three attacks upon Israel. There is no question but that his help would have assured an Arab victory. Walter Price writes:

   "The Israeli forces experienced some initial setback from the Russian equipped army of Egypt which occupied territory east of the Suez Canal. However, in the north, Israel began to drive toward Damascus. Soon, Israeli troops were able to invade Egypt also. When the United Nations finally was able to enforce a ceasefire, the Israeli troops were within twenty miles of Damascus. They had also established a bridgehead into Egypt, where they occupied territory on the west bank of the Suez Canal . . ." (*Next Year in Jerusalem*, p. 94)

6. On October 25, 1973, the fourth (and by far, the biggest) Middle East War came to an end. Arab casualties exceeded 15,000. Israeli losses were over 4,000.

Introduction to Bible Individuals

Some have been troubled over those "sordid" passages in the Bible which depict (often in some detail) crimes of rape, incest, adultery, bloodshed, suffering, and murder. Why, they ask, would a holy and loving God even permit such things, let alone publish them for everyone to read? Here it should be immediately pointed out that the Bible is *not* an edited book by any account! It is rather the full story of the outworking of God's eternal plan and purpose in the world of men. Because of this, sinful human beings have been allowed to play an important part in the history of this plan. The faults and merits of both sinners and saints are included. It therefore becomes vital if one is to understand the Bible to recognize at least by name the more important individuals described within its pages. Thus, to know God's dealings with people is (to a great measure) to know God himself!

300 Individuals in the Bible

There are over 6000 people who walk across the pages of the Bible. Of this number, I have selected just over 300 names, based on their historical, spiritual, or human interest significance. Each chosen person has then been placed in one of six basic categories. These are:

A. Positive Old Testament people. (Those whose lives were marked by the good.)
B. Negative Old Testament people. (Those whose lives were marked by evil.)
C. Positive New Testament people.
D. Negative New Testament people.
E. Carnal (backslidden) people in both Testaments.
F. Unnamed people in both Testaments.

A. POSITIVE OLD TESTAMENT PEOPLE.
   Aaron: Israel's first high priest (Lev. 8).
   Abel (son): the world's first martyr (Gen. 4).
   Abiathar (father of excellence): a priest loyal to King David (1 Sam. 22).
   Abigail (mother of joy): David's second wife (1 Sam. 25).
   Abishai (father of gift): a loyal and brave warrior of King David (1 Sam. 26).
   Abraham (father is exalted): father of the Hebrew race (Gen. 12).
   Adam (man): first human being (Gen. 1-2).
   Ahijah (the Lord's brother): prophet who advised Jeroboam (1 Ki. 11, 14).
   Ahimelech (the king is my brother): the high priest who befriended David (1 Sam. 21).
   Amos (burden): author of the book of Amos.
   Asa (created): the first saved king of Judah (1 Ki. 15).
   Azariah (whom God aids): the high priest who rebuked King Uzziah (2 Chron. 26).
   Barak (lightning): the Hebrew commander who defeated the Canaanites (Jdg. 4).
   Baruch (blessed): Jeremiah's faithful scribe (Jer. 36, 45).

Barzillai (iron-maker): an old Gileadite citizen who befriended David during Absalom's revolt (2 Sam. 17, 19).

Bathsheba (daughter of the oath): the favorite wife of David and mother of Solomon (2 Sam. 12).

Benaiah (the Lord has built): a brave warrior of King David (2 Sam. 23).

Bezaleel (in the Lord's shadow): chief designer of the tabernacle (Ex. 31).

Boaz (strength): husband of Ruth, and great-grandfather of David (Ruth 4).

Caleb (dog): one of the two faithful spies at Kadesh (Num. 13).

Cyrus (son): the great Persian king who issued the return decree (Ezra 1).

Daniel (God is my judge): Hebrew prime minister in Babylon (Dan.).

Darius (he who upholds the good): Persian governor over Babylon in Daniel's time (Dan. 6).

David (commander, hero): Israel's greatest king (1 Sam. 16).

Deborah (bee): the Hebrew prophetess who helped Barak defeat the Canaanites (Jdg. 4).

Ehud (God of praise): a left-handed judge who killed a Moabite king (Jdg. 3).

Eldad and Medad: two men who prophecied during the Exodus wilderness experience of Israel (Num. 11).

Eleazar (God has helped): Israel's second high priest after Aaron (his father) died (Num. 20).

Eli (uplifted): Israel's first high priest after the Jordan crossing (1 Sam. 1).

Eliezer (help of God): Abraham's faithful servant (Gen. 15, 24).

Elihu (he is my God): preacher boy advisor to Job (Job 32).

Elijah (my Lord is Jehovah): greatest nonwriting Old Testament prophet (1 Ki. 17).

Eliphaz, Bildan, Zophar: Job's three critical friends (Job 2:11).

Elisha (God is salvation): successor of Elijah (2 Ki. 2).

Enoch (dedicated): first human being not to die (Gen. 5).

Esther (star): the beautiful Hebrew queen in Persia who saved the Jews from destruction (Est.).

Eve (life): the world's first woman (Gen. 2).

Ezekiel (the strength of God): great Hebrew writing prophet in the city of Babylon during the captivity period (Ezek.).

Ezra (help): a Hebrew scholar and scribe who ministered in Jerusalem during the reconstruction days of the return stage (Ezra).

Gad (fortune): a prophet advisor of King David (1 Sam. 22; 2 Sam. 24).

Gedaliah (God is great): Hebrew governor of Judah after the Babylonian captivity (2 Ki. 25).

Gershon, Konath, and Merari: three sons of Levi, whose descendants became the caretakers of the tabernacle (Num. 3).

Gideon (hewer): Hebrew judge who defeated the Midianites with 300 men (Jdg. 7).

Habakkuk (basil plant): author of the book bearing his name.

Haggai (festal): author of the book of Haggai.

Hanani (gracious): brother of Nehemiah and keeper of the gates of the rebuilt city of Jerusalem (Neh. 1, 7).

Hannah (grace): godly mother of Samuel (1 Sam. 1-2).

Hezekiah (strength of God): the second greatest Judean (southern) king (2 Ki. 18).

Hilkiah (God's portion): high priest during Josiah's time who discovered the Law of Moses in the Temple (2 Ki. 22).

Hiram of Naphtali: Hebrew contractor of the Temple of Solomon (1 Ki. 7).

Hiram of Tyre: Phoenician king who supplied the wood material for the Temple construction (1 Ki. 5).

Hosea (salvation): author of the book of Hosea.

Huldah (weasel): a prophetess in Josiah's court (2 Ki. 22).

Hur (noble): helper to Moses and possible husband of Miriam (Ex. 17).

Hushai (my brother's gift): David's counterspy in Absalom's court (2 Sam. 16).

Isaac (laughter): Abraham's promised heir (Gen. 21).

Isaiah (God's salvation): author of the book of Isaiah.

Ithamar (island of the palm tree): youngest priest son of Aaron, in charge of transporting and erecting the tabernacle (Num. 4).

Ittai (with me): the Philistine warrior who with 600 soldiers joined with David against Absalom (2 Sam. 15).

Jacob (supplanted): son of Isaac and founder of Israel's twelve tribes (Gen. 25).

Jael (deer): a Kenite woman who killed Sisera (Jdg. 4).

Japheth (he enlarges): third son of Noah and ancestor of the Gentile people (Gen. 9-10).

Jeduthun (praiseworthy): a Levite appointed by David to head up the music in the Temple (1 Chron. 16).

Jehoiada (the Lord knows): the high priest who hid the young prince Joash during the reign of bloody queen Athaliah (2 Ki. 11).

Jehoshaphat (God has judged): a godly, but at times compromising, king of Judah (1 Ki. 22).

Jephthah (set free): an Israelite judge who made a rash vow (Jdg. 11).

Jeremiah (God will elevate): author of the books of Jeremiah and Lamentations.

Jesse (the Lord is): father of David (1 Sam. 16).

Jethro (excellence): father-in-law of Moses (Ex. 4).

Job: suffering patriarch from the land of Uz.

Jochebed (the Lord is glory): mother of Moses (Ex. 2, 6).

Joel (the Lord is God): author of the book of Joel.

Jonadab (the Lord is bounteous): a godly and separated nomad referred to by Jeremiah as an example of religious purity (Jer. 35).

Jonah (dove): reluctant prophet and author of the book of Jonah.

Jonathan (given by God): godly son of Saul and beloved friend of David (1 Sam. 18).

Joseph (may God add children): son of Jacob and prime minister of Egypt (Gen. 41).

Joshua the leader (God is salvation): the man who led Israel into the Promised Land (Josh. 3).

Joshua the priest: Judah's first high priest after the Babylonian captivity (Ezra 3; Zech. 3).

Josiah (God-healed): the greatest Judean king (2 Ki. 22).

Keturah (incense): the final wife of Abraham who bore him six sons (Gen. 25).

Leah (gazelle): first wife of Jacob and mother of six of his twelve sons (Gen. 29).

Malachi (my messenger): author of the final book in the Old Testament.

Manoah (rest): father of Samson (Jdg. 13).

Melchizedek (king of righteousness): the godly and mysterious king of Salem who blessed Abraham (Gen. 14).

Mephibosheth (contender against shame): the crippled son of Saul befriended by David (2 Sam. 9).

Methuselah (when he is dead it shall be sent): the oldest man that ever lived (Gen. 5).

Micah (who is like God): author of the book of Micah.

Micaiah (who is like God): a fearless Old Testament prophet, imprisoned by wicked Ahab, but who nevertheless predicted his doom (1 Ki. 22).

Miriam (bitterness): sister of Moses (Ex. 2, 15; Num. 12).

Mordecai (consecrated to Merodach): cousin (or uncle) and guardian of Esther (Est. 2).

Moses (to draw out): great Hebrew leader and lawgiver.

Naaman (pleasantness): the Syrian commander who was healed of leprosy by washing himself in the Jordan river at the order of Elisha (2 Ki. 5).

Naboth (fruits): a godly Jezreelite who was murdered by Jezebel for refusing to sell his vineyard to Ahab (1 Ki. 21).

Nahum (comforted): author of the book of Nahum.

Naomi (my pleasure): mother-in-law of Ruth (Ruth 1).

Nathan (he gave): the prophet who rebuked David for his sin with Bath-sheba (2 Sam. 12).

Nehemiah (God has consoled): great Jewish wall builder and author of the book of Nehemiah.

Noah (rest): builder of the ship that preserved eight human beings during the universal flood (Gen. 6-8).

Obadiah (servant of God): author of the book of Obadiah.

Othniel (my strength is God): first of the Israelite judges (Jdg. 1, 3).

Phinehas (negro): high priest son of Eleazar and grandson of Aaron (Num. 25).

Rachel (ewe): second (and favorite) wife of Jacob (Gen. 29).

Rahab (wide): converted harlot who aided Israel in their victory over Jericho (Josh. 2).

Rebekah: wife of Isaac (Gen. 24).

Reuben: first of Jacob's twelve sons. The others are: Simeon, Levi, Judah, Dan, Naphtali, Gad, Asher, Issachar, Zebulun, Joseph, and Benjamin (Gen. 29, 30, 35).

Ruth (beloved): wife of Boaz and great-grandmother of David (Ruth 1, 4).

Sarah (princess): wife of Abraham (Gen. 11-12).

Seth (founder): third son of Adam and Eve and the successor of Abel (Gen. 4).

Shadrach, Meshach, Abednego: three Hebrew men thrown into a furnace for their testimony (Dan. 3).

Shem (renown): eldest son of Noah and founder of Semitic race (Gen. 9).

Shemaiah (God hears): prophet who advised Rehoboam (1 Ki. 12).

Solomon (peaceable): son and successor of David (1 Ki. 1).

Uriah (God is my light): soldier husband of Bath-sheba, murdered by David (2 Sam. 11).

Uzziah (God is my strength): good Judaean king later struck with leprosy for his sin of intruding into the office of the priesthood (2 Chron. 26).

Zadok (just): high priest in the time of David and Solomon (2 Sam. 15; 1 Ki. 1).

Zechariah the priest (God has remembered): martyred Hebrew priest (slain by his own countrymen) for fearlessly denouncing sin (2 Chron. 24).

Zechariah the writer: author of the book of Zechariah.

Zephaniah (God has protected): author of the book of Zephaniah.

Zerubbabel (seed of Babylon): a political leader who led the first return of the Jews back to Jerusalem (Ezra 3).

Zipporah: wife of Moses (Ex. 2).

B. NEGATIVE OLD TESTAMENT PEOPLE.

Abimelech (the king is my father): murderous son of Gideon (Jdg. 8-9).

Abner (father of light): King Saul's cousin and the commander of his army (1 Sam. 26).

Absalom (my father is peace): rebellious son of David who attempted to take over the throne (2 Sam. 15).

Achan (troublemaker): the Israelite whose disobedience caused the defeat of the Jewish army at Ai (Josh. 7).

Achish (the king gave): Philistine king of Gath with whom David, in a backslidden state, twice took refuge (1 Sam. 21, 27-29).

Adonijah (my Lord is God): son of David who attempted to steal the throne from Solomon (1 Ki. 1).

Adonizedek (Lord of righteousness): the king of Jerusalem who formed an alliance of Canaanites to fight against Joshua (Josh. 10).

Agag: the king of Amalek who was defeated (but spared) by King Saul (1 Sam. 15).

Ahab (father's brother): husband of Jezebel and wicked ruler of the northern kingdom in the days of Elijah (1 Ki. 16:31-34).

Ahasuerus (mighty): Persian king and husband of Esther (Est. 1-2).

Ahaz (he grasped): wicked king who sacrificed his own children to devil gods (2 Ki. 16).

Ahaziah (God sustains): a king of northern Israel who attempted to kill Elijah (2 Ki. 1).

Ahithophel (God is my brother): David's leading counselor who betrayed him and joined in with Absalom during the rebellion (2 Sam. 17).

Amasa: David's nephew who commanded the revolt forces of Absalom (2 Sam. 17-20).

Amnon (trustworthy): David's eldest son who raped his half-sister Tamar (2 Sam. 13).

Anak (long-necked): founder of a race of giants who frightened the spies of Moses by their size (Num. 13).

Athaliah (God is exalted): wicked daughter of Jezebel and murderous queen of Judah (2 Ki. 11).

Balaam (ruin): a corrupt prophet who attempted to curse Israel (Num. 22-24).

Belshazzar (Bel protect the king): Babylonian king whose divine judgment was written by a supernatural hand on the wall behind him (Dan. 5).

Bera (son of evil): homosexual king of Sodom who attempted to bribe Abraham (Gen. 14).

Cain (spear): world's first murderer (Gen. 4).

Canaan (purple): son of Ham who sinned against his grandfather Noah (Gen. 9).

Chedorlaomer: Mesopotamian king who captured Lot, Abraham's nephew (Gen. 14).

Delilah: Philistine woman who betrayed Samson (Jdg. 16).

Doeg (fearful): Saul's Edomite chief herdsman who murdered eighty-five priests of God at Nob (1 Sam. 22).

Eglon (calf-like): a fat Moabite king oppressor of Israel, slain by Ehud (Jdg. 3).

Er and Onan: two sons of Judah the patriarch who were slain by the Lord for their wickedness (Gen. 38).

Esau (hairy, shaggy): firstborn son of Isaac (Gen. 25).

Goliath: Philistine giant killed by David (1 Sam. 17).

Gomer (ember): unfaithful wife of the prophet Hosea (Hosea 1–2).

Ham (hot): second son of Noah (Gen. 5, 9).

Haman: the Adolf Hitler of the Old Testament who attempted to kill all the Jews in the time of Esther (Est. 3–7).

Hananiah (the Lord is gracious): false prophet who attempted to undermine the ministry of Jeremiah (Jer. 28).

Hanun (gracious): Ammonite king who ridiculed David's ambassadors of good will (2 Sam. 10).

Hazael (God sees): a Syrian king who shed much Israelite blood (2 Ki. 8).

Hophni and Phinehas: two wicked priest sons of Eli (1 Sam. 2–4).

Ishbosheth (a man of shame): Saul's son who took over at the death of his father the battle against David (2 Sam. 2).

Ishmael (God hears): son of Abraham through Hagar (Gen. 16).

Jabin (he understands): the king of Hazor who was defeated by Joshua at the waters of Merom (Josh. 11).

Jehoiakim (God established): a wicked Judean king who persecuted Jeremiah and burned the Word of God (Jer. 36).

Jehoram (God is exalted): wicked son of Ahab and king of northern Israel during the ministry of Elisha (2 Ki. 3).

Jeroboam (the people increased): first king of the ten northern tribes (1 Ki. 12).

Jezebel (chaste): wicked queen, wife of Ahab (1 Ki. 16).

Joab (God his father): David's nephew and commander of the king's armies (2 Sam. 2–3).

Joel and Abijah: wicked priest sons of Samuel (1 Samuel 8).

Korah (baldness): a Levite who led a rebellion against Moses and Aaron in the wilderness march (Num. 16).

Laban (white): tricky and heartless father-in-law of Jacob (Gen. 29).

Lamech (strong): world's first recorded polygamist and second recorded murderer (Gen. 4).

Maacah: idol-worshiping queen, mother of Asa (1 Ki. 15).

Manasseh (forgetting): son of Hezekiah, ruler of Judah, and possibly the most wicked man (before his conversion) in the entire Bible (2 Chron. 32–33).

Mesha (freed): Moabite king who sacrificed his own son in a futile attempt to win a battle (2 Ki. 3).

Micah (who is like God): a money-hungry, idol-worshiping thief who became a priest for the backslidden tribe of Dan (Jdg. 17–18).

Michal (who is like God): Saul's youngest daughter and David's first wife (1 Sam. 19).

Nabal (fool): drunken sheep farmer, barely saved from David's wrath by Abigail his wife (1 Sam. 25).

Nadab and Abihu: eldest priest sons of Aaron, killed by God for offering strange fire (Lev. 10).

Nahash (serpent): Ammonite king defeated by Saul after his stated plans to torture the besieged Israelite city of Jabesh-gilead (1 Sam. 11).

Nebuchadnezzar: greatest of all Babylonian kings and the one who captured Jerusalem (Dan. 1–4).

Nimrod: great grandson of Noah (through Ham) and probable builder of the Tower of Babel (Gen. 10–11).

Og: giant king of Bashan who fought against and was defeated by Moses (Num. 21).

Pashhur (freedom): chief priest who persecuted Jeremiah (Jer. 20).

Pharaoh Amenhotep: king during the ten plagues (Ex. 5–12).

Pharaoh Thutmose III: king who attempted to kill all Hebrew male babies (Ex. 1–2).

Rabshakeh (chief cupbearer): Sennacherib's head propaganda expert (2 Ki. 18–19).

Rehoboam (increase of the nation): Solomon's successor son whose stupidity caused the Israelite civil war (1 Ki. 12).

Sanballat: a pagan troublemaker who attempted to prevent Nehemiah from building the walls of Jerusalem (Neh. 2, 4).

Saul (loaned): Israel's first king (1 Sam. 9).

Sennacherib: Assyrian king who lost 185,000 troops in his futile attempt to destroy Jerusalem by God's death angel (2 Ki. 18–19).

Sheba: a Benjaminite who stirred up a rebellion against David after the revolt of Absalom had been quelled (2 Sam. 20).

Shimei (famed): a member of Saul's family who cursed David and threw rocks at him during Absalom's rebellion (2 Sam. 16).

Sihan (a sweeping away): Amorite king who refused Israel passage during the Exodus journey (Num. 21).

Sisera: Canaanite commander, defeated by Barak, and later killed by Jael (Jdg. 4).

Tobiah (the Lord is good): a Jew who joined with Sanballat in opposing the wall-building activities of Nehemiah (Neh. 4).

Zeresh (gold): wife of Haman who encouraged him to hang the Jew Mordecai (Est. 5–6).

C. POSITIVE NEW TESTAMENT PEOPLE.

Aeneas (praise): a paralytic, bedridden for eight years, who was healed by Peter (Acts 9).

Agabus (to love): a prophet in the days of Paul the apostle (Acts 11, 21).

Ananias (God is gracious): the believer who ministered to the blinded Saul in Damascus (Acts 9).

Andrew (manly): one of Jesus' first disciples and the brother of Peter (Jn. 1).

Anna (grace): an elderly prophetess who worshiped the Christ child when he was dedicated in the Temple (Lk. 2).

Apollos: an eloquent Jewish preacher and contemporary of Paul (Acts 18–19).

Aquila and Priscilla (eagle; ancient): a godly couple who greatly aided Paul (Acts 18).

Archippus (master of the horse): close friend of Paul in Colosse, and possible son of Philemon (Col. 4; Philemon 1).

Aristarchus (the best ruler): a faithful fellow traveler and constant companion of Paul (Acts 19, 20, 27; Col. 4).

Barnabas (son of exhortation): Paul's partner during the first missionary journey (Acts 13).

Bartimaeus: blind Jericho beggar healed by Christ (Mk. 10).

Chloe (verdant): Corinthian woman who informed Paul of the trouble in her church (1 Cor. 1).

Cleopas: one of the disciples to whom the resurrected Christ appeared on the road to Emmaus on the first Easter Sunday (Lk. 24).

Cornelius (of a horn): Gentile centurion led to Christ by Peter at Caesarea (Acts 10).

Crispus (curled): ruler of the Jewish synagogue in Corinth, led to Christ by Paul (Acts 18).

Elisabeth (God is my oath): mother of John the Baptist (Lk. 1).

Epaphras: a probable "preacher boy" student of Paul who evangelized the area in and around Colosse (Col. 1, 4).

Epaphroditus (lovely): a messenger from the Philippian church who brought Paul a gift during his first Roman imprisonment (Phil. 2, 4).

Erastus (beloved): a helper of Paul during his missionary journeys (Acts 19; Rom. 16; 2 Tim. 4).

Eunice (conquering well): mother of Timothy (Acts 16; 2 Tim. 1).

Eutychus (fortunate): a young man raised from the dead by Paul at Troas (Acts 20).

Gamaliel (reward of God): renowned Hebrew Pharisee who gave the Pharisees some sound advice (Acts 5).

Gaius: the addressee of the last letter of John (3 Jn. 1).

Jairus (whom God enlightens): Sanhedrin leader whose little daughter was raised from the dead by Christ (Mk. 5).

James the apostle: brother of John the apostle and the first of the twelve to be martyred (Lk. 5; Acts 12).

James, the half-brother of Christ: pastor of the Jerusalem church and writer of the New Testament book (Acts 15:13-21; Jas.).

Joanna: a woman who helped Jesus in a financial way (Lk. 8).

John the apostle: brother of James and author of John, Revelation, 1 John, 2 John, and 3 John (Lk. 5).

John the Baptist: forerunner of Christ (Lk. 1, 3).

Joseph of Arimathea: wealthy follower of Christ who, with Nicodemus, claimed the body of Christ from Pilate (Jn. 19:38-42).

Joseph of Nazareth: husband of Mary and legal (only) father of Jesus (Mt. 1).

Julius: a Roman centurion who showed consideration to and later saved the life of Paul during the journey to Rome (Acts 27).

Lazarus the beggar: the saved man in Jesus' account of the rich man and Lazarus (Lk. 16).

Lazarus, the brother of Mary and Martha: Jesus raised him from the dead (Jn. 11).

Lois: grandmother of Timothy (Acts 16; 2 Tim. 1).

Luke: Paul's beloved Greek physician; author of Luke and the book of Acts.

Lydia: merchant woman from Thyatira led to Christ by Paul in Philippi (Acts 16).

Mark (large hammer): author of the book of Mark.

Martha (lady): sister of Lazarus and Mary (Jn. 11).

Mary of Bethany: sister of Lazarus and Martha (Jn. 11).

Mary Magdalene: converted harlot who became the first human being to see the resurrected Christ (Jn. 20).

Mary of Nazareth: mother of Christ (Lk. 2).

Matthew (gift of God): one of the twelve apostles and author of the book of Matthew (Mt. 9).

Matthias (gift of Jehovah): the man elected to take the place of Judas (Acts 1).

Nathanael (God has given): one of Christ's earliest apostles (Jn. 1).

Nicodemus (victor over the people): rich Pharisee ruler who came to Christ by night (Jn. 3).

Onesimus (useful): runaway slave from Colosse, converted to Christ by Paul in Rome (Philemon).

Onesiphorus (profit-bringer): loyal friend of Paul who comforted the apostle during the difficult days preceding his martyrdom in Rome (2 Tim. 1, 4).

Paul (little): greatest Christian who ever lived and author of at least thirteen New Testament books.

Peter (rock): spokesman for the twelve and author of 1 and 2 Peter.

Philemon (loving): owner of the runaway slave Onesimus, and close friend of Paul (Philemon).

Philip the apostle: an original disciple of John the Baptist and one of the first disciples of Christ (Jn. 1).

Philip the evangelist: one of the original seven deacons in the early church and a great soul-winner (Acts 6, 8).

Phoebe (bright, radiant): a friend of Paul and bearer of the epistle to the Romans, which she carried from Corinth to Rome (Rom. 16).

Publius: chief official on the island of Malta who befriended Paul after his terrible shipwreck ordeal (Acts 28).

Rhoda (rose): servant-girl who recognized the voice of Peter outside the door (of the house in which prayer was going on for his release) but in her joy failed to let him in (Acts 12).

Salome (peaceful): mother of James and John (Mt. 20; Mk. 15-16).

Silas (asked of God): Paul's traveling companion during his second missionary journey (Acts 15-16).

Simeon (hearing): an ancient and devout Jew who recognized the Christ child during his Temple dedication as Israel's Messiah (Lk. 2).

Simon of Cyrene: a passerby compelled by the Roman soldiers to carry the cross of Christ to Golgotha (Mt. 27; Mk. 15; Lk. 23).

Simon the tanner: owner of the house in Joppa where Peter lived for awhile (Acts 9).

Sosthenes: former ruler of the synagogue in Corinth and later companion of Paul (Acts 18; 1 Cor. 1).

Stephen (crown, wreath): one of the original seven deacons and the first recorded martyr to die for Christ (Acts 6-7).

Susanna (lily): a woman who helped Jesus financially (Lk. 8).

Tabitha: a godly woman who was raised up from the dead at her own funeral by Peter (Acts 9).

Theophilus (lover of God): addressee of both the Gospel of Luke and the book of Acts.

Timothy (honoring God): a Jewish "preacher boy" coworker of Paul to whom he wrote two New Testament epistles.

Titus: a Greek "preacher boy" co-worker of Paul to whom he wrote the book of Titus.

Trophimus (nourishing): a Gentile Ephesian Christian who accompanied Paul on his final trip to Jerusalem (Acts 20:4; 21:29; 2 Tim. 4:20).

Tychicus (fortuitous): an Ephesian convert who carried some of Paul's New Testament epistles to their respective churches (Acts 20:4; Eph. 6:21; Col. 4:7-9; 2 Tim. 4:12; Titus 3:12).

Zacchaeus (pure): a small tax collector who climbed a sycamore tree to see Christ pass by (Lk. 19).

Zacharias (whom God remembers): father of John the Baptist (Lk. 1).

D. NEGATIVE NEW TESTAMENT PEOPLE.

Alexander the apostate: a heretical teacher in the Christian community in Asia Minor, condemned by Paul (1 Tim. 1:20; 2 Tim. 4:14, 15).

Annas (merciful, gracious): the wicked high priest who condemned Christ to Calvary's cross (Jn. 18).

Barabbas (son of a teacher): Jewish prisoner who was released at the trial of Christ (Mk. 15).

Bar-Jesus (son of Jesus): a Jewish sorcerer who opposed Paul on the island of Cyprus (Acts 13).

Caiaphas: co-high priest with his father-in-law Annas who aided in the crucifixion of Christ (Mt. 26).

Demetrius: pagan defender of the goddess Diana; led a riot against Paul in Ephesus (Acts 19).

Diotrephes: an arrogant troublemaking and self-centered leader to whom Gaius, the recipient of 3 John, belonged.

Felix (happy): Roman procurator who trembled with conviction upon hearing Paul preach (Acts 24).

Festus (joyful): Roman procurator, successor of Felix, who accused Paul of being mad with much learning (Acts 26).

Herod Agrippa I: grandson of Herod the Great who killed James, imprisoned Peter, and was himself struck dead by God (Acts 12).

Herod Agrippa II: great grandson of Herod the Great, before whom Paul preached while imprisoned in Caesarea (Acts 26).

Herod Antipas: son of Herod the Great; he killed John the Baptist (Mt. 14).

Herod the Great: king who attempted to murder the infant Christ (Mt. 2).

Herodias: Herod the Great's granddaughter who plotted the death of John the Baptist (Mk. 6).

Hymenaeus (the god of marriage): a heretical teacher within the Christian community, condemned by Paul (1 Tim. 1, 2 Tim. 2).

Judas: notorious apostle who betrayed Christ (Mt. 26).

Pilate: procurator of Judea who sentenced Christ to death (Mt. 27).

Salome (peaceful): daughter of wicked Herodias, whose sensuous dance paved the way for John's execution (Mk. 6).

Sceva: false Jewish exorcist whose evil ways backfired upon him and his sons in Ephesus (Acts 19).

Simon the Pharisee: hypocritical Jewish leader rebuked by Christ during a meal in his own home (Lk. 7).

Simon the sorcerer: materialistic Jewish opportunist rebuked by Peter at Samaria (Acts 8).

Tertullus: Roman prosecuting attorney employed by the Sanhedrin to present their case against Paul before Felix at Caesarea (Acts 24).

E. CARNAL (BACKSLIDDEN) PEOPLE IN BOTH TESTAMENTS.

Ananias and Sapphira: husband and wife in the early church who lied to the Holy Spirit (Acts 5).

Cleopas: one of the disciples Jesus appeared to on the road to Emmaus during the first Easter Sunday (Lk. 24).

Demas (popular): a companion of Paul who forsook the apostle during his second Roman imprisonment (2 Tim. 4).

Dinah (judged): loose daughter of Jacob (Gen. 34).

Elihu: young "preacher boy" who criticized Job (Job 32).

Eliphaz, Bildad, and Zophar: Job's three critical friends (Job 2).

Euodias and Syntyche (fragrance and fortunate): two quarreling ladies in the church at Philippi (Phil. 4).

Gehazi (valley of visions): the manservant of Elisha (2 Ki. 5-6).

Hagar (one who fled): Sarah's Egyptian slave-maid and second wife of Abraham (Gen. 16).

Johanan (God's mercy): Judean official after the Babylonian captivity who took Jeremiah with him to Egypt (Jer. 43).

Judah (God will lead): fourth son of Jacob (Gen. 38).

Levi (joined): third son of Jacob (Gen. 34).

Lot (a covering): nephew of Abraham (Gen. 13, 19).

Obadiah (servant of God): head of King Ahab's royal household (1 Ki. 18).

Reuben (see a son): eldest son of Jacob (Gen. 35:22).

Samson (man of the sun): Hebrew strong man from the tribe of Dan (Jdg. 13-16).

Simeon (God has heard): second son of Jacob (Gen. 34).

Tamar (date): wife of Judah's two eldest sons (Gen. 38).

Thomas (twin): doubting (but loyal) apostle of Christ (Jn. 11, 20).

F. UNNAMED PEOPLE IN BOTH TESTAMENTS.

Cain's wife (Gen. 4).

Lot's wife (Gen. 19).

Lot's two daughters (Gen. 19).

Potiphar's wife (Gen. 39).

Jephthah's daughter (Jdg. 11).

Witch of Endor (1 Sam. 28).

Queen of Sheba (1 Ki. 10).

Widow of Zarephath (1 Ki. 17).

Widow and her pot of oil (2 Ki. 4).

Shunammite woman (2 Ki. 4).

Naaman's wife (2 Ki. 5).

Naaman's wife's servant (2 Ki. 5).

Job's wife (Job 2).

Ezekiel's wife (Ezek. 24).

Wise men (Mt. 2).

Shepherds (Lk. 2).

Ruler of the feast at Cana (Jn. 2).

Nobleman (Jn. 4).

Woman of Samaria (Jn. 4).

Woman taken in adultery (Jn. 8).

Infirm man (Jn. 5).

Man born blind (Jn. 9).

Prodigal son (Lk. 15).

Elder brother (Lk. 15).

Loving father (Lk. 15).

Good Samaritan (Lk. 10).

Rich fool (Lk. 12).

Rich fool (Lk. 16).

Father and his demon-possessed son (Mt. 17).
Rich young ruler (Mt. 19).
Maniac of Gadara (Mk. 5).
Lad who gave his lunch to Christ (Jn. 6).
One thankful leper (Lk. 17).
Peter's wife and mother-in-law (Lk. 4).
The woman who anointed Jesus in Simon's house (Lk. 7).
Woman with an issue of blood (Mt. 9).
The Syro-phoenician woman (Mt. 15).
Woman with two mites (Lk. 21).
Widow of Nain (Lk. 7).
Jairus' daughter (Lk. 8).
Woman bound for eighteen years (Lk. 13).
A sincere scribe (Mk. 12:32).
The young man at Gethsemane (Mk. 14:51).
The Capernaum centurion (Lk. 7).
The Calvary centurion (Mt. 27).
The two false witnesses (Mt. 26:60).
Pilate's wife (Mt. 27:19).
The servant who slapped Christ (Jn. 18:22).
The two thieves on the cross (Mt. 27:38).
The bribed soldiers at the resurrection (Mt. 28).
The lame man at the gate beautiful (Acts 3).
The Ethiopian eunuch (Acts 8).
The cripple at Lystra (Acts 14).
The Philippian jailer (Acts 16).
The Philippian demoniac girl (Acts 16).

Introduction to Cross-Reference List

One cannot even casually read the New Testament without being aware of the tremendous amount of Old Testament material quoted therein. Our Lord began his ministry and ended it by quoting from the Old Testament. Compare Matthew 4:4, 7, 10 with Deuteronomy 8:3; 6:16, 13 and Matthew 27:46 with Psalm 22:1. In fact, it is estimated that over 10 percent of his recorded words were taken from the Old Testament. Every single Old Testament book is either directly or indirectly referred to in the New Testament. It thus becomes not only *difficult,* but indeed *impossible* to properly understand the New Testament without some basic knowledge of the Old Testament.

The purpose therefore of this study is to give ready cross-reference listing to all the Old Testament verses found in the New Testament.

It is divided into nine sections, corresponding to the nine basic historical and chronological stages.

A quick check, for example, shows that fifty-four passages from the Creation Stage (Genesis 1-11) are quoted (and requoted) some eighty-seven times in eighteen of the New Testament books!

Old Testament and New Testament Cross-Reference List

CREATION STAGE

Genesis

1:1	Heb. 11:3	1:27	Mt. 19:4;
1:3	2 Cor. 4:6		Mk. 10:6;
1:6-9	2 Pet. 3:5		Acts 17:29;
1:11	1 Cor. 15:38		1 Cor. 11:7;
1:26	Eph. 4:24		1 Tim. 2:13
1:26, 27	Col. 3:10;	1:29	Rom. 14:2
	Jas. 3:9	1:31	1 Tim. 4:4

2:2	Heb. 4:4, 10	4:3-10	Heb. 11:4
2:7	1 Cor. 15:45, 47;	4:7	Rom. 6:12
	1 Tim. 2:13	4:8	Mt. 23:35;
2:9	Rev. 2:7; 22:2, 14, 19		Lk. 11:51; 1 Jn. 3:12
2:17	Rom. 5:12	4:10	Heb. 12:24; Jas. 5:4
2:18	1 Cor. 11:9	4:25—5:32	Lk. 3:36-38
2:21-23	1 Cor. 11:8	5:1	Mt. 1:1; 1 Cor. 11:7
2:22	1 Tim. 2:13	5:2	Mt. 19:4; Mk. 10:6
2:24	Mt. 19:5; Mk. 10:7, 8; 1 Cor. 6:16; Eph. 5:31	5:3	1 Cor. 15:49
3:4	Jn. 8:44	5:24	Heb. 11:5
3:6	Rom. 5:12; 1 Tim. 2:14	5:29	Rom. 8:20
3:13	Rom. 7:11; 2 Cor. 11:3; 1 Tim. 2:14	6:1—7:24	1 Pet. 3:20
		6:5	Rom. 7:18
3:15	Lk. 10:19; Rom. 16:20	6:5-12	Lk. 17:26
		6:9-12	Mt. 24:37
3:16	1 Cor. 11:3; 14:34; Eph. 5:22; Col. 3:18	6:13-22	Heb. 11:7
		6:13—7:24	Mt. 24:38-39
		7:1	Heb. 11:7
3:17, 18	Heb. 6:8	7:6-23	Lk. 17:27
3:17-19	Rom. 8:20; 1 Cor. 15:21	7:11-21	2 Pet. 3:6
3:19	Rom. 5:12; Heb. 9:27	8:18	2 Pet. 2:5
		8:21	Rom. 7:18; Phil. 4:18
3:22	Rev. 22:2, 14, 19	9:3	Rom. 14:2; 1 Tim. 4:3
3:22, 24	Rev. 2:7	9:4	Acts 15:20, 29
4:3-8	Jude 11	9:6	Mt. 26:52; 1 Cor. 11:7
		11:10-26	Lk. 3:34-36

PATRIARCHAL STAGE

Genesis

12:1	Acts 7:3	17:7	Lk. 1:55, 72, 73; Gal. 3:16
12:1-5	Heb. 11:8		
12:3	Acts 3:25; Gal. 3:8	17:8	Acts 7:5
12:5	Acts 7:4	17:10, 11	Rom. 4:11
12:7	Acts 7:5; Gal. 3:16	17:10-13	Jn. 7:22
		17:10-14	Acts 7:8
13:15	Acts 7:5; Gal. 3:16	17:12	Lk. 1:59; 2:21
		17:17	Rom. 4:19
14:17-20	Heb. 7:1, 2	17:19	Heb. 11:11
14:19	Rev. 10:6	18:1-8	Heb. 13:2
14:20	Lk. 18:12	18:4	Lk. 7:44
14:22	Rev. 10:6	18:10	Rom. 9:9
15:5	Rom. 4:18	18:11	Lk. 1:18
15:5, 6	Heb. 11:12	18:11-14	Heb. 11:11
15:6	Rom. 4:3, 9, 22; Gal. 3:6; Jas. 2:23	18:12	1 Pet. 3:6
		18:14	Mt. 19:26; Mk. 10:27; Lk. 1:37; Rom. 9:9
15:13, 14	Acts 7:6, 7		
15:16	1 Thess. 2:16	18:18	Acts 3:25; Rom. 4:13; Gal. 3:8
15:18	Acts 7:5		
16:1	Acts 7:5		
16:11	Lk. 1:31	18:20, 21	Lk. 17:28; Rev. 18:5
16:15	Gal. 4:22		
17:5	Rom. 4:17	18:20—19:28	Mt. 10:15

Genesis

18:25	Heb. 12:23
19:1-3	Heb. 13:2
19:1-14	Lk. 17:28
19:1-16	2 Pet. 2:7
19:4-25	Jude 7
19:15-29	Lk. 17:29
19:17	Lk. 17:31, 32
19:24	2 Pet. 2:6;
	Rev. 14:10;
	20:10; 21:8
19:24, 25	Lk. 10:12
19:24-28	Mt. 11:23
19:26	Lk. 17:31, 32
19:28	Rev. 9:2
21:2	Gal. 4:22;
	Heb. 11:11
21:3	Mt. 1:2;
	Lk. 3:34
21:4	Acts 7:8
21:9	Gal. 4:29
21:10	Gal. 4:30
21:12	Mt. 1:2;
	Rom. 9:7;
	Heb. 11:18
22:1-10	Heb. 11:17
22:2	Mt. 3:17;
	Mk. 1:11;
	12:6
22:9, 12	Jas. 2:21
22:16	Heb. 6:13
22:16, 17	Lk. 1:73, 74
22:17	Lk. 1:55;
	Heb. 6:14;
	11:12
22:17, 18	Rom. 4:13
22:18	Mt. 1:1;
	Acts 3:25
23:2-20	Acts 7:16
23:4	Heb. 11:9, 13
24:7	Acts 7:5;
	Gal. 3:16
25:21	Rom. 9:10
25:23	Rom. 9:12
25:26	Mt. 1:2;
	Lk. 3:34
25:33, 34	Heb. 12:16
26:3	Heb. 11:9
26:4	Acts 3:25
27:27-29, 39, 40	Heb. 11:20
27:30-40	Heb. 12:17
28:12	Jn. 1:51
28:15	Heb. 13:5
29:35	Mt. 1:2;
	Lk. 3:33
30:23	Lk. 1:25
32:12	Heb. 11:12
33:19	Jn. 4:5;
	Acts 7:16
35:12, 27	Heb. 11:9
37:11	Acts 7:9
37:28	Acts 7:9

38:8	Mt. 22:24;
	Mk. 12:19;
	Lk. 20:28
38:29, 30	Mt. 1:3
39:2, 3, 21, 23	Acts 7:9
41:37-39	Acts 7:10
41:40-44	Acts 7:10
41:54	Acts 7:11
41:55	Jn. 2:5
42:1, 2	Acts 7:12
42:5	Acts 7:11
45:3, 4	Acts 7:13
45:4	Acts 7:9
45:9-11	Acts 7:14
45:16	Acts 7:13
45:18, 19	Acts 7:14
46:5, 6	Acts 7:15
46:27	Acts 7:14
47:9	Heb. 11:13
47:31	Heb. 11:21
48:4	Acts 7:5
48:15, 16	Heb. 11:21
48:22	Jn. 4:5
49:9, 10	Rev. 5:5
49:10	Heb. 7:14
49:29, 30	Acts 7:16
49:33	Acts 7:15
50:7-13	Acts 7:16
50:24, 25	Heb. 11:22

Job

1:1, 8	1 Thess. 5:22
1:9-11	Rev. 12:10
1:20	Mt. 26:65
1:21	1 Tim. 6:7
2:3	1 Thess. 5:22
2:6	2 Cor. 12:7
2:12	Mt. 26:65
3:21	Rev. 9:6
4:9	2 Thess. 2:8
4:19	2 Cor. 5:1
5:11	Lk. 1:52;
	Jas. 4:10
5:13	1 Cor. 3:19
12:7-9	Rom. 1:20
12:14	Rev. 3:7
12:19	Lk. 1:52
13:16	Phil. 1:19
15:8	Rom. 11:34
16:9	Acts 7:54
22:29	Mt. 23:12;
	1 Pet. 5:6
23:10	1 Pet. 1:7
34:19	Jas. 2:1
38:3	Lk. 12:35
38:17	Mt. 16:18
39:30	Lk. 17:37
40:7	Lk. 12:35
41:11	Rom. 11:35
42:2	Mt. 19:26
	Mk. 10:27

THE EXODUS STAGE

Exodus

1:6	Acts 7:15
1:7, 8	Acts 7:17, 18
1:10, 11	Acts 7:19
1:22	Acts 7:19;
	Heb. 11:23
2:2	Acts 7:20;
	Heb. 11:23
2:3-10	Acts 7:21
2:10-12	Heb. 11:24
2:11, 12	Acts 7:23, 24
2:13, 14	Acts 7:26-28
2:14	Lk. 12:14;
	Acts 7:35
2:15	Acts 7:29;
	Heb. 11:27
2:21, 22	Acts 7:29
3:2	Mk. 12:26;
	Lk. 20:37;
	Acts 7:35
3:2, 3	Acts 7:30, 31
3:4-10	Acts 7:31-34
3:6	Mt. 22:32;
	Mk. 12:26;
	Lk. 20:37;
	Acts 3:13;
	Heb. 11:16
3:12	Acts 7:7
3:14	Rev. 1:4, 8;
	4:8; 11:17;
	16:5
3:15	Mt. 22:32;
	Mk. 12:26;
	Acts 3:13;
	Heb. 11:16
3:16	Mt. 22:32;
	Mk. 12:26
4:5	Heb. 11:16
4:19	Mt. 2:20
4:21	Rom. 9:18
4:22	Rom. 9:4
6:1, 6	Acts 13:17
7:3	Acts 7:36;
	Rom. 9:18
7:11	2 Tim. 3:8
7:17-21	Rev. 16:3
7:17, 19, 20	Rev. 11:6
7:19-24	Rev. 16:4
7:20, 21	Rev. 8:8
7:22	2 Tim. 3:8
8:19	Lk. 11:20
9:10	Rev. 16:2
9:12	Rom. 9:18
9:16	Rom. 9:17
9:23-25	Rev. 8:7
9:24	Rev. 11:19;
	16:21
10:12, 15	Rev. 9:3
10:21	Rev. 16:10
12:1-27	Mt. 26:2;
	Lk. 22:1
12:3-20	1 Cor. 5:8
12:6	Mk. 14:12;
	Lk. 22:7

12:8-11	Lk. 22:8
12:11	Lk. 12:35
12:14	Lk. 22:7
12:14-20	Mt. 26:17
12:15	Mk. 14:12;
	Lk. 22:7
12:16	Lk. 23:56
12:21	1 Cor. 5:7
12:21-30	Heb. 11:28
12:24-27	Lk. 2:41
12:40	Gal. 3:17
12:46	Jn. 19:36
12:51	Acts 13:17;
	Heb. 11:27;
	Jude 5
13:2	Lk. 2:23
13:7	1 Cor. 5:7, 8
13:9	Mt. 23:5
13:12	Lk. 2:23
13:15	Lk. 2:23
13:19	Heb. 11:22
13:21, 22	1 Cor. 10:1
14:4, 17	Rom. 9:18
14:21	Acts 7:36
14:21-31	Heb. 11:29
14:22-29	1 Cor. 10:1
15:1	Rev. 15:3
15:11	Rev. 15:3
15:18	Rev. 11:15;
	19:6
16:4	Mt. 6:34;
	1 Cor. 10:3
16:7	2 Cor. 3:18
16:15	Jn. 6:31
16:18	2 Cor. 8:15
16:33	Heb. 9:4
16:35	Acts 13:18;
	1 Cor. 10:3
17:6	1 Cor. 10:4
17:7	Heb. 3:8
18:3, 4	Acts 7:29
19:1-6	Acts 7:38
19:5	Titus 2:14;
	1 Pet. 2:9
19:6	1 Pet. 2:5, 9;
	Rev. 1:6;
	5:10; 20:6
19:12, 13	Heb. 12:20
19:16	Rev. 4:5;
	11:19
19:16-19	Rev. 8:5;
	16:18
19:16-22	Heb. 12:18, 19
19:18	Heb. 12:26;
	Rev. 9:2
19:20, 24	Rev. 4:1
20:1-17	Acts 7:38
20:5	Jn. 9:2;
	Jas. 4:5
20:8-10	Mk. 2:27
20:9, 10	Lk. 13:14
20:10	Mt. 12:2;
	Lk. 23:56

20:11	Acts 4:24; 14:15; Rev. 10:6; 14:7
20:12	Mt. 15:4; Mk. 7:10; Lk. 18:20; Eph. 6:2, 3
20:12-16	Mt. 19:18, 19; Mk. 10:19
20:13	Mt. 5:21; Jas. 2:11
20:13-15	Rom. 13:9
20:13-16	Lk. 18:20
20:14	Mt. 5:27; Jas. 2:11
20:17	Rom. 7:7; 13:9
20:18-21	Heb. 12:18, 19
21:2	Jn. 8:35
21:12	Mt. 5:21
21:17	Mt. 15:4; Mk. 7:10
21:24	Mt. 5:38
21:32	Mt. 26:15
22:1	Lk. 19:8
22:11	Heb. 6:16
22:28	Acts 23:5
23:4, 5	Mt. 5:44
23:20	Mt. 11:10; Mk. 1:2; Lk. 7:27
24:3	Heb. 9:19
24:6-8	1 Cor. 11:25; Heb. 9:19
24:8	Mt. 26:28; Mk. 14:24; Lk. 22:20; 1 Cor. 11:25; 2 Cor. 3:6; Heb. 9:20; 10:29
24:12	2 Cor. 3:3
24:17	2 Cor. 3:18
25:9	Acts 7:44
25:10-16	Heb. 9:4
25:16	Heb. 9:4
25:18-22	Heb. 9:5
25:23-30	Heb. 9:2
25:31-40	Heb. 9:2
25:40	Acts 7:44; Heb. 8:5
26:1-30	Heb. 9:2
26:31-33	Lk. 23:45; Heb. 9:3
26:31-35	Mt. 27:51
27:21	Acts 7:44
28:1	Heb. 5:4
28:21	Rev. 21:12, 13
29:18	Eph. 5:2; Phil. 4:18
29:37	Mt. 23:19
29:38	Heb. 10:11
30:1-3	Rev. 8:3; 9:13
30:1-6	Heb. 9:4
30:7	Lk. 1:9
30:10	Heb. 9:7
30:13	Mt. 17:24
31:18	Jn. 1:17; 2 Cor. 3:3
32:1	Acts 7:40
32:4-6	Acts 7:41
32:6	1 Cor. 10:7
32:9	Acts 7:51
32:13	Heb. 11:12
32:23	Acts 7:40
32:32	Lk. 10:20; Rom. 9:3
32:32, 33	Phil. 4:3; Rev. 3:5; 13:8; 17:8; 20:12, 15; Rev. 21:27
33:3, 5	Acts 7:51
33:19	Rom. 9:15
33:20	Jn. 1:18; 1 Tim. 6:16
34:1	2 Cor. 3:3
34:6	Jas. 5:11
34:28	Mt. 4:2; Jn. 1:17
34:29, 30	2 Cor. 3:7, 10
34:33	2 Cor. 3:13
34:34	2 Cor. 3:16
36:35	Lk. 23:45; 2 Cor. 3:13
38:21	Rev. 15:5
38:26	Mt. 17:24
40:34	Rev. 15:5, 8

Leviticus

3:17	Acts 15:20, 29
6:16, 26	1 Cor. 9:13
7:6, 15	1 Cor. 10:18
9:7	Heb. 5:3; 7:27
11:1-47	Acts 10:14
11:2	Heb. 9:10
11:25	Heb. 9:10
11:44, 45	1 Pet. 1:16
12:3	Lk. 1:59; 2:21; Jn. 7:22; Acts 15:1
12:3, 6	Lk. 2:22
12:8	Lk. 2:24
13:46	Lk. 17:12
14:2	Mt. 8:4
14:2, 3	Lk. 17:14
14:2-32	Mk. 1:44; Lk. 5:14
14:4	Heb. 9:19
14:4-32	Mt. 8:4
15:18	Heb. 9:10
15:25	Mt. 9:20
16:2	Heb. 9:7
16:2, 3	Heb. 6:19
16:3	Heb. 9:13
16:6	Heb. 5:3; 7:27
16:12	Heb. 6:19; Rev. 8:5
16:14	Heb. 9:7; 9:13
16:15	Heb. 6:19; 7:27; 9:7, 13; 10:4
16:21	Heb. 10:4
16:27	Heb. 13:11
16:29	Acts 27:9
17:10-14	Acts 15:20, 29
17:11	Heb. 9:22
18:5	Mt. 19:17; Lk. 10:28; Rom. 7:10; 10:5; Gal. 3:12
18:7, 8	1 Cor. 5:1
18:15	Heb. 9:21
18:16	Mt. 14:3, 4; Mk. 6:18
18:19	Heb. 9:21
18:22	Rom. 1:27
19:2	Mt. 5:48; 1 Pet. 1:16
19:12	Mt. 5:33
19:13	Mt. 20:8; Jas. 5:4
19:15	Jn. 7:24; Acts 23:3
19:17	Mt. 18:15
19:18	Mt. 5:43; 19:19; 22:39; Mk. 12:31, 33; Lk. 10:27; Rom. 12:19; 13:9; Gal. 5:14; Jas. 2:8
19:32	1 Tim. 5:1
20:7	1 Pet. 1:16
20:9	Mt. 15:4; Mk. 7:10
20:10	Jn. 8:5
20:13	Rom. 1:27
20:21	Mt. 14:3, 4
21:9	Rev. 17:16; 18:8
23:15-21	Acts 2:1; 1 Cor. 16:8
23:29	Acts 3:23
23:34	Jn. 7:2
23:36	Jn. 7:37
24:5-8	Mt. 12:4
24:5-9	Mk. 2:26; Lk. 6:4
24:9	Mt. 12:4
24:16	Mt. 26:65, 66; Mk. 14:64; Jn. 10:33; 19:7
24:17	Mt. 5:21
24:20	Mt. 5:38
25:35, 36	Lk. 6:35
25:43, 53	Col. 4:1
26:11, 12	Rev. 21:3
26:12	2 Cor. 6:16
26:21	Rev. 15:1, 6
26:41	Acts 7:51
26:42	Lk. 1:72, 73
27:30	Mt. 23:23; Lk. 11:42

Numbers

1:50	Acts 7:44
6:2-5	Acts 21:26
6:3	Lk. 1:15
6:5	Acts 21:23, 24
6:13-18	Acts 21:23, 24
6:13-21	Acts 21:26
6:18	Acts 18:18
6:21	Acts 21:23, 24
6:25, 26	Rom. 1:7
9:12	Jn. 19:36
11:4	1 Cor. 10:6
11:7-9	Jn. 6:31
11:29	1 Cor. 14:5
11:34	1 Cor. 10:6
12:7	Heb. 3:2, 5
12:8	2 Jn. 12; 3 Jn. 14
14:1-35	Heb. 3:16-18
14:2	1 Cor. 10:10
14:3	Acts 7:39
14:6	Mt. 26:65; Mk. 14:63
14:16	1 Cor. 10:5
14:21-23	Heb. 3:11
14:22, 23	Heb. 3:18
14:23	1 Cor. 10:5
14:29	Heb. 3:17
14:29, 30	1 Cor. 10:5; Jude 5
14:33	Acts 7:36
14:34	Acts 13:18
14:35	Jude 5
14:36	1 Cor. 10:10
15:17-21	Rom. 11:16
15:38, 39	Mt. 23:5
16:5	2 Tim. 2:19
16:19-35	Jude 11
16:22	Heb. 12:9
16:26	2 Tim. 2:19
16:41-49	1 Cor. 10:10
17:8-10	Heb. 9:4
18:2-6	Heb. 9:6
18:8	1 Cor. 9:13
18:21	Heb. 7:5
18:31	Mt. 10:10; 1 Cor. 9:13
19:6	Heb. 9:19
19:9	Heb. 9:13
19:13	Heb. 9:10
19:17-19	Heb. 9:13
20:2-5	Heb. 3:8
20:11	1 Cor. 10:4
21:5, 6	1 Cor. 10:9
21:9	Jn. 3:14
22:7	2 Pet. 2:15; Jude 11

Numbers

22:28	2 Pet. 2:16
23:19	Rom. 9:6;
	2 Tim. 2:13;
	Heb. 6:18
24:17	Mt. 2:2;
	Rev. 22:16
25:1, 2	Rev. 2:14, 20
25:1, 9	1 Cor. 10:8
27:16	Heb. 12:9
27:17	Mt. 9:36;
	Mk. 6:34
28:9, 10	Mt. 12:5
30:2	Mt. 5:33
31:16	Jude 11;
	Rev. 2:14

Deuteronomy

1:10	Heb. 11:12
1:16	Jn. 7:51
1:17	Jas. 2:9
2:5	Acts 7:5
4:2	Rev. 22:18, 19
4:7, 8	Rom. 3:2
4:11, 12	Heb. 12:18, 19
4:15–19	Rom. 1:23
4:20	Titus 2:14;
	1 Pet. 2:9
4:24	Heb. 12:29
4:35	Mk. 12:32
4:35, 39	1 Cor. 8:4
5:4–22	Acts 7:38
5:12–14	Mk. 2:27
5:13, 14	Lk. 13:14
5:14	Mt. 12:2;
	Lk. 23:56
5:16	Mt. 15:4;
	Mk. 7:10;
	Lk. 18:20
5:16–20	Mt. 19:18, 19;
	Mk. 10:19
5:17	Mt. 5:21;
	Jas. 2:11
5:17–19	Rom. 13:9
5:17–20	Lk. 18:20
5:18	Mt. 5:27;
	Jas. 2:11
5:21	Rom. 7:7;
	13:9
5:22–27	Heb. 12:18, 19
6:4	Mk. 12:32;
	Rom. 3:30;
	1 Cor. 8:4
6:4, 5	Mk. 12:29, 30
6:5	Mt. 22:37;
	Mk. 12:33;
	Lk. 10:27
6:7	Eph. 6:4
6:8	Mt. 23:5
6:13	Mt. 4:10
6:13, 14	Lk. 4:8
6:16	Mt. 4:7;
	Lk. 4:12

6:20–25	Eph. 6:4
7:1	Acts 13:19
7:6	Rom. 9:4;
	Titus 2:14;
	1 Pet. 2:9
7:9	1 Cor. 1:9;
	10:13
8:3	Mt. 4:4;
	Lk. 4:4;
	1 Cor. 10:3
8:5	Heb. 12:7
9:3	Heb. 12:29
9:4	Rom. 10:6–8
9:10	Acts 7:38
9:10, 11	2 Cor. 3:3
9:19	Heb. 12:21
10:3–5	Heb. 9:4
10:12	Lk. 10:27
10:15	1 Pet 2:9
10:17	Acts 10:34;
	Rom. 2:11;
	Gal. 2:6;
	Eph. 6:9;
	Col. 3:25;
	1 Tim. 6:15;
	Rev. 17:14;
	19:16
10:22	Acts 7:14;
	Heb. 11:12
11:14	Jas. 5:7
11:29	Jn. 4:20
12:5–14	Jn. 4:20
12:32	Rev. 22:18, 19
13:1–3	Mt. 24:24;
	Mk. 13:22
13:2–4	Rev. 13:14
13:3	1 Cor. 11:19
14:1, 2	Rom. 9:4
14:2	Titus 2:14;
	1 Pet. 2:9
15:7, 8	1 Jn. 3:17
15:11	Mt. 26:11;
	Mk. 14:7;
	Jn. 12:8
15:12	Jn. 8:35
15:16	Eph. 6:2, 3
16:1–8	Lk. 2:41
16:3	1 Cor. 5:8
16:9–11	Acts 2:1;
	1 Cor. 16:8
17:6	Jn. 8:17;
	1 Tim. 5:19;
	Heb. 10:28
17:7	Jn. 8:7;
	1 Cor. 5:13
18:1–3	1 Cor. 9:13
18:13	Mt. 5:48
18:15	Mt. 17:5;
	Mk. 9:7;
	Lk. 24:27;
	Jn. 5:46; 7:40;
	Acts 7:37
18:15, 16	Acts 3:22
18:15, 18	Jn. 1:21; 6:14
18:18	Jn. 1:45

18:19	Acts 3:23
19:15	Mt. 18:16;
	Jn. 8:17;
	2 Cor. 13:1;
	1 Tim. 5:19;
	Heb. 10:28
19:19	1 Cor. 5:13
19:21	Mt. 5:38
21:6–9	Mt. 27:24
21:22	Acts 10:39
21:22, 23	Mt. 27:57, 58;
	Jn. 19:31
21:23	Gal. 3:13
22:21	1 Cor. 5:13
22:22	Jn. 8:5
22:24	1 Cor. 5:13
22:30	1 Cor. 5:1
23:21	Mt. 5:33
23:24, 25	Mt. 12:1
23:25	Mk. 2:23;
	Lk. 6:1
24:1	Mt. 5:31; 19:7
24:1, 3	Mk. 10:4
24:7	1 Cor. 5:13
24:14	Mk. 10:19
24:14, 15	Jas. 5:4
24:15	Mt. 20:8
25:3	2 Cor. 11:24
25:4	1 Cor. 9:9;
	1 Tim. 5:18
25:5	Mt. 22:24;
	Mk. 12:19;
	Lk. 20:28
27:20	1 Cor. 5:1
27:26	2 Cor. 3:9;
	Gal. 3:10
28:4	Lk. 1:42
28:35	Rev. 16:2
29:4	Rom. 11:8

CONQUEST STAGE

Joshua

1:5	Heb. 13:5
2:4	Jas. 2:25
2:11, 12	Heb. 11:31
2:15	Jas. 2:25
3:14–17	Acts 7:45
6:12–21	Heb. 11:30
6:17	Jas. 2:25
6:21–25	Heb. 11:31
7:19	Jn. 9:24
8:33	Jn. 4:20
14:1	Acts 13:19

JUDGES STAGE

Judges

2:10	Acts 13:36
2:16	Acts 13:20
5:4	Heb. 12:26
5:19	Rev. 16:16
5:24	Lk. 1:42
13:3	Lk. 1:31
13:4	Lk.1:15
13:5, 7	Mt. 2:23
14:6, 7	Heb. 11:33

29:18	Acts 8:23
30:4	Mt. 24:31;
	Mk. 13:27
30:6	Rom. 2:29
30:11	1 Jn. 5:3
30:12–14	Rom. 10:6–8
31:6	Heb. 13:5
31:7	Heb. 4:8
31:8	Heb. 13:5
31:26, 27	Jn. 5:45
32:4	Rom. 9:14;
	Rev. 15:3;
	16:5
32:5	Mt. 17:17;
	Acts 2:40;
	Phil. 2:15
32:6	Jn. 8:41
32:8	Acts 17:26
32:17	1 Cor. 10:20;
	Rev. 9:20
32:20	Mt. 17:17
32:21	Rom. 10:19;
	11:11;
	1 Cor. 10:22
32:29	Lk. 19:42
32:35	Lk. 21:22;
	Rom. 12:19;
	Heb. 10:30
32:36	Heb. 10:30
32:40	Rev. 10:5, 6
32:43	Rom. 15:10;
	Rev. 6:10;
	19:2
33:2	Jude 14
33:3, 4	Acts 20:32;
	26:18
33:9	Mt. 10:37;
	Lk. 14:26
33:12	2 Thess. 2:13

18:1	Acts 7:45
22:4	Heb. 4:8
22:5	Mt. 22:37;
	Mk. 12:29,
	30; 12:33;
	Lk. 10:27
23:9	Acts 7:45
24:18	Acts 7:45
24:32	Jn. 4:5;
	Acts 7:16

Ruth

4:12	Mt. 1:3
4:13	Mt. 1:4, 5
4:17–22	Mt. 1:4, 5;
	Lk. 3:31–33
4:17, 22	Mt. 1:6
4:18, 19	Mt. 1:3

1 Samuel

1:11	Lk. 1:48

1:17	Mk. 5:34
2:1-10	Lk. 1:46-55
2:5	Lk. 1:53a
2:26	Lk. 2:52
3:20	Acts 13:20
4:8	Rev. 11:6

CHAOTIC KINGDOM STAGE

1 Samuel

8:5, 19	Acts 13:21
10:20, 21, 24	Acts 13:21
11:15	Acts 13:21
12:3	Acts 20:33
12:22	Rom. 11:1, 2
13:14	Acts 13:22
14:45	Mt. 10:30; Lk. 21:18; Acts 27:34
15:22	Mk. 12:33
15:29	Heb. 6:18
16:1	Lk. 3:31, 32
16:7	Jn. 8:15
16:12, 13	Acts 13:22
16:13	Lk. 3:31, 32
17:34-36	Heb. 11:33
20:42	Mk. 5:34
21:1-6	Mt. 12:3, 4; Mk. 2:25, 26; Lk. 6:3, 4

2 Samuel

3:39	2 Tim. 4:14
5:2	Mt. 2:6
5:14	Lk. 3:31
7:2-16	Acts 7:45, 46
7:8	2 Cor. 6:18
7:12	Jn. 7:42; Acts 13:23
7:12, 13	Lk. 1:32, 33; Acts 2:30
7:14	2 Cor. 6:18; Heb. 1:5; 12:7; 21:7
7:16	Lk. 1:32, 33
12:24	Mt. 1:6
13:19	Mt. 26:65
14:11	Acts 27:34
15:9	Mk. 5:34
15:35	Mk. 2:26
22:6	Acts 2:24
22:9	Rev. 11:5
22:28	Lk. 1:51
22:50	Rom. 15:9
23:2	Mt. 22:43

1 Kings

2:10	Acts 2:29; 13:36
5:11	Acts 12:20
6:1, 14	Acts 7:47
8:1, 6	Rev. 11:19
8:10, 11	Rev. 15:8
8:13	Mt. 23:21
8:17, 18	Acts 7:45, 46
8:19, 20	Acts 7:47
8:27	Acts 17:24
9:7, 8	Mt. 23:38
10	Mt. 6:29
10:1-10	Mt. 12:42; Lk. 11:31
10:4-7	Lk. 12:27

1 Chronicles

1:1-4	Lk. 3:36-38
1:24-27	Lk. 3:34-36
1:28	Lk. 3:34
1:34	Mt. 1:2; Lk. 3:34
2:1-14	Lk. 3:31-33
2:4, 5, 9	Mt. 1:3
2:10-12	Mt. 1:4, 5
2:13-15	Mt. 1:6
3:10-14	Mt. 1:7-10
3:15, 16	Mt. 1:11
3:17	Lk. 3:27
3:17, 19	Mt. 1:12
11:2	Mt. 2:6
16:35	Acts 26:17
17:1-14	Acts 7:45, 46
17:11	Mt. 1:1
17:13	Heb. 1:5
24:10	Lk. 1:5
29:11	Rev. 5:12
29:15	Heb. 11:13

2 Chronicles

3:1	Acts 7:47
5:1	Acts 7:47
5:7	Rev. 11:19
5:13, 14	Rev. 15:8
6:2	Acts 7:47
6:7, 8	Acts 7:45, 46
6:10	Acts 7:47
6:18	Rev. 21:3
9	Mt. 6:29
9:1-12	Mt. 12:42; Lk. 11:31
9:3-6	Lk. 12:27

Psalms

2:1	Rev. 11:18
2:1, 2	Acts 4:25, 26
2:2	Rev. 19:19
2:7	Mt. 3:17; 15:5; Mk. 1:11; Lk. 3:22; 9:35; Jn. 1:49; Acts 13:33; Heb. 1:5; 5:5
2:8	Heb. 1:2
2:8, 9	Rev. 2:26, 27
2:9	Rev. 12:5; 19:15
2:11	Phil. 2:12
4:4	Eph. 4:26
5:9	Rom. 3:13
6:3	Jn. 12:27
6:8	Mt. 7:23; Lk. 13:27
7:9	Rev. 2:23
7:12	Lk. 13:3, 5
7:13	Eph. 6:16
8:6	1 Cor. 15:27; Eph. 1:22
9:8	Acts 17:31
10:7	Rom. 3:14
10:16	Rev. 11:15
11:6	Rev. 14:10; 20:10; 21:8
14:1-3	Rom. 3:10-12
14:7	Rom. 11:26, 27
16:8-11	Acts 2:25-28
16:9	Jn. 20:9
16:10	Acts 2:31; 1 Cor. 15:4
17:15	Rev. 22:4
18:2	Lk. 1:69
18:4	Acts 2:24
18:6	Jas. 5:4
18:49	Rom. 15:9
19:1	Rom. 1:20
19:4	Rom. 10:18
19:9	Rev. 16:7; 19:2
21:9	Jas. 5:3
22	1 Pet. 1:11
22:1	Mt. 27:46; Mk. 15:34
22:1-18	Mk. 9:12; Lk. 24:27
22:5	Rom. 5:5
22:7	Mt. 27:39; Mk. 15:29
22:7, 8	Mt. 26:24; Lk. 23:35, 36
22:8	Mt. 27:43
22:15	Jn. 19:28
22:16	Phil. 3:2
22:16-18	Mt. 26:24
22:18	Mt. 27:35; Mk. 15:24; Lk. 23:34; Jn. 19:24
22:20	Phil. 3:2
22:21	2 Tim. 4:17
22:22	Heb. 2:12
22:23	Rev. 19:5
22:28	Rev. 11:15; 19:6
23:1	Jn. 10:11; Rev. 7:17
23:2	Rev. 7:17
23:5	Lk. 7:46
24:1	1 Cor. 10:26
24:3, 4	Mt. 5:8
25:11	1 Jn. 2:12
25:20	Rom. 5:5
25:21	Lk. 6:27
26:6	Mt. 27:24
26:8	Mt. 23:21
28:4	Mt. 16:27; 2 Tim. 4:14; 1 Pet. 1:17; Rev. 20:12, 13; 22:12
29:3	Acts 7:2
31:5	Lk. 23:46; Acts 7:59; 1 Pet. 4:19
31:24	1 Cor. 16:13
32:1, 2	Rom. 4:7, 8
32:2	Rev. 14:5
32:5	1 Jn. 1:9
33:2, 3	Eph. 5:19
33:3	Rev. 5:9; 14:3
33:6, 9	Heb. 11:3
34:8	Heb. 1:14; 1 Pet. 2:3
34:12-16	1 Pet. 3:10-12
34:13	Jas. 1:26
34:14	Heb. 12:14
34:15	Jn. 9:31
34:19	2 Cor. 1:5; 2 Tim. 3:11
34:20	Jn. 19:36
35:8	Rom. 11:9, 10
35:13	Rom. 12:15
35:16	Acts 7:54
35:19	Jn. 15:25
36:1	Rom. 3:18
36:9	Rev. 21:6
37:4	Mt. 6:33
37:11	Mt. 5:5
37:12	Acts 7:54
38:11	Lk. 23:49
39:1	Jas. 1:26
39:12	Heb. 11:13; 1 Pet. 2:11
40:3	Rev. 5:9; 14:3
40:6	Eph. 5:2; Heb. 10:8
40:6-8	Heb. 10:5-7
40:7	Lk. 7:19; Heb. 10:9
41:9	Mt. 26:23; Mk. 14:18; Lk. 22:21; Jn. 13:18; 17:12; Acts 1:16
41:13	Lk. 1:68; Rom. 9:5
42:2	Rev. 22:4
42:5, 11	Mt. 26:38; Mk. 14:34; Jn. 12:27
43:5	Mt. 26:38; Mk. 14:34
44:22	Rom. 8:36
45:6, 7	Heb. 1:8, 9
46:2, 3	Lk. 21:25
46:6	Rev. 11:18

Psalms

47:8	Rev. 4:2, 9, 10; 5:1, 7, 13; 6:16; 7:10, 15; 19:4; 21:5
48:2	Mt. 5:35
50:6	Heb. 12:23
50:12	Acts 17:25; 1 Cor. 10:26
50:14	Heb. 13:15
50:16-21	Rom. 2:21
50:23	Heb. 13:15
51:1	Lk. 18:13
51:4	Lk. 15:18; Rom. 3:4
51:5	Jn. 9:34; Rom. 7:14
53:1-3	Rom. 3:10-12
55:22	1 Pet. 5:7
62:10	Mt. 19:22; 1 Tim. 6:17
62:12	Mt. 16:27; Rom. 2:6; 2 Tim. 4:14; 1 Pet. 1:17; Rev. 2:23; 20:12, 13; 22:12
65:7	Lk. 21:25
66:10	1 Pet. 1:7
66:18	Jn. 9:31
67:2	Acts 28:28
68:8	Heb. 12:26
68:18	Eph. 4:8
69:4	Jn. 15:25
69:9	Jn. 2:17; Rom. 15:3
69:21	Mt. 27:34, 48; Mk. 15:23, 36; Lk. 23:36; Jn. 19:29
69:22, 23	Rom. 11:9, 10
69:24	Rev. 16:1
69:25	Acts 1:20
69:28	Phil. 4:3; Rev. 3:5; 13:8; 17:8; 20:12, 15; 21:27
72:10, 11	Mt. 2:11; Rev. 21:26
72:15	Mt. 2:11
72:18	Lk. 1:68
74:2	Acts 20:28
75:8	Rev. 14:10; 15:7; 16:19
78:2	Mt. 13:35
78:4	Eph. 6:4
78:8	Acts 2:40
78:15	1 Cor. 10:4
78:24	Jn. 6:31; Rev. 2:17
78:24-29	1 Cor. 10:3
78:31	1 Cor. 10:5
78:37	Acts 8:21
78:44	Rev. 16:4
79:1	Lk. 21:24; Rev. 11:2
79:3	Rev. 16:6
79:6	1 Thess. 4:5; 2 Thess. 1:8
79:10	Rev. 6:10; 19:2
82:6	Jn. 10:34
86:9	Rev. 15:4
88:8	Lk. 23:49
89:3, 4	Jn. 7:42
89:4	Jn. 12:34
89:10	Lk. 1:51
89:11	1 Cor. 10:26
89:20	Acts 13:22
89:26	1 Pet. 1:17
89:27	Rev. 1:5
89:36	Jn. 12:34
89:50, 51	1 Pet. 4:14
90:4	2 Pet. 3:8
91:11	Lk. 4:10; Heb. 1:14
91:11, 12	Mt. 4:6
91:12	Lk. 4:11
91:13	Lk. 10:19
92:5	Rev. 15:3
93:1	Rev. 19:6
94:1	1 Thess. 4:6
94:11	1 Cor. 3:20
94:14	Rom. 11:1, 2
94:19	2 Cor. 1:5
95:7, 8	Heb. 3:15; 4:7
95:7-11	Heb. 3:7-11
95:11	Heb. 3:18; 4:3, 5
96:1	Rev. 5:9; 14:3
96:11	Rev. 18:20
96:13	Acts 17:31; Rev. 19:11
97:1	Rev. 19:6
97:3	Rev. 11:5
97:7	Heb. 1:6
98:1	Rev. 5:9; 14:3
98:3	Lk. 1:54; Acts 28:28
98:9	Acts 17:31
99:1	Rev. 19:6
102:4, 11	Jas. 1:10, 11
102:25-27	Heb. 1:10-12
103:3	Mk. 2:7
103:7	Rom. 3:2
103:8	Jas. 5:11
103:13, 17	Lk. 1:50
104:2	1 Tim. 6:16
104:4	Heb. 1:7
104:12	Mt. 13:32
105:8, 9	Lk. 1:72, 73
105:21	Acts 7:10
105:40	Jn. 6:31
106:10	Lk. 1:71
106:14	1 Cor. 10:6
106:20	Rom. 1:23
106:25-27	1 Cor. 10:10
106:37	1 Cor. 10:20
106:45, 46	Lk. 1:72
106:48	Lk. 1:68
107:3	Mt. 8:11; Lk. 13:29
107:9	Lk. 1:53
107:20	Acts 10:36
109:4, 5, 7, 8	Jn. 17:12
109:8	Acts 1:20
109:25	Mt. 27:39; Mk. 15:29
109:28	1 Cor. 4:12
110:1	Mt. 22:44; 26:64; Mk. 12:36; 14:62; 16:19; Lk. 20:42, 43; 22:69; Acts 2:34, 35; Rom. 8:34; 1 Cor. 15:25; Eph. 1:20; Col. 3:1; Heb. 1:3, 13; 8:1; 10:12, 13; 12:2
110:4	Jn. 12:34; Heb. 5:6, 10; 6:20; 7:3, 17, 21
111:2	Rev. 15:3
111:4	Jas. 5:11
111:9	Lk. 1:49, 68
112:9	2 Cor. 9:9
112:10	Acts 7:54
113—118	Mt. 26:30
114:3-7	Rev. 20:11
115:4-7	Rev. 9:20
115:13	Rev. 11:18; 19:5
116:3	Acts 2:24
116:10	2 Cor. 4:13
116:11	Rom. 3:4
117:1	Rom. 15:11
118:6	Rom. 8:31; Heb. 13:6
118:18	2 Cor. 6:9
118:20	Jn. 10:9
118:22	Lk. 20:17; Acts 4:11; 1 Pet. 2:4, 7
118:22, 23	Mt. 21:42; Mk. 12:10, 11
118:25, 26	Mk. 11:9; Jn. 12:13
118:26	Mt. 21:9; 23:39; Lk. 13:35; 19:38
119:46	Rom. 1:16
119:137	Rev. 16:5, 7; 19:2
119:165	1 Jn. 2:10
122:1-5	Jn. 4:20
125:5	Gal. 6:16
126:5, 6	Lk. 6:21
128:6	Gal. 6:16
130:8	Titus 2:14; Rev. 1:5
132:1-5	Acts 7:45, 46
132:11	Acts 2:30
134:1	Rev. 19:5
135:1	Rev. 19:5
135:14	Heb. 10:30
135:15-17	Rev. 9:20
137:8	Rev. 18:6
137:9	Lk. 19:44
139:1	Rom. 8:27
139:14	Rev. 15:3
139:21	Rev. 2:6
140:3	Rom. 3:13; Jas. 3:8
141:2	Rev. 5:8; 8:3, 4
141:3	Jas. 1:26
143:2	Rom. 3:20; 1 Cor. 4:4; Gal. 2:16
144:9	Rev. 5:9; 14:3
145:17	Rev. 15:3; 16:5
145:18	Acts 17:27
146:6	Acts 4:24; 14:15; 17:24; Rev. 10:6; 14:7
147:8	Acts 14:17
147:9	Lk. 12:24
147:18	Acts 10:36
147:19, 20	Rom. 3:2
149:1	Rev. 5:9; 14:3

Proverbs

1:16	Rom. 3:15-17
2:3, 4	Col. 2:3
2:3-6	Jas. 1:5
2:4	Mt. 13:44
3:3	2 Cor. 3:3
3:4	Lk. 2:52; 2 Cor. 8:21
3:7	Rom. 12:16
3:11, 12	Heb. 12:5, 6
3:12	Rev. 3:19
3:27, 28	2 Cor. 8:12; 1 Pet. 5:5
7:3	2 Cor. 3:3
8:15	Rom. 13:1
8:22	Rev. 3:14
10:9	Acts 13:10
10:12	1 Cor. 13:7; Jas. 5:20; 1 Pet. 4:8
11:24	2 Cor. 9:6
15:29	Jn. 9:31
16:33	Acts 1:26
17:3	1 Pet. 1:7
18:4	Jn. 7:38
19:17	Mt. 25:40
19:18	Eph. 6:4

20:22	1 Thess. 5:15	**27:1**	Jas. 4:13, 14	**Isaiah**		**11:15**	Rev. 16:12
20:27	1 Cor. 2:11	**27:20**	1 Jn. 2:16	**1:9**	Rom. 9:29	**12:2**	Heb. 2:13
22:6	Eph. 6:4	**28:13**	1 Jn. 1:9	**1:10**	Rev. 11:8	**13:8**	Jn. 16:21
22:9	2 Cor. 9:6	**28:22**	1 Tim. 6:9	**1:15**	Jn. 9:31	**13:10**	Mt. 24:29;
23:4	1 Tim. 6:9	**29:3**	Lk. 15:13	**1:16**	Jas. 4:8		Mk. 13:24,
24:12	Mt. 16:27;	**29:23**	Mt. 23:12	**2:3**	Jn. 4:22		25;
	Rom. 2:6;	**30:4**	Jn. 3:13	**2:5**	1 Jn. 1:7		Lk. 21:25;
	2 Tim. 4:14;	**30:8**	1 Tim. 6:8	**2:10, 19,**	2 Thess. 1:9;		Rev. 6:12, 13;
	1 Pet. 1:17;	**31:17**	Lk. 12:35	**21**	Rev. 6:15		8:12
	Rev. 2:23;			**5:1**	Lk. 20:9	**13:21**	Rev. 18:2
	20:12, 13;	**Ecclesiastes**		**5:1, 2**	Mt. 21:33;	**14:12**	Lk. 10:18;
	22:12	**1:2**	Rom. 8:20		Mk. 12:1		Rev. 12:9
24:21	1 Pet. 2:17	**5:15**	1 Tim. 6:7	**5:9**	Jas. 5:4	**14:13, 15**	Mt. 11:23;
25:6, 7	Lk. 14:8-10	**7:9**	Jas. 1:19	**5:21**	Rom. 12:16		Lk. 10:15
25:21	Mt. 5:44	**7:20**	Rom. 3:10-12	**6:1**	Jn. 12:41;	**19:2**	Mt. 24:7;
25:21, 22	Rom. 12:20	**11:5**	Jn 3:8		Rev. 4:2, 9,		Mk. 13:8;
26:11	2 Pet. 2:22	**12:14**	2 Cor. 5:10		10; 5:1, 7,		Lk. 21:10
					13; 6:16;	**19:12**	1 Cor. 1:20
DIVIDED KINGDOM STAGE					7:10, 15;	**21:3**	Jn. 16:21
					19:4; 21:5	**21:9**	Rev. 14:8;
1 Kings				**6:2**	Rev. 4:8		18:2
16:31	Rev. 2:20	**4:43, 44**	Mt. 14:20	**6:3**	Rev. 4:8	**22:13**	1 Cor. 15:32
17:1	Jas. 5:17;	**4:44**	Lk. 9:17	**6:4**	Rev. 15:8	**22:22**	Rev. 3:7
	Rev. 11:6	**5:1-14**	Lk. 4:27	**6:9, 10**	Mt. 13:14, 15;	**23**	Lk. 10:13, 14
17:1, 7	Lk. 4:25	**5:10**	Jn. 9:7		Mk. 4:12;	**23:1-8**	Mt. 11:21, 22
17:9	Lk. 4:26	**5:19**	Mk. 5:34		Lk. 8:10;	**23:8**	Rev. 18:23
17:9-24	Mt. 10:41	**9:1**	Lk. 12:35		19:42;	**23:17**	Rev. 17:2;
17:17	Lk. 7:12	**9:7**	Rev. 6:10;		Acts 28:26,		18:3
17:17-24	Heb. 11:35		19:2		27	**24:8**	Rev. 18:22
17:18	Mt. 8:29;	**9:13**	Lk. 19:36	**6:10**	Jn. 12:40	**24:15**	2 Thess. 1:12
	Mk. 5:7	**9:22**	Rev. 2:20	**7:14**	Mt. 1:23;	**24:17**	Lk. 21:35
17:21	Acts 20:10	**9:27**	Rev. 16:16		Lk. 1:31;	**24:23**	Rev. 4:4
17:23	Lk. 7:15	**12:9**	Mk. 12:41		Jn. 1:45;	**25:8**	1 Cor. 15:54
18:1	Lk. 4:25	**23:29**	Rev. 16:16		Rev. 12:5		Rev. 7:17;
18:12	Acts 8:39	**24:12-16**	Mt. 1:11	**8:12-13**	1 Pet. 3:14,		21:4
18:17	Acts 16:20				15	**26:3**	Phil. 4:7
18:24-39	Rev. 13:13	**2 Chronicles**		**8:14**	Lk. 2:34;	**26:11**	Heb. 10:27
18:42-45	Jas. 5:18	**13:9**	Gal. 4:8		Rom. 9:32;	**26:17**	Jn. 16:21
18:46	Lk. 12:35	**15:6**	Mt. 24:7;		1 Pet. 2:8	**26:19**	Eph. 5:14
19:10, 14	Rom. 11:3		Mk. 13:8;	**8:18**	Heb. 2:13	**26:20**	Mt. 6:6
19:18	Rom. 11:4		Lk. 21:10	**8:22**	Rev. 16:10	**27:9**	Rom. 11:27
19:20	Mt. 8:21;	**15:7**	1 Cor. 15:58	**9:1, 2**	Mt. 4:15, 16	**27:13**	Mt. 24:31
	Lk. 9:61	**18:16**	Mt. 9:36;	**9:2**	Lk. 1:78, 79;	**28:11, 12**	1 Cor. 14:21
22:17	Mt. 9:36;		Mk. 6:34		2 Cor. 4:6;	**28:16**	Rom. 9:38;
	Mk. 6:34	**18:18**	Rev. 4:2, 9,		1 Pet. 2:9		10:11;
22:19	Rev. 4:2, 9,		10; 5:1, 7,	**9:6**	Jn. 1:45;		1 Cor. 3:11;
	10; 5:1, 7,		13; 6:16;		Eph. 2:14		Eph. 2:20;
	13; 6:16;		7:10, 15;	**9:7**	Lk. 1:32, 33;		1 Pet. 2:4, 6
	7:10, 15;		19:4; 21:5		Jn. 12:34	**29:10**	Rom. 11:8
	19:4; 21:5	**18:25, 26**	Heb. 11:36	**10:3**	1 Pet. 2:12	**29:11**	Rev. 5:1
22:26, 27	Heb. 11:36	**19:7**	Acts 10:34;	**10:22, 23**	Rom. 9:27, 28	**29:13**	Col. 2:22;
			Rom. 2:11;	**11:1**	Mt. 2:23;		Mk. 7:6, 7
2 Kings			1 Pet. 1:17		Acts 13:23;	**29:14**	1 Cor. 1:19
1:8	Mt. 3:4;	**19:17**	Eph. 6:9;		Heb. 7:14;	**29:16**	Rom. 9:20
	Mk. 1:6		Col. 3:25		Rev. 5:5;	**30:33**	Rev. 19:20;
1:10	Rev. 11:5;	**20:7**	Jas. 2:23		22:16		20:10, 15;
	20:9	**24:20, 21**	Mt. 23:35;	**11:2**	Eph. 1:17;		21:8
1:10, 12	Lk. 9:54		Lk. 11:51		1 Pet. 4:14	**32:17**	Jas. 3:18
2:11	Mk. 16:19;	**24:21**	Heb. 11:37	**11:3**	Jn. 7:24	**33:14**	Heb. 12:29
	Rev. 11:12	**29:31**	Heb. 13:15	**11:4**	Jn. 7:24;	**33:18**	1 Cor. 1:20
4:8-37	Mt. 10:41	**30:17**	Jn. 11:55		Eph. 6:17;	**33:24**	Acts 10:43
4:25-37	Heb. 11:35	**36:10**	Mt. 1:11		2 Thess. 2:8;	**34:4**	Mt. 24:29;
4:29	Lk. 10:4;	**36:15, 16**	Lk. 20:10-12		Rev. 19:11		Mk. 13:24,
	12:35	**36:16**	Mt. 5:12;	**11:5**	Eph. 6:14		25;
4:33	Mt. 6:6		Lk. 6:23;	**11:10**	Rom. 15:12;		Rev. 6:13, 14
4:36	Lk. 7:15		Acts 7:52		Rev. 5:5;		
					22:16		

Isaiah

34:10	Rev. 14:11; 19:3	**45:15**	Rom. 11:33	**53:4, 5**	Rom. 4:25	**60:19, 20**	Rev. 21:23; 22:5
34:11	Rev. 18:2	**45:17**	Heb. 5:9	**53:5**	Mt. 26:67; 1 Pet. 2:24	**60:21**	2 Pet. 3:13
35:3	Heb. 12:12	**45:21**	Mk. 12:32	**53:5, 6**	Acts 10:43	**61:1**	Mt. 11:5;
35:5	Lk. 7:22; Acts 26:18	**45:23**	Rom. 14:11; Phil. 2:10, 11	**53:6**	1 Pet. 2:25		Lk. 7:22; Acts 4:27; 10:38
35:5, 6	Mt. 11:5; Mk. 7:37	**46:13**	Lk. 2:32	**53:6, 7**	Jn. 1:29	**61:1, 2**	Lk. 4:18, 19
35:10	Rev. 21:4	**47:7-9**	Rev. 18:7, 8	**53:7**	Mt. 26:63; 27:12, 14;	**61:2, 3**	Mt. 5:4
37:19	Gal. 4:8	**47:9**	Rev. 18:23		Mk. 14:60, 61; 15:4, 5;	**61:3**	Lk. 6:21
38:10	Mt. 16:18	**48:10**	1 Pet. 1:7		1 Cor. 5:7;	**61:6**	1 Pet. 2:5, 9;
40:1	Lk. 2:25	**48:12**	Rev. 1:17; 2:8; 21:6;		1 Pet. 2:23; Rev. 5:6, 12;		Rev. 1:6; 5:10; 20:6
40:2	Rev. 1:5		22:13		13:8	**61:10**	Rev. 19:8; 21:2
40:3	Mt. 3:3; Mk. 1:3;	**48:13**	Rom. 4:17	**53:8, 9**	1 Cor. 15:3	**62:2**	Rev. 2:17;
	Lk. 1:76; Jn. 1:23	**48:20**	Rev. 18:4	**53:9**	Mt. 26:24; 1 Pet. 2:22;		3:12
40:3-5	Lk. 3:4-6; Acts 28:28	**49:1**	Gal. 1:15		1 Jn. 3:5; Rev. 14:5	**62:6**	Heb. 13:17
40:6, 7	Jas. 1:10, 11	**49:2**	Eph. 6:17; Heb. 4:12;	**53:11**	Rom. 5:19	**62:11**	Mt. 21:5; Rev. 22:12
40:6-8	1 Pet. 1:24, 25		Rev. 1:16; 2:12, 16;	**53:12**	Mt. 27:38; Lk. 22:37;	**63:1-3**	Rev. 19:13
40:10	Rev. 22:12		19:15		23:33, 34;	**63:3**	Rev. 14:20; 19:15
40:11	Jn. 10:11	**49:3**	2 Thess. 1:10		Heb. 9:28;	**63:10**	Acts 7:51;
40:13	Rom. 11:34; 1 Cor. 2:16	**49:4**	Phil. 2:16		1 Pet. 2:24		Eph. 4:30
40:18-20	Acts 17:29	**49:6**	Lk. 2:32	**54:1**	Gal. 4:27	**63:11**	Heb. 13:20
41:4	Rev. 1:4, 8; 4:8		Jn. 8:12; 9:5; Acts 13:47;	**54:11, 12**	Rev. 21:19	**63:16**	Jn. 8:41
41:8	Lk. 1:54; Jas. 2:23		26:23	**54:13**	Jn. 6:45	**63:18**	Lk. 21:24; Rev. 11:2
41:8, 9	Heb. 2:16	**49:8**	2 Cor. 6:2	**55:1**	Rev. 21:6; 22:17	**64:4**	1 Cor. 2:9
41:10	Acts 18:9, 10	**49:10**	Rev. 7:16, 17	**55:3**	Heb. 13:20	**64:8**	Jn. 8:41; 1 Pet. 1:17
42:1	Mt. 3:17; Mk. 1:11;	**49:13**	Lk. 2:25; 2 Cor. 7:6;	**55:6**	Acts 17:27	**65:1**	Rom. 10:20
	Lk. 9:35		Rev. 18:20	**55:8**	Rom. 11:33	**65:2**	Rom. 10:21
42:1-4	Mt. 12:18-21	**49:18**	Rom. 14:11	**55:10**	2 Cor. 9:10	**65:15**	Rev. 2:17; 3:12
42:5	Acts 17:24, 25	**49:23**	Rev. 3:9	**56:7**	Mt. 21:13; Mk. 11:17;	**65:17**	2 Pet. 3:13; Rev. 21:1
42:6	Lk. 2:32; Acts 26:23	**49:24**	Mt. 12:29		Lk. 19:46	**65:19**	Rev. 21:4
		49:26	Rev. 16:6	**56:8**	Jn. 10:16	**65:23**	Phil. 2:16
42:7	Acts 26:18	**50:6**	Mt. 26:67; 27:30	**56:12**	1 Cor. 15:32	**66:1**	Mt. 5:34, 35; 23:22
42:10	Rev. 5:9; 14:3	**50:8**	Rom. 8:33	**57:19**	Acts 2:39; Eph. 2:13, 17	**66:1, 2**	Acts 7:49, 50
42:12	1 Pet. 2:9	**51:17**	Eph. 5:14	**57:20**	Jude 13	**66:5**	2 Thess. 1:12
42:16	Acts 26:18	**51:17, 22**	Rev. 14:10; 15:7; 16:19	**58:5**	Mt. 6:16	**66:6**	Rev. 16:1, 17
42:18	Mt. 11:5	**52:1**	Mt. 4:5; Eph. 5:14;	**58:6**	Lk. 4:18, 19; Acts 8:23	**66:7**	Rev. 12:2, 5
43:4	Rev. 3:9		Rev. 21:2, 27	**58:7**	Mt. 25:35, 36	**66:14**	Jn. 16:22
43:5	Acts 18:9, 10	**52:5**	Rom. 2:24; 2 Pet. 2:2	**58:8**	Lk. 1:78, 79	**66:15**	2 Thess. 1:8
43:6	2 Cor. 6:18	**52:7**	Acts 10:36; Rom. 10:15;	**58:11**	Jn. 7:38	**66:22**	2 Pet. 3:13; Rev. 21:1
43:18	2 Cor. 5:17		2 Cor. 5:20	**59:7, 8**	Rom. 3:15-17	**66:24**	Mk. 9:48
43:20	1 Pet. 2:9		Eph. 2:17; 6:15	**59:17**	Eph. 6:14, 17; 1 Thess. 5:8		
43:21	1 Pet. 2:9	**52:9**	Lk. 2:38	**59:18**	1 Pet. 1:17; Rev. 20:12,	**Jeremiah**	
43:25	Mk. 2:7; Lk. 5:21	**52:10**	Lk. 2:30, 31		13; 22:12	**1:5**	Gal. 1:15
44:6	Rev. 1:17; 2:8; 21:6;	**52:11**	2 Cor. 6:17; Rev. 18:4	**59:20, 21**	Rom. 11:26, 27	**1:7**	Acts 26:17
	22:13	**52:13**	Acts 3:13	**60:1**	Eph. 5:14	**1:8**	Acts 18:9, 10
44:10-17	Acts 17:29	**52:15**	Rom. 15:21; 1 Cor. 2:9	**60:1, 2**	Lk. 1:78, 79; Jn. 1:14	**1:10**	Rev. 10:11
44:23	Rev. 18:20	**53**	Lk. 24:27, 46;	**60:1, 2**	Rev. 21:11	**1:17**	Lk. 12:35
44:25	1 Cor. 1:20		1 Pet. 1:11	**60:3, 5**	Rev. 21:24	**2:11**	Gal. 4:8
44:27	Rev. 16:12	**53:1**	Jn. 12:38; Rom. 10:16	**60:6**	Mt. 2:11	**2:13**	Rev. 7:17; 21:6
44:28	Acts 13:22	**53:2**	Mt. 2:23	**60:7**	Mt. 21:13	**3:19**	1 Pet. 1:17
45:3	Col. 2:3	**53:3**	Mk. 9:12	**60:11**	Rev. 21:25	**4:4**	Rom. 2:25
45:9	Rom. 9:20	**53:4**	Mt. 8:17;	**60:14**	Rev. 3:9	**4:29**	Rev. 6:15
45:14	1 Cor. 14:25; Rev. 3:9		1 Pet. 2:24	**60:19**	Rev. 21:11	**5:14**	Rev. 11:5
						5:21	Mk. 8:18

5:24	Acts 14:17; Jas. 5:7
6:10	Acts 7:51
6:14	1 Thess. 5:3
6:16	Mt. 11:29
7:11	Mt. 21:13; Mk. 11:17; Lk. 19:46
7:34	Rev. 18:23
8:2	Acts 7:42
8:3	Rev. 9:6
8:11	1 Thess. 5:3
9:15	Rev. 8:11
9:24	1 Cor. 1:31; 2 Cor. 10:17
9:25	Rom. 2:25
9:26	Acts 7:51
10:6, 7	Rev. 15:4
10:14	Rom. 1:22
10:25	1 Thess. 4:5; 2 Thess. 1:8; Rev. 16:1
11:20	1 Thess. 2:4; Rev. 2:23
12:3	Jas. 5:5
12:7	Mt. 23:38
13:25	Rom. 1:25
14:12	Rev. 6:8
14:14	Mt. 7:22
15:2	Rev. 13:10
15:3	Rev. 6:8
16:9	Rev. 18:23
16:19	Rom. 1:25
17:10	1 Pet. 1:17; Rev. 2:23; 20:12, 13; 22:12
17:21	Jn. 5:10
18:6	Rom. 9:21
19:13	Acts 7:42
20:2	Heb. 11:36
20:9	1 Cor. 9:16
21:7	Lk. 21:24
22:5	Mt. 23:38
23:1, 2	Jn. 10:8
23:5, 6	1 Cor. 1:30
23:18	Rom. 11:34
23:23	Acts 17:27
25:10	Rev. 18:23
25:15	Rev. 14:10; 15:7; 16:19
25:29	1 Pet. 4:17
25:30	Rev. 10:11
25:34	Jas. 5:5
26:11	Acts 6:13
27:15	Mt. 7:22
27:20	Mt. 1:11
31:9	2 Cor. 6:18
31:15	Mt. 2:18
31:25	Mt. 11:28; Lk. 6:21
31:31	Mt. 26:28; Lk. 22:20; 1 Cor. 11:25; 2 Cor. 3:6
31:31-34	Heb. 8:8-12
31:33	2 Cor. 3:3; Heb. 10:16
31:33, 34	Rom. 11:27; 1 Thess. 4:9
31:34	Acts 10:43; Heb. 10:17; 1 Jn. 2:27
32:6-9	Mt. 27:9, 10
32:38	2 Cor. 6:16
32:40	Lk. 22:20; 1 Cor. 11:25; 2 Cor. 3:6; Heb. 13:20
36:24	Mt. 26:65
37:15	Heb. 11:36
38:6	Heb. 11:36
43:11	Rev. 13:10
46:10	Lk. 21:22
49:11	1 Tim. 5:5
49:36	Rev. 7:1
50:6	Mt. 10:6
50:8	Rev. 18:4
50:15	Rev. 18:6
50:25	Rom. 9:22
50:29	Rev. 18:6
50:34	Rev. 18:8
50:38	Rev. 16:12
50:39	Rev. 18:2
51:6	Rev. 18:4
51:7	Rev. 14:8; 17:2, 4; 18:3
51:8	Rev. 14:8; 18:2
51:9	Rev. 18:4, 5
51:13	Rev. 17:1
51:36	Rev. 16:12
51:45	Rev. 18:4
51:48	Rev. 18:20
51:49	Rev. 18:24
51:63, 64	Rev. 18:21

Lamentations

1:15	Rev. 14:20; 19:15
2:15	Mt. 27:39; Mk. 15:29
3:45	1 Cor. 4:13

Hosea

1:6, 9	1 Pet. 2:10
1:10	Rom. 9:26-28
2:1	1 Pet. 2:10
2:23	Rom. 9:25; 1 Pet. 2:10
6:2	Lk. 24:46; 1 Cor. 15:4
6:5	Eph. 6:17
6:6	Mt. 9:13; 12:7; Mk. 12:33
9:7	Lk. 21:22
10:8	Lk. 23:30; Rev. 6:16; 9:6
11:1	Mt. 2:15
12:8	Rev. 3:17
13:14	1 Cor. 15:55
14:2	Heb. 13:15
14:9	Acts 13:10

Joel

1:6	Rev. 9:8
2:2	Mt. 24:21
2:4, 5	Rev. 9:7
2:5	Rev. 9:9
2:10	Mt. 24:29; Mk. 13:24, 25; Rev. 6:12, 13; 8:12
2:11	Rev. 6:17
2:23	Jas. 5:7
2:28	Acts 21:9; Titus 3:6
2:28-32	Acts 2:17-21
2:30, 31	Lk. 21:25
2:31	Mt. 24:29; Mk. 13:24, 25; Rev. 6:12
2:32	Acts 2:39; 22:16; Rom. 10:13
3:4-8	Mt. 11:21, 22; Lk. 10:13, 14
3:13	Mk. 4:29; Rev. 14:15, 18; 19:15
3:15	Mt. 24:29; Mk. 13:24, 25; Rev. 6:12, 13; 8:12
3:18	Rev. 22:1

Amos

1:9, 10	Mt. 11:21, 22; Lk. 10:13, 14
3:7	Rev. 10:7; 11:18
4:11	Jude 23
5:10	Gal. 4:16
5:13	Eph. 5:16
5:15	Rom. 12:9
5:25-27	Acts 7:42, 43
8:9	Mt. 27:45; Mk. 15:33; Lk. 23:44, 45

Obadiah

21	Rev. 11:15

Jonah

1:17	Mt. 12:40; 1 Cor. 15:4
3:5	Mt. 12:41
3:6	Mt. 11:21
3:8	Mt. 12:41
3:8, 10	Lk. 11:32
4:9	Mt. 26:38; Mk. 14:34

Micah

4:7	Lk. 1:33
4:9	Jn. 16:21
4:10	Rev. 12:2
5:2	Mt. 2:6; Jn. 7:42
6:8	Mt. 23:23
6:15	Jn. 4:37
7:6	Mt. 10:21, 35, 36; Mk. 13:12; Lk. 12:53
7:20	Lk. 1:55; Rom. 15:8

Nahum

1:6	Rev. 6:17
1:15	Acts 10:36; Rom. 10:15; Eph. 6:15

Habakkuk

1:5	Acts 13:41
2:3	2 Pet. 3:9
2:4	Rom. 1:17; Gal. 3:11
2:18, 19	1 Cor. 12:2
3:17	Lk. 13:6

Zephaniah

1:3	Mt. 13:41
3:8	Rev. 16:1
3:13	Rev. 14:5
3:15	Jn. 1:49

CAPTIVITY STAGE

Ezekiel

1:1	Rev. 19:11
1:5-10	Rev. 4:6, 7
1:13	Rev. 4:5; 11:19
1:18	Rev. 4:8
1:22	Rev. 4:6
1:24	Rev. 1:15; 14:2; 19:6
1:26, 27	Rev. 4:2, 9, 10; 5:1, 7, 13; 6:16; 7:10, 15; 19:4; 21:5
1:26-28	Rev. 4:3
2:1	Acts 26:16
2:8	Rev. 10:9, 10
2:9, 10	Rev. 5:1
3:1-3	Rev. 10:9, 10
3:17	Heb. 13:17
4:14	Acts 10:14
5:12, 17	Rev. 6:8
7:2	Rev. 20:8
9:2	Rev. 1:13
9:4	Rev. 7:3; 9:4; 14:1
9:6	1 Pet. 4:17
9:9	Lk. 22:31
9:11, 12	Acts 15:16, 17

Ezekiel

10:12	Rev. 4:8
10:14	Rev. 4:6, 7
11:19	2 Cor. 3:3
12:2	Mk. 8:18
13:10	1 Thess. 5:3
13:10-12	Mt. 7:27
13:10-15	Acts 23:3
14:21	Rev. 6:8
16:61, 63	Rom. 6:21
17:23	Mt. 13:32; Mk. 4:32; Lk. 13:19
18:20	Jn. 9:2
18:23	1 Tim. 2:4
20:34, 41	2 Cor. 6:17
20:41	Eph. 5:2; Phil. 4:18
21:26	Mt. 23:12
22:27	Mt. 7:15
22:31	Rev. 16:1
24:7	Rev. 18:24
26-28	Mt. 11:21, 22; Lk. 10:13, 14
26:13	Rev. 18:22
26:16	Rev. 18:9
26:17	Rev. 18:10
26:21	Rev. 18:21
27:12, 13	Rev. 18:12, 13
27:17	Acts 12:20
27:22	Rev. 18:12, 13
27:27-29	Rev. 18:17
27:30-34	Rev. 18:19
27:30-35	Rev. 18:9
27:32	Rev. 18:18
27:36	Rev. 18:11, 15
28:2	Acts 12:22; 2 Thess. 2:4
28:13	Rev. 17:4; 18:16
31:6	Mt. 13:32; Mk. 4:32; Lk. 13:19
32:7	Mt. 24:29; Lk. 21:25
32:7, 8	Mk. 13:24, 25; Rev. 6:12, 13; 8:12
33:5	Mt. 27:25
33:27	Rev. 6:8
34:2, 3	Jn. 10:8
34:5	Mt. 9:36
34:5, 6	1 Pet. 2:25
34:8	Mk. 6:34; Jude 12
34:11	Lk. 15:4
34:15	Jn. 10:11
34:16	Lk. 15:4; 19:10
34:17	Mt. 25:32
34:23	Jn. 1:45
34:23	Jn. 10:16; Rev. 7:17

36:20	Rom. 2:24
36:23	Mt. 6:9
36:25	Heb. 10:22
36:26	2 Cor. 3:3
36:27	1 Thess. 4:8
37:5	Rev. 11:11
37:9	Rev. 7:1
37:10	Rev. 11:11
37:12	Mt. 27:52, 53
37:14	1 Thess. 4:8
37:23	Titus 2:14
37:24	Jn. 10:16
37:26	Heb. 13:20
37:27	2 Cor. 6:16; Rev. 21:3
38:2	Rev. 20:8
38:19, 20	Rev. 11:13
38:22	Rev. 8:7; 14:10; 20:9, 10; 21:8
39:6	Rev. 20:9
39:17-20	Rev. 19:17, 18
39:17, 20	Rev. 19:21
40:2	Rev. 21:10
40:3	Rev. 11:1
40:3, 5	Rev. 21:15
43:2	Rev. 1:15; 14:2; 19:6
44:4	Rev. 15:8
44:7	Acts 21:28
44:30	Rom. 11:16
47:1	Rev. 22:1
47:12	Rev. 22:2, 14, 19
48:16, 17	Rev. 21:16, 17
48:30-35	Rev. 21:12, 13
48:35	Rev. 3:12

Daniel

1:12, 14	Rev. 2:10
2:28	Lk. 21:9
2:28, 29	Mt. 24:6; Rev. 1:1, 19; 4:1; 22:6
2:34, 35	Mt. 21:44
2:44	1 Cor. 15:24; Rev. 11:15
2:44, 45	Mt. 21:44
2:45	Rev. 1:1, 19; 4:1; 22:6
2:47	1 Cor. 14:25; Rev. 17:14; 19:16
3:4	Rev. 10:11
3:5, 6	Rev. 13:15
3:5	Mt. 4:9
3:6	Mt. 13:42, 50
3:10	Mt. 4:9
3:15	Mt. 4:9
3:23-25	Heb. 11:34
4:2	Jn. 4:48

4:12, 21	Mt. 13:32; Mk. 4:32; Lk. 13:19
4:30	Rev. 18:10
4:34	Rev. 4:9
4:37	Jn. 4:48
5:20	Acts 12:23
5:23	Rev. 9:20
6:1-27	Heb. 11:33
6:21	2 Tim. 4:17
6:26	1 Pet. 1:23; Rev. 4:9
7:2	Rev. 7:1
7:3	Rev. 11:7; 13:1; 17:8
7:4-6	Rev. 13:2
7:7	Rev. 11:7; 12:3, 17; 13:7
7:8	Rev. 13:5
7:9	Rev. 1:14; 20:4
7:9, 10	Mt. 19:28; Rev. 20:11, 12
7:10	Rev. 5:11
7:13	Mt. 26:64; Mk. 14:62; Lk. 21:27; Rev. 1:7, 13; 14:14
7:13, 14	Mt. 24:30; Mk. 13:26
7:14	Mt. 28:18; Lk. 1:33; Jn. 12:34; Rev. 10:11; 11:15; 19:6
7:18	Rev. 22:5
7:20	Rev. 13:5
7:21	Rev. 11:7; 12:17; 13:7
7:22	Lk. 21:8; 1 Cor. 6:2; Rev. 20:4
7:24	Rev. 17:12
7:25	Rev. 12:14; 13:5

RETURN STAGE

Ezra

3:2	Mt. 1:12; Lk. 3:27
4:3	Jn. 4:9
9:1—10:44	Jn. 4:9
9:3	Mt. 26:65
9:7	Lk. 21:24

Nehemiah

9:6	Rev. 10:6
9:15	Jn. 6:31
9:36	Jn. 8:33
10:37	Rom. 11:16
11:1	Mt. 4:5

7:27	Rev. 20:4; 22:5
8:10	Rev. 12:4
8:16	Lk. 1:19
8:26	Rev. 10:4
9:6, 10	Rev. 10:7; 11:18
9:21	Lk. 1:19
9:24	Acts 10:43
9:26	Lk. 21:24
9:27	Mt. 24:15; Mk. 13:14
10:5	Rev. 1:13
10:6	Rev. 1:14, 15; 2:18; 19:12
10:13, 21	Jude 9; Rev. 12:7
11:31	Mt. 24:15; Mk. 13:14
11:36	2 Thess. 2:4; Rev. 13:5
11:41	Mt. 24:10
12:1	Mt. 24:21; Mk. 13:19; Phil. 4:3; Jude 9; Rev. 3:5; 7:14; 12:7; 13:8; 16:18; 17:8; 20:12, 15; 21:27
12:2	Mt. 25:46; Jn. 5:29; 11:24; Acts 24:15
12:3	Mt. 13:43; Eph. 2:15
12:4	Rev. 10:4; 22:10
12:7	Lk. 21:24; Rev. 4:9; 10:5, 6; 12:14
12:9	Rev. 10:4
12:11	Mt. 24:15; Mk. 13:14
12:12	Jas. 5:11

Esther

4:1	Mt. 11:21
5:3, 6	Mk. 6:23
7:2	Mk. 6:23

Haggai

1:13	Mt. 28:20
2:6	Heb. 12:26
2:6, 21	Mt. 24:29; Lk. 21:26

Zechariah

1:1	Mt. 23:35
1:3	Jas. 4:8

1:6	Rev. 10:7; 11:18	**12:12**	Rev. 1:7	
1:8	Rev. 6:2, 4; 19:11	**12:14**	Mt. 24:30; Rev. 1:7	
2:1, 2	Rev. 11:1	**13:4**	Mk. 1:6	
2:6	Mt. 24:31	**13:7**	Mt. 26:31, 56 Mk. 14:27, 50; Jn. 16:32	
2:6, 10	Mk. 13:27			
2:10	Rev. 21:3			
3:1	Rev. 12:10	**13:9**	1 Pet. 1:7	
3:2	Jude 9; 23	**14:5**	Mt. 25:31; 1 Thess. 3:13; 2 Thess. 1:7; Jude 14	
4:2	Rev. 4:5			
4:3	Rev. 11:4			
4:10	Rev. 5:6	**14:7**	Rev. 21:25; 22:5	
4:11-14	Rev. 11:4			
6:2	Rev. 6:4, 5	**14:8**	Rev. 22:1	
6:3	Rev. 6:2; 19:11	**14:9**	Rev. 11:15; 19:6	
6:5	Rev. 7:1	**14:11**	Rev. 22:3	
6:6	Rev. 6:2, 5; 19:11			
		Malachi		
8:16	Eph. 4:25	**1:2, 3**	Rom. 9:13	
8:17	1 Cor. 13:5	**1:6**	Lk. 6:46	
8:23	1 Cor. 14:25	**1:7**	1 Cor. 10:21	
9:2-4	Mt. 11:21, 22; Lk. 10:13, 14	**1:11**	2 Thess. 1:12; Rev. 15:4	
9:9	Mt. 21:5; Jn. 12:15	**1:12**	1 Cor. 10:21	
		2:7, 8	Mt. 23:3	
9:10	Eph. 2:17	**2:10**	1 Cor. 8:6	
9:11	Mt. 26:28; Mk. 14:24; Lk. 22:20; 1 Cor. 11:25 Heb. 13:20	**3:1**	Mt. 11:3, 10; Mk. 1:2; Lk. 1:17, 76; 7:19, 27; Jn. 3:28	
10:2	Mt. 9:36; Mk. 6:34	**3:2**	Rev. 6:17	
11:12	Mt. 26:15	**3:3**	1 Pet. 1:7	
11:12, 13	Mt. 27:9, 10; Rev. 11:2	**3:5**	Jas. 5:4	
		3:7	Jas. 4:8	
		4:2	Lk. 1:78	
12:10	Mt. 24:30; Jn. 19:37; Rev. 1:7	**4:5**	Mt. 11:14	
		4:5, 6	Mt. 17:10, 11; Mk. 9:11, 12; Lk. 1:17	
12:11	Rev. 16:16			

Introduction to Holy Land Statistics

These Holy Land statistics accurately bear out the glowing description of Jerusalem given by the Psalmist.

"Great is the Lord, and greatly to be praised in the city of our God, in the mountain of his holiness. Beautiful for situation, the joy of the whole earth, is mount Zion, on the sides of the north, the city of the great King. God is known in her palaces for a refuge. As we have heard, so have we seen in the city of the Lord of hosts, in the city of our God: God will establish it for ever. Selah. We have thought of thy lovingkindness, O God, in the midst of thy temple. According to thy name, O God, so is thy praise unto the ends of the earth: thy right hand is full of righteousness. Let mount Zion rejoice, let the daughters of Judah be glad, because of thy judgments. Walk about Zion, and go round about her: tell the towers thereof. Mark ye well her bulwarks, consider her palaces; that ye may tell it to the generation following. For this God is our God for ever and ever: he will be our guide even unto death" (Ps. 48:1-3, 8-13).

Holy Land Statistics

I. General Facts About the Various Nations.
  A. Organization of Petroleum Exporting Countries (OPEC nations).
    1. Saudia Arabia.
      a. square miles—829,995
      b. population—9,800,000
      c. gross national product—$45 billion
      d. capital—Kiyadh
    2. Iran.
      a. square miles—636,296
      b. population—34,200,000
      c. gross national product—$69.7 billion
      d. capital—Teheran
    3. Iraq.
      a. square miles—167,924
      b. population—12,350,000
      c. gross national product—$16.6 billion
      d. capital—Baghdad
    4. Kuwait.
      a. square miles—6880
      b. population—1,190,000
      c. gross national product—$18.5 billion
      d. capital—Al-kuwait
  Note: The combined wealth of the four small OPEC nations is staggering. Their gross national product is nearly 80 percent of Great Britain's and 25 percent of mighty Russia's. Their profit margins along with the other OPEC nations could buy:
  —The Bank of America in six days.
  —IBM in 143 days.
  —General Motors in ninety days.
  —All the companies on the world's major stock exchanges in fifteen and a half years.
  B. Non-OPEC nations.
    1. Egypt.
      a. square miles—386,661
      b. population—39,500,000
      c. gross national product—$10.5 billion
      d. capital—Cairo
    2. Syria.
      a. square miles—71,498
      b. population—8,000,000
      c. gross national product—$6 billion
      d. capital—Damascus
    3. Jordan.
      a. square miles—37,738
      b. population—2,080,000
      c. gross national product—$1.6 billion
      d. capital—Amman
    4. Lebanon.
      a. square miles—4,015
      b. population—3,165,000
      c. gross national product—unavailable
      d. capital—Beirut
    5. Israel.
      a. square miles—8,019 (not counting area taken in 1967)
      b. population—3,700,000
      c. gross national product—$14 billion
      d. capital—Jerusalem
II. Specific Facts About Israel.
  A. Boundaries (bordered by four Arab states: Lebanon, Syria, Jordan, and Egypt).
    1. length of border with Jordan—298 miles

2. Egypt—112 miles
3. Lebanon—65 miles
4. Syria—50 miles

B. Size. The territory before the 1967 June Six-Day War was 8,019 square miles. After the war it included a total of 34,493 square miles.

C. Lay of land.
1. These geographical land areas are immediately recognizable, all running north and south.
   a. The coastal zone—including:
      (1) the Plain of Acco
      (2) the Jezreel Valley
      (3) Sharon
      (4) the Philistine Coast
      (5) the Shephelah
      (6) the Western Negeb
   b. The central mountain range—including:
      (1) Galilee
      (2) Mt. Ephraim
      (3) Judean Hill Country
      (4) Eastern Negeb
   c. The Jordan Rift—including:
      (1) the Hulah Valley
      (2) the Sea of Galilee
      (3) the Jordan River
      (4) the Dead Sea
2. In Jesus' day the land was divided into three basic areas.
   a. Galilee (northern area)
      (1) 1600 square miles
      (2) width—35 miles
      (3) length—60 miles
   b. Samaria (middle area)
      (1) 1,590 square miles
      (2) width—47 miles
      (3) length—56 miles
   c. Judea
      (1) 2,000 square miles
      (2) width—55 miles
      (3) length—45 miles

D. Population.
1. Jews—approximately 3,200,000
2. Arabs—475,000
3. Christians—90,000 (75 percent Catholic, 25 percent Protestant)
4. Druze—46,000
5. Samaritans—400

E. Houses of worship.
1. 400 churches and chapels—staffed by 2,500 clergymen, including 160 monks and 600 nuns
2. 100 Moslem mosques, staffed by 200 clergy
3. 6,000 synagogues, cared for under the supervision of 387 officially appointed rabbis

F. Chief cities.
1. Jerusalem—population 450,000
2. Tel Aviv—population 375,000
3. Haifa—population 250,000

G. Bodies of water.
1. Mediterranean Sea
2. Sea of Galilee
   a. breadth (greatest)—6-7 miles
   b. length—14 miles
   c. depth—200 feet

   d. surface—112 square miles
   e. circumference—32 miles
   f. below sea level—690 feet
3. Jordan River
   a. breadth—100 to 200 feet
   b. length—due to its curving, 200 miles from Sea of Galilee to the Dead Sea (actual distance, 65 miles)
4. Dead Sea
   a. breadth—10 miles
   b. length—48 miles
   c. depth—1,300 feet (NE)
   d. below sea level—1,292 feet
   e. salt and chemical content—29 percent (as opposed to the 5 percent average of the oceans)—the Dead Sea contains 45 billion tons of valuable chemicals
5. the Red Sea (Gulf of Eliot)

H. Mountains.
1. Carmel—1,800 feet high
2. Ebal—3,077 feet high
3. Gerizim—2,849 feet high
4. Gilboa—1,625 feet high
5. Gilead—3,600 feet high
6. Hermon—9,500 feet high
7. Hor—4,360 feet high
8. Nebo—2,643 feet high
9. Olivet—2,700 feet high
10. Sinai—8,700 feet high
11. Tabor—1,843 feet high

I. Wars (since 1947).
1. War of Independence. From November 29, 1947 to 1949. Took place simultaneously on four fronts: Lebanon, Transjordan, Syria, Egypt. Cost of Jewish life—6,000.
2. Sinai War. From October 29, 1956, to November 5, 1956. Less than 200 Jews killed.
3. Six Day War. From June 5-10, 1967. Less than 800 Jews killed.
4. War of Attrition. From 1968 to August 8, 1969. Loss of Jewish life—400.
5. Yom Kippur War. From October 6 to October 24, 1973. Nearly 3,000 Jews killed.

J. Distances from the Holy City.
Outside Israel
1. New York—5,600 miles
2. Chicago—6,200 miles
3. Rome—1,400 miles
4. London—2,100 miles
5. Geneva—1,700 miles
6. Ottawa—5,400 miles
7. Buenos Aires—7,700 miles
8. Cairo—260 miles
9. Bombay—2,500 miles
10. Tokyo—5,600 miles
11. Amman—50 miles
12. Peking—4,400 miles
13. Damascus—150 miles
14. Moscow—1,600 miles
15. Istanbul—700 miles
Inside Israel
1. Hebron—23 miles
2. Beersheba—54 miles
3. Emmaus—8 miles

4. Joppa—38 miles
5. Caesarea—64 miles
6. Samaria—40 miles
7. Nazareth—88 miles

8. Capernaum—94 miles
9. Jericho—21 miles
10. Bethany—2 miles
11. Bethlehem—6 miles

ACKNOWLEDGMENTS

I am grateful to the following publishers for the kind permission to quote from the books listed below.

Baker Book House, Grand Rapids, Michigan
James L. Boyer, *For a World Like Ours,* 1971.
Reginald M. Daly, *Earth's Most Challenging Mysteries,* 1972.
John Davis, *Conquest and Crisis,* 1969.
————, *Moses and the Gods of Egypt,* 1971.
Frederick A. Filby, *The Flood Reconsidered,* 1971.
John Whitcomb, *The Early Earth,* 1972.
————, *Solomon to the Exile,* 1971.

Brethren Missionary Herald, Winona Lake, Indiana
John Davis, *The Birth of a Kingdom,* 1970.
Herman A. Hoyt, *The End Times,* 1967.
————, *Revelation,* 1966.
Homer Kent, *The Epistle to the Hebrews,* 1972.
————, *From Jerusalem to Rome,* 1972.

Creation-Life Publishers, San Diego, California
Viola Cummings, *Noah's Ark,* 1973.
Duane T. Gish, *Evolution? The Fossils Say No,* 1973.
Henry Morris, *The Bible Has the Answers,* 1976.
————, *The Genesis Record,* 1976.
————, *The Remarkable Birth of Planet Earth,* 1972.
————, *Scientific Creationism,* 1974.

William B. Eerdmans Publishing Company, Grand Rapids, Michigan
Donald G. Barnhouse, *God's Remedy,* Vol. III, 1952.
Erich Sauer, *The Dawn of World Redemption,* 1955.
Merrill C. Tenney, *New Testament Survey,* 1953.
Kenneth S. Wuest, *Ephesians and Colossians,* 1953.
————, *First Peter,* 1953.
————, *In These Last Days,* 1952.

Gospel Light Publications, Glendale, California
Henrietta C. Mears, *What the Bible Is All About,* 1966.
Ray Stedman, *What More Can God Say?* 1975.

Moody Press, Chicago, Illinois
Gleason L. Archer, *A Survey of Old Testament Introduction,* 1964.
Maxwell Coder, *Jude, the Acts of the Apostates,* 1958.
Allen Johnson, *The Freedom Letter,* 1974.
Homer Kent, *Glory of the Church,* 1971.

Rene Pache, *The Return of Jesus Christ,* 1955.
J. D. Pentecost, *Prophecy for Today,* 1969.
————, *Will Man Survive?* 1971
John Phillips, *Exploring Romans,* 1969.
————, *Revelation,* 1974.
Charles Ryrie, *Balancing the Christian Life,* 1969.
————, *Dispensationalism Today,* 1955.
————, *First and Second Thessalonians,* 1959.
————, *Revelation,* 1968.
Merrill Unger, *Unger's Bible Handbook,* 1977.
John Walvoord, *Revelation,* 1966.

Through the Bible Publications, Pasadena, California
J. Vernon McGee, *Genesis, Exodus, Numbers, Deuteronomy, Ruth, Psalms, Luke, Ephesians, Second Timothy, Jude, Revelation,* 1971-77.

Victor Books, Wheaton, Illinois
Richard DeHaan, *Good News for Bad Times,* 1975.
Warren Wiersbe, *Be Free,* 1978.

Zondervan Publishing House, Grand Rapids, Michigan
Donald G. Barnhouse, *Genesis,* 1970.
————, *Revelation,* 1971.
W. A. Criswell, *Revelation,* 1969.
Arthur C. Custance, *Genesis and Early Man,* 1975.
————, *Noah's Three Sons,* 1975.
Henry H. Halley, *Halley's Bible Handbook,* 1965.
S. F. Lodgson, *Profiles in Prophecy,* 1971.
John Walvoord, *The Holy Spirit,* 1970.
————, *The Thessalonian Epistles,* 1973.
Leon Wood, *A Survey of Israel's History,* 1970.

Also, I acknowledge permission to reprint from:
J. Sidwell Baxter, *Explore the Book,* Marshall, Morgan, & Scott, London, England, 1958.
L. Strauss, *Daniel,* Loizeaux, Neptune, N.J., 1969.
J. Patten, *The Biblical Flood and the Ice Epoch,* Pacific Meridian Publishing Co., Seattle, Washington, 1966.
Tim LaHaye, *Revelation,* Publishers of Scriptural Truth, La-Mesa, California, 1968.
Hal Lindsey, *There's a New World Coming,* Vision House, Santa Ana, California, 1973.
W. McDonald, *Letters to the Thessalonians,* Walterick Publishers, Kansas City, Kansas, 1969.

INDEX
A BRIEF INDEX OF EVENTS AND
PERSONS IN THE CHRONOLOGICAL STUDY

INDEX
A BRIEF INDEX
OF TOPICAL SUMMARIES

GENERAL STUDIES

OLD AND NEW TESTAMENT STATISTICS

BIBLE INDIVIDUALS SUMMARIZED IN THIS STORY

THE PERSON AND WORK OF JESUS CHRIST AS DESCRIBED IN THIS BOOK